HISTORY OF THE THIRD INFANTRY DIVISION

IN WORLD WAR II

HEADQUARTERS THIRD INFANTRY DIVISION
OFFICE OF THE COMMANDING GENERAL
APO No. 3

    On this Memorial Day of 1945, the 3d Division remembers you for the contribution you have made to America and all it stands for in the loss of your loved one.

    These things are hard to understand, but in a war such as this one where the gain to be had was so great and the destruction of the evil force so necessary, great sacrifice was inevitable.

    We who are living know that the success of the Division, and our own very existence is due mainly to those who unselfishly gave their lives in battle. This realization will be with us always.

    Now that the German Army is destroyed, you can well feel proud that through your great contribution, our nation may live as was intended: in freedom and goodness.

    As Division Commander of the 3d Division, I speak from the bottom of my heart for all of us when I say be of good cheer and be ever proud that his sacrifice makes it possible for our country to be great and free forever.

JOHN W. O'DANIEL
Major General, U. S. Army
Commanding

HISTORY OF
THE THIRD INFANTRY DIVISION
In World War II

Edited by
DONALD G. TAGGART

THE BATTERY PRESS
NASHVILLE

Reprinted by
THE BATTERY PRESS
P.O. Box 3107, Uptown Station
Nashville, Tennessee 37219
Thirty-first in the Divisional Series
1987
ISBN: 0-89839-101-6
Printed in the United States of America

*TO OUR FALLEN COMRADES
WHEREVER THEY MAY LIE
AND TO THE MEMORY OF
THEIR VALIANT DEEDS*

This history was compiled by the 3d Infantry Division
Office of the A. C. of S., G-2
Historical Section

and

Office of the A. C. of S., G-3
Information & Education

Lt. Col. Grover Wilson, GSC	A. C. of S., G-2
Major Hugh A. Scott, GSC	Officer in Charge
Major Frederick C. Spreyer Lieutenant Donald G. Taggart	Editors
Lt. Col. Walter T. Kerwin	Custodian of History
T/4 James E. Claunch	Custodian of Records
T/4 Merrill S. Harrison Pvt. Edward A. Fetting	Editorial Assistants
Pfc. Emil Hunt Pvt. William L. Cunningham	Clerk-Typists
Master Sgt. George S. Carr T/4 William D. Cooper Staff Sgt. Orville Sheldon	Maps
T/3 John D. Cole T/5 Howard B. Nickelson Pfc. Robert S. Seesock T/5 William J. Toomey T/4 William Heller	Photographers

Preliminary sketches by T/4 Henry McAlear and Cpl. Richard Gaige

Finished paintings by Corporal Gaige of the Recruiting Publicity Bureau, Governors Island, N. Y.

Contents

PREFACE		xxi
ACKNOWLEDGMENTS		xxiii
I.	PREPARATION FOR WAR	
	"Coming Events Cast Their Shadows Before"; We Prepare for the Showdown	3
II.	CASABLANCA	
	We Storm the Beaches of North Africa and Capture a White-Walled City	13
III.	NORTH AFRICAN INTERLUDE	
	We Learn the "Truscott Trot" and Prepare to Invade Sicily	37
IV.	SICILY	
	"In Which We Carve Our Name"	51
V.	SOUTHERN ITALY	
	We Battle in the Craggy Apennines	79
VI.	ANZIO	
	1. The First Battle of Cisterna di Littoria	105
	2. The Tide of Battle Turns	121
	3. The Big War of Little Battles	139
VII.	THE PUSH TO ROME	
	1. The Second Battle of Cisterna di Littoria	153
	2. Cisterna–Rome Operation: 26 May to 5 June	173
	3. Interlude: Rome	189
VIII.	SOUTHERN FRANCE	
	From the Riviera to the Vosges in Thirty Days	199
IX.	THROUGH THE VOSGES	
	The Summer War Gives Way to Bitter Combat in the Forests of France's "Impassable" Mountains	237
X.	THE COLMAR POCKET	
	We Move in the Lead Again to Crack the "Frozen Crust"	283
XI.	GERMANY	
	The Long Trail from the Rugged Shores of Morocco Ends Deep in the Hartland	327

Appendix

DECORATIONS AND AWARDS
- Medal of Honor 378
- Distinguished Service Cross 389
- Silver Star 389
- Legion of Merit 403
- Soldier's Medal 404
- Bronze Star 405
- Distinguished Unit Citations 431
- Meritorious Service Unit Plaque 435
- Battle Credits, 3d Infantry Division 437

THIRD (REGULAR ARMY) DIVISION, WORLD WAR I 438

ROSTERS OF PERSONNEL, WORLD WAR II
- Commanders and Staff 442
- Headquarters & Headquarters Company 443
- 7th Infantry Regiment 446
- 15th Infantry Regiment 478
- 30th Infantry Regiment 507
- 3d Infantry Division Artillery 534
- 9th Field Artillery Battalion 536
- 10th Field Artillery Battalion 539
- 39th Field Artillery Battalion 542
- 41st Field Artillery Battalion 545
- 3d Reconnaissance Troop 548
- 10th Engineer Combat Battalion 550
- 3d Medical Battalion 554
- 3d Signal Company 556
- 3d Quartermaster Company 558
- 703d Ordnance Company 560
- 3d Infantry Division Band 561
- 441st Antiaircraft Artillery Battalion 562
- 601st Tank Destroyer Battalion 566
- 756th Tank Battalion 571

"THE DOGFACE SOLDIER" 575

Maps

Fedala to Casablanca	20
3d Division in North African Theater	47
D-day Objectives and Landing Beaches	55
Sicily: 10 July to 18 August 1943	62
Battle of San Fratello	67
Battle of Acerno	82
Southern Italy: 18 September to 18 November 1943	84
Crossing the Volturno	89
Approaching the Winter Line	98
Attack on the Flank: 22 January 1944	106
Landing Area and D-day Objectives, Anzio	107
Attack Against Cisterna di Littoria	114
3d Division Positions: 31 January 1944	118
Enemy Attack Against 3d Division Line: 16 February 1944	129
Enemy Attack Against 3d Division: 29 February–3 March 1944	134
Anzio–Rome: 22 January–6 June 1944	141
Operation "Mister Black": Development of Attack	145
Area Seized in 3d Division Limited Objective Attacks	147
Plan of Attack Against Cisterna	155
Breakout at Cisterna to Highway 6	172
Landing Area and D-day Objectives, Southern France	203
Southern France: 15 August to 12 September 1944	204
Battle of Brignoles	215
Advance Against Montelimar	222
Attack Against Besancon	227
Advance in the Vosges Mountains	246
Reaching the Meurthe River	254
The Advance to Strasbourg	267
Cracking the Winter Line	273
Crossing the Ill and Fecht Rivers	304
The Colmar Pocket	306
Crossing the Colmar Canal	314
Isolation and Fall of Neuf Brisach	319
Smashing the Siegfried Line	335
Germany–Austria: 15 March to 8 May 1945	340
Crossing the Rhine	344
Battle of Nürnberg	355
3d Infantry Division Positions at the End of Active Hostilities	371

General of the Army George C. Marshall

Foreword by the Chief of Staff

I have a very special interest in the history of the 3d Division. My first assignment in the Army was with the 30th Infantry, later I commanded the 15th Infantry in China, and my last command in the field was the 5th Infantry Brigade, then a part of the Division.

As a staff officer in the AEF with the First United States Army, I had many opportunities personally to observe the 3d Division during the bitter fighting in the Meuse-Argonne.

But all this is ancient history to the men who represent the Division today. The names which will stir their memories in the years to come are Port Lyautey and Casablanca in French Morocco, Licata in Sicily, Paestum's beaches on the Italian mainland, Acerno, the Volturno, Mount Rotondo and bloody Cassino. They will speak of those days at Anzio, where they held the beachhead from the January landings until the breakthrough to Rome.

Last August the Division was selected for the amphibious assault on the south coast of France which led to its rapid pursuit of the retreating Germans up the valley of the Rhône. As I write, the Division is engaged in a grand assault on the German homeland.

There is no comradeship so close as that which is born of long campaigns, of hardship and bravery, of danger and sacrifice. From such experiences as the Division has recently gone through, there grows a realization that the men who compose our democratic army are strong and fine. From such experiences arises a fuller meaning of the principles for which we fight.

The 3d Division has undergone a magnificent development and growth since those dark morning hours in November 1942 when its men dropped into the assault boats to storm the Moroccan coast for their baptism of fire. In expressing my gratitude to all ranks, I wish them God's protection and, when their part in this war is done, the years of full enjoyment of their honors and of peaceful happiness. There will always be our deep sorrow that so many comrades of the battlefield will be denied the privileges for which their final sacrifice was made.

Washington, D. C.
November 23, 1944

General of the Army Dwight D. Eisenhower

Foreword by the Supreme Commander

The Third U. S. Infantry Division entered World War II with a reputation for gallantry and reliability already established by its brilliant performance in the first World War. Never once in World War II, either in the Mediterranean or in the Western European theater, has the Division failed to add a still greater luster to its record. My own service in the Division covered just slightly more than the year 1940. Three years later, in Tunisia, it was a rare privilege, during an inspection of the Division, to meet on a foreign battleground many of the officers and men who had been my comrades on the West Coast of the United States.

The Third Division now adds to its battle streamers the names of many fierce engagements in French Morocco, in Sicily, in Italy and in Western Europe. None of these names will ever recall a single instance when the Division gave up a foot of ground or failed to attain the objectives assigned it by its commander.

The most pleasant thing that old soldiers can talk about among themselves is the memory of successful battles; the future reunions of the Third Division will be most enjoyable affairs.

Dwight D Eisenhower

Major General Jonathan W. Anderson

Nothing in my military career has given me the pleasure, satisfaction and pride than has my service with the 3d Infantry Division—both in World War I and in World War II.

JW Anderson

Fort Bragg, North Carolina
8 May 1946

Lieutenant General Lucian K. Truscott, Jr.

To Those Who Served With the Third Division

Yours has been a gallant group and proud your record! Morocco, Tunisia, Sicily, Italy, France, Germany have known your conquering steps. No condition of war has been unknown to you—barren beaches, desert sands, rugged mountains, vine-clad slopes, dense forests, marshy plains, torrid heat, torrential rains, winter snows, mud, ice—you knew them all. Attack and pursuit were your familiar forms of combat. Defense you learned. Only withdrawal and retreat you never needed. Truly your achievements merit well the grateful appreciation of your countrymen.

This record of your exploits is a monument to our comrades who paid the supreme sacrifice, a bond of comradeship between us who served with them, and an inspiration to all who follow in your footsteps.

L. K. Truscott Jr.

Washington, D. C.
18 April 1946

Major General John W. O'Daniel

Message from the Commanding General

This history is about the 3d Infantry Division in World War II.

It tells of the events that made possible the final victory for which we fought so long.

It describes the feats of heroism and valor that were the spark plugs which helped make our combat successful.

It is dedicated to the men of the 3d Infantry Division who gave their lives that the principles on which our country is founded might live forever. It was their sacrifice that made the victory over Italy and Germany possible.

No officer ever commanded a finer group of men, more loyal group of men or finer fighters than it has been my privilege to command in the 3d Division.

As you read the lines in this book, memories of days gone by will return. You will again live through Fedala, Sicily, Acerno and Anzio. You will again land in Southern France and dash northward up the Rhône Valley. You will drive through the Vosges Mountains and eliminate the Colmar Pocket. You will smash the Siegfried Line and bridge the Rhine. You will storm Nürnberg and capture Munich. Finally, you will speed on to Austria, capture Salzburg and be in on the kill at Berchtesgaden. You will again live with those fighting men who belong to the Brotherhood of Arms, to which only men of combat can belong.

My congratulations to you all for the way you brought this phase of the war to a close, and may we all see to it that such a war never occurs again.

Well done, 3d Division!

John W. O'Daniel

Salzburg, Austria
8 May 1945

Preface

This is the story of the United States 3d Infantry Division in World War II. It is dedicated to "our fallen comrades . . . and to the memory of their valiant deeds." It is addressed to and written for you, the 3d Division soldiers, of whose many experiences in war it tells.

The main purpose in view and the chief intent of those concerned in the presentation of this book was to set down in words for the pleasure and enjoyment of all 3d Infantry Division veterans the story of the 3d Infantry Division in war; to recapture therein from fading memory a perception of the bond of comradeship that was then ours; to recall the varied emotions we knew in battle and to perpetuate the esprit and traditions of the Division to whose accomplishments we all contributed.

The major part of this history was written by Donald G. Taggart, 1st Lieutenant, Infantry, AUS. Many other people within and without the Division contributed in part to the realization of the project. The information it contains was compiled from several sources: viz., the Daily Periodic and Special Reports from the Offices of the A Cs of S, G-2 and G-3, the Monthly Reports of Operations and After Action Reports of all 3d Infantry Division units, reports of the U. S. Fifth and Seventh Armies and the French First Army, reports of the U. S. II, VI, XV and XXI Corps and the French II Corps, War Department publications and records, newspaper articles and personal interview with officers and soldiers who commanded units and fought in the battles described. The separate rosters were compiled by Unit Personnel Sections.

It can be presumed that there may be inaccuracies in some of the sources mentioned. Many of the original reports were made and written during the confusion of battle; they were hastily scribbled journals of telephone conversations, situation reports, verbal orders. Some reports were false. It has been attempted to review all the available material, compare reports, interview participants in the action concerned and thereby strive to arrive as near to the truth as possible. If the editor has fallen short of the truth, the fault lies not in the honesty and genuineness of his effort, but in the untruth of the information that comes out of battle.

The story tells of the Division's campaigns in French Morocco, Tunisia, Sicily, Southern Italy, at Anzio, in Southern France; it traces the course of the Division over the Vosges Mountains, through the Colmar Pocket and across Germany to Berchtesgaden in Bavaria and Salzburg in Austria; it describes the amphibious assaults against Casablanca in French Morocco, Licata in Sicily, Anzio in Italy and Cavalaire and St. Tropez in Southern France; it relates the saga of the seemingly endless days of combat and the ever-increasing toll of casualties; it describes the heroic deeds of the Division's thirty-seven recipients of the Medal of Honor. It relates the story of the Division's operation in the Colmar Pocket, for which the entire Division was awarded the Distinguished Unit Citation and the sixteen different actions for which component units of the 3d Infantry Division were awarded the Distinguished Unit Citation. It tells of the Division's campaign in France, in gratitude for and recognition of which the Provisional Government of the French Republic (by Decision No. 975, signed at Paris,

27 July 1945, by General Charles de Gaulle, President of the Provisional Government of the French Republic and Commander-in-Chief of the Armed Forces of France) authorized the members of the 3d Infantry Division to wear the fourragere in the colours of the Croix de Guerre 1939-1945.

This history, made by you, is written for you. May it afford you many pleasant hours and hold for you the memories of a soldier's life.

FREDERICK C. SPREYER
Major, FA

Washington, D. C.

Acknowledgments

Of valuable services rendered in the preparation of the 3d Infantry Division History to the following persons and establishments:

To Col. Joseph I. Greene, Editor of the *Infantry Journal,* for valuable counseling, and for the benefit of his comprehensive editorial experience in preparing the book for publication.

To Lt. Col. Mark A. Rollins, in charge of production for the *Infantry Journal* for performing the major task of preparing the material for printing and performing the actual task of bookmaking.

To Major Frederick C. Spreyer, FA, for having written the preface and having made the final edit of the text.

To Mr. Nicholas J. Anthony, Assistant to the Editor of the *Infantry Journal* for numerous acts of helpfulness.

To Col. Arthur Symons of the *Infantry Journal* for a painstaking and thoroughly comprehensive job of editing the narrative text.

To Mr. Jack LaBous and Mr. Jacob Guenther, artists, *Infantry Journal,* for revision of the map work.

To Mr. Felix Jager of *Look* Magazine for prompt and courteous forwarding of photographs requested, and to *Look* Magazine for permission to use photographs in this history.

To Miss Marion Lippincott of *Time-Life,* Inc., and to *Time-Life,* Inc., for photographs and permission to use them in this history.

To Army Pictorial Service, U.S. Army Signal Corps, for many fine photographs.

To Willys-Overland Motors, Inc., and to the *San Francisco Chronicle* for photographs.

To Col. LeRoy W. Yarborough, Commanding Officer, Recruiting Publicity Bureau, Fort Jay, N. Y., for valuable assistance in obtaining illustrations.

To Lt. Col. Walter T. Kerwin, FA, for his voluntary expenditure of time and effort in addition to his normal duties in the supervision of the financial problems attendant upon the preparation and publication of this history.

To Cpl. Richard Gaige and T/4 Henry McAlear of the Art Department, Recruiting Publicity Bureau, Fort Jay, N. Y., for the fine color illustrations.

To correspondents, too numerous to mention by name, whose graphic writings have been "lifted" wholesale and piecemeal to liven the pages of this book.

To families of the Medal of Honor winners, for graciously permitting the 3d Infantry Division to borrow photographs of their sons and husbands—in many cases the only photograph in the family's possession—for inclusion in this history.

I
PREPARATION FOR WAR

"Coming Events Cast Their Shadows Before"
We Prepare for the Showdown

December 7, 1941!

THE day started like any ordinary Sunday. Most married officers, noncommissioned officers and enlisted men of the 3d Infantry Division, then stationed at Fort Lewis, Washington, were at home with their families. A large percentage of the remainder of the command was away from the post on pass. There had been no hint of impending hostilities through any official channels, and only by press accounts of events in the Far East, and the apparent lack of success of the Kurusu mission in Washington, was there any suspicion that war against Japan might break out in the immediate future.

Just before noon, all scheduled radio programs went off the air and fantastic accounts of the Jap attack on Pearl Harbor began to come through. Jap bombs had hit many of our warships lying in the harbor; Jap planes had bombed and strafed Hickam and Wheeler fields, damaging United States aircraft, hangars and barracks. Men of the 3d, who for months had been preparing for a theoretical war against a theoretical enemy, were as surprised and stunned as the rest of the western world.

Almost immediately Headquarters IX Army Corps, of which the 3d Infantry Division was a part, sent out instructions for all members of the command to report to their organizations.

From homes, churches, theaters and clubs, the move to the post began. Officers and men entering Fort Lewis by bus and private car found a traffic jam at the gates where military police were inspecting the occupants of all vehicles as they entered. Machine guns were set up at post entrances and at various points about the post for antiaircraft protection. So unexpected was the Pearl Harbor attack that the possibility of an invasion, or at least of raids against the Pacific coast, was uppermost in everyone's mind.

Blackout measures at the post were initiated almost immediately, and from the first day of the war until the Division left Fort Lewis, blackout was normal. For a time the blackout fixtures—tarpaper and shelter halves—could be removed only with difficulty, so office personnel worked by artificial light even during the daytime. Later, removable blackout panels were installed.

Every morning at dawn, observation planes from Gray Field, adjoining the barracks area, roared over the post on routine patrol of Pacific waters.

To guard against glider or air-landing attacks, tactical vehicles of the Division were dispersed on the parade ground at night as obstacles to such an enemy attempt. The fact that nearby Gray and McChord fields were not similarly blocked, or that the Division would have experienced great difficulty in sorting out its trucks in the event of an emergency move illustrates the lack of tactical perception which prevailed at that stage of the war.

On Monday, the day after the Pearl Harbor attack, combat elements of the Division went into concealed bivouac on the Fort Lewis reservation, partly as a "shakedown" in the event of immediate hostilities and partly to get away from the vulnerable barracks area. As the first week passed and the capabilities and intentions of the enemy became clearer, organizations returned to their permanent quarters in barracks.

* * *

The 3d Infantry Division's role in World War I, ended in August, 1919, when the Division completed its occupational duties at Andernach, on the Rhine, and entrained for Brest, France, where it embarked for the United States. For the following three years the Division was scattered at various posts throughout the country. In September, 1922, Division Headquarters moved to Fort Lewis, Washington, and other elements of the command were stationed in the west.

In 1939 and 1940, when the War Department triangularized all infantry divisions, several major changes in the Division's organization occurred.

Infantry and artillery brigade headquarters were disbanded. The 4th and 38th Infantry Regiments, both of which fought with great distinction during the first war, were lost to the Division, and the 15th Infantry, hoary with the tradition of twenty-six years' occupational duty in China, was added. The 18th and 76th Field Artillery Regiments departed; the 10th was broken up into three separate light battalions: the 10th, 39th and 41st; and one battalion of the 9th Field Artillery, redesignated the 9th Field Artillery Battalion, became the Division's medium artillery unit. The 2d Battalion of the 6th Engineer Regiment, renamed the 10th Engineer Battalion, remained with the division. Division Headquarters was reorganized. Medical, signal and quartermaster units were reactivated in the new triangular organization. The old 3d Tank Company was taken away, and a new unit, the 3d Reconnaissance Troop, was organized around a cavalry cadre.

These changes, occurring under the mounting pressure of the international crisis, also saw the Division

3d Infantry Division doughboys simulate a bayonet attack during training.

concentrated at Fort Lewis. At the outbreak of the war, the following units composed the division:

Headquarters and Headquarters and MP Company.
7th Infantry Regiment.
15th Infantry Regiment.
30th Infantry Regiment.
Headquarters and Headquarters Battery, 3d Infantry Division Artillery.
9th Field Artillery Battalion.
10th Field Artillery Battalion.
39th Field Artillery Battalion.
41st Field Artillery Battalion.
10th Engineer Battalion.
3d Medical Battalion.
3d Quartermaster Battalion.
3d Reconnaissance Troop.
3d Signal Company.

In addition, the 603d Tank Destroyer Battalion, attached, had been formed from divisional infantry and artillery units and was regarded as part of the division.

Only two changes in the organic composition of the division occurred prior to movement overseas. The 3d Quartermaster Battalion was reduced to company size, and the 703d Ordnance Company was added (due to transfer of motor vehicle responsibility from the quartermaster to the ordnance branch); also, the MP platoon was made separate from Headquarters Company, but remained attached to it.

One month before the outbreak of war, the War Department assigned to the 3d Infantry Division the primary mission of training in landing operations. For tactical purposes, the Division was assigned to Amphibious Corps Pacific Fleet, a Navy-Marine headquarters located in San Diego, California.

This new training mission did not alter the Division's basic composition as a triangular infantry division, nor its responsibility for remaining capable of triangular land operations. Amphibious training did, however, consume most of the Division's training time during the remainder of its stay in the United States.

A training-camp area was obtained at Henderson's Inlet, eight miles north of Olympia, Washington on Puget Sound. Here a pier, workshops, orderly room and messhall were constructed, and a boat detachment of some 200 officers, noncommissioned officers and enlisted men, drawn from divisional units, was established. Captain Glenn Wood, on special duty from the 15th Infantry, commanded the detachment during its period at Henderson's Inlet, and later on, in California.

Forty Higgins landing craft (LCP's) and a few old-type motor sailers, sufficient to embark an entire battalion landing team at one time, were available for training. During November, 1941, the first battalion exercises were held, in which the battalion landing teams traveled to Henderson's Inlet from Fort Lewis (about fourteen miles), loaded into landing boats, proceeded to a rendezvous point, and returned to the pier for unloading.

About December 1 the exercises were made tactical, with the battalion landing teams traveling from Henderson's Inlet by water to McNeil Island, landing on a steep gravelly beach on the north side of the island, and continuing a few hundred yards inland to a coordinating line. All nine battalion landing teams of the Division completed this problem.

Training of battalions in actual loading upon and disembarkation from transports began the last week in January, when the 1st Battalion Landing Team, 7th Infantry, combat-loaded the *USS Zeilin* at Tacoma and sailed to San Diego, where the battalion remained two weeks engaged in landing exercises and practice disembarkations. From San Diego the battalion moved north to Fort Ord, near Monterey, California, to which the Division had received a warning order to move.

Following this training of the 1st Battalion Landing Team, 7th Infantry, other battalions of the Division went to San Diego in numerical order, with the 7th completing training first, followed by battalions of the 15th and 30th Infantry Regiments. Regimental headquarters units and other elements of the RLGs (Regimental Landing Groups) made the journey with one of their battalions and went through the same type of training. This training continued all through the spring and summer, with at least one of the Division's infantry battalions, with its attached amphibious elements, at San Diego at all times.

There was only one interruption of this continuous training program. In mid-February, the 41st Infantry Division, which had been made responsible for security of industrial plants and communications in the Northwestern Sector, as well as for coastal defense of the sector extending from the Canadian border to the Oregon-California line, was ordered to prepare for overseas movement. On February 15 the 3d Infantry Division took over these defensive missions, using the 15th Infantry in the area from Seattle northward, and the 30th Infantry on the Olympic Peninsula and southward. This duty continued little more than a week, when the division was relieved by the 44th Infantry Division, a former New York-New Jersey National Guard unit.

From the beginning of training in landing operations, in which many personnel of the Division had taken part during the spring of 1940, development of Tables of Organization and Tables of Basic Allowances was continuous. It became apparent that even before a unit could practice loading dummy boats on dry land, some sort of decision had to be made as to the personnel and equipment which would compose the unit. While frequent changes were made in boat assignments and detailed items of equipment and methods of loading, the basic composition of the battalion landing team remained fairly constant, including: battalion headquarters, three rifle companies, heavy weapons company, attached artillery battery, attached engineer platoon, attached medical platoon, attached antitank platoon, and battalion shore party.

The RLG normally contained three battalion landing teams, regimental Headquarters and Headquarters Company, other regimental units, headquarters of the attached artillery battalion, engineer and medical company headquarters, and a regimental shore party.

While no attempt will be made to relate in detail the hundreds of decisions made on organization and equipment, and the reasons for them, the following basic principles became increasingly clear with the advance in training:

1. Combat-loading of transports and landing craft must be 100 per cent; that is, tactical units must be complete on transports and in boat teams, and weapons, vehicles and ammunition must be loaded in the correct priority on the same transports as the using units.

2. Landing-boat crews must be trained in landing and retracting their boats in surf.

3. Individual equipment must be light, and the minimum amount required for the first phases of the operation carried by the individual.

4. Actual practice-loading of transports, preferably those to be used in the operation itself, and the training of personnel in debarkation with equipment and supplies, is vital.

5. Supply must conform to the peculiarity of the operation, bearing in mind the transportation which will be available after the landing is made.

Any veteran of the landings in Sicily, at Anzio and in Southern France will smile as he reads of these things which harassed the best minds of the Division, and which appear to be almost axiomatic in the light of historical retrospect. Yet it must be remembered that the division was then preparing for a hypothetical ship-to-shore operation, in which the whole array of specialized landing craft, developed later, capable of carrying all the Division's transportation and supporting armor, was almost wholly absent. Indeed, the feeling of many junior officers and noncoms, following their first exposure to amphibious training, was that once a soldier had learned to clamber down a cargo net while carry-

Heavy machine-gun crew in training.

ing full kit, he was a trained artist in amphibious warfare.

Some of the larger aspects of amphibious operations, such as the question of command responsibility between the Army and Navy commanders, the determination of the appropriate hour for attack, means of prior reconnaissance of the landing area, and the coordination of naval gunfire and air support, were somewhat beyond the scope of the Division's training at Fort Lewis and Fort Ord, although these questions engaged the constant attention of the Division staff and were frequently discussed by them with Amphibious Corps headquarters at San Diego.

A source of considerable pride to the Division was the boat detachment, previously mentioned, which began its training in the relatively calm waters of Puget Sound but which later made numerous landings in heavy ocean surf and never lost a boat. The consequent insistence by the Division on the proven ability of trained operators to beach a landing craft and retract it even under unfavorable conditions was subject to incredulity on the part of those who had never seen it done successfully. The boat detachment never failed to fulfill its mission in superior fashion in consequence of thorough training.

In order to include larger headquarters in exercises using amphibious organization and equipment, an imaginary "island" known as Taongi Island was laid out on the Fort Lewis reservation and regimental problems by the 15th and 30th Infantry Regiments were conducted along the "beach line" formed by Muck Creek. The 3d Reconnaissance Troop acted as the defenders. Boat teams were carried in trucks, disembarking on the south side of the creek and crossing on foot with their equipment, except personnel carried in vehicles which would normally be borne ashore in landing craft.

The commander of the Division from the outbreak of the war until March 21, 1942, was Maj. Gen. John P. Lucas, who left on that date to take command of the III Army Corps. Brig. Gen. Jonathan W. Anderson, commanding division artillery, assumed command of the Division and was promoted to major general shortly afterward.

While still at Fort Lewis, the Division staged two simultaneous parades on Army Day, April 6, 1942, in Tacoma and Seattle, with the 30th Infantry combat team marching in Tacoma and the 15th Infantry combat team in Seattle. Demonstrations of weapons and equipment were given in both towns, and luncheons were given honoring the staff officers of the combat teams involved.

On February 16, 1942, the Division was electrified by a warning order to be prepared to move by February 23. The move was first stated by higher headquarters to be a temporary change of station to a staging area at Fort Ord preparatory to going overseas, as the 41st Infantry Division had done. Division personnel immediately started making arrangements to vacate their quarters and move their household goods. Organizations sold much of their company- and battery-fund property, and a general shakedown of office equipment and supplies took place.

Within a few days it was announced that the move would not take place February 23, and that the change of station would be a permanent one for training purposes, rather than a temporary one prior to overseas movement. Even so, the flurry caused by the sudden preparations for departure was a short sensation in the Fort Lewis area, largely because the Division had been so long established there, and the news of the impending move was an ill-guarded secret.

During March and April the Division stayed at Fort Lewis, awaiting orders to move, while more and more of its units were going to San Diego for training and moving on to Fort Ord to await the remainder of the Division. The entire 7th Infantry and 10th Field Artillery Battalion were concentrated there by the time the Division finally moved, between April 28 and May 5.

The move was made by train and motor vehicle and was over familiar terrain, as the Division had twice been to California in the preceding two years. The 30th Infantry, indeed, had made the move between San Francisco and Fort Lewis several times independently of the Division, as its permanent station had been the Presidio of San Francisco for many years.

The Division had been at Fort Ord only three weeks when the coast-wide alert which preceded the Battle of Midway was sounded. Word from Fourth Army indicated that a large Japanese task force had left Jap bases and was headed eastward, but its mission was not known at that time. Consequently, on the night of May 29-30 the Division moved into dispersed bivouac on the Fort Ord reservation, returning to barracks at noon Memorial Day. Five days later the Battle of Midway began, and the enemy attack on Dutch Harbor, Alaska, took place.

On the Fourth of July the Division participated in two parades, the 7th Infantry combat team marching in San Francisco and elements from other units marching in Monterey.

During July a series of battalion GHQ tests was held, each test being an identical problem for battalion landing teams involving embarkation from the pier at Monterey, and an advance inland to an objective on Grant Ewing Ridge on the Fort Ord reservation. A demonstration of overhead artillery fire with 75mm pack howitzers was part of each problem. These tests, under the

The 3d Infantry Division passes in review in front of Major General Thompson at Fort Lewis, Washington.

direction of Brig. Gen. William W. Eagles, assistant division commander, were given to each of the nine BLT's in the division.

A special phase of amphibious training was undertaken by 3d Reconnaissance Troop, which trained as commandos or raiders. The men, their fatigue suits dyed black and with black felt covering their helmets, wore rubber-soled shoes and carried knives and tommy guns during their many rubber-boat landings. They practiced reaching objectives at night by the most direct overland routes.

Until the first part of August, the Division's amphibious training remained merely a phase of its training as a triangular infantry division. This placed a burden on all personnel because all planning, training and supply had to include not only the normal triangular requirements but also similar requirements for amphibious training, and in many cases the two differed greatly. At one time, for instance, the field artillery battalions were equipped with four sets of tubes—the regular 105mm howitzers, 75mm guns, 75mm pack howitzers and 37mm subcaliber guns. Only the 75mm pack howitzers were amphibious equipment, but they placed an additional maintenance burden on the organizations.

However, in early August, the Division began to feel the tremendous suction of the battle fronts in dead earnest. Until this time it had been assumed that any operation in which the Division might participate would be in the Pacific theater, inasmuch as the Division was assigned to the Amphibious Corps, Pacific Fleet. A great deal of material in the way of maps and literature on the Pacific theater and Japanese army had been collected with this in mind. The Division was now told to prepare for a mission in the Atlantic; and to train intensively in amphibious warfare, since the first task in combat would probably be a landing operation.

The work of drawing up the tables by which the Division was to be organized and equipped was speeded up. These tables had existed in tentative form since early spring as a basis for training, but it now became necessary to freeze them, embodying the lessons learned in practice.

The largest exercise conducted on the west coast was a practice operation in which the 7th Regimental Landing Group embarked in three transports at San Francisco August 15, swung out into the Pacific and returned to Monterey Bay for a landing during the morning of August 17. They were preceded ashore by the 3d Reconnaissance Troop landing from a destroyer in rubber boats about midnight. The opposition was represented by 2d Battalion, 30th Infantry, reinforced.

The main landing was made at 1100 and was supported by naval aircraft flown from San Diego. The planes laid a smoke screen and executed simulated strafing missions. Two destroyers accompanied the task force during the maneuver, since the threat of enemy submarines was always present.

Two battalions were landed from transports and the third, initially in reserve, landed behind the first two from the *"USS Pier"* (the pier in Monterey Bay from which training was ordinarily conducted). The regiment succeeded in establishing its beachhead, and in theoretical cooperation with other elements of the Division, in driving the enemy off the southern end of the "island," which was assumed to be surrounded by water on the inland side.

Other amphibious maneuvers involving the same "island," but with no actual landings except those from the pier, using the boat detachment, were held during the latter part of August. The staff and separate companies received valuable training in division operation, since the Division had not been in the field as a tactical unit since the preceding summer at Fort Lewis.

During August, Major General Anderson and many members of his staff went to Washington, D.C. and to Camp Pickett, Va., where they were given some details of the impending operation, and where they organized Amphibious Corps, Atlantic Fleet. Toward the end of August the Division was ordered to prepare for a move to Camp Pickett, and the move was begun Sunday, September 6. The final order for the move was received two hours before Saturday midnight. The last train left Fort Ord Monday, September 14 and reached Camp Pickett Sunday, September 20. This was a temporary change of station prior to overseas movement.

Camp Pickett was virtually a new post, having been occupied only a few months by the 79th Infantry Division prior to the arrival of the 3d Division. Sidewalks had not been laid and the frequent rains left paths, motor parks and drill areas a sea of mud. Housing facilities in nearby communities were scarce and poor. Nevertheless many families accompanied the Division to Camp Pickett.

The new location was actually a staging area for the Division, which remained there only a month. The only event of importance during this period was a practice loading and landing operation called "Exercise Quick." In this exercise, which began at Norfolk September 29, most of the elements of Sub-Task Force Brushwood (3d Infantry Division reinforced for landing operations) were loaded aboard thirteen transports, proceeded north up Chesapeake Bay, and made a landing in the vicinity of Solomon's Island, using a tactical plan modeled on that projected for the actual operation in North Africa.

The work of preparing the division for a "wet run" in such a short period was of staggering proportions. As an example, consider that the following units, most of which were unknown to the Division, much less included in previous plans and tables, were attached to the sub-task force for the operation:

9½ platoons, 443d AAA AW Bn
436th AAA AW Bn CA Bn
36th Engr Regt (less 2d Bn and shore parties; plus Det 71st Sig Co)

3d Infantry Division soldiers en route by troop train from Fort Ord, California to Camp Pickett, Virginia.

Camp Pickett, Virginia, the Division's staging area prior to movement overseas.

2d Bn 20th Engrs (less certain elements) (Plus Regt Hq and Serv Co)
204th MP Co
1st Bn LT, 67th Armd Regt, 2d Armd Div

Until this time, the division had planned on the assumption that it would have to organize and equip its own shore parties. Now it was learned that this vital task would be performed by an engineer unit which, until the time of Exercise "Quick," was totally strange to the division.

In addition, the following units were attached for overseas movement only:

Det Air Task Force, XII GASC
Det 66th Engr Co (Topo)
Det 1st Armd Sig Bn
Det 239th Sig Co (Opr)
Det 122d Sig Co (RI)
Det 163d Sig Co (Photo)
Det 1st Broadcasting Sta (Opr)

Counterintelligence Group
Prs Inter Group
Censorship Unit
Cvl Govt Pers
Task Force "A" Hq Elements
Task Force "A" Sig Det

Companies A and C of the 756th Tank Battalion, which had been attached to the Division at Fort Ord, accompanied the Division on the operation, but the 603d Tank Destroyer Battalion did not. The remainder of the tank battalion remained with Group Three (administrative and other elements of the Division which did not accompany the assault convoy).

A few of the other problems which had to be worked out included the following:

Establishment at Norfolk of an advance detachment for the purpose of supervising loading and the preparation of necessary tables.

Reception of a few hundred replacements, both officers and enlisted men, to bring the division up to authorized strength for the operation. Few, if any of the replacements had had prior amphibious training.

Receipt, processing and loading of a large amount of new or special equipment which came flooding in virtually at the last moment. One weapon, the antitank rocket launcher (also called the "bazooka" or "Buck Rogers" gun) was never fired by any divisional troops prior to embarkation, and it was held such a closely-guarded secret that instructions for its use were not made available until after the troops had boarded the transports.

Waterproofing of all vehicles.

Completion of all necessary administrative processes prior to overseas movement. Combat-loading of vessels and the leaving behind of Group Three personnel greatly complicated the normal procedures. Handling of service records, preparation of safe-arrival cards and identification tags, handling of sick and absent personnel, provision for physical examination and immunization were additional problems.

Distribution of tactical plans, intelligence data and maps for all units. The fact that none of this information could be disseminated or studied prior to sailing meant that every item had to be broken down and tallied against the loading plan for every unit, segment and detachment.

Arrangements for all types of supply, and supervision of loading of supplies and equipment to conform to tactical plans. The ammunition problem alone was a major one, and was rendered more difficult by two facts: First, the force which loaded at Norfolk before the 3d Division, had been compelled to load some of the ammunition intended for the Brushwood force, and second, plans for loading several units were changed, with the result that ammunition shipped to certain berths had to be diverted into a common pool and redistributed. The pool system was found to be the only one that would work without too great loss of time.

In consideration of the brief period available for preparation and the newness and complexity of the problems involved, the division's effort to load its own personnel, equipment and supplies, as well as those of many miscellaneous attachments within a specified period was attended by well-deserved success.

The clatter and hum of winches ceased. The great gray transports, mysterious in the subdued glare of essential loading lights, stopped taking on inert cargo as the human shipments arrived by train on the piers: the doughboys of the 3d Infantry Division. Tired, patient, they waited endless hours, sleeping on the concrete with their heads on their packs until it came their turn to have their names checked on the sailing lists, to mount the gangplank, to seek a bunk in the hot, moist troop compartments. The dockworkers watched for a while, then drifted into the night. They were tired too, from a week's steady manhandling of vehicles, ammunition, water cans, medical chests, deadweight of all descriptions. The hawsers slackened, tightened, slackened, tightened. . . . The last troops were aboard. . . .

Sub-Task Force Brushwood, under command of Major General Anderson, set sail from Norfolk, Va., as part of Naval Task Force 34 on October 24, 1942. Destination: French Morocco.

II
CASABLANCA

We Storm the Beaches of North Africa and Capture a White-Walled City

TROOP LIST—Operation "Torch" Third Infantry Division (Reinf)

Organization for Combat

1. *Hq & Hq Co, 3d Inf Div*
2. *7th Inf Regt*
3. *15th Inf Regt*
4. *30th Inf Regt*
5. *3d Inf Div Artillery*
    9th FA Bn(-LT)
    10th FA Bn(-LT)
    39th FA Bn(-LT)
    41st FA Bn(-LT)
6. *3d Rcn Troop*
7. *3d QM Bn*
8. *3d Signal Co*
9. *3d Med Bn*
10. *10th Engr Bn*
11. *Attached Units*
    756th Tk Bn
    443d AAA AW Bn
    436th AAA AW Bn
    36th Engr Regt
    2d Bn, 20th Engrs
    Co A, 204th MP Bn

Armd Bn LT 67th Armd Regt 2d Armd Div
Det ATF 12th GASC
562d Sig Bn ATF
16th Obsn Sq
21st Engr Bn(Avn)
68th Obsn Gp ATF
122d Obsn Sq ATF
12th Serv Cmd ATF
41st Serv Gp ATF
Det 1st Armd Sig Bn
Det 239th Sig (Opr)
Det 122d Sig Co (RI)
Det 163d Sig Co (Photo)
Det C, 829th Sig (Opr)
Sp Rad Co (1st Bdc)
Ctr Rad Co (1st Bdc)
Prs Interr Group
Cvl Govt Pers
Det 66th Engrs
Pub Rel Officers
Counterintelligence Group

IN the pitch-black hours preceding the dawn of a memorable African morning a mighty armada of ships lay offshore the resort town of Fedala, French Morocco.

It was November 8, 1942.

Three months earlier United States Marines, in the United States' first offensive effort of World War II, had assaulted the beaches at Guadalcanal and struck at the enemy in the Pacific. Now was the time for the United States to commit her strength in another theater, against the enemy whom almost all had privately acknowledged to be the common foe prior to the beginning of the war against Japan on December 7, 1941—Nazi Germany.

To engage the enemy initially where planned gave rise to a paradox. It was necessary first to fight a people who always had been—and again would be—our ally. It was necessary to establish ourselves solidly in North Africa in order to carry our share of the fight to Rommel's *Afrika Korps,* even then fleeing before the hammer blows of a rejuvenated, victorious British Eighth Army in Egypt. So arose the necessity of attacking and seizing the French garrisons at Fedala, Casablanca, Safi, and Port Lyautey on the Atlantic coast, and Oran and Algiers and the surrounding area on the Mediterranean coast.

The 3d Infantry Division was one of five divisions which began the United States' offensive against Hitler's far-flung empire.

United States pilots and seamen had been battling German aircraft, submarines and warships for many months; United States tank crews had supported the British in the African desert; but the United States doughboy did not begin his steady, unremitting fight until that chill morning on the beaches of French North Africa.

This landing, which fittingly enough was designated "Operation Torch," was made while the vast array of special amphibious craft and equipment, later to carry our troops ashore in dozens of smashing blows, was still on drawing boards or factory production lines. There were no LSTs, LCIs or "ducks" at Fedala; only big gray transports and their small transport-borne landing craft. This meant that the Division's heavy supporting weapons and trucks had to be painfully ferried ashore, one or two at a time, in LCMs (Landing Craft Mechanized) designed to carry one light tank each. It meant also that transportation had to be scaled down drastically to conform to the "Amphibious Tables of Organization" previously developed by the Division.

Even the artillery complement was affected; light battalions were equipped with 75mm pack howitzers, which were broken down and carried in LCPs (Landing Craft, Personnel, known familiarly as "Higgins boats"), while the medium battalion used halftrack 105's ferried ashore in LCMs.

In effect, each battalion landing team was a small task force—a separate entity in itself, the theory being that each battalion commander had at his disposal all the elements of a force that would be self-sustaining for several days. This was later basically altered to follow a theory of more interdependence with regiment and Division.

Supply was predicated on bringing rations, ammunition and gasoline ashore by small-boat shuttle, although it was hoped the port of Fedala would be freed at least by the second day, enabling transports to come in one at a time and unload at the pier.

Operation Torch had the strategic aim of cutting North Africa out from under the Axis' European edifice, opening the Mediterranean to Allied shipping, and providing a base for later offensive operations against the continent of Europe. Casablanca, Oran, Algiers, Bizerte and Tunis were all big ports, and there were enough potential air-base sites in eastern Algeria and Tunisia to accommodate all the planes the Allies could put onto them.

The tactical mission of the 3d Infantry Division was to capture the great city of Casablanca, largest port on the west coast of Africa, the only one on the Atlantic Coast of French Morocco capable of being used as a base of operations for large bodies of troops. It was farthest of the five ports from Axis bomber bases.

Reinforcing the Division were the 67th Armored Battalion Combat Team from the 2d Armored Division; two companies of the 756th Tank Battalion (light); elements of the 443d AAA AW Battalion, 436th AAA AW Battalion, 36th Engineer Regiment (C); and one battalion of the 20th Engineer Regiment and several smaller attachments.

To accomplish this mission, the Division was directed to land on beaches in the vicinity of Fedala, a small port sixteen miles northeast of Casablanca; seize Fedala as a temporary base of operations; and attack toward Casablanca. Landings by other units were to be made at Safi, 120 miles southwest of Casablanca, which had a small harbor suitable for landing armor, and at Port Lyautey, eighty miles northeast of Casablanca, which had an airfield on which could be landed planes from the United Kingdom to support the attack on Casablanca itself.

Fedala, in normal times, has a population of about 2500 Europeans and 13,000 natives. Cape Fedala at the west end of town projects northward from the coast about 1000 yards, providing some protection for the harbor and serving as a base for one of the two jetties which enclose the harbor.

About three miles northeast of Fedala, and immediately north of the deep-cut ravine of Wadi Nefifikh, is Batterie du Pont Blondin, at that time a defended locality and seacoast gun emplacement. Pont Blondin itself is a highway bridge across the Wadi Nefifikh.

Immediately west of Fedala another stream empties into the sea. A few hundred yards inland the course of this stream flows between steeply sloping banks which form the Wadi Mellah. The terrain between Fedala and Casablanca is gently rolling, largely cultivated, and ideal for motor and mechanized operation, since there is a good network of roads and trails.

Information furnished by the War Department and other sources indicated that the attitude of the French armed forces was highly uncertain; many high French officers were known to be friendly to the Allied cause; yet others were known to be solidly under Vichy control or even pro-Axis, so that the places where the enemy would defend and the extent of his resistance could not be accurately estimated beforehand. It was believed, however, that the navy was under a strong Vichy influence but would strongly resist any attack, whether Axis or Allied.

Intelligence reports showed about a battalion and a half of infantry in Fedala, two or three antiaircraft batteries and a coastal gun battery on Cape Fedala, a field artillery battery and two troops of Moroccan Spahis (cavalry). In Casablanca there were believed to be three or four infantry battalions, four troops of Spahis (one mechanized), and four battalions of field artillery.

In devising the tactical plan for the landings, the Division Planning Staff recognized the necessity of destroying, at the earliest possible moment, the powerful enemy batteries on Cape Fedala and north of Pont Blondin. Until this was done, no craft could safely approach shore nor could the port of Fedala be used to supply troops in their push on Casablanca. The 7th Infantry was assigned the mission of capturing the town and cape of Fedala, and neutralizing the guns on the Cape. The 30th Infantry received the mission of attacking and reducing Batterie du Pont Blondin and protecting the rear and left flank of the Division. The 15th Infantry was to land as the Division's reserve regiment, prepared to pass inland on the left of the 7th Infantry and, in company with the latter, take up the drive on Casablanca.

To avert unnecessary fighting in case the French were of a mind to welcome us ashore, President Roosevelt and the Allied High Command broadcast to the people of North Africa at 0100, November 8, before any of our troops had touched foot on shore, telling them to expect us and to stack their arms and point their searchlights in the air if they desired to cooperate with us.

A special mission had also been assigned to Col. W. H. Wilbur, who was to drive to Casablanca in a jeep, protected by a white flag, and offer friendly armistice terms to the French authorities there. United States flag arm bands were worn by all personnel and United States flag transfers were applied to all vehicles so there would be no doubt as to the identity of the assailant-liberators.

On November 7, the day before the landing, the powerful Western Task Force convoy, composed of nearly eighty transports, warships and airplane carriers, turned northeast from a deceptive course laid toward Dakar and began deploying before dark as the groups destined for Safi, Fedala and Port Lyautey made for their respective transport areas.

Some difficulty was encountered by vessels in the 3d Infantry Division convoy (known as Sub-Task Force Brushwood) during the evening of November 7 when two 45-degree turns were made while approaching the transport area, and some vessels misinterpreted the signals for the turn. At 0200 the Division Commander, Maj. Gen. Jonathan W. Anderson, and his staff, aboard the *Leonard Wood,* were informed by the Navy that four ships had moved into the assigned areas, and were assumed to be those bearing the four assault battalions. This later turned out not to be the case, as one of the ships was carrying a reserve unit.

It was now just two hours before H-hour.

The boat-employment plan had envisaged borrowing small boats from transports which did not carry assault battalions and as these ships were then only slowly finding their way into the transport area and sending their landing craft to be loaded in small driblets, the question of whether the assault waves could be formed in time to hit the beaches at 0400 became critical.

At 0415 word was received from the destroyers marking the line of departure that some of the assault battalions had only one wave present for dispatch to shore. It thus became imperative to set H-hour back in order to give the four battalions concerned time to get at least four waves ashore without interruption.

The new H-hour was set at 0445, and the change announced to all vessels.

The landing plan was fairly simple, and may be generalized as follows:

On the extreme left, or northeast flank of the Division, Company L, 30th Infantry, was to land on Beach Blue 3, beyond Batterie du Pont Blondin, and assist in its capture by attacking from the rear. The 2d Battalion, 30th Infantry, was to land on Beach Blue 2, immediately southwest of the battery, and assault it from the Fedala side.

Next in order was 1st Battalion, 30th Infantry, scheduled to land on Beach Blue 1, proceed inland and seize the remainder of the beachhead line in the 30th Infantry sector.

The 2d Battalion, 7th Infantry, had a mission similar to that of its neighbor on the left, 1st Battalion, 30th Infantry, which was that of advancing inland and seizing the bulk of the regimental beachhead. The 1st Battalion, 7th Infantry, was prepared to land on Beach Red 2, immediately northeast of Fedala, then turn to the right, capture the town, and reduce the coastal battery on the Cape.

The Reconnaissance Troop and Company L, 7th Infantry, were both to land at Yellow Beach southwest of Fedala. The Reconnaissance Troop was to assist 1st Battalion, 7th Infantry, by attacking defenses on the Cape, while Company L was to advance inland and seize a crossing over the Wadi Mellah.

The grinding of ships' engines dies away and the quiet seems strange after so many days at sea, just as the absence of gunfire after days of continuous combat becomes a silence strong enough to be heard in the ears of the battle-weary soldier. The anchor chain rattles loudly.

There is suddenly the sound of many footsteps and voices topside; gear being kicked around; sailors stumbling over Army equipment and cursing all landlubbers (some of whom have spent as much time afloat as ashore for several preceding months); power winches starting up preparatory to lowering landing craft into the water; clanging, apparently meaningless bells; orders shouted in that strange Navy idiom: "Sea detail report to aft steering"; and the sleepy soldiers in green herringbone twill with a United States flag armband around the left sleeve—some with faces painted black—in close company in the stuffy holds, each trying to get his equipment and put it on in the dim blue lamplight; belt, haversack with full field pack, rifle, tommy gun, or some with that strange new weapon already dubbed "bazooka," which was so secret prior to embarkation that no one had the chance to fire it.

Chest bumps rear of the man next higher up on the steel steps, with somebody pressing closely behind and making the blue light a little bluer when a canteen slaps against his face; gripping the handrail on either side for support and aid in pulling the weight of man and equipment upward. There are low-toned imprecations against the restrictions of space with so many soldiers and much equipment packed into that space; constant urging from N.C.O.'s and officers to keep moving

Down the net of the dipping transport and into the landing craft below.

onto the already jammed deck which is milling with silent soldiers and harassed sailors.

Over the rail eventually, slowly, feeling for the rope net first with the feet, then the hands; descent to the waiting boat which is pitching on the high swells and provides a momentary test of balance as each soldier poises on the gunwale before helping hands assist him in getting down to the deck. Soon it's all loaded and somebody yells "Shove off!" The coxswain accelerates the motor a little to clear the steel sides of the ship, then feeds it a little more gas, and the endless cruising begins.

Presently a thousand men will say to themselves the pertinent cliché "This is it," and shake a little with cold as each downward lurch of the craft propels a cold spray skyward to descend a moment later on the huddled, shivering figures. A chronic whine in the engine rises to a shrill scream over the roar of the engine, and the run to the beach begins.

Correspondent Harold V. (Hal) Boyle, landing with the 30th Infantry, pictured the following scene:*

Our section of the convoy reached its journey's end in a light rain. Darkest Africa was only a dim glow as we pulled away from the transport and circled toward our rendezvous point.

Phosphorescent flecks gleamed briefly in the water and were gone like drowning fireflies when the boats assembled. We turned suddenly toward shore at full speed with motors roaring.

We were in the third assault wave. The first two waves, which preceded us by a matter of moments, landed safely on a four-mile stretch of beach between Cape Fedala and the Pont du Blondin area known as the Riviera of French Morocco.

They had reached shore in the darkness, completely surprising French batteries at each end of the beach. As we neared the coastline, however, a bright searchlight stabbed the skies at Pont du Blondin and then swept seaward, catching our assault wave.

In a bright glare that dazzled the coxswains, we ducked to the bottom of the boat. Machine-gun bullets ripped across the water at us. A naval support boat on our left flank opened fire at the searchlights with .50-caliber machine guns.

We could clearly see, in quick glimpses, the red path of the tracer bullets striking above, below, and to the right of the shining target.

Then came a grinding crash as our landing boat smashed full speed into a coral reef which has helped to win this shore the name of Iron Coast.

The craft climbed futilely, then fell back in the water.

From its ripped front ramp the water climbed to our shoetops, then surged to our knees.

"Every man overboard," said the boat commander.

We plunged from the sides of the settling craft up to our armpits in the surf and struggled to the reef. Waves washed over our heads, doubling the weight of our 60-pound packs with water, but sweeping us nearer safety.

I grabbed an outcropping of coral.

A soldier, there before me, lay on it completely exhausted. He was unable to move and was blocking me. Twice the surf pulled me loose and twice it returned me.

My strength was ebbing fast when another soldier pulled up the man before me and lent me a wet hand to safety.

When I could stand again I saw about scores of dripping soldiers, their legs weary and wide-braced.

Staff Sergeant John Anspacher, my public relations escort, and I discarded our lifebelts and turned toward the

_____
*Harold V. (Hal) Boyle, in an Associated Press release.

shore. We had to clamber across a 100-yard patch of spike-sharp coral reef and wade to the shore.

The way those soaked men, a few moments before so weary they could not stand, forgot their fatigue on seeing their objectives is a never-to-be-forgotten example of soldierly fortitude.

Forlorn on a hostile coast, with much of their heavy equipment fathoms under the salt water, they quickly organized and turned to their assigned tasks when we had crossed the beach and flung ourselves beneath a covering grove of pepper trees.

I found I had a two-inch gash on my right thumb and a lacework of cuts on both hands to remember our soggy trek through the coral.

Our grove quickly became dangerous. We were caught between our own fire and the batteries of Pont du Blondin above us. After one shell showered dirt only a few yards behind us we split away from the beach and turned toward Cape Fedala. . . .

The actual places of landing bore only a faint resemblance to those laid down on paper, due to the blackness of the night, the lack of landmarks, failure of transports to rendezvous at the proper locations, and insufficient training and briefing of small-boat crews. To make matters tougher for the infantry, there was a fairly heavy surf running and many small boats broached and were overturned upon beaching. At some points the boats struck offshore bars, and many went aground on a coral reef which lay between Beaches Red 2 and 3, northeast of Fedala.

In spite of these difficulties infantry units were able to reorganize and proceed to their objectives, with the exception of the two flanking companies, whose experiences will be discussed later. Thorough instruction of all personnel in their missions and duties and determination to get ashore and reach their objectives enabled commanders to collect scattered elements of their units and to accomplish their missions.

The 1st Battalion Landing Team, 7th Infantry, commanded by Lt. Col. Roy E. Moore, started landing at approximately 0500 on the beach and reefs about one mile east of Fedala. Many of the boats struck the reefs separating Beaches Red 2 and 3 with the result that personnel were battered and cut getting ashore on the rocks through the surf, equipment was soaked or lost, and organization of the advance was rendered extremely difficult.

The first two waves apparently landed without opposition, but from that time on the beach was covered intermittently by an enemy searchlight and by artillery and machine-gun fire from Fedala and Pont du Blondin. The bulk of the initial waves went ashore at Beach 3 instead of 2 because of the unfamiliarity of the coxswains with pre-designated landing places together with the other difficulties mentioned.

At about 0530 Colonel Moore's wave (the third) landed on the rocks east of Beach Red 2. After spending a half hour getting from the rocks to the beach he found elements of his two assault companies, A and C. Both companies were ordered to proceed toward their objectives as planned. Advance guards were ordered out to precede the advance of the two companies, and a patrol sent to cover the left flank. The advance on Fedala began.

The battalion had not proceeded far when Company A observed enemy Senegalese troops "skylined" against a ridge. The two assault platoons immediately took cover. When the Senegalese, about a company in strength, became aware of the presence of Americans they became disorganized and were captured without resistance. Company A proceeded rapidly toward Fedala. It entered the town, passing on the way small groups of Senegalese who gave no trouble.

The 1st platoon, Company A, surrounded and entered the Miramar Hotel. It was intent on capturing the members of the German Armistice Commission in Fedala, known to have been staying at the hotel. The Commission had escaped in the confusion, so the platoon gathered what papers were left. A C.I.C. detachment completed the search of three floors of the hotel, finding documents of military value, equipment, and money.

While elements of Company A and the C.I.C. detachment were in the Miramar, friendly naval shells began to fall on the building and at least two direct hits on the hotel served to speed them in rejoining their company, which had proceeded through town and made its way to an area just above a Casino, where the men took cover from the shelling.

The 3d platoon, Company C, meanwhile, had intercepted the fleeing Commission by stopping their cars.

The members, ten German officers and men, were disarmed and searched.

Colonel Moore arrived at Boulevard Moulay Youssef, the first street in town, shortly after the first elements of the battalion had passed through the town, and encountered a small group of Senegalese who promptly surrendered. He proceeded to his battalion CP near the Miramar Hotel, and at about 0700 his CP group began to arrive. He sent his executive officer, Capt. Everett W. Duval, back to the rear in an attempt to get the Navy to cease firing. Captain Duval found the Assistant Division Commander, Brig. Gen. William W. Eagles, and gave him the information.

General Eagles immediately got in touch with the *Leonard Wood* and sent the following message: "Stop shelling Fedala."

Shortly thereafter Colonel Moore was guided to Gen-

Landing craft carrying waves of reserve troops off the Moroccan coast.

eral Eagles, and there gave him the situation, repeating the request for a cessation of naval fire.

The Division Commander on the *Wood,* fearing an enemy transmission for purposes of deception, asked for a verification on the previous message. General Eagles sent him the following: "For God's sake stop shelling Fedala—you're killing our own men and friendly French groups—the shells are falling all over town—if you stop they will surrender."

The shelling was finally halted although Col. A. H. Rogers, commanding the 30th Infantry, desired to have it continued in order to interdict two light artillery pieces on Cape Fedala which were firing northeast upon Beaches Red 3, Blue 1 and 2.

At about 0900 four tanks of the 2d platoon, Company A, 765th Tank Battalion, went by the Miramar Hotel in the direction of Cape Fedala. Riding on the foremost tank was Colonel Wilbur, who had completed his mission to Casablanca. He had taken command of the tanks with the idea of attacking the Cape and silencing the gun which was giving the landing waves much trouble and causing casualties. He had just come from the beach.

The 1st Battalion, 7th Infantry was prepared to attack twenty minutes after the tanks had arrived at a forward position, where the battalion commander had gone to reconnoiter for his attack on the Cape.

At 1030 Capt. C. C. Crall reported to Colonel Moore and said that Company B was in its reserve position.

The fire-control station of the battery on Cape Fedala was on a small hill. Between the hill and Company A was open ground, and the station was well protected with bands of barbed wire. Company A opened fire on it with all weapons.

When some of the wire had been cut one of the light tanks started to go through it, but hit an embankment and turned over. The enemy immediately opened fire, which was returned by the assaulting troops. The station was reached and overcome. There were twenty-two prisoners and approximately five dead.

After going through town, Company C's 1st platoon had moved rapidly, and had advanced to within 150 yards of the battery without opposition, when the naval barrage came down. After about twenty minutes of shelling, Capt. Herman E. Wagner, the company commander, was able to get forward and contact the platoon, telling its leader to withdraw about 300 yards to the rear, where the balance of the company was. When the naval barrage failed to lift, it was decided to move the company to the south, in the vicinity of a racetrack, to avoid further casualties. The company immediately came under direct fire from an enemy antiaircraft battalion stationed there. The company shifted about to attack this new menace to its security.

The company maneuvered into position and opened fire, and individuals began working their way forward. A lieutenant and a sergeant moved in close with a rocket launcher and fired a few rounds. A white flag was raised, but when the two stood up to take the surrender they were cut down by a fusillade of fire. The company resumed fire on the enemy and shortly thereafter there was an actual surrender. The sergeant and lieutenant died a short time afterward.

At the battery, the tanks had arrived at the fire-control station. The French officer who had been in command insisted on lowering the French flag, so at 1201 Capt. Albert Brown hoisted a United States flag while the United States and French soldiers stood at present arms or hand salute.

Colonel Moore arrived at the station and ordered Captain Brown to prepare for an attack on the tip of the Cape, on which remained some enemy fortifications, and which had to be taken in accordance with the original battalion plan.

Company A was organizing for this attack, to jump off at 1330, preceded by a five-minute mortar concentration of battalion heavy weapons, and to be accompanied by the tanks . . . when a French civilian arrived from the tip of the Cape. He said the French there wished to surrender, providing the rights of prisoners of war be granted them, and that if a United States officer came with him, the French commander would discuss the surrender. Captain Brown went alone, where he found an officer and fifty or sixty men who had already piled their arms and ammunition on the ground and were lined up. Captain Brown sent back for ten men to guard the prisoners. Col. Harry McK. Roper, War Department observer attached to the 3d Division, arrived at this time and ordered that a search be made of the surrounding buildings. Twenty more prisoners were taken as a result of this search.

Company B, less the 2d platoon, which had been sent on battalion order to reinforce the attack on the Cape, dug in on its objectives which it had reached much earlier. One squad entered in a fire fight with French marines on a patrol boat mounting a machine gun. The enemy was driven off the boat and retreated. The remainder of the platoon assaulted and captured a warehouse containing arms and ammunition.

Battery A of the 10th Field Artillery Battalion came ashore at 0900, its four gun sections landing on four separate beaches. The 1st section opened fire on sandbagged emplacements on Cape Fedala shortly thereafter, and was joined at 0930 by the 3d section. The 2d and 4th sections landed in the 30th Infantry area and joined Battery B, 41st Field, until they could be moved into their own battery position. The battery commander and his party had landed at dawn on the reefs between Beaches Red 2 and 3 under artillery and machine-gun fire.

The 75mm guns at the base of the oil tank on the Cape were taken under fire and silenced by one section of Battery A under the direction of Maj. Walter T. "Dutch" Kerwin, S-2 of 3d Infantry Division Artillery, who had come ashore to supervise operation of the shore fire-control parties working with the warships.

In connection with the action of the 1st Battalion, the report of Col. W. H. Wilbur is interesting. Colonel Wilbur came ashore in one of the boats of the 1st Battalion, in an amphibious jeep which had been equipped with a radio, a United States flag, and a white flag. He carried letters signed by Maj. Gen George S. Patton and approved by the President, directed to the Commanding General of the Casablanca Division.

According to his report he reached land about 0530. Before reaching the beach a searchlight was turned on the boat and a .50-caliber machine gun opened fire. When the beach was reached, the motor of his jeep would not start so he commandeered the next jeep to land, transferred the flags and set off for the line of dunes with his own chauffeur driving the jeep. He contacted the French without being fired upon and drove into Casablanca followed by a French captain in a civilian car.

At Division Headquarters he found the French General Desré and Admiral Ronarc'h, whom he told he had a letter from the President of the United States. Neither would take the letter, both saying that an Admiral Michelier was in command, so he placed it on General Desré's desk and left.

He was then guided by the French captain to the French admiralty, in the attempt to confer with Admiral Michelier. As the party approached the admiralty friendly naval shells, and bombs from United States planes, began falling. Another French captain (naval or army unspecified) stopped him, apparently angry at the shelling and bombing. He refused to admit the colonel to Admiral Michelier's office, continuing to refuse after twice entering the office to consult with the Admiral. When Colonel Wilbur remonstrated he was told to get out.

Colonel Wilbur drove back to Fedala, encountering French sailors whose attitude was very threatening. They passed numerous groups of French soldiers.

He stopped at the command post of 1st Battalion, 7th Infantry, and was told that the battalion had come ashore as planned.

He then moved to 3d Division Headquarters which was then established, and sent the following message by voice radio to General Patton: "Letter to the Commanding General Casablanca Division has been deliv-

3d Division soldiers, one of whom carries a United States flag, run across the beaches toward the Fedala shore.

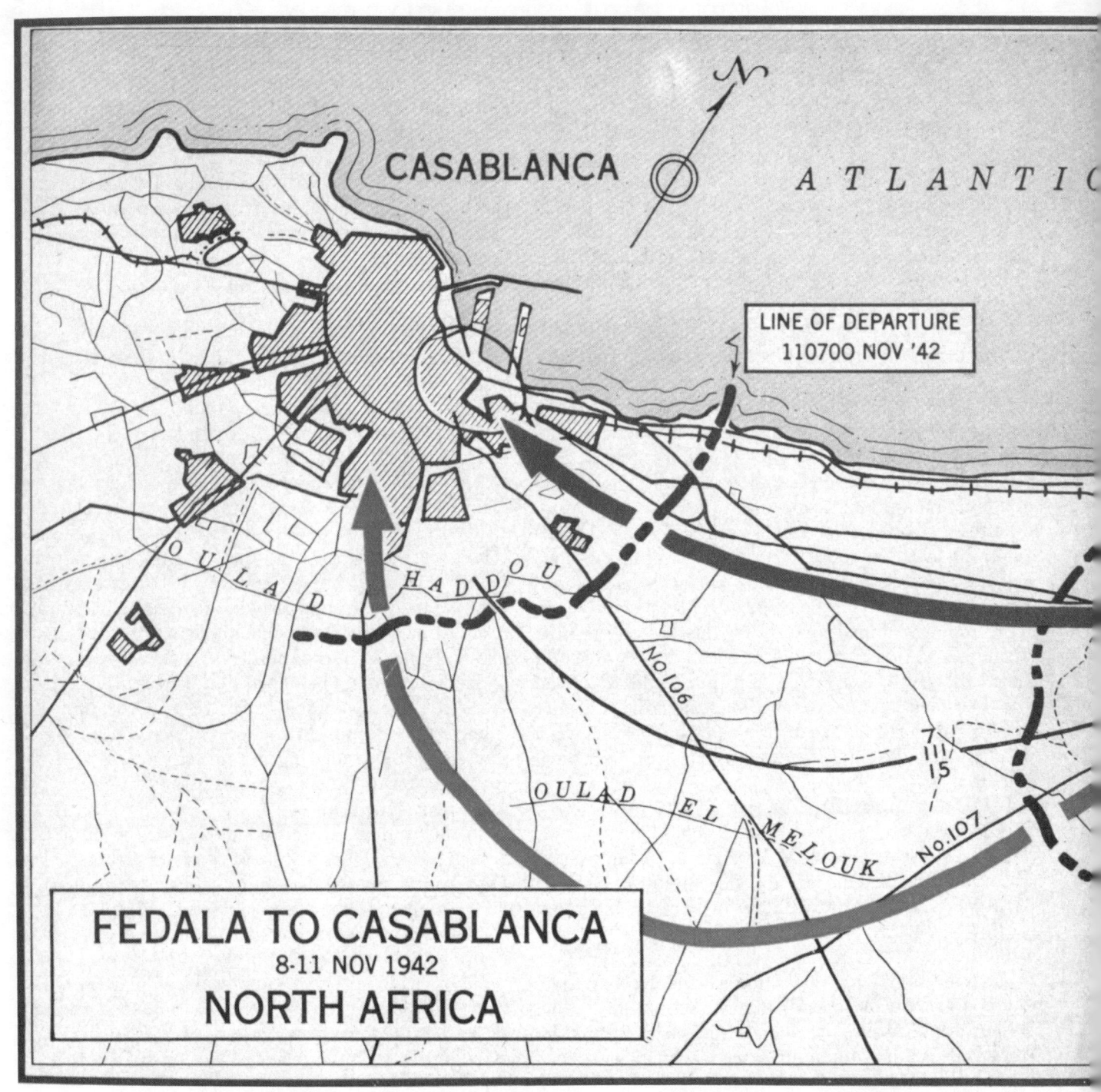

ered to him. I went to the Admiralty in Casablanca, but Admiral Michelier refused to receive me. The French Army does not want to fight. I will report to you on the *Augusta*."

Moving along the beaches in an attempt to find a boat to return him to the *Augusta,* he came to the beach where small boats were being fired on by the gun from the battery on the Cape. He decided to organize an attack to capture the battery.

He commandeered 1st Lt. John M. Rutledge's platoon of light tanks, which was attached to the 7th Infantry. Riding on the leading tank, he encountered Col. Robert C. Macon, regimental commander of the 7th, whom he informed he intended to guide the tanks into Fedala. He shortly thereafter contacted Colonel Moore, and when Company A took the battery he was still riding the tank.

For his participation in the battle of Fedala and the delivery of the President's letter, Colonel Wilbur later received the Congressional Medal of Honor.

The request for cessation of naval fire, once confirmed, was ordered by the Navy. The additional shell-

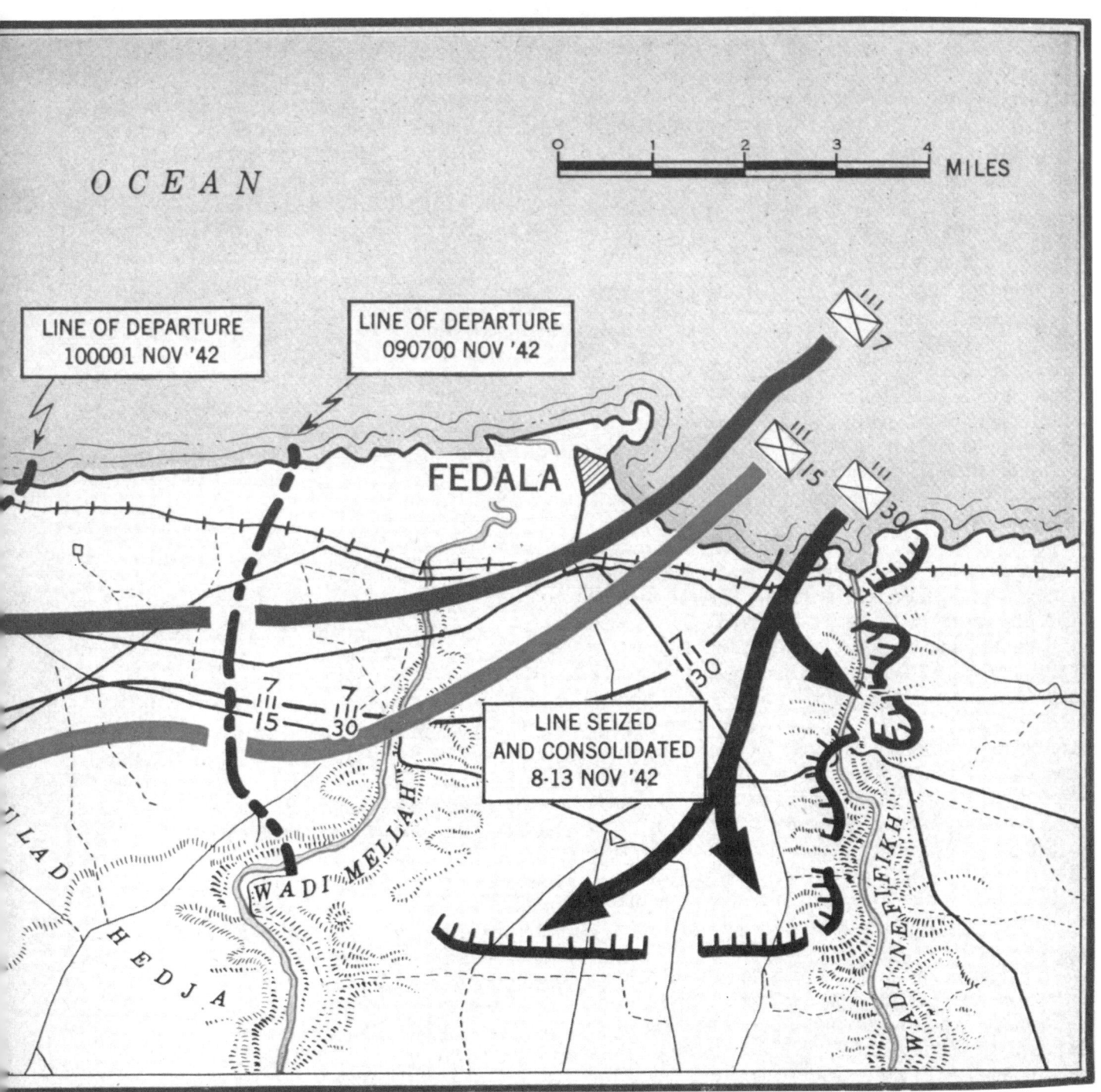

ing in the vicinity of Cape Fedala was done by one destroyer which apparently had not received the cease-fire order.

The 2d Battalion Landing Team, 7th Infantry, commanded by Lt. Col. Rafael L. Salzmann, was less fortunate even than the 1st Battalion in the location at which it was landed.

Companies E and F, the two assault companies, were landed on a beach east of the Mansouriah railroad station, about twelve kilometers east of their assigned objective, against no opposition but on rough, rocky reefs which damaged many boats and caused much equipment to be lost. After organizing, the companies moved west along the railroad toward Fedala. They crossed the Wadi Mellah and continued on toward their objectives under occasional strafings by single enemy aircraft which were, however, kept off by rifle fire. At 1430 they were met by the battalion commander north of Fedala and led to their initial objectives which were the road and railroad crossings over the Wadi Mellah.

Company G was scheduled to land at Beach Red 3

A close-up of one of the 128mm coast defense guns at Pont du Blondin.

in battalion reserve. Instead, part of the third wave landed on a beach northeast of Fort Blondin, and the remainder landed farther to the east and out of sight of the right group. Part of the fourth wave landed at Beach Red 3 and the remainder at Beach Red 2 with one squad near Fort Blondin.

Those who landed nearest Fort Blondin—four squads of Company G and a section of heavy machine guns and a section of mortars of Company H, proceeded to attack the fort. Their landing had been made under naval gunfire and some fire from the fort. When the naval gunfire ceased, the fire from the fort was very weak. Under the covering fire of the heavy weapons, the small unit led by Colonel Salzmann personally attacked the fort. They captured some prisoners and turned them over to the 30th Infantry, which had attacked and entered the fort first from the other side.

After Colonel Salzmann had conferred briefly with Maj. Edner J. Nelson, executive of 2d Battalion, 30th Infantry, who was in the fort with other personnel of the 30th, the elements of the 2d Battalion, 7th Infantry withdrew to move to their own objectives on the Wadi Mellah.

The 3d platoon of Company G less one squad, landed at Beach Red 2. The platoon leader knew that part of the battalion's objective was the railroad crossing over the Wadi Mellah, so he led his platoon there, in advance of any elements of our forces. He was joined by a section of Company H's machine guns. Upon arriving at the crossing it was necessary to drive out detachments of the enemy.

The entire battalion was on its objectives by 1700.

Battery B, 10th Field Artillery Battalion, was landed at 1600 and went into position west of the Wadi Mellah in the area of the 2d Battalion, 7th Infantry.

The first wave of 1st Battalion Landing Team, 30th Infantry, commanded by Lt. Col. Fred W. Sladen, Jr., hit the beach at 0510 and was not detected by the enemy. The second wave three minutes later received machine-gun fire, probably "overs" from Fort Blondin aimed at 2d Battalion units landing to the east. The third wave, which hit the beach at 0535, was illuminated before landing by the searchlight on the point and was machine-gunned from the same place. The light was shot out at 0530 by assault boats and scout boats.

In spite of a lack of small boats, all rifle companies were ashore by 0600. Most of the boats landed on Beach Blue, but part of Company C and part of Headquarters Company were landed east of the battery at Pont du Blondin. Colonel Sladen and some of the shore party landed east of the beach on the rocky point. The boat was wrecked and everyone had to swim ashore. Part of Company D landed on the reef west of the beach. In spite of the mixup, boat groups quickly rejoined their companies and all units pushed rapidly toward their objectives.

At 0700 a squad from Company B; the 2d platoon, Company C; and one section of the 2d platoon and a section of the mortar platoon, Company D, halted an electric train moving toward Rabat, about two kilometers west of the Wadi Nefifikh. Seventy-five French military, naval, and air corps personnel were made prisoners. At 0800 identification and information from these prisoners were obtained by the regimental interrogation team.

By 0830 Companies A and B had reached the Division objective on the high ground southeast of the beach and began organizing it for defense. During the day Companies C and D and other elements of the battalion established bivouac areas, established a roadblock on Route No. 1 at St. Jean de Fedala, set up antiaircraft and antitank security, and organized the command post near Route No. 1, southeast of Fedala. Nearly all units were subjected to artillery fire, strafing and bombing on their way to objectives.

During the morning a Company C roadblock halted a car and captured three French colonels who were attempting to escape.

The first of the four gun sections of Battery A, 41st Field Artillery Battalion, landed shortly before 0700 and was put into position 500 yards off the beach. Its first four rounds were fired at the Batterie du Pont Blondin. Another round was fired at the electric train heading into the 1st Battalion sector, hitting behind it and uprooting a rail.

After bringing up ammunition and establishing an observation post, the battery began adjusting on the Cape Fedala battery, but ceased firing when the Navy opened up on the same target.

The experience of the 2d Battalion Landing Team, 30th Infantry, commanded by Lt. Col. Lyle W. Bernard, was similar to the 1st Battalion's in getting its personnel away from the transport, because none of the boats scheduled to report to the transport *Dickman* had arrived by 0430. The reassignment of some personnel and shifting of equipment which was necessary as a result of the shortage of boats took considerable time.

The first 30th Infantry unit to set foot on Moroccan shores was the assault wave of Company B, commanded by Capt. Charles C. Nalle, which landed on the west side of Beach Blue 2. As this company and succeeding waves were coming ashore—at about 0500—a searchlight from Fort Blondin came on, shining in the air. The troops had been informed that a searchlight pointed at a 90-degree angle and held stationary would indicate that the French units at that point were friendly and ready to surrender without fighting, but this soon proved to be false. (It is believed the French placed the light in the air because they thought the landing boats' roar was that of airplane motors.)

Just before the second wave landed on the east bank of the Wadi Nefifikh at 0530 the Fort Blondin searchlight came on again and this time was directed at Beaches Blue 1 and 2, and at advancing landing boats. Naval support boats and several landing boats directed machine-gun fire at the light which was destroyed in short order.

A few minutes later, as Company C's assault wave was debarking and as units of the 3d platoon and weapons platoon, Company B, were wading the Wadi toward its bank, machine-gun fire from Fort Blondin began crisscrossing the beach.

Among the units which were finally organized for the attack were the bulk of Company F, under Capt. Walter A. Cromer, most of the 3d platoon and mortar section of Company E, led by 2d Lt. Jesse G. Ugalde, together with a squad from Company F, all three coordinated and led by Capt. Mackenzie E. Porter, commander of Company F; a boat group of Company G under 1st Lt. C. L. Elmore, and the 1st mortar section of Company H, the mortar platoon of which was commanded by 1st Lt. Charles W. Morse, Jr.

As the bulk of Captain Cromer's company organized and began advancing for the assault on the fort from the east, heavy naval gunfire opened on the fort, with "overs," "shorts," and "wides" hitting all around the various advancing troops of the 2d Battalion LT-30. Heaviest casualties from this fire were suffered by Company F troops—six killed, three wounded. (First 3d Division soldier to die in action in World War II was Pvt. Earl F. Takala of Company F, who was killed in this barrage. In his honor the Division's bivouac camp at Rabat, and later another bivouac at Port Lyautey, were named Camp Takala.)

Throughout this prolonged naval fire and the .50-caliber machine-gun fire which opened the assault on Fort Blondin, Capt. Elmer Egleston, 2d Battalion surgeon, and 1st Lt. James P. Flynn, battalion chaplain, were doing more than their duty of finding and caring for the wounded. Both officers encouraged the men to go forward, take proper cover, break up huddled groups, and find their parent units. In general they displayed qualities of courageous leadership that stand above the ordinary.

When the naval fire let up slightly—toward 0700—Captain Cromer organized his men for an assault from the northeast. At about the same time Captain Porter, having his own heavy weapons company emplaced, obtained permission from Maj. Edner J. Nelson, 2d Battalion executive officer, to organize a scattered group of disorganized and officerless men from Companies E and F into a three-pronged assault on the fort from the west and southwest. Meanwhile Captain Porter's 81mm mortar section, led by Sgt. Franklin H. McNeeley, from a position south of the Fedala-Mansouriah highway bridge was lobbing shells into the fort. Before receiving the "cease fire" order—when advancing foot troops were observed within 200 yards of the fort—the section had lobbed seventeen shells into the battery. Observing and sensing of bursts was extremely difficult due to the simultaneous fall of naval gunfire. That the shells had their effect, however, was beyond doubt, and it was believed that one or more was responsible for destroying the fort fire-control mechanism.

In addition to this shelling, Battery A, 41st Field Artillery Battalion, from its position in the 1st Battalion LT-30 sector, fired four 75mm howitzer shells into the fort during the same period.

Maj. Robert D. Henriques of the British Army, an observer attached to Western Task Force, materially aided the organization of the assault from the southwest, for which important action he was later awarded the Distinguished Service Cross.

As Captain Porter's group was preparing to hit from the southwest, Captain Cromer's leading elements reached the open ground about fifty yards west of the buildings at Chergui, and were fired on by a machine gun placed near the Fort Blondin entrances. One man was wounded. The company's mortar section was then placed in position near the Chergui restaurant.

At 0700 Captain Cromer sent up a green star parachute flare and at about the same time, from the other side, Captain Porter ordered two yellow smoke grenades set off, both men attempting to signal the Navy to cease firing on the fort, in order that the final assault might begin. The naval spotter planes either failed to see the signals, didn't recognize them, or chose to ignore them as being contrary to their own orders. At any rate the fire did not cease. Nevertheless Captains Porter and Cromer ordered the advance to continue.

At 0715, as the detachment led by Porter was approaching from the southwest, the Navy ceased firing.

Small-arms fire punctuated the continuing advance. At the same time Company F's 60mm mortars opened fire on the building from which the machine-gun fire was issuing. After four rounds had plunked on the target a white flag on a rifle was thrust from the window.

As the white flag appeared, Captain Porter entered the fort, followed immediately by Lieutenant Ugalde and his men from Companies E and F. The French commander and his men came into the court, their hands high in the air, and surrendered to Porter. The time was 0730.

Men from Companies E and F were immediately ordered to remove enemy personnel from the four gun positions and gather all prisoners in one spot in the center of the emplacement, which was done. The commanding officer and his seventy-one remaining enlisted men, including four wounded, were made prisoners.

Major Nelson arrived at 0740, followed closely by Cromer and the bulk of his company, together with Lieutenant Gibson's 3d Platoon, Company E. The 2d platoon, Company E, which was also heading for the fort at the time of the final assault, stopped its advance when the white flag was raised and took up a defensive position east of the highway at once. At the same time a Company G boat group, consisting of a machine-gun squad and 3d platoon rifle squad, both led by Lieutenant Elmore, which had participated in the firing on the fort, entered the emplacement.

About fifteen minutes after Major Nelson's arrival, eight enlisted men from 2d Battalion, 7th Infantry, entered, followed by Lt. Col. Rafael Salzmann. Colonel Salzmann, who spoke fluent French, conversed freely with the defeated fort commander and conveyed many of the commander's requests for burying the French dead, caring for the wounded, and disposing of effects to Major Nelson, who was then in charge of the battery.

At about 0755, just after Colonel Salzmann stepped into the fort, Lt. Col. Lyle W. Bernard, 2d Battalion, 30th Infantry, commander, came on the scene and found the fort being organized for defense by Captain Cromer. Captain Egleston, Battalion Surgeon, was caring for the French wounded. Colonel Bernard thereupon directed Cromer to take charge of the position, the 3d platoon, Company E, to rejoin its parent unit, and the 2d platoon to take up a defensive position along the west bank of the Wadi Nefifikh south of the Fedala-Mansouriah highway.

A portion of Company E had gone up the Wadi Nefifikh looking for a garrison which was thought to be located at the rear of Fort Blondin on the east side of the Fedala-Mansouriah highway. After searching the area thoroughly, and being showered with "overs" from the Navy shelling of Fort Blondin, the patrol found the garrison to be no longer there. Two detachments were sent out to take over the Moroccan railroad and Route Principale highway bridges in case Company G had not already done so.

The landing of Company L, 7th Infantry and the 3d Reconnaissance Troop, which were to have come in together on Beach Yellow 2 at H-hour, was one of several instances in which units were entirely unable to perform their missions because of the time and place of landing. Because their transport was hours late in reaching the transport area, these units were not put into landing craft until approximately 0500, fifteen minutes after they should have been on the beach. Dawn was breaking before they finally approached their landing place. As they came in toward the beach, however, they got caught in heavy naval gunfire—believed to have originated with French cruisers at Casablanca—firing at our warships, and the small-boat crews circled and headed back.

The 3d Reconnaissance Troop was on the water approximately seven hours before being returned to their transport, where they remained until the evening of November 10, taking no part in the action. The fact that they would have been landed by daylight when all chance of surprise had been lost would have greatly reduced their value in the fight for Cape Fedala.

The same lack of surprise applied to Company L, 30th Infantry, which finally landed at Beach Blue 2 south of Pont Blondin at about 1030, in roughly the same spot where the 2d Battalion had landed earlier. The company rejoined its battalion, which was in regimental reserve near the Villa Velozza, immediately after landing.

The 3d Battalion Landing Team, 7th Infantry, commanded by Maj. E. H. Cloud, began landing on regimental order at about 0930 and went into assembly area southeast of Fedala near the Regimental command post.

Company I landed at about 0815 on Beach Red 3 under fire of a battery of French 75's. In about an hour they had assembled and reorganized.

Company K also landed at Beach Red 3.

Company M landed at the wrong beach in the face of heavy artillery fire and was just beyond the line of dunes when an enemy plane dived and strafed it. The company reached the prearranged coordinating line at about 1000 or 1015.

At about 1100 the battalion, less Company L, was assembled and within the next two hours the missing company had rejoined. The battalion, with Company L as advance guard, moved down Route Secondaire to the Wadi Mellah. Company L secured the high ground in front of the highway bridge over the Wadi, and Company I secured the bridge.

Orders were then received from the regimental commander to proceed south toward Casablanca and go into assembly area prior to continuing the attack at daylight. The battalion reached the assembly area at about 0130, and security was established by all companies.

3d Battalion Landing Team, 30th Infantry, commanded by Maj. Charles E. Johnson, landed troops as follows:

0830: Battalion commander and headquarters
        Red 2
0930: Company M   Red 3 & Blue 1
1030: Company K   Red 3
1030: Company I   Red 2 & 3

The battalion commander with his headquarters personnel marched to the predesignated assembly area in the vicinity of the landing beach and across the Wadi Nefifikh from Batterie du Pont Blondin. By 1130 the other three companies had arrived. (Company L, commanded by Capt. Paul E. Doherty, had received permission to land on Beach Blue 2 instead of Blue 3 about 1030.) The battalion was intact, dug in, and ready for a move in any direction.

While in the boats and on the beaches the battalion was subjected to intermittent artillery fire from Cape Fedala, strafing, and aerial bombardment, which resulted in a few casualties. It later received another bombing and several strafings.

When the situation in Fedala became sufficiently clarified around noon November 8, it was decided to land the 15th Infantry Regimental Landing Group, commanded by Col. Thomas H. Monroe, on Beaches Red 1 and 2 as rapidly as possible. The 1st Battalion Landing Team, which received orders to land on Beach Red 2, was actually put ashore on several different beaches because of the unfamiliarity of the naval coxswains with the shore line. Immediately upon landing the battalion was directed to move to, and hold, the bridge by which Route No. 1 crossed the Wadi Mellah.

The battalion, maintaining contact with the 7th Infantry on its right, moved into an assembly area east of the bridge, and sent outposts across the bridge with the mission of holding the crossing. This was done just prior to darkness November 8.

At 1600 Colonel Monroe was directed to land the remaining element of the regiment as rapidly as possible. That evening the remainder of the landing group was landed in darkness all along the beaches from Fedala northward.

In contrast to the token resistance or quick capitulation on the part of most of the land forces resisting our invasion, the French naval forces, as expected, put up a wicked, last-ditch fight.

John A. Moroso, III, Associated Press, described it from a grandstand seat aboard the light cruiser *Augusta,* General Patton's command ship, in a dispatch dated November 8:*

The audacious and well-trained Vichy French naval force today staged a furious, reckless and soul-searing battle against American ships attempting to land troops at Fedala, French Morocco.

The American force, the greatest of its kind in history, had crossed the Atlantic without casualty. With more than 100 ships and thousands of men determined to open the long-awaited second front we waded through Axis submarines.

Here is the battle as I logged it until the order to cease fire reached the crew:

11:25 p. m.—We arrived at the designated area for operations in Stygian darkness and a slight rain squall. We are surprised that all navigation lights are on.

11:45 p. m.—At Casablanca and Fedala the lights go out suddenly and village blacks out. We are six miles offshore and we make several whistle signals. They know something is wrong.

12:05 a. m.—Our first motorboat leaves the transport and we start loading troops into landing barges.

4:45 a. m.—Destroyers go almost to the beach to help barges land. The swell is heavy and some boats are damaged. Overhead the big and little dipper and Orion stand out brilliantly as the Rev. Father O'Leary of Boston offers prayer. Lt. Comdr. George K. Williams of Salt Lake City gives last-minute instructions.

4.55 a. m.—Our troops machine-gun a searchlight that appears on the beach. Red tracer bullets scream through the night air. Minutes later a destroyer machine-guns and then shells the French tanker *Lorraine* which disobeyed a command to stop. The *Lorraine* fires back and then gives up to a boarding party. Hell starts popping off in the dark.

5:47—The captain asks for the range on the powerful Chergui battery.

6:00—Heavy firing is heard dead ahead.

6:12—Chergui opens with a terrific cannonading and our ships reply instantly. The sky fills with flame and smoke.

6:20—A destroyer says Chergui has his range and he will need help. We give him plenty after closing to 11,500 yards.

6:35—We give Chergui rapid fire that obliterated our target in smoke and dust.

6:45—We give Chergui a round of drum-firing. An oil storage tank and two buildings break into fire, our plane spotter tells us. Three of four guns have been knocked out. Suddenly I note that our landing boats, loaded with soldiers, are making their way ashore in the midst of this inferno.

6:53—Our plane reports the fourth gun smashed. Three minutes later two of their guns reopen fire. The Army reports no resistance was offered to landing.

7:01—Chergui is silent again and we close to 10,000 yards

---
*John A. Moroso, III, Associated Press, Nov. 8.

making fifteen knots. Later, one gun puts a shell 400 yards from us and water cascades skyward.

7:08—Seventeen American planes approach us.

7:10—Scores of landing boats are now in the water, heading shoreward. We fire fifty rounds in five minutes.

7:18—Eleven friendly planes zoom over us. We need them because shells are coming closer and submarines have been detected.

7:21:—A tremendous salvo shatters the glass on our bridge.

7:25—Chergui has been silent five minutes, Lt. Eugene Bertram, senior aviator from Spokane, Wash., reports.

7:30—Our planes are bombing and strafing Chergui. Thirteen Grummans, United States Navy fighter planes, join them.

7:32—The French battleship *Jean Bart* begins a long-range duel with one of the battle wagons. Huge flashes spring up and the *Jean Bart* takes a few pot shots at us from a distance of twelve miles. More glass shatters on the bridge.

7:36—My head is reeling from the blast.

7:39—They have fixed the gun at Chergui and are shooting at us again. We pound them brutally and in two minutes score a direct hit.

7:41—These Frenchmen are tough. Two of Chergui's guns are going and we silence them with a round of rapid fire.

7:58—One of our destroyers fires at one of our planes and we warn him.

7:59—Our starboard 5-inch batteries blast away at French planes strafing soldiers on the beach and men in small boats.

8:00—Planes begin attacking transports and all hell breaks loose. Right in the middle of this those obstinate Frenchmen at Chergui get another gun going.

8:05—We put up two more planes for spotting.

8:10—They report Chergui is silenced.

8:14—The planes tell us the location of the French antiaircraft guns ashore. We blaze away at them.

8:19—The French ships escape from Casablanca under a smoke screen. We are ordered to destroy two cruisers coming our way and steam away at twenty-five knots.

8:28—Our destroyer screen reports the cruisers are firing on them. Most of us are scared as hell, but we all try to hide it.

8:35—We fire two batteries at the cruisers. We hear that some French ships have headed for the open sea.

8:50—We make contact with the French cruisers. Shells begin to fall all around us and we and our flagship give them plenty. The cruiser lookouts report one French cruiser is hit and possibly the other.

8:59—After a furious action the Frenchman reverses his course toward Casablanca. We speed up to thirty knots to chase them. Right in the middle of this the Army sends us this message: "Admiral refused to see me. I delivered message to him at Casablanca. French army does not wish to fight. Citizens welcome us and hold us in high esteem." We learned later that only the French navy wants to continue the battle and they fight like mad dogs. A shell plunks into the water twenty feet from me.

9:05—We fire away with renewed energy and our lookout reports we have twenty-three hits on one cruiser. She is smoking, but continues to fire at us. She is doing a fine job. We hear later that both the cruisers we have engaged are beached, but this is not confirmed.

9:30—A submarine is spotted off our starboard bow, but the captain tells us to ignore him. We are zigzagging at thirty-two knots, too fast for him to hit us—we hope. A few minutes later another submarine is sighted to port.

9:35—We are ordered to return to Fedala to protect our transports. This makes us mad as hell.

9:49—We are told French destroyers are coming out of Casablanca. Our orders told us to destroy them. Our battleship smacked a French cruiser, setting her ablaze.

10:01—We are doing a wonderful job, radio message says.

10:09—Shells appear from nowhere. Their bursts are a peculiar magenta color. I think we are gone this time. Shells whistle over my head. They are shortening range now. They have us. That last one hit about twenty feet away to port. We turn. Their range is short by 400 yards. We open with rapid fire and straddle a destroyer behind a smoke screen. These cagey Frenchmen are hiding in the sun and all we have to fire at is flashes. They are giving us fits.

10:20—Their subs are in on us, firing torpedoes. We hit a destroyer as a torpedo goes by our port side.

10:25—Two French submarines have periscopes up. Five torpedoes head at us. Watching their wakes, we reel into a zigzag and luckily go in between them.

10:29—They straddled us again and we can't see them. We go into furious rapid fire. Our ship is reeling from our own gunfire. I suddenly notice a number of birds swimming in the water. They are totally unaware of the battle. How I envy them.

10:47—Lookout reports periscope to port. Boy, how we could use some planes. They must be somewhere else. Somebody reports a torpedo wake, but we are too busy with the destroyers to watch it.

10:57—A battleship is coming to help us. We are going to box in those destroyers and let them have it from all sides. Our guns thunder steadily and my head is a mass of pain.

11:30—The French ships appear to be running away. Thank God we are returning to Fedala to guard transports.

11:40—From ashore the Army sends word our officers are conferring with the French on whether naval gunfire must cease during an armistice. I run down to the captain's cabin—where I am living. I find blood all about. However, our four wounded are not in critical shape.

12:17 p.m.—We scatter from general quarters. We had been firing since six o'clock this morning, and have had no food. Our fliers return and tell us how we pounded the Chergui battery to pieces.

12:55 p.m.—The French navy is ignoring the armistice at Fedala. Two cruisers and two destroyers just left Casablanca and are heading for us. In addition a French bomber attacked the beach during the armistice.

1:08—We contact the French squadron and blaze away. It turns back toward Casablanca—and lets us have it. Our

The French battleship *Jean Bart* in Casablanca harbor after having been dive-bombed by United States Navy planes.

flagship falls back and we find ourselves fighting all four ships. The bursts are coming nearer and nearer.

1:30—Our flagship gets in the battle. Our planes depth-charge a submarine off our port bow. The French are using submarines with their surface ships, but they have had no luck. Some Navy dive-bombers appear and we shout with joy. One of the French destroyers is reported dead in the water. Our dive-bombers roar in on the French ships and one of the destroyers is hit.

2:03—Planes report that the French cruiser is being towed toward Casablanca and fifteen minutes later the planes tell us a French destroyer has been beached inside the harbor. We believe we hit at least three ships.

2:26—The Army tells us Fedala has been taken and that minesweepers have been ordered to clear out the French minefields. The officers and I limp below for coffee and sandwiches.

3:20—French bombers attack our soldiers on the beach.

4:27—We don't even get up when planes drop depth charges off the starboard bow. We want to rest and eat. We expect a night riddled with submarine attacks and French planes at dawn.

The situation at midnight was generally as follows:

The Division and its attachments had succeeded in landing all the important units of the three regimental landing groups, and were in the process of bringing in the Armored Battalion Combat Team; had seized all its initial objectives but had stopped short of its D-day objectives because of lack of transportation for moving troops and supplies; and had brought ashore sufficient supply and control personnel to make possible continued coordinated operations the following day.

The biggest disappointment, amounting almost to a catastrophe, which threatened the entire operation was the realization that because of the terrific undertow and heavy surf all plans for unloading equipment and supplies over beaches were absolutely impossible of accomplishment. Hundreds of landing craft were beached, only to find that retraction was impossible. LCM's and Higgins boats were turned end-over-end by the raging surf. The morning of November 9 disclosed a scene on the beaches of waste and destruction that was symbolic of total war. The obvious solution to unloading was the maximum use of the port of Fedala. This was exploited to the utmost.

It was believed not much resistance could be expected from ground forces during the advance on Casablanca, but there was good reason to believe that all naval elements in Casablanca, including ships based there, marines, coast defense guns, and antiaircraft batteries would provide stiff and determined resistance.

Orders were issued to all regiments as follows: 7th Infantry was to advance toward Casablanca on the right,

15th Infantry on the left; Division reserve was 3d Battalion, 30th Infantry. The remainder of the 30th Infantry stayed on its objectives of November 8 and performed local missions.

The 7th Infantry jumped off at 0730, the 15th at 0700. Both continued without opposition until halted by Division order, the 15th at 1100, the 7th around 1400. This order was issued because of the extremely critical supply situation caused by lack of transportation, and it was not desired to over-extend the supply lines. The advance was to continue at 2400 that day. The 7th was to reach a coordinating line on the outskirts of Casablanca at 0700 November 10. The 15th was to move onto high ground extending from Bled Oulad Cheikh eastward through Hill 92 and high ground in the vicinity of Oulad el Melouk.

A description of the march that night, written by the commanding officer of Company H, 7th Infantry, Capt. Gilbert C. St. Clair, is presented here to illustrate the condition of most of the men at this time:

> ... In column of companies, at 0001 of the 10th of November Company H was again on the move; tired men shifted their loads and groaned very quietly; the silence in which the battalion moved was worthy of real veterans; and the knowledge that we were approaching the objective, with the probability of real action and, incidentally, expending a good part of all that heavy ammunition we had been carrying since early morning of the 8th, encouraged every one.
>
> Tired legs stretched out, bent backs straightened, deep breaths could be heard; and across the Bled (open country) toward Casablanca marched the battalion. After a while we were on the smooth pavement of a highway.
>
> In the darkness of that night, with a thin rain coming down persistently, and a chill wind that penetrated to the very bones, no man but could appreciate the smooth walking of a surfaced road, after all that stumbling, shuffling, sinking, on plowed fields, and climbing walls and fences.
>
> All the length of the column, long as it was, and wide, no sound could be heard other than a low rustling of shoe leather meeting asphalt, but off the front and to right and left, hundreds of dogs howled a continuous alert, keeping up with the column, never quite dying down, gaining in volume occasionally.
>
> Periodically, almost monotonously, the batteries of Ain El Diab roared, accompanied by a great flash. The rush of wind and the scream of shells passed over our heads. After a while the men forgot to duck. That instinctive shrinking of heads into shoulders had not been due to fear but to unfamiliarity with the sound.
>
> Now, from time to time, a new noise could be heard; a man would stumble, fall forward on his face, get up, and try to pick up his load again, but though the spirit was strong, endurance had reached its limit. This was particularly true in this company. Heavy machine guns and the corresponding load of ammunition, heavy mortars and their heavy shells, were never meant to be man-carried day after day, night after night, by soldiers who had their own individual weapons.
>
> They kept up, and they fell, not once, but many times on that march to Ain Sebah, and always they got up again and walked some more, and were grateful for the rests that had to come more and more frequently now.

As the order to advance was being issued around 2300, patrols of the 15th Infantry encountered enemy patrols south of the battalion positions and encountered an enemy defense line organized north of the Tit Mellil crossroad. The commanding officer informed Division Headquarters that a night march across country on unfamiliar ground against hostile automatic weapons and organized defense would be extremely hazardous. He was ordered to hold up until dawn.

The 7th Infantry, despite intensified shelling from land and naval artillery, commenced moving at 0030 and moved steadily until shortly after daylight, when hostile artillery and small arms halted the advance of all but Company L, which continued in the face of fire received from small enemy forces.

During the morning platoons of Companies I and K, 7th Infantry, attacked and captured a battery of antiaircraft guns located about 1200 yards southeast of Point Oukacha.

The 2d Battalion, on the left, had moved more rapidly during the approach march, but a half hour prior to daylight began receiving machine-gun, rifle and artillery fire from front and flanks. A short time later the battalion commander ordered the elements in contact to move to the left (south) flank. The companies became somewhat disorganized, largely as a result of losing the commanding officer of Company E, who was wounded, and the commanding officer of Company F, who was killed. The battalion commander led the bulk of the battalion to the south, clearing out hostile riflemen and a number of machine guns en route, to high ground near Route Secondaire No. 106. Leading elements of the battalion, principally two platoons of Company E and one of Company G, remained in contact with the enemy all day. During the progress of the morning one hostile artillery piece was captured, its crew destroyed, and the crews of two other field pieces driven from their guns.

The platoon of Company G undertook to envelop the hostile left flank but was unable to advance over the open terrain. It later withdrew to a line formed to provide protection for the 10th Field Artillery Battalion guns in the rear.

As soon as the situation of the 2d Battalion was clarified, the 1st Battalion was directed to attack, with tank and artillery support, in the previous zone of action of the 2d Battalion and to capture the military barracks

The United States flag waves over a sand dune on the coast of French Morocco where 3d Division soldiers secure the beach

area on the outskirts of Casablanca. It crossed the line of departure at 1200 and at darkness held a line immediately in front of the barracks area, which was held during the night.

The 15th Infantry, meanwhile, had jumped off at dawn, and immediately encountered enemy positions. Enemy rifle and machine-gun fire was heavy; it was estimated that the hostile positions were held by a squadron of cavalry, organized in depth, with machine-gun crossfire covering their front.

Under covering artillery, machine-gun, and 81mm mortar fire, enemy positions were finally enveloped and the hostile forces withdrew to the south and west of Tit Mellil. The enemy, as they withdrew, mounted horses which had been held in the rear. A tentative enemy attempt to establish a line was discouraged by accurate long range machine-gun and 37mm antitank fire, employing high-explosive shell. Thereafter enemy cavalry withdrew toward Casablanca and contact was lost. The 15th Infantry suffered only slight casualties in the engagement.

By 1300 the 15th Infantry had pushed south of Tit Mellil and reorganized. At 1400 a platoon of light tanks was attached to the 1st Battalion. By 1700 the battalions were on their objectives.

Just prior to this time the 2d Battalion received a 30-minute artillery concentration fired from a park in the center of Casablanca. The battalion withdrew about 500 yards out of the impact area and spent the night there.

The 3d Battalion, 30th Infantry, which was in Division reserve, stayed near the Division command post at Villa Coigny until morning of November 10 when it moved to an assembly area about halfway from the Route No. 1 intersection on Route No. 7 to Tit Mellil.

This battalion was not committed on the 9th or 10th although strafed on the 9th and subjected to artillery fire believed to have been observed by civilians on nearby hills. On the 11th Company L and a machine-gun platoon was sent to high ground southwest of Tit Mellil with the mission of protecting the Division against French troops reportedly moving north from Marrakech. News of an armistice was received as soon as this company arrived in position. The remainder of the 30th Infantry underwent a small local patrol action during which there were a night attack from a Goum patrol in which four men of Company B were stabbed and two taken prisoners, a platoon-sized counterattack and a major armor scare.

The latter scare with which the regiment made extensive preparations to deal, never materialized because naval dive bombers, called into action by Lt. (j.g.) J. B. Furstenberg, naval air liaison officer with the regiment, strafed the column, destroying several tanks and completely disrupted the enemy and rendered him unable to attack.

At Division Headquarters preparations for the assault on Casablanca began about 1400 November 10. Arrangements had been made for naval gunfire and dive bombing support during the attack, and the details were discussed with the commanders concerned. The attack was to employ all the striking power then available to the Division—the armored battalion, all the Divisional artillery except that supporting the 30th

Infantry, Cannon and Antitank Companies of the 7th and 30th in addition to the organic infantry firepower. H-hour was set for 0730.

During the night prisoners were taken by the regiments, all of whom stated that orders had been issued them to cease firing pending an armistice.

At 0230 a telephone call was received from the 30th Infantry. Two French officers and four enlisted men in a French car, flying a white flag and sounding a bugle, had entered Company G's area and stated that they had authority from the Commanding General in French Morocco to seek an armistice.

They were directed to Task Force Headquarters at the Miramar Hotel in Fedala. Task Force Headquarters was notified, and General Campbell, in Fedala, was called and directed to represent the Division at the parley. Similar reports later came from 7th and 15th Infantry Regiments.

One French officer, picked up by the Division Ordnance Officer and brought to the command post, carried a copy of orders issued by General Desré, commanding the Casablanca Division, directing the cessation of hostilities. This officer arrived under guard at 0620.

Units were notified of the possibility of an armistice. When General Patton arrived at the CP at 0655 with definite word of the truce, immediate orders were issued calling off the attack. Some elements of the Armored Battalion had moved to the line of departure and delivered a brief attack against an artillery position, but broke off when they received word of the situation.

Artillery attached to the 7th and 15th began registration, the former resulting in the death of several French soldiers, but aside from these instances, it is believed there was no other fighting or firing.

Naval dive bombers were circling above their carrier with ready lights on when word of the armistice was put through to them. They came in and circled the northeastern outskirts of Casablanca and were over their targets at H-hour, but apparently received word in time to avoid delivering the attack.

After General Patton had arrived at the advance Division CP at Villa Coigny and gave the order to cease hostilities, General Eagles, Maj. Albert A. Connor and Col. Harry McK. Roper left for Casablanca to arrange for the capitulation of the French. On the way they stopped at the 15th Infantry CP, picked up Capt. Burton S. Barr and 1st Lt. Walter Millar and took them to Casablanca with them. Captain Barr carried a United States flag into Casablanca. On the outskirts of town they met some French officers whom General Desré had sent to lead them into the French headquarters. The Frenchmen said they wanted to clear out some mines along the road before the party proceeded. The 15th Infantry sent some troops to assist with the clearing of the mines, and the group went ahead with a white flag on the French car. All the way into Casablanca the crowds lining the streets cheered and clapped.

At French headquarters General Eagles arranged with Admiral Ronarc'h to call Admiral Michelier and tell him to be present at 1030 to go to Fedala, where they were to be at 1130. Prior to 1030 General Anderson arrived and had a conference with General Desré and Admiral Ronarc'h. They discussed mutual release of prisoners, which was arranged; return of certain French troops from Casablanca to Mediouna; obtaining of American dead from the French morgue where they were being held, and the use of part of the European cemetery for burial of American dead.

General Eagles by this time had departed with Admiral Michelier for Fedala, where the meeting was delayed until the arrival of General Nogues from Rabat in the afternoon. Certain terms of armistice had been previously prepared by General Patton's staff, but when information was received from Lt. Gen. Dwight D. Eisenhower's headquarters concerning terms of the armistice arranged by Eastern Task Force they were found to differ so widely that the armistice could not be concluded in Fedala at that time.

However, hostilities were definitely ended with the exception of action by submarines in sinking our transports, and it is probable that the subs were German. Local movements of French troops were not restricted, and no incidents were reported between them and the occupying United States forces. Elements of Sub-Task Force Brushwood went into defensive positions in Casablanca and Fedala, and began the job of unloading remaining transports in Casablanca harbor. The operation was ended.

"Thanks for the birthday present, Andy!" General Patton had said to General Anderson when he stopped into the Division CP that morning. The second armistice, twenty-fourth anniversary of the first Armistice, and the General's birthday were all rolled into one on that November 11, 1942.

That afternoon and evening the Division CP was moved forward to the Villa Mas in Casablanca.

It is desirable to mention here the activities of some of the component units of the Division as well as those attached, in tribute to the yeoman service performed by them during the three-day operation. Some already have been mentioned. Elements of the 39th Field Artillery Battalion were in close support of the 15th Infantry. The battalion commander came ashore with the regimental commander at 1530 November 8, and a short while later led Battery A, which landed at 1600, to a new position three miles inland. This battery later displaced all its guns at once with a jeep and a civilian truck and on the morning of November 10 placed fire on the enemy at Tit Mellil positions and aided in destroying resistance at that point. Shortly after, with a liaison officer conducting the adjustment, the battery neutralized enemy cavalry firing from a building in a field. Several rounds of counterbattery fire fell on the battery in this action.

The other two batteries did not get into action in time to aid the advance. The battalion, however, was in position with eleven guns the morning of November 11 with survey and registration complete, ready to support the attack of the 15th Infantry when hostilities were called off.

Battery B, 9th Field Artillery Battalion, did salvage work along the beach until it landed two self-propelled 105mm howitzers the morning of November 11. These were immediately dispatched to the front and were in firing position at 0800, too late to participate in the action as the armistice had already gone into effect. A third gun was later landed but the fourth was lost in the surf.

The 1st Battalion Combat Team, 67th Armored Regiment, 2d Armored Division, commanded by Maj. R. E. Nelson, and consisting of an armored battalion reinforced by armored infantry, artillery, engineer and reconnaissance elements, landed one platoon of tanks from Company A the night of November 8. This platoon immediately proceeded to the high ground east of the railroad station at Fedala.

As the other elements of the unit were unloaded, they were assembled in the same general area. Due to the swell and the shortage of tank lighters, unloading of the transports *Arcturus* and *Biddle* was slow, but most of the vehicles were unloaded by 1900 November 9. The process was hastened by moving the *Arcturus* into the port of Fedala at 1300 November 9, and unloading directly onto the pier.

The mortar and assault platoons of Headquarters Company, and Battery A, 78th Armored Field Artillery Battalion, were actually the only United States troops who began the attack as scheduled on the morning of November 11, but as mentioned before, their fire on a gun position was broken off immediately upon receipt of word of the armistice.

On November 9 the Division Engineer and the Signal Officer checked the railroad telegraph in Fedala, located prospective water points and obtained wrenches from the town engineer, and reconnoitered for crossings of the Wadi Mellah. A detail under the 10th Engineer Battalion supply sergeant checked the city and beaches for engineer supplies. At about 1900 the battalion command post was set up in the port area of Fedala.

On November 10 details were sent along the beaches to salvage all possible equipment. Repair of the shunting-engine and railway in the port area was commenced under the Assistant Division Engineer. Power on the Fedala-Casablanca line was found to be interrupted. That evening the Division Engineer went to the Division command post to discuss plans for the demolition of water aqueducts and power lines leading into Casablanca, and the company commander and one platoon of Company C were ordered to stand by at the battalion command post to perform this mission, which was never found necessary. A water point was established at Tit Mellil.

The chief work of the 3d Medical Battalion, other than that of the collecting companies which were assigned to regimental landing groups, was in establishing and operating Division clearing stations. The work was made enormously difficult by the shortage of equipment and transportation. Coupled with this hampering factor was the burden of casualties caused by the sinking of four transports off Fedala November 11 and 12 probably by German submarines.

For this operation, the battalion was divided into amphibious collecting companies with the assault landing groups, and one such company under Division control; two clearing platoons; and headquarters and headquarters detachment, which remained with Group 3 at Camp Pickett. Equipment and supplies were reduced to those absolutely necessary for the amphibious operation. The Division Surgeon's office was likewise split into an "A" and "B" group, corresponding with the method used in landing the Division Headquarters.

The abbreviated collecting companies with the assault landing groups landed and functioned as prescribed, as did the two clearing stations, one at the Casino and the other at a winery about six miles southeast of Fedala, closer to the front. The collecting company, under Division control, was landed and attached to Regimental Landing Group 15 after it was committed to action.

The 3d Signal Company had a difficult time. Prior to 0900 November 9, when the first wire net was laid, all communications had been by runner, radio or direct liaison. The company came ashore on the afternoon of the 9th, and that night and the following night vehicles and equipment were landed. It had been impossible to land them before this. Until the evening of the 9th the company had only one jeep, three SCR-284 radios hand-carried, and hand-carried wire and telephone equipment. One radio team was attached to each of the assault landing groups and one radio operated as net control at Division Headquarters.

Maximum use was made of existing wire facilities such as open-wire lines and switchboards. One of two major problems was the destruction of lines by shelling and the other was the foreign construction of wire, switchboards and telephone circuits.

Elements of the 3d Quartermaster Battalion were embarked on three vessels: the *Leonard Wood, Rutledge,* and *Procyon.* The Division Quartermaster and eleven enlisted men landed at 0600 November 8 and at 1400 the officers aboard the *Rutledge* were sent ashore to meet the Quartermaster's party in the vicinity of the Casino. Reconnaissance was undertaken for Class I, II, III, and IV dumps. The office of the Quartermaster was established at La Compagnie du Port de Fedala adjacent to the west dock.

The 436th AAA AW Battalion was landed at Fedala November 10, although some officers and men had preceded it on November 8 and 9. The thirty-two 40mm guns on truck-drawn mounts were emplaced for the temporary protection of Fedala. The one officer and forty-eight men who remained aboard ship for unloading were among those torpedoed November 12 and suffered many casualties.

On November 11 Batteries C and D moved to Casablanca to provide antiaircraft defense of the airport while Batteries A and B consolidated their positions in Fedala.

The 36th Engineer Regiment (Combat), which underwent extensive training in the organization and operation of shore party installations before leaving the United States, provided these services for Sub-Task Force Brushwood. One battalion was attached to the assault landing groups, with the companies sub-attached to the battalion landing teams for initial phases of the landing.

The 2d Battalion, 20th Engineer Regiment, commenced landing in Fedala the afternoon of November 8, and by the next day had completed taking over police and local security missions in the town. Throughout the operation they continued to perform these functions. They relieved the 1st Battalion, 7th Infantry, which was enabled to go into regimental reserve.

The 204th Military Police Company suffered one of the most unfortunate disasters of the entire operation. Four landing craft filled with officers and men were disembarked at 0200 November 9, and before daylight had entered Casablanca harbor, instead of Fedala. The boats were in column about a hundred yards apart. Second Lt. Edward W. Wellman, who was in one of the boats tells about it:

We were supposed to land on the beaches of Fedala, but through error, the assault boats headed toward Casablanca, fifteen miles away, where the French fleet was quartered.

It was not until we were in Casablanca harbor that we realized that the fire toward which we were headed was not from oil tanks on Cape Fedala, but a French ship hit by our naval fire.

Two of our boats drew back.

The other two had drawn near the vessel, which, in the darkness, they thought was a United States destroyer.

I was in one. When the men in the other hailed the vessel, a foreign voice answered. They shouted back, "We are Americans."

A burst of machine-gun fire came from the destroyer, then only fifteen yards away, and the first burst fatally wounded the Captain (Capt. William H. Sutton, the Commanding officer).

Realizing that resistance was useless against a destroyer, the men stood up and threw up their hands—some even tearing off their undershirts and waving them.

The destroyer, perhaps thinking they were up to a trick, immediately opened fire with 3-inch shells.

Some men in the boat were killed by the shells and machine-gun bullets. Then Sgt. Claude Cunningham, of Memphis, Tenn., sent the survivors over the side into the water.

The French kept on pumping shells into the boat until it sank. Under international law, they could do this, since it was an assault vessel.

I was in the second boat, only twenty yards behind the first, and we shouted to the third and fourth boats to get away. Then we too turned and tried to escape by zigzagging.

The destroyer was pouring 3-inch shells our way.

A splinter took away the front of one of my shoes splitting two toes.

Another shell blew a leg off the coxswain.

The air was full of metal. A second lieutenant jumped up to take the wheel. A moment later he got a machine-gun slug through a thigh.

As I started to climb up for the wheel, a shell crossed my lap and blew up the motor. Burning gasoline spread over the boat so I gave the order for the men to go over the side. A destroyer picked us up.

The men in the first boat swam for the shore. Hundreds of French civilians waded out to drag them to safety. They chased away the Moroccan police and took off their own coats to wrap our dripping soldiers.

A French officer grabbed me and asked how many boats there were in the attack group. I told him I could tell nothing but my name, rank and number. The officer ran excitedly to the bridge. They apparently thought the whole invasion was being centered at Casablanca, instead of Fedala, and steamed back to port.

There were no doctors on the destroyer but our six wounded didn't let out a whimper . . . We were taken to a French military hospital jammed with their own wounded.

Lieutenant Wellman added that the commanders of the two boats which escaped, Lts. Arthur Erwin and Thomas W. Kelly, Jr., of the 20th Engineers, refueled and landed at Fedala Beach as originally planned.

The lieutenant and twenty-four men, the only survivors of the two boats which did not escape (four

Smashed landing craft litter the coastline.

other men were captured), reported to the Division CP at 1000 November 9 and were attached to the Provost Marshal's office for duty.

On the evening of November 11 between 1930 and 2030 the transport *Hewes* was torpedoed, presumably by a German submarine. About fifty casualties were received at the Casino clearing station at Fedala, most of the men suffering from exposure, cuts, and bruises. Up until Thursday evening the clearing stations continued to receive army casualties and wounded native and French civilians, including some severe injuries which involved amputation. Among them were cases of natives who had picked up fragmentation hand grenades and pulled the pins.

At about 1730 November 12 the *Scott, Bliss* and *Rutledge* were torpedoed. Some 1500 wet survivors, some of them terribly burned, came ashore by 2200. The quartermaster battalion at once issued at least 1200 woolen blankets to the clearing station, and issued food and coffee all during the night. The battalion surgeon assisted in attending the wounded, of which there were about 355.

That the 3d Infantry Division succeeded in accomplishing its mission in French Morocco is a tribute to the perspicacity of its commanders, and to the courage and tenacity of its soldiers. Consider these facts:

Some of the transports became lost, initially.

H-hour had to be changed virtually at the last minute, and all commanders did not receive this information.

Coxswains were not familiar with the coastline and did not become familiar with it even after several trips to the beaches. This resulted in repeated landings of units on the wrong beaches.

The bulk of the landing boats hit the rocks, rather than the beaches. Many of those boats that did not broach-to or capsize were left on the beaches to be hammered to pieces by the tide.

The original plan of landing supplies by small boats was virtually impossible because 219 out of 320 small boats were lost during the first day of operation.

Transportation was almost nil, seriously hampering bringing up those supplies that did get ashore, again traceable to the shortage of small boats.

There was no transportation for wire, curtailing

The United States Military Cemetery at Fedala, French Morocco, where 3d Division dead lie.

communications almost to the zero point, making imperative the maximum use of runner and radio.

Despite these handicaps, Casablanca *was* taken, and the United States had her port on the Atlantic Coast of French Morocco through which to move the men and material which played such a large part in the subsequent defeat of the Axis in Africa.

Outside reaction to the African landing was varied. Hitler publicly promised "terrible vengeance." Allied peoples were very enthusiastic, in many cases wildly optimistic. The invasion was hailed by many newspapers in the United States as the "Second Front," an event for which the occupied countries of Europe, the Russians, and the citizens of Britain and the United States had so long and eagerly waited. It was not.

Only a few leaders, civil and military, actually knew how many bitter months yet remained before the actual Second Front was finally to open in Normandy on June 6, 1944.

There yet remained much "blood, sweat, tears and toil," not only for the 3d Infantry Division but for all the United States Army in the Mediterranean Theater.

The bitter days of Kasserine and Faïd Pass and Hill 609 lay ahead for those in the gallant 34th Infantry and 1st Armored Divisions.

The "Fighting First" and the 9th Divisions were yet to participate in the bloody fights at El Guettar and Mateur.

Bloody Ridge in Sicily for the 45th Division.

Salerno for the 36th Division.

The desperate, disheartening, almost hopeless battling for the mountain heights of the Gustav Line in Italy—Mignano and Cassino.

The Anzio Beachhead.

Yet, the battle had been joined. It was against the French, true, who immediately after the Armistice became our staunch, and in time strong, ally. Still, the 3d Infantry Division, and all those who made the landings on the morning of November 8, had been blooded for the bitter battles that were yet to come. and from which they were finally to emerge triumphant.

That is why the landing at Fedala was so important in spite of its short duration. The revelation of the great number of mistakes made by an organization in its first action, and the overcoming of all difficulties to attain the final objective was prophetic of the future career of the Division in all its battles in World War II. The first action is usually the most important from the standpoint of the quantity of lessons learned, and that is why so much space has been devoted here to telling about Casablanca and Fedala.

Confident in its newly acquired maturity born of battle, the 3d Infantry Division looked ahead.

TABLE OF CASUALTIES*
North Africa
(Oct. 23, 1942 through July 9, 1943)

KIA	WIA	MIA	Total Battle Casualties	Non-Battle Casualties
66	234	11	311	3299

Reinforcements & Hospital return-to-unit personnel

Reinf		Hosp RTUs	
Off	EM	Off	EM
173	5004	127	4302

KNOWN ENEMY CASUALTIES

Killed	Wounded	Captured
Not recorded	Not recorded	9

*These figures were provided by the A C of S, G–1, 3d Infantry Division.

III
NORTH AFRICAN INTERLUDE

We Learn the "Truscott Trot" and Prepare to Invade Sicily

THE battle for Casablanca, like a brief, feverish nightmare, was over. Hardly had the men of the Division become accustomed to the sights and sounds of battle when they found themselves again faced with a long period of marking time. During the eight months before they were again committed to combat, however, their eyes were turned to the east where the slow, terrible drama of Tunisia was being enacted; and finally toward Sicily, where the Division itself was to participate in one of the great amphibious assaults in World War II.

Meanwhile there were the sights, sounds—and smells—of a fascinating new country to keep the men occupied. They learned about medinas—the old native towns which squatted anachronistically amid the modern cities of western Morocco; about French food and customs, French men and women; about mangy burros, wooden plows, Arab beggars; about gasogenes, chicory coffee, and the thousand subterfuges by which a people accustomed to colonial luxury attempted to shore up their living standards.

When Casablanca fell on November 11 at 0655, units of the 7th and 15th Infantry Regiments, poised on the outskirts of the city, entered, without firing a shot, and occupied the port area, the power plant, and other strategic objectives. Gazes airport on the southeastern edge of town was taken under protection by the 436th AAA AW Battalion. The two regiments took over guard duties in the city and port, while the 30th Infantry and 36th Engineer Regiments remained in Fedala to guard and operate the port under the supervision of a rear Division CP, commanded by Brig. Gen. William A. Campbell.

The main Division CP was established in the fashionable Anfa district in the southwestern outskirts of Casablanca. The CP itself was in the luxurious Villa Mas, home of Pierre Mas, wealthy publisher of *Le Petit Marocain* and other Moroccan newspapers. The nearby Italian and Japanese consulate buildings were also used for offices while the swank Anfa hotel and Villa Mirador on top of the hill were used as residential quarters for the staff.

During its stay in Casablanca the Division completed unloading the vessels of its convoy in Casablanca harbor, established liaison with French Army authorities, provided some security for the Casablanca area and straightened out problems of personnel and equipment occasioned by the landing, insofar as facilities permitted.

Transports which had brought the Brushwood force to Africa were still lying off the port of Fedala. As previously noted, one was torpedoed and sunk the evening of November 11, and three more the following evening. On November 13 the ships were moved into Casablanca harbor, and unloading began immediately, with at least one infantry battalion being constantly on duty to perform this work. The reason for the urgency was that another convoy was expected on D-plus-five (November 13). It actually arrived two or three days late, and lay off the port one day before being brought in.

From the close of the Casablanca operation until April 28, 1943, the 30th Infantry was destined to be scattered throughout French Morocco and western Algeria, serving as border, school, and line-of-communication guard troops.

The 1st Battalion, under command of Lt. Col. Fred W. Sladen, marched from its positions near Fedala on November 12 to Rabat, colorful, historical Moroccan port, where for almost a month its companies guarded the Rabat airport, the city of Rabat and all roads leading to the vicinity.

On November 12 the first issue of the *Daily News Summary* was published by the G-2 office, and this summary continued to appear daily until the Division began loading for the Sicilian operation. It is believed to be the first news sheet published by United States troops in the North African theater.

During the next week and a half there was very little training activity, units being occupied in guard and labor duties, care of equipment, completing reports on the operation, and taking in the sights of the strange new country.

Relationships with French military personnel rapidly changed from cool correctness at the moment of surrender to warm cooperation. Pro-Germans and Vichyites, of whom there were a small number, found it expedient to hide their sentiments as the great majority of French officers began studying American organization and methods, with the unconcealed intention of some day joining the battle against the "Boche." Capt. Donald H. Lieb was sent to Casablanca Division headquarters as American Liaison Officer, while Capt. Anthony du Pradel joined the 3d Division as French Liaison Officer.

A striking illustration of the new spirit was the visit of Major General Anderson to the headquarters of General de Division Henri Martin in Marrakech, in accordance with the desire of Major General Patton, Western Task Force commander. On the afternoon of November 17 General Anderson, accompanied by Col. Harry McK. Roper, Lt. Col. Edgar C. Doleman, Maj. Albert O. Connor, and Capt. William H. Ellsworth, flew to Marrakech by Army transport.

There the American party was entertained by General Martin and by his Excellency Hadji Thami El Glaoui, Pasha of Marrakech. Both the Pasha and General Martin welcomed General Anderson's party warmly, and vowed that North African forces would soon be in the fight on the Allied side. History knows how soon their promises were made good; before the year's end French troops had drawn German blood along the Grande Dorsale in central Tunisia.

Further to seal the rift caused by the brief hostilities, joint ceremonies for American and French soldiers killed during the operation were held in Casablanca November 23. Chaplains from the Division participated in both the Catholic and Protestant services. Meanwhile many of the Division's wounded had been evacuated to the United States aboard vessels of the D-day convoy, while nontransportables and those with superficial wounds remained behind in the French military hospital, which had been taken over by United States authorities.

Much of the administrative work during this period was done with the aid of equipment left behind by the German Armistice Commission, which had hastily evacuated the Villa Mas, Anfa Hotel and Villa Mirador. Mimeograph machines, paper, ink, stencils, notebooks, and office supplies of all descriptions virtually kept the Division offices going when American supplies were not to be had. Oddly, planning for the operation apparently had not contemplated that any administrative work would have to be done for a long time after the landing, and such things as American envelopes were very scarce for months following November 8.

On November 25 the Division CP was moved from Casablanca to the Casino in Fedala, a large, drafty wooden structure whose western windows overlooked the beaches on which the original landings had been made. The nearby Miramar hotel, from which the German Armistice Commission had fled on the first morning, was taken over for staff quarters.

Units of the Division made the trip from Casablanca to the Fedala area in a one-day march, as organic transportation was still on a slim amphibious basis. The move was made to get troops into training areas and away from Casablanca, which was already beginning to fill up with service troops.

(On November 27 the French fleet was scuttled at Toulon. In Tunisia Allied advance units were locked in combat with Germans around Tebourba, almost within sight of Tunis. The Germans were rapidly reinforcing, and hopes for the quick seizure of Tunis and Bizerte were approaching the vanishing point. But in Libya, the gallant British Eighth Army was rolling in high gear following its successful drive from El Alamein, October 23.)

The Division was not by any means on a non-tactical basis, even in Fedala. The favored German capability at the moment was to make a lightning move into Spanish Morocco, occupied by Franco troops, and attack out of the almost trackless Rif hills against the thinly-held Allied supply line running from Casablanca through Port Lyautey, Meknes, Fez, Taza and Oudjda to Oran and eastward. Terrain studies of western Spanish Morocco were initiated; order-of-battle of Spanish troops was plotted and brought up to date. The Division itself moved to Rabat on December 5, sending patrols up toward the Spanish Moroccan border, and checking strength and dispositions of French troops on border duty.

On December 4, 30th Infantry, less 3d Battalion, was transferred to control of Western Task Force, commanded by Maj. Gen. George S. Patton, and alerted for movement by air, rail and motor to Oudjda, French Morocco. Company C, commanded by Capt. George Abbott, was placed in air transports and flown to Oudjda to guard the airport there against possible German parachute invasion or land invasion through Spain and Spanish Morocco.

On December 5-6 the remainder of 1st Battalion was moved to Oudjda by truck and train to reinforce Company C and to strengthen the defenses of northern French Morocco and protect the vital line-of-communication supply line from Casablanca to Tunisia.

The 2d Battalion, 30th Infantry, and special units, less the platoon of Cannon Company with 1st Battalion, remained in the Fedala area until December 6, when they were moved by truck and train to Guercif, French Morocco, an old French Foreign Legion post used during the Rif Campaign of the French in the mid-twenties.

The battalion and regimental special units remained in the Guercif area, guarding the airport and maintaining motor, rail, and air patrols, the last consisting of one Division Artillery and one I Armored Corps cub plane in the Taza-Guercif-Taourirt-Spanish Moroccan border areas, and necessitating a daily flight of over 200 miles. The 2d Battalion patrols met 1st Battalion patrols at various contact points between Guercif and Oudjda.

Col. Arthur H. Rogers' staff had prepared an elaborate "staff study" of enemy capabilities, one of which was a paratroop attack from Spanish Morocco, against which an alert system was established, in addition to preparations made for dealing with land attack. A joint French-American system of guarding and patrolling, also under Colonel Rogers' command, was established in late February and March, continuing until April 19, when full responsibility was assumed by the French.

The 3d Battalion, 30th Infantry, under Maj. Charles E. Johnson, remained on guard and labor-battalion duty in the Fedala area from November 12 until the first week of January, serving one week in late December as Casablanca port battalion troops—a desperate measure adopted to speed ammunition and supply shipments from that crowded port to the hard-pressed Tunisian front.

In Rabat, Division headquarters was established in the Chamber of Commerce building, while the smart Balima hotel was taken over for staff quarters. Enlisted men were put up at the Grand Hotel. The troops, most of whom had marched from Fedala, were initially bivouacked in the outskirts of Rabat, but were soon moved to the cork-oak Forêt de Mamora about eight miles east of Sale, twin city of Rabat.

Because there were no administrative or base section troops in Rabat, the Division headquarters was split in order to establish a headquarters for Third Military Area, which included a part of western Morocco with Rabat as its capital. Col. Walter E. Lauer, Division chief of staff, was placed in command of the area headquarters, which administered nondivisional units and handled civil affairs.

On December 14, the Division opened a school for twenty-eight French officers and fifty noncommissioned officers, to train them in use of American weapons, motor vehicles and armor. The school was well-planned, competently run, and resulted in a thorough grounding of the French students in the subjects taught, as well as improved relationships between the two armies. The French quickly earned respect because of their knowledge of weapons and their excellence as artillerists. A second school, identical in subject matter but with new students, opened on January 11. This day there was a demonstration for the French press, in which all divisional weapons were fired.

December 20 saw another outburst of Franco-American solidarity, when the 3d Infantry Division, together with elements of the 2d Armored Division, and French troops, paraded through downtown Rabat. Large cheering crowds watched the parade, which was lavishly written up in the press.

On December 23 the Group Three convoy, which had remained at Camp Pickett, arrived at Casablanca. This convoy brought the Division's transportation virtually up to normal strength, and partially answered the query of a disillusioned Frenchman upon seeing the Division's earliest North African road march, "But where are all your big American trucks?" The four-ton prime movers of the medium artillery battalion and the big wreckers of the Ordnance Company looked good after several weeks of moving in half-tons and a tiny fleet of "two-and-a-halfs." Arrival of personnel sections, the APO, and other administrative units also took a great burden off the harassed tactical sections of unit headquarters.

(On the evening of December 30 an estimated six to ten enemy bombers came in over Casablanca and dropped several bombs, doing slight damage in the port and killing some Arabs in the New Medina. Two planes were reported shot down. Those who were in Casablanca at the time said the ack-ack was like a Fourth of July demonstration. Except for the Fedala torpedoings, this was the only direct enemy action against western Morocco during the Division's entire stay.)

On January 29 ceremonies were held in the lovely cathedral in Rabat for 1st Lt. Clement Falter, Catholic chaplain who was killed on the beach at Fedala. He was believed to be the first American chaplain killed in action during the war.

The 3d Infantry Division was present at the making of world history on Thursday, January 21. On this day President Franklin D. Roosevelt reviewed troops of the 3d Infantry and 2d Armored Divisions on the main highway leading north from Sale. He was accompanied by many dignitaries, civil and military, including his secretary, Stephen T. Early; Harry Hopkins, personal agent and adviser; Lt. Gen. Mark W. Clark, commanding Fifth Army; Maj. Gen. George S. Patton, Jr., commanding I Armored Corps; Maj. Gen. Jonathan W. Anderson, commanding 3d Infantry Division; Maj. Gen. Ernest Harmon, commanding 2d Armored Division; and Maj. Gen. Manton Eddy, commanding 9th Infantry Division.

The President, wearing a gray business suit and gray felt hat, with a black band around his left arm, in mourning for his mother, rode in the front seat of an army jeep down the long line of troops, which extended about one mile along the tree-lined highway, and which represented all separate units of the Division. General Clark and General Anderson were in the rear of the jeep during its progress past 3d Infantry Division troops.

Soldiers were in full field uniform with bayonets fixed, and heavy weapons and some organic transportation from each unit was lined up behind the troops east of the highway.

After passing the length of the column, the President met and congratulated heroes of the November landing operation from both the 2d Armored and 3d Infantry Divisions, and ate lunch at a mess prepared by Service Battery, 39th FA Battalion. Bands of the 7th Infantry and 3d Infantry Division Artillery took part in the ceremonies.

The visit was such a closely-guarded secret that no one, with the exception of those concerned with the planning, knew he was to see the President until shortly before his arrival.

As he passed the President returned the salutes of the units and spoke words of greeting to those along the way.

P-40 pursuit planes were over the line of march much of the time.

The President came by automobile with his party from Casablanca, arriving at the head of the 3d Infantry Division troops about 1140 and completing his visit at about 1205. A strong, chilly wind sprang up about the time the President arrived, so that those who took part were well-chilled by the time the Commander-in-Chief had departed around 1200.

A number of Army and Navy officers, in addition to those named, as well as secret servicemen, military police, press correspondents, and cameramen accompanied the President on his tour. The party left for Port Lyautey after lunch, presumably to put the President aboard a plane for Casablanca.

It was later learned that the President had attended the historic conference at the Anfa Hotel, together with British Prime Minister Winston Churchill. Basic plans were laid there for the 1943 offensive against the European continent, and this second of many well-publicized meetings between these two public figures made front page headlines in every newspaper in the world as the "Unconditional Surrender" Conference, so dubbed when Roosevelt and Churchill borrowed a famous phrase from General Ulysses S. Grant, and upon the President's insistence, announced that the Axis powers would feel the full force of Allied power until they should surrender unconditionally.

Guard of the conference area was assigned to 3d Battalion, 30th Infantry, under command of Lt. Col. Charles E. Johnson. From January 8 to 23 the battalion provided security for the area, inspecting houses in the vicinity and keeping a close check on personnel entering and leaving the Anfa.

Personages who attended the Conference read like a military Who's Who. The complete roster of the United States delegation included:

President Roosevelt;
General George C. Marshall, Chief of Staff;
Admiral Ernest J. King, COMINCH, USN;
Lt. Gen. Henry H. Arnold, Commanding General USAAF;
Lt. Gen. Brehon B. Somervell, Commanding General, SOS;
Mr. Harry Hopkins;
Lt. Gen. Dwight D. Eisenhower, Commanding General, NATOUSA and Allied Force Headquarters;
Lt. Gen. Mark W. Clark, Commanding General, Fifth Army;
Maj. Gen. Carl Spaatz, Commanding General, MAAF;
Lt. Gen. Frank M. Andrews, Commanding General US Forces, Middle East;
Mr. William Averill Harriman, Lend-Lease representative in London;
Lt. Col. Elliott Roosevelt, USAAF.

The British delegation, headed by Prime Minister Winston Churchill included:

Admiral Sir Dudley Pound, Chief of Naval Staff;
General Sir Alan Francis Brooke, Chief of the Imperial General Staff;
Air Chief Marshal Sir Charles Portal;
Vice-Admiral Lord Louis Mountbatten, Chief of Staff, Combined Operations;
Field Marshal Sir John Dill;
Lt. Gen. Sir Harold Alexander, Commander-in-Chief, Middle East;
Maj. Gen. Sir Bernard Montgomery, Commanding General, Eighth Army;
Sir Arthur Tedder, Air Chief Marshal, Middle East.
Also present were:
General Charles de Gaulle;
General Honoré Giraud.

On January 23 the Division G-2 and G-3 offices moved into the field, in preparation for the commencement of training.

On February 18 Assistant Secretary of War John J.

French artillery-men learn to service the United States 105mm howitzer.

Archbishop Spellman of New York at the grave of Lt. Clement Falter, Catholic chaplain killed on the beach at Fedala.

McCloy visited the Division CP in the field southeast of Port Lyautey. The 3d Reconnaissance Troop formed the guard of honor and the 3d Infantry Division Band provided music for the occasion. General and Special Staff officers of the Division, as well as General Anderson and unit commanders, formed a receiving line for the guests.

Meanwhile General Anderson had received orders re-assigning him to the United States. On February 20, following a ceremony at the Division CP, Col. Robert C. Macon was presented with the stars of a brigadier general. General Anderson said farewell to his staff. He left for the United States on February 22, and General Campbell assumed temporary command of the 3d Division.

(On February 16, the German 10th Panzer Division, which had made an undetected move north from the Mareth line sector, attacked inexperienced United States units deployed on and between three or four isolated hills west of Faid Pass. In two or three days the attack rolled past Sidi Bou Zid, Sbeitla, through Kasserine Pass—and the Germans were bearing down on the advanced Allied base at Tebessa, also the location of II US Corps headquarters. Whole infantry and artillery battalions were swallowed up in this enemy drive; scores of tanks were lost. The commander of a United States airfield, hearing a distant ammunition dump go up, interpreted this as a withdrawal signal, and ordered his planes destroyed and abandoned the field. The attack was finally halted by the combined action of tank destroyers and artillery units which had been rushed into the area southeast of Tebessa. But at least two United States divisions had suffered telling losses, and a great blow had been delivered to Allied morale.)

To make good the heavy casualties in men and material suffered in Tunisia—and the name "Kasserine" will long be remembered as the token of a black day—the 3d Infantry Division and 2d Armored Division were tapped for replacements. About 3,400 men, most of them volunteers, and all but 400 of them infantrymen, left the Division for Tunisia during the last week in February. The 3d sent its best men and officers, and thereby earned an enduring reputation for excellence among the units which it reinforced. Later, during preparations for the Sicilian landing, many of these men had a chance to come back to the 3d, and several hundred did so. Battle-wise and competent, they provided valuable stiffening at a propitious moment.

Maj. Gen. Lucian King Truscott, who had seen the fighting around Kasserine Pass as General Eisenhower's deputy, arrived March 7 to take command of the 3d Division, and brought with him Col. Don E. Carleton as Chief of Staff. One of General Truscott's first acts was to gather his officers together and tell them, in unvarnished language, what had happened in Tunisia. His cardinal point: the "Boche" were not supermen. They could be beaten by applying known principles of warfare with aggressiveness and daring.

On March 15 the 15th Infantry commenced its move to Fifth Army's Invasion Training Center at Arzew, there to begin amphibious training in preparation for the invasion of Sicily.

The training in Africa could not be confined merely to the normal Army Ground Force training, for the Sicilian operation was to be a combined operation, calling for the closest cooperation between ground, sea and air forces. "Intensive amphibious training" was the name applied to the program. It had to be intensive because time was growing short.

On April 28 the 30th Infantry rejoined the 3d Division for the first time since conclusion of the Casablanca operation and reassembled as a regiment at Arzew.

The complete Division had now closed in at Arzew. Here General Truscott introduced something new in training methods. Soon dubbed the "Truscott Trot," the innovation proved to be a marching speed of five miles an hour for one hour, four miles an hour for the next two hours, and three and one-half miles an hour for the remainder of a 30-mile march.

Companies D and I, 30th Infantry, commanded by Capts. Eugene A. Salet and Edward G. Paar, respectively, served as School and Demonstration Troops at Arzew, training other elements of the Division in amphibious tactics and simulating the enemy in maneuvers.

Other training at Arzew, which stressed coordination of all arms from airborne infantry to naval units, was emphasized from the beginning but physical conditioning was the immediate need. In addition to the speed marches there was log-rolling, obstacle-course running, bayonet training and training in hand-to-hand combat. Men who couldn't meet the standards were immediately eliminated.

The late President Franklin D. Roosevelt during the playing of the United States national anthem at a Guard Mount held by 3d Division troops in his honor during the Casablanca Conference. In the background are the late Gen. George S. Patton, Jr. and the Commanding Officer of Troops.

Camp Takala in the Forêt de Mamora near Rabat, named in honor of Pvt. Earl F. Takala.

Infantry and artillery also began to learn to work together more closely than ever before. Doughboys learned to follow artillery barrages closely, sometimes to within 100 yards, and thereby gained confidence in the accuracy of artillery during these firing problems.

Battle conditions were also simulated by using mortars and machine guns. There were naturally some casualties as a result of this training with live ammunition but it is undeniable that the training resulted in saving many lives later in combat.

Lessons that other United States soldiers were learning the hard way in Tunisia at this time were also taught the men. They became familiar with all types of mines and booby traps that the Germans and Italians were using in Tunisia and gained confidence in their ability to avoid or overcome these weapons.

There was also training with the Navy. This included practice landings and training in controlling fire of naval vessels by shore groups. Every type of landing craft, from LSTs and LCMs to rubber boats, was tested. This meant "dry-run," after "dry-run," until men of the 3d were ready to swear they had spent more time afloat than many of the men in the Navy.

Training in the firing of naval guns utilizing shore observation posts was a continuation, with improvements, of the methods that were first tried in the landings in Morocco. Picked groups of Division officers and enlisted men were assigned to work with Navy personnel, forming Shore Fire Control Parties. Under control of the 3d Infantry Division Artillery, their function was similar to that of the usual observation teams of field artillery.

Concurrent with the training, the Division had conceived and put into operation something new for staff work on division level, called a Planning Board. This method of preparation for a combined operation was designed to insure the utmost in cooperation between all branches of the services involved. It was named Joss Force Planning Board, after the code reference name for 3d Infantry Division Reinforced. It was headed by Lt. Col. Albert O. Connor, Deputy Chief of Staff; staffed by Lt. Col. Ben Harrell, A C of S, G-3; Maj. Grover Wilson, A C of S, G-2; Lt. Col. Robert D. Henriques of the British Army (a member of the Combined Operations Staff of Allied Force Headquarters); Lt. Col. Charles E. Johnson, A C of S, G-4; Maj. George H. Revelle, Assistant A C of S, G-4; Capt. Robert C. Shaw, G-4 liaison officer and Lt. Col. Bruce C. Price, Adjutant General. There were also representatives from 36th Engineer Regiment (C), 2d Armored Division, 3d Ranger Battalion and the Navy.

As time went on and the planning grew more detailed a number of other men, representing all component elements which go to make up a combined operations task force, were added to the Planning Board. It can truthfully be said that one of the main factors in what was to prove the phenomenally successful Sicilian campaign was the careful, coordinated planning of infinitely numerous details.

A vital part of the work was the gathering of intelligence of the enemy. Part of the success of the coming operation hinged on our knowing where the enemy was and in what strength; his available reserves, and the nature of his defenses. From the time the Division was given the mission of landing in Sicily until the last possible moment before D-day and H-hour, the G-2 Section worked night and day gathering and fitting together every scrap of information about the Axis

The 10th Engineers construct a road through the Division's bivouac area in the forest.

Colonel Thomas H. Monroe, commanding the 15th Infantry.

defenders. The bulky sheaf of papers that was called the Intelligence File finally included everything known about Sicily pertinent to the operation both from the military and civilian points of view.

Information on terrain, communications and customs of the people and towns was gathered. Information concerning enemy fixed defenses was compiled. The Navy supplied most of the information on beach defenses. This mass of information was then employed to build relief models for the benefit of commanders and leaders of units down to squads and platoons.

Early in the planning phase it was recognized that for a force the size of Joss (three times the normal strength of the Division with approximately fifty attached units) a special organization, other than the Division service troops, would be necessary for supply, evacuation and embarkation. This fact was emphasized by the directive that the force would be prepared to sustain itself on Sicily for from twenty-one to thirty days. It was obvious also that the formation of this special organization could not wait until the actual landing but that it must be formed if possible prior to the concentration of the force in the staging area.

Accordingly, the concept of supply control through three agencies was developed. These agencies were Force Depot, Near Shore Control, and Beach Group. Force Depot consisted of all the quartermaster, ordnance, chemical, medical, and signal supply troops attached to the Division other than the Beach Group. It was controlled by the Division Quartermaster, Col. B. M. James, who was assisted by an executive officer from G-4 and a specially selected officer for each of the Division Services.

The mission of Force Depot was to furnish to the Joss forces all those services and evacuation normally supplied to a division in the field by an Army headquarters. The depot was set up to operate on the Near Shore (Tunisia) exactly as it would be on the Far Shore of Sicily. It was capable of establishing truckheads and railheads anywhere on the island of Sicily and was charged with maintaining these installations at all times within fifteen miles of the Division rear boundary. This was to result in the unique but highly satisfactory arrangement of having the command of a higher echelon of supply and evacuation directly vested in the unit being supplied.

Near Shore Control was a provisional headquarters set up to plan, control, and supervise the embarkation of all organizations and to load all supply ships. It included the Division Embarkation Officer, the Division Transport Quartermaster (TQM) and was also the headquarters for all subordinate TQMs. This organization worked in close harmony with the corresponding organization of the Navy and with the 1st Embarkation Group of Eastern Base Section which was charged by higher headquarters with the responsibility of the supply and embarkation of Joss Force.

The Beach Group consisted of the 36th Combat Engineer Regiment, a battalion of the 540th Engineer Regiment (Port) and attached medical and supply troops.

Colonel Robert C. Macon, commanding the 7th Infantry.

Soldiers of the 3d Recon Troop during a training exercise in North Africa.

The purpose of this group was to organize three of the four landing beaches so as to facilitate the landing of the force, to unload supplies and establish dumps, and, upon capture of a port, to repair and operate the port.

As the downfall of the German and Italian forces in Tunisia approached, the Allied command decided to exploit the successes of II U. S. Corps by committing a fresh U. S. division.

At noon on April 30 the Commanding General, 3d Infantry Division, received a warning order from the Commanding General, I Armored Corps, to be prepared to move the Division immediately to the Tunisian zone of action, reporting upon arrival to the Commanding General, II U. S. Corps. Purpose of the move, and the mission of the Division, was to provide II U. S. Corps with fresh reinforcements in order to effect the rapid destruction of the Axis army then being pushed back against the Mediterranean coast. The Division was to be relieved from assignment to I Armored Corps upon commencement of its move.

Training was halted immediately. At 2200 April 30, the order was received to begin the movement. The Division's movement order had already been prepared and was issued immediately. The 15th Infantry moved out as scheduled at 0300 May 1, five hours following receipt of the movement order from higher headquarters.

The Division's order intended that all elements of the Division be on the road by 0900 May 2 and be concentrated in the Constantine area by the evening of May 4 or morning of May 5. However, difficulty was immediately experienced in placing this density of vehicles on the road, due to the requirements of other movements, and the Division was limited to 800 vehicles per day past a given point.

This practically doubled the time required for getting the Division on the road. RCT 7 passed its initial point at 1200 May 1, RCT 30 at 0800 May 2, and Division Headquarters at 0400 May 3, followed by Division Artillery (minus three light battalions), 10th Engineer Battalion and Division rear echelon.

Other units followed the same route and, with

Major General Lucian K. Truscott, commanding 3d Infantry Division.

minor exceptions, occupied the same bivouac areas on successive nights. By Friday afternoon, May 7, the Division was entirely concentrated in the Ghardimaou-Wadi Melis area just inside the Tunisian border.

On May 7, General Truscott visited II U. S. Corps CP and received oral instructions to move one combat team behind the 1st Infantry Division, prepared to pass through the 18th Infantry and attack the enemy on its front. At that time elements of the *Barenthin* regiment, which was part of the hastily-formed German *Manteuffel* Division, was dug in on the high ground eight miles southeast of Mateur and was causing the 1st Infantry Division considerable trouble.

In the early morning of May 8, RCT 15 left the Wadi Melis bivouac and moved to a new bivouac about fourteen miles south of Mateur, prepared to execute its combat mission. Meanwhile General Truscott had gone to the 1st Infantry Division CP to keep abreast of the situation. While he was there, at about 2300 May 8, he received instructions to move the remainder of the Division into the Ferryville area, and also received a new attack mission—namely, to attack eastward from the base of the Metline-Porto Ferina peninsula and mop up any remaining resistance. Combat attachments for this operation included the 13th FA Brigade, 5th Armored Artillery Group, RCT 39, 601st Tank Destroyer Battalion, and 106th AAA AW Battalion. The 15th Infantry was instructed to move to a position west of the junction of the Ferryville-Bizerte-Tunis highways, and the Division rear CP at Wadi Melis was instructed to order 7th Infantry to move immediately to the Mateur area.

At this time the only known enemy forces in the peninsula east of the Tunis-Bizerte road were elements of the *Barenthin* regiment which may have been withdrawn from the high ground west of the road, and a few tanks which had been driven back into this area by the 1st Armored Division. There were other pockets of unimportant enemy units, notably a company of the *Hermann Goering* Division on Djebel Ichkeul whose commander refused to surrender until one of his superiors personally ordered him to do so.

At 0730, May 9, the advance Division CP was opened in an olive grove one mile south of Ferryville on Route C-54. Reconnaissance had been sent to the Tunis-Bizerte highway to look for a truck turn-around, and at about 0800 the head of the RCT 15 truck column passed the Division CP headed for the front.

At this time General Truscott was with General Harmon, Commanding General, 1st Armored Division, on reconnaissance along the Tunis-Bizerte highway. The attack of the 1st Armored had made such progress that the attack of the 3d Infantry Division was unnecessary. At 0830 General Truscott reported the facts to Commanding General, II U. S. Corps, and upon instructions from II U. S. Corps, released the Division's combat attachments. An attempt was made to halt RCT 7 before it left Wadi Melis, but as it could not be reached until it had got within a short distance of its bivouac south of Mateur it was permitted to close in the new area.

On May 10 the entire Division, with the exception of the rear echelon, RCT 30, and certain service detachments, was concentrated in the Ferryville area. Still under the control of II U. S. Corps, the Division was given a mission of operating the PW cage west of Mateur, where approximately 38,000 prisoners were collected in three or four days, and of collecting captured matériel into designated salvage dumps and guarding it. One company of the 15th Infantry was placed in charge of the PW cage initially, but on the evening of May 9 the entire 3d Battalion, 15th Infantry, was detailed to take over the cage, and the battalion continued to run the cage until the Division departed for the Jemmapes–Philippeville area May 15. So ended the 3d Infantry Division's brief participation in the Tunisian campaign. Training was immediately resumed.

Training in the reduction of beach fortifications, and the Division's proposed plan of maneuver, were the two most important items on the docket. Jemmapes was not ideal for this work, since the area was covered with heavy underbrush, but at the moment it was the best area available.

As a general objective all the units prepared for a landing on defended beaches and an advance inland of about five miles. Here at Jemmapes four units were picked for the specific task of assaulting the beaches. They were: 1st Battalion, 7th Infantry; 3d Battalion, 15th Infantry; 2d Battalion, 30th Infantry and the attached 3d Ranger Battalion. Other infantry battalions trained to accomplish their missions of passing through the assault battalions and seizing inland objectives. One other battalion also underwent specialized training in street fighting. Most of the training of the assault battalions and of the street fighting unit was carried on at night.

On June 1 the Division began concentrating in an area near Lake Bizerte in northern Tunisia. Here it was joined daily by other units comprising Task Force Joss. Training at Lake Bizerte stressed co-ordination with the Navy in all phases of the operation, from the fire control of naval guns prior to and during the actual landing to the smooth disembarkation of troops on the beaches. This training of the combined forces proved effective as later shown by the manner in which all units worked during the actual operation.

Specialized training at Lake Bizerte included the removal of beach obstacles and mines, the attack against

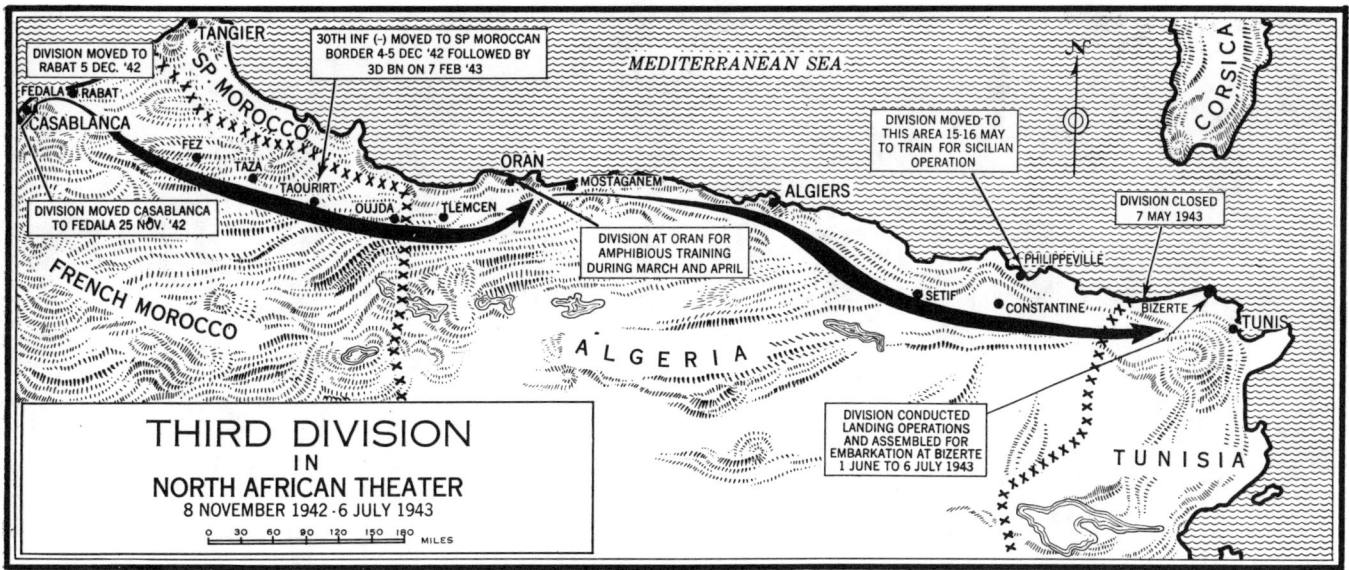

genuine, German-built pillboxes, mortar firing from landing craft, and the firing of grapnels to remove beach wire. Speed marches remained the rule to and from training areas.

After three weeks of this tough work the big dress rehearsal, Operation "Copybook," was held. It included nearly every unit in Joss Force and followed the actual plans for the landing as closely as possible. So realistic were the preparations for "Copybook" that the majority of men half believed the actual operation to be underway, and refused to be convinced otherwise until the morning for the landing found the landing craft still off African beaches.

This huge "dry-run" brought to light some faults which were corrected in time for the actual operation. There was increased confidence among men of the Division in the ability of the Navy to land all troops on the proper beaches. This spirit of harmony with the Navy was encouraged to the extent that a Division order stated that commanders of Naval craft would be invited by the 3d Division officer of each unit, representing the Naval officer's "opposite number," to a meal ashore at each army unit officers' mess.

Following the rehearsal the men were given a rest. Intensive training came to an end. Drill hours were shortened, and there was more time allowed for recreation. The speed marches and physical conditioning continued, however, in order to prevent a drop in the already high physical standards attained.

Never, anywhere, was a combat division more fit for combat . . . more in readiness to close with the enemy, than the 3d Infantry Division at this time.

The evening sun had dropped behind the tired, dusty green olive trees, but the heat driven into the ground by its piercing rays during the day was still radiating upward, bringing perspiration to the tanned faces of the men sitting in a large group toward the northeast edge of the Division bivouac area.

The group sat in a large semicircle. It was composed of every officer of the 3d Division. To the front a line of chairs conformed to the shape of the formation, and upon these chairs sat the ranking officers—the regimental commanders and the two brigadier generals. The majority of the officers sat on the upturned edges of their steel helmets.

It was not a particularly noisy gathering. The prevailing heat forbade exuberance. Rather it was a silent, somewhat speculative group. On O.D.-clad backs, white salt stains of dried perspiration indicated the exertion of the foregoing weeks.

A loudspeaker microphone had been placed in front of the group. A large red-faced man with a bushy moustache—Col. Don E. Carleton, Division Chief of Staff—stepped up to it. Before he began to speak a sudden rush of withering hot air struck the assembled officers.

"Gentlemen," said the Colonel, "the first Sirocco. A hot wind that sweeps north across the sands of the Sahara, with the heat of a furnace, to die over the Mediterranean. A good omen."

There was a slight murmur of laughter, which was quickly stilled. There was a silence. The Colonel fidgeted slightly, waited. Then he looked to his right, straightened, and called out, "Attention!" The officers scrambled to their feet.

"Gentlemen, the Commanding General."

General Truscott, heavy-set, steel-gray haired, took his place at the microphone. A beam of light from the dying sun shot through an opening in the olive trees and rested on his face, causing him to wrinkle his features in a characteristic grimace. He looked the entire assemblage over, slowly.

"Gentlemen," he began, speaking very deliberately,

Soldiers of the 3d Infantry Division march aboard the landing craft at Bizerte, Tunisia, which are to transport them to Sicily.

"we are on the eve of a great adventure. We are about to set forth upon the greatest amphibious expedition the world has ever known. We are going forth to engage the enemy and to defeat him. . . .

"I say to you, as I look upon you, that we are ready. Let us review briefly the training of the last few months. . . .

"You have engaged in five-mile-an-hour marching—which my staff officers tell me is commonly referred to as the 'Truscott Trot'—until you are now able to march great distances over long periods of time, and arrive at your destination ready for combat. . . .

"You have learned what it is to follow closely your supporting artillery, and your men have learned not to be afraid of it. . . .

"You have learned how to land on your assigned beaches, quickly disembark, and move inward rapidly to seize your objectives. . . .

"I repeat, we are ready. . . .

"On the eve of this great adventure, we find ourselves anticipating success or—failure? No, instead we anticipate success, or success beyond our utmost expectations. We do not know the word 'failure.' We know only that we will be successful, or that we will be successful beyond our utmost expectations. . . ."

It was nearly dark when the General ended his speech.

The following day was July 4. The 3d Infantry Division staged a review. Certain men were decorated for actions they had performed in the Fedala landing. This time General Truscott spoke for the benefit of the whole Division. The speech was shorter, less comprehensive. It was designed to put the men in the final aggressive spirit so necessary for combat.

It concluded: "You are going to meet the 'Boche'! Carve your name in his face!"

The Division commenced loading on its invasion convoys the following morning. The United States Army was about to teach the Axis an overwhelmingly crushing lesson in blitz warfare.

IV
SICILY

"In Which We Carve Our Name"

TROOP LIST—Operation "Joss" Third Infantry Division (Reinf)

Organization for Combat

1. *Hq & Hq Co, 3d Inf Div*
    Det CIC Pers
    Two IPW Teams
    Det Civ Affairs Pers
    Det Pub Relations Pers
    Censorship Det
    Boadcasting Det
    Naval Party (Liaison Only)
2. *7th Inf Regt*
3. *15th Inf Regt*
4. *30th Inf Regt*
5. *3d Inf Div Artillery*
    9th FA Bn
    10th FA Bn
    39th FA Bn
    41st FA Bn
    5th Armd FA Gp
    77th FA Regt
    2d Bn, 36th FA Rgt
    Btry B, 1st FA Obsn Bn (S&F) (–Flash Det)
    Survey Plat, Co B, 66th Engr Bn (Topo)
    Naval Shore Fire Control Parties
6. *10th Engr Bn*
    Det, 2658th Engr Co (Map Dep)
    3d Plat, Co B, 601st Engr Bn (Cam)
    20th Engr Regt
    815th Engr Bn (Avn)
7. *3d Ranger Bn*
8. *4th Tabor Goums*
9. *3d Cml Bn Mtz (Mortar)*
10. *3d Rcn Troop*
11. *3d Med Bn*
    Det, 3d Aux Surg Gp
    Vet Det, 8580th GG
    20th Malarial Control Unit
12. *3d QM Co*
    1st Plat, 48th QM Co
13. *3d Signal Co*
    2d Gen Assnmt Co, 196th Sig Photo Co
    Two Rad Rep Secs & one Tp Rep Sec, 177th Sig Rep Co
    Det, 128th R & I Sig Co
    Co A, 51st Sig Bn (–)
14. *Hq & Hq Btry, 105th AAA AW Gp, with attchd units*
15. *CC "A", 2d Armd Div (Hq & Hq Det), with attchd units*
16. *703d Ord Co*
    1st Plat, 235th Ord Co (Bomb Disp)
17. *Administration Center, 3d Inf Div, Rear Echelon*
    32d Fin Disbursing Sec
    APU No 547
18. *Far Shore Control*
    Force Depot, Beach Group and their attchd units
19. *Near Shore Control and attchd units*
20. *Air Officer, XII ASC*
    Administration & Liaison Det
    Air Support Parties
    Fighter Control
        Advance Landing Ground Party
        Hq Control and Plotting Sec
    Two radar dets, Prov AW Bn

SOMEWHERE in the gloomy interior of a captured enemy emplacement a bell rang. Correspondent Michael Chinigo of International News Service picked up the receiver of an Italian field telephone, and spoke a word of question, in Italian. A worried "brasshat," volubly querulous, had received a disturbing report that United States troops were then landing in force all along the Southern coast of Sicily, and this, signor, was most disquieting. Please, I beg of you, say it isn't so.

When the flood of words had subsided somewhat, Chinigo seized his opportunity to break in. In firm tones he assured his questioner that all was quiet, the situation well under control. The "brasshat," his fears allayed, hung up. Chinigo, amused, did likewise. Then he went out to watch the LSTs unload.

Unfortunately for the Italian general's later peace of mind he had been only too well informed the first time. At 0200 that morning, July 10, 1944, the seaborne invasion of Sicily had commenced. The investment of the outer fringe of *Festung Europa* was underway. It was to carry the Allies almost nonstop into the inner bastions of Germany's defenses, eliminating almost parenthetically along the way the junior Axis partner, Italy. It was to pile on an additional crushing loss of prestige to a nation which had two months before lost an entire army in the tip of Tunisia. It was to give the Allies an invaluable base for further operations in the Mediterranean

Theater, including the final, brilliantly executed invasion of southern France.

The wresting of Sicily from the Axis meant much more than the mere seizure of enemy territory. A popular military cliché has it that "he who controls Sicily controls the Mediterranean." Since the days of the ancient Romans and Cathaginians the island has been the traditional stepping stone from Europe to Africa, and its people have known many conquerors. One inherited characteristic of the Sicilians, springing from the constant infusion of the warrior blood of new races, is the fiery Latin temperament, unsurpassed for sheer intensity anywhere on the Continent; the temperament which has given the country so much colorful notoriety and internal dissension.

In this war Great Britain held Gibraltar, Suez, and Malta, but Axis-controlled Sicily in the center of the Mediterranean was a constant threat to Allied shipping. From Italian naval bases at Palermo, Syracuse and Catania, packs of German and Italian submarines, plus a few surface vessels, constantly harassed Allied ships carrying supplies for operations against the enemy in Egypt, Libya, Tripolitania, and Tunisia. Ships bearing cargoes destined for the Near, Middle, and Far East continually ran the gantlet of enemy air squadrons whose fields were on Sicily. Sicilian-based Axis bombers made little Malta a hell on earth—"the most bombed spot in the world"—at least up until the time the RAF and AAF intensified their pilgrimages to Berlin.

A lesser reason for the invasion of Sicily was economic. Despite its square miles of mountain "badlands," the island is fertile and its people primarily agricultural. Deprived of its possession the Axis aggressors would lose not only a large quantity of tribute in the form of agricultural products, levied annually against the populace, but also a certain amount of mineral resources and industrial products, a triple blow not necessarily crippling, but not helpful to the industries of Italy and Germany, battered as they were even then by the Allies' aerial blows.

It is only three miles across the Straits of Messina (where, according to Homer's Odyssey, the twin monsters Scylla and Charybdis jealously mount guard against unwary voyagers) to the Italian province of Calabria. The capture of Sicily would aid the Allies in gaining a literal "toehold" on the boot of Italy. Possession of Sicilian airfields would mean increased bombing of targets in southern Europe, extended fighter range. When the nearest fighter bases were in Africa, long-range bombers of the MAAF were obliged to fly unescorted over long, dangerous round-trip missions and their casualty figures reflected the need for fighter escort. Possession of the airfields was also vital to the eventual support and fighter protection of our landings on the Italian mainland.

Thus it was that the pre-dawn of July 10, 1943, found the 3d Infantry Division, powerfully reinforced, forcing its second assault beachhead in World War II, in the region of Licata, near the center of the south Sicilian coast.

We were traveling in excellent company. Several miles to the East in the vicinity of Gela the 1st U.S. Infantry Division established its foothold on the island. To the right of this force was a combat team of the 9th U.S. Infantry Division and the entire 45th U.S. Infantry Division. The latter division, shortly to prove itself a first-class assault formation, was previously untried in combat. Its mission was to drive inland and contact the left elements of the Eighth British Army which landed between Pozzalo, around Cape Passero, and northeast to Syracuse.

On the night of D-minus-one paratroopers of the 82d U.S. Airborne Division landed behind enemy lines. Their primary mission was to seize an enemy airfield, then to destroy enemy communications and harass the enemy's attempts to move up reinforcements. In its initial "jump in anger" many of the paratroopers were dropped in locations widely scattered from each other, bearing little resemblance to previously scheduled DZs (drop zones) because of faulty navigation on the part of the C-47 crews. Worse than this, however, was the tragic occurrence when the twenty-three fully-loaded transports were shot down off the Gela area. Due to failure in coordination, a large flight of C-47s flew over friendly naval vessels which had just undergone a severe enemy air attack. The recognition code for the night of July 11-12 was "red-red," two colors indistinguishable from the streams of upward-bound anti-aircraft tracer. The AA gunners, quite naturally assuming that another enemy bombing was in progress, turned the full force of their combined firepower on the low-flying, lumbering '47s. Many of the paratroopers and plane crews never had a chance to escape the vicious welter of hot metal.

Principal military objectives of the 3d Infantry Division after clearing the beaches, were the port of Licata and the nearby airfield. Licata, a town of approximately 30,000 in normal times, lies near the center of the south Sicilian coast at the mouth of the Salso River. To the west, paralleling the coast, is a long steep ridge, topped by Monte Sole. On the eastern end of the ridge is Castel Sant' Angelo, a relic of former days and a prominent landmark. (Future visitors in Rome, veterans of Sicily, were destined to wonder at the familiar ring to the name of the Eternal City's famous relic and tourist attraction, the Castel Sant' Angelo.) Except for this ridge the ground around Licata is flat or low and rolling for a radius of about six miles, with a few minor hills immediately to the northeast of town.

Surrounding the Licata plain is a ring of hills ranging in height from 1200 to 1600 feet. There are many rocky ridges and steep-walled ravines in these hills which favor the defense, but as later events showed, the enemy was never able to make full use of this peculiarity of terrain. The port itself is a small one, completely enclosed by three breakwaters. The airfield was an uncompleted strip about two miles nothwest of the town. This field had never been used by the enemy, but was a potential base for speedy development and exploitation.

The invasion convoy sailed in three echelons. The first echelon left Bizerte on July 6, and made a short stopover at Sousse, Tunisia. The fighting doughboys here got the chance to stretch their amphibious legs and to undergo a few limbering-up speed marches, after which they reembarked. The medium speed convoy of LSTs and a slow convoy of LSTs composed the other two echelons, and set sail July 7. The three convoys took separate routes for purposes of deception, as well as for achieving a successful compromise between the varying speeds of the type of ship in each echelon. The final rendezvous was made on July 9, off Gozo Island, near Malta.

For a short time then, it seemed as though the gods of Fortune were leagued against the Allies. Perhaps the ancient deities of the Mediterranean were determined that the upstart mortals should at least taste of the type of weather which those all-powerful beings could invoke even over that notably calm, watery arena of age-old naval battles. For the sky clouded over, the wind commenced to blow, and the sea began acting as though it were *en rapport* with its mammoth sister to the west. The elements seemed bent on proving themselves "mightier than them all." The success of the entire operation hung by a thread. It seemed for a space as though the months of laboriously-conceived work and planning might be entirely wasted, and more terrible yet it appeared the entire invasion convoy might enter battle under absolutely adverse and highly hazardous conditions to the jeopardy of thousands of lives. The brand-new landing craft were as yet untested. There was one thought paramount in the minds of every person aboard each of them: "Will they be able to withstand the fury of the storm?" Luckily they were.

An apocryphal story has been told in at least one place of Seventh Army Commander Patton's decisive conference with his meteorological officer.

"How long will this storm last?" asked the General.

"It will calm down by D-Day," replied the weatherman.

"It had better," replied the General.

Despite the unspoken promise contained in General Patton's words (or perhaps because of it) the weather miraculously reverted to its habitual calm just in the nick of time.

In the 3d Division fleet a master stroke by Rear Admiral R. L. "Push-'em-in-closer" Conolly recovered the time lost by the LCTs in the storm. They were ordered to take a new and much shorter course, which they did, and the flotilla did not stop until it reached the Sicilian beaches—on time within seconds.

There were many seasick boys looking forward to seeing land by this time, even hostile land. Perhaps the reason for the untamed fury with which the 3d Division hit the Sicilian beaches can be traced partly to the fact the majority of soldiers were so damned sick that the prospect of hastening what seemed a lingering death was almost welcome. The thought that we were soon to be fighting against the very persons whose former aggressions had indirectly caused all this misery was almost certainly a strong contributing factor to the forbidding mood of the invaders. There was little mercy, and likewise a negligible quantity of thought, wasted over the coming doom of many Italian and German defenders.

The final estimate of enemy strength in Sicily that could be mustered against the Division at H-hour or thereafter included:

> 207th Coastal Division, in the Licata area;
> 26th (Arietta) Division, in the vicinity of Sciacca, 65 miles west of Licata;
> 4th (Livorno) Division, at Caltagirone;
> 54th (Napoli) Division, believed near Catania;
> 26th (Aosta) Division, in the Marsala-Trapani area;
> Army and Corps troops, mainly manning heavy guns around Caltanissetta, Campobello, Agrigento, and Porto Empedocle;
> About 34,000 German troops known to be in the vicinity of Palermo, and on the major airfields.

Enemy air strength in Sicily and Italy was estimated at 945 modern-type combat planes, of which in late June only 552 were believed serviceable. In addition there were several hundred obsolete German and Italian planes of various designs.

From the foregoing estimates of enemy strength on land and in the air, it appeared that the defenders of Sicily could put up a stubborn fight. The type of fortifications and annotation of defenses seemed to justify the expectation on our part of a tenacious, all-out battle to get ashore and hold.

By 0135, July 10, the Division Headquarters Ship, USS *Biscayne,* had dropped anchor off the coast. It was safely and correctly assumed aboard the *Biscayne* that

The town of Licata, Sicily, near where the Joss Force assaulted the beaches.

all other craft had reached their areas and were preparing to disembark the troops, since the units had been instructed to break radio silence and report only in case of emergency.

Just before 0200 heavy gun and antiaircraft fire was heard coming from the direction of Gela, where the 1st Division had met resistance. Despite a column of German tanks which at a later hour actually drove between two regiments of the 1st, the division succeeded in repulsing the attack, to secure firmly its beachhead.

As the 3d Infantry Division was preparing to debark its troops, searchlights from Licata and the surrounding heights to the west suddenly blinked on, and their dazzling beams swept over the sea off Yellow and Blue Beaches. From the bridge of the *Biscayne* the craft in the transport areas stood out in dark, ominous relief.

Without warning four searchlights converged on the *Biscayne*. The ranking naval officer made a quick decision to open fire, but withheld execution of the order to confer with General Truscott. Outcome of this brief parley was the abeyance of fire until the enemy should open up in proof that the ship had been observed. Amazingly, the lights soon went off. It seems apparent that although the *Biscayne* had been caught in the cone of four powerful searchlights for ten minutes at a distance of only 7,000 yards it had not been seen. At least the shore batteries did not fire, and the landing operation went forward as planned.

At H minus 30 minutes units of the U. S. Navy shattered the fearful silence of the black morning, when the two cruisers, USS *Brooklyn* and *Birmingham,* protected by a part of the invasion fleet's destroyer force, steaming up and down the coastline, began a pre-arranged bombardment of enemy positions in a diversionary demonstration outside the assault area in the vicinity of Agrigento. After the assault waves of the division had landed, the cruisers mentioned stood off the assault area firing on call at pre-arranged targets, while the U. S. destroyers *Buck, Ludlow, Roe, Swenson, Edison, Woolsey, Wilkes* and *Nicholson,* together with nineteen smaller British craft, curved shoreward, firing as they went, to destroy targets as requested by the infantry and cover its landing.

By 0340 reports began sifting in to the headquarters ship that flotillas were all in proper position and that small boats were off and away. This was followed by reports that small craft had landed and were returning. At 0440 a message was sent to General Patton to the effect that the first waves had landed on Blue, Yellow and Red Beaches.

No word had been received from Green Beach. At 0500 the Division Artillery Air OP aboard an LST was contacted by radio and told to have a Cub plane stand by. Through a misunderstanding two Cubs took off from the improvised flight deck and were on the way inland by daylight. Shortly afterward one Cub observer reported that our troops could be seen climbing the hills back of Green Beach. For two hours these planes, piloted by 1st Lts. Oliver P. Soard and Julian W. Cummings, continued to spot enemy artillery positions and report progress of our troops.

Prior to the landing, seven areas were thoroughly analyzed for defenses. These included the four beaches, Blue, Yellow, Green, and Red, on which the landings actually were made. The entire width of the Division zone, including the all-important terrain to the flanks, had been subdivided for purposes of study and planning into seven parts, although not so designated by either number or color. Enemy static defenses consisted of beach obstacles, barbed wire, pillboxes, trenches, fortified blockhouses, and antitank ditches. Defending these were machine-gun positions, rifle pits, emplaced antiaircraft guns, and registered artillery batteries.

The initial assault was carried out by only four battalions: one from each regiment and the 3d Ranger Battalion, attached. The 2d Battalion, 30th Infantry, landed on the right over Beach Blue; 3d Battalion, 15th Infantry, landed on Beach Yellow. The 3d Ranger Battalion went ashore at Beach Green, and 1st Battalion, 7th Infantry, landed on the left at Beach Red.

During this time, commencing shortly after 0100, enemy planes were over the flotillas, periodically discharging red flares. Brilliant yellow chandelier flares followed, but no other hostile action was taken at that time.

Greatest difficulty in landing was experienced by Lt. Col. Roy E. Moore's 1st Battalion, 7th Infantry, where machine-gun and artillery fire were received for some time. The attackers began landing at 0400 and received no fire until they had crossed the beach and reached the foot of the bluff rising from it. Then the enemy opened fire. The men ran through gullies to the top of the bluff and within an hour had overcome resistance in the immediate beach area. Over this beach the Navy was able to claim one of a number of valuable assists. In one instance, naval gunners on an LCI slugged it out with a couple of enemy machine-gun nests above the beach and destroyed both of them. Then enemy 47mm guns on the left flank scored hits on two LCIs. Naval guns promptly got the range and silenced the enemy position. By 1000 7th Infantry had taken all its objectives.

The 3d Infantry Division Artillery also took part in the fight on Red Beach. By 0630, 10th Field Artillery Battalion, commanded by Lt. Col. Kermit L. Davis, with the 62nd Armored FA Battalion and Battery A, 9th FA Battalion, had landed and gone into position from 500 to 1500 yards inland. Once set up, these guns fired on every target the observers could spot for them, including enemy mortars, infantry, an enemy gun battery, machine-gun nests, and an OP.

The 3d Ranger Battalion began disembarking on Green Beach at 0300, achieving tactical surprise. The men were able to cross the beach and pass through a wide band of defensive wire before the enemy was aware of the situation. When he opened fire the gun flashes gave away locations of the enemy weapons and the Rangers were easily able to subdue them.

Lt. Col. William N. Billings' 2d Battalion, 15th Infantry, following the Rangers, landed without opposition, reorganized immediately and begun pushing eastward along the Monte Sole hill pass toward Licata. At 0735 a United States flag, carried specifically for that purpose, was raised over Castel Sant' Angelo. Then, after the naval shelling of Licata, the 2d Battalion and other regimental units together with the Rangers approaching from the east entered and captured the town by 1130. The first major objective was taken.

The 3d Battalion, 15th Infantry, commanded by Lt. Col. Ashton H. Manhart, made its regiment's initial assault over Beach Yellow, commencing at 0345. The landing was not opposed until the boats actually beached, at which time the enemy opened fire with machine guns and small arms. The battalion quickly cleared the beach defenses, seized the spurs overlooking the beach, and then reorganized to move west. The battalion entered Licata at about 1130, at about the same time 2d Battalion and Rangers entered from the west and 1st Battalion from the north.

The 1st Battalion, commanded by Maj. Leslie A. Prichard, landed at 0445, pushed a mile inland to its assembly area, then advanced on its first objective, the high ground immediately northeast of Licata at 0600. The objective was reached at 0800 and at 0930 the battalion received orders to advance on Licata. One platoon, however, was detached to protect the un-

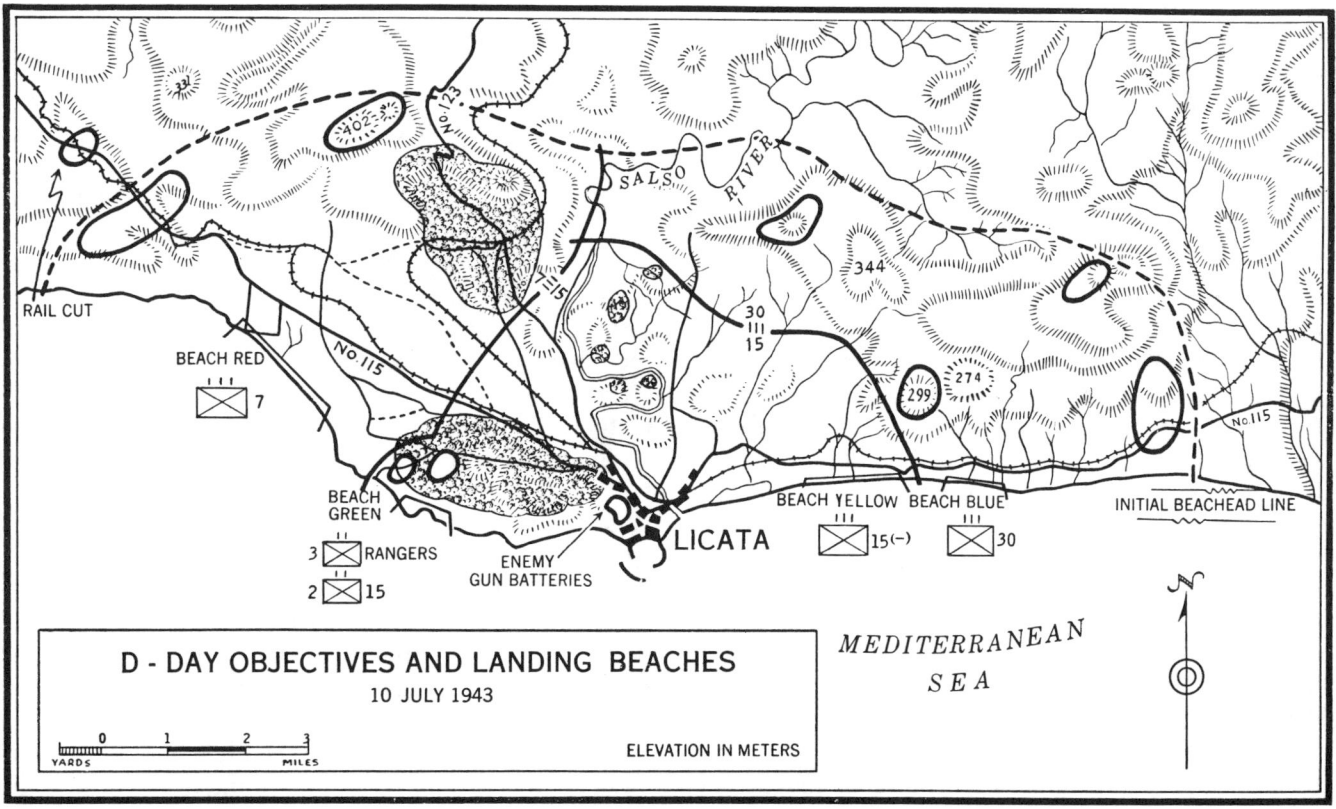

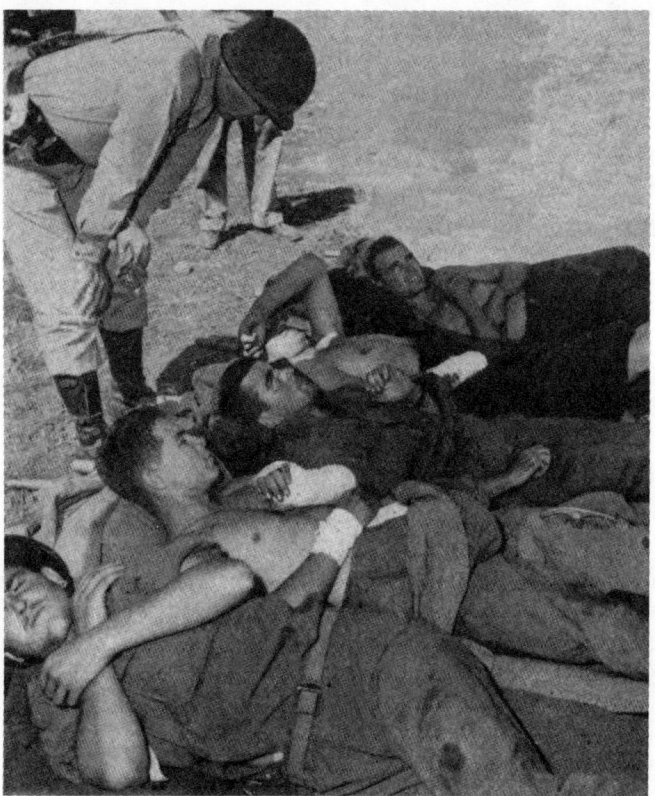

Lieutenant-General Patton, CG Seventh Army talks with wounded soldiers on the beach.

damaged bridges over the Salso River and the remainder of the battalion forded the Salso about two miles upstream from the town and moved on Licata from the north.

The assault group for Beach Blue—2d Battalion, 30th Infantry—began landing at 0330. Like the other assault waves this unit, commanded by Lt. Col. Lyle W. Bernard, achieved tactical surprise. The force, however, soon met rifle and machine-gun fire from pillboxes on the beach and artillery fire from a strongpoint east of the beach. Prearranged naval gunfire soon neutralized this enemy artillery. The battalion, employing its 10-man antipillbox squads, cleared the beach head in its sector and advanced against the enemy strongpoint at Poggio Lungo, which it occupied at 0845. Meanwhile, the 1st and 3d Battalions, 30th Infantry, commanded by Lt. Cols. Fred W. Sladen and Edgar C. Doleman, respectively, landed approximately on schedule and moved inland to take and hold their initial objectives.

The same held true for 2d Battalion, 7th Infantry, under the command of Maj. Everett N. Duval, and 3d Battalion, 7th, commanded by Lt. Col. John A. Heintges.

All units received necessary field artillery support at the right time. With minor exceptions, all battalions of Division Artillery landed on schedule and went into position, firing where and when needed. In addition, Cannon Company, 30th Infantry, and Company I, 66th Armored Regiment, both supporting the 30th's 2d Battalion, moved in and destroyed several enemy strongpoints.

Before evening the eight-by-fifteen-mile beachhead had been secured, and supplies and reinforcements were pouring in through the captured port of Licata. Aggressive reconnaissance already was being pushed to the front and flanks. Nearly 3000 prisoners, preponderantly Italian, were taken by the Division on D-Day

The next twelve days were to be hectic ones for the 3d Division. Under the influence of the personalities of two hell-for-leather generals, one the ex-cavalryman Truscott, the other the ex-tanker Patton, the Division was about to "carve itself a slice of Sicilian real estate" from Licata to the capital city, Palermo, on the north coast; a distance of over 120 miles.

On July 11, D-plus-one, two regimental combat teams, the 7th and 15th, each captured a town. The 7th took Palma di Montechiaro against uncertain Italian resistance, and the 15th, Campobello. By seizing Palma, the 7th forced the enemy to withdraw in the direction of Agrigento and also opened up another north-south highway for the Division.

In the fight for Campobello the 15th Infantry met the first organized German opposition in Sicily. The regiment broke through this resistance to take the town, destroying in the process two Italian 90mm. self-propelled guns and an Italian light tank. Following seizure of Campobello the 15th contacted Combat Command A (CCA) of the 2d Armored Division at Naro and the 30th Infantry at Riesi.

Two spectacular actions took place on July 11, one credited to the 30th Infantry, the other to an officer of the 15th Infantry. The 30th was holding its original position after the landing, but was concentrated and alerted for movement, when a patrol was sent out with the mission of contacting Headquarters, II Corps at Gela. This group, consisting of one rifle platoon, a platoon of medium tanks, and two platoons of the regimental Cannon Company, set out eastward along the coastal road.

En route the patrol fought its way through three enemy positions, taking 400 prisoners. The patrol leader, Maj. Lynn D. Fargo, contacted General Patton, commanding the Seventh Army, at Gela at 1430 and began the return trip. On the way back the patrol reduced another enemy strongpoint and captured an additional 153 prisoners.

It was the same day, July 11, that 2nd Lt. Robert Craig, a member of the 15th Infantry, performed the action for which he was later awarded the Congressional Medal of Honor. It was at Favarotta that Lieutenant Craig's company was blocked by fire from a concealed gun. With the aid of Cpl. James Hill, Craig located the gun and crawled to within thirty-five yards of the emplacement before the enemy saw him. The lieutenant shouted for Hill to cover him, while he ran head on through the machine-gun fire until he reached the gun, whose three-man crew he killed with his carbine. This allowed the company to continue the advance. Later in the day Craig and his platoon found themselves on a slope on which there was no cover, ambushed by a large group of Germans. Craig ordered his men to withdraw to the cover of the hill crest while he himself charged forward about seventy-five yards, and opened fire. He killed five enemy and wounded three more before he fell under the concentrated fire of an estimated one hundred enemy guns.

By midnight of July 12 the entire Division and attached units had completely reorganized and was systematically enlarging the beachhead. Units boldly moved forward, capturing several towns and establishing strong contact in all sectors. The 7th Infantry had contacted CCA near Naro; 15th Infantry had captured Ravenusa and Sommatino; the 3d Battalion 30th Infantry had taken Riesi, and the regiment minus 3d Battalion occupied Naro. CCA took Delia and Canicatti. In the action around Naro the 30th Regiment destroyed and captured four 40mm AT guns and considerable small arms and equipment.

Two other accomplishments had been marked up by midnight of D-plus-two. The first LCIs that had landed were back again, this time with material and follow-up troops, and men of the 815th Aviation Engineer Battalion had begun work on the uncompleted German landing strip outside of Licata.

The following day, July 13, saw the beginning of one of the many spectacular moves of the 3d Infantry Division in Sicily. General Patton told General Truscott that he did not desire a major effort made at this time to capture Agrigento, but that he had no objection to a "reconnaissance in force." To this reconnaissance mission, then, General Truscott committed the 7th Infantry Regiment, with the reservation that it was not to become involved in a battle from which it could not be readily withdrawn.

The 1st and 2d Battalions of the 7th occupied high ground east of the Naro River and patrolled to the front while the other battalion remained in assembly northwest of Palma di Montechiaro. The advance was begun on July 16, with 2d Battalion moving around to the north of Agrigento and 1st Battalion attacking directly to the west, crossing the Naro River north of the main highway. At 1430 3d Battalion entered the scrap, attacking west along the highway toward Porto Empedocle.

Although communications between 2d and 3d Battalions were sketchy and out completely much of the time, the gamble succeeded largely because of the speed and daring of the maneuver. The appearance of 2d Battalion on the high ground north of Agrigento took the defenders by surprise and 3d Battalion met little opposition in its rapid advance west along the highway.

The 3d Ranger Battalion, which had moved out ahead of 2d Battalion, 7th Infantry, was able to circle Agrigento on the northeast and enter Porto Empedocle at 1900 against little opposition en route. The 3d Battalion, 7th, however had been in Porto Empedocle since 1430, entering the town from along Highway 115.

The 1st Battalion advanced directly into Agrigento from the east, overcoming scattered strongpoints and engaging in some street fighting. The city was captured and outposted by 0300 July 17.

While success of the maneuver was in great measure due to the audacity of its planning and the speed and endurance of the infantry, credit is also due to the attached artillery units who worked with 7th Infantry during the time. For at 1410, July 16, large enemy reinforcements were spotted by artillery observers moving by motor toward Agrigento. Guns of the 10th Field, 58th and 65th Armored FA Battalions, and 77th FA Regiment caught the convoy coming down from Aragona and when the shooting stopped it was apparent that the convoy had been broken up with an estimated loss of fifty vehicles and at a cost to the enemy of about a hundred killed and wounded.

The capture of Agrigento gave the Division about 6000 prisoners, and the most important city in that part of southern Sicily, plus the port of Empedocle. It also cost the enemy besides human casualties, many destroyed transports and guns, about fifty assorted field pieces and a hundred vehicles captured.

During the fight for Agrigento another member of the Division, 1st Lt. David C. Waybur of the 3d Reconnaissance Troop, performed the action for which he was later awarded the Congressional Medal of Honor, marking up the second of two such caliber deeds within one week. While leading a three vehicle patrol on a volunteer mission to contact an isolated unit of Rangers, Waybur found himself and his group waylaid at night by four Italian light tanks. Men of the patrol immediately opened fire with their machine guns, despite the fact they were combating armor, and soon most of them were wounded. Waybur, himself severely hit, took up a tommy gun and, standing but a few yards from the leading tank and in its direct line of fire in bright moonlight, opened up. By firing through the

"Chips," the beloved war-dog of the 30th Infantry, later the possession of the Division MPs.

ports he killed two of the crew. The driverless tank veered erratically and toppled over into a creek bed. The patrol remained in position all night. Just before reinforcements arrived the tanks withdrew.

Between the capture of Agrigento on July 17 and 1800 July 18 when Joss Force, which was the 3d Infantry Division reinforced, was dissolved, the Division and its attachments also captured Serradifalco, San Cataldo, and Raffadali. As a result of the breaking up of Joss Force on the 18th the Division reverted to its normal combat strength, plus a tabor (about a battalion) of Moroccan Goumiers. At the same time Joss Force was dissolved the Division was incorporated into Provisional Corps.

The first order from Provisional Corps directed the advance on Palermo. For battalions of the 3d, taking a short rest following the quick slashes northwest from Licata in the harrowing heat, it was a dramatic announcement which was relayed to them from General Truscott: "I want you to be in Palermo in five days."

Palermo! The city was over one hundred miles by chokingly dusty road, under the fiery Sicilian sun, with water scarce and hard to supply rapidly moving battalions.

Nevertheless the Division prepared for a most spectacular move; the breathtaking dash across Sicily to capture the island's capital and leading city . . . a race then unprecedented by foot soldiers in either of two World Wars, and comparable only in relatively modern war to several of the rapid cleavages of Sherman or Stuart in the Civil War. At that, Stuart at least had moved on horseback. This was a rugged hundred miles even if traversed strictly by road, that was scheduled to feel the tramp of doughboy brogans every foot of the way.

Plan of the general advance was simple in itself but, because of the speed, offered tremendous difficulties in the way of supply, communications and artillery support.

With the 7th Infantry in Division reserve, the first phase of the drive to Palermo was borne by the 15th and 30th Infantry Regiments and 3d Ranger Battalion. The 15th advanced north of Aragona toward Casteltermini, meeting scattered resistance and some artillery fire. South of Casteltermini demolitions in the form of blown bridges and tunnels impeded the advance, but not for long.

The 30th moved forward from Aragona toward San Stefano Quisquina, also encountering demolitions. One of these was particularly difficult; the enemy had blown a section of a road along a cliff just south of the Platani River, necessitating hard work by Lt. Col. Leonard L. Bingham's 10th Engineer Battalion to make the route passable for jeeps. Despite the magnitude of the job, by midnight jeeps of the regiment had passed the obstacle.

Moving northwest from Raffadali toward Cattolica the Rangers met no resistance and continued on toward Calamonica where they outposted the left flank of the Division. During the day they also made and maintained contact with the 82d Airborne Division, operating on the 3d's left.

Next day, the 20th, 15th Infantry continued the advance on the right, passing through Casteltermini and Castronuovo and occupying the area just southwest of Lercara Friddi, where it covered the assembly of the 7th Infantry. Resistance again was light, taking the form mainly of armored vehicles, artillery, and mines. Many prisoners were captured and much equipment was taken.

The 30th Infantry captured San Stefano Quisquina, but had a fight doing it.

At 2215, July 19, Colonel Rogers, on orders of General Truscott, ordered his 3d Battalion to move cross-country and seize high ground northeast of town. No roads existed, therefore during the marching over mountainous terrain the battalion was unable to receive rations or additional water for July 20 (a situation which later became familiar along the island's north coast). The battalion set a record for marching that perhaps still stands for World War II: 54 miles in 33 hours, cross-country, to reach the assembly area for the attack on San Stefano Quisquina at 0945, July 20.

Commencing at 0500, July 20, 1st Battalion moved cross-country west of Highway 118 to attack the west side of San Stefano, and 2d Battalion moved along Highway 118 in regimental reserve to an approach south of the city. The 41st Field Artillery Battalion, regimental Antitank and Cannon Companies, and attached artillery moved by bounds from the vicinity of the road north of the stream crossing of the Platani River to positions from which they were prepared to support the attack of infantry battalions on San Stefano.

At 1130, 3d Battalion, having overcome intermittent resistance, reached the east outskirts of San Stefano to encounter strong resistance, including machine-gun and artillery fire. The heights were immediately attacked, but progress was slow until a coordinated attack was launched from the west.

Meanwhile the motorized advance guard of the regiment, consisting of a platoon of the 82d Reconnaissance Battalion, 2d Armd Division, led by Lt. James Fontone, a platoon of the 3d Reconnaissance Troop under 1st Lt. William Gunter, and the 30th Regimental I & R Platoon commanded by 2d Lt. Samuel W. Riley, had by-passed blown-out bridges and skirted minefields to reach a position a hundred yards from San Stefano.

At about 1200 Colonel Rogers joined Lieutenant Riley and four men of his platoon at the I & R observation post which was located 700 yards from an Italian roadblock position before the city. Here he discovered two enemy batteries going into position to fire on our approaching infantry when they came within range. Organizing a fire unit from his reconnaissance elements, consisting of three 37mm guns, one 75mm gun, three 60mm mortars, one 81mm mortar, five .50-caliber machine guns, four .30-caliber machine guns and fifteen riflemen, Colonel Rogers ordered them to open fire at the maximum rate. The sudden hail of fire achieved complete surprise. The gunners abandoned their pieces without firing a shot, as did the gunners of thirty-two machine guns, all of them making off toward San Stefano, several hundred yards to the rear. Pressure on the 3d Battalion on the right was relieved. Rogers ordered 1st Battalion to attack east of Highway 118.

The 1st Battalion drove toward the southern entrance of the city, assisting 3d Battalion in its difficult task of clearing the eastern slopes of the mountains which bordered San Stefano.

Once again under the personal direction of the 30th regimental commander, the 41st Field Artillery Battalion, with one battery initially, and subsequently with the entire battalion, placed heavy concentrations on the highway north of the city, preventing the escape of enemy personnel and transportation. Regimental Antitank Company also placed direct 57mm fire on retreating vehicles, and Company D laid 81mm mortar fire to the same effect. The intense fire destroyed numerous enemy vehicles and trapped at least a hundred pieces of transportation. The better vehicles captured in this haul were used by the 30th to speed movement of the regiment northward.

Immediately following this action the hard-pressing reconnaissance and battalion elements rounded up at least 750 prisoners.

The coordinated attack on San Stefano had begun at 1330 and continued throughout the afternoon. The city was entered by 3d Battalion at about 1700, followed by 1st Battalion.

The 2d Battalion, which had reached the southern city outskirts at about 1600, was ordered to prepare to push on to Prizzi, while 1st and 3d Battalions were to hold positions on the mountains north, northeast and northwest of San Stefano. The 41st Field Artillery Battalion, in position south of the city, commenced registering on all routes leading north from it.

Next day the 7th Infantry led the advance on the Sicilian capital. Attacking west from Castronuovo at 0555 with two battalions abreast, the regiment captured Prizzi and seized the high ridge beyond it by 0930, taking 500 prisoners in this area. The battalions then reorganized and continued the advance to the north, the 3d moving on Corleone at 1400 followed by the 1st at 1500. The 2d Battalion, which had left its area near Raffadali at 0130, arrived in the assembly area beyond Castronuovo and after being held in trucks as a mobile reserve, then moved on to Prizzi. At 1840 3d Battalion entered the town of Corleone, most important city between Agrigento and Palermo, and by 2100 the entire regiment was concentrated north of Corleone. At 2200 the 2d Battalion had moved forward by truck, detrucked just north of the town and then begun an advance toward Marineo.

The 15th Infantry, with the 4th Tabor of Goumiers attached, followed in the trace of 7th Infantry, one battalion passing through the 7th and starting up the secondary road which runs through Piana del Gresi toward Palermo.

At 1017 30th Infantry sent Company F (reinforced)

Troops of the 3d Division passing through Palermo.

north and west to Roccamena with the mission of securing the high ground in that vicinity and protecting the Division's left flank. The remainder of the regiment, with two battalions of field artillery in addition to the 41st Field, 65th Armored Field, and the 1st Battalion, 77th Field, was ordered to move to Roccamena to await further orders.

The regiment moved as ordered but a change in the plan was caused by an order from Provisional Corps changing the left boundary of the Division. The regiment was ordered to concentrate in an area about two miles south of Corleone, leaving Company F, reinforced, at Roccamena. This order necessitated a retracing of the line of march of 2d Battalion, which had been in the lead, from a position eight miles north of Campoflorita to the new area south of Corleone.

July 22 was one of the great days for the 7th Infantry, commanded throughout the Sicilian campaign by Col. Harry B. Sherman. By 0300 2d Battalion had reached a point two miles southwest of Marineo, meeting very light resistance. At the same time the Division field order was issued for the advance on Palermo.

The 1st Battalion entrucked and passed through 2d Battalion just north of Marineo. The 3d Battalion entrucked at Corleone at 1115 and after detrucking passed through 1st Battalion at Misilmeri at 1300. Supporting artillery, the 10th, 65th and 77th Field, moved forward also to support the attack.

At Misilmeri 1st Battalion moved northwest across the mountains in order to enter the Palermo plain from the south. Some resistance was encountered and sixty German port troops were taken prisoner. At 1445 orders were received from General Patton that no troops other than patrols were to pass the line extending from Villabate through Belmonte to Monreale until further orders. The 7th Infantry, having sent motor patrols into the city at 1400, occupied posisitions along this line, prepared to move forward on order. At 1900 civilians representing the people of Palermo offered the surrender of the city to Brig. Gen. William W. Eagles, assistant division commander. At 2030 3d Battalion, 7th Infantry, was sent into the city to guard important installations.

The entire phase just concluded was well summed up by Will Lang in *Life* Magazine:*

... The "Truscott Trot," as his men dubbed their gruelling pace, proved more prescient than sadistic once the 3d Division had landed at Licata in Sicily. There followed an operation which is already classic in military annals for speed and success. After seven days' fighting the division captured Agrigento ... and five days after that its patrols entered Palermo, fully 100 miles to the north. The bulk of this latter distance was covered by all three regiments in three days. On the 14th day the Division rested after having slyly gained for Truscott one of his most memorable firsts—the entry into Palermo.

As the various American forces approached Palermo, Patton defined a "blue phase line" just four miles short of the city beyond which no infantry excepting patrols, were to go. Patton's tanks had been chosen to make the victorious entry into the island's capital. This they did, with banners flying and cameras grinding. But inside the city they found the 3d Division's Lt. Col. John Heintges and his entire battalion quietly patrolling the streets ...

While 7th Infantry was busily herding thousands of Italian and German prisoners together, the other two regiments were mopping up pockets of enemy resistance. The 15th Infantry, following in the wake of the 7th, reached the Seventh Army limiting line and was on the heights overlooking Palermo at 1445. Light resistance encountered north of Piana dei Greci was neutralized by the regiment's Cannon Company and attached artillery.

*Will Lang, *Life*, Oct. 2, 1944.

At 1400 the same day 30th Infantry had moved out from its area south of Corleone, following in the route of the 7th. The regiment concentrated just south of Misilmeri where it was prepared to move on short notice to any point desired by higher headquarters. The race to Palermo was over and the Division was allowed to rest for a few days before resuming pursuit of the faltering but still strong German and Italian armies.

Second Phase

By the time 3d Division captured Palermo, 2d Armored Division had cleaned up all of western Sicily west of the 3d's boundary. II Corps had moved north, east of the 3d, so that its front extended on a line from Montemaggiore through Petralia to Nicosia. Over in the eastern part of the island the British Eighth Army was fighting on a front from south of Nicosia through Catenanuova to just south of Catania. The stage was set to push east along the north coast to Messina. The United States 45th Infantry Division was chosen to lead the advance while the 3d Division enjoyed a well-earned rest.

The 45th pushed off but met heavy resistance and by the time the division got to San Stefano di Camastra, on the north coast road, it was decided that the 3d would relieve it. The relief began July 31.

The weather by this time, if it were possible, had grown hotter. At the peak of the day, around 1100, temperatures soared to between 100 and 110 F. It was muggy, sticky. The sun dawned each morning in an absolutely flawless blue sky, and before it was well into the zenith, men began sweating and cursing its relentless, burning rays. Not a breath of air stirred but that it was hotter than the normal motionless air and felt as though it had been piped through a blast furnace.

The single ribbon of road leading along the north coast of the island between Palermo and Messina was often as not thoroughly chewed up, cratered, and mined. On either side the broad shoulders were covered with finely ground dust which rose to tree-top height under the churning treads of the constant two-way traffic of supply vehicles and ambulances.

Water, which until Palermo had been scarce, was now to become more precious as relief for alkaline throats than the finest of aged beverages. It was a common sight to approach large groups of men clustered around a small pipe cemented into the side of a rocky cliffside, from which a small trickle of cold water flowed. These men would edge their way in in the attempt to fill their canteens, then double-time for several hundred yards to arrive, soaked with perspiration and covered with a film of dust, back in place in their rapidly-marching colunms. Foresighted soldiers carried

Colonel Don E. Carleton, Chief of Staff.

as many as four canteens, often one or two U. S. style, with possibly Italian or German models which had larger capacities.

It was a case of sanitation be damned. The drinking of unchlorinated spring water was at no time officially condoned. All men knew they were supposed to dissolve halazone tablets into unpurified water before drinking it, but it was hard to tell that to thousands of soldiers, constantly thirsty, when water points were so few and far between. More than once it became literally a life-and-death matter to various forces, isolated on forbidding heights, to get water. That the barest minimum necessary to sustenance was achieved is a tribute to many anonymous men, stout-hearted and strong of back, who carried five-gallon cans over heart-breakingly steep, rugged slopes; to the persistence of the men of the 3d Provisional Pack Train who led their mules as far as those agile animals could go, and then carried the precious cans the remainder of the way on their backs. It was also a commentary on human nature that men, deprived of water in inaccessible places, yet knowing the enemy ahead controlled watering spots, would fight like supercharged demons, preferring—if it became a matter of hard choice—to stop a piece of flying metal than to die agonizingly with their throats choking for moisture.

The single road was generally quite narrow. It wound between sea and mountain. At times the north side of the road edged gently into flat ground, covered

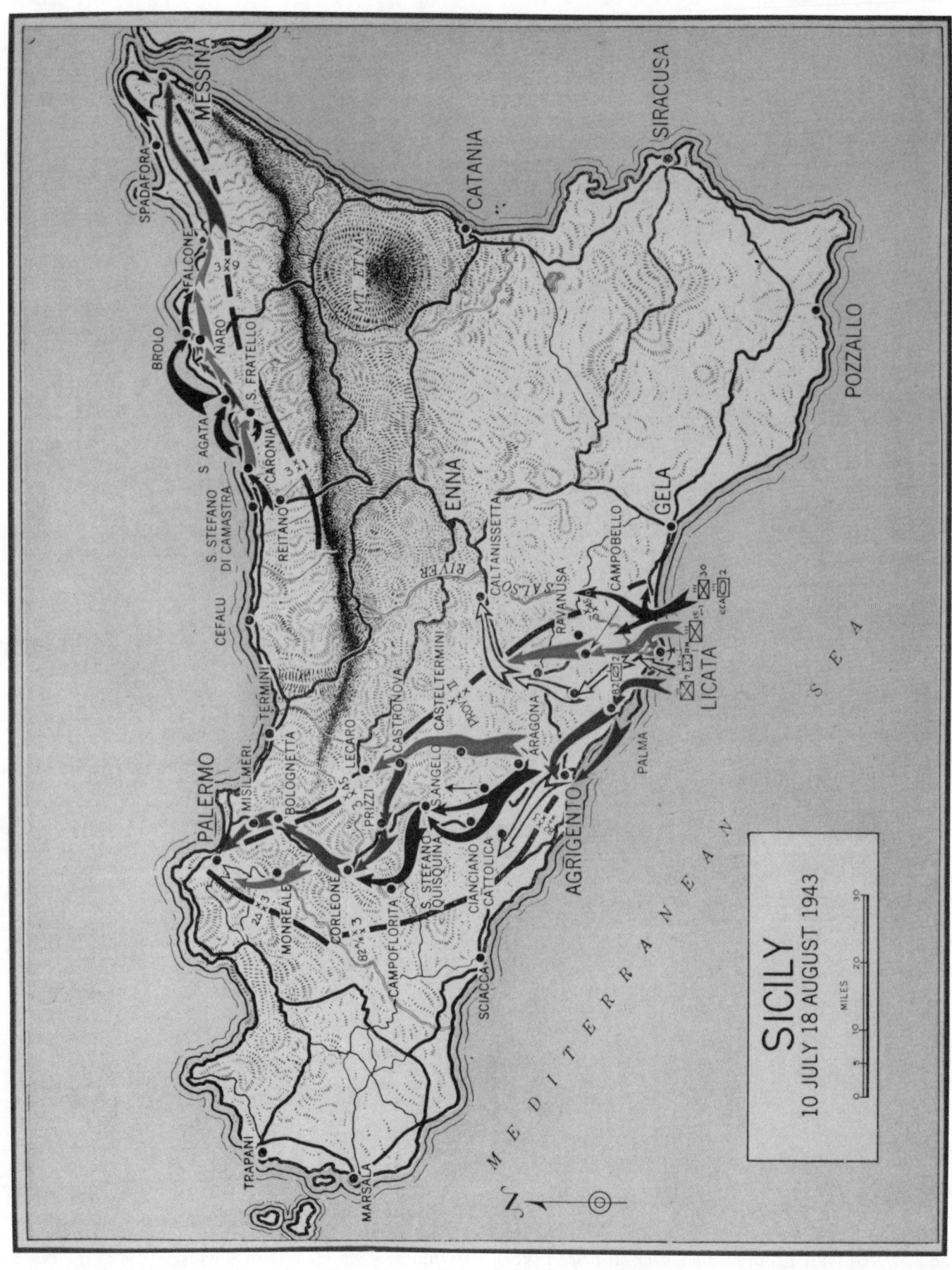

War and the civilian: An Italian funeral procession at the environs of Palermo. Probably a victim of artillery fire.

with olive trees, to slope gently to the water's edge. The opposite side might ascend gently into higher ground, then rise abruptly to lofty peaks. Along the greater part of the route however, the terrain was sharply defined, and on one side sheer hundred-foot drops to rock-lined surf confronted the unwary driver, while on the island's side great, towering rock cliffs, presenting few toeholds, jutted toward the sky. In such places the road was carved from the mountainside itself.

On the maps each projection of terrain is referred to as a "hill," in many cases probably the cartographers' little joke. To the men who had to climb them the humor was salted with plenty of sweat.

Is it any wonder then that an enemy who, with the exception of a couple of notable battles, was fighting a delaying action could defend with such relative ease, deploy a minimum number of men, and still make the fight of the 3d Infantry Division as harrowing as any fought anywhere? It is to the everlasting credit of the doughboys that the ninety miles from San Stefano di Camastra to Messina was covered in seventeen days following completion of the relief.

The 30th Infantry led the advance initially along the north coast. The 1st Battalion detrucked in the San Stefano di Camastra area at 1115, July 31, and marched south to Reitano where it contacted the 179th Infantry of the 45th Division. The 2d Battalion completed detrucking at 1315 and moved east along Highway 113 toward San Stefano, effecting contact with the 157th Infantry of the 45th Division one and one-half miles west of the town.

At the riverbed just west of the town a blown bridge and mines were encountered and at this point the battalion left the road and moved to positions about 4,000 yards southeast of San Stefano. All that night the 10th Engineers, supervised by Colonel Rogers, worked to ready the by-pass to enable the Division timetable to be met. A combat and reconnaissance patrol entered San Stefano and proceeded two miles east, meeting no enemy activity other than sporadic artillery fire. By 2130 the battalion had moved along steep mountain trails to a point six miles southeast of San Stefano.

The 3d Battalion, 30th Infantry, detrucked at 1505 and remained in an assembly area near the detrucking point, moving east at 2100. Company C, 10th Engineer Battalion, moved immediately from the detrucking area and began the repair of by-passes in the San Stefano area.

The 15th Infantry, meanwhile, had gone into bivouac in the area just east of Castel di Tusa and prepared to move on to the east. By midnight of August 1 the entire Division was concentrated in the San Stefano area, poised to begin its relentless drive to the east. Effecting this concentration was not an easy matter. The highway and bridge situations already men-

The north coast of Sicily in vicinity of San Stefano di Camastra.

Waiting for the mines to be swept from a river bed ahead.

tioned were bad in that they hindered the orderly relief of the 45th Division. Order was soon formed from seeming chaos, however, and the Division began its attack hampered only by Germans, heat, and miserable communications caused by the one, lone road.

At 0500, August 2, 30th Infantry attacked to the east over steep cliffs and extremely rugged terrain. Its mission was to seize the bridge west of Caronia, to capture the town itself, and to cut the road east of the town. The 41st FA Battalion supported the attack. The 1st Battalion reached its objective by 0900 and sent a patrol to the northeast of Highway 113 and thence back through Caronia. The 2d Battalion attacked from its position to seize the high ground just south of Caronia, arriving at its objective by 1500, although advance patrols entered the town at 1430. The 3d Battalion moved down the highway and advanced to the east along it.

The 3d Battalion seized the bridge and Company L entered the town at 1215. The enemy reaction was violent, and took the form of copious artillery and mortar fire, long-range machine-gun fire and treacherous minefields. This was the first German resistance of any nature met by the 30th Infantry since landing overseas. From 1000 to 1030, and then intermittently until 1100, the regimental command post, but 800 yards behind 3d Battalion, underwent an intensive enemy artillery concentration, which resulted in two killed and eleven wounded. General Truscott was there to "sweat it out," and among the casualties was Lt. Col. Lionel C. McGarr, executive officer, who was seriously wounded by a mine explosion while he was en route to Caronia.

Blown bridges hindered moving up organic transportation. Mortar, artillery, and machine-gun fire inflicted approximately forty casualties in the 3d Battalion as it assaulted Caronia across rugged, shrub-covered terrain.

The 2d Battalion, 15th Infantry, now moved out along the coast road to the vicinity of Caronia, followed by the remainder of the regiment. Progress was extremely slow because of the numerous blown bridges, minefields, and the slow movement of the troops in front.

The 2d Battalion moved through the 30th Infantry at 1545 and continued east along Highway 113. Foot troops were able to by-pass the blown and mined bridges but the vehicles had to wait until the engineers constructed by-passes. The 2d Battalion reached its objective at 2345 and patrols were sent forward to the east. The 3d Battalion, 15th Infantry, passed through the 30th Infantry at 1730 and started cross-country at 1845 to a position two miles west of San Fratello. The first of the two bloodiest battles on the north coast of Sicily was about to begin. Again, however, during this day resistance mainly took the shape of enemy minefields.

Sergeant Jack Foisie, *Stars and Stripes* correspondent, graphically described this "minefield resistance."

You march in extended order and you keep looking for snipers in the hills, and mines under your feet. Your eyes soon get tired from looking but you keep on looking first at the hills and then the road.

A jeep passes you by; it is the first vehicle through the by-pass and you think it is going to get into town before you. You curse the mobility of the army.

The jeep enters a tunnel and there is a muffled explosion. The medics start to run down to the tunnel and someone says, "Yeh, you'd better let me go first" and an engineer with a mine detector begins sweeping a path for them. You are suddenly glad you are an infantry man—but only for a minute . . .

On the bend in the road are what look like small shell craters in the asphalt surface. You wonder who did the nice shooting, and then a smart sergeant says, "watch out for those soft spots, they're antitank mines." Sure enough, an engineer comes along and probes with a bayonet and it strikes metal.

"Take it easy, Joe," says the guy who's working with him, "those things are touchy." The two get down on their knees around the mine and from a few yards off it looks like they're shooting craps. If you're a damn fool you come closer and, looking over their shoulders, you see them dig out the dirt around the mine and then work their hands under the mine to see if it's boobied, that is, if it will explode when lifted up. Satisfied, the engineer called Joe lifts out the German Teller mine and the other guy unscrews the caps and defuses it. "Now it's completely harmless," says Joe, and he lays it down very carefully way off the road. There are a pile of these Teller mines; they look just like an oversize discus.

You've been walking over an hour now and the white lines of salt begin to appear on your sweat-soaked shirt. Your canteen is still half-full but the water is more than lukewarm. There is a spout of cool mountain water emptying into a cement basin in the shade of a grove of big-leafed trees. "How about a ten-minute break?" Okay, but you'd better jump from the asphalt to the bank; those shoulders are always mined.

So you leap over the soft shoulder and land on the bank; you lean back and relax. The weight of the pack leaves your shoulders. The grass is cool and soft. You stretch out flat—and that saves your life. The guy who had been marching out in front of you—yes, the fellow carrying a Browning Automatic Rifle—had been the first to refill his canteen from that spout of cool water, and the first to find that the Germans had put a ring of S-mines around the foot of the basin.

You are tempted to take to the railroad tracks which go straight across into town but then you remember the jeep in the tunnel . . . It is decided to reconnoiter the roadblock at the entrance to the bridge. Two men are selected and you are not one of them. A halt is called while they go ahead. . . . One of the two scouts comes running back.

"Mines. All around the bridge. A patrol from another company coming down from the hills ran into them. Got quite a few. They need a doctor," the scout reports.

"Doctor up front! Pass the word back!" orders the point commander. The word is passed back: "Doctor up front!" There is more talk on a walkie-talkie; it is decided to try and get the doc through; the engineers will be up shortly but there is no time.

You reach the other bank and there above you on the ledge is an Italian civilian, all smiles and a mixture of languages. He is wearing sandals made out of rubber tires. Naturally, he announces right off that he lived twenty-three years in Brooklyn—they all have, it seems.

"Okay, Joe, tell us about that later. What we want to know, can you lead us around that minefield?"

He leads you along the bank until you come onto the wounded and the dead about fifty yards in front of you. You were taking the same path that these men had taken.

The file backs up. This time the Italian who had once lived in Brooklyn is ordered to take us up over the ridge and then swing around to the road. The old man explains that he is very old and cannot make the hill. There is nothing to do but go on without a guide. Shoot the old man, you say. No, remember that he was in the lead and would have been the first one to go. Blame it on the fumblings of an old man's mind.

You climb the terraced ridge and turn toward the road. Your eyes are glued to that soil. You follow in the exact footsteps of the man in front of you. The man in the lead —perhaps he follows in the footsteps of God. Every snap of a twig, each rattle of a pebble, makes you twitch and shiver. If you think at all it is perhaps about what you said in your last letter home.

The leader reaches the bank overlooking the road. He jumps and lands on the firm asphalt surface. He is safe. The next one jumps. He is safe. Each one jumps and is safe. You jump and you are safe.

The doctor walks in the middle of the road down to the bridge. There is a cart at the end of the bridge. It was touching this cart that set off the first of the mines. The doctor goes to work.

Monte San Fratello is a 2200-foot peak standing on the east bank of the Furiano River, close to the Mediterranean. A saddle joins it to higher ridges to the south and in the saddle lies the village of San Fratello. A road winds up the western side of the mountain from the coastal highway to the village and continues on south. A short distance inland from the village the Furiano forks, forming two deep gorges with a lofty, steep-sloped nose standing between the branches.

The crest of Monte San Fratello is a high, rocky escarpment and the western slope is irregular, with many hummocks and draws. The Germans occupied dug-in positions east of the river. In addition they had thickly sown the bed of the Furiano with "S" and Teller mines and had demolished the bridge which carried the main highway across the river.

The problem thus facing the Division was by no means easy. The Germans were in position to make a strong bid to stop the advance of the 3d and these Germans were not ready to start running again. It was up to the Division to outmaneuver and outfight them.

The 2d Battalion, 15th Infantry, following a terrific two-and-one-half hour artillery barrage beginning at 0830 August 3, advanced along Highway 113 until it reached the west bank of the Furiano River where it encountered strong opposition. It reorganized and attempted to continue the attack but was halted by heavy artillery, machine-gun, and mortar fire from the east of the river and minefields in the river bed.

During the evening of the same day the 1st Battalion moved up on the south flank of the 2d Battalion and 3d Battalion advanced cross-country to positions west of San Fratello, well south of 1st Battalion.

The advance of the 3d Battalion was slow and grueling. During the long march, exhausted soldiers plodded on across deep gorges and over mountain trails so precipitous, that the mules bearing rations and ammunition were often unable to negotiate the steep ascent, lost footing and tumbled to their death hundreds of feet below. The 3d Battalion skirted two enemy minefields to find the enemy in the mountainous terrain and carry the battle to him. Ammunition, food and water supply was precariously low. Yet the advance on Hill 673 continued.

Patrols went out and preparations were made to continue the attack in the morning.

At 0600 the 1st and 2d Battalions attacked again; again they were halted. The 2d then changed direction of advance, made a lunge toward the right, but got only to the east side of the river bed when heavy enemy fire drove it back. The 1st Battalion tried several times to cross the river at a more southern point but was driven back each time.

At this point General Truscott ordered a coordinated attack on San Fratello and patrols spent the night of August 4-5 vigorously probing enemy defenses to obtain additional information concerning their strength and locations.

The 15th and 30th Infantry Regiments attacked at 0600 the following morning, the 30th minus its own 2d Battalion but reinforced by the 3d Battalion of the 15th. Moving from a line of departure that ran along the ridge from Di Nicoletta to Santa Maria, the 1st Battalion of the 30th was taken under terrific enemy artillery and mortar fire that lasted for an hour. The battalion withdrew with heavy losses.

The entire attack was destined to the same fate—every step toward the objective was made at high cost. The advance down on our slope, the crossing of the river bed, the advance up the enemy slope, offered nothing but obstacles and clear enemy observation.

Even mule packs had difficulty negotiating the hills and maintenance of communications proved almost impossible, although mounted messengers furnished by the Provisional Horse Cavalry Troop were indispensable aids.

The terrain was so rough that it took five hours for the 3d Battalion of the 30th to reach the 3d Battalion of the 15th, which had moved secretly into positions on the Santa Maria ridge prior to the attack. Contact with our own units which were not over 1,000 yards away was frequently broken.

Like that of the 30th the advance of the 15th, which was veiled in a heavy smokescreen laid down by our artillery and Chemical Battalion, was extremely slow.

After an all-day fight that at times was disheartening, the 15th minus the 3d Battalion, which was still attached to the 30th, had reached only half way up the ridge when it was ordered to hold its positions till dark and withdraw back across the river. The 2d Battalion of the 7th aided in this withdrawal, which was completed under cover of darkness.

The coordinated attack had hardly punctured the enemy positions during the whole day and after reorganization the units were set to continue the mission the following day, August 6. The 7th Infantry, which had been held in readiness near Caronia also was to move forward with the mission of passing through the 15th, crossing the Furiano and pushing east along Highway No. 113 toward the sea.

The 7th struck early in the morning, by-passed the San Fratello action and reached Acquedolci at 0753. By 1115, the regiment was in Sant' Agata and an hour later had made contact with the 2d Battalion of the 30th, which had made a successful amphibious landing three miles east of Sant' Agata.

The San Fratello objective fell during a night assault.

At 1830, one platoon of Company C, 30th Infantry, attacked with the mission of clearing out machine-gun and mortar fire which had retarded previous advances. Company D covered the platoon with machine-gun and mortar fire but suffered heavily from an enemy artillery and mortar concentration. The platoon, though badly disorganized, continued on and succeeded in reaching the top of the hill just south of San Fratello.

The 3d Battalions of both the 30th and 15th encountered stiff resistance at Hill 673 but had fought their way nearly to the crest at daybreak, when it was discovered that part of the ground was exposed to enemy enfilade fire from a ridge to the south and most of the men had to be shifted to other positions.

Company I of the 30th however, commanded by 1st Lt. George K. Butler, continued the attack toward San Fratello but was stopped by artillery, machine-gun and cannon fire from tanks in San Fratello. The company held its position all day while the rest of the 3d Battalion was reorganizing.

At 1930, the 3d Battalion struck again, with Company L in the assault, supported by Company K and an 81mm mortar platoon from the 15th Infantry. The hitherto indomitable enemy defense finally cracked and at 2330 Hill 673 was captured by Company L. A fierce counterattack was repelled, adding considerably to the already high total of casualties that the enemy had suffered.

It was the weary 3d Battalion of the 15th Infantry which was hardest hit by the enemy counterattack. For more than 45 minutes it was subject to a violent TOT-artillery concentration, after which it met the several waves of counter-attacking enemy, committing all service troops in the attempt to stop the on-rushing foe.

A large number of machine guns and mortars were also destroyed and captured during the two-day engagement. Company L, leading 3d Battalion, 30th Infantry, entered San Fratello proper at 0800. Moving from there to Monte Fratello, the battalion took 500 prisoners.

The 3d Battalion, 15th Infantry was committed to attack another hill mass, which they stormed under a protecting mortar concentration and seized. It then descended on San Fratello in the valley and in house-to-house fighting, fought through the town to contact elements of Co. L, 30th Infantry.

For its action from 3-8 August, the 3d Battalion 15th Infantry was awarded the Distinguished Unit Citation.

The crossing of the Furiano, the struggles in the high hills and finally the seizure of the San Fratello ridge were the bitterest operations the Division had encountered since Licata.

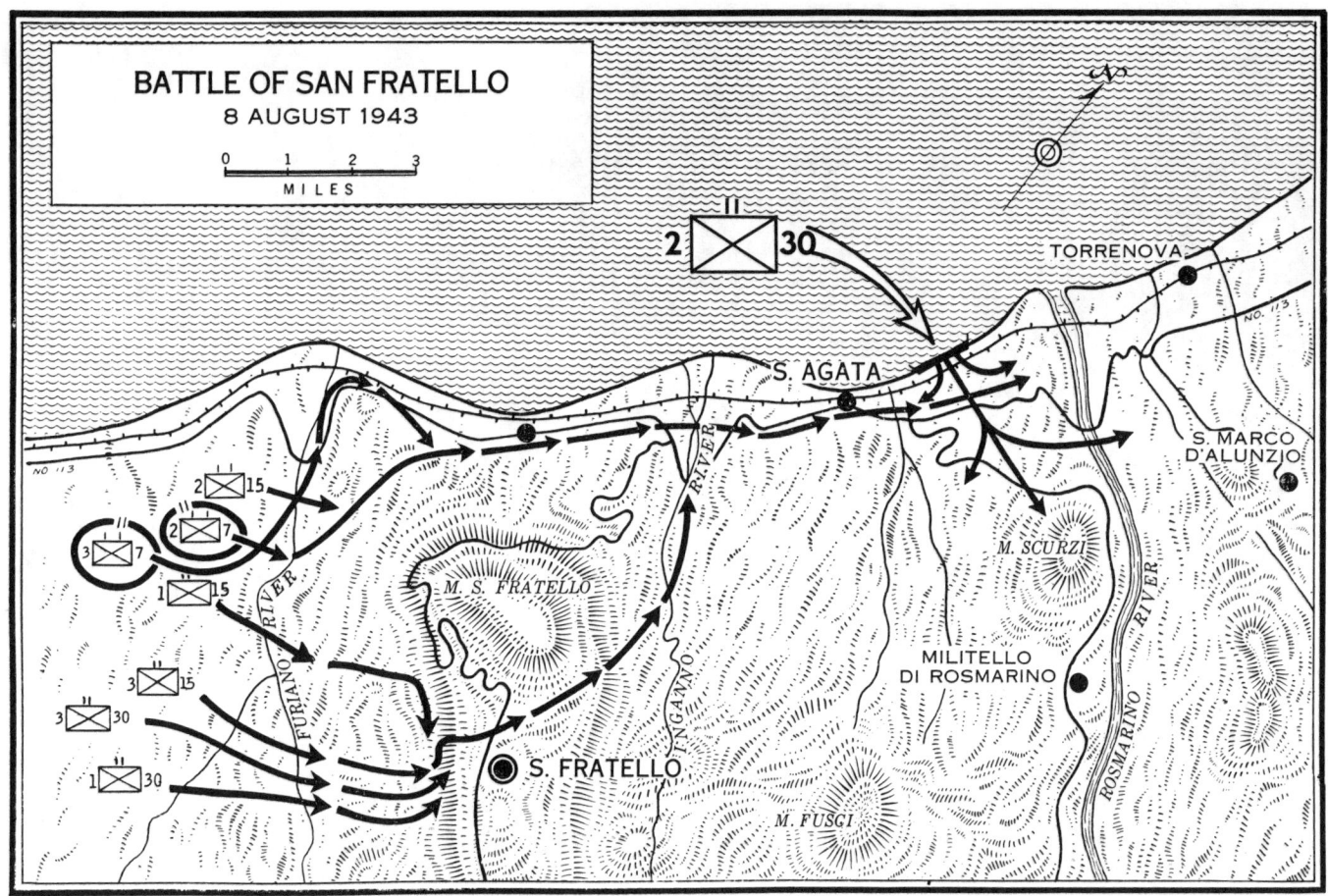

During the night of August 7, while the rest of the regiment was making its successful attack against San Fratello by land, the 2d Battalion, 30th Infantry, with tanks, armored artillery and other attachments, loaded into several landing craft and early on the morning of August 8 made a successful, almost unopposed landing near Sant' Agata, a short distance east of San Fratello on the north coast.

Certain passages from a story by Foisie in the *Stars & Stripes* help to tell of the results attained by this "minor" amphibious landing:

We landed seven miles behind the enemy lines at 0300 hours Sunday morning.

Our mission was to fight our way through the beach defenses to a high tableland a mile inland, there to cut the coastal highway leading to Sant' Agata and isolate the entrenched Germans holding up the American advance along the north Sicilian coast. Alone and without hope of reinforcements we were for twenty-four hours to hold off the bulk of the Axis forces to the east, at the same time keeping the net tightly closed around the enemy caught between us and the main lines.

"It is the chance that few outfits get, so let's cut the rug and knock them all the way back to Messina," were the final words of the raider commander, Lt. Col. Lyle W. Bernard.

Five hours after the first assault boat had touched sand we were firmly entrenched in the hills, had smeared all German traffic going in either direction. By noon the town of Sant' Agata had fallen. At 1241 hours, contact was established with the advanced elements of the main American forces, ahead of schedule.

The unparalleled success of the daring knifelike thrust at the enemy's rear resulted in the complete collapse of their strong defense line on the 2200 ridge east of Sant' Agata and sent them reeling back without being able to depend upon minefields and other Nazi tricks for delaying action. . . .

There was virtually no opposition to the landing but the battalion was later counterattacked strongly by the enemy, supported by machine guns and artillery. All positions were held. As a result of this landing 250 enemy were killed, one hundred were captured, four tanks were disabled and fourteen trucks and four motorcycles were destroyed.

The 7th Infantry passed through the 15th Infantry about daylight August 8 and advanced along the costal road meeting little opposition. The enemy, yielding to heavy pressure from south of San Fratello, and disorganized by the landing of 30th Infantry's 2d Battalion in his rear, had withdrawn from all his forward positions and could not offer further effective delaying action here. Contact between 7th Infantry and 2d Battalion, 30th Infantry, was made at 1236 August 8 and a gain of more than twelve miles was the second important result of this audacious operation.

The 39th FA passes through the rubble of Sant' Agata on their way along the northern Sicilian coast.

From Sant' Agata the attack was pressed vigorously by 7th Infantry along the coast with 15th Infantry moving up and attacking cross-country on its right on August 10. The 2d Battalion, 30th Infantry, in the meantime, without any rest, was preparing for another amphibious operation. This time the mission was to land fifteen miles behind the enemy lines and cut the highway at Brolo, halfway between Cape Orlando and Cape Calava.

On August 11, 30th Infantry, minus the 2d Battalion, continued the attack along the coastal road, while the 7th Infantry swung inland. Both 7th and 15th reached and secured positions along the important Orlando-Randazzo road that day, across extremely difficult terrain, and against increasingly strong enemy resistance.

On August 11 Colonel Bernard's force struck again. This second landing, like the first, was unopposed in the beginning. The landing craft hove to about 3000 yards off the landing beach and by 0310 the landing craft from the LST and the sixteen ducks were in their rendezvous circles. The run into the beach commenced immediately and at 0243 the first wave landed without a shot being fired. Rapid, quiet work landed the entire assault force on the beach without loss by 0400.

By daylight not a trace remained on the beach or to seaward to indicate that a landing of infantry troops had occurred, but the absence of exits from the beach to the highway was a very serious drawback to wheeled and tracked vehicles. It was necessary for the tanks and mobile artillery to go through a lemon grove, traversed by numerous ditches, then up to a steep embankment to reach the highway; moreover, there were only a few ways the vehicles could get up the embankment, namely by going under the bridges at either end of the beach.

Immediately upon landing Company E began clearing the lemon grove. Within forty-five minutes after disembarking, the grove, between the embankment and the road, was reported clear of enemy. Companies F and G had reached the road at 0345 when the leading elements heard a vehicle moving along the road from west to east. This vehicle was allowed to pass as the secrecy of the operation had not yet been lost. About five minutes later the put-put of a motorcycle broke the silence. Overanxious riflemen shot and killed the driver. A few seconds later another small car came down the road and was destroyed by an antitank rocket shell. As a result of this shooting the enemy opened up with flares and tracer fire in the darkness.

As the two rifle companies, followed by battalion headquarters and the supporting weapons, crawled up the steep slope at the eastern tip of the mountain, rifle and machine-gun flashes lit the night about them. Four machine guns and several rifles were quickly identified. These were put out of action by the advancing infantry who had to grab and hold on to the bushes to ascend the slope. Enemy fire, however, was not well directed. The bulk of the landing team was still obviously undetected. Two German prisoners were taken during the climb.

By 0530 the top of Monte Creole had been reached and within an hour all units reported by radio that they were in position and reorganized. The few men who attempted to scale the tip of the mountain after that drew heavy fire from the machine guns and 20mm guns located across the river in the hills south of Brolo. With daylight, movement of any kind became extremely hazardous. About fifteen men were killed trying to climb this slope with messages or equipment.

Before daylight Battery A of the 58th Armored FA Battalion had taken up positions in the lemon grove, firing toward Brolo. Battery B took position to fire on targets of opportunity to the west. Both batteries gave extremely effective supporting fire until they were destroyed in the late afternoon.

Their location in the lemon grove, which was dominated by high ground to the west, their proximity to the enemy on the east; and hampered by lack of direct observation on close-in targets, made their task very difficult. In spite of these limitations they succeeded in preventing the enemy from emplacing any supporting artillery on the eastern end of the position, and harassed the enemy a great deal on the west end, where the situation and terrain were more favorable to enemy action.

The tanks were also hampered, even more seriously, by the number of ditches in the lemon grove, as well as by a stone wall along the edge of the road which limited their movement. They were also under observation, and, although they were able to fire as fixed guns, they were not able to maneuver effectively, and so were relatively useless in the engagement which was about to follow.

By 0700 the enemy had recovered from his surprise and began to initiate reconnaissance. The first of these probing attempts came in the form of a motorized patrol. This force came roaring down the road from Naso. The concentrated rocket and machine-gun fire which greeted them set the two leading vehicles on fire and scattered the enemy personnel.

Shortly after this a large patrol of about thirty men began working its way down the bed of the Brolo River and was kept under observation until it got to within 700 yards. It was engaged by heavy machine-gun fire from the platoon on top of Monte Creole. The force was decimated. Its members returned again only to drag away their casualties.

About an hour later a company of enemy was located marching boldly down the bed of the Naso River. This group was caught in machine-gun and 60mm mortar fire and was pinned down. All three of these attempts having proved both abortive and costly to them, the Germans made no further attempts to attack from the south. The sector was relatively quiet until after dark.

At 0900 enemy vehicles were seen moving westward along the road from Cape Orlando, about five miles east of Brolo. The Navy opened fire. No direct hits were observed, but the enemy was forced to dismount. At about the same time one light tank and one Mark IV moved along this same road, accompanied by a small detachment of infantry. Artillery fire forced the tank to seek cover, and the infantry moved into the woods north of the road.

By this time the lack of mortar ammunition, with

Lieutenant Colonel Lyle W. Bernard, commanding 2nd Battalion, 30th Infantry.

which these enemy soldiers could have been taken under fire, was beginning to be felt. Only harassing fire was possible. Since sixteen mules had been brought along, the mule train attempted to bring ammunition up on the hill, but was caught by machine-gun fire when it came under observation from the hills south of Brolo. All but two mules were killed. These two mules reached the top of Monte Creole late in the afternoon. Hand carry of ammunition was attempted but was only partially successful, since the trip was so long and the losses prohibitively high.

While reconnaissance of the eastern flank was carried out by the enemy, a strong attack was obviously in preparation from the direction of Brolo. At least two companies arrived in personnel carriers; several tanks came down the road and entered the town. Small groups of men also could be seen in the woods east of the town.

At 1300 the artillery fired on Brolo, intense naval gunfire was placed west of the town, and 2d Battalion dumped heavy mortar shells into the town. An hour later a friendly air mission came over and dropped bombs over a large area covering the roads and assembly areas east of Brolo.

From all appearances this bombardment from three directions and from the air ended any attempt to assault the position from the east and a column of enemy troops could be seen moving to the east in great confusion. Friendly planes which came over again at 1430 disabled many of these.

Three Mark IV tanks remained concealed in the town, however, and at about 1500 began working their way across the bridge over the Brolo River. Because of the high wall at this point and the limited observation for direct fire the artillery was unable to engage these tanks, which succeeded in penetrating the position and destroying two of the ammunition half-tracks and two of the artillery pieces. One of the tanks was destroyed in this battle. The others made good their escape.

During the course of this action an especially heavy concentration of enemy artillery fire fell on Monte Creole, and kept up for an hour, causing several casualties. The tanks which had penetrated the western end of the position also delivered considerable direct fire against buildings, walls, clumps of trees and other likely places for congregation or concealment of our men.

Enemy tracer set fires on the northern slopes of Monte Creole which burned out telephone lines. The repair crews which were sent down in an attempt to fix them suffered severe losses by machine-gun fire from the German tanks and were forced to withdraw.

The volume of enemy fire was rapidly increasing on the western end of the position. Naval fire support was called to lay a concentration on the woods just west of the Naso River. An air mission on this area had been requested previously, but had not yet materialized. It was then discovered that communication with the naval support had been disrupted by the burning of the telephone lines. The naval craft did not respond.

An attempt was made to move the artillery pieces to positions from which they could lay fire on the enemy assembly areas. This resulted in their being detected by the enemy tanks. Three of our pieces were destroyed. Troops on the hill placed as much rifle fire as possible in the area but without much effect as it was primarily plunging fire. Mortar and machine-gun ammunition, beyond a very small last contingency reserve which was being held out on orders of the battalion commander, Lt. Col. Lyle W. Bernard, was exhausted and replenishment, although attempted, resulted in considerable casualties.

To remedy this situation Company F was ordered down into the flats to relieve elements of Company E on the east flank, who would then reinforce the west flank position. The one remaining gun of Battery A was placed to cover the road west of Brolo and the bridge across the Brolo River.

This movement began about 1500 and soon relieved the pressure on the west flank. In spite of this the enemy had been able to get small groups into the position.

At about this time the requested air attack materialized all too surprisingly. Seven A-36s swooped in low over the southern hill and planted two heavy bombs in the battalion CP and the remainder on the artillery in the lemon grove in the flats below the road. Here the lack of dispersion resulted in all four guns of Battery B's being destroyed by 1630. All supporting weapons were now gone and the infantry in the flats stood alone.

At this point the battalion executive officer, Maj. Lynn D. Fargo, returned to the CP from the flats with word that Company E had been badly disorganized by the tank fire from the rear, the enemy attacks from the front, and by the ammunition exploding in the half-tracks of the artillery, two of which were now burning.

It appeared now that the position in the flats would soon become untenable. The elements there were ordered to withdraw to the hill and organize a defensive position which would be held for the night. The remaining mortar ammunition was expended in a concentration placed in the woods just west of the Naso River and machine-gun and rifle fire was directed at the bridge to prevent infiltration on that side, and to cover the disengagement.

About this time a message over the 511 radio from an unknown source was received by Colonel Bernard. It gave the electrifying news that 7th Infantry was on a hill just beyond Naso and that help was on the way. So, with the groans of the wounded in the aid station and the scraping sound of steady digging coming from all directions on the beleaguered hill, the battered battalion settled down to hold the position to the last.

A small patrol of the enemy started up the hill about midnight but was driven off by heavy machine-gun fire. In the early part of the night, bursts of small-arms fire and an occasional grenade-burst testified eloquently that those who had been left on the flats were fighting their way back to the battalion. From dark until early morning hours, the movement of tracked and wheeled vehicles could be heard on the road below the position and in the town of Brolo.

At 0600 survivors on the hill looked to the west and a welcome light greeted their eyes. Friendly troops were approaching. Contact with them was made at 0830. They proved to be elements of 1st Battalion, 30th Infantry. They continued marching down the highway, passing through 2d Battalion. The hungry, dirty, tired and thirsty men were relieved. An immediate check was made of the battalion and results summarized, while the battalion and attached units moved to a bivouac area in the grove just west of the Naso River, where the battalion remained in Division reserve for the next two days.

The results of the Brolo operation were realized more in morale effect on the retreating enemy than in the punishment actually inflicted, although that in itself was quite severe. No longer could he move with any freedom in his rear areas along the remaining distance to Messina.

At any time a large force was likely to land in his rear and cut off and destroy his entire command.

As one example, a mere feint with a larger group a few days later contributed to a very hasty withdrawal of all enemy forces across the Straits of Messina, since any successful breaching of the north coast would have laid the other elements spread across the island of Sicily open to attack from the flank.

(Foregoing material on 2d Battalion (reinforced) 30th Infantry, in its landing at Brolo is from the report submitted by Capt. Walter K. Millar, Jr., A.D.C., and later of the 45th Infantry Division, who participated in the entire engagement.)

In tallying up losses at Brolo both sides were seen to have paid heavily, with the Division losing more heavily in personnel and materiel than the Germans, but gaining on the strategic side of the ledger.

The Germans lost two Mark IV tanks destroyed and two disabled; one 77mm gun with 1½-ton prime-mover destroyed; four personnel carriers destroyed; two motorcycles destroyed; twelve Germans captured; and an estimated 100 killed.

United States losses were four officers and 37 men killed; three officers and 75 men wounded; three officers and 55 men missing. We lost also seven M-7's (105mm full-track) destroyed, one M-7 disabled, two half-tracks (ammunition carriers) destroyed, and 14 mules killed.

According to the Distinguished Unit Citation which was later awarded the battalion, ". . . The action of the 2d Battalion was marked by gallantry, fearlessness and profound devotion to duty in the successful accomplishment of two vital missions."

During the night of August 9-10, while the 2d Battalion of the 30th was slipping through the waters of the Tyrrhenian in its second amphibious operation, the remainder of the Division had started a parallel land march east, the 7th Infantry skirting Highway 113, the 15th moving cross-country south of the highway and the 1st and 3d Battalions of the 30th edging up the coast behind the 7th.

Our artillery, displaced in positions east of Sant' Agata, supported the advance of the regiments, although enemy artillery countered on their positions frequently and with good effect. Maj. Edward C. Robertson, commanding the 41st Field Artillery Battalion, was killed during an early-morning reconnaissance just before the infantry started advancing.

Reaching the Di Zappulla river, the 7th encountered heavy resistance and Company B sustained unusually severe losses from mines in the bed of the river, which the company crossed at daybreak. Shortly after Companies A and C had crossed the river to occupy Hill De Morco, the enemy launched a terrific counterattack and the whole 1st Battalion withdrew across the river after inflicting heavy losses on the enemy in a five-hour battle.

The 3d Battalion of the 7th attacked again that night and by 1945 was firmly established on Hill De Morco.

The 15th Infantry moved through the hills unopposed in the early hours of its march but came under heavy artillery fire after reaching Mirto and had to infiltrate across open, observed ground to cover the final steps to the Di Zappulla.

The 7th and 15th initiated attacks early on the morning of the 11th.

The 7th, veering south of Highway 113, struck at Malo, which was taken at 1030 despite heavy enemy mortar and machine-gun fire and at 1145 Pernicchia was occupied. The regiment then turned northeast toward Brolo to disrupt an enemy counterattack which was forming against the 2d Battalion of the 30th, which had made its amphibious landing at 0300 that morning. Contact with the 30th's battalion was made at noon.

Lacking artillery preparation, the 15th moved slowly behind patrols as it crossed the Di Zappulla. The 1st Battalion occupied Naso late in the afternoon and the rest of the regiment moved into the area surrounding Castel Umberto. The enemy was withdrawing rapidly in front of the 15th and steady progress was only lightly contested.

The 1st and 3d Battalions of the 30th, meanwhile, had taken Cape Orlando, which juts out into the sea midway between Sant' Agata and Brolo. Learning that the 2d Battalion was in dire straits after the seaborne landing, the 30th immediately began a speed march toward Brolo. Arriving at Monte Creole, between the Naso and Erelo rivers, contact was made with the beleaguered battalion, which was relieved by the 1st and 3d and went into concealed bivouac.

By August 12 the Division had advanced to a line running from Brole to Castel Umberto but the march had been costly, slow and difficult. An approximate casualty report submitted by the 7th Infantry on that date indicated the regiment had fifteen officers and 400 men killed, wounded and missing during the period August 7-12 and this figure approximated these of the other units in the Division.

The Division resumed the mountainous pursuit the following day with the 30th headed toward Cape Calava on the coast and the 15th pointing to Patti, a little town on Highway 113 just east of Cape Calava. The route of the 15th lay through treacherous country and all heavy weapons were loaded onto pack mules at San Angelo. The trek ahead required it. Although the march was uninterrupted insofar as enemy resistance was concerned, it took eight hours to cover the distance, a little over five miles. The men and animals were so worn that they were given a four-hour rest when they reached Highway 113, just outside Patti.

Our artillery and air bombarded the advance route of the 30th as the regiment made its coastal march toward Cape Calava. The enemy, however, was withdrawing as rapidly as possible and the retreat had become so hasty that large stores of supplies and guns were scattered along the escape route. For instance, an enemy dump on Highway 113 yielded the following equipment, all new: 50 light MGs, 40 heavy MGs, 20 light mortars and 15 truckloads of hand grenades, ammunition flares, rockets and explosives. Coast defense batteries and other heavy guns were found undamaged in many places. Mark IV tanks were being employed to cover rear-guard engineers as they hastily prepared demolitions and laid mines along highway 113, just ahead of our advancing troops.

While no direct enemy fire was received when the 30th approached Cape Calava, the advance was halted abruptly where a section of highway was blown off the face of a cliff directly above the Tyrrhenian and at a point where Highway 113 cut through a tunnel on the tip of the cape.

Col. Arthur H. Rogers, the regimental commander, with Lt. John C. Perkins, Communications Officer, and some communications personnel, loaded two amphibious 2½-ton trucks with water and signal equipment and "by-passed" the obstruction via the Tyrrhenian Sea while the 10th Engineer Battalion began the task of restoring the highway, one of the most notable feats of engineering performed during World War II.

Stripped to the waist in heat that was almost unbearable, the engineers worked without rest literally to "hang a bridge from the sky," as the late Ernie Pyle described the job in his book *Brave Men*.

Jeep traffic crossed the gap eighteen hours after the engineers started the job and within twenty-four hours the larger trucks were moving over the ledge in perfect safety. General Truscott, to accelerate the operation and to lend heart to the weary engineers, spent the entire night at the site.

"I'm going to stay here and look impatient until they get the job done," said the General.

Pyle told of a busy engineer, engaged with an air hose, who tripped over the General's feet.

"Why don't you get the hell out of here if you're not working," suggested the irritated soldier to the anonymous figure sitting in the dark.

The General moved out of the way without a word.

General Truscott, in his jeep, was first to cross the completed structure.

The 30th continued to advance without incident to Patti. Considerable heavy equipment, such as tanks and guns, was ferried around Cape Calava while the hastily built bridge along the cliff road was being reinforced for heavier traffic.

On August 13 the 15th and 30th Infantry regiments were moving out of the Patti area. The 7th loaded its Cannon Company on LCTs in the vicinity of Brolo while the foot troops moved out from the Cresta di Naso and advanced along Highway 113 to an area near Falcone, where the Cannon Company rejoined after landing at Patti.

Hugging the coast, the 15th moved steadily along, passed through Cape Tendari and Oliveri and occupied the high ground east and south of Oliveri. The 3d Reconnaissance Troop located four enemy pillboxes across the Mazara River in the vicinity of Castroreale Station and the Cannon Company of the 15th destroyed them by direct fire from 75mm SPs. Pack howitzers also took part in the neutralization.

The 30th passed its second day of light action as it moved to positions north of Furnari.

On the morning of August 15 the 7th passed through the 15th and in an all-day drive took Barcellona, Mari and San Lucia and by night had enveloped the enemy at Spadafora, forcing a withdrawal from the town after considerable street fighting.

The 3d Reconnaissance Troop was especially active in front of the 7th along Highway 113 and encountered many minefields and small pockets of resistance, which were eliminated by their own pack howitzers or by on-rushing 7th Infantry men. The troop also came under occasional fire from Mark IV tanks that the enemy was using as roving artillery to cover the retreat and to blow bridges. Strong positions on Cape di Milazzo, which jutted like a finger into the sea, were abandoned without a fight. A large 88mm ammunition dump, several coast defense batteries, about 150 undamaged vehicles, several thousand gallons of gasoline and oil and huge quantities of lumber were taken on Cape di Milazzo. A lighthouse off the Cape yielded several long-wave transmitters and a complete radio direction-finder was located at the seaplane base nearby.

Four ME-109s bombed Milazzo the following day, apparently bent on destroying the spoils which already had fallen into our hands.

The last day of enemy resistance in Sicily, August 16, found the 7th moving rapidly through the hills to Rometta, then to the high ground overlooking Messina. The enemy put up stiff resistance at a road junc-

The 3d Division's 10th Engineers "hang a bridge from the sky" at Cape Calava. (1) an engineer drills into the rock with a jackhammer. (2) a heavy timber is wrestled into position. (3) the flooring is laid. (4) General Truscott is the first to cross the span.

tion joining Highways 113 and 133 and the infantry by-passed the stronghold, which was later reduced by Company A of the 753d Tank Battalion, which destroyed one 88mm gun, two 77mm guns, one pillbox and a Mark IV tank. The tank, incidentally, had set afire a freight car filled with ammunition near Rometta early in the day, holding up traffic on Highway 113 for several hours.

The 15th and 30th Infantry Regiments closed in with little resistance and occupied positions beyond Messina.

The enemy completed his evacuation of Sicily during the night of August 16-17 and enemy guns from the Italian mainland hindered our convergence on the city with sporadic fire laid on roads and in the city itself.

Formal surrender of Messina was made at 1000 August 17, by Colonel Michele Tomasello, senior military authority of the city. The 3d Battalion of the 7th was the first unit to reach the town, which had been reported clear at 0500 that morning by a patrol led by 2d Lts. Ralph Yates of Company L and Jeff McNeely of 3d Battalion Headquarters. The first British patrols entered the city shortly after the 3d Battalion's patrol. General Patton, with a motorcycle escort and accompanied by General Truscott, entered the city at 1000.

The clearance of Sicily took thirty-eight days and was a well-coordinated campaign which ended in the enemy's being literally squeezed off the island. As the 3d pounded along the north coast, the II U. S. Corps had broken through all defenses west of Mt. Etna and the British, after taking Catania, had smashed through on the eastern slope of the Etna hill mass and were rushing pell-mell up the eastern coast intent on trapping the Germans southeast of Messina.

The infantryman is proud to say, and few will disagree, that all other arms and services are fundamentally in a support role to the infantry. Sicily was primarily an infantryman's campaign. If it was the almost perfect example of a well-executed military campaign, it is because the conquest of the island demonstrated how all branches of all services can work in the smoothest coordination so that the man who carries the M-1 rifle can fight the enemy at close range, destroy him, and move forward to occupy territory—and no war can be won without occupying the ground.

Before the first soldier could step ashore at Licata the problem of keeping him supplied had to be worked out. While the campaign was expected to be rapid, it was not expected that troops could or would move as swiftly as they did. That the entire supply setup managed to operate as well as it did, despite the handicaps of a swiftly-moving operation and the lack of good roads, was not the miracle it appeared to be, but rather the end result of sound logistical planning.

It has been related in the previous chapter in the preparation for Sicily of the formation of Force Depot, Near Shore Control, and Beach Group. It is time to mention their excellent work in connection with the successful campaign conducted by the fighting troops.

Force Depot continued operation in Africa until after the departure of the assault forces. The first groups of Force Depot landed in Sicily on D-plus-3 and D-plus-4, took over central dumps and warehouses already established by the Beach Group near Licata, reconnoitered for other installations and operations on D-plus-5. This marked the end of direct supply of troops by Beach Group and resumption of normal supply of the force.

The depot established railhead supply for all troops west of Licata and continued the operation of a daily train and advance railhead at Campobello which had been initiated on D-plus-4 by the Division Quartermaster and Division Ammunition Officer.

The 10th Field Hospital and 11th Evacuation Hospital were landed and placed in operation east of Licata under control of Force Depot.

During its period of operation the Depot supplied, in addition to Joss Force, a regimental combat team of the 9th Infantry Division, major elements of the 82d Airborne Division, and the entire 2d Armored Division. Thus, for a short period the reinforced 3d Infantry Division supplied more than 60,000 troops.

At midnight, July 17, orders were received from Seventh Army detaching all attached supply, medical and ordnance troops from the Division and attaching them to the newly created Special Engineer Brigade. This occurred nine days after the landing, just as the rapid push from Agrigento to Palermo began. Some of the units which had formerly operated under control of Force Depot, including ammunition and truck units, were removed entirely from the Division area and were no longer available to perform the necessary supply and transportation functions.

The Special Engineer Brigade, suddenly and unexpectedly thrust into the picture while the combat operation was in full swing, was unable to coordinate the remaining units to fill the gap left vacant by the dissolution of Force Depot. As a result, the entire burden of supply was placed squarely on the Division, which did not have sufficient organic transportation to maintain its own supply over the long distances which prevailed.

Near Shore Control worked in close harmony with the corresponding organization of the Navy and with the First Embarkation Group of Eastern Base Section which was charged by higher headquarters with the responsibility of the supply and embarkation of Joss Force.

The Beach Group landed before daylight with the combat troops. Shortly after daylight Beaches Yellow and Blue were organized and prepared to unload any type of craft; including LSTs, which could not be beached and had to be unloaded by a 300-foot ponton dock.

In three days Beach Group had landed at least 188 craft and had unloaded and placed in beach supply dumps about 7000 tons of supplies of all classes. On one occasion fourteen LSTs were unloaded in five hours. On D-plus-7 the advance detachment of Beach Group entered Porto Empedocle with the combat troops and within twenty-four hours had the port in operating condition. This shortened the supply line of the Division nearly forty miles. Both Licata and Porto Empedocle continued to handle the traffic of supplies and troops throughout the entire campaign.

The very success of the operation in Sicily increased the problems of supply and transportation. Combined with the breaking up of the Force Depot, Division supply units were faced with a difficult situation. To exploit the initial success of the operation and to keep fresh troops in contact with the enemy General Truscott therefore directed the organization of a special troop movement platoon of thirty-five 2½-ton trucks. These were employed continually on the drive to Palermo in shuttling infantry battalions. After carrying our troops forward, the trucks were used to haul prisoners of war to the Prizzi enclosure. The normal procedure of having empty supply trucks for this job was not feasible as there were too many prisoners. Consequently, in addition to normal supply vehicles other vehicles had to be used for this purpose.

The greatest drain on transportation was the necessity for carrying supplies from the beach dump at Agrigento to the advance Division supply dumps. This continually-lengthening supply line eventually involved a round trip of 175 miles, taking twenty hours. "The Battle of Transportation" was won only by the twenty-four-hour operation of all Division transportation and by using thirty 2½-ton trucks of the 3d Chemical Battalion. The victory was a tribute to the quality of the trucks which operated continually over the poorest roads without developing any serious maintenance trouble and to the drivers who drove day and night, in blackout and through numerous by-passes, with few vehicle accidents.

Greatest surprise to the Germans, and a feature upon which the support of later, more ambitious, amphibious operations was predicated, was the excellence of the naval gunfire support. In his report of naval gunfire, Lt. (jg) Hubert C. Manning, Navy liaison officer, was enthusiastic over the coordination of Navy and 3d Infantry Division.

For the first time in any operation, naval gunfire was directed successfully from an artillery fire-direction center, in this case the FDC of 10th FA Battalion. Direct hits were made on the railway battery on the mole of Licata and on gun positions northeast of Licata. In all, the Navy effectively screened and protected the assault forces and delivered smashing blows at enemy shore installations during the initial phase of the assault. When the push to Palermo began the Navy continued to assist the Division. When fire was needed during the fight for Agrigento, field artillery units could not reach their targets unless they went into positions lacking both cover and concealment. The Navy fired the missions. The missions were successful.

When the 3d Infantry Division began the advance along the north coast of the island the Navy was again available. All during the drive, especially in the engagements at San Fratello, Sant' Agata, and Brolo, naval gunfire proved tremendously effective. Crowning achievement of the Navy, according to many enlisted personnel, was the direct gunfire on the north coast which destroyed a Mark IV Tank at a critical moment.

The civilian reaction was interesting. In a country supposedly tightly controlled by, and wholeheartedly in favor of, the Fascist political rule, the "enemy" was greeted with open arms (and palms). As units moved through the towns and villages the civilians lined the streets, clapping and cheering—and begging for *"mangiare, caramelli, un sigaretto."* In the beginning the troops took pity on the obvious poverty and squalor and gave freely of their rations, candy, and cigarettes. Later the ascending prices of wine and eggs, which were the reward of generosity, began to change the attitude of the troops. Generally, however, the people were glad to see the Americans. The Fascist regime, it seemed, contained more slogans than food. *"Credere—Obedire—Combattere"* (Believe—Obey—Fight) was a little hard to digest without spaghetti and Marsala wine as the main course.

From the perspective of time, what were the visible results of the whirlwind campaign?

First, the Division played an outstanding role in clearing the island of enemy and making it usable as a base for further operations.

Second, the Division demonstrated conclusively that a well-planned operation placed in rapid and smooth execution, coordinated with naval and air forces, can overwhelm the enemy by not giving him a chance to get set. Once he is on the run he can be kept on the run if sufficient pressure is continually exerted.

Third, the Division demonstrated that small-scale amphibious operations in the enemy's rear can disrupt his entire defensive setup and force him to withdraw, sometimes more rapidly than if he were subjected to land or air attack only.

Fourth, the Division helped materially to eliminate Italy from the war. The Italian was not a good soldier, had no stake in the war, and no interest in continuing to fight it. Only the dyed-in-the-wool Fascists, as a rule, made a serious effort to provide determined resistance. The remainder surrendered in large numbers on the slightest pretext. The vast numbers who did give up with little or no struggle proved conclusively that Germany could depend little on her junior partner when the going got tough, and revealed upon what a foundation of sand the "Sawdust Caesar," Mussolini, had erected his grand castles in the air.

The campaign over, the 3d Infantry Division moved to western Sicily, near Marsala and Trapani, for a rest. Some portentous event, unnamable, indefinable, was even then rushing toward its bloody, hairbreadth fulfillment—the Battle of Salerno.

There were small hints dropped here and there from the airmen. "There was a funny thing happened over on one of the eastern fields yesterday. A big black Italian plane came in, and none of the ack-ack opened up on it. They say Eisenhower himself was there to meet it. . . ." From the paratroopers: "This is strictly on the Q.T., of course, but we got a big deal on, and its coming up pretty damn quick . . ." From the higherups: "Tonight we expect a lot of planes over. Unless they commit a hostile act, instruct your men not to fire on them. . . ."

The Gethsemane of Mussolini and his Mediterranean Empire was rapidly approaching. The chickens of unwarranted invasion, rapacious seizure, and cruel domination had come home to roost. The crumbling of empire was about to shift the entire role of Italy in World War II from that of an opportunist aggressor to that of a bewildered, internally-torn bystander. The mountainous, narrow peninsula, infrequently studded with low, rolling plains—famed in song and legend as a land of sparkling wines, sunshine, flashing signorinas, gay and colorful opera, was about to turn into the bitterest, most heartbreaking, most cursed battlefield of the longest-fought campaign in Europe in the Second World War.

The 3d Infantry Division was even then destined to play a prominent part in the coming ill-starred struggle. Now, men of the Division rested, took light training, and absorbed at a more leisurely pace the sights and sounds of Sicily, which before they had had time only to observe in passing. But Italy loomed as visibly from Trapani and Marsala almost as plainly as it had to those soldiers of the 3d who shortly before gazed at it across the turbulent waters of the Straits of Messina.

TABLE OF CASUALTIES*

Sicily

(July 10, 1943 through Sept. 19, 1943)

KIA	WIA	MIA	Total Battle Casualties	Non-Battle Casualties
381	1398	146	1925	2983

Reinforcements and Hospital return-to-unit personnel

Reinf		Hosp RTUs	
Off	EM	Off	EM
50	676	13	665

KNOWN ENEMY CASUALTIES

Killed	Wounded	Captured
Not recorded	Not recorded	50,104

*These figures were provided by the A C of S, G–1, 3d Infantry Division.

V
SOUTHERN ITALY

We Battle in the Craggy Apennines

NOT eagerly, not with the curiosity of tyros, but rather with the almost detached and very comprehensive first glance of an engraver at a difficult photograph on which he will shortly begin work, men of the 3d Division, lined at the rails looked forward. Ahead lay the beaches of Salerno.

Where the layman would discern only flat sandy beaches, backed by a low, almost imperceptible dirt ridge beyond which the terrain lay almost as flat as a billiard table; tall trees lining the main roads; some olive groves, some farmhouses; in the distance foothills and back of them the blue of mountains . . . the doughboy visualized, almost as though he had been here a few days before, enemy fire whipping in red slashes or invisibly across the hot fields . . . the terrain offering little or no natural cover; sparse foliage, lightly wooded hills and rugged mountains.

Naval officers made mental reconnaissances of the shifting line where sand disappeared beneath water, and of the color of the sea near shore; studied their hydrographic charts and scanned the blue skies for enemy planes which might come out of the sun in screaming, death-dealing power dives. The sailors' main concern was with how far inshore the craft and ships could get and still be able to retract after unloading. The doughboys thought in terms of, "How close can these things go here? Maybe we won't have to get our feet wet, for once."

A few correspondents thought in terms of the recently opened front, this time on the mainland of Italy: "At the point to which Seventh Army has carried the battle against the Nazis the newly-committed Fifth Army now enters the fray, and a new phase in the Mediterranean War at this point begins to unfold before our eyes."

To the doughboys the thought occurred and sometimes found articulation that something was now starting of which no one, not even the most optimistic nor belligerent could see the finish. "Where will it end? When will it end? Will I be there when it does end?"

The last week of August and the first week of September, 1943, was an extremely tense period. A large juggling of government, conducted on a high diplomatic level, with strong military overtones, was taking place, and lives and the outcome of battles hung in the balance.

The Badoglio government, which on July 25 had taken over the reins of Italian government from Mussolini, was dickering with the Allied governments through General Eisenhower for peace. Neither side, however, held the trump card, militarily speaking. This belonged to the Germans, and how much it meant was yet to be disclosed. The major questions of the moment were, how firmly were the Germans entrenched in Italy, technically still an Axis ally; and from the positions they held, how quickly could they move once their partners' defection became known? A lot depended on the answers to these two questions.

It has since been uncovered that Badoglio was possessed of an optimism which almost resulted in a catastrophe for the Allies. It was the belief of the aged Marshal (the man who won the war in Ethiopia for Mussolini) that there was enough Italian strength in and around Rome to seize and hold the capital city following the announcement of Italian surrender, until Allied troops could land amphibiously somewhere in the vicinity of Lido di Roma, or elsewhere near, and push on to the Eternal City. Badoglio underestimated both *Wehrmacht* intelligence and German sagacity.

The enemy knew that Italy had been ruled by a strong man and strong party. Once that man had been overthrown the fall of the party could not be long delayed, and with the collapse of Fascism in Italy any power the military had once possessed must certainly collapse under the Allied weight. The Germans, therefore, were prepared for just such a contingency, and were fully willing and able to take up the fight alone at the first hint that the Italian army was through.

A parachute drop on, first, Naples, then the main airfield at Rome, were called off at the last moment on the advice of a United States delegation headed by a brigadier general which was secretly in Rome in early September, when it was discovered that the *Wehrmacht* was almost completely in control of Rome and environs, and already had taken measures toward disarming the two or three Italian divisions stationed in and around the city. Military disaster for the Allies was thus avoided only by the narrowest of margins.

The Badoglio government signed final, unconditional surrender terms on September 3, the day which the Allied High Command had selected for the initial landings by the British 8th Army on the toe of the boot; at Calabria opposite Messina.

The main United States invasion effort, however, came on September 9, at Salerno. The story of Salerno has been told time and again, in other places. It is sufficient to say that Salerno was deemed the only practical place for the Fifth Army to land and that the Germans knew it; that some of the landing troops (which included a strong force of British troops) were deceived by the news of the Italian surrender; and that the enemy was fully prepared for the invasion convoy when it reached the beaches. Outstanding also, are the facts that Allied courage and tenacity went ahead to win the battle anyway, and that by September 18, when the first elements of the 3d Infantry Division went ashore, the battle of Salerno was finished. It remained for the 3d Division to help exploit the initial victory.

To backtrack: On September 5, Major General Truscott; his Chief of Staff, Col. Don E. Carleton; G-2, Lt. Col. Walter C. Mercer; Col. Richard L. Creed; Maj. Frederick Boye, Assistant G-3; Lt. Col. Charles E. Johnson, G-4; Division Signal Officer, Maj. Jesse F. Thomas; and Division Artillery S-3, Lt. Col. Walter T. Kerwin, Jr.; flew to Algiers for a conference with Fifth Army Commander, Lt. Gen. Mark W. Clark. The party was given details of the pending landing operation at Salerno and informed that 3d Infantry Division would probably be under Fifth Army control for the operation. The party returned to the CP at Trapani on September 7.

When news of the Italian surrender reached the Heaquarters, 7th Infantry and 1st and 2d Battalions of the 30th Infantry were immediately dispatched to guard several airports in the vicinity of Trapani. Part of the Division already had been stationed at these fields, but since word had been received that major units of the Italian air force might fly in to surrender that night, the additional units were employed and the guard doubled. Nothing materialized, however.

The 3d Battalion, 30th Infantry, commanded by Lt. Col. Edgar C. Doleman, established, maintained, and guarded a staging area in the vicinity of Castellamare del Golfo, midway between Trapani and Palermo, where elements of the British 10 Corps were staged prior to the assault landing at Salerno September 9.

The Salerno landing on the 9th found the U. S. 36th Infantry Division on the right, and British 10 Corps on the left. The situation there quickly became critical, and at 2115, September 13, a message was received by General Truscott from General Patton for the 3d's CG to take a small staff to Salerno for a conference with General Clark. Hard on the heels of this message, at 2356, came word from the 15th Army Group: 3d Division was to be "lifted" and moved to Salerno as soon as possible to meet the urgent situation there.

On September 14 General Truscott and Colonel Carleton took a plane to Palermo, and a PT boat from there to Salerno, where they conferred with General Clark. The 30th Infantry, meanwhile, left Trapani about 1330 the same day, and arrived at a newly-constructed staging area just outside Palermo around 2000. The Division CP was established in a former Italian schoolhouse.

Wholesale movement of the Division was continued and completed on September 15. As time permitted, equipment was obtained and issued. Two thousand replacements were received from 1st and 9th Infantry Divisions and assigned to units. General Truscott and the Chief of Staff returned at 2300 with some reassuring news. The situation at Salerno had improved considerably; 36th Division had reorganized and was now holding. Shipping was to be available the following day. Key personnel worked feverishly the rest of the night to complete loading arrangements.

The 30th Infantry, Division Headquarters, Division Artillery, and parts of service units loaded on LSTs at Palermo on September 16. The ships commenced pulling out at midnight and shortly thereafter rendezvoused. General Truscott, with a small staff, left again for Salerno by PT boat.

The following day, as loading of the remainder of the Division continued, the first convoy sailed at 0700. At 1500 a BBC broadcast gave the news that patrols of the 8th Army, advancing from the south, had made contact with 5th Army patrols. The Battle of Salerno had ended victoriously.

The LSTs which contained the first elements of the 3d Division began beaching at about 0900 September 18 south of the Sele River. It was planned for the 3d to go in on the left of the 45th Division, which had broken the beachhead stalemate a day or two earlier in a drive to the east. At that time, the area north between the beach and Battipaglia was held by the British 10 Corps while U. S. Rangers and British Commandos held the high ground west of Salerno. The 45th Division was on the right flank.

Battipaglia, an important rail and highway center some fifteen miles north of the beach, had fallen to the British that afternoon.

After officer patrols of the 30th Infantry had reconnoitered assembly areas and approach routes in the vicinity of Battipaglia, the 30th Infantry and Division Artillery units moved into positions near the beaches for the night.

By the morning of September 19 it was learned that the enemy had withdrawn north toward Acerno and the bivouac areas that night were established just south and southwest of Battipaglia, with patrols out toward Olevano.

About midnight, the I & R Platoon of the 30th, with Capt. Richard M. Savaresy, serving as Division advance guard, passed through the ruins of Battipaglia and moved north on the road toward Acerno—the first elements of the 3d Infantry Division to enter the treacherous range of the Apennine Mountains.

Three hours later, at a road fork that led to Montecorvino Rovella on the left and to Acerno on the right, the platoon engaged and defeated a small enemy infantry detachment.

The next opposition led to the Division's first real engagement in Italy.

3d Division's 10th Engineers reconstruct a demolished bridge near Salitto, Italy.

On a reverse curve northeast of Salitto and some two miles southwest of Acerno, the platoon approached a blown bridge which spanned a 60-foot gorge where the Isca della Serra plunges from a narrow canyon into the Tusciano far below in the valley.

German machine gunners and riflemen, later identified as members of the 1st Battalion, 9th *Panzer Grenadier* Regiment, commanded the curve of the road from almost impregnable positions on a hilltop across the valley to the east.

It was clear that the enemy intended to defend Acerno.

Captain Savaresy established an observation post, obtained all available information and returned to headquarters with his men to report on his mission. The fight for Acerno was in the mold.

At 0730, September 20, the Division received its mission, boundaries and objectives. The left boundary ran north and northwest from Battipaglia to a point just west of Montecorvino Rovella and Avellino. The right comprised the high ground east of the Acerno-Montello road.

The order to advance came at 1100.

The 30th Infantry, commanded by Col. Arthur H. Rogers, with Company A, 601st TD Battalion; Company B, 751st Tank Battalion; Company B, 84th Chemical Battalion; and Company C, 10th Engineer Battalion, attached, moved north in the Division zone of advance.

The 30th's 3d Battalion, under Lt. Col. Edgar C. Doleman, was the first to leave Battipaglia, followed by the 2d Battalion, commanded by Lt. Col. Lyle W. Bernard, which was to reconnoiter the west flank of the advance route. The 1st Battalion took the right flank under command of Maj. Oliver W. Kinney.

Only minor skirmishes marked the advance of the regiment, which halted for the night with 3d Battalion occupying the most northern position, a saddle just west of Tusciano. The march continued at daybreak September 21, just before enemy artillery shells began falling in 3d Battalion's bivouac area.

General Truscott had ordered the 30th to advance on Acerno at once.

Company I, under 1st Lt. Robert M. Boddy, started

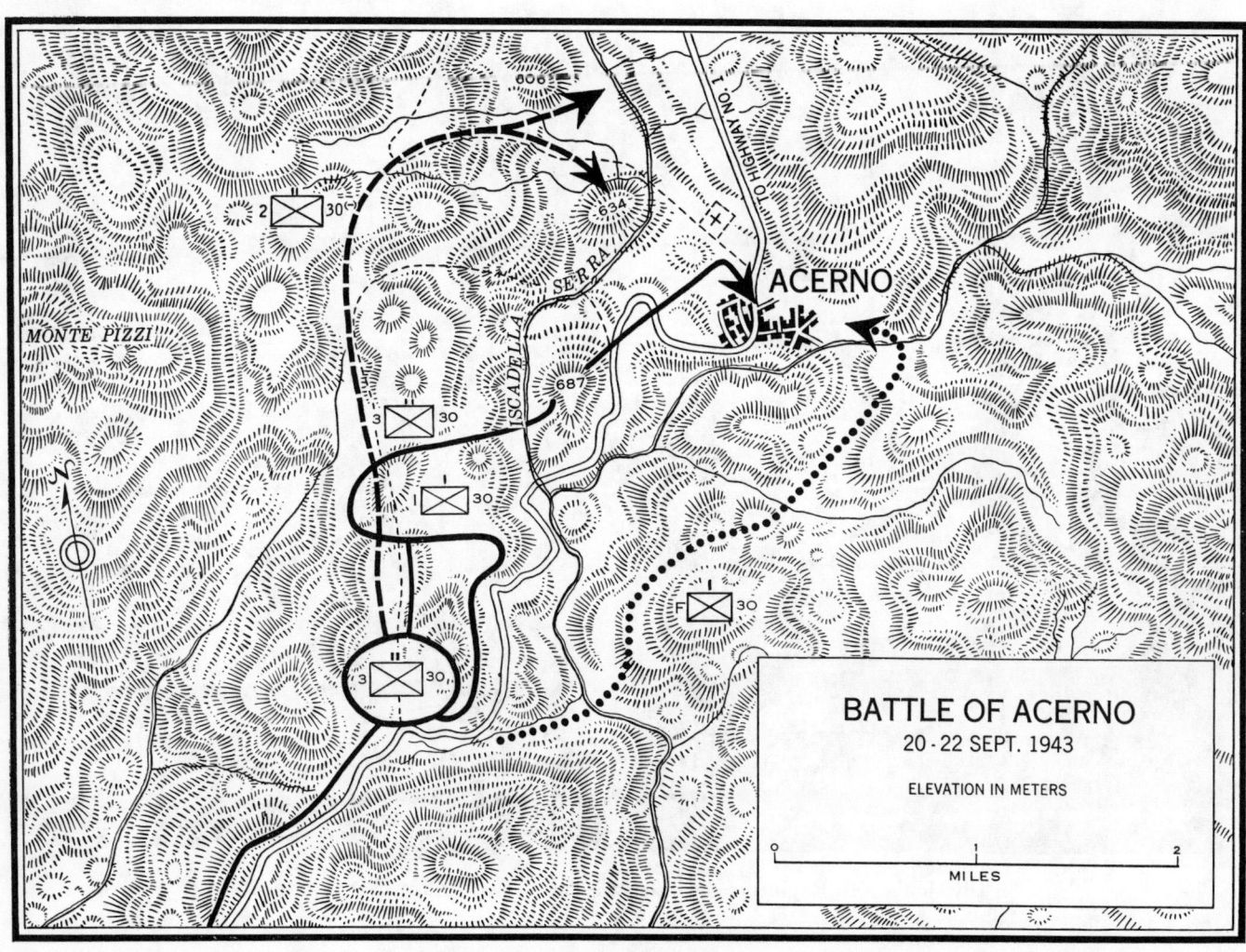

BATTLE OF ACERNO
20-22 SEPT. 1943
ELEVATION IN METERS

up the Acerno road but harassing fire from enemy artillery positions just north of the village, coupled with German command of the curve south of the demolished bridge, made this route impracticable and the company soon joined Company L, whose men were clambering over the wild mountains west of the road. Company L was commanded by 1st Lt. Maurice L. Britt. By 1800 Company I had taken the lead and reached the southern nose of Hill 687, north of the bridge.

Meanwhile, the bulk of the 2d Battalion was moving up past 3d Battalion, with the mission of by-passing Acerno and cutting the German escape route north of town. Company F, with Capt. Burleigh T. Packwood commanding, veered off to the east side of the road, scaled down the precipitous slopes into the Tusciano Valley and climbed another hill to be in position to drive out any delaying force and attack Acerno from the south.

All through the night these stalwarts of the 3d Division stole toward their objectives and by daybreak of September 22 the entire 3d Battalion rested on Hill 687, Company F was on high ground east of the Tusciano, one platoon of Company C commanded Hill 606 near the main road north of Acerno and the remainder of 2d Battalion held Hill 634, northwest of the city. Division Artillery occupied positions along the ridge north of Olevano and 1st Battalion was in assembly at a point two miles south of Montecorvino.

Meantime, while the 30th was pushing into enemy territory, the rest of the 3d Division was landing on the beaches at Salerno.

The 7th Infantry, commanded by Col. Harry B. Sherman, had debarked at 2100 on September 19 and had occupied the area south of Battipaglia. With the 7th were the remainder of Division Headquarters, 3d Signal Company, Companies A and B of the 10th Engineer Battalion, Companies A and B, 3d Medical Battalion; 3d Reconnaissance Troop, 703d Ordnance Company, and the remainder of Division Artillery, including the 441st AAA AW Battalion, attached.

On the following day the 7th Infantry moved to high ground north of Montecorvino and the 15th Infantry, under Col. William L. Ritter, landed and moved into the Battipaglia area. The entire 3d Division was now in Italy.

The attack on Acerno by the 30th Infantry began at 0800, September 22. The 3d Battalion proceeded due east toward the village while the 2d, on the 3d's left flank, headed toward the road running north out of the town.

The 3d met stiff opposition in an olive grove infested with enemy light and heavy machine guns just at the town's edge and, after bitter fighting with hand grenades and bayonets, took the grove and continued

Colonel Rogers, CO 30th Infantry, explains the Acerno situation to General Clark, CG, 5th Army.

northeast into a clearing outside the woods. They were stopped by fire from a 75mm battery in position behind a church. Heavy mortar fire was also falling in the area, further retarding their progress and keeping open the enemy escape route to the north. The Germans were pulling back and covering their withdrawal with savage counterattacks, which were habitually beaten off.

All morning, Division Artillery kept enemy mortar positions and traffic north of the town under constant fire while the 2d Battalion was moving up to positions within machine-gun and mortar range of the escape road. Company F occupied high ground south of Acerno.

At noon the regiment ordered a coordinated attack— a knockout blow which would start at 1300.

The 3d Battalion, with two companies abreast, one in reserve, was to attack east through the town. The 2d Battalion, minus one company, would advance east along an intermittent stream and cut the north-south road out of Acerno. Company F, reinforced by one platoon from the 1st Battalion, was to strike due north from its present position.

Came H-Hour. The 10th, 39th and 41st Field Artillery Battalions, under Lt. Cols. Kermit L. Davis, John D. Byrne and James R. Wendt, respectively, opened up with a concentration which battered the town and sent Germans streaming out the northern

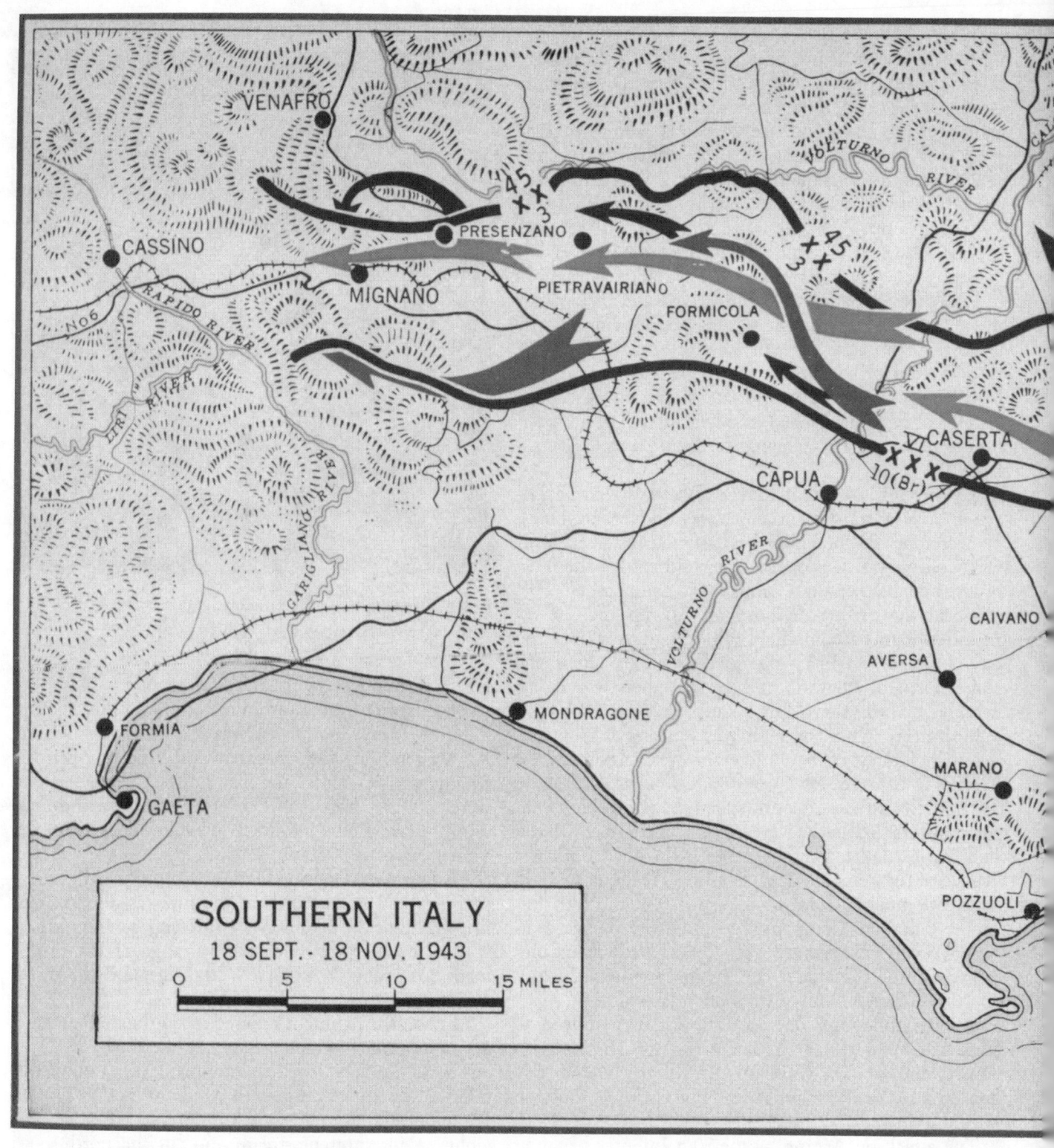

exit in armored vehicles. The Artillery, with Battery C. 36th Field Artillery and 441st AAA AW Battalion attached, fired a total of 1,016 rounds into Acerno from 1252 to 1325 that afternoon.

The 3d Battalion was pinned down for some time by enemy mortar and artillery fire from strong positions in the hills north of the city while the 2d continued to advance slowly over the rugged terrain north-west of the city, intent on cutting off the enemy retreat.

At 1525, the 3d Battalion struck dagger-like at the northwest corner of the village and Company F, with the attached platoon, simultaneously stabbed from the south. Opposition faded under this attack and at 1700 the 3d Battalion entered battered Acerno, which yielded thirty-four prisoners.

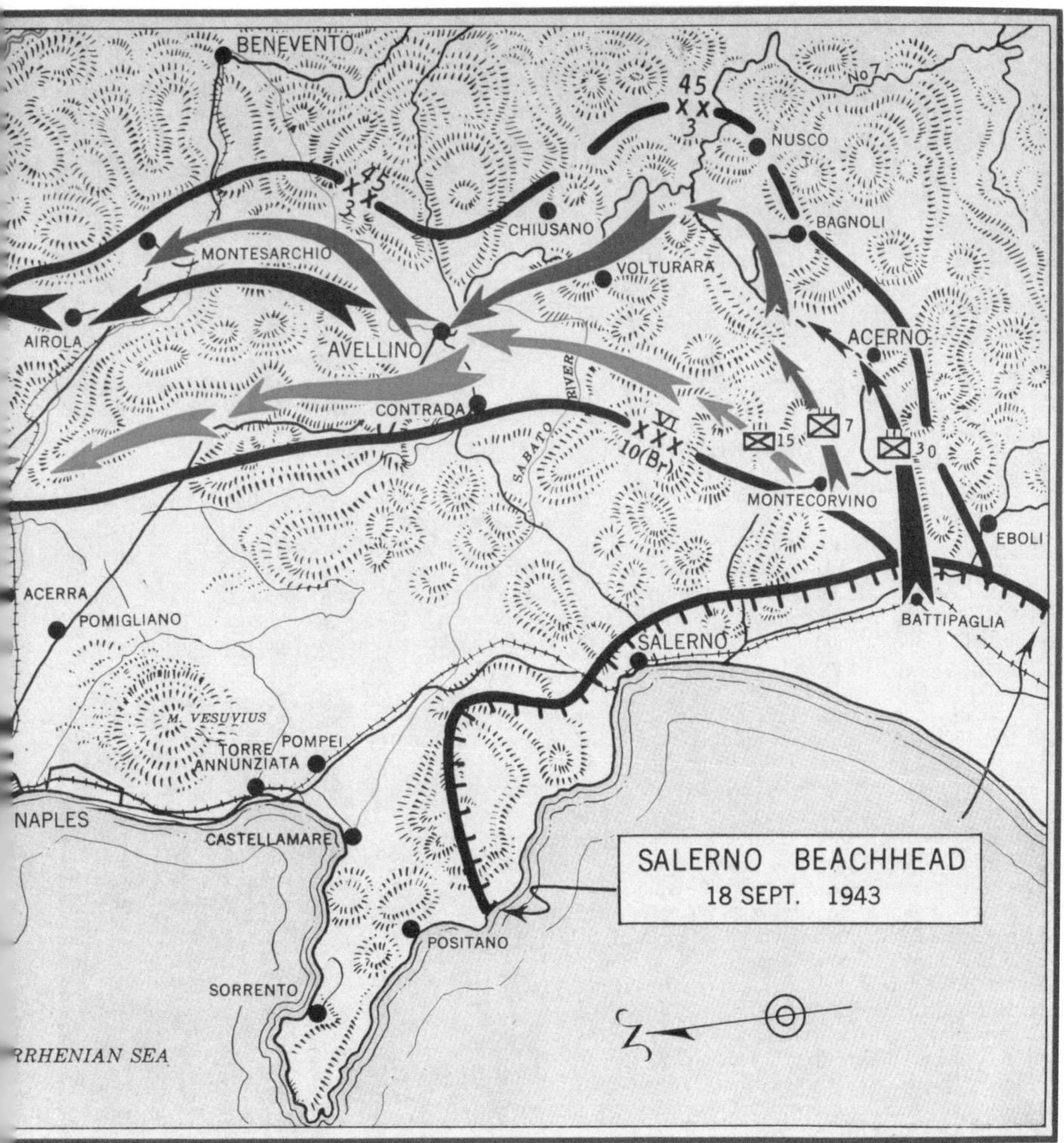

SALERNO BEACHHEAD
18 SEPT. 1943

The main German body had escaped under heavy protective fire but the opening round of the Division's "Boot Campaign" was won.

The Volturno River was the next Division objective—and the road that led to it was a series of obstacles designed to tax the ingenuity, vitality and endurance of every man, mule and vehicle in the entire organization.

Nature and the ages had provided impregnable defensive positions for enemy motorized infantry and self-propelled guns. Lone roads that cut through passes, skirted ledges and wrapped the lofty peaks with rough-surfaced ribbon, afforded secure avenues for German escape.

But the Volturno loomed and Acerno was only an-

The infantry moves its supplies through Acerno, which was captured after a two-day battle.

other milestone as the Division renewed the enemy chase September 23.

Augmenting the defenses set up by Nature, the Germans strengthened the delaying action which they effected after Acerno with innumerable demolitions that commanded all the resourcefulness of the 10th Engineer Battalion and supporting elements of the 36th Engineer Battalion. The Division Engineers were commanded by Lt. Col. Charles F. Tank.

No less than five bridges in a 2,200-yard stretch of road leading north from Acerno had been demolished by the enemy. Company C of the 10th, under Capt. Stanley E. Larson, rebuilt the demolished bridge on the main road just south of Acerno in two days. It was a two-story, two-bent trestle span eighty feet long, capable of carrying eighteen tons.

The engineers also swept the roads for mines, operated supply dumps, maintained water points, repaired road craters and even constructed a landing strip for Divisional artillery planes at Acerno.

At one point during their retreat, the Germans not only destroyed the bridge that spanned a canyon, but also blew away a cliffside, completely eliminating the road for about a hundred feet. In two days, Company A, 10th Engineers, with Capt. Edwin H. Swift commanding, reopened the road with a 40-foot steel treadway bridge and joined it to a stretch of roadway that had to be cut out of the sheer cliffside.

Fall rains, which frequently turned into mountain cloudbursts, added more difficulty to the transportation problems and made the route of the foot-weary doughboys more boggy and miserable.

The roads were so bad that units on many occasions could be supplied only by mule trains which had been brought from Sicily, and on one occasion even mules were unequal to the task and supplies were carried by human pack trains provided from personnel of reserve companies.

Despite these obstacles, the Division advanced twenty-eight miles, from Battipaglia to Highway No. 7, in eight days. The detoured route made the actual distance even greater.

Leaving Acerno, the movement was generally north

Pvt. Paul Oglesby stands in reverence before the altar of a ruined Catholic church on September 23, 1943.

and northwest, with the 45th Division on the right flank and the British 10 Corps on the left. The 30th Infantry was to lead the Division, followed in order by the 7th and 15th Infantry Regiments.

Little resistance was encountered until the 1st Battalion of the 30th reached Le Croci de Acerno, a village situated in a saddle along the main axis of advance. The 30th, with Division Artillery support and assisted by the 1st Battalion of the 7th, under command of Lt. Col. Frank M. Izenour, attacked at 1530. Within three hours, the enemy had been cleaned out and the push resumed.

The 7th passed through the 30th and assumed the lead on the following morning. The 3d Battalion, under Lt. Col. John A. Heintges, overcame resistance in the difficult terrain near Mt. Sovero that afternoon and by dark the battalion had secured the high ground and had sent night patrols into Bagnoli. A detachment of sixty American parachutists was contacted shortly after dark. Members of the 509th Parachute Infantry Battalion, they had been fighting behind enemy lines for nearly two weeks. They stated that the Germans were methodically withdrawing to the north bank of the Volturno.

The Division met additional light resistance in the vicinity of Salza and Nusco, but the principal enemy contact was maintained by the 15th Infantry in the advance up the Sabato Valley, which they had entered after crossing the mountains north of Curticello.

The 7th Infantry took Volturrara with little trouble as it continued westward through the hills from the Acerno road.

On September 27, the 30th on the right flank of the 7th, occupied Montemarano on Highway No. 7, thus completing an arc around Avellino, an important road junction and the next objective.

Wiremen of the 3d Signal Company lay wire in the Italian mud.

A jeep grinds its way forward over a mud-bottom road.

Elements of the 34th Division, which had begun landing on the beaches at Paestum September 21, had moved up parallel with the 30th, with the mission of cutting the main road that ran north from Avellino to Benevento. The 45th Division, meanwhile, guarded the 3d's right flank.

The swoop on Avellino began at 2200 September 29, when the arc comprising the 7th, 15th and 30th Infantry Regiments suddenly contracted, squeezing the Germans out of another mountain position, which was occupied the next morning with only light casualties.

The partial envelopment of Avellino and the night marches that preceded it and Acerno, were models for future night operations by the Division. The tendency to string out and lose control, with an overestimation of speed obtainable in cross-country marches after dark, was conquered. Enemy resistance was by-passed in the Avellino encirclement under cover of darkness and the German positions so completely infiltrated that at daybreak small fights were in progress over a considerable area.

Truly the 3d was learning lessons as the advance into "Fortress Europe" progressed. New battle tricks were being introduced every day. Short-cuts of all kinds appeared in every echelon and Division Headquarters launched one of the first right after the landings at Salerno, when a War Room was organized to meet the need for a simplified, more streamlined command post.

In the War Room was gathered all information concerning the Division, adjacent units and the enemy as well as the G-2 and G-3 operations maps, G-4 situation map concerning ammunition and ration supply, Engineer road situation map and G-1 information relative to losses and replacements. Here was centered, for the use of the Commanding General, all necessary information on which to base prospective plans and orders for the Division. It was an innovation which was later widely copied by other divisions.

And while the Division was literally "learning to walk" in new surroundings, the enemy was rapidly losing ground. The great but badly damaged port of Naples had fallen to the British October 1 without opposition. Although Naples, some thirty miles northwest of Salerno, was the prime objective of the Allied invasion scheme, its occupation did not alter the original plans to push the Germans back across the mouth of the Volturno, which is within about twenty miles of the Neapolitan metropolis.

After Avellino, the 3d branched off into two directions toward the Volturno. The 30th Infantry, moving north, subdued light enemy resistance as it took San Angelo, continued the march through San Martino and reached the high ground north of Airola. The 3d Battalion of the 7th had moved up along the right flank of the 30th and aided in the capture of another village, Montesarchio.

The 15th Infantry, advancing northwest from Avellino, met weak opposition on a ridge east of Cancello and pressed on through Baiano and Maddaloni to mountainous positions north of Caserta.

This thrust-by-thrust advance ended October 6—the 3d Division had reached the banks of the Volturno.

In falling back from Avellino to the river, the Germans had employed their usual delaying tactics but their retreat had been considerably hastened by the excellent work of the 3d Reconnaissance Troop under Capt. Alvin T. Netterblad, Jr., and the ability of the 10th Engineer Battalion to keep roads open through quick construction of by-passes and bridges.

So close was the chase that many structures prepared for demolition by the enemy lacked explosive charges. However, elaborately prepared roadblocks and the continued appearance of boobytraps, coupled with almost daily downpours of rain, made the final steps to the Volturno both difficult and dreary.

Established in high ground overlooking the river, the Division immediately initiated continuous and extensive reconnaissance and patrolling and the few remaining Germans were eliminated after light engagements. By the morning of October 8 the entire Division sector south of the river was clear.

The Volturno crossing came next.

The Volturno is not a formidable looking stream. Rising high in the Apennines, it follows a devious ninety-five mile course through steep mountains and pleasant valleys to its terminus at Castel Volturno, where it empties into the Tyrrhenian Sea. It runs generally south and southwest from its headwaters to a point just below Amerosi where it joins the Calore and meanders the rest of the way in a southwesterly direction through the Campanian Plain.

The river ran due east-west along the 3d Division front, was about 150 feet wide and varied in depth from three and a half to six feet. The banks ranged from two to fourteen feet in height while the terrain back of the banks was flat and unusually soft due to recent heavy rains.

Two bridges which formerly spanned the river had been blown by the Germans. Thus the crossing would have to be made by equipment and plans conceived, manufactured and executed by 3d Division officers and men, and they dedicated themselves to this objective.

Intelligence patrols cautiously selected crossing points, then waded and swam the river at night, probed enemy defenses, felt out the terrain, located strongpoints and marked logical spots for fordings that were to come later. These hazardous missions were accomplished in the face of an alert, dug-in enemy and not without casualties.

It was soon determined that a sufficient number of assault boats would not be available. So units improvised boats from life rafts obtained from the Navy, used rubber pontons from treadway bridges and made rafts with gasoline tins and water cans as floats. A supply of Italian life jackets found in a warehouse was appropriated.

The 3d Division was to bear the brunt of the main effort of VI Corps in the crossing of the Volturno, the second phase of the Allied campaign in Italy. This was indeed an important assignment. And it was common knowledge among the men that the defenders were the *Mauke* Battle Group of the *Hermann Goering Panzer* Division, one of Germany's proudest.

It was a great moment for General Truscott and the 3d Division when the mission was announced—to attack across the Volturno River between Triflisco and a point south of Caiazzo, secure a bridgehead and assist in the advance of the British 10 Corps.

A certain tenseness prevailed as preparations for the crossing were carried on around the clock.

All units were in concealed bivouac—the 7th just east of Caserta, the 30th in the vicinity of Casagiove and the 15th hidden behind a slope looking over the river.

Each unit conducted vigorous patrolling missions every night. The daily report of October 11 revealed the intense efforts that were being exerted to obtain all the details concerning enemy strength, positions and the nature of terrain that confronted the Division. Nothing was overlooked.

The 7th Infantry report of that date said: "Patrol crossed N261823; good crossing waist deep, seventy-five yards wide. Patrol crossed at N259829, waist deep, heavily defended on north side. Patrol crossed at N255817, four feet deep, bottom firm, no mines."

The 15th Infantry report stated: "Patrol crossed on debris of bridge at N267820, received MG fire from house on north bank, also hand grenades thrown at them. Another patrol crossed 500 yards east of that point and received MG fire. Patrol at N213810 received MG fire. Other patrols went to river vicinity 287-290 grids."

The 30th Infantry reported: "Guard patrol went down sunken road at N209991, received harassing long-range MG fire. Patrol went to N196805 opposite sand bar in river. Reconnaissance patrol reconnoitered upstream to power line, heard MG and mortar fire east of position, saw three lights across river."

By the next day, all Division Artillery except the 10th Field Artillery Battalion had been brought up to the vicinity of Balzi-Grottole and was in concealed positions behind a hill just south of the river.

The Engineers had completed construction of a tank road that led to the river's edge and had assembled and loaded all bridging material, including a prefabricated cableway built with material salvaged from a railroad yard and torpedo-assembly plant.

An improvised jeep bridge was constructed by using six regular floats supporting treads made of two strips of narrow gauge railroad track overlaid with Irving matting.

Nearly five miles of guide rope was ready for use by foot troops who were to ford the river.

Most vehicles of the 751st Tank Battalion, commanded by Lt. Col. Louis A. Hammack, had been waterproofed, as had those of the 601st Tank Destroyer Battalion, under Maj. Walter R. Tardy. A number of wire-laying jeeps had also been made "seaworthy."

The 84th Chemical Battalion, supervised by the Division Chemical Officer, Capt. Albert L. Safine, was prepared to employ smoke pots and mortars in order to hinder enemy observation of the crossing, while artillery units were to lay down additional smokescreens.

General Truscott had decided that the crossings, all enemy-held high ground, and our tentative bridge sites were to be completely enveloped in smoke at H-Hour.

And H-Hour was at hand—0200 October 13, 1943.

Aware that the Germans anticipated a plunge at Triflisco Gap, the Division Commander staged a fake attack on the left flank, which faced the gap.

At midnight, two hours before jump-off time, the fireworks began. The 1st Battalion, 15th Infantry, commanded by Maj. Thomas R. Davis, and the heavy weapons companies of the 30th Infantry, opened up with all their available fire, directed at enemy positions

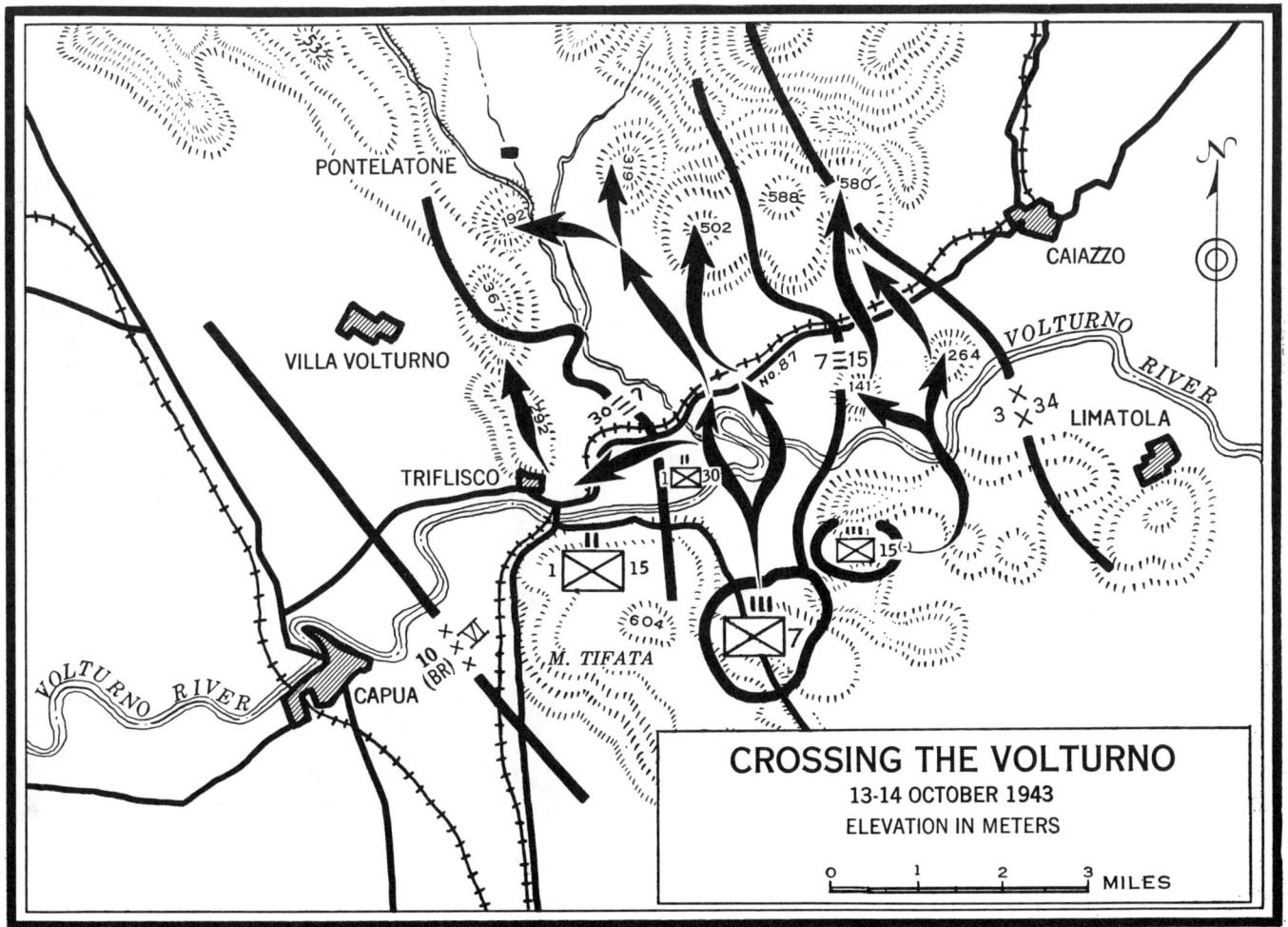

CROSSING THE VOLTURNO
13-14 OCTOBER 1943
ELEVATION IN METERS

Brigadier General William A. Campbell, CG 3d Div. Arty.

across the gap. The weapons companies, which fired throughout the night, were commanded by: Capt. Claude R. Streb, Company D; 1st Lt. William G. Stucky, Company H; and 1st Lt. James L. Osgard Company M.

The 2d Battalion, 30th Infantry, stood ready for a dash across the river in event the Germans weakened under this fire and showed signs of withdrawing. However, failure of the British to effect a crossing at Capua on the preceding night, which would have weakened the enemy position if successful, made this crossing impracticable.

One hour after this diversion fire began, Division Artillery, commanded by Brig. Gen. William A. Campbell, let loose with a terrific bombardment of all enemy positions across the river.

Bedlam reigned until five minutes before H-Hour, when smoke shells were mixed with high explosives and began bursting all over the area, laying a thick pall over the Volturno and enemy positions beyond it. It was a fitting prelude to events that quickly followed.

The night was clear and cool and the smoke-filled darkness, splotched with myriad flashes from artillery bursts, provided a protective cloak that covered the three battalions of the 7th Infantry Regiment as they moved down the valley between Mount Tifata and Mount Castellone. The main assault of the 3d Division was under way.

The feint on the left flank was being coordinated with the 7th Infantry's drive at the center and the 15th Infantry's simultaneous effort on the right.

The 7th headed for the river at a hairpin loop southwest of Piana di Caiazzo and the 15th was assigned a point directly south of the city.

At 0200 the 1st Battalion of the 7th, commanded by Lt. Col. Frank M. Izenour, crossed just west of the loop; 2d Battalion, under Lt. Col. Everett Duvall, crossed east of the turn and the 3d Battalion, with Lt. Col. John A. Heingtes commanding, followed in the traces of the 2d.

The Volturno was literally filled with assault boats, rafts and soldiers, some of whom crossed with life preservers and others who forded the stream clinging to guide ropes.

The Germans opposed the crossing with everything they had. Enemy machine-gun, artillery and mortar fire continually blazed away, but in less than two hours the 2d Battalion was across and by 0640 the entire 7th Infantry was anchored on the north bank of the river.

The regiment's attached tanks and tank destroyers were unable to make an early crossing because of heavy enemy fire that kept our bulldozers out of action, thus preventing the cutting of approaches in the high river bank. Despite the absence of armor, the 7th expanded

Brigadier General William W. Eagles, Assistant Division Commander.

its bridgehead and pushed north toward Mount Majulo.

By 0800 forward elements of the 1st Battalion had reached the foot of the mountain and within a short time held the flat ground to the left of it, south of Highway 87. This highway, the best in the 3d Division zone, runs from Naples through Caserta, crosses the Volturno at Triflisco and again at Amerosi and goes northeast to Pontelandolfo.

The 2d Battalion quickly moved across country toward the objective at Mount Majulo. Many enemy machine-gun nests could not be located in the dark and were by-passed. The 3d Battalion, advancing behind the 2d, engaged these positions at daybreak and, after a series of aggressive fire fights, had cleared the river bank and the irrigation ditches leading to Highway 87. After the 3d had crossed Highway 87, the enemy still remaining in these strongpoints, aware that they were cut off, surrendered.

The 2d Battalion was reorganizing on Mount Majulo, when the 3d Battalion arrived on the western slope. At this time K Company reported six enemy tanks approaching its position. Antitank guns were not yet across the river and the majority of the bazooka teams were out of ammunition. The situation appeared critical. Lt. Jenkin R. Jones, forward observer, 10th Field Artillery, set up his radio and called for artillery fire from the 10th and 39th Field Artillery Battalions, which stopped the enemy armored attack only after the lead tank had approached to within 50 yards of the 3d Battalion's left flank. For his gallantry and quick thought in the face of the enemy Lieutenant Jones was credited with having stopped a serious enemy threat and was awarded the Silver Star. He was killed later on the Anzio Beachhead.

By this time our attached armor had crossed the river at a ford which the 10th Engineers had improved under fire with hand tools, giving the 7th added strength to beat off an expected armored counterattack from the northwest. This threat never materialized.

The tremendous success of this vitally important operation by the 7th Infantry was attested to when Lt. Gen. Mark W. Clark, Commanding General of the Fifth Army, called Colonel Sherman the following morning and personally congratulated him on the achievement of his regiment.

The 15th Infantry, under temporary command of Brig. Gen. William W. Eagles, Assistant Division Commander, met stubborn resistance as it fought desperately to take the high ground beyond the river at its front.

The 2d Battalion, commanded by Lt. Col. John J. Toffey, had crossed the river at the west end of Mount Castellone and quickly seized Hill 141, its first objective.

The 3d Battalion, under Lt. Col. Charles F. Frederick, forded the river at a little island at the foot of Mount Castellone after climbing down the steep slopes that almost dipped into the stream. Hill 246 was the objective and it was taken from a determined enemy.

The two battalions, astride the promontories in the valley, came under intense enemy fire from dug-in positions on the north. Colonels Toffey and Frederick reorganized their units and the Germans were shoved back to the slopes beyond Piana di Caiazzo before dark.

With the 7th and 15th Infantry Regiments securely on their objectives, the main action focused around the high ridge above Triflisco, where the Germans were firmly entrenched. This ground had to be taken at any cost—and it was taken, by the 30th Infantry, under command of Col. Arthur H. Rogers. The regiment, however, suffered several setbacks before accomplishing the mission.

A number of patrols sent to the river before daybreak were driven back by heavy machine-gun fire but one from Company F succeeded in crossing at about 0440 and returned after capturing five prisoners.

Resistance was so strong and enemy fire so heavy that 2d Battalion, which was making the initial effort to cross the river, was ordered to delay in making the crossing. That night 1st Battalion cut back and crossed a jeep bridge which had been built across the river near the hairpin loop in the 7th Infantry zone and, under cover of darkness, stormed the hill from the east and drove the Germans out.

The 2d Battalion, 30th Infantry, followed by 1st Battalion, 15th Infantry, crossed early next morning. This meant that all the infantry battalions were now on the north side of the Volturno.

The attack had been executed exactly as planned by General Truscott and his staff and in approximately twenty-four hours of hard fighting the 3d Division had won control of the Volturno Valley from Triflisco Gap to Piana di Caiazzo.

Amidst the heroism during that time the actions of Capt. Arlo L. Olson, commanding Company F, 15th Infantry, especially stand out. Company F crossed near Scaffa di Caiazzo at approximately 0200 October 13. When nearly across the river a machine gun opened fire, killing the scout who had gone forward of Captain Olson to locate a path up the bank. The enemy opened fire on the captain, but he continued on until he reached the base of the bank and threw two hand grenades directly into the gun position, killing the crew.

"The enemy had placed a machine gun to cover the trail and laid a continuous band of grazing fire which temporarily prevented us from advancing toward our objective," T/Sgt. Robert F. Witham said later. "Captain Olson . . . divided the company into two parts and personally led one group in an envelopment from the left. At this point five Germans came toward us, and commenced throwing hand grenades at him. In the brief scrap which ensued the enemy were either all killed or wounded, and Captain Olson got a machine pistol from one of the casualties.

"This obstacle out of the way, Captain Olson advanced on the enemy position, crossing the intervening 150 yards in a slow, deliberate walk, in spite of aimed machine-gun fire which was striking the ground within two feet of him. When he got to a point about twenty-five yards from the enemy, he took aim with the German machine pistol and killed the machine-gun crew. He then turned his attention to the riflemen occupying foxholes nearby and killed six of them. Although Captain Olson had half a rifle company at his immediate disposal, he effected the destruction of this enemy strongpoint single-handed. . . ."

The advance up the valley now awaited bringing up supplies and artillery.

The 10th Engineers had built the jeep span and an 8-ton bridge over the river during the first day of the assault and had suffered many casualties as they worked under constant enemy fire and observation at sites that afforded no natural cover.

Their work on the heavy bridge was slowed considerably by enemy machine-gun, rifle and direct artillery fire. Much of the equipment was damaged by shell fragments and many rubber floats had to be repaired during the construction. The bridge and a detail of maintenance men were bombed and strafed the following day but damaged parts were quickly replaced and the bridge was kept open for two weeks. Seven of the attacking planes were shot down by the attached 441st AAA AW Battalion.

At daybreak October 14, the 39th FA Battalion, commanded by Lt. Col. John D. Byrne, displaced across the river and a section of Battery A, under Capt. Fred P. Stevens, immediately captured two German 150mm guns and six men and set up their own gun in the enemy's former position.

This capture was but one of many outstanding feats performed by Division Artillery at the Volturno as is attested to by the fact that 12,000 rounds of ammo were fired by the light batteries during the 24-hour period starting with H-Hour.

Upon completion of a 30-ton bridge by Company B, 16th Armored Engineer Battalion, the problem of moving heavy transport across the river was solved and consolidation of the Division bridgehead, which was now virtually secure, rested on the success attained in pushing the Germans further north.

This push was to continue relentlessly.

At noon October 14, the 15th Infantry was on the heights northeast of Piana di Caiazzo, the 7th was in the hills east of Pontelatone and the 30th was on the left flank driving along the ridges from Triflisco toward Formicola.

The 7th was planning an attack on Pontelatone when orders were received changing the direction of the Division advance. The altered route sent the 7th northeast through Liberi and Majorano to Dragoni, with the latter the main objective.

The sun was sinking when the 3d Battalion, with attached tanks and tank destroyers, began to advance over the hills toward Mount Fallano with the view of capturing Liberi before dark. These plans were upset when an all-night fight was encountered at Cisterna (*not* Cisterna di Littoria) a little village which the enemy stubbornly yielded early next morning.

While the 3d was engaged at Cisterna, the 2d Battalion pushed through the darkness along the slopes of Mount Friento where German tanks, committed as roving artillery, caused some delay. By daybreak, the 2d had reached the high ground above Prea and was headed toward Liberi.

In detail, the account of the action is as follows:

The 2d Battalion had moved around the 7th's left flank and captured Mount Friento. Company F's bazooka teams destroyed an enemy antitank gun and two armored halftracks, which were firing on the 3d Battalion. The maneuver of the 2d Battalion had surprised the enemy on Mount Friento and made him give ground. Further advance was stopped by heavy enemy fires from machine guns, mortars and a 20mm Flakwagon located in Villa and on the northern slopes of Hill 561.

Meanwhile the 3d Battalion had resumed its attack astride the road to capture the crossroads at Villa and to assist the 1st Battalion in its advance toward Liberi. Hill 561 was captured but the enemy counterattacked immediately. Five enemy attacks inflicted severe losses on the 3d Battalion and particularly Company K, in which company one platoon had a strength of four men. Yet the 3d Battalion yielded no ground. Late in the afternoon the enemy broke off the fight and withdrew his battered infantry under the protection of a tremendous mortar concentration.

The 1st Battalion moved up through Strangolagalli, by-passed Cisterna on the right and encountered some stiff opposition at Hill 581, a ridge running northwest from Sasso through Villa.

The scrub-covered ridges around Sasso afforded good ground for resistance and the 1st Battalion fought all night before the enemy was finally subdued.

The 2d Battalion, meantime, moved steadily forward on the 7th's left flank but was stopped shortly after midnight by strong resistance at a point southwest of Villa, which lay between Hill 561 and Hill 524. The battalion suffered many casualties in driving the enemy out of this area.

On the morning of October 16, the 7th was engaged in sharp fighting around Liberi. The Division intelligence section (G-2), under Maj. Grover Wilson, had learned that the 29th and 115th *Panzer Grenadier* Regiments were established on the far slopes of Hill 524 and were determined to wreck the plans to take Liberi or, at least, any hope of taking it without maximum cost. The 3d Battalion, 15th Infantry, had come from the Pontelatone area to join the 7th in the mission.

Liberi was the target for thrusts from all sides. All day long these thrusts were met with fierce counterattacks. Continuously the Germans charged back. First at Hill 524, then Hill 561. It was a bloody engagement and it continued far into the night. When dawn came the 7th attacked with renewed vigor and entered the town but found that the bulk of the Germans had retreated under cover of darkness.

Dragoni was the next objective and to reach it required covering the roughest terrain encountered since the march from the Volturno began. Even the Provisional Reconnaissance and Pack Train and the Provisional Pack Battery attached to the infantry units had difficulty in negotiating the slopes and steep hills that were encountered. The natural obstacles, with demolitions and mines that the enemy employed in his withdrawal, made it difficult to maintain contact at times.

By the night of October 17, the 2d Battalion had pushed its way to Mount Lungo, just west of Dragoni, and the 3d Battalion was on Hill 371, just south of the city. At this point, General Truscott ordered the 7th to stop its advance in order to rest the men and pack animals.

The 15th Infantry, joined by its 3d Battalion, moving on the left of the 7th, also negotiated a long stretch of tiresome hill-climbing to reach the ridges east of Pietramelara. The 1st Battalion made its way to Hill 446, above Roccaromana, that night and the following morning swooped down the hillside to capture the town, after having overrun enemy resistance-pockets on the slopes and in the valley where the town was situated. The occupation of Roccaromana was, however, only partial and temporary.

The 2d Battalion moved over Hill 446 and drove on to the Roccaromana-Statigliano-Latina road.

The 3d Battalion moved north across the Roccaromana–Statigliano–Latina road to seize the Mount della Costa and prevent the enemy from using the Latina–Baja-e-Latina–Pietramelara road farther north. The 3d Battalion succeeded in occupying the mountain mass, chiefly through the efforts of Company L. Company L,

A 3d Division aid-man merely glances at the dead German as he advances.

alone on the northern edge of Mount della Costa, overlooking the strategic enemy supply route to Baja-e-Latina, held its position for eight days, despite severe enemy shellings and counterattacks by numerically superior forces. The attrition of the battle on the slopes of Mount della Costa reduced Company L's strength to a handful of men. For three days and two nights the Company was without food and water. Yet the Company doggedly held the position and directed artillery fire upon the German line of supply to Baja-e-Latina. The enemy was, because of his inability to drive Company L from Mount della Costa, forced to withdraw from the Baja-e-Latina area. For this action, Company L, 15th Infantry was later awarded the Distinguished Unit Citation.

The 30th Infantry, meanwhile, had a hard tussle with the Germans in the vicinity of Formicola.

Monte Grande, a high ridge southeast of Formicola, lay in a gap that separated the 3d Division from the British 10 Corps and it was under alternate attacks by the 30th Infantry and British 56th Division when the 30th disengaged and moved to a position in Division reserve northeast of ͞ ͞lla.

The 7th, af͞ ͞ ͞ ͞, struck at Dragoni on the morning of October ͞9 but the 34th Division, on the right flank, stabbed sharply at dawn in a surprise attack from the south and entered the city a few minutes be-

A 3d Division wounded soldier is hastened rearward on the hood of a jeep.

fore the first troops of the 7th Infantry Regiment arrived.

The 7th then turned north from Dragoni toward Mount degli Angeli and Mount Monaco, two high formations that rise northwest of Baja e Latina.

The 15th, headed toward high ground beyond Pietramelara, was delayed several days at Roccaromana, which the enemy finally relinquished October 22, the same day that the 7th reached Mount degli Angeli. Baja e Latina had been occupied by the 7th in its march from Dragoni after Co. L, 15th Infantry's position on Mount della Costa had forced the enemy to withdraw from the town.

After three days of tough fighting, the 7th drove the enemy from the slopes of Mount Monaco, the last natural point of resistance that was available to the Germans in this area. On the morning of October 25, the 30th moved up to an assembly area near Baja e Latina, thus completing occupation of high ground that gave the 3d Division command of everything overlooking its bridgehead at the Volturno.

Hill by hill the *Hermann Goering Panzer* Division fell back—with the 3d always at its heels. Mignano Gap beckoned from the north.

Taking up the pursuit October 26, the Division veered to the northwest with the mission of sweeping its sector and securing the left flank of 10 Corps. The British were still on our left, with the 34th Division on the right flank. Monte San Nicola was attacked by elements of 7th and 30th Infantry Regiments.

Under command of Lt. Col. Lionel C. McGarr (who had assumed his new post on hospitalization of Colonel Rogers October 21), 30th Infantry jumped off in an attack on Mt. Nicola and Pietravairano at 0900 October 26, following a four-hour artillery concentration.

All three battalions of the 30th were committed, with 3d Battalion on the left, 2d Battalion on the right, and 1st Battalion echeloned to the right rear. The 7th Infantry supported the initial attack by fire.

As the three battalions crossed the flats of the valley leading up to Mount Nicola from the east, all troops came under heavy enemy mortar fire. Approaching the great hill mass 30th Infantry found the Germans had made intensive preparations and had dug in along the crest and not along the forward slopes. Throughout the entire day of October 26 the battalions battled enemy infantry, encountering "S" mines, demolition tripwire boobytraps, thick brush that had to be cut to make paths, and enemy *Nebelwerfer* fire. By nightfall 3d Battalion had captured the first of the three highest knolls along the crest of the ridge.

That night the front lines were but five yards apart in places, heavy brush and rain making visibility nil. All the next day grenade and tommy-gun battles raged as 3d Battalion, encountering the brunt of the enemy opposition, along with one company of 2d Battalion, forged forward to capture the two other high points which the Germans had made into almost impregnable machine-gun positions. By 2100 the evening of October 27 Company L and the 3d Battalion command group entered the city of Pietravairano to find it filled with Teller-mine boobytraps and "S" mines. The battalion had killed at least twenty-six Germans, wounded scores more, and captured thirty. In addition it had suffered numerous casualties, including six killed, in the two-day fight. Throughout the entire action, the battalion went practically without food and water as the 1200-meter climb over rugged, mountainous, brush-covered, slippery, and boobytrapped terrain made movement, supply, and evacuation almost man-killing. The 1st Battalion, after being relieved on the northern edge of the ridge by elements of the 7th Infantry, moved behind the 2d Battalion and then, after touching the eastern outskirts of Pietravairano, went north to occupy and hold the town of Vairano. The 15th swept up the valley and drove the Germans from San Felice and Mount Gaievola, meeting little opposition en route. Part of the 7th took the Monticello feature, thus establishing an unbroken front in the Division sector, which had been cleared in avalanche fashion.

October 27 saw the culmination of Capt. Arlo L. Olson's deeds. For thirteen days he had constantly been in the lead of Company F, 15th Infantry, leading combat patrols or acting as number-one scout.

"... at about 1200 hours the company was attacking enemy positions north of San Felice," said Radioman Pfc. Lawrence E. Adkins later. "... a reconnoitering

3d Division Infantrymen moving into position for the attack on Pietravairano on October 26, 1943.

party . . . returned with information that the enemy had a strongpoint about fifty yards from the base of the hill.

"Captain Olson, upon receiving the above information, called for one of his platoons to follow him and moved down the slope in an attack on the enemy. When he reached the base of the hill he crawled to within twenty-five yards of the enemy strongpoint whereupon he charged the enemy machine-gun which was in the center of the enemy position. Despite continuous fire which barely missed him as he ran, Captain Olson reached the enemy machine-gun and dispatched the crew with his pistol. When his men saw the Captain make his head-on charge against the machine-gun they followed him and completely overran the enemy. When the shooting stopped I counted twelve dead Germans and seven prisoners.

"Captain Olson sent for the balance of the company and led the company in an advance on the next objective, a mountain about 2000 yards across the flat. . . ."

Olson moved across toward the hill and two-thirds of the way up the hill, when strong enemy fire was received. At this point he organized his company into an assault line and moved forward in the lead, disdaining cover. The assault was successful and the hill was taken.

"With the hill completely in our hands," said Sgt. Anthony Trisolini, "Captain Olson posted one platoon as security and began to reorganize the company behind the cover of the crest. At this time we were subjected to a severe concentration of enemy mortar fire which killed one of our officers, our radioman and fatally wounded the Captain.

"Although mortally wounded, Captain Olson kept going and moved about the crest of the hill completely disregarding his wounds in order that the company might be placed in position to withstand successfully any possible future counterattack. After satisfying himself that the objective was properly defended he supervised evacuation of his casualties, refusing medical aid for himself until all of his men had been cared for. Captain Olson died before he could be evacuated."

Said his battalion commander, Lt. Col. John J. Toffey: "Captain Olson's intrepidity, exemplary conduct, and demonstrated professional skill served as a model for his officers and men and enabled the company to accept casualties without weakening the desire to close with the enemy and destroy him. This spirit, instilled by Captain Olson, has never left the company."

Captain Olson was awarded the Medal of Honor posthumously for his heroism from 13-27 October.

October 28 marked the first day in weeks that our men were not confronted with hills. Pack animals got a second breath for the first time since the Volturno and as October ended patrols were as far north as

General Eisenhower, Supreme Commander Allied Forces in the Mediterranean Theater, Lieutenant General Clark, CG Fifth Army and Major General Lucas leave the 3d Division War Room during a tour of the front in Italy.

Presenzano, where the 3d was to assist the 45th Division in effecting another crossing of the Volturno. The 34th Division, which had been on our right flank, had turned northeast and was moving along Bava Creek on the right of the 45th.

During this period 2nd Lt. Harold E. Greer, S-2 of the 2d Battalion, 30th Infantry, volunteered for a hazardous mission. He led a six-man patrol seven miles past his battalion front lines to a preselected Italian farmhouse within the German lines near Presenzano, Italy, the night of October 28-29. After establishing his OP listening post in the upper story of the farm building, Lieutenant Greer reconnoitered the outskirts of Presenzano, coming under the fire of friendly artillery that scored a direct hit on a German ammunition dump seventy-five yards away, scattering debris that narrowly missed him.

Observing the enemy preparing to withdraw, building final defensive positions and roadblocks and destroying bridges, Lieutenant Greer reported this information to his battalion by SCR 284 radio. He narrowly escaped death for a second time when American planes dive-bombed his farmhouse OP the morning of October 29. Bombs burst as close as fifty yards from the building. While this took place, Greer located an enemy field kitchen unit bivouacked along a draw 500 yards from the house and directed artillery fire on the area, inflicting heavy damage. The night of October 29 a 10-man German patrol entered the ground floor of his OP and remained there for forty-five minutes, but failed to discover him. When he saw the patrol lay mines along the roadbed forty yards from his OP, Greer recorded the fact and later informed advance friendly engineers who removed them before friendly tanks reached the city.

He also sighted an enemy convoy evacuating troops

and equipment toward the German rear on October 30, and quickly radioed the information to his battalion CO who in turn notified Division Headquarters.

Early on the morning of November 1, Lieutenant Greer met 15th Infantry troops as they entered Presenzano. His timely information had materially aided in speeding the advance.

Nearly two months had elapsed since the 3d had started its drive up the Italian boot from Battipaglia. Enemy activity had been characterized throughout the advance by deliberate withdrawal, covered by mining and demolition. He had consistently infiltrated our forward positions with night combat patrols; he came back to reoccupy positions which our patrols previously penetrated; he ambushed our supply trains and booby-trapped trails and bivouac areas; he employed armor frequently but sparingly, using tanks in twos and threes to work with small groups of infantry; he sited self-propelled guns in defiladed positions and towns where they were difficult to find. And he took full advantage of the rugged terrain, the greatest asset of defensive warfare.

All the enemy's tricks had been solved by the men of the Marne Division. All his innovations had been countered with improvisations of our own. The difficult access to certain mountain heights was conquered by the use of the Provisional Pack Train and Provisional Mounted Reconnaissance Troop. Divisional Cub planes were used for hitherto unknown purposes, as in the instance where a pack train became lost in the mountains and a plane searched it out and led it to its destination, where it arrived with ammunition just in time to save a battalion. Coordination with air support was so precise that prisoners of war taken in the Pietravairano area claimed the air bombardment was more accurate and terrifying than any they had ever experienced before.

And the mountain range that now faced us (the German Winter Line of 1943-44, or Gustav Line) presented even higher peaks, more precipitous cliffs, and less passable roads than those which the 3d had just crossed. The range skirted the Volturno Valley from Isernia, through Venafro to Mignano, which was located in a gap that temporarily broke the string. At places the peaks reached a height of one mile. Increasing rains and colder weather joined hands to make the operations more difficult as November 1 arrived and the drive on Mignano was begun.

With Highway No. 6 as the axis of advance, the Division moved forward with the 7th Infantry on the left, the 15th Infantry, now under command of Lt. Col. Ashton H. Manhart, in the center and the 30th, commanded by Lt. Col. Lionel C. McGarr, on the right.

The crossing of the Volturno by the 45th Division during the night of November 3-4 was aided by the 3d during the next three days, when a strong demonstration was conducted toward Terra Corpo in the 7th's sector and a swift seizure of the high ground back of Presenzano was effected.

The 15th met heavy resistance in the Presenzano area but after a bitter struggle drove the enemy out of the valley between Presenzano and Mignano and followed up with the capture of Mount Cesima.

The 7th, in its action near Terra Corpo, succeeded in cutting the road between Roccamonfina and Mignano and took Mount Friello. Mount Friello was a key terrain feature, affording us observation up the Mignano valley. The Camino–Difensa–Maggiore range was still in possession of the enemy. It was here that the 7th encountered an astounding example of German obstacle construction. Mount Friello was hardly large enough to conceal the 3d Battalion. Yet the enemy had laid over 3000 S mines along every trail, ditch or break in the thick underbrush. The hill was to have been taken in a night attack. Interrogation of Italian civilians revealed the presence of the mines and saved the 3d Battalion from a possible disaster. The doughfeet of the 3d Battalion, 7th Infantry, named Mount Friello, "Mine Hill," and rightfully so.

On November 5, the Division was poised to make its attack on Mignano, which is situated in a wide gap, protected from the east and west by lofty peaks. Mount Lungo and Mount Rotundo, formidable barriers in themselves, rise like two camel humps from the level of the gap north of Mignano. Reconnaissance patrols reported that both of these terrain features were covered with gun positions, minefields and tank traps, thus making an attack through the southern opening to the gap impracticable.

General Truscott's strategy was to attack the Mignano gap from the mountains on its flanks.

This operation proved to be the most heart-breaking, nerve-wracking venture that the 3d Division had undertaken since its baptism of fire at Casablanca. It was here that the offensive prowess of every member of the Division crystallized into a shining brilliance. Mignano's tremendous value to the enemy as a communication center and a defensive hub to the plains beyond had to be destroyed, and with it the defending enemy, who held the peaks that look down upon the gap.

The 30th Infantry, which had been in reserve and blocking to the northeast, moved northwest from Presenzano during the night of November 5-6, passed through elements of the 45th Division en route and opened an attack through Rocca Pippirozzi at 0530 November 6.

The 15th Infantry at that time was moving down the northwestern slope of Mount Cesima and through Mignano toward Mount Rotundo and Mount Lungo.

The 7th Infantry was fighting its way down the northern slope of Mount Camino toward Mount la Difensa.

All three regiments were fighting under the worst of conditions. They were attacking a battle-wise and vicious enemy, who held the commanding terrain features. He was dug in in solid rock and had the entire approach area covered with artillery, mortar, machine-gun, automatic-weapon and rifle fire. Mines were sown thickly through the entire area. It was cold and damp. The mist hung low over the mountainside and visibility was so bad at times that it was impossible to see a man 20 feet to the front. Thus the attack began.

The 30th Infantry attacked westward from Rocca Pippirozzi at 0530, November 6, with the mission of seizing Mount Rotundo. It advanced in a column of battalions, 1st leading, followed by the 2d and 3d. The advance was difficult. Men, physically exhausted by five weeks of continuous campaigning in the Apennines, crawled up steep and slippery "hills" on their hands and knees. Sure-footed mules and burros carrying food and ammunition fell from narrow trails which led up the precipitous and treacherous Apennines, to their death below. The 1st Battalion contacted the enemy at 0920 and engaged him in a small-arms fire fight. The fight continued as the 1st Battalion advanced. By late afternoon it had taken its objective, the nose of Mount Cannavinelle, where it was subjected to murderous concentrations of artillery and mortar fire at 1315.

At 1530, the 2d Battalion passed through the 1st Battalion which secured its line of departure, and attacked Mount Rotundo. The enemy on Mount Rotundo was quick to take up the challenge. Extremely intense small-arms, machine-gun, mortar and artillery fire poured forth from well dug-in positions, magnificently camouflaged and protected by anti-personnel minefields and barbed wire, on Mount Rotundo. The 2d Battalion was unable to take its objective because of this terrible opposition.

The 15th Infantry, during the 30th's advance, moved down the forward slopes of Mount Cesima. The 2d Battalion pushed north to attack Mount Rotundo from the south and the 3d Battalion passed through enemy-deserted Mignano and pressed north up the gap toward Mount Lungo. Here, too, enemy resistance was immediate and intense. Enemy on Mount Lungo, Mount Rotundo and Hill 253, which is directly south of Mount Lungo, brought fire to bear on the attackers with such intensity and accuracy that it was beyond the human ability of the men to advance.

Across the gap, on the Division left flank, the 7th

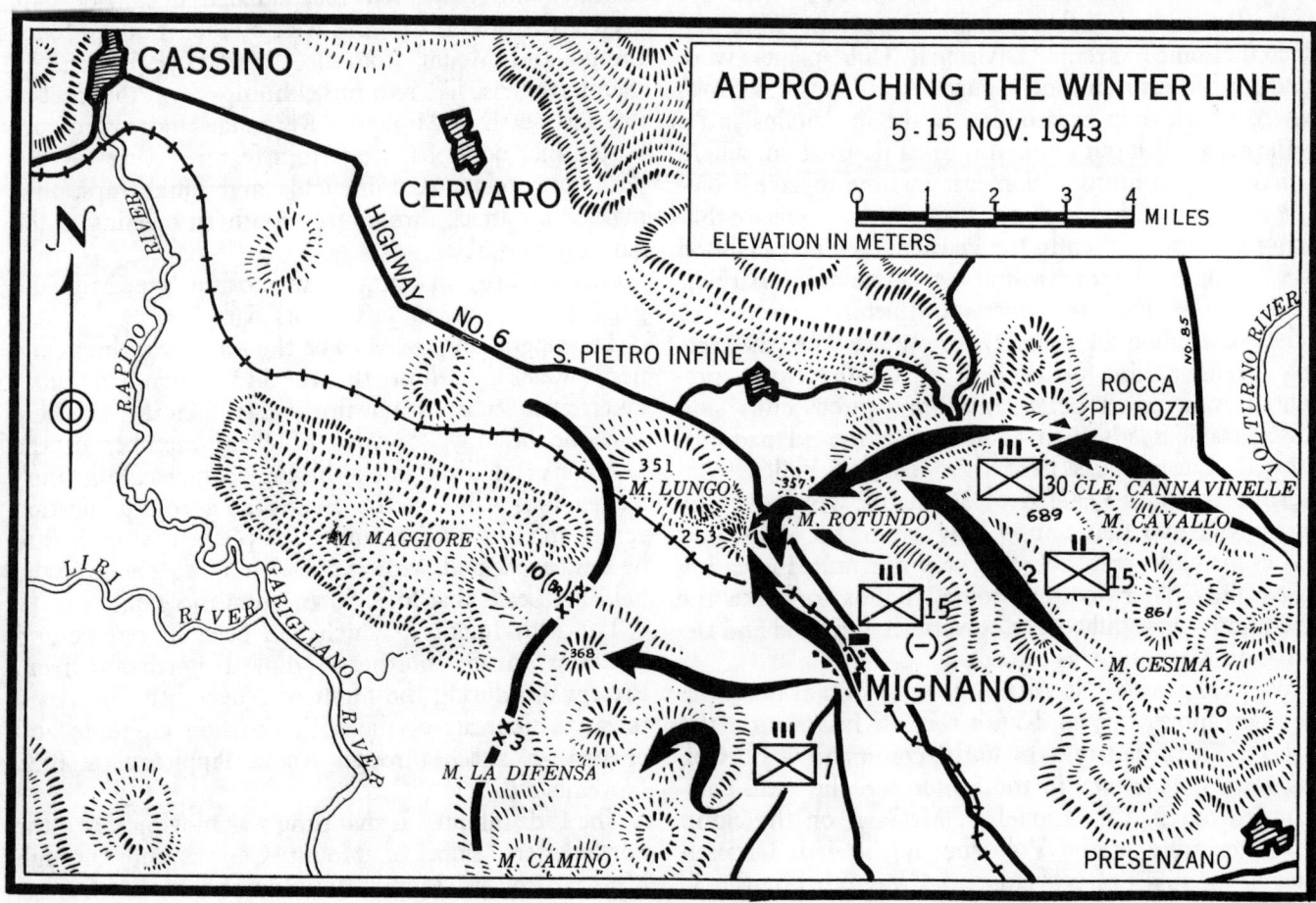

Infantry was wrapped in a terrific struggle to wrest the towering Mount la Difensa from the enemy. The 2d Battalion had attacked on 5 November, through Caspoli and Casale toward the high ridge between the jagged peaks of Mount Camino and the perpendicular cliffs of Mount la Difensa. The 3d Battalion assisted on the right flank by cleaning out the enemy in the 7th's zone of action on the Mignano Valley floor and clearing the southeastern slopes of Mount la Difensa. The 1st Battalion passed around the right flank of the 3d Battalion and attacked the northeastern slope of la Difensa. This maneuver pinched out the 3d Battalion and placed the 1st and 2d Battalions abreast, and in control of the northeastern and southeastern slopes of Mount la Difensa. During the next ten days these battalions tried in vain to scale the heights and secure the top of the mountain. Their every effort was balked by a cliff sixty feet high, following north and south some 1500 yards along the top of the mountain. In the sector of the 2d Battalion, only one path could be found up the cliff and this was commanded by two enemy machine guns, firing from positions blasted out of rock, only the firing apertures visible. Action along the entire line held by the 7th Infantry was stalemated. Yet the fire fight was continuous and savage. From his positions the enemy laid down deadly fires against our every attempt to move forward. In the sector of the 1st Battalion the enemy paid a heavy price to retain his position. His counterattacks were often costly, too, but he managed to shift his reserves and replace his losses.

Supplying the combat troops in the 7th, 15th and 30th Infantry Regiments' zones was a major problem in this terrain, cut by deep gorges and precipitous ridges. Even the valuable pack mules and burros were useless, and food, ammunition and water had to be carried by carrying parties, equipped with improvised packboards. A man could manage only a small amount, for he needed both hands for climbing. The trip up required a full day and the evacuation of the dead and wounded was accomplished in an average of six-seven hours. The soldiers suffered severely from exposure to rain and cold and from a lack of proper food and clothing. Yet the priceless ammunition was always adequate. No definition of the word "Teamwork" could explain the full significance of the word there in the Apennines. The spirit that was tacitly present, between the hard-pressed infantrymen at the crest of the mountain and the carrying parties that labored night and day to sustain them, defies to be set down in words.

On 12 November, Company K, commanded by Lt. Frank Petruzel, reinforced by the 2d (MG) Platoon of Company M, moved out to relieve the depleted 2d Battalion. On 16 November Company K, after a fifteen-minute artillery, Cannon Company and chemical mortar concentration placed on enemy positions, jumped off to give it one more try. The dense fog and occasional clouds, which, it was hoped, would reduce visibility to our advantage, suddenly cleared, and the enemy stopped the attack ten yards from the line of departure and fifty feet from the top of the mountain. It was the last attempt, for on 17 November, troops of the 36th Infantry Division began the relief of the 3d Infantry Division.

Meanwhile the 30th Infantry was engaged in front of Mount Rotundo. When the advance of the 2d Battalion was stopped on 6 November, it was decided that the 2d and 3d Battalions would make a coordinated attack at 1330 November 7. Due to the great difficulties of reorganizing under continual enemy fire and the trouble caused by the infiltration of a wily and crafty enemy, determined to withstand all efforts to seize this vital outpost of the Cassino Line, the attack was postponed. In the interim the 2d Battalion was forced to repulse a counterattack and thwart enemy attempts to cut its line of communication. The 1st Battalion, too, repulsed a bitter enemy counterattack during the night of 7-8 November.

The 15th Infantry, meantime, had pressed its attack strongly but without success. Every attempt to seize the southern slope of Mount Rotundo and Mount Lungo met with bitter, determined resistance. At 0845 November 8 a coordinated attack, by the 15th and 30th Infantry Regiments, was launched after a fifteen-minute preparation, fired by eight battalions of artillery. The 1st Battalion of the 15th Infantry advanced around the southwest side of Mount Rotundo to seize Hill 193, which occupies the center of a horseshoe curve in Highway 6. The 3d Battalion of the 15th Infantry fought its way to and captured Hill 253, which is the southern nose of Mount Lungo. The 2d Battalion fought up the southern slope of Mount Rotundo.

The 3d Battalion, 30th Infantry, attacked Mount Rotundo from the east. At 1100 November 8, Companies I and L, less one platoon, had taken the objective. The attack had struck the enemy in the flank and rear and had taken him by surprise, while he was engaged with the 15th Infantry.

Enemy counteraction was immediate. A series of local counterattacks began within an hour of the capture of the hill and continued in mounting intensity for forty-eight hours.

Both the 15th and the 30th dug in on their objectives and were counterattacked by the enemy day and night for a period of five or six days. Attacks were launched by both units to improve their positions, which brought counterattacks by the enemy each time.

On the morning of November 10, 3d Battalion, 30th Infantry, was occupying captured Mount Rotundo with two depleted companies on the hill mass and Company

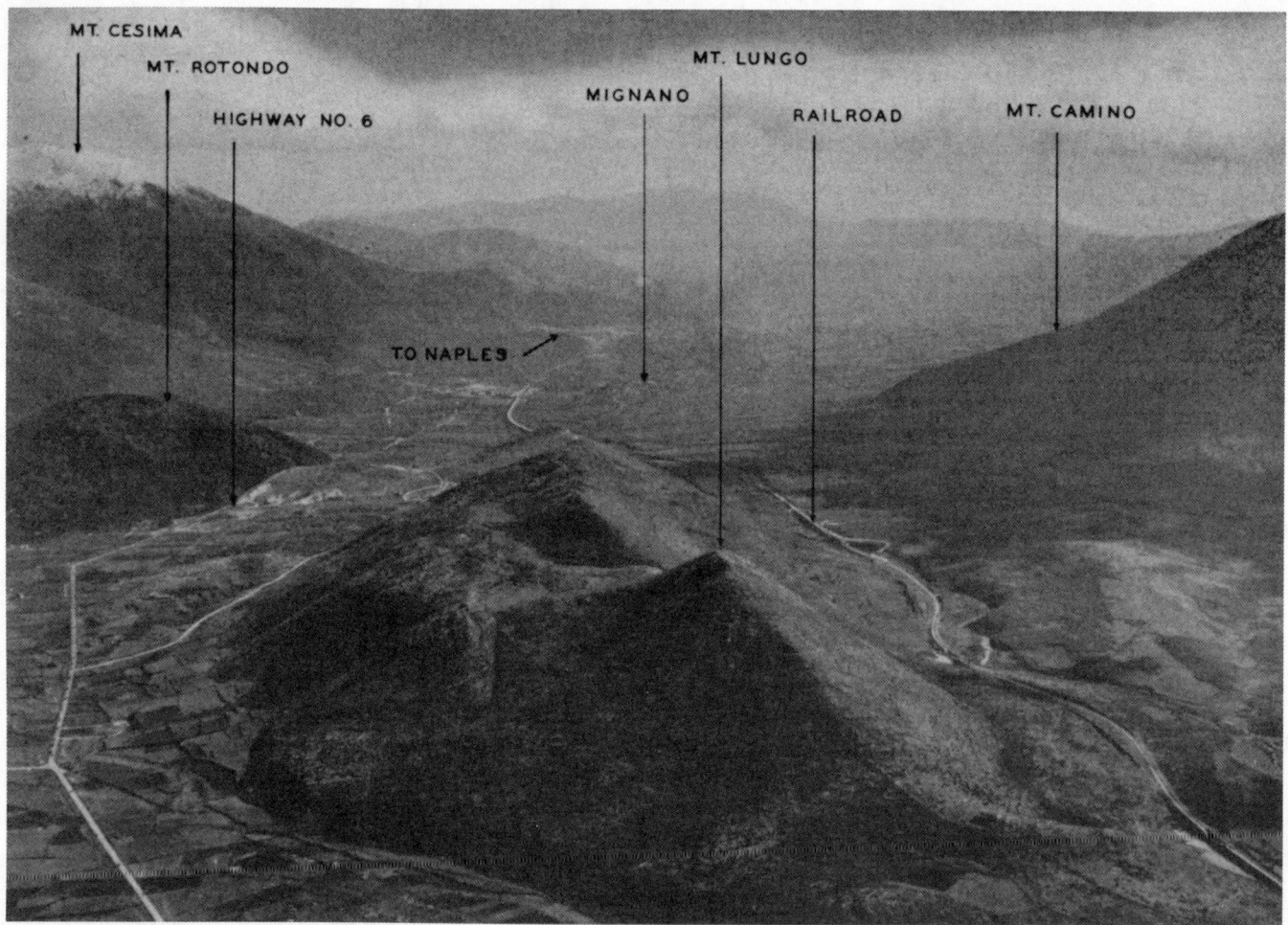

This view of the Mignano corridor, from the German side, shows the importance of Mount Lungo as a block at the exit from the corridor.

L in the pass to the east. The company's right flank extended to the lower nose of Mount Cannavinelle. The main line of resistance ran across the mouth of the gap up the northwest slope of Mount Rotundo through heavy brush and trees, Company L's left flank toward the right flank of Company K. "Company L's combat strength of fifty-five men," stated Battalion CO Lt. Col. Edgar C. Doleman, "made it impossible to maintain contact across the 600 yards of densely wooded slope except by patrols and listening posts. One section of heavy machine guns was attached to Company L and was in position on the left (west) flank protected by four riflemen."

The deeds of two men during the latter part of the drive are particularly deserving of note. One of these men was 1st Lt. Maurice L. Britt, the other Pfc. Floyd K. Lindstrom.

"At 0830 the morning mentioned, the Germans counterattacked over the north nose of Mount Rotundo southeast toward the gap between Company L and Company K, turned down the slope, hit Company L's left flank and captured the machine-gun section and four riflemen by a ruse. The counterattackers, later estimated from PW reports as a company of approximately one hundred men, had as their mission the retaking of Mount Rotundo. When Company L's left-flank men opened fire, the enemy hit them in force and pushed them southeast toward the gap between the mountains. . . ."

Said Cpl. John Syc: ". . . The Germans attacked our left flank and captured some Americans whom they placed in front of them as a shield. We couldn't see the Americans, but we could hear them shouting down to us not to shoot. When they were about fifty yards away, Lieutenant Britt yelled, 'Take off! They can't hurt you! We're going to fire anyway!' All of us then opened fire and the Germans fired back with rifles, machine pistols and machine guns, too. The American prisoners scattered, some later escaping. . . . During the fire fight, which was intense, a mortar section ammo man near me was wounded and his weapon knocked out. Lieutenant Britt, while firing his carbine, suddenly yelled, 'Ow' and put his hand on his side saying he thought he was hit, but ordering me to fire my machine gun faster. . . ."

"He ran from side to side of our machine gun of which I was assistant gunner," said Pfc. Fred E. Marshall, "firing at every sound and sight of Germans. . . .

Later, I saw Lieutenant Britt, slightly bleeding on the face, having run out of carbine ammo, grab the M-1 rifle from a badly wounded man lying near me, and continue to fire with it. He also grabbed some hand grenades and with the rifle and grenades went ahead into a wooded area ahead of our position looking for Germans. A few minutes later I saw him throwing grenades, disregarding machine-pistol bursts hitting all around him. I marveled that he wasn't hit. Concussion grenades, too, were bursting all about him...."

Said Sgt. James G. Klaes: "... All in all ... I saw him throw approximately ten to twelve grenades, German automatic fire and grenades coming back all the time. At times we thought we would be overrun. Always I saw Lieutenant Britt out in front firing his carbine, throwing hand grenades, first from one position, then from another...."

"... I saw his canteen was pierced with bullet holes and his shirt covered with water; his field glasses case, too, was pierced with bullet holes," said T/5 Eric B. Gibson (Cf. Push to Rome). "... I was throwing hand grenades at Germans and Lieutenant Britt asked me for some as he had thrown all he had. During the morning he must have thrown at least thirty-two hand grenades...."

At about 0930 Britt and Gibson went toward the left to find what had become of the two mortars which had been to the left of the attacking Germans. There was another encounter with a machine gun and the lieutenant threw a couple of grenades, saving Gibson's life, according to Gibson's testimony. They returned, then once more Britt went into the woods and had another encounter with an enemy machine gun.

"... Lieutenant Britt greeted me in my aid station," said 3d Battalion Surgeon Capt. Roy E. Hanford. "I was busy with a couple of casualties at the time ... about a half hour later I asked Lieutenant Britt if there was anything I could do for him. His reply was 'No, Doc, go ahead and finish with your other casualties. *I got a little scratch here that I want you to look at when you get time.*'

"Lieutenant Britt's scratch turned out to be an elliptical avulsion of skin down to the muscle about one inch long and one-half inch wide on his left side. There were a number of other visible small superficial wounds on his face and hands.... I asked Lieutenant Britt if he would like to go into the hospital. He replied, 'No,' calmly and determinedly, 'I got to get back up on the hill to help those boys.' ... There were several remarks from some casualties from his company after he left. 'I'd give anything to be like that guy.' 'That guy is a one man army....'"

Lieutenant Britt was subsequently awarded the Medal of Honor for his action.

For the November 7-12 period 3d Battalion, 30th Infantry, later received the Distinguished Unit Citation. "With fire sweeping its ranks from the rear and from an exposed flank, the battalion launched its attack up the forward slope of the mountain (Rotundo) and doggedly advanced to the crest in the face of stubborn enemy resistance," read the citation, in part. "Although depleted heavily in effective strength and having neither food nor water for a period of two days, the intrepid infantrymen of the 3d Battalion met the onslaught of the enemy (over a six-day period) and repelled each assault with heavy losses to the attackers...."

Later honored with the Medal of Honor for actions during the same period was Pfc. Floyd K. Lindstrom.

On November 12 the 2d platoon of Company H, 7th Infantry, was attached to Company E. The platoon had been depleted to a total of fourteen men and two serviceable guns. Pfc. Lindstrom was the gunner of one gun.

At about 0900 approximately forty enemy launched a counterattack against the left flank of the company. Lindstrom's machine-gun section received the greater weight of the attack.

"... The enemy, from his position on the commanding heights," said Pvt. Marvin D. Crone, assistant gunner, "had excellent observation and when he opened fire on us he was deadly accurate. The bulk of the enemy were 200 yards above us when he attacked. E Company withdrew about 150 yards, because there was not enough cover for them at this point, leaving our machine-gun section out in front.

"Even though he saw the rifle company withdraw, Pfc. Lindstrom nevertheless instantly and without orders immediately set up a defensive position and opened fire with his machine gun. The enemy fire became intense as they started dropping a great number of mortar shells in our 'section' area and commenced to rake our positions with machine-gun, machine-pistol, and rifle fire.

"... Lindstrom insisted on moving forward alone another ten yards for a better field of fire. He picked up the machine gun bodily and moved uphill over the rocky ground with his 112-pound load. In doing this he became the direct target of machine-gun and small-arms fire from some of the enemy who weren't more than fifteen to twenty yards away ... at least thirty-five hand grenades of the concussion variety were thrown at Pfc. Lindstrom in an attempt to silence his gun.

"Lindstrom was aiming for one German machine gun and crew in particular when he singlehandedly carried his heavy machine gun forward because he saw that it was the chief supporting weapon in the German counterattack. Despite the heavy fire from their mortars and machine pistols, he moved to within about fifteen yards of this machine gun even though it was firing at him and missing him only by inches.

"I could hear the Jerries yelling at him in pidgin English, 'American soldier—you give up—we treat you fine—you no surrender, plenty trouble—we got you surrounded.' This was repeated time and again and each time Lindstrom answered 'Go to Hell!' and gave them another burst of fire from his machine gun. . . .

"When Lindstrom saw that the attack was likely to succeed if the enemy machine guns were not put out of action, he yelled at me to cover him with my rifle, that he was going to 'get that machine gun,' and armed only with the .45-caliber pistol which he always had at his hip, he frontally assaulted the machine gun in a mad uphill dash. The Germans saw him coming and let go a continuous stream of fire which kicked up the dirt inches behind his heels as he ran at them. Somehow he miraculously escaped being hit by the continuous chain of automatic fire from the machine gun, got right on top of the gunners and shot them to death with his pistol. He then returned, dragging the German machine gun behind him, after which he braved more enemy fire to go back to their position and return with two full boxes of ammo which he directed us to emplace and put to use in countering the enemy attack. We received no support from our other machine gun during the counterattack because it was unable to fire on the enemy from its position. . . ."

Said Sgt. Nicholas Alfier: "Lindstrom gave the gun to me telling me to use it on the German infantry, and he immediately went back to his gun and opened fire.

"Lindstrom's spectacular action and withering machine-gun fire completely demoralized the Germans and their counterattack seemed to disintegrate. . . ."

"The rifle company and the other machine gun of our section attempted to come to our aid while the attack was going on," said Pvt. Sam G. Rohan, "But Pfc. Lindstrom so effectively handled the situation that it was all over before they could get into action. . . ."

The exhausted warriors of the 3d Infantry Division by November 15, deserved the needed rest that was to come when higher headquarters called a halt to the advance that night.

In two days all elements of the Division had been relieved and were en route to San Felice, tired, bearded, and dirty, but flushed with victory and justly proud that they had penetrated the German Winter Line and forced the first approaches to Cassino.

The 3d Infantry Division was holding the trumps when relief by the 36th Division was effected November 17, 1943.

TABLE OF CASUALTIES*

Southern Italy

(Sept. 14, 1943 through Jan. 21, 1944)

KIA	WIA	MIA	Total Battle Casualties	Non-Battle Casualties
683	2412	170	3265	12,959

Reinforcements and Hospital return-to-unit personnel

Reinf		Hosp RTUs	
Off	EM	Off	EM
438	8616	241	7295

KNOWN ENEMY CASUALTIES**

Killed	Wounded	Captured
265	86	547

*These figures were provided by the A C of S, G–1, 3d Infantry Division.

**Throughout this history, statements of enemy casualties as compiled from records of A C of S, G–1, 3d Infantry Division, are those enemy dead actually buried in 3d Division cemeteries and those enemy wounded actually processed through 3d Division medical installations. It is estimated that these figures reflect not more than five per cent of the casualties inflicted on the enemy by the 3d Division and its attached units. Statements of enemy captured are those prisoners of war actually processed through 3d Division cages under supervision of the Provost Marshal.

VI
ANZIO

1: The First Battle of Cisterna di Littoria
January 22 to February 1

TROOP LIST—Operation "Shingle" Third Infantry Division (Reinf)

Organization for Combat

1. *Hq & Hq Co, 3d Inf Div.*
2. *7th Inf Regt (Reinf)*
    10th FA Bn
    Plat Co A, 751st Tk Bn
    Plat Co A, 601st TD Bn
    Co A, 3d Med Bn (Coll)
    Det 10th Engr Bn
    Det 3d Sig Co.
3. *15th Inf Regt (Reinf)*
    39th FA Bn
    Plat Co A, 751st Tk Bn
    Plat Co B, 601st TD Bn
    Co B, 3d Med Bn (Coll)
    Det 10th Engr Bn
    Det 3d Sig Co.
4. *30th Inf Regt (Reinf)*
    41st FA Bn
    Plat Co A, 751st Tk Bn
    Plat Co C, 601st TD Bn
    Co C, 3d Med Bn (Coll)
    Det 10th Engr Bn
    Det 3d Sig Co.
5. *Division Artillery*
    (—10th, 39th & 41st FA Bns)
    69th Armd FA Bn (105 SP)
    Btry B, 36th FA Bn (155 G)
    Det, Btry B, 15th Obsn Bn (Sound)
6. *3d Rcn Troop*
    Prov Mtd Troop
    Prov Pack Btry
    Dets, 10th Engr Bn.
7. *441st AAA AW Bn*
8. *84th Chemical Bn*
9. *504th Parachute Inf Regt.*
10. *3d QM Co*

CASABLANCA was the baptism and the proof that the 3d Infantry Division could and would measure up to the most rigid standards of modern combat. Sicily was the gratifying fruition of an idea which held that a good United States division could move fast, and strike hard bewildering blows to confound the enemy and help to bring about his quick capitulation. Lower Italy, until the crossing of the Volturno River, was almost a continuation of the Sicilian campaign. Fording the Volturno to carry the bitter fight into the mountain fastness of an essentially mountainous country, over peaks whose sides were sown with thousands of deadly antipersonnel mines, in the teeth of lethal crossfires from an enemy imbedded in rock—minor fortresses carved into the very mountain sides—twenty-four hours a day in rain and snow, proved something again that needed proof only for the layman: When every other weapon bogs down the infantryman can still move and fight, although it costs him terribly.

The ultimate test, and the battle from which the 3d Infantry Division was to emerge as one of the great divisions of World War II, however, had yet to be fought. The name of a rather obscure hamlet; a former watering spot where Nero once had come to soak his tyrannical bones and where a latter-day, would-be Nero had come to pitch hay, bare-chested, for the benefit of the newsreels, was destined to be brought prominently into the consciousness of the world. This small port on the Tyrrhenian coast, about twenty miles below the Lido di Roma, where the Tiber River empties its waters, was to have its name written in letters of fire: Anzio.

The bitter series of battles for the mountain passes around Cassino, and for the town itself, had been going on for about two months; since the 3d Division spearheaded the crossing of the Volturno River the fighting had become fiercer and progress slower for United States troops than at any time since the first landings were made in the Mediterranean Theater. When the Division was withdrawn from the lines after the bitter fights for Mount Lungo and Mount Rotundo, and almost immediately commenced training in amphibious warfare, everyone concerned suspected that an "end run" was about to take place in an attempt to break the stalemate.

On December 28, the Commanding General, Fifth Army, Lt. Gen. Mark W. Clark, informed the Commanding General, 3d Infantry Division, Maj. Gen. Lucian K. Truscott, that the Division would take part in an amphibious operation to be known by the code name of "Shingle," scheduled for about January 20, 1944. This operation had already been under consideration for several weeks and had been postponed or discarded on previous occasions because the troops and shipping believed necessary to success had not been available.

The broad purpose of the landing, which was initially to be made by this Division and the 1st British Division, was to debark on beaches north and south of the towns of Nettuno and Anzio, about twenty-five miles in a direct line south of Rome, with the intention of quickly driving inland, cutting Highway 7, by which the enemy supplied his forces on the Garigliano-Minturno front, and with the eventual purpose of cutting Highway 6 at Valmontone, trapping the German forces who opposed the bulk of Fifth Army on the front at, and around, Cassino.

Few foresaw a bitter, four-month struggle, in which our stalemated beachhead was to battle for its life on three separate occasions against fanatically attacking Germans who had orders from Hitler himself to eliminate this threat completely, destroying or capturing its defenders. Few contemplated the fruitless, holding warfare of World War I type; doughboys standing for hours and days at a time in water up to their ankles; crouching in the foxholes in the daytime because of the almost complete lack of defilade; front lines that faced each other at distances no greater than fifty yards; above all, the devastating artillery barrages from weapons up to and including 280mm pieces that were apt to land at any time on any part of the beachhead.

Within the lifetime of surviving veterans of the beachhead there will be endless arguments as to "What did Anzio accomplish?," and in military textbooks and service schools the discussions will probably outlast the lifetime of any of the soldiers who engaged in the fighting there. The military student may ponder every aspect of it in the future. The why and wherefore of the situation are not such a major matter of interest to us now, however; the fact remains that when the explanations, accusations, and fulminations of the people and newspapers of the United States and Great Britain died down we still had the beachhead, and we had to live there, and give lives in order that it remain a beachhead. In short, we had a bear by the tail and could not let go.

Against this is to be held the undoubted fact that many German divisions, badly needed to stem the Allied effort on the southern front, were tied down; several divisions were brought into Italy at a time when Germany was scraping the bottom of the barrel for enough strength to counter the impending invasion which finally took place on the Normandy coast on June 6; and also the fact that the beachhead, as long as it remained intact, was in the nature of a cocked

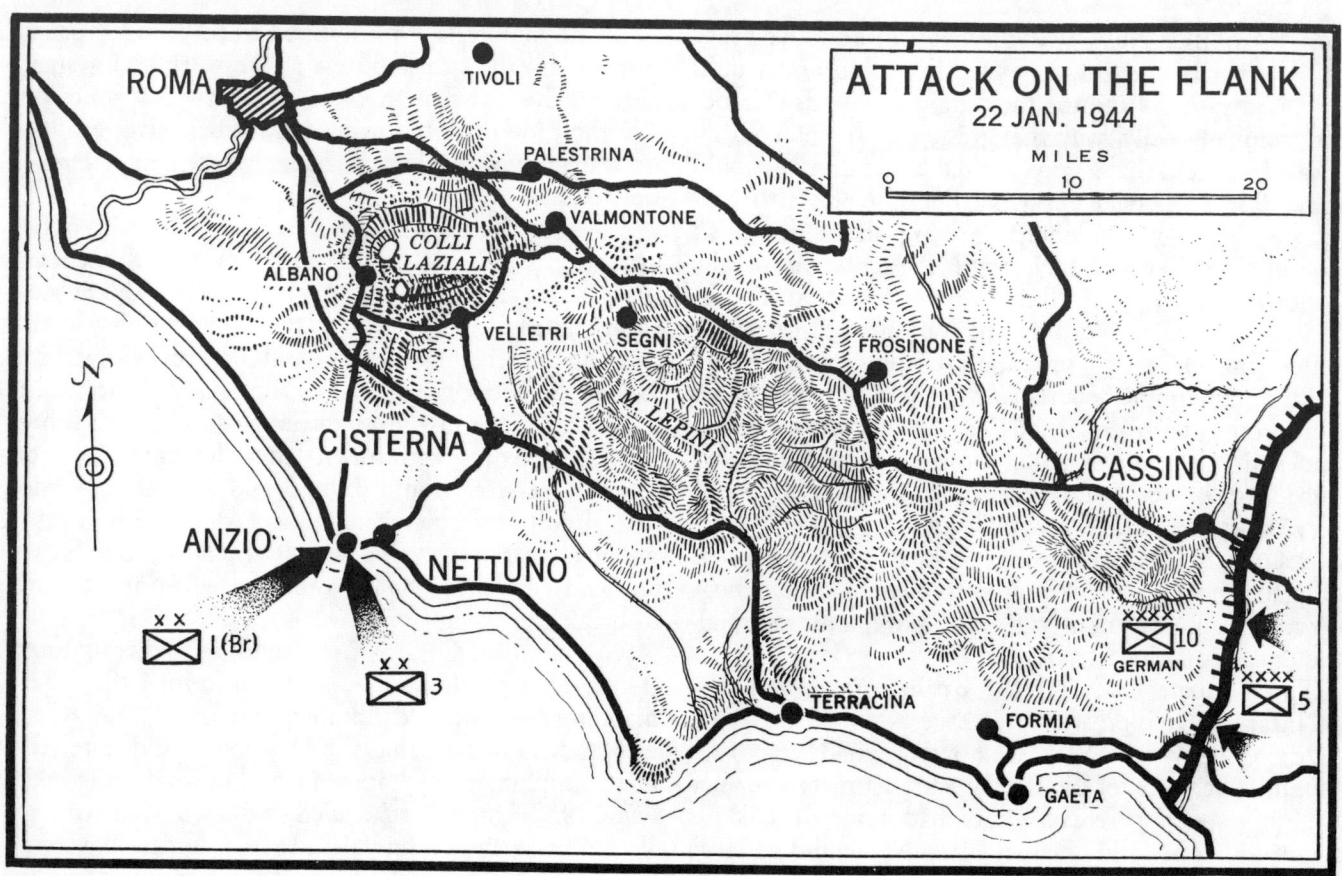

and loaded pistol pointed at the back of Field Marshal Kesselring's forces at Cassino. It represented a staging area for the major assist in the Allied drive that eventually carried to Rome and beyond.

Together with its companion divisions, the 1st, 5th, and 56th British, and the United States 45th, 34th Infantry and 1st Armored Divisions; Special Service Force; 504th Parachute Infantry Regiment, and 509th Parachute Infantry Battalion, the 3d Infantry Division was to add a brilliant chapter in defensive warfare to its already bright record of achievements. This new feat—rarely equalled by a United States division engaged in defensive warfare—occurred when, on two occasions, the 3d bore the brunt of attack across its entire front, and not only did it give no ground, but each time cost the enemy extremely serious losses in men and matèriel. As in 1918, when it had been the "Rock of the Marne," it became the "Rock of Anzio" in 1944. It was once mentioned in official dispatches as stemming the main force of the enemy's most determined attempt to eliminate the beachhead.

It is interesting to note the short time allowed for the planning, training, and mounting of Operation "Shingle"—an amphibious landing, the most complex of all military operations. The same phase of the Sicilian operation had taken a full three months. Only past experience and an expeditious and enthusiastic approach to all problems enabled the Division to accomplish its assigned task in the three weeks allotted. The landing itself was the proof of the pudding. Never before in amphibious warfare had carefully laid plans been executed so letter perfect by the Army Ground Force-Navy-Army Service Force team that mounts every operation of this type. As it developed, men and equipment were to pour ashore with almost monotonous regularity and strictly on schedule in the fulfillment of a logician's favorite dream.

The plan called for landing of the 3d Infantry Division (reinforced) and one brigade of the 1st Division (British) on the beaches north and south of Nettuno, with remaining elements of 1st Division as floating reserve; 3d Division landing on beaches south of Nettuno and 1st Division landing on beaches north of Anzio. As soon as the beachhead was established, U. S. 1st Armored and 45th Infantry Divisions were to follow ashore, prepared to move quickly in continuation of the attack.

The 3d Infantry Division's mission was to land, destroy enemy beach defenses, and capture an initial beachhead line extending generally to the line of Musso-

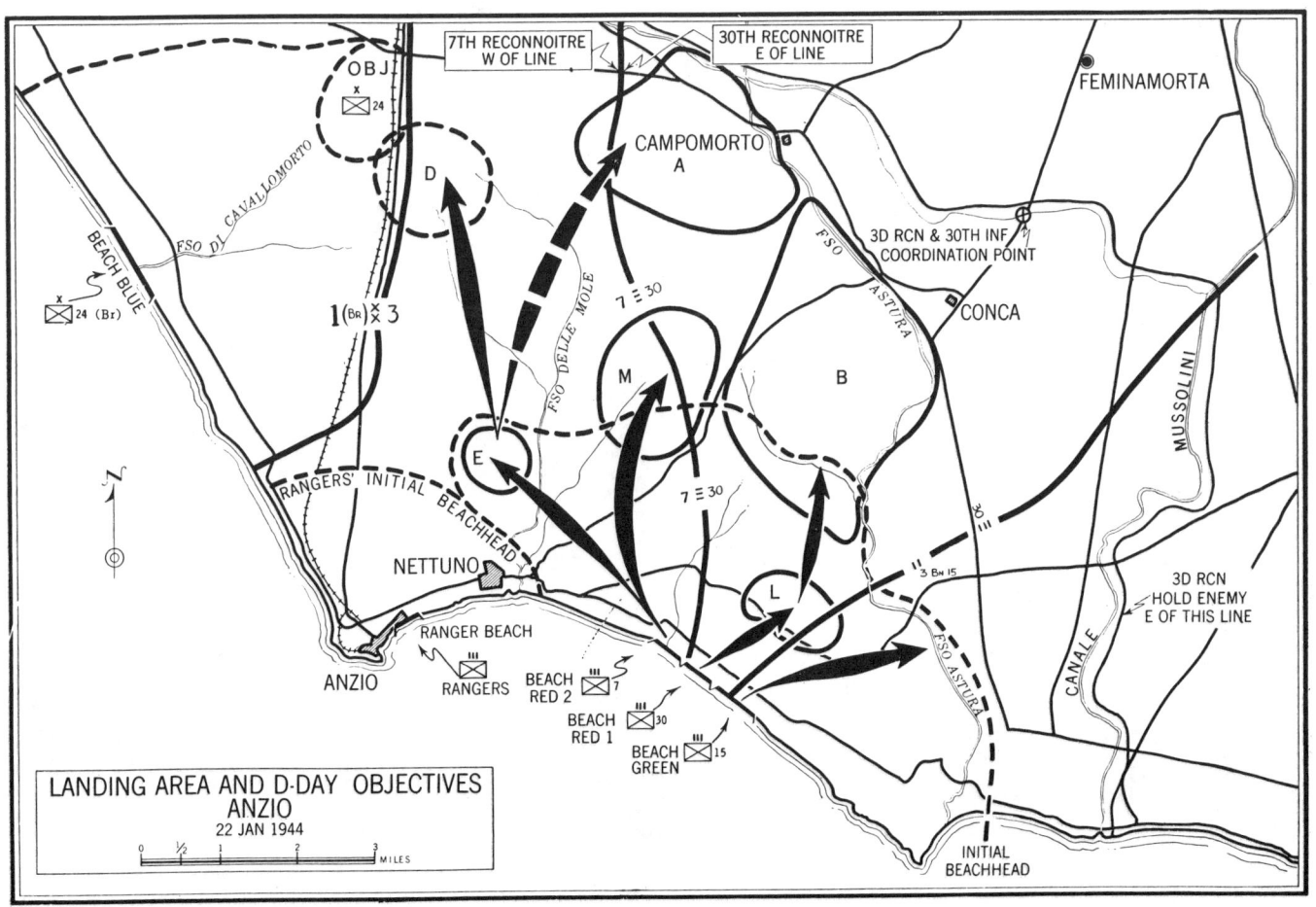

LANDING AREA AND D-DAY OBJECTIVES
ANZIO
22 JAN 1944

lini Canal and its northwest branch. The Division's left boundary was the main highway between Anzio and Albano. The assault plan called for landing assault battalions of all three regiments of the Division simultaneously, as well as a battalion of Rangers just east of Anzio. The Rangers were to be tactically attached to the Division as soon as contact was physically established ashore.

Order of landing was 7th, 30th, and 15th Infantry Regiments from left to right. The assault battalions were 1st Battalion, 7th; 2d Battalion, 30th; and 3d Battalion, 15th. These battalions were organized and trained as units and sub-units or teams specifically designed and trained to attack and destroy pillboxes, fortifications and coast defense weapons and to cross beach wire and minefields.

Following the assault battalions, the other two battalions of each regiment were to be landed in column from LCIs. These battalions of the 7th and 30th Infantry Regiments were to be advanced to the north, northwest, and northeast sectors and clear and occupy the beachhead in the Division sector; 15th Infantry, on the 30th Infantry's right, was to relieve elements of the 3d Reconnaissance Troop on crossings over the Mussolini Canal, protect the right flank of the Division, and be prepared to pass to the west with remaining forces behind the 30th Infantry and 7th Infantry.

Elements of the 601st Tank Destroyer Battalion and the 751st Tank Battalion were attached to regiments, to be loaded on LCTs and landed before daylight. The 441st Antiaircraft Battalion was likewise to land prior to daylight and protect the beaches until Corps antiaircraft could be debarked and set up. Naval gunfire preparation, once scheduled, was cancelled at the last minute in favor of surprise, although two rocket boats accompanied the convoy to fire barrages on the Division's beaches at H-Hour minus ten minutes. Actually there were no enemy targets ashore which suffered from these barrages.

The 504th Parachute Infantry Regiment, whose previously scheduled drop on a flat rise north of Anzio had been cancelled, was to be landed from LCIs on Division beaches as Corps troops.

Late in the afternoon, January 21, 1944, the invasion convoy set sail from Naples. H-Hour had been finally set for 0200 on the following day.

The following, though fragmentary, gives some idea of the ease with which the actual landing was accomplished. It is an extract from the Division staff (War Room) journal as of January 22:

0145: Rocket Ships fired.
0220: 2d wave hit Red Beach. Landed dry.
0229: No opposition met by 1st or 2d waves.
0245: From 15th Infantry: Landed on Green Beach. Left company advancing rapidly. Right company fair. 4th wave has hit the beach.
0300: LCIs are using LCVPs. (*Unloading onto LCVPs*: Ed.)
0330: Message from Liaison Officer, 30th Infantry: "Our leading elements are at . . . (*Location in code*: Ed). No opposition.
0335: 15th Infantry reports: Initial operation believed successful. Now regrouping.
0335: 1st Battalion, 7th Infantry Reports: All companies now fairly well together. No opposition. Five boat waves have landed.
0350: 1st Battalion, 7th Infantry, reorganizing on road directly behind Red Beach.

Enemy planes bomb the landing-craft off shore at Anzio-Nettuno on D-Day morning.

Men and materiel move inland across the beaches of Anzio on D-Day.

0405: 1st Battalion, 7th Infantry, advancing from coordination line to objective "E."
0410: Intercept from 3d Battalion, 15th Infantry: "Sabotage the transportation and put the krauts under guard."
0430: 30th Infantry; No MG, mines, or artillery encountered.
0430: All six waves landed on Green Beach.
0450: Congratulatory message from Commanding General, VI Corps.
0515: 1st Battalion, 7th Infantry now fording stream at . . . (*Gave location in code*: Ed.). Bridge OK.
0548: Message from 15th Infantry: Our progress satisfactory. We are not yet hull down (*not yet dug in*. Ed.).
0550: From Assistant Commanding General: Prisoners report one battalion extending 25 miles north of this point.
0600: Tanks, TDs, artillery landed successfully on Red 1.
0615: 2d Battalion, 7th Infantry moving toward objective.
0625: 30th Infantry reports companies in positions between 3d parallel road and . . . (*Code location name*: Ed.).
0915: Division command post opened.

Except for a few mines and elements of an understrength enemy battalion on beach-watching duty, the operation went off like a well executed maneuver. The enemy had been entirely surprised, indicating that the secret of the operation was well kept beforehand. (It was subsequently discovered that the area around the Lido di Roma to the north, at the mouth of the Tiber, and the shores of the Golfo di Gaeta to the south, were heavily mined and fortified. It is probable that the enemy *had* expected a landing but did not accurately determine where it was to strike.)

By daylight main elements of the infantry regiments, artillery, and some armored units were ashore. By noon of D-Day the infantry regiments had consolidated on initial objectives and were reconnoitering to the front and flanks. The 3d Reconnaissance Troop and 3d Provisional Reconnaissance Troop had reached and prepared for demolition all bridges on the Mussolini Canal from the sea to Bridge 7. Bridges 1, 3, 4, and 5 were demolished. Guards were placed on all bridges.

In order to understand the series of attacks and counterattacks, patrol actions and defensive measures undertaken during the 3d Infantry Division's nightmarish stay on Anzio Beachhead, it is necessary to become acquainted with the natural setting, and to learn the names of a few places which figured prominently in all these actions.

The beachhead, in the form it was finally to assume following the main German counterattack of February 16-19, comprised an area of little more than a hundred square miles, being about ten miles deep and fifteen miles wide in its greatest dimensions. The twin towns of Anzio and Nettuno lay in the southwestern corner, about two miles apart, Nettuno being farther east along a curving bay.

The eastern boundary of the beachhead lay generally along the Mussolini Canal, which was a wide, shallow man-made trough about 120 feet across at the top but with only a six-foot water gap in its bed. It had orig-

It was approximately from this point North where troops of the 3d Division landed. Nettuno is in the background.

inally been dug to drain the area and reclaim the marshy ground for farm land. The result was a series of model farms. Just south of the beachhead line lay the Pontine Marshes.

About six miles inland the canal branched. One fork ran northeast toward the mountains back of Cisterna di Littoria. The other ran west and slightly north for another six or seven miles, where it finally petered out into a small, natural stream. This western fork was a natural defensive line inasmuch as it provided defilade against ground observation, and a small wet gap which was impassable to tanks and vehicles.

There was no true high ground on the beachhead, the only significant elevation being a gentle rise just south of the town of Le Ferriere which reached a maximum height of 220 feet above sea level. Elsewhere the terrain was flat or very gently rolling, except for small ravines formed by the streams. North of the western fork of the Mussolini Canal, where the terrain sloped gradually upward toward the foothills of the Colli Laziali, these ravines assumed greater proportions, being forty to sixty feet in places and very steep-sided, but generally carrying a trickle of water in the bottom.

The perfectly flat terrain immediately north of the canal was further crisscrossed by a series of drainage ditches, which varied from small scratches in the ground to a twenty or thirty-foot width, and fifteen or twenty-foot depth.

Aside from Anzio and Nettuno, there were no real towns, as such, on the beachhead. In the 3d Infantry Division sector there were clusters of buildings at Acciarella, Conca (Borgo Montello on some maps), consisting of an old castle, a church, and two or three houses and sheds, Le Ferriere (a group of large buildings clustered around a woolen mill with a prominent, high smokestack), Campo Morto, Carano, and Feminamorta—"Dead Woman"—(Isola Bella on some maps). For a time in the early part of February, the British held the little settlement of Aprilia, famous in news stories as the "factory area," which lay due north of Anzio at the western edge of an absolutely flat plain, and the railway station at Campoleone, still farther north.

Immediately back of the beachhead line were several larger towns: Littoria, on the eastern flank; Cisterna di Littoria, usually called simply Cisterna, an important road junction on Highway 7 (Appian Way) just northeast of Feminamorta; Cori, a few miles northeast of Cisterna, which nestles low on the western slopes of the Monti Lepini, and Velletri, on the slopes of the Colli Laziali mountains. Both could be plainly seen on a clear day (of which there were all too many) from almost any part of the beachhead.

There must be kept in mind also, in order to understand the development of the situation at Anzio, the following points. The knowledge that the build-up of friendly forces on the beachhead would of necessity be slow, together with the lack of knowledge of the enemy's ability to counteract our action, cautioned the Division not to overextend itself and thereby lose its ability to defend itself against counterattack from any direction. At the same time it was necessary that the Division advance and seize the terrain most favorable both to its defensive position and to its ability to continue the attack forward. Therefore the Division rushed inland boldly to secure its objectives within the initial beachhead line and thereafter consolidated its won positions and continued the advance only in consideration of the above-mentioned factors. The enemy was surprised but was quick to become aware of the threat, occasioned by the landing, to his forces in the south. His immediate concern was to dispatch as rapidly as possible to the threatened area all available units in an effort to contain the beachhead in as small a space as possible, until such time as he could arrive there with forces in strength capable of effecting a counterattack that would destroy the invader. Thus there took place initially a series of meeting engagements which gained in intensity as the forces increased in strength.

On the morning of January 23, just twenty-four hours after the landing, enemy elements began efforts to establish themselves on bridgeheads over the Mussolini Canal. It is likely that these were the *Hermann Goering* Division, an old "friend" of the 3d Division, which had engaged it twice before. This was in an area which had been almost entirely free of enemy troops the day before. It gives some indication of the speed with which the enemy reacted. The 1st Battalion, 30th, engaged infantry and tanks during the night and morning. During the afternoon the enemy crossed the canal at Bridges 2, 5, 6, 7 and 8 with strong combat patrols. Most of these patrols were supported by tanks. During the evening our units began counterattacking these enemy bridgeheads with the mission of destroying them and clearing the area south and west of the canal. It was an ominous harbinger of the trial of strength that was shortly to take place.

The 504th Parachute Infantry Regiment began moving into an area adjacent to the Mussolini Canal between the sea and Bridge 5, to relieve the 3d Reconnaissance Troop and to retake some bridge sites. The 4th Ranger Battalion relieved the 1st Battalion, 7th Infantry, from the position it had reached the day before. The 1st and 2nd Battalions, 7th Infantry, were assembled in Division reserve in the vicinity of a road junction on the Nettuno-Le Ferriere road.

January 24 the attacks against the enemy bridgeheads were continued and by 1010 the last bridge site was cleared. Two infantry companies of the 15th Infantry, with tank reinforcements, were ordered north across the canal at Bridges 6 and 8, and similar forces from the 30th Infantry were to cross at Bridges 12 and 13 with instructions to advance as far as possible without taking excessive casualties, and to take and hold the ground so gained.

The companies of the 15th Infantry did not move out in time to accomplish their mission prior to an attack by the 2d Battalion the following morning. The companies of the 30th Infantry moved north and became involved in fire fights at key road junctions north of the Mussolini Canal. One of these became famous as "Britt's Corner," so named in honor of Capt. Maurice L. Britt, commanding Company L, winner of the Congressional Medal of Honor for gallantry in southern Italy.

After the 3d Division had driven the enemy from his small defensive bridgeheads across the Mussolini Canal, and had established strong forces north of the canal, the enemy undertook a vigorous program of defensive works, with the object of halting our advance on flat ground and eventually building up reserves behind these defenses for a counterattack which was to drive us into the sea.

To accomplish this, we learned from later information, the enemy began to organize an MLR (main line of resistance) along the railroad line running northwest from Cisterna. This line crossed several low, rolling rises in the ground by means of alternating cuts and embankments, leaving few good level crossings for tanks and vehicles. This MLR terminated at the town of Cisterna as the enemy did not then dispose enough troops to attempt the extension southeast of Cisterna.

Having got this work started, the enemy began pushing his outposts down toward the canal in an effort to stop us and hold us as far south of his MLR as possible. With one or two companies he dug in along the road which looped down from Cisterna through Ponte Rotto and Carano, while other units were pushed down along the roads running south from Ponte Rotto and Cisterna. The German early realized the value of the masonry farmhouses, barns, silos and outdoor ovens for defensive purposes. He dug fire trenches around the outside foundations of the houses and put his machine guns inside the houses and the ovens (invariably located fifteen to twenty yards from the house), where they had blast protection and overhead cover against artillery time and percussion fire, and protection against small-arms fire. Only tanks, TDs and heavy artillery proved effective against these positions.

On January 25 the 4th Ranger Battalion and 3d Battalion, 7th Infantry, moved north and occupied a line, keeping contact with the British on their left. The 504th Parachute Infantry Regiment moved across the Mussolini Canal to the east in several groups, the 2d Battalion reaching Borgo Piave without much resistance prior to dark. The 2d Battalion, 15th Infantry, and 1st Battalion, 30th Infantry, attacked northeast at 0500. Heavy resistance was encountered by both battalions about a mile and a half north of the canal. Plans were made for 1st Battalion, 15th, to attack up the Conca-Cisterna road on the left of the 2d Battalion, which was ordered to hold an outpost position. The 1st Battalion, 30th Infantry, had a vicious fight to capture an important road junction on the Ponte Rotto road. After Company F, 30th Infantry, had driven to within 300 yards of the junction on the 24th, the 1st Battalion next day drove through and captured the junction, losing two tanks in the attack. The enemy was able to look down the throats of the attackers as the junction was open. The attack flanked enemy positions to the east. Having reached this junction (thereafter known throughout the 30th as "Kinney's Corner" after Maj. Oliver G. Kinney, 1st Battalion CO) the battalion was ordered to outpost the position astride the road.

On January 26, the 2d Battalion, 15th Infantry, and 1st Battalion, 30th Infantry, held and improved their positions. A road junction was captured by Company L, 30th Infantry, and Company K, 7th Infantry. The 504th Regiment withdrew its battalion from Borgo Piave, where it had withstood a counterattack during the night. The 1st Battalion, 15th Infantry, was to attack northeast. The battalion attacked at 1400 and met heavy resistance. It reached a line and held there during the night. Some enemy was driven out by enfilade fire from the 2d Battalion, 15th Infantry. The 7th and 30th Infantry Regiments remained in position and began to prepare to dig defensive positions along the canal.

January 27 the 3d Battalion, 7th Infantry, and the Ranger Force advanced. Infantry elements of the Division south of the Mussolini Canal line were instructed to begin work on the defensive positions along the canal in order to provide a firm base for further operations as well as to provide security against a counterattack. The 3d Battalion, 15th Infantry, attacked through the 2d Battalion with the mission of cutting the Conca-Cisterna road north of the 2d Battalion which it relieved. The 2d Battalion moved south of the canal in regimental reserve. The 1st Battalion, 15th Infantry, demonstrated with fire to assist the attack of the 3d Battalion. The 3d Battalion, 30th Infantry, relieved 1st Battalion, 30th Infantry. Patrols which reached the line of the railroad track west of Cisterna reported enemy digging in.

This maneuvering and displacing—small, stiff fights and small patrol actions—were the prelude to the bloody January 30-31, February 1 full-scale Division attack. The first zephyrs did not indicate the full fury of the coming storm.

By the morning of January 28, it was apparent that our front was too wide. If further advances toward Cisterna were to be made, the now-strong enemy resistance dictated a narrower zone of advance in order that maximum force should be concentrated for the attack. This was discussed with the Corps Commander, who agreed, and accordingly the Division boun-

Aerial view of the town of Nettuno with Anzio in the distance.

dary was moved to the stream north and south through Carano, and the 504th Parachute Infantry Regiment was relieved as far north as Bridge 5 by elements of the 179th Infantry of the 45th Division.

The Ranger Force and 3d Battalion, 7th Infantry, were relieved on the left by the 509th Parachute Infantry Battalion.

This still left the Division (reinforced) front at nearly ten kilometers, which had to be held even during the attack.

Company A, 15th Infantry, repelled an enemy counterattack of platoon or company strength at daylight, January 28, destroying two armored vehicles.

On the right flank of the 30th Infantry there was an enemy pocket which would have to be eliminated prior to the Division attack against Cisterna. At 1100, January 28, Company I, 30th Infantry, moved out toward the line of departure to destroy the enemy pocket. Under a heavy concentration of friendly artillery fire the infantry penetrated the enemy position. Enemy reaction was quick and determined, a dense concentration of heavy machine-gun, mortar and artillery fire being called down upon our advancing infantry, which caused them to take cover after having suffered many casualties. Captain Boddy, the company commander, rallied his men quickly and assaulted the enemy position through a hail of deadly fire. His attack destroyed six enemy machine-gun positions, killed at least 23 enemy, captured 19 and wounded an estimated 35 more. While this attack was progressing, the 2d Squad, 2d Platoon, protecting the company's left flank, was engaged in ejecting the enemy from the Fossa Feminamorta.

In previous campaigns T/5 Eric G. Gibson, a company cook, had often volunteered for combat assignments.

In Sicily Gibson had voluntarily led a pack train several miles across rugged mountainous terrain. His mission accomplished, he acted as number-one scout, locating several enemy positions. The following day he had killed one and wounded another enemy. At Acerno, Formicola, and Mt. Rotundo, Gibson had likewise distinguished himself.

Said Rifleman Pvt. Joseph E. Chilcoat: "The attack (of January 28) began at 1200. By 1215 our squad had moved forward 400 yards and we had just entered the ditch, T/5 Gibson leading. . . . One of the men said Fossa Feminamorta meant the 'Ditch of Dead Women.' We were afraid it would be the 'Ditch of the Dead Men' before we got out of it. T/5 Gibson told us to stay fifty yards behind him, while he went ahead and found the Germans for us . . ."

The squad had proceeded only a few steps when a blast of machine-pistol fire opened up from a clump of brush along the ditch bank. Gibson did not even take cover, but ran twenty yards up the ditch, firing his tommy gun from the hip as he went. He poked the gun muzzle into the brush and finished the German hidden there.

Under a heavy artillery concentration the squad again moved out. Knocked flat under the concussion of one close shell, Gibson had no sooner risen than he was fired upon by a machine pistol and rifle. Again he charged down the ditch, to fire his submachine gun into another pile of brush.

"When we came up to T/5 Gibson this time he had killed one German in the hole and another just climbing out with his hands up," related Pfc. John J. Slattery. "I wondered if we would have to do any fighting at all while T/5 Gibson was leading us."

Once again the squad took up the trek down the ditch. Instead of ordering his squad to assault the next machine gun which opened fire, Gibson ordered the men to build a base of fire while he crawled along the top of the ditch and flanked the position. Over the protestations of his squad he climbed the ditch bank and crawled 125 yards across the corner of an open field under the fire of artillery and two machine guns. When he reached a point within thirty-five yards of the machine gun positions in the ditch he threw two hand grenades, arising before the second went off to charge the position. Here he killed two more Germans and captured another.

Down the ditch again, until the bend was reached. Gibson told his men to stay behind until he found if there were any Germans around the bend. The tensely waiting squad heard a machine pistol, followed by Gibson's tommy gun. When they ran around the bend they found two bodies—Gibson and that of the enemy soldier who had opened fire. Gibson lay fallen in a firing position.

"T/5 Gibson brought his squad through its first combat safely," said BAR-man Pfc. Joseph W. Fiebelkern, "though he died doing it. . . . There isn't very much you can say about T/5 Gibson except that there are very, very few like him."

In less than an hour he had eliminated four German emplacements, killed five of the enemy and captured two more.

For this action T/5 Gibson was posthumously awarded the Medal of Honor.

For its action on January 28-29, Company I, 30th Infantry was later cited. During its overwhelming attack Company I destroyed six enemy machine-gun emplacements and killed 23 and wounded at least 35 enemy soldiers. Elements on the flank eliminated four-enemy outpost positions. After attacking continuously for one and a half hours, Company I reached a point within 50 yards of its objective and was met with intense machine-gun fire from enemy positions in a house on the right flank which enfiladed the ranks. Elements of the company assaulted this enemy strongpoint, killing six and capturing 27 enemy, and enabling the company to reach its objective.

Patrols over the night of January 28-29 met enemy dug-in positions, especially along a line south of the railroad tracks west of Cisterna, and along the 15th Infantry front. On January 29, preparations were begun for the attack on Cisterna.

Plans for our attack on Cisterna were carefully worked out and discussed at a meeting of all unit commanders the afternoon of January 29. The 7th Infantry was assigned objectives astride Highway 7 northeast of town; 15th Infantry was assigned similar objectives southeast of the town on the highway. The Ranger Force was to capture and clean out the town itself by infiltration of two battalions one hour before H-hour. The 7th and 15th Infantry Regiments were to start one battalion each moving by infiltration at H-hour, following up with armor and more infantry prior to daylight, at an hour selected by each regimental commander. H-hour was 0200. The 30th Infantry was to hold the line between 7th and 15th Regiments, act as Division reserve, and assist the other regiments by fire.

Corps order directed the attack and capture of the town, cutting of the highway, and preparation for resumption of the attack toward Velletri.

At 0100, January 30, the 1st and 3d Ranger Battalions advanced from their line of departure, infiltrated through the enemy strongpoints and met virtually no resistance. It was a paradoxical beginning of a day that was to witness their complete destruction before noon.

At daylight they were 800 yards south of Cisterna.

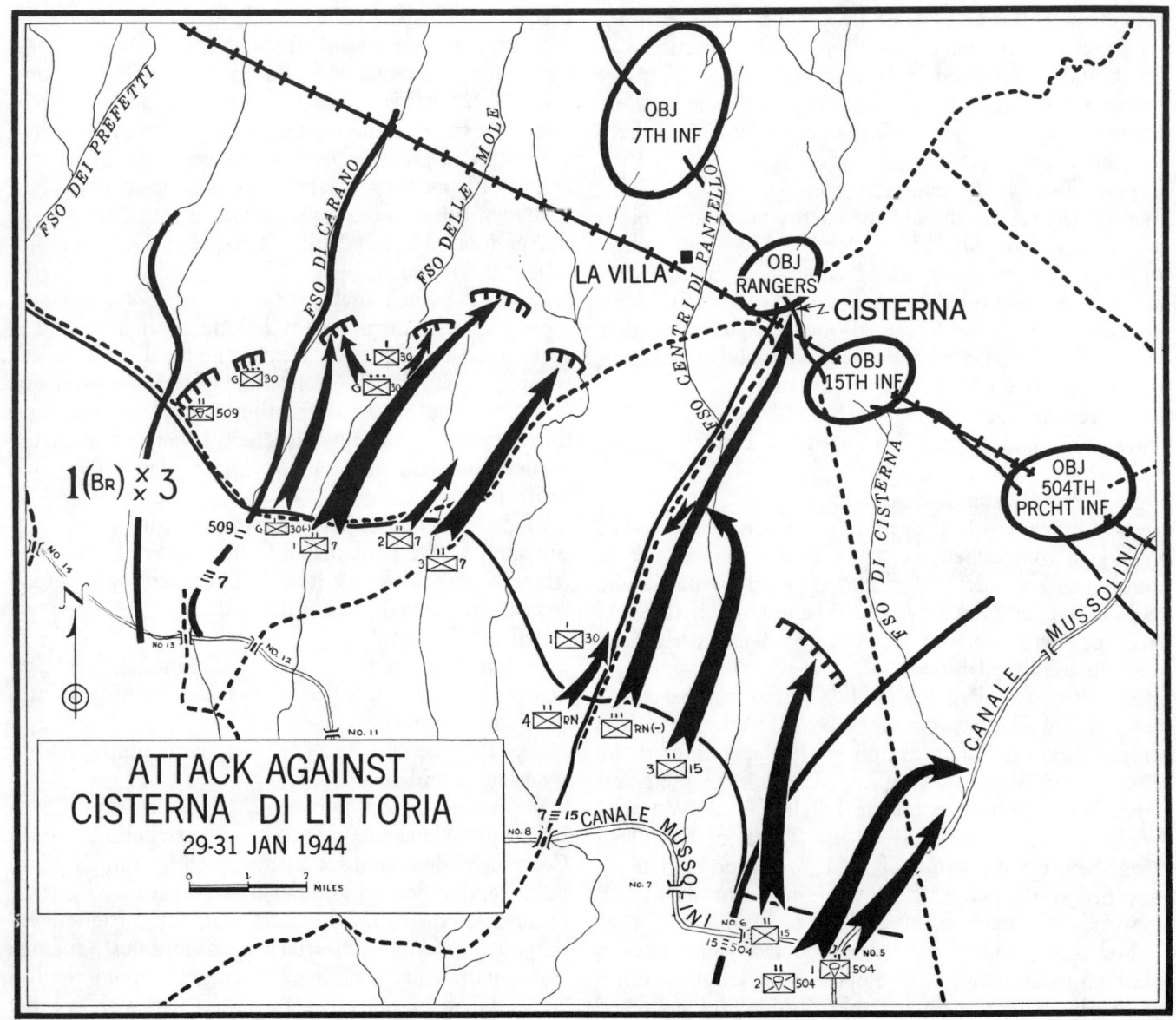

ATTACK AGAINST CISTERNA DI LITTORIA
29-31 JAN 1944

Here a wave of fire from tanks and self-propelled guns hit them and they were immediately pinned down in ditches. They were attacked by tanks and Flakwagons which debouched from Cisterna, infantry of an enemy parachute battalion which also emerged from the town, and by enemy machine-gun fire from every one of the houses that lined the roads into town. Almost immediately they were surrounded and the capture of two battalions of some of the finest troops in the United States Army began.

Behind them the Commanding Officer of the Ranger Force was trying to shove his 4th Battalion through to them.

Part of what happened to all three battalions may be found in the pages of the War Room journal, with its record of telephone conversations:

0415: No news from 1st and 3d Battalions. Apparently OK. 4th Battalion is getting fire from all houses along the road.

0450: Still out of contact with two battalions. Things are going well. 4th Battalion is definitely held up on road. Commanding Officer of Rangers says he will send up tanks and TDs if things don't break soon.

0610: Hasn't heard from 1st and 3d Battalions. Artillery trying through forward observer. 4th Battalion having a tough time. 3d Reconnaissance Troop platoon attached to Rangers passed through them in jeeps, came back, were fired upon (a survivor reported that "a solid sheet of machine-gun fire and hand grenades struck them!") and hit truck driven onto road by enemy; most of personnel killed or captured. (*There were approximately forty men and officers in this group*: Ed.)

0820: Halftracks and TDs being sent up by Rangers hit artillery and mines south of road block.

0835: Call received from 1st and 3d Battalions, in south edge of Cisterna completely surrounded. Both battalion COs out, one killed, one wounded. Can't adjust fire; enemy in buildings; town strongly held.

1030: 4th Battalion well shaken up.

1210: Commanding Officer, Rangers, informs party with radio near Cisterna that a company of American PWs have been seen marching north toward town, instructed Rangers to try and rescue them.

1210: 504th Parachute Regiment, on right flank of Division, told to get its attached tanks down to rescue PWs if possible.

Sometimes a fragmentary conversation composed of jerky sentences and half sentences can tell more than fifty thousand words. There is on record such a conversation, mostly one-sided, in the journal. It is the Commanding Officer, Colonel William O. Darby, Ranger Force, talking by radio to his old Sergeant Major who was with a small group that had the only radio left in operation. It is a poignant conversation.

1215: *Sgt:* Nobody is giving up. . . . Shoot them if they come any closer. *Darby:* Issue some orders but don't let the boys give up! . . . who's walking in with their hands up? Don't let them do it! Get the officers to shoot! . . . Don't let them do it! . . . Do that before you give up! . . . Get the old men together and lam for it. . . . We're coming through. Hang onto this radio until the last minute. How many men are still with you? Stick together. . . . Who's with the 1st Battalion? Use your head and do what is best. . . . You're there, and I'm here, unfortunately, and I can't help you, but whatever happens, God bless you!

1215: *From Commanding Officer, Rangers:* They came and got them at the last minute. My old sergeant major stayed with the last ten men. It was apparently too much for them.

The prosaic journal closes its account on the 1st and 3d Ranger Battalions, Ranger Force, United States Army. They were then, to all intents and purposes, written off by the War Department as "destroyed."

The plight of the 4th Ranger Battalion, meanwhile, was almost as desperate. It is also best revealed by a telephone conversation:

0820: I am afraid we have had some bad luck. They (tanks and TDs) got up past 4th Battalion's position and down the road to the roadblock, tried to outflank the roadblock and ran into artillery fire and minefields. One halftrack and M-10 knocked out. We got the men out of the M-10. The machine-gun fire is terrific from both flanks. The shells are landing all over the place. Look like 170s. 4th Battalion is the boy that is in the jam. All of his communications are out. An officer just came in and apparently he is pinned down badly. He is trying to work them out by **fours**.

Meanwhile, every effort was also being made by the 1st and 3d Battalions, 15th Infantry, to push north and contact the surrounded battalions. An attempted breakthrough by halftracks and M-10s was halted south of Feminamorta and our infantry was held to a slow rate of advance by enemy well-entrenched in and around all the houses along the roads.

The flat, coverless nature of the terrain was ideal for infantry defense and our troops advanced through dense bands of fire. The enemy had to be cleaned out house by house; even so, small enemy detachments were unintentionally by-passed and held their positions and fired on our troops from the rear.

By noon, 3d Battalion, 15th Infantry, was about 2000 yards from the last reported position of the ill-fated Ranger battalions.

The 1st Battalion, 7th Infantry, moved out on schedule but gained not more than 3000 yards that day, and the 2d Battalion, committed on the right of the 1st Battalion, was stopped with even less gain. The 3d Battalion was committed the night of January 30-31, to advance along the axis of the Ponte Rotto—Cisterna road, and succeeded in reaching the stream west of Ponte Rotto the morning of January 31.

The 1st Battalion, 15th Infantry, also made slow progress the same day in the face of heavy resistance almost from the line of departure, and by nightfall had done well to gain 2000 yards. The 3d Battalion was attacking, by-passing this resistance on the right, toward a road junction from the east; this mission was accomplished successfully and the battalion had seized the crossroad before dark of January 30.

The 1st Battalion, 30th, battling against the most intense Flak, tank, artillery, mortar, *Nebelwerfer*, and small-arms fire encountered to that point, gained 1500 yards after having had to fight 500 yards to secure its own line of departure. The battalion drove to within 1500 yards of Cisterna, the closest any battalion of the 3d Division was to get until the breakthrough in May. When ordered slightly later to withdraw from his exposed and most forward position, Major Oliver G. Kinney, commanding, said, "Hell, no! We can hold!"

The Commanding General could afford to take no chances, however, and Major Kinney was ordered to withdraw to protect his exposed flanks and come within range of supporting artillery.

It was on January 30 at 1500 that Pfc. Lloyd C. Hawks, Medical Detachment, 30th Infantry, brought great glory to himself and to the combat medical man. He braved an enemy counterattack to rescue two wounded soldiers near Carano, who were lying helpless in an exposed position within thirty yards of the enemy. Two riflemen had previously attempted to reach their wounded comrades but had been driven back by the fierce fire of the enemy. An aid man had been critically wounded in a similar attempt. The citation of War Department General Orders No. 5, dated January 15, 1945, awarding Pfc. Hawks the Medal of Honor, best describes his deed of heroism and is quoted here in part:

". . . Private Hawks nevertheless crawled fifty yards through a veritable hail of machine-gun bullets and flying mortar fragments to a small ditch, administered first aid to his fellow aid man who had sought cover therein, and continued toward the two wounded men fifty yards distant. An enemy machine-gun bullet penetrated his helmet, knocked it from his head and momentarily stunned him. Thirteen bullets passed through his helmet as it lay on the ground within six inches of his body. Private Hawks crawled to the casualties, administered first aid to the more seriously wounded man, and dragged him to a covered position 25 yards distant. Despite continuous automatic fire from positions only 30 yards away and shells which exploded within 25 yards, Private Hawks returned to the second man and administered first aid to him. As he raised himself to obtain bandages from his medical kit his right hip was shattered by a burst of machine-gun fire and a second burst splintered his left forearm. Displaying dogged determination and extreme self-control despite severe pain and his dangling left arm, Private Hawks completed the task of bandaging the remaining casualty and with superhuman effort dragged him to the same depression to which he had brought the first man. Finding insufficient cover for three men at this point, Private Hawks crawled 75 yards in an effort to regain his company, reaching the ditch in which his fellow aid man was lying."

The 504th Parachute Infantry Regiment captured crossings over the Mussolini Canal, both bridges having been demolished by the Germans before they could be seized and destroyed by our troops.

A member of 1st Battalion, 7th Infantry, particularly distinguished himself during the night of January 30-31. By the evening of January 30, all assault battalions had suffered heavily, and the 1st of the 7th was no exception.

Said 1st Lt. Jan Capron, CO of Company B "The battalion took up a defensive position behind the crest of a small ground rise, in a horseshoe formation. Company B was occupying the center sector, with the battalion command post about 100 yards behind it.

". . . Automatic weapons were at a premium . . . Company B had only one machine gun for its sector. This weapon was in position about twenty-five yards in front of our riflemen, overlooking about 600 yards of clear area between us and the enemy, who was occupying another section of the high ground to our front.

"Sgt. Truman C. Olson . . . was in charge of the six-man crew manning this . . . one machine gun."

The enemy counterattacked continually throughout the night. Sergeant Olson's machine-gun crew bore the brunt of the counterattacks and fired intermittently all night. When morning came five of Sergeant Olson's six men were casualties. At daybreak the enemy launched another counterattack. For two hours Sergeant Olson beat off the enemy almost single-handedly, operating his weapon without assistance. He was the sole barrier between Company B and the enemy. There the Germans concentrated all types of fire in an effort to eliminate him.

After the fight, it was learned by Lieutenant Capron that Sergeant Olson had received severe mortar-shell fragment wounds in his back and leg. Though suffering terrible pain and losing blood constantly he continued to man his machine gun and to beat off the enemy for an hour and a half, until the counterattack was broken and the enemy repulsed.

Said T/Sgt. John H. Earl: "... I brought the medics to Sergeant Olson. He had serious shell-fragment wounds in his back and left leg and was just about done for when we arrived to evacuate him. His wounds were so severe that he died while being carried to the rear.

"... It is only because he carried on when he knew his life was slowly ebbing away from his grievous wounds that others of us are alive today."

Sergeant Olson was posthumously awarded the Medal of Honor.

On January 31, the attack was continued by 1st Battalion, 30th Infantry, attacking through 3d Battalion, 7th Infantry, on the Ponte Rotto–Cisterna axis and by 2d Battalion, 15th Infantry, on the Conca–Cisterna axis. The attack was launched at 1400 and both battalions encountered strong opposition. The 1st Battalion, 30th, made about 1500 yards, and 2d Battalion, 15th Infantry, made about 2500 yards.

The storm, having spent most of its full fury, began to die away in rapidly diminishing smaller actions. January 30 was the day its vortex fully swept over the 3d Division.

An attack by 1st Battalion, 15th Infantry, on February 1, toward a vital road junction was stopped before dark without attaining its objective. Two counterattacks, one against 3d Battalion, 15th, and one against 1st Battalion, 30th Infantry, were both repulsed with heavy casualties to the enemy.

Pfc. Alton W. Knappenberger of Company C almost singlehandedly repulsed the latter attack. During the attack all officers in the area were killed or captured and every noncommissioned officer either killed, wounded, captured, or dispersed. Eight men remained on the company's right flank, which was on the battalion left. One man had a bazooka, and the other, Knappenberger, had a BAR.

"During the counterattack, Pfc. Knappenberger took up a firing position on a small exposed knoll," said Pfc. Charles McGregor. "At about 0900 his position was rushed by a German platoon in strength, all of them armed with automatic weapons, fire from which struck all around his knoll."

A German machine-gun crew moved into position about sixty-five yards to Knappenberger's flank. He took his BAR and rose to a kneeling position, placing several well-aimed bursts into the crew of four, which killed two, wounded a third, and forced another of the enemy to flee. "As Pfc. Knappenberger was firing his BAR at the machine gun, two Germans attempted to kill him with potato masher grenades, which burst but a few feet away," said S/Sgt. Ralph W. Moody. "A Flak gun, also, was covering the area with 20mm shells, Flak from which flew right over his knoll. As soon as he had destroyed the machine-gun crew, Pfc. Knappenberger fired at the two grenade-throwing Germans and killed them. ..."

A grenade went off, killing the third. Said Pfc. Daniel P. Vasien: "A little later a Flakwagon opened fire on Pfc. Knappenberger and just missed him by inches. His position was attacked at about 0900 by a platoon. He kept a continual stream of lead pouring out of his BAR. He killed and wounded several of the enemy and stopped the platoon attack."

"... But for the determined resistance against overwhelming odds of the small group of which Pfc. Knappenberger was most outstanding," stated Lt. Col. Edgar C. Doleman, "much more serious losses would probably have been suffered. Had the enemy attack not been disrupted by these men for approximately two and one-half hours its continuation could have had a serious effect on later operations by forcing occupation of less advanced and less favorable defensive positions. ..."

For his action Pfc. Knappenberger was awarded the Medal of Honor.

The 7th Infantry's 2d Battalion relieved the 1st Battalion, which was considerably reduced in strength, and the regiment repulsed a counterattack on the morning of February 2. Aggressive patrolling and continuation of defensive preparations were the main activity of February 2. About fifty PWs were taken in cleaning out small pockets of resistance behind the lines. A counterattack against 2d Battalion, 7th Infantry, at 1600 was stopped without any loss of ground. Engineers took over the guarding of bridges across the northwest branch of the Mussolini Canal.

The Division prepared on February 3 to hold forward positions with outposts and to construct and occupy a main line of resistance along the northwest branch of the Mussolini Canal.

We now know that the enemy Order of Battle on the 3d Infantry Division front on February 1, when our attack on Cisterna had been definitely stopped included:

1st Battalion, 104th *Panzer Grenadier* Regiment, 15 *PG Division*

1st Battalion, 1st Parachute Regiment, 1st Parachute Division

171st Reconnaissance Battalion, 71st Infantry Division

356th Reconnaissance Battalion, 356th Infantry Division

Parachute Machine Gun Battalion

114th Reconnaissance Battalion, 114th Infantry Division

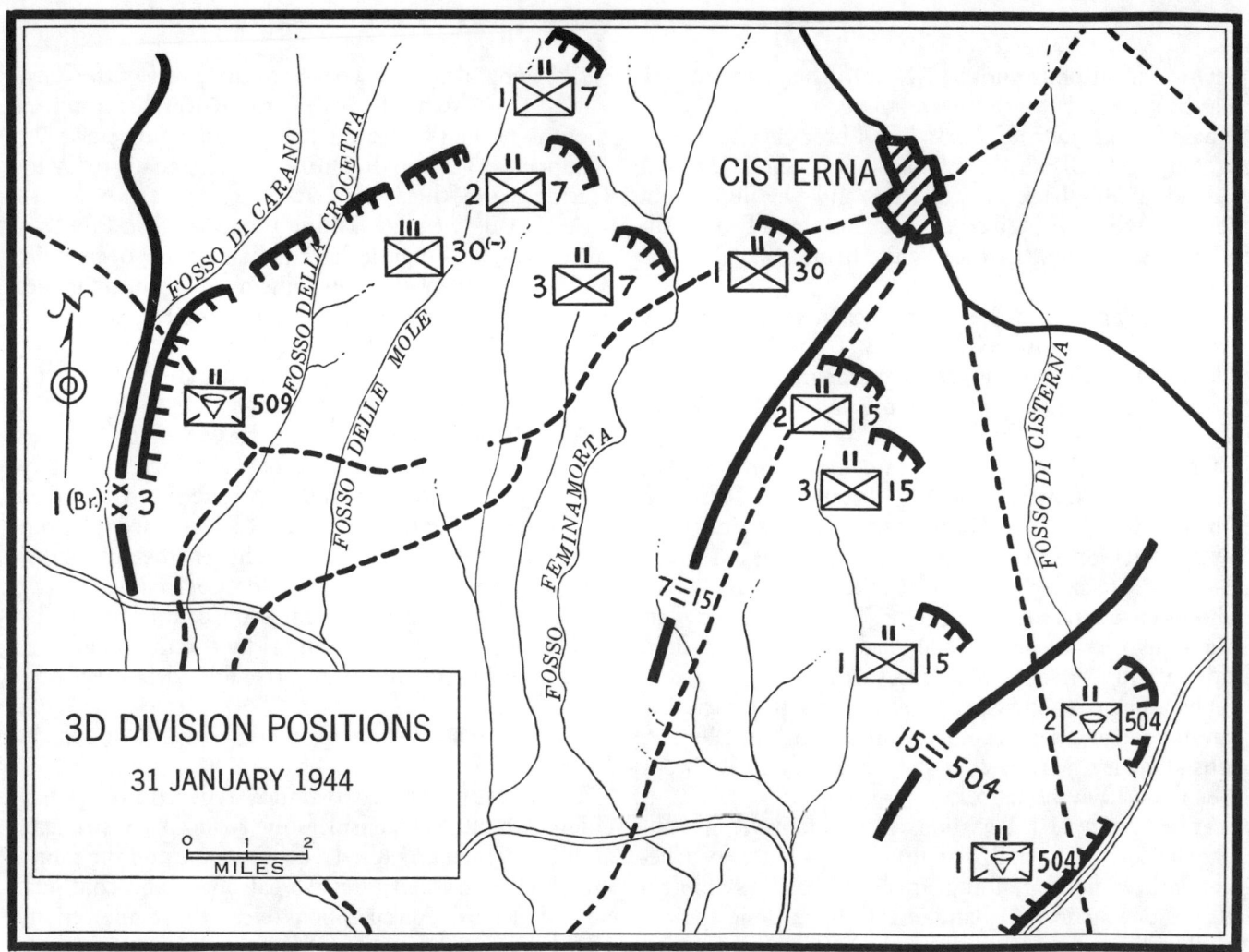

2d Battalion, 1st *Panzer Grenadier* Regiment, *Hermann Goering* Division.
Luftwaffe Jaeger Battalion *zbV* 7
Assumed reserves: 67th *Panzer Grenadier* Regiment, 26th *Panzer* Division. *Schutzstaffel Brigade Reichsfuehrer*
Hermann Goering Engineer Battalion

Thus the enemy had seven divisions represented by eleven battalions with which to oppose our attack, and roughly half of this total had not even been identified in our sector at the time our attack started. It will be noted that five of these battalions were reconnaissance units, which were speeded into action because of their mobility and comparatively heavy fire power. All but the *Hermann Goering* Reconnaissance Battalion were far away when we landed on January 22. The enemy had indeed moved swiftly.

Nor should one overlook the enemy artillery, which was brought up rapidly and was already present in strength at the time of the first attack on Cisterna. This consisted of 105mm howitzers and rifles, 150mm howitzers, 170mm rifles, 88mm antiaircraft-antitank self-propelled and towed rifles, and six-barrelled *Nebelwerfers*.

But—what happened on January 30? Overwhelming opposition was not the only explanation.

Perhaps the lessons learned that day, bitter as they were, help best to explain the halting of our attack.

To begin with, infiltration tactics were chosen in the hope of establishing strong infantry forces in the enemy rear, isolating his forward defenses, and avoiding the necessity of attacking by daylight through interlocking machine-gun and observed artillery fire. Great emphasis was placed on moving up supporting armor and antitank weapons prior to daylight.

The tactics used were not those best adapted to the attack on a numerous enemy, well dug in on a more or less continuous line. Later beachhead operations showed that these defenses could be penetrated only by overwhelming them from the front in a series of violent, carefully coordinated attacks against forward positions. Elements which infiltrate the forward positions are apt to find themselves cut off without succor, because, to reach them, other troops have to attack and eliminate the intervening defenses anyhow.

Second: Flat, treeless terrain is tough on the daylight attacker unless he has overwhelming artillery and air superiority, a carefully devised smoke plan, and a pinpoint knowledge of enemy positions and weaknesses. These elements were simply not present in sufficient degree on January 30, 1944.

Third: The enemy house-silo-oven defenses were virtually new to the Division and proved tremendously effective. Later when we learned about them more fully we learned how to cope with them successfully.

Fourth: For the first time in the Division's World War II history, the enemy was employing everything he had in defense, and not merely delaying. Thus, a battalion of parachutists not known to be in Cisterna provided one nasty surprise; counterattacking enemy who became more numerous in spite of heavy casualties another, copious and expertly-handled artillery still a third.

In spite of all these adverse factors, the Division's attack was delivered with great violence, and gained a good deal of important ground, while inflicting enormous casualties on the enemy, probably more than the Division took itself. Actions of our magnificent infantry battalions during that two-day period will remain long in the memory of the Division.

There was the 1st Battalion, 7th Infantry, commanded by Lt. Col. Frank B. Izenour. This battalion had been chosen to infiltrate to Highway 7 northwest of Cisterna starting at H-hour. Almost from the line of departure it ran into strong, stubborn resistance, so that its "infiltration" movement rapidly became a sticky infantry fire fight with all companies heavily engaged. Late in the morning the battalion had made only 1000 yards and was being fired at from the front and the two flanks. It was decided to commit the 2d Battalion on the right to clear the flank and enable it to keep rolling.

The afternoon witnessed the near-destruction of the 1st Battalion—but it also witnessed the killing of an estimated 200 enemy at the very least and the wounding or capture of many more. Colonel Izenour was himself wounded in the shoulder by machine-pistol bullets. In an orchard the battalion over-ran two enemy 105s. Led by Capt. William Athis, commander of Company D, about twenty men turned the weapon around and used it to good effect on the enemy. Shortly before dusk it was reported that the battalion's leading elements had crossed the railroad track, a feat that was not repeated until the breakthrough of May 23. Maj. Frank C. Sinsel, who assumed command following Colonel Izenour's wound, received the Distinguished Service Cross for his actions during this engagement.

A witness (a fighting soldier of the 1st Battalion) described the kind of an afternoon all the battalions had:

"Hollywood would have paid five million dollars to have had that on film. Here we were, *walking* in on the enemy and he had every weapon from machine guns on up zeroed in on us. Small arms and artillery were intense. Men were dropping all around. It made you wonder when you were going to get it. The rest of the men never even hesitated, just kept walking forward, only stopping to shoot. The tanks and TDs were moving right along with us, shooting hell out of houses and haystacks. When we got in on the Jerry positions they couldn't take it. They poured out of those foxholes. So then it was our turn. The fellows with their rifles and BARs and the TDs and tanks with their .30 and .50-caliber machine guns went to work on them. We knocked off a hell of a lot of kraut. In the orchard they were practically piled one on top of each other. The Marines at Tarawa had nothing on the 3d Division at Cisterna that day."

The battalion had gained about 3000 yards since H-hour against violent opposition. Unfortunately, it was reduced to 150 effectives, and the battalion commander was compelled to withdraw about 400 yards south of the track and set up a defensive position for the night. Later he was ordered to fall back even farther, approximately to the 2d Battalion position because of the exposed salient he occupied.

Patrols which visited this area later told of the carnage and loss of equipment on both sides in the area covered by this battalion. It was an example outstanding among examples of fighting quality, ferocity in the attack and will to achieve an objective.

There was the 3d Battalion, 15th Infantry. Ordered to attack north across country, east of the Cisterna—Conca road in an effort to relieve the surrounded Rangers, this battalion organized in an area occupied by the 4th Ranger Battalion (which was to have followed the infiltration of the 1st and 3d Ranger Battalions) and, under heavy fire from the start, moved 2000 yards across flat terrain and succeeded in capturing Feminamorta by nightfall, although this crossroad settlement was held in strength by enemy well equipped with antitank weapons. This attack might never have succeeded but for the heroic work of our armor, especially TDs which closed in on the built-up area, destroyed three enemy antitank guns with pointblank fire and neutralized many of the most strongly-held houses by pumping high-velocity projectiles right through them.

There were the 2d Battalion, 15th Infantry, and the 1st Battalion, 30th Infantry, which made a gallant bid to smash their way into Cisterna the afternoon of January 31. Each battalion got to within about 2000 yards of the city in slashing attacks. The 2d Battalion of the 15th approaching from Feminamorta, got within

2000 yards of Cisterna, and the 1st Battalion of the 30th, attacking from Ponte Rotto, got within 1500 yards. Both battalions were rolling forward when halted by Division because the stiffness of the opposition, coupled with the advanced positions reached by these battalions, made it questionable whether their forward elements could be supported or reinforced. Some of their gains had to be sacrificed in order to hold a stable line later on, but this does not detract from the brilliant work they performed that day.

There was the 1st Battalion of the 15th which emerged from the three-day battle with an average of eighteen to twenty men per company remaining.

These battalions are mentioned, not because their conduct was the exception, but rather the rule, of all the battalions and attached units during that period.

No newspaper accounts have ever been given a reasonable explanation of what happened to the 1st and 3d Ranger Battalions in the first Battle of Cisterna. But in light of what was later learned about the enemy, and in light of the Division's most determined efforts to relieve the Rangers, it is possible to view their tragic isolation and destruction as a sober military fact rather than only as a gallant but unsuccessful struggle against overwhelming odds.

First: A prisoner from the 356th Reconnaissance Battalion, defending the Feminamorta sector, later said his unit had been orderd to allow our leading elements to pass through unmolested, in the expectation that they would be cut off and destroyed by enemy troops further back. This may explain why the Rangers' infiltration succeeded initially, as they reached the outskirts of Cisterna without having to fire a shot.

Secondly: The Rangers, having been originally organized for fast-moving individual operations on foot, were not strong in automatic weapons, mortars, and communications equipment as the ordinary infantry battalion. They were actually primed for house-to-house fighting in Cisterna rather than for a defense against enemy tanks south of the city.

Thirdly: The tanks and TDs which were to have reached the Rangers by daylight scarcely got started before one M-10 and one halftrack hit mines and were immobilized, and the others were unable to move forward until they had reached Feminamorta with the 3d Battalion, 15th Infantry, later in the day. The 4th Ranger Battalion, which was to attack north with the armor, was disorganized by intense enemy shelling and machine-gun fire at the line of departure and was unable to progress beyond this point.

Fourth: Enemy armor and Flakwagons which debouched from Cisterna and attacked the Rangers on flat country shortly after daylight, succeeded in cutting them up into small uncoordinated groups which were later mopped up piecemeal. Success of our venture actually depended on the Rangers getting into Cisterna before daylight, as it was known that the *Hermann Goering* Division had tanks available for the town's defenses and could easily stand off the Rangers outside the build-up area. Presence of the enemy parachute battalion was an additional reinforcement over and above the tanks.

Commendations later awarded individuals and units of the 3d Infantry Division reflect the spirit of these tremendous battles more truly than any prose.

That was the first battle of Cisterna. It was the most savage and disappointing action the Division had fought up to that time, and the first time the 3d had ceased to move forward in 100 days of action. But in accepting that setback, and withstanding the most terrible assaults the Germans could hurl against it in the months that followed, the Division took its place beside the greatest fighting units in our country's history.

The beachhead siege, which was to last four months to the day from the first landing on January 22, had set in.

2. The Tide of Battle Turns

February 2 to March 3

THE people of the United Nations, had they been completely informed on the situation, might have realized that between February 2 and March 3, 1944 a basically simple question was being hammered out in terrific strife and mental agony of thousands of men and women, on a ten-by-fifteen-mile patch of ground in Italy.

The question was simple because it boiled down to this: Were the British War Office and the United States War Department going to have to write off some of their most experienced combat divisions with the notation . . . "Destroyed" as happened in the case of the 1st and 3d Battalions, Ranger Force?

There were also the Special Service Force, the 504th Parachute Infantry Regiment, the 4th Ranger Battalion, 36th and 39th Combat Engineer Regiments, the 509th Parachute Infantry Battalion, thousands of service troops, doctors, nurses, airmen, and ground crewmen. Were they to be doomed to confinement in German prison camps or consignment to military cemeteries? Was a quantity of material to be lost in a military debacle such as the Allies had not known since the days of Gallipoli? The threat of all this was, unfortunately, all too real and absolutely not to be underestimated in considering our position on the Anzio Beachhead in February and early March, 1944.

Anyone who was on the beachhead had a pretty fair idea of the fate that awaited if the beachhead line had not held. The better part of thirteen German divisions sat in a watchful ring about that little patch of ground and did their best to make it the sort of Inferno such as a native son of Italy had once described as awaiting the souls of those who sinned on earth. Danté's descriptions, however, were imaginary. Anzio unfortunately, was not.

February was the most crucial month the 3d Infantry Division experienced since it began fighting in World War II. We were fighting for our lives and we knew it. There was no place to go if the Germans broke through our lines and no one was in a better position to know it than we. If the Germans made a serious penetration and were able to exploit that penetration quickly, it is hard to say what mercy we would have been shown, but it took no master mind to say accurately what would have been the military fact of the matter. In front of us was the enemy, behind us the Tyhrrenian Sea. It was a long swim back to Naples.

The enemy, who had begun his counteraction against the newly-formed beachhead with as unlikely a conglomeration of units as could be formed anywhere, had nevertheless acted with unexpected rapidity in getting units into the line first to stop, then to counterattack the Allied forces.

We were fortunate in having gallant British allies, and worthy comrades in other United States divisions. They contained much of the enemy punch. But the ultimate trial of strength took place between some of the best troops in the German Army and the *"Sturm"* —United States—3d Infantry Division. It ended in a complete defensive victory for the 3d.

While the first enemy units in contact were slowing, then holding the attack toward Cisterna di Littoria and the vital Rome-Naples Highway 7, the Germans were pouring reinforcements of men and artillery into the beachhead sector at a very rapid rate. Orders had gone out from the High Command to stop—stop at any cost —the threat to the German Army's rear in the south, and at considerable cost to the enemy it *was* stopped. But by February 3 we had more than evened the score. We had lost two battalions of the United States Ranger Force; one battalion of each of the regiments had taken terrific punishment, and the others in lesser, but still heavy, degree, as had the remaining 4th Ranger Battalion and the attached parachutists of the 504th Regiment and 509th Battalion. But the enemy had absorbed much greater punishment from our combined artillery, bombing, naval artillery, tank and tank-destroyer onslaught, combined with the magnificent way in which the doughboys had moved in on enemy positions.

We know now, from completely reliable sources, that Adolf Hitler gave orders to push the beachhead into the sea. Let us see how the enemy went about attempting this:

For more than two weeks in February his attitude was chiefly defensive. He began by reorganizing and replacing his shattered units. Segments of organizations which had been hurled into various gaps in his defensive line were withdrawn or supplemented by more elements of the same organizations, in order better to reform his lines. He perfected his defenses in our sector, his main line of resistance following the line of the railroad track northwest of Cisterna on the line of Fosso di Cisterna-Mussolini Canal south of the town. Then he continued to regroup his forces for his first big offensive.

February 3 and 4 found the 3d Infantry Division improving and consolidating its positions. Aggressive patrolling and continuation of defensive preparations was the main activity. On February 4, as the main line of resistance along the Mussolini Canal neared completion, weapons were sited and manned in forward areas, and these positions were stocked with ammunition and rations, in preparation for enlarging the beachhead line by the difference in distance between the canal positions and the forward positions. Erection of wire obstacles and the laying of defensive minefields began. Although their use signified defense rather than attack (attack had characterized the United States Army in the Mediterranean Theater since commencement of operations in French North Africa) a couple of vicious new antipersonnel mines which the Ordnance Department had developed gave us our first chance to strike back at the enemy with one of his own predominantly favorite weapons.

One company each from the 1st and 2d Battalions, 7th Infantry, remained on forward positions attached to the 30th Infantry. The remainder of the regiment moved to Division reserve in the vicinity of Le Ferriere. The 15th Infantry redisposed its forces, with about one-third of each battalion on the forward outpost line of resistance, one-third on the secondary line, and the remaining one-third on the main line of resistance.

Elements of the 1st Battalion, 30th Infantry, in the 15th Infantry sector, remained on forward positions attached to the 15th (southwest of Ponte Rotto). The remainder of the 1st Battalion occupied primary and secondary defensive lines in the 30th Infantry sector. The 2d Battalion, 30th Infantry, moved to the vicinity of Le Ferriere and began working on MLR defenses. The 3d Battalion was released from Division reserve and moved to the vicinity of Campo Morto. The 504th Parachute Infantry Regiment was organized on three defensive lines in its sector.

The reason for the scheme was obvious. We needed a defense in depth, and the only way to secure it was to have three separate lines which could be defended in their turn. If it became necessary to fall back from the first, the second could be defended, and if that had to be abandoned there was always the main line of resistance, behind which there was no retirement. The main line of resistance, if ever reached, would mark the turn of balance in the enemy's favor, and absolutely had to be defended to the last man. As it turned out it was never necessary to abandon even the first line.

At 1700 February 5 an estimated company of enemy hit our outpost line, preceded by a short, intense artillery preparation, which caused the outpost line of resistance to fall back. The 7th Infantry found enemy Mark III tanks in its sector. This attack broke off shortly after it had started, and the enemy withdrew under cover of his own artillery. Elements of the 2d Battalion, 7th Infantry, scheduled for relief by the 30th Infantry, reassembled south of the Mussolini Canal and rejoined the regiment. Company K, 7th Infantry, counterattacked and restored all positions by 0230, February 6.

February 6 the 2d Battalion, 7th Infantry, moved into positions along the canal vacated by the 3d Battalion, 30th Infantry. The remainder of the 7th Infantry was in assembly southwest of Le Ferriere.

At 0420 the 15th Infantry repulsed a platoon-size counterattack. Over the night of 6-7 the 3d Reconnaissance Troop and 3d Provisional Reconnaissance Troop patrolled, probing enemy positions.

During that night Divisional units were regrouped. The 15th, 30th and 504th Regiments were to defend forward areas with two battalions each, holding one battalion each in regimental reserve. The 7th Infantry was to organize and occupy a line on the northwest branch of the Mussolini Canal.

Company E, 15th Infantry, attacked on the evening of February 7, with the objective of taking the farm at Ponte Rotto. Strong opposition was encountered, and the fight continued until midnight. The company took four bitterly contested houses but did not reach its objective. Company F also attacked, going east toward Ponte Rotto with the mission of clearing the road junction there. The enemy was driven 1000 yards west of Ponte Rotto and out of some houses, but this attack also stopped short of its objective.

During the night the enemy attacked the 15th Infantry along the Cisterna-Isola Bella axis, and reached the crossroad at Isola Bella (Feminamorta), but withdrew before daylight. The enemy also attacked down the west bank of Fosso delle Mole, but was driven off. An enemy platoon attacked Company K, 30th Infantry, at midnight and was repulsed.

On February 8 the 509th Parachute Infantry Battalion repelled an attack northeast of Carano. In this action, Cpl. Paul B. Huff of Company A particularly distinguished himself. His company came under fire from its right flank which was exposed due to the company's forward position. Huff volunteered to lead a six-man patrol to investigate and determine the strength and location of the enemy forces.

Commencing at 0730, the patrol advanced toward a draw which was covered by fire from three enemy machine guns and a 20mm gun. In addition to being mined it was the only route of approach offering any cover whatsoever, and the patrol was forced to take it.

"As the patrol proceeded toward the objective the men came under small-arms and machine-gun fire and a concentration of mortar fire," said 1st Lt. Joseph J. Winsko. "Moving ahead of his patrol, Cpl. Huff came under the fire of the machine guns and the 20mm gun covering the draw. Realizing the danger to his patrol, he had them wait while he advanced through the minefield along the edge of the draw to within seventy-five yards of the nearest machine-gun position, having traveled 275 yards under fire of these guns."

Said 1st Lt. Albert L. Kinderknecht, "Still under fire, which was striking all around him, he crawled the final seventy-five yards to the enemy machine gun and poking his weapon into the emplacement, killed the crew and destroyed the gun. Upon returning to the patrol he was continually under mortar, machine-gun and small-arms fire.

"Cpl. Huff reported back to his company with his entire patrol, suffering no casualties and giving valuable information. . . ."

"At 1300 hours," said Pfc. John E. Pumphrey, "without rest and under sniper fire, Cpl. Huff accompanied a combat patrol, led by Sgt. Kelly C. Bath, into position. The patrol attacked, killed 27 Germans, captured 21 prisoners and forced the remaining enemy to flee in disorder. His leadership of one section of this later patrol was a deciding factor in the success of the mission.

"The terrain was favorable to the enemy. With the exception of one ditch under enemy mortar fire there was no cover or concealment. The enemy had a clear field of observation and fire.

"Enemy sniper and mortar fire was heavy for much of the two patrols; mortar shells were landing within five to ten yards of the men and bullets were striking within two to three feet of them. During the attack enemy machine-gun fire and sniper fire were heavy. Visibility was excellent from 0730 hours to 1630 hours and the enemy were dug in 400 yards from our lines."

Corporal Huff was awarded the Medal of Honor for this action.

At this time an enemy force estimated at two divisions was beginning the first big effort to knock in the left flank of the beachhead in the British sector. Fighting for the "factory" at Aprilia was fierce, and although the line gave at some points the enemy did not succeed in penetrating it seriously enough to cause a major threat to the entire beachhead. Casualties were high on both sides. This attack died down after about three days of furious attacking by the enemy and intensive counterpreparations of the famed "meat grinder" British artillery fire. The lines held.

Between the last attacks early in the month and the time of the first big attack directed at the 3d Division there was somewhat of a lull. No description has yet been given of the more human visual aspects of the beachhead. Perhaps the viewpoint of a replacement who came to join the Division at this time should be included:

Our LST was sitting in the harbor about 3000 yards offshore when most of us came on deck that morning. There were several hundred of us, mostly replacements and return-to-unit men of the Division. Most of us were pretty curious about the beachhead, and scared, because we'd already heard a lot about it in the two and a half weeks since it was first made.

We got a typical greeting. There was a swishing sound, a vicious crack, and a geyser shot up about 400 yards from our ship, sending some of us back into the hold after our helmets. Several of us looked to some of the veterans of lower Italy and Sicily; hell, we didn't know the score.

A young kid of a sailor standing near me, so young he couldn't have found it necessary to shave more than once a week, said: "They got a couple of railroad guns sitting back by those hills that they can't spot. The Air Corps has been trying to get them for two weeks. Mostly the guns shoot into the town. That last one was about as far out into the water they can reach. Boy, I'll be glad when we get turned around and headed back for Naples."

I looked where he pointed. The hills were large mountains against country that was flat as a sand table—our territory. The air was clear as a bell and they loomed up there as though they were cut from blue cardboard.

"Have we got those hills?" I asked.

"No, that's Jerry's territory," said the sailor.

I found out later that it was the Monti Lepini, a foremost tip of the Apennine Mountains. On its side was a cluster of buildings—Cori. To the left—north—was a pass through the "hills" and there was another mass of rugged high ground that ran back toward the sea ending before reaching it to leave another flat space along the water. This was the Colli Laziali, and on the side of it I could see another town, higher up than Cori. I found out later that this was Velletri.

Anzio was a mass of masonry behind which was a small rise and some trees. Even from where we were I could see there was considerable damage done to it. It was of about thirty feet elevation, rising away from the water. It fronted on a narrow sandy beach which seemed to run south for at least a couple of miles. Along that beach the ground away from the beaches rose into a cliff that was about a hundred feet at its greatest height. Farther the ground smoothed out again and a pine forest hugged the water.

About eleven o'clock we were moving toward shore. There were thirty or so barrage balloons rising over and around the town. The gun had not fired again.

We docked at a paved-over stone jetty sticking out like an arm into the water. It took about half an hour to get our group off the LST.

The officer in charge led us off in groups of platoon size, taking interval in a single column on either side of the street. I got a good look at Anzio. It *was* hammered, but as we got into it further I could see there were a lot of buildings which were fairly intact. There was a lot of

Immediately after the burst of a 280mm shell near the stone jetty at Anzio. Five men were killed.

the usual rubble around, of course, timbers, crumbled plaster and glass. We walked several hundred yards and turned left to follow a road along the sea. There were frequent antiaircraft emplacements sandbagged in. The crews looked us over as we marched by. There were a few British M.P.s and a lot of signs pointing to ration dumps, unit headquarters, different towns, and listing orders on traffic restrictions.

When we had gone about half a mile we came to a large, open field. There were about twenty six-by-six trucks dispersed around the field. An officer met the officer commanding our group and had us deployed over the field.

Finally we got called together again and assigned to regiments. We were packed into the trucks and they got moving. We started down the road back through part of the town. We drove over a black-top road lined with evergreen trees. We got out into a clear stretch and then went into Nettuno. The trucks barreled right along.

We had no sooner got out of town than a hell of a racket sprung up all around us. It was antiaircraft fire of all calibers. We looked up, and there, streaking through the sky were three planes. There was a flock of black puffs around them. They headed right for the harbor, and when they got near it they went into a shallow dive. You could see the glint of bombs. Then they turned north and streaked away as they'd come, with the guns still shooting at them. Around one of the LSTs in the harbor there were several terrific explosions and huge waterspouts, but when the water had settled back down, the ship was still there and looked undamaged.

A few minutes later and six or seven friendly planes were flying circles over the harbor.

After a couple of miles along a rutted road the trucks turned off into a field. On the right was a large patch of scrub oak. We could see quite a few men and tents scattered through it. We unloaded. It was the regimental service company and rear command-post area.

The men there were all wearing brown overall-like combat suits and jackets of the same color, most of them tucked inside the suits. Most of the suits were mud-stained; everyone wore helmets and most of them carried sidearms or rifles.

We all had overcoats and a two-blanket roll. We were told that we would be assigned to battalions and taken up the next day, after the regimental commander had spoken to us. So we slept in the open that night and damn near froze.

While we were still trying to thaw out the next day, we were lined up by an officer doing his best to sound tough, and pretty soon the regimental commander came up in his jeep. He was rough, and he didn't waste any words.

"Close in so you can hear me," he barked. When we had closed in the Colonel looked around. "You're now part of the —th Infantry," he said. "You're going up as replacements to the best goddamn regiment in the United States Army. You're joining a crack unit of a crack division. You will be expected to live up to the traditions of that regiment and that division.

"You're going to suffer. You came here to suffer. You're going to suffer everything that the Boche can throw at you and you're going to suffer everything that goes with a miserable goddamn climate. But you're going to take it like men.

"We've quit playing games. This is serious business. The Boche is sitting out there with seven or eight divisions and trying to shove us into the ocean. Upon you men depends the future of every living soul on this beachhead. Don't make any mistake about it. It's men like you that're going up into front-line foxholes and stop the attack that the Boche is going to throw within a week. And you're going to get up there with the idea that you will kill as many of them as possible. That's the only thing that's going to keep us from being shoved into the sea, is killing Boche.

"Listen to what the men up there have got to tell you about how to kill Boche, but don't listen to any defeatist talk from any of 'em. You're new, but as far as we're concerned you're every bit as good a man, each one of you, as the best man in the division, until or unless you show us otherwise."

There was some more on the same line. Then the colonel saluted and got into his jeep and drove off.

I joined my battalion on the side of a hill. They had dug in there. We got sent out to our companies. The one I was assigned to was on the other side of that hill. They were just out of the lines for a short time, and there weren't many of them. They'd just finished a big attack on Cisterna and a lot of them had been killed and wounded. The men looked tired, and most of them were unshaven.

They didn't say much when we came in, clean and shiny in our new overcoats, packs, and helmets. They just looked at us. But they came in close to see what we were like.

The company commander, a young second lieutenant, grouped us into a semi-circle and made us a little speech right there on the side of the hill. He said we were welcome and that we were badly needed. He said he was glad we were so well equipped because there was a big supply problem, and while we could get anything we needed it was better to start with it than have to requisition it. He said we only had a few days before we would probably return to the lines. He said we only had a few combat suits that the hospitals had taken off the casualties and sent back to us, so until we could get us one we had better hang on to our overcoats. He said keep your weapons in good order and pay attention to all the pointers the old men could give us. He said, last, that he hoped we were glad to be joining a first-class fighting outfit and good luck to all of us.

We got assigned to platoons and squads.

We stuck around that area for a week. The weather turned rainy, and the holes we dug filled up with water. We were a miserable bunch. The only thing to be done was bail out, get some straw, and try to get the bottom of the hole dry enough to lay on. The wind was sharp and ice-cold. The old men told us it wasn't so bad here, to wait until we got into the line where we couldn't get out of our holes. It was bad enough already for us.

We moved up into the line starting about six o'clock one evening. It was black as pitch and you had to watch the man ahead. I don't know where the road led, all I know is that we marched for about five or six miles, with a couple of halts.

You could tell when you were getting close to the line. You passed most of the artillery, which was popping away from time to time. You looked off to the front and flank and every once in awhile you could see a squirt of white tracer and it seemed to float its way toward our lines. That was Jerry. Ours answered with bursts that had red tracer in them. They seemed to be steadier. Then, from far off there was the blurt of a machine rifle, or the tack-tack-tack of one of our machine guns. It got louder as we got closer.

Once we heard a couple of shells coming in and hit the dirt, but they landed quite a ways away. The old men told us in whispers that it was a pretty quiet night and for us to hope it stayed that way. We were spread out, of course, and keeping a good interval between us.

Pretty soon we got off the road and on to a plowed field. It was rough and muddy and hard going. Pretty soon it was all you could do to keep going. After some time we halted and the word was passed to spread out and get down. After marching we were pretty warm, but when we lay on that wet ground we began to get cold almost right away. After a while the squad leader rounded us up and led us forward. We waded a creek and got told, in whispers, not to make so goddam much noise. We got to the top of a little rise and we were in the front line.

It was pretty quiet, but that only made us all the more nervous. When a Jerry flare popped about a quarter mile away we all hit the dirt. The squad leaders took two of us to a two-man foxhole. We could just barely see a couple of boys rounding up some equipment. They climbed out and said, "Here it is. You're welcome to it." Then we climbed in.

The bottom was squashy. It wasn't a very big hole, about chest deep. Part of it was boarded over. At the front was a dirt ledge. I felt around this and found a bandolier of ammunition and five hand grenades.

The squad leader came around a few minutes later and said that one of us had to be awake at all times, and for Christ's sake if we heard or saw anything in front of us, not to challenge too loud or hesitate to shoot if we didn't get the right answer.

It was cold as usual the rest of that night, but it was pretty hard staying awake. All through the night there were flares going up from the Jerry lines. Once Jerry threw in a terrific artillery barrage which landed about five hundred yards behind us. I was scared.

We were around for ten days. It was just plain hell all through the day, and the nights were worse. We had five days of rain. The hole got about six inches of water, and you couldn't do anything but try to bail it out with your helmet. We wrapped shelter halves and blankets around us but they didn't do much good. They got soaked with rain and then you sat on a piece of wood or something and shivered and cussed. If you "had to go," you had to think about it before daylight because you couldn't get out of that hole once the sun came up, or ever show the top of your head.

At night we got canned "C" rations. Toward the last they brought them up warmed up a little, and coffee, only a little warm by the time it got to us, and once in a while a beef sandwich or some doughnuts. Those did more to help our morale than anything else, except mail. But it was pretty fierce.

You had to get out of the hole when it got dark for several reasons, one of which was to get some circulation back into your feet. A lot of the boys went to the medics with bad cases of trench foot, but I wasn't that lucky.

Jerry threw in a lot of artillery and mortars. The best thing to do was pull in your head and pray. Some of that big stuff would cave in the side of a wet foxhole like it was sand, and a couple of the boys got buried right in

The breechblock of a captured German 280mm gun.

their hole fifty yards away from me. We had two or three casualties every day, mostly from artillery and mortars. If you got it at night you were lucky, because they could get you out right away. God help you if you got hit in the daytime, because you might have to lay there all day before somebody could get to you. A couple of our medics got Silver Stars for going out in the daytime to help wounded men. One of them got his posthumously.

We stayed there through the first big attack around the middle of February. . . .

The 504th Parachute Infantry Regiment repelled an attack northeast of Bridge 5 on February 9. February 10 the attack was resumed with one or two companies, but was repulsed. The 3d Battalion, 7th Infantry, moved up to the canal to be ready to meet the threat against the 504th. The 4th Ranger Battalion was attached to the 504th.

At 0330 February 12 an enemy company attacked Company C, 15th Infantry. The outposts were temporarily forced back, but positions were restored by 0505.

On February 13, 7th and 30th Regiments reconnoitered each other's positions in preparation for relief of the 30th Infantry by the 7th. Two enemy platoons attacked Company D, 504th Regiment at 0315, but were driven off. A few enemy penetrated the outpost position but were all either killed or captured.

The night of February 14-15 the 1st Battalion, 7th Infantry, relieved the 1st Battalion, 30th Infantry, and was attached to the 30th. The 1st Battalion, 30th, moved to the other's old position and was attached to the 7th.

The frequency of patrol clashes and small-scale counterattacks had the appearance of probing for weaknesses in our lines. It seemed certain that the enemy was shortly to mount a large-scale attack in our sector, something he had not yet attempted. It is possible that he found the standpat defenses of the British a nut too tough to crack and hoped, by a sudden shift, to catch us off balance and drive through our lines, splitting the beachhead down the middle, following which would be a mere cleaning out of the entire beachhead.

Before going into the description of that day, his method of attack should be briefly examined. As it was to develop, his main effort on February 16 took place along the Albano-Anzio road axis, and the full force of it enveloped the 45th Infantry Division on our left flank. At the same time, however, he struck at seven separate places in the sector of the 3d Infantry Division, and any weaknesses displayed in our lines could have been quickly exploited by reserves who were waiting for just that chance. If he had succeeded in his major effort, the beachhead would have been effectively cut in two, the British and the 45th Division on one side, and the 3d Division, its attachments, and the Special Service Force on the other.

Added to our knowledge that the Germans had moved in troops and men to the immediate beachhead area was the fact that now was the time for the enemy to strike. If he waited any longer, we would be stronger in minefields, barbed-wire entanglements, and antitank and machine-gun emplacements. He knew that, and we knew that. Thus an attack was expected by our Intelligence almost hourly, as February 16 approached.

Enemy armor continued to build up in the Cisterna area. For several days during early February the daily Intelligence summary carried the following warning: "His (the enemy's) attitude is that of active, aggressive defense, with attacks being launched on any Allied penetration that threatens the security of his main defense position. Active reconnaissance, similar to the attack on our front on 5 February and limited objective counterattacks may be expected frequently as he attempts to determine our dispositions, strength, and consequent intentions. Enemy strength in the 3d Division sector is now believed to be such that should he appreciate a change on our part from an offensive to a defensive attitude, he would well be able to contain a large portion of the front with light forces and mass considerable strength for an attack in any chosen sector."

On the eve of the attack the following units had been identified at one time or another in the beachhead sector: elements of 71st Infantry Division, *Schutzstaffel Reichsfuehrer* Division, 26th *Panzer* Division, 715th Infantry Division, 3d *Panzer Grenadier* Division, 114th Light Division, 1st Parachute Division, *Hermann Goering Panzer* Division, 65th Infantry Division, and 4th Parachute Division. In addition there had, at one time or another, been identified the following, or elements thereof: *Luftwaffe Jaeger* Battalion, *zbV* 7 (a special mission group), Parachute *Lehr* Regiment, 356th *Fusilier* Battalion, and 1028th Grenadier Regiment.

Naturally, not all of these units were in the line. But their presence at some time in the beachhead sector indicated the mass of men available to the enemy for his major effort.

While the 2d Battalion, 7th Infantry, was relieving the 2d Battalion, 30th Infantry, information of heavy vehicular traffic toward Cisterna was beginning to sift into the Division Headquarters War Room. This began in the late afternoon, February 15.

At 0735: A report came in from PW interrogaters at VI Corps that a captured German said his officer had told him to "take a good look at the terrain, because something big is coming off February 16." The PW said there was a rumor of a big attack, the object being to reduce the bridgehead and split it down the center.

At 0005, February 16: A radar report received at the War Room told of a big concentration of armor in the vicinity of Cisterna.

0035: Call from 30th Infantry: "A patrol just returned and they said they thought the enemy might be forming for an attack."

An intercepted radio message revealed that a big attack was planned to begin just about daylight. Quickly a VI Corps artillery "shoot" (or "Bingo") was arranged for 0430. The total weight of every piece of artillery on the beachhead would be brought to bear on targets all around the beachhead to last half an hour. Further fires would be on call from observer.

At 0430 the skies split wide open. Cannon roared and argued; it was like a huge eruption, and brought to mind moving pictures of the first World War. It was the greatest artillery concentration that had yet been fired on the Anzio Beachhead. German front lines were pounded. At the same time known routes of supply, enemy artillery emplacements, road junctions, likely assembly areas, and reserve assembly areas were also hit.

About the time the sky grew gray with light the German artillery began to interject its note of returning fire. Intermingled with the solid crack and thunder of "outgoing mail" was the whine and crash of incoming shells. And about the time our barrage began to slacken off the enemy fire reached its vicious peak. Artillery of all calibers fell on our front lines and worked its way back to our secondary line. Greatest caliber was 170mm. From distances as great as a half mile these shells sounded as though they were landing right next to one. Huge geysers of wet earth blossomed and descended on the torn ground. The earth was churned up yard by yard. As this preparation began to lift, the German infantry attack began.

0545: Call from 30th Infantry: "Just received word from F Company, 7th Infantry, that there was approximately a company of enemy moving toward their position and that artillery fire had ceased."

0635: Call from SSF: "Jerries have a little show up here coming toward our lines. They're putting some heavy barrages on our left."

0645: Call from VI Corps: "45th Infantry Division just called that heavy artillery just started on their front and from the way the thing just started, it looks like today should be the day."

0655: Call from 509th: "We have a PW who stated that the general attack was to take place down the draw between 509th and 30th. There has been a large patrol reported in front of us. 1st Battalion, 7th, reported an impending attack, but it seems to have slowed down."

0715: Call from 504th: "We need some more artillery help here. Called Divarty (Division Artillery) and they allotted me half a battalion. I need more—they're out in front of E and F company. Using our own artillery."

0730: Call from 30th: "Seem to be having a little activity. Talked to I Company and he said that about one-half hour ago about a hundred Germans came over that hill out of Ponte Rotto and they laid mortar and machine gun on them and about forty of them kept coming. They are in defilade now in that little creek. Another group tried to come over from the northwest above the little tip 83 (*Refers to Hill*: Ed.) and they've got them under fire and they are pinned down by that. That seems to be fairly well under control. Company K met an attack of approximately a hundred men and they have been taken under artillery fire. Also had a report of an uncounted number of tanks in the K Company area. Have alerted the TDs and ordered the AT defense in that area. In front of F Company the same situation, but no armor. Got a PW taken by the Para who claims that there was a battalion of tanks supposed to come down the draw by the graveyard. They had an 88 SP gun attached to the battalion. Said they had armor, about thirty 'Tigers' and forty 'Panthers.' This man was a private and that is a lot of information for a private. Everything seems to be pretty well under control."

0730: Call from 15th: "Enemy artillery concentration along 1st Battalion front. Small infantry action in front of B Company."

0745: Call from SSF: "The actual size of opposition is not fully determined. No penetration as yet."

0810: Call from 30th: "There has been a penetration of K Company's position by approximately a company. L Company, the reserve, is alerted and is going to have to hit it on the point or take it in the flank if possible. K Company forward positions are holding. Tanks are reported to the left of K Company—are being taken under fire by TDs at the present time."

0815: Call from 509th: "The Germans are laying smoke all along the front . . . We have been in contact with the enemy and killed a few and the enemy seemed to withdraw. We are putting mortar on them now."

0825: Call from 601st TD: "I have some information from my people in 30th sector. They fired on some tanks. They said observation was poor and the tanks seem to have gone into a defiladed position. They are keeping close watch for them. I also have some information from a PW. He states that at the graveyard there is a battalion that is going to make an attack. If it is not successful, they have 30 Mark VIs and 40 Mark IVs which will try to make a breakthrough."

0830: Call to Divarty: "The attack seems to have moved up north."

0835: Call from VI Corps: "CO, SSF, says it has died down on his front."

0955: Call from Bridge 5: "There are two ME 109s hedgehopping over the canal keeping spaced and trying to knock down the 3d Division Cub plane."

1050: Call to VI Corps: "Slight penetration between K Company, 30th, and E Company, 7th, that they are restoring with a local counterattack. Still fighting along the front, but it has died down."

1115: Call from 30th: "Element of G Company is moving over to retake that area in E Company. C Company is moving up behind our 3d Battalion and will push in through K Company positions to restore the two front line platoons . . . C Company of the 7th is going to go through L and K Companies and push on the positions held by the two platoons and clear the Germans out of that house . . ."

By noon it was clear that our artillery counterpreparation delivered at daylight had greatly succeeded in breaking the attack before it got into full swing. That will be brought out later. Two slight penetrations had been made. The enemy had succeeded in driving a wedge between Company E, 7th Infantry, and Company K, 30th Infantry. Company C, 7th Infantry was preparing to counterattack to wipe that out. A small part of Company E, 7th Infantry, had been pushed off position. Company G moved over rapidly to retake this ground.

1300: Call to Asst. CG from CG: *CG*: "What is the score over there?" *Asst. CG*: "C Company attack is about to jump off. The left of the 3d Battalion is receiving another attack on the left flank of K Company. Estimated to be a company. The other attack is about to go. We are starting from behind K Company and will go through it with concentrations prepared to lay on the objective, which is a house . . ."

1410: "The attack is going off but slowly . . ."

1605: "This attack is moving along and it looks like we have it straightened out . . ."

1630: Call from CG 45th Division: "We are all set over here. Our lines are pretty well restored over by that factory (Aprilia) now. The Boche had quite a lot of men clear across the area down to the sea and there were some tanks in there. We've had some good shooting today—I believe they've taken quite a few casualties (the enemy)."

1630: Call from SSF: ". . . Everything is quiet now . . ."

1825: Call from 504th: "As a result of the action in front of D Company this morning, there was a mixup this afternoon. A truce was declared to enable the dead and wounded to be collected and one of our medics who speaks German was out talking with the kraut medics. They told him that the attack was made by one company. He was smart enough to take a count of the bodies, and he counted thirty-eight of them . . . He says they are all very young. The wounded casualties would be in proportion to the dead so they must have taken quite a beating."

1800: Call from 509th: "Small enemy groups have been trying to infiltrate through our left forward position, around A Company, which have been driven off."

2020: Call from Asst. CG: "I've contacted CO 2d Battalion, 7th Infantry, and CO 3d Battalion, 30th Infantry . . . 2d Battalion CO states his right flank is in vicinity of where it was this morning . . . The whole of companies C and G with two tanks are cleaning it up."

During the night of February 16 the Division completed cleaning up elements of attacking enemy units remaining on the front and restoring the salient along Fosso delle Mole. Patrols maintained contact with the enemy during the night. Enemy attacks of February 16 were estimated to have involved five battalions on the 3d Infantry Division front and to have cost the enemy 150 dead and 250 wounded.

During the course of the day's action the 15th Infantry's Company "J", a provisional company made up of drivers, cooks, and mechanics of the 15th Infantry, repulsed an attack of about a hundred enemy, inflicting many casualties.

Except for the penetration between the 2d Battalion, 7th Infantry, and 3d Battalion, 30th Infantry, and the other slight salient before mentioned, the enemy had been completely repulsed at all points. The two slight enemy successes were both wiped out before midnight of February 16.

The diary of a captured German officer of the 29th Artillery Regiment revealed that the main drive was along the Anzio-Albano axis, with three objectives: Fosso di Carocetto, a lateral road in that sector, and Bosco di Padiglione. The first wave was to consist of the 114th *Jaeger* Division on the left, the 153d Infantry Division in the center, and the 3d *Panzer Grenadier* Division on the right. The second wave was to be formed on the 26th *Panzer* Division and 29th *Panzer Grenadier* Division. According to this diary, the method of the attack was to be: first, radio controlled tanks with 450 kilograms of explosives; second, a "break-in"; and third, a tank attack by 20 Mark VI tanks and 80 Mark V tanks supported by self-propelled guns and howitzers.

Second Lieutenant Carl J. Kasper, a FA Battalion forward observer with the 30th Infantry, during the morning's attack adjusted artillery fire on his own position when that position was threatened. His last fire adjustment order came over the radio: "Five Zero Over" (indicating to Fire Direction Center to shorten range by fifty yards).

"Someone in fire direction must have pointed out that he was firing on his own position," said T/5 Jack H. McDurman, "for he came back with, 'I know—fire on me.'

"Lieutenant Kasper set fire to his map and a few personal papers and then told us to destroy the radio. As soon as the radio was put out of commission he told us to leave, if we wanted to.

"The last time I saw Lieutenant Kasper, he was shooting his pistol out the front door at a group of enemy soldiers who had made their way to within fifteen yards of the house. I wasn't wasting any time and ran for the drainage ditch which I knew to be about fifty yards back of the house. Just as I reached

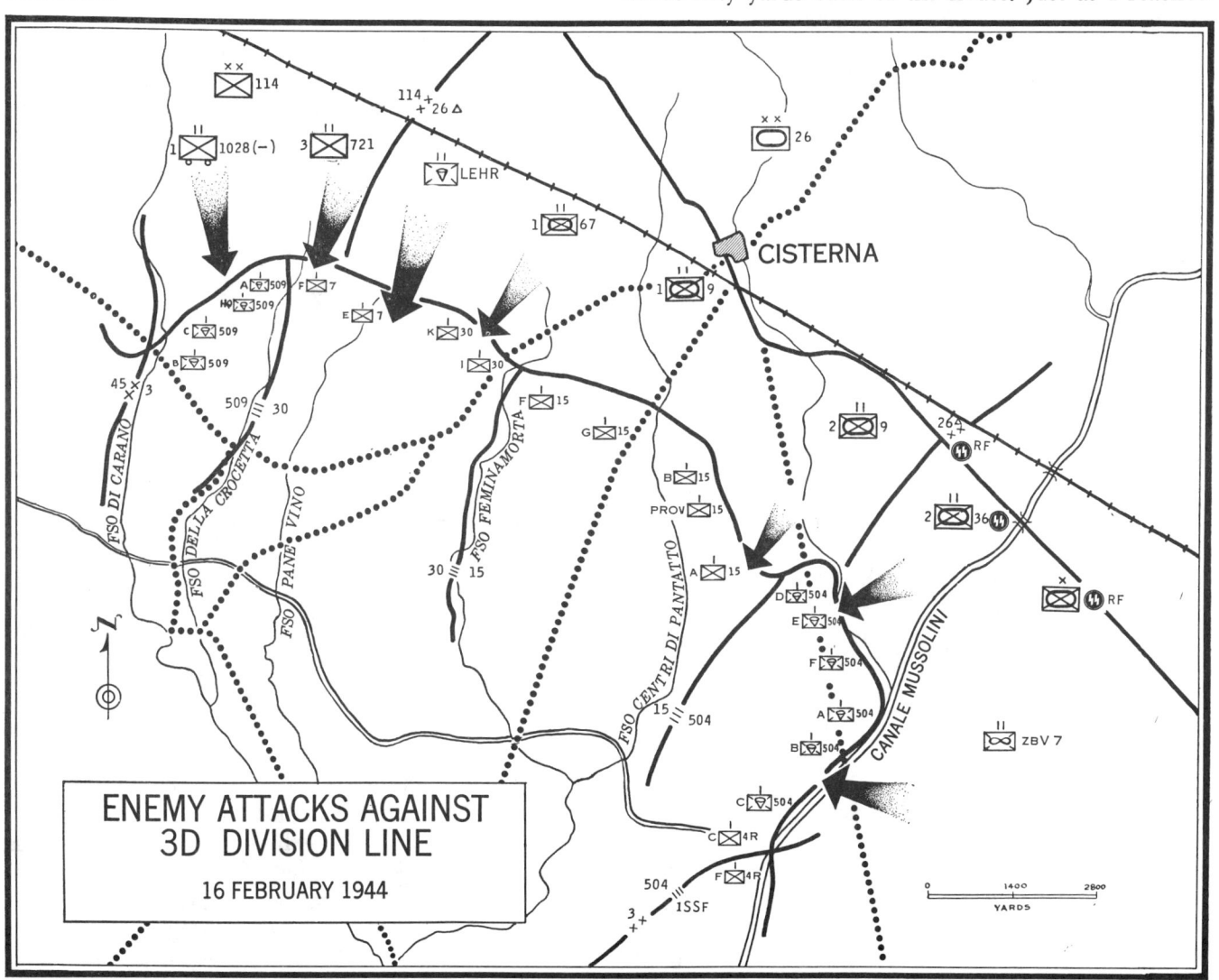

ENEMY ATTACKS AGAINST 3D DIVISION LINE
16 FEBRUARY 1944

Brigadier General Whitfield P. Shepard, Assistant Division Commander.

the ditch I looked back toward the house; shells were landing all around it. There must have been at least eight direct hits—the house was just one big cloud of smoke and dust . . . When I looked back the last time, there was only one wall left standing; the rest of the house was only rubble."

Lieutenant Kasper was captured. He was later awarded the Distinguished Service Cross.

The main attack was a limited success on February 16 against the 45th Infantry Division on our left flank. The enemy succeeded in making a penetration of several hundred yards. The following day, February 17 he continued the attack in this sector and succeeded in enlarging his gains to about 3000 yards. It thus became urgent to commit a strong force in this sector to gain back the lost ground. Any further gains would constitute a serious threat to the security of the entire beachhead. The 3d Battalion, 30th Infantry, had just been relieved by the 3d Battalion, 7th Infantry, a relief that had been delayed one night by February 16's attack. The entire 30th Infantry was now in Division reserve south of Le Ferriere. Accordingly, on February 18 the 30th Infantry was attached to the 1st Armored Division and instructed to plan for a counterattack in the 45th Division sector for the following day.

Continuation of February 16's attack in the 45th Division sector also brought a small attack between the 7th Infantry and the 509th Parachute Infantry Battalion on its left, over the night of February 17, but this was repulsed.

At this time the 3d's Commanding General, Maj. Gen. Lucian K. Truscott, was ordered by the Commanding General, Fifth Army, to take command of the VI Corps, which then included the 1st and 56th British Divisions, the United States 45th, and 3d Infantry and 1st Armored Divisions, the 36th and 39th Combat Engineer Regiments, United States-Canadian Special Service Force, 4th Ranger Battalion, 504th Parachute Infantry Regiment, and 509th Parachute Infantry Battalion. In addition to these combat organizations, VI Corps had thousands of organic and attached special and service troops. General Truscott had commanded the 3d Division since its training period at Port Lyautey, French Morocco, in 1943, eleven months before. Brig. Gen. John W. "Iron Mike" O'Daniel, Assistant Division Commander, was assigned as commander of the Division and Col. (a few days later Brigadier General) Whitfield P. Shepard became the Assistant Division Commander.

In his published farewell order, General Truscott ended by saying "The memory of your fine spirit, your self-confidence, your devotion to duty, and your splendid discipline that brought about your many victories in the last year will be with me always and I will cherish that memory as one of my most priceless possessions.

"Good luck and Godspeed to victory to you all."

Just before daylight on February 19 the 2d Battalion, 30th, crossed the line of departure on the right of the 6th Armored Infantry Regiment of the 1st Armored Division, to take part in what was to be one of the most smashing successes of all limited-objective counterattacks on the beachhead. The 1st Battalion, 30th Infantry, followed at 0700. They were preceded by an intense artillery preparation. Initially only long-range machine-gun fire and antitank fire was received, but resistance shortly got very stiff. Company F proceeded against little opposition, but Company E found the going extremely difficult.

Despite this, at 1030 the 2d Battalion was 1200 yards forward of the line of departure and still moving. The regimental plan contemplated passing the 1st Battalion through the 2d Battalion in continuation of the attack. The VI Corps Commanding General, however, decided that any further gains would put the 30th Infantry in a dangerously exposed salient into the enemy lines, and at 1645, as the 1st Battalion was preparing to pass through, the attack was called off and the 2d Battalion was ordered to consolidate the ground gained.

During the day, the 2d Battalion had taken about 200 prisoners and killed many more enemy. The regiment was still moving when the attack was called off, and casualties suffered were low in comparison with the ground retaken, with its significance to the security of the beachhead.

The attack also proved costly to the 2d Battalion, for the commanding officer, Lt. Col. Lyle W. Bernard, was wounded one-half hour after the jumpoff and replaced by Lt. Col. Woodrow W. Stromberg, who was at the time observing from Division Headquarters. Every officer in Company E, as well as the First Sergeant was killed; every officer in Company F, but one, as well as the First Sergeant, was killed or wounded, and the losses among the other enlisted men in these companies was proportionately high.

The outpost line established upon the ordered withdrawal of 2d Battalion was held by Company G, some 1,400 yards ahead. During the two days this company remained on outpost, a line was prepared behind them for occupation by 45th Infantry Division elements.

Prisoners for several days afterward continued to talk of the intensity of United States artillery fire, losses suffered by their individual units, and the low quality of their own replacements.

At 1210 on the same day (February 19), an estimated enemy battalion hit strongly between the left flank of the 2d Battalion, 7th Infantry, and the right flank of the 509th Parachute Infantry Battalion. It was immediately taken under a devastating artillery barrage and small-arms fire and the attack was stopped within an hour. The enemy took a breathing space, regrouped, and at 1545 three or four tanks followed by infantry resumed the attack. This was repulsed with no penetration within two hours.

1650: Call from VI Corps: "They did a wonderful job out there today. Took plenty of prisoners and knocked them around a bit."

2100: Call from VI Corps: "Swell work today. Keep after them. General Lucas."

Major General Harmon, 1st Armored Division Commanding General, also praised the 30th Infantry for its outstanding role in his successful counterattack, stating that this attack had "saved the beachhead." The same sentiment was echoed on high level at VI Corps.

On the same day the 504th Parachute Infantry Regiment also had a fire fight, but no attack developed.

The usual aggressive patrolling marked February 20 and 21. The 30th Infantry was detached from 1st Armored Division and placed in Corps reserve, in the vicinity of Campo Morto and Le Ferriere.

On February 22, the 3d Battalion, 30th Infantry, was released from Corps reserve and attached to the 509th Parachute Infantry Battalion, moving into positions extending from Carano 1500 yards northward. A forming attack by an enemy battalion in front of the 509th was broken up by artillery.

From February 23-28 the Division continued to hold on to all positions and the usual aggressive patrolling was carried out.

The enemy had by no means exhausted his resources, nor his will to attack with the intention of destroying the beachhead. The Intelligence Summary for February 27 warned:

"The enemy has now had eight days since the attack down the Albano-Anzio axis in which to regroup and reorganize his badly disorganized forces. During this period there has been some indication that he has displaced his artillery, in part, to alternate positions. The bulk of his artillery still, however, remains in the western sector of the beachhead, from where it can support a resumption of the attack in the Carrocetto area. Replacements have been received in some of the units; and sufficient time has elapsed to have permitted the enemy to bring up additional ammunition and other supplies. It is believed that he is now capable of continuing the attacks on the beachhead; and that, when the weather affords him artillery observation and is suitable for the employment of armor, he will resume his offensive action. The increase in activity along the eastern flank of the beachhead makes it seem likely that some diversionary effort may be made at this time, possibly in the vicinity of Bridge No. 5, in conjunction with the main effort, which will, in all probability, be continued on the western flank. It can be logically assumed that the *Hermann Goering Panzer* Division, the chief elements of which have been out of the line resting for some days past, will spearhead this effort. *The offensive capabilities of troops now in contact in the 3d (US) Infantry Division sector are not believed great enough to lend much assistance to this effort.*"

In reality, the enemy was shifting considerable strength to this sector in preparation for his huge attack of February 29. He was also employing a process of attrition, or infringement on the beachhead line. In the British sector, where he held Carrocetto and the "factory," wherever he could seize a small portion of ground he immediately moved up enough troops to hold it, laying wire and mines. Every salient point he could take he deemed worthy of holding.

He had available for the attack of February 29 the following divisions or elements thereof:

362d Infantry Division
26th *Panzer* Division
715th Infantry Division
Hermann Goering Panzer Division
29th *Panzer Grenadier* Division
114th Jäger Division

In addition he had a battalion-sized force, called "*zbV 7*", and the 1028th Grenadier Regiment (Motorized).

That he used strong forces from all of these divisions against the 3d Infantry Division during the period February 29-March 3 we know from identifications of the large numbers of prisoners captured in our sector during that time. Five divisions against one.

The enemy now intended to force a decision.

February 28—1600: Call from Divarty: "Report of three enemy tanks . . . We're firing on them with the 9th Field Artillery . . . ."

1745: Call from VI Corps: ". . . PW said there was quite a few tanks coming into Cisterna and the attack would come very shortly."

2007: Call from VI Corps: "77th Field Artillery reports trains running in and out of Velletri. Smokescreen laid on front and troops moving up . . . Company or more observed in this group. Personnel running around there all day. PW said he had heard that tanks were rolling forward for a new attack . . . Another PW . . . said 300 tanks, mostly Tigers, are nearing Cisterna and that an attack will come very shortly" (*this was a prisoner estimate and not to be taken too literally*: Ed.).

Beginning at 2130 the Commanding General called all regiments and informed them to be especially alert, and to be sure that patrols were active and alert. During the night enemy artillery increased noticeably.

0500: Call from 7th Infantry: "Both of our frontline battalions are receiving a hell of an artillery barrage which started fifteen minutes ago. . . ."

At first light the enemy attacked in the area of Fosso Carano, against the 509th Parachute Infantry Battalion, and south of Cisterna against the 15th Infantry, and in the center of the Division sector against the 7th Infantry. The attacks were supported by a total of forty Mark IV and VI tanks, and the 362d Infantry Division was identified for the first time as spearheading the attack. Elements from *Hermann Goering Panzer* Division, 26th *Panzer* Division, and at least a regiment each from the 715th Infantry Division and 114th Jäger Division also took part in the assault.

At 0605 the first infantry attack hit between 2d and 3d Battalions, 7th Infantry, and an hour later the left flank of the 2d Battalion came under attack. Company F was immediately shifted to back up Company E on the left flank.

0643: Call from 7th Infantry: "There is a 20-man penetration between L and A companies of our outfit. Reported to 300 yards behind L Company, which report is unconfirmed so far."

0650: Call from 7th Infantry: "2d Battalion is being attacked on both flanks but they said situation was in hand. Had report that few enemy got in vicinity of K Company and are being cleaned up."

0735: Call from 7th Infantry: "Just lost contact with 509th. Understood they withdrew a unit. Would like further information. The 2d Battalion CO thinks they have broken through over there but he doesn't know for sure. I've ordered F Company to move on that flank and C Company to back them up."

0745: Call from 7th Infantry: "Received radio message from 509th: 'Breakthrough on our lines—need tanks—urgent!' "

A great battle lies behind the cryptic lines. In some sectors of the 2d Battalion, 7th Infantry, an old German battle tactic was being used—rush in closely packed, screaming. The machine gunners were having a field day. It was a dirty, bitter fight, however. The morning was miserable, wet, and cold. Shivering soldiers stood in water-filled holes and forced themselves to hold rifles steady enough to shoot. From one artillery OP could be seen figures in gray-green long overcoats, carrying shiny messgear, infiltrating down draws. The observer waited until the draw had filled, then gave orders for a concentration of fire. When the smoke had cleared, green figures lay still, or writhing, on the ground.

Lt. Col. John A. Heintges of the 3d Battalion, 7th Infantry, saw about 200 Germans formed in defilade, about to attack the 2d Battalion on his left, and ordered artillery on them, completely smashing the attack and leaving dozens of dead enemy lying on the ground.

Tank destroyers of the 601st Battalion pulled out from behind sheltering houses and blasted away, almost pointblank, at attacking tanks. Gunners from the regimental antitank companies stood their ground with their comparatively small 37mm and 57mm antitank guns and shot until their targets, or they themselves, were destroyed.

Most serious situation developed in the 509th sector where the lines were stretched extra thin. The enemy had attacked at daylight in battalion strength and penetrated about 700 yards on a 1000-yard front, with a maximum penetration of 1500 yards. The 2d Battalion, 30th Infantry, was given orders to prepare for a counterattack to regain the lost ground.

A 40-man patrol infiltrated into a 15th Infantry position. The bulk of the patrol was captured, and the remainder killed or driven out. About noon, fourteen enemy tanks supported by a company of infantry attacked Isola Bella and drove a platoon of Company G, 15th Infantry, out of position north of the crossroad, but other positions were held. Company F, 15th Infantry, moved up and relieved Company G at Isola Bella, digging in immediately south of the crossroad, astride the road. Company G moved a short distance south on the Conca-Cisterna road and took up position.

Said Lt. Col. Jack Toffey, CO 2d Battalion, 15th Infantry: ". . . A German company, with machine guns and tank support, assaulted our outposts near Ponte Rotto. Control of this tiny settlement was essential to our operations and the machine gunners and riflemen lodged in the houses around it were ordered, although outnumbered, to hold at all costs. . . ."

"The brunt of the kraut attack struck at a house some 800 yards beyond the company CP," said MG squad-leader Robert L. Jones, "which was held by Pfc. John B. Silva . . ., his machine-gun crew, and about half a dozen riflemen. Through the haze and mist, a whole company of krauts, backed with two machine guns, approached our position and opened up with a terrific volume of fire."

Silva waited until advance enemy elements were within fifty yards, then opened fire, mowing down every German who exposed himself.

The enemy continued to advance. Two machine guns laid down intense fire on the barricaded window which Silva was using for a gun position. Rifle-grenadiers opened fire, while others rushed up to within a few yards of the house and hurled hand grenades.

"In spite of the odds and the terrific punishment he was taking," said Sergeant Jones, "Pfc. Silva kept his gun going continuously. As long as we could hear the fire of our machine gun, we were able to forget our fear and keep on sniping at the enemy."

The enemy was stopped for two hours, at the end of which time he brought up a Mark VI tank and placed it in turret defilade in an irrigation ditch about a hundred yards from the house.

The tank fired eight rounds, from its 88mm gun, at point-blank range. The house, seriously weakened by previous artillery concentrations, came tumbling down in a rain of masonry, rafters, and other debris. Silva, in spite of the shaking up and the cuts and bruises he sustained, dug himself out of the mess, and found his machine gun buried beneath the mass of rubble. He commenced cleaning and checking its serviceability.

Said Sergeant Jones, "Picking myself up in the midst of the dust and rubble, I saw Pfc. Silva frantically removing debris which had covered his machine gun. Bleeding and bruised, he rapidly wiped the barrel and slot with a rag and *ran a cleaning rod through the dust-covered barrel.*"

". . . The Germans were advancing," said Sgt. (then Private) Willard Plegge, "believing that the Mark VI had knocked out our machine gun and that all they had to do was mop up. Pfc. Silva quickly disillusioned them. He dragged his machine gun to the opposite corner of what had been the building and set up a new firing position in the mass of rubble. I heard his machine gun go into action a second time; again the kraut was stopped dead."

Silva, in this newly-exposed position, continued to fire his gun until he had exhausted his ammunition. Then, instead of withdrawing, he ran through the wreckage of the house, found four boxes of ammunition, carried them back to the gun and resumed fire.

Said 2d Lt. (then S/Sgt.) William H. Trachimewicz, "All day he operated his machine gun single-handed, holding off the strong enemy force. At twilight, he exhausted his ammunition for the second time. Instead of taking advantage of semidarkness to withdraw, Pfc. Silva seized a carbine and continued to fire at the enemy. In this way he managed to hold off the Germans until fresh supplies of machine-gun ammunition came up from the rear.

"After thirteen hours of virtually single-handed combat, he turned over his gun to a relief crew. Through his gallant action he had thwarted an attack by approximately a hundred Germans, killing about thirty of them. The house was held. We had broken a powerful enemy attack without yielding ground."

Another epic defense that day was put up by Pfc. Frederick Vance and Pfc. Eugene Procaccini of Company I, 30th Infantry, in which both men lost their lives.

"At about 0530 hours, the enemy attacked in great strength," said Capt. Maurice Rothseid, CO of Company I, "utilizing at least two companies of infantry, supported by artillery, in their first wave. After fighting for about twenty minutes, the left flank and center outposts withdrew to the MLR. However, the right flank outpost, which was manned by Pfc. Vance . . . assistant BAR man and his gunner, Pfc. Eugene Procaccini, held fast in the face of the enemy onslaught."

About sixty enemy concentrated their efforts in an attempt to eliminate the outpost, using heavy concentrations of mortar and artillery fire to "soften it up." When the fire was lifted the enemy began advancing in short rushes and succeeded in reaching to within twenty yards of the position. Meanwhile another wave of Germans struck the left flank, forcing the company to divert most of its firepower to that sector, leaving Vance and Procaccini unassisted. Nevertheless they remained in position and cut down enemy who charged. Suddenly a figure arose from the outpost and began crawling back to the MLR.

"As the figure got closer, I saw that it was Pfc. Vance," related Squad Leader S/Sgt. William C. Beeson. "He was moving as fast as a man can on his belly and elbows, coming right through an artillery concentration. He had left his rifle back in the outpost."

Procaccini, meanwhile, having run out of BAR ammunition, opened fire with Vance's M-1 rifle.

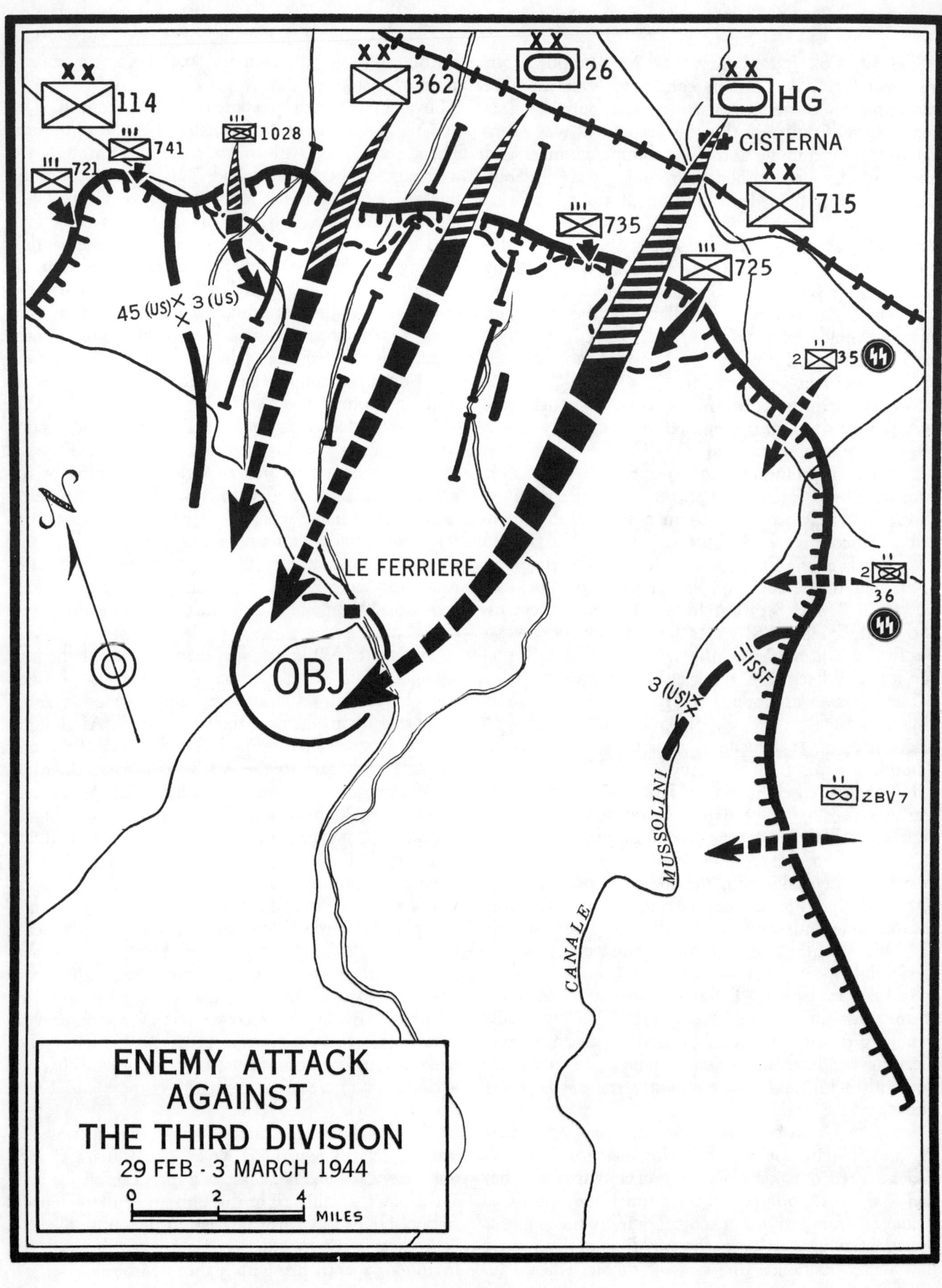

Captain Rothseid told Vance that he had done his job and that it was time for the two men to abandon the outpost, but Vance merely continued stuffing a couple of sandbags with ammunition. When he had filled them he picked up another M-1 from a nearby casualty and commenced crawling back toward the outpost. When he had got about halfway an enemy machine gun opened fire from a range of about seventy-five yards, the bullets tearing through his pack. Vance stopped crawling, worked his M-1 into firing position, and with two shots disposed of the enemy gunner and his assistant. Then he continued his slow crawl until he had reached the emplacement.

During his absence Procaccini had been keeping the Germans at bay with his M-1 by standing up despite withering small-arms fire, and firing at every enemy soldier he saw, but they had continued to infiltrate toward him. With the increased firepower, the two men again began to hold their own.

After about an hour the enemy abandoned hopes of an infantry assault and wheeled a self-propelled gun into position. Said Rifleman Pfc. Herman E. Johnson, ". . . While the gun was getting the range, Pfc. Vance and Pfc. Procaccini turned their attention to the attack on our MLR and directed intense and effective fire on the flank of the attacking krauts, throwing them into confusion. Finally, the SP gun scored a direct hit, which killed them both instantly."

"Their unselfish heroism held back an overpowering enemy attack for over two hours, giving the rest of the company time to adjust artillery fire which completely stopped it," said Sgt. Beeson. "Later, when we went to the outpost, I saw these two men had fired the M-1 until its rifling had been completely worn out; the weapon was absolutely useless. In all, these men had killed eighteen krauts and wounded at least eighteen more. Five of the krauts they had killed lay within ten feet of their emplacement."

Both Pfc. Procaccini and Pfc. Vance were posthumously awarded the Distinguished Service Cross.

The 504th Parachute Infantry Regiment stopped two attacks, one of small scale against Company A, and one of company size against the 4th Ranger Battalion, attached.

The attacks against the 7th Infantry were heaviest, but nowhere did the enemy gain and hold any ground. In the afternoon the 2d Battalion, 30th Infantry, and Company C, 7th Infantry, both initiated counterattacks, Company C attacking up the Fosso della Crocetta on the right of the 2d Battalion's attack through Carano. The company attack continued until nightfall, and succeeded in clearing out some infiltration down that stream, which was just to the left of 2d Battalion, 7th Infantry.

The 2d Battalion, 30th Infantry, jumped off on its second large-scale counterattack within ten days, at 2130, February 29. It was a bloody affair for both sides, but the attack was absolutely essential to the security of the beachhead.

The attack reached its first phase line 1,200 yards beyond the line of departure by 0130, March 1, when the battalion encountered extremely heavy small-arms and automatic-weapons fire in pitch darkness and heavy rain. At 0545, after reorganizing in the dark, and coordinating all three companies under trying weather, the attack resumed. By 0815 the entire enemy penetration attacks had been eliminated, and 2d Battalion, 30th Infantry, took over the 509th position.

How dangerous the situation had been prior to the attack was revealed when the regimental commander of the 30th, Lieutenant Colonel McGarr, inspected the ground over which the attack had been made and found German bodies a bare hundred yards north of Carano.

Nothing has yet been said of the artillery in the day's attack. When all the accounts of the day's action were finally compiled, it was clearly evident that the artillery was the instrumental arm in breaking the force of the attack. Principal employment was against enemy reserves. PWs taken revealed that practically all communications had been cut, reserves scattered and demoralized, attacking units severely cut up and further reduced by accurate small-arms and machine-gun fire. The fire of over 1200 pieces of artillery was employed that day, and several batteries fired a total of shells during the period exceeding any number they had ever before fired.

During the day the enemy lost fourteen tanks, more than 150 prisoners, and several hundred killed and wounded in the 3d Infantry Division sector. By noon of March 1 the PW count had swelled to over 300.

Engineers cratered and mined roads leading into our sector over the night of February 29-March 1. The 3d Battalion, 1st Armored Regiment, moved into the 3d Division area in general support.

Three enemy attacks, one supported by tanks, were repulsed during the afternoon of March 1. Artillery fire broke up an attack of 200 men against the 2d Battalion, 7th Infantry. An attack of two companies supported by tanks against the 3d Battalion, 7th Infantry was repulsed only after six tanks had broken into the platoon positions of Company K and fired pointblank at the men in their foxholes. Artillery fire repulsed an enemy push against the 2d Battalion, 30th Infantry. During the night of March 1-2 our positions were consolidated, wire and mines placed, and cratering and mining of roads leading into enemy territory continued. Prisoners continued to stream in, a total of 153 being counted in the 24-hour period between noon of March 1 and noon of March 2. During the same period twenty tanks were destroyed.

On March 2 and 3, several small-scale enemy attacks supported by tanks were repulsed successfully, except southwest of Ponte Rotto where two tanks ran right up the road and got into platoon positions of Company L, 7th Infantry, and behind one of their forward platoon positions. This forced an element of Company I on the right of the road to fall back, and the abandonment of the forward position on the left of the road by L Company.

Companies A and B, 7th Infantry, formed for a counterattack, Company A on the right of the road, and Company B on the left. From the beginning A Company came under terrific *Nebelwerfer,* artillery self-propelled, and small-arms and machine-gun fire, and Company B likewise received a good deal of artillery and time-fire from self-propelled weapons, but nevertheless pushed as far forward as was practicable. Company A received very heavy casualties, but after nightfall was able to reconsolidate the ground lost by Company I.

The line again rejoined and rested on the Ponte Rotto road, although 300 yards remained in enemy hands, and could not be retaken on account of intense artillery and small-arms and machine-gun fire. That night the road was cratered and mined.

An attack of eight enemy tanks and a company of infantry was repulsed by the 15th Infantry the same day. Two tanks were destroyed. From noon of March 2 to noon of March 3, eight enemy tanks were put out of action.

"Hospital Row" on the Anzio beachhead more frequently than not under long range artillery fire or night-bombing attacks.

This day marked the end of the enemy's offensive effort and his return to the defense.

Prisoners taken from February 29 to March 3 included men from the following units:

Hq. Company, 1st, 2d, 3d, 4th Companies, 954th Regiment, 362d Infantry Division

1st, 2d Companies, 362d *Fusilier* Battalion, 362d Infantry Division

Hq. Company, 2d, 3d, 5th, 6th, 7th Companies, 1028th Grenadier Regiment (Motorized)

Engineer Company, 1028th Grenadier Regiment (Motorized)

5th, 6th Companies, 67th *Panzer Grenadier* Regiment, 26th *Panzer* Division

1st and 3d Batteries, Artillery Regiment, 715th Infantry Division

Hermann Goering "Alarm" Companies: *"Alarich," "Pauke," "Vesuv"*

Hermann Goering Light Weapons *Jaeger* Battalion.

2d, 3d, 4th Companies *zbV 7*.

1st and 2d Companies, 715th Engineer Battalion, 715th Infantry Division

7th Company, 35th *Schutzstaffel PGR SS Reichsfuehrer Division*

1st, 2d, 3d Companies, *PGR 2, Hermann Goering Panzer* Division

Hq., 955th Regiment, 362d Infantry Division

Hq., 2d Battalion, 955th Regiment, 362d Infantry Division

1st, 2d, 3d, 5th, 6th, 7th, 8th, 13th Companies, 955th Regiment, 362d Infantry Division

1st Company, 60th Engineer Battalion (General Headquarters)

1st Company, 362d Engineer Battalion

5th Company *PGR 9*, 26th *Panzer* Division

4th Battery Artillery Regiment, *Hermann Goering* Panzer Division

3d Company *PGR 129*, 15th *Panzer* Division

1st Company, 2d Company, Engineer Battalion, 715th Division

GERMANS' ANZIO OFFENSIVE A COSTLY FAILURE; FORTS BOMB RAIL YARDS

ALLIES REGAIN ALL LOST GROUND

3D DIVISION BORE BRUNT OF ATTACK; FINAL NAZI TANK BLOWS REPULSED*

*By the Associated Press***

Allied Headquarters, Naples, March 3—A strong German drive into the center of the Anzio beachhead this

---
*Headlines in the Philadelphia Evening Bulletin, March 4, 1944.
**Associated Press dispatch dated March 3, 1944.

Lieutenant Colonel Albert O. Connor, Division G-3.

week was described officially today as a "costly failure." Allied Headquarters said defense positions remained intact with all lost ground regained.

The enemy offensive, the third large-scale attempt to drive the American and British forces into the sea, had now collapsed. Two final German assaults with tanks and infantry late Wednesday were repulsed, it was announced, and no new attacks came yesterday.

U. S. Troops of the 3d Infantry Division bore the brunt of the attack and scored "a complete defensive success," a headquarters spokesman said. Less than a week ago, the 3d, originally composed chiefly of troops from the Pacific Coast, was officially commended for previous exploits on the beachhead.

"Rock of the Marne"

(Graham Hovey in a dispatch from the beachhead today said the 3d's stand was a brilliant repetition of the performance which won it the title of "The Rock of the Marne" in July, 1918, when it played a major part in repulsing the last great German offensive of the last war.)

(A Regular Army unit, the Fighting 3d landed in French Morocco on November 8, 1942, and played an important role in the quick success of the American Expeditionary Force. Later the division paced Lt. Gen. George S. Patton's march through Sicily and has carried a big share of the Fifth Army's fighting in Italy since shortly after Salerno.)

Hovey said the 3d took 430 prisoners and left hundreds of enemy dead on the beachhead in this week's battle . . .

Campo Morto, the Division Forward Command Post on the beachhead. The tower served daily as a check point for enemy artillery.

ITALIAN ALLIED HEADQUARTERS, NAPLES. (UP)*

The German 14th Army has abandoned its third major attempt to crush the Allied beachhead below Rome, it was disclosed officially today, after taking a savage, 36-hour beating from the veteran American 3d Infantry Division and a record concentration of Allied planes and cannon.

Counting their dead in the hundreds, the . . . (Germans) . . . fell back to their initial jumping-off place yesterday as the Americans completed the liquidation of the 1500-yard salient won and lost by the Germans at a staggering cost. . . . (Lt. Gen. Mark W.) Clark paid tribute to the American 3d Division—the Rock of the Marne—whose doughboys smashed the last Hindenburg offensive in France in July, 1918.

The 3d, supported by a number of other units, took on the full weight of the German attack and broke it in embittered, hand-to-hand fighting. . . ."

Truly, the 3d Infantry Division had earned its niche in military history. From the ashes of this great defeat, the *Wehrmacht* could not, or at any rate did not, mount another attack of the same proportions against the Anzio Beachhead. The terrible losses inflicted against the enemy were sufficient to make him realize that we were on Anzio to stay. As the months wore on in their monotonous bitterness, the area became a supply dump bristling with munitions and materiel, and before the German hold was broken in May around the edge of the beachhead line, two more United States divisions came to swell our strength sufficiently to be of major value in the drive on Rome.

Said the Commanding General, 1st British Division: "Congratulations on your work out there today. Our lads have been bucked up quite a bit."

---
*United Press dispatch dated March 3, 1944.

3: The Big War of Little Battles

March 4 to May 21

THE ill-fated German attack proved to be the last kick of a do-or-die German effort to push the Anzio Beachhead back into the sea—Kesselring's hopes for destroying our beachhead had vanished forever.

Breathing heavily, the enemy retired to the security of his prepared positions, which he immediately began to strengthen.

Brig. Gen. John W. "Iron Mike" O'Daniel, the new Division Commander, well aware of the enemy impotency at this time, ordered that all front-line men be given a two-day rest beginning March 8, and a rest camp under the supervision of Maj. Robert E. Mitchell, Division Special Service Officer, was set up in a clump of woods about five miles south of the "hot" zone. The rest period was also devoted to unit reorganization. Infantry units took advantage of the opportunity to rest a company at a time.

The camp was not in a quiet zone by any means but the men were given new uniforms to wear (and no forms to fill out), they had hot showers, they went to the movies (even during blackout hours), they had barber service (including shaves) and, most important of all, they had two nights of uninterrupted sleep, for many the first in seven weeks.

Although the usual lull that follows all storms prevailed, there was no let-down in patrolling, consolidation of position and the laying of harassing and interdictory fires.

For the first time in its combat experience in this war, the Division had been required to hold a defensive sector after seizing an objective and the assignment was made doubly difficult by the tremendous importance which the enemy attached to the destruction of our beachhead.

Even in the wake of his setback, the enemy continued to move his outposts nearer our lines. Our combat patrols, always active, seldom failed to find resistance somewhere, as on March 8 when a patrol of the 15th Infantry, working along the canal near the Cisterna-Sessano road, was engaged in two fire fights. On the same day an enemy patrol of platoon size tried to infiltrate our positions and was brought under artillery, mortar and machine-gun fire southwest of Ponte Rotto and forced to withdraw.

A German wire-laying detail was surprised while operating near our front line the following day and two prisoners were taken by members of Company B, 7th Infantry. The 30th Infantry captured the pilot of an enemy plane that crashed in its sector the same day.

Many attempts to probe our defenses and infiltrate our positions added to the population of the Division PW cage, where interrogaters obtained much information during the somewhat quiet days that marked the month of March.

The stone houses of standard design that lined the few roads to our front were fortified centers of resistance and generally contained bunkers dug into floors. When the houses were destroyed, the debris fell on top of the bunkers and served to increase camouflage and protection.

Ovens, built in every yard, were used as machine-gun nests while manure piles and straw stacks frequently served as positions for automatic weapons.

The situation became such a see-saw affair that every house in the Division sector was pin-pointed on the War Room map, with each dwelling designated by number, i.e., 1, 2, 3, 4, etc.

The houses numbered 5 and 6, northwest of Carano, became objects of special attention. Houses 1, 2, and 3, or what remained of them, were in our hands, House No. 3 being on the rim of the Division outpost line. House No. 4 was in "no man's land." Beyond lay Houses 5 and 6.

On March 10 a strong combat patrol of the 30th Infantry made a sneak attack on the houses and ran into terrific fire from both inside the houses and from concealed positions around them. A tank also came out of hiding to take part in the melee.

The battle raged for two hours but the odds were too great against the patrol, whose members were caught in cross-fires of machine guns and automatic weapons. The patrol fought until its ammunition ran out and withdrew.

On the same morning 15th Infantry sent out a patrol from Company L, commanded by 1st Lt. James W. Coles, to attack House No. 7, about 300 yards from House No. 6. Again, well-protected machine guns and automatic weapons were met in abundance. This patrol also fought to the end of its ammunition and caused one German to emerge from the house with upraised hands. One of his own machine guns cut him down as he advanced toward the patrol to surrender.

Fights similar to these were frequent.

In the early hours of March 12, 1st Lt. Richard B. Peckinpaugh, commanding Company K, 30th Infantry, led a combat patrol into a draw and headed northeast into enemy territory.

The men encountered an enemy machine gun guarding a road junction and destroyed it with an AP rifle grenade, killing three men. They continued up the road a few hundred yards and destroyed another enemy machine gun with the same tactics, this time killing two. Machine-gun and rifle fire from nearby houses drove the patrol to cover and Lieutenant Peckinpaugh and his men were making their way back through another draw when they caught an enemy position by surprise, killing six and capturing twelve. The patrol's record for the day: eleven enemy killed, twelve captured, two machine-gun nests destroyed.

Houses 5 and 6 were still operating when the 509th Parachute Infantry Battalion received orders to silence the inhabitants who for weeks had resisted attempt after attempt to evict them. Once before the 509th had tried to take House No. 5 but didn't succeed. This time it would be different. The plan for attack was arranged, the 'chutists fully briefed on their mission.

On the night of March 13-14 the battalion's mortar and machine-gun crews moved out under cover of darkness and stole into positions within range of Houses 5 and 6. All night long they dug with muffled sound, placed their guns, built up a supply of ammunition. They spent the following day in concealment near their guns, studying the targets, ranging in.

Company L, 30th Infantry, sent an outpost to the vicinity of House No. 6 to assist in securing a line of departure for the 509th's attack.

The attack had been minutely planned before Company C moved out to the attack at 0100, March 15, followed by Company A in reserve. The inevitable occurred when the attackers neared their objective. Machine guns, pistols and small arms spat from the houses with a spontaneity that turned the night's darkness into a sieve of white and black.

Tracers screamed across the marshes from House No. 7. Enemy artillery and mortar fire was brought into play and the horizon blazed as two *Nebelwerfer* batteries opened up from positions along a railroad track 5,000 yards to our front. Four German 81mm mortars that had been spilling death in our area of attack fell into silence when Corps Artillery answered a call for counterbattery with perfect accuracy. Even the Long Toms (155mm. gun) couldn't reach the *Nebelwerfers*, however.

A bake oven in the back yard of House No. 6 suddenly came to life, but it wilted quickly when two fragmentation grenades hit their mark. White phosphorus smoke from grenades sent over to shield our positions added to the stench, which was made somewhat more unbearable by the light drizzle that had started when the attack began. House No. 6 fell at 0430, ending a terrific two-hour struggle that brought death and injury to many paratroopers, but which reflected much credit on the entire battalion. House No. 5 still hung by a thread.

At 0530 the enemy started a counterattack at our left flank with an estimated two platoons. This was smashed in its infancy by a terrific barrage from our 105s.

All during the night a 4.2 mortar company of the 84th Chemical Battalion and the 60mm mortars of the parachute battlion kept surrounding houses under fire, notably House No. 7, which later was the starting point for another counterattack that was stopped at its inception, mainly by BARs employed at close range.

The Germans in House No. 5 surrendered late in the afternoon, just as the 'chutists were preparing to level the house with pole charges and bangalore torpedoes.

The 509th had avenged a previous setback, and moved the 3d Division front line 500 yards nearer Rome by taking Houses 5 and 6.

The night of March 15 saw 3d Battalion, 30th Infantry, relieving 509th Parachute Infantry Battalion completely. Company L, under Capt. Robert B. Pridgen, was ordered to take over the two houses. Relieving the parachutists in House 6, the company moved to take over 5 and found that the enemy, in the process of counterattacking both houses, had again seized number 5. This counterattack was repulsed after vicious nightlong fighting, in which Company L sustained eighteen casualties, including two officers wounded.

After Company L had secured House 5 and occupied House 6, it and the remainder of 3d Battalion began outposting all houses to prevent enemy infiltration from the north; improved the positions with barbed wire and hasty minefields, and placed guns at strategic points to defend against another counterattack. The rears of the houses were broken out to enable tanks to take up positions inside. The houses had been a tough objective to take and the doughboys of the 3d did not intend to lose them—and they didn't, although the Germans made several futile attempts to regain them.

The strong defenses set up around Houses 5 and 6 demonstrated the value of ground on the beachhead. The situation was best described by Colonel Yarborough when he briefed the 'chutists prior to their attack.

"The price of ground here is skyrocketing like the price of Scotch whiskey—high as hell and just as hard to get," he said.

The miserly affection with which the ground was coveted is shown by the fact that during March the Division Engineers, assisted by infantrymen, erected no less than 17,400 yards of double-apron fence and laid some 7,000 antitank mines in the Division area. Triple-concertina and barbed wire entanglements enmeshed all infantry positions while bridges within our control were kept prepared for demolition at all times. Road craters were used extensively as antitank measures and on one occasion an enemy SP gun,

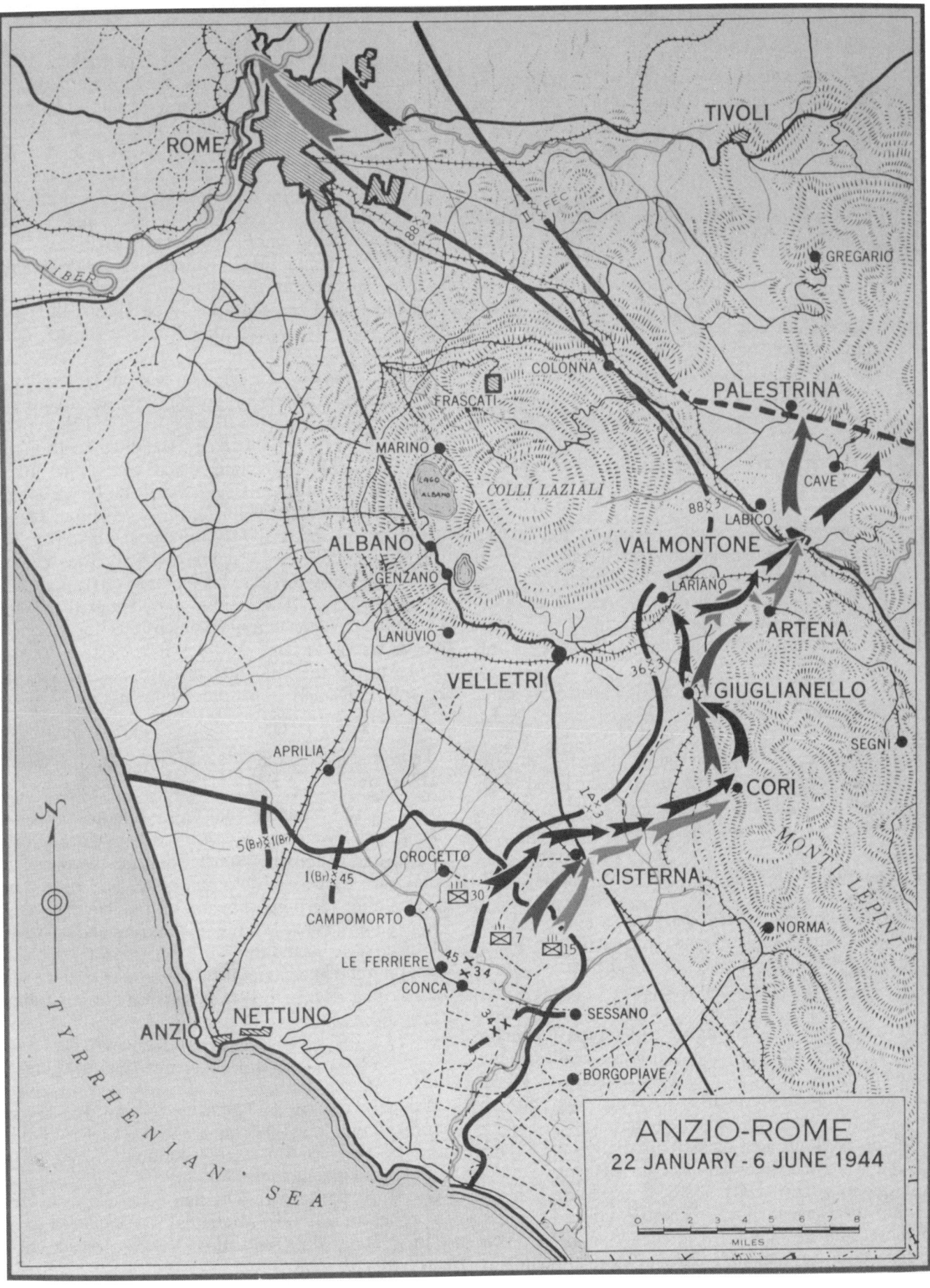

stopped at a crater, was knocked out by AT fire and a Mark IV tank which tried to by-pass it suffered the same fate. Varied antiparachutist defenses dotted our rear areas.

Daylight movements were held to a minimum, due to excellent enemy observation. Messenger runs, except in emergency, were invariably made under cover of darkness. Despite this handicap more than 22,000 runs were made during the month by the operations platoon of the 3d Signal Company. More than 400 miles of wire circuits were maintained, and much of the wire was placed under ground, especially in the forward areas. Lt. Col. Jesse F. Thomas was the Division Signal Officer.

The 3d Division learned that to seize a beachhead was one thing—to hold it indefinitely was another.

As the end of March drew near the conquered ground was well nigh impregnable. In fact, it was so secure that activities took on the appearance of garrison life right under the nose of Kesselring's forces.

A naturalization ceremony in which thirty-seven members of the Division became citizens of the United States, was held on the beachhead. Thomas S. Estes, United States vice-consul at Algiers and special representative of the United States Department of Justice, conferred the citizenship upon men whose residences were listed from fifteen states.

A romance which began in Sicily ended in a sandbagged hospital tent in the battle zone when 2d Lt. Genevieve Clark, an Army nurse, was married to 1st Lt. Thomas G. Rose of the 3d Signal Company. A pair of improvised candelabra, stained red with iodine, added dignity to the setting as some 300 nurses, officers and enlisted men sat on cartridge cases and cots to witness the nuptials. There was a reception after the wedding and the bride cut the 25-pound cake with a trench knife.

The Division started relinquishing its portion of the beachhead line March 22 and units withdrew piecemeal from their positions as units of the 34th Infantry Division moved in to replace them.

The final week in this area also marked the dissolution of the pack trains commanded by Capt. Raymond E. Baker. The departure of the animals recalled many outstanding deeds performed by the mounted reconnaissance and pack troops in the long trek through mountains in Sicily and Southern Italy.

In the Avellino area of southern Italy, 1st Lt. Jack Hallett had led a reconnaissance detachment on a 30-mile scouting trip which took his men fifteen miles behind the German lines seeking demolished bridges, pillboxes and strongly fortified enemy positions. Their radio stopped functioning far up in the mountains and each bit of information was sent back to headquarters by runner. When the detachment returned, two men had been lost to enemy action and sixteen had been sent back as individual messengers.

Their main mission, however, was to harass the enemy, screen the Division movement and protect our flanks. How well they did this job was reflected by the sadness that marked the passing of the 3d Provisional Reconnaissance Troop, 3d Provisional Pack Train, 3d Provisional Pack Battery and the Provisional Mortar Platoon from the 3d Infantry Division.

The men who had comprised these outfits, all volunteers for the duty, were returned to their former status in the Division.

At 0900 March 28 the Division was officially relieved of command of the sector, ending sixty-seven consecutive days in the line from 0200 January 22, 1944.

The units enjoyed a two-day breathing spell at the rest camp which was interrupted by an air attack March 29. Men of the 441st AAA AW Bn hit six enemy ME 109s and FW 190s during the fight. From D-day to the rest period, the 441st, under command of Lt. Col. Thomas H. Leary, downed twenty-three enemy planes, damaged three and had three probables.

The Division, after its rest, moved into the Torre Astura area where it trained intensively for the next two weeks on defense and limited-objective attacks.

On April 7, the following message was received by General O'Daniel from the Commanding General of VI Corps:

To the Officers and Men of the Third Infantry Division:

Upon the relief of the Third Infantry Division from front-line duty, where it has been since D-day, I desire to express my appreciation for the complete and loyal cooperation of every officer and man. The outstanding accomplishments of the Division during the entire battle since 22 January and, particularly, the outstanding work in connection with stopping the final German attack on 29 February and succeeding days, will be a bright page in our future history.

(Signed) L. K. TRUSCOTT, JR.,
Major General, U. S. Army, Commanding.

While enemy harassing tactics continued throughout the training period, reports from adjacent units indicated the Germans were continuing a defensive attitude throughout the sector.

On April 9 the 34th Division reported that four remote-controlled tanks (Goliaths) had exploded close to their front lines and that a rifle grenade had destroyed a fifth one.

The British, on the left flank of the 34th, reported that a "rocket-like projectile with a 3,000-foot-long streak" had been observed but unidentified.

After a two-week layoff from combat, the 3d began to move into position to relieve the 45th Division on April 11. By 0600 April 16, the Division had completed the relief and was in command, with a mission to straighten out its lines, relieve enemy pressure on vital strong points and improve its defensive positions.

The 7th and 30th Infantry Regiments occupied the new front-line positions, with the 15th in reserve. The 7th's sector, on the left, was wooded and cut with draws, affording the enemy good opportunity for infiltration into our positions. The 30th's front was more open, although it was cut with one unusually deep draw, the Spaccasassi Creek, down which the enemy was to attempt several attacks.

The regiments spent the first day locating sniper posts, improving their defensive works, and establishing outposts and listening posts. The 7th sent out a combat patrol to find approach routes for infiltrating troops to more favorable positions.

On the following day, the 2d Battalion of the 30th celebrated its return to combat by firing all its organic weapons on known enemy positions in a five-minute barrage that shook the lethargic beachhead. That night, the 191st Tank Battalion, attached, fired 120 rounds in a single shoot and started a large fire in the enemy area. The Division had returned to action, blazing away.

The Germans were intent on containing the 3d in its present position and the 3d was determined to straighten the weaving front that offered opportunities for enemy flank attack.

Our combat patrols annoyed the enemy for several days but with no noticeable effect—the scalloped front still remained. On April 21, three combat patrols tried in vain to oust four enemy machine guns that created a bulge in the 7th's sector between Companies K and L. A limited objective attack, the kind the Division had been training for at Torre Astura, was launched against the positions at 2200 April 22 with Company G, supported by four tanks, assaulting. Companies K and L were in support. It was an all-night fight but by daybreak the enemy positions had been destroyed and twenty-seven prisoners had been taken.

Two other plans for raids into enemy territory had been completed and were ready for execution—the operations known as "Mr. Black" and "Mr. Green."

The enemy had made three attacks down the Spaccasassi Creek bed against Company B, 30th Infantry on April 22, so General O'Daniel decided to forestall future pushes by taking the ground to the immediate

This is a "fosso," the Italian word for ditch. The beachhead was covered with "fossi" of various sizes.

front of the 1st Battalion of the 30th, in the initial operation.

The "Mr. Black" operation was an attack by Company A of the 30th that developed into one of the bloodiest small encounters that the Division had ever known.

The assault, which began at midnight April 23, was preceded by artillery and mortar fire and introduced the "scorpion" as an advance road-clearer for foot troops. The scorpion, a medium tank with a rotating flailing device made of chains and designed to detonate land mines, led the attack across "no man's land" and up the road that led into the enemy lair. The scorpion, as well as the radio-equipped light tank which followed it as a guide, was quickly put out of action by enemy antitank rocket launchers and two T-2 recovery vehicles were disabled trying to retrieve them and clear the advance route.

Following closely behind the scorpion the company attacked in column of platoons, each platoon supported by a medium tank from the 191st Tank Battalion.

Two houses, located about 400 yards apart on alternate sides of the road, were objectives of two of the platoons. The third platoon was to cross the open fields, drive the enemy from the banks of Spaccasassi Creek and establish an outpost near the bend in the river.

The attack was to be "fast, aggressive and ruthless," but the medium tank with the leading 3d platoon struck a mine and the advance was temporarily halted. Enemy mortar and artillery fire caused numerous casualties among our bunched-up infantry, mostly members of the 1st platoon, which was following the 3d.

With their platoon leader, two squad leaders, the platoon guide and radio operator wounded and out of action, the remaining members of the 1st platoon joined with the 2d platoon, which by now had by-passed the 3d platoon and was crossing the open fields toward the Spaccasassi.

Fire from machine guns and small arms was turned on the men from all directions as they headed for the creek—from houses far up the road, from ruins of battered dwellings in the vicinity, from the irrigation ditches and from the numerous shell holes that pocked the area. These hideouts, unoccupied in daylight, had become centers of destruction at night.

One squad reached the river bank and plunged down the 25-foot slope that led to the bed, screaming, shouting, and shooting. Several Germans were killed and a number were captured by this audacious act. Other members of the raiding force who had lived through the withering fire in the open field slid down the river bank. The group was being reassembled when point-blank fire from enemy guns placed in the river bend drove them back with more casualties. The 3d Division men stood toe-to-toe and slugged until the enemy withdrew to a point of safety beyond the bend.

The enemy had converted the high river banks into a system of foxholes and dugouts that were interconnected by narrow footpaths which afforded convenient avenues of approach and exit. Facing an emplaced enemy, the platoon came under heavy artillery fire at this point and was forced to move north up the gully out of range.

This "battle of the river bed" continued all night but fire gradually subsided because neither force could see the enemy positions on account of the intervening river bend. During the night a platoon from Company K, 15th Infantry, arrived and one squad took positions in the river bed while two evacuated the wounded.

The first light of day revealed an unoccupied ditch with a clear field of fire into the enemy's foxholes and dugouts. It was here that Pfc. John C. Squires particularly distinguished himself. Squires, at the time 18 years old and engaged in his first combat, had been performing far above and beyond the normal call of duty all through the night's hellish activity. When Company A's 1st platoon was badly hit during the night, Squires volunteered to go forward and see what had become of it, returning to report that its platoon leader and platoon sergeant were wounded, and that his platoon could go around and carry on the fight.

"Not many of us thought very much of the idea," said Radioman Pfc. James T. Simmons. "There was nothing ahead except high explosive and lead all the way to the creek. Nevertheless, our platoon leader gave the order to move out."

The platoon moved forward under a terrific concentration of fire, suffering along the way. When it reached Spaccasassi Creek the situation became nearly intolerable. In addition to heavy fire which converged on the creek the enemy was within hand-grenade range.

One after another each NCO became wounded. Squires thereupon took charge and coolly placed the remaining men of the platoon in firing positions as though it were a tactical exercise and the battlefield miles away. Following this he volunteered to return to the company CP for reinforcements, which he did, returning about an hour later with his trousers ripped to shreds from enemy fire, but bringing with him Company A's 2d platoon, a light machine gun, and a bazooka squad from Company K, 15th Infantry.

" . . . The Germans counterattacked our outpost three times in the early morning of April 24," said Pvt. Cleo A. Toothman, "from our front, both flanks, and our rear, using every weapon at their command . . . I should like to express the opinion that Pfc. Squires was in great part responsible for our successful defense. In the first attack he operated a German Spandau machine gun until it jammed, then used both a rifle and BAR just as effectively. In the second, he used the borrowed BAR. Before the third attack he obtained information concerning the operation, assembly, and disassembly of his Spandau machine gun from a captured German officer, reduced the stoppage in his weapon, and surrounded himself with ammunition. When the counterattack developed Pfc. Squires fired three full belts of ammunition (750 rounds) into the oncoming enemy, inflicting heavy casualties. He was, in every sense of the word, an inspiration to all of us.

"After the third counterattack Pfc. Squires went down the Spaccasassi Creek bed alone in a personal manhunt for Germans who still remained in their holes. One by one he silenced enemy machine pistols which opened up on him, setting up his Spandau in the midst of the enemy fire which missed him by only a few inches each time, and firing his weapon until the Germans were forced to surrender. Alone, Pfc. Squires captured twenty-one prisoners in this unique manner, and collected thirteen more Spandau machine guns. These he distributed among the men in the outpost, placed them in firing position, and instructed his comrades in their cleaning and operation."

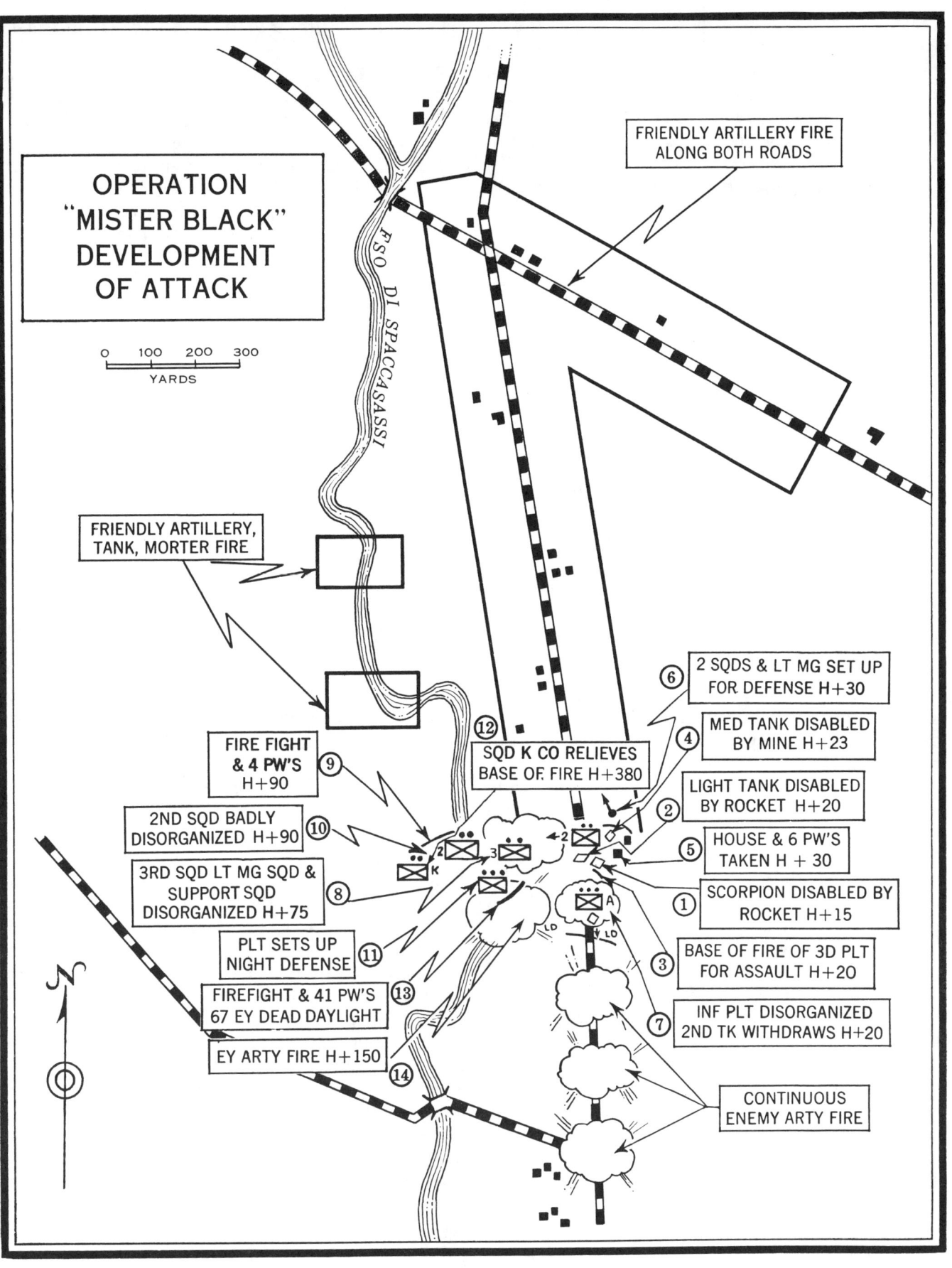

Said Rifleman Pvt. Aubra Smith, "The desire to close with and eliminate the Jerries whenever and wherever he could find them inspired confidence in me as this was my first taste of real offensive fighting and I was not overly confident. Although it was Pfc. Squires' first fighting, too, he couldn't wait to get at the Jerries and clean them out of their holes.

"Pfc. Squires was an inspiration to all of us. His fearlessness showed us what a determined man could do to the so-called Nazi superman."

Pfc. Squires was killed in a subsequent action. He was posthumously awarded the Congressional Medal of Honor.

The "battle of the river bed" successfully completed the Division's first limited-objective, infantry-tank attack, since the 3d platoon had seized its objective early, capturing a number of prisoners, an 88mm antitank rocket launcher, and fourteen machine guns in the process.

Operation "Mr. Black" extended our outpost line, resulted in penetration of the strongly fortified Spaccasassi Creek banks, brought in forty-seven PWs and marked the decimation of two companies of the 29th *Panzer Grenadier* Division.

While the Division prepared to execute Operation "Mr. Green" another small, but important, objective was seized; an objective that had become a symbol of German resistance and a stubborn target for our troops.

It was an ordinary country windmill of the type that dots the rural areas all over the United States and it was located in a farmyard only a few hundred yards to our front. The enemy had used it for weeks as an outpost and we had tried many times to take it without success. Few Daily Operations Reports were issued that didn't mention the windmill in some manner.

". . . windmill at (906299) attacked by our combat patrol which withdrew under heavy S/A and MG fire." This was a common notation in our records for more than a week.

The doughboys wanted this picturesque, but lethal, windmill; so, on April 24 a heavily armed combat patrol of the 7th Infantry stormed it, killed four Germans in the ensuing fire fight, captured two machine guns and took possession.

The enemy tried desperately to retake it the next day and several times thereafter but we posted it with one officer, eight men and a section of machine guns and flanked it on both sides by protective outposts manned in strength. A serious enemy hotbed had been eliminated and we had added a picturesque outpost to our line.

"Mr. Green" operation was awaited with anxiety since details about it had been circulated among the men in advance. It was to be something new and different.

It was to be the first "psychological attack" ever conducted by United States forces since the war began and it was the first time that words instead of bullets were to be used by the 3d Division against the enemy, although the verbal barrage made up only a small part of the attack. Several loud speakers directed toward the enemy lines were to be used in urging the Germans to surrender at a psychological moment during the attack.

Like "Mr. Black," it was a small-scale offensive, directed against the 362d *Fusilier* Battalion, which occupied a defensive position west of Cisterna.

The 2d Battalion, 30th Infantry, commanded by Lt. Col. Woodrow W. Stromberg, made the assault, with Company F, under Capt. Paul W. Stanley, actually staging the attack. The remainder of the battalion was in support.

At 0300 April 25, the usual sporadic night fighting which was common to the beachhead was sharply punctured when our 155s awakened the enemy with a thirty-five-minute concentration designed to set his nerves on edge.

This harassing fire suddenly stopped at 0405 and the beachhead seemed to start rocking as nine battalions of field artillery, reinforced with fire from tanks and self-propelled guns, cut loose. For nearly five minutes the projectiles from all these guns hit their target simultaneously. The roar was terrific. Designed to impress the enemy with the amount of artillery at our disposal, it also impressed the inhabitants of Anzio, some seven miles away.

Instantly, at 0407, all firing ceased.

A voice that could be heard 1,000 yards away blasted forth from the loud-speakers hidden in the weeds along the front lines. In their own language, the Germans heard that more and heavier artillery was to come. They were told about the impending attack that faced them. And they were urged to lay down their arms and enter our lines at once, or "else." Over and over they heard the words repeated. Then the loudspeakers became silent—and the artillery again took up the "appeal" with a deafening roar.

The fire of our artillery placed the enemy positions in a "box." The sides of the box remained stationary as our shells fell continuously and precisely along the edges, 1,000 yards apart. The rear wall moved forward like the lid of a roll-topped desk, to force the enemy out of their holes and toward our lines. This barrage lasted twenty minutes and finally gave way to harassing fire placed on known enemy positions to soften them further and provide noise to cover the movement of our tanks into position.

Again our guns were silenced, at 0445, and the loudspeakers blared forth a final chance for surrender. With monotonous repetition came the "Surrender! Surrender!" as German NCOs raced from hole to hole threatening death to any *Landser* who heeded the words. The last words died in the renewed thunder of artillery as Company F, with tank reinforcement, moved out of the area in the vicinity of Campo Morto and went into attack at 0500.

Advancing by rushes, our men dropped to their knees to fire tommy guns into German positions at close range, stuck M-1s into dark foxholes and pulled the triggers, and took and generally overran their objective by 0520, the time set in advance plans for the attack to cease. Captain Stanley and his men stayed five minutes overtime "just in case," but they were ordered to withdraw according to plan.

The withdrawal of the company, which ordinarily would have been a difficult operation under the circumstances, was made easy by the close support given by the remainder of 2d Battalion.

Company E, commanded by Capt. James H. Greene, operated the smoke pots that created a covering screen which enveloped the area and hid the men from enemy view as they withdrew. The company also placed small-arms fire on the enemy during the withdrawal.

Members of Company G, under Capt. Hugh E. Wardlaw, Jr., guided the attacking troops and tanks in and out of the zone of action, pointing out the openings in our own and enemy wire and minefields which had been gapped by Division Engineers the night before the attack. The engineers also marked the clear lane with luminous buttons.

As the attack came to a close, Company H, commanded by Capt. Eric W. Tatlock, laid 81mm smoke shells on predesignated points and the Cannon Company, under 1st Lt. Norwood L. Snowden, maintained continuous fire as the company withdrew down Fosso delle Bove.

The attackers were happy and proud of their achievement—they captured nine PWs and killed some fifty Germans.

"Mr. Green" is perhaps the most unforgettable character that Company F and the remainder of 2d Battalion, 30th Infantry, ever met.

The stabilized situation which existed in the 3d Division sector was a perfect setting for such limited-objective operations as "Mr. Black" and "Mr. Green" and the Division learned to employ them effectively.

Late April found the Division still attacking in small groups while the enemy continued to probe our defenses, looking for the opening that never appeared.

Enemy aircraft became especially active just when we were being relieved by the 45th Division.

During the night of April 28 about forty planes dropped high-explosives, antipersonnel and rocket bombs on our front lines and in the beach area. Nine planes were shot down. Some fifteen enemy craft bombed and strafed the area the following night, our last in the line, and four of them were brought down.

On the following day, at 0600 May 1, 1944, the Division passed control of the sector to the 45th and moved back into the dune area near Torre Astura to prepare for an offensive that would break the beachhead stalemate.

The period of fighting that came to a close with the relief of the 3d Infantry Division by the 45th Infantry Division is known as the "Big War of Little Battles." When the "little" battles were over, however, and the stage was being set for the big battle that was about to be fought, it was known in high staff and command circles that this "Big War of Little Battles" carried on chiefly by the 3d Infantry Division from March 4 until May 1, had accomplished much more than a straightening of the lines, than killing, wounding and capturing enemy and destroying enemy equipment. It had made for one of the chief factors that was to attain its full importance and recognition in the great battle pending. It had raised the morale of all troops on the beachhead and had changed the attitude of the Allied soldiers from one of defense to one of offense.

For nearly four months the beachhead forces had served as a poised dagger, ever threatening to stab into the right flank of the German army that was slowly being pushed north up the Italian boot by other elements of the United States Fifth Army.

The 3d Division was to be the dagger's point. It was the instrument that would penetrate the enemy's defenses and cut rapier-like through his fixed positions. In anticipation of the stab, the first three weeks of May were devoted to sharpening the dagger.

All phases of training centered on the attack with emphasis placed on storming of pillboxes and other in-

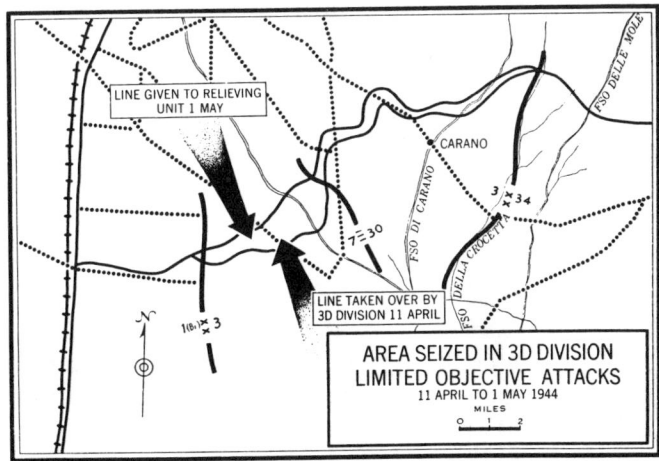

3d Division infantrymen practice "tank-busting" tactics during the training in early April on the beachhead.

fantry emplacements, use of battle-sleds, street fighting, coordination of the infantry-tank team, defense against tanks, attack over open country and attack against protected "fossi."

The training of all three regiments of the Division was similar, excepting the 7th Infantry, which spent a short period in Nettuno, where live ammunition and explosives were used in training for street fighting. Two battalions of the regiment were employed in this phase, which stressed the use of rifle grenades, maintenance of control and use of supporting weapons. The 7th had the mission of assaulting Cisterna di Littoria and no stone was left unturned in preparing for the task.

Infantry-tank cooperation similar to that involved in the operations "Mr. Black" and "Mr. Green" received the special attention of all regiments and additional hardening exercises were given members of the battle patrols which previously had been organized in each regiment, and the Division Reconnaissance Troop. The patrols comprised forty-five to sixty men and were heavily armed for special assault missions.

A battle-sled team of sixty men was organized in each regiment and the innovation created much interest in the Division. The sleds, invented by Maj. Gen. John W. O'Daniel, were narrow steel tubes mounted on flat runners and were wide enough to carry one armed infantryman lying down. One medium tank towed twelve of them, which meant that a regimental team comprised one platoon of tanks and sixty sleds. They were used to transport personnel through enemy barrages to the front, the armored tubes serving as protection against shell fragments and small-arms fire.

The artillery units reconnoitered all the area available for gun positions so that when D-day arrived gun pits had been dug, surveys completed, camouflage erected and communication lines laid.

A nightly "cover preparation" program, fired by all artillery on the beachhead, started May 12 and was highly successful in inducing the enemy to expend much protective fire which could have been used later when the real preparation was fired.

Another innovation created for the breakthrough was the organization of a provisional machine-gun battalion, using all the .50-caliber machine guns in the Division. Applying artillery methods, the battalion was trained to place interdictory and harassing fire on known enemy assembly points and routes of advance during the early stages of the attack.

The 10th Engineer Battalion built wooden bases for the machine guns that provided stable supports for the tripods.

In fact, the engineers made many nonroutine contributions to the advance preparations.

They built a splinterproof Division CP in a quarry just south of Borgo Montello, where they also erected a predesigned PW cage for reception, segregation, interrogation and evacuation. It had a capacity of 5,000.

Each regimental sector was provided with two additional footbridges across the Mussolini Canal, safe from interdictory fire, while great stores of "fascines" (compact bundles for improving traction on soft ground) were placed at appropriate spots for use by armored vehicles.

Personal reconnaissance, study of air photographs and the knowledge of all the surrounding terrain gained after four months on the beachhead, led to experiments in running vehicles along creek bottoms.

Mines no longer needed for defense of the Mussolini Canal were removed and methods devised for breach-

General O'Daniel directs a training manoeuvre in the employment of "battle-sleds," while Generals Clark and Truscott observe.

ing enemy minefields quickly and safely. One of these devices comprised twelve connected 100-foot lengths of primacord with one attached to a 60mm mortar and the other end held stationary at the gun position. The cord was detonated after being propelled to its destination by the mortar shell. The cord would detonate antipersonnel mines that lay along its path and clear a way into enemy territory. Another contrivance, called the "M-2 Snake," was a steel trough filled with bangalore torpedoes laid end to end along its 200-foot length, which could be shoved into an enemy antitank field by a tank.

These mechanical aids, however, did not reduce the amount of training that the Engineers received in breeching minefields by hand, the method which proved highly successful during the Cisterna attack.

Six tank crossings were made at the Fosso Feminamorta and Fosso di Battagone, draws that criss-crossed our area and averaged sixty-five feet in width and thirty-five feet in depth.

A new road, to supplement the two main arteries that were used by adjacent units, was built between Borgo Montello and the rear beachhead area, a distance of five miles.

The first warning order to move up came during the day of May 20, but by evening it had proved to be a false alarm. The day of attack, however, was imminent. At night it was now possible to see gun flashes from the southern front in the clear Italian skies. The push north from Cassino started May 12, and was destined for clear-cut success from the beginning. Sure enough, the next day the order came out "The regiments will move up tonight."

The coincidence of dates was unintended. It was now May 21. On January 22 units of the 3d Infantry Division had first touched ground below Nettuno. It was the eve of the first landings which touched off the ill-starred campaign.

That evening, May 21, 3d Infantry Division moved out from the pine forest in full marching order.

It was a balmy evening. As if to justify, finally, the cognomen "Sunny Italy" after so many months of nothing but rain, wind, and snow, all the days had been warm lately, even hot. There were few clouds in the sky this evening and it was still full daylight when the leading Division elements were to be seen emerging from the protective concealment of the wooded bivouac. The smoke-fog machines were going full blast, and the sickly-sweet streams of man-made mist merged into a low-hanging blanket which screened the telltale rear areas of the beachhead.

The 15th Infantry, from its encampment on the sandy wastes north of the pine forest, took its route through the forest, then struck out up the road for the front. The 7th and 30th Infantry Regiments followed.

In the green fields which fronted the wooded area, a few sheep were grazing. Their Italian herders looked at the troop-filled roads with interest.

Along the main road which skirted the forest's edge the 3d Division Band under the leadership of Chief Warrant Officer Eugene Kusmiak had taken a vantage point. As the doughboys moved past, the band played "Dogface Soldier," and a selection of marches.

As judged from the attitudes and remarks of the passing columns, never had the men been in finer fettle; never had the morale been higher.

They joked with the bystanders, the bandsmen, the MPs along the route and themselves. They sang or whistled. They held their heads high.

The price of Victory. This is a portion of the Allied Cemetery at Nettuno, where many 3d Division soldiers are buried.

To those persons who had been at Bizerte the soldiers' attitude was reminiscent of the condition and mental attitude of the same Division just prior to embarkation for Sicily. Of those men then it has been said that, "never, anywhere, was a division of any army better equipped, mentally or physically, for combat."

Ahead but a short distance were the front lines which for four months had been braced and strengthened to a point almost unparalleled in the war of movement which prevailed from 1939-1945. There were thousands of antitank and antipersonnel mines laid by both sides. The enemy had sited his weapons in order to cover most favorably all routes of approach. The ground was flat, with few folds and a scarcity of ditches.

Added to all these disadvantages for the attacker was the fact that the southern front was rapidly moving north. Kesselring's intelligence knew that the Anzio front was soon to move into action. If ever it was to be of value, now was the time. Surprise, therefore, could only be the limited surprise of exact date and exact place.

The steadily marching men of the 3d Infantry Division advanced toward one of the bloodiest single encounters fought by any Division in one day in World War II and what might well be classed as the greatest victory of its total combat career. The sky darkened, and still the columns lined the roads. The artillery commenced its nightly serenade and the gun flashes merged their fire, like chain lightning.

TABLE OF CASUALTIES*

Anzio Beachhead

(Jan. 22, 1944 through May 22, 1944)

KIA	WIA	MIA	Total Battle Casualties	Non-Battle Casualties
1074	4302	919	6295	6455

Reinforcements and Hospital return-to-units personnel

Reinf.		Hosp. RTU	
Off	EM	Off	EM
249	6755	197	7967

KNOWN ENEMY CASUALTIES

Killed	Wounded	Captured
433	255	1588

*These figures were provided by the A C of S, G-1, 3d Infantry Division.

VII
THE PUSH TO ROME

1: The Second Battle of Cisterna di Littoria

TROOP LIST— Operation "Buffalo" Third Infantry Division (Reinf)

Organization for Combat

1. *Hq and Hq Co, 3d Inf Div*
2. *7th Inf Regt*
3. *15th Inf Regt*
4. *30th Inf Regt*
5. *3d Inf Div Artillery*
   9th FA Bn
   10th FA Bn
   39th FA Bn
   41st FA Bn
   24th Armd Field Regt (105H) (Br)
6. *441st AAA AW Bn*
7. *3d Rcn Trp*
8. *3d QM Co*
9. *3d Signal Co*
10. *3d Med Bn*
11. *10th Engr Bn*
12. *84th Chem Bn*
13. *601st TD Bn*
14. *751st Tk Bn*
15. *703d Ord Co*

AT about dusk May 25, 1944, a rather slack-appearing German officer, wearing a lieutenant colonel's uniform, appeared in the interrogation room at the 3d Infantry Division's cage just south of Borgo Montello, on what had been the Anzio beachhead. He was the commanding officer of the 955th Infantry Regiment, which had been charged with the defense of the city of Cisterna di Littoria and its immediate environs.

At this moment, his regiment no longer existed as a fighting force; Cisterna was in United States hands, and only small, disorganized groups and individual soldiers were falling back in front of our forces, or fleeing in an effort to reach previously selected areas and reorganize.

The presence of the German lieutenant colonel in our cage was symbolic of the two salient facts of the Second Battle of Cisterna: first, the tactics of the German defenders, which were to defend in place and face the alternatives of success or destruction; second, the total triumph of the Division's attack, which in three days had fulfilled that portion of the familiar directive contained in the field order for the operation which read: "To destroy the enemy in the Division's zone of action."

Next morning's headlines carried the news that the southern Fifth Army and the beachhead forces had met on the swampy flat-lands of the Pontine marshes; less attention was given to the fact that Cisterna, after nearly four months of intermittent siege, was at last firmly in United States hands. Yet this latter item contained the story of one of the greatest attacks ever delivered by an infantry division, without which the advance on Rome might well have been delayed for days or even weeks.

It was one of the strange coincidences of war that the victors of the Second Battle of Cisterna had been the losers of the First Battle of Cisterna nearly four months before. On January 30, 1944, the 3d Infantry Division, reinforced by Ranger and Parachute units, fought a gallant, heartbreaking and unsuccessful battle to capture Cisterna. The Division staff learned on that day, from prisoners of war, what it could not have learned previously from any normal intelligence source: that Hitler had ordered the beachhead destroyed, and that enemy reinforcements were streaming toward Anzio from northern Italy, southern France and the Balkans. Enemy numbers plus the flat, coverless terrain defeated the 3d Division that day and foreshadowed the long, near-stalemate that followed. The destruction of two Ranger battalions in the space of eight hours at Cisterna was a somber detail in a dark picture.

The situation was vastly different in May. Not the smallest difference was the fact that our forces had the enemy completely "cased" for the latter attack, almost down to each machine-gun nest and firepit. Long and careful interrogation of prisoners, detailed study of air photos, and constant patrol activity gave our staff an intimate knowledge of where the enemy was located and how he defended his positions.

The enemy, likewise, enjoyed many advantages. He still had perfect observation of the entire beachhead area from many vantage points. He had three and a half months in which to dig in, lay wire and mines, sandbag his positions, erect tank obstacles and coordinate his fields of fire. His artillery was registered on every worthwhile target and road junction in the battle area. His troops knew every wrinkle in the ground, and knew that a major Allied attack was coming.

Yet this position was broken in three days, and every living German killed or chased from the battle area.

Terrain, in the battle of Cisterna, played a largely

negative role. In many small sectors, the battle might as well have been fought on a billiard table, the ground was so flat and devoid of cover. There were, however, certain interesting irregularities worth a brief review.

Several ditches (Italian "fosso") cut the battle area into compartments, running generally north to south, with anywhere from a few hundred to several thousand yards between ditches. These "ditches" are actually small canyons in many cases, sometimes reaching a depth of sixty feet or more, representing absolute barriers to vehicle movement and serious obstacles to infantry movement. South of Cisterna they are not so important, the ground being flatter and the ditches shallower; north of the town, however, the ground rises and the ditches become deeper and their banks steeper. In addition, there are many minor drainage ditches which intersect the fields and prevent cross-country vehicle movement.

The area around Cisterna was well-settled and there were numerous farm buildings of concrete or masonry construction. Most of these buildings had been totally or partially destroyed by artillery fire, and were very useful to the enemy as strongpoints or gun emplacements, as the walls and rubble offered considerable protection against small-arms fire and shell fragments.

By the time of the attack in late May, field grasses and grain had grown to a considerable height in places, affording some concealment to creeping men. Scattered patches of woods, well chewed up by artillery fire, still concealed enemy strongpoints, supply distributing points or tank-assembly areas. Nowhere did the vegetation offer any particular barrier to movement.

The ground itself, muddy and covered with patches of standing water during the early spring, had dried out sufficiently at the time of the attack to permit the passage of tanks almost anywhere.

Back of the battlefield itself, to the north and northeast, was the real high ground which gave the enemy his observation and defilade. North beyond Velletri were the Colli Laziali, or Alban Hills; northeast were the Monti Lepini, whose nearest peak, Monte Arrestino, was obviously the key terrain feature in the entire sector and actually was the first hill captured by the beachhead forces.

The road network in the battle area was fairly good, but it was discovered after the breakthrough that German road maintenance was far worse than ours, due to our air superiority and the greater intensity of our shelling. Highway 7, the only first-class road in the area, ran diagonally across the battlefield from southeast to northwest, passing through Cisterna.

The Rome-Cisterna-Naples rail line, which also passed through Cisterna itself, was a feature of some importance. In January the Germans had begun to prepare this line as their MLR, but when the front solidified two or three thousand yards south of the railroad, nothing further was done to improve the positions which had been begun along it. The physical barrier of the railroad embankments and cuts, remained, however, as well as the weapon pits and dugouts which already had been prepared.

Division headquarters as well as higher headquarters, had been hard at work for many weeks on a series of plans to resume the offensive and break out of the beachhead. Everyone recognized that our defensive attitude was purely temporary, and that as soon as sufficient strength in troops and supplies had been built up, the big attack would be unleashed. Earlier hopes had depended on the first two abortive efforts to break through the southern front at Cassino, but when these attempts failed, the Allies raised their sights to a grand offensive in which every unit which could be spared would be hurled into the Italian drive.

The beachhead forces had three principal lines of action in mind, each dependent on the speed with which the southern campaign proceeded. They were:

First, in the event of a slow, grinding advance from the south, beachhead troops planned to drive due east to high ground south of Cori, in the Monti Lepini, and then push southeast to effect a union with our units in the south.

Second, in the event of a steady, assured advance on the southern front, beachhead forces would smash enemy defenses at Cisterna and push due north toward Valmontone in order to cut Highway 6 and contribute to the defeat of Kesselring's southern forces.

Third, in the event of a German debacle and hasty withdrawal to the north, beachhead troops would hasten the push on Rome by cracking through the factory area at Carroceto and attacking northwest along the Albano-Rome axis. In all these plans, 3d Infantry Division played a key part in the assault.

The second of these alternatives was ultimately adopted, as the Germans in late May were being steadily forced back but had not yet been knocked off their feet.

In this attack, the 3d Infantry Division's assignment was to assault Cisterna frontally with one regiment and to by-pass it with a regiment on each side, continuing the advance northeast to Cori and anchoring the VI Corps right flank on high ground behind Cori. Special Service Force, operating independently, was on the Division's right flank, and 1st Armored Division on the left. Early capture and reduction of Cisterna was the key to success, as the main roads to Cori and Velletri passed through it. Once Cori was captured, the attack was to turn north toward Valmontone, and eventually toward Rome.

Responsibility for the defense of the Cisterna sector was divided between two German infantry divisions, the 362d and 715th. Neither was up to full strength; heavy casualties and the gradual shriveling of the German divisional organization (each division had only six battalions of infantry) left them with a probable frontline combat strength of about 2500-3000 men apiece. However—and this is important—the enemy was well supplied with automatic weapons and mortars, and had enough ammunition stacked on his positions to keep shooting as long he could hold out, barring a long siege. By the time we attacked, our artillery superiority was marked, and in this department the enemy suffered possibly his greatest disadvantage.

The 362d Infantry Division was responsible generally for the sector west of the Borgo Montello-Cisterna road (Borgo Montello is called Conca on some maps), and the 715th Infantry Division, reinforced by 1028th *PGR*, for the sector between the road and the coast to the southeast. Battalion sectors normally covered a frontage of about 2,000 yards; our Division, attacking on a 7,000-yard front, therefore found about four enemy battalions in its path, with the equivalent of two or three battalions in reserve.

The enemy defense consisted of a series of platoon strongpoints based on clusters of buildings or terrain features such as clumps of woods, knolls, ravines, etc. These were backed up by similar strongpoints organized to a depth of about 3,000 yards; these positions were of such density that they presented a continuously occupied zone across the front of the Division, with hardly a spot in the entire zone that could not be brought under the fire of automatic weapons from at least two directions, if not from all sides at once. The enemy had virtually completed a belt of double-apron or concertina wire across his entire front, using the wire chiefly to prevent the approach of foot troops to his strongpoints. Antipersonnel and antitank mines were thickly sown along all avenues of approach, both in front of and between his positions.

Each strongpoint was organized for all-around defense, utilizing three to six machine guns and outlying rifle pits to hold off our threats from any direction. Automatic weapons were generally sited close to the ground in order to get maximum effect against crawling or crouching troops. Overhead cover was provided for many, but not all of the positions.

Firing positions had been prepared for, and employed by, the tanks and SP guns which the Germans had in fair quantity. The enemy was very clever in staking out these positions so that the weapons could deliver effective harassing fire, even at night, then pull out and return to a safe spot before our counterbattery could attack them. The enemy was not especially strong, however, in towed antitank weapons, which

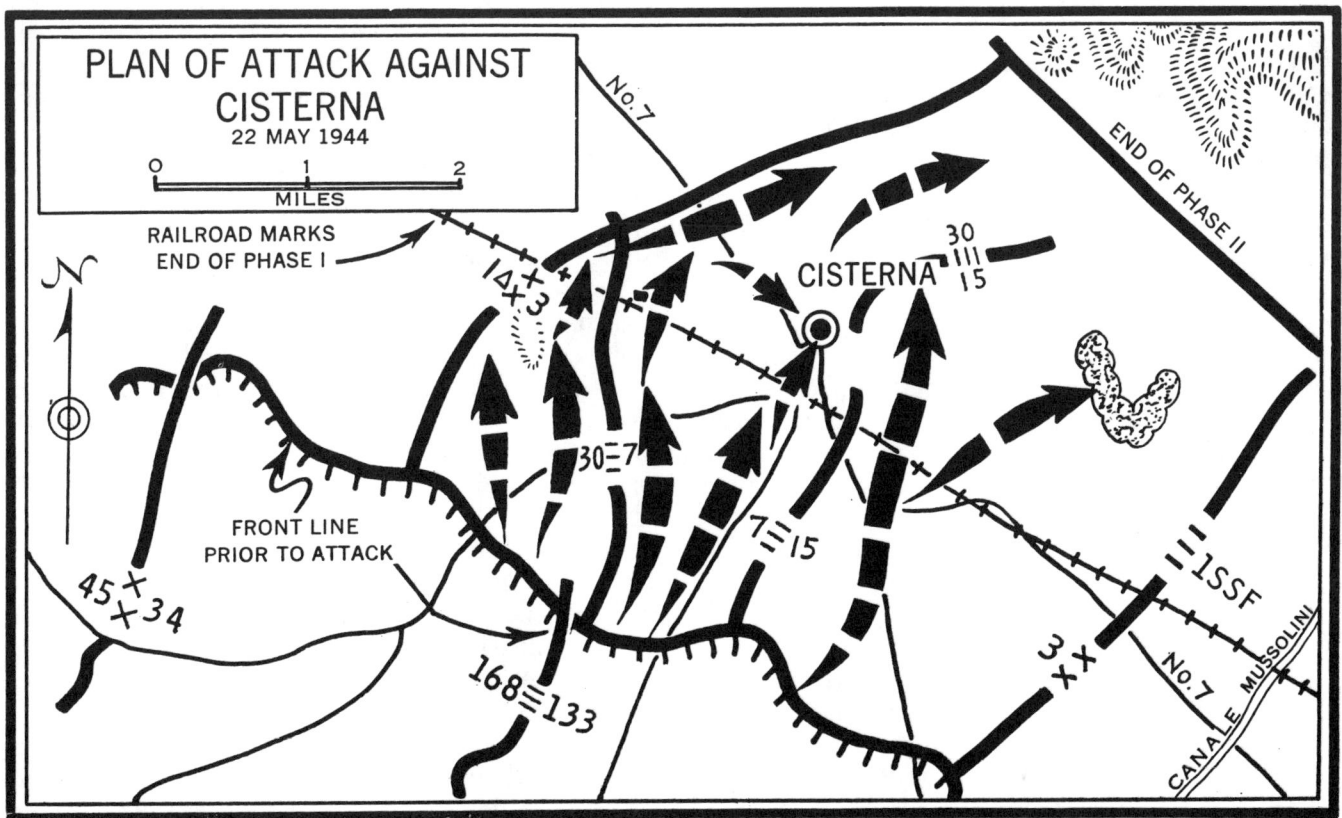

would have been of great advantage to him in well-dug-in forward positions.

It was known that enemy strategy called for a defense on his positions, even at the expense of annihilation, because the successful extrication of his troops on the southern front depended absolutely upon his ability to contain the beachhead. It was upon this basis that our plans for attack were made.

Promptly at 0545 May 23 the artillery preparation for the attack began. For the next forty-five minutes, ten battalions of light, medium and heavy artillery poured high explosives into enemy fortifications and gun positions. Dive bombers, hampered by low clouds, began a counterbattery program which was frequently interrupted by poor visibility.

At 0630 the doughboys attacked. Their movements were covered locally by smoke and seconded by fire of tanks and TDs which initially occupied static firing positions.

For the preceding two nights, troops, trucks, tanks, guns and supplies had been moved into assembly areas in ditches and draws on the flat ground south of Isola Bella, and along the Mussolini Canal. The slightest movement in daylight would have aroused enemy suspicion and drawn a hail of artillery fire—yet these large-scale preparations were carried out without a flaw, and a very real element of surprise was gained.

30TH INFANTRY

The 30th Infantry commanded by Col. Lionel C. McGarr, making the Division main effort on the left, attacked north from a line of departure along the road running west from Isola Bella, thence northwest across the Fosso Feminamorta and the road southwest of Ponte Rotto. The regiment advanced with 2d Battalion west of Fosso Feminamorta, and 3d Battalion (with Company A attached) was astride the ditch and east of it. 1st Battalion (less Company A) was in regimental reserve, occupying an assembly area in Fosso Feminamorta about two miles south of Ponte Rotto.

Enemy reaction to the attack was immediate and violent. The 2d Battalion met strong fire from small arms, SP and artillery before it hit the line of departure. The battalion was in column of companies in the order G, E and F. Company G fought its way about 300 yards north of the Ponte Rotto road, at a point 500 yards west of that settlement, where it received fire from both flanks as well as the front, since friendly units on the flanks had not caught up. At this point a hundred Germans in a quarry were surrounded but could not be routed out as it was impossible to place fire on them. They surrendered the following afternoon. Wardlaw's Wadi (named after Capt. Hugh E. Wardlaw, G Company's commander), a small creek running parallel to Company G's axis of advance proved difficult to clean out; during the process, heavy fire was received from Ponte Rotto.

Company E passed through Company G and continued to meet strong opposition as it fought its way about 800 yards farther north. The company then turned east and wiped out an enemy strongpoint in a group of buildings just west of Fosso Feminamorta. In these buildings, concealed in the rubble, the enemy had placed automatic weapons, SP guns and dispersed riflemen.

The extent of the enemy defense in depth was revealed when Company F passed through Company E and headed for the next objective about 1000 yards due north. Strong fire was received all along the front from well-entrenched enemy. The company moved up a series of small ditches, wiping out enemy opposition, and by nightfall it was attached to 1st Battalion for an attack on enemy positions along the railroad track.

A brief consideration of this attack will make clear the reasons for 2d Battalion's difficulty in maintaining control during the night. Each company ran into strong and continuing opposition; even while Company F was preparing to cross the railroad tracks from its lately-won position, Company E and Company G to the rear were still engaged by scattered groups of enemy in fossi, cellars, dugouts and isolated sniper posts. The battalion was thus strung out in a depth of about 2500 yards, and was fighting bitter, small-scale engagements over the entire area. Elements of 6th Armored Infantry, attacking on the Division's left, made slow initial progress but later arrived at the railroad track prior to the 2d Battalion; some of the armored infantry personnel who accidentally crossed into 2d Battalion's sector assisted in the reduction of some enemy positions.

Company L, the left company of 3d Battalion, assigned to clean out Fosso Feminamorta as far north as Ponte Rotto, had one of the most bitter experiences of the entire attack. About 700 yards southwest of Ponte Rotto, at a point where Fosso Feminamorta swings sharply south, the enemy had installed a company strongpoint based on machine-gun positions dug into the shoulders of the ravine, outlying rifle pits, concertina and double-apron wire, and similar positions stretching northwest across the road. Company L moved rapidly up the stream until reaching the bend, where withering fire was received from the enemy weapons. A light tank, which was to have accompanied Company L up the ditch and to have attacked the enemy positions with 37mm canister, entered the ditch too far south and got bogged down in about five feet of water. Two M-4 medium tanks were also to assist in the attack, one going up each side of the creek. One of these tanks never showed up; the other hit a mine before reaching the line of departure and was of no value in the attack. The company finally moved into the position by sending one platoon up the creek and one platoon along the crest of each bank, and was later reinforced by a platoon of riflemen from the battle-sled group, whose tow-tanks had been immobilized by mines. After a struggle lasting nearly twenty-four hours, during which five separate attacks were made, Company L finally cracked the position and took the last remaining enemy prisoners although the bulk of the defenders had been killed or wounded. An enemy battalion CP, well dug-in and equipped, was found in the ditch just northeast of the strong point, and was later occupied by 3d Battalion as its CP.

Company A, attached to 3d Battalion for the attack, enjoyed the most rapid initial success of any unit of the division. Attacking north along the east side of the road running south from Ponte Rotto, the company rapidly overcame resistance in the houses on its side of the road, killing 16 enemy and capturing 6 in the open fields, besides taking 15 prisoners in the first house, 17 in the second and 13 in the third. It was not until after the company had passed through this zone that the enemy laid down his defensive artillery fire, which fell well behind the company as it advanced. Attacking the strongpoint in the house southeast of the Ponte Rotto road junction, the company captured two officers and 13 soldiers, as well as two 75 mm antitank guns. This objective was captured and organized for defense shortly after 0730, only one hour after moving out; success was due chiefly to following friendly artillery fire very closely, at an interval of 50 to 100 yards.

Company I had reached its objective at Ponte Rotto road junction seven hours ahead of time with its radio out of order. Friendly artillery was falling, since higher headquarters had no way of knowing that the company was so far ahead of schedule. In addition to this the enemy was firing direct fire with an 88mm mobile gun and three machine guns, and a large group of enemy riflemen about 300 yards distant were also adding their fire.

"We had been sitting there about 30 minutes, helpless, unable to do a thing about the situation, when the BAR man in my squad, Pfc. John Dutko, shouted to me, 'Toothman, I'm going to get that 88 with my heater!'" related S/Sgt Cleo A. Toothman, adding, "He always called his BAR a 'heater.'

"Before I could say a word he took off like a ruptured duck. He made the first hundred yards in a dead run. Machine-gun bullets were striking the ground only a foot or two behind him but he was running faster than the krauts could traverse. The kraut 88 crew let a couple of fast shells go at him also, but they exploded about thirty yards from him, and he dived into a shell hole which one of our own big guns had conveniently made a split second before he got there. I told myself that he would never make it. The enemy fire, coupled with our own artillery, was the heaviest that I had ever seen in such a small area. The enemy machine gunners converged their fire on the shell-hole occupied by Pfc. Dutko, making it, in my opinion, impossible for him to advance farther."

This was not the case. After a short rest Dutko jumped from his hole and ran in a wide circle toward the 88mm gun, followed by Pvt. Charles R. Kelley. By flanking the gun Dutko had succeeded in aligning the machine guns so that only one could fire at him, which it continued to do in long, murderous bursts. After running about 175 yards Dutko hit the dirt and threw a hand grenade into the machine-gun position, killing the two-man crew.

Kelley speaking: "Pfc. Dutko was a madman now. He jumped to his feet and walked toward the 88mm firing his BAR from his hip. He had apparently forgotten the other two machine guns; at least he was ignoring them. When he had gone about halfway to the 88mm he reached a point within ten yards of the weapon and wiped out the five-man crew with one long burst of fire. Pfc. Dutko then wheeled on the second German machine gun and killed its two-man crew with his BAR.

"The third German machine gun opened fire on Pfc. Dutko. This gun was only twenty yards away and its first burst of fire wounded him, making him stagger, but like a wounded lion he charged this gun in a half run. Pfc. Dutko killed both the gunner and the assistant gunner of the enemy weapon with a single burst from his BAR and, staggering forward, fell across the dead German machine gunner. When I reached him he was dead."

Pfc. Dutko's heroism won him a posthumous Congressional Medal of Honor.

The enemy launched three counterattacks against the company's defenses. The first was repulsed by small-arms fire, the second by artillery, and the third by small-arms and mortar fire.

After reaching this objective, the company was subjected to all types of fire from the front and both flanks during most of the day, but was well dug in and did not suffer unduly.

Company K suffered many casualties, possibly fifty, before crossing the line of departure, as the enemy had opened up with artillery and mortars as soon as our artillery preparation started; the company was also under machine-gun fire coming from the left and left

3d Division Infantrymen in house to house encounter with the enemy in the Battle of Cisterna di Littoria.

rear. The company commander, 1st Lt. Arnold Spillman, and executive, 2d Lt. Ben Seward, were among those hit.

Company K's mission was to attack up the west side of the road running south of Ponte Rotto, keeping abreast of Company A on the east side of the road. Upon the loss of the two ranking officers, Lieutenant Ethridge took over the company and led his men over 600 yards of flat terrain, exposed to searing machine-gun fire, by crawling through small ditches in the field. The company reached its initial objective at the Ponte Rotto crossroad in this manner, then attacked north, across the road to seize high ground immediately above Ponte Rotto. The platoon of tanks towing battle sleds, as indicated previously, was committed in this attack, but the tanks were immobilized by mines at the dog-leg in the road south of Ponte Rotto, and the personnel were attached to Company L for its attack on the strong point in Fosso Feminamorta. The battalion was never able to employ the sleds.

Company I, in reserve, was committed about 1400 to move around the right flank of Company A and attack objective F, a short distance northeast of Ponte Rotto. The company, commanded by 1st Lt. Norbert B. Sauer, accomplished this mission by crawling across open ground around Company A's flank. By late evening K, I and A Companies occupied a bulge north of the Ponte Rotto-Cisterna road, just east of Ponte Rotto. This position was organized by Capt. Kenneth A. Noseck, A Company commander. The battalion suffered about 300 casualties during the day's fighting.

About midafternoon May 23, 1st Battalion was ordered to move north, pass through 2d Battalion (which was fighting for objectives between the Ponte Rotto road and the railroad track) and seize high ground on both sides of the railroad just west of Fosso Feminamorta.

Artillery and mortar fire began falling on 1st Battalion after it crossed the road west of Ponte Rotto, and shortly after passing through 2d Battalion, Company E which was leading, began meeting heavy resistance from enemy dug in around ruined masonry houses on two small hills south of the railroad track. Large numbers of automatic weapons were employed against our troops, and artillery and mortar fire were continuous.

As Company E, 30th Infantry came abreast of Ponte Rotto, an enemy machine gun opened fire on the company's left flank from a position about a hundred yards away. Four men were killed almost instantly, and the rest took cover.

"Pfc. Patrick L. Kessler, an antitank grenadier in my platoon," related Pfc. Nicholas Rusinko, "ran fifty yards through a hail of machine-gun fire to a point where three of us were huddled in a ditch and suggested that we form an assault team to knock out the gun, which we instantly agreed to. Using us as a base of fire, Pfc. Kessler climbed out of the ditch and began to crawl toward the machine-gun position. He succeeded in making his way about 50 yards forward before the krauts spotted him and fired directly at him. Bullets struck so close to him that Kessler was almost obscured by the dust. Later I learned that he had been lightly wounded."

Charging forward, side-stepping like a broken field runner in a football game Kessler got to within two yards of the enemy emplacement. Here he kneeled and shot both the enemy gunner and assistant gunner with his '03 rifle. He then jumped into the gun position, overpowered one more soldier, and wounded a fourth attempting to make a getaway.

No sooner had he accomplished this deed than two machine guns and a group of enemy riflemen opened fire from a position about 175 yards to the rear. Ten men who had left covered positions when the first machine gun was eliminated were killed. Mortar and artillery concentrations began to fall in the area. The picture looked black. Two men attempting to assault the machine guns were also killed.

Kessler, who had been escorting his prisoner to the rear, turned him over to a nearby soldier and crawled thirty-five yards to the side of a BAR man to secure the BAR and ammunition belt. Then, under shellfire, the concussion of which rolled him over several times, Kessler kept up his steady crawl, passing through the length of an antipersonnel minefield. The enemy, who had spotted Kessler shortly after he had left the BAR man, converged the fire of both guns on him, yet he kept going for seventy-five yards.

Said Pvt. Alan C. Smith: "Just as he crawled out of the minefield, Pfc. Kessler occupied a position in a ditch about fifty yards from the kraut strongpoint and engaged in a duel with the two machine guns. Throughout this action, the German artillery and mortar fire kept coming in. Pfc. Kessler had fired about four magazines into the krauts when an artillery shell landed almost directly on top of him. For a moment we all thought that his number was up yet, when the smoke had cleared away, Pfc. Kessler had risen to his feet and was walking toward the machine guns, firing his BAR from his hip as he advanced."

Reaching the enemy strongpoint under continuous fire directed at him, Kessler killed the gunner of each of the two machine guns and took thirteen enemy prisoners. But he was not quite through.

"Pfc. Kessler had not traveled more than 25 to 30 yards to the rear with his prisoners before he was fired on by two snipers, who had infiltrated to positions to the rear of the company and about 100 yards away from him," said Pvt. Richard J. Alexander. "When this happened, several of the prisoners made a break for it; however, Pfc. Kessler fell to the ground and placed a burst of fire to either side of the prisoners, forcing them to hit the ground. Then he fired at each of the two snipers, causing them to surrender."

This heroic deed was later recognized by award of the Congressional Medal of Honor.

Both sides employed flares during the night, the enemy to illuminate our attacking troops, our units to light up enemy fortifications and to facilitate control. The night was very black, and during the attack parts of Company F, as well as one company of the 6th Armored Infantry, were fighting in the 1st Battalion zone.

Company B, led by Capt. Samuel B. Seetin, attacked frontally against the eastern of the two hills, which was immediately south of the railroad and west of Fosso Feminamorta. Upon receiving fire from the other hill to the west, one platoon of Company B was sent to attack the hill and reduce the machine-gun position which was causing the trouble. Enemy resistance on both hills was overcome at about 0200 or 0300 May 24.

Company C, following Company B, swung to the right before reaching the Company B objectives and attacked east across Fosso Feminamorta, which was a deep gorge at this point, presenting a considerable obstacle to movement. The company successfully crossed the gorge and succeeded in taking its objective with the assistance of direct fire support from tanks and TDs at about daylight May 24. The objective was high ground southeast of the railroad bridge over Fosso Feminamorta. Some casualties were suffered from the company's own direct-fire support weapons.

On the preceding day, the battalion had had a brief

Enemy run out of Cisterna with hands raised in sign of surrender.

fight for Objective C, about 1200 yards north of the Ponte Rotto road, which had already been partially occupied by elements of 2d Battalion. Constant enemy artillery and mortar fire failed to cause disproportionate casualties, as the advance was conducted with men well dispersed. Ditches were used for movement whenever possible. Enemy positions on the final objective were reduced by direct assault, with tommy guns, BARs, rifle grenades and hand grenades the principal weapons used. Rifle grenades were particularly effective; the grenadier would normally crawl within twenty-five to forty yards of a position before firing. NCOs equipped with carbines did good work, shooting rapid-fire at troublesome spots from wherever they happened to be. Coordination of fire support weapons —tanks, TDs and cannon company weapons—was a big factor in the success of the attack. A battalion staff officer was normally forward with each company, his chief duty being to see that these weapons were properly and effectively employed.

Artillery fire supporting 30th Infantry was delivered chiefly by the 41st FA Battalion. Infantry officers normally adjusted fire over infantry radios to battalion CP, from where the artillery liaison officer relayed adjustments to the fire direction center. Most of the fire was observed, insofar as this was possible at night. Artillery was used to a greater extent than mortars in smothering enemy fire while the infantry was closing in on enemy positions.

Control was excellent, and no important element of the battalion was out of touch with battalion headquarters, or with its own company, for any length of time.

7TH INFANTRY

The 7th Infantry had the mission of attacking Cisterna di Littoria frontally, with the Borgo Montello-Cisterna road as the main axis of advance. The 2d Battalion was designated to attack northeast astride the road with 3d Battalion on its left, adjacent to 30th Infantry. 1st Battalion was in reserve.

The 3d Battalion attacked in column of companies, in the order L, I and K, with machine guns from Company M sited to deliver fire from both flanks.

In order to escape the enemy's retaliatory shelling in answer to our preparation preceding H hour, Company L crossed the line of departure two hours before H-hour and waited at a 34th Division outpost for the time of attack. The line of departure was the lateral road running northwest from Isola Bella; the ground rose gradually north of the road and provided no cover and little concealment.

The initial objective was the crest of the slope, about 1800 yards due north of Isola Bella; however, the first resistance was encountered at a strongpoint located in a stream junction about 500 yards north of the line of departure. In addition the company received fire from houses on the right flank, in the 2d Battalion sector. The company was unable to advance until these houses had been captured by 2d Battalion troops. One platoon then worked its way to the objective, by-passing the strong point under cover of a smokescreen and an early morning fog. Unfortunately the fog and smoke cleared before the rest of the company moved up, and the enemy strongpoint had to be attacked and reduced before the company could continue. The company joined its leading platoon on the objective by crawling up the stream bed. Heavy enemy fire from the north caused several casualties and forced the company to dig in on the south slope of the objective for the remainder of the day.

After Company L reached its objective, Company I was sent around its left flank with the mission of advancing up a nose due north of Company L. Company I, however, advanced about 300 yards too far west, entering a draw to the left of its objective. Here it ran into a hornet's nest of opposition, getting fire from both flanks and the front. Company K was committed between Companies I and L but was likewise stopped by enemy fire, most of it coming from the railroad track. The commanding officer of Company K was killed, and the officer who replaced him was killed later. The battalion remained generally in this position during the night, fighting a continuous action against enemy who were attempting to infiltrate. The night was extremely dark, adding to the difficulty of reorganizing and supplying the battalion. This was accomplished, however, and the battalion was prepared to continue the fight the following morning.

The 2d Battalion attacked on the right of the 3d Battalion from a line of departure along the first small stream northwest of Isola Bella, and the road running east from Isola Bella. Company E was designated to attack along the west side of the Isola Bella-Cisterna road and Company F along the east side, with Company G in a reserve position along the ditch running south from Isola Bella. The battalion was supported by a platoon of medium tanks.

Before the attack the battalion suffered casualties from enemy artillery, which opened up before our own preparation was completed. As soon as our troops rose up out of their ditches and foxholes to attack, they began to receive intense automatic weapon and tank fire from two enemy strongpoints. One was in a group of three buildings west of the road and 500 yards beyond the line of departure; the other was organized around a single house east of the road and 700 yards

3d Division Infantrymen take cover from enemy fire during the Battle of Cisterna.

beyond the line of departure. Both had excellent fields of fire toward our lines, across flat terrain. The strongpoints were surrounded with barbed wire and Italian box mines; both had numerous automatic weapons and outlying rifle protection, besides the support of tanks. As the attack started, the fire of all our supporting weapons—five tanks, 37mm guns, heavy and light mortars, heavy and light machine guns and individual weapons, was placed on the two strongpoints.

Company E, attacking the strongpoint west of the road, sent one platoon around to the west in a flanking maneuver. This platoon had difficult going, advancing over absolutely flat terrain, and reached the objective two hours after moving out with only eighteen men left of its original thirty-four. The five tanks supporting the action were all immobilized by antitank mines shortly after moving out.

Company F attacked the strongpoint east of the road in a frontal assault with troops widely deployed; and reached its objective in forty minutes. After consolidating on the objective Company F organized a task force consisting of a rifle platoon reinforced, one tank destroyer, one medium tank and one light tank, with the mission of assaulting two further points of resistance. The first was on the Fosso di Fantano about 1200 yards northeast of Isola Bella; the second was 300 yards farther up the creek, where it was bridged by the Isola Bella-Cisterna road. The medium tank became mired in several feet of mud and water in the creek and the TD was destroyed by enemy SP fire, hence only the light tank aided in the attack. However, both points were overcome, and the enemy withdrew along the creek to the north. Meanwhile Company E advancing from its first objective, attacked enemy positions on a slight knoll just across the road from Company F, and occupied the knoll by 1130.

Company F had suffered severe casualties, so Company G was committed east of Company F to clean out resistance on the right flank among some houses about 700 yards east of Company F's last positions. Resistance was heavy, and fighting lasted through the afternoon and into the night. During hours of darkness several groups of enemy attempted to infiltrate the battalion's positions and intermittent fighting resulted; however, the battalion was able to supply itself in preparation for the next day's fighting.

The 1st Battalion, 7th Infantry, was not committed in the attack during the first day's action, but was employed in mopping up pockets of resistance which had been by-passed by the other two battalions. Very light casualties were suffered by 1st Battalion in this action.

15TH INFANTRY

The 15th Infantry had an initial mission complementary to that of the 30th Infantry, that of attacking on the right of the 7th Infantry, by-passing Cisterna to the southeast and seizing objectives along Highway 7 and the railroad embankment. The initial plan was to attack with two battalions abreast, 3d Battalion on the left and 2d Battalion on the right, with 1st Battalion in reserve; however, so much resistance was expected on the right flank, in the gap between 3d Infantry Division and Special Service Force, that a special task force built around Company A, 15th Infantry, commanded by the 1st Battalion executive, was constituted to operate in the gap. This task force was called Task Force Paulick, after its commander, Maj. Michael Paulick.

The 3d Battalion attacked at H-hour in column of companies, in the order L, K and I, with its first objective a road junction 1500 yards east of Isola Bella. The terrain was perfectly flat but was crossed by a series of drainage ditches, most of which ran north and south. Along the road running east from Isola Bella was a series of houses, usually in pairs facing each other across the road, and located 100 to 200 yards apart. One house, just southwest of the initial objective, was very strongly held with machine guns in the ruins of the house and nearby positions. Oddly, there were no antipersonnel mines south of the junction, although both roads were lined with antitank mines.

Company L, in the lead, started east from an assembly position in a drainage ditch about 1000 yards east of Isola Bella. Almost immediately, the company ran into fire of every description—from small arms, machine guns, mortars, artillery, and SP guns. By a series

German Infantrymen rush out of their shelters in Cisterna to surrender.

"Chateau Woods," 1000 yards east of the junction, in addition to fire from the frontal sector along the road. At this time the battle-sled team was ordered into action. Tanks hauling infantrymen in battle sleds moved up the north-south road to the junction which formed the previous objective, then turned east on the right side of the east-west road. About 200 yards east of the junction the tanks encountered a drainage ditch too wide to cross, so the infantry personnel left the sleds and moved on foot against the houses 200 yards away. This move was coordinated with the continuation of the attack by the remainder of the battalion, and the front started moving forward again.

Company L's commander was wounded at this time and the remainder of the company stayed at the first objective to reorganize. It was later attached to I Company.

K Company moved up a ditch running generally parallel to the road and hit a number of antipersonnel mines, suffering about ten casualties. The rest of the day was spent cleaning out "Kraut Woods" and adjacent houses; the enemy was well dug-in with machine guns in mutually supporting positions, and as usual he took full advantage of ruined houses for use as strongpoints. All positions were wired in, necessitating a separate assault on each one. The battalion Ammunition and Pioneer platoon built a road from near the line of departure to the woods, in order to bring the TDs into position without their traveling over mine-filled roads. The battalion remained in this area during the night.

First objective of 2d Battalion on D-Day was the patch of trees known as "Chateau Woods," just southwest of the first main road junction south of Cisterna on the road to Sessano. The battalion began its attack in column of companies, with E Company leading, followed by F and G in order. Company E advanced slowly across flat terrain and was subjected to powerful ground opposition. The enemy had established his strongest line of defense along the south edge of the woods, and was supported by SP guns, tanks, and registered artillery fire. Company E was halted by fire about 1000 yards beyond the line of departure, and F Company was committed to the west, on E Company's left flank. While Company F was drawing fire from the woods, E Company reorganized rapidly and launched one of the most successful *bayonet attacks* of the war. The attack was ordered because the company was low on ammunition; in the charge, fifteen Germans were killed in their holes and eighty more were captured. An unestimated number managed to escape to the northwest.

Company E was well supported by tanks in this charge. Originally the battalion had no allotment of

of rushes Company L took the first two houses, and almost immediately afterward patrols reached the next two, making it impossible for our artillery to fire on the houses. However, supporting TDs delivered fire on the houses and aided in their reduction.

In the first two or three hours of the attack, Company L's strength was cut from 150 men to only thirty or forty effectives, and the company was so badly disorganized that the attack lagged for the next three hours. The battalion was then redisposed in echelon formation to the right rear, with remnants of Company L guiding on the south edge of the road about 400 yards beyond the junction. Fire was received from tanks, but one platoon of mediums was made available in the afternoon. The tanks advanced to within a short distance of the woods, where they were halted by mines, but were able to support the attack by fire. When Company E entered the woods, Company F moved forward and assisted Company E in cleaning out the last enemy resistance.

While the other two companies were fighting for the woods, G Company by-passed that fight and moved north to the next objective, the road junction at the northeast corner of the woods. Light resistance was encountered, so the company continued north to clean out Fosso di Cisterna. In this deep ditch G Company found and captured more than a hundred enemy, who were cowering in deep caves and surrendered when approached. The caves were well prepared as living quarters and were immune to air attack or artillery fire, but were useless as fighting positions.

After "Chateau Woods" were cleaned out, F and E Companies followed Company G, with Company E being in reserve. Company G reached the point where Highway 7 crosses Fosso di Cisterna and moved out across the flat ground toward the railroad. Here the opposition increased considerably. The company received direct fire from the vicinity of the railroad track and was able to make little headway during the night. In spite of the intensity of the fighting and the blackness of the night, battalion headquarters was able to maintain contact with Company G with W-130 wire. The fighting was still going on as daylight approached.

Because it was necessary to keep the bulk of the 1st Battalion in regimental reserve, Task Force Paulick was organized to fill the 3000-yard gap on the Division's right flank. The Task Force consisted of Company A, 15th Infantry, a platoon of medium and a platoon of light tanks from 751st Tank Battalion, a section of TDs from 601st TD Battalion, the regimental Battle Patrol, a platoon of machine guns and a section of heavy mortars from D Company, a platoon of Cannon Company, a medical detachment and a squad of engineers. The Task Force attacked at H-hour and immediately encountered bitter opposition.

Enemy machine guns, antitank guns, and SP guns from the left flank, in vicinity of "Chateau Woods," hit the company and its supporting armor heavily. Other machine guns and an antitank gun fired south into the force's flank from the direction of Cisterna, along the north-south road which the Task Force had to cross. A ditch which ran northwest-southeast across a flat field immediately south of Chateau Woods had been converted into a strongpoint, with excellent fighting holes rendering the enemy virtually immune to artillery fire. Machine guns on the enemy flanks afforded crossfire against our troops, and for about 600 yards along the Cisterna road every house had been converted into a strongpoint protected by rifle, machine-gun and tank fire.

The commander of Company A was killed early on D-Day. German tanks were so skillfully placed to cover antitank mine fields that in the first day the Task Force lost two medium tanks and one light tank from this cause, while one TD and one medium tank were lost on improperly marked friendly mine fields prior to the attack. Company A, however, managed to reach Fosso di Cisterna by dark, and worked its way north to its initial objective, the bridge just southeast of "Chateau Woods."

Although unable to get ammunition or food because of the bitter fighting, the long haul, and lack of personnel, the Task Force continued after dark to clear out the houses along a road running parallel to, and 600 yards east of Fosso di Cisterna. The houses finally fell when two medium tanks were sent across the Fosso di Cisterna over the next bridge to the south, in the Special Service Force sector, thus flanking the strongpoints. Firing down the road into the enemy positions, the tanks forced the enemy infantry to withdraw and A Company occupied the area.

Immediately afterward the Task Force attacked east, against "88 Woods," about 600 yards east of the road just referred to. Little opposition was encountered here, but the Task Force's right flank was endangered when an enemy Mark VI tank counterattack forced the Special Service Force, which had no heavy antitank weapons, to give up a position on Highway 7 and the railroad line to the east. After Company A had cleaned out the woods, the Battle Patrol passed through the woods toward a road junction just 300 yards to the east. There was no opposition between the woods and the road junction, but upon arriving at the latter point, the patrol discovered an estimated reinforced enemy platoon moving down the road in column of twos, apparently to take up a defensive position, unaware that United States troops were so near. A two-minute fire fight followed, during which the Battle Patrol killed approximately twenty enemy and took thirty-seven prisoners. The next day they rounded up six more wounded enemy. An ammunition dump was discovered and set on fire, and an SP gun destroyed by the patrol.

Mission of Battle Patrol, 15th Infantry, was to cut Highway 7 southeast of Cisterna. To reach the highway it was necessary to clear the enemy from a large area, protect the regimental right flank, cross a long wheat field, a road, move through a woods and cover some more open terrain before reaching the objective.

The 53-officer-and-man Patrol encountered its first task when it reached a ditch beside the road it had to cross. Enemy small-arms fire was already being directed on the men. Suddenly four snipers opened fire from the patrol's rear.

Pfc. Henry Schauer, whom S/Sgt. Joseph M. Brown calls "the best BAR-man I have ever seen," climbed out of the ditch and walked slowly toward the snipers. Two of them were at the base of a house 200 yards to the rear, one on a road near the house, and the fourth concealed in the wheat field to the left of the house. "Pfc. Schauer was made of ice," said Sergeant Brown admiringly. "He stood upright, raised his BAR to his shoulder, and went to work. The snipers 170 yards away alongside the house were low to the ground, blending in with the grass. Two bursts from the BAR killed both snipers. Pfc. Schauer turned his body slightly. The sniper lying on the shaded road was only a dark shadow. One burst from the BAR finished him. The last sniper, the one in the field, was almost impossible to spot. Pfc. Schauer fired again. One burst was enough.

"As Pfc. Schauer ran to catch up with us he glimpsed another sniper hiding behind the chimney on the roof of a house 150 yards to our front. He stopped, aimed, and his burst of fire tumbled the sniper's body off the roof."

Crossing the tree-lined road, the patrol proceeded up the ditch on the right side of the road. Another smaller patrol moved out to the right in a parallel ditch. Schauer was fourth in line in the latter formation. Two German machine guns opened fire, one, sixty yards to the front, the other, about 500 yards to the right of the road. Everyone took cover except Schauer.

"The man acted as though nothing could kill him," according to 2d Lt. James M. Dorsey, Jr. "He assumed the kneeling position on the bank of a ditch. Bullets from both machine guns swept about him, miraculously missing him by inches. Fragmentation from enemy shells which burst no more than fifteen yards from him, hit the ground all around him. He permitted none of this fire to ruffle his composure. Pfc. Schauer engaged the first machine gun, the one sixty yards away, opening up on it with a full clip of ammunition. In one long burst of fire he killed the gunner and the man alongside him. He put a new magazine in his BAR, fired two short bursts and killed the two remaining Germans who ran to man the weapon."

Schauer jammed another magazine into the BAR, aimed, and with one burst killed the gunner of the second machine gun, plus three other soldiers near the gun.

On May 24, after pushing on to Highway 7 the patrol moved south, paralleling the highway. An enemy machine gun opened fire when the men had proceeded about 800 yards south. At the same time an enemy Mark VI tank began pumping shells at the patrol from a position 600 yards to the left.

Schauer climbed out of the ditch and crawled toward the machine gun. After twenty yards of this, he stood up. The tank fired four rounds directly at him, and the enemy machine gun kept up its vicious rate of fire.

"But looking at Pfc. Schauer," stated 2d Lt. Max R. Hendon, "you would think he was taking aim at target practice on the firing range. He fired a full clip of twenty at the enemy machine gun. The entire crew of four enemy were riddled by his bullets and fell dead.

"Pfc. Schauer's calm courage, his remarkable skill and accuracy, removed three enemy machine guns which hindered our advance, killed the entire crew in each case, and killed five enemy snipers."

For his deeds Pfc. Schauer was later justly awarded the Congressional Medal of Honor.

The part played by the engineers in the operation was largely completed during the preparational phase; however, their line companies were subattached on the basis of one squad per battalion, with an additional platoon attached to Task Force Paulick. They worked in close support of the infantry, clearing mines from roads and road shoulders, gapping tactical wire and minefields, with advancing troops. Enemy employment of mines and boobytraps was on a far heavier scale than anything previously encountered; there were even instances reported in which the Germans booby-trapped their own dead, in the hope of killing our medical personnel.

As the first twenty-four hours' fighting drew to a close, the shape of victory was already beginning to appear. While there was still contact with fixed enemy defenses all along the front, except in the sector of Task Force Paulick, the main enemy positions were known to have been broken through, with only reserve elements in previously prepared positions trying to keep the back door shut. Remaining resistance was strongest in front of Cisterna, but faded away progressively to the flanks.

Battle casualties on May 23 had been 995, believed to be the largest number suffered by any single United States Army division in one day in World War II, even though the attack was successful. The figure reveals in some measure the wholesale ferocity of fighting on both sides. During the next two days—May 24 and 25—the battle for Cisterna unfolded exactly according to plan, as though an invisible power, holding a copy of the field order, were directing the actions of both sides. Yet it must not be forgotten that the actual course of the battle was not the result of the foreordination of fate, but of meticulous planning, objective training, and above all, fiery execution and dogged hammering at objectives in the face of last-ditch opposition.

3d Division Infantrymen cautiously advance into a portion of the ruins of Cisterna.

The role of the 30th Infantry during this period was to implement its breakthrough west of Cisterna by continuing its drive northeast across Highway 7, toward Cori.

The last phase of the breakthrough occurred when Company F, attached to 1st Battalion, succeeded in driving north across the railroad track and overcoming enemy opposition there, at a point about two miles northwest of Cisterna. The enemy had tanks, SP guns and automatic weapons covering the rail bed with enfilade fire and every possible route for crossing the tracks was zeroed in with artillery and mortars. The Germans were extremely well dug-in (this was the old MLR dating from January and February), and automatic-weapon positions were protected by other weapons. Company F casualties in advancing to the railroad were not heavy, because numerous ditches provided favorable routes of approach.

Coordination between our tanks and infantry during the crossing was poor, and Company F suffered casualties from its supporting armor. The tanks were not informed when the infantry was forced out of its zone of advance, and fired into the foot troops when they changed course to outflank enemy weapons. However, the attack, carried on entirely during hours of darkness, was finally successful.

During the morning of May 24, Company F was returned to 2d Battalion, which was ordered to follow the 1st and 3d Battalions in their wide flanking drive north and east of Cisterna. While there was virtually no opposition from enemy in position along the route of advance, many enemy falling back from the 7th Infantry's attack retreated into 2d Battalion columns, forcing our troops to deploy locally and deal with them. Enemy in isolated positions around La Villa, which had already been passed through by the 7th Infantry, caused considerable trouble. Fire was also received from the Cisterna cemetery, which the battalion by-passed on the north. During the evening of May 24, fire was received from both front and rear, as the battalion reached and occupied its objectives, but the opposition was overcome during the night.

The morning of May 25 the battalion reverted to regimental reserve, both 1st and 3d Battalions having passed through it and begun the advance on Cori. The 2d Battalion moved out for Cori during the afternoon, following the other two battalions. About 800 yards short of the line of departure, which was a crossroad two miles northeast of Cisterna, the battalion received some casualties from friendly artillery fire. Shortly afterward six Allied planes flew over and bombed and strafed the road, causing casualties. This was blamed on the rapid advance of our forward elements, and the fact that the planes were apparently aiming at a battery of 88mm guns which had been recently abandoned and were still smoking. The planes flew perpendicular to the marching column, instead of parallel to it, which would have been the case had the troops been the target; also, only three planes dropped their bombs. The battalion went into an assembly area short of Cori that night.

During the morning May 24, 3d Battalion was alerted to move north up the Fosso Feminamorta, following 2d Battalion, to pass through 2d Battalion north of Cisterna and capture objectives 1000 yards northeast of the town. The battalion moved out about 1630, following 2d Battalion north to the railroad track, then southeast to La Villa. Along the eastern side of La Villa there was a small ditch, and two or three hundred yards farther east was a larger ditch; 2d Battalion started up this larger ditch, planning to cross Highway 7 and then move east cross-country to its objectives, thus by-passing Cisterna. Company L, following 2d Battalion, ran into a strong concentration of friendly artillery fire just after passing La Villa, and drew back to the protection of the smaller ditch. When the column moved forward again, it crossed Highway 7 just north of the cemetery. At this time, 7th Infantry launched an attack toward Cisterna from the northwest; the German reaction was the general firing of machine guns and mortars from the north edge of town. It was dark by this time, and the enemy had no observation, yet the battalion suffered several casualties. The battalion then drew back west of Highway 7, reorganized, moved several hundred yards north, crossed the highway, and proceeded east toward its objectives on a compass bearing. Company I was then leading.

The battalion reached its objectives (the crossroad two miles northeast of Cisterna, and high ground immediately northwest of the crossroad) and put in a defensive position prior to daylight May 25. The battalion had orders to attack at 0630 that morning toward Cori, with 1st Battalion on its right between it and the Cori-Cisterna road. However, the attack could not be coordinated by that time, due to difficulties of supply, so the battalion remained in position.

The attack got under way at 1600, with no opposition encountered. At 1700, however, the troops were caught in the same air attack that hit 2d Battalion, and Lieutenant Colonel Bennett, the battalion commander, was injured and evacuated. Lieutenant Colonel (then Major) Neddersen assumed command. The battalion had a series of objectives en route to Cori, and moved through the objectives without difficulty. The battalion reached the road junction just west of Cori at 2030, then moved due north to the Cori-Giuglianello road, closing and completing organization for defense by 2300.

By evening of May 24, Company A, which had captured twenty-six Germans in caves while clearing Fosso Feminamorta, had been returned to 1st Battalion, which assembled astride the railroad just east of Fosso Feminamorta. The battalion CP was in the ditch itself. Shortly after midnight the battalion received orders to move to the crossroad two miles northeast of Cisterna, relieve 3d Battalion there, and prepare for a coordinated attack toward Cori the following morning. The 3d Battalion had already moved out toward the crossroad; 1st Battalion was to follow roughly the same route, by-passing Cisterna on the north, and assemble on the objective, while 3d Battalion was to move a short distance to the north, prepared to attack toward Cori on the left of 1st Battalion. The Cori-Cisterna road was designated as the boundary between 30th Infantry on the left and 15th Infantry on the right.

Officers of the 1st Battalion, reaching the crossroad shortly after daylight on reconnaissance, found small elements of 3d Battalion at the crossroad with a squad outpost to the northeast. The battalion itself initiated its march in column of companies, in the order B, C. D (—), Headquarters and A. The battalion passed immediately beyond the northwestern limits of Cisterna, moving east, and received considerable fire (mostly mortar) from enemy in Cisterna prior to daylight. During the morning, Germans made continuous efforts to escape from Cisterna by infiltrating to the north and northeast along draws and ditches, and it was necessary to leave Company A behind to stop this infiltration and cover the battalion's rear. However, the battalion was able to reach the crossroad, relieve 3d Battalion and organize for the attack toward Cori. One company was placed west of the crossroad and patrols were sent to contact the 15th Infantry.

The battalion had not been in position long when it began receiving strong enemy artillery fire from medium and heavy guns to the north and northwest, and other artillery fire from Cori; there was some 88mm fire mixed in, but the bulk of the fire came in battalion concentrations of thirty to forty rounds. A group of friendly tanks in an assembly area just north of 1st Battalion doubtlessly drew the fire. Casualties in the 1st Battalion were light, as the men were well dispersed and dug-in, but movement and control were difficult.

The enemy artillery apparently began displacing

Cori, perched high upon the forward slopes of Monti Lepini was captured by the 3d Division in its "Push to Rome."

during the afternoon, as the intensity of fire diminished, and at about 1600 the battalion attacked as planned, with 3d Battalion on its left and 15th Infantry on the right. Enemy resistance had faded away during the day as scattered groups of Germans, cut off from their units and driven from their positions, retreated into the hills. There was virtually no resistance as the battalion advanced and after crossing the north-south railway east of Cisterna the battalion was moved out onto the highway, with only a patrol operating on the left flank. High ground immediately north of Cori was reached just before dark. One company was stationed in the mountains one mile north of Cori, but there were no enemy there. All personnel were greatly fatigued, and only minimum security personnel were kept alert while others slept.

During the 1st Battalion advance toward Cori, Company A passed through and continued on to Cori where it took eighteen prisoners. The battalion was then assembled north and east of Cori and outposts established.

The heaviest fighting during May 24 and 25 was done by 7th Infantry, which had the mission of capturing Cisterna itself and cleaning out the city. The 1st Battalion, which had been in reserve all during D-day, was committed to attack at daylight May 24. The battalion took its first objective, a nose north of the Cisterna-Ponte Rotto road about half way between those towns, with little difficulty, and immediately moved north to capture La Villa. Shortly before reaching the railroad track, at about 0930, Company C encountered fierce enemy fire and was halted. The enemy was dug in all along the railroad bed and on the high ground to the rear. The railroad bed itself was crisscrossed by enfilade fire from machine guns, rifles and 88mm guns. The approaches to the railroad were covered with antipersonnel and antitank mines.

By working one platoon across the railroad track at a time, Company C overran German positions and occupied a point north of the railroad shortly before noon. The company was rather disorganized, however, and in order to occupy La Villa, Company A was sent around Company C's right flank to take high ground east of La Villa. It reached its objective with only scattered rifle and machine-gun fire opposing it, and by its occupation of high ground outflanking La Villa on the east, forced the enemy to withdraw. Company C then moved in and cleaned out the area.

While a platoon of tanks and a platoon of TDs remained at La Villa and assisted by fire, Company B attacked and occupied the Cisterna cemetery 1000 yards northwest of town by 1600. The area was heavily pounded by our tanks and TDs and by Division Artillery, and the advance of 3d Battalion, 30th Infantry, to the north of the cemetery assisted in causing an enemy withdrawal into Cisterna. Company B had little trouble taking the cemetery, where it stopped and reorganized. The battalion organized a defensive position in this area, and repulsed one counterattack during the night, which came from the direction of the city. At 2200, 3d Battalion passed through 1st Battalion to assault Cisterna on the axis of Highway 7.

At 1400 May 25, 1st Battalion began its advance into Cisterna, following 3d Battalion. The battalion moved in column of companies in the order A, C and B. Seven medium tanks assisted the battalion in its move into the town. Many enemy strongpoints were encountered in buildings, in the streets and in Fosso di Cisterna. The enemy had taken full advantage of the four-month lull to build strong positions in the rubble caused by our bombing and shelling. Enemy at the north edge of town provided strong opposition for the tanks but were finally neutralized. Company A met the greatest resistance, but suffered only moderate casualties. Company C, which swung to the right of Company A, cleaned out opposition in its sector and then took up a defensive position in the east edge of town. While 3d Battalion was left in the city to clear out the last remaining enemy, 1st Battalion left town at 1700 May 25 and moved to an assembly area two miles north of Cisterna.

The 2d Battalion, which had advanced 1500 yards up the axis of the Isola Bella-Cisterna road during the first day, continued the attack astride the road on May

The remains of the statue that adorned the village square of Cisterna.

25, with Company G on the right of the road and Company E on the left. Enemy strongpoints on the immediate front had been evacuated during the night, and the only initial opposition was in the form of harassing artillery fire. When it was about 600 yards south of Cisterna, however, the enemy opened up with machine-gun, SP-gun, rifle and mortar fire from the railroad, and artillery fire increased greatly. The battalion was unable to advance during the remainder of the day.

At 2100, Companies E and G attacked abreast across the railroad and both got across after heavy close combat. The enemy was thoroughly dug-in and Company G suffered several casualties from mines around the Cisterna railroad station. In spite of extreme darkness and heavy resistance, the attack progressed well because it had been planned in every particular and previously rehearsed. After the railroad line was breached, Company F was sent into town at 0300 May 25, and by daylight had one-third of the town in its hands. Casualties crossing the railroad line were not excessive, probably because the battalion crossed on a wide front at six different places. German lines were then attacked from the rear and most of the enemy killed.

During the morning of May 25 the battalion was joined by eight light tanks, two medium tanks and two platoons of Cannon Company. Company F was halted by resistance in a large castle at the center of the town, so Company G was sent around the south side of the castle with two platoons of tanks as assault guns. Company G advanced along the Fosso di Cisterna, but it too was held up by fire from the castle. The castle had only one entrance, and it was covered by an antitank gun. Company F placed a machine gun on top of a house across from the castle; while the machine gun fired on the enemy antitank gun and kept the crew away from it, a medium tank roared through the castle entrance and destroyed the gun. Company F closed in and routed 250 prisoners from a cave underneath the castle. Included were the commanding officer of 955th Infantry Regiment and his staff. Company G was then able to push through the town and took sixty more prisoners from caves north of Cisterna. The 1st and 3d Battalions were contacted, and resistance in the town was completely wiped out by dusk May 25.

The 3d Battalion, 7th Infantry, spent the first night of combat—May 23-24—south of the Cisterna-Ponte Rotto highway, and a few hundred yards east of Ponte Rotto. Next morning, 1st Battalion passed through 3d Battalion, and the latter followed in column of companies in the order L, I, K and M. Upon reaching the Cisterna-Ponte Rotto road, moving north, the battalion headquarters group came under a concentration of twenty-five rounds of enemy 88mm air-burst, wounding two officers and six men. The battalion executive was wounded and evacuated, and the Company M commander took his post.

The battalion passed through 1st Battalion at La Villa, having suffered few other casualties. During the evening it moved out toward high ground across Highway 7, and northwest of the Cisterna cemetery. Some elements of the battalion became mingled with 3d Battalion, 30th Infantry, but no other trouble was encountered as 1st Battalion had cleaned out all enemy resistance.

Upon reaching its objective, the battalion swung southeast to attack Cisterna along the axis of Highway 7. With Company I on the right and Company K on the left, the battalion attacked at 2000 May 24. A half-hour before the attack the battalion commander was wounded, and the former commander of Company M, Capt. Glenn Rathbun, took command of the battalion. Resistance at the cemetery was heavy (although Company B had previously captured it—most probably, enemy retreating from Cisterna had bumped into the 1st Battalion around the cemetery and had gone into temporary defensive positions). The enemy still had positions east of the cemetery, and delivered strong mortar and artillery fire. The two leading companies fought all night and into the next day, coordinating a second attack at 1630, when they received excellent support from a platoon of tanks and a platoon of TDs. Between the Fosso Centri di Pantano and the highway the battalion received a small amount of fire, but this was followed by the prompt surrender of 120 prisoners, including several officers. Cisterna had already been taken but there was considerable by-passed resistance to be cleaned up. The enemy had taken to numerous caves and abandoned dugouts which were prepared against attack from the south or west, but could not hold out against the drive from the northwest.

The battalion moved to the northwest end of town to complete its occupation, then moved to an assembly area about three miles above Cisterna. During the last phase of the attack a platoon of Company L, which was intended to be used in battle sleds following medium tanks, was out of the fight altogether after the tanks were disabled shortly after H-hour. The platoon did not rejoin the company until May 28.

Resistance on the front of the 15th Infantry lasted longer than that against the 30th, possibly because the attack of both the 7th and 30th Infantry Regiments passed to the west of the town, although resistance was lighter during the second day than during the first. Early May 24, 3d Battalion reached the road junction two miles south of Cisterna which 2d Battalion had captured the evening before, and immediately attacked up the improved road toward Cisterna. There were about thirty-five houses lining this stretch of road, but none was strongly held. Chief resistance came from SP and artillery fire from pieces located northeast of the railroad. As the battalion approached the intersection with Highway 7, it received fire from an open field to the west, and from Fosso di Cisterna to the east. This fire was neutralized by mortar and artillery fire, plus mortar fire from 2d Battalion which was fighting in Fosso di Cisterna. The 7th Infantry Battle Patrol was contacted at the road junction, and the Patrol assisted 2d Battalion in cleaning out resistance between Highway 7 and the railroad.

Meanwhile two companies of 3d Battalion advanced north along Highway 7, reaching the railroad overpass at the southern edge of the city. The battalion went into position along the railroad shortly after dark and sent outposts across the railroad. Enemy fire during the night was moderate. TDs took up positions south of the battalion area, and a platoon of tanks, which had joined the battalion during the day, occupied positions in "Kraut Woods."

At 0530 May 25 the battalion left its position, moved southeast about 2,000 yards on Highway 7, then turned northeast and completed the encirclement of Cisterna by occupying an assembly area 2,000 yards northeast of town, adjacent to 30th Infantry positions. At 1000, the battalion moved out toward Cori, in an attack coordinated with 1st Battalion and 30th Infantry, 3d Battalion advancing along the southeast side of the Cisterna-Cori highway. There was virtually no resistance at 2000 and the battalion remained in this position during the night, sending patrols into Cori from the south and west.

The 2d Battalion had more trouble May 24 than did 3d Battalion. At first light Company F was sent up Fosso di Cisterna, crossing under the railroad bridge and moving onto open ground north of the railroad. Here, too, the ground was flat, and foot-high wheat provided the only concealment. When the company reached a point about 500 yards north of the railroad the enemy opened up with fire from an estimated three tanks. Enemy infantry was well dug in to the north, immediately east of Cisterna, and occupied several house strongpoints that swept the company with cross fire.

Company F moved out at about 1330 to seize and hold a large strongly-fortified house 600 yards beyond our foremost elements. It was situated in the center of a flat open field, and all approaches to it were covered with interlocking bands of grazing machine-gun fire. Prior reconnaissance had indicated the advisability of proceeding along a narrow draw which appeared to lead directly to the objective, in order to minimize what seemed must inevitably be numerous casualties.

Pvt. James H. Mills, in his second day of combat, was the leading man of the foremost platoon, as number one scout. After proceeding about 300 yards, he disappeared around a sharp turn in the fosso. A vicious burst of machine-gun fire was heard, followed by a single rifle shot. Second Lieutenant Arthur J. Mueller, foremost man, rushed around the corner. There he saw Mills leaning against the steep bank covering an enemy soldier with his rifle. Crumpled over a machine gun lay another enemy soldier, dead, shot between the eyes.

"I had to do it, sir, he almost got me," said Mills apologetically. Then he turned on his heel and struck out down the ditch once more, with Lieutenant Mueller close behind.

First, Mills captured a German in the act of pulling the pin from a potato masher grenade. As the prisoner was being searched by others, Mills spotted another soldier immediately above the men's position, and killed him as he was in the act of pulling the pin of a grenade. The advance then continued, with Mills still leading.

Once more he rounded a bend, to engage in a duel with six enemy soldiers. He charged.

"The sheer guts displayed by Private Mills must have unnerved the enemy, for when he had reached a point within about ten feet of them they threw their helmets to the ground and chorused 'Kamerad!' as loud as they could shout," narrated S/Sgt. Dewey A. Olsen. "Six heavily-armed Germans had surrendered to one lone United States soldier."

Enemy mortar fire began plastering the edges of the draw. Mills pointed out a shallow drainage ditch which ran from the draw to within fifty yards of the house-objective. It was pointed out also that although the ditch was too shallow to permit passage without being observed by the enemy, a strong diversion by fire might allow a force to proceed up the ditch while the enemy's attention was centered elsewhere.

So . . . Mills took it upon himself as a one-man task force to create the diversion. He climbed from the cover of the draw under heavy enemy fire and emptied his M-1 toward the enemy, shouting defiance all the while. Then he sought cover and reloaded. A small group, meanwhile, began working its way toward the house.

Said Pfc. Charles L. Hyson, Jr.: "I do not know how many times Private Mills repeated this process but he was still standing out there firing when we reached the closest point to the house and began our assault.

"The enemy had been completely taken in by Private Mills' plan and we caught the enemy with his 'pants down,' taking the position and forcing his surrender before he knew what was happening. We captured twenty-two enemy soldiers, three machine guns, and three heavy mortars without a single casualty. Private Mills was directly responsible for our success."

Private Mills later received the Congressional Medal of Honor.

Supporting TDs played an important part in the attack. They moved to a point near the railroad southeast of the battalion and fired across the battalion front at strongpoints on the left front. At this time Company E was committed in an effort to outflank the enemy on the right, but flat terrain continued to work against the battalion and little progress was made.

Under cover of darkness, antitank guns were brought up, and just after first light they were brought to bear on enemy strongpoints, neutralizing most of them. The remainder of the enemy withdrew and the battalion advanced to a crossroad about a mile and a half northeast of Cisterna.

The battalion then received orders to move to a U-shaped patch of woods on flat ground two miles due east of Cisterna. The battalion displaced by company, Company C arriving first with no opposition. There reorganization was completed and the battalion marched to Cori, taking a route well to the right of the Cisterna-Cori road, and spent the night in an assembly area on the northern slopes of Monte Arrestino.

As dawn broke May 24, the 15th Infantry Battle Patrol was engaged in front of Task Force Paulick in a successful action against an enemy platoon. Company A reorganized preparatory to continuing the attack, with its objective a road junction 1000 yards north of the woods occupied the previous night. The Battle Patrol reported the location of an extensive minefield 300 yards short of the junction, and extending 300 yards on either side of it. A heavy concentration of artillery and tank fire was laid on enemy positions, and under its protection the squad of engineers cleared three paths through the mines. The artillery fire continued while the infantry went through the left gap and the tanks through the center, reducing the outpost at the road junction and taking five prisoners.

Company A continued to a strongpoint 600 yards farther north, where twelve enemy and two machine guns were captured. One platoon remained at this position and supported by fire another platoon, which moved southeast to a point where Highway 7 contacts the railroad bed. The platoon encountered strong artillery and small-arms fire and was forced to move back south of the railroad embankment. At 1430 the remainder of the battalion joined Task Force Paulick in order to force a crossing of the railroad. Attached armor remained with the battalion. Company A casualties had been high, with one officer and eight enlisted men killed, three officers and fifty-four enlisted men wounded and two enlisted men missing.

The railroad embankment was the enemy's strongest line of defense. It was covered with enfilade fire by automatic weapons and SP guns, and was completely blanketed by prepared artillery and mortar concentrations. All the enemy's fire was brought to bear on Company B, the first to storm the tracks, and although fire was heavy the company got nearly 700 yards north of the tracks before it was stopped. There it drew fire from two enemy tanks, one of which was destroyed by our TDs.

Another heroic action was performed the same day by Sgt. Sylvester Antolak, in which he lost his life. Mission of Company B, 15th Infantry, was to cut the railroad near Cisterna and capture commanding terrain on the far side.

The 1st platoon crossed the railroad bed without encountering enemy fire and it appeared that the Germans had fled. As the lead scouts of the 2d platoon were about to follow, a hail of enemy machine gun, machine pistol and rifle fire burst on them from an enemy strongpoint about 200 yards to the right front. The German plan was evident: to bar the advance of the 2d platoon, then seal off and destroy the 1st platoon.

Antolak saw the impending danger and, ordering a base of fire set up, called on his men to follow him as he charged the German position, fully thirty yards ahead of his squad. As he moved forward in short rushes across the bare, coverless terrain he became a prime target for the enemy's concentrated fire.

After advancing a few dozen yards he was hit by automatic-weapons fire and knocked to the ground. Jumping to his feet he again charged, his shoulder gashed and bleeding. Again he was hit and knocked to the ground, and again he picked himself up to resume the advance.

Said S/Sgt. Audie L. Murphy: "The 200-yard interval was narrowing; the Germans were firing their machine gun, their "spit" pistols, and rifles about as fast as they could squeeze the triggers. They must have sensed that Sergeant Antolak was sparking the charge and that he was the man they had to knock out."

With but fifty yards to go Sergeant Antolak was hit and thrown to the ground a third time, his right arm shattered by the burst of automatic fire. He wedged his submachine gun into his left armpit, staggered to his feet, and continued his grim charge. He advanced to within fifteen yards of the enemy strongpoint and killed both the gunner and assistant gunner with a long burst of fire. The remaining ten Germans surrendered to this man whom their bullets could not stop.

Another German strongpoint 100 yards to the right immediately opened fire. "We urged Sergeant Antolak to take cover in the machine-gun emplacement he had just captured," said Cpl. William H. Harrison, "while we arranged to get him medical aid. He looked too weak from his wounds and loss of blood to keep on going."

Antolak refused to consider this proposition. Again he led the attack against this new strongpoint, with the remainder of his men following at an interval of several yards. He made sixty yards before being hit by the concentrated firepower. By sheer will power he managed to stagger forward another ten yards before collapsing. The squad pushed forward, assaulted the German position and overran it, taking eight prisoners. When the men returned to Sergeant Antolak he was dead.

"His heroic action had enabled the squad to kill or capture twenty Germans, wipe out the last enemy pockets in the area and prevent the 1st platoon from being cut off," stated Pfc. Marion Ellis.

Sergeant Antolak was awarded posthumously the Congressional Medal of Honor.

Enemy were detected forming on Company F's right flank, apparently for a counterattack, so the Battle Patrol was committed. It met approximately a company of Germans in a small woods north of the tracks, and it was found necessary to commit Company A again. Company A received heavy fire while crossing the tracks and suffered further casualties, so Company C was sent across the tracks to the left of Company B. Company C provided the necessary manpower to overcome the enemy, and after two hours of moderate firing reached a U-shaped patch of woods two miles east of Cisterna, which 2d Battalion was to pass through later. Long-range fire harassed Company C in the woods during the night.

Meanwhile, Company A had eliminated the threatened counterattack, and joined the remainder of the battalion in the woods at 0400 May 23. Tanks had been unable to cross the tracks during the daylight May 24, so during the night the engineers bulldozed two crossings and the armor rejoined the battalion at dawn May 25.

At 0800 the battalion attacked toward Cori with the mission of occupying high ground immediately south of town and protecting the Division's right flank. Company C led the attack and encountered strong machine-gun fire from enemy who had withdrawn the previous day. The terrain was rolling at the beginning of the attack but became steeper as the troops moved northeast. One tank was lost in the morning from enemy artillery fire. Both the 3d Division and 15th Infantry Battle Patrols were operating with the battalion, to maintain contact with SSF on the right and provide flank security.

Company C's drive slowed down about half way to the objective, and Company A was passed through. Advance patrols of the battalion were on the objective by 1500, and the battalion had occupied the entire objective by 1900. This position was held during the night.

With the capture of Cisterna and Cori at approximately the same time—late afternoon of May 25—the breakthrough was complete. No organized resistance remained in the Division zone of advance. While the Division had suffered heavily—approximately 1400 killed and wounded in three day's fighting—the enemy had suffered far more heavily, losing nearly 1600 prisoners to the 3d Division alone, and probably an equal number in killed and wounded. The 362d Infantry Division, ordered to defend in place, had been annihilated by the combined attack of the 3d Division and 1st Armored Division, and the 715th Infantry Division had lost at least half its front-line effectives.

In considering the success of this attack, it is noteworthy that there was little straggling. Hospitals reported that wounded 3d Division personnel were anxious to rejoin their units in combat, a not commonly-encountered phenomenon. This not only bespeaks high morale, but explains why companies, although greatly reduced in strength, could continue to attack and move forward in the face of terrific fire. Troops advanced well-deployed, minimizing losses, but every man was imbued with the desire to close with the enemy, and it was unnecessary to drive or push the men forward. This also bespeaks leadership of highest caliber, which was demonstrated time and again by junior officers who suddenly found important commands thrust upon them, and who turned in performances which could not be excelled.

Thus ended the Second Battle of Cisterna.

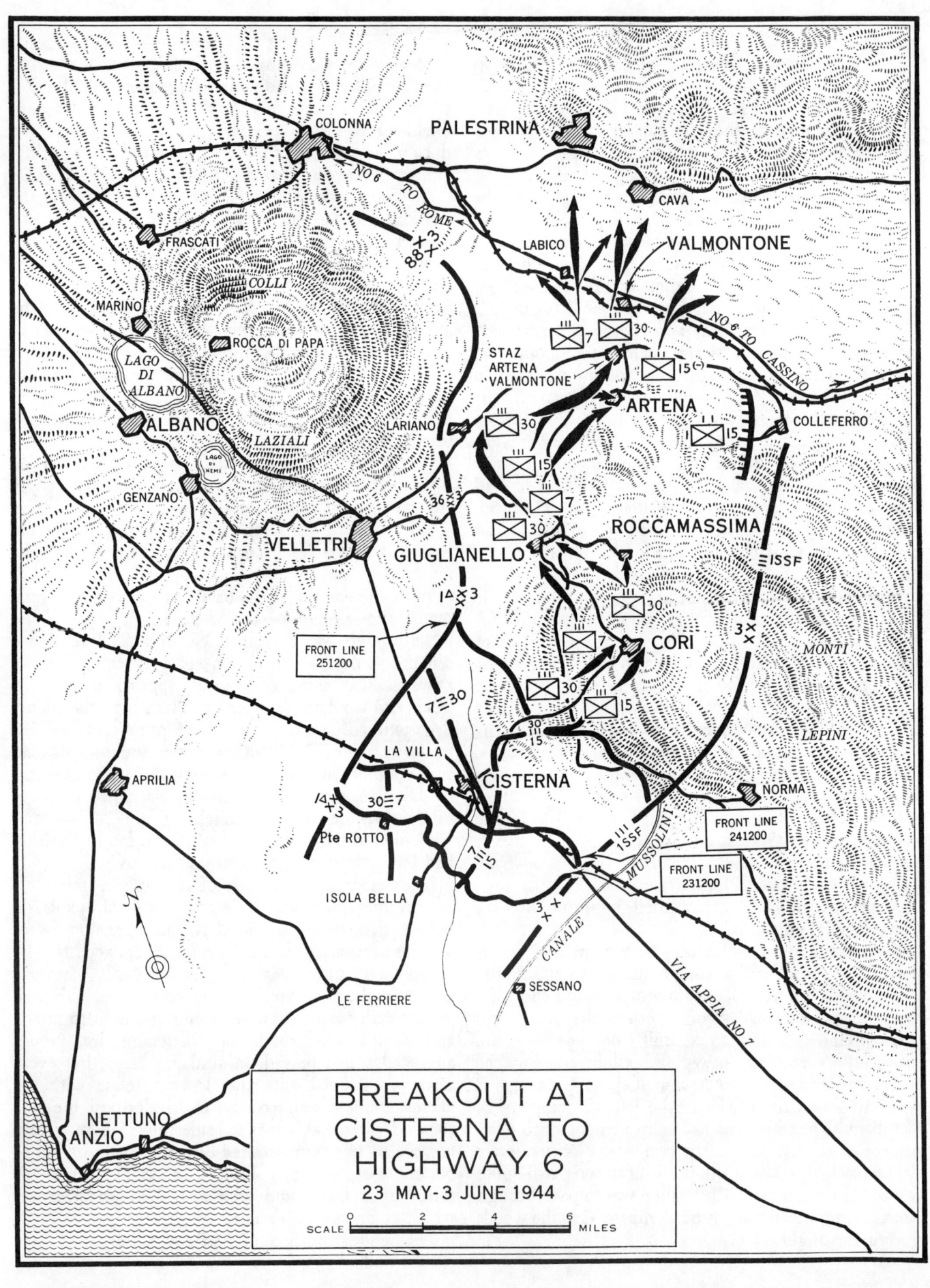

2: Cisterna—Rome Operation

26 May to 5 June

THE morning of 26 May marked the beginning of the Division's rapid pursuit of the enemy after German defenses around Cisterna had crumbled. Following the night of May 25-26, spent in assembly areas in the vicinity of Cori, the Division headed northward with 2d Battalion, 15th Infantry, in the lead. Because there was practically no enemy opposition, the battalion moved on foot on the Cori-Giuglianello road with patrols protecting the flanks. Shortly after noon, while rounding a sharp curve at the outskirts of Cori, the battalion column was bombed and strafed by five United States P-40 fighter-bombers. The first three planes of the flight dropped their bombs, scoring direct hits on the highway. More than a hundred men were killed or wounded, including seventy from the 2d Battalion, 15th Infantry, and the Adjutant and S-2 of the 30th Infantry. A number of jeeps loaded with ammunition were hit, and additional casualties were caused by exploding 37mm antitank and small-arms ammunition.

A considerable number of individual acts of heroism took place during this incident by soldiers who braved the fires and exploding shells to assist wounded comrades. Several jeeps were hit alongside abandoned German tanks in a narrow defile about 300 yards from the curve, tying up traffic for five or six hours.

Following the bombing the battalion reorganized and moved on foot toward Giuglianello, arriving there about 1800 hours.

Three large by-passes were constructed by the engineers between Cori and Giuglianello to replace bridges demolished by the enemy. The bridges were sighted by artillery liaison planes, reported to the engineers, and work was under way shortly after elements of the 2d Battalion reached the river. The gap was fifty feet deep and sixty feet wide. Bulldozers were put across the gap shortly after work began and two other by-passes were finished a half hour after the first was completed.

Later a supply road from Cisterna to Cori was built for the 1st Battalion of the 15th Infantry.

The engineers also cleared the road of abandoned enemy vehicles and inspected for boobytraps. Four boobytrapped 88mm guns between Cisterna and Giuglianello were made harmless and 150 vehicles were cleared from the road.

The other two battalions of the 15th Infantry followed the 2d Battalion to Giuglianello, with the bombing incident at Cori the only obstacle. The three battalions assembled around Giuglianello at 1800 hours and about an hour and a half later entrucked for Artena. The truck column moved with 3d, 1st and 2d Battalions in that order, and had traveled only three or four miles when it came under intense German artillery fire. The 3d and 1st Battalions halted in that position for the night while the 2d Battalion, led personally by Brig. Gen. Whitfield P. Shepard, Assistant Division Commander, continued on wheels toward Artena, with the belief that Artena was in friendly hands, a false report by an adjoining unit commander.

Night had fallen when General Shepard halted the column about 700 yards west of Artena and went forward to seek a truck "turnaround." The General was fired on by enemy small arms and his aide slightly

Behind Cori, the Germans had placed a cemetery, where they had buried their Beachhead dead.

Villagers probe about the ruins of the village of Roccamassima.

wounded, so he ordered the battalion to organize a defense west of the town. Meanwhile rear elements of the motor column had become separated from the forward units, so Major Potter, Battalion Executive Officer halted the rear vehicles and sent out a contact patrol to find the forward part of the column. At that time enemy aircraft came over the column and the men hastily detrucked to escape the bombing and strafing. In detrucking, the men ran headlong into three German machine-gun positions covering that sector of the road. The enemy could have caused more confusion among the already frightened men by opening fire, but apparently taken completely by surprise by the headlong rush from the trucks, they gave up without firing a shot.

The remainder of the battalion was contacted shortly thereafter and a defense organized along the road facing north and east, with Company G on the right, Company F on the west and Company E behind F on the south side of the road. That position was held until morning.

The 30th Infantry followed the 15th on May 26, with the 1st Battalion protecting the Division's right flank. Shortly after noon the 1st Battalion with Company A leading, marched up the mountain trail leading due north from Cori, passing through the 1st Special Service Force, which was assembled in the northern outskirts of Cori. The SSF then followed the 1st Battalion toward Roccamassima, a small town sitting atop a high peak overlooking the Division's main route of advance. About 1500 yards south of Roccamassima, two enemy were seen in the woods down the mountainside to the west. A squad from Company A was sent down to investigate, and heavy machine-gun fire was placed on the vicinity where the enemy had been seen. The fire brought several Germans running out, and the remainder of the 1st Battalion platoon was sent down to assist the squad in attacking them. The enemy showed no disposition to fight however, and the platoon took about ninety-four prisoners, who stated their mission was to go to Cisterna, reinforce the garrison there, and fight to the last. Three enemy were killed in this action. The battalion reached Roccamassima at about 1600 hours May 26 and organized a defensive position there before dark, covering the Division's right flank. During this period the Special Service Force started passing through to the north, all three regiments marching in column over the mountain trail.

The 2d Battalion moved to a position north and east of Cori the morning of May 26, where it spent the day regrouping and recovering from the losses it suffered around Cisterna. The 3d Battalion was ordered at 0700 hours to proceed north to Giuglianello and establish a defensive position west of that town. The battalion moved into position along a north-south ridge, extending to the main road about a mile west of Giuglianello. This was accomplished by 1400 hours and the rest of the day was spent organizing the position for all-around defense and laying wire on the final protective line.

The 7th Infantry, held up while it cleaned out Cisterna, followed the Division to the north. It moved in column along the railroad bed west of Cisterna in advance-guard formation, with 1st, 2d and 3d Battalions in that order. The regiment was held up by a fire fight between the enemy and 6th Armored Infantry Regiment along the Colli Rotundo, about two miles from Artena. At dusk the 3d Battalion moved cross-country and took up a position on the regimental right flank west of Artena, on the forward slope of a large hill mass south of the town. During the move, with Company K in the lead, about thirty-five Germans were encountered in a meeting engagement. A 30-minute fight resulted, with four enemy killed, three wounded and three captured. The battalion then moved into position on the slope, picking up straggler enemy prisoners during the night.

Shortly after daylight of May 27, the 2d Battalion, 15th Infantry, began its attack against Artena. At about the same time a roadblock held by Company G west of town captured an enemy amphibious jeep containing two staff officers from the *Hermann Goering Panzer* Division. They were on reconnaissance prior to bringing their unit into combat, and provided the 3d Division its first contact with the *Panzer-Fallschirmjäger* since the Anzio beachhead days of March.

Still under command of General Shepard, the 2d Battalion attacked toward Artena with G and F Companies abreast and Company E following F.

Both Companies G and F were halted outside Artena by fire from enemy Flakwagons, heavy artillery and small-arms fire, although Company G was able to cut the Artena-Valmontone road north of Artena. The enemy was well established in the town and it wasn't until Company E was sent through Company G on the right that the battalion was able to break into the town. It took nearly seven hours to cover the 500-600 yards distance. Casualties were relatively high, with more than seventy men killed or wounded.

While the 2d Battalion fought for Artena, the 3d Battalion, 15th Infantry, marched toward the town and went into an assembly area in a 30-foot ditch at 1800 hours. A lucky enemy artillery shell landed in the ditch and caused thirteen casualties in Company M, wiping out an entire machine-gun section. Before dark the battalion was to have moved to Artena while the 2d Battalion regrouped. Company K got its forward elements into town but most of the company was under perfect enemy observation and was held up. At nightfall the company fell back to its assembly area in the ditch, then later the night of May 27-28 moved back into the town, which had previously been cleared of enemy. The 1st Battalion went into position west of the town, at daylight May 27, where it remained to protect the regiment's left flank during the attack.

The 30th Infantry moved but little during the 27th. The 3d Battalion moved its defensive position 1000 yards further west to close a gap between the 3d Division and elements on the left, and a new defensive position was organized. Wire was laid and a patrol sent along a road toward Velletri for about a mile, then swung south around the lower end of the small lake. The patrol returned and reported contact with a patrol from the 36th Division. The battalion commander, Major R. H. Neddersen, and S-3, Capt. James L. Osgard, then went to contact units of the 36th personally to determine the exact location of the latter's forward elements.

The 2d Battalion ran into considerable fire from enemy retreating north and other enemy units moving south to reinforce their retreating comrades. This resulted in a number of meeting engagements, with neither side able to use prepared positions. Instead both the 2d Battalion and enemy relied on available terrain features.

At about 1000 hours the 1st Battalion (minus Company A, which was left on the mountain as security), moved to a position northwest of Giuglianello, reaching positions there during the afternoon without opposition. The battalion was placed in regimental reserve and remained in the one location during the 28th.

In the morning of May 27th the 7th Infantry moved toward Artena and in the afternoon took up a position southwest of the town. The regiment had three battalions on a line, with the 1st Battalion in the center, 3d Battalion on the right and 2d Battalion on the left. The position was organized for all-around defense, wire was laid, some mines were laid, and automatic weapons were sited to cover the rolling terrain. The 3d Battalion was ordered to contact the SSF on top of a hill mass south of Artena. The SSF arrived about dusk and the battalion (less Company L) went into position on the northern slope of the mass. Company L was detached to help Task Force Howze's tanks in their establishment of road blocks on the Division's left flank.

During the morning of the 28th, 7th Infantry received orders to oust the enemy from his positions along the railroad tracks between Artena and Valmontone. The 1st and 3d Battalions spearheaded the attack. Lt. Col. Frank M. Izenour started his 1st Battalion with A Company on the right and Company B on the left, Company C in reserve and Company D supporting the attack. Company A ran into extremely heavy opposition, for the *Hermann Goering Panzer* Division, fresh from the north, had had two days in which to get set for our battle-weary soldiers.

The enemy was dug-in on the reverse slope of the rolling hills and was getting a great deal of assistance from self-propelled guns and artillery. From noon until 2000 hours Company A fought without letup, at which time it reached its objective 2,000 yards from the line of departure. Enemy automatic weapons refused to move from their positions until blasted out by supporting tank fire, hand grenades or point-blank small-arms fire. The only concealment provided our attacking forces was the two-foot high wheat. In the words of Colonel Izenour, "Company A was able to reach its objective only because my boys wanted that ground worse than Goering's did."

The position taken by Company A was at a junction of the highway and railroad tracks. Immediately after reaching its objective Company A dug in. Company B, on the left, had a great deal less trouble during its attack. Its main trouble was caused when the right platoon wandered too far to the north and encountered a column of enemy troops marching down the road. A fire fight resulted. Company B's platoon suffered a few casualties and captured ten prisoners. After the brief skirmish the company moved without opposition into position near the railroad to the left of Company A. Although it had little trouble moving forward, Company B was prevented from giving more than a small amount of assistance to Company A because the rolling hills obscured vision.

Meanwhile the 3d Battalion was meeting the same kind of resistance as Company A. With Company I on the right and Company K on the left (Company L was still with Task Force Howze's tanks) the battalion crossed the road west of Artena and moved out without too much opposition at first. At a point 200 yards south of the east-west railroad north of Artena the enemy opened up with all he had. Heavy machine-gun fire, from German positions on the high ground north of the railroad, stopped I Company. The company reorganized early in the afternoon and without additional help started out again. Meanwhile Company E had been able to move about 400 yards beyond the battalion objective, which was a hill mass nearly 1500 yards wide extending from a road junction east to a large knoll. However, the company was forced to pull back to the objective because of intense fire received from the same enemy that was firing on Company I. Company I, advancing by fire and movement, contacted Company K on the objective early in the evening and the two companies set up a defense on the objective.

At this time Company L rejoined the battalion, under the command of 1st Lt. Ralph Yates, who had taken over when Capt. Blaikie was wounded on the 24th. Lieutenant Yates personally led a patrol from his company three miles to the west along the railroad without contacting the Special Service Force or the enemy. Contact with friendly units was finally made the morning of the 29th when Company C came up on the left and the SSF on the right.

Except for the 3d Battalion which reverted to Division control behind the 30th Infantry, the 15th Infantry remained in its original positions during the 28th. Company I was detached and established road blocks in the mountains east of the Giuglianello-Artena road preparatory to the attack on Valmontone of June 1.

The 2d Battalion, 30th Infantry, remained on the high ground west of Giuglianello the 28th to protect the north-south highway from Giuglianello to Artena against enemy attack from the west. The 3d Battalion received orders to attack toward Lariano and to go as far as the ridge 500 yards east of the Velletri-Artena railroad and set up a defense. Patrols had already reported that no enemy was short of the objective, and when the battalion reached the ridge without opposition, the commanding officer, Major Nedderson, obtained permission to move forward to the railroad track and organize a defense there. This was done without incident. Company I put an outpost on the south flank, tied in with the 36th Division, and Company L established a platoon outpost just south of Lariano.

During the night of May 28-29 enemy patrols and larger units began moving down into Lariano and attempting to infiltrate our forward positions.

The Division received badly-needed replacements during the night of May 28-29, each battalion getting from 150 to 200 new men. These men were needed to replace the losses suffered by all the battalions at Cisterna, by the 15th Infantry at Artena and the 7th Infantry in its push north of Artena.

The 30th Infantry moved toward Lariano the morning of the 29th with the mission of covering the Velletri-Artena road and protecting the Division's main supply route (the Cori-Giuglianello-Artena road). The regiment attacked to the northwest with the 1st Battalion, now commanded by Lt. Col. Allen F. Bacon, in the center, 3d Battalion on the left and the 2d on the right. The 1st Battalion reached and occupied positions between the Velletri-Artena road and the railroad which paralleled the road to the east.

Other units had preceded the 1st Battalion into Lariano, and reported no enemy there. However, when 1st Battalion sent its patrols into the town they were severely shelled from the direction of Velletri, and began meeting aggressive German patrols well equipped with automatic weapons and camouflaged uniforms. Enemy tanks and armored cars also came into Lariano in small numbers, but did not remain there. A period of weird, difficult fighting in the vineyards and terraces around Lariano followed. The 1st Battalion had succeeded in passing through, without resistance, a complete system of previously prepared enemy field works, dug by Italian labor and carefully camouflaged, forming part of the enemy's Velletri-Valmontone line. Enemy patrols first encountered were the advance elements of the *Hermann Goering* Division, which had come down from the north to man this defense line. The Goering troops never assaulted our positions east of Lariano, but made continuous efforts to infiltrate our lines and reach their own prepared defenses. There was a great deal of sniping and fighting by individuals and small groups; in one case, one of our 37mm anti-tank guns in a forward position "picked off" an enemy sniper. First Battalion patrols went into Lariano, as the enemy did also; sometimes these patrols would meet and exchange fire there. Neither side made an initial effort to occupy the town, however.

The Germans, unable to occupy their prepared positions, were forced to dig in hastily west of Lariano. Our patrols reported many of these locations, and our continuous mortar fire was later learned to have produced heavy enemy casualties.

The 2d Battalion attacked in a column of companies —E, F, G and 3d Battalion's Company I, which was attached to 2d Battalion for the mission. The terrain was rolling and wheat fields provided little cover, especially since the battalion's right flank was open. Tanks were not used in force but were committed piecemeal and in the opinion of the battalion's commanding officer, Lt. Col. Woodrow W. Stromberg, were not far enough forward to support the infantry satisfactorily. In many cases hostile machine-gun nests could have been more easily eliminated if tank support had been closer. Two tanks were put out of action by enemy artillery.

The 3d Battalion experienced little trouble moving into position, but was bothered by the enemy's infiltration tactics after the regiment's objective had been reached. Fifty enemy attacked Company L's outpost the evening of May 29 but were driven off with the aid of artillery and mortar fire. Several small patrol skirmishes took place in the area between the battalion's outposts.

The 1st and 3d Battalions of the 7th Infantry remained in place the night of May 28-29 after their attack, but the 2d Battalion moved northeast to establish a roadblock at a point where the road and railroad cross. Companies E and G moved abreast and ran into enemy opposition at the objective. After an hour's battle, the infantry fire supported by mortars and artillery, the enemy withdrew and the battalion went into position with G on the left, E on the right, F in reserve.

All during the day the 3d Battalion could see German tanks moving into position on the high ground to the north. The battalion located its heavy machine guns and antitank guns on high ground south of the main line and fired long-range, harassing fire at the enemy. More than 2,000 rounds of 81mm mortar ammunition were fired during the day at enemy moving into position, plus additional artillery. Four enemy *Nebelwerfers* were silenced by our artillery fire. Two platoons of Company L moved to the right to fill in the gap between the 3d Battalion and the SSF on the right. This continual exchange of fire between our artillery and mortars and the enemy's artillery and SP guns continued through the night of 29-30 May.

The entire 15th Infantry remained in position north of Artena during this period to prevent the loss of the town in case of an enemy counterattack from the northwest.

Only action during the night of 29-30 May was an enemy counterattack along the axis of the Artena-Valmontone road. The bulk of this attack hit the SSF and did not affect the 3d Battalion, 7th Infantry. The 1st Battalion, 15th Infantry, was also hit, but received assistance from 2d Battalion, 15th Infantry, and the enemy's attempt to break through our line was repulsed all along the front.

The next morning the 2d Battalion of the 15th attacked northward astride the Artena-Valmontone road to push its defensive line farther north from Artena and pull up even with the rest of the Division's front. The tank-infantry team was at its best in this attack. Tanks moved abreast of the infantry, blasting enemy positions with 75mm and small-arms fire while the infantry mopped up stragglers. The attack halted short of a woods, about halfway between Artena and Valmontone, facing the enemy who was well dug-in along the wood line.

The rest of the Division remained in position from the 29th to the 31st, improving its defensive positions, laying wire and mines and improving all installations. Aggressive patrolling was carried out to the east, north and west to maintain contact with the enemy and to gain information about his positions. All this time the enemy worked on his own positions, laying a great deal of wire, and hastened to completion construction of positions on the ridge line just south of Highway 7 east and west of Valmontone. The 2d Battalion, 7th Infantry was relieved by a battalion of the 88th Infantry Division the night of May 30-31 and went into an assembly area well behind the front. It was attached to the 30th Infantry for the forthcoming attack on the 1st of June.

Shortly after noon of May 31, the 7th Infantry was ordered to push forward in an effort to maintain contact with the 88th Division on the left, which was attacking to the north. At 1400 hours the 1st Battalion commander sent C Company ahead to occupy Hill 331 against scattered but strong enemy resistance. A platoon of Company C reached the hill and outposted the position while the remainder of the battalion moved up.

At the same time a platoon of Company L was ordered to move out about 400 yards beyond the main line of resistance to occupy a piece of high ground. The platoon reached its objective in less than fifteen minutes, but twenty minutes later was subjected to a terrific enemy artillery barrage followed by a German counterattack down the nose of the high ground. In addition the platoon had both flanks exposed and received fire from both sides. The platoon leader was killed shortly after the counterattack got started, when an enemy artillery shell landed in his hole. The same shell also killed the officer's radio operator and left the platoon out of communication with the rest of the battalion. At 1600 hours four tanks were sent out to screen the platoon's withdrawal, and one was almost immediately destroyed by enemy antitank fire. Company K was alerted to help the stranded platoon but shortly thereafter, a change of orders sent it to cover an objective of the 1st Battalion. A second tank was destroyed and the platoon was forced to withdraw with the supporting fire of only two tanks. Of the forty-two men and one officer sent out only nineteen men returned. Five were captured and the rest killed. One of the remaining two tanks was lost just after dark when attempting to withdraw.

The successes of the attacks of both the main forces of the US Fifth Army in the South and the Allied Beachhead Forces driving out of Anzio threatened the rout and almost complete destruction of the German Army in the south of Italy. In order to permit the orderly disengagement of their Beachhead forces and to prevent the Allied Beachhead Force from advancing to the northeast in an attempt to arrive at the rear of the forces retreating in front of the main US Fifth Army force coming up from the South, the Germans had moved the *Herman Goering Panzer* Division from the vicinity of the port Civitavecchia south into the Artena Gap. It was the apparent intention of the enemy to occupy a position on the eastern slopes of Colli Laziali, that followed across the Artena Gap and anchored its eastern flank on the western side of the Artena hill mass. Fortunately the enemy was heavily attacked before he was able to establish and organize his desired position. However, before the enemy was ejected and driven back from the positions he finally occupied, it was necessary for the 3d Infantry Division to make a coordinated major attack, which attack should be considered a very definite phase in the elimination of the Anzio Beachhead.

The Division was detached from VI Corps and attached to II Corps for the attack of June 1st and remained with II Corps until relieved from the line after Rome had fallen. All elements of the Division were relieved by the 85th Division prior to the night of May 31 and June 1, except the 1st and 3d Battalions, 7th Infantry. Those two battalions held their portion of the line while the 15th and 30th passed through.

The 15th attacked along the axis of the Artena-Valmontone road, 1st, 2d and 3d Battalions on line left to right and the 30th Infantry on the left. The 1st Battalion of the 15th Infantry moved almost directly north with the road on its left. Included in its sector was the Artena railroad station, which had been turned into a strongpoint by the enemy. Five Mark IV tanks were located at the railroad and made the battalion's advance exceedingly difficult. Company A led the attack, and though suffering a large number of casualties, succeeded in reaching the high ground beyond the station. A mist hampered visibility, making it difficult to observe artillery fire. Nonetheless two enemy tanks were destroyed—one while right in the middle of Company A. Medium tanks, supporting the attack, moved down the road. The lead tank was hit by enemy tank fire from the station and three enemy tanks retreated with the enemy infantry.

Company B passed through Company A, but shortly after moved forward under intense enemy fire from the left flank. This resulted from the unit on the left being held up about 2000 yards to the rear. A considerable amount of *Nebelwerfer* fire from the vicinity of Labico was received, but Company B reached its objective—about halfway between the railroad station and Valmontone—at 1700 hours.

Shortly thereafter eight enemy machine guns and one tank began firing at the battalion and enemy infantry formed for a counterattack from the north. Major Paulick called for Division artillery, 81mm mortar and 4.2 chemical mortar fire, and for the next forty-five minutes dropped fifty-five rounds of high explosive per minute on the enemy. The tank was destroyed and two captured Germans said all their comrades who were alive after the concentration got up and ran. Company C had no trouble moving on to the objective. Company A went to the left flank and held the high ground there.

The 2d Battalion jumped off in the attack with its direction of attack east of the Artena railroad station. Company G led and moved in the cover of a ditch. It was stopped when almost due east of the station by enemy fire from the west. The enemy was well dug-in and had supporting fire from SP guns and tanks. Further advance during daylight hours was impossible because the already-inhabited ditch provided the only cover in the battalion's zone of advance. Company F maneuvered to the left during the night of June 1-2 and drew an additional hail of 20mm Flakwagon and artillery fire as well as small-arms fire. Companies G and F continued to battle during the night, moving into enemy positions by infiltration, and by daylight had cracked the German defenses. In spite of the heavy fighting, control and communications were handled expertly. On the morning of June 3 the battalion captured the ridge line south of Highway 6, cut the road and moved into position to defend against any enemy efforts to break back across the highway. Following the original breakthrough the enemy withdrew rapidly and failed to muster anything more than token resistance.

The 3d Battalion, 15th Infantry, remained in an assembly area at a junction of five roads northeast of Artena and sent a patrol out to the initial objective, on the western nose of a slight hill, during the night prior to the jump-off hour. Therefore the battalion was bothered only by sniper fire until the next morning when it moved out. From the first objective, Company K led across the railroad tracks north of Artena. Company I followed K and both met considerable resistance from high ground north of the tracks while crossing the tracks. Both companies had to move across the ridge line of the tracks in small-group rushes.

Serious enemy resistance ceased once the railroad had been crossed and the 3d Battalion moved against only harassing sniper and SP-gun fire to cut Highway 6 by midafternoon. A defensive position was set up on the ridge overlooking the road from the south before dark and the antitank guns of the battalion were sited to stop any enemy vehicles moving into Valmontone from the east. This position was held until 1300, June 3. During this time no enemy was encountered; the battalion contacted the SSF and later the French.

On the left flank of the 15th Infantry was the 30th Infantry, making the Division main effort, with the Artena-Valmontone road serving as the right boundary for the 30th's 1st Battalion. The battalion moved up to attack with Company A on the left, Company B on the right and Company C behind the two in reserve. A machine-gun platoon from Company D was with each assaulting company; heavy mortars were placed in the railroad bed. Casualties were suffered by forward elements as they descended the slope into the railroad bed before reaching the line of departure, from enemy artillery and mortar fire. The enemy at the time held the second ridge north of the railroad track. In the 1st Battalion sector this ridge was divided into two hills, a small hill just west of the Artena-Valmontone road, and a long hill extending to the west, forming part of the same ridge. There was a six-foot bank just at the crest of the long hill, and heavy woods commenced a short distance north of this bank. The enemy main line of resistance was in the woods, but within view of the open terrain over which our troops had to attack.

The enemy was heavily supplied with automatic weapons, and had mortars in defilade directly behind the ridge; besides, the period of four days required for us to bring in the 85th and 88th Divisions, and regroup for the attack, had enabled the enemy to do considerable digging and to improve his excellent position.

The attack did not begin auspiciously. Company B managed to get a platoon onto the small hill near the Artena-Valmontone road, but Company A, moving across exposed terrain on a forward slope facing the enemy position, had soon lost all but one of its officers. 1st Lt. Randolph Bracey, leading a platoon of Company A to the northwest in order to attack the long ridge from its west flank, was killed and the platoon was wiped out. Enemy machine guns located farther west placed enfilade fire on all elements of Company A to add to its difficulties. 1st Lt. James Packman, commanding officer of Company D, was placed in command of Company A; 1st Lt. Ray Young took command of Company D.

All of our available artillery was placed on the long ridge. Enemy positions were so well concealed in the woods that at times the effect of artillery fire had to be sensed by its success in reducing the activity of automatic weapons. Our infantry creeping down the north slope of the hill on the line of departure received bursts whenever they moved.

The only factor which made a continuation of the attack possible was the arrival of a platoon of tanks and a few tank destroyers, some of which moved up on the left of the battalion and some through a saddle in the ridge from which the battalion was attacking. In conjunction with the attack, Company C, having lost both its commander and executive, led by 1st Lt. Rex Metcalf, passed through Company A, while the latter returned to the reverse slope of the friendly ridge to reorganize. Enemy artillery, machine-gun and mortar fire was the most severe in the experience of any of the officers taking part. Enemy snipers were also active.

Our tanks finally gained the top of the enemy-held ridge and cruised among the enemy positions, while Company C's men succeeded in storming the bank and shooting and grenading the enemy, who took to their holes when our tanks appeared. Lack of enemy mines and barbed wire was a great factor in the final success of our attack; otherwise the enemy was well dug-in, and naturally was very strong. The 1st Battalion suffered about 150 casualties during the day.

The battalion continued to move north against sporadic resistance during the night of the 1st and 2d of June and finally attained its objective—high ground southwest of Valmontone, although our own artillery twice prevented them from occupying the hill.

The 2d Battalion was faced with steep hills more

3d Division Infantrymen, supported by 1st Armored Division tanks, battle the Hermann Goering Panzer Division in the Artena Gap.

than enemy infantry in its advance, and received terrific artillery fire all during its attack. Although the progress was slow, it was mostly because of the terrain and the battalion's casualties were not excessive. Company I, commanded by Capt. Lloyd K. Jensen, had been attached to the battalion and was committed at about 1330 hours on the 1st, passing through the 2d Battalion and seizing several objectives about 2000 yards west, and 1000 yards south, of Valmontone. Fourteen prisoners were taken, including a company commander whose defense was wiped out. The 3d Battalion was then ordered to continue the attack, with objectives north of Highway 6 and east of Labico. Company I rejoined the 3d Battalion on the march to the new objectives.

On the way north to Highway 6 the battalion encountered two serious obstacles—the first was a sunken road with high banks, the second a cliff which bordered Highway 6 on the south. These features did not show up on the map and the cliff cost the battalion three hours of hard work in making the descent. Formation for the advance was Companies L and K abreast, with a platoon of heavy machine guns from Company M attached to each, sweeping the area, and Company I in reserve with Company M's mortars.

After reaching the bottom of the cliff, one platoon was sent north across the highway to the high ground north of the road to see if the objective was clear. The platoon was starting up the slopes of the hill when a Corps Artillery "Time on Target" concentration fell on the objective. Fortunately the platoon was clear of friendly artillery and no damage was done. This objective was occupied by 0600 hours June 2, with one enemy straggler captured. The other objectives to the north were taken shortly thereafter. Almost immediately orders were received to proceed to new objectives north and west of Valmontone. The only opposition encountered en route to these objectives was occasional sniper fire and machine-gun fire from a roadblock formed by a squad of enemy. The machine guns fired on Company I, which returned the fire, and the enemy evacuated the roadblock by using three combat vehicles marked with red crosses. There were three enemy wounded and one captured in this action.

The battalion had just reached and organized the west end of the two objectives when an enemy SP gun, located to the east where a power line crossed the highway, opened up with damaging fire. Our troops tried to get artillery fire on it, but it moved in under a cliff, still firing too close to our positions. The 3d Battalion sent bazooka men after the SP gun but they were confronted by about a hundred yards of clear ground, and machine guns mounted in the SP chassis kept them away. Meanwhile friendly tanks and tank destroyers were being held up in Valmontone by mines. The 3d Battalion was never able to neutralize the gun, but it was forced out of the area by the 2d Battalion, which relieved the 3d Battalion about nightfall. The gun caused fifteen casualties in the 3d Battalion. The battalion remained on the west end of the two objectives during the night and all day of the 2d.

The 2d Battalion, 7th Infantry, attached to the 30th Infantry for the attack, was committed at 0800 hours and told to cross the line of departure at the railroad west of the Artena-Valmontone road and take two pieces of high ground located just east of a three-way road crossing. Company F suffered eighteen casualties during an artillery concentration before reaching the line of departure. The attack was made with Company E on the left, Company F on the right and Company G in reserve, and the two hills were taken by 1800 hours. Opposition consisted mainly of enemy rear-guard action; that is, SP guns and Flakwagons.

The hills northwest of Valmontone were the next objective and the battalion started out after dark with E on the right and G on the left. The only opposition came from enemy aircraft dropping antipersonnel bombs, but the battalion had difficulty keeping contact and maintaining control due to the nature of the terrain and the darkness. The railroad west of Valmontone and Highway 6 were reached at 0500 hours June 2 and cut in the face of some scattered small arms fire and heavy *Nebelwerfer* fire. Company F went through to take high ground west of Valmontone, and the battalion commander then sent a nine-man patrol from the battalion intelligence section into the town. It was found cleared of enemy but the patrol ran into Flakwagon fire at the northeast edge and suffered seven casualties. Immediately after ascertaining that Valmontone was cleared, the battalion headed north to high ground about 5000 yards north of Valmontone on the road to Palestrina. There were some enemy with automatic weapons on this high ground but they withdrew as the battalion advanced.

Here the battalion was resupplied, and at 1800 hours Company G jumped off to take the crossroads south of Palestrina. This crossroads was located about 700 yards southwest of the town, which sat on high ground. Companies E and F followed Company G up the road. Some Flakwagon, SP and small-arms fire was met, but not a great deal and by 2000 hours Company G was at a cemetery about 1000 yards south of the crossroads. On reaching this point Company G was subjected to heavy tank and SP fire from the crossroads, so Company F went into a firing position west of the road and Company E deployed astride the road between Companies F and G. The battalion remained in this position during the night and the morning of June 3, sending patrols to the east and west.

The 3d Battalion, 7th Infantry, did not take part in the attack until 0230 hours on June 2, at which time it moved toward Valmontone in advance guard formation, and by daylight had reached a position on the flat ground southwest of the town. At 1045 hours it moved farther north to a new objective, where it halted for a brief rest and at 1615 started for a cross road to the south and east of the 2d Battalion's objective. Company I led the attack, supported by tanks and followed by Company K. Company L was attached to Task Force Ellis. Company I received a great deal of artillery fire and tank fire while still about 2000 yards short of the objective and the battalion went into attack formation with Company I on the right and Company K on the left. The battalion received fire from hostile machine guns and Mark VI tanks from south of the crossroads. At 0500 hours on June 3,

The battered ruins of Valmontone rise above the little figures in the plain below Highway 6.

Companies I and K were still 700 yards short of their objective, held up by a couple of Mark VI tanks which couldn't be hit by supporting tanks because they were well hidden behind a small ridge.

While the 2d and 3d Battalions were moving north of Valmontone to prevent enemy from counterattacking against Highway 6, the 1st Battalion was attached to Task Force Howze. The remainder of the Task Force consisted of the 3d Battalion, 13th Armored Infantry, one troop of the 1st Armored Division Recon Squadron, and a company of tank destroyers. It was joined June 3 by a battalion of the 88th Division and by the 751st Tank Battalion. The 1st Battalion's mission was to protect the tanks from enemy infantry and wipe out infantry pockets by-passed by the tanks. Task Force Howze was organized to provide a large, mobile striking force and to protect the gap between the 3d Division and the 88th Division during the attack to Highway 6.

The Task Force jumped off with two tank companies abreast. A Company of 1st Battalion, 7th Infantry, followed behind the right tank company and had little trouble reaching its part of the battalion objective. It advanced straight north toward Labico then swerved over to the left as it neared the highway.

Company B ran into considerably more trouble. In the first place one platoon was detached and given the mission of contacting the 88th Division on the left. The remainder of Company B failed to contact its company of tanks and ran into a fight alone in a group of low hills. It was hit by snipers from a house on the left, received intermittent machine-gun fire from a knoll to the right and then ran into a line of enemy riflemen armed with rifle grenades. Company C was committed at 1500 hours to gain contact with the left company of tanks and help Company B. By flanking the resistance which was holding up Company B, Company C forced the enemy to withdraw and Company B was able to advance. Resistance slackened and during the early morning of June 2 Companies B and C were assigned to front-line tank companies. By noon, meeting only scattered sniper, mortar and artillery fire, the Task Force reached the railroad tracks west of Labico. During the afternoon the battalion crossed the highway to an assembly area, where it remained until the morning of the 3d.

While the 2nd and 3d Battalions of the 7th Infantry were protecting the Division against a possible enemy thrust from the north, it was imperative that enemy units withdrawing in the face of the French push from the east not be allowed to hit the Division from the east. Hence, the 2d Battalion, 30th Infantry was sent toward Cave, a small town located about four miles east of Palestrina. Moving under cover of darkness the night of June 2-3, the battalions took a position on high ground to the southwest of Cave overlooking the town and the road to Palestrina. The battalion had to move almost noiselessly, as it was deep in enemy territory without flank protection.

During the night the battalion was hit by small-arms fire, antipersonnel bombs, SP guns, Flakwagons and mortars, but casualties were surprisingly light considering the amount of fire received.

The battalion formed in a huge semicircle, with a perimeter of about 2000 yards. Company E faced north and east, Company F faced north and west and Company G protected against an enemy move from the south. All day the battalion was subjected to enemy fire, Company E receiving direct fire from enemy tanks to the north. The battalion was too far to the north to get support from our artillery, but did receive some aid from two tanks and two tank destroyers that arrived shortly after daylight on the 3d. The battalion's roadblock destroyed an enemy tank and two other vehicles. Tanks fired into Cave most of the day, and a 14-man group of Germans was sighted near the town. The group was the advance part of a German unit that was to have moved into the area. They were taken without a fight.

The 1st Battalion, 30th Infantry, took over for the 2d Battalion when the latter went to Cave, and remained in an assembly area north and west of Valmontone until June 4.

June 3 was the date of one of the most stirring tales of courage and self-sacrifice in the annals of United States military history. The way it came into being was a minute incident of the push to Rome, which otherwise would now be lost in the larger picture. Sgt. Raymond Bunning begins the epic story:

"On 2 June my patrol, an element of Battle Patrol, 15th Infantry, was ordered to cross Highway 6 . . . and proceed 1500 yards north, scouring the area for enemy dispositions. We moved out at about 2300 hours and proceeded on our mission. By 0100, June 3, we had covered the greatest part of our assignment without making contact with the enemy.

"We made our way through a lightly-wooded area and had started to cross a large clearing when we came under severe fire from our front, both flanks, and slightly to the rear. Three tanks raked us with 20mm slugs and machine-gun fire. Three machine guns traversed across our position and approximately sixty enemy riflemen fired directly on us. The patrol leader was killed almost instantly; a burst of machine-gun fire caught him squarely. The rest of us hit the dirt. The enemy had prepared an ambush and had sprung the trap, catching us entirely by surprise.

"The only way out was to the rear. Inasmuch as I was the second in command, I took over and ordered that everyone lie low until I could figure the lay of the land. While we were lying there, I saw two of my men jump up and walk toward the enemy. Pvt. Elden Johnson, my BAR man, and Pfc. Herbert Christian, a tommy gunner, had elected to sacrifice themselves in order that the rest of us could withdraw from the trap. They motioned to me, indicating that I was to take the remainder of the patrol to the rear."

"Almost at once," continued T/5 Douglas Bragg, "Pfc. Christian was hit just above the right knee by a 20mm slug which completely severed his right leg. The flares made it as bright as day and I was almost sickened by the sight. Blood was gushing from the stump. Shreds of flesh dangled from his leg. The pain must have been intense. This man Christian was like a wounded animal; instead of calling for aid he took his Thompson submachine gun and made his way forward on one knee and the bloody stump, firing his weapon as rapidly as possible. He was raking the kraut and succeeding in killing or wounding at least three.

"These two men, determined to sell their lives as dearly as possible, attracted all of the fire of the entrenched enemy group. So audacious was their attack that the kraut forgot about the rest of us for the moment. The sight of these two men out there, each one heading for a machine gun, not seeking cover as any normal human would do, almost hypnotized the enemy."

Said Pvt. Robert Wriston: "Private Johnson advanced a total of about twenty yards, reaching a point within five yards of the enemy. He killed the crew of the machine gun which had killed our patrol leader, with one burst of fire from his BAR. Reloading his weapon, he turned on the riflemen to the left and fired directly into their position, either killing or wounding four of the enemy. A burst of machine-gun fire struck Private Johnson, causing him to slump forward; however he caught himself and balanced on his knees long enough to kill another German before he fell forward, dead.

"Meanwhile, Pfc. Christian had continued forward, despite obvious pain, to a point within ten yards of the enemy. He traveled about twenty yards in all. Intent on covering us to the last, Pfc. Christian emptied his tommy gun into a German machine-pistol man, hastily reloaded his weapon, and sprayed one last burst of fire. About this time the enemy seemed to have completely recovered from his initial surprise and concentrated his fire on Pfc. Christian. Machine-gun, 20mm, machine-pistol and rifle fire was concentrated on him as the enemy vented his anger over the now-obvious ruse. Pfc. Christian fell forward, dead.

"The courage and self-sacrifice displayed by Pfc. Christian and Private Johnson was all that saved our lives. That's something that none of the rest of us will ever forget."

Both men were posthumously awarded the Medal of Honor.

On the 3d of June the 15th Infantry started a dash west on Highway 6 toward Rome. The 1st Battalion had relieved the SSF on June 2 to protect the Division's right flank, then on the morning of the 3d it moved by motor to the west. The battalion detrucked at Colonna and from there patrolled on foot to the north of Highway 6. No enemy was met and the battalion contacted the French coming south from Highway 6 on the latter's drive into Rome. The battalion continued on to the Aniene River, reaching there about 2200 hours.

At 0400 hours on the 4th, 1st Battalion resumed its march, this time heading for the Tiber River. By 0600 hours it was along a small north-south creek when it received tank fire from a road about 1000 yards to the northwest. At this time the battalion was north of Monte Sacro, which is located at the northeastern outskirts of Rome. One of our tank destroyers was lost in the ensuing fight and the rest of the day was spent trying to overcome enemy rear-guard action. The enemy was putting up fierce rear-guard action in this sector in an effort to get his troops out of Rome and to the north. The battalion moved west slowly, cutting Highway 4 at Castel Giubbile, about four and a half miles due north of Rome at a point where the Tiber swings away from the highway. A platoon of the 3d Recon Troop was contacted at this point. The enemy was firmly entrenched in the bluffs across the river, making it impossible for the battalion to cross, but fire was placed on Highway 3 and the enemy was unable to withdraw along that route.

The French reported at 1300 hours to take over the sector but battalion patrols had reported enemy coming out of Rome along Highway 4 so Major Paulick retained control for an additional four hours. His battalion ambushed three tanks and six trucks and scattered enemy infantry on the trucks. Eighty prisoners were rounded up and command of the sector was turned over to the French.

The 2d Battalion, 15th Infantry, followed closely behind the 1st Battalion in the move by motor the 3d of June, but stopped for reorganization in a flat open field near Colonna, a small town about half way between Valmontone and Rome, remained there during the night and continued toward the Italian capital the next day. The 3d Battalion stopped at San Cesarso, another small town on the way to Rome. The battalion then split, Company I moving to Monte Massino, Company L to a road block on high ground farther east and Company K with the battalion CP in a central position. The CP was about fourteen miles from Rome.

At daylight of the 4th the 3d Battalion returned to San Cesarso, remained there an hour and started on foot to Rome. It reached a vineyard four miles out of Rome due east of the city shortly after dark, then later walked to the Aniene River, where it was supposed to establish a bridgehead across the river. Here it ran into considerable artillery fire, the first enemy fire of any concentration it had received in two days. The 1st and 2d Battalions passed through the 3d Battalion and went into positions north of Rome. The 2d Battalion was bombed on the road, and suffered some casualties in Companies F and H. Following the bombing Company E got in a small fire fight after which the battalion established roadblocks for the night in conjunction with the rest of the regiment. Except for occasional sniping there was no opposition on the 5th and in the afternoon the entire regiment assembled in Rome after all three battalions had been relieved by the French. Throughout the regiment's pursuit along Highway 6 there was little or no opposition. Only when the 1st and 2d Battalions cut off the enemy's escape route to the north of the city did it meet any kind of resistance and then it was mainly rear-guard action of SP guns and a few snipers.

While the 15th Infantry was heading for Rome, the 2d and 3d Battalions of the 7th Infantry continued their battle south of Palestrina. Their tactics were really an aggressive defense, for the Division did not want Palestrina other than to prevent the enemy from counterattacking against Highway 6 and cutting off our forward elements from their supplies. Because the main road leading to 3d Battalion positions were under perfect enemy observation, engineers constructed a cross-country tank road and tanks and tank destroyers were brought into position. At 1030 hours on the 3d the platoon of tanks was sent around to the left while the platoon of tank destroyers made a base of fire south of the enemy and German tanks were forced to withdraw. Because of the hilly terrain it took the tanks several hours to get into position, but once the enemy armor was endangered it withdrew immediately. Company I moved on to the crossroads at 1700 hours. Company K, receiving fire from the enemy in front of the 2d Battalion, was disorganized and unable to move forward. Its company commander was killed during an enemy artillery barrage. Lt. Col. Toffey,* regimental executive officer, was killed and Lt. Col. Snyder, tank battalion commander, was wounded by the same enemy shell during the tank action. After dark Company K was reorganized and put into position south of Company I in a defense in depth.

The 2d Battalion didn't get its attack started until 1300 hours, but once it got started it made short work of the enemy and reached its crossroads in an hour and a half. Supported by fire from two tanks, three tank destroyers and two battalions of artillery, Company G stormed the position. One Flakwagon and one Mk IV tank were destroyed, six enemy were killed, five taken prisoner and the rest forced to withdraw into Palestrina. During the night the remainder of the enemy that had withdrawn, estimated at a platoon, counterattacked but were driven off by artillery and mortar fire before they reached our front lines.

Both battalions of the 7th were relieved by units of the French by 0800 hours on the 4th; they assembled during the morning and entrucked for Rome. The 3d Battalion spent the night at Tor Sapienza, a small settlement at the outskirts of Rome and the 2d Battalion established a company at each of three roadblocks a short distance north of Highway 6. The morning of the 5th both battalions moved by truck into Rome without further enemy contact.

As a part of Task Force Howze, the 1st Battalion of the 7th was the first full combat unit of the Allied armies to enter Rome, moving into the city during the afternoon of June 4. On June 3, preceding other II Corps units, the Task Force attacked to the left of Highway 6, guiding on the road, cleaning out pockets of enemy resistance. Armor from the 751st Tank Battalion moved out in the lead, followed by Lt. Col. Frank M. Izenour's battalion on foot. The enemy had set up a series of automatic weapon emplacements which were neutralized, and a large number of prisoners were taken at little cost to the 1st Battalion.

At 1700 hours the battalion was ordered to set up three roadblocks, a company of tanks and a company of infantry at each, between Highways 6 and 5. Company B, riding on the tanks, moved to its block without trouble and went into position. Shortly thereafter Company A, also mounted on tanks, was ambushed by an enemy roadblock. The first two tanks got past the enemy block, but the third was hit by antitank fire and thirteen infantrymen were wounded. The tanks and infantry halted, deployed in the field and drove off the enemy, then set up a roadblock at this point instead of going to its original position. Company G followed with fourteen tanks and set up the third roadblock. Shortly before dark it ambushed an enemy convoy of nearly thirty vehicles, captured all the vehicles—including two mobile 88mm guns—and 130 prisoners, including an antiaircraft battalion commander. Four of the enemy were killed. Company G had no casualties.

The battalion moved on foot to Tor Sapienza and at 1400 was ordered to move into Rome with SSF on its left. The SSF was held up at the outskirts of the city, so 1st Battalion moved ahead into Rome, outflanking the enemy in front of the SSF and forcing him to withdraw. The battalion reached the San Lorenzo railroad yards about 1700 hours without any opposition, remained there the night after setting up a defense in the streets around the station, and joined the remainder of the regiment in a Rome bivouac the next day. From June 3 until June 5 the battalion met only light enemy resistance and suffered few casualties.

All three battalions of the 30th Infantry were relieved from their defensive positions the morning of June 4, and immediately entrucked toward Rome. A number of likely points of enemy resistance—crossroads and railroad stations—were investigated, but only scattered

---

*Lt. Colonel Toffey had formerly commanded the 2d Battalion of the 15th Infantry but had been transferred and made executive of the 7th just prior to the breakout from the Beachhead. Toffey was one of the best-loved and most colorful characters in the Division, if not in our entire Army. He was famous for wise-cracking and coolness under fire. The tougher the spot the more exuberant he became and the dryer his humor. The story of how he got into the Division is epic. His application for transfer to the 3d from his old division—the 9th—having been disapproved, Toffey proceeded to disappear for a 48-hour period without leave. Upon his return to military control he was informed that nothing stood in the way of his transfer to the 3d any longer. General Truscott, who had known him since he participated in the landing with him at Port Lyautey, French Morocco, welcomed him with a battalion command. No one was missed more than this mad, genial Irishman. ED.

enemy snipers were encountered. The regiment detrucked a few kilometers outside Rome and moved west to the outskirts of the city expecting resistance but meeting none. Tanks, tank destroyers and cannon company M-8 self-propelled howitzers were attached to each battalion and plans made to move into Rome during the night of June 4-5. However the plan was cancelled in order to forestall any heavy fighting in the streets at night.

Jumping off from the railroad tracks, which ran north and south on the outskirts of the city, the regiment attacked toward the Tiber River at dawn of the 5th with the 1st Battalion on the right, 3d on the left and 2d in reserve. All the regiment's companies had been split up into separate task forces, with objectives, the bridges across the Tiber. Except for Companies A and G, the regiment had no trouble.

Company A, advancing to the Aniene River on Highway 4, met resistance from an estimated platoon of enemy north of the river, reinforced by two tanks. Fire of M-8's, machine guns and mortars was placed on the enemy, and when communications were established with artillery, enabling us to shell him, the enemy withdrew. Company G got into a fire fight near the Villa Savoia, between Highway 4 and the Tiber at the north edge of town. The enemy used tank and small-arms fire, but Company G was limited to the use of small arms so as not to destroy the city wantonly. The fight lasted until mid-afternoon, when the enemy withdrew because of pressure from elements of the 15th Infantry to the north. Twenty-two prisoners were picked up and Company G continued to its bridge objectives.

Soon after our rifle companies reached the bridges, to prevent the enemy from destroying them, engineers were brought up to check all bridges and later all public buildings for mines, boobytraps, and other demolitions. Not a single mine was found, so rapid had been the enemy's retreat and so disorganized his forces.

The entire Division was relieved from the line by the afternoon of the 5th, after having taken the longest route to Rome.

On 7 June, General O'Daniel received a teletype which read:

Please give to my old Division, the Third, my thanks, and to my first regiment in the Army, the Thirtieth, and the Seventh of my Vancouver days and especially to my old China regiment, the Fifteenth, for cutting Highway Six

GEORGE C. MARSHALL
Chief of Staff
U. S. Army

THIRD RECON TROOP IN CISTERNA-ROME OPERATION

Nothing has been said in the foregoing account of the operations of the Division's principal Reconnaissance Troop, and its attached Battle Patrol. This omission was intentional, since the operations of the troop were of an independent nature and could not easily be described concurrently with the infantry action, as could the operations of the artillery, engineers and armor, without causing unnecessary confusion. However, the work of the troop was of such importance to the successful accomplishment of the Division's mission that it is described here in detail.

During most of the Anzio beachhead operation, in fact since the first week in February, the 3d Recon Troop did little but patrol Division rear areas and man three Division observation posts. The operation at Cisterna, however, brought forth a need for motorized reconnaissance and from May 26, when the enemy's defensive ring around Cisterna was broken, until June 5 the three platoons of the Recon Troop plus the Division Battle Patrol were in almost constant use.

The Battle Patrol was an organization formed during the stagnant days of the beachhead to give the Division an extra "company," especially trained in scouting and patrolling, to work either with the Recon Troop or independently. It consisted of two officers and fifty-six men, all volunteers, armed with the following weapons: eight Browning Automatic Rifles, eight '03 rifles for grenade launching, twenty-eight Thompson submachine guns, two bazookas, eight M-1 semi-automatic rifles and a demolition crew.

It was sent into action the second day of the attack, filling a gap between the 1st Battalion of the 15th Infantry and the Special Service Force. When the 15th Infantry cut the railroad south of Cisterna the second day of the attack, the Battle Patrol pushed ahead and were the first United States troops into Cori. A platoon of the Recon Troop was sent through the breach in the enemy's lines on May 25, initially to clear a road junction north of Cisterna and immediately thereafter to proceed directly to Cori. The platoon was held up on high ground short of Cori by a barrage from our own artillery, then moved into Cori shortly after the Battle Patrol had cleared the town.

On the move into Cori the first platoon met an enemy strongpoint, destroyed a 105mm assault-gun howitzer, took twenty-six prisoners and captured two 88mm guns. Meanwhile the third platoon reconnoitered for another route into Cori. It too got into a fire fight and killed eight enemy and took ten prisoners. The third platoon continued on toward Giuglianello and ran into an enemy position beyond the town where it killed nineteen, and took fifty-eight prisoners.

Curious Italians crowd about the first 3d Division troops entering Rome.

On the 27th all three platoons of the Recon Troop moved out to the west and north of Giuglianello. The 2d platoon went into action for the first time and cut the Velletri-Artena road, engaged in a short fire fight west of Artena, then later in the day retired behind the 30th Infantry's antitank gun positions. The Battle Patrol conducted dismounted reconnaissance toward Artena for the 15th Infantry. The 1st platoon moved toward Velletri in the morning, remained there during the night, and met an enemy force the next morning. As the platoon dismounted and moved through the underbrush to deploy, the platoon leader and one enlisted man, on foot reconnaissance, were captured by the enemy. Their jeep was hit by enemy antitank fire and was destroyed by 37mm fire from the platoon's armored car to prevent its falling into German hands. The platoon remained in that position during the day, pulled back to a night position at dark and was relieved by the 2d platoon. The 3d platoon, with a platoon of tank destroyers, put in a roadblock northeast of Velletri.

The 1st platoon relieved the 3d platoon at the roadblock shortly before dark on the 29th, then pulled off the block at 2200 hours. The troop located and operated a Division OP from the 29th until the 1st of June, when the Division's attack toward Highway 6 began.

While the Division remained north of Artena, the Battle Patrol worked in front of and on both flanks of the Division to maintain contact with the enemy and friendly units. During the night of the 31st patrols went east of Roccamassima and the next day discovered enemy along a ridge west of Segni.

With the 30th Infantry on the left and 15th Infantry on the right, the Battle Patrol was given the mission of clearing Valmontone the morning of June 2. The town was cleared by 0600 hours and six hours later the Patrol was 8000 yards north of town. The troop's 3d platoon started north of the town toward Palestrina but was held up for an hour and a half until the streets could be cleared of debris. At noon it encountered an enemy roadblock consisting of an antitank gun, two machine guns and ten riflemen. The platoon killed twelve enemy enlisted men and one officer.

The 2d platoon covered the road net south of Highway 6 west of Valmontone, and suffered six casualties from heavy enemy *Nebelwerfer* and artillery fire.

Mission of the 1st platoon was to move west on Highway 6 to the road junction 3000 yards west of Labico. As the platoon reached Valmontone its armored car was fired on by an enemy antitank gun but was not hit. It turned west on Highway 6 at Valmontone and started for Labico. The highway between the two towns is in deep defilade, with steep, wooded banks rising in height to seventy-five feet on either side of the road, necessitating careful attention to flank protection in order to avoid the typical "mouse trap" frequently employed by the Germans.

The platoon reached the eastern edge of Labico by 1100 hours without incident, then noted ten Germans moving through the undergrowth 150 yards short of the city limits and within fifty yards of the platoon's point. The platoon leader brought his armored car into position thirty yards from the enemy and opened fire. Two Germans were taken prisoner, seven were killed and one escaped into town.

Immediately following this action the platoon received fire from two enemy machine guns and several rifles from the rear, and five minutes later received additional enemy fire from the left flank. The fire fight lasted for an hour; eleven prisoners were taken and an undetermined number killed. The platoon suffered no casualties. The prisoners said they had been withdrawing from positions to the south when they struck the rear of the Recon platoon.

During the early afternoon the platoon received aerial-burst fire from an enemy 20mm Flakwagon located in Labico, and *Nebelwerfer* fire from the north. At 1800 hours a mixed platoon of tanks and tank destroyers arrived and began an assault of the town in conjunction with the Recon platoon. However immediately after the attack got under way the Recon platoon was ordered to return to Valmontone and reconnoiter to a point approximately 4500 yards northeast of town.

The Battle Patrol was given the mission of clearing out Labico and had wiped out enemy resistance by 0500 hours of the 3d. The 1st platoon, which had been held up five hours on its mission northeast of Valmontone, returned to Labico, contacted the Battle Patrol and continued to the road junction 3000 yards west of the town—the same road junction it had been ordered to take the day before.

It was thought best to continue until contact with the enemy was made, so the platoon moved without delay to San Cesarso, reaching that point in the morning. Here it received harassing enemy artillery fire. After a short reconnaissance west along Highway 6, the platoon established a roadblock at San Cesarso until late in the afternoon when it was relieved by the 2d platoon. The 3d platoon meanwhile continued its reconnaissance from Valmontone to Palestrina.

The 4th of June was a busy day for the Troop. Two platoons and the battle patrol cut Highways 5 and 4 physically and Highway 3 by fire and the 1st platoon moved into Rome. The 2d platoon, on reaching Highway 5, was fired on by an enemy Flakwagon. This Flakwagon was destroyed by the coordinated work of the mounted platoon and foot Battle Patrol, and a roadblock was set up on the highway. Several enemy vehicles were fired on by the platoon. These vehicles turned tail and sped east—into the area of the advancing French troops.

While the 2d platoon remained at the roadblock, the 3d platoon moved to Highway 4, cut it, and continued to a small knoll overlooking the Tiber River. Here it contacted a tank destroyer that had become lost from its unit. This tank destroyer was employed in firing on Highway 3—it was impossible to cut the road because the enemy was too well entrenched on high bluffs west of the river. Suddenly six enemy tanks and several personnel carriers loaded with troops counterattacked from the east, the platoon's rear. All fire, including that of the tank destroyer, was brought to bear on this counterattack and the enemy was

United States Army officers and men pay tribute to their dead comrades at Nettuno, on Memorial Day, 1944.

quickly stopped. The Germans lost two tanks and at least two tracked personnel carriers.

Attention was returned to the west. Four machine guns were spotted and neutralized with four shots from the armored car's 37mm gun. The platoon was relieved that afternoon by elements of the 15th Infantry.

While the 2d and 3d platoons cut the three highways, the 1st platoon started early in the morning of June 4 west on Highway 6 to Rome. Several members of the platoon, including the platoon leader, got into the city limits of Rome, dismounted, at 0830 hours. In doing so they had passed a number of snipers—actually stragglers using up their last ammunition, but at the point where Highway 6 entered the city at the crest of a hill, very real opposition was met in the form of a roadblock placed on the reverse slope of the hill.

The block consisted of a Mk IV tank, placed squarely in the middle of the road 150 yards below the crest of the hill, and adequately protected by machine guns and riflemen; and 500 yards beyond this was a 40mm antitank gun perfectly camouflaged. This block was reinforced by four self-propelled 150mm howitzers mounted on Mk IV chassis (Grizzly Bears). Mines were concealed beneath the pavement in front of the tank.

Two Sherman tanks were destroyed attempting to force the roadblock, one by the enemy tank and one by mines. Finally, in the late afternoon, this point was outflanked by infantrymen, the roadblock was neutralized and Task Force Howze rolled into the city. The Recon's 1st platoon, after reporting the roadblock to higher headquarters, watched the tank-infantry action against the block from a ridge just outside the city limits.

On June 5 units of the Recon Troop raced into Rome to secure bridges across the Tiber River before they could be destroyed by the enemy. All bridges were found unharmed, including a 75-foot railroad span. When foot troops arrived to take over the bridge guard the Recon Troop was relieved.

By the time the 3d Division entered Rome, approximately 3000 German prisoners of war had passed through the Division cage. Added to the 1800 prisoners previously captured on the Anzio beachhead, this made a total of nearly 5000 prisoners taken by the Division in four and one-half months of operation. During the last stages of the campaign the prisoners were from a weird variety of units—corps headquarters, base section dumps, Flak-units, assault-gun battalions, and scatterings from more than a dozen divisional formations. This spoke eloquently of the enemy's complete disorganization and the complete success of our attack.

These facts stood out following the operation:

The Division's frontal assault and breakthrough at Cisterna, against fortified and strongly-manned positions, was a monument not only to the excellence of planning and coordination at every level, but also to the indomitable spirit and sheer fighting ability of the troops. These story-book situations—bayonet assaults, daring patrol ambushes, deep reconnaissance missions, perfectly-coordinated infantry-tank-artillery attacks—actually occurred during this operation.

The rapid advance to Artena upset the enemy's timetable for withdrawal up Highway 6, and greatly hastened the fall of Rome.

The breakthrough at Valmontone, accomplished against fresh German troops by the 3d Division after having suffered so heavily at Cisterna, was overshadowed by the earlier attack only in scope and duration.

The shrewd development of the situation around Lariano, denying the enemy the benefit of an excellent and long-prepared defensive position, aided in the outflanking of Velletri by the 36th Division and the subsequent advance to the west across the Colli Laziali.

Knowing the enemy to be virtually without reserves, boldness in pushing attacks even with troops tired to the point of bogging down paid rich dividends and set up a clean breakthrough both at Cisterna and Valmontone.

The 3d Infantry Division settled down and prepared to garrison Rome.

TABLE OF CASUALTIES*

Breakthrough to Rome

(May 23, 1944 through Aug. 14, 1944)

KIA	WIA	MIA	Total Battle Casualties	Non-Battle Casualties
511	2575	235	3321	6783

Reinforcements and Hospital return-to-unit personnel

Reinf		Hosp RTUs	
Off	EM	Off	EM
90	1430	98	6612

KNOWN ENEMY CASUALTIES

Killed	Wounded	Captured
1034	245	2903

*These figures were provided by the A C of S, G–1, 3d Infantry Division.

3: Interlude: Rome

ROME—civilization. The two words were synonymous. Rome, one of the most beautiful cities on the European Continent (or anywhere for that matter) was like a haven to tired, sweat-soaked, sore-footed infantrymen of several divisions. The 3d was no exception.

Late the afternoon of June 4, electrifying news reached the large tent which housed the Division War Room about five miles from the city's outskirts. It was from Fifth Army Headquarters and read: "Third Infantry Division will garrison Rome!" (Exclamation ours.) It was the most welcome news since the fall of Messina. It seemed to herald a long rest in one of Europe's most scenic capitals.

The morning of June 6 found the CP comfortably ensconced in the spacious buildings of Rome University, with most regimental, battalion, and even company headquarters equally well-housed throughout the city. It was then that the flash announcement for which all the world had been waiting first came over millions of radios in dozens of tongues: "The Allies have landed in Normandy!" That was all, but it was enough. Added to the liberation of the Eternal City, it was enough to justify a double celebration among men of the Allied Armies in Italy, but it was also a very sobering announcement. Now, shortly, we would know whether the so-called Atlantic Wall, the strength and impregnability of which the Germans had been trumpeting for years, was reality or something less. At the 3d's most triumphant moment to date, probably the entire fate of Western civilization rested with the men, arms, and machinery then struggling for the victory on France's Channel coast.

The tremendous fact of invasion, The Invasion, all but overshadowed Fifth Army's barely-won conquest; the magnificent battle fought north from Cassino and the Beachhead. In countless newspapers everywhere, printers had hurried to tear out front pages telling of the capture of Rome, and to replace the already huge headline type with even larger letters announcing the long-awaited invasion of France.

From that moment on, Italy became the Forgotten Front.

There was a lot to be seen in Rome. The opinion among fighting men was unanimous that it had almost everything needed to qualify for a place among United States cities except United States civilians. The quality and quantity of the women were especially impressive to doughs who, for the previous four and one-half months, had seen nothing but mud, blood and death. "Gawdamighty, they even got redheads!" was a common exclamation.

There was a definite task awaiting. The city needed to be policed. It was the seat of Fascism but a few months before, and if trouble was to be expected anywhere in Italy, it seemed commonsense reasoning to suppose that it would pop up in liberated Rome.

With this in view the 3d's task was to establish guard over every important installation which might be considered worthy of sabotage by disgruntled Fascists. Bridges, aqueducts, electric power installations, and communications centers were priority "targets" (as a later code word described centers to be guarded). The streets themselves had to be policed. It was necessary for armed guards to patrol regular beats, working in conjunction with the Italian carabinieri. Riot squads roamed the city in jeeps, tanks, and halftracks. The city was divided into zones, each of which was allotted to a regiment of the 3d Division. Unit operations officers made preparation to deal immediately with any contingency arising in the form of Fascist-hoodlum uprisings, German-inspired hysteria, or acts of sabotage.

Amazingly, despite a few small "incidents" occurring among a suddenly-liberated populace during the first few days, nothing arose which might have been termed "untoward." The same situation with respect to Fascism that had been encountered throughout Sicily and Italy was found to prevail at Fascism's seat. The word and the political movement had suddenly become unpopular, terminating a gradual swing away from it which had begun with the entry of Italy into the war in June 1940, and the subsequent military reverses, coupled with an increase in food and clothing rationing, and the ever-increasing presence of numbers of German troops in and around the city. Since the country's surrender some atrocities had turned most Italians even further from the occupying enemy.

The United States soldier has never had much trouble making friends among either civilians or women of

An Italian wedding takes place in the environs of Rome, despite the war at the gates.

Italians crowd the streets to view the victorious Yanks.

any nationality, and Rome provided a heretofore-unparalleled opportunity to test that sanguine ability. Men of Italian descent suddenly found themselves popular among their comrades beyond all explanation of personal charm; many soldiers, undyed deceivers that they were, discovered that an interpreter in the crowd is always a welcome asset.

There were those rugged individualists, however, who scorned such underhanded methods, preferring a combination of "pidgin" Italian, Basic English, and universal language to sell the desirability of their companionship. The more practical among them even went to the extent of assisting budding friendships by the judicious use of such small tidbits as chocolate, C Rations, and chewing gum, to mention nothing of the more solid rations, originally destined for United States Army consumption, which circuitously went to cement Italo-United States cobelligerency.

Along with the policing and relaxation was the resumption of a limited amount of training. This consisted largely of close-order drill, calisthenics, organized athletics, and orientation lectures. Although operations officers are notoriously never in doubt as to improvisation of training, it was not known immediately what the Division's next active participation in the war would be.

The German retreat, which actually began in the hills north of Cassino, and received a tremendous boost with the successful breaking of the Anzio "iron ring," was still in progress. With breath-taking rapidity, Allied units of several nationalities, among them United States, British, Indian, Canadian, and French divisions, had continued to force the issue with the hastily-withdrawing Germans. Rome, which but a few days before had been ahead of, then directly on, the front lines, became rear-echelon with a speed that was no less breathtaking to the frontline combat troops. Almost before skinned feet had recovered from the devastating effect of practically continuous marching, the Base Section had moved in lock, stock, and barrel.

The first day of entry into the city had seen a hastily improvised *Stars & Stripes* with crude, black letters advertising the fact that "WE'RE IN ROME." This special edition featured the services of such high-caliber correspondents as Milton Bracker and Herbert Matthews of *New York Times,* Will Lang of *Time-Life,* Ken Dixon and Edward Kennedy of Associated Press, and Reynolds and Eleanor Packard of United Press. The combination covered every angle from the breakthrough at Velletri to a husband-wife reaction upon returning to a city which they had left just slightly more than two years before.

"A bearded, dust-grimed U. S. infantryman, holding his helmet in his hand, stepped inside the vast, vaulted coolness of St. Peter's Cathedral at 3:15 this morning, only a few hours after Allied troops had entered Rome," began one *Stars & Stripes* story.

"He stood looking straight ahead and then up and he gulped and blinked his eyes and said in a quiet, shaky voice: 'I never thought there was a place in the world as wonderful as this. I didn't know there was anything so beautiful.'

"He would not give his name, his organization or anything else. 'I'm just here,' he said, 'and I know what I'm seeing is too big to talk about.' And he walked out, down under the great high ceiling toward the tomb of St. Peter I, at the far end of the great entrance way. . . ."

Lt. Gen. Mark W. Clark took time out to pay brief, oral tribute to "the men and women of the Fifth Army who made the supreme sacrifice so that we could keep going to Rome and beyond."

"This great day for the Fifth Army was made

possible by the combined efforts of French, British and American troops," he said.

And, keynoting a small, but ironic (though hardly unfamiliar) twist was the Italian carabiniere's words as quoted in the *Stars & Stripes*: "I watched the American bravely kill five Tedeschi in an old stone house. The Germans stole my oil and typewriter. The Americans are good and kind. *Do you have a cigarette?*"

General Clark attended a party given in the ballroom of the Grand Hotel a few nights after the Rome entry and pinned the second star of a Major General on the shoulders of Commanding General John W. "Iron Mike" O'Daniel, at the same time congratulating him and his command for the outstanding part played by both in the big push.

Notable among the sights to be seen were, of course, St. Peter's Cathedral (including mass audiences with Pope Pius XII), the Vatican, the Coliseum, Castel Sant' Angelo, the ruins of the Roman Forum, Mussolini's monument and balcony, Victor Emmanuel's monument, any one of several Christian catacombs, and many of the lesser-known, but no less beautiful, basilicas and churches throughout the city.

The Normandy invasion, meanwhile, had proved successful. Emerging from the flood of statements about "strategic reserves," "breakthroughs," and "build-up period" was the solid fact, undisputed even by the enemy, that the Allies had got ashore and were in a position to hold. The beachhead was secure, and a wave of optimism had set in in the allied camp which was not entirely confined to civilians.

Although few officers or men in the 3d Division knew it, our future part in the war had long been scheduled. Rome was merely a breathing period.

The seeming lap of luxury into which the 3d had been suddenly dumped was to prove only a resting place between campaigns—and a very short one at that. The doubts that it was too good to be true shortly materialized. Orders were received on June 13 that the Division would move south of Castel Prezinano, near the Lido di Roma on the Tyrhennian Coast about twenty miles from Rome, preparatory to returning to Naples. The order crystallized in most minds as having but one significance—amphibious training. What else? The Division had never failed to commence practicing for landing operations in its several withdrawals from combat, and battle-wise veterans of Casablanca, Sicily, and Southern Italy summarized the prevalent feeling in very few words: "Where the hell's it going to be this time?"

The move commenced June 14 and was completed June 16.

Upon arrival in the new bivouac area, all units established and improved their areas and commenced a training program covering close-order drill, military

A British officer runs out of the building, from whose balcony Mussolini once delivered his orations.

courtesy, calisthenics, hardening marches, scouting and patrolling and small-unit problems.

Also included were athletics, ceremonies, and the care and cleaning of equipment.

Plans were immediately formulated by the various headquarters for the move to the Naples area. Some organizations were scheduled to move by motor, some by boat.

Castel Sant' Angelo, an historic Italian landmark on the Tiber River.

The move was undertaken commencing June 19. All wheeled vehicles and all personnel, except infantry foot elements moved overland to the vicinity of Pozzuoli (which is about five miles from the heart of Naples). Ninety-six tracked vehicles of the 756th Tank Battalion and sixty-six "ducks" of the 52nd QM Battalion were loaded aboard six LSTs at Civitavecchia, north of Rome, for shipment to Pozzuoli.

In addition to organic personnel and equipment, and attachments besides the ones enumerated above, the following were attached to 3d Infantry Division for the move: 601st TD Battalion, 441st AAA AW Battalion (two of the three "regular" attachments): 39th Engineer Combat Regiment; 235th QM Truck Company; 3334th QM Truck Company; Headquarters and Headquarters Detachment, 56th Medical Battalion; 885th, 886th, 887th, and 891st Medical Collecting Companies; 14th Ordnance MM Company; one-half of each of 3353d and 3355th QM Truck Companies; and one platoon of the 94th QM Railhead Company.

The move was carried to completion by June 24. Upon arrival at its new bivouac area near Pozzuoli the Division began preparations for intensive training for large-scale amphibious operations. Training was divided into three periods of five days each, followed by a day of rest. The first five-day period got under way on June 28.

As in past operations, a Planning Board was immediately set up. This functioned at VI Corps Headquarters at the "blockhouse" in downtown Naples. The board consisted of Lt. Col. Albert O. Connor, G-3; Lt. Col. Grover Wilson and Capt. Frederick C. Spreyer, G-2; Maj. Robert Shaw, G-4; Lt. Col. Walter T. Kerwin, S-3, Division Artillery; Maj. Robert L. Petherick, Division Engineer; and representatives from the Signal, Ordnance, QM sections, and Beach Group. Later the S-3's of infantry regiments were added and shortly prior to loading each large unit of the Division set up its own planning room in its bivouac area in order to complete unit orders and to brief staff personnel and unit commanders.

An AG Detachment at the Planning Board Headquarters handled incoming and outgoing documents, and reproduced all operational publications. A rigid system of passes was maintained at the Headquarters, and all planning rooms were guarded by MP's.

Unit training was generally similar to that which had become familiar to all 3d Division veterans, with one important difference. Departing from the former practice of having one battalion per regiment trained as a beach-assault battalion, all infantry personnel were given training in the assault of beach defenses. In addition two of the Division's four special battle patrols were allotted to 7th Infantry and two to 15th Infantry for the purpose of assaulting and destroying enemy gun emplacements on the flanks of both beaches. These patrols were increased to a strength of five officers and 150 men each for the assignment.

The scheduled naval gunfire support for the Division

was: one battleship in general support of both the Division's beaches, and six light cruisers and five destroyers assigned to support individual beaches. Smaller craft carrying guns or rockets were also given missions of firing on beach defenses. Primary mission of the warships was to neutralize enemy land-based artillery. No important enemy interference from the sea was expected.

A prearranged bombardment of known battery positions was to begin at H-minus-90 and continue until H-plus-15 minutes, when the warships were to take over certain sectors of responsibility in support of the landing, and fire on targets observed by spotting planes and shore fire-control parties. There were nine of these parties, tied in not only with their respective ships but also with the Naval liaison officer at Division Artillery Headquarters. This arrangement in effect gave the Division a naval fire-direction center, by which the fire of all supporting warships could be massed on suitable targets.

The Corps air plan provided for a detailed schedule of attack for ten days preceding the operations by a powerful force of planes, as well as strong general support on D-Day by counterbattery missions, pre-H-hour bombardment of enemy beach defenses, and attack of nearby enemy airdromes.

To a few, carefully-considered individuals—top commanders—the word by now had gone out that the landings were to be conducted over the beaches of southern France. Companion divisions were the 45th on the immediate right and 36th on VI Corps right flank.

July wore on. The training program carried on and approached its conclusion. Physical conditioning was attained primarily through speed marches and night marches. Training, following the procedure which had paid such rich dividends on previous landings, included attack of pillboxes and fixed fortifications, gapping and crossing wire, mine removal, use of flamethrowers, bangalore torpedoes, rifle grenades, bazookas and similar specialized equipment, and infantry-tank cooperation. Assault troops were drilled in loading and disembarking from landing craft. Several landing exercises were conducted over beaches of Mondragone, about thirty miles north of Pozzuoli.

The 10th Engineer Battalion drew the nastiest assignment of the period. Previous experience dictated the necessity of a full-scale "dress rehearsal," omitting nothing but the presence of enemy troops. There was only one area within practical distance which closely resembled the actual landing area—the Formia-Gaeta sector north of the mouth of the Garigliano.

This area was directly behind the German lines all during the previous winter's campaign, having been back of the "Winter Line." German engineers had mined everything so completely that it was one of the most fortified areas in all of Italy. Friendly troops who eventually overcame enemy resistance in the push north took time only to demine the immediate roadside areas. The remainder bristled with every fiendish design of explosive and boobytrap known to the mine-conscious German Army. It fell to the 10th Engineers to clear the beaches and hills between the road and shoreline, in order for 3d Infantry Division to hold its exercise.

The battalion, in completing this mission, suffered a total of eighteen men killed and forty-three wounded;

The University of Rome, Headquarters of the United States 3d Infantry Division when it garrisoned the city.

Lieutenant General Alexander Patch, CG Seventh U. S. Army reviews the entire 3d Infantry Division near Naples immediately prior to embarkation for France.

3d Infantry Division Artillery liaison planes on the improvised flight deck of an LST off Naples harbor prior to the invasion of Southern France.

ironical to a unit at that time "out of combat." From one small knoll on the right flank of the left beach—"Beach Yellow"—alone, 750 "S"-mines were cleared before the area was given up as being hopelessly covered. When the landing operation—the final rehearsal—was conducted toward the end of July, the Formia-Gaeta area had still much hidden death in wait for the Division, and a few casualties were suffered in order that many more lives might be saved later. The last "bugs" were ironed out of landing plans on this exercise, and the Division was again at the peak of condition . . . ready for anything.

Security as to exact time and place of the coming operation was excellent, but the fact could not be disguised from German agents and sympathizers among the Italians that a large-scale amphibious expedition was shortly to set sail. There were still too many pro-Nazis and unconverted Fascists in order for our large-scale preparations to remain a secret. Consequently, the mission coming up was probably "sweated out" by the men who were to accomplish it, more than any other since the initial landings in Africa. For several days, in the latter part of July and early August, the Axis radio trumpeted nervously that a new invasion was ready to strike at southern France. Only the fact that such shots had been apparently "called" by the enemy on previous occasions, and then subsequently carried successfully to completion anyway, prevented our forces from a too overbearing concern over the enemy's feigned knowledge of coming events. Southern France *was* a logical target, and it was much more so now that the beachhead forces in Normandy had broken loose and were in the process of overrunning the Brittany Peninsula.

The "Bomb Plot" against Hitler broke during the latter part of July. So much elation was evidenced in the Division that it was necessary for General O'Daniel to issue a memorandum reminding all personnel of the danger of overoptimism. Salerno's eve had brought news of the Italian surrender, he cautioned, but did not alter the course of the bloody battle there, except possibly to make it even worse.

The final combat landing got under way toward the end of July. The 3d Infantry Division was the first of three divisions to load, and practically all vehicles were aboard the ships and craft before the Formia exercise. There were four ports out of which to load: Baia for LCTs, Pozzuoli for LCIs, Nisida for LSTs, and Naples for naval transports and cargo ships, Merchant Marine Liberty Ships, and British Indian Ocean passenger vessels (AP, AK, MT, & LSI, respectively).

Because of the priority on landing the Division had more time for loading adjustments, with the consequence that instead of the originally scheduled 3,337 vehicles estimated by higher headquarters as the maximum load, over 4,500 vehicles were loaded on the assault convoy.

A final briefing of all commanders of battalions and higher units took place on August 7. All naval commanders were present, all commanding generals. General Truscott opened the meeting with a brief summary of amphibious warfare: ". . . Determined men can get ashore anywhere." Division commanders then outlined their respective Task Forces' plans of assault.

Sitting quietly in the bottom row of seats was a medium-sized, trim man in Naval uniform—summer khakis, black tie, black shoes—minus insignia of rank. He was practically unnoticed until the briefing was over. Then he stood up at the invitation of Vice Admiral H. K. Hewitt.

For a moment there was puzzlement among the assembled officers. Then recognition dawned, with the speaker's words. It was Secretary of the Navy James V. Forrestal. He spoke briefly and appreciatively of the parts played by all arms in the fight against the Axis. He mentioned the coming operation with confidence. As he talked his unassuming manner and calm poise completely won the group. His speech was short and to the point. When he sat down the meeting was at an end.

Final loading of troops was completed on August 8, and various units of the convoy began getting under way, to rendezvous later.

As yet only a few of the troops knew their final destination.

VIII
SOUTHERN FRANCE

From the Riviera to the Vosges in Thirty Days

TROOP LIST—Operation "Anvil" Third Infantry Division (Reinf)

Organization for Combat

1. *Hq & Hq Co, 3d Inf Div*
   Naval Combat Int Team
   Air Support Control Party
   Order of Battle Personnel
   CIC Personnel
   Sécurité Militaire
   OSS Personnel
   Photo Interpreters
   Civil Affairs Personnel
   IPW Det

2. *7th Infantry*
   Co A, 756th Tk Bn
   Co A, 601st TD Bn
   Co A, 3d Chem Bn
   Co A, 10th Engr Bn (Initially)
   Co A, 3d Med Bn
   10th FA Bn (Initially)
     Naval Shore Fire Control Party
   Det 6617th Mine Clr Co (Gapping Team)
   Det 3d Sig Co
   IPW Team

3. *15th Infantry*
   Co B, 756th Tk Bn
   Co B, 601st TD Bn
   Co B, 3d Chem Bn
   Co B, 10th Engr Bn (Initially)
   Co B, 3d Med Bn
   39th FA Bn (Initially)
     Naval Shore Fire Control Party
   Det 6617th Mine Clr Co (Gapping Team)
   Det 3d Sig Co
   IPW Team

4. *30th Infantry*
   Co C, 3d Chem Bn
   Co C, 3d Med Bn
   Det 3d Sig Co
   IPW Team

5. *3d Division Artillery*
   9th FA Bn
   41st FA Bn
   441st AAA AW Bn
   634th FA Bn (155mm How)
   69th Armd FA Bn
   36th FA Bn (155mm Gun)
   Det 2d FA Obsn Bn
   Naval Gunfire Liaison
   Naval Shore Fire Control Parties

6. *3d Rcn Troop*
7. *Troop C (Reinf) 117th Cav Rcn Sq (Mczd)*
8. *756th Tank Bn (–Cos A & B)*
9. *601st TD Bn (–Cos A & B)*
10. *3d Chemical Bn (–Cos A, B & C)*
    Det 6th Chem Dep Co
    Det 11th Chem Maint Co
11. *3d Signal Co (–Dets)*
    Det 163d Sig Photo Co
    Det D-1 SIAA 3151st Rcn Sq (Mczd)
12. *10th Engr Bn (–Cos A & B)*
    2nd Bn, 343d Engr GS Regt
    Det Treadway Bridge Co (378th Engr Bn) (Sep)
13. *703d Ord Co*
14. *Hq & Hq Det 43rd Ord Bn*
    14th Ord (MM) Co
    3432d Ord (MM) Co
    64th Ord Ammo Co
    143d Ord Bomb Disp Sq
    Det 261st Ord (MM) Co (AA)
    Det 87th Ord (Hv M) Tk Co
15. *3d Med Bn (–Cos A, B & C)*
    10th Fd Hosp (–Hosp Unit) (–12 Nurses)
      6703d Blood Transfusion Unit (Fwd Dist Sec)
    Det 2d Aux Surg Group (–12 Nurses)
      5 Gen Surg Teams (Nos 2, 3, 10, 12, 21)
      1 Thoracic Team (No. 1)
      1 Neuro Team (No. 2)
      1 Orthopedic Team (No. 1)
      1 Maxille Facial Team (No. 1)
      1 Dental Prosthetic Team
16. *95th Evac Hosp (– 24 Nurses)*
17. *3d QM Co*
    1st Plat, 46th QM GR Co
    379th Rpl Co (600 Repl)
18. *Beach Group*
    36th Engr (c) Regt
    1st Naval Beach Bn
    72d Sig Co (Spec)
    Det 207th Sig Rep Co + Det 177th Sig Rep Co
    Hq & Hq Det 52d Med Bn

376th Med Coll Co
377th Med Coll Co
378th Med Coll Co
682d Med Clr Co
616th Med Clr Co (—1 Plat)
1 Sec 377th PW Esct Gd Co
Det Boat Guards
   157th MP PW Det
   706th MP PW Det
   790th MP PW Det
Co A, 759th MP Bn
1st Plat 21st Cml Decon Co (Smoke Troops)
Det 63d Cml Dep Co
3d Plat 450th Engr Dep Co
Hq & Hq Det, 530th QM Bn
   4133d QM Sv Co
   4134th QM Sv Co
   4135th QM Sv Co
   4136th QM Sv Co
   3277th QM Sv Co
3357th QM Trk Co
3634th QM Trk Co
Det 6690th Regulating Co
Hq & Hq Det, 52d QM Bn (Mbl)
   3333d QM Trk Co (DUKW)
   3334th QM Trk Co (DUKW)
   3335th QM Trk Co (DUKW)
   3336th QM Trk Co (DUKW)
   3353d QM Trk Co (DUKW) (Personnel Only)
   3355th QM Trk Co (DUKW) (Personnel Only)
1 Sec 3856th QM Gas Sup Co
Plat 93d QM Rhd Co
332d Air Force Sv Gp (Beach Detail)
111th RAF Beach Sec (Beach Unit)
69th Ord Ammo Co
3407th Ord M Auto Maint Co (DUKW)
Det 77th Ord Dep Co
Det 977th Ord Dep Co

19. *Navy Troops*
   16 Combat Demolition Units

THE end of the tortuous trail was not yet in sight, but the beginning of the end was.

Men of the 3d Infantry Division, doubly heartened by the victorious conclusion of the push on Rome and the successful amphibious invasion of France's Normandy coast, began to see where that trail had been leading all this time.

Sometimes it had seemed there was no pattern to its crazy wanderings. There was no end—not even a remembered beginning, lost in too many endless days and sleepless nights—just the awful, eternal middle. Shells, mountain peaks, destroyed villages, and mud were the only milestones to mark the journey.

Men of the 3d, and its brother divisions in the Mediterranean Theater, for a long time bore most of the United States' ground effort in the European war. Sometimes they took staggering casualties. They froze, sweated, and cursed, by turn. They fought, died, and wept without tears for dead comrades. They looked for hope when often there seemed nothing for which to hope. About the only thing left to them was faith, which was equally divided—faith in God and faith in the fighting qualities of the men on either flank.

The men who lived like rats in the ruins of Cassino and dodged death day and night were hard put to it to see the grand scale of a strategical map. The soldiers who smashed across the Rapido River, to get smashed right back, could not with a casual wave of the hand say, "Well, we took a bit of a reverse today." The men who carefully kept even the tops of their helmets from showing over the parapets of Anzio foxholes were in no position to predict the end of the war by "Oh, say, Christmas."

But the beginning of the end suddenly materialized. The tentative start, gradually evolved into full-scale warfare, now fitted neatly into a single picture which could be viewed from one perspective. That France, and eventually Germany, had been the ultimate objectives, everyone had known. It was the method of getting to those objectives that had sometime been obscured for the fighting soldiers.

When, with the invasion convoy in mid-journey, it was announced that the destination was Southern France, the pattern was now complete.

Africa, Sicily, Southern Italy, Anzio . . . it had taken the 3d Infantry Division a long time to get there.

It is interesting to note how strongly events in the Mediterranean Theater exercised influence over the planned invasion of Southern France.

In Vice Admiral H. K. Hewitt's report as Naval Commander, Western Task Force, on the Invasion of Southern France, there is to be found the following:

The preliminary directive* received from Commander-in-Chief, Mediterranean, on December 28, 1943, embodied the following mission:

Task
To establish the army firmly ashore;
To continue to maintain and support the army over

---
*Section 1.3, Invasion of Southern France, Report of Naval Commander, Western Task Force.

beaches until all need for maintenance over beaches had ceased.

Purpose

To support the invasion of Northern France.

As a basis for planning, the preliminary directive gave the following points:

(1) Preparation for the invasion of Northern France was in progress and it was expected to take place during the first suitable day in May, 1944;

(2) Decision had been made that a beachhead would be established on the south coast of France in conjunction with the invasion of Northern France for the purpose of supporting it;

(3) Composition of the army forces for the invasion of Southern France had not been decided but would probably consist of ten divisions: three or four US divisions, and the balance French divisions.

The date *December 28, 1943,* is especially important to members of the 3d Infantry Division. It clearly indicates how far ahead Allied leaders had laid definite plans. At a time when the 3d was nearly ready to jump off on the Anzio operation, plans were being formulated for an operation which was to place United States troops on the shores of Southern France, a program actually not put into effect until August 15, 1944, nearly eight months later.

In line with this, the selection of Army forces for the operations is discussed in Admiral Hewitt's report:*

The question of the identity of the military forces to be made available for the operations was of great concern to the naval planners inasmuch as three major problems depended on the final assignments. In the first place, it was desired that the assault divisions each be thoroughly trained in amphibious assault with the naval attack forces until the army and navy elements were firmly welded into a finished amphibious attack unit. Secondly, the broad problem of mounting and transporting the assault and follow-up forces required considerable planning, assignment of ships, and construction in the many mounting ports. This problem was jointly considered by the Movements and Transportation Section of AFHQ, Service of Supply, North African Theater of Operations (SOS NATOUSA), the G-4 section of the Seventh Army, and the Eighth Fleet planning and logistics sections. Lastly, after having the assault divisions assigned, it was necessary for these commands to work out their tactical assault plans with respect to definite assault beaches.

During the early period of planning, since the two or possibly three US infantry divisions having the necessary qualifications were found only in the US Fifth Army, it was necessary to remove them from the Italian front. This withdrawal from the Allied Armies in Italy (AAI) raised the problem of where the divisions should be moved for training, refitting and mounting. Originally, it was proposed to train the two US infantry divisions, the 3rd and the 45th, in the Salerno area, beginning as soon as the Pisa-Rimini line was established. In order to meet the original invasion date, May 1944, promulgated in the preliminary directive issued by the Commander-in-Chief, Mediterranean, on 28 December, it was imperative that these two infantry divisions be withdrawn from combat sometime in April. At the same time, the 85th US Infantry Division was training in North Africa in the Oran area.

French divisions at this time had not yet been nominated, but they also would have to be withdrawn from the front, trained, refitted, and mounted. It was considered that training in the Salerno area might congest the port of Naples. Therefore Sicily and the "heel" ports were considered as suitable places for refitting some of the French divisions.

Because of the distance the 85th Division would have to travel from Oran to the assault area, it was determined that that movement should be a ship-to-shore assault from combat-loaded personnel and cargo ships. The 3d and 45th Divisions would then make the assault on a shore-to-shore basis in craft, probably staging in Ajaccio.

Army operations in Italy, south of the Pisa-Rimini line, were not stabilized in time to meet the requirements for an operation in May. Consequently, craft and ships assigned for the invasion of Southern France were withdrawn for the invasion of Northern France. By the middle of June, the 3d and 45th Divisions were released from the Italian front and, instead of the 85th Division, the 36th US Infantry Division was withdrawn from the Italian front for participation in the invasion of Southern France.

While the amphibious operation against the Riviera coast was to be the fourth major landing against a hostile shore by the 3d Infantry Division, and the sixth for 2d Battalion, 30th Infantry, the operation was by no means a purely routine performance. There were several important ways in which it differed from past operations.

In the past, certain elements of surprise had been major features of the success of our landings. In this case, the Normandy landing had been carried out two months previously, giving the enemy access to information on all our latest techniques and equipment. The enemy could reasonably assume that we had employed all our major new tricks in the all-important Normandy landing and had no surprises in store. In that event we had to depend solely on the surprises of time and place.

For the first time in its experience, the Division was faced with a daylight landing. This called for changes in many of the plans which had previously been successfully employed in night landings.

There was clear evidence that the enemy had constructed offshore obstacles along the Division's beaches, which had never been encountered on any previous operation.

The tremendous concentration of shipping in the Naples area preceding our attack, and the shifting of

---

*Section 1.4, Invasion of Southern France, report of Naval Commander, Western Task Force.

the bulk of our air strength to Corsica, combined with the limited area of coast upon which we were likely to land, minimized our chance for obtaining surprise. Added to this problem was the tremendous difficulty of maintaining security on the Italian mainland, where the majority of the planning and mounting was done.

(Practice landings had been made in Nisida harbor, within full view of hundreds of Italian bathers. Full-scale assaults had been mounted at Mondragone and Formia. For days on end quantities of material had flowed into the holds and onto decks of ships through the docks at Naples, Nisida, Pozzuoli, and Baia.)

All these factors, weighed together, meant only one thing—that we could not depend on surprising the enemy with small, scattered landings, but would have to plan on stunning him with all the firepower and concentrated mass of men and material that we could direct against a small number of closely grouped beaches. The naval gunfire and air support plans were coordinated with the Division's own attack plan to achieve this effect, and this in turn fitted into the Corps scheme of maneuver, which contemplated putting more infantry battalions ashore at H-hour than were put ashore in the Normandy landing.

Stated simply, the Division's mission in Southern France was to land on beaches in the vicinity of St. Tropez and Cavalaire, some 30 miles east of Toulon, clear the enemy from the beaches and from adjacent high ground, and advance rapidly inland, preparatory to assisting in Seventh Army's attack to the west against the ports of Toulon and Marseille. Clearing of St. Tropez peninsula, maintaining contact with the 45th Infantry Division on the right and with French troops on the left, were among subsidiary initial missions.

Since it was part of the Division's mission to advance inland and seize high ground in the vicinity of Cogolin at the head of the gulf of St. Tropez, it was decided to land two battalions of the 15th Infantry initially on Yellow Beach (lying between Cap de St. Tropez and Cap Camarat, on the east side of the St. Tropez peninsula) and two battalions of the 7th Infantry on Red Beach (Gulf of Cavalaire), using the 30th Infantry to land on Red Beach after it had been cleared, with a mission of exploiting to the north and seizing objectives deep in the enemy's rear to the west, north and northeast of Cogolin. The 7th and 15th Infantry Regiments were organized as combat teams, with artillery battalions, TD, tank, chemical and medical companies, mine-gapping and signal detachments attached, while the 30th Infantry had only chemical and medical companies and a signal detachment with it.

"A soldier named Patelli stood up on the crowded deck. 'Take it from me,' he said, 'the first wave onto the beach is the best one to be in. Why, you gotta choice on the first wave! If you don't like the pillbox on the right you just move over and take the pillbox on the left. But if you gotta come in later you get no choice. You gotta take the pillbox that the first wave passed!'

"The soldiers around him grinned and kept on playing cards. A little later when someone said, 'Okay, you jokers, take your last look at Italy!', only a few of the men looked up. Even when a small radio was tuned in to 'Axis Sally,' the Nazi propagandist, and she boasted that the Germans knew all about the coming invasion of Southern France, the soldiers kept on playing cards or talking quietly. Finally, the ship's chaplain couldn't stand it any longer. 'This bunch of men is awfully unexcited,' he complained. 'I just had a normal crowd at services this morning. On the way across the Channel from England almost *everybody* turned out.'

"These men were different. They were 3d Division men. . . .'"*

On the evening of August 12, a long convoy of LSTs stretched almost as far as the eye could see over a choppy sea, off the port of Naples. The sky, darkening from its midday brightness, was faultlessly blue.

A few soldiers, lining the afterdecks of each LST, stared toward the last ship in the convoy. A small speck, distinguishable as some sort of craft, was rapidly approaching. It drew closer and the soldiers could make it out to be a speedy launch. One figure was prominent in the forepart. He stood erect, disdaining to maintain his balance by a handhold.

As the boat approached to within a few hundred yards of each LST, a few soldiers stared unbelievingly. Then the cry went up: "It's Churchill!" The cry was taken up and echoed throughout the ship. Soldiers and sailors crowded to that side of the vessel.

The short, stubby figure stood straight. His thinning white hair blew awry. As the launch drew nearly abreast, he waved. Then the doughty little warrior raised his right hand to form with two fingers the V-for-Victory sign—the symbol of hope and determination which, two years and more before, he had raised and flaunted at the power of the then mighty German war machine. The United States soldiers cheered and waved back.

Prime Minister Winston Churchill, in Italy to confer with Italian Minister Bonomi, had been unable to resist seeing off the invasion convoy, and to wish God-speed and a quick, successful victory to the United States troops. It was a favorable omen.

Admiral Hewitt on August 9 had promulgated D-Day as August 15, and H-hour as 0800. The assault troops of the 7th and 15th Infantry Regiments debarked at Ajaccio, Corsica, for the planned staging, then once again

---

*Will Lang, *Life*, Oct. 2, 1944.

embarked. By the morning of August 15, all the units of the 3d Infantry Division flotilla were in place off the coast of Cavalaire and St. Tropez.

D-Day, as do all such days, began early. In the wheelhouse of each LST a naval rating kept his attention fixed on a fascinating pattern of concentric light circles. His particular LST was the constant, the hub of his own universe, the pole around which revolved the blobs of dim light which were the other ships and craft. As the vessels slowly maneuvered through the darkness into their final positions, the magic of radar kept them safe from collision.

The captain stood on the bridge with the officer of the watch, and now and then spoke a few words to him, some of which the officer relayed through the speaking tube to the engine room.

Under dim blue lights in the crowded troop compartments men lay warm under a single thickness of blanket, and slept—most of them. Some, unable to overcome wakefulness, pondered at what the day might bring, tossed restlessly, and countless thoughts coursed through their minds: thoughts of the sound of bursting shells . . . letters from home . . . buddies they had known . . . last minute briefings: beaches, objectives, routes of advance. But most of them still slept.

In wardrooms sleepy Navy fliers cupped their hands around mugs of hot "jamoke" and pondered the coming day, their part in it, and the imminence of their return to friendlier waters and more hospitable anchorages.

At airfields on nearby Corsica, fliers were crawling from their bunks and shivering in the predawn chill. Outside, on the airstrips, ground crews already were busily warming up the motors of the bombers. The man-made thunder spoke the promise of a busy day, and of coming hell for the enemy beach defenders.

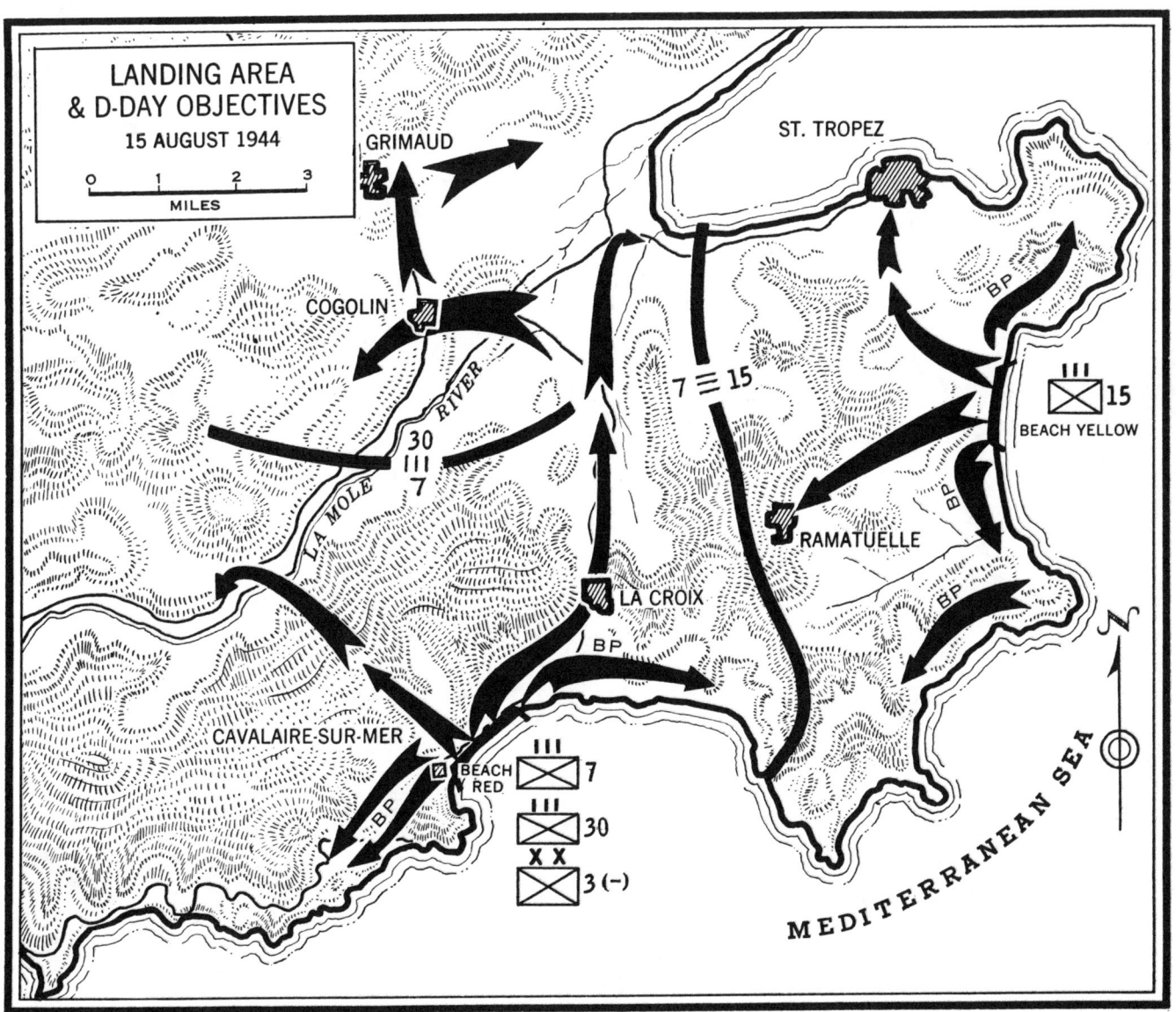

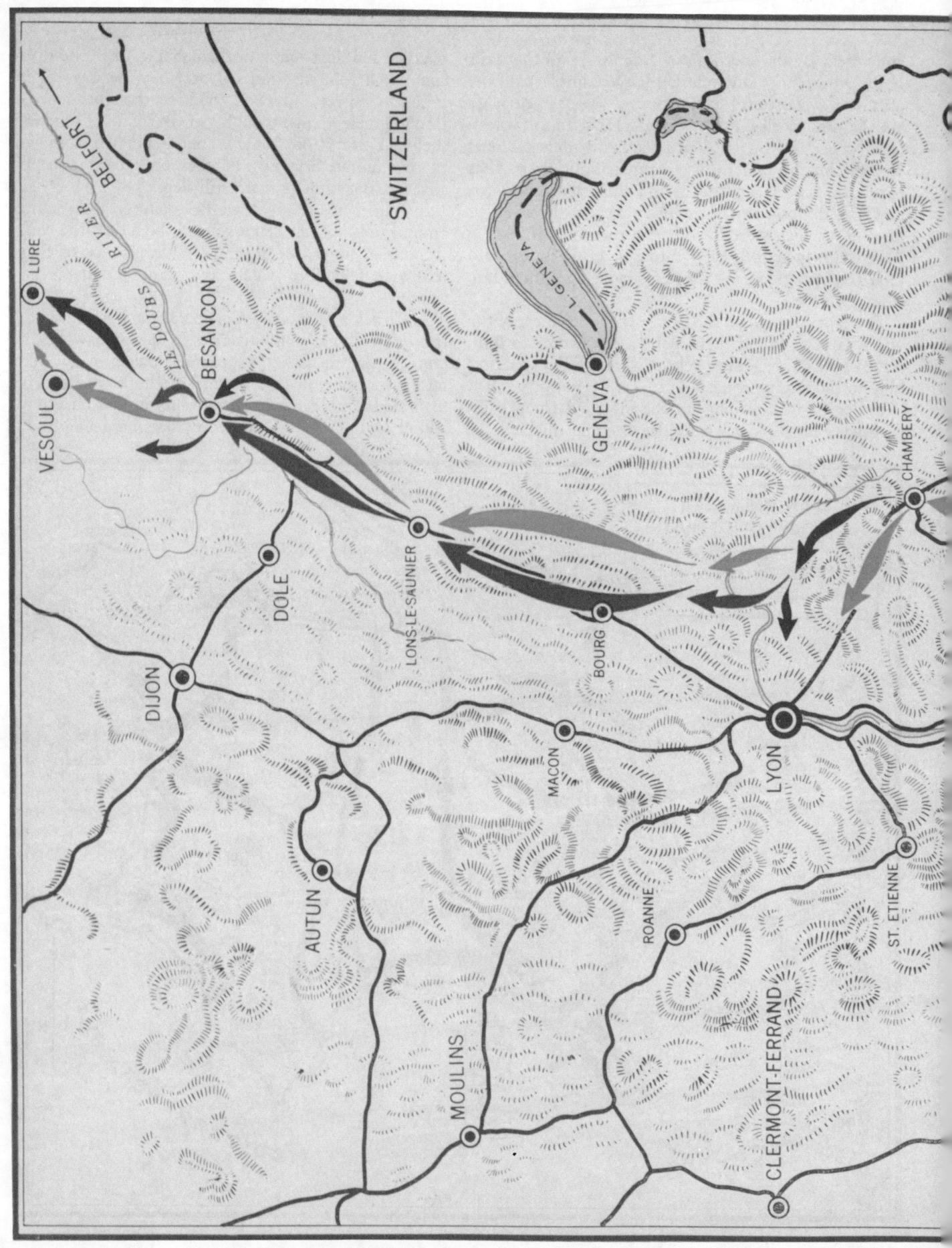

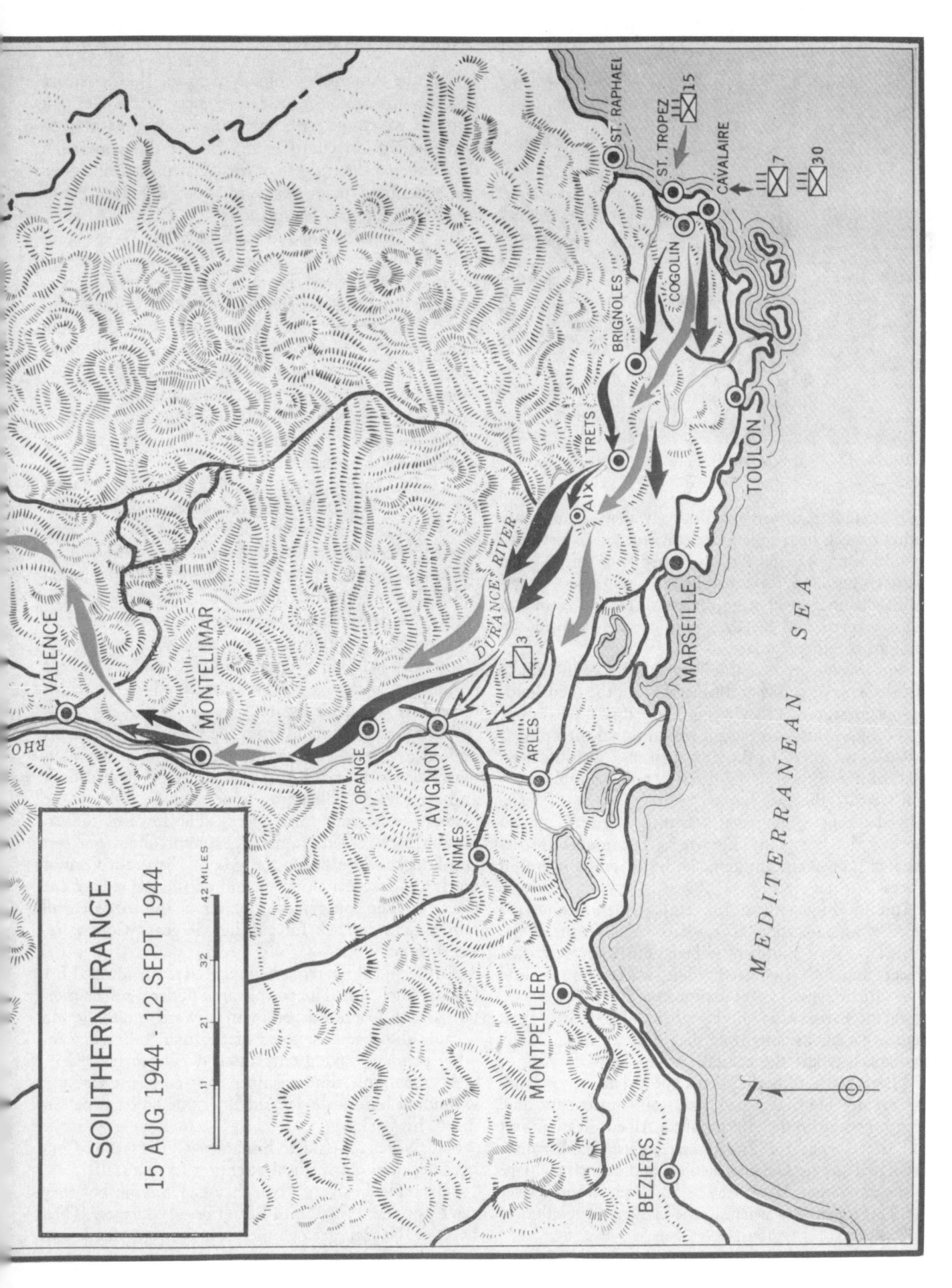

A British LCT turns toward shore and prepares for the run in.

Commanders aboard the ships, awakened early, ate without much interest, and speedily turned to last-minute discussion of plans. Details, settled long before, once again cropped up for attention and reminder. Broad outlines of maneuver were reviewed. Mental estimates of time, space, and distance were checked against the opinions of others.

Soon the queues of half-asleep soldiers would move past the cans of coffee and pans of food, the men holding out messgear as they went. The jolt of a portion of food dropped into a meat can would signal the individual to move along to the next pan and waiting mess attendant, and then down the slippery, food-splattered iron steps to the messroom.

In the supporting naval warships, gunnery officers checked the fire plans. Elsewhere, last-minute inspections of guns, ammunition, and fire tables were in process.

And in dugouts and fire emplacements ashore, a weird conglomeration of Russians, Turcomans, Poles and Slavs, their numbers spiked with a few German officers and NCOs effected reliefs, walked patrols, and turned their eyes to a still-darkned sea. There was an attitude of expectation among them. There had been stepped-up air assaults over the previous week. Many civilians had left the coastal regions between August 12-14, stating frankly that they expected an Allied landing at any hour. German radio announcements had been broadcast to the effect that an Allied invasion fleet had left Corsica for France on August 14. A rumor circulated among German soldiers and French civilians to the effect that Allied leaflets had been dropped over the St. Tropez area warning the civilian population to leave the coastal regions.

"Let the Americans come," many of the defenders probably thought. "We are foreigners to the German army. If we escape with our lives, we have nothing to lose—perhaps much to gain." But at the same time they fingered the triggers of the German machine guns and rifles, and made ready to shoot if today should prove to be the day of invasion.

It can be stated unequivocally that the D-day landings on the shores of southern France by the 3d Infantry Division were the most successful ever undertaken by the Division in its entire history in the Mediterranean Theater. Even the landings at Nettuno, smooth as they were, did not compare with those of August 15 in smoothness of execution.

Scattered resistance on the beaches was quickly overcome. The specially-trained, reinforced, Battle Patrols which landed on the flanks of both beaches speedily smashed enemy resistance with only one of them, that of the 7th Infantry, encountering strong opposition. Mission of this Battle Patrol was: to proceed about 2000 yards west from its landing point to the town of Cavalaire-sur-Mer and to clean out the town and the entire peninsula on which it is situated. The peninsula overlooks the entire beach where a major portion of the landings were scheduled to be made. It was the enemy's only available position for interfering with landing operations by flanking fire; it also furnished an excellent position for directing observed artillery fire, for which the enemy was utilizing it.

"As we started inland from the water ... I suddenly noticed a wire just above my head," said S/Sgt. Herman F. Nevers, leader of the 1st squad. "I looked back and ... saw ... a hanging mine explode and tear the platoon leader into small pieces. The force of the explosion blew S/Sgt. James P. Connor about ten feet and knocked him flat to the ground. Sergeant Connor received a fragmentation wound on the left side of the neck ... The commanding officer of the battle patrol told him to go back for aid, but Sergeant Connor refused to go."

As the squad neared a bridge a German jumped up. Connor shot him. The patrol came under a severe mortar barrage. Connor urged them forward and the group became disorganized, some of the men following another platoon, leaving only about twenty men.

At about this time a sniper shot Sergeant Connor, wounding him in the left shoulder, the bullet penetrating to his back.

Said Nevers, "I said to him, 'For Christ's sake, Connor, stop and get medical attention for yourself!'

"He replied, saying, 'No, they can hit me but they can't stop me. I'll go until I can't go any farther.' Then he said, 'Nevers, get out there on the right flank and

A soldier holds taut a line on which his comrades of the 3d Medical Battalion support themselves as they make their way toward the shore.

get those men rolling! We've got to clean out these snipers before we can advance farther!'

"Sergeant Connor told the men, 'If there's only one of us left, we've got to get to that point (the objective) and clean it up, so the guys coming in after us can get in safely with no fire on them.'"

The platoon started forward again. Connor was in the lead again. A German rose from a hole not more than thirty feet to Sergeant Connor's front and shot him in the leg. Nevers fired over Connor as he fell, killing the German.

"Sergeant Connor called me over and told me to give him a hand to help him on his feet so he could go on with the fight. I helped him up but he couldn't stand on his leg and fell down again. I wanted to give him first aid, but he wouldn't even let me look at the wound, saying there wasn't time. He told me to take the rest of the men, about fifteen now, and to carry on, and that he hoped he would see me sometime. Sergeant Connor told me that even if I had to get down and dig the bastards out with my bare hands to go ahead and dig them out . . ."

Then, according to Sgt. Edward G. Collins, the group started out to carry out Connor's instructions. Too many men started around the right flank and Connor called some of them back and sent them around to the left. In carrying out his orders the platoon cleaned out the entire area, killing three or four of the enemy and capturing approximately forty more.

Said 1st Lt. William K. Dieleman, Battle Patrol com-

3d Infantry Division troops debark from LCIs onto the beaches of Southern France on D-Day.

General "Iron Mike" O'Daniel discusses unloading with the commanding officer of the 36th Engineers' shore party on the beaches of Southern France on D-Day.

mander, "But for the outstanding example set by Sergeant Connor in the face of tremendous odds in fire power and men, the critically important mission of the whole Battle Patrol might have been delayed for a considerable time, or might even have failed entirely."

Major John R. Darrah, Special Troops surgeon, examined the area of wounds received by Sergeant Connor, two months later, and testified that the second wound must have caused him excruciating pain at the slightest movement.

Sergeant Connor received the Congressional Medal of Honor.

The 3d Reconnaissance Troop Battle Patrol, upon landing, found twenty prisoners awaiting the pleasure of their captors. The fire delivered by BARs and rifles of the Battle Patrol, shooting from their landing craft, had converted them to the Allied cause before any United States soldier set foot in Southern France. Within a short time 115 more were added and by 1030 the Battle Patrol had returned to 3d Reconnaissance Troop control, having completely accomplished its mission.

The 7th Infantry landed with 3d Battalion on the left, 2d Battalion on the right. There were concrete tetrahedra offshore, and mines and wire on the beach and inland for distances up to 500 yards, yet little resistance was encountered. The naval rocket barrage which had immediately preceded the assault had apparently had good effect, as a dense, even, pattern of bursts was observed inshore, and the first prisoners taken were well shaken up. Shortly after landing, 2d Battalion, moving up the road toward La Croix, received mortar and small-arms fire from the right, and this fire continued sporadically for about two hours with little effect. By 1045, 2d Battalion had passed through La Croix and was on its way north to its objective on the high ground astride the road west of Gassin, and by 1430 had reached the objective and contacted 30th Infantry.

The 3d Battalion had very light opposition also, and reached its first two objectives by 1345.

Both assault battalions of the 15th Infantry—3d on the right and 1st on the left—hit Yellow Beach at 0800, reduced all beach defenses within forty minutes, and moved inland to their objectives on high ground 3000 to 5000 yards back from the beach. These objectives were occupied about noon against little enemy opposition.

Leading elements of the 30th Infantry landed behind 7th Infantry on Red Beach at H-plus-80 minutes and struck rapidly inland. Overtaking a battalion of

A tank destroyer of the 3d Division's 601st TD Battalion is guided down the ramp toward the shore by a crew member.

the 7th Infantry, the 30th moved through and took objective W, and proceeded to objective D. By 1400 2d Battalion was east of the road north of La Croix, and 3d Battalion was moving toward Cogolin, which Company K reached and entered at 1415.

Landing at H-hour in support of each assault regiment were a smoke detail from the 3d Chemical Battalion (attached), four DD tanks (tanks made amphibious by canvas flotation aprons) from the 756th Tank Battalion, and on Yellow Beach four tank destroyers from the 601st TD Battalion.

By noon almost all units were on the Division's initial beachhead line.

During the afternoon 1st Battalion, 7th Infantry, passed through 3d Battalion on its objective and advanced to Highway 98 east of La Mole and turned west on the highway. The 2d Battalion, relieved by 30th Infantry on its objective, followed 1st Battalion. 1st Battalion was assembled, and moved west along the coast road, meeting no resistance until about 2300 when it encountered a strongpoint of six or eight machine guns, three AT guns, and several riflemen, covering a wire-and-mine roadblock. This strongpoint was still under attack at noon of the following day.

The 2d Battalion, 15th Infantry, swung north through 3d Battalion, 15th Infantry, and attacked St. Tropez, reducing the last resistance there and taking nearly 100 PWs by 1945. The entire regiment then assembled and moved west through Cogolin behind the 30th Infantry.

The 1st Battalion, 30th Infantry, followed 3d Battalion, 30th, through Cogolin. Company G contacted 15th Infantry at 1500 and at 1640 the regimental Battle Patrol contacted 15th Infantry Battle Patrol on the peninsula between Red and Yellow Beaches. The 1st Battalion, 30th Infantry, entered Grimaud at 1710 against little but sniper resistance, with a reinforced platoon protecting its flank. The 3d Battalion rode on tanks west from Cogolin to Grimaud at 1755. The first enemy contacted by 3d Battalion was about one and one-half miles east of Collobrières at 2240.

This resistance was overcome and 3d Battalion had closed in Collobrières by 0300 August 16.

By 0435 1st Battalion had passed through La Garde

Dead 3d Division comrades are laid on stretchers along the beach.

A shallow water mine is exploded near shore by the 3d Division Engineers while unloading is proceeding.

like a man trying to keep two determined intruders from entering a stolen house which he had taken for his home, and running back and forth alternately attempting to hold two doors shut. Suddenly he hears noises which sound like a third party about to come in through the cellar. He is powerless to do anything about this new threat.

From subsequent interrogation it was learned that the enemy had expected the main landing effort to be made in the vicinity of Toulon and Marseille. He knew that we must have in short order at least one good port through which to pour supplies to keep the advance continuous. The bulk of the enemy's force, therefore, was disposed farther west, and was in no position to intervene until after we were well ashore. But even then it was too late. The provisional airborne division, under Brig. Gen. Robert T. Frederick, which landed in the vicinity of Le Muy; the rapid advances inland of all three United States divisions; the harassment of naval gunfire along the coast; the disrupting of the enemy's lines of communications and movement of enemy reserves by well-organized and well-armed French resistance groups; the bombing "strangle"—all these prevented the enemy from making the ghost of a showing of countermeasure or even offering effective resistance.

The enemy high command issued one amazing statement about three days following the landings. "No counterattack will be launched against the invasion forces," said the enemy in an intercepted radio broad-

Freinet and was in Les Mayons reducing resistance, and taking twenty-two prisoners.

An hour after that time the reinforced platoon from 1st Battalion, on flank-protection duty, was relieved by elements of the 45th Division.

By noon of August 16, D-plus-one, leading elements of the 3d Infantry Division were twenty miles inland.

Its gains were surprising, and gratifying, in comparison with its former landing operations below Nettuno.

In retrospect, here is what had happened:

A harassed German High Command was even then stretching its forces nearly to the breaking point between the long Russian front and the fluid battlefield which all of France from the Seine River to the Brittany Peninsula had become on the west. It was

The Grand Hotel at Cavalaire-sur-Mer near where 3d Division troops landed.

Aid-men of the shore party tend to the wounds of a 3d Division soldier on the beach awaiting evacuation.

cast, "until they have driven inland far enough so as to be out of effective range of the support of their own naval gunfire." In effect, this was equivalent to a flat admission of German impotence.

"We broke a very thin crust," said one high-ranking United States officer "and behind the crust there was nothing that could stop us."

So, with scarcely a pause, the 3d Infantry Division prepared to make its longest advance in the shortest length of time that it had ever made—or ever would make—in Europe. There was no warning such as, "I want you to be in Palermo in five days." Movement and attack orders were, for the most part, to be issued verbally by the VI Corps commander, Maj. Gen. Lucian K. Truscott, to General O'Daniel; General O'Daniel's orders were usually issued the same way to his regimental commanders. The confirming orders, on paper, would be sent along later, but right now it was "to hell with written orders, let's get going." The enemy had been maneuvered back on his heels, and every man in VI Corps, weary though he might be, could not help but sense that keeping the enemy off-balance was a sure way to keep casualties to the bare minimum. The Division moved west against only scattered, unorganized resistance.

Improvisation paid dividends. It was found that an entire infantry battalion could be completely loaded on transportation within a regiment, including tanks, TDs, jeeps, and other assorted vehicles without having recourse to non-organic vehicles.

It was a common sight to see a whole rifle battalion moving down a road—doughboys draped over the

A conglomeration of eastern nationalities and a few German soldiers are herded together as prisoners of war at the beach entrance.

211

Wounded comrades of the 3d Division are carried along the beach by aid-men to the evacuation area.

3-inch guns of tank destroyers, clinging to the slippery-sided tanks of the 756th, or loaded sixes-and-sevens to trailer-hauling jeeps.

Of the 1627 prisoners taken on D-day, the overwhelming majority were from the 242nd Infantry Division, with a few hundred more from fortress and coast defense battalions, and miscellaneous numbers of them from labor, naval, air and signal organizations.

Company G, 30th Infantry, with armor, occupied Carnoules, southeast of Gonfaron, by 0530 August 16 while 2d Battalion attacked and occupied Gonfaron by 1400. Company K, 30th Infantry, captured Pierrefeu by 1819, August 16, against self-propelled and small-arms fire—the westernmost advance of the 30th. The company took thirty-five prisoners.

The leading battalions, 1st and 3d, of the 7th Infantry, overcame enemy strongpoints. By noon of August 17 our front lines ran generally from Cuers-Carnoules-Gonfaron-Le Luc, inclusive. Tanks and tank destroyers were being used with infantry to patrol and clear roads linking battalion sectors. Towns captured in twenty-four hours included Le Lavandou, Bormes, Leoube, Pierrefeu, Pignans, Carnoules, Puget Ville, Rocbaron, and Flassans.

At 1350 August 17, 2d Battalion of the 7th Infantry forward elements received small-arms fire from a road junction on the approaches to La Londe. Intense artillery and machine-gun fire also delayed the battalion's advance. The battalion engaged the enemy in an all-night fire fight, during which forty to fifty Germans were killed. Patrols into La Londe during the morning of August 18 reported the town clear.

It was in this fight that S/Sgt. Stanley Bender of Company E particularly distinguished himself. The three bridges which spanned the Maravennes River just beyond the town had to be taken intact, otherwise the advance would have been slowed for hours, when every minute counted in pursuing the retreating Germans.

Said 1st Lt. George H. Franklin, "At about 1400 hours, just as we were about to round the last bend in the road . . . We were stopped by a Frenchman who advised us that there was a roadblock about 200 yards beyond us and that the town was full of enemy troops. We instantly dismounted from four M-10 TDs and three M-4 tanks and went into a squad column on either side of the road and then went cross-country in an effort to surprise the enemy."

After going only a short distance the company was fired upon by machine guns and small arms from well-concealed positions to the left. At the same time an enemy antitank gun opened fire and destroyed one of the tanks which had left the road and was advancing with the infantry. All remaining TDs and tanks moved into firing position from where they attempted to engage the antitank guns.

"We all took cover as rapidly as possible," said S/Sgt. Edward C. Havrila. ". . . I saw that . . . Sergeant Bender . . . hadn't taken cover with the rest of us. The crazy guy was standing up on top of the knocked-out tank, in full view of the kraut, shading his eyes and looking around trying to pick out the source of the enemy fire. Bullets were bouncing off that tank right beside him, but he nevertheless stayed right there until he found the kraut position . . ."

When Bender located the position he jumped to the ground and ran to a ditch in which two squads had taken cover. He ordered them to engage the enemy while he took his squad forward in an effort to destroy the strongpoint. Then, without waiting for instructions or orders, Sergeant Bender ran forward, motioning for his squad to follow. The intrepid squad leader reached the ditch under machine-gun fire which

General Shepard, Assistant Division Commander, supervises activities along the beaches at Cavalaire-sur-Mer in Southern France.

wounded four of his men. The enemy tried to throw grenades into the ditch, but Bender did not move until his squad had joined him. Said Sgt. Forest M. Law: "The next time I saw Sergeant Bender he was in the act of crawling from the ditch at a point between seventy-five and one hundred and fifty yards beyond the Kraut strongpoint. He was all alone and was making no effort to conceal himself. Walking erect ... he made a fine target and one of the kraut machine gunners picked up his gun and turned it around in an effort to get him. However Sergeant Bender continued his wide end sweep in a rapid walk. He was too far away for me to see his facial expression, but his manner looked as calm and unperturbed as a soldier on pass."

Bender walked the entire forty to fifty yards, directly up to a gunner who, during Bender's entire "stroll," had had a clear field of fire. Bender shot the man with his tommy gun.

Following this, he walked another twenty-five yards to the second machine-gun emplacement and killed the gunner and his assistant. He called his squad out of the ditch and walked another thirty-five yards to kill an enemy rifleman who was in the act of firing. The squad joined him in the slaughter.

As a result of Sergeant Bender's actions, and the inspiration they caused, all bridges over the Maravennes were taken intact, a roadblock was destroyed, and the dominating high ground was seized. Sergeant Bender was later awarded the Congressional Medal of Honor.

The 15th Infantry regrouped during the period of 2d Battalion, 7th's action, and pushed west along the Besse-Forcalqueiret road, clearing out the hills south of the road. Opposition was light for the most part and the regiment moved swiftly. At 1900 3d Battalion pushed through St. Anastasie and across the high ground west of Besse. At the same time, 2d Battalion began a truck shuttle movement toward the regimental zone of advance after being relieved by 7th Infantry at Pierrefeu. The 3d Battalion was held up for a short period at Anastasie by about fifty enemy, but these were soon forced to withdraw. At 2100 1st Battalion was south of Forcalqueiret and 2d Battalion was east of the same town.

The 30th Infantry, led by 2d Battalion, under the command of Maj. Frederick R. Armstrong, reached the vicinity of Brignoles, where it was delayed by enemy opposition from 1840 August 17, until the morning of the 18th. The enemy brought up his 1st Company, 757th Regiment, 338th Infantry Division, and other units totalling two battalions in strength, to hold the town. The forces occupied a position west of the town, covering a 300-meter front, protected by sharp terrain on both sides. At 1825 a patrol from the 3d Reconnaissance Troop was stopped by the enemy on Highway 7 with 3d Battalion about 1000 yards behind.

The 2d Battalion, which had taken Flassans by 1200, August 17, was on its way to Brignoles two hours later. Although the 30th did not know it, the capture of Brignoles was to be the regiment's first big fight in southern France.

Plan of the attack was to move astride the Flassan-Brignoles road with 1st Battalion on the right on a flanking mission, and 2d Battalion on the left. H-hour was set for 0600 August 18.

The attack got away as planned and Company B swung north to Le Val to protect the regiment's right flank, as Company G moved west from Besse to the high ground dominating Le Celle, protecting the 30th's left flank. The attack moved forward against stubborn resistance. During August 18 Company F got around

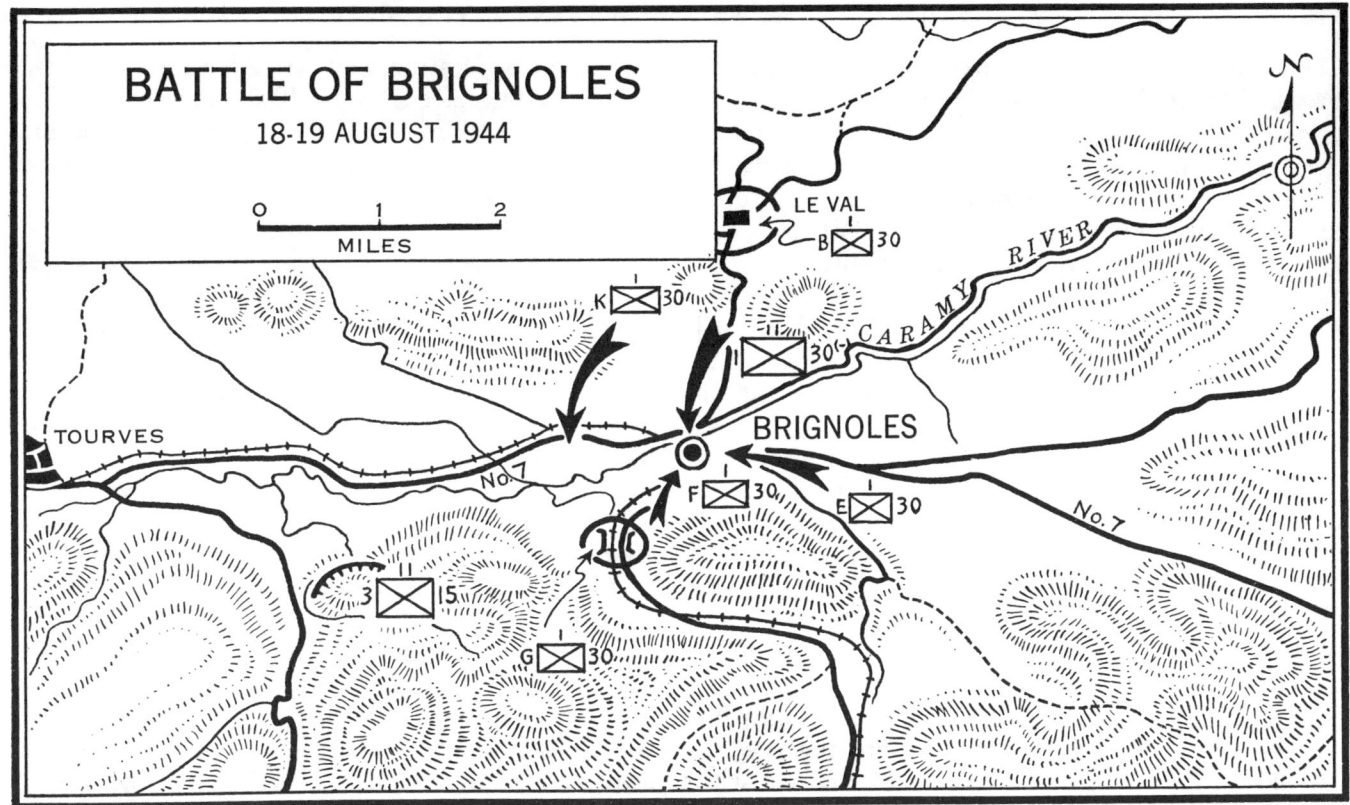

south of the town and cut the road to the west. Company E drove to the center of Brignoles by 1900. The 1st Battalion ran into heavy resistance just north of the city.

During the night of August 18-19 3d Battalion was committed in an envelopment to the north to cut the road west of town and continue toward Bras, as 1st Battalion (minus Company B at Le Val) and 2d Battalion (minus Company G at La Celle) worked into the town.

The attack began again at 0600, August 19. Lt. Col. Allen F. Bacon's 1st Battalion, spearheaded by Company A, came in from the north, while Company E drove from the west and Company F from the southwest, to meet in the center of the town. This, coupled with the wide 3d Battalion flanking attack, broke enemy resistance and the town was completely cleared by 1030. The 3d Battalion continued toward Bras.

Elements of the 338th Infantry Division were now being counted through the cages, although the bulk of opposition, such as it was, was still being provided by 242nd Infantry Division, in addition to dozens of "spare parts" organizations, such as handfuls from the 189th Reserve Division and 244th Infantry Division.

Between noon of August 19 and noon August 20 the Division advanced nearly thirty miles, moving both on foot and by motor. Towns liberated during the 24-hour period were, besides Brignoles: Meounes, Gareoult, Neoules, La Roquebrussane, Camps, La Celle, and Le Val.

A Task Force consisting of Company C, 15th Infantry, plus four tanks, two TDs, and three trucks moved from Mazauges. The 1st Battalion followed the Task Force; then on August 20, continued the advance toward Auriel. No resistance was encountered. From Tourves, 2d Battalion, 15th, continued the advance toward Trets, which was found clear, and on the morning of the 20th the battalion continued the advance toward Gardanne. The 3d Battalion had taken Tourves early in the afternoon of the 19th after a 45-minute attack, and Company L pushed on toward St. Maximin. The battalion occupied La Defenos and terrain in the vicinity. On the morning of the 20th 3d Battalion moved by truck to Trets, thence southwest toward Peynier.

The 30th Infantry reorganized in the vicinity of Brignoles following its fight there and moved out with 1st Battalion in the lead. By 1430, August 19 1st Battalion had gone beyond La Censies. The 2d Battalion was on high ground to the south of 1st Battalion and 3d Battalion was on high ground to the south of Bras. At 1900 3d Battalion left St. Maximin for Ollières on foot and arrived there prior to midnight. Shortly thereafter it moved out for Pourcieux. The 2d Battalion remained in reserve near Brignoles until 0400, when it moved out along Highway 7. At noon 30th Infantry had still encountered no opposition.

During the same period (August 19-20) 1st Battalion, 7th Infantry, remained in defensive positions near Pierrefeu, except for Company B, which outposted

Cuers. Company A was relieved by units of the 1st French Division at 1405. By 0800 1st Battalion had begun shuttling toward La Celle, and upon arriving there prepared to move by vehicle to the regimental assembly area. The 2d Battalion, 7th Infantry, moved to a defensive position in the vicinity of Meounes and Forcalqueiret during the night of August 19-20. By noon, August 20, French troops were relieving the 2d Battalion. The 3d Battalion was completely relieved by French troops by 1405 August 19 and moved first to assembly near St. Honoré, then by vehicle to the vicinity of La Celle.

Summary of localities liberated again read like a Michelin guidebook to the area: Masaugnes, Tourves, Rougiers, Seillons, Ollières, Pourcieux, St. Zacharie, Pourrierers, Trets, Peynier, Rousset, and Puyloubier.

The move against the most important town in the vicinity, Aix-en-Provence, began on the afternoon of August 20.

The 2d Battalion, 30th Infantry, met opposition as it moved into position east of Aix. At 2215 Company G was astride Highway 7 leading into town while the entire 2d Battalion was engaged in a firefight with the enemy until 0130, when the fire died down. During the night the regiment established blocks to the west and south of town. The 3d Battalion, meanwhile, was driving west north of Highway 7, and reached the outskirts of Aix before being fired on about dark of August 20. From this position, 1st Battalion swung north, then west, cutting across four to five "hub" roads leading into Aix, fifteen kilometers to the north of the city, in the dark, fighting bicycle-mounted Germans who came in from the north. The 1st Battalion then established blocks on roads, placing themselves to the northwest of Aix. The 3d Battalion established blocks to the north of their zone of attack.

By dawn 1st Battalion, which had moved farthest, so as to be on 3d Battalion's right as it faced south, was ready to attack, and had a strong block at Celoney, astride Highway 7 (7th and 15th were not far enough west to establish these blocks as planned).

By daylight 3d Battalion, too, was poised to attack, having swung northwest inside 1st Battalion.

The coordinated attack got away at 0600. The 2d Battalion provided a base of fire as 1st Battalion attacked from the northwest and 3d Battalion pushed in from the north. Bulk of the attached armor was with 3d Battalion.

Just as the attack commenced 1st Battalion was attacked by enemy infantry with strong armor support down Highway 7 from vicinity of Celoney. The entire battalion was ordered to block to the northwest and deal with this threat while 3d Battalion continued with its mission of clearing the city. Aix-en-Provence was completely free of enemy by 1000, August 21.

The 3d Battalion, 7th Infantry, began a shuttling movement toward Chateauneuf following the fall of Aix-en-Provence.

The 1st Battalion, 15th Infantry, had overcome opposition in front of Auriel, and by 0200, August 21, entered and cleared the town. The 2d Battalion, advancing toward Gardanne, met resistance. Company G moved against it and by 1515 had a patrol into the town. The battalion was generally held up, however, by an enemy pocket estimated to be from 400 to 600 men in strength. The battalion moved out at daylight, August 21, attacked approximately 1500 yards, and had the town by 1000.

Towns liberated were Aix-en-Provence, Gardannes, Chateauneuf, Vaubenargues, St. Mare, and Le Lollonet.

Following its capture of Aix and Gardannes, the two most important towns in the area, the Division conducted vigorous patrolling up to ten miles to the west, northwest, and southwest and established a series of roadblocks in the three directions. Reconnaissance elements entered Berre and patrolled to the lake near it.

The broad scheme of maneuver, in which 3d Infantry Division drove to the west, might be explained at this time. Originally, rather than make a direct assault by sea on the highly fortified area of Toulon-Marseille, VI Corps had chosen to land farther to the east. Early seizure of both of them was necessary, however, to gain a port before October's unfavorable weather set in, making maintenance over the beaches extremely difficult.

Toulon had to be reduced because the port there, in addition to being strongly fortified with big guns which could seriously interfere with shipping bound for Marseille, was a warship and submarine base whose possession by the enemy would enable him to send out damaging naval units against unprotected convoys; or, tie up and hinder our supply lines by forcing the Navy to convoy every LST and Liberty ship which sailed from Naples to Marseille. Marseille was the needed port since, in peacetime, it had handled the largest amount of tonnage of any harbor city on the Mediterranean.

French units which began landing over Red and Yellow beaches on D-plus-one relieved our elements along the coast—that is, 7th Infantry—narrowing the Division's then 20-mile frontage. The 3d Division then continued the rapid advance to the west, flanking from the north both Toulon and Marseille while French units undertook the task of cleaning them out.

By this time, therefore, all roads leading north and northwest from the city had been blocked.

Over August 22-23 1st Battalion, 7th Infantry, was

sent by truck to the vicinity of Lambesc, then moved northwest of the town and set up a defense along the highway. A motorized patrol was sent into Pelissane and found the town clear of enemy. The 3d Battalion left for La Roque and relieved elements of 180th Infantry (45th Division), going into position on the road about 1000 yards east of the town. A roadblock was set up in the town.

The 15th Infantry's 1st Battalion remained in defensive positions around Gardannes and to the south and southwest. The 2d Battalion continued its blocking role also, with the CP at La Fare. At 0910, August 23, the battalion moved to its final phase line, which included Gignac, Marignane, and Martigues. An L Company patrol investigated the airport north of Marignane and found mines on the field marked with flags.

The 30th Infantry sent out a motorized patrol shortly after noon on August 22, to Lançon, which came from the south through La Fare and reported no enemy. The 3d Battalion began a motor movement toward Salon at 2030, and by 0515 had set up roadblocks in that vicinity. The 2d Battalion remained in reserve and 1st Battalion stayed in position with roadblocks covering all approaches.

Towns liberated during the period were Marignane, St. Victoret, Vitrelles, Rognac, Coudoux, La Fare, Cornillon-Confoux, Lançon, St. Cannat, Labarben, Palissanee, Salon, Vernegues, Alleins, Mullemort, and Charleval.

The swing north to parallel the Rhone River was about to begin, together with the most rapid phase of Division's most rapid advance in Europe. The German 19th Army was now almost completely disorganized. Up until noon of August 23 the Division had taken 4165 prisoners. Elsewhere in the VI Corps zone the German commander of the coastal defense area had been captured, along with most of his staff, and this early disruption of enemy communications left the 19th Army with no choice but to begin its rapid backpedalling toward Germany.

A major factor aiding the speed and success of our movement was the activity of the French resistance groups. Four years of Nazi subjugation had left many ardent French patriots with a strong urge to take to the "underground," a word loosely used in connection with resistance activities—that is to say, to go into hiding from the German Gestapo. At the time of our landing there were about seventeen of these groups which had attained a high degree of organization by consolidating, selecting common leaders, and formulating strict rules of conduct. Any man who wished to be a member of the F.F.I. (*Forces Francaise D'Interieure*—the common, but by no means only, name for the resistance groups) had to renounce completely his ties with home and family and devote his time and energies toward aiding in the liberation of France.

Strict rules of conduct did not mean that a man would be put on extra duty in the kitchen for failure to keep his shirt buttoned or his cap straight on his head, but it did mean that his comrades would put him to death if he lost his rifle. Weapons, seized from ambushed German *Wehrmacht* units, or dropped by parachute from British bombers, were bought with blood, and were too precious to waste through carelessness. Other governing restrictions were equally as severe, although, with typical Gallic logic, applied only to things having mainly to do with life and death.

The motivating spirit was patriotism and a burning desire for freedom. The harsh conditions of service were entirely in keeping with the ascetic singleness of purpose which had dictated the groups' formation.

In certain cities, notably Grenoble, Avignon, and Lyons, and in scores of lesser localities, the F.F.I. swung into decisive action with the landings in southern France. Sometimes under the leadership of United States or British members of the O.S.S. (Office of Strategic Services), more often led by Frenchmen, whole towns were seized and held to await our coming. In addition to this sabotage activities were coordinated with our movements. If the Air Force failed to destroy a bridge, that bridge might be demolished anyway—from the ground and with hand-laid demolitions. Speeding convoys of enemy reserves ran into mysteriously laid roadblocks, and ambush. Small, isolated German pockets were sometimes wiped out to the last man, and lone enemy soldiers, if they escaped retribution at the hands of the patriots, surrendered to the first United States soldier to present himself, in preference to being the quarry in a relentless manhunt.

It is true there were a few summer patriots in the ranks of the F.F.I. These were the heroes who put on white armbands after the Germans had been cleared out, and some of them were the leading spirits in the head-shaving parties which accompanied each liberation of new territory. But these persons were in a very small minority. Most of the patriots fought behind the lines, and rendered us valuable assistance in our clean sweep from the Riviera coast north up the Rhone Valley.

Beginning on August 23 our reconnaissance elements patrolled up to fifteen miles in front of the Division, reaching Arles on the Rhone River as a move was begun to the northern banks of the Durance River.

The 2d Battalion, 30th Infantry, relieved 7th Infantry, which was in position with its 1st Battalion near Aliens and Mallemont, 2d Battalion in Division reserve at St. Cannat, and 3d Battalion located between La Roque and Charleval. The 7th Infantry, in turn be-

Pont du Cavaillon, the immensity of whose pillars is here indicated, was demolished by the enemy.

gan a relief of the 157th Infantry (45th Division) north of the Durance River. Goums began relieving 3d Battalion, 15th Infantry, on the Division left flank, and 1st Battalion, 15th Infantry, was assembled in the vicinity of St. Cannat as Division reserve.

At 1710, August 23, 1st Battalion, 30th Infantry, moved north to Lamonen against no resistance, and had reached its objective by 2130.

The move across the Durance River continued. The 15th Infantry moved during the night of August 24-25, following relief by units of the 1st French Armored Division. 30th Infantry commenced its move on the morning of the 25th. The 7th Infantry, meanwhile continued patrolling the terrain to its front and, upon finding it unoccupied, moving forward. By 1000 2d Battalion had a patrol into Cavaillon, and during the morning of August 25 reconnaissance elements passed through the battalion to patrol the road northwest toward Avignon, which was later entered by elements of the 3d Reconnaissance Troop.

Moves of the Division had now begun to resemble the pattern left on an ice rink by the skates of busy hockey players as successive objectives were reached, found unoccupied, and new ones assigned.

7th Infantry sent a motorized patrol on August 25th from Segonce to Montlaux, Cruix, Stetienne, and to Ongles without making contact with the enemy. The 2d Battalion sent a patrol into Caumont and picked up two straggler prisoners. The 3d Battalion sent Company L (less one platoon) to Sault, and from there to Vaison. The platoon set up a roadblock at a road junction 1000 yards north of Montbrun. Remainder of the battalion remained in Division reserve near Apt. The 1st Battalion moved through Pernes and occupied the town of Orange. It remained there until all elements of the 15th Infantry had passed through it, meanwhile contacting the French to the south.

The 15th Infantry moved from its assembly area in the vicinity of Apt by motor to another in the vicinity of Carpentras. At 0500, August 26, the regiment advanced to the northwest with 1st Battalion on the left and 3d Battalion on the right, making no contact with the enemy.

The 30th Infantry, after moving by truck from Salon to Vaison, was given the mission of clearing out the area northwest of Vaison and south of the Aigue River. The regimental I & R platoon had occupied Vaison before dark of August 25 after reconnoitering north out of Sault. The 1st Battalion trucked from Salon to an assembly area near Apt. The 2d Battalion followed the 1st, then moved by motor to Carpentras, from which point it moved to clear the area south of the Aigue River and northwest of Vaison. The 1st Battalion moved abreast, clearing between the river and the Mirabel-Vaison road.

The 1st platoon of the 3d Reconnaissance Troop contacted elements of the 36th Infantry Division in Nyons at 1350, August 25. The 2d Platoon had entered Carpentras unopposed at 1715. The 3d platoon captured sixty-one prisoners in the vicinity of Orange at 1035, August 26.

This rubber ponton bridge over the Durance River near Mirabeau was built by the 3d Division's 10th Engineer Battalion.

The Division was now moving into positions preparatory to launching an attack northwest toward Montelimar.

The 7th Infantry advanced north along Highway 7, paralleling the Rhone, to Bourg St. Andeol, 1st and 2d Battalions abreast. At Bourg the regiment was passed through by 15th Infantry, which reached Donzere after a terrific battle at a bridge 1000 yards south of the town. Several AT guns and a strong force of infantry with artillery support had to be overcome at this point. The battle lasted seven hours. On the morning of the 27th the regiment continued along Highway 7 toward Montelimar. Company L encountered enemy resistance from approximately thirty enemy on the regiment's right, armed with one machine gun and some rifles, besides an antitank gun. The enemy withdrew after a short fight. The 30th Infantry finished the job of clearing south of the Aigue River, and from Vaison to Mirabel, and continued the attack on the morning of the 27th between 15th Infantry and the 36th Infantry Division. Toward noon screening reconnaissance elements encountered an enemy strongpoint in the vicinity of Grignan. The 1st Battalion, between 1400 and 1430 of the previous day, had been bombed and strafed by four planes identified as P-47s. The 2d Battalion started at 0700, August 27, reached Valreas at 0900 and continued along its zone of advance. The 3d platoon, 3d Reconnaissance Troop, after engaging in a fight which netted eighty-five PWs, entered Bollene.

During this period one of Mauldin's characters ruefully remarked something to the effect that, "We try like hell to catch the enemy and when we catch him we try like hell to get him on the run." It was at Montelimar that the 3d Division once more caught him. By the time the brief battle was over, a considerable weight of enemy materiel and more than a thousand prisoners were prevented from making any further progress in their headlong rush backward.

The 15th Infantry continued to advance north along Highway 7 on the approaches to the town. On August 27, the 1st Battalion, moving on the regimental left flank, had first encountered enemy resistance in the vicinity of Donzere. The 3d Battalion advanced on the right flank, with Company L first meeting enemy opposition. The 2d Battalion, in reserve, followed 3d Battalion.

The 3d Battalion, 7th Infantry, had moved to the 30th Infantry sector at 1915, August 27, passing through Begude-de-Mazenc en route, which placed it east of Montelimar.

The 30th Infantry on August 27 had cleared the enemy out of strongpoints and rear-guard localities along the Nyons-Montelimar road and west to Grignan. The 2d Battalion, after cleaning out Grignan, moved to Salles-en-Bois during the night. At 0800 the battalion moved out in two columns to rejoin at Rochefort, where it ran into some small-arms opposition.

A coordinated attack at 0800 found 3d Battalion, 7th Infantry, on the right side of the road leading west into Montelimar, with 3d Battalion, 30th Infantry, on the left, and 1st Battalion, 30th, echeloned to the left rear. The 3d Battalion, 7th, encountered continuous rear-guard resistance, but 3d Battalion, 30th, met none until 1030, when it was fired on from the vicinity of La Batie Rollande. The 1st Battalion, 7th Infantry, advanced behind 3d Battalion, while 2d Battalion remained in Division reserve near Grillon.

The 1st Battalion 15th Infantry drove relentlessly for-

Members of the F.F.I. guard German prisoners captured by French Army forces in the city of Marseille.

Part of an enemy truck convoy which was partly destroyed south of Montelimar. The chief scene of destruction was north of the town.

ward into the enemy resistance. The enemy force now trapped in the Montelimar area resorted to violent and incessant counterattacks to break out of the cordon. The 1st Battalion drove forward and smashed every German counterattack against it, repulsing at one time the attack of an entire regiment of infantry. It pounded the enemy force with concentrations of artillery and mortar fire.

The 15th Infantry pressed its attack during the afternoon of the 28th. The 1st Battalion encircled the town and attacked with Company A from the east, Company C from the northeast, and Company B from the north. The 2d Battalion attacked from the southeast, squeezing out 3d Battalion, which then reverted to regimental reserve. The town was entered at 1430 by Company F, supported by Company G. During the afternoon and night the 1st and 2d Battalions continued to clear the town of enemy snipers, drawing enemy small-arms, sniper, and artillery fire—the last from an enemy gun located right in town. All roads

One of the two 380mm German railway guns abandoned by the enemy in the battle of Montelimar. There were also four 280mm guns abandoned.

leading into the city were blocked, and the area between it and the Rhone River cleared. Elements of the 3d Battalion screened to the southeast. Company C repulsed an enemy counterattack of estimated company strength from the north at 2030. The job of cleaning out Montelimar was finally completed by 1145, August 29.

During this three-day action, the 1st Battalion took 804 prisoners, killed and wounded 485 enemy, captured or destroyed at least 500 vehicles and an estimated 1,000 horses. For this action the 1st Battalion was awarded the Distinguished Unit Citation.

The 1st Battalion, 30th Infantry, had continued its attack along the south side of the east-west road into Montelimar. At 1255, August 28, the battalion moved southwest through Portes-en-Valdane, then proceeded to La Touche, where it engaged the enemy in a firefight at Hill 304. Here, forty-one prisoners were taken after a fifteen to twenty minute fight. At 1255 3d Battalion was located on the outskirts of Puygeron and 2d Battalion was advancing toward Rochefort, which was entered by Company G by 1415.

The 7th Infantry continued attacking west and northwest, and entered Montelimar shortly before noon, August 29, as well as contacting elements of the 36th Division and occupying the important hill mass generally northeast of the town. The 3d Battalion was the unit which took La Batie Rollande; the 2d Battalion moved during the night of August 28-29 to Cardineau from which it launched its attack to the west and northwest at 0600.

The small river east of Montelimar was crossed during the morning of August 29 by 3d and 1st Battalions, 7th Infantry, and 3d Battalion, 30th Infantry.

Following clearance of the town itself, 7th and 30th Infantry Regiments took up the advance north along Highway 7, with 30th Infantry on the right.

Attacking on the left of the Division zone, 7th Infantry assaulted north along Highway 7 and the high ground to the immediate east of the highway. There was no organized resistance, but 2d Battalion met considerable sniper fire while clearing the hills, and Flakwagon, mortar, and small-arms fire from a column of enemy vehicles which was halted along the road. The 2d Battalion relieved 3d Battalion, 143d Infantry on high ground north of the town at 1300, August 29. At the same time 3d Battalion was moving north of the 2d, with 1st Battalion following to the right rear.

A Division Artillery forward observer with 2d Battalion, 7th Infantry, 1st Lt. Robert W. Metz, first spotted a huge enemy convoy moving up Highway 7 north of Montelimar. What he saw made him call for all the artillery that could be brought to bear. This was practically all of the Division's organic gunfire, plus guns

This stretch of road north of Montelimar lined with about 1,000 dead horses was "an avenue of stenches."

of the attached 69th Armored FA Battalion. The 2d Battalion observed fire on the enemy convoy; then directed additional artillery fire on a train pulling a railroad gun, stopping the train and wrecking three or four boxcars. 2d Battalion occupied the west slope of a ridge; 3d Battalion was in position directly south, and 1st Battalion put a platoon on a hill to the east to prevent enemy from infiltrating to the rear of the regiment's leading elements.

The 1st Battalion, 7th Infantry, then started to move to the right of 2d Battalion, with its objective to cut the enemy column. This move commenced at 1700, and the battalion advanced without opposition to be on its objective by 2100. The 1st and 2d Battalions contacted each other on the highway at 0330, August 30, and at 0600 continued the attack to the north with 1st Battalion on the right and 2d Battalion on the left. All objectives were reached at 1130.

The 30th Infantry, meanwhile, had advanced abreast of 7th Infantry, over the hills north to make contact with elements of the 36th Infantry Division. Task Force Butler (Elements of VI Corps) was contacted at 1130, August 29. Then, under orders to send a battalion to protect the left flank of the 7th Infantry from infiltration, 2d Battalion was moved by motor from Sauzet to Marsanne, then advanced by foot and was on its objective before dawn of August 30. Before noon Company G had occupied Mirmande.

In 7th Infantry's initial advance the enemy, under the mistaken impression that the road had been cut north of Montelimar by the 36th Infantry Division, surrendered in large numbers, although many of them organized small pockets which had to be cleaned out.

Outstanding feature about the area north of Montelimar, however, was the enemy motor convoy. It stretched from the northern outskirts of town for approximately 14 kilometers. It was composed of all sorts of vehicles, from German heavy cargo trucks to numerous requisitioned French sedans—about 2000 vehicles in all. For the most part traffic had been double-banked—

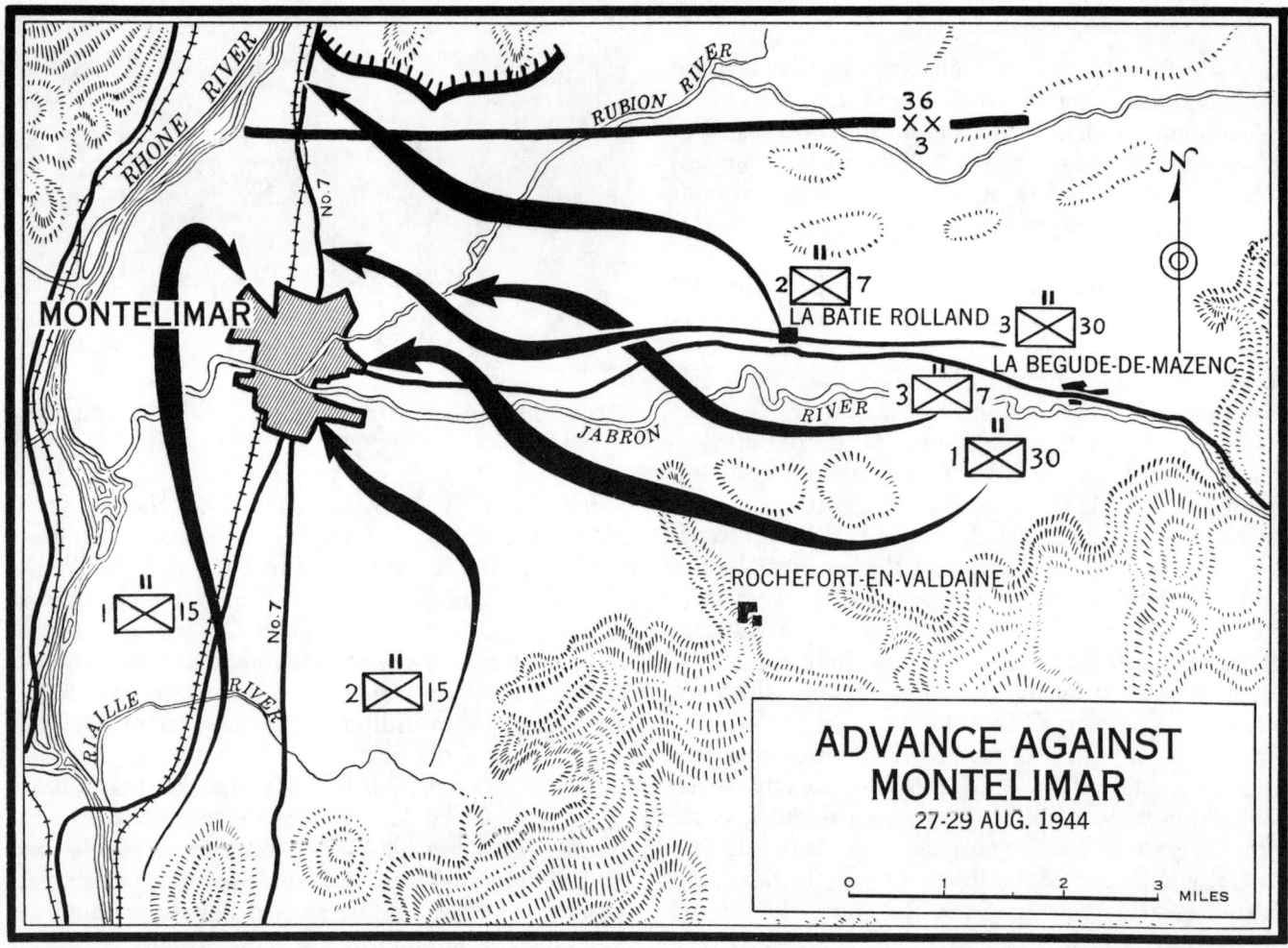

ADVANCE AGAINST MONTELIMAR
27-29 AUG. 1944

in some places triple-banked—with vehicles facing both north and south.

The drivers and personnel had, for the most part, abandoned their vehicles and made for the Rhone River.

The 36th Division artillery had also taken the convoy under fire, and friendly fighter-bombers took several swipes at it, as well. As 3d Infantry Division troops advanced through the debacle they saw almost unbelievable carnage. An estimated 1000 horses were pulling carts, or trailing behind motor vehicles, tied by ropes. Many of them had been taken from the French. When the shells came down, most of them were killed. A few, some with entrails dragging or otherwise wounded, had to be put out of the way with merciful bullets. Some were unharmed, and nosed incuriously about the bodies of their dead fellows, or grazed peacefully in the pastures next to the road.

Smashed, fire-blackened trucks, halftracks, and sedans—some still burning or smouldering—clogged the road. The bodies of dead Germans, many of them also fire-blackened, lay among the ruins, or alongside the road where they had been cut down by artillery while trying to make good their escapes.

On the railroad which paralleled the highway at a distance of several hundred yards sat six giant railway guns. Four of them were the familiar 280mm monsters, sisters to the "Anzio Express." Two of them were gigantic 380mm pieces. All had been left standing, intact. Along the entire length of the scene of destruction an outrageous odor of burned and burning wood, scorched metal, stinking dead and singed flesh and clothing assailed the nostrils. Even the "avenues of smells" along some of the roads on the Anzio Beachhead in late April and early May, with their dead sheep and cattle, had not been such an affront to the nose.

Enemy materiel captured or destroyed also included 20 75mm AT guns, 12 88mm AA guns, and 8 or 10 self-propelled guns. Prisoner total for the three days was over 1000. As it had been all the way up from the coast the enemy order of battle, as indicated by units of PWs, was still a miscellaneous assortment from 338th Infantry Division, 198th Infantry Division, 189th Reserve Division, with the recent addition of 11th *Panzer* Division, 716th Infantry Division, 148th Reserve Division, and 244th Infantry Division. There were also other elements, too numerous to mention.

The Battle of Montelimar had been costly for the German 19th Army.

Thus far nothing had been said regarding the reception of American troops by the French populace.

Veterans of Africa, Sicily, and Italy suddenly found themselves in a country in which sincere friendship and joy at liberation was expressed so vividly as to leave no doubts regarding the feelings which prompted these emotions. It was the wholehearted, warm conveyance of gladness of a proud, individualistic race once again made free.

After nearly two years of association with Italians, Sicilians, and Arabs, the genuineness displayed by Frenchmen high and low was like fresh air in a cave. Always it was tonic to morale.

When a Frenchman offered a soldier his bottle of wine there was a slight deference in his manner, but there was also apparent pride and happiness at being able to do something for his liberators. It was as if he said "Here, m'sieu, it is about all I can offer you. I cannot give you strength when you face the enemy, although I wish I could. I cannot sustain you when you falter on the long march. That, too, I wish I could do. I can but offer you this wine, and with it try to convey the feeling of gratitude which I and my countrymen have for you." This attitude, throughout, could not but help give most soldiers some realization of why they were fighting. Freedom must be a wonderful thing. Here were those who had once had and lost it, once again to have it restored to them. The sight of their happiness was a thing to behold.

Since elements of the 45th Infantry Division had patrolled as far northeast as Voiron and found no enemy there, the 3d Infantry Division prepared itself for an administrative move of over ninety miles.

Intelligence from the F.F.I. (which proved very accurate) at this time was as follows "Civilians report that the enemy has pulled the bulk of his infantry out of Lyon, and that the city contains only scattered rear guard armored units. Many enemy troops were withdrawn west of the Rhone. Two civilian reports indicate the enemy is building up his forces along the Loue and Doubs Rivers, sixty miles north of Bourg. All bridges across the Doubs are guarded, and Frenchmen are not permitted to cross to the north (probably because F.F.I. forces are stronger in the south). The enemy is reported to have sizable garrisons in Dijon, Dole, Besançon, and Belfort. The last three towns are on the Doubs River and lie in the enemy's apparent escape corridor to Mühlhaus (Mulhouse)."*

The 15th Infantry's 3d Battalion moved out at 1915, August 31, to relieve the 45th Division roadblock at St. Etienne and to screen the road net to Bourgoin. The 2d Battalion relieved 179th Infantry (45th Division) at Bourgoin, and 1st Battalion left its assembly area, but remained in regimental reserve.

The 30th Infantry entrucked and moved by motor to an assembly area northwest of Voiron. All units had closed in by 0035, September 1. At 1130 the regiment began a move by motor to the vicinity of Cremieu, preparatory to moving west on Division order.

The 7th Infantry remained, guarding the smashed motor column until shortly after noon, September 1, when the regiment entrucked and moved first to an assembly area near Trepts, then re-entrucked and moved to a new area east of Leyment, where it closed in by 2400.

The 15th Infantry, 3d Battalion leading, commenced moving at 1930 to an assembly area near Lagnieu. Company I rode on tank destroyers. 1st Battalion followed and 2d Battalion commenced its move during the morning of September 2.

Meanwhile 30th Infantry already had swung back into action. The 3d Battalion engaged the enemy in a firefight at Pont de Churuy, killing seven enemy and taking two prisoners. At Janneyrieas, while 3d platoon, 3d Reconnaissance Troop engaged the enemy, Company L flanked the enemy position and captured ninety-nine prisoners, an AT gun, and three trucks. The fight lasted until about 2100, September 1. 3d Battalion protected a front from Loyettes through Charvieu, with a strong outpost at Colonbier. Contact was made with the 143d Infantry in Catzian at 2100. The 2d Battalion, at 0600, moved out from regimental reserve to relieve 3d Battalion, 179th Infantry, on the regimental right flank.

The 1st platoon, 3d Reconnaissance Troop, after outposting Cote La Andre, moved out on the morning of September 2 to investigate the roads southwest of that town, and was recalled at 0700 to reconnoiter the road northwest of Amberieu to Chalamon, Villers, Striver, and Chatallon, during which reconnaissance it encountered some light enemy resistance.

During September 2-3, 15th and 7th Infantry Regiments remained in assembly areas with reinforcing trucks, prepared to move out on Division order. The 30th Infantry assembled during the same period. The 7th Infantry sent patrols to the north during the night but failed to make contact with the enemy. A patrol from 30th Infantry went north on a main highway through Neuville-sur-Ain and contacted a platoon of the 3d Reconnaissance Troop and a unit of 180th Infantry. The patrol continued north and found the bridge across the Suran River blown; continued on to Villereversure, Simandre-sur-Suran and Treffort, and was told by the F.F.I. that Cruislat was also clear of enemy. A patrol from Company I crossed the bridge at Villereversure, and failed to make enemy contact. Another patrol went northwest on the road to Charlamonte with the same results. The 1st platoon, 3d Recon,

---

*3d Infantry Division G-2 Periodic Reports No. 17, 2 Sept., 1944.

Tank destroyers of the 601st TD Battalion move through Lons-le-Saunier in pursuit of the retreating enemy.

continued on its mission of September 2. It was held up at a bridge across the Ain River. The Division Battle Patrol outflanked the resistance by crossing the river south of the bridge; and took and held the town of Gevrieu across the river.

The enemy apparently was still rapidly withdrawing. The 3d Infantry Division once again entrucked and conducted a march of over seventy-five miles to contact the enemy.

At 1345, September 3, 7th Infantry led the move. The march objective was north of Lons-le-Saunier. The 3d Battalion closed into position at 2300, September 3, 1st Battalion at 0050, and 2d Battalion at 0055, all without incident and without the slightest contact with the enemy. Upon arrival the regimental Battle Patrol conducted reconnaissance to the north and northeast from Poligny to investigate reports of enemy, but failed to make contact.

15th Infantry moved in order 1st, 2d, and 3d Battalions, crossing its initial point near Lagnieu at 2200, and closing into its new area northeast of Lons-le-Saunier at 0615. It advanced from St. Denis to Amberieu to Poncin; thence to Granges through Arinthod, Orgelet and from there to its area. During the morning of September 4, 1st Battalion established roadblocks of company strength near Montrond and on the road between Vers and Les Pasquier. The 2d Battalion put in roadblocks east of Equievillon and south of Champagnole on Highway 6.

The 30th Infantry remained in assembly area south of Lagnieu until 1045, September 4, when it entrucked for its area in the vicinity of Lons-le-Saunier. The regiment closed in at about noon of that day.

The 3d Reconnaissance Troop preceded the advance of 7th and 15th Infantry Regiments on their march to Lons-le-Saunier, making no contact with the enemy.

The Division continued its attack to the northeast. The 1st Battalion, 7th Infantry, moved from a defensive position near Arley at 1845, September 4, to the vicinity of Arbois. Vigorous patrols maintained contact with the Battle Patrol at Mont-sous-Vaudrey. The 2d Battalion moved to the vicinity of Arbois, with one company going to Mouchard. At 2100 2d Battalion, reinforced, moved by vehicle to Argue, southwest of Besançon, arriving there at 0100, September 5. The battalion detrucked and began an attack toward Besançon at 0530. Company F encountered resistance at a bridge near Beure. Company E, at 0830, moved in a southeast direction to within 200 yards of Highway 73 near St. Ferjeux and fired on an enemy truck convoy. The battalion continued to fight during the September 5-6 period to secure bridges and destroy enemy motor movement along the highway southwest and south of Besançon. The 3d Battalion remained in position protecting the regiment's left flank.

The objective was now Besançon. A key communication and road net center, as well as an important industrial city of approximately 80,000 persons in peacetime, Besançon is divided by the Doubs River, with the industrial and most valuable section situated in the loop south of the river. This loop has a bottleneck opening, solidly guarded by a huge Vauban-designed fort, La Citadelle, which in turn is supported by four minor forts—Fort Tosey on the southwest, Fort des Trois Chatels on the southeast, and two other forts at a high elevation across the river: Fort Bregille on the northeast and Fort Chaudanne on the west. These forts were built in the 17th Century. La Citadelle alone took six years to complete (1667-1673). Its aspect is formidable to an attacker, presenting extremely thick walls surrounded by moats, and being situated on high ground which commands all avenues of approach.

The 15th Infantry moved from its position near Champagnole on the afternoon of September 4, 3d Battalion moving to a position south of Besançon. Company I attacked to a position south of Beure, with Company K farther south and Company L at Quingey. The 2d Battalion was disposed along the Ornans-Besançon road, and 1st Battalion remained in regimental reserve near Mouchard.

The 30th Infantry made no contact during the period.

The 1st platoon of the 3d Recon moved ahead of 15th Infantry en route to Besançon and by noon, September 5, was standing by for 15th Infantry on the main routes south of Besançon. The 2d platoon was attached to 7th Infantry, and reconnoitered in front of that regiment south of Besançon. At Sanitorium de la Tilleroy the platoon reported a large concentration of troops and a large convoy on the main highway. An air mission was requested, granted, and good results were reported. At 1600 many Germans were reported in the town, and an enemy roadblock one-half mile south of town was also reported. The platoon screened to the west while the artillery dug in and commenced firing at the roadblock. The 3d platoon, 3d Recon, screened before 7th Infantry northwest of Poligny and reported enemy in Mont-sous-Vaudrey. An F.F.I. patrol reported 700 enemy in the town. This platoon, too, spotted an enemy convoy leaving town and called down a successful air mission on it. The platoon was moving toward Dole when recalled to the Troop CP for another mission in the vicinity of Besançon.

At 1900 1st Battalion, 7th Infantry, arrived at Mouchard. The 2d Battalion was deployed south and west of Besançon in the vicinity of Beure, engaged in cleaning out enemy on the high ground and along the Doubs River, and firing into Besançon. The Battalion relieved 1st Battalion, 30th Infantry at Mouchard, to patrol to the Division front and left flank. The 2d Battalion, attached to 15th Infantry, reached a position 800 yards south of a key ridge, receiving considerable enemy fire. At 2400 Company E was north of Beure with the other two rifle companies adjacent. These positions were held during the night. On the morning of September 6 the battalion was relieved by 1st Battalion, 15th Infantry.

The Division was continuing its attack to occupy all high ground on three sides of Besançon. The 15th Infantry continued its northerly assault. The 30th Infantry advanced on the Division right boundary, neutralizing enemy roadblocks southeast of Besançon. The 1st and 3d Battalions moved to the north by motor, starting at 1025, to cut the roads to the north and northeast and to enter the town from those directions. The 2d Battalion, 30th Infantry, followed to the rear of, and assisted, the 15 Infantry.

Company B, 15th Infantry, attacked and captured Fort Fontain during the afternoon of September 5, and Company A seized adjacent high ground, while Company C remained in battalion reserve in the vicinity of Fontain. The 2d Battalion, 7th Infantry, attached to the 15th Infantry, captured high ground to the northwest with Company G leading. Shortly after 0800 2d Battalion reverted to 7th Infantry control.

The 1st Battalion, 15th Infantry, cleared the ridge between Companies A and C and sent reconnaissance patrols to Besançon. The battalion was ordered to block the two roads in its sector leading south and southeast from the city. The 2d Battalion was attached to 30th Infantry on the right. At 2300 Company E was having a fight with a Mark VI tank and an unknown number of infantry, and drawing some self-propelled fire. Company G blocked the highway in the vicinity of Tarcenay. The 30th Infantry continued moving on the right flank against slight opposition. At 1950, September 6, 1st Battalion was located south of Salins and 2d Battalion was at Mouchard. The two battalions closed out of these positions by 0115. By 0830 2d Battalion was located north of Tarcenay and 3d Battalion was in the vicinity of Mamirolle. The 3d Battalion then passed to regimental reserve at Lachevelotte, and 2d Battalion's leading elements were at Morre, advancing from the southeast on Besançon.

Explanation of the action was described in the G-2 report*: "To protect his escape route along Highway 73 through Besançon the enemy occupied the high ridge south of the Doubs River. The high ground was held by infantry, occasionally supported by tank fire and artillery. Most of the bridges across the Doubs were

---
*3d Infantry Division G-2 Report No. 21, 6 Sept., 1944.

La Citadelle, a Vauban-constructed fortress, situated at the loop in the Doubs River at Besançon.

Soldiers of the 3d Division move through Larnod-Dorines for the assault on Besançon.

blown and roadblocks established on the north side of the river. Our troops began to flank the city from the west during daylight, September 5, and the enemy was driven off or withdrew from the advantageous terrain during the night 5-6 September. Roadblocks southeast of Besançon, active during the afternoon of 5 September, offered but little resistance to our attacks during the evening."

Again: "Almost continual fire was received from enemy units occupying the high ground south of Besançon. Most of the enemy positions consisted of small enemy detachments who put up stiff resistance to our attack during afternoon and evening of 5 September, but who pulled out or were overrun during the night of 5-6 September. . . . On the left of the Division sector the enemy occupied positions north of important bridges across the Doubs River after having blown the bridges. He had positions at Belmont, Orchamps, and Dole. The latter bridge was not blown, probably because the enemy was still using that route as an axis of withdrawal."

During the night of September 6-7 the 3d Battalion, 7th Infantry, forward CP came under attack by a platoon of German infantrymen who, supported by 20mm Flak guns and machine guns, had infiltrated between the assault companies and the Battalion CP, virtually surrounding the latter. The Battalion Commander, Lt. Col. Lloyd B. Ramsey, and his S-3, being present in the CP, were in danger of being captured. Said Col. Ramsey: "Also, a rupture of communications with the assault companies, which were then meeting strong resistance, might easily have been disastrous."

The platoon advanced to within fifteen yards of the house in which the CP was situated. It occupied an old railroad draw, paralleling the wall which the CP's defenders were using for cover, and fired at everything within sight. It raked the doors and windows.

"Through all this fire," said Radio Operator Pvt. James P. Soblensky, "there was one man who just sat there calmly observing out into the darkness, taking pot shots at every kraut he saw. It was T/5 Robert D. Maxwell, one of the wire corporals. He was the coolest customer I've ever seen. Tracer bullets were just barely clearing his head, yet he didn't seem to notice it."

The Germans worked their way to within about ten yards and began throwing grenades. There was a chicken-wire extension over the wall, which saved those inside. The grenades struck it, bounced to the other side, and exploded harmlessly.

Maxwell continued calmly to take aim and fire his .45. Most of the rest of the men had "taken off," despite Maxwell's urging them to stay. One man who did stay was killed a few minutes later.

Said Wire Chief T/4 Cyril F. McCall: "The Battalion Commander saw that he would be unable to hold the CP with the small force available and ordered that it be moved to another location. While the evacuation was begun under cover of our fire, the enemy intensified his attack in a determined effort to overwhelm our position."

Suddenly a grenade came over the wall and landed in the group's midst. Maxwell, clutching a blanket to his body, dove upon it without a second's hesitation. An instant later there was an explosion. "I lay still for a few seconds," said Wireman Pfc. James P. Joyce, "partially stunned by the concussion; then I realized that I wasn't hurt. T/5 Maxwell had deliberately drawn the full force of the explosion on himself in order to protect us and make it possible for us to continue at our posts and fight."

Colonel Ramsey summed up: "T/5 Maxwell's zeal in the maintenance of military communications, his instantaneous acceptance of dangers which no soldier is obligated to incur, and his lofty sacrifice of self in behalf of his fellow soldiers made possible the orderly withdrawal of the CP personnel, contributed in high degree to the eventual capture of Besançon, and are a continuing inspiration to the officers and men of the 3d Battalion."

Maxwell was severely wounded in the face and his right foot was permanently maimed, but he lived to be awarded the Congressional Medal of Honor.

The enemy indicated his strong desire to hold the city and to prevent our forces from crossing the Doubs River by moving into Besançon elements of the 159th Reserve Division which had been diverted from their route of withdrawal. Lengthy fire fights with small arms, machine guns, and mortars took place in front of each of the forts and bunkers on the south and east of town. On the north side of the city scattered self-propelled and tank fire opposed the 7th Infantry.

At 1400 September 7, 1st Battalion, 7th Infantry,

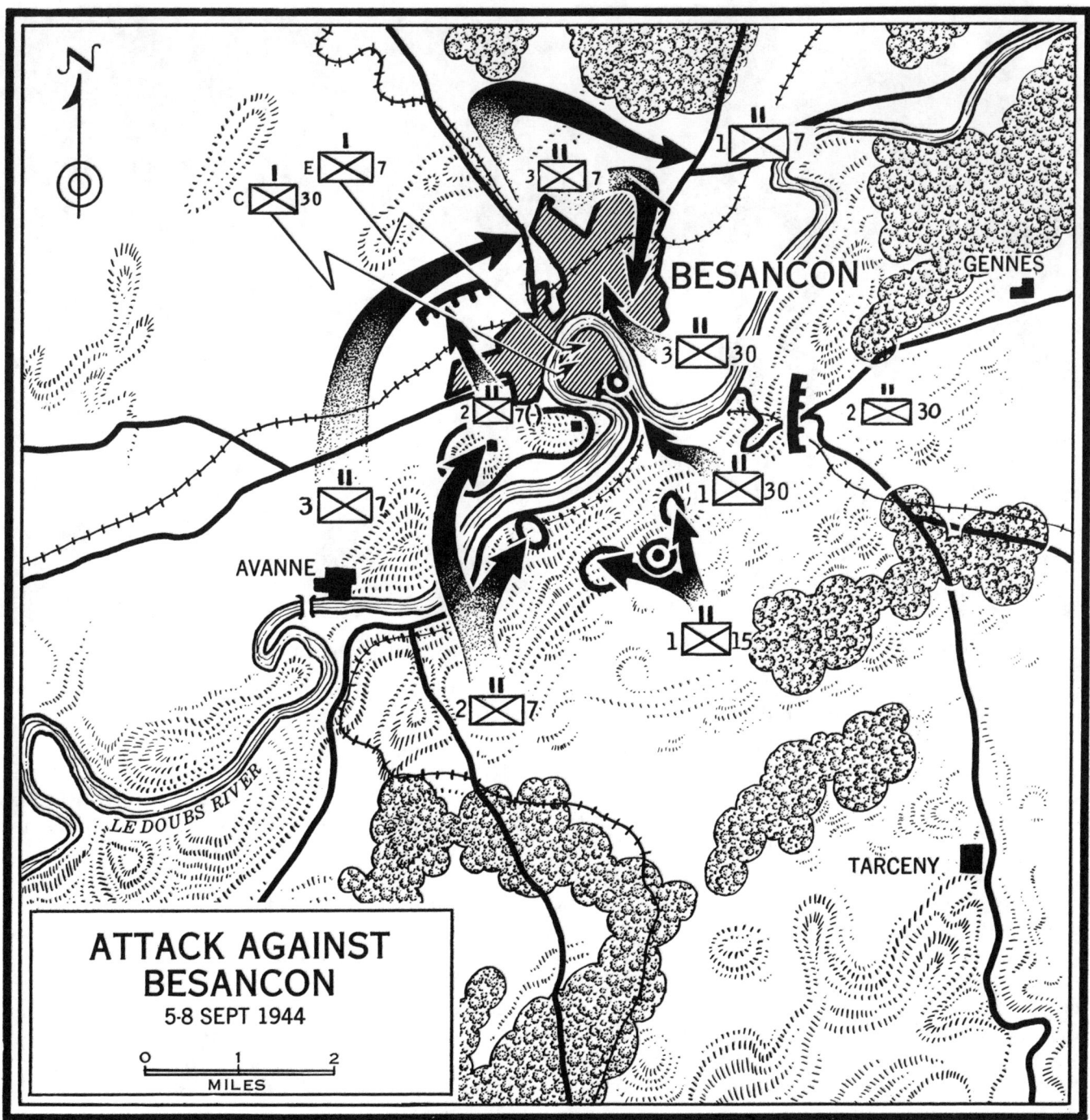

crossed the line of departure and attacked east. Enemy action consisted of scattered strongpoints supported by machine-gun and artillery fire. The battalion halted overnight and protected the regiment on its north flank. The 3d Battalion continued its attack and by 1530 reached la Baraque. At 2315 3d Battalion again advanced against enemy small-arms and mortar fire, until security patrols reported no enemy to the front. At 2100 contact was established with 2d Battalion. The 3d Battalion pulled out of Besançon and at 0930 the next morning attacked an enemy convoy, destroying ten vehicles.

The 30th Infantry, meanwhile, had been divided into two groups. 1st Battalion was assigned the difficult mission of neutralizing the formidable Citadelle and of clearing the southern section of Besançon, which was situated in the loop of the river, and 3d Battalion was to cross the Doubs at Avanne, circle completely behind the city and come in from the northeast.

At 0030, 1st Battalion, commanded by Captain Christopher W. Chaney, jumped off to clear the Doubs loop. On reaching the Chapelle des Bois, contact was made with 1st Battalion, 15th Infantry, and the advance continued northwest toward the Besançon goose-egg. The battalion came under fire at 0338.

As Companies C and B continuing in column reached

Infantrymen of the 3d Division rest beside a railroad near the town of Larnod, after having been relieved.

the high ground south of the Citadelle, they came under more fire from two hitherto unknown forts guarding the right and left approaches to the Citadelle.

Aided by tanks of Company C, 756th, under 1st Lt. Rex Metcalfe, Company C, 30th, battled for four hours against fanatical *Hitlerjugend* inductees and took the fort on the west side of the neck with fifty-three prisoners. While Company B attacked by fire, Company A was moved in, and after a stiff fight, took the east guard fort and about twenty-five prisoners. In a coordinated attack, using all weapons of the battalion, and even employing the direct fire of a 9th FA Battalion 155mm howitzer at a range of about 500 yards, Captain Chaney maneuvered his battalion into a final assault on the Citadelle. While Company C moved around to the northwest and rear of the fort, Company A assaulted frontally, and with the aid of close mortar fire support forced the surrender of the fort by 1830.

Troops which entered the Citadelle to handle the more than 200 prisoners (which included one battalion CO and two company CO's) reported that the massive walls had been barely more than chipped by the high explosive 155 shells, but the terrific muzzle blast combined with the terrifying sound of shell bursts had been too much for the defenders' nerves. Seventeen casualties, most of them wounded, were taken from the fort. All of these had been wounded by mortar fire.

By 2205 1st Battalion, 30th Infantry, had closed on its objective, the Doubs River loop, from the south.

For its outstanding performance of duty in action during the period September 6-7 at Besançon, the 1st Battalion, 30th Infantry, was awarded the Presidential Unit Citation.

During the fight for, and capture of, the Citadelle, 3d Battalion, 30th Infantry, had been relieved by Company F at 1420 and moved out on trucks via the Avanne bridge to a position northeast of Besançon to join in the coordinated attack on the city. The attack was launched at 2005 that night. By 2130 Company L had met resistance near the city's railroad station. Company K was moved to assist Company L, and at daylight was in contact with the enemy while Company L was engaged in clearing enemy from the city. Both companies continued to work on this strong pocket of enemy resistance throughout the day of September 8 while Company I moved to establish a roadblock. By 1220 resistance was broken and over 100 prisoners taken. By 1645 the battalion was assembled and moved to a regimental assembly area, where it closed in at 1900 and prepared to push to the north.

The 2d Battalion had been in reserve during most of the fight. At 0810 that morning the battalion crossed the Doubs River Bailey bridge into the city and at 1050 was held up by continuing fighting within the city. Company F held the high ground overlooking the city and was committed to assist 3d Battalion in its street-fighting assignment. Company F took 196 prisoners in this work and in the later afternoon moved to the regimental assembly area, closing there with the rest of 2d Battalion at 1900.

Cost to the enemy in the Battle of Besançon had been about 653 prisoners, not including wounded (and taken prisoner), and killed. Numbered among the latter was a Brig. Gen. Schmidt, who was killed at a roadblock of Company A, 7th Infantry, on the afternoon of September 6. His orderly, who was taken prisoner, said that the general was 56 years old, had fought in Russia, and had been commanding an artillery school at Autun from April 26, 1943, to September 2, 1944. He supposedly had been en route to take command of a division (probably the 159th) in the Besançon area when the four cars in his party took the wrong road and the general stopped an M-1 bullet.

Following the axis of two main roads to the north, the Division continued its attack in the direction of Vesoul. The 7th Infantry advanced to the northeast to Rigney, then turned west toward Rioz. It moved against slight resistance until enemy were encountered at Traitie Fontaine. The 2d Battalion led this advance, followed by 3d Battalion.

The 15th Infantry continued to advance north toward Rioz against strong resistance in the form of organized defenses as well as a number of by-passed pockets of enemy forces. The 1st Battalion reached Tallenay without resistance. After fighting all through the night of September 8-9 Company F captured Ecole and Company E captured Miserey-Salines. By noon, September 9, Company G had reached a point just south of the Ornan River. The 3d Battalion continued its advance against strong resistance to the vicinity of Chatillon-le-Duc. By 1005, September 9 Companies I and L were abreast near Devecey, continuing the attack.

In Besançon, 30th Infantry made a thorough sweep of the town until, by 1400, September 8, it had been determined that the last enemy soldier was rounded up. The regiment moved out during the night of September 8-9. The 1st Battalion encountered considerable resistance during the morning of September 9, but overcame it. The 3d Battalion followed the 1st Battalion.

At 2000, September 9, Company G moved to the northeast side of Rioz and was 2000 yards from its outskirts. Three hours later the company was 800 yards from a road north of the town and 500 yards from the town itself. During the fight it captured prisoners from the 634th Guard Regiment which had been moved into the sector to assist in the disengagement of elements of the 198th and 338th Divisions and to reinforce the positions. The 2d Battalion did not enter Rioz in force, but early in the morning of September 10 contacted elements of 15th Infantry in town. The 3d Battalion, 7th Infantry, sent a platoon of Company I to Loulans, then reinforced the position with the entire company. Remainder of the battalion was located in the vicinity of Cirey during the night, then assembled at Loulans, and at noon, September 10, was moving northeast against light resistance. The 1st Battalion was located at Regney, with Companies A and C on the outskirts of Vandeland to screen the Division's right flank. The 2d Battalion assembled in the vicinity of Cirey and at 1000 crossed the line of departure moving northeast.

The 1st Battalion, 15th Infantry, moved by truck to Neuville-de-Cromary, then moved by foot to Sorans-

FFI in Besancon stand guard over several German prisoners, whom they apparently ferreted out somewhere in the city.

This bridge spanned the Doubs River. While it was being repaired the Infantrymen made use of ladders to move across the gap on their way north from Besançon.

les-Breury on September 9. On the morning of the 10th the battalion resumed the attack toward Vesoul, moving out at 0700. At 1015 Company A encountered an estimated platoon of enemy, reinforced by a tank and SP gun, but soon took care of the trouble. The 2d Battalion moved against a series of enemy roadblocks near Voray, and at 1545, September 9, was at Sorans-les-Breury after destroying three strong roadblocks and capturing three 88mm guns. The battalion moved on toward Rioz, aided in clearing the town, and set up roadblocks. The 3d Battalion, 15th Infantry, moved by truck through Traitie Fontaine and assisted 2d Battalion in clearing Rioz, and also set up roadblocks.

The 30th Infantry was originally on the Division's left flank in contact with the 36th Division. One company of the 1st Battalion crossed the Ornan River between Cussey and Boulot to protect the crossing of the rest of the battalions. Company B forded the river and at 2000, September 9, was on the outskirts of the Boulot. The 3d Battalion, at 1940, had a platoon in Bussieres, and 2d Battalion closed in an area near Voray on the north side of the Ornan River. At 0600, 3d Battalion led the regiment in a move to the north. Company K headed the battalion, moving to the left of Voray. The 2d Battalion pushed through Rioz on trucks while 3d Battalion moved cross-country to Boult on the Division left flank. At 1115 3d Battalion was moving north against scattered small-arms and machine-gun fire.

Enemy rear guard and delaying forces south of Vesoul made our advance difficult during September 10-11. The 1st Battalion, 15th Infantry, advancing toward Vesoul, was held up by strong enemy resistance in Quenoche, encountering small-arms, machine-gun, antitank, Flakwagon, tank, and artillery fire. By 1500, September 10, the battalion was on the outskirts of the town, and by 1900 the town of Quenoche was in our hands, although some mopping-up remained to be done. The 2d Battalion, following the first, was on the left flank at 1335. The battalion moved to Hyet and contacted the enemy. By 2000 Hyet was completely in our hands and the battalion moved north to Pennesieres. On the morning of September 11, 2d Battalion continued the advance through Courboux without resistance, while 1st Battalion advanced until it received enemy Flakwagon fire, which it eliminated.

The 2d Battalion, 30th Infantry, detrucked northwest of Rioz and advanced toward Tresilley over the September 10-11 period. Slight opposition was encountered and at 1730 artillery fire was directed on enemy personnel and vehicles. The 1st and 2d Battalions continued to advance against slight resistance.

At 0600, September 11, 1st Battalion, 7th Infantry, attacked north toward Filain. The battalion encountered enemy resistance toward noon and engaged in a fire fight southwest of Vy-le-Aubertans. The 2d Battalion, during the afternoon of September 10, had encountered strong enemy resistance south of Aubertans. The resistance was overcome during the night of September 10-11 and at 0630 Company G moved out toward Authoison against heavy machine-gun fire. Toward noon, however, the battalion was advancing without opposition.

During the same 24-hour period 3d Battalion overcame strong enemy resistance at Ormemans to encounter an enemy strongpoint at Roche-sur-Linotte at about 2000. At 0730 the battalion attacked north, encountered strong resistance, and pushed on into it.

The objectives of Vesoul and the road nets east of the city were being stubbornly defended.

The 1st Battalion, 7th Infantry, advanced through Filain, while 2d Battalion left Authoison, and 3d Battalion engaged in a fire fight outside Dampierre. The 7th Infantry finally occupied Hills 418 and 405 after attacking through the Bois de Dampierre.

The 30th Infantry advanced northeast toward Presle, meeting strong enemy resistance all the way. The wooded, hilly terrain necessarily made advances slow.

The 3d Battalion moved by motor from its assembly area near Mariox to its line of departure for the attack on Presle. At 2000 the battalion, having cleared out machine-gun and rifle outpost positions on the way, prepared to attack Presle at daylight September 12.

During September 12 the attack on Presle was continued by 3d Battalion. Because of the dogged resistance and heavy enemy fire it became necessary to commit the 1st and 2d Battalions on a flanking movement to encircle the town.

The 3d Battalion jumped off at daylight as planned, but was immediately met with fire from three sides, and the attack was halted. A combat group of infantry, tanks, and TDs was sent to clear the enemy from a ridge on the left flank. This was accomplished, but heavy fire from Presle as well as observed artillery fire

After the battle was over, citizens of Besançon crowded the streets to watch the remaining elements of the 3d Division pass through on their way North.

from Mt. Jesus, and machine-gun and sniper fire from the Bois de Petit Pas continued to halt the attack. Company I moved to Thieffrans at 2130.

The 1st Battalion was committed at 1715 with the mission of outflanking and cutting off the determined enemy from the north. The battalion entrucked and advance elements met and fired on about seventy-five enemy at a cross road. At 2000, the balance of the battalion jumped off in the attack on Esprels. The battalion moved forward without opposition but met many unmanned roadblocks which the 10th Engineers cleared to permit the advance of attached armor.

The 2d Battalion was committed at 1645, September 12. Company E was sent by truck with the mission of clearing the roadblock on the main highway by attacking it from the rear. The balance of the battalion moved down the main highway through Dampierre to assault Presle via Trevey. Trevey was occupied by 2010.

In face of pressure exerted by this three-battalion attack, the enemy withdrew on September 13. Presle, Vallerois-le-Bois, Les Patey, Chassey-les-Montboxon, and Esprels were all occupied.

The 3d Battalion, 15th Infantry was committed on the regiment's left flank, by-passing 2d Battalion, and advancing to the southern outskirts of Vesoul. By noon of September 12 it was in the first few buildings there. The 1st Battalion advanced against constant enemy resistance with a mission of advancing north and flanking the town from the east. The 2d Battalion advanced through La Demie with a mission of blocking a road in that vicinity.

Vesoul finally fell during the afternoon of September 12 to elements of the 15th Infantry and two battalions of the 36th Division.

Two heroic actions especially marked the September 12-13 period.

Second Lt. Raymond Zussman of Company A, 756th Tank Battalion, was a platoon leader. As his tank and another of his platoon were approaching Noroy-le-Bourg at about 1900, they were in front of 3d Battalion, 7th Infantry. The intercommunication system was out between tanks and throughout the subsequent action Lieutenant Zussman directed the tank from outside, either verbally or by signals.

Zussman went forward on foot to reconnoiter the highway. He disappeared from sight; there was the sound of small-arms fire and the lieutenant reappeared, to motion the tank to the highway. Several infantrymen proceeded forward with the group.

After directing the tank through a boobytrapped roadblock, the group was fired upon by an enemy machine gun and some riflemen about forty yards to the right front. Lieutenant Zussman stood on the right of the tank, directing fire on the enemy positions, and in a matter of seconds three of the enemy were killed and eight had surrendered. After collecting these prisoners, Zussman again directed fire, this time on a German *Volkswagen* at a road junction; three more enemy were killed and seven or eight surrendered.

Lieutenant Zussman then obtained a tommy gun, being out of carbine ammunition, and started toward town, across a field paralleling the road to town. The tank followed. Again he was fired upon. Again he returned under intense fire to direct the tank in neutralizing the opposition. Standing up straight he pointed out the enemy, and within a few minutes twenty more had surrendered.

"Lieutenant Zussman had the infantrymen collect these prisoners while he went ahead alone to investigate some houses on our side of the road about fifty yards in front of us," said Cpl. Theodore Coller, a crew member of the tank.

Added Pvt. Calvin E. Eaton: ". . . I saw Lieutenant Zussman approach the back of the house, running and firing his tommy gun en route. A few wild small-arms shots were taken at him, and as he neared the far corner several hand grenades were thrown in his direction but he was unharmed and beckoned us forward. He directed our fire through a back door of the house and into a small shed nearby, and twelve more Jerries who were in and around the house hastily surrendered."

Reconnoitering for a route for the tank out to the highway, a storm of fire and a grenade came Zussman's way. He returned fire and the enemy ceased. He called the tank up again; by the time the tank had neared the house he had gone to the front again, and by the time the tank had rounded the corner, Lieutenant Zussman had returned with fifteen more prisoners.

He directed the tank's fire on a house across the road, toward which a number of the enemy were scurrying in an attempt to escape. At least two or three were killed and several wounded.

The miniature armored force continued down the main street of Noroy, Zussman still leading. A wagon started across an intersection to the front; the tank fired on it and killed eight or ten enemy. "Lieutenant Zussman figured the intersection might be zeroed in for antitank fire, so he had us wait while he went around the corner to investigate," said T/5 Espiridion Guillen. "We heard Lieutenant Zussman repeatedly yelling, 'Hände hoch! Hände hoch!' and heard frequent bursts from his tommy gun. In a few minutes he stepped out in the intersection where we could see him, and a string of about thirty prisoners filed around the corner and were taken into custody by the infantrymen. Lieutenant Zussman said he routed them out of a basement."

As night fell, Zussman again went forward alone to a truck. There was another hand-grenade explosion, but when the smoke cleared away he returned with another prisoner.

The results of his actions were seventeen enemy killed, ninety-two captured, and two antitank guns, one 20mm Flak gun, two machine guns, and two trucks captured.

Lieutenant Zussman was killed in a subsequent action, but was awarded the Congressional Medal of Honor.

Another officer, 1st Lt. John J. Tominac, of Company I, 15th Infantry, also especially distinguished himself during this same time.

The 3d Battalion, having captured the hill mass south of Saulx-de-Vesoul, drove down the hillsides toward the city in the face of stubborn resistance. Forces in the hills north of Saulx-de-Vesoul hammered the German positions with artillery, mortar and machine-gun fire. In this operation the other forces were the anvil, the 3d Battalion, the hammer.

As Tominac's platoon neared a bend in the road down which they were proceeding, an enemy machine gun opened fire, raking the highway with bursts of knee-high fire.

Lieutenant Tominac sized up the situation and shouted back to bring up tank support. Within a matter of minutes an M-4 came up and halted just ahead of the platoon's leading elements.

Under heavy fire Tominac ran forward ten yards to direct fire on the enemy machine-gun nest, as two squads of his platoon worked their way forward into firing positions on the road, protected from the enemy by the tank's hull.

A second enemy machine-gun nest remained, following the neutralization of the first. Working his left squad to within fifty yards of the weapon, Tominac halted the men and rushed headlong into the weapon, firing his tommy gun. He killed the three men manning it.

This action alerted the main enemy defensive force. The occupants of this position were about 200 yards to the left front. Tominac led a squad against the enemy strongpoint. Although the area was swept by infantry fire of every type, Tominac rushed back and forth from one squad to the other, supervising and directing the one he led personally, and one which he had directed to clean out any enemy who might be in a group of nearby houses.

He and his men overran the hostile strongpoint, killing about thirty of the enemy. The squad resumed the advance. After proceeding a few yards, Tominac spotted a concealed 77mm self-propelled gun in a "V" intersection of the road, about 200 yards to the front.

He ordered his men to halt, and went ahead, alone and on foot, followed by the tank. The SP opened fire on the tank and neutralized it. The tank caught fire and the crew bailed out.

Driverless and burning, it began to roll down the road toward the German position. Tominac ran and jumped on it; stood boldly upright, silhouetted against the sky, grasping the M-4's .50-caliber machine gun. As he opened fire on the 77's crew, a rain of bullets from hostile machine guns, machine pistols and snipers ricocheted off the turret and hull of the tank, with the 77 also still firing at it.

Tominac fired burst after burst at the SP gun and the infantry foxholes around it. After raking the area with fire he jumped down from the steadily accelerating tank.

Joined by S/Sgt. John B. Shirley, one of his squad leaders, it was noted that Tominac was painfully wounded in the shoulder. Shirley took out his pen knife and removed a dollar-sized fragment from the shoulder. At about the same time the tank crashed in the midst of a group of German gun pits, bursting into flames as its gasoline and ammunition exploded.

Again Tominac led his men forward. The enemy had been forced to abandon his roadblock. The SP gun withdrew into Saulx-de-Vesoul. Refusing medical aid, Lieutenant Tominac sent Shirley's squad to clean out a group of houses in the city, while he led the remainder of the platoon against a strongly-fortified group of buildings which contained about a company of Germans. Despite his painful wound, he took his men to within pointblank range of a wall which surrounded the buildings from which the enemy was firing. Hurling hand grenades into the enemy's midst and simultaneously deploying a portion of his force around to the rear of the buildings, Tominac compelled thirty-one enemy soldiers and one officer to surrender, captured at least half a dozen enemy vehicles, together with machine guns and a quantity of other materiel.

At the cost of only four casualties, he had led his men in overcoming four successive enemy strongpoints, killing at least thirty of the enemy, taking thirty-two prisoners and capturing the platoon's sector of Saulx-de-Vesoul. For this he later received the Congressional Medal of Honor.

By straight-line distance it is more than 400 miles from Cavalaire and St. Tropez to Vesoul. The American VI Corps, advancing not in a straight line, but tacking first to the west, then north, then northeast, back to the northwest, finally, north and northeast, as the tactical situation required, had covered the distance in less than a month—truly an amazing feat. In a war of movement, this accomplishment stood out as an example of speed and mobility. The 3d Infantry Division had played a prominent part in making that feat possible.

French forces, coming up from the rear, reinforced and emphasized the rapid cleavage, but the spearhead was always VI Corps.

There were immediate and telling results of the avalanche which rolled north from the Riviera beaches. Somewhere south of the Loire River, in western France, 20,000 enemy soldiers surrendered to a United States platoon. Four United States correspondents drove a jeep through supposedly enemy-infested territory, from south to north, and did not encounter a single German soldier. Isolated enemy pockets were swiftly wiped out by avenging F.F.I. bands. When French forces joined those of Lt. Gen. George S. Patton's Third Army near Dijon in early September, all of Central and Western France, with the exception of a few western ports, was automatically freed. Instead of a slow slugging-match to liberate France the United States armies were now free to concentrate on the western approaches to Germany. The ultimate end of the war in Europe was probably speeded many months. And in the zone of VI Corps the German 19th Army received a blow from which it never recovered.

Probably the outstanding difficulty of the rapid move had been the ever-present bugaboo of supply, magnified many times over. Even the most optimistic planners had not foreseen moving so far, so fast.

Initially, while preinvasion beach reconnaissance had indicated that Red Beach at St. Tropez would be excellent for beaching craft, only one section was good enough to beach LCIs, and this was so heavily protected with underwater mines that it could not be used until H-plus-8 hours. These unexpected difficulties would have been extremely serious had more than slight resistance been met by the infantry, as supporting tanks and artillery were not ashore and assembled until late on D-day and the Beach Group reacted slowly to changes occasioned by the difficulties. However, late on D-day the Group became better organized, and by H-plus-20 hours all small craft except the five supply LCTs were completely discharged.

Unloading of the ocean-type ships lagged far behind schedule, primarily because all Liberty ships arrived at the transport area behind schedule. Due in the transport area at noon of D-day, seven of the ten Liberties arrived at noon of D-plus-one and the other three not until the forenoon of D-plus-two.

While the delay in unloading caused considerable difficulty due to lack of transportation, its most serious implication was the almost complete lack of supply. Through unforeseen difficulties, a critical gasoline shortage existed by H-plus-30 hours when supply LCTs were finally beached.

Normally Army supply bases keep within twenty miles of Division rear. Initially Division transportation was used exclusively to move supplies from the beaches to supply dumps, reaching a round trip of 400 miles before Army was able to establish forward dumps at St. Maximin. This relief was short-lived, as Division was called upon to furnish forty trucks to Corps for special missions, and 3d Infantry Division began a 150-mile move from Aix to Montelimar, which again eventually put Army dumps 150 miles behind the troops. That the supply problem was whipped is a credit to the men who worked 24-hour days for days on end to keep the supplies flowing.

Some measure of what it takes to make a move of the proportions of VI Corps' move north is furnished by a look at the wire summaries of the Division Signal Officer. During the sixteen days from August 15 to 31, alone, 2207 miles of wire were laid, and only 190 recovered. Communications, at that, were often solely by radio.

The 3d Infantry Division continued its push, and found itself at the approaches to the Vosges Mountains. It was still mid-Autumn—on the calendar—but the cold winds already had begun to blow, and the weather had turned rainy. It seemed only a short time ago that the Anzio sun came out to stay and ended the long, cold, wet Italian winter. Now the seasons had once more rolled around, and with the annual change came winter fighting in France's Vosges Mountains.

The Vosges Mountains had never been crossed by a military force opposed by an enemy. That solid fact stood out as the divisions of VI Corps set out to commence the fight. Miles ahead lay the Rhine River and the frontier of Germany.

TABLE OF CASUALTIES*

Southern France

(Aug. 15, 1944 through Sept. 14, 1944)

KIA	WIA	MIA	Total Battle Casualties	Non-Battle Casualties
218	1072	401	1691	1583

Reinforcements and hospital return-to-unit personnel

Reinf		Hosp RTUs	
Off	EM	Off	EM
16	307	17	967

KNOWN ENEMY CASUALTIES

Killed	Wounded	Captured
330	1005	9003

*These figures were provided by the A C of S, G-1, 3d Infantry Division.

IX
THROUGH THE VOSGES

The Summer War Gives Way to Bitter Combat in the Forests of France's "Impassable" Mountains

"DENSE clouds hang between the mountains of the lower Vosges. The roads glisten with rain and the wind sweeps cold over the plains. The soldiers who bathed for a long time in the warming sun of the Riviera coast freeze in the unaccustomed climate. The shelter halves over their shoulders are wet because they had no chance to dry them out at any of the roadside farmhouses. There has hardly been a pause during the arduous march of the last two or three weeks, during those disengaging movements which brought so much grief in its various phases.

"Now the Army which used to stand guard in the sunny south, many hundreds of miles away, stands at the frontier of the Reich and the thunder of the guns already echoes in the peaceful dales and the villages beyond.

"The conversation of the soldiers these days centers around the question: 'When shall we hold a definite line again?' They talk about it frankly without false hopes, without defeatism, with the clear perception and the straight opinion of soldiers who see things as they are and will not be influenced by the black prophets who are present in any situation, who form their own honest opinions which it is their right to do. For whoever has experienced the ordeal of the withdrawal through the Rhone Valley, the withdrawal which often turned into a veritable hell, has proved that he knows no fear and no despair. . . ."*

Those words were written by the enemy.

The 3d Infantry Division, without perceptible pause, found itself in its second winter campaign. There seemed to be no dividing line. One week we were racing through Southern and Central France in the middle of a temperate Autumn; the next, fighting in difficult, wooded terrain in rain and cold. The local inhabitants, as local inhabitants will the world over, said, "This is very unusual weather for this time of year," whatever that means.

During September enemy action passed through three definite phases. First phase was his rapid withdrawal, leaving only small, disorganized forces to attempt delaying action. As this phase reached its climax he turned and attempted the stand at Besançon. Our troops attacked Besançon September 6, and two days later all enemy resistance in the city ceased.

From Besançon to the Moselle River the enemy put up definite resistance, although in the main it was delaying action, and each day's fighting usually ended with the enemy's falling back to prepared positions in the rear. There was a gradual build-up of enemy artillery during this phase. The first counterattack was launched September 15 at Longevelle, east of Lure. As the enemy fell back toward the Moselle River his daily withdrawals became shorter and his positions gave an indication of considerable work prior to occupation. As artillery fire increased, so did the employment of mines, boobytraps and log roadblocks.

The Division was about to enter this final phase, which was to prevail until the crossing of the Meurthe River. On the high ground east of the Moselle River the enemy finally occupied a definite line of resistance, ceased his withdrawals and held on tenaciously, counterattacking when overrun. He resorted to jungle tactics in the heavily-wooded terrain between the Moselle and Mosellette Rivers and frequently infiltrated behind our lines, ambushing supply trains. When the Moselle River line was taken, the enemy occupied a second, definite, well-organized position northeast of St. Amé and in the vicinity of Cleurie. Here the enemy resisted fiercely, counterattacking and infiltrating to retake ground lost to our attacks and bringing in both reinforcements and replacements.

The granite massif of the Vosges rises steeply from the Plain of Alsace, lies northeast-southwest, and blocks easy entrance to the Rhine Valley from the west. The Vosges consist of low, generally rounded mountains from 1000 to 4000 feet in height, arranged in parallel ridges which individually tend more to the northeast than does the range as a whole.

This is an area of forested mountains forming the southern part of the Vosges chain which lies along the Franco-German frontier and reaches from Belfort in the south to Kaiserslautern in the north. The Saverne Gap divides the High Vosges from its northern extension, the Low Vosges. To the south, the High Vosges terminate abruptly in a series of summits towering above the Belfort Gap.

Average height of the Vosges eastern ridge line is about 3000 feet, but many summits rise about 4000 feet, with elevation increasing southward where the highest point is the Grand Ballon (over 4600), lying northeast of Belfort. The Hohneck, the highest point on the main watershed, rises 4400 feet just north of Grand Ballon. The long ridge lines are usually flat topped, fairly level, and carry stretches of moor, coarse pasture, and peat bog, as well as large amounts of rock debris. Many granite tors rise above the level surface. The ground drops sharply to the east but slopes more gradually to the west, falling in a series of plateaus toward the Lorraine Plain.

---

*Die Wacht, German Nineteenth Army Newspaper "On the Threshold of the Reich," September 13, 1944.

A feature of the Vosges is its number of valleys. Main valleys stand at right angles to the main ridges and tend to lie northwest on the western side and east or east-northeast on the eastern side. Tributary valleys parallel the ridges, lead far into the range, and terminate in a series of headstreams on the slopes of the main ridges. Valley bottoms within the Vosges itself are sometimes poorly drained and long narrow lakes and swampland areas often result.

In autumn, the evergreens are in sharp contrast with the changing colors of the deciduous trees and the yellow and brown of the stubble fields.

In winter, the reds of the sandstone rocks and some of the granite become more noticeable after the forest leaves have fallen. Forests remain green at higher levels, but on the lower slopes browns and russets predominate.

The road net in the Vosges is somewhat constricted by terrain. Main routes often bottleneck in narrow village streets. Sharp turns and steep gradients are common in the Vosges and very winding roads are found in the lake areas near Belfort. Secondary and local roads tend to be narrow and sometimes muddy. In wet weather, they are generally unsuited to military traffic. They are often bordered by ditches or embankments and the crown on old cobbled roads is often so great that vehicles are required to travel at reduced speeds.

Above moderate heights, winters, particularly in the Vosges, may be long and hard, with drastic and sudden changes in temperatures. At all seasons bad weather is more persistent over the mountains than in areas 300-400 miles north because there is a decided tendency for "fronts" to slow up as they approach the Alps barrier; frequently a "front" becomes stationary along the line of the Alps, creating a broad belt of rain and cloud over the foothills which lasts for a day or two.

The 3d Infantry Division was on the western foothill approaches to the Vosges Mountains when Vesoul fell on September 12.

The 2d Battalion, 15th Infantry, which was one element of the forces which took the town, did not pause but continued through, and by 1645 September 12 was on Hill 349, a dominating feature northeast of the town in the direction of Velleminfroy. Movement of the Division at this time was pivoting to the northeast on 30th Infantry, the hub of which was generally at the town of Vallerois le Bois.

Shortly after noon September 12, 1st Battalion, 15th Infantry, moved to Hill 360, with two companies occupying the position at 1325. Company A, leading, encountered enemy machine-gun and small-arms fire at 1446, but outflanked the enemy and was near Quincy at 1640 with roadblocks to the southeast, northeast and northwest. At 1720 1st Battalion was prepared to continue the advance to the north, and at 1930 moved out, shortly to encounter small-arms fire. The 1st Battalion continued to advance during the night and at 0345 reported the town of Calmoultier clear of enemy.

The 30th Infantry, which attacked initially in a north and northeast direction on the Division's right flank, later moved to the southeast toward Esprels, maintaining contact with the 45th Infantry Division. Shortly after noon of September 12, 3d Battalion captured thirty-six enlisted enemy soldiers and one officer, obtaining information on other enemy locations that aided in a successful advance. During the afternoon of September 12, 1st Battalion went to Dampierre, flanked to the left, then began a movement to the southeast against Hill 309. Late in the night of September 12-13, 1st Battalion began encountering enemy opposition, plus log barriers placed at intervals of twenty-five yards along the road to slow 1st Battalion's armor. Despite this, the advance continued.

The 2d Battalion, 15th Infantry, moved from Hill 349, which it had captured previously, and continued to advance against scattered enemy opposition through Comberjon to Moncey. Moncey was cleared at 0645 September 13 and the battalion moved on through Colombotte toward Velleminfroy, toward noon meeting about a platoon of enemy armed with small arms and machine guns.

During the same period the 7th Infantry, in the center of the Division sector, occupied high ground past Noroy-le-Bourg, which it cleaned out en route. The 3d Battalion performed this task during the night of September 12-13, taking 100 to 150 prisoners and killing and wounding an unknown number. At 1830 2d Battalion had been ordered into Division reserve, and 1st and 3d Battalion had advanced toward Hill 452 past Noroy-le-Bourg. By 2030 the 1st Battalion had captured the hill, with 3d Battalion almost directly to the north. At 1000 September 13, 3d Battalion attacked toward Hill 410 and Montjustin. Company C attacked from Hill 459 at 1030 and pushed toward Hill 430. There was scattered, unorganized small-arms and machine-gun fire in opposition to the morning attacks of 1st and 3d Battalions.

The enemy was driven out of Maras and Melmay by patrols from 1st Battalion, 30th Infantry, while the bulk of the battalion was still three or four kilometers short of Esprels on September 13.

The 2d Battalion, 30th Infantry, attacked Presle and by 2115 September 12 was in the corner of the woods near Trevey. At 2300 2d Battalion began its move toward Presle and at 2400 Company F entered the town, with Company E generally to the northeast and Company G to the southeast. There was little resistance at the town, but there were indications that the enemy had just pulled out. Companies F and G remained in Presle while Company E blocked to the northeast until 0700, when the battalion moved out toward Vallerois-le-Bois. The 3d Battalion's Company I, which had been on a flank-protection mission at Thieffrans, was relieved by a company of the 180th Infantry and at 0850 attacked to the northeast toward Montbozon. The remainder of the 3d Battalion prepared for an attack on Mt. Jesus, moving in from the west.

During the foregoing period, 1st Platoon, Company B, 601st TD Battalion, scored a notable success by catching a column of enemy foot troops and killing seventy-five to a hundred enemy.

During the afternoon of September 13 the entire Division advance continued against strong enemy opposition, but the Division occupied all immediate objectives before dark. The 3d Battalion, 7th Infantry, sent one company on to Hill 410 while the remainder of the battalion moved to the east flank. The 1st Battalion advanced through Cerre-les-Noroy and started up the slopes of Hill 430. The 2d Battalion was released from Division control at 1445 and returned to regimental control. The 3d Battalion's remaining two rifle companies moved southeast to Autrey-les-Cerre. The 1st Battalion encountered considerable opposition and at 1915 some enemy still held on Hill 430. The 3d Battalion, meanwhile continued pushing until its leading company ran into heavy artillery, small-arms and mortar fire. The 2d Battalion rested during the latter part of darkness and resumed its advance at 0400, toward Borey and Arpenans. The battalion moved against light opposition. The 1st and 3d Battalions moved out at 0830 and by noon 3d Battalion had occupied Montjustin without making contact with the enemy and was sending a company toward Arpenans. The 1st Battalion moved ahead steadily on 3d Battalion's flank.

Company A, 15th Infantry, occupied Lievans during the evening of September 13 and one platoon was left in the town until relieved by the 7th Infantry. On the morning of September 14 Company B, followed by Company A, moved to Mollans without resistance. Company C moved northwest toward Pomoy and Company B moved toward Genevreuville toward noon September 14. The 2d Battalion, Companies F and G leading, entered Velleminfroy at 0920, September 14 and upon occupation of the town went into regimental reserve.

The 3d Battalion's Company L occupied Hill 289 and on the morning of September 14 followed Company I into reserve. Company K attacked Saulx-de-Vesoul, meeting enemy small-arms and machine-gun fire, but had the town cleared at 1855 September 13. Elements of the 141st Infantry relieved Company K, which then moved to Creveny and Chateney. Toward noon Company K was advancing toward Colombe-le-Bithaine. Company I moved from Chatenois and occupied La Creuse at 0945 September 14 against practically no resistance. Toward noon 3d Battalion was continuing the advance toward Adelans.

The 1st and 2d Battalions, 30th Infantry, began their attack at 1530 September 13, 1st Battalion located about 1000 yards beyond Esprels and 2d Battalion on the left (northeast) flank. The 3d Battalion moved up to Les Patey. Both battalions advanced against small-arms fire. The 3d Battalion sent a platoon to Autrey-le-Vay in conjunction with a platoon from the 45th Division to protect the sector between divisions. At 0630 September 14, 2d Battalion, from its position reached the night before, resumed its attack due east toward Oppenans and advanced without meeting enemy resistance. 1st Battalion fired interdictory machine-gun fire into Marast during the night, and on the morning of September 14 moved into the town against no opposition.

During September 14-15 the Division continued its steady pace toward Lure, swinging to the north and east against enemy resistance that became increasingly stronger during the afternoon of September 14 and which continued strong. The 15th Infantry, on the Division left flank, occupied Pomoy, Genevreuille and Mollans against strong resistance and moved toward Lure from the northwest. The 7th Infantry had contact with the enemy throughout the period, receiving small-arms, machine-gun, and mortar and artillery fire as it advanced to Arpenans, Les Aynans, and headed toward Vy-les-Lure.

Company C, 15th Infantry, entered Pomoy at 1200 September 14, then moved on toward Genevreuille. At 1315 a patrol encountered enemy artillery, mortar, machine-gun and small-arms fire, but the company continued its advance against well-prepared enemy positions and dug-in enemy and at 1830 reached the outskirts of Genevreuille in spite of heavy casualties. The company was pulled back from the town and an artillery barrage laid down. Company B was relieved at Mollans by a company from 30th Infantry at 2245 and moved to rejoin the battalion at Pomoy.

At 1245 3d Battalion was located at Colombe-le-Bithaine, from where it moved to Danbenoit. Company K occupied Citers and patrolled to Quers.

Company A, 30th Infantry, entered the town of Aillevans at 1310 against no opposition, then moved to the east, Company B moving to the northeast. Company A crossed L'Oignan River and reached Hill 324 at 1600. Company C cleared the town of Longeville after overcoming considerable sniper fire. Patrols were sent north of Longeville and to the northeast up to 1000 yards, making negligible contact.

At 2125 the 2d Battalion, 15th Infantry, was ordered

to move to Bithaine and to send a reinforced company to Hill 412. Company F reached the hill at 0925 September 15.

After continuous fighting over September 14 and during the night, 1st and 2d Battalions, 7th Infantry, continued to advance on the morning of September 15. At 0840 2d Battalion was in contact at Les Aynans, our troops on the west side of L'Oignan River, the enemy on the other side. The 1st Battalion by noon had sent patrols toward Vy-les-Lure, ready to attack the town from the northwest.

The 3d Battalion, 15th Infantry, assembled during the morning in the vicinity of Citers. Company K attacked Quers in the face of considerable enemy fire and occupied the town by 1750 that evening. Remainder of the battalion moved toward Lure from the northwest. The 1st Battalion, 15th Infantry, moved on Genevreuille and at 1210 Company B entered against little opposition. The battalion continued toward Amblans, which was occupied in the face of moderate resistance.

The 2d Battalion, 30th Infantry, was assembled at Aillevans. At 0115 September 15 the battalion moved by truck to Lievans, closing in at 0345.

The 3d Battalion moved from Les Patey to Mollans, its last company closing in at 0200, and remained in regimental reserve. The 2d Battalion was in Division reserve.

The 1st Battalion, 7th Infantry, entered La Grange du Veau shortly after noon, September 15 and prepared a defensive position around the town. Strong enemy harassing fire was received, and at 2015 the battalion launched an attack toward high ground to the east. Enemy resistance was strong and the Germans had to be routed from their holes with bayonets and grenades. The battalion dug in for the night about halfway between La Grange du Veau and its objective.

The 2d Battalion, 7th Infantry, secured two bridges near Les Aynans at 1310. One platoon of Company E, assisted by fire from Company G, attacked Hill 383. Patrols were sent into Gouchenans during the night and reported enemy in the town, which Company G took the next morning.

At 1410 3d Battalion, 7th Infantry, attacked Vy-les-Lure and at 1500 Company L was almost in the outskirts with Company I on its right flank. Determined enemy resistance, supported by considerable machine-gun, artillery and mortar fire prevented I and K companies from entering the town.

Company L, led by Capt. Ralph J. Yates, advanced through heavy artillery and mortar concentration, to seize a cluster of houses on the outskirts of the town. The company was swiftly surrounded by an enemy which outnumbered the men three to one. For seven hours the company beat off savage counterattacks one after another, as artillery and mortar fire scored eight direct hits on the company CP, tearing down a corner of the house and demolishing an adjacent shed.

At the cost of 37 casualties the company repulsed all counterattacks and inflicted heavy casualties—18 dead, 70 wounded—on the enemy.

At 0150 a patrol from Company K entered Vy-les-Lure and contacted elements of Company L. The 3d Battalion entered the town in strength at 0900, September 16.

For the foregoing action Company L was later awarded the Distinguished Unit Citation.

The 1st Battalion, meanwhile, resumed its attack toward the high ground east of La Grange du Veau at 0710 and reached its objective at 0945. Toward noon the battalion was moving toward Lure.

The 2d Battalion, 15th Infantry, in its attack on Adelans during the afternoon of September 15, met considerable resistance. Patrols were sent into the town during the night and the attack was resumed the morning of September 16. The town fell before noon. Company K, 15th Infantry, moved to Francheville during this time and protected the regiment's left flank while the remainder of 3d Battalion moved toward Lure from the northwest.

The 1st Battalion, 30th Infantry, sent a patrol toward Gouchenans, which engaged approximately forty enemy in a fire fight on the afternoon of September 15. At 0015 four enemy infiltrated into Company B lines, killing one man, but losing one captured, and two killed. The other escaped. Later Company B patrols captured nine enemy who were asleep and at 0804 September 16, patrols captured six more. The 2d and 3d Battalions remained in Division and regimental reserve, respectively.

Lure was entered first by 1st Battalion, 15th Infantry shortly after noon September 16; 1st Battalion, 7th Infantry, following shortly after.

The capture of Lure ended the toughest battle that the Division had had for some time and the series of coordinated attacks over a wide front that was required in the operation was an indication that the Germans were stiffening their defense.

The actual occupation of Lure was unopposed insofar as enemy infantry was concerned but considerable artillery fell in the city all day September 16, coming from positions north of the town.

At this point, the Division's right zone was taken over by the 1st French Armored Division and the 3d veered almost straight north in the direction of Faucogney.

The 15th Infantry had just moved out of Lure when the 2d Battalion was hit first by artillery fire and then

Gunners of the 3d Division's 441st AAA AW Battalion, their half-track carrier camouflaged, keep an alert watch for enemy aircraft near Remiremont.

by five machine guns at a strongly defended roadblock in a dense woods just northeast of the city.

Hand grenades bounced from tree to tree and the clash of bayonets rang through the forests as the two forces met in this eerie setting, shrouded in pitch darkness. Maj. John O'Connell's men never fought more savagely as the enemy fell, one by one, in individual fights. The Germans retreated after about an hour and the battalion moved on toward St. Germain shortly before midnight.

The 30th moved generally in the same direction as the 15th but the advance was slowed by an increasing number of mines along the roads. The 1st Battalion attacked and occupied the villages of Linexert and Lantenot by noon the following day, repulsing a strong enemy counterattack in the vicinity of Lantenot.

The 7th Infantry occupied Lure and the vicinity south and east of the village, and spent the next three days in patrolling and establishing road blocks in that area.

The 1st Battalion of the 15th, attacking east from Francheville, had many fights before it finally gained the next objectives September 18, when St. Germain, Froideterre and Lemont were taken without opposition. The 2d Battalion encountered heavy resistance including Flak, mortar and artillery fire just south of Froideterre but, as in the battle for the roadblock on the previous day, the enemy was decisively defeated, after which the battalion went into regimental reserve near Lure.

The 30th, after taking Lantenot, met a strong defense when the 3d Battalion, commanded by Lt. Col. Richard H. Neddersen, attempted to take Raddon, a small village about three miles west of Faucogney.

Attacking north, Company L, under Capt. Robert B. Pridgen, reached a ridge and began defensive preparations along a low, rock wall overlooking Raddon. Shortly after noon, heavy enemy tank and 20mm fire swept over the ridge and the concentration was immediately followed by an assault by some 200 frenzied, shouting Germans, many of whom yelled in English that "they wanted to die for Hitler."

Captain Pridgen, later describing the counterattack, said, "They rushed into our fire in an insane manner, as if they had been given liquor or drugs before the assault."

The right flank squad of Company L, led by Sgt. Harold O. Messerschmidt, bore the brunt of the charge and was subjected to a hail of fire from machine guns, machine pistols, rifles and grenades. Firing his submachine gun as he went (180 rounds in all), Sergeant Messerschmidt passed from man to man, encouraging and instructing them as he went.

Sgt. Bob J. Tucker, one of the squad members, stated that Messerschmidt was struck down by automatic fire early in the battle, shot through the chest and shoulder.

"Although badly wounded, he laid burst after burst of fire on everything moving up that slope," Tucker said, continuing, "I saw him grab his tommy gun by the barrel when he ran out of ammunition and kill a kraut by crashing the stock on his head. He sure killed a lot of Germans that day."

First Lt. Glenn Shuler, who brought a squad to relieve the beleaguered men, said that Messerschmidt was fighting alone when he arrived, all other members of the squad having been killed or wounded.

"I saw the sergeant run to the rescue of a wounded comrade who was being overpowered," the Lieutenant said. "Messerschmidt got the kraut and then I saw him disappear down the slope, flailing his empty gun at another fleeing German. The sergeant's body was later found at the bottom of the hill."

Colonel Neddersen said that the Nazi group which attacked our numerically inferior force was "the most determined and fanatical that we encountered." True, these SS Panzer troops, wearing long black overcoats, gave an excellent account of themselves.

Sergeant Messerschmidt was awarded the Congressional Medal of Honor posthumously.

Captain Pridgen's men fought off the enemy for several hours before they received reinforcements from Company I, commanded by Capt. Thomas A. Dawson.

The Distinguished Unit Citation which was later awarded to Company L for its gallant stand stated: "For six hours, the heavily outnumbered company fought on without respite, repulsing the German assault forces time and again with heavy loss despite the enemy's immense superiority in firepower. . . . When the last wave of counterattack was rolled back, the men of Company L, their ammunition almost entirely expended, their ranks reduced by casualties and their situation apparently hopeless, prepared to assault and break through the German lines, although they had but four rifle squads with which to do it. But the enemy had already withdrawn, battered and beaten, abandoning his broken line to attempt a new stand at the Moselle."

By 2000, the enemy counterattacking force, which comprised Flakwagons, armor, an antitank gun and several bazooka teams in addition to the large infantry group, was driven from the slopes and at daylight of September 18 Company K, commanded by Capt. M. B. Etheredge, Jr., moved into Raddon, which the badly-mauled Germans elected not to defend.

The retreating enemy fell back rapidly after the fight at Raddon and the next two days were spent in setting up a series of roadblocks in the Division zone and in maintaining vigorous patrols.

The 3d was now only a short distance from the headwaters of the Moselle River, which rises on the north face of Ballon d'Alsace. The Moselle is the most important river in this area and it captures all other streams in the vicinity as it courses northeast toward the Lorraine Plain.

While awaiting relief by French units, the Division on September 20 launched an early morning attack northeast toward the Moselle, guided along the main road out of Faucogney, which the Germans had deserted in their flight.

The route of advance was through a semi-valley edged on both sides by hills which the enemy employed to good advantage in slowing our movement. Snipers, defended roadblocks, concealed machine guns, and mortars lined the route.

With the 7th Infantry on the left, the 30th on the right and two battalions of the 15th in reserve, the Division moved steadily forward, overcoming continuous resistance from the hills.

Company I of the 30th felt the brunt of a counterattack in the vicinity of Melay, where the 3d Reconnaissance Troop, commanded by 1st Lt. Allen R. Kenyon, also suffered heavily when it ran into a minefield just as the enemy opened fire on the troop from a hill near Melay. Company I withdrew and our artillery then laid a terrific concentration on the area.

During the period September 20-26, the 30th Infantry engaged in some of the most bitter and exhausting fighting in its entire history and contributed materially to the 3d Division's outstanding role in the Seventh Army's flanking attack on the Belfort gap.

Jumping off in the attack to the northeast at 0630 September 20, the 2d Battalion, in fog and rain, moved forward with Company F in the lead, followed by Company E, with G Company in reserve. Objective was the village of Voleaux, eight miles distant and north of Faucogney. Route of the battalion led through a valley with rugged wooded high ground on either side. At 1145 elements of the enemy defense system outside the village began a harassing action and by 1400 had built up sufficient resistance, using small arms, machine guns, and mortars, to force the battalion to deploy and bring up artillery and mortars to soften enemy positions preliminary to frontal assault.

As Company E attacked under this fire it almost reached the ridge, only to be forced back by a violent counterattack. Company F launched an attack directly up the south slope of the high ground but was cut in half by a German thrust from the flanks and forced to pull back. At 1600 G Company, in reserve, was sent one mile to the north, across a waist-deep stream, through heavily wooded, mountainous country to a point 500 yards southeast of the objective to prepare for an attack early in the morning.

At 0700, September 21, Company G attacked forward, northeast along the ridge, meeting intense opposition, including much close-range grenade fighting, but the company succeeded in capturing its objective.

Bitterly counterattacked without rest the company and a reinforcing platoon from Company F beat off no less than nine counterattacks in as many hours in one period. Numerous counterattacks were launched by fanatical Nazis who yelled allegiance to Hitler as they attacked.

Relief reached the company late September 21 when Company E finally broke through the enemy positions which had been established across the rear of Company G. In the bitter action the Germans lost an estimated 140 men killed or wounded and twelve as pris-

3d Infantry Division infantrymen "take a break" in the town of Faucogney, France, which despite the ruins, has been decorated by its citizens.

oners. Company G lost twenty-nine killed, wounded and missing. For this action Company G received the Distinguished Unit Citation.

Throughout the September 20-21 period, the 1st and 3d Battalions, 30th Infantry, were engaged in bitter fighting with the enemy in the vicinity of Melay and La Mer. Mined roads prevented extensive use of armor, and heavy mortar and artillery fire caused numerous casualties. Heavy rains made the poor road net impassable.

The advance of the 7th, which was generally north, met only harassing fire as it moved forward to occupy Hill 753 after silencing several machine guns on the hill, which overlooked the Moselle River.

Turning its attack to the southeast, the Division advanced steadily against decreasing opposition, then turned sharply northeast. This sudden shift took the Germans by surprise and the badly disorganized enemy abandoned trucks, field pieces and other material as they broke and fled by whatever transportation they could jump onto, and by foot, across the bridge at Rupt-sur-Moselle.

The bridge had been prepared for demolition with nineteen cases of TNT but the 1st Battalion of the 7th Infantry, commanded by Lt. Col. Jesse F. Thomas, struck so quickly that the baffled Germans who remained to fight were killed or captured and the others retreated across the river. Company B, under 1st Lt. William K. Dieleman, effected the bridge capture and repulsed numerous attempts of the enemy to infiltrate back to detonate the explosives during the night. The company also beat off several efforts to recapture the bridge and by daylight of September 24, the entire 1st Battalion had crossed the bridge and was engaging the enemy in a fire fight in Rupt-sur-Moselle, which lay just east of the Moselle.

A platoon of the 3d Battalion, 7th Infantry, made another crossing of the river at Maxonchamp, about one mile north of Rupt-sur-Moselle, at noon. The 3d Battalion of the 15th was attached to the 7th to protect its right flank during the river-crossing operation.

Meanwhile the 1st and 3d Battalions, 30th Infantry, following relief by the 117th Reconnaissance Squadron, assembled in Faucogney the morning of September 22 and at 1200 jumped off in a coordinated attack, the 3d on the left and 1st on the right—the 2d holding the line of departure. Objective of the attack, which was straight northeast on the east side of the Faucogney-Remiremont highway, was the high ground east of Corravillers-le-Plain.

Opposition was immediate. All roads in the rugged regimental sector were mined and blocked by trees. Fog and rain added to the difficulties. Every type of enemy fire was encountered. When the 1st Battalion reached the vicinity of Evouhey and encountered a well-prepared enemy line, the advance was halted for coordination purposes, preparatory to a renewal of the attack. The 2d Battalion, meanwhile, cleared the roads to Esmoulieres.

Throughout September 23 the advance continued, with the two assault battalions jumping off at 0645, the 1st Battalion securing Evouhey at 0717 and the 3d Battalion moving up on the left only to encounter stiff resistance from by-passed enemy positions in the 7th Infantry sector. The 3d Battalion continued its blocking mission to the right flank and east of the regiment.

At 1400 September 24 a strongly held enemy roadblock on the main road, manned by enemy infantry, with a Flak gun in the woods behind, prevented a further advance by the 3d Battalion. When it appeared that a battalion from the 7th Infantry could not clear this area before dark, the 3d Battalion, 30th Infantry, by-passed the resistance, leaving K Company as a blocking force, and proceeded to clear out the enemy in its assigned sector. Company F meanwhile was attached to the battalion, abreast of the left flank positions on the Le Chene road.

At 0630, September 25, the 30th Infantry jumped off in an attack to the southeast to secure high ground overlooking Le Thillot, which was to serve as a springboard for French armor to attack that important city and continue on toward Belfort.

The 3d Battalion advanced on the left and the 1st Battalion on the right of the Corravillers-Chateau Lambert road. The 3d Battalion, whose left flank on the Moselle River was exposed to enemy fire, found the going through dense woods and over the rough terrain very slow, enemy small-arms fire being extremely persistent. Company F attacked and found the Le Chene road almost entirely blocked by fallen trees and heavily mined. By 1620, however, the company had reached the outskirts of Le Chene.

The 1st Battalion, although making no contact initially, ran into well-defended positions at 1305, with mortar, self-propelled artillery and Flak guns composing the opposition. The assault companies forced their way slowly through pouring rain, dense woods, and numerous roadblocks, with visibility very low, to reach the final objective at 1910. The battalion barely missed capturing an enemy divisional commander, but took a German battalion command post with telephones intact which was in communication with the German division command post. More than 150 prisoners, including three officers, were taken in this outstanding action.

At 1845 Company L was sent to assist Company F in the attack on Le Chene, which had proved in early efforts to be too large a job for one company.

The 3d Battalion, having continued throughout the night of September 25-26, reached its objective at 0930 September 26, after killing, wounding, or capturing fifty-two more enemy soldiers.

On the same day 2d Battalion, less Company G, captured Le Chene after a 40-minute fight, taking twenty more prisoners.

That afternoon the 30th Infantry was relieved by French troops and closed in assembly areas at La Longine and Corravillers. During the afternoon of September 27 the regiment moved by motor to Remiremont, and spent the following day in preparation for the attack toward Le Tholy.

Rupt-sur-Moselle was cleared of all resistance by noon September 25 and Hill 867, which rose directly behind the village and served as a vantage point from which the enemy fired on traffic crossing the bridge, was occupied. The high ground east of Maxonchamp likewise served the enemy well until it was cleared by the 7th, which had expanded its area by fanning out north to Dommartin and south to La Roche.

The 15th Infantry, meanwhile, had moved out from positions in the vicinity of Remiremont and attacked northeast from St. Amé, with the 7th Infantry protecting its right flank south of the Moselette, from a high wooded area containing many enemy gun positions.

With nature as the greatest obstacle to progress, the 15th moved steadily forward after the attack began early September 27 but on the next day the enemy, in well dug-in and previously prepared positions between Le Syndicat and Cremanvillers, put up a terrific fight.

Two night counterattacks, coupled with constant infiltrations after dark, taxed the 15th's strength to the utmost and on September 28 the 30th joined in the attack, going into position between the 15th and the 36th Infantry Division on the 3d's left flank.

The 7th continued to clean out the Germans between the Moselle and Mosellette Rivers and occupied Ferdrupt, east of the Moselle and a little north of Le Thillot, shortly after noon.

It was at Ferdrupt that Company F of the 7th Infantry particularly distinguished itself. For six consecutive days it had advanced in chilling rain up the precipitous slopes of a 2,500-foot hill mass against determined opposition to seize its objective. Fighting at hand-to-hand range raged for days in the densely wooded terrain. German infiltration attempts through the wooded area and enemy counterattacks were repulsed time and time again. Having secured the top of the hill mass the weary, thinned-out ranks of the company continued to drive off German attacking forces to hold the terrain feature they had so dearly won in the fog and cold. For this grim battle and victory the Distinguished Unit Citation was later awarded the doughty warriors of Company F.

The 15th Infantry approached one of its greatest battles in the Vosges (and the entire war) as it neared the Cleurie Quarry. During the afternoon of September 26 the 1st Battalion relieved elements of the 36th Infantry Division in the vicinity of St. Amé. The enemy still held a roadblock on the bridge crossing the stream south of the town, which was covered by fire from positions a mere 300 yards from the bridge. The battalion immediately seized it and the crossroads there in the face of heavy enemy fire, just in time to prevent the enemy from detonating 250 pounds of dynamite laid to demolish the bridge. The 1st Battalion had thus secured the southern extremity of the line of departure for the following day's attack, and seized an important bridge.

The same afternoon, 2d and 3d Battalions moved into positions in preparation for the attack; 2d Battalion to an area just west of St. Amé, and 3d Battalion farther to the north.

At daylight, September 27, the 2d Battalion attacked east through the densely wooded sector following a 15-minute artillery concentration. The battalion pushed through the gloomy, rain-soaked foothills and almost at once the leading elements drew enemy mortar fire. The first group of enemy was contacted immediately north of St. Amé and was protecting the secondary road leading north from the town, from the woods west of the road. Elements of the 2d Battalion surprised the enemy from the rear and there was a brief skirmish, during which thirty-two prisoners were captured.

The battalion continued to the northeast through small-arms, machine-gun, and mortar fire, and booby-trapped roadblocks. By 1400 it had reached the secondary road running southeast from Bemont. Resistance then slacked off and the 2d Battalion pushed rapidly to its objective on the high ground northeast of St. Amé.

The 3d Battalion, which had held back initially to support the 2d's advance with fire, attacked at mid-morning toward Cleurie, from the vicinity of Putiéres, and moved along the ridge to the northeast without opposition. In the afternoon the advance was punctuated by bitter hand-to-hand fighting, but the battalion battered its way to positions on the high ground south of Cleurie.

At dusk about 150 Germans launched a counterattack against Company K. This attack was preceded by a short, intense, artillery barrage, but was repulsed within three hours.

The fight for the Cleurie Quarry was in the mold. Company I attacked all night and secured Bemont. Company G continued toward Cremanvillers, held up in the woods, and sent patrols to the town. At 0230 the enemy hit Company G with a heavy counterattack, which was beaten off. Daylight found the company again heavily engaged just northeast of Cremanvillers. Company C was attached to the 2d Battalion to aid G Company, and pushed east from St. Amé, where it was counterattacked by the enemy in the wooded areas.

The enemy was now completely aroused. He struck again at K Company and again was beaten off. The constant, driving rains, the fog and mist, cut visibility almost to the zero point and the Germans used this to advantage to move between our elements in attempts to disorganize our lines and demoralize the men.

Company F, moving south from the 2d Battalion hill position toward G, again was heavily attacked, and fought throughout the day. Other enemy groups pushed through the gaps between the companies of the 2d and 3d Battalions, one group even penetrating almost to the 3d Battalion command post.

By dawn, September 28, the entire effective strength of the 15th Infantry was committed. Elements of the 1st Battalion were pushing toward Cremanvillers and Bemont to assist the other two battalions, moving out to attack north through the woods in the zone east of the road leading north out of St. Amé. As the 1st moved north into the clearing east of Bemont, it drew heavy fire of all descriptions from the woods to the east, and consequently it attacked northeast through the woods to outflank the enemy positions from which the fire was coming. 1st Battalion remained heavily engaged throughout the day.

Enemy tanks were encountered for the first time in several days. One moved south almost to Bemont, where it was beaten off by artillery. Two others fired on the houses east of Bemont.

Ration details were forced to run a gantlet of roving enemy tanks and snipers while hand-carrying their heavy loads up slippery, wet slopes. Even litter teams were not exempt. Many a wounded doughboy had to be carried through small-arms and mortar fire.

The ferocious fighting continued throughout the day and through the night of September 28-29. In the early morning hours five enemy tanks moved in to shoot up F Company positions in a group of houses, and before the armor could be turned away with artil-

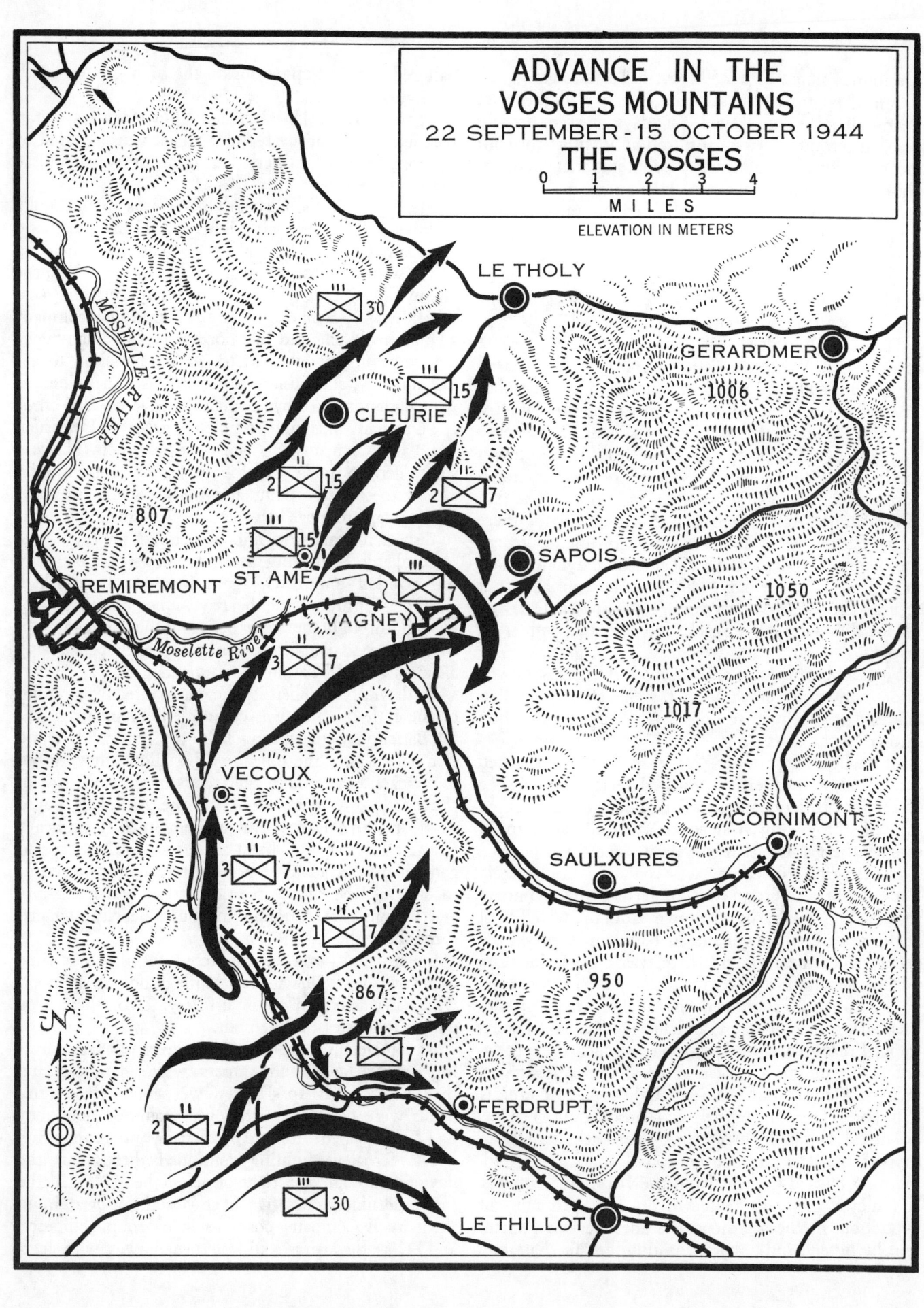

lery the company had become badly scattered, the Commanding Officer and much of company headquarters either killed, wounded, or captured. Only seventy men could be accounted for by the time the attack was beaten off.

Company E was counterattacked and forced to fight for four hours to hold its positions. The attack was finally broken.

Company L, fighting south toward K Company, was hit by 250 enemy and engaged in a furious battle to hold its hill. Two platoons of the company were split and scattered and it was daylight before about seventy or eighty men could be rounded up, organized and moved up to the original hill positions.

The 1st Battalion continued its drive as the remainder of the regiment cleaned out the enemy who had infiltrated everywhere into the regimental sector. Company I was attached to the battalion. From the area east of Bemont the 1st drove up the main road, against small-arms and mortar fire. Our artillery raked enemy strongpoints near Cleurie and in the buildings south of town. The battalion made good progress and turned east along the edge of the woods. Late September 29, the forward elements were hit with fire from about forty enemy who were lodged in the vicinity of Cleurie Quarry. It was then that the great battle began.

Company B held up—then pushed on. A few hours later the enemy launched a light counterattack. At midnight, a full-force counterattack hit the tired company. Capt. Paul Harris and his men groped their way toward the top of "Great Rock," to reach the crest and hole up, but under the thick night fog the enemy once more slammed back. Closing in, feeling their way along like blind men, the enemy approached behind a heavy artillery preparation to within fifty yards. Slinging potato-masher grenades and blasting away with machine pistols, he hit B Company's right flank. Fanatical young Nazis pressed the attack for five hours. The attack mounted in fury. Then, just before the dawn of September 30, the enemy withdrew. Although the right flank platoon of B Company, which had borne the brunt of the savage battle, had been forced to pull back, the bulk of the company was still holding firm.

In the remainder of the 15th Infantry zone, the constant attempts at infiltration had continued. One group of enemy had probed its way between G and C Companies; another counterattacked E Company, and still another struck at G Company twice during the day, and the night of September 29-30. All attempts finally were repulsed with the help of prepared concentrations from mortar batteries and the regimental Cannon Company. But the battle was not yet over.

On September 29 the 30th Infantry assumed offensive action, with the objective of seizing Hill 781, high

This statue in Remiremont serves as a signpost for traffic control signs.

ground overlooking Le Tholy. The 3d Battalion led the attack, crossing the line of departure at 0700 and continuing without resistance until 0835, when strong resistance in the form of small-arms and artillery fire was met from well-defended all-around positions, which blocked maneuvering elements at every point. The 2d Battalion, following to the right rear, found it could not pass through 3d Battalion without becoming engaged in a fire fight, and 1st Battalion was then committed. The 2d Battalion became the reserve battalion and established roadblocks.

Company A relieved Company K, 15th Infantry. Later A Company was relieved by E Company. It took part in a cross-country march with 1st Battalion which began at 1500 September 29 and continued until 0020 September 30, when the entire battalion relieved 3d Battalion, 141st Infantry (36th Division).

At 0715 that morning, 1st Battalion jumped off in the attack again, and began receiving heavy fire at 0810, initially from machine guns, mortars, and small arms, but which was intensified with the addition of heavy artillery concentrations at 0945. Severe casualties, numbering up to 150, were received. Company B, under 1st Lt. Lysle Standish, attempted to maneuver and flank enemy positions, and was met with heavy automatic-weapons fire, which slowed the advance. The 3d Battalion resumed its attack at 0915, September 30, but strongly-entrenched enemy in commanding positions held up the advance. Another attack at 1815 secured a line and gained strategic ground, while the 2d Battalion remained in regimental reserve.

As the month of September closed, the Division was embroiled in heavy fighting. Enemy counterattacks were characterized by a ferocity hitherto encountered only in Italy the previous winter. Increased artillery

The 3d Division's 10th Engineers begin construction of a ponton bridge north of Remiremont in the Vosges.

fire from 75s, 88s, and 105s was evidence that the German commander had received reinforcements in this all-important branch as October came and actual winter began to set in.

The Division was well into the first phase of October, with the three regiments battling for important ground in its over-all attack northeast toward Le Tholy in conjunction with the move east to overrun Vagney and Sapois. The second phase was to come following the capture of these important centers, and consisted of an attack through elements of the 45th Infantry Division that carried across the Mortagne River and to the high ground overlooking the important enemy communications center of St. Dié. The latter attack was to begin at noon, October 20, and result in a breakthrough of the enemy's strong defensive line based on the Mortagne River. But much fighting remained before this could be achieved.

By September 30 the 7th Infantry had taken Ferdrupt and was pushing on toward Vagney to come up on the 15th Infantry's right flank. While the remainder of the 15th was forced to halt and clean out its zone of infiltrating Germans, the 1st Battalion continued to batter away against the quarry positions.

The quarry was a major thorn in our side and had to be cleaned out, although it was proving a tough obstacle. It controlled the main route of advance, the Le Tholy-Gerardmer road, which itself had to be cleared before the Division could continue on the over-all mission of penetrating the Vosges proper. The quarry was the anchor point of the enemy main line defending the important St. Amé hill mass, and the largest hill in the area which controlled the entire situation all the way back to Remiremont.

There were several reasons for the difficult mission that the quarry proved to be. First, it was situated on the slopes of the large, thickly-wooded hill mass. The only approaches to it were up the steep, almost clifflike sides of this mountain. On the north and south sides of the quarry were steep cliffs covered by machine guns. In order to gain entrance to the interior, our men had to charge up the sides in the face of furious fire. East and west ends were blocked by huge, stonewall roadblocks constructed by the Germans. The steep cliffs on either side made it impossible to by-pass these, and thus the only way left open was to go over the top of them which again, was covered by terrific concentrations of small-arms fire.

The quarry was honeycombed with passageways, tunnels and walls, rendering the defenders virtually safe from mortar fire. Another difficulty was that it was impossible for us to use artillery after the companies had closed in around the position, since our guns in position in the flat lands near St. Amé had to fire over the top of the hill mass, and with our troops so close to the enemy, tree bursts often fell within our own lines.

As October came, prisoners reported that there were

two companies, approximately 100 men each in strength, with orders to fight to the death for the position. The regimental plan now was to coordinate with the drive of the 30th Infantry in a house-to-house push down the valley toward Gerardmer, the VI Corps objective, where the enemy was known to be entrenched in strength.

All three battalions of the 30th Infantry during the period October 1-8 continued an unrelenting pressure toward the northeast. On October 1 the 3d Battalion, 30th Infantry, resumed its attack at 0700, and the 1st Battalion jumped off at 0800. The 2d Battalion patrolled into the valley, encountering and charting minefields, and taking and occupying fifteen houses. Despite enemy artillery concentrations and counterattacks the 1st and 3d Battalions continued to advance.

On October 2, the 2d Battalion was moved by motor to the extreme left of the regimental sector, behind Hill 769, to outflank enemy positions on the high ground and open the route across the Tendon-Le Tholy highway to the high ground beyond. The 1st Battalion, meanwhile, continued a yard-by-yard advance against well dug-in and held enemy positions, sustaining heavy casualties and overrunning one enemy mortar platoon. The battalion also captured four mortars, two antitank guns, two Flak guns, and fifteen soldiers plus an artillery observer. Throughout the day the 2d Battalion continued the slow advance through heavily mined areas, and was relieved by 15th Infantry and 10th Engineer Battalion elements at 2010, following which the battalion entrucked and moved to an assembly area, prepared to attack on October 3.

In the 15th zone, virtual stalemate had set in by the morning of October 2. In some places the lines were barely seventy-five yards apart. It was jungle warfare, with thick nests of enemy snipers and infiltrating German parties. At the mouth of the quarry the enemy now had constructed a rock wall squarely across both entrances, then covered them with fire from positions in the rock piles. During the night of October 2-3, Companies C and I were returned to their battalions, and took up positions in their respective zones.

The all-out drive got underway October 3. At first light two tank destroyers and two tanks mounting 105mm assault guns were moved into position across the valley from the quarry, from where they pumped 500 rounds of high explosive into the tunnels and main part of the quarry. At the same time, 1st Battalion mortars laid in a terrific concentration. When the fire lifted, patrols from all three rifle companies of the 1st Battalion ranged out to probe the quarry. Opposition still remained, and brisk fighting raged throughout the day. Company B patrols were hit by an enemy machine gun immediately in front of its lines short of the quarry, and captured a sniper. Other prisoners indicated that a complete company of sharpshooters, eighty men strong, had been brought into the area, each man carrying a rifle equipped with telescopic sight. One squad of marksmen was attached to each regular rifle platoon of the 601st *Schnelle* Battalion, defending the quarry, for employment as snipers.

Contact with the enemy was constant throughout the day. Plans to launch the cleanup attack the following day were made. While on his way to an observation post, Col. Richard G. Thomas, regimental commander, was stricken with a heart attack, and command of the 15th Infantry passed to Regimental Executive Lt. Col. Hallett D. Edson. In the 3d Battalion, Lt. Col. Frederick Boye, commanding, left for the United States on temporary duty and his executive officer, Maj. Russell Comrie, replaced him.

At 0530, October 4, the 3d Battalion launched an outflanking attack. In conjunction with the 30th Infantry, the battalion drove northeast down the valley from positions just northwest of L'Omet, and sent Company I around west of the quarry to cut the road. The other two battalions remained in blocking positions.

Despite the fact that the enemy had poured strong reinforcements into the quarry and prepared for a bitter stand, Company I surprised the first positions short of the quarry and the enemy here withdrew.

Behind the supporting fire of three battalions of artillery, the 3d Battalion drove on. In less than two hours L Company had destroyed two machine guns, captured a crew of six, and driven two other machine-gun crews back. By noon Company I was halfway around the quarry on the west side and was meeting heavy sniper fire, while L Company was overrunning the houses in the valley and bringing up tanks to blast them.

All afternoon and during most of the night the fight went on. By dark I Company had cleared the enemy from the western approaches to the quarry, after bringing up tanks to blast down the stone-wall roadblock at that entrance with their guns.

The 3d Battalion had now established a line from the main road just west of Hazintray, bending around almost to the western edges of the quarry. Before midnight one platoon-sized patrol from I Company pushed into the eastern end of the quarry after men of the 10th Engineer Battalion had been committed to blast the stone wall blocking the road at that end.

The fight was at a climax and the job completed on October 5. Mortars of the 1st Battalion opened up with an 1100-round continuous creeping barrage. Then combat patrols from the battalion, plus the 3d Battalion Battle Patrol, and a platoon of Company I pushed out to destroy the last positions. By midafternoon, the Battle Patrol, under Sgt. John J. Shermetta, came up to the

Defeated, dejected, enemy file out of the Cleurie quarry after its reduction by 3d Division troops.

quarry from the west and met S/Sgt. John D. Shirley's I Company platoon coming from the east.

The quarry had now fallen after a gruelling six-day fight.

The Medal of Honor was awarded to 1st Lt. (then 2d Lt.) Victor L. Kandle for his action performed during the last days of the fight for the quarry. While leading a reconnaissance patrol in the vicinity of La Forge in enemy territory, Lieutenant Kandle engaged in a daylight duel at point-blank range with a German field officer and killed him. Having taken five enemy prisoners during the morning, he led his skeleton platoon of sixteen men, reinforced by a light machine-gun squad, through fog and over precipitous mountain terrain to fall on the rear of the approach positions of the German quarry stronghold, which had checked the advance of the 1st Battalion. The citation of Lieutenant Kandle reads in part:

". . . Rushing forward several yards ahead of his assault elements, Lieutenant Kandle forced his way into the heart of the enemy strongpoint and by his boldness and audacity forced the Germans to surrender. Harassed by machine-gun fire from a position which he had by-passed in the dense fog, he moved to within fifteen yards of the enemy, killed a German machine gunner with accurate rifle fire, and led his men in the destruction of another machine-gun crew and its rifle security elements. Finally he led his small force against a fortified house held by two German officers and thirty enlisted men. After establishing a base of fire, he rushed forward alone through an open clearing in full view of the enemy, smashed through a barricaded door, and forced all thirty-two Germans to surrender. His intrepidity and bold leadership resulted in the capture or killing of three enemy officers and fifty-four enlisted men, the destruction of three enemy strongpoints and the seizure of . . ."

Meanwhile the 30th Infantry had jumped off on October 3, with the 2d Battalion now committed in a new attack on the regiment's extreme left with the final objective of seizing Hill 781, north of Le Tholy. At 0700 the attack was well under way, with the 2d Battalion coordinating with the 1st Battalion on the right. Throughout the bright moonlight night of October 3-4 the regiment continued its determined attack. At 0500 the 1st Battalion was counterattacked on its exposed right flank. Company B beat off the attack and at 1320 the enemy counterattacked this battalion again, but failed to dent it. The 2d Battalion's attack met equally fierce resistance, but the 3d Battalion reached its objective by 1230, taking eight prisoners and a mortar position, using the mortars to fire back at the enemy. Casualties for the period October 1-3 totalled more than 400.

Throughout October 4, the enemy continued to make limited attacks against the 1st Battalion's right flank. Both the 1st and 2d Battalions continued to press the attack, but enemy resistance was determined and progress was slow. During this period enemy artillery increased considerably with several three-gun batteries firing simultaneously at 30th Infantry troops.

The 1st Battalion maintained its pressure on the enemy, and advanced slowly toward the objective. The 2d Battalion, by late afternoon of the 6th, placed fire on enemy positions astride the main Tendon-Le Tholy highway, driving the Germans out. During the night this position was occupied by 2d Battalion troops.

At 0730, October 7, the 1st Battalion jumped off in an attack which gained the crest of the objective by 0930, while the 3d Battalion moved Company I to reinforce the 1st Battalion's sector.

On the 8th the 1st Battalion launched a concerted cleanup attack at 1515, coordinated with tanks and TDs to drive all the enemy from the ridge by dark, despite heavy enemy 150mm artillery opposition.

Remaining in position on the 9th, and consolidating its positions, the regiment took its final objectives on October 10, with the 2d Battalion pushing Companies E and F across the Tendon-Le Tholy road under cover of darkness and seizing the objectives by 0700. The entire battalion was consolidated on the high ground north of Le Tholy that night and the 3d Battalion moved up to occupy positions left by the 2d Battalion.

The 7th Infantry, in this tedious fight for control of the Vosges, entered Vagney after overcoming stubborn resistance. The 1st Battalion, which had borne the brunt of the fighting, established its CP approximately in the center of town. The regimental command post was set up just north of Vagney, and the 3d Battalion CP was also moved into town. A dense fog covered the area on October 7 and small, by-passed groups of enemy still held out in the hills and pine forests that flanked the narrow valley floor on which Vagney was located.

The decision to displace 7th Infantry headquarters units forward while Vagney was still receiving strong shell fire involved a deliberate sacrifice of security, but the necessity of establishing and maintaining control over the combat elements required it. Vagney was still under observation from high ground in the direction of Sapois.

Terrain, the weather conditions and the progress of the offensive all conspired to create perfect conditions for a hostile counterattack and the Germans took advantage of one of the darkest and foggiest nights of the early winter to conduct a raid on the 3d Battalion CP.

T/Sgt. Gerald T. Hennings, the battalion sergeant-major, later described the action.

"I heard a terrific roar as a tank came down the road and stopped in front of the house next to the CP," Hennings said. "I knew that some of our tanks were expected to return to the rear areas for a short rest and naturally thought that this was one of them. I heard the sound of a grenade as it exploded in the next house. Then another came through our own window in the CP!"

A supporting tank platoon, under command of 2d Lt. James L. Harris, was in the town square at the time. The noise brought immediate action from the lieutenant's crew.

"There was confusion as to the identity of the tank at first," Hennings continued, "and Lieutenant Harris elected to go forward afoot in an effort to identify it. The first burst of machine-gun fire from the enemy tank caught the Lieutenant squarely, knocking him to the ground. The next burst killed a man beside me. We were really in a bad spot.

"Lieutenant Harris didn't forget his mission and despite his painful wounds, he crawled thirty yards through a hell of machine-gun fire to his tank, where he ordered the tank into a covered archway, but it burst into flames, struck by five direct hits, while still in the center of the street."

Pvt. Burton B. Roberts, a medic attached to the 1st Battalion, said that Lieutenant Harris refused medical aid until the sole survivor of his tank had been cared for.

"After I had evacuated the enlisted men I returned to help Lieutenant Harris," Roberts stated. "He asked me if I had taken care of his men and I told him I had. He seemed relieved. He told me he was done for and I saw that his right leg had been cut off at the crotch, apparently by the flying pieces of armor plate from his tank. He was in bad shape. I don't see how he lived as long as he did."

Col. Ben Harrell, commanding officer of the 7th, commented, "The Germans had struck at the heart of a vital command area. As a result of Lieutenant Harris' heroism and single-minded devotion, the force

Colonel Lionel C. McGarr, CO 30th Infantry Regiment pauses beside his jeep to study his map somewhere in the Vosges.

General "Iron Mike" O'Daniel briefs General Marshall on the situation during the latter's inspection of the division in the Vosges near Remiremont. General Devers, CG Sixth Army Group looks on.

of their blow was warded off; the battalion command post was saved from possible destruction and an interruption of offensive operations in that sector of the Vosges was averted."

The posthumous award of the Congressional Medal of Honor that followed Lieutenant Harris' act was the recognition of many similar deeds performed by the 756th Tank Battalion during the battle for the Vosges and Lieutenant Harris' heroism was typical of many other officers and enlisted men during the bitter winter warfare.

The 1st Battalion of the 7th repulsed a strong tank-supported counterattack at Vagney while another that isolated Companies E and I from the rest of the regiment for a short time was beaten off after a bitter fight in the same vicinity.

The 7th Infantry occupied Sapois and completed the occupation of Zainvillers, clearing out many sniper nests in the process. The regiment was taken out of the line October 11 and began a five-day training schedule in the vicinity of Eloyes. On the same day, Peck Force (elements of the 15th Infantry) took LaForge and the rest of the regiment continued its march to the northeast while the 30th remained in the vicinity of Le Tholy where the Germans were firmly dug in.

Regimental raider platoons and reinforced combat patrols raided enemy positions frequently during the next few days and although no major gains were made during the period, the Division maintained a continuous pressure that was slowly pushing the enemy back.

The Porter Force of the 30th, led by 1st Lt. Morris C. Porter, commander of the regimental raider platoon, and including a platoon of the division battle patrol, led by 2d Lt. Walter Gill, who was captured in the action, engaged in a torrid fight in the early morning hours of October 16 when another raid was conducted against Le Tholy. Lieutenant Porter's men suffered heavily when they were caught from the front and flanks upon entering the town. The battle lasted for several hours and the force withdrew at daylight.

The 15th was relieved by French units October 17, leaving only the 30th in the line. The latter regiment maintained contact with the enemy through vigorous patrolling until October 20, when the Division renewed the attack northeast toward Vervezelle and Brouvelieures.

The setting for this action was generally as follows:

VI US Corps was still fighting with the same divisions which had landed on the Riviera two months before—the 3d, 36th, and 45th. All had been continuously engaged. Now, with winter approaching and the rugged terrain adding to the difficulties imposed by the weather, our tired troops were finding it increasingly difficult to keep up their day-to-day advances. Meanwhile the enemy's lines of supply had shortened, his replacements were becoming more numerous and frequent, and above all he now had time to emplace and employ his artillery.

Against this, the Allies had in their favor the slow but steady buildup of troops and supplies which everyone knew spelled eventual victory, but which was powerless to offset the temporary enemy advantages. It was part of the Allied build-up that the French were to come into the line opposite Belfort, and relieve United States troops as far north as Le Tholy; the slowness of the Allied build-up was emphasized by the fact that our troops could not be relieved fast enough to build up a really large striking force, strong enough, say, to break through and reach the Rhine.

Thus the 7th and 15th Infantry Regiments, relieved by the French in the Vagney and St. Amé areas, were able to effect a breakthrough at Brouvelieures, and the 30th, relieved around Le Tholy, was able to exploit the breakthrough nearly as far as St. Dié. But there the advance momentarily stopped, while our forces regrouped and our build-up continued, augmented next by the 100th and 103d Infantry Divisions, recently arrived from the United States.

The shape of the battle was roughly as follows:

The 7th and 15th Infantry regiments attacked abreast at noon October 20, the 7th on the right heading due east for Vervezelle, the 15th on the left swinging to the northeast toward Brouvelieures. The enemy had previously stabilized his positions on the high ground west of Brouvelieures, where the 45th Infantry Division, strung out as far as Rambervillers on the north, had been unable to concentrate enough force to penetrate the enemy line. (As a matter of fact, a strong enemy counterattack with armored support had hurt the 45th badly in this very area the previous week).

Now, with the 36th Infantry Division engaged in a successful attack on Bruyéres, and the 45th continuing to attack farther north, the added kick provided by the 3d caused the enemy line to give way completely, and by the end of the second day a definite breakthrough had been accomplished.

The 3d Battalion of the 15th Infantry, commanded by Maj. Russell Comrie, helped the campaign tremendously by seizing a bridge over the Mortagne River just north of Brouvelieures before the enemy could demolish it. The regiment crossed as rapidly as possible at this point, and began an attack to the east along the ridge on which the town of Mortagne was situated. The 15th met many strong detachments of enemy trying to escape over the few roads leading away from this ridge-top to the east and northeast, and fought a series of spirited engagements during this advance.

The 7th meanwhile had captured Vervezelle and Domfaing in two powerful attacks, and had then swung east up the south side of the valley leading to Les Rouges Eaux. In night marches over the heavily forested hills the 7th secured valuable ground, although control was so difficult that the 1st Battalion on one occasion had a hard time locating itself on the map when daylight came. On the high ridge southeast of Etival, and south of Les Rouges Eaux, the regiment first made contact with the 201st Mountain Battalion, a fresh formation of well-equipped Austrian mountaineers, some 600 men strong. Fortunately the 7th hit this unit before it had a chance to get well dug-in, and smashed it so badly the first day of contact that it never gained its full fighting efficiency.

It was in this vicinty north of Les Rouges Eaux, on October 25, that S/Sgt. Clyde L. Choate, Company C, 601st TD Battalion, engaged a German Mark IV tank in a one-man battle, with Choate stalking the tank until he finally destroyed it just as it was about to break through to an infantry battalion CP area.

"The Germans had launched a surprise attack on densely wooded positions on a hilltop occupied by our forces," related Lt. Col. Walter E. Tardy, Commanding Officer of the 601st, "and the enemy struck with force and decision.

"The only tank destroyer available in this sector was knocked out before it could open fire. The German tank proceeded straight down a wagon road, slashing through the infantry positions and shooting the soldiers in their foxholes.

"Sergeant Choate couldn't find all of our crew and he believed the driver was trapped in the burning TD. Choate ran through a rain of enemy fire to the M-10, which was empty. Kraut infantry followed the Mark IV as it headed toward the infantry battalion CP about 400 yards to our rear," added Sgt. Thomas L. Langan, who was a gunner in the ill-fated TD.

"The German tank cruised through the woods, firing down into the foxholes of the doughboys and crushing soldiers to death under its tracks. Grabbing a bazooka from one of the foxholes, Choate immobilized the enemy tank, which the Germans then converted into an armored pillbox.

"Choate ran back to our infantrymen again, got another rocket and closed in on the tank to within ten yards, always under heavy enemy fire. The shot was a bull's eye and Germans began piling out of it, with Choate shooting them with his revolver."

T/4 Jay W. Shively, who also witnessed the event, said that Choate "winged" at least two Krauts and threw a hand grenade into the tank to be certain there were no more live ones in it.

Losing their tank, the German infantry became dis-

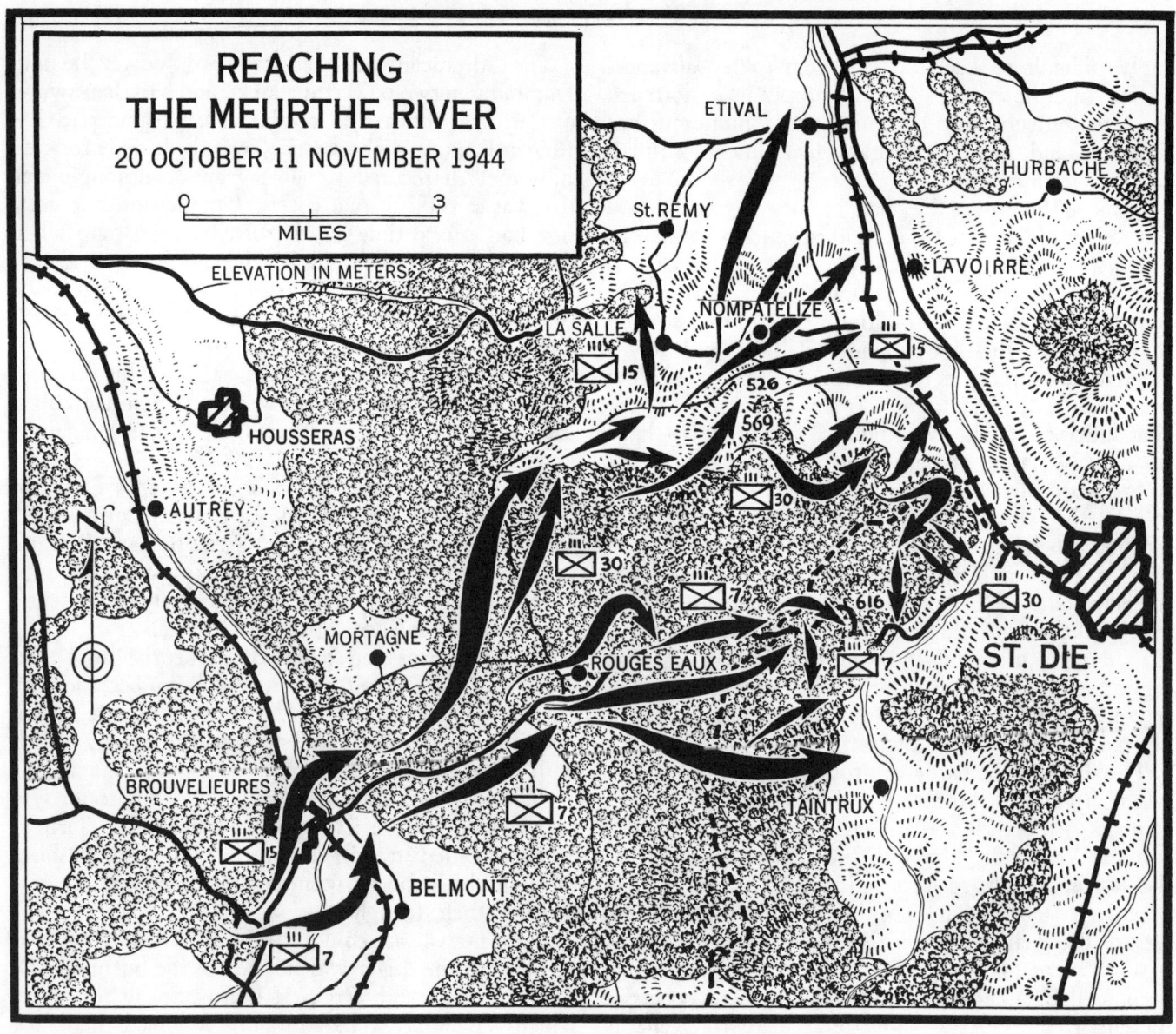

organized and the melee ended with thirty Germans killed, wounded or captured.

How Sergeant Choate "got his man" and stopped enemy armor without a tank destroyer is legend in the 601st TD Battalion.

For this action Sergeant Choate was awarded the Medal of Honor.

The determination displayed by Choate was characteristic of the Battalion's efforts ever since it was first attached to the 3d Infantry Division at Monte Corvino, Italy on September 20, 1943. Lt. Col Tardy was commanding throughout the period of the attachment, except for short periods.

The Commanding General at this time decided to commit the 30th Infantry, with the mission of attacking through the 7th Infantry and driving east. Col. Lionel C. McGarr, regimental commander, directed patrols be sent between the 7th on the south and 15th Infantry on the north, which got through the lines to a depth of 600 yards. Colonel McGarr then recommended that the regiment not batter against the strong resistance which was holding up the other two regiments, but drive through what apparently was a soft spot. The Commanding General approved the suggestion.

The 1st Battalion led off, followed by the 2d, which swung from a road "spiderweb" north to a mill near the south side of the Nompatelize Valley. It was there that armor attached to the 2d Battalion encountered enemy armor and shot it up.

Lt. Col. Eugene Salet's 2d Battalion of the 15th followed the 30th here, swung in behind and took a hill to the northeast of the crossroads at which the 15th Infantry had been held up for several days. This maneuver allowed the 15th to flank and clear a strongly-held road junction halfway between Les Rouges Eaux and La Bourgonce for which it had been battling

The Chief of Staff of the U. S. Army, General Marshall addresses the Division staff at Remiremont. Generals O'Daniel, Truscott and Devers are seen in the background.

A dead German is evacuated to the rear on top of the hood of a jeep.

fiercely. On the last day of this road-junction battle, Company I of the 15th, attacking from the east destroyed nine enemy machine guns in a few hours, and provided the flanking punch that drove the enemy clear out of the position.

Both the 1st and 2d Battalions of the 30th were committed along the ridge-top to support the 3d, the 1st taking over the left half of the zone in the area dominated by Les Jumeaux, or twin peaks, which jutted into the plain south of Nompatelize, and the 2d going into the right half of the zone, holding a long east-west line north of Le Haut Jacques.

The type of battle that was being waged during these days resulted in a situation of October 28 that brought the 3d Infantry Division another Congressional Medal of Honor.

The 30th Infantry was pressing through the Mortagne Forest toward the heights overlooking St. Dié when elements of the German 201st Mountain Infantry Battalion, which had been by-passed, succeeded in cutting the supply line of the 3d Battalion, disrupting the flow of ammunition and food to the unit.

Company I, commanded by 1st Lt. Maurice Rothseid, was in reserve position when it was called on to drive the enemy out. Going into the attack at 1400 that afternoon, the company was immediately subjected to intense fire from automatic weapons and small arms coming from an enemy that was well concealed in the dense undergrowth and woods.

At this point, S/Sgt. Lucian Adams, a squad leader of the 2d platoon, under 2d Lt. Frank H. Harrell, took charge of the situation and began a one-man assault that ended after he had killed nine Germans and captured two singlehanded. The number that he wounded as he dashed from tree to tree with his BAR was not determined.

He engaged an enemy machine gun at twenty yards and succeeded in killing the gunner.

Lieutenant Harrell described Adams' action, saying, "Sergeant Adams moved so fast and had such a head start on the rest of us that he killed a great number of them before we could maneuver to shoot at the enemy without endangering him by our fire."

Adams' charge disorganized the enemy in their strong defensive positions and was mainly responsible for the quick manner in which Company I cleared the supply line to the assault companies of the 3d Battalion.

For this action Sergeant Adams was awarded the Medal of Honor.

By this time the exploitation phase had ended, and during the closing days of October the Division fought a bitter, costly action against a constantly-reinforced, infiltrating foe. The 2d platoon of the 3d Reconnaissance Troop, commanded by 2d Lt. John Begovich, holding a hillside position just north of Le Haut Jacques, fought almost nightly actions against enemy who came up draws both from the east and west. All three battalions of the 30th had "hot corners" where two enemy seemed to spring up for every one shot down. This was almost literally true, as the enemy, sensing the threat posed by the 3d Division to St. Dié, robbed other sectors of the front to throw in the 291st and 292d Special Employment Battalions, the 737th Infantry Regiment, the 726th Infantry Regiment, and finally introduced another fresh mountain battalion, the 202d. By this time the German 16th Infantry Division, whose 221st, 223d and 225th Infantry Regiments had opposed our initial attack west of Brouvelieures, had virtually disappeared from the picture, although the division's General Haeckel still commanded the sector opposite the 3d.

The fighting in the western Vosges was weirder than any engaged in before or since by the Division. Crushing concentrations of 120mm mortar fire smashed into the wooded ridges without warning, sometimes wiping out half a company in a comparatively few minutes. Casualties mounted rapidly, largely because of these tree-bursts of artillery and mortars. The nights, chilly before, suddenly turned cold, and frost gave way to snow on the ridge-tops. The artillery airstrip had to be corduroyed because of the deep mud. Logging trails which ran the ridges had to be rebuilt by the engineers in order to support the supply traffic which ran nightly to the farthest units. There was only one area prac-

The chain of command at the 3d Division War Room somewhere in the Vosges: General Truscott, CG VI Corps. General Patch, CG 7th Army and General Devers, CG 6th Army Group.

ticable for gun positions—the plateau south of Mortagne—and nightly it was constantly lit up by flashes from scores of artillery pieces.

With a bit of improvisation, Maj. Norman C. Tanner, Division Artillery Air Officer, provided his spotter planes a landing field during the difficult weather which characterized the Vosges throughout the whole campaign there.

It took the form of a 250- by 15-yard wooden runway, and at the time it was built it was 6000 yards from the enemy front lines. To camouflage it, Major Tanner had it painted olive drab.

Capt. Alfred W. Schultz, Assistant Air Officer, commented after his first landing, "I checked my map twice to make sure that I had the correct coordinates, for that little strip looked like a ribbon up there," to which Pilot 1st Lt. Warren T. Ries rejoined, "Yes, a very tiny ribbon."

Meanwhile the Division faced the enemy on three sides—the north, east, and south. Enemy armor showed up in unexpected places—one Mark IV tank was destroyed by one of the enemy's own mines several hundred yards north of Le Haut Jacques, on the crest of a wooded ridge. Friendly supply parties were ambushed. Small groups of enemy, cut off by our rapid advance, showed up in our rear and fought with CP groups and wire crews. One whole company of the enemy, cut off by the 7th Infantry, surrendered after negotiations which covered an entire night.

October 25 saw the first issue of the Division weekly newspaper, the *Front Line*.

In an opening statement written for the paper, Commanding General O'Daniel declared: "It is fitting that this paper is being published today for the first time. It is the mouthpiece of a fighting Division, and as we are now in the midst of a great attack, we can say that the 3d Division *Front Line* was born in battle.

"We shall therefore be able to submit very soon additional reports on more deeds of valor as performed by our fighting men. This paper is one way we can let them know what we think of them. Therefore the names of all men who are cited in orders of this division will be published in this paper. We salute them all."

At first crude in form, the paper rapidly acquired polish, and by June 1945, was able to announce proudly that it had been adjudged by Camp Newspaper Service the second best overseas letter-press organizational paper.

November began with fights for Hill 256, near Les Jumeaux, and for the crossroads town of Le Haut Jacques.

Survivors of the battle for the crossroads at Le Haut Jacques were later to refer to it as "The Crossroads of Hell." Anzio veterans said that at times the fighting was worse than any they had seen all during the beachhead siege and the drive to Rome.

To advance a few hundred yards took the 7th Infantry five days. The enemy had—and used—every weapon in the book: 120mm mortars, Flakwagons, mines and booby-traps, machine guns, artillery, and small arms.

The hot spot was first encountered on October 31st. All three battalions were on line: 1st, under Capt. Kenneth W. Wallace, on the north (left) flank; 2d, commanded by Lt. Colonel Clayton C. Thobro, to right (slightly back); and Maj. Glenn E. Rathbun's 3d Battalion on the regimental right and echeloned somewhat to the rear.

On the 31st, 1st Battalion moved slowly along the St. Dié road. Company A moved north behind a mortar preparation, with the intention of flanking the town from that direction, Company B was in reserve, and Company C attacked due east. Companies E and G of the 2d Battalion took Hill 652, which they had fought for the entire previous twenty-four hours, and continued east slowly. The 3d Battalion, which was

Colonel Harrell, CO 7th Infantry Regiment (center) studies the Le Haut Jacques situation with Lieutenant Colonels Izenour, Exec., and Duncan, S-3 in the 7th Inf. War Room.

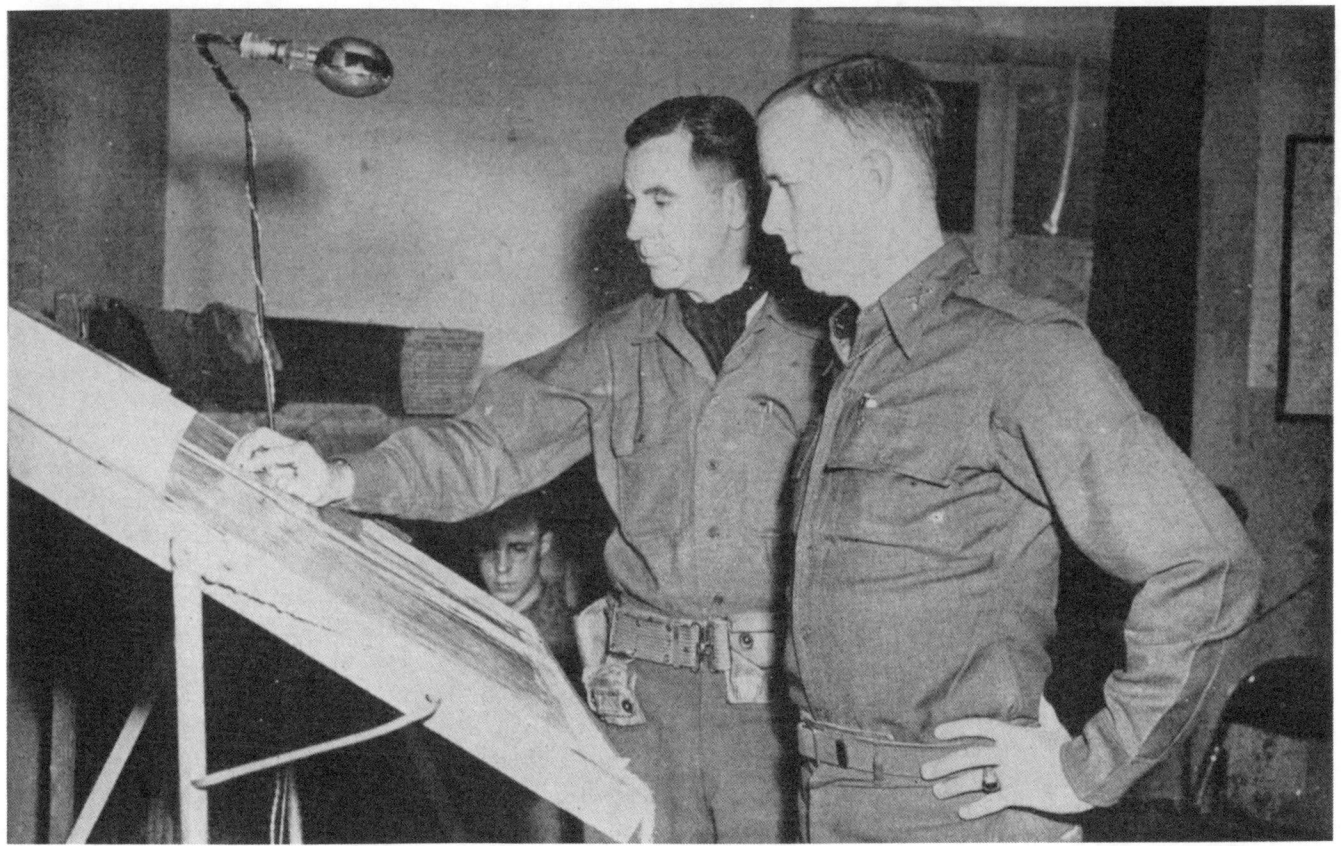

General Sexton, CG 3d Division Artillery discusses an artillery problem with his S-3, Lieutenant Colonel Kerwin, somewhere in the Vosges.

attacking southeast, had been stopped the day before by heavy fire in the vicinity of an enemy roadblock. The area, in addition, was found to be heavily mined. On the morning of the 31st the attack was resumed, but initially only Company K made any progress, due to slightly lighter resistance than that encountered by L Company. Hill 499 was taken by K—its second objective. In the afternoon, however, some slight progress was made as Company K engaged the enemy in a moving fire fight. Company L found itself, likewise, in a strong exchange of fire.

The 2d Battalion, under extremely heavy mortar and artillery on its company areas and OP, nevertheless shoved forward, but it was slow, painful going.

The following day, November 1, this same inching forward continued. Every bit of firepower available to the 7th was called down on Le Haut Jacques and the vital crossroads, but the enemy more than matched it with the combined fire of every emplaced weapon. That afternoon the enemy fired a heavy artillery concentration at the 2d Battalion at 1500, and followed up with a counterattack at Company G. which was repulsed. Company C was forced to beat off a counterattack at 1615. During this time mines were encountered throughout the zone of both 1st and 2d Battalions.

The 3d Battalion continued the attempt to push to the southwest. Company L destroyed an enemy machine-gun nest during the morning of November 2.

The 2d Battalion was counterattacked about noon of the same day and repulsed it. Company F was relieved by the 7th Infantry Battle Patrol at 1230 and in turn relieved Company C, which moved further north toward the remainder of 1st Battalion. Relief of the 3d Battalion was started during the afternoon by 2d Battalion, 141st Infantry.

Meanwhile, 1st and 2d Battalions had launched an all-out attack at 1415, but failed to make any appreciable gains. The enemy fire was of an intensity rarely encountered before in the entire war by the 7th Infantry. The 3d Battalion joined this attack on November 3, and worked further toward the achievement of getting to the east of the village for the final assault. The 2d Battalion would have to attack directly east as 1st Battalion pushed in from the north.

As the attack went into its fifth day, the bloody battle reached its climax. The entire regiment (less one company) moved out at 0615, determined to smash the enemy at Le Haut Jacques. The enemy, aggressive in the defense, almost immediately made a counterattack at Company A and 1st Battalion was held up. Company I encountered withering fire from four well-emplaced machine guns and also stopped, but K Com-

A wounded 3d Division comrade is evacuated on the hood of a jeep near Nompatelize in the Vosges.

pany continued moving on against strong resistance.

To Companies E and F—commanded by 1st Lt. James F. Powell and 2d Lt. Earl E. Swanson, respectively—and especially to E company, fell the task of moving in directly from the west. By 0940 Company F had control of one house in the village and E was taking prisoners.

By 1150, after weathering murderous mortar and artillery, 2d Battalion had cleared the village. Companies I and K still had a fight on their hands, but the back of the enemy resistance was broken. Over a hundred prisoners were taken. The regiment had suffered 125 casualties in the final push. Le Haut Jacques was a costly objective.

"It seemed to me that we were just a handful of men trying desperately to push the whole top away from that mountain," said Pvt. Alfonso Pesko of E Company, later. "It was worse than Anzio, because we were steadily going up hill and were in such a confined area."

Although the entire regiment had experienced grim fighting E Company had been especially outstanding and those members who survived were later awarded the Distinguished Unit Citation.

With the village occupied, the 7th moved east and north.

During the attack by the 7th Infantry on Le Haut Jacques, the 30th Infantry helped greatly by flanking the town from the north—with Task Force Kenyon and Task Force Greer, and without this help 7th Infantry might never have taken Le Haut Jacques.

On October 30, while the bulk of the 30th Infantry was passing through the Mortagne Forest, Company G, 30th Infantry, passed through Company F to press the battle on Hill 616, north of and part of the Le Haut Jacques position which the 7th Infantry had been attacking from the west. The attack of Company G was made through cross machine-gun fire against enemy established in deep dugouts and bunkers along the forward slope of the hill. The attack progressed to within two hundred yards of the company's objective where it was halted because of the frightful number of casualties exacted by the defending enemy. The company dug in under harassing enemy fire. Private Wilburn K. Ross had placed his light machine gun in a position ten yards in advance of the foremost supporting riflemen. Shortly thereafter the enemy counterattacked. Thirty-three men remained in the company, fifty-five having been lost in the attack. Private Ross, exposed to machine-gun and small-arms fire of the attacking force, fired with deadly effect upon the assaulting enemy troops and repelled the counterattack. Despite the hail of automatic-weapons fire and the explosions of rifle grenades within a stone's throw of his position, he continued to man his machine gun alone, repulsing six more German attacks. The citation of the award of the Medal of Honor to Private Ross is quoted here in part:

". . . When the eighth assault was launched, most of his supporting riflemen were out of ammunition. They took position in echelon behind Private Ross and crawled up during the attack, to extract a few rounds of ammunition from his machine-gun ammunition belt. Private Ross fought on virtually without assistance, and, despite the fact that enemy grenadiers crawled to within four yards of his position in an attempt to kill him with hand grenades, he again directed accurate and deadly fire on the hostile force. . . . After expending his last round, Private Ross was advised to withdraw to the company command post, together with the eight surviving riflemen, but as more ammunition was expected he declined to do so. . . . As his supporting riflemen fixed bayonets for a last-ditch stand, fresh ammunition arrived. . . . Having killed and wounded at least fifty-eight Germans in more than five hours of continuous combat and saved the remnant of his company from destruction, Private Ross remained at his post . . ."

Such was the fury of the battles fought at the hell-hole, Le Haut Jacques.

The 15th, which had a tough day in attacking Hill 526, occupied its objective the next morning with no resistance as the Germans had evacuated their positions during the night. Les Faignes and Nompatelize, villages in the path of the 15th's advance, were also yielded without a fight but definite resistance was met in the attack on La Salle.

General Truscott, VI Corps commander, beside General O'Daniel, 3d Division commander, says farewell to the Division staff in the Vosges, prior to his assuming command of the Fifth Army in Italy.

The 2d Battalion, commanded by Maj. Eugene A. Salet, hit La Salle from three directions. Company E, under 1st Lt. Charles E. Adams, closed in from the south, Company F, commanded by Capt. Hugh H. Bruner, advanced from the northwest and Company G, under Capt. Richard B. Dorrough, assaulted the village from the west.

All companies were halted at well dug-in positions which surrounded the village and after these were overrun, a house-to-house fight ensued as the Germans were occupying every building in the settlement. Heavy artillery and mortar fire was laid down on the attackers but Company G finally broke through and entered the town at noon on the second day of the battle. By 1200 hours, November 3, the town was cleared.

The 1st Battalion of the 30th Infantry, commanded by Maj. Mackenzie E. Porter, attacked the town of Sauceray. In a perfectly coordinated attack, employing machine guns, mortars, and artillery, the battalion closed in from south and west. There was a sharp 30-minute fight, but the prebattle conception had been excellent and the town fell. This attack was the first of a series of battalion attacks in which the regiment had to pull a battalion from a defensive position and extend it over the other two battalion fronts in order to close up a large gap and make an attack.

During the days of the 7th Infantry's fight for Le Haut Jacques the 30th Infantry's 2d Battalion, under Lt. Col. Frederick R. Armstrong, launched and completed a successful coordinated attack on Hill 616, a key terrain feature for the defense of St. Dié. The regiment had been battling for this hill even before the 7th Infantry encountered the defenses of Le Haut Jacques, but previous attacks met with furious fire and fanatical resistance. The final attack the enemy also resisted fiercely, and with reinforcements. Enemy artillery fire caused a number of casualties when the command post of Company C, commanded by 1st Lt. Rex Metcalfe, was struck on the third day of the attack. Much air activity, both friendly and enemy, was present during the days that the Division fought on the hills in front of the Meurthe River and our forces were strafed many times by enemy planes. Hill 616 was occupied by the 2d Battalion on November 5 when elements of the 7th Infantry entered the attack.

The day witnessed also the seizure of Biarville by the 15th Infantry. This attack was short lived but it demonstrated great determination.

Biarville was fairly covered by fire when it was attacked by a force comprising Company A of the 15th, one platoon of light tanks, a platoon of mediums, one platoon of tank destroyers and a platoon of engineers. The withering fire brought quick results and the town fell in a short time.

The Germans by now had started a real flight rearward and although the Division was still subjected to heavy artillery and mortar fire during its continued advance, the resistance became more scattered and

Howitzers of the 3d Division's 9th FA Battalion send death hurtling through the air at the enemy in France's Vosges Mountains near Les Rouges Eaux.

sporadic as the 3d Battalion neared the Meurthe River.

The towns of Brehimont and La Vacherie, overlooking St. Michel, were weakly defended and most of the defenders were taken prisoner when the 3d Division occupied them. The PW total mounted rapidly as scattered pockets of left-behinds were cleared.

One by one, the towns fronting on the hills along the Meurthe were occupied with the chief action in the Division zone being waged in the 15th and 30th Infantry sectors. Enemy troops in a draw and in the woods to the north opposed the 15th's advance toward Le Menil, while at the same time the 30th Infantry was clearing the St. Dié hill mass by battalion attacks around its entire perimeter which, in addition, helped the 15th Infantry by covering its right flank. The 2d Battalion, 30th Infantry, took Chalet on the morning of November 10, and the 3d Battalion took La Bolle after an afternoon and all-night fight on November 10-11, with Companies I and K in the assault. Fighting ended the morning of November 11 when the bridge across the Taintrux River was taken and the Chalet-Saucerey highway was completely cleared.

On the afternoon of November 8, Companies E and F of the 15th attacked Le Menil, supported by tanks of the 756th Tank Battalion, commanded by Lt. Col. Glenn F. Rogers. There were four light tanks from Company D under Capt. Robert F. Kremer, and two mediums from Company B, commanded by Capt. David D. Redle with the 2d Battalion, when it launched its drive. As at Biarville, the attack was well-planned and vicious and lasted but a short time since the Germans withdrew in the face of the onslaught.

While the 2d Battalion was entering Le Menil, the 3d attacked Deyfosse, a short distance to the south. A wooded area outside Deyfosse gave the enemy convenient emplacement positions but Company K, commanded by 1st Lt. John J. Tominac, wore down the resistance after Companies I and L had made a house-to-house clearance of the south part of the village. Company K completed clearing the village late that night.

The 15th continued the Division advance while elements of the 7th were being relieved by the 103d Infantry Division. Etival, a small village located on the edge of the Meurthe, was taken by the 15th with little resistance.

At a conference conducted at VI Corps headquarters at Grandvillers on the afternoon of November 10, Corps Commander General Brooks outlined to his division commanders the operations incident to the Corps mission of proceeding east through the Vosges from the

Battle-tired soldiers of the 3d Infantry Division eagerly swallow a hot meal near Bult after having been relieved after seemingly endless days of combat in the Vosges.

St. Dié area, capturing Strasbourg, and destroying the enemy west of the Rhine River in its zone. He presented three plans, all of which involved crossings of the Meurthe River by the 3d Infantry Division.

Plans "A" and "B" called for the 3d to cross the Meurthe in the vicinity of St. Michel, and to establish an initial bridgehead on the east bank. In plan "A" the 3d proceeded due east on the axis Saales-Schirmeck-Strasbourg, with the 100th Infantry Division operating on its left, and the 103d Infantry Division on its right, following an administrative crossing behind the 3d and subsequent passage through its right to the south and southeast. In plan "B" the missions of the 3d and 103d Divisions were interchanged after the establishment of the initial bridgehead by the 3d. Plan "C" called for the 3d Infantry Division and the 103d Infantry Division to cross the Meurthe River abreast, with the 3d on the left. The action of each division following establishment of the initial bridgehead conformed to the maneuver outlined for plan "A," which was favored.

General Brooks indicated that the probable date for the 3d Division crossing would be November 20. This date was contingent upon the progress of the 100th Infantry Division in its action southeast from Baccarat, and of the progress of the 103d on the right of the 3d in seizing the high ground southwest of St. Dié. Successsful consummation of these operations would serve to draw enemy reserves from the front of the 3d, thereby weakening the enemy in the zone of crossing.

At the time of the issuance of the Corps Commander's plans, the 3d was in the process of undergoing relief by the 103d Division of its center and right regiments (30th and 7th Infantry Regiments). At the same time 15th Infantry was carrying out an operation to the northeast to clear the enemy from the west bank of the Meurthe as far north as Clairfontaine. Necessarily, then, the 7th and 30th were earmarked for the assault, whereas 15th Infantry was to hold the west bank of the Meurthe in the Division zone and to cover all preparations incident to the river crossing, then assemble in Division reserve following the crossing.

Men of the Division heard many explosions during the next few days as the Germans methodically began destroying St. Dié. This town, seat of the Congress which named America in honor of the Italian, Amerigo Vespucci, had been shelled to some extent but was not nearly as thoroughly battered as Bruyéres, for example. But now reports were received at the Division headquarters from front-line infantrymen and artillery forward observers that "St. Dié is in flames."

It was revealed later that the enemy, without reasons justifiable even on the grounds of military necessity, had ordered St. Dié destroyed. Giving scant notice to the occupants of the town's houses and business structures, the Germans reduced the greater part of the town to ashes; the wall skeletons which were left standing intact testified that high explosive played little part in the needless destruction of St. Dié, but rather that it was gutted by German-started fires. General Haeckel, German 16th Infantry Division CG, was responsible for the destruction of St. Dié and surrounding villages.

"Powerhouse I" was the name given the Meurthe crossing operation. On the face of it, this was an extremely difficult job.

Division engineers had made careful map, photo and ground reconnaissance, but had failed to locate good bridge sites except where hard-surfaced approaches reached the river at points where bridges had been demolished. The Meurthe twisted northwest across a flat bottomland several hundred yards wide which was flooded north of Etival, and boggy everywhere else.

The city of St. Dié on the Meurthe River in the Vosges was burned and gutted by the Germans.

3d Division infantrymen train in river-crossing operations in the Vosges in preparation for the crossing of the Meurthe River.

The river itself, swollen by fall rains, was everywhere too deep and swift to be forded by foot troops.

Worst of all, the "winter line," a solid chain of prepared enemy defenses, ran all the way from Fraize to Raon L'Etape, especially strong in the sector opposite the 3d. These defenses consisted of trenches, barbed wire, weapons pits, AT gun positions, AT ditches, and mines, and had been under construction since early fall. Our machine gunners on the west bank could see many of these defenses clearly.

Rather than make a frontal assault against these defenses behind an artillery heavy barrage, General O'Daniel decided to try to gain surprise by infiltration in force under cover of darkness. Plans were made therefore to throw footbridges across the river at last light, move the foot elements of the 7th and 30th regiments across during the night, and attack from the *east bank* at daylight with strong preparatory fires. Caliber .50 machine guns, Flakwagons, tanks, TD's and all available weapons were to provide fire support from the west bank.

The 15th Infantry held the line of departure (the west bank of the river) for several days prior to the attack, and patrolled vigorously to determine the conditions of the river and the nature of enemy opposition on the far bank. The patrols confirmed the fact that fording for any large body of troops was out of the question, and that employment of boats and rafts would be difficult because of the current. It was then that the use of prefabricated footbridges was decided upon.

Enemy reaction to the patrolling, however, was surprisingly weak, and although no prisoners were taken it was fairly clear that (1) the enemy held the east bank very thinly, and (2) enemy troops who were present were neither aggressive nor alert. The enemy was compelled to keep his line thin by continuing attacks on the part of the 103d Infantry Division in the Taintrux area, on the 3d's right, and the 100th Infantry Division's attack southeast through Raon L'Etape, on the 3d's left.

Then, for two or three days prior to the attack, friendly planes strafed and dropped fire bombs all along the enemy's line of prepared positions, to further lower the already low morale of the German soldiers holding those positions.

While plans went forward for the crossing, 7th and 30th Infantry regiments were engaged in training with their respective combat-team engineer companies. Since the crossing plan had been communicated to the appropriate commanders at the outset of the five-day period, it was possible to make all training objective in nature. To this end full emphasis was placed on engineer training in assault-boat operation and in construction of footbridges of the prefabricated type. Infantry received training in assault boats and in crossing over

General Brooks, CG VI Corps stops on an inspection of the front to question a 3d Division soldier.

footbridges. This training was conducted on a battalion basis. Half of the training was conducted at night with a view to developing speed, coordination, and control. Directional aids such as luminous markers, telephone wire, engineer tape, ropes, and markings on the rear of helmets were stressed. Finally, special exercises were conducted for the assault platoons earmarked for covering footbridge construction.

In order to deceive the enemy as to the date and time of our crossing, the Commanding General directed the artillery commander, Brig. Gen. William T. Sexton, to increase harassing fires on the Division front during the three days prior to the crossing. In addition, he prescribed for these three days a 15-minute pre-daylight shoot plus a 15-minute after-darkness shoot. It developed later from prisoner accounts that this program served as an effective cover plan for the main preparation which was fired from H-minus-30 to H-hour, since the enemy had become accustomed to heavy firing at this time.

On November 18 notification was received from Corps to the effect that the splendid progress of the 100th Infantry Division southeast of Baccarat warranted cancellation of crossing plans for the 3d Infantry Division in the interest of passing the 3d through the 100th to exploit its progress. Immediately upon receipt of these instructions, the concentration plan for the crossing which had been underway for two days was cancelled, and the assault regiments were directed to reconnoiter forward assembly areas in the zone of the 100th Division in the vicinity of Raon L'Etape. A movement order was issued covering concentration in forward assembly areas preliminary to passage through the 100th Infantry Division. Movement was to be initiated on Corps order during the night of November 19-20.

At a meeting on the 18th, originally intended to be a final review of crossing plans, General O'Daniel made the announcement of the new plan and initiated discussion on it.

The original plan was destined to carry through, however. For, on the morning of November 19, word was received from General Brooks that the progress of the 100th Division for the preceding twenty-four hours had been considerably retarded, and that instead of passing the 3d through the 100th in the face of increasing resistance, the 3d would effect its crossing of the Meurthe as originally planned.

Fortunately, the thorough preparation pertaining to both the concentration and crossing plans enabled the Division to resume its concentration and complete all preparations without incident. It was impossible, however, due to the loss in time, to emplace all tanks, TD's and smoke generators originally scheduled to move into position during the three nights prior to D-Day. The tanks and TDs were instead tied in with artillery fire-direction centers and used in an indirect fire role to support the crossing.

The Division drew a damp, moonless night for the crossing—the night of November 19-20. A platoon of Company I, 15th Infantry, had crossed two nights before by boat in the 7th Infantry's zone and occupied a house immediately in front of the enemy's main position without being detected. This platoon had radioed back several reports on the 19th, all of which indicated that

The bodies of the dead near the mine sign at St. Die attest to the truth of the sign.

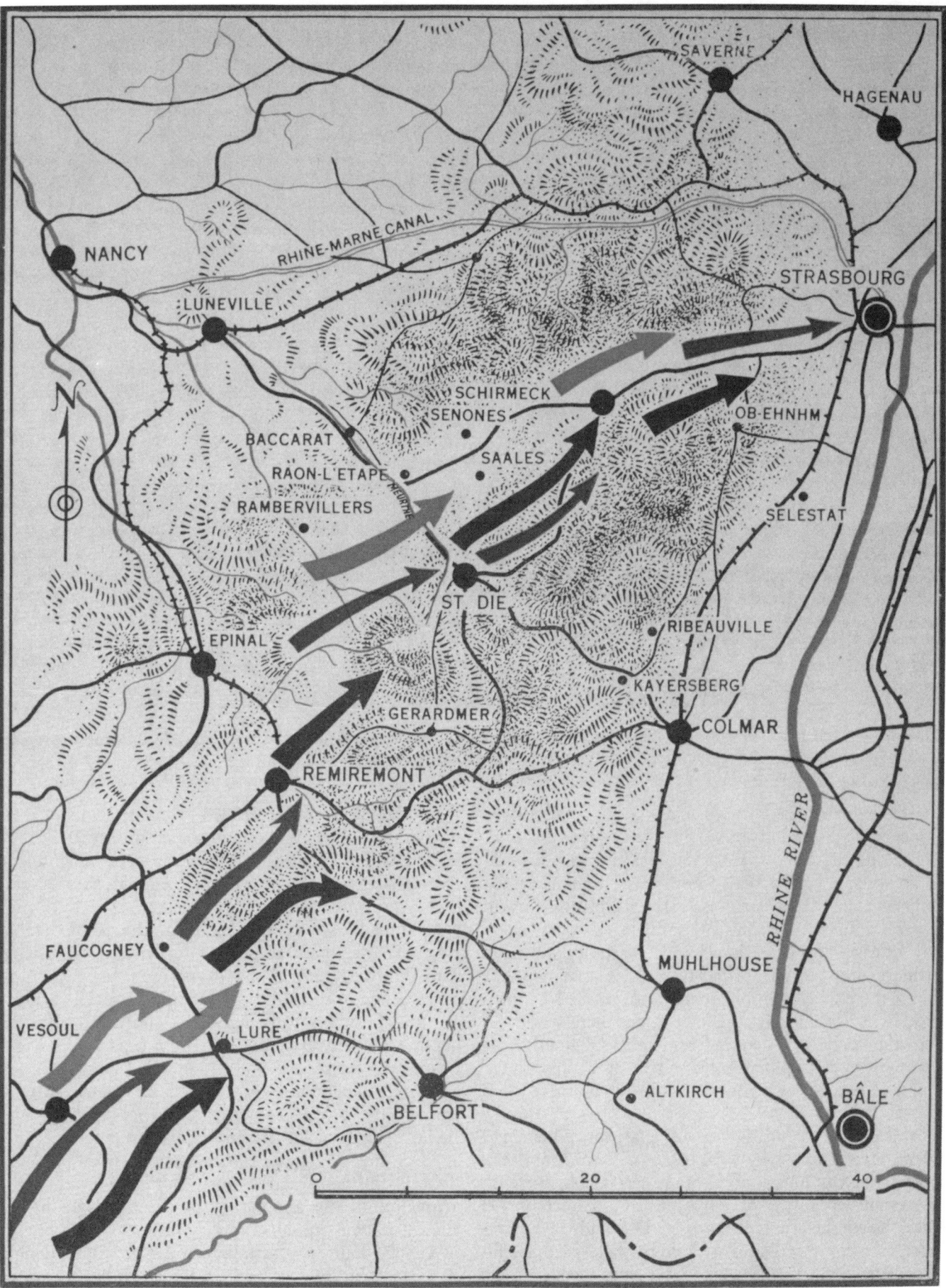

This piece of 3d Division's 9th FA Battalion is well camouflaged in its position in the coniferous forest near Bourgonne in the Vosges Mountains.

the enemy was holding his main position with light forces, who appeared entirely to be occupying buildings along the Raon L'Etape–St. Dié highway.

To observers not actually on the river line, it seemed unbelievable that a large-scale river crossing was in progress. There was hardly as much shooting as on any quiet night of ordinary patrol activity. Division artillery dropped its normal quota of harassing shells along the enemy's supply routes with studied haphazardness; rifles cracked occasionally, but there was nothing approaching a genuine fire fight. Obviously, the enemy was totally unaware that two of United States' finest regiments were moving onto his doorstep on a narrow front.

By 2400 the footbridge assault platoons, which had been ferried across by Company A, 10th Engineers, under the command of Capt. Albert Cook, were in possession of a line of departure approximately 300 yards from the Raon L'Etape–St. Dié highway. Footbridges were installed with exceptional speed, being completed by approximately 2359. Foot troops of the main assault forces proceeded from detrucking areas to the footbridges without incident. Immediately they started over—riflemen, BAR men, machine gunners, mortar squads, communication men, aid men—everybody who walks in the infantry team.

Meanwhile the bridge trains of the 36th Combat Engineer Regiment were moving toward St. Michel and Clairefontaine, to be in position for beginning construction of the Bailey and treadway vehicle bridges as soon as the far bank had been cleared to sufficient depth. Company B of the 10th Engineers, under Capt. Daniel A. Raymond, and Company C, under Capt. Homer M. Lefler, also ferried advance troops and took part in the bridge construction. The treadway and Bailey bridges at St. Michel drew intermittent enemy artillery fire all during the first day, but this did not prevent the construction and continuous use of the bridges until the approaches of the treadway bridge finally became unusable.

At 0600 hours, five battalions of United States doughboys stood on the east bank of the river, having won a

struction of a wide-track armored force treadway bridge in the vicinity of St. Michel. After initial progress the work was suspended for several hours due to accurate enemy mortar and self-propelled fire on the bridge site. Although efforts were made to smoke the sites by means of generators, smoke pots, and chemical mortars, shifting winds and the fact that the enemy had registered on the bridge sites minimized the effect of the smoke.

At approximately noon orders were received from Corps that two regimental combat teams of the 103d Infantry Division were to be crossed over 3d Division footbridges at the earliest possible moment and, following assembly on the far bank, were to pass through the right of the 3d and continue the attack to the southeast. Immediate contact was made with the 103d, and it was ascertained that the two regimental combat teams (409 and 410) were in assembly areas on our right rear in the vicinity of the town of La Bourgonce. The 103d was requested to send its reconnaissance forward to the footbridges and to the CPs of the assault regiments of the 3d. Brig. Gen. Robert N. Young, As-

Brigadier General Robert N. Young, Assistant Division Commander, 3d Infantry Division.

solid victory by their quiet crossing before even beginning the attack.

It was now time for Division artillery, with Corps artillery and several other battalions in support, to raise the mask of secrecy and fire an all-out preparation. Tanks, TDs and Flakwagons stationed on the west bank of the river opened direct fire on houses and strongpoints known to be in the enemy main line of resistance. Under cover of this fire, infantrymen of the Division struck, and in less than an hour the 7th had seized Le Voivre while the 30th had captured La Hollande and Himbaumont, preparatory to springing a trap on Clairefontaine.

It was one of the smoothest operations ever conducted by the 3d Division. It was easily the quickest and most successful large-scale river crossing we had ever made.

The Winter War of Movement was under way.

The 36th Engineer Combat Regiment, together with certain personnel of the 10th Engineer Combat Battalion, initiated reconnaissance of the four heavy bridge sites at daylight of November 20. Reconnaissance of the two Clairefontaine sites was rendered impossible by small-arms, mortar and self-propelled fire from the town. At the two St. Michel sites, however, reconnaissance proceeded satisfactorily and by midmorning engineer material had been moved to the vicinity of the bridge sites. Work was initially concentrated on con-

Lieutenant Colonel Petherick, CO 10th Engineer Bn.

sistant Division Commander, was designated as coordinator of crossing and was stationed at the footbridge sites.

Quickly exploiting the crossing, 7th and 30th Infantry Regiments moved to the east. The 1st Battalion, 7th Infantry, shoved on toward Hurbache. Second Battalion, 30th Infantry, entered the town at 1635 in conjunction with Company C, 7th Infantry, and the village was shortly cleared. The 2d Battalion 7th, leaving Company G to block on the right flank, continued to advance without opposition. The 1st Battalion, 30th Infantry, cleared Clairefontaine on the afternoon of the 20th.

The 15th Infantry moved from its defensive positions on the west bank of the Meurthe River to the vicinity of La Hollande commencing with the 3d Battalion at 1530 and followed by 1st Battalion at 1600. Both battalions crossed on the northern footbridges in 30th Infantry sector.

The 3d Battalion, 7th Infantry, had seized Denipaire by 2100.

Meanwhile on the "engineer front" the progress of front-line troops was such that by late afternoon the enemy was unable to bring fire to bear upon the bridge sites. At darkness, therefore, work progressed in earnest and continued steadily through the night. The light assault bridge at the footbridge crossing area, which had been completed prior to daylight of the 20th, had passed approximately seventy-five ¼-ton loads

Sgt. Joseph Powell, 41st FA Battalion relaxes on a real bed at Bourbonne-les-Bains rest center in France.

prior to 2300, at which time the approaches to the bridge were rendered impassable by rising water and mud. Had it not been for this bridge, the Division resupply and emergency evacuation at the most critical time would have been imperiled.

With daylight on November 21 work on all four heavy bridge sites was intensified. By 0645 the wide-track armored force treadway bridge at the St. Michel site was completed and promptly passed seventeen armored vehicles and about twenty other tactical vehicles. At this time a tank bogged down at the exit of the bridge because of flooding of the approach by rising water, and the bridge was inoperative from this time on.

During the night the two combat teams of the 103d Infantry Division had crossed the Meurthe over 3d Division footbridges, and during the morning of the 21st passed through Company G, 7th Infantry, to the south.

On the morning of the 21st Denipaire became the assembly area for the 1st Battalion, 7th Infantry, and 2d Battalion, 30th Infantry. The 3d Battalion, 30th Infantry, which had been pushing steadily, despite Company I's meeting small-arms fire a good part of the way, was still moving. Company I cleared La Paire. Companies I and K followed Company L toward La Chapelle. The 3d Battalion, 7th Infantry, which had captured Denipaire the night before, shoved on toward St. Jean d'Ormont.

The 2d Battalion, 15th Infantry, was the last of that regiment to cross the Meurthe, which it did at Etival at 0715, after which it closed in its assembly area at La Hollande before noon.

The 3d Battalion, 7th Infantry, seized St. Jean d'Ormont on the afternoon of the 21st.

Task force Whirlwind was activated on that same

Lieutenant Colonel Walter E. Tardy, CO 601st Tank Destroyer Battalion.

afternoon. This consisted of the 1st Battalion, 15th Infantry; Company C (minus one platoon) of the 756th Tank Battalion; a platoon of Company C, 601st TD Battalion; 3d Recon Troop minus one platoon; B Battery of the 93d Armored FA Battalion; a platoon of Company B, 10th Engineers, with an armored bulldozer; and the 2d platoon of Company D, 756th Tank Battalion. Division provided twenty-five 2½-ton trucks to motorize the battalion of infantry.

The 1st Battalion, 7th Infantry, scarcely paused in its rapid move as it seized La Fontanelle, Launois, and Maire. Its fight carried over to November 22, when it encountered strong resistance at Nayemont.

The 3d Battalion, 30th Infantry, pushing east, sent its Company I into La Chapelle without opposition, at 1230, November 21. At 1300 Companies K and L moved from La Chapelle and headed for Menil which they entered at 1500, meeting no opposition. The 1st Battalion moved by marching from Clairefontaine to La Paire, with Company C moving on to La Chapelle. The remainder of the battalion closed into La Chapelle during the afternoon, reverting to regimental reserve. The 2d Battalion continued its attack, attaining successive objectives before Laitre, which fell at 1700.

By late afternoon of November 21, the attack of the 103d Division on our right (south) flank, which had commenced at 0900 that morning and moved out to the southeast through elements of 2d Battalion, 7th Infantry, had progressed from two to four kilometers on its entire front. At 1430 the 103d was given traffic priority over the St. Michel bridge. Upon completion of the crossing of the 103d Infantry Division tactical transportation, the 103d's passage phase as applied to the 3d Division was complete.

During the night of November 21-22 3d Battalion, 7th Infantry, occupied Baltant de Bourras.

Task Force Whirlwind moved out of its assembly area at 0730 November 22 and passed through 7th In-

Soldiers of the 3d Infantry Division make merry while they may with French companions at the Division rest center at Bourbonne-les-Bains.

Concrete mixers and steel carts used to build the "Winter Line" at Saales.

fantry along the route La Hollande-Hurbache-Denipaire, north to a road junction, and then southeast toward Launois. The 3d Battalion of the 15th moved from the vicinity of La Hollande at 0800 and followed the Task Force by shuttling. Task Force Whirlwind had reached Launois (which had fallen to 1st Battalion, 7th) by noon and was prepared to continue the advance.

The 3d Battalion, 7th Infantry, during the morning seized Hill 619 and drew enemy fire from a nearby crossroad.

The 1st Battalion, 7th Infantry, had run into a definitely tough battle at Nayemont. Here the enemy "Winter Line" positions were first encountered by 7th Infantry elements. These consisted of elaborately-constructed zigzag fire trenches, machine-gun emplacements, and partially-finished concrete bunkers. These positions had been under construction for several months preceding, and it was here that the enemy had planned on spending the rest of the winter. The VI Corps attack, spearheaded by 3d Infantry Division in its surprise crossing of the Meurthe and rapid advance eastward, gave the Germans no opportunity to utilize fully the well-built positions. The 103d and 100th Divisions (the latter attacking on our left) had helped draw enemy strength from our zone and stretch his reserves to the breaking point.

The positions were so formidable, however, that 1st Battalion was engaged in a harrowing fight that lasted several hours before the line was cracked and the German remnants forced to withdraw. Nayemont was occupied at 1650.

The 2d Battalion, 30th Infantry, took Le Roaux in its stride, reaching the town by 0820 November 22 and continuing to Chatas, which was cleared at 0945. By 1010 the battalion had reached a further phase line and was still pushing.

The 3d Battalion's Company I reached Grandrupt and was still clearing the town at noon.

The 2d Battalion, 7th Infantry, engaged an enemy roadblock force in the village of Le Fraiteux during the afternoon and, after reducing it, continued east on the Saales road, but was passed through by the 3d Battalion at 1600. The 7th Infantry Battle Patrol advanced east on the Saales road after Nayemont was taken and encountered a mined enemy roadblock.

Task Force Whirlwind had shoved off from Launois at 1200, and made good progress until it encountered enemy resistance in the early morning hours of November 23, when it halted for the night.

The 2d Battalion, 15th, assembled in La Fontanelle and moved to Grandrupt at 1625, establishing roadblocks on main roads leading into town upon arrival.

At 1645 2d Battalion, 30th Infantry, continued its advance and seized the high ground overlooking Saales.

The Division advance scarcely paused during the night of November 22-23. The 3d Battalion, 7th Infantry, by-passed the roadblock on the Saales road which the regiment's Battle Patrol had encountered during the afternoon of the 22nd and at 0100 Company I seized the town of La Grande Fosse. While 2d Battalion, 30th Infantry, sent patrols into Saales which destroyed an 88mm gun and actually cleared the northwest corner of town, Company K, 7th Infantry, spearheaded its battalion's attack on the town, entering at dawn and promptly becoming engaged in a fire fight. The 3d Battalion was engaged in this mission all the morning of November 23 and into the afternoon. Capture of the town symbolized entrance of the Division into Alsatian territory, but still more important was the fact that one of the two principal hinges of the Winter Line, (the other being Saulxures) had been taken and that now the enemy could not hope to stop us short of the Rhine River.

The 2d Battalion, 7th, eliminated the roadblock in the wake of 3d Battalion. The 1st Battalion en-

This deep pit near Saales was probably intended as the base of a large concrete pillbox.

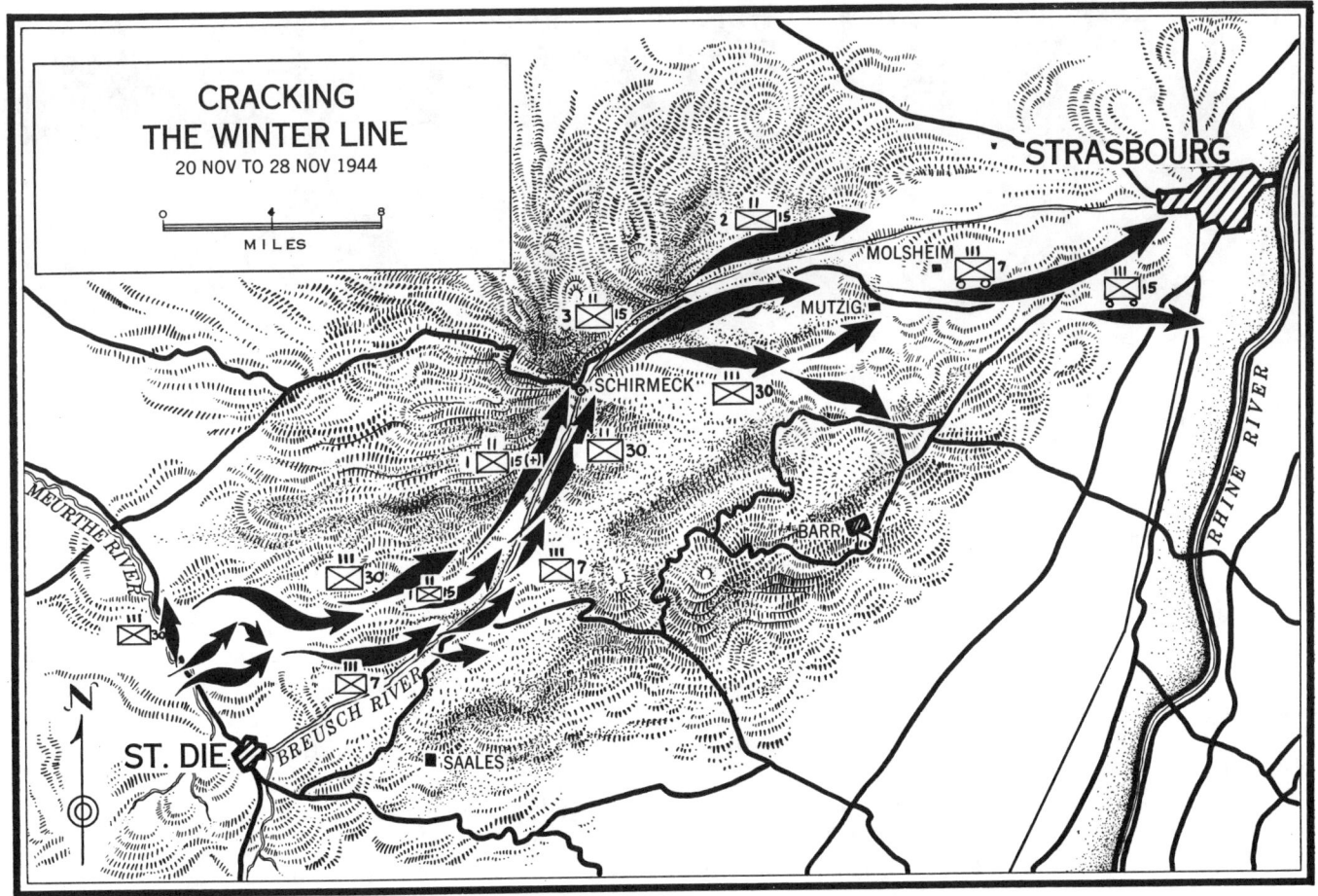

trucked at Nayemont and moved to a point near St. Barbe, north of Saales, where the men detrucked and marched to the heights of St. Barbe, from which point the battalion moved south to assist 3d Battalion in clearing Saales. Upon entry into the town the afternoon of November 23, 1st Battalion found that Saales had been cleared by 3d Battalion at 1535. The 1st Battalion thereupon headed east again, toward Bourg-Bruche.

Task Force Whirlwind had been held up by an enemy roadblock and small-arms fire from the vicinity of Saulxures. At 1400, in conjunction with 3d Battalion, 30th Infantry, it attacked Saulxures. Companies I and L, 30th Infantry, attacked the town while Company K went over the high ground east of town and there seized Hill 512. Companies I and L entered town, along with elements of Whirlwind, at 1400, and had cleared the town at approximately 1630 against stubborn enemy resistance. The Winter Line was now completely broken. The condition of prisoners captured both in Saales and Saulxures indicated that they had been expecting a protracted stay behind what their superiors fondly imagined to be a secure line. Many of the rear-echelon personnel had acquired such appurtenances as skis and snowshoes, in anticipation of moments of relaxation. The skis found new owners and the dispossessed would-be skiers found exercise in marching back to the PW cages, hands clasped firmly and resting lightly on top of the head.

Only disconnected battles along the route to Strasbourg now remained. One of the toughest of these was encountered by 1st Battalion, 7th Infantry, at Bourg-Bruche. It was here that the Germans had marshalled a striking force and were on the verge of counterattacking the 3d Battalion in an attempt to recapture Saales. At 1730, November 23, 1st Battalion moved out to attack Bourg-Bruche.

Approximately 150 yards beyond Saales elements of Company B encountered heavy machine-gun and rifle fire from both sides of the road. S/Sgt. James P. Wils, a squad leader, immediately rushed an S-shaped communications trench from which a storm of enemy fire was issuing, jumped inside it and fired eight clips of M-1 ammunition, coming out with twenty prisoners. The company's 3d platoon on the other side of the road wounded and killed another sizable number of enemy, putting the rest to flight.

At 1930 the battalion resumed its advance along the highway. A mile along machine-gun and rifle-grenade fire flayed the assault company. Reconnaissance disclosed that a strong German force was defending a railroad overpass which had been partially demolished by explosives.

Lieutenant Colonel Donald E. Long, a 3d Division soldier in World Wars I and II, receives, as Division Civil Affairs Officer, thanks from the Mayor of Saales for liberation of the town.

Riflemen of Company B worked their way forward, firing at enemy muzzle blasts in the gloom. Soldiers of an enemy platoon attempting to strike at the company's left flank silhouetted themselves on the embankment and were decimated by a prompt fusillade of M-1 fire.

After tough fighting the enemy was gradually driven from the embankment. At 2300 the 1st Battalion resumed the advance toward Bourg-Bruche. Spearhead elements of Company B worked their way from building to building upon reaching the town, toward a crossroads in the center of town. A pair of building strongpoints held up the advance. Flakwagon and 88mm gun fire deluged the intersection.

A tank was brought forward by 1st Lt. Wendell D. Leavitt, who rode it up to direct cannon fire on the enemy 88mm guns and Flakwagons. The assault platoons then charged forward into the building strongpoints to

At Natzwiller Concentration Camp SS guards and trained dogs patrolled between the fences.

A German AT gun destroyed this 3d Recon Troop scout car near Mutzig.

destroy or put to flight the German occupants.

Company C drove up the right side of the highway and penetrated into the eastern section of Bourg-Bruche. The 3d platoon, with a strength of nine men, held its gains against strong enemy pressure for five hours. A squad of Germans assaulted the house in which the platoon had taken cover and demanded that the platoon surrender, only to be greeted and repulsed by fragmentation hand grenades.

Another group similarly held out in a nearby house throughout the night.

In the morning Company C's 1st and 3d platoons joined forces and proceeded to clean out the houses on the right side of the east-west road through Bourg-Bruche, leaving the 2d platoon in support. This attack took place under strong enemy artillery, emplaced on a ridge running north-south and masking the eastern portion of the town. The ridge contained a long communications trench and heavily fortified emplacements.

The two platoons pressed their attack and reached a tavern near the railroad overpass, where they remained under concentrated fire and from which they directed artillery on the German gun emplacements, destroying an 88mm gun, blowing up an ammunition dump, and destroying a dug-in 20mm Flak gun.

During this time the Battalion CO, Lt. Col. Kenneth W. Wallace, committed Company A in an attack on the eastern section of town. As the company advanced it came under fire from two machine guns and a 20mm gun emplaced on a ridge, but these weapons were silenced by tanks and a tank destroyer after a duel which lasted several minutes.

Rounding a curve in the road, the company resumed the advance. The men drew furious blasts of Flak and machine-gun fire from the right. The enemy opened fire with an intensive mortar concentration. The company halted, having had five casualties. An unsuccessful assault on the enemy positions in which a platoon leader was killed and two men wounded followed; then a bazooka team crept forward and placed three rockets on the position, killing two Germans and crippling the position. The 3d platoon assaulted and destroyed it.

Companies B and C occupied positions in a cluster of buildings and rained fire on the Germans emplaced on the ridge. By midafternoon of the 24th they had killed between forty and fifty of the enemy and silenced two machine guns.

At about 1500 the third platoon of Company C assaulted the communications trench which was dug into the ridge. As the platoon surged up the hill slope the effect of the M-1, machine-gun, and intense artillery fire, added to the assault, convinced the Germans of the uselessness of the struggle. Approximately eighty-five prisoners were taken. Remnants of the battered German garrison fled from Bourg-Bruche only to be captured in large numbers by the 3d Battalion, which had maneuvered into position beyond the town. By 1630 Bourg-Bruche was firmly in our hands, lacking only the clearance of isolated snipers. Approximately 200 prisoners had been taken and seventy-five of the enemy killed.

3d Division infantrymen moving up near Schirmeck pass a dead enemy.

The 3d Division's 756th Tank Battalion cautiously enters the environs of Strasbourg.

The 2d Battalion, 15th Infantry, had moved from St. Stail to Chateau St. Louis. Company G remained in St. Stail and sent patrols north to Le Vermont, contacting the 398th Infantry of the 100th Division. The 3d Battalion, 15th Infantry, remained in assembly in the vicinity of La Fontelle, alerted to move.

The 1st Battalion, 30th Infantry, was in flank-blocking positions along the regiment's route of advance over the 24-hour period from noon to noon of November 23-24. The 2d Battalion's Company E reported Sanatorium clear at 1540 November 23, after a brief fire fight, while Companies G, F, and H were assembled and moved toward the town. At 0700 of the 24th the battalion moved out toward St. Blaise, sweeping the edge of the woods en route.

The 3d Battalion, 7th, passed through 1st Battalion in Bourg-Bruche and encountered enemy north of the town on the afternoon of the 24th. This resistance was taken care of and the battalion had pushed on to an assigned phase line by 1840. The 2d Battalion moved north from Lehan and cut the Bourg-Bruche–La Saales Road, leaving Company F there to block. Remainder of the battalion pushed north and assembled.

Task Force Whirlwind continued to push east until 0550 the next morning when it made contact with an isolated group of enemy. By 0830 this group had been cleared up and the Task Force, its mission accomplished, was dissolved and its elements returned to control of parent units.

The last phase in the Meurthe-Rhine River push was a sweep out onto the Alsatian plain, clearing scores of towns en route. There were only brief fire fights with bewildered, isolated enemy groups. At the town of Mollkirch there were nearly a hundred Germans who wanted neither to fight nor surrender. They finally decided to fight a little, then surrendered almost wholly. Taken prisoner, most of them stated that their only hope had been to make their way back across the Rhine.

The 30th Infantry took Grendelbruch. The 2d Battalion, commanded by Lt. Col. Frederick R. Armstrong, had an all-night house-to-house fight at Grendelbruch. Shortly before midnight Company E, under Capt. Ralph R. Carpenter, moved around to the right of the town, sweeping out the woods as it went. The company then attacked from the east as Company F, commanded by Capt. Marshall T. Hunt, struck simultaneously from the west. By 1000 November 26 the battalion headquarters was doing business at a CP situated in the center of the town.

The 3d Battalion, 15th Infantry, had advanced from La Broque to Schirmeck, Wisches, Schwartzbach, Urmatt, and Dinsheim, to west of Mutzig, along the main road to Strasbourg by noon of the 26th. On the afternoon of November 26, 3d Battalion cleared Mutzig.

Combat Command A, 14th Armored Division, passed through the 3d Infantry Division, moving from Schirmeck at 0700, following two routes. One column followed the route Schirmeck-Mutzig-south to Obernai east in the direction of Erstein. The second column followed the route Schirmeck-east to Russ-Grendelbruch-Obernai south to Coxwiller.

On the night of November 26-27, 1st and 2d Battalion, 7th Infantry, assembled and moved by truck to an assembly area in the vicinity of Strasbourg, to which patrols had gone and met elements of the French 2d Armored Division which reached the town ahead of the 3d Division, having come in from the northwest. The 1st Battalion, 15th Infantry, also moved by motor to take up defensive positions along the Rhine River south of Strasbourg that same night, and 2d Battalion prepared to join it.

The 1st Battalion, 30th Infantry cleared Rosheim, and moved on to establish defensive positions in the vicinity of Dorlisheim by 0330 of November 27. The 2d Battalion established roadblocks during the same period to protect 1st Battalion's flank. Company G patrols cleared Laubenheim and Mollkirch.

The 3d Battalion, 30th Infantry, captured Boersch, Klingenthal, and Obernai. Roadblocks were established on all roads leading out of Obernai.

On our north flank the 117th Cavalry Reconnaissance Squadron, attached, screened the last move into Strasbourg. Isolated enemy elements occasionally offered resistance, but the squadron encountered no real fight until it approached the vicinity of Gambsheim, where determined SS troops made a stand. After much tentative probing of the strong positions here, the 117th settled down and awaited stronger forces to attack the town.

Strasbourg is the great communications and market center and capital of the Bas-Rhin Department, located on the Rhine River. The 7th prepared to relieve General Jacques Le Clerc's famed 2d French Armored Division which had taken Strasbourg and held positions in the city in the vicinity of the Kehl Bridge, which crosses the Rhine east of Strasbourg.

The port of Strasbourg, third largest in all France, stretches east to northeast between the Rhine and Kleiner Rhine (small Rhine) opposite the Kehl Bridge and has a peacetime annual capacity of ten million tons.

Strasbourg's peacetime population was nearly 200,000 persons. The Ill River crosses the city in two branches, one along the northeast edge and the other along the southwest. Upstream, the Ill joins the Rhone-Rhine Canal and the Breusch River whereas downstream, the river receives the waters of the Rhone-Rhine Canal.

The 7th Infantry took up defensive positions on the western outskirts of Strasbourg, the 15th occupied positions south of the city along the Rhine River and the 30th continued to scour the rear sector of the Division for straggler groups that had been by-passed in the rush to the Rhine and that had taken refuge in some old forts near Mutzig.

In one of them some 200 Germans, armed with bazookas, machine guns and small arms, offered stubborn resistance to all efforts to dislodge them. Benko Force of the 2d Battalion, 30th Infantry, commanded by 1st Lt. John F. Benko, spent several days searching caverns and hammering the strongpoints with fire from our TDs which had little effect on the occupants.

These forts had been a part of the Maginot Line. This one had been built in the late 1800s and later modernized, completely equipped with generators, water supply, and ample ammunition. In its location and structure the fort posed a perplexing problem in reduction to the 30th Infantry, artillery, and 10th Engineer Battalion. Special interest was manifested in it owing to the fact that the VI Corps command post wished to move into Mutzig, but thought it inadvisable to locate with such proximity to the enemy.

The fort was built below ground level on the crest of the highest terrain in the area and was enclosed by a moat thirty feet wide and thirty feet deep. Any attempt to enter the fort could be frustrated by fire covering all angles of the moat. Direct fire could be brought to bear only on the steel turrets housing 150mm guns, and the entrance, which was set at an angle to the fort proper. Tanks could not approach the edge of the moat to pound the walls because of extremely accurate *Panzerfaust* fire from slits in the walls.

Lt. Col. John A. Heintges, 30th Infantry executive officer, was in charge of operations, and Company E was charged with maintaining a cordon around the fort. A 155mm Long Tom was first employed in an attempt to batter down the entrance, only to find that entrance to the fort proper was still blocked by

The 3d Infantry Division Command Post at Koenigshofen near Strasbourg.

a series of steel doors and compartments, each of which could be sealed off from other sections. The second measure taken was to call on the Air Corps, and two missions with dive bombers, using heavy, delayed-action and fire-bombs, were flown—but with scant success because of the planes' inability to register successive direct hits. Company E maintained its vigil and Company H pounded the fort steadily with mortar fire.

Colonel Heintges finally devised a plan. First, he announced in German to the garrison over a loudspeaker that the men had one-half hour in which to surrender, or else to be subjected to something new in secret weapons. This failed to budge them. At the end of the elapsed time Company H resumed its 88mm mortar fire to cover the work of a tank-dozer which was cutting a driveway to the edge of the moat. When the driveway was completed a captured halftrack personnel carrier loaded with four tons of explosive was started by Company C, 10th Engineer Battalion, and sent driverless toward the driveway. The vehicle toppled over and fell into the moat with its load of explosive resting against the wall.

The electrical detonator was disconnected by the plunge, so mortars fired on the vehicle. There was an explosion which rattled windows in Strasbourg, thirty miles away, and when the dust had settled a fifteen-foot hole marred the side of the fort.

During the night of December 4-5 the garrison endeavored to break out through the fire of Company E. After three unsuccessful attempts the detachment of eight-four men and officers surrendered at 0900, December 5. Only the commander, a major, escaped and he was rounded up at a roadblock a few days later.

Company E guarded the fort until it could be sealed by the 10th Engineers and rendered useless. On December 7 Company E rejoined its battalion at Oberhausbergen.

As November ended, the 79th Infantry Division was on the 3d's left flank and the 103d was on the right.

The 3d Infantry Division of World War II now began its "Watch on the Rhine." The first day of December found the 7th Infantry launching an attack to reduce the German bridgehead at the eastern outskirts of Strasbourg, opposite the town of Kehl, while other elements of the Division began police and guard duty in Strasbourg.

The 7th met stubborn resistance when it attacked on the morning of December 1. Small-arms, automatic-weapon, machine-gun and rocket-launcher fire from dug-in positions on the west side of the river and mortar and artillery fire from the east side comprised the enemy defense.

The 2d Battalion, commanded by Lt. Col. Clayton C. Thobro, took up the "Battle of the Apartment Houses" in the eastern section of the city while Company C, commanded by Capt. Beverly G. Hays, continued the street fight which it started shortly after midnight. Members of Company C will long remember the hand-to-hand battles that were staged in the vicinity of the Hippodrome and in the railroad yards on the edge of town. Sniper fire from across the river also added to the misery.

Organized resistance began to dwindle with daylight of December 2 after the 2d Battalion had cleared the peninsula between the Bassin De L'Industrie and the Rhine River. The entire area rocked late that afternoon as demolitions set off by the Germans destroyed all three bridges across the river. The last Germans to leave the bridgehead escaped by boat.

While the 7th was chasing the Germans from the west bank of the Rhine, the 1st Battalion of the 30th, attached to the 2d French Armored Division, veered suddenly south and crossed the southern branch of the Ill River between Sermersheim and Kogenheim. The mission was to secure a site for the French to build an armor-carrying span.

At about midnight, Colonel Porter's battalion crossed in boats and came under a concentration of heavy mortar and artillery fire. Company B, commanded by 1st Lt. Lysle E. Standish, made the crossing at Kogenheim and Company C, under 1st Lt. Charles H. Skeahan, Jr., landed at Sermersheim, about a half mile upstream. The two companies came under more artillery fire in the towns, where an estimated 600 rounds of heavy enemy shells fell the next morning. Supported by French artillery and tanks, the attackers pushed the Germans out of the villages and carried the assault into the woods east while Company A, commanded by 1st Lt. Willard C. Johnson, took over blocking positions to the southeast.

Action described by a veteran doughboy as the "toughest three days I have ever spent" came to a close when a French colonel announced that the battalion attached to him by the 30th Infantry "is the finest outfit of its kind I have ever seen."

So satisfied were the French forces with the job that they awarded twenty-three Croix de Guerre to members of the 30th's 1st battalion from CO Major Mackenzie E. Porter down to the privates of the front ranks, who received most of the decorations.

In the same way the French 2d Armored Division's plaudits were passed out to Company C. At Company C, 1st Lt. Rex Metcalfe accepted the tribute by passing credit on to his doughfeet, who ended their 48-plus hours of fighting by sitting on the division objective for fourteen hours alone.

The 15th Infantry continued to maintain defensive positions, check the numerous pillboxes that the enemy had evacuated, and provide antiparachute alert units. Our troops occupied many of the pillboxes as outposts.

Marnemen will recall the guard duty in the old Alsatian capital—the Physics Building, Adolf Kosmier, Matford Factory, Hotel De Ville, the Pioneer Gasno, the laboratories at Fort Ney, and the interminable strings of railroad cars that filled the yards.

Many will remember the worship services that were held in the world-famous Strasbourg Cathedral . . . the first since the Germans came in 1940. Others will recall the burial given Pfc. Simon Quiroz of the 15th Infantry, who was the only 3d Division man to die in the liberation of the little village of Mutzig. M. Haller Eugene, mayor of St. Maurice, was given permission to conduct the services, which were attended by a guard of honor from VI Corps artillery. After eulogizing Quiroz and paying high tribute to the 3d Division, the mayor announced that a plaque would be erected in honor of the fallen soldier.

Strasbourg, as the largest and most important city occupied by the 3d Division in France, called for special attention from the occupying forces. The 1st Battalion, 7th Infantry, for instance, guarded intelligence targets prescribed by Sixth Army Group's T-Force, which had the mission of protecting and exploiting anything that might yield information of the enemy's army or war industry. Included in the targets were an amphibious-motor-vehicle plant, an important naval munitions experimental plant, and the notorious laboratory at the University of Strasbourg, whose doctors were accused of performing experiments with poison gas and disease cultures on living humans.

Before reaching Strasbourg, the Division also liber-

The facade, and famous rose-window of the Strasbourg Cathedral as seen from the approach street.

boat being sent downstream on the loose, and many other measures were perpetrated, designed to make the Germans believe that the 3d was going to cross the Rhine in the Strasbourg sector.

Once the restoration of some degree of order, if not normality, was well under way in Strasbourg, the 3d had some chance to reflect upon its recent accomplishments. The effect of the sullenly-bitter Vosges battle manifested itself in several ways.

LeClerc's 2d Armored Division, the outfit which had been first to enter Paris the previous autumn, and which had moved on Strasbourg from a general northwest direction in the recent drive with characteristic celerity, had spearheaded that effort to crack German defenses before the Rhine River. Enemy elements west of the river were already partially frustrated in their efforts to hold a sizable salient when elements of the French First Army reached the Rhine just above Basle, Switzerland, and moved up to liberate a section of territory which included Mulhouse. This occurred a short time before our own all-out push from the Meurthe.

The 3d Infantry Division had broken through the enemy's intended winter line, spearheading Seventh Army's push through the central Vosges in the latter stages of the drive, to widen the breach made by the first breakthrough to Strasbourg, and to help reduce

ated one of the most brutal of the Nazi concentration camps—that at Natzwiller, northeast of Schirmeck.

The Division established a supervisory city administration (G-5) under the A C of S, G-2, Lt. Col. Grover Wilson. Until the arrival of French 10th Military District headquarters under the French General Schwartz, the Division was responsible for guarding food dumps, utilities and warehouses, arranging for transportation and distribution of food, and other functions performed by military government personnel.

Prize PW of the Strasbourg episode was General Major (equivalent: Brig. Gen.) Vaterrodt, the town commandant, who was described by interrogators as cringing, totally opportunistic, and only too willing to give information if it might improve his position wth his captors.

On December 8, the Division started a program of deception, designed to assist the VI Corps in its attack in the north toward Germany.

Artillery registration on points east of the Rhine River, apparently "careless" revealing of rubber assault boats on the banks of the river with an occasional

Chaplain Ralph Smith, 3d Infantry Division celebrates mass in the Strasbourg Cathedral on the Feast of the Immaculate Conception.

The 10th Engineers outfitted these assault boats for reconnaissance work on the Rhine. This is the Kleiner Rhein.

German forces west of the Rhine in our sector and split them into two groups: a large pocket which included Colmar on the south and a German foothold on Alsatian soil to the north which was rapidly dwindling under continued Seventh Army pressure.

The recent drive had been record-making in several ways. In a congratulatory message, VI Corps Commander Major General Edward H. Brooks made note of one precedent-shattering fact:

"Since the beginning of the military history of Europe, to force a successful passage of the Vosges Mountains has been considered by military experts as an operation offering such small opportunity for success as to forestall consideration of such effort. [No military force had ever before crossed the Vosges against organized resistance.]

"To march, supply and maintain a large body of troops through these natural obstacles, without hostile opposition, is a major problem in itself.

"To fight cross-country, in the face of unreasoning, stubborn Nazi resistance, at times supplying over snow-covered mountain roads and trails, through this region and at this season of the year, is a military achievement of which all who participated can be justly proud.

"To those men of the 100th and 36th Divisions who battered the flanks, to those of the 3d and 103d Divisions and of the 14th Armored Division who poured onto the Alsatian Plain, to those supporting combat troops of the Corps, and to those indispensable elements of supply, maintenance, and evacuation, I extend my thanks and congratulations. Teamwork, throughout to a superlative degree.

"It is with pride and humility that I realize the pinnacle and the magnitude of this concerted achievement of American soldiery—your achievement. I have every confidence that the future of the VI Corps rests secure and bright in your capable hands."

Bare statistics pointed up another important feat. From the beginning of the attack on the morning of November 21 to the time leading elements of the 7th Infantry entered Strasbourg on the night of the 26th, the distance covered was at least fifty miles, measured by road. The troops who ended the long march in the vicinity of Strasbourg were very near exhaustion.

They were not particularly articulate about their great success. The trail was too rocky. Even at the finish, when the Rhine forced a temporary halt, the job was not done. There had been the grinding, nerve-wracking "Battle of the Apartment Houses" under small-arms, machine-gun, and *Panzerfaust* fire, and heavy caliber artillery from Germany for the 2d and 3d Battalions, 7th Infantry. There was the temporary attachment of 1st Battalion, 30th Infantry to LeClerc, and Company E's battle to reduce the Mutzig fort.

There was to be no sustained period of rest in Strasbourg. On the north the bulk of Seventh Army was continuing to force the issue with the enemy remaining in Alsace in that sector. The 36th and 103d (the latter very shortly relieved and sent to rejoin the Seventh) were still in strong contact with the Germans to the south. The French 2d Armored slowed down in its attack toward Colmar as the enemy, anticipating a pincers between I French Corps on the south and II French Corps on the north flank, demolished bridges along every possible route of approach and offered tenacious resistance to the attackers. The 36th Division was attached to II French Corps.

There was much speculation in regard to 3d Division's next assignment. Cross the Rhine? Go north and into Germany through the old Maginot Line? Or south, to join the French . . . ?

TABLE OF CASUALTIES*

Vosges Mountains and Early Colmar
Sept. 15, 1944 through Jan. 21, 1945

KIA	WIA	MIA	Total Battle Casualties	Non-Battle Casualties
1277	4852	108	6237	7895

Reinforcements and Hospital return-to-unit personnel

Reinf		Hosp RTUs	
Off	EM	Off	EM
195	5667	196	6563

KNOWN ENEMY CASUALTIES

Killed	Wounded	Captured
1151	655	7258

*These figures were provided by the A C of S, G–1, 3d Infantry Division.

X
THE COLMAR POCKET

We Move in the Lead Again to Crack the "Frozen Crust"

TROOP LIST

1. Hq & Hq Co, 3d Inf Div
2. 7th Infantry
3. 15th Infantry
4. 30th Infantry
5. 3d Inf Div Arty
    9th FA Bn
    10th FA Bn
    39th FA Bn
    41st FA Bn
    141st FA Bn
    II/62d FA Bn (Fr)
    802d FA Bn
    773d (4.5) FA Bn
6. 254th Inf Regt (—)
7. 3d Bn, 112th Inf Regt
8. 441st AAA AW Bn
9. 2d Plat, Btry A, 353d (S/L) Bn
10. 10th Engr Bn (C)
    3d Bn, 40th Engr Regt.
11. 256th Engr (C) Bn
12. 3d Rcn Troop
13. 3d Med Bn
14. 3d Signal Co
15. 756th Tank Bn
16. 601st TD Bn
17. 99th Cml Mortar Bn
    168th Cml Co (SG)
    21st Cml Co
18. 5 DB (Fr)
19. Air Support

ALTHOUGH many units of the 3d Division seized the opportunities offered them to rest and rehabilitate in and near Strasbourg, at no time was the Division off the front lines or out of contact with the enemy.

Following elimination of the Kehl bridgehead (with the weird "Battle of the Apartments," and the end, by German surrender, of the publicized Mutzig *"Ostfort"*), nightly contacts in the form of vicious exchanges of fire across the Rhine punctuated the 7th and 15th Infantry Regiments' otherwise almost monotonous vigil along the banks of the river.

The 3d Infantry Division was on the defensive for the second time in the war, but despite the lack of face-to-face contact it was an uneasy period. Through no direct connection with our activities, stalemate had overcome the Division as a whole. A crossing in strength of the Rhine River was not then feasible nor contemplated; consequently a good deal of wonderment was in store as to the immediate future.

To the north, other units of the Seventh Army were pushing into southern Germany. To the south, First French Army, with the U. S. 36th Infantry Division attached, found, with a growing realization that it still had on its hands an embarrassing German bulge west of the Rhine, and that temporarily it was unable to do anything about it. As the Germans, to preserve Colmar, pushed back some French units and elements of the 36th Division around Selestat, the fact emerged that here was no mere line on the situation map to be wiped out at leisure, but a stubbornly-fighting pocket of enemy who were becoming fortified more strongly daily, and that a full-scale coordinated army-sized attack was going to be required to eliminate them.

At first it was called "the bridgehead around Colmar," but as it persisted, a name was given it which stuck: "Colmar Pocket." The 3d Infantry Division was to learn that it was a pocket bulging with fortifications and sudden death; and an area whose elimination was to develop into our second greatest fight of the entire war—some said the greatest—in the same degree of ferocity as the attack to break the Anzio "iron ring." Yet, even following the elimination of the Colmar Pocket, comparatively few persons on the outside knew Colmar—if they knew of it at all—as anything more than the name of an upper Alsatian city whose liberation came only after a lengthy period of waiting.

Following receipt of the Seventh Army order that 3d Infantry Division would relieve 36th Infantry Division, 30th Infantry was designated as the vanguard, and commenced moving south on the afternoon of December 13, to be attached to the 36th.

The complete force was dubbed "Task Force McGarr" —so named because Col. Lionel C. McGarr (then acting Assistant Division Commander) was ordered to lead it into the Colmar Pocket action. Lt. Col. Richard H. Neddersen commanded the 30th Infantry. Initially the force was composed of the complete 30th Infantry; 41st Field Artillery Battalion; Company C of the 10th Engineers; Battery D, 441st Antiaircraft Battalion; a section of tanks from Company B, 753d Tank Battalion; and a platoon of tanks and a section of tank destroyers

The exterior of the 3d Infantry Division's Officers' Club in Strasbourg.

from Combat Command IV, 5th French Armored Division (*Cinquiéme Division Blindée*).

(The attack, which was coordinated with that of a regiment of the 36th Division, commenced one day before the enemy in the north launched the tremendous counter-offensive in the Ardennes-Schnee Eiffel area, although this was not known until two day later.)

The 30th Infantry, of all the 3d Division units, had had the least rest. During its 15-day stay in Strasbourg the 1st Battalion had been attached to the 2 DB (LeClerc's famed 2d Armored) for the five-day engagement near Kogenheim for which twenty-three officers and men had been awarded the Croix de Guerre. Company E, in addition, had been assigned the mission of neutralizing the Mutzig fort, which it accomplished successfully.

The regiment's attack, following its commitment in the Colmar Pocket, got off between 0700 and 0800, December 15, the three battalions attacking simultaneously from assembly areas in the vicinity of Aubure and Freland. The 2d and 3d Battalions moved through the mountainous forest of Sigolsheim into firing positions near Ursprung. The first opposition was encountered by Company I, which received intense enemy machine-gun fire at 1300 from a force emplaced on Hill 651, an irregular mountainous mass which dominated the then critically important Toggenbach-Alspach area. After a 25-minute fire fight, Company I destroyed three machine guns, and killed several enemy riflemen.

The two assault battalions moved across the twin hill-masses flanking Toggenbach. At 1417 approximately fifty Germans, manning concrete and earthwork emplacements of World War I type on Hill 672, opened fire on Company E with machine guns, machine pistols, and rifles. Company E accepted the challenge. In a swift flanking movement it overwhelmed this segment of the German outpost line of resistance and swept southwest along the rugged wooded ridge toward Hill 621. The movement of the battalion along the ridge line which pointed like an arrow at Kaysersberg directly to the south was harassed by continuing small-arms and automatic fire, but the advance was uninterrupted.

The 3d Battalion meanwhile advanced on Toggenbach, a cluster of houses between Aubure and Kaysersberg. A roadblock, manned by a determined German force, was reported 1300 meters north of the village, and a combat patrol was dispatched to demolish it. Sgt. William A. Nagowski was instrumental in clearing this roadblock. Another 3d Battalion patrol sliced the highway south of Toggenbach at 1500 after a brisk fire fight.

While Company G was pounded by heavy howitzer fire along the high ground north of Hill 666, Company E organized night positions to the east of the Toggenbach road and plans were completed for the final assault on the village. One platoon of Company K guided on the ridge line for the attack, but encountered a large force of determined enemy on the hillside due west of the village. Fighting in dim light in deep weeds at almost hand-to-hand range, the platoon took eighteen prisoners and killed or wounded the remainder of the German force.

Company G moved through a tempest of howitzer fire to establish night positions at the north base of Hill 666. Companies E and G were deluged by heavy artillery concentrations during the night, in one of which 2d Battalion CO Lt. Col. Frederick R. Armstrong was killed while personally assisting his most advanced assault unit—Company G—in its forward drive. Maj. James L. Osgard succeeded him.

General Young, Acting CG, 3d Division receives General Schwartz, CG 10th French Military District, in Strasbourg.

had taken Hill 672, establishing a line of departure to attack Hills 666 and 621.

On December 16 the Task Force was strengthened by the addition of Companies C of: 756th Tank Battalion, 601st Tank Destroyer Battalion, and 3d Medical Battalion, all normal attachments to the 30th.

The three battalions of the 30th were now ready to join in the assault on Kaysersberg, located on the rim of the Rhine plain where the Weiss River flows through a narrow channel between rugged, forested mountain masses, which flank the town to the north and south. East is the flatland of the Rhine; west the valley winds upward through the hills toward the La Bonhomme pass, one of the main corridors through the Vosges.

The 1st Battalion drew the assignment of crossing the Weiss and ascending the steep slopes of Hill 512, south of the town. The 2d Battalion was to thrust its way down the precipitous, oblong mountain mass to the north of Kaysersberg, consisting of Hills 616 and 612. The 3d Battalion had the assignment of driving into Kaysersberg itself, to clear the town.

There were confused clashes between patrols and isolated enemy groups as the 30th Infantry moved silently forward to join the battle in the early morning hours of December 16.

By 0630 Company B had moved through the factory area of Kaysersberg and found no enemy. The battalion attack on Hill 512 commenced. The main force was preceded by a screen of scouts, especially coached by Maj. Mackenzie E. Porter to be on the alert to report all evidences of enemy activity. Aim of the battalion commander was to gain his objective by stealth, avoiding all fighting until the troops were established on the crest of the hill.

Using circuitous routes, the 1st Battalion reached the trail net on Hill 512, which constituted the point agreed

Lieutenant Colonel Donald E. Hoffmeister, Commanding Officer, 10th Field Artillery Battalion.

At 2200 Company M headquarters repulsed a 10-man enemy patrol, wounding six of the attackers.

As engineers cleared the Toggenbach-Kaysersberg road of mines, tanks thrust their way through Toggenbach. At 1835, patrols of Company B established contact with Company I inside the village. Tanks and engineers with bridging materials moved up to await patrol reports on suitable crossing sites over the Weiss River. The report came back at 2250 that the stream could be crossed without difficulty near the Kaysersberg road, although the stream was swift and elsewhere the banks steep.

Two separate reconnaissance patrols, one from Company I, the other from the 1st Battalion I & R Platoon, thrust into Kaysersberg, heart of the enemy defensive position, engaged an antitank strongpoint and drew withering fire from the buildings.

In the first day's action Toggenbach had been captured, the Toggenbach-Alspach road cleared, a vital bridge site over the Weiss seized, and the first five houses in Kaysersberg taken. In addition 2d Battalion

Lieutenant Colonel Paulick and Major Potter, 15th Exec. and S-3 discuss the situation over a map.

upon with French Goums. By 0930 the entire hill was cleared with no contact other than overrunning a five-man enemy observation post. The enemy began pounding the hill with mortar fire. The 1st Battalion sent out patrols to guard its positions and repel all counterattacks.

Meanwhile Company I had thrust aggressively into Kaysersberg from the southeast, followed by Company K and supporting armor. The hard, bloody work of house-clearing began. Withering small-arms fire whipped up and back the narrow streets as our troops advanced. Company I changed commanders twice during the battle for the town.

By 1300, footholds had been gained in the heart of the town, at heavy cost. The 3d Battalion CP set up in Kaysersberg, and the work of clearing snipers continued. Suddenly, the enemy launched an all-out counterattack to regain his principal stronghold. Tanks opened fire on 3d Battalion troops in the town, while at the same time Companies I and L were hit from the east by a force of 300 Germans. Heavy artillery, mortar, tank, and machine-gun fire poured in on the troops in the town.

The counterattack continued for two hours, during which numerous separate acts of heroism stood out. The attack was repulsed, but the powerful German force, still determined to regain Kaysersberg, estab-

Colonel Charles E. Johnson, Chief of Staff, 3d Infantry Division.

lished and entrenched itself around the city, gathering its strength for new counterblows.

Meanwhile, 2d Battalion had commenced its attack on the hill mass north of Kaysersberg and east of the Toggenbach-Kaysersberg road. At 1300, Company E's 1st platoon moved to the nose of the long hill which ended at Kaysersberg while Companies F and G continued their slow advance along the wooded slopes of Hill 666 against heavy opposition.

The enemy held the oval hill mass with a determined force of crack troops, abundantly supplied with all types of weapons, and greatly aided by the concrete and earthwork strongpoints originally built by the French in the early part of the war.

The way was prepared by Cannon Company fire on Ammerschwihr and systematic pounding of the hostile hill positions with mortar rounds and machine-gun fire. The battalion then moved toward the crest. By midafternoon Company G was halted by fire from three concrete machine-gun emplacements, which were difficult to locate due to the dense vegetation in which they were sited. At approximately the same time Company F found its attack interrupted by intense fire from six defiladed enemy machine guns.

The 2d Battalion decided to postpone its attack and made preparations for a full-scale assault the following day. The engineers began to clear roads to the hill

Lieutenant Colonel William B. Rosson, G-3, 3d Infantry Division.

positions so that three tanks, assigned to the battalion from the 756th, could be brought into action. While diversionary fire was laid on the west side of the hill Company E was to attack from the east. Clearing of these two hills was considered the key to the position and the central objective of Task Force McGarr.

The 1st Battalion, which had seized its objective swiftly and without strong opposition, rained artillery, mortar, and small-arms fire from Hill 512 on the Germans fleeing from Kaysersberg. A decision was made to strike southward from the hill crest, setting up a roadblock at Bridge 267, commanding an important east-west highway leading from Ammerschwihr. First Lt. Charles P. Murray, Jr., CO of Company C, led the two platoons which performed this mission and in accomplishing it performed an outstanding deed of gallantry and intrepidity to the successful accomplishment of the mission.

Unwilling to risk his men in the attack, Murray went forward with an SCR 536 to a suitable vantage point. Here he attempted to place artillery on the withdrawing enemy, but found his radio out of commission. Returning to his platoon he borrowed an M-1 with grenade-launcher attachment, returned to his exposed position, and opened fire on the enemy. The German force of 200 replied with intense fire, but Lieutenant Murray stayed at his post until all of his ten grenades had been thrown. He withdrew to secure a BAR and returned to his hazardous position to engage the enemy in a half-hour attack. Fighting alone, he compelled the Germans to withdraw leaving three 120mm mortars, then directed mortar fire on the withdrawing enemy with devastating effect; he led his men forward in an assault from foxhole to foxhole although wounded in eight places by an exploding grenade. He personally killed twenty and captured eleven of the enemy, for which he later received the Nation's highest award—the Congressional Medal of Honor.

On December 17, fighting in the Kaysersberg salient reached a climax. The 2d Battalion continued its difficult drive to seize the hill masses north of the city, and 1st Battalion weathered a furious German counterattack which was delivered with great power and determination. The 3d Battalion drove deeper into Kaysersberg under accelerated enemy artillery and mortar fire. Company I directed tank-destroyer fire on a medieval tower north of Kaysersberg which the enemy was employing as an observation post. Companies K and L advanced to the south and southwest of town and toward the base of Hill 512. Tank and bazooka fire was received from the northwest edge of the city, but the battalion directed artillery on the tanks, destroying one.

The fighting still continued unabated at noon. Heavy

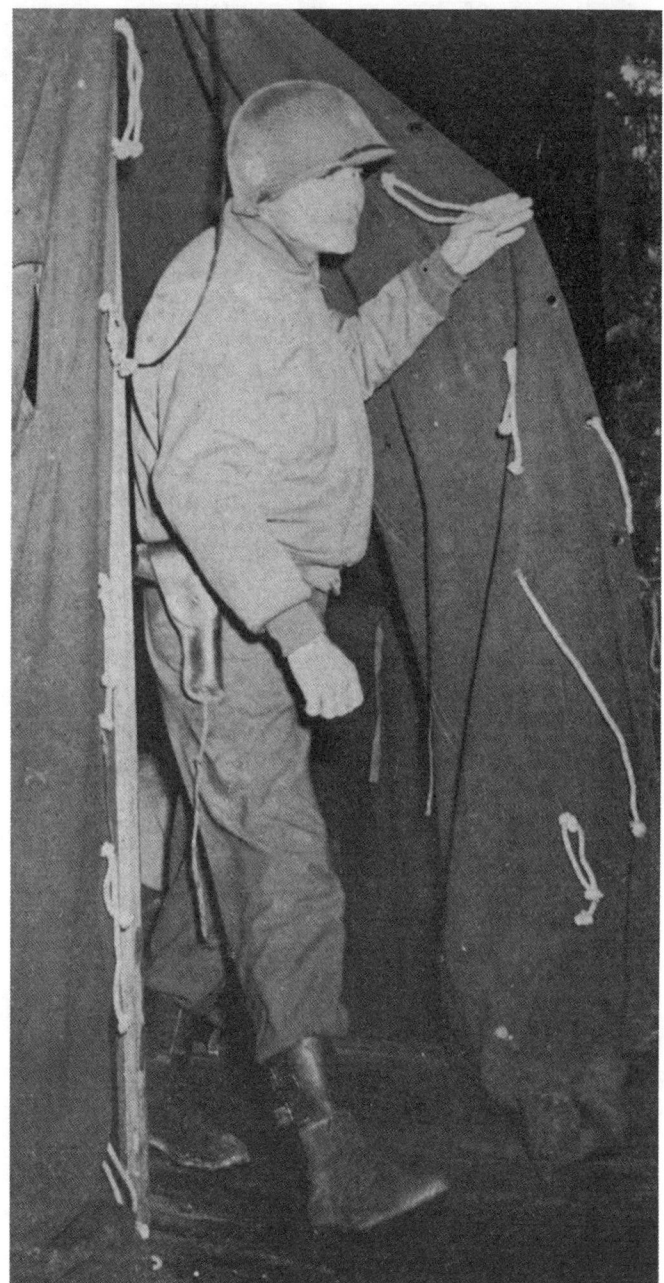

Lieutenant Colonel James R. Wendt Jr., commanding officer, 41st Field Artillery Battalion.

fighting also occurred at the Weiss River bridge. The enemy jabbed at 3d Battalion's positions with small-scale tank-infantry attacks. Attack and counterattack continued throughout the day with unflagging violence. By midnight the enemy was definitely losing his hold.

The 2d Battalion jumped off on its all-out attack at 0645, December 17. Three tanks from the 756th Tank Battalion supported Company F in its attack on Hill 621 as Companies E and G drove on Hill 666, making such rapid progress that the section from Bat-

Brigadier General William Sexton, CG, 3d Infantry Division Artillery.

tery D, 441st AAA ("anti-anything, anytime") Battalion, which had fired sixty-three rounds of 37mm high-explosive shells and 2660 rounds of cal. .50 ammunition, was obliged to lift fire. Company E scaled the precipitous slope, losing eight men killed and seventeen wounded, but reaching the summit and killing, wounding, or capturing all Germans there. Simultaneously Company G made its frontal assault on the hill through a screen of enemy howitzer, mortar, machine-gun, and *Panzerfaust* fire.

Hills 666 and 621 were cleared by 1130, with at least fifty Germans killed and a hundred wounded, plus thirty prisoners. Twenty machine guns were destroyed, and three mortars captured, as well as a vast quantity of small arms and ammunition.

Companies E and G regrouped and drove southeast toward Company F on Hill 621, encountering strong enemy opposition. In the fierce fight to make this linkup, troops of the battalion destroyed five more machine guns. They also killed thirty and captured forty-five more Germans in the all-afternoon fight, and themselves took heavy casualties. Contact was made with Company F at 1545 by Company G. The companies immediately began to organize night defensive positions. Despite incessant German infiltration and savage patrol combat in the forests, the battalion succeeded in maintaining its grip on the high ground.

The 1st Battalion's daylong fight had commenced with a German counterattack, delivered by an entire regiment, driving from three directions at once. The enemy swarmed toward Hill 512 from Ammerschwihr and Kaysersberg, hitting Company B's line at 0811.

The battalion had not had time to consolidate its hill positions and tie in closely with the remainder of the Task Force. There was but one mountain trail to the summit of Hill 512. No armor had been able to get to the summit and the battalion requirements of ammunition, food, and water had to be hand-carried up the trail, necessitating a four-hour trip each time.

At 0825 approximately a hundred enemy advanced from the southeast to drive a wedge between Companies B and C on the high ground designated Objective "X." By 0840 the three prongs of the enemy counterattack had overrun the eastern nose of the battalion position.

The Battalion CO, Major Porter, placed artillery fire on the enemy's rear to prevent reinforcement of the counterattack and pounded the Germans with a mortar concentration. The enemy, however, continued to gain ground, overrunning the eastern end of Company C's position.

Major Porter consolidated his forces and ordered the battalion to hold the high ridge line at all costs. The nose of the hill had been temporarily lost, but the crucial ridge line and the road net junction were firmly in our hands. The reinforced platoon at Bridge 267, finding itself isolated by the sudden counterattack, now fought its way back through hostile lines, finally reaching the ridge to join the defense.

The battalion engaged the Germans from its high ground position in a fire fight that lasted all day and all night. The enemy forces were composed of German officer candidates, who had been promised that once they regained Kayserberg and the surrounding hills they would be returned to Germany to complete their courses. Fresh, fanatical, and more intelligent than the average *Landser,* these men fought with skill and determination. By the end of the day an estimated fifty had been killed and twice that number wounded.

The German recapture of Bridge 267 was disastrous —for the enemy. Mortar and artillery fire placed on the bridge and roadblock was so intense that the enemy retreated leaving behind twenty-five dead.

On December 18 Task Force McGarr was further strengthened by the addition of Company B, 99th Chemical Battalion, but the battalion's tank and tank-destroyer support from the French CC4 and 753d Tank Battalion was withdrawn.

At daybreak 1st Battalion was still weathering furious counterattacks. It was noticed by Major Porter that the enemy chose the same avenues of assault; accordingly, he regrouped his forces so that they could effectively control with enfilading small-arms and machine-gun fire and mortars, the draws and pathways along which the enemy so persistently advanced.

The supply problem grew more acute. The battalion rear echelon was mobilized, almost entirely, to carry ammunition. Supplies were thus assured for the rest of the day.

Patrols were sent from the beleaguered hill position. First Sgt. Nicholas F. Kiwatisky of Company B reflected the temper of several valorous actions by leading his small patrol deep into enemy territory, killing a machine gunner and assistant with M-1 fire at 200-yard range, and moving straight into the core of the German position to silence a second machine gun and kill seven enemy soldiers singlehandedly.

By 1300 the battalion had repulsed three counterattacks; from the east, from Ammerschwihr, and from the southeast, each of them consisting of from 200 to 300 men supported by tank and self-propelled-gun fires. Three more counterattacks were hurled against the battalion during the afternoon and all were repelled. By 1845, after bringing the combined weight of all fires on the enemy, the counterattacks ceased. At 2055 a check revealed that 1st Battalion had not lost an inch of ground during the day's counterattacks.

During the morning of the 18th, the 2d Battalion expelled the Germans from their last remaining positions around Hill 621, then continued its drive to the southwest to link up with the Task Force positions in Kaysersberg. Company F remained behind to eliminate a small German pocket.

The 3d Battalion received counterattacks during the day but pressed forward, tightening its control over Kaysersberg and establishing patrol contact with the French CCV at approximately 1300. Company L, having cleared its sector of Kaysersberg, was ordered to move up the hill south of town to join 1st Battalion and reinforce its west flank. Preparations were made for the final attack to eliminate the enemy from his remaining positions on and around Hill 512.

The primary task of December 19 was to smash the German positions in the 1st Battalion sector. Tremendous preliminary fires deluged the enemy line. At 0815 1st Battalion, with Companies B and C in the assault, fell on the German force. By 0920 the enemy was driven in confusion from the nose of the hill which he had fought so desperately to retain. Dazed by the furious fire, the Germans put up little more than token resistance. Then, at 1115, Company C reported the establishment of contact with the French in Ammerschwihr and set up and manned a roadblock at Bridge 267.

Company F eliminated the pocket in its zone after a fierce fire fight, destroying eight machine guns and three mortars and taking eleven prisoners, then con-

This scene looking west from the Rhine Plain toward the foothills of the Vosges depicts typical terrain fought over in the Colmar Pocket.

tinued over Hill 21 and entered Kayserberg at 1100.

At 1845 two battalions of enemy were sighted approaching Task Force positions from the west. Company C set up a roadblock on the Alspach-Kaysersberg road to thwart this move and brought a section of Flakwagons up for its defense.

At daybreak on December 20, the 441st Flakwagons fired 4,900 rounds of .50 caliber ammunition and 170 rounds of 37mm HE ammunition, saturating the woods where the Germans were preparing their counterattack. The 30th Infantry, with the aid of this fire, shattered this counterattack before it got under way.

At 1030 another and final enemy blow was reported in preparation, this time from the south in the vicinity of Bridge 267. Again the Task Force deluged the assembly areas of the Germans with artillery, mortar, and cannon fire.

Results of the entire mission, now completed, were striking. A 5,000-meter German penetration between the 3d French DIA (*Division Infanterie Algerienne*) and the 36th U. S. Infantry Division had been sealed off and smashed, opening a vital supply artery from St. Dié to the Rhine Valley for the passage of troops and materiel. A preliminary battle to the major offensive that was to obliterate the Colmar Pocket had been waged and won.

The accomplishment of this task involved the most exacting type of mountain warfare in icy weather. Scaling steep slopes, their passage barred by a tangled undergrowth and a maze of forest, subjected to harrowing fire from German casemates of timber, earthwork, and concrete, the men of Task Force McGarr had fought with determination and quiet heroism.

Prisoner interrogation revealed that nine battalions of German infantry, two of engineers, a specialized support battalion and a minimum of four artillery battalions had been shattered.

The victory was accomplished at a cost to the Task Force of fifty-eight killed, eighteen missing, and 190 wounded. In comparison, known enemy losses were

The 3d Signal Company posted similar signs throughout the area to aid the campaign to keep in communications.

298 killed, 327 prisoners, and an estimated 1185 wounded. In addition the enemy lost four tanks, twelve mortars, two Flakwagons, forty machine guns, and a large number of artillery pieces.

The 41st Field Artillery Battalion fired 7226 rounds of 105mm howitzer ammuntion in seventy-four concentrations and ten TOTs (time on target, a system whereby the fire of all guns of a given number of artillery units is brought to bear simultaneously). Cannon Company fired 5864 rounds of 105 and 75mm ammunition, and a total of ninety-nine rounds of 4.2 mortar ammunition were expended by Company B, 99th Chemical Battalion.

(Beginning December 16, the Fifth and Sixth *Panzer* Armies of Field Marshal von Rundstedt lashed out in a counteroffensive in Belgium and Luxembourg which stunned the entire Allied camp. Known later as "Battle of the Bulge," German elements achieved a maximum penetration of approximately fifty-five miles before the tide of battle turned and Third and Ninth Armies to either flank of the attacked United States First Army began slashing at the sides of the Bulge. Colmar Pocket, in the big picture, was an irritating little red grease-pencilled twist on the lower end of the situation map, only a minor battle—unless one was there.)

On December 17 the 3d Infantry Division began moving south for the continuance of the relief of 36th Infantry Division. The 2d Battalion, 15th Infantry, was first relieved, to commence its move to the vicinity of Riquewihr, where it closed in on the following day. It was followed by the 3d and 1st Battalions on December 19. The 1st and 2d Battalions, 7th Infantry, were completely relieved on defensive positions in Strasbourg by other elements of the 36th Division, and command of the former 36th sector passed to Brigadier General Robert N. Young (commanding the Division in the absence of General O'Daniel, on temporary duty in the United States) at 1430, December 21.

Two days later, December 23, the 15th Infantry launched an attack against the two towns of Bennwihr and Sigolsheim, as the first step in securing a more stable line of defense. Defense was the keynote at this time. Seventh Army had received a sizable German counterattack against its barely-won positions in southern Germany and was forced to withdraw to a more tenable line in lower Alsace. It was known that the Germans had announced their intentions of retaking Strasbourg, if possible, as a "Christmas present" for *der Führer,* and a pincers between the forces opposing Seventh Army forces and those opposing French First Army, of which the 3d Infantry Division was now a part, was considered a definite possibility. Our first step, therefore, was to secure Bennwihr and Sigolsheim, the last two towns of any size between that part of our line and the key city of Colmar, and to drive the Germans from all high ground north of a line Sigolsheim-Kayersberg.

Sigolsheim and Bennwihr are located at the extreme western edge of the Alsace Plain and just east of the last high slopes of the Vosges. Advance reconnaissance indicated that Sigolsheim in particular was strongly occupied by the enemy, and later events proved this to be entirely true.

Besides drawing the assignment to take the two towns, 15th Infantry also had the mission of clearing Hill 351, a high mass that lies between them.

The 15th's drive was directed east from positions in the vicinity of Kientzheim, which was held by the 2d Battalion, 30th Infantry. The 1st Battalion, commanded by Lt. Col. Keith L. Ware, was to capture Sigolsheim; the 3d Battalion, under Maj. John O'Connell, to attack Bennwihr, and the 2d Battalion, under Lt. Col. Eugene A. Salet, was to block and support the attack of the other battalions from positions on the northern slope of Hill 351.

At H-hour, 0730, Companies A and C attacked. Particularly stiff resistance was encountered just before reaching the town when a convent just north of it was found to be an enemy stronghold, with enemy manning machine guns, mortars, and small arms. After a stiff two-hour fight Company A succeeded in pressing through and past this opposition to reach the edge of town at noon.

The entrance of Company A into the town of Sigolsheim was only a forerunner to a terrific fight that lasted five days. The small village was a shambles, having been reduced by our bombers and artillery, and by tank and tank-destroyer fire provided by the 601st and 756th attachments to 1st Battalion, 15th Infantry, under command of Lt. Colonel Ware.

The 3d Battalion, meanwhile, had marched south from Mittelwihr in the morning and attacked Bennwihr from the north and west. Companies I and K under command of Capts. Warren M. Stuart and Robert W. Hahn, respectively, moved into the town at 0800, and it seemed as if resistance would be light until Company K suddenly came under terrific fire from a school near the center of the village.

Accepting the challenge, Company K stormed the school. The enemy was entrenched in the rubble of houses and cellars, and resisted bitterly. Finally Company K drove the enemy from the school and established the buildings as a temporary PW cage. The conquest, however, was short-lived. A desperate enemy counterattack was launched that afternoon and the Germans retook the school and some sixty prisoners who were being held in it. Enemy armor figured strongly in this attack and a Mark IV tank was reported to have withstood several bazooka and rifle-grenade shots which apparently struck it squarely. As darkness came the 3d Battalion withdrew slightly to prepare for another attack the following morning.

In Sigolsheim, too, there was a bitter fight. Several armored vehicles of the 756th Tank Battalion, under command of Lt. Col. Glenn F. Rogers, bogged down in the muddy terrain, thus reducing the striking power of our force.

Complete penetration into the village had not been accomplished and the battalion was still attempting to gain a good toehold in Sigolsheim when the enemy counterattacked from the center of town with infantry and armor late that night, and from the direction of Hill 351 to the north, with mortar and artillery fire. The position became untenable and 1st Battalion relinquished its slender hold on Sigolsheim and, under orders, withdrew to Kientzheim and Riquewihr for the night.

It was now apparent that before any position in Sigolsheim could be held the enemy must be driven completely from Hill 351, or else the same thing would happen again.

During darkness Companies K and L, the latter commanded by 1st Lt. Earl B. Hobbs, struck Bennwihr again in an early morning thrust, this time from the east. Each company destroyed an enemy tank shortly after the attack got underway and this seemed to help demoralize the enemy, who always had placed a good deal of faith in his supporting armor. Moving in, the 3d Battalion again commenced the grinding, dangerous, physically-exhausting work of eliminating the enemy from the basements and house-fragments of Bennwihr. By 1225 a major portion of the town had been cleared.

Intent on eliminating the harassing interference from Hill 351, 1st Battalion attacked up the northwestern slope of the hill on the morning of December 24, from the direction of Riquewihr. Company B, commanded by 1st Lt. George W. Mohr, encountered a heavy fire fight en route, coming under machine-gun and small-arms fire from well dug-in and concealed positions. This pocket was eliminated and the company proceeded. Company A, under Capt. Elmo F. Tefanelli, reached the top of the hill twice, but was badly disorganized on the barren slopes by heavy flanking fire and concentrations of mortar and artillery, and was forced to withdraw. Company C, commanded by Capt. Samuel H. Roberts, took up the fight and, with Company B, succeeded in reaching the northeast slope of the hill at noon.

At this point Lt. Col. Keith L. Ware, 1st Battalion commander, reviewed the situation and decided that a vigorous display of personal leadership was necessary to invigorate the troops with an offensive spirit that had been dampened by the extremely heavy losses that had been sustained, the icy-cold weather, and the continuous fighting.

After a two-hour personal reconnaissance, he led a handful of men and a tank in a daring assault on the enemy positions on top of the hill, which was crowned with six enemy machine guns.

In describing Colonel Ware's action, Capt. Merlin C. Stoker, S-3 of the 1st Battalion and himself a member of the group that went with the Colonel, said: "It is my opinion that Colonel Ware's display of icy courage was an act, not only of heroism, but of necessity. It was essential that the deadlock in the Sigolsheim sector be broken and that the discouraged troops be given a new injection of the offensive spirit."

Capt. Vernon L. Rankin, commanding Company D, who directed mortar fire on the hill during the assault, said that Colonel Ware personally killed five Germans and captured about twenty others. Tank fire which the Colonel directed accounted for four of the six machine guns that comprised the hard core of the German hill position.

At the end of the assault, twenty German dead were counted, thirty captured, and about 150 crack SS troops, were put to flight.

Colonel Ware was awarded the Congressional Medal of Honor for this feat.

The 2d Battalion coordinated its fires with the attack

A German Mark IV tank destroyed in the battle at Bennwihr.

of the 1st in the final clearing of all-important Hill 351.

The 3d Battalion, having cleared all but a few houses on the south edge of Bennwihr, proposed to turn southeast out of the city but again struck a stronghold at a road junction on the edge of town. A platoon of Company K, which had been deployed in the vicinity of the junction, was attacked from two directions—from the southern edge of Hill 351 and from the basements of houses that lined the roads at the intersection. As the Germans closed in from Hill 351 the others, apparently in a prearranged plan, jumped yelling from the basement windows. The remainder of Company K, with a tank destroyer, took up the fight, but the enemy also brought in reinforcements and forced the company back. Captain Stuart then reorganized his men, launched them into a fierce counterattack, and by 1600 the company had killed a great number of Germans and retaken control of the road junction.

This terrific fight over a mere road junction was typical of the entire fight over the small area. Bennwihr and Hill 351 were still the scenes of great violence as night came on—the eve of the birth of the Prince of Peace.

The roast turkey, creamed potatoes, and other supplementary items which the Division Quartermaster had received for the Yule dinner were not to be consumed on Christmas Day by the 15th Infantry. On the contrary, the day was to be only another fierce episode which saw the Germans resisting with a fanaticism generated partly by the exaggerated version of the Rundstedt drive to the north given them by their superiors. Statements from prisoners indicated that the enemy morale, especially that of the younger and more fanatical soldiers, had been greatly raised by such statements as, "The U. S. First Army has been completely destroyed," and which led them to believe that help from northern Germany would soon be on the way.

[West of Echternach the Germans had been engaged at two points near the frontier. The columns of the enemy had been halted some thirty miles from Namur, Liège, and Sedan Gap.

On the north flank the enemy had failed to take his objectives. The shoulder of the salient above Stavelot was beaten back some six miles. In Belgium, the advance was not halted but was being well canalized. Elements of the 1st SS Divsion were cut off with the loss of fifteen tanks, 200 prisoners taken. The two regimental combat teams of the U. S. 106th Infantry Division that had been cut off during the initial phases of the counteroffensive, had made contact and were still fighting. They were being supplied from the air.

The 84th Infantry Division had just been committed south of Maffe. The 2d Armored and 75th Infantry Divisions were assembled just to the north. Some 7,000 Allied air sorties were flown December 24. Ten thousand tons of bombs were dropped. One hundred and sixteeen enemy aircraft were destroyed. Enemy movements were limited to darkness. One spectacular raid blew up a hundred vehicles loaded with gasoline.

Goebbels told the Germans that is was the worst Christmas of the war. He also told them not to worry, that the *Führer* was filled with plans and visions for the future.

On the main street of Bennwihr, a small figure was implanted in the ground in front of a ruined church. It was a reproduction of Christ crucified. The head was missing.]

Although Company K held the road junction at the dawn of Christmas Day, enemy snipers and machine gunners in the houses near the junction wrought death and injury to a number of our men in that area. At 1700, flame throwers were brought into use and several houses were fired. In a little more than an hour, over fifty Germans had surrendered and the other occu-

A solitary 3d Division soldier patrols the streets of Bennwihr.

pants were either casualties or had retreated to a safer place to spend the rest of the holiday.

Hill 351, Bennwihr, the little road junction outside Bennwihr, and a large number of prisoners constituted the holiday gift that Brig. Gen. Robert N. Young, acting division commander, received from the 15th Infantry.

Sigolsheim remained as the only uncaptured objective of the regiment's offensive, and it was attacked from the east on December 26-27.

The 1st Battalion, after clearing out some of the diehards on Hill 351, tied in with 2d Battalion on the left. Company G moved to the road east of the town and joined with Companies K and L, which had been driven back after attacking the east side of the village Christmas night.

The coordinated attack began at 0930, December 26, with Company K advancing along the north road into town from the east, Company L moving along the center road and Company G taking the south road. Air-support missions were also being flown.

The enemy put up a suicidal defense as he fell back from house to house in the streets of Sigolsheim. It was not unusual to see a German standing completely exposed in the center of the street, firing a bazooka or sometimes only a rifle, at our tanks as the armor relentlessly mowed him down or the doughboys took pot shots at him.

The fighting continued unabated all day throughout the night and into the next day. Company K was the first unit to report its zone "all clear," and when the company finished mopping up the northern part of the town at 1450, it swung north toward the convent, which like Hill 351, had been a thorn in the side of the regiment's operations ever since the attack began.

Company L found opposition stiffest in the center of town but continually kept pounding at strongpoints behind rubble, stone fences and pillboxes until the enemy finally began disintegrating and retreating from the city in small groups.

During Company I's bitter fight to clear the enemy from the houses they held in the fire-swept streets of Sigolsheim, 1st Lt. Eli Whiteley particularly distinguished himself and earned the Medal of Honor. In the midst of the savage street fighting, he was hit and badly wounded in the arm and shoulder. Despite this, he attacked alone a house on the street, fire from which was delaying the advance of the company. He killed its two defenders. Hurling smoke and fragmentation grenades, he charged a second house, killed two and captured eleven enemy. He continued to lead his platoon down the battle-crazy street, eliminating house after house. Finally he reached a building held by fanatical Nazis. ". . . Although suffering from painful wounds which had rendered his left arm useless, he advanced on this strongly defended house and, after blasting out a wall with bazooka fire, charged through a hail of bullets. Wedging his sub-machine gun under his uninjured arm, he rushed into the house through the hole torn by his rockets, killed five of the enemy and forced the remaining twelve to surrender. As he emerged to continue his fearless attack, he was hit again and critically wounded. In agony and with one eye pierced by a shell fragment, he shouted for his men to follow him to the next house. He was determined to stay in the fighting and did remain at the head of his platoon until forcibly evacuated . . ."

Company G met the same fanatical resistance in the south part of the city but cleared its section shortly before Company L.

Late that night the town was completely cleared of Germans and the 15th Infantry had captured another hundred prisoners. The regimental I and R platoon, under 1st Lt. Robert Wann, was attached to 3d Battalion for the battle, and distinguished itself in combat.

The convent fell to Company K early the following morning after an all-night siege. The monastery gave up fifty more prisoners, in addition to about 150 civilians hiding in the basement.

While the remainder of the regiment was concentrating on the Sigolsheim attack Company E, commanded by Capt. Charles Adams, cleared the enemy from the area north of the Weiss River, which was the right boundary of the regiment. This mission in itself resulted in many fire fights in which the enemy used mortars, machine guns, and Flakwagons. More than twenty Germans were killed in one of these engagements.

In this area, however, the enemy proved himself particularly obstinate. His infiltration back into the area along the Weiss became a nightly process, and it was necessary to work the vicinity over again and again, since the Weiss was easily forded.

A nasty surprise awaited our troops on Hill 216. Previously reported clear of enemy, the enemy soon proved in occupation of the crest (which was east of the road leading south from Bennwihr) in sizable strength and determined to hold.

Throughout 15th Infantry's occupation of the Bennwihr-Sigolsheim area, and 30th Infantry's subsequent control of the sector, Hill 216 with its sizable, determined forces of enemy defenders, was a salient into our lines. The western side was cleared only after a series of small attacks by 15th and 30th Infantry, but the enemy remained in control of the east side up until the full-scale Division attack which commenced January 22, when the 254th Infantry drove him from it. The crest was no-man's land.

A 3d Division soldier, Technical Sergeant Joe Hodgins is chosen man of the year by *Yank*.

In addition to capturing Bennwihr and Sigolsheim, the 15th Infantry had annihilated the *Zeiher* Battle Group and the SS Battle Group *Braun*, taking nearly 500 prisoners during the last ten days of December.

Following clearance of the 15th Infantry sector to the Fecht River on the east, the Division began regrouping, and received as an attachment the 254th Infantry of the 63d Infantry Division to assist in defending the Division front, which had been broadened by the removal of the 3d Algerian Division, the unit that occupied our right flank during the Sigolsheim-Bennwihr offensive. Purpose of attaching the 254th was to add to the Division's strength and to give the regiment combat seasoning.

On New Year's day the Division sector in the Vosges Mountains covered a frontage of approximately fifteen miles between Chatenois (west of Selestat) and Orbey, which is just south of La Poutroie.

The 15th Infantry held the longest front, its line running from Chatenois, through Bennwihr, to a point west of Alspach. The 7th Infantry's line began at Alspach and terminated at Orbey.

There were numerous adjustments to the Division boundary during the first three weeks of January, chief of which was the extension of the Division front about six miles west into high Vosges.

[These were the days of the "great scare." Even though the enemy had by now been definitely stopped in the Ardennes and the Bulge was being slowly whittled away; although the Seventh Army had temporarily halted with considerable loss the renewed offensive toward the south —the enemy still held the initiative in most areas of the front. A decision to move administrative elements out of Strasbourg, pending the necessity of withdrawing tactical troops to the Vosges, precipitated a panic in the Alsatian Capital. A large number of loyal Frenchmen were fleeing

Two 3d Division mortar men fire a routine 81mm barrage from Beblenheim on 31 December.

Over frozen and ice-covered roads the supply trucks crept over the crests of the Vosges to supply the troops in the pocket on the plain.

the city in terror of their lives should the Germans return. United States and French flags disappeared from the windows, to be replaced in some instances with the swastika. Two men from the Strasbourg staff of the *Stars and Stripes* and three members of the 3d Division's *Front Line* staff formed the only U. S. administrative establishment remaining in the city. (The CP and some troops of 42d Infantry Division, in tactical control of the area, remained in Strasbourg throughout this period.) The two newspaper groups worked together in producing a *Stars and Stripes* with a special, boxed daily column in French for the benefit of the panic-stricken population. It and the daily presence of six Americans did much to dispel many of the Alsatians' fears. The *Front Line* likewise continued to make its regular weekly appearance.]

Division Order of Battle personnel had some difficulty in piecing together some of the rag, tag and bobtail which opposed the Division on its long front. Upon moving into the sector, we inherited from the 36th Division the following Battle Groups (each of about

Brigadier General Robert N. Young, Acting Division Commander, briefs General DeGaulle on the situation in the Colmar Pocket in the War Room at Ribeauville.

battalion size): *Ayrer, Bermann, Backe, Braun,* SS *Dietrichs, Eberle, Fischer, Fuhrguth, Geiser, Herbrechtsmeier, Hock, Huth, Krebs, Landeberger, Lang, Probst, Reimers, Remmes, Schaefer, Scheck, Schweitzer, Wallner, Wasser, Zeiher,* and *Winter*.

As the Division took its own prisoners, however, these elements shook down and sorted themselves generally into members of regular divisions, principal of which were the 198th Infantry Division, 708th *Volksgrenadier* Division, 16th and 189th Infantry Divisions. Toward the end of December two battalions of the 40th *Panzer Grenadier* Replacement Training Battalion made their appearance. Also known to be on the bridgehead, and against some of whom the 3d Infantry Division later fought were: 269th VG Division, 159th VG Division and 338th Infantry Division.

The 254th Infantry, attached to the 3d, was assigned a defensive sector during the adjustments and the 290th Engineer Combat Battalion, a unit with no previous battle experience, was attached for use as infantry. A French parachute battalion was also attached.

Winter weather was present with all its mountain fury with the coming of January and many frostbite cases were added to the trenchfoot casualties brought by cool, rainy days during the previous three months.

Generally speaking, the situation in the first three weeks was characterized by defensive actions and patrolling on both sides, with the east slopes of Hill 216 occupying the most important role.

It was a snowy and cold New Year's Eve and the 10th Engineer Battalion was busy all night keeping roads passable. Company A, commanded by Capt. Albert H. Cook, spread cinders and sand on the road from Kaysersberg; Company B, under Capt. Daniel A. Raymond, de-iced and drained the Riquewihr-Kientzheim road while Company C, commanded by 1st Lt. Robert L. Bangert, continued the never-ending task of erecting triple-concertina wire around and in front of our positions.

Late that night Company E of the 30th Infantry, commanded by 1st Lt. Douglas W. Chambers, engaged a strong enemy patrol in a small arms fight in the woods north of the Weiss River and another German patrol overran the outposts of Company F, commanded by 1st Lt. Richard N. Hagelin. These outposts, located south of Hill 216, were reestablished before daylight, however.

At about midnight of January 2, Companies E and F of the 15th Infantry attacked south along the eastern slopes of Hill 216, intent on clearing the hill and the area south to the Weiss River. The 30th Infantry assisted the attack by sending out three strong combat patrols with artillery support.

Company E of the 15th met heavy resistance at a road curve northeast of the hill and suffered heavy casualties when the enemy set up a searing defense with machine guns, *Panzerfaust,* small arms, mortars, and hand grenades. The attack, originally scheduled as a strong raid supported by tanks, quickly turned into a bloody full-scale pitched engagement. Two of the supporting tanks were almost immediately destroyed by either *Panzerfaust* or antitank fire as they crossed the rise of

Armored bulldozers became snow plows in the Colmar Pocket.

the next several days. Our own troops, without camouflage clothing, improvised by using mattress covers.

On January 4 the Division sector was extended on the right to include Le Rudlin and abandoned on the left to exclude Zellenberg and Ostheim. The 15th Infantry, which had occupied the extreme left of the Division front, moved to the extreme right, putting our troops deeper into the heights of the Vosges.

A strong German counterattack against the 1st French Motorized Infantry Division, on the Division's left flank, was launched January 7 and resulted in the extension of the 3d Division's zone farther north, and the 254th Infantry was regrouped to take over the newly acquired sector in the vicinity of Ribeauville.

Assisted by diversionary fire by the 7th Infantry's field artillery, chemical, tank, tank-destroyer, and antiaircraft attachments, the 30th Infantry staged two attacks on January 8, the purpose being to divert the

3d Division Artillery Liaison pilots flew missions from snow covered strips.

the crest, and the company commander, Capt. Charles E. Adams, went forward to supervise his men personally. While he was moving forward he stepped into a hole in which there was an enemy soldier, who immediately shot and killed him. The company was disorganized and forced to fall back.

Company F, commanded by Capt. Hugh H. Bruner, proceeded well down the forward slopes of the hill but was hit by a strong enemy counterattack early in the morning. A heavy fire fight ensued but Company F held its ground. A short time later, the Germans launched another counterattack supported by tanks and Captain Bruner's men fell back to the road leading to Bennwihr. The two companies took sixteen prisoners in the attack. The enemy's reluctance to abandon any of the terrain under his control was proving costly to both forces and the pocket of resistance on Hill 216 developed into a bloody battlefield.

Enemy patrols, clad in white garments as camouflage in the snow, were little less aggressive than our own, and continuous clashes between them took place during

A Tabor of Goums move along the road toward their position.

Staff Sergeant Charles E. Steiner, Sergeant Nicholas A. Lynch and Pfc John H. Stokes read "The Front Line" near the front line in the Colmar Pocket.

enemy's attention from the fact that an Allied division was being replaced in another sector of the perimeter surrounding the enemy Colmar bridgehead.

Company A, commanded by 1st Lt. Willard C. Johnson, moved through Company C at 1430, under cover of smoke from 4.2 chemical mortars and 81mm mortars, and reached the crest of Hill 216 after overcoming resistance from dug-in infantry using small arms and machine guns. After killing and capturing a number of Germans, Company A was relieved in its new positions by Company C, commanded by 1st Lt. Charles P. Murray, Jr.

Simultaneously Company I, under 1st Lt. Darwyn E. Walker, attacked south from Ammerschwihr toward Hill 616, which lies just west of Katzenthal. Company C of the 756th Tank Battalion, commanded by Capt. John W. Heard, was in close support of the attackers.

After a difficult 45-minute climb through the heavy snow, the company came under enemy fire from German positions halfway up the hill and about eighty-five yards to the front. A Flakwagon on a hill 500 yards southwest of Hill 616 poured extremely accurate fire on Lieutenant Walker's men and they were forced back to cover in a clump of trees. A second attack ended in the same manner and the company swung around the hill out of range of the Flakwagon and attacked for the third time.

It was here that S/Sgt. Russell E. Dunham, acting platoon sergeant of the 3d platoon and commonly known to his buddies as "The Arsenal," performed the actions that earned him the Congressional Medal of Honor.

Dunham carried a dozen hand grenades that hung from his suspenders, from the buttonholes in his clothes and from his belt. And he had eleven full magazines of carbine ammunition, four in pouches, seven more in his pockets.

The enemy machine guns had a clear, snow-covered field of fire from solidly-built emplacements covered with logs hidden by recent heavy snows. Two-man foxholes protected the machine-gun position from all sides.

Dunham's platoon moved forward, with the sergeant far out in front, crawling from small bush to tree stump into the very face of the German fire. A machine gun on the left of his platoon front received first attention and Dunham edged his way toward it until he reached a point about ten yards away. Jumping to his

Staff Sergeant Herman Nevers and his non-functioning Beretta pistol with which he escaped from the enemy.

feet, he charged the position, throwing hand grenades, firing his carbine from the hip and yelling as he went. A second machine gun on the right fired a full clip at him and Dunham fell, a 10-inch gash ripped across his back.

The doughty sergeant rolled fifteen feet down the hill, arose, and charged again as his mattress-cover uniform turned red with blood. An enemy egg grenade fell at his feet, was quickly kicked aside and exploded in the snow several yards away. Dunham continued to fire, killed the machine gunner and his assistant, and yanked a third German from the emplacement when his carbine was empty.

Refusing evacuation by the medics, Dunham led the advance on the second machine gun some seventy-five yards up the hill. Again he was the lone figure out in front, leaving a crimson trail in the snow as he crept toward the blazing gun. Rifle fire and rifle grenades raked his path. Dunham got within throwing range and tossed a grenade that bounced off a tree a little to the right of the machine gun emplacement. His next heave was a bull's eye which killed the entire gun crew.

Two Germans raised their heads from a nearby foxhole to take a bead on Dunham. The sergeant promptly killed one and wounded the other, winging a third who tried to escape.

The mattress cover was rosy as Sergeant Dunham briefed his platoon for the attack on a third machine gun hidden about a hundred yards up on the side of the hill. Again he was the platoon's "advance element" as he sneaked to the kill.

This time he was favored with a deserving stroke of luck when a German fired point blank at him and missed after Dunham had just tossed a grenade that neutralized the gun. The poor-shooting rifleman fell dead from a Dunham bullet. Another shouted *"Kamerad"* and gave up.

Dunham continued his maniacal attack on enemy foxholes, killed one more German, shot five others as they attempted to flee, and took another prisoner.

Dunham's total was: three enemy machine guns destroyed, nine dead Germans, seven wounded, and two prisoners. He had fired 175 rounds of ammunition and tossed eleven of his twelve hand grenades.

Praise was later heaped upon Dunham by Lieutenant Walker, his company commander, by 2d Lt. James M. Beck, Company I platoon leader, and by 2d Lt. Glenn A. Black who had been Dunham's first sergeant on the day of the attack, prior to receiving a battlefield promotion.

The next few days featured the normal fire fights that come with vigorous patrolling and in addition some of the bitterest give-and-take small engagements the Division ever had encountered. Frequent efforts were made by the enemy to infiltrate our positions to obtain information concerning the shifts that were being made in the front lines of the 3d Division.

The nights were moonless and bitterly cold; the days chilly and misty and both forces were using houses scattered throughout the area in "no-man's land" as outposts. The Division Operations Report rarely failed to record an account of an attack on one or more of them, either by our patrols or by the enemy.

Preceded by an artillery and mortar barrage, a strong enemy patrol staged a midnight raid January 9 on a platoon CP near La Baroche and took one officer and seven men, retiring under cover of artillery fire.

A patrol leader of Company L, 7th Infantry, S/Sgt. Herman F. Nevers, reported the same night that he had been seized and taken to a house in the La Baroche vicinity and effected an escape while he was being questioned, when he drew a small non-functioning pistol which he had concealed in one of his boots. He held the surprised Germans at bay and backed out of the building into the darkness.

A 254th Infantry outpost was also attacked that night by a patrol of superior force and had to withdraw from its position until the next morning.

An enemy propaganda truck, interspersing subversive words with popular American "hillbilly" music, turned its loud speakers toward the 7th Infantry sector while the men were sweating "chow" on the night of January 10. Our artillery answered with well-placed fire that silenced the music.

Our artillery also stopped a sizable attack by an infiltrating group that reached a point west of Ammerschwihr on January 15. A similar attack on an outpost near Ostheim was staged the next morning and the Germans took thirteen prisoners. This latter attack, however, was overshadowed by a highly successful raid conducted the same morning by the 3d Battalion of the 7th Infantry, commanded by Lt. Col. Lloyd B. Ramsey.

Company L, commanded by Capt. Phillip T. Perry, crossed its line of departure at 0630 and immediately encountered heavy enemy mortar and small-arms fire near La Baroche, and a concentration of eight German machine guns north of this point held up the company's advance.

A house which contained about thirty enemy was blown up when one of Captain Perry's men placed a satchel charge in it. Three enemy machine guns also were silenced before the raiders withdrew.

Companies I and K, under Capts. Edward J. Brink and Francis J. Kret, respectively, attacked south at a point east of Company L's effort. Company I headed

3d Infantry Division soldiers attack the enemy on the snow-covered plain of Alsace.

toward the little village of Braderhau, neutralized a machine gun, and captured a few prisoners en route. A heavy fire fight ensued when a strong enemy force was encountered just north of Braderhau. Four more German machine guns were destroyed in this battle.

Company K also silenced four enemy machine guns, killed a large number of Germans, and forced the foe to desert his positions in the area.

The regimental Battle Patrol assisted the 3d Battalion's raid with a diversionary attack on Hill 806, near La Rochette. This raid, which was started and ended before daylight, brought several casualties to the Patrol when it came under heavy artillery fire. The Patrol closed with the Germans, however, and inflicted severe losses on them before withdrawing just prior to dawn.

The raiding companies all withdrew early in the morning. All had accomplished their mission of locating enemy strongholds and measuring their strength.

The tacit understanding which had existed among officers and men of the Division that the defensive was not our style, well though the 3d had performed that role (Cf. Anzio—February) when assigned to it, was sometimes expressed by a shrug, a grimace, and the unanswerable question, "How long before . . . ?" To an outsider these cryptic signs would have meant nothing. To veterans indoctrinated in the 3d Infantry Division this restlessness when confronted with stalemate spoke volumes, but translated might be stated very simply. "How long before we start another attack? How long before they shove us in to knock out this damn pocket?"

By the same token, the restlessness could not be interpreted as eagerness. Such an assumption would have been foolish. The cold, bone-chilling winds; the quality and spirit of the German defenders as evidenced during the grim fights for Kaysersberg, Sigolsheim and Bennwihr, and the day-and-night bitterly-fought patrol clashes; the trenchfoot and the frostbite; all precluded any tendency toward individual desire to tangle again full-scale with the enemy. But the restlessness persisted. "We'll have to be at it soon." The feeling pervaded every platoon and squad.

"As long as there's a war and as long as there's a 3d Division, the 3d Division will be in that war." Variations on this same theme were repeated many times by nearly every wearer of the blue-and-white patch. The knowledge was omnipresent. The thought was conveyed in various shades of tone—cynically, bitterly, disgustedly . . . or, confidently, resignedly, cockily . . . or in any combination. But in nearly every case there was a matter-of-fact acceptance of the fact that soon we would return to the offensive. Coupled with this was the feeling of surety, born of success in battle, that the 3d would accomplish successfully any task given it. And that is the feeling that wins battles.

Withdrawal from the lines in preparation for an offensive began with the 7th Infantry during the night of January 17-18. The 3d Battalion, 254th Infantry, moved from Ribeauville to the vicinity of Kaysersberg and during the hours of darkness relieved the 1st Battalion, 7th, on positions, to become attached to the 7th Infantry. This relief was completed by 0200, and 1st Battalion, 7th, moved into Alspach. The 290th Combat Engineer Battalion moved from St. Croix to the vicinity of Hachimette and relieved 2d Battalion and Antitank Company, 7th Infantry, likewise coming under the command of 7th Infantry. By 0450 this relief was complete and the 2d Battalion, with AT Company, assembled in La Poutroie. The battalion moved to Kaysersberg by motor during the morning.

The 28th Infantry Division, after participating in the initial stages of the Ardennes counteroffensive and suffering great losses, had been relieved from attachment to Twenty-first Army Group and sent south to join Sixth Army Group, which in turn assigned the division to assist, in a minor role, in the attack against the north flank of the Colmar Pocket. As the 3d shifted and regrouped in preparation for withdrawing the bulk of its striking force to the east, in the general vicinity of Guemar, elements of the 28th slipped into position on the right of the 254th Infantry, which held down the 3d's right flank.

There was no time to lose in preparing for the coming operation. On the same day that relief of the 3d was completed by the 28th, January 20, French I Corps launched its drive against the south side of the Pocket from long-held positions immediately to the north of Mulhouse. We had learned at Anzio of the invaluable need for coordination between the Cassino and beachhead forces, and if the German defenders of the Colmar Pocket were to be kept from shifting their strength from one dangerous sector to another, repelling individual attacks in sequence, our attack must get away on time. The date was already set—January 22.

Individual units had begun conducting as much training as was practical under the circumstances, upon their separate reliefs from the line. All armor and all combat vehicles were painted white. Mattress covers, sheets, pillowcases, everything available in the way of white cloth—was set upon and redesigned into "spook suits" for camouflage in the snow. The infantry regiments also undertook limited training programs in small-unit problems, speed marches, weapons training, field firing, night problems, river crossing technique, and use of the German *Panzerfaust*.

The 10th Engineer Battalion assembled bridging materials for the operation.

The narrow zone which we faced was characterized by a front line which followed for the greater part, a river—the Fecht. This stream splits the town of Ostheim and forms the southeast boundary of Guemar. The primary move, therefore, was a crossing of its flooded, icy waters. Although the Division's "target" was not announced to any but important commanders until the latest possible date in the interests of security, regimental and smaller-unit intelligence officers had long concentrated on gathering information relative to the width, depth, steepness of banks, and conditions and swiftness of water, of all streams which lay along a possible future zone of advance. The Fecht had been thoroughly "cased" in preparation for the unnamed eventuality, as had the Weiss. Information was also sought from left-flank French elements as to the same conditions prevailing with respect to the Ill River. Possible marshy areas had also come under the same critical scrutiny: "Is it frozen? How deep is the water? Is it possible to go around it without going too far out of the way?"

In addition to the all-important terrain study, of course, there was the never-ending quest for enemy dispositions and order of battle. The best information available prior to the attack placed the 748th *VG* Regiment of the 708th *VG* Division, and a battalion of the 760th *VG* Regiment, from the same division, to our front. An additional battalion of the 760th and elements of the 728th *VG* Regiment, same division, were suspected but lacked definite confirmation.

The enemy's counteroffensive possibilities were well summed up in the January 17 Division G-2 Report: "While the new Russian offensive in Poland may seem to be a long way from our front-line infantry platoon positions, it is bound to have an immediate and profound effect on the enemy capabilities in the Alsace pocket.

"This effect stems directly from the priorities on reinforcements (both men and materiel) which will have to be reshuffled among the various fronts. Heretofore top priority has gone to the Belgium front, with the Upper Rhine not far behind. Now, however, Poland is bound to absorb everything the Germans can throw into it, at least until the Russian drives are well stopped. The result should be a decline in enemy ability to send important reinforcements, especially for offensive purposes, into the Colmar Bridgehead. *Under pressure, the enemy will always be able to find scratch units to try to keep us from reaching important objectives,* but fresh divisions are a luxury he can hardly afford in a sector like this when he needs them for fire-fighting purposes in other parts of his household . . ."

Substantially, that was the picture of the enemy's *offensive* capabilities. His defensive capabilities, however, were to prove an entirely different story. For, in telling the story of the Colmar Pocket, it must be emphasized that terrain and weather were the equal of the worst any unit ever contended with anywhere. From Guemar to Neuf-Brisach there was hardly a depression in the ground worthy of the name, with the exception of a few stream beds (the Fecht, the Ill, the Colmar, and Rhone-Rhine Canals), the basements of houses in the captured towns and old Maginot Line emplacements—from all of which the enemy had to be driven—and finally a few bomb and shell holes, the impressions of which were much less deep than could normally be expected, due to the frozen solidity of the ground.

The mercury in thermometers constantly stood at minus 10 degrees C. (14° F) which was about the highest point reached during the day. In the late afternoon, early morning, and during each night the temperature dropped lower and stayed there. This may not seem extremely cold weather to inhabitants of the northern and eastern parts of the United States, but it must be remembered that men were fighting, attempting to sleep, fording streams—and dying—in constant exposure to these temperatures. To experience a few seconds' exposure of nose and ears to the icy gusts of wind which constantly swept down from the high Vosges was almost unbearable.

Over-all plan of the Division attack was as follows: To attack on D-day, H-hour, force crossings of the Fecht and Ill Rivers in the Guemar-Ostheim area; to pivot to the south, force crossings over the Colmar Canal in the Wickerschwihr area, block to the southwest in the area southwest of Houssen, and *isolate* Colmar on the east. (It was known that the capture of Colmar was assured once it became isolated from the main road feeding it with supplies and reinforcements via the two bridges over the Rhine near Neuf-Brisach.)

Upon completion of this action, the Division was to group the bulk of its infantry in the Holtzwihr-Riedwihr area, and the bulk of its attached Armored Combat Command in the Horbourg-Bischwihr-Andolsheim area, prepared to:

One: Capture Colmar and block the Fecht Valley immediately west of Turckheim, or

Two: Assist 5 DB (5th French Armored Division) in the capture of Neuf-Brisach.

Separate missions of the regiments were:

30th Infantry (Attached: Company C, 756 Tank Battalion; Company C, 601st Tank Destroyer Battalion; Company B, 99th Chemical Battalion; Reconnaissance Company, 601st Tank Destroyer Battalion; 3d Reconnaissance Troop and Division Battle Patrol; 3d platoon, Company D, 756th Tank Battalion; three sections, 441st AAA AW Battalion (SP)):

To force a crossing of the Fecht River in its zone, advance with all possible speed to clear the east-west road in its zone through Colmar Forest (*Foret Communale de Colmar*), and seize objectives indicated on the Ill River.

To force a crossing of the Ill River at the earliest possible moment and continue the advance to seize objectives indicated (along a line running east from the Ill River south of Maison Rouge bridge).

To extend south to another phase line, blocking to the east.

On Division order, to be prepared to regroup in the Horbourg-Bennwihr area prepared to execute Maneuver 1 and capture Colmar from the east, or to pass to Division reserve.

In addition, 30th Infantry was to protect its own left throughout the advance south along the east side of the Ill; to protect the Division left; to maintain contact with 1 DMI and 5 DB on the left flank, and to reinforce its supporting engineers with one rifle company from the regiment's reserve battalion for the purpose of carrying an infantry footbridge from the Fecht River to the Ill.

7th Infantry (Attached: Company A, 756th Tank Battalion; Company A, 601st Tank Destroyer Battalion; Company C, 99th Chemical Mortar Battalion (—one platoon); Company D, 756th Tank Battalion (—two platoons); and three sections of the 441st AAA):

To force a crossing of the Fecht in its zone; advance with all possible speed to seize objectives in a line to the west of 30th Infantry's first phase line across the Ill.

To clear the east-west road in its zone through the Colmar Forest and the road running east from Ostheim in its zone.

To extend its line further south, seizing and holding the objectives taken within the boundary defined.

To push strong combat patrols to the southwest in the direction of Ingersheim and to the south in the direction of Colmar.

On Division order to assemble on last line gained, and to be prepared:

To attack toward Neuf-Brisach and objectives in that vicinity.

To execute Maneuver 1 and capture Colmar, or

To execute Maneuver 2; isolate Colmar on the south, capture Wintzenheim and Turckheim, and block to the southwest as indicated.

254th Infantry (Attached: one platoon, Company B, 756th; one platoon, Company B 601st; one platoon, Company A, 99th Chemical; two sections, 441st AAA Battalion):

Attack through 28th Infantry Division north of Hill 216 at daylight of D + 1, isolate and capture Hill 216, seize Line A-B (extension of 30th and 7th first phase line, to the west), in zone, and seize and hold bridge over the Fecht River immediately west of its junction with the Weiss River.

Push strong combat patrols to the south on Ingersheim.

On Division order following the forcing of the Fecht River, assemble 2d Battalion in the Beblenheim area under regimental control.

On Division order, undergo relief of positions on line A-B in zone, by elements of 28th Infantry Division.

On Division order following relief of positions on line A-B, relieve elements of 7th Infantry on line C-D (second phase line) between the Fecht and Ill rivers, prevent enemy movement northeast of this line, and patrol vigorously to the south on Colmar and to the southwest in Ingersheim.

Protect Division right.

Maintain contact with 28th Infantry Division on right.

Coordinate directly with commanding officer of regiment on right in reference to passage and assistance.

15th Infantry was assigned the mission of crossing the Fecht immediately behind 30th Infantry to assemble in Division reserve, or

On Division order from present assembly area or the Colmar Forest, be prepared to assume the mission of either the 7th or 30th Infantry Regiments.

The remainder of the order pertaining to 15th Infantry specified several alternatives, duplicating those found in orders for the 7th and 30th, providing the 15th took over for either of them.

French II Corps Artillery was to support the 3d Infantry Division attack by reinforcing direct-support fires, and by supplementing interdiction, counterbattery, and harassing fires of the Division Artillery.

In addition a powerful air program was to be conducted in support of the Division attack in conjunction with an over-all air program in the entire First French Army zone.

CC4 of the French 5th Armored Division (5 DB) was attached to 3d Infantry Division for the attack.

Attacking on our left at daylight of D-plus-1 was 1st *Division Motorisé Infanterie*.

The attack was scheduled to begin three hours after darkness on January 22, the first anniversary of the landing of the Division below Nettuno. During the morning of January 22 units began moving to the forward assembly areas, and footbridges and heavy bridging material were moved to proposed crossing sites at Guemar and Ostheim during the night. Company A, 10th Engineers, under the command of 1st Lt. Robert K. Fleet, hid a preconstructed 84-foot span in a cemetery north of Guemar.

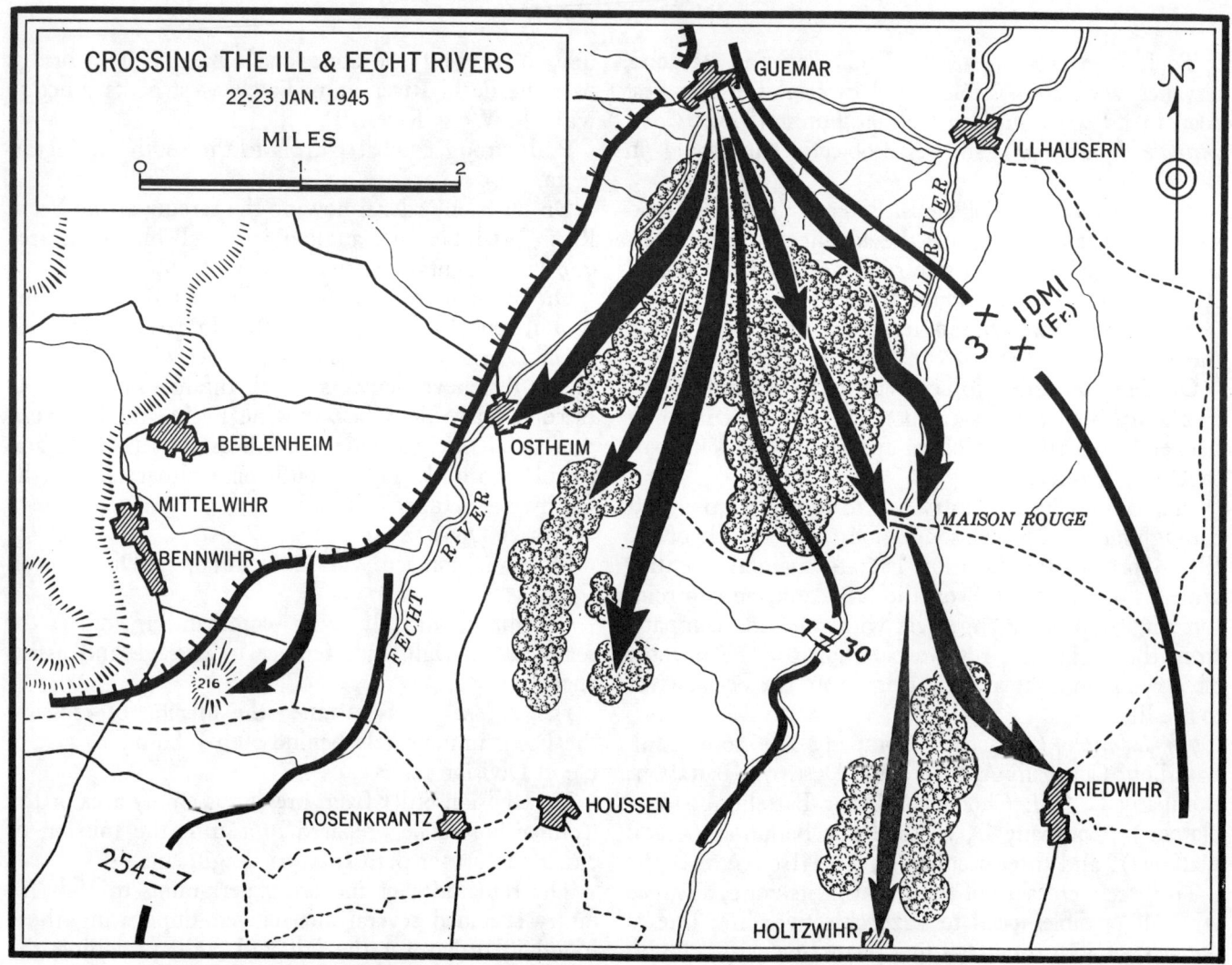

The 7th and 30th Infantry Regiments, commanded by Lt. Col. John A. Heintges and Col. Lionel C. McGarr, respectively, began their crossing of the Fecht River by stealth at Guemar at 2100, on a front measuring less than 1000 yards in width. It was a repetition of the Meurthe stunt, and it worked. In the 7th zone two platoons crossed just prior to H-Hour and seized bridgeheads. Artillery fell on both bridges of the 7th, and enemy heavy mortar fire fell on 1st Battalion, 30th Infantry, but enemy infantry resistance was negligible.

The 3d Battalion, 7th Infantry, commanded by Lt. Col. Lloyd B. Ramsey, after crossing the river swung southeast and encountered enemy small-arms and machine-gun fire in the *Bois Communale de Guemar*. After overcoming this resistance the battalion, with Company I on the right and Company L on the left, moved swiftly across the east-west road which runs along the northern edge of the *Foret Communale de Colmar*.

Clearing the woods as they advanced, Colonel Ramsey's men continued past Ostheim and to a small wooded area, Brunnwald, where they beat off an enemy counterattack consisting of tanks and infantry which came from the east. Our artillery and mortar fire played an important part in stopping the German counterthrust while elements of Lt. Col. Glenn F. Rogers' 756th Tank Battalion supported the battalion all along the route of advance. Company A, under Capt. Orlando A. Richardson, Jr., and elements of Company D, commanded by Capt. Robert F. Kramer, were attached to the 7th Infantry throughout.

Maj. Kenneth W. Wallace's 1st Battalion turned directly south after crossing the river and suffered some casualties as the troops moved through a wooded area filled with wire obstacles and mines. The battalion entered Ostheim from the north at 0400 and engaged the Germans in a heavy small-arms and machine-gun battle that lasted for five hours.

The enemy continued to resist fiercely in the southern part of the town, where every window was a potential sniper's nest. By 1730, however, the last vestige of resistance had ended and the battalion was in full possession of the city.

The Maison Rouge Bridge and the camouflaged tank which went crashing through it when it attempted to cross the Ill River.

The 2d Battalion, which had followed in the wake of the assault battalions, moved rapidly south to the Bois dit de Rothleible after engaging in a hot fire fight en route.

The 30th Infantry crossed the Fecht with the 1st Battalion, under the command of Lt. Col. Mackenzie E. Porter, on the left and 3d Battalion, commanded by Maj. Robert B. Pridgen, on the right.

Meeting little opposition, 1st Battalion continued through the *Foret Communale de Colmar* to the east and had elements across the Ill River by daybreak. By 0900 the entire battalion had crossed the Ill and moved south along the east bank of the stream, heading for the Maison Rouge bridge, at the southeast corner of the forest.

The 3d Battalion, 30th, cut southeast through the forest, and encountered a *schu*-minefield and two enemy strongpoints during its advance. A brisk fire fight was staged at Niederwald, a crossroad settlement in the *Foret Communale,* but the doughboys soon eliminated this obstacle.

Closing in on the Maison Rouge bridge, Major Pridgen's battalion had it, intact, by 1155.

That little wooden bridge figured greatly in the 30th Infantry's plans, and around it revolved one of the most fateful moments of the regiment or Division in the entire war.

Foreseeing the possibility of capturing the bridge, Division engineers had ordered reinforcing treadway to be delivered as soon as possible to the bridge site once it was captured in order to get armor across in the minimum possible time. Traffic along the roads to the rear was heavy. The engineers, having already allocated most of the available treadway to other bridge projects, sent forward all the remaining treadway to the Maison Rouge site. When they had a chance to look the bridge over and measure it, the amount was just fifteen feet short.

Traffic over the roads to the rear was heavy. The time required to obtain an extra fifteen feet might be prohibitive. After a certain number of tactical vehicles of the 30th had passed over the bridge, it was closed to traffic and the treadway was laid on either side. A 15-foot gap remained in the center.

The order had been given: "Get armor across the Ill with all possible speed." The engineer officer in charge was dubious, but did not want to delay the armor. One tank started across. The bridge shook a bit, but that was nothing unusual. The driver stopped. Engineers, watching tensely, decided the bridge was stable. They waved the tank on. The full weight of the tank passed on to the nonreinforced section of the bridge. There was a rending crash and the bridge collapsed to the level of the river, the tank staying just above water. The crew clambered out. A few minutes passed. A truck, bearing an amount of treadway sufficient to have bridged the gap arrived on the scene.

While the 7th and 30th Infantry regiments were attacking their objectives, the 254th Infantry assaulted Hill 216 at daylight. This long-time salient in our lines proved as difficult as ever, with one important difference. It was no longer the sole point of attack, but only one of many. By noon the 254th had routed the Germans from well dug-in positions on the eastern slopes, which were protected by *schu*-mines and booby-traps, plus the fire of machine guns, small arms, and *Panzerfaust*. This clearing of the enemy from the far side of Hill 216 eliminated a strongpoint that jeopardized the flank of our attacking units and deprived the Germans of an extraordinary observation post.

Following the capture of Hill 216, 254th Infantry continued its mission of clearing the area south to the Weiss River, and of capturing a bridge across the Fecht River, in conjunction with joining the 7th Infantry in that area, once the enemy had been cleared from the

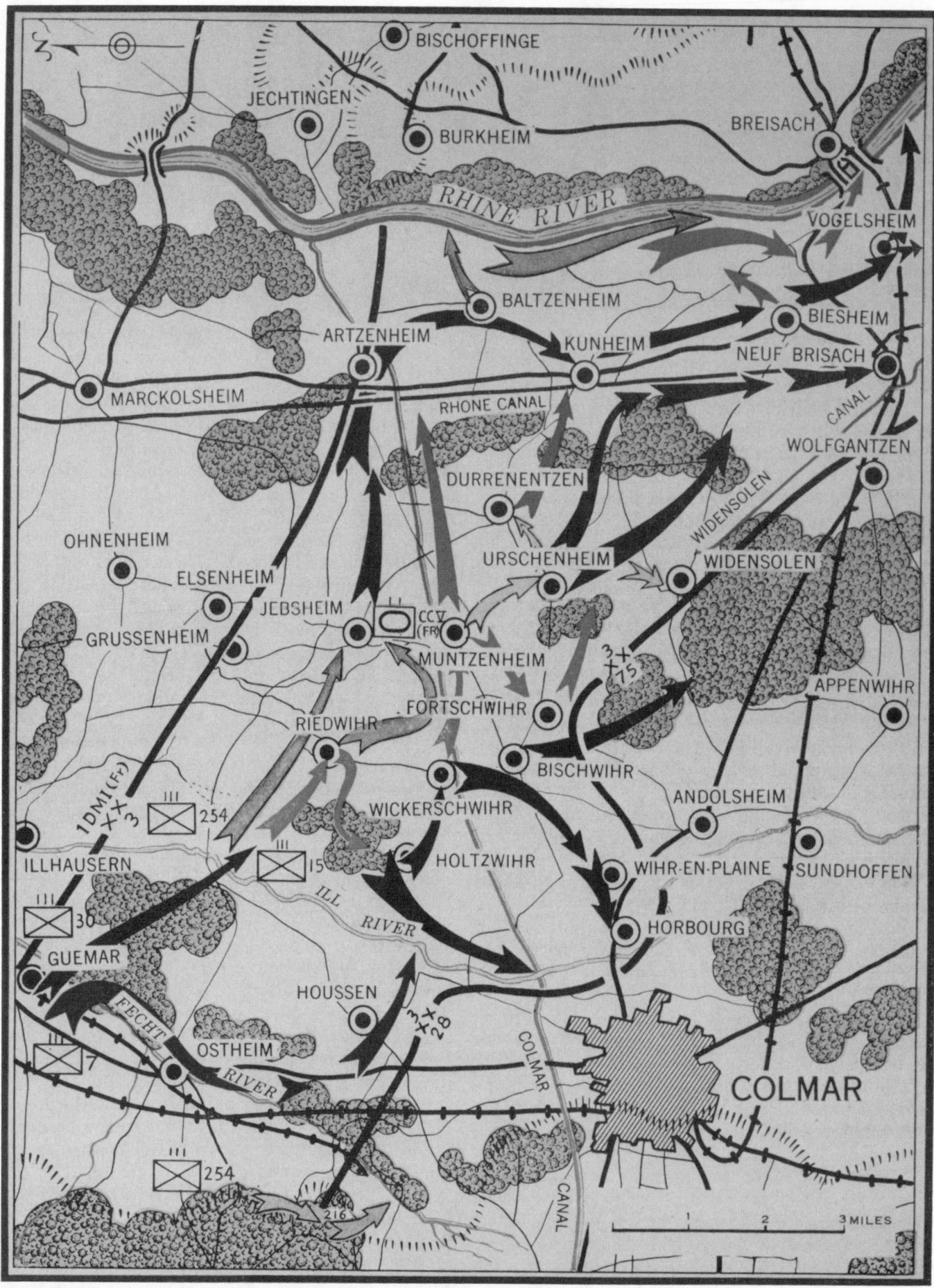

lower Fecht stream bank near its juncture with the Weiss.

Heavy fighting here carried into the following day. The 1st Battalion, leading the attack, became stalled and the 3d Battalion was committed around its right flank. Troops of the 254th were forced virtually to ferret the Germans out of their dug-in positions in a yard-by-yard advance that was bitterly contested all the way.

The Germans had nearly recovered from the initial shock of the surprise attack. The enemy was marshalling every tank and automatic weapon at his command to stem the tide of our advance. The battle of armor and infantry that was waged in and around the wooded areas in the vicinity of Houssen, Riedwihr, Holtzwihr, and Wickerschwihr will be remembered as one of the most bitterly fought engagements, and without doubt one of the most important, that the 3d Division ever encountered.

During the afternoon of the 23rd, 30th Infantry forward elements reached the outskirts of Riedwihr and Holtzwihr and held the clump of woods known as Bois de Riedwihr.

Companies I and K had moved into the northern edge of Holtzwihr. Position of the 1st and 3d Battalions at this time was like a finger sticking deep into enemy territory. Opposition had been so light up to this point that the 30th had lanced ahead and was completely exposed on the left flank, resistance against the French having prevented them from advancing rapidly, and ahead of 7th Infantry on the right, which was also encountering very tenacious resistance.

At 1650 the first blow struck. Companies I and K of the 30th under 1st Lts. Darwyn E. Walker and Ross H. Calvert, respectively, without armor, advanced into Holtzwihr. Ten enemy tanks and TDs accompanied by at least a hundred foot troops, moved into and beyond Holtzwihr from the southeast. The tanks broke up into groups of two's and three's and sliced the 30th's positions into several pockets. Tank machine-gun fire whipped along the snow-covered ground in murderous grazing fire and the tanks and tank destroyers fired as they came.

The 3d Battalion had just completed a rapid move and, even had the men had time to dig in they would have been completely frustrated. The ground was frozen solid. It would have taken TNT charges to blow holes in it. And—it was perfectly flat. There was not a vestige of cover as 3d Battalion, struck from three sides and without even one tank or tank destroyer to shoot at the oncoming assortment of power, vainly tried to repel the counterattack. Also important was the fact that artillery FOs with the 30th had not yet established radio communication.

The result was a foregone conclusion. 3d Battalion, badly disorganized, was forced to make its way back—back toward the Ill and the protection afforded by its banks.

At 1720, as the 1st Battalion was about to reach Riedwihr, the blow fell on it as it had on the 3d. The enemy hit with all he had. Men sought in vain for cover. Bands of grazing machine-gun fire criss-crossed in vicious, cracking streams. As in the case of 3d Battalion, 1st Battalion had nowhere to go but to the rear—if possible—nothing with which to combat the thick-sided enemy tanks and the *Jagdpanzer* tank destroyers, and above all no holes from which to fight.

During the withdrawals, handfuls of brave men in each company braved almost certain death or capture to stick it out on the hopeless positions. Despite open flanks on the right and left, small, bitter and last-ditch actions were fought by isolated groups, such as those led by 1st Lts. Darwyn E. Walker and Ross H. Calvert, who were last seen on that day entering a patch of woods from which two enemy tanks shortly thereafter emerged. In the Orchbach stream bed, east of the Ill by several hundred yards, a group of 30th Infantry men was still in position the next day when a

Pfc Steven R. Lakos, 3d Infantry Division takes a look at the winter equipment of a dead enemy.

Colonel John A. Heintges, commanding officer, 7th Infantry Regiment.

counterattack was launched and the ground was regained!

At the Maison Rouge bridge site, bystanders gazed ruefully at a Sherman tank sitting in the center of the Ill River, icy waves lapping at the base of its turret.

The 2d Battalion, 30th, under Maj. James L. Osgard, had crossed the Ill at the southeast corner of the Colmar Forest, but had hardly had time to get reorganized before it, too, was counterattacked by enemy tanks and infantry and was forced back across the river, where it set up temporary positions in the Colmar woods. Approximately 350 men, most of whom were captured, were lost by the 30th in this counterattack. However, during the withdrawal machine-gun sections from H and D Companies and small groups of infantrymen, chiefly from Companies A, B, C and E held on the east side of the Ill and covered the remainder of the battalion.

As night drew on the enemy was completely in possession of the east bank of the Ill, with this important exception. Lt. Colonel MacKenzie Porter and Capt. William F. Stucky organized a group and stuck it out on the east side, north of Maison Rouge. It was the 3d Infantry Division's sole bridgehead during that dark night of January 23-24.

The 30th Infantry was in a bad way. A hurry-up call went out for pyramidal tents, stoves, blankets, clothes, and hot coffee and food. Regimental supply personnel scoured their stocks and brought these items forward. Division G-4 also got an urgent call: "Send us dry clothes, rifles, and machine guns." A good proportion of the entire regiment was nearly frozen from its terrible exposure to the Ill River and the icy blasts of wind which greeted the men as they clambered from the water.

Straggler posts were set up along all possible routes to the rear, to direct the men back into the line. Although terribly chilled, the offensive spirit was still present in many of them. When collected by the officers they moved up into defensive positions west of the Ill supported by their massed armor and covered by their riflemen and machine guns east of the river. The attitude of some of the men was expressed by several who were wringing out their wet clothes, their weapons at their sides: "Yes, sir, we can hold! No goddamn kraut is going to kick the hell out of us and get by with it! We'll be here in the morning."

The tenure of 7th Infantry troops in Ostheim was even threatened for a time when the enemy organized for a strong counterattack from Houssen but our artillery massed heavy concentrations on the enemy force and broke up the attack at its inception.

The 15th Infantry was also very busy during the night of January 23-24. The attack must be pushed at all costs. It was obvious that 30th Infantry would need some time in which to reorganize. The 3d Battalion, 15th Infantry, was chosen to cross the Ill first, to seize a bridgehead around Maison Rouge to enable the engineers to get the all-important bridge in. Enemy tanks had ranged to within as close as a quarter-mile, firing direct fire on the bridge site.

The 3d Battalion jumped off at 0300, with Company I on the left and Company K on the right. The attack made good progress east of the Ill until Company I was counterattacked by four tanks and large numbers of enemy infantry. Again, still lacking armor pending a suitable bridge across the Ill, Company I was forced back in much the same manner as had been 30th Infantry the previous day. Three tanks supporting the 15th Infantry from the west bank of the river were neutralized in a few minutes. The 1st Battalion, 15th Infantry, moving up to the line of departure by 1000, was about to attack in conjunction with 3d Battalion when the counterattack hit the latter.

The 1st Battalion was temporarily held up, but by noon was ready to deliver its attack. The advance rapidly moved through 3d Battalion at Maison Rouge bridge, to the woods northeast of Riedwihr. Here, however, enemy tanks and infantry were encountered and forced 1st Battalion—without armor as had been its predecessors—to withdraw from the woods. At any rate we now held a bridgehead, and the engineers went forward with all possible speed, completing the bridge. It was more than obvious that the attack east of the Ill would get nowhere if supporting armor was not in close support of our infantry troops.

The enemy taunted us with a special propaganda leaflet sent over by enemy artillery, claiming that over one hundred members of Company I, 30th Infantry, including 1st Lt. Darwyn E. Walker—whom the leaflet named—had been captured on May 23. (In Walker's case, at least, it was true. Both he and 1st Lt. Ross H. Calvert, Company K commander, were later liberated by United States troops in Germany. Walker was liberated by his own Division.)

After completing the clearance of Ostheim, the 1st Battalion of the 7th Infantry, commanded by Maj. Kenneth W. Wallace, had attacked shortly after midnight of January 24 toward Chateau de Schoppenwihr. A strong counterattack consisting of enemy infantry and six tanks came at daybreak. Three of the tanks were destroyed, but the fighting continued all day. It was not until 1830 that night that the Germans were finally driven from their positions in the Chateau area and in the woods between the railroad tracks and west to the Fecht River. Company C, 99th Chemical Battalion, laid down a heavy smoke screen while the fight was at its height, thus enabling Company A, 7th, to rejoin its battalion by crossing the open under cover of smoke at Bois dit de Rothleible. The additional strength was both timely and necessary.

The 3d Battalion, 7th Infantry, had a fierce fight in the Brunnwald woods, where the enemy had infiltrated while the struggle for the Chateau was in progress. The infiltration was followed by reinforcements after dark and when the 3d raided the positions at about midnight the enemy was prepared to resist with great strength. Mortars, machine guns and small arms provided stiff opposition to the raiders.

Company L, commanded by 1st Lt. Orville L. Dilley, moved around the tip of the woods and ran into German machine guns and Flakwagons. Company A, 756th Tank Battalion, under Capt. Orlando A. Richardson, Jr., and Company A of the 601st TD Battalion, with Capt. Francis X. Lambert commanding, were supporting the 7th in the attack and our armor fought the enemy tanks and tank destroyers to a standstill.

Concealed German bazookamen, mechanized and horse-drawn antitank guns, Mark IV and Mark V tanks, were strewn throughout the area. Our casualties also were high and included six or seven pieces of armor.

At the end of the first forty-eight hours an important identification among enemy units had been made. As suspected, we were opposed by the two battalions of the 760 *VG* regiment, as well as elements of 748th, 225th, 308th, and 728th *VG* regiments. An additional unit, the 602nd Mobile Battalion, was almost wiped out during the period. The new identification, however, was that of the enemy 67th Reconnaissance Battalion from the 2d Mountain Division, previously identified in Norway. This was combined with the recognition of another element of the same division, the 137th Mountain Regiment, in the I French Corps zone. It provided an indication that the enemy was not going to let the Colmar Pocket be eliminated without a determined effort to prevent it. The 2d Mountain Division actually was earmarked for the pocket to replace the 269th Infantry Division, which previously had been sneaked out and sent to the Russian front. The enemy vainly hoped the switch could be completed before any Allied offensive could be started against the pocket.

Also known to be opposing our advance were: Battle Group *Diemer* and 235th Engineer Battalion. Suspected were elements of the 40th *PG* (*Panzer Grenadier*) Replacement Battalion in the 254th Infantry zone, and a possible addition of elements of the 137th Mountain Regiment opposing the 7th Infantry.

By 2010 of the night of January 24, the 254th Infantry's 3d Battalion, which had been committed around the right flank of 1st Battalion in the regiment's attack south toward the Weiss River from Hill 216, reached the Weiss. The regiment thus held the river line east to its juncture with the Fecht, although north of that point, along the Fecht stream line the area was not completely clear of enemy.

Company K, 7th Infantry, commanded by Capt. Francis J. Kret, was still in close contact with the enemy in the woods when the 7th struck south in an all-out attack, with three battalions abreast, at daybreak January 25. Company I, under 1st Lt. William D. Anthone, was left to contain the enemy in the forest while the bulk of the regiment made the attack, which began after a heavy artillery and mortar concentration had been placed on Houssen and the surrounding area.

Meanwhile, across the Ill, the 2d and 3d Battalions, 15th Infantry, took up the fight at 0300 the morning of January 25. They encountered enemy small-arms, machine-gun, 20mm, tank, and mortar fire about 300 yards northwest of Riedwihr. Two tanks and a tank destroyer with the 2d Battalion (a bridge strong enough for armor had finally been put in several hundred yards north of Maison Rouge) became stuck, and the battalion withdrew about 700 yards. The men were not in the confusion that our elements had been the previous two days, however, when there was no supporting armor whatsoever. The battalion was quickly reorganized. Maj. John O'Connell's 3d Battalion, with

Companies K and L in the assault, encountered enemy in the vicinity of a road junction northeast of Riedwihr. Company K was disorganized and forced to withdraw. Company L succeeded in driving the enemy from some buildings there, and by noon the 3d Battalion was awaiting relief by elements of the French CC4, preparatory to attacking Riedwihr.

The very relentlessness of the Division attacks slowly wore the Germans down and the towns of Riedwihr, Rosenkranz, and Houssen fell during the torrid fighting of January 25-26.

The 7th Infantry inflicted terrific losses on the enemy when the Germans launched a strong counterattack during the afternoon of January 25. The 1st Battalion, beating back the onslaught, turned the counterattack into an enemy rout and drove along the east-west road into Rosenkranz while 3d Battalion was holding firm against strong enemy armor and infantry pressure.

During the night of January 25 near Rosenkranz, Pfc. Jose F. Valdez gave his life in sacrifice. He was on outpost duty with five other soldiers, when the enemy counterattacked with overwhelming strength. From his position near some woods about five hundred yards beyond his lines, he observed a hostile tank about 75 yards away and raked it with automatic-rifle fire until it withdrew. Soon afterwards, he saw three enemy stealthily approaching through the woods. At thirty yards' distance he engaged in a fire fight with them until he had killed all three. The enemy quickly launched an attack with two full companies of infantrymen, blasting the patrol with murderous concentrations of automatic and rifle fire and beginning an encircling movement which forced the patrol leader to order a withdrawal. Private Valdez volunteered to cover the maneuver, and as the patrol, one by one, plunged through the enemy fire toward their own lines, Private Valdez fired burst after burst into the swarming enemy. The citation of his Medal of Honor award reads in part:

"... he was struck by a bullet which entered his stomach, and, passing through his body, emerged from the back. Overcoming agonizing pain, he regained control of himself and resumed his firing position, delivering a protective screen of bullets until all others of the patrol were safe. By field telephone, he called for artillery and mortar fire on the Germans and corrected the range until he had shells falling within fifty yards of his position. For fifteen minutes he refused to be dislodged by more than two hundred of the enemy, then seeing that the barrage had broken the counterattack, he dragged himself back to his own lines. He later died as a result of his wounds ..."

Final mopping-up of Houssen was done the same day by the 2d and 3d Battalions.

Colonel Heintges' regiment took 166 prisoners, including three officers, and killed and wounded a great number of Germans during the 24-hour period beginning at noon, January 25. The 67th Reconnaissance Battalion of the German 2d Mountain Division, being fed into the line as it moved down from Norway, was caught by several stray artillery TOT's fired into Houssen prior to the attack, and was completely disorganized. Although this battalion contained 700 men, it was no opposition for the 7th's attack.

The 1st Battalion of the 15th, commanded by Maj. Kenneth B. Potter, with the 2d Battalion, under Lt. Col. Eugene F. Salet, on its flank, advanced into the woods west of Riedwihr during the afternoon of the 25th and actually fought until its ammunition ran out after they had penetrated some 600 yards into the forest against tree-to-tree resistance. Major Potter stopped the advance of his battalion until ammunition could be brought up and the attack was resumed at 0200 in the morning.

The 2d Battalion, 15th Infantry, moving from positions northwest of Riedwihr, also expended all its ammunition late that night and after being resupplied continued the advance and reached its objective on the south edge of the woods at 0930 the next morning.

The 3d Battalion fought its way to the outer edge of Riedwihr at about midnight and within an hour had cleared the Germans out of the city and had patrols out toward Wickerschwihr to the south.

While the 7th and 15th attacked their objectives, the 254th had been relieved by the 28th Division's 112th Infantry by 0700 of January 25 on the Division right. After coordinating with 7th Infantry in cleaning out the Fecht River bed, the 254th was committed on the Division left, to attack Jebsheim. The end of its first day's fighting found the regiment temporarily stopped by bitter resistance, and temporary defensive preparations were made along an intermittent stream that ran just west of Jebsheim. An old mill on the stream was a landmark of the area.

The 1st and 2d Battalions of the 15th were holding a line along the south edges of Le Schmalholtz and Brunnwald woods on the afternoon of the 26th, and occupied the Bois de Riedwihr on the north. Enemy infantry, reinforced by armor, struck the 1st Battalion positions on the west side of the woods. An enemy 88mm gun caught one of our tank destroyers flush in the middle, and a swarm of German armor overran the positions of Company B, thus threatening the Division's control of the forest which dominated the German stronghold of Holtzwihr, to the south.

It was here that 1st Lt. Audie L. Murphy stopped an attack practically singlehandedly.

Lt. Col. Keith L. Ware, 15th Infantry Executive

Officer, said later: "Control (of the Bois de Riedwihr) had been wrested from the enemy at a heavy cost in blood. Its possession was of cardinal importance.

"Accordingly, on the afternoon of January 26 the enemy launched a determined counterattack, hurling two companies and six heavy tanks at Company B's position in an effort to retake the woods at any cost."

1st Lt. Walter W. Weispfenning, a Field Artillery forward observer, said "The woods were sparse and there was practically no underbrush. I could see everything that happened. The kraut tanks rumbled past Murphy's position, passing within fifty yards of him and firing at him as they went by. They did not want to close in for the kill because they wanted to give our tank destroyer, which was burning but not in flames, as wide a berth as possible.

"While we tried to hold off the tanks with directed artillery fire and bazooka rockets, the German infantry line, consisting of two full-strength companies of 125 men each, surged across the open meadow in a wide arc. They fired at Murphy with machine pistols and rifles as they advanced.

"Then I saw Lieutenant Murphy do the bravest thing that I had ever seen a man do in combat. With the Germans only a hundred yards away and still moving up on him, he climbed into the slowly-burning tank destroyer and began firing the .50-caliber machine gun at the krauts. He was completely exposed and silhouetted against the background of bare trees and snow, with a fire under him that threatened to blow the destroyer to bits if it reached the gasoline and ammunition. Eighty-eight millimeter shells, machine-gun, machine-pistol and rifle fire crashed all about him.

"Standing on top of the tank destroyer, Murphy raked the approaching enemy force with machine-gun fire. Twelve Germans, stealing up a ditch to flank him from his right, were killed in the gully at 50-yard range by concentrated fire from his machine gun. Twice the tank destroyer he was standing on was hit by artillery fire and the Lieutenant was enveloped in clouds of smoke and spurts of flame. His clothing was torn and riddled by flying shell fragments and bits of rock. Bullets ricocheted off the tank destroyer as the enemy concentrated the full fury of his fire on this one-man strongpoint."

Sgt. Elmer C. Brawley added: "The enemy tanks, meanwhile, returned because Lieutenant Murphy had held up the supporting infantry and they were apparently loath to advance further without infantry support. These tanks added their murderous fire to that of the kraut artillery and small-arms fire that showered the Lieutenant's position without stopping.

"The German infantrymen got within ten yards of the Lieutenant, who killed them in the draws, in the meadows, in the woods—wherever he saw them. Though wounded and covered with soot and dirt which must have obscured his vision at times, he held the enemy at bay, killing and wounding at least thirty-five during the next hour.

"Lieutenant Murphy, worn out and bleeding profusely, then limped forward through a continuing hail of fire and brought the company forward. Refusing to be evacuated, he led us in a strong attack against the enemy, dislodging the Germans from the whole area. When the fight was over, he allowed his wound to be treated on the field."

Pfc. Anthony V. Abramski, a member of Company

The northern fringe of the city of Colmar, which was isolated from the east by the drive of the 3d Infantry Division during the reduction of the Colmar Pocket.

The village of Urschenheim was wrested from the enemy at great cost. The tanks shown here were lost by the French. The snow has thawed.

B, added that the company was ordered to withdraw to prepared positions inside the woods when an enemy artillery concentration that preceded the attack began.

"Lieutenant Murphy remained at his command post under a tree so that he could direct artillery fire on the advancing tanks," Abramski said. "Together with a tank destroyer, which was across the main road through the woods and about ten yards to his right rear, he held that rear-guard position under raking fire from the German tanks.

"From my position in the woods, I saw a direct hit on our tank destroyer from a *Jagdpanther* carrying an 88mm gun. The crew piled out as fast as they could and withdrew toward the company position in the forest. And that is when Lieutenant Murphy took over," concluded Abramski. For his action, Lieutenant Murphy later was awarded the Congressional Medal of Honor.

Simultaneously with the smash against 1st Battalion, 15th Infantry, the enemy, attacking north from Holtzwihr, struck at 2d Battalion positions on the south rim of the forest. Our artillery, however, laid some excellent concentrations on the advancing Germans and marked the area with smoke for friendly fighter-bombers which strafed the enemy forces and attacked their assembly areas in Holtzwihr. The attack came as though planned by a scenario writer. All day the skies had been cloudy. A few minutes before the German counterattack began, the area over the woods became clear enough for our fighter-bombers to strike, caus-

Pictured from the air are the many enemy pillboxes protecting the road to Biesheim. Tank and motor vehicle tracks form the crazy pattern.

This study in black and white is the result of an attack made under searchlights by 3d Division troops near Neuf-Brisach.

ing many casualties and proving instrumental in forcing a complete German withdrawal. Then the clouds closed in once more.

During the struggle a number of enemy entered the woods from the east and got behind 2d Battalion positions. A hurriedly-gathered task force of doughboys, with a Flakwagon in support, was organized, and the enemy was put to flight after a stiff engagement.

The 254th Infantry jumped off at 1630 in resumption of its attack toward Jebsheim; 1st Battalion was on the right, 2d Battalion on the left. The 1st Battalion encountered strong enemy resistance from a pillbox 500 yards north of Jebsheim, which was seven feet high and manned by twelve men. Following its reduction the advance continued. The 2d Battalion entered Jebsheim at 2355, following a 15-minute artillery barrage, and 1st Battalion followed. Stiff house-to-house fighting lasted through the night and into the morning.

The 3d Battalion, 254th Infantry, attacked at 1750,

The shape of Neuf-Brisach from the air resembles that of the grids of a waffle iron.

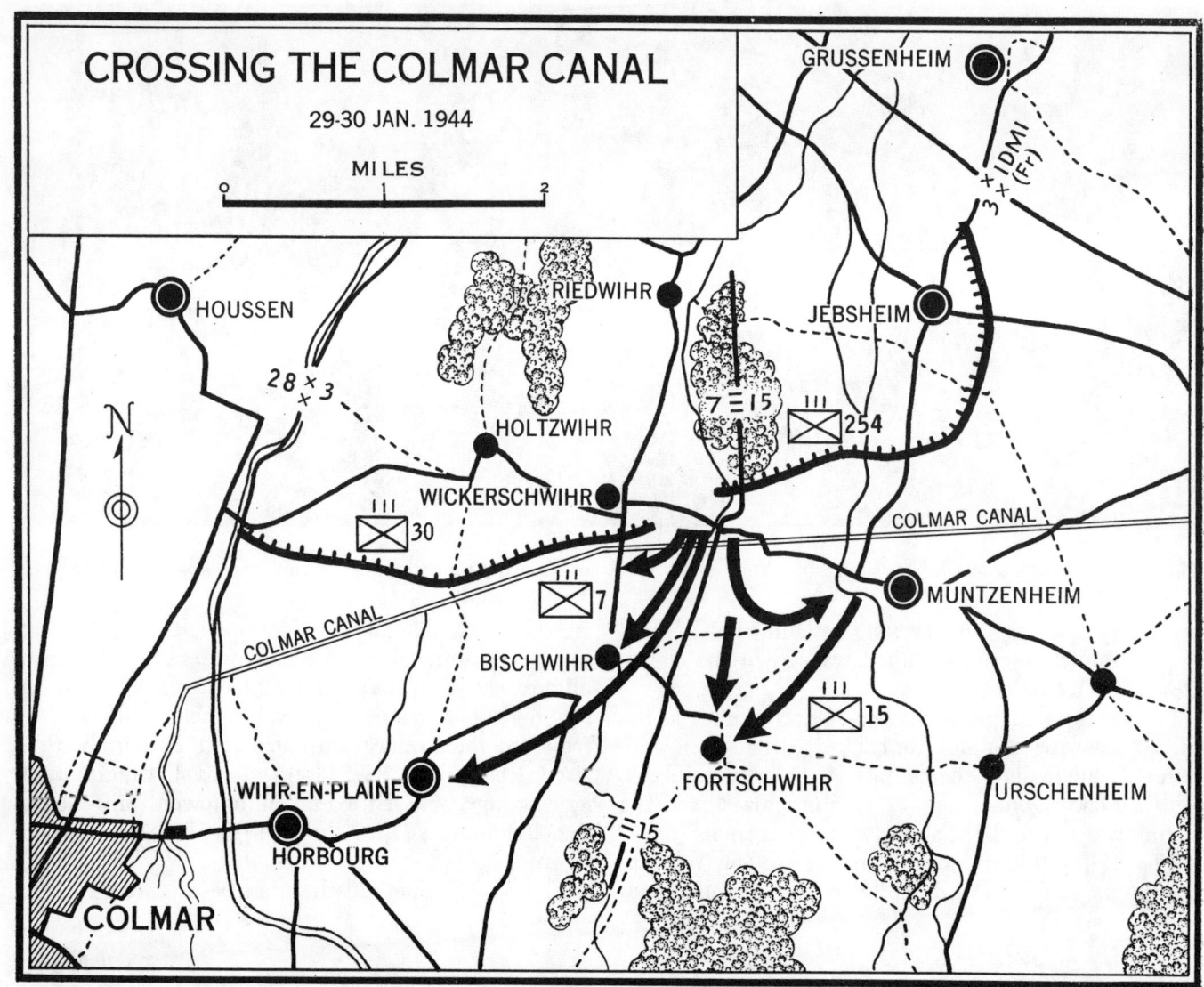

January 26, with the mission of advancing southeast and clearing the Bois de Jebsheim from the south. Prepared enemy positions were encountered along a stream line and the advance was slow, likewise continuing throughout the night into the next day.

The 7th Infantry's 1st and 2d Battalions made local attacks during the afternoon of the 26th to improve their positions preparatory to relief. The 3d Battalion, following artillery preparation, attacked south from Brunnwald woods at 1300, with the Battle Patrol attacking east of Houssen. This got away at 1300 with the purpose of clearing some enemy who were well-intrenched between a dike and the Ill River on the left flank. Company I was particularly successful in its mission, although it was a very bloody small attack. During the night 28th Division's 109th Infantry elements relieved 7th Infantry, which went into Division reserve after having attacked continuously since the night of January 22.

The morning of January 27th saw a reorganized, vengeful 30th Infantry in the fight once again. The 2d Battalion left its assembly area at 0445 in an attack toward the Colmar Canal which was coordinated with French units on its flank. The 1st Battalion moved out, crossing its line of departure and clearing across the road leading southwest from Riedwihr to an area in the vicinity of west of Wickerschwihr by 0510. The 3d Battalion blocked east of the Ill River. By 0845 Company E reported the east side of Holtzwihr clear. Company F, after losing a tank to enemy bazooka fire, withdrew to its line of departure to reorganize, and attacked again, to report the remainder of Holtzwihr clear by 0950. The 1st Battalion cleaned out Wickerschwihr by noon.

The Division Commander later praised the 30th Infantry for its rapid reorganization and resumption of the offensive. In his own words: "It took a fighting regiment to make the gains you made on January 22-23, but it took a great regiment to come back after the reverses you suffered and kick hell out of the kraut at Holtzwihr and Wickerschwihr."

By noon of the 27th all but the southern tip of

A rather thorough job of demolition was done by the enemy on the railroad bridge over the Rhine River at Neuf-Brisach.

Jebsheim was reported clear by the 254th Infantry. Elements of 5 DB moved in to take charge of the southern part of the town, and strong German elements infiltrated back in. The task of clearing them out the French then handed back to the 254th because of their lack of infantry. Fierce fighting continued in that small tip for two more days and it was nearly midnight of January 29th before the 254th Infantry could finally and authoritatively report Jebsheim free of Germans. The regiment, new to combat prior to joining the 3d in the Colmar Pocket, acquitted itself with distinction, first in clearing troublesome Hill 216 and then mopping up in Jebsheim, taking a total of nearly 1,000 prisoners in three days. (The importance of Jebsheim was that it was one of a string of fortified towns on the enemy's main north-south communication artery.)

It now remained for the 15th and 30th Infantry regiments to clear out a few scattered German elements north of the Colmar Canal and the next large phase of the operation was ready to be initiated. During that two-day period, thorough preparations were made to slam across the canal in force, and to move far and fast. This time there was to be no repetition of the grinding battle of attrition which had characterized the fighting so far.

Patrols to the Canal reported that it was about fifty feet wide and five feet deep, its steep banks being some twelve feet high and about eight feet wide at the top and fifteen at the bottom. The water was slow-moving, but not frozen.

At 2100, January 28, the 3d Infantry Division passed from control of II French Corps to control of XXI American Corps, which was commanded by Maj. Gen. F. W. Milburn.

Reconnaissance along the north bank of the Colmar Canal was continuous during the hours of darkness January 28-29. Huge trucks hauling engineer bridging equipment clogged the roads behind the forward areas.

The entire French 5 DB was attached to the 3d Division as of 1635, January 29.

That evening, with the coming of darkness, 7th and 15th Infantry Regiments stole to the edges of the Colmar Canal with engineer rubber boats, and waited.

Heavy concentrations of preparatory fire of all weapons broke loose just preceding the crossing. During a 24-hour period beginning at 1800, the artillery

Within the walls of Neuf-Brisach these bunkers provided shelter to the enemy and citizens against our bombing and artillery.

Twenty-eight men and a guidon remain of the original Company I, 30th Infantry, which received the Distinguished Unit Citation for its action at Cisterna on 28-29 January, 1944.

battalions fired 16,438 rounds of ammunition, most of which was fired at the beginning of the attack, while the 441st AAA Battalion, under command of Lt. Col. Thomas H. Leary, fired 22,300 rounds of .50-caliber ammunition during the first three hours of the attack. The antiaircraft gunners sent a continuous hail of shells into enemy positions across the canal and into the towns of Bischwihr, Fortschwihr, and Muntzenheim.

Operation "Krautbuster" was initiated at 2100. Behind the furious screen of preparatory shells, leading elements of the 7th Infantry moved down the steep banks of the canal and paddled across. Enemy resistance was surprisingly light. The 1st and 3d Battalions of the 7th were completely across by 2205; the 15th Infantry had its bridging supplies held up by heavy traffic, but began crossing at 2145 with the 2d and 3d Battalions in the lead. By midnight the 7th and 15th were completely across.

Company B, 7th Infantry, engaged some enemy in a fire fight while the remainder of 1st Battalion moved into Bischwihr at 2245. The 3d Battalion on the right,

After the battle of the Colmar Pocket was over the thaws came and the terrain was under water in the valleys and on the plain.

also attacking Bischwihr, encountered some resistance in the town but reported the town clear at 2400.

No less speedy was the 15th Infantry's rapid attack upon Muntzenheim. The 2d and 3d Battalions reorganized after the canal crossing, with 1st Battalion crossing behind them. The 2d and 3d then attacked Muntzenheim from the west with 3d Battalion on the left. Company K was reported on its objective by 0110 and the first elements of the 2d Battalion were reported in the town at 0130.

After Muntzenheim was cleared, the 3d Battalion remained in the town and the 2d Battalion attacked Fortschwihr from the northeast in conjunction with 1st Battalion (less certain elements) which attacked south to the town from assembly areas. The town was cleared in short order. During the attack on the two villages approximately 200 prisoners were taken; a 105mm gun with crew, an 88mm gun with crew and two 120mm mortars were captured intact.

The 2d Battalion, 7th Infantry, now did some broken-field running. Having crossed the canal on footbridges at 2330, the battalion moved rapidly toward Wihr-en-Plaine, and was approaching it by 0130 in the face of tank fire and some small-arms resistance. Companies F and G entered the town at 0205 as two enemy tank destroyers penetrated between the two companies and the battalion OP group, a member of which was Maj. Jack M. Duncan, the battalion commander. A phenomenal 500-foot bazooka shot by Pfc. Joseph L. Bale destroyed one of the tank destroyers, setting it on fire. The other fled as did the accompanying enemy infantry.

By 0315 the battalion was meeting scattered resistance in Wihr-en-Plaine. At 0630 there was a strong counterattack of enemy armor and infantry. Fierce fighting ensued. By noon the battalion controlled the northern half of the town and was fighting in the southern portion.

During this time 254th Infantry had launched an attack south from Jebsheim to the Colmar Canal and east toward the Rhone-Rhine Canal. At the time 7th Infantry began its crossing of the Colmar Canal, all resistance in Jebsheim had ceased. Five hundred and seventy-five prisoners were taken there the last day of fighting.

The bitter fight in Wihr-en-Plaine conducted by 2d Battalion, 7th Infantry, with Company L attached, continued on through the 30th of January. After repulsing a second counterattack early in the afternoon, 2d Battalion and Company L attacked south at 1430, with the 7th Infantry Battle Patrol also participating. Some more of Wihr-en-Plaine was cleared after a hard, close-in fight, and another counterattack at 1830 was repelled. The artillery placed a TOT on Horbourg,

Colonel (then Lt. Col.) Hallett D. Edson, commanding officer, 15th Infantry Regiment.

adjoining. The 2d Battalion jumped off to attack Wihr-en-Plaine's southwest edge at 2230 followed by elements of CC4, which were to pass through the battalion and enter Colmar providing a bridge were seized.

The 1st Battalion, 15th Infantry, assembled east of captured Fortschwihr at 1640, January 30, and attacked the woods to the southeast. Little or no enemy resistance was encountered by the battalion. Company B was reported on its objective at 1830, Company A on its objective by 1835.

The 1st Battalion remained in position until noon the following day. The 2d Battalion, minus Company F, which was guarding a bridge across the Canal, remained in Fortschwihr.

Elements of the French CC5 attacked Urschenheim from Muntzenheim at 1700. After an extremely stiff fight the town was reported clear at 2000 and Company I, 15th Infantry was ordered to take it over, which it did at 2200.

The 30th Infantry held and cleared the south bank of the Colmar Canal, blocking to the east and west. It was shot at from the south where enemy groups still held out. The 28th Division had not yet attacked south into Colmar, leaving the regiment's right flank open.

The 1st Battalion, 30th Infantry, remained in blocking positions to the east in Wickerschwihr, with Company A outposting bridges. Company A was relieved of these positions early on January 31 by elements of the 75th U. S. Infantry Division, which had been brought down from the northern Allied front and was in the process of being placed into position between the 3d and 28th Divisions.

The 2d Battalion also remained in position for the January 30-31 period, as did 3d Battalion, although the latter, and especially Company L, was subjected to very heavy artillery, Flakwagon, machine-gun, and rifle fire in its mission of blocking and clearing. At 1500 an enemy group of about forty men began an attack toward Company L, but artillery and mortar fire stopped them.

The 1st Battalion, 7th Infantry, moved south from Bischwihr at 1700 and entered the Niederwald woods. The battalion encountered only light resistance. At 0700 next morning a reported 200 enemy approaching the southern edge of the woods were taken under artillery fire and routed. An armored infantry force from CC4 joined 1st Battalion. The 1st Battalion continued scouring Le Niederwald for isolated groups of enemy.

The 2d Battalion, 7th Infantry, continued its fight throughout the night of January 30-31. At 0120 Companies E and L (attached) were 300 yards short of a key road junction in Wihr-en-Plaine, near Horbourg, encountering stiff enemy resistance. They had made only fifty yards and were held up by an antitank ditch at 0435. Company E received a counterattack at 0700 and repulsed it only after bitter fighting.

The 3d Battalion (minus Company L) entered the woods northwest of 1st Battalion and encountered strong small arms resistance. Company I followed 3d Battalion and engaged the enemy in the woods in a firefight, killing many enemy and taking sixteen prisoners.

The 2d Battalion seized the road junction in Wihr-en-Plaine by noon and pushed on to Horbourg.

French CC5 pushed on from Urschenheim to Durrenentzen, and engaged the enemy there in a hard fight. Before the town was taken the French lost nine tanks.

The 2d Battalion and Company L, 7th Infantry, together with CC4 attacked Horbourg shortly after noon January 31. By 1435 they were in the town fighting a stubbornly resisting foe. By 1535 they held half the town and were fighting from house-to-house as the French armor drove on through. Artillery was directed on enemy withdrawing from the town. A TOT was placed on the west side of the Ill River and advance elements of the 2d Battalion reached the Ill at midnight putting the town completely in our hands.

The attack was about to go into its final phase. The 15th and 30th Infantry Regiments concentrated on clearing out all enemy west of the Rhone-Rhine Canal which ran north from Neuf-Brisach. The 1st Battalion, 15th Infantry, attacked east from Urschenheim to clear the woods and secure a bridge across the Rhone-Rhine Canal near Kunzheim. During the advance, which was led by Company B with armor, 1st Battalion destroyed two enemy tanks and damaged one. The 2d Battalion attacked at 0100, February 1, on the regimental left flank, and advanced to the east along the Colmar Canal, reaching a position from which it could cover the bridge with fire. The 3d Battalion prepared to make an attack to clear the woods between the 1st and 2d Battalions.

The 1st Battalion, 30th Infantry, moved out at 0100, February 1, to clear a stretch east of the Rhone-Rhine Canal. Company A, in the lead, reached its objective at 0625 and fired on enemy vehicles with Cannon Company and artillery fires. At 0637 Companies B and C reached the west side of the canal. Company C crossed the canal on locks at 0717. At 0722 Company A repulsed a two-tank attack. The battalion took 124 prisoners in the twenty-four hours ending noon of February 1.

The 2d Battalion, 30th Infantry, continued clearing objectives west of the Rhone-Rhine Canal during the February 1-2 period. The 3d Battalion repulsed a 40-man, two-tank counterattack, shortly after noon of February 1.

The next play belonged to 7th Infantry. During the night of January 31-February 1, the regiment was relieved from its newly-won positions by elements of the 75th Infantry Division and assembled in Urschenheim. From here the battalions moved to Wickerschwihr, and foot elements moved by marching to the Rhone-Rhine Canal.

Artzenheim, on the east side of the Rhone-Rhine Canal, had been taken by the French 1 DMI. The plan now was for 7th Infantry to attack south from Artzenheim in the direction of Neuf-Brisach, which lay close to the Rhine River and east of which were the two bridges over which the Germans had been supplying the bulk of their bridgehead forces for so long.

The attack got off at 0500 February 2, 2d and 3d Battalions abreast. By 0615 Company I had penetrated to the northern edge of Kunzheim. The 2d Battalion became engaged in a small arms and machine gun fight for Baltzenheim at 0800, while 3d Battalion fought to clear Kunzheim. By 0900 both towns were cleared.

With Kunzheim taken, next step was Biesheim, then the final objective, Neuf-Brisach. Leading elements of the 30th Infantry were cleaning out the southern edges of the Schaeferwald woods, a southwestern projection of Bois de Biesheim, directly east of Widensolen. To the south, athwart the 30th Infantry's path which was clearly outlined and guided by the converging lines of

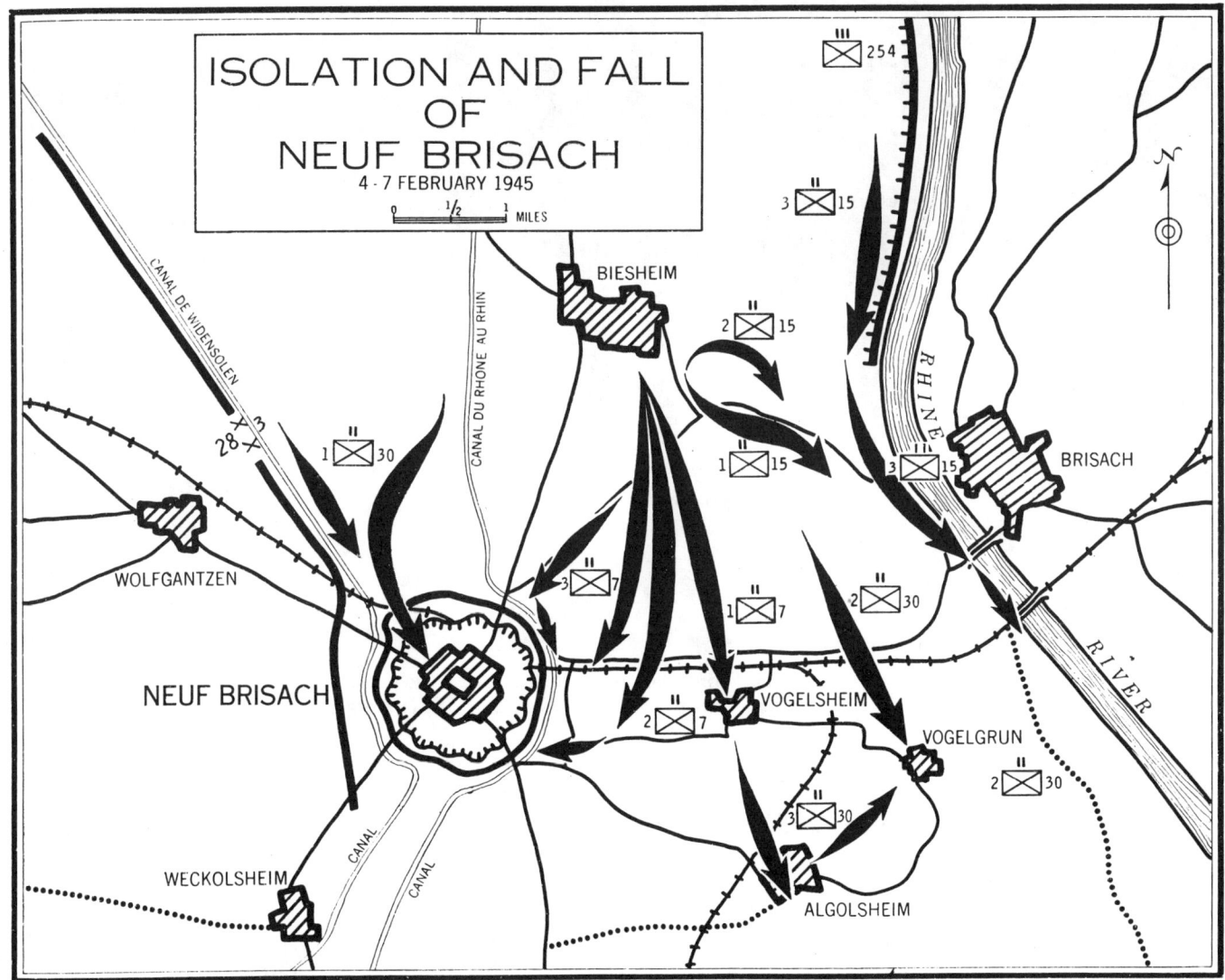

the Widensolen and Rhone-Rhine Canals, were the northern moats and city wall of Neuf-Brisach.

The 15th Infantry moved behind 7th Infantry into Kunzheim, ready to follow the 7th, then to continue branching out to the southeast, to clean out the enlarged zone of advance caused by the southeast bend of the Rhine in the vicinity of Fort Mortier.

At 0230, February 3, Col. Heintges' 2d and 3d Battalions attacked, 3d Battalion on the right following the east bank of the Rhone-Rhine Canal. The 1st Battalion was in reserve, and followed at 0600.

The 2d Battalion passed through enemy in trenches north of Biesheim in the darkness, and entered Biesheim at 0400. The battalion's hardest fight was encountered in these trenches.

It was in the light of a waning moon that the advancing infantry was ambushed. Enemy forces outnumbering the infantry point four to one poured withering artillery, mortar, machine-gun and small-arms fire into the stricken men from the flanks, forcing them to seek the cover of a ditch which they found already occupied by enemy foot troops. As the opposing infantrymen struggled in hand-to-hand combat, T/5 Forrest E. Peden, an artillery forward observer from Battery C, 10th Field Artillery Battalion, accompanying the infantry, courageously went to the assistance of two wounded soldiers and rendered them first aid under heavy fire. With radio communications inoperative, he realized that the unit would be wiped out unless help could be secured from the rear. On his own initiative he ran eight hundred yards to the battalion command post through a hail of bullets, which pierced his jacket, and there secured two light tanks to go to the aid of his hard-pressed comrades. Knowing the terrible risk involved, he climbed upon the hull of the lead tank and guided it into battle. The tank lumbered on through a murderous concentration of fire until it reached the ditch. A direct hit struck the tank, just as it was about to go into action, turning it into a burning pyre and killing T/5 Peden. His death was not in vain. The remainder of the battalion was guided to the scene of action by the flames and relieved their embattled com-

Captain Claude Lazard, French Liaison Mission, pins the Croix de Guerre on the colors of the 3d Division's 756th Tank Battalion for actions performed in the Colmar Pocket operation.

rades. Peden was posthumously awarded the Medal of Honor.

The 3d Battalion, on the other hand, became involved with enemy along the canal, and initially only Company I succeeded in entering Biesheim. Enemy in the "Jewish Cemetery" also took Lt. Col. Lloyd B. Ramsey's assault elements under fire from their east flank. Maj. Kenneth W. Wallace's 1st Battalion, following the 2d Battalion under Maj. Jack M. Duncan, discovered when daylight came that the hardest enemy opposition had actually been by-passed and that a very determined group held out in the Jewish Cemetery and in pillboxes echeloned in depth between that point and the Rhine. The 1st Battalion was involved in a stiff fight all day and half the night of February 3-4, when the cemetery and surrounding area finally were reported clear. At 0400 the battalion was ordered to return to Kunzheim, pending further action.

During most of February 3 the 3d and 2d Battalions continued to work on Biesheim and it was cleared of Germans by 1700. The 3d Battalion captured 250 prisoners and 2d Battalion took about 150.

Meanwhile the 30th Infantry had attacked south along the west bank of the Rhone-Rhine Canal on February 3 and elements of the 1st Battalion, under Lt. Col. Mackenzie E. Porter, reached the canal bridge east of Biesheim, where enemy fire was received.

Maj. Kenneth B. Potter's 1st Battalion, 15th Infantry, attacked east during the early morning hours of February 4 to assist the 1st Battalion, 7th Infantry, in clearing the cemetery area. A small task force from the battalion then moved north from Biesheim to clear up scattered enemy resistance elements along the Kunzheim-Biesheim road, and it was this that shortly thereafter enabled Major Wallace's Battalion to return to Kunzheim.

During the night of February 3-4 and February 4-5, 2d Battalion, 30th Infantry, commanded by Maj. James A. Osgard, sent patrols toward Neuf-Brisach, as did the 1st Battalion. Elements of the 1st Battalion encountered some enemy pillboxes at 1925, February 3, succeeded in eliminating two of them by 2100, and at 2340 sent a platoon from Company A to occupy the pillboxes.

At 0435 a five-man patrol from Company A went to a point approximately 500 meters north of Neuf-Brisach and succeeded in returning with twenty-four German prisoners. Major Osgard's 2d Battalion, and 3d Battalion, under Maj. Christopher W. Chaney, maintained aggressive combat patrols to the front and flanks during the 24-hour period beginning noon February 3.

At 0015, February 5, 7th Infantry left the line of departure at Biesheim. The 1st Battalion's mission was to seize the crossroads north of Vogelsheim; 3d Battalion on the right had the mission of seizing the railroad station and sealing the northeast and east entrances to Neuf-Brisach. The 2d Battalion was then to pass through 3d Battalion and seize the hospital and factory area southeast of Neuf-Brisach.

General de Lattre de Tassigny decorates General "Iron Mike" O'Daniel with the Legion d'Honneur, 3d degree and the Croix de Guerre with Palm for his superb generalship in the Colmar Pocket operation.

The 15th Infantry already had moved to the southeast of Biesheim, where elements of 1st Battalion had seized a crossroads there. Maj. John O'Connell's 3d Battalion cleared the Boulay Woods along the banks of the Rhine and was then moved south to continue clearing the woods to the south. Lt. Col. Eugene Salet's 2d Battalion, 15th Infantry, also worked on the territory along the banks of the Rhine, operating south of the 3d Battalion.

The 7th Infantry succeeded in clearing Vogelsheim by 0630, February 5, and 2d Battalion moved through on schedule, clearing out the hospital and factory area with little trouble. During the night of February 5-6 a patrol from Company K, led by Sgt. Chester M. Owens, reconnoitered to the east and northeast of Neuf-Brisach, and succeeded in reaching the northeast wall without being fired upon.

The 15th Infantry encountered considerable trouble at Fort Mortier, southeast of Biesheim, on the afternoon of February 5, but the fort was cleared out by 2100. The 1st Battalion accomplished this mission. The 3d Battalion continued to move south. By 1730 Company K had cut the main highway bridge approach, and Company I had moved even further south and cut the railway bridge approach.

Neuf-Brisach was now nearly sealed off. During the night of February 5-6 the enemy began evacuating the fortress city. Preparatory to this, however, there was a stiff fight north of the city. The 1st Battalion, 30th Infantry, during the night of February 4-5 assigned Company C the mission of ascertaining the condition of a bridge across the Widensolen Canal just east of Petite Hollande Ferme. At 0430 the four men of the point of 1st Lt. Louis J. Lombardi's 2d platoon were fired upon by machine guns in the vicinity of the bridge and from machine guns at the farm. The platoon thereupon withdrew slightly and dug in along the east bank of the canal.

Company B, 30th Infantry, attacked through Company A along the west bank of the Rhone-Rhine Canal a few minutes after 1500, February 5, with predesignated phase lines. The attack was successful. The company "peeled off" to the right by platoons, with armor support, and took seventy-eight prisoners, wounded fourteen more, and killed four.

The company set up an outpost line between canals and shortly thereafter Company C, moving south along the Widensolen Canal, contacted Company B's right elements, and the two companies set up their defense.

That same night of February 5, 2d Battalion, 30th Infantry, moved by marching to Biesheim and at 2030 the battalion attacked toward Vogelsheim in column of companies. The area east and south of Vogelsheim was interdicted by our artillery as the battalion advanced. Light opposition was encountered and the town of Vogelgrun was reported clear by 2315.

After the 2d Battalion's successful attack on Vogelgrun, the 3d Battalion launched an attack on Algolsheim. The enemy here was supported by at least three tanks, and intense artillery fire was received from enemy Flak guns east of the Rhine. Under the command of Lt. Col. Christopher W. Chaney, the battalion fought through the afternoon of February 6 and into the morning of February 7 to clear the town, beating off one enemy counterattack after the town was taken.

Pfc. Kenneth E. LaRue of Company B led a patrol to the northeast wall of Neuf-Brisach during the night of February 5-6, with a mission of determining the condition of the railroad bridge in that vicinity. The men found strong demolition charges laid, but the bridge was intact. The patrol drew four or five rounds of sniper fire and observed about five men in a nearby grape vineyard. These were captured the following morning by Company C personnel.

At 0900, February 6, elements of the 2d Battalion, 7th Infantry, reported heavy enemy traffic evacuating from the town on the southeast road leading from Neuf-Brisach. Major Duncan ordered artillery, tank, and infantry weapons fire laid on this traffic.

At 0800 Sgt. Elbert Tapley of Company C, 30th Infantry, led a three-man patrol to the north wall of town and was fired on by an enemy machine gun. However, the patrol remained in wait and at about 1000 observed a white flag above the arch entrance way into the town. Sergeant Tapley returned to find his company moving one platoon down to the northwest wall.

At about 0930 a Company B platoon under S/Sgt. Richard B. Weiler moved south in column. As the men neared the railroad bridge they observed a civilian who, after some persuasion, jumped down into the dry moat and led the platoon to a narrow, low-ceilinged 60-foot tunnel which led through the wall into the town.

The 3d platoon, Company C, under 1st Lt. Hennon Gilbert, however, had preceded the Company B Platoon. Led by Sergeant Tapley the platoon approached a blown bridge on the northwest edge of town, and two young French children went down into the moat to guide them through the archway into town.

Since this platoon entered first, it took all the prisoners. In one building in the north part of town there were thirty-eight. The others drifted in in groups of three and four until a total of seventy-six had been accounted for. There was no fighting in the town.

By 1115 it was radioed that the town was clear of enemy.

The ending was as anti-climactic as the fighting which preceded it had been fierce. The fact that entry into the town was made easily did not detract from the work of the regiments in Neuf-Brisach's near vicinity.

Thus fell Neuf-Brisach, entered by 1st Battalion, 30th Infantry. Built in 1472, and first destroyed by the Germans in 1870, the town had been built to withstand a siege. The 3d Infantry Division's chosen method of attack made direct assault unnecessary. The Division's work was done.

PRESIDENTIAL UNIT CITATION

As authorized by Executive Order 9396 (sec. I, WD Bul. 22, 1943), superseding Executive Order 9075 (sec. III, WD Bul. 11, 1942), the following unit is cited by the War Department for outstanding performance of duty in action during the period indicated, under the provisions of section IV, WD Circular 333, 1943, in the name of the President of the United States as public evidence of deserved honor and distinction. The citation reads as follows:

The *3d Infantry Division* with the following-attached units:

254th Infantry Regiment,
99th Chemical Battalion,
168th Chemical Smoke Generator Company,
441st Antiaircraft Artillery Automatic Weapons Battalion,
601st Tank Destroyer Battalion (SP),
756th Tank Battalion,
IPW Team 183,

fighting incessantly, from 22 January to 6 February 1945, in heavy snow storms, through enemy-infested marshes and woods, and over a flat plain criss-crossed by numerous small canals, irrigation ditches, and unfordable streams, terrain ideally suited to the defense, breached the German defense wall on the northern perimeter of the Colmar bridgehead and drove forward to isolate Colmar from the Rhine. Crossing the Fecht River from Guemar, Alsace, by stealth during the late hours of darkness of 22 January, the assault elements fought their way forward against mounting resistance. Reaching the Ill River, a bridge was thrown across but collapsed before armor could pass to the support of two battalions of the 30th Infantry on the far side. Isolated and attacked by a full German Panzer brigade, outnumbered and outgunned, these valiant troops were forced back yard by yard. Wave after wave of armor

DECISION No 508

The President of the Provisional Government of the French Republic, Commander-in-Chief of the Armed Forces, cites:

TO THE ORDER OF THE ARMY:

3rd US INFANTRY DIVISION:

An elite division which has remained faithful to the traditions of courage and sacrifice which it had already acquired during the last war, when it was known as the "ROCK OF THE MARNE".

Under the vigorous command of General O'DANIEL, an energetic and resourceful leader, it fought continuously for 169 days, from the MEDITERRANEAN beaches to the banks of the RHINE.

Placed under the command of the Commanding General, First French Army, for the operations in the ALSACE pocket, by the power of its repeated attacks, it played a large part in the victorious battle for COLMAR.

During the night of 23-24 January 1945, it succeeded in making a surprise crossing of the FECHT and the ILL and capturing the first enemy position, in spite of a snowstorm and terrain strewn with obstacles.

Giving no respite to the enemy, and increasing the strength of its attack, it crossed the COLMAR Canal in order to surround and take the town of NEUF-BRISACH after heavy fighting, thus cutting one of the only two escape routes available to the German troops still defending the COLMAR area.

During these actions it captured over 4,000 prisoners, thus bringing to a brilliant conclusion the series of outstanding operations which took place from the MEDITERRANEAN to the RHINE.

The present Citation carries award of the Croix de Guerre with Palm.

PARIS, 15 March 1945

/s/ /t/ C. de GAULLE

1ere ARMEE FRANCAISE

ETAT-MAJOR - 1er BUREAU

No. 1799 CH/DC

TRUE COPY TRANSMITTED TO:
CO, French Liaison Mission, Seventh Army.

2 copies, including one for transmission to CG, Seventh Army.

CP, 13 April 1945.

For General d'Armee de LATTRE de TASSIGNY, Commander-in-Chief, First French Army:

Lt. Colonel LEGRAND, Chef du 1er Bureau:
/s/ R. LEGRAND

AG Section
Translation and Coordination
T-1957   18 April 1945

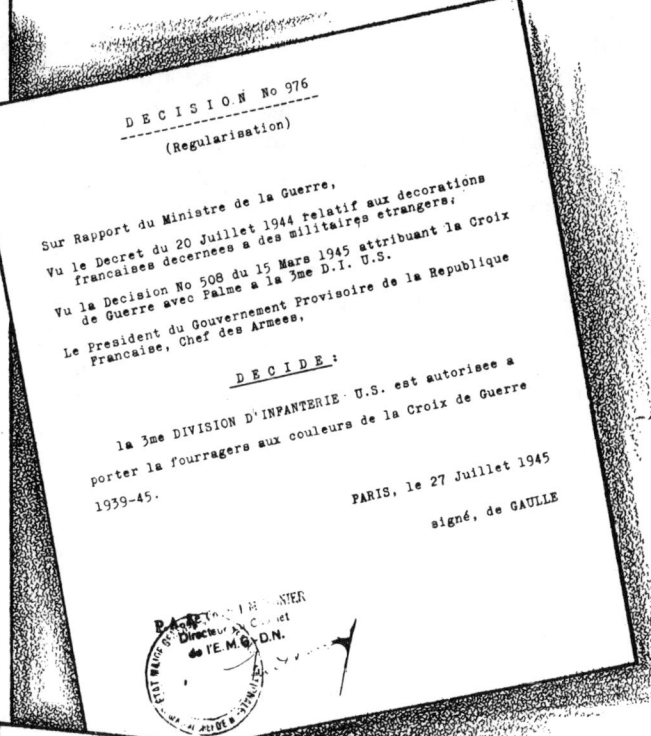

DECISION No 976
(Decision)

On the report of the Minister of War,

Noted the Decree of 20 July 1944 relative to French decorations awarded to Foreign Military personnel,

Noted Decision No 508, 15 March 1945 awarding the Croix de Guerre with Palm to the 3rd U.S. Infantry Division,

The President of the Provisional Government of the French Republic, Chief of Armies,

DECIDED:

the 3rd U.S. INFANTRY DIVISION is authorized to wear the fourragere of the colors of the Croix de Guerre 1939-45.

PARIS, the 27th July 1945

Signed, de GAULLE

SEAL OF THE CHIEF OF STAFF
OF THE MINISTRY OF WAR

DECISION N° 508

Le Président du Gouvernement Provisoire de la République Française, Chef des Armées, Cite :

A l'ORDRE DE L'ARMEE :

3ème DIVISION D'INFANTERIE U.S.

Division d'élite qui est restée fidèle aux traditions de courage et de sacrifice qu'elle avait déjà faites siennes pendant la dernière guerre où elle s'était acquis le surnom de "ROC DE LA MARNE".

Sous la vigoureuse impulsion d'un Chef énergique et manoeuvrier le Général O'DANIEL, a combattu sans interruption pendant 169 jours, des plages de la Méditerranée aux rives du RHIN.

Placée sous le Commandement du Général Commandant la Ière Armée Française, pour les opérations de la poche d'ALSACE, a, par la puissance de ses attaques renouvelées, pris une large part à la victorieuse bataille de COLMAR.

Dans la nuit du 23 au 24 JANVIER 1945, a réussi à traverser par surprise la FECHT et l'ILL et à s'emparer de la première position ennemie, malgré la tempête de neige et un terrain semé d'obstacles.

N'a laissé aucun répit à l'adversaire et poussant de plus en plus fort son action, a franchi le Canal de COLMAR pour venir entourer et conquérir de haute lutte la ville de NEUF-BRISACH coupant ainsi l'une des deux seules voies de retraite aux troupes allemandes défendant encore la région de COLMAR.

A capturé au cours de ces actions plus de 4.000 prisonniers, concluant ainsi brillamment la série de ses opérations glorieuses qui se sont déroulées depuis la Méditerranée jusqu'au RHIN.

La présente Citation comporte l'attribution de la Croix de Guerre avec Palme.

PARIS, le 15 MARS 1945
Signé : C. de GAULLE.

I° ARMEE FRANCAISE

ETAT - MAJOR - I° BUREAU

N° 1799 CH/DC

RO/13

COPIE CONFORME NOTIFIEE :

à Monsieur le Capitaine, Chef de la Mission Française de Liaison auprès de la 7ème Armée U.S.

-2 exemplaires dont 1 pour remise à M. le Général Commandant la 7° Armée U.S.

P.C. le 13 AVR 1945

Le Général d'Armée de LATTRE de TASSIGNY, Commandant en Chef de la I° Armée Française,

P.O. Le Lt Colonel Legrand
Chef du 1er Bureau

and infantry was hurled against them but despite hopeless odds the regiment held tenaciously to its bridgehead. Driving forward in knee-deep snow, which masked acres of densely sown mines, the *3d Infantry Division* fought from house to house and street to street in the fortress towns of the Alsatian Plain. Under furious concentrations of supporting fire, assault troops crossed the Colmar Canal in rubber boats during the night of 29 January. Driving relentlessly forward, six towns were captured within 8 hours, 500 casualties inflicted on the enemy during the day, and large quantities of booty seized. Slashing through to the Rhone-Rhine Canal, the garrison at Colmar was cut off and the fall of the city assured. Shifting the direction of attack, the division moved south between the Rhone-Rhine Canal and the Rhine toward Neuf-Brisach and the Brisach Bridge. Synchronizing the attacks, the bridge was seized and Neuf-Brisach captured . . .

GO 44 WD 6 June 1945

Maj. Gen. John W. O'Daniel, who had commanded 3d Infantry Division since February 17, 1944—through the push to Rome, Southern France, and the Vosges Mountains, had this to say to the Division upon the completion of the 16-day attack against the Colmar Pocket:

"In crossing the Fecht and Ill Rivers, the Colmar and Rhone-Rhine Canals, and your attacks toward Neuf-Brisach, culminating in the routing of the Germans and the capture of the Neuf-Brisach area, you have participated in the *most outstanding* operation in the career of your Division.

"You drove on relentlessly day and night through the worst of weather. Your action not only enabled you to advance, but also made possible the advance of all other forces in the bridgehead and hastened the collapse and elimination of the German-held Colmar Pocket.

"As your commander, I congratulate you on your outstanding performance and am proud of the honor of being in command of such a superb group of fighting men."

Said Maj. Gen. F. W. Milburn, XXI Corps Commander: "The operations of the XXI Corps in the Colmar area have been successfully completed. Colmar has been liberated and the enemy has been driven to the east of the Rhine.

"The success of these operations has been due to the loyalty, the gallantry, and the unselfish devotion to duty of the many thousands of officers and enlisted men of the units that constitute the XXI Corps.

"*The 3d Infantry Division was particularly outstanding in these operations.* It performed its assigned missions with great enthusiasm. It completed these missions successfully, contributing materially thereby to the great victory achieved by our units.

"I wish to commend you, the officers, and enlisted men of the 3d Infantry Division for the superior manner in which they performed during these operations. Their actions were superb, and they reflect the finest traditions of the Armies of the United States."

". . . This commendable operation," said Lt. Gen. Jacob Devers, Sixth Army Group Commander, "is in the best tradition of the 3d Infantry Division and has added another glorious chapter to your outstanding record which includes almost 400 combat days and nineteen Medals of Honor. I congratulate each officer and man on this fine organization of which you should all be justly proud."

Bare statistics shed further light on the Colmar accomplishment. The 3d Infantry Division, reinforced, during the 16-day period, captured twenty-two towns, over 4,200 prisoners, and killed an enemy total disproportionately high to the total number captured. It virtually destroyed the 708th *VG* and 2d Mountain Divisions, badly mauled the 189th and 16th *VG* Divisions, and destroyed a great amount of all types of enemy materiel.

General Charles de Gaulle, head of the Provisional French Government, chose another way of saying, "Thanks." On February 20, 1945, there was a notable ceremony in Colmar. The 1st Battalion, 30th Infantry, represented the 3d Division's infantry; a battery of the 41st FA Battalion, the artillery. The 3d Reconnaissance Troop was also represented by a platoon.

General Jean de Lattre de Tassigny, commander of the First French Army, pinned the Order of the Croix de Guerre to the Division's colors. He then conferred the Legion D'Honneur, 3d Degree, and the Croix de Guerre with Palm on the 3d's Commanding General, John W. "Iron Mike" O'Daniel.

TABLE OF CASUALTIES*
Colmar Pocket
(Jan. 23, 1945 through March 14, 1945)

KIA	WIA	MIA	Total Battle Casualties	Non-Battle Casualties
317	1410	323	2050	2550

Reinforcements and hospital return-to-unit personnel

Reinf		Hosp RTU	
Off	EM	Off	EM
93	2405	106	2265

KNOWN ENEMY CASUALTIES

Killed	Wounded	Captured
713	297	4016

*These figures were provided by the A C of S, G-1, 3d Infantry Division.

XI
GERMANY

The Long Trail from the Rugged Shores of Morocco Ends Deep in the Heartland

TROOP LIST

1. *Hq & Hq Co, 3d Inf Div*
2. *7th Infantry*
3. *15th Infantry*
4. *30th Infantry*
5. *9th FA Bn*
6. *10th FA Bn*
7. *39th FA Bn*
8. *41st FA Bn*
9. *10th Engr Bn*
    540th Engr Gp (C)
    1109th Engr Gp (C)
10. *3d Signal Co*
11. *3d Rcn Troop*
12. *3d Inf Div Arty*
    250th FA Bn
    693d FA Bn
13. *441st AAA AW Bn*
    2d Plat, Btry A, 353d AAA S/L Bn
    Btry C, 353d S/L Bn
14. *756th Tank Bn*
15. *601st TD Bn*
16. *3d Med Bn*
17. *106th Cav Gp*
18. *87th Cml Mortar Bn*

WITH the capture of Neuf-Brisach, the end of the Colmar Pocket was assured. The enemy was now unable to supply or reinforce his troops. As the 3d Infantry Division inexorably closed on the two bridges over the Rhine east of Neuf-Brisach the enemy demolished them.

The United States 12th Armored Division raced south from Colmar and made contact with I French Corps elements at Houffach. The mop-up of the remaining elements of the German Nineteenth Army took only a few days. And again the 3d took up its Watch on the Rhine.

Limited training was undertaken almost immediately as the Division outposted and patrolled, and made plans to deal with any German attempts to recross the river. The 7th and 30th Infantry Regiments handled this task, while 15th Infantry remained in reserve.

The 254th Infantry was completely relieved on February 9 and reverted to control of its parent organization, the 63rd Infantry Division.

By February 10 a subparagraph in the G-2 Periodic Report noted that: "Organized enemy resistance west of the Rhine River between Strasbourg and the Swiss border is reported to have ceased."

The 99th Chemical Mortar Battalion remained in Division reserve, registering, firing on targets of opportunity, and firing smoke missions across the Rhine. The 168th Chemical Company continued smoke operations along the river, screening our movements from the enemy in Germany until the morning of February 12, when a detachment from the 21st Chemical Company relieved it.

Commencing on February 16, elements of the 4th *Regiment Tirailleurs Marocain* of the 2d *Division Infanterie Motorisé* reconnoitered 7th and 30th Infantry positions, preparatory to relief of the entire Division. "You're going back so far you'll be able to eat ice cream," a happy General Devers had promised the Division at the finish of the attack, and the 3d was ready to take the Sixth Army Group Commander at his word.

The relief commenced on February 17 and at 1800, February 18 control of the sector passed from the Commanding General, 3d Infantry Division, to the Commanding General of the 2d DIM.

The 3d assembled and made preparations to move to prearranged areas in Lorraine near Nancy, after 188 days of continuous contact with the enemy.

Pont-a-Mousson is almost exactly halfway between Nancy and Metz. There is a sign which reads, "Nancy 27 km" and directly below it with an arrow pointing in the opposite direction the legend says, "Metz 28 km." It was here that the Division CP set up for business. The regiments disposed themselves in small towns all along the Nancy-Metz highway. The 7th Infantry's 1st Battalion was stationed in Belleville, and 2d at Dieulouard, and the 3d at Marbache, all between Pont-à-Mousson and Nancy. Near Pont-à-Mousson the 30th Infantry set up housekeeping: 1st Battalion near Eulmont, 2d at Bouxieres, and 3d Battalion at Lay St. Christopher. The 15th Infantry bivouacked in towns north of Pont-à-Mousson, in the vicinity of Pagny.

Official status of the Division was now SHAEF reserve, but there were few who doubted that recommitment to combat would long be delayed. Meanwhile rest, rehabilitation, and then, inevitably, training, were the order of the day. The infantry regiments began training new replacements, just as did the 601st TD

This is a smoke-fog generator emplaced near the banks of the Rhine at Neuf-Brisach to afford concealment for our movements on the west side.

Battalion and 756th Tank Battalion. The armored attachments had suffered heavier casualties in the Colmar attack than in any campaign since the push to Rome. New tanks, New TDs, and reinforcements were received to be absorbed into the framework of organizations. The 441st AAA AW Battalion's Battery C was immediately set to work providing antiaircraft protection for lines of communications, bivouac areas, and bridges, while the other two lettered batteries underwent rehabilitation.

The 10th Engineer Battalion and 3d Reconnaissance Troop likewise began rehabilitation and reception of reinforcements.

Along with the commencement of training, recreation was introduced to an organization which had known little recreation since its stay in Pozzuoli, near Naples, six months before. Pass trucks began making regular runs to Nancy, which by now was a large hospital and base-section strongpoint, and the locale of *beaucoup femmes,* always a subject of considerable interest to soldiers. Nancy, in many places virtually untouched by bombs and shells, was a sight for eyes weary of scarred, razed Alsatian villages.

But the war, as always, soon predominated and subordinated all other efforts. As February passed into March the training program rounded off. This consisted of intensive practice in street fighting, the attack of permanent fortifications, weapons firing, intelligence, night operations, and the technique of river crossings.

Effective March 12 the Division became a part of XV Corps, under the command of Maj. Gen. Wade H. Haislip, and plans were formulated for a forthcoming operation. Although plans for the operation were secret, oldtimers with the faculty of sensing preparations for reentry into combat, knew an operation was scheduled. This time no one doubted the destination or purpose. As one of the very few United States divisions which had fought against Germany almost continuously since July 10, 1943, what was more logical than action in the homeland of the enemy himself? Germany it was to be, and before the war ran its course the 3d Infantry Division was to have the distinction of playing a prominent part in seizing the very place in which Naziism had first arisen to plague the world.

On March 13 the Division began moving to assembly areas near Etting, Schmittviller, and Bining. The move was entirely secret. Numbers on vehicle bumpers were covered over. Shoulder patches were blotted out with strips of adhesive, as were the blue-and-white diagonal patches which decorated either side of each steel helmet.

The Division was poised on the Franco-German border, awaiting the signal for attack. It was not long coming. The date was set—March 15. The hour—0100.

In a special, last minute briefing, Iron Mike told his regimental commanders: "Within one hour after the jumpoff you will be in Germany."

Events proved him right. The 3d Infantry Division reached the fringe of its long-sought goal exactly thirty-one minutes after its leading elements crossed the line of departure.

The path into Germany was necessarily a thorny one. For the third push to the Rhine River also marked the third time that the division had been assigned to a highly-fortified area and given the task of reducing all obstacles that lay in the path. The two other times

Sgt. Horgan, Pvt. Theole and Sgt. Saridski, 601st TD Battalion inspect their TD at Pont-a-Mousson.

A race-track in Pont-a-Mousson was the scene of many decoration ceremonies during the rest period.

were against the "iron ring" of Anzio and the "frozen crust" of the Colmar Pocket.

Other United States units had faced the enemy in this area for more than two months. Shortly following the beginning of the German Ardennes–Eiffel offensive in the north there had been an attack against the Seventh Army. When this push was stopped, no further offensives were mounted in this area by either side. Stalemate developed. As usual, the Germans promptly mined every possible spot accessible to their engineers; fortified their lines by digging zig-zag fire trenches and siting their weapons with the expert eye to terrain for which they were noted.

Elements of the crack German 17th SS *Panzer* Division occupied a major portion of the sector through which lay our zone of advance at the time of our attack. Although morale of the average German soldier was not, on the average, high, that of the NCOs and officers was still unbroken, and the over-all fighting ability of enemy troops could still be termed no less than "excellent."

The ground was gummy, sticky, following recent rains.

Promptly at 0100, March 15, the 1st and 2d Battalions of the 7th Infantry and 1st and 3d Battalions of the 30th Infantry pushed off; the 7th from Rimling and the 30th from the vicinity of Schmittviller, passing through elements of the 44th Infantry Division. Division Artillery simultaneously opened fire with ten battalions, plus an additional six battalions of XV Corps artillery supporting. The initial barrage lasted twenty minutes.

Advancing on the left flank of the regiment the 1st Battalion of the 7th Infantry, commanded by Lt. Col. Kenneth W. Wallace, moved northward rapidly and aggressively, overcoming small-arms resistance which was supported by mortar and artillery defensive fire.

At 0135 Company B led the 3d Infantry Division into Germany about one mile south of Utweiler. First Scout Pfc. Wayne T. Alderson was the first man across. Minus Company A, the battalion crossed the Bickenalbe stream and seized crossroads 304, one kilometer east of Baumbusch woods. By noon, despite increasing enemy resistance, Company C was in the eastern edge of the woods, while Company B had pushed through moderate resistance to occupy Erching. Company A, which had swung left after progressing about one and one-half miles from the line of departure, stormed Guiderkirch from the north and had it cleared by 0400, taking sixty-one prisoners.

The 3d Division had had many attacks in which temporary disaster, as it sometimes must to the best formations, came to one battalion. In practically all cases it had resulted from enemy armor counterattacking a temporarily armorless unit. As it was at Maison Rouge bridge in the attack against the Colmar Pocket, so it was on the first day of the attack with Lt. Col. Jack M. Duncan's 2d Battalion of the 7th.

Advancing on the regiment's right flank the battalion encountered thick *schu*-minefields as well as antitank minefields and sustained serious casualties at the outset. Four tanks were disabled and the balance of attached armor halted. In spite of its crippling losses, plus heavy enemy resistance, the battalion forged its way into Utweiler and captured the town, taking many prisoners. At 0730 strong enemy Flakwagon and self-propelled gunfire was received and two hours later a battalion of enemy infantry, supported by nine tank destroyers and four Flakwagons, were observed on the high ground that ringed the town on three sides. Men of the isolated battalion watched the hostile armor roll into town, methodically leveling every house in its path. With no supporting armor, the only alternative to annihilation was withdrawal. Only a portion of the battalion managed to reach the high ground south of the town. There was a heavy toll in killed, wounded and captured, a good part of which was suffered prior to the withdrawal.

The 1st and 3d Battalions, 30th Infantry, also encountered intensely-sown *schu*-minefields from the outset and in addition 1st Battalion drew automatic fire from pillboxes. The 3d reported a stream of small-arms fire on the narrow gaps in minefields and extremely heavy, casualty-inflicting self-propelled gunfire.

Because of their maneuverability and the ease with which they crossed antipersonnel minefields, tanks of the 756th Battalion were employed to great advantage by the 30th both in smashing pillboxes and evacuating wounded.

3d Infantry Division infantrymen move up to the line of departure prior to the attack against Germany itself.

A tank-infantry attack, led by 1st Lt. Richard Rosebury of the regimental raider platoon attached to the 3d Battalion, was outstandingly successful in securing the dominating crest of a hill whose possession was absolutely essential to the battalion.

While the 1st and 3d Battalions of the 30th were rolling up the field defenses, the 2d was in "reserve" near Volmunster, if such can be called the role of a unit which found it necessary in a 26-hour period to clean out at least fifty pillboxes in an adjacent division's area, rather than endure a hail of fire from these positions.

The 7th Infantry's 3d Battalion, under Maj. Ralph J. Flynn, was committed at 0400. It pulled up behind the 2d Battalion and formed an arc around Utweiler running south to east. Companies I and L, and AT Company

The first group of enemy prisoners taken by the 3d Infantry Division on enemy soil move back to the PW cage on 15 March, 1945.

Rimschwiller village was the scene of a hard-fought battle. When this photo was taken enemy and friendly forces were both under cover.

(organized as a bazooka unit), supported by fifteen pieces of armor, launched a counterattack on Utweiler behind an artillery preparation. By 1540 assault elements of Company I had penetrated enemy defenses and entered the town. Armor of the task force destroyed seven enemy tanks and tank destroyers and all four of the enemy's Flakwagons. Fighting in Utweiler continued until 1800 hours that first day before the town was ours.

First element of the 15th Infantry to be thrown into the fight was the 1st Battalion, which shoved off from its area near Bining at noon, to attack Ormersviller. The battalion moved along the axis of the Rimling-Epping Urbach road to Epping Urbach, then swung north toward Omersviller. Near midnight, March 15, Company A had pushed to within 1000 yards of the town with no contact save for enemy artillery and mortar fire.

Division artillery, as always, played a very important part in the initial attack. From 0100 until daylight, March 15, the battalions fired a hundred concentrations in support of the attacking infantry units, in addition to the opening barrage.

At 0135 Company A, 15th Infantry, reported that it was entering Ormersviller, now against heavy artillery and mortar fire although there was very little small-arms resistance. Less than an hour later the company had occupied the left side of the town, with Company B on the east side. Ormersviller was captured—first town to fall to the 15th Infantry in the new drive.

The 1st and 3d Battalions, 7th Infantry, resumed the attack to the north and east toward the Siegfried Line at 0130. Against scattered but determined rearguard resistance, Company I took Hill 370 while Company L pushed into the Dackerwald woods. The 1st Battalion infiltrated into Medelsheim against stubborn enemy delaying action during the hours of darkness and during the early hours of daylight cleared the town, taking many prisoners.

By noon 1st Battalion, 15th Infantry, had got to within 800 yards of Loutzviller, where its lead element, the 2d Platoon of Company A, was held up by small-arms fire from a house on the outskirts. One member of the platoon here killed one and captured nine Germans to eliminate this obstacle, and the town fell shortly after.

The 3d Battalion had moved from its assembly area near Epping Urbach that morning and passed through 1st Battalion elements at Ormersviller, attacking southeast toward Volmunster. The town fell to Company I within two and a half hours as Company L swung toward Eschviller, which it and elements of Compny K took during the morning.

During the rest of the day and for part of the next, 15th Infantry continued to advance. The 1st Battalion overran Scheidberg and stepped into Germany to follow up with the capture of Hornbach, against small-arms and machine-gun fire. One platoon of Company A fought two hours in taking Hornbach. The 1st Battalion moved on to capture Mauschbach.

Dietrichingen fell to the 2d Battalion while a patrol found Brensschelbach clear. The 3d Battalion took the main road junction east of Loutzviller, then swept through Windhof, Schweyen, Ohrenthal, and pressed on to Rolbing where Company I crossed an unnamed river. In the battle for the road junction, Pfc. Buster D. Robertson, first scout in an assault platoon, distinguished himself by walking forward under heavy

Cpl. Edward Keeler and T/Sgt. Paul Mayer reconnoitre possible targets on the approaches to the Siegfried Line from a forward observation post.

Typical defenses of the Siegfried Line. In the foreground an anti tank ditch; behind, a band of dragon's teeth; to the left fire trenches.

fire and indicating enemy positions to be destroyed. He himself was killed with a burst of machine-gun fire, but the assault platoons inflicted approximately fifty casualties on the enemy causing his forces to withdraw leaving behind eleven machine guns.

At 1400 March 16, the 1st and 3d Battalions, 7th Infantry, resumed the attack in their zone. Troops of the 1st Battalion broke into Neu-Altheim and engaged the enemy in a bitter small-arms fight. In slightly more than an hour, despite furious attempts on the part of two enemy tanks or self-propelled guns to stem the assault, the town was cleared. The 3d Battalion, in an aggressive attack, seized Riesweiler, closed in and took the *Nasserwald* and *Grosserwald* woods and by 1700 advanced to a road junction and patch of woods a mile east of Altheim.

This is a close-up of a single band of dragon's teeth fronted by an anti-tank ditch. Bulldozers filled the gaps and engineers demolished the obstacles after the infantry took the position.

This aerial photo, taken from south of Zweibrücken shows one of the places through which the infantry, followed by armor and transportation, broke.

At 0020, March 17, 1st Battalion pushed out again in the attack, while the 3d Battalion dispatched patrols. Altheim fell without resistance to the 1st Battalion. Companies K and L attacked Stuppacheshof and occupied it within three-quarters of an hour. Patrols moved into Mittelbach unopposed but found the town heavily mined, and boobytrapped with 75mm shells.

The 3d Infantry Division was now at the first fortifications of the vaunted Siegfried Line.

A task force consisting of a rifle platoon from 1st Battalion, 7th Infantry, a bazooka platoon from the

This aerial photo shows part of the German defensive position south of Zweibrücken. These defenses posed a difficult problem to the infantry, who eliminated them.

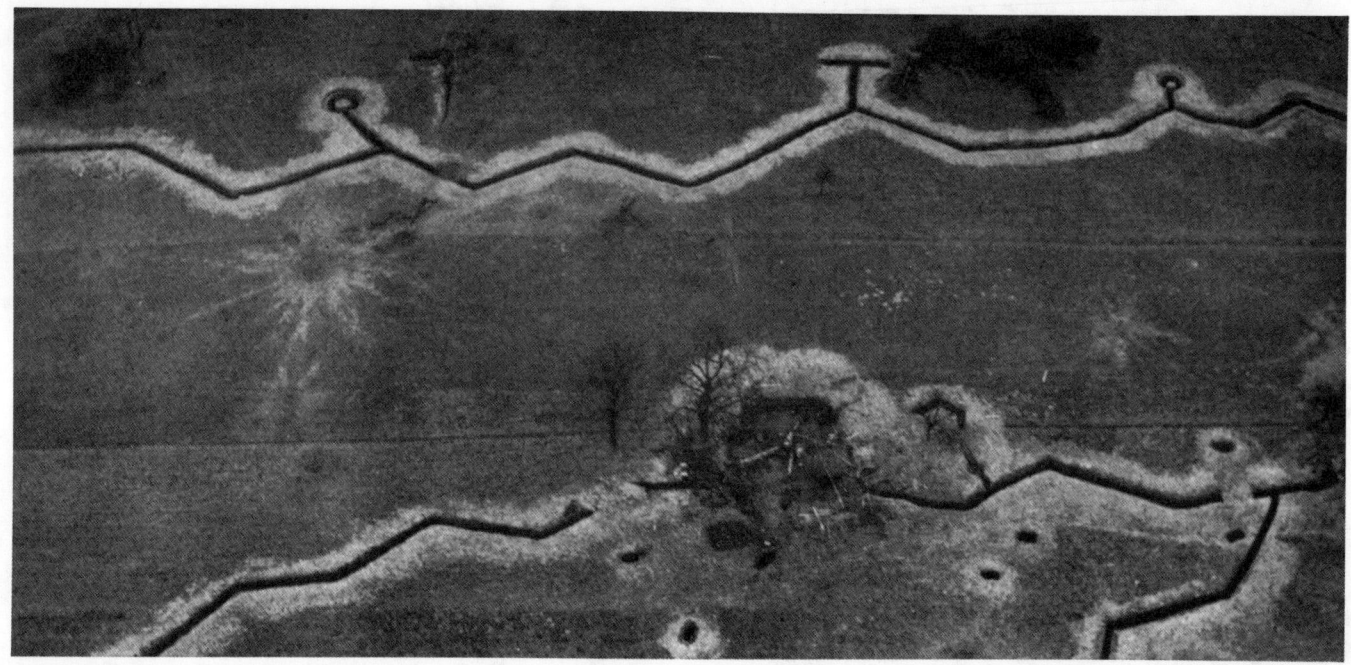
Part of the Siegfried Line south of Zweibrücken. An anti-tank gun (slightly to the right of center) is sited behind a zigzag fire trench.

regimental Antitank Company, and five light tanks from the 756th Tank Battalion set out for Mittelbach from Altheim.

During the night of March 17-18 a small, carefully-briefed patrol from 1st Battalion, 15th Infantry, was sent out to the first row of the Siegfried Line's "dragon's teeth," and drew small-arms, artillery, and self-propelled-gun fire, indicating that the sector was extremely sensitive.

Maj. Gen. John W. O'Daniel at this time ordered a two-regiment attack against the Siegfried Line, 7th and 15th, with the 15th on the right, to breach the line, push rapidly to the Schwarzbach River, secure two bridges and the high ground immediately to the north; then mop up from the flank and rear of the Siegfried defenses east of the breach. H-hour was set for 0545, March 18.

The 7th Infantry moved to an assembly area in the vicinity of Althornbach during the night of March 17-18 and the 15th likewise completed its operations.

The 30th Infantry was still in reserve.

Assault battalion was the 1st in each of the regiments.

At 0545, following a strong artillery preparation, the two battalions jumped off. The 1st Battalion, 7th Infantry, penetrated the first three belts of dragon's teeth, by-passing many enemy groups in pillboxes, each of which thereafter became an objective of its own, to reach the Muhlthalderhof Ferme, about a mile-and-a-half southeast of Zweibrücken, at 0630, where the battalion was engaged in a fire fight by the enemy.

The 1st Battalion, 15th Infantry, followed by the 2d, while the 3d performed a blocking mission on the right flank of the Division and regiment, got away at 0545 and likewise advanced behind the massed fire of nine battalions of artillery and was supported by engineers with bulldozers and demolitions.

The battalion immediately drew fierce small-arms fire and picked its way ahead slowly, closing in on the woods to the front. As it advanced, the enemy opened fire with heavy concentrations of artillery fire.

By 0930 Company C was in the woods, with Company A on the right, moving toward the first row of dragon's teeth. The resistance was now furious. Brisk fire fights raged throughout the course of the morning and the enemy succeeded in preventing the battalion from reaching the dragon's teeth until 1130, when Company C forced its way in. Four hours later the company was barely inside the obstacles and commencing to mop up against tenacious resistance that slowed the advance to a yard-by-yard pace. In this sector the enemy was fighting with everything he could muster to hold the Westwall and keep the last great man-made barrier before the Reich intact.

The 7th Infantry, at 0730, committed the 3d Battalion, which initially was without armor because the engineers had been unable to blow the dragon's teeth sufficiently for tanks of the 756th and tank destroyers of the 601st to operate. At 0930 Company I, assault company of the battalion, encountered stiff resistance from by-passed enemy groups 500 yards south of the 1st Battalion. The balance of the 3d Battalion further south also engaged formidable enemy elements by-passed by the 1st. The 2d Battalion meanwhile mopped up and secured the flanks of the advance.

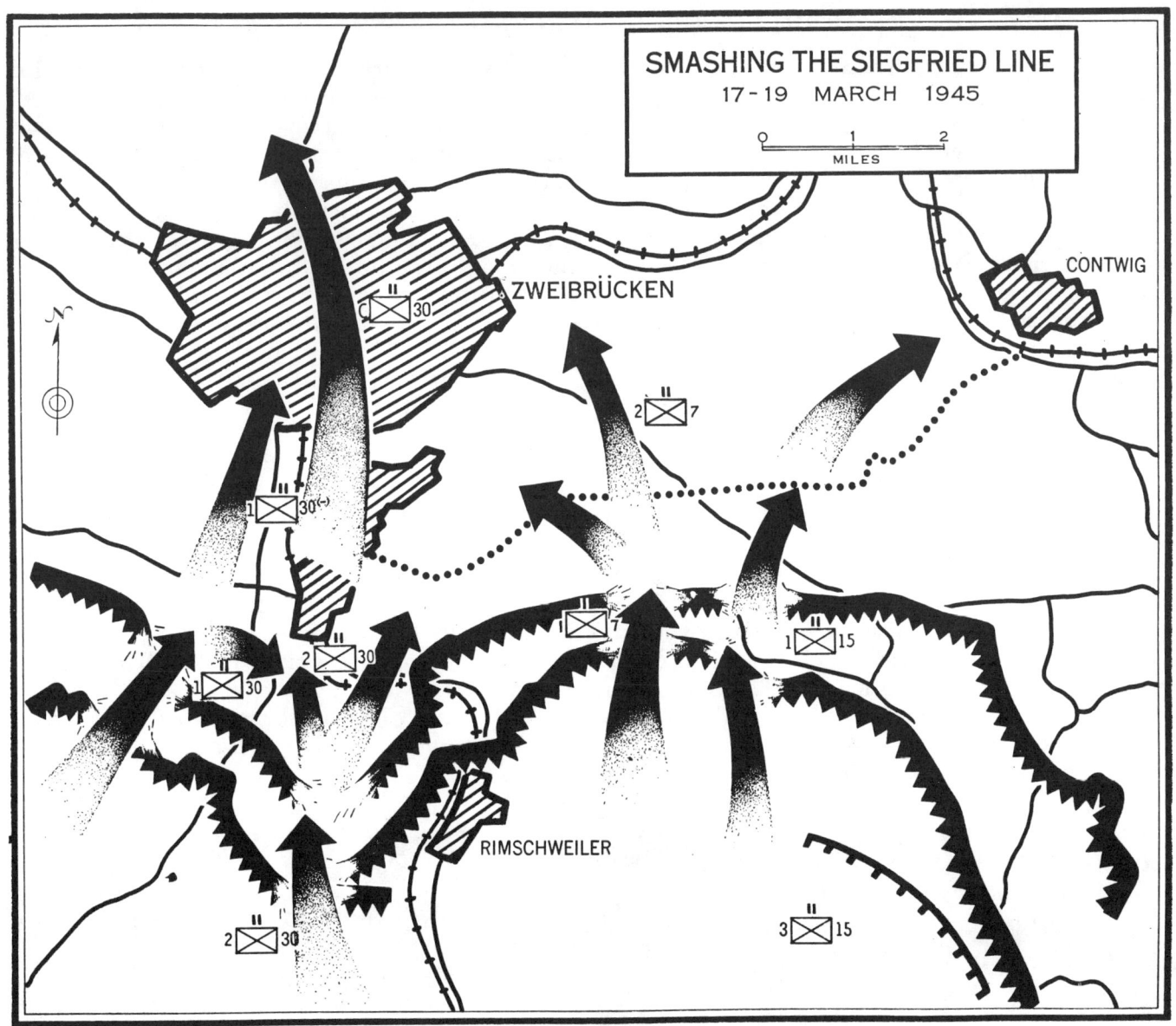

Company B, 15th Infantry, passed through the weary Company C and pressed the attack with renewed force. Fierce fighting raged the length of the Division front.

At about 1900 a reinforced company of enemy infantry counterattacked the 1st Battalion, 7th Infantry, the brunt of which was taken and repulsed by Company A. The battalion in turn launched counterthrusts that drove the enemy back with many losses. By the end of the day the 7th Infantry had driven a thin wedge 1500 yards in depth through the first and second rows of dragon's teeth and was within sight of Zweibrücken, fighting the enemy on three sides. Shortly after midnight, March 18, Company I repulsed a determined counterattack at Wallerscheid. By this time the 1st Battalion had almost exhausted its ammunition and supplies. Armor was held up by the antitank ditches and one tank was stuck in the "teeth." A task force, consisting of Company I and engineers commanded by the 3d Battalion S-3, Captain Harold Wigetman, succeeded in supplying the 1st Battalion during the night, although the task force received and repulsed a strong counterattack from the northeast just before it contacted rear elements of the 1st.

The fighting continued all night in the 15th zone also. The 2d Battalion, standing by all the previous day ready to move up and renew the attack, had been held up by furious artillery fire. However, it passed through the 1st Battalion in the early morning hours of March 19 with Company F in the lead, followed by Company E.

The Commanding General decided that the attack needed additional impetus and committed the 30th Infantry to the left of the 7th Infantry in a new sector on the morning of March 19. At 0515 the 2d and 1st Battalions in the assault, preceded by a thunderous half-hour artillery barrage, blasted their way into the dragon's teeth.

Maj. Kenneth B. Potter, commanding 1st Battalion, 15th Infantry, in the absence, due to injury, of the battalion commander, Lt. Col. Michael Paulick, was caught in an antitank ditch while the enemy fired down the portion of the ditch that ran off at right angles on either flank. Thus trapped and unable to crawl out because of a hill, the major and his party remained there until nightfall directing the fight by radio.

The 1st Battalion, 15th Infantry, assumed the job of blocking to the east and west the morning of the 19th. The 2d's Company G was thrown into the battle and during the morning eliminated four pillboxes. By noon however, the battalion was approximately 2000 yards southeast of Contwig and receiving direct antitank-gun fire. In addition, hundreds of antitank and antipersonnel mines were hampering the advance—one of the greatest mine concentrations the regiment had ever faced.

The 3d Battalion, 7th Infantry, had moved north at 0800 to contact advance elements (1st Battalion) of the regiment, despite enemy-manned pillboxes on both flanks of the line of advance which tried vainly to break up the operation.

The grinding, slashing, grueling fight continued that whole day of March 19. The Germans had provided obstacles by demolishing every bridge in the path of advance. The line was a maze of reinforced concrete pillboxes with interlocking fields of fire, barbed-wire entanglements, entrenchments and deep antitank ditches, in addition to the omnipresent dragon's teeth.

The enemy facing Seventh Army was rapidly being cut off in the rear by elements of the advancing Third Army at this time, but this was nowhere apparent in the quality and ferocity of opposition offered the 3d Infantry Division. The crackup, however, was not far away. General O'Daniel, sensing this, ordered the attack ruthlessly pressed. It went on through the night.

In one small action, Cpl. Henry Mount of 15th Infantry's Company G placed pointblank machine-gun fire on a pillbox from an exposed position, although he could hardly have hoped to neutralize it. After a short time the occupants ceased firing and friendly riflemen, having got next to the fortification unobserved, blew the door with TNT charges and took eight prisoners. In another instance one rifleman killed five snipers with five shots within a very few minutes.

The breakup came on the morning of the 20th. Prisoners began to swarm in, over-run by the relentless attack.

The railroad yards at Zweibrücken had been the target for the airforce long before the 3d Division entered the city.

A 3d Infantry Division patrol cautiously enters the devastated city of Zweibrücken.

At 0230 Company E, 7th Infantry, seized and occupied a pillbox 300 yards south of the Muhlthalderhof Ferme. An hour later 3d Battalion had cleaned out six pillboxes. The enemy's defense began to dissolve and patrols quickly pushed out to the front.

The 1st Battalion, 30th Infantry, under Lt. Col. Mackenzie E. Porter, had a bridgehead across the Hornbach River by 0545. As the 1st and 2d Battalions continued their assault, plans were being laid for 3d Battalion to widen the corridor which the assault units were making through the fortifications, and to mop up scattered pockets of resistance.

In front of the 15th, likewise, the breakthrough was obviously successful and the enemy was moving out in double time. Companies F and G were attacked from the rear at 0400 but by dawn the resistance had been mopped up and the 2d Battalion moved ahead toward Contwig without enemy contact save for scattered groups of Germans which surrendered without creating trouble.

Leaving a platoon to protect engineers at the Hornbach River crossing site the 1st Battalion, 30th Infantry, capitalizing on the Siegfried breakthrough in the 30th Infantry zone, rushed patrols to the bridges leading into Zweibrücken, the first large and well-known German city yet encountered. The 2d Battalion, after detailing troops to block exposed positions, was ordered to clear the city in its zone. To take Zweibrücken was entirely a 30th Infantry assignment, which the regiment rapidly proceeded to do.

The 1st and 3d Battalions, 7th Infantry, advanced to the north at the same time. By 0825 thirty-five prisoners had been taken. At 1100 a task force, consisting of Company E and tank destroyers, contacted elements of the 30th Infantry one kilometer southwest of Muhlthalderhof Ferme. By noon the 7th Infantry was engaged in mopping-up operations.

During the remainder of the 20th, the 30th Infantry concentrated on clearing Zweibrücken, as the 7th relieved the 30th in Ixheim, and took Nieder-Auerbach. The 1st and 2d Battalions, 30th, moved to high ground north of Zweibrücken following its capture, where the 1st Battalion had a stiff fight with numerous dug-in enemy infantry liberally supported by 88mm guns. The battalion destroyed two of these guns and captured sixty prisoners to secure the high ground, which then served as a line of departure for the 6th Armored Division.

All regiments, during the night of the 20th and over the 21st, re-checked and completed clearing isolated sections of the Siegfried Line, and made ready for some blitz warfare in the style to which the 3d Infantry Division had long ago become so well accustomed.

The deed was done. The Siegfried Line, not engaged until March 18, was breached in the 3d Division zone in three days—start to finish. Despite the fact that the Third Army was threatening the German rear, the

Two 3d Division infantrymen rush forward, crouched low, to avoid fire from their left in a village near the Siegfried Line.

enemy defenders seemingly were not affected by the menace, and the resistance offered to our attack was as tenacious as that encountered anywhere.

During the late afternoon of March 21 the 7th Infantry moved to an assembly area in the vicinity of Contwig, and at 2100 attacked to the northeast. Without firing a shot the 1st Battalion cleared the towns of Battweiler, Schmittenhausen, Reifenberg, Herschberg, Schauer-Berg, and Hoheinod, capturing more than a hundred prisoners in the process. Operating in the right half of the regimental sector, the 3d Battalion cleared Thalischweiler after a hard fight against automatic weapons and small-arms resistance. The 3d Battalion seized more than fifty prisoners, two anti-tank guns and one Flakwagon.

At 2350, March 22, 1st Lieutenant Elmer J. Becker, 2d Battalion S-2, led a task force consisting of a bazooka platoon from Antitank Company and a reinforced rifle platoon from 2d Battalion plus two demolition engineers and two radiomen in a rapid move by vehicle through Schmitthausen, Wallhalben and Saalstadt to Harsberg, where contact was made with elements of the 106th Cavalry Group. From Harsberg the task force moved on foot across country to Steinalben, where the bridge over the Moosalbe River was seized intact and demolitions removed from the span.

By the end of the day, the regiment had accounted for 203 prisoners, including three officers. Over one hundred slave laborers had been freed and evacuated to the rear.

The 30th Infantry had been completely motorized on the previous day. The regiment was chosen to follow up the 6th Armored Division's dash to the Rhine—the Division's third trip to the river in World War II.

The 30th covered the sixty miles in three days, to assemble in the vicinity of Ludwigshafen. The *Autobahn*, built originally for military traffic, served its purpose well. After the first day, the 30th's move was largely administrative as Third Army units had already cleared the route of the *Autobahn*.

The 15th Infantry, meanwhile, had pushed off to the east on March 21, led by the 1st Battalion, and entered Walshausen by 1600 against spotty resistance; then shoved on to take Winzeln while Company C moved due east to Windsberg and Company A to the southeast. The battalion was on the move all night, taking fifty prisoners and inflicting casualties whenever it encountered the enemy. There were brief, but frequent, encounters.

The 3d Battalion jumped off in midafternoon of the 21st, advancing along the axis of the main road running southeast from Stambach. The battalion plowed ahead with a company on either side of the road and Company L moving astride it. Six tanks supported the attack. Company I reached Nunschweiler before midnight with virtually no opposition. However by midnight the enemy brought up troops and engaged the company in a lively fight using small-arms, machine-gun, mortar and self-propelled gun fire. After two hours the fight subsided; the town fell and Company I pushed on to clean up the woods immediately to the east.

Company L then passed through Nunschweiler, attacking toward Hoheidschweiler. Reaching the town, our assault squads were working their way through the streets when the Germans launched a strong counterattack and directed intense machine-gun fire down the streets. The enemy forces were supported by two tanks. After a short fight one was destroyed and the enemy withdrew.

Company K, in the meantime, had taken the town of Hoh and was ready to forge on to Froschen and south to Petersburg, while Company L attacked toward Fohbach and Hengsberg. By early morning of March 22, Company K had reached Thal and Company I had captured Petersburg.

The 15th Infantry regrouped and early in the evening of March 22 moved out from the vicinity of Contwig to reach Kaiserslautern. The 2d Battalion remained at Kaiserslautern while the remainder of the regiment, following in the wake of the 7th and 30th Infantry Regiments, went on to bivouac in the vicinity of Hardenburg to the northeast. On the following day the battalions pushed on to the Rhine.

The 7th Infantry, after resting on March 22, made an administrative move to the vicinity of Carlsberg, and during the night of March 24-25 moved to the Frankenthal area in preparation for the crossing of the Rhine.

The 30th Infantry was ordered to an assembly area near Herxheim-am-Berg.

The Division immediately began practicing boat drills and made preparations for crossing. Even while training, one 30th Infantry company captured four Germans and forced them to finish a speed march with them.

The tremendous Seventh-Third Army pocket was now completely eliminated with the exception of a number of stragglers and small groups, and Seventh Army was being grouped for the plunge across the river.

The Wehrmacht now reeled like a punchdrunk boxer, unable either to duck or parry. Armored spearheads of other United States armies already had broken loose east of the Rhine and were wheeling, almost without opposition, deep into Germany.

Supreme Commander Dwight D. Eisenhower's pre-

Capt. L. H. Bishop, 163d Engineers (attached) helps anchor one end of a ponton bridge being built across the Rhine.

diction that the war would be won west of the Rhine River was becoming fact.

Shortly after dusk on March 25 the 10th Engineers began bringing boats and river-crossing material to the water front. Because of the high dikes south of the unfinished *Autobahn* bridge it was necessary for the troops to hand-carry their boats to the water's edge. Work was considerably hampered by mortar fire coming from the town of Sandhofen in the 7th Infantry zone and several boats were lost, as well as nine casualties sustained before the enemy fire was silenced by counterbattery and smoke from Division Artillery.

H-hour was set for 0230, March 26. The 7th and 30th Infantry Regiments were to make the assault. On the left (north) flank the 45th Infantry Division was to cross at the same time.

Division Artillery, with the 250th and 693d FA Battalions attached, opened fire at 0152. It was a terrific barrage. Approximately 10,000 rounds were fired in a 38-minute period. Corps artillery fired a program on towns, enemy artillery, and road nets.

For over half an hour, as assault troops of the 3d Infantry Division tensely crouched on the western bank, shells from friendly artillery burst on the other side, less than 300 yards away, painting the skyline a lurid red. In the 7th Infantry Zone, a chance hit by an enemy incendiary shell on a barn in the vicinity of the regimental CP lit up the crossing area, silhouetting the men and boats, and rendering them excellent targets for the enemy.

As H-hour approached, the boats of the first assault wave were at the water's edge in an inferno of fire. Many boats were splintered to kindling before they could be launched. Those men who could pick up their boats ran quickly to the water, shoved them in and climbed aboard. The boats got off. Some were hit, some capsized. Motors sputtered and died and engineers and men paddled frantically through the smoky, murky haze to the far shore. As the first wave hit the opposite bank a heavy concentration of mortar and self-propelled-gun fire awaited it. Both banks were zeroed in by the enemy. Quickly men of the 7th Infantry reorganized and headed east with the 1st and 3d Battalions abreast.

Ahead lay an open field. Powder smoke burned the nostrils of the men. A bright moon cast eerie shadows against the high bank of the *Autobahn* as numerous but scattered enemy machine guns, forming the final protective line for Sandhofen, opened up on the troops. Within a few minutes the 3d Battalion, 7th Infantry, minus Company L, was at the cloverleaf north of Sandhofen, while Company L was moving north toward the castle. By 0500 hours, the 1st Battalion closed in on Sandhofen against determined resistance. Forty minutes later the 3d Battalion was at Scharhof, sending elements in a flanking move to the north to take Kirschgartshausen. Without pause 3d Battalion continued to the east until it ran into the direct fire of four enemy tanks, supported and protected by infantry firing from the factories deep in the Viernheimer woods.

Against initially light enemy resistance and artillery fire on the near bank, 30th Infantry, with 2d and 3d Battalions in the assault, had hurdled the Rhine at 0230. The regiment found the east bank defended by a position of double foxholes and squad positions, with a light machine gun in each squad.

By early morning real resistance was encountered in each battalion sector and it became imperative that the movement inland be swift, and the all-essential high ground secured. However, hardened soldiers of the 30th refused to be stopped by anything the enemy could offer.

By midmorning engineers and regimental vehicles as well as tank destroyers and tanks at the 7th Infantry crossing site were under an almost constant barrage of 88mm fire. This continued to midafternoon.

At noon elements of the 1st Battalion, 7th Infantry, were in Sandhofen fighting fiercely for the town. Every

The heavy ponton bridge constructed across the Rhine near **Worms.**

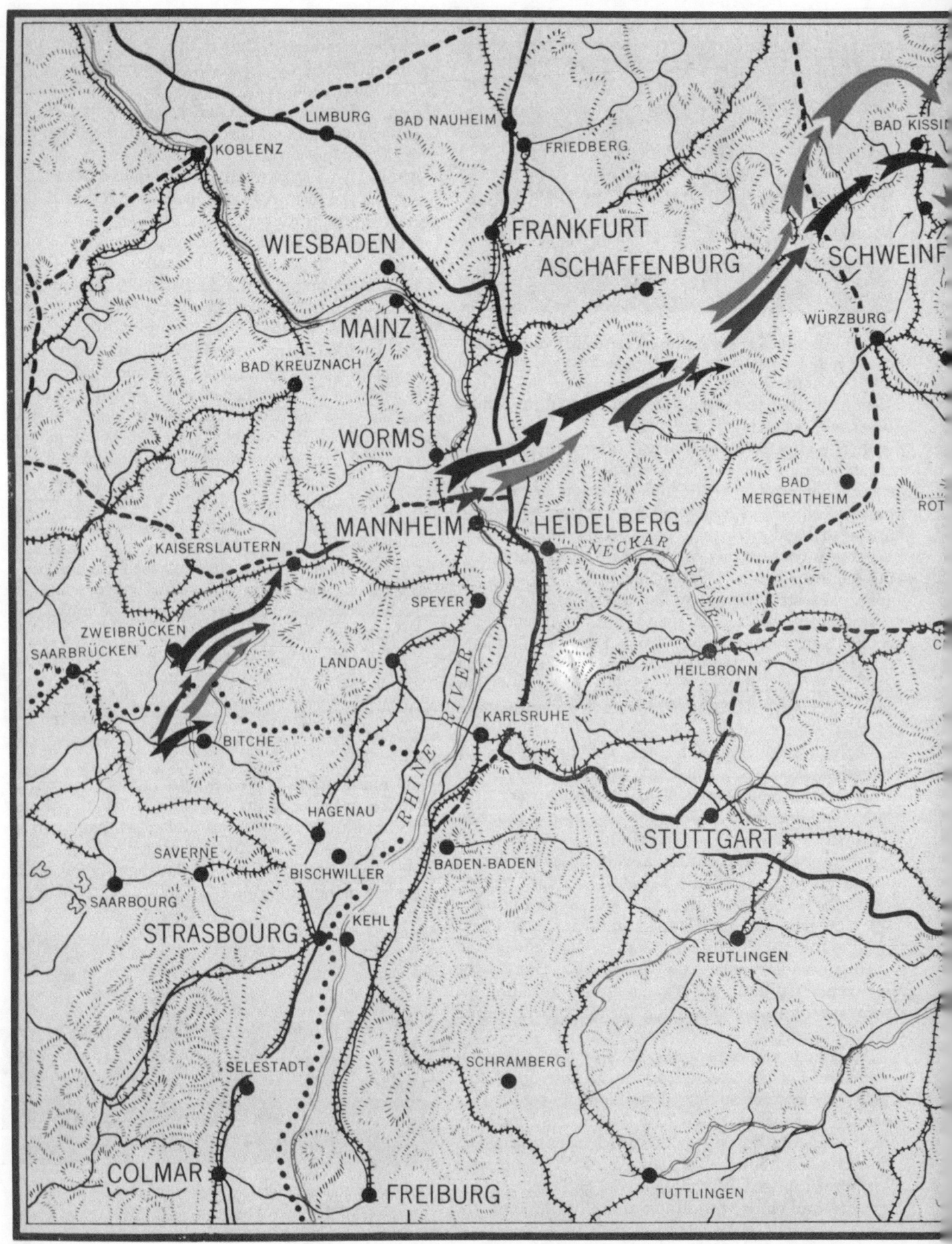

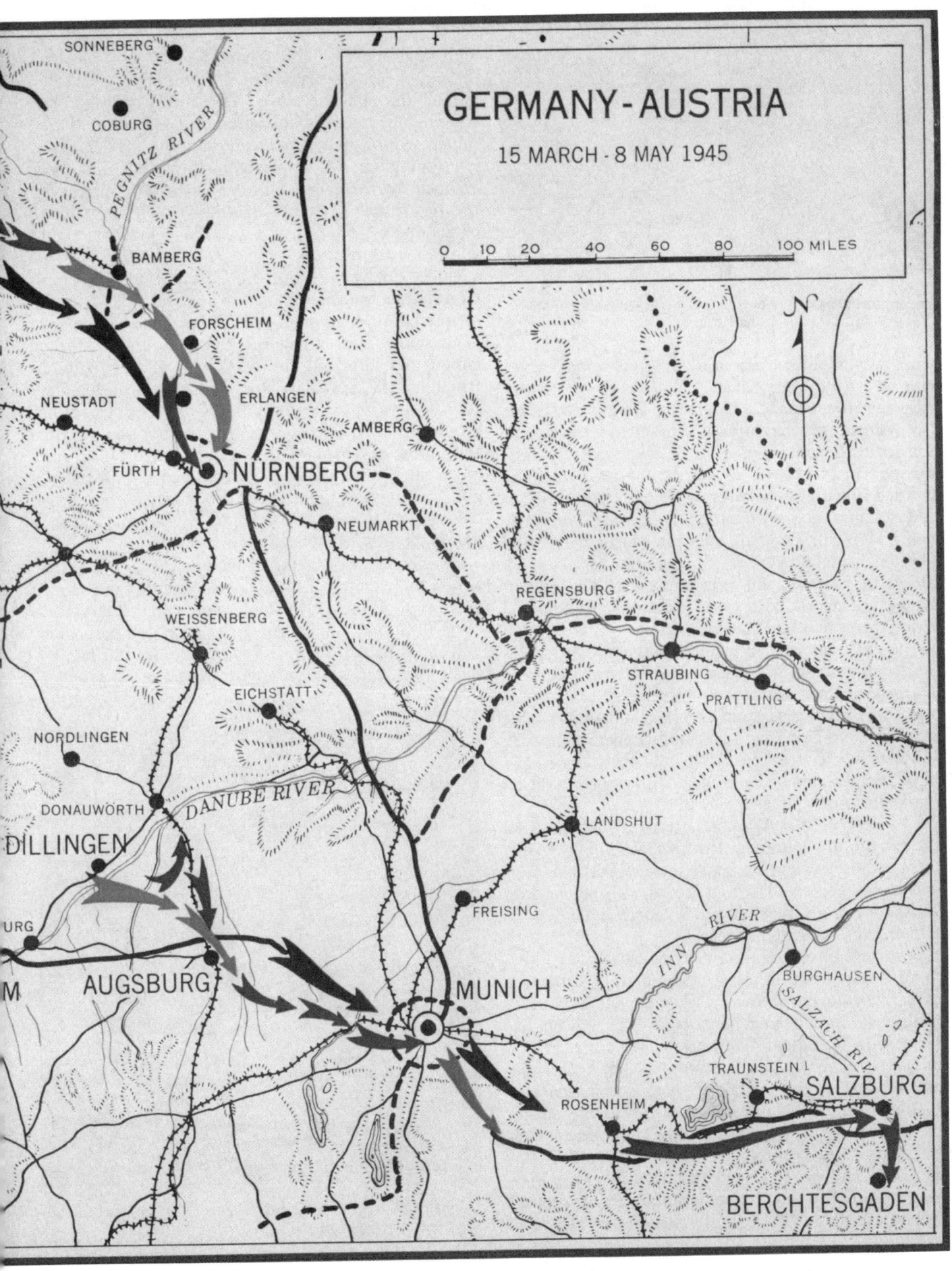

An engineer assault boat tows a ponton back upstream after it had broken away.

house was a pillbox that had to be destroyed, along with its fanatical occupants.

Enemy troops made a number of attempts to pierce the positions of 3d Battalion, but each fresh assault was repulsed and prisoners were taken continuously. Moving out of reserve, 2d Battalion crossed the river and tied in with 1st Battalion in Sandhofen at 1415.

Most opposition encountered by the 30th Infantry was in Hofheim, Bobstadt, Burstadt, and Lampertheim. The 1st Battalion, crossing behind the 2d and 3d, circled to Bobstadt and took the town in a brilliant maneuver against withering small-arms, 40mm, and 88mm direct fire. One company drove straight through on the flank and came around from the rear; after this the frontal attack was launched. All Germans in the town were either killed or captured. Eighteen generators and searchlights from German antiaircraft units were captured along with much other enemy materiel.

Bobstadt, reported cleared by another army, had never been entered by United States troops before the 1st Battalion fought for and took it.

By 1000 the 2d Battalion had reached Hofheim and cleared the town immediately thereafter. The enemy then withdrew what he could toward Burstadt, near which town he combined his troops with other forces withdrawn from the Rhine, and counterattacked with armor and Flakwagon support.

Company F took the brunt of this counterattack. Although hampered by lack of supporting armor or other attachments, because they were hit before the bridge was in and after heavy ponton ferry boats had just begun operating, Company F and other 2d Battalion elements fought tigerishly. Using *Panzerfaust* and bazookas; receiving aid from their battalion anti-tank-platoon bazooka teams, the company dealt the enemy a decisive blow and repulsed the counterattack. Subsequent interrogation of prisoners revealed that Hofheim had been defended by 200 infantry with Flakwagons and five dual-purpose 88mm guns in support.

The 7th Infantry's fight for Sandhofen continued with unabated fury throughout the day and far into the night as 1st Battalion slowly but aggressively pushed through the town. The enemy resisted the cleaning-up process with mortar and sniper fire, later supplementing it with machine-gun and artillery fire. Every building was employed for protection and concealment by the enemy and our forces. The success of the regimental operation depended upon the taking of Sandhofen, which stuck into the regiment's right flank like a knife.

Under cloudy skies, the 15th Infantry, in Division reserve, crossed during the morning of March 26. During the preceding evening 2d and 3d Battalions had moved to assembly areas along the river just south of the famous old cathedral city of Worms and at 0330 2d Battalion had moved out for the crossing site on the edge of the city followed by the 3d. At 0900, troops of the 3d Battalion piled out of their rubber assault rafts and up the east bank of the river, followed by 2d Battalion an hour later. Both encountered self-propelled-gun and mortar fire during the crossings, but little damage was done. The 1st Battalion, assembled in the woods south of Worms, crossed at noon.

Once on the east bank, 3d Battalion was committed almost immediately to clean out the island in the Rhine northwest of Lampertheim. Enemy forces there had been firing on the crossing site with self-propelled-gun and small-arms fire, and so effective was the harassment that engineer operations on the bridges under

Colonel McGarr, CO 30th Infantry, confers with two of his staff by the banks of the Rhine.

The first tank destroyer of the 3d Division's 601st TD Battalion crosses the heavy ponton bridge at Worms to aid the infantry on the far side of the Rhine.

construction had to be suspended for two hours. Several assault craft also had been sunk.

Attacking from the south, the bridge was seized, and within an hour Company K was on the island making good progress, having taken twenty prisoners. By 1400 the entire east side was cleared, and three hours later the entire island was cleared and seven Flak guns captured.

At Lampertheim, five miles from the Rhine, 3d Battalion, 30th Infantry, had met 500 infantry supported by 88s, Flakwagons, and armor, all determinedly resisting. While Companies K and I placed a pincers on the town from the northwest and northeast respectively, Company I undertook the main enveloping role. Company K attacked from the right, bearing into the city almost frontally. Company L, which was defending the battalion left flank and blocking to the north at vital road intersections, ran into intense opposition.

In the attack on the city itself the Company I commander, 1st Lt. Gerald G. Mehuron, directed artillery fire that landed on all sides of him and even fired it to the rear of his position with great effect.

First Lt. Eldon North of the regiment's Cannon Company, attached to Company L, destroyed a complete battery of 88mm guns with fire from his unit's guns. In addition, Company L bazooka men destroyed two tanks which attempted to counterattack their position. After clearing the woods beyond Lampertheim, the 3d Battalion passed into regimental reserve.

During the early morning crossing, the second tank of Company C, 756th Tank Battalion, which had attempted to cross was stuck on the river bank. The remaining tanks of an original fourteen in support of the 30th Infantry had "swum" (having been fitted with canvas flotation aprons) across successfully between 0930 and 1130. Of the seven tanks attached to 7th Infantry one was hit and destroyed by enemy artillery fire prior to the crossing. Shell fragments ripped the canvas flotation aprons on the remaining two, which sank, and two more were unable to float on the hastily-repaired aprons.

The remainder of the tanks in the battalion were ferried across at intervals during the rest of the day.

The 601st TD Battalion supported the crossings with fire and awaited facilities to be ferried across the river.

By nightfall the backbone of the enemy defense in the factory area in the Viernheimer woods was smashed by the 7th Infantry, and shortly before midnight 3d Battalion, 7th, with its attached armor, attacked southeast through the 1st Battalion in Sandhofen, encountering small-arms fire.

The 3d Battalion, 15th Infantry, after mopping up the island, had sent a patrol to Santdorf, just southeast of Lampertheim, where it was greeted with self-propelled-gun fire from the crossroads. Artillery was called for, the strongpoint smashed, and Company L moved in on the town followed by the remainder of the battalion. More enemy fire was met and artillery fire was once more directed on the enemy. Again the attack was launched and by 1935 the town fell.

Morning of March 27 saw 1st Battalion, 7th Infantry, in control of Sandhofen as the enemy sought to blast down every building with concentrated artillery fire. As the men reached the Alt Rhine dike to the southeast, all organized enemy resistance in the sector ceased.

Morning also saw 2d Battalion, 30th Infantry, in control of both Burstadt and Lorsch. The entire battalion

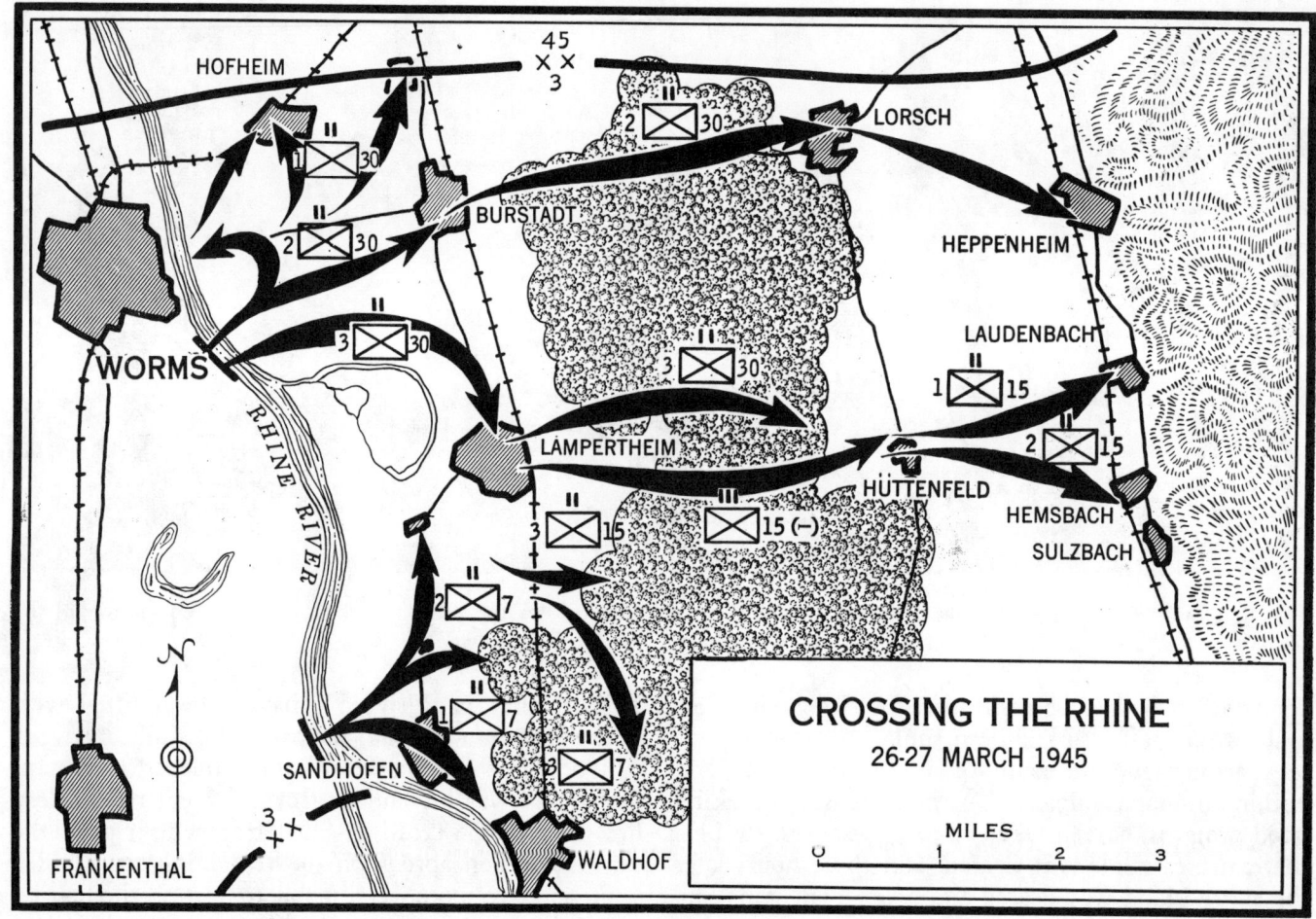

CROSSING THE RHINE
26-27 MARCH 1945

then mounted trucks, "ducks," and armor and dashed toward Heppenheim.

A patrol of Company E, under Capt. Ralph R. Carpenter, reached the hospital town first and with Company G, commanded by Capt. John H. West, took the town and liberated 300 American hospital patients, including several 3d Division officers and men and some 800 other Allied prisoners in other hospitals. The town was cleared by 1030 that morning.

During the afternoon of March 27, after clearing its sector, the 7th Infantry was relieved by the 71st Infantry (44th Infantry Division) and moved north to Lorsch. The following day, the regiment moved to Winkel and on the 29th made a third move to Reischelsheim.

The 30th Infantry within thirty-six hours after reaching the far bank of the Rhine, had taken 1250 prisoners, an enormous amount of equipment, a number of small towns, and had secured positions on vital high ground.

Appropriating all captured enemy transportation, the regiment became completely motorized and, with attached armor, continued the chase of the major German elements to its front, by-passing numerous small groups as it sped pell-mell eastward from Heppenheim. The terrific pace carried the 1st Battalion, commanded by Lt. Col. Mackenzie E. Porter, 40 kilometers (25 miles) in one day, and at 0230 March 29, the battalion raced into Lindenfels. When a German force sent to defend the city arrived, the 1st Battalion had secured all road junctions and entrances to the city and the Germans fell back with many casualties.

Late that afternoon, the 30th reached the west bank of the Main River. Company A of the 1st Battalion, commanded by Capt. Hugh S. Montgomery, had seized the town of Wörth and 2d Battlion had cleared Trennfurt.

On the second day of the river crossing attack, the 15th, like the other regiments, pushed rapidly ahead, clearing Laudonbach, Bonsweiher, Hembach, Sulzbach and Viernheim and numerous pockets of resistance. A six-man motorized reconnaissance patrol of the 3d Battalion, operating on the highway east of Heppenheim, found elements of the 39th FA Battalion held up by enemy machine-gun and Flakwagon fire some 200 yards outside the town. The patrol worked its way to observation points and was soon engaged in a heavy fire fight, during which the members killed ten Germans, wounded the same number and captured three others as well as putting to flight the rest of the group of forty who were manning the roadblock.

The regiment's attack began shortly after midnight, with the 1st and 2d Battalions jumping off from Lampertheim. Swinging southeast through the woods, the two battalions moved rapidly ahead while the 3d followed closely behind, mopping up by-passed groups of enemy.

Company A, under 1st Lt. Michael J. Daly, cut the north-south *Autobahn* just west of Huttenfeld shortly after the attack got under way and Company C, commanded by Capt. Samuel H. Roberts, moved into Huttenfeld just before daybreak. The enemy retreated so fast that numerous bridges over canals in the area were all left intact, although Company A, leading the push, destroyed an occasional enemy machine gun left to guard them.

The battalion was on the objective of Laudenbach before noon. Company G, under 2d Lt. William T. Nickerson of the 3d Battalion, met heavy opposition outside Hemsbach but tanks and tank destroyers laid a concentration on the town and the battalion moved in. Suddenly the enemy opened up with a hail of Flak fire from the high ground east of the village and Company F, which had just left the battalion and was headed for Sulzbach, was driven to cover. Again the tanks and tank destroyers were sent into action and their deadly fire neutralized the enemy guns. Company F, under 1st Lt. Charles O. Wigmore, then continued on to Sulzbach, overcame 40mm fire on its outskirts, and took the objective late that night.

All three battalions of the 15th were in the attack as it was continued on the morning of March 28.

The 1st Battalion overran Juhoe and cleared Bonsweiher while the 2d occupied Nieder-Liebersbach and drove into Morlenbach in time to capture five boxcars loaded with Germans. A sharp fight in Morlenbach and on the high ground in the vicinity was the first organized infantry resistance that the 15th had met since the crossing of the Rhine.

The 3d Battalion, which had been blocking to the south in the Lorsch woods for two days, quickly occupied Rimbach, Burth and Ober Ostern and on the 29th enemy resistance before the 15th had melted away as Hammelbach, Litzelbach and Gros Ellenbach were occupied.

By noon, March 29, the regiment's mission had been completed and it moved into Division reserve in the vicinity of Kirch Brombach and Bollstein.

The 7th Infantry moved out of its positions near Reichelsheim on the morning of March 29 and without resistance occupied Rohrbach, Ober Mossau, Rehbach, Steinbach, Zell, Momant and Kimbach. The 3d Battalion also moved rapidly and occupied Mickelstadt, where 525 enemy in three hospitals were put under guard. The 1st Battalion passed through the 3d and reached the Main River at Laudenbach after capturing a huge ammunition dump en route over a detour made necessary by bad roads.

Resistance in the Division zone was entirely disorganized and only small battle groups were encountered during the final day of the drive to the banks of the Main.

The 3d was now poised for a forced crossing of the Main at Wörth, which lies southeast of the large industrial city of Frankfurt.

Although our advance reconnaissance of the river banks in the vicinity of Wörth drew considerable small-arms, machine-gun and artillery fire from the enemy, the crossing itself, which began at 0300 on the morning of March 30, was surprisingly unopposed.

The advance plan called for the initial crossing by the 30th Infantry and the securing of the bridgehead by that regiment, which would be followed by the 15th and 7th Infantry Regiments in order.

The crossing was made virtually without incident as the 1st Battalion of the 30th, commanded by Lt. Col. Mackenzie Porter, took to the assault boats and skimmed across the river under cover of darkness. Captain Montgomery led Company A across first, followed by Company C, commanded by 1st Lt. Charles P. Murray.

The battalion captured a number of German gunboats tied up on the east bank of the river and within three hours had cleared out Erlenbach, which is located directly across the river from Wörth.

The 2d Battalion, under Maj. James L. Osgard, crossed the river north of Wörth, the bridge having been demolished by the Germans shortly before midnight, when the last remnants of the German force evacuated Wörth. Company C, 10th Engineer Battalion, commanded by Capt. Robert L. Bangert, quickly threw a footbridge over the wreckage and it was in operation the next day.

The 2d Battalion swung south and east and secured the high ground east of Erlenbach and Klingenberg, destroying three *Nebelwerfers* in the process.

The 3d Battalion, committed to reserve in the crossing, met more difficulty than the assault battalions when it engaged the enemy in a strong fight at Trennfurt.

After his battalion had destroyed a tank and two Flakwagons and had killed a large number of German snipers, Lt. Col. Christopher W. Chaney, the battalion commander, procured a captured German barge that carried the entire battalion across the river the following day.

The 30th went into Division reserve at 0500 March 31.

The crossing of the Main by the 15th Infantry came at noon March 30 and although some small-arms fire

Pvt. John J. Flynn, 3d Military Police Platoon, directs traffic onto the ponton bridge across the Maine River near Wörth.

was received, the 1st Battalion, commanded by Maj. Kenneth B. Potter, continued without halting and turned south to occupy Rollfield, Gros Heubach, Miltenberg and Rollbach.

At Miltenberg, the enemy counterattacked after resisting with small arms, and recaptured six German prisoners before being driven back. Two military hospitals, in which there were four Americans and more than 200 German patients, were seized intact with staff and equipment. More than a hundred prisoners were taken at Gros Heubach.

Crossing the river later in the day, the two other battalions of the 15th drove east and southeast. The 2d Battalion, commanded by Maj. Burton S. Barr, pushed through the woods and took the town of Reistenhausen after moving down from the high ground north of the village to defeat the enemy in a short fire fight. Occupation of Fechbach was accomplished without resistance.

The 3d Battalion, under Maj. John O'Connell, captured Smachtenberg and with it a valuable airport that yielded a dozen gliders, a German glider instructor and a number of his students.

The 7th Infantry, last of the Division's regiments to make the crossing, passed through elements of the 30th at about midnight of March 30 and attacked east.

By daylight, the 1st Battalion, under Lt. Col. Kenneth W. Wallace, had cleared Eschau and was headed northeast, while the 2d Battalion, commanded by Lt. Col. Jack M. Duncan, had ended the resistance in Wildensee and Hofwildensee, which had been evacuated by the enemy. The 2d had a bitter fight against small arms and automatic weapons at Krausenbach which lasted until noon the following day, when the Germans pulled out after losing a large number of men.

In the meantime, the 1st pushed rapidly through Unter Aulenbach, Wildenstein, Hobbach and Wintesbach.

The entrance into Germany brought strange sights —the white token of capitulation that greeted the Men of the Marne as they crashed through town after town with unrelenting power and speed. Panties, bed sheets, nightgowns—anything that was white—flew from windows that for years had displayed the Nazi swastika. A farmer plowing in the field near Wörth attached a white flag to the harness on his horse.

In towns where civilian groups had been organized and armed with *Panzerfaust* and rifles, and resistance was offered when the doughboys started their house-to-house "canvass." Our tanks and tank destroyers laid down short concentrations and the resistance quickly ended.

As in France and all other countries that the 3d Division had touched, people lined the streets and roads to stare at the oncoming troops, some out of curiosity, some to express their relief at the end of the Nazi regime and some to glare in open hostility.

Many townspeople smiled as the 3d tore through and around the German roadblocks in pursuit of the fleeing enemy army. They called the obstructions "61-minute blocks" because, they said, "It will take the Americans sixty-one minutes to get past them. They will look at them and laugh sixty minutes and then tear them down in one."

This derision of German military might and leadership was also demonstrated by the increasing number of deserters and stragglers that poured into the Division PW cage, which handled 6,146 prisoners from March 15 to March 31. Most of these prisoners were taken in battle, but many were Germans who surrendered after seeing their home towns lost or destroyed in the wake of their retreat.

With the crossing of the Main completed and all obectives secured, the 3d Division was assigned a new sector as the April campaign began. Elements of the 42d Infantry Division relieved the 15th Infantry on the Division's right and the 15th replaced elements of the 45th Infantry Division on the left flank.

The 30th Infantry was in Division reserve when the 7th and 15th turned the axis of the Division advance to the northeast April 1.

The advance of the 15th went well until the lead elements reached the spiderweb road junction southwest of Weibersbrunn, a little village hidden in a dense wooded area. The enemy had determined to hold the road net with a company armed with machine guns, small arms and *Panzerfaust*. The fight continued for several hours before Company L, commanded by 1st Lt. John H. Toole, broke through the defense and entered Weibersbrunn, closely followed by Company I, under 2d Lt. Daniel J. Shulkatis. The companies quickly suppressed the opposition in the town, which was cleared shortly after noon, yielding twenty-five prisoners.

The 1st Battalion passed through the 3d after Weibersbrunn was taken and engaged in a hard fight at Rothenbuck, which was occupied at midnight after two "88's" that had held up the attack were neutralized. Company C, under 1st Lt. Wilmer L. Lee, entered the town first.

The 7th Infantry began the month with the 1st Battalion moving northeast of Lichtenau, intent on seizing Rechtenbach. Moving through the 3d Battalion in Lowenstein Park, the 1st neutralized a roadblock at Bischenbernerhof and occupied its objective after overcoming strong small-arms and antitank resistance. An enemy 155mm gun was destroyed during the melee but not before it had disabled one of the tanks of Company A, 756th Tank Battalion, commanded by 1st Lt. William R. Engger. The 756th, under Maj. Oscar S. Long (and later Maj. Edwin Y. Arnold) played a major role in the 3d Division's dash through the Siegfried Line and into Germany.

Rodenbach and Wombach, on the banks of the Main, were the 7th's next objective and the 2d Battalion moved to the attack early in the morning of April 2. A spirited battle for Rodenbach took place against an enemy force comprising officer candidates, Luftwaffe pilots and other personnel. The battalion took 160 prisoners and chased the remnants of the enemy force south along the Main River, returning to establish the battalion command post in the town, after which the assault elements moved northwest for an attack on Wombach.

While the remainder of the troops were fighting in Wombach, a reinforced platoon of Germans attempted to destroy Lt. Col. Jack M. Duncan's headquarters at Rodenbach but the personnel of the CP fought off the attack; they killed at least five enemy and captured fifteen others.

Movement of the Division came to an almost complete standstill April 2-4 while the 14th Armored Division passed through the 7th on April 3 to seize Lohr, located about a mile north of Wombach on the Main. The armored unit made the capture after losing several tanks at the town's approaches. The 7th occupied the high ground on three sides of the town, after Wombach fell late on the night of April 2.

The 1st Battalion, 7th Infantry, remained in Rechtenbach until noon of April 3, when it moved north and took Steinhalerhof without opposition after a difficult march over hilly, densely-wooded terrain.

Without incident, the 2d Battalion crossed the Main River south of Lohr in "ducks" and assault craft to occupy Pflochsbach the same afternoon, and completely cleared the peninsula formed by the loop of the Main River northeast of Lohr the following day. The battalion remained on the peninsula during the night of April 4-5, prepared to shield and cover proposed bridging operations of the 14th Armored Division but the plans were changed and the battalion crossed the Main for the third time during the morning of April 5, following an intensive artillery preparation. A great deal of trouble was experienced in getting the "ducks" into the water, for the enemy had felled a number of large trees along the river bank at one point.

The battalion was across the river east of Gemunden at 1400 hours and immediately set out for the town, meeting stubborn resistance along the railroad tracks south of the town from well dug-in Germans equipped with *Panzerfaust*. After taking seventy prisoners during the morning battle outside the town, the 2d entered the village under heavy mortar fire shortly after noon and by 1530 hours had cleared the village, capturing a number of German marines and sailors committed as infantry.

Early in the morning of April 4, Company G of the 15th pushed down the valley of the Main River and secured a bridge west of Langenbrozelten while the rest of the 1st Battalion occupied Wohnroth, Fellen and Aura.

The 3d Battalion of Col. Hallett D. Edson's 15th Infantry, however, met one of its stiffest fights in weeks at Rieneck, just west of the Sinn River, moving southeast from Rengersbrunn. Maj. John O'Connell's 3d Battalion completely surprised the enemy who were digging in on the western slopes of two bald hills that guarded the town from the west. Tanks, TDs and *Flakwagons*, placed on the wooded nose of the hill along which the battalion had advanced, added to the slaughter that followed the assault. The German officer who surrendered his troops found only two of his men unaccounted for. By actual count, eighty-five had been killed, the remainder wounded or captured.

Following the surrender, Company I, commanded by 1st Lt. Robert L. Hawkins, remained behind and dug out a number of civilian snipers who persisted to the end.

After being in Division reserve for five days, the 30th Infantry went back into the line April 5, leaving its assembly area west of Rieneck early that morning. Attached "ducks" were used as infantry carriers and with the available armor and organic vehicles, the regiment spent the day seeking fire fights and strongpoints as it proceeded rapidly northeast toward Wolfmunster, which forward elements of the 3d Battalion entered late that night.

The 15th Infantry, like the 30th, swept through village after village that day and the 1st Battalion, spearheading, took Detter and Seissenbach before noon almost without a fight.

In the afternoon the 1st swept through Modlos, Bruckenau, Breitenbach and Mitgenfeld while the 2d moved out from Fellen to Heiligkreuz, cleared through the 1st Battalion and attacked toward Heckmuhle. A small delaying force was met and overcome outside Heckmuhle, which had been evacuated by the enemy; the battalion pushed elements through Ober Geiersnes and by the following morning had reached Ober Leichterbach.

Meanwhile, the 3d Battalion had blocked for other regiments of the Division from positions near Rieneck and had pulled stakes to join in the 3d's mad rush through western Germany. Passing through Reidenbach and Oberbach, which had been cleared by the 14th Armored Division, the 3d Battalion won another short fight at Wildflecken, which purportedly was to be defended by SS troops. The defense melted before Major O'Connell's battlers and the short fight that ensued ended as all other German resistance had ended in the last several weeks—with the Marnemen in complete control of the situation. A huge German chemical warfare plant and great quantities of guns and other war materiel were taken in Wildflecken, which was also the site of an enemy army camp capable of housing approximately 40,000 men. Striking southeast from Wildflecken, Company L quickly occupied the nearby town of Langeleiten.

Late that night, the 2d Battalion moved up to Wildflecken and attacked northeast to Ober Weissenbrunn, from where Company G, commanded by 2d Lt. William Nickerson, struck out to seize the village of Frankenheim, which was protected by a roadblock manned with small arms and self-propelled guns, designed to delay our advance. The battalion deployed and wiped out the enemy force; Company G entered the town before noon of April 7.

Early in the morning of April 6, the 7th Infantry had driven north, with the 2d Battalion riding "ducks" to a point where it seized the high ground in the vicinity of Michelau and continued on to the area near Schonau, while the remainder of the regiment, in successive marches, moved to the vicinity of Geroda, preparing to force a crossing of the Saale River.

Under cover of darkness and with the 1st and 3d Battalions abreast, the 7th turned sharply east and advanced over bad roads, strong enemy roadblocks and blown bridges during the rest of the night. Company A, commanded by 2d Lt. Floyd W. Clark, had a sharp fight before seizing Aschbach but found no opposition at Grossenbach. Company B, under Capt. James B. Rich, Jr., crossed the Saale River with only slight resistance and occupied Bocklet, one mile northeast of Aschbach. The enemy infiltrated our positions later from the north and attacked the Company CP in Bocklet, burning the building to the ground. This adventure cost the Germans dearly as virtually every member of the attacking force was either killed or captured in the fight that followed and in which Company A took part. The rest of the battalion entered Frauenroth and Stralsbach and found both towns clear.

Major Flynn's 3d Battalion picked its way over the rough roads and rugged terrain to Stangenroth, from where it jumped off to take the deserted villages of Premich and Steinach. Continuing north, the battalion approached a roadblock consisting of three Mark V tanks, three antitank guns and nearly a battalion of enemy troops southwest of Steinach. The battle raged all night long and into the next day, when two of the three tanks were destroyed by accurate fire of Company A, 601st Tank Destroyer Battalion, commanded by 1st Lt. George Philipovich. The Germans brought down artillery and salvos of *Nebelwerfer* fire and rushed additional armor into the fray in an effort to stem the tide but finally retreated before the continuous pressure of the 3d Battalion. In all, the enemy lost twelve Mark V tanks during the struggle.

The advance of the 30th Infantry had been a succession of occupations and small fire fights for two days and the regiment gathered several hundred prisoners en route. The battalions seemed to be spread out like so many claws and when they contracted they were filled with German PWs. For instance, one patrol of Company E, under Capt. Ralph R. Carpenter, engaged in a fire fight northwest of Hammelberg at 1715 hours April 6 and one hour later reported back with thirty-five prisoners.

Windheim, Unter Thulba, Elfershausen, Seeshof,

Witternhausen, Hetzlos, Thulba, Albertslauter and Lauter all were seized by Col. Lionel C. McGarr's regiment, although three of the towns did not fall without resistance.

Company I, commanded by 2d Lt. Gerald G. Mehuron, fought a small enemy group before entering Hetzlos; Company L, under 1st Lt. Phillip B. Larimore, shoved the enemy out of Ober Thulba after a 25-minute tussle while Company G, commanded by Capt. John H. West, met determined opposition and called for supporting fires before Seeshof was finally cleared.

Leaving Ober Thulba, Company L pushed directly east, with patrols out toward Bad Kissingen, a world-famed watering place noted for its fine springs and numerous resort hotels, twenty-eight of which had been converted into German military hospitals, whose red-crossed roofs had saved the city from Allied bombing.

One of the patrols, led by 2d Lt. Emil T. Byke, moved along a road leading into the city and met an officer delegation from the hospital community whose spokesman announced a desire to surrender the city intact.

After summoning Lt. Col. Christopher W. Chaney, 3d Battalion commander, Lieutenant Byke placed his men at advantageous points on the hills surrounding the town while Company M, commanded by 1st Lt. Harold J. Saine, brought up mortars and placed them in firing position "just in case."

Colonel Chaney, with Capt. Carroll McFalls, Jr., 3d Battalion S-3, went to the city hall with the delegation and laid down surrender terms to a ranking German field officer who had been recuperating at one of the hospitals.

Bad Kissingen is an important rail and highway center and its spacious buildings could easily accommodate corps and army troops, making it a highly desirable military prize. Thus, Colonel Chaney made it clear that the 3d Division would not accept Bad Kissingen as an "open city" but that it would be used as a military base for United States troops. This being acceptable to the negotiators, the colonel sent for Col. Lionel C. McGarr, regimental commander of the 30th, who, accompanied by two Division staff officers, Major F. C. Spreyer and Capt. Henry Huguenin, restated the American's conditions and accepted the surrender of the city and 2825 German soldier-patients as prisoners.

As a denouement, the battalion moved through the city to an assembly area on the outskirts of town while Company F, commanded by Capt. Robert L. Fleet, was brought in from Witterhausen to guard the public buildings and hospitals.

The Saale River divides Bad Kissingen into halves and both vehicular bridges that connect them were destroyed by German demolition crews who always worked in small groups, hiding in areas until our troops were within striking distance before detonating their charges. Company C of the 10th Engineers, commanded by Capt. Robert L. Bangert, had one of the bridges replaced a few hours after the city surrendered.

While the 3d was taking Bad Kissingen, the 1st Battalion, moving on the regiment's north flank, ran into a battery of "88's" that was silenced by our artillery and by the regimental Cannon Company, commanded by Capt. Norwood L. Snowden. The 2d Battalion, meanwhile, encountered artillery fire falling in Aura; and destroyed an enemy antitank gun in Euerdorf.

After winning the armor-infantry battle at the crossroads outside Steinach, the 3d Battalion of the 7th Infantry met more enemy armor at the edge of town and another pitched battle took place, featuring an increased amount of enemy artillery and *Nebelwerfer* fire. After several hours of bitter fighting, the resistance weakened and when the tussle ended the enemy had lost the remainder of his twelve Mark V tanks to our TDs and bazookamen, who led the battalion into the city.

The 2d Battalion moved down from the heights near Schonau and rejoined the regiment with the mission of taking the town of Haard. At 1010 hours, the battalion was in the western outskirts of the town, where a one-hour fire fight was staged with members of a German cavalry training battalion and of the 2d *Panzer* Division, who had been committed as infantry. Moving through Haard, the battalion continued east to clear the high ground beyond the village; the advance was speeded up considerably and was only lightly contested because the 14th Armored Division was just ahead of the 2d and was leaving only scattered enemy remnants in its wake.

Around midnight, the 3d Battalion's command post

A 3d Signal Company officer stares at the destroyed jeep of General Young, Assistant Division Commander, after it was hit by an enemy shell.

and OP was attacked by a large number of reassembled German stragglers intent on making an opening for an enemy artillery unit to pass through. In the early stages of the surprise attack, the enemy took five prisoners, shot up four jeeps and destroyed one of our TDs. At daylight a great number of German dead were found, fifty-five prisoners had been taken and the battalion had acquired four German horse-drawn 155mm howitzers.

After passing through the 2d Battalion at Weichtungen, the 1st Battalion on April 9 seized the towns of Thundorf, Rothhausen, Stadtlauringen, Altenmunster and Fuchstadt and halted while the 2d Battalion passed through. The regiment stopped at this point and spent most of April 9-10 patrolling and cleaning rear areas of stragglers, who were becoming more numerous each day.

The 2d Battalion of the 15th Infantry, after clearing Frankenheim, moved out to attack Bischofsheim, the Division objective. But, like Bad Kissingen, it was surrendered by a group of civilians who met the leading elements of the battalion some distance outside the town. It was coincidental that both towns were being handed over to the 3d Division at about the same hour on the same day, as both surrenders were negotiated shortly after noon.

South of Bischofsheim, the 3d Battalion ripped through light opposition after the main part of the battalion had joined Company L at Langenleiten and swept southeast in the direction of Neustadt. The remarkable pace that the battalion maintained was attributed in a large measure to the work of Company C, 10th Engineer Battalion, commanded by Capt. Daniel A. Raymond, which cleared the debris-covered roads ahead of Major O'Connell's battalion. All highways were literally strewn with German vehicles that had been hit by our armor, artillery and air support.

Company L struck northeast to Waldberg, through Sandberg and on to Kilianshof, where the company turned southeast to Hohenroth. Company I, followed by Company K, moved east from Sandberg to Schmalwassen, where Company I came under enemy fire from self-propelled guns, which were silenced that night. After taking Schmalwassen, the two companies drove unopposed through Windhausen, Leuterhausen and to Hohenroth. Company K, commanded by 1st Lt. Walter H. Kropp, attacked Strahlungen, where the enemy resisted for a short time with small-arms fire which was effectively suppressed with the capture of sixty-five PWs.

The 1st Battalion, acting as infantry support for the 14th Armored Division, moved rapidly east along the main road to Neustadt from south of Bischofsheim.

Company A, commanded by 1st Lt. Michael J. Daly, quickly cleared Unter Weissenbrunn, Wegfurt and Schonau. Company B, under 1st Lt. Harold M. Patterson, swung northeast off the main road, passed through Weisbach and Sondernau and pushed several miles to a point just north of Neustadt, where a strong roadblock was established.

The 15th Infantry was now closed in on Neustadt and the time was ripe for its capture. In a two-pronged thrust, Colonel Edson, the regimental commander, shot one column out from Schonau and another from the south, with Neustadt as the target.

Company C passed through Company A at Schonau and cleared the towns of Reyersbach, Braidbach and Rodles, which lie directly north of Neustadt. Company A, riding "ducks" whipped through Brendlorenzen, right outside the northern edge of Neustadt, and was met by heavy small-arms, sniper, *Nebelwerfer* and *Panzerfaust* fire coming from the southeast section of the town. Company B went north to occupy Weisbach and Sondernau and then struck southeast to an intersection near Wollbach, where a strong roadblock was established. Elements of the 1st Battalion entered the northern part of the city shortly after noon while the 3d Battalion's Companies K and L closed in from the south, Company K taking Strahlingen and Company L taking Ebersbach en route with a total of approximately 100 prisoners.

Resistance to the 15th's attack buckled late in the afternoon and the town fell with the bridges across the Frank Saale still intact. In less than twenty-four hours, the regiment had captured nineteen villages and nearly 300 prisoners, had destroyed at least ten enemy tanks and had neutralized a number of enemy guns.

With the capture of Neustadt, the 15th went into Division reserve and on the morning of April 9 moved into assembly areas near Schweinfurt, a city which once was known as the "graveyard" of Allied airmen because of the huge Flak concentrations that came from the city's numerous antiaircraft installations.

After the fall of Bad Kissingen, the 30th Infantry moved east and southeast and met considerable artillery and antitank fire from the vicinity of Hambach and Maibach, outer defensive points protecting Schweinfurt. The excellent coordination between our field artillery units and infantry elements was never better demonstrated than when the forward observer of the 41st FA Battalion, commanded by Lt. Col. Barney D. White, called for a concentration in the Maibach area that neutralized two tanks and a Flakwagon and drove off three other enemy tanks in less than an hour of firing.

It was obvious at this time that the Germans were trying once more to slow the 3d Division's relentless attack, either to make a stand along one of the few remaining natural lines of defense or to give the Nazi "bigwigs" a chance to withdraw to safety to the Redoubt area in the high Austrian Alps.

While the 42d Infantry Division was taking Schweinfurt, the 30th Infantry, which had gotten ahead of friendly elements on the flanks, was forced to slow down and confine its activities during April 10-11 to semidefensive warfare, consisting mainly of mopping-up and eliminating enemy roadblocks.

Many roads leading into Schweinfurt, a main industrial center, were heavily mined and several regimental vehicles were ambushed by isolated German resistance groups.

The 7th Infantry, commanded by Col. John A. Heintges, struck southeast from positions near Fuchstadt with the 2d Battalion, under Lt. Col. Jack M. Duncan, on the right, 3d Battalion, commanded by Maj. Ralph M. Flynn, on the left, and 1st Battalion, under Lt. Col. Kenneth W. Wallace, in regimental reserve.

Very little artillery and mortar fire, but much small-arms resistance was encountered as the 2d seized Kleinsteinach, Kleinmunster, Mechenreis, Holzhausen, Uchenhofen, Ober Hohenreid and Unter Hohenreid. The Germans attempted to make a stand at Uchenhofen, a few miles northwest of Haszfurt, but it was only suicidal and the battalion brushed on to Unter Hohenreid, overlooking Haszfurt.

The 3d Battalion captured Heilingen and Romershofen, receiving light artillery, small-arms, mortar and automatic-weapons fire designed primarily to slow the attack but actual defense of the towns was not made. The battalion seized Prappach and the high ground in that area and when 2d Battalion took Augsfeld in an early morning attack, it gave the 7th Infantry all the high ground surrounding the city and paved the way for 1st Battalion to move into Haszfurt at noon the following day with only a few roadblocks to impede the advance.

Continuing southeast along the banks of the Main, Colonel Wallace's men passed through Zeil, which the 2d Battalion had previously taken, and moved on through Zieglander to Steinbach, where the march was temporarily halted because the next two battalion objectives, Gleisenau and Ebelsbach, had already been taken by elements of the 45th Infantry Division. The retreat of the German forces at this point was matched only by the drive of the 3d Division doughboys and by the maintenance of our ever-lengthening supply routes and constant movement of our artillery and antiaircraft units, whose frequent changing of position kept the personnel digging in around the clock.

Hundreds of German stragglers, many of whom had changed into civilian clothes, were picked up by our

German prisoners of war are herded across an infantry footbridge near Haszfurt by 3d Division soldiers.

rear elements and the Division Intelligence Section reported that two German officers and a master sergeant had bicycled into one of our outposts near Madenhausen and stated that they were "going home."

On April 11, the Division crossed the Main River for the fourth time at points east of Schweinfurt and the drive for Nürnberg (Nuremburg), important German bastion and symbol of Naziism, was on. The 45th Infantry Division was on our left flank and the 42d (Rainbow) Division was on the right.

The Division's crossing was effected by the 30th Infantry, with 1st Battalion taking the lead in assault boats at a point near Unter Theres. Company A, commanded by Capt. Hugh S. Montgomery, met enemy Flakwagon and other fire near the village of Dampfach shortly after making the crossing but our artillery placed effective fire on the enemy positions and silenced the only display of resistance that marked the crossing.

The 3d Battalion crossed the river at Ober Theres on a footbridge constructed by Company A of the 10th Engineers, commanded by 1st Lt. Robert K. Sleeth, and turned east into the enemy-deserted village of Wonfurt.

Numerous *Panzerfaust* with tripcords attached were laid by the enemy in the path of the 30th but most of the roadblocks that were encountered were either entirely unmanned or poorly manned with only small delaying groups. In the 24-hour period from noon April 12 to April 13, the regiment captured no less than forty German "88's," testimony to the disaster that the 3d was wreaking on enemy forces.

The 15th Infantry moved out of its reserve positions northeast of Schweinfurt on the afternoon of April 11 and attacked south toward the Main with the 3d Battalion leading the advance into Mainburg, which was occupied without a fight. Schonungen, Forst, Gadheim, Ottendorf, Bayerhof, and Gresshausen all fell to the battalion by the next day and the PW count was increased by 265.

The 2d Battalion pushed on to Kleinmunster and cleared the woods between that town and the Main as it rushed into Wulflingen, a river-bank village.

Both battalions crossed the river at Ober Theres on foot April 12, passed through 30th Infantry, and boarded every available vehicle to assume the spearhead of the Division's attack along the banks of the Main and to the southeast.

The 2d Battalion, commanded by Lt. Col. Keith L. Ware, moved along the river and seized Limbach and Eltman, and Maj. John O'Connell's 3d Battalion drove southeast to occupy Zell and Unter Schleichach. The enemy forces were completely disorganized and occasional small-arms fire presented the only opposition to the regiment as it sped on almost without pause to Bamberg, a sizable city located at the junction of the Main and Regnitz (or Pegnitz) Rivers. En route, the following towns were occupied and quickly cleared, giving the 15th control of the southern part of Bamberg and all entrances to that section of the city: Priesendorf, Walsdorf, Gaustadt, Muhlendorf, Höfer, Reundorf, Pettstadt, and Sassanfahrt. The German retreat was so hasty that it was becoming more difficult each day for the Division to maintain contact with the enemy. The 3d Reconnaissance Troop, commanded by Capt. Allen R. Kenyon, roved the left flank of our units with abandon, capturing many towns, numerous prisoners, and much enemy equipment. The daily report of the 2d platoon for the 24-hour period beginning at noon, April 12, revealed the capture of six villages and 112 PWs, and the destruction of two machine-gun nests. This report was repeated in its generalities day after day as the Division maintained its pursuit.

The 2d Battalion, 15th Infantry, captured four enemy artillery pieces and a large ammunition dump and destroyed a Mark V tank at Gaustadt, just west of Bamberg, while elements of the 3d Battalion recalled the days of Anzio when a large number of Goliath tanks (miniatures loaded with high explosive) were encountered in the vicinity of Erlau, southwest of Bamberg. Ten Goliaths were captured but not until two had detonated, killing two 3d Division men and wounding two others.

At 1835, April 13, less than twenty-four hours after the 15th had been committed across the Main River, 2d Battalion had entered Bamberg, a German hospital city containing some 200 enemy medical installations. In two days the regiment had occupied forty-four villages and captured more than 1,000 prisoners, including many German officers.

In sheer desperation and with utter disregard for the German patients in the city's hospitals, the *Luftwaffe* that night attacked the town, spilling numerous bombs on the hospitals and in the area occupied by the 2d Battalion, which suffered many casualties and lost a number of vehicles. This apparently was a token raid, mustered as a final kick of a dying enemy.

Only slight resistance to the occupation of the town was offered by the German troops and the officer in command had been taken with hundreds of other prisoners when 2d Battalion entered the city.

The 7th Infantry, in assembly areas near Frenshof, also received the full blast of an air raid on the night of April 14 and antipersonnel bombs dropped in the area occupied by the regiment's Cannon Company, commanded by Capt. George E. Guckert, Jr., caused a number of casualties.

The 30th Infantry, which was on the right flank of the 15th, met little opposition as it proceeded southeast. The complete confusion which permeated the German ranks as the regiment drove forward was illustrated at a small town which Capt. George S. Peck, 2d Battalion S-3, entered on April 13. Unaware that the town was held by a company of Germans, Captain Peck acted under the pretext that he had come to accept a previously proffered surrender and to his amazement a majority of the defending officers and men gave up without a struggle, unsure that a surrender offer had been made but glad to accept Captain Peck's declaration as fact.

Although the advance of the 30th was only slightly restricted by the enemy, small fire fights were encountered at a few of the many towns that the regiment occupied during its headlong drive.

At Hochstadt, a hastily-organized town command put up a short fight that resulted in the capture, among other Germans, of the German colonel in command. At Millersdorf, southwest of Bamberg, a platoon-sized counterattack was repulsed and reconnaissance elements had fire fights in the vicinity of Greinendorf while some of our troops west of the Pegnitz River received enemy artillery fire coming from Forchheim, which was later taken by a small Division task force.

The force that took Forchheim was led by 1st Lt.

3d Infantry Division soldiers ride the 756th Tank Battalion's tanks in pursuit of the enemy near Erlangen.

Richard W. Rosebury, Jr., and was composed of Battle Patrols from all three of the Division's regiments, three demolition men from the 10th Engineer Battalion, a radio team from the 3d Signal Company, a forward observation party from Division Artillery and one mechanic from the 703d Ordnance Company. All members of the force volunteered for the special assignment.

Moving six miles behind enemy lines, this daring group had the mission of securing the railroad and highway bridges across the Pegnitz in the vicinity of Baiersdorf. A motor-driven railroad engine captured by the Division was carried to the narrow-gauge railroad that ran between Bamberg and Hausen and the six-car "train" had to be jacked over several bombed-out stretches that were met en route to the marshalling yards of Forchheim, where a house-to-house battle netted the raiders twenty prisoners. After a thorough reconnaissance in this unusual vehicle, the lieutenant and his group returned to Division headquarters with seventy-five PWs and much information for the Intelligence section.

By April 15 the entire 3d Division was poised on the west side of the Pegnitz ready for a lunge toward Nürnberg. The 30th Infantry made the initial crossing, overrunning many small towns and capturing numerous 88mm guns en route. It also included the crossing of the Ludwigs Canal at points in the vicinity of Baiersdorf, with 3d Battalion under Lt. Col. Christopher W. Chaney leading the attack, followed closely by the 2d Battalion, under Lt. Col. James L. Osgard.

The crossing, made under cover of darkness, was met with only slight opposition and the rest of the Division moved across the river on the following day and struck south toward Nürnberg, overrunning many small towns en route. Erlangen, Brück, Eltersdorf, Gründlach, Steinach, and Stadein fell to the Division but many casualties were suffered at the hands of a strengthening German defense and more frequent reappearances of the *Luftwaffe*.

At Erlangen, which offered a poorly-conducted defense, the German colonel in command committed suicide after agreeing to terms surrendering the city.

The 1st Battalion of the 7th Infantry encountered small-arms, automatic-weapon, and self-propelled-gun fire in the fight for Tennenlohe, and 1st Battalion, 15th Infantry, received similar opposition in taking Heroldsberg. The 3d Battalion of the 15th also ran into strong 88mm artillery concentrations at Kalchreuth as the Division neared the outskirts of Nürnberg.

The Germans were determined to make a strong bid to defend the shrine of Naziism and members of the 441st AAA Battalion, commanded by Lt. Col. Thomas H. Leary, fired thousands of rounds of ammunition at enemy ME 109s and FW 190s during the advance on Nürnberg.

Our troops came under heavy fire from hundreds of German antiaircraft guns located in small villages that surrounded the big city. Entrance into the political capital was to prove little less costly than anticipated.

The 7th Infantry, for instance, was held up for some time at the small town of Kraftshof, just north of Nürnberg, by stubborn resistance and the villages of Kleinrueth and Thon were also taken against stiff opposition.

The 3d Battalion, 15th Infantry, met strong resistance as it moved through Bueckenbuhl while the 1st Battalion battered down the defenses of a large garrison of SS troops and drunken *Volkssturm* at Heroldsberg.

During the advance of the 15th Infantry, Pvt. Joseph F. Merrell performed the heroic action in a hill position near Lohe for which he was awarded the Medal of Honor. He made a gallant one-man attack against vastly superior forces in an effort to drive the disorganized enemy forces from the hills dominating Nürn-

This aerial photo taken while the fighting was in progress in Nűrnberg indicates the degree of destruction that was visited upon the city.

berg. His company was pinned down by brutal fire from rifles, pistols and two heavy machine guns.

". . . Entirely on his own initiative, Private Merrell began a single-handed assault. He ran a hundred yards through concentrated fire, barely escaping death at each stride, and, at point-blank range, engaged four German machine-pistol men with his rifle, killing all of them while their bullets ripped his uniform. As he started forward again, his rifle was smashed by a sniper's bullet, leaving him armed only with three grenades, but he did not hesitate. He zigzagged two hundred yards through a hail of bullets to within ten yards of the first machine gun, where he hurled two grenades and then rushed the position, ready to fight with his bare hands, if necessary. In the emplacement, he seized a Luger pistol and killed all Germans who had survived the grenade blast. Rearmed, he crawled toward the second machine gun, located thirty yards away, killing four Germans in camouflaged foxholes on the way, but receiving a critical wound in the abdomen. He went on staggering, bleeding, and disregarding bullets which tore through the folds of his clothing and glanced off his helmet. He threw his last grenade into the machine-gun nest and stumbled on to wipe out the crew. He had completed this self-appointed task when a machine-pistol burst killed him instantly . . ." (General Orders No. 21, War Department, 26 February 1946.)

The coordinated Division attack on Nürnberg was worked out in minutest detail. Major General O'Daniel issued comprehensive orders for the forthcoming operation.

Although the fighting in Nürnberg itself was fierce, it was no worse than in the little villages that edged the city proper and where enemy infantry, antiaircraft, artillery and machine gunners were imbedded in bombed-out structures that now served as strongpoints of defense.

Penetration of Nürnberg was made doubly difficult by the fact that the city was a "city within a city" in that a century-old wall surrounded the inner section, which once was the fortified Nürnberg of feudal days.

Although the entire 3d Division was committed in the siege, elements of the 15th Infantry were the first to enter the outer, or "new" city, shortly after noon of April 17, after Division troops had overrun at least fifty "88s" in the drive through the outskirts of the city on the previous night.

It was on April 17 that 1st Lt. Frank Burke, transportation officer of the 1st Battalion, 15th Infantry, fought with such extreme gallantry in the war-torn

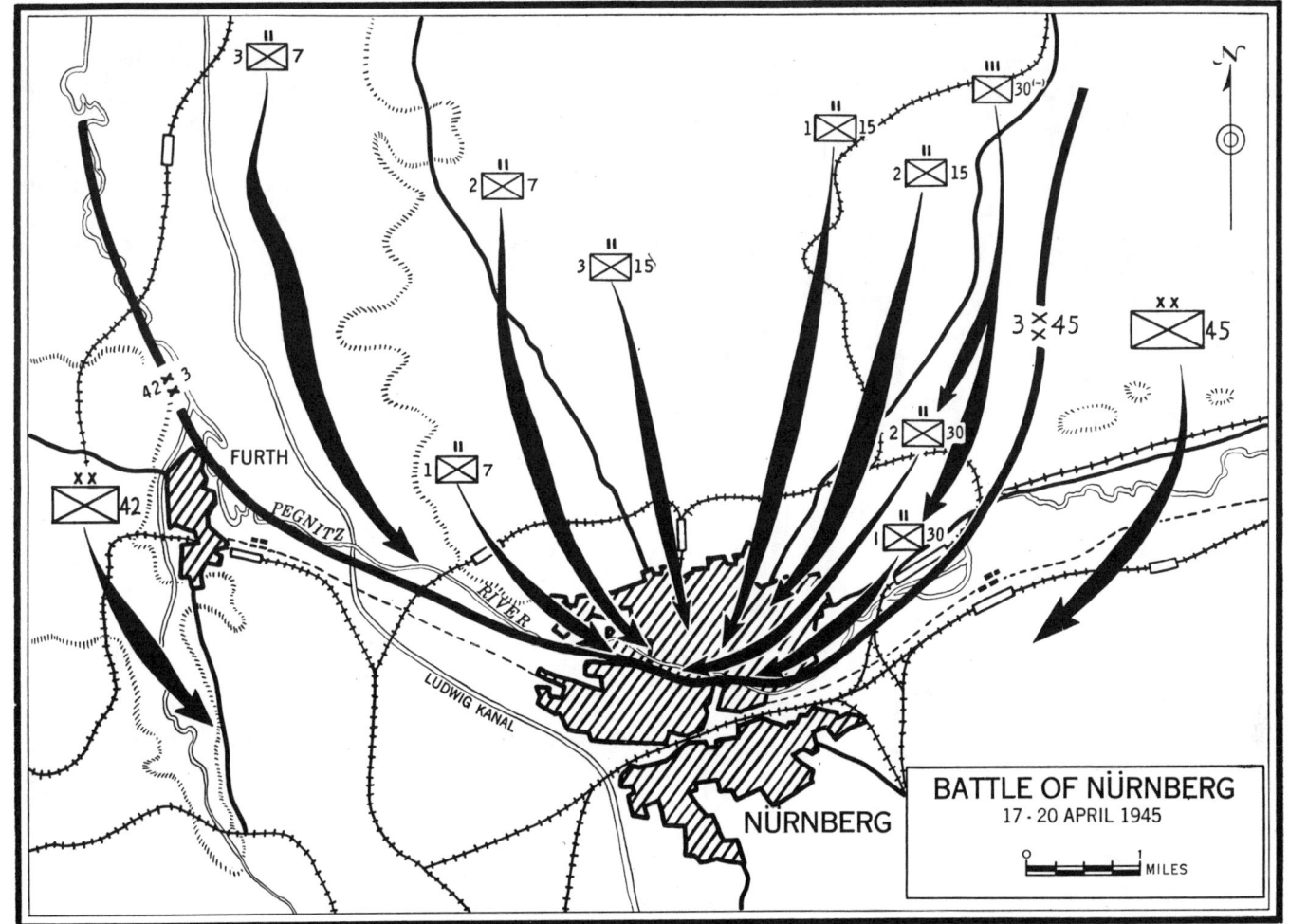

streets of Nürnberg that he was later awarded the Medal of Honor. Lieutenant Burke had gone forward to select a motor-pool site, when in a desire to perform more than his assigned duties and take part in the fight, he advanced beyond the lines of the forward riflemen. Detecting a group of enemy making preparations for a local counterattack, he rushed back to a nearby friendly company and obtained a light machine gun, with which he engaged the superior enemy force. A fire fight ensued in which Lieutenant Burke succeeded in driving off the force after having killed a machine-gun crew of the attacking unit. Lieutenant Burke then picked up a rifle, dashed about a hundred yards through intense enemy fire and from a position behind an abandoned tank engaged the enemy. Lieutenant Burke finally disposed of the majority of enemy riflemen in and about his position with a hand-grenade assault. He continued on fighting his way forward along the battle-crazy street aiding our units to advance by his heroic example of willingness to close with the enemy. His citation reads in part: "... In four hours of heroic action Lieutenant Burke single-handedly killed eleven and wounded three enemy soldiers and took a leading role in engagements in which an additional twenty-nine enemy were killed or wounded."

However, it was the 30th Infantry that entered the "old" or walled city first, a little later, and it was through a hole breached by the 30th that the remainder of the Division entered.

Three solid German battle groups defended the old town in addition to many civilians, including a group of about 150 city firemen who were holed up in the eastern section of the town.

One of the defending units was the Battle Group *Dirnagel,* made up mainly of SS troopers organized in Rothernberg, southeast of Wurzburg; the Battle Group *Rienow,* consisting of air force personnel and officer candidates from an airfield at Roth, south of Nürnberg and the 1st Battalion, 38th SS *Panzer Grenadier* Regiment. Although armor was not available to a great extent, the enemy employed all kinds of small arms in defense of the city as well as great numbers of *Panzerfaust,* which destroyed several of our vehicles in the drive through the outer edges of the bastion and on the road leading from Heroldsburg, where many Hungarian box mines had been laid.

Hundreds of snipers holed up in debris in the city

This ancient tower in Nürnberg yielded 125 Germans to a 3d Division patrol, after having been blasted with TD fire.

attack very costly but all three regiments drove on in their zone of advance as house after house, park after park and even every immobilized streetcar was taken with a fight.

Civilian snipers hid in spider holes, let our troops pass, then opened fire at their backs.

The 15th Infantry, in its march toward the Pegnitz River, which runs through the heart of the town, captured a German general and several hundred German patients in a number of hospitals that were taken intact with their staffs.

Through the early days of the attack on Nürnberg the 30th Infantry had been in Division reserve with the 1st Battalion blocking to the Division right rear on the west bank of the Pegnitz River and the 2d and 3d Battalions blocking to the left rear or east bank of the river.

On April 19 the regiment was committed to the final drive to clear Nürnberg in a wide flanking movement driving in from the northeast. The 1st Battalion led the 30th Infantry's advance through the outer city, with Companies A and B spearheading the drive, and by noon of April 19 the battalion had captured 150 prisoners and reached the walled old city of Nürnberg.

That afternoon, 2d Lt. Telesphor C. Tremblay and his antitank platoon engaged in a spectacular action at the Laufer tower, on the edge of the walled city.

caused numerous casualties and it was a step-by-step fight to ferret out the defenders in the northeastern part of the city, where they occupied individual holes effectively concealed in the tall grass in that area.

Four blocks of apartments between Bismarck Strasse and Sulzbacher Strasse were strongpoints that took several hours to clear and the fighting went into the second day with the city and its adjacent small towns converted into a giant inferno.

Company K of the 15th hit fierce resistance at the settlement of Klein and was forced to withdraw and call for artillery to blast out the buildings and other strong points.

The Germans used every trick in the book to hold the city. Mines, boobytrapped German bodies, civilians with *Panzerfaust* and rifles, all combined to make the

3d Division soldiers feel their way down a Nürnberg street, wary of snipers.

An aerial photo of Nűrnberg depicts clearly the scene where the 3d Division fought one of its bitterest fights in Germany.

Advancing toward the tower, Lieutenant Tremblay and his men engaged in a hot pistol duel with a large number of Germans whom they kept imprisoned in the tower until bazooka and TD fire was placed on the structure. The ensuing concentration brought out a white flag and some 125 prisoners and the last resistance in the residential and factory district had ended in the 30th's zone.

The 2d Battalion, 30th Infantry, commanded by Lt. Col. James Osgard, was the first to enter the inner city after a coordinated regimental attack on the evening of April 19.

At 0400 hours the next morning, however, Company F was hit by a fierce enemy counterattack and the first fire hit the Company CP group, causing a number of casualties. This fanatical attack came from the island which was the 1st Battalion's objective and was led by the *Gauleiter* of the city.

The attackers were armed with automatic weapons, grenades and *Panzerfaust* but Capt. Robert L. Fleet's company stood them off in an hour-long battle that at times threatened the entire battalion positions in that section of the city. Although some casualties were suffered by Company F, a five-to-one ratio of losses was inflicted on the attacking force, which withdrew around daylight.

Many individual feats of heroism were performed in the attack on Nürnberg and 1st Lt. Michael J. Daly was one of the many officers who led their men into the face of well-protected enemy positions in order to conquer the seat of the German political party.

Maj. Burton S. Barr, executive officer of the 1st Battalion, stated later that Lieutenant Daly had gone without sleep for two days and nights during the attack, "advancing ahead of his men into blistering fire, destroying German gun positions single-handedly and fighting with an unfaltering heroism that won the admiration and amazement of all who witnessed it."

First Sgt. Roy A. Kurtz said: "We had advanced as far as the *Nordost* railroad station when Lieutenant Daly, moving far ahead of us as usual, found that the twisted wreckage of a railroad bridge lay across the Bayreutherstrasse, the principal highway into the city. Swinging around to the right of the bridge, Lieutenant Daly had just begun to climb upon a low embankment along the railroad when a machine gun suddenly opened up on us from the other side of the Leipziger Platz. We were caught out in the open by rapid traversing fire. Our men were killed left and right.

"Realizing that the whole company was threatened with annihilation, the lieutenant ran toward the machine gun, a conspicuous target as he crossed the tracks to a position in some rubble within fifty yards of the enemy gun. He killed all the German gunners with his carbine and he pushed on forward, ahead of his company, until he sighted an enemy antitank detachment which was 'zeroed in' on our attached armor units."

S/Sgt. Ivan Ketron said that Lieutenant Daly signalled for the company to halt and again struck out alone.

"He was taking his life in his hands and we all knew it," Ketron said, adding, "I saw the Lieutenant work his way forward to what was left of a house and open fire with his carbine.

"The krauts replied with a rain of automatic fire

Probably the most devastated and ruined section of the ancient city of Nűrnberg is shown here.

that sent up eddies of fine white dust from the building he was shooting from. Then *Panzerfaust* rockets began to slam against the furthest wall of the building. Although the whole kraut patrol was concentrating on him, Lieutenant Daly kept firing his carbine until he killed six Germans and silenced the enemy fire.

"Leading his men forward once more, he entered a public park, well ahead of his troops. As he paused to place his platoons in position, two Germans rushed forward from concealment and set up a machine gun only ten yards from the Lieutenant. An American sergeant fell dead at the first burst and Lieutenant Daly seized the M-1 that was lying on the ground and took up a pointblank fire fight which resulted in the killing of the enemy MG crew."

Major Barr said that in four singlehanded fire fights with a strong enemy Lieutenant Daly "had killed fifteen Germans, destroyed three machine guns and wiped out an entire enemy patrol.

"During two days and nights of bitter hand-to-hand fighting he served as first scout of the company, taking all the major risks himself and fearlessly disregarding deadly enemy fire. His heroism during the battle for Nürnberg will never be forgotten by the officers and enlisted men who fought there," Major Barr concluded.

Lieutenant Daly was awarded the Medal of Honor for this deed of heroism.

Just before noon on April 20, 1945—Adolf Hitler's birthday—the 2d Battalion of the 30th reached the Adolf Hitler Platz in the center of the town after taking its ground in a building-to-building fight. The street markers in the square were replaced by others bearing the name "Eiserner Michael Platz" (Iron Mike Square) in honor of the 3d Division's Commanding General, Maj. Gen. John W. O'Daniel, who was known to his intimate friends and to thousands of Marnemen as "Iron Mike."

The 7th Infantry, which reached the center of town at about the same time as the 30th, attacked directly south from the area northwest of Nürnberg, including the villages of Schnepfenreuth, Kleinreuth and Thon. After neutralizing a great deal of small-arms opposition at these points, 2d Battalion, in the regimental lead, moved slowly south through the outskirts of the city and by noon of April 18 the front elements were some 600 yards south of the railroad tracks and the left flank of the battalion was along the main road leading from Thon into Nürnberg. Fanatical resistance was encountered and an actual room-by-room battle was fought in one apartment house which finally yielded fifty PWs. Several small counterattacks were launched by the Germans but they were all repelled by Colonel Heintges' battalions, who fought amazingly and with utter disregard for their own safety.

A storeroom completely filled with machine guns and machine pistols was captured in Ruckert Strasse. The materiel was quickly demolished by our troops who were taking no chances with the boobytrapped contrivances that the Germans used so freely in defense of the city. Friendly tanks that roved the streets were kept constantly on the alert by *Panzerfaust* fired by Germans from upstairs windows. This was an innovation first introduced by the enemy, but which in the end proved costly to him. The standard procedure was to turn the fire of the nearest tank against the source of trouble.

The push down Ruckert Strasse by 2d Battalion was slow but devastating. When day broke April 19, its forward elements had reached the park at Wieland and Roritzer Strassen, where a road block covered by heavy machine guns held up the advance to the Pegnitz River.

By noon, Company G, commanded by 1st Lt. Louie R. Van Hoy, was in the municipal park of Unter Perkheimer; Company E, under Capt. James F. Powell, was cleaning out the buildings on Judg Strasse and eliminating another roadblock in front of Company F, commanded by 1st Lt. Willis B. Conklin.

Close contact was maintained by all units of the Division as the block-by-block cleanup proceeded. Members of Company E found themselves firing at the same targets as the 15th Infantry, Company E moved onto Wieland Strasse.

In the vicinity of Frommann Strasse, Company E had a hard fire fight as it moved down Graben Bucher Strasse. The street was lined with old stone walls which the enemy utilized to the fullest extent as protection. The old city rang with shellfire and smouldered in its ruins as the 7th fought into the second night of the siege. At 2000 April 19, Company E crossed Burgschmeit Strasse and was hit on both flanks by small-arms and machine-gun fire and one of the company's platoons was cut off by a sharp counterattack that was staged by *Luftwaffe* trainees in Johannes Strasse. Two platoons of Company F were sent to relieve the beleaguered outfit and in a short time the Germans were driven back.

At about noon, when the large castle north of Adolf Hitler Platz fell to the 15th Infantry, 7th Infantry was in the famed square, withdrawing from the old city

A group of 3d Division soldiers move down one of the rubble-lined streets of Nürnberg near the close of the battle.

late that afternoon to assembly areas north of the Pegnitz River and west of Graben Bucher Strasse. Here the men got their first real rest and sleep in four days.

The 1st Battalion, 7th, in its battle for Nürnberg, attacked from positions in the vicinity of Reutles and Gross Grundlich, hitting the northwest section of the city. The movement of Lieutenant Colonel Wallace's battalion was hindered in the early stages of the attack by unusually heavy small-arms and machine-gun fire that came from dug-in positions in a cemetery and from across the Pegnitz River.

During the early hours of the battle, 140 members of the Nürnberg police department, who had been fighting as infantrymen, surrendered when attached tank destroyers moved into view.

By 1430 April 19 Company C, commanded by Capt. M. Morris, had taken two vehicle bridges and one foot bridge intact and had crossed the Pegnitz River. Within four hours the entire area west of Kern and Will Strasse had been cleared and more than 200 prisoners taken.

The United States flag is raised in Adolf Hitler Platz, Nürnberg, by troops of the 3d Infantry Division in the presence of General O'Daniel.

Late that night, Company C had a hot fire fight about 600 yards west of the clock in the old tower. This was overcome, and the company entered the walls of the old city at Max Pi early the next morning.

The 3d Battalion, 7th Infantry, had a hectic time before it entered Nürnberg and took several hundred prisoners en route from positions in the vicinity of Erlangen.

A large ammunition manufacturing plant at Brück, surrounded by hastily-abandoned antiaircraft positions, was taken by Major Flynn's battalion, which successively occupied Tennenlohe, Klein Grundlach, Gross Grundlach and Steinach after coming under heavy "88" and artillery fire en route.

Company L, commanded by 1st Lt. Sherman W. Pratt, was in Steinach when the lieutenant, acting as fire control officer for the 10th FA Battalion, saw fourteen German Flak guns firing on Company E positions from the vicinity of Bislohe, Sack, and Braunsbach. His call for artillery resulted in a 20-battalion concentration on the three towns, two of which surrendered without a fight, although slight resistance appeared at Braunsbach.

Continuing to Poppenreuth, Company L captured twelve "88's" and their sleeping crews and drove southeast through Wetzendorf, Schniegling, and Muggenhof, taking much radar and searchlight equipment that had been abandoned by the enemy.

Pressing on in the wake of the remainder of the regiment, the 3d Battalion accumulated vast stores of war materiel as well as hundreds of prisoners before it moved into Nürnberg following capitulation of the city.

The battle for Nürnberg cannot be described without mention of the Antitank Company of the 15th Infantry, which fought as infantrymen from the 18th to the 20th of April. Numbering only 52 officers and men, weary from continuous marching and fighting, after two nights without sleep or rest, these infantrymen blasted their way through the Nürnberger Stadtpark, destroyed a heavily manned roadblock in a rifle-grenade assault, broke through a block of sniper-infested apartment houses, and finally reached the massive Innerstadtmauer and moat which girded the old city. In the sector assigned to them this unit broke the back of enemy resistance. For this action it was awarded the Presidential Unit Citation.

Officially, at 1400, April 20, Nürnberg—"the most

On April 22, 1945, Lt. Gen. A. M. Patch, Seventh Army commander, conferred the Medal of Honor on five 3d Division officers and men. Left to right: Lt. Col. Keith L. Ware, Lt. John J. Tominac, T/Sgt. Russell E. Dunham, S/Sgt. Lucian Adams, and Pfc. Wilburn K. Ross.

German of all cities"—fell, and all resistance north of the Pegnitz River had ceased.

At 1830, in the battered Adolf Hitler Platz, a rifle platoon from each regiment, as well as tanks, TDs, and Flakwagons, stood in silent array. Old Glory ascended an improvised flagpole and the band played the National Anthem. Maj. Gen. John W. O'Daniel then spoke.

"Again the 3d Division has taken its objective," he said. "We are standing at the site of the stronghold of Nazi resistance in our zone. Through your feats of arms, you have smashed fifty heavy antiaircraft guns, captured four thousand prisoners, and driven the Hun from every house and every castle and bunker in our part of Nürnberg.

"I congratulate you upon your superior performance...."

The band broke into "Dogface Soldier." A few be-

The Zeppelinfeld at Nürnberg is the scene of the raising of "Old Glory" which eclipses the Hakenkreuz.

wildered civilians contemplated the red, white, and blue banner flying at half-mast in mourning for President Franklin Delano Roosevelt.

On the following day an impressive military ceremony was conducted and the United States flag was officially raised over the city of Nürnberg, while still another ceremony was held on April 22 when Lt. Gen. Alexander M. Patch, Commanding General of the 7th Army, presented five members of the Division with the Congressional Medal of Honor in an impressive display witnessed by many of the famous news correspondents and radio announcers of the European Theater of Operations. The awardees were: T/Sgt. Ralph Dunham, S/Sgt. Lucian Adams and Pfc. Wilburn K. Ross of the 30th Infantry, and Lt. Col. Keith L. Ware and 1st Lt. John J. Tominac of the 15th Infantry.

The 3d Battalion, 30th Infantry, all blitzed up with new infantry jackets, painted helmets and new boots, represented infantrymen of the Division at both ceremonies. The 3d Battalion was Division reserve at the time.

The latter ceremony was held at the famous Nürnberg Zeppelin stadium, site of great rallies in the more halcyon days of the National Socialist German Workers' Party.

The fall of Nürnberg rocked Nazidom. The center of distribution for Nazi laws and Nazi propaganda was gone, the last-ditch fight which was exerted in defense of the city had been for naught and the relentless drive of the 3d Division and other United States units was no longer to be denied nor halted.

The Division was now about to go into Seventh Army reserve. However, in a dramatic move south, the 12th Armored Division, which had broken loose while the Marnemen were cleaning up Nürnberg, fought its way across the Danube River, last barrier before Munich, and captured a bridge intact near Dillingen, to the southwest.

The last chance for the Germans to develop a line west of Munich had now vanished. The 15th Infantry was rushed to that vicinity to reinforce and hold the bridgehead while the remainder of the Division stayed in Nürnberg on guard duty until relief by the 80th Infantry Division was effected.

After an all-night move, the 15th crossed the Danube near Dillingen and assembled in the Kicklingen-Holzheim area early on April 24.

The 3d now was poised to strike toward Munich, Germany's third largest city and key to the entire southern part of the country and to the Redoubt area, in which many military authorities thought the Germans would make a last determined stand.

Passing through the 12th Armored Division at Binswangen, the 15th Infantry attacked toward Weringen, with the 1st Battalion, commanded by Maj. Kenneth B. Potter, taking the lead following a heavy artillery concentration on dug-in enemy positions.

With Company A on the right and Company C on the left, the battalion pushed ahead but was met with a counterattack just outside the village and a six-hour fight against small arms, machine guns and antitank weapons ensued. The town was cleared, the blocks established by midmorning, and Company A moved on to occupy Roggden before nightfall.

The 2d Battalion, meanwhile, was conducting guard

Brigadier General Fehn (left) Stadtskommandant of Augsburg, with two officers, after his surrender.

duties in and around Dillingen and the 3d Battalion blocked in the vicinity of Holzheim, Weisengen, Altenbaindt and Eppisburg.

The 3d Battalion of the 30th Infantry also had a blocking mission in support of the 12th Armored Division in the vicinity of Crailsheim while the armored units exploited the brilliant capture of the Dillingen bridge.

The bridgehead situation was precarious for several days and what was expected to be a two-day "breather" for the 30th turned out to be an active period of blocking that finally developed into an all-out attack by the regiment to clear troublesome Germans from woods on the left flank.

The 1st Battalion, meanwhile, crossed the Danube on the right of the established front and cleared a salient

A German youth views probably without understanding the wreckage of a Jagdpanther near Eisenach.

after establishing another bridgehead shortly after midnight of April 25-26.

This crossing was made northeast of Augsburg while the 7th and 15th Infantry Regiments fought through that portion of the city west of the river.

Crossing the Lech River and then the Werk Canal, on the early morning of April 28, the 1st and 3d Battalions of the 30th ran into some of the heaviest artillery fire witnessed since Anzio. The 3d Battalion, crossing behind the 1st Battalion, came under intense artillery fire as it was crossing the bridge. It was learned later that the massed artillery fire of two German divisions had been turned on the crossing site in addition to much 20mm Flak and tank fire. Numerous battle groups, supported by fifty dual-purpose "88s" and a large number of "Tiger Royal" tanks carrying 120mm guns, were astride the *Autobahn* facing the river and poured hundred of shells into our attacking force. This was the last organized German defensive position protecting Munich.

The site chosen for the installation of a bridge was at the *Autobahn,* but the troop crossing site was 500 yards north over a spillway where the canal and river meet.

The intense enemy fire precluded the building of

United States soldiers liberated from the enemy.

A view of some of the Anti-aircraft gun positions that ringed the city of Munich in the environs and at the approaches.

bridges and no ferry could be put into use. Every five minutes a heavy concentration of at least fifty guns was placed on the river crossing site and not until the doughboys overran the German positions did the firing cease.

Company C, under 1st Lt. Charles P. Murray, broke a German counterattack, cut through the enemy lines, and took a large number of "88's" in an attack from the rear. The pitched battle continued all day of April 28, with 1st Battalion taking 24 "88's" and 3d Battalion netting 16. Company A alone captured 18 of the dreaded German field pieces.

Late that day, Company L, under 1st Lt. Abraham Fitterman, left the rest of the battalion and proceeded to clear the vital suburbs of Augsburg, east of the Lech River including Lechhausen, where contact was made with 15th Infantry, which had taken several hundred prisoners in its dash through Hettlingen, Gerashofen, Laugna, Asbach, Osterbuch, Reidsend, Wengen, Sontheim, Marzelstetten, Willenback, Rischgan, and Zusamaltheim. Company A captured a completely equipped airplane-parts plant at Roggden.

Frequent small groups of Germans were encountered during the rapid advance but there was no organized resistance such as was met at Wertingen, although the *Luftwaffe* came over at intervals. These raids did little more than harass our hard-driving troops.

The 2d Battalion of the 15th pushed through Affaltern, Feigenhofen, Lutzelburg, and Gablingen and the 3d raced into Bocksberg, Heretried, Holzhausen, Rettenbergen and Lautersbrunn on the morning of April 27; Company K, in front, was nearing Edenbergen on the Munich *Autobahn*.

Pushing north and northeast over a 20,000-yard front toward Therhaupten and Mertingen, the 1st and 3d Battalions of the 7th crossed the Lech River and the Werk Canal, turned south and southeast and, over a 4,000-yard front, moved into position for entrance into Augsburg.

The 1st Battalion encountered stubborn small-arms

Hundreds of German prisoners of war walk along this street in captured Munich under guard of 3d Division soldiers.

German prisoners by the thousands stream onto the Autobahn south of Munich to begin their long trek back to the 3d Division PW cage.

resistance as it moved out of Wortingen but the enemy fire was soon silenced and the town of Gottmannshofen was cleared. Company B, commanded by 1st Lt. Aldo F. Dal Molin, moved into Frouerstetten and Company C, under Capt. Victor M. Morris, took Bleinsbach. Hohenreichen, Prettelshofen and Hirschbach were taken without a fight but members of Company A had to eliminate the defenders of a roadblock before they could occupy Rieblingen and Company C was forced to inspect forty-two Storch planes that the enemy had destroyed near Langenreichen. Company A came under enemy artillery fire at Biberbach after the Germans had evacuated the city.

All during the night of April 26-27, the 1st Battalion received artillery fire from enemy positions across the Werk Canal and many casualties were suffered. Early the next morning, Company C was in Markt, Company B was in Erlingen and Company A was in Eistenbrechtshofen, en route to Theringen, the jumping-off position for the attack on Augsburg from the west.

One of the most memorable liberations of the war was celebrated at the small town of Unter Thurheim, which was entered by Company K, under 1st Lt. Herman Ramer.

Fifty-two Americans, some of whom were members of the 3d Division who had been captured by the Germans at Anzio Beachhead more than a year before, were set free when the Marnemen entered the town. A wilder celebration and more genuine greeting had never before been received by 3d Infantry Division men who captured the town.

The men had heard the 3d Division Artillery for several days and all of them had "sweated out" the liberation.

"When I saw those guys out of the window, my knees started to knock and I didn't know whether to jump or fly," said Pvt. Frank Parco, one of the liberated Anzio veterans. "Everybody was out in the street hugging and slapping each other, and I even kissed the first infantryman I saw, because I had been swearing for the last fourteen months that I would do so." Most of the 150 Germans defending the town were taken prisoner after a short fire fight, and Company K continued on to Vord Reid, Greggenhof, and Allmanshofen, where the company secured a bridge intact. Company I, commanded by 1st Lt. Eli Levy, took Pfaffenhofen, Buttenwiesen, Druisheim, and Mertigen, destroying three 150mm guns that had caused several delays to the advance of the battalion. Company L, under 1st Lt. Sherman W. Pratt, cleared Westendorf, Ellgau, Ostendorf and Waltershofen, coming under machine-gun and Flakwagon fire from across the Werk Canal while in the process.

Main over-all enemy resistance in the 7th Infantry area was centered on the north-south road leading from Nordendorf to Mertingen which the enemy attempted to deny our forces by frequent concentrations of self-propelled-gun fire on the highway.

The regiment's 2d Battalion, which had been in mobile reserve, moved from its bivouac area in the vicinity of Langenreichen and Company F attacked Langweid, where the enemy put up one of the few organized-resistance fights that the 7th had encountered in recent days. Twelve "88's" were captured on the outskirts of the village and the attacking force was brought under heavy small-arms and mortar fire directed from woods north and east of the town.

Lieutenant Conklin's men overran ten 105s whose crews withheld their fire until the attackers reached a close range.

The remainder of the battalion met stubborn delaying action as it proceeded through Achsheim and Stettenhofen but the enemy gradually withdrew along the railroad tracks running into Augsburg.

At Obersalzburg, the Nazis' retreat near Berchtesgaden, the RAF bombs had caused considerable destruction as evidenced by this photo.

The push to the south continued and Company G moved into Augsburg along the railroad right-of-way.

A civilian delegation offered to surrender the city to Lt. Col. Jack M. Duncan, Commanding Officer of the 2d Battalion, late that night, but while negotiations were under way elements of 2d Battalion, 15th Infantry, swept into the town from another direction—also with civilian assistance—and the 30th threw a ring around the city, completely cutting off any possible escapes and making a surrender unavoidable.

A hastily-organized task force of the 15th had passed through elements of the 7th at Krigshaber early that day, taking Rettenbergen, Edenbergen, Batzenhofen, Westheim, and Stadtbergen in a whirlwind drive into Augsburg. Col. Hallett D. Edson, the regimental commander, devised a surrender plan for the differing groups of civilians and military authorities.

The military commander of the city, a Brigadier General Fehn, desired to capitulate "honorably" but members of the German "Freedom Party" wanted to hand over the city without a fight, so Colonel Edson directed that the German garrison in the city of 200,000 population be surrendered in small groups, which was quickly accomplished to the satisfaction of all concerned, including the "honorable" German commander who also became a PW.

With the fall of Augsburg, the seizing of a bridgehead over the Lech River and the liquidation of the strong enemy defensive position astride the *Autobahn* to the east of the city, the 3d Division hardly paused in its sweep to Munich, whose Rosenheim Strasse beer hall was the scene of Hitler's famous "putsch" in 1923.

The 15th remained in Augsburg as the garrison unit while the other two regiments of the Division took up the pursuit of the disintegrating German army.

Passing through elements of the 30th Infantry at Friedberg, the 7th attacked on the right flank with Task Force Horton, commanded by Capt. Robert Horton of the 3d Battalion, in the van as the regiment raced down a road parallel to the *Autobahn* in quest of new towns to conquer.

Hegnenberg, Horbach, Eitelsreid, Galgen and Puch all fell before the Horton Force, which was comprised of a platoon of the Reconnaissance Company of the 601st TD Battalion, a section of the regimental Battle Patrol, a platoon of light tanks from Company D of the 756th Tank Battalion and a platoon of mediums from Company A; an armored advance guard of two platoons of medium tanks and a platoon of TDs; one tank dozer from Company A, 10th Engineer Battalion; and all the personnel of Company L of the 7th mounted on the armored vehicles; followed by other elements of the 3d Battalion utilizing organic and reinforcing transportation.

It was no wonder that the Germans surrendered by the hundreds upon seeing these fast-moving forces sweeping over the country.

Twelve "88's," a huge searchlight, and much radar equipment were taken with a large number of prisoners between Friedberg and Mering. Some enemy machinegun and antitank fire was met on the road between Mering and Merching. Kiefersbrunn, Steinach and Hochsdorf were also occupied by noon but a large crater and blown water main at a railroad crossing on the *Autobahn* held up progress shortly before midnight of April 29. The force moved slowly past the wreckage and was in Puchheim at 0200 the next morning. At Germering, fourteen "88's" were taken, in addition to numerous prisoners, after a fight that lasted almost until daybreak. Driving into Neaubing, the battalion detrucked, distributed its tanks and TDs to the other battalions of the regiment and continued the advance on foot, all Task Force missions having been completed and accomplished.

All the towns that were by-passed during the rapid advance of Task Force Horton were secured and cleaned out by the 1st Battalion while 2d Battalion, marching on foot, covered approximately twenty-five miles on the first day's trek toward Munich.

Rederzhausen, Mergenthau, Bachern, Holzburg, Harmonsburg, Ried, Zillenberg, Eismansberg, Sichenried, Baierberg, Tegernbach and Baindlkirch all fell to the 2d Battalion. At Holzberg, 800 prisoners were taken while another 500 were gathered up at Mittelstatten, Langenmoos, Hanshofen, Vogach and Gunzelhofen. By 0230 hours, April 30, the battalion had reached Unter Malching where it went into regimental reserve.

The 1st Battalion struck a strong resistance pocket at Pullach, where several hundred *Hitler Jugend* and SS troops fought for several hours before surrendering. Several bridges over the Isar River in the vicinity of Pullach were destroyed.

After clearing the suburban districts south of Munich to the Isar on May 1, 7th Infantry was placed in Division reserve and moved to the area east of the Isar.

Task Force Osgard, named after its commander, Lt. Col. James L. Osgard, commander of the 2d Battalion, 30th Infantry, jumped off on its race to Munich at 0130 hours on the morning of April 29 with the other two battalions close behind mopping up by-passed German groups.

Moving down the Munich *Autobahn* at breakneck speed, Task Force Osgard liquidated or captured a great number of Germans in carrying out its mission to secure approaches to Munich and clear the suburbs around the southwestern side of the city.

Before noon, the force was at a slight rise before the last barrier, the Amper River, where only one of a large number of bridges had not been blown. This lone bridge was discovered by Col. Lionel C. McGarr and Lt. Col. James L. Osgard on a personal reconnaissance well forward of the advance units of the regiment.

The United States flag is raised at Obersalzburg, above Berchtesgaden, by Pvt. Bennet A. Walter and Pfc. Nick Urich of the 3d Division's 7th Infantry, after capture of the village.

The much-publicized front window of Hitler's chalet at Obersalzburg above Berchtesgaden.

Late in the afternoon, Company F, commanded by Capt. Robert L. Fleet, moved across the bridge with supporting armor, and after overcoming stiff early resistance established a bridgehead. The remainder of 2d Battalion followed by the 1st Battalion moved across the river later in the evening.

At 0945 hours, April 30, Company C, under 1st Lt. Charles P. Murray, entered the city and the rest of the 1st Battalion moved in around noon, after overcoming a force of 300 enemy with machine guns who had arrived in the southwest corner of the city from the east almost simultaneously with the 30th's advance units from the west.

Capt. Gilbert Hunt, 1st Battalion Adjutant, reported that civilians had pointed out hiding places of stubborn enemy troops and that United States soldiers and vehicles had been showered with flowers by some civilians.

Resistance in Munich was indeed weird, with flower-throwing in some parts of the city and last-ditch fighting taking part in other sections. There were numerous antiaircraft guns protecting Munich and most of them were employed against the invading infantry of the 3d Division. The 30th Infantry encountered much small-

The gateway to the main entrance to the Schloss Klessheim, Hitler's Guesthouse for visiting foreign plenipotentiaries.

arms fire as it worked its way through the city's streets toward the center of the town, where a suicide squad of about twenty-five German Elite Guards held out in a building until one of our artillery pieces tore the structure down with several well-directed shots.

There was no official surrender at Munich such as in Nürnberg and many other smaller towns for the very simple reason that all the city's officials had left before General O'Daniel rode into the main part of town at 1600 hours, April 30.

The General talked with three men who held minor jobs in the city government but none of them felt sufficiently responsible to offer up the city, although they were Nazi party members and had been ordered by party leaders to remain behind to care for the 450,000 persons in Munich.

With Nürnberg and Munich in our hands, pursuit of the German army by the 3d Division was converted into a campaign of mopping up scattered points of resistance and running thousands of PWs through the cages, which now were so full that it was almost impossible to keep an accurate check on their numbers.

One of the spacious magnificently-furnished rooms of the Schloss Klessheim near Salzburg.

Leaving Augsburg April 30, the 15th Infantry assembled in the area near Rottbach, northwest of Munich,

The 3d Infantry Division Honor Guard passes in review before Secretary of War Patterson, Lieut. Gen. Patch, CG 7th Army and Lieut Gen Haislip, CG XV Corps (none is visible under archway of Schloss Klessheim.)

and organized small, hard-hitting task forces that quickly pushed past Munich, moved south along the Isar River to Grunwald then southeast along the axis Grunwald-Strasslach-Pullach-Oden-Kreuz and Ober Haching.

Task Force Ware, named after Lt. Col. Keith L. Ware, commanding officer of the 2d Battalion, led the regiment's attack as it took Otterloh, Sauerlach, Bergham, Holzham, Foching, Unter Darching and Unter Laindern during the drive of May 1-2, when 1478 prisoners were taken. German units were surrendering in their entirety and hundreds of enemy marched into our lines to give themselves up.

The closing days of the war were some of the most spectacular that the Division had encountered and the 30th Infantry, after leaving Munich, engaged in some stirring episodes during these final phases.

Task Force Chaney, named after Lt. Col. Christopher W. Chaney, 3d Battalion commander, was running hell-bent down the *Autobahn* to cut off escaping Germans in Rosenheim and to secure bridges across the Inn River, last natural barrier to the area leading into the Redoubt country.

It was May Day and a freak snow storm had blanketed the countryside. A cold, damp wind reminiscent of the Vosges whipped across the highways from the Tyrolean Alps as the task force pushed rapidly on, capturing one airport that held more than 300 German planes, many of which were "warmed up" and ready for flight when the raiders swooped down on the field.

Through Feldkirchen, the force reached Rosenheim where Company I and two platoons of Company L slipped through four enemy battalions and secured two of the three bridges in the city.

The third, and most strategically-located bridge, a two-lane structure that reached 135 yards across the Inn, was reconnoitered by 2d Lt. Emil T. Byke's 1st platoon of Company L.

A fire fight arose when the platoon neared the bridge site and when the Germans fled; the Marnemen took up the chase only to be stopped by a great number of mines that had been strewn along the bridge flooring. At this point, Lieutenant Byke saw a smoldering fuse beneath the bridge, rushed down and cut the primacord (an instantaneous type fuse) on a huge amount of demolitions just in time to save the bridge and many of his men's lives.

The lieutenant's alertness and quick action saved the only bridge in that area capable of carrying the armored units on their drive south, and without it the entrance of the 3d Division into Salzburg and Berchtesgaden would have been delayed several days.

While Company L was securing the bridges, Company I, commanded by 2d Lt. Gerald G. Mehuron, cleaned out the sentinels and outguards of the Rosenheim garrison.

By making the German commander believe that the United States forces were much larger than they were Lieutenant Mehuron won the surrender of nearly 1500 men and 125 officers in a slick ruse.

Task Force Chaney was held up at Traunstein when French and 20th Armored Division elements passed through, creating a traffic tie-up that was also agitated by a blown bridge over the Salzach River. After tak-

Lieutenant General Geoffrey Keyes, CG U. S. II Corps, pins the Distinguished Unit Citation to the colors of the 3d Division near Salzburg, awarded for action in the Colmar Pocket.

ing Bergen, the entire 30th Infantry assembled in the vicinity of Traunstein, from where it moved to Salzburg to perform guard duty in that historic old city until May 10.

The 7th Infantry took up the chase along the *Autobahn* east of Bergen. A blown bridge over the Tirolger Achen River near Stegenhauser held up the forces until a crossing could be effected east of Moosen. A surprisingly stiff fight was encountered by Company I in Ober Siegsdorf but the resistance was short-lived and ended with the killing or capture of all the defending Germans.

During the night of May 2-3, the 2d Battalion passed through the 3d in the vicinity of Ober Siegsdorf but was held up at the Saalach River, west of Salzburg, because all three bridges spanning the river had been destroyed.

On the following night, the battalion crossed the river in assault boats to be the first troops of the 3d Division to enter Austria.

Brig. Gen. Robert N. Young, Assistant Division Commander, accompanied advance elements of the 106th Cavalry Group, which was the first unit officially to enter Salzburg. General Young accepted the surrender of the city.

The German collapse was so complete that the 1st Battalion, 15th Infantry, commanded by Major Kenneth B. Potter, cleaning up behind advance formations, took over 3,000 prisoners including three Generals.

One member of the battalion who had become separated from his company was called upon to accept the surrender of a completely equipped German battalion. While he was preparing to have the Germans march to the PW cage, twenty more enemy officers came down from the hills and joined the surrender group.

Although Berchtesgaden was beyond the Division zone, General O'Daniel ordered the 7th Infantry to continue on through the hills to Hitler's mountain retreat, with the 1st and 3d Battalions following the regimental Battle Patrol in the attack.

Smouldering ruins of Hitler's Der Berghof Obersalzburg greeted the 3d Division. The Allied bombings of previous days had left little to defend, although the subterranean caves later proved interesting to sightseers who swarmed over the grounds for several weeks after the war's end.

During the afternoon of May 5, an American flag was raised over the charred buildings by members of the 7th Infantry in a ceremony that put the final touch to the 3d Division's pursuit that had began at Fedala, French Morocco, more than two years before.

The last act of *Nazidämmerung* was played out beginning May 3, before an appreciative 3d Infantry Division, the division which had fought over a longer trail than any other organization of comparable size in the European Theater of Operations. It was a fitting climax to the brilliant career of the Division which suffered 35,000 battle casualties in its almost solid twenty-two months' campaigning against the Axis.

An armistice commission representing Field Marshal Albert Kesselring, commander of all German forces on what had been the Western Front until the Russians and Americans met along the River Elbe and cut that front in two, had been reported in the Salzburg area for the past forty-eight hours.

In a small, rock-walled room, some hundred feet below the street level and at the bottom of a shaft sunk into the depths of the Mönchsberg close by the Klausen Tor in Salzburg, several United States officers, Brig. Gen. Robert N. Young; his staff officer, Major Frederick C. Spreyer; and Lt. Col. Jack M. Duncan, CO of the 2d Battalion, 7th Infantry, were discussing and attempting to solve the many problems attendant upon the surrender of the city of Salzburg with the *Stadtskommandant;* Colonel Lepperdinger, and his staff. Suddenly the radiotelephone in an alcove off the main room rings and the German *Feldwebel* responds with, "*Jawohl, Herr General . . . Jawohl!*" Colonel Lepperdinger is summoned to the phone and after a few minutes returns to inform the United States officers that he is in communication with Lieutenant General Zimmerman, Field Marshal Kesselring's chief of staff. General Zimmermann wishes to know if Salzburg is in United

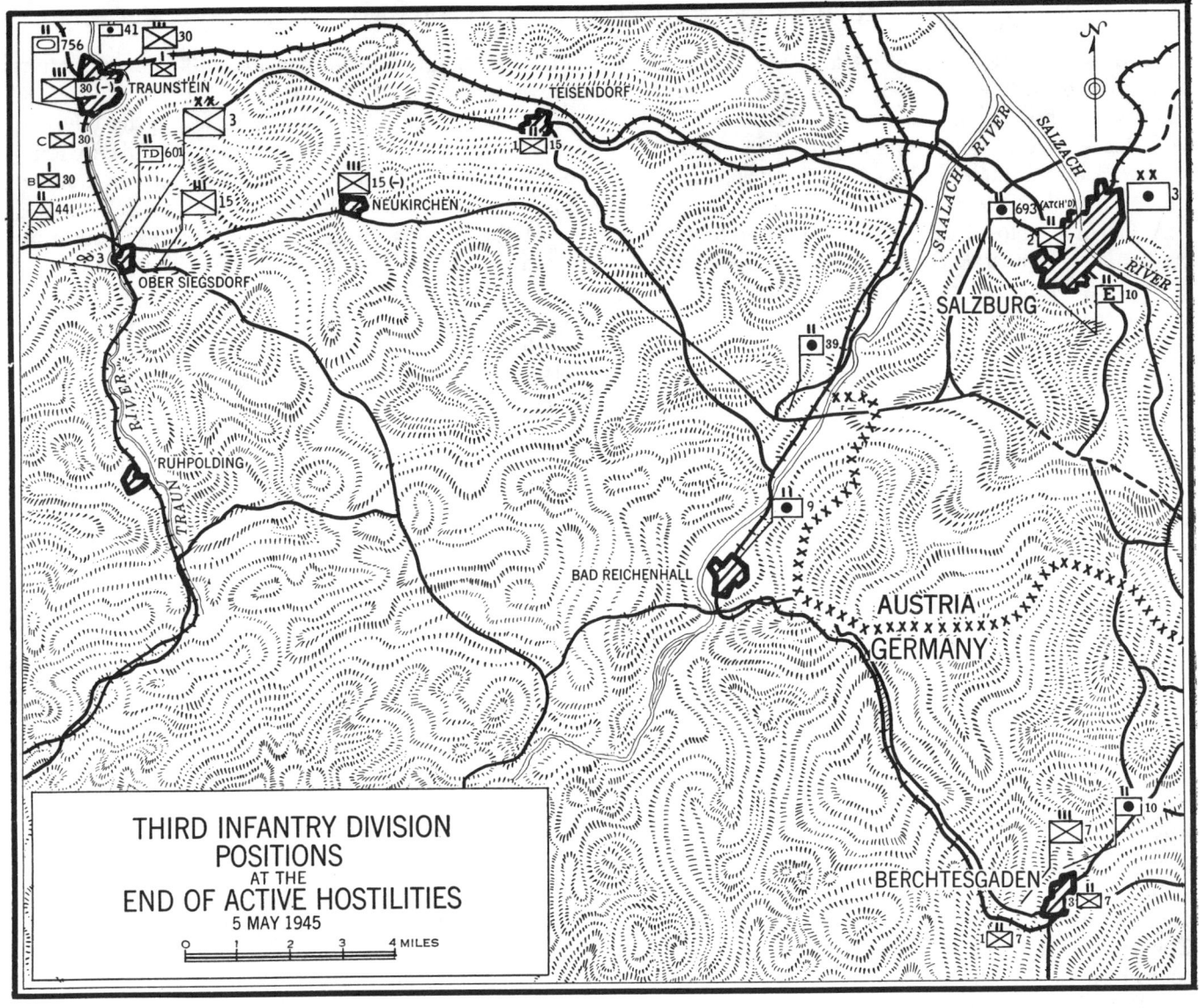

States hands. If so, would the United States commanding general receive a German armistice delegation from Field Marshal Kesselring's headquarters? German officers begin to talk *sotto voce* in little groups; General Young confers with his staff officers; English is translated into German, and German into English. Finally arrangements are agreed upon and relayed to Lieutenant General Zimmerman. The German armistice delegation will proceed from Field Marshal Kesselring's headquarters in motor vehicles plainly marked with white flags of truce via Hallein to Salzburg and will be met by General Young at the Osterreicher Hof.

In Room 49 at the Osterreicher Hof General Young and Major Spreyer await the arrival of the German delegation. Col. Bernard Wilson, commander of the 106th Cavalry Group, is ordered to send out parties in reconnaissance cars to aid the delegation in passing the lines. A British captain, recently released from a German prison camp by the U.S. 3d Infantry Division, joins in the search.

That afternoon a German major drove through the lines and requested to be conducted to an American headquarters. He brought the information that a Lt. Gen. Foertsch was heading the party, which was on the way.

"Shortly after 1900, Major Thomas Howard and Lt. Herbert Heldt burst into Room 49 of the Osterreicher Hof," reported AP's Howard Cowan, ". . . and said, 'They blew the bridge up right in our faces!'

"The bridge near Hallein south of Salzburg had been dynamited by SS troops and it was feared the armistice party was trapped.

"'Maybe they've been picked up by some of our men and taken to the PW cage,' said General Young. 'We'd never find them'.

"The deal had been given up as a bad job as the sun went down and no sign of the German officers. Room 49 cleared. . . .

"I left and got down one flight of stairs when I was almost knocked down by Foertsch and his party striding up the stairs two steps at a time. The party was covered with white chalk dust which gave their faces a deathly pallor and grayed their hair. They were loaded with brief cases and parcels of paper...."

The British captain had located the delegation and guided it to the Osterreicher Hof.

A German colonel said: "Do you want to see our credentials?" General Young nodded and the colonel began fumbling for the papers as General Foertsch began speaking in German with Maj. Frederick C. Spreyer.

"I have come to ask an armistice as soon as possible to complete arrangements for unconditional surrender of the German army, navy, and air forces," said Foertsch. "I have full authority to act for the German army and German government. It is imperative that I see your Sixth Army Group commander immediately. The meeting should be as near this spot as possible because of the state of our communications."

[The communications were in worse state than Foertsch suspected. Surrender negotiations were also being conducted in other parts of the dissected Reich.]

The party left immediately for the Division CP at Ober Siegsdorf. The Germans travelled in their own vehicles, sandwiched in between armored cars and jeeps bristling with machine guns. White flags flew from the radiator of the touring car in which Foertsch was a passenger. Behind him a huge American flag was folded on the lap of a German lieutenant.

"All along the route, which was cleared of heavy tank and truck traffic by scouts speeding ahead," said Cowan, "parties of doughboys lined the roads and you could hear the babble of comments as we passed by.

"'Von Kesselring!' one ejaculated.

"'Is it over?' was shouted scores of times."

The mission arrived in Ober Siegsdorf shortly after midnight, after detouring most of the way. The German general spent the rest of the night at the CP.

Foertsch and his party left in the morning and went back to XV Corps headquarters to surrender to General Devers.

Following the meeting the German party passed through the 3d Division on its way to Kesselring's headquarters.

A United States party headed by Captain Rhoman Clem of Division Headquarters accompanied the German delegation on its quest for the headquarters. In the party were: 1st Lts. Joseph A Mercer, George Allen, and Harold Willingham; Sgt. George Allen and a group of twenty-one other men.

SS fanatics held up the combined party on the first day's try, blowing up roads and one whole mountainside. The 3d Division personnel present were treated to the rare spectacle of an SS 2d lieutenant arguing with a German lieutenant general, and actually getting abusive.

Captain Clem's detachment returned to the Division CP, which had moved into Salzburg, while negotiations were held up for a day. Then a German Colonel Zelling led the party along the road to Zell-am-See, "an idyllic Austrian lake resort where Nazi big-shots alternately played and planned their next conquests," according to Edgar Snow of Saturday Evening Post.

On the night of May 8, Captain Clem met Marshal Kesselring on his private train, the "Brunswick," which had moved to the south of the lake. From that time on communication was constant with the Allied high command, including General Eisenhower, and remained constant until the following day, when representatives of Sixth Army Group headquarters appeared to receive the Marshal's final surrender. This historic act, involving the submission of more than one million enemy troops, took place in the "Brunswick" at the little town of Saalfelden. The last German force in Europe had surrendered.

(At 2:41 A.M., Monday, May 7 at Reims, France, General of the Army Dwight D. Eisenhower turned to his deputy commander, British Air Marshal Tedder and said, "Thank you very much, Arthur." Then he held up the two pens with which surrender had been signed and made a "V" for victory. Peace had officially come to Europe.

(Russian ratification of the final surrender came in Berlin, a little later in the day of May 8 when Field Marshal Keitel capitulated to Stalin's deputy, Marshal Gregory Zhukov.)

As far as the 3d Infantry Division was concerned, however, the war was not quite over.

A few days after the official V-E proclamation, 15th and 30th Infantry Regiments suddenly got the order to move, in full battle equipment. A group of SS troops was supposedly still holding out in the Redoubt area.

"A hell of a time to be shot—after all them speeches," grumbled the men, many of whom had well above the announced "critical score" necessary for a trip to the United States and possible discharge. According to C.I.C. information Himmler, the notorious SS leader who was still at large, was supposed to be in charge of the force.

The information proved erroneous, however, and men of the two regiments breathed sighs of relief. "For," said Jack Bell of the Chicago *Tribune,* "men do not want to be killed, even while playing cops and robbers."

The 3d Infantry Division apprehended the notorious Skorzeny, SS leader who had "rescued" Mussolini following the Italian dictator's downfall in 1943, and who had organized the abortive assassination missions against high-ranking allied military leaders during the

Ardennes counteroffensive and breakthrough—a very much-sought war criminal.

Probably one of the most valued comments was made by Kesselring. The German Field Marshal, who commanded troops on the Italian Front during the entire time that 3d Infantry Division fought in Italy, and who succeeded Marshal von Rundstedt as commander of the German West Front, was asked directly by Seymour Korman, war correspondent for the Chicago *Tribune*: "What was the best American division faced by troops under your command on *either* the Italian or Western Fronts?" Without hesitation, Kesselring named four American divisions, two infantry and two armored. The 3d Infantry Division he placed first on the list.

The incidents relative to the downfall of an entire nation only punctuated the fact that the fighting was finished. As men who have been living in constant apprehension of physical injury for the better portion of two and a half years, veterans of the 3d's total campaigning were almost skeptical, at first, of the fact that the war, indeed, was over. The ultimate goal of every soldier who had ever fought, the end had seemed like the pot of gold at the end of the rainbow. It had been wonderful to dwell upon, but it would never materialize. Then, suddenly, it was upon them all and the impact of the fact was a thing that failed to register—like the sudden death of a loved one—an idea, like some involved bit of philosophical reasoning that had to be taken again and again, in small doses. The sure knowledge of the fact was there, but the full implication of it needed much time and serious consideration to sink in.

Only after the connotations of the word "peace" began to manifest themselves in such realities as the absence of shot and shell, enough food to eat and enough time to sleep, did the end of hostilities effect the fullest benefit on the minds of all men.

Then, and only then, did the transition reach full cycle. It was sad that so many thousands of 3d Division men slept in places so far from the scenes of rejoicing.

It is with pride that the men of the 3d Infantry Division point to their record of combat, of campaigns, of landings, of victories [said the Division *Front Line*]. The route from Casablanca to Berchtesgaden is strewn with the wreckage of the shattered *Wehrmacht*. Never did the 3d Infantry Division falter or fall back in its thirty months of combat. All of this is indeed glorious and in Army language can be said to be, "in keeping with the highest traditions of the service."

But there is another side to the picture. Now that the active campaigning is over in Europe we must look back and tally the cost of all this glory.

The Division has its heroes, its Footsie Britts. It has its thousands of unsung heroes, the infantry and engineers, the artillerymen, the medics, signalmen and QM, its ordnance and tankers, its pencil-pushers and staff officers. From the privates to the generals they are heroes, all of them. They did their job. Some of them never saw the Germans; some of them saw too many. But it was teamwork that made the 3d what it was and is.

But the cost of the reputation—it cannot be tallied. The cost cannot be added in terms of cash, materiel, time. Nor can it be a statistical report of so many killed, injured, missing, prisoners. For the cost has too personal a significance to each of us to permit it to be summarized as a statistical report. All of us have lost someone in this war; a friend, a brother, a son, someone whom we loved.

It is to these men that we look back today in our moment of triumph. We cannot look back to them if we do not look forward to the future for which they fought—and died.

The cost has been great—almost at times, it seemed, too great. It is now our task to build the future on the solid foundation laid by those who have left us forever. That future may keep us in Europe, for a time, send us home, send us to the Pacific. No one knows. But we are still the 3d Division—the Division that has never failed. We shall go forward, in our traditional way, never forgetting those who march with us in memory.

TABLE OF CASUALTIES*

Germany

(March 15, 1945 through May 8, 1945)

KIA	WIA	MIA	Total Battle Casualties	Non-Battle Casualties
373	1744	416	2533	1909

Reinforcements and Hospital return-to-unit personnel

Reinf		Hosp RTUs	
Off	EM	Off	EM
56	1970	63	1278

KNOWN ENEMY CASUALTIES

Killed	Wounded	Captured
381	1020	101,201

*These figures were provided by the A C or S, G-1, 3d Infantry Division.

3D INFANTRY DIVISION MONUMENT AT FEDALA

Location: At Fedala, on the beach esplanade at a point midway between the Casino property and the Hotel Miramar property. The site is on the shoreward side of the esplanade in a semicircular revetment surrounded by a white wall. The inscription, translated from the French, reads:

NOVEMBER 8, 1942

U. S. THIRD INFANTRY DIVISION MADE AN ASSAULT AMPHIBIOUS LANDING IN THIS VICINITY. THE ENTRANCE INTO CASABLANCA MARKS THE DAY ON WHICH THE DIVISION TOOK ITS PLACE AT THE SIDE OF ITS FRENCH COMRADES-IN-ARMS IN THE LONG, HARD STRUGGLE THAT TERMINATED IN THE LIBERATION OF FRANCE AND THE DEFEAT OF GERMANY.

3D INFANTRY DIVISION BEACHHEAD MONUMENT AT LICATA

Location: On a triangular piece of ground located at the intersection of three streets on the northeastern edge of the city of Licata, adjacent to the city park and overlooking the beach. Licata is located on Highway No. 115 at the southern termination of Highway No. 123. The inscription, translated from the Italian, reads:

JULY 10, 1943

U. S. THIRD INFANTRY DIVISION, REINFORCED, MADE AN ASSAULT AMPHIBIOUS LANDING IN THIS VICINITY, ESTABLISHED A FIRM BEACHHEAD, AND COMMENCED AN HISTORIC ATTACK, CULMINATING IN THE CAPTURE OF AGRIGENTO, PALERMO, AND MESSINA.

3D INFANTRY DIVISION BEACHHEAD MONUMENT AT ANZIO

Location: The site is located in the edge of a grove of trees on the Anzio–Nettuno–Littoria paved highway adjacent to the site of the old 3d Division rear CP area. The inscription, translated from the Italian, **reads:**

JANUARY 22, 1944

U. S. THIRD INFANTRY DIVISION MADE AN ASSAULT AMPHIBIOUS LANDING IN THIS VICINITY, ESTABLISHED A BEACHHEAD WHICH WAS MANTAINED FOR FOUR MONTHS AT GREAT SACRIFICE OF HUMAN LIFE, AND WITH INDOMITABLE COURAGE. IN A VALIANT AND SANGUINARY ATTACK, THE DIVISION LED AN OFFENSIVE THAT DESTROYED THE STRONG GERMAN DEFENSES AND CULMINATED IN THE LIBERATION OF ROME.

3D INFANTRY DIVISION BEACHHEAD MONUMENT AT ST. TROPEZ–LA CROIX

Location: On Highway No. 559, at an intersection of three roads five kilometers southeast of the town of La Croix and about three hundred yards from the La Croix–Vollmer beach. The inscription, translated from the French, reads:

AUGUST 15, 1944

U. S. THIRD INFANTRY DIVISION MADE AN ASSAULT AMPHIBIOUS LANDING IN THIS VICINITY, ESTABLISHED A FIRM BEACHHEAD, AND TOGETHER WITH ITS ALLIES, BEGAN A RAPID ADVANCE UP THE RHÔNE VALLEY, CULMINATING IN THE LIBERATION OF PROVENCE, THE VALLEY OF THE RHÔNE, FRANCHE COMTÉ, THE VOSGES, AND ALSACE.

3d Infantry Division Headquarters at Bad Wildungen, Germany, 1945-46.

APPENDIX

The Medal of Honor is awarded in the name of the Congress to each person who, while an officer, noncommissioned officer, or private of the Army, in action involving actual conflict with an enemy, distinguishes himself conspicuously by gallantry and intrepidity at the risk of his life above and beyond the call of duty.

In order to justify an award of the Medal of Honor, the individual must perform in action a deed of personal bravery or self-sacrifice above and beyond the call of duty, so conspicuous as clearly to distinguish him for gallantry and intrepidity above his comrades, involving risk of life or the performance of more than ordinarily hazardous service, the omission of which would not justly subject him to censure as for shortcoming or failure in the performance of his duty. The recommendations for the decoration will be judged by this standard of extraordinary merit and incontestable proof of the performance of the service will be exacted. (Act of 9 July 1918, 40 Stat. 870; 10 U. S. C. 1403; M. L. 1939, sec. 903).

      Adams   Antolak   Bender   Britt

S/SGT. LUCIAN ADAMS, 38417252, Company I, 30th Infantry. For conspicuous gallantry and intrepidity at the risk of his life above and beyond the call of duty. On 28 October 1944 near St. Dié, France, when his company was stopped in its effort to drive through the Mortagne Forest to reopen the supply line to the isolated 3d Battalion, *Sergeant Adams* braved the concentrated fire of machine guns in a lone assault on a force of German troops. Although his company had progressed less than 10 yards and had lost three killed and six wounded, *Sergeant Adams* charged forward dodging from tree to tree, firing a borrowed BAR from his hip. Despite intense machine-gun fire which the enemy directed at him and rifle grenades which struck the trees over his head, showering him with broken twigs and branches, *Sergeant Adams* made his way to within 10 yards of the closest machine gun and killed the gunner with a hand grenade. An enemy soldier threw hand grenades at him from a position only 10 yards distant; however, *Sergeant Adams* despatched him with a single burst of BAR fire. Charging into the vortex of the enemy fire, he killed another enemy machine gunner at 15 yards range with a hand grenade and forced the surrender of the two supporting infantrymen. Although the remainder of the German group concentrated the full force of their automatic-weapons fire in a desperate effort to knock him out, he proceeded through the woods to find and exterminate five more of the enemy. Finally, when the third German machine gun opened up on him at a range of 20 yards, *Sergeant Adams* killed the gunner with BAR fire. In the course of action, he personally killed nine Germans, eliminated three enemy machine guns, vanquished a specialized force which was armed with automatic weapons and grenade launchers, cleared the woods of hostile elements, and reopened the severed supply line to the assault companies of his battalion.

SGT. SYLVESTER ANTOLAK, 3503502, Company B, 15th Infantry, on 24 May 1944 near Cisterna di Littoria, Italy, charged 200 yards over flat, coverless terrain to destroy an enemy machine-gun nest during the second day of the offensive which broke through the German cordon of steel around the Anzio beachhead. Fully 30 yards in advance of his squad, he ran into withering enemy machine-gun, machine-pistol, and rifle fire. Three times he was struck by bullets and knocked to the ground, but each time he struggled to his feet to continue his relentless advance. With one shoulder deeply gashed and his right arm shattered, he continued to rush directly into the enemy fire concentration with his submachine gun wedged under his uninjured arm until within 15 yards of the enemy strongpoint, where he opened fire at deadly close range, killing 2 Germans and forcing the remaining 10 to surrender. He reorganized his men and, refusing to seek the medical attention he needed so badly, chose to lead the way toward another strong point 100 yards distant. Utterly disregarding the hail of bullets concentrated on him, he had stormed ahead nearly three-fourths of the space between strong points when he was instantly killed by hostile rifle fire. Inspired by his example, his squad went on to overwhelm the enemy troops. By his supreme sacrifice, superb fighting courage, and heroic devotion to the attack, *Sergeant Antolak* was directly responsible for eliminating 20 Germans, capturing an enemy machine gun, and clearing the path for his company to advance.

S/SGT. STANLEY BENDER, 6920404, Company E, 7th Infantry, for conspicuous gallantry and intrepidity at risk of life, above and beyond the call of duty, in action involving actual conflict. On 17 August 1944, near La Londe, France, *Staff Sergeant Bender* climbed on top of a knocked-out tank, in the face of withering machine-gun fire which had halted the advance of his company, in an effort to locate the source of this fire. Although bullets ricocheted off the turret at his feet, *Staff Sergeant Bender* nevertheless remained standing bolt upright in full view of the enemy for over two minutes. Locating the enemy machine guns on a knoll 200 yards away, he ordered two squads to cover him and led his men down an irrigation ditch, running a gantlet of intense machine-gun fire, which completely blanketed 50 yards of his advance and wounded four of his men. While the Germans hurled hand grenades at the ditch, *Staff Sergeant Bender* stood his ground until his squad caught up with him, then advanced alone, in a wide, flanking approach, to the rear of the knoll. He walked deliberately a distance of 40 yards without cover in full view of the Germans and under a hail of both enemy and friendly fire, to the first machine gun, 25 yards distant. As he neared it, its two-man crew swung the machine gun around and fired two bursts at him, but *Staff Sergeant Bender* walked calmly through the fire, and, reaching the edge of the emplacement, dispatched the crew. Signalling his men to rush the rifle pits, he then walked 35 yards further to kill an enemy rifleman and returned to lead his squad in the destruction of the eight remaining Germans in the strong-point. His audacity so inspired the remainder of the assault company that the men charged out of their positions, shouting and yelling, to overpower the enemy roadblock and sweep into town, knocking out two antitank guns, killing 37 Germans and capturing 26 others.

CAPT. MAURICE L. BRITT, 0-410196 (then First Lieutenant), commander, Company L, 30th Infantry. For conspicuous gallantry and intrepidity at the risk of his own life above and beyond the call of duty. Disdaining enemy hand grenades and close-range machine-pistol, machine-gun, and rifle fire, *Lieutenant Britt* inspired and led a handful of his men in repelling a bitter counterattack by approximately 100 Germans against his company positions north of Mignano, Italy, the morning of 10 November 1943. During the intense fire fight, *Lieutenant Britt's* canteen and field glasses were shattered; a bullet pierced his side; his chest, face, and hands were covered with grenade wounds. Despite his wounds, for which he refused to accept medical attention until ordered to do so by his battalion commander following the battle, he personally killed five and wounded an unknown number of Germans, wiped out one enemy machine-gun crew, fired five clips of carbine and an undetermined amount of M1 rifle ammunition, and threw 32 fragmentation grenades. His bold, aggressive actions, utterly disregarding superior enemy numbers, resulted in capture of four Germans, two of them wounded, and enabled several captured Americans to escape. *Lieutenant Britt's* undaunted courage and prowess in arms were largely responsible for repulsing a German counterattack, which, if successful, would have isolated his battalion and destroyed his company.

LIEUT. FRANK BURKE, 0-1288033, 15th Infantry, fought with extreme gallantry on 17 April 1945 in the streets of war-torn Nürnberg, Germany, where the 1st Battalion, 15th Infantry Regiment, was engaged in rooting out fanatical defenders of the citadel of Naziism. As battalion transportation officer, *Lieutenant Burke* had gone forward to select a motor-pool site, when, in a desire to perform more than his assigned duties and participate in the fight, he advanced beyond the lines of forward riflemen. Detecting a group of about 10 Germans making preparations for a local counterattack, he rushed back to a nearby American company, secured a light machine gun with ammunition, and daringly opened fire on this superior force, which deployed and returned his fire with machine pistols, rifles, and rocket launchers. From another angle a German machine gun tried to blast him from

Photograph not Available	Photograph not Available		
Burke	Choate	Christian	Connor

his emplacement, but *Lieutenant Burke* killed this gun crew and drove off the survivors of the unit he had originally attacked. Giving his next attention to enemy infantrymen in ruined buildings, he picked up a rifle, dashed more than 100 yards through intense fire and engaged the Germans from behind an abandoned tank. A sniper nearly hit him from a cellar only 20 yards away, but he dispatched this adversary by running directly to the basement window, firing a full clip into it and then plunging through the darkened aperture to complete the job. He withdrew from the fight only long enough to replace his jammed rifle and secure grenades, then reengaged the Germans. Finding his shots ineffective, he pulled the pins from two grenades, and, holding one in each hand, rushed the enemy-held buildings, hurling his missiles just as the enemy threw a potato-masher grenade at him. In the triple explosion the Germans were wiped out and *Lieutenant Burke* was dazed; but he emerged from the shower of debris that engulfed him, recovered his rifle, and went on to kill three more Germans and meet the charge of a machine-pistol man, whom he cut down with three calmly delivered shots. He then retired toward the American lines and there assisted a platoon in a raging, 30-minute fight against formidable armed hostile forces. This enemy group was repulsed, and the intrepid fighter moved to another friendly group which broke the power of a German unit armed with a 20mm gun in a fierce fire fight. In 4 hours of heroic action *Lieutenant Burke* singlehandedly killed 11 and wounded 3 enemy soldiers and took a leading role in engagements in which an additional 29 enemy were killed or wounded. His extraordinary bravery and superb fighting skill were an inspiration to his comrades, and his entirely voluntary mission into extremely dangerous territory hastened the fall of Nürnberg in his battalion's sector.

S/SGT. CLYDE L. CHOATE, Company C, 601st Tank Destroyer Battalion, for conspicuous gallantry and intrepidity at risk of life, above and beyond the call of duty, in action involving actual conflict. On 25 October, 1944, at 1730 hours, near Bruyeres, France, when a Mark IV tank knocked out his destroyer, crashed through infantry positions and threatened the battalion command post, *Sergeant Choate* dashed through automatic fire which pierced his jacket and knocked off his helmet, seized his bazooka and stalked the tank. Passing through the enemy infantry line, he immobilized the German tank with a rocket, then ran back to reload and destroy the tank with rocket fire from 30 feet. After shooting two of the fleeing tank crew, he threw a grenade into the tank. His bold, singlehanded assault shattered the counterattack.

PFC. HERBERT F. CHRISTIAN, 35592775, Company E (Battle Patrol), 15th Infantry, for conspicuous gallantry and intrepidity at risk of life, above and beyond the call of duty, in action involving actual conflict. On 2-3 June 1944 at 0100 hours, near Valmontone, Italy, *Private First Class Christian* elected to sacrifice himself in order that his comrades might extricate themselves from an ambush. Braving the massed fire of 60 riflemen, three machine guns and three tanks from positions only thirty yards distant, he stood erect and signaled to the patrol to withdraw. Although his right leg was severed above the knee by 20mm cannon fire, *Private First Class Christian* advanced on his left knee and the bloody stump of his right thigh, firing his submachine gun. Despite excruciating pain, *Private First Class Christian* continued on his self-assigned mission and succeeded in distracting the enemy, enabling his 12 comrades to escape. He killed three enemy soldiers almost at once. Leaving a trail of blood behind him, he made his way forward twenty yards, halted at a point within ten yards of the enemy, and, despite intense fire, killed a machine-pistol man. Reloading his weapon he fired directly into the enemy positions. The enemy, enraged at the success of his ruse, concentrated 20mm, machine-gun, machine-pistol and rifle fire on him, yet he refused to seek cover. Maintaining his erect position, *Private First Class Christian* fired his weapon to the very last. Just as he emptied his submachine gun, the enemy bullets found their mark and *Private First Class Christian* slumped forward, dead. The courage and spirit of self-sacrifice displayed by this soldier is true to the highest traditions of the American Army.

SGT. JAMES P. CONNOR, 32066575, Battle Patrol (SD from Company K), 7th Infantry, for conspicuous gallantry and intrepidity at risk of life, above and beyond the call of duty, in action involving actual conflict. On 15 August 1944, at 0800 hours, *Sergeant Connor*, through sheer grit and determination, led his platoon in clearing an enemy vastly superior in numbers and firepower from strongly entrenched positions on Cape Cavalaire, removing a grave enemy threat to his division during the amphibious landings in Southern France, and thereby insured safe and uninterrupted landings for the huge volume of men and matériel which followed. Battle Patrol landed on Red Beach at H-hour, with the mission of destroying the strongly fortified enemy positions of Cape Cavalaire peninsula with utmost speed. From the peninsula, the enemy had commanding observation and seriously menaced the vast landing operations taking place. Though knocked down and seriously wounded in the neck by a hanging mine which killed his platoon lieutenant, *Sergeant Connor* refused medical aid and with his driving spirit practically carried the platoon across several thousand yards of mine-saturated beach through intense fire from mortars, 20mm flak guns, machine guns and snipers. En route to the Cape, *Sergeant Connor* became platoon leader. Receiving a second wound, which lacerated his shoulder and back, he again refused evacuation, expressing determination to carry on until physically unable to continue. He reassured and prodded the hesitating men of his decimated platoon forward through almost impregnable mortar concentrations. Again emphasizing the prevalent urgency of their mission, he impelled his men toward a group of buildings honeycombed with enemy snipers and machine guns. Here, he received his third grave wound, this time in the leg, felling him in his tracks. Still resolved to carry on, he relinquished command only after his attempts proved it physically impossible to stand on his legs. Nevertheless, from his prone position he gave the orders and directed his men in assaulting the enemy. Infused with *Sergeant Connor's* dogged determination, the platoon, though reduced to less than one-third of its original 36 men, out-flanked and rushed the enemy with such furiousness that they killed 7, captured 40, seized 3 machine guns and considerable other matériel, and took all their assigned objectives, successfully completing their mission. By his own repeated example of tenaciousness to purpose and indomitable spirit *Sergeant Connor* had transmitted his heroism to his men until they had become a fighting team which could not be stopped.

LIEUT. ROBERT CRAIG, O-13101959, Company L, 15th Infantry, for conspicuous gallantry and intrepidity at risk of life, above and beyond the call of duty, on 11 July 1943, near Favoratta, Sicily. *Lieutenant Craig* voluntarily undertook the perilous task of locating and destroying a hidden enemy machine gun which had halted the advance of his company. Attempts by three other officers to locate the weapon had resulted in failure, with each officer receiving wounds. *Lieutenant Craig* located the gun and snaked his way to a point within 35 yards of the hostile position before being discovered. Charging headlong into the furious automatic fire, he reached the gun,

Craig   Daly   Dunham   Dutko

stood over it, and killed the three crew members with his carbine. With this obstacle removed, his company continued its advance. Shortly thereafter, while advancing down the forward slope of a ridge, *Lieutenant Craig* and his platoon, in a position devoid of cover and concealment, encountered the fire of approximately 100 enemy soldiers. Electing to sacrifice himself in order that his platoon might carry on the battle, he ordered his men to withdraw to the cover of the crest while he drew the enemy fire to himself. With no hope of survival, he charged toward the enemy until he was within 25 yards of them. Assuming a kneeling position, he killed five and wounded three enemy soldiers. While the hostile force concentrated fire on him, his platoon reached the cover of the crest. *Lieutenant Craig* was killed by enemy fire, but his intrepid action so inspired his men that they drove the enemy from the area, inflicting heavy casualties on the hostile force.

LIEUT. MICHAEL J. DALY, 0-1692630, Commanding Officer, Company A, 15th Infantry, for conspicuous gallantry and intrepidity at risk of life, above and beyond the call of duty, in action involving actual conflict. At 0500 hours on 18 April 1945, while leading his company through the shell-battered, sniper-infested wreckage of Nürnberg, Germany, *Lieutenant Daly* dashed through blistering fire to assault a German machine gun singlehandedly and kill its three-man crew with carbine fire. Again charging alone through *Panzerfaust* and automatic fire, he wiped out a six-man German patrol, then boldly engaged a second machine gun at 10 yards range. Fighting for two days and nights without sleep, *Lieutenant Daly* destroyed three machine guns and killed 15 Germans.

T/SGT. RUSSELL DUNHAM, 16015617 (then Staff Sergeant), Company I, 30th Infantry, at about 1430 hours on 8 January 1945, during an attack on Hill 616 near Kaysersberg, France, singlehandedly assaulted three enemy machine guns. Wearing a white robe made of a mattress cover, carrying 12 carbine magazines, and with a dozen hand grenades snagged in his belt, suspenders and buttonholes, *Sergeant Dunham* crawled in the attack up a snow-covered hill under fire from two machine guns and supporting riflemen. His platoon 35 yards behind him, *Sergeant Dunham* crawled 75 yards under heavy, direct fire toward the timbered emplacement shielding the left machine gun. As he jumped to his feet 10 yards from the gun and charged forward, machine-gun fire tore through his camouflage robe and a rifle bullet seared a 10-inch gash across his back, sending him spinning 15 yards down hill into the snow. When the indomitable sergeant sprang to his feet to renew his one-man assault, a German egg grenade landed beside him. He kicked it aside and, as it exploded 5 yards away, shot and killed the German machine gunner and assistant gunner. His carbine empty, he jumped into the emplacement and hauled out the third member of the gun crew by the collar. Although machine-gun bullets kicked up the dirt at his heels and blood was seeping through his white coat, *Sergeant Dunham* proceeded 50 yards through a storm of automatic and rifle fire to attack the second machine gun. Twenty-five yards from the emplacement he hurled two grenades, destroying the gun and its crew; then fired down into the supporting foxholes with his carbine, despatching and dispersing the enemy riflemen. Although his coat was so thoroughly blood soaked that he was a conspicuous target against the white landscape, *Sergeant Dunham* again advanced ahead of his platoon in an assault on enemy positions further up the hill. Coming under machine-gun fire from 65 yards to his front, while rifle grenades exploded 10 yards from his position, he hit the ground and crawled forward. At 15 yards range, he jumped to his feet, staggered a few paces toward the timbered machine-gun emplacement and killed the crew with hand grenades. An enemy rifleman fired at pointblank range, but missed him. After killing the rifleman, *Sergeant Dunham* drove others from their foxholes with grenades and carbine fire. Killing nine Germans, wounding seven and capturing two, firing about 175 rounds of carbine ammunition and expending 11 grenades, *Sergeant Dunham*, despite a painful wound, spear-headed a spectacular and successful diversionary attack.

PFC. JOHN W. DUTKO, 13022501, Company A, 30th Infantry. For conspicuous gallantry and intrepidity at the risk of his life above and beyond the call of duty on 23 May 1944 near Ponte Rotto, Italy. *Private Dutko* left the cover of an abandoned enemy trench at the height of an artillery concentration in a single-handed attack upon three enemy machine guns and an 88mm mobile gun. Despite the intense fire of these four weapons which were aimed directly at him, *Private Dutko* ran 100 yards through the impact area, paused momentarily in a shell crater, and then continued his one-man assault. Although machine-gun bullets kicked up the dirt at his heels and 88mm shells exploded within 30 yards of him, *Private Dutko* nevertheless made his way to a point within 30 yards of the first enemy machine gun and killed both gunners with a hand grenade. Although the second machine gun wounded him, knocking him to the ground, *Private Dutko* regained his feet and advanced on the 88mm gun, firing his Browning automatic rifle from the hip. When he came within 10 yards of this weapon he killed its five-man crew with one long burst of fire. Wheeling on the machine gun which had wounded him, *Private Dutko* killed the gunner and his assistant. The third German machine gun fired on *Private Dutko* from a position 20 yards distant, wounding him a second time as he proceeded toward the enemy weapon in a half run. He killed both members of its crew with a single burst from his Browning automatic rifle, continued toward the gun and died, his body falling across the dead German crew.

T/5 ERIC G. GIBSON, 36004320, Company I, 30th Infantry. For conspicuous gallantry and intrepidity at the risk of his life above and beyond the call of duty. On 28 January 1944 near Isola Bella, Italy, *Technician Gibson*, company cook, led a squad of replacements through their initial baptism of fire, destroyed four enemy positions, killed five and captured two German soldiers, and secured the left flank of his company during an attack on a strongpoint. Placing himself 50 yards in front of his new men, *Technician Gibson* advanced down the wide stream ditch known as the Fossa Femminamorta, keeping pace with the advance of his company. An enemy soldier allowed *Technician Gibson* to come within 20 yards of his concealed position and then opened fire which barely missed him. *Technician Gibson* charged the position firing his submachine gun every few steps. Reaching the position *Technician Gibson* fired pointblank at his opponent, killing him. An artillery concentration fell in and around the ditch and the concussion from one shell knocked him flat. As he rose to his feet *Technician Gibson* was fired on by two soldiers armed with a machine pistol and a rifle from a position only 75 yards distant. *Technician Gibson* immediately raced toward the foe. Halfway to the position a machine gun opened fire on him. Bullets came within inches of his body yet *Technician Gibson* never paused in his forward movement. He killed one and captured the other soldier. Shortly after, when he was fired upon by a heavy machine gun 200 yards down the ditch, *Technician Gibson* crawled back to his squad and ordered it to lay down a base of fire while he flanked the

| Gibson | Harris | Hawks | Huff |

emplacement. Despite all warning *Technician Gibson* crawled 125 yards through an artillery concentration and the cross-fire of two machine guns which showered dirt over his body, threw two hand grenades into the emplacement, and charged it with his submachine gun killing two of the enemy and capturing a third. Before leading his men around a bend in the stream ditch *Technician Gibson* went forward alone to reconnoiter. Hearing an exchange of machine-pistol and submachine-gun fire *Technician Gibson's* squad went forward to find that its leader had run 35 yards toward an outpost, killed the machine-pistolman and had himself been killed while firing at the Germans.

LIEUT. JAMES L. HARRIS, O-1703032, Company A, 756th Tank Battalion, for conspicuous gallantry and intrepidity at risk of life, above and beyond the call of duty, in action involving actual conflict. On 7 October 1944, in Vagney, France, *Lieutenant Harris*, an M-4 tank platoon leader, drew machine-gun fire upon himself at pointblank range in order to ascertain the location of an enemy tank which threatened to destroy an infantry battalion CP; crawled through devastating enemy fire, while fatally wounded, to direct his tank in an attack, and, though bleeding profusely from a second wound, persevered until the enemy withdrew. At 2100 hours, an enemy raiding party, comprising a tank and two platoons of infantry, infiltrated through the lines under cover of mist and darkness and attacked an infantry battalion CP with hand grenades, retiring a short distance to an ambush position on hearing the approach of the M-4 tank commanded by *Lieutenant Harris*. Realizing the need for bold, aggressive action, *Lieutenant Harris* ordered his tank to halt while he proceeded on foot, fully 10 yards ahead of his six-man patrol and armed only with a service pistol to probe the darkness for the enemy. Although struck down and mortally wounded by machine-gun bullets which penetrated his solar plexus, he crawled back to his tank, leaving a trail of blood behind him, and, too weak to climb inside it, issued fire orders while lying on the road between the two contending armored vehicles. Although the tank which he commanded was destroyed in the course of the fire fight, he stood the enemy off until friendly tanks, preparing to come to his aid, caused the enemy to withdraw and thereby lose an opportunity to kill or capture the entire battalion command personnel. Suffering a second wound, which severed his leg at the hip, in the course of this tank duel, *Lieutenant Harris* refused aid until after a wounded member of his crew had been carried to safety. He died before he could be given medical attention.

PFC. LLOYD C. HAWKS, 37019945, Medical Detachment, 30th Infantry. For gallantry and intrepidity at the risk of his life above and beyond the call of duty. On 30 January 1944 at 1500 hours near Carano, Italy, *Private Hawks* braved an enemy counterattack in order to rescue two wounded men who, unable to move, were lying in an exposed position within 30 yards of the enemy. Two riflemen attempting the rescue had been forced to return to their fighting holes by extremely severe enemy machine-gun fire, after crawling only 10 yards toward the casualties. An aid man, whom the enemy could plainly identify as such, had been critically wounded in a similar attempt. *Private Hawks* nevertheless crawled 50 yards through a veritable hail of machine-gun bullets and flying mortar fragments to a small ditch, administered first aid to his fellow aid man who had sought cover therein, and continued toward the two wounded men 50 yards distant. An enemy machine-gun bullet penetrated his helmet, knocked it from his head, and momentarily stunned him. Thirteen bullets passed through his helmet as it lay on the ground within 6 inches of his body. *Private Hawks* crawled to the casualties, administered first aid to the more seriously wounded man, and dragged him to a covered position 25 yards distant. Despite continuous automatic fire from positions only 30 yards away and shells which exploded within 25 yards, *Private Hawks* returned to the second man and administered first aid to him. As he raised himself to obtain bandages from his medical kit his right hip was shattered by a burst of machine-gun fire and a second burst splintered his left forearm. Displaying dogged determination and extreme self-control despite severe pain and his dangling left arm, *Private Hawks* completed the task of bandaging the remaining casualty and with superhuman effort dragged him to the same depression to which he had brought the first man. Finding insufficient cover for three men at this point, *Private Hawks* crawled 75 yards in an effort to regain his company, reaching the ditch in which his fellow aid man was lying.

CPL. PAUL B. HUFF, 34142155, Company A, 509th Parachute Infantry Battalion, for conspicuous gallantry and intrepidity at risk of life above and beyond the call of duty in action on 8 February 1944, near Carano, Italy. *Corporal Huff* volunteered to lead a six-man patrol with the mission of determining the location and strength of an enemy unit which was delivering fire on the exposed right flank of his company. The terrain over which he had to travel consisted of exposed, rolling ground, affording the enemy excellent visibility. As the patrol advanced, its members were subjected to small-arms and machine-gun fire and a concentration of mortar fire, shells bursting within 5 to 10 yards of them and bullets striking the ground at their feet. Moving ahead of his patrol, *Corporal Huff* drew fire from three enemy machine guns and a 20mm weapon. Realizing the danger confronting his patrol, he advanced alone under deadly fire through a minefield and arrived at a point within 75 yards of the nearest machine-gun position. Under direct fire from the rear machine guns, he crawled the remaining 75 yards to the closest emplacement, killed the crew with his submachine gun, and destroyed the gun. During this act he fired from a kneeling position which drew fire from other positions, enabling him to estimate correctly the strength and location of the enemy. Still under concentration of fire, he returned to his patrol and led his men to safety. As a result of the information he gained, a patrol in strength sent out that afternoon, one group under the leadership of *Corporal Huff* succeeded in routing an enemy company of 125 men, killing 27, and capturing 21 others.

PVT. ELDEN H. JOHNSON, 31353962, Company H (Battle Patrol), 15th Infantry, for conspicuous gallantry and intrepidity at risk of life, above and beyond the call of duty, in action involving actual conflict. On 2-3 June 1944, at 0100 hours, near Valmontone, Italy, *Private Johnson* elected to sacrifice his life in order that his comrades might extricate themselves from an ambush. Braving the massed fire of sixty riflemen, three machine guns and three tanks from positions only twenty-five yards distant, he stood erect and signaled his patrol leader to withdraw. Then, despite 20mm, machine-gun, machine-pistol and rifle fire, aimed directly at him *Private Johnson* advanced upon the enemy in a slow deliberate walk. Firing his BAR from the hip, he succeeded in distracting the enemy, enabling his 12 comrades to escape. Advancing to within five yards of a machine gun, *Private Johnson* killed its crew, emptying his weapon. Standing there, in full view of the enemy, he reloaded his BAR and turned on the riflemen to the left and fired directly into their positions, either killing or wounding four of them. A burst of machine-gun fire tore into *Private Johnson* and he dropped to his knees. Fighting to

Johnson   Kandle   Kessler   Knappenberger

the very last, he steadied himself on his knees and sent a final burst of fire crashing into another German; with that he slumped forward, dead. *Private Johnson* had willingly given his life in order that his comrades might live.

LIEUT. VICTOR L. KANDLE, 0-1324419, Company I, 15th Infantry, for extraordinary heroism in action. On 9 October 1944, at about 1200 hours, near La Forge, France, *Lieutenant Kandle*, while leading a reconnaissance patrol into enemy territory, engaged in a duel at pointblank range with a German field officer and killed him. Having already taken five enemy prisoners that morning, he led a skeleton platoon of 16 men, reinforced with a light-machine-gun squad, through fog and over precipitous mountain terrain to fall on the rear of a German defensive stronghold which had checked the advance of his company for two days. Rushing forward several yards ahead of his advance assault element, *Lieutenant Kandle* fought his way into the heart of the quarry stronghold and, by his boldness and audacity, forced the Germans to surrender. Harassed by machine-gun fire from a strongpoint which he had bypassed in the dense fog, he again moved to within 15 yards of the enemy, killed a German machine gunner with accurate rifle fire and led his men in the destruction of another machine-gun crew and its rifle support elements. Finally, he led his small force against a fortified house held by two German officers and 30 enlisted men. Having established his base of fire, he rushed forward alone through an open clearing under enemy observation, smashed through a barricaded door and forced all 32 Germans to surrender. His intrepidity and bold combat leadership resulted in the capture and destruction of three enemy officers and 54 enlisted men, the annihilation of three enemy strongholds and the seizure of the quarry defensive positions which had halted a battalion's advance.

PFC. PATRICK L. KESSLER, 35473422, Company K, 30th Infantry. For conspicuous gallantry and intrepidity at the risk of his life above and beyond the call of duty on 23 May 1944 near Ponte Rotto, Italy. *Private Kessler*, acting without orders, raced 50 yards through a hail of machine-gun fire, which had killed five of his comrades and halted the advance of his company, in order to form an assault group to destroy the machine gun. Ordering three men to act as a base of fire he left the cover of a ditch and snaked his way to a point within 50 yards of the enemy machine gun before he was discovered, whereupon he charged headlong into the furious chain of automatic fire. Reaching a spot within 6 feet of the emplacement he stood over it and killed both gunner and his assistant, jumped into the gun position and overpowered and captured a third German after a short struggle. The remaining member of the crew escaped, but *Private Kessler* wounded him as he ran. While taking his prisoner to the rear this soldier saw two of his comrades killed as they assaulted an enemy strongpoint, fire from which had already killed 10 men in the company. Turning his prisoner over to another man *Private Kessler* crawled 35 yards to the side of one of the casualties, relieved him of his Browning automatic rifle and ammunition, and continued toward the strong point 125 yards distant. Although two machine guns concentrated their fire directly upon him and shells exploded within 10 yards, bowling him over, *Private Kessler* crawled 75 yards, passing through an antipersonnel minefield to a point within 50 yards of the enemy and engaged the machine guns in a duel. When an artillery shell burst within a few feet of him he left the cover of the ditch and advanced upon the position in a slow walk, firing his Browning automatic rifle from the hip. Although the enemy poured heavy machine-gun and small-arms fire at him, *Private Kessler* succeeded in reaching the edge of their position, killed the gunners, and captured 13. Then, despite continuous shelling, he started for the rear. After going 25 yards *Private Kessler* was fired on by two snipers only 100 yards away. Several of his prisoners took advantage of this opportunity and attempted to escape; however, *Private Kessler* hit the ground, fired on either flank of his prisoners, forcing them to take cover, and then engaged the two snipers in a fire fight and captured them. With this last threat removed Company K continued its advance, capturing its objective without further opposition. *Private Kessler* was killed in a subsequent action.

PFC. ALTON W. KNAPPENBERGER, 33618556, Company C, 30th Infantry. For conspicuous gallantry and intrepidity at the risk of life above and beyond the call of duty in action involving actual conflict with the enemy, on 1 February 1944, near Cisterna di Littoria, Italy. When a heavy German counterattack was launched against his battalion, *Private Knappenberger* crawled to an exposed knoll and went into position with his automatic rifle. An enemy machine gun 85 yards away opened fire and bullets struck within 6 inches of him. Rising to a kneeling position *Private Knappenberger* opened fire on the hostile crew, knocked out the gun, killed two members of the crew, and wounded the third. While he fired at this hostile position, two Germans crawled to a point within 20 yards of the knoll and threw potato-masher grenades at him, but *Private Knappenberger* killed them both with one burst from his automatic rifle. Later a second machine gun opened fire upon his exposed position from a distance of 100 yards, and this weapon also was silenced by his well aimed shots. Shortly thereafter, an enemy 20mm antiaircraft gun directed fire at him, and again *Private Knappenberger* returned fire to wound one member of the hostile crew. Under tank and artillery shell fire, with shells bursting within 15 yards of him, he held his precarious position and fired at all enemy infantrymen armed with machine pistols and machine guns which he could locate. When his ammunition supply became exhausted, he crawled 15 yards forward through steady machine-gun fire, removed rifle clips from the belt of a casualty, returned to his position, and resumed firing to repel an assaulting German platoon armed with automatic weapons. Finally, his ammunition supply being completely exhausted, he rejoined his company. *Private Knappenberger's* intrepid action disrupted the enemy attack for over 2 hours.

PFC. FLOYD K. LINDSTROM, 37349634, Company H, 7th Infantry. For conspicuous gallantry and intrepidity at risk of life above and beyond the call of duty. On 11 November 1943 this soldier's platoon was furnishing machine-gun support for a rifle company attacking a hill near Mignano, Italy, when the enemy counterattacked, forcing riflemen and half the machine-gun platoon to retire to a defensive position. *Private First Class Lindstrom* saw that his small section was alone and outnumbered five to one yet he immediately deployed the few remaining men into position and opened fire with his single gun. The enemy centered fire on him with machine gun, machine pistols, and grenades. Unable to knock out the enemy nest from his original position, *Private First Class Lindstrom* picked up his own heavy machine gun and staggered 15 yards up the barren, rocky hillside to a new position, completely ignoring enemy small-arms fire which was striking all around him. From this new site only 10 yards from the enemy machine gun, he engaged it in an intense duel. Realizing that he could not hit the hostile gunners because they were behind a large rock, he charged up hill under a steady stream of fire, killed both gunners with his pistol, and dragged their gun down to his own men, directing them to

Lindstrom

Maxwell

Merrell

Messerschmidt

employ it against the enemy. Disregarding heavy rifle fire he returned to the enemy machine-gun nest for two boxes of ammunition, came back, and resumed withering fire from his own gun. His spectacular performance completely broke up the German counterattack. *Private First Class Lindstrom* demonstrated aggressive spirit and complete fearlessness in the face of almost certain death.

T/5 ROBERT D. MAXWELL, 37330616, Headquarters Company, 3d Battalion, 7th Infantry. For conspicuous gallantry and intrepidity at the risk of his life above and beyond the call of duty on 7 September 1944 near Besançon, France. *Technician Maxwell* and four other soldiers, armed only with .45 automatic pistols, defended the battalion observation post against an overwhelming onslaught by enemy infantrymen in approximately platoon strength, supported by 20mm flak and machine-gun fire, who had infiltrated through the battalion's forward companies and were attacking the observation post with machine-gun, machine-pistol and grenade fire at ranges as close as 10 yards. Despite a hail of fire from automatic weapons and grenade launchers, *Technician Maxwell* aggressively fought off advancing enemy elements and, by his calmness, tenacity, and fortitude, inspired his fellows to continue the unequal struggle. When an enemy hand grenade was thrown in the midst of his squad, *Technician Maxwell* unhesitatingly hurled himself squarely upon it, using his blanket and his unprotected body to absorb the full force of the explosion. This act of instantaneous heroism permanently maimed *Technician Maxwell*, but saved the lives of his comrades in arms and facilitated maintenance of vital military communications during the temporary withdrawal of the battalion's forward headquarters.

PVT. JOSEPH F. MERRELL, 42179711, a scout with Company I, 15th Infantry Regiment, made a gallant, one-man attack against vastly superior enemy forces near Lohe, Germany, on 18 April 1945. His unit, attempting a quick conquest of hostile hill positions that would open the route to Nürnberg before the enemy could organize his defense of that city, was pinned down by brutal fire from rifles, machine pistols, and two heavy machine guns. Entirely on his own initiative, *Private Merrell* began a single-handed assault. He ran 100 yards through concentrated fire, barely escaping death at each stride, and, at point-blank range, engaged four German machine pistolmen with his rifle, killing all of them while their bullets ripped his uniform. As he started forward again, his rifle was smashed by a sniper's bullet, leaving him armed only with three grenades, but he did not hesitate. He zigzagged 200 yards through a hail of bullets to within 10 yards of the first machine gun, where he hurled two grenades and then rushed the position, ready to fight with his bare hands if necessary. In the emplacement he seized a Luger pistol and killed all Germans who had survived the grenade blast. Rearmed, he crawled toward the second machine gun located 30 yards away, killing four Germans in camouflaged fox holes on the way, but receiving a critical wound in the abdomen. Yet he went on, staggering, bleeding, and disregarding bullets which tore through the folds of his clothing and glanced off his helmet. He threw his last grenade into the machine-gun nest and stumbled on to wipe out the crew. He had completed this self-appointed task when a machine-pistol burst killed him instantly. In the spectacular one-man attack, *Private Merrell* killed 6 Germans in the first machine-gun emplacement, 7 in the next, and an additional 10 infantrymen who were astride his path to the weapons which would have decimated his unit had he not assumed the burden of the assault, and stormed the enemy positions with utter fearlessness, intrepidity of the highest order, and a willingness to sacrifice his own life so that his comrades could go on to victory.

SGT. HAROLD O. MESSERSCHMIDT, 33779438, Company L, 30th Infantry, on 17 September 1944 near Raddon, France, displayed conspicuous gallantry and intrepidity above and beyond the call of duty. Braving machine-gun, machine-pistol, and rifle fire, he moved fearlessly and calmly from man to man along his 40-yard squad front, encouraging each to hold against the overwhelming assault of a fanatical foe surging up the hillside. Knocked to the ground by a burst from an enemy automatic weapon, he immediately jumped to his feet, ignoring his grave wounds, fired his submachine gun at the enemy, which was now upon them, killing five and wounding many others before his ammunition was spent. Virtually surrounded by a frenzied foe and all of his squad now casualties, he elected to fight on alone, using his empty submachine gun as a bludgeon against his assailants. Seeing friendly reinforcements running up the hill, he continued furiously to wield his empty gun against the foe in a new attack, and it was thus he made the supreme sacrifice, fighting his way deep into the enemy line. *Sergeant Messerschmidt's* sustained heroism in hand-to-hand combat with superior enemy forces was in keeping with the highest traditions of the military service.

PVT. JAMES H. MILLS, 34792609, Company F, 15th Infantry, for conspicuous gallantry and intrepidity at risk of life, above and beyond the call of duty, in action involving actual conflict. On 24 May 1944, at 1330 hours, near Cisterna di Littoria, Italy, *Private Mills*, undergoing his baptism of fire, preceded his platoon down a draw to reach a position from which an attack could be launched against a heavily fortified strongpoint. After advancing about 300 yards *Private Mills* was fired on by a machine gun only 5 yards distant. *Private Mills* killed the gunner with one shot and forced the surrender of the assistant gunner. Continuing his advance, he saw a German soldier in a camouflaged position behind a large bush. This man was in the act of pulling the pin of a potato-masher grenade. *Private Mills* covered the German with his rifle, forced him to drop the grenade and captured him. When another enemy soldier attempted to throw a hand grenade into the draw, *Private Mills* killed him with one shot. Shortly afterward, when *Private Mills* was brought under fire by a machine gun, two machine pistols and three rifles at a range of only fifty feet he charged headlong into the furious chain of automatic fire shooting his M-1 from the hip. Tracers whipped past his body barely missing him, and thudded into the bank of the draw. The enemy was completely demoralized by *Private Mills'* daring charge and when he reached a point within 10 feet of their position all six surrendered. As he neared the end of the draw, *Private Mills* was brought under fire by an enemy machine gunner only 20 yards distant. Despite the fact that he had absolutely no cover, *Private Mills* stopped in his tracks and with bullets striking the bank within three or four inches of him, took careful aim and killed the gunner with one shot. Two enemy soldiers who were near the machine gun fired wildly at *Private Mills* and then fled. *Private Mills* fired twice, killing one of the enemy. Continuing onto the position he captured a fourth enemy soldier. When it became apparent that an assault on the strongpoint would, in all probability, cause heavy casualties in the platoon, *Private Mills* volunteered to cover the advance down a shallow ditch to a point within 50 yards of the objective. Standing on the bank in full view of the enemy less than 100 yards away, *Private Mills* shouted at the enemy and

| Mills | Murphy | Murray | Arlo L. Olson |

then fired his rifle directly into the position. His ruse worked exactly as planned; the enemy centered his fire on *Private Mills.* Tracers passed within inches of his body; rifle and machine-pistol bullets ricocheted off the rocks at his feet barely missing him, yet he stood there firing until his rifle was empty. Intent on covering the movement of his platoon, *Private Mills* jumped down into the draw, reloaded his weapon, climbed out again and continued to lay down a "one-man" base of fire. Repeating this action four times he enabled his platoon to reach the designated spot undetected, from which position it assaulted and overwhelmed the enemy, capturing 22 Germans and taking its objective without casualties.

LIEUT. AUDIE L. MURPHY, 0-1692509, Company B, 15th Infantry, for conspicuous gallantry and intrepidity at risk of life, above and beyond the call of duty, in action involving actual conflict. At 1400 hours on 26 January 1945, near Holzwihr, France, when his company was savagely counterattacked by six enemy tanks and two German infantry companies, *Lieutenant Murphy* remained at an advanced outpost, braving furious tank and automatic fire, to direct artillery concentrations on the enemy assault force. When a tank destroyer was set afire at his side, he climbed on the turret of the burning vehicle and, despite a painful shell wound, fired his .50-caliber machine gun, killing or wounding approximately 50 Germans, some of them at 10 yards range, and beating back every enemy assault.

LIEUT. CHARLES P. MURRAY, JR., 0-13178, commanding Company C, 30th Infantry, displayed supreme courage and heroic initiative near Kaysersberg, France, on 16 December 1944, while leading a reinforced platoon into enemy territory. Descending into a valley beneath hilltop positions held by our troops, he observed a force of 200 Germans pouring deadly mortar, bazooka, machine-gun, and small-arms fire into an American battalion occupying the crest of the ridge. The enemy's position in a sunken road, though hidden from the ridge, was open to a flank attack by *Lieutenant Murray's* patrol, but he hesitated to commit so small a force to battle with the superior and strongly disposed enemy. Crawling out ahead of his troops to a vantage point, he called by radio for artillery fire. His shells bracketed the German force, but when he was about to correct the range his radio went dead. He returned to his patrol, secured grenades and a rifle to launch them and went back to his self-appointed outpost. His first shots disclosed his position; the enemy directed heavy fire against him as he methodically fired his missiles into the narrow defile. Again he returned to his patrol. With an automatic rifle and ammunition, he once more moved to his exposed position. Burst after burst he fired into the enemy, killing 20, wounding many others, and completely disorganizing its ranks, which began to withdraw. He prevented the removal of three German mortars by knocking out a truck. By that time a mortar had been brought to his support. *Lieutenant Murray* directed fire of this weapon, causing further casualties and confusion in the German ranks. Calling on his patrol to follow, he then moved out toward his original objective—possession of a bridge and construction of a roadblock. He captured 10 Germans in foxholes. An eleventh, while pretending to surrender, threw a grenade which knocked him to the ground, inflicting eight wounds. Though suffering and bleeding profusely, he refused to return to the rear until he had chosen the spot for the block and had seen his men correctly deployed. By his single-handed attack on an overwhelming force and by his intrepid and heroic fighting, *Lieutenant Murray* stopped a counterattack, established an advance position against formidable odds, and provided an inspiring example for the men of his command.

CAPT. ARLO L. OLSON, 0-383969, 15th Infantry. For conspicuous gallantry and intrepidity at the risk of life above and beyond the call of duty. On 13 October 1943 when the drive across the Volturno River began, *Captain Olson* and his company spearheaded the advance of the regiment through 30 miles of mountainous enemy territory in 13 days. Placing himself at the head of his men, *Captain Olson* waded into the chest-deep water of the raging Volturno River and despite point-blank machine-gun fire aimed directly at him made his way to the opposite bank and threw two hand grenades into the gun position, killing the crew. When an enemy machine gun 150 yards distant opened fire on his company *Captain Olson* advanced upon the position in a slow, deliberate walk. Although 5 German soldiers threw hand grenades at him from a range of 5 yards, *Captain Olson* dispatched all of them, picked up a machine pistol, and continued toward the enemy; advancing to within 15 yards of the position he shot it out with the foe, killing 9 and seizing the post. Throughout the next 13 days *Captain Olson* led combat patrols, acted as Company number one scout, and maintained unbroken contact with the enemy. On 27 October 1943 *Captain Olson* conducted a platoon in attack on a strongpoint, crawling to within 25 yards of the enemy and then charging the position. Despite continuous machine-gun fire which barely missed him *Captain Olson* made his way to the gun and killed the crew with his pistol. When the men saw their leader make this desperate attack they followed him and overran the position. Continuing the advance, *Captain Olson* led his company to the next objective at the summit of Monte San Nicola. Although the company to his right was forced to take cover from the furious automatic and small arms fire which was directed on him and his men with equal intensity, *Captain Olson* waved his company into a skirmish line and despite the fire of a machine gun which singled him out as its sole target led the assault which drove the enemy away. While making a reconnaissance for defensive positions *Captain Olson* was fatally wounded. Ignoring his severe pain, this intrepid officer completed his reconnaissance, supervised the location of his men in the best defense positions, refused medical aid until all of his men had been cared for, and died as he was being carried down the mountain.

SGT. TRUMAN O. OLSON, 36246624, Company B, 7th Infantry, for conspicuous gallantry and intrepidity at risk of life, above and beyond the call of duty, in action involving actual conflict. Near Cisterna di Littoria, Italy, *Sergeant Olson*, a light machine gunner, elected to sacrifice his life to save his company from annihilation. On the night of 30 January 1944, after a 16-hour assault on entrenched enemy positions in the course of which over one-third of Company B became casualties, the survivors dug in behind a horseshoe elevation, placing *Sergeant Olson* and his crew, with the one available machine gun, forward of their lines and in an exposed position to bear the brunt of the expected German counterattack. Although he had been fighting without respite, *Sergeant Olson* stuck grimly to his post all night, while his gun crew was cut down, one by one, by accurate and overwhelming enemy fire. Weary from over 24 hours of continuous battle and suffering from an arm wound received during the night engagement, *Sergeant Olson* manned his gun alone, meeting the full force of an all-out enemy assault by approximately 200 men supported by mortar and machine-

| Truman O. Olson | Peden  | Ross  | Schauer 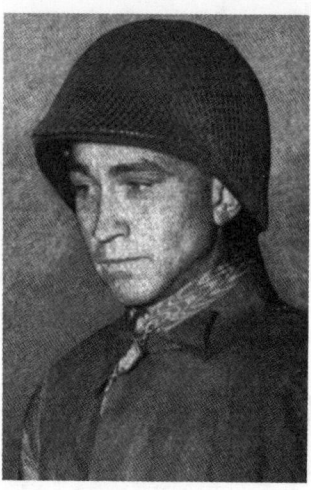 |

gun fire which the Germans launched at day-break on the morning of 31 January. After thirty minutes of fighting, *Sergeant Olson* was mortally wounded; yet, knowing that only his weapon stood between his company and complete destruction, he refused evacuation. For an hour and a half after receiving his second and fatal wound, he continued to fire his machine gun, killing at least 20 of the enemy, wounding many more, and forcing the assaulting Germans to withdraw. He died before he could be given medical attention.

T/5 FORREST E. PEDEN, 37503529, Battery C, 10th Field Artillery Battalion, was a forward artillery observer near Biesheim, France, on 3 February 1945, when the group of about 45 infantrymen, with whom he was advancing, was ambushed in the uncertain light of a waning moon. Enemy forces outnumbering the Americans by four to one poured withering artillery, mortar, machine-gun, and small-arms fire into the stricken unit from the flanks, forcing our men to seek the cover of a ditch which they found already occupied by enemy foot troops. As the opposing infantrymen struggled in hand-to-hand combat, *Corporal Peden* courageously went to the assistance of two wounded soldiers and rendered first aid under heavy fire. With radio communications inoperative, he realized that the unit would be wiped out unless help could be secured from the rear. On his own initiative, he ran 800 yards to the battalion command post through a hail of bullets, which pierced his jacket, and there secured two light tanks to go to the relief of his hard-pressed comrades. Knowing the terrible risk involved, he climbed upon the hull of the lead tank and guided it into battle. Through a murderous concentration of fire, the tank lumbered onward, bullets and shell fragments ricocheting from its steel armor within inches of the completely exposed rider, until it reached the ditch. As it was about to go into action, it was turned into a flaming pyre by a direct hit which killed *Corporal Peden*. However, his intrepidity and gallant sacrifice were not in vain. Attracted by the light from the burning tank, reinforcements found the beleaguered Americans and drove off the enemy.

PVT. WILBURN K. ROSS, 35668451, Company G, 30th Infantry. For conspicuous gallantry and intrepidity at the risk of his life above and beyond the call of duty near St. Jacques, France. At 1130 hours on 30 October 1944, after his company had lost 55 out of 88 men in an attack on an entrenched, full-strength German company of élite mountain troops, *Private Ross* placed his light machine gun 10 yards in advance of the foremost supporting riflemen in order to absorb the initial impact of an enemy counterattack. With machine-gun and small-arms fire striking the earth near him, he fired with deadly effect on the assaulting force and repelled it. Despite the hail of automatic fire and the explosion of rifle grenades within a stone's throw of his position, he continued to man his machine gun alone, holding off six more German attacks. When the eighth assault was launched, most of the supporting riflemen were out of ammunition. They took positions in echelon behind *Private Ross* and crawled up, during the attack to extract a few rounds of ammunition from his machine-gun ammunition belt. *Private Ross* fought on virtually without assistance and, despite the fact that enemy grenadiers crawled to within 5 yards of his position in an effort to kill him with hand grenades, he again directed accurate and deadly fire on the hostile force and hurled it back. After expending his last round, *Private Ross* was advised to withdraw to the company command post, together with the eight surviving riflemen, but, as more ammunition was expected, he declined to do so. The Germans launched their last, all-out attack, converging their fire on *Private Ross* in a desperate attempt to destroy the machine gun which stood between them and a decisive breakthrough. As his supporting riflemen fixed bayonets for a last-ditch stand, fresh ammunition arrived and was brought to *Private Ross* just as the advance assault elements were about to swarm over his position. He opened murderous fire on the oncoming enemy, killed 40 and wounded 10 of the attacking force, broke the assault single-handed, and forced the Germans to withdraw. Having killed and wounded at least 58 Germans in more than 5 hours of continuous combat and saved the remnants of his company from destruction, *Private Ross* remained at his post that night and the following day, for a total of 36 hours. His actions throughout this engagement were an inspiration to his comrades and maintained the high traditions of the military service.

PFC. HENRY SCHAUER, 39600219, Company E (Battle Patrol), 15th Infantry, for conspicuous gallantry and intrepidity at risk of life, above and beyond the call of duty, in action involving actual conflict. On 23 May 1944 at 1200 hours, near Cisterna di Littoria, Italy, *Private First Class Schauer* left the cover of a ditch to engage four German snipers who opened fire on the patrol from its rear. Standing erect, he walked slowly and deliberately 30 yards toward the enemy, stopped amid the fire from four rifles centered on him, and with four bursts from his BAR, each at a different range, killed all of the snipers. Catching sight of a fifth sniper waiting for the patrol behind a house chimney, *Private First Class Schauer* brought him down with another burst. Shortly after, when a heavy enemy artillery concentration and two machine guns temporarily halted the patrol, *Private First Class Schauer* again left cover to engage the enemy weapons single-handed. While shells exploded within 15 yards, showering dirt over him, and strings of grazing German tracer bullets whipped past him at chest-level, *Private First Class Schauer* knelt, killed the two gunners of the machine gun only 60 yards from him with a single burst from his BAR, and crumpled two other enemy soldiers who ran to man the gun. Calmly inserting a fresh magazine in his BAR, *Private First Class Schauer* shifted his body to fire at the other weapons 500 yards distant and emptied the weapon into the enemy crew, killing all four Germans. Next morning, 24 May, when shells from a German Mark VI tank and a machine gun only 100 yards distant again forced the patrol to seek cover, *Private First Class Schauer* crawled toward the enemy machine gun, stood upright only 80 yards from the weapon as its bullets cut the ground around him and four tank shells fired directly at him burst within 20 yards. Raising his BAR carefully to his shoulder, *Private First Class Schauer* killed the four members of the German machine-gun crew with one burst of fire, bringing his total to 17 enemy killed in 17 hours.

SGT. JOHN C. SQUIRES, 35706627 (then Private First Class), Company A, 30th Infantry. For conspicuous gallantry and intrepidity at risk of life above and beyond the call of duty. At the start of his company's attack on strongly held enemy positions in and around Spaccasassi Creek, near Padiglione, Italy, on the night of 23-24 April 1944, *Private First Class Squires*, platoon runner, participating in his first offensive action, braved intense artillery, mortar, and antitank-gun fire in order to investigate the effects of an antitank-mine explosion on the leading platoon. Despite shells which burst close to him, *Private First Class Squires* made his way 50 yards forward to the advance element, noted the situation, reconnoitered a new

Squires

Tominac

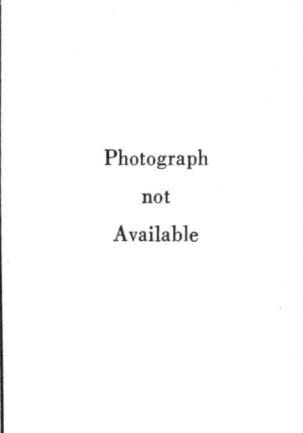
Valdez

Ware

route of advance, and informed his platoon leader of the casualties sustained and the alternate route. Acting without orders, he rounded up stragglers, organized a group of lost men into a squad, and led them forward. When the platoon reached Spaccasassi Creek and established an outpost *Private First Class Squires,* knowing that almost all of the noncommissioned officers were casualties, placed eight men in position on his own volition, disregarding enemy machine-gun, machine-pistol, and grenade fire which covered the creek draw. When his platoon had been reduced to 14 men he brought up reinforcements twice. On each trip he went through barbed wire and across an enemy mine field under intense artillery and mortar fire. Three times in the early morning the outpost was counterattacked. Each time *Private First Class Squires* ignored withering enemy automatic fire and grenades which struck all around him and fired hundreds of rounds of rifle, Browning automatic, and captured German Spandau machine-gun ammunition at the enemy, inflicting numerous casualties and materially aiding in repulsing the attacks. Following these fights he moved 50 yards to the south end of the outpost and engaged 21 German soldiers in individual machine-gun duels at point-blank range, forcing all 21 enemies to surrender and capturing 13 more Spandau guns. Learning the function of this weapon by questioning a German officer prisoner, he placed the captured guns in position and instructed other members of his platoon in their operation. The next night, when the Germans attacked the outpost again, he killed three and wounded more Germans with captured potato-masher grenades and fire from his Spandau gun. *Private First Class Squires* was killed in a subsequent action.

FIRST LIEUT. JOHN J. TOMINAC, 0-1321210 (then Second Lieutenant), Company I, 15th Infantry, for conspicuous gallantry and intrepidity at risk of life, above and beyond the call of duty, in action involving actual conflict. On 12 September 1944, at about 1630 hours, in the attack of Saulx-de-Vesoul, France, *Lieutenant Tominac* charged alone over 40 yards of exposed terrain into an enemy roadblock to despatch the three-man crew of a German machine gun with a single burst from his Thompson submachine gun. After smashing this enemy outpost, he led one of his squads in the annihilation of a second hostile strongpoint, defended by mortar, machine-gun, automatic-pistol, rifle and grenade fire, killing about 30 of the enemy. Reaching the suburbs of the town, he advanced 50 yards ahead of his men to reconnoiter a third enemy position, which commanded the road with a 77mm SP gun supported by infantry elements. The SP gun opened fire on his supporting tank, setting it afire with a direct hit. A fragment from the same shell painfully wounded *Lieutenant Tominac* in the shoulder, knocking him to the ground. As the crew abandoned the M-4, which was rolling down hill toward the enemy, *Lieutenant Tominac* picked himself up and jumped onto the hull of the burning vehicle. Despite withering enemy machine-gun, machine-pistol and sniper fire which ricocheted off the hull and turret of the M-4, *Lieutenant Tominac* climbed to the turret and gripped the .50-caliber antiaircraft machine gun. Plainly silhouetted against the sky, painfully wounded and with the tank burning beneath his feet, he directed bursts of machine-gun fire on the roadblock, the SP gun and the supporting German infantrymen which forced the enemy to withdraw from his prepared position. Jumping off the tank before it exploded, *Lieutenant Tominac* refused evacuation despite his painful wound. Calling on a sergeant to extract the shell fragment from his shoulder with a pocket knife, he continued to direct the assault, led his squad in a hand grenade attack against a fortified position occupied by 32 of the enemy, armed with machine guns, machine pistols and rifles, and compelled them to surrender. His outstanding heroism and exemplary leadership resulted in the distruction of four successive enemy defensive positions, the seizure of a vital sector of the city of Saulx-de-Vesoul, and the death or capture of at least 60 of the enemy.

PFC. JOSE F. VALDEZ, 38352446, Company B, 7th Infantry, was on outpost duty with five others near Rosenkrantz, France, on 25 January 1945, when the enemy counterattacked with overwhelming strength. From his position near some woods 500 yards beyond the American lines, he observed a hostile tank about 75 yards away and raked it with automatic rifle fire until it withdrew. Soon afterward, he saw three Germans stealthily approaching through the woods. Scorning cover as the enemy soldiers opened up with heavy automatic-weapons fire from a range of 30 yards, he engaged in a fire fight with the attackers until he had killed all three. The enemy quickly launched an attack with two full companies of infantrymen, blasting the patrol with murderous concentrations of automatic and rifle fire and beginning an encircling movement which forced the patrol leader to order a withdrawal. Despite the terrible odds, *Private Valdez* immediately volunteered to cover the maneuver, and, as the patrol, one by one, plunged through a hail of bullets, toward the American lines, fired burst after burst into the swarming enemy. Three of his companions were wounded in their dash for safety and he was struck by a bullet which entered his stomach and, passing through his body, emerged from his back. Overcoming agonizing pain, he regained control of himself and resumed his firing position, delivering a protective screen of bullets until all others of the patrol were safe. By field telephone, he called for artillery and mortar fire on the Germans and corrected the range until he had shells falling within 50 yards of his position. For 15 minutes he refused to be dislodged by more than 200 of the enemy, then seeing that the barrage had broken the counterattack, he dragged himself back to his own lines. He later died as a result of his wounds. Through his valiant, intrepid stand and at the cost of his own life, *Private Valdez* made it possible for his comrades to escape and was directly responsible for repulsing an attack by vastly superior enemy forces.

LT. COL. KEITH L. WARE, 0-1288333, Executive officer (then Commanding Officer, 1st Battalion), 15th Infantry, for conspicuous gallantry and intrepidity at risk of life, above and beyond the call of duty, in action involving actual conflict. At about 1200 hours on 26 December 1944, near Sigolsheim, France, *Colonel Ware* braved the fire of six enemy machine guns to dislodge 200 fanatical SS troops from formidable defensive positions. Finding that one of his companies had been repeatedly halted in its efforts to assault a bleak, rocky hill, which dominated the neighboring towns of the Southern Alsatian Plain with artillery, mortar, and machine-gun fire, *Colonel Ware* advanced 150 yards beyond the positions of his foremost riflemen to reconnoiter the terrain, determine enemy gun locations and find a feasible route of attack. Disdaining to seek cover, ignoring shells which exploded within 20 yards of him he engaged in a two-hour reconnaissance, deliberately drawing enemy fire to ascertain hostile depositions. Returning to the company and finding the men reluctant to resume the attack, *Colonel Ware* seized a BAR, called for one platoon to follow him, and advanced boldly toward the enemy positions. Striding forward 20 yards ahead of

Waybur

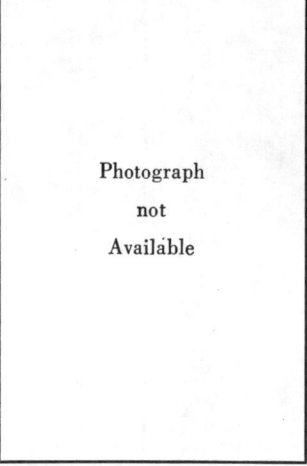
Whiteley

Zussman

his puny force of two officers, nine enlisted men, and a tank, *Colonel Ware* advanced 200 yards through uninterrupted and furious fire which inflicted five casualties on his men. While white tracers from 6 enemy machine guns ricocheted off the rocks at his side, forming jagged patterns of fire, a mortar and artillery concentration deluged the area over which the assault group was advancing. Approaching to within 20 yards of an enemy machine gun, *Colonel Ware* dashed forward into a hail of automatic fire despatched two riflemen with his BAR and fired tracers into the machine-gun emplacement, enabling his tank to make the kill. Inserting a new magazine in his BAR, *Colonel Ware* charged a second machine gun 80 yards to his right. Killing two of the support riflemen and forcing others to surrender, he engaged the machine gun in a duel at 30 yards' range. Guided by the strike of his bullets, the tank opened fire and administered the *coup de grâce*. His BAR ammunition spent, *Colonel Ware* seized an M-1, killed a German rifleman and attacked the third machine gun 50 yards away with rifle fire. His tank then entered the fight, knocking out the hostile gun. While one of the officers destroyed two more machine guns, *Colonel Ware* charged forward 20 yards into withering fire to grapple with the last enemy machine gun. As he approached to within 40 yards of the gun, the supporting riflemen surrendered in panic; he fearlessly engaged the machine gun; his tank destroyed it. *Colonel Ware's* relentless assault sent the remaining German force in headlong flight. He was wounded in the hand, but refused treatment or evacuation until all positions on the hill were properly placed. Personally killing 5 Germans and capturing approximately twenty, *Colonel Ware* had fought for an hour, to disintegrate a well emplaced force of 200 crack German troops and seize the hill position they had been ordered to hold to the death.

LIEUT. DAVID C. WAYBUR, O-452653, 3rd Reconnaissance Troop. For conspicuous gallantry and intrepidity at the risk of life above and beyond the call of duty, in action involving actual conflict with the enemy on 17 July 1943, near Agrigento, Sicily. Commander of a reconnaissance platoon, *Lieutenant Waybur* volunteered to lead a three-vehicle patrol into enemy-held territory to locate an isolated Ranger unit. Proceeding under cover of darkness, over roads known to be heavily mined, and strongly defended by roadblocks and machine-gun positions, the patrol's progress was halted at a bridge which had been destroyed by enemy troops and was suddenly cut off from its supporting vehicles by four enemy tanks. Although hopelessly outnumbered and outgunned, and himself and his men completely exposed, *Lieutenant Waybur* quickly despersed his vehicles and ordered his gunners to open fire with their .30 and .50 caliber machine guns. Then with ammunition exhausted, three of his men hit and himself seriously wounded, he seized his .45 caliber Thompson machine gun, and standing in the bright moonlight directly in the line of fire, alone engaged the leading tank at 30 yards and succeeded in killing the crew members, causing the tank to run onto the bridge and crash into the stream bed. After despatching one of the men for aid, he rallied the rest to cover and withstood the continued fire of the tanks until the arrival of aid the following morning.

LIEUT. ELI WHITELEY, O-1310907, Company L, 15th Infantry, for conspicuous gallantry and intrepidity at risk of life, above and beyond the call of duty, in action involving actual conflict. At 0900 hours on 27 December 1944, in Sigolsheim, France, *Lieutenant Whiteley* dashed through withering automatic and shell fire to assault an enemy-held house single-handedly and despatch its garrison. Hurling smoke and fragmentation grenades before him, he charged, although wounded, down a fire-swept street and battered his way alone into a second building, killing two and capturing 11 Germans. Though his wounded arm dangled uselessly, he blasted down the wall of a third house with bazooka fire and charged inside to kill five and capture 12 Germans. When blinded by another shell wound, he kept on fighting until forcibly evacuated.

LIEUT. RAYMOND ZUSSMAN, O-1014997, Cavalry, Company A, 756th Tank Battalion, for conspicuous gallantry and intrepidity at risk of life above and beyond the call of duty, in action involving actual conflict. On 12 September 1944, at 1900 hours, *Lieutenant Zussman* dismounted from his command tank and proceeded on foot, armed only with a carbine and followed by a lone M-4 tank, and assaulted Nory-le-Bourg, France. Forging ahead of the tank into blazing small-arms fire, he located and neutralized an improvised roadblock which had been booby trapped. Although intense enemy machine-gun and small-arms fire from a German position only 50 yards distant ricocheted off the hull and turret of the tank, *Lieutenant Zussman* stood beside it, fully exposed, firing on the enemy with his carbine and directing the tank's fire. When three Germans fell dead, the remaining eight surrendered to *Lieutenant Zussman*, who immediately proceeded to direct the fire of the tank on another center of resistance, killing three and compelling an additional seven to surrender. Having already exhausted his carbine ammunition, he seized a Thompson submachine gun from a member of the tank crew and advanced well in front of the tank, toward a group of houses occupied by the enemy. Machine-gun and small-arms fire opened up on him from another enemy strongpoint 75 yards to his right front. Disregarding bullets which kicked up the dirt at his feet, he again stood in an exposed position and directed the fire of his tank until resistance was broken and 20 Germans surrendered. Leaving the tank behind, he rushed toward an enemy strongpoint in a house, firing his submachine gun as he ran, while the Germans tried to stop him with small-arms fire and threw hand grenades in his path. After a brief fire exchange, he brought up the tank and directed its fire on the house, forcing 11 more Germans to give up. His submachine gun blazing, *Lieutenant Zussman* again dashed forward into rifle and automatic weapons fire to another German held house, emerging after a short exchange of fire with 15 more prisoners. As the Germans fled before his whirlwind attack accurate tank fire accounted for 11 more killed. Noting an ideal antitank position, he plunged forward alone to reconnoiter. His submachine gun fired; his voice was heard above the tumult, shouting *"Hände hoch!"* and in a few minutes 30 prisoners, including the crews of two AT guns, filed around the corner. As night fell, he again went forward alone, to a truck; there was a hand grenade explosion, but when the smoke cleared *Lieutenant Zussman* returned with another prisoner. With lightning rapidity, *Lieutenant Zussman* had overwhelmed one enemy position after another. Fighting against heavy odds and on his own volition, he had blasted his way into and through the strongly defended town ahead of the infantry, killing 17 and capturing 92 enemy soldiers, and capturing two antitank guns, one 20mm flak gun, two machine guns, and two trucks. *Lieutenant Zussman* was killed in a subsequent action.

DISTINGUISHED SERVICE CROSS

Adams, Patrick, A., 2d Lt, Co. I 7th Inf, Montelimar, France 29 Aug. 1944
Amundson, Oscar M., S/Sgt, Co. L 15th Inf, Cisterna Di Littoria, Italy 1 Feb. 1944
Athas, William P., Capt, Co. D 7th Inf, Liberi, Italy 16 Oct. 1943
Balbaton, Anthony J., Sgt, Co. K 7th Inf, Thalesweiler, Germany 22 Mar. 1945
Bale, Joseph L., Pfc, Hq. Co. 2d Bn. 7th Inf, Wihr-en-plaine, France
Belanger, Alfred, 2d Lt, 751st Tank Bn., Mignano, Italy 4 Nov. 1943
Bitar, Emil S., Capt, Co. E 15th Inf, San Fratello, Sicily 4 Aug. 1943
Borrelli, Charles T., Sgt, Co. A 7th Inf, Artena, Italy 1, June 1944
Boyer, Thomas W., Pfc, 30th Inf, Lariano, Italy 28 May 1944
Blumhagen, Robert F., 1st Lt, Co. F 15th Inf, Nompatelize, France 3 Nov. 1944
Bracey, Randolph, 2d Lt, Co. A 30th Inf, Padigione, Italy 24 Apr. 1944
Braden, Roy A., Cpl, 10th Engr., Nettuno, Italy 23 Jan. 1944
Branch, Winifred R., Pfc, Co. B 15th Inf, 11 July 1943
Britt, Maurice L., Capt, Co. L 30th Inf, 26 Jan. 1944
Brooks, Emery, Pfc, Co. E 7th Inf, Cisterna Di Littoria, Italy 23 May 1944
Brown, Joseph M., S/Sgt, 15th Inf, San Tropez, France 16 Aug. 1944

Calvert, Ross H., 1st Lt, Hq. Co. 30th Inf, Taulignan, France 28 Aug. 1944
Campagna, Robert A., S/Sgt, Co. E 15th Inf, San Felice, Italy 26 Oct. 1943
Ciancanelli, Arco Anthony, S/Sgt, Co. L 15th Inf, Vesoul, France 12 Sept. 1944
Choate, Clyde L., S/Sgt, Co. C 601st TD Bn., Bruyeres, France 25 Oct. 1944
Cohen, Marvin, Pfc, Co. E 15th Inf, LaDemie, France 11 Sept. 1944
Coles, James W., Capt, Co. L 15th Inf, Allan, France 27 Aug. 1944
Conner, Garlin M., 1st Lt, 3d Bn. 7th Inf, Houssen, France 24 Jan. 1945
Conway, Claude, Pvt, MD 30th Inf, Cave, Italy 3 June 1944
Cook, Eugene W., Pfc, Co. K 30th Inf, Germany 26 Mar. 1945
Cosson, Edgar A., Pvt, Co. H 7th Inf, Le Haut Jacques, France 4 Nov. 1944
Cotter, Lloyd H., 1st Lt, Cn Co. 15th Inf, Nompatelize, France 3 Nov. 1944
Crawford, Joseph B., Lt Col, Hq. 15th Inf, Niscemi, Sicily 11 July 1943
Culver, Arthur P., T/Sgt, Co. A 30th Inf, La Mer, France 21 Sept. 1944
Cummings, Julian W., 2d Lt, 10th FA Bn., Locita, Italy 10 July 1943

Davila, Rudolph B., 2d Lt, 7th Inf, Artena, Italy 28 May 1944
Delmonico, Dominick, S/Sgt, Co. L 15th Inf, Allan, France 27 Aug. 1944
Dezarn, William R., 2d Lt, Co. A 7th Inf, France 3 Nov. 1944
Doleman, Edgar C., Lt Col, 30th Inf, Acerno, Italy 22 Sept. 1943
Donnelly, Earl F., Sgt, Co. B 756th Tank Bn., Algolsheim, France 6 Feb. 1945
Drolla, Charles P., Sgt, 30th Inf, San Fratello, Sicily 7 Aug. 1943
Duncan, Duell M., 1st Lt, Co. K 30th Inf, Kaysersberg, France 16 Dec. 1944

Ernst, Michael A., S/Sgt, Co. C 7th Inf, Dom faing, France 22 Oct. 1944
Elling, James C., Pfc, Co. A 15th Inf, Germany 30th Mar. 1945
Evans, Willie C., Pvt, Co. G 30th Inf, Aix, France 20 Aug. 1944
Ezzell, James C., Sgt, 601st TD Bn., Hyeres, France 17 Aug. 1944

Fairclo, Carroll E., Sgt, 15th Inf, Mignano, Italy 9 Nov. 1943
Felerski, Russell F., 1st Lt, Co. F 15th Inf, San Fratello, Sicily 4 Aug. 1943
Firestone, Clarence, Pfc, Co. B 7th Inf, Erohingen, Germany 15 Mar. 1945
Floto, Kenneth B., 1st Lt, Co. C 15th Inf, Cisterna Di Littoria, Italy 29 Feb. 1944
Forbes, Sanford F., Sgt, Hq. Co. 7th Inf, Fedala 8 Nov. 1942

Gallardo, Macario J., Pvt, Co. L 7th Inf, Maramossa, France 28 Oct. 1944
Gardner, Madison D., 2d Lt, Co. A 30th Inf, Sauceray, France 4 Nov. 1944
Goerlitz, Adam, T/4, MD 30 Inf, Caronia, Sicily 2 Aug. 1943
Grando, George A., S/Sgt, Co. L 7th Inf, Marmossa, France 31 Oct. 1944
Grant, Charles I., Sgt, 10th Engr., Nettuno, Italy 23 Jan. 1944
Griffith, Sylvan W., S/Sgt, 3d Rcn Trp., St. Die, France 20 Oct. 1944
Groden, Raymond, S/Sgt, Co. C 30th Inf, Kogenheim, France 2 Dec. 1944
Guffey, Bennie L., Sgt, 7th Inf, Capua, Italy 13 Oct. 1943

Hambelton, Frank E., Pfc, Co. I 15th Inf, Rieneck, Germany 4 Apr. 1945
Haselwood, Leroy A., Capt, 7th Inf, Majorano, Italy 18 Oct. 1943
Haught, James M., Pfc, Co. A 7th Inf, Rupt-sur-Moselle, France 27 Sept. 1944
Havens, Harry E., T/Sgt, Co. G 7th Inf, Houssen, France 25 Jan. 1945
Hellinger, Peter J., Sgt, Co. C 15th Inf, La Forge, France 25 Oct. 1944
Henderson, Torsten E., Pvt, Co. H 30th Inf, Nurnberg, Germany 20 Apr. 1945
Hendon, Max R., 2d Lt, 15th Inf, Pietrovairano, Italy 11 Nov. 1943
Hobbs, James M., S/Sgt, Co. H 15th Inf, Isola Bella, Italy 31 Jan. 1944
Hodgdon, Fred, 1st Lt, Co. F 15th Inf, Bourgonce, France 23 Mar. 1945
Hodgdon, George E., 1st Lt, 15th Inf, Cisterna Di Littoria, Italy 30 Jan. 1944
Horyt, Edward S., Pvt, Co. E 7th Inf, Hyeres, France 17 Aug. 1944

Hosea, Ernest W., S/Sgt, Co. F 15th Inf, Sigolsheim, France 26 Dec. 1944
Howey, Harold G., S/Sgt, Co. B 15th Inf, Licata, Sicily 10 July 1943
Hudspeth, James R., S/Sgt, Co. D 756th Tank Bn., Houssen, France 26 Jan. 1945

Jacoby, Robert S., T/4, MD 30th Inf, Caronia, Sicily 2 Aug. 1943
Jones, James W., Pfc, Co. B 30th Inf, Kayersberg, France 17 Dec. 1944

Kalinowski, Walter J., Pvt, Cn Co. 30th Inf, St. Die, France 28 Oct. 1944
Kaplan, Louis, S/Sgt, Co. K 30th Inf, Faucogney, France 22 Sept. 1944
Kasper, Carl J., 2d Lt, Div. Arty, Carano, Italy 16 Feb. 1944
Kellum, William L., Pvt, Co. A 15th Inf, Cisterna Di Littoria, Italy
Kirtley, Herman C., S/Sgt, 756th Tank Bn., Brignoles, France 27 Aug. 1944
Kostrisak, John A., Sgt, Co. E 30th Inf, Padiglone, Italy 18 Feb. 1944
Kunert, George C., S/Sgt, Co. F 15th Inf, Bennwihr, France 2-3 Jan. 1945

Larson, Stanley E., Capt, 10th Engr., Anzio 23 May 1944
Lawlor, Harry J., S/Sgt, Co. L 7th Inf, Ponte Rotto, Italy 3 Mar. 1944
Lindsley, Merl C., 1st Lt, AT Co. 15th Inf, Nurnberg, Germany 18 Apr. 1945

Masitis, George, T/Sgt, Co. F 30th Inf, Carano, Italy 25 Apr. 1944
Megown, John N., Jr., Pfc, Co. A 7th Inf, Cisterna Di Littoria, Italy 25 May 1944
McBride, Robert J., Co. E 15th Inf, Etival, France 10 Nov. 1944
McGarr, Lionel C., Col, CO 30th Inf, Besancon, France 6 Sept. 1944
McNamara, William W., Pfc, Co. L 15th Inf, St. Tropez, France 15 Aug. 1944
Mishakas, Joseph, T/Sgt, Co. I 30th Inf, Ponte Rotto, Italy 23 May 1944
Morris, Victor M., 1st Lt, Co. C 7th Inf, Vogelsheim, France 5 Feb. 1945
Morrow, William C., Maj, Hq. Co. 30th Inf, San Fratello, Sicily 7 Aug. 1943
Murphy, Audie L., 2d Lt, Co. B 15th Inf, Ramatuelle, France 15 Aug. 1944

Neshiem, Ernest B., S/Sgt, Co. B 15th Inf, San Fratello, Sicily 6 Aug. 1943
Nickerson, Philip E., Pfc, Co. F 30th Inf, Campo Morto, Italy 29 Feb. 1944

Ong, Donald G., T/Sgt, Co. E 30th Inf, Brignoles, France 18 Aug. 1944

Paulick, Michael, 15th Inf, Cisterna Di Littoria, Italy 30 Jan. 1944
Pollard, Samuel W., Sgt, Co. F 7th Inf, Cisterna Di Littoria, Italy 25 May 1944
Praeger, Emil, Sgt, Co. L 15th Inf, Sigolsheim, France 27 Dec. 1944
Preece, Wendell M., Pvt, MD 30th Inf, Campo Morto, Italy 30 Jan. 1944
Pridgen, Robert B., Maj, CO 3d Bn. 30th Inf, Raddon, France 17 Sept. 1944

Reisinger, Belere R., Pfc, Co. E 15th Inf, La Bourgonce, France 26 Oct. 1944
Reynolds, Wayne O., S/Sgt, Cn Co. 30th Inf, Aix, France 21 Aug. 1944
Rosson, William B., Lt Col, 7th Inf, Ponte Rotto, Italy 31 Jan. 1944

Schultz, George J., Pfc, Co. A 30th Inf, Ponte Rotto, Italy 23 May 1944
Schwalbach, James E., Pfc, Co. K 30th Inf, Taulignan, France 28 Aug. 1944
Schwab, Donald K., 1st Lt, Co. E 15th Inf, Lure, France 17 Sept. 1944
Sherman, Harry B., Col, Hq. 7th Inf, Acerno, Italy 24 Sept. 1943
Silva, John B., Pfc, Co. E 15th Inf, Ponte Rotto, Italy 29 Jan. 1944
Sinsel, Frank C., Maj, 1st Bn. 7th Inf, Cisterna Di Littoria, Italy 31 Jan. 1944
Smerillo, Michael J., Sgt, Co. H 7th Inf, Les Aynans, France 15 Sept. 1944
Smith, John E., S/Sgt, Co. E 15th Inf, Bourgonce, France, 26 Oct. 1944
Smithson, Kenneth L., Sgt, Co. E 7th Inf, Ostheim, France 25 Jan. 1945
Stanley, Paul W., Capt, Hq. Co. 3d Div., Carano, Italy 25 Apr. 1944
Stanton, John H., Sgt, Co. L 7th Inf, Noroy Le Bourg, France 13 Sept. 1944
Stefek, Emil, Jr., Pfc, Co. K 7th Inf, Salles, France 23 Nov. 1944
Stoodley, Robert P., Pfc, Co. F 15th Inf, Cisterna Di Littoria, Italy 23 May 1944
Swanson, Earl E., Capt, Co. F 7th Inf, Cisterna Di Littoria 25 May 1944

Tatko, Walter A., Pfc, Co. A 30th Inf, Begude, France 27 Aug. 1944
Thobro, Clayton C., Lt Col, 7th Inf, Ferdrupt, France 25 Sept. 1944

Varner, William R., Cpl, Hq. Co. 30th Inf, Brolo, Sicily 11 Aug. 1943
Valentino, Nicholas F., S/Sgt, Co. M 7th Inf, Ponte Rotto, Italy 31 Jan. 1944
Vance, Frederick, Pfc, Co. I 30th Inf, 29 Feb 1944

Wallace, Kenneth W., Lt Col, 1st Bn. 7th Inf, 22 Jan. 1945
Wendt, Herman A., Pvt, MD 7th Inf, Cape d'Orlando, Sicily 10 Aug 1943
Wilson, Joseph F., 2d Lt, Co. M 30th Inf, Kayersborg, France 6 Dec 1944
Zalewski, Frank C., Pfc, Co. A 30th Inf, Begude, France 27 Aug. 1944

POSTHUMOUS AWARDS OF DISTINGUISHED SERVICE CROSS

Allen, George A., 2d Lt, 30th Inf, Rotundo, Italy 9 Nov. 1943
Bray, William H., Pvt, Co. L, 7th Inf, Italy 10 Nov. 1942
Davis, Moffett D., Pfc, Co. K, 15th Inf, France 25 Oct. 1944
Kelly, John J., Sgt, Co. F, 7th Inf, Strasbourg, France 1 Dec. 1944
Moritz, Martin, T/4, Med Det, 30th Inf, Brolo, Sicily 11 Aug. 1943

Ritso, John C., S/Sgt, Co. E, 601st TD Bn, Carano, Italy 25 Jan. 1944
Sessa, Silvio, Pfc, Co. G, 30th Inf, St. Jacques, France 30 Oct. 1944
Pompanio, Mario, Pvt, Co. E, 7th Inf, Wihr-en-Plaine, France 30 Jan. 1945
Tapley, Elbert, Cpl. Co. C, 30th Inf, Kogenheim, France 2 Dec. 1944
Thomas, Clifton C., Pvt, Co. B, 7th Inf, Colmar, France 25 Jan. 1945

DISTINGUISHED SERVICE MEDAL

Anderson, Jonathan W., Major General, 3d Infantry Division
O'Daniel, John W., Major General, 3d Infantry Division
Truscott, Lucian K., Major General, 3d Infantry Division

SILVER STAR

▲Aaron, Hubert L., S/Sgt, Co. E 7th Inf, Italy 16 Feb. 1944
Abbott, Harvey F., 1st Lt, Inf Co. D 756th Tk Bn., Jebsheim, France 31 Jan. 1945
Abramson, Merle R., Pfc, Med. Det. 15th Inf, France 26 Dec. 1944
Acker, Frank, Pfc, Co. G 7th Inf, Italy 23 Apr. 1944
Adam, Gustav G., Pfc, Co. A 3rd Med. Bn., French Morocco 8 Nov. 1942
▲(4) Adams, Charles E., Capt, Co. L 15th Inf, La Bourgonce, France 27 Oct. 1944

Adams, Clarence E., Pfc, Co. C 15th Inf, Althornbach, Germany 18 Mar. 1945
Adams, Floyd W., T/Sgt, Co. F 7th Inf, Italy 17 Feb. 1944
Adams, Morgan K., Capt, MC Med. Det. 41st FA Bn., Sicily Aug. 1943
Addison, William C., S/Sgt, Hq. Co. 15th Inf, Tresvilley, France 6 Sept. 1944
Aemmer, Herman M., T/Sgt, Co. L 7th Inf, Italy 27 Jan. 1944
Akers, Willis B., Pfc, Co. L 30th Inf, Italy 20 Apr. 1944
Albertson, Carl U., 1st Lt, Co. E 7th Inf, France 20 Nov. 1944
Allain, Carl N., S/Sgt, Co. F 30th Inf, France 23 Jan. 1945

▲ Oak Leaf Cluster.

Allan, Harvey T., T/4, Cn. Co. 15th Inf, Sicily Aug. 1943
Alldredge, William B., Pfc, Co. K 15th Inf, Germany 9 Apr. 1945
Allen, Leroy W., S/Sgt, Co. A 30th Inf, Nurnberg, Germany 20 Apr. 1945
Allison, Albert E., Jr., S/Sgt, Co. L 30th Inf, Siegfried Line 20 Mar. 1945
Alpert, Samuel, Sgt, Co. F 7th Inf, Italy 15 Oct. 1943
Alpheus, George I., S/Sgt, Co. C 30th Inf, Italy 26 Apr. 1944
Altemus, Ronald A., Pvt, Med. Det. 30th Inf, France 20 Aug. 1944
Alto, Donald A., Sgt, Co. F 7th Inf, Italy 17 Feb. 1944
Alton, Clyde J., S/Sgt, Co. L 30th Inf, Italy 29 May 1944
Altshuler, Robert L., 1st Lt, Inf Co. F 7th Inf, Humprechthausen, Germany 12 Apr. 1945
Alvarez, Ygnacio D., Pvt, Co. M 30th Inf, Italy Aug. 1943
Amicone, Albert F., Pvt, 3d Rcn Trp., Italy 25 May 1944
Ananich, John, Jr., 1st Lt, Inf Co. H 7th Inf, Wombach, Germany 3 Apr. 1945
Ancavage, Joseph S., 2d Lt, Inf Cn. Co. 7th Inf, Italy 3 Mar. 1944
Anderson, Charles M., Pvt, Hq. Co. 1st Bn. 15th Inf, Italy 12 Nov. 1943
Anderson, Elmer C., Sgt, Btry A 10th FA Bn., Sicily 5 Aug. 1943
Anderson, Everette R., 2d Lt, Co. K 15th Inf, Italy 29 Feb. 1944
Anderson, Fred G., S/Sgt, Co. L 7th Inf, Germany 18 Mar. 1945
Anderson, James J., Pvt, Co. E 30th Inf, France 23 Nov. 1944
Anderson, Jesse L., Jr., S/Sgt, Co. B 15th Inf, Germany 28 Mar. 1945
Anderson, Paul, Sgt, Co. H 7th Inf, Italy 30 Jan. 1944
Andy, Leo, Cpl, Co. 15th Inf, Italy 29 Feb. 1944
Angell, William W., Pfc, Hq. Co. 3d Bn. 15th Inf, Rischgau, Germany 26 Apr. 1945
Angelle, Roy P., Sgt, Co. M 30th Inf, Italy 5 June 1945
Angle, Chesley S., Cpl, Hq. Co. 2d 15th Inf, Anzio, Italy 19 Feb. 1944
Anglin, Jess W., Pfc, Co. I 15th Inf, France 15 Jan. 1945
Anstey, Jack W., Pfc, Co. C 15th Inf, France 23 Dec. 1944
▲Anthony, William D., 1st Lt, Co. I 7th Inf, Houssen, France 26 Jan. 1945
Antonucci, Salvatore A., T/Sgt, Co. E 7th Inf, Ostheim, France 23 Jan. 1945
Anzalone, Angelo, Pfc, Co. A 30th Inf, Vosges, 5 Dec. 1944
Argo, Charles R., Sgt, Co. L 7th Inf, French Morocco 10 Nov. 1942
▲(2) Armstrong, Frederick A., Major, Co. 2d Bn. 30th Inf, Italy 1 June 1944
Armstrong, John B., 1st Lt, Inf 15th Inf, Italy 10 Nov. 1943
Asher, William H., T/4, Hq. Co. 3d Bn. 7th Inf, Althornbach, Germany 18 Mar. 1945
Ashford, Lee S., S/Sgt, Co. A 7th Inf, France 23 Jan. 1945
Ashton, Charles E., S/Sgt, Co. A 30th Inf, Rhine 1 Feb. 1945
▲Asin, Carlos C., Pvt, Co. D 7th Inf, Sicily July 1943
Asman, Rudolph K., S/Sgt, Hq. & Hq. Co. 2d Bn. 30th Inf, Italy 24 May 1944
Atterbury, John H., T/5, Co. B 10th Engr. Bn., Italy 13 Oct. 1943
Auld, Thomas, Pfc, Co. F 15th Inf, Nurnberg, Germany 17 Apr. 1945
Aulisio, Anthony, T/5, Med. Det. 11th Inf, France 27 Sept. 1944
Aven, Bruce A., S/Sgt, Hq. Co. (BP) 7th Inf, France 17 Sept. 1944

Babincsak, Jesse C., Pfc, Co. H 7th Inf, Italy 24 Mar. 1944
Babiyan, Andrew L., Pfc, Co. C 15th Inf, Nurnberg, Germany 17 Apr. 1945
▲Backus, Floyd J., T/Sgt, Co. K 7th Inf, Germany 5 Apr. 1945
▲Bacon, Allen F., Major, Ex O 3d Bn. 30th Inf, Italy Aug. 1943
Bacon, Eugene F., Capt, Co. H 7th Inf, France 23 Jan. 1945
Badalamento, Sam, T/Sgt, Co. L 15th Inf, Nauheim, Germany 1 Apr. 1945
Bagley, William D., 1st Lt, 601st TD Bn. El Guettar, Tunisia, Africa 9 Mar. 1944
Bah, Wallace K., S/Sgt, Co. H 7th Inf, Italy 25 May 1944
Bahr, John W., Pvt, Co. H 15th Inf, Italy 12-13 Oct. 1943
▲Bailey, Alvie P., S/Sgt, Co. D 30th Inf, France 1 Feb. 1945
Bailey, Reid S., T/5, Hq. Btry 9th FA Bn., Italy 17 Nov. 1943
Bailey, Urbine A., Pvt, Med. Det. 7th Inf, Italy 30 Jan. 1944
Bailey, William L., S/Sgt, Co. M 7th Inf, Italy 1 Mar. 1944
Baird, R. L., S/Sgt, Co. L 30th Inf, France 21 Sept. 1944
Baker, Francis J., 1st Lt, CWS Co. A 84th Cml Bn. Italy 30 Jan. 1944
Balkovitz, John G., S/Sgt, Co. D 7th Inf, France 16 Sept. 1944
Ball, Earl, Pfc, 3d Ren Trp., Sicily July 1943
Ball, Lester, Sgt, Co. A 30th Inf, Nurnberg, Germany 19 Apr. 1945
Balogh, Eugene J., T/5, Med. Det. 15th Inf, France 26 Dec. 1944
Balogh, Michael S., Pfc, Co. H 7th Inf, Italy 1 Feb. 1944
Balun, Vincent W., Pfc, Co. K 15th Inf, Strahlungen, Germany 8 Apr. 1945
Bancks, Robert W., Pvt, Co. B 30th Inf, Italy 19 Feb. 1944
Banek, Stanley C., Sgt, Co. E 15th Inf, Italy 23 May 1944
Bangert, Robert L., Capt, Co. C 10th Engr. Bn., Siegfried Line, 19 Mar. 1945
Barkhaus, Anthony J., T/5, Med. Det. 15th Inf, Sicily Aug. 1943
Barnes, Chester B., S/Sgt, Co. K 7th Inf, Italy 15 Nov. 1943
Barnes, Donald H., Pfc, Hq. Co. 15th Inf, Bois de Riedwihr, France 26 Jan. 1945
Barnes, Paul V., 1st Sgt, Co. F 7th Inf, Sicily Aug. 1943
▲Barr, Burton S., Major, Inf Hq. 1st Bn. 15th Inf, Germany 1 Apr. 1945
Barr, Everett E., S/Sgt, Co. D 7th Inf, Italy 31 Jan. 1944
Barrett, James A., Pvt, Co. A 3d Med. Bn., Sicily Aug. 1943
Barrett, Francis R., Pfc, Co. C 30th Inf, Germany, 8 May 1944
Barrett, Thomas J., Pfc, Hq. Co. 1st Bn. 15th Inf, Mellrichstadt, Germany 7 Apr. 1945
Barth, Clifford U., T/Sgt, Hq. Co. 2d Bn. 15th Inf, France 10 Nov. 1944
Bass, Fred W., Pfc, Co. A 15th Inf, Brouvilieres, France 22 Oct. 1944
▲(2) Bass, James E., T/Sgt, Co. I 15th Inf, Italy 30 Jan. 1944
Bassett, Frederick J., Pfc, Co. C 7th Inf, Italy 28 May 1944
Bates, William C., 2d Lt, Inf Co. C 30th Inf, Worth, Germany 29 Mar. 1945
Baumann, William, Pfc, Med. Det. 15th Inf, Sicily Aug. 1943
Baumgartner, Anthony R., Pfc, Co. M 30th Inf, Vosges 5 Dec. 1944
Bautch, Frank D., Sgt, Btry C 10th FA Bn., Sicily Aug. 1943
Bear, Frederick Turning, Sgt, Co. C 7th Inf, French Morocco 10 Nov. 1942
Beard, Clarence J., Jr., Pfc, Hq. Co. 1st Bn. 15th Inf, Bruyeres, France 25 Oct. 1944
Beaty, Clarence W., Sgt, Co. G 2d Bn. 7th Inf, Sicily Aug. 1943
Beaudoin, Joseph A. A., Pfc, Hq. Co. 2d Bn. 7th Inf, France 25 Jan. 1945
Beaverson, Donald H., Pfc, Co. F 30th Inf, Voleaux, France 21 Sept. 1944
Beck, John J., T/5, Med. Det. 15th Inf, Sicily July 1943
Beck, Vernon H., T/4, 3d Rcn Trp., Germany 20 Mar. 1945
Begenwald, William F., Pfc, Med. Det. 7th Inf, Hyeres, France 19 Aug. 1944
Begovich, John C., S/Sgt, Cavalry 3d Rcn Trp., Italy 11 Nov. 1943
Bell, Clifton, Pfc, 3d Sig. Co., Italy 29 Feb. 1944
Bell, James W., Pfc, Co. E 15th Inf, France 28 Dec. 1944
Bell, Wallace A., Jr., 1st Lt, Co. B 30th Inf, France 19 Nov. 1944
Bellish, John E., T/Sgt, Co. K 30th Inf, Italy 12-13 Mar. 1944
Bello, Joseph, Pfc, Med. Det. 15th Inf, France 27 Dec. 1944
Bemis, Amos J., Sgt, Co. K 7th Inf, French Morocco 8 Nov. 1942
Bene, Andrew, Jr., Sgt, Co. K 30th Inf, Italy 23 May 1944
▲Benjamin, Arthur, Pvt, Co. A 7th Inf, Germany 26 Mar. 1945
Benjamin, Robert P., Cpl, Co. C 10th Engr. Bn., France 18 Dec. 1944
Benko, John F., 1st Lt, Co. E 30th Inf, France 11 Nov. 1944
Bennett, Cecil G., T/Sgt, Co. A 30th Inf, France 30 Sept. 1944
Bennett, Charles R., S/Sgt, Co. F 7th Inf, Italy 29 Feb. 1944
Bentley, Eugene W., Pfc, Co. A 30th Inf, Wickerschwihr, France 28 Jan. 1945
Berg, Edward E., Pfc, Co. E 7th Inf, Hodenbach, Germany 2 Apr. 1945
Berg, William K., Sgt, BP 15th Inf, Italy 3 Mar. 1944
Bergandi, Ernest, S/Sgt, Co. I 15th Inf, Cleurie Quarry, France 2 Oct. 1944
Berger, Vernon S., S/Sgt, Co. A 15th Inf, France 22 Oct. 1944
Berlin, Enoch E., Pvt, Co. F 15th Inf, France 29 Jan. 1945
Bernard, Lyle W., Lt Col, Inf 30th Inf, Sicily July 1943
Berube, Edward F., Pfc, Co. D 30th Inf, Valmontone, Italy 1 June 1944
Besonday, Harold J., Cpl, Co. K 7th Inf, Italy Oct. 1943
Bickel, John F., S/Sgt, Co. K 30th Inf, Cleurie, France 30 Sept. 1944
Bickford, David G., T/5, 3d Rcn Trp., Germany 17 Mar. 1945
Bielski, Matthew F., Pvt, Co. F 7th Inf, Italy 2 Feb. 1944
Bierchen, Theodore F., Cpl, Co. D 15th Inf, Italy 27 Jan. 1944
Biesiada, Stanley F., Sgt, Co. F 7th Inf, France 1 Oct. 1944
Biggers, Marcus D., Capt, Inf Co. K 7th Inf, Sicily July 1943
Bilby, Kenneth W., Major, Inf, Hq. 2d Bn., Siegfried Line 19 Mar. 1945
Bishop, Harold C., 1st Lt, Co. I 30th Inf, Italy 22 Sept. 1943
Bitka, Chester W., Pfc, Co. D 7th Inf, Italy 28 May 1944
Black, Albert W., S/Sgt, Co. G 15th Inf, Italy 31 Jan. 1944
Black, Dale R., Pfc, Co. K 15th Inf, France 15 Dec. 1944
▲(3) Black, Glenn A., 2d Lt, Co. I 30th Inf, Germany 15 Mar. 1945
Blackburn, Jack, Sgt, Co. C 7th Inf, France 11 Sept. 1944
▲Blackman, Harold L., Pfc, Co. A 7th Inf, Sapais, France 9 Oct. 1944
Blackwood, Arthur J., T/Sgt, Co. H 7th Inf, 8 Mar. 1944
Blaikie, John W., Capt, Hq. 3d Bn. 7th Inf, France 15 Aug. 1944
Blair, George T., Pfc, Co. C 10th Engr. Bn., France 17 Dec. 1944
Blanford, Forrest M., 1st Lt, Inf Co. B 756th Tank Bn., Nurenberg, Germany 18 Apr. 1945
▲Blankenship, Chester, Sgt, Co. H 15th Inf, Isola Bella, Italy 29 Feb. 1944
Bledsoe, Raymond L., Pfc, Co. G 15th Inf, Nurnberg, Germany 17 Apr. 1945
Blissit, Charley N., T/5, 3d Trp., Zweibrucken, Germany 20 Mar. 1945
Blixt, Rudolph E., Pfc, Co. C 15th Inf, Italy 15 Feb. 1944
Block, David, Pfc, Co. I 30th Inf, Waldhausen, Germany 24 Apr. 1945
Bloom, Weldon E., S/Sgt, Co. C 7th Inf, Italy 17 Feb. 1944
Bloomingburg, Windell N., Pfc, Med. Dept. Med. Det. 7th Inf Regt., France 31 Oct. 1944
Blumhagen, Robert F., 1st Lt, Co. F 15th Inf, France 8 Sept. 1944
Blythe, Melvin V., Sgt, Co. I 15th Inf, Italy 2 Mar. 1944
Board, Oliver P., 2d Lt, CE 41st FA Bn., Sicily July 1943
Boardman, Foster, 2d Lt, Co. L 15th Inf, Germany 22 Mar 1945
Boddy, Robert M., Capt, Hq. & Hq. Co. 3d Bn. 30th Inf, Italy 28 Jan. 1944
Boerstler, Montie H., 2d Lt, Inf Co. A 30th Inf, Urbach, Germany 15 Mar. 1945
Bogner, Milden E., S/Sgt, Co. A 15th Inf, Sicily 6 Aug. 1943
Bolson, Frank W., S/Sgt, Co. I 7th Inf, Italy 16 Nov. 1943
Bonner, David T., Sgt, Co. F 30th Inf, France 16 Aug. 1944
Bonner, Forrest L., T/5, Co. A 10th Engr. Bn., Italy 20 Mar. 1944
▲Bonner, Vincent H., 2d Lt, FA Rcn Co. 601 TD Bn., Besancon, France 8 Sept. 1944
Bonnes, John, Jr., Pfc, Hq. Co. 30th Inf, Rhine River 25-26 Mar. 1945
Boomer, Walter H., Pfc, Hq. Co. 2d Bn. 7th Inf, Italy 19 Feb. 1944
Boone, Carl W., S/Sgt, Co. K 7th Inf, Sicily July 1943
Booze, Kenneth R., S/Sgt, Co. D 751st Tank Bn., Italy 31 Jan. 1944
Borick, John S., Pfc, Co. H 30th Inf, France 20 Sept. 1944
Boros, Steve P., T/Sgt, Co. C 30th Inf, Sauceray, France 1 Nov. 1944
Bosack, Thomas A., Pfc, Co. H 15th Inf, Sicily Aug. 1943
Bostwich, John J., T/4, Co. C 756th Tank Bn., Pasing, Germany 29 Apr. 1945
Bothee, Herbert E., 1st Lt, Inf Co. K 7th Inf, Ormersvillers, France 15 Mar. 1945
Botkin, Samson, Pfc, Co. F 30th Inf, France 18 Dec. 1944
Bousquet, Edward O., Pfc, Co. D 15th Inf, France 8 Nov. 1944
Bowen, Arvo P., Pfc, Co. E 30th Inf, Vosges 5 Dec. 1944
Bowers, Ralph T., Pfc, Co. L 7th Inf, Ostheim, France 23 Jan. 1945
Bowers, Wilson F., T/5, Med. Det. 15th Inf, France 6 Nov. 1944
Bowles, Alfred, Pvt, Co. D 7th Inf, French Morocco 8 Nov. 1942
Bowles, Carl, Pfc, Co. B 15th Inf, Wortingen, Germany 26 Apr. 1945
Bowling, Lincoln, Pfc, Co. A 30th Inf, France 3 Nov. 1944
Boy, Glenn L., Pfc, Med. Det. 15th Inf, Sicily July 1943
Boyce, Eugene S., Pvt, Hq. Co. 1st Bn. 15th Inf, France 12 Oct. 1944
Boye, Frederic W., Jr., Lt Col, 15th Inf, Italy 30 Jan. 1944
Boyle, Joseph J., T/Sgt, Co. I 30th Inf, Cleurie, France 2 Oct. 1944
Boysen, Bernhard E., Pfc, Co. B 15th Inf, Wertingen, Germany 25 Apr. 1945
Bozeman, Charles E., S/Sgt, Co. K 30th Inf, Sicily July 1943
Braak, John A., Pfc, Med. Det. 15th Inf, Italy 16 Oct. 1943
▲Bradburn, Morin, S/Sgt, Co. A 756th Tank Bn., Germany 17 Apr. 1945
Bradshaw, Calvin T., Pfc, Co. C 7th Inf, Italy 24 May 1944
▲Brandenberg, Philip A., Pfc, Co. A 7th Inf, France 23 Jan. 1945
Brandon, Van I., Sgt, Co. K 15th Inf, Italy 8 Nov. 1943
Brandt, Benjamin, T/5, Btry A 10th FA Bn., Sicily 6 Aug. 1943
Branscombe, Merrin A., Pvt, Co. G 30th Inf, Colmar 20 Feb. 1945
Brawley, Elmer C., S/Sgt, Co. B 15th Inf, France 26 Jan. 1945
Breen, Walter W., Pfc, Co. B 7th Inf, Vagney, France 7 Oct. 1944
Brennan, James A., 2d Lt, Inf, 15th Inf, Italy 8 Nov. 1943
Brewer, Ira V., Jr., S/Sgt, Hy. Btry 9th FA Bn., France 15 Aug. 1944
Bridges, Willie, S/Sgt, Co. F 15th Inf, Nurnberg, Germany 17 Apr. 1945
Brier, James O., Pvt, Co. M 7th Inf, Italy Nov. 1943
Brimmer, Marvin L., 1st Sgt, Btry C 41st FA Bn., Italy 26 Oct. 1943
Brink, Edward J., Capt, Inf Hq. 7th Inf, Hachimette, France 16 Jan. 1945
Britt, John W., Jr., Pfc, Co. M 30th Inf, France 29 Oct. 1944
Britt, Maurice L., 1st Lt, Co. L 30th Inf, Italy 22 Sept. 1943
Broadhurst, Harris, Pvt, Co. I 30th Inf, France 17 Dec. 1944
Brogan, Emmett B., Pfc, Co. C 10th Engr. Bn., Sicily Aug. 1943
▲Brohel, Joseph E., Pvt, Co. I 7th Inf, Germany 26 Mar. 1945
Broide, Macy D., T/5, Serv. Co. 30th Inf, Munich, Germany 29 Apr. 1945
Brooks, Bert, Jr., Sgt, Co. G 15th Inf, France 30 Jan. 1945
Brookshear, James W., S/Sgt, Co. K 7th Inf, Cavalaire, France 16 Aug. 1944
Brothers. Vernon W., Sgt, Co. B 10th Engr. Bn., Italy 20 Dec. 1943
Broussard, Julian J., Sgt, Co. B 30th Inf, France 21 Aug. 1944
Brower, Eaker C., Pfc, Co. F 30th Inf, Italy 29 Feb. 1944
Brown, Albert, Capt, Inf 7th Inf, French Morocco 9 Nov. 1942

▲ Oak Leaf Cluster.

Brown, Bedford M., T/5, Co. A 756th Tank Bn., Rosendrantz, France 25 Jan. 1945
Brown, Carrolton L., Sgt, Co. B 7th Inf, Italy 28 May 1944
Brown, Charles A., 1st Lt, Inf Co. L 7th Inf, Utweiler, Germany 15 Mar. 1945
Brown, Hobert B., Pvt, Med. Det. 7th Inf, Rimling, France 15 Mar. 1945
Brown, Norton L., Pvt, Hq. Btry 9th FA Bn., Italy 16 Nov. 1943
Brown, Ralph M., S/Sgt, Hq. Co. 1st Bn. 7th Inf, Germany 18 Mar. 1945
Brown, Richard, 1st Sgt, Hq. Co. 2d Bn. 15th Inf, Sicily Aug. 1945
Brown, William E., T/Sgt, Co. G 7th Inf, Italy 24 May 1944
Brozek, William E., Pfc, Co. G 30th Inf, France 9 Nov. 1944
Bruhl, Guido, Pvt, Med. Det. 30th Inf, Germany 15 Mar. 1945
▲Bruner, Hugh H., Capt, Co. F 15th Inf, Bois de Riedwihr, France 29 Jan. 1945
Bruns, Paul E., Pvt, Hq. Co. 1st Bn. 7th Inf, French Morocco 8 Nov. 1942
Brunstad, Irving O., Capt, FA Hq. Btry 39th FA Bn., Italy 30 Jan. 1944
Bryan, James E., Sgt, Co. B 10th Engr. Bn., St. Blaise, France 23 Nov. 1944
Bryant, Jack R., Pfc, Co. D 30th Inf, Italy 6 Nov. 1943
Bubnic, Mirko J., Sgt, Co. B 751st Tank Bn., Italy 22 Oct. 1943
Buchanan, Gerald C., 1st Lt, Co. I 30th Inf, France 16 Dec. 1944
Buckley, Thomas P., Pfc, Co. H 15th Inf, Sicily Aug. 1943
Bucsa, Alexander, T/Sgt, Co. F 7th Inf, France 7 Sept. 1944
Budrevich, Joseph E., Sgt, Co. A 601st TD Bn., France 16 Aug. 1944
Buelna, Alvard R., Pfc, Co. D 7th Inf, Italy Oct. 1943
Buff, Roy M., Pfc, Co. B 15th Inf, Wertingen, Germany 25 Apr. 1945
Bultrewicz, Edward A., T/5, Co. H 7th Inf, La Croix, France 15 Aug. 1944
Bunker, Rufus P., Jr., Pfc, Co. E 30th Inf, Vosges 5 Dec. 1944
Bunte, August H., T/Sgt, Co. A 15th Inf, France 3 Oct. 1944
Burgess, Robert W., Pfc, Co. I 30th Inf, Italy 28 Jan. 1944
Burgess, William R. E. L., T/Sgt, Co. I 7th Inf, Italy 23 May 1944
Buriak, John, S/Sgt, 3d Sig. Co., France 18 Nov. 1944
Burns, Ernest H., Pfc, Co. G 7th Inf, Besancon, France 5 Sept. 1944
Burns, John J., Pfc, Serv. Co. 7th Inf, Scharof, Germany 27 Mar. 1945
Burr, Arthur F., Pfc, Co. B 7th Inf, Colmar, France 24 Jan. 1945
Burris, Joseph B., Sgt, Co. A 601st TD Bn., Steinach, Germany 7 Apr. 1945
Burton, Joseph A., T/Sgt, Co. F 15th Inf, Anzio, Italy 3 Mar. 1944
Burud, William N., 1st Lt, Inf 15th Inf, Italy 2 Feb. 1944
Buscher, Louis E., 1st Sgt, Co. F 15th Inf, Sicily 6 Aug. 1943
Bushaw, Charles S., Pfc, Co. H 30th Inf, Italy 18 Mar. 1944
▲Busk, Merrill L., 1st Sgt, Co. B 7th Inf, Italy 30 Jan. 1944
▲(2) Buss, Fred, Sgt, Co. D 30th Inf, France 2 Dec. 1944
Busse, Herman A., T/Sgt, Co. G 30th Inf, Erlangen, Germany 16 Apr. 1945
Butcher, John L., 1st Sgt, Hq. Co. 3d Bn. 7th Inf, Italy 24 Sept. 1943
Butler, George K., 1st Lt, Inf 30th Inf, Sicily Aug. 1943
Butler, William E., Pvt, Hq. Co. 15th Inf, Italy 1 Mar. 1944
Butterworth, Paul R., Pvt, Med. Det. 30th Inf, Sicily Aug. 1943
Bux, William E., Pfc, Hq. Co. 1st Bn. 15th Inf, France 26 Jan. 1945
▲(3) Byke, Emil T., 2d Lt, Co. L 30th Inf, Germany 2 May 1945
Byrne, John D., Lt Col, 39th FA Bn., Italy 21 Oct. 1943

Caldwell, James T., 1st Lt, 10th Engr. Bn., Bamberg, Germany 13 Apr. 1945
Caldwell, Melvin P., Pfc, Co. E 30th Inf, Sicily Aug. 1943
Caldwell, Paul D., Capt, FA Hq. Btry 41st FA Bn., France 12 Sept. 1944
Caley, Robert W., Jr., 2d Lt, Co. F 30th Inf, Italy 25 Jan. 1944
Callahan, Rolland P., S/Sgt, Co. G 7th Inf, Nurnberg, Germany 18 Apr. 1945
Calva, Rafael, Pvt, Co. E 15th Inf, Italy 29 Feb. 1944
Calvert, Ross H., Jr., 1st Lt, Co. I 30th Inf, Italy 17 Mar. 1944
Cameron, Clarence A., Sgt, Co. G 30th Inf, Sicily July 1943
Campbell, Charles O., Pfc, Co. K 30th Inf, Bairesdort, Germany 16 Apr. 1945
Campbell, George W., Jr., Pfc, Btry C 9th FA Bn., Sicily July 1943
▲Campbell, Herbert L., Pfc, Co. A 30th Inf, Italy 16 Oct. 1943
Campbell, John A., 1st Lt, FA Co. A 601st TD Bn., Rosencrantz, France 25 Jan 1945
Campbell, Robert J., T/5, Med. Det. 39th FA Bn., Italy 21 Oct. 1943
Caplan, Martin, Sgt, Hq. Co. 3d Inf Div., French Morocco 8 Nov. 1942
Cappiello, Dante, Sgt, Co. A 601st TD Bn., Rosencrantz, France 25 Jan. 1945
Capps, Leslie H., Sgt, Co. G 7th Inf, Gemunden, Germany 5 Apr. 1945
Caravella, Manual R., Pfc, Co. C 30th Inf, Anzio 27 Apr. 1944
Cardullo, Everett P., Pfc, Hq. Co. 1st Bn. 7th Inf, French Morocco 8 Nov. 1942
Carlson, Ralph E., Pfc, Hq. Co. 30th Inf, Italy 1 Mar. 1944
Caron, Roland, 2d Lt, Inf Co. E 30th Inf, Vogelgrun, France 6 Feb. 1945
▲Carpenter, Ralph R., Capt, Co. B 30th Inf, Germany 8 May 1944
Carothers, Charles A., Pfc, Co. L 7th Inf, Utweiler, Germany 15 Mar. 1945
Carreira, Manual, Pfc, Inf Co. D 30th Inf Regt., France 2 Oct. 1944
Carroll, David M., 1st Sgt, Co. E 7th Inf, Utweiler, Germany 15 Mar. 1945
Carter, George L., Pfc, Co. G 15th Inf, Nurnberg, Germany 18 Apr. 1945
Carter, Willard L., Pfc, Co. L 30th Inf, Italy 10 Nov. 1943
Carty, William J., Pfc, Co. L 30th Inf, Le Tholy, France 4 Oct. 1944
Casella, Stanley A., Pfc, Co. H 30th Inf, Italy 29 Feb. 1945
Casey, Floyd S., S/Sgt, Co. E 7th Inf, Italy 10 Nov. 1943
Cassell, William H., S/Sgt, Hq. Btry 9th FA Bn., Italy Nov. 1943
Castaneda, Edward V., Pfc, Co. E 30th Inf, So. France 18 Nov. 1943
Castenon, Paul L., Sgt, Co. D 7th Inf, France 5 Oct. 1944
Castillo, Jesus, Pfc, Co. E 15th Inf, Nurnberg, Germany 17 Apr. 1945
Castro, Abundio, Pfc, Co. D 7th Inf, Nurnberg, Germany 20 Apr. 1945
Castro, Max, Pfc, Hq. & Hq. Btry 10th FA Bn., Fedala, French Morocco 8 Nov. 1942
Catalano, Santo J., S/Sgt, Co. E 15th Inf, Nurnberg, Germany 17 Apr. 1945
Caudell, Roy C., Pfc, Co. G 15th Inf, Germany 19 Apr. 1945
Caudill, Lloyd R., Pfc, Co. A 10th Engr. Bn., Sicily July 1943
Caulkins, Dane V., Pvt, Co. K 7th Inf, Italy 29 Feb. 1944
Ceasar, Ruben, Pfc, Co. M 7th Inf, Saales, France 22 Nov. 1944
Cessna, Dale E., Pfc, Co. G 7th Inf, Italy 30 May 1944
Chamblee, Francis L., Pvt, Co. A 30th Inf, French Morocco 8 Nov. 1942
Chambless, Bonnie J., T/Sgt, Co. L 7th Inf, France 5 Feb. 1945
Chandler, James H., S/Sgt, Co. C 7th Inf, France 16 Aug. 1944
▲Chandler, John T., Pvt, Hq. Co. 2d Bn. 30th Inf, Sicily July 1943
▲Chaney, Christopher W., Major, 1st Bn. 30th Inf, Italy 1 June 1944
Chaney, Marvin L., Sgt, 601st TD Bn., Italy 22 Oct. 1943
Chappell, Lloyd, Pfc, Co. G 7th Inf, Italy 23 May 1944
Chase, John P., Co. A 15th Inf, Biesheim, France 5 Feb. 1945
Chase, Kenneth W., Pvt, Hq. Btry 3d IDA, Italy 2 Mar. 1944
Chiarelli, Peter F., 2d Lt, Amd Co. C 756th Tank Bn., Gross Dechsendorf, Germany 15 Apr. 1945
Chipp, Augustine R., T/5, Serv. Co. 30th Inf, Anzio, Italy 5 June 1944
Chism, Harry D., Pfc, Hq. Co. 3d Bn. 30th Inf, Germany 9 Apr. 1945
Choike, Joseph S., S/Sgt, Co. I 30th Inf, Italy 30 May 1944
Cholewa, Samuel, Co. D 7th Inf, Riedwihr, France 29 Jan. 1945
Christ, Bennie S., Sgt, Hq. Co. 3d Bn. 30th Inf, Italy 16 Feb. 1944
Christansen, Edward, 2d Lt, Inf 30th Inf, Sicily July 1943
Christian, Edward S., Sgt, Cn Co. 15th Inf, Sicily July 1943
▲Christian, John D., S/Sgt, Co. B 601 TD Bn., Italy 29 Feb. 1944
Churack, Matt J., T/Sgt, Co. M 7th Inf, Italy 29 Feb. 1944
Cilley, George B., Jr., Cpl, 3d Rcn Trp., Italy 27 May 1944
Clam, Clyde N., Pfc, Co. 1 30th Inf, Sicily July 1943
Clapp, Dean W., Pvt, Co. G 30th Inf, Sicily July 1943
Clark, David E., S/Sgt, Co. E 30th Inf, Zweibrucken, Germany 19 Mar. 1945
Clark, Eldred B., Pvt, Co. D 7th Inf, Italy 1 Feb. 1944
Clark, Floyd W., 2d Lt, Co. A 7th Inf, France 21 Sept. 1944
Clark, John E., S/Sgt, Co. B 7th Inf, Sandhofen, Germany 26 Mar. 1945
Clark, Kenneth J., S/Sgt, Co. H 7th Inf, La Croix, France 15 Aug. 1944
Clary, Randal R., T/Sgt, Co. L 7th Inf, Kirklingberg, Germany 29 Apr. 1945
Claypool, Russell B., Cpl, Hq. Btry 39th FA Bn., Italy 2 Feb. 1944
Clayton, J. C., 2d Lt, Inf Co. 1 15th Inf Regt., France 17 Mar. 1945
Clayton, James L., S/Sgt, Co. F 7th Inf, Utweiler, Germany 15 Mar. 1945
Clayton, Johnie T., Pfc, Co. C 7th Inf, Strasbourg, France 1 Dec. 1944
▲Clemens, Maurice D., T/Sgt, Co. K 30th Inf, Italy 23 May 1944
Clever, Paul D., Jr., Sgt, Co. M 7th Inf, France 7 Sept. 1944
Cline, Jacob B., T/Sgt, Co. E 30th Inf, Italy 27 Oct. 1943
Closmore, Alfred G., T/4, Cn Co. 15th Inf, Sicily July 1943
Cloutier, Napoleon E., Pfc, Co. F 7th Inf, Cisterna, Italy 23 May 1944
Cmorey, Andrew B., T/Sgt, Co. D 15th Inf, Italy 29 Feb. 1944
Coats, Wendell J., Lt Co., FA Bn., France 13 Sept. 1944
Coaty, Leo V., Sgt, Co. G 30th Inf, Sicily July 1943
Coburn, Henry, Pfc, Co. D 7th Inf, French Morocco 8 Nov. 1942
Cockerill, Frank R., Jr., S/Sgt, Co. B 756th Tank Bn., Siegfried Line 19 Mar. 1945
Cochran, Andrew, Cpl, Co. D 30th Inf, Anzio, Italy 5 June 1944
Coffee, Henry G., Pvt, Co. L 15th Inf, Sicily July 1943
Coffin, Arthur L., Pfc, Co. D 30th Inf, Riedwihr, France 27 Jan. 1945
Coffman, Donald, Pfc, Co. K 15th Inf, Italy 29 Feb. 1944
Cohen, Benjamin, Pfc, Co. F 30th Inf, Sigolsheim, France 31 Dec. 1944
Cohen, Seymour, Pfc, Co. L 30th Inf, Wolfstein, Germany 1 Apr. 1945
Colandro, Thomas L., Pfc, Co. D 15th Inf, France 1 Feb. 1945
Colbert, Reford W., 2d Lt, Inf Co. E 30th Inf, Ixheim, Germany 19 Mar. 1945
Colburn, Edward L., Pfc, Co. F 15th Inf, Sicily Aug. 1943
Colburn, Kenneth D., Pfc, Co. A 15th Inf, Montelimar, France 28 Aug. 1944
Colburn, Robert J., Pfc, Hq. Co. 2d Bn. 30th Inf, France 23 Jan. 1945
Coleman, Clyde J., S/Sgt, Co. G 30th Inf, Italy 30 Jan. 1944
Coles, James W., 2d Lt, Co. L, 15th Inf, Italy 22 Sept. 1943
Collins, Edward G., Pfc, Hq. Co. 7th Inf, France 15 Aug. 1944
Collins, Francis J., S/Sgt, Co. G 7th Inf, Sicily July 1943
Collins, Thomas W., Sgt, Co. M 15th Inf, Gadheim, Germany 12 Apr. 1945
Collison, Robert O., Sgt, Co. E 15th Inf, Italy 20 Feb. 1944
Colombo, Frank J., Pfc, Hq. Co. 1st Bn. 7th Inf, Germany 18 Mar. 1945
Colon, Milton E., Pfc, Co. C 7th Inf, Strasbourg, France 1 Dec. 1944
Conklin, Willis B., 1st Lt, Co. E 7th Inf, France 22 Nov. 1944
Conn, Clyde M., Cpl, Co. K 7th Inf, French Morocco 10 Nov. 1942
▲Connolly, Joseph S., 1st Lt, Co. E 15th Inf, France 5 Feb. 1945
▲(3) Connor, Garlin M., 1st Lt, 3d Bn. 7th Inf, Biesheim, France 3 Feb. 1945
Constantin, James M., Sgt, Co. G 15th Inf, 26 Jan. 1945
Converse, Edward E., Pfc, Co. H 15th Inf, France 2 Sept. 1944
Converse, Glen E., T/4, Med. Det. 7th Inf, Italy Nov. 1943
Conway, Denzil B., Cpl, Co. H 15th Inf, Sicily Aug. 1943
▲Cook, William, S/Sgt, Co. L 30th Inf, Besancon, Siegfried Line 20 Mar. 1945
Coon, William G., Pfc, Co. H 7th Inf, France 25 Jan. 1945
Copeland, Leonard E., S/Sgt, Co. E 15th Inf, France 30 Jan. 1945
Copenhaver, Franklin L., Jr., Pvt, BP 3d Rcn Trp., Italy 4 June 1944
Copley, John R., T/Sgt, Co. E 30th Inf, France 3 Oct. 1944
▲Corbe, William J., Sgt, Co. A 7th Inf, Nurnberg, Germany 18 Apr. 1945
Corbin, Earl, Sgt, Co. G 7th Inf, Italy 2 Nov. 1943
Cormanick, Michael W., Pfc, Co. L 15th Inf, Italy 31 Jan. 1944
Cornelius, Harold J., Sgt, Co. 1 30th Inf, Italy 4 Feb. 1944
Coronel, Rudolph J., Pvt, Btry C 41st FA Bn., Italy 26 Oct. 1943
Corrigan, Charles B., Pfc, Hq. Co. 2d Bn. 15th Inf, France 13 Sept. 1944
▲Costa, Antone V., Pfc, Co. M 7th Inf, Italy 28 Jan. 1944
Costa, Arthur J., Pfc, Co. M 7th Inf, Italy 28 Jan. 1944
Costa, Vincent J., Pfc, Co. D 7th Inf, France 29 Jan. 1945
Costas, George C., 1st Lt, FA 41st FA Bn., France 18 Aug. 1944
▲Cotter, Lloyd H., 1st Lt, Cn Co. 15th Inf, France 23 Oct. 1944
Covington, Robert L., Jr., Pvt, Co. E 30th Inf, France 17 Dec. 1944
Cox, Ernest P., Cpl, Co. C 15th Inf, Italy 18 Oct. 1943
Cox, Herman W., Sgt, Co. C 7th Inf, France 25 Sept. 1944
Craig, Clayton C., Capt, Inf 15th Inf, Sicily Aug. 1943
Cramp, Edmund L., S/Sgt, Co. K 30th Inf, Italy 16 Feb. 1944
Crandall, Raymond K., Cpl, Hq. Btry 9th FA Bn., Italy 17 Nov. 1943
Crane, Robert E., S/Sgt, Med. Det. 7th Inf, La Voivre, France 20 Nov. 1944
Crawford, Arden L., S/Sgt, Hq. Co. 2d Bn. 30th Inf, Sicily 18 Aug. 1943
Crawford, James H., T/Sgt, Co. D 7th Inf, Italy 30 Jan. 1944
▲Crawford, Joseph B., Lt Col, Inf, 17th Inf, French Morocco 8 Nov. 1942
Crepeau, Victor, 1st Lt, BP 7th Inf, Italy 27 May 1944
Crews, Hilman V., Cpl, Co. D 7th Inf, Italy 10 Dec. 1943
Crissman, Samuel S., Jr., 1st Lt, Hq. & Hq. Co. 1st Bn. 15th Inf, Sicily 11 July 1943
Croatti, Michael L., Pfc, Co. M 7th Inf, Erlangen, Germany 19 Apr. 1945
Cromer, Walter A., Capt, Inf, 30th Inf, French Morocco 8 Nov. 1942
Crooks, Raymond M., T/5, 3d Sig. Co., Italy 29 Feb. 1944
Crouch, Joseph, Sgt, CWS Co. C 84th Cml Bn., Italy 21 Oct. 1943
▲(2) Crough, James A., 2d Lt, Inf Co. E 7th Inf Regt., France 4 Nov. 1944
Crowell, Christopher J., S/Sgt, Co. G 15th Inf, Nurnberg, Germany 18 Apr. 1945
Cruz, Raymond, Pfc, Co. F 7th Inf, French Morocco 10 Nov. 1942
Cucciniello, William S., S/Sgt, BP 7th Inf, Italy 25 Mar. 1944
Cuicello, James W., S/Sgt, Co. C 10th Engr. Bn., France 31 Dec. 1944
Cullen, Patrick, Pfc, Co. H 7th Inf, Italy 2 Feb. 1944
Culp, Johnnie W., Pvt, Co. L 15th Inf, France 27 Dec. 1944
Cunningham, Earl W., T/4, Co. B 756th Tank Bn., France 23 Dec. 1944
Cuny, Arthur E., 1st Lt, Co. D 7th Inf, Italy 23 Apr. 1944
Cupka, John L., Pfc, Co. C 7th Inf, French Morocco 8 Nov. 1942
Currence, Howard P., Jr., Pvt, Cn Co. 15th Inf, France 24 Aug. 1944
Cusick, Alvania, S/Sgt, Co. K 15th Inf, France 15 Sept. 1944
Czar, Joseph F., Pfc, Btry B. 41st FA Bn., Sicily 4 Aug. 1943
Czarniawski, Edward M., Pfc, Co. I 30th Inf, Colmar 20 Feb. 1945

▲ Oak Leaf Cluster.

Dakauskas, Leon V., Pfc, Med. Det. Co. B 10th Engr. Bn., Italy 29 Feb.1944
Dalton, James J., S/Sgt, Hq. Co. 1st Bn. 15th Inf, La Bourgonce, France 30 Oct. 1944
Daly, Byrne M., Major, MC Regt'l Surgeon Med. Det. 30th Inf, Italy 25 Jan. 1944
▲(2) Daly, Michael J., 1st Lt, Inf Co. 15th Inf, Bieshiem, France 4 Feb. 1945
Daly, William F., Jr., Pfc, Co. D 7th Inf, France 23 Jan. 1945
Daly, William L., Pfc, Co. I 30th Inf, Cisterna, Italy 29 Jan. 1944
Dana, Richard H., Cpl, Hq. Co. 2d Bn. 7th Inf, Italy 16 Oct. 1943
D'Angelo, Thomas, Pfc, Co. D 7th Inf, Italy 31 Jan. 1944
Darkow, Emanuel W., Pvt, Med. Det. 30th Inf, Sicily Aug. 1943
Darrah, John R., Major, MC Med. Det. 30th Inf, Sicily Aug. 1943
Dash, Clarence E., Pfc, Co. M 30th Inf, Italy 7 Mar. 1944
Daugird, Joseph J., Pfc, Co. G 30th Inf, Germany 29 Mar. 1945
Davenport, Milburn L., Pvt, Hq. Co. 3d Bn. 30th Inf, Sicily Aug. 1943
Davies, Thomas, Capt, Hq. 1st Bn. 30th Inf, Germany 8 May 1944
Davis, Chester F., Pfc, Co. A 7th Inf, France 22 Nov. 1944
Davis, Chester H., Pfc, Hq. Co. 1st Bn. 15th Inf, Italy 12 Nov. 1943
▲Davis, Herbert R., Sgt, Co. G 7th Inf, Italy 30 May 1944
Davis, Jean C., S/Sgt, Co. E 7th Inf, Italy 10 Nov. 1943
Davis, Kermit L., Lt Col, FA Hq. VI Corps Artillery Beaulieu Ain Seba, North Africa 10 Nov. 1942
Davis, Leonard D., S/Sgt, Btry C 9th FA Bn., Sicily, Aug. 1943
Davis, Lucius S., 1st Lt, Co. M 7th Inf, Italy 30-31 Jan. 1944
Davis, Quinton D., S/Sgt, AT Co. 15th Inf, Cleurie Quarry, France 3 Oct. 1944
▲Davis, Rondal N., Pfc, Co. C 30th Inf, Germany 13 Apr.1945
Davis, Russell, Pvt, Co. K 30th Inf, Sicily, July 1943
Dawson, Howard R., Pvt, Med. Det. 7th Inf, Italy 5 Mar. 1944
▲Dawson, Richard C., S/Sgt, Hq. Co. Bn. 30th Inf, Kaysersburg, France 16 Dec. 1944
Day, Kenneth L., Capt, MC Med. Det. 15th Inf, Sicily July 1943
Daze, David J., 2d Lt, Co. L 30th Inf, France 10 Oct. 1944
Dean, Everett L., 2d Lt, Co. F 7th Inf, Italy 23 Sept. 1943
Dean, Jesse A., Sgt, Co. B 7th Inf, Italy 30 Jan. 1944
Deatherage, Earnie E., T/4, Co. C 751st Tank Bn., Italy 24 Jan. 1944
Deerkop, Bernal J., Pfc, Btry C 41st FA Bn., Italy 6 Mar. 1944
De Francisco, Albert A., S/Sgt, AT Co. 15th Inf, Biesheim, France 6 Feb. 1945
Dehart, Harold K., Pvt, Co. K 15th Inf, Italy 1 June 1944
Dellinger, Lewis A., 2d Lt, Inf, Co. H Inf, Italy 2 Nov. 1943
Dellinger, Marvin J., Sgt, Co. A 601st TD Bn., France 25 Jan. 1945
Delooze, Thomas P., Pfc, Co. H 15th Inf, France 18 Oct. 1944
DeLorenzo, Enrico H., S/Sgt, Co. E 30th Inf, St. Die, France 29 Oct. 1944
▲Deltieure, Rene, Sgt, Co. M 7th Inf, Neroy le Bourg, France 11 Sept. 1944
Del Torto, Nicholas J., 2d Lt, Inf Co. E 7th Inf, Salzburg, Austria 3 May 1945
DeLuca, Alfred, S/Sgt, Co. B 30th Inf, France 8 Nov. 1944
Demutis, Cecil A., Pvt, Med. Det. 30th Inf, Burstadt, Germany 27 Mar. 1945
Denten, Dwight D., Capt, Co. M 15th Inf, Italy 24 Apr. 1944
Depasquale, Dominick, S/Sgt, Co. C 30th Inf, Besancon, France 7 Sept. 1944
DePaul, Samuel, Pvt, Btry C 41st FA Bn., France 7 Sept. 1944
Derrickson, Wayne R., S/Sgt, Co. K 15th Inf, Nurnberg, Germany 20 Apr. 1945
Derosier, Gerald A., Capt, Hq. 1st Bn. 7th Inf, France 1 Dec. 1944
Derrough, Roger A., 1st Lt, Co. L 15th Inf, Narzelstetten, Germany 26 Apr. 1945
▲Derryberry, Hugh C., Sgt, 601st TD Bn, Italy Sept. 1943
▲(2) Desforge, William V., 1st Lt, Rcn Co. 601st TD Bn., Verre, France 8 Sept. 1944
▲DeVisch, Kamiel G., Sgt, Co. I 30th Inf, France, Biesheim 4 Feb. 1945
De Voss, Albert A., Cpl, Co. B 10th Engr. Bn., Italy 5 Nov. 1943
Diamond, Irving, S/Sgt, Co. G 39th Inf, France 30 Oct. 1944
▲Dick, John A., 1st Lt, Inf, AT Co. 15th Inf, Robersdorf, Germany 15 Apr. 1945
Dickensauge, Cesar, Pfc, Co. M 15th Inf, Sicily 7 Aug. 1943
Dickson, Billy, Pfc, Co. F 15th Inf, Italy 1 Feb. 1944
Dickson, William A., Lt, Hq. Co. 1st Bn. 15th Inf, Sigolsheim, France 23 Dec. 1944
Dietrich, John J., Pfc, Co. H 15th Inf, Biesheim, France 2 Feb. 1945
Dietz, Alex J., Pfc, Co. L 7th Inf, Italy 1 Mar. 1944
Diggs, Jesse F., III, 2d Lt, Inf 30th Inf, Sicily July 1943
▲Digiovanni, Joseph C., Pfc, Hq. Co. 15th Inf, Nompatelize, France 24 Oct. 1944
Dill, George R., Cpl, Co. C 7th Inf, Italy 24 Oct. 1943
Dillie, Luther, Pfc, Co. L 15th Inf, Italy 1 Feb. 1944
DiMattesa, Joseph D., Pvt, Co. K 7th Inf, Italy 2 Feb. 1944
Dimedio, Richard P., Pfc, Co. C 7th Inf, Hollande, France 20 Nov. 1944
Dierio, Jack A., Pvt, Co. I 15th Inf, Italy 24 May 1944
Ditzler, William H., S/Sgt, Co. G 30th Inf, France 20 Aug. 1944
Dodson, Guy W., Pfc, Med. Det. 7th Inf, France 20 Nov. 1944
Dolaway, Chester W., S/Sgt, Hq. Co. 2d Bn. 15th Inf, France 4 Nov. 1944
▲Doleman, Edgar C., Lt Co, Ex Off. 30th Inf, Italy 5-6 Feb. 1944
Dombrouski, Stanley R., Sgt, Co. K 7th Inf, Italy Oct. 1943
Dominguez, Valentine, Pfc, AT Co. 15th Inf, Nurnberg, Germany 20 Apr. 1945
Dominski, Tyrus, S/Sgt, Co. I 30th Inf, France 2 Feb. 1945
Donnelly, Robert W., Capt, MC Med. Det. 7th Inf, La Voivre, France 20 Nov. 1944
Dooley, Harry L., Sgt, Co. E 7th Inf, Italy 24 May 44
Dorato, Anthony J., T/Sgt, Co. K 7th Inf, Wermichshausen, Germany 9 Apr. 1945
Dorman, Jessie O., T/Sgt, Co. L 30th Inf, Anzio, Italy 23 Feb. 1944
Dorrico, Anthony F., Sgt, Co. H 30th Inf, France 18 Dec. 1944
Dorrough, Richard P., Capt, Co. G 15th Inf, France 29 Sept. 1944
Dotson, Lloyd H., Pfc, Co. H 15th Inf, France 4 Nov. 1944
Doty, William L., Sgt, Co. G 30th Inf, Sicily July 1943
Doubet, Harold D., Pvt, Co. K 15th Inf, France 25 Dec. 1944
Dougherty, Millard F., 1st Lt, Inf, Hq. Co. 3d Bn., 30th Inf, Rosenheim, Germany 2 May 1945
Dowling, Edwin S., Jr., Co. A 7th Inf, French Morocco 8 Nov. 1942
Downard, Donald E., Major, Inf 15th Inf, Sicily Sept. 1943
Downer, Robert P., Sgt, Co. C 30th Inf, S. France, 12 Sept. 1944
Doyle, John R., S/Sgt, Co. B 15th Inf, France 21 Aug. 1944
Doyle, Lawrence W., Pfc, Co. L 30th Inf, Guemar, France 23 Jan. 1945
Drake, Harris B., Capt, Inf Co. M 15th Inf, Italy 5 Nov. 1943
Draper, James H., Pfc, Co. M 7th Inf, Italy 26 May 1944
Draper, Willard T., 1st Lt, Co. C 30th Inf, Italy 24 Apr. 1944
▲Drayton, Frederick R., Jr., 2d Lt, Co. C 7th Inf, Germany 19 Mar. 1945
Drescher, Lawrence E., Sgt, Co. C 10th Engr. Bn., Italy 23 May 1944
Drill, Wallace G., Pfc, Co. I 7th Inf, Italy 23 May 1944
Driscoll, William D., Pfc, Co. B 7th Inf, Le Haut Jacques, France 4 Nov. 1944
Droll, Robert L., Pfc, Co. I 30th Inf, Waldhausen, Germany 24 Apr. 1945
Drozd, Henry R., S/Sgt, Co. I 30th Inf, France 30 Sept. 1944
Duckworth, James E., Pfc, Co. L 30th Inf, Italy 23 May 1944
Dudik, Andrew S., Pfc, Co. E 30th Inf, Italy 22 Jan. 1944
Duffy, Edward F., 1st Lt, CWS Co. D 84th Cml Bn., Italy 22 Feb. 1944
Dugger, Robert S., Pfc, Hq. Co. 2d Bn. 30th Inf, Kayserberg, France 16 Dec. 1944
Dumais, Henry, Pfc, Co. E 30th Inf, Les Haut Jacques, France 29 Oct. 1944
Dumanski, Charles A., T/3, Co. F 30th Inf, Nurnberg, Germany 20 Apr. 1945
▲Duncan, Jack M., Major, Hq. 2d Bn. 7th Inf, Germany 18 Apr. 1945
Dunham, Ralph, Sgt, Co. I 30th Inf, France 28 Oct. 1944
Dunham, Russell, S/Sgt, Co. I 30th Inf, Italy 2 June 1944
Dunlap, Nelson L., S/Sgt, Co. G 30th Inf, Sicily Aug. 1943
Dunn, Herbert A., 1st Sgt, Co. C 7th Inf, Neu Altheim, Germany 17 Mar. 1945
Durfey, James F., Sgt, Btry B 41st FA Bn., Sicily, Aug. 1943
Durgen, John, T/5, Co. A 10th Engr. Bn., France 18 Dec. 1944
Durik, Michael J., S/Sgt, Med. Det. 15th Inf, Sicily July 1943
Dutra, John, Pvt, Co. M 30th Inf, France 23 Sept. 1944
Duvall, Everett W., Lt Col, 2d Bn. 7th Inf, Italy 11 Nov. 1943
Duwe, Arthur E., Jr., S/Sgt, Co. K 30th Inf, France 16 Aug. 1944
Dye, Diamond A., Sgt, Co. A 601st TD Bn., Houssen, France 25 Jan. 1945
Dye, Elmont E., T/5, Co. A 3d Med. Bn., French Morocco 8 Nov. 1942
Dyer, John W., Pfc, Co. I 15th Inf, Buchenbuhl, Germany 15 Apr. 1945
Dykes, Samuel M., 1st Lt, Hq. 3d 30th Inf, France 10 Sept. 1944
Dykstra, Peter, Cpl, Co. B 601st TD Bn., Italy 30 May 1944
Dylewski, Withold F., Capt, Co. D 7th Inf, France 24 Jan. 1945

▲Earnest, Charles E., Sgt, Co. C 30th Inf, Cissy, Brisach, France 6 Feb. 1945
Easter, Raleigh D., Pfc, Co. F 7th Inf, France 30 Sept. 1944
Eastmond, Frank T., Pfc, Co. B 30th Inf, Sicily July 1943
Eddy, Charles W., 2d Lt, Hq. Co. 756th Tank Bn., France 30 Sept. 1944
Edick, Arthur C., Pvt, Co. K 15th Inf, France 25 Dec. 1944
Edmondson, James T., Sgt, Co. F 30th Inf, France 6 Sept. 1944
Edmondson, William K., 1st Lt, Co. A 15th Inf, France 28 Aug. 1944
▲Edson, Hallett D., Lt Col, 15th Inf, Bois-de-Wikr, France 26 Jan. 1945
Edwards, Cletus W., Sgt, Co. L 7th Inf, Munich, Germany 25 Apr. 1945
Edwards, Nelson C., S/Sgt, Co. E 7th Inf, Italy 16 Feb. 1944
Edwards, Phillip H., Cpl, 3d Rcn Trp., Italy 27 May 1944
Edwards, Sidney L., 1st Sgt, Co. H 15th Inf, Italy 13 Oct. 1943
Egebergh, Carl C., Pvt, Co. I 7th Inf, Italy 25 May 1944
▲Egleston, Elmer F., Capt, Mc 30th Inf, Fedala, French Morocco 8 Nov. 1942
Egurrolo, Ramon C., T/4, Med. Det. 30th Inf, France 17 Dec. 1944
Ehlke, Arlan H., Pfc, Co. L 15th Inf, Nurnberg, Germany 19 Apr. 1945
Ehret, Robley W., 1st Lt, Co. B 15th Inf, France 28 Aug. 1944
Eifler, Oliver W., T/5, Med. Det. 15th Inf, France 10 Nov. 1944
Eike, Maurice E., Pfc, Co. K 15th Inf, France 7 Nov. 1944
Elder, Luther B., Pvt, Co. M 30th Inf, Italy 16 Feb. 1944
Elliott, Gordon A., Pfc, Rcn Co. 601st TD Bn., Italy 21 Oct. 1943
▲Elliott, Lewis P., 1st Lt, Co. C 601st TD Bn., Brignolis, France Aug. 1944
Ellis, James H., 2d Lt, Co. F 7th Inf, Italy 2 Feb. 1944
Ellis, John F., Sgt, Hq. & Hq. Co. 1st Bn. 30th Inf, Italy 9 Feb. 1944
Elmore, E. L., Capt, Co. Off. Co. E 30th Inf, Anzio, Italy 5 June 1944
Elmore, Lester C., 2d Lt, CE Co. A 10th Engr. Bn., France 29 Jan. 1945
Elston, Robert B., T/Sgt, Co. L 15th Inf, Italy 31 Jan. 1944
▲(2) Elterich, John A., Major, Hq. 2d Bn. 7th Inf, Italy 13 Nov. 1943
Enders, Theobald L., S/Sgt, Co. F 30th Inf, Italy 23 May 1944
Engfer, William R., 1st Lt, Co. A 756th Tank Bn., France 24 Jan. 1945
Engom, Arthur C., Cpl, Btry B 39th FA Bn., Italy 21 Oct. 1943
Eoff, James C., Pfc, Hq. Co. (BP) 7th Inf, France 15 Aug. 1944
Eosefow, John, Pfc, Co. E 15th Inf, Nurnberg, Germany 17 Apr. 1945
Epperson, Walter E., S/Sgt, Co. I 15th Inf, Italy 27 Jan. 1944
Ernst, Michael A., S/Sgt, Co. C 7th Inf, France 23 Nov. 1944
Ernstes, Herman C., Sgt, Co. B 10th Engr. Bn., Italy 13 Oct. 1943
Esenwein, Erich K., Pvt, Med. Det. 30th Inf, Vosges 5 Dec. 1944
Esparaza, Manuel M., S/Sgt, Co. L 7th Inf, France 15 Sept. 1944
Esquibel, Julio G., Pfc, Co. M 7th Inf, LaVoivre, France 20 Nov. 1944
Estes, Charles T., Pvt, Co. D 30th Inf, France 17 Dec. 1944
Etheridge, James E., Pvt, Med. Det. 2d Bn. 7th Inf, Sicily Aug. 1943
▲(3) Etheridge, M. B., Capt, Co. K 30th Inf, Pierrefeu, France 16 Aug. 1944
Etzel, George, Jr., Pvt, AT Co. 15th Inf, Italy 29 Feb. 1944
Evans, Ambrass R., Cpl, Co. D 30th Inf, Carano, Italy 14 Apr. 1944
Evans, Willard D., S/Sgt, Co. D 15th Inf, Biarfille, France 8 Nov. 1944
Ewing, Raymond D., 2d Lt, Co. M 7th Inf, Italy Oct. 1943
Eye, Bennie A., S/Sgt, Co. A 7th Inf, France 22 Nov. 1944
Eyles, Robert R., 1st Lt, Btry C 39th FA Bn., Italy 14 Oct. 1943
Ezzell, James C., T/5, Rcn Co. 601st TD Bn., France 8 Sept. 1944

Fabiano, John N., T/Sgt, Co. I 30th Inf, Italy 23 May 1944
Fagan, Charles, Jr., Pfc, Co. L 30th Inf, Italy 16 Apr. 1944
Fahey, Bernard D., 2d Lt, Co. D 756th Tank Bn., Otterloh, Germany 1 May 1945
Fajkowski, Leo S., Pfc, Co. M 7th Inf, Vy-les-Lure, France 15 Sept. 1944
Falcone, Carl, Pfc, Co. E 30th Inf, France 23 Jan. 1945
Falkenberg, Walter R., Sgt, Co. C 15th Inf, Germany 21 Apr. 1945
Fallsdown, Wesley, Pfc, Hq. Co. 1st Bn., Fuchestadt, Germany 8 Apr. 1945
Falvey, Robert E., Pfc, Hq. Co. 3d 30th Inf, 26 Oct. 1944
▲Fanelli, Michael C., S/Sgt, Co. F 7th Inf, Nurnberg, Germany 17 Apr. 1945
▲Fargo, Lynn D., Major, Inf 30th Inf, Sicily July 1943
Farley, Ed., Sgt, Co. B 756th Tank Bn., France 25 Sept. 1944
Farner, Dwight M., Cpl, 3d Rcn Trp., Sicily 17 July 1943
Farquar, James C., Sgt, Co. C 7th Inf, Italy 24 Oct. 1943
Farr, Dell A., Jr., Pvt, Co. I 30th Inf, France 16 Dec. 1944
Farrell, Robert F., Capt, Inf Co. G 30th, Italy 29 Jan. 1944
Faubion, Driskill C., S/Sgt, Co. F 30th Inf, France 25 Nov. 1944
Faust, Francis S., Pfc, Co. I 30th Inf, Italy 28 Jan. 1944
Faustino, Harry J., Pfc, Co. A 30th Inf, France 17 Dec. 1944
▲Fechtman, Robert H., 1st Lt, Inf 30th Inf, French Morocco 10 Nov. 1942
Federico, Frank B., Pvt, Co. I 30th Inf, Italy 29 Feb. 1944
Federmeyer, Bernard P., T/Sgt, Co. A 15th Inf, Sicily 3 Aug. 1943
Fee, James B., Sgt, Co. L 15th Inf, Italy 29 Jan. 1944
Feingold, Albert H., Pfc, Co. G 30th Inf, Sicily July 1943
Fell, Alvin S., Pfc, Hq. Co. 2d Bn. 15th Inf, Nurnberg, Germany 18 Apr. 1945
▲Fell, Russell C., S/Sgt, Co. F 30th Inf, Grendelbruch, France 25 Nov. 1944
Fennessy, Francis J., Pfc, Hq. Co. 2d Bn. 15th Inf, France 10 Nov. 1944

▲ Oak Leaf Cluster.

Ferguson, William R., S/Sgt, Co. D 15th Inf, Bonsweihur, Germany 28 Mar. 1945
Fernald, Harold L., Jr., Cpl, Co. K 7th Inf, Italy 2 Nov. 1943
Ferraro, Anthony, Sgt, Co. F 7th Inf, Italy 25 May 1944
Ferro, Samuel J., Sgt, Co. K 30th Inf, Weiskirch, Germany 16 Mar. 1945
Fetto, August F., Pvt, Hq. Co. 7th Inf, Sicily 10 Aug. 1943
Fifer, Harry G., Pfc, Co. B 30th Inf, France 17 Dec. 1944
▲(2) Fifield, William H., S/Sgt, Co. A 30th Inf, France 4 Feb. 1945
Finch, Ned, S/Sgt, Co. L 7th Inf, France, 15 Sept. 1944
Finch, Ralph E., T/Sgt, Co. L 30th Inf, Mittlebach, Germany 19 Mar. 1945
Finken, Stillman W., T/5, Co. C 10th Engr. Bn., Italy 23 May 1944
Firestone, Clarence, Pfc, Co. B 7th Inf, Sandhofen, Germany 26 Mar. 1945
Fisher, Alvin E., Sgt, Co. E 30th Inf, Sicily July 1943
Fisher, Fred, S/Sgt, Co. G 30th Inf, Erlangen, Germany 16 Apr. 1945
Fisher, Henry, Pfc, Co. C 7th Inf, Germany 26 Mar. 1945
Fisher, Richard L., T/Sgt, Co. G 7th Inf, Italy 10 Nov. 1943
Fiske, Warren, Pvt, Co. G 15th Inf, France 5 Sept. 1944
Fitterman, Abraham, 1st Lt, Inf Co. L 30th Inf, Germany 5 Apr. 1945
Fitzgerald, Roland J., Sgt, Btry B 39th FA Bn., Italy 21 Oct. 1943
Fitzimmons, Sam S., 1st Lt, Co. I 7th Inf, Germany 15 Mar. 1945
Flaherty, Edward J., S/Sgt, Hq. Co. 15th Inf, Sigolsheim, France 27 Dec. 1944
Flaten, Clifford O., Cpl, Co. A 30th Inf, Italy 24 Apr. 1944
Fleet, Robert L., Capt, Inf Co. F 30th Inf, Lorsch, Germany 27 Mar. 1945
Flender, Stanley J., Pfc, Co. E 30th Inf, France 27 Aug. 1944
Fler, Glen P., T/Sgt, Co. M 15th Inf, Italy 2 Feb. 1944
Flickinger, Ray M., S/Sgt, Co. M 15th Inf, Italy 23 May 1944
▲Flinner, Albert L., Jr., S/Sgt, Co. C 7th Inf, Germany, 19 Apr. 1945
Flynn, Ralph M., Capt, Hq. 3d 7th Inf, Italy 29 Feb. 1944
Fodi, Martin, Pfc, Co. F 15th Inf, Italy 5 Mar. 1944
Foister, Shelby, Pfc, Co. F 30th Inf, France 29 Sept. 1944
Foley, Ross R., Pvt, Co. E 30th Inf, Sicily July 1943
Follin, Lee M., Sgt, Co. G 30th Inf, Zweibrucken, Germany 19 Mar. 1945
Formato, Aurelius A., Pfc, Co. H 7th Inf, Ferdrupt, France 29 Sept. 1944
Forstner, Paul, Cpl, Co. K 30th Inf, Sicily July 1943
Forsyth, Ira R., 1st Sgt, 3d Rcn Trp., France 22 Sept. 1944
Foster, Winfield L., Pvt, Cn Co. 30th Inf, Italy 8 Nov. 1943
Fotsch, Laverne P., T/5, Med. Det. 7th Inf, France 4 Oct. 1944
Fournier, Ernest J., Pfc, Btry C 441st AAA (AW) Bn., Italy 15 Oct. 1943
Fowler, Dewey E., Pfc, Co. G 15th Inf, Germany 19 Mar. 1945
Foy, George F., Pfc, Hq. Co. 15th Inf, Tresvilley, France 6 Sept. 1944
Fox, James R., Sgt, Co. E 7th Inf, Wihr-en-Plaine, France 29 Jan. 1945
Franck, Ralph W., Pfc, Co. A 30th Inf, Sicily July 1943
Franckowiak, Thomas A., Sgt, Co. M 7th Inf, Erlangen, Germany 17 Apr. 1945
Frecentese, William, Pfc, Med. Det. 7th Inf, France 1 Oct. 1944
Frederick, John J., 1st Lt, Hq. Co. 30th Inf, Germany 21 Mar. 1945
Freeland, Frankie L., Sgt, Hq. Co. 3d Bn. 7th Inf, France 7 Sept. 1944
Freeman, Donald A., Jr., Sgt, Co. C 756th Tank Bn., France 7 Sept. 1944
Freeman, Willard L., Pvt, Med. Det. 10th FA Bn., Sicily Aug. 1943
Frega, Nicholas J., Cpl, Co. H 7th Inf, Fordrupt, France 1 Oct. 1944
French, Clayton C., Pvt, Co. D 7th Inf, Italy 16 Oct. 1943
Fretwell, John D., Cpl, Co. F 15th Inf, Sicily 6 Aug. 1943
Fritz, Frank J., 2d Lt, Inf Co. M 15th Inf, Italy 2 Mar. 1944
Frost, Eugene A., T/Sgt, Co. I 15th Inf, Italy 13 Oct. 1943
Fuchs, Charles F., S/Sgt, Co. I 15th Inf, Italy 23 May
Fuhrman, Oscar F., Pfc, Co. M 7th Inf, Italy 29 Feb. 1944
Fulkersen, James W., Pfc, Co. I 30th Inf, Italy 23 May 1944
Funk, Christian A., Pfc, Co. H 7th Inf, Neunhof, Germany 17 Apr. 1945
Furlan, Martin, Pfc, Co. M 30th Inf, Italy 18 Mar. 1944
Futuluychuk, Steve, 1st Sgt, Co. C 601st TD Bn., Reidwihr, France 26 Jan. 1945

Gable, George R., T/4, Co. A 30th Inf, Romathal, Germany 8 Apr. 1945
Gabriel, Arthur C., T/5, Med. Det. 7th Inf, Cisterna, Italy 3 Mar. 1944
Gackowski, Gerald J., Pfc, Hq. Co. 3d Bn. 30th Inf, Lechhausen, Germany 28 Apr. 1945
Gaddis, Carl E., Pfc, Hq. Co. 1st Bn. 30th Inf, France 16 Aug. 1944
Gair, Donald O., 2d Lt, Inf Co. I 30th Inf, Grosskichen, Germany 24 Apr. 1945
Gallegos, Manual, Cpl, Co. G 30th Inf, France 25 Nov. 1944
Gallinoto, Michael R., 1st Lt, Inf AT Co. 15th Inf, Schonau, Germany 8 Apr. 1945
Gallernani, Louis D., Pvt, Co. D 7th Inf, France 3 Nov. 1944
▲Gancos, Steve M., S/Sgt, 3d Rcn Trp., Italy 6 Oct. 1943
Gane, Donald W., S/Sgt, Co. E 30th Inf, Italy 1 Mar. 1944
Ganos, Thomas, Cpl, Med. Det. 15th Inf, Mortagne, France 25 Oct. 1944
Garcia, Jacinto M., Pfc, Co. D 7th Inf, France 3 Nov. 1944
Garcia, Juan E., Pvt, Co. H 7th Inf, Italy 3 Feb. 1944
Garcia, Nash A., Pfc, Co. C 15th Inf, Nurnberg, Germany 20 Apr. 1945
Gardner, Eugene M., T/5, 3d Rcn Trp., Italy 26 Aug. 1944
Gardner, Leslie E., T/Sgt, Co. G 30th Inf, France 21 Sept. 1944
Garo, Louis W., Pvt, Co. A 30th Inf, France 18 Aug. 1944
Garvy, Andrew C., Jr., Capt, MC Surg. 9th FA Bn., Cori, Italy 30 May 1944
Gaugler, Bernard H., 1st Lt, Co. C 756th Tank Bn., France 4 Dec. 1944
Gavron, Steve, Sgt, Co. F 7th Inf, France 2 Dec. 1944
Gayda, Mike, T/5, Med. Det. 15th Inf, Sicily Aug. 1943
Gaydos, Michael, Pvt, Co. C 15th Inf, Nurnberg, Germany 17 Apr. 1945
Geissler, Jerome W., Sgt, Co. G 7th Inf, France 15 Aug. 1944
Genger, Edward P., 1st Lt, Inf Co. M 30th Inf, Holtzwihr, France 23 Jan. 1945
Gensler, Donald W., 1st Lt, Inf Co. D 15th Inf, Besancon, France 8 Sept. 1944
George, Donald F., Cpl, Co. I 30th Inf, Germany 14 Apr. 1945
George, Wilburn W., 1st Lt, Serv. Co. 15th Inf, Sicily 12 July 1943
▲Gerber, Joseph J., S/Sgt, Co. B 15th Inf, Italy 24 May 1944
Gerhardt, Charles F., Pfc, Co. G 30th Inf, Italy 29 Jan. 1944
Germershausen, Joseph P., Pfc, Med. Det. 7th Inf, Germany 15 Mar. 1945
Gertz, Jack L., T/5, Co. E 30th Inf, Nurnberg, Germany 19 Apr. 1945
Gettman, Peter, Pvt, Med. Det. 7th Inf, French Morocco 10 Nov. 1942
Giannini, Gene L., Pfc, Co. K 15th Inf, Volmunster, France 16 Mar. 1945
Gilbert, Lloyd M., Pfc, Co. B 15th Inf, Germany 17 Mar. 1945
Gilden, Bert D., 2d Lt, Co. A 756th Tank Bn., France 3 Feb. 1945
Gillespie, Paul A., Pfc, Co. I 30th Inf, Urbach, Germany 15 Mar. 1945
Gilliland, Vivian C., Pvt, Co. K 30th Inf, Anzio, Italy 5 June 1944
Ginwright, Wilson L., S/Sgt, Co. K 15th Inf, Italy 23 May 1944
Gioia, Joseph A., 1st Lt, 601st TD Bn., El Guetter, Tunisia 23 Mar. 1943
Giuliani, Richard A., Pfc, Co. D 15th Inf, Nurnberg, Germany 18 Apr. 1945
Giza, Frank J., 2d Lt, Co. L 30th Inf, France 17 Sept. 1944
Gladden, Noel A., S/Sgt, Co. G 7th Inf, Ostheim, France 23 Jan. 1945
Glatzmaier, Andrew, T/5, Med. Det. 30th Inf, Italy 8 Oct. 1943

Glenn, Cap A., Cpl, Co. B 10th Engr. Bn., Italy 5 Nov. 1943
Glerum, Cornelius, Jr., 1st Lt, Btry C 41st FA Bn., France 21-22 Jan. 1945
Godfrey, Tom F., Sgt, Co. B 15th Inf, Morsch, Germany 26 Mar. 1945
Goebel, Murray J., 1st Sgt, Co. I 30th Inf, Germany 15 Apr. 1945
Goercke, Forrest W., S/Sgt, Hq. Co. 2d Bn. 7th Inf, Italy 16 Oct. 1943
Goff, Curtis B., Sgt, Cn Co. 15th Inf, Italy 5 June 1944
Gojmerac, John, Pfc, Co. B 7th Inf, France 24 Nov. 1944
Gokey, George, S/Sgt, Co. K 15th Inf, Italy 29 Feb. 1944
Goldberg, David, Pvt, Co. C 751st Tank Bn., Italy 24 Jan. 1944
Goldberg, Loel H., Pfc, Hq. & Hq. Co. 1st Bn. 30th Inf, Italy 26 Jan. 1944
Goldberg, William, Pfc, Co. F, 30th Inf, St. Die, France 28 Oct. 1944
Golemba, Stanley, Jr., Pfc, Co. I 15th Inf, Italy 23 May 1944
Golman, Francis J., T/5, Hq. Co. 15th Inf, Tresvilley, France 6 Sept. 1944
Gondek, Gilbert J., Pfc, Co. C 15th Inf, Nurnberg, Germany 17 Apr. 1945
Gonzales, Anselmo, Jr., Co. L 7th Inf, Vidonchamp, France 28 Oct. 1944
Gonzales, Gonzalo J., Pvt, Med. Det. 30th Inf, Italy 23 May 1944
Gonzales, Manuel V., Sgt, Co. C 15th Inf, Nurnberg, Germany 17 Apr. 1945
Goodin, Hayward, S/Sgt, Co. L 30th Inf, Italy 5 Mar. 1944
Goodwin, James A., Sgt, Co. A 7th Inf, Italy 1 Feb. 1944
Goodwin, James P., Sgt, Co. E 7th Inf, Italy 9 Nov. 1943
Goodwine, Leo A., Cpl, Co. I 15th Inf, Sicily Aug. 1943
Gordon, Francis L., Pvt, Hq. Co. 3d Bn. 30th Inf, France 9 Sept. 1944
▲Gore, Charles J., Pvt, Inf Co. L 30th Inf Regt., Germany 6 Apr. 1945
Gorobetz, Milton L., Pvt, Hq. Co. 1st Bn. 30th Inf, French Morocco 10 Nov. 1942
Gossett, Lamar, Sgt, Co. L 30th Inf, France 10 Nov. 1944
Gourley, Donald F., Capt, Inf Co. C 756th Tank Bn., Solacciano, Italy 13 May 1944
▲Graham, Frank R., 1st Lt, Co. A 15th Inf, Heroldsburg, Germany 15Apr. 1945
Grant, Charles I., Sgt, Co. C 10th Engr. Bn., Italy 4 Mar. 1944
Grant, Clarence J., 2d Lt, Co. E 7th Inf, Italy 29 Feb. 1944
Grant, James A., 1st Lt, Co. B 10th Engr. Bn., Italy 28 Jan. 1944
Grasso, Charles J., Pvt, AT Co. 15th Inf, Italy 7 Nov. 1943
Grasso, Frank J., Sgt, Co. G 7th Inf, Italy 23 Apr. 1944
Gravel, Edgar J., Pfc, Co. C 15th Inf, France 28 Aug. 1944
Gray, Harold, Pfc, Co. M 30th Inf, Germany 26 Mar. 1945
Greager, Thomas F., S/Sgt, Co. L 30th Inf, Italy 22 Mar. 1944
Greathouse, Cecil, Pfc, Co. A 30th Inf, La BiHay, France 6 Nov. 1944
Green, Robert J., T/Sgt, Co. A 7th Inf, Sicily 16 July 1943
Greene, John J., 2d Lt, Inf, Italy 23 Apr. 1944
Greer, Frederic R., T/5, Med. Det. 7th Inf, Sicily Aug. 1943
Greer, Harold E., Capt, Hq. Co. 30th Inf, Vosges 5 Dec. 1945
Griebel, Floyd H. W., T/Sgt, AT Co. 15th Inf, Nurnberg, Germany 20 Apr. 1945
Grik, Glen D., 1st Lt, Inf Co. M 15th Inf, Italy 28 May 1944
Griffiths, Hamlet, Pfc, Co. E 30th Inf, Italy 3 June 1944
Griffiths, Jack D., 1st Lt, FA Btry A 39th FA Bn., Sicily 12 Aug. 1943
Griggins, Anthony A., 2d Lt, Inf Co. A 30th Inf, Sicily July 1943
▲Grimes, Leonard R., Cpl, Hq. Co. 1st Bn. 7th Inf, Sicily 7 Oct. 1943
▲Groden, Raymond, T/Sgt, Co. C 30th Inf, Germany 30 Apr. 1945
Grose, Jack B., Sgt, Co. G 15th Inf, Italy 29 Feb. 1944
Grosso, James, S/Sgt, Co. D 756th Tank Bn., Germany 15 Apr. 1945
Grubb, Ernest H., Co. B 10th Engr. Bn., Sicily Aug. 1943
Grubbs, Molder M., Pfc, Co. A 30th Inf, France 3 Nov. 1944
Guanci, Peter P., S/Sgt, Co. H 7th Inf, Rupt-sur-Moselle, France, 25 Sept. 1944
▲Guckert, George E., Jr., 1st Lt, Cn Co. 7th Inf, Noroy le Bourg, France 13 Sept. 1944
Guckian, John J., Pfc, Co. C 30th Inf, Boulot, France 9 Sept. 1944
Guimont, Wilfred F., S/Sgt, Co. G 7th Inf, Italy 23 Apr. 1944
Gullett, Lewis W., Pfc, Co. E 7th Inf, France 6 Oct. 1944
Gunderson, Orville, Pfc, Med. Det. 7th Inf, Sicily Aug. 1943
Gunn, Robert E., Pvt, Co. K 15th Inf, Italy 29 Feb. 1944
Gunning, Leroy G., 2d Lt, Inf 30th Inf, Sicily July 1943
Gunst, Otto E., Capt, Co Co. F 15th Inf, Isola Bella, Italy 2 Feb. 1944
Gunter, William B., 1st Lt, CAV 3d Rcn Trp., Sicily July 1943
Gupton, Edward C., Pfc, Co. E 7th Inf, Italy 5 Feb. 1944
Gusler, Noel, Jr., Pfc, Co. I 30th Inf, France 1 Feb. 1945
Gutierrez, Angel, Jr., Pfc, Co. H 15th Inf, France 2 Nov. 1944
Gutowski, Edwin S., Pfc, Hq. Co. 3d Inf Div., Italy 2 Mar. 1944
Guzman, John R., Pfc, Co. M 15th Inf, France 25 Aug. 1944
Guzzo, Ralph G., Pvt, Hq. Co. 2d Bn. 30th Inf, Italy 3 June 1944

Habermeyer, Herbert H., Pfc, Hq. Co. 1st Bn. 15th Inf, Italy 13 Feb. 1944
Hack, Arthur J., Jr., Pfc, Hq. Co. 1st Bn. 7th Inf, Artena, Italy 28 May 1944
Hackbarth, Elmer A., S/Sgt, Co. B 15th Inf, Italy 1 Feb. 1944
Hacker, Raymond A., Pfc, Hq. Co. 3d Bn. 30th Inf, Anzio, Italy 5 June 1944
Hacker, Samuel E., Cpl, Co. M 30th Inf, Italy 3 Nov. 1943
Hagel, Clarence J., 1st Lt, Co. F 15th Inf, St. Amek, France 6 Oct. 1944
Hagelin, Richard H., 1st Lt, Inf Hq. Co. 2d Bn. 30th Inf, Sigolsheim, France 25 Dec. 1944
Hagen, Curtis G., Pvt, Med. Det. 7th Inf, Sicily Aug. 1943
Hagenberg, Andrew R., T/Sgt, Co. B 15th Inf, France 1 Nov. 1944
Hagstrom, Ralph A., Pfc, Hq. Co. 15th Inf, Italy 20 Dec. 1943
Haimowitz, Samuel I., Capt, MC 2d Bn. 30th Inf, Sicily Aug. 1943
Haines, Harold H., Capt, Inf Hq. Co. 1st Bn. 7th Inf, Italy 30-31 Jan. 1944
Haire, Charlie C., Pfc, Co. M 7th Inf, Steinach, Germany 8 Apr. 1945
Hale, Gordon R., S/Sgt, Co. A 15th Inf, Sicily 15 July 1943
Hale, James L., Pfc, Co. E 7th Inf, Italy 15 Oct. 1943
Hale, Kenneth B., Pfc, Co. G 7th Inf, Nurnberg, Germany 20 Apr. 1945
Haley, Theodore W., Pfc, Co. G 7th Inf, Nurnberg, Germany 22 Apr. 1945
Hall, Carl R., Sgt, Co. G 7th Inf, Italy 24 May 1944
Hall, Eugene, Pvt, Co. F 15th Inf, Nurnberg, Germany 17 Apr. 1945
Hall, Milton J., Pfc, Co. F 7th Inf, Italy 23 May 1944
Hall, Ralph D., Sgt, Co. C 15th Inf, Fort Mortier, France 6 Feb. 1945
Hall, William H., Sgt, Co. C 15th Inf, Riedwihr, France 24 Jan. 1945
Hamilton, Conrad J., T/Sgt, Co. M 30th Inf, Holtzwihr, France 28 Jan. 1945
Hamilton, Leroy E., T/Sgt, Co. C 7th Inf, Italy 21 May 1944
Hammett, John W., Sgt, Btry A 9th FA Bn., Sicily 10 Aug. 1943
Hammonds, Robert W., Sgt, Co. G 30th Inf, Italy 1 Mar. 1944
Hammons, Harless, S/Sgt, Co. B 7th Inf, Vogelsehim, France 4 Feb. 1945
Hanauer, Henry L., Pvt, Co. I 30th Inf, Vosges 5 Dec. 1944
Hancock, Henry H., 1st Lt, MC Med. Det. 7th Inf, Sicily July 1943
Hancock, John (NMI), Pvt, 3d Rcn Trp., Italy 28 Oct. 1943
Haneline, Norman E., S/Sgt, Co. E 15th Inf, Germany 17 Apr. 1945
Haney, Donald, S/Sgt, Co. K 15th Inf, France 25 Oct. 1944

▲ Oak Leaf Cluster.

▲Hanford, Roy E., 1st Lt, Med. Det. 30th Inf, Sicily Aug. 1943
Hann, George J., Pfc, Co. I 30th Inf, Steppach, Germany 14 Apr. 1945
Hanney, Leonard D., Capt, Co. G 7th Inf, France 23 Jan. 1945
Hansen, Olaf C., T/5, Co. A 10th Engr. Bn., France 6 Nov. 1944
Harbison, Derian A., Pvt, Co. E 7th Inf, Nurnberg, Germany 18 Apr. 1945
Harding, Delbert W., Pfc, Co. D 30th Inf, Carano, Italy 14 Apr. 1944
▲(2) Hardy, James C., Pfc, Co. M 30th Inf, Anzio, Italy 5 June 1944
Hargens, George A., S/Sgt, Co. E 601st TD Bn., Worth, Germany 29 Mar. 1945
Harper, Bill R., S/Sgt, Co. C 601st TD Bn., Alt. Erlauger, Germany 17 Apr. 1945
Harper, William W., 2d Lt, Inf Co. G 30th Inf, Heppenheim, Germany 27 Mar. 1945
Harrell, Ben, Co. I Inf 7th Inf, France 23 Nov. 1944
Harrell, Thomas E., Pfc, Co. H 30th Inf, Le Tholy, France 6 Oct. 1944
Harrington, Cecil C., Pfc, Co. A 7th Inf, French Morocco 8 Nov. 1942
Harrington, John R., Pfc, Co. K 7th Inf, Italy 26 Jan. 1944
Harris, Francis L. A., S/Sgt, Hq. Co. 30th Inf, France 25 Sept. 1944
Harris, Jack S., 1st Lt, Co. G 15th Inf, Nurnberg, Germany 17 Apr. 1945
Harris, Paul G., Capt, Hq. 3d Bn. 15th Inf, France 5 Feb. 1945
Harrison, Woodrow W., Pfc, Hq. Co. 1st Bn., 30th Inf, France 30 Sept. 1944
Hart, James D., Pfc, Co. A 30th Inf, France 17 Dec. 1944
Hart, Leon M., Capt, MC Srgn. 2d Bn. 15th Inf, France 27 Aug. 1944
Hart, Walter D., Sgt, Btry B 9th FA Bn., Sicily Aug. 1943
Hartman, Henry M., Cpl, Co. A 601st TD Bn., Houssen, France 24 Jan. 1945
Hartnagle, Paul F., T/Sgt, Co. F 15th Inf, Cremonvillers, France 2 Oct. 1944
Harvey, William S., S/Sgt, Co. E 7th Inf, Rodenbach, Germany 2 Apr. 1945
▲Harwell, Edward M., 1st Lt, Inf Co. A 15th Inf, Binswangen, Germany 24 Apr. 1945
Haug, Emil, Jr., Sgt, Inf Co. G 30th Inf Regt., France 28 Jan. 1945
Havens, Harry E., Jr., T/Sgt, Co. Gm 7th Inf, France 20 Nov. 1944
Havens, Wayne L., S/Sgt, Co. L 30th Inf, Italy 11 Mar. 1944
Hawes, George W., Cpl, Co. A 601st TD Bn., Germany 15 Mar. 1945
Hawkins, Alan W., Pfc, Co. A 30th Inf, France 17 Dec. 1944
Hawkins, Charles E., Pfc, Med. Det. 30th Inf, Sicily July 1943
Hawks, Lloyd C., Pfc, Med. Det. 30th Inf, Italy 28 Oct. 1943
Hawks, Robert A., Sgt, FA Co. B 601st TD Bn., Italy 29 Feb. 1944
Hawthorn, Floyd C., Pfc, Inf Antitank Co. 15th Inf Regt., France 30 Sept. 1944
Hayes, Paul L., 1st Lt, S-2 1st Bn. 30th Inf, France 24 Jan. 1945
Haynes, Donald L., 1st Lt, Co. H 30th Inf, Anzio, Italy 5 June 1944
Hayslett, Leroy B., T/5, Hq. Co. 15th Inf, Italy 29 Feb. 1944
Hayward, John L., Pvt, Co. F 15th Inf, Italy 24 May 1944
Heater, Edward J., Pfc, Anti-tank Co. 30th Inf, Vosges 5 Dec. 1944
Heagerty, Patrick D., Pfc, Co. I 15th Inf, France 15 Oct. 1944
Hebert, Nolan J., Pfc, Hq. Co. (BP) 30th Inf, France 28 Oct. 1944
Hebner, Robert H., Pfc, Co. K 15th Inf, Italy 29 Feb. 1944
Heckmann, Gerald T., 1st Sgt, Co. F 30th Inf, Munich, Germany 29 Apr. 1945
Hedberg, Arthur J., T/4, Hq. Btry 41st FA Bn., Sicily Aug. 1943
Heidebrink, Frank L., Cpl. Inf Co. A 504th Para Inf Regt., Italy 31 Jan. 1944
Heins, Paul E., Pfc, Co. D 7th Inf, Italy 28 May 1944
▲(2) Heintges, John A., Col, Co. 7th Inf, Germany 15 Mar. 1945
Heisler, Jesse W., Pfc, Co. M 15th Inf, Italy 23 May 1944
Heidemann, Bernard W., Pvt, Co. B 7th Inf, Sicily Aug. 1943
▲Helms, Paul E., Sgt, Co. G 7th Inf, France 23 Jan. 1945
Hemmenway, William, Pvt, Co. F 7th Inf, French Morocco 10 Nov. 1942
Henault, Edward A., Pfc, Co. M 30th Inf, France 1 Oct. 1944
Henderson, Gleatus E., Pfc, Co. D 7th Inf, Italy 28 May 1944
▲(2) Hendon, Max R., 1st Lt, Inf Hq. 3d Bn. 15th Inf, Italy 1944
Hendrickson, James C., S/Sgt, Co. L 15th Inf, Italy 20 Oct. 1943
Hendrix, Forrest W., Sgt, Co. C 7th Inf, Italy 24-25-Apr. 1944
Hendrixson, Waldo, S/Sgt, Co. H 15th Inf, France 28 Sept. 1944
Hennings, Gerald T., Sgt, Co. C 7th Inf, Italy 31 May 1944
▲Henrich, John A., Cpl, Co. D 7th Inf, France 23 Nov. 1944
Henry, Kenneth H., Cpl, Btry B 39th FA Bn., Italy 21 Oct. 1943
Henshaw, Otis H., T/Sgt, Co. F 30th Inf, France 5 Oct. 1944
Hensley, Noah P., Pfc, Co. G 15th Inf, Italy 31 Jan. 1944
Herbert, Noland J., Pfc, Hq. Co. 30th Inf, Vosges 5 Dec. 1944
▲Herman, Adam, Sgt. Rdr Plt Co. C 30th Inf, France 28 Oct. 1944
Hernandez, Arthur A., Pfc, Co. E 30th Inf, Nurnberg, Germany 19 Apr. 1945
Hernandez, Elias A., Pfc, Co. L 7th Inf, Germany 15 Mar. 1945
Hershey, William G., Pfc, Co. D 15th Inf, Le Tholy, France 6 Oct. 1944
▲Hess, John W., T/5, Co. A 30th Inf, Le Tholy, France 17 Oct. 1944
Hess, Kenneth H., T/Sgt, Co. G 15th Inf, Muntzenheim, Germany 3 Feb. 1945
Hester, Edward J., Pfc, AT Co. 30th Inf, France 28 Oct. 1944
Heyman, Henry, Pvt, Med. Det. 15th Inf, Italy 12-13 Oct. 1943
Hickerson, Jessie O., Sgt, Co. L 15th Inf, Italy 15 Feb. 1944
Hicks, Boris A., 1st Lt, Hq. Co. 3d Bn., Italy 16 Mar. 1944
Higgins, Robert A., T/Sgt, Co. L 7th Inf, France 26 Jan. 45
Hill, Carl D., Pfc, Co. G 30th Inf, France 30 Oct. 1944
Hill, Sterling L., Capt, FA Hq. 3d Div., Rieneck, Germany 4 Apr. 1945
Hinman, Daniel S. T., Major, Hq. 601st TD Bn., Italy 25 Jan. 1944
Hinspeter, William C., Pfc, Co. M 7th Inf, Bischwihr, France 29 Jan. 1945
Hird, John A., Pfc, Btry A 441st AAA (AW) Bn., Italy 29 Oct. 1943
Hisaw, John M., Pfc, Co. B 30th Inf, France 15 Sept. 1944
Hise, Edward, S/Sgt, Co. G 30th Inf, France 30 Oct. 1944
Hites, Louis G., T/5, Hq. Btry 9th FA Bn., Mignano, Italy 17 Nov. 1943
Hobbs, Orville, Pvt, Co. E 7th Inf, France 1 Dec. 1944
Hodge, Forrest W., S/Sgt, Co. L 30th Inf, Raddon, France 17 Sept. 1944
Hodgins, Joseph V., T/Sgt, Co. F 7th Inf, France 20 Nov. 1944
Hodin, Joseph, Pfc, Btry C 9th FA Bn., Maxonschamp, France 25 Sept. 1944
Hodlick, Chester J., Pvt, Btry A 10th FA Bn., Italy 30 Jan. 1944
Hofelich, Richard G., T/Sgt, Co. C 7th Inf, Sicily 21 July 1943
Hoffman, Arthur L., Pfc, Co. G 7th Inf, France 15 Sept. 1944
Hoffner, Albert F., Pfc, Hq. Co. 1st Bn. 7th Inf, France 8 Sept. 1944
Holbrook, Howard C., Cpl, Co. H 30th Inf, Guemar, France 23 Jan. 1945
Holcomb, Frederick C., Pvt, Co. A 7th Inf, Sicily July 1943
Holder, David F., S/Sgt, Co. H 7th Inf, Wihr-en-Plaine, France 28 Mar. 1945
Holder, Oral W., S/Sgt, Co. K 30th Inf, France 23 Jan. 1945
Holder, Walter C., S/Sgt, Hq. Co. 2d Bn. 30th Inf, France 23 Jan. 1945
Holderman, Charles E., Pfc, Hq. Co. 3d Bn. 30th Inf, Guemar, France 23 Jan. 1945
▲Hollen, Norman O., Sgt, Co. B 15th Inf, Sigolsheim, France 26 Dec. 1944
Hollon, Troy B., Cpl, Cn Co. 7th Inf, France 14 Sept. 1944
Hollon, Paul H., 2d Lt, Inf Co. D 7th Inf, Italy 24 May 1944
Holmes, Eldon S., T/5, Med. Det. 30th Inf, Sicily Aug. 1943
Holst, Arne J., Sgt, Co. K 7th Inf, Italy Oct. 1943
Holt, Guy D., Pfc, Co. H 15th Inf, France 2 Sept. 1944
Hommel, Roger C., Jr., Pfc, Co. M 7th Inf, Italy 26 May 1944
Hoobs, Robert E., Sgt, Co. K 15th Inf, Italy 6 Feb. 1944
Hoover, Herbert C., Sgt, Co. E 7th Inf, France 23 Jan. 1945
Hooper, Cpl, Co. B 751st Tank Bn., Italy 23 Oct. 1943
Horan, Philip G., 1st Lt, Co. F 30th Inf, Southern Italy 18 Nov. 1943
Horne, James S., Pfc, Co. B 7th Inf, France 23 Nov. 1944
Horral, Junior N., Pfc (then Pvt),Btry A 9th FA Bn., Sicily 10 Aug. 1943
Horstman, Clarence W., T/Sgt, Co. H 30th Inf, Italy 1 Mar. 1944
Horten, Harold I., Pfc, Co. E 30th Inf, Heppenheim, Germany 27 Mar. 1945
Horton, Rovert V., Capt, Cn Co. 7th Inf, France 7 Sept. 1944
Hosmer, Rawson F., 1st Lt, MC Co. C 3d Med. Bn., Sicily Aug. 1943
Houghtaling, Reid L., T/Sgt, Co. L 15th Inf, Italy 27 Feb. 1944
Houle, Henry J. W., Sgt, Co. A 30th Inf, Italy 5 Feb. 1944
Houlette, Kenneth N., 1st Lt, Inf Hq. Co. 1st Bn. 30th Inf, Eppingh Urbach, Germany 15 Mar. 1945
Howe, David M., Jr., 2d Lt, Co. L 30th Inf, Italy 20 Apr. 1944
Hozan, Martin A., Jr., Cpl, Co. K 30th Inf, Sicily July 1943
Hruska, Lambert J., Capt, Inf 7th Inf, French Morocco 10 Nov. 1942
Hubbs, Clifford L., Pfc, Co. E 7th Inf, 7 Nov. 1944
Hudspeth, Elbert, Sgt, Co. H 7th Inf, Italy 30 Jan. 1944
Huff, Ernest E., S/Sgt, 3d Rcn Trp., Italy, 25 May 1944
Huff, Franklin W., Pfc, Co. F 15th Inf, Nurnberg, Germany 17 Apr. 1945
Huff, Verne R., Sgt, Co. G 30th Inf, France 30 Oct. 1944
Hull, Ellis P., Sgt, Co. G 7th Inf, Houssen, France 25 Jan. 1945
Hulsey, Arthur J., Pfc, Co. K 7th Inf, Italy Oct 1943
Humbert, Robert B., Sgt, Co. F 7th Inf, Utweiler, Germany 15 Mar. 1945
Humiston, LeRoy M., Sgt, Co. F 30th Inf, Zweibrucken, Germany 19 Mar. 1945
▲(2) Hungerford, Grover E., Pfc, Med. Det. 7th Inf, France 25 Jan. 1945
Hunt, Gilbert B., 2d Lt, Co. A 30th Inf, France 18 Aug. 1944
Hurdelbrink, Michael W., Capt, Hq. 15th Inf, Sicily 20 July 1943
Hurl, Charles W., Jr., Pfc, Co. B 30th Inf, France 17 Dec. 1944

Imtroni, Bruno J., Sgt, Co. I 30th Inf, France 18 Aug. 1944
Ingram, Frank J., Pvt, Hq. Co. 2d Bn. 15th Inf, France 26 Oct. 1944
Irelan, Lowell, Pvt, Hq. Co. 30th Inf, Sicily Aug. 1943
Irwin, J. D., S/Sgt, Co. C 30th Inf, France 17 Sept. 1944
Irvin, George O., Pfc, Btry C 35th FA Bn., Sicily 10 July 1943
Isaac, Thomas J., 1st Lt, Hq. 2d Bn. 15th Inf, Italy 29 Feb. 1944
Iuliano, Victor A., Sgt, Co. B 30th Inf, Nurnberg, Germany 19 Apr. 1945
Izenour, Frank M., Lt Col, 1st Bn. 7th Inf, Italy 13 Oct. 1943

Jaber, Edward F., Pfc, Btry B 9th FA Bn., Sicily 5 Aug. 1943
Jablonski, Francis X., Pfc Co. G 7th Inf, France 25 Jan. 1945
Jablonski, Walter M., Pfc, Rcn Co. 601st TD Bn., Italy 29 Feb. 1944
Jachimski, Joseph, Pfc, Hq. Co. 30th Inf, Italy 1 Mar. 1944
Jackson, David P., Pfc, Co. D 7th Inf, Zweibrucken, Germany 18 Mar. 1945
Jackson, Harry R., 1st Lt, FA Btry C 41st FA Bn., France 23 Jan. 1945
Jacobs, Leonard L., 1st Sgt, Co. G 30th Inf, Biesheim, France 1 Feb. 1945
Jacques, Robert E., Sgt, Co. A 15th Inf, Bruyeres, France 21 Oct. 1944
▲Jaffe, Abraham S., 1st Lt, Co. B 7th Inf, France 26 Jan. 1945
▲Jaffe, Abraham S., 1st Lt, Co. B 7th Inf, France 26 Oct. 1944
James, Curtis H., Jr., S/Sgt, Hq. Co. 1st Bn. 7th Inf, Cisterna di Littoria, Italy 1 May 1945
James, Gilbert I, S/Sgt, AT Co. 15th Inf, Nurnberg, Germany 18 Apr. 1945
James, Lawrence A., T/5, Co. A 10th Engr. Bn., Sicily July 1943
Janczuk, Anthony, Pfc, Co. D 15th Inf, St. Ame, France 29 Sept. 1944
Jannone, Michael J., S/Sgt, Co. A 30th Inf, Kayserberg, France 17 Dec. 1944
Janos, John, Pfc, Co. F 30th Inf, Italy 19 Feb. 1944
Janoski, Joseph M., Sgt, Co. M 30th Inf, France 8 Jan. 1945
Janowsky, Bernard B., Pfc, Hq. Co. 3d Bn. 30th Inf, France 27 Oct. 1944
Jarnecke, Lawrence, Cpl, Hq. & Hq. Btry 41st FA Bn., Italy 7 Nov. 1943
Jarvis, John J., Capt, Inf Co. H 7th Inf, Rupt-sur-Moselle, France 28 Sept. 1944
Jeffe, Maxwell S., Sgt, Inf Co. L 30th Inf Regt., Germany 26 Mar. 1945
Jeffs, Owen L., T/Sgt, Co. L 7th Inf, Italy 29 Feb. 1944
Jensen, Jens H., S/Sgt, Co. D 30th Inf, French Morocco 8 Nov. 1942
Jenson, Lloyd K., Capt, Inf S-3 3d Bn. Co. I 30th Inf, Italy 1 June 1944
Jernigan, James C., 1st Lt, Inf AT Co. 7th Inf, Besancon, France 9 Sept. 1944
Jerzyk, Theodore A., Sgt, Rcn Co. 601st TD Bn., Italy 29 Feb. 1944
Jewell, Jesse, Pvt, Co. A 7th Inf, Zweibrucken, Germany 18 Mar. 1945
Jividen, Denver C., Sgt, Co. I 7th Inf, France 15 Sept. 1944
Job, Eugene E., Pfc, Co. G 7th Inf, La Chapelle, France 8 Jan. 1945
Joffe, Maxwell S., Pvt, Co. L 30th Inf, Germany 8 May 1944
▲(2) Johns, Kenneth W., T/Sgt, Co. A 15th Inf, Bois-de-Reidwihr, France 25 Jan. 1945
Johns, Louis L., Cpl, Hq. Co. 30th Inf, Italy 27 May 1944
Johnson, Edwin G., 2d Lt, Hq. Co. 3d Bn. 7th Inf, Italy 31 Jan. 1944
Johnson, Edwin H., S/Sgt, Co. M 30th Inf, Herbeville, France 30 Oct. 1944
Johnson, George W., Pfc, Btry B 39th FA BN., Marshiano, Italy 14 Oct. 1943
Johnson, Herbert G., T/5, Co. D 7th Inf, France 15 Mar. 1945
Johnson, Herman, Pfc, Co. A 7th Inf, Le Haut Jacques, France 5 Nov. 1944
▲Johnson, John J., Pvt, Co. I 15th Inf, Italy 2 Mar. 1944
▲(3) Johnson, Robert E., 1st Lt, Hq. Co. 1st Bn. 30th Inf, Kayserberg, France 4 May 1945
Johnson, Roy, Pfc, Co. I 15th Inf, Sicily Aug. 1943
Johnson, Willard C., 1st Lt, Co. A 30th Inf, France 10 Sept. 1944
Johnson, William T., Cpl, Co. 2d Bn. 30th Inf, France 18 Dec. 1944
Jojola, Joseph R., Pvt, Co. L 7th Inf, Sicily July 1943
Jolley, James E., S/Sgt, Co. F 30th Inf, Germany 8 May 1944
Jones, A. D., S/Sgt, Co. A 30th Inf, France 10 Nov. 1944
Jones, Doyle, 1st Lt, CE Co. B 10th Engr. Bn., France 29 Oct. 1944
Jones, Frank P., 1st Lt, Co. K 15th Inf, Italy 7 Feb. 1944
Jones, Jenkin R., 2d Lt, Btry C 10th FA Bn., Italy 13 Oct. 1943
Jones, Joe B., 2d Lt, Co. I 7th Inf, France 16 Aug. 1944
Jones, John P., S/Sgt, Co. H 7th Inf, France 23 Nov. 1944
Jones, Lewis L., Sgt, Co. I 30th Inf, Italy Aug. 1943
Jones, Ottis M., Pfc, Co. M 15th Inf, Gadheim, Germany 12 Apr. 1945
Jones, Robert C., Sgt, Co. A 10th Engr. Bn., Italy 2 Feb. 1944
Jones, Robert M., 1st Lt, FA Hq. Btry 39th FA Bn., Anzio, Italy 28 Feb. 1944
Jones, Robert V., Pfc, Co. M 15th Inf, France 25 Jan. 1945
Jones, Thomas A., S/Sgt, Co. A 30th Inf, France 16 Dec. 1944
Joppa, Andrew, 1st Sgt, Co. C 15th Inf, France 4 Feb. 1945
Jordan, John J., S/Sgt, Co. D 7th Inf, Anzio, Italy 29 Feb. 1944
Josephs, Clarence E., T/4, Med. Det. 10th Engr. Bn., Italy 24 Oct. 1943
▲Josowitz, Edward L., 1st Lt, Rcn Co. 601st TD Bn., Sollis Point, France 19 Aug. 1944

▲ Oak Leaf Cluster.

Joyner, Alton, Pfc, Anti-tank Co. 30th Inf, Colmar 20 Feb. 1945
Juarez, Frank M., Pfc, Co. D 7th Inf, Sicily July 1943
Juarez, Paz M., Pfc, Co. D 3d Med. Bn., Sicily July 1943
Juliano, Jennarino S., T/5, Co. I 30th Inf, Waldhausen, Germany 24 Apr. 1945
Jurgensen, Robert H., Pfc, Co. K 7th Inf, Ormersvillers, France 15 Mar. 1945

Kalmanowitz, Morris, S/Sgt, Co. A 7th Inf, Italy 3 Mar. 1944
Kane, Hayden W., S/Sgt, Co. C 30th Inf, Sermersheim 1 Dec. 1944
Karbowski, John R., Sgt, Co. A 15th Inf, France 31 Oct. 1944
Karls, Sylvester C., Sgt, Co. A 15th Inf, Italy 5 June 1944
Karrib, Louis J., Pvt, Hq. Co. 84th Cml. Bn., Italy 14 Feb. 1944
Karten, Everett (NMI),Pfc, Hq. Co. 2d Bn. 7th Inf, Sicily Aug. 1943
Kavachevich, Leo M., Pfc, Co. H 15th Inf, Sicily Aug. 1943
Kazaroff, Albert, Pfc, Co. L 30th Inf, Guemar, France 23 Jan. 1945
Keator, Harry D., T/Sgt, Co. C 15th Inf, France 25 Jan. 1945
Keene, William F., 2d Lt, Inf Co. B 30th Inf, Epping Urbach, Germany 16 Mar. 1945
Keith, Elmer M., S/Sgt, Co. A 15th Inf, France 5 Oct. 1944
Kelsey, Robert M., Pvt, At Co. 30th Inf, France 19 Aug. 1944
Keller, Charles L., Pfc, Med. Det. 15th Inf, France 24 Dec. 1944
Keller, Charles L., S/Sgt, Co. D 7th Inf, France 4 Nov. 1944
Keller, James E., S/Sgt, Co. M 15th Inf, Italy 2 Mar. 1944
Kelley, Andrew, S/Sgt, Co. G 15th Inf, France 3 Nov. 1944
Kelley, Irving B., S/Sgt, Co. B 15th Inf, France 26 Jan. 1944
▲Kelley, Thomas J., 1st Lt, Co. A 601st TD Bn., France 3 Feb. 1945
Kemp, James L., M/Sgt, 3d Sig. Co., Italy Nov. 1943
Kemper, William H., S/Sgt, Co. L 30th Inf, Colmar 20 Feb. 1945
Kennedy, Edward H., CWO, 3d Sig. Co., Mannheim, Germany 26 Mar. 1945
Kennedy, Frank J., Hq. Co. 30th Inf, Italy 20 Feb. 1944
Kennelly, Patrick C., Sgt, Co. D 7th Inf, Grandrupt, France 20 Nov. 1944
Kent, Royal P., 2d Lt, Inf Co. A 15th Inf, France 25 Nov. 1944
Kent, William K., Sgt, Co. C 756th Tank Bn., Germany 21 Mar. 1945
Kenyon, Allen R., 1st Lt, 3d Rcn Trp., Italy 23 Jan. 1944
Kerns, Delbert D., Pfc, Co. C 30th Inf, Wickerschwihr, France 27 Jan. 1945
Kesner, Sam, Capt, CWS Hq. 3d Inf Div., San Tropez, France 15 Aug. 1944
Ketcher, Clyde, Pvt, Co. B 15th Inf, Italy 24 May 1944
▲Ketron, Ivan, S/Sgt, Co. A 15th Inf, Germany 7 Apr. 1945
▲(2) Ketron, Ivan, S/Sgt, Co. A 15th Inf, Nurnberg, Germany 7 Apr. 1945
Keyes, Robert R., Jr., Cpl, Co. C 601st TD Bn., Unter Steinbach, Germany 13 Apr. 1945
Kilduff, Thomas C., Pfc, Co. M 30th Inf, France 28 Oct. 1944
Killian, James H., Pfc, Co. C 30th Inf, Germany 8 May 1944
Kimbrell, Donald L., T/Sgt, Co. H 15th Inf, Hot de Tot, France 10 Oct. 1944
Kinderman, George T., Pfc, Hq. Co. 3d Bn. 15th Inf, Germany 28 Apr. 1945
King, Delbert W., S/Sgt, Inf Co. E 7th Inf, Regt., France 23 Jan. 1945
King, John E., 2d Lt, Co. H 15th Inf, Italy 5 Mar. 1944
▲Kinney, Oliver G., Lt Col, Inf, 30th Inf, Italy 30 Jan. 1944
▲Kinter, Kenneth E., 2d Lt, Co. I 15th Inf, Germany 20 Apr. 1945
Kinunen, Raino H., Pfc, 3d Rcn Trp., Italy 28 Oct. 1943
Kirk, Arthur T., Pvt, Bp 15th Inf, Italy 16 Mar. 1944
Kirchner, Patrick M., Pfc, Co. C 30th Inf, Vosges 5 Dec. 1944
Kirschbaum, Lester H., Cpl, Co. A 30th Inf, Sicily July 1943
Kirtley, Herman C., 2d Lt, Inf, Co. C 756th Tank Bn., St. Die, France 17 Oct. 1944
Kitchin, Joseph O., T/4, Hq. Co. 2d Bn. 7th Inf, Utweiler, Germany 15 Mar. 1945
Kitchens, Emory H., Pfc, Co. F 7th Inf, Hohemreichen, Germany 25 Apr. 1945
Kiwatisky, Nicholas F., T/Sgt, Co. B 30th Inf, Colmar 20 Feb. 1945
Kizer, Lee T., Sgt, Co. D 15th Inf, Nurnberg, Germany 19 Apr. 1945
Klaes, James E., Sgt, Co. L 30th Inf, Italy 22 Sept. 1943
Klaus, Robert W., T/5, Co. C 30th Inf, Germany 8 May 1944
Kleaver, Otis, Pfc, Co. E 30th Inf, Hofheim, Germany 26 Mar. 1945
Kleeman, Arthur E., Co. A 30th Inf, France 25 Dec. 1944
Klein, Edward H., S/Sgt, Co. A 7th Inf, France 29 Jan. 1945
Kleinschmidt, Robert J., T/Sgt, Co. F 15th Inf, Italy 29 Feb. 1944
Klementowicz, Joseph S., Pvt, Co. C 30th Inf, Sicily Aug. 1943
Klemetnowicz, Leon, Pfc, Co. D 30th Inf, France 17 Dec. 1944
Klinger, Leroy L., Pvt, Co. G 15th Inf, Italy 31 Jan. 1944
Klinkenborg, Ray J., 1st Lt, Co. E 15th Inf, Italy 29 Feb. 1944
Knapp, Marlin R., Pfc, Co. M 30th Inf, France 18 Dec. 1944
Knight, Robert, S/Sgt, Co. C 15th Inf, Althornbach, Germany 18 Mar. 1945
Knox, Lawrence E., Sgt, Co. A 7th Inf, Italy 30 Jan. 1944
Knudson, Harold E., Sgt, Hq. Btry 39th FA Bn., Italy 22 Jan. 1944
Kobernick, John W., T/4, Co. B 30th Inf, Italy 24 Apr. 1944
Koering, Arthur C., T/4, Med. Det. 15th Inf, Mortagne, France 25 Oct. 1944
Kohrmann, Virgil J., S/Sgt, Co. E 7th Inf, Italy 23 May 1944
Kokaszka, Louis J., Pfc, Co. E 15th Inf, France 17 Sept. 1944
Kopatick, Louis J., Sgt, Serv. Co. 7th Inf, Kunehim, France 13-14 Feb. 1945
Koss, Fred, S/Sgt, Co. M 30th Inf, Herbaville, France 30 Oct. 1944
Koss, Walter S., S/Sgt, Co. M 30th Inf, Lampertheim, Germany 26 Mar. 1945
Kotz, Raymond, Sgt, Co. F 7th Inf, French Morocco 10 Nov. 1942
▲Kovatch, Merle S., Sgt, Co. B 7th Inf, Zweibrucken, Germany 18 Mar. 1945
Kramlich, Ewald, S/Sgt, Co. L 15th Inf, Italy 23 May 1944
Krause, Harry F., Sgt, Co. D 15th Inf, France 7 Nov. 1944
▲Kreis, Jonnie F., Sgt, Co. D 7th Inf, Guiderkurch, 15 Mar. 1945
Kresoya, Leonard, 1st Lt, CWS, Co. D 84th Cml. Bn., Italy 1 Mar. 1944
▲Krichbaum, Milo D., 1st Lt, 15th Inf, Italy 27 Jan. 1944
Krichbaum, Milo D., 1st Lt, Inf, 15th Inf, Italy 7 Nov. 1943
Krieger, Alfred R., S/Sgt, Hq. & Hq. Co. 1st Bn., 15th Inf, Bois de Durrenentzen, France 1 Feb. 1945
Krueger, William C., T/Sgt, Co. L 30th Inf, Anzio, Italy 28 Feb. 1944
Krug, Charles E., Jr., S/Sgt, Co. C 30th Inf, France 7 Sept. 1944
Kuckkan, Edward H., Pvt, Hq. Co. 2d Bn. 7th Inf, 2 June 1944
Kuhns, Edwin C., Cpl, Co. B 3d Med. Bn., Sicily Aug. 1943
Kukis, Anthony J., 1st Lt, Co. A 756th Tank Bn., 25 Jan. 1945
Kunde, Arthur A., S/Sgt, Co. B 10th Engr., France 11 Sept. 1944
▲Kvaas, Martin G., 1st Lt, Inf Co. A 7th Inf, Sandhofen, Germany 26 Mar. 1945
Kyle, Woods B., Jr., 2d Lt, Co. L 15th Inf, France 9 Sept. 1944

La Boch, Harry, Pfc, Co. F 15th Inf, Nurnberg, Germany 17 Apr. 1945
Labuta, George J., Sgt, Co. G 15th Inf, Italy 27 Jan. 1944
LaDouce, Edward H., S/Sgt, Co. M 30th Inf, Colmar 20 Feb. 1945
Laeser, Walter E., S/Sgt, Hq. Co. 1st Bn. 30th Inf, Nurnberg, Germany 19 Apr. 1945
Lafata, William, Pfc, Co. F 7th Inf, Germany 31 Mar. 1945
La. Fevre, Lawrence C., 1st Lt, Co. H 7th Inf, La Croix, France 15 Aug. 1944
Laha, Milburn E., Pfc, Med. Det. 30th Inf, Sicily Aug. 1943
Lahr, Charles, Jr., 1st Lt, Co. H 30th Inf, France 18 Aug. 1944
Lambert, Joseph G., 1st Lt, Hq. Co. 2d Bn. 7th Inf, Germany 2 Apr. 1945
Lambert, Lauren D., 1st Lt, FA Hq. Btry 41st FA Bn., Sicily Aug. 1943
Landucci, Oscar, Pvt, Co. I 30th Inf, Italy 1 June 1944
Lane, Victor K., Pfc, Co. K 15th Inf, Italy 29 Feb. 1944
Lang, Lawrence J., 2d Lt, Co. A 756th Tank Bn., Rimschweiler, Germany 19 Mar. 1945
Langston, Roy, Sgt, Co. G 7th Inf, Sicily July 1943
Lanier, Charles M., Pvt, Med. Det. 7th Inf, Italy 1 Feb. 1944
Larence, Robert J., Pfc, Co. A 15th Inf, France 21 Aug. 1944
Large, William E., Cpl, Hq. Btry 3d IDA, France 3 Nov. 1944
Larger, Charles, Jr., Sgt, Btry C 441st AAA (AW) Bn., Italy 15 Oct. 1943
▲Larimore, Philip B., Capt, Co. L 30th Inf, Germany 8 Apr. 1945
LaRose, Murray K., T/5, 3d Rcn Trp., Ober Thulba, Germany 12 Apr. 1945
Larrabee, Robert A., Pfc, Med. Det. 30th Inf, France 31 Jan. 1945
Larsen, Kenneth C., Sgt, Co. E 30th Inf, Sicily July 1943
Larsen, Ward F., T/4, Med. Det. 30th Inf, Sicily Aug. 1943
Larson, John W., Pfc, Co. F 30th Inf, French Morocco 8 Nov. 1942
Larson, Rudolph E., Sgt, Co. B 601st TD Bn., Italy 30 May 1944
Larson, Thomas A., 1st Lt, Co. C 15th Inf, Italy 24 May 1944
Larweck, Franklyn A., Pvt, Co. E 15th Inf, Germany 17 Apr. 1945
LaSala, Patsy, Pfc, Co. 30th Inf, Siegfried Line 19 Mar. 1945
Lauderdale, George W., Capt, Co. K 7th Inf, France 24 Sept. 1944
Lauffer, William P., T/5, Co. C 10th Engr. Bn., France 17 Dec. 1944
Laughlin, Virgil V., 2d Lt, Co. M 15th Inf, Sicily Aug. 1943
Laughlin, William H., S/Sgt, Co. I 30th Inf, Italy 28 Jan. 1944
Laurent, Harry E., Sgt, Inf Co. M 30th Inf, Italy 23 May 1944
Lavalley, Alfred, Pvt, Co. G 30th Inf, France 9 Nov. 1944
▲LeVasseur, Joseph L. M., Pfc, Co. A 30th Inf, Roussit, France 27 Aug. 1944
Lavin, Douglas E., Pfc, Rcn Co. 601st TD Bn., Italy Sept. 1943
Lavner, Nathan, Pfc, AT Co. 30th Inf, Ill River, France 23 Jan. 1945
Law, Bobby L., Pfc, Co. F 15th Inf, Contwig, Germany 23 Mar. 1945
Laweka, Bicuwa, Cpl, Co. D 30th Inf, Riedwihr, France 24 Jan. 1945
▲Lawing, Elmer H., Pfc, Co. C 30th Inf, France 19 Aug. 1944
Leas, John B., 2d Lt, Inf BP 7th Inf, France 15 Aug. 1944
Leassner, John F., S/Sgt, Co. D 7th Inf, France 5 Oct. 1944
Leavitt, Edwin, Sgt, Co. A 3d Med. Bn., Sicily Aug. 1943
Leavitt, Wendell D., 2d Lt, Co. B 7th Inf, France 24 Nov. 1944
Le Blanc, Gerald C., T/Sgt, Co. A 15th Inf, Froteyles Vesoul, France 12 Sept. 1944
Lebo, Leonard, 1st Lt, Co. A 601st TD Bn., France 24 Jan. 1945
Lebowitz, Julian L., S/Sgt, Co. A 15th Inf, Riedwihr, France 24 Jan. 1945
Lee, Rabum A., Sgt, Co. M 30th Inf, Anzio, Italy 5 June 1944
Lee, Wilmer L., 1st Lt, Inf Co. B 15th Inf, Althronbach, Germany 18 Mar. 1945
Lefler, Homer M., Capt, Co. C 10th Engr. Bn., Italy 3 Nov. 1943
Lehman, Jack B., 2d Lt, Co. L 7th Inf, Italy 5 Mar. 1944
Leithner, Joseph W., Jr., S/Sgt, Co. L 15th Inf, France 27 Aug. 1944
▲Leitner, Eric F., S/Sgt, Bt. Patrol 7th Inf, Italy 26 Mar. 1944
Leo, Arman F., Sgt, Co. M 30th Inf, Italy 29 Feb. 1944
Leonard, Alton A., Jr., S/Sgt, Co. F 7th Inf, France 1 Dec. 1944
Leppar, Frank D., Pvt, Co. A 7th Inf, French Morocco Nov. 1942
Lesnieski, Raymond, T/5, Co. C 10th Engr. Bn., France 17 Dec. 1944
Letendre, Lawrence A., Pfc, Co. H 30th Inf, Holtzwihr, France 27 Jan. 1945
LeValley, Alfred, Pfc, Co. G 30th Inf, Vosges 5 Dec. 1944
Levin, Joseph I., Pfc, Co. F 15th Inf, Germany 7 Apr. 1945
Levy, Eli, Capt, Inf Co. I 7th Inf, Saales, France 22 Nov. 1944
Levy, Harold, 1st Lt, Co. C 756th Tank. Bn., Seigfried Line 17 Mar. 1945
Lewis, Abel, Sgt, Co. E 30th Inf, Nurnberg, Germany 19 Apr. 1945
Lewis, Byon P., T/Sgt, Co. I 15th Inf, Italy 2 Feb. 1944
Lewis, Donald E., Pfc, Co. G 15th Inf, Achsheim, Germany 29 Apr. 1945
Lewis, Wilbur F., 2d Lt, Co. L 30th Inf, S. France 12 Sept. 1944
Lian, Luverne, Pfc, Co. F 15th Inf, Nurnberg, Germany 17 Apr. 1945
Licht, Edmund F., Pfc, Co. B 30th Inf, Aix, France 22 Aug. 1944
Liggett, Delbert E., S/Sgt, Co. B 30th Inf, France 20 Aug. 1944
Light, Paul B., Cpl, 3d Rcn Trp., Sicily July 1943
Lile, Irvin M., Sgt, 3d Rcn Trp., Sicily July 1943
Lilevjen, Hugh A., S/Sgt, Cn Co. 7th Inf, France 3 Oct. 1944
Lillie, Roy L., Pfc, Co. B 15th Inf, Sicily 6 Aug. 1943
Lilly, Daniel T., Pfc, Co. E 7th Inf, Italy 23 May 1944
Lindert, Gordon O., 1st Sgt, Co. F 7th Inf, Ferdrupt, France 30 Sept. 1944
Lindsay, Floyd E., S/Sgt, Co. M 7th Inf, Regheim, Germany 11 Apr. 1945
Lindsay, Frank E., Pfc, Co. M 15th Inf, Riedwihr, France 25 Jan. 1945
Lindsay, Joseph F., Pfc, Hq. Co. 7th Inf, Italy 24 May 1944
Lindstrom, Floyd K., Pvt, Co. K 7th Inf, Sicily July 1943
Linville, Wayne A., Cpl, Hq. Co. 15th Inf, Sicily July 1943
Livingston, Robert B., T/4, Btry B 9th FA Bn., Sicily 5 Aug. 1943
Locascio, Peter, Pfc, Co. M 7th Inf, Italy Nov. 1943
Loeser, Edgar C., Pfc, Btry C 9th FA Bn., Sicily Aug. 1943
Lohman, Richard H., Pfc, Co. B 30th Inf, France 17 Dec. 1944
Lombard, William E., Pfc, Hq. Co. 30th Inf, Sicily July 1943
Long, Billy M., Pfc, Co. M 30th Inf, Anzio, Italy 5 June 1944
Long, Roland G., 1st Lt, Inf Hq. Co. 1st Bn. 15th Inf, Bois de Riedwihr, France 25 Jan. 1945
Long, William A., S/Sgt, AT Co. 15th Inf, Fome, Italy 4 June 1944
Long, William G., 1st Lt, Co. A 15th Inf, France 25 Jan. 1945
Longcrier, Herbert H., S/Sgt, Hq. Co. 3d Bn. 7th Inf, Italy 23 Apr. 1944
Loomis, Robert C., Sgt, Co. A 30th Inf, France 18 Aug. 1944
Looman, Victor, Pfc, Co. F 30th Inf, Italy 25 Apr. 1944
Looney, Leon P., Pfc, Co. H 7th Inf, Houssen, France 24 Jan. 1945
Lopez, John J., Pfc, Co. H 30th Inf, France 19 Sept. 1944
Lopez, John O., Sgt, Co. B 30th Inf, Italy 22 Oct. 1943
Lorah, Henry, Pvt, Hq. Co. 30th Inf, Sicily July 1943
Lostumbo, Dominick J., 1st Lt, Co. L 7th Inf, Noroy le Bourg 13 Sept. 1944
▲(2) Lottman, Vernon G., S/Sgt, Co. D 30th Inf, Riedwihr, France 23 Jan. 1945
Lotze, Milton R., Cpl, Co. F 30th Inf, France Nov. 1944
Loup, Benjamin E., Pfc, Co. F 7th Inf, Montelimar, France 30 Aug. 1944
Lovaas, Bernie V., T/5, Co. A 3d Med. Bn., Sicily Aug. 1943
Lovell, Ottice, T/4, 3d Sig. Co., Italy 29 May 1944
Lovington, Albert E., T/5, 30th Inf, 11 Aug. 1943
Lowery, Lewis O., Sgt, Co. H 7th Inf, Cisterna, Italy 30 Jan. 1944

▲ Oak Leaf Cluster.

Lowman, Richard M., Pvt, Co. H 7th Inf, Italy 22 Feb. 1944
Lucas, Robert R., Pfc, Co. M 30th Inf, La Bolle, France 30 Oct. 1944
Lucima, Jeroma, Pfc, Hq. & Hq. Btry 41st FA Bn., Italy 7 Nov. 1943
Lucisano, Frank A., Sgt, Hq. Co. 2d Bn. 15th Inf, France 2 Nov. 1944
Lukatch, John J., Pvt, Hq. Co. 2d Bn. 15th Inf, Italy Aug. 1943
Lukenbill, Alfred L., S/Sgt, Co. E 7th Inf, Biesheim, France 3 Feb. 1945
Lutterman, Vincent J., T/4, Co. D 7th Inf, Anzio, Italy 29 Feb. 1944
Lutz, Kenneth R., Pfc, 3d Rcn Trp., Sicily July 1943
Lynch, Clyde R., Cpl, Co. I 7th Inf, French Morocco 9Nov. 1942
Lynch, Edward J., Pfc, Hq. Co. 30th Inf, Vosges 5 Dec. 1944
Lynch, James C., 1st Lt, Co. C 7th Inf, Italy 2 June 1944
Lynch, James C., Cpl, 3d Rcn Trp., Sicily July 1943
Lyons, Harold L., Pfc, Co. I 30th Inf, Kaysersberg, France 1 Jan. 1945
Lyons, William J., S/Sgt, Co. F 7th Inf, Italy 25 May 1944

Mackerchar, John A., Sgt, Hq. Co. 1st Bn. 15th Inf, France 8 Nov. 1944
Mackey, John C., Sgt, Hq. Co. 2d Bn. 30th Inf, Sicily July 1943
MacLean, Angus B., 2d Lt, Inf Co. L 30th Inf, Germany 16 Mar. 1945
▲Macklin, Lenny A., Pfc, Co. I 7th Inf, Italy Oct. 1943
MacPherson, John S., Sgt, Co. F 30th Inf, Burstadt, Germany 27 Mar. 1945
MacPherson, Kenneth W., Pfc, Co. B 30th Inf, France 17 Dec. 1944
Macon, Robert C., Col, Inf 7th Inf, French Morocco 10 Nov. 1942
Maddox, Earl E., Pfc, Co. A 15th Inf, France 28 Aug. 1944
Madey, Walter S., T/4, Hq. Co. 3d Bn. 7th Inf, Artena, Italy 26 May 1944
Madrid, Thomas R., T/4, Co. H 30th Inf, Guemar, France 23 Jan. 1945
Madsen, Harold, S/Sgt, Co. I 15th Inf, Italy 26 Jan. 1944
Magnuson, Edwin L., Sgt, Co. L 15th Inf, Italy Oct. 1943
▲Magurany, William A., 1st Lt, Inf Co. A 756th Tank Bn., Germany 17 Apr. 1945
Mahony, John E., Jr., Pfc, Co. C 7th Inf, France 6 Oct. 1944
Mai, Clarence W., Sgt, Co. G 7th Inf, Utweiler, Germany 15 Mar. 1945
Main, Robert R., 1st Lt, Co. I 15th Inf, France 26 Oct. 1944
Majerus, Joseph F., Pvt, Co. B 30th Inf, France 17 Dec. 1944
Malaussena, James E., S/Sgt, Co. A 15th Inf, France 15 Aug. 1944
Mancuso, Vincent J., Sgt, Co. C 7th Inf, Nurnberg, Germany 19 Apr. 1945
Mandit, Joseph, T/5, Med. Det. 15th Inf, Italy 23 May 1944
Maness, William H., S/Sgt, 3d Rcn Trp., Italy 5 June 1944
Mangina, Frank, Pfc, Co. L 15th Inf, France 21 Oct. 1944
Manhart, Ashton H., Lt Col, Inf 15th Inf, Italy 10 July 1943
Marchant, Julian M., 1st Lt, Inf Co. K 15th Inf, Salz, Germany 8 Apr. 1945
Marchel, Benjamin J., Pfc, Co. E 30th Inf, France 27 Jan. 1945
Marchunsky, Albert J., Pfc, Co. D 7th Inf, Rupt-sur-Moselle, France 4 Oct. 1944
Marcum, Donald, S/Sgt, Co. L 15th Inf, Italy 30 Jan. 1944
Marcus, Philip W., Capt, Co. B 30th Inf, Sicily 6 Aug. 1943
Marek, Delfin E., 1st Lt, Inf Co. C 15th Inf, Nurnberg, Germany 20 Apr. 1945
Marek, Roger V., Jr., Pfc, Med. Det. 39th FA Bn., Borgo, Italy 24 Jan. 1944
Marella, John J., Pfc, Co. G 7th Inf, Cisterna, Italy 25 May 1944
Marinelli, Carmine D., Pfc, Med. Det. 30th Inf, Sicily Aug. 1943
Marion, Elbert R., Pfc, Co. B 10th Engr., France 11 Sept. 1944
▲Marion, Grady W., Pfc, Co. D 15th Inf, France 1 Oct. 1944
Marker, Dale M., Pfc, Co. L 15th Inf, France 21 Oct. 1944
Marmillion, Norman J., 1st Lt, Co. G 15th Inf, France 2 Feb. 1945
Maroney, Frederick B., Pfc, Co. F 15th Inf, Contwig, Germany 23 Mar. 1945
Marsh, Robert D., Capt, Ind. 2d Bn. 7th Inf, La Rosierie, France 23 Sept. 1944
Marsh, Ted L., Pfc, Hq. Co. (BP) 7th Inf, France 2 Nov. 1944
Marshall, Edward L., Pfc, Hq. Co. 2d Bn. 30th Inf, Sicily 11 Aug. 1943
Marshall, Fred E., Pfc, Co. L 30th Inf, Italy 10 Nov. 1943
Marshall, Robert P., T/5, Btry A 39th FA Bn., Sicily Aug. 1943
▲(2) Marszalek, Frank J., Sgt, Co. D 30th Inf, Riedwihr, France 23 Jan. 1945
Martin, Chester L., Pfc, Hq. Co. 30th Inf, Italy 29 Feb. 1944
Martin, Joseph E., Capt, Hq. Co. 2d Bn. 7th Inf, Rodenbach, Germany 2 Apr. 1945
Martin, Numa E., Pfc, Co. G 30th Inf, Italy 18 Mar. 1944
Martin, Roy E., Pvt, Med. Det. 30th Inf, Italy Oct. 1943
Martinez, John H., Pvt, Med. Det. 7th Inf, French Morocco 10 Nov. 1942
Martinez, Max R., Sgt, Co. E 30th Inf, Italy 3 June 1944
Martinez, Raul M., Pfc, Co. F 7th Inf, Italy 17 Feb. 1944
Martinson, Ole M., T/Sgt, Co. E 7th Inf, Italy 2 Feb. 1944
Marvel, Roland J., Sgt, Co. E 30th Inf, Germany 19 Apr. 1945
Marvin, Robert A., S/Sgt, Co. A 7th Inf, French Morocco 10 Nov. 1942
Marvin, Robert J., Cpl, Cavalry, 3d Rcn Trp., Italy 2 Feb. 1944
Marzalek, Frank J., Pfc, Co. D 30th Inf, S. France 12 Sept. 1944
Mason, Maurice J., S/Sgt, Co. L 15th Inf, Italy 13 Oct. 1943
Matlcok, Henry A., 1st Lt, Btry B 30th FA Bn., Italy 21 Oct. 1943
Matuszewski, Louis, Pvt, Hq. Co. 3d Bn. 15th Inf, Italy 11 Nov. 1943
Maulshagen, Adolph J., Jr., S/Sgt, Co. K 30th Inf, France 27 Oct. 1944
Maxfield, Robert J., S/Sgt, Co. G 15th Inf, France 9 Sept. 1944
▲Maxwell, Robert D., Pfc, Hq. Co. 3d Bn. 7th Inf, Besancon, France 7 Sept. 1944
Mayer, John J., 1st Lt, Co. I 30th Inf, Italy 29-30 Jan. 1944
Mayhew, John R., 1st Lt, Hq. Co. 1st Bn. 7th Inf, France 23 Jan. 1945
Mayhew, Ralph E., T/Sgt, Co. C 15th Inf, Italy 27 Jan. 1944
Mayhugh, Delbert P., Pfc, Hq. Co. 2d Bn. 7th Inf, Sicily Aug. 1943
Mayne, Ernest L., Sgt, Med. Det. 30th Inf, Sicily Aug. 1943
Mayo, Hershel V., Pfc, Co. B 30th Inf, St. Die, France 28 Oct. 1944
Mayo, John Arthur, Sgt, Co. B 7th Inf, Sicily July 1943
Mays, Howard A., S/Sgt, Armored Co. B 756th Tank Bn., Germany 19 Mar. 1945
McAllister, Wallace B., T/Sgt, Hq. Co. 3d Bn. 30th Inf, Italy 16 Feb. 1944
McBee, Roy C., Pfc, Co. I 30th Inf, France 8 Jan. 1945
McBride, R. J., Sgt, Co. E 15th Inf, Germany 17 Apr. 1945
McCallum, Garvice H., S/Sgt, Co. B 30th Inf, Italy 27 Apr. 1944
McCarry, Earl J., Sgt, Co. I 7th Inf, French Morocco 9 Nov. 1942
McCarty, Winn, Sgt, Co. A 7th Inf, Ostheim, France 23 Jan. 1945
McClelland, George D., 1st Lt, Chc 7th Inf, French Morocco 10 Nov. 1942
McConaghey, David L., T/4, Co. A 756th Tank Bn., France 27 Aug. 1944
McConnell, John P., 2d Lt, 1st Bn. 7th Inf, France 29 Sept. 1944
McCord, Clarence F., S/Sgt (then T/4), Med. Det. 30th Inf, Italy 8 Oct. 1943
McCrea, Paul J., Pvt, Med. Det. 2d Bn. 7th Inf, Sicily Aug. 1943
McCullough, Addison F., Sgt, Hq. Co. 30th Inf, Sicily 20 July 1944
McCullough, John D., 1st Lt, Inf Co. I 30th Inf, Kayserberg, France 16 Dec. 1944
McDavid, Lewis L., Pvt, Med. Det. 30th Inf, Italy 11 Feb. 1944
McDermid, Alton J., Cpl, Co. C 7th Inf, French Morocco 10 Nov. 1942
McDermott, Robert J., Sgt, Co. C 10th Engr. Bn., Italy 26 May 1944
McDonald, Richard F., T/Sgt, Co. M 30th Inf, Italy 29 Jan. 1944
McDonald, Thurman V., T/5, 36th FA Bn., Sicily 10 July 1943
McDonough, James V., 1st Lt, Co. L 30th Inf, Italy 23 May 1944
McDougall, John J., Pfc, Co. K 15th Inf, Nurnberg, Germany 19 Apr. 1945
McEiroy, Robert C., S/Sgt, Co. C 601st TD Bn., France 18 Aug. 1944
McElhose, Harold M., Pvt, Co. K 30th Inf, Sicily Aug. 1943
McEnvoy, Robert R., Pfc, Co. G 30th Inf, Germany 15 Apr. 1945
McFalls, Carroll, Jr., 1st Lt, Co. M 30th Inf, Italy 17 Feb. 1944
McFeeley, Charles J., T/5, 3d Rcn Trp., Zweibrucken, Germany 18 Mar. 1945
▲McGarr, Lionel C., Lt Co, Co. 30th Inf, Italy 25 Jan. 1944
McGee, James, 1st Lt, 3d Rcn Trp., France 15 Sept. 1944
McGhan, Paul V., 1st Lt, Co. K 7th Inf, Italy 31 Jan. 1944
McGinnis, James F., S/Sgt, Co. F 7th Inf, Cisterna Di Litorria, Italy 16 Feb. 1944
McGowan, George A., 2d Lt, Inf 30th Inf, Sicily July 1943
McGregor, Charles, Sgt, Co. C 30th Inf, Italy 1 Feb. 1944
McGregor, Charles, Sgt, Co. B 30th Inf, Anzio, Italy 5 June 1944
McGregor, Richard W., S/Sgt, Hq. & Hq. Btry 41st FA Bn., Sicily Aug. 1943
McGrew, Senia N., 1st Lt, Co. M 30th Inf, Italy 23 May 1944
McGuire, Francis J., Pvt, Med. Det. 15th Inf, Italy 8 Nov. 1943
McGuire, Lloyd, T/Sgt, Med. Det. 30th Inf, Sicily Aug. 1943
McIntosh, Jackson, Sgt, Co. F 7th Inf, Neunhof, Germany 17 Apr. 1945
McIntyre, James L., S/Sgt, Co. F 7th Inf, Houssen, France 25 Jan. 1945
McKinney, Charles W., Sgt, Co. L 30th Inf, Ober Thulba, Germany 7 Apr. 1945
McKinney, Lee K., S/Sgt, Co. E 30th Inf, Nurnberg, Germany 19 Apr. 1945
McLavid, Lewis L., Pvt, Med. Det. 30th Inf, Anzio, Italy 5 June 1944
McLean, Parrish M., Pfc, Co. E 7th Inf, Gemunden, Germany 6 Apr. 1945
McNutt, John T., S/Sgt, Med. Det. 9th FA Bn., Sicily Aug. 1943
McPhaill, James C., 1st Lt, Co. D 30th Inf, La Bihay, France 7 Nov. 1944
McQueen, Harry L., T/4, Hq. Co. 30th Inf, Italy 20 Feb. 1944
McQueen, Howard L., 1st Lt, Hq. Co. 2d Bn. 30th Inf, Italy 3 June 1944
Meachum, Hubert J., 2d Lt, Co. A 30th Inf, France 21 Aug. 1944
Meador, Howe, S/Sgt, Hq. Co. 1st Bn. 15th Inf, Mellrichstadt, Germany 7 Apr. 1945
Medeiros, Joseph, T/5, Co. H 7th Inf, Italy 29 Feb. 1944
Medina, Jose D., Pfc, Co. I 15th Inf, Italy 8 Feb. 1944
Medina, Lorenzo, Pfc, Co. F 7th Inf, Utweiler, Germany 15 Mar. 1945
Meek, William R., Sgt, Co. A 10th Engr. Bn., France 24 Sept. 1944
Mees, Arthur C., Cpl, Hq. Co. 3d Bn. 15th Inf, Sicily Aug. 1943
Mehl, William W., Sgt, Co. B 7th Inf, Italy 30 Jan. 1944
Mehuren, Gerald G., 2d Lt, Inf Co. I 30th Inf Regt., Germany 15 Mar. 1945
Meindl, Albert S., Pvt, Co. K 30th Inf, Sicily July 1943
Meisky, Richard D., Capt, Inf Co. A 751st Tank Bn., Italy 4 Nov. 1943
Melcher, Donald F., Pfc, Med. Det. 30th Inf, Lampertheim, Germany 26 Mar. 1945
Melchor, Ysabel, Pfc, Co. D 7th Inf, Nurnberg, Germany 18 Apr. 1945
Melgard, William J., 2d Lt, Co. C 7th Inf, Italy 16 Oct. 1943
▲(2) Mellard, Robert B., T/Sgt, Co. D 30th Inf, Germany 26 Mar. 1945
Mellert, Roger J., Sgt, Co. M 30th Inf, France 17 Dec. 1944
Merashoff, Robert, T/Sgt, Co. G 30th Inf, France 30 Oct. 1944
Meredith, Elaon O., Pfc, Co. M 7th Inf, Italy 31 Jan. 1944
Merrick, Charles D., Pfc, Co. B 30th Inf, Italy 27 Jan. 1944
Messina, Angelo L., Pfc, Co. A 15th Inf, France 15 Aug. 1944
Meszaros, Stephen W., Pfc, Med. Det. 15th Inf, France 24 Dec. 1944
Metcalf, Charles E., 2d Lt, Inf Hq. Co. 2d Bn. 30th Inf, Sicily Aug. 1943
Metz, Robert L., 1st Lt, FA Btry C 10th FA Bn., Anzio, Italy 11-22 Mar. 1944
Meyers, George, Pfc, Co. C 7th Inf, French Morocco 10 Nov. 1942
Meyers, Maurice, Pfc, Co. C 7th Inf, Sandhofen, Germany 26 Mar. 1945
▲Meyer, Otto C., Pfc, Co. B 30th Inf, France 17 Dec. 1944
Miceli, Albert, Pvt, Co. M 7th Inf, Italy 26 May 1944
Michael, Clifford H., S/Sgt, Co. G 30th Inf, Italy 1 Mar. 1944
Michak, Andrew A., Sgt, Co. E 7th Inf, Italy 26 Sept. 1943
Middendorf, Arnold J., Pvt, Med. Det. 15th Inf, Sicily July 1943
Milisitis, Stephen F., Pfc, Co. I 30th Inf, Italy 29 Feb. 1944
Millar, Walter K., Capt, Inf Hq. 3d Inf Div., Sicily Aug. 1943
Miller, Arthur F., T/5, Hq. Btry 9th FA Bn., Sicily Aug. 1943
▲Miller, Aubry D., T/Sgt, Co. H 7th Inf, Germany 16 Mar. 1945
Miller, Claude R., Pfc, Med. Det. 7th Inf, Sicily July 1943
Miller, Charles P., Pfc, Co. I 30th Inf, Anzio, Italy 5 June 1944
Miller, George E., Pfc, Co. H 7th Inf, Neunhof, Germany 17 Apr. 1945
Miller, Jack, Pfc, Hq. Co. 3d Bn. 7th Inf, Italy 5 July 1944
Miller, Orville L., Pfc, Inf Co. 7th Inf Regt., France 8 Oct. 1944
Miller, Raymond C., Sgt, Co. M 15th Inf, Italy 30 Jan. 1944
Miller, Raymond J., Pfc, Med. Det. 7th Inf, Sicily July 1943
Miller, Talmadge, Sgt, Co. C 7th Inf, French Morocco 8 Nov. 1942
Miller, William B., 1st Lt, Inf Hq. Co. 7th Inf, Bamberg, Germany 15 Apr. 1945
Millman, Richard B., Sgt, Co. K 7th Inf, Omersvillers, France 15 Mar. 1945
Milward, John I., Pfc, Raider Pltn, 30th Inf, Siegfried Line 16 Mar. 1945
Mishakes, Joseph, T/Sgt, Co. I 30th Inf, France 8 Jan. 1945
Miskinis, Peter F., Sgt, Co. M 15th Inf, France 24 Jan. 1945
Misterkiewicz, Edward W., Cpl, Co. C 7th Inf, Italy 16 Oct. 1943
Mistretta, Onfrio, Pvt, Co. H 7th Inf, Italy Oct. 1943
Misurelli, Frank, S/Sgt, Co. D 30th Inf, France 5 Nov. 1944
Mitchell, Robert G., Pfc, Med. Det. 15th Inf, Italy 28 Jan. 1944
Mitchusson, Vernice, Pfc, Co. I 30th Inf, Germany 15 Mar. 1945
Mittge, Merrill L., Sgt, Co. D 756th Tank Bn., Nurnberg, Germany 18 Apr. 1945
Moergen, Herman A., Sgt, Co. K, 30th Inf, Sicily July 1943
Moffitt, Orville, S/Sgt, Co. D, 30th Inf, Anzio, Italy 5 June 1944
Moffitt, Raleigh, Sgt, Co. E 15th Inf, Sigolsheim, France 27 Dec. 1944
Mohr, George W., 1st Lt, Co. A 15th Inf, France 17 Aug. 1944
Mole, Robert A., 1st Lt, CAC, Btry C 441st AAA (AW) Bn., Meutzig, France 23 Nov. 1944
Moll, Arthur, Sgt, 3d Sig. Co., Italy 8 Mar. 1944
Molldrem, Clifford R., T/Sgt, Co. E 30th Inf, Italy 19 Feb. 1944.
Mollenkopf, John R., Sgt, Hq. Co. 2nd Bn. 15th Inf, France 13 Sept. 1944
Moller, Carl R., Pfc, Co. H 7th Inf, Gemunden, Germany 6 Apr. 1945
▲Molnar, Julius, Sgt, Co. C 15th Inf, Biarville, France Nov. 5, 1944
Moloney, Robert C., 1st Lt, Co. A 751st Tank Bn., Italy 29 Jan. 1944
Mondelli, Hugo J., 1st Lt, Co. I 7th Inf, France 15 Sept. 1944
Mongold, Fred O., Sgt, Co. H 7th Inf, Houssen, France 25 Jan. 1945
Montague, Russell B., S/Sgt, Co. E 30th Inf, Germany 8 May 1944
Montesano, Anthony, Pfc, Co. B 30th Inf, Frenchville, France 16 Sept. 1944
Montgomery, Neil L., Pfc, Co. H 30th Inf, Sicily Aug. 1943

▲ Oak Leaf Cluster.

Montgomery, Orel L., Sgt, Co. G 30th Inf, Sicily July 1943
Montoy, Armen L., Pfc, Hq. Co. 3d Bn. 30th Inf, Lampertheim, Germany 26 Mar. 1945
Moody, Jasper G., Pfc, Co. L 15th Inf, France 27 Dec. 1944
Moody, Ralph W., S/Sgt, Co. C 30th Inf, Italy 1 Feb. 1944
Moody, Theodore M., Cpl, Hq. Co. 30th Inf, Sicily 20 July 1943
Mooney, William C., 2d Lt, Co. L 15th Inf, Sicily July 1943
Mooneyham, Clifton W., 1st Lt, EA Co. C 601st TD Bn., Jebsheim, France 27 Jan. 1945
Moore, Aubrey T., S/Sgt, Co. A 15th Inf, France 26 Jan. 1945
Moore, Clayton H., 1st Lt, Co. F 30th Inf, Germany 8 May 1944
Moore, Duward H., S/Sgt, Co. B 7th Inf, Sicily 10 Aug. 1943
Moore, George D., Jr., S/Sgt, Co. C 7th Inf, Zweibrucken, Germany 19 Mar. 1945
Moore, Harry D., S/Sgt, Co. H 30th Inf, Italy 3 Mar. 1944
Moore, James G., Pfc, Co. L 30th Inf, Obernheim, France 26 Nov. 1944
Moore, John J., T/5, 3d Rcn Trp., France 15 Aug. 1944
Moore, Roy E., Lt, Co. Inf 7th Inf, Italy 13 Oct. 1943
Moore, Wallace R., Pfc, Co. L 15th Inf, France 9 Sept. 1944
Moran, Edward J., T/5, Hq. Co. 3d Bn. 30th Inf, Kayserberg, France 18 Dec. 1944
Moran, Frank J., Jr., S/Sgt, Hq Co. 3d Bn. 15th Inf, Rischgau, Germany 26 Apr. 1945
Moree, Edgar A., Pfc, Hq. Co. 1st Bn. 15th Inf, Aveleno, Italy 27 Sept. 1943
Moreschi, Bruno G., Pfc, Co. L 15th Inf, France 27 Dec. 1944
Moretti, Cesare A., Pfc, Strategic Serv. Section, G-2 Sec. 3rd Inf Div., France 20-21 Aug. 1944
Moretti, Frank A., 1st Lt, Inf AT Co. 30th Inf, Colony, France 21 Aug. 1944
Morgan, Charles E., Capt, Co. E 15th Inf, Italy 23 May 1944
Morgan, Perry A., Pvt, Co. M 30th Inf, Italy 15 Oct. 1943
Morgan, Stanley, Pvt, Co. G 30th Inf, Anzio, Italy 5 June 1944
Morgan, Walter D., T/5, Hq. & Hq. Btry 41st FA Bn., Sicily Aug. 1943
Moriber, Leonard, 1st Lt, Co. F, 30th Inf, France 16 Aug. 1944
Morris, James M., 2d Lt, Co. K 15th Inf, France 23 Dec. 1944
Morris, Jim H., Pfc, Co. E 7th Inf, Cisterna Di Litorria, Italy 23 Sept. 1944
Morris, John A., 1st Lt, Co. M 15th Inf, France 26 Oct. 1944
Morris, Thomas, Pvt, Co. F 30th Inf, Italy 29 Feb. 1944
Morris, Victor M., Capt, Inf Co. C 7th Inf, Zweibrucken, Germany 19 Mar. 1945
Morrison, Brenton J., Pfc, Co. F 7th Inf, Neunhof, Germany 17 Apr. 1945
Morrison, Hugh E., T/4, Med. Det. 30th Inf, Sicily Aug. 1943
Morrow, John L., Cpl, Hq. Co. 1st Bn. 7th Inf, Zweibrucken, Germany
Morrow, Paul E., Pfc, Co. E 30th Inf, Saales, France 23 Nov. 1944
Morrow, Robert L., Pfc, Co. L 30th Inf, Italy 7-8 Mar. 1944
Morse, Robert L., Pfc, Co. D 30th Inf, Italy Nov. 1943
Morton, William F., Pfc, Co. F 7th Inf, Italy 1 June 1944
Mosely, Cecil E., Sgt, Co. F 7th Inf, Nurnberg, Germany 19 Apr. 1945
Mottweiler, Richard H., 1st Lt, 3d Rcn Trp., France 18 Aug. 1944
Mowery, Harlan R., Pfc, Hq. Co. 2d Bn. 15th Inf, Nurnberg, Germany 18 Apr. 1945
Moyer, Harold R., Pfc, Hq. Co. 2d Bn. 30th Inf, La Hollande, France 20 Nov. 1944
Mudd, William C., 1st Lt, Inf Co. B 30th Inf, Horhausen, Germany 12 Apr. 1945
Mueller, Eugene H., Pfc, Co. H 30th Inf, Holtzwihr, France 27 Jan. 1945
Mulshagen, Adolph J., S/Sgt, Co. K 30th Inf, Vosges 5 Dec. 1944
Mullen, Orval H., Sgt, Co. L 11th Inf, Italy Oct. 1943
Mullen, Richard D., 1st Lt, Btry A 39th FA Bn., Anzio 29 Jan. 1944
Mullen, Robert D., S/Sgt, Co. E 30th Inf, St. Die, France 5 Nov. 1944
Mullins, Sam, Pfc, Med. Det. 15th Inf, Italy 12 Oct. 1943
Munderville, Peter T., Pfc, Co. A 7th Inf, France 25 Jan. 1945
Muniz, Hilario, Pfc, Co. L 30th Inf, France 10 Nov. 1944
Munson, Allan A., S/Sgt, Hq. Co. 1st Bn. 30th Inf, Sicily July 1943
Murk, Edward J., T/Sgt, Co. M 15th Inf, Italy 2 Mar. 1944
▲Murphy, Audie L., 1st Lt, Co. B 15th Inf, France 2 Oct. 1944
Murphy, Jack H., Co. H 30th Inf, France 19 Sept. 1944
▲(2) Murray, Charles, Jr., 1st Lt, Co. C 30th Inf, Colroy, France 24 Nov. 1944
Murvin, Garland G., 1st Lt, Inf, Co. G 15th Inf, Contwig, Germany 19 Mar. 1945
Muskey, Eugene T., Pfc, Co. H 7th Inf, Italy 13 Oct. 1943
Mutschler, Edward C., Pfc, Hq. Co. 1st Bn. 15th Inf, Germany 13 Oct. 1944
Myatt, Elvin E., Pfc, Co. E 15th Inf, Italy 29 Feb. 1944
Myers, Robert L., Pfc, Co. E 15th Inf, France 28 Oct. 1944
Myers, Roy J., Pvt, Co. M 30th Inf, Colmar 20 Feb. 1945

Nacey, John A., Pfc, Co. M 30th Inf, Augsburg, Germany 26 Apr. 1945
Nagler, George H., Cpl, Co. K 30th Inf, Sicily July 1943
Nalle, Charles C., Capt, Co. H 30th Inf, Sicily Aug. 1943
Nastari, Augustus, S/Sgt, Co. M 7th Inf, Italy 1 Mar. 1944
Nash, Clarence H., Jr., T/Sgt, Co. H 30th Inf, Mittlebach, Germany 19 Mar. 1945
Nathanson, Benjamin, Pfc, Inf, Co. I 7th Inf Regt., France 16 Jan. 1945
▲Neddersen, Richard H., Lt Col, Inf Co. 3d Bn. 30th Inf, France 11 Sept. 1944
Neese, George R., Pfc, Co. F 7th Inf, Nurnberg, Germany 17 Apr. 1945
Neff, William J., Pfc, Hq. Co. 2d Bn. 15th Inf, France 13 Sept. 1944
▲Nelson, Albert L., Pfc, Co. K 7th Inf, Italy 1 Mar. 1944
▲Nelson, Alfred W., Jr., 1st Lt, Co. A 30th Inf, Italy 23-24 Apr. 1944
Nelson, Donald N., Cpl, Med. Det. 39th FA Bn., Italy 21 Oct. 1943
Nelson, John A., Pvt, Co. L 7th Inf, Wihr-en-Plaine, France 30 Jan. 1945
Nelson, Marion W., 1st Sgt, Hq. Co. 3d Bn. 15th Inf, France 8 Sept. 1944
Nelson, Winston R., S/Sgt, Co. B 7th Inf, Italy 28 May 1944
Nemeth, Stephen J., Pfc, Co. H 7th Inf, Italy 1 Feb. 1944
Nerthling, Carl H., Sgt, Co. A 601st TD Bn., Houssen, France 26 Jan. 1945
Neswoog, Olaf K., S/Sgt, Co. A 15th Inf, Germany 18 Mar. 1945
Nevers, Herman F., S/Sgt, Hq. Co. (BP) 7th Inf, France 16 Aug. 1944
Newby, Knarf S., Pfc, Co. K 30th Inf, Germany 26 Mar. 1945
Newby, Lexer D., Pfc, Co. E 30th Inf, France 17 Dec. 1944
Newell, John R., Pfc, Hq. Co. 30th Inf, France 26-28 Oct. 1944
Newell, Richard C., Sgt, Hq. Btry 39th FA Bn., Osterbuck, Germany 26 Apr. 1945
Newton, Earl, Pfc, Co. G 15th Inf, Nurnberg, Germany 17 Apr. 1945
Newton, Orien S., T/Sgt, Co. D 15th Inf, Italy 27 Jan. 1944
Nichols, Edwin A., Maj, Inf Exec. O 30th Inf, Italy 23 Jan. 1944
Nicholson, Howard E., 1st Lt, Co. B 15th Inf, Italy 24 May 1944
Nicholas, James F., Pvt, Hq. Co. 2d Bn. 15th Inf, France 2 Nov. 1944
▲(2) Nicholson, Harry L., 2d Lt, Inf Co. M 30th Inf, France 1944
Niles, Charles F., Pvt, Co. K 7th Inf, Italy 2 Nov. 1943
Nisi, Frank J., 1st Lt, Inf Hq. Co. 2d Bn. 7th Inf, Ferdrupt, France 27 Sept. 1944
▲Noel, Jack W., Sr., S/Sgt, Hq. Co. 3d Bn. 15th Inf, Germany 4 Apr. 1945
Noga, John J., Pfc, Co. B 30th Inf, Frencacheville, France 16 Sept. 1944
Nolan, Jack T., Cpl, Btry C 9th FA Bn., Italy 31 Oct. 1943
Normand, Lee J., Pfc, Co. K 15th Inf, Nurnberg, Germany 19 Apr. 1945
Norrick, Joseph T., T/Sgt, Co. A 15th Inf, Beisheim, France 5 Feb. 1945
Northrip, Ray E., 1st Lt, Inf Co. E 15th Inf, Kirschfurt, Germany 31 Mar. 1945
Norve, Lester H., 1st Lt, Co. F 7th Inf, France 25 Jan. 1945
Norwood, Furman E., Pfc, Hq. Co. 1st Bn. 15th Inf, France 26 Jan. 1945
Noseck, Kenneth A., Capt, Inf Co. A 30th Inf, Italy 23 May 1944
Nosko, Mike R., Pvt, 9th FA Bn. Med. Det. atchd to Btry B 9th FA Bn., Sicily Aug. 1943
Nottingham, Lucius S., Jr., Pfc, Hq. Co. 30th Inf, Riedwihr, France 26 Jan. 1945
Nurnberger, Roy H., Sgt, 3d Sig. Co., Sicily Aug. 1943
Nusbaum, Arthur H., 1st Lt, Co. F 30th Inf, France 18 Dec. 1944
Nussbaum, Melvin F., Sgt, Co. A 7th Inf, Rieblingen, Germany 26 Apr. 1945

Oakes, Edward G., S/Sgt, Co. B 15th Inf, France 15 Aug. 1944
Oakley, Everett E., S/Sgt, Co. I 15th Inf, France 12 Sept. 1944
O'Brien, Francis T., Pfc, Hq. Co. 3d Bn, 15th Inf, Rischgau, Germany 26 Apr. 1945
O'Brien, Mark P., T/4, Hq. Btry 39th FA Bn., France 23 Aug. 1944
O'Brien, Patrick J., Pfc, Co. M 30th Inf, France 28 Oct. 1944
Ochs, Jack, Pvt, Co. E 15th Inf, Nurnberg, Germany 17 Apr. 1945
Ockerhausen, James R., S/Sgt, Co. K 30th Inf, Italy 23 May 1944
Ockman, Andre J., Sgt, Co. K 30th Inf, Sicily July 1943
O'Connell, Frank M., Pvt, Co. I 30th Inf, Italy 29 Feb. 1944
▲OConnell, John, Maj, 3d Rcn Trp., Italy 23 Dec. 1944, Bennwihr, France
Oddson, Marlin S., Pvt, Co. A 15th Inf, Germany 30 Mar. 1945
▲Odom, Sol R., S/Sgt, Co. M 15th Inf, Gadheim, Germany 12 Apr. 1945
Odland, Clifford, Pfc, Btry B 10th FA Bn., Sicily Aug. 1943
Oglesby, David H., Jr., T/Sgt, Co. A 30th Inf, Italy 23-24 Apr. 1944
O'Hara, Wallace B., Sgt, Btry A 10th FA Bn., Sicily 5 Aug. 1943
O'Kane, Robert M., S/Sgt, Co. B 7th Inf, Nurnberg, Germany 18 Apr. 1945
Oliver, Haskell O., S/Sgt, Co. B 756th Tank Bn., Italy 4 June 1944
Oliver, James, Pfc, Co. C 15th Inf, France 26 Dec. 1944
Oliver, Raymond L., S/Sgt, Co. C 7th Inf, Italy 18 Oct. 1943
Oliver, William H., Pfc, Co. L 15th Inf, France 3 Jan. 1945
Olsen, Frank I., Cpl, Co. M 30th Inf, Sicily Aug. 1943
Olsen, John V., Pvt, Co. H 7th Inf, Houssen, France 25 Jan. 1945
Olsen, Robert A., S/Sgt, Co. L 7th Inf, Althornbach, Germany 19 Mar. 1945
Olson, Beauford L., T/5, Med. Det. 7th Inf, Ostheim, France 23 Jan. 1945
Olson, Philip J., Pfc, Med. Det. 30th Inf, Sicily 7 Aug. 1943
Olson, Raymond F., S/Sgt, Co. M 30th Inf, France 22 Nov. 1944
O'Neill, Robert J., Pfc, Co. C 15th Inf, Rothenbach, Germany 1 Apr. 1945
Ong, Donald C., S/Sgt, Co. E 30th Inf, France 15 Oct. 1944
O'Rourke, Edward J., Jr., 1st Sgt, Co. G 30th Inf, Germany 8 May 1944
Orr, George R., Pfc, Co. F 7th Inf, France 30 Sept. 1944
Orr, William R., 1st Lt, Co. B 30th Inf, Zweibrucken, Germany 21 Mar. 1945
Ortiz, Dominick, Pfc, Co. L 15th Inf, France 15 Aug. 1944
Osbeck, Harry C., Pfc, Co. E 15th Inf, France 28 Dec. 1944
Osborne, Paul E., T/Sgt, Co. A 7th Inf, Sandhofen, Germany 26 Mar. 1945
Osborne, Vernon L., M/Sgt, Hq. & Hq. Btry 41st FA Bn., Sicily 8 June 1944
Osborne, Walter B., Co. E 30th Inf, Le Haut Jacques, France 29 Oct. 1944
Osment, James, Pvt, Co. H 30th Inf, Germany 8 May 1944
Ostrander, Frank J., Pfc, Co. G 30th Inf, Zweibrucken, Germany 19 Mar. 1945
Ott, Alexander, Pfc, Co. A 30th Inf, Italy 25 Jan. 1944
Otto, Raymond, Sgt, Co. A 7th Inf, Sapois, France 8 Oct. 1944
Overskei, Ernest O., Pfc, Co. A 15th Inf, Germany 7 Apr. 1945
Overton, Mays G., T/Sgt, Co. I 7th Inf, Italy 29 Feb. 1944
Oxner, Fred L., S/Sgt, Co. L 30th Inf, Italy Aug. 1943
Ozwirk, Joseph F., Pvt, Co. I 30th Inf, Italy 29 Feb. 1944

Pace, Willie E., S/Sgt, Co. L 30th Inf, Weiskirch, Germany 16 Mar. 1945
Packman, James L., Capt, Co. A 30th Inf, Italy 1 June 1944
Packwood, Burleigh T., Capt, S-3 2d Bn. 30th Inf, Italy 26 Jan. 1944
Palley, Harold I., Pfc, Co. G 7th Inf, France 7 Oct. 1944
Palmer, Saymour L., Pfc, Co. B 30th Inf, Epping Urbach, Germany 16 Mar. 1945
Palyszeski, George, Pfc, Med. Det. 7th Inf, Italy 24 May 1944
Panetta, James L., Pfc, Co. C 30th Inf, Italy 1 June 1944
Papanek, Carl P., S/Sgt, Co. H 7th Inf, French Morocco 8 Nov. 1942
Parham, Donald E., 1st Lt, Hq. Co. 3d Bn. 15th Inf, Italy 30 Jan. 1944
Parisi, Carlo A., Pvt, Co. D 7th Inf, France 25 Jan. 1945
Parker, William C., Jr., 1st Lt, 3d Rcn Trp., Italy 27 May 1944
Parkinson, Gilbert N., 1st Lt, SC 3d Sig. Co. St. Remy, France 18 Nov. 1944
Partin, John T., S/Sgt, Co. K 7th Inf, Italy 2 Feb. 1944
Parziale, Charles J., Capt, Inf 15th Inf, Italy 13 Oct. 1943
Pascual, Nicolas, 1st Lt, Co. D 30th Inf, Germany 8 May 1944
Pase, Arnold R., Sgt, Co. I 30th Inf, France 17 Dec. 1944
Patnoe, Tuffield T., T/Sgt, Co. M 15th Inf, France 22 Aug. 1944
Patten, Moultrie, 1st Lt, Inf Co. A 756th Tank Bn., Rosenkrantz, France 25 Jan. 1945
Patterson, Glen I., Sgt, Co. B 15th Inf, Sicily July 1943
Patterson, Howard L., S/Sgt, Co. K 7th Inf, Italy 30 Jan. 1944
Patterson, James H., Sgt, Co. E 15th Inf, Italy 29 Jan. 1944
▲Patton, Charlie Y., Jr., Sgt, Co. H 15th Inf, France 26 Jan. 1945
Patton, James E., S/Sgt, AT Co. 30th Inf, France 23 Jan. 1945
Paul, Walter P., 2d Lt, CWS, Co. D Chem Mortar Bn., France 7 Oct. 1944
▲Paulick, Michael, Maj, Inf Hq. 1 Bn. 15th Inf, Italy 2 Feb. 1944
Paulson, Kermit P., Pfc, Med. Det. 2d Bn. 7th Inf, Sicily Aug. 1943
Pauson, Arthur C., Pvt, Med. Det. 30th Inf, Fedala 11 Nov. 1942
Pawlen, Joseph E., Jr., Med. Det. 7th Inf, La Chin, France 16 Jan. 1945
▲Payne, Leland B., Pfc, Co. A 15th Inf, France, Burnstedt, Germany 26 Mar. 1945
Peairs, Douglas D., 1st Lt, FA Hq. 41st FA Bn., Italy 23 May
Pearson, Charlie T., Pvt, Med. Det. 7th Inf, Sicily Aug. 1943
▲Peck, George S., 2d Lt, Co. E 30th Inf, Riedwihr, France 23 Jan. 1945
Peckham, Albert F., Pfc, Co. A 30th Inf, France 17 Dec. 1944
▲(2) Peckham, George M., Capt, MC 30th Inf, Sicily Aug. 1943
Peckinpaugh, Richard, 1st Lt, Co. K 30th Inf, Italy 12 Mar. 1944

▲ Oak Leaf Cluster.

Peckman, Herbert M., Pfc, Co. K 15th Inf, Kalchreuth, Germany 16 Apr. 1945
Pellegrino, Anthony J., Pfc, Co. H 30th Inf, Le Tholy, France 6 Oct. 1944
Pellman, Harry A., Pfc, Co. C 30th Inf, Germany 8 May 1944
Pelzer, Harold J., Sgt, Hq. Co. 1st Bn. 15th Inf, Sicily July 1943
Pena, John T., S/Sgt, Co. G 30th Inf, Italy 20 Feb. 1944
Pender, Horace E., Sgt, Co. K 30th Inf, Sicily July 1943
Pennell, Clyde W., Sgt, 3d Rcn Trp., France 23 Oct. 1944
Pennell, Donald N., T/5, Med. Det. 15th Inf, Althornbach, Germany 18 Mar. 1945
Pennuto, Lawrence B., Pfc, Co. F 30th Inf, Holtzwihr, France 27 Jan. 1945
Perez, Eduardo, Pvt, Co. C 30th Inf, Sicily Aug. 1943
Perkins, Lee H., S/Sgt, Co. E 7th Inf, Sicily July 1943
Perrine, Bernard F., Sgt, Co. E 30th Inf, France 25 Nov. 1944
▲Perry, Morton H., 1st Lt, Co. M 7th Inf, Italy 29 May 1944
Perry, Vernon C., Pfc, Co.C 7th Inf, French Morocco 10 Nov. 1942
Perry, Victor J., Pfc, Hq. Co. 30th Inf, France 26 Oct. 1944
Pestka, Raymond, Pfc, Hq. & Hq. Btry 10th FA Bn., Sicily Aug. 1943
Peters, Herman W., Pfc, Co. K 30th Inf, Lampertheim, Germany 26 Mar. 1945
Peterson, Lyman K., Capt, 41st FA Bn., French Morocco 8-11 Nov. 1942
Peterson, Celon A., Capt, Inf Co. A 7th Inf, Sicily July 1943
Petree, William H., Jr., Cpl, Co. K 30th Inf, Italy 16 Feb. 1944
Petrovich, John J., Pfc, Co. G 15th Inf, Riedwirh, France 26 Jan. 1945
Petrozzello, Thomas J., T/4, Btry B 10th FA Bn., Utweiler, Germany 15 Mar. 1945
▲Petruzel, Frank, Capt, Inf Co. K 7th Inf, Italy 31 Jan. 1944
Pfeffer, Roman L., Pfc, Co. L 30th Inf, Holzwihr, France 30 Jan. 1945
Phillips, Frederick J., 1st Lt, Co. M 7th Inf, Italy 31 Jan. 1944
▲Phillips, Frederick J., 1st Lt, Co. M 7th Inf, Italy 30 Jan. 1944
Phillips, Hoyt G., 2d Lt, Inf Co. L 30th Inf, France 17 Sept. 1944
Phillips, James T., Jr., Pvt, Co. E 7th Inf, Italy 25 May 1944
Phillips, Malcolm H., 1st Lt, Co. F 7th Inf, Italy 16 Oct. 1943
Phillips, Michael P., Pfc, Co. L 30th Inf, Italy .10 Nov. 1943
Phillips, Roger N., 2d Lt, Co. K 15th Inf, Italy 13 Oct. 1944
▲Phillips, Rose E., Pfc, Co. G 15th Inf, Sigolsheim, France 27 Dec. 1944
Phillips, Wendel M., 2d Lt, Inf 30th Inf, Sicily July 1943
▲Phillips, Wiley W., Pfc, Co. C 30th Inf, Germany 19 Apr. 1945
Picaso, Jose H., Pfc, Co. H 30th Inf, Holtzwihr, France 27 Jan. 1945
Pierce, Ervan B., T/Sgt, Co. L 15th Inf, Italy 30 Jan. 1944
Pierce, William W., Pvt, Hq. Co. 2d Bn. 15th Inf, Italy 29 Feb. 1944
Pierce, Winston F., S/Sgt, Co. D 7th Inf, France 20 Nov. 1944
Pilcher, Luther L., Sgt, Btry C 9th FA Bn., Italy 29 Feb. 1944
Pilgrim, James, S/Sgt, Co. L 15th Inf, Italy 29 Jan. 1944
Pindyski, Michael J., Sgt, Co. B 7th Inf, Germany 26 Mar 1945
Piper, Raymond H., Pvt, Med. Det. 7th Inf, Sicily July 1943
Pisano, Salvatore S., Pfc, Co. F 30th Inf, Nurnberg, Germany 20 Apr. 1945
Pittaluga, Joseph A., S/Sgt, Co. C 7th Inf, France 20 Oct. 1944
Pitts, Floyd E., S/Sgt, Co. C 30th Inf, France 2 Nov. 1944
Pixley, Erwin W., Pvt, Med. Det. 7th Inf, France 21 Sept. 1944
Plegge, Willard, Pfc, Co. E 15th Inf, Italy 29 Feb. 1944
▲Pletzke, George C., S/Sgt, Co. C 7th Inf, Italy 2 June 1944
Poinsett, Edgar H., Capt, Inf Co. G 7th Inf, Italy 23 Apr. 1944
Pointer, Woodrow W., Pvt, Co. H 15th Inf, Sicily Aug. 1943
Pollack, Clifton M., Pfc, Co. C 30th Inf, Epping Urbach, Germany 15 Mar. 1945
Pontarelli, Anthony C., T/5, Med. Det. 7th Inf, Italy 24 Sept. 1943
Pontzer, Lloyd L., S/Sgt, Co. M 30th Inf, Anzio, Italy 16 Feb. 1944
Poorman, Donald J., S/Sgt, Co. G 7th Inf, Italy 1 Feb. 1944
Popovich, William, Pfc, Co. A 30th Inf, Italy 24 Apr. 1944
▲(3) Porter, MacKenzie E., Maj, Inf 30th Inf, Fedala, French Morocco 8 Nov. 1942
Porter, Morris C., 1st Lt, Hq. Co. 30th Inf, France 28 Oct. 1944
Porter, Sedric E., S/Sgt, Co. K 15th Inf, France 27 Aug. 1944
Potaczek, Alois J., S/Sgt, Co. E 15th Inf, Italy 30 Jan. 1944
Potash, Philip, Sgt. Co. M 30th Inf, Sicily July 1943
Potter, Kenneth B., Maj, Inf, Hq. 1st Bn. 15th Inf Regt., Nurnberg, Germany 17 Apr. 1945
Potterfield, Clarence A., 2d Lt, 7th Inf, French Morocco 10 Nov. 1942
Potts, Charles D., Pvt, Co. I 15th Inf, Germany 4 Apr. 1945
Potts, Phillip R., Pfc, Co. M 7th Inf, Italy 23 May1944
Powell, Elmer A., Pvt, Co. D 15th Inf, France 1 Oct. 1944
Powell, Harry A., Pfc, Co. G 15th Inf, Nurnberg, Germany 17 Apr. 1945
▲Powell, James F., Capt, Co. E 7th Inf, Ostheim, France 23 Jan. 1945
Powell, Maynard S., Jr., Pfc, Hq. Co. 1st Bn. 15th Inf, Mellrichstadt, Germany 7 Apr. 1945
Praeger, Emil, T/Sgt, Co. L 15th Inf, Weibersbrunn, Germany 1 Apr. 1945
Prario, Henry S., 2d Lt, Co. C 7th Inf, Italy 31 May 1944
▲Prather, Herman E., T/Sgt, Co. B 30th Inf, Italy 24 Apr. 1944
Prenderville, Joseph P., S/Sgt, Co. A 30th Inf, French Morocco 8 Nov. 1942
Presson, Durwood E., Pfc, Co. B 15th Inf, Italy 9 Nov. 1943
Preston, Morgan O., 2d Lt, Co. E 15th Inf, Italy 17 Mar. 1944
Price, Walter E., S/Sgt, Co. C 30th Inf, France 7 Oct. 1944
Price, William A., Sgt, Co. G 30th Inf, Holtzwihr, France 27 Jan. 1945
Pridgen, Robert B., Capt, Co. L 30th Inf, Italy 17 Mar. 1944
Prigge, Ray W., Cpl, Co. H 15th Inf, Italy 12 Oct. 1943
Pringle, James A., 2d Lt, Co. H 30th Inf, France 18 Nov. 1944
Prior, Richard, Pvt, Co. E 15th Inf, Italy 10 Nov. 1943
Pritt, Raymond L., Pfc, Co. E 15th Inf, France 10 Sept. 1944
Proctor, James V., Pfc, Co. L 30th Inf, Kaysersberg, France 16 Dec. 1944
Proctor, William W., T/Sgt, Co. C 15th Inf, France 23 Dec. 1944
Proehl, Frank J., Pfc, Co. B 30th Inf, Sicily Aug. 1943
Prohme, Rupert, Capt, Co. L 30th Inf, Anzio, Italy 5 June 1944
▲Prunier, Henry, S/Sgt, Co. G 15th Inf, Italy 27 May 1944
Psyzbys, Michael J., Pfc, Co. D 30th Inf, Italy 23 Apr. 1944
Purdy, Kenneth E., S/Sgt, Co. C 15th Inf, Italy 15 Feb. 1944
Purdy, Melvin J., Pfc, Co. C 30th Inf, France 16 Dec. 1944
Puszko, John A., Sgt, Co. K 15th Inf, France 28 Dec. 1944
Putman, Loyal L., Pfc, Co. M 15th Inf, Italy 28 May 1944
Pyatt, Miles K., S/Sgt, Co. A 7th Inf, France 21 Sept. 1944
Pye, Warner W., Pvt, Med. Det. 7th Inf, Italy 6 Nov. 1943
Pyeatt, Jewel W., Pfc, Co. G 15th Inf, France 9 Sept. 1944
Pyles, Albert L., Sgt, Co. B 15th Inf, France 21 Aug. 1944
▲Pysz, Charles F., S/Sgt, Co. C 30th Inf Bn., St. Die, France 7 Nov. 1944

Quaale, Joseph, S/Sgt, Co. G 15th Inf, Germany 19 Apr. 1945
Quarles, Lee W., Pfc, Serv. Btry 41st FA Bn., Sicily 4 Aug. 1943
Quast, Clifford A., T/5, Med. Det. 30th Inf, Italy 8 Oct. 1943
Quigg, Vincent F., Pfc, Co. G 15th Inf, Zweibrucken, Germany 18 Mar. 1945
Quinby, Ronald V., Pvt, Co. K 30th Inf, Italy 16 Feb. 1944

Rabe, William M., T/5, Hq. Co. 2d Bn. 15th Inf, Sigolsheim, France
Rabun, Lee A., Sgt, Co. M 30th Inf, Italy 16 Feb. 1944
Rackey, George H., Pfc, Co. L 30th Inf, Rosenheim, Germany 2 May 1945
Rachiele, Frederick J., Capt, MC, 7th Inf, Le Haut Jacques, France 31 Oct. 1944
Radosevich, Mathew S., 1st Sgt, Co. B 30th Inf, France 3 Dec. 1944
Raeth, Ervin F., S/Sgt, Hq. Co. 2d Bn. 15th Inf, France 30 Jan. 1945
Raezer, Donald C., Cpl, AT Co. 15th Inf, France 1 Jan. 1945
Rall, Clarence E., Pfc, Co. K 7th Inf, Italy 2 Feb. 1944
Ramer, Herman, Capt, Inf Co. K 7th Inf, Krum, Germany 13 Apr. 1945
Ramos, Agustin, Pfc, Co. L 15th Inf, France 24 Dec. 1944
Ramsey, Boyd W., T/5, Med. Det. 84th Cml Bn., Italy 14 Feb. 1944
▲Ramsey, Lloyd B., Lt Col, Hq. 3d Bn. 7th Inf, France 16 Aug. 1944
Raney, Arthur L., Pfc, Co. L 30th Inf, France 17 Sept. 1944
Rankin, Vernon H., Capt, Co. D 15th Inf, France 26 Dec. 1944
Rathbun, Glenn E., Capt, Co. M 7th Inf, Italy 13 Oct. 1943
▲Rathbun, Glenn E., Capt, Inf Co. M 7th Inf, Italy 30 Jan. 1944
Ratini, John B., 2d Lt, Co. H 15th Inf, France 12 Sept. 1944
Ratledge, Gordon V., Pvt, Btry C 9th FA Bn., Italy 30 May 1944
Raue, John H., S/Sgt, Co. E 15th Inf, Italy 9 Nov. 1943
Ravenscroft, Earl H., S/Sgt, Co. K 15th Inf, Italy 29 Feb. 1944
Raymond, George E., 1st Lt, Hq. 2d Bn. 30th Inf, France 17 Dec. 1944
Raymond, Normand E., Pvt, Co. H 7th Inf, Italy 16 Oct. 1943
Reaves, Joseph A., Pvt, Med. Det. 15th Inf, Italy 20 Oct. 1943
Reck. Howard M., Pfc, Btry A 39th FA Bn., Sicily 10 July 1943
Redle, David D., Capt, Co. B 756th Tank Bn., France 25 Jan. 1945
Reed, James L., Pvt, Med. Det. 15th Inf, Italy 2 Feb. 1944
Reed, Lewis A., S/Sgt, Co. A 15th Inf, Germany 2 Apr. 1945
Reed, William, Sgt, Co. A 15th Inf, France 5 Feb. 1945
Reedy, John M., Pfc, Med. Det. Med. Det. 30th Inf Regt., Germany 15 Mar. 1945
Reeve, Arnold M., 1st Lt, Co. L 7th Inf, Italy 4 Mar. 1944
Reeves, Williard H., 1st Lt, Inf Hq. 1st Bn. 15th Inf, Sicily 6 Aug. 1943
Reilman, John D., S/Sgt, Cn Co. 15th Inf, Sicily July 1943
▲Reinhardt, Victor E., Pfc, BP 15th Inf, Nompatelize, France 24 Oct. 1944
Relyea, Wilbur T., Cpl, Co. M 7th Inf, France 25 Oct. 1944
Rendon, Mauro M., Pfc, Co. C 15th Inf, France 25 Dec. 1944
Renfro, James M., S/Sgt, Hq. Co. 10th Engr Bn., Italy 4 Mar. 1944
Reno, Sterling, Pfc, Co. K 7th Inf, Italy 31 Jan. 1944
Restivo, Peter, Pvt, Co. H 7th Inf, France 15 Sept. 1944
Retherford, Carl E., 2d Lt, Inf Co. I 7th Inf, Utweiler, Germany 15 Mar. 1945
Reynolds, Buren V., 1st Sgt, Co. G 7th Inf, Italy 15 Oct. 1943
Reynolds, Edgar Z., Sgt, Co. D 30th Inf, Italy 25 Jan. 1944
Reynolds, John E., Sgt, Co. C 15th Inf, Rothenbach, Germany 1 Apr. 1945
Reynolds, Victor D., 2d Lt, Inf 7th Inf, Italy 2 Nov. 1943
Rhoads, George L., T/5, Hq. Co. 3d Bn. 30th Inf, Colmar 20 Feb. 1945
Rhoads, Paul M., 1st Lt, CE Co. B 10th Engr. Bn., Les Rouge Eaux, France 23 Oct. 1944
Rice, Budd, 1st Sgt, Co. E 7th Inf, Italy 1 Feb. 1944
Rice, Timothy J., Pfc, Co. K 7th Inf, Italy 2 Mar. 1944
Rice, Walter M., 2d Lt, Inf. Co. C 7th Inf, Italy 1 June 1944
Rich, James B., Jr., Capt, Co. B 7th Inf, Bocklet, Germany 8 Apr. 1945
Richter, Arthur F., 1st Lt, Inf Co. A 756th Tank Bn., Utweiler, Germany 16 Mar. 1945
Rider, Edward R., S/Sgt, Co. L 15th Inf, Italy 23 May 1944
Rider, Walter E., Pfc, Hq. Co. 2d Bn. 30th Inf, Italy 9 Mar. 1944
Ridgway, William O., WOJG, Serv. Co. 30th Inf, Germany 19 Apr. 1945
Rieke, Chester V., 1st Lt, Inf Co. F 30th Inf, Italy 25 Apr. 1944
Riggs, Dan E., Capt, FA Btry B 178th FA, Italy 15 Nov. 1943
Rigling, Roy S., S/Sgt, Co. K 15th Inf, France 22 Oct. 1944
Riley, Lewis C., Pvt, Hq. Co. 1st Bn. 7th Inf, Sicily Aug. 1943
Riley, Samuel W., 2d Lt, Inf Hq. Co. 30th Inf, Sicily July 1943
Riportella, Joseph C., Sgt, Co. G 15th Inf, Hornbach, Germany 17 Mar. 1945
Ristuccia, Frank A., Pfc, Co. I 30th Inf, France 28 Oct. 1944
Ritchey, John E., Jr., Pvt, Co. G 30th Inf, Sicily July 1943
▲Ritchie, Harry J., Sgt, Co. B 601 TD Bn., Italy 29 Feb. 1944
Ritenour, Mervin K., Pfc, Co. L 30th Inf, Rosenheim, Germany 2 May 1945
Ritter, Rudolph R., Pfc, Med. Det. 7th Inf, Sicily Aug. 1943
Rivera, Zoila F., Sgt, Co. F 7th Inf, Italy 1 June 1944
Rivers, Troy B., Sgt, Co. B 3d Med. Bn., Sicily Aug. 1943
Rizo, Barbarito M., Sgt, Co. M 15th Inf, Italy 13 Oct. 1943
Roark, John T., S/Sgt, Co. G 30th Inf, France 20 Sept. 1944
Robbins, Lewis T., T/Sgt, Co. F 30th Inf, France 26 Jan. 1945
▲Robbolino, Frank, Pvt, Co. C 30th Inf, France 7 Nov. 1944
Roberts, Kenneth, Pfc, Co. M 30th Inf, Germany 26 Mar. 1945
Roberts, Lee R., Pfc, Co. L 30th Inf, Rosenheim, Germany 2 May 1945
Roberts, Samuel H., Capt, Inf Co. C 15th Inf, Rathau, France 18 Nov. 1944
Roberts, William J., 1st Lt, Inf Co. H 15th Inf, St. Ame, France 28 Sept. 1944
Robertson, Alexander, 1st Lt, CE Co. A 10th Engr. Bn., France 23 Oct. 1944
Robertson, Anderville, Pvt, Med. Det. 41st FA Bn., Sicily Aug. 1943
Robertson, Edward C., Capt, FA 41st Bn., French Morocco 8 Nov. 1942
Robertson, James H., Pvt, Co. L 7th Inf, Saales, France 22 Nov. 1944
Robinson, Cline J., S/Sgt, Co. C 756th Tank Bn., Stambach, Germany 20 Mar. 1945
Robinson, Hugh, Pfc, Co. G 15th Inf, France 26 Jan. 1945
▲Robinson, Lewis H., Pfc, Co. G 7th Inf, Le Hart Jacques, France 20 Oct. 1944
Robinson, Raymond M., Cpl, AT Co. 15th Inf, Nurnberg, Germany 18 Apr. 1945
Rode, John S., 1st Lt, Co. E 30th Inf, Germany 8 May 1944
Rodenbough, Francis C., Pvt, Co. M 30th Inf, France 13 Sept. 1944
Roderick, To G., Jr., Pfc, Co. I 7th Inf, France 25 Jan. 1945
Rodgers, Malcolm W., T/5, Co. A 10th Engr. Bn., Italy 20 Mar. 1944
Rodgers, Thomas R., 1st Lt Hq. Co. 2nd Bn. 30th Inf, July 1943
▲Rodman, Bert A., Pfc, Co. D 7th Inf, Valmentone, Italy 28 May 1944
Rodriguez, Frank Pvt, Cn Co. 15th Inf, Sicily July 1943
Roesslein, Theodore A., 2nd Lt, Btry A 39th FA Bn., Italy 18 Oct. 1943
Rogan, Richard J., Jr., Pfc, Co. I 30th Inf, France 17 Dec. 1944
Rogel, Albert, Pfc, Co. I 30th Inf, Germany 15 Mar. 1945
Rogers, Arthur H., Col, Inf 30th Inf, French Morocco 8 Nov. 1942
Rogers, Emil Jr., Pfc, Co. M 30th Inf, France 13 Sept. 1944
Rogers, Lawrence B., Sgt, Co. L 7th Inf, Sicily July 1943

▲ Oak Leaf Cluster.

Rogers, Rolan C., Pfc, Co. E 30th Inf, France 4 Nov. 1944
Rohkar, Charles H., Cpl, Hq. Co. 2d Bn. 15th Inf, Italy Aug. 1943
Roif, Harold, Pvt, Co. A 30th Inf, Italy 25 May 1944
Rolak, Joseph J., Pfc, Co. I 30th Inf, French Morocco 8 Nov. 1942
Rolen, Craig A., Pfc, Co. I 30th Inf, Lampertheim, Germany 26 Mar. 1945
Rolli, Aldo, Sgt, Co. C 601st TD Bn., El Guettar, Tunisia 23 Mar. 1943
Roman, Joseph J., Sgt, Co. C 15th Inf, Althornbach, Germany 17 Mar. 1945
Roper, Hubert L., Pfc, Med. Det. 30th Inf, Biesheim, France 1 Feb. 1945
Rosas, Steven O., S/Sgt, Co. F 15th Inf, Contwig, Germany 23 Mar. 1945
Roscart, Charles W., Pfc, Co. K 7th Inf, Scharof, Germany 26-27 Mar. 1945
Rose, Albert L., Pfc, Co. F 30th Inf, Sicily July 1943
Rose, David J., S/Sgt, Co. E 30th Inf, Italy 15 Apr. 1944
Rose, Frederick, Pfc, Hq. Co. 30th Inf, Sicily Aug. 1943
Rose, Lewis E. Jr., Pfc, Co. L 30th Inf, France 28 Aug. 1944
Rose, Loranzo M., S/Sgt, Co. C 30th Inf, France 2 Nov. 1944
▲Rosebury, Richard M., Jr., 1st Lt, Hq. Co. 30th Inf, Germany 15 Apr. 1945
Rosenfeld, Arthur H., Pfc, Hq. Co. 3d Bn. 30th Inf, Melay, France 20 Sept. 1944
Rosinski, Henry J., Pfc, Co. C 7th Inf, Strasbourg, France, 1 Dec. 1944
Rosloof, James H., Pfc, Co. K 7th Inf, Italy 31 Jan. 1944
Rosplock, Joseph F., 2d Lt, Inf, Co. K 7th Inf, Italy 16 Oct. 1943
Ross, Addison L., 1/Sgt, Co. H 7th Inf, La Croix, France 15 Aug. 1944
Ross, Gerald C., Pfc, AT Co. 15th Inf, Nurnberg, Germany 18 Apr. 1945
Ross, Lawrence B., Sgt, Co. K 15th Inf, Sicily July 1943
Rothseid, Maurice, Capt, Hq. 3d Bn. 30th Inf, France 1 Sept. 1944
Rowe, John C., T/Sgt, Co. E 7th Inf, Ostheim, France 23 Jan. 1945
Rowe, Perry E., 1st Lt, MC 7th Inf, French Morocco 10 Nov. 1942
Rowland, Orvin C., S/Sgt, Co. L 15th Inf, France 7 Oct. 1944
Rowles, Donald F., Pfc, BP Hq. Co. 7th Inf, France 30 Jan. 1945
Roy, Lionel E., Pvt, Hq. Btry 9th FA Bn., Sicily Aug. 1943
Rubick, Allen J., T/Sgt, Co. F 30th Inf, Vosges 5 Dec. 1944
Rubicky, Martin J., S/Sgt, Co. C 7th Inf, Cisterna di Litorria, Italy 29 Feb. 1944
Ruddle, Ralph H., Pfc, Co. M 15th Inf, Italy 29 Feb. 1944
Ruderman, Barney B., 1st Lt, Co. C 601st TD Bn., France 18 Aug. 1944
Rush, Lloyd N., Pvt, Co. G 15th Inf, France 26 Jan. 1945
Rushing, Marion D., Jr., Pfc, Co. A 15th Inf, France 30 Mar. 1945
Russ, Kenneth L., S/Sgt, Co. A 7th Inf, France 23 Jan. 1945
Russeau, Lawrence R., Pfc, Co. A 7th Inf, France 15 Mar. 1945
Russell, Jay N., Pfc, Hq. Co. 2d Bn. 15th Inf, Sigolsheim, France 24 Dec. 1944
Russo, Frank P., Pfc, Hq. Co. 15th Inf, Sigolsheim, France 27 Dec. 1944
Ryan, Bernard J., Pfc, Co. L 7th Inf, France 15 Mar. 1945
Ryan, Daniel J., Pfc, Co. M 30th Inf, France 16 Dec. 1944

Safstrom, Norman W., Pfc, Co. A 15th Inf, France 31 Oct. 1944
▲Sage, Marvin C., T/Sgt, Co. E 15th Inf, Nurnberg, Germany 17 Apr. 1945
Sain, Dick M., 1st Lt, Btry C 9th FA Bn., Italy 3 June 1944
Saine, Harold J., 1st Lt, Co. M 30th Inf, France 20 Dec. 1944
St. Clair, Gilbert C., Capt, Inf 7th Inf, French Morocco 10 Nov. 1942
St. George, Joseph D., S/Sgt, Co. L 15th Inf, Riedwihr, France 26 Jan. 1945
St. Pierre, Philip T., Pvt, Co. D 7th Inf, Sicily Aug. 1943
Sakaris, John, Pfc, AT Co. 30th Inf, Ill River, France 23 Jan. 1945
Salazar, Philbert, T/Sgt, Co. M 30th Inf, Vosges 5 Dec. 1944
Salet, Eugene A., Lt Col, CO 2d Bn. 15th Inf, France 5 Jan. 1945
Salfen, Ambrose G., Capt, Co. B 601st Td Bn., Italy 30 Jan. 1944
Salisbury, Oakley, S/Sgt, Co. D 7th Inf, Guiderkurch, France 15 Mar. 1945
Sallette, William F., Jr., S/Sgt, Co. K 15th Inf, France 25 Dec. 1944
Salley, Dan N., Pvt, Med. Det. 7th Inf, Althornbach, Germany 18 Mar. 1945
Salzmann, Rafael L., Lt Col, Inf 7th Inf, French Morocco 10 Nov. 1942
Sanvoff, James, Pfc, Co. G 15th Inf, Achsheim, Germany 29 Apr. 1945
Sanders, George, S/Sgt, Co. H 30th Inf, Italy 14 Oct. 1943
Sanders, Aubrey B., Pfc, Co. I 30th Inf, Germany 16 Mar. 1945
Sandidge, Sam D., T/Sgt, Co. K 30th Inf, Italy 28 Jan. 1944
Sandler, Harold L., 2d Lt, Hq. 2d Bn. 7th Inf, Italy Oct. 1943
Santers, Joseph V., Pvt, Co. D 7th Inf, Sicily Aug. 1943
Sargent, Rufus V., Sgt, Co. H 15th Inf, Italy 8 Nov. 1943
Sarrah, John E., Sgt, Co. L 30th Inf, Germany 15 Mar. 1945
Sarten, Edmon L., Pvt, Co. K 30th Inf, Sicily July 1943
Sasavage, Peter W., S/Sgt, Co. C 7th Inf, Le Haut Jacques, France 28 Oct. 1944
Sasse, Leroy F., 1st Lt, Co. C 10th Engr. Bn., Italy 4 Mar. 1944
Satuloff, Danford M., 1st Lt, CA Co. C 441st AAA AW Bn., Bois de Riedwihr, France 26 Jan. 1945
Sauer, Norbert B., 1st Lt, CO Co. I 30th Inf, Italy 23 May 1944
Sayers, Carroll S., Pfc, Co. K 30th Inf, France 16 Aug. 1944
Saylors, Isaac C., Sgt, Co. C 15th Inf, Sicily Aug. 1943
Scales, Howard A., Pfc, Co. E 15th Inf, Nurnberg, Germany 17 Apr. 1945
Scarpa, Fred, S/Sgt, Co. L 15th Inf, Nurnberg, Germany 19 Apr. 1945
Schake, Howard, Jr., Pvt, Co. C 7th Inf, France 25 Sept. 1944
Schermbeck, Robert E., 2d Lt, Co. I 15th Inf, France 5 Sept. 1944
Schiele, Bert D., Cpl, Co. G 7th Inf, Sicily July 1943
Schilz, Leonard J., S/Sgt, Co. K 15th Inf, Italy 29 Feb. 1944
Schlicher, William R., S/Sgt, AT Co. 30th Inf, Colmar 20 Feb. 1945
Schmerbauch, Emery L., Pfc, Co. L 30th Inf, Italy 20 Apr. 1944
Schmidt, Herman L., T/Sgt, Co. F 30th Inf, Germany 20 Apr. 1945
Schmuhl, Wayne H., S/Sgt, Co. L 15th Inf, Munt Zenheim, France 29 Jan. 1945
Schneiber, Harold J., Pfc, Co. H 30th Inf, Germany 8 May 1944
Schneider, Delvin H., T/Sgt, Co. A 30th Inf, Italy 9 Feb. 1944
Schneider, Eugene E., 1st Lt, Btry B 41st FA Bn., Anzio 21 Feb. 1944
Schoenfeld, Woodrow J., Pvt, Co. I 7th Inf, Beisheim, France 15 Mar. 1945
Schoop, Arthur Pfc, Co. F 30th Inf, Italy 29 Feb. 1944
Schorkopf, William M., Pfc, Co. G 15th Inf, Germany 19 Apr. 1945
Schrader, Arthur F., Pfc, Co. L 15th Inf, France 28 Sept. 1944
Schultz, Henry J., 1st Lt, FA Btry B 10th FA Bn., Italy 9 Mar. 1944
Schultz, James W., Pfc, Co. A 7th Inf, France 8 Oct. 1944
Schwartz, Alex, Pvt, Co. A 30th Inf, Sicily July 1943
Schwartz, James R. 1st Sgt, Co. I 30th Inf, France 17 Dec. 1944
Schwartz, Walter, Pfc, Hq. Co. 1st Bn., 30th Inf, Colmar 20 Feb. 1945
Schwartz, William A., 1st Sgt, Btry A 9th FA Bn., Sicily 10 Aug. 1943
Scott, Dave F., Pvt, Co. D 7th Inf, Italy Oct. 1943
Scott, Richard W., T/5, Co. E 30th Inf, Zweibrucken, Germany 19 Mar. 1945
Scott, Walter C., Pfc, Med. Det. 15th Inf, France 27 Dec. 1944
Scura, Sunday, Pfc, Co. K 15th Inf, Kalreuth, Germany 17 Apr. 1945
Sczyepanowski, Karol, S/Sgt, Co. A 30th Inf, S. France 12 Sept. 1944

▲Searls, Pearl E., S/Sgt, Co. D 15th Inf, Briarville, France, 5 Nov. 1944
Sedwick, Harold H., Pfc, Co. D 30th Inf, Italy 5 June 1944
Seehafer, Erwin C., 1st Lt, Inf Co. B 15th Inf, Miltenberg, Germany 30 Mar. 1945
Seely, John W., Pfc, Co. K 7th Inf, Italy 2 Feb. 1944
Seifarth, Charles K., 2d Lt, Hq. Co. 7th Inf, France 28 Sept. 1944
Seifert, Milton E., Pfc, Co. L 15th Inf, Bocksberg, Germany 26 Apr. 1945
Seivers, Orville H., Cpl, Btry B 41st FA Bn., French Morocco 10 Nov. 1942
Self, Charles H., T/5, Co. D 7th Inf, Nurnberg, Germany 18 Apr. 1945
Sepulvado, Wilburn, Pvt, Btry C 10th FA Bn., France 28 Jan. 1945
Sereno, Francis C., Pfc, AT Co. 7th Inf, Italy 13 Oct. 1943
Sessa, Jerry, Pfc, Co. G 30th Inf, France 30 Oct. 1944
Severinsky, Michael, Pvt, Co. B 30th Inf, Italy 21 Oct. 1943
Shackleford, Thomas T., S/Sgt, Co. K 15th Inf, Italy 23 May 1944
Shade, Ernest, S/Sgt, Co. F 30th Inf, France 9 Sept. 1944
▲Shaffer, J. D., S/Sgt, Hq. & Hq. Btry 41st FA Bn., Le Tholy, France 8 Oct. 1944
▲Shaffer, William O., Jr., Pvt, Med. Det. 30th Inf, France 2 Oct. 1944
Shapiro, Bernard, Sgt, Co. L 7th Inf, Italy 2 Mar. 1944
Sharoff, Robert L., Capt, Med. Det. 15th Inf, Italy 28 Jan. 1944
Sharp, Jim C., S/Sgt, Hq. Btry 39th FA Bn., Italy 21 Oct. 1943
Sharp, Ralph R., Pvt, Co. L 30th Inf, Italy 7 Mar. 1944
Shaw, Ferris L., S/Sgt, Co. F 30th Inf, France 18 Dec. 1944
Sheen, Glen S., T/Sgt, Co. F 15th Inf, Nurnberg, Germany 18 Apr. 1945
Shepherd, Elmer V., Pvt, Med. Det. 7th Inf, Italy 1 Feb. 1944
Sheppard, Louis M., Pvt, Co. M 7th Inf, Italy 16 Oct. 1943
Shinnamon, George E., Sgt, Co. C 7th Inf, Vagney, France 7 Oct. 1944
Shipp, James R., S/Sgt, Co. H 7th Inf, France 15 Aug. 1944
Shipp, Lloyd L., Pvt, Co. K 7th Inf, Sicily July 1943
Shirley, John B., 2d Lt, Co. I 15th Inf, France 23 Dec. 1944
Shiro, Samuel H., 1st Lt, FA 9th FA Bn., Sicily Aug. 1943
Shook, Gordon, Pfc, Co. F 7th Inf, French Morocco 10 Nov. 1942
Shores, Elmer E., T/4, Med. Det. 30th Inf, Sicily Aug. 1943
Shulkatis, Daniel J., 1st Lt, Co. L 15th Inf, Sandtorf, Germany 28 Mar. 1945
Sieczek, John J., Cpl, Hq. Co. 15th Inf, Italy 1 Apr. 1944
Sicina, Florina, S/Sgt, Co. D 30th Inf, France 3 Oct. 1944
Sigel, Franz, 2d Lt, Co. A 7th Inf, Sapois, France 9 Oct. 1944
Sigmon, Maymon E., Sgt, Co. B 7th Inf, Sandhofen, Germany 26 Mar. 1945
Silberman, Jack, Cpl, Co. D 7th Inf, France 22 Jan. 1945
Silcox, Jack, Pfc, Co. C 15th Inf, Althornbach, Germany 18 Mar. 1945
Silva, Antonio L., Cpl, 3d Rcn.Trp., Ober Thulba, Germany 12 Apr. 1945
Silverstein, George, Pfc, Co. E 30th Inf, Kaysersberg, France 18 Dec. 1944
Simkins, Henry B., Cpl, Co. F 15th Inf, Sicily Aug. 1943
Simmons, James T., Pfc, Co. A 30th Inf, Italy 23-24 Apr. 1944
Simokausks, William F., Pfc, Hq. Co. 2d Bn. 7th Inf, Besancon, France 6 Sept. 1944
Simonson, Kenneth R., 1st Lt, FA 39th Bn., Monte Rotundo, Italy 6 Nov. 1943
Simpkins, Algie H., Pvt, Med. Det. 30th Inf, French Morocco 8 Nov. 1942
Simpkins, Bob, T/Sgt, Co. H 30th Inf, Italy 8 Nov. 1943.
Simpson, John B., Jr., T/5, Co. C 10th Engr. Bn., Zweibrucken, Germany 19 Mar. 1945
Sinclair, Edmond B., Maj, MC 7th Inf, Sandhofen, Germany 26 Mar. 1945
Singer, Melvin S., S/Sgt, Co. L 15th Inf, France 15 Aug. 1944
Siwek, Charles, Pfc, Co. L 7th Inf, Cisterna di Litorria, Italy 29 Feb. 1944
Skarwecki, Joseph J., 2d Lt, Co. L 7th Inf, France 1 Nov. 1944
Skeahan, Charles H., Jr., 1st Lt, Co. C 30th Inf, France 27 Jan. 1945
Skinner, Ivan L., Pvt, Med. Det. 7th Inf, Sicily Aug. 1943
Skjefte, Arley, Sgt, Co. L 15th Inf, Italy 11 Nov. 1943
Sladen, Fred W., Lt Col, Inf 1st Bn. 30th Inf, Sicily July 1943
Slattery, Donald J., Pfc, Med. Det.15th Inf, Sicily Aug. 1943
Slaughter, Robert B., Sgt, Co. D 7th Inf, France 21 Oct. 1944
Sloan, Arthur M., T/5, Med. Det. 7th Inf, Germany 18 Mar. 1945
Slusher, Cecil B., Pvt, Co. F 30th Inf, Germany 27 Mar. 1945
Smith, Albinus H., Sgt, Co. G 30th Inf, France 21 Sept. 1944
Smith, Benjamin F., Pfc, AT Co. 15th Inf, Italy 29 Feb. 1944
▲(2) Smith, Claude E., 1st Sgt, Co. K 15th Inf, Germany 22 Mar. 1945
▲Smith, Cleo I., Pfc, Co. A 30th Inf, France 30 Jan. 1945
Smith, Cyril E., T/4, Med. Det. 7th Inf, Sicily Aug. 1943
Smith, Emerald M., T/5, Med. Det. 7th Inf, Sicily Aug. 1943
Smith, Forrest L., Jr., S/Sgt, Co. A 7th Inf, Sicily 17 July 1943
Smith, George F., S/Sgt, Co. D 30th Inf, Sicily July 1943
Smith, Murian F., 2d Lt, AT Co. 7th Inf, Italy Oct. 1943
Smith, Ralph V., Jr., Pfc, Cn Co. 15th Inf, Achsheim, Germany 27 Apr. 1945
Smith, Reno, Pfc, Co. B 7th Inf, Germany 31 Mar. 1945
Smith, Robert C., Pvt, Co. M 30th Inf, France 26 Nov. 1944
Smith, Robert L., S/Sgt, Co. C 30th Inf, France 7 Sept. 1944
Smith, Roland C., Sgt, Co. G 15th Inf, Nurnberg, Germany 17 Apr. 1945
Smith, Rudolph, Sgt, Hq. Co. 2d Bn. 30th Inf, France 16 Aug. 1944
Smith, Wesley J., S/Sgt, Co. C 30th Inf, Pasing, Germany 30 Apr. 1945
Smith, William H., Pfc, Cn Co. 15th Inf, Italy 5 June 1944
▲Smith, Willis B., Sgt, Co. B 601st TO, Italy 3 Feb. 1944
▲Smitherman, Robert W., 1st Lt, Co. G 7th Inf, France 4 Nov. 1944
Smithers, Charles E., Pfc, Co. F 15th Inf, France 26 Jan. 1945
Snead, Earnest (NMI), Pfc, Co. C 7th Inf, Italy 13 Oct. 1943
Snowden, Forest C., Pvt, Co. F 30th Inf, Sicily July 1943
Snowden, Norwood L., Capt, Inf Cmdr Cn Co. 30th Inf Regt, France 18 Aug. 1944
Snow II, George L., Capt, Hq. Btry 3d IDA, Sicily 5 Aug. 1943
Snyder, Arthur, Lt Col, FA 751st Tank Bn., Italy 25 May 1944
Snyder, Bernard R., S/Sgt, Co. L 15th Inf, France 19 Aug. 1944
Snyder, Harry B., Pvt, 3d Sig. Co., Sicily Aug. 1943
Snyder, James R., Pfc, Co. E 7th Inf, France 1 Dec. 1944
Snyder, Morris F., Sgt, Co. L 7th Inf, Italy 29 Feb. 1944
Snyder, Walter H., T/Sgt, Co. C 30th Inf, Nurnberg, Germany 19 Apr. 1945
Sobolewski, Frank, S/Sgt, Co. K 7th Inf, French Morocco 10 Nov. 1942
Sobuta, Edward A., S/Sgt, Co. K 7th Inf, Italy 1 Mar. 1944
Socie, George R., Sgt, Hq. Co. 2d Bn. 7th Inf, Cisterna, Italy 1 Mar. 1944
Soderquist, Richard W., Capt, Hq. 1st Bn. 15th Inf, Sicily Aug. 1943
Solch, Joseph W., Capt, Co. G 15th Inf, Italy 26 May 1944
Solomon, Warren M., Capt, Inf Hq. Co. 1st Bn. 7th Inf, Besancon, France 7 Sept. 1944
Sonefelt, John F., AT Co. 15th Inf, Nurnberg, Germany 18 Apr. 1945
Soskil, Morris, Pfc, Co. G 7th Inf, Utweiler, Germany 15 Mar. 1945
Sosnowski, Alexander, Pvt, Hq. Co. 2d Bn. 7th Inf, Italy 19 Feb. 1944
Soules, John H., 2d Lt, Co. K 7th Inf, Germany 1 Apr. 1945
Soyster, Russell J., Sgt, Co. C 7th Inf, France 6 Oct. 1944

▲ Oak Leaf Cluster.

Spaeth, Dean W., S/Sgt, Co. E 7th Inf, Wirh-en-Plaine, France 12 May 1945
Spain, Joe, Pvt, Med. Det. 7th Inf, Italy 31 May 1944
Spann, Manual O., Pfc, Co. H 30th Inf, Italy 2 Mar. 1944
Sparks, Richard M., Cpl, Co. L 7th Inf, Sicily July 1943
Spell, James E., Cpl, Armd. Comd. Hq. Co. 751st Tank Bn., Italy 16 Feb. 1944
Spicer, George K., 1st Lt, Inf Co. L 30th Inf, Taulignan, France 19 Aug. 1944
Spinks, Garlen, Pfc, Med. Det. 30th Inf, Germany 7 Apr. 1945
Spisak, Andrew, Cpl, Co. C 30th Inf, Italy 8 Nov. 1943
Sporacio, Anthony J., Pvt, Med. Det. 7th Inf, French Morocco 10 Nov. 1942
Spota, Anthony F., Pvt, Co. L 30th Inf, Rosenheim, Germany 2 May 1945
▲Sprague, Wilbur F., Pfc, Co. L 15th Inf, Germany 9 Apr. 1945
Springer, Wilbur D., Sgt, Co. M 7th Inf, France 7 Sept. 1944
Staats, Garrett R., S/Sgt, Co. C 15th Inf, France 12 Oct. 1944
Stafford, Elmer A., Sgt, Hq. 3d Bn. 15th Inf, Italy 28 Feb. 1944
Stage, Shirley E., S/Sgt, Co. E 7th Inf, France 5 Oct. 1944
Stanek, Millard J., Capt, Hq. 41st FA Bn., France 16 Oct. 1944
Staniford, Archie V., Pfc, Hq Co. 2d Bn. 30th Inf, Italy 4 Mar. 1944
Stanley, Alvin W., T/5, Med. Det. 15th Inf, Miltenberg, Germany 30 Mar. 1945
▲Stanley, Howard E., T/Sgt, Co. K 15th Inf, Italy 29 Feb. 1944
Stanley, Paul W., Capt, Co. F 30th Inf, Italy 29 Feb. 1944
Stanton, John J., T/3, Co. C 30th Inf, Nurnberg, Germany 18 Apr. 1945
Staples, Frank E., Cpl, Hq. Btry 9th FA Bn., Sicily Aug. 1943
Starkey, Elvyn H., Pfc, 3d Rcn Trp., Germany 24 Apr. 1945
Starkey, George G., Jr., T/Sgt, Co. B 30th Inf, France 26-28 Oct. 1944
Starr, Esmund S., Jr., Pvt, Co. G 15th Inf, Italy 26 Jan. 1944
Steele, Robert H., Sgt, Cn Co. 15th Inf, Achsheim, Germany 27 Apr. 1945
Steenback, Kurt, Pfc, Co. E 7th Inf, French Morocco 10 Nov. 1942
Stegmann, Donald F., 2d Lt, Co. K 7th Inf, France 20 Nov. 1944
Stein, Gilbert B., Pfc, Co. G 7th Inf, Italy 29 Feb. 1944
Stephens, Wilfred R., Capt, Co. L 15th Inf, Sicily July 1943
Sternberg, Raymond L., Pfc, Co. I 7th Inf, France 29 Oct. 1944
Stevens, Alfred H., Pfc, Hq. Co. 30th Inf, Vosges 5 Dec. 1944
Stevens, Howard L., Pfc, Co. D 7th Inf, Langenreich, Germany 26 Apr. 45
Stevenson, Earl K., Pvt, Co. B 7th Inf, Utweiler, Germany 15 Mar. 1945
Stewart, Graham, Sgt, Co. L 7th Inf, France 16 Jan. 1945
Stewart, William B., Capt, Hq. 3d Bn., Italy 2 June 1944
Stezar, William A., T/Sgt, Co. D 15th Inf, France 26 Dec. 1944
Stillson, George G., Jr., Pfc, Co. L 30th Inf, France 17 Sept. 1944
Stobaugh, Elbert O., Pfc, Cn Co. 30th Inf, France 21 Aug. 1944
Stocker, John A., Pfc, 3d Sig. Co., France 19-20 Nov. 1944
Stockman, Perry J., 2d Lt, Inf 7th Inf, French Morocco 10 Nov. 1942
Stoessell, Carl A., Cpl, Co. D 7th Inf, Italy Oct. 1943
Stoker, Merlin C., Capt, Hq. 1st Bn. 15th Inf, France 14 Sept. 1944
Stoner, Edward W., Pfc, Co. E 30th Inf, Anzio, Italy 5 June 1944
Stoodley, Robert P., S/Sgt, Co. F 15th Inf, Nurnberg, Germany 18 Apr. 1945
Stouffer, Wilferd, Sgt, Co. B 30th Inf, Italy 1 June 1944
Stromberg, Woodrow W., Lt Col, Co. 2d Bn. 30th Inf, Italy 19 Feb. 1944
Struckmeyer, Frederick C., 1st Lt, Co. K 15th Inf, France 12 Sept. 1944
▲Stuart, Warren M., Capt, Inf Co. I 15th Inf, France 12 Sept. 1944
Stout, Irvin P., Sgt, Co. I 30th Inf, Vamontone, Italy 1 June 1944
Stranahan, Herbert B., 2nd Lt, Inf 30th Inf, Sicily July 1943
Strauley, Raymond C., Pfc, Co. L 30th Inf, Italy 23 May 1944
Strauss, Daniel F., Pvt, Co. F 30th Inf, Germany 27 Mar. 1945
Strausser, Charles, Pfc, Co. D 30th Inf, France 30 Sept. 1944
Streff, Robert A., Sgt, Co. F 30th Inf, Italy 2 Mar. 1944
Strickland, Melvin C., Pfc, Co. B 7th Inf, France 6 Oct. 1944
Strickler, William C., Pfc, Co. E 7th Inf, French Morocco 10 Nov. 1942
Stripling, Gordon A., Pfc, Co. G 30th Inf, Vosges 5 Dec. 1944
Stripp, George E., 1st Lt, Co. E 7th Inf, France 6 Sept. 1944
▲Stucky, William, Capt, Inf Hq. 3d Inf Div., Woret de Colmar 24 Jan. 1945
Suek, Sylvester C., T/5, Med. Det. 30th Inf, Italy 15 Oct. 1943
Sugarman, Robert M., Pfc, Co. C 30th Inf, Colmar 20 Feb. 1945
Sugg, Raymond M., S/Sgt, Hq. Co. 2d Bn. 15th Inf, Nompatelize, France 4 Nov. 1944
Sulinski, John W., S/Sgt, Co. K 7th Inf, Scharof, Germany 28 Mar. 1945
Sullivan, Daniel T., Pfc, Co. C 30th Inf, Italy 1 Feb. 1944
Sullivan, James C., Sgt, AT Co. 15th Inf, Italy 29 Feb. 1944
Sullivan, Walter G., S/Sgt, Hq. Co. 2d Bn. 30th Inf, Italy 22 May 1944
Sullivan, Woodard H., Co. A 30th Inf, France 3 Nov. 1944
Suman, Kenneth L., Pfc, Hq. Co. 3d Bn. 7th Inf, Althornbach, Germany 18-19 1945
Sumers, Pete A., S/Sgt, 3d Rcn Trp., Sicily July 1943
Summers, William B., Pvt, Med. Det. 7th Inf, Italy 30-31 Jan. 1944
Sumner, William A., 1st Lt, Co. I 30th Inf, France 1 Feb. 1945
Sundby, Harold R., S/Sgt, Co. B 7th Inf, France 23 Sept. 1944
Sutton, Carl S., Pfc, Co. L 15th Inf, Nurnberg, Germany 17 Apr. 1945
Sweet, Earl L., Pvt, Co. I 15th Inf, France 24 Jan. 1945
Sweeney, Carl C., Cpl, Hq. & Hq. Btry 41 st FA Bn., Italy 7 Nov. 1943
▲Sweeney, Frank E., Jr., S/Sgt, Co. A 30th Inf, France 31 Jan. 1945
Sweeney, Hugh A., 1st Lt, Cn Co. 30th Inf, France 4 Feb. 1945
Swickerath, Carl J., Capt, Co. E 30th Inf, Italy 19 Feb. 1944
Swanson, Chester R., T/Sgt, Co. C 7th Inf, Sicily 16 July 1943
Swanson, Earl E., 1st Lt, Co. F 7th Inf, France 3 Nov. 1944
Swanson, Stanley M., Pvt, Hq. Co. 1st Bn. 30th Inf, French Morocco 10 Nov. 1942
Syc, John W., Cpl, Co. L 30th Inf, Italy 10 Nov. 1943
Sylvis, Cecil A., Sgt, Co. F 15th Inf, Wildensorg, Germany 13 Apr. 1945
Szczepanowski, Karol, S/Sgt, Co. A 30th Inf, France 21 Aug. 1944
Szladek, Frank J., Capt, MC Co. A 3d Med. Bn., Kaysersberg, France 22 Jan. 1945

▲Tait, George R., Jr., Pfc, Co. L 30th Inf, Germany 2 May 1945
Talbert, Earl H., Pvt, Med. Det. 30th Inf, Italy 5 Mar. 1944
Talbert, James, Pfc, Co. H 30th Inf, Sicily July 1943
Talgo, George L., Sgt, Inf Co. A 30th Inf Regt., France 2 Oct. 1944
Tancredi, Vincent A., Pfc, Co. M 30th Inf, Italy 7 Mar. 1944
Tank, Charles F., Lt Col, CE. 10th Engr. Bn., France 7 Sept. 1944
Taphorn, Francis J., Sgt, FA Co. A 601st TD Bn., France 24 Jan. 1945
Taphorn, Francis J., S/Sgt, Co. A 601st TD Bn., Steinach, Germany 7 Apr. 1945
Tardif, Joseph M., S/Sgt, Co. B 601st TD Bn., France 27 Jan. 1945
Tarrant, Hugh L., Pfc, Co. M 7th Inf, Mehlingerhoff, France 15 Mar. 1945
Tatro, Howard U., Pfc, Co. M 7th Inf, Italy 23 May 1944
▲Taylor, Keith L., Sgt, Hq. Co. 30th Inf, Italy July 1943
Teague, Dearl N., T/5, Med. Det. 15th Inf, Bennwihr, France 26 Dec. 1944
Teague, Norris M., Jr., 1st Lt, Co. B 7th Inf, Italy 30 Jan. 1944
Tedrow, Odell, T/4, Med. Det. 30th Inf, French Morocco 8 Nov. 1942
Tee, Wilbert M., S/Sgt, Co. I 30th Inf, Waldhausen, Germany 24 Apr. 1945
Teekell, Milan J., 1st Lt, Co. I 7th Inf, France 16 Jan. 1945
Teets, Francis, Pvt, Co. A 15th Inf, Italy 7 Feb. 1944
▲Telseth, Orie H., S/Sgt, Co. F 7th Inf, Germany 26 Apr. 1945
▲Terry, Milford A., Sgt, Co. D 15th Inf, Le Tholy, France 4 Oct. 1944
Tetreault, Albert J., 2d Lt, Hq. Co. (BP), France 15 Aug. 1944
Theiss, Walter G., Sgt, Hq. Co. 1st Bn. 15th Inf, French Morocco 9 Nov. 1942
Theodore, Teddy E., T/5, Hq. Co. 7th Inf, Sicily Aug. 1943
▲Thierolf, Dwight R., S/Sgt, Co. C 7th Inf, Villers, Le Sec, France 12 Sept. 1944
Thobro, Clayton C., Lt Col, Inf 7th Inf, France 4 Nov. 1944
▲Thomas, Carl W., 2d Lt, Hq. Co. 2d Bn. 15th Inf, Italy 21 Sept. 1943
Thomas, Cecil B., Jr., 1st Lt, FA Btry B 39th FA Bn., France 17 Oct. 1944
Thomas, Quentin C., T/5, Hq. Co. 1st Bn. 7th Inf, Italy 30-31 Jan. 1944
Thomas, John, S/Sgt, Med. Det. 7th Inf, Italy 24 Sept. 1943
Thomas, Virgus C., Pfc, Med. Det. 7th Inf, Italy 22 Apr. 1944
Thompson, Ben M., S/Sgt, Co. L 15th Inf, Italy 30 Jan. 1944
Thompson, Calvin F., T/5, Hq. Btry 9th FA Bn., Mortagne, France 1 Nov. 1944
Thompson, Clifford B., 1st Lt, FA 601st TD Bn., Walhausen, Germany 23 Mar. 1945
Thompson, Dale D., Sgt, 3d Sig. Co., Sicily Aug. 1943
Thompson, Theodore F., Jr., T/5, Med. Det. 7th Inf, Italy 23 April 1944
Thorn, Henry H., Pfc, RDR Pltn. Co. A 30th Inf, Italy 25 May 1944
Thorpe, George, Cpl, AT Co. 15th Inf, Nurnberg, Germany 18 Apr. 1945
Thull, Herbert J., Sgt, Hq. Btry 9th FA Bn., Italy 16 Nov. 1943
Tickler, Peter A., Sgt, Hq. Co. 30th Inf, Sicily 20 July 1944
Tiffany, Hiero G., Jr., 1st Lt, Co. D 30th Inf, France 27 Jan. 1945
Tijerina, Charlie T., Pvt, Co. D 7th Inf, Italy Oct. 1943
Tillman, Robert L., 2d Lt, MAC Med. Det. 7th Inf, France 23 Jan. 1945
▲Tilseth, Orie H., S/Sgt, Co. F 7th Inf, Germany 26 Apr. 1945
Todd, Jimmie L., Pfc, Hq. Co. 3d Bn. 30th Inf, Schwarzelbach, Germany 6 Apr. 1945
▲Todd, Merl H., S/Sgt, Co. I 15th Inf, Italy 2 Mar. 1944
▲Tofanelli, Elmo F., Capt, Co. A 15th Inf, Sigolsheim, France 23 Dec. 1944
▲Toffey, John J., Jr., Lt Col, Inf, 7th Inf, Italy 3 June 1944
Tomlinson, Harold H., Pfc, Co. C 15th Inf, Roccoromana, Italy 18 Oct. 1943
Tompkins, Harold L., Pvt, Hq. Co. 2d Bn. 15th Inf, France 22 Oct. 1944
Toney, Malcolm B., 1st Lt, Hq. Co. 1st Bn. 7th Inf, Germany 18 Mar. 1945
Toole, Frederick W., 1st Lt, Co. A 15th Inf, France 27 Aug. 1944
Toole, John H., 1st Lt, Inf Co. L 15th Inf, Nurnberg, Germany 19 Apr. 1945
Toomer, Harold K., 1st Lt, Co. F 7th Inf, France 26 Aug. 1944
Toomey, Jacob C., Pfc, Co. K 15th Inf, Kalchreuth, Germany 16 Apr. 1945
▲Toothman, Cleo A., Pfc, Co. D 30th Inf, Germany 26 Mar. 1945
Torchia, Joseph R., Pvt, Co. B 756th Tank Bn., Germany 5 Apr. 1945
Torman, John, Pfc, Co. D 15th Inf, Besancon, France 8 Sept. 1944
Torres, Ceasar R., Jr., S/Sgt, Co. L 15th Inf, Moheisweiler, Germany 22 Mar. 1945
Trapani, Charles, Sgt, Co. L 30th Inf, Italy 24 Jan. 1944
▲Travis, Ragan W., Sgt, Co. I 15th Inf, Benniwhr, France 28 Dec. 1944
▲Treadway, Charles L., 1st Lt, Co. I 7th Inf, Vagney, France 6 Oct. 1944
▲Tremblay, Telesphor C., 2d Lt, Hq. Co. 1st Bn., Germany 19 Apr. 1945
Trippett, Thurman, S/Sgt, Co. B 7th Inf, Sicily July 1943
Trost, Louis R., 1st Sgt, Co. K 30th Inf, France 23 Jan. 1945
Troyer, Orve J., T/Sgt, Co. D 7th Inf, Italy 31 Jan. 1944
Truax, Edward, Sgt, Hq. Co. 7th Inf, Rougeville, France 6 Nov. 1944
Trumbley, Bert E., Cpl, Co. C 10th Engr. Bn., Italy 23 May 1944
Tucker, Alfred V., Cpl, Co. D 7th Inf, Italy 31 Jan. 1944
▲Tumulty, Vincent A., T/Sgt, Co. I 15th Inf, France 3 Oct. 1944
Turpin, Herman L., S/Sgt, Co. A 756th Tank Bn., Houssen, France 26 Jan. 1945
Tussey, Joe W., S/Sgt, Hq. Co. 7th Inf, Houssen, France 27 Jan. 1945
Tyler, Robert V., S/Sgt, Co. L 15th Inf, France 27 Dec. 1944
Tylinski, Stanley A., Cpl, 3d Qm Co., Italy 7 Oct. 1943
Tyrer, David L., Pvt, Co. E 30th Inf, Sicily Aug. 1943

Uecker, Daniel R., Pfc, Co. K 15th Inf, Bennwihr, France 20 Dec. 1944
▲Ugade, Jesse G., Capt, Inf 30th Inf, 1 June 1944
▲Ugalde, Jesse G., 2d Lt, Inf 30th Inf, Fedala, French Morocco 8 Nov. 1942
Ulanski, Chester P., S/Sgt, AT Co. 30th Inf, France 23 Jan. 1945
Ung, Charles A. W., Pfc, Co. E 30th Inf, Zweibrucken, Germany 19 Mar. 1945
Urban, Joe F., Pfc, Co. B 30th Inf, Germany 8 May 1944
Uschold, Raymond C., Pfc, Co. B 7th Inf, Latona, Italy 18 Apr. 1944
Uttecht, Ruben A., Pfc, Cn Co. 15th Inf, France 2 Nov. 1944

Vail, James M., Pvt, Co. L 30th Inf, Italy Sept. 1943
Valdespino, Emilio J., Cpl, Btry C 10th FA Bn., Sicily Aug. 1943
Valenzuela, Olegario L., Pvt, Co. E 7th Inf, Italy Oct. 1943
Van Brunt, Billie V., T/5, Btry B 9th FA Bn., Italy 17 Mar. 1944
Van Demark, Kenneth R., Pfc, Co. H 7th Inf, Besancon, France 5 Sept. 1944
▲Vander Ende, Charles T., S/Sgt, Co. D 30th Inf, France 16 Dec. 1944
Van Dyke, Lester, Pfc, Co. B 30th Inf, Kaysersberg, France 17 Dec. 1944
Van Horn, Boyd, S/Sgt, Co. D 15th Inf, Italy 16 Feb. 1944
Van Hoy, Louie R., 1st Lt, Co. F 7th Inf, Italy 2 Feb. 1944
Vanover, Ralph B., S/Sgt, Co. B 30th Inf, France 15 Sept. 1944
Van Wey, William S., Capt, Inf Co. M 7th Inf, Hyeres, France 19 Aug. 1944
Vario, Joseph, Pfc, Co. B 30th Inf, Nurnberg, Germany 18 Apr. 1945
Vernarelli, Arnold F., 1st Lt, Hq. 1st Bn. 30th Inf, France 25 Sept. 1944
Vasilakis, Thomas, S/Sgt, Co. M 15th Inf, Thal, Germany 22 Mar. 1945
Vasquez, Gilbert E., Pvt, Co. M 7th Inf, Italy 24 May 1944
Vasion, Daniel P., Pfc, Co. C 30th Inf, Italy 1 Feb. 1944
Venable, Everette, Pfc, Co. H 30th Inf, France 18 Dec. 1944
Ventimiglia, Benedetto, 1st Sgt, Co. K 30th Inf, Sicily 2 Aug. 1943
Villella, Louis, Pfc, Co. D 15th Inf, France 1 Feb. 1945
Vilt, Edward J., Pvt, Co. A 7th Inf, France 15 Mar. 1945
Vogel, Robert B., S/Sgt, Co. F 7th Inf, Italy 15 Oct. 1943
Vong, Leonard E., T/5, Med. Det. 30th Inf, Sicily 7 Aug. 1943
Von Kahle, Vancino, Pfc, Co. B 30th Inf, St. Die, France 6 Nov. 1944
Vowell, Earl P., Sgt, Co. G 7th Inf, Italy 29 Feb. 1944

Waddell, William E., Capt, MC Med. Det. 15th Inf, Italy 26 Jan. 1944
Waddell, Otis J., Sgt, Co. M 15th Inf, Italy 1 June 1944

▲ Oak Leaf Cluster.

Wade, John E., Jr., 1st Lt, Co. M 15th Inf, Italy 2 Mar. 1944
Wadkins, Emanuel F., T/Sgt, Co. C 7th Inf, Sicily 10 Aug. 1943
Wagner, Adolph, Pfc, Med. Det. 15th Inf, France 7 Nov. 1944
Wagner, Sherman J., Pvt, Med. Det. 15th Inf, Italy 16 Feb. 1944
Wagner, Willard F., S/Sgt, Hq. Co. 3d Bn. 7th Inf, France 8 Sept. 1944
Waldner, Stanley C., 2d Lt, Co. B 15th Inf, France 26 Jan. 1945
Waldrop, James D., Pvt, Co. K 15th Inf, Italy 23 Apr. 1944
Walker, Darwin E., 1st Lt, Co. I 30th Inf, Colmar 20 Feb. 1945
Walker, William J., Pfc, Med. Det. 30th Inf, Hornbach, Germany 18 Mar. 1945
Walker, George W., Jr., Pfc, Co. K 30th Inf, Italy 5 Feb. 1944
▲Walker, Bennett O., S/Sgt, Co. L 7th Inf, Germany 18 Apr. 1945
Wall, Stephen J., S/Sgt, Co. M 7th Inf, Houssen, France 25 Jan. 1945
Wallace, Charles C., Pfc, Co. A 10th Engr. Bn., France 5 Feb. 1945
Wallace, Kenneth W., Capt, Hq. 1st Bn. 7th Inf, Italy 30 Jan. 1944
Wallace, Sherry R., 2d Lt, Co. F 30th Inf, Vosges 5 Dec. 1944
Walters, Charles L., Pvt, Med. Det. 7th Inf, France 4 Nov. 1944
Walters, Raymond C., S/Sgt, Co. M 30th Inf, Siegfried Line 19 Mar. 1945
Walters, Richard T., Pfc, Co. M 15th Inf, Nurnberg, Germany 12 Apr. 1945
Wang, Laverne E., Cpl, Co. E 7th Inf, Sicily Aug. 1943
Wann, Robert A., Capt, Inf Co. E 15th Inf, Sigolsheim, France 27 Dec. 1944
Wanner, William A., T/5, Co. L 7th Inf, Steinach, Germany 8 Apr. 1945
Ward, Bascom Z., Pfc, Co. M 15th Inf, Nurnberg, Germany 20 Apr. 1945
Ward, Hershel, Co. C 30th Inf, Colmar 20 Feb. 1945
▲Wardell, William T., T/Sgt, Co. B 30th Inf, Chalet, France 9 Nov. 1944
Wardlaw, Hugh E., Jr., Maj, Hq. 2d Bn. 30th Inf, France 21 Sept. 1944
Ware, Keith L., Capt, Inf Hq. 1st Bn. 15th Inf, Sicily 11 Aug. 1943
Warne, Walter R., 1st Lt, Co. D 7th Inf, France 23 Jan. 1945
Warner, Edward P., Cpl, Hq. Co. 2d Bn. 30th Inf, Germany 23 Jan. 1945
Warren, Arnold E., S/Sgt, Co. G 30th Inf, Munich, Germany 30 Apr. 1945
Watson, Herman O., Pfc, Co. C 30th Inf, Vosges 5 Dec. 1944
Watkins, George W., Pfc, Hq. Co. 3d Bn. 15th Inf, Germany 4 Apr. 1945
Watts, Otis, Pfc, Co. C 30th Inf, Colmar 20 Feb. 1945
Wax, Leslie C., Pfc, Co. C 30th Inf, France 7 Nov. 1944
Wayrynen, Reino, Pvt, Co. D 7th Inf, French Morocco 8 Nov. 1942
▲Weakley, Leonard, Sgt, Co. I 15th Inf, Bennwihr, France 23 Dec. 1944
Weaver, Herchel H., S/Sgt, Co. B 30th Inf, France 14 Sept. 1944
▲Webb, Charles W., 1st Lt, Co. H 7th Inf, Naussen, France 25 Jan. 1945
Webb, William R., Pfc, Btry A 9th FA Bn., Sicily Aug. 1943
Webb, William W., Pvt, Co. M 7th Inf, Italy Nov. 1943
Webber, Edward W., S/Sgt, Co. L 30th Inf, Lapertheim, Germany 26 Mar. 1945
Webber, Robert M., Capt, Hq. & Hq. Btry 41st FA Bn., Italy 26 Jan. 1944
Weber, Edward H., S/Sgt, Co. L 15th Inf, France 9 Nov. 1944
Weber, John, 2d Lt, Inf Co. A 30th Inf, Urbach, Germany 15 Mar. 1945
Weber, Martin, S/Sgt, Co. G 7th Inf, Nurnberg, Germany 18 Apr. 1945
Weber, Sterl W., Cpl, Co. A 601st TD Bn., Steinach, Germany 7 Apr. 1944
▲Weese, Floyd, Pfc, Co. C 30th Inf, France 7 Sept. 1944
Weimar, David A., Sgt, Co. F 30th Inf, Italy 13 Dec. 1943
Weimaster, Floyd V., S/Sgt, Co. G 7th Inf, Womach, Germany 2 Apr. 1945
Weiner, Abraham, 1st Lt, Inf Serv. Co. 15th Inf, Italy 18 Oct. 1943
Weingarden, Aldfred, T/Sgt, Co. G 7th Inf, Krausenbach, Germany 1 Apr. 1945
Weisenburg, Leonard E., Capt, 10th FA Bn., Italy 29 Feb. 1944
Weisman, Simon A., Pvt, Co. H 30th Inf, Italy 28 Feb. 1944
▲Welch, Thomas P., 1st Lt, FA Co. B 601st TD Bn., Durrenentzen, France 2 Feb. 1945
Wells, Dorsie S., Pfc, Co. M 7th Inf, Italy 19 Feb. 1944
Wells, Harry L., Pfc, Med. Det. 15th Inf, Sicily Aug. 1943
Werkheiser, Raymond T., Pvt, Co. F 30th Inf, France 21 Sept. 1944
Wero, Henry B., Pfc, Co. K 15th Inf, Italy 26 Sept. 1943
▲West, Jim D., Pfc, Med. Det. 15th Inf, Sicily Aug. 1943
▲West, John H., Capt, Inf Co. G 30th Inf Regt., France 30 Oct. 1944
Westberry, Clifford, Pfc, Co. K 15th Inf, Italy 24 May 1944
Westenheffer, William W., Pvt, Co. A 7th Inf, Sicily Aug. 1943
Weverstad, Stanley W., S/Sgt, Co. L 7th Inf, Hornbach, Germany 16 Mar. 1945
Weylandt, William A. J., S/Sgt, Co. K 30th Inf, France 13 Sept. 1944
Wheat, Ellis F., 2d Lt, Co. I 15th Inf, France 5 Aug. 1944
Wheat, Paul G., S/Sgt, Co. C 30th Inf, Kosbach, Germany 15 Apr. 1945
Wheaton, Rendell L., Pfc, Co. A 30th Inf, Italy 8 Feb. 1944
Wheeler, James B., Pfc, Co. G 30th Inf, Hoppenheim, Germany 27 Mar. 1945
Wheeler, Melvin O., Pfc, Co. K 15th Inf, Germany 9 Apr. 1945
White, Allen H., Pvt, Co. M 7th Inf, Italy 31 May 1944
White, Leland P., S/Sgt, Co. F 30th Inf, Nurnberg, Germany 19 Apr. 1945
▲White, Robert A., S/Sgt, Hq. Co. 1st Bn. 7th Inf, Italy 30 Jan. 1944
▲White, Frank I., Pfc, CW Co. D 2d Chem Bn., Italy 13 Nov. 1944
Whitehouse, John F., Sgt, Co. K 30th Inf, France 17 Dec. 1944
Whitfield, Alonzo B., S/Sgt, Co. F 15th Inf, Sicily 8 Aug. 1943
Whitley, Clifton E., Pfc, Co. L 7th Inf, French Morocco 10 Nov. 1942
Whitlow, Malon L., Pvt, Co. E 7th Inf, Italy 2 Mar. 1944
Whitney, Burleigh F., Pfc, Co. L 15th Inf, France 3 Jan. 1945
Widman, Albert A., S/Sgt, Co. C 30th Inf, 19 Aug. 1944
Wiederhoeft, George W., Pfc, Co. B 15th Inf, Germany 30 Mar. 1945
▲Wigetman, Harold, 1st Lt, Hq. Co. 3d Bn. 7th Inf, Houssen, France 26 Jan. 1945
Wiggins, Alton E., Pfc, Co. G 15th Inf, Achsheim, Germany 29 Apr. 1945
Wiggins, Cecil W., Pfc, Co. C 30th Inf, Italy 17 Dec. 1943
Wilcox, Sherman R., Pfc, Co. F 15th Inf, Italy 3 Mar. 1944
Wilcoxson, William J., Pfc, Co. E 30th Inf, Germany 16 Apr. 1945
Wiles, Charles J., Pfc, Co. H 30th Inf, France 17 Sept. 1944
Wilk, Walter, Pfc, Co. E 7th Inf, Le Haut Jacques, France 30 Oct. 1944
Willbanks, Robert R., Sr., Pvt, Hq. Co. 1st Bn. 7th Inf, France 15 Mar. 1945
Willeford, Lloyd E., Sgt, Co. I 30th Inf, Italy Aug. 1943
Willette, William L., 1st Lt, Co. B 756th Tank Bn., Germany 9 Apr. 1945

Willey, Duane E., S/Sgt, Co. G 30th Inf, France 17 Dec. 1944
▲Williams, Earl B., S/Sgt, Co. C 30th Inf, Bennwihr, France 28 Dec. 1944
Williams, Edward B., 1st Lt, FA Btry A 41st FA Bn., France 24 Jan. 1945
Williams, Garvis P., Pfc, Co. G 7th Inf, Nurnberg, Germany 18 Apr. 1945
Williams, Glenn F., S/Sgt, Co. I 30th Inf, Germany 26 Mar. 1945
Williams, Harold, Pvt, Hq. Co. 2d Bn. 30th Inf, Sicily Aug. 1943
Williams, Maurice L., S/Sgt, Co. F 7th Inf, Italy 7 Mar. 1944
Williams, Sidney L., Sgt, Co. A 3d Med. Bn. French Morocco 10 Nov. 1942
▲Williams, Warren B., S/Sgt, Co. I 7th Inf, Italy 30 Jan. 1944
Williamson, Aubrey L., S/Sgt, Co. K 7th Inf, 24 May 1944
Williamson, Thurman, Pfc, Co. F 15th Inf, Italy 23 May 1944
Willigar, Lawrence L., Pfc, Co. K 7th Inf, France 15 Sept. 1944
Willingham, George H., Pfc, Hq. Co. 2d Bn. 15th Inf, Le Haut Jacques, France 28 Sept. 1944
Wils, James P., S/Sgt, Inf Co. B 7th Inf Regt., France 23 Nov. 1944
Wilson, Daniel R., 1st Sgt, Co. A 30th Inf, Munich, Germany 29 Apr. 1945
Wilson, James E., Pvt, Rcn Co. 601st TD Bn., Sbeitla, Tunisia 18 Feb. 1943
Wilson, Joe, Pfc, Co. K 7th Inf, Italy 20 Mar. 1944
Wilson, Rex E., Sgt, Co. E 7th Inf, Italy 16 Feb. 1944
Wilson, William H., S/Sgt, Co. G 30th Inf, Sicily July 1943
Winans, Richard C., S/Sgt, Hq. Co. 7th Inf, Sicily Aug. 1943
Winchell, Edward H., S/Sgt, Co. K 7th Inf, Munich, Germany 29 Apr. 1945
▲Winiarski, Edward T., Pfc, Co. A 7th Inf, Germany 18 Mar. 1945
Wiseley, George W., Sgt, Co. H 30th Inf, France 19 Sept. 1944
Wisinski, Norbert J., 1st Lt, Co. I 15th Inf, Italy 23 May 1944
Wisner, James O., S/Sgt, Co. A 15th Inf, France 25 Oct. 1944
Woeik, Albert, T/5, Co. B 10th Engr. Bn., France 8 Oct. 1944
Wojtowicz, Eugene H., Pfc, Co. I 7th Inf, Lampertheim, Germany 26 Mar. 1945
Wolf, Herbert F., 1st Sgt, Co. L 15th Inf, Sicily Aug. 1943
Wolf, Theodore J., Pfc, Inf Co. G 15th Inf Regt., France 5 Feb. 1945
Wolfe, Coy R., S/Sgt, Co. G 15th Inf, Italy 25 May 1944
Wolfe, Roy W., 2d Lt, 3d Rcn Trp., France 18 Sept. 1944
Wonderling, Eugene C., Pfc, Co. G 7th Inf, St. Die, France 9 Nov. 1944
▲Wood, Elmer W., S/Sgt, Co. G 30th Inf, France 30 Oct. 1944
Wood, George C., Pfc, Co. F 30th Inf, Germany 20 Apr. 1945
Wood, George E., S/Sgt, Co. G 7th Inf, Italy 23 Apr. 1944
Wood, John W., S/Sgt, Co. I 30th Inf, France 1 Feb. 1945
▲Wood, Leonard H., Pfc, Med. Det. 7th Inf, Italy 13 Oct. 1943
Woodley, Leroy B., 1st Lt, FA Prov Pack Btry 3d Inf Div., Italy 30 Jan. 1944
Wooldridge, Gerald V., Pfc, Co. B 30th Inf, France 17 Dec. 1944
Works, Walton M., 1st Sgt, Co. L 15th Inf, France 26 Dec. 1944
Wotherspoon, Samuel G., S/Sgt, Co. G 30th Inf, France 17 Dec. 1944
Wright, Chester O., T/5, Hq. & Hq. Co. 2d Bn., 30th Inf, Sicily Aug. 1943
Wright, Elam W., Jr., 1st Lt, Inf Co. G 30th Inf, Kaysersberg, France 16 Dec. 1944
Wright, Thomas M., T/Sgt, Co. A 30th Inf, Italy 31 Jan. 1944
Wright, Walter L., 2d Lt, Inf 30th Inf, Sicily July 1943
Wright, William K., Sgt, Hq. Btry 39th FA Bn., Italy 27 May 1944
Wright, William T., 1st Lt, Inf Co. C 7th Inf, Zweibrucken, Germany 19 Mar. 1945
Wriston, Robert, Pvt, Serv. Co. (BP) 15th Inf, France 13 Sept. 1944
Wroblewski, Chester F., Pfc, Co. D 15th Inf, Mellrichstadt, Germany 7 Apr. 1945
Wunderlich, Edward, Jr., 2d Lt, Co. E 15th Inf, France 3 Nov. 1944
Wyatt, Carl R., 2d Lt, Co. G 15th Inf, Italy 1 Mar. 1944
Wysoglad, Vincent J., S/Sgt, Co. K 30th Inf, Heppenheim, Germany 26 Mar. 1945

Xiques, George M., Pvt, Co. K 30th Inf, Germany 27 Mar. 1945

Yandell, David R., 2d Lt, Co. A 30th Inf, France 4 Nov. 1944
Yarnall, George W., Capt, MC Med. Det. 7th Inf, Utweiler, Germany 15 Mar. 1945
Yates, Garland P., Pvt, Co. F 30th Inf, Germany 20 Apr. 1945
▲Yates, John R., S/Sgt, Co. A 15th Inf, France 1 Feb. 1945
Yates, Ralph J., Capt, Co. L 7th Inf, France 15 Sept. 1944
Yeager, Richard H., S/Sgt, Co. L 15th Inf, Italy 20 Oct. 1943
Young, Charles R., Sgt, Co. B 30th Inf, Germany 18 Apr. 1945
Young, Leonard, S/Sgt, Co. F 30th Inf, France 10 Sept. 1944
Young, Oscar E., Sgt, Co. A 30th Inf, Italy 12 Nov. 1944
Young, Ray, Capt, Inf Co. H 30th Inf, Cisterna, Italy 28 Jan. 1944
Young, Robert N., Brig Gen, U.S.Army, Ass't to Com Gen 3d Inf Div., France 30 Jan. 1945
Young, Walter L., Pfc, Co. A 30th Inf, St. Die, France 30 Oct. 1944
Young, Willie M., Pfc, Co. C 10th Engr. Bn., France 18 Dec. 1944
Yurik, Martin A., Pfc, Co. C 30th Inf, Vosges 5 Dec. 1944

Zabinski, Leo S., S/Sgt, Co. C 756th Tank Bn., Nurnberg, Germany 18 Apr. 1945
Zalanka, Frank E., Pvt, Med. Det. 30th Inf, Italy 10 Dec. 1943
▲Zawacki, John H., Pfc, Co. 7th Inf, Rupt-sur-Moselle, France 26 Sept. 1944
Zeichner, Edward, Pvt, Hq. Co. 30th Inf, Italy 22 Feb. 1944
Zentner, Burnell L., T/Sgt, Co. G 15th Inf, France 25 Jan. 1945
Zeuli, John P., T/4, Cn Co. 15th Inf, Italy 2 Feb. 1944
Zimmerman, Isidore, Pfc, Co. L 30th Inf, France 17 Sept. 1944
Zingo, Frank B., Pfc, Co. G 15th Inf, Contwig, Germany 18 Mar. 1945
Zinn, Ernest E., T/5, Hq. Co. 15th Inf, Italy 31 Jan. 1944
Zinn, William M., Cpl, Cn Co. 30th Inf, France 8 May 1944
Zitlow, Wyman R., Sgt, Hq. & Serv. 10th Engr. Bn., France 4 Dec. 1944
Zito, Richard, Pfc, Co. E 15th Inf, France 28 Dec. 1944
Zoppa, Jerry T., S/Sgt, Co. E 7th Inf, France 17 Aug. 1944
Zucker, George C., Pfc, Med. Det. 41st FA Bn., Sicily Aug. 1943

POSTHUMOUS AWARDS OF SILVER STAR

Albright, Donald C., Pvt, 3d Rcn Trp., Italy 26 May 1944
Alexander, Cecil G., S/Sgt, Co. I 15th Inf, Italy 4 Feb. 1944
Alexander, Richard J., Sgt, Co. K 30th Inf, France 29 Oct. 1944
Alfier, Nicholas, T/Sgt, Co. H 7th Inf, Italy 11 Nov. 1944
Anzalone, Angelo, Pvt, Co. A 30th Inf, France 7 Nov. 1944
Archabal, John R., Pvt, Co. K 7th Inf, Italy Oct. 1943

Atkins, Levi, T/5, Med. Det. 15th Inf, Nurnberg, Germany 18 Apr. 1945
Avant, Joe R., Pfc, Co. B 30th Inf, Italy 24 Apr. 1944
Avila, John H., Sgt, Co. E 30th Inf, Sicily July 1943

Bailey, Mason E., Pvt, Co. A 601st TD Bn., Steinach, Germany 7 Apr. 1945
Baker, Victor W., Pvt, Hq. Btry 41st FA Bn., France 26 Jan. 1945

▲ Oak Leaf Cluster.

Bakus, Joseph, Pfc, Hq. Co. 2d Bn. 30 Inf, Italy 8 Nov. 1943
Barber, David H., S/Sgt, Co. C 30th Inf, France 21 Aug. 1944
Barko, Andy S., Pfc, Co. K 7th Inf, Italy 31 Jan. 1944
Bazille, Leonard H., Pvt, Co. F 30th Inf, Sicily July 1943
Bell, Owen D., Pfc, Co. L 15th Inf, France 28 Sept. 1944
Bernander, Edwin A., Capt, Inf Hq. Co. 3d Bn. 15th Inf, Italy 18 Jan. 1944
Bernwasser, Charles P., Pfc, Co. B 7th Inf, Italy 31 Jan. 1944
▲Bisbee, Eldon R., T/Sgt, Co. H 15th Inf, France 25 Feb. 1945
Blanchard, Ellie J., Jr., Pvt, Co. A 15th Inf, France 4 Feb. 1945
Blaskowski, Leonard J., Pvt, Co. M 7th Inf, Siegsdorf, Germany 3 May 1945
Bliss, Mile V., Pfc, Co. K 7th Inf, Italy 25 Jan. 1944
Block, Robert O., S/Sgt, Co. L 30th Inf, Italy 22 Nov. 1943
Bond, Jerald R., Pfc, 3d Rcn Trp., France 18 Aug. 1944
Boyer, Floyd M., Sgt, Co. L 15th Inf, Italy 15 Feb. 1944
Brannon, Russell E., Pfc, Co. E 7th Inf, Italy Oct. 1943
Branscembe, Merlin A., Pfc, Co. G 30th Inf, France 16 Dec. 1944
Breau, Hermidas J., Sgt, Co. E 15th Inf, France 5 Sept. 1944
Brewer, Henry C., T/Sgt, Co. I 30th Inf, France 9 Feb. 1945
Bridgeman, George H., Pfc, Co. I 30th Inf, France 8 Sept. 1944
Brooke, Dillon D., Pfc, Co. G 7th Inf, Italy 24 May 1944
Bryant, John J., S/Sgt, Co. L 30th Inf, France 7 Feb. 1945
Bubb, Ralph R., Sgt, Co. K 15th Inf, France 6 Nov. 1944
Burkhardt, Richard L., 1st Lt, Co. D 7th Inf, France 21 Aug. 1944
Bush, Ernest T., S/Sgt, Co. L 30th Inf, France 10 Nov. 1944
Butler, Richard J., Pfc, Med. Det. 254th Inf, France 23 Jan. 1945

Caine, Lloyd C., S/Sgt. Co. G 30th Inf, Italy 29 Jan. 1944
Campbell, Tyler, Capt, Co. A 7th Inf, France 13 Sept. 1944
Carico, Hugh V., Capt, Inf 7th Inf, Sicily Aug. 1943
Carmichael, Wilbur N., Pfc, Co. D 30th Inf, Italy 3 Mar. 1945
▲Carpenter, Ralph R., Capt, Co. E 30th Inf, Germany 19 Mar. 1945
Carragher, Matt, Pvt, Med. Det. 30th Inf, Italy 28 Jan. 1944
Carter, Harold J., Pfc, Hq. & Hq. Btry 41st FA Bn., Italy 13 Oct. 1943
Castaneda, Edward V., Pfc, Hq. Co. 2d Bn. 30th Inf, Italy 8 Nov. 1943
Chaves, William M., Jr., Sgt, Inf Co. D 7th Inf Regt., Nayemont, France 22 Nov. 1944
Chewiwi, Joe A., Pfc, Med. Det. 7th Inf, Seigfried Line 18 Mar. 1945
Chief, Timothy Tall, Pfc, Co. L 30th Inf, Italy Sept. 1943
Chipley, Clarence L., Pfc, Co. F 30th Inf, France 8 Nov. 1944
Clark, Clifford I., Sgt, Co. F 7th Inf, Cisterna, Italy 25 May 1944
Clark, George W., Pfc, Co. G 7th Inf, France 25 Jan. 1945
Clukey, Julian P., T/5, Btry B 39th FA Bn., Italy 3 Mar. 1944
Coffin, Cecil B., Pvt, Co. D 7th Inf, Guiderkurch, France 15 Mar. 1945
Cooper, Lloyd S., III, Pvt, Co. C 7th Inf, Italy 16 Feb. 1944
Corse, Americo, 1st Lt. FA Btry C 41st FA Bn., France 17 Dec. 1944
Cowan, Bruce D., Sgt, Co. L 15th Inf, Italy Oct. 1943
Crumpler, Woodard W., Pvt, Co. G 15th Inf, France 9 Sept. 1944
Cyr, Normand M., Pvt, Co. F 7th Inf, Italy 2 Feb. 1944

Daniel, Samuel L., 2d Lt, Co. I 17th Inf, Germany 27 Mar. 1945
Deeke, Norman H., Sgt, BP Hq. Co. 7th Inf, Wihr-en-Plaine, France 30 Jan. 1945
Demetriou, Fotois D., Sgt, CIC CIC Det. Hq. 3d Inf Div., 22 Jan. 1944
DeNimo, Patsy, Pvt, Co. K 30th Inf, France 22 Sept. 1944
Dimmitt, Ellsworth W., Capt, Inf 15th Inf, Sicily Aug. 1943
Dolsen, Fred R., 1st Sgt, Co. E 30th Inf, Italy 23 Jan. 1944
Domingo, Joseph A., Jr., S/Sgt, Co. G 7th Inf, Italy 28 Jan. 1944
Donish, William J., Sgt, Co. I 15th Inf, Germany 4 Apr. 1945
Dubey, Joseph E., S/Sgt, Co. E 30th Inf, France 29 Mar. 1945
Durkee, Charles R., Jr., 2d Lt, Co. C 7th Inf, Italy 1 Mar. 1944

Epps, Calvin B., 2d Lt, Co. L 15th Inf, Italy 3 May 1944
Escalante, Augustin N., S/Sgt, Co. I 30th Inf, France 18 Aug. 1944
Esenwein, Erich K., Pvt, Med. Det. 30th Inf, France 29 Sept. 1944
Evans, Robert E., 1st Lt, Inf Co. A 7th Inf, France 22 Nov. 1944
Evans, Vernon H., 1st Lt, CE 10th Engr. Bn., Sicily Aug. 1943

Fettenbury, Otis O., 2d Lt, Co. M 7th Inf, Italy 28 May 1944
Fockler, Harvey D., Pfc, Co. A 15th Inf, Italy 23 May 1944
Foley, William C., Cpl. AT Co. 7th Inf, Italy Oct. 1943
Foote, Glenn S., S/Sgt, Co. C 7th Inf, Sicily Aug. 1943
Frank, Harry E., Jr., Pfc, Co. E 7th Inf, Faucogney, France 20 Sept. 1944
Frank, Leon, Sgt, Co. B 30th Inf, France 17 Dec. 1944
Frederick, Charles E., Lt Col, 3d Bn. 15th Inf, Monte Della Costa, Italy 19 Oct. 1943
Freeman, Julian H., 1st Lt, FA Btry B 9th FA Bn., Italy 6 Oct. 1943
Fuller, Julius, Pfc, Co. C 7th Inf, Strasbourg, France 1 Dec. 1944

Garcia, Fernando F., Pvt, Co. D 15th Inf, Biarville, France 5 Nov. 1944
Gebing, Howard V., 2d Lt, Co. I 7th Inf, Italy 16 Nov. 1943
Germain, George D., 1st Lt, Inf Co. B 30th Inf, Guemar, France 23 Jan. 1945
Giermann, Alfred J., Jr., 3d Lt, Inf Co. C 15th Inf, Nurnberg, Germany
Gilliland, Vivian C., Pvt, Co. K 30th Inf, Italy 16 Feb. 1944
Gilman, Herbert R., 2d Lt, Co. M 7th Inf, Italy 31 Jan. 1944
Goldsby, Orrin E., Pfc, Co. C 30th Inf, France 7 Sept. 1944
Gordon, Clifford G., 1st Lt, Co. K 7th Inf, Italy 31 Jan. 1944
▲Greene, John J., 1st Lt, Inf Co. L 7th Inf, France 13 Sept. 1944
Grieshaber, Russell J., Sgt, Inf Co. D 15th Inf, France 1 Oct. 1944
Gross, Joseph J., 2d Lt, Co. B 7th Inf, France 24 Nov. 1944

Hall, Cloyse E., Pfc, AT Co. 15th Inf, Nurnberg, Germany 18 Apr. 1945
Hanauer, Henry L., Pfc, Co. I 30th Inf, France 21 Sept. 1944
Hardy, James C., Pfc, Co. M 30th Inf, Italy 5 Feb. 1944
▲(2) Hardy, James C., Pfc, Co. M 30th Inf, Italy 6 Apr. 1944
Harris, Walter J., T/Sgt, Co. I 15th Inf, 15 Aug. 1944
Hart, James S., Pfc, Co. L 15th Inf, France 26 Oct. 1944
Hart, John D., Pfc, Hq. Co. 2d Bn. 30th Inf, Germany 26 Mar. 1945
Hatten, Robert J., 1st Lt, Co. K 30th Inf, Italy 23 May 1944
Held, Leslie J., T/Sgt, Co. E 15th Inf, France 25 Jan. 1945
Heller, Lawrence A., Sgt, Co. A 10th Engr. Bn. Sicily 16 July 1944
Hennrikus, Walter F., Pfc, Co. D 15th Inf, France 1 Oct. 1944
Hernandez, Alfonse M., Pvt, Co. G 7th Inf, Italy 24 Apr. 1944
Hess, Mike, Sgt, Co. G 7th Inf, Italy 15 Oct. 1943
Holm, Robert E., Sgt. Co. F 30th Inf, France 5 Oct. 1944
Holt, Russell D., S/Sgt, Co. K 30th Inf, 16 Aug. 1944
Hombis, John, Pvt, Co. K 30th Inf, Sicily Aug. 1943
Hudock, Peter, Pfc, Co. K 7th Inf, Italy 1 Feb. 1944
Hudolin, Edward, S/Sgt, Co. A 30th Inf, Rhine 1 Feb. 1945
Hunt, James R., Pfc, Hq. Co. 2d Bn. 30th Inf, Germany 26 Mar. 1945
Husing, John C., 1st Lt, AT Co. 7th Inf, France 25 Oct. 1944

Iadarola, Lee A., Sgt, Co. E 7th Inf, Italy 25 May 1944

Janus, Joseph, Pvt, 3d Rcn Trp., France 18 Dec. 1944
Jobe, William L., Pfc, Co. A 15th Inf, Italy 28 Feb. 1944
Johnson, Raymond C., 1st Lt, Co. A 15th Inf, Italy 1 June 1944
Jones, Leonard A., T/Sgt, Co. K 7th Inf, France 24 Sept. 1944
Jones, Morris E., 2d Lt, Co. G 15th Inf, France 24 Oct. 1944
Jordan, Hilary R., 1st Lt, Co. I 30th Inf, Italy 28 Jan. 1944
Joyal, Henry, Pfc, Med. Det. 30th Inf, Italy Sept. 1943
Judy, George F., S/Sgt, Co. B 15th Inf, France 15 Aug. 1944

Kandle, Victor L., 1st Lt, Co. I 15th Inf, Bennwihr, France 29 Dec. 1944
Keim, Robert L., Pfc, Co. L 15th Inf, France 27 Dec. 1944
Kefurt, Gus J., S/Sgt, Co. K 15th Inf, France 23 Dec. 1944
Kelly, Carl E., Pfc, Co. K 15th Inf, France 26 Feb. 1945
Kemper, William H., S/Sgt, Co. L 30th Inf, France 15 Dec. 1944
Kershaw, Paul E., 1st Lt, Co. G 15th Inf, France 27 Dec. 1944
Kiely, Joseph J., 1st Lt, Co. C 15th Inf, Italy 29 Feb. 1944
King, Raymond D., Sgt, Inf Co. M (BP) 15th Inf, France 8 Sept. 1944
King, William C., Pfc, Co. G 7th Inf, France 26 Jan. 1945
Kirkpatrick, Seba W., 1st Lt, Hq. Btry 39th FA Bn., Sicily 5 Aug. 1943
Kirtley, Kenneth W., Maj, Inf Hq. 3d Bn. 15th Inf, Italy 18 Jan. 1944
Klish, Chester B., Cpl, Co. D 30th Inf, Sicily 7 Aug. 1943
Knoll, Arthur A., Jr., 2d Lt, Co. G 15th Inf, Germany 21 Mar. 1945
Koshkin, Eugene S., 2d Lt, Inf Co. I 15th Inf, Riedwihr, France 24 Jan. 1945
Kossman, William C., S/Sgt, Co. H 504th Prcht Inf, Italy 22 Jan. 1944
Krevchuck, William E., Pvt, Hq. Co. 2d Bn. 7th Inf, France 4 Sept. 1944
Kuzyk, Myron, 1st Lt, Co. G 30th Inf, Heppenheim, Germany 27 Mar. 1945
Kyte, George J., Jr., 1st Lt, Hq. 10th FA Bn., Wihr-en-Plaine, France 29 Jan. 1945

LaChance, George B., S/Sgt, Co. F 30th Inf, France 8 Nov. 1944
Lahna, Lee, Pvt, Co. L 7th Inf, Italy 1 Nov. 1943
Laney, William M., Jr., Cpl, Co. C 751st Tank Bn., Italy 22 Jan. 1944
Larsen, Hans, S/Sgt, Serv. Co. 7th Inf, Sicily Aug. 1943
Lawson, Edward W., 2d Lt, CE Co. C 10th Engr. Bn., Minschweiler, Germany 19 Mar. 1945
Lehmann, Ralph J., Pfc, Btry A 39th Bn., Italy 2 Feb. 1944
Linebarger, Sterling F., T/5, Hq. & Hq. Co. 3d Bn. 30th Inf, Italy 25 Jan. 1944
Loftis, Howard D., S/Sgt, Co. K 15th Inf, France 5 Nov. 1944
▲Lombardi, Louis J., 1st Lt, Co. C 30th Inf, Germany 15 Mar. 1945
Long, Billy M., Pfc, Co. M 30th Inf, Italy 7 Mar. 1944

Maier, Alvin, Sgt, Co. M 15th Inf, France 9 Nov. 1944
Mangels, Darrel J., Sgt, Co. F 15th Inf, Italy 28 Oct. 1943
Mannett, John J., Pfc, Hq. Co. 2d Bn. 30th Inf, Sicily July 1943
Marchetti, Raymond, S/Sgt, Co. A 15th Inf, Sicily 15 July 1943
Martin, William R., T/5, Btry B 10th FA Bn., France 28 Dec. 1944
Maynard, Carl H., Pfc, Co. A 15th Inf, France 6 Oct. 1944
McCracken, James H., 1st Lt, Inf Co. K 7th Inf, Italy 21 Apr. 1944
McCoy, James W., Pvt, Co. I 15th Inf, Italy 1 Nov. 1943
McCoy, Leinster W., Jr., Pfc, Hq. Co. 3d Bn. 30th Inf, France 4 Nov. 1944
McDermott, Edward J., Sgt, Co. L 7th Inf, France 24 Sept. 1944
McFarland, Beryl E., Sgt, Co. E 7th Inf, France 30 Oct. 1944
▲McHarg, James J., T/Sgt, Co. A 30th Inf, Riedwihr, France 22 Jan. 1945
McLaughlin, Frank J., Pvt, Hq. Co. 2d Bn. 15th Inf, Sicily Aug. 1943
▲McMahen, William E., 1st Lt, Co. K 15th Inf, France 24 Dec. 1944
Mendoza, Joseph, Co. D 30th Inf, Sicily Aug. 1943
Miele, John J., Pfc, Co. G 7th Inf, France 23 Jan. 1945
Miller, Mevin R., S/Sgt, Co. B 15th Inf, Biesheim, France 4 Feb. 1945
Miller, Paul N., Sgt, Co. L 30th Inf, France 1 Sept. 1944
Mills, Thomas K., S/Sgt, Co. M 7th Inf, Italy 23 May 1944
Mitchum, Clarence, Pfc, Co. L 7th Inf, Wihr-en-Plaine, France 29 Jan. 1945
Moffitt, Orville A., S/Sgt, Co. D 30th Inf, Cisterna, Italy 30 Jan. 1944
Moore, Ralph W., Pfc, Co. M 7th Inf, France 3 Feb. 1945
Mott, Courtland D., T/5, Co. A 30th Inf, Nurnberg, Germany 19 Apr. 1945

Nault, Benjamin J., Sgt, Co. G 30th Inf, Italy 29 Jan. 1944
Nelson, Arnold G., Cpl, Co. B 7th Inf, Sicily Aug. 1943
Neville, Ben W., 2d Lt, Inf 7th Inf, Italy Oct. 1943
Newton, Arthur C., 2d Lt, Co. E 30th Inf, France 9 Mar. 1945
Nock, Edwin B. S/Sgt, Co. L 15th Inf, Muntzenheim, Germany 29 Jan. 1945

O'Donnell, John E., Pfc, Co. G 7th Inf, Italy15 Oct. 1943
Ooton, Charles H., S/Sgt, Co. C 30th Inf, France 24 Sept. 1944
Ostmeyer, Earl H., 2d Lt, CE Co. C 10th Engr. Bn., France 30 Dec. 1944

Panse, Arthur F., Pfc, Hq. Co. 3d Bn. 30th Inf, France 7 Feb. 1945
Pasquale, Urbane Di, Sgt, Co. A 7th Inf, France 27 Aug. 1944
Pearson, Robert L., S/Sgt, Co. G 15th Inf, France 18 Aug. 1944
Pennell, Frank J., S/Sgt, Co. A 15th Inf, Italy 27 Jan. 1944
Person, Claude A., S/Sgt, 41st FA Bn., Italy 16 Feb. 1944
Pertiner, Everett L., Pfc, Co. L 15th Inf, Italy 13 Oct. 1943
Petrey, Edgar, S/Sgt, Co. K 7th Inf, France 3 Feb. 1945
Petrizzi, Marice P., Sgt, Co. K 15th Inf, France 24 Dec. 1944
Peyton, Harold T., T/Sgt, Co. G 30th Inf, France 19 Aug. 1944
Pifer, Nevin W., S/Sgt, Co. L 30th Inf, France 10 Nov. 1944
Place, Lloyd C., Jr., Pvt, Co. L 15th Inf, Almoshof, Germany 20 Apr. 1945
Powers, Forest F., Cpl, Co. A 601st TD Bn., Steinach, Germany 7 Apr. 1945
Prassas, Constantinos, Sgt, Co. H 15th Inf, Requewihr, France 26 Jan. 1945
Primmer, Donald B., Pfc, Btry C 39th FA Bn., Sicily 10 July 1943

Rains, Onis L., Sgt, Co. L 7th Inf, France 30 Oct. 1944
▲Raney, John S., 1st Lt, Co. M 7th Inf, Italy18 July, 1944
Reece, Bennie G., 1st Lt, Co. G 15th Inf, Italy 25 Jan. 1944
Reece, Billie, Pvt, Co. E 30th Inf, Germany 8 May 1944
Rethermund, Earl R., Sgt, Co. F 7th Inf, France 30 Sept. 1944
Ridout, Arnold B., Pfc, Co. E 30th Inf, France 17 Dec. 1944
▲Ritse, John C., S/Sgt, Co. B 601st TD Bn., Italy 8 June 1944
Rivera, Edward A., S/Sgt, Co. F 7th Inf, Italy 23 May 1944
Robertson, Buster D., Pfc, Co. I 15th Inf, France 17 Mar. 1945
Robledo, James R., Cpl, Hq. Co. 2d Bn. 15th Inf, Sicily Aug. 1943
Rodarte, Lee P., T/Sgt, Co. C 30th Inf, France 7 Nov. 1944

▲ Oak Leaf Cluster.

Ross, Robert A., 2d Lt, Inf 15th Inf, Italy 13 Oct. 1943
Rowe, Rolland W., Sgt, Hq. Co. 1st Bn. 15th Inf, Italy 1 June 1944
Rumrill, Herman F., Sgt, Co., F 15th Inf, France 2 Oct. 1944
Russell, Geran B., S/Sgt, Co. E 7th Inf, Italy 2 Feb. 1944
Ryan, Donald A., Cpl, Btry C 41st FA Bn., France 17 Dec. 1944

Sallander, Gordon N., Pfc, 3d Rcn Trp., Germany 25 Aug. 1945
Schreiner, Howard K., Pfc, Co. G 30th Inf, France 20 Aug. 1944
Schweizer, John J., Pfc, Rcn Co. 601st TD Bn., Gersorenz, Germany 28 Mar. 1945
Selph, Israel E., Cpl, Co. A 10th Engr. Bn., Sicily 3 Aug. 1943
Seman, Thomas, Pfc, Co. B 30th Inf, France 30 Oct. 1944
Sharel, Ted, W., Sgt, Co. F 7th Inf, Germany 16 Apr. 1945
Shea, Edward P., Jr., S/Sgt, Co. C 15th Inf, France 13 Sept. 1944
Shields, Charles P., Pfc, Cavalry 3d Rcn Trp., Sicily 17 July 1943
Silski, Anthony, Pfc, Co. H 15th Inf, Requewihr, France 26 Jan. 1945
Smith, Richard T., T/5, Co. B 601st TD Bn., Bemberg, Germany 14 Apr. 1945
Sneckenberger, Robert J., Sgt, Co. G 7th Inf, France 7 Oct. 1944
Stafford, Clarence E., Pfc, Co. L 15th Inf, France 27 Dec. 1944
Staines, Ira B., Pvt, Co. F 30th Inf, Nurnberg, Germany 20 Apr. 1945
Shaw, Lloyd W., S/Sgt, Co. B 30th Inf, S. France 12 Sept. 1944
▲Standish, Lysle E., Capt, Co. B 30th Inf, Germany 26 Mar. 1945
Stebleton, Bryan M., Pfc, Co. I 30th Inf, Waldhausen, Germany 24 Apr. 1945
Steere, Raymond J., 1st Lt, Co. C 15th Inf, France 25 Jan. 1945
Stencil, James C., Pfc, Hq. Co. 1st Bn. 30th Inf, Pfandhausen, Germany 9 Apr. 1945
Stiles, Leslie E., 1st Lt, Hq. Co. 1st Bn. 7th Inf, Italy 3 Mar. 1944
Stratten, Jesse, S/Sgt, Co. E 7th Inf, Italy 4 Feb. 1944
Stripling, Gordon A., Pfc, Co. G 30th Inf, France 17 Sept. 1944
Stutchbury, Bruce F., Pfc, Co. K 7th Inf, Ormersvillers, France 15 Mar. 1945
Sutton, Charles W., 1st Lt, Co. L 15th Inf, Brouvelieurs, France 25 Oct. 1944
Swatzberg, Gerald H., 2d Lt, Co. I 30th Inf, Sicily Oct. 1943
Szczotka, John F., T/5, Rcn Co. 601st TD Bn., Ellerbach, Germany 25 Apr. 1945

Tatlock, Eric W., 1st Lt, CO Co. H 30th Inf, Italy 24 May 1944
Taylor, George T., Pfc, Co. D 30th Inf, France 23 Jan. 1945
Taylor, Robert L., Pfc, Co. I 30th Inf, Urbach, Germany 15 Mar. 1945
Tester, Charles L., Pvt, Med. Det. 7th Inf, Italy 31 Jan. 1944
Thompson, Allen N., T/4, Btry C 41st FA Bn., Italy 7 Feb. 1944
Thompson, John B., Cpl, Co. G 30th Inf, Sicily July 1943
Thompson, Russell L., S/Sgt, Co. K 15th Inf, France 5 Oct. 1944
Thompson, Welden G., Pfc, Co. D 7th Inf, Italy Oct.1943
Toffey, John J., Jr., Lt Col, Inf 7th Inf, Italy 3 June 1944
Tomaiolo, Angelo J., Sgt, Co. M 15th Inf, Italy 3 Jan. 1943
Truman, Patrick W., Pfc, Co. D 15th Inf, Sicily 6 Aug. 1943
Tucker, Gordon I., 1st Lt, Co. G 15th Inf, France 2 Feb. 1945

Ulmer, Nevin R., Pfc, Co. H 7th Inf, Italy Sept. 1943

Wagner, Herman E., Capt, Inf 7th Inf, Sicily July 1943
Wagoner, Lloyd S., Pvt, Co. F 30th Inf, Nurnberg, Germany 20 Apr. 1945
Wallace, Sherry R., 2d Lt, Co. F 30th Inf, France 28 Oct. 1944
Watson, Robert, S/Sgt, Co. G 15th Inf, France 26 Dec. 1944
Weaver, Clifton, Pvt, Co. H 30th Inf, France 28 Dec. 1944
Weber, Harry, Pfc, Co. L 15th Inf, Italy 13 Oct. 1943
Wellingham, Alan H., Cpl, Co. B 7th Inf, Sicily Aug. 1943
Werbie, Thomas J., Pfc, Co. L 7th Inf, Italy 23 Apr. 1944
Westburg, John H., Jr., Pfc, Co. A 15th Inf, France 24 Dec. 1944
Whittington, Albert E., Pvt, Hq. Co. 1st Bn. 7th Inf, France 16 Mar. 1945
Wiener, Raymond, 1st Lt, Btry C 39th FA Bn., France 13 Sept. 1944
Wilmer, William L., Sgt, Co. M 15th Inf, France 26 Dec. 1944
Wilson, Cecil J., S/Sgt, Co. L 15th Inf, Italy 30 Sept. 1943
Wingle, Lawrence E., Pvt, Med. Det. 15th Inf, France 19 Dec. 1944
Wounaris, Steve W., T/5, Med. Det. 15th Inf, Sicily Aug. 1943

Yeatts, Claude A., Pfc, Co. F 30th Inf, France 20 Nov. 1944
York, Howard J., Cpl, Hq. Co. 2d Bn. 15th Inf, Sicily 7 Aug. 1943
Yurik, Martin A., Pfc, Co. C 30th Inf, France 8 Nov. 1944

Zinn, William M., Cpl, Cn Co. 30th Inf, Lindenils, Germany 27 Mar. 1945
Zotos, Stephen, Pvt, Co. B 15th Inf, Italy 22 Feb. 1944
Zullo, Michael A., Pvt, Co. A 7th Inf, France 30 Jan. 1945

SILVER STAR
MISSING IN ACTION

Albritton, Walter V., Sgt, Co. G 7th Inf, France 25 Jan. 1945
Alexander, William A., 1st Lt, Plt Ldr, Co. B 10th Engr. Bn., Italy 24 May 1944

Brzezinski, Marion V., S/Sgt, Co. A 15th Inf., France 23 Nov. 1944

▲Costa, Antone V., Pfc, Co. M 7th Inf, Italy 28 Jan. 1944
Courtney, William J., 1st Lt, Co. I 15th Inf, France 23 Dec. 1944
Crape, Andrew, Pfc, Co. C 7th Inf, Italy 17 Feb. 1944
Cummins, Lloyd J., S/Sgt, Co. I 7th Inf, Italy 26 May 1944
Czarniawski, Edward M., Pfc, Co. I 30th Inf, France 15 Dec. 1944

Dively, Ned E., S/Sgt, Co. G 7th Inf, Italy 1 Feb. 1944

Elmore, C. L., Capt, Inf Co. E 30th Inf, Italy 23 Jan. 1944
Ewell, Vivian S., Pfc, Hq. Co. 1st Bn. 15th Inf, France 30 Dec. 1944

Hartstein, George H., Sgt, Co. G 7th Inf, Germany 23 Jan. 1945
Hellars, Ralph D., S/Sgt, Co. G 7th Inf, France 25 Jan. 1945
Hensey, Arlie C., Pfc, Co. G 15th Inf, Italy 21 Feb. 1944

Kelly, Carl E., Pfc, Co. K 15th Inf, France 24 Dec. 1944
Kennedy, Gordon H., Pfc, Co. H 15th Inf, France 2 Nov. 1944
Krizan, Fred A., S/Sgt, Inf Co. F 7th Inf., France 1 Dec. 1944

McKane, Weston S., 1st Lt, Co. G 7th Inf, France 23 Jan. 1945
McKibben, Donald H., 2d Lt, Co. F 7th Inf, 2 Nov. 1944
Marder, Samuel, S/Sgt, Co. K 30th Inf, France 24 Nov. 1944

Mauser, Curtis N., S/Sgt, Co. I 30th Inf, France 16 Dec. 1944
Meegelin, William M., 2d Lt, Co. C 7th Inf, 23 Jan. 1945
Miller, Charles P., Pfc, Co. I 30th Inf, Italy 30 Jan. 1944
Miner, Francis H., Pfc, Co. I 30th Inf, France 8 Jan. 1945
Monks, Earl A., Pfc, Co. I 30th Inf, France 18 Dec. 1944
Motz, Philip G., Sgt, Co. I 30th Inf, France 17 Dec. 1944

Nagowski, William A., Sgt, Co. L 30th Inf, France 15 Dec. 1944
Nyers, Roy J., Pvt, Co. M 30th Inf, France 17 Dec. 1944

Petruzziello, Mario, T/Sgt, Co. I 30th Inf, France 8 Jan. 1945

Rawlings, Kenneth, Pfc, Co. K 15th Inf, France 5 Oct. 1944
Redman, John R., T/Sgt, Co. F 15th Inf, France 6 Oct. 1944
Ross, Earnest N., Pfc, Co. G 7th Inf, Italy 23 Apr. 1944

Schmidt, Joseph J., Pfc, Co. M 30th Inf, France 18 Dec. 1944
Showers, Howard L., S/Sgt, Co. C 30th Inf, Velletri, Italy 1 June 1944
Smith, Emden G., Cpl, Co. E 15th Inf, Italy Oct. 1943
Stoner, Edward W., Pfc, Co. E 30th Inf, Italy 9 Feb. 1944
Strange, Thomas J., S/Sgt, Co. F 7th Inf, 29 Feb. 1944

Tidwell, Jack N., 1st Lt, 3d Rcn Trp., Italy 21 Mar. 1944

Vanderbilt, Frank H., S/Sgt, Co. E 7th Inf, Italy 1 Feb. 1944
Via, Herbert W., Pfc, Co. A 15th Inf, France 23 Nov. 1944

Walker, Darwyn E., 1st Lt, Co. I 30th Inf, France 8 Jan. 1945
Wilson, Oscar D., Sgt, Co. I 30th Inf, France 16 Dec. 1944

LEGION OF MERIT

Alder, Willis F., Sgt, Co. H 7th Inf, 4 June 1944
Anderson, Robert, T/4, 10th Engr., 18 Nov. 1943
Arnold, Edwin Y., Maj, 756th Tank Bn., 11 June 1944
Austin, Ben R., S/Sgt, Hq. Co. 7th Inf, 17 Nov. 1943

Baker, Tom A., S/Sgt, Serv. Co. 7th Inf, 4 June 1944
Basila, Basil F., Capt, Hq. 3d Div., 23 July 1943
Bentzel, Donald M., T/Sgt, Serv. Co. 15th Inf, 4 June 1944
Bernard, Lyle W., Lt Col, 30th Inf
Biesmann, Marcus C., 1st Sgt, Serv. Co. 30th Inf, 5 June 1944
Bilby, Kenneth W., Maj, 30th Inf, 4 June 1944
Bingham, Leonard L., Lt Col, 10th Engr. Bn.
Boddy, Robert M., Capt, 30th Inf, 22 Feb. 1944
Bonham, William H., S/Sgt, Hq. Co. 2d Bn. 7th Inf, 15 Aug. 1944
Branstetter, Ross W., 1st Sgt, 7th Inf, 18 Aug. 1943
Brown, Joseph M., S/Sgt, 15th Inf, 4 June 1944

Carleton, Don E., Col, Hq. 3d Div., July 1943
Campbell, William A., Brig Gen, 3d Div Arty, 28 Mar. 1944
Churack, Matt J., T/Sgt, Serv. Co. M 7th Inf, 4 June 1944
Connor, Albert O., Lt Col, Hq. 3d Div., 23 July 1943
Cooper, Sammy, T/5, 7th Inf, 1 Jan. 1944
Cotton, Melvin K., S/Sgt, Hq. Co. B 30th Inf, 20 Feb. 1945
Coyne, Christopher C., Lt Col, 3d Div. Arty, 21 Jan. 1944
Crawford, Joseph B., Lt Col, 15th Inf

Devol, Brenton A., Jr., Capt, 3d Div. Arty, 23 July 1943

Dielman, William K., 1st Lt, Co. H 7th Inf, 17 Sept. 1944
Dundee, Morris G., 1st Lt, 3d Sig. Co., 15 Sept. 1944
Dwan, John E., Capt, Hq. 30th Inf, 20 Feb. 1945

Eakin, John I., CWO, Hq. 3d. Div., 15 Sept. 1944
Elwell, Alfred M., Capt, 3d Med. Bn., 27 Nov. 1944
Faist, William H., Maj, Sig. Hq. Div., 5 Sept. 1944
Fergerson, Harold M., Pfc, 15th Inf, 15 Mar. 1944
Fezell, George H., Maj, Serv. Co. 30th Inf, 5 Sept. 1944
Flynn, Ralph M., Maj, 3d Bn. 7th Inf, 26 Nov. 1944
Foster, James L., Capt, 751st Tank Bn., 18 Nov. 1943

Gibson, Eric G., T/5, 30th Inf, 18 Nov. 1943
Goodwin, Benjamin F., Maj, 3d QM Co., 20 Aug. 1944
Greer, Harold E., Capt, Hq. 30th Inf, 30 Oct. 1943

Haney, George B., WOJG, 15th Inf, 15 Dec. 1944
Hanson, Richard E., Capt, 39th FA Bn., 3 Nov. 1943
Harrell, Ben, Lt Col, Hq. 3d Div., 23 July 1943
Harrison, William R., Capt, 601st TD Bn., 6 June 1944
Heile, Ralph C., S/Sgt, Serv. Co. 30th Inf, 14 Sept. 1944
Heintges, John A., Lt Col, 7th Inf, 4 Dec. 1944
Heipel, Lorne W., M/Sgt, Serv. Co. 30th Inf, 5 June 1944
Henson, Earl O., Lt Col, Hq. 3d Div., 26 July 1943
Horn, Myron D., T/Sgt, 15th Inf, 18 Feb. 1945
Householder, Clyde C., Cpl, 30th Inf, 9 Jan. 1944
Hovda, Roger H., WOJG, 15th Inf, 4 June 1944
Hovern, Alton A., M/Sgt, Serv. Co. 15th Inf, 4 June 1944

▲ Oak Leaf Cluster.

Howell, Clifton, T/Sgt, 756th Tank Bn., 25 Sept. 1944
Hughes, Ben B., M/Sgt, Hq. Co. 3d Div., 10 Nov. 1942

Iacuzzi, Joe T., T/4, Co. A 10th Engr. Bn., 23 May 1944
Izenour, Frank M., Lt Col, 7th Inf, 4 June 1944

Jagels, Fred H., T/Sgt, Hq. Co. 601st TD Bn., 14 Sept. 1944
Johnson, Charles E., Lt Col, Hq. 3d Div., 23 June 1943
Johnson, Edwin G., 1st Lt, Serv. Co. 7th Inf, 30 Sept. 1944
Johnston, Robert J., S/Sgt, 703d Ord, 17 Oct. 1945

Kaufman, Carl F., 1st Lt, 30th Inf, 18 Nov. 1943
Kennedy, Oran J., 1st Sgt, Hq. Btry 41st FA Bn., June 1944
Kerwin, Walter T., Lt Col, Div. Arty, 19 Jan. 1944
King, Dick A., Lt Col, Hq. 3d Div., 5 June 1944
Kingston, George R., Maj, Hq. 3d Div., 5 June 1944
Klipfel, Myles H., S/Sgt, Hq. Btry 9th FA Bn., 26 May 1944
Kriedberg, Marvin A., Maj, 15th Inf, 7 July 1943

Lang, Clarence W., T/4, C Btry 39th FA Bn., 14 Aug. 1944
Larson, Stanley M., Capt, 10th Engr. Bn., 29 Mar. 1944
Larson, Stanley R., Sgt, Hq. Co. 3d Div., 18 Nov. 1943
Lau, Frederick G., T/3, 3d Sig. Co., 15 Jan. 1944
Lembke, Orlan P., Pvt, 7th Inf, 11 Nov. 1942
Lewis, Robert L., S/Sgt, 10 FA Bn., 18 Mar. 1944
Lewis, Ruel E., 2d Lt, Serv. Co. 30th Inf, 5 June 1944
Lunsford, Frank J., T/Sgt, Co. D 15th Inf, 18 Feb. 1945

McCarty, William J., Lt Col, 3d Med. Bn., 12 Oct. 1943
McCoy, George V., M/Sgt, Hq. Co. 3d Div., 23 July 1943
▲McGarr, Lionel C., Col, 30th Inf, 5 June 1944
McGehee, James L., Lt Col, Hq. 3d Div., 8 Aug. 1944
McCloskey, John J., 1st Lt, 3d Rcn Trp., 6 Oct. 1943
Massey, Clarence, S/Sgt, Hq. Co. 1st Bn. 7th Inf, 26 Nov. 1944
Meyer, Harley E., Pfc, Co. I 30th Inf
Meyer, William E., Pvt, 3d QM, 18 Nov. 1943
Millican, Burr, 1st Lt, Div. Arty, 26 Feb. 1944
Mitchell, Robert E., Maj, 3d Div. Hq., 5 June 1944
Moore, Denis C., Capt, 15th Inf, 18 Aug. 1943
Murphy, Audie L., 1st Lt, Co. B 15th Inf, 18 Feb. 1945
Murr, Clyde E., T/Sgt, 703d Ord, 10 May 1944

Neddersen, Richard H., Lt Col, 30th Inf, 3 Dec. 1943
Netterblad, Alvin T., Capt, 3d Rcn, 18 Aug. 1943
Nofal, Henry E., 1st Lt, Serv. Co. 7th Inf, 5 June 1944
Noonan, Eugene M., S/Sgt, 751st Tank Bn., 18 Nov. 1943

O'Daniel, John W., Brig Gen, Hq. 3d Div.
Oliver, Garnet W., 1st Lt, 30th Inf, 11 Mar. 1944
Ott, Daniel B., T/4, Serv. Co. 30th Inf, 5 June 1944

Parke, Charles T., T/4, Hq. Btry 9th FA Bn., 5 June 1944
Perkins, John C., 1st Lt, 30th Inf, 12 Apr. 1944
Personeni, John L., S/Sgt, 703d Ord, 29 Sept. 1943
Petherick, Robert L., Capt, 10th Engr. Bn., 13 Oct. 1943
Petruzel, Frank, Capt, 7th Inf, 18 Aug. 1943

Pinkard, Calvin M., Capt, 3d Div. Arty, 1 Jan. 1944
Porter, Mackenzie E., Maj, 30th Inf, 5 June 1944
Price, Bruce C., Lt Col, Hq. 3d Div., 5 June 1944
Pugsley, Matthew C., Lt Col, Hq. 3d Div., Sept. 1943

Ramsey, Carl D., Capt, 30th Inf, 30 Nov. 1944
Ransom, Henry R., Maj, MD 15th Inf, 8 Nov. 1943
Ratekin, Jason E., S/Sgt, 30th Inf, 10 Nov. 1943
Reed, Ralph A., Capt, 7th Inf, 26 June 1944
Reinertsen, Paul A., Sgt, 7th Inf, 10 Oct. 1944
Revelle, George H., Jr., Maj, Hq. 3d Div., 23 June 1943
Richardson, Edward G., S/Sgt, 30th Inf, 19 Nov. 1943
Roles, Everett A., CWO, 7th Inf, 1 Dec. 1944
Rogers, Arthur H., Col, 30th Inf, 23 May 1943
Rogers, William B., Maj, 7th Inf
Rosson, William B., Maj, 7th Inf, 5 June 1944
Russell, William K., 2d Lt, 9th FA Bn., 18 Nov. 1943

Safine, Albert L., Maj, Hq. 3d Div., 5 June 1944
Salet, Eugene A., Maj, 15th Inf, 4 June 1944
Sanders, Edmund M., Capt, 30th Inf
Saylor, Samuel L., Maj, Div. Surgeon, 18 Nov. 1943
Schmidt, William R., Maj Gen, 9 May 1945
Scott, Hugh A., Maj, Hq. 3d Div., 24 Oct. 1944
Seiffert, Frank H., M/Sgt, 601st TD Bn.
Sevacool, John K., T/5, Hq. Co. 3d Div., 6 June 1944
Shaw, Robert C., Capt, Hq. 3d Div., 23 July 1943
Shephard, Whitfield P., Brig Gen, Hq. 3d Div., 27 Aug. 1944
Sherman, Harry B., Col, 7th Inf, 23 July 1943
Smith, John A., Sgt, 601st TD Bn., 28 Nov. 1944
Smith, Richard A., Capt, 7th Inf, 18 Aug. 1943
Snellenberger, Lenn A., T/Sgt, 7th Inf, 16 Aug. 1943
Snowden, Wayne H., Maj, Hq. 3d Div., 5 June 1944
Spangler, George C., 1st Lt, 30th Inf, 4 Jan. 1945
Spreyer, Frederick C., Capt, Hq. 3d Div., 14 Sept. 1944
Swaim, Allen L., 1st Lt, 15th Inf, 4 June 1944

Tardy, Walter E., Lt Col, CO 601st TD Bn., 5 June 1944
Taylor, Keith L., 1st Lt, 30th Inf, 22 Oct. 1944
Tedrow, Odell, S/Sgt, 30th Inf, 11 Mar. 1944
Thobro, Clayton C., Maj, 7th Inf, 4 May 1944
Treby, Harold E., Capt, Hq. 3d Div., 8 Aug. 1944
Truscott, Lucian K., Maj Gen, Hq. 3d Div.

Walter, Mercer C., Lt Col, Hq. 3d Div., 23 July 1943
Weber, William E., T/4, 703d Ord
Weispfenning, Walter W., T/Sgt, 39th FA Bn., 12 Nov. 1943
Wendt, James R., Jr., Lt Col, 41st FA Bn., 5 June 1944
Wilson, George M., CWO, 15th Inf, 4 June 1944
Wilson, Grover, Lt Col, GSC Hq. 3d Div., 5 June 1944
Woebkenberg, Eugene F., M/Sgt, 3d Sig. Co., 18 Aug. 1944
Woelpern, Frederick R., S/Sgt, Serv. Co. 30th Inf, 14 Sept. 1944
Wuis, Thomas R., WOJG, 30th Inf, 5 June 1944

Yarborough, William P., Lt Col, 509th Para. Inf
Young, Robert N., Brig Gen, Hq. 3d Div., 14 Mar. 1943

SOLDIER'S MEDAL

Abbott, Royal L., Cpl, Co. C 441st AAA Bn. (SP), Baia, Italy 24 July 1944
Accorsi, Robert, T/Sgt, Co. I 15th Inf, La Forge, France 9 Oct. 1944
Adams, Charles E., 1st Lt, Co. L 15th Inf, Phillipville, Tunisia 3 June 1943
Anderson, Harold K., T/Sgt, Serv Btry 9th FA Bn., Acciarella, Italy 12 Apr. 1944
Aycock, William B., 1st Lt, Co. A 15th Inf, Nettuno, Italy 9 May 1944

Bassett, Frederick J., Pfc, Co. C 7th Inf, Poppenlaver, Germany 8 Apr. 1945
Berescik, John J., Sgt, Hq. Co. 751st Tank Bn., Conca, Italy 9 May 1944
Bess, Eugene G., T/Sgt, AT Co. 30th Inf, Padiglione, Italy 20 Feb. 1944
Bramwell, Gordon, Pfc, Btry B 441st AAA Bn. (SP), Pozzuoli, Italy 15 July 1944
Broskey, Robert H., Pvt, Co. M 30th Inf, Anzio, Italy 22 June 1944

Casanova, Joseph G., Sgt, Serv. Btry 9th FA Bn., Acciarella, Italy 12 Apr. 1944
Case, Arthur D., S/Sgt, Hq. Co. 7th Inf, Tyrrhenian Sea, Italy 28 June 1944 (Posthumous Award)
Comstock, Walter, Pfc, Co. H 30th Inf, Ponte Rotto, Italy 19 May 1944
Crozier, Wilfred L., Pfc, Hq. 1st Bn. 30th Inf, Italy 22 Jan. 1944

Dawes, Charles H., Pfc, Hq. Btry 3d IDA, Port Lyautey, French Morocco 11 Apr. 1943
Deleon, Pedro, Pfc, Co. A 15th Inf, St. Ansiste, France 17 Aug. 1944

Earl, John H., T/Sgt, Co. B 7th Inf, Italy 1 July 1944
Edson, Hallet D., Lt Col, Inf CO 15th Inf, Saint Pilt, France 20 Dec. 1944
Escott, James, Pfc, Btry A 39th FA Bn., Salerno, Italy 18 Jan. 1944
Evanosky, Getty, Pfc, Co. C 7th Inf, France 21 Aug. 1944 (Posthumous Award)

Fair, Gordon N., T/5, Serv. Co. 15th Inf, Tannenkirch, France 2 Jan. 1945
Feldkamp, Rudolph C., Pfc, AT Co. 30th Inf, Cisterna, Italy 20 May 1944
Fuhrmann, Oscar R., Sgt, Co. M 7th Inf, Volturna River, Italy 27 Dec. 1943

Garcia, Fernando B., Pfc, Btry C 10th FA Bn., Cisterna, Italy 10 Mar. 1944
Groneveld, James A., Pvt, Co. D 7th Inf, Cisterna Di Littoria, Italy 27 Feb. 1944

Hall, William M., T/5, Hq. Co. 30th Inf, Rome, Italy 7 June 1944
Hatcher, Daniel W., Sgt, Cn Co. 30th Inf, Carpentras, France 27 Aug. 1944
Heavner, Gordon W., Pfc, Hq. Co. 15th Inf, Anzio, Italy 4 May 1944
Heintges, John A., Lt Col, Hq. 3d Bn. 7th Inf, Termini Immerse, Italy 30 July 1943
Henley, Charles R., Sgt, Btry A 39th FA Bn., Demel Begrat, N. Africa 5 June 1943

Hickerson, Jessie O., S/Sgt, Co. L 15th Inf, Etival, France 19 Nov. 1944
Hinman, Daniel S. T., Maj, Hq. 601st TD Bn., Salerno, Italy 21 Sept. 1943
Houston, David L., Pvt, Co. D 3d Med. Bn., Sicily July 1943

Irons, Kurt C., Pvt, Hq. 3d Bn. 7th Inf, France 24 Aug. 1944
Isaacson, Gerald, T/5, Serv. Co. 15th Inf, Salzburg, Austria 8 May 1945

Jameson, Dale W., S/Sgt, Btry A 9th FA Bn., Qualiano, Italy 21 June 1944
Jenkins, Gerwin, Pfc, Med. Det. 7th Inf, St. Nazaire, France 21 Aug. 1944
Joffe, Maxwell S., Sgt, Co. L 30th Inf, Zweibrucken, Germany 21 Mar. 1945

Kane, Francis C., 1st Lt, MC Co. D 3d Med. Bn., Sicily 1943
Kehoe, Joseph E., S/Sgt, Hq. Co. 30th Inf, Rome, Italy 7 June 1944

Lang, Paul, T/5, Serv. Co. 7th Inf, Aragona, Sicily 24 July 1943
Lent, Robert P., Pfc, Btry A 41st FA Bn., Bizerte, Tunisia 5 July 1943
Levy, Harry, Pvt, Serv. Co. 7th Inf, Italy 5 Aug. 1944
Lodle, Elwood G., 1st Lt, CAC Btry B 441st AAA Bn. (SP), Pozzuoli, Italy 15 July 1944
Lowe, Howard D., Capt, Co. A 30th Inf, Tunisia June 1943

McFalls, Carroll, Jr., Capt, Inf Hq. 3d Bn. 30th Inf, Worth, Germany 30 Mar. 1945
McGuire, Jim, Pvt, Co. D 30th Inf, Algeria Apr. 1943
Malecki, Anthony, Pfc, 3d QM Co., Acerno, Italy 28 Sept. 1943
Malone, Robert F., Pvt, Serv. Co. 30th Inf, San Tropez Bay, France 16 Aug. 1944
Marks, William F., Pfc, Med. Det. 30th Inf, Italy 20 Feb. 1944
Marsh, Charlie A., Pfc, Cn Co. 30th Inf, Salzburg, Austria 30 May 1945
Martin, Chester L., Pfc, Hq. Co. 30th Inf, Italy 16 May 1944
Meccariello, Edward P., Pfc, Hq. 3d Bn. 7th Inf, France 24 Aug. 1944
Mecke, Theodore H., Jr., Pvt, Hq. Co. 3d Div., Italy 14 Aug. 1944
Milam, Irvin L., Cpl, AT Co. 30th Inf, Anzio, Italy 24 Mar. 1944
Miller, Jack N., T/5, Hq. 3d Bn. 7th Inf, France 24 Aug. 1944
Miller, William H., Pvt, Serv. Co. 7th Inf, Termini Immerse, Italy 30 July 1943
Milner, Homer, T/Sgt, Serv. Co. 30th Inf, St. Croix, France 21 Jan. 1945
Morris, James M., 1st Lt, Inf Co. K 15th Inf, Artena, Italy 28 May 1944

Nethken, Lloyd H., AT Co. 30th Inf, Anzio, Italy 24 Mar. 1944
Newell, Richard W., 2d Lt, AT Co. 30th Inf, Algeria May 1943
Nielson, Ernest W., Pfc, Hq. Co. MP Pltn, Conca, Italy 17 Feb. 1944
Null, John C., T/4, Co. C 756th Tank Bn., Seicheprey, France 13 Mar. 1945

Oder, Charles, Pvt, 3d QM Co., Acciarella, Italy 27 May 1944
Oliver, Raymond L., S/Sgt, Co. C 7th Inf, St. Nazaire, France 21 Aug. 1944

▲ Oak Leaf Cluster.

Owen, Charles B., Pfc, Btry A 39th FA Bn., Salerno, Italy 18 Jan. 1944
Oxley, Charles K., Pfc, AT Co. 30th Inf, Padiglione, Italy 20 Feb. 1944

Poythress, Sam J., Jr., 1st Lt, Cn Co. 15th Inf, Italy 15 June 1944
Punska, Joseph, T/Sgt, Hq. 3d Bn. 7th Inf, Termini Immerse, Italy 30 July 1943

Rapoza, Victor, T/Sgt, Co. F 30th Inf, Monte Dragona, Italy 20 July 1944
Robinson, F. D., Pfc, Btry A 9th FA Bn., Presinzano, Italy 6 Nov. 1943
Rosenfeld, Arthur H., Pvt, Co. M 30th Inf, LaBanca, Italy 7 May 1944

Santella, Samuel J., Pfc, Co. F 30th Inf, Monte Dragona, Italy 20 July 1944
Sease, James R., Pfc, Co. M 30th Inf, Nettuno, Italy 22 Jan. 1944
Scholl, Elmer A., Cpl, Co. I 15th Inf, Palermo, Sicily 28 July 1943
Sherry, Nicholas J., T/5, 3d Sig. Co., Sicily 12 Sept. 1943
Smith, Hobert C., 1st Lt, QMC Co., Acciarella, Italy 27 May 1944
Snyder, Arthur, Lt Col, 751st Tank Bn., Conca, Italy 17 Feb. 1944
Sudlow, Robert D., Pfc, Btry A 39th FA Bn., Demel Begrat, N. Africa 5 June 1943

Tate, William H., Sgt, Co. D 441st AAA Bn. (SP), San Stefano, Italy 11 Aug. 1943
Tenny, Flao L., Pfc, Co. K 15th Inf, Artena, Italy 28 May 1944

Vaillancourt, Ernest J., Pfc, Cn Co. 7th Inf, Campo Morto, Italy 8 Mar. 1944
Votruba, Kenneth E., Serv. Co. 7th Inf, French Morocco 16 Feb. 1943

Wakefield, Robert L., Sgt, Btry A 9th FA Bn., Cononia, Sicily 21 Sept. 1943
Wall, John P., Pvt, Hq. 3d Bn. 7th Inf, Italy 25 June 1944
Wallner, Gilbert F., Pfc, Btry B 9th FA Bn., Cori, Italy 26 May 1944
Williams, Burl, Sgt, Co. D 30th Inf, Algeria Apr. 1943
Wimmer, Ray E., S/Sgt, Hq. 1st Bn. 30th Inf, Cori, Italy 26 May 1944
Withman, Louis W., S/Sgt, Co. I 30th Inf, Le Tholy, France 10 Oct. 1944
Worthington, Elbert T., Pfc, Co. I 7th Inf, Termini Immerse, Italy 30 July 1943 (Posthumous Award)

Zeiger, Alfred A., Pfc, Cn Co. 7th Inf, Rupt-sur-Moselle, France 26 Oct. 1944

BRONZE STAR

Aaron, Paul S., Jr., Co. L 30th Inf, Colmar
Aaronson, Max, 1st Lt, Hqs. 7th Inf, Italy & France 11 Feb. 1945
Abbott, Royal L., Sgt, Btry C 441 AAA AW Bn., Sicily, Italy, France, Germany 8 May 1945
Abernethy, Charles H., S/Sgt, Co. E 30th Inf Regt., France 25 Dec. 1944
Abraham, Kurt, T/3, Hq. 3d Inf Div., France, Germany 5 May 1945
Abrahamson, Arthur, 1st Lt, Cav. Hq. Co. 756th Tank Bn., Germany 29 Apr. 1945
Ackerman, Walter R., S/Sgt, Serv. Co. 756th Tank Bn., France, Germany 6 Apr. 1945
Adams, Charles D., 1st Lt, Co. E 15th Inf, San Fratello, Sicily 6 Aug. 1943
Adams, Darrell V., Pfc, Co. C 7th Inf, Lavilla 27 May 1944
Adams, Francis C., T/4, Hq. 3d Div., Italy 23 May 1944
▲Adams, Howard P., T/5, Hq. Co. 1st Bn. 7th Inf Regt., Germany 18 Mar. 1945
Adams, James R., Pfc, 3d Rcn Trp, Rome 5 June 1944
Adams, John E., Pfc, Hq. Co. 3d Bn. 30th Inf, France 23 Jan. 1945
Adams, Lucian, Pfc, Co. I 30th Inf, Ponte Rotto 23 May 1944
Adams, Raymond A., Cpl, Hq. Btry 3d IDA, Anzio, Italy 29 Feb. 1944
Adams, Steve, Pfc, Serv. Co. 756th Tank Bn., Germany 19 Mar. 1945
Adams, Vernon L., T/5, Btry A 441 AAA AW Bn., Italy 29 Oct. 1943
Adams, Walter M., Pfc, Co. H 7th Inf, Cisterna Di Littoria 23 May 1944
Adamski, Raymond, S/Sgt, Co. G 30th Inf, Carano 22 Apr. 1944
Adaskin, Saul, S/Sgt, Co. M 7th Inf, France 30 Jan. 1945
Addison, William C., Sgt, Hq. Co. 1st Bn. 7th Inf Regt., Anzio, Italy 4 Mar. 1944
▲Adelson, Bernard, Pfc, Hq. Co. 1st Bn. 30th Inf Regt., France 17 Dec. 1944
Adkisson, Charles C., T/5, Serv. Co. 30th Inf Regt., Italy, France, Germany, Austria 8 May 1945
Adlard, Ithel R., Sgt, Hq. Co. 756th Tank Bn., France 4 Oct. 1944
Africano, Salvatore J., T/4, Rcn Co. 601st TD Bn., N. Africa, Italy, France, Germany, Austria 8 May 1945
Agne, Herbert G., Med. Corps, Co. A 3d Med. Bn., France, Germany, Austria 8 May 1945
Ahlcrim, Everett R., M/Sgt, Hq. 3d Inf Div., N. Africa, Sicily, Italy, France, Germany, Austria 8 May 1945
Aho, Arthur M., T/4, Btry A 41st FA Bn., Venafro 8 Nov. 1943
Aho, Douglas R., T/5, Hq. Btry 39th FA Bn., Italy 2 June 1944
Aiken, John H., S/Sgt, CIC Det. 3d Inf Div., Germany, Austria 8 May 1945
Ailen, Wilbur E., Sgt, Btry B 10th FA Bn., Cisterna 19 Feb. 1944
Aimone, Otto, T/5, Co. B 601st TD Bn., Isola Bella 29 Feb. 1944
Airheart, Onclo M., Pfc, Co. B 15th Inf Regt., Germany 26 Mar. 1945
Akers, Willis B., Pfc, Co. L 30th Inf Regt., Raddon 17 Sept. 1944
▲Alarie, John B., Capt, Inf Hq. Co. 7th Inf Regt., Germany 4 May 1945
Albaugh, Gordon A., Pvt, Btry C 10th FA Bn., Cisterna 8 May 1944
Albensi, Joseph W., T/5, Co. C 601st TD Bn., Cisterna 24 May 1944
Albro, Robert W., T/5, Hq. Btry 9th FA Bn., N. Africa, Sicily, Italy, France, Germany 8 May 1945
Alder, Willis F., Sgt, Co. H 7th Inf, Ferdrupt 30 Sept. 1944
Aldridge, Marion G., Cpl, Btry B 39th FA Bn., Italy 10 Oct. 1943
Alexander, George, Pfc, 3d Sig. Co., N. Africa, Sicily, Italy, France 31 Jan. 1945
Alexander, William E., Pvt, Co. B 601st TD Bn., Isola Bella 29 Feb. 1944
Alf, Leonard F., Pfc, Co. B 7th Inf, Cisterna Di Littoria 24 May 1944
Alfano, Anthony, Jr., Sgt, Co. F 15th Inf, Anzio, Italy 29 Feb. 1944
Alfano, Joseph A., Pfc, Hq. Co. 1st Bn. 7th Inf Regt., Italy 20 Apr. 1944
Aline, Robert F., Capt, Inf Serv. Co. 7th Inf Regt., Italy 4 June 1944
Alkire, Raymond B., Sgt, Hq. Btry 69th Armd FA Bn., Anzio, Italy 31 Jan. 1944
Allard, Albert, Jr., T/5, Hq. Co. 2d Bn. 7th Inf Regt., France 4 Feb. 1945
Allard, Howard A., T/5, Co. D 756th Tank Bn., Germany 26 Apr. 1945
Allen, Clarence B., Pfc, Co. H 30th Inf, Les Jacques 18 Oct. 1944
▲Allen, George E., 1st Lt, Corps of MP, MP Platoon, 3d Inf Div., Germany 8 May 1945
Allen, Harold E., M/Sgt, Hq. Co. 30th Inf Regt., Sicily, Italy Mar. 1944
Allen, James M., Pfc, Co. G 7th Inf, Anzio, Italy 23 Apr. 1944
Allen, Raymond S., Sgt, Co. G 15th Inf Regt., France 24 Dec. 1944
Allen, Roy E., T/4, Hq. Co. 3d Div., France, Germany, Austria 7 May 1945
Allen, Thomas A., T/5, Serv. Btry 41st FA Bn., San Fratello, Sicily 5 Aug. 1943
Allen, Walter P., S/Sgt, Btry A 39th FA Bn., Campo Belle, Sicily 11 July 1943
Allender, Maurice B., S/Sgt, Co. K 30th Inf, Anzio, Italy 23 Jan. 1944
Allinger, Robert V., Pfc, Hq. Co. 30th Inf Regt., N. Africa, Sicily, Italy, France Oct. 1944
Almon, William F., S/Sgt, Hq. Co. 2d Bn. 7th Inf Regt., Germany 15 Mar. 1945
Alonge, Sam F., T/5, Serv. Co. 756th Tank Bn., Germany 19 Mar. 1945
Alton, O'Neil R., Cpl, 3d Rcn Trp., Ponte De Cheruy, France 1 Sept 1944
▲(2) Altschuld, Max, Cpl, Co. B 601st TD Bn., Anzio, Italy 11 Mar. 1944
Altum, Marion L., Pfc, Co. A 30th Inf, Ponte Rotto 23 May 1944
Alvarez, Louis A., T/5, Hq. Btry 9th FA Bn., Africa, Sicily, Italy, France, Germany 8 May 1945
Alvarez, Pedro A., Pfc, Btry C 441st AAA AW Bn., Germany 27 Mar. 1945
Alvarino, Gerard R., Pfc, Co. D 30th Inf Regt., Italy 29 Apr. 1945

Amarnte, Stephen, T/5, Hq. Co. 1st Bn. 7th Inf Regt., Italy 2 Mar. 1944
Amburgey, Haymond, Pfc, AT Co. 15th Inf, France 2 Jan. 1945
Amundson, Willis O., Pfc, Co. H 15th Inf, Italy 13 Oct. 1943
Amunso, Michael J., Pvt, Hq. Co. 3d Bn. 7th Inf, Padiglione 25 Apr. 1944
Anders, John V., Pvt, Co. A 601st TD Bn., Ponte Rotto 23 May 1944
Anderson, Albert, T/5, Co. B 10th Engr. Bn., Cisterna 24 May 1944
Anderson, Arnold L., Hq. Btry 9th FA Bn., Sicily, Italy, France, Germany, Austria 8 May 1945
Anderson, Ben F., Cpl, AT Co. 30th Inf, Valmontone 2 June 1944
Anderson, Edward L., T/4, Btry C 10th FA Bn., N. Africa, Sicily, Italy, France, Germany 8 May 1945
Anderson, George E., Sgt, Co. M 30th Inf Regt., Sicily, Italy, France, Germany, Austria May 1945
▲Anderson, Harley, Sgt, Co. D 756th Tank Bn., Germany 17 Apr. 1945
Anderson, Harold K., T/Sgt, Serv. Btry 9th FA Bn., N. Africa, Sicily, Italy 5 June 1944
Anderson, Harold L., Pfc, Hq. Co. 2d Bn. 7th Inf Regt., Italy 15 Mar. 1944
Anderson, Henry, 1st Lt, Co. C 601st TD Bn., Presle, France 13 Sept. 1944
Anderson, James T., Pfc, Hq. Co. 2d Bn. 30th Inf, Colmar
Anderson, John W., Maj, 39th FA Bn., N. Africa, Sicily, Italy, France, Germany 8 May 1945
Anderson, Lester K., M/Sgt, Hq. Btry 3d Div. Arty., Italy, France, Germany 7 May 1945
Anderson, Merritt W., Pvt, Hq. Btry 3d Div. Arty., Guilianello 28 May 1944
Anderson, Murl O., Maj, Med., Sicily, Italy 31 June 1944
Anderson, Nathan K., 2d Lt, Hq. Co. 7th Inf, Italy 29 Feb. 1944
Anderson, Orland A., T/5, Hq. Btry 3d Inf Div. Arty., N. Africa, Italy, France, Germany 8 May 1945
Anderson, Roy L., S/Sgt, Co. B 756th Tank Bn., France 15 Sept. 1944
Anderson, Thomas G., T/4, Serv. Co. 7th Inf, N. Africa, Sicily, Italy, France Germany 6 May 1945
Anderson, Vernon A., 2d Lt, Btry C 9th FA Bn., Italy 12 Mar. 1944
Anderson, William D., Pfc, Co. G 7th Inf, Cisterna Di Littoria 5 Apr. 1944
Anderson, Wilson L., Pfc, Hq. Co. 10th Engr. Bn., Le Ferriere 29 Feb. 1944
Anistrateko, Peter P., T/Sgt, Hq. Co. 1st Bn. 30th Inf Regt., France 26 Jan. 1945
Andreasen, Stanley C., T/5, Btry C 10th FA Bn., N. Africa, Sicily, Italy, France, Germany 8 May 1945
Andress, Max A., Pfc, Co. A 601st TD Bn., Cisterna Di Littoria 6 Mar. 1944
Andrews, Francis F., 1st Sgt, Hq. Co. 1st Bn. 7th Inf Regt., France 7 Oct. 1944
Andrews, Roland C., Pfc, Hq. Co. 2d Bn. 7th Inf, France 7 Oct. 1944
Andrus, Alton L., S/Sgt, 3d Sig. Co., France 20 Dec. 1944
▲Andy, Leo, T/Sgt, Co. C 15th Inf Regt., France 30 Jan. 1945
Angelle, Roy P., Sgt, Co. M 30th Inf, Italy 29 Feb. 1944
Angerer, Bennie B., T/5, Hq. Co. 756th Tank Bn., France, Germany 8 May 1945
Anglin, Suel C., S/Sgt, Serv. Co. 756th Tank Bn., France, Germany, Austria 8 May 1945
Annis, William W., S/Sgt, Btry D 441st AAA AW Bn., Sicily, Italy, France, Germany 8 May 1945
Ansell, Earl G., T/4, Co. A 601st TD Bn., Italy, France Mar. 1945
Ansell, Dale W., 1st Lt, Hq. 3d Div. FA, Italy 18 Nov. 1943
Antaya, Joseph E., Pfc, Hq. Co. 3d Bn. 30th Inf, Le Tholy 16 Oct. 1944
Anthony, Louis R., Pfc, Hq. Btry 39th FA Bn., France 23 Aug. 1944
Araujo, Clarence L., S/Sgt, Hq. Co. 3d Bn. 30th Inf, France 23 Jan. 1945
Arceneaux, Arthur, Pfc, Co. B 30th Inf Regt., Germany 26 Mar. 1945
Archbold, Edgar B., Jr., Pfc, Hq. Co. 2d Bn. 30th Inf, Colmar
Arena, Louis L., Pvt, Btry A 41st FA Bn., Lontenat, France 17 Sept. 1944
Armel, Julian K., T/5, Serv. Co. 7th Inf, Italy, France Feb. 1944
Armetta, Sam M., Pfc, Co. B 15th Inf, Cisterna Di Littoria 24 May 1944
Armstrong, Burton, Pfc, Co. D 15th Inf, Anzio, Italy 17 Apr. 1944
Arndt, Daniel, Cpl, Hq. Co. 756th Tank Bn., France 2 Dec. 1944
Arnold, Archie L., Sgt, Co. G 7th Inf, Italy 23 May 1944
Arnold, Austin L., Cpl, Co. A 601st TD Bn., Tunisia 23 Mar. 1943
Arnold, Edwin Y., Maj, CO, 756th Tank Bn., Italy, France 10 Oct. 1944
Arnold, Lawton R., Pfc, Rcn Co. 601st TD Bn., Italy 10 Mar. 1944
Arp, Arch W., Pfc, Hq. Co. 1st Bn. 30th Inf, Germany 11 Apr. 1945
Ashbaugh, Carroll D., T/Sgt, Hq. 3d Inf Div., Italy 7 June 1944
Asher, William H., T/4, Hq. Co. 3d Bn. 7th Inf Regt., France 25 Oct. 1944
Ashford, Lee S., S/Sgt, Co. A 7th Inf Regt., France 28 Dec. 1944
Ashton, Charles E., S/Sgt, Co. A 30th Inf Regt., Germany 15 Apr. 1945
Ashton, John G., Pfc, Hq. Co. 3d Bn. 7th Inf, Germany 16 Mar. 1945
Atkins, Levi, T/5, Med. Det. 15th Inf Regt., France 27 Dec. 1944
Aubel, Harvey J., S/Sgt, Co. D 7th Inf, Magiorano 16 Oct. 1943
▲Auld, Henry C., Jr., Capt, Inf Hq. Co. 15th Inf Regt., France, Germany 8 May 1945
Aulisio, Anthony, Pfc, Co. G 15th Inf Regt., France 28 Sept. 1944
Austin, Ben R., T/5, Hq. Co. 30th Inf, Sicily 27 June 1944
Austin, Hubert L., T/5, Serv. Co. 15th Inf Regt., France, Germany 20 Apr. 1945
Austin, Lovell D., T/4, Btry A 39th FA Bn., San Fratello, Sicily 3 Aug. 1943

▲ Oak Leaf Cluster.

Awen, Joseph H., S/Sgt, 703d Ord. Co. N. Africa, Sicily, Italy, France, Germany, Austria 1 May 1945
Ayala, Esteban, Sgt, Co. A 7th Inf Regt., France 8 Oct. 1944
Ayala, Frank V., Pfc, Co. M 15th Inf, La Forge, France 25 Aug. 1944
Aycock, William B., 1st Lt, Co. A 15th Inf, Cisterna Di Littoria 28 Feb. 1944
Ayotte, Clifford, Pvt, Co. A 30th Inf Regt., France 27 Oct. 1944
Ayres, Harmon N., T/4, Med. Det. 601st TD Bn., Anzio, Italy 2 Mar. 1944
Azevedo. Tony L., T/4, Hq. Btry 9th FA Bn., France 16 Dec. 1944

Baars, Donald A., T/5, Serv. Btry 10th FA Bn., N. Africa, Sicily, Italy, France, Germany, Austria 8 May 1945
Babb, Harley G., Jr., Pvt, Co. K 30th Inf Regt., Germany 26 Mar. 1945
Babcock, Godfrey, Pfc, Co. E 7th Inf Regt., France 1 Dec. 1944
Bachert, Hadley J., Pfc, Co. A Cisterna Di Littoria 24 May 1944
Bacon, Allen F., Lt Col, CO, 1st Bn. 30th Inf, Italy 27 June 1944
Bacon, Eugene F., 1st Lt, Co. E 7th Inf, Artena 29 May 1944
Bagley, Ross T., Pfc, Co. B 7th Inf Regt., Germany 8 Apr. 1945
Bahe, Alfred H., Pvt, Hq. Co. 2d Bn. 30th Inf, Anzio, Italy 19 Apr. 1944
Bailey, Guy M., Pfc, Co. M 30th Inf, N. Africa, Sicily, Italy, France, Germany May 1945
Bailey, Lester R., Pfc, Btry C 39th FA Bn., Cisterna 10 Mar. 1944
Bailey, Lewis T., Pfc, Hq. & Hq. Btry, 41st FA Bn., Conca 31 Jan. 1944
Bailey, Roland W., Capt, Hq. Btry 39th FA Bn., N. Africa 5 June 1944
Bailey, Ulysses G., Pfc, Co. D 30th Inf, France 17 Sept. 1944
Baird, Carl W., Pfc, Co. M 15th Inf, Benoit 15 Sept. 1944
Baird, Joseph E., Sgt, Co. M 7th Inf, Artena 29 May 1944
▲Bajek, Gilbert W., S/Sgt, Co. K 30th Inf Regt., Germany 8 Apr. 1945
Baker, Allen K., Pfc, Hq. Btry 9th FA Bn., Anzio, Italy 29 Feb. 1944
Baker, Alvin G., Pvt, Co. B 7th Inf, Artena 28 May 1944
Baker, Jesse R., S/Sgt, Co. F 30th Inf Regt., France 26 Nov. 1944
Baker, Frederick E., Pfc, Hq. Co. 7th Inf, France 23 Jan. 1945
Baker, Howard J., Pfc, Btry A 9th FA Bn., Casablanca, French Morocco 10 Nov. 1942
Baker, Lowell W., T/5, Hq. Co. 1st Bn. 7th Inf Regt., Italy 24 May 1944
Baker, Ronald L., 1st Lt, Coast Arty. Corps, Hq. 441st AAA AW Bn., Sicily, Italy, France, Germany 8 May 1945
Baker, Victor W., Pvt, Hq. Btry 41st FA Bn., Campo Morto 20 Feb. 1944
Baker, Wilburn D., Pfc, Co. C 10th Engr. Bn., Faucogney 21 Sept. 1944
Bakey, Russell F., 1st Lt, Hq. Co. Cav., Italy 25 Feb. 1944
Baldwin, Clarence F., Pfc, Med. Det. 7th Inf Regt., Germany 20 Apr. 1945
Baliantini, Elmer, T/5, Co. C 601st TD Bn., Italy, France, Germany, 8 May 1945
Balkenbush, Adrian F., Cpl, MP Pltn Hq. 3d Div., France 6 Feb. 1945
Balkus, Joseph W., Pfc, Med. Det. 15th Inf, France 5 Feb. 1945
Ball, Donald E., Pfc, Co. C 7th Inf, Rupt Sur-Moselle 29 Sept. 1944
Ballard, Russell W., Pvt, Co. A 756th Tank Bn., France 25 Jan. 1945
Ballestero, Manuel, Pfc, Co. I 15th Inf Regt., France 31 Dec. 1944
Balog, William L., T/3, 3d Sig. Co., Italy 4 June 1944
Balsama, Joseph, Pfc, Co. A 7th Inf Regt., France 2 Nov. 1944
Bambaok, Roland J., S/Sgt, Hq. Co. 1st Bn. 30th Inf Regt., Italy 11 Nov. 1943
Bandera, Kenneth E., T/4, Hq. Co. 756th Tank Bn., France 29 Jan. 1945
Baran, John S., Sgt. Co. A 601st TD Bn., France 1 Mar. 1945
Barber, August F., Pfc, Hq. Co. 1st Bn. 7th Inf Regt., France 7 Oct. 1944
Barber, David H., S/Sgt, Co. C 30th Inf, Besancon, France 7 Sept. 1944
Barber, Steve C., Pfc, Hq. Co. 30th Inf, Cisterna Di Littoria 20 May 1944
Barber, Thomas M., T/5, Co. B 756th Tank Bn., France 13 Sept. 1944
Barclay, Louis L., Pfc, Hq. Co. 2d Bn. 30th Inf Regt., Italy 1 Mar. 1944
Barco, Barney M., 1st Lt, FA Btry C 41st FA Bn., Germany 7 Apr. 1945
Barker, Harold O., Jr., 2d Lt, 3d CIC Det. 3d Inf Div., France 15 Feb. 1945
Barnard, George R., T/4, Med. Det. 7th Inf Regt., France 1 Dec. 1944
Barnes, James D., Pfc, Co. D 30th Inf Regt., Italy 1 June 1944
Barnes, John E., 1st Sgt, Co. A 3d Med. Bn., N. Africa, Sicily, Italy 1 July 1944
Barnes, Norman P., Maj, Hq. 3d Div., Italy 10 Aug. 1944
Barnes, Russell E., T/Sgt, Co. M 15th Inf, France, Germany, Austria 8 May 1945
Barnes, Vernon E., Pfc, Co. F 30th Inf Regt., Anzio, Italy 4 Mar. 1944
Barnett, Carlos R., Pfc, Co. A 7th Inf, France 22 Nov. 1944
Barnett, Charles E., Sgt, Co. A 756th Tank Bn., Germany 18 Apr. 1945
▲Barr, Burton S., Maj, Inf, 1st Bn. 15th Inf, Germany 24 Apr. 1945
Barr, J. Y.,S/Sgt, Co. A 3d Med. Bn., Sicily, Italy, France, Germany, Austria 8 May 1945
Barrett, Francis J., Pfc, Co. E 7th Inf, Artena, 28 May 1944
Barron, Eugene D., T/5, Hq. Btry 39th FA Bn., France 4 Nov. 1944
Barrows, Henry R., Pvt, Btry B 39th FA Bn., Cisterna 10 Mar. 1944
Barry, Alfred R., 1st Sgt, Rcn Co. 601st TD Bn., Italy, France, Germany, Austria May 1945
Barth, Edward J., S/Sgt, Rcn Co. 601st TD Bn., El Guettar 23 Mar. 1943
Bartosiak, Joseph R., Pvt, Hq. 3d Bn. 7th Inf Regt., France 27 Jan. 1945
▲Basila, Basil F., Lt Col, Gen. Staff Corps, Hq. 3d Inf Div., Italy, France 14 Sept. 1944
Basile, Frank, T/5, Btry A 441st AAA AW Bn., Sicily, Italy, France, Germany 8 May 1945
▲Basquez, Manuel, Cpl, Hq. Btry 41st FA Bn., France 28 Aug. 1944
Basso, Louis L., S/Sgt, Co. D 15th Inf, Anzio, Italy 23 Mar. 1944
Bastian, Henry G., Pfc, Co. D 15th Inf Regt., Anzio, Italy 29 Feb. 1944
Batdorff, Emerson L., 1st Lt, Inf, 3d Bn. 30th Inf, France, Germany 11 Apr. 1945
Bateman, John F., Hq. & Hq. Det. 3d Med. Bn., France, Germany 8 May 1945
Batrick, Stacy T., Pvt, Hq. & Hq. Btry 41st FA Bn., Conca 31 Jan. 1944
Batson, Hugh A., S/Sgt, Serv. Co. 7th Inf Regt., France 4 Jan. 1945
Baudouin, Eugene V., Sgt, Co. B 7th Inf, France 8 Nov. 1944
Bauer, Raymond P., Pvt, Co. K 15th Inf Regt., France 26 Oct. 1944
Bauer, Roy E., T/4, Hq. Btry 441st AAA AW Bn., Sicily, Italy, France, Germany 8 May 1945
Baugh, John W., 1st Lt, Inf, Hq. Co. 2d Bn. 7th Inf Regt., Italy, France 27 Nov. 1944
Baukair, Akle N., Pfc, QM Co., Morocco 10 Nov. 1942
Baul, Rogue C., T/4, 3d Inf Div. Band, N. Africa, Sicily, Italy 31 Dec. 1943
Bauman, Jack L., T/4, Hq. 3d Inf Div., Italy, France, Germany, Austria May 1945
Baumgartner, Anthony R., Pfc, Co. M 30th Inf Regt., France 27 Oct. 1944
Baunach, Joseph R., Jr., Pvt, Co. D 30th Inf, Sicily 1 Aug. 1943
Bay, Walter A., Pfc, Hq. Co. 2d Bn. 15th Inf, Italy, 24 May 1944
Baylard, Elden D., Jr., T/5, Hq. Co. 1st Bn. 30th Inf, France 23 Jan. 1945

Bazelewski, Bruno J., Pfc, Co. B 10th Engr. Combat Bn., France 22 Jan. 1945
Beal, George C., S/Sgt, Co. L 30th Inf, France 10 Nov. 1944
Beal, Ivan W., T/5, Btry C 9th FA Bn., Artena 30 May 1944
Bean, Wesley V., Jr., Pvt, Hq. Btry 3d IDA, Anzio, Italy 29 Feb. 1944
Beard, Clarence J., Jr., Pvt, Co. A 15th Inf, Saint Anaista, France 17 Aug. 1944
Beard, Samuel I., Pfc, Co. K 30th Inf Regt., Germany 28 Mar. 1945
▲Beardslee, Owen C., S/Sgt, 1st Bn. 30th Inf, France 25 Oct. 1944
Beasley, Lee A., T/4, Hq. 3d Inf Div., Italy, France, Germany, Austria 6 May 1945
Beaton, Donald R., Pvt, Hq. Co. 1st Bn. 7th Inf Regt., France 20 Oct. 1944
Beauchene, Oliver D., M/Sgt, Serv. Co. 7th Inf, Italy, France, Germany May 1945
Beaver, Clifford R., T/Sgt, AT Co. 15th Inf Regt., near Riedwihr, France 27 Jan. 1945
Becenti, Ned, Pfc, Hq. Co. 3d Bn. 30th Inf, Le Tholy 16 Oct. 1944
Bechard, Walter S., Pvt, Co. H 15th Inf, Ponte Rotto 1 Mar. 1944
Beck, Dwight, Pfc, Med. Det. 41st FA Bn., Le Ferriere 31 Jan. 1944
Beck, James A., T/5, Med. Det. 7th Inf, La Londe, France 18 Aug. 1944
Beck, James M., 2d Lt, Inf Co. I 30th Inf Regt., France 8 Jan. 1945
Becker, Elmer C., 1st Lt, Inf Hq. 2d Bn. 7th Inf, France 4 Feb. 1945
Becker, William C., S/Sgt, Hq. & Hq. Co. 2d Bn. 30th Inf, Cisterna Di Littoria 24 May 1944
Beckerleg, John, 1st Sgt, Hq. & Serv. Co. 10th Engr. Combat Bn., Italy 15 Feb. 1944
Beckstrand, Wendell E., T/4, Hq. Co. 3d Bn. 30th Inf Regt., France 23 Jan. 1945
Bee, Stanley P., T/4, Hq. Co. 3d Inf Div., N. Africa, Sicily, Italy, France, Germany 8 May 1945
Beer, Jack W., Co. D 7th Inf Regt., France 24 Oct. 1944
▲Behr, Alexander T., 1st Lt, Hq. Co. 30th Inf, Cisterna Di Littoria 25 May 1944
▲Beifield, Martin P., T/4, Serv. Co. 7th Inf Regt., Italy, France, Germany May 1945
Bell, Charles O., Pfc, Serv. Co. 15th Inf Regt., France, Germany 7 May 1945
Bell, Charles R., 1st Lt, FA Co. B 601st TD Bn., Germany 1 Apr. 1945
Bell, Clayton R., T/5, Rcn Co. 601st TD Bn., Sollgis Pont, France 18 Aug. 1944
Bell, George E., Pfc, Hq. Btry 441st AAA AW Bn., Marseilles, France 18 Sept. 1944
Bell, John A., Pfc, Co. E 30th Inf Regt., France 17 Dec. 1944
Bellrose, Walter C., Btry A 441st AAA AW Bn., Costello 29 May 1944
Benadom, Max, S/Sgt, Hq. Co. 756th Tank Bn., France, Germany 8 May 1945
Bencenti, Ned, Pfc, Hq. Co. 3d Bn. 30th Inf, Vosges
Bendt, Clarence A., Cpl, Co. M 30th Inf Regt., N. Africa, Sicily, Italy, France, Germany 8 May 1945
Benedict, Robert O., Sgt, Hq. Co. 2d Bn. 7th Inf Regt., France 3 Nov. 1944
Benko, John F., 1st Lt, Inf Hq. 2d Bn. 30th Inf, Italy, France, Germany 8 May 1945
Bennett, Bryan E., Pfc, MP Pltn. 3d Inf Div., Germany 8 May 1945
Bennett, Fred W., Cpl, Co. B 10th Engr., France 8 Nov. 1944
Bennett, Lawrence M., T/3, Med. Det. 30th Inf, Italy 23 May 1944
Bensing, Floyd A., S/Sgt, Hq. Btry 39th FA Bn., N. Africa, Sicily, Italy, France, Germany, Austria 8 May 1945
Benson, Oster A., Pfc, Btry C 10th FA Bn., Artena 28 May 1944
Bentley, Eugene W., S/Sgt, Co. A 30th Inf Regt., France 10 Jan. 1945
Bentley, John H., T/5, Btry C 9th FA Bn., France 21 Aug. 1944
Berard, Stanley J., Pfc, Co. H 7th Inf, France 25 Jan. 1945
Berg, Edward E., Pvt, Co. E 7th Inf, Cisterna Di Littoria 1 Feb. 1944
Bergbower, Roy J., T/5, Serv. Co. 756th Tank Bn., France, Germany, Austria 8 May 1945
Bergman, Antone A., Pfc, Co. E 15th Inf, Isola Bella 29 Feb. 1944
Bergsten, Boyd T., T/4, Hq. Co. 15th Inf, Anzio 4 June 1944
Berk, Morris, Pfc, Hq. Btry 41st FA Bn., Le Perriere 25 Feb. 1944
Berkouski, John E., 1st Sgt, Co. A 756th Tank Bn., France 15 Feb. 1945
Berndt, Alvin D., S/Sgt, Hq. Btry 39th FA Bn., Italy 8-9 Oct. 1943
Berner, Lester L., T/4, Co. B 601st TD Bn., France 23 Jan. 1945
Bernhard, George W., Sgt, Co. A 756th Tank Bn., France 15 Sept. 1944
Bernice, Peter C., Cpl, Co. C 10th Engr., Cisterna 23 May 1944
Berry, Clarence W., T/Sgt, 703d Ord. Co., Italy, France 1 Jan. 1945
Berry, Clifton A., Pfc, Co. H 7th Inf, France 5 Feb. 1945
Berry, Glen W., M/Sgt, Serv. Co. 756th Tank Bn., France, Germany, Austria 8 May 1945
Berryman, Richard J., Sgt, Hq. Special Troops, 3d Inf Div., Italy 5 June 1944
Bester, Anthony V, T/5, Med. Det. Special Troops, 3d Inf Div., N. Africa, Sicily, Italy, France, Germany 8 May 1945
Betbeze, Charles A., Capt, AGD, Hq. 3d Inf Div., Italy, France, Germany, Austria 8 May 1945
Bethany, Charlie H., Pfc, Hq. Co. 2d Bn. 7th Inf, Anzio, Italy 19 Feb. 1944
Betteley, Paul J., Pfc, Co. D 15th Inf, Italy 27 May 1944
Bettis, Nathan W., S/Sgt, Co. D 756th Tank Bn., Germany 16 Mar. 1945
Betz, Joseph H., Sgt, 3d QM Co., Sicily, Italy 6 June 1944
Bianchi, Anthony J., 1st Lt, FA Rcn Co. 601st TD Bn., Germany 2 May 1945
Bickrest, Paul D., Pfc, Hq. Co. 2d Bn. 7th Inf, Italy, France 26 Nov. 1944
Bieder, Chester, Pfc, Co. C 10th Engr. Bn., Cisterna 23 May 1944
▲Bieganowski, Edwin A., Pfc, Hq. Co. 2d Bn. 30th Inf Regt., France 6 Feb. 1945
Bielenberg, Robert E., 1st Sgt, Co. D 15th Inf Regt., Germany 25 Apr. 1945
Biernet, Ben W., T/Sgt, Cn Co. 15th Inf, France 8 Feb. 1945
Biladeau, James E., Pfc, Hq. & Hq. Co. 601st TD Bn., Tunisia 9 May 1943
Bilby, Kenneth W., Maj, Hq. 2d Bn. 30th Inf
Bilda, Gerald J., Pfc, Hq. Co. 1st Bn. 30th Inf, France 24 Jan. 1945
Billings, William H., Lt Col, 15th Inf, Licata 13 July 1943
Binder, Howard W., Pfc, Co. K 15th Inf Regt., Germany 11 Apr. 1945
Binstock, Ernest W., Pfc, Serv. Btry 9th FA Bn., Valmontone 1 June 1944
Bird, Luman A., Pvt, Co. C 10th Engr. Bn., Valmontone 2 June 1944
Birt, Robert J., S/Sgt, Hq. Co. 3d Div., Italy, France, Germany 8 May 1945
Bischoff, John A., Pvt, Hq. Co. 30th Inf, Campo Morto 26 Apr. 1944
Bisson, Joseph L., Pvt, Co. F 15th Inf, Cisterna Di Littoria 24 May 1944
Biss, Richard L., T/5, Co. H 30th Inf, Anzio, Italy
Bixby, Allen J., 1st Sgt, Hq. Co. 601st TD Bn., Tunisia, Italy, France, Germany 20 Mar. 1945
Bixby, Lewis F., 2d Lt, I & R Pltn. Hq. Co. 30th Inf Regt., Italy 26 Jan. 1944
Black, Albert W., Pfc, Hq. Co. 1st Bn. 7th Inf Regt., Germany 19 Apr. 1945
Black, Glenn A., 2d Lt, Co. I 30th Inf Regt., France 8 Jan. 1945
Black, Leslie H., Pfc, Co. M 30th Inf, N. Africa, Sicily, Italy, France, Germany 8 May 1945
Black, Richard C., Pfc, Hq. Co. 1st Bn. 30th Inf, France 23 Jan. 1945
Black, Richard G., S/Sgt, Hq. Btry 39th FA Bn., N. Africa, Sicily, Italy, France, Germany 8 May 1945

▲ Oak Leaf Cluster.

Blackwell, James R., Pfc, Cannon Co. 30th Inf Regt., Germany 28 Apr. 1945
Bladow, Roy H., Med. Det. 30th Inf Regt, France 13 Sept. 1944
Blaikie, John W., Maj, Inf Hq. 7th Inf Regt., Germany, Austria 4 May 1945
Blaine, Billy M., Pfc, QM Co. 7th Inf, Italy 1 Dec. 1942
Blake, Dolan, Pfc, Hq. Co. 1st Bn. 7th Inf Regt., France 28 Sept. 1944
Blake, Frank A., Jr., 1st Lt, Inf AT Co 30th Inf, France 6 Nov. 1944
Blakeley, William E., S/Sgt, Hq. Btry 3d Div. Arty, Castel Morrong 11 Oct. 1943
Blaker, John W., 1st Lt, Hq. Co. 2d Bn. 30th Inf, Cisterna Di Littoria 23 May 1944
Blakley, Richard C., T/4, Co. C 756th Tank Bn., Germany 26 Apr. 1945
Blalock, John R., T/5, Btry C 441st AAA AW Bn., Sicily, Italy, France, Germany 8 May 1945
Blanford, Forrest M., 1st Lt, Inf Co. B 756th Tank Bn., Germany 26 Mar. 1945
Blankenburg, Edward W., Pfc, Hq. Co. 1st Bn. 7th Inf, France 24 Jan. 1945
Blankenship, James R., Pfc, Hq. Co. 1st Bn. 7th Inf Regt., Italy 24 May 1944
▲Blaumuller, George J., T/5, Co. A 601st TD Bn., Anzio, Italy Mar. 1944
Bless, Herman E., Sgt, Btry C 10th FA Bn., Artena 28 May 1944
Bliss, Alfred, T/5, Btry B 39th FA Bn., Sicily 11 July 1943
Bliss, John N., M/Sgt, Hq. 3d Inf Div., Italy, France, Germany 8 May 1945
Bliss, Richard L., T/5. Co. H 30th Inf. Italy 29 Feb. 1944
Bloom, Meyer, Pfc, Hq. Co. 1st Bn. 7th Inf Regt., France 5 Feb. 1945
Bloomingburg, Wayne C., Pfc, Co. M 7th Inf, Vagney, France 7 Oct. 1944
Blossom, Charles C., Jr., 1st Lt, Inf Hq. 3d Inf Div., Italy, France 31 Jan. 1945
Blount, George W., S/Sgt, Co. K 15th Inf Regt., Germany 3 May 1945
▲Blum, Charles K., 1st Lt, Inf Co. G 7th Inf Regt., Germany 6 Apr. 1945
Blumhagen, Robert F., 2d Lt, Co. F 15th Inf, Valmontone 1 June 1944
Blyshak, John, Pfc, A-T Co. 30th Inf, Colmar
Bochenek, Stanley I., Pfc, Co. G 15th Inf Regt., France 2 Nov. 1944
Boerner, Fred W., M/Sgt, Hq. Co. 15th Inf Regt., France, Germany 8 May 1945
Boffanil, Clebert B., Sgt, Co. B 30th Inf Regt., France 19 Oct. 1944
Bogner, Charles, Maj, Hq. 41st FA Bn., Italy 5 June 1944
Bogosewski, William S., Pfc, Hq. Co. 2d Bn. 7th Inf, Anzio, Italy 29 Feb. 1944
Bogusz, John M., Sgt, Co. G 30th Inf Regt., France 21 Nov. 1944
Bohannon, Carl G., S/Sgt, Co. C 7th Inf Regt., France 20 Oct. 1944
Bohler, Robert E., Pfc, MP Pltn 3d Inf Div., Germany 26 Mar. 1945
Bohmer, Howard E., Pfc, Hq. Co. 1st Bn. 30th Inf, France 2 Feb. 1945
Bohn, Leslie A., Pfc, Hq. Co. 2d Bn. 30th Inf, Colmar
Bohner, Dale A., T/4, Serv. Co. 30th Inf Regt., Italy, France, Germany May 1945
Bojanek, Walter J., T/5, Btry C 441st AAA AW Bn., Germany 30 Apr. 1945
Bolte, Willis H., Pfc, Hq. Co. 1st Bn. 30th Inf Regt., Germany 9 Apr. 1945
Boltjes, Herman, T/5, 3d Rcn Trp., Germany 8 May 1945
Bolton, Joseph J., Pfc, Co. C 30th Inf Regt., France 27 Oct. 1944
Bolton, Keith D., T/4, Hq. Co. 601st TD Bn., Italy 8 Feb. 1944
Bonham, William H., S/Sgt, Hq. Co. 2d Bn. 7th Inf, Anzio, Italy 1 Mar. 1944
▲Bonham, Raymond L., Pfc, Hq. Co. 2d Bn. 30th Inf Regt., France 6 Feb. 1945
Bonkowski, Gerald F., T/5, Co. C 3d Med. Bn., France 19 Dec. 1944
Bonner, Forrest L., Sgt, Co. A 10th Engr. Combat Bn., France 29 Oct. 1944
Bonner, Howard, T/5, Serv. Co. 30th Inf, Italy 18 Aug. 1943
Bonner, Vincent H., 1st Lt, Rcn 601st TD Bn., Germany, Austria 4 May 1945
Bonnes, John, Jr., Pvt, Hq. Co. 30th Inf, Velletri 28 May 1944
Boor, Howard D., Sgt, MP Pltn, 3d Inf, France 12 Feb. 1945
Boos, Richard O., T/Sgt, Hq. & Hq. Btry 41st FA Bn., N. Africa, Sicily, Italy, France, Austria 8 May 1945
Booth, Frank S., Cpl, Hq. Co. 30th Inf, Cisterna Di Littoria 20 May 1944
Borcheller, Darl H., Pfc, Hq. Co. 30th Inf Regt., France 10 Nov. 1944
Borchers, Victor D., Pvt, Co. C 10th Engr. Bn., Carano 5 Mar. 1944
Borda, William P., Pfc, Hq. Co. 30th Inf Regt., Germany 19 Mar. 1945
Borders, Joe B., Sgt, Co. F 30th Inf Regt., France 10 Jan. 1945
Borkowski, Edward J., Sgt, Hq. Co. 3d Bn. 15th Inf, San Fratelo 8 Aug. 1943
Boros, Steve P., Jr., T/Sgt, Co. C 30th Inf Regt., Germany 26 Mar. 1945
Borson, Oscar, T/4, Hq. Btry 9th FA Bn., N. Africa, Sicily, Italy, France, Germany 8 May 1945
Bosch, Samuel, Pfc, Co. E 30th Inf, France 1 Jan. 1945
Boston, William W., Cpl, Co. C 756th Tank Bn., Germany 30 Apr. 1945
Boulay, Raymond A., Pfc, AT Co. 30th Inf, 19 Feb. 1945
▲Boutilier, George A., S/Sgt, Co. A 756th Tank Bn., Germany 19 Mar. 1945
Bouton, Vernon W., CWO, Hq. 3d Div., Italy 8 July 1943
Bowden, John N., Pvt, Co. A 756th Tank Bn., France 15 Sept. 1944
Bowen, Arvo P., Pfc, Co. E 30th Inf Regt., France 9 Nov. 1944
Bowen, Brian H. M., 1st Lt, Co. A 10th Engr., France 29 Jan. 1945
Bowen, James E., Pfc, Co. C 15th Inf Regt., Italy 29 May 1944
Bowers, Howard J., T/4, Serv. Co. 756th Tank Bn., Italy 28 Jan. 1944
Bowles, Earl, Pfc, 3d Sig. Co., Germany 8 May 1945
Bowles, Earl H., Pfc, Co. A 756th Tank Bn., France 26 Jan. 1945
Bowman, Allen H., Pfc, Rcn Co. 601st TD Bn., Germany 5 May 1945
Boyce, Beryl L., Capt, 9th FA Bn., N. Africa, Sicily, 5 June 1944
Boyd, Clarence A., 1st Sgt, Co. D 7th Inf Regt., Germany 27 Mar. 1945
Boyd, George, Jr., T/Sgt, Co. I 30th Inf Regt., France 8 Jan. 1945
Boyd, Jackson, T/5, 3d Rcn Trp., Germany 8 May 1945
Boyda, Henry A., T/4, Ord. Co., Volturno 26 June 1944
Boyer, Edward H., Pfc, Co. A 7th Inf Regt., France 22 Nov. 1944
Boyer, George C., Sgt, Co. B 601st TD Bn., Germany 15 Apr. 1945
Boyle, Andy E., S/Sgt, Hq. Co. 756th Tank Bn., France, Germany 8 May 1945
Boyle, Hugh P., T/4, Co. B 601st TD Bn., N. Africa, Italy, France 15 Jan. 1945
Boyle, Joseph J., T/Sgt, Co. I 30th Inf Regt., France 17 Dec. 1944
Boysen, Bernhard E., Pfc, Co. B 15th Inf, Germany 25 Apr. 1945
Braak, John A., T/5, Med. Det. 15th Inf, France 26 Dec. 1944
Bracewell, Eltve, S/Sgt, Serv. Co. 7th Inf, France 11 Feb. 1945
Bradke, George J., Pfc, Co. A 7th Inf Regt., France 5 Feb. 1945
Brady, Joseph D., Capt, Hq. 441st AAA AW Bn., Sicily, Italy, France, Germany 8 May 1945
Bragg, Douglas E., Pfc, Med. Dept. Btry Ptrl 15th Inf, Italy 24 May 1944
Braidich, Henry M., Cpl, Btry B 441st AAA AW Bn., Sicily, Italy, France, Germany 8 May 1945
Braley, Elton B., Pfc, Co. H 7th Inf, Artena 29 May 1944
Brandel, Earl H., T/5, Hq. Co. 7th Inf, Palestrina 23 June 1944
Brashears, Charlie, Pfc, Co. A 15th Inf, Cisterna Di Littoria 29 Feb. 1944
Braswell, Walter B., Pfc, Co. A 756th Tank Bn., Germany 19 Mar. 1945
Braudrick, Thomas J., T/5, Med. Det. 30th Inf, Mt. Rotundo, 8 Nov. 1943
Braun, Robert L., T/4, Co. D 756th Tank Bn., France 2 Feb. 1945
Braun, William B., Pfc, Co. D 7th Inf, Besancon, France 6 Sept. 1944
Brawley, Elmer C., Sgt, Co. B 15th Inf Regt., France 25 Dec. 1944

Bray, Edgar L., T/5, Btry C 441st AAA AW Bn., France 9 Nov. 1944
▲Breaux, Alvin J., T/4, Med. Det. 7th Inf Regt., France 8 Oct. 1944
Brecher, Nicholas, Pfc, Co. I 30th Inf, Sicily 17 Aug. 1943
Brecheisen, William R., Pfc, AT Co. 30th Inf, France 6 Feb. 1945
▲(3) Breed, Allen L., S/Sgt, Co. C 601st TD Bn., France 22 Aug. 1944
Breitmeier, John F., T/5, Btry C 39th FA Bn., Sicily 17 Aug. 1943
Brenke, Edwin H., Pvt, QM Corps, 3d QM Co., Italy 6 June 1944
Brennan, James A., 2d Lt, Co. E 15th Inf, Isola Bella 21 Mar. 1944
Brese, Robert, Pfc, Hq. Co. 2d Bn. 30th Inf, Colmar
Brewer, Ellis M., T/Sgt, Co. B 30th Inf, Valmontone 1 June 1944
Brewer, Elto H., WOJG, US Army, 3d Sig. Co., France, Germany, Austria 8 May 1945
Brewer, Harold W., CWO, Hq. Co. 3d Inf Div., Sicily 18 Aug. 1943
Brewer, Ira V., 2d Lt, Btry B 41st FA Bn., France, Germany, Austria 8 May 1945
Brewer, Jacob H., Pfc, Serv. Co. 7th Inf, Germany 15 Mar. 1945
Brewer, Kibbie E., Sgt, Co. A 7th Inf Regt., Germany 18 Mar. 1945
Brewer, Robert S., T/5, Hq. Co. 30th Inf Regt., France 10 Nov. 1944
Bridge, William T., Pfc, Hq. Co. 30th Inf Regt., Germany 16 Mar. 1945
Bridges, Cosper J., Pvt, Co. B 751st Tank Bn., Anzio, Italy 12 Feb. 1944
Bridges, Frank B., Jr., 1st Lt, Hq. Co. 1st Bn. 7th Inf, Vagney, France 7 Oct. 1944
Brien, James J., T/Sgt, Co. M 7th Inf Regt., Germany 26 Mar. 1945
Brigance, Felton, S/Sgt, Co. F 30th Inf Regt., Germany 30 Apr. 1945
Brignall, William J., Cpl, Co. D 3d Med. Bn., N. Africa, Sicily, Italy, France 19 Feb. 1945
Briggs, Erwin W., T/Sgt, Co. M 15th Inf Regt., Germany 4 Apr. 1945
Brin, Martin, Pvt, Hq. Co. 1st Bn. 30th Inf, France 24 Jan. 1945
Britt, Maurice L., 1st Lt, Co. L 30th Inf, Dietravairano 29 Oct. 1943
Brocks, George, T/5, Co. B 10th Engr. Combat Bn., Germany 18 Apr. 1945
Brody, Michael, S/Sgt, Co. A 756th Tank Bn., France, Germany, Austria 8 May 1945
Brohel, Joseph E., Sgt, Co. I 7th Inf Regt., France 5 Feb. 1945
Broide, Macy I., T/5, Serv. Co. 30th Inf, France Nov. 1944
Brooks, Calvin, Sgt, Serv. Btry 10th FA Bn., N. Africa, Sicily, Italy, France, Germany 8 May 1945
Brooks, Glenn D., Sgt, Co. C 7th Inf Regt., France 20 Oct. 1944
Brooks, Merle E., T/5, Co. B 756th Tank Bn., Germany 27 Apr. 1945
Brooks, Philip R., Capt, Military Govt. Sec Hq. 3d Inf Div., France, Germany, Austria 8 May 1945
Brooks, Walter A., Sgt, Hq. Co. 3d Bn. 30th Inf, Anzio, Italy 16 Feb. 1944
Brough, Ferris T., Pvt, Hq. Btry 9th FA Bn., Anzio, Italy 29 Feb. 1944
Broughton, James R., Cpl, Co. D 7th Inf Regt., Italy 24 May 1944
Browder, Clyde M., Pfc, Hq. 3d Inf Div., France, Germany 8 May 1945
Brown, Albert S., S/Sgt, Co. H 30th Inf, France 30 Jan. 1945
Brown, Alfred M., S/Sgt, Co. C 7th Inf Regt., France 22 Nov. 1944
Brown, Clifford C., Sgt, Btry C 9th FA Bn., Anzio, Italy 6 Mar. 1944
Brown, Frank F., Jr., Pvt, Co. B 601st TD Bn., Isola Bella 29 Feb. 1944
Brown, Howard N., Pfc, Rcn Co. 601st TD Bn., France 8 Sept. 1944
Brown, Isaac W., S/Sgt, Btry C 9th FA Bn., N. Africa, Sicily, Italy, France, Germany 8 May 1945
Brown, Jack, Pfc, Co. I 7th Inf Regt., Italy 2 June 1944
Brown, Kenneth W., 1st Lt, Med. Corps Hq. 3d Inf Div., Italy, France, Germany 8 May 1945
Brown, Paul J., Pfc, Med. Det. 30th Inf Regt., France 20 Nov. 1944
Brown, Philip C., Pvt, Serv. Co. 15th Inf, Pomoy, France 17 Sept. 1944
Brown, Thomas G., Pfc, Co. G 7th Inf, Padiglione 22 Apr. 1944
Browneller, Kenneth E., Capt, Hq. 7th Inf, Sicily, Italy, France 6 Dec. 1944
Browning, John H., T/5, Co. E 30th Inf, France 1 Nov. 1944
Brozowski, John J., Pfc, Co. E 30th Inf Regt., France 10 Nov. 1944
Bruce, George M., S/Sgt, Co. A 30th Inf, Cussey-Sur L'Ognen, France 10 Sept. 1944
Bruce, John R., S/Sgt, Co. M 30th Inf, France 19 Dec. 1944
Brudnicki, Edward J., Cpl, Btry A 39th FA Bn., France 15 Oct. 1944
Bruneau, Henry S., Sgt, Co. L 30th Inf Regt., France 8 Sept. 1944
Brunni, Donald W., M/Sgt, Hq. 3d Div., Italy 12 Aug. 1944
Brush, James E., Jr., Sgt, Co. M 30th Inf Regt., Germany 15 Mar. 1945
Brusin, Gunnar L., Pfc, Co. M 30th Inf, Baraques, France 29 Oct. 1944
Bruzdzinski, Casimer E., Pfc, Co. B 7th Inf, Artena 28 May 1944
Bruyere, Patrick D., T/4, Btry B 39th FA Bn., Germany 14 Apr. 1945
Bryan, Sidney, Pvt, Med. Det. 7th Inf, Ponte Motto 16 Feb. 1944
Bryant, Amos, Pfc, Btry B 634th FA Bn., Cisterna Di Littoria 28 May 1944
Bryant, James S., 1st Lt, Hq. Btry 441st AAA AW Bn., Sicily, Italy, France, Germany 8 May 1945
Bryant, Walter C., Cpl, Cn Co. 30th Inf, France 27 Aug. 1944
Bryant, William H., Jr., Sgt, MP Pltn, Hq. Co. 3d Inf Div., France, Germany 8 May 1945
Bryson, Herbert D., Pfc, Hq. Co. 1st Bn. 7th Inf, France 15 Mar. 1945
Bucca, Joseph S., Pfc, Med. Det. 7th Inf, Cisterna Di Littoria 24 May 1944
Bucholz, Clayton S., T/Sgt, Co. G 7th Inf, Artena 28 May 1944
Buchman, Arthur H., Cpl, Co. A 601st TD Bn., France 3 Oct. 1944
Buckalew, Jay R., T/4, 3d Sig. Co., Anzio, Italy 29 Feb. 1944
▲Buckley, Benjamin A., Sgt, Co. C 601st TD Bn., France 21 Aug. 1944
Buckley, Joseph M., S/Sgt, Btry C 10th FA Bn., France 20 Sept. 1944
Buckely, Paul P., Sgt, Hq. 3d Div., Sicily, Italy, France, Germany 10 May 1945
Buffington, Alfred P., Cpl, Cn Co. 30th Inf, France 19 Aug. 1944
Bukoske, Henry C., T/4, Co. K 7th Inf, Germany 15 Mar. 1945
Bulen, Bertie L., T/4, Co. B 756th Tank Bn., France 15 Sept. 1944
Bulich, Robert, S/Sgt, Btry B 41st FA Bn., Italy, France, Germany 8 May 1945
Bullard, Oscar, Pfc, AT Co. 30th Inf, Colmar
Bullian, Henry E., Cpl, Btry B 39th FA Bn., France 30 Jan. 1945
Bullins, Kelly D., Sgt, Co. I 30th Inf Regt., France 8 Jan. 1945
Bunk, Donald J., T/4, Co. D 3d Med. Bn., Italy, France, Germany 8 May 1945
Burchfield, Glenn E., Cpl, Btry B 39th FA Bn., Dampvalley-Les-Colombe, France 13 Sept. 1944
Burchell, James, Sgt, Btry A 9th FA Bn., Artena 30 May 1944
Burchett, Samuel J., Pvt, Co. C 10th Engr. Bn., Carano 5 Mar. 1944
Burdenski, Henry E., T/4, Hq. 3d Inf Div., Italy, France, Germany, Austria 6 May 1945
Burger, Carl J., T/4, Med. Det. 15th Inf, Italy 14 Oct. 1943
Burger, Jack E., T/5, Co. B 756th Tank Bn., Germany 28 Apr. 1945
Burgess, John D., T/Sgt, Co. I 30th Inf, Germany 27 Mar. 1945
Burgett, Don M., Pfc, Co. A 30th Inf, S. France

▲ Oak Leaf Cluster.

Buriak, Don M., Pfc, Co. A 30th Inf, 21 Aug. 1944
Buriak, John, T/5, 3d Sig. Co., Conca 1 Mar. 1944
▲Burke, Frank, 1st Lt, Inf 1st Bn. 15th Inf, France 8 May 1945
Burkell, James J., Pfc, Co. H 7th Inf Regt., France, Germany 8 May 1945
Burks, George S., 1st Lt, Co. L 15th Inf, Cisterna Di Littoria 24 May 1944
▲Burnasky, Peter, T/Sgt, Co. D 30th Inf Regt., France 3 Oct. 1944
Burneau, Henry S., Sgt, Co. L 30th Inf, France
Burnett, Paul G., Pfc, Rcn Co. 601st TD Bn., France, Germany 8 May 1945
Burns, Francis X., Cpl, Btry B 39th FA Bn., Cisterna 6 Feb. 1944
Burns, George J., T/5, Serv. Co. 7th Inf Regt., Sicily, Italy 10 Dec. 1943
Burr, Leonard W., T/5, Serv. Btry 10th FA Bn., N. Africa, Sicily, Italy, France, Germany 8 May 1945
Burr, Lloyd C., Pfc, Co. K 7th Inf, Cisterna Di Littoria 2 Feb. 1944
Burrill, Henry W., T/5, Hq. Btry 39th FA Bn., Germany 16 Apr. 1945
Burton, Joseph A., T/Sgt, Co. F 15th Inf, France 1 Feb. 1945
Bushong, James R., Pfc, Hq. Co. 1st Bn. 7th Inf, Vagney, France 7 Oct. 1944
Buss, Fred, S/Sgt, Co. D 30th Inf, Vosges
Busse, Herman A., T/Sgt, Co. G 30th Inf Regt., France 17 Dec. 1944
Buswell, Dennis G, Pfc, Co. L 15th Inf Regt., France 18 Feb. 1945
Butler, Bryan, Pfc, Btry B 39th FA Bn., Cisterna 10 Mar. 1944
Butler, Decatur P., Capt, Inf Hq. Co. 7th Inf Regt., France 4 Feb. 1945
Butler, Donald A., 1st Lt, MP Pltn 3d Inf Div., Anzio, Italy 11 Feb. 1944
Butcher, Matthew V., Sgt, Co. M 30th Inf Regt., Germany 26 Mar. 1945
Butkus, Walter J., S/Sgt, Co. I 30th Inf, Mt. Rotundo 5 Nov. 1943
Buzzell, Frederick P., S/Sgt, Co. C 601st TD Bn., Sicily, Italy, France, Germany May 1945
Byerly, Philip J., Pvt, Co. L 15th Inf, San Fratelo, Sicily 6 Aug. 1943
Byrd, David A., Pfc, Hq. Btry 39th FA Bn., Anzio, Italy 23 Mar. 1944
Byrd, Elmo F., T/4, Serv. Btry 41st FA Bn., Anzio, Italy 23 Mar. 1944
Byrd, Reecie R., T/5, Btry C 441st AAA AW Bn., Germany 30 Apr. 1945
Byrne, Arthur J., Pfc, Co. A 10th Engr. Combat Bn., France 2 Nov. 1944
Byrne, John D., Lt Col, Co. 39th FA Bn., Italy 5 June 1944

Cabibi, Dave, Pfc, Inf AT Co. 30th Inf Regt., France 7 Feb. 1945
Cable, George F., T/5, Co. E 7th Inf, Cisterna Di Littoria 24 May 1944
Cable, William N., T/4, H Btry 39th FA Bn., N. Africa, Sicily, Italy, France, Germany, Austria 8 May 1945
Cade, Robert, T/4, Hq. Co. 30th Inf Regt., Sicily, Italy 18 Nov. 1943
Caden, Paul J., Pfc, Hq. Co. 2d Bn. 30th Inf, France 24 Dec. 1944
Cahill, Arthur M., T/5, Co. D 30th Inf Regt., France 20 Dec. 1944
Cahill, Phillip E., T/Sgt, Hq. Co. 1st Bn. 30th Inf
Cailahan, Francis L., T/5, Med. Det. 15th Inf, Italy, France 8 Feb. 1945
▲Cain, Lillion W., Capt, Chap. Corps Hq. 3d Bn. 30th Inf, France 23 Jan. 1945
Calderon, Isabel, Pfc, Co. I 30th Inf Regt., France 28 Oct. 1944
Caldwell, Paul D., 1st Lt, Hq. 41st FA Bn., Radon-et Chapgnou, France 17 Sept. 1944
Calhoun, Harvey F., Sgt, Hq. Co. 756th Tank Bn., Italy 10 Feb. 1944
Calzetta, John J., Pfc, Hq. Co. 1st Bn. 30th Inf, Colmar
Call, Clelland C., Cpl, Co. C 601st TD Bn., Cisterna 23 May 1944
Callahan, Harry B., 1st Sgt, Cn Co. 30th Inf, N. Africa, Sicily, Italy, France, Germany, Austria 8 May 1945
Callahan, Lloyd E., T/4, Co. B 601 TD Bn., 23 Jan. 1945
Calloway, Jack F., Sgt, Co. C 3d Med. Bn., Italy 24 Oct. 1943
Calvert, Ross H., Jr., 1st Lt, Hq. 3d Bn. 30th Inf, Ponte Rotto, 23 May 1944
Camp, Perry, Cpl, Co. F 15th Inf, Italy 27 May 1944
Camp, Robert L., Pfc, AT Co. 30th Inf Regt., France 25 Dec. 1944
Campbell, Alvin W., 1st Sgt, Co. C 601st TD Bn., Germany 19 Apr. 1945
Campbell, Claude C., T/Sgt, 441st AAA AW Bn., Sicily, Italy, France, Germany, Austria 8 May 1945
Campbell, Dexter, Cpl, Co. A 10th Engr. Combat Bn., France 23 Nov. 1944
▲(2) Campbell, Earl, Cpl, Rcn Co. 601st TD Bn., Germany 27 Apr. 1945
Campbell, Harry V., Pfc, Hq. Co. 3d Bn. 30th Inf, Le Tholy 16 Oct. 1944
Campbell, James C., Sgt, Co. K 7th Inf Regt., France 31 Jan. 1945
Campbell, John A., 1st Lt, FA Co. A 601st TD Bn., France, Germany, Austria 8 May 1945
▲Campbell, J. Robert, Maj, Med. Corps Hq. 3d Inf Div., France, Germany, Austria 8 May 1945
▲Campbell, Tyler, 1st Lt, Co. A 7th Inf, Artena 28 May 1944
Campbell, William A., Brig Gen, Italy 5 June 1944
Campbell, Woodrow T., T/Sgt, AT Co. 30th Inf, Vosges
Canant, Ermer O., Pfc, Hq. Co. 1st Bn. 30th Inf Regt., France 24 Jan. 1945
Canty, William P., 2d Lt, Btry C 441st AAA AW Bn., Dampvalley, France 15 Sept. 1944
Cantley, Jehu R., T/5, Hq. Co. 3d Bn. 7th Inf, France 9 Nov. 1944
Cappiello, Dante, Sgt, Co. A 601st TD Bn., Carano 29 Feb. 1944
Capron, Jon, 1st Lt, Inf Hq. 7th Inf Regt., France 29 Oct. 1944
Carassco, Conrado, Pfc, Co. B 10th Engr. Combat Bn., France 22 Jan. 1945
Carbalieira, Manuel J., Capt, Med. Corps 601st TD Bn., Isola Bella 3 Mar. 1944
Card, Ralph L., Jr., Pfc, Co. A 15th Inf, Germany 18 Mar. 1945
Cardwell, Ross, S/Sgt, Co. A 756th Tank Bn., Africa, Italy, France, Germany, Austria 8 May 1945
Carey, Francis W., Cpl, 3d CIC Det., Germany, Austria 8 May 1945
Carey, Frederick D., Pfc, Rcn Co. 601st TD Bn., Beja Latina 23 Oct. 1944
▲Carey, Joseph J., Cpl, Co. B 601st TD. Bn., France 5 Sept. 1944
Cargill, William, Jr., 1st Lt, Btry A 441st AAA AW Bn., Cori 24 May 1944
Carlson, Alton E., T/5, Hq. Co. 3d Bn. 30th Inf
Carlson, Charles H.,Pfc, Co. A 30th Inf, Colmar
Carlyle, Deo G., Pfc, Hq. Co. 2d Bn. 15th Inf, Anzio, Italy 16 Feb. 1944
Carmello, Michael A., T/5, Med. Det. 7th Inf Regt., France 2 Feb. 1945
Carney, Eugene G., Pfc, Co. A 30th Inf Regt., France 31 Jan. 1945
Carr, Almon E., S/Sgt, Btry B 441st AAA AW Bn., Sicily, Italy, France, Germany 8 May 1945
Carr, George M., Jr., M/Sgt, Hq. 3d Inf Div., Sicily, Italy, France, Germany 8 May 1945
Carr, Seigle A., T/5, Hq. Btry 9th FA Bn., Mignano, 17 Nov. 1943
Carrin, Thomas R., Sgt, Co. F 30th Inf Regt., France 18 Dec. 1944
Carroll, Alex B., Sgt, Co. G 15th Inf Regt., France 24 Dec. 1944
Carroll, Bill W., Cpl, Co. H 30th Inf Regt., France 16 Sept. 1944
Carter, Allan B., T/4, Hq. Co. 756th Tank Bn., Italy 16 Feb. 1944
Carter, John F., S/Sgt, Co. D 30th Inf Regt., Germany 15 Apr. 1945 24 May 1944
Carter, Joseph T., Pvt, Co. A 15th Inf. Cisterna Di Littoria
Carter, William R., T/4, 3d Sig. Co., Sicily, Italy, France 31 Jan. 1945
Carty, Edwin F., T/5, Btry A 441st AAA AW Bn., Sicily, Italy, France, Germany 8 May 1945

Cate, Kenneth P., Pfc, Cn Co. 30th Inf, Colmar
Carver, John S., Jr., 1st Lt, Co. L 15th Inf Regt., Germany 21 Mar. 1945
Casanova, Edward V., T/5, Hq. 3d Div., Italy 23 May 1944
▲Casbolt, Frank J., Pvt, Hq. Co. 1st Bn. 7th Inf Regt., Italy 20 Apr. 1944
Casertano, Angelo, J., T/5, Btry C 441st AAA AW Bn., Germany 27 Mar. 1945
Casey, George C., 1st Sgt, Co. D 30th Inf, Italy 12 Feb. 1944
Casiano, Carlos, Pfc, Co. I 15th Inf Regt., France 18 Sept. 1944
Casieski, Albin J., Jr., T/4, 3d Sig. Co., Germany 8 May 1945
Casillas, Bernard J., Pfc, Co. H 30th Inf, France 18 Dec. 1944
Cassel, Robert S., Sgt, Co. E 30th Inf Regt., N. Africa, Sicily, Italy, France 31 Dec. 1944
Castellaw, Charles R., Pfc, Co. E 30th Inf Regt., France 10 Nov. 1944
Castelunova, Eugene B., Pvt, Co. A 10th Engr. Bn., La Villa 26 May 1944
Castilow, John E., Pvt, Co. F 15th Inf, Feminamorta 27 Mar. 1944
Casterchino, Ralph A., Pfc, Hq. Co. 3d Bn. 30th Inf, France 7 Feb. 1945
Catalano, Santo J., S/Sgt, Co. E 15th Inf Regt., Germany Apr. 1945
Caton, June E., 1st Lt, Inf Aide-de-Camp Hq. 3d Inf Div., France 31 Jan. 1945
Caudie, Frank A., S/Sgt, Co. G 15th Inf Regt., Germany 29 Apr. 1945
▲Caughey, Donald E., Maj, Dnt Corps Hq. 3d Div., France, Germany, Austria 8 May 1945
Ceizyk, Casimer J., Cpl, MP Pltn 3d Inf Div., Germany 8 May 1945
Cella, James F., Hq. Co. 3d Bn. 30th Inf., St. Mare, France 1 Oct. 1944
Cervanek, George F., Pfc, Hq. Co, 2d Bn. 7th Inf, Anzio, Italy 17 Feb. 1944
Cespiva, Edward, T/Sgt, Hq. Btry 9th FA Bn., Sicily, Italy, France, Germany 8 May 1945
Chahl, John M., Cpl, Btry A 441st AAA AW Bn., Sicily, Italy, France, Germany 8 May 1945
Chaikin, Milton, Cpl, Hq. Co. 2d Bn. 7th Inf Regt., Italy 24 May 1944
Chain, Frank D., Pfc, Hq. Btry 9th FA Bn., Anzio, 29 Feb. 1944
Chambers, Douglas W., 1st Lt, Co. H 30th Inf, Brignoles, France 19 Aug. 1944
Champ, Harry W., Sgt, Hq. Btry 39th FA Bn., N. Africa, Sicily, Italy, France, Germany 8 May 1945
▲Chaney, Christopher W., Lt Col, Inf Hq. 3d Bn. 30th Inf Regt., Germany 1 May 1945
Chandler, Andrew P., Pfc, Co. A 7th Inf Regt., France 23 Jan. 1945
Chandler, James H., S/Sgt, Co. C 7th Inf, La Villa 24 May 1944
Chaney, Christopher J., Lt Col, Inf Hq. 3d Bn. 30th Inf Regt., France 16 Dec. 1944
Chapman, Edgar E., Pfc, Co. H 7th Inf Regt., Italy, France Mar. 1945
Chavez, Ernesto A., Sgt, Co. D 756th Tank Bn., France 1 Feb. 1945
Cheever, Francis L., 1st Lt, Med. Det. 756th Tank Bn., Italy, France, Germany 8 May 1945
Cheperka, Donald M., T/5, Serv. Co. 7th Inf, Italy, France, Germany 8 May 1945
Cherne, Fred W., Cpl, Co. D 30th Inf Regt., France 9 Sept. 1944
Cherry, E. L., Pfc, Hq. Co. 2d Bn., 7th Inf, Anzio, Italy 29 Feb. 1944
Chesnavich, Vincent J., Sgt, Btry A 441st AAA AW Bn., France 19 Nov. 1944
Chew, Art F., T/5, Hq. Co. 3d Inf Div., Italy, France 31 Jan. 1945
Chewiwi, Jose A., Pfc, Med. Det. 7th Inf Regt., France 24 Nov. 1944
Chiapella, Karl J., Capt, MC Co. D 3d Med. Bn., Acciarella 29 Feb. 1944
Chiarella, Joseph, Pfc, Co. L 30th Inf, Germany 15 Mar. 1945
Chiarelli, Peter F., 2d Lt, Inf Co. D 756th Tank Bn., Germany 29 Apr. 1945
Chiarini, Thomas, Pfc, Co. L 7th Inf Regt., France 20 Nov. 1944
Chichura, Michael, S/Sgt, Btry C 39th FA Bn., N. Africa, Sicily, Italy, France, Germany 8 May 1945
Chiffriller, George F., T/5, Hq. Co. 2d Bn. 7th Inf, Anzio, Italy 2 Mar. 1944
Childress, Edgar H., Pfc, Co. E 7th Inf, Cisterna Di Littoria 2 Feb. 1944
Chingman, Louis, Pvt, Hq. Btry 9th FA Bn., Mignano 17 Nov. 1943
Chipka, Joseph J., Pfc, MP Pltn 3d Inf, Italy 14 May 1944
Chittenden, Frederick M., Pfc, Co. G 15th Inf, Germany 7 Apr. 1945
Choate, Clyde L., T/5, Co. C 601st Tank Bn., Isola Bella 2 Mar. 1944
Choate, John D., Capt, FA Hq. 10th FA Bn., France 24 Jan. 1945
Chop, Thomas J., S/Sgt, Co. M 30th Inf Regt., Germany 10 Apr. 1945
Christ, Charles L., T/5, Btry A 441st AAA AW Bn., France 23 Jan. 1945
Christensen, James, Pfc, Hq. & Serv. Co. 10th Engr. Combat Bn., Italy 10 Mar. 1944
Christian, Donald R., Pvt, Hq. Co. 30th Inf, Italy 5 June 1944
Christianson, Albert A., Pfc, Btry A 41st FA Bn., France 24 Jan. 1945
Christie, Elmer W., Pfc, Hq. & Serv. Co. 10th Engr. Combat Bn., Italy 10 Mar. 1944
Christmas, Clyde E., Pfc, Rcn Co. 601st TD Bn., Donzerg 27 Aug. 1944
Christopher, George M., Pfc, Co. C 7th Inf Regt., Germany 19 Mar. 1945
Chromek, Paul, Jr., Pfc, Hq. Co. 3d Bn. 30th Inf Regt., France 3 Nov. 1944
Churchill, David R., 1st Lt, Sig. Corps 3d Sig. Co., France, Germany 20 Feb. 1945
Ciancanelli, Arco A., Pvt, Co. L 15th Inf, Isola Bella 3 Feb. 1944
Ciavaglia, Gidio, Pfc, Hq. Co. 2d Bn. 30th Inf, Colmar
Cichalski, Stanley J., M/Sgt, Serv. Co. 7th Inf Regt., Italy, France, Germany May 1945
Citara, Fred A., Cpl, Btry C 441st AAA AW Bn., Germany 16 Apr. 1945
Clack, William L., Cpl, Btry A 441st AAA AW Bn., Costello 29 May 1944
Clapp, Edgar W., T/4, Co. A 756th Tank Bn., Germany 18 Mar. 1945
Clark, Arthur G., Jr., Pfc, Hq. Co. 1st Bn. 30th Inf, France 24 Jan. 1945
Clark, Clell, T/4, Co. H 7th Inf Regt., Africa, Sicily, Italy 22 May 1944
Clark, Doyle S., 2d Lt, Co. C 3d Med. Bn., Italy 6 June 1944
Clark, Floyd W., 2d Lt, Inf Co. A 7th Inf Regt., France 25 Dec. 1944
Clark, Harry S., M/Sgt, Med. Det. Hq. 3d Inf Div., France, Germany, Austria 8 May 1945
Clark, John E., S/Sgt, Co. B 7th Inf Germany 26 Mar. 1945
Clark, Merwin R., Pvt, Btry A 9th FA Bn., Anzio 25 May 1944
Clark, Norman A., Sgt, CIC Det. 3d Inf Div., France 15 Mar. 1945
Clark, Percy A., T/5, AT Co. 7th Inf Regt., Italy 17 Feb. 1944
Clark, Thomas L., Jr., S/Sgt, Co. H 30th Inf Regt., France 2 Nov. 1944
▲Clark, Thomas W., Sgt, Rcn Co. 601st TD Bn., Germany 27 Apr. 1945
Clark, Verne D., S/Sgt, Co. C 10th Engr., N. Africa, Sicily, Italy, France, Germany, Austria 8 May 1945
Claunch, James E., Pfc, Hq. Co., Italy June 1944
Clauss, Arthur L., T/4, Hq. Btry 441st AAA AW Bn., Borgo Montello 29 Feb. 1944
Claxton, Daw A., Pvt, Hq. Co. 30th Inf Regt., Italy 26 Jan. 1944
Claypool, Russell B., Cpl, Hq. Btry 39th FA Bn., Sicily 5 June 1944
Clayton, Calvin C., Pfc, AT Co. 30th Inf, Colmar
Clayton, James A., WO, Staff JA Sec 3d Inf Div., Metousa 14 Sept. 1944
▲Clayton, John M., T/4, Hq. 3d Div., Germany, Austria 8 May 1945
Claytor, Eugene C., Cpl, Co. A 601st TD Bn., Ponte Rotto 23 May 1944

▲ Oak Leaf Cluster.

Clegg, Elijah, Pfc, Med. Det. 30th Inf Regt., Germany 19 Apr. 1945
▲Clem, Rhoman E., Capt, Inf Hq. 3d Inf Div., Germany, Austria 8 May 1945
Clift, Lawrence E., 1/Sgt, Hq. Co. 3d Bn. 30th Inf
Clingerman, Vernal H., S/Sgt, Armd Comd Co. B 751st Tank Bn., 31 Jan. 1944
Clise, James W., Sgt, Co. B 7th Inf, France 6 Sept. 1944
Cloer, Clyde C., T/5, Hq. Co. 3d Bn. 7th Inf Regt., Germany 16 Mar. 1945
Cloer, Russell W., 1st Lt, Inf Hq. Co. 7th Inf Regt., France 10 Feb. 1945
Coats, Wendell J., Lt Col, FA Co. 39th FA Bn., Italy 10 Nov. 1943
Cochran, Andrew H., Jr., Cpl, Co. D 30th Inf, Anzio, Italy
Cochran, Carl C., Pfc, Med. Det. 7th Inf Regt., Germany 15 Mar. 1945
Cochran, Johnnie L., Pvt, B.P. 7th Inf, Anzio, Italy 26 Jan. 1944
Cockerill, Ernest F., Cpl, Hq. Co. 2d Bn. 15th Inf Regt., France 19 Dec. 1944
Cockrell, Earnest F., T/5, Hq. & Serv. Co. 10th Engr. Combat Bn., Italy 15 Feb. 1944
▲Coday, Bernard F., 2d Lt, Co. A 7th Inf, France 28 Oct. 1944
Coe, Ernest E., Pfc, Co. A 30th Inf Regt., Germany 12 Apr. 1945
Coe, William F., T/5, Med. Det. 15th Inf, Anzio, Italy 10 Mar. 1944
Cogar, Manfred F., T/5, 3d QM Co., Italy, France, Germany Apr. 1945
▲Cohagen, John R., 1st Lt, CE Co. A 10th Engr. Combat Bn., Italy, France 2 Mar. 1945
Cohen, Bernard, Capt, DC 30th Inf Regt., France, Germany May 1945
Cohen, Jacob, Pvt, Hq. Co. 2d Bn. 7th Inf Regt., Italy 23 May 1944
Cohn, George G., Capt, Inf Per Off 15th Inf Regt., France, Germany 18 Feb. 1945
Cohn, Julius, Pfc, Hq. Btry 41st FA Bn., France 28 Aug. 1944
Coker, Leon J., S/Sgt, Co. A 15th Inf, N. Africa, Sicily, Italy, France, Germany, Austria 8 May 1945
Coldwell, Allen J., Pfc, Med. Det. 7th Inf Regt., France 15 Mar. 1945
Cole, John D., T/3, 3d Sig. Co., Italy, France, Germany Apr. 1945
Cole, Robert J., Pvt, Btry C 41st FA Bn., Anzio 28 Feb. 1944
Coleman, Warren C., 1st Lt, Inf Cn Co. 30th Inf, France 20 Nov. 1944
Colley, Raymond W., Sgt, Co. B 756th Tank Bn., France 15 Sept. 1944
▲Collins, Henry, M/Sgt, Hq. 3d Inf Div., France, Germany, Austria 8 May 1945
Collins, John D., Cpl, Btry B 9th FA Bn., Italy 21 Oct. 1944
Collins, Richard D., Jr., T/4, Hq. Co. 1st Bn. 15th Inf Regt., Italy 24 Feb. 1944
Collins, Roy, 2d Lt, FA Co. A 756th Tank Bn., France, Germany, Austria 8 May 1945
Colvin, Ansel M., T/4, Hq. Co. 756th Tank Bn., France 2 Dec. 1944
Colquette, Charles W., Sgt, Co. E 30th Inf, France 11 Oct. 1944
Colombaro, Natalino A., T/4, Med. Det. 30th Inf, Germany
Combs, Bill, Pvt, Hq. Btry 41st FA Bn., France 11 Nov. 1944
Comerford, Vincent P., 1st Sgt, Hq. Btry 41st FA Bn., Italy, France, Germany 8 May 1945
Compton, Howard L., S/Sgt, Btry C 41st FA Bn., N. Africa, Sicily, Italy, France, Germany 8 May 1945
Comrie, Russell M., Maj, Hq. 15th Inf, Rome 4 June 1944
Comstock, Vernon T., T/4, Co. E 7th Inf, Anzio, Italy 24 Mar. 1944
Comstock, Walter L., Pfc, Co. H 30th Inf, France 18 Dec. 1944
Conant, Karl E., Sgt, Co. H 15th Inf, France 3 Jan. 1945
Conder, Boyce L., T/5, Hq. Co. 1st Bn. 30th Inf, N. Africa, Sicily, Italy, France, Germany, Austria 8 May 1945
Condie, James P., S/Sgt, Co. I 7th Inf, Italy 5 June 1944
Condon, Gurnwey R., M/Sgt, Serv. Co. 15th Inf Regt., Italy 5 June 1944
Condon, Jack F., Pfc, Btry B 41st FA Bn., France 26 Jan. 1945
Cone, Oris C., Pfc, Co. C 7th Inf, Agristno, Sicily 14 July 1943
Cone, Wallis D., Capt, MC Co. B 3d Med. Bn., France, Germany, Austria 8 May 1945
▲(2) Conklin, Willis B., 1st Lt, Co. F 7th Inf, Germany 26 Mar. 1945
Connelly, Eugene F., T/5, Med. Det. 751st Tank Bn., Italy 13 Oct. 1943
Connelly, William B., Hq. Det. 3d Inf Div., Africa, Sicily, Italy 21 May 1944
Conner, Jewel L., Pfc, Co. H 30th Inf Regt., France 27 Aug. 1944
Conner, Karl, Maj, Co. 9th FA Bn., Africa, Sicily 5 June 1944
Connor, Albert O., Lt Col, GSC Ass't Chief of Staff G-3 3d Inf Div., Italy 20 Jan. 1944
▲Connor, Albert O., Lt Col, Hq.VI Corps, Italy 16 June 1944
▲Conover, Lewis J., 2d Lt, Co. F 15th Inf, Tarcenay, France 5 Sept. 1944
Conrad, Loren L., Pvt, Hq. Co. 7th Inf, Loulans, France 12 Sept. 1944
Conrey, William J., Pvt, Med. Det. 7th Inf, Cisterna Di Littoria 26 May 1944
Conte, Dante A., 1st Lt, Inf Hq. Co. 2d Bn. 7th Inf Regt., France 12 Nov. 1944
Contreras, Rudolph, Pfc, Hq. Co. 30th Inf, Padiglione 19 Feb. 1944
Contrino, Frederick W., Pfc, Hq. Co. 30th Inf
Conway, Gerald T., Pfc, Btry A 39th FA Bn., Italy 1 June 1944
Cook, Albert H., Capt, CE Comdt. Co. A 10th Engr. Combat Bn., France 11 Jan. 1945
Cook, Arnold, S/Sgt, Co. K 30th Inf, Anzio, Italy 20 Apr. 1944
Cook, Cloyce L., Cpl, Hq. Co. 756th Tank Bn., Italy 16 Feb. 1944
Cook, Denton F., T/Sgt, Co. M 7th Inf, France 30 Jan. 1945
Cook, Gerald A., Sgt, Co. B 15th Inf, Montelimar, France 30 Aug. 1944
Cook, Leo G., Cpl, Co. C 601st TD Bn., El Guettar, Tunisia 23 Mar. 1943
Cook, William W., Pvt, Armd Comd Co. B 751st Tank Bn., Anzio, Italy 31 Jan. 1944
Cooke, Carl, Pfc, MP Pltn 3d Inf Div., France Feb. 1945
Cooke, John R., S/Sgt, Serv. Co. 7th Inf, Sicily, Italy, France, Germany May 1945
Cooke, Stanley J., Capt, MC Co. B 3d Med. Bn., Italy 14 Nov. 1944
Cooklin, Clarence J., S/Sgt, Btry A 39th FA Bn., France 24 Aug. 1944
Coombs, Richard S., T/5, Co. B 756th Tank Bn., Germany 17 Apr. 1945
Coons, David C., Pfc, Co. C 15th Inf Regt., Germany 18 Mar. 1945
Cooper, Donald K., S/Sgt, Hq. Co. 30th Inf
Cooper, Lewis V., S/Sgt, Co. K 7th Inf Regt., France 23 Nov. 1944
Cooper, William D., T/4, Hq. 3d Div., France, Germany 25 Mar. 1945
Copley, John R., T/Sgt, Co. E 30th Inf Regt., France 4 Dec. 1944
Corak, Nick, Sgt, Co. A 756th Tank Bn., France 24 Jan. 1945
Corbett, Lawrence F., Pfc, Hq. Co. 2d Bn. 30th Inf, Colmar
Corbin, Willie L., T/5, Co. A Engr. Combat Bn., France 5 Nov. 1944
Cordick, Charles F., 1st Lt, Hq. Co. 3d Div., Italy 7 July 1944
Cordova, Anthony C., Pvt, Hq. & Serv. Co. 10th Engr. Combat Bn., France 23 Jan. 1945
Cordova, Ralph W., T/5, Co. L 30th Inf Regt., France 8 Sept. 1944
▲Cores, Thomas R., S/Sgt, Co. F 30th Inf, France 23 Jan. 1945
Corley, Paul D., 1st Sgt, Hq. Co. 3d Div., Italy 2 June 1944
Corn, Charles E., Cpl, Hq. Btry 39th FA Bn., Artena 27 May 1944
Corn, Ernest, Pvt, Rcn Co. 601st TD Bn., Citero, France 15 Sept. 1944
Cornell, Gene M., Sgt, Co. C 601st TD Bn., France 6 Feb. 1945
Cornish, Joseph L., T/5, Serv. Co. 7th Inf Regt., Italy, France, Germany May 1945
Coronel, Rudolph J., Pvt, Btry C 41st FA Bn., Ponte Roto 23 May 1944
▲Corr, Joseph J., 1st Lt, Btry A 441st AAA AW, Sicily, Italy, France, Germany 8 May 1945
Cortese, Dominic, T/5, Serv. Co. 7th Inf, France, Germany 5 May 1945
Corvino, Angelo, Pfc, Hq. Co. 1st Bn. 30th Inf Regt., France 17 Dec. 1944
Corwin, William W., Capt, Con Co. 30th Inf, Acerno 23 Sept. 1943
Cory, Mark E., Jr., Maj, Hq. 3d Bn. 7th Inf, Sicily 17 Aug. 1943
Cosat, John W., Pvt, Co. C 10th Engr. Bn., Carano 5 Mar. 1944
Cosgrove, Robert F., Pvt, Co. D 15th Inf, Cisterna Di Littoria 24 May 1944
Costello, Emmett M., M/Sgt, Hq. Btry 441st AAA AW Bn., Borgo Montello 29 Feb. 1944
Costello, Joseph J., T/Sgt, Co. K 15th Inf Regt., France 18 Sept. 1944
Costello, William J., Sgt, Co. B 30th Inf, France 17 Sept. 1944
Costen, John, Sgt, Hq. Co. 30th Inf Regt., France 10 Nov. 1944
Costley, Lloyd J., Pfc, Med. Det. 15th Inf, France 23 May 1944
Cotoia, Frank J., Cpl, Hq. Co. 15th Inf, Nompatelize 4 Nov. 1944
Cotter, Lloyd H., 1st Lt, Cn Co. 15th Inf, France 27 Aug. 1944
Cotter, Paul G., T/5, Serv. Co. 30th Inf, Colmar
Cotingim, Randolph, Pfc, Co. C 756th Tank Bn., Germany 26 Mar. 1945
Cotton, Melvin K., S/Sgt, Hq. Co. 3d Bn. 30th Inf Regt., Italy 1 June 1944
Cottone, Paul, Pfc, Hq. Co. 7th Inf Regt., Italy 30 May 1944
Courtney, Sylvester R., Pvt, BP Co. A 7th Inf, Anzio, Italy 24 Apr. 1944
Covey, Edwin O., 1st Sgt, Btry B 39th FA Bn., Cisterna 16 Apr. 1944
Cowan, Lynn F., T/4, Serv. Co. 756th Tank Bn., Italy 28 Jan. 1944
Cowart, Thomas L., Pfc, Hq. Co. 7th Inf, France 23 Jan. 1945
Cox, Chester H., T/4, 3d Inf Div. Band, N. Africa, Sicily, Italy 31 Dec. 1943
Cox, John L., Pfc, Btry A 39th FA Bn., San Fretello, Sicily 7 Aug. 1943
Cox, Ned S., T/4, Co. A 756th Tank Bn., France 25 Jan. 1945
Cox, Ross C., S/Sgt, Serv. Co. 7th Inf, Anzio, Italy 23 Mar. 1944
▲(2) Coyne, Christopher C., Col, FA Hq. 3d Inf, France, Germany 8 May 1945
Cozzens, Richard D., T/Sgt, Hq. Co. 3d Bn. 7th Inf Regt., Germany 19 Mar. 1945
Crabtree, Roy G., Sgt, Co. C 7th Inf Regt., France 9 Sept. 1944
Craig, Harvey L., 1/Sgt, 3d Sig. Co., near Le Ferriere, Italy 10 Mar. 1944
Craig, Joseph E., S/Sgt, Co. C 7th Inf, France 16 Aug. 1944
Cramer, Bernnie L., Cpl, Co. C 10th Engr. Bn., Carano 5 Mar. 1944
Crandall, Calvin L., T/5, AT Co. 30th Inf, Colmar
Crane, David, Pfc, Btry A 441st AAA AW Bn., Italy 29 Oct. 1943
Crane, Jess, Jr., Pfc, Co. C 10th Engr., Cisterna 23 May 1944
Crapps, John W., T/5, Btry D 441st AAA AW Bn., Sicily, Italy, France, Germany, Austria 8 May 1945
Crawford, Arden L., Sgt, Hq. Co. 2d Bn. 30th Inf, Licata, Sicily 10 July 1943
Crawford, Clayton E., T/Sgt, Co. H 30th Inf, Anzio, Italy 29 Feb. 1944
Crawford, Herman C., Sgt, Co. B 15th Inf, Ramatuello, France 15 Aug. 1944
Crawford, Woodrow W., Pfc, Co. E 7th Inf, Anzio, Italy 25 Mar. 1944
▲Creager, James H., S/Sgt, Co. D 30th Inf Regt., Italy 25 Jan. 1944
Creamer, Roy C., Pfc, Hq. Co. 30th Inf Regt., Italy, France Nov. 1944
Creed, Marvin W., Pfc, Cn Co. 30th Inf, France 23 Dec. 1944
Creiman, Garry R., 1st Lt, Inf Hq. Co. 30th Inf Regt., Italy, France, Germany, Austria 5 May 1945
Crenshaw, Oscar T., S/Sgt, Co. B 756th Tank Bn., France, Germany, Austria 8 May 1945
Crescenzi, Columbo E., Pvt, Co. C 10th Engr. Bn., Valmontone 2 June 1944
Cress, Donald, Pfc, Co. H 15th Inf Regt., Germany 18 Mar. 1945
Cressotti, Carlo B., Pfc, Btry C 441st AAA AW Bn., Germany 30 Apr. 1945
Crnofevich, Charles, Sgt, AT Co. 7th Inf Regt., Austria 1 May 1945
Cromartie, John D., T/4, Hq. Btry 39th FA Bn., Italy 27 May 1944
Cronan, Joseph D., 1st Lt, CA Corp Btry B 441st AAA AW Bn., Germany 2 Apr. 1945
Crook, James L., Jr., T/5, 3d QM Co., Italy, France 28 Feb. 1945
Cropp, Albert E., Jr., T/Sgt, Co. I 15th Inf, France 29 Dec. 1944
Crosby, Elmore L., 2d Co. B 15th Inf, France 26 Jan. 1945
Crosley, Willard D., Sgt, Co. H 15th Inf, Isola Bella 25 Jan. 1944
Cross, Luther A., Pvt, Hq. Btry 3d IDA, Anzio, Italy 29 Feb. 1944
Crossley, Martin E., Jr., 1st Lt, Inf Co. H 15th Inf Regt., Germany 17 Apr. 1945
Crotty, John J., T/4, Hq. 3d Div., Italy 23 May 1944
Crounk, Samuel M., Sgt, Btry C 441st AAA AW BN., Germany 30 Apr. 1945
Crouse, Glen J., Pfc, Co. A 756th Tank Bn., France 26 Jan. 1945
Crowe, Robert O., S/Sgt, Co. H 30th Inf Regt., Germany 27 Mar. 1945
Crozier, Wilfred L., Pfc, Hq. Co. 1st Bn. 30th Inf Regt., Anzio, Italy 25 Jan. 1944
Cubbage, Emery N., Pfc, Btry B 10th FA Bn., Cisterna Di Littoria 15 Feb. 1944
Culler, William O., Cpl, Co. A 756th Tank Bn., France 26 Jan. 1945
Cullifer, Leslie B., 1st Sgt, Serv. Co. 30th Inf, Italy 25 Feb. 1944
Cullins, Edwin W., Pvt, Co. G 15th Inf Regt., Germany 18 Mar. 1945
Cummings, Chester A., Pvt, Co. D 7th Inf, France 5 Feb. 1945
Cummins, Lloyd A., 1st Lt, Inf Co. G 30th Inf Regt., Germany 17 Apr. 1945
Cundiff, Gordon P., 1st Lt, QM Corps 3d QM Co., France 30 Jan. 1945
Cunningham, Doile R., Pfc, Co. C 7th Inf, Anzio, Italy 16 Feb. 1944
Cunningham, Ernest S., Jr., Capt, Med. Det. 15th Inf, Anzio, Italy 18 Feb. 1944
Cunningham, Francis J., Pfc, Hq. Btry 39th FA Bn., France 23 Aug. 1944
Cunningham, Lionel J., 1st Lt, Inf Serv. Co. 756th Tank Bn., France, Germany, Austria 6 May 1945
Cunningham, Theodore R., Pfc, Hq. Btry 39th FA Bn., 23 Mar. 1944
Cunningham, William H., Cpl, Hq. Co. 2d Bn. 7th Inf, Cisterna Di Littoria 23 May 1944
Cuny, Arthur E., Sgt, Co. D 7th Inf, Anzio, Italy 6 Mar. 1944
Curran, James P., Pvt, Btry C 9th FA Bn., Artena 30 May 1944
Curtaccio, Dan O., Pfc, Med. Det. 30th Inf Regt., France 23 Jan. 1945
Curtin, Stanley J., S/Sgt, 3d QM Co., N. Africa, Sicily, Italy, Germany France, Austria 8 May 1945
Curtis, Vincent V., S/Sgt, Hq. Btry 9th FA Bn., Sicily, Italy, France 28 Feb. 1945
Curvin, Lymon H., S/Sgt, Co. L 30th Inf Regt., France 8 Sept. 1944
Cusic, Marshall E., Capt, Hq. Btry 69th Armd FA Bn., Italy 11 July 1944
Cusick, Alvania, S/Sgt, Co. K 15th Inf, France 24 Dec. 1944
Cussen, John B., Sgt, 3d Sig. Co., France, Germany 6 May 1945
Cuzzo, Joseph J., T/5, Co. D 756th Tank Bn., France 12 Feb. 1945

▲ Oak Leaf Cluster.

Cychosz, Clarence, Sgt, Co. I 30th Inf
Cyphers, William E., Pfc, Hq. Co. 3d Inf Div., France, Germany 8 May 1945
Czarniawski, Edward M., Pvt, Co. I 30th Inf, Harbaville 4 Nov. 1944
Czeck, Ambrose A., S/Sgt, Hq. Co. 2d Bn., 7th Inf, Italy 15 Oct. 1943

Dale, Henry, Pfc, Co. H 7th Inf, Cisterna Di Littoria 23 May 1944
Dalmonego, Albin A., Pvt, Co. C 10th Engr., Faucogney 21 Sept. 1944
Dalton, James J., S/Sgt, Hq. Co. 1st Bn. 15th Regt., France 15 Aug. 1945
Daly, Byrne M., Capt, Med. Det. 30th Inf, Italy 17 Nov. 1943
Daly, Michael J., Capt, Inf Co. A 15th Inf Regt., Germany 18 Mar. 1945
Dandrea, Charles J., Pvt, Co. H 15th Inf, Isola Bella 31 Jan. 1944
Daniel, Evrette L., Pfc, Btry A 9th FA Bn., Anzio, Italy 25 May 1944
Daniel, Samuel L., S/Sgt, Co. K 7th Inf Regt., France 7 Nov. 1944
Danilson, Charles E., Pfc, Co. E 7th Inf, Cisterna Di Littoria 24 May 1944
Danner, Robert B., Sgt, Co. B 756th Tank Bn., France 18 Feb. 1945
Darchi, Alfonso P., Jr., Pfc, Co. E 7th Inf Regt., France 7 Oct. 1944
Darrah, John R., Maj, MC Hq. 3d Inf Div., Italy, France 25 Dec. 1944
Daub, David L., 1st Lt, SC 3d Sig. Co., Italy, France 20 Feb. 1945
Dauby, Gervase F., T/5, Co. L 15th Inf, Isola Bella 12 Mar. 1944
Daugherty, William J., Sgt, Hq. Co. 30th Inf, Italy, France, Germany 8 May 1945
Davidson, Thomas A., Pvt, Btry C 10th FA Bn., Cisterna Di Littoria 7 Mar. 1944
Davies, David L., Cpl, Serv. Co. 15th Inf, Italy 2 June 1944
Davies, John N., Pfc, Serv. Btry 41st FA Bn., Italy 18 Nov. 1944
Davies, Thomas, Capt, Inf 1st Bn. 30th Inf Regt., France 23 Jan. 1945
Davila, Tony A., Pfc, Co. G 30th Inf Regt., France 21 Sept. 1944
Davis, Alfred R., Pfc, Co. D 30th Inf Regt., Italy 23 Jan. 1944
Davis, Arthur L., Cpl, Serv. Btry 41st FA Bn., San Stefano, Sicily 5 Aug. 1943
Davis, Charles W., S/Sgt, Co. M 7th Inf, Italy 5 June 1944
Davis, Ervin L., S/Sgt, Btry B 41st FA Bn., Italy 19 Jan. 1944
Davis, George C., Pfc, Co. B 756th Tank Bn., France 15 Sept. 1944
Davis, John C., T/Sgt, Co. B 7th Inf, France 26 Jan. 1945
Davis, John M., T/4, Hq. & Serv. Co. 10th Engr. Combat Bn., Italy, France, Germany 8 May 1945
▲Davis, Kermit L., Lt Col, VI Corps, Volturno, 13 Oct. 1943
▲Davis, Marion A., Cpl, Co. A 756th Tank Bn., Germany 7 Apr. 1945
▲Davis, Ralph E., Capt, FA Hq. 39th FA Bn., Germany 4 Apr. 1945
Davis, Richard C., S/Sgt, Hq. Co. 1st Bn. 15th Inf, Italy, France 18 Feb. 1945
▲Davis, Rondal N., S/Sgt, Co. C 30th Inf Regt., Germany 15 Mar. 1945
Davis, Ross E., Pvt, Co. C 756th Tank Bn., Germany 10 Apr. 1945
Davis, Thomas R., Lt Col, CO 2d Bn. 15th Inf, S.E. Rome 4 June 1944
Davis, Thomas V., T/5, Co. M 30th Inf Regt., N. Africa, Sicily, Italy, France, Germany 8 May 1945
Davis, Wesley N., 1st Sgt, Hq.—Serv. Co. 10th Engr., N. Africa, Sicily, France, Italy, Germany, Austria 8 May 1945
Davis, Wilfred H., T/5, Co. A 3d Med. Bn., Sicily, Italy, France 10 Jan. 1945
Davis, William G., T/5, Rcn Co. 601st TD Bn., Italy 10 Mar. 1944
Dawes, Ivan J., S/Sgt, AT Co. 30th Inf, Anzio, Italy 29 Feb. 1944
Dawkins, Howard, Pfc, Co. M 30th Inf Regt., France 20 Dec. 1944
Dawson, Alvin M., M/Sgt, Hq. Det. 3d Inf Div., Italy, France Feb. 1945
Dawson, Richard C., Pfc, Hq. Co. 3d Bn. 30th Inf, Tauligan 28 Aug. 1944
Day, Ernest E., Pvt, BP 7th Inf, Anzio, Italy 20 Apr. 1944
Dean, Everett L., 2d Lt, Co. G 7th Inf, Padiglione 23 Apr. 1944
DeAngelo, Frank T., Pfc, Co. C 30th Inf Regt., France 24 Nov. 1944
Deatherage, Virgil V., S/Sgt, Co. C 7th Inf, Campo Di Morto 17 Feb. 1944
DeChambeau, Maurice H., Cpl, Cn Co. 30th Inf Regt., Italy 2 Mar. 1944
De Coster, Joseph J., T/5, Hq. Btry 39th FA Bn., Caiazzo 14 Oct. 1944
Deem, Robert B., T/Sgt, Hq. 3d Inf Div., France, Germany, Austria 8 May 1945
Deen, Carl H., T/Sgt, Co. C 7th Inf Regt., Germany 26 Mar. 1945
Deenihan, John J., Cpl, Co. A 756th Tank Bn., Germany 18 Mar. 1945
Deering, Fred, T/5, AT Co. 15th Inf Regt., France 28 Oct. 1944
Dees, William P., S/Sgt, Co. G 15th Inf, Germany 19 Mar. 1945
DeFinis, Michael J., T/4, Hq. Btry 441st AAA AW BN., Borgo Montello 29 Feb. 1944
Dehart, William E., Pfc, Hq. Co. 2d Bn. 7th Inf Regt., France 20 Nov. 1944
De Hirmida, Eugene A., 1st Lt, Cav. Co. B 756th Tank Bn., France 25 Oct. 1944
Dehetre, Real F., Sgt, Co. C 7th Inf, France 16 Aug. 1944
DeJardin, Robert P., Pfc, Co. K 30th Inf, Nelay, France 28 Sept. 1944
Delaney, James M., Pvt, Co. H 30th Inf, Anzio, Italy 3 Mar. 1944
DeLange, Harold J., Pfc, Co. G 30th Inf Regt., Germany 19 Mar. 1945
DeLay, James W., Sgt, Co. A 601st TD Bn., Tor Sapienze 5 June 1944
DeLeon, Pedro, Pfc, Co. A 15th Inf, Nompatelize, France 31 Oct. 1944
Delgado, Joe W., Pvt, Rcn Co. 601st TD Bn., Sollies Pont 18 Aug. 1944
DeLibero, Frank C., Sgt, Btry D 441st AAA AW Bn., France 10 Nov. 1944
Dell, Joseph, 1st Lt, MC Hq. & Hq. Det. 3d Med. Bn., France, Germany 8 May 1945
Dellinger, Paul F., Pfc, Co. B 10th Engr., France 8 Nov. 1944
Delooze, Thomas P., Pfc, Co. H 15th Inf, France 2 Jan. 1945
Deltieure, Rene P. J., S/Sgt, Co. M 7th Inf Regt., near Wihr-en-Plaine, France 30 Jan. 1945
DeLuca, Bart J., T/5, Btry B 39th FA Bn., France 30 Jan. 1945
Demangate, Homer, Pfc, Hq. Btry 39th FA Bn., Anzio 18 Mar. 1944
De Marcus, John D., 2d Lt, Co. I 30th Inf, Carano 29 Apr. 1944
DeMars, Robert E., Sgt, Co. I 30th Inf Regt., France 23 Jan. 1945
De Martini, Loring A., Capt, DC Hq. 3d Inf Div. Arty, N. Africa, Sicily, Italy, France, Germany 8 May 1945
Demersseman, Donald, Pvt, Btry A 9th FA Bn., France 22 Sept. 1944
De Moine, Arthur L., Pvt, Btry C 9th FA Bn., Italy 10 Mar. 1944
DeMouchel, Leo J., T/Sgt, Co. K 30th Inf Regt., Germany 15 Mar. 1945
Dempsey, Frank, 1st Sgt, Serv. Co. 7th Inf, French Morocco, Fedala 11 Nov. 1942
Dempsey, Horace L., Cpl, Co. C 601st TD Bn., Anzio, Italy 7 Feb. 1944
Denbo, William C., Pfc, Btry C 10th FA Bn., N. Africa, Sicily, Italy, France, Germany, Austria 8 May 1945
Dennin, Robert A., T/4, Co. B 601st TD Bn., N. Africa, Italy, France, Germany, Austria 8 May 1945
Dennington, James J., 1st Lt, QMC 3d QM Co., France, Germany, Austria 1 May 1945
Dennis, Joe R., T/5, Hq. Co. 2d Bn. 15th Inf Regt., France, Germany 8 May 1945
Dennis, Loyd T., Pvt, 3d Sig. Co., Melisey 21 Sept. 1944
Dennison, Arthur, S/Sgt, Btry C 9th FA Bn., Conca 11 Mar. 1944
Denton, Author M., Sgt, Co. H 7th Inf, Cisterna Di Littoria 21 Feb. 1944
De Paepe, Raymond H., Pfc, Co. H 7th Inf, Anzio, Italy 19 Feb. 1944
DeRienzo, Leonard, Jr., Pfc, Btry B 441st AAA AW Bn., France 25 Jan. 1945
Derosier, Gerald A., Capt, Inf Hq. 1st Bn. 7th Inf Regt., France 2 Nov. 1944
Derrick, Carl S., Sgt, Co. G 15th Inf, Germany 7 Apr. 1945
D'Errico, Augustine B., Pfc, Co. H 7th Inf Regt., France 1 Nov. 1944
Derrickson, Wayne R., Sgt, Co. K 15th Inf Regt., France 21 Dec. 1944
DeSantis, Orazio J., Capt, Med. Det. 30th Inf, Aix, France 20 Aug. 1944
Desfosses, Philippe R., Cpl, Hq. Co. 601st TD Bn., Italy 22 May 1944
DeShields, Ernest L., Sgt, Co. C 7th Inf, Germany 7 Apr. 1945
Des Laurier, Lauren H., 2d Lt, Med. Adm. Corps Med. Det. 7th Inf Regt., Africa, Sicily, Italy 4 June 1944
Desrosiers, Leo H., Pvt, AT Co. 30th Inf, France 24 Dec. 1944
Dethman, Frank E., 1st Sgt, Hq. Btry 10th FA Bn., N. Africa, Sicily, Italy, France, Germany 8 May 1945
DeTienne, Earl L., T/4, Co. C 601st TD Bn., France 27 Oct. 1944
Detrie, James F., Pvt, Co. M 7th Inf, Aprilia 25 Apr. 1944
Dettlaff, Frank J., Jr., S/Sgt, 3d QM Co., N. Africa, Sicily, Italy, France, Germany 8 May 1945
Dever, Eugene C., 1st Lt, Btry B 41st FA Bn., France 22 Jan. 1945
▲Devlin, Raymond J., Pfc, Hq. Btry FA 3d Div. Arty, Cajazzo 13 Oct. 1943
Devlin, Raymond J., Pfc, Hq. Btry 3d IDA, Anzio, Italy 29 Feb. 1944
Devlin, Thomas F., Pfc, Co. B 756th Tank Bn., France 1 Nov. 1944
Deweese, Hurshell T., Pfc, Co. E 7th Inf, Cisterna Di Littoria 1 Feb. 1944
Dial, Luther, Sgt, Co. M 7th Inf Regt., France 25 Nov. 1944
DiBartolo, Joseph V., Pfc, Btry A 441st AAA AW Bn., Italy 29 Oct. 1943
Dibbert, Orin H., Pfc, Btry B 39th FA BN., Cisterna 10 Mar. 1944
Di Bona, Gildo L., T/Sgt, Co. A 7th Inf, Italy 28 May 1944
Dick, Leo L., Pfc, MP Pltn 3d Inf Div., France Feb. 1945
Dickerson, Kenneth L., T/Sgt, Serv. Btry 10th FA Bn., N. Africa, Sicily, Italy, France, Germany 8 May 1945
Dickey, Clarence, Pfc, Hq. Co. 3d Inf Div., France, Germany 8 May 1945
Dickey, John R., S/Sgt, Co. F 30th Inf, France 16 Aug. 1944
Dickinson, Raymond E., T/4, Hq. Co. 1st Bn. 7th Inf Regt., Germany 26 Mar. 1945
▲Diehl, Earl H., 2d Lt, Inf Co. I 30th Inf Regt., Germany 2 May 1945
Diehl, Francis H., Pfc, Cn Co. 7th Inf Regt, France 3 Nov. 1944
Dieleman, William K., Capt, Inf Hq. Co. 2d Bn. 7th Inf Regt., France 5 Feb. 1945
Dietrick, John J., Pfc, Co. H 15th Inf, Isola Bella 31 Jan. 1944
Dietz, George J., Sgt, Co. C 601st TD Bn., Germany 19 Apr. 1945
Dietz, George J., Pfc, Btry C 41st FA Bn., Italy 3 June 1944
Difiore, John J., S/Sgt, Co. G 30th Inf, Germany
Digerness, Alvin R., Sgt, AT Co. 7th Inf, Cisterna Di Littoria 26 May 1944
Digregorio, Oscar, Pfc, 3d Inf Div. Band, Italy, France, Germany 8 May 1945
Diiro, Orval W., Pfc, Co. G 15th Inf, Lacelle, France 18 Aug. 1944
Di Laura, Fernaldo, Pfc, Hq. Co. 7th Inf, France 7 Oct. 1944
Dill, Orlin W., Pfc, Co. E 7th Inf Regt., Germany 18 Apr. 1945
Dillon, Claude O., Pfc, Med. Det. 30th Inf, 23 Jan. 1945
Dillon, Gordon K., Pfc, Hq. Co. 7th Inf, Loulans, France 12 Sept. 1944
Dillon, William P., Cpl, Hq. Btry 39th FA Bn., Anzio, Italy 23 Mar. 1944
DiMario, Carmen, Pvt, Hq. Co. 30th Inf, S. France
DiMeglio, Benedetto J., Pvt, Btry D 441st AAA AW Bn., France 10 Nov. 1944
DiNucci, John J., Sgt, Hq. Co. 1st Bn. 15th Inf Regt., Italy 22 Feb. 1944
Diomandes, Diamond A., Pfc, Med. Det. 15th Inf Regt., France 1 Feb. 1945
Dirienzo, William W., Pfc, Hq. Co. 3d Bn. 30th Inf Regt., France 29 Jan. 1945
Dittoe, George H., S/Sgt, Co. I 15th Inf, France 29 Dec. 1944
Diveley, Wilbur B., M/Sgt, Serv. Co. 30th Inf Div., N. Africa, Sicily, Italy, France, Germany, Austria 8 May 1945
Dix, Arthur M., 1st Lt, Btry B 634th FA Bn., Cisterna Di Littoria 28 May 1944
Dobbins, Richard F., Pfc, Co. B 7th Inf Regt., Germany 31 Mar. 1945
Dobbs, Malcolm C., 1st Lt, Inf Co. H 7th Inf Regt., France 28 Oct. 1944
Dobrosky, Michael J., Pfc, Co. E 30th Inf Regt., Germany 5 Apr. 1945
Dockery, Willard J., T/5, Co. C 601st TD Bn., Anzio, Italy 26 Mar. 1944
Dodd, Marcus W., 1st Lt, Cn Co. 15th Inf Regt., France, Germany 8 May 1945
▲Doherty, Joseph C., 1st Lt, FA Btry C 41st FA Bn., France 30 Jan. 1945
Doherty, Paul E., Capt, Hq. 3d Inf, Italy 10 Aug. 1944
Dolan, Thomas J., 1st Lt, FA Hq. 3d Inf Div., France, Germany, Austria 8 May 1945
Dolaway, Chester W., Sgt, Hq. Co. 2d Bn. 15th Inf, Cori 26 May 1944
▲Doleman, Edgar C., Lt Col, Inf Hq. 3d Bn. 30th Inf Regt., Italy 12 Nov. 1943
Doloway, Chester W., S/Sgt, Hq. Co. 2d Bn. 15th Inf, Lure, France 18 Sept. 1944
Dombrowski, Chester C., Pfc, Co. M 7th Inf, Artena 31 May 1944
Dominguez, Robert, Pfc, Hq. Co. 3d Bn. 30th Inf Regt., Germany 28 Apr. 1945
Dominiak, William W., T/5, Hq. Co. 30th Inf Regt., France 24 Nov. 1944
Donaldson, Charles K., Pfc, Co. L 15th Inf Regt., France 27 Dec. 1944
▲Donegan, Winfred S., Pfc, Hq. Co. 3d Bn. 30th Inf Regt., France 25 Sept. 1944
Doney, Charles, Pfc, Co. B 7th Inf, Artena 28 May 1944
Donovan, Gerard C., Pfc, Hq. Co. 2d Bn. 30th Inf, France 30 Dec. 1944
Donovan, Joseph E. R., 1st Sgt, 601st TD Bn., N. Africa, Italy, France 15 Jan. 1945
Donovan, Robert E., Pfc, Med. Det. 30th Inf, Anzio, Italy 16 Apr. 1944
Donowski, Stanley W., 2d Lt, Co. M 7th Inf, Italy 27 June 1944
Dooling, John B., Pfc, Co. B 30th Inf, Anzio, Italy 30 Apr. 1944
Doris, Thomas, Cpl, Btry D 441st AAA AW Bn., France 21 Oct. 1944
Dorr, Martin, Pfc, MP Pltn 3d Inf Div., France Feb. 1945
▲Dorr, Milton E., Pfc, Hq. Co. 2d Bn. 30th Inf Regt., France 31 Oct. 1944
Dorrell, Edward L., T/5, Med. Det. 30th Inf, Germany
▲Dorschler, Eugene, Sgt, MP Pltn Hq. Co. 3d Inf Div., France, Germany 8 May 1945
Dostal, Vladimir M., 1st Lt, Inf Hq. 7th Inf, France, Germany 8 May 1945
Dostman, George S., 1st Sgt, Hq. Co. 1st Bn. 30th Inf Regt., Italy 1 June 1944
▲Dotson, Lloyd H., Pfc, Co. H 15th Inf Regt., France 21 Dec. 1944
Doty, Vernon H., Pfc, Co. B 10th Engr. Combat Bn., France 29 Oct. 1944
Dougan, Robert O., Jr., Pfc, Co. C 10th Engr. Combat Bn., France 8 Oct. 1944
Dougherty, Millard F., 1st Lt, Inf Co. L 30th Inf, France 6 Feb. 1945
Dowdy, Hershel H., Pfc, Co. E 30th Inf Regt., France 23 Jan. 1945
▲Dowling, William D., S/Sgt, Rcn Co. 601st TD Bn., Germany 27 Apr. 1945
Doyle, Herbert L., T/4, Hq. Co. 7th Inf, France 23 Jan. 1945
Doyle, James B., Pfc, Co. E 7th Inf, Cisterna Di Littoria 1 Mar. 1944
▲Doyle, James E., Jr., S/Sgt, Co. I 15th Inf, France 29 Dec. 1944

▲ Oak Leaf Cluster.

Doyle, John W., Pfc, Co. E 7th Inf Regt., France 3 Nov. 1944
Doyle, Ward, S/Sgt, Co. F 30th Inf, Faucogney, France 20 Sept. 1944
Drabczyk, Edward L., Pfc, Co. L 30th Inf Regt., France 16 Dec. 1944
Drega, Henry F., Pfc, Cn Co. 30th Inf Regt., France 18 Aug. 1944
▲Drake, Frank R., Lt Col, MC Div. Surgeon Hq. 3d Inf Div., France 6 Feb. 1945
Drake, Silas B., Sgt, Co. C 601st TD Bn., France 22 May 1944
Draucek, Joseph D., Sgt, Co. E 30th Inf, Vosges
Drayton, Frederick R., Jr., Pvt, Co. C 7th Inf Regt., Italy, France 1 Nov. 1944
Dreadfulwater, Levi, Pfc, Rcn Co. 601st TD Bn., France 8 Sept. 1944
Drennan, Harold, Pfc, Co. D 15th Inf, Cisterna Di Littoria 12 Feb. 1944
Drenner, Jesse E., Pvt, 3d QM Co., French Morocco 1 Dec. 1942
Drescher, Lawrence E., S/Sgt, Co. C 10th Engr. Combat Bn., France 22 Jan. 1945
Dresp, Fred C., Pfc, Co. B 7th Inf, France 30 Oct. 1944
Driggers, Irvin L., Pvt, Co. D 15th Inf Regt., 2 June 1944
Drossner, Jacob L., Capt, Med. Det. 30th Inf, France 5 Feb. 1945
Duckworth, Leland R., Pfc, Hq. Co. 7th Inf, Anzio, Italy 29 Feb. 1944
Due, Paul A., Pfc, AT Co. 30th Inf, Anzio, Italy 6 Mar. 1944
▲Duenn, Albert E., T/5, Cn Co. 30th Inf, France 27 Aug. 1944
Duewler, Robert W., Sgt, Co. G 15th Inf, Hautontot 13 Oct. 1944
Duffy, William L., T/4, Co. D 756th Tank Bn., Germany 13 Apr. 1945
Duggan, Thomas V., T/Sgt, Hq. Co. 756th Tank Bn., Italy, France, Germany, Austria 8 May 1945
Dugger, Troy R., T/5, Hq. Co. 3d Bn. 15th Inf Regt., France 9 Sept. 1944
Duke, Leland, T/4, Hq. Co. 7th Inf, France 10 Feb. 1945
Duket, Joseph E., Sgt, Co. K 15th Inf, Italy 15 Oct. 1943
DuMouchel, Leo J., T/Sgt, Co. K 30th Inf, Germany
Dunbar, Burton L., T/4, 3d Div. Band, Sicily, Italy, France, Germany, Austria 8 May 1945
Dunbar, John C., Hq. Btry 39th FA Bn., Germany 16 Apr. 1945
Duncan, Elmer S., Pfc, Med. Det. 39th FA Bn., Italy 26 May 1944
Duncan, Herbert L., Capt, AGD Ass't AG Hq. 3d Inf Div., Africa, Sicily, Italy, France, Germany, Austria 8 May 1945
Duncan, Jack M., Capt, Hq. 7th Inf, Cape Orlando, Sicily 10 Aug. 1943
Dunham, Ralph, T/Sgt, Co. I 30th Inf, France 1 Feb. 1945
▲Dunham, Russell, T/Sgt, Co. I 30th Inf Regt., France 17 Dec. 1944
Dunkerley, William J., Pfc, Co. I 7th Inf Regt., Germany 25 Apr. 1945
Dunn, Ernest B., Cpl, Cn Co. 7th Inf, Anzio, Italy 17 Mar. 1944
Dunn, Patrick, Pfc, Co. A 7th Inf Regt., France 28 Dec. 1944
Dunn, William G., Sgt, MP Pltn 3d Inf, France 12 Oct. 1944
Dupere, Albert H., Pfc, Co. A 7th Inf, France 27 Sept. 1944
Duprey, Arthur J., Pfc, Hq. Co. 7th Inf, Valmontone 1 June 1944
Duranleau, Robert J., Pvt, Btry Bm 39th FA Bn., Cisterna 22 Apr. 1944
Dutra, John, S/Sgt, Co. M 30th Inf Regt., France 23 Jan. 1945
Duvall, Everett W., Lt Col, Hq. 2d Bn. 7th Inf, Cisterna Di Littoria 25 May 1944
Duvinski, Chester A., Sgt, Co. A 756th Tank Bn., Germany 17 Apr. 1945
Dvorak, Wesley G., T/Sgt, Hq. Btry 39th FA Bn., Italy 26 May 1944
Dvores, Morton, Pvt, 3d Med. Bn., French Morocco 15 Nov. 1942
Dye, Eurie G., Pfc, Med. Det. 7th Inf Regt., Germany 26 Mar. 1945
Dyer, Samuel N., Pfc, Co. B 30th Inf Regt., Germany 19 Apr. 1945
Dyerson, Delmar L., Capt, Chap. Corps, Sicily 17 Aug. 1943
Dykes, Samuel M., 1st Lt, Co. M 30th Inf, Anzio, Italy 22 Apr. 1944
Dykstra, Peter, Pvt, Co. B 601st TD Bn., Ponte Rotto 29 Feb. 1944
Dylewski, Withold F., 1st Lt, Co. D 7th Inf, Ruptsur-Moselle, France 24 Sept. 1944
Dymock, Lee L., Capt, Hq. 7th Inf, La Mole, France 18 Aug. 1944
Dymond, William H., Pfc, Co. C 756th Tank Bn., France 7 Sept. 1944
Dysert, Russell C., Sgt, Hq. Btry 441st AAA AW Bn., Sicily, Italy, France, Germany 8 May 1945
Dyvad, Bert H., T/4, Co. A 30th Inf Regt., France 30 Dec. 1944
Dziedzic, Edward J., Pvt, Med. Det. 30th Inf, Anzio 23 May 1944
Dziura, Joseph F., 1st Lt, FA Btry B 9th FA Bn., Italy 4 Feb. 1944

Eakin, John K., 2d Lt, Inf Hq. 3d Inf Div., France, Germany, Austria 8 May 1945
Eaton, Douglas B., Sgt, 3d Rcn Trp., France 20 Aug. 1944
Eaton, Louis, Pfc, Co. M 30th Inf, Anzio, Italy 24 Apr. 1944
Eberle, Fred I., T/4, Hq. Btry 41st FA Bn., Sicily 12 Aug. 1943
Ebling, John, Pfc, Med. Det. 30th Inf, France 31 Jan. 1945
Echeverria, Oscar C., Sgt, Co. K 15th Inf Regt., France 18 Sept. 1944
Eddy, J. S., Sgt, Co. C 601st TD Bn., Germany 11 Apr. 1945
Edick, Kenneth G., 1st Lt, FA Hq. & Hq. Co. 601st TD Bn., France, Germany, Austria 8 May 1945
▲(3) Edson, Hallett D., Col, CO 15th Inf, Germany 20 Apr. 1945
Edwards, George H., T/Sgt, Hq. Btry 9th FA Bn., France 5 Sept. 1944
Edwards, Richard B., Pfc, Co. K 30th Inf, Germany 16 Mar. 1945
Egan, Pvt, Hq. Co. 601st TD Bn., Kassering 22 Feb. 1944
Egizio, Florie, Sgt, Btry A 10th FA Bn., France 22 Oct. 1944
Eifler, Oliver W., Pvt, Med. Det. 15th Inf, Isola Bella 28 Feb. 1944
▲Eiland, Robert G., WOJG, US Army Serv. Co. 7th Inf Regt., Sicily, Italy, France, Germany 28 Mar. 1945
Eilers, Norbert B., T/5, 3d QM Co., Sicily 18 Aug. 1943
Ek, Manfred L., T/Sgt, Hq. & Hq. Det. 3d Med. Bn., France, Germany 8 May 1945
Eldridge, Roy M., Pvt, Co. A 15th Inf, Cisterna Di Littoria 24 May 1944
Elkins, Emuel H., Serv. Btry 41st FA Bn., Italy 17 Aug. 1943
Elliott, Earl H., Pfc, Co. F 30th Inf Regt., France 9 Nov. 1944
Elliott, Gerald L., Sgt, Co. C 15th Inf Regt., Germany 18 Mar. 1945
Elliott, Howard N., T/5, Btry B 39th FA Bn., N. Africa, Sicily, Italy, France, Germany 8 May 1945
Elliott, Lewis P., 1st Lt, Co. C TD Bn., Mignano 18 Nov. 1943
▲Ellis, Calvin C., Maj, MC Hq. 3d Inf Div. Arty, N. Africa, Sicily, Italy, France, Germany, Austria 8 May 1945
▲(2) Ellis, John F., 2d Lt, Hq. 1st Bn. 30th Inf, France 12 Sept. 1944
Ellis, Raymond E., T/5, Serv. Co. 756th Tank Bn., Germany 19 Mar. 1945
Ellis, Richard G., Pvt, Btry B 41st FA Bn., Italy 5 June 1944
Ellison, Irving J., 1st Lt, Inf Cn Co. 30th Inf, Italy, France, Germany 8 May 1945
Ellison, Robert B., Capt, FA Btry C 9th FA Bn., N. Africa, Sicily, Italy, France, Germany, Austria 8 May 1945
▲Ellsworth, William H., Lt Col, JAGD Staff JA Hq. 3d Inf Div., Italy, France, Germany, Austria 8 May 1945

Elrod, Cecil E., T/4, Co. A 756th Tank Bn., France, Germany, Austria 8 May 1945
Elwell, Alfred M., Capt, Co. C 3d Med. Bn., France 19 Dec. 1944
Emmel, John F., Pfc, MP Pltn 3d Inf Div., Italy 5 Mar. 1944
Emberger, Joseph H., 1st Lt, Inf Hq. Co. 3d Bn. 7th Inf Regt., France 6 Oct. 1944
Emery, Chester F., T/5, Btry D 441st AAA AW Bn., Guilianello 31 May 1944
Emery, Norman D., T/4, Btry B 39th FA Bn., Italy 21 Oct. 1943
Engebretson, Herman O., Sgt, Hq. Det. 3d Inf Div., Sicily, Italy, France Germany 8 May 1945
Engerbriston, Gisle G., Pfc, Co. G 30th Inf Regt., France 4 Sept. 1944
Engfer, William R., Capt, Co. A 756th Tank Bn., Germany 4 May 1945
Engle, Donald R., T/4, 3d Rcn Trp., France 30 Nov. 1944
Enser, Edward W., T/5, Hq. Co. 601st TD Bn., Italy 22 May 1944
Entwistel, Sherwood R., 1st Lt, Co. G 15th Inf, Anzio, Italy 20 Apr. 1944
Epps, Arthur G., Pfc, 3d Rcn Trp., Germany 8 May 1945
Erickson, Evarts C., Pfc, Btry B 39th FA Bn., Cisterna 6 Feb. 1944
Erickson, Gunnar E., T/4, Hq. Co. 601st TD Bn., Italy 1 June 1944
Erickson, Wendell E., Sgt, Co. G 7th Inf Regt., France 12 Nov. 1944
Ericsson, Carl W., T/5, Btry B 41st FA Bn., Italy 30 May 1944
Ernest, Fred W., S/Sgt, Hq. Co. 3d Bn. 30th Inf Regt., France 20 Nov. 1944
Ernst, Michael A., S/Sgt, Co. C 7th Inf Regt., France 9 Sept. 1944
Ernst, Wilbur L., T/5, Hq. Co. 30th Inf
Ertman, Joseph, Pfc, Co. B 30th Inf, France 8 Jan. 1945
Esparza, Manuel M., S/Sgt, Co. L 7th Inf, Anzio, Italy 23 Apr. 1944
Espeland, Arthur M., Capt, FA Btry A 9th FA Bn., Italy, France, Germany 8 May 1945
Esposito, John, S/Sgt, Co. C 601st TD Bn., France 19 Mar. 1945
Esquibel, Alarino, Cpl, Btry C 10th FA Bn., N. Africa, Sicily, Italy, France, Germany 8 May 1945
Esser, Edmund V., S/Sgt, Hq. Co. 2d Bn. 7th Inf Regt., France 1 Dec. 1944
Essy, Victor M., T/4, Serv. Co. 756th Tank Bn., Germany 19 Mar. 1945
Estes, Ambrose C., Capt, MC Co. C 3d Med. Bn. 15th Inf Regt., Italy, France 14 Mar. 1945
Estes, Hayden R., Pvt, Hq. Co. 30th Inf, France 23 Jan. 1945
Estep, Kenneth P., Pvt, Btry A 441st AAA AW Bn., Costello 29 May 1944
Etheredge, M B., Jr., Capt, Co. K 30th Inf, France 8 Oct. 1944
Ethridge, Cecil O., S/Sgt, Med. Det. 601st TD Bn., Anzio, Italy 28 Mar. 1944
Eureyecko, Michael, T/5, Co. A 756th Tank Bn., Italy, France, Germany 8 May 1945
Evans, Evan P., 1st Sgt, Btry C 39th FA Bn., Sicily 17 Aug. 1943
Evans, Howard D., Maj, FA Hq. 41st FA Bn., N. Africa, Sicily, Italy, France 14 Sept. 1944
Evans, Roy E., Pvt, BP 7th Inf, Anzio, Italy 20 Apr. 1944
Evans, Samuel G., T/4, Btry C 10th Engr. Combat Bn., Italy, France 15 Sept. 1944
Even, Francis A., 1st Lt, 10th Engr. Bn., Italy 28 Mar. 1944
Everhart, James E., Cpl, Hq. Btry 39th FA Bn., Statigliano 21 Oct. 1943
Ewing, Charles G., M/Sgt, Hq. Det. 3d Inf Div., N. Africa, Sicily, Italy, France 31 Dec. 1944
Eyerdam, John W., Capt, MC Hq. 3d Med. Bn., France, Germany, Austria 8 May 1945
Eyermann, Charles A., Sgt, Co. F 30th Inf, Italy 5 June 1944
Ezzi, John L., Pfc, 3d Rcn Trp., France 9 Sept. 1944

Fadale, Charles J., T/4, Hq. 3d Inf Div., Italy, Germany 8 May 1945
Fagan, Charles J., Jr., Pfc, Co. L 30th Inf Regt., France 8 Sept. 1944
Fain, Joseph R., Pfc, Hq. Co. 3d Bn. 7th Bn., Ponte Rotto 31 Jan. 1944
Fair, Gordon, N., T/5, Serv. Co. 15th Inf, Italy, France, Germany 8 May 1945
▲Faisst, William H., Maj, Inf Serv. Co. 30th Inf, France, Germany 8 May 1945
Fajkowski, Leo S., Pvt, Co. M 7th Inf, Cisterna Di Littoria 26 May 1944
Falardeau, Roland F., Cpl, Btry B AAA AW Bn., Germany 2 Apr. 1945
Falconetti, Danielle W., Pvt, Co. E 7th Inf, Anzio, Italy 8 June 1944
Falkoski, Zigmund S., S/Sgt, Serv. Co. 756th Tank Bn., Italy 28 Jan. 1944
Falvey, Robert E., Pfc, Hq. Co. 3d Bn. 30th Inf Regt., France 16 Dec. 1944
Fanell, Joseph A., Pvt, Hq. Co. 2d Bn. 7th Inf, Anzio, Italy 29 Feb. 1944
Fankhauser, Edward, Sgt, 3d Rcn Trp., Guilianello 26 May 1944
Fankhauser, Walter E., Jr., 1st Lt, Inf Serv. Co. 15th Inf, Italy 8 Aug. 1944
Farkas, James, S/Sgt, Co. M 7th Inf Regt., France 26 Dec. 1944
Farkas, Joseph W., Pfc, Co. C 7th Inf, Villers L Sec 12 Sept. 1944
Farlaino, Jakie, T/5, 3d Sig. Co. Anzio, Italy 7 Mar. 1944
Farley, Henry J., T/5, Co. A 756th Tank Bn., France 26 Jan. 1945
Farnack, Frank T., Pvt, Med. Det. 15th Inf, Anzio, Italy 25 Mar. 1944
Farrell, Addison S., Capt, Hq. Co. 1st Bn. 30th Inf, Anzio, Italy 3 Mar. 1944
Farrington, Don R., Pfc, MP Pltn 3d Inf, Sicily 18 July 1943
▲Faubion, Albert J., T/5, Med. Det. 15th Inf Regt., France 5 Feb. 1945
▲Faucher, Oliver J., Lt Col, Inf Hq. 3d Inf Div., Germany, Austria 8 May 1945
Faul, James F., Pfc, Hq. Co. 1st Bn. 15th Inf Regt., Italy 1 June 1944
Faull, Truran M., 1st Lt, Hq. Co. 2d Bn. 15th Inf Regt., Anzio, Italy 25 Jan. 1944
Fawcett, Robert M., Capt, MC 756th Tank Bn., Campagna Di Roma 7 June 1944
Feagle, Clarence S., Sr., Pfc, Co. I 15th Inf, France 29 Dec. 1944
Feely, Carl W., Pvt, Co. G 7th Inf, Cisterna Di Littoria 28 Jan. 1944
Feeney, Elmer T., S/Sgt, Hq. Co. 2d Bn. 15th Regt., France 5 Feb. 1945
Feigel, William, M/Sgt, 3d Inf Div. Band, Italy, France, Germany 7 May 1945
Feldman, Wilmer O., T/Sgt, AT Co. 7th Inf, N. Africa, Sicily, Italy, France, Germany, Austria 5 May 1945
Feller, Stephen H., T/3, Med. Det. 30th Inf Regt., Italy, France, Germany, Austria 8 May 1945
Felt, Lawrence E., 1st Sgt, Hq. Co. 1st Bn. 7th Inf Regt., Italy 12 Nov. 1943
Fennell, Gerald T., 2d Lt, Inf Hq. Co. 756th Tank Bn., France 11 Feb. 1945
Ferenz, Ferdinand R., T/4, Hq. Co. 3d Bn. 7th Inf, Italy 24 Sept. 1943
Ferguson, George X., 1st Lt, Inf Serv. Co. 15th Inf, France 8 Feb. 1945
Ferguson, Hal, Capt, MC 3d Med. Bn., France 7 Feb. 1945
Fernald, Harold L., Jr., S/Sgt, Co. K 7th Inf, Ponte Rotto 1 Mar. 1944
Fernicola, William, Sgt, Co. C 7th Inf, Libico 27 May 1944
Ferraro, Anthony, T/5, Co. F 7th Inf, La Mole, France 18 Aug. 1944
▲Fezell, George H., Lt Col, Div. Sig. Officer 3d Sig. Co., France, Germany, Austria 8 May 1945
Fick, George F., Cpl, Co. B 756th Tank Bn., France 15 Sept. 1944
Field, Harold G., Jr., Pvt, Hq. Co. 15th Inf, Cisterna Di Littoria 29 Jan. 1944

▲ Oak Leaf Cluster.

Fields, John L., T/4, Hq. Co. 601st TD Bn., N. Africa, Italy, France, Germany, Austria 8 May 1945
Fife, James R., Cpl, Co. H 30th Inf, Sicily 8 Aug. 1943
Filipek, George, Cpl, Btry C 39th FA Bn., Sicily 17 Aug. 1943
Fillion, Norbert P., Pvt, Hq. Co. 601st TD Bn., Italy 22 May 1944
Finch, Ralph E., T/Sgt, Co. L 30th Inf Regt., Germany 26 Mar. 1945
Finley, William W., 1st Lt, Co. B 601st TD Bn., France 25 Jan. 1945
Fischlein, Otto J., S/Sgt, Btry C 441st AAA AW Bn., Sicily, Italy, France, Germany 8 May 1945
Fisher, Cecil R., 2d Lt, Co. K 30th Inf Regt., France 5 Mar. 1945
Fisher, James H., Jr., Pfc, Co. C 30th Inf, France 3 Oct. 1944
Fisher, John W., T/5, Btry B 441st AAA AW Bn., Artena 1 June 1944
Fisher, Joseph F., Pfc, Co. K 30th Inf Regt., France 10 Nov. 1944
Fisher, Louis H., Sgt, Co. A 756th Tank Bn., Germany 19 Mar. 1945
Fisher, Raymond L., Pfc, Hq. Co. 1st Bn. 7th Inf, Anzio, Italy 31 Jan. 1944
Fisler, Benjamin H., Jr., C Arty Corps Btry B 441st AAA AW Bn., France, 25 Jan. 1945
Fiss, David B., M/Sgt, Hq. 41st FA Bn., France 18 Feb. 1945
Fittgerald, Edward P., 1st Lt, Serv. Btry 69th Armd FA Bn., Italy 10 Nov. 1944
Fitzgerald, Thomas W., Pfc, Cn Co. 15th Inf, Germany 27 Apr. 1945
Fitzsimmons, Fred A., Pfc, Co. L 30th Inf Regt., France 15 Dec. 1944
▲Flaherty, Francis D., Pfc, Co. A 7th Inf Regt., Germany 2 Apr. 1945
Flaherty, George M., Pfc, Co. M 30th Inf, N. Africa, Sicily, Italy, France, Germany 8 May 1945
Flammia, Michael, Pfc, Cn Co. 7th Inf Regt., Italy 4 June 1944
Fleet, Robert L., Capt, Inf Cmdr Co. F 30th Inf Regt., France 23 Jan. 1945
Flehan, Henry, Pfc, Co. B 10th Engr. Combat Bn., France 23 Jan. 1945
Fleischman, Ervin C., T/4, Hq. Co. 3d Bn. 15th Inf, Anzio 22 Jan. 1944
Fleming, James S., Sgt, Co. A 15th Inf, Italy 8 Oct. 1944
Fleming, Bernard T., T/5, Med. Det. 39th FA Bn., N. Africa, Sicily, Italy, France, Germany, Austria 8 May 1945
▲Flender, Stanley J., Pfc, Co. E 30th Inf Regt., France 20 Nov. 1944
Flesher, Walter D., Jr., T/5, Serv. Co. 30th Inf, France Nov. 1944
Flesik, Martin, Jr., Pfc, Btry C 39th FA Bn., Italy 27 Feb. 1944
Flick, Wayne L., S/Sgt, Hq. Co. 3d Bn. 30th Inf
Flinner, Albert, Jr., S/Sgt, Co. C 7th Inf Regt., France 2 Dec. 1944
Floch, Walter, Pvt, Co. E 7th Inf, Cisterna Di Littoria 24 May 1944
Floto, Kenneth B., 1st Lt, Hq. VI Corps, France 1 Nov. 1944
Flynn, Hugh J., T/5, Co. M 7h Inf, France, Germany 5 May 1945
▲Flynn, Ralph M., Maj, Hq. 3d Bn. 7th Inf, France 25 Jan. 1945
Flynn, Stephen E., T/Sgt, Hq. 3d Inf Div., Italy, France, Germany 8 May 1945
Fochesato, Roger A., T/4, Btry B 39th FA Bn., France 23 Aug. 1944
Folliett, Earl C., Sgt, Med. Det. 751st TD Bn., Artena 1 June 1944
Forcey, Samuel A., Cpl, Co. D 30th Inf, La Begude De Mazing, France 27 Aug. 1944
Ford, Buster E., Pfc, Hq. Co. 3d Inf Div., France 6 Feb. 1945
Forehand, Edgar E., S/Sgt, Co. K 30th Inf, Ponte Rotto 23 May 1944
Forgue, William E., Pvt, Btry C 9th FA Bn., Artena 30 May 1944
Forman, William P., T/Sgt, Hq. 3d Inf Div., Italy, France, Germany 8 May 1945
Forsyth, Ira R., Pvt, 3d Rcn Trp., Rome 4 June 1942
Foster, Charles G., Capt, MC Med. Det. 15th Inf, Germany 13 Apr. 1945
Foster, Flavus M., Cpl, Btry C 10th FA Bn., N. Africa, Sicily, Italy, France, Germany 8 May 1945
Foster, Russell J., 1st Lt, Btry B 39th FA Bn., Ponte Rotto 12 Apr. 1944
Foster, Stanley E., Pfc, Co. G 30th Inf Regt., Germany 28 Mar. 1945
Fotis, Spiro, T/Sgt, Hq. Co. 3d Bn. 30th Inf Regt., France 20 Nov. 1944
Fotsch, Laverne P., Pvt, Med. Det. 7th Inf, Palestrina 31 May 1944
Fotta, John J., Sgt, Co. A 15th Inf, France 5 Nov. 1944
Foulds, Robert A., 1st Lt, CAC Btry D 441st AAA AW BN., France 31 Dec. 1944
▲(2) Foulk, John D., Capt, Inf Hq. 7th Inf Regt., Germany 4 May 1945
Fowler, Dewey E., Pfc, Co. G 15th Inf, Germany 7 Apr. 1945
Fox, Rolland L., T/4, Hq. 3d Inf Div., N. Africa, Sicily, Italy, France, Germany 8 May 1945
Frady, Richard J., Pfc, Co. E 15th Inf Regt., Germany 18 Apr. 1945
Fraime, Guy L., Pvt, Btry B 39th FA Bn., Cisterna 10 Mar. 1944
Frame, John, Pvt, Co. C 7th Inf Regt., Aix 25 Aug. 1944
Francher, Roy B., Sgt, AT Co. 30th Inf, Vosges
Franklin, Dell W., Sgt, Hq. Co. 15th Inf, France 15 Aug. 1944
Franks, Dan R., T/4, Hq. Co. 3d Bn. 30th Inf, N. Africa, Sicily, Italy, France, Germany 8 May 1945
Franks, Durell, Pfc, Co. H 7th Inf, Cisterna Di Littoria 23 May 1944
▲Franyish, Stephen J., S/Sgt, Co. M 7th Inf Regt., Germany 8 May 1945
Frazer, John, Jr., Pfc, Co. L 15th Inf Regt., France 25 Oct. 1944
Frederick, Edward, S/Sgt, Co. I 30th Inf Regt., France 8 Jan. 1945
Frederick, Robert E., Pfc, Hq. Btry 39th FA Bn., Italy 2 June 1944
Frederickson, Albin, Cpl, Btry B 39th FA Bn., Cisterna 10 Mar. 1944
Freed, Marion J., S/Sgt, Co. A 3d Med. Bn., Africa, Sicily, Italy, France 6 Jan. 1945
Freed, Orville, W., T/5, Co. B 601st TD Bn., Isola Bella 29 Feb. 1944
Freeman, Robert R., T/4, Med. Det. 30th Inf Regt., France 23 Jan. 1945
▲French, Eugene F., S/Sgt, 3d Sig. Co., France 20 Dec. 1944
French, Lester E., T/4, Med. Det. 15th Inf, Sicily, Italy, France 18 Feb. 1945
Frensley, Robert R., Pfc, Co. M 7th Inf, France 3 Feb. 1945
Freson, Robert J., Pfc, Hq. Co. 30th Inf Regt., France 10 Nov. 1944
Frey, Clark E., Pfc, Hq. Co. 1st Bn. 15th Inf, France 1 Feb. 1945
▲Frey, Harold W., Cpl, Btry C 441st AAA AW Bn., Sicily, Italy, France, Germany 8 May 1945
Frey, Kelvey N., Pfc, Co. M 30th Inf Regt., Germany 27 Apr. 1945
Friedrich, Daniel E., Sgt, Co. D 7th Inf Regt., France 22 Jan. 1945
Friederich, Lambert P., 1st Lt, Inf Co. E 30th Inf Regt., France 30 Jan. 1945
Friery, Michael G., Pvt, Hq. Co. 3d Bn. 15th Inf, Isola Bella 1 Mar. 1944
Fries, Ruben F., Pfc, Co. B 756th Tank Bn., France 15 Sept. 1944
Fritz, Melvin H., Co. C 601st TD Bn., Italy, France, Germany 8 May 1945
Frohman, Warner B., 1st Lt, MC Hq. 3d Inf Div., Germany 5 May 1945
Frost, Eugene A., T/Sgt, Co. I 15th Inf, Artena 27 May 1944
Frye, Kenneth I., Pfc, Co. I 7th Inf, Anzio, Italy 14 Mar. 1944
Fulde, Karl F., S/Sgt, Co. L 15th Inf Regt., France 27 Dec. 1944
Fuller, Curtis A., Pvt, Btry C 39th FA Bn., Dampvalley Les Colombe, France 13 Sept. 1944
Funk, Clifford L., Pvt, Co. A 10th Engr. Combat Bn., 5 Nov. 1944
Futrelle, Rollin L., T/3, Hq. 3d Inf Div., Sicily, Italy, France, Germany 8 May 1945
Fuqua, Jack D., Cpl, Btry B FA 41st Bn., Anzio, Italy 23 Mar. 1944

Gabel, Lee F., Cpl, MP Pltn 3d Inf, 20 July 1943
Gabig, Jack F., T/5, 3d QM Co., Sicily, Italy, France, Germany 8 May 1945
Gabin, Herman L., Cpl, Co. B 756th Tank Bn., Germany 13 Apr. 1945
Gabriel, Arthur C., T/5, Med. Det. 7th Inf, France 30 Sept. 1944
Gabner, William W., Pfc, Co. D 756th Tank Bn., Germany 1 May 1945
Gabrielli, John E., Cpl, MP Pltn 3d Inf Div., France Feb. 1945
Gage, Charles D., 1st Lt, FA 41st FA Bn., France 21 Sept. 1944
Gage, Ward E., Capt, Corps of Chaplains Hq. 30th Inf Regt., Sicily, Italy, France 22 Jan. 1945
Gail, Norbert V., S/Sgt, Co. A 3d Med. Bn., Italy 5 June 1944
Galanos, John, T/5, Rcn Co. 601st TD Bn., Kassering 22 Feb. 1943
Gale, James H., Sgt, Co. I 30th Inf Regt., France 5 Nov. 1944
Gale, Meade B., T/5, MP Pltn 3d Inf Div., Germany 8 May 1945
Gallagher, William T., Pfc, Hq. Co. 1st Bn. 7th Inf, France 23 Sept. 1944
Gallaher, William, Pfc, Co. B 7th Inf Regt., France 25 Oct. 1944
Gallups, Henry H., Sgt, Hq. Btry 9th FA Bn., France 4 Feb. 1945
Galonsky, Max, Pfc, Co. L 15th Inf Regt., Germany 4 Apr. 1945
Gambrell, Roderick D., Capt, Hq. 39th FA Bn., Italy, France 25 Jan. 1945
Games, Richard E., Pfc, Co. B 10th Engr. Combat Bn., Alsace 23 Dec. 1944
Gamous, Bonnie T., Jr., 2d Lt, Co. G 7th Inf, Cisterna Di Littoria 28 Jan. 1944
Gann. Cecil, Pfc, Co. C 7th Inf Regt., Germany 19 Mar. 1945
Ganoe, Grant E., T/5, Med. Det. 41st FA Bn., Le Ferriere 31 Jan. 1944
Ganos, Thomas, Pvt, Med. Det. 15th Inf, Valmonte 2 June 1944
Garcia, Paul V., Pfc, Btry C 441st AAA AW Bn., Germany 30 Apr. 1945
Garcia, Paul R., Pfc, Co. F 30th Inf Regt., Germany 26 Mar. 1945
Garcia, Randolph O., Sgt, Co. E 30th Inf, San Agata Siou 8 Aug. 1943
Garcia, Roberto, Pfc, Rcn Co. 601st TD Bn., Germany 1 Apr. 1945
Garcia, Tomas S., Sgt, Co. A 756th Tank Bn., France 15 Sept. 1944
Gardella, William J., Pfc, Co. H 7th Inf Regt., France 1 Dec. 1944
Gardner, Earl C., Jr., Capt, Med. Det. 30th Inf, S. Italy
Gardner, Floyd H., 1st Sgt, Co. D 756th Tank Bn., Germany 3 May 1945
Gardner, George, 1st Sgt, Hq. & Serv. Co. 10th Engr. Bn., Italy, France 22 Jan. 1945
Gardner, Gerald L., Pfc, Hq. Co. 3d Bn. 30th Inf, Mt. Rothnoo 11 Nov. 1943
Garman, Selvie D., Pfc, Hq. Co. 1st Bn. 30th Inf, Germany 11 Apr. 1945
▲Garman, Wayne C., Sgt, MP Pltn Hq. Co. 3d Inf Div., France, Germany 8 May 1945
Garner, Irby, Sgt, Btry A 9th FA Bn., Africa, Sicily, Italy 5 June 1944
Garner, Joseph N., S/Sgt, Co. H 30th Inf, Germany 20 Apr. 1945
Garner, Ray E., Pvt, Hq. Co. 2d Bn. 7th Inf, Cisterna Di Littoria 20 May 1944
Garoch, Paul M., Pfc, Co. M 15th Inf Regt., Germany 4 Apr. 1945
Garrett, Luther, Cpl, Hq. Co. 1st Bn. 30th Inf, Anzio, Italy
Garrett, Willard M., 2d Lt, Hq. Co. 1st Bn. 7th Inf, Anzio, Italy 28 Feb. 1944
Garrison, Roy, Pfc, Co. M 30th Inf Regt., N. Africa, Sicily, Italy, France, Germany, Austria May 1945
Garritano, Nicholas, Pfc, Hq. Co. 2d Bn. 30th Inf, Colmar
Garrity, Hugh F., Pfc, Co. H 7th Inf Regt., Italy 23 May 1944
Garwood, William, Jr., T/4, Btry B 441st AAA AW Bn., Sicily, Italy, France, Germany 8 May 1945
Gaskin, Hubert, T/Sgt, Hq. Det. 3d Med. Bn., N. Africa, Sicily, Italy, France, Germany May 1945
Gassman, George E., Pfc, Serv. Co., 7th Inf, Sicily, Italy 18 May 1944
Gasperich, John R., Cpl, MP Pltn 3d Inf, Germany 8 May 1945
Gates, Franklin F., Field Dir. Amer. Red Cross, Hq. 3d Inf Div., N. Africa, Sicily, Italy, France 31 Jan. 1945
Gates, Raymond L., 2d Lt, Co. K 7th Inf Regt., France 23 Nov. 1944
Gatto, John A., Capt, DC Med. Det. 30th Inf, N. Africa, Sicily, Italy, France 20 Feb. 1945
Gaugler, Bernard H., 1st Lt, Co. C 756th Tank Bn., France 27 Dec. 1944
▲Gauldin, Lester F., T/4, Btry A 41st FA Bn., France 24 Oct. 1944
Gauthier, Conrad A., Sgt, Co. B 601st TD Bn., N. Africa, Italy, France 15 Jan. 1945
Gaunt, Donald E., T/5, Serv. Co. 15th Inf Regt., Italy 4 June 1944
Gavalas, John P., T/5, Btry A 441st AAA AW Bn., Costello 29 May 1944
Gavenda, George F., Jr., T/5, Co. C 756th Bn., Germany 14 Apr. 1945
▲Gdowski, Joseph L., T/Sgt, Med. Det. 30th Inf Regt., France 15 Mar. 1945
Gedacht, Isidore, Pfc, Co. D 7th Inf Regt., France 15 Aug. 1944
Gee, Merrill T., T/4, Co. B 601st TD Bn., France 23 Jan. 1945
Gehret. Kenneth G., Pfc, Hq. Co. 30th Inf Regt., Sicily, France, Italy 15 Mar. 1945
Geiss, Oliver E., T/Sgt, 3d Sig. Co. Italy, France, Germany 30 Apr. 1945
Geist, Glenn W., T/4, Hq. Btry 3d Inf Div. Arty, Sicily, Italy, France, Germany 8 May 1945
Gelade, Benjamin, Cpl, Co. B 601st TD Bn., Ponte Rotto 29 Feb. 1944
Gell, James E., S/Sgt, Co. A 7th Inf Regt., Germany 18 Mar. 1945
▲Gelsi, Walter A., Pfc, Med. Det. 7th Inf, Cisterna Di Littoria 4 Feb. 1944
Genger, Edward P., 1st Lt, Inf Co. M 30th Inf Regt., France 1 Feb. 1945
▲Genito, Nicholas H., Pvt, Hq. Co. 2d Bn. 30th Inf Regt., France 6 Feb. 1945
Gensler, Donald W., 1st Lt, Co. D 15th Inf, Valmontone 1 June 1944
Gentiluomo, Nicholas J., T/4, Hq. Co. 30th Inf Regt., France 6 Feb. 1945
Gentry, Maxie L., Pfc, Co. D 7th Inf, France 30 Oct. 1944
George, Clarence E., S/Sgt, Rcn Co. 601st TD Bn., N. Africa, Sicily, Italy, France, Germany 5 May 1945
Georgelas, John G., Maj, 3d Div., Volturno 14 Oct. 1943
Geraghty, John F., T/5, Co. A 756th Tank Bn., France 15 Sept. 1944
Geren, Olen G., Pfc, Co. E 30th Inf Regt., France 3 Jan. 1945
Gerety, John H., Lt Col, Inf Spec Trps 3d Inf Div., Italy, France 15 Mar. 1945
Gerg, Robert H., 1st Sgt, Co. I 15th Inf, 18 Sept. 1944
Gerovac, John C., T/Sgt, Cn Co. 15th Inf, Germany 27 Apr. 1945
Gerstein, Harry, S/Sgt, Co. M 7th Inf Regt., France 15 Sept. 1944
Gette, Luther M., Capt, DC Hq. 7th Inf Regt., France, Germany 8 May 1945
Getz, Arlington C., Sgt, Co. A 7th Inf, France 3 Feb. 1945
Giampa, Joseph N., Jr., Pfc, Hq. Co. 30th Inf, Anzio, Italy
Giannico, Anthony, T/5, Hq. Co. 30th Inf, France, Italy 18 Feb. 1945
Gibbons, Charles E., 1st Lt, AGD,Ass't Adj. Gen., Hq. 3d Inf Div., Italy 8 Aug. 1944
▲Gibson, Curtis C., Cpl, Co. C 601st TD Bn., Germany 5 Apr. 1945
Gifford, Dale F., Cpl, Btry A 9th FA Bn., Italy 5 June 1944
Gifford, Coy E., T/Sgt, Co. F 30th Inf, Anzio, Italy 20 Feb. 1944
Gilberg, Ragnar F., Pfc, Co. K 15th Inf, France 13 Sept. 1944
Gilbert, Hennon, 1st Lt, Inf Hq. 1st Bn. 30th Inf, France 5 Feb. 1945

▲ Oak Leaf Cluster.

Gilden, Bert D., 2d Lt, Inf Co. A 756th Tank Bn., France 6 Feb. 1945
▲Gile, Floyd H., S/Sgt, Co. G 30th Inf Regt., France 30 Oct. 1944
▲Giles, Joseph M., 2d Lt, Co. A 756th Tank Bn., Germany 20 Apr. 1945
Gill, Joseph M., Pvt, Hq. Co. 30th Inf, Anzio, Italy 13 Mar. 1944
Gillett, Robert W., T/5, 3d Rcn Trp., France 6 Feb. 1945
Gilliland, Robert L., Cpl, Med. Det. 69th Armd FA Bn., Mignano 28 Dec. 1943
Gillmartin, Russell, Sgt, Serv. Co. 7th Inf, Sicily, Italy 11 Dec. 1943
Ginwright, Wilson L., S/Sgt, Co. K 15th Inf, France 25 Oct. 1944
Giordano, Anthony V., 1st Lt, Co. E 15th Inf, Ponte Rotto 7 Feb. 1944
Giovanni, Joseph C., Pvt, Co. M 15th Inf, Torpes, France 8 Sept. 1944
Girton, Ferol Z., Pvt, Hq. Co. 3d Div., Anzio 18 Mar. 1944
Giusto, Guy, Pfc, Serv. Co. 15th Inf Regt., France 18 Feb. 1945
Giza, Frank J., S/Sgt, Co. L 30th Inf, Carano 25 Apr. 1944
Gladney, Winston T., Pfc, AT Co. 30th Inf Regt., Italy, France, Germany, 8 May 1945
Glantz, Melvin N., Capt, FA MG Sec. 3d Inf Div., France, Germany 8 May 1945
Glass, Carl A., Sgt, Btry C 441st AAA AW Bn., Sicily, Italy, France, Germany 8 May 1945
Glass, Edward B., S/Sgt, Cn Co. 30th Inf, Germany
Glaze, Andrew J., Jr., Sgt, Hq. Det. 3d Inf Div., Italy, France, Germany 8 May 1945
Gleeson, Paul L., Pfc, Co. F 7th Inf Regt., Germany 7 May 1945
▲Glos, Karl F., Lt Col, IG Dep Hq. 3d Inf Div., Italy, France, Germany, Austria 8 May 1945
Glover, Elbert E., T/4, Hq. Co. 1st Bn. 7th Inf Regt., France 22 Jan. 1945
Gnadt, Charles L., 1st Sgt, Co. A 15th Inf, Anzio 24 Mar. 1944
Gnatek, Stanley W., Sgt, Btry A 9th FA Bn., Italy 30 May 1944
Goad, Lawrence T., T/5, Med. Det. 30th Inf Regt., France 23 Jan. 1945
Gochnour, Dwain T., Sgt, Hq. Co. 2d Bn., 15th Inf, Sicily 18 Aug. 1943
Goddard, Roy W., S/Sgt, Btry B 41st FA Bn., France, Germany, Austria 8 May 1945
Godfrey, Samuel W., S/Sgt, Co. F 30th Inf, Carano 8 Feb. 1944
Godlewski, Henry E., Cpl, Co. B 601st TD Bn., Isola Bella 29 Feb. 1944
▲Goehl, George E., T/Sgt, AT Co. 15th Inf Regt., France 28 Oct. 1944
Goercke, Forrest W., 1st Sgt, Co. E 7th Inf Regt., Italy 25 May 1944
Goff, Arthur, Pfc, Co. L 30th Inf, Cisterna Di Littoria 8 Feb. 1944
Goff, Hallie L., Pfc, Hq. Co. 1st Bn. 30th Inf, France 1 Oct. 1944
Goff, Olden M., Pfc, Hq. Co. 1st Bn. 15th Inf, France 26 Dec. 1944
Goldberg, David, Pfc, Hq. Co. 2d Bn. 7th Inf Regt., Italy, France 5 Feb. 1945
Goldberg, William, Pfc, Co. F 30th Inf Regt., Germany 19 Apr. 1945
Golden, Nathan L., M/Sgt, Photo Int. Unit Hq. 3d Inf Div., France, Germany, Austria 5 May 1945
Goldman, Hyman, Pvt, Med. Det. 30th Inf, France 29 Oct. 1944
Goldsmith, James F., Col, Co. B 601st TD Bn., Isola Bella 29 Feb. 1944
Goldstein, Edward, Pfc, Btry D 441st AAA AW Bn., France 1 Feb. 1945
Golichowski, Richard R., Cpl, Med. Det. 7th Inf, France 6 Oct. 1944
Golnick, Kenneth A., T/5, Hq. Btry 9th FA Bn., Sicily, Italy, France 15 Sept. 1944
Gonter, Charles C., T/5, Co. A 601st TD Bn., Tunisia 23 Mar. 1943
Gonzales, Gonzalo J., Pfc, Med. Det. 30th Inf, Faucogney 21 Sept. 1944
Gonzales, Oscar T., Pfc, Med. Det. 30th Inf Regt., France 17 Dec. 1944
Gonzales, Hector, Sgt, Co. B 30th Inf Regt., France 4 Dec. 1944
▲Goodman, Robert H., T/Sgt, Co. E 30th Inf Regt., Germany 26 Mar. 1945
Goodrich, Donald A., S/Sgt, AT Co. 30th Inf, Vosges
▲Goodson, Elbert R., Pfc, Hq. Co. 3d Bn. 7th Inf Regt., France 24 Oct. 1944
Goodwin, Benjamin F., Lt Col, 3d QM Co., France, Germany, Austria 8 May 1945
Gordon, Oscar, S/Sgt, Btry B 441st AAA AW Bn., Sicily, Italy, France, Germany 8 May 1945
Gordy, Richard S., Pfc, Cn Co. 15th Inf Regt., France 28 Jan. 1945
Gorecki, Edward T., S/Sgt, AT Co. 30th Inf, France 24 Dec. 1944
Gorman, Howard G., Pfc, Co. M 15th Inf, Cisterna Di Littoria 2 Feb. 1944
Goslin, Henry B., Pfc, Co. C 30th Inf, Vosges
Goulet, Robert R., T/5, Hq. Btry 3d Inf Div. Arty, France 16 Aug. 1944
Gourley, Donald F., Capt, Inf Co. C 756th Tank Bn., Italy 27 May 1944
Gorzelanczyk, Ladislaus F., Pvt, Co. H 7th Inf Regt., France 1 Dec. 1944
Gover, Jack W., Jr., Pfc, Med. Det. 7th Inf Regt., France 3 Nov. 1944
Grace, Cornelius J., Jr., 1st Lt, CO Co. H 30th Inf, La Croix, France 15 Aug. 1944
Graham, Eugene B., 1st Lt, Hq. Co. 30th Inf, Germany
Graham, Frank R., 1st Lt, Co. A 15th Inf Regt., France 16 Mar. 1945
Granado, Tomas D., Pvt, Co. A 10th Engr. Combat Bn., France 5 Nov. 1944
Grande, Gilbert B., Pfc, Co. C 10th Engr., Cisterna 23 May 1944
Grandmaison, Robert J., Pfc, Co. C 7th Inf Regt., Germany 16 Mar. 1945
Grant, Clarence J., 1st Lt, Inf Hq. 2d Bn. 7th Inf Regt., France 21 Sept. 1944
Grasser, Lester S., Pfc, Co. D 3d Med. Bn., N. Africa, Sicily, Italy, Germany, Austria 8 May 1945
Grasso, Paul, Sgt, Btry A 441st AAA AW Bn., Cori 24 May 1944
Grasso, Constantino, Cpl, Co. I 15th Inf Regt., France 18 Nov. 1944
Graves, John E., T/5, Btry C 441st AAA AW Bn., Italy, France, Germany 8 May 1945
Graves, Vance E., Serv. Btry 10th FA Bn., N. Africa, Sicily, Italy, France, Germany 27 Apr. 1945
Gray, Breece E., Pfc, Co. B 30th Inf Regt., Germany 16 Mar. 1945
Gray, Frederick R., Pfc, Co. A 30th Inf, France 3 Nov. 1944
▲(2) Gray, Samuel L., Cpl, Btry C 441st AAA AW Bn., France 20 Nov. 1944
Gray, Thomas F., Sgt, Co. B 30th Inf Regt., Germany 20 Mar. 1945
Grecni, Emil, T/Sgt, Co. E 751st Tank Bn., Italy 18 Nov. 1943
Greco, Guiseppe V., Sgt, Co. A 30th Inf Regt., Germany 28 Apr. 1945
Grefe, John H., Pfc, Co. A 15th Inf, Cisterna Di Littoria 24 May 1944
Green, Daniel H., Jr., T/Sgt, Co. C 601st TD Bn., Germany 10 Apr. 1945
Green, Richard R., T/5, Hq. & Hq. Det. 3d Med. Bn., N. Africa, Sicily, Italy, France, Germany, Austria 8 May 1945
▲Green, Roy J., T/5, Med. Det. 7th Inf, Cerre Les Nordy, France 13 Sept. 1944
Green, U. L., Pvt, Med. Det 7th Inf, Artena 1 June 1944
Greenwood, Lawrence W., Sgt, Co. K 30th Inf Regt., France 17 Dec. 1944
Greer, Frederick R., T/5, Med. Det. 7th Inf Regt., Anzio, Italy 22 Jan. 1944
Greer, Harold E., Maj, Inf S-3 Inf Regt., France 30 Oct. 1944
Greer, Hohn T., Pfc, Co. H 7th Inf Regt., France 1 Dec. 1944
Gregoire, Leo P., Pfc, Co. A 15th Inf Regt., France 25 Oct. 1944
Gregory, Chester H., S/Sgt, Co. C 7th Inf Regt., Germany 16 Mar. 1945
Gregory, Clyde R., Pfc, MP Pltn 3d Inf Div., Anzio, Italy 10 Feb. 1944
Gresak, Matthew P., Pfc, Co. D 7th Inf, France 22 Jan. 1945
Gribinas, John, Pvt, Hq. Btry 3d IDA, Anzio, Italy 29 Feb. 1944
Griek, Glen D., 2d Lt, Co. M 15th Inf, Isola Bella 2 Mar. 1944
Griffiths, Robert A., T/4, 3d Inf Div. Band, N. Africa, Sicily, Italy 31 Dec. 1943
Grimes, Leonard R., S/Sgt, Hq. Co. 7th Inf, Sicily, Italy 18 Nov. 1944
▲Grimes, Lyle C., Lt Col, Finance Dept. Hq. 3d Inf Div., Italy, France, Germany, Austria 8 May 1945
Grimitt, Billy, Pfc, Co. C 3d Med. Bn., France, Germany 8 May 1945
Grinnell, Sidney G., Pfc, Hq. Btry 9th FA Bn., Anzio, Italy 29 Feb. 1944
Griswold, George W., T/5, Hq. Co. 30th Inf Regt., Italy, France 15 Sept. 1944
Groden, Raymond, Pfc, Co. C 30th Inf Regt., France 7 Feb. 1945
Groeger, John P., Cpl, Interp. 3d Div., Germany 8 May 1945
▲Groff, Howard W., Pfc, Hq. Co. 2d Bn. 15th Inf, Cori 26 May 1944
▲Groden, Raymond, T/Sgt, Co. C 30th Inf, Germany
Grondin, Robert J., Pfc, Hq. Co. 1st Bn. 30th Inf, Lariano 27 May 1944
Gronewald, Gail J., Sgt, Co. G 7th Inf, Besancon 4 Sept. 1944
Gross, Raymond L., T/5, Btry B 10th FA Bn., France 26 Jan. 1945
▲Grossman, Nathan H., 1st Sgt, Co. D 30th Inf, France 7 Sept. 1944
Groves, Cleburn F., T/4, MP Pltn 3d Inf, France 10 Oct. 1944
Growcock, Walter J., T/4, Btry C 441st AAA AW Bn., France 26 Nov. 1944
Gruber, David P., 1st Lt, Serv. Btry 39th FA Bn., Cisterna 24 May 1944
Grumbacher, Ernst, Pvt, Hq. Co. 2d Bn. 30th Inf, Cisterna Di Littoria 24 May 1944
Grumelot, Ivan M., Cpl, Co. B 601st TD Bn., France 25 Jan. 1945
Guard, Charles A., Pvt, Hq. Co. 30th Inf, Italy 5 June 1944
Guard, Ernest K., 2d Lt, AT Co. 7th Inf, Orchi, France 3 Oct. 1944
Guber, Alfred M., M/Sgt, Hq. Co. 3d Inf Div., Anzio, Italy 1 May 1944
Guelker, Frederick John, Pvt, Co. I 7th Inf Regt., France 6 Oct. 1944
Guild, Clyde W., Cpl, Co. B 756th Tank Bn., France 6 Feb. 1945
Gulizia, John J., Pfc, Co. M 30th Inf Regt., Italy 23 May 1944
Gulowacz, Thomas, Pfc, Co. E 7th Inf, Cisterna Di Littoria 1 Mar. 1944
Gumley, Wayne I., T/4, Serv. Co. 7th Inf Regt., France 5 Jan. 1945
Gunderson, Orville M., S/Sgt, Hq. Btry 39th FA Bn., France 13 Sept. 1944
Gurley, Arley B., Pfc, Hq. Co. 15th Inf, Germany 17 Mar. 1945
Gursky, Edward S., Pfc, Co. B 756th Tank Bn., France 29 Sept. 1944
Gusler, Noel, Jr., Pfc, Co. I 30th Inf, Valmontone 2 June 1944
Gustafson, Elmer W., Cpl, Btry B 10th FA Bn., Cisterna 19 Feb. 1944
Gustafson, Frank Q., Jr., S/Sgt, Hq. Btry 9th FA Bn., Sicily, Italy, France 15 Sept 1944
▲Guyre, Leonard J., 1st Lt, Inf Hq. Co. 2d Bn. 7th Inf Regt., Italy, France, Germany 26 Mar. 1945

Haase, Clement L., Jr., 1st Lt, MC Co. B 3d Med. Bn., France, Germany, Austria 8 May 1945
Haase, Robert S., T/Sgt, 3d QM Co., Dragoni 27 Oct. 1943
Hacker, Raymond A., Pfc, Hq. Co. 3d Bn. 30th Inf Regt., Italy 10 Mar. 1944
Hadle, Joseph C., Pvt, Serv. Btry 9th FA Bn., Valmontone 1 June 1944
Hadsell, Francis P., Co. C 7th Inf, France 16 Aug. 1944
Haene, Walter H., Capt, Co. D 751st TD Bn., Italy 4 June 1944
Haglund, Wesley C., Pfc, Hq. Btry 39th FA Bn., France 19 Mar. 1945
Hagman, James A., T/3, Hq. 3d Inf Div., Italy, France, Germany 21 Mar. 1945
Hahn, Frederick G., T/5, Hq. Co. 1st Bn. 15th Inf Regt., France 25 Sept. 1944
Hahn, George, Pfc, Hq. Co. 30th Inf Regt., France 29 Dec. 1944
Hain, Russell L., Pfc, Co. M 15th Inf, Artena 2 June 1944
Haines, John R., Pfc, Hq. 3d Inf Div., France, Germany 25 Mar. 1945
Hall, Bert, Jr., Pfc, Co. D 7th Inf, Anzio, Italy 15 Apr. 1944
Hall, Charles W., Sgt, Co. A 601st TD Bn., Germany 15 Mar. 1945
▲Hall, Fred E., S/Sgt, Co. G 15th Inf, France 5 Feb. 1945
Hall, Gerald V., T/5, Hq. Co. 1st Bn. 7th Inf, Anzio, Italy 31 Jan. 1944
Hall, Quince S., Capt, Hq. Btry 41st FA Bn., Sicily 6 Aug. 1943
Hall, Ralph E., T/Sgt, Hq. Co. 3d Bn. 7th Inf, France 6 Oct. 1944
Hall, Russell B., Hq. Btry 41st FA Bn., Coronia, Sicily 5 Aug. 1943
Hall, Russell C., Pfc, Co. K 15th Inf, France 27 Dec. 1944
Hall, William H., T/5, Hq. Co. 30th Inf Regt., France 19 Nov. 1944
Halley, Walter E., Sgt, Co. B 7th Inf, Anzio, Italy 26 Apr. 1944
Halstad, Anton S., S/Sgt, Co. E 30th Inf, Italy 30 June 1944
Hamill, Alfred D., T/5, Btry A 39th FA Bn., France 30 Jan. 1945
Hamilton, Francis E., Pvt, Hq. Co. 1st Bn. 15th Inf, Cisterna Di Littoria 12 Feb. 1944
Hamilton, George W., Pfc, Co. H 15th Inf Regt., France 21 Dec. 1944
Hamilton, John F., S/Sgt, 3d CIC Det., France 14 Sept. 1944
Hamilton, John M., 1st Lt, Co. B 756th Tank Bn., France 22 Nov. 1944
Hamilton, Robert B., Cpl, Hq. Btry 3d IDA, Anzio, Italy 29 Feb. 1944
Hammond, James A., Jr., T/4, Co. A 601st TD Bn., Italy, France, Germany 5 June 1945
Hammons, Harless, S/Sgt, Co. B 7th Inf Regt., France 1 Nov. 1944
▲Haney, Sigsby C., Pfc, Co. D 15th Inf, Germany 26 Apr. 1945
▲Hanley, John F., Capt, Chaplain Hq. 2d Bn. 30th Inf Regt., France 12 Oct. 1944
Hanly, John R., T/5, Btry A 441st AAA AW Bn., Costello 29 May 1944
Hanna, Beauford L., Pfc, Co. K 7th Inf Regt., France 23 Nov. 1944
Hannah, Loring A., Pfc, Hq. Co. 30th Inf, Cisterna Di Littoria 20 May 1944
Hannah, William C., Pfc, Hq. Btry 41st FA Bn., Anzio, Italy 17 Feb. 1944
Hanner, Orvil M., Sgt, Co. M 7th Inf, Cisterna Di Littoria 26 May 1944
Hansberry, Charles A., Sgt, Co. B 30th Inf Regt., near Guemar, France 23 Jan. 1945
Hansen, Clifford C., T/4, Hq. Btry 9th FA Bn., Sicily, Italy, France, Germany 8 May 1945
Hansen, Edwin L., Pfc, Co. B 15th Inf, Anzio, Italy 2 Feb. 1944
Hansen, John A., Sgt, Serv. Co. 7th Inf, Sicily 10 July 1943
Hansen, John L., Pfc, Hq. Co. 1st Bn. 7th Inf, France 6 Sept. 1944
Hansen, Wilford H., T/3, Med. Det. 39th FA Bn., N. Africa, Sicily, Italy, France, Germany 8 May 1945
Hapanowich, Paul, Pfc, Co. C 10th Engr. Combat Bn., France 8 Oct. 1944
Harbour, David E., Sgt, Btry A 39th FA Bn., S. France 5 Oct. 1944
Harder, Fitzgerald F., Pfc, Hq. Co. 2d Bn. 15th Inf Regt., Anzio, Italy 22 Mar. 1944
Hardy, Norman L., T/5, Co. B 756th Tank Bn., France 6 Feb. 1945
Hargens, George A., T/5, Co. C 601st TD Bn., Anzio, Italy 7 Feb. 1944
Harless, Richard A., Cpl, Btry B 39th FA Bn., Cisterna 10 Mar. 1944
Harmon, Bernis H., Pfc, Co. 7th Inf, France 16 Aug. 1944
Harmon, John F., 1st Lt, Co. C 756th Tank Bn., Presle, France 13 Sept. 1944
Harper, Audie N., 1st Lt, Btry B 39th FA Bn., Statigline 21 Oct. 1943
▲Harrell, Ben, Col, CO 7th Inf, France 15 Nov. 1944
Harrell, Frank H., 2d Lt, Co. I 30th Inf, Herbaville 4 Oct. 1944

▲ Oak Leaf Cluster.

Harrell, Thomas E., Pfc, Co. H 30th Inf Regt., France 9 Jan. 1945
Harris, Aaron G., Capt, Sig. Corps Ass't Div. Sig. Off. 3d Inf Div., France, Germany, Austria 8 May 1945
Harris, Emmett, Pfc, Co. C 7th Inf Regt., Germany 15 Mar. 1945
Harris, Glenn W., 1st Lt, Inf Hq. Co. 2d Bn. 15th Inf Regt., France 20 Jan. 1945
Harris, Hunter L., Pfc, Co. C 7th Inf, France 29 Jan. 1945
Harris, John T., Pvt, Co. A 601st TD Bn., Carano 19 Feb. 1944
Harris, Paul G., Capt, Co. B 15th Inf, Beuandon, France 13 Sept. 1944
Harris, Robert E., M/Sgt, Hq. Det. 3d Inf Div., Africa, Sicily, Italy 19 Nov. 1943
Harrison, Howard W., 1st Lt, AT Co. 30th Inf, Colmar
Harrison, Merrill S., T/5, Hq. Co., Italy 27 June 1944
Harrison, William H., S/Sgt, Co. B 15th Inf, France 30 Jan. 1945
▲Harrison, William R., Maj, CO 601st TD Bn., Germany 20 Apr. 1945
Hart, Darwin S., S/Sgt, Co. D 30th Inf, N. Africa, Sicily, Italy, France, Germany, Austria 8 May 1945
Hart, James D., S/Sgt, Co. A 30th Inf Regt., France 6 Feb. 1945
Hart, James H., S/Sgt, Hq. Co. 1st Bn. 15th Inf Regt., France 24 Jan. 1945
Hart, John R., Pvt, Hq. Co. 601st TD Bn., Dussgltis 16 Feb. 1943
Hart, Leon M., Capt, MC Med. Det. 2d Bn. 15th Inf Regt., France 9 Feb. 1945
Hartley, Willis E., Pfc, Hq. Co. 3d Inf Div., French Morocco 15 Nov. 1942
Hartline, Taylor N., Sgt, Co. A 756th Tank Bn., France 15 Sept. 1944
Hartstein, Theodore, T/4, Hq. Co. 30th Inf Regt., Africa, Sicily, Italy, France 22 Oct. 1944
Hartstern, Carl J., Pfc, Co. E 7th Inf, Cisterna Di Littoria 1 Mar. 1944
Haskins, Richard D., Pvt, Co. I 15th Inf, France 29 Dec. 1944
Haspel, James E., 2d Lt, Inf Co. B 756th Tank Bn., France 27 Dec. 1944
Hassett, Charles J., Cpl, Hq. Co. 30th Inf, Valmontone 1 June 1944
Hastings, Earie G., Jr., Capt, Btry A 41st FA Bn., Anzio 23 May 1944
Hatch, Floyd G., 1st Lt, Serv. Btry 39th FA Bn., Rocca Romana 10 Nov. 1943
Hatch, Smith E., Pfc, Hq. Co. 756th Tank Bn., France 4 Oct. 1944
Hatcher, Daniel W., Sgt, Cn Co. 30th Inf Regt., France 18 Aug. 1944
Hatton, James W., Pvt, Co. C 10th Engr. Bn., Cisterna 23 May 1944
Hatzimagari, George J., Pfc, Co. I 7th Inf Regt., France 24 Oct. 1944
Haupert, Paul E., T/5, Btry C 39th FA Bn., N. Africa, Sicily, Italy, France, Germany, Austria 8 May 1945
Havel, William H., Pvt, Co. M 15th Inf, Isola Bella 3 Mar. 1944
Hawbaker, Dale K., Pfc, Co. I 15th Inf, France 29 Dec. 1944
Hawks, Robert A., Sgt, Co. B 601st TD Bn., Ponte Rotto 3 Mar. 1944
Hawkins, Alfred, Cpl, Btry B 441st AAA AW Bn., Cisterna 22 Mar. 1944
Hawkins, Paul E., Pfc, Co. L 30th Inf, France 11 Nov. 1944
Hawkins, Robert L., 1st Lt, Inf Cn Co. 15th Inf Regt., France 23 Dec. 1944
▲Haycraft, Wilbert O., Sgt, Co. A 756th Tank Bn., Germany 29 Apr. 1945
Haydel, Otis J., Cpl, Btry B 39th FA Bn., Dampvalley-Les-Colombe, France 13 Sept. 1944
Hayden, James E., Capt, Hq. 10th Engr. Bn., Sicily, France 8 Apr. 1944
Hayes, Edward J., 1st Lt, Inf Hq. Co. 1st Bn. 30th Inf Regt., France 24 Jan. 1945
Hayes, J. B., Sgt, Co. K 30th Inf Regt., Germany 28 Mar. 1945
Hayes, Louis E., Pfc, Co. C 7th Inf Regt., France 20 Oct. 1944
Hayes, Paul L., Capt, Inf Co. B 30th Inf, France, Germany 15 Mar. 1945
Haymond, Summers C., Pfc, Hq. Co. 3d Bn. 7th Inf Regt., France 16 Jan. 1945
Haynes, Donald L., 1st Lt, Co. H 30th Inf, Anzio, Italy 23 May 1944
Haynes, Glenn, Sgt, Hq. Btry 30th FA Bn., France 4 Nov. 1944
Head, Warren, T/5, Hq. 3d Inf Div., France, Germany 8 May 1945
Heard, John B., Pfc, Co. H 30th Inf Regt., France 12 Oct. 1944
Heard, John W., Capt, Co. C 756th Tank Bn., Germany 14 Apr. 1945
Hearn, Leonard E., S/Sgt, Hq. Co. 601st TD Bn., Ponte Rotto 3 Mar. 1944
Heath, Ralph S., Jr., Capt, Hq. 3d Inf Div. FA Btry, Sicily 6 Aug. 1943
Heath, Virgil L., T/5, Hq. Co. 2d Bn. 7th Inf Regt., France 25 Jan. 1945
Heathcoe, Edwin J., T/4, Hq. Btry 9th FA Bn., N. Africa, Sicily, Italy, France, Germany 8 May 1945
Hedberg, Arthur J., T/4, Hq. & Hq. Btry 41st FA Bn., France 17 Dec. 1944
Hegedus, Gene J., T/3, 3d Sig. Co., Italy, France, Germany 8 May 1945
Heidrick, Benny J., T/5, Co. A 756th Tank Bn., Germany 19 Mar. 1945
Hein, Frederik C., T/5, Hq. Btry 9th FA Bn., Sicily, Italy, France 31 Dec. 1944
Heiman, Arthur H., S/Sgt, Co. A 30th Inf, Begude, France 28 Aug. 1944
▲(3) Heintges, John A., Col, Inf CO 7th Inf, Germany 20 Apr. 1945
Heinz, Sylvester H., Pfc, Co. K 15th Inf, Italy 15 Oct. 1943
Heiser, Raymond B., Pfc, Btry C 9th FA Bn., Artena 30 May 1944
▲Heistand, Joseph T., Pfc, Hq. Btry 39th FA Bn., France 13 Sept. 1944
Heitkamp, Hugh H., Sgt, Hq. Det. 3d Inf Div., France 23 Dec. 1944
Helfer, Abe, Pvt, Co. D 7th Inf, Germany 15 Mar. 1945
Heller, William, T/4, 3d Sig. Co., France, Germany, Austria 8 May 1945
Hemann, Henry A., T/5, Hq. Co. 7th Inf, Palestrina 3 June 1944
Hemel, Julian S., Pfc, Btry C 41st FA Bn., France 12 Sept. 1944
Hempleman, Marvin, Pfc, MP Pltn 3d Inf Div., France Feb. 1945
Henderson, Billy, Pfc, Co. F 7th Inf Regt., France 14 Sept. 1944
Henderson, Marvin J., CWO, Hq. Btry 3d Div. Arty, Sicily, Italy, France, Germany 8 May 1945
Hendrixson, Waldo, S/Sgt, Co. H 15th Inf, Germany 19 Mar. 1945
Henkelman, Edward G., T/5, Btry D 441st AAA AW Bn., France 10 Nov. 1944
Henley, Charles R., Sgt, Btry A 39th FA Bn., San Fratello, Sicily 3 Aug. 1943
Henneberry, William F., Pfc, Co. M 30th Inf, France 28 Aug. 1944
Hennings, Gerald T., T/Sgt, Hq. Co. 1st Bn. 7th Inf Regt., France 7 Oct. 1944
▲Henry, Glenn, Pfc, Med. Det. 30th Inf Regt., France 1 Feb. 1945
Henry, John E., Cpl, Btry C 9th FA Bn., N. Africa, Sicily, Italy, France, Germany, Austria 8 May 1945
Henry, Kenneth H., Pvt, Btry B 39th FA Bn., Vagney 25 Jan. 1944
Henshaw, Otis H., T/Sgt, Co. F 30th Inf, Faucogney, France 21 Sept. 1944
Henson, Edwin L., Sgt, MP Pltn Hq. Co. 3d Inf Div., France, Germany 8 May 1945
Herman, Clarence J., S/Sgt, Hq. Co. 2d Bn. 30th Inf Regt., France 22 Nov. 1944
Hern, Joseph F., Pfc, Co. K 30th Inf, Anzio, Italy 20 Apr. 1944
Herr, Allen J., Pfc, MP Pltn Hq. Co. 3d Inf Div., France, Germany, Austria 8 May 1945
Herlihy, John P., 1st Lt, Btry C 441st AAA AW Bn., Germany 30 Apr. 1945
Heroman, William L., T/Sgt, Serv. Co. 7th Inf Regt., N. Africa, Sicily, Italy, France, Germany 4 May 1945
Herrera, Laurencio, T/5, Btry C 441st AAA AW Bn., Germany 27 Mar. 1945
Herring, Charles J., Pfc, Cn Co. 30th Inf, Colmar
Herrmann, Donald H., Pfc, Co. D 30th Inf Regt., Germany 19 Apr. 1945
Hershatter, Milton A., Pfc, Hq. Co. 3d Bn. 30th Inf, France 7 Feb. 1945
Hertel, Arthur D., Cpl, Cn Co. 7th Inf, Cisterna Di Littoria 24 Mar. 1944
Hess, Frank P., Jr., 1st Sgt, Hq. Btry 441st AAA AW Bn., Sicily, Italy, France, Germany 8 May 1945
Hess, Kenneth H., S/Sgt, Co. G 15th Inf, Adelans, France 16 Sept. 1944
Hetzner, Herbert J., T/5, 3d Rcn Trp., France 28 Oct. 1944
Heydon, William T., T/5, Btry A 441st AAA AW Bn., Borgo Montello 4 Feb. 1944
Hiatt, Charles C., Pfc, Co. D 7th Inf Regt., France 23 Jan. 1945
Hicks, Boris A., 1st Lt, Inf Hq. 3d Bn. 30th Inf Regt., Italy 8 Mar. 1944
Hicks, Clarence S., Pfc, Co. F 30th Inf Regt., Germany 20 Apr. 1945
Hicks, Leo L., 1st Sgt, Co. C 7th Inf Regt., France 12 Sept. 1944
Hicks, William R., Capt, Inf Hq. 3d Inf Div., Italy, France, Germany, Austria 8 May 1945
High, John J., S/Sgt, Co. K 30th Inf, Presle, France 13 Sept. 1944
Hilderbrand, Joe B., Pfc, Co. L 7th Inf, Torre De Padaglione 25 Apr. 1944
Hilkey, Robert E., T/4, Co. B 10th Engr. Combat Bn., France 5 Feb. 1945
Hilkey, Robert E., T/4, Co. B 10th Engr. Combat Bn., France 5 Feb. 1945
Hill, Chester W., 1st Lt, FA Hq. 10th FA Bn., France 24 Jan. 1945
▲Hill, Dennis H., T/4, 3d Sig. Co., Italy, France, Germany Apr. 1945
Hill, Henry F., S/Sgt, Med. Det. 30th Inf, Germany
Hill, Sterling L., Capt, Inf Hq. 3d Inf Div., France, Germany 25 Mar. 1945
Hill, Walter A., Jr., Pvt, Hq. Co. 3d Div., France 2 Nov. 1944
Hilton, Charles D., Capt, Coast Arty Corps 441st AAA AW Bn., Italy, France, Germany, Austria 8 May 1945
Hilts, Richard B., Sgt, Co. I 30th Inf, St. Die 28 Oct. 1944
Hilvick, Anthony, S/Sgt, Hq. Co. 3d Bn. 30th Inf
Himmelfarb, Joseph, Pvt, Hq. Co. 1st Bn. 15th Inf Regt., Germany 18 Mar. 1945
Hinch, John F., Pfc, Co. L 30th Inf Regt., France 8 Sept. 1944
Hindman, Paul L., Pvt, Hq. Btry 41st FA Bn., Le Ferriere, Italy 2 Mar. 1944
Hines, Daniel C., Pfc, Co. A 15th Inf Regt., France 23 Dec. 1944
Hinote, Clyde H., Pvt, Co. M 7th Inf, Anzio, Italy 3 Mar. 1944
Hinton, David G., Pvt, 3d Sig. Co., Italy 5 June 1944
Hipple, Robert E., T/5, Btry B 10th FA Bn., N. Africa, Sicily, Italy, France, Germany 8 May 1945
Hiritz, Steve, S/Sgt, Co. A 30th Inf, Colmar
Hirschhorn, Solomon, Cpl, Btry C 441st AAA AW Bn., Germany 27 Mar. 1945
Hirshkovitz, Jacob J., T/5, Co. B 3d Med. Bn., Germany 20 Mar. 1945
Hite, John B., M/Sgt, Hq. 3d Inf Div., N. Africa, Sicily, Italy, France, Germany, Austria 8 May 1945
▲Hixson, James C., Sgt, Co. H 30th Inf Regt., France 9 Jan. 1945
Hoadley, Carl, Pvt, Med. Det. 7th Inf, Cisterna Di Littoira 24 May 1944
Hoefke, Robert C., S/Sgt, Co. A 7th Inf Regt., France 23 Jan. 1945
Hodge, Forrest W., S/Sgt, Co. L 30th Inf
Hoerstman, Robert W., Pfc, Co. H 15th Inf, Isola Bella 25 Jan. 1944
Hoey, Frederick E., Pfc, Co. L 15th Inf, Cisterna Di Littoria 23 May 1944
Hoff, Louis R., T/4, Med. Det. 15th Inf, France 8 Feb. 1945
Hoffman, Charles M., T/5, AT Co. 7th Inf Regt., Italy 22 May 1944
Hoffman, Harry, Ist Lt, Co. L 30th Inf, France 16 Dec. 1944
Hoffman, Richard, Pfc, Co. H 15th Inf, Anzio, Italy 26 Jan. 1944
Hoffmeister, Donald E., Lt Col, CO 10th FA Bn., Italy 5 June 1944
Hoffner, Albert F., Pfc, Hq. Co. 1st Bn. 7th Inf, Italy 30 Jan. 1944
Hogan, Dennis D., Capt, FA Ass't S-3 Hq. 3d Inf Div. Arty, N. Africa, Sicily, Italy, France, Germany, Austria 8 May 1945
Hogue, Archie F., Jr., Pvt, Co. H 30th Inf, Sicily 11 Aug. 1943
▲(2) Hollenbaugh, Russell W., 2d Lt, Co. B 7th Inf, Padiglione 23 Apr. 1944
Holder, Sorrelle, T/Sgt, Co. B 30th Inf, Padiglione 20 Feb. 1944
Holder, Walter C., Pvt, Hq. Co. 2d Bn. 30th Inf, Brelo, Sicily 11 Aug. 1943
▲Holderbaum, Edward, Pfc, Hq. Co. 1st Bn. 30th Inf Regt., France 17 Dec. 1944
Holley, Jessie W., T/5, Co. G 7th Inf Regt., France 16 Jan. 1945
Hollis, Hosea T., Cpl, Hq. Co. 7th Inf, France 18 Feb. 1945
Hollis, James H., Pfc, Co. M 30th Inf Regt., Italy 23 May 1944
Hollis, Walter R., Sgt, Co. A 30th Inf, Colmar
Holstein, Earnest B., Sgt, Co. A 601st TD Bn., France 1 Feb. 1945
Holt, Guy D., Sgt, Co. H 15th Inf, France 27 Dec. 1944
Holt, Joe T., T/4, 3d Inf Div. Band, N. Africa, Sicily, Italy 31 Dec. 1943
Holtje, Arthur M., Pfc, Btry B 9th FA Bn., Italy 25 May 1944
Holton, John J., Pfc, Btry D 441st AAA AW Bn., France 29 Dec. 1944
Homer, Allan V., Pvt, Btry C 9th FA Bn., Artena 30 May 1944
Hoover, James B., T/4, Btry A 441st AAA AW Bn., France 23 Jan. 1945
Hopkins, Donald E., Pvt, Co. H 30th Inf Regt., France 30 Oct. 1944
Hopper, Deroy, Sgt, Co. B 30th Inf Regt., France 10 Dec. 1944
Horan, Lawrence T., T/5, Hq. Co. 756th Tank Bn., France, Germany 8 May 1945
▲Horan, Philip G., 1st Lt, Co. F 30th Inf, Campo Morto 9 Feb. 1944
Horaney, George R., Sgt, Co. C 601st TD Bn., Italy, France, Germany, Austria May 1945
Horder, William H., Sgt, Co. D 30th Inf, Anzio, Italy
Horne, Ammie W., Pfc, Rcn Co. 601st TD Bn., El Guettar, Tunisia 23 Mar. 1943
Horne, Chevis F., Capt, Chap. Corps Hq. 7th Inf, Sicily, Italy, Anzio 29 Feb. 1944
Horner, William H., Sgt, Co. D 30th Inf Regt., Italy 28 May 1944
Horowitz, Sam, T/4, Hq. Co. 2d Bn. 30th Inf, Anzio, Italy 10 Mar. 1944
Horton, George H., Pfc, Hq. Co. 1st Bn. 30th Inf, Colmar
Horton, Robert L., Pfc, Hq. Co. 30th Inf Regt., France 10 Nov. 1944
Horton, Robert V., Capt, Inf 3d Bn. 7th Inf Regt., Germany 25 Apr. 1945
Horvatt, John S., Pvt, Med. Det. 7th Inf, Germany 20 Apr. 1945
Horvath, Stephen J., T/4, Co. C 756th Tank Bn., France 1 Feb. 1945
Horvath, William S., Pfc, Batl Ptrl 15th Inf, Roccamassima 28 May 1944
Horwedel, Arnold V., Pfc, Co. A 7th Inf Regt., France 27 Sept. 1944
Hosmer, Rawson R., Capt, MC 30th Inf, Montelimar, France 28 Aug. 1944
Hostetter, John A., Pfc, Co. M 30th Inf, Baraques 29 Oct. 1944
▲Houlette, Kenneth N., 1st Lt, Hq. Co. 1st Bn. 30th Inf, France 19 Nov. 1944
Hounshell, Anderson H., Cpl, Btry C 441st AAA AW Bn., Germany 30 Apr. 1945
Houp, Ben W., Pfc, Co. H 30th Inf Regt., France 23 Jan. 1945
House, Arthur L., T/3, 3d Sig. Co., Italy 22 Mar. 1944
Houseman, David P., Cpl, Co. C 10th Engr. Combat Bn., France 4 Dec. 1944
Hovis, Guy W., Sgt, Co. B 7th Inf, Sapois, France 9 Oct. 1944
Howard, Jessie R., Pfc, Serv. Co. 756th Tank Bn., France, Germany, Austria 8 May 1945

▲ Oak Leaf Cluster.

Howard, William R., T/3, Med. Det. 7th Inf, Italy, France, Germany May 1945
Howell, George W., Pvt, Co. B 7th Inf, Artena 28 May 1944
Howell, Harley L., T/Sgt, Hq. Co. 3d Bn. 15th Inf Regt., France 9 Sept. 1944
Howland, Henry U., Capt, Hq. 15th Inf, France 25 Aug. 1944
Hoza, Rudolph G., Pfc, Hq. Co. 2d Bn. 7th Inf Regt., France 9 Nov. 1944
Hrin, Paul, Pvt, Hq. Co. 15th Inf, France 26 Oct. 1944
Hritz, Steve, S/Sgt, Co. A 30th Inf, France 28 Dec. 1944
Huba, Joseph G., T/4, Med. Det. 751st Tank Bn., Italy 13 Oct. 1943
Huback, Raymond C., Pfc, Hq. Co. 2d Bn. 7th Inf Regt., Germany 2 Apr. 1945
Hubbard, Harry S., Pfc, 3d Rcn Trp., Rome 4 June 1944
Hubbarth, David J., Jr., Pfc, Serv. Co. 756th Tank Bn., France 16 Aug. 1944
Hudson, Charles E., 2d Lt, Inf Serv. Co. 756th Tank Bn., France 13 Feb. 1945
Hudson, Dewey L., S/Sgt, Co. H 30th Inf Regt., France 19 Oct. 1944
Hudson, Ira A., Pvt, Btry A 39th FA Bn., Italy 31 May 1944
▲Hudson, Irvin L., Pfc, Co. K 15th Inf Regt., France 26 Dec. 1944
Hudson, Roy L., Pvt, Co. L 7th Inf, Germany 20 Apr. 1945
Hudy, Joseph D., T/5, 3d Sig. Co., Melisey 21 Sept. 1944
Huelsmann, Edwin B., Pfc, Med. Det. 7th Inf Regt., France 15 Mar. 1945
Huffam, Richard R., Pfc, Co. A 30th Inf, Cussey-Sur-L'Ognen, France 10 Sept. 1944
Huff, Charles W., T/4, Co. A 756th Tank Bn., France, Germany 8 May 1945
Huggins, Harold H., T/5, Co. C 30th Inf Regt., Italy 1 June 1944
Hughes, Ben G., WOJG, US Army Hq. 3d Inf Div., Italy, France, Germany 8 May 1945
Hughes, Elwyn, Pfc, Co. M 30th Inf Regt., N. Africa, Sicily, France, Germany May 1945
Hughes, Francis P., S/Sgt, Co. K 15th Inf, Isola Bella 29 Feb. 1944
Hughes, Harold F., Capt, MC Co. D 3d Med. Bn., France 19 Feb. 1945
Hughes, J. T., Pfc, Co. E 7th Inf, Cisterna Di Littoria 24 May 1944
Hughson, David N., 1st Lt, FA Hq. 601st TD Bn., Italy, France 15 Mar. 1945
Huguenin, Henry, Capt, Inf Hq. 3d Inf Div., Italy, France, Germany 31 Mar. 1945
Hull, George A., T/5, Btry D 441st AAA AW Bn., France 8 Sept. 1944
Hull, Levi F., Jr., T/5, Co. A 756th Tank Bn., Germany 20 Apr. 1945
Hulstine, Quinton L., WOJG, US Army Hq. & Serv. Co. 10th Engr. Combat Bn., France, Germany, Austria 8 May 1945
Humes, Ollie A., Pfc, Hq. Co. 3d Bn. 15th Inf, Mt. Lungo 10 Nov. 1943
Humiston, LeRoy M., Sgt, Co. F 30th Inf Regt., France 23 Jan. 1945
Hummel, Clarence J., T/4, MP Pltn 3d Inf Div., France Feb. 1945
▲Humphreys, Leslie L., S/Sgt, Co. I 7th Inf Regt., Germany 18 Mar. 1945
Hungerford, Grover E., Pvt, Med. Det. 7th Inf Regt., France 29 Oct. 1944
▲Hunt, Francis W., Pvt, Hq. Co. 30th Inf, La Salle 26 Oct. 1944
▲Hunley, Jesse N., Jr., 1st Lt, FA Co. C 601st TD Bn., France 4 Dec. 1944
Hunsaker, Horace D., T/4, Co. A 756th Tank Bn., France 6 Feb. 1945
▲Hunt, Albert L., T/Sgt, Hq. Co. 30th Inf Regt., France 10 Nov. 1944
Hunt, Marshall T., Capt, Inf Co. F 30th Inf Regt., France 8 Nov. 1944
Hunter, James R., S/Sgt, Hq. Co. 3d Div., N. Africa, Sicily, Italy, France, Germany, Austria 8 May 1945
Huntley, Robert M., 1st Sgt, Serv. Co. 30th Inf, N. Africa, Sicily, Italy 4 Apr. 1944
Hupfer, William M., Pvt, Btry A 9th FA Bn., Italy 5 June 1944
Hursyz, John C., Pfc, Hq. Btry 3d Inf Div. Arty, Italy, France, Germany 8 May 1945
Huseck, James H., Pfc, Co. B 30th Inf Regt., near Guemar, France 23 Jan. 1945
Hutchinson, Virgil C., Pfc, Co. L 30th Inf, Germany 19 Mar. 1945
Hutt, John H., T/5, Med. Det. Hq. Co., Italy 4 June 1944
▲Huttman, Frank, T/Sgt, 3d Rcn Trp., Italy, France, Germany, Austria 8 May 1945
▲Hutton, Ralph E., Pfc, Hq. Co. 3d Bn. 30th Inf Regt., France 3 Nov. 1944
▲Hutton, Walter A., Sgt, Btry C 441st AAA AW Bn., France, Germany 8 May 1945
Hybert, William J., 1st Lt, Hq. Co. Inf, Italy 6 June 1944
Hymers, Stuart C., T/5, 3d Sig. Co., Italy, France, Germany, Austria 8 May 1945

Ihrig, Albert W., Pfc, Serv. Co. 15th Inf, Italy 4 June 1944
Ilacqua, Norman S., Pfc, Co. I 30th Inf Regt., France 27 Oct. 1944
Indahl, Harry B., T/Sgt, Hq. 3d Div., France, Germany 25 Mar. 1945
Infelise, Thomas A., Cpl, Hq. Btry 3d IDA, Anzio, Italy 29 Feb. 1944
Ingham, Walton C., Capt, Co. D 3d Med. Bn., Anzio 5 June 1944
Inglis, Walter, CWO, 41st FA Bn., Nettuno 19 Jan. 1944
Ingram, Charles, Jr., T/5, Hq. Co. 3d Inf Div., Italy, France 15 Sept. 1944
▲Interrante, Charles W., S/Sgt, Co. F 15th Inf Regt., France 3 Feb. 1945
Irey, Lester J., T/4, Btry A 9th FA Bn., N. Africa, Sicily, Italy, France, Germany 8 May 1945
Irwin, Edward M., S/Sgt, Serv. Co. 7th Inf Regt., N. Africa, Sicily, Italy, France, Germany, Austria May 1945
Isaac, Edwin A., S/Sgt, Co. B 30th Inf Regt., France 18 Dec. 1944
Isaac, George D., Pfc, Co. L 30th Inf, France 23 Jan. 1945
Isaac, Ralph W., Maj, MC 7th Inf, Cori 31 May 1944
Isenberg, Hayes D., Pfc, Hq. Co. 2d Bn. 30th Inf, Vosges
Ison, Berthel, Pfc, Co. H 7th Inf, Cisterna Di Littoria 21 Feb. 1944
Italiano, Jasper, Pfc, Co. M 30th Inf, Anzio, Italy
Ivancic, Frank, Pfc, AT Co. 30th Inf, Cisterna Di Littoria 24 May 1944
Iverson, Alvin J., Sgt, Btry A 39th FA Bn., Artena 28 May 1944
Ivey, Jeroutha, Pfc, Co. E 7th Inf, Artena 1 June 1944
Izenour, Frank M., Lt Col, Hq. 7th Inf, La Mole 16 Aug. 1944

Jack, Lloyd E., Pvt, Co. K 30th Inf, France 2 Feb. 1945
Jackson, Claude A., Capt, MC Co. D 3d Med. Bn., Acciarella 29 Feb. 1944
Jackson, Eugene A., Sgt, Rcn Trp. (3), Cisterna Di Littoria 2 Feb. 1944
Jackson, Harry R., 1st Lt, Btry B 41st FA Bn., Anzio, Italy 19 Mar. 1944
Jackson, Herbert V., Jr., S/Sgt, Cn Co. 30th Inf Regt., France 20 Feb. 1945
Jackson, Isaac W., Pvt, Co. D Inf Regt., France 16 Aug. 1944
Jackson, Robert R., Pfc, Med. Det. 30th Inf, 1 Feb. 1945
Jackson, Walter, T/5, Serv. Btry 10th FA Bn., N. Africa, Sicily, Italy, France, Germany 8 May 1945
Jaco, Ora G., Cpl, Btry B 9th FA Bn., Di Buzza, Sicily 4 Aug. 1944
Jacob, Walter H., S/Sgt, Cn Co. 30th Inf, Campo Morto 29 Feb. 1944
Jacobs, Bernard H., Pfc, Co. K 7th Inf, France 15 Mar. 1945
Jacobs, S. Herman, Sgt, Co. K 30th Inf, Germany 27 Mar. 1945
Jacobs, Leonard L., 1st Sgt, Co. G 30th Inf, Anzio, Italy 5 Feb. 1944
Jacobs, Raymond S., T/5, Hq. Co. 2d Bn. 30th Inf, Campo Morto 2 Mar. 1944
Jacobs, Thomas A., Pvt, Med. Det. 30th Inf Regt., Anzio, Italy 19 Feb. 1944
Jacobson, Lloyd S., Pfc, Serv. Co. 7th Inf, Sicily, Italy 18 May 1944
Jacobson, Meyer J., T/4, Co. A 756th Tank Bn., France 25 Jan. 1945
Jacobson, Robert D., Sgt, Cn Co. 30th Inf Regt., Italy, France, Germany 8 May 1945
Jaeger, Jack J., 1st Sgt, Hq. Btry 10th FA Bn., N. Africa, Sicily, Italy, France, Germany 8 May 1945
James, Francis H., Pfc, Hq. Co. 1st Bn. 30th Inf, Germany
James, Grover Q., T/5, Co. A 756th Tank Bn., France 15 Sept. 1944
James, Ronda J., Pfc, Co. A 15th Inf, Cisterna Di Littoria 2 Feb. 1944
Jamieson, Russell A., 1st Sgt, Btry C 10th FA Bn., N. Africa, Sicily, Italy, France, Germany 8 May 1945
Jamison, Alfred A., Capt, Hq. Co. C 751st Tank Bn., Artena 1 June 1944
Jamison, John F., Jr., Sgt, Co. B 756th Tank Bn., Germany 12 Apr. 1945
Janczuk, Anthony J., Pvt, Co. D 15th Inf, Cisterna Di Littoria 25 May 1944
Janowsky, Bernard B., Pfc, Hq. Co. 3d Bn. 30th Inf Regt., France 16 Dec. 1944
Jantz, Rudolph A., Pfc, Co. L 15th Inf, Cisterna Di Littoria 1 Feb. 1944
January, Steve, Pfc, Hq. Co. 30th Inf, Montelimar 29 Aug. 1944
Jarrett, Harold B., T/5, Co. C 601st Tank Bn., El Ghettar, Tunisia 23 May 1943
Jarvis, John J., 1st Lt, Co. H 7th Inf, Mignano 11 Nov. 1943
Jasinski, Edward I., Sgt, Co. F 15th Inf, Isola Bella 24 Jan. 1944
Jaskierny, Arthur, CWO, US Army Ass't AG 3d Inf Div., Italy, France Feb. 1945
Jeffries, James M., Pvt, Btry B 39th FA Bn., France 30 Dec. 1944
Jeffs, Owen L., T/Sgt, Co. L Inf, Cisterna Di Littoria 30 Jan. 1944
Jehling, Gilbert, S/Sgt, Hq. Btry 3d Div. Arty, Sicily, Italy, France, Germany 8 May 1945
Jelinsky, Zigmund J., T/5, Serv. Co. 30th Inf
Jenkins, Alvin R., 1st Lt, Inf Hq. Co. 30th Inf Regt., Italy 28 Jan. 1944
Jenkins, Wilburn D., T/5, Btry B 39th FA Bn., N. Africa, Sicily, Italy, France, Germany 8 May 1945
Jensen, Christian M., T/5, Hq. Co. 30th Inf Regt., N. Africa, Sicily, Italy, France Dec. 1944
Jensen, Harvey W., Sgt, Hq. Det. 3d Inf Div., Sicily, Italy, France, Germany 8 May 1945
Jensen, Ingeman A., Sgt, Btry C 41st FA Bn., Italy, France 21 Feb. 1945
Jenson, Lloyd K., Capt, 3d Bn. 30th Inf, S. France 13 Oct. 1944
Jersey, William H., Pfc, Co. C 30th Inf, France 23 Jan. 1945
Jevsevar, James F., Pfc, Hq. Co. 1st Bn. 7th Inf Regt., France 28 Sept. 1944
Jewell, Grover C., T/4, Hq. Btry 9th FA Bn., N. Africa, Sicily, France, Germany 8 May 1945
Jewell, Melvin W., T/4, 3d Sig. Co., N. Africa, Sicily, Italy, France, Germany 1 May 1945
Jilka, Frank A., S/Sgt, Hq. Btry 3d Dis. Arty, France, Germany, Austria 8 May 1945
▲Jividen, Denver C., 1st Lt, Hq. 3d Bn. 7th Inf Regt., 16 Apr. 1945
Joens, Cornelius J., Jr., T/4, Btry A 39th FA Bn., France 15 Oct. 1944
Joffe, Maxwell S., Sgt, Co. I 30th Inf Regt., Germany 11 Apr. 1945
Johansen, Thorvald L., Jr., Pfc, Btry A 9th FA Bn., France 5 Nov. 1944
Johns, Louis L., T/5, Hq. Co. 30th Inf, San Stephano, Sicily 20 July 1943
▲(3) Johnson, Charles E., Col, Hq. 3d Div., France, Italy 1 Nov. 1944
Johnson, Charles R., S/Sgt, Co. L 30th Inf, Germany
Johnson, Chester J., S/Sgt, Btry B 10th FA Bn., Cisterna Di Littoria 15 Feb. 1944
Johnson, Earle R., 1st Lt, Hq. 3d Bn. 7th Inf, France 14 Sept.
Johnson, Edwin G., 1st Lt, Inf Serv. Co. 7th Inf, France 7 Sept. 1944
Johnson, Edward L., T/4, 3d Inf Div. Band, N. Africa, Sicily, Italy, France, Germany 8 May 1945
Johnson, Emmett L., Pfc, Med. Det. 15th Inf, Cisterna Di Littoria 23 May 1944
Johnson, Gustaf J., Pfc, Co. M 30th Inf Regt., France 19 Aug. 1944
Johnson, Harold L., S/Sgt, Hq. 3d Inf Div., N. Africa, Sicily, Italy, France 28 Feb. 1945
Johnson, Henry, T/Sgt, Hq. Btry 441st AAA AW Bn., Sicily, Italy, France, Germany 8 May 1945
Johnson, Herman E., Pfc, Co. I 30th Inf, Valmontone 2 June 1944
Johnson, Herbert A., Pvt, Hq. Co. 30th Inf, Italy 5 June 1944
Johnson, Huston L., Pvt, Hq. 3d Inf, Anzio, Italy 29 Feb. 1944
Johnson, James L., Pfc, Co. H 7th Inf, Germany 2 Apr. 1945
Johnson, L. V., Pfc, Hq. Btry 41st FA Bn., Italy 5 June 1944
Johnson, Lyle R., Pvt, Btry A 441st AAA AW Bn., Costello 29 May 1944
Johnson, Oliver T., Sgt, Btry B 39th FA Bn., Cisterna Di Littoria 16 Apr. 1944
Johnson, Richard J., S/Sgt, AT Co. 30th Inf, Italy Oct. 1944
Johnson, Solvin E., Cpl, Co. A 751st Tank Bn., Carano 29 Feb. 1944
Johnson, Winfield G., Sgt, Co. F 7th Inf Regt., Germany 16 Apr. 1945
Johnston, Howard E., Cpl, Hq. Co. 7th Inf, Anzio, Italy 3 Feb. 1944
▲Johnston, Robert L., Pfc, Hq. Co. 30th Inf Regt., France 6 Feb. 1945
▲Joines, George C., Pfc, Co. A 15th Inf Regt., France 25 Jan. 1945
Jolly, James I., T/5, 3d QM Co., Sicily 18 Aug. 1943
Jones, Alvin F., Pfc, Co. A 10th Engr. Combat Bn., France 29 Jan. 1945
Jones, Cary E., Jr., Cpl, Btry B 39th FA Bn.,Sicily 10 Aug. 1943
Jones, Charles H., Jr., S/Sgt, Co. A 7th Inf Regt., Italy 30 May 1944
Jones, Clarence H., Sgt, Co. K 15th Inf, France Nov. 1944
Jones, Doyle, 2d Lt, Co. B 10th Engr. Bn., Italy 5 June 1944
Jones, Earl L., Pfc, Co. D 756th Tank Bn., Germany 15 Apr. 1945
Jones, Frank P., 1st Lt, Co. K 15th Inf Regt., Italy 21 Mar. 1944
Jones, James D., Jr., Pfc, Hq. Co. 1st Bn. 30th Inf, Italy 1 June 1944
Jones, James W., Pfc, Serv. Co. 30th Inf Regt., Germany 26 Mar. 1945
Jones, John A., S/Sgt, 3d Rcn Trp., France 12 Sept. 1944
Jones, John P., Sgt, MP Pltn 3d Inf Div., French Morocco 21 Nov. 1942
Jones, John Z., Pfc, Co. F 7th Inf Regt., Germany 26 Mar. 1945
Jones, Keith A., Pvt, Hq. Co. 30th Inf, Ponte Rotto 23 May 1944
Jones, Leslie R., T/3, 3d Sig. Co., France, Italy 31 Jan. 1945
Jones, Murphy C., Pfc, Co. M 30th Inf, Carano 22 Apr. 1944
Jones, Paul J., Pfc, Hq. Co. 30th Inf Regt., France 6 Feb. 1945
Jones, Paul, Jr., Pfc, Hq. Co. 1st Bn. 7th Inf, France 22 Nov. 1944
▲Jones, Wilber N., S/Sgt, Co. H 7th Inf Regt., Germany 16 Apr. 1945
Jordan, George R., Capt, FA Hq. & Hq. Btry 41st FA Bn., Sicily 12 Aug. 1943
Jordan, Hubert L., Pfc, Co. L 30th Inf Regt., Germany 20 Mar. 1945
Jordan, Hugo J., Pvt, Hq. Co. 2d Bn. 30th Inf, Voleaux, France 21 Sept. 1944
Jordan, Vernon C., Pfc, Co. F 30th Inf Regt., France 26 Nov. 1944

▲ Oak Leaf Cluster.

Jordan, Warren G., Cpl, Hq. Btry 39th FA Bn., N. Africa, Sicily, Italy, France, Germany 8 May 1945
Joseph, George P., Pfc, Co. B 30th Inf, Anzio, Italy 26 Apr. 1944
Joslin, Morris B., 1st Lt, Co. A 10th Engr. Bn., Anzio 23 May 1944
▲Josowitz, Edward L., 1st Lt, FA Co. C 601st TD Bn., Germany 27 May 1945
Josten, Thomas W., Pfc, Co. M 15th Inf Regt., Germany 18 Apr. 1945
Joyce, Arthur C., Pfc, Co. A 601st TD Bn., near Rome, Italy 5 June 1944
Joyce, James P., Pfc, Hq. Co. 3d Bn. 7th Inf, France 29 Jan. 1945
Jozwiak, Alex C., Pfc, Hq. Btry 41st FA Bn., Le Ferriere 25 Feb. 1944
Juknis, Carl J., Sgt, Co. H 30th Inf, Sicily 11 Aug. 1943
Julian, Rosaire M., T/5, Med. Det. 30th Inf Regt., France 22 Sept. 1944
Jumper, William D., T/5, Co. F 30th Inf, Germany 21 Apr. 1945
Juneau, Maxwell A., 2d Lt, Inf Co. D 30th Inf Regt., N. Africa, Sicily, Italy, France 30 Nov. 1944
Just, Kenneth G., Pfc, Co. B 30th Inf Regt., France 15 Jan. 1945
Justice, Clarence H., S/Sgt, Co. M 30th Inf, Sicily 17 Aug. 1943

Kaczmarek, Leo P., Pfc, Co. C 7th Inf Regt., France 25 Jan. 1945
Kaehler, Herbert W., Pfc, Co. B 30th Inf, Colmar
Kalb, Merrill B., Sgt, Hq. 3d Inf Div., France, Germany 25 Mar. 1945
Kalhagen, Alvin M., Pfc, AT Co. 30th Inf, Italy 27 June 1944
Kalisiak, Morris, 1st Sgt, Co. M 7th Inf, Anzio, Italy 5 June 1944
Kalwite, Kenneth D., Sgt, Co. C 601st TD Bn., Artena 27 May 1944
Kamp, Warren L., Pfc, Hq. Co. 1st Bn. 15th Inf, Anzio, Italy 28 Jan. 1944
Kane, Francis C., Capt, Med. Det. 39th FA Bn., N. Africa, Sicily, Italy, France, Germany 8 May 1945
Kanthack, John R., Pfc, Hq. Co. 7th Inf, Anzio, Italy 5 Feb. 1945
Kapaun, Ralph O., Pfc, Hq. Co. 1st Bn. 30th Inf, France 2 Feb. 1945
Karier, John A., Pvt, Co. K 7th Inf, Germany 28 Mar. 1945
Karls, Sylvester C., Sgt, Co. A 15th Inf, Auriol, France 20 Aug. 1944
Karow, Kenton J., T/5, Cn Co. 30th Inf, Acerno 23 Sept. 1943
Kartheiser, Theodore A., S/Sgt, Hq. Co. 756th Tank Bn., Italy, France, Germany 8 May 1945
Kartis, Frank S., T/5, Co. C 756th Tank Bn., Germany 27 Apr. 1945
Kasel, Joseph H., Pfc, Btry A 9th FA Bn., Acerno 23 Sept. 1943
Kasparovitch, Eugene, 1st Lt, Rcn Co. 601st TD Bn., Germany 6 Apr. 1945
Kaszewicz, Edward F., S/Sgt, 3d Sig. Co., Italy, France, Germany Apr. 1945
Katcher, Glen W., Pvt, Serv. Btry 39th FA Bn., Guilianello 31 May 1944
Katz, Sidney, Pfc, Hq. Co. 3d Bn. 7th Inf, Anzio, Italy 1 Mar. 1944
Kauffman, Gael F., Capt, Inf Serv. Co. 30th Inf Regt., Italy, France 20 Feb. 1945
Kaufmann, Herman J., Capt, Inf Co. D 756th Tank Bn., Italy, France 25 Jan. 1945
Kaufman, Loren R., Cpl, Hq. Btry 3d Inf Div. Arty, N. Africa, Sicily, Italy, France, Germany 8 May 1945
Kawa, Henry P., Pfc, Hq. Co. 3d Inf Div., Italy, France, Germany 8 May 1945
Kazaroff, Albert, Pfc, Co. L 30th Inf Regt., France 25 Nov. 1944
Kazda, James C., S/Sgt, Btry C 9th FA Bn., Italy 10 Mar. 1944
Keane, Daniel F., Pfc, Hq. Co. 2d Bn. 15th Inf Regt., France 3 Feb. 1945
Keane, John V., Pfc, Med. Det. 39th FA Bn., Italy 31 Oct. 1944
Kearney, Thomas A., Pfc, Co. B 30th Inf Regt., near Guemar, France 23 Jan. 1945
Keeler, Harvey R., Pfc, Hq. Co. 3d Bn. 7th Inf, Italy 5 June 1944
Keeler, Rovert C., Pvt, Btry A 441st AAA AW Bn., Costello 29 May 1944
Keene, William F., 2d Lt, Inf Co. B 30th Inf Regt., Germany 18 Apr. 1945
Keeter, Leo, T/5, Serv. Co. 30th Inf, Italy 5 June 1944
Kehoe, Joseph S., Pfc, Bn. B 9th FA Bn., France 5 Feb. 1945
Keilbach, Russell J., Pfc, 3d Sig. Co., Italy 22 Jan., 5 June 1944
Keller, Harold W., Pfc, Co. B 30th Inf, France 7 Sept. 1944
▲Keller, Robert R., Pfc, Hq. Co. 1st Bn. 30th Inf Regt., France 20 Nov. 1944
Keller, Walter, T/5, 3d Sig. Co., Italy, France 31 Jan. 1945
Kellerman, Henry B., Cpl, Btry C 10th FA Bn., N. Africa, Sicily, Italy, France, Germany 8 May 1945
Kelley, Loran L., Pfc, Co. M 30th Inf Regt., France 25 Nov. 1944
Kelley, William R., Pfc, Co. F 7th Inf, Licata, Sicily 10 July 1942
Kellner, Maurice A., Pfc, Hq. Co. 3d Bn. 30th Inf, France 18 Jan. 1945
Kelly, Thomas J., 1st Lt, Co. A 601st TD Bn., France 15 Mar. 1945
Kelly, William H., Pfc, Co. A 7th Inf Regt., France 15 Mar. 1945
Kelly, William J., T/5, Med. Det. 441st AAA AW Bn., Anzio, Italy 7 Feb. 1944
▲Kelsey, Walter E., 1st Lt, AT Co. 30th Inf Regt., France 17 Dec. 1944
Kelso, Goins, T/4, Co. I 30th Inf, Carano 22 Apr. 1944
▲Kempf, Marvin E., Cpl, Co. A 756th Tank Bn., Germany 19 Mar. 1945
Kemppel, Walter R., Pfc, Hq. Co. 1st Bn. 7th Inf Regt., Germany 20 Apr. 1945
Kenaston, Douglas A., T/5, Med. Det. 30th Inf, Campo Morto 28 Feb. 1944
Kendall, Maurice W., 1st Lt, Inf Hq. 3d Bn. 15th Inf Regt., France 27 Dec. 1944
Kendizior, Alexander F., S/Sgt, Co. I 15th Inf, Italy 23 May 1944
Kendrick, Loomis C., Pvt, Med. Det. 30th Inf, Ponte Rotto 23 May 1944
Kennedy, Alvan E., Pfc, 3d Sig. Co., Italy 22 Jan., 5 June 1944
Kennedy, Benjamin T., T/4, Hq. Co. 2d Bn. 7th Inf Regt., Italy 3 June 1944
Kennedy, Charles D., Pfc, Hq. Det. 3d Med Bn., Italy 23 May 1944
Kennedy, Donald J., Sgt, Btry A 39th FA Bn., Artena, Italy 30 May 1944
Kennedy, John A., 1st Lt, CAC, Btry D 441st AAA AW Bn., France 29 Dec. 1944
Kennedy, Kenneth M., T/Sgt, Hq. Co. 756th Tank Bn., Italy, France, Germany 8 May 1945
Kent, Royal P., 1st Lt, Co. A 15th Inf Regt., France 5 Nov. 1944
Kenvin, James, Pvt, Btry A 41st FA Bn., Cisterna di Littoria, Italy 1 Feb. 1944
Kenyon, Allen R., Capt, 3d Rcn Trp., Germany 20 Mar. 1945
▲Keogh, Claude R., 1st Lt, Hq. Co. 7th Inf, France 22 Jan. 1945
Kephart, Alfred B., T/5, Italy, France 31 Jan. 1945
Kerley, Samuel R., Sgt, Co. M 7th Inf Regt., Germany 8 Apr. 1945
Kerns, William F., Sgt, Co. D 756th Tank Bn., Germany 1 May 1945
Kerwin, Walter T., Lt Col, Hq. FA, Italy 5 June 1944
Kesner, Sam, Ist Lt, Chem Wrf Serv., Italy 20-25 Apr. 1944
Kesselschmidt, Abraham, Pfc, Btry D 441st AAA AW Bn., France 5 Feb. 1945
Kesterson, Wayne N., S/Sgt, Co. A 10th Engr. Bn., Carano 6 Mar. 1944
Ketchum, Charles M., Sgt, Hq. Co. 1st Bn. 15th Inf Regt., Italy 30 Oct. 1943
Ketterling, Harold, T/5, Btry B 41st FA Bn., Anzio, Italy 29 Feb. 1944
▲Kiblen, Charles J., Capt, Fin. Dept. Hq. 3d Inf Div., France 28 Feb. 1945
Kicklighter, Rylch, Pfc, Co. G 15th Inf, Germany 7 Apr. 1945
Kielar, Edward C., Pfc, Co. B 15th Inf Regt., Germany 26 Apr. 1945

Kienle, Helmut O., Pfc, Hq. & Hq. Btry 41st FA Bn., France 22 Jan. 1945
Kiernan, Edward P., M/Sgt, Serv. Co. 7th Inf Regt., French Morocco 31 Dec. 1942
▲Kigg, Dick A., Lt Col, Div. Hq., Italy, France 20 Nov. 1944
Killian, Leland E., S/Sgt, Co. B 30th Inf, Anzio, Italy 30 Apr. 1944
Kimbrel, Melvin E., Pfc, Hq. Co. 3d Bn. 30th Inf Regt., France 25 Sept. 1944
Kimbrough, James, Pfc, Co. A 10th Engr. Combat Bn., France 5 Nov. 1944
Kimmel, Donald M., Pvt, Hq. Co. 30th Inf, Carano 15 Mar. 1944
Kincaid, Clifford B., T/4, 3d Div. Band, N. Africa, Sicily, Italy, France 31 Dec. 1944
Kindel, Harold, T/5, Btry B 441st AAA AW Bn., France 25 Jan. 1945
Kindiarski, Joseph, Cpl, Hq. Co. 2d Bn. 15th Inf, Mt. Casema 8 Nov. 1943
King, Alger C., Pfc, AT Co. 7th Inf, Sicily, Italy 18 Nov. 1943
King, Buck N., 2d Lt, Co. H 15th Inf, Haut-Du-Tot, France 12 Oct. 1944
King, Delbert W., S/Sgt, Co. E 7th Inf Regt., France 24 Jan. 1945
King, Denver W., S/Sgt, Co. K 30th Inf, France 1 Feb. 1945
▲(3) King, Dick, A., Lt Col, GSC G-4 Hq. 3d Inf Div., France, Germany, Austria 8 May 1945
King, Edward T., Pvt, Med. Dept. Co. C 3d Med. Bn., Pontelatone 16 Oct. 1944
King, George E., Pfc, Btry A 9th FA Bn., Acerno 23 Sept. 1943
King, George P., Cpl, Co. A 15th Inf Regt., France 5 Nov. 1944
King, George W., 1st Lt, Hq. Co. 3d Div., Italy 7 June 1944
King, Grover N., T/4, Btry B 9th FA Bn., France 24 Jan. 1945
King, Herman E., Pvt, Hq. Co. 1st Bn. 30th Inf Regt., France 20 Aug. 1944
King, Jack, T/5, Serv. Co. 30th Inf
King, Warren A., Pfc, Co. B 30th Inf, Colmar
Kinney, Oliver G., Lt Col, Inf Hq. 1st Bn. 30th Inf Regt., Italy 5 Nov. 1943
▲(2) Kinter, Kenneth E., 1st Lt, Co. I 15th Inf Regt, France 17 Mar. 1945
Kirby, Edward P., Sgt, Co. M 30th Inf, Cisterna Di Littoria 25 May 1944
Kirchner, Edward R., T/4, Serv. Co. 30th Inf, Anzio, Italy 17 Mar. 1944
Kirchner, Patrick M., Sgt, Co. C 30th Inf Regt., France 9 Sept. 1944
Kirk, John N., 1st Lt, Inf AT Co., France 20 Nov. 1944
▲Kirkland, Clifford E., Cpl, Co. C 756th Tank Bn., France 25 Jan. 1945
Kirkland, William C., Sgt, Co. H 30th Inf, Sicily 8 Aug. 1943
Kirkpatrick, George E., T/5, Hq. Det. 3d Med. Bn., France, Germany 8 May 1945
Kirkpatrick, Gerald R., T/5, 3d QM Co., Sicily 18 Aug. 1943
Kish, George, T/5, Co. M 30th Inf, N. Africa, Sicily, Italy, France, Germany 8 May 1945
Kissen, Martin D., Capt, Btry Surg. 1st Bn. 15th Inf Regt., France 28 Nov. 1944
Kitt, Clyde, Jr., Cpl, Btry C 10th FA Bn., N. Africa, Sicily, Italy, France, Germany, Austria 8 May 1945
Kittinger, Robert H., S/Sgt, Hq. Co. 7th Inf, France, Germany 28 Mar. 1945
Kitts, Arthur C., T/5, Btry C 10th FA Bn., N. Africa, Sicily, Italy, France, Germany 8 May 1945
Kiwatisky, Nicholas F., T/Sgt, Co. B 30th Inf Regt., France 23 Jan. 1945
Klappich, Walter S., 1st Lt, Corps Engr Act. Ass't AG 3d Inf, N. Africa, Sicily, Italy 7 June 1944
Klaren, Donald A., T/4, Hq. Co. 30th Inf Regt., France 10 Nov. 1944
Klein, Edward B., Pvt, Cn Co. 15th Inf, France 26 Dec.
▲Klein, Seymour H., Pfc, Hq. Co. 30th Inf Regt., Germany 15 Mar. 1945
Klysa, Michael, S/Sgt, Hq. Co. 2d Bn. 15th Inf Regt., France 4 Feb. 1945
Kniesel, Edward M., S/Sgt, Serv. Btry 9th FA Bn., Sicily 18 Aug. 1943
Knight, Robert E., Pfc, Co. L 15th Inf, Statigliano 21 Oct. 1944
Kniola, Richard A., Pfc, Hq. Co. 3d Bn. 30th Inf Regt., France 3 Nov. 1944
Knois, Cecil A., Sgt, Co. C 30th Inf Regt., France 9 Sept. 1944
Knoll, Raymond J., 1st Lt, FA Hq. Btry 10th FA Bn., N. Africa, Sicily, Italy, France, Germany 8 May 1945
Knotts, Richard E., Pfc, Hq. Co. 1st Bn. 7th Inf Regt., Italy 2 Mar. 1944
Knowles, Haston E., Pfc, Co. D 7th Inf Regt., Germany 19 Apr. 1945
Knowles, James J., Pfc, Co. F 15th Inf, Anzio, Italy 10 Feb. 1944
Knudson, Harold E., Sgt, Hq. Btry FA, Isola Bella 30 Jan. 1944
Knutson, Neil I., S/Sgt, Serv. Btry 39th FA Bn., France 18 Feb. 1945
Kobernick, John W., 1st Sgt, Co. B 30th Inf Regt., Germany 29 Apr. 1945
Kochera, Joseph T., Sgt, Hq. Co. 2d Bn. 15th Inf Regt., Anzio, Italy 27 Jan. 1944
Kocken, Cornelius, S/Sgt, Co. C 15th Inf, Anzio, Italy 25 Jan. 1944
Koeneman, Walter H., Pfc, Co. A 601st TD Bn., Ponte Rotto 3 Mar. 1944
Koetting, Earnest M., S/Sgt, Hq. Btry 9th FA Bn. N. Africa, Sicily, France, Italy, Germany, Austria 8 May 1945
Koffman, David, Pfc, Serv. Co. 30th Inf, Italy 2 June 1944
Kohrmann, Virgil J., S/Sgt, Co. E 7th Inf, Cisterna Di Litteria 25 Mar. 1944
Komanekin, Joseph G., Pvt, Co. C 10th Engr, Melay, France 21 Sept. 1944
Konopka, Frank S., T/4, Co. B 601st TD Bn., N. Africa, Italy, France 15 Jan. 1945
Konopka, Joseph S., Pvt, Co. B 7th Inf, Artena 28 May 1944
Kontorchik, Stanley L., T/5, Btry C 441st AAA, Germany 30 Apr. 1945
Korenbaum, Israel J., 1st Lt, Inf Serv. Co. 7th Inf Regt., France, Germany, Austria 5 May 1945
▲Kostikos, John Z., Pfc, Hq. Btry 9th FA Bn., Borgo Montello 29 Feb. 1944
Kostryk, Steve, S/Sgt, Co. A 7th Inf Regt., France 8 Oct. 1944
Kouba, Edward J., T/Sgt, Hq. Co. 1st Bn. 7th Inf Regt., France 21 Jan. 1945
Kovach, Jerome P., Pfc, 3d Sig. Co., France, Germany 8 May 1945
Koyama, Raymon M., Pvt, Co. K 7th Inf, Ponte Rotto 1 Mar. 1944
Kozlowski, Chester R., Pvt, Btry C 9th FA Bn., Cesareo 3 June 1944
Kral, Charles E., S/Sgt, Co. H 7th Inf, Italy, France 6 Feb. 1945
Kraus, John C., Jr., 1st Lt, Hq. 9th FA Bn., Italy 15 Feb. 1944
Krause, Earle G., S/Sgt, Hq. Co. 30th Inf Regt., Sicily 18 Aug. 1943
▲Kravitz, Hilard L., Capt, MC Med. Det. 30th Inf Regt., France 8 Jan. 1945
Kravos, Joseph F., Sgt, Hq. Co. 1st Bn. 7th Inf Regt., France 2 Nov. 1944
Krebsbach, Henry J., Pfc, Btry C 9th FA Bn., Italy 30 May 1944
Kremer, Robert F., Capt, Inf Co. D 756th Tank Bn., France 6 Feb. 1945
Krenn, Arthur C., Pfc, Co. C 30th Inf Regt., Germany 13 Apr. 1945
Kret, Francis J., Capt, Inf Co. I 7th Inf, France 10 Sept. 1944
Krieger, Alfred R., S/Sgt, Hq. Co. 1st Bn. 15th Inf, France 1 Feb. 1945
Krieger, Wilbert E., S/Sgt, Co. K 15th Inf, Rome 4 June 1944
Krintz, Loyd C., Pvt, Co. C 10th Engr., Cisterna 23 May 1944
▲Krok, John S., S/Sgt, Co. L 15th Inf Regt., France 25 Oct. 1944
Krolick, Frank J., Pfc, Co. M 15th Inf Regt., France 21 Oct. 1944
Krom, Arthur D., Jr., Pvt, Co. D 15th Inf Regt., France 28 Aug. 1944
Kropp, Walter H., 1st Lt, Inf Co. M 15th Inf Regt., France 12 Sept. 1944
Krovchick, William E., Pvt, Hq. Co. 2d Bn. 7th Inf, Carano 2 Mar. 1944
Krueger, William C., T/Sgt, Co. L 30th Inf
Kruszka, Floyd J., Sgt, Btry C 9th FA Bn., Conca 11 Mar. 1944
Kryger, James A., Pfc, Med. Det. 7th Inf Regt., France 5 Jan. 1945

▲ Oak Leaf Cluster.

Kubicek, Edward, T/5, Btry C 441st AAA AW Bn., Sicily, Italy, France, Germany 8 May 1945
Kucinski, William B., S/Sgt, Co. K 30th Inf, Anzio, Italy 19 Apr. 1944
Kucz, Theodore, Pfc, Co. M 30th Inf Regt., N. Africa, Sicily, Italy, France, Germany 8 May 1945
Kuehling, Lester G., S/Sgt, Hq. Co. 2d Bn. 30th Inf Regt., Italy 19 Feb. 1944
Kuhn, Frederick A., Pfc, Co. L 30th Inf Regt., Germany 16 Mar. 1945
Kuhn, Marshall L., M/Sgt, 3d Sig. Co., France 8 May 1945
Kunz, William J., Sgt, Hq. Btry 9th FA, Italy 1 Feb. 1944
Kushner, George, Jr., Pvt, Hq. Co. 30th Inf, Cisterna Di Littoria 25 May 1944
▲Kusmiak, Eugene, CWO, US Army 3d Inf Div. Band, Italy, France, Germany 7 May 1945
Kuzbecki, Frank H., Pvt, Serv. Btry 41st FA Bn., Carroceto 29 Feb. 1944
Kuzel, John S., Sgt, Co. D 30th Inf, Anzio, Italy
▲Kuzma, John J., Sgt, Co. C 3d Med. Bn., France 30 Sept. 1944

La Bella, Verdi P., Pfc, Co. H 15th Inf Regt., Germany 18 Mar. 1945
LaBelle, Edward C., 1st Lt, Inf Co. C 30th Inf, France 27 Jan. 1945
Labelle, John P., Pfc, Co. A 10th Engr. Combat Bn., France 5 Nov. 1944
Labosky, Raymond, Sr., Pfc, AT Co. 30th Inf Regt., France 25 Dec. 1944
Labuta, George J., S/Sgt, Co. G 15th Inf, France 1 Nov. 1944
Lach, John E., Cpl, Cn Co. 30th Inf, Colmar
Lachmund, Herman A., Pfc, Co. L 7th Inf, Cisterna Di Littoria 4 Mar. 1944
Lackman, Elwood E., Sgt, Co. D 30th Inf, Anzio, Italy
Lackwool, Arthur L., Sgt, Hq. Co. 30th Inf, Vosges
Lacy, Paul, Jr., Pfc, MP Pltn 3d Inf, France 6 Feb. 1945
Lacy, Robert J., T/4, Hq. Btry 39th FA Bn., Italy 21 Oct. 1943
▲LaDouce, Edward H., S/Sgt, Co. M 30th Inf Regt., France 25 Nov. 1944
▲Ladwig, Charles P., T/5, Btry C 41st FA Bn., France 31 Jan. 1945
▲Laeser, Walter E., S/Sgt, Hq. Co. 1st Bn. 30th Inf Regt., France 25 Oct. 1944
Lafelice, Joseph J., S/Sgt, Co. G 30th Inf Regt., Germany 27 Mar. 1945
Lafferty, Henry J., Pfc, Co. D 7th Inf, Anzio, Italy 23 Feb. 1944
LaFleur, Jevese M., 2d Lt, Inf Co. L 7th Inf Regt., France 25 Dec. 1944
LaFrance, Omer, T/5, Rcn Co. 601st TD Bn., N. Africa, Sicily, Italy, France, Germany 8 May 1945
Laird, Harvey L., S/Sgt, Co. B 7th Inf, Rigney, France 9 Sept. 1944
Lais, Richard R., Capt, Btry A 69th FA Bn., Italy 11 July 1944
▲(2) Lakey, Ralph H., Cpl, Hq. Co. 7th Inf Regt. Div., Germany 27 Mar. 1945
Lamb, Alvin H., Jr., Pfc, Co. E 15th Inf, Anzio, Italy 29 Feb. 1944
Lambert, Jacob I., T/5, Btry C 441st AAA AW Bn., Germany, Austria 8 May 1945
Lambert, James H., 2d Lt, Hq. Co. 7th Inf, Anzio, Italy 31 Jan. 1944
Lampe, Nathan C., S/Sgt, Btry C 39th FA Bn., N. Africa, Sicily, Italy, France, Germany, Austria 8 May 1945
Lampton, John S., Jr., Pvt, Co. C 7th Inf, Villers L Sec 12 Sept. 1944
Lander, Luther E., T/5, Serv. Co. 15th Inf Regt., France 17 Sept. 1944
▲Landman, Henry, Pfc, Hq. Co. 1st Bn. 30th Inf Regt., France 24 Jan. 1945
Landowski, Alexander T., Sgt, Med. Co. C 3d Med. Bn., France 17 Nov. 1944
Lane, Elijah H., Pvt, Btry B 9th FA Bn., Borgo Montello 29 Feb. 1944
Lane, Robert C., Pfc, Hq. Btry 39th FA Bn., France 24 Dec. 1944
Langan, Thomas L., Cpl, Co. C 601st TD Bn., El Guettar, Tunisia 23 Mar. 1943
Langeliers, Leslie J., T/5, Btry C 10th FA Bn., N. Africa, Sicily, Italy, France, Germany 8 May 1945
Langenmayr, Robert, Pfc, Hq. Btry 9th FA Bn., Anzio 29 Feb. 1944
Langford, Lloyd E., Maj, Chap. Corps, Sicily 18 Aug. 1943
Langston, Autry, T/5, Med. Det. 30th Inf, Padiglione 20 Feb. 1944
Lanning, Virgil E., S/Sgt, Btry B 9th FA Bn., N. Africa, Sicily, Italy, France, Germany, Austria 6 May 1945
LaPine, Glenn H., Pfc, Co. M 30th Inf, Carano 24 Apr. 1944
La Point, Joseph, Pfc, Hq. Co. 7th Inf, France 23 Jan. 1945
Larence, Robert J., Pfc, Co. A 15th Inf Regt., France 5 Nov. 1944
Large, William E., Cpl, Cn Co. 15th Inf, Valmontone 2 June 1944
Larger, Charles, Jr., Sgt, Btry C 441st AAA AW Bn., France 26 Nov. 1944
▲Larrimore, Phillip B., Capt, Co. L 30th Inf, France 1 Feb. 1945
Larrabee, Robert A., Pfc, Med. Det. 30th Inf Regt., France 8 Jan. 1945
Larsen, Gilbert E., S/Sgt, 3d Rcn Trp., Germany 19 Mar. 1945
Larsen, Thomas A., 1st Lt, Inf Co. A 15th Inf, France 23 Oct. 1944
Larson, Gilbert, Pvt, 3d Rcn Trp., Germany 18 Mar. 1945
Larson, Kenneth V., 1st Sgt, Co. D 3d Med. Bn., Italy 19 Feb. 1945
Larson, Rudolph E., Cpl, Co. B 601st TD Bn., Ponte Rotto 29 Feb. 1944
Larson, Stanley MD., Pfc, Hq. Co. 1st Bn. 15th Inf, France 1 Feb. 1945
Larson, Sterling E., Capt, Hq. 9th FA Bn., Sicily 9 Aug. 1943
Lashua, Melvin G., Cpl, Btry A 41st FA Bn., St. Die, France 27 Oct. 1944
Lasko, Arthur S., Sgt, Co. F 15th Inf Regt., France 7 Nov. 1944
Latham, Arthur A., 1st Lt, Inf Hq. 2d Bn. 30th Inf Regt., France 3 Nov. 1944
Latham, Royal W., Pvt, Co. F 15th Inf, Anzio, Italy 5 Mar. 1944
Latta, Raymond E., Cpl, Co. C 601st TD Bn., Mignano 13 Nov. 1943
Lauderdale, George W., 1st Lt, Serv. Btry 39th FA Bn., Cisterno Di Littoria 30 Jan. 1944
Lauer, Charles E., Pfc, Co. K 15th Inf, Isola Bella 30 Jan. 1944
Laughlin, Virgil V., Capt, Hq. 3d Bn. 15th Inf, Anzio 6 June 1944
Lavelle, James I., Pfc, Hq. Det. 3d Inf Div., N. Africa, Sicily, Italy, France, Germany 8 May 1945
▲Lavinski, Chester, Pfc, Co. A 756th Tank Bn., Germany 19 Mar. 1945
Lavoi, Richard R., Pvt, Co. M 7th Inf, France 3 Feb. 1945
Law, Forest M., S/Sgt, Co. E 7th Inf Regt., France 5 Oct. 1944
Lawless, Joseph L., Pfc, Co. L 7th Inf, Padiglione 26 Apr. 1944
Lawrence, Hazen G., Sgt, Hq. Btry 39th FA Bn., Africa, Sicily, Italy, France, Germany 8 May 1945
▲Lawrence, Houston R., Pfc, Hq. Co. 2d Bn. 7th Inf Regt., Germany 20 Mar. 1945
Lawton, William T., Sgt, MP Pltn 3d Inf, Germany 8 May 1945
Lazar, John, Pfc, Btry C 39th FA Bn., Italy 27 Dec. 1943
Lazaroff, Dimitar A., T/4, Co. B 7th Inf Regt., Germany 12 Apr. 1945
La Zerda, Alfredo P., Pfc, Co. F 15th Inf, Ecots, France 8 Sept. 1944
Lazrine, Robert, T/Sgt, Hq. Co. 3d Bn. 7th Inf, France 22 Nov. 1944
Lazzaro, John E., Sgt, Btry C 441st AAA AW Bn., Sicily, Italy, France, Germany 8 May 1945
Leaming, Andrew W., Capt, Co. L 15th Inf, Cisterna Di Littoria 30 Jan. 1944
▲Leary, Thomas H., Lt Col, CO 441st AAA AW Bn., Germany 20 Apr. 1945
Leatherman, Thomas E., T/5, Serv. Btry 10th FA Bn., N. Africa, Sicily, Italy, France, Germany 8 May 1945
LeBlanc, Irvine, S/Sgt, AT Co. 30th Inf, Germany
Lechner, Leo W., Sgt, Co. C 756th Tank Bn., France 23 Jan. 1945
▲Ledbetter, Leonard, T/4, Med. Det. 30th Inf, Anzio, Italy 21 Apr. 1944
Ledet, Charles J., T/5, Co. A 756th Tank Bn., Germany 18 Mar. 1945

Lee, George C., T/5, Hq. Btry 3d Div. Arty, Italy 23 Feb. 1944
Lee, William G., Pvt, Hq. Co. 2d Bn. 30th Inf, Voleaux, France 21 Sept. 1944
Leedy, Charles R., S/Sgt, Btry A 441st AAA AW Bn., Sicily, Italy, France, Germany 8 May 1945
Lees, Donald G., T/5, Co. B 601st TD Bn., Ponte Rotto 29 Feb. 1944
Lefelice, Joseph J., S/Sgt, Co. G 30th Inf, Germany
▲Lefevre, Robert C., Pfc, Med. Det. 15th Inf Regt., France 12 Oct. 1944
LeFore, Aaron, T/5, Hq. Co. 1st Bn. 15th Inf Regt., France 24 Nov. 1944
Legg, Robert L., Capt, DC 3d Med. Bn., France, Germany 8 May 1945
Lehman, Jack B., 1st Lt, Hq. Co. 3d Bn. 7th Inf, Padiglione 24 Apr. 1944
Lehnert, James D., Pfc, Co. C 30th Inf Regt., France 2 Nov. 1944
Leibold, Robert V., Sgt, Co. A 751st Tank Bn., Italy 13 Oct. 1943
Leichty, Raymond, Pvt, Med. Det. 15th Inf, Cisterna Di Littoria 24 May 1944
Leistritz, Kenneth E., S/Sgt, Cn Co. 30th Inf, Sicily, France Sept. 1944
Leitner, Eric F., S/Sgt, B. P. 7th Inf, Anzio, Italy 30 Jan. 1944
Lemar, Carl R., Pfc, Hq. Co. 7th Inf, France 24 Jan. 1945
▲Lemay, Alfred J., Pfc, Hq. Co. 2d Bn. 7th Inf Regt., France 20 Nov. 1944
Lemons, Wendell G., T/5, Btry C 441st AAA AW Bn., Sicily, Italy, France, Germany 8 May 1945
▲Lenaham, Daniel W., Maj, Inf Hq. 3d Inf Div., France, Germany 25 Mar. 1945
Lenta, Mario, Pvt, Med. Det. 10th Engr. Bn., Cisterna 23 May 1944
Leo, Arman F., Sgt, Co. M 30th Inf, Ponto Rotto 23 May 1944
Leong, Dick M, T/4, Serv. Co. 30th Inf Regt., Italy, France 16 Jan. 1945
Leroy, Clarence G., Pfc, Co. H 30th Inf, France 15 Oct. 1944
Lesica, Francis R., T/5, Hq. Co. 3d Bn. 30th Inf
Levesque, Lucien A., Pfc, Hq. Co. 2d Bn. 30th Inf, Germany
Levesque, Francis J., Cpl, Hq. Co. 2d Bn. 30th Inf, Germany
▲Levin, Hyman S., Sgt, Cn Co. 30th Inf, Colmar
Levin, Hyman S., Pfc, Cn Co. 30th Inf, France 25 Jan. 1945
Levitt, Monte, Pfc, Btry C 9th FA, Italy, Anzio 29 Feb. 1944
Levy, Harold, 1st Lt, Inf Co. C 756th Tank Bn., France 1 Feb. 1945
Lewallen, William L., T/4, Med. Det. 7th Inf Regt., France 23 Dec. 1944
Lewandowski, Alexander J., S/Sgt, Co. A 10th Engr. Combat Bn., France 6 Nov. 1944
Lewinski, John D., Sgt, Hq. Co. 3d Bn. 7th Inf Regt., France 27 Jan. 1945
Lewis, Abel, Sgt, Co. E 30th Inf Regt., France 7 Feb. 1945
Lewis, French G., Maj, Inf Hq. 756th Tank Bn., France 8 Feb. 1945
Lewis, Gilbert, S/Sgt, 7th Inf Regt., France 28 Oct. 1944
Lewis, Harold E., 1st Lt, Serv. Co. 15th Inf, Anzio 6 June 1944
Lewis, William E., Pfc, Co. C FA 601st TD Bn., Isola Bella 7 Feb. 1944
Lewis, William R., Pfc, MG Sec. 30th Inf, Germany
Ley,Robert P., Pvt, Hq. Btry 3d IDA, Anzio, Italy 29 Feb. 1944
Liberti, Bert A., Pfc, Co. H 30th Inf Regt., France 22 Sept. 1944
Lichtenegger, Seibold, Jr., 1st Lt, Coast Arty Corps Btry D 441st AAA AW Bn., France 4 Feb. 1945
Lieberman, Henry, 1st Lt, Coast Arty Corps Btry A 441st AAA AW Bn., Italy, France, Germany, Austria 8 May 1945
▲Liebold, Robert V., Sgt, Co. A 751st Tank Bn., Sessano 14 Mar. 1944
Lightcap, George A., Pfc, Co. E 7th Inf Regt., Italy 23 May 1944
Lima, Wallace F., Pfc, Co. M 30th Inf Regt., N. Africa, Sicily, Italy, France, Germany 8 May 1945
▲Limprecht, Hollis J., 1st Lt, Hq. 3d Div., Italy 30 Sept. 1944
Lind, Harold, Pfc, Co. A 15th Inf Regt., France 4 Feb. 1945
▲(2) Lind, Nels E., T/5, Med. Det. 15th Inf, La Providence 11 Sept. 1944
Lind, Nes E., Pfc, Med. Det. 15th Inf, Cisterna Di Littoria 23 May 1944
Lindberg, Edward M., Pfc, Co. A 15th Inf, Saint Anaista, France 17 Aug. 1944
Lindeen, Eskil C., 1st Sgt, Co. M 30th Inf, Anzio, Italy 29 Feb. 1944
Linder, General W., Pfc, Btry B 39th FA Bn., Cisterna 22 Apr. 1944
Lindgren, Leslie J., T/4, Hq. Btry 3d Inf Arty, Guilinello 29 May 1944
Lindi, Bill A., Pvt, Med. Det. 15th Inf, Italy 3 Mar. 1944
▲Lindley, Robert B., 2d Lt, Corps Engr. Hq. & Serv. Co. 10th Engr. Combat Bn., France 10 Nov. 1944
Lindow, Norman S., S/Sgt, Hq. Co. 756th Tank Bn., Germany 3 May 1945
Lindsey, Theodore A., Cpl, Btry B 39th FA Bn., N. Africa, Sicily, Italy, France, Germany 8 May 1945
Lineback, Roy M., Pvt, Met. Det. 15th Inf, Cleurie 27 Sept. 1944
Ling, William S. M., Capt, Med. Det. 751st Tank Bn., Anzio, Italy 28 Mar. 1944
Linkey, Ernest W., 2d Lt, F A Co. B 601st TD Bn., N. Africa, Italy, France 15 Jan. 1945
Linsey, Paul D., Capt, JA Det. Hq. 3d Div., Nov. 1944
Lipstein, Milton E., Pfc, Co. L 30th Inf, France 15 Oct. 1944
▲Littreal, Jacob D., S/Sgt, Co. A 756th Tank Bn., Germany 17 Apr. 1945
Livinghouse, Frederick J., Pvt, Co. C 10th Engr., Cisterna 23 May 1944
▲Lockwood, Arthur L., Sgt, Hq. Co. 3d Bn. 30th Inf, France 17 Dec. 1944
Lodato, John J., Capt, Hq. 39th FA Bn., Italy 3 Aug. 1943
Lodle, Elwood G., 1st Lt, Btry B 441st AAA AW Bn., France 5 Feb. 1945
Loeb, David, Capt, Inf Serv. Co. 756th Tank, France, Italy 13 Feb. 1945
Loewer, Henry G., Cpl, Hq. Co. 1st Bn. 30th Inf Regt., France 24 Jan. 1945
Lofgren, William H., T/4, Co. B 3d Med. Bn., N. Africa, Sicily, Italy, France 1 Jan. 1945
Loftus, Milton R., Pfc, Btry C 39th FA Bn., N. Africa, Sicily, Italy, France, Germany 8 May 1945
Logan, George E., Pfc, Hq. Btry 39th FA Bn., Anzio, Italy 23 Mar. 1944
▲Logsdon, Jessie M., Pfc, Co. C 7th Inf, Germany 7 Apr. 1945
Logue, Donald J., Sgt, Co. E 30th Inf, Vosges
Loibl, Mathew, Cpl, Co. M 30th Inf, N. Africa, Sicily, Italy, France, Germany 8 May 1945
Lombardi, Severino S., Pvt, Co. B 601st TD Bn., N. Africa, Italy, France 15 Jan. 1945
London, Kenneth M., Sgt, Co. B 30th Inf Regt., Germany 26 Mar. 1945
▲Long, Donald E., Lt Col, Chief MG Off. 3d Inf Div., France 4 Feb. 1945
Long, Oscar S., Maj, Inf CO Off. Tank Bn., Italy, France 14 Sept. 1944
Long, Runar A., Cpl, Btry B 39th FA Bn., Germany 17 Apr. 1945
Longcrier, Herbert H., 1st Sgt, Hq. Co. 3d Bn. 7th Inf Regt., France 27 Jan. 1945
Longo, Michael J., T/4, Hq. Co. 7th Inf Regt., France, Germany, Austria 4 May 1945
Longoria, Jesus, Pfc, Co. I 15th Inf Regt., France 17 Mar. 1945
Loofboro, Elmer L., Pvt, Med. Det. 7th Inf, Cisterna Di Littoria 25 May 1944
Looney, J. D., Pfc, Hq. Co. 3d Bn. 15th Inf Regt., Italy 29 May 1944
Lorenz, Marvin P., 1st Sgt, Hq. Btry 39th FA Bn., Anzio 26 Feb. 1944
Lorusso, Daniel P., T/Sgt, Hq. Btry 39th FA Bn., Italy
Losh, Elmer E., Pfc, Btry B 39th FA Bn., Cisterna 26 May 1944
Loss, John R., Pfc, Co. H 30th Inf, Le Tholy, France 6 Oct. 1944

▲ Oak Leaf Cluster.

Lottmann, Vernon G., T/Sgt, Co. D 30th Inf Regt., Germany 19 Apr. 1945
Love, Robert A., S/Sgt, Co. F 15th Inf, Isola Bella 1 Feb. 1944
Loveless, Gilbert C., Cpl, Co. F 15th Inf, Anzio, Italy 10 Mar. 1944
Lovell, Edward R., Capt, Btry A 9th FA Bn., Anzio 29 Feb. 1944
Lovell, Ottice, T/4, 3d Sig. Co., Italy 29 May 1944
Lovvorn, J. B., S/Sgt, Co. F 30th Inf, Anzio, Italy 24 Mar. 1944
Lucas, Harold E., T/5, Hq. Co. 3d Bn. 30th Inf
Lucas, Grady F., Pfc, Co. I 15th Inf, France 17 Mar. 1945
Luciatta, Raymond R., Pvt, Hq. Co. 30th Inf, Italy 5 June 1944
Lucide, Mario, Sgt, Hq. Co. 1st Bn. 30th Inf, Vosges
Lucidom, Mario, Sgt, Hq. Co. 1st Bn. 30th Inf Regt., France 7 Nov. 1944
Ludemann, John, Pvt, Co. D 15th Inf, Cisterna Di Littoria 23 May 1944
Ludtke, John H., Sgt, Co. H 7th Inf Regt., Italy, France 12 Nov. 1944
Ludwig, Fred A., T/5, Btry B 441st AAA AW Bn., Sicily, Italy, France, Germany, Austria 8 May 1945
Lukaszek, Edward N., Pvt, Serv. Co. 756th Tank Bn., France, Germâny, Austria 8 May 1945
Lunceford, Ernest L., Pfc, Co. M 30th Inf, N. Africa, Sicily, Italy, France, Germany 8 May 1945
Lundblad, John P., 1st Lt, Co. B 756th Tank Bn., Germany 28 Apr. 1945
Lunde, Kenneth H., T/4, Btry B 41st FA Bn., Artena 2 June 1944
Lunsford, Harold W., Pfc, Co. F 30th Inf Regt., France 23 Jan. 1945
Lupinski, Bronislaw S., Pfc, Co. C 7th Inf Regt., France 22 Nov. 1944
Luporini, Angelo J., Pvt, Co. F 30th Inf, Artena 1 June 1944
Lusby, William D., Pvt, Hq. Btry 3d IDA, Anzio, Italy 29 Feb. 1944
Luther, James M., Pfc, Hq. Co. 2d Bn. 30th Inf Regt., Germany 27 Mar. 1945
Lutz, Christian C., T/4, Serv. Co. 756th Tank Bn., Italy 28 Jan. 1944
Lykins, Eugene C., Pfc, Hq. Co. 3d Bn. 15th Inf, France 8 Jan. 1945
Lynch, Carl J., S/Sgt, 3d Rcn Trp., France 15 Jan. 1945
Lynch, Edward J., Pfc, Hq. Co. 30th Inf Regt., France 28 Oct. 1944
Lynch, Martin, T/4, Serv. Co. 30th Inf, Anzio, Italy 17 Mar. 1944
Lynch, Milford S., Pfc, Btry B 41st FA Bn., Italy 2 June 1944
Lynn, Orval R., Pfc, Btry B 9th FA Bn., Borgo Montello 29 Feb. 1944
Lynch, Thomas J., Jr., Pfc, Co. I 30th Inf, Ponte Rotto 23 May 1944
Lynch, Wayne W., T/4, Serv. Co. 30th Inf Regt., France 25 Dec. 1944
Lyons, Brian V., S/Sgt, Co. C 601st TD Bn., France, Germany May 1945

Maas, Robert L., Pvt, Hq. Co. 2d Bn. 30th Inf, Voleaux, France 21 Sept. 1944
MacAfee, Donald R., Pvt, SS Sec. 3d Div. Hq., Macon, France 3 Sept. 1944
Macedo, James, T/Sgt, Co. K 7th Inf Regt., France 15 Mar. 1945
Mackey, Ernest C., 1st Sgt, Hq. 3d Bn., 30th Inf
Mackey, Robert L., S/Sgt, Cn Co. 7th Inf, Anzio, Italy 9 May 1944
MacIntosh, Robert P., Pfc, Hq. Co. 2d Bn. 30th Inf, Anzio, Italy 21 Apr. 1944
▲Macklin, George F., Capt, Hq. 601st TD Bn., France, Germany Mar. 1945
MacTavish, Jack W., Pfc, Hq. Co. 3d Bn. 30th Inf Regt., France 3 Nov. 1944
Manijak, Frank J., Pfc, Co. K 15th Inf, France 27 Dec. 1944
Maddalozzo, John, T/5, Co. A 10th Engr. Combat Bn., France 2 Nov. 1944
Mader, Merrill T., T/5, Hq. Co. 601st TD Bn., Italy 8 Feb. 1944
Maegher, Michael T., Cpl, AT Co. 30th Inf, Vosges
▲Madriaga, William H. D., T/Sgt, Co. C 756th Tank Bn., France 5 Feb. 1945
Maher, Daniel W., Sgt, Co. C 30th Inf, Colmar
Maguire, William H., Capt, Inf Hq. 1st Bn. 7th Inf Regt., Germany 26 Apr. 1945
▲Maham, Ralph E., S/Sgt, Hq. Co. 2d Bn. 7th Inf, Anzio, Italy 16 Mar. 1944
Mahler, George C., Sgt, Serv. Co. 30th Inf Regt., Sicily, Italy, France 16 Jan. 1945
▲Mahoney, Robert H., T/5, Hq. Co. 3d Bn. 30th Inf, Raddon, France 17 Sept. 1944
Maier, Alvin, Cpl, Co. M 15th Inf, Isola Bella 11 Feb. 1944
Maier, Elmer A., Capt, Vet. Corps Hq. 3d Inf Div., Italy, France 22 Dec. 1944
Main, Emmet L., S/Sgt, AT Co. 7th Inf Regt., France 9 Sept. 1944
Main, Robert R., 1st Lt, Inf Co. I 15th Inf, France 29 Dec. 1944
Majewski, Lawrence L., 1st Sgt, Hq. Co. 3d Bn. 15th Inf, France 15 Aug. 1944
▲Malinowski, Adam A., Pvt, Hq. Co. 3d Bn. 30th Inf, Anzio, Italy 17 Mar. 1944
Malloy, George F., Pvt, Co. A 10th Engr. Combat Bn., France 29 Oct. 1944
Maloney, Bob E., Co. C 756th Tank Bn., Germany 30 Apr. 1945
▲Maloney, Joseph G., Pfc, Co. A 15th Inf, Montelimar, France 28 Aug. 1944
Manasco, Simon C., Pfc, Co. H 30th Inf, Brignoles, Frances 19 Aug. 1944
Manbeck, William W., S/Sgt, Co. H 30th Inf, France 22 Sept. 1944
Mancini, Orlando J., Pfc, Hq. Co. 756th Tank Bn., France 2 Dec. 1944
Mandalski, Frank J., Pfc, Co. B 756th Tank Bn., France 15 Sept. 1944
Maners, Earl W., Pfc, 3d Sig. Co., N. Africa, Sicily, Italy, France 31 Jan. 1945
Maniello, Frank E., S/Sgt, Btry C 441st AAA AW Bn., Sicily, Italy, France, Germany 8 May 1945
Mann, Travis, Jr., Pvt, Co. K 15th Inf, Italy 15 Oct. 1943
Mann, Wiley J., T/5, Rcn Co. 601st TD Bn., Sollgis Pont, France 18 Aug. 1944
Mannella, Joseph W., Pvt, Co. H 7th Inf, Ferdrupt 30 Sept. 1944
Manetta, Joseph J., Pvt, Hq. Btry 9th FA Bn., Anzio 29 Feb. 1944
Manning, Frank P., Capt, Btry C 69th Armd FA Bn., Italy 11 July 1944
Mapes, Terrance S., Pvt, Btry B 39th FA Bn., Cisterna 22 Apr. 1944
Manuska, Joseph J., Jr., Pfc, Co. C 30th Inf Germany
March, William A., Pvt, Hq. Co. 30th Inf, Volturno 15 Oct. 1943
Marchak, Joseph T., T/5, Btry B 441st AAA AW Bn., Cisterna 22 Mar. 1944
Marchesin, Enrico, Sgt, 3d Rcn Trp., Germany 8 May 1945
Marchiano, Lucas, S/Sgt, Co. M 30th Inf, France 1 Feb. 1945
Margritz, Robert M., Jr., Pvt, Co. H 7th Inf Regt., France 30 Oct. 1944
Marchunsky, Albert J., Pfc, Co. D 7th Inf Regt., Italy 24 May 1944
Marciszewski, Steve A., Pfc, Co. A 10th Engr. Combat Bn., France 5 Nov. 1944
Marini, Loreto, S/Sgt, Co. A 756th Tank Bn., France, Germany, Austria 8 May 1945
Mario, Carmen, Pvt, Hq. Co. 30th Inf, Flassans, France 18 Aug. 1944
Markes, William, Pvt, Hq. Co. 1st Bn. 7th Inf, Germany 18 Mar. 1945
Marochi, Greno J., T/5, Btry A 9th FA Bn., Italy 30 May 1944
Marotta, Carmine A., Sgt, Co. H 30th Inf Regt., France 5 Feb. 1945
Marquering, Joseph E., Sgt, Co. B 30th Inf Regt., France 20 Nov. 1944
Marquez, Gilbert H., Sgt, Co. K 7th Inf, Anzio, Italy 4 Feb. 1944
Marsh, Charles O., 1st Sgt, Btry A 9th FA Bn., Germany 18 Mar. 1945
Marszalek, Frank J., Pvt, Co. D 30th Inf, Aiz, France 21 Aug. 1944
Martell, John W., Cpl, Co. B 601st TD Bn., Miganao 9 Nov. 1943
▲Martin, Albert E., Maj, Hq. 441st AAA AW Bn., Italy, France 30 Nov. 1944
Martin, Andrew, Sgt, Co. E 7th Inf, Artena 28 May 1944
Martin, Courtney K., Jr., T/5, Serv. Co. 756th Tank Bn., France 2 Feb. 1945
Martin, Douglas M., Jr., T/Sgt, Hq. Co. 756th Tank Bn., N. Africa, Sicily, Italy, France, Germany, Austria 8 May 1945
Martin, Edward L., T/4, 3d Inf Div. Band, N. Africa, Sicily, Italy 31 Dec. 1943
Martin, John A., Sgt, Co. B 601st TD Bn., Germany 1 Apr. 1945
Martin, Joseph E., 1st Lt, Co. E 7th Inf Regt., Italy 12 Oct. 1943
Martin, Joseph S., T/Sgt, Co. E 30th Inf Regt., France 17 Dec. 1944
Martin, Kenneth G., S/Sgt, 3d QM Co., Sicily, Italy, France 14 Sept. 1944
Martin, Lionel A., Sgt, Co. A 30th Inf Regt., France 14 Oct. 1944
Martin, Lyle W., Sgt, SB Btry 9th FA Bn., Italy 3 June 1944
Martin, Max A., 1st Lt, Co. C 15th Inf, Cisterna Di Littoria 12 Feb. 1944
Martineau, Harvey R., Cpl, Btry B 9th FA Bn., Isola Bella 5 Feb. 1944
Martinez, Alfonso O., Pvt, Hq. Co. 30th Inf, Besancon, France 7 Sept. 1944
Martinez, Santiago M., S/Sgt, Co. A 15th Inf, Ramatuelle, France 15 Aug. 1944
Martino, Vincent A., T/5, Btry A 441st AAA AW Bn., Italy 29 Oct. 1943
Martinson, Frank L., T/5, Btry C 41st FA Bn., Sicily, Italy, France, Germany, Austria May 1945
Martowski, Patrick S., S/Sgt, CIC Det. 3d Inf Div., France 16 Feb. 1945
Martuch, George J., T/5, Hq. Co. 2d Bn. 30th Inf
▲Masi, Alfred, Pfc, Hq. Co. 2d Bn. 15th Inf Regt., France 5 Feb.. 1945
Mason, J K., 1st Lt, Sig. Corps 3d Sig. Co., Germany 26 Mar. 1945
Massey, Burrell T., S/Sgt, Btry B 10th FA Bn., Vittroles, France 24 Aug. 1944
Massey, Clarence, S/Sgt, Hq. Co. 1st Bn. 7th Inf, Cisterna Di Littoria 31 Jan. 1944
Masterton, Lennert D., Pfc, Hq. Co. 30th Inf, Germany 26 Mar. 1945
Matheny, Charles A., Pfc, Hq. & Hq. Btry 10th FA Bn., France 30 Jan. 1945
Mathewson, Kenneth C., Pfc, Rcn Co. 601st TD Bn., France 24 Nov. 1944
Mathile, Gerald D., Pfc, Co. I 7th Inf Regt., France 6 Oct. 1944
Matlock, Henry A., Capt, FA Btry B 39th FA Bn., France 23 Aug. 1944
Matte, Cecil J., Sgt, Rcn Co. 601st TD Bn., Italy, France, Germany 8 May 1945
Matter, Lester D., Jr., Capt, Co. C 601st TD Bn., Artena 29 May 1944
Matthews, Marion J., T/5, Btry D 441st AAA AW Bn., Guillianello 31 May 1944
Mauk, William H., Capt, MC Hq. Det. 3d Med. Bn., France 11 Dec. 1944
Maulshagen, Adolph J., Jr., S/Sgt, Co. K 30th Inf Regt., France Sept. 1944
Mauser, Curtis N., S/Sgt, Co. I 30th Inf, Colmar
Maxwell, Kenneth, T/5, Btry D 441st AAA AW Bn., France 29 Dec. 1944
Maxwell, Nelson S., Pfc, Co. H 7th Inf Regt., France 19 Jan. 1945
May, Joe N., Pfc, Hq. Co. 1st Bn. 30th Inf, France 5 Oct. 1944
May, Marks L., T/Sgt, Co. D 30th Inf Regt., Italy 5 Nov. 1943
May, Peter P., Jr., Pfc, Hq. Co. 30th Inf Regt., France 10 Nov. 1944
Mayfield, Cullen D., S/Sgt, Co. M 7th Inf, Italy 23 May 1944
Mayer, John J., Capt, Inf Co. K 30th Inf Regt., Germany 5 Apr. 1945
Mayes, William D., Pfc, 3d Inf Div. Band, Italy, France, Germany 8 May 1945
Maynard, Robert A., Capt, FA Co. B 601st TD Bn., France 15 Mar. 1945
Maynard, Robert E., Capt, FA Bn. Btry 41st FA Bn., Italy, France, Germany 8 May 1945
Mayo, Henry W., Jr., Capt, Med. Det. 41st FA Bn., France 8 Dec. 1944
Mazepa, Walter J., Pvt, Btry B 39th FA Bn., Cisterna 10 Mar. 1944
▲Mazner, Joe J., Sgt, MP Pltn 3d Div., France, Germany 8 May 1945
Mazor, John V., S/Sgt, Hq. Btry 39th FA Bn., Italy 26 May 1944
Mazur, John M., S/Sgt, Rcn Co. 601st TD Bn., Germany 6 Apr. 1945
▲McCall, Cyril F., S/Sgt, Hq. Co. 3d Bn. 7th Inf Regt., France 25 Oct. 1944
McCallie, John R., S/Sgt, 3d Rcn Trp., Germany 2 May 1945
McClain, Orris L., Pfc, Hq. Co. 3d Bn. 30th Inf, N. Africa, Sicily, Italy, France, Germany 8 May 1945
McClain, Paul E., S/Sgt, Co. I 15th Inf Regt., Germany 30 Mar. 1945
McClanahan, Maurice W., T/5, Hq. Btry 9th FA Bn., Sicily, Italy, France, Germany 8 May 1945
McClellan, Kenneth M., T/5, 3d Sig. Co., Artena 1 June 1944
McClung, George R., Cpl, Hq. Btry 39th FA Bn., Anzio, Italy 23 Mar. 1944
McClure, Edward S., T/5, Co. A 601st TD Bn., Rome 5 June 1944
McConnell, Sgt, Co. A 7th Inf, Artena 28 May 1944
McConnell, Russell B., Capt, Btry B 41st FA Bn., Italy 5 June 1944
McCrady, Jack R., Pfc, Hq. Co. 3d Bn. 30th Inf, Germany
McCurley, Alfred C., 2d Lt, Cn Co. 30th Inf
McCutchan, Charles O., S/Sgt, Btry B 39th FA Bn., Sicily 6 Aug. 1943
McDade, James E. A., T/4, Med. Det. 30th Inf, Germany
McDaniels, Victor, Pfc, Hq. Co. 2d Bn. 30th Inf, France 25 Dec. 1944
McDermott, Thomas M., Pvt, Btry A 41st FA Bn., Campo Morto 12 May 1944
McDonald, Durwood C., Pfc, Hq. Co. Med. Bn. 30th Inf, Italy 7 Nov. 1943
McDonald, Jack N., Pfc, Co. C 30th Inf, Brignoles, France 19 Aug. 1944
McDonald, Richard F., T/Sgt, Co. M 30th Inf, Campo Morto 25 Jan. 1944
McDurman, Jack H., T/5, Btry A 41st FA Bn., Aiz, France 20 Aug. 1944
McElroy, Robert C., Sgt, Co. C 601st TD Bn., Isola Bella 18 Mar. 1944
McEneany, Gerard J., Pfc, Hq. Co. 30th Inf Regt., France 10 Nov. 1944
McEwen, Orville S., Pfc, MP Pltn 3d Inf, Germany 8 May 1945
▲McFalls, Carroll, Jr., Capt, Inf Hq. 3d Bn. 30th Inf Regt., Germany 28 Apr. 1945
McFarland, Beryl E., Sgt, Co. E 7th Inf Vagney, France 17 Sept. 1944
McFerrin, Thomas L., 1st Sgt, Hq. Co. 751st TD Bn., Artena 1 June 1944
▲(4) McGarr, Lionel C., Col, Inf CO 30th Inf, Germany 20 Apr. 1945
McGaughey, Edward, S/Sgt, Cn Co. 30th Inf, Colmar
McGee, Walter D., 2d Lt, Btry D 441st AAA AW Bn., Sicily, Italy, France, Germany 8 May 1945
McGlothlin, Carlos M., S/Sgt, Co. F 7th Inf Regt., France 1 Oct. 1944
McGorvin, Raymond, Pfc, Serv. Btry 41st FA Bn., Sicily, Italy, France, Germany 8 May 1945
McGourty, Henry J., Jr., Pfc, Hq. Co. 3d Bn. 30th Inf, Taulignan 27 Aug. 1944
McGovern, James F., Capt, Btry A 441st AAA AW Bn., Italy 5 June 1944
McGraw, Alton J., Pfc, Co. I 7th Inf, Vagney 6 Oct. 1944
McGreevey, James E., Capt, MC Co. D 3d Med. Bn., N. Africa, Sicily, Italy, France, Germany 16 Mar. 1945
McGregor, Charles, Pfc, Co. C 30th Inf, France 18 Aug. 1944
McGregor, Kenneth C., Pfc, Co. B 7th Inf, Anzio, Italy 21 Apr. 1944
McGrew, Russell A., Pvt, Co. I 30th Inf Regt., Germany 28 Mar. 1945
McGuire, Francis L., T/5, Med. Det. 15th Inf Regt., France 11 Sept. 1944
▲(2) McGuire, Loyd, 1st Lt, Med. Det. 7th Inf Regt., France 23 Dec. 1944
McGuire, Russell A., Sgt, Hq. Btry 10th FA Bn., France 25 Jan. 1945

▲ Oak Leaf Cluster.

IN WORLD WAR II 419

McIlwain, Billy F., Sgt, Hq. Co. 2d Bn. 30th Inf Regt., France, Italy, Germany 8 May 1945
McIntire, Charles V., 1st Sgt, Co. H 30th Inf Regt., Germany 19 Mar. 1945
McIntyre, Delmar P., Cpl, Co. B 756th Tank Bn., France 15 Sept. 1944
McIntyre, William C., Jr., Capt, Hq. 3d Div. Arty, San Stephano, Sicily Aug. 1943
McKeown, Gordon, T/5, Btry C 41st FA Bn., France 24 Jan. 1945
▲McKinney, Lee K., Sgt, Co. E 30th Inf, France 23 Dec. 1944
McKirgan, Lowell T., Pfc, Hq. Co. 2d Bn. 7th Inf Regt., Germany 2 Apr. 1945
McLean, Luther C., T/5, Hq. Co. 2d Bn. 30th Inf, Colmar
McMahan, Roy S., T/5, Hq. Co. 30th Inf, France 10 Oct. 1944
McManus, Leo J., Pfc, Hq. Co. 3d Bn. 30th Inf, St. Mare, France 1 Oct. 1944
McMillan, John F., Sgt, Co. M 30th Inf, N. Africa, Sicily, Italy, France, Germany 8 May 1945
McMurray, Carroll D., T/5, Cn Co. 30th Inf, Mignano 4 Nov. 1944
McNabb, Paul R., S/Sgt, 3d QM Co., France 15 Oct. 1944
▲McNee, William W., Pfc, Hq. Co. 7th Inf, Germany 27 Mar. 1945
McNeel, Merton J., Pvt, Hq. Co. 1st Bn. 30th Inf, France 3 Oct. 1944
McPherson, Alan W., T/Sgt, 3d QM Co., France, Germany Mar. 1945
Meaders, James H., Pfc, Co. C 7th Inf, France 6 Feb. 1945
Meador, Howe, Sgt, Hq. Co. 1st Bn. 15th Inf, Anzio, Italy 6 Mar. 1944
Meagher, Michael J., Cpl, AT Co. 30th Inf, Aix, France 21 Aug. 1944
Meccariello, Edward P., Pfc, Hq. Co. 3d Bn. 7th Inf Regt., France 15 Aug. 1944
Meckley, William J., T/5, Hq. Co. 3d Bn. 7th Inf Regt., France 6 Oct. 1944
Medeiros, Manual J., Pvt, Co. B 30th Inf, France 3 Oct. 1944
Medina, Peter P., Pfc, Hq. Btry 3d IDA, Anzio, Italy 29 Feb. 1944
Mehl, John F., S/Sgt, Co. C 601st TD Bn., N. Africa, Italy, France 19 Feb. 1945
Mehuron, Gerald G., 1st Lt, Inf Co. I 30th Inf Regt., Germany 2 May 1945
Meier, Leopold J., T/Sgt, Hq. Co. 7th Inf Regt., Italy, France, Germany, Austria May 1945
Mellard, Robert B., S/Sgt, Co. D 30th Inf, Lantenot, France 17 Sept. 1944
Melfi, Michael A., Sgt, 703d Ord Co., N. Africa, Sicily, Italy, France 1 Jan. 1945
Mellinger, Leonard, Pfc, Hq. Btry 39th FA Bn., France 24 Jan. 1945
Mello, Anonc J., Sgt, Co. B 601st TD Bn., Ponte Rotto 29 Feb. 1944
Menter, Merle W., Cpl, Med. Det. 30th Inf, France 19 Dec. 1944
Mercer, Joseph A., 1st Lt, Inf Hq. 3d Inf Div., France, Germany, Austria 8 May 1945
Mercurio, Alphonse T., Pfc, Co. K 7th Inf, Padiglione 25 Apr. 1944
Mercurio, Peter P., Pfc, Serv. Co. 30th Inf, France 23 Jan. 1945
Meredith, Peyton W., Pvt, Hq. Btry 10th FA Bn., Italy 25 Mar. 1944
Meridith, Edward J., S/Sgt, AT Co. 30th Inf Regt., France 7 Nov. 1944
Merrell, James E., Pfc, Btry B FA Bn., Italy 14 Oct. 1943
Merrill, William B., 1st Sgt, Co. B 3d Med. Bn., N. Sicily, Italy, France, 24 Dec. 1944
Merritt, Leo H., T/4, Co. D 756th Tank Bn., Germany 1 May 1945
▲Merritt, Leo R., T/4, Co. D 756th Tank Bn., Germany 16 Mar. 1945
Mertsching, Frank R., Cpl, Btry B 39th FA Bn., France 11 Oct. 1944
Mersy, John G., Pfc, Co. E 7th Inf, Cisterna Di Littoria 29 Feb. 1944
Messick, Charles W., Pvt, Hq. Co. 1st Bn. 30th Inf, Le Tholy 30 Sept. 1944
Metcalfe, Charlie B., Capt, AC, Italy, France 15 Jan. 1945
Metcalfe, Rex, 1st Lt, CO Co. C 30th Inf, Valmontone 1 June 1944
▲Metzler, Roland N., Pfc, Co. M 30th Inf Regt., France 13 Sept. 1944
Meyer, Leonard F., Pvt, Hq. Btry 39th FA Bn., France 13 Sept. 1944
Meyer, Paul L., T/Sgt, Cn Co. 15th Inf Regt., France 8 Feb. 1945
Meyer, Wilbur H., S/Sgt, Serv. Btry 10th FA Bn., N. Africa, Sicily, France, Italy, Germany 8 May 1945
Meyers, Harlan A., T/5, Hq. Btry 3d Inf Div. Arty, N. Africa, Sicily, Italy, France, Germany 8 May 1945
Meyers, Mark W., Pfc, MP Pltn 3d Inf Div., France Feb. 1945
Michael, Donald P., Capt, Hq. Btry 69th Armd FA Bn., Italy 11 July 1944
Michalek, Clemence J., T/4, Cn Co. 15th Inf Regt., Italy, France 8 Feb. 1945
Michaud, Louis P., Pvt, Co. C 30th Inf Regt., France 2 Nov. 1944
Michehl, Milton C., Cpl, Co. M 30th Inf, N. Africa, Sicily, Italy, France, Germany 8 May 1945
Mihalic, Louis D., Sgt, Hq. & Serv. Co. 10th Engr. Combat Bn., Italy 6 June 1944
Milanowycz, Joseph A., Pfc, Co. G 15th Inf, Maillanfaing 24 Oct. 1944
Milburn, George W., Cpl, Co. C 601st TD Bn., France, Germany 8 May 1945
Milburn, Vernon M., S/Sgt, Co. E 7th Inf Regt., Italy 23 Jan. 1944
Miliczky, George A., T/5, Serv. Co. 30th Inf.
Miller, Albert E., Pfc, Hq. Co. 30th Inf. Regt., N. Africa, Sicily, Italy, France, Germany 8 May 1945
Miller, Aubry D., T/Sgt, Co. H 7th Inf, France 30 Oct. 1944
Miller, Carlyle E., Capt, 3d Bn. 15th Inf Regt., Germany 23 Mar. 1945
Miller, Elmer H., Cpl, Co. M 15th Inf, Cisterna Di Littoria 31 Jan. 1944
Miller, Francis E., T/4, Hq. Co. 601st TD Bn., Italy 1 June 1944
Miller, Frank I., Pfc, Co. F 7th Inf, Volmontone 2 June 1944
Miller, James W., Jr., Sgt, Co. C 756th Tank Bn., France 22 Feb. 1945
Miller, John B., Pfc, Co. L 7th Inf Regt., Germany 8 Mar. 1945
Miller, John B., 1st Lt, FA Co. C 601st TD Bn., Germany 29 Mar. 1945
Miller, John J., Jr., Pfc, Co. L 7th Inf Germany 30 Apr. 1945
Miller, John S., S/Sgt, Btry D 441st AAA AW Bn., Guillianello 31 May 1944
Miller, Joseph, Pfc, Rcn Co. 601st TD Bn., Germany 27 Apr. 1945
Miller, Machull, T/4, Hq. Btry 39th FA Bn., N. Africa, Sicily, Italy, France, Germany, Austria 8 May 1945
Miller, Morris E., S/Sgt, Co. E 30th Inf, San Agata, Sicily 8 Aug. 1943
Miller, Richard E., T/4, Cn Co. 30th Inf, Italy, France 15 Nov. 1944
Miller, Robert A., 2d Lt, Inf Cn Co. 7th Inf Regt., Germany, Austria 4 May 1945
Miller, Robert W., Pfc, Co. H 15th Inf, France 4 Feb. 1945
Miller, Roy E., S/Sgt, Hq. Co. 7th Inf Regt., France 29 Sept. 1944
Miller, Shelby, Pfc, Co. F 30th Inf, Sicily 8 Aug. 1943
Miller, William, Jr., 1st Lt, Inf Hq. Co. 7th Inf Regt., Germany 4 May 1945
Millican, Burr, Capt, Chap. Corps Hq. 441st AAA AW Bn., France, Germany 8 May 1945
Milligan, George F., Pfc, Hq. Btry 39th FA Bn., France 4 Nov. 1944
Milligan, Thomas R., S/Sgt, Co. I 7th Inf Regt., Germany 18 Apr. 1945
Milliken, Eugene V., Pfc, Hq. Co. 3d Bn. 15th Inf, Nettuno, Italy 22 Jan. 1944
Millis, Galen E., Pfc, Hq. Co. 3d Bn.15th Inf, France 18 Jan. 1945
Miner, Frederick C., Maj, FA S-3 601st TD Bn., Italy, France 14 Mar. 1945
Minerva, Frank D., Capt, MC 15th Inf, Volturno River 14 Oct. 1943
Minkler, Robert, T/4, AT Co. 7th Inf Regt., Italy 28 Apr. 1944
Minnick, George W., Jr., Sgt, Co. B 756th Tank Bn., France 27 Dec. 1944
Mirabello, Anthony H., Pfc, Hq. Co. 3d Bn. 7th Inf Regt., Padiglione 25 Apr. 1944
Miramontes, Salvador C., Pvt, Co. C 10th Engr., Cisterna 23 May 1944
Mironchik, Alexander J., T/4, AT Co. 15th Inf, France 4 Jan. 1945
▲Mishakas, Joseph, Sgt, Co. I 30th Inf, Boult 14 Nov. 1944
Mitcheli, Stephen W., T/4, Hq. Btry 3d Div., Arty, N. Africa, Sicily, Italy, France, Germany, Austria 8 May 1945
▲Mitchell, Jim, Pfc, Hq. Co. 7th Inf Regt., Germany 27 Mar. 1945
Mitchell, Joe E., T/5, Med. Det., France, Germany 30 Apr. 1945
Mitchell, Joseph H., T/5, Med. Det. 601st TD Bn., Anzio, Italy 28 Mar. 1944
Mitchell, Lewis H., Pfc, Co. A 7th Inf, France 30 Oct. 1944
Mitchell, Robert E., Maj, Inf Hq. 3d Inf Div., France, Germany, Austria 8 May 1945
Mitchusson, Vernice, Pfc, Co. I 30th Inf, Germany 26 Mar. 1945
Mitstifer, Francis R., Pvt, Hq. Co. 2d Bn. 7th Inf, Anzio, Italy 29 Feb. 1944
Mizinski, Frank R., Pfc, AT Co. 30th Inf, Germany
Moen, Lloyd P., Pfc, Hq. Co. 30th Inf, N. Africa, Sicily, Italy, France 18 Feb. 1945
Mohar, Norman M., Pvt, Hq. Co. 2d Bn. 30th Inf Regt., France 16 Aug. 1944
Mohr, George W., 1st Lt, Co. A 15th Inf, Rome 5 June 1944
Moldenhauer, Heinz D., Pvt, Co. E 7th Inf, Cisterna Di Littoria 23 May 1944
Mole, Joseph P., T/4, Hq. Co. 3d Inf Div., France 24 Jan. 1945
Molina, Ralph P., T/4, Hq. Co. 3d Inf Div., Italy, France 15 Sept. 1944
Moll, Arthur, T/5, 3d Sig. Co., France 28 Jan. 1945
Mollers, Lee V., Pfc, Med. Det. 30th Inf Regt., Germany 26 Mar. 1945
Molloy, Paul F., T/Sgt, Hq. Co. 7th Inf, N. Africa, Sicily, Italy, France, Germany 4 May 1945
Molnar, Julius, S/Sgt, Co. D 15th Inf Regt., France 20 Aug. 1944
Molnar, Zigmond, T/Sgt, Co. B 30th Inf Regt., France 23 Jan. 1945
Monaco, Thomas, Pvt, Co. K 7th Inf Regt., France 15 Mar. 1945
Monaghan, James E., S/Sgt, Co. K 7th Inf Regt., Germany 28 Apr. 1945
Monceaux, Dallas, S/Sgt, Co. M 30th Inf Regt., N. Africa, Sicily, Italy, France, Germany 8 May 1945
Moniz, Francis J., Sgt, Co. K 30th Inf Regt., Germany 26 Mar. 1945
Monks, James, Sgt, Hq. Co. 1st Bn. 30th Inf, Italy 24 Apr. 1944
Monnett, Lester R., Cpl, QM Co., Volturno 26 June 1944
▲Monohan, Joseph W., T/5, Co. B 601st TD Bn., Ponte Rotto 20 Feb. 1944
Monson, John H., T/4, Hq. Btry 9th FA Bn., N. Africa, Sicily, Italy, France, Germany 8 May 1945
Montano, Jose D., Pfc, Med. Det. 7th Inf Regt., Italy 5 Mar. 1944
Montano, Porfirio, Pfc, Co. D 7th Inf, France 22 Jan. 1945
Montemayor, Nemecio S., Pfc, Co. C 15th Inf Regt., Germany 20 Apr. 1945
Montesano, Anthony, Pfc, Co. B 30th Inf Regt., near Guemar, France 23 Jan. 1945
Montoya, Albert, 1st Lt, Hq. Btry 41st FA Bn., Coronia 5 Aug. 1943
Monturo, Joseph P., T/5, Hq. Btry 10th FA Bn., France 16 Aug. 1944
Moon, George R., Jr., 1st Lt, Co. A 601st TD Bn., Ponte Rotto 25 Feb. 1944
Moon, John V., T/Sgt, Hq. Sp. Trp. 3d Inf Div., France 30 Jan. 1945
Moon, Walter C., Pvt, Rcn Co. 601st TD Bn., Italy 21 Oct. 1943
Mooney, Earl S., Capt, Serv. Co. 30th Inf Italy, France 10 Feb. 1945
Moore, Carlisle C., Sgt, Hq. Co. 2d Bn. 7th Inf Regt., France 17 Jan. 1945
Moore, Denis G., Capt, Chap. Corps 15th Inf, Italy 9 Nov. 1943
Moore, Clarence H., Pfc, Med. Det. 30th Inf, Germany
Moore, Clayton H., Jr., 1st Lt, Inf Co. F 30th Inf Regt., near Burstadt, Germany 26 Mar. 1945
Moore, George H., S/Sgt, Hq. Btry 41st FA Bn., S. France 6 Oct. 1944
Moore, George L., Pfc, Co. C 15th Inf Regt., Germany 1 Apr. 1945
Moore, James H., Pfc, Co. M 30th Inf Regt., N. Africa, Sicily, Italy, France, Germany, Austria May 1945
Moore, John D., Cpl, Med. Det. 15th Inf Regt., Germany 7 Apr. 1945
Moore, Richard T., Pfc, Co. C 3d Med. Bn., Italy, France, Germany 8 May 1945
Moore, Robert B., T/5, Med. Det. 30th Inf, Anzio, Italy
▲Moore, Robert E., Pvt, Med. Dept. 30th Inf, Carano 25 Jan. 1944
Moore, Robert L., S/Sgt, Co. C 601st TD Bn., Cisterna 24 May 1944
Moore, Robert L., S/Sgt, Co. C 601st TD Bn., Conca 2 Mar. 1944
Morales, Mariano, T/Sgt, 3d Inf Div. Bn., Sicily 31 Dec. 1943
Moran, Edward J., Pfc, Hq. Co. 2d Bn. 30th Inf, Colmar
Morelli, Leo M., Pvt, Co. C 10th Engr. Bn., Faucogney 21 Sept. 1944
Moretto, Salvatore J., Pfc, Co. H 30th Inf Regt., France 18 Dec. 1944
Morgan, Elvin R., 1st Lt. Hq. 1st Bn. 7th Inf, Sicily 19 Aug. 1943
Morgan, James T., Cpl, Bn. B 9th FA Bn., Italy 6 Oct. 1943
Morgan, Leonard D., 2d Lt, Co. C 756th Tank Bn., Germany 21 Mar. 1945
Morgan, Paul R., 1st Lt, Corps Engr. Hq. & Serv. Co. 10th Engr. Combat Bn., France, Germany, Austria 8 May 1945
Morgan, Stanley, Pvt, Co. K 30th Inf, Vittoria 29 Jan. 1944
Morgan, Walter D., T/5, Hq. Btry 41st FA Bn., Cori 24 May 1944
Morgan, William A., Pfc, Co. G 7th Inf Regt., Italy 24 May 1944
Moriber, Leonard, 1st Lt, Inf Co. F 30th Inf Regt., France 8 Nov. 1944
Morina, Louis, Sgt, Co. B 10th Engr., France 8 Nov. 1944
Moro, Antonio, Pvt, Co. E 30th Inf, Anzio, Italy
Morris, Aaron E., T/4, Btry B 39th FA Bn., N. Africa, Sicily, Italy, France, Germany 8 May 1945
Morris, Bennie, T/5, Btry A 441st AAA AW Bn., Italy 29 Oct. 1943
Morris, Earl, Pvt, Co. C 10th Engr. Bn., Carano 5 Mar. 1944
Morris, Frane E., Pfc, MP Pltn 3d Inf, Germany 8 May 1945
▲(2) Morris, James M., 1st Lt, Inf Co. K 15th Inf Regt., France 6 Feb. 1945
Morris, Robert J., Pfc, Hq. Co. 30th Inf, Italy 1 June 1944
Morris, William W., Sgt, Co. B 30th Inf, France 2 Feb. 1945
Morrison, Hugh E., 1st Lt, Med. Det. 30th Inf, Germany 26 Mar. 1945
Morrison, John E., Sgt, Co. K 7th Inf, Ponte Rotto 9 Mar. 1944
Morrongiello, Salvatore J., S/Sgt, Co. M 15th Inf, Isola Bella 29 Feb. 1944
Morrow, Vincent J., T/4, Hq. Btry 3d Div. Arty, Sicily, Italy, France, Germany 8 May 1945
Morton, Carl A., T/5, Hq. Co. 30th Inf Regt., Italy, France, Germany 8 May 1945
▲Mosher, Francis C., 2d Lt, Co. G 7th Inf, Padiglione 22 Apr. 1944
Moss, Robert D., Cpl, Hq. Btry 9th FA Bn., Anzio, Italy 28 Mar. 1944
Motes, Clyde, Pfc, Co. G 7th Inf, Cisterna Di Littoria 24 May 1944
Mott, Harold, Pfc, Btry A 441st AAA AW Bn., Italy 29 Oct. 1943
Motteberg, Melvin, S/Sgt, Co. E 7th Inf Regt., Italy 5 June 1944
Mottor, Arthur F., Pfc, Co. H 15th Inf Regt., France 11 Oct. 1944
Mount, Henry F., Cpl, Hq. Co. 15th Inf, Nompatelize 4 Nov. 1944
Mousseau, Lyle C., Sgt, Serv. Btry 41st FA Bn., Castonia, Sicily 3 Aug. 1943

▲ Oak Leaf Cluster.

Moynihan, Francis D., Pfc, Med. Det. 7th Inf Regt., France 21 Oct. 1944
▲(2) Mozzer, Thotant J., Jr., Pfc, Co. H 15th Inf, France 2 Jan. 1945
Mudd, William C., 2d Lt, Inf Co. B 30th Inf Regt., France 23 Jan. 1945
Mudry, Metro, T/Sgt, Hq. Co. 3d Bn. 7th Inf Regt., Italy 5 June 1944
Muething, Gerald F., Capt, Btry B 441st AAA AW Bn., France 29 Jan. 1945
Mulhern, Charles E., Pvt, Med. Det. 15th Inf, Cisterna Di Littoria 23 May 1944
Mullen, Clyde F., S/Sgt, Hq. Sp. Trp. 3d Inf, France 30 Jan. 1945
Mullen, Richard D., 1st Lt, Serv. Btry 39th FA Bn., France 6 Sept. 1944
Mullen, Robert, T/5, Co. A 601st TD Bn., Tunisia 9 May 1943
Mullen, Robert D., S/Sgt, Co. E 30th Inf Regt., Germany 30 Mar. 1945
Mullens, Roy M., Pvt, Co. F 30th Inf Regt., Germany 20 Apr. 1945
Mullins, John J., Pvt, Hq. Co. 2d Bn. 30th Inf, Anzio, Italy 5 Mar. 1944
Mullins, Samie, T/5, Med. Det. 15th Inf, France, N. Africa, Sicily, Italy 8 Feb. 1945
Mullins, William K., Pfc, Co. A 7th Inf Regt., France 25 Sept. 1944
Mulshagen, Adolph J., Jr., S/Sgt, Co. K 30th Inf, Vosges
Mulvey, James J., Pvt, Hq. Co. 7th Inf, Palestrina 3 June 1944
Munro, John P., Cpl, 3d QM Co., Sicily, Italy, France, Germany, Austria 8 May 1945
▲Munsey, Giles R., 1st Lt, Hq. Co. 1st Bn. 30th Inf, France 20 Dec. 1944
Munson, Virgil L., Cpl, Cn Co. 30th Inf, Anzio, Italy
Murach, Andrew J., Pfc, Serv. Btry 41st FA Bn., Carroceto 29 Feb. 1944
Murdock, Court L., Cpl, AT Co. 30th Inf, Aix, France 21 Aug. 1944
Murk, Edward J., T/Sgt, Co. M 15th Inf, Anzio, Italy 27 Feb. 1944
Munrnahan, Oscar, Jr., Pvt, Co. A 7th Inf, France 27 Sept. 1944
Murphy, Albert W., Pfc, 3d Rcn Trp., Ponte Rotto 1 Mar. 1944
Murphy, Audie L., 1st Lt, Inf Co. B 15th Inf Regt., Italy 2 Mar. 1944
Murphy, Charles, Pfc, Co. H 15th Inf, France 4 Feb. 1945
Murphy, Francis J., Sgt, Co. F 30th Inf Regt., France 9 Nov. 1944
Murphy, James C., T/5, Btry A 441st AAA AW Bn., Italy 29 Oct. 1943
Murphy, Ramond P., Pvt, Hq. Co. 15th Inf, Cisterna Di Littoria 29 Feb. 1944
Murray, Charles P., Jr., 1st Lt, Inf Co. C 30th Inf Regt., France 24 Jan. 1945
Murray, Leo H., Sgt, Hq. Co. 756th Tank Bn., Italy 16 Feb. 1944
Murray, Louis H., Pfc, Co. D 15th Inf Regt., France 28 Aug. 1944
Musano, Jerry, Pfc, Hq. Co. 3d Bn. 7th Inf Regt., France 31 Dec. 1944
Muzzy, Edward J., Sgt, Btry B 441st AAA AW Bn., Italy 16 Feb. 1944
Myatt, Elvin E., 1st Sgt, Co. E 15th Inf Regt., Germany 18 Apr. 1945
Myers, Thomas R., Pfc, Serv. Co. 15th Inf Regt., Italy 4 June 1944
Mytkowicz, John, Pvt, Hq. Co. 30th Inf, Cisterna Di Littoria 23 May 1944

Nadler, Bernard, T/Sgt, Co. A 7th Inf, Cisterna Di Littoria 30 Jan. 1944
Nagy, Frank J., Cpl, Cn Co. 30th Inf, Colmar
▲Nanegos, Willard G., Pvt, Hq. Co. 7th Inf, Palestriana 3 June 1944
Naples, Nick, Pfc, Co. I 15th Inf, France 29 Dec. 1944
Napoli, Louis M., Pfc, Hq. Co. 3d Bn. 7th Inf, Italy 4 June 1944
Nardi, William A., Cpl, Hq. Btry 3d Div. Arty, Conca 26 Jan. 1944
Nardini, Freddie J., Pfc, Co. B 10th Engr. Combat Bn., France 22 Jan. 1945
Narodzonek, Stanley E., Sgt, Co. D 30th Inf, France 9 Nov. 1944
Natoli, Bartolo, T/4, Co. B 601st TD Bn., France 26 Jan. 1945
Naugle, George F., S/Sgt, Med. Det. Co. C 3d Med. Bn., France 17 Nov. 1944
▲Nault, Lionel J., Sgt, Co. F 30th Inf Regt., France 28 Jan. 1945
▲(3) Navarro, Joseph, Jr., Sgt, MP Pltn 3d Div., Germany 8 May 1945
Neary, Thomas A., S/Sgt, Co. A 601st TD Bn., N. Africa, Sicily, Italy, France, Germany 25 May 1945
▲(2) Neddersen, Richard H., Lt Col, Inf 30th Inf Regt., France 2 Nov. 1944
▲Needham, George W., Pvt, Hq. Co. 7th Inf, Palestrina 3 June 1944
Neelands, Marshall W., S/Sgt, Co. A 15th Inf, France 1 Feb. 1945
Neeson, George F., Pfc, Hq. & Serv. Co. 10th Engr. Combat Bn., Italy 10 Mar. 1944
Neilson, LaVar, Pfc, Co. M 30th Inf Regt., N. Africa, Sicily, Italy, France, Germany, Austria 8 May 1945
Neino, John, Pvt, Co. C 10th Engr., Carano 5 Mar. 1944
Nejia, Elliott, Pvt, 3d Rcn Trp., Germany 8 May 1945
Nelson, Earl E., T/4, Co. M 30th Inf Regt., N. Africa, Sicily, Italy, France, Germany 8 May 1945
Nelson, Clifford F., T/4, Hq. Co. 3d Inf Div., Italy, France 15 Sept. 1944
Nelson, Donald N., 2d Lt, Med. Det. 15th Inf, France 25 Jan. 1945
Nelson, John R., T/5, Btry B 39th FA Bn., Italy 10 Oct. 1945
Nelson, Lloyd N., Cpl, Btry B 41st FA Bn., Anzio, Italy 23 Mar. 1944
Nelson, Palmer C., Cpl, Serv. Btry FA, Italy 18 Nov. 1943
Nemec, Joseph C., Jr., Pfc, Hq. Co. 1st Bn 7th Inf Regt., France 24 Sept. 1944
Ne Smith, Albert N., 2d Lt, Inf 3d CIC Corps Det., Italy, France, Germany 28 Apr. 1945
Ness, Arden J., T/4, Med. Det. Hq. Co., Sicily 17 Apr. 1944
▲Neswoog, Olef K., S/Sgt, Co. A 15th Inf Regt., Germany 19 Apr. 1945
Neuens, Joseph L., Pfc, Btry B 39th FA Bn., Italy 8 Feb. 1944
Neumann, Robert D., Pfc, Hq. Btry 9th FA Bn., Germany 16 Apr. 1945
Newell, Dwight H., Sgt, Hq. Co. 3d Bn. 30th Inf, Anzio, Italy
Newell, Richard W., Capt, Inf Hq. 3d Inf Div., Italy, France 31 Jan. 1945
Newman, Earl L., Pfc, Hq. Btry 3d IDA, Anzio, Italy 29 Feb. 1944
Newman, Rushton M., Pfc, Co. M 15th Inf, Isola Bella 5 Feb. 1944
Newsom, John A., 1st Lt, 3d QM Co., Dragoni 27 Oct. 1943
Newton, William B., T/5, 3d Rcn Trp., Germany 21 Mar. 1945
Nicoli, Albert L., T/5, Hq. Co. 30th Inf Regt., Italy, France 10 Sept. 1944
Nicoll, Kenneth S., Cpl, Hq. Co. 2d Bn., Cisterna 14 Feb. 1944
Nicpon, Stanley, Pfc, MP Pltn 3d Inf, Germany 8 May 1945
▲Nichols, Harold E., 1st Lt, Btry B 39th FA Bn., Montelimar, France 28 Aug. 1944
Nichols, Lee R., S/Sgt, Co. D 30th Inf, France 21 Aug. 1944
Nichols, Leonard R., Sgt, Co. A 15th Inf, Germany 1 Apr. 1945
▲Nicholson, Harry L., 2d Lt, Co. M 30th Inf, Raddon, France 17 Sept. 1944
Nicholson, Joseph F., S/Sgt, Hq. Co. 3d Bn. 30th Inf Regt., France 23 Jan. 1945
Nicks, Clifford W., 1st Lt, Co. M 30th Inf, Ponte Rotto 21 May 1944
Nicoli, Albert L., T/5, Hq. Co. 30th Inf
Niedringhaus, Kimsey R., Pfc, Hq. Co. 3d Bn. 30th Inf, France 6 Feb. 1945
Nienow, Erwin C., T/5, Hq. Co. 7th Inf, Anzio, Italy 25 Feb. 1944
Nitzel, Kenneth E., Sgt, Co. L 30th Inf Regt., France 10 Nov. 1944
Nix, Otis, Pfc, Co. G 15th Inf, Germany 26 Mar. 1945
Noble, Harold J., Pfc, Co. L 15th Inf, Cisterna Di Littoria 23 May 1944
Nofal, Henry E., 1st Lt, Inf Serv. Co. 7th Inf Regt., France, Germany, Austria 5 May 1945
Noga, John J., Pfc, Co. B 30th Inf, Germany
Noland, Daniel B., Pvt, Co. K 15th Inf, Valmontone 30 May 1944
Noreuil, Louis O., Pfc, Co. M 7th Inf, Cisterna Di Littoria 23 May 1944
Norfolk, Albert A., Pfc, Co. A 15th Inf Regt., Germany 7 Apr. 1945
▲Norfolk, Robert G., Sgt, Co. H 7th Inf, Germany 7 Apr. 1945
Normoyle, Benedict F., Pfc, Hq. Btry 39th FA Bn., Anzio, Italy 23 Mar. 1944
Norris, John M., Pfc, MP Pltn 3d Inf Div., France 20 Oct. 1944
Norris, Warren P., Pfc, Co. C 30th Inf Regt., Germany 6 Apr. 1945
Norris, William E., T/4, Hq. & Serv. Co. 10th Engr. Combat Bn., Italy 10 Mar. 1944
Norrish, Frank W., T/Sgt, Co. E 7th Inf, Cisterna Di Littoria 28 May 1944
▲North, Eldon F., 2d Lt, Inf Cn Co. 30th Inf Regt., France 23 Jan. 1945
Norton, George E., T/5, Serv. Co. 30th Inf Regt., Italy, France, Germany, Austria 8 May 1945
Norton, Lowell D., Sgt, 3d Rcn Trp., Germany 8 May 1945
Norvell, William J., Pfc, Med. Det. 39th FA Bn., France 13 Sept. 1944
Norwood, Furman E., Pfc, Hq. Co. 1st Bn. 15th Inf Regt., France 11 Oct. 1944
▲(2) Noseck, Kenneth A., Capt, 1st Bn. 30th Inf, Le Tholy, France 30 Sept. 1944
Nottingham, Lucius S., Jr., Pfc, Hq. Co. 30th Inf Regt., France 10 Nov. 1944
Novak, Frank, Pfc, Btry A 441st AAA AW Bn., Italy 29 Oct. 1943
Nowicki, Raymond S., T/5, Med. Det. 15th Inf, St. Tropez 15 Aug. 1944
Nowosielski, Casimer F., Pfc, Co. B 7th Inf, Germany 18 Mar. 1945
Numainville, Woodrow W., Pfc, Co. C 3d Med. Bn., Italy 24 Oct. 1943
Nusz, Alvin, 1st Sgt, Co. B 756th Tank Bn., France 15 Feb. 1945
Nuzel, John S., Sgt, Co. D 30th Inf Regt., Italy 28 May 1944
Nylund, Leonard O., Pvt, Co. L 30th Inf Regt., France 10 Nov. 1944

Oakland, Gordon S., T/4, Hq. Co. 7th Inf Regt., France 22 Sept. 1944
Oates, Calvin W., T/3, Med. Det. 30th Inf, France 11 Nov. 1944
▲Obadowski, Joseph J., 1st Lt, Inf Co. F 30th Inf, Italy, France, Germany May 1945
▲Obelieiro, Ferdinand E., Pfc, Med. Det. 7th Inf Regt., France 15 Mar. 1945
Obler, Edward I., 1st Lt, Corps Engr. Co. B 10th Engr. Combat Bn., Germany 20 Apr. 1945
O'Block, Victor J., Pfc, Hq. Co. 3d Inf Div., Italy, France, Germany 8 May 1945
O'Brien, Cyril P., Sgt, Co. G 7th Inf Regt., France 16 Feb. 1945
O'Brien, Edward E., S/Sgt, 3d QM Co., Italy June 1944
O'Brien, Francis T., Pfc, Hq. Co. 3d Bn. 15th Inf Regt., Germany 4 Apr. 1945
O'Brien, John F., Cpl, Hq. Co. 3d Bn. 30th Inf, N. Africa, Sicily, Italy, France, Germany 8 May 1945
O'Brien, Mark P., T/4, Hq. Btry 39th FA Bn., France 13 Sept. 1944
▲O'Brien, Patrick J., Pfc, Co. M 30th Inf, Anzio, Italy 10 Mar. 1944
O'Brien, Robert J., Pfc, Btry A 39th FA Bn., N. Africa, Sicily, Italy, France, Germany, Austria 8 May 1945
O'Brien, Russell E., Pfc, Co. M 30th Inf Regt., France 30 Oct. 1944
Ochs, Thomas V., Pfc, Hq. Co. 2d Bn. 30th Inf Regt., France 31 Dec. 1944
▲O'Connell, Frank M., S/Sgt, Co. I 30th Inf Regt., near Weiskirch, Germany 16 Mar. 1945
O'Connel, James J., Pfc, MP Pltn 3d Inf Div., France May 1945
O'Connell, John Maj, Inf CO 3d Bn. 15th Inf Regt., France 28 Jan. 1945
O'Daniel, John W., Maj Gen, US Army 3d Inf Div., France 24 Oct. 1944
Odegard, Arnold B., Pvt, Co. B 10th Engr. Combat Bn., France 22 Jan. 1945
▲(2) O'Donnell, John C., Cpl, Co. B 601st TD Bn., France 23 Jan. 1945
O'Hara. William J., Cpl, 3d QM Co., Italy, France, Germany 18 Feb. 1945
Ohlemacher, Russell R., T/5, Med. Det. 7th Inf Regt., France 30 Nov. 1944
Olander, Edwin J., 1st Lt, 3d Sig. Co., Italy 9 Mar. 1944
Olds, Kendell A., Pvt, Co. G 30th Inf Regt., Germany 27 Mar. 1945
Olecki, Joseph F., Pfc, Cn Co. 30th Inf Regt., Germany 2 May 1945
Olenik, Andrew B., Pfc, Med. Det. 7th Inf Regt., France 22 Jan. 1945
Olevich, Victor J., Pfc, Hq. Co. 1st Bn. 15th Inf, France 1 Feb. 1945
Oliver, John, T/5, Btry A 441st AAA AW Bn., Italy 29 Oct. 1943
Oliver, Coy E., Pvt, Hq. Co. 2d Bn. 7th Inf Regt., France 20 Nov. 1944
▲Oliver, Haskey O., S/Sgt, Co. B 756th Tank Bn., France 15 Sept. 1944
Olsen, Clyde W., Pvt, Btry C 9th FA Bn., Borgo Montello 29 Feb. 1944
▲Olson, Alfred S., Pfc, Hq. Co. 2d Bn. 7th Inf Regt., Germany 20 Mar. 1945
Olson, Arthur B., T/4, 3d Rcn Trp., France 18 Jan. 1945
Olson, Charles M., T/5, Co. A 756th Tank Bn., France 15 Sept. 1944
Olson, Edwin B., Capt, Inf Hq. 756th Tank Bn., France 13 Feb. 1945
Olson, Emil A., Sgt, Co. M 30th Inf, Anzio, Italy 17 Feb. 1944
Olson, Gordon E., T/5, 3d Inf Div. Band. N. Africa, Sicily, Italy 31 Dec. 1943
▲Olson, Raymond F., Sgt, Co. M 30th Inf, Carano 9 Apr. 1944
Olszewski, Joseph M., Sgt, Serv. Btry 69th Armd FA Bn., Italy 10 Mar. 1944
O'Mears, Philip G., S/Sgt, Hq. Btry 39th FA Bn., Artena 2 June 1944
▲O'Mohundro, Wiley H., Col, Inf, France, Italy 22 Aug. 1944
O'Neill, Hugh A., Capt, Co. A 3d Med. Bn., Italy 10 Oct. 1944
Ong, Donald C., Sgt, Co. E 30th Inf Regt., France 10 Nov. 1944
Onofrietti, Philip, Pfc, Co. E 7th Inf Regt., France 20 Nov. 1944
Oppek, Florian J., T/3, Med. Det. 30th Inf Regt., Italy, France, Germany 8 May 1945
Oppenhimer, John S., 1st Lt, Hq. 3d Inf Div. Atry, France, Germany 8 May 1945
Oppio, Santino, S/Sgt, Hq. Co. 2d Bn. 7th Inf Regt., Italy, France 11 Feb. 1945
Ording, Lowell H., Pfc, 3d Inf Div. Band, N. Africa, Sicily, Italy, France, Germany 8 May 1945
Orlando, Tony, Pfc, Med. Det. 10th Engr. Bn., Anzio, Italy 2 Feb. 1944
O'Rourke, Edward J., S/Sgt, Co. G 30th Inf Regt., France 17 Dec. 1944
O'Rourke, John J., Pfc, Btry A 39th FA Bn., France 27 Jan. 1945
Orr, Delmar D., Pfc, Co. C 601st TD Bn., France 16 Aug. 1944
Ortega, Peter, Cpl, Co. B 10th Engr. Combat Bn., Germany 18 Mar. 1945
Osborn, James W., Cpl, Btry C 39th FA Bn., N. Africa, Sicily, Italy, France, Germany, Austria 8 May 1945
▲Osborne, Arthur, T/Sgt, Co. B 30th Inf Regt., Germany 19 Apr. 1945
Osborne, James H., S/Sgt, Btry C 10th FA Bn., N. Africa, Sicily, Italy, France, Germany, Austria 8 May 1945
Osborne, Paul E., T/Sgt, Co. A 7th Inf Regt., Germany 18 Mar. 1945
Osborne, William H., Pfc, Co. H 15th Inf, Isola Bella 31 Jan. 1944
▲(3) Osgard, James L., Lt Col, Inf Hq. 2d Bn. 30th Inf Regt., Germany 29 Apr. 1945
O'Shaughnessy, Francis J., Pvt, Btry B 39th FA Bn., Cisterna 10 Mar. 1944
O'Shea, Patrick J., S/Sgt, Co. A 3d Med. Bn., France 20 Nov. 1944
Ostrobinski, Stanley J., Cpl, Med. Det. 601st TD Bn., El Guettar, Tunisia 23 Mar. 1944
Ostrosky, Bruno J., Pfc, Co. H 7th Inf Regt., France 13 Sept. 1944
Ostrowski, Walter J., Pfc, Btry D 441st AAA AW Bn., Germany 27 Mar. 1945

▲ Oak Leaf Cluster.

Osuchowski, William W., S/Sgt, Hq. Co. 601st TD Bn., N. Africa, Italy, France, Germany 18 Apr. 1945
Oswald, Raymond C., Capt, FA Hq. 3d Inf Div. Arty, Italy, France, 6 Feb. 1945
Ottinger, Loyd M., Pvt, Co. E 15th Inf Regt., France 19 Dec. 1944
Ovellett, Clement P., T/5, Serv. Co. 30th Inf
Overstreet, Marvin E., Pfc, Serv. Co. 30th Inf Regt., N. Africa, Sicily, Italy, France 13 Dec. 1944
Overton, Mays G., T/Sgt, Co. I 7th Inf, France 16 Jan. 1945
Owen, Alfred W., T/4, Co. K 15th Inf, France 27 Dec. 1944
Owen, William T., T/5, Co. C 601st TD Bn., Mignano 8 Nov. 1943
Owens, Jack D., Pfc, Btry A 9th FA Bn., Italy 29 May 1944
Owsinski, Joseph, Sgt, Co. E 7th Inf, Anzio, Italy 29 Feb. 1944

Pace, Willie, Pfc, Med. Det. 10th Engr. Bn., Carano 13 Mar. 1944
Packman, James L., Capt, CO Co. A 30th Inf, Cussey, France 9 Sept. 1944
Pacunas, Alban A., CWO, US Army Serv. Co. Inf Regt., N. Africa, Sicily, Italy, France 20 Feb. 1945
Padolak, Walter J., Sgt, Co. M 7th Inf, France 31 Oct. 1944
Page, George H., Capt, FA Btry B 10th FA Bn., N. Africa, Sicily, Italy, France, Germany 8 May 1945
Page, Lewis J., T/5, Serv. Co. 756th Tank Bn., France, Germany, Austria 8 May 1945
Page, Warren L., Pfc, Hq. Co. 3d Bn. 30th Inf Div., France 16 Dec. 1944
Pagenkopf, Charles A., S/Sgt, Serv. Co. 15th Inf, France 26 Dec. 1944
Paine, John H., T/Sgt, Hq. 3d Inf Div., Sicily, Italy, France, Germany 8 May 1945
Palmer, Allan L., S/Sgt, Co. B 10th Engr. Combat Bn., Italy, France, Germany 8 May 1945
Palmer, Robert G., Pvt, Hq. Btry 39th FA Bn., Anzio, Italy 23 Mar. 1944
Palumbo, Sam, Pfc, Hq. Btry 39th FA Bn., France 19 Mar. 1945
Panek, Thomas, Jr., Co. G 30th Inf Regt., France 21 Nov. 1944
Panico, Ralph, Sgt, Co. C 601st TD Bn., France 23 Jan. 1945
Panicko, Stanley, Pfc, Med. Det. 15th Inf Regt, France 16 Mar. 1945
Panning, Alvin E., T/Sgt, Co. C 751st Tank Bn., Isola Bella 16 Feb. 1944
Parent, Leo E., Pfc, Co. C 7th Inf, France 30 Oct. 1944
Parini, Harley D., T/5, Serv. Btry 41st FA Bn., San Stephano, Sicily 5 Aug. 1943
Parisi, Daniel T., Pfc, Co. B 7th Inf, France 30 Oct. 1944
Parish, Howard L., Pvt, Co. A 30th Inf Regt., France 1 Oct. 1944
Parisi, Joseph A., T/5, Co. D 7th Inf Regt., France 23 Oct. 1944
▲Parizo, Norman R., Pvt, Med. Det. 15th Inf, Germany 12 Apr. 1945
Parker, Arthur Y., Pvt, Hq. Co. 30th Inf, Italy 5 June 1944
Parker, Frank M., M/Sgt, Serv. Co. 7th Inf Regt., Italy, France, Germany 4 May 1945
Parks, Jack, Pfc, Co. M 30th Inf Regt., Sicily, Italy, France, Germany, Austria May 1945
Parks, John M., T/Sgt, Co. L 7th Inf Regt., France 1 Jan. 1945
Parlegreco, Thomas A., Sgt, Btry B 39th FA Bn., Cisterna 10 Mar. 1944
Parmelee, Luke W., T/5, Med. Det. 10th FA Bn., Cisterna 10 Mar. 1944
▲Parslow, Clifford D., Pfc, Hq. Co. 1st Bn. 15th Inf, France 1 Feb. 1945
Parsons, Lowell D., 1st Lt, Co. E 30th Inf, Germany
Partin, John T., Sgt, Co. K 7th Inf, Ponte Rotto 29 Feb. 1944
Partridge, Oscar R., M/Sgt, Serv. Btry 10th FA Bn., Sicily 17 Aug. 1943
Parulski, Walter S., Pfc, Btry B 41st FA Bn., Artena 2 June 1944
Parziale, Charles J., Capt, Hq. 3d Bn. 15th Inf, Isola Bella 1 Feb. 1944
Pascoe, Albert B., Pfc, Co. G 7th Inf, Cisterna Di Littoria 5 Apr. 1944
▲Pascual, Nicholas, 1st Lt, Co. D 30th Inf, France 7 Sept. 1944
Passon, Walter, Pfc, Hq. Btry 10th FA Bn., Italy 25 Mar. 1944
Patchell, Donald, Pfc, Co. E 30th Inf, Germany 19 Apr. 1945
Pate, Herbert, Pvt, Hq. Btry 9th FA Bn., Anzio 29 Feb. 1944
Patnoe, Tuffield T., S/Sgt, Co. M 15th Inf, Anzio, Italy 20 Feb. 1944
Patrick, Charles J., 2d Lt, Co. G 7th Inf, France 20 Nov. 1944
Patrick, Jack B. E., Pfc, Co. K 15th Inf Regt., Germany 3 May 1945
Patrick, John W., Pfc, Co. M 30th Inf Regt., France 22 Nov. 1944
▲(2) Patrick, Richard B., S/Sgt, Co. K 15th Inf Regt., France 24 Dec. 1944
Patrizio, Vincenzio T., Pfc, Hq. Co. 1st Bn. 7th Inf, France 15 Mar. 1945
Patterson, Carl D., Jr., Capt, Serv. Btry 69th Armd FA Bn., Italy 10 Aug. 1944
Patterson, Dale M., Sgt, Co. H 15th Inf Regt., Germany 18 Mar. 1945
Patterson, Graham L., 1st Lt, Ord. (703d), Italy 15 Sept. 1944
Patterson, Harry E., 2d Lt, Co. F 7th Inf, Anzio, Italy 20 Apr. 1944
Patterson, Howard L., S/Sgt, Co. K 7th Inf, Anzio, Italy 26 Jan. 1944
Patterson, Howard J., Pfc, Co. G 30th Inf Regt., France 21 Sept. 1944
Patterson, James A., T/5, Btry A 10th FA Bn., Rupt-Sur-Moselle, France 1 Oct. 1944
Patsey, Edward G., T/5, Btry 39th FA Bn., Italy 1 June 1944
Patton, James E., 1st Sgt, AT Co. 30th Inf, Colmar
Paul, Frank S., Jr., T/5, Hq. Co. 3d Bn. 15th Inf, France 27 Dec. 1944
Pauley, William H., Pfc, BP 7th Inf, Italy 2 June 1944
Paulick, Michael, Lt Col, CO 1st Bn. 15th Inf, France 31 Aug. 1944
Paulson, Bernard D., T/5, Hq. Btry 41st FA Bn., Coronia, Sicily 5 Aug. 1943
Paukst, Joseph J., T/4, Serv. Co. 7th Inf Regt., France 5 Jan. 1945
Pauly, Levien C., Pfc., Co. M 30th Inf Regt., N. Africa, Sicily, Italy, France, Germany 8 May 1945
Pavlovich, Elroy G., 1st Lt, Hq. Co. 2d Bn. 15th Regt., Italy, France 21 Nov. 1944
Pavonetti, Pardo A., T/5, Hq. Co. 2d Bn. 15th Inf Regt., Germany 18 Mar. 1945
Payne, Howard T., Pfc, Co. A 30th Inf, Anzio, Italy
Payne, Ralph W., 1st Lt, Inf Co. K 7th Inf, France 20 Nov. 1944
Paz, Michael M., Pfc, Hq. Co. 2d Bn. 7th Inf, Italy 15 Oct. 1943
Peairs, Douglas D., 1st Lt, FA 41st Bn., Italy 2 Mar. 1944
Pearce, Henry N., T/5, Hq. Co. 601st TD Bn., N. Africa, Italy, France, Germany, Austria 8 May 1945
Pearson, Cecil, Pfc, Hq. & Hq. Co. 2d Bn. 15th Inf Regt., France 29 Oct. 1944
▲Peck, George S., Capt, Inf Hq. 2d Bn. 30th Inf Regt., Germany 12 Apr. 1945
Peckham, Julian F., Jr., T/5, Co. D 756th Tank Bn., Italy, France, Germany, Austria 8 May 1945
Pederson, Henry M., Sgt, Btry B FA, Cisterna Di Littoria 29 Feb. 1944
▲Peebles, William R., Capt, CAC Hq. 3d Inf Div., Italy 5 June 1944
▲Pendleton, Verl L., S/Sgt, Hq. Co. 1st Bn. 7th Inf, Italy 10 Mar. 1944
Pellagrini, Nadzarini, Pfc, Btry C 41st FA Bn., Italy 3 June 1944
Pellicciari, Nicholas J., 1st Lt, Inf Hq. 7th Inf Regt., Italy, France 7 Oct. 1944
Pellis, Alexander, S/Sgt, Co. M 7th Inf Regt., France 23 Oct. 1944
Peluso, Rocco, Sgt, Co. C 756th Tank Bn., Germany 21 Mar. 1945
Penna, Denver T., Sgt, Co. L 15th Inf, France 24 Dec. 1944
Pennell, Clyde W., Pfc, 3d Rcn Tp., France 28 Oct. 1944
Penny, William J., Cpl, Med. Det. 601st TD Bn., Anzio, Italy 28 Mar. 1944
Pentiak, Peter R., S/Sgt, Serv. Co. 7th Inf, Italy, France, Germany May 1945
▲Pepchinski, Bonivent J., Pfc, Co. E 15th Inf Regt., France 5 Feb. 1945
Pepper, Green L., Sgt, Co. K 7th Inf Regt., Germany 18 Apr. 1945
Peraset, Charles, T/4, Btry A 444st AAA AW Bn., Sicily, Italy, France, Germany 8 May 1945
Perchan, Harold W., Sgt, Hq. Co. 7th Inf Regt., France 22 Aug. 1944
▲Pergament, Hyman, 1st Lt, Inf Co. H 30th Inf, France 26 Jan. 1945
Perkins, John C, Maj, Inf S-2 30th Inf, France, Germany May 1945
Perkins, Lester O., Pvt, Hq. & Hq. Btry 41st FA Bn., Le Ferriere 8 Apr. 1944
Perry, Buster, Cpl, Btry 39th FA Bn., France 4 Nov. 1944
Perry, John C., Capt, FA Hq. Co. 601st TD Bn., France 28 Feb. 1945
Perry, Victor J., Pfc, Co. L, 30th Inf Regt., France 28 Oct. 1944
Perschbacher, Edward H., Pfc, Hq. Co. 1st Bn. 30th Inf Regt., France 17 Dec. 1944
Peters, Edgar E., Cpl, Med. Det. 7th Inf Regt., Italy, France 26 Nov. 1944
Peters, Frank J., Pfc, MP Pltn 3d Inf Div., Italy 23 May 1944
Peterman, Daniel V., Sgt, Co. D 7th Inf Regt., France 30 Jan. 1945
Petersen, Louis C., Sgt, Hq. 3d Div., Italy, France, Germany 1 May 1945
Peterson, Bernard J., S/Sgt, Hq. Btry 10th FA Bn., St. Tropez, France 15 Aug. 1945
Peterson, Charles E., Pfc, Co. F 30th Inf, Volturno 13 Oct. 1943
Peterson, Irving C., Pfc, Hq. Co. 1st Bn. 15th Inf Regt., Italy 22 Feb. 1944
Peterson, James C., Pfc, Co. M 7th Inf, Anzio, Italy 1 Mar. 1944
▲Peterson, Orville S., T/5, Med. Det. 30th Inf, Anzio, Italy 21 Apr. 1944
Peterson, Palmer, T/5, Btry A 9th FA Bn., Germany 18 Mar. 1945
Peterson, Robert L., Pfc, Co. A 10th Engr. Combat Bn., France 5 Nov. 1944
Peterson, Vincent L., Pfc, Co. B 15th Inf Regt., France 26 Jan. 1945
Peterson, Wesley F., T/Sgt, Hq. 3d Inf Div., France, Germany 8 May 1945
▲(2) Petherick, Robert L., Maj, Engr. Corps Co. 10th Engr. Combat Bn., Germany 20 Apr. 1945
Petitbon, Leon A., 1st Lt, FA Co. B 601st TD Bn., Germany 19 Apr. 1945
Petrak, James H., Cpl, Btry D 441st AAA AW Bn., France 29 Dec. 1944
Petrarca, Ernest, Pvt, Co. A 756th Tank Bn., France 15 Sept. 1944
Petrella, Daniel D., T/Sgt, Hq. Co. 3d Bn. 30th Inf Regt., France 23 Jan. 1945
Pettijohn, James A., T/Sgt, Hq. Co. 756th Tank Bn., N. Africa, Sicily, Italy, France, Germany 8 May 1945
Petty, Leo, 1st Sgt, Co. C 756th Tank Bn., France, Germany, Austria 8 May 1945
Peyton, Levi G., Pvt, Co. H 15th Inf, Torpes, France 8 Sept. 1944
Pezzati, Albert, S/Sgt, CIC Det. 3d Inf Div., Germany, Austria 8 May 1945
▲Phalen, James B., Cpl, Hq. Co. 3d Bn. 15th Inf, Cisterna 26 May 1944
▲Phelps, Jim S., Capt, Inf Hq. 2d Bn. 30th Inf, Germany 7 Apr. 1945
Philipp, Edward H., T/5, Hq. Co. 2d Bn. 30th Inf, France 23 Jan. 1945
Philip, Philip, T/4, Co. C 601st TD Bn., France 13 Oct. 1944
Phillips, Carlos E., Pfc, Hq. Btry 9th FA Bn., Germany 16 Apr. 1945
Phillips, Clinton O., Pfc, Serv. Co. 30th Inf Regt., Germany 26 Mar. 1945
Phillips, Hoyt G., 1st Lt, Serv. Co. 30th Inf Regt., Germany 26 Mar. 1945
Phillips, James A., Pfc, MP Pltn 3d Div., Germany 8 May 1945
Phillips, James F., Sgt, Co. C 7th Inf, Germany 7 Apr. 1945
Phillips, James T., Jr., S/Sgt, Co. E 7th Inf Regt., France 28 Sept. 1944
Picard, Ovila H., 1st Sgt, Co. A 601st TD Bn., Germany 6 Apr. 1945
Pichot, Emil, Pfc, Hq. Btry 39th FA Bn., France 24 Jan. 1945
Pickard, Floyd J., Pvt, Co. D 15th Inf, Artena 28 May 1944
Pickett, Samuel R., S/Sgt, Co. F 15th Inf Regt., France 27 Jan. 1945
Pier, Gerald L., Pfc, Cn Co. 15th Inf, Allan, France 28 Aug. 1944
Pierce, Joe M., Pfc, Co. I 30th Inf Regt., France 8 Jan. 1945
Pierce, Maurice E., T/4, Hq. 3d Div., N. Africa, Sicily, Italy, France, Germany, Austria 8 May 1945
Pierson, Julius B., Pfc, Co. C 10th Engr. Combat Bn., France 7-8 Oct. 1944
Pimental, James H., Cpl, MP Pltn 3d Inf, Sicily 22 July 1943
Pion, Louis J. B., Pvt, Hq. Co. 1st Bn. 7th Inf Regt., Germany 19 Apr. 1945
Piper, John H., T/4, Hq. Btry 441st AAA AW Bn., Sicily, Italy, France, Germany 8 May 1945
Pipes, Melvin, Pfc, Co. F 30th Inf Regt., France 10 Jan. 1945
Pirrone, John B., T/4, Hq. Btry 3d Inf Div. Arty, Italy, France, Germany 8 May 1945
Piscitelli, Clemente P., S/Sgt, Co. L 30th Inf Regt., France 10 Nov. 1944
Piskor, Stanley T., T/4, Hq. Co. 3d Bn. 15th Inf Regt., Sicily 4 Aug. 1943
Pistilli, John J., Pfc, Co. G 7th Inf, Italy 23 May 1944
Pitcher, Elmer B., Pfc, Co. C 30th Inf
Pitz, Harland W., T/4, Btry B 41st FA Bn., N. Africa, Sicily, Italy, France, Germany 8 May 1945
Pixley, Erwin W., Pvt, Med. Det. 7th Inf Regt., France 23 Jan. 1945
Platt, Louis I., T/5, Hq. Co. 3d Inf Div., Italy, France 21 Jan. 1945
Plunkett, Robert L., T/Sgt, Hq. Co. 1st Bn. 15th Inf Regt., France 24 Oct. 1944
Podemski, Ervin, T/Sgt, Hq. Co. 3d Bn. 15th Inf, Italy 18 Nov. 1943
Poe, William S., Sgt, Co. D 756th Tank Bn., France 22 Nov. 1944
Poindexter, Robert A., T/4, Co. A 601st TD Bn., Germany 15 Mar. 1945
Pointer, Grant, Cpl, Btry C 39th FA Bn., Italy 23 Dec. 1943
Pola, Orlando M., Pfc, Hq. Co. 3d Bn. 15th Inf, France 17 Sept. 1944
Poland, Jack L., Sgt, Co. K 7th Inf Regt., France 15 Mar. 1945
Polek, Micheal P., Sgt, Btry C 39th FA Bn., Sicily 17 Aug. 1943
Polenchar, Joseph E., Pfc, Co. C 30th Inf, Brignaoles, France 19 Aug. 1944
Poli, Constantine J., Pfc, Med. Det. 7th Inf Regt., Germany 18 Apr. 1945
Polich, George B., T/Sgt, Cn Co. 15th Inf, Conca 29 Feb. 1944
Polk, Tom R., Sgt, Serv. Co. 15th Inf, Italy 2 June 1944
Poltiske, Anton, Pfc, Co. I 30th Inf, Carano 28 Feb. 1944
Pompei, Daniel R., Pfc, Co. E 7th Inf, Cisterna Di Littoria 29 Feb. 1944
Pompilio, Vincent E., Pfc, Med. Det. 756th Tank Bn., Italy 4 June 1944
Pond, Fred L., Pvt, Co. G 30th Inf, Cisterna Di Littoria 20 May 1944
Pontarelli, Anthony C., T/5, Med. Det. 7th Inf, France 25 Oct. 1944
Pool, Lewis R., Cpl, Co. K 15th Inf Regt., Germany 3 May 1945
Poole, Tim F., Pvt, Btry B 9th FA Bn., Germany 18 Mar. 1945
Pope, William C., Pfc, Hq. Co. 2d Bn. 15th Inf, France 3 Nov. 1944
Popple, James C., 1st Lt, Inf S-2 2d Bn. 15th Inf Regt., France 26 Dec. 1944
Porch, Harold M., Pfc, Hq. Co. 3d Bn. 7th Inf Regt., Germany 17 Apr. 1945
Porks, Jack, Pfc, Co. M 30th Inf
Porter, Clarence I., Jr., S/Sgt, Co. C 15th Inf, Vesoul, France 10 Sept. 1944
Porter, George I., S/Sgt, 3d Sig. Co., France 31 Jan. 1945
▲Porter, Mackenzie E., Lt Col, CO 1st Bn. 30th Inf, France17 Feb. 1945
Porter, Mark F., Pfc, Co. K 15th Inf, Italy, France Nov. 1944
Porter, Sedric E., S/Sgt, Co. K 15th Inf Regt., France 26 Jan. 1945
Porter, Vincent J., Pfc, Co. A 15th Inf, Cisterna di Littoria 31 Jan. 1944
Porterfield, Edwin G., Pfc, Co. M 7th Inf, Isola Bella 23 May 1944

▲ Oak Leaf Cluster.

Porth, John F., Pfc, Btry C 441st AAA AW Bn., France, Germany 8 May 1945
Porucznik, Stanley A., S/Sgt, Co. A 15th Inf Regt., Germany 7 Apr. 1945
Posaski, Chester, Pfc, Btry C 441st AAA AW Bn., Germany 27 Mar. 1945
Poss, Urban M., Pfc, Co. C 15th Inf Regt., Germany 20 Apr. 1945
Potelunas, Clement B., Capt, Co. D 3d Med. Bn., N. Africa, Sicily, Italy, France, Germany, Austria 8 May 1945
Potkoski, Bruno, Pfc, Hq. Co. 2d Bn., Vitellara 5 Feb. 1944
Potter, Charlie G., Pvt, Btry A 441st AAA AW Bn., Costello 29 May 1944
Potter, Kenneth B., Maj, Inf CO 1st Bn. 15th Inf Regt., France 26 Jan. 1945
Potter, William J., Jr., T/4, Co. B 756th Tank Bn., Germany 19 Mar. 1945
Potty, Joseph C., Pfc, 3d Rcn Trp., Germany 8 May 1945
Poulin, Alcide G., Pfc, Co. L 30th Inf Regt., France 8 Sept. 1944
Powell, Cary B., S/Sgt, AT Co. 30th Inf, Italy 9 Nov. 1944
Powell, Ira M., Pfc, Hq. Co. 2d Bn. 30th Inf Regt., Germany 12 Apr. 1945
Powell, James A., S/Sgt, Btry B 441st AAA AW Bn., Sicily, Italy, France, Germany, Austria 8 May 1945
Powell, James F., Capt, Inf Co. E 7th Inf Regt., Germany 18 Apr. 1945
Powell, Joseph P., Sgt, Hq. 41st FA Bn., La Lonbine, France 23 Sept. 1944
Powell, Philip J., S/Sgt, Hq. Co. 2d Bn. 7th Inf Regt., France 3 Nov. 1944
▲Powell, Troy N., M/Sgt, Serv. Co. 7th Inf, Sicily 18 Aug. 1943
Powell, William A., Pfc, Hq. Co. 2d Bn. 30th Inf, Anzio, Italy 10 Mar. 1944
Powers, Stanley, Pfc, Co. C 30th Inf, Lariano 28 May 1944
▲Poythress, Sam J., Jr., 1st Lt, Cn Co. 15th Inf, Artena 27 May 1944
Pratt, Howard J., T/5, Co. C 601st TD Bn., Artena 27 May 1944
Pratt, Sherman W., S/Sgt, AT Co. 7th Inf, Italy 18 Nov. 1943
Precht, Harold L., T/5, Hq. Btry 9th FA Bn., Sicily, Italy, France 10 Feb. 1945
▲Preston, George, 1st Sgt, Co. K 7th Inf Regt., Germany 27 Mar. 1945
Preston, Neil W., T/5, Hq. Co. 2d Bn. 30th Inf
Preuss, Charles W., S/Sgt, Co. C 756th Tank Bn., France 28 Nov. 1944
Prevo, Randall M., Pvt, 3d Sig. Co., Conca 10 Mar. 1944
Price, Carroll J., Pvt, Hq. Co. 30th Inf, Carano 15 Mar. 1944
Price, Fred J., Pfc, Hq. Co. 2d Bn. 7th Inf Regt., Germany 15 Mar. 1945
Price, Myles A., Pfc, Btry A 441st AAA AW Bn., Italy 29 Oct. 1943
Price, William A., Sgt, Co. G 30th Inf Regt., France 30 Jan. 1945
Pridgen, Robert B., Capt, CO Co. D 30th Inf, Tauling van, France 28 Aug. 1944
Prince, Jacob, Jr., Sgt, MP Pltn 3d Inf Div., Germany 8 May 1945
Pringle, James A., 1st Lt, Inf Co. H 30th Inf Regt., France 15 Aug. 1944
Printy, Thomas, Pvt, Co. B 10th Engr. Combat Bn., France 22 Jan. 1945
Pritzel, Gilbert V., Cpl, Co. D 15th Inf, Cistena di Littoria 12 Feb. 1944
Proegler, Walter H., Jr., Pfc, Med. Det. 15th Inf, France 17 Mar. 1945
Proctor, Edward F., Pvt, Hq. Co. 3d Div., N. Africa, Sicily, France 15 Aug. 1944
Proctor, James V., Co. L 30th Inf Regt., France 8 Sept. 1944
Prohme, Rupert, 1st Lt, Hq. 30th Inf, Italy Nov. 1944
Propst, Homer E., 1st Sgt, Co. A 7th Inf Regt., Germany 26 Mar. 1945
Prosser, Darel E., T/4, Serv. Co. 30th Inf Regt., Africa, Sicily, Italy, France 8-12 Nov. 1944
Proud, Harry S., Capt, Hq. 3d Med. Bn., Italy 6 June 1944
Provengana, Peter J., S/Sgt, Co. L 15th Inf Regt., Germany 17 Apr. 1945
Pruitt, Pleamon H., 1st Sgt, Co. B 601st TD Bn., N. Africa, Italy, France, Germany 1 Mar. 1945
Prunier, Henry S., Sgt, Co. G 15th Inf, Cisterna di Littoria 26 May 1944
Pryor, Joseph E., Pfc, Co. E 15th Inf Regt., Anzio, Italy 29 Feb. 1944
▲Przada, Julian J., Cpl, Hq. Btry 39th FA Bn., Germany 25 Apr. 1945
Puacz, Thaddeus T., 1st Lt, Btry A 69th Armd FA Bn., Borgo Bainsizza 28 Jan. 1944
Pucci, Raymond C., T/Sgt, Hq. Co. 1st Bn. 30th Inf, Vosges
Pucciarelli, Ellis, Pfc, Btry B 9th FA Bn., France 23 Jan. 1945
Puchala, Stanley G., Pfc, MP Pltn 3d Inf Div., Sicily 8 Nov. 1942
Puckett, Herman V., Jr., Cpl, Cn Co. 30th Inf, Anzio, Italy
Pugh, John H., T/5, Co. M 30th Inf Regt., N. Africa, Sicily, Italy, France, Germany, Austria 8 May 1945
Pulaski, Charles J., Pfc, Co. L 5th Inf, Germany 26 Mar. 1945
Punska, Joseph, T/Sgt, Hq. Co. 3d Bn. 7th Inf Regt., Italy 30 Jan. 1944
Purvis, Eual L., S/Sgt, Co. G 30th Inf Regt., France 2 Nov. 1944
Puszko, John A., Pfc, Co. K 15th Inf, Cisterna di Littoria 23 May 1944
Purdue, Paul M., Pfc, Hq. Co. 2d Bn. 7th Inf Regt., Italy 3 June 1944
Purdy, Roy B., Sgt, Serv. Btry 9th FA Bn.,Valmontone 1 June 1944

Quarrels, James C., T/5, Co. A 756th Tank Bn., France 15 Sept. 1944
Quick, Lester C., Pfc, Hq. 3d Inf Div., France, Germany 8 May 1945
Quirk, Edward A., T/5, Co. L 15th Inf, Statigliano 22 Oct. 1943

Rabe, Robert A., Pvt, Co. C 30th Inf, Germany 26 Mar. 1945
Rabil, Emil P., Pfc, Hq. Co. 3d Inf Div., Sicily, Italy, France, Germany, Austria May 1945
Rachal, Leonard, T/5, Serv. Co. 756th Tank Bn., France, Germany, Austria 8 May 1945
▲Rachiele, Frederick J., Capt, MC Med. Det. 7th Inf Regt., France 20 Nov. 1944
Radomski, Henry F., Pvt, Co. I 15th Inf Regt., Germany 7 Apr. 1945
Radosevich, Matthew S., 1st Sgt, Co. B 30th Inf, Anzio, Italy 30 Apr. 1944
Raezer, Donald C., S/Sgt, AT Co. 15th Inf Regt., Germany 18 Apr. 1945
Rafferty, Thomas F., T/5, Co. B 3d Med. Bn., Anzio, Italy 5 June 1944
Rafferty, William E., Pfc, Co. D 30th Inf, France 23 Jan. 1945
Ragland, Bourland T., Pfc, Co. A 15th Inf Regt., France 18 Feb. 1945
Rains, Denver C., S/Sgt, Co. L 30th Inf Regt., France 20 Oct. 1944
Rainwater, Elbert, T/5, Co. B 756th Tank Bn., France 15 Sept. 1944
Ramer, Herman, 1st Lt, Inf Co. K 7th Inf Regt., France, Germany 2 Feb. 1945
Ramsey, Roger W., Pfc, MP Pltn 3d Inf, France 6 Feb. 1945
Ramsey, Lloyd B., Lt Col, Inf Hq. 3d Bn. 7th Inf Regt., France 12 Sept. 1944
Ramsier, Ivan F., T/5, Hq. Co. 3d Bn.30th Inf, France 7 Feb. 1945
Ranalla, Frank H., T/5, Co. C 3d Med. Bn., France 19 Dec. 1944
▲Randall, Frank E., T/5, Hq. Co. 7th Inf, France 24 Oct. 1944
Randolph, Blaine P., Pfc, 3d Inf Div. Band, Italy, France, Germany 8 May 1945
Rankin, W. T., S/Sgt, Hq. Co. 3d Bn. 30th Inf, France 1 Oct. 1944
Ranta, Arnold I., Sgt, Co. M 15th Inf, Anzio, Italy 29 Feb. 1944
Rapoza, Victor, S/Sgt, Co. F 30th Inf, Brilo, Sicily 11 Aug. 1943
Ratcliff, Charlie H., T/Sgt, Co. F 30th Inf Regt., France 20 Nov. 1944
▲Rath, Howard W., 2d Lt, MAC Med. Det. 30th Inf Regt., Germany 19 Mar. 1945
Rathbun, Glenn E., Capt, Hq. 3d Bn. 7th Inf, Cisterna Di Littoria 25 May 1945
Ratliff, James A., Jr., Sgt, Co. G 15th Inf Regt., France 5 Feb. 1945

Ravenscroft, Earl H., S/Sgt, Co. K 15th Inf, Julienrupt, France 6 Oct. 1944
Raymond, Daniel A., Capt, S-4 10th Engr. Combat Bn., Germany 28 Apr. 1945
Raymond, George E., 1st Lt, Inf Co. F 30th Inf Regt., France 7 Oct. 1944
Raymond, Raymond E., 1st Lt, Co. E 30th Inf, Vosges
Raymond, William R., Sgt, Co. A 30th Inf, France 21 Aug. 1944
Raynor, Howard D., Pvt, Btry C 41st FA Bn., Anzio, Italy 16 Feb. 1944
Reardon, Edward J., 1st Lt, 3d QM Co., S. France 15 Oct. 1944
Reavis, Randall A., T/4, Hq. Co. 7th Inf, Anzio, Italy 3 Feb. 1944
Rebovich, George, 2d Lt, Inf Hq. Co. 1st Bn. 7th Inf Regt., France 15 Mar. 1945
Reddick, John R., S/Sgt, Co. G 7th Inf, Cisterna Di Littoria 28 Jan. 1944
Reddish, Joseph R., Pvt, Cn Co. 30th Inf
Redfern, John H., Pvt, Hq. Btry 10th FA Bn., Italy 25 Mar. 1944
Redle, David D., Capt, Inf CO Co. B 756th Tank Bn., France 13 Feb. 1945
Reed, Hardy W., Pfc, Btry C 441st AAA AW Bn., Germany 27 Mar. 1945
Reed, Toliver E., Pfc, Hq. Co. 1st Bn. 30th Inf Regt., France 7 Nov. 1944
Reeser, Clarence C., Pvt, Co. D 30th Inf, Sicily 1 Aug. 1943
Regnier, Earl A., Sgt, Co. B 756th Tank Bn., Germany 17 Apr. 1945
Reichard, David A., Jr., Pfc, Co. H 15th Inf, Anzio, Italy 26 Feb. 1944
Reichow, Howard R., 1st Lt, FA Hq. 3d Inf Div. Arty, Italy, France, Germany 8 May 1945
Reid, Robert E., Sgt, Co. B 756th Tank Bn., France 5 Feb. 1945
Reidenbach, Robert C., Pfc, Co. A 15th Inf Regt., France 12 Oct. 1944
Raiff, Fred H., Pvt, Co. A 10th Engr. Combat Bn., France 2 Mar. 1945
Rapoza, Victor, T/Sgt, Co. F 30th Inf, Sicily
Reisenauer, Anton A., T/5, Co. B 10th Engr. Combat Bn., France, Germany 8 May 1945
Renfrew, John R., T/5, Med. Det. 756th Tank Bn., Italy 4 June 1944
Renzi, Settimio A., T/5, Med. Det. 7th Inf Regt., Franee 2 Nov. 1944
Reppert, Jack, T/5, Med. Det. 3d Inf Div. Arty, Germany 8 May 1945
Restivo, Frank H., Pvt, Hq. Co. 30th Inf Regt., France 10 Nov. 1944
Rettig, Pfc, Co. H 15th Inf, Isola Bella 25 Jan. 1944
Reynolds, Fred E., T/5, Btry C 441st AAA AW Bn., Germany 27 Mar. 1945
Reynolds, Robert H., T/5, Btry C 441st AAA AW Bn., France, Germany 8 May 1945
Rhodes, Charles R., 1st Lt, Hq. Btry 9th FA Bn., France 17 Sept. 1944
Rhodes, Edward J., Cpl, Co. C 601st TD Bn., Anzio, Italy 2 Mar. 1944
Rhodes, Russell R., S/Sgt, Co. A 7th Inf, France 28 Dec. 1944
Rhodes, Ralph L., Pfc, Co. B 30th Inf, Colmar
Rice, Bruce A., 1st Sgt, AT Co., N. Africa, Sicily, Italy, France 20 Feb. 1945
Rice, Budd, 1st Sgt, Co. E 7th Inf, Villa 15 Oct. 1943
Rice, Carmon H., T/5, Co. A 601st TD Bn., Carano 6 Aug. 1943
Rice, Harold E., Pvt, Hq. Co. 10th Engr. Bn., Le Ferriere 29 Feb. 1944
Rice, Vernon W., Capt, Chap. Corps, N. Africa, Sicily, Italy 13 Oct. 1943
Rice, Walter M., 1st Lt, Co. C 7th Inf, Aix 25 Aug. 1944
Richard, Francis L., T/5, Btry D 441st AAA AW Bn., Germany 24 Mar. 1945
▲Rich, James B., Jr., Capt, Inf Co. B 7th Inf Regt., France 22 Nov. 1944
Richardson, Bruce D., Pvt, Co. I 30th Inf, Cremigu, France 27 Aug. 1944
Richeson, Eugene, Cpl, Hq. Btry 3d Div, Atry, Italy, France, Germany 8 May 1945
▲Richardson, Samuel G., Capt, FA Co. C 601st TD Bn., France 19 Aug. 1945
Richter, Arthur F., 1st Lt, Inf Co. A 756th Tank Bn., Germany 7 Apr. 1945
Richter, Julius, Jr., Pvt, Co. C 10th Engr. Bn., Valmontone 2 June 1944
Rickart, Elmer, Sgt, Co. A 756th Tank Bn., France 15 Sept. 1944
Rickerson, Jesse B., Jr., T/4, Co. B 756th Tank Bn., France 15 Sept. 1944
Riddell, Charles G., Pfc, Co. I 30th Inf, Vosges
Ridel, Adam S., Pfc, Hq. Co. 2d Bn. 15th Inf Regt., France 1 Nov. 1944
Riedel, Warren F., T/4, Rcn Co. 601st TD Bn., France, Germany 8 May 1945
Rieke, Chester V., 1st Lt, Co. F 30th Inf, Anzio, Italy 24 Mar. 1944
Riendeau, Roland E., Pfc, Co. E 7th Inf, Cisterna Di Littoria 1 Mar. 1944
Rifkin, Charles, 1st Lt, Inf Serv. Co. 30th Inf, France 20 Feb. 1945
Rigby, Paul T., Maj, Hq. 41st FA Bn., Sicily 6 Aug. 1943
Riggins, Herman F., Pfc, Co. A 7th Inf Regt., France 15 Jan. 1945
Rihner, Philip O., T/5, Btry A 41st FA Bn., Anzio, Italy 1 Feb. 1944
Riley, Charles H., Cpl, Co. A 10th Engr. Combat Bn., France 29 Oct 1944
Rincon, Roberto G., S/Sgt, Btry B 9th FA Bn., Italy 27 May 1944
Rineer, Clarence E., Pfc, Co. M 30th Inf, France 15 Oct. 1944
Ring, Alex, Pfc, 3d Sig. Co., N. Africa, Sicily, Italy, France 31 Jan. 1945
Ring, Creighton F., T/5, Co. C 30th Inf Regt., France 24 Nov. 1944
Riordan, Daniel F., Sgt, Co. C 601st TD Bn., Sicily, Italy, France, Germany 8 May 1945
Rios, Abel, Pfc, Hq. Co. 2d Bn. 15th Inf Regt., Germany 18 Mar. 1945
Risdahl, Magnus, S/Sgt, 3d Rcn Trp., Italy 13 Oct. 1943
Risdal, Carroll S., S/Sgt, Co. K 7th Inf, Palermo, Sicily 22 July 1944
Ritchie, Harvey E., Sgt, Serv. Co. 7th Inf Regt., Italy, France 1 Dec. 1944
Rittner, John F., Sgt, Btry C 39th FA Bn., Sicily 17 Aug. 1943
Rivett, Donald I., 1st Lt, Inf Serv. Co. 30th Inf Regt., Germany 26 Mar. 1945
Roach, John P., WOJG, Hq. 30th Inf
Robards, John T., Pfc, MS 41st FA Bn., Italy 26 Oct. 1943
Robb, Kenneth R., Capt, AT Co. 30th Inf, N. Africa, Sicily, Italy, France 20 Feb. 1945
Robbin, Burdette C., S/Sgt, Btry A 39th FA Bn., N. Africa, Sicily, Italy, France, Germany, Austria 8 May 1945
Robbins, Ray, Pvt, Hq. Btry 3d IDA, Anzio, Italy 29 Feb. 1944
▲Roberts, Burton B., Cpl, Hq. Co. 1st Bn. 7th Inf Regt., France 7 Oct. 1944
Roberts, Carter, Pfc, Hq. Co. 2d Bn. 7th Inf, 20 Jan. 1945
Roberts, Clayton, Pfc, Hq. Co. 1st Bn. 15th Inf, France 1 Feb. 1945
Roberts, James B., Pfc, Serv. Co. 15th Inf Regt., Italy 25 May 1944
Robards, John T., Pfc, MC 41st FA Bn., Italy 26 Oct. 1943
Roberts, Oscar B., 1st Lt, CAC Btry B 441st AAA AW Bn., France 9 Feb. 1945
Roberts, Samuel H., Capt, Inf Co. C 15th Inf Regt., Italy 25 May 1944
Roberts, Samuel J., Pfc, Hq. Co. 1st Bn. 30th Inf, Colmar
Robertson, Alexander, 1st Lt, Co. A 10th Engr., France 30 Jan. 1945
Robertson, William B., T/Sgt, Co. L 30th Inf
Robinette, William J., Pfc, AT Co. 15th Inf, Isola Bella 4 Mar. 1944
Robinson, Elbert M., Jr., Pfc, Co. M 30th Inf, France 23 Jan. 1945
Robinson, Hugh, Pfc, Co. G 15th Inf, Germany 7 Apr. 1945
Robinson, John D., Pfc, Btry A FA, Cisterna Di Littoria 29 Feb. 1944
▲Robustelli, Joseph A., S/Sgt, Serv. Co. 15th Inf, France, Germany 8 May 1945
Roccabruna, Mario J., Sgt, Co. H 15th Inf, Lure, France 17 Sept. 1944
Rocco, Guy T., Pfc, Co. B 15th Inf, Amblans, France 15 Sept. 1944
Roche, John D., Pfc, Co. K 30th Inf, France 7 Feb. 1945
Rochmis, Max, 1st Lt, MP Hq. 3d Div., France 30 Nov. 1944
Rockwell, Arthur R., Pfc, Co. K 30th Inf Regt., Germany 8 Apr. 1945

▲ Oak Leaf Cluster.

Roddy, Francis J., Maj, CA Corps Hq. 441st AAA AW, Sicily, Italy, France, Germany 8 May 1945
Roddy, Robert C., 1st Lt, Co. C 7th Inf, Agrigento, Sicily 13 July 1943
Roderick, Tom G., Jr., Pfc, Co. I 7th Inf, Germany 1945
Rodgers, Arthur J., T/5, Co. B 756th Tank Bn., Germany 13 Apr. 1945
Rodgers, George F., Pfc, 756th Tank Bn.,France, Germany 15 Apr. 1945
Rodgers, Nelson J., Pfc, MP Pltn 3d Inf Div., Italy 2 Mar. 1944
Rodriquez, Eleuteric, S/Sgt, 3d Inf Div. Band, N. Africa, Sicily, Italy 31 Dec. 1943
Rodriquez, Milton, S/Sgt, Co. L 30th Inf, Vosges
Rodriquez, William, T/5, Hq. Co. 3d Bn. 7th Inf Regt., France 1 Oct. 1944
Rogan, Richard J., Jr., Pfc, Co. I 30th Inf Regt., France 28 Oct. 1944
Rogers, Arthur H., Brig Gen, 30th Inf, San Stefano, Sicily 20 July 1943
Rogers, Glenn F., Lt Col, Cav. Co. 756th Tank Bn., France 25 Jan. 1945
Rogers, Homer C., S/Sgt, AT Co. 7th Inf Regt., N. Africa, Sicily, Italy, France, Germany 8 May 1945
Rogers, Jack H., Pfc, Co. F 30th Inf, Faucogney, France 21 Sept. 1944
Rogers, Raymond, S/Sgt, Co. C 30th Inf Regt., France 1 Dec. 1944
▲Rogers, Stephen J., Lt Col, AGD, Adj Gen Hq. 3d Inf Div., France, Germany, Austria 8 May 1945
Rogers, William S., T/Sgt, Co. I 7th Inf, Cisterna Di Littoria 23 May 1944
Rogowski, John P., S/Sgt, 3d Sig. Co., N. Africa, Sicily, Italy, France, Germany 8 May 1945
Rohr, Joseph J., Pfc, Hq. Co. 7th Inf, France 24 Jan. 1945
Rohrer, Wilbur K., T/Sgt, Cn Co. 30th Inf Regt., near Rocheforteon-Valdane, France 27 Aug. 1944
Roles, Everett A., CWO, Serv. Co. 7th Inf, Anzio, Italy 27 June 1944
Rolli, Aldo, Sgt, Co. C 601st TD Bn., Artena 30 May 1944
Romain, William B., Sgt, 3d Sig. Co., France 20 Dec. 1944
Roman, Victor A., T/5, Hq. Co. 3d Bn. 30th Inf Regt., France 30 Nov. 1944
Romano, Lino N., S/Sgt, Co. F 30th Inf
Romer, John, Pfc, Cn Co. 7th Inf, Pompiere, France 12 Sept. 1944
Rominger, Arthur D., Pfc, Co. F 30th Inf Regt., France 18 Dec. 1944
Romo, Henry J., Jr., Capt, Hq. Btry 10th FA Bn., Italy 18 Nov. 1943
Romero, Heberto G., S/Sgt, Hq. Co. 3d Bn. 15th Inf Regt., Germany 18 Apr. 1945
Ronning, Eugene R., Pvt, Serv. Btry 41st FA Bn., Italy 23 Mar. 1944
Rook, Franklin H., T/5, AT Co. 7th Inf Regt., Italy, France, Germany 8 May 1945
Rosas, Franco A., Pfc, Med. Det. 7th Inf Regt., Germany 16 Apr. 1945
Rose, Vernon E., Cpl, MP Pltn 3d Inf, France 28 Jan. 1945
Rosenbaum, Harry A., WOJG, US Army 3d Sig. Co., N. Africa, Sicily, Italy, France, Germany 8 May 1945
Rosenberg, Burton, Sgt, Hq. Co. 15th Inf Regt., France, Germany 8 May 1945
Rosenblum, Philip, Sgt, Co. G 30th Inf, Italy 24 May 1944
Rosenfeld, Arthur H., Pfc, Hq. Co. 3d Bn. 30th Inf Regt., Italy 28 Apr. 1944
▲Rosick, Michael, Cpl, Co. C 601st TD Bn., France 24 Nov. 1944
Rosner, Adolph C., Jr., 1st Lt, Co. C 30th Inf, San Fratelo, Sicily 7 Aug. 1943
Ross, Alzie, Pfc, Btry A 9th FA Bn., Anzio, Italy 30 Apr. 1944
Ross, Harley P., Pfc, Cn Co. 30th Inf, Anzio, Italy 22 Apr. 1944
Ross, James A., Cpl, Btry C 441st AAA AW Bn., Germany 30 Apr. 1945
Ross, Kenneth R., Capt, AT Co. 30th Inf, Colmar
Rossi, Michael P., Pfc, Co. A 30th Inf Regt., France 20 Dec. 1944
▲(2) Rosson, William B., Lt Col, AC of S G-3 Hq. 3d Inf Div., France 5 Feb. 1945
Roth, Albert R., 1st Sgt, Btry C 10th FA Bn., Artena 28 May 1944
Roth, Bernard E., Pfc, Co. F 30th Inf Regt., France 27 Jan. 1945
Roth, Harry L., S/Sgt, Co. M 30th Inf Regt., N. Africa, Sicily, Italy, France 8 May 1945
Rothseid, Maurice, 1st Lt, Co. I 30th Inf, Sauceray 24 Oct. 1944
Row, Ivan F., Pfc, Hq. Co. 3d Bn. 30th Inf Regt., France 15 Sept. 1944
Rowe, John C., T/Sgt, Co. E 7th Inf Regt., Germany 19 Mar. 1945
Rowson, Roy W., T/Sgt, Hq. & Serv. Co. 10th Engr. Bn., Italy, France, Germany 8 May 1945
Royal, Richard R., T/Sgt, Hq. Btry 441st AAA AW Bn., Sicily, Italy, France, Germany 8 May 1945
Rosselle, Harry R., Pfc, Co. F 30th Inf Regt., France 18 Dec. 1944
Rozzelle, Henry R., Pfc, Co. E 30th Inf, Colmar
Rubick, Allen J., T/Sgt, Co. F 30th Inf Regt., France 25 Nov. 1944
Rubinfeld, Allen J., T/5, Hq. 3d Inf Div., France, Germany 25 Mar. 1945
Rucken, George J., T/5, MG Sec. 30th Inf, Germany
Rudolph, John B., Pfc, Hq. & Hq. Btry 10th FA Bn., France Feb. 1945
Rudy, John V., S/Sgt, Rcn Co. 601st TD Bn., N. Africa, Sicily, Italy, France, Germany 8 May 1945
Ruggles, Claude R., Pfc, Co. K 15th Inf Regt., France 18 Sept. 1944
▲Rusak, Nicholas, S/Sgt, Co. G 30th Inf Regt., France 23 Dec. 1944
Russell, James E., T/Sgt, Hq. Co. 3d Bn. 7th Inf Regt., France 29 Aug. 1944
Russell, William F., T/Sgt, Co. E 15th Inf, France 5 Feb. 1945
Russo, Joseph F., Pfc, Med. Det. 30th Inf, Valmontone 1 June 1944
Russo, Rocco, Pvt, Hq. Co. 30th Inf, Italy 5 June 1944
Rutherford, Clyde W., T/4, Hq. Co. 3d Div., Italy 1 May 1944
Rutherford, Lloyd, Jr., T/4, 3d Sig. Co., France, Germany 8 May 1945
Rutzen, Ralph A., Sgt, Co. B 756th Tank Bn., Vesoul 11 Sept. 1944
Ruud, Edwin H., T/4, Btry A 9th FA Bn., Sicily 5 Aug. 1943
Ryan, John F., Pvt, Rcn Co. 601st TD Bn., Volturno 13 Oct. 1943
Ryan, Robert W., 1st Lt, Inf AT Co. 7th Inf Regt., France 20 Nov. 1944
Rybicki, Raymond, Cpl, Co. M 15th Inf, Isola Bella 30 Jan. 1944
Ryder, Emmett R., T/5, Co. C 601st TD Bn., Artena 27 May 1944
Ryder, Lawrence J., Sgt, Co. B 7th Inf, Ponte Rotto 24 Feb. 1944
Rydman, Robert H., Capt, Inf Hq. 756th Tank Bn., France 13 Feb. 1945
Ryduchowski, Edward J., T/Sgt, AT Co. 30th Inf, France 24 Dec. 1944
Rysz, Edmund P., Cpl, Co. C 601st TD Bn., Carano 1 Mar. 1944

Sabastian, Clayton, S/Sgt, Co. B 10th Engr. Combat Bn., France 22 Jan. 1945
Saddler, John T., T/5, Btry C 441st AAA AW Bn., France 20 Nov. 1944
Sadler, Cleo K., T/5, Hq. Co. 30th Inf, France 28 Nov. 1944
Sadowski, Edward J., T/5, Co. B 756th Tank Bn., France 15 Sept. 1944
Sadowski, Frank C., Pvt, Co. K 15th Inf, Torre Di Padiglione 24 Apr. 1944
▲Safine, Albert L., Maj, CWS Hq. 3d Inf Div., France 6 Feb. 1945
Saine, Harold J., Capt, Inf Co. M 30th Inf, Germany 15 Mar. 1945
St. Denis, Maurice A., Pfc, Co. D 756th Tank Bn., Germany 16 Mar. 1945
St. Jacque, John S., S/Sgt, Hq. Co. 7th Inf Regt., France, Germany, Austria 4 May 1945
Sakariason, Martin O., Sgt, Btry A 10th FA Bn., Velletri 1 June 1944
Salazar, Elcy S., Pfc, Co. B 10th Engr. Combat Bn., France 5 Feb. 1945
Salazar, Eulojio, Pfc, Btry C 10th FA Bn., N. Africa, Sicily, Italy, France, Germany 8 May 1945
Salazar, Philburt H., T/Sgt, Co. M 30th Inf, Baraques, France 29 Oct. 1944
Salazar, Toby, Sgt, Co. C 7th Inf, Libico 27 May 1944
Salet, Eugene A., Lt Col, Inf, 2d Bn. 15th Inf Regt., France 8 Nov. 1944
Salfen, Ambrose G., 1st Lt, Co. B 601st TD Bn., Mignano 9 Nov. 1943
Sallee, Orville C., S/Sgt, Serv. Co. 7th Inf, Anzio, Italy 28 Apr. 1944
Salette, William F., Jr., S/Sgt, Co. K 30th Inf, Cleurie 27 Sept. 1944
Salter, Melvin R., Pfc, Co. K 15th Inf, France 25 Oct. 1944
Salvagio, Louis T., Pvt, Btry A 441st AAA AW Bn., Costello 29 May 1944
Samolowitz, Jacob I., Pfc, Co. D 15th Inf Regt., France 6 Feb. 1945
Samson, James, S/Sgt, Co. F 7th Inf, Mt. Defenso 8 Nov. 1943
Sanchez, Davis C., T/5, Serv. Co. 15th Inf, Anzio 29 Feb. 1944
Sanders, Lloyd A., Pvt, Med. Det. 7th Inf, Valmontone 1 June 1944
Sanders, Raymond T., 1st Lt, MC Med. Det. 30th Inf Regt., France 23 Jan. 1945
Sanders, Ryndal L., 1st Lt, Rcn Co. 601st TD, Sedjenang, Tunisia 29 Apr. 1943
Sanders, Thomas W., Cpl, Co. C 756th Tank Bn., France 2 Feb. 1945
Sanderson, Aubrey B., Pfc, Co. I 30th Inf, Germany 26 Mar. 1945
Sandor, Sandor A., Sgt, 3d QM Co. 3d Inf Div., France, Germany 6 Apr. 1945
Sands, Ralph B., T/4, Hq. Btry 41st FA Bn., Coronia 6 Aug. 1943
Sanford, Leland F., Capt, QM Corps 3d QM Co., Italy June 1944
Sanford, Robert H., Sgt, Cn Co. 15th Inf Regt., Italy, France 22 Jan. 1944, 8 Feb. 1945
Sansone, Robert P., T/5, Btry B 441st AAA AW Bn., France 25 Jan. 1945
Santerre, Delphis J., Pfc, Co. L 15th Inf Regt., Germany 1 Apr. 1945
Sapinsky, Louis, T/4, Serv. Co. 756th Tank Bn., France, Germany, Austria 8 May 1945
Sapiro, Saul J., Capt, Inf MP Pltn 3d Inf Div., France 15 Aug., 30 Dec. 1944
Sardelich, Peter J., Cpl, Co. D 15th Inf, France 4 Feb. 1945
▲Sarginson, Kenneth J., Pfc, Co. I 30th Inf, Germany 26 Mar. 1945
Sarno, Anthony M., Capt, MC 756th Tank Bn., Italy 12 June 1944
Sarver, Harry H., Pfc, Hq. Co. 1st Bn. 15th Inf Regt., Germany 1 Apr. 1945
Satterfield, Ralph E., Pvt, Rcn Co. 601st TD Bn., Kassering 22 Feb. 1944
▲Satuloff, Sanford M., 1st Lt, Coast Arty Btry C 441st AAA AW Bn., Germany 18 Apr. 1945
Saunders, Zebulon V., Co. I 30th Inf, Colmar
Sauter, George J., S/Sgt, 15th Inf Regt., Italy, France 29 Nov. 1944
Savaresy, Richard M., Capt, Hq. 30th Inf, Sicily 2 Aug. 1943
▲Savaresy, Richard M., Maj, Hq. 30th Inf, Besancon, France 6 Sept. 1944
Savitski, Augustine W., T/4, Hq. Co. 601st TD Bn., N. Africa, Italy, France, Germany May 1945
▲Sayer, Ralph E., Pfc, Cn Co. 30th Inf, Colmar
Sayer, Ralph E., Pfc, Cn Co. 30th Inf, France 25 Jan. 1945
Sayler, Willard P., Pfc, Btry A 9th FA Bn., Anzio 22 May 1944
Saylor, Donald J., 1st Lt, MC Med. Det. 441st AAA AW Bn., France, Germany 8 May 1945
Scalera, Peter V., Pfc, Co. B 7th Inf, Rupt Sur Moselle, France 24 Sept. 1944
Scarpa, Fred, Sgt, Co. L 15th Inf, France 9 Nov. 1944
Schaefer, William F., S/Sgt, Btry B 441st AAA AW Bn., Sicily, Italy, France, Germany 8 May 1945
Schaffer, Virgil C., T/5, Co. A 756th Tank Bn., France, Germany 8 May 1945
Schank, Clarence V., Pvt, Med. Det. 30th Inf, Artena 1 June 1944
▲Schapp, Marvin, T/Sgt, Co. F 7th Inf Regt., France 6 Nov. 1944
Schauer, Henry, Pvt, Co. F 15th Inf, Anzio, Italy 17 Mar. 1944
Scheer, Chester A., Pvt, Hq. Btry 3d Div. Arty, Conca 2 Mar. 1944
Scheflo, Ove H., T/3, Med. Det. 441st AAA AW Bn., Cisterna 26 Feb. 1944
Schenck, Walter R., T/4, Med. Det. 15th Inf Regt., France 26 Dec. 1944
Schepker, Dietrich, Jr., Pfc, Hq. & Hq. Btry 10th FA Bn., France 20 Jan. 1945
Schiefer, Edward J., Pfc, Co. M 7th Inf Regt., France 15 Sept. 1944
Scheiring, Harry C., Sgt, Med. Det. 3d Inf Div. Arty, Italy, France, Germany 8 May 1945
Schihl, Clarence R., Pfc, Serv. Co. 7th Inf Regt., Italy 24 Apr. 1944
Schipper, James A., Pfc, Hq. Co. 3d Bn. 7th Inf Regt., France 31 Jan. 1945
Schirmer, Carl F., Sgt, Btry C 9th FA Bn., Italy 30 May 1944
Schirmer, Charles W., Pfc, Co. C 601st TD Bn., Anzio, Italy 1 Mar. 1944
Schirracher, Walter A., Pfc, Co. H 30th Inf, Campo Morto 29 Feb. 1944
Schkerke, Robert E., T/5, Hq. Co. 3d Bn. 7th Inf, France 14 Sept. 1944
Schlegel, Carl H., S/Sgt, Cn Co. 7th Inf Regt., Italy, France, Germany 30 Apr. 1945
Schlegel, Charles J., S/Sgt, Med. Det. Co. D 3d Med. Bn., Africa, Sicily, Italy, France, Germany 5 May 1945
Schleifer, Lavern C., T/4, Co. C 10th Engr. Bn., France 7 Feb. 1945
Schlicher, William R., S/Sgt, AT 30th Inf, Anzio, Rome
Schlicter, Robert J., Capt, Inf Adj Spec Trps. 3d Inf Div., Italy, France 22 Jan. 1944
▲Schmidt, Arthur D., 2d Lt, Inf Co. D 30th Inf, France, Germany 8 May 1945
Schmidt, Fred L., Capt, Inf Hq. 756th Tank Bn., France 13 Feb. 1945
Schmidt, Henry, T/5, Btry B 10th FA Bn., N. Africa, Sicily, Italy, France, Germany 8 May 1945
Schmidt, Robert G., Cpl, 3d Rcn Trp.,near Riedlingen, Germany 24 Apr. 1945
Schmit, Roland A., T/5, 3d Sig. Co., Italy, France, Germany 8 May 1945
▲Schmitt, Bernard J., T/Sgt, Cn Co. 30th Inf Regt., N. Africa, Sicily, Italy, France 8 Nov. 1942, 25 Jan. 1945
Scheibner, Alfred A., Pvt, Btry C 39th FA Bn., Italy 29 Feb. 1944
Schneider, Eugene E., 1st Lt, Hq. 41st FA Bn., France 3 Feb. 1945
Schneider, John E., S/Sgt, Btry B 9th FA Bn., N. Africa, Sicily, Italy, France, Germany, Austria 8 May 1945
Schneider, Joseph M., Cpl, Hq. Co. 3d Bn. 7th Inf, Moffans 17 Sept. 1944
Schnettler, Alton E., T/Sgt, Hq. Btry 3d Div. Arty, France 10 Feb. 1945
Schoenfeld, Melvin E., S/Sgt, Cn Co. 7th Inf, Anzio, Italy 8 May 1944
Schoenwolf, William L., Sgt, MP Pltn Hq. Co. 3d Inf Div., France, Germany 27 Apr. 1945
Schreiner, John W., Cpl, Btry A 41st FA Bn., France 18 Dec. 1944
Schuch, Ivan C., Pfc, Btry B 30th FA Bn., Anzio 27 Feb. 1944
Schuder, Max E., Pfc, Hq. Co. 756th Tank Bn., Italy 16 Feb. 1944
▲Schuffler, William L., Pfc, 3d Sig. Co., Italy 22 Jan., 5 June 1944
Schulte, Elmer F., Pfc, MP Pltn 3d Inf Div., Italy 26 May 1944
Schultz, Vernon B., Pfc, Hq. Co. 1st Bn. 15th Inf, France 26 Dec. 1944
Schumacher, Donald J., 1st Lt, Co. K 30th Inf, France 1 Feb. 1945
Schwamm, Howard R., Pfc, Btry C 10th FA Bn., N. Africa, Sicily, Italy, France, Germany 8 May 1945
Schwabland, Howard J., T/5, Btry A 41st FA Bn., Italy 24 May 1944
Schwartz, Max, Pvt, Hq. Co. 3d Bn. 7th Inf, Besancon, France 7 Sept. 1944

▲ Oak Leaf Cluster.

Schweighardt, Andrew F., T/5, Btry A 441st AAA AW Bn., Costello 27 June 1944
Schwetke, William E., Sgt, 3d Rcn Trp., N. Africa, Sicily, Italy, France, Germany, Austria 8 May 1945
Schwinn, Murrow D., Sr., T/5, Co. M 15th Inf, Anzio, Italy
Scoggins, Joseph W., T/5, Co. C 601st TD Bn., Cisterna 24 May 1944
Score, Frank B., Pfc, Co. L 30th Inf, Germany
Scott, Charles B., 1st Sgt, Hq. Co. 30th Inf Regt., N. Africa, Sicily, Italy 17 Nov. 1943
▲Scott, Hugh A., Maj, GSC Act. C. of S. Act. G-2 Hq. 3d Inf Div., France, Germany, Austria 8 May 1945
Scott, Marion H., Pfc, Co. M 7th Inf Regt., Germany 18 Mar. 1945
Scott, Thomas L., Pfc, Co. A 30th Inf, France 22 Oct. 1944
Scott, Willis, Pvt, Btry C 441st AAA AW Bn., Germany 8 May 1945
Scroozak, Walter, S/Sgt, Co. L 30th Inf, France 23 Jan. 1945
Seabrook, Lynville G., Pfc, Co. L 30th Inf Regt., Germany 8 Apr. 1945
Searls, Pearl E., Sgt, Co. D 15th Inf, France 1 Feb. 1944
Searls, Sidney F., T/4, Serv. Co. 15th Inf Regt., Italy, France, Germany 26 Mar. 1945
Sears, Paul R., Sgt, Co. F 15th Inf Regt., France 26-27 Dec. 1944
Seaton, Thomas W., S/Sgt, Cn Co. 7th Inf, Anzio, Italy 29 Feb. 1944
Secchirtti, Mario, Pfc, Serv. Co. 15th Inf, Italy, France, Germany 8 May 1945
Secrist, Harold C., Pfc, MP Pltn 3d Inf Div., Germany 26 Mar. 1944
▲Sedlak, Michael J., Pfc, Hq. Co. 2d Bn 7th Inf, France 7 Oct. 1944
Seegar, Frank A., Pvt, Co. B 30th Inf Regt., Germany 19 Apr. 1945
Seehafer, Erwin C., 1st Lt, Inf Co. B 15th Inf Regt., Germany 1 Apr. 1945
Seel, Harlow W., T/5, Co. A 756th Tank Bn., Germany 7 Apr. 1945
Seesock, Robert S., Pfc, 3d Sig. Co., France, Germany, Austria May 1945
Segala, Henry, T/5, Btry A 441st AAA AW Bn., France 15 Jan. 1945
Segar, Raymond J., Pfc, Btry C 39th FA Bn., Cisterna 31 Jan. 1944
Segit, Joseph A., S/Sgt, Co. C 601st TD Bn., Mt. Rotundo 10 Nov. 1943
Seems, Chalmer J., Pvt, Btry C 9th FA Bn., Anzio, Italy 7 Mar. 1944
Seider, Camilla H., Sgt, Co. C TD Bn., Isola Bella 2 Mar. 1944
Seifarth, Charles K., 2d Lt, Hq. Co. 7th Inf, France 25 Jan. 1945
Seiffert, Frank H., 1st Lt, FA Hq. 601st TD Bn., France 15 Mar. 1945
Seitz, Glenn L., Pfc, Med. Det. 15th Inf, France 23 May 1944
Self, Carl F., Pfc, Co. D 15th Inf, France 17 Sept. 1944
Self, Harmon E., S/Sgt, Co. H 7th Inf, Cisterna di Littoria 23 May 1944
Selfridge, Richard J., S/Sgt, Serv. Btry 10th FA Bn., N. Africa, Sicily, Italy, France, Germany 8 May 1945
Selman, Joe C., Pvt, Co. K 30th Inf Regt., France 15 Dec. 1944
Semerdjian, Mardious, Sgt, Co. C 756th Tank Bn., Germany 26 Mar. 1945
Senecal, Joseph S., Pfc, Cn Co. 30th Inf Regt., Italy 25 May 1944
Sepanski, Michael J., Sgt, Hq. Co. 601st TD Bn., Italy, France, Germany 21 Mar. 1945
Serdan, William M., S/Sgt, Med. Det. 756th Tank Bn., Italy 4 June 1944
▲Serena, Joseph V., T/5, 3d Sig. Co., Italy, France, Germany, Austria 8 May 1945
Sergakis, Emanuel, Pfc, Btry B 10th FA Bn., Cisterna 29 Feb. 1944
Serrano, David G., Pvt, Hq. Co. 7th Inf, Italy 31 May 1944
Serva, Caesar J., 1st Sgt, Hq. Btry 9th FA Bn., Mignano 17 Nov. 1943
Sessoms, Harvey R., Pfc, Hq. Co. 2d Bn. 15th Inf Regt., Italy 26 May 1944
Sesto, Anthony, Pfc, MP Pltn 3d Inf, France 3 Jan. 1945
Seulowitz, Isidore T., Pfc, 3d QM Co. Italy 24 Jan. 1944
Seymour, Willard K., S/Sgt, Co. L 7th Inf Regt., Germany 2 May 1945
Sexton, William T., Col, Div. Arty Com., Italy, France 15 Nov. 1944
▲(3) Sexton, William T., Brig Gen, U. S. Army CG 3d Inf Div. Atry, Germany 20 Apr. 1945
Shadley, Miles L., Jr., S/Sgt, Co. B 3d Med. Bn., Italy 5 June 1944
Shaffer, J. D., S/Sgt, Hq. Btry 41st FA Bn., Italy 27 June 1944
Shaheen, Ralph, M/Sgt, Hq. Co. 601st TD Bn., Italy 1 June 1944
Shale, William A., Pfc, Co. F 7th Inf Regt., Germany 26 Mar. 1945
Shane, Charles S., Cpl, Btry A 441st AAA AW Bn., Italy 29 Oct. 1943
Shanks, Don E., Pfc, Hq. Btry 39th FA Bn., Germany 24 Apr. 1945
Shannon, Robert M., 1st Lt, Inf Co. K 7th Inf Regt., France 26 Oct. 1944
▲Shapovnick, Morris, 2d Lt, Co. I 30th Inf, Germany 26 Mar. 1945
Sharp, Casewell A., Pfc, Co. M 30th Inf Regt., France 23 Jan. 1945
Sharp, Jim C., T/Sgt, Hq. Btry 39th FA Bn., N. Africa, Sicily, Italy, France, Germany 8 May 1945
Sharp, Ralph R., 1st Sgt, Co. L 30th Inf
Shaw, Ferris L., S/Sgt, Co. F 30th Inf Regt., France 23 Jan. 1945
Shaw, John Y., Jr., S/Sgt, Btry A 441st AAA AW Bn., France 9 Jan. 1945
Shaw, Lawrence V., Cpl, Btry C 10th FA Bn., Vagney, France 1 Oct. 1944
▲(2) Shaw, Robert C., Maj, GSC Hq. 3d Inf Div., France, Germany, Austria 8 May 1945
Sheeley, Johnny R., Pfc, Co. L 15th Inf, France 27 Dec. 1944
Shefchik, Harry F., Sgt, Hq. Co. 1st Bn. 15th Inf, France 31 Jan. 1945
Sheilds, George D., Jr., Hq. Btry 441st AAA AW Bn., Italy, France, Germany, Austria 8 May 1945
Sheldon, William P., T/4, Hq. Btry 39th FA Bn., N. Africa, Sicily, Italy, France, Germany 8 May 1945
Shelton, Arthur E., Pfc, Med. Det. 30th Inf, France 8 Jan. 1945
Shepherd, Elmer V., T/3, Med. Det. 7th Inf Regt., Germany 2 Apr. 1945
Shepard, Joseph E., 1st Lt, Inf Hq. 7th Inf Regt., Italy 1 Mar. 1944
Shepherd, Donald G., Pvt, Hq. Btry 3d IDA, Anzio, Italy 29 Feb. 1944
Sheppard, James D., S/Sgt, Co. G 30th Inf Regt., France 8 Jan. 1945
Sherbondy, Wilbur E., Pvt, Co. E 7th Inf, Anzio, Italy 25 Mar. 1944
Sherfey, Hall O., Pvt, Co. E 30th Inf Regt., Germany 20 Apr. 1945
Sheridan, Lloyd M., Cpl, Cn Co. 7th Inf Regt., France 3 Nov. 1944
Sherry, Nicholas R., T/5, 3d Sig. Co., N. Africa, Sicily, Italy 3 June 1944
Shiels, Robert H., T/5, Hq. Co. 2d Bn. 15th Inf, Italy 24 May 1944
Shimer, Paul S., Jr., Sgt, Co. K 15th Inf Regt., France 24 Dec. 1944
Shinnamon, George E., Pfc, Co. C 7th Inf Regt., France 9 Sept. 1944
Shipp, James R., S/Sgt, Co. H 7th Inf, France 23 Jan. 1945
Shirk, John R., Pfc, Co. E 30th Inf, France 29 Jan. 1945
Shirley, John B., S/Sgt, Co. I 15th Inf, Bemont, France 28 Sept. 1944
Shirley, Stanley W., Pfc, Hq. Co. 2d Bn. 30th Inf, Colmar
Shively, Jay W., T/4, Co. C 601st TD Bn., Italy, France, Germany May 1945
▲(2) Shockley, Dewey D., Pfc, Co. A 15th Inf Regt., France 24 Dec. 1944
Shoemaker, Myrl W., Pfc, Co. D 15th Inf Regt., Germany 1 Apr. 1945
Shoemaker, Warren A., Pfc, Co. K 7th Inf Regt., France 15 Mar. 1945
Shonka, Donald G., Pfc, Med. Det. 756th Tank Bn., Germany 14 Apr. 1945
Shope, William A., Jr., Cpl, Rcn Co. 601st TD Bn., Germany 1 Apr. 1945
Short, Willis E., T/4, Hq. Co. 2d Bn. 30th Inf, Anzio, Italy 26 Mar. 1944
Shrader, Royal G., Pvt, Hq. Co. 30th Inf, Italy 5 June 1944
Shuler, Glenn, Capt, Inf, Co. L 30th Inf Regt., France 16 Dec. 1944
Shumchenia, Michael, Sgt, Rcn Trp. 601st TD Bn., Mignano 2 Nov. 1943
Shure, David L., Pfc, Co. H 7th Inf Regt., Germany 7 Apr. 1945
Shustick, Cecil, Capt, Dent Corps 69th Armd FA Bn., Nettuno 25 May 1944
Shutt, Samuel W., 1st Lt, Hq. 1st Bn. 30th Inf, Anzio, Italy 1 Feb. 1944
Siegal, Louis, Pfc, Hq. Btry 9th FA Bn., Italy 27 May 1944
Siegel, Marvin, Pfc, Hq. Co. 7th Inf, Germany 27 Mar. 1945
Siembab, John A., Sgt, Hq. Co. 3d Bn. 30th Inf
Sigelmier, George C., Pfc, Co. E 30th Inf Regt., France 10 Nov. 1944
Sigler, Kenneth J., Pfc, Btry C 441st AAA AW Bn., France, Germany 8 May 1945
Sigrist, Donald R., Sgt, Co. D 15th Inf, Allen, France 27 Aug. 1944
Silva, Antonio, T/Sgt, Hq. Co. 601st TD Bn., N. Africa, Italy, France 15 Jan. 1945
Silva, Antonio L., Pvt, 3d Rcn Trp., Cori 25 May 1944
Silvey, Donald S., S/Sgt, 3d Inf Div. Band, N. Africa, Sicily, Italy 31 Dec. 1943
Sim, Gee H., Pfc, Hq. Co. 3d Inf Div., Italy, France Mar. 1944, 31 Jan. 1945
Simi, Roy J., 1st Lt, Coast Arty Corps Btry C 441st AAA AW Bn., Italy, France, Germany 8 May 1945
Simon, Michael A., S/Sgt, AT Co. 15th Inf, Isola Bella 4 Mar. 1944
Simon, Theodore E., T/5, Co. A 756th Tank Bn., Germany 15 Mar. 1945
Simonda, George E., S/Sgt, Btry C 39th FA Bn., N. Africa, Sicily, France, Germany, Austria 8 May 1945
Simmons, George D., T/5, Btry C 441st AAA AW Bn., France 26 Nov. 1944
Simmons, James E., S/Sgt, Co. K 30th Inf, Baraques 30 Oct. 1944
Simmons, James T., Pfc, MG Sec. 30th Inf, Germany
Simmons, Lee D., Pfc, Hq. Co. 15th Inf, France 27 Dec. 1944
Simmons, Milton L., 1st Lt, Inf Co. K 15th Inf Regt., Germany 21 Mar. 1945
Simon, Anatole J., Jr., S/Sgt, Co. A 30th Inf Regt., France 20 Nov. 1944
Simon, Floyd W., T/5, Btry C 10th FA Bn., N. Africa, Sicily, France, Germany 8 May 1945
Simpson, George W., Pfc, Co. H 7th Inf, France 7 Oct. 1944
Simpson, Leonard P., Pfc, Co. C 7th Inf, Rupt-Sur-Moselle 29 Sept. 1944
Simpson, Lowell C., Cpl, Btry A 9th FA Bn., Italy 4 June 1944
▲Simpson, William R., Jr., Cpl, Co. H 7th Inf Regt., Germany 16 Mar. 1945
Sinclair, Edmond B., Maj, MC Med. Det. 7th Inf Regt., France, Germany 8 May 1945
Singer, Earl H., Capt, Inf Hq. Co. 2d Bn. 7th Inf Regt., Italy 23 May 1944
Singer, Melvin S., S/Sgt, Co. L 15th Inf Regt, Germany 5 Apr. 1945
Sink, Paul J., Pfc, Co. A 15th Inf, St. Anaista, France 17 Aug. 1944
Sir, Kenneth O., T/5, Hq. Co. 1st Bn., 30th Inf, Vosges
Sirabella, Ericardo, Pfc, Co. K 15th Inf, Italy 16 Oct. 1943
Sirbaugh, Conrad H., Pfc, Co. K 7th Inf, Germany 13 Apr. 1945
Siskaninetz, Frank, Pfc, Btry A 39th FA Bn., Italy 1 June 1944
Sissel, George W., Pfc, Hq. Btry 9th FA Bn., Artena 1 June 1944
Sitton, Elmer F., T/5, Co. A 7th Inf Regt., Italy 30 May 1944
Sivess, Theodore A., S/Sgt, Hq. 3d Div., France, Germany May 1945
▲Skeiber, Stanley C., Capt, Inf Hq. Const. 30th Inf Regt., France 13 Mar. 1945
Skelton, Carl M., T/5, Rcn Co. 601st TD Bn., Germany 3 Apr. 1945
Skila, Mike, Pfc, Co. A 15th Inf Regt., France 31 Oct. 1944
Skinner, Edward C., Pfc, Co. B 756th Tank Bn., France 15 Sept. 1944
Skinner, John A., Pvt, Hq. Btry 10th FA Bn., Italy 25 Mar. 1944
Skopkowski, Stanley S., Pfc, Btry C 39th FA Bn., Sicily Aug. 1943
Skrzypczyk, Ladislaus J., T/4, Hq. 3d Inf, France, Germany 25 Mar. 1945
Slade, Bruce, T/Sgt, Co. F 30th Inf, Sicily 10 July 1943
Sladen, Fred W., Jr., Col, Hq. 1st Bn. 30th Inf
Sladky, Robert C., T/5, Btry C 10th FA Bn., France 8 Oct. 1944
Slater, Joseph M., Sgt, Rcn Co. 601st TD Bn., Italy, France, Germany 8 May 1945
Slatt, Tom, Pvt, Co. M 7th Inf Regt., Anzio, Italy 16 Feb. 1944
Slawter, Oliver J., Sgt, Co. G 15th Inf, Anzio, Italy 2 Mar. 1944
Sleep, Harold L., Pvt, Co. I 30th Inf, Artena 1 June 1944
▲(2) Sleeth, Robert K., Capt, CE Co. A 10th Engr. Combat Bn., Austria 4 May 1945
Sliva, Michael J., Pfc, Co. C 30th Inf, Colmar
Slothower, William R., Pfc, Co. L 30th Inf Regt., France, Germany, Austria 8 May 1945
Slusser, Ralph E., T/5, Co. B 756th Tank Bn., Germany 14 Apr. 1945
Small, Thomas R., Pfc, Co. C 7th Inf Regt., France 9 Sept. 1944
Smallwood, Harry M., Sgt, Hq. Co. 3d Bn. 7th Inf, France, Germany 8 Feb. 1945
Smartt, James E., T/5, Co. G 7th Inf Regt., Italy, France, Germany, Austria
Smith, Alan C., Pfc, Co. K 30th Inf, Vosges
Smith, Bill B., Sgt, Hq. Co. 2d Bn. 30th Inf, Anzio, Italy 26 Mar. 1944
Smith, Carlos F., Pfc, Hq. Co. 1st Bn. 15th Inf Regt., Italy 22 Feb. 1944
Smith, Claude E., 1st Sgt, Co. K 15th Inf Regt., France 6 Feb. 1945
Smith, Dee, Pfc, Co. D 7th Inf, Anzio, Italy 30 Jan. 1944
Smith, Delbert W., S/Sgt, Hq. Co. 601st TD Bn., Italy 1 June 1944
Smith, Dewey E., Pfc, Co. C 751st Tank Bn., Anzio, Italy 25 Jan. 1944
Smith, Donald E., Pfc, Hq. Co. 3d Inf Div., France, Germany 8 May 1945 8 May 1945
Smith, Donlad E., Pfc, Hq. Co. 3d Inf Div., France, Germany 8 May 1945
Smith, Earl H., S/Sgt, 3d Sig. Co., Italy 4 June 1944
Smith, Frank, Pfc, Co. M 30th Inf Regt., France 22 Nov. 1944
Smith, Fred A., S/Sgt, Co. G 7th Inf Regt., Italy, France 7 Feb. 1945
Smith, Freddie R., S/Sgt, AT Co. 7th Inf, Volturno River 13 Oct. 1943
Smith, Gerald H., Pfc, Co. A 7th Inf, Germany 18 Mar. 1945
Smith, George W., Pfc, Med. Det. 7th Inf Regt., France 21 Sept. 1944
Smith, Harold L., Pfc, Hq. Co. 3d Bn. 7th Inf, Capri di Orlando, Sicily 10 Aug. 1943
Smith, Hermit S., Pfc, Btry C 441st AAA AW Bn., Germany 30 Apr. 1945
Smith, Herman A., M/Sgt, Serv. Co. 30th Inf Regt., N. Africa, Sicily, Italy, France 20 Feb. 1945
Smith, James A., Jr., Sgt, Btry A 9th FA Bn., Italy, France, Germany 5 May 1945
Smith, James T., Pfc, Hq. Co. 2d Bn. 30th Inf, Padiglione 19 Feb. 1944
Smith, Joe C., Pfc, Co. M 7th Inf Regt., France 20 Nov. 1944
Smith, John D., T/5, Btry A 10th FA Bn., France 28 Oct. 1944
Smith, John H., Pvt, Co. A 3d Med. Bn., Cisterna 30 Jan. 1944
Smith, Joyce M., Pfc, MP Pltn 3d Inf, Italy 23 May 1944
Smith, Leonard R., T/Sgt, 3d Sig. Co., Sicily, Italy, France, Germany, Austria 8 May 1945
Smith, Merlin F., T/4, Btry C 10th FA Bn., N. Africa, Sicily, Italy, France, Germany 8 May 1945
Smith, Paul S., Pvt, 3d Rcn Trp., Germany 8 May 1945

▲ Oak Leaf Cluster.

▲Smith, Ralph J., Lt Col, Chap. Corps Hq. 3d Div., Eloyes, France 8 Oct. 1944
Smith, Robert R., S/Sgt, AT Co. 7th Inf Regt., Germany 9 Apr. 1945
Smith, Reno, Pfc, Co. B 7th Inf, France 26 Jan. 1945
▲Smith, Richard A., Maj, Serv. Co. 7th Inf, France Jan. 1945
Smith, Rudolph, 2d Lt, Hq. Co. 2d Bn. 30th Inf, So. France
Smith, Thomas G., Pfc, Co. M 7th Inf, Ponte Rotto 12 Mar. 1944
Smith, T. W., T/5, Hq. Co. 7th Inf, Anzio, Italy 5 Feb. 1944
Smith, Toliver R., Pvt, Hq. & Hq. Btry 41st FA Bn., Conca 31 Jan. 1944
Smith, W. C., Pfc, Co. E 7th Inf, Cisterna di Littoria 16 Feb. 1944
Smith, Warren A., Sgt, Co. A 601st TD Bn., France 25 Jan. 1945
▲Smith, Wesley J., S/Sgt, Co. C 30th Inf Regt., France 1 Dec. 1944
Smith, William A., 1st Sgt, Serv. Btry 9th FA Bn., Africa, Sicily, Italy, France, Germany, Austria 7 May 1945
Smith, William E., T/4, Btry B 10th FA Bn., N. Africa, Sicily, Italy, France, Germany, Austria 8 May 1945
Smith, William H., T/5, Btry C 441st AAA AW Bn., Sicily, Italy, France, Germany 8 May 1945
Smith, Willie G., T/5, Rcn Co. 601st TD Bn., France 23 Nov. 1944
Smith, William R., Pfc, Hq. Co. 30th Inf Regt., France 16 Aug. 1944
Smithson, Kenneth L., Pfc, Co. E 7th Inf, Cisterna di Littoria 29 Feb. 1944
Smock, Donald R., Sgt, Co. C 756th Tank Bn., France 2 Feb. 1945
Smolinski, Frank E., Pvt, Co. C 15th Inf, France 11 Sept. 1944
Smyth, Richard E., Sgt, Btry A 441st AAA AW Bn., Costello 29 May 1944
Sneed, Charles E., Cpl, Btry A 9th FA Bn., Italy 1 June 1944
Snell, Hugh F., T/5, Btry D 441st AAA AW Bn., Sicily, Italy, France, Germany, Austria 8 May 1945
▲Snowden, Norwood L., Capt, Inf Cn Co. 30th Inf Regt., France 20 Feb. 1945
Snyder, Bernard L., Pfc, 3d Sig. Co., N. Africa, Sicily, Italy, France, Germany 8 May 1945
Snyder, Nelson L., Pvt, Co. K 30th Inf Reg., France 29 Oct. 1944
Snyder, Richard A., T/5, Co. E 7th Inf Regt., Italy 4 June 1944
Snyder, Richard C., Pfc, Hq. Co. 2d Bn. 30th Inf, Anzio, Italy
Sodano, Thomas C., Pfc, Cn Co. 7th Inf Regt., Italy 12 & 22 Mar. 1944
Sofranko, Raymond J., T/5, Hq. Co. 3d Bn. 15th Inf Regt., Germany 19 Mar. 1945
Solberg, Harold L., Pvt, Co. A 10th Engr. Combat Bn., France 5 Nov. 1944
Solberg, Walter P., T/4, Co. 756th Tank Bn., Italy 16 Feb. 1944
Soloman, Irving I., T/5, Hq. & Hq. Btry 41st FA Bn., France 17 Dec. 1944
Solomon, Warren M., Capt, Inf Hq. Co. 1st Bn. 7th Inf Regt., Italy 28 Feb. 1944
Soltis, John G., Pfc, Co. M 15th Inf, Anzio, Italy 30 Jan. 1944
Somers, David D., T/4, Hq. Btry 9th FA Bn., N. Africa, Sicily, Italy, France, Germany 8 May 1945
Somers, Francis D., S/Sgt, 3d Sig. Co., France, Germany 8 May 1945
Soos, Frank W., S/Sgt, Btry A 9th FA Bn., N. Africa, Sicily, France, Germany, Austria 8 May 1945
Sorenson, William M., Sgt, Co. F 7th Inf, France 18 Jan. 1945
Soroczak, Walter, Pfc, Co. L 30th Inf, Colmar
Sorrell, Clinton L., Pfc, MP Pltn 3d Inf, France 12 Oct. 1944
Sorrell, Curtis K., M/Sgt, Serv. Co. 15th Inf, France, Germany 8 May 1945
Sosnowski, Alexander, Cpl, Hq. Co. 2d Bn. 7th Inf, Cisterna di Littoria 23 May 1944
Soto, Clarence E., Pfc, Serv. Co. 7th Inf Regt., Italy, France, Germany May 1945
Soules, John H., Jr., T/Sgt, Co. K 7th Inf, Italy 18 Nov. 1943
Soza, Frankie E., Pfc, Co. M 15th Inf, Cisterna di Littoria 29 Jan. 1944
Spangler, George C., T/Sgt, Med. Det. 30th Inf, Italy 28 Nov. 1943
Spanhake, George W., Hq. Co. 3d Bn. 7th Inf Regt., Germany 27 Mar. 1945
Spear, John J., Pfc, Co. B 601st TD Bn., Germany 1 Apr. 1945
Spencer, Verdon V., Pvt, Hq. Btry 41st FA Bn., Coronia 6 Aug. 1943
▲Spicer, George K., Capt, Inf 3d Bn. 30th Inf Regt., France 23 Jan. 1945
Spicer, Kermit B., T/4, Serv. Co. 30th Inf, Italy 1 June 1944
Spilker, Carl J., S/Sgt, Hq. Co. 3d Bn. 7th Inf Regt., France 26 Jan. 1945
Spillard, Albert F., 1st Lt, Inf Hq. Co. 756th Tank Bn., France, Germany 8 May 1945
Spindler, Edward A., S/Sgt, Co. C 15th Inf, France 5 Feb. 1945
Spinrad, Walter I., Capt, MC 7th Inf, Cisterna Di Littoria 31 Jan. 1944
Spitler, Charles H., Pfc, Co. E 7th Inf Regt., France 30 Jan. 1945
Spivey, Thomas W., Jr., Pfc, Co. B 30th Inf Regt., near Guemar, France 23 Jan. 1945
Splinter, Earl E., S/Sgt, Btry A 9th FA Bn., N. Africa, Sicily, Italy, France, Germany 8 May 1945
Sporar, Harold A., Pfc, Co. H 30th Inf, France 18 Dec. 1944
Spoto, Sebastian J., T/5, Hq. Co. 2d Bn. 30th Inf, Brolo 11 Aug. 1943
Spotts, Paul F., Pfc, Co. M 7th Inf, France 6 Jan. 1945
Sprague, Warren, Pfc, Hq. Co. 756th Tank Bn., Italy 19 Feb. 1944
Spreigl, Clarence T., T/4, Hq. Btry 9th FA Bn., Sicily, Italy, France 15 Sept. 1944
Spreyer, Frederick C., Maj, FA Hq. 3d Inf Div., France, Germany, Austria 8 May 1945
Spriggs, Robert L., Sgt, Btry C 9th FA Bn., Italy, Anzio 13 Feb. 1944
Springer, Alex, T/Sgt, Hq. Co. 601st TD Bn., N. Africa, Italy, France, Germany, Austria 8 May 1945
Spruill, Charles, Pfc, Co. I 15th Inf Regt., France 3 Jan. 1945
Spurlin, Wesley J., Pvt, Med. Det. 15th Inf, Femingamorta 15 Mar. 1944
Spurrier, Lawrence G., Pvt, Hq. Co. 30th Inf, Campo Morto 26 Apr. 1944
Spurrier, Paul J., Pvt, 3d QM Co., French Morocco 1 Dec. 1942
Squires, Weller J., Cpl, Co. A 10th Engr. Combat Bn., France 2 Nov. 1944
Sromovski, Andrew, Pfc, Co. D 7th Inf, Cisterna Di Littoria 31 Jan. 1944
Stack, John J., Pvt, Co. E 7th Inf Regt., Germany 19 Apr. 1945
Stackhouse, Charles L., Jr., 1st Lt, FA Hq. 41st FA Bn., Italy 24 Apr. 1944
Stacy, Henry D., 1st Lt, MAC Co. C 3d Med. Bn., Italy 17 Nov. 1943
Stadler, Louis, T/5, Btry B 441st AAA AW Bn., France 25 Jan. 1945
Stafford, Elmer A., S/Sgt, Hq. Co. 3d Bn. 15th Inf Regt., France 24 Oct. 1944
Stage, Shirley E., S/Sgt, Co. E 7th Inf Regt., France 12 Jan. 1945
▲Stallsmith, Lewis E., T/4, Med. Det. 15th Inf, France 27 Dec. 1944
Stamler, Maurice, Capt, MC 41st FA Bn., Baia E Latina 26 Oct. 1943
Standerfer, Robert J., 1st Lt, Co. M 15th Inf, San Fratelo, Sicily 7 Aug. 1943
Standley, Charles L., Pvt, Co. L 7th Inf, Anzio, Italy 28 Feb. 1944
Stanek, Millard J., Capt, FA Hq. Btry 41st FA Bn., France 23 Aug. 1944
Stanich, Peter C., T/5, Co. M 30th Inf Regt., N. Africa, Sicily, Italy, France, Germany 8 May 1945
Stapleton, Samuel J., M/Sgt, Hq. 3d Div., Italy, France 30 Nov. 1944
Starkweather, Chester K., Pvt, Hq. Btry 39th FA Bn., Anzio, Italy 23 Mar. 1944
Starnick, Rudy, 1st Sgt, AT Co. 7th Inf, N. Africa, Sicily, Italy, France, Germany, Austria 8 May 1945
Stasion, Henry, Pfc, Btry D 441st AAA AW Bn., France 5 Feb. 1945
Stasser, Godfrey P., III, T/Sgt, Cn Co. 7th Inf Regt., France, Germany 5 May 1945
Stebbins, Thomas J. V., T/5, Hq. Btry 9th FA Bn., Sicily, Italy, France, Germany 8 May 1945
Steeb, John, Cpl, Btry A 441st AAA AW Bn., Costello 29 May 1944
Steel, Bertram N., Pfc, Co. I 15th Inf Regt., France 12 Sept. 1944
Steele, Robert H., Pfc, Cn Co. 15th Inf, Campo Bella 12 July 1944
Steele, William D., Pvt, Med. Det. 30th Inf Regt., Anzio, Italy 10 Feb. 1944
Steenberg, Walter F., Pfc, Hq. Co. 3d Bn. 30th Inf
Steger, James R., T/4, Hq. Btry 39th FA Bn., Italy 10 Oct. 1943
Stegmann, Donald F., 1st Lt, Co. K 7th Inf Regt., France 20 Nov. 1944
Steinitz, Henry J., Cpl, Btry A 441st AAA AW Bn., Italy 29 Oct. 1943
Stelmack, John H., Pfc, Hq. Co. 1st Bn. 30th Inf, Cisterna Di Littoria 25 May 1944
Stein, John F., Maj, Hq. 9th FA Bn., Sicily 18 Aug. 1944
Steinbach, Martin A., Sgt, Btry C 41st FA Bn., Italy 4 Mar. 1944
Steinborn, Ralph F., M/Sgt, Hq. Co. 3d Inf, N. Africa, Sicily, Italy, France, Germany 8 May 1945
▲Steiner, Earl F., T/3, 3d Sig. Co., Artena 27 May 1944
Stepanski, Eugene F., Pfc, Btry A 41st FA Bn., Valmontone 3 June 1944
Stephens, Ben T., Capt, Cav. Serv. Co., France 8 Feb. 1945
Stephens, James D., Pfc, Hq. Btry 3d Div. Arty, San Agata, Sicily 10 Aug. 1943
Stephens, Herbert S., 2d Lt, Inf Co. A 30th Inf Regt., Germany 19 Apr. 1945
Stephens, Robert C., Pfc, Co. F 30th Inf Regt., Germany 19 Apr. 1945
Sterner, Gunnar A., Pfc, Co. L 30th Inf Regt., France 27 Oct. 1944
Stevens, Alfred H., Pfc, Hq. Co. 30th Inf Regt., France 28 Oct. 1944
Stevens, John, Pfc, Hq. Co. 3d Bn. 7th Inf, France 24 Jan. 1945
Stevens, Red P., Capt, Btry A 39th FA Bn., Anzio 11 Mar. 1944
Stevenson, Lloyd, Pfc, Hq. Co. 1st Bn. 30th Inf Regt., France 24 Jan. 1945
Steward, Buford A., S/Sgt, Co. M 15th Inf Regt., France 15 Sept. 1944
Stewart, Connie B., Cpl, Hq. Co. 7th Inf, Cisterna Di Littoria 25 May 1944
Stewart, Jack A., S/Sgt, 3d Sig. Co., Italy 1 Oct. 1944
Stickney, William C., S/Sgt, Cn Co. 30th Inf Regt., Italy 2 Mar. 1944
Stienstra, Floyd, Pfc, Co. M 30th Inf Regt., France 17 Dec. 1944
Stone, Loren F., Capt, FA Btry C 41st FA Bn., Italy 6 Mar. 1944
Stout, Erman, S/Sgt, Serv. Co. 7th Inf, Anzio, Italy Mar. 1944
Strand, Donald A., T/4, Hq. Btry 3d Div. Arty, N. Africa, Sicily, Italy, France, Germany 8 May 1945
Strausner, Carl F., Pvt, Hq. Co. 30th Inf, Valmontone 1 June 1944
Streb, Claude R., Capt, Inf Hq. 1st Bn. 30th Inf Regt., Italy 29 Jan. 1944
Strebe, Richard W., T/4, 3d Inf Div. Band, N. Africa, Sicily, Italy, France 31 Dec. 1944
Streible, Joseph A., Sgt, Btry C 41st FA Bn., Herbaville 29 Oct. 1944
Streid, Delmar C., Sgt, Hq. Btry 39th FA Bn., Anzio 9 Feb. 1944
Strezempek, Ted J., S/Sgt, Btry A 41st FA Bn., Italy 20 May 1944
Stilwell, Harold R., Cpl, Hq. Co. 756th Tank Bn., Italy 16 Feb. 1944
Striscko, Michael J., 1st Lt, FA Hq. & Hq. Co. 601st TD Bn., Italy, France 15 Mar. 1945
Strouss, Irvin W., Cpl, FA Btry C FA Bn., Kembs, Alsaco, France 25 Feb. 1945
Stocker, John A., T/5, 3d Sig. Co., Conca 10 Mar. 1944
▲(2) Stoker, Merlin C., Capt, Inf Hq. 1st Bn. 15th Inf Regt., France 7 Feb. 1945
Stoll, James W., S/Sgt, Btry B 39th FA Bn., San Stefano, Sicily 6 Aug. 1943
Stoller, Jacob, T/4, Hq. Co. 3d Bn. 30th Inf Regt., France 23 Jan. 1945
Stoltz, Edwin I., Pvt, Hq. Co. 1st Bn. 30th Inf Regt., France 30 Sept. 1944
Stomel, Samuel, Pfc, Hq. Co. 3d Bn. 7th Inf, France 25 Jan. 1945
Stone, Charles H., S/Sgt, Co. C 756th Tank Bn., France 2 Feb. 1945
Stone, Cloford J., Pfc, Co. K 7th Inf Regt., Germany 22 Mar. 1945
Stone, Goerge F., T/5, Serv. Co. 15th Inf, France 18 Feb. 1945
Sotne, Roy, Pfc, Hq. Co. 30th Inf, Vosges
▲Stone, Walter L., T/5, Co. F 15th Inf Regt., France 1 Nov. 1944
Stool, Henry E., Cpl, Hq. Btry 39th FA Bn., Anzio Beachhead, Italy 8 June 1944
Stout, Lloyd R., Sgt, Co. B 756th Tank Bn., France 15 Sept. 1944
▲Stromberg, Woodrow W., Lt Col, CO 2d Bn. 30th Inf, Ponte Rotto 24 May 1944
Stroth, Arthur C., T/5, Co. F 7th Inf Regt., Italy, France, Germany 7 May 1945
Stroyan, Jacob L., Cpl, Hq. Btry 39th FA Bn., N. Africa, Sicily, Italy, France, Germany 8 May 1945
Stuart, Warren M., Capt, Inf Co. I 15th Inf Regt., France 26 Nov. 1944
Stubbings, Gordon G., T/5, Co. C 756th Tank Bn., France 5 Feb. 1945
Stucky, William G., Capt, Inf Hq. 1st Bn. 30th Inf Regt., Germany 9 Apr. 1945
Sturdivant, Leonard H., T/5, Co. C 10th Engr. Bn., Carano 5 Mar. 1944
Sturgeon, Wilbur L., Pfc, Co. M 7th Inf Regt., France 5 Jan. 1945
Sturzl, Budd F., 1st Lt, Serv. Btry 39th FA Bn., Sicily 18 Aug. 1943
Stych, Henry, Cpl, Med. Det. 41st FA Bn., Anzio, Italy 2 Mar. 1944
▲Stych, T/3, 41st FA Bn., France 18 Dec. 1944
Suchanek, John F., T/Sgt, Hq. Btry 9th FA Bn., N. Africa, Sicily, Italy, France, Germany 8 May 1945
Suckley, George A., Cpl, Btry A 441st AAA AW Bn., Italy 29 Oct. 1943
Sudlow, Robert D., Pfc, Btry A 30th FA Bn., Germany 18 Mar. 1945
Suhayda, Sylvester E., S/Sgt, Co. I 15th Inf, France 29 Dec. 1944
Sulantich, Mike J., T/4, Med. Det. 756th Tank Bn., Italy 4 June 1944
Sullivan, Daniel P., Pfc, Co. C 30th Inf, France 18 Aug. 1944
Sullivan, Francis C., WOJG, Serv. Co. 30th Inf, France, Germany 8 May 1945
Sullivan, James A., M/Sgt, Hq. Btry 9th FA Bn., Sicily, Italy, France, Germany 8 May 1945
Sullivan, Thomas J., Sgt, Hq. Co. 2d Bn. 7th Inf, Cisterna Di Littoria 20 May 1944
Sumner, William A., 1st Lt, Co. I 30th Inf, Germany 26 Mar. 1945
Summers, Marion A., T/3, Hq. 3d Inf Div., Italy, France, Germany 8 May 1945
Summers, Robert W., 1st Lt, Hq. 10th FA Bn., Anzio 4 Mar. 1944
Summerville, Harold R., T/4, Co. B 601st TD Bn., N. Africa, Italy, France 15 Jan. 1945
▲Super, Alexander, T/5, Btry C 441st AAA AW Bn., Germany 26 Apr. 1945
Sustarich, John W., T/5, Hq. Btry 9th FA Bn., Anzio 29 Feb. 1944
Sutherland, Donald H., Pfc, Hq. Co. 3d Bn. 7th Inf, Ponte Rotto 29 Feb. 1944

▲ Oak Leaf Cluster.

Sutker, Leonard, Sgt, Co. B 7th Inf Regt., France 25 Oct. 1944
Svaco, John, Pfc, Co. K 30th Inf Regt., Germany 27 Mar. 1945
Svoboda, Joseph S., Pfc, Co. E 30th Inf Regt., France 17 Dec. 1944
Swan, Thayne J., Pfc, Hq. Co. 3d Bn. 15th Inf Regt., France 19 Dec. 1944
Swanberg, Charles, Jr., Capt, Hq. 3d Div., France 15 Sept. 1944
Swanberg, Harold A., Cpl, Hq. Co. 3d Bn. 30th Inf Regt., N. Africa, Sicily, Italy, France, Germany, Austria 8 May 1945
Swanson, Ralph B., Pfc, Co. E 30th Inf, Germany 19 Apr. 1945
Swart, John W., Pfc, Btry C 10th FA Bn., N. Africa, Sicily, Italy, France, Germany, Austria 8 May 1945
Sweat, Lomis P., Cpl, Co. A 10th Engr. Combat Bn., France 5 Nov. 1944
Sweatt, Willie M., Pfc, Co. F 15th Inf, Ecots, France 8 Sept. 1944
Sweeney, Frank E., Jr., S/Sgt, Co. A 30th Inf, France 13 Oct. 1944
Sweeney, William L., Pfc, Hq. Co. 1st Bn. 15th Inf Regt., Italy 22 Feb. 1944
Swendsen, Paul O., S/Sgt, Btry A 10th FA Bn., France 17 Aug. 1944
Swenson, George O., T/5, Btry C 10th FA Bn., Cisterna Di Littoria 9 Mar. 1944
▲Swenson, John A., Sgt, Hq. Co. 2d Bn. 30th Inf, Carano 25 Mar. 1944
Swiatek, Stanley E., 2d Lt, Co. E 7th Inf, Piano Di Ciazzo 12 Oct. 1944
Swigert, John J., Cpl, Co. C 601st TD Bn., France 15 Aug. 1944, 8 Jan. 1945
Swol, Stanley W., T/5, Hq. Co. 2d Bn. 7th Inf Regt., Italy 24 May 1944
Swontek, Stanley A., S/Sgt, Co. E 7th Inf Regt., Italy 22 Jan., 5 June 1944
Sydelo, Michael P., Pfc, MP Pltn 3d Inf, Italy 23 May 1944
Sykes, Eldon C., Pfc, Hq. Co. 30th Inf Regt., Italy, France 11 Nov. 1944
Syreika, Stanley C., T/5, Hq. Co. 7th Inf, France 24 Oct. 1944
Szczepanowski, Karol, S/Sgt, Co. A 30th Inf Regt., France 14 Oct. 1944
Szekeres, John G., Pfc, Co. H 7th Inf, France 21 Oct. 1944
Szladek, Frank J., Capt, MC Co. A 2d Med. Bn., France 25 Oct. 1944

Tacito, Antonio, Pfc, Btry C 10th FA Bn., Cisterna 1 Mar. 1944
Tackett, Carl P., 2d Lt, Co. C 3d Med. Bn., Germany 26 Mar. 1945
Taffit, Morton A., Pfc, Btry B 441st AAA AW Bn., Cisterna 22 Mar. 1944
▲Taggart, Donald G., 1st Lt, Inf Hq. 3d Inf Div., France, Germany, Austria 8 May 1945
Taggart, George B., Pfc, Co. A 30th Inf Regt., France 29 Sept. 1944
Tait, Ernest E., Pfc, Co. B 7th Inf, Italy 12 Feb. 1944
Talbert, Clyde L., T/5, Btry B 39th FA Bn., Cisterna 6 Mar. 1944
Talbert, Howard C., Pfc, Hq. Co. 2d Bn. 15th Inf, France 3 Nov. 1944
Tamayo, Andrew S., Pfc, Hq. Btry 39th FA Bn., Artena 27 May 1944
Tamburello, Joseph B., Pvt, Med. Det. 7th Inf, Cisterna Di Littoria 26 May 1944
▲Tank, Charles F., Lt Col, CE Engr. Off. 3d Inf Div., Italy 14 Oct. 1943
Tannatt, Willard C., Pfc, Hq. Co. 2d Bn. 30th Inf, Anzio, Italy 15 Apr. 1944
Tanner, James W., S/Sgt, Cn Co. 30th Inf Regt., France 20 Feb. 1945
Tanner, Norman C., Maj, FA Hq. 3d Inf Div. Arty, France 6 Feb. 1945
Tanner, Virgil L., T/Sgt, Co. I 7th Inf, France 24 Oct. 1944
▲Tapley, Elbert, Sgt, Co. C 30th Inf, France 7 Feb. 1945
Tapp, Ralph E., Pfc, Hq. Co. 3d Bn. 7th Inf, Franould, France 5 Oct. 1944
Tartaglia, Frank, Pfc, Hq. Co. 2d Bn. 7th Inf, Anzio, Italy 27 Feb. 1944
Tardif, Joseph M., S/Sgt, Co. B 601st TD Bn., France 29 Aug. 1944
▲Tardy, Walter E., Lt Col, FA Co. 601st Bn., France 6 Feb. 1945
Tarrance, James P., Pvt, Hq. Co. 2d Bn. 7th Inf, Italy 15 Oct. 1943
Tasdad, Ervin E., S/Sgt, Hq. Co. 2d Bn. 15th Inf, Isola Bella 26 Jan. 1944
Tatar, Robert, Pfc, Co. C 30th Inf, France 30 Sept. 1944
Tatlock, Eric W., 1st Lt, Co. H 30th Inf Regt., Italy 7 Nov. 1943
Taurino, Romer M., Sgt, Co. B 15th Inf Regt., France 26 Nov. 1944
Taylor, Eliajh, 1st Sgt, Serv. Btry 41st FA Bn., Coronia, Sicily 3 Aug. 1943
Taylor, Frank C., Pfc, Co. A 756th Tank Bn., Germany 7 Apr. 1945
Taylor, Fred C., 2d Lt, Hq. 7th Inf Regt., French Morocco 25 Dec. 1942
Taylor, James P., Pfc, AT Co. 7th Inf Regt., France 20 Nov. 1944
▲Taylor, James W., Capt, Gen. Staff Corps 3d Inf Div., France, Germany, Austria 8 May 1945
Taylor, Leroy G., T/4, Serv. Co. 756th Tank Bn., Italy 28 Jan. 1944
Taylor, Lyle, Pfc, Hq. Co. 2d Bn. 7th Inf, France 25 Jan. 1945
Taylor, Paul M., Pfc, Co. I 7th Inf Regt., France 29 Aug. 1944
Taylor, Roy A., Sgt, Co. F 30th Inf, Sicily 10 July 1943
Taylor, R. B., S/Sgt, Co. H 15th Inf, France 27 Dec. 1944
Taylor, Robert L., S/Sgt, Btry A 441st AAA AW, Sicily, Italy, France, Germany 8 May 1945
Taylor, Roy C., T/4, Co. C 10th Engr. Combat Bn., France 8 Oct. 1944
Teague, Dearl N., Pfc, Md. Det. 15th Inf, Anzio, Italy 11 Feb. 1944
Tedrow, Odell, S/Sgt, Med. Det. 30th Inf, Anzio, Italy 18 Feb. 1944
Teets, Fred J., T/4, Hq. Co. 601st TD Bn., Italy 8 Feb. 1944
Tegan, Warren A., Maj, Inf Hq. 15th Inf Regt., Italy, France 15 Aug. 1944
▲Telecky, Richard C., S/Sgt, Co. B 601st TD Bn., France 28 Aug. 1944
Telleck, Anthony, 1st Lt, Inf Serv. Co. 7th Inf Regt., Italy, France, Germany 4 May 1945
Tench, Ray, T/5, 601st TD Bn., Isola Bella Mar. 1944
TenEyck, John F., T/Sgt, Hq. Btry 441st AAA AW Bn., Sicily, Italy, France, Germany 8 May 1945
Tenney, Flao L., Pfc, Hq. Co. 15th Inf Regt., France 9 Nov. 1944
Terock, John, Pfc, Btry B 10th FA Bn., Cisterna 9 Mar. 1944
Terral, William J., Pfc, Co. C 7th Inf, Mont Justine 15 Sept. 1944
Terrarosa, Edmund A., Pfc, Co. I 15th Inf, France 18 Sept. 1944
Terribilini, Robert S., Pfc, Med. Det. 9th FA Bn., Italy, France, Germany 8 May 1945
Terry, Gerald C., Pfc, Hq. Co. 3d Bn. 30th Inf Regt., Germany 27 Apr. 1945
Terry, James W., 1st Lt, FA Btry C 9th FA Bn., Italy, France 6 Dec. 1944
Tesch, Roz R., Sgt, Co. L 15th Inf, France 21 Oct. 1944
Tessier, Ernest W., 2d Lt, Hq. Co. 15th Inf Regt., Artena 27 May 1944
Testa, Falco A., S/Sgt, Co. F 15th Inf Regt., France 1 Nov. 1944
Tetreault, Albert J., S/Sgt, BP Co. K 7th Inf, Anzio, Italy 24 Apr. 1944
Tharp, Howard C., Sgt, Co. K 7th Inf Regt., France 24 Jan. 1945
Thayer, Robert H., Sgt, Co. A 756th Tank Bn., Germany 7 Apr. 1945
Theis, Norbert A., T/Sgt, Med. Det. 7th Inf, France, Germany May 1945
Theophile, John T., Pvt, Co. C 10th Engr. Combat Bn., Italy 25 Apr. 1944
▲Thobro, Clayton C., Lt Col, Inf Hq. 7th Inf Regt., France 22 Nov. 1944
Thomas, Carl R., Pfc, Co. C 30th Inf Regt., Italy 19 Apr. 1944
Thomas, Daniel W., 1st Lt, Btry A 441st AAA AW Bn., Sicily, Italy, France, Germany 8 May 1945
Thomas, James C., Pfc, Co. C 30th Inf, France 23 Jan. 1945
Thomas, Jesse F., Lt Col, Sig. Co., Italy June 1944
Thomas, Richard E., S/Sgt, Co. I 7th Inf Regt., France 10 Sept. 1944
▲Thomas, Richard G., Col, 15th Inf Regt., Italy, France 30 Sept. 1944
Thomas, Robert M., T/5, Hq. Co. 10th Engr. Bn., Le Ferriere 29 Feb. 1944
Thomas, Walter A., WOJG, US Army Serv. Co. 7th Inf Regt., France, Germany, Austria 5 May 1945
Thomas, Wilbur, Cpl, Co. A 30th Inf, Artena 1 June 1944
Thomason, Walter D., Sgt, Co. G 7th Inf, France 2 Jan. 1945
Thome, John J., Pfc, Co. K 7th Inf, Ponto Rotto 29 Feb. 1944
Thome, Paul I., Jr., Sgt, Hq. Co. 2d Bn. 30th Inf, Colmar
Thompson, Charles S., Pfc, Co. E 7th Inf, Cisterna Di Littoria 23 May 1944
Thompson, Clifford B., 1st Lt, Rcn Co. 601st TD Bn., France 8 Sept. 1944
Thompson, Floyd W., T/4, Hq. Co. 3d Inf Div., Italy, France 15 Sept. 1944
Thompson, George M., Cpl, Hq. Btry 41st FA Bn., Presig, France 11 Sept. 1944
Thompson, Henry H., T/5, Rcn Co. 601st TD Bn., France 14 Sept. 1944
Thompson, James J., Pfc, Hq. Co. 7th Inf, France 24 Oct. 1944
Thompson, John W., T/5, Rcn Co. 601st TD Bn., Tunisia 15 Feb. 1943
Thompson, Marion E., Pfc, Co. M 30th Inf, Boult 10 Sept. 1944
Thompson, William A., Sgt, Co. C 7th Inf Regt., Germany 19 Mar. 1945
Thomson, Chester D., T/5, Serv. Co. 15th Inf Regt., Anzio Beachhead, Italy 4 June 1944
Thorell, Clarence M., T/5, Hq. Btry 9th FA Bn., Sicily, Italy, France 15 Sept. 1944
Thornton, Ellis S., Pfc, Co. C Medics, Le Ferriere 2 Mar. 1944
Thornburg, Herby A., Pvt, Hq. Btry 3d IDA, Anzio, Italy 29 Feb. 1944
Thornburg, Leon, Pvt, Co. M 15th Inf, Isola Bella 29 Feb. 1944
Thuilliez, Raymond R., S/Sgt, Co. E 30th Inf, Colmar
Thurber, Harlow, Cpl, Co. L 30th Inf Regt., France 27 Oct. 1944
Thurman, Maurice K., T/Sgt, Co. M 30th Inf, Anzio, Italy 10 Mar. 1944
Tickler, Peter A., Sgt, Hq. Co. 2d Bn., Cisterna Di Littoria 9 Feb. 1944
Ticknor, Arthur R., T/5, Hq. Btry 9th FA Bn., Sicily, Italy, France, Germany 8 May 1945
Tidwell, Phillip, Sgt, Co. C 756th Tank Bn., France 25 Jan. 1945
Tierney, George A., T/5, Hq. Btry 39th FA Bn., Sicily, Italy, France, Germany 8 May 1945
Tiffany, Hiero G., Jr., 1st Lt, Co. D 30th Inf, France 27 Jan. 1945
Tigue, Robert T., T/5, Hq. Btry 39th FA Bn.,Italy 2 June 1944
Tikkanen, Emil A., T/4, Co. B 756th Tank Bn., France 15 Sept. 1944
Tiller, Jack B., Sgt, Co. F 30th Inf Regt., France 27 Oct. 1944
Tilley, Delmar O., Cpl, MP Pltn 3d Inf, France 6 Feb. 1945
Tilliman, John W., Sgt, 3d Rcn Trp., Molay, France 20 Sept. 1944
Timmons, Leonard L., Pfc, 3d Inf Div. Band, France, Germany 8 May 1945
Timoney, Joseph L., Pvt, Med. Det. 7th Inf Regt., France 15 Mar. 1945
Tin Wah Chin, Pfc, Hq. Co. 3d Inf Div., Italy, France, Germany 8 May 1945
Tinker, Samuel M., Pfc, Hq. Co. 2d Bn. 30th Inf, Anzio, Italy 19 Apr. 1944
Tinsely, Calvin H., Pfc, Co. K 15th Inf Regt., France 26 Dec. 1944
Tinti, George J., Cpl, AT Co. 30th Inf, France 24 Dec. 1944
Tipton, Lattie, Pfc, Co. B 15th Inf, Anzio, Italy 6 Feb. 1944
Tirko, John, Pfc, Co. K 7th Inf, Artena 28 May 1944
Titus, William L., Pfc, Co. C 7th Inf Regt., Germany 19 Mar. 1945
Tobiczyk, John E., Cpl, Rcn Co. 601st TD Bn., near Fronois, France 7 Sept. 1944
Tobin, William P., Pfc, Cn Co. 15th Inf Regt., Italy 4 June 1944
Todaro, Samuel F., Pfc, Co. H 30th Inf Regt., France 18 Dec. 1944
Todd, Lucian B., Co. M 7th Inf Regt., Italy 28 Feb. 1944
Toivonen, Louis E., T/4, Btry C 41st FA Bn., Italy, France, Germany 8 May 1945
Toland, Herbert, CWO, US Army 7th Inf Regt., French Morocco 31 Dec. 1942
Toll, Vincent M., Cpl, 3d QM Co., Italy, France, Germany 8 May 1945
Tomczak, Edward C., S/Sgt, Cn Co. 7th Inf, Sicily 17 Aug. 1943
Tominac, John J., 1st Lt, Co. K 15th Inf, France 6 Nov. 1944
Tomlin, Jack L., 1st Lt, Inf Cn Co. 30th Inf, Sicily 11 July 1943
Tomlinson, Herbert J., Pfc, Co. E 7th Inf, Cisterna Di Littoria 29 Feb. 1944
Tomlinson, LeRoy H., Pfc, Btry B 39th FA Bn., Cisterna 25 Jan. 1944
Tonucci, Romolo, T/5, Hq. Co. 7th Inf Regt., France, Germany, Austria 4 May 1945
Toole, John H., 1st Lt, Co. K 15th Inf, France 25 Oct. 1944
Toole, John T., Pfc, Btry D 441st AAA AW Bn., Germany 27 Mar. 1945
Toomer, Harold D., 1st Lt, Co. F 7th Inf, Cisterna Di Littoria 24 May 1944
Toomey, William J., Pfc, 3d Sig. Co., France, Germany, Austria 8 May 1945
Toot, Dean A., Sgt, Co. G 15th Inf Regt., Italy, France, Germany, Austria 8 May 1945
Toothman, Elmer D., T/5, Cn Co. 15th Inf, France 10 Jan. 1945
Torjanowski, Thomas J., T/4, Hq. Btry 39th FA Bn., N. Africa, Sicily, Italy, France, Germany 8 May 1945
Torkelson, Raymond F., 2d Lt, Co. K 30th Inf Regt., France 7 Feb. 1945
Torman, John, Pfc, Co. D 15th Inf Regt., Italy 28 May 1944
Torres, Bennie L., Pfc, Hq. Co. 3d Bn. 15th Inf, Anzio 23 May 1944
Torten, Archie C., Pfc, Hq. Co. 1st Bn. 7th Inf Regt., France 24 Sept. 1944
Torza, Camille W., Cpl, Co. M 30th Inf, Colmar
Tosteson, Anthony M., Pfc, Co. G 15th Inf, Germany 7 Apr. 1945
Toth, Stephen R., Pfc, Co. E 15th Inf, Hyet, France 10 Sept. 1944
Tower, Owgood, Capt, Cav. Hq. Co. 756th Tank Bn., France, Germany 1 Apr. 1945
Townsend, George R., 1st Lt, Inf Co. I 7th Inf Regt., Germany 26 Mar. 1945
Tracey, Orrin A., Capt, Hq. Co. 7th Inf, Italy 8 Oct. 1943
Trafton, Willis A., Jr., 1st Lt, Inf Co. C 756th Tank Bn., France 11 Dec. 1944
Trapani, Rosario J., Cpl, Btry A 39th FA Bn., Germany 24 Mar. 1945
Travis, Ragan W., Sgt, Co. I 15th Inf, France 29 Dec. 1944
Travis, Raymond J., T/5, Btry A 9th FA Bn., Sicily 10 Aug. 1943
▲(3) Trazinski, Edward F., Pfc, Co. C 30th Inf Regt., Germany 13 Apr. 1945
Treadway, Charles L., Capt, Inf Co. M 7th Inf Regt., France 7 Oct. 1944
Treadwell, Chandler H., Pfc, Co. F 30th Inf Regt., Germany 19 Apr. 1945
Treby, Harold E., Capt, Medics 3d Div., France, Germany 8 May 1945
Tremblay, Telesphor C., 2d Lt, Inf Hq. Co. 1st Bn. 30th Inf Regt., France 25 Oct. 1944
▲Trembienski, Florian F., T/5, 3d Sig. Co., Germany 8 May 1945
Trenkamp, Edward J., Sgt, Co. F 15th Inf Regt., France 7 Nov. 1944
Trethewey, Thomas G., T/5, Btry A 39th FA Bn., Anzio 26 Jan. 1944
Triden, Fred A., S/Sgt, Hq. Co. 3d Bn. 7th Inf, Italy 25 May 1944
Trine, Jerry B., Pfc, MP Pltn 3d Div., Germany 8 May 1945
Trisolini, Anthony, Pfc, Co. F 15th Inf, Cisterna, Femina, Morta 29 Jan. 1944
Tritico, Louis A., 1st Lt, Inf Hq. 30th Inf, France 20 Feb. 1945
Troje, Bernard M., WOJG, US Army Hq. 10th Engr. Bn., Italy, France, Germany 6 May 1945
Trost, Louis R., 1st Sgt, Co. K 30th Inf Regt., France, Germany, Austria 8 May 1945
Troum, Norman G., Pvt, Co. H 15th Inf, Ponte Rotte 1 Mar. 1944
Trout, Harold E., Pfc, Hq. Co. 2d Bn. 30th Inf, Camp Morto 2 Mar. 1944

▲ Oak Leaf Cluster.

Troxell, Billy F., T/5, Hq. Btry 9th FA Bn., Germany 16 Apr. 1945
Truesdell, William A., Pvt, Hq. Co. 3d Bn. 7th Inf, Capri, Di Orlando, Sicily 10 Aug. 1943
Truitt, William O., Cpl, Med. Det. 39th FA Bn., Dampvalley-Les-Colombe, France 13 Sept. 1944
Trulillo, Jack R., Pfc, Cn Co. 30th Inf, Anzio, Italy
Trzeciak, Edward J., Pfc, Co. G 7th Inf Regt., France 4 Sept. 1944
Tschoerner, Arthur R., Cpl, Hq. Btry 10th FA Bn., Cisterna 23 May 1944
Tschudy, Fred, M/Sgt, Order of Battle Team 76, MIS 3d Inf Div., France, Germany 8 May 1945
Tubb, Robert L., 1st Lt, Hq. 1st Bn. 15th Inf, France 26 Jan. 1945
Tubek, Edward J., Sgt, Btry A 441st AAA AW Bn., Sicily, Italy, France, Germany 8 May 1945
Tucker, Bob J., S/Sgt, Co. L 30th Inf Regt., Germany 30 Mar. 1945
Tucker, Buford L., Jr., T/4, Btry D 441st AAA AW Bn., Sicily, Italy, France, Germany 8 May 1945
Tucker, Charles J., Jr., Pfc, Co. M 30th Inf, France 1 Sept. 1944
Tucker, Gordon I., T/Sgt, Co. H 15th Inf, Anzio, Italy 29 Feb. 1944
Tuggle, James E., Pfc, Co. C 30th Inf Regt., France 31 Dec. 1944
Tumlison, James R., S/Sgt, Co. H 7th Inf Regt., Italy 2 Feb. 1944
Turcotte, Raymond L., T/5, 3d Inf Div. Band, N. Africa, Sicily, Italy, France, Germany 8 May 1945
Turekian, Samuel, S/Sgt, 3d Sig. Co., N. Africa, Sicily, Italy, France 31 Jan. 1945
Turk, Wilson C., T/5, Hq. Co. 2d Bn. 7th Inf Regt., Italy 23 May 1944
Turnbull, Joseph W., S/Sgt, Co. I 15th Inf, France 29 Dec. 1945
Turner, Hiram, T/5, AT Co. 30th Inf, Colmar
Turner, William R., S/Sgt, Co. D 7th Inf Regt., France 11 Oct. 1944
Tussey, Joe W., S/Sgt, Hq. Co. 7th Inf Regt., France 2 Nov. 1944
Tuttleman, Stanley C., 1st Lt, FA Btry C FA Bn.,25 Feb. 1945
Tyler, Robert V., S/Sgt, Co. L 15th Inf Regt., France 26 Dec. 1944

Uecker, John G., T/4, Hq. Co. 7th Inf Regt., N. Africa, Sicily, Italy Jan. 1944
Ugalde, Jesse G., 1st Lt, Co. E 30th Inf, San Agata, Sicily 8 Aug. 1943
Uliana, Nisio L., S/Sgt, Btry B 441st AAA AW Bn., Germany 2 Apr. 1945
Ulloa, Atanasio, Pfc, Hq. Co. 1st Bn. 30th Inf, Germany 11 Apr. 1945
Ulrich, Wayne T., S/Sgt, 3d Div. Band, N. Africa, Sicily, Italy, France, Germany, Austria 8 May 1945
Underwood, Jack R., Pvt, Btry C 41st FA Bn., Isola Bella 25 May 1944
Underwood, William A., Cpl, Btry C 441st AAA AW Bn., Germany 27 Mar. 1945
Unser, Edgar, T/5, Co. A 10th Engr. Combat Bn., France 5 Nov. 1944
Upchurch, Shelton W., Pfc, Btry D 441st AAA AW Bn., France 10 Nov. 1944
Uschold, Raymond C., Pfc, Co. B 7th Inf, Artena 28 May 1944
Usrey, James D., Cpl, Hq. & Hq. Btry 41st FA Bn., Conca 31 Jan. 1944
Utter, Harley D., T/5, Serv. Btry 41st FA Bn., San Stephano, Sicily 4 Aug. 1943

Vaccaro, Charles L., Pfc, Co. L 7th Inf Regt., Italy 4 June 1944
Vaccaro, Frank N., 1st Lt, Hq. MP Corps, Sicily 18 Nov. 1943
Vagg, Bryon, Pvt, Rcn Co. 601st TD Bn., Acerno 21 Sept. 1943
Vail, Ralph J., T/5, Btry D 441st AAA AW Bn., France 10 Nov. 1944
Valdez, Augustine, Pvt, Co. C 3d Med. Bn., Campo Morto 29 Feb. 1944
Valenti, Isadore L., T/4, Med. Det. 7th Inf Regt., Italy 1 June 1944
Valenzuela, Olegario L., S/Sgt, Co. E 7th Inf, Cisterna Di Littoria 25 Mar. 1944
Vallero, Sam L., Pfc, Hq. Btry 441st AAA AW Bn., Borgo Montello 29 Feb. 1944
Vanatta, Elmer L., Pvt, Co. H 7th Inf, Campo Morto 18 Mar. 1944
Van Bogart, Bernel, Pfc, Hq. & Hq. Btry 41st FA Bn., Italy 18 Nov. 1943
Vance, Alma E., Sgt, Co. H 7th Inf, Valmontone 1 June 1944
▲Vander Ende, Charles T., S/Sgt, Co. D 30th Inf Regt., Germany 6 Apr. 1945
Vandervort, Francis H., Sgt, AT Co. 7th Inf, Volturno 13 Oct. 1943
Van Emmerick, Wynand, S/Sgt, Co. A 756th Tank Bn., France, Germany, Austria 8 May 1945
Van Every, William G., Cpl, Btry C 10th FA Bn., N. Africa, Sicily, Italy, France, Germany 8 May 1945
Van Horn, Charles R., Sgt, Btry D 441st AAA AW Bn., France 29 Dec. 1944
Van Hoy, Louie R., 1st Lt, Inf Co. G 7th Inf Regt., Germany 18 Apr. 1945
Van Hyning, Dale, 1st Lt, FA Btry C 10th FA Bn., France 7 Feb. 1945
VanMeeteren, William A., Cpl, Btry C 441st AAA AW Bn., Italy, France, Germany 8 May 1944
▲Van Sickle, Robert E., 1st Lt, Inf MP Pltn 3d Inf, Germany 8 May 1945
Vasey, Johnnie E., S/Sgt, Btry B 39th FA Bn., Sicily 14 Aug. 1943
Vasquez, Reynaldo, Pfc, Btry C 441st AAA AW Bn., Germany 30 Apr. 1945
Vay, Henry M., S/Sgt, Btry A 441st AAA AW Bn., Italy, France, Germany 8 May 1945
Venhaus, Arthur B., Pfc, Btry B FA, Isola Bella, Italy 19 Feb. 1945
Vergano, Frank D., S/Sgt, Hq. Btry 41st FA Bn., France 19 Feb. 1945
VerMeulen, Edward F., Pfc, Co. G 7th Inf, Padiglione 23 Apr. 1944
▲Vermillion, Eugene, Capt, Gen. Staff Corps Hq. 3d Inf Div., France 2 Mar. 1945
Verneris, Arthur H., Pvt, Hq. Co. 3d Bn. 30th Inf Regt., France 20 Nov. 1944
Vernillo, Jerry J., Sgt, Serv. Co. 756th Tank Bn., France, Germany, Austria 8 May 1945
Vesey, Francis L., Jr., Pfc, Co. A 15th Inf Regt., France 25 Jan. 1945
Vial, Joseph R., S/Sgt, Hq. Co. 30th Inf, N. Africa, Sicily, Italy, France 20 Feb. 1945
Vickey, Jack M., Pvt, Hq. Co. 30th Inf Regt., Italy 26 Jan. 1944
Viehland, Hugo A., S/Sgt, Co. B 30th Inf Regt., France 29 Nov. 1944
Vignolo, Armando V., Sgt, Co. B 756th Tank Bn., Germany 9 Apr. 1945
Viherek, Stephen J., Pfc, Co. D 30th Inf, France 21 Sept. 1944
Villa, Mario H., Pfc, Co. B 10th Engr. Combat Bn., France 27 Oct. 1944
Villagran, Edward, S/Sgt, Btry B 41st FA Bn., France 6 Oct. 1944
Villane, Alphonse J., Pfc, Co. M 7th Inf, Germany Mar. 1945
Villanueva, Santiago E., Pfc, Btry C 441st AAA AW Bn., Germany 27 Mar. 1945
Villegas, Mike V., T/Sgt, Hq. Spec Trps. 3d Div., Italy, France Mar. 1945
Vincent, Loren G., Pfc, Cn Co. 7th Inf, Anzio, Italy 29 Feb. 1944
Vinicki, Joseph S., Pfc, Hq. Co. 3d Bn. 30th Inf, France 18 Jan. 1945
Vint, Raymond E., Capt, Chap. Corps 7th Inf Regt., Germany 15 Mar. 1945
Viola, John J., Pvt, Hq. & Serv. Co. 10th Engr. Combat Bn., Italy 15 Feb. 1944
Virelli, Louis J., T/4, Co. B 756th Tank Bn., Germany 13 Apr. 1945
Virgin, Lyndon L., Pfc, Co. A 30th Inf, France 8 Nov. 1944

▲ Oak Leaf Cluster.

Visconti, Lino L., Pfc, Co. H 7th Inf Regt., Italy, France, Germany 7 May 1945
Viteo, Stephen, Pfc, Co. G 15th Inf, Anzio, Italy 26 Feb. 1944
Vogt, Nelson W., Pfc, Co. C 7th Inf Regt., France 25 Jan. 1945
Vogt, William O., S/Sgt, Co. M 30th Inf Regt., France 17 Dec. 1944
▲(2) Voigts, Walter E., Sgt, Co. H 7th Inf Regt., Germany 2 Apr. 1945
Volpicella, Leonardo, Pfc, Hq. Btry 3d IDA, Anzio, Italy 29 Feb. 1944
Von Holtz, Edward F., Pvt, Hq. Co. 30th Inf, Cisterna Di Littoria 20 May 1944
Von Kahle, Vancino A., Pfc, MG Sec. 30th Inf, Germany
Voss, James R., 1st Sgt, Co. A 30th Inf Regt., France 7 Oct. 1944
Votruba, Kenneth E., T/4, Serv. Co. 7th Inf Regt., Italy, France, Germany 4 May 1945
Vowell, Earl P., S/Sgt, Co. G 7th Inf, St. Honore, France 17 Aug. 1944
Voyles, Thomas M., Jr., T/4, Co. A 751st Tank Bn., Pratone 29 Feb. 1944
Vrain, Hyman S., S/Sgt, Co. A 7th Inf Regt., France 30 Sept. 1944
Vrana, Randolph L., T/4, Hq. 3d Inf Div., Italy, France, Germany 10 May 1945
Vratarie, Nicholas C., Sgt, Co. M 7th Inf Regt., France 23 Nov. 1944
Vreeland, Edward L., Sgt, Serv. Co. 7th Inf Regt., Italy 5 June 1944

Wade, Levi, Cpl, Btry C 441st AAA AW Bn., Germany 16 Apr. 1945
Wagenhogger, Stephen H., T/5, Btry B 441st AAA AW Bn., 27 Jan. 1945
Waggoner, Dallas L., T/5, Hq. Co. 2d Bn. 15th Inf Regt., Anzio, Italy 27 Jan. 1944
Wagner, Bernard K. G., Pvt, Hq. Co. 3d Bn. 7th Inf, Besancon, France 7 Sept. 1944
Wagner, Frank W., CWO, U. S. Army Hq. Co. 601st TD Bn., N. Africa, Sicily, Italy, France, Germany 8 May 1945
Wagner, George F., Sgt, Co. M 30th Inf Regt., N. Africa, Sicily, Italy 6 June 1944
Wagner, Howard M., Pfc, Hq. Co. 7th Inf Regt., France 27 Jan. 1945
Wagner, Stanley R., Pfc, Hq. Co. 10th Engr. Bn., Le Ferriere 29 Feb. 1944
Wagner, Wilbur W., T/4, Hq. Co. 756th Tank Bn., Germany 2 May 1945
Wagner, Willard F., S/Sgt, Hq. Co. 3d Bn. 7th Inf, France 6 Sept. 1944
Walker, Bennett O., Pvt, Co. L 7th Inf, By-Les-Lure, France 16 Sept. 1944
Walker, Carl E., 1st Sgt, Btry C 9th FA Bn., N. Africa, Sicily, Italy, France, Germany 8 May 1945
Walker, Thomas J., Sgt, Co. C 30th Inf Regt., France 18 Aug. 1944
Walkowski, Edward H., T/4, Hq. Co. 601st TD Bn., Italy 22 Jan. 1944
Wall, Norbet, T/Sgt, Serv.Co. 756th Tank Bn., France, Germany, Austria 8 May 1945
Wallace, Elmer J., S/Sgt, Co. M 15th Inf, France 4 Nov. 1944
Wallace, James F., Pfc, Co. M 1st Bn. 15th Inf, N. Africa, Sicily, Italy, France, Germany 8 May 1945
▲(2) Wallace, Kenneth W., Lt Col, Hq. 1st Bn. 7th Inf Regt., Germany 3 May 1945
Wallace, Willard C., T/5, Co. B 10th Engr. Combat Bn., France 23 Jan. 1945
Wallin, Tage H. S., S/Sgt, Btry B 441st AAA AW Bn., Sicily, Italy, France, Germany 8 May 1945
Wallner, Gilbert F., Pfc, Btry B 9th FA, Anzio, Italy 2 Mar. 1944
Walowitz, Alex, Pvt, Co. M 15th Inf, Isola Bella 2 Feb. 1944
Walsh, Edward L., S/Sgt, Co. L 15th Inf, France 1 Oct. 1944
Walsh, Edward P., Jr., S/Sgt, Co. M 7th Inf, Ponte Motto 1 Apr. 1944
Walsh, Leneus E., Cpl, Cn Co. 30th Inf, Campo Morto 29 Feb. 1944
Walsh, Roger J., Sgt, Btry A 9th FA Bn., Italy 4 June 1944
Walters, Henry J., Sgt, Co. L 30th Inf, France 27 Oct. 1944
Walters, James T., Pfc, Co. C Medics, Le Ferriere 2 Mar. 1944
▲Wann, Robert A., 1st Lt, Inf Co. E 15th Inf Regt., France 29 Jan. 1945
Ward, Carroll A., CWO, US Army 3d Med. Bn. 3d Inf Div., France, Germany 8 May 1945
Ward, Herschel O., Pfc, Co. C 30th Inf Regt., Germany 13 Apr. 1945
Ward, Robert E., S/Sgt, 3d Rcn Trp., near Kaysersburg, France 10 Jan. 1945
Wardlaw, Hugh E., Jr., Capt, Co. G 30th Inf Carrocetto 19 Feb. 1944
Ware, Frank M., Cpl, Co. B 756th Tank Bn., France 15 Sept. 1944
Ware, Keith L., Lt Col, Inf Exec. Off.1st Bn. 15th Inf Regt., France 22 Oct. 1944
Wark, Earl C., T/4, Co. C 756th Tank Bn., France 5 Feb. 1945
Warming, Stanford L., Cpl, Hq. Co. 2d Bn. 7th Inf Regt., Italy 25 May 1944
Warner, Floyd E., T/Sgt, Co. H 7th Inf Regt., Sicily 17 Nov. 1943
Warner, Edward P., T/Sgt, Hq. Co. 3d Bn. 30th Inf, Colmar
Warner, Floyd E., T/Sgt, Co. H 7th Inf Regt., Sicily 17 Nov. 1943
▲Warner, Kenneth D., Cpl, Hq. Co. D 15th Inf Regt., France 13 Feb. 1945
Warner, LeRoy L., Pvt, AT Co. 15th Inf, France 30 Jan. 1945
Warren, Delbert F., Cpl, Cn Co. 15th Inf, San Agata Di Militello, Sicily 6 Aug. 1944
Warren, Kenneth P., Pfc, Co. C 7th Inf, Mont Justine 15 Sept. 1944
Wasco, John, Cpl, Btry C 41st FA Bn., Germany 26 Mar. 1944
Wasilini, John J., Sgt, Hq. Co. 30th Inf, Vosges
Wasko, Mike, M/Sgt, Rcn Co. 601st TD Bn., Tunisia 26 Apr. 1943
Washington, Wilson S., Jr., Pfc, Co. F 30th Inf
Wasyluk, Joseph, Pfc, Btry B 441st AAA AW Bn., France 2 Feb. 1945
Waters, Charles H., T/5, Hq. Co. 3d Bn., N. Africa, Sicily, Italy, France, Germany 8 May 1945
Waters, Paul R., Sgt, Hq. Co. 3d Bn. 30th Inf, St. Die 11 Nov. 1944
Waters, William J., Pvt, Med. Det. 601st TD Bn., El Guettar, Tunisia 23 Mar. 1943
Watkevitch, Peter M., Pfc, Co. M 7th Inf Regt., Germany 8 Apr. 1945
Watson, Leonard O., S/Sgt, Hq. Co. 751st Tank Bn., Italy 20 Dec. 1943
Watson, Thomas J., 2d Lt, Co. E 30th Inf, Colmar
▲Watts, Geater, Pfc, Co. H 30th Inf Regt., Germany 27 Mar. 1945
▲Watts, James K., Maj, MP Corps Hq. 3d Div., France 30 Nov. 1944
Weatherford, Thomas H., Pfc, Co. B 7th Inf, Artena 28 May 1944
Weaver, Augusta, Pfc, Co. F 30th Inf Regt., Germany 27 Mar. 1945
Weaver, Herchel H., S/Sgt, Co. B 30th Inf, France 23 Jan. 1945
Webb, Earl E., S/Sgt, Hq. Btry 9th FA Bn., N. Africa, Sicily, Italy, France, Germany 8 May 1945
Webb, Robert A., Pfc, Co. C 30th Inf Regt., France 15 Jan. 1945
Webb, Thomas C., Pfc, Co. E 7th Inf, Cisterna Di Littoria 24 May 1944
Weber, Edwin W., S/Sgt, Co. L 30th Inf, Germany
Weber, Thomas R., Pvt, Med. Det. 30th Inf, Anzio, Italy 10 Mar. 1944
Webster, Theodore R., Sgt, Co. C 601st TD Bn., Isola Bella 18 Mar. 1944
Weddell, James R., Capt, Med. Det. 7th Inf, Cisterna Di Littoria 25 May 1944
Wedding, Vincent D., 1st Sgt, Co. K 7th Inf, Nettuno, Italy 22 Jan. 1944
Wedlake, Glenn W., Cpl, Co. D 30th Inf, Italy 12 Feb. 1944

Weeks, Loyz B., Pfc, 3d Rcn Trp., near Zwiebrucken, Germany 20 Mar. 1945
▲Weeks, Walter L., Pfc, Co. F 30th Inf, Carano 25 Apr. 1944
Weese, Albert P., Pfc, Hq. Co. 2d Bn. 30th Inf Regt., Germany 12 Apr. 1945
Weese, Floyd, Pfc, Co. C 30th Inf Regt., France 9 Sept. 1944
Weiler, Richard B., S/Sgt, Co. B 30th Inf Regt., France 21 Nov. 1944
Weingarden, Alfred, Sgt, Co. G 7th Inf, France 25 Jan. 1945
Weir, Howard J., S/Sgt, Co. C 15th Inf Regt., Germany 17 Apr. 1945
Weisman, Simons A., S/Sgt, Co. H 30th Inf Regt., France 6 Oct. 1944
Weiss, Homer L., T/4, Rcn Trp., Italy 5 June 1944
Welch, Fred C., Sgt, Co. C 30th Inf Regt., France 7 Feb. 1945
Welch, Thomas P., 1st Lt, Co. B 601st TD Bn., Presenzano 1 Nov. 1943
Welliver, Clyde N., Cpl, Co. H 7th Inf, Cisterna Di Littoria 30 Jan. 1944
Wells, Richard F., S/Sgt, Co. I 7th Inf Regt., Italy 2 June 1944
Wells, Vories H., Sgt, Hq. Co. 3d Inf Div., Italy, France 7 Dec. 1944
Wendel, Edmund, Jr., Capt, Hq. Btry 69th Armd FA Bn., Italy 11 July 1944
Wendschlaf, Lenhard W., T/5, Hq. Co. 1st Bn. 15th Inf Regt., France 18 Feb. 1945
▲Wendt, James R., Lt Col, FA Hq. 3d Inf Div., Arty, France, Germany 8 May 1945
Wenzel, Donald R., T/5, Serv. Co. 756th Tank Bn., France, Germany, Austria 8 May 1945
Werth, Leonard J., M/Sgt, Hq. Btry 441st AAA AW Bn.(SP),Sicily, Italy, France, Germany, Austria 8 May 1945
Wertman, Willard A., T/Sgt, Co. K 30th Inf, France, Germany 7 Apr. 1945
Wessels, Robert D., Pfc, Co. E 30th Inf Regt., Germany 26 Mar. 1945
West, John H., Capt, Co. G 30th Inf Regt., France 21 Nov. 1944
Westerfield, William J., Sgt, Co. H 7th Inf, Dragoni 17 Oct. 1944
Westerlund, Bacil C., T/4, Hq. & Hq. Det. 3d Med. Bn., France 15 Feb. 1945
Westlake, Bernard P., Pvt, Btry C 9th FA Bn., Artena 30 May 1944
Westmorlan, Leroy, Pvt, Co. F 30th Inf, Sicily 8 Aug. 1943
Westwal, Jerome J., Pfc, Med. Det. 9th FA Bn., Conca 6 Mar. 1944
Wetzel, Paul R., S/Sgt, Serv. Co. 30th Inf Regt., N. Africa, Sicily, Italy 4 June 1944
Werthmann, Edward H., Cpl, Hq. Co. 756th Tank Bn., Italy 20 Feb. 1944
West, Harold R., T/5, 3d Inf Div. Band, N. Nfrica, Sicily, Italy 31 Dec. 1943
West, Luther, Pfc, Co. F 30th Inf, Anzio, Italy 25 Apr. 1944
Westberry, Clifford, Pfc, Co. K 15th Inf Regt., France 26 Oct. 1944
Westerman, Homer, T/5, Btry C 441st AAA AW Bn., France 9 Nov. 1944
Wexler, Leo A., Pfc, MP Pltn 3d Inf Div., Italy 23 May 1944
Weygant, Vincent R., T/5, Btry B 10th FA Bn., Ferdrupt, France 20 Sept. 1944
Whaley, Leslie A., Pfc, Co. E 30th Inf, Germany
▲Whall, Winston G., Capt, Inf Serv. Co. 7th Inf Regt., Italy 6 June 1944
Wheat, Paul G., Pfc, Co. C 30th Inf, Germany
Whedbee, Richard M., Pfc, Co. B 15th Inf Regt., Germany 18 Mar. 1945
Wheeler, Dalton W., T/Sgt, Cn Co. 30th Inf Regt., near Rome, Italy 4 June 1944
Wheeler, Donald B., T/Sgt, Med. Det. 3d Med. Bn., Italy 23 May 1944
Wheeler, Ivan E., Cpl, Co. E 30th Inf, Germany
Wheeler, William J., S/Sgt, Co. E 7th Inf, Artena 29 May 1944
Whipps, John A., Jr., 1st Lt, Btry B 9th FA Bn., San Fratelo, Sicily 5 Aug. 1943
White, Arnold L., Pvt, 3d Rcn Trp., Germany 8 May 1945
White, Arthur F., T/4, Cn Co. 15th Inf, Anzio 1 Apr. 1944
White, Barney D., Maj, Hq. 39th FA Bn., Castel Morrone 11 Oct. 1943
White, Charles E., Jr., Sgt, Co. I 30th Inf Regt., Italy 26 Mar. 1944
White, Charlie C., Pvt, Btry D 441st AAA AW Bn., Guilianello 31 May 1944
White, Clarence H., Jr., Maj, Inf Hq. 2d Bn. 7th Inf Regt., France, Germany, Austria 4 May 1945
White, Daniel R., Jr., Pfc, Co. C 30th Inf Regt., France 3 Nov. 1944
White, Gerald S., T/5, Co. D 30th Inf, Anzio, Italy
White, Leland P., Sgt, Co. F 30th Inf Regt., France 3 Nov. 1944
White, Marshall C., Pvt, 3d Rcn Trp., Italy 6 June 1944
White, Nathan W., 1st Lt, Inf Hq. 7th Inf Regt., France, Germany, Austria May 1945
White, Richard L., Sgt, Co. M 15th Inf, Isola Bella 30 Jan. 1944
Whitehead, Fred W., Pfc, Med. Det. 30th Inf Regt., France 26 Nov. 1944
Whitelock, Kenly W., Capt, Btry C 39th FA Bn., Mignano 24 Dec. 1943
Whitley, Herson L., Sgt, Hq. Co. 3d Div., Italy, France, Germany, Austria 8 May 1945
▲Whitlock, Lee D., Sgt, Co. H 30th Inf Regt., Germany 19 Mar. 1945
Whittle, Glen, T/4, Co. D 756th Tank Bn., Germany 30 Apr. 1945
▲Whittle, John H., S/Sgt, Cn Co. 30th Inf, Anzio, Italy 22 Apr. 1944
Whittle, Roger L., Pfc, Co. H 7th Inf, Palestrina 2 June 1944
▲Wickersham, Daniel L., Maj, Inf Hq. 3d Inf Div., France 25 Jan. 1945
Wickey, Jack H., Pvt, Hq. Co. 30th Inf, Anzio, Italy
Widejkis, Stanley J., Pfc, Co. H 7th Inf, France 30 Jan. 1945
Wieder, James F., Pfc, Co. A 30th Inf, Germany
▲Wieg, Dwain O., T/5, 3d Sig. Co., Italy 5 June 1944
Wiener, Raymond, 1st Lt, Btry C 39th FA Bn., Statigliano 21 Oct. 1943
Wierschem, Joseph F., Sgt, Serv. Co. 30th Inf, Italy 5 June 1944
Wiese, Walter W., T/5, Btry A 39th FA Bn., Italy 31 May 1944
Wieting, Earl K., T/5, Hq. & Serv. Co. 10th Engr. Combat Bn., N. Africa, Sicily, Italy, France, Germany 8 May 1945
Wiggins, Howard A., Sgt, Btry C 441st AAA AW Bn., France 25 Nov. 1944
Wiggins, Lloyd, Jr., Sgt, Co. A 7th Inf, France 5 Feb. 1945
Wiiusz, Edward J., Sgt, Co. A 10th Engr. Combat Bn., France 5 Nov. 1944
Wilander, Thomas E., T/5, Serv. Co. 756th Tank Bn., France 6 Jan. 1945
Wilbanks, Cletis A., Pfc, Hq. Co. 3d Bn. 30th Inf, Germany
Wilberger, Roy C., Cpl, Hq. Btry 39th FA Bn., France 27 Dec. 1944
Wilcheck, Casimer A., T/5, Med. Det. 756th Tank Bn., Italy 4 June 1944
Wilensky, Sidney R., T/Sgt, Serv. Co. 7th Inf, Italy June 1944
Wiles, Charles J., Pfc, Co. H 30th Inf, Colmar
Wilhelm, George J., Cpl, Co. M 30th Inf Regt., Sicily, Italy, France, Germany, Austria May 1945
Wilk, Venceslaw W., Sgt, AT Co. 15th Inf, France 4 Jan. 1945
Wilkinson, Edward L., Capt, 39th FA Bn., Italy, France, Germany 8 May 1945
Willers, Carl A., Pvt, Co. A 10th Engr. Combat Bn., France 5 Nov. 1944
Willette, William L., 1st Lt, Co. B 756th Tank Bn., Germany 7 Apr. 1945
Williams, Charles S., Capt, Med. Det. 30th Inf, Anzio, Italy 20 Apr. 1944
Williams, Colie W., Pfc, Co. F 30th Inf, Italy 31 May 1944
Williams, Dewel W., Pvt, Co. C 10th Engr., Melay, France 21 Sept. 1944
Williams, Duart M., S/Sgt, 3d QM Co., N. Africa, Sicily, Italy, France, Germany, Austria 8 May 1945
Williams, Frank L., Capt, Co. E 7th Inf, Artena 1 July 1944
Williams, Freddie L., S/Sgt, Co. I 7th Inf, Morocco 10 Nov. 1942
Williams, Leonard F., T/Sgt, AT Co. 30th Inf, Vosges
▲Williams, Ralph R., S/Sgt, MP Pltn, France, Germany 8 May 1945
Williams, Robert, Cpl, Btry C 9th FA Bn., N. Africa, Sicily, Italy, France, Germany 8 May 1945
Williams, Rolla R., Cpl, Med. Det. 1st Bn. 15th Inf, Cisterna Di Littoria 25 May 1944
▲(2) Williams, Warren B., S/Sgt, Med. Det. 30th Inf, Cisterna Di Littoria 23 May 1944
Williamson, John B., 1st Lt, 10th FA Bn., France 4 Feb. 1945
Willigar, Lawrence H., Sgt, Co. H 7th Inf Regt., France 30 Jan. 1945
Willingham, Harold L., 2d Lt, Sig. Corps 3d Sig. Co., Germany 8 May 1945
Willis, Emerson C., Pfc, Hq. Co. 1st Bn. 7th Inf, France 22 Nov. 1944
Willis, William M., Jr., Pvt, Co. D 756th Tank Bn., Germany 25 Apr. 1945
Willsey, Frank M., 1st Lt, CE Co. G 10th Engr. Combat Bn., France 23 Jan. 1945
▲Wilm, Mathew M., Sgt, 9th FA Bn., France 10 Oct. 1944
Wilson, Buster B., Pvt, Co. A 10th Engr. Combat Bn., France 5 Nov. 1944
Wilson, Carlyle H., 1st Inf Co. E 7th Inf Regt., Germany 18 Apr. 1945
Wilson, Charles W., Sgt, Co. H 30th Inf, Brignoles, France 19 Aug. 1944
▲Wilson, Grover, Lt Col, AC of S G-2 Hq. 3d Inf Div., France 5 Jan. 1945
Wilson, Howard R., Cpl, Btry A 39th FA Bn., Italy 9 Oct. 1943
Wilson, Joseph H., S/Sgt, Co. G 7th Inf Regt., France 2 Nov. 1944
Wilson, Webster W., 1st Lt, FA Btry C 10th FA Bn., France 7 Oct. 1944
Wilson, Gwyn E., Pfc, Hq. Co. 3d Bn. 7th Inf Regt., Germany 27 Mar. 1945
Wilson, Harry T., T/5, Btry A 441st AAA AW Bn., Costello 29 May 1944
Wilson, Hyman, Sgt, Co. C 30th Inf, Italy 27 Apr. 1944
Wilson, Joseph F., S/Sgt, Co. M 30th Inf, Carano 30 Jan. 1944
Wilson, Robert L., Pfc, Co. C 30th Inf Regt., Germany 13 Apr. 1945
Wilson, Sidney L., Pfc, Co. H 7th Inf, Anzio, Italy 17 Feb. 1944
Wilson, Soule R., T/4, Med. Det. 7th Inf Regt., Germany 2 Apr. 1945
Wilson, William L., Pfc, Cn Co. 7th Inf, Guilianello 28 May 1944
Winchell, Donald C., 1st Lt, Btry A 441st AAA AW Bn., Italy, France, Germany 8 May 1945
Winey, Charles W., Pfc, Co. C 7th Inf, Cerre Les Nordy, France 13 Sept. 1944
Wing, Clinton H., Sgt, Btry A 41st FA Bn., San Fratelo, Sicily 4 Aug. 1944
Winkler, Thurston N., Pfc, Co. F 30th Inf Regt., Germany 20 Apr. 1945
Winters, Harry D., Pvt, Btry A 10th FA Bn., France 22 Jan. 1945
Winters, John, T/5, Med. Det. 7th Inf Regt., Germany 9 Apr. 1945
▲Wisdom, Joseph, Jr., S/Sgt, Co. I 30th Inf, Italy 15 Nov. 1943
Wise, Merlin W., T/4, Hq. Co. 756th Tank Bn., Italy 18 Feb. 1944
Wiseley, George D., Sgt, Co. H 30th Inf, Germany 20 Apr. 1945
Wiseman, Louis, 1st Lt, Btry D 441st AAA AW Bn., Guilianello 31 May 1944
▲Wiseman, Willis M., T/4, Hq. Co. 1st Bn. 30th Inf, France 24 Jan. 1945
Wisinski, Norbert J., 2d Lt, Co. I 15th Inf, Anzio, Italy 3 Mar. 1944
Wisniewski, Eugene, T/5, Serv. Co. 756th Tank Bn., France 24 Jan. 1945
Wisuri, Leslie W., Pfc, Cn Co. 30th Inf Regt., France 23 Jan. 1945
Witbeck, Allen B., Pfc, Co. E 30th Inf Regt., France 3 Jan. 1945
With, Alex H., Jr., T/4, Med. Det. 15th Inf, Italy, France 18 Feb. 1945
Witinski, Joseph, Pvt, 3d Sig. Co., Anzio, Italy 7 Mar. 1944
Witcher, Clarence V., Sgt, 3d QM Co., Sicily 18 Aug. 1943
Witham, Eugene B., Pvt, Hq. Co. 1st Bn. 30th Inf Regt., France 17 Dec. 1944
Witmer, Roy H., Pfc, Hq. Btry 39th FA Bn., France, Germany, Austria 8 May 1945
Wittig, Richard, Pfc, Co. B 10th Engr. Combat Bn., France 22 Jan. 1945
Witulski, John J., Cpl, Co. C 756th Tank Bn., France 24 Jan. 1945
Wockman, William L., Pvt, Hq. Co. 1st Bn. 15th Inf, Germany 17 Mar. 1945
Wojcik, Edwin S., Pfc, Co. C 30th Inf Regt., France 7 Feb. 1945
Wolfe, George D., T/3, Med. Det. 7th Inf, France, Germany May 1945
Wolfe, Howard, Pfc, Co. L 30th Inf, France 15 Oct. 1944
Wolfert, Dave I., T/5, 39th FA Bn., Italy 16 Feb. 1944
Wolfert, Frederic F., Lt Col, Div. QM 3d Inf Div., Italy 24 Oct. 1943
Wolff, Robert C., Pfc, Btry A 9th FA Bn., Artena-Guilianello Hiway 29 May 1944
Wolford, Wilbur W., T/5, Btry C 9th FA Bn., Artena 30 May 1944
Wong, James K., Pfc, Hq. Co. 3d Inf Div., France, Germany 8 May 1945
Wood, Elmer W., Sgt, Inf Co. G 30th Inf Regt., France 20 Nov. 1944
Wood, John W., S/Sgt, Co. I 30th Inf Regt., France 23 Nov. 1944
Wood, Levi E., T/5, Co. F 15th Inf, Italy 27 Mar. 1944
Wood, Raymond J., Pvt, Btry A 441st AAA AW Bn., Borgo Montello 22 Feb. 1944
Woodall, James E., T/5, Co. B 601st TD Bn., Germany 1 Apr. 1945
Wooden, F. A., Pfc, Cn Co. 30th Inf, France 27 Aug. 1944
▲Woods, John F., S/Sgt, Co. B 601st TD Bn., France 23 Jan. 1945
Woods, Roy E., T/5, Hq. Co. 3d Bn. 30th Inf
Woods, Thomas W., Pfc, Hq. Co. 3d Bn. 30th Inf, Le Tholy 16 Oct. 1944
Woodward, Marcus C., CWO, U.S.A. Hq. 3d Inf Div., Italy, France Feb. 1944
Woodward, Williard N., Pfc, Hq. Co. 1st Bn. 7th Inf Regt., Germany 20 Apr. 1945
Wooldridge, Gerald V., Pfc, Co. B 30th Inf Regt., France 4 Oct. 1944
Woosley, Charles E., Pfc, Co. A 30th Inf, Anzio, Italy 24 Apr. 1944
Works, Walton W., 1st Sgt, Co. L 15th Inf, Valmontone 1 June 1944
Wright, Elam W., Jr., 2d Lt, Co. G 30th Inf, France 23 Jan. 1945
Wright, Roy J., T/5, Hq. Btry 41st FA Bn., Italy 5 June 1944
Wright, Seymour C., T/Sgt, Cn Co. 7th Inf, Cisterna Di Littoria 24 Mar. 1944
Wuis, Thomas R., WOJG, US Army Serv. Co. 30th Inf Regt., Italy, France, Germany 20 Feb. 1945
Wurm, Frank A., Cpl, Btry B 9th FA Anzio, Italy 3 Mar. 1944
Wyatt, Carl R., 1st Lt, Inf Hq. 2d Bn. 30th Inf Regt., France 30 Dec. 1944
Wyatt, Lloyd T., S/Sgt, Co. M 7th Inf, Anzio, Italy 3 Mar. 1944
Wyatt, Robert H., T/5, Co. G 7th Inf Regt., Italy, France 5 Feb. 1945
Wysoglad, Vincent J., Pfc, Co. K 30th Inf Regt., France 29 Oct. 1944
Wyss, Maurice, 1st Lt, Hq. Co. IPW Interrogator 30th Inf, Italy, France 20 Feb. 1945

Xavier, Joseph, Pvt, Hq. Co. 3d Bn. 7th Inf Regt., Italy 24 Apr. 1944

Yager, Harold D., Pfc, Hq. Co. 1st Bn. 30th Inf, France 2 Feb. 1945
Yarte, Gordon A., Pfc, Hq. Co. 2d Bn. 15th Inf Regt., France 5 Feb. 1945
Yates, Ralph J., 2d Lt, Co. L 7th Inf, Palermo, Sicily 22 July 1944
Yates, William J., T/5, Med. Det. 30th Inf, Anzio, Italy 8 Feb. 1944
Ybanez, Gilberto, Pfc, Hq. Btry 39th FA Bn., Italy 2 June 1944
Yeager, Verol F., Pvt, Sig. Co., Le Ferriere 1 Mar. 1944
Yefchak, John, Jr., T/4, Co. A 10th Engr. Combat Bn., France 12 Jan. 1945

▲ Oak Leaf Cluster.

Yendrek, Louis E., T/Sgt, Co. A 15th Inf Regt., 26 Dec. 1944
Yetter, Charles F., 1st Sgt, Cn Co. 7th Inf, Anzio, Italy 29 Feb. 1944
Yoakum, John D., T/Sgt, Co. L 7th Inf Regt., France 22 Dec. 1944
York, Tommy W., Pfc, Co. F 30th Inf, Bonne Fontaine 19 Oct. 1944
▲Young, Charles R., Sgt, Co. B 30th Inf Regt., France 3 Dec. 1944
Young, Charlie, Pfc, Co. G 15th Inf, Germany 7 Apr. 1945
Young, Grady L., T/Sgt, Hq. Co. 3d Bn. 30th Inf, Germany
Young, John M., Cpl, Btry A 9th FA Bn., Italy 5 June 1944
Young, Loys E., M/Sgt, Serv. Co. 756th Tank Bn., France 14 Feb. 1945
Young, Ray, Capt, Hq. 2d Bn. 30th Inf, Sicily
▲Young, Richard T., Maj, Inf Hq. 7th Inf Regt., France 7 Feb. 1945
▲Young, Robert N., Brig Gen, US Army Ass't OG 3d Inf Div., France 1 Nov. 1944, 6 Jan. 1945
Young, William, T/5, Med. Det. 7th Inf Regt., Germany 15 Mar. 1945
Younker, Christian A., Pfc, Co. A 756th Tank Bn., France 30 Jan. 1945
Yourey, Michael, AT Co. 30th Inf, Colmar
Yurko, Peter P., T/5, Serv. Co. 756th Tank Bn., France, Germany, Austria 8 May 1945
Younkin, Glenn, S/Sgt, Hq. Co. 2d Bn. 30th Inf

Zabinski, Leo S., S/Sgt, Co. C 756th Tank Bn., Germany 19 Apr. 1945
Zachwieja, Joseph S., Pvt, Hq. Co. 7th Inf, Palestrina 2, 3 June 1944
▲(2) Zaida, Charles G., T/4, Hq. Co. 30th Inf, Germany 29 Dec. 1944
Zaleski, Alfred, Pfc, Hq. Co. 2d Bn. 30th Inf, Sicily 11 Aug. 1943
Zawacky, Chester P., Pfc, Co. B 7th Inf Regt., France 15 Mar. 1945
Zeifman, Sol S., Cpl, Co. I 7th Inf Regt., Sicily 18 Aug. 1943
Zemke, Clarence A., S/Sgt, Sb Btry 10th FA Bn., France 19 Feb. 1945
Zicopula, James, Pvt, Hq. Co. 30th Inf, La Salle 26 Oct. 1944
Ziegler, Elwood W., 1st Lt, Hq. Btry 39th FA Bn., Sicily 3 Aug. 1943
Zielke, Alvin A., Pfc, Serv. Btry 41st FA Bn., Sicily 17 Aug. 1943
Zimmerman, Fritz, Cpl, Hq. Btry 39th FA Bn., Anzio 9 Feb. 1944
Zimmerman, George H., S/Sgt, Co. B 7th Inf, Messina, Sicily 10 Aug. 1943
Zirkle, Robert R., T/4, Co. A 10th Engr. Combat Bn., France 29 Jan. 1945
Zlatnick, Arthur, Sgt, Co. F 30th Inf
Zoeller, Louis G., Sgt, 3d Rcn Trp., Germany 18 Mar. 1945
Zombotti, David J., Pfc, Hq. Co. 1st Bn. 15th Inf Regt., France 29 Oct. 1944
Zulisky, Henry, Pfc, Co. B 10th Engr. Combat Bn., France 5 Feb. 1945
Zwick, Nathan L., T/5, Hq. Co. 1st Bn. 30th Inf, Germany 11 Apr. 1945

POSTHUMOUS AWARDS OF BRONZE STAR

Acosta, Jesus P., Sgt, Co. A 30th Inf, France 10 Jan. 1945
Alexakos, James G., S/Sgt, Co. A 7th Inf, Italy 31 Jan. 1944
Armstrong, Frederick R., Lt Col, CO 2d Bn. 30th Inf, France 21 Sept. 1944

Barbour, Will P., Jr., 2d Lt, Co. B 30th Inf, France 17 Sept. 1944
Barys, Stanley O., S/Sgt, Co. M 7th Inf, Italy 24 Apr. 1944
Beatrice, Louis, Pfc, Hq. Btry 41st FA Bn., Italy 4 Feb. 1944
Beck, Harley D., T/5, Co. C 10th Engr. Bn., Italy 5 Mar. 1944
Bell, Harvey H., T/Sgt, Co. F 30th Inf, Italy 8 Feb. 1944
Bilski, Joseph J., Pvt, Hq. Co. 2d Bn. 7th Inf, Italy 29 Feb. 1944
Birchmier, Robert L., Pfc, Co. H 30th Inf, France 23 Dec. 1944
Bischoff, Willard F., Pvt, Btry B 39th FA Bn., Italy 11 Nov. 1944
Bond, Kermit A., Pfc, Hq. Co. 2d Bn. 7th Inf, Anzio, Italy 27 Feb. 1944
Boettcher, Roy M., Pfc, Co. G 30th Inf, Germany 26 Mar. 1945
Bonnett, Rhienhold E., Pfc, Co. L 15th Inf, Italy 15 Feb. 1944
Boyer, Thomas W., Pfc, Hq. Co. 3d Bn. 30th Inf, France 28 Aug. 1944
Branch, Robert L., 2d Lt, Inf Co. I 30th Inf, Germany 15 Mar. 1945
Brewer, Charles R., Pvt, Co. B 756th Tank Bn., Germany 19 Mar. 1945
Bridgers, Wilson R., Cpl, Co. C 601st TD Bn., Italy 25 May 1944
Brinkey, Harry J., Pfc, Co. E 7th Inf, France 1 Dec. 1944
Brinson, Logan G., T/Sgt, Co. I 15th Inf, France 29 Dec. 1944
Burrage, Ronald P., Jr., Pfc, Med. Det. 15th Inf, Italy 23 May 1944
Busby, Edward K., 1st Lt, Co. I 7th Inf, French Morocco 10 Nov. 1942
Butcher, Phillip, Sgt, Co. C 15th Inf, France 26 Nov. 1944
Butrim, George S., S/Sgt, Co. I 30th Inf, France 22 Sept. 1943

Carlson, Charles H., Pfc, Co. A 30th Inf, France 31 Jan. 1945
Carmichael, Wilbur N., Pfc, Co. D 30th Inf, Italy 28 May 1944
Clark, Howard F., S/Sgt, Co. B 15th Inf, Italy 24 May 1944
Collison, Robert O., Pfc, Co. E 15th Inf, Italy 23 May 1944
Crotis, Lawrence L., T/5, 3d Sig. Co., Italy 31 May 1944
Current, George A., 1st Lt, Co. B 756th Tank Bn., France 23 Nov. 1944

Davis, John W., Co. B 756th Tank Bn., France 23 Dec. 1944
Decker, John R., Pvt, Co. C 15th Inf, France 28 Aug. 1944
Deletis, Patsy, Pvt, Co. A 3d Med. Bn., Italy 3 Nov. 1943
Demko, Emil E., Pvt, Co. A 7th Inf, France 28 Dec. 1944
Dersch, Frank E., Pvt, Co. A 30th Inf, France 28 Oct. 1944
Dishner, Dual F., Pvt, Co. B 756th Tank Bn., France 27 Aug. 1944
Donnelly, John J., Sgt, Co. D 30th Inf, Anzio, Italy 21 Apr. 1944
Draughn, Harvey G., T/5, Co. A 756th Tank Bn., France 21 Sept. 1944
Dries, Joseph O., Pfc, Co. F 30th Inf, Italy 1 June 1944
Drosch, Oscar A., Pfc, Co. D 30th Inf, Sicily 1 Aug. 1943
Dunning, Raymond, Sgt, Co. G 15th Inf, Italy 3 June 1944
Durkee, Louis H., 1st Lt, Co. M 7th Inf, Anzio, Italy 24 Apr. 1944

Eastbury, Herbert C., Pvt, 3d Rcn Trp., Italy 2 June 1944
Eggemeyer, Clyde L., Pfc, Hq. Co. 7th Inf, France 24 Jan. 1945
▲Elliott, Lewis P., 1st Lt, FA 601st TD Bn., France 26 Nov. 1944
English, Bert L., 1st Lt, Serv. Btry 39th FA Bn., France 29 Feb. 1944
Evans, Robert E., 1st Lt, Inf Co. A 7th Inf, France 25 Nov. 1944

Fanning, Thomas F., Pfc, Co. L 7th Inf, France 30 Jan. 1945
Farina, Patrick F., Pfc, Co. I 7th Inf, France 10 Sept. 1944
Flynn, James P., 1st Lt, Hq. Co. 30th Inf, French Morocco 12 Nov. 1942
Flynn, Frank J., Pfc, Med. Det. 7th Inf, France 20 Nov. 1944
Froneberger, Leonard D., Jr., Sgt, Co. B 756th Tank Bn., France 15 Dec. 1944
Fuller, Norman C., S/Sgt, Co. A 756th Tank Bn., France 15 Aug. 1944

Gabriel, Paul E., Pvt, Co. A 10th Engr. Bn., Italy 26 May 1944
Garrett, Luther, Cpl, Hq. Co. 1st Bn. 30th Inf, Anzio, Italy 28 Jan. 1944
Gibson, Byron N., Pfc, Hq. Co. 2d Bn. 15th Inf, N. Africa, Sicily, Italy 27 May 1944
Gidcumb, Alfred W., Pvt, Hq. Co. 2d Bn. 7th Inf, Italy 23 May 1944
Goodloe, Everett M., Pfc, Co. I 7th Inf, Germany 3 May 1945
Goldsby, Orrin E., Pfc, Co. C 30th Inf, Italy 1 June 1944
Gross, Joseph J., 2d Lt, Co. B 7th Inf, France 23 Nov. 1944
Grzyb, Stanley J., Pvt, Co. C 10th Engr. Bn., Italy 21 Sept. 1944

Hale, William P., T/5, Co. A 601st TD Bn., Italy 5 June 1944
Hall, Foster, Pfc, Co. F 15th Inf, Germany 19 Mar. 1945
Hamberg, Leo, Jr., Pfc, AT Co. 30th Inf, France 22 Dec. 1944
Hanson, Ralph L., 1st Lt, Inf Co. A 756th Tank Bn., France 16 Sept. 1944
Hardy, William H., Sgt, Co. C 10th Engr. Bn., Italy 23 May 1944
Herring, Francis M., 1st Sgt, Co. A 7th Inf, France 8 Oct. 1944
Hestley, Charles S., Pfc, Btry B 39th FA Bn., Anzio, Italy 4 Feb. 1944
Hoffman, Alfred, Cpl, Rcn Co. 601st TD Bn., Tunisia 5 May 1943
Hoffman, Alfred, Sgt, Rcn Co. 601st TD Bn., France 21 Aug. 1944
Hollis, Walter R., Sgt, Co. A 30th Inf, France 22 Dec. 1944

Hutto, Eldridge J., Pfc, Co. M 7th Inf, Italy 23 May 1944

Isaacson, Walter A., Sgt, Co. B 30th Inf, France 17 Dec. 1944

▲Jarrett, Harold B., Sgt, Co. C 601st TD Bn., Italy 1 June 1944
Jenson, Erik L., Sgt, Hq. Btry 39th FA Bn., N. Africa, Sicily, Italy 2 Mar. 1944
Jones, Jenkin B., 1st Lt, FA 10th FA Bn., Sicily 22 July 1943
Jones, Leonard A., S/Sgt, Co. K 7th Inf, Italy 3 June 1944

Kaplan, Louis, S/Sgt, Co. E 30th Inf, France 10 Nov. 1944
Kerby, Earl L., Pfc, Co. D 30th Inf, Sicily 1 Aug. 1943
Klang, Bernard, 1st Lt, Btry C 39th FA Bn., Italy 27 Oct. 1943
▲Kline, Leon W., Jr., Pvt, Med. Det. 7th Inf, France 29 Sept. 1944
Knight, Albert H., Pfc, Co. F 15th Inf, Anzio, Italy 16 Feb. 1944
Kosse, Roman L., Pfc, Co. L 30th Inf, France 10 Nov. 1944
Kramer, Laurence P., Pfc, Hq. Co. 2d Bn. 30th Inf, Italy 6 Nov. 1943

Lake, Robert J., Pfc, Med. Det. 30th Inf, Italy 9 Feb. 1944
Lamken, Russell, Pvt, Med. Det. Co. D 3d Med. Bn., Italy 29 Feb. 1944
Larson, Stanley E., Capt, Co. C 10th Engr. Bn., Italy 23 May 1944
Leake, William J., S/Sgt, Co. E 15th Inf, Italy 20 Feb. 1944
Leverich, Edward K., Pvt, Hq. Btry 9th FA Bn., Italy 29 Jan. 1944
Limoncelli, Matthew G., Sgt, AT Co. 15th Inf, Italy 4 Mar. 1944
Lindsey, James W., Pfc, Co. D 30th Inf, Sicily 1 Aug. 1943
Logue, James F., Cpl, Hq. Co. 1st Bn. 7th Inf, France 7 Oct. 1944

McCrite, William C., S/Sgt, Btry A 9th FA Bn., Italy 23 Sept. 1943
McGee, Emery J., Sgt, Hq. Co. 3d Bn. 7th Inf, Germany 19 Mar. 1945
▲McHarg, James J., T/Sgt, Co. A 30th Inf, France 4 Feb. 1945
McKenzie, Hugh D., Maj, Hq. 3d Bn. 30th Inf, Italy 23 Sept. 1943
Maczka, Marion J., S/Sgt, Co. M 7th Inf, Anzio, Italy 2 Mar. 1944
Magaro, Peter N., Pfc, Co. B 7th Inf, Anzio, Italy 21 Apr. 1944
Moravec, Frank J., Pfc, Cn Co. 30th Inf, Italy, France 31 Dec. 1944
Multer, Malcolm E., Pfc, Co. M 30th Inf, France 1 Feb. 1945
Myers, Robert E., 2d Lt, FA Co. C 601st TD Bn., Italy 27 May 1944

Newman, George M., Pvt, Co. F 30th Inf, France 28 Jan. 1945

Orient, Andrew D., 2d Lt, Inf Co. B 756th Tank Bn., France 23 Aug. 1944
Ortiz, Michael J., Pfc, Hq. Co. 3d Bn. 7th Inf, France 25 Oct. 1944

Palette, Fred W., Pfc, Hq. Co. 2d Bn. 15th Inf, Germany 18 Mar. 1945
Petropolis, Stanley, 2d Lt, Hq. 7th Inf, France 17 Nov. 1944
Pinkstaff, Thomas W., Cpl, Co. A 756th Tank Bn., France 5 Sept. 1944
Piquet, Paul K., Pfc, Co. L 15th Inf, France 25 Dec. 1944
Putman, John E., 1st Lt, Co. M 7th Inf, Sicily 10 Aug. 1943

Richardson, Orlando A., Jr., Capt, Inf Co. A 756th Tank Bn., France 28 Jan. 1945
Robinett, Clarence I., S/Sgt, Btry B 39th FA Bn., Italy 21 Oct. 1943
Rodkey, George L., T/5, Hq. Co. 3d Bn. 7th Inf, France 25 Oct. 1944
Rogers, Jefferson S., Pvt, Co. B 601st TD Bn., Germany 1 Apr. 1945
Russell, Larry J., Pfc, Co. L 30th Inf, France 30 Jan. 1945

Scarbrough, Charles E., Sgt, Co. L 15th Inf, Anzio, Italy 29 Feb. 1944
Schepkowski, Theodore V., S/Sgt, Co. K 7th Inf, France 16 Jan. 1945
Schleicher, Ray V., Sgt, Co. A 756th Tank Bn., France 5 Feb. 1945
Schubert, Otto J., Pfc, Co. M 7th Inf, France 20 Nov. 1944
Shaw, Lloyd W., Pfc, Co. B 30th Inf, France 21 Aug. 1944
Shirley, Elmer R., Pfc, Co. E 30th Inf, France 20 Oct. 1944
Slocum, George W., Pvt, Btry A 41st FA Bn., France 1 Feb. 1945
Smith, Richard T., T/5, Co. B 601st TD Bn., Germany 14 Apr. 1945
Smock, Burdtt W., S/Sgt, Cn Co. 7th Inf, Italy 24 May 1944
Spark, Albert J., Sgt, Co. H 7th Inf, Italy 25 May 1944
Spicer, Lynn A., Cpl, Co. B 601st TD Bn., Tunisia 22 Feb. 1943
Standish, Lyle E., Capt, Inf Co. B 30th Inf, France 23 Jan. 1945
Stone, Kenneth H., S/Sgt, Rcn 601st TD Bn., Italy 26 Apr. 1943
Swan, Leland, T/5, Btry B 10th FA Bn., N. Africa, Sicily, Italy, France, Germany 8 May 1945

Taylor, John C., Sgt, Co. B 7th Inf, France 25 Oct. 1944
Tacker, Calvin R., Pvt, Co. I 15th Inf, France 16 Mar. 1945
Thompson, Chester E., Pfc, Hq. Co. 3d Bn. 15th Inf, France 30 Oct. 1944
Torrence, Norman M., S/Sgt, Co. B 15th Inf, France 15 Aug. 1944
Tuomie, Toivo T., Pvt, Co. C 30th Inf, Italy 20 Aug. 1944

Van Son, John H., Pfc, Hq. Co. 3d Bn. 30th Inf, Anzio, Italy 25 Mar. 1944

▲ Oak Leaf Cluster.

Vargo, Frank A., Sgt, Co. B 601st TD Bn., Germany 1 Apr. 1945
Vargo, Steve, Cpl, Co. B 756th Tank Bn., France 27 Aug. 1944

Weaver, Robert E., Sgt, Co. B 7th Inf, France 24 Jan. 1945
Wilkins, Paul N., Pvt, Hq. Btry 39th FA Bn., Italy, France 22 Oct. 1944
Williams, Robert J., Sgt, Co. G 7th Inf. Italy 23 Apr. 1944

Wittkopp, Arthur, Pfc, Btry B 10th FA Bn., Italy 29 Feb. 1944
Wood, John J., Pvt, Co. A 756th Tank Bn., Germany 18 Mar. 1945
Wytewa, Vincent, Pvt, Co. L 15th Inf, France 20 Nov. 1944

Zeltsman, Jacob, Pfc, Co. A 15th Inf, Germany 27 Mar. 1945

BRONZE STAR
MISSING IN ACTION

Allen, Ray A., Pfc, Med. Det. 30th Inf, France 8 Jan. 1945
Armijo, Francis C., S/Sgt, Co. K 7th Inf, Italy 30 Jan. 1944

Bennett, George W., Sgt, Co. K 15th Inf, France 18 Sept. 1944

Cenko, Steve, Jr., Pfc, Co. D 30th Inf, France 23 Jan. 1945
Christian, Olice, Pfc, Co. D 30th Inf, France 23 Jan. 1945
Coles, James W., 2d Lt, Co. L 15th Inf, Italy 13 Aug. 1943
Collins, Owen K., Sr., Pfc, Co. L 30th Inf, France 15 Dec. 1944

Deemer, William H., Sgt, Co. I 30th Inf, France 5 Nov. 1944
Dickey, Freeman L., Pfc, Co. M 30th Inf, France 20 Dec. 1944

Gill, Walter L., 1st Lt, 3d Rcn Trp., Italy 5 June 1944
Gravenish, Lawrence T., Cpl, Co. I 15th Inf, France 29 Dec. 1944

Huebsch, Norman F., Co. M 7th Inf, Italy 31 May 1944

Joines, George C., Pfc, Co. A 15th Inf, France 27 Aug. 1944
▲Julian, Rosaire M., T/5, Med. Det. 30th Inf, France 8 Jan. 1945

Lee, Everett L., Pfc, Co. I 15th Inf, France 29 Dec. 1944
▲Lister, Harold, Pfc, Hq. Co. 1st Bn. 30th Inf, France 17 Dec. 1944
Lowry, Damon C., Pfc, Co. H 30th Inf, France 18 Dec. 1944

Mauser, Curtis N., S/Sgt, Co. I 30th Inf, France 8 Jan. 1944
Messine, Frank A., Pfc, Med. Det. 30th Inf, France 17 Dec. 1944

▲ Oak Leaf Cluster.

Miner, Francis H., Pfc, Co. I 30th Inf, France 23 Nov. 1944
Morales, Jose I., Pfc, Btry B 39th FA Bn., Italy 26 Mar. 1944
Moro, Antonio, Pvt, Co. E 30th Inf, Italy 20 Feb. 1944

Payne, Howard T., Pfc, Co. A 30th Inf, Anzio, Italy 25 Jan. 1944
Prince, Floyd E., 1st Sgt, Co. F 30th Inf, France 20 Sept. 1944

Reeves, William E., Pfc, Co. H 7th Inf, Italy 1 June 1944
Riddell, Charles G., Pfc, Co. I 30th Inf, France 1 Nov. 1944

Sanislow, Henry J., Sgt, Co. B 756th Tank Bn., France 27 Dec. 1944
Saunders, Zebulon V., Pfc, Co. I 30th Inf, France 17 Dec. 1944
Sheats, James B., Pvt, Med. Det, 7th Inf, Italy 1 June 1944
Slack, Zigmund C., Pfc, Co. F 15th Inf, Italy 8 Sept. 1944
Smith, Alan C., Pfc, Co. K 30th Inf, France 30 Oct. 1944
Spencer, Edward S., S/Sgt, Co. L 7th Inf, Anzio, Italy 4 Mar. 1944
Stanton, Loren L., Capt, Chap. Corps Hq. Bn. 30th Inf, France, Germany 26 Mar. 1945

Turner, David H., Pvt, Hq. Co. 30th Inf, Italy 26 Jan. 1944

Varns, Lewis A., Pvt, Co. A 7th Inf, France 22 Nov. 1944
Velykis, Peter, Pfc, Hq. Co. 2d Bn. 7th Inf, Italy 1 June 1944

Wiles, Charles J., Pfc, Co. H 30th Inf, France 18 Dec. 1944
Wilson, Oscar D., Sgt, Co. I 30th Inf, France 8 Jan. 1945

DISTINGUISHED UNIT CITATIONS

3d Infantry Division
Company E, 7th Infantry
Company F, 7th Infantry
Company L, 7th Infantry
1st Battalion, 15th Infantry
3d Battalion, 15th Infantry
Company L, 15th Infantry
Anti-Tank Company, 15th Infantry

1st Battalion, 30th Infantry
2d Battalion (Reinf), 30th Infantry
3d Battalion, 30th Infantry
Company G, 30th Infantry
Company I, 30th Infantry
Company L, 30th Infantry
441st AAA AW (SP) Battalion
756th Tank Battalion

601st Tank Destroyer Battalion

GENERAL ORDERS
No. 44

WAR DEPARTMENT
Washington 25, D. C., 6 June 1945

* * *

As authorized by Executive Order 9396 (sec. I, WD Bul. 22, 1943), superseding Executive Order 9075 (sec. III, WD Bul. 11. 1942), the following unit is cited by the War Department for outstanding performance of duty in action during the period indicated, under the provisions of section IV, WD Circular 333, 1943, in the name of the President of the United States as public evidence of deserved honor and distinction. The citation reads as follows:

The *3d Infantry Division* with the following attached units:

254th Infantry Regiment,
99th Chemical Battalion,
168th Chemical Smoke Generator Company,
441st Antiaircraft Artillery Automatic Weapons Battalion,
601st Tank Destroyer Battalion (SP),
756th Tank Battalion,
IPW Team 183,

fighting incessantly, from 22 January to 6 February 1945, in heavy snow storms, through enemy-infested marshes and woods, and over a flat plain crisscrossed by numerous small canals, irrigation ditches, and unfordable streams, terrain ideally suited to the defense, breached the German defense wall on the northern perimeter of the Colmar bridgehead and drove forward to isolate Colmar from the Rhine. Crossing the Fecht River from Guemar, Alsace, by stealth during the late hours of darkness of 22 January, the assault elements fought their way forward against mounting resistance. Reaching the Ill River, a bridge was thrown across but collapsed before armor could pass to the support of two battalions of the 30th Infantry on the far side. Isolated and attacked by a full German Panzer brigade, outnumbered and outgunned, these valiant troops were forced back yard by yard. Wave after wave of armor and infantry was hurled against them but despite hopeless odds the regiment held tenaciously to its bridgehead. Driving forward in knee-deep snow, which masked acres of densely sown mines, the *3d Infantry Division* fought from house to house and street to street in the fortress towns of the Alsatian Plain. Under furious concentrations of supporting fire, assault troops crossed the Colmar Canal in rubber boats during the night of 29 January. Driving relentlessly forward, six towns were captured within 8 hours, 500 casualties inflicted on the enemy during the day, and large quantities of booty seized. Slashing through to the Rhone-Rhine Canal, the garrison at Colmar was cut off and the fall of the city assured. Shifting the direction of attack, the division moved south between the Rhone-Rhine Canal and the Rhine toward Neuf Brisach and the Brisach Bridge. Synchronizing the attacks, the bridge was seized and Neuf Brisach captured.... In one of the hardest fought and bloodiest campaigns of the war, the *3d Infantry Division* annihilated three enemy divisions, partially destroyed three others, captured over 4,000 prisoners, and inflicted more than 7,500 casualties on the enemy.

GENERAL ORDERS
No. 21

WAR DEPARTMENT
Washington 25, D. C., 30 March, 1945

* * *

Company E, 7th Infantry Regiment, is cited for outstanding performance in combat during the period 31 October 1944 to 4 November, 1944, near Le Haut Jacques, France. On 31 October 1944, *Company E,* led by Captain George R. Ellis, spearheaded a five-day offensive to seize the strategic crossroads and pass commanding the Taintrux Valley, a corridor to the fortress city of St. Die. Fighting their way forward through the steep, forested mountains of the Vosges in cold, rain and fog, the men of *Company E* engaged fanatical, well-trained German infantry, heavily equipped with automatic weapons and occupying prepared positions in depth, guarded by minefields. Although subjected to terrific concentrations of mortar and artillery fire and to heavy, defensive small arms and machine gun fire, *Company E* nevertheless closed with the enemy and slowly pushed him back. So tenacious was German resistance that the foe had to be killed in their foxholes and dugouts with hand grenades and point-blank small arms fire before ground could be won. Although the Company Commander was wounded and the company had run so dangerously low on ammunition that captured German weapons had to be employed, the troops pressed the attack relentlessly. Assuming command, First Lieutenant James F. Powell led the company in dislodging the enemy from his successive strongholds and seizing one intermediate objective after another. On the fifth day, *Company E* battered through the German main line of resistance and, though almost surrounded, fought to take and hold the crossroads dominating the mountain pass. With over half of its riflemen killed or wounded, *Company E* accomplished its mission, having killed thirty-seven, wounded one hundred and thirty, and captured seventy-eight of the enemy, and opened a gateway to St. Die and the Meurthe River crossing.

GENERAL ORDERS
No. 109

WAR DEPARTMENT
Washington 25, D. C., 24 November 1945

* * *

Company F, 7th Infantry Regiment, is cited for outstanding performance in action during the period 25-30 September 1944 near Ferdrupt, France. In a 6-day offensive operation to seize and hold high ground dominating a critically important sector of the Moselle Valley, *Company F,* commanded by Captain Robert D. Marsh, fought its way in chilling rain up the precipitous slopes of a 2,500-foot hill mass against savage and determined opposition. Scaling slippery 15-foot rock ledges under withering machine-gun and small-arms fire, hacking their way through dense woods and undergrowth to close with a strong and heavily armed enemy force, the valiant men of *Company F* gradually pressed the Germans back from their prepared defensive positions. After seizing the hill crest, the company fought for days at hand-to-hand range in rugged, densely wooded terrain to extend its hold on the high ground, killing Germans in their foxholes who were too stubborn to retreat. Launching six desperate counterattacks with as many as 200 men at a time, the enemy approached to within 15 yards of the company line, but could neither penetrate nor break it. Neither heavy artillery preparation nor assault by stealth availed to break through positions held by men with iron determination not to yield ground. Forward observers drew mortar fire down on their own positions to halt German counterattacks which seemed on the brink of victory. Weary, exhausted, chilled, and drenched to the bone, without food for 24 hours, their ammunition supplies dwindling, the intrepid soldiers of *Company F* summoned their last reserves of strength and will power to hold the high ground they had conquered. In this grim, savage, 6-day battle in the mountains and fog, *Company F, 7th Infantry Regiment*, killed 81, wounded an estimated 283, and captured 39 of the enemy. (General Orders 322, Headquarters 3d Infantry Division, 3 September 1945, as approved by the Commanding General, European Theater (Main).)

GENERAL ORDERS }
No. 34 }

WAR DEPARTMENT
Washington 25, D. C., 3 May 1945

* * *

Company L, 7th Infantry Regiment, is cited for outstanding performance in combat on 15 September 1944 at Vy-Les-Lure, France. On 15 September 1944, *Company L*, led by Captain Ralph J. Yates, advanced through heavy artillery and mortar concentrations to seize a cluster of houses on the outskirts of Vy-Les-Lure, a focal communications point in that sector defended by five hundred fanatical Germans, supported by mortar, machine gun and artillery fire. The gallant men of *Company L* were swiftly surrounded by an enemy which outnumbered them three to one; most of the mortar and machine gun crews were unable to run the gantlet of withering and continuous enemy fire. While machine gunners and mortarmen lay on exposed ground for seven hours, fighting off savage counterattacks, the men in the houses held the enemy at bay with their BAR's, rifles, carbines and hand grenades. Mortar and artillery fire scored eight direct hits on the Company command post, tearing down a corner of the house and demolishing an adjacent shed. Three houses were set ablaze by hostile artillery, and the men occupying them were obliged to dash through fire to the undamaged buildings. Unable to reach the Battalion, cut off from all support forces, their ranks depleted by heavy casualties and their ammunition almost expended, the soldiers of this heroic Company refused to yield ground or surrender. Beating off wave after wave of savage counterattack, the men killed Germans at point-blank range; when the last assault was shattered and driven back in confusion, enemy dead, clutching their hand grenades, lay sprawled within twenty feet of the command post. Reduced to less than a clip of rifle ammunition apiece, the men of *Company L* stood on the alert all night, their bayonets fixed, waiting for another counterattack which the enemy was unable to deliver. Leaving two prisoners, eighteen dead and an estimated seventy wounded, the defeated enemy withdrew during the night from the Vy-Les-Lure position which he had determined to defend to the last. At the cost of thirty-seven casualties, *Company L* had held its ground with indomitable valor against overwhelming odds and all the massive pressure that a determined foe could bring to bear.

GENERAL ORDERS }
No. 21 }

WAR DEPARTMENT
Washington 25, D. C., 30 March, 1945

* * *

The *1st Battalion, 15th Infantry Regiment*, is cited for outstanding performance in combat. On 27 August 1944, the *1st Battalion*, commanded by Lieutenant Colonel Michael Paulick, approached the town of Montelimar, France, by shuttle and forced march, to come to grips with the major part of the German 338th Infantry Division and elements of four or five other enemy divisions. Marching and fighting in unbearable heat, weary from the twelve days of strenuous offensive combat which followed the Riviera landings, the *1st Battalion* drove relentlessly forward, compressing the numerically superior hostile force into an ever smaller space. Caught in the Montelimar-Orange-Nyon triangle, its left flank pinned against the Rhone River and its escape routes to the north and northeast dominated by other units of the Seventh Army, the German force resorted to violent and incessant counterattacks to break through the Allied cordon that was suffocating it. Constricting the major part of the enemy force within the immediate vicinity of Montelimar, the *1st Battalion* drove forward in three days of continuous battle and smashed every German counterattack, including an assault by an entire enemy regiment. Pounding the enemy force with concentrations of artillery and mortar fire, withstanding frenzied German efforts to break out from the trap, the *1st Battalion* penetrated into Montelimar and completed the annihilation of the German force. During this action the Battalion took eight hundred and four prisoners, killed and wounded four hundred and eighty-five others, captured or destroyed at least five hundred vehicles and an estimated one thousand horses. Inflicting the most disastrous blow of the Southern France Campaign on the German Nineteenth Army, the *1st Battalion* was mainly responsible for destroying German resistance south of the Drone and east of the Rhone Rivers and for annihilating a major portion of the mechanized and motorized equipment available to the enemy.

GENERAL ORDERS }
No. 15 }

WAR DEPARTMENT
Washington 25, D. C., 5 February 1946

* * *

The *3d Battalion, 15th Infantry Regiment*, is cited for outstanding performance in combat during the period 3-8 August 1943 near San Fratello, Sicily. Scaling steep mountains and sheer rock walls, the *3d Battalion*, commanded by Lieutenant Colonel Ashton H. Manhart, marched for 14 hours across deep gorges and over mountain trails so precipitous that mules, bearing rations and ammunition were unable to negotiate the ascent and fell hundreds of feet to the ravine floor. Skirting two minefields, attacking, storming, and utterly disintegrating a powerful Italian delaying force in an 8-hour battle in the mountains, the troops of the *3d Battalion* continued their advance under a broiling sun to seize Hill 673, a dominating terrain feature guarding the Palermo-Messina Highway. The men of the *3d Battalion* held this hill position on short rations, with water virtually unobtainable, ammunition supplies at a low ebb and the mule pack trains subject to decimation by the powerful enemy force surrounding them. After weathering a 45-minute TOT-artillery concentration, these valiant soldiers met and broke three successive counterattacks delivered by one of the elite regiments of the Italian Army reinforced with Wehrmacht elements. As the fourth counterattack surged forward, the *3d Battalion* Command hurled all service troops into the line and distributed the light machine-gun and BAR-ammunition among the riflemen to conserve every round and ensure that every bullet would count. The enemy onslaught was repelled, but only after 2 hours of savage, hand-to-hand fighting with grenades, bayonets, and even with rocks. The weary *3d Battalion* clung all night to the hard-won hill, digging in the wounded to prevent their being killed by shell fire, trapping goats, sheep, and cows to stave off hunger. As daybreak came on 7 August, battle-weary elements of the *3d Battalion* were committed to attack another precipitous and strongly defended hill-mass, which they stormed under a protecting mortar concentration and with weapons seized from the enemy. With the major prominent terrain features in their hand, the troops of the *3d Battalion* swept down on the key town of San Fratello, spurred to their utmost by the prospect of obtaining food and water from the enemy supply dumps, captured it in fierce, house-to-house fighting, and then marched 16½ miles into reserve. Displaying the utmost in tenacity, fortitude, and physical endurance, this gallant *3d Battalion, 15th Infantry Regiment*, shattered an enemy regiment, killed, wounded, or captured 1,175 Italians and Germans, and broke the chain of mountain defenses that barred the advance to the Messina straits and to the continental mainland of Europe. (General Orders 393, Headquarters 3d Infantry Division, 11 December 1945, as approved by the Commanding General, Headquarters Seventh Army.)

GENERAL ORDERS }
No. 75 }

WAR DEPARTMENT
Washington 25, D. C., 18 September, 1944

* * *

Company L, 15th Infantry Regiment, is cited for outstanding performance of duty in action from 19 to 26 October 1943 near Statigliano, Italy. Assigned the mission of assaulting and holding the strategically important Mount Della Costa, *Company L* captured the mountain and succeeded in holding it for 8 days despite severe enemy shelling and extremely savage counterattacks by numerically superior enemy forces ranging up to battalion strength. The enemy subjected *Company L* to continuous artillery and mortar fire, intermittent tank and intense machine gun, machine pistol, and rifle fire. Although outnumbered five to one, often forced to replenish its ammunition from the bodies of its casualties, with neither food nor water for 3 days and 2 nights, *Company L* met the onslaughts of the enemy and repelled them with heavy losses. Despite all enemy efforts the company clung to its position overlooking the main supply route to German forces which were containing an entire regiment in the Baja e Latina sector, 2,000 yards to the east. The hill mass prevented supporting fire by friendly artillery, yet *Company L* doggedly held the mountain and directed artillery fire upon the enemy's line of supply. With his source of supply shut off, the enemy was forced to withdraw from the Baja e Latina sector, enabling friendly forces to occupy the town and surrounding territory without opposition. The intrepidity displayed by members of *Company L, 15th Infantry Regiment,* was the principal factor in forcing a German withdrawal from a strategic sector, and their feat will be inscribed indelibly in the annals of the American Infantryman.

GENERAL ORDERS }
No. 123

WAR DEPARTMENT
Washington 25, D. C., 22 December 1945

* * *

Antitank Company, 15th Infantry Regiment, is cited for outstanding performance of duty in action during the period 18 to 20 April 1945 in Nuremberg, Germany. Pitted against a desperate, well-armed, and fanatical Nazi Force, which was determined to hold its positions to the last, *Antitank Company, 15th Infantry Regiment* commanded by First Lieutenant Merle C. Lindsley, 02055121, fought its way from the environs to the heart of the strategic city of Nuremberg in a 2½-day running battle. Numbering only 52 officers and men, *Antitank Company* fought as a rifle unit against a numerically superior enemy, with courage, tenacity, and superb offensive spirit. Although weary from continuous marching and fighting, after 2 nights without sleep or rest, these infantrymen blasted their way through the Nuremberg Stadtpark, destroyed a heavily manned roadblock in a spectacular rifle grenade assault, broke through a block of sniper-infested apartment houses, and finally reached the massive 11th-Century wall and moat which girded the Old City. They crossed the moat under fire and fought as a spearhead force through the labyrinthine underground passageways of the medieval fortifications, engaging the enemy in hand-to-hand struggles, despite semidarkness and the continuous danger of infiltration, and destroying every unit they encountered. In 2½ days of fierce and incessant combat, the valiant *Antitank Company* killed, wounded, or captured approximately a thousand enemy soldiers, seized large stores of material, and broke the backbone of German resistance in the sectors assigned them. (General Orders 384, Headquarters 3d Infantry Division, 14 November 1945, as approved by the Commanding General, 3d Infantry Division.)

GENERAL ORDERS }
No. 18

WAR DEPARTMENT
Washington, D. C., 15 March 1945

* * *

The 1st Battalion, 30th Infantry Regiment, is cited for outstanding performance of duty in action during the period 6 September 1944 to 7 September 1944, at Besancon, France. Assigned the mission of reducing the giant Citadelle fortress, key defense bastion of Besancon, and clearing the enemy from the vital southern industrial section of that important roadnet center, the *1st Battalion* jumped off on a night frontal attack. Pushing forward aggressively against dogged German resistance, the *1st Battalion* climbed slippery hills through pouring rain under murderous grazing machine gun, machine pistol, mortar and flak wagon fire to assault and destroy strong enemy forces entrenched in three rock-walled, supposedly impregnable forts situated on high ground commanding all approaches to the bottlenecked Doubs River loop section of the city. One by one the Battalion reduced two lesser forts and finally the mighty Citadelle, employing skillful flanking maneuvers, and masterfully coordinating the heavy fires of infantry supporting weapons with those of attached armor and artillery. Although it had moved hundreds of miles and fought two major engagements during the preceding twenty-two days and although it had been moving thirty-six hours without rest prior to launching the twenty-two hour attack, the *1st Battalion,* with aggressive, inspired leadership and outstanding individual heroism, overcame all opposition and seized its objectives. A fresh, reinforced enemy battalion was wiped out, fifty Germans killed, seventy wounded, three hundred and twenty-eight enlisted men and eight officers captured, and vast quantities of German materiel, including enough mortars, machine guns, rifles and pistols to equip a battalion were seized or destroyed during the brilliant action. The *1st Battalion's* achievement frustrated the German intention to hold the Citadelle until 15 September, pierced the heart of the enemy's defenses of Besancon, crumbling their entire system of mutually supporting forts, materially assisted the *3d Infantry Division* in blocking a vital escape route to German units trapped to the west and speeded pursuit of remnants of the battered Nineteenth German Army fleeing to the Belfort Gap. The heroic performance of the officers and men of the *1st Battalion* reflects the finest traditions of the Army of the United States.

GENERAL ORDERS }
No. 44

WAR DEPARTMENT
Washington 25, D. C., 30 May, 1944

* * *

The 2d Battalion (Reinforced), 30th Infantry Regiment, is cited for outstanding performance of duty in action during the period 8 August 1943 to 12 August 1943. When a determined enemy was successfully withstanding the attack of an American Army the *2nd Battalion (Reinforced)* made an amphibious landing near San Agata, Sicily, eight miles behind the German lines. This battalion forced a breach in the enemy positions, inflicted heavy casualties upon him in men and materiel, and advanced the American positions ten miles. Forty-eight hours later, without rest or normal preparation, the *2d Battalion* made a second amphibious landing, this time fifteen miles behind the German lines, in order to seize Mount Creole, a dominating terrain feature between the Naso and Brolo Rivers. In the face of murderous fire from all types of weapons, and tanks, the battalion, without supporting artillery, doggedly fought its way up the precipitous heights of its objective. The soldiers of this organization maintained their captured positions for nineteen and one-half hours, despite constant shelling and repeated counterattacks, until the balance of the division drove through fifteen miles of enemy territory to their relief. In seizing Mount Creole, the *2d Battalion* inflicted and suffered heavy losses in men and materiel, but forced the enemy to withdraw fifteen miles and denied him the use of a lateral supply line to his inland positions. The action of the *2d Battalion* was marked by gallantry, fearlessness and profound devotion to duty in the successful accomplishment of two vital missions.

GENERAL ORDERS }
No. 79

WAR DEPARTMENT
Washington 25, D. C., 4 October, 1944

* * *

The *3d Battalion, 30th Infantry Regiment,* is cited for outstanding performance of duty in action during the period 7 to 12 November 1943 near Mignano, Italy. The *3rd Battalion* was assigned the mission of wresting the strategically important Mount Rotondo from a determined and numerically superior German force which had withstood all previous attacks. With fire sweeping its ranks from the rear and from an exposed flank, the Battalion launched its attack up the forward slope of the mountain and doggedly advanced to the crest in the face of stubborn enemy opposition. The assaulting troops killed or captured enemy groups holding the forward slope and immediately reorganized in preparation for clearing the southern slope of the hill. Immediately the enemy launched a series of attacks designed to drive the *3d Battalion* from its positions. For 6 days, against severe shelling and savage counterattacks by fanatical enemy paratroopers, the Battalion held its ground. Although depleted heavily in effective strength and having neither food nor water for a period of 2 days, the intrepid infantrymen of the *3d Battalion* met the onslaughts of the enemy and repelled each assault with heavy losses to the attackers. Throwing headquarters personnel into the line at crucial points, the *3d Battalion* clung tenaciously to its positions until the enemy abandoned his attempt to regain the hill. The heroic performance by officers and men of the *3d Battalion* resulted in the capture of an important terrain feature and in flanking many fortified positions in the enemy's defenses. Their courage and fighting determination reflect the finest traditions of the Army of the United States.

GENERAL ORDERS }
No. 1   }

WAR DEPARTMENT
Washington 25, D. C., 1 January 1946

* * *

Company G, 30th Infantry Regiment, is cited for outstanding performance of duty in action from 20-22 September 1944 near Faucogney, France. In a 2-day battle waged on the steep, densely wooded slopes of "Potato Masher Hill" in cold, fog, and rain against a battalion of fanatical enemy troops, *Company G, 30th Infantry Regiment,* commanded by Captain Hugh E. Wardlaw, Jr., smashed into an iron ring of German defense and held on grimly and tenaciously, despite overwhelmingly unfavorable odds and the absence of armored or artillery support. Although two other companies had attempted the assault on this rocky hill mass only to be hurled back to their line of departure, the men of *Company G* drove forward with such impetus and fury that they seized a spearhead position on the slopes, but were promptly encircled and isolated by the ubiquitous enemy. Completely surrounded, their wire communications slashed, cold, wet, and weary, with only a day's supplies available, the troops weathered five counterattacks of fanatical violence. With all officers except the company commander dead or wounded, they battered their way forward against a wall of mortar and automatic fire, then dug in on the summit of the irregular hill position and held it against every weapon and stratagem the enemy could bring to bear on them. Fighting hand to hand against an enemy of such fanatical temper that one German blew himself to bits with a hand grenade rather than surrender, the men of *Company G* held on with resolute intrepidity. Under incessant tree bursts, surrounded, unable to protect their wounded and dying, they clung to the high ground with epic tenacity until reinforcements arrived. Through their steadfastness and heroism, 152 of the enemy were killed, wounded or captured, the German defending battalion was shattered, and the *30th Infantry Regiment* was able to roll up a powerful enemy ridge line of defenses which had barred the advance of the Allied forces into that sector of the Vosges. (General Orders 383, Headquarters 3d Infantry Division, 14 November 1945, as approved by the Commanding General, 3d Infantry Division.)

GENERAL ORDERS }
No. 79   }

WAR DEPARTMENT
Washington 25, D. C., 4 October, 1942

* * *

Company I, 30th Infantry Regiment, is cited for outstanding performance of duty in action on 28 and 29 January 1944 near Cisterna di Littoria, Italy. *Company I* launched a daylight attack on strongly fortified positions occupied by a reinforced German rifle company. Advancing across bare, flat terrain through heavy artillery fire, the company became subjected to intense machine gun cross-fire from enemy positions 100 yards distant. Dense mortar fire coupled with a heavy artillery concentration caused heavy casualties among the attacking elements, but the two assault platoons were rallied and advanced through a hail of small arms and machine gun fire. In an overwhelming attack, *Company I* destroyed six enemy machine gun emplacements, killed 23 and wounded at least 35 German soldiers. Elements on the left flank eliminated four enemy outpost positions. After attacking continuously for 1½ hours, *Company I* reached a point within 50 yards of its objective and was met by intense machine gun fire which enfiladed the ranks from enemy positions in a house on the right flank. Elements of *Company I* assaulted this enemy strongpoint, killing 6, capturing 27 enemy soldiers, and enabling the company to reach its objective. The determination of this single company sustained a 1,000-yard drive over enemy emplacements, under severe concentrations of artillery and mortar fire, through the German main line of resistance. Forty-six Germans were killed, at least 35 wounded, 52 captured, and the enemy resistance was neutralized completely. The performance by the intrepid infantrymen of *Company I* reflects the finest traditions of the Army of the United States.

GENERAL ORDERS }
No. 55   }

WAR DEPARTMENT
Washington 25, D. C., 13 July, 1945

* * *

Company L, 30th Infantry Regiment, is cited for outstanding performance in action on 17 September 1944, near Raddon, France. Advancing through fog and rain in a tortuous ascent over heavily forested terrain, the men of *Company L,* under the command of Captain Robert B. Pridgen, seized a key ridge which dominated a roadnet essential to the maintenance of the German Main Line of Resistance. Fighting desperately to regain this vital ground, two hundred fanatical German troops, abundantly supplied with automatic firepower and supported by a tank and heavy artillery, pounded the gallant men of *Company L* in wave after wave of savage counterattack. For six hours, the heavily outnumbered company fought on without respite, repulsing the German assault forces time and again with heavy loss despite the enemy's immense superiority in firepower. At times completely surrounded and cut off, with only a few dozen rounds of pistol and carbine ammunition left, the soldiers of *Company L* resisted and repelled every enemy attempt to overrun their line. Battling hand to hand, killing Germans with their rifle butts, these valiant men held their ground. When the last wave of counterattack was rolled back, the men of *Company L,* their ammunition almost entirely expended, their ranks reduced by casualties and their situation apparently hopeless, prepared to assault and break through the German lines, although they had but four rifle squads with which to do it. But the enemy had already withdrawn, battered and beaten, abandoning his broken line to attempt a new stand at the Moselle.

GENERAL ORDERS }
No. 35   }

WAR DEPARTMENT
Washington 25, D. C., 9 May, 1945

* * *

The *601st Tank Destroyer Battalion** is cited for outstanding performance in combat on 23 March 1943, near El Guettar, Tunisia. Filling a two and one-half mile gap in the American lines, the Battalion absorbed the shock of an all-out onslaught by the German 10th Panzer Division, and materially assisted divisional and attached artillery units in definitely stopping two successive, determined enemy tank attacks, launched in great strength. Although greatly outnumbered and outgunned, the Battalion traded shot for shot with the overwhelming enemy force. Doggedly holding its ground, harassed by enemy dive bombers and long-range artillery, with ammunition running dangerously low, the Battalion prepared to hold out to the end despite the loss of twenty-seven of its thirty-seven guns. The German tanks approached to within one hundred yards of its positions only to be thrown back with heavy losses. When the enemy reformed for a second assault, the Battalion placed such intense fire on the advancing German soldiers that the attack was stopped before it could get well under way. The *601st Tank Destroyer Battalion* contributed materially to this outstanding victory of the *1st Infantry Division,* wherein, with other units of the Division, it fought with such ferocity and intense determination that at least four hundred enemy casualties were left on the field, thirty-seven enemy tanks destroyed, and numerous other enemy armored vehicles evacuated in a disabled condition.

---

* Included because of 601st TD Battalion's later attachment to the 3d Infantry Division. The Battalion was not attached to the 3d Division at the time the action was performed for which the citation is awarded.

MERITORIOUS SERVICE UNIT PLAQUE

3D MEDICAL BATTALION

22 January to 6 June, 1944

3D MEDICAL BATTALION. For superior performance of duty in the performance of exceptionally difficult tasks in Italy from 22 January 1944 to 6 June 1944. The battalion, on 22 January 1944, participated in the amphibious assault which secured the beachhead at Anzio, Italy. Thorough planning, training, indoctrination, and a high standard of discipline enabled the battalion to render outstanding medical service to the 3d Infantry Division and attached troops throughout the period on the beachhead and the breakthrough. The entire beachhead was under continuous direct enemy observation and all roads received frequent interdictory fire. The Battalion's installations were shelled on 26 occasions and subjected to 16 bombing attacks. This sustained enemy activity destroyed 33 tents, damaged 45 vehicles, inflicted 59 casualties upon the battalion, and necessitated the digging in of the entire medical battalion. Absolute blackout prevailed and most ambulance runs were made at night to prevent the disclosure of forward positions. At times it was necessary to drive ambulances to the infantry company command posts during daylight hours to evacuate the seriously wounded. The litter squads were repeatedly used forward of the battalion aid stations rather than in their normal zone to the rear of the battalion aid stations. The personnel of the battalion, by their exemplary endurance, determination, and devotion to duty, prevented untold suffering and saved an inestimable number of lives among the 19,653 patients cared for during the period.

3D QUARTERMASTER COMPANY

1 January to 30 June 1944

The 3D QUARTERMASTER COMPANY displayed outstanding devotion to duty in completing all assigned missions in a superior manner, from 1 January to 30 June 1944, during the Italian campaign. All members, whether truck driver, laborer or clerk, did their utmost to increase the standard of service afforded the combat troops. Throughout the entire period there was a shortage of personnel, yet despite this handicap many additional duties which raised morale and safeguarded the health of all members of the 3d Infantry Division were accomplished. The soldierly and efficient manner in which the 3D QUARTERMASTER COMPANY conducted itself throughout the entire period was in keeping with the finest traditions of the military service.

3D INFANTRY DIVISION BAND

1 January to 30 June, 1944

The 3D INFANTRY DIVISION BAND, from the time of its organization on 1 January 1944 to 30 June 1944, during the campaign in Italy, displayed outstanding devotion to duty and performed in a superior manner, often under difficult and trying conditions. Its members, most of whom previously had actively participated in combat, without exception strived to the utmost in providing needed and highly appreciated entertainment to combat troops of the 3d Infantry Division and other units. By continuous application, the exercise of initiative, and complete cooperation, a high standard of musical performance was achieved and maintained. Exercising their worthy talents to the full, and devoting themselves whole-heartedly to their work, the members of the 3D INFANTRY DIVISION BAND deservingly received the admiration and thanks of the entire Division.

3D INFANTRY DIVISION BAND

15 August 1944 to 15 February 1945

The 3D INFANTRY DIVISION BAND performed in a superior manner in carrying on various activities at rest centers, reinforcement depots and ceremonial functions, and maintained an exceptionally high standard of discipline during the period 15 August 1944 to 15 February 1945. Throughout the campaigns from Southern France to the River, the noteworthy service of the Band assisted materially in maintaining the morale of the 3d Infantry Division at a consistently high level.

MILITARY POLICE PLATOON

1 January to 30 June 1944

MILITARY POLICE PLATOON, 3d Infantry Division, distinguished itself by outstanding and courageous performance of duty during the period, 1 January 1944 to 30 June 1944, throughout training for and participation in the Anzio Beachhead operation in Italy and the breakthrough culminating in the capture of Rome. Landing early the morning of D-Day on Anzio, the Military Police immediately drove inland, established traffic-control posts and greatly facilitated the movement of traffic from the beaches. From posts at road junctions and bridges constantly interdicted by enemy fire, they observed and reported enemy activity, apprehended stragglers, collected prisoners of war, prevented unauthorized civilians from circulating, and controlled military traffic. In the breakthrough operation, traffic-control post teams were kept well forward and rendered invaluable assistance in the rapid advance of the Division from Anzio to Rome. Upon reaching Rome, they policed the city in a highly efficient manner. By its constant devotion to duty and efficient performance of all its tasks, the MILITARY POLICE PLATOON materially assisted in the successful accomplishment of the missions of the 3d Infantry Division.

3D SIGNAL COMPANY

1 January to 30 June 1944

Throughout preparations for an participation in the Anzio Beachhead campaign and the breakthrough operation culminating the capture of * * * Italy, the 3D SIGNAL COMPANY rendered invaluable service to the Division by installing and maintaining vital communication lines and services. Although subjected to constant enemy artillery and occasional small-arms fire, and despite obstacles of terrain and weather, the personnel performed their tasks in a superior manner, insuring continuous efficient communication among all the elements of the Division at all times. Among the many services rendered was the establishment and operation of a photographic section, which proved of great value in the speedy processing of aerial photos. By their initiative, resourcefulness, and untiring efforts, the personnel of the 3D SIGNAL COMPANY contributed materially to the successful accomplishment of the missions of the Division.

703D ORDNANCE (LM) COMPANY

1 January to 30 June 1944

The 703D ORDNANCE (LM) COMPANY, 3d Infantry Division, displayed constant devotion to duty and performed outstanding service from 1 January to 30 June 1944, during the campaign in Italy. In combat and out, the Company maintained all ordnance equipment in repair, utilizing spare parts on hand, and improvising and manufacturing those not available. Many items needed by combat personnel in the conduct of their operations, but unobtainable through normal supply, were constructed by the Ordnance Company. The initiative, skill, and perseverance of the personnel of the 703D ORDNANCE (LM) COMPANY contributed materially to the successful accomplishment of the missions of the 3d Infantry Division.

703D ORDNANCE (LM) COMPANY

15 August 1944 to 15 February 1945

Throughout the period 15 August 1944 to 15 February, 1945, the 703D ORDNANCE (LM) COMPANY rendered invaluable assistance to the combat units of the 3d Infantry Division by maintaining all ordnance matériel in an excellent condition. The many difficulties inherent in the fast-moving campaign in Southern France, as well as those arising from unfavorable terrain and weather during the Meurthe River crossing, the drive through the Vosges Mountains and the campaign in Southern Alsace, were overcome by the personnel of the Company who, by their resourcefulness, constant devotion to and outstanding performance of duty contributed in large measure to the effectiveness of the Division's armament and automotive matériel.

SERVICE COMPANY, 7TH INFANTRY REGIMENT
1 January to 30 June 1944

In the preparation for and during the Anzio Beachhead operation in Italy, for the six months' period beginning 1 January 1944. SERVICE COMPANY, 7th Infantry Regiment, distinguished itself by outstanding and courageous performance of duty. The component sections of Service Company carried out many additional as well as normal functions in a superior manner under adverse tactical, weather, and terrain conditions. Despite hostile mines, bombings, and shell and small arms fire, the personnel of SERVICE COMPANY discharged their varied responsibilities with exemplary devotion to duty and inaugurated services which contributed immeasurably to the well-being and the successful operations of the 7th Infantry Regiment.

SERVICE COMPANY, 7TH INFANTRY REGIMENT
1 July to 31 December 1944

In the preparation for and during the campaigns in France, SERVICE COMPANY, 7th Infantry Regiment, displayed unusual devotion to duty in order to carry out difficult supply missions. Covering enormous distances over greatly extended supply lines, Service Company secured and delivered rations, ammunition, and equipment to combat elements of the Regiment, sacrificing rest and sleep until each assignment was completed. With great resourcefulness, the Company found substitutes for shortages of matériel, and used captured enemy equipment to excellent advantage.

BATTLE CREDITS 3D INFANTRY DIVISION

ALGERIA–FRENCH MOROCCO

Combat zone. Algeria, French Morocco, and adjacent waters.

Time limitation. 8 to 11 November 1942.

TUNISIA

Combat zone. Tunisia and Algeria east of a north-south line through Constantine (inclusive), and adjacent waters.

Time limitation. 12 November 1942 (air), 17 November 1942 (ground), to 13 May 1943.

SICILY

Combat zone. Sicily and adjacent waters.

Time limitation. 14 May 1943 (air), 9 July 1943 (ground), to 17 August 1943.

NAPLES–FOGGIA

Combat zone. Italy (exclusive of Sicily and Sardinia), Corsica, and adjacent waters.

Time limitation. 18 August 1943 (air), 9 September 1943 (ground), to 21 January 1944.

ANZIO

Combat zone. Mussolini Canal–Sessano, Cisterna, Campoleone, Carroceto, Moletta River, and adjacent waters.

Time limitation. 22 January to 24 May 1944.

ROME–ARNO

Combat zone. Italy (exclusive of Sicily and Sardinia), Corsica, and adjacent waters, to 15 August 1944; thereafter, that portion of the Italian mainland and adjacent waters north of 42 degrees north latitude, except that the area of the Anzio combat zone is excluded from 22 January to 24 May 1944.

Time limitation. 22 January to 9 September 1944.

SOUTHERN FRANCE

Combat zone. Those portions of France (exclusive of Corsica) occupied by forces assigned to the North African Theater of Operations, and adjacent waters.

Time limitation. 15 August to 14 September 1944.

RHINELAND

Combat zone. Belgium, Holland, Luxembourg, Germany, and France east of the line: Franco-Belgian frontier to 4 degrees east longitude, thence south along that meridian to 47 degrees north latitude, thence east along that parallel to 5 degrees east longitude, thence south along that meridian to the Mediterranean coast, except that the area of the Ardennes–Alsace combat zone is excluded from 16 December 1944 to 25 January 1945.

Time limitation. 15 September 1944 to 21 March 1945.

ARDENNES–ALSACE

Combat zone. Euskirchen, Eupen (inclusive), Liège (exclusive), east bank of the Meuse River to its intersection with the Franco-Belgian border, thence south and east along this border to the western border of Luxembourg, thence to Metz (inclusive), east bank of the Moselle River to Epinal (inclusive), Strasbourg (inclusive).

Time limitation. 16 December 1944 to 25 January 1945.

CENTRAL EUROPE

Combat zone. The areas occupied by troops assigned to the European Theater of Operations, east of a line 10 miles west of the Rhine River between Switzerland and the Waal River until 28 March 1945, and thereafter east of the east bank of the Rhine.

Time limitation. 22 March to 11 May 1945.

THIRD (REGULAR ARMY) DIVISION
WORLD WAR I

5th Infantry Brigade   6th Infantry Brigade

4th Infantry Regiment	30th Infantry Regiment
7th Infantry Regiment	38th Infantry Regiment
8th Machine Gun Battalion	9th Machine Gun Battalion

3d Field Artillery Brigade

10th FA Regiment (75mm)	76th FA Regiment (75mm)
18th FA Regiment (105mm)	3d Trench Mortar Battery

Divisional Troops

7th Machine Gun Battalion	6th Engineer Regiment
5th Field Signal Battalion	Headquarters Troop

Trains

The 3d Division, Regular Army, was organized in November, 1917, with headquarters at Camp Greene, North Carolina.

Division elements were gathered from 11 camps and posts but were never concentrated at one station before departure for France. The 6th Engineer Regiment, first unit to leave the United States, left Hoboken, N. J., December 4-5, 1917, and arrived at Brest and St. Nazaire December 21-22. Remainder of the Division sailed during the period March 14 to April 30, 1918, from Halifax, Hoboken, Newport News and New York, and landed at St. Nazaire, Brest, Liverpool and Glasgow.

The Division reached its greatest war-time strength in September, 1918, when it numbered 27,714 officers and men.

The 6th Engineers, serving with a British engineer unit, were the first 3d Division troops to see action in World War I. Occupying a defensive position east of Amiens, the 6th Engineers, on orders to hold to the last against the German offensive launched March 21, stood their ground so well that the retreating British forces on March 27 retired behind this line, which then became the front line. The Engineers held their position until relieved on April 3.

The 3d Division as a whole went into action for the first time on May 30, 1918, when it was placed at the disposal of the French Group of Armies of the North for the purpose of defending the passages of the Marne River from Chateau-Thierry to Damery. It was in this engagement that the 3d Division, by its gallant stand in defeating powerful German attacks, earned its proud sobriquet, "Rock of the Marne."

During World War I, one or more units in the 3d Division were awarded battle honors by the War Department for participation in the following:

Somme Defensive, March 21–April 6; Aisne Offensive, June 1-15; Chateau-Thierry Sector, June 6-July 14; Champagne-Marne Defensive, July 15-17; Aisne-Marne Offensive, July 18-29; Aisne-Marne Offensive (6th Inf. Brig.), August 3-6; Visle Sector (6th Inf. Brig.), Aug. 7-11; St. Mihiel Offensive, Sept. 12-15; Meuse-Argonne Offensive, Sept. 26-Nov. 1.

Following the armistice the Division, on Nov. 17, began to move as part of the Army of Occupation to the district of Mayen, 30 miles west of Coblenz. On March 9, 1919, the 3rd Trench Mortar Battery sailed from St. Nazaire for the United States. Sailings for the remainder of the Division began August 10 and by August 28 the last elements had arrived in the United States.

ROSTERS

OF PERSONNEL WHO SERVED OVERSEAS IN WORLD WAR II

3D INFANTRY DIVISION COMMANDERS & STAFF*

Commanding General

(Highest rank held)	Held pos. from	To
Maj. Gen. Jonathan W. Anderson		22 Feb 1943
Brig. Gen. Wm. A. Campbell (Actg)	23 Feb 1943	6 Mar 1943
Maj. Gen. Lucian K. Truscott, Jr.	7 March 1943	17 Feb 1944
Maj. Gen. John W. O'Daniel	17 Feb 1944	2 Dec 1944
Brig. Gen. Robert N. Young (Actg)	3 Dec 1944	7 Jan 1945
Maj. Gen. John W. O'Daniel	7 Jan 1945	

Assistant Division Commander

Brig. Gen. William W. Eagles		23 Nov 1943
Brig. Gen. John W. O'Daniel	1 Dec 1943	16 Feb 1944
Brig. Gen. Whitfield P. Shepard	26 Feb 1944	25 Aug 1944
Brig. Gen. Robert N. Young	14 Oct 1944	3 Dec 1944
Col. Lionel C. McGarr (Actg)	13 Dec. 1944	7 Jan 1945
Brig. Gen. Robert N. Young	8 Jan 1945	

Chief of Staff

Col. Walter E. Lauer		3 Jan 1943
Lt. Col. Edgar C. Doleman (Actg)	4 Jan 1943	9 Feb 1943
Col. Harry McK. Roper	10 Feb 1943	17 Feb 1943
Lt. Col. Ben Harrell (Actg)	18 Feb 1943	6 Mar 1943
Col. Don E. Carleton	7 Mar 1943	25 Feb 1944
Col. Charles E. Johnson	26 Feb 1944	

Assistant Chief of Staff, G-1

Maj. Jeremiah F. Van Wakeman		15 Dec 1942
Lt. Col. Albert O. Connor	16 Dec 1942	21 June 1943
Lt. Col. Basil F. Basila	22 June 1943	12 Oct 1944
Maj. Daniel L. Wickersham (Actg)	13 Oct 1944	25 Jan 1945
Lt. Col. Basil F. Basila	26 Jan 1945	25 Feb 1945
Maj. Daniel L. Wickersham	16 Feb 1945	

Assistant Chief of Staff, G-2

Lt. Col. Mercer C. Walter		21 Jan 1943
Maj. Grover Wilson	22 Jan 1943	31 July 1943
Lt. Col. Mercer C. Walter	1 Aug 1943	11 Sept 1943
Lt. Col. Grover Wilson	12 Sept 1943	4 Jan 1945
Maj. Hugh A. Scott (Actg)	5 Jan 1943	

Assistant Chief of Staff, G-3

Lt. Col. Ben Harrell		1 Sept 1943
Lt. Col. Albert O. Connor	2 Sept 1943	23 Oct 1944
Lt. Col. William B. Rosson	24 Oct 1944	

Assistant Chief of Staff, G-4

Lt. Col. Carroll T. Newton		21 Jan 1943
Lt. Col. Charles E. Johnson	22 Jan 1943	25 Feb 1944
Lt. Col. Dick A. King	26 Feb 1944	

Engineer Officer

Lt. Col. Leonard L. Bingham		30 Aug 1943
Lt. Col. Charles Tank	31 Aug 1943	19 Sept 1944
Lt. Col. Robert L. Petherick	20 Sept 1944	

Signal Officer

(Highest rank held)	Held pos. from	To
Lt. Col. James F. Brook, Jr.		6 Sept 1943
Lt. Col. Jesse F. Thomas	7 Sept 1943	18 Oct 1944
Lt. Col. George H. Fezell	19 Oct 1944	

Division Quartermaster

Col. Boyce James	Nov 1942	Aug 1943
Lt. Col. Fred Wolfer	Aug 1943	Oct 1944
Lt. Col. Benjamin Goodwin	Oct 1944	May 1945

Ordnance Officer

Lt. Col. James McGehee

Adjutant General

Lt. Col. Bruce C. Price		30 June 1944
Lt. Col. Stephen J. Rogers	1 July 1944	

Inspector General

Lt. Col. Karl Glos

Staff Judge Advocate

Lt. Col. William H. Ellsworth

Finance Officer

Lt. Col. Clarence A. Frank		31 Mar 1943
Capt. L. C. Grimes	1 Apr 1943	13 May 1943
Lt. Col. D. J. Nielson	14 May 1943	4 July 1943
Lt. Col. L. C. Grimes	5 July 1943	

Division Chaplain

Lt. Col. Patrick J. Ryan		16 Feb 1943
Lt. Col. Ralph J. Smith	17 Feb 1943	

Chemical Officer

Maj. Albert L. Safine

Division Surgeon

Col. Matthew C. Pugsley		4 Dec 1943
Lt. Col. William J. McCarty	5 Dec 1943	31 Dec 1943
Lt. Col. Frank R. Drake	1 Jan 1944	

Provost Marshal

Capt. M. N. Mikalak	7 Oct 1942	15 July 1943
Maj. Paul T. Gerard	15 July 1943	6 Oct 1943
Lt. Col. Richard L. Creed (Killed in Action 18 Nov 1943)	6 Oct 1943	16 Nov 1943
Lt. Col. Arthur Snyder	16 Nov 1943	15 Apr 1944
Lt. Col. James K. Watts	15 April 1944	15 June 1945

Headquarters Commandant

Maj. Paul T. Gerard		6 Feb 1943
Maj. James K. Watts	7 Feb 1943	12 April 1944
Lt. Col. John H. Gerety	13 Apr 1944	

*The names and positions held apply only from Nov. 8, 1942 to May 8, 1945 (V-E Day). Neither opening nor closing dates of service are listed.

HEADQUARTERS AND HEADQUARTERS COMPANY 3D INFANTRY DIVISION

The Headquarters and Headquarters Company was organized January 1, 1918, at Chickamauga Park, Georgia. Within three months the company was in France, and experienced its first combat at Chateau Thierry on July 14, 1918. It later participated in the Aisne Offensive, Aisne-Marne Offensive, capture of the St. Mihiel Salient, and the Meuse-Argonne Offensive.

Abbott, George R., Capt.,
Adamonis, Walter F., Pvt,
Adams, Francis C., T/3,
Adolphson, Emil E., 1st Sgt,
Ahlgrim, Everett R., T/Sgt,
Ahrens, Walter V., S/Sgt,
Alday, Albert, Pfc,
Alford, James S., Pfc,
Allen, George E., 1st Lt,
Allen, Roy E., T/4,
Althoetmar, August P., Sgt,
Alttroggen, Rudolf O., 2nd Lt,
Alves, Vernon J., T/5,
Ames, Joseph E., 2nd Lt,
Anderson, J. W., Maj Gen,
Anderson, Shelley A., Cpl,
Anthony, Robert E., Pfc,
Ark, Huie, Pfc,
Arkema, Clyde H., Pvt,
Arney, Norman E. T/3,
Ashbaugh, C. D., Jr., T/Sgt,
Atwood, Oliver W., M/Sgt,
Ayoub, Edward J., 1st Lt,

Babior, Martin, Pfc,
Back, Herschel P., T/5,
Bagnulo, Gillis H., Pvt,
Bailey, Kenneth C., M/Sgt,
Bailey, Richard K., Sgt,
Baker, Raymond F., Capt,
*Balaber, Sidney, T/5,
Balkenbush, Adrian F., Cpl,
Ball, William E., S/Sgt,
Banahan, Timothy C., Pvt,
Baranko, William, Sgt,
Barber, John T., Pfc,
Barchesky, Lester V., Pfc,
Barna, Louis, Pvt,
Barnes, Norman P., Maj,
Barnette, Walker E., 1st Sgt,
Barr, Roy, Pfc,
Bartash, Jack E., Capt.,
Basila, Basil F., Lt Col,
Battain, Primo F., T/4,
Bauman, Edward C., T/5,
Bauman, Jack L., T/4,
Bear, Jack W., Pvt,
Beargeon, Edward J., T/4,
Beasley, Lee A., T/4,
Bee, Stanley P., T/4,
Beel, Wayne R., Cpl,
Bella, Mario J., Cpl,
Bellino, Daniel J., Pfc,
Belt, George L., Pfc,
Benedict, Kenneth G., Cpl,
Bennett, Bryan E., Pfc,
Bennett, Eugene, Pvt,
Benoschek, Jay K., Pfc,
Bergstrom, Carl G., Pfc,
Berkholz, Clarence O., Pvt,
Berman, Samuel, Pvt,
Bernal, Pablo P., Pfc,
Berryman, Richard J., Sgt,
Bertschinger, Harold W., T/5,
Bester, Anthony V., T/5,
Betbeze, Charles S., Capt,
Bickers, Melvin H., Pfc,

Billingsley, John W., Pfc,
Bird, Raymond C., Sgt,
Birt, Robert J., S/Sgt,
*Black, Thomas R., Pfc,
Bleimeister, Frank E., Pfc,
Bliss, John N., M/Sgt,
Blosnich, Rudolf S., Pvt,
Blossom, C. C., Jr., 1st Lt,
Blumenthal, Rolf S., Pvt,
Bohler, Robert E., Pfc,
Bonner, William A., Capt,
Boor, Howard D., T/4,
Bosworth, Frank M., T/4,
Boulden, James E., Pfc,
Bouton, Vernon W., CWO,
Boyce, Clarence E., S/Sgt,
Boyd, James W., Pfc,
Boyd, Wallace T., WOJG,
Boyda, Henry A., Pfc,
Boye, Frederic W., Maj,
Boylan, Raymond A., T/5,
Boylen, James E., T/5,
Bracken, John H., T/4,
Braganza, Jose D., Pfc,
Brdar, Vincent J., T/5,
Breth, James E., Lt Col,
Brewer, Harold W., CWO,
Brewer, Robert T., Pfc,
Brischler, John, Pfc,
Bristow, Ivan P., S/Sgt,
Britton, Robert H., Pvt,
Brodie, Norman, T/5,
Brooks, Philip R., 1st Lt,
Brothers, William W., Maj,
Browder, Clyde M., Pfc,
Brown, Allen H., III, 2nd Lt,
Brown, Elvin L., Pfc,
Brown, Franklin C., Pvt,
Brown, Jack D., Pfc,
Brown, James H., Pfc,
Brownfold, William F., Pfc,
Brunni, Donald W., T/Sgt,
Bryant, William H., Jr., Sgt,
Buckley, Paul P., Sgt,
†Bunger, George T., Pvt,
Burdenski, Henry E., T/4,
Burgess, Okey T., Pvt,
Burkhard, Donald J., Pvt,
Burkell, James J., Pfc,
Butler, Donald A., 1st Lt,
Buttgen, George A., T/Sgt,
Byrd, Thomas J., T/4,

Cain, Lillion W., Capt,
Caldwell, Walter E., Jr., T/4,
Callaway, Alma J.,
Campbell, Robert J., Maj,
Camy, Robert M., Pfc,
Canady, George M., Pfc,
Caplan, Martin, Pfc,
Carleton, Don E., Col,
Carlisle, Glen D., 2nd Lt,
Carlson, Carl E., Pfc,
Carpenter, Edwin H., Jr., Pfc,
Carr, George M., Jr., M/Sgt,
Carver, John H., Pfc,
Casanova, Edward V., T/4,

Caton, June C., 1st Lt,
Caughey, Donald E., Maj,
Ceizyk, Casimer, J., Cpl,
Cella, Eugene W., Pfc,
Cenko, Steve, Jr., Pfc,
Chambers, William H., 1st Lt,
Chambliss, Clifton D., Pfc,
Chapman, Lawrence W., Pfc,
Chatfield, Philip H., Pfc,
Chaudron, David L., Pfc,
Chavez, Gonzalo, A., Pfc,
Cheaney, Louis B., Jr., Cpl,
Chee, Joe M., Pvt,
Chestnut, Louis L., Pvt,
Chew, Art F., T/5,
Chin, Tin W., Pfc,
Chipka, Joseph J., Pfc,
Chockla, Mitchel, Pfc,
Cholewinski, Eugene D., Pfc,
Church, Robert I., Pfc,
Cibulka, Howard F., Pvt,
Cieplinski, Anthony J., Pvt,
Cischke, Donald W., Pfc,
Clark, Harry S., T/4,
Clark, Martin F., Pfc,
Clarke, Milton C., Pfc,
Claunch, James E., T/4,
Clayton, John M., Sgt,
Clem, Rhoman E., Capt,
Clement, John F., T/5,
Collier, Howard S., Pfc,
Colligan, James, Pfc,
Collins, Archie B., Pfc,
Collins, Henry, M/Sgt,
Colombo, Charles, Pfc,
Conley, Berton B., Pfc,
Conley, John P., 2nd Lt,
Connelly, William B., Sgt,
Connor, Albert O., Lt Col,
Connor, William C., T/5,
Conrad, Jerry C., 1st Lt,
Conway, Theodore J., Lt Col,
Conz, George J., S/Sgt,
Cook, Roy E. Capt,
Cooke, Carl M., Pfc,
Cooley, Edwin R., Capt,
Cooper, Arthur T., Pfc,
Cooper, William D., T/4,
Corder, William E., Pfc,
Cordick, Charles F., 1st Lt,
Corley, Paul D., 1st Sgt,
Cornelius, Forrest L., Pfc,
*Cottrell, James A., Pfc,
†Craft, William H., Pfc,
Crain, Floyd W., 2nd Lt,
Crandall, Lloyd R., T/5,
Crandall, Robert W., Maj,
†Creed, Richard L., Col,
Cross, Ted W., Pfc,
Crook, Arba W., Maj,
Crotty, John J., T/4,
Cullinan, Edward P., Pfc,
Cunningham, R. E., Pvt,
Cunningham, Wm. L., Pvt,
Curl, Jerome J., T/5,
Cushing, Cecil W., Pfc,
Cutuli, Santo L., Pfc,

Cardillo, Albert, Pfc,
Cyphers, William E., Pfc,

Damato, Daniel F., Pfc,
Daniel, Dale R., Pfc,
Da Polito, Steven A., Pfc,
D'Aprile, Michael D., Sgt,
Dare, Hoon, Pfc,
Darling, Glenwood B., 2nd Lt,
Darlington, James P., T/5,
Darrah, John R., Maj, Cody,
Daugherty, Robert H., Pfc,
Dautel, Alfred G., Pvt,
Davis, Edwin E., Sgt,
Davis, Leo, F., Pvt,
Dawson, Alvin M., M/Sgt,
Dawson, Howard R., Pfc,
Dea, Wing, J., Pvt,
Deatherage, Robert W., Pfc,
Decker, Timothy F., T/5,
Deem, Robert B., T/3,
Delaney, James M., Cpl,
Dempsey, Norman S., M/Sgt,
Devaney, Patrick E., T/4,
Diaz, Joseph J., Pfc,
Dick, Leo L., Pvt,
Diebold, Kenneth G., S/Sgt,
Donica, Wayne W., Pfc,
Dorr, Martin H., Pfc,
Dorschler, Eugene F., Sgt,
Doyle, Raymond J., T/4,
Drake, Frank R., Lt Col,
Dragneff, Nicholas W., Maj,
Drotos, Fred N., Pvt,
Dunbar, Jack W., Pvt,
Duncan, Herbert L., Capt,
Dunn, William G., Cpl,
Dvores, Morton, Pvt,
Dyckman, Harry, Pfc,

Eagles, William W., Brig Gen,
Eakin, John K., 2nd Lt,
Eastberg, James E., S/Sgt,
Easterday, Dan C., Capt,
Eavey, Robert L., Pfc,
Egbert, Dan M., Pfc,
Eisenstein, Harold L., S/Sgt,
Elliott, Charles W., T/5,
Ellsworth, William H., Lt Col,
Emmel, John F., Pfc,
Engebretson, Herman O., T/5,
Engel, Bert C., 1st Lt,
Engman, Carl D., Pfc,
Erickson, Ernest R., Pfc,
Erickson, John A., T/4,
Ertl, Wolfgang G., Pvt,
Everett, Clyde, Pfc,
Ewing, Charles G., M/Sgt,
Ewonus, William, T/4,
Earls, Raymond, T/5,

Fadale, Charles J., T/4,
Fall, Jack T., Pfc,
Fall, Millard C., T/4,
Fallot, Pierre L., Pfc,
Farnham, Robert H., 2nd Lt,
Farr, Dell A., Jr., Pvt,

Farrington, Don R., Pfc,
Faucher, Oliver J., Lt Col,
Fecicz, Nicholas, Pvt,
Feld, Joseph G., T/5,
Ferriell, Joseph C., Pfc,
Ferrier, Derreld E., Pfc,
Fink, Wilmen C., Pvt,
Fish, Charles J., 1st Lt,
Fitzgerald, George L., Pfc,
Fitzpatrick, Kenneth, Pfc,
Fleischmann, Edward D., Pfc,
Flora, James A., T/Sgt,
Floto, Kenneth B., 1st Lt,
Flynn, John J., Col,
Flynn, Stephen E., T/Sgt,
Foley, Patrick T., Pfc,
Ford, Buster E., Pfc,
Forman, William P., T/3,
Foster, Joe, Pfc,
Fouts, Gilbert W., T/5,
Fowler, Morris L., Pfc,
Fox, Rolland L., T/4,
Fraker, Joseph W., Pfc,
Frame, George L., T/4,
Francis, Franklyn W., Pvt,
Franklin, Albert S., Pvt,
Franz, Robert W., Capt,
Fratt, Clarence E., T/4,
Fredenburg, George, Pvt
Frederick, Charles E., Lt Col
Freeland, Robert E., Pvt,
Freemore, Robert E., Pfc,
Friedman, Joseph, T/5,
Fritzke, Robert P., T/5,
Froom, William P., Pfc,
Futrelle, Rollin L., T/3,

Gabel, Lee F., Cpl,
Gabrielli, John E., Pfc,
†Gadoury, Phillip L., T/5,
†Gagnon, Albert J., T/4
Gale, Meade B., Pfc,
Galloway, Joseph R., T/4,
Garcia, Orencio, Pvt,
Gardner, Gerald L., Pfc,
German, Wayne C., Sgt,
Garrett, Howard, Pfc,
Gasperich, John R., Cpl,
Geier, Robert C., Sgt,
Geighes, John J., T/5,
Geisert, Earl V., Sgt,
Geitgey, Alvin J., T/4,
Gentile, Robert P., Pvt,
Gerard, Paul T., Maj,
Gerety, John H., Lt Col,
†Gerlin, Louis W., Cpl,
Gersh, Philip, T/5,
Gettinger, Daniel N., 2nd Lt
Ghilarducci, Bruno V., S/Sgt,
Gibbons, Charles E., 1st Lt,
Gibbs, Jack, Pfc,
Gierut, Stanley G., Pfc,
Girton, Ferol Z., Pfc,
Giuntolli, William M., 2nd Lt
Glantz, Melvin N., Capt.
Glaze, Andrew J., Jr., T/5,
Gleason, Thomas G., Jr., T/4,

† Killed in Action.   * Prisoner of War.   ‡ Missing in Action.   § Died of Wounds.

Glos, Karl F., Lt Col,
Glover, Alfred W., Pfc,
Goding, William H., Pvt,
Goins, Kelso, T/4,
Gozales, Fred, T/5,
Goodman, Owen F., Capt,
Goodman, Stanford D., Jr.,
Goodson, Hoyt R., Pvt,
Goodson, Thomas J., Pvt,
Goss, Gunther F., Pfc,
Graff, John F., Pfc,
Graneri, Daniel F., Pvt
Grant, Davis H., 1st Lt,
Gray, Wilbur D., Pfc,
Green, Clifford R., Pfc,
Gregory, Clyde R., Pfc,
Griffis, John W., T/4,
Griffith, Frederick W., Pfc,
Grimes, Lyle C., Lt Col,
Grove, Leon H., Pfc,
Groves, Cleburn F., T/4,
Guber, Alfred M., M/Sgt,
Guensberg, Gerold, T/5,
Guillory, Thomas F., Pvt,
Gum, Harold E., Pfc,
Gutowski, Edwin S., Pfc,
Guy, Harold C., Sgt,
Guzlow, Albert L., Sgt,

Hackman, William L., Pfc,
Hadler, Robert F., Pfc,
Haegelin, Hilmer B., Lt Col,
Hagen, Arnold C., T/4,
Haggard, Edwin C., Maj,
Hagman, James A., T/3,
Haines, John R., T/4,
Hallett, Jack D., 2nd Lt,
Hamilton, Burger W., Capt,
Hamm, Walter S., Pfc,
Hanson, Raymond H., Pfc,
Hardy, Jerry L., Pvt,
Haritos, James N., Cpl,
Harms, Walter J., Pfc,
Harrell, Ben, Lt Col,
Harris, James A., Pvt,
Harris, Robert E., M/Sgt,
Harrison, Merrill S., T/4,
Harter, Ellis W., 1st Sgt,
Hartley, Willis E., Pfc,
Hatfield, Arthur A., Jr., T/5,
Hawks, Earl E., S/Sgt,
Haworth, Leonard S., 2nd Lt,
Hayden, Caskie V., Pvt,
Haynie, Guy W., Pfc,
Heckman, Omer H., Pfc,
Hectorne, F. Nolan, T/Sgt,
Heidinger, Jack, S/Sgt.
Heintges, John A., Lt Col,
Heitkamp, Hugh H., Sgt,
Heitmiller, Raymond A., Pfc,
Henico, Henry, Pfc,
Hempelman, Marvin K., Pfc,
Henson, Edwin L., Sgt,
Herr, Allen J., Pfc,
Hicks, William R., Capt,
Hill, Walter A., Jr., Pfc,
Hill, Sterling L., Capt,
Hite, Daniel P., T/5,
Hite, John B., T/Sgt,
Hockman, William L., Pfc,
Hoflund, Arnold M., T/4,
Hoge, David W., Pfc,
Hohenfels, Arthur P., Pvt,
Holbrook, Vance H., T/3,
Holicky, John, Pfc,
Holland, Clifton E., Pvt,
Hollier, Edgar, Jr., Pfc,
Holt, George G., T/5,
Hom, Wing M., Pvt,
Homola, Elmer P., M/Sgt,
Hong, Taw S., Pfc,
Hoober, Joe M., T/4,
Hor, Charles L., Pfc,
Hoss, Vernon W., T/5,
House, Thomas R., T/5,
Howard, Charles M., Pfc,
Howe, Harold E., Pfc,
Howell, Joseph E., T/4,
Howell, Lawrence E., S/Sgt,
Hrabosky, Leonard O., Pfc,
Hubbard, Boyd, Jr., Lt Col,
Huebner, Joseph F., Jr., Pfc,
Huff, Gerald B., Pfc,
Huffman, Ralph E., T/5,
Huge, Robert H., Pvt,
Hughes, Ben J., WOJG,
Huguenin, Henry, Capt,
Hummel, Clarence J., Pfc,
Humphries, John R., Pfc,
Hunn, Charles J., Pvt,
Hunt, Clint, T/5,
Hunt, Emile, T/5,
Hunter, James R., S/Sgt,
Hunter, John M., M/Sgt,
Hutchins, Sherman C., T/5,

Hutt, John H., T/5,
Hylbert, William J., 1st Lt,

Indahl, Harry B., M/Sgt,
Ingram, Charles D., Jr., T/5,
Ingrim, Mervyn H., Pfc,
Isaacson, Alfred S., Pfc,
Ivonen, Larry, Pvt,
Iyoob, John M., T/4,

Janssen, William G., T/5,
Jarvis, Gordon C., T/5,
Jaskierny, Arthur, CWO,
Jensen, Harvey W., Sgt,
Jew, Guey K., Pfc,
John, William K., WOJG,
Johnson, Albert C., Pfc,
Johnson, Charles E., Col,
Johnson, Gunnard L., Pvt,
Johnson, Harold L., S/Sgt,
Johnston, William P., Cpl,
Joissains, Andre, 2nd Lt,
Jones, Burton R., Jr., Pvt,
Jones, Jay L., 2nd Lt,
Jones, John P., Sgt,
Jones, Robert C., T/3,
Jordan, Lawrence W., Pvt,
Joslin, Robert V., T/4,
Joung, Joe, Pfc,
Jukich, Russell J., Pvt,
Juneau, Charles G., Capt,
Jung, Raymond A., T/5,
Juraska, Robert E., T/4,
Jursch, Carl C., Pfc,

Kahlke, James H., T/4,
Kaiser, William B., Pfc,
Kalb, Merrill B., T/Sgt,
Kaplish, Murray J., M/Sgt,
Kaporis, James J., Pfc,
Karr, Howard H., Pfc,
Katz, Norman, T/5,
Kawa, Henry P., Sgt,
Keels, Harry, Pfc,
Kellas, William W., Pfc,
Keller, Marshall C., Cpl,
Keller, Ted B., M/Sgt,
Keller, William W., T/5,
Kellers, Newell R., Cpl,
Kendall, James G., Pfc,
Kennedy, Edward J., Pvt,
Kerr, Gerald J., 1st Lt,
Kerr, Richard L., 1st Lt,
Kesner, Sam, Capt, Dallas,
Kiblen, Charles, Capt,
Kiesecker, Gilbert G., T/3,
King, Dick A., Lt Col,
King, George W., Capt,
Kingston, George R., Maj,
Kirkland, Homer D., S/Sgt,
Kirschbaum, Robert F., T/Sgt,
Kittleson, Laurence L., Pvt,
Klenk, Julius J., Pfc,
Knoop, Elbert B., Pvt,
Koberstein, Henry F., Capt,
Koppelman, Harry, Cpl,
Koprowski, M. J., 1st Lt,
Krepky, Morris, Pfc,
Krill, Marlin P., S/Sgt,
Krochmal, Arnold, 2nd Lt,
Krupansky, Stephen F., T/5,
Kuchukian, Ohan, Pfc,

Lacey, Victor E., Pfc,
Lacy, Paul, Jr., Pfc,
La Dam, George W., Sgt,
Laha, Milburn E., T/5,
Lalaian, Suren, Cpl,
Lamanna, Alexander, T/5,
Lander, Irvin, Pfc,
Langford, Lloyd E., Maj,
Lapin, Sam, T/3,
Lapine, David W., Pfc,
Larson, Stanley R., M/Sgt,
LaVelle, James, I., Pfc,
Lawrence, David L., Pvt,
Lawton, William T., Sgt,
Layton, Hoyt H., T/4,
Leavitt, Edwin, Sgt,
Leavitt, Le Roy S., T/5,
Ledford, Oscar L., Pfc,
Lee, Arlie L., Jr., Pfc,
Lee, Charles J., T/5,
Lemke, Howard D., Pfc,
LeMoine, Joseph W., Pfc,
Lenahan, Daniel W., Jr., Maj,
Leong, George C., T/5,
Leptuch, Adam M., Pfc,
Levi, Robert L., Sgt,
Lewandowski, Erwin F., T/5,
Lieb, Donald H., Capt,
Lieberman, Gerald, Pfc,
Limprecht, Hollis J., Capt,
Lindsey, Paul D., Capt,
Lissauer, Hans J., T/5,

Logar, Anthony S., Sgt,
Lokey, William H., Maj,
Long, Donald E., Lt Col,
Long, Eddie L., Pfc,
Losh, Elmer E., Pfc,
Loughery, Francis X., Pfc,
Lowry, Roye L., T/5,
Loyd, Charles, W., Cpl
Lucas, Ecklor C., T/5,
Lumpkin, Raymond, Sgt,
Lunde, Kenneth E., M/Sgt,
Lundeen, Edward P., T/5,
Lytle, Marvin C., Pfc,
Lytle, William P., T/4,

Mader, Luke W., S/Sgt,
Magart, Robert E., Pfc,
Magewski, Walter J., Pfc,
Maier, Elmer A., Capt,
Mallozzi, Anthony J., Jr., Pvt,
Mangler, Harold J., T/5,
Mangrum, Wayne, S/Sgt,
Mannesto, William R., Pfc,
Marina, Joseph, Cpl,
Marquette, Richard A., T/4,
Marshall, Robert J., Pfc,
Martin, Herman, Pvt,
Martowski, Patrick A., S/Sgt,
Marx, Phillip, Pfc,
Mason, Bruce, 2nd Lt,
Mason, Charles R., Pfc,
Mason, Richard L., T/5,
Matlack, Edwin W., Cpl,
Mayer, John J., Pfc,
Mazner, Joe J., Sgt,
Mazza, Joseph S., S/Sgt,
McCabe, Joseph J., T/5,
McCafferty, Clair C. T., T/3,
McCarthy, Marion C., Capt,
McCarthy, Millard, Pfc,
McCauley, Marco A., Pfc,
McClurg, Ray F., Pfc,
McComber, Hester F., T/4,
McCourt, Thomas J., Jr., Pvt,
McCoy, George V., M/Sgt,
McDaniel, Charles W., T/5,
McDermott, Jack F., Cpl,
McEwen, Orville S., Pfc,
McGettigan, Edward W., Cpl,
McGrew, Thomas W., T/4,
McKinley, Elliot L., Pvt,
McKnight, Wendell L., S/Sgt,
McPherson, Alan W., Pvt,
Mears, Roy A., T/5,
Mecke, Theodore H., Sr., T/4,
Meek, Bernard F., Pfc,
Merchant, Adrian, Pvt,
Meyers, Mark W., Pfc,
Michella, John R., Pvt,
Mikos, Paul, Pfc,
Millar, Walter K., Jr., Capt,
Miller, Aubrey, T/5,
Miller, Coolie, Pfc,
Miller, John W., Pvt,
Miller, Robert L., T/4,
Miller, Sidney, Pvt,
Mills, Jimmie E., Sgt,
Minerva, Frank D., Major,
Minkus, Sam M., T/4,
Mintz, Edward, Pvt,
Mitchell, Harold D., Pvt,
Mitchell, Robert E., Major,
Mitsakow, Constantine C., Pvt,
Mizin, Anthony J., Pfc,
Mobley, Thomas A., Pvt,
Mol, James R., T/5,
Mole, Joseph P., T/5,
Molina, Ralph P., T/4,
Mollison, John C., Pfc,
Monahan, Robert C., Pvt,
Montimurno, Vincent, Pfc,
Moon, John V., T/Sgt,
Moore, Johnie, T/5,
Moore, Harold S., Jr., T/5,
Moore, Miles O., Pvt,
Moore, Wm. H., Pfc,
Morgan, Marion O., Pfc,
Morris, Frank E., Pfc,
Morrow, Owen W., T/4,
Mosher, David E., S/Sgt,
Mosher, Herbert, T/5,
Mottweiler, Richard H., 2nd Lt,
Moy, Baker, Pvt,
Moya, Octavio, Pvt,
Muguerza, Raime G., Pfc,
Mullen, Clyde F., S/Sgt,
Munro, Dale R., T/3,
Myers, George C., Pvt,

Nagle, Gabriel, Pfc,
Naslund, George M., Capt,
Nassar, Edward A., T/4,
Navvarro, Joseph, Jr., Sgt,
Naylor, William E., Pfc,
Neiheisel, Gilbert C., Pfc,

Nelsen, Curtis A., Pfc,
Nelson, Clifford F., T/5,
Nelson, William J., Pfc,
Ness, Arden J., M/Sgt,
Nethken, Lloyd H., Pfc,
Nevins, Donald I., T/5,
Newell, Richard W., Capt,
Newman, Norbert C., T/5,
Nicholls, Russelll A., Pfc,
Nicpon, Stanley, Pfc,
Nielson, David J., Lt Col,
Nielson, Earnest W., Pfc,
Noethlich, Robert M., Pfc,
Noin, Fernando, Pfc,
Norelius, George, T/5,
Norris, John M., Pfc,
Norton, Lowell E., T/5,

O'Barr, W. A., Jr., 1st Lt,
O'Brien, Patrick J., Pfc,
O'Connell, James J., Pfc,
O'Daniel, John W., Major Gen,
O'Dell, Clarence E., Pfc,
O'Neill, Gerald F., Pfc,
Ong, Fred, Pfc,
Orbach, Manfred, Pfc,
Owend, Thomas, Sr., Sgt,

Page, Woodrow P., Pfc,
Paine, John H., T/Sgt,
Parachini, Mario A., Pfc,
Parker, Wm. C., Jr., 2nd Lt,
Parkinson, Peter A., 2nd Lt,
Parsons, William C., Pfc,
Patterson, John D., Pfc,
Paul, Donald M., Pvt,
Payne, Jack A., S/Sgt,
Pearlman, Sidney, Sgt,
Pedinoff, Murray M., Pfc,
Penrod, Keith E., Pfc,
Peters, Keith E., Pfc,
Petersen, Louis C., Sgt,
Peterson, Wayne A., Pfc,
Peterson, Wesley F., T/Sgt,
Petroni, Leonard L., Pfc,
Pettigrew, Aubrey W., 2nd Lt,
Petzke, Theodore W., Pvt,
Pewitt, Robert L., Pfc,
Phillips, James A., Pfc,
Phinsey, Gordon T., Pfc,
Picrell, Gordon C., Pfc,
Pierce, Frank B., Cpl,
Pierce, Maurice E., T/3,
Pierce, William W., Cpl,
Pitcamer, Stanley P., Pfc,
Platt, Louis I., T/5,
Plumb, Wm. C., Pfc,
Podgur, Julian, Pfc,
Poinsert, Edgar H., Capt,
Polly, Willis R., Pfc,
Pope, Robert E., Pfc,
Poy, Tom H., Pfc,
Pravitz, Russell C., Pfc,
Predoehl, Walter R., T/5,
Pribble, Harry M., Pfc,
Price, Bruce C., Lt Col,
Price, Stanley P., Pfc,
Prince, Jacob, Jr., Cpl,
Proctor, Elward F., Pfc,
Proud, Harry S., Capt,
Proulx, Raymond I., Pfc,
Puchala, Stanley G., Pfc,
Pugsley, Matthew C., Colonel,

Quan, Fong, Pfc,
Quinn, Donald S., 1st Lt,

†Raatz, Carl G., Pfc,
Rabil, Emil P., Pfc,
Rami, Victor M., Pfc,
Ramsey, Lloyd B., Capt,
Ramsey, Roger W., S/Sgt,
Raskosky, John M., T/5,
Rath, Louis F., Pfc,
Reese, Lawrence L., Pfc,
Rehbany, Nicholas M., Pfc,
Reimers, Carl, T/5,
Reis, Gregory P., T/4,
Renne, Lynn, Major,
Restivo, Andrew P., Pfc,
Restivo, Joe J., Pfc,
Revelle, George H., Jr., Major,
Riback, Bernard J., T/4,
Rice, Walter M., 2nd Lt,
Riecken, George J., T/5,
Roach, James E., Sgt,
Rochmis, Max, Capt,
Rodgers, Nelson J., Pfc,
Rogers, Stephen J., Lt Col,
Roland, James T., Sgt,
Romano, Tony A., Pfc,
Roney, James L., 1st Sgt,
Rosati, William H., Pfc,
Rose, Anthony J., Pfc,
Rose, Vernon E., Cpl,

Rosenzwog, Harold W., S/Sgt,
Ross, Elmer J., T/5,
Rubinfeld, Allen J., T/4,
Runyan, Hugh W., T/4,
Runyon, Donald E., Pfc,
Russell, Robert E., T/5,
Rutherford, Clyde W., T/5,
Ryan, Richard, Pfc,

Sabbadini, Alex, Pfc,
Safine, Albert L., Major,
Samsel, Edward, Pfc,
Sanders, Robert W., Capt,
Sapiro, Saul J., Capt,
Saraver, Alvin R., T/4,
Sarazin, Charles H., Jr., Pfc,
Saunders, Robert A., WOJG,
Savacool, John K., T/5,
Saylor, Samuel L., Major,
Scagliarini, George, Pfc,
Schafer, Robert F., T/4,
Schear, Dwight B., T/4,
Scherer, John W., Jr., Pfc,
Scheuer, Frank E., Pfc,
Schlichter, Robert J., Capt,
Schmidt, Eduardo Z., Pfc,
Schmidt, Eldon W., CWO,
Schownwolf, William L., Pfc,
Schueneman, Wilbur C., Pfc,
Schuller, Wm. J., Pfc,
Schulte, Elmer F., Pfc,
Schultz, George H., Pfc,
Schulz, Donald W., Pfc,
Schwalb, Junior C., T/5,
Scott, Hugh A., Major,
Seal, William J., Pfc,
Secrist, Harold C., Pfc,
Seibt, Lawrence H., Pfc,
Seigler, Walter J., Pfc,
Seminara, Phillip C., Pfc,
Sesto, Anthony, Pfc,
Seymour, Lawrence C., Pfc,
Shaffer, Walter A., Sgt,
Sharp, William D., Pfc,
Shaw, Robert C., Major,
Sheldon, Clyde L., Pfc,
Shell, Thomas E., Cpl,
Shelton, Crowell B., Major,
Shepard, W. P., Brig Gen,
Sherman, Harry B., Col,
Sherman, Jack W., Pvt,
Sherman, Warren L., T/Sgt,
Sheilds, Derrill E., Major,
Shields, Robert F., Pfc,
Shively, Clair C., Pfc,
Shuman, Preston N., Pfc,
Siblini, Mohammed, Pfc,
Sicinski, Stanley J., Cpl,
Siegel, Joseph, Jr., T/4,
Sigler, Douglas J., Pvt,
Silver, Irwin, Pfc,
Sim, Gee H., Pfc,
Simigi, Arthur E., Sgt,
Simons, Raymond G., T/5,
Sims, Howard W., Pfc,
Siporin, Mitchell, Pfc,
Sipple, James W., Pfc,
Sivess, Theodore A., Pfc,
Skrzypcyk, Ladislaus J., T/4,
Smart, Alvin L., Pfc,
Smith, Donald E., Pfc,
Smith, Donald S., M/Sgt,
Smith, Harold L., Pfc,
Smith, Henry C., Pfc,
Smith, Jobie R., Pfc,
Smith, Joyce M., Sgt,
Smith, Lavern P., Pfc,
Smith, Lawrence O., Pfc,
Smith, Lewis B., Pfc,
Smith, Ralph J., Lt Col,
Smith, Tommy C., Pfc,
Smith, William G., Pvt,
Smith, William T., T/5,
Snyder, Arthur, Lt Col,
Snyder, John M., Pfc,
Soderstrom, Harold C., T/4,
Sorrell, Clinton L., Pfc,
Spain, Paul T., Pfc,
Spangler, James E., Pfc,
Spoelstra, Gael G., Pfc,
Sporleder, Wilbur R., T/4,
Spott, Wm. A., Jr., T/5,
Spreyer, Frederick C., Major,
Sproesser, Nils A., M/Sgt,
Staffen, Edward P.,
Stanley, Dale P., Pfc,
Stanley, Paul W., Capt,
Stapelton, Samuel J., Pfc,
Stark, Orville B., Pfc,
Starr, Lawrence B., Pfc,
Stasyshyn, Lawrence B., Pfc,
St. Clair, Gilbert C., Capt,
Steich, Harold E., Pfc,
Steinborn, Ralph F., M/Sgt,
Steinborn, Ralph T., Pfc,

† Killed in Action. * Prisoner of War. ‡ Missing in Action. § Died of Wounds.

Steiner, Harold B., Pfc,
Stepanon, John B., Pfc,
‡Stern, Ernest, Pfc,
Stewart, Charles E., Major
Stoffer, Leward D., Pfc,
Stoll, Henry C., S/Sgt,
Storey, Earl W., T/5,
Strickland, William F., Pfc,
Sticker, Joseph W., Pfc,
Stroud, William F., Pvt,
Struckmeyer, Frederick C., 2nd
Sturgill, Willie, Pfc,
Sullivan, Edward J., CWO,
Sullivan, David E., Cpl,
Summers, Marion A., T/4,
Sunday, Levi L., Pvt,
Sutton, Roy L., Pvt,
Swanberg, Charles, Jr., Capt,
Swarthout, Glendon F., T/4,
Sweigard, Harold H., Pfc,
Sybouts, Lawrence, T/3,
Sydelo, Michail P., Pfc,
Sykes, Stanley M., Pfc,

Tabor, William C., Pfc,
Taggart, Donald G., 1st Lt,
Tait, Ernest E., Pfc,
Talarico, Albert, S/Sgt,

Taylor, James W., Capt,
Taylor, Lawrence, Pfc,
Telleck, Anthony, 1st Lt
Terrall, James, 1st Lt
Thomas, Felix A., S/Sgt,
Thomas, Jesse F., Major
Thompson, Floyd W., T/4,
Thompson, M. C., Jr., Sgt,
Thrall, Leo, T/5,
Tidwell, Jack N., 1st Lt,
Tilghman, Marion E., Pvt,
Tilley, Delmar O., Cpl,
Tomczak, Theodore, Pfc,
Tompkins, Chester E., Pfc,
Trapp, Ernst W., Pfc,
Traylor, Jesse R., T/4,
Treby, Harold E., Capt,
Trine, Jerry B., Pfc,
Troje, Bernard M., Pfc,
Troth, Edward A., T/4,
Truscott, Lucian K., Maj Gen
Turkovich, Albert P., Pfc,
Turner, Hiram, T/5,
Tuton, George R., Cpl,
Twachtman, Paul, 1st Lt
Tyler, Howard L., S/Sgt,
Tyler, James M., T/5,
Tyler, James P., CWO,

Uhlmann, F. F., Jr., Pvt,
Ullenberg, Ralph J., Pfc,

Vaccaro, Frank N., 1st Lt,
Vaclavek, William, Pfc,
Valdez, Augustine, Pfc,
Vancampen, Benjamin H., Pfc,
Vanderwalde, Herbert, Pfc,
Van Sickle, Robert E., 1st Lt,
Varley, Thomas S., Pfc,
Vaught, Carl M., Pfc,
Venezia, Anthony A., Pfc,
VerMeer, Henry, Cpl,
Villegas, Mike V., T/Sgt,
Visko, George W., Pfc,
Vogt, Oswald R., Pfc,
Voight, Erich G., Sgt,
Vranka, Randolph L., S/Sgt,
Vroaman, Albert L., Pfc,

Wake, Arthur H., Jr., Pfc,
Walden, Ernest A., Pfc,
Wallace, Charles R., T/5,
Wallack, Samuel, T/4,
Walter, Mercer C., Lt Col
Ward, Carroll A., WOJG,
Washburn, William C., 1st Lt
Waters, Charles H., T/5,
Watts, Frank M., T/3,

Weidanz, Theodore, Jr., Pfc,
Weisner, Gordon R., Pvt,
Weitzel, William A., Lt Col
Weitzman, William, S/Sgt,
Welch, Albra D., Pfc,
Wells, George, Pfc,
Wells, Jones, Sgt,
Wertman, Harry F., Pfc,
Wexler, Leo A., T/5,
White, Eugene D., 2nd Lt
White, George M., T/5,
Whitley, Herson L., Sgt,
Whitley, Daniel L., Pfc,
Wickersham, Daniel L., Major,
Wigetman, Harold, 1st Lt
Wilk, Anthony, Pfc,
Williams, Clyde J., Cpl,
Williams, Clyde T., Pfc,
Williams, Duart M., S/Sgt,
Williams, Irving B., 1st Lt,
Williams, Ralph R., S/Sgt,
Williams, Troy, Pfc,
Wilson, Evan K., Pvt,
Wilson, Grover, Lt Col
Wilson, James M., 1st Lt
Winegar, Charles A., Pfc,
Wing, Paul W., Pfc,
Winter, Arthur A., Pfc,

Witbracht, Donald R., T/5,
Wojeik, Ted, Pfc,
Wolfe, Jack H., T/Sgt,
Wong, James K. Y., Pfc,
Wong, Roland C., Pfc,
Wong, Sing, Pfc,
Woo, Sun Y, T/5,
Woodley, LeRoy B., 1st Lt,
Woods, John F., Pfc,
Woodward, Marcus C., CWO,
Woodyard, Williard A., Capt
Works, Bill B., Pfc,
Wright, Woodrow J., 2nd Lt,
Wyss, Maurice, 1st Lt

Yackle, Herbert W., Pfc,
Yatsco, Andrew T., Pfc,
Yee, Wing S., Pfc,
You, Chin, Pfc,
§Young, Arthur L., Pfc,
Young, Frank, Pfc,
Young, Robert L., Pfc,
Young, Robert N., Brig Gen,

Zarb, Ferdinand F., Pfc,
Zell, William R., Pfc,
Zernich, Wallace, Pvt,
Zinn, Rudolph P., M/Sgt,
Zylberburg, David, Pfc.

† Killed in Action.   * Prisoner of War.   ‡ Missing in Action.   § Died of Wounds.

7TH INFANTRY REGIMENT

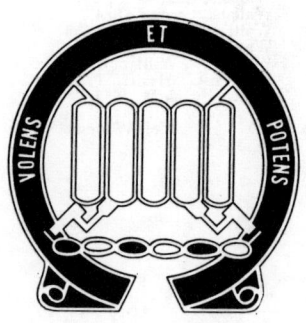

The "Cotton Balers," who gained that nickname for the use they made of cotton bales in the battle for New Orleans during the war with Britain 1812-1814, were first organized in 1798, mustered out in 1800, and re-organized in 1808, with continuous service dating from that time. As such they are the second oldest regiment in the United States Army.

The 7th received its baptism of fire against the British at Villiere's Plantation, Louisiana, in December, 1814. Two weeks later it won undying fame in the Battle of New Orleans. From 1815 to 1846 the regiment was stationed at Fort Gibson, now the site of Muskogee, Okla., and participated in numerous operations against the Indians.

Between 1839 and 1842 it took part in the Florida War against the Seminoles and their chief Osceola.

In 1846, when difficulties with Mexico became serious, the 7th Infantry was concentrated at Corpus Christi, Texas, then moved to the Rio Grande. The regiment next went to Monterrey. It joined in the siege of Vera Cruz, which ended in the Mexican capitulation in March, 1847. The 7th marched into the interior, winning recognition for capturing the heights of Cerro Gordo, carrying the entrenchments of Contreras and Churubusco, and finally the works of Chapultepec. It entered Mexico City on Sept. 14, 1847.

The 7th Infantry served throughout the Civil War, and participated in the following engagements: Mesilla, 1861; Valverde, Corinth, Fredericksburg and Murfreesboro, 1862; Chancellorsville, Hoover's Gap, Gettysburg, Chickamauga, Siege of Chattanooga and Missionary Ridge, 1863; Resaca, New Hope Church, Neal Dale Station and Siege of Atlanta, 1864.

It also participated in many Indian campaigns and is remembered as the regiment which was sent to relieve Custer. The 7th Infantry's last operation against the Indians was in 1891.

During the war with Spain the 7th fought in Cuba, at El Caney and San Juan Heights, and followed that with service in the Philippines and Alaska.

On Nov. 23, 1917, the 7th Infantry became part of the 3d Division and has been a member of the Division ever since. In World War I it fought with distinction in the Aisne Defensive, Champagne-Marne Defensive, Aisne-Marne Offensive and the Meuse-Argonne Offensive. For its great fighting on French soil the regiment was awarded the Croix de Guerre with Star by a grateful French government.

After serving in the Army of Occupation in Germany the regiment returned to the United States in August, 1919. Following brief stays at a number of posts the 7th moved to Vancouver Barracks and was stationed at Fort Lewis, Wash., when war was declared Dec. 8, 1941.

7TH INFANTRY*

Regimental Commander

(Highest rank held)	Held pos. from	To	(Highest rank held)	from	To
Col. Robert C. Macon		18 Feb 1943	Col. Wiley H. O'Mohundro	11 Mar 1944	21 Aug 1944
Col. Harry B. Sherman	19 Feb 1943	16 Feb 1944	Col. Ben Harrell	22 Aug 1944	1 Dec 1944
Col. William O. Darby	17 Feb 1944	18 Feb 1944	Lt. Col. Frank M. Izenour	2 Dec 1944	3 Dec 1944
Col. Wiley H. O'Mohundro	19 Feb 1944	26 Feb 1944	Lt. Col. Clayton C. Thobro	4 Dec 1944	4 Dec 1944
Col. Harry B. Sherman	27 Feb 1944	10 Mar 1944	Col. John A. Heintges	5 Dec 1944	

Regimental Executive Officer

(Highest rank held)	from	to	(Highest rank held)	from	to
Lt. Col. John O. Williams		11 Feb 1943	Lt. Col. Wiley H. O'Mohundro	27 Feb 1944	10 Mar 1944
Lt. Col. Rafael L. Salzmann	12 Feb 1943	28 Feb 1943	Lt. Col. John J. Toffey, Jr.	13 Mar 1944	2 June 1944
Lt. Col. John O. Williams	1 Mar 1943	15 July 1943	Lt. Col. Victor E. Sinclair	17 June 1944	1 Sept 1944
Maj. William B. Rosson	16 July 1943	24 July 1943	Lt. Col. Jesse F. Thomas	2 Sept 1944	14 Sept 1944
Lt. Col. Roy E. Moore	25 July 1943	6 Jan 1944	Lt. Col. Frank M. Izenour	15 Sept 1944	4 Dec 1944
Lt. Col. James E. Breth	7 Jan 1944	10 Jan 1944	Lt. Col. Clayton C. Thobro	5 Dec 1944	25 Feb 1945
Lt. Col. Roy E. Moore	11 Jan 1944	4 Feb 1944	Lt. Col. Lloyd B. Ramsey	26 Feb 1945	
Lt. Col. Ashton H. Manhart	5 Feb 1944	13 Feb 1944			

1st Battalion Commander

(Highest rank held)	from	to	(Highest rank held)	from	to
Lt. Col. Roy E. Moore		11 Feb 1943	Lt. Col. Frank M. Izenour	13 Mar 1944	14 Sept 1944
Maj. Everett W. Duvall	12 Feb 1943	28 Feb 1943	Lt. Col. Jesse F. Thomas	15 Sept 1944	14 Oct 1944
Lt. Col. Roy E. Moore	1 Mar 1943	24 July 1943	Maj. Benjamin C. Boyd	15 Oct 1944	30 Oct 1944
Lt. Col. Frank M. Izenour	25 July 1943	29 Jan 1944	Lt. Col. Kenneth Wallace	31 Oct 1944	
Maj. Frank C. Sinsel	30 Jan 1944	12 Mar 1944			

2d Battalion Commander

(Highest rank held)	from	to	(Highest rank held)	from	to
Lt. Col. Rafael L. Salzmann		3 Mar 1943	Lt. Col. Everett W. Duvall	23 Oct 1943	10 Nov 1943
*Maj. Everett W. Duvall	13 April 1943	28 June 1943	Maj. John A. Elterich	11 Nov 1943	9 Jan 1944
Maj. John A. Elterich	29 June 1943	3 July 1943	Lt. Col. Everett W. Duvall	10 Jan 1944	15 July 1944
Maj. Everett W. Duvall	4 July 1943	23 Sept 1943	Lt. Col. Clayton C. Thobro	16 July 1944	3 Dec 1944
*Lt. Col. Everett W. Duvall	5 Oct 1943	17 Oct 1943	Maj. Robert D. Marsh	4 Dec 1944	5 Dec 1944
*Maj. John A. Elterich	18 Oct 1943	22 Oct 1943	Lt. Col. Jack M. Duncan	6 Dec 1944	

3d Battalion Commander

(Highest rank held)	from	to	(Highest rank held)	from	to
Maj. Eugene H. Cloud		11 Nov 1942	Maj. Lloyd B. Ramsey	13 Mar 1944	25 Mar 1944
Lt. Col. Robert C. Williams, Jr.	12 Nov 1942	11 Feb 1943	Lt. Col. William A. Weitzel	26 Mar 1944	21 April 1944
Maj. Carroll A. Plaquet	12 Feb 1943	28 Feb 1943	Lt. Col. Arthur J. Smith, Jr.	22 April 1944	24 May 1944
Maj. Carroll A. Plaquet	4 Mar 1943	24 April 1943	Maj. Glenn E. Rathbun	25 May 1944	21 June 1944
Maj. Mark E. Cory, Jr.	25 April 1943	27 April 1943	Maj. Lloyd B. Ramsey	22 June 1944	2 Oct 1944
Maj. Carroll A. Plaquet	28 April 1943	31 May 1943	Maj. Ralph M. Flynn	4 Dec 1944	15 Dec 1944
Lt. Col. Frank M. Izenour	1 June 1943	3 July 1943	Capt. Robert V. Horton	16 Dec 1944	17 Dec 1944
Lt. Col. John A. Heintges	4 July 1943	17 Nov 1943	Maj. Ralph M. Flynn	18 Dec 1944	19 Dec 1944
Lt. Col. William B. Rosson	18 Nov 1943	23 Feb 1944	Lt. Col. Lloyd B. Ramsey	20 Dec 1944	25 Feb 1945
Lt. Col. John A. Heintges	24 Feb 1944	3 Mar 1944	Maj. Ralph M. Flynn	26 Feb 1945	4 May 1945
Maj. Clayton C. Thobro	4 Mar 1944	12 Mar 1944	Capt. Robert V. Horton	5 May 1945	

*The names and positions held apply only from Nov. 8, 1942 to May 8, 1945 (V-E Day). Neither opening nor closing dates of service are listed.

7TH INFANTRY REGIMENT

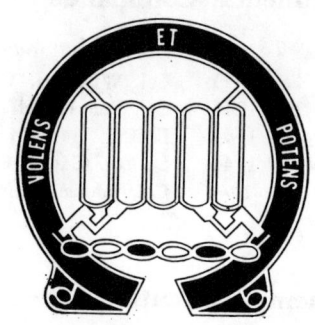

Aalderks, John A., Sgt,
Aaron, Arlice O., Pfc,
Aaron, Hubert L., S/Sgt,
Aaron, Juland A., Pfc,
Aaronson, Max, 1st Lt,
Abandt, James H., Pfc,
Abbott, Howard I., Pvt,
Abele, Chester H., Pvt,
Abelson, Leonard, Pvt,
‡Abercrombie, Irby, Pvt,
Abernathy, Herrod H., Pvt,
Abernathy, James, T/5,
Abernathy, John C., S/Sgt,
Abendroth, Joseph R., Pvt,
†Abernathy, Thomas C., Pvt,
*Abernathy, Walter T., Pfc,
†Abney, Alvie, Pfc,
Abraham, Frank J., Pfc,
Abraham, Philip E., Pvt,
Abraham, Philip E., Pvt,
Abrams, Michael, Pfc,
Abrams, Robert E., Pvt,
Abrams, Sollie, Pfc,
Abrescia, Anthony J., Sgt,
Abt, Theodore R., Pfc,
Accurio, Joseph W., Pfc,
Acedo, Usbaldo C., Pvt,
Ach, Vernon E., Pvt,
Achenbach, William T., Pfc,
†Achorn, Elmer A., Pvt,
§Acker, Frank, T/Sgt,
Ackerman, Raymond S., Pvt,
Ackerman, Sam, Pvt,
†Ackley, Kenneth R., Pvt,
Ackerman, Robert W., Pvt,
Acord, Wilbur W., Pvt,
Acosta, Julio S., Pfc,
Acuna, Juan V., Pvt,
Acy, Charles F., Pvt,
Adair, John H., S/Sgt,
Adair, Virgil D., Pfc,
†Adam, Armand, Pvt,
Adam, Harry J., Pvt,
Adam, Hubert B., Sgt,
†Adamaitis, Frank J., Pvt,
†Adamian, Vahey A. J., Pvt,
Adamonis, Walter F., Pvt,
Adams, Car K., Pfc,
Adams, Clyde E., Jr., Pfc,
Adams, Darrell V., Sgt,
Adams, Edmond M., Pfc,
Adams, Eugene B., S/Sgt,
Adams, Floyd W., T/Sgt,
Adams, George G., Pvt,
Adams, Harold L., Pfc,
Adams, Howard P., T/5,
Adams, James E., Pvt,
†Adams, John R., Pvt,
Adams, Lee S., Pvt,
Adams, Lewis E., Pfc,
Adams, Luis P., S/Sgt,
Adams, Morris M., Pvt,
Adams, Oscar R., Pfc,
Adams, Patrick E., 2nd Lt,
†Adams, Paul E., Pfc,
Adams, Ray S., Pfc,
Adams, Raymond, Pvt,
Adams, Robert P., 2nd Lt,
Adams, Rollen D., Pfc,
Adams, Thomas C., Sgt,
‡Adams, Walter M., Cpl,
Adams, William B., Pvt,
Adams, William P., Pfc,
Adams, William W., Pfc,
Adamski, Mathew A., Pfc,
*Adamson, Leonard M., Pfc,
Adamus, Andrew T., Pvt,
Adaskin, Saul, S/Sgt,

Adcock, Lee A., Sgt,
†Addis, Gerald J., S/Sgt,
Addison, Sherman, Pvt,
Addor, Blair F., Sgt,
Addy, Gordon R., Pfc,
Ade, John J., T/5,
Adelstein, Harold S., Pvt,
†Aderhold, Calvin D., Pfc,
†Adkins, Clyde J., Pfc,
‡Adkins, Earl, Jr., Pvt,
*Adkins, George D., Cpl,
Adkins, Herbert, Pfc,
†Adkins, James K., Pfc,
Adkins, Oscar T., Cpl,
Adler, Harold, Pfc,
Adler, Sidney, Pfc,
Adolphson, Emil E., 1st Sgt,
Adrian, Edward, Pvt,
Aemmer, Robert M., T/Sgt,
Aeschliman, Karl K., Pfc,
Affholter, John A., Pvt,
Affinito, Clement P., Cpl,
‡Agee, Henry L., Pfc,
Agee, William S., Pvt,
Ager, Clair P., Pfc,
Agostine, Rocco M., Sgt,
Agresta, Dominic, Pvt,
Agrista, Dominic S., Cpl,
*Aguirre, Emelio, Pvt,
Aguirre, Pablo N., Jr., Pvt,
Ahlers, Joseph H., Pfc,
Ahlfs, John H., T/4,
Ahrman, Frank H., Pvt,
Aimonetti, John J., Pfc,
Aicher, Charles F., Pvt,
†Aiello, Frank T., Pvt,
Ainsworth, James L., Jr., Pvt,
‡Airis, Robert M., Pvt,
Airth, Edward W., Pfc,
Akagi, Joseph, Sgt,
*Ake, James W., Pfc,
Aker, Ga, Cpl,
*Akerblom, Gastav H., Pfc,
Akers, Leonard E., S/Sgt,
Albano, Anthony J., Pfc,
Alarie, John B., Capt,
Albee, Clarence V., Pfc,
Albert, Hilmore B., Pvt,
Albert, Hyman, Pvt,
†Albert, Thomas A., Pvt,
Alberts, Stephen J., Pfc,
Albertson, Alfred R., Pfc,
Albertson, Carl U., 2nd Lt,
†Albertson, Orville C., Sgt,
*Albright, Wayne O., Pfc,
Albrightson, Harry E., T/5,
Albrightson, Joe, Pfc,
†Albritton, Joe C., 1st Lt,
†Albritton, Walter V., Sgt,
†Albus, Richard F., Pfc,
Alcoe, Edgar L., 2nd Lt,
Alday, Albert, Pfc,
†Alder, Arthur H., T/5,
Alder, Melvin D., Pvt,
Alder, Willis F., S/Sgt,
Alderman, Jesse G., Pvt,
Alderman, Woodrow W., Pvt,
Alderson, Wayne T., Pfc,
‡Aldis, Wallace R., Pvt,
Aldous, Vincent A., Pvt,
Aldrich Byron A., Pfc,
Aldridge, Ambers T., Pfc,
Aldridge, Elwood L., Pfc,
Alesandrini, Raymond E., Pvt,
Alex, Edward A., Pfc,
‡Alexakos, James G., 1st Sgt,
Alexander, Dan R., Pfc,
Alexander, Frank J., Pfc,

Alexander, Harold I., 1st Lt,
Alexander, Henry, Pvt,
Alexander, Jimmie L., Pfc,
†Alexander, John F., T/5,
Alexander, Johnny E., Pvt,
Alexander, Raymond G., Pfc,
Alexander, Vernol E., S/Sgt,
Alexandresen, Carl A., Pvt,
Alf, Leonard F., S/Sgt,
Alfano, Joseph A., Pfc,
†Alfier, Nicholas, T/5,
Alfieri, Louis P., Pvt,
Alford, Curtis E., Pfc,
Alger, John F., Pfc,
Aline, Robert F., Capt,
Alix, Rodolphe A., S/Sgt,
Alkire, Pete R., S/Sgt,
Allan, George R., Jr., Pvt,
Allard, Albert, Jr., T/5,
Allard, Joseph F., Pvt,
*Allardise, John D., 1st Lt,
Alle, Harold W., Pvt,
Allen, Alonze, Pvt,
Allen, August A., Pvt,
Allen, Donald C., T/4,
Allen, Doyle, Pfc,
Allen, Earl L., Pfc,
†Allen, Elvin C., Pvt,
Allen, Gerald F., T/5,
Allen, Harry W., Sgt,
Allen, James D., T/4,
Allen, James M., Pfc,
Allen, John H., Pvt,
Allen, John F., Pfc,
Allen, Joseph P., Pfc,
Allen, Malcolm L., T/4,
Allen, Robert M., Pfc,
Allen, Robert C., Pfc,
Allen, Richard, Pvt,
Allen, Stanley N., Pvt,
Allen, Victor W., Pvt,
Allen, William E., Pfc,
Allen, William S., T/Sgt,
‡Allenmand, John E., Pvt,
Alley, Clyde W., Pvt,
†Alley, Willis D., Pfc,
†Allford, Roy H., Pvt,
Allhands, Quentin C., Pfc,
Allie, John, Jr., Pfc,
Allison, Floyd O, Cpl,
†Allison, George G., T/Sgt,
Allison, Herman L., Pfc,
Allison, William J., Pvt,
Allison, William F., Pfc,
Allman, Loyal C.,
Allred, John W., Pvt,
‡Allshouse, Gladwin E., Pfc,
*Allyn, James L., Pfc,
Almon, William F., S/Sgt,
Almquist, J. H., Jr., 2nd Lt,
Alonze, Joe L., Pfc,
Alpert, Samuel, Sgt,
Alterski, Henry J., Jr., Pvt,
†Althouse, Robert E., Pvt,
Altman, Ben, Pvt,
Altman, Enos R., Sgt,
Altmayer, Arthur J., Pvt,
‡Alto, Donald A., Sgt,
Alton, Chester M., Pvt,
Altorfer, Kenneth J., 1st Lt,
Altshuler, Robert L., 1st Lt,
Alvarez, Angel, Pvt,
†Alverson, Clyde H., Pvt,
*Alyne, Alfred E., Pvt,
Amador, Arthur P., Sgt,
Amarante, Stephen, T/5,
Amato, Salvatore J., Pfc,
†Amatucci, Severino, Pvt,

Ambrose, Augustus M., Pvt,
Amburgey, Billie, S/Sgt,
Amen, Robert C., Pvt,
†Amendola, Julio F., Pfc,
Ames, Adrian D., Pfc,
Amici, Anthony C., Pvt,
Amolsch, James E., Pvt,
†Amore, George L., Pvt,
Amrein, Albert G., T/5,
Amrheim, Paul F., T/Sgt,
Amundson, Ernest M., Sgt,
Amuso, Michael J., Pfc,
Ananich, John, Jr., 1st Lt,
Anaya, Jose D., Pvt,
†Ancanage, Joseph S., 2nd Lt,
Andenno, Anthony J., Pfc,
Andercyk, Frank, Pvt,
Anderegg, Charles, Pvt,
†Andersen, Thomas J., Pvt,
Anderson, Aubrey H., Pfc,
Anderson, Benjamin R., Pvt,
Anderson, Casper J., Pfc,
Anderson, Charles A., Pvt,
Anderson, Charles B., Pfc,
†Anderson, Chester A., Pvt,
Anderson, Clarence, Pvt,
†Anderson, Claude E., Pvt,
Anderson, Donald C., S/Sgt,
Anderson, Dwaine W., Pfc,
Anderson, Ebbie L., Sgt,
Anderson, Edward C., Pfc,
Anderson, Elmer A., Pfc,
Anderson, Elmer H., Pvt,
Anderson, Franklin K., Sgt,
Anderson, Fred G., S/Sgt,
Anderson, General G., Pfc,
Anderson, George W., Pvt,
Anderson, Harold L., Pfc,
†Anderson, Gordon A., Sgt,
Anderson, George, Pvt,
Anderson, Harry B., Jr., Pfc,
Anderson, Hilmer E., Pvt,
Anderson, James F., Pvt,
Anderson, James H., Cpl,
Anderson, John E., Pfc,
Anderson, John M., Pvt,
Anderson, Kenneth B., Pfc,
Anderson, Kent C., Pvt,
Anderson, Lee L., Pfc,
Anderson, Marion W., Pvt,
Anderson, Marvin J., T/4,
Anderson, Maurice E., Pfc,
Anderson, Merle A., Pfc,
†Anderson, Nathan E., Pfc,
Anderson, Nathan K., 2nd Lt,
Anderson, Olaf A., Pfc,
Anderson, Paul, S/Sgt,
Anderson, Oliver J., Pfc,
Anderson, Otis C., 2nd Lt,
Anderson, Paul, Pvt,
Anderson, Percy L., S/Sgt,
Anderson, Raymond C., Pfc,
Anderson, Raymond W., Pfc,
Anderson, Robert, Sgt,
†Anderson, Robert L., Pfc,
Anderson, Robert P., Pfc,
Anderson, Rufus W., Pfc,
Anderson, Russell C., Pvt,
Anderson, Ruthford A., Pvt,
Anderson, Thomas G., T/4,
Anderson, Victor A., Pfc,
Anderson, Wallace P., Pfc,
‡Anderson, William D., Sgt,
Anderson, Joseph L., T/4,
Andreski, Edward M., Pvt,
*Andress, Floyd J., Sgt,
Andrews, Arthur C., Pfc,
Andrews, Francis F., 1st Sgt,

Andrews, James W., Pfc,
Andrews, Leo V., Pvt,
Andrews, Lloyd J., T/4,
Andrews, Roland C., Pfc,
Andrews, Walter W., Pvt,
Androsian, Sarkis, Pfc,
Andruski, Edward F., Pfc,
Angel, Elmer, T/Sgt,
Angeles, John A., Pvt,
Ange, Lloyd C., Pvt,
*Angel, Luther E., Pvt,
†Angley, Carl J., Pvt,
Anglim, William F., Pvt,
†Anglin, James H., Pvt,
Annable, Kenneth M., Sgt,
Annen, Forrest D., 1st Lt,
Anshe, Norton, Pfc,
†Anson, Charles K., Cpl,
Antebi, Joseph, Pfc,
Antelope, George W., Pfc,
Anthony, Alvin W., Pfc,
Anthony, Buri W., Pvt,
Anthony, Robert E., Pvt,
Anthony, William D., Capt,
Anthony, William J., Pfc,
Antill, Robert A., Pvt,
Antkowiak, Anthony S., Pvt,
Antolik, John A., Pfc,
Anton, Arthur H., Pfc,
Antonson, Charles R., Pvt,
Antonucci, Salvatore A., S/Sgt,
Anzalone, Romeo T., Pfc,
Apkarian, Richard B., T/5,
Apoldite, Andrew F., Pfc,
Apostolakes, Louis, Pfc,
Appel, Robert S., Pfc,
Appice, John J., Pfc,
Apple, Raymond E., Pfc,
*Appleby, Gerald V., Pfc,
Appleby, William C., Pvt,
Applegate, Charles L., Pvt,
*Aprimis, Frank M., Pfc,
‡Aragon, Cecilio L., Pvt,
Aragon, Filiberto, Pvt,
Arambula, John M., T/5,
Arb, Weldon E., Pvt,
Arcaro, Joseph N., 2nd Lt,
†Archabal, John R., Pvt,
Archambault, Albert, Cpl,
†Archer, Davis M., Cpl,
Archer, Urban M., Cpl,
Archuleta, Esequel Z., Pvt,
Arcoren, Alfred M., Pvt,
Arena, Joseph, Pvt,
Arends, Thomas, Pvt,
Arendt, Richard G., Pfc,
Argo, Charles, Sgt,
Ariail, Thomas M., Capt,
Arledge, Charlie, Pfc,
Armel, Julian K., T/5,
Armentrout, Harold J., Sgt,
Armes, Eldred, Pvt,
Armetta, Manuel F., Pfc,
*Armijo, Francis C., S/Sgt,
Armoian, Aram Y., Pvt,
‡Arms, Radford L., Pfc,
Armstrong, Charles A., S/Sgt,
Armstrong, William J., T/5,
Arndt, Emil H., Pfc,
Arndt, Roland J., Pfc,
†Arnett, Archie W., Sgt,
Arnett, Blaine A., T/Sgt,
Arnett, James H., Pvt,
Arnold, Archie L., Sgt,
†Arnold, Bryan L., Pvt,
Arnold, Clarence W., T/Sgt,
Arnold, Willie C., Sgt,
Arnold, William E., Pvt,

† Killed in Action.   * Prisoner of War.   ‡ Missing in Action.   § Died of Wounds.

Arnold, William L., Pfc,
Arnone, Frank C., Sgt,
Arnopp, John T., Pfc,
Arrington, John D., Pfc,
Arruda, John, Pfc,
†Arrowsmith, Stanley,1/Sgt,
Arslanian, Paul T., Pfc,
†Arsenault, George C., Sgt,
Arthur, Omer E., T/5,
Arthur, Wayne R., Sgt,
Arvin, Martin L., S/Sgt,
Arredono, Guadalupe Q., Pvt,
Arwood, Ernest C., Sgt,
Asberry, Omer G., Pfc,
Ascienzo, John L., Pvt,
†Ascolese, Dominick S., Pfc,
Ash, Ameil M., Cpl,
Ash, Donald F., Pvt,
Ashby, Tuell D., Pfc,
Ashcraft, William A., Pfc,
Asher, Lester J., T/4,
Asher, William H., T/4,
Ashford, Lee S., S/Sgt.
‡Ashforth, George Jr., Pfc,
Ashley, Charles S., Pfc,
Ashton, John G., Pfc,
†Asimus, Earl E., Pfc,
Asin, Carlos C., Pfc,
Aswegan, Luke, Jr., Pfc,
‡Atencie, Armando S., Pvt,
Athhas, William P., Capt,
Atherton, Paul R., 2nd Lt,
†Atkins, Charles L., Pvt,
Atkins, George P., T/5,
Atkins, Nathaniel, Pfc,
Atkins, Tillman A., Cpl,
Atkins, Wylie C., Pfc,
Atkinson, Atley A., Pvt,
Attenberg, Joseph G., Pfc,
Atte, Walter F., Pvt,
Atwater, Bennie M., S/Sgt,
Aubel, Harvey J., S/Sgt,
Auclair, Armand J., Pvt,
Auger, Roy J., Pvt,
Aughtman, John T., Pfc,
Augustino, Albert G., T/5,
Augustson, Leslie G., Sgt,
†Augustyn, Anthony S., Sgt,
Aurand, Hoover B., Pfc,
Aurness, James K., Pvt,
Ausburne, Robert L., Pvt,
Austin, Ernest E., Pvt,
†Austin, Marvin T., Pvt,
Austin, Reginald T., Pfc,
Austin, Relle B., Pfc,
Austin, Robert C., Pvt,
Austin, Robert W., Pvt,
Austin, Roswell P., Pfc,
Austin, Willard M., Pfc,
†Austrick, Albert B., Pvt,
Auteri, Leonard J., Pvt,
Autilio, Emanuel R., Pfc,
Auwarter, Henry D., Pvt,
Avallone, Anthony V., Pvt,
Aven, Bruce A., S/Sgt,
Averett, Vergil H., Pfc,
Avery, William D., Sgt,
†Avilla, Salvador S., Pfc,
Avina, Victor V., Pvt,
Ayala, Esteban, Sgt,
Aycock, Ernest C., Jr., S/Sgt,
Ayers, Eugene C., Pvt,
‡Ayers, James W., Pfc,
Ayers, Lowell F., Pvt,
Ayres, Rolland W., Pvt,
Axelson, Robert J., Pfc,
†Azzata, Frank, Pvt,

†Babbs, Charles E., Pvt,
Babcock, Frank E., Pfc,
Babcock, Godfrey, Pfc,
Babcock, Joseph, S/Sgt,
Babcock, Paul F., Pvt,
†Baber, John M., Jr., Pvt,
Babey, Michael P., Pfc,
Babich, Morris L., Pvt,
Babincsak, Jesse C., Pvt,
†Babineaux, Curley, Pfc,
Babinka, Michael, Jr., Pfc,
Baccash, George, Pvt,
Bachenberg, Harold, T/5,
Bachmeyer, Raymond N., Pfc,
Bachert, Joseph P., Pvt,
Bacigalupa, Louis A., Sgt,
Back, John E., Cpl,
Backa, Sulo A., Pfc,
Backman, Emil A., T/5,
Backus, Floyd J., T/Sgt,
Backus, Calvin A., Pvt,
Bacon, Eugene, Capt,
Bacon, Joe B., Pfc,
Bacon, Paul E., Pfc,
Bacon, Samuel R., S/Sgt,
Baden, Elton, Pfc,
Baete, Maurice F., Pfc,
Bagatini, Alfred V., Pfc,
†Baggs, Robert W., Pvt,
Bagley, Ross T., Pfc,
Bagwell, Clifton C.,Pvt,
Bah, Wallace K., S/Sgt,
‡Bahia, Francis J., Pvt,
Baier, George W., Pvt,
Bailey, Alfred B., Pvt,
*Bailey, Amos, T/4,
Bailey, Herman B., Pfc,
Bailey, Horace J., Pvt,
Bailey, Howard L., Pfc,
Bailey, Leo B., Jr., Pfc,
Bailey, Mac W., Pfc,
Bailey, Marvin L., Pfc,
Bailey, Quentin W., Cpl,
Bailey, Roland, T/5,
Bailey, Roy, Pfc,
§Bailey, Theodore, Pfc,
Bailey, Thomas, Pvt,
Bailey, Urbine A., Pvt,
Bailey, William L., Pvt,
Bailey, William L., T/Sgt,
Bailey, Willis, Pvt,
†Baillargeon, Maurice, Pvt,
Bain, George E., Pfc,
Bain, Paul L., S/Sgt,
Baird, Forrest W., T/5,
Baird, George B., Pfc,
Baird, James H., Pvt,
Baird, Joseph E., Pvt,
Baird, William D., Pfc,
Bajner, Rudolph C., Pvt,
*Bak, Edward P., Pfc,
Bakalyar, Arthur C., Pvt,
Baker, Alvin G., Pfc,
Baker, Arnold J., Pfc,
Baker, Brown, Pfc,
†Baker, Donald J., Sr., Pfc,
Baker, Douglas M., Pfc,
Baker, Edsel R., Pfc,
Baker, Ellis J., Pvt,
Baker, Floyd C., Pvt,
Baker, Fred, T/5,
Baker, Frederick E., Pfc,
Baker, George B., Jr., Pvt,
†Baker, George J., Pvt,
Baker, George W., Pvt,
Baker, Jack E., Pvt,
Baker, James B., Pfc,
Baker, James H., Pfc,
Baker, Jarrett J., Pvt,
Baker, Jay L., Pfc,
Baker, John T., T/5,
†Baker, Kenneth W., Pfc,
Baker, Leo S., Pvt,
Baker, Lester A., Pvt,
Baker, Lowell W., T/5,
‡Baker, Max, Cpl,
†Baker, Raymond R., Pfc,
†Baker, Robert D., Pvt,
Baker, Robert L., Sgt,
Baker, Tom A., S/Sgt,
†Baksanskas, Victo, Pfc,
Balbach, Erwin L., Pfc,
Balbaton, Anthony J., T/Sgt,
Balchus, Frank E., Pvt,
Baldesseri, Joseph P., Pfc,
Baldridge, Leonard, Pvt,
Baldwin, Clarence F., Pfc,
Baldwin, Paul, Cpl,
Baldyga Stanley W., Pfc,
†Bale, Joseph L.,
Bales, Harrell L., T/5,
Bales, Isaac P., Pfc,
Balestrieri, Edward B., Pfc,
Balicki, Joseph J., Sgt,
Balint, Louis A., Pfc,
†Balkovec, Nicholas L., Pfc,
Balkovitz, John G., T/Sgt,
Ball, Donald E., Pfc,
Ball, John W., S/Sgt,
Ball, Nelson G., Sgt,
Ball, Orville, Pvt,
†Ball, William J., Pvt,
Ballard, Clifford E., Sgt,
Ballard, George H., Cpl,
*Ballard, Thomas, Pvt,
Ballard, Wayne E., Pvt,
Ballenger, Fred K., Pvt,
Ballentine, Edwin R., Pfc,
Ballesteros, Agustin J., Pfc,
Ballew, Billy D., Pfc,
Balog, Edward, Sgt,
Balogh, James E., Pfc,
Balogh, Michael S., Pfc,
Balsama, Joseph, Pfc,
Balnu, Vincent W., Pvt,
Bamburg, Jesse J., Pfc,
†Bamburak, Joseph W., Pfc,
Banas, Michael, Pvt,
Banasiak, Eugene, Pvt,
Banazak, Stanley S., Pfc,
Bancroft, Varney M., T/5,
Bandy, Clarence W., Jr., Sgt,
Bangen, Quentin R., Pfc,
Banker, Raymond E., Pfc,
‡Bankes, Edgar E., Pvt,
Banks, Joseph J., Pvt,
Banks, Stacy O., Pvt,
Banks, Wurth W., T/5,
Banks, Wesley R., Pvt,
Bankston, Orville J., Pvt,
‡Banninger, J. W., Pfc,
Bannister, George G., Pvt,
†Bansemer, Theodore C., T/Sgt,
Banuelos, Adam, Pvt,
Barabasz, Boleslaus T., Tec 5,
Baragona, Louis A., Pfc,
†Baran, Thomas S., Pfc,
‡Barath, Gaza, Pfc,
Baratta, Thomas G., Pvt,
Barbagallo, Joseph M., T/4,
†Barbara, Stephen T., T/5,
Barber, Adam H., Pvt,
Barber, August F., Pfc,
Barber, Jake A., Pfc,
Barber, Joseph C., Pvt,
*Barber, Marvin, Sgt,
†Barbour, Will P., Jr., 2nd Lt,
Barchesky, Lester B., Pfc,
Barcus, John, Jr., Pvt,
Barcus, Nich, Pvt,
‡Bard, Donat F., Pvt,
Bard, Robert H., Pfc,
Bardell, Clarence L., Pvt,
†Bardoni, Julius J., Pvt,
†Bare, Paul W., Pvt,
†Barich, John A., S/Sgt,
Barker, Acle H., Pfc,
Barker, Alvin R., T/5,
Barker, Jack C., Pvt,
Barker, Garland E., Pfc,
Barker, Meril A., Pfc,
†Barker, Perry W., Pvt,
Barker, Oscar L., Pfc,
*Barket, Albert A., Pfc,
Barkley, Hugh E., Pfc,
Barkley, Leslie, Jr., Pvt,
†Barko, Andy S., Pfc,
Barkowski, Chester F., Pfc,
Barletta, Anthony M., Pvt,
Barletta, Arthur C., Pvt,
Barley, Wilbur E., S/Sgt,
Barlow, Hansel R., Pvt,
Barna, Wassil, Jr., S/Sgt,
Barnack, David L., Pfc,
Barnard, George R., T/4,
Barnackie, Leon J., Pfc,
Barnes, Burton H., Pfc,
Barnes, Chester B., S/Sgt,
Barnes, Clement A., Pfc,
Barnes, Cletus G., Pvt,
‡Barnes, George, T/5,
Barnes, Howard F., Pfc,
†Barnes, Lloyd C., S/Sgt,
Barnes, Lloyd C., Pvt,
Barnes, Paul V., 1st Sgt,
Barnes, Paul V., 2nd Lt,
‡Barnes, Reginald C., Pvt,
Barnes, Samuel L., Pvt,
Barnes, Stanley J., Pfc,
Barnett, Carlos R., Pfc,
Barnett, Dean W., Sgt,
Barnett, Jessie B., S/Sgt,
Barnett, Thomas B., Pfc,
Barnett, George E., Pvt,
Barnett, Marvin. M., Pvt,
Barnett, Robert J., Pvt,
Barney, Willard G., Sgt,
Barnhart, Wayne M., Pfc,
Baron, Charles J., S/Sgt,
†Barone, Joseph J., Pvt,
Barquist, Stanley A., Pfc,
Barr, Burl, Cpl,
Barr, Everett E., T/Sgt,
Barr, Hugh, Sgt,
Barr, John W., Pvt,
Barr, Leroy S., Pfc,
Barr, Ray, Pfc,
Barr, Roy, Pfc,
‡Barra, Vincent R., Pfc,
Barranger, John E., Pfc,
Barraza, Liborio N., Pfc,
Barrentine, Malcom V., Pfc,
Barrett, Clarence D., Cpl,
Barrett, Francis J., Pfc,
Barrett, Joseph T., Pfc,
Barrett, Paul J., Pfc,
Barrett, Ray E., Pvt,
Barroll, Edward K., Pvt,
Barros, Joe O., Sgt,
Barrows, Frederick W., Pvt,
Barry, John Q., Sgt,
Barry, Peter P., T/5,
Barry, William J., Pfc,
†Barsamian, Souren, Pvt,
Barsh, George E., Pvt,
Bartaldo, Joseph, Tec 5,
†Bartel, Edward H., Pfc,
Bartells, Donald F., Tec 4,
†Bartelson, John L., Pvt,
Bartlet, Milton J., Pvt,
Bartholomew, Galvin H., Tec 5,
Bartholomew, Harvey M., Cpl,
†Bartilucci, James J., Sgt,
Bartosiak, Joseph R., Pfc,
†Bartkowiak, Benedict M., Pfc,
Bartkowiak, Frank, Pvt,
†Bartlett, Anrdew F., Pfc,
Bartlett, Charles H., 2nd Lt,
Bartlett, Charles R., S/Sgt,
†Bartlett, Edward O., Pvt,
Bartlett, Harold M., Pfc,
Bartolotta, Michael J., Pvt,
Barton, Ray, Pvt,
†Barys, Stanley P., S/Sgt,
Basala, Nestor, Pvt,
†Basco, Stephen J., Cpl,
Basil, Robert B., Pfc,
Basile, Patrick J., Pvt,
Basileo, Frank H., Cpl,
Basler, John W., Pfc,
‡Bass, Leymer D., Pvt,
Bassett, Earl J., Pfc,
Bassett, Frederick J., Pfc,
†Bassett, Harvey H., S/Sgt,
Bassett, Oswald G., Pfc,
Bassett, Wallace R., Tec 5,
Bassett, Winton A., Pfc,
Bassler, Carl E., Pfc,
Bassler, Roy H., Pfc,
†Bast, Alvin E., Pfc,
Basta, Frank J., Pfc,
Bastean, Herbert H., Pvt,
†Bastian, Daniel R., Pvt,
Bastien, Paul J., Pfc,
Bateman, Clyde F., S/Sgt,
†Bateman, Edward A., Pfc,
Bates, Fred W., Pvt,
Bates, Hershel G., Pvt,
Bates, Lenos H., Pvt,
Bates, Marvin E., Pvt,
Bates, Pirtle, Pvt,
‡Bates, Russell, Jr., Pfc,
*Bates, Thomas, Pfc,
Batson, Earl C., Pvt,
Batson, Hugh A., S/Sgt,
*Battaglia, Vincent, Pvt,
Battain, Primo F., Pfc,
Batters, Wesley P., Pfc,
Battey, Gerald R., Pfc,
Battishill, Bert C., Cpl,
Baty, Donald G., Pvt,
*Baty, Ralph R., Tec 5,
Bauder, Harold H. P., Pfc,
Baudouion, Eugene V., Sgt,
Bauer, Helmut, Pfc,
Bauer, John H., Pfc,
Bauer, Manford H., Cpl,
Bauer, Roland E., Pvt,
Bauer, Russell D., Sgt,
Bauerle, Alfred G., S/Sgt,
Baugh, John W., 1st Lt,
Baughman, Lester L., Pfc,
†Baughman, Willie E., Pvt,
Baughman, Charles J., Pfc,
Baughman, Raymond F., Pfc,
Bauguess, Ervin E., Pvt,
Baul, Roque C., T/Sgt,
Baulo, Joseph, Pvt,
†Bauman, Louis, T/5,
Bauman, Louis, Pfc,
†Bauman, William R., Pfc,
Baumgart, Alfred E., Cpl,
Baumgartner, Adam J., T/5,
Baurle, Raymond H., Pfc,
Baxa, James, Sgt,
Baxter, A. D., Pfc,
Baxter, Charlie, Sgt,
Baxter, Henry E., Pfc,
Baxter, Joe J., Pfc,
Bayer, Edward A., Pfc,
Bayless, Burland L., Pfc,
*Baylor, Charles N., Jr., Pvt,
†Bayne, James E., Pvt,
Baynes, Clyde, Pvt,
†Baynum, Leroy W., Pvt,
Bayones, Ferdinand A., Sgt,
Bazany, John C., Pfc,
†Beader, Gordon C., Pvt,
Beadle, Claude K., Pfc,
Beahm, Lewis W., Pvt,
Beal, Bion N., Pvt,
Beale, William C., T/5,
Beam, John, Pvt,
Bean, Johnie G., Pfc,
†Bean, Ray T., Sgt,
Bean, Robert L., Pfc,
‡Bean, Walter S., Jr., Pfc,
Bean, Willard M., Pfc,
Beando, Anthony J., Pfc,
Bear, Clarence H., Sgt,
Bear, Jack W., Pfc,
†Beard, Davis M., Pvt,
Beard, James A., Cpl,
Beard, James R., Pfc,
Beardslee, Wilfred A., Pfc,
Beasley, John M., Pvt,
Beaton, Donald R., Pfc,
†Beatrice, John J., Pvt,
Beaty, Clarence W., Sgt,
Beauchamp, Leonard M., T/5,
Beauchamp, Ralph, T/5,
Beauchene, Oliver D, Sgt,
†Beaudet, Marcel, R., Pvt,
Beaudoin, Joseph A., Pfc,
Beauprey, Louis J., Pfc,
Berber, Jacob L., Pfc,
Beck, Deon E., Pvt,
Beck, Fred C., Pfc,
Beck, James A., T/5,
Beck, James F., Pfc,
Beck, Otto J., Pvt,
Becker, Albert V., Jr., 2nd Lt,
*Becker, Arthur W., Pvt,
Becker, Danald J., Pvt,
Becker, Elmer C., 1st Lt,
Becker, Raymond C., Pfc,
†Becker, Richard A., Pvt,
Becker, Rudolph, Pfc,
Becker, Walter, Pvt,
Beckham, Pruitt T., Pvt,
Beckman, George L., Pvt,
Beckman, Junior F., Pfc,
*Beckman, Vincent, Pfc,
Bedonie, Chee, Pvt,
Bedsole, John B., S/Sgt,
*Beefa, Amos F., Pvt,
†Beeler, Thomas O., Pvt,
Beem, Frank C., 1st Sgt,
†Beemer, Robert J., S/Sgt,
Beernaert, George A., Cpl,
Beers, Jack J., Sgt,
Beesley, Harley R., Pfc,
†Beever, John D., Pvt,
Beglau, Herbert G., Pfc,
Begenwald, William E., Pfc,
Behar, Manny N., Pvt,
Behr, Rovert E., Pfc,
Behrens, Edward C., Pvt,
Beifield, Martin P., T/4,
Beisch, Louis J., Pfc,
Beistle, Ward, E., Pvt,
‡Belander, Mauno H., Pvt,
Belcher, Carl, Pfc,
Belcher, Jese W., Pfc,
Belcher, Thurmon E., S/Sgt,
Belcourt, Victor F., Pfc,
Belfonti, John J., Pvt,
Belilin, Harold L., T/5,
Beliveau, Roland W., Pfc,
Belknap, Robert A., Pfc,
Bell, Alfred S., Pfc,
Bell, Arnold W., Pfc,
†Bell, Carl M., Cpl,
Bell, Elmer J., Jr., Pfc,
Bell, Elvin W., Cpl,
Bell, Ernet L., Pvt,
Bell, Freddie H., Pfc,
Bell, Harry S., Pfc,
Bell, Irving, 2nd Lt,
Bell, James C., Pfc,
§Bell, James I., Pfc,
‡Bell, Kenneth C., Pvt,
§Bell, Vergil G., Pvt,
†Belland, Robert M., Pfc,
†Bellavigna, John, Pfc,
Belleri, Anthony T., Pvt,
†Bellettine, Tony, Pfc,
Bellis, Clarence E., Pvt,
*Bello, Joseph, Jr., Pfc,
*Bellomo, Andrew, Pfc,
Bellrose, George L., Pvt,
Bellucci, Pat J., Pvt,
Belofi, John M., Pvt,
Belovitz, Walter J., Pfc,
Belot, Marcel F., Pvt,
Belnerio, George A., Pfc,
Bolt, Junior O., Pvt,
Belter, Fred F., Pvt,
Beltran, Joe C., Pvt,
Belvees, Joseph L., Pfc,
Belvin, Thomas E., Pvt,
Bemis, Amos J., Sgt,
Bemis, Donald, Sgt,
Benas, Nick G., Pvt,
Benda, Douglas P., Tec 5,
Bender, Paul L., Pfc,
Bender, Stanley, T/Sgt,
‡Bender, Victor A., Pvt,
Benderman, Curv F., Pvt,
†Bendigo, Elmer J., 1st Lt,
Benedic, Theodore, Pvt,
†Benedict, Clifford J., Pfc,
Benedict, George O., Pfc,
Benedict, Kenneth G., Pfc,
Benedict, Morris, Pfc,
Benedict, Robert O., S/Sgt,
Benefiel, Lawrence D., Cpl,

† Killed in Action. * Prisoner of War. ‡ Missing in Action. § Died of Wounds.

Benefield, Ray O., T/5,
*Benenson, Laurence L., Pfc,
*Benge, Carl J., Pfc,
Benham, William F., Pfc,
Benicak, Francis J., Sgt,
Benigar, Matt C., Pfc,
Benjamin, Arthur, Sgt,
Benjamin, Walter R., Pvt,
Benn, Dwight, Pfc,
Bennett, Arthur L., Pvt,
Bennett, Burnal C., Pfc,
Bennett, Charles R., S/Sgt,
Bennett,Charles R., Pvt,
Bennett, Gerald R., T/4,
Bennett, Harold L., Pfc,
Bennett, Harold L., 1st Sgt,
†Bennett, Jerome W., Pvt,
Bennett, Joe H., Pvt,
Bennett, Julian W., Jr., Pfc,
Bennett, Royce E., S/Sgt,
Bennett, Stephen F., Pfc,
Bennett, Talmadge, Pvt,
Bennett, Virgil R., Pfc,
Benoit, Alfred, Pfc,
Benoit, Joseph A., Pfc,
Benson, Arthur, WOJG,
†Benson, Calvin S., Pfc,
Benson, John H., Pvt,
Benson, Joseph C., Pfc,
Benson, Karl H., Pfc,
Benson, Odas, Pvt,
Benson, Wayne E., Pfc,
Bentlage, James W., Sgt,
Bentley, Clarence, Pfc,
†Bentley, Ray, Pvt,
Bentley, Otis H., T/Sgt,
Benton, Harry W., Pvt,
Benvenuto, Robert W., Pvt,
Berard, Stanley J., Pfc,
†Berardi, Frank J., Pfc,
§Berardi, Nello L., Pvt,
Berardinelli, Michael N., Pvt,
†Berchiolly, Thomas F., S/Sgt,
§Berdou, Henry D., Pfc,
Berelo, Stanley L., Pvt,
Berens, William J., Pfc,
Berezowski, Stefan, Pvt,
Berg, Edward E., Pfc,
†Berg, Leonard, S/Sgt,
Berge, Frank J., Pfc,
Bergeman, Isidore, Pvt,
Bergen, Isaac W., Pvt,
Berger, Franklin A., Pfc,
Berger, Fritz N., Pfc,
‡Berger, Robert L., Pvt,
Bergman, James J., Pfc,
Berhalter, Frank J., Pfc,
Berkenkopf, Robert O., Pvt,
Berkholz, Clarence O., S/Sgt,
Berkholz, Harry L., T/4,
Berkner, Earl M., Pfc,
Berkofsky, Morris, Pvt,
Berkowitz, Samson, Pvt,
§Berkshire, Arthur B., S/Sgt,
Berkshire, James A., Pfc,
Berley, Grady L., Pfc,
Berlin, Raymond E., Sgt,
*Berman, David, Pvt,
Bernaciak, Raymond, Pvt,
Bernardo, Albert J., Pvt,
Bernat, John, Pfc,
Berner, Joseph L., Pfc,
Berner, Russell F., Pfc,
Berner, William J., Pfc,
Bernhardt, Charles M., Sgt,
‡Bernier, Arthur W., Pvt,
Bernier, Paul H., Pfc,
Bernoski, Benjamin, Pfc,
Bernstein, Harry I., Pvt,
Beron, Dwight E., Pfc,
Berquist, Roger K., Pvt,
Berridge, Albert, Pfc,
‡Berry, Bernard H., Pvt,
Berry, Calvin A., T/5,
Berry, Clifton A., Pfc,
Berry, Edmund, Pfc,
Berry, Ervin H., Jr., S/Sgt,
Berry, Jefferson F., Cpl,
Berry, William E., Pfc,
Berry, William J., Pfc,
Berryman, Richard J., Sgt,
Berst, Albert J., Pvt,
Bertel, Sylvester W., Pfc,
*Bertella, Guido J., Pvt,
Bertelsen, Harry W., Pvt,
Berteotti, Louis F., Pfc,
‡Berthiaume, Eldon J., Pvt,
Bertoncelli, George, Pfc,
Bertos, Charles J., Pvt,
§Bertram, Elmo, Pvt,
Bertrand, Edward E., T/5,
‡Berthume, Addison A., Pfc,
Berube, Louis J., Pvt,
†Berumen, Tony F., S/Sgt,
Besaw, Dallas P., 1st Sgt,
Besheres, Donald R., Pfc,
Besko, John, Pvt,
Besonday, Harold J., S/Sgt,
†Best, Lowell E., T/5,
Best, Samuel F., T/4,
Bethany, Charles H., T/5,
Bethell, Robert L., Pvt,
Bethune, Clifford M., Sgt,
Bethune, Percy L., Pvt,
Betten, Evert H., Sgt,
Betters, Herbert D., Pfc,
Bettinger, George E., Pvt,
Betts, Frank J., S/Sgt,
Betts, William A., Pvt,
Betza, George, Pfc,
Beukema, Garrett W., T/3,
Bevan, Donald, Pfc,
*Beverly, Roscoe G., Pvt,
Bevin, Donald R., Pvt,
†Bevins, Edward J., Sgt,
Beyer, Frank, Pfc,
‡Beyer, Frederick F., Pvt,
Bezio, Alfred J., Pvt,
†Biadasz, Alfred L., Pvt,
†Biaga, Stanley J., Cpl,
Biancuzzo, Joseph P., Pfc,
Biasella, Frank A., T/4,
Bibby, Marion H., Pfc,
Bibeault, Robert M., Pvt,
†Bibinski, Anthony J., Pfc,
Bible, John T., Pvt,
Bice, Carl M., Pvt,
Bickel, Charles G., Pfc,
Bicking, John W., Pfc,
Bickrest, Paul D., Pfc,
Biedrzycki, Arthur M., Pvt,
Biehn, Claude W., T/5,
Biehn, Roy R., Sgt,
Bielski, Mathew F., Pfc,
Bienkiewicz, John P., Sgt,
†Bier, Arthur A., Pvt,
Bierhaus, John S., Pvt,
Bierley, Wesley A., T/4,
Biernacki, Zimund F., Pfc,
Biesiada, Stanley F., Sgt,
Biggers, Marcus D., Capt,
§Biggs, Howard R., Pvt,
Bigler, Berthel O., Pfc,
Bigler, Vernon E., Pfc,
Bika, Joe J., Pfc,
Bila, Victor M., Pvt,
Biles, Denzil E., Pvt,
*Biley, George M., Pvt,
Billings, Clarence, Pvt,
Billings, Harold J., Pvt,
Billings, Theodore F., Pfc,
Billingsley, John W., Pfc,
Billington, Clarence W., Pfc,
†Bills, Charles R., Pfc,
*Billuni, Simone, Pvt,
§Bilski, Joseph J., Pvt,
Binda, Joseph, Pfc,
Binder, Arthur J., Pfc,
†Binegar, Robert E., Pfc,
†Bing, Bradford L., Pfc,
Bing, Franz Joseph B., Pvt,
Bingham, Lynn J., Pfc,
Binkowski, Albert C., Pvt,
*Birch, Gene E., Pvt,
Birchenough, Francis G., Pfc,
†Bird, Charles R., Pvt,
Bird, Ellis H., Pvt,
†Bird, George, Pvt,
Bird, Raymond, T/4,
Birdsall, Joseph C., Pfc,
Birdsall, Robert V., Pfc,
Biri, Loyd J., Pfc,
Birt, Harvey C., Cpl,
Bisher, Russell W., Pfc,
Bishop, Alfred W., Pvt,
Bishop, Carl E., S/Sgt,
Bishop, Clifford D., 2nd Lt,
‡Bishop, Eugene R., Pvt,
Bishop, Frank G., Pvt,
Bishop, George L., Pvt,
Bishop, Harold W., Pvt,
Bishop, Harry W., Pvt,
†Bishop, Joseph L., Pvt,
Bishop, Melvin L., Pvt,
Bishop, Truman A., Cpl,
†Bishop, Stanley V., Sgt,
‡Bishop, Walter E., Pfc,
†Bispham, Edward J., Pvt,
Bisson, Joseph B., Pvt,
Bissonnette, Norman J., Pvt,
Bitka, Chester W., Pfc,
Bivins, Lester G., Cpl,
Bixel, Virgil J., Cpl,
Bizzozero, Alfred N., Pvt,
Bjornebo, Fritjor, Pfc,
Black, Bryce D., Pfc,
Black, Christian A., Pfc,
‡Black, Claud R., Pfc,
Black, Conard, Pfc,
†Black, Dean P., Pfc,
Black, Fred C., Pvt,
Black, James B., 2nd Lt,
Black, Jay E., Pvt,
Black, Merle E., T/5,
Black, Orville M., Pfc,
†Black, Paul D., Pvt,
Black, Saul, Pfc,
Blackader, Joseph B., Pvt,
Blackburn, David D., Pvt,
Blackburn, Jank, Sgt,
‡Blackenburg, William J., Pfc,
Blackford, Franklin T., Pfc,
Blackledge, Kenneth E., Pfc,
Blackledge, Richard, Sgt,
Blackman, Harold L., Pfc,
Blackman, Herbert, Pvt,
Blackwell, J. D., Pfc,
Blackwell, William C., Pvt,
†Blackwood, Arthur J., 2nd Lt,
Blackwood, E. C., Jr., Pvt,
Blackwood, William F., 2nd Lt,
Bladh, Peer L., T/Sgt,
†Blaha, Richard J., Pfc,
Blaikie, John W., Major,
Blair, Angus, Pvt,
Blair, Edgar J., Pvt,
†Blair, Leonard O., Sgt,
Blair, Virgil, Pvt,
Blais, Fred A., Pvt,
Blaiwes, Samuel A., Pvt,
Blake, Dolon, Pfc,
Blake, King J., Pvt,
Blake, Marvin L., Pfc,
Blake, Shirley L., Pfc,
†Blake, Tommy S., Pvt,
Blake, Wayne O., Pfc,
Blakesley, Merville, Cpl,
Blakley, James D., Pfc,
†Blalock, Coy, Pfc,
‡Blalock, Luther R., Pvt,
Blanchard, John E., Pfc,
Blanckenburg, William L., Pvt,
Blanco, Henry F., Pfc,
Bland, Charlie C., Pfc,
Bland, Lonnie R., Pvt,
†Blandeburgo, Sal, Pvt,
Blankenburg, Edward W., Pfc,
Blankenship, Delmer E., Pfc,
‡Blankenship, Edmond L., Pvt,
Blankenship, Floyd R., Sgt,
Blankenship, James R., Pfc,
Blankenship, Samuel G., Pfc,
*Blankenship, William P., Pfc,
Blanton, Jesse D., Pvt,
Blaski, Mike, Sgt,
†Blaskowski, Leonard J., Pvt,
Blaylock, Cloyce M., Pfc,
Blaylock, Gerald, T/5,
Bldor, Frank T., Pvt,
Bleau, Earl L., T/4,
Bledsue, Herbert C., Pfc,
Bleich, Herbert, Pfc,
Bleicker, Frederick E., Pvt,
Blenkinson, Robert M., Cpl,
Blessing, Earl D., Pvt,
Blevins, Andrew J., Pvt,
Blevins, Robert E., 1st Lt,
†Blevins, William F., Sgt,
Blight, William L., Sgt,
†Bliss, Milo V., Pfc,
Blitz, Saul, Pvt,
†Blizzard, Elwood S., Pvt,
§Blizzard, John E., Sgt,
Bloch, Alfred, Pvt,
Blocher, Philip J., Pvt,
Block, Donald J., Pvt,
Block, Harold B., Pvt,
Block, Joseph E., Pvt,
Blodgett, Frederick W., Pfc,
Blomker, Lyall G., Pfc,
Bloom, Joseph, Pvt,
Bloom, Milton, Pfc,
Bloom, Weldon E., S/Sgt,
Bloom, William, Pvt,
Bloomfield, Preston G., Pvt,
Bloomingburg, Wayne C., Pfc,
Bloomingburg, W. H., Pfc,
Bloomquist, Roger E., Pvt,
Blosch, David F., S/Sgt,
Blount, Ronald D., Pvt,
Bloyed, Dale E., Pvt,
Bloyer, Jack H., Pvt,
Blum, Charles K., 1st Lt,
Blum, Peter H., Pvt,
Blume, Kenneth R., Sgt,
Blumenkrantz, Walter, Pvt,
Blunck, Walter V., Pfc,
Blunk, Murrel, Pfc,
Bly, George E., T/Sgt,
Boanini, Roy J., Pfc,
Board,Fayne B., Pvt,
Board, Lebert W., Pvt,
Board, Thomas P., Capt,
‡Boatright, Thomas, Pfc,
†Boatwright, J. W., Jr., Pfc,
Bobb, John E., Cpl,
Bobbitt, Felix, S/Sgt,
Bobrowski, Walter C., S/Sgt,
‡Bocchino, John A., Pvt,
†Bockholt, Luverne M., Pvt,
Bodenheimer, Gradie A., Pfc,
Bodenstadt, Grover L., Pfc,
Bodin, Ralph C., Pvt,
Bodislaw,Harry J., Pvt,
Boelter, Leslie W., Pvt,
Boen, Lonial D., Pvt,
Bogart, Charlie T., 2nd Lt,
Bogart, Theodore F., Lt Col,
Bogdonoff, John G., Pfc,
Bogenholm, Wilfred, Pfc,
†Boger, Arthur O., Pvt,
Bogess, Glenn R., Pfc,
Boggs, Grady O., Pvt,
Boggs, William A., Sgt,
Boglino, John, Pvt,
Bogosewski, William S., Pfc,
Bohannon, Carl G., S/Sgt,
Bohm, Robert C., Cpl,
‡Bohms, Max E., Pvt,
*Bohna, Frank Jr., Pfc,
Bohner, Robert I., Pvt,
Bohy, Jack C., Pfc,
Boice, Fred H., T/5,
†Boisjoli, Rolland O., Pfc,
Boisvert, Herbert L., Pvt,
†Bokedon, George, Jr., Pfc,
Boker, Ethelmer J., S/Sgt,
†Bolen, Charles I., Pvt,
Boley, George W., Pfc,
Boleyn, Robert F., Pfc,
Bolin, William W., Pfc,
†Bollen, Chester H., Pvt,
Boller, John L., Pvt,
Bolles, Floyd M., Pfc,
Bolsonn, Frank W., T/Sgt,
Bolte, Willis H., Pfc,
Bolton, Harold R., Pfc,
Bolton, Theodore G., Pfc,
Boltz, Edward G., Cpl,
Boltze, Fred C., Pfc,
Bolz, Clifford L., Pfc,
*Bombardier, Raymond W., Pfc,
Bona, Jerome M., Pvt,
Bonagura, Emil, Pfc,
Bonagura, Hugo P., Pfc,
Bonanni, Angelo S., Cpl,
Bond, Chester E., Pfc,
Bond, Elmer E., Pfc,
†Bond, Kermit A., Pfc,
Bond, Mozelle, Pvt,
Bond, Robert M., Pfc,
Bonds, Doyal A., Pvt,
Bonds, James E., Pvt,
Bonecutter, Donald E., Pfc,
Bonham, William H., S/Sgt,
Bonislawski, Stanley J., Pfc,
†Bonner, Andrew L., Jr., Pfc
†Bonner, Daniel T., Pvt,
Bonner, James P., Pvt,
†Bonoyer, Francis T., Sgt,
†Book, Eugene O., Pfc,
Boomer, Walter H., Cpl,
§Boone, Carl W., S/Sgt,
Boone, James H., Pfc,
Booth, Albert C., Pfc,
§Booth, Everett J., Pvt,
Booth, Harold L., Pvt,
Booth, Joseph E., S/Sgt,
Borawski, Peter W., Sgt,
Borchers, Victor D., Pvt,
Bordeaux, Daniel L., Pfc,
†Borel, Paul G., Pfc,
Borden, Raymond R., Sgt,
Borden, William F., S/Sgt,
Borer, Fred J., Cpl,
Borez, Nelson A., Pvt,
Borgel, William F., Pvt,
Borghese, Salvatore, Pvt,
Borgilt, Ralph W., Sgt,
†Borgmann, John W., Pfc,
Boring, Byron V., Pvt,
Boriss, Ernest J., Pvt,
Borland, Jack, Cpl,
Borland, Loren J., Pvt,
Bornwasser, Charles P., Pfc,
Boros, Andrew P., Pvt,
‡Borow, Joseph M., Pvt,
†Borowski, Walter J., S/Sgt,
Borrasi, Roland, Pfc,
Borrelli, Charles T., Sgt,
Borshowski, Peter, Pvt,
Borst, Donald J., Pvt,
Borst, Jack T., Pvt,
Bortz, John, T/4,
Borycz, Edward, Pfc,
†Borzewski, Edward M., Pvt,
§Bosak, Michael C., Cpl,
Bosch, Balzar N., T/5,
Bosch, Peter J., T/5,
Boschult, William D., Pvt,
Boscono, Louis, Pfc,
Bosela, Paul N., Pfc,
Bosiger, Norbert A., Pvt,
*Bosio, Charles P., Sgt,
Boss, Benedict C., Pvt,
Boss, Eugene, Cpl,
Boss, John J., Jr., Pvt,
Bosshardt, Robert L., Pfc,
Bossie, Joseph C., Jr., Pvt,
Bossler, Ernest B., Pfc,
Bostner, Stanley J., Cpl,
Botelho, James A., Sgt,
Botes, Gus G., Pfc,
Bothes, Herbert E., 1st Lt,
Botsford, William H., Pvt,
Bottelson, Russell C., Pfc,
Botti, John A., Pfc,
Bottone, Frank J., Pvt,
Botts, Robert G., Pvt,
Boucher, Edward C., Sgt,
Boucher, George H., Pvt,
Boucher, Joseph R., Sgt,
Boudoin, Joseph C., Pfc,
Boudreau, Alfred J., Pvt,
Boudreau, David A., Pfc,
Bouer, Allie, Pvt,
†Boulanger, Adrien A., Pvt,
Boulden, James E., Pfc,
Boull, Oakley E., Pfc,
Boulton, Clark H., Pvt,
†Bouman, Paul D., S/Sgt,
Bourgault, Eugene J., Pfc,
Bourgeois, Wilfred J., Sgt,
Bourget, Thomas J., Pfc,
Bouten, Victor, Cpl,
Boutross, George M., Pfc,
Bowden, Arthur C., Sgt,
Bowels, Russell T., Pvt,
Bowen, Harvey, Jr., Pfc,
Bowen, Joseph N., Pfc,
†Bowen, Thomas D., Jr., Pvt,
Bower, Charles H., Pvt,
Bowers, Charles D., Pfc,
Bowers, Donald L., 1st Lt,
Bowers, Ralph T., Pfc,
Bowles, Alfred, Pfc,
Bowles, Alva, Pvt,
Bowles, Donald R., Pvt,
Bowles, James A., Cpl,
Bowles, James W., Pfc,
Bowles, Willard L., Sgt,
Bowley, Robert J., Pfc,
Bowlin, Hiram Butler, Sgt,
Bowling, Robert D., Pvt,
Bowling, Joseph A., Pfc,
Bowman, Alfred L., Pvt,
†Bowman, Charles, Pfc,
Bowman, Darrell C., Pvt,
Bowman, Edward P., Pvt,
†Bowman, Glen M., Pfc,
†Bowman, James, Pvt,
§Bowman, Stanley H., Jr., Pvt,
Bowser, Charles R., Pvt,
Bowstring, Billy, Pfc,
Bowsza, Leonard B., Pfc,
†Bowyer, Cloyd A., Cpl,
Bowyer, Odell G., Pfc,
Boyce, Clarence E., Cpl,
Boyce, Raymond H., Pfc,
Boyd, Benjamin C., Maj,
Boyd, Clarence A., Sgt,
‡Boyd, Ernest M., Pfc,
†Boyd, James A., Capt,
Boyd, Junior, T/5,
*Boyd, Robert C., Pfc,
Boyd, Robert J., Sgt,
†Boyer, Earl W., Pfc,
Boyer, Edward H., Pfc,
Boyer, Harry I., T/5,
Boyer, Johnnie, Pfc,
Boyer, Norman W., Pfc,
†Boyer, Walter L., Pfc,
Boyington, Alfred E., Pvt,
Boykin, Dock, Pvt,
Boyle, Joe P., Sgt,
Boyles, Harold J., Pfc,
Boyles, Houston C., T/4,
Boynton, Richard, Jr., Pvt,
*Boyuka, John, Pfc,
§Bozeman, William T., Pfc,
Bracewell, Eltvee, Sgt,
Brack, Lawrence M., Pfc,
Brackbill, Albert J., Pvt,
Bracken, Fairel O., Pvt,
Brackett, Maurice, Pfc,
Bracy, Claude R., Pfc,
Bradac, William A., Pfc,
*Bradish, Thomas M., Pfc,
Bradke, George J., Pfc,
*Bradford, John A., Sgt,
Bradford, Kermit H., Pfc,

† Killed in Action. * Prisoner of War. ‡ Missing in Action. § Died of Wounds.

IN WORLD WAR II 451

Bradford, Thomas W., Pvt,
Bradish, Louis J., Pfc,
Bradley, James, Pfc,
Bradley, James D., Pfc,
Bradley, James, Jr., T/5,
Bradley, Jesse G., Pfc,
Bradley, Lercy, Pvt,
Bradley, Victor A., Pfc,
Bradley, Victor M., Pfc,
Bradshaw, Calvin T., Sgt,
Bradshaw, John T., Jr.,
†Bradshaw, Marion M., Pfc,
Brady, Alfred R., Pfc,
Brady, Edward, Pfc,
Brady, John F., Pfc,
Bragalone, Annello J., T/5,
Brainard, Charles W., Pvt,
Brainerd, Russell H., Pfc,
Brakeall, Milton E., T/5,
Brakefield, Joseph D., Pfc,
Braley, Elton B., Pfc,
Bramlett, Alfred L., T/4,
Branch, Ernie L., Pvt,
Brand, James L., Cpl,
Brandel, Earl H., T/5,
Brandenburg, Philip A., Pfc,
Brandes, Lawrence F., Pfc,
Brandhoff, Edward B., Pfc,
Brandt, Lyle D., Jr., Pvt,
*Branham, Lonnie, Pfc,
Brannon, Arthur L., Pfc,
Brannon, Dale F., T/5,
Brannon, Harry F., Sgt,
‡Brannon, Russell E., Pfc,
Brannum, John W., Pvt,
Branstetter, Ross W., 1/Sgt,
Brantley, Richard B., Pfc,
‡Brantner, Thomas J., Pvt,
Brasco, Sam, Pvt,
Bratcher, Earl J., Pvt,
Bratsakis, Andrew J., Pvt,
†Bratsos, Harry P., Pfc,
Brattin, Joseph T., S/Sgt,
Branz, Aldo, Pvt,
Braun, Charles E., 2d Lt,
Braun, Clemens, Pfc,
Braun, William G., Pfc,
Braxton, Jack D., Pvt,
Braucher, Donald A., Sgt,
‡Braus, Dallas, T/4,
Brawner, Macon C., Pvt,
†Bray, Herman E., Pvt,
Bray, James G., Pfc,
Bray, Lewis M., Pfc,
§Bray, William H., Pfc,
Brcich, Joseph M., Pvt,
Breaux, Alvin J., T/4,
Breazeale, Vernon E., Pvt,
†Breazier, Louis W., Pvt,
Brecke, Arnold W., Cpl,
‡Brede, Earl L., Pvt,
Bredimus, John F., 2nd Lt,
Breen, Walter W., Pfc,
Brekhus, Adolph H., Sgt,
Brekken, Carl W., Pvt,
Bremer, August H., Pfc,
Brenaman, Walter H., Pfc,
§Brengel, James F., Pfc,
Brening, Herman H., Pvt,
Brennan, Charles J., Jr., Pfc,
Brennan, E. H., Jr., S/Sgt,
Brennan, Emmet E., Pfc,
Brennan, Thomas P., Pfc,
‡Brennan, William F., Pfc,
†Brennan, William L., Pvt,
Brenner, Henry, Pvt,
Brenner, Lyman E., Pfc,
Brennick, Lawrence M., Pvt,
§Breon, Parse H., Pvt,
Bresh, Felix J., Pvt,
Breth, James E., Lt Col,
Brett, John J., Pvt,
Bretz, Frederick L., Pvt,
Bretz, Harold G., Pfc,
Brewer, Clifford C., Pvt,
Brewer, Delbert R., Pvt,
Brewer, Edward A., Pfc,
Brewer, Jacob B., Pfc,
Brewer, Kebbie E., Sgt,
Brewer, Leon L., Pfc,
Brewer, Sidney T., Pvt,
Brewster, George G., Pvt,
Brevard, Robert E., Pvt,
Brezavar, Edwin F., Pfc,
Briano, Nicolas A., T/5,
Bricker, Frank L., Jr., Pvt,
Bricker, LeRoy C., Pfc,
Bridges, Delmas D., Sgt,
†Bridges, Maurice W., Pfc,
Brien, James J., Sgt,
Brier, James O., Pvt,
Brigadier, Karol N., Pvt,
Brigance, Kenneth W., S/Sgt,
Briggs, Donald L., Pfc,
Briggs, Geary E., Pvt,
Briggs, John D., Pfc,
Briggs, Robert G., Pvt,
‡Briggs, William N., Pfc,
Bright, Milford V., Pvt,
Bright, Ross V., Pfc,
Brignac, Woodrow W., Pfc,
Briley, Richard, Pvt,
Brill, Hugh G., Pfc,
Brilla, Joseph N., Sgt,
†Brin, Nathan H., Pvt,
Brindle, Ralph L., Pfc,
Briner, William S., S/Sgt,
Brink, Edward J., Capt,
†Brinkey, Harry J., Pfc,
Brining, Elmer G., Sgt,
Brisbois, Wilmer L., Pfc,
Brischler, John, Pvt,
Briskey, Harry J., Pfc,
Brita, Genero A., Pfc,
Broadt, Donald H., Pfc,
Broadus, James, Pfc,
†Brobst, Charles W., Cpl,
Brocious, John H., Pfc,
Brock, John D., Pfc,
Brock, Julian P., Pvt,
Brock, Willard C., Pfc,
Brockwell, James E., T/5,
†Broderick, Raymond J., Pfc,
Brodeur, Roland F., Pvt,
Brodie, Daniel J., Cpl,
Brodo, Nathaniel I., Pvt,
Brody, Edward P., Pvt,
Brohel, Joseph E., S/Sgt,
Broich, Kenneth R., 1/Sgt,
Brokenshire, William L., Sgt,
Bromberg, Sandy A., Pvt,
Bronner, William R., Pvt,
Bronson, Alan L., Pvt,
Bronstein, Milton L., WO(JG),
Bronzo, Sylvio J., Pvt,
Brooke, Charles E., Pfc,
†Brooke, Dillon D., Pfc,
Brooker, Clarence E., S/Sgt,
Brooks, Aldis W., Pvt,
Brooks, Charles H., Pfc,
Brooks, Dale E., S/Sgt,
§Brooks, Eldridge H., Pvt,
‡Brooks, Emery, Pfc,
†Brooks, Glenn D., Sgt,
†Brooks, Harold R., Jr., Pvt,
Brooks, Harry J., Pvt,
Brooks, Hermit O., Pvt,
Brooks, Jack, T/4,
Brooks, James D., Pfc,
Brooks, Kenneth H., Pvt,
Brooks, Marion C., Pfc,
Brooks, Ralph L., Pvt,
Brooks, Richard J., Pvt,
Brooks, Wilbur F., Pvt,
Brookshear, James W.,
Brooksher, Donice A., Pfc,
Brooksher, Edward C., Pfc,
†Brophy, Arthur C., Jr., Pvt,
Brotzman, Johnathan, Sgt,
Brough, Richard F., 2nd Lt,
Broughton, Billy T., S/Sgt,
Broughton, James R., Cpl,
†Brouillard, Alcide J., Pvt,
†Brouthers, Addison F., Pfc, J
Brouthers, Carl F., Pvt,
†Brower, Herman, Pfc,
Brown, Albert, Capt,
Brown, Albert J., Pfc,
†Brown, Alexander A., Pvt,
Brown, Alfred M., S/Sgt,
*Brown, Allan W., Pvt,
Brown, Amos, Pvt,
†Brown, Armand V., Pvt,
Brown, Byron C., Pfc,
Brown, Calvin R., Pfc,
Brown, Carolton I., S/Sgt,
†Brown, Carson E., Pvt,
Brown, Charles G., Pvt,
†Brown, Clement H., Cpl,
†Brown, Curtis V., Pvt,
Brown, Delmar A., Pfc,
Brown, Dennis F., Pvt,
Brown, Donald C., Cpl,
Brown, Eddie H., Pfc,
Brown, Edward, Sgt,
Brown, Eugene R., Pfc,
Brown, George W., Pfc,
Brown, Guy D., Pfc,
Brown, Harold T., Pfc,
Brown, Harry H., Pfc,
Brown, Herbert A., Jr., Pvt,
Brown, Hewell, Pfc,
Brown, Hobert B., Pvt,
Brown, Howard E., Pfc,
Brown, Jack, Pfc,
Brown, Jack W., 1st Lt,
†Brown, James A., Sgt,
Brown, John C., Pfc,
Brown, John K., Pfc,
Brown, John W., Pfc,
Brown, Joseph E., Jr., Pvt,
Brown, Joshua W., Pvt,
Brown, Miland F., T/4,
Brown, Oswald F., Pvt,
Brown, Owen C., Pfc,
Brown, Paul C., Pfc,
Brown, Ralph D., Pfc,
†Brown, Ralph E., Pfc,
Brown, Ralph M., S/Sgt,
Brown, Raymond C., Pfc,
Brown, Reuben H., Capt,
†Brown, Richard S., 2nd Lt,
†Brown, Richard S., Sgt,
‡Brown, Richard W., Pvt,
Brown, Robert E., Pvt,
Brown, Robert F., T/5,
Brown, Robert R., Pfc,
Brown, Roger R., Pfc,
Brown, Ross W., Pfc,
Brown, Saul, Pfc,
Brown, Sumner B., Pfc,
Brown, Thomas G., Pfc,
§Brown, Truman L., Sgt,
Brown, Wade E., Pfc,
Brown, Walter F., T/5,
Brown, Walter H., Pfc,
Brown, William, Pvt,
Brown, William D., Pvt,
Brown, William D., Pvt,
Brown, William E., T/Sgt,
Brown, Willie L., Pfc,
†Brownback, James R., S/Sgt,
‡Browne, William L., Pvt,
Browneller, Kenneth E., Capt,
*Browning, John W., Pvt,
Brownlee, Walter J., Sgt,
Brownlow, William, Jr., T/4,
Brozo, Frank J., Pvt,
Brubaker, John S., Pvt,
Bruce, Charles W., Pvt,
Bruce, Hayden L., T/4,
Bruce, John L., Pvt,
Bruce, Robert P., Pfc,
Bruce, Roy B., Sgt,
Bruggeman, Charles J., S/Sgt,
Bruffee, Arthur L., Pvt,
Bruhn, Ramon R., Pfc,
Bruhy, Bill B., 1st Lt,
Brumm John, T/4,
Brummerstedt, Charles R., Pvt,
Brummett, Denver, Pvt,
Brummett, Leslie M., Pfc,
Brunet, Earl A., Pvt,
Bruno, Alfred T., Pfc,
Bruno, Joseph N., Cpl,
Bruno, Salvatore, Pvt,
‡Bruns, Paul E., Pfc,
Brustkern, Joseph H., Cpl,
Bruzdzinski, Casimer E., Pfc,
Bruzzese, Orland J., Cpl,
Bryan, Sydney, Pfc,
Bryan, Wilbert, T/4,
†Bryank, Charles R., Pvt,
Bryant, Hassell, Pvt,
Bryant, Tommie W., Pvt,
Bryant, Walter L., Pvt,
Brylo, Steve, Sgt,
Bryner, Edward R., Pfc,
Bryowsky, Joseph W., Pfc,
Bryson, Herbert D., Pfc,
Bucca, Joseph S., Pfc,
Buchalew, Joseph L., Cpl,
Buchanan, Paddy H., Pvt,
Buchholz, Charles L., Pfc,
Buchholz, Clayton S., T/Sgt,
†Buck, Clovis C., Pvt,
Buck, Howard A., Pvt
Buckenroth, Albert, Pvt,
Buckhannon, Homer, Pfc,
Buckley, James H., Pvt,
Buckley, John J., Pvt,
Buckley, Philip G., Pfc,
Buckner, Marvin G., Cpl,
Bucsa, Alexander, T/Sgt,
*Bucy, Claire H., Pfc,
Buda, Alex J., T/Sgt,
Budd, Arthur D., 2d Lt,
Buddy, Gorden E., Pfc,
Budnicki, John F., Pfc,
Budzyn, Eugene J., Pfc,
Buelna, Albert R., Pvt,
Buelna, Alvaro R., Cpl,
Buffington, James E., Pfc,
Bugal, Frank J., Pfc,
†Bugalia, Edward J., Pvt,
†Buganski, Bert, Pfc,
Bugg, J. H., Pfc,
Buikema, John, Pvt,
Buist, Charles A., T/5,
Bukoske, Henry C., T/4,
Bukowski, Edward J., Pfc,
Bulger, Ira W., T/4,
†Bull, Harry E., Pvt,
Bull, Herman P., Cpl,
Bullard, John W., Pvt,
Bullen, Ralph L., Pfc,
†Buller, Vernon H., Sgt,
Bullerwell, Keith M., Pvt,
Bullington, Claude G., Pfc,
Bullis, Francis J., Pfc,
Bullock, Harold A., Pvt,
Bultrowicz, Edward A., T/5,
†Bumbarger, William J., Pvt,
Bumgarner, Arnold J., Pvt,
Bumm, Edwin A., Pfc,
Bunco, Joseph J., Pvt,
Bundyk, Joseph T., Sgt,
†Bunting, Herbert J., Pfc,
†Buran, Steve L., Pfc,
Burch, Edward H., Sgt,
Burch, Robert A., Pvt,
Burchill, Alfred J., Pfc,
Burdette, Glenn A., Sgt,
Burdick, Lavalla, Pfc,
Burger, Albert E., T/5,
Burger, Herman, Pvt,
Burger, Spencer W., Sgt,
Burgess, Gordon C., Pvt,
Burgess, Jessey O., Pfc,
Burgess, Okey T., Pfc,
Burgess, William, T/Sgt,
Burghart, Paul F., Cpl,
Burgher, Homer H., Pfc,
Burk, Ora, Pvt,
†Burke, Charles O., T/Sgt,
Burke, Harold L., T/5,
Burke, James J., S/Sgt,
Burke, James W., Cpl,
*Burke, John F., Pfc,
Burke, Joseph J., Pfc,
Burke, Martin J., Pvt,
†Burke, Melon J., Pvt,
Burke, Mitchel D., Pfc,
Burke, Ralph A., Cpl,
Burke, Robert J., Cpl,
Burke, William R., Pvt,
†Burke, Woodrow, Pfc,
Burkell, James J., Pfc,
Burkett, Francis A., Pfc,
Burkett, James A., Pvt,
Burkett, Leroy R., Pfc,
†Burkhardt, Richard L., 1st Lt,
Burkholder, Arthur E., Pfc,
Burki, Harry J., Pvt,
Burkitt, Robert B., Pfc,
Burks, Q. P., Pfc,
Burleson, Dorris A., Pvt,
Burley, George R., Sgt,
*Burley, James G., Pvt,
Burlison, Dwight E., Pvt,
Burman, Samuel W., T/5,
Burnell, John T., Pfc,
Burnell, Ralph W., Pvt,
Burnes, Edward J., Pfc,
Burnett, Oscar A., Pvt,
Burnett, Walter W., Pfc,
‡Burnette, Oliver B., Pvt,
Burnham, Gordon G., Pfc,
Burnight, Francis J., T/5,
Burns, Archer T., Pvt,
Burns, Buford L., Pfc,
Burns Ernest H., Pfc,
Burns, George J., T/5,
†Burns, James G., Pfc,
Burns, John J., Sgt,
Burns, John J., Pfc,
†Burns, Owen V., Pfc,
†Burns, Ray E., Pfc,
Burns, Robert, Pfc,
Burns, Thomas F., Pvt,
Burowicz, John Z., Pfc,
Burr, Arthur F., Pfc,
Burr, Lloyd C., Pfc,
§Burrgess, William A., Pfc,
Burris, Gordon, Pfc,
†Burris, Othie, Pvt,
Burroughs, Birl F., Pvt,
Burroughs, J. W., Pvt,
Burrows, Lee A., Pvt,
Burrows, Ralph S., Pfc,
Burson, John H., Pfc,
Burton, Aubrey L., S/Sgt,
Burton, Bernard, Pfc,
Burton, Jerrel V., Pfc,
Burznski, Thaddeus J., Pfc,
Burzynski, Chester J., Pfc,
Busby, Addison D., Pvt,
†Busby, Edward V., 1st Lt,
Busch, John J., Pvt,
†Busch, Richard Raymond, Pfc,
Bush, Edgar A., Pvt,
Bush, Elbert, Pvt,
Buschel, Leonard, 1st Lt,
†Bush, James H., Pvt,
§Bushby, William E., 2nd Lt,
Bushong, James R., Pfc,
Busk, Merrill L., 1st Sgt,
Buss, Leroy L., Pfc,
Bussard, Eugene W., Pfc,
Bussard, John H., Pfc,
Bussing, Richard A. F., Pfc,
‡Bustad, Leo K., Capt,
Bustoz, Fernando P., Pfc,
Bustrom, William J., Pvt,
Buswell, Gerald E., Pvt,
Butcher, James F., Pvt,
Butcher, John L., 1st Sgt,
Butcher, Marion G., Cpl,
Butler, Calvin D., Pfc,
Butler, Charles M., Sgt,
Butler, Columbus T., Pfc,
Butler, Decatur P., Capt,
Butler, Donald E., T/4,
Butler, Earl, Pfc,
Butler, George E., T/5,
Butler, William H., Pvt,
Butsika, Dhimitri, Pvt,
Butters, Deryl E., Cpl,
Buttimer, John B., Pvt,
Butts, Clement W., Pfc,
†Butts, Willis E., Pfc,
Butz, Franklin I., Pfc,
†Buwen, Frank D., Pvt,
Buxton, Francis W., Pvt,
Buzzard, LaVerne L., Pfc,
Byars, Charles B., Sgt,
Bye, George B., Jr., Pfc,
†Byers, Omer S., S/Sgt,
Byker, John J., Jr., Pfc,
Byrd, Cecil, Pfc,
*Byrd, Henry P., Pfc,
Byrd, Lehmann T., S/Sgt,
Byrd, Russell H., Pvt,
Byrne, Charles P., Pfc,
Byrne, Vincent, Sgt,
Byrnes, William T., Sgt,
Bystrzynski, Frank W., T/5,
Bzdak, John C., Pfc,

†Cabala, Francis, Pfc,
Cabana, Robert J., Pfc,
Cable Charles A., Pfc,
Cable, George F., T/5,
Caddell, Lester C., Pvt,
‡Cadmes, Victor W., Pvt,
Cadwallader, George, Pfc,
Cadwallader, Warren, Pfc,
Cafazzo, Frank, Pvt,
Caffee, Walter, Pfc,
Caferey, Bernard L., Cpl,
Cagnina, Frank, Pfc,
Cahill, John F., Pfc,
Cahill, Robert S., Sgt,
Caiazza, Gerald, Pfc,
Cain, Harvey R., Pfc,
Cain, Lee C., Pfc,
Cain, Robert L., Pvt,
*Cains, Sheldon, Pvt,
Cairns, Hugh L., Pvt,
Cak, Joseph S., Pvt,
Calabrese, Perry, Sgt,
†Calderella, Anthony V., Pvt,
Calderone, Paul A., Pvt,
Calderwood, Kenneth, Cpl,
Caldwell, James C., Pvt,
Caldwell, Walter,Jr., T/4,
Caldwell, Warren J., Sgt,
†Cale, James E., Cpl,
Call, Robert D., Pfc,
†Callagy, Ambrose J., Pfc,
Callahan, Edward M., Pfc,
Callahan, Gerald J., Sgt,
Callahan, Peter E., Capt,
Callahan, Roland P., Sgt,
Callahan, Thomas A., S/Sgt,
Callaway, Timothy F., Pvt,
Callahan, Walter C., Pvt,
Callahan, William J., Sgt,
Callaway, William C., Pfc,
Callis, Joseph, Jr., Pvt,
Calloway, George M., 1st Sgt,
Calogeras, Arthur, Pvt,
Caltagirone, Nicholas J., Pvt,
Camarata, William J., Pfc,
Cambria, Joseph, Pfc,
Cambridge, Charles L., Pvt,
Camden, Clyde, Pvt,
Cameron, Donald A., Jr., Pvt,
Cameron, James, Pfc,
Cameron, Leonard G., Pfc,
Cameron, Malcom C., 2nd Lt,
†Camp, Byron, Pfc,
Camp, Charles W., S/Sgt,
Camp, Edward, Pvt,
†Camp, George, Pfc,
Camp, Paul, Pfc,
Camp, Walter, Pvt,
Campagnari, Victor, Cpl,
Campanini, John J., Pvt,
†Campbell, Charles B., Pfc,
Campbell, Charles, Jr., Pvt,
Campbell, Charles W., Pfc,
Campbell, Clarence E., Pfc,
Campbell, Dallas W., Pfc,
Campbell, Douglas R., Pfc,

† Killed in Action. * Prisoner of War. ‡ Missing in Action. § Died of Wounds.

†Campbell, Edward G., Pfc,
Campbell, Forrester, Pfc,
Campbell, Howard E., Pvt,
Campbell, James C., Sgt,
Campbell, John B., Pfc,
Campbell, John H., Pfc,
Campbell, Lewis E., Pvt,
Campbell, Raymond L., Pfc,
*Campbell, Robert E., Pvt,
*Campbell, Roger H., Pvt,
†Campbell, Tyler, Capt,
Campbell, Walter J., Pfc,
Campbell, Walter L., Pvt,
†Campbell, William F., Pvt,
‡Campbell, Woodrow, Pvt,
Campeau, Arthur J., T/5,
Campillo, Robert S., Pfc,
Campise, Marion S., Cpl,
Camporeale, L. W., Pfc,
‡Campos, Robert, Pvt,
Camprini, Roderick P., 2nd Lt,
Camy, Robert M., Pfc,
†Canale, William T., Pfc,
Canales, Vicente R., Pfc,
†Cancela, Justo, Pvt,
Candito, Carmen J., Pvt,
Caniglia, Benedetto O., Pvt,
Canini, Benjamin A., Pfc,
†Canis, John P., Pfc,
Cannaday, Claude R., Pfc,
Canniff, Ralph I., Pfc,
Canning, Earl, S/Sgt,
Cannistra, James L., Pfc,
*Cannon, Dean L., Pfc,
Cannon, Roy L. J., Pvt,
†Canonica, Edmund M., Pvt,
Cantini, Alberto E., Pvt,
Cantley, Jehu R., T/5,
Cantor, Harry, Pvt,
*Cantrell, Clifford O., Pfc,
Cantwell, Clarence C., Pvt,
Cap, Charles, Pfc,
Capalbe, Nicholas, Pvt,
Caples, Joseph R., Pfc,
Caplet, Louis, Pvt,
Capogna, Nicholas, Pvt,
Capone, Anthony, Pfc,
Caponecchia, Joseph V., Pvt,
Cappadona, Anthony D., Pfc,
Cappello, Salvatore J., Pfc,
Capps, Connard L., Pvt,
Capps, Leslie H., Sgt,
Capriano, Everett F., Pvt,
†Caprio, Dante A., Pfc,
Capron, Jon, 1st Lt,
Capstik, Lincoln S., Pfc,
Caradonna, Frank, Pfc,
Caramoney, Isaac, Pvt,
Carano, Salvatore J., Pvt,
Caravan, Vincent R., Pvt,
Carcelli, William G., Cpl,
‡Carchietta, Lawrence J., Pfc,
Carchrie, Burnham W., Pvt,
Carden, Clyde R., Pfc,
Carden, Robert G., Pfc,
*Cardenas, Daniel, Pvt,
†Cardenas, Raymond H., Pvt,
*Cardenas, Robert M., S/Sgt,
Cardilino, Santa, Pfc,
†Cardillo, Carmelo, Pvt,
†Cardillo, Guy, Pfc,
Cardos, Robert, Pvt,
Cardullo, Everett P., Cpl,
*Cardwell, Preston, Pvt,
§Care, William H., Pfc,
Carew, Gordon R., Jr., Pfc,
†Carico, Hugh V., Capt,
Caristo, Dominik, Pvt,
Carl, Victor D., Pfc,
Carlascio, Anthony J., Pvt,
*Carlascio, James A., Pvt,
Carleton, J. C., Pfc,
‡Carlin, John, Pvt,
Carling, Jack L., Pfc,
Carlisle, Charles E., Pvt,
Carlson, Albert R., Pfc,
Carlson, Cal E., Pfc,
Carlson, Carl E., T/5,
†Carlson, Cecil H., Cpl,
†Carlson, Dale, Pvt,
Carlson, Daniel J., Pfc,
Carlson, Ernest F., S/Sgt,
Carlson, Harold A.,
*Carlson, Richard N., Pvt,
Carlson, Robert L., 2nd Lt,
‡Carlton, James D., Pfc,
Carmack, Theodore A., Pfc,
Carman, Jesse L., Pfc,
Carman, Robert C., Pfc,
Carmello, Michael A., Pfc,
Carmichael, Arthur B., Cpl,
Carmon, Hoyt L., Pfc,
Carmon, Lester G., Pvt,
Carnahan, Tony, Pfc,
Carneal, Ernest H., Pvt,
Carnevale, Patrick A.,
Carney, Carroll E., Pfc,
Carney, Donald J., Cpl,
Carney, Harold E., Pvt,
Carney, Stephen A., Pfc,
Carofano, Pasquale G., T/4
Carothers, Charles A., Pfc,
Carpenter, Archie W., Cpl,
Carpenter, Carl, T/5,
‡Carpenter, Jessie M., Jr., Pvt,
Carpenter Leonard B., S/Sgt,
Carpenter, Lynn, T/5,
Carpenter, William A., Pvt,
Carpenter, William H., Pvt,
†Carr, Andrew J., Pfc,
Carr, Charlie B., Jr., Pfc,
Carr, Donald A., Pfc,
Carr, Edward V., S/Sgt,
†Carr, George F., Pfc,
§Carr, James, Pvt,
Carr, John J., Pvt,
Carr, Newton E., Pfc,
Carr, Rider W., Pvt,
Carr, Thomas D., Jr, Pfc,
Carrell, Ray A., Sgt,
Carrick, Cuther E., Pfc,
Carrigan, Edmund D., Pfc,
‡Carrigan, Joseph D., Pvt,
Carriveau, Paul E., Pfc,
Carroll, Daniel J., Pvt,
Carroll, David, 1st Sgt,
†Carroll, James E., T/5,
Carroll, James V., Sgt,
Carroll, Otis G., Pvt,
†Carroll, Silas, Jr., Pvt,
†Carrow, Louis G., Pvt,
†Carrubba, Harry J., Pvt,
Carson, Herman F., Pvt,
§Carson, Joseph C., Pfc,
Carson, William H., Pvt,
†Carstens, George H., 1st Lt,
Cartelli, Joseph R., Pfc,
*Carter, Albert R., S/Sgt,
Carter, Alfred I., Pfc,
‡Carter, Delmas, Pvt,
Carter, Elbert W., Pfc,
Carter, Herbert L., Pvt,
Carter, Jack D., Pvt,
Carter, Lyman M., Pfc,
Carter, Milin L., Pfc,
Carter, Richard B., Pfc,
Carter, Roy, Pvt,
Carter, Stacy L., Pvt,
Carter, Walter, Pfc,
§Cartier, Albert G., Pfc,
Cartwright, John A., Pvt,
Caruth, Robert J., Pfc,
Carver, Shirley, Pfc,
Cary, Nelson F., 1st Lt,
Casbolt, Frank J., Pvt,
Casciola, Amil, Pvt,
†Case, Arthur D., S/Sgt,
Case, Daniel F., Pvt,
Case, Eugene M., Pvt,
Case, Lawrence L., Sgt,
Case, Ralph L., Pfc,
Case, Robert W., Pfc,
Case, Velton T., Sgt,
Case, Virgil W., T/5,
Casey, Floyd S., S/Sgt,
Casey, Thomas F., S/Sgt,
Casey, William B., Jr., Pvt,
Cash, Harrison F., Pfc,
Cashman, John C., Pvt,
Casiday, Jake E., Sgt,
Caskey, Robert H., Pfc,
Cason, Frank P., Pvt,
Casper, John, Pfc,
Casquilho, Manuel R., Jr., Sgt,
‡Cass, Ernest C., Pfc,
Cass, Lewis C., Sgt,
Cassano, Frank J., Pvt,
Cassidy, Edwin H., T/5,
Cassidy, George R., T/5,
†Cassidy, James H., Pfc,
Cassino, William, Pvt,
Cassulo, Pete D., Pvt,
Castagna, Joseph S., Pfc,
Castagnola, Joseph J., Pfc,
Castagnolo, Joseph A., Sgt,
Castanon, Paul L., Sgt,
Casteel, Richard W., Pfc,
Castellano, Peter, Pvt,
†Castellaw, Aaron S., T/Sgt,
Castillo, Ernest, Pfc,
Castner, John C., Pvt,
Caston, Talmadge L., Pvt,
†Castonguay, R. J., S/Sgt,
Castro, Abundio, Pfc,
Castro, Henry F., Pfc,
†Castrovinci, Thomas, Pvt,
Castrovilla, Joseph S., Pvt,
Caswell, Harold R., Pfc,
†Caswell, Henry J., Pvt,
†Catalono, Angelo J., S/Sgt,
Castalono, Stephen J., Pvt,
Cataldi, Anthony J., Pvt,
Catania, John F., Pvt,
Catena, Vincent J., Pfc,
Cathey, Thomas F., Pfc,
Cato, Louis B., Pfc,
Cattaruzza, Irto C., Pfc,
Catterall, William V., Sgt,
*Cattey, Lucien H., Jr., Pfc,
†Catts, William L., Pfc,
Caulfield, Andrew J., Pfc,
*Caulkins, Dane V., Sgt,
Causey, Rufus C., Pvt,
Cavallo, Dante S., Pvt,
Cavalieri, Dominick R., Cpl,
Cavanaugh, William J., Pvt,
Cave, Robert E., S/Sgt,
Cavello, Constantine A., Pfc,
Cayer, Arthur M., Pvt,
Ceasar, Ruben, Pfc,
†Ceberek, Stanley A., Pvt,
Cebetic, Albert J., Pvt,
Cebuhar, Anthony, Cpl,
Cecil, Milford J., Pvt,
Cedoz, Russell W., Cpl,
Cegonko, John, Pvt,
Cenicola, Vincent J., Pfc,
Cerneka, Carl G., Pfc,
Cernighia, James J., 1st Lt,
‡Certo, Michael J., T/4,
Cervenak, George F., T/5,
Cervenka, James F., Pvt,
‡Cesareo, Stellario, Pfc,
§Cessna, Dale E., Sgt,
*Chacks, Anthony B., Jr., Pvt,
Chacon, Maxcimiliano, Pvt,
Chacon, Rafael F., Pfc,
†Chadd, John A., Pvt,
Chaffee, Edward E., Pfc,
Chaffin, Marvin B., Pfc,
Chaikin, Milton, Cpl,
Chalcraft, Chas. R., Pfc,
Challoner, Edgar M., Pvt,
Chaloux, Jessie J., Pfc,
Chamberlin, Stuart N., Sgt,
Chambers, Raymond D., Pfc,
Chamberlain, W. J., Jr., 1st Lt,
†Chamberlain, Willard, Pfc,
Chambers, Arthur M., Pfc,
Chambers, Charles T., Pfc,
†Chambers, John M., Pvt,
Chambless, Bonnie J., T/Sgt,
†Champagne, Leon J., Pvt,
Champion, Leonard, Pvt,
Chan, Ernest R., Pfc,
†Chan, John J., Pvt,
Chance, Robert F., Sgt,
Chandler, Andrew P., Pfc,
Chandler, Dean C., Sgt,
‡Chandler, Fred L., Pvt,
Chandler, Henry F., Pfc,
Chandler, James H., S/Sgt,
†Chandler, Walter R., S/Sgt,
†Chaney, Charles, Pfc,
Chaney, Henry, Jr., T/Sgt,
Chaney, Howard W., Pvt,
Chaney, Richard C., Pvt,
Channing, Donald F., Sgt,
Channing, Robert J., Sgt,
Chapek, Norman R., Pfc,
Chapel, Leo C., Pvt,
Chapman, Donald S., Pfc,
Chapman, Edgar E., Pfc,
Chapman, Lawrence W., Pfc,
Chapman, Leon A., Jr., Pfc,
†Chapman, Lionel E., Pvt,
Chapman, Robert E., T/4,
Chapmen, Clarence C., Pfc,
Chapmen, Donald A., Pfc,
Chappa, Rudolph, Pvt,
‡Chappell, James A., Cpl,
Chappell, Jesse W., Pvt,
Chappell, Lloyd, S/Sgt,
Chappie, Michael F., Pfc,
Charbonneau, Leo M., Pvt,
Chard, Thomas A., Pfc,
Charek, Arthur R., Pfc,
Charetsky, Ben, S/Sgt,
Charles, Roswell S., Pvt,
Charlton, Joseph F., Pfc,
Charlton, William R., Pfc,
†Charzyinskim, Ray F., Pvt,
Chase, Charles N., Pvt,
Chase, Harry N., S/Sgt,
Chase, Howard M., Pvt,
Chase, Ralph A., Jr., Pfc,
Chase, Raymond H., Pvt,
‡Chase, Robert M., Pvt,
†Chasing, Vernon P., S/Sgt,
*Chason, Ronald, Pfc,
Chastain, Clay, Sgt,
Chatfield, Robert F., Sgt,
Chaudron, David L., Pfc,
†Chavers, W. L., Pfc,
Chaves, Bengnino, Pvt,
Chaves, Ruben M., Pfc,
Chavez, Gonzalo A., Pvt,
Chavez, Leandro, Jr., Pfc,
Chavis, Albert D., Pfc,
Chavis, Hobson H., S/Sgt,
Cheaney, Louis B., Pvt,
Chechotka, Joseph J., Pvt,
Chee, Joe M., Pvt,
Cheek, Joseph H., Pvt,
†Cheek, Paul H., Pfc,
Cheever, Jack M., Pvt,
Chelhowski, Joseph A., T/Sgt,
Chemiski, Chester J., Pfc,
Chenevey, Joseph E., Pfc,
Cheney, Harlan R., Pvt,
Cheney, Robert A., Pfc,
§Cherney, Robert H., 1st Lt,
†Chernitzky, Seymour, Pfc,
Cherubini, Warren B., Pfc,
Chescavage, Peter J., Pfc,
Cheshire, George B., Pfc,
Cheshire, Gordon V., T/5,
Chesley, Harry E., Pfc,
Chestnut, Raymond, T/5,
Cheuvront, Eugene J., Pvt,
†Chewiwi, Jose A., Pfc,
Chiapuso, John J., Pfc,
Chiarini, Thomas, Pfc,
Chichetto, James J., 2nd Lt,
Chick, Frank P., Pfc,
Chicotel, Robert A., Pfc,
Chidester, Roy L., Pvt,
Chiffriller, George F., S/Sgt,
Chila, Walter A., Pvt,
Chilcote, Clyde E., Cpl,
†Childers, Francis M., Pfc,
Childers, James H., T/5,
Childers, Leonard, Jr., Pvt,
Childers, Max L., Sgt,
Childers, Raymond R., Pfc,
Childress, Edgar H., Pfc,
Childress, John D., Pfc,
Childs, Chester M., Pfc,
Childs, Clyde F., Pfc,
†Chilensky, John, 2nd Lt,
Chilson, Allen H., Pvt,
Chin, Lun, Pvt,
Chin, Tin W., Pvt,
†Chinchilla, John J., Pvt,
†Chine, Joseph, Pvt,
Chisholm, Arthur H., Pvt,
Chism, John P., Pfc,
†Chismer, Edward T., Pvt,
Chitwood, Bill H., Sgt,
Chivers, Alfred, Cpl,
Chmela, Charles J., Pfc,
Cholewa, Samuel, Cpl,
Chouinard, Maurice L., Pfc,
Chown, Harold M., Pfc,
†Chrapek, Walter T., Cpl,
Chrisman, Othel C., T/5,
Christenson, Dave, Sgt,
§Christian, Clarence A., Pvt,
Christianson, Cato P., Pvt,
Christianson, Harold B., Cpl,
Christianson, Henry J., Cpl,
Christenson, Kenneth P., Pfc,
Christianson, Lowell D., Pvt,
Christley, William B., Pvt,
Christman, Everett E., Pfc,
Christner, Paul J., Pfc,
Christo, George, Pfc,
Christoff, Nick, Pvt,
Christopher, George M., Pfc,
Christy, Delbert S., Sgt,
Chmura, Henry W., Pvt,
Chockla, Mitchel, Sgt,
Chojnowski, John E., Pvt,
*Choromanski, Stanley, Pvt,
Chouinard, William A., Pvt,
Chrymko, Horace O., Pfc,
Chryst, Jasper B., Pfc,
Chrzan, Henry J., Pfc,
Chuck, Edward L., Pfc,
Chuntz, Hyman, Pvt,
Churack, Matt J., T/Sgt,
Church, Ariel J., Pfc,
Church, Louis D., Pfc,
Church, William C., Pfc,
Church, Woodrow R., Pvt,
Churchfield, Charles D., Cpl,
Churchill, Robert C., Pfc,
Churchman, John E., Pfc,
Ciaccia, Michael, Pfc,
Ciamarra, Vincent J., Pvt,
Ciampichini, Cyril R., Pfc,
Ciarelli, Joseph N., Pfc,
Ciaravino, Vito J., Pfc,
‡Ciaschini, Domenic J., T/5,
Cicale, Louis, Pvt,
Cichalski, Stanley J., M/Sgt,
‡Cienfuegos, Joe C., T/4,
‡Ciensie, Francis W., Pfc,
Cieplik, Walter, Pvt,
Cieply, Thomas S., Pfc,
Cierny, Paul A., Pfc,
Cieszynski, Ray C., Pvt,
Ciezki, Erwin A., Pfc,
Cikel, Rudolph, Sgt,
Cincoski, James L., Pvt,
Cinque, George S., Pvt,
Cioffi, Anthony D., Pvt,
‡Cioffi, Dominick P., Pfc,
Ciolfi, Othello M., Pvt,
Cipolla, Pasquale P., Pvt,
Cipollone, Lawrence V., Pvt,
Cipra, Stephen J., Pvt,
Ciresi, Joseph F., Pvt,
Cis, Anthony J., Pvt,
Cisek, Frank P., Pvt,
Ciszon, William J., Pvt,
Clancy, Hugh P., Pvt,
‡Clanto, Pink R., Jr., Pfc,
‡Clark, Brainard K., Jr., Pvt,
Clark, Charles L., Pfc,
†Clark, Charles L., Pvt,
†Clark, Charles W., Pvt,
Clark, Clell, Pfc,
Clark, Clifford I., Sgt,
Clark, Cristal O., T/5,
Clark, Donald M., Pvt,
†Clark, Edward H., Pvt,
Clark, Eldred B., Cpl,
Clark, Elvin R., Pfc,
Clark, Floyd W., 2nd Lt,
†Clark, George W., Pfc,
Clark, Harland M., Pvt,
Clark, Harry M., Pvt,
Clark, Henry N., Pvt,
Clark, Horace E., Pfc,
Clark, Howard C., Pfc,
Clark, John E., S/Sgt,
Clark, John T., Pvt,
Clark, Kenneth H., Sgt,
Clark, Kenneth J., S/Sgt,
Clark, LaVerne C., Pvt,
Clark, Lester W., Pfc,
Clark, Percy A., Pfc,
Clark, Raymond F., Pfc,
Clark, Richard A., Pvt,
Clark, Roy W., Pfc,
†Clark, Winnie W., Pvt,
Clarke, Joseph B., Pvt,
Clarke, Robert M., Pfc,
Clarke, Samuel H., Jr., Pfc,
†Clarke, Walter N., T/Sgt,
‡Clarkson, Jess, Jr., Pvt,
Clarkson, Lester E., Sgt,
Clary, Randal R., Sgt,
Claude, Ernest, Pvt,
Claus, Adelbert W., Pvt,
Clausen, Henry A., Pvt,
Claussen, Buril M., Pvt,
Claussen, Melvin, Pvt,
†Claxton, John H., Pfc,
†Clayton, Calvin C., Pfc,
Clayton, James L., S/Sgt,
Clayton, John S., Pfc,
Clayton, Johnie T., Pfc,
Clayton, Woodrow K., Pfc,
Cleary, William J., Jr., Pfc,
Cleghorn, John L., Pvt,
Clem, Rhoman E., Capt,
Clem, William M., 2nd Lt,
Clemens, Richard, Cpl,
Clement, William A., Pfc,
Clements, Vernon, Pvt,
Clementi, Gregory, Pvt,
Clements, Thomas J., Pfc,
Clemons, Clark F., Pvt,
‡Clesos, Nicholas, Pfc,
†Clevenger, Benjamin W., Sgt,
Clever, Paul D., Jr., Sgt,
Clifford, LaVerne D., Pvt,
Cline, David A., T/5,
Cline, Garnet S., Pfc,
Clinkenbeard, Bob F., Pfc,
Clise, James W., Pfc,
Clodfelter, William J., Pfc,
Cloer, Arthur D., Pvt,
Cloer, Clyde C., T/5,
Closer, Russell W., 1st Lt,
Clonce, Robert K., Pfc,
*Clontz, George L., Pvt,
Clontz, William D., Pfc,
Clough, Jackson, Pfc,
Cloutier, Napoleon F., Pfc,
Clunen, Frederick T., Pvt,
Cluss, Edwin A., Pvt,
*Clute, Robert A., Pvt,
†Clyburn, Luther J., Pvt,
Clyde, Ralph B., Pfc,
Coady, Chandler G., Pvt,
Coakes, James R., S/Sgt,
Coates, Frederick R., Pvt,
Cobb, Billy J., Pvt,
Cobb, Charles W., Sr., Pvt,
Cobb, John W., Pvt,
Cobb, Richard P., Pvt,
Coburn, Estil F., Pfc,

† Killed in Action. * Prisoner of War. ‡ Missing in Action. § Died of Wounds.

IN WORLD WAR II 453

Coburn, Hager, T/5,
Coburn, Lois G., Cpl,
Coburn, Perry, Cpl,
*Coburn, Stanley W., Pvt,
Cocciardi, Frank, Pfc,
Coccio, Nicholas A., Sgt,
†Cochenour, Howard G., Pfc,
Cochran, Carl C., Pfc,
Cochran, Henry D., Pvt,
Cochran, James E., Pvt,
Cochran, James O., Pfc,
Cochran, Johnie L., Pvt,
‡Cochran, Raymond W., Pvt,
‡Cochran, William L., Pvt,
Cochrane, Clayton, Pfc,
‡Cochrane, Robert M., Pvt,
Cockerham, Robert P., Cpl,
‡Coco, Richard L., Pvt,
Cocopoti, Anthony J., Pvt,
Coday, Bernard F., 2nd Lt,
Codding, Blake H., Pfc,
Coddington, Preston H., Pfc,
Coe, John R., Pfc,
Coffee, Buck H., Jr., Pfc,
Coffey, Jesse J., Pvt,
†Coffin, Cecil B., Pvt,
Coffin, Charles B., Pvt,
†Coffman, Paul R., Pvt,
†Cogar, Fred, Pfc,
Cogar, Orda M., Pfc,
Coger, Christian C., T/5,
*Coghlan, Lowell W., Pfc,
Cohen, David, Pfc,
†Cohen, David, Pvt,
‡Cohen, Jacob, S/Sgt,
Cohen, Jacob, Pfc,
Cohen, Lawrence, Pvt,
Cohen, Lawrence H., Pfc,
Cohen, Maurice D., Pfc,
Cohen, Max, Pvt,
Cohen, Nathan N., T/4,
†Cohen, Ralph L., Pvt,
†Cohen, Samuel R., Pvt,
Cohn, Howard, Pvt,
Cohn, Perry E., S/Sgt,
Cohn, Sidney, 2nd Lt,
Coile, Odelle, Pfc,
Coke, Harry J., Pvt,
‡Coker, Kenneth R., Pfc,
Coker, Paul L., Pvt,
‡Colabufo, August, Pvt,
Colasuonno, Nicholas M., Pvt,
†Colbath, Chester G., Pvt,
Cole, Charles J., S/Sgt,
Cole, Edward W., Pvt,
Cole, Franklin J., Pfc,
‡Cole, James R., Pfc,
Cole, Leroy, Pfc,
Cole, Loell, Pfc,
Cole, Louie, Sgt,
Cole, Paul E., Pfc,
Cole, Vernon W., Cpl,
Cole, Wayne O., Pfc,
Cole, William L., Pvt,
Colegrove, Joe B., Pfc,
Coleman, Dewey V., Pvt,
Coleman, Donald E., Pfc,
†Coleman, Forrest H., Jr., 1st Lt
Coleman, Laman R., Pfc,
Coleman, Harry L., Pfc,
‡Coleman, Hyrum P., Cpl,
Coleman, Jesse, Pvt,
Coleman, John H., Sgt,
Coleman, John H., Pvt,
‡Coleman, John T., Jr., Pvt,
Coleman, Victor V., Pvt,
Coleman, William C., Pfc,
Coles, Ray C., Pfc,
Colesanti, Angelo L., Pvt,
Colin, John A., T/5,
Coll, Bernard A., Sgt,
†Collett, George F., Pfc,
Collette, Donald H. L., Pvt,
Collier, Homer J., Jr., Pvt,
Collier, Howard S., Pvt,
*Collier, Richard E., Jr., Pfc,
Collier, Royce L., Pfc,
Colligan, Henry L., Pvt,
‡Colling, William F., Pfc,
Collingnon, Louis R., Pvt,
Collingwood, Robert C., Pvt,
Collins, Bud, Pvt,
‡Collins, Cecil, Pfc,
Collins, Charles R., Pfc,
*Collins, Charley G., Pvt,
Collins, Clifford C., Pfc,
Collins, Edward G., Pfc,
Collins, Francis J., S/Sgt,
Collins, George A., Pvt,
Collins, George B., Pvt,
§Collins, Gordon A., Sgt,
Collins, Leo O., Pfc,
Collins, Merle J., Pvt,
†Collins, Wallace D., Pvt,
Collins, Warren D., S/Sgt,
Collins, Wilford H., Pfc,
Collins, William A., Pvt,
Collins, William H., Pfc,
‡Collins, William R., Pvt,
Colombo, Frank J., Pfc,
Colombo, Louis, Pfc,
Colon, Milton E., Pfc,
Colson, Charles D., Pfc,
Colson, Robert B., Cpl,
Colter, Grover E., Pvt,
*Colville, Henry W., S/Sgt,
Colwell, Albert P., Pvt,
Colwell, Allen J., Pfc,
†Colwell, Robert B., Pvt,
Colyer, Harold H., Pvt,
Combs, Donald W., Pvt,
‡Combs, Gene L., Pfc,
Combs, John R., Pfc,
Combs, Ova, Pfc,
Comer, Raymond J., Pvt,
Comp, Kenneth A., Pfc,
Comparato, Vincent J., Pvt
Compitello, Michael, Pvt,
‡Compton, Hiram A., T/5,
Comstock, Buster J., Pfc,
Comstock, Harold A., Pvt,
Comstock, Harry E., Pfc,
Comstock, John D., Pfc,
Comstock, Russell L., T/5,
Comstock, Vernon T., T/4,
‡Cona, Leonard D., Pvt,
Conca, Joseph L., S/Sgt,
Condie, James P., S/Sgt,
Condiff, Alexander H., T/5,
†Condon, Robert W., Pvt,
Condurso, Dominick F., Pvt,
Cone, Lester E., Pfc,
Cone, Marion, Pfc,
Cone, Oris C., S/Sgt,
Conger, Frederick D., Pvt,
Congleton, Frank, Jr., Pvt,
Congleton, James M., Jr., Pfc,
Conklin, Willis B., Capt,
Conley, John F., Pfc,
Conley, John H., Pfc,
Conley, Paul E., Pfc,
Conley, Sanford L., Pvt,
Conklin, Bernard C., Pfc,
‡Conklin, Eddie E., Pfc,
Conklin, Roscoe E., Pfc,
†Coley, Ed, Pvt,
Conley, Hanford A., Pvt,
†Conlon, Donald, Jr., Pfc,
Conlon, Edmond H., Pvt,
Conn, Clyde M., S/Sgt,
‡Conn, Noah F., Pfc,
†Connell, Jessie W., Pvt,
Connell, John J., Pvt,
Conner, Garlin M., 1st Lt,
‡Conner, Ralph E., Pfc,
Conner, Rex A., Cpl,
Conner, James S., Pvt,
‡Conner, Simon R., S/Sgt,
Conners, John, Pvt,
Conners, John J., Pvt,
Conners, Louis F., Pvt,
Conners, Michael T., Pfc,
Connett, Lester V., Pvt,
Connor, James P., Jr., Sgt,
Connor, Raymond L., Pfc,
Conover, Francis, Pfc,
Conover, James W., Pvt,
Conrad, Howard C., Pfc,
Conrad, Howard H., 1st Lt,
Conrad, James B., Pfc,
Conrad, Jerry C., 1st Lt,
Conrad, Keith B., Cpl,
Conrad, Loren L., Pfc,
Conrey, William J., Pfc,
Conron, Edward C., Pvt,
†Constable, Robert L., Pfc,
Constantin, Clifford R., Pfc,
Constantine, Joseph W., Pfc,
Contadino, Joseph J., Pvt,
Contaldo, Tony P., Pvt,
Conte, Dante A., 1st Lt,
Conti, Alphonso, Pvt,
*Conti, Antonio, Pvt,
Conti, Peter A., Sgt,
†Contreras, William R., Cpl,
Converse, Glen E., Sgt,
Converse, Raymond V., Pfc,
Conway, Edward T., Sgt,
*Conway, Harold, Pfc,
Conway, John L., 2nd Lt,
Conway, Martin J., Pfc,
†Conway, Minos T., Pvt,
Conway, Robert L., Pfc,
Conwell, William E., Pfc,
Cook, Alfred, Pvt,
†Cook, Charles R., Pfc,
Cook, Denton F., T/Sgt,
§Cook, Dexter M., Pfc,
Cook, Eugene A., Pfc,
Cook, George, Sgt,
*Cook, George E., Pvt,
Cook, George R., Pfc,
‡Cook, Harold N., Pvt,
Cook, Henry M., Pvt,
Cook, John, Jr., Pvt,
*Cook, John D., Pvt,
*Cook, Joseph J., Pfc,
Cook, Leslie R., T/5,
Cook, Raymond H., Cpl,
†Cook, Robert O., Cpl,
‡Cook, Robert W., Pfc,
†Cook, Roy E., Capt,
Cook, Russell J., Sgt,
Cook, Wilbert C., Pvt,
Cook, William E., Pfc,
Cook, William F., Jr., Pvt,
Cooke, Aaron T., Pfc,
Cooke, John R., Sgt,
Cooksey, Earl L., Pfc,
Cooksey, Hiram C., Pvt,
Cookson, Raymond L., Pfc,
†Cool, Truman A., S/Sgt,
§Cooley, Fred W., Pvt,
Cooley, Harold E., Pfc,
Cooling, John E., Pvt,
Coombe, Charles D., Sgt,
Coon, Delbert E., T/5,
Coon, Wallace R., Pvt,
Coon, William G., Pfc,
§Coons, Walter S., Pvt,
Coontz, Omer L., Pvt,
Cooper, Alfred C., Pfc,
Cooper, Arthur W., Pfc,
Cooper, Burnis, Pfc,
Cooper, Charles R., Pfc,
Cooper, Jackson, Cpl,
†Cooper, James E., Pfc,
Cooper, James G., Pvt,
Cooper, James W., Pfc,
Cooper, Leslie J., Pvt,
Cooper, Lewis V., S/Sgt,
†Cooper, Lloyd S., Pvt,
Cooper, Norman J., Pvt,
Cooper, Orrin K., Pvt,
Cooper, Sammy, S/Sgt,
Cooper, Walter C., 2nd Lt,
Cooper, Warren T., Pfc,
Cooper, Wilbert W., Sgt,
†Cooperberg, Harold, Pfc,
Cooperman, Fred, Pvt,
Coovert, Dave, Jr., Cpl,
Cope, Edgar J., Pvt,
Copeland, Herbert R., Pfc,
†Copen, Carl L., S/Sgt,
Copen, Marshall E., III, Pvt,
Copher, Griffith J., S/Sgt,
Copp, Clarence W., T/Sgt,
Coppee, Arthur, Pfc,
Coppola, Mario, Pfc,
Coram, Roscoe L., Pfc,
Corbe, William J., Sgt,
Corbett, George Q., T/5,
Corbett, Raymond J., T/5,
Corbett, Robert E., Pvt,
Corbin, Curtis H., Pfc,
Corbin, Earl, 2nd Lt,
Corbin, Earl, T/Sgt,
†Corbin, Frank A., Jr., Pfc,
Corbin, Wilford C., S/Sgt,
‡Corbin, Willard, Pfc,
Corcimiglia, Joseph B., Pvt,
Corcoran, Joseph B., Jr., Pfc,
*Corcoran, William F., Pvt,
Cordero, John, Sgt,
Cordero, Maure B., Pvt,
Cordier, Henry T., Pfc,
Cordova, Faustin N., Pfc,
Corey, Bernard W., Sgt,
§Corey, Elliott L., Pfc,
Corley, Thomas J., Pvt,
Cormier, Edward, Pvt,
Cornelius, Abe, Pvt,
†Cornelius, Howard F., Jr., Pfc
Cornett, Roy W., Pfc,
Cornish, Joseph L., T/5,
Cornwell, James R., 2nd Lt,
‡Corona, Tony A., Pfc,
Corona, William, Pfc,
‡Corpis, George P., Pvt,
Corr, Harold V., Sgt,
Corrao, Joseph A., Pvt,
Correia, Anthony, Pvt,
Corridan, Edward T., Pvt,
‡Corrigan, Joseph, Pvt,
†Corsaro, James, Pvt,
Corsi, Frank B., Pvt,
Corson, Elton B., Pvt,
†Corson, Joseph G., Pvt,
Cortese, Dominic, Pfc,
Cortez, Jesus O., Pvt,
Cortez, Joseph R., Pvt,
§Cortez, Luis, Pfc,
Cortinas, Esteban, Pvt.
Cortvrient, Albert J., Pfc,
Corviazier, Eugene J., Pfc,
Corwin, Marlin D., Pfc,
Cory, Mark E., Jr., Maj,
Coryea, Nelson H., Pvt,
Cosentino, Anthony, Pvt,
†Cosharek, Nicholas, Pvt,
Cosio, Gustave M., Pvt,
Cossett, John W., Pfc,
Cosson, Edgar A., Pvt,
*Costa, Antone V., Pfc,
Costa, Arthur J., Pfc,
Costa, Raymond L., Pvt,
Costa, Vincent J., Pfc,
Costa, William J., Pfc,
Costantino, Charles J., Pvt,
Costello, Francis R., Pfc,
Costilow, Charlie E., Pfc,
Costulis, Joseph J., Pvt,
Cota, Harry W., Pvt,
Cota, Lawrence, Pvt,
Cote, Alfred H., Pfc,
Cote, Alfred J., Pfc,
Cotter, Fred N., Pvt,
Cotton, Richard L., Pvt,
Cottone, Paul, Pfc,
Cottongim, Elmore, Pfc,
Coughlin, Earl G., Pfc,
†Coughlin, Francis X., Pvt,
Coughlin, Thurman F., Pvt,
Coulson, Carl A., T/5,
Coultas, Robert E., 1st Lt,
Countryman, Albert W., Pvt,
Court, Robert E., Pvt,
Courtney, Leston, Cpl,
Courtney, Marion R., Pvt,
Courtney, Sylvester R., Sgt,
Cousens, Charley F., Pfc,
Cousineau, Robert J., Pfc,
Coutu, Wilfred J., Pvt,
Couvillier, John J., Pvt,
Covello, Marciano, Pvt,
Cowan, Fred A., Pfc,
Cowart, Thomas L., Pfc,
Cowell, George W., Pfc,
†Cowling, James W., T/Sgt,
Cowls, Chester C., Sgt,
Cox, Charles A., Pvt,
Cox, Chester H., T/5,
Cox, Claude, Pvt,
Cox, Don W., Pvt,
Cox, Earl E., Pvt,
Cox, Edgar E., Jr., 1st Lt,
Cox, Floyd E., Pfc,
Cox, Harry E., Pvt,
Cox, Herman W., Sgt,
Cox, Hubert, Pfc,
Cox, Joseph J., Cpl,
†Cox, Kenneth R., T/4,
Cox, Layton A., S/Sgt,
Cox, Manford, Pfc,
Cox, Marion L., Pfc,
Cox, Ross C., 1st Sgt,
Cox, Walter W., 1st Sgt,
Coxsey, Abner L., Pfc,
Coy, Alvin G., Pfc,
Coy, Arthur D., Pfc,
Coy, Edward C., Pvt,
‡Coyle, Harold E., 2nd Lt,
Coyle, Joseph J., Pvt,
Cozort, Lancer, Pfc,
Cozzens, Richard D., S/Sgt,
Cozzolongo, Anthony J., Pvt,
Cozzolongo, Nicholas C., Pvt,
Crabtree, Robert E., Pfc,
Crabtree, Roy G., Sgt,
Craddock, T. B., Pvt,
Craft, Thomas L., Pvt,
Craft, William B., S/Sgt,
Craig, Francis, Pfc,
Craig, James W., Sgt,
†Craig, Johnnie S., Pfc,
Craig, Joseph E., S/Sgt,
Craig, Robert, Cpl,
Craig, Robert D., Pfc,
Craigen, Patrick M., Pvt,
Craigo, Leonard V., Pfc,
Crain, Floyd W., 2nd Lt,
Craker, Robert L., Pfc,
Crall, Charles C., Capt,
Cramer, Miles M., Pfc,
Cramer, Wallace R., Pfc,
†Crampton, Merle O., Pfc,
Crandall, Lloyd R., Pvt,
*Crandall, Robert W., Maj,
Crane, Charles C., Pvt,
Crane, Forest K., Pfc,
Crane, Robert E., S/Sgt,
†Crapo, Andrew, Pfc,
Crates, Calvin E., Pvt,
Craven, Lawrence E., T/5,
Cravens, Royal G., Pfc,
Crawford, Gene J., T/4,
†Crawford, George W., T/Sgt,
Crawford, Harold G., Sgt,
Crawford, Hugh W., Pfc,
Crawford, James H., Sgt,
†Crawford, John B., Pfc,
Crawford, Lee R., T/4,
†Crawford, Melvin L., T/5,
†Crawford, Richard E., S/Sgt,
Crawford, Robert E., Pvt,
§Crawford, Vincent G., Pvt,
†Crawford, Woodrow W., Pfc,
†Crawford, W. H., Pvt,
†Creagh, John J., 2nd Lt,
Creager, Paul S., Pfc,
Creamer, Guy R., Pfc,
Creaser, Lewis J., Sgt,
†Creasy, Stewart W., Sgt,
Creech, Ben W., Pfc,
†Creegan, John T., Pvt,
Creek, Howard W., Pfc,
Creel, Clarence, Pfc,
Creelman, Benjamin L., Pvt,
*Crenshaw, Carl E., Pfc,
Crenshaw, Doyle T., Pfc,
Crenshaw, James D., Sgt,
Crepeau, Victor, 1st Lt,
Cretella, Arnold, Pvt,
†Creviston, Marvin W., Pfc,
‡Crews, Ernest D., Cpl,
†Crews, Hilman V., S/Sgt,
Crews, James C., Pfc,
Crews, Leslie B., Pfc,
Cribbs, Cecil C., Pvt,
Crichton, James H., Cpl,
Crippen, Daniel A., Pfc,
Crider, James T., Pvt,
Cridge, Edward S., Pfc,
Crilly, Francis X., Pvt,
Crim, Bruce M., Pvt,
Crim, Lee, Sgt,
Crimaldi, Joe, Pfc,
Crippen, Daniel A., Pfc,
Crislip, Kenneth W., Pfc,
Crisp, Otis L., Pvt,
Criss, Edward E., Pvt,
Criswell, James A., Pvt,
*Critchley, Charles O., Pfc,
Crnojevich, Charles, Cpl,
Croas, William B., Pvt,
Croatti, Michael L., Pfc,
‡Crocker, John G., Pvt,
Croft, Edward H., Pvt,
Croman, John Q., Pfc,
Cromer, Jarvis, T/5,
Crone, Marvin D., Pvt,
Cronemiller, George R., Pvt,
Cronin, Andrew F., Jr., Pvt,
Cronk, Charles B., Pfc,
Crook, Fred, Pfc,
Crook, John H., Jr., T/4,
Crook, Miles S., Pfc,
Crooks, William R., Pfc,
Cross, Nye R., Pfc,
Cross, Richard B., 2nd Lt,
Cross, Ted W., Pvt,
Crotty, John J., Pvt,
Crough, James A., 2nd Lt,
Crouse, Franklin D., 1st Sgt,
Crow, Jim W., S/Sgt,
Crowe, James D., S/Sgt,
Crowe, Walter M., Cpl,
*Crowley, Martin V., Pfc,
Crowley, Thomas D., Pfc,
Croy, Charles, Pfc,
Crozier, Robert L., Capt,
Crudup, Edgar, T/5,
Crum, Leonard A., T/5,
Crump, Joe, Pvt,
Cruppenink, Joseph L., Pfc,
Cruz, Epimenio T., Pfc,
Cruz, Marcelo, Pfc,
Cruz, Raymond F., Pfc,
†Cruz, Rodolfo G., Pvt,
Cruzen, James B., Capt,
Csepcsar, Stephen J., Pvt,
†Cucciniello, William S., S/Sgt,
Cuculich, Thomas F., Pfc,
Cuellar, Arthur, Pfc,
Cuiffreda, Frank A., T/5,
Cullen, Patrick, Cpl,
Cullen, Thomas J., Pfc,
Cullop, Roy W., Pfc,
†Culp, Adam, Pfc,
Culpepper, Charles C., Pvt,
‡Culvahouse, Odis F., Pfc,
Culverson, Robert A., Pvt,
Cummings, Chester A., Pvt,
Cummings, Hollis A., Cpl,
†Cummings, James T., Pfc,
Cummings, Oliver D., Pfc,
†Cummins, Albert B., Pvt,
Cummins, Lloyd J., S/Sgt,
Cundell, Robert K., S/Sgt,
Cunic, Robert F., Pvt,
Cuniglio, Arthur A., Pvt,
†Cunningham, Alvy L., Pvt,
Cunningham, Doile R., Pfc,
†Cunningham, Edward H., Pvt,
‡Cunningham, Glenn C., Pfc,

† Killed in Action. * Prisoner of War. ‡ Missing in Action. § Died of Wounds.

Cunningham, Hubert D., Pfc,
Cunningham, Jack, Pvt,
†Cunningham, Joe R., Jr., Pfc,
Cunningham, John D., Pvt,
Cunningham, Thomas P., Pvt,
Cunningham, Wm. H., S/Sgt,
Cunningham, William J., Pvt,
Cunningham, William L., Pvt,
Cup, Paul R., Pvt,
Cuny, Arthur E., 2nd Lt,
§Cupka, John L., Cpl,
Curcio, Philip, Pvt,
Curiale, Alfonso, Pvt,
†Curl, Ralph W., Jr., T/4,
Curl, Willis O., Pvt,
Curnutte, Adam, Pvt,
†Curr, Charles H., Pfc,
Curran, Joseph D., Pfc,
†Curran, Louis F., Jr., Pvt,
Currie, Bramon J., Pfc,
Currier, Clifford E., Pvt,
*Currier, Phillip J., Pvt,
Currin, John S., Jr., Pvt,
†Curry, Glendie M., Sgt,
‡Curry, Mulford C., Pfc,
†Curry, William J., Cpl,
*Curtin, Clarence C., T/5,
‡Curtis, Billie, Pvt,
Curtis, Burroughs L., Pvt,
*Curtis, Grafton D., Pfc,
Curtis, Joseph T., Pvt,
Curtis, William L., Pfc,
Curtiss, Kenneth A., Pfc,
Curtsinge, Richard S., Pvt,
Cushman, Alexander V., Pvt,
*Custer, Howard W., Pfc,
Custer, Myrtus A., Pfc,
Cutler, Coleman, Pvt,
Cutler, Ralph L., Pvt,
Cwienk, Frank, Jr., T/5,
Cwienk, George T., Pfc,
Cybyske, Donald R., Pvt,
Cyhers, William E., Pfc,
Cynarski, Theodore J., T/5,
Cyran, Joseph F., Pvt,
†Cyr, Normand M., Pvt,
Czajka, Henry L., Sgt,
*Czaka, Stephen M., Pvt,
Czapski, Harry A., Pfc,
Czeck, Ambrose A., S/Sgt,
Czekner, Stephen J., Pvt,
Czepiel, Stanley, Sgt,
Czerniak, Sigmund J., Pfc,
Czinski, Stanley J., Cpl,
Czyzyk, Stanislaw K., Pvt,

Daar, Clarence J., Jr., Pvt,
Daebler, Clarence H., Pvt,
D'Agnese, Anthony T., Pfc,
Dagy, Elmer H., Pvt,
Dahl, John A., Pfc,
Dahl, Sidney R., T/4,
Dahlgren, Carl I., Pfc,
*Dahling, Frederick W., Pvt,
Dahlman, Klyde, Pvt,
D'Aiello, Joseph J., Pvt,
†Dailey, Donald L., Pfc,
Dailey, George, Jr., Pvt,
Dailey, Howard C., Pfc,
Dailey, Jack E., Pfc,
Dalbec, Francis E., Cpl,
Dale, Henry, S/Sgt,
D'Alesandro, Bostiano, Pvt,
Dalessandro, Arthur, Pfc,
D'Alessandro, Patsy C., Pvt,
§D'Alessio, Antonio, Pvt,
*Dalke, Felix E., Pvt,
Dal Molin, Aldo F., 1st Lt,
Dalton, Terry J., Jr., T/Sgt,
Daly, William F., Jr., Pfc,
D'Ambrise, Rocco L., Jr. Pvt,
Damiano, Philip, Pfc,
D'Amico, Louis A., Pvt,
Damman, Robert E., Pvt,
Damron, John, Jr., Sgt,
‡Damron, Leroy, Pvt,
Dana, Richard H., Cpl,
Dana, Robert R., Cpl,
Danborn, Edward C., Pfc,
Dancer, Harold H., Pfc,
Dancik, Mitchell, Pfc,
Dando, Louis M., Pfc,
†Dandos, Pete, Pvt,
D'Andrea, Mario A., Sgt,
Dane, Raymond E., Pfc,
Danek, Earl R., Pfc,
Danforth, Floyd G., Pfc,
D'Angelo, Bartolo J., Pvt,
†D'Angelo, Melvin, Pfc,
D'Angelo, Michael, Pfc,
†D'Angelo, Thomas, Pfc,
D'Angelo, Vincent A., Pfc,
Daniel, Dale R., T/5,
Daniel, Edward A., Pfc,
Daniel, James P., Jr., Sgt,
Daniel, Joseph P., Pfc,
†Daniel, Samuel L., 2nd Lt,
Daniel, Willis E., Pfc,
Daniel, Woodrow W., Pfc,
D'Aniello, Charles A., Pfc,
Daniels, Andrew A.,
Daniels, Christopher C., Pfc,
Daniels, Howard W., Pfc,
Daniels, John C., Pfc,
Daniels, Mathew, Pfc,
Daniels, Ray P., S/Sgt,
†Danihlik, Steve, Pvt,
Danilson, Charles E., Sgt,
†Danko, Steve P., Pfc,
Danlovich, Dan W., Pvt,
Danner, Leroy, Pvt,
Danton, Joseph A., Pfc,
†Danzer, Harry, Pvt,
Danzig, Leonard S., Pvt,
Darby, William O., Col,
Darchi, Aleonso P., Jr., T/5,
†D'Ardia, Fred R., Pfc,
§Dare, Samuel E., T/5,
†Darlack, Stanley G., Pvt,
Darling, Russell E., 1/Sgt,
Darlington, James P., Pvt,
Darnell, Henry L., Pfc,
Darrow, Raymond C., Pvt,
Darsey, Curtis H., Pvt,
Darst, Homer C., Pfc,
Darst, Raymond J., Pvt,
‡Dashnau, Sidney I., Pvt,
†Dashner, Merton D., Pvt,
Datria, Anthony R., Pfc,
Daugherty, Adrian, Pvt,
Daugherty, Hiram G., Pvt,
Daugherty, Zena S., T/3,
†Daum, Bathasar L., Pvt,
Davenport, Bernard A., Pfc,
Davenport, Claude, Sgt,
Davenport, Fred P., Sgt,
Davenport, Glenn, Jr., Pfc,
Davenport, Harold B., Pfc,
†Davenport, Harry I., Pfc,
Daverin, John J., Pfc,
Daverin, John J., Cpl,
†Davey, John J., Pvt,
Davey, Joseph D., Pvt,
†Davidovitz, Alfred, Pvt,
Davidhiser, Lester M., 2nd Lt,
Davidson, George, Pfc,
†Davidson, George H., Pvt,
Davidson, Harold S., Pfc,
Davidson, James A., Sr., Pfc,
Davidson, Philip W., Pvt,
Davidson, Robert F., Pvt,
†Davidson, Russell G., Pvt,
Davidson, Ted, Pfc,
Davies, Luren W., Pfc,
*Davies, Ward R., Pfc,
Davila, Rudolph B., 2nd Lt,
Davis, Alfred E., S/Sgt,
Davis, Archibald H., Pfc,
Davis, Carvey G., Pfc,
Davis, Charles A., Pfc,
Davis, Charles E., Pfc,
Davis, Charles W., S/Sgt,
Davis, Chester F., Sgt,
†Davis, Cleborn S., Pvt,
Davis, Clyde W., Pvt,
Davis, Coley B., Pvt,
Davis, Esmond L., Cpl,
Davis, Donald W., Pvt,
Davis, Earl C., Pvt,
Davis, Edgar, Pfc,
Davis, Edward M., Pfc,
Davis, Elroy Lewis, T/4,
Davis, Eugene, Pvt,
†Davis, Eugene A., S/Sgt,
Davis, Everett R., Pvt,
Davis, Frank H., Pvt,
Davis, George E., Pfc,
Davis, George W., Jr., Pfc,
Davis, George W., Pvt,
Davis, Harold A., Pvt,
Davis, Herbert R., S/Sgt,
Davis, Homer N., Pfc,
Davis, Homer W., T/5,
Davis, Howard D., Pvt,
Davis, James A., Pvt,
†Davis, James, Pvt,
Davis, James E., Pvt,
†Davis, Jean C., T/Sgt,
†Davis, Jefferson W., 2nd Lt,
Davis, Jess W., Pvt,
Davis, Joe, Pfc,
Davis, John C., T/Sgt,
Davis, Lee A., Cpl,
Davis, Leo P., Sgt,
§Davis, Lucius S., Jr., Capt,
Davis, Marvin E., S/Sgt,
Davis, Mulford R., Pvt,
†Davis, Raymond M., Jr., Pfc,
Davis, Richard F., T/4,
†Davis, Richard H., Pvt,
Davis, Robert A., Pfc,
*Davis, Robert F. O., Sgt,
Davis, Robert J., Pvt,
Davis, Robert J., Cpl,
*Davis, Robert L., Pvt,
Davis, Rudenn D., Pfc,
†Davis, Sammie, Pvt,
Davis, Stanford H., Pvt,
Davis, Stuart A., Pvt,
Davis, Wayne M., T/Sgt,
†Davis, William J., 2nd Lt,
‡Davis, William J., Jr., 2nd Lt,
Davis, William P., Pvt,
Davis, William R., Pvt,
Davisson, Ralph W., Pvt,
Dawdy, Charles M., Cpl,
Dawson, Douglas I., Pvt,
Dawson, Harold E., Pfc,
‡Dawson, Henry, Jr., Pvt,
*Dawson, Herbert L., Pfc,
Dawson, Howard R., Pfc,
Dawson, Stanley R., Pfc,
†Day, Ernest E., Sgt,
†Day, Morris G., Pfc,
Dea, Wing J., Pvt,
Deal, Darby O., Pfc,
Deal, Haskel G., Pvt,
Deal, James H., Jr., Pfc,
Deambrogio, Joseph, Pvt,
Deamer, Clifford B., Pvt,
Deamud, Wilder S., Jr., 1st Lt,
Dean, Carroll P., Pfc,
Dean, Charles W., Pvt,
Dean, Edward V., Pfc,
Dean, Everett L., 2nd Lt,
*Dean, Ezra, Pfc,
Dean, Fred, Pfc,
Dean, George A., Pfc,
†Dean, Harlan E., Pfc,
†Dean, Harold M., Pfc,
Dean, Jesse A., Sgt,
Dean, Julius, Pfc,
De Angelis, Edward, Pvt,
Dearie, Nathaniel F., Jr., Pvt,
Deater, Clifford J., Pvt,
Deatherage, Charles D., Pvt,
§Deatherage, Virgil V., Cpl,
Deaton, Everett J., Pfc,
Deaton, Olin J.,
†De Beney, Richard, Pvt,
Debnar, Edward V., Pfc,
†Debo, Ralph V., Pfc,
De Boer, Worthington, Pvt,
De Bray, Jules H., Pfc,
De Broeck, Gerard R., Cpl,
De Broka, Charles, Cpl,
De Bruicker, V. P., 2nd Lt,
De Busk, Donald M., Sgt,
†Dec, Walter A., Sgt,
Decarolis, Vito C., Pfc,
De Castro, Robert, Pvt,
Dechmerowski, Edward, Cpl,
Decker, Andrew J., Pfc,
Decker, Duane H., Cpl,
Decker, George S., S/Sgt,
Decker, Joe S., Pvt,
Deckert, Harry E., Pfc,
Deckman, Jasper W., Jr., Sgt,
De Costa, Lawrence, Pfc,
De Courcy, John P., Pvt,
Dedor, Zigmund P., T/4,
Dedousis, Nicholas P., Pvt,
Dedrick, Cyrus P., Pfc,
Deebanks, Kenneth J., Pvt,
†Deegan, Thomas J., Jr., Pvt,
†Deeke, Norman H., Sgt,
†Deemer, Howard K., Pvt,
Deemer, William H., Jr., Pfc,
Deen, Carl H., T/Sgt,
Deenick, John M., Pvt,
Deering, Ralph, Pfc,
†Deese, Lee L., Pvt,
De Fatta, Joseph A., Pfc,
†De Filippo, Anthony J., Pvt,
De Ford, James L., Pvt,
De Franco, Santo, Pvt,
Defren, David R., Pvt,
De George, R. N. P., Pfc,
De Gilio, Michael, Pfc,
De Giorgio, Bert, Pvt,
De Gonia, Gerald, Pvt,
De Graeve, Leo P., Pvt,
†De Gregory, Henry R., Pfc,
De Groff, Harold W., Pvt,
De Haan, Siebren, Sgt,
De Hart, William E., Pfc,
De Hetre, Real F., Sgt,
De Horde, Arthur W., Pfc,
Dehm, Louis A., Pvt,
Deigert, Philip J., Pfc,
De Josia, Anthony F., Pvt,
De Kett, Burton G., Sgt,
De Lacy, Daniel J., Pvt,
Delacy, James I., Pfc,
De Ladurantaye, R. F., T/3,
Delaney, Elbert A., Pvt,
Delaney, Orvis I., T/5,
†Delaney, Paul J., Jr., 1st Lt,
Delano, Clarence E., Jr., Pvt,
Delano, Ernest W., Pvt,
Delano, Russell G., Pfc,
De Lao, Max B., Pvt,
Delaportas, John, Pfc,
‡Delaquila, Frank J., T/5,
†De La Ronde, Frederic R., Pvt,
Del Balse, Nicholas, Pfc,
De Leeuw, Henry, Pvt,
§Delella, Thomas, Pfc,
Deleo, Joseph, Pvt,
De Leon, John E., Capt,
De Leonardo, Michael P., Cpl,
Delfarro, Charles, Pvt,
Delgado, Luis A., Pvt,
Delgiudice, Frank J., Pvt,
Del Guercio, John J., Pfc,
†D'Elia, Pasquale, Pfc,
DeLisle, Albert S., Pfc,
‡Dell, Carl M., Pfc,
Dell, William A., Pvt,
Della-Mae, Carl, Pfc,
Dellagatta, Gennaro, Pfc,
Dell'anno, Salvatore, Pfc,
*Delligatti, John P., Pvt,
Del Naigo, Angelo P., Pvt,
†Delong, Lewis R., Pfc,
†DeLonge, John H., Pfc,
†Delpra, Leonard, Pvt,
Del Priore, Joseph, T/5,
Delseno, Patrick, Pvt,
Deltieure, Rene P. J., S/Sgt,
Del Torto, Mecholas J., 2nd Lt,
Del Vecchio, Armondo, Pvt,
De Masse, Stephen P., Pvt,
De Marco, John, Pfc,
Demaree, Herald A., Jr., Pfc,
Demattro, William R., Pvt,
Dembeck, Francis A., Pfc,
Dembinski, John J., Pfc,
†Demchock, Theodore T., Pvt,
†De Meglio, Jerry A., Pfc,
De Mello, John G., Pfc,
De Meo, Sammy S., Pfc,
§Demetre, Alexander S., Pvt,
Deming, Albert H., Pvt,
†Demko, Emil E., Pvt,
Demmie, Peter, Pfc,
DeMott, Melvin W., Pfc,
Dempsey, Frank, 1st Sgt,
Demski, Alexander, Pvt,
Demsky, John M., Pvt,
†Denehy, George A., Pvt,
Denial, Roy, Pfc,
Denise, Gale D., Pvt,
Denison, Clarence C., Pfc,
Denk, Walter J., Pvt,
Denlinger, Richard H., Pfc,
Denman, Joseph W., Pfc,
†Denning, Adrian I., Jr., T/Sgt,
Dennington, James J., 1st Lt,
Dennis, Frank L., Pvt,
†Dennis, Neal W., Pvt,
*Dennis, Ralph A., Jr., Pvt,
Dennison, Donald J., Cpl,
Dennison, Gove E., Sgt,
Denno, Orvalle J., T/5,
Denny, Edward, Pfc,
Denny, Lawrence E., Pvt,
Denny, Thomas J., Pvt,
De Noyer, Orvil E., Pfc,
Densmore, Thomas F., T/5,
Dent, Loren E., Sgt,
Dentel, William V., T/5,
‡Denton, Arthur M., S/Sgt,
Denton, Jack V. C., 1st Lt,
Denton, Warren L., Pfc,
De Nucci, Anthony, Pfc,
Denver, John W., T/4,
Depaepe, Raymond H., Sgt,
De Palma, John R., Pfc,
DePalma, Paul, Pfc,
Depatsy, Alfred, Pfc,
Depew, Harold L., Pfc,
DePillo, Patsy J., Pfc,
De Pover, Vernon F., Pvt,
DePriest, James C., Pvt,
Deprimio, Dominic J., Pfc,
De Prospo, Ettore A., Pvt,
Deras, Martin W., 2nd Lt,
D'Eredita, Marco C., Pfc,
De Remer, Fred G., Pfc,
Derivan, Francis J., Sgt,
‡Derose, Pete, Pvt,
Derosier, Gerald A., Maj,
Derosiers, Wilfred N., Sgt,
†Derr, Howard H., Pfc,
D'Errico, Augustine B., Pfc,
‡Derry, Philip O., Pfc,
Derryberry, Dale H., Pvt,
DeRushia, Emery J., Pfc,
De Sanio, Carmen M., Pfc,
†De Santi, Michael, Pfc,
De Santis, Frank V., Pfc,
Desantis, Salvatore J., T/5,
*De Sarbo, Frank M., Pvt,
De Savigny, George M., Pfc,
Deschaw, Angus W., Pvt,
De Shetler, Louis K., Pvt,
De Shields, Ernest L., Sgt,
Deshotel, Godrey, Pvt,
Desiderio, Joseph J., Pfc,
DeSimone, Armando T., Pfc,
De Sino, Alfred A., Pfc,
‡DeSisto, Mario, Pvt,
Des Laurier, L. H., 2nd Lt,
Desmoines, Anthony J., T/4,
Desorcy, Romeo M., Cpl,
Despins, Wilfred C., Pfc,
Desrosiers, Donald A., Pfc,
†Des Vergnes, Thomas, Pfc,
Deteso, Dante E., Pvt,
Detrie, James F., Pvt,
Dettbarn, Merle M., Pfc,
†Detty, Arthur C., T/5,
Detwiler, Harold, Pfc,
†Detwiler, Richard E., Pvt,
Deubner, William R., Jr., Pfc,
†Deutschman, Alfred J., Sgt,
Devita, Alexander, Pvt,
De Vito, John C., Pvt,
†Devine, John H., Pfc,
Devlin, William C., Pvt,
Devor, Samuel A., Pfc,
Devos, Charles E., Pvt,
Dewberry, Lee R., S/Sgt,
Deweese, Franklin W., Pfc,
Deweese, Hurshell T., Pfc,
Dewey, Vernon A., Pfc,
†DeWinter, Frank J., Pfc,
De Witt, Donald L., Pfc,
Dewyn, Robert J., Pvt,
Dexter, Grant S., Pvt,
†Deyle, Forrest B., Cpl,
Deyo, Burt B., Pfc,
Deyo, Floyd S., Pfc,
DeYoe, Melvin H., Pfc,
Deyoung, Dick, Pvt,
De Young, Richard, Pfc,
Dezarn, William R., 2nd Lt,
Dezotell, Alfred P., Pvt,
Diak, Nick, Pvt,
Dial, Luther, Sgt,
Dials, John, Sgt,
Diano, Francisco, Pfc,
†Diaz, Benny C., Pfc,
Diaz, Danny V., Pvt,
*Diaz, Fernando, Pvt,
Diaz, Frank M., Pfc,
Diaz, Joseph J., Pfc,
Diaz, Rafael C., Pvt,
†Di Bartolomeo, Sebastian R.,
Dibble, Thomas L., Pvt,
Di Belle, James W., Pvt,
De Benedetti, Nat V., Pfc,
De Benedetto, R. S., Jr., Pvt,
DiBona, Gildo L., T/Sgt,
Dicarlo, Rocco J., Pfc,
Dichtel, Charles F., Pfc,
Dicicco, Alfred M., Pfc,
Dick, Edwin B., Pvt,
Dick, Frederick L., Pfc,
Dick, Lewis, Pvt,
Dick, Walter L., Sgt,
Dick William, Jr., Pfc,
Dickerson, Gaige O., Pfc,
Dickerson, Jessie E., Pvt,
Dickerson, Luther M., Pvt,
Dickerson, Tommy, Pfc,
†Dickey, Burl E., Pfc,
Dickey, Clarence, Pfc,
Dickey, Douglas A., Capt,
Dickey, Leonard, Pvt,
Dickie, Kenneth R., Pfc,
*Dickinson, Byron K., Pfc,
Dickinson, Edgar M., Pvt,
Dickinson, Harold W., Pfc,
Dickinson, Raymond F., Pfc,
Dickson, Thomas E., Pfc,
‡Dicsko, John, Pfc,
Dicurcio, Michael A., Pfc,
Didbarzdis, John, Pvt,
†DiDonato, William J., Pfc,
DiDucca, Alfred, Pvt,
Diederich, John P., Pfc,
Diehl, Francis H., Pfc,
Diehl, Leonard F., 1st Sgt,
†Diehl, William H., Pfc,
Dielman, William K., Capt,
Dienslake, Paul B., Sgt,
Dienstman, Benjamin, Pvt,
‡Dietz, Alex J., Pfc,
Dietz, Thomas H., Pvt,
Dietzel, George, Pfc,
DiFazio, Dominic, Pvt,
†Di Filippo, Carmen, Pfc,
Di Franza, Michael, Pvt,

† Killed in Action. * Prisoner of War. ‡ Missing in Action. § Died of Wounds.

IN WORLD WAR II 455

Digerness, Alvin R., S/Sgt,
Digilio, Frank T. A., Pvt,
Di Giovanni, Aldo G., Pfc,
Di Gregorio, Oscar, Pfc,
Di Laura, Fernaldo P., Pfc,
Dile, Lester E., Pvt,
Di Lello, Gastano J., Pfc,
Di Lello, Joseph A., Pvt,
Di Leo, Nicholas, Pfc,
Dilks, James J., Jr., Sgt,
Dilks, Walter T., S/Sgt,
†Dill, George R., Jr., S/Sgt,
Dill, Gordon L., T/5,
Dill, John A., Pfc,
Dill, Kenneth E., Pvt,
Dill, Orlin W., Pfc,
†Dillard, Barney P., Cpl,
Dillard, James C., Pfc,
Diller, Max B., Pfc,
†Dilley, Orville L., 1st Lt,
†Dillman, Roger M., Pvt,
Dillon, Barney L., Sgt,
‡Dillon, Gordon K., Pfc,
Dillon, Joseph R., Pfc,
Di Marcantonio, Albert J., Pvt,
Dimaria, Eugene, Pfc,
Di Marzo, Gaetano S., Pfc,
†Di Matteo, Joseph M., Pfc,
Di Mattesa, Joseph D., Pfc,
Di Medio, Richard P., Pfc,
Di Michele, Anthony C., Pvt,
Dimitriou, George, Pvt,
Dimm, George R., Pfc,
Dimston, Sylvain B., Pfc,
†Di Mura, Phillip, Pfc,
Di Napoli, Anthony N., Pvt,
Di Nardo, Samuel F., Pfc,
Di Natle, Paul V., Pvt,
†Dingus, Henry M., Pfc,
Dinkines, Troy B., Jr., Pfc,
Dinkle, James L., T/4,
Dinsmore, Harry G., Cpl,
†Dioguardi, Joseph C., Sgt,
Dion, George E., Pvt,
Diorio, Michael R., Pfc,
†Di Pasquale, Urbano, Sgt,
Di Persio, Flavio A., Sgt,
†Dipietra, Mariano J., Pvt,
Di Prima, Salvatore C., Pfc,
Di Roma, Michael A., Pfc,
†Di Sanzi, Oreste J., Pfc,
Dishon, Jesse H., Cpl,
Disotelle, Seth H., Cpl,
Distano, Carmen A., Pfc,
Ditchek, Eli, Pvt,
†Ditsworth, La Verne E., Pfc,
Ditsworth, Ralph W., Pvt,
Ditteurth, Raymond, Pfc,
‡Dively, Ned E., T/Sgt,
Divine, Gene B., Pvt,
DiVito, Anthony, Pvt,
Dix, Alfred T., Pfc,
†Dixon, Dewey W., Pfc,
Dixon, Harold A., Pfc,
‡Dixon, Luverne F., Sgt,
Dixon, Robert L., Pvt,
Dixon, William E., Jr., S/Sgt,
Doak, Kermit E., Pfc,
Doan, Herman J., Pvt,
Dobbins, David F., 1st Sgt,
Dobbins, Richard F., Pfc,
Dobbs, Gilbert F., Cpl,
Dobbs, Logan, L., Sgt,
Dobbs, Malcolm C., 2nd Lt,
†Dobek, Frank P., Pfc,
Dobes, John, Jr., Pvt,
†Dobiecki, Mathew T., Pfc,
Doble, Paul C., Sgt,
Dobrovolskis, Frank M., T/4,
Dobson, Gerald A., Pfc,
Dobson, Kenneth A., Pfc,
Dobson, William M., Pvt,
Doby, James O., Pvt,
Dockery, William, Pfc,
Dodd, Homer L., Pvt,
Dodds, Gilbert I., Pfc,
Dodds, Joel L., Pvt,
Dodge, Charles R., Pfc,
Dodge, Donald G., Sgt,
Dodge, Frederick N., 2nd Lt,
Dodge, Richard L., 1st Sgt,
Dodint, Edward F., Pfc,
Dodson, Guy W., Pvt,
Dodson, Harold E., Pfc,
Dodson, James O., Pfc,
‡Dodson, John H., Jr., Pfc,
Dodson, Usters B., Sgt,
Doerfler, Richard G., Pfc,
†Doerner, Wayne, Pfc,
†Doherty, Joseph A., Cpl,
Doherty, Philip D., Jr., Pfc,
Doherty, Timothy J., Pvt,
†Dolak, John M., Pvt,
Dolan, Lawrence E., Pvt,
Dold, George M., Pvt,
Doldan, Manuel, Cpl,
Dolinski, John, Pvt,
Dolton, Herbert F., Pfc,
Dombrosky, Anthony, Pfc,
Dombrouski, Stanley R., Sgt,
Dombrowski, Chester G., Pfc,
Dombrowski, Leonard R., Pvt,
Domek, Nicholas, Jr., Pfc,
Domier, Joseph B., Pfc,
†Domingo, Joseph A., Jr., S/Sgt,
†Dominguez, Anthonio B., Pvt,
Dominguez, Crecencio V., Pfc,
Dominick, Armand J., Pfc,
Dominisk, Edward T., Pfc,
Dommel, Chester W., Cpl,
Domurat, Sigmund A., Pvt,
Donahey, Robert L., Pfc,
Donaldson, Henry W., T/5,
Donaldson, James W., Pfc,
Donaldson, Robert C., Pfc,
Donchez, William, Pvt,
Dondalski, Edward J., Pfc,
Donegan, Timothy J., Pfc,
Doney, Charles, Pfc,
Doney, Richard E., Pvt,
Donica, Wayne W., Pfc,
Donigan, Gerald P., Pfc,
Donlay, Harold W., Pfc,
Donnary, Charles A., Jr., Pfc,
Donnell, Hart B., T/5,
Donnely, Joseph H., Pvt,
Donnelly, James H., Pfc,
Donnelly, Robert E., Pvt,
Donnelly, Robert W., Capt,
Donner, Clement J., Pfc,
Donofrio, Eugene V., Pfc,
Donohue, Daniel V., Jr., Pvt,
Donovan, James P., Pvt,
Donowski, Stanley W., 2nd Lt,
Dooley, Donald G., Pfc,
†Dooley, Frank J., T/4,
Dooley, Harry L., Sgt,
Doorley, James P., Pfc,
‡Doran, James R., Pvt,
Doran, Thomas F., Pfc,
Dorato, Anthony J., T/Sgt,
Dorazo, Francis N., T/5,
*Dorfman, Samuel, Pvt,
Doria, Santino V., Pvt,
Doris, Frank J., Pfc,
Dority, John D., Pvt,
Dorman, Gordon, 1st Lt,
Dorman, Judd P., Pvt,
Dorman, Robert P., Pvt,
*Dorminey, William R., Pvt,
Dorn, Clarence B., Pvt,
Dorner, Chester D., Pfc,
Dorr, Martin H., Pfc,
Dorrian, Daniel G., Pfc,
Dorrier, Walter J., Pfc,
*Dorriety, Emmet H., Pfc,
*Dorsch, George T., Pvt,
Dorsey, Robert L., Pvt,
Dorward, Stuart E., Pvt,
Dose, Kurt, Pfc,
Doskus, Theodore J., Pvt,
Doss, Fred, Pfc,
Doss, Raymond H., Pvt,
Dostal, Vladimir M., 1st Lt,
‡Dostie, Fernand P., Pvt,
Doubler, James L., Pfc,
Doucette, William L., Pfc,
Dougherty, Bruce F., Pfc,
Dougherty, James, S/Sgt,
Dougherty, John E., Cpl,
Dougherty, Thomas J., Pvt,
Douglas, Charles E., Pfc,
Douglas, James W., Pfc,
Douglas, John D., Pfc,
Douglas, Millard A., Sgt,
*Douglas, Walter A., Sgt,
Douglas, William H., Jr., Pfc,
Dover, Henry E., Pvt,
Dowd, John N., Pfc,
Dowdy, Avery F., Pfc,
Dowdy, Curtis F., Pvt,
Dowdy, Leon, Pfc,
Dowell, Kenneth G., Pfc,
Dowell, Raymond R., Pvt,
Dowen, Woodrow W., Pvt,
†Dowling, Edwin S., Jr., Pfc,
‡Dowling, John R., Jr., Sgt,
†Downey, Thomas E., Jr., Sgt,
Downing, John P., Pfc,
Downing, Verl D., Pfc,
Dowrick, Stephen A., Pfc
Doyen, Walter J., Pfc,
Doyle, Herbert L., T/4,
Doyle, James B., Jr., Pvt,
Doyle, John E., Cpl,
Doyle, John W., Pfc,
Doyle, Leroy W., Pfc,
†Draben, Melvin H., T/5,
Drake, Walter R., Pfc,
Drapalski, Frank J., Pfc,
†Draper, James H., Cpl,
Drasner, Jack, Pvt,
Draughon, Hardy R., Pfc,
†Drauszewski, Henry, Pvt,
Dreher, Ralph G., Pfc,
§Dreher, Thomas H., Pfc,
†Dreibelbies, Robert A., S/Sgt,
Dresp, Fred C., Pfc,
Drew, Harry F., Pfc,
Drexler, Steve, Jr., Pfc,
Dreyfuss, Lester, Pvt,
Drezek, Edward, Pvt,
Drill, Wallace G., Pfc,
Drinkard, Arthur G., Pvt,
Driscoll, Walter M., Pvt,
Driscoll, William D., Pfc,
Drnak, Emil S., Pvt,
§Drobniewski, Chester G., Pfc,
†Drobnik, Frank S., Sgt,
Drollinger, Alfonzo, Pvt,
†Droney, John, Pfc,
Drossner, Jacob L., Capt,
Droyton, F. R., Jr., 1st Lt,
Drozd, Frank, Pvt,
Drozda, John A., Pfc,
†Drucker, Simon, Pfc,
Druet, Arthur L., T/4,
Drum, Fred E., Pfc,
Drummond, Robert T., Pvt,
†Drury, Charles M., Pfc,
§Drury, Vernon A., Pfc,
†Druyos, James, Pvt,
Drzyga, Henry J., T/5,
†Duart, James F., Pvt,
Dubberly, Jack, Pfc,
Dube, Andre J., Pvt,
‡Dube, Lowell C., Pfc,
Dubish, Joseph A., Pvt,
†Dubruiel, Wilfred A., Pfc,
Dubuc, Joseph E., Pvt,
†Duby, Bernard L., Pvt,
Duby, Wesley J., Pfc,
*Duch, Joseph J., Jr., Pvt,
Ducharme, Henry J., Pfc,
Duchesne, Roland J., Pvt,
Duckworth, Leland R., T/5,
Duclos, Rodger T., Pvt,
Ducute, I., Cpl,
Duda, Richard, Sgt,
Dudderar, Lee A., Sgt,
†Duddleston, William J., Pvt,
Dudek, Chester A., Pvt,
§Dudik, John, Jr., Pfc,
Dudley, Gene B., Cpl,
Dudley, Jim L., S/Sgt,
Dudley, Joseph L., T/5,
Dudley, Leo E., Pvt,
§Dudley, Leonard P., Pfc,
†Dudley, Nobel F., Pvt,
Dudley, Owen R., Pvt,
†Dudley, Stanley J., Pvt,
Dudley, Warren G., Sgt,
Dudon, Andrew A., Cpl,
Duell, George A., Pfc,
‡Duerkes, Henry W., Pfc,
Duerr, Errol W., Pfc,
Duffany, Charles E., Pvt,
†Duffy, Daniel T., Pfc,
Duffy, William C., Pfc,
Dufresne, Armand H., Pvt,
Dugan, David J., Pfc,
Dugan, Edward P., Jr., Pvt,
Duggan, John J., Pvt,
Duhamel, Anatole J., Pvt,
Dukart, Jacob, Jr., S/Sgt,
Dukart, Lawrence J., Sgt,
Duke, Claude R., Pvt,
Duke, Harry C., Pvt,
Duke, John W., Pvt,
Duke, Leland, T/4,
Duke, Robert W., Pfc,
Dulac, Marcel C., Pfc,
Dulin, Dock, Pvt,
Dull, Lance W., Pfc,
Dumas, Edgar J., S/Sgt,
Dumbaugh, Max L., Pfc,
Dumont, Donald J., Pvt,
Dunaway, John R., Pfc,
Dunay, Augustine J., Pfc,
Duncan, Carl L., Pfc,
Duncan, Charles R., Pfc,
Duncan, Elmer S., Pfc,
Duncan, Fred, Pfc,
Duncan, Harless W., Pfc,
Duncan, Jack M., Lt Col,
Duncan, James F., Pvt,
Duncan, Julius A., Capt,
†Duncan, Kenneth A., Pvt,
Duncan, Onis L., Pfc,
Duncan, Samuel B., Pfc,
Duncan, William A., Sgt,
Dunford, Leonard T., Pfc,
Dungan, Vernon E., Pfc,
§Dunham, Donald F., Pfc,
Dunham, Harold C., Jr., Pfc,
Dunitz, Charles, Cpl,
Dunk, Arthur H., Pfc,
†Dunkelberger, D. L., 1st Lt,
Dunkerley, William J., Pfc,
Dunleavy, John F., Pvt,
Dunlop, Hugh D., Pvt,
Dunn, Arthur M., 1st Lt,
Dunn, Carl R., Pfc,
Dunn, Ernest B., S/Sgt,
Dunn, Herbert A., S/Sgt,
Dunn, Patrick, Pfc,
Dunn, William A., 1st Lt,
Dunn, William F., Pvt,
Dunnagan, William L., 2nd Lt,
Dunnam, Joe W., Pvt,
Dunne, William F., Sgt,
Dunnett, Harry A., Sgt,
Dunnigan, Chris J., 1st Sgt,
Dupere, Albert H., Pfc,
Du Pont, Walter G., Pvt,
Duprey, Arthur J., S/Sgt,
Duran, Trinidad T., Pvt,
Durand, John L., Pfc,
†Durando, Thomas J., Pvt,
Durbin, Clyde P., Pfc,
Durbin, Dewey O., Pvt,
†Durdon, Stephen, Pvt,
Durga, Charles A., Pfc,
‡Durham, Charles F., Pvt,
Durham, Floyd W., Pfc,
*Durham, Frank H., Pfc,
Durham, Joseh E., Pfc,
Durham, Robert M., Pvt,
†Durkee, Charles R., Jr., 2nd Lt,
†Durkee, Louis H., 1st Lt,
Durkin, John P., Pvt,
Duronio, Ennio, Pfc,
Durrance, Lawton J., S/Sgt,
Dusch, Walter H., Pfc,
Duskey, Charles, Jr., Pvt,
§Dutchak, Joseph E., Pvt,
Dutcher, Albert H., Pvt,
Dutil, Elisee A., Pfc,
Dutil, Robert A., Pfc,
Dutkowski, Adam S., Cpl,
‡Dutra, Carl E., Pvt,
Dutton, Henry H., Pvt,
Duval, George F., Jr., Pvt,
Duval, Leon P., Pvt,
Duvall, Everett W., Lt Col,
Duvall, Isadore E., Pfc,
Dvonch, Elmer, Sgt,
Dvoracek, George F., 1st Lt,
Dvoulety, Cyril K., Pvt,
§Dwyer, Joseph E., Pfc,
Dwyer, Joseph M., S/Sgt,
Dwyer, Otis C., Pvt,
Dwyer, William M., S/Sgt,
Dyckman, Harry, Pvt,
Dye, Charles, Pvt,
Dye, Charles L., Jr., Pfc,
Dye, Claude, Pvt,
Dye, Eurie G., Pfc,
Dye, Joffrey B., Pfc,
Dye, Paul H., Jr., Pvt,
Dyer, Mason S., Pvt,
Dyett, Joe, Jr., Pvt,
†Dyke, Lawrence, Pvt,
Dykes, Francis, Pfc,
Dylewski, Withold F., Capt,
Dymock, Lee L., Capt,
Dyreson, Delmar L., Capt,
Dzbanski, John J., Pfc.,
‡Dziak, Thomas F., Pvt,
†Dziak, Walter, S/Sgt,
*Dziamba, Peter, Pfc,
Dziedzi, Robert P., Pfc,
Dzieginski, Aloysius J., Pvt,
Dzula, Edward J., Pfc,

Eades, Lawrence, Pfc,
Eads, Harry L., Pfc,
Eads, Jack W., Pfc,
Eagan, John J., Jr., Pvt,
Eagan, Lloyd E., Sgt,
Eakes, Robert E., Cpl,
Earl, John H., T/Sgt,
Earl, Wilbur M., Pfc,
*Earle, Erwin I., Pvt,
§Earle, Howard, Cpl,
Earles, John W., Pfc,
Early, Raymond W., Pvt,
Early, Robert M., Sgt,
Earp, Claude R., Pfc,
§Earp, Otis C., Pfc,
Easley, John R., 1st Sgt,
East, Bill W., Pvt,
†East, Harry F., Pvt,
East, Plemer L., Sgt,
Eastburn, Alfred H., Pfc,
Easter, Clyde E.,
Easter, Raleigh D., Pfc,
Easterday, Dan C., Capt,
Eastham, Kenneth L., Pfc,
Eastman, James B., Sgt,
Eaton, Arch, Jr., Pvt,
Eaton, Earl V., Pfc,
Eaton, Marvin D., S/Sgt,
Eaton, Robert F., Pfc,
Eaton, Roy L., Pfc,
†Eazor, John, Pvt,
†Eberhardt, Donald W., Sgt,
Eberle, Morris E., Pfc,
Eberle, Robert C.,
Ebinger, Kenneth A., Pvt,
Ebright, Neale F., Capt,
Eccles, Arthur T., Pfc,
†Eccles, Charles J., Pfc,
*Eccles, Clifford, Pvt,
Echko, Joseph, T/5,
Echols, Woodrow, Pfc,
Eck, John S., Pvt,
Eckenrode, Paul F., Cpl,
Eckenrode, Vincent J., S/Sgt,
Eckert, Albert M., S/Sgt,
Ecklar, Willard T., Pfc,
Eckler, Walter H., Pfc,
Eckwert, Vernon P., Pvt,
Eddins, Lonnie, Jr., Pfc,
Eddy, Walter A., Pvt,
Edelen, Carl H., 1st Lt,
Edelstein, Herman, Pvt,
Edgington Verne J., Pfc,
§Edmark, Percy G., Pfc,
Edmiston, William D., Jr., Pvt,
Edmonds, Thurman M., Pfc,
Edmondson, L. M., Pvt,
Edmondson, Oscar O., Pfc,
Edwards, Carl L., Sgt,
Edwards, Charles T., Pfc,
†Edwards, Charles W., Jr., Capt,
Edwards, Cletus W., Sgt,
Edwards, Donald C., Pvt,
Edwards, Everett L., Pvt,
Edwards, Garnnet E., Pfc,
Edwards, Harold L., Pvt,
*Edwards, Harry S., Jr., Pvt,
Edwards, James E., Pfc,
Edwards, James L., Pfc,
†Edwards, John, Pvt,
Edwards, John A., Pfc,
Edwards, John S., Pfc,
Edwards, Joseph M., Pvt,
Edwards, Joseph P., Pfc,
Edwards, Joseph W., Pfc,
Edwards, Leslie G., Cpl,
§Edwards, Nelson C., S/Sgt,
‡Edwards, Norman E., Pvt,
*Edwards, Robert L., Pvt,
Edwards, William, Pfc,
†Eeckhout, Leonard P., Pvt,
Effinger, Clarence J., Cpl,
Egan, Edward J., Pfc,
Egan, Frank J., 1st Lt,
Egan, Joseph F., Pfc,
Egan, Thomas R., Pfc,
Ege, John D., S/Sgt,
Egebergh, Carl C., Pvt,
Egerton, Robert M., S/Sgt,
§Eggemeyer, Clyde L., Pfc,
Eggert, George L., Jr., S/Sgt,
†Egglefield, William R., Sgt,
Eggler, Edward F., Pfc,
Eggleston, Woodrow W., Pvt,
†Eglitz, Arturs, Pfc,
†Egy, Orvile D., S/Sgt,
Ehlers, Bennie L., T/5,
‡Ehmling, Ralph J., Pvt,
†Ehrhart, Charles E., Pvt,
†Ehrlich, Howard N., Pfc,
Ehrsam, Herbert L., T/5,
Eibl, Joseph G., Pfc,
Eichman, Daniel J., Pfc,
Eichstedt, John H., Pfc,
Eickelmann, Harold W., Pfc,
Eidson, Floyd E., Pfc,
†Eidson, James W., Pfc,
†Eidson, Wyman, Pvt,
Eigelbach, Allen Z., Pvt,
Eiland, Robert G., WO(JG),
Eilers, Earl E., Pfc,
Einbu, Sigmund, Pvt,
Eirtle, Jack L., S/Sgt,
Eitzenhoefer, Stephan A., Sgt,
Ekberg, Vernon J., Pvt,
Ekenstam, Harold F., Pvt,
Ekstrand, Karl L., Pfc,
Ekwall, Elmer F., Pfc,
Elasky, Daniel D., Pfc,
Elbers, Theodore P., Pfc,
Elchlinger, John, Pfc,
Elder, Carl L., Pvt,
Eldridge, Alfred S., Pfc,
§Eldridge, Robert J., 1st Lt,
†Eldridge, Walter C., Pfc,
Elekman, Melvin L., Pvt,
Elford, Frank W., Pfc,
Elia, Domenick V., Pvt,
†Elick, Russell W., S/Sgt,

† Killed in Action. * Prisoner of War. ‡ Missing in Action. § Died of Wounds.

Elkind, William, Pfc,
†Elkins, Eddie, Cpl,
Elkins, Floyd R., Pfc,
Elledge, Thomas H., Pvt,
Ellerbrock, Richard A., Pfc,
Ellington, George W., Jr., Pvt
Elliot, Edward S., Sgt,
Elliott, James, Pvt,
Elliott, John W., Pvt,
Elliott, Leroy J., T/4,
Elliott, Linn L., Pfc,
Elliott, Ralph H., Pfc,
†Elliott, William F., Pvt,
Ellis, Billy D., Cpl,
Ellis, Clifford, Pfc,
Ellis, Donald F., Cpl,
Ellis, Franklin S., Pfc,
Ellis, George R., Capt,
Ellis, James H., 1st Lt,
Ellsworth, Howard I., Pvt,
Elluzzi, Dominick J.,
Ellyson, Otis E., Pfc,
Ellzey, Irvin L., Sgt,
†Elmes, John D., Sgt,
Elmore, Joe R., Pvt,
Elmore, Marvin E., Sgt,
Elms, Harold B., Pfc,
Elsevier, John, S/Sgt,
Elsner, George H., Pvt,
Elson, Paul L., Pvt,
Elterich, John A., Maj,
Ely, Orville B., Pvt,
Ely, William, Pfc,
Elzey, Roy E., Pfc,
Emberger, Joseph H., 1st Lt,
Emig, Nelson C., Pfc,
Emil, Sanford J., Pvt,
Emmons, Chester T., Pfc,
Emond, Michael O., Sgt,
Emond, Walter Jr., Pfc
Emory, William H., Pvt,
Enberg, David E., Pfc,
Encinas, Charles M., Sgt,
Endrizzi, Julius M., S/Sgt,
Engebretson, Irwin O., Pfc,
Engel, Blaine N., Pfc,
Engel, Robert J., S/Sgt,
‡Engel, Roland H., Pvt,
Engel, Sam, Pvt,
‡Engels, Henry W., Pvt,
England, Billy V., Pfc,
Engle, Charles M., Pvt,
*Engle, Edward E., Pvt,
Englert, Joseph F., Pfc,
Engwis, Lawrence P., Pvt,
Enloe, Lawrence J., Pfc,
Ennamorati, James, Pfc,
Enos, Charles M., Pvt,
Enos, Warren G., Pfc,
Ensley, Clint E., Pvt,
Ensweiler, Clements B., Cpl,
Ent, George H., Pfc,
Enterline, Quimby C., Sgt,
Eoff, James C., Pfc,
Epelbaum, Rubin, Pvt,
Epler, Herbert J., Pvt,
Epperly, Robert T., Pfc,
Epps, Marvin A., T/4,
Erb, George J., Pfc,
Erb, Jack W., Pfc,
Erby, William J., Pfc,
Erdely, Carl J., Pfc,
Erdman, Harold C., Pvt,
Eremita, Nunsio, Pfc,
§Erhardt, Harold W., 1st Lt,
Erickson, Carl R., Pfc,
Erickson, Raymond L., Pfc,
Erikson, Robert H., T/Sgt,
Erickson, Roy W., Pvt,
†Erickson, Rudolph M., S/Sgt,
Erickson, Theodore, Pfc,
Erickson, Wendell E., Sgt,
Erlandson, Jack E., S/Sgt,
‡Erlewine, Samuel O., Pvt,
Erne, Walter F., 2nd Lt,
Ernst, Michael A., S/Sgt,
Eroh, Robert E., Pvt,
Erwin, Ora A., Pfc,
Eshia, John, Pvt,
Esche, Alban E., Sgt,
Esparza, Manuel M., 2nd Lt,
Esposo, Jose A., Pvt,
Esquibel, Julio G., Pfc,
Essell, Amor, Pfc,
Esser, Edmund V., Sgt,
Essig, William T., Pfc,
Estep, Arvin O., S/Sgt,
Estep, Jack B.,
Ester, Joseph L., Pvt,
Estes, Calvin H., Pfc,
Estes, Bascom F., Pfc,
Estes, Edward H., Pfc,
Estrada, Pantaleon V., Pfc,
Estrada, Patrick, Pvt,
Eternicka, Joseph L., Pfc,
Etheridge, Everett F., Pfc,
Ethier, Arthur C., Pfc,
Ethridge, Harold C., 2nd Lt,
Etter, Kenneth E., Pfc,
§Etzold, James J., Sgt,
†Evanosky, Getty, Pfc,
Eudy, Claude, Pfc,
Eunice, Donald A., T/Sgt,
Eusanio, Robert P., Pvt,
†Evanich, Andy, Jr., Pfc,
Evans, Donald E., T/4,
Evans, Earl W., Sgt,
§Evans, Harold Y., Pfc,
Evans, John F., Pfc,
Evans, John W., Pfc,
Evans, Kulby, S/Sgt,
‡Evans, Leroy J., Sgt,
Evans, Robert, Pfc,
†Evans, Robert E., 1st Lt,
Evans, Roy E., Sgt,
†Evans, Rufus, Jr., Pfc,
Evans, Thomas A., Jr., Pvt,
Evans, Thomas W., Jr., Pfc
Evans, Virgil B., Pfc,
Evans, Walter, Pfc,
Evans, William H., Pvt,
Evans, William R., Pfc,
Evans, Winston C., Cpl,
†Evenson, Orville J., Pvt,
Everett, Edward J., Pfc,
†Everett, George F., Pvt,
Everett, John K., Pfc,
Evleth, Richard L., Pfc,
Ewald, William, R., Pfc,
Ewan, James M., Sgt,
Ewankovich, John, Pvt,
Ewer, John A., Pvt,
§Ewing, James F., Pvt,
Ewing, Raymond D., 1st Lt,
†Ewing, Robert E., Pvt,
Ewing, William R., M/Sgt,
Eye, Bennie A., S/Sgt,
Ezell, Frank J., Pfc,

Fabbro, Bruno M., Pvt,
Fabian, Frank J., Pfc,
Fabjancic, Joseph F., Sgt,
§Fabry, Charles A., Pvt,
Facemyers, Duffy C., S/Sgt,
†Fachet, Adolph F., Sgt,
Fadale, Charles J., Pfc,
†Fadel, Salih M., Pvt,
Fadell, Angelo A., Pvt,
Fadness, Ivan S., Pvt,
Faeo, John, Pvt,
Faerman, Isidore, Pfc,
Fagan, Vincent T., Pfc,
Fagen, William G., Jr., Sgt,
†Fagenbaum, Joseph S., Pfc,
Fagerlie, Wayne D., Sgt,
Fahr, Charles M., Pfc,
Faia, Joseph A., Pfc,
Faidley, Carl M., Pfc,
Faillace, Carlo C., Pvt,
Fain, Joseph R., T/5,
Fain, Robert M., Pvt,
†Fairchild, James W., Cpl,
†Faircloth, James W., Pfc,
Fairclough, Earl H., Pfc,
Fajans, Irving, 2d Lt,
Fajkowski, Leo S., Pfc,
Falck, Walter L., Pvt,
†Falco, Anthony J., Pvt,
Falco, William C.,
Falcon, Robert C., Pvt,
Falconetti, Daniel W., Pfc,
Faletti, Joseph R., Pfc,
Falk, Charles E., Pvt,
Falkowski, Frank W., Pfc,
§Falkowski, John S., Pfc,
Fallowfield, Frank C., Pfc,
Falls Down, Welsey, Pfc,
Falls, Paul W., Pvt,
Falter, Gerard F., Pfc,
Fanell, Joseph A., Pvt,
Fanelli, Joseph G., Pvt,
Fanelli, Michael C., S/Sgt
Fanion, Paul F., Pfc,
Fanning, John J., Pvt,
Fanning, Leo F., Pfc,
†Fanning, Thomas F., Pfc,
†Faranda, John A., Pvt,
Faraone, Henry J., Pvt,
†Farina, Eugene J., Pfc,
†Farina, Patrick F., Pfc,
Farkas, James, Jr., Cpl,
Farkas, Joseph W., Sgt,
Farmer, Charles W., Pvt,
†Farmer, Leslie H., Pfc,
‡Farley, D. C., Pfc,
Farmer, Jason M., Sgt,
Farner, Donald J., Pfc,
Farnham, Alton, Pfc,
Farnsworth, Donald C., Pfc,
Farnsworth, Francis O., T/4,
Farquer, James C., Sgt,
Farraday, David L., Jr., Pvt,
Farran, Ross B., Sgt,
Farrell, Francis E., Pfc,
‡Farrell, Francis R., Pvt,
Farrell, Harry P., Jr., Pfc,
Farrell, James E., S/Sgt,
†Farrell, John P., Pfc,
Farrell, Robert J., Pfc,
Farrington, Don R., Pfc,
†Farris, Henry T., Jr., Pvt,
Farrow, Robert F., Pvt,
†Farwell, Irving A., Pfc,
Fasano, John, Cpl,
Faubion, William J., Pvt,
Faucher, Oliver J., Lt Col,
Faught, John, Pfc,
Faulkner, Donald L., T/5,
Faulkner, Homer J., Pfc,
*Faultersack, Robert, Pvt,
*Fausnaught, Russell W., Sgt,
Faust, Charles W., Pfc,
Faustino, Bernardino, Pfc,
Favazza, Frank, Pfc,
‡Favreau, Leo A., Pvt,
Fay, Carl T., Pvt,
Fazzio, Vincent, Pfc,
Fecca, Orlando J., Pfc,
†Fecicz, Nicholas, Pfc,
Fedeli, Alfred, Sgt,
Feehan, Martin J., T/5,
Feeley, James, Pfc,
§Feely, Carl W., Pfc,
Feigel, William, T/Sgt,
Feightner, Lester U., T/5,
Feine, Harry, S/Sgt,
Feinstein, Bernard, Pvt,
Feinstein, Morris, Pfc,
Feld, Joseph G., Cpl,
Felder, Forest G., Pvt,
†Feldman, Harry, Sgt,
Feldman, Nathan, Pfc,
Feldman, Wilmer O., T/Sgt,
§Felicko, John, Cpl,
†Felkel, Absalom C., Pfc,
Feller, John W., Pvt,
Felt, Lawrence E., 1st Sgt,
‡Feltes, Edward J., Pvt,
†Feltner, Herman, Pvt,
Felts, Charlie O., Pfc,
Fendler, Vernon M., Pvt,
Fendrick, Rudolph V., Pfc,
Fendt, Herbert W., Pvt,
Fennell, Charles A., Sgt,
Fennell, Ray, Pvt,
Fenoglio, Ansel J., Pfc,
†Fenstermacher, Irvin O., Pvt,
‡Fenstermacher, N. E., Sgt,
Feole, Edward R., T/Sgt,
Ferenz, Ferdinand R., T/4,
Ferguson, Charles L., Pfc,
Ferguson, Charles M., Pfc,
Ferguson, Fred, Pfc,
Ferguson, Howard L., Pfc,
Ferguson, Walter A., Pvt,
†Fernald, Harold L., Jr., T/Sgt,
Fernandes, Harold L., T/Sgt,
Fernandez, Joe L., Pfc,
Fernandez, Julio F., Pvt,
Fernandez, Michael J., Pfc,
Fernicola, William, S/Sgt,
Feroleto, Salvatore A., Pfc,
Ferrante, Joseph H., Pvt,
Ferrara, John, Pvt,
Ferrara, Joseph P., Pfc,
Ferraro, Anthony, Sgt,
Ferraro, Nicholas P., Pvt,
Ferraro, Saro G., Cpl,
*Ferreira, Edward, Pvt,
Ferreira, Frank M., Pvt,
Ferrier, Careld, Pvt,
Ferrier, Hugh E., Jr., Pvt,
Ferrell, Ralph S., Pvt,
Ferretti, John F., T/4,
Ferrick, James J., Pfc,
Ferrigno, Sebastian J., Jr., Pvt,
Ferris, Carl F., Pvt,
Ferro, Gaetano, Pvt,
Ferro, Vincent, Pvt,
Ferro, William E., Jr., Pfc,
Ferrucci, Frank L., Pfc,
Ferry, John C., Pvt,
Fertitta, Rosario S., Pvt,
Festa, Tony A., Pvt,
Fesler, Willard, Sgt,
Fesperman, Larkin D., Pvt,
Fessler, Frank J., Pfc,
Festa, Ernest J., Pfc,
Fetcenko, John E., Pfc,
Fetting, Edward A., Pvt,
†Fetto, August F., Pvt,
Fetz, Joseph J., Pfc,
Feulner, Louis H., 1st Lt,
Fey, Edward C., Pvt,
Ficara, Bruno, Pvt,
Fickert, Edward C., T/5,
†Fidler, Eugene F., Pvt,
Field, James B., Pvt,
Fields, George E., Pvt,
†Fiero, Oscar H., Jr., Pvt,
Fife, Albert E., Jr., Pvt,
‡Figeroa, Siego S., Pvt,
Figone, John, Pfc,
Figueroa, Martin G., T/5,
Filipski, Tony F., Cpl,
§Finch, Ned, T/Sgt,
†Fine, William, Pvt,
Fini, Wallace G., Pfc,
†Fink, John F., Pvt,
Fink, Sol A., Pvt,
Finkel, Saul, Pvt,
Finklestein, Arthur, S/Sgt,
Finlayson, Willie M., Pfc,
Finley, Paul J., Pvt,
Finley, Warren C., Pfc,
Finn, Allan T., Sgt,
Finn, Bernard J., Sgt,
Finn, Francis J., Pvt,
Finnegan, Robert W., Pfc,
Finnell, Herman L., Pvt,
Finney, Bruce C., Cpl,
†Finocchiaro, Fred E., Cpl,
Finucan, Robert A., T/5,
Fiore, Francesco P., Jr.,
Fiorentino, Michael, Pfc,
§Fipps, Bailey, Pfc,
Firestone, Clarence, Pfc,
Firlik, Thomas C.,
Fischer, Anthony C., 2nd Lt,
Fischer, Francis J.,
Fischer, Harvey J., 2nd Lt,
Fish, Floyd, S/Sgt,
†Fish, Joseph H., Pfc,
Fish, Opie R., Pvt,
§Fisher, Allen R., Pfc,
Fisher, Burl, Pvt,
†Fisher, Charles P., Pfc,
Fisher, Earnest O., Pvt,
Fisher, Henry, Pfc,
*Fisher, John J., Pfc,
Fisher, John W., Pfc,
*Fisher, Julius, Pfc,
†Fisher, Lloyd N., Pfc,
Fisher, Raymond L., T/4,
Fisher, Raymond M., Pvt,
Fisher, Richard L., T/Sgt,
§Fisher, Robert L., Pfc,
Fisher, Samuel, Pvt,
Fisher, Vernon A., Pvt,
Fisher, Virgil D., S/Sgt,
†Fishun, Andrew, Pfc,
‡Fisk, Blake E., Cpl,
Fisk, Donald J., Pvt,
Fitch, Robert, Pvt,
Fitterer, John F., Pfc,
Fittery, Eugene C., Pfc,
Fitzanko, Walter E., Sgt,
†Fitzgerald, Francis J., Pfc,
Fitzgerald, George L., Pvt,
Fitzgerald, Matthew F., Pvt,
Fitzhugh, Paris M., Pfc,
Fitzpatrick, Robert E., Pfc,
Fitzpatrick, William F., Pvt,
Fitzsimmons, Sam S., 1st Lt,
†Fix, John W., Pvt,
*Fizer, Eugene L., Pvt,
Flachsmann, Matthew J., Pvt,
Flaherty, Francis D., Pfc,
Flaherty, Harry J., Pvt,
Flaherty, Robert J., Pfc,
Flake, James A., Jr., T/5,
Flammia, Michael, Pfc,
†Flanagan, J. C., Pvt,
Flanagan, Lawrence J., Cpl,
Flanagan, Norman E., Pvt,
Flanagan, Robert E., Pvt,
†Flanigan, James R., Pfc,
Flanigan, John F., S/Sgt,
Flannery, Arnold W., Pvt,
Flatley, Russell J.,
Flaugher, James H., Pfc,
Flaver, John F., Pfc,
†Flavin, Lawrence W., Pfc,
Flax, Harold, Pfc,
Fleek, Floyd, Pfc,
Fleeman, David B., Capt,
Fleeman, George E., Pvt,
Fleeman, Jerome, Capt,
†Flege, Emil W., Pfc,
Fleming, Carlyle, Pvt,
†Fleming, Charles W., Pvt,
†Fleming, Jearold B., Pvt,
Fleming, Jerry M., Pfc,
Fleming, John E., Cpl,
*Fleming, Wilbur A., Pvt,
Flener, Osburn R., Pvt,
Flerchinger, Hubert P., Pfc,
Flerry, Kenneth E., Sgt,
†Fletcher, Adrian S., Pvt,
Fletcher, Daniel J., Sgt,
Fletcher, Henry H., S/Sgt,
Fletcher, Kyle C., S/Sgt,
Fletcher, Milton S., Pvt,
*Fletcher, Robert J., Pfc,
†Fletke, Gilbert E., Sgt,
Fleury, Jule A., Pfc,
Flinn, Robert W., Pvt,
Flinner, Albert, Jr., S/Sgt,
Flint, Arthur F., Pvt,
Flint, Nathan A., T/4,
Floch, Walter, Pfc,
Flohrs, Harold, Pfc,
Flomer, Robert E., Pvt,
Flora, Ellis, Pvt,
Florence, Walter J.,
Flores, Guadalupe R., Pfc,
‡Flores, Luis L., Pfc,
Flores, Paul, Pvt,
†Flournoy, Edward O., Pfc,
Flowers, Dale, Pvt,
Flowers, John D., Pvt,
Flowers, Raymond L., Pvt,
Floyd, Acie O., Pvt,
*Fluder, Joseph S., Pfc,
Fluharty, Hugh, Pvt,
Flury, Ernest G., Pvt,
Fluss, Milton, Pfc,
Flynn, Bernard J., Pfc,
Flynn, Bernard J., Jr., Pfc,
Flynn, Bernard J., Jr., Pvt,
Flynn, Christopher E., Pvt,
†Flynn, Francis P., Pfc,
†Flynn, Frank J., Pfc,
Flynn, Henry T., Pfc,
Flynn, Hugh J., T/5,
‡Flynn, James, Sgt,
Flynn, John J., Pvt,
Flynn, Leonard, Sgt,
Flynn, Martin L., Pvt,
Flynn, Ralph M., Maj,
Fogarty, Kenneth H., Pvt,
Fogleman, Kenneth R., Pvt,
Fogt, Harold A., Pfc,
*Foisy, Francis J., Pfc,
Foland, Harley, Pvt,
Foley, Johnny, Pvt,
Foley, Joseph W., Pfc,
†Foley, William C., Cpl,
Folger, Nelson C., Pvt,
Folks, Betram, Pvt,
Follen, Walter M., Pvt,
Follett, Earl W., Pvt,
Follett, Mahlon, Pvt,
Fontana, Edward J., Pvt,
Fontenot, Johnie, Pvt,
Fontenot, Nelson J., Sgt,
Foon, Igai Yeu, Pfc,
Foote, Francis, Pvt,
§Foote, Glenn S., S/Sgt,
Foppema, Sidney B., Pvt,
†Foran, John C., Pvt,
Forbes, Dale E., Pfc,
†Forbes, Henry G., Pfc,
Forbes, Kenneth W., Pfc,
†Forbes, Sanford M., Sgt,
Forcella, Gus J., Pvt,
Ford, Albert J., Pfc,
‡Ford, Charles W., Pvt,
*Ford, Doyle H., Pfc,
Ford, Harold M., T/5,
Ford, John E., Pvt,
Ford, Patrick, Pvt,
Fordham, Daniel J., Pfc,
Fordham, James K., Pvt,
Fore, Cecil, Pvt,
Fore, Leo W., Pvt,
†Forestal, Bernard J., Pvt,
Forgue, William E., Pfc,
†Forister, William G., Pvt,
†Forkey, John H., S/Sgt,
Forlinano, Vincent, Pvt,
Forman, Andy, 1/Sgt,
Formato, Aurelius A., Pfc,
†Forni, Louis C., Pfc.
Fornnarino, George M., Pfc,
‡Forrest, Greig K., Pfc,
Forsaith, Fred J., Jr., Pfc,
Forsgren, Odeen L., Pfc,
Forst, William F., Pvt,
Forsyth, Ira R., Pvt,
†Fortin, Delmar R., Pfc,
*Fortin, Roland M., Pfc,
†Fortuna, William B., Pfc,
Fortunate, Guy P., Pvt,
Fortunato, Arthur P., Pfc,
Fosse, Alvin J., Pfc,
Fossett, John, Pfc,
Fosso, Trygve N., Pfc,
*Foster, Anson E., Pfc,
§Foster, Charles R., Cpl,

† Killed in Action. * Prisoner of War. ‡ Missing in Action. § Died of Wounds.

IN WORLD WAR II 457

*Foster, Chester C., Jr., Pfc,
Foster, Clifford W., Pvt,
Foster, James E., Pfc,
Foster, Joe, Pfc,
Foster, Richard K., 1st/Sgt,
Foster, Robert A., Pfc,
Foster, Robert A., Pvt,
Foster, Wesley J., Pvt,
Foster, William M., Pfc,
*Foster, William W., Pvt,
Fotsch, Laverne P., T/5,
†Fottenbury, Otis O., 2nd Lt,
Fouhy, Bernard J., Pvt,
Foulk, John D., Capt,
*Fountain, Davis H., Pvt,
Fournier, Joseph A., Pvt,
§Fournier, Leon W., Pfc,
Fournier, Thomas A., Sr., Pfc,
†Foussard, Gaston J., Pvt,
Foutty, Andrew D., T/Sgt,
Fowler, Clifford H., Pvt,
*Fowler, Earl H., Pvt,
Fowler, Floyd L., Cpl,
†Fowler, Herman G., Sgt,
Fowler, James B., Pfc,
Fowler, John J., S/Sgt,
Fowler, William L., Jr., Pfc,
Fowler, Woodrow W., T/5,
Fowles, Richard G., Pfc,
†Fox, Alex, Pvt,
Fox, Carl, T/5,
†Fox, Charles E., Pvt,
Fox, Donald F., Pfc,
Fox, George O., Pfc,
Fox, Glenn H., Pvt,
Fox, James M., Pfc,
Fox, James R., Sgt,
Fox, Marvin R., Sgt,
Fox, Patrick J., Pvt,
Fox, Robert L., Pvt
Fox, Russel N., Pvt,
Fox, Thomas A., Jr., 2nd Lt,
Foy, John P., Pvt,
Frabotta, Ovie R., Pfc,
Fradella, Joseph S., Pfc,
†Fraley, Lloyd J., Pvt,
†Frame, John, Pfc,
Franc, Joseph W., Pfc,
France, Robert H., T/4,
Franchak, Michael, T/Sgt,
Francione, John A., Sgt,
Francis, Charles, Pvt,
Francis, Clair L., Pfc,
Francis, Joseph W., Sgt,
Francis, William A., Pfc,
Franckowiak, Thomas, Sgt,
Francks, William G., Pvt,
Franco, Frank T., Pvt,
Frank, Albert, Pfc,
Frank, Carl C., Pfc,
Frank, Charles J., Pvt,
†Frank, Delmer A., Pvt,
§Frank, Harry E., Jr., Pfc,
Frank, James R., Pfc,
Frank, Julius, Pfc,
Frank, Junior, Sgt,
Franke, Werner C., Pvt,
Frankenstein, Ralph W., Pfc,
Franklin, George H., 1st Lt,
Franklin, Kenneth W., Pfc,
Franklin, Walter D., Pfc,
Frankowski, Raymond J., Pvt,
†Franks, Albert W., 1st/Sgt,
Franks, Charles E., Pfc,
Franks, Durell, S/Sgt,
Franks, George C., Pvt,
Franks, William R., Jr., Pvt,
Frankum, Ventner L., Pvt,
†Frankwich, Joseph M., T/5,
Franson, Arthur T., Pvt,
Franyish, Stephen J., S/Sgt,
Franzblau, Sidney P., Pfc,
Franzen, Bertil C., Pfc,
Franzen, Hester C., Pfc,
Fraser, George J., Pfc,
Fraser, Harry L., Pfc,
Fraser, John A., Pfc,
Frasl, Martin, Cpl,
Frassetto, Frank J., Pvt,
Frattolillo, Raymond, Pvt,
Frawley, Clarence J., Pvt,
Frawley, John F., Pvt,
Frayser, Roy V., Pfc,
Fraysur, Charles F., Pvt,
Frazee, Dorsey R., Pfc,
Frazer, William H., Pvt,
Frazier, Albert, Pfc,
Frazier, John J., Jr., Pfc,
Frazier, Leon E., Pvt,
Frazier, Lewis N., Pvt,
†Freano, Joseph W., Sgt,
Freas, John E., Pvt,
Frecentese, William, Pfc,
†Fredell, William L. A., Pvt,
Frederick, Charles, T/5,
Frederick, John P., Pvt,
Frederick, Joseph W., Pfc,
Frederick, William J., Pfc,
*Fredericks, Frank, S/Sgt,
Fredette, Eugene C., Pfc,
Fredlund, Clarence, S/Sgt,
Free, William A., Pfc,
Freed, Howard, Pvt,
§Freedman, Bernard M., Pvt,
Freedman, Jesse E., Pvt,
Freels, Eugene W., Pvt,
Freeman, Curtis R., Pvt,
†Freeman, Daniel E., Sgt,
Freeman, Donald M., Pfc,
Freeman, Edgar P., Pfc,
Freeman, Eugene E., Pfc,
†Freeman, Gilbert H., 2nd Lt,
Freeman, Irving, Pfc,
Freeman, J., Pvt,
Freemore, Robert E., Pfc,
Freeze, Marion J., Pfc,
Frega, Nicholas J., Cpl,
Freidus, Edward F., Pvt,
Frein, Melvin D., Pfc,
Freitag Raymond C., Pvt,
Frelier, Roger L., Sgt,
†French, Charles E., Pfc,
French, Clayton C., S/Sgt,
†French, James H., Sgt,
†French, William H., Pvt,
Frensley, Robert R., Pfc,
Frerichs, Herman F., Pvt,
†Frese, Wallace E., Pvt,
Fretlose, James L., Pfc,
Fretz, John W., Jr., Sgt,
Freunscht, James D., T/5,
Frey, Benjamin E., Pfc,
Frey, Gustave H., Pvt,
Frias, Raymond, Pvt,
Fricke, Francis A., Sgt,
Fricker, William E., Pfc,
†Friday, Charles J., Jr., Pfc,
‡Fridberg, Walter F., Pfc,
Fridley, Ira B., Pfc,
Fridley, Marshall E., Pvt,
Fried, Irwin E., Sgt,
Friedl, Arthur J., Pvt,
‡Friedlander, Herman H., Pvt,
Friedlander, Myron, Pvt,
Friedman, Nathan S., Pvt,
Friedman, Sam, Pfc,
Friedrich, Daniel E., Sgt,
Friel, Jack E., Pfc,
Frieling, Walter A., Sgt,
Friend, Paul H., Pfc,
Friend, Ward W., Pvt,
Frisbie, Hubert L., S/Sgt,
Frisby, Charles A., Pvt,
Frisicaro, Louis J., Pvt,
Fritz, Herbert L., Pfc,
Fritz, Jessie F., Pfc,
‡Fritz, Joseph F., Jr., Pvt,
Fritz, Raymond A., Pvt,
Fritz, Willis J., Cpl,
Fritzke, Robert P., Cpl,
Frix, Clarence R., Pfc,
Frix, Troy W., Pvt,
Frock, Clarence R., Pvt,
Frohbergh, John R., 1st Lt,
Fromer, David, Pfc,
Fromhart, Wilbur B., Pvt,
*Fronczak, Chester A., T/5,
Froncsak, Walter J., Pfc,
Fronek, Joseph, Jr., Pfc,
Fronius, George M., T/5,
Frost, Ernest R., Pfc,
Frost, Walter J., Pvt,
Frowine, Richard F., Pvt,
†Fruback, Anthony, Sgt,
Fruchtman, Philip M., Pfc,
Fry, Abram J., Pvt,
†Fry, Cecil O., Pvt,
Fry, John B., T/5,
Fry, Paul E., Pvt,
Fry, Ralph F., Pfc,
Fry, Thomas A., Pvt,
Fry, Wilbert W., Pvt,
Frye, Edward F., Sgt,
Frye, John C., 2nd Lt,
Frye, Kenneth I., S/Sgt,
Frye, Marvin J., Pvt,
Fryer, John C., Pvt,
Fuchs, Adrian V., Sgt,
†Fuchs, Herbert B., Pvt,
Fuchs, John R., Sgt,
Fuentes, Antonie, Pfc,
Fuentes, Gustavo A., Pfc,
Fugate, Scott L., Pfc,
Fugitt, Walter R., T/4,
Fuermann, Oscar F., Sgt,
†Fulbright, Golden J., Pfc,
Fulcher, Elbert C., Pfc,
Fulford, Seabron A., Pfc,
Fulkerson, Elmer R., Pfc,
Fulks, Ira J., Cpl,
†Fuller, Julius, Pfc,
Fuller, Luther H., Pfc,
Fuller, Perry E., Pvt,
Fullerton, Adrian H., Pvt,
†Fulton, Robert R., Pfc,
Fultz, Bill M., Pvt,
Funderburk, Darrell J., Pfc,
Funk, Christian A., Pfc,
Funkhauser, Purman A., Pvt,
Furlow, Daniel R., Pfc,
Furniss, James C., T/5,
Furr, Esta S., Pfc,
Furstenberg, Henry, Pfc,
Fusco, Charles J., Jr., Pfc,
Futrell, Jack B., Jr., Pfc,

Gabbard, Andrew, Pvt,
Gabel, Ambrose V., Pvt,
Gabel, Roy H., Pvt,
Gable, Myron L., Pfc,
Gabriau, Frank J., Pfc,
Gabriel, Arthur C., T/5,
Gabriel, Joseph S., Pvt,
†Gabrynowicz, Richard C., Pvt,
Gac, Chester N., Cpl,
Gaccione, Vincent, Pfc,
Gadberry, John T., Pfc,
Gade, Robert E., Pvt,
Gadjusek, Rudolph F., Pvt,
Gaffin, Daniel J., Pvt,
Gaffney, William D., Pvt,
Gage, Anthony Jr., Pfc,
Gage, Richard A., Pfc,
Gage, Willard L., Pfc,
Gaglio, John A., Pvt,
*Gagne, Alfred, Jr., Pvt,
Gagne, Cephas A., Pfc,
Gagne, Edgar C., Pfc,
Gagne, Edgar R., Pfc,
Gagne, Raymond G., Pvt,
Gagnon, Samuel G., Pvt,
Gagnon, William J., Pvt,
Gago, Benito, Pvt,
Gahagan, Harold J., Pfc,
†Gaines, Delbert, Pvt,
Gaines, James R., T/4,
†Gainor, Summers H., Jr., Pvt,
Gaiton, Trinidad S., Pvt,
‡Gaj, Alfred J., Pvt,
Galante, Anthony, Pfc,
†Galfre, Vincent A., Pfc,
Galgon, Edward J., Cpl,
Galie, Carl V., Sgt,
Galindo, Ismael N., Pfc,
Galkus, Walter J., Pvt,
†Gall, Harry, Pvt,
Gall, William B., Pvt,
†Gallagher, Bernard J., Pfc,
Gallagher, Earl P., Pfc,
Gallagher, Edward R., Pvt,
Gallagher, Frank M., Jr., Pfc,
Gallagher, Le Roy, Pvt,
Gallagher, Oliver I., Pfc,
†Gallagher, Robert B.,
Gallagher, William T., Pfc,
Gallaher, William, Pfc,
Gallant, Lionel A., Pvt,
†Gallardo, Macario, Jr., Pvt,
Gallardo, Moises, Pvt,
Gallegos, Gilbert, Pvt,
Gallello, Dominic, Pvt,
‡Gallentine, James, Pvt,
Gallerani, James, Pvt,
Gallerani, Louis D., Pvt,
Gallic, John M., Pfc,
Gallion, Clifton L., Pfc,
Gallo, James V., Pfc,
Gallo, Kelly J., Pfc,
†Gallo, Nicholas R., Pfc,
Gallo, Peter J., Pfc,
Gallucci, Andrew A., Pvt,
Gallup, Clarence D., Cpl,
‡Gallup, Russell D., Pfc,
Galovic, Frank Z., Pvt,
*Galusha, Clarence, Pfc,
Galvagni, Victor J., S/Sgt,
Galvez, Ricardo A., Pfc,
Galvin, William E., Pvt,
Galyean, Charles D., Pfc,
Gamble, Boyd V., Pfc,
Gamble, Glenn W., Pvt,
Gamble, Laurence J., Sgt,
Gamble, Stanley M., Pfc,
†Gamble, William C., Pvt,
Gambrell, James H., Jr., 1st Lt,
†Gamelin, Arthur J., Pvt,
Gamillo, Laurence F., Pvt,
Gamon, Willis D., Pfc,
†Gamperl, Frank, Cpl,
Gane, Edgar J., Pvt,
Ganguzza, Sebastian B., Pfc,
*Ganley, Richard J., 1st Lt,
Gann, Cecil, Pfc,
Gann, Hobert E., Pvt,
Gann, John W., Pfc,
Gannon, Richard D., Sgt,
Ganous, Bonnie T., Jr., 2nd Lt,
Gapen, Leo M., Pvt,
Gapienski, Joseph, Pfc,
Garbaccio, Joseph, Pvt,
Garber, Charles A., Sgt,
Garber, Donald J., Pfc,
Garcia, Anthony H., Pfc,
Garcia, Cesar A., Pvt,
Garcia, David A., Pfc,
Garcia, Edward, Pfc,
†Garcia, Emilio E., Pvt,
Garcia, Fernando F., Pvt,
Garcia, Jacinto M., Pfc,
Garcia, Joe C., Pvt,
†Garcia, Jose M., Pvt,
Garcia, Joseph, Pvt,
Garcia, Juan E., Pfc,
Garcia, Maximino, Pfc,
Garcia, Orencie, T/5,
Garcia, Raymond, Pvt,
Garcia, Raymond T., Pfc,
Garcia, Trinidad R., Pvt,
*Gardella, William J., Pfc,
Gardener, Gerald L., Pvt,
Gardiner, Daniel C., Pfc,
Gardpipe, Jacob, Pvt,
†Gardner, Calvin R., Pfc,
Gardner, Frank, Pvt,
Gardner, Gerald L., Pvt,
Gardner, James E., Pvt,
Gardner, Roy E., Cpl,
Gardner, Russell A., Pfc,
Garellick, John J., Pvt,
‡Gargano, Tony, Pvt,
Gargiulo, Albert, Pfc,
Gari, Louis H., Pfc,
Garifalos, James, Pfc,
Garland, Boyd, Pfc,
Garland, James N., Pvt,
Garner, Carlton T., Pfc,
Garner, Dillard L., Pfc,
Garner, James H., Pfc,
Garner, Robert F., Pvt,
Garner, Roy E., Pfc,
*Garner, Shirley, Pvt,
Garnot, Frank M., Pvt,
Garnsey, Earl F., Pfc,
Garone, Leo N., T/5,
Garrett, Ebon A., T/5,
†Garrett, Ira B., Pvt,
Garrett, Ray A., Pvt,
Garrett, Virgil L., Pfc,
Garrett, Willard M., 1st Lt,
Garrigan, Leo J., S/Sgt,
Garrison, Herbert A., Pvt,
§Garrison, Thomas S., Pfc,
Garrity, Hugh F., Pfc,
Garrity, John J., S/Sgt,
Garrow, Edward O., T/4,
Gartman, Jullian W., Pfc,
Gartner, Herman P., Pfc,
Garton, Raymond E., Pvt,
Garves, Edward A., Pfc,
†Garvey, Kenneth J., Pvt,
Garvey, Thomas A., 2nd Lt,
†Garvey, William J., Pfc,
Garvin, Kenneth E., Pfc,
Garzia, Armand A., Pfc,
Gasper, Matthew C., T/4,
Gasser, James E., T/4,
Gassman, George E., T/4,
Gastiger, Ralph C., Pfc,
Gaston, Billy C., Pvt,
*Gaston, Harold, Pvt,
‡Gateley, Arthur L., Pvt,
Gates, Doyle D., T/Sgt,
Gates, Raymond L., 2nd Lt,
Gates, Virgil A., Pfc,
Gatewood, Charles E., Pfc,
Gatewood, John R., Pfc,
Gatlin, Milton E., Pvt,
*Gaudet, John E., Pvt,
Gaudiosi, Charles, Pfc,
Gaul, William J., Pvt,
Gauna, Crecencio, Pfc,
Gauna, Lancho P., Pvt,
Gauthier, Arthur J., Pvt,
Gauthier, Paul R., Pfc,
Gavron, Steve, Sgt,
Gay, Bryan W., S/Sgt,
Gay, Lynn C., Pfc,
†Gebhart, Nickolas H., Sgt,
‡Gebing, Howard V., 2nd Lt,
Gedacht, Isidore, Pfc,
Gedeon, Frank J., Pvt,
Gedney, Frank, Pvt,
Gedrich, Jerome E., Pvt,
†Gee, Albert, Pvt,
Geer, Donald C., Pfc,
Geers, Paul E., 2nd Lt,
Geesey, Stewart W., Pfc,
Gegenheimer, W. T., Pfc,
†Gehman, Webster, Pfc,
Geier, Clemens, Pvt,
Geiger, Mathias R., Pfc,
Geisler, Robert R., Pfc,
‡Geissler, Jerome W., S/Sgt,
Geldart, Richard W., Pfc,
Geldmyer, Albert J., Pvt,
Gell, James E., S/Sgt,
Gellerman, John P., T/5,
Gelman, Delmore R., Pvt,
Gelski, Walter A., T/5,
Gemmiti, Mario F., Pfc,
Genatempo, Patrick J., Pfc,
Gennari, Thomas L., Pvt,
†Gens, August W., Jr., Pvt,
Gentile, Michael J., Pvt,
Gentile, Robert P., Pvt,
Gentleman, Francis I., Pfc,
Gentry, Maxie L., Pfc,
*Gentry, Roy W., T/4,
Gentry, Ruford, Pfc,
Gentry, Wayne M., Pvt,
George, Bernard T., Pfc,
George, Doyle L., Pvt,
George, Ernest J., Pfc,
George, Frederick B., S/Sgt,
George, Manuel F., Pfc,
George, Modeste M., T/5,
George, Raymond, Jr., Pfc,
George, Robert J., Pfc,
Georgeoff, Alexander, Pfc,
Gerber, Harry, Pfc,
†Gerhardt, Elmer E. K., Pvt,
†Gerhart, John M., Jr., Pvt,
§Gerhart, Michael M., Jr., Pvt,
Gerlach, Chester J., Pvt,
Gerlach, Richard J., Pfc,
German, Benson W., Pfc,
German, Fillmore, Pvt,
German, Peter P., Pfc,
Germano, Mario A., Pfc,
†Germany, Roy B., Pfc,
Germershausen, J. B., Pfc,
Gernazio, Mike, Pvt,
Gerrich, Robert H., Pvt,
Gerry, George, Pvt,
Gerstein, Harry, S/Sgt,
Gessele, Raymond C., Pfc,
Geter, Oner J., Pvt,
Gette, Luther M., Capt,
Gettings, Claiborne W., Pvt,
†Gettys, Wilbur G., Pvt,
Getz, Arlington C., S/Sgt,
Gewirtz, Norman, Pfc,
Gherardi, Silveo, Pvt,
Ghoogasian, Stephen, Pvt,
Giabidino, Robert A., Pvt,
Giammateo, Robert, S/Sgt,
Giammona, Sam, Pfc,
†Gianaris, Louis N., Pvt,
Giardiello, Arthur, Pvt,
‡Giardino, Vincent F., Pvt,
Gibbons, Edward G., Pfc,
*Gibbons, John B., Pfc,
Gibbons, Nicholas J., Pvt,
†Gibbs, Harold L., Pvt,
Gibbs, Jack, Pfc,
Gibbs, Preston B., Pfc,
Gibbs, William R., Pfc,
*Giberson, George A., Pvt,
Giblin, Vincent F., Pfc,
Gibouleau, Edward F., S/Sgt,
Gibson, Arnold J., T/Sgt,
Gibson, Carl V., Pvt,
Gibson, Noah C., Sgt,
†Gibson, Paul D., Pvt
Gibson, Paul J., Pfc,
Gibson, Paul R., Pfc,
Gibson, Robert C., Pvt,
Gibson, Robert L., Pfc,
Gibson, Wallace C., Sgt,
Gibson, William T., Pvt,
†Gidcumb, Alfred W., Pvt,
Giedris, Walter A., Pvt,
Giello, Carmen E., Pvt,
Gierhart, Charles E., Pvt,
†Giffin, Edgar R., 2nd Lt,
†Gifford, Alwyn R., Pvt,
†Gifun, Donald E., Pvt,
‡Gilbert, Earl R., Jr., Pvt,
Gilbert, George B., Cpl,
Gilbert, Harold A., Pvt,
Gilbert, James F., Jr., Pvt,
Gilbert, James H., Jr., Pfc,
†Gilbert, James J., Pvt,
Gilbert, Lee R., Pvt,
Gilbert, Oscar M., Jr., Pvt,
Gilbert, Sidney, Pvt,
Gilbertson, Jervin G., S/Sgt,
†Gilbertson, Richard A., Pfc,
Gilchrist, Edward L., Pfc,
Gildenberg, Morris, Pvt,
Gildner, Reginald H., Pfc,
Giles, Ernest G., S/Sgt,
Giles, Merrill H., Pfc,
Gilge, Ellsworth L., Pvt,
Gilkerson, Densel, Pvt,

† Killed in Action. * Prisoner of War. ‡ Missing in Action. § Died of Wounds.

Gill, John M., Pfc,
†Gill, Michael P., Pfc,
Gillan, Alexander K., Pvt,
‡Gille, Donald H., Pfc,
Gille, Harold J., S/Sgt,
Gillespie, Clifford W., Pfc,
Gillespie, Ellis F., Pfc,
Gillespie, George W., Pfc,
*Gillespie, Ralph L., Pfc,
Gilley, Fred J., Pfc,
Gilley, John R., Sgt,
Gillies, Murray, Pvt,
†Gilliland, Henry O., Pfc,
Gilliland, William, Pvt,
Gillin, Edward J., Pvt,
Gillis, John J., Pvt,
Gillispie, William, Pfc,
Gilman, Donald H., Pfc,
§Gilman, Herbert R., 2nd Lt,
Gilman, James W., Pvt,
Gillmartin, Russell, Sgt,
Gilmer, John H., Pfc,
†Gilmore, John C., Pvt,
Gilmore, Patrick G., Pvt,
‡Gilmore, Ralph, Pvt,
Gilpin, Barney T., Pvt,
Gilpin, James R., Pfc,
†Gilbreath, James A., Pvt,
Gilbreath, William C., Pfc,
Gilson, George T., Pvt,
Gilutin, Joseph, T/4,
Ginsberg, Abraham A.,
Gioio, Ernest H., Pvt,
†Gioitta, Anthony G., Pvt,
Giombetti, Amiedio V., Pfc,
Giongrete, Frank A., Pfc,
Giordano, Carl, Pvt,
Giovanacci, Wilson, Sgt,
Giovanni, John, Pfc,
‡Gipson, Ernest L., Pfc,
Gipson, Roy, T/5,
Girocco, Amedia J., Pvt,
Girouard, Edmond J., Pvt,
Gisondi, Dan, Pvt,
Gissarelli, Luke, Cpl,
Gitchell, Harvey H., Pvt,
Gittins, Robert N., Pfc,
†Gittlen, Joseph J., Cpl,
‡Giuga, Mariano T., Pvt,
‡Giza, John A., Pfc,
Gizynski, Joseph, Pfc,
Gjunnanaritz, Alex J., Pvt,
Gladden, Noel A., S/Sgt,
†Glade, Keith E., Pvt,
Gladwell, Gordon W., Pfc,
Glahe, Lawrence W., Pfc,
Glancy, Fletcher H., Jr., Pvt,
Glantz, Ervin R., Cpl,
Glasco, Ray B., T/4,
Glascoe, Floyd M., Pfc,
Glasgow, Isadore, Pvt,
*Glass, Albert D., Pvt,
Glass, Charles, Pfc,
Glass, William F., T/4,
Glasscock, Arue, Pfc,
Glasser, William B., Pfc,
Glassgow, James C., Pfc,
Glassner, Kenneth C., Pfc,
Glasure, Earl L., Pfc,
Glavey, James, Pfc,
Glaze, Andrew J., Jr., Pvt,
Glaze, Edward L., 2nd Lt,
Glazer, David W., Pvt,
Glazer, Lester, Pvt,
Gleason, Robert E., Pvt,
†Gleaves, James G., Pvt,
Gleeson, Joseph J., Pfc,
Gleeson, Paul L., Pfc,
†Gleich, Frederick L., Pfc,
Glena, Robert F., Pfc,
*Glenn, Charles H., Pvt,
Glenn, Elmer H., Jr., Pvt,
Glenn, Leo V., T/5,
Glenn, Vernon C., Sgt,
Glenny, Hoyt, Pvt,
Glewwe, Alfred E., S/Sgt,
*Gliniecki, Joseph F., Pvt,
Glock, Leo E., S/Sgt,
Glock, Werner E., Pfc,
†Glosner, James V., Pvt,
Glosto, Edward J., Pfc,
Glover, Earl W., Pfc,
Glover, Elbert E., T/4,
Glover, Luther J., Pfc,
Glowa, Paul M., Sgt,
‡Glum, Walter W., Pfc,
Gnoinski, Joseph J., Pvt,
Goad, Calvin H., Pfc,
Goans, Franklin K., Jr., Pfc,
Gobrogge, Albert C., S/Sgt,
Gochis, Constantine, 2nd Lt,
†Goda, David, Pvt,
Goddard, Donald D., Pvt,
Goddard, Ernest, Pvt,
Goddard, John B., 1st Lt,
Goddard, John H., Pfc,
Godek, John F., Pfc,
Godfrey, Louis J., Pvt,
Godfrey, Robert J., T/5,
Godin, Frank A., Pfc,
Godlewski, Victor J., Jr., Pfc,
†Godsey, Clarence, Pfc,
Godwin, Cameron H., Sgt,
Godwin, William J., Sgt,
Goedde, Frank E., Pfc,
Goercke, Forrest W., 1st Sgt,
Goetz, Carl A., Pvt,
Goetz, Louis C., Pvt,
Goetzman, Maurice B., Pvt,
Goff, George L., Pvt,
Goff, Louis H., T/5,
Goff, Sidney R., Pvt,
‡Goffinet, Andrew J., Pvt,
Goforth, Quinton, Pvt,
Goham, Joseph C., Pfc,
Gohl, John E., Pfc,
Goida, John, Pfc,
Goin, Pat O., Pfc,
Goin, Valda L., Pfc,
Gojmerac, John, Pfc,
Golab, Walter F., Sgt,
Golabek, William J., Pfc,
Goldberg, David, Pfc,
Goldberg, Martin, Pfc,
Goldberg, Murray, Pvt,
Golden, Joseph, Pvt,
‡Golder, George, Pfc,
Goldhaber, David L., Pvt,
Goldhagen, Herbert W., Pvt,
Goldman, Alvin C., Pfc,
†Goldner, Herman A., Pfc,
Goldrick, Michael P., Jr., Pvt,
†Goldsmith, James H., Pvt,
Goldstein, Joseph, S/Sgt,
Goldstein, Walter, Pfc,
Golichowski, Richard R., Cpl,
Golis, Anthony J., Pfc,
†Golladay, Floyd W., Pfc,
Golochowicz, Joseph J., Pfc,
Gomberg, Richard, 1st Lt,
Gomez, Joe B., Pvt,
Gomez, Mauchelino G., Pvt,
Gompers, Charles, S/Sgt,
‡Gona, Richard, Pfc,
Gondola, Anthony J., Pvt,
Gonsalves, James, Pvt,
Gonsalves, Manuel J., Sgt,
Gonzales, Anselmo, Jr., Pfc,
Gonzales, Aurelio, Pfc,
Gonzales, Fred, T/5,
Gonzales, Ramond M., Pfc,
Gonzales, Victor R., Pfc,
Gonzalez, Aureliano B., Pfc,
†Gonzalez, Dimas S., Pvt,
Gonzalez, Edmundo, T/4,
Gonzalez, Joseph, Pfc,
Gonzalez, Leopoldo, Jr., Pvt,
§Gonzalez, Pedro, Cpl,
Gonzalez, Rudolph, Pfc,
Gooch, Adelbert O., Pfc,
Good, Carl L., Pfc,
Good, Frank S., Sgt,
Goodhue, Raymond E., Pvt,
†Gooding, Francis X., Pvt,
†Goodloe, Everette M., Pfc,
*Goodman, Charles F., 1st Lt,
Goodman, Eric, Pvt,
Goodman, Frank, Pvt,
Goodman, Henry G., Pfc,
Goodman, Herbert, Pvt,
Goodman, Morris, Pfc,
Goodman, Wayne C., Pfc,
Goodmon, Robert C., Sgt,
†Goodnite, Glenn N., Sgt,
Goodpaster, George F., Pfc,
Goodrich, Carl D., Pfc,
Goodrich, Harold E., Pvt,
Goodrich, Russell H., Pfc,
Goodrich, Warren C., T/5,
§Goodson, Elbert R., Pfc,
Goodwald, Clyde H., Pfc,
†Goodwin, C. P., Jr., 1st Lt,
†Goodwin, Cornelius A., Pfc,
†Goodwin, James A., Sgt,
†Goodwin, Harold H., Pfc,
†Goodwin, James P., S/Sgt,
†Goodwin, Lawrence E., Pfc,
Goolsby, Bobby K., Pvt,
‡Goolsby, John T., Pvt,
Goraj, Anthony S., Pfc,
Goraj, John C., Cpl,
†Gordon, Clifford G., 1st Lt,
Gordon, Earl A., Cpl,
Gordon, Fred G., T/5,
Gordon, Giles T., Pfc,
*Gordon, Harold, Pvt,
Gordon, Walter J., Pvt,
Gorman, Fred D., Pfc,
Gorman, George G., Pfc,
Gorman, William J., Jr., Pfc,
Gormley, Charles M., Pvt,
Gorwelanczyk, L. F., Pvt,
Gose, Ralph D., Pfc,
Goskowicz, Alois, Cpl,
*Gosnell, Grady R., Pfc,
Goss, Everett, Pfc,
†Goss, Floyd E., Pvt,
Gosselin, Gerard M., Pfc,
Gossett, James R.,
Gotbeter, Henry, Pvt,
Gotta, John B., Pfc,
Gottberg, John N., Pfc,
Gottlieb, David, Pfc,
§Gottschald, Arthur H., Pfc,
Goucher, Burton G., Pvt,
‡Gough, William P., Pvt,
†Goulette, Cheshawgan H., Capt,
Gourley, Joseph H., Pvt,
Gouse, William E., Pfc,
Gover, Jack W., Jr., Pfc,
Goveronski, Victor A., Cpl,
Govetche, Joseph D., Pfc,
†Gower, Clyde A., Pfc,
‡Gowker, Arthur R., Pvt,
†Grabarek, Frank J., Sgt,
Grabarz, Charles C., Pfc,
Grabitsky, Marcellus A.,
Grabner, George P., S/Sgt,
Grabo, Arthur J. W., Pvt,
Grace, Edward J., Pfc,
Graceffo, Charles C., Pfc,
Grady, David J., Jr., Pvt,
Grady, Earl H., Pvt,
†Grady, Joseph M., Sgt,
Grady, Percy F., Pfc,
Graeser, Gilbert L., Pfc,
Graff, Lawrence W., T/Sgt,
Gragg, Hobert, Pvt,
Graham, Harry L., Jr., T/4,
Graham, Hobart P., Pfc,
Graham, Jack, Pfc,
Graham, James H., Pfc,
Graham, John L., Pfc,
Graham, Leo O., Pfc,
Graham, Leonard F., Pvt,
†Graham, Philip S., Pvt,
Graham, Richard E., Pfc,
Graham, Robert D., Pfc,
Graham, Robert W., Pfc,
†Graham, Roland H., Pfc,
Grahek, Edward F., Pfc,
†Grama, John G., Pvt,
Gramm, Harold, Pfc,
Gramse, Harland A., Sgt,
Granato, Fred A., Pvt,
Grand, Robert, Sgt,
Grande, Joseph E., Pfc,
Grandin, Horace J., Pvt,
Grandmaison, Robert J., Pfc,
†Grando, George A., Sgt,
†Granger, Percival H., Jr., Pvt,
Granice, Antonio J., T/5,
Granillo, Carlos D., Cpl,
‡Grant, Clarence J., 1st Lt,
†Grant, Daniel J., Pfc,
Grant, Donald D., Pfc,
Grant, Thomas L., Sgt,
Grant, William R., Pvt,
Grass, James W., Pvt,
‡Grassia, Pasquale, Pfc,
Grasso, Frank J., S/Sgt,
†Grasty, Charles F., Pfc,
Grasz, Albert T., Sgt,
Grau, Charles O., Pfc,
Graves, Albert P., Pfc,
Graves, Fred R., Jr., Pfc,
Graves, Hollis, T/Sgt,
†Graves, Robert J., Pfc,
‡Gray, Alvin V., T/Sgt,
Gray, Charles W., Cpl,
‡Gray, Herbert L., S/Sgt,
Gray, Howard M., Pfc,
Gray, Thomas R., Sgt,
‡Graziano, Anthony A., Pfc,
Grazio, La, Ralph W., Pfc,
Greco, Frank P., Pfc,
†Greco, Thomas J., Pvt,
Green, Alan M., 2nd Lt,
Green, Albert L., Sgt,
Green, Claude A., Pvt,
Green, Edgar M., Pvt,
Green, Ernest J., 1st Lt,
Green, Herman L., Pfc,
Green, James T., Pvt,
Green, John A., Pvt,
*Green, Johnny S., Pfc,
Green, Lloyd L., Pvt,
Green, Luther M., T/Sgt,
†Green, Robert A., Pvt,
Green, Robert J., T/Sgt,
Green, Roy J., T/5, Flint,
†Green, Samuel T., Jr., Pfc,
Green, U. L., Pfc,
†Green, Wesley L., Pfc,
Green, William A., Pvt,
Green, William H., Pfc,
Greene, Clyde R., Pvt,
Greene, James D., T/5,
†Greene, John J., 1st Lt,
†Greene, Julian F., S/Sgt,
Greene, Lavaughn H., T/Sgt,
Greene, Seymour, Pfc,
Greenfield, Saul, Pvt,
Greengtski, Arnold A., Sgt,
Greenhill, Raymond F., Pfc,
Greening, William B., Pfc,
Greenlee, William E., Pfc,
†Greenman, Robert E., Pvt,
†Greenwald, Robert L., Pfc,
Greenwold, Vernon R., Pfc,
Greenwood, James R., Pfc,
†Greenwood, John F., Pfc,
†Greenwood, Percy J., Pfc,
Greenwood, Roy F., Pfc,
Greenwood, Samuel A., Pvt,
Greer, Frederick R., Pfc,
Greer, John A., Cpl,
‡Greer, John T., Pfc,
Greeson, Wayne L., Pvt,
Greff, Leo J., Pvt,
†Greggerson, Robert G., Pvt,
Gregoire, Romeo J., Pvt,
Gregorczyk, Bernard M., Pvt,
Gregory, Chester M., S/Sgt,
†Gregory, Hugh N., Sgt,
Gregory, James A., Pfc,
Gregory, Lee L., Pfc,
†Gregory, Lewis S., 2nd Lt,
Gregware, John P., Pvt,
†Greider, Harold L., Pvt,
Greig, James, Pfc,
Greinier, Vincent L., Pfc,
Greinke, Edwin, Pvt,
Greinki, Le Roy G., Pvt,
Greising, George L., S/Sgt,
Grennen, George H., Pfc,
Grenough, Gerald O., Pvt,
Gresak, Matthew P., Pfc,
Gresh, Homer H., Pfc,
Gresham, Robert N., Pfc,
Greshel, Joseph J., Pfc,
Gress, Leslie I., Pfc,
*Greyzck, Lawrence M., Pfc,
Gribbin, Thomas F., Pvt,
Grice, Carl F., Pvt,
Grice, Thomas C., Pfc,
Grider, William E., Pfc,
†Griebstein, Alfred, Pfc,
Grier, Arthur, Pfc,
Grier, Clyde H., Pvt,
Grieser, Bruce E., Pfc,
Grifaitis, Edmund J., T/5,
†Griffin, Anthony N., Pvt,
Griffin, Edward T., Pfc,
Griffin, George L., Sr., Pvt,
Griffin, George M., Pfc,
Griffin, Homer C., Pvt,
Griffin, Hubert, Sgt,
Griffin, Jasper N., Jr., Pvt,
Griffin, Norwood G., Pvt,
†Griffin, Virgil R., T/5,
Griffin, Willard, Pfc,
Griffin, William E., Pvt,
Griffin, William T., Jr., Pvt,
Griffith, Ambrose, 2nd Lt,
Griffith, George J., Pfc,
Griffith, Leslie U., Pvt,
Griffith, Sylvan W., S/Sgt,
Griffith, Warren G., Pfc,
Griffith, Warren W., Pvt,
Griffith, Wilbur H., Pfc,
Griffiths, Robert A., T/5,
Grigsby, Ernest, Pvt,
Grigsby, Onnie R., Pvt,
Grimes, Francis M., T/4,
*Grimes, Howard L., Pvt,
Grimes, Leonard R., S/Sgt,
Grimm, Oley O., Pvt,
Grimme, William R., Pvt,
Grindle, Howard R., Pvt,
Grindstaff, Earl H., Pfc,
Grindstaff, Howard S., Pfc,
Grinnan, John F., Pvt,
Grisso, Paul A., Pfc,
Grissom, Hugh B., Pfc,
Griswold, William R., S/Sgt,
Grob, Howard G., Sgt,
Groccia, Nathan J., Pfc,
Grochowski, Matthew H., Pvt,
Groegler, Alois L., Pfc,
†Groeneveld, James A., Pvt,
‡Groff, Charles R., S/Sgt,
†Groff, David L., Pvt,
Groff, William W., Pfc,
†Grogg, Claude R., Jr.,
Groh, John, Pfc,
Gronewald, Gail J., Sgt,
*Gronkiewicz, Raymond H., Pvt,
Grooms, Glenn, S/Sgt,
Groot, Melvin L., 1st Lt,
Grosfeld, William, Pvt,
Gross, Anthony, Cpl,
Gross, Earl E., Pvt,
Gross, Edward, Pvt,
Gross, Emil G., Pvt,
Gross, Harry A., Sgt,
Gross, Harry L., Pfc,
Gross, Joseph A., Pfc,
§Gross, Joseph J., 2nd Lt,
Gross, Marvin, P., 2nd Lt,
†Gross, Peter, Pfc,
Gross, Thomas A., T/4,
Grossman, Ivan, Pvt,
Grossman, Leo, Pfc,
Grossman, Ralph E., Pvt,
Grossnickle, Walter R., Pvt,
Grotto, Pasquale J., Pfc,
Grove, Edward R., Jr., Pfc
Grove, John A., Pfc,
Grover, William T., Pvt,
‡Grubb, Myron E., Pvt,
Grubb, Paul B., Pvt,
Grubbs, Warren P., Pfc,
Grube, Everett N., Pfc,
Grube, Ralph D., Pfc,
Grudzien, Alexander J., Pfc,
Grueber, William H., Pfc,
Gruel, Clarence E., Pvt,
Grund, Erwin W., Pvt,
‡Grunwald, Harold C., Pvt,
Grunzweig, Nicholas J., 1st Lt,
Gruwell, Merlin W., Pfc,
Grzywacz, Chester A., Sgt,
Guanci, Peter P., S/Sgt,
†Guard, Ernest K., 1st Lt,
Guber, David, Pvt,
Guckert, George E., Jr., Capt,
Guelker, Frederick J., Pvt,
Guentherman, Henry J., Pvt,
Gueringer, Clifton E., Pfc,
Guerra, Peter, Pvt,
Guerrieri, Emilio, Pvt,
Guertin, Leo F., Pfc,
Guessnier, Warren J., Pvt,
Guevara, Raymond M., Pfc,
Guffey, Bennie L., Sgt,
Guglielmo, Arthur, Pfc,
Guida, Anthony A., Pfc,
Guidinger, Dayton, Pvt,
Guidone, Salvatore P., Sgt,
Guigliano, Sam P., Pvt,
Guild, Harold L., Pvt,
Guillaume, Henry C., Pfc,
Guillou, Jean L., Pvt,
Guimont, Wilfred F., S/Sgt,
Guin, Boyd E., Pvt,
Guinn, George J., Pvt,
Gukeisen, Silas J., Pfc,
Gula, John, Jr., Pvt,
Gulentz, John D., Sr., Pfc,
Gulick, Mike, Pvt,
Gullett, Earl, Pfc,
Gullett, Lewis W., Pfc,
Gullo, Joseph J., Pfc,
Gulowacz, Thomas, Pfc,
‡Gumble, Howard C., Pvt,
Gumley, Wayne I., S/Sgt,
Gunderson, Orville L., Pfc,
§Gunkel, Raymond B., Pvt,
Gunnells, Thomas J., Pvt,
†Gunsallus, Russell C., Pvt,
Gunter, Ernest E., Pvt,
†Gunter, Lawrence W., Pvt,
Gupton, Edward C., Pfc,
Gurchiek, William H., Pfc,
Gurley, Willie J., Pfc,
†Gurski, Joseph A., Pfc,
Gustafson, Robert O., T/5,
Guthrie, Albert E., Cpl,
Guthrie, Buford A., Pfc,
§Guthrie, Willie D., Pvt,
†Gutierrez, Jose, Pfc,
Gutierrez, Rudolph G., Pvt,
Gutshall, Avis R., Pvt,
Guy, Robert E., S/Sgt,
Guyer, Donald L., Pfc,
Guyre, Leonard J., 1st Lt,
Guzicki, Aloysius C., 1st Lt,
Guzzetta, Arthur A., Pvt,
Gynan, Dexter N., Pvt,

Haas, Kenneth L., Pfc,
Haberstroh, August, T/5,
Habitz, Edward, Sgt,
Hablutzel, Robert C., Pfc,
Hack, Arthur J., Jr., Pfc,
†Hack, Charles C., Pfc,
Hack, James R., Pfc,
†Hacker, John L., Pvt,
Haddock, Philip, Pvt,
†Haddock, Wayman J., Pvt,
Haddon, James C., Pvt,
Hadley, Kenneth W., Cpl,
Hadley, William C., Sgt,
Hadsell, Francis P., Sgt,

† Killed in Action. * Prisoner of War. ‡ Missing in Action. § Died of Wounds.

IN WORLD WAR II 459

Haedike, William D., Capt,
†Haeni, Robert, Pvt,
Hafer, Howard W., Jr., Pfc,
Hagman, Robert R., Jr., T/Sgt,
Hagan, Earl J., T/5,
Hagan, Frank L., Pfc,
†Hagan, James R., Pfc,
†Hagan, Stephen J., Pvt,
Hagedon, Ralph T., Pfc,
Hagedorn, Lawrence F., Pfc,
†Hagemeyer, Ralph O., S/Sgt,
Hagen, Anthony J., T/5,
Hagen, Anton A., Cpl,
†Hagen, Curtis G., Pfc,
Hagen, George E., Pfc,
Hagenow, Sidney R., Pvt,
Hager, Grover C., Jr., Pfc,
Hager, Russell M., Pfc,
Hagerty, Carl J., T/4,
Hagerty, George V., Pfc,
Haggard, Lyle W., Pfc,
Haggerty, James A., Jr., Pvt,
Haggerty, James F., Pfc,
Haggitt, Vern F., Pfc,
Hagle, Clarence, Pvt,
Hagood, Leon D., Pfc,
Hahl, Erich K., Pvt,
Hahler, Robert J., Pfc,
†Hahn, Joseph D., Pvt,
Haier, George A.,
Haigh, Charles D., T/5,
Haire, Charlie C., Pfc,
Haines, Charles F., S/Sgt,
Haines, Harold H., Capt,
†Haines, John E., Pvt,
§Hainey, Bogan, Pfc,
Hainey, James, Pvt,
Hake, Tod M., Sgt,
Hakki, Edward M., Pfc,
Hakki, Henry P., Pfc,
Hakki, William T., Pfc,
Halackna, Chris, Pfc,
Hale, Cecil T., Sgt,
†Hale, James L., S/Sgt,
Hale, Joe, Jr., Sgt,
Hale, Kenneth B., Pfc,
‡Hale, Max E., Pvt,
Hale, Titus G., Pfc,
†Halek, Edward F., Pvt,
Hales, William A., Pvt,
Haley, John H., Pvt,
Haley, Theodore W., Pfc,
Hall, Arthur G., Pvt,
Hall, Bert, Pfc,
Hall, Bert M., Cpl,
Hall, Carl R., Sgt,
Hall, Clifford A., Pvt,
Hall, Earnest A., Cpl,
Hall, Estil, Pvt,
†Hall, Francis G., Pfc,
Hall, Frank H., Pvt,
Hall, H. D., Jr., Pfc,
Hall, Gerald V., T/4,
Hall, George W., Pvt,
Hall, Jack S., Pfc,
Hall, Kellis, Pvt,
‡Hall, Lawrence D., Pvt,
Hall, Mark R., Jr., Pfc,
Hall, Milton J., Pfc,
†Hall, Noah B., Pfc,
Hall, Otho L., Pfc,
Hall, Ralph E., Sgt,
Hall, Ross D., Pfc,
Hall, Roy W., Cpl,
†Hall, Sterling C., Pfc,
Hall, William R., Cpl,
§Hall, Zehnor, T/4,
†Hallet, Linn W., Jr., Pvt,
Halley, Walter E., S/Sgt,
Hallman, Otis H., S/Sgt,
Hallmark, Ernest F., Pfc,
Halsey, Ellsworth L., T/Sgt,
Halterman, Joseph M., Sgt,
Ham, John W., Jr., Pvt,
Hambrick, Hoyt Z., S/Sgt,
Hamel, Albert J., Pvt,
Hamel, Louis H., Pvt,
Hamilton, Clayton W., Pfc,
Hamilton, LeRoy E., T/Sgt,
Hamilton, Marvin E., Pfc,
Hamilton, Milton E., Pfc,
†Hamilton, Paul V., Pvt,
Hamilton, Robert B., Pvt.
Hamilton, William A., Pfc,
*Hamlett, Eugene J., Pfc,
†Hamlin, Everett, Pfc,
Hamlin, John H., Pvt,
†Hamm, Clayton E., Pvt,
Hamm, Raymond M., Pvt,
Hamm, Rudolph P., Pfc,
Hamm, Wilbur V., 2d Lt,
Hamme, Ervin G., Jr., Cpl,
Hammer, Maurice, Pfc,
Hammerlund, George H., Pfc,
Hammerstone, L. E., Pvt,
Hammett, William C., 2d Lt.,
Hammock, Charles R., Pfc,
†Hammon, Frank E., Pfc,
Hammond, Leslie W., Pvt,
†Hammons, Clifford D., Sgt,
Hammons, Harless, S/Sgt,
Hammons, Lester R., Pvt,
Hampel, Tyrus W., Pvt,
Hampson, Russell A., Pfc,
Hampton, Arthur C., Pvt,
†Hampton, Oren R., Pvt,
Hampton, William R., Sgt,
Hamrick, Dave, Pfc,
‡Hamrick, Don F., T/5,
Hamrick, Silas B., Pfc,
Hanberry, James J., S/Sgt,
Hance, Walter, Pfc,
Hancock, Charles E., Jr., Pvt,
Hancock, Clifton D., 1st Lt,
Hancock, Grady E., Pvt,
Hancock, Henry H., Capt,
Hancock, Wallace L., Pvt,
Hancox, Gordon M., Pvt,
‡Hand, Floyd F., Pvt,
†Handley, Charles W., T/5,
Handley, Clarence P., Jr., Pvt,
Haney, Walter J., Jr., Sgt,
Haney, William F., Pfc,
Hanish, Reginald J., Pvt,
Hanley, Edward J., Pvt,
Hanley, John W., Pfc,
Hanna, Beauford L., Pfc,
Hanna, James C., Pfc,
†Hannah, Walter W., Pvt,
Hanne, Leonard D., Capt,
Hanner, Benjamin N., Sgt,
Hanner, Orvil M., S/Sgt,
Hannewald, Emery G., Sgt,
Hannin, William F., Pvt,
†Hannon, Ernest E., Pfc,
Hansen, Archie, Pfc,
Hansen, Budd L., S/Sgt,
Hansen, Clarence R., Pfc,
Hansen, Clifford L., Pfc,
Hansen, Edmund J., Pvt
Hansen, Edward H., Pfc,
Hansen, Edward H., Pfc,
Hansen, Frank R., Sgt,
Hansen, Gordon E., T/4,
Hansen, John A., S/Sgt,
Hansen, John L., Cpl,
Hansen, Lloyd F., Pvt,
Hansen, Milton L., Pvt,
Hansen, Niels A., Pfc,
Hansen, Robert W., Sgt,
†Hansen, Thomas E., Pfc,
Hansford, Virgil E., Pvt,
Hanson, Cecil E., Sgt,
Hanson, Elmer E., Pfc,
‡Hanson, Norman L., Pfc,
Hanson, Raymond H., Pvt,
Hanson, Walter E., Pfc,
Harahush, Peter, Pvt,
Haraway, Luther W., Pfc,
Harber, Joseph J., Pfc,
Harbin, James A., Pfc,
Harbison, Derlan A., Pvt,
†Harbison, Frank, Pfc,
Harbridge, Thomas E., Pfc,
Harchar, Henry J., Pfc,
Hardeman, Glenn E., Pvt,
Hardeman, Harold L., Pvt,
Harden, Elmer L., Pfc,
Harders, Raymond, Pvt,
Hardesty, Ray D., Pfc,
Hardie, Edward W., Pvt,
Hardigree, William R., T/5,
Hardin, Howard, Pfc,
Hardin, James W., T/4,
Harding, Edmund D., Pfc,
Harding, Perry E., Pfc,
Hardman, Melvin, Pfc,
†Hardwick, Willis J., Pfc,
Hardy, Lewis W., Pfc,
Hardy, Llewellyn L., Pvt,
Hare, Victor B., Pfc,
Hargett, Robert E., Pfc,
Hargis, Tom, Pvt,
*Hargrove, Robert L., Jr., Pvt,
Haring, John J., Pfc,
Harkins, William J., Jr., Pvt,
‡Harlan, Donnie W., Pvt,
Harley, Everett L., Pvt,
Harlon, William M., Pfc,
†Harlow, Arthur F., Pvt,
Harmala, Raymond, Sgt,
Harman, Samuel A., Pfc,
Harmon, Bernis H., Pfc,
‡Harmon, J. V., Cpl,
Harms, Otto H., Pfc,
Harner, James R., Pvt,
Harner, Milton E., Pfc,
Harness, Herbert L., Pvt,
†Harnett, Thomas M., S/Sgt,
§Harnicar, Joseph R., Pvt,
Harp, Carl M., Pfc,
Harp, Otis L., Pvt,
Harper, Covington C., Pvt,
Harper, Dennis G., Pvt,
Harper, Jesse H., Sgt,
Harper, Harvey H., Jr., Pfc,
Harper, Melvin D., Pfc,
Harrell, Ben, Col,
†Harrell, Paul F., Pfc,
Harrigan, Lawrence J., Sgt,
Harrigan, Robert D., Pvt,
Harrington, Cecil C., Cpl,
Harrington, John J., Pfc,
Harrington, John R., Pfc,
Harrington, John R., Pvt,
‡Harrington, Kenneth G., Pvt,
Harrington, Richard O., Pfc,
Harris, Carl H., Pfc,
Harris, Clyde E., Pfc,
Harris, Emmett, Pfc,
Harris, Frank A., Pvt,
Harris, George E., Pvt,
Harris, George L., Jr., 1st Lt,
Harris, Gerald W., Cpl,
Harris, Harlan H., Sgt,
Harris, Hobert, Jr., S/Sgt,
Harris, Howard S., Pvt,
Harris, Hunter L., Pfc,
Harris, James A., Pfc,
Harris, James W., Pfc,
Harris, Jennings L., Pvt,
†Harris, John W., Pfc,
Harris, Kyle R., Pvt,
†Harris, Lonnie M., Pfc,
Harris, Luther A., Cpl,
Harris, Noel W., Cpl,
Harris, Orbie G., S/Sgt,
Harris, Orville R., Pfc,
Harris, Robert H., Pvt,
*Harris, Travis J., Pfc,
*Harris, Vernon R., Pfc,
Harris, Walter G., Pfc,
Harris, Wendell W., T/4,
†Harris, Woodward, Pvt,
Harrison, Carl W., T/5,
Harsch, Walter H., S/Sgt,
Harrison, Bryce A., Pfc,
Harrison, Charles, Pfc,
Harrison, Eldridge C.,
Harrison, Franklin C., Pvt,
*Harrison, George R., Jr., Pvt,
Harrison, Herbert H., Pvt,
Harrison, Vinson, Pfc,
Harry, Edwin P., Sgt,
Hart, Edman M., Pvt,
Hart, George, Pvt,
Hart, George H., Pfc,
Hart, Harold A., Pfc,
Hart, Harvey, Pfc,
Hart, Howell H., Capt,
Hart, James G., Sgt,
†Hart, Loraon S., Pvt,
Hart, Other W., Pvt,
Hart, Ralph B., Pvt,
Hart, Reginald C., Pvt,
Hart, Robert E., Pvt,
Hart, Thomas B., Pfc,
Harter, Lyle N., Pfc,
Hartfield, Donald G., Pvt,
Hartin, Robert, T/4,
Hartless, Lloyd W., S/Sgt,
Hartley, James W., Pfc,
Hartman, Rudolph, Sgt,
Hartronft, James A., Pvt,
†Hartill, Fred E., Pvt,
Harting, Donald, Pvt,
Hartley, Elden G., Pvt,
Hartman, Louis W., Pfc,
†Hartman, Robert R., Pvt,
†Hartman, William C., Sgt,
‡Hartstein, George H., Sgt,
Hartstern, Carl J., Pfc,
‡Hartwell, Edwin D., Pvt,
Hartwig, Wilbur R., Pvt,
‡Harvey, Adam, Pvt,
†Harvey, Donald A., Pfc,
Harvey, Frank D., Pfc,
Harvey, Howard Edmond, Pfc,
Harvey, Joseph G., T/4,
Harvey, Rolland, Pvt,
Harvey, William S., S/Sgt,
Harvey, Zollie R., Pvt,
†Harvill, Edward E., Sgt,
Harvill, William P., Pfc,
Harward, James E., Jr., Pfc,
Harwood, Chester L., Pfc,
Haschak, Joseph, Pfc,
Haselberger, James J., T/5,
†Haselwood, Leroy A., Capt,
Hash, Cecil R., Pfc,
Hash, Elisha P., Pfc,
Haskell, Albert E., Sgt,
‡Haskett, James, Pfc,
†Haskew, Sam T., Pvt,
Hass, Stanley R., T/5,
†Hastings, Claude H., Pvt,
Hastings, Kenneth R., S/Sgt,
Hatala, Cyril P., Pfc,
†Hataway, Willie B., Pvt,
Hatch, Robert C., Pfc,
Hatch, Ronald G., Pfc,
Hatcher, Edward A., Pfc,
Hatcher, William P., Sr., Pvt,
Hatcher, William R., Pvt,
Haten, Solomon S., Pfc,
Hatfield, Edward, 2nd Lt,
Hatfield, James E., Pfc,
†Hathaway, Ernest V., Pfc,
Hathaway, Lawrence J., Pvt,
Hathorn, George S., Pfc,
Hatten, Sam, Pfc,
Hatter, Melvin E., Pfc,
Hatzimagari, George J., Pfc,
Haubrich, Irving J., Jr., Pvt,
Haugen, Einer M., T/4,
Haugh, James D., Pvt,
Haugh, Roy, Pfc,
†Haught, James M., Pfc,
Haultcoeur, Hippolyt, T/5,
Haulsee, Andrew R., Pfc,
‡Hauschild, Harry G., 2nd Lt,
Hauser, Albert C., Pvt,
Hauser, Harold H., S/Sgt,
Hausner, Edward, Pfc,
Hausvater, Jacob N., Pvt,
†Hautala, Arne J., Pfc,
‡Havens, Harry E., Jr., Sgt,
Haversat, Earl W., Pvt,
Havrila, Edward G., T/Sgt,
Hawk, Hugh K., Pfc,
Hawkinberry, Junior N., Pvt,
Hawkins, Albert G., Pvt,
Hawkins, Charles E., Pvt,
*Hawkins, Fay L., Pfc,
Hawkins, Hubet C., S/Sgt,
Hawkins, Joe B., Pfc,
Hawkins, Jonnie H., Pvt,
Hawkins, Lawrence E., Pvt,
Hawkins, Lee V., Sgt,
Hawkins, Samuel R., Pfc,
Hawthorne, John W., Pvt,
Hay, Arthur R., Pvt,
Haye, Edward F., Jr., Pfc,
†Hayes, Clayton J., Pvt,
†Hayes, Frank, Pfc,
Hayes, Harold D., Pvt,
†Hayes, Henry C., Pvt,
Hayes, Ira D., Pvt,
Hayes, James E., Jr., Pfc,
Hayes, Louis E., Pfc,
§Hayes, Otis E., Jr., Pvt,
Hayes, William A., Jr., Pfc,
*Hayes, William R., Cpl,
Haymond, Summers C., Pfc,
Haynes, Elmo L., Pvt,
†Haynes, Robert E., S/Sgt,
Haynes, Roger G., Pvt,
†Hays, Beverly G., Capt,
Hays, Elvin E., Sgt,
Hays, Rayman W., Pvt,
Hays, Raymond L., Pfc,
Hays, Thomas B., T/5,
Hayward, James S., T/5,
†Hayward, William A., Pvt,
Hazel, James G., 1st Lt,
Hazelden, Robert, T/5,
Hazelwood, Charles, Pfc,
†Hazen, James W., Jr., Pfc,
†Hazlewood, Leonard A., Pfc,
Heacock, Frank, Pfc,
Heacox, Wilfred J., Pvt,
§Head, Earl, Jr., Sgt,
Head, Herbert W., Jr., Sgt,
Head, Vincent G., Cpl,
Head, Warren A., Pfc,
Heald, Howard A., Pvt,
Healey, Paul U. V., Pfc,
Healy, Dennison F., Pfc,
Healy, George V., 1st Lt,
Healy, Jeremiah P., Pfc,
Healy, John A., Jr., Pvt,
†Healy, Milton H., Pfc,
Healy, William H., T/5,
‡Heard, Robert M., Sgt,
Heater, Robert C., S/Sgt,
†Heater, Wallace W., T/Sgt,
Heath, Charles S., Pfc,
Heath, James L., Pvt,
Heath, Virgil E., T/5,
Heath, William C., Pvt,
Heath, William E. F., Pvt,
Heaton, George A., Pvt,
Heaton, Harold A., Pvt,
Heaver, Marion F., Pfc,
Heavens, Elvin L., Sgt,
Heavey, James F., Jr., Pvt,
Hebbeler, Henry H., Pvt,
†Hebert, Clifford O., Pvt,
†Hebert, Joseph J., Pvt,
Hebert, Joseph P., Pfc,
†Hebert, Norman A., Pvt,
Hebron, George D., Jr., Cpl,
Heck, Maxwell R., Pfc,
Heckendorf, Royal H., Pvt,
Heckmann, Eugene M., Pfc,
Hedberg, Robert A., Cpl,
Hedden, Ralph F., S/Sgt,
†Heden, Harold G., Pfc,
Hedge, Orval E., Pfc,
Hedges, Robert H., Pfc,
Hedges, Theodore G., Pvt,
Hedrick, Elbert R., Pvt,
Hedrick, Jesse H., T/5,
Heffington, Charles W., Pvt,
Hefling, Morris J., Pfc,
Hegedus, Gene J., Pvt,
Hegel, Wilbert A., Pfc,
Hegllund, William O., Pfc,
†Heglund, Dale L., Pvt,
Heidemann, Bernard W., Pfc,
†Heidenfelder, John J., Jr., Pvt,
Heidt, Walton B., Pfc,
§Heigold, Gene G., Pvt,
Heil, Roy M., Pfc,
Heina, Edward O., Pfc,
Heinbaugh, Ira D., Pvt,
Heine, Reinhold E., Pfc,
Heinlein, Walter F., Pfc,
Heintges, John A., Col,
†Heintz, Louis E., Pfc,
Heinz, William E., Pfc,
Heisick, Raymond J., Sgt,
†Heisler, Arthur W., Pvt,
Heissner, Henry F., T/4,
Heithoff, Alvin J., Pvt,
Heitmeyer, John A., Pfc,
Heitzman, Robert T., Pfc,
*Hejduk, Nelson S., Pvt,
Helbling, Lee, Pfc,
Held, Cletus A., Pvt,
Helfrick, Paul J., T/5,
Heller, Ralph R., Pfc,
Heller, Robert E., Pfc,
Hellingson, Lyle F., Pvt,
Helm, Alford H., Pfc,
Helman, David L., Pfc,
Helms, Jack S., Pfc,
Helms, Paul E., Sgt,
Helstetter, Harold J., Pfc,
‡Helt, Paul A., Pfc,
Helton, Lonnie, Cpl,
Helzerman, Willard W., Pfc,
Hemann, Henry A., T/5,
Hembleben, Edwin C., Pvt,
Hembree, Joe J., Pvt,
Hembrook, Kenneth J., Pfc,
Hemmenway, William F., Pfc,
Hemner, Vernon L., Pfc,
†Henbest, Henry G., Pvt,
Henbest, Laverne L., Pfc,
*Henderlight, Fred K., Pvt,
Henderlite, Garland R., Pvt,
Henderson, Billy, Pfc,
Henderson, Cleatus E., 2nd Lt,
Henderson, Harry G., Pvt,
Henderson, Leroy, Pfc,
Henderson, Robert W., Pfc,
Henderson, Russell J., S/Sgt,
Hendrick, Donald R., Pvt,
‡Hendricks, G. W., Jr., 2nd Lt,
Hendricks, Robert C., Pfc,
Hendricks, Roger P., Pfc,
Hendricksen, George A., Pfc,
Hendrickson, Oliver R., Cpl,
‡Hendrix, Forrest W., S/Sgt,
‡Henerlau, Paul R., II, Pvt,
Henesler, James C., T/5,
Henico, Henry, Pvt,
Hennessee, Edgar F., Pfc,
Hennessey, William A., Pvt,
Hennick, Lloyd R., S/Sgt,
Hennigh, John W., Pfc,
Henning, William, Pfc,
Hennings, Gerald T., T/Sgt,
Henningson, William C., Pvt,
Henrich, Conrad A., Pfc,
Henrich, John A., Cpl,
*Henrie, George, Cpl,
Henritze, Robert T., Sgt,
Henry, Anson C., Sgt,
Henry, Frank D., Pvt,
Henry, Garland, Pvt,
†Henry, James, Pvt,
Henry, J. T., Pvt,
*Henry, Turner T., T/Sgt,
Henry, Walter, Jr., Pfc,
†Henry, William C., Pvt,
Henry, William M., Pvt,
Hensen, Frederick T., Pvt,
Henslee, Howard L., Pfc,

† Killed in Action. * Prisoner of War. ‡ Missing in Action. § Died of Wounds.

Hensley, Earl, Pvt,
Hensley, Frank R., T/5,
Hensley, Lester W., Pvt,
Hensley, Robert N., T/4,
†Henson, Delma, Pfc,
Henson, Hirstle L., S/Sgt,
Henson, Melvin W., Pvt,
*Henthorn, James J., Pvt,
Hepler, William I., Pvt,
Herbaugh, Cecil A., Pfc,
*Herber, Harlan H., Pvt,
†Herbin, Harry J., Pfc,
Herbranson, Morris W., Sgt,
Herbst, Donald F., Pfc,
Herlihy, Robert E., Sgt,
Herman, Elton H., Sgt,
Herman, Forrest C., Pvt,
Hernandez, Albaro, Pvt,
†Hernandez, Alfonso M., Sgt,
Hernandez, Elias A., Pfc,
Hernandez, Leonard G., Pfc,
Hernandez, Rodolfo L., Pfc,
Hernandez, Salvador, Pfc,
†Herndon, Robert, Pvt,
Herndon, Virgil R., Pfc,
Herndon, William E., Pvt,
†Herndon, Willis E., Pvt,
Heroman, William L., S/Sgt,
Herr, Lloyd S., Pvt,
†Herrera, John A., Pfc,
†Herring, Francis M., 1/Sgt,
Herring, James S., Pfc,
Herring, Jessie E., Sgt,
Herring, Roy J., Pfc,
Herring, William C., Pfc,
Herrington, Weldon R., Pfc,
Herrlich, William F., Pfc,
*Herron, Earl P., Pvt,
Hershkowitz, Max, Pfc,
*Herstein, Edward J., Sgt,
Hertel, Arthur D., Cpl,
Hertz, Leonard B., Pvt,
†Hertzen, Harold G., Pfc,
†Heskitt, Floyd L., Jr., Sgt,
Hess, Bradburn H., Pfc,
†Hess, James R., Pvt,
†Hess, Mike, Sgt,
Hess, Russell L., Pfc,
Hess, Steven C., T/Sgt,
†Hesser, Norman C., Pvt,
†Hessey, Benjamin F., Pvt,
Hessney, Michael C., Pfc,
Hester, C. E., Pfc,
Heston, Garrett W., Pfc,
Hetherington, Delmar W., Cpl,
Hetterscheidt, William A., Pfc,
Hewell, Carl J., Pfc,
†Hewitt, Thomas L., Pfc,
†Heylmun, Leroy J., Pvt,
Heywood, William F., Pvt,
Hiatt, Charles C., Pfc,
*Hibbard, Darrell, Pvt,
Hibbs, Robert T., Pvt,
†Hickey, Avon H., Pvt,
Hice, Howard C., Pfc,
Hickey, Estel L., Pfc,
Hickle, Leroy L., Jr., Pfc,
Hicklin, Clifford B., Pfc,
Hickman, Alton L., Pvt,
Hickman, Charles T., Pfc,
Hicks, Brownie, Sgt,
*Hicks, Cecil, Pvt,
Hicks, Crawford N., Pfc,
Hicks, James W., Pvt,
Hicks, Leo L., 1/Sgt,
Hicks, Richard G., Pfc,
Hicks, Thomas L., Pvt,
Hicks, William E., Pvt,
Hicks, William R., Capt,
Hieber, Arthur E., Jr., Cpl,
Hiett, Alva J., Pfc,
†Higdon, Howard J., Pvt,
Higdon, James R., Pfc,
Higgins, Ervine, Pfc,
Higgins, James A., Pfc,
Higgins, Joseph, Pvt,
Higgins, Robert A., T/Sgt,
Hightower, Thomas M., Pvt,
Hightowitz, Ellis, Pfc,
†Hiland, Vincent E., Pfc,
Hilbert, John J., Pvt,
†Hilbert, Waldo B., Pvt,
Hildebrand, Alezander J., Pfc,
Hilderbrand, Joe B., S/Sgt,
Hildreth, Luther T., Pvt,
Hiley, Art L., S/Sgt,
Hill, Armour R., Pvt,
†Hill, Baxter L., Pvt,
Hill, Bobbie E., Pvt,
Hill, Charles A., T/5,
Hill, Douglas E., Pfc,
Hill, Edward J., Pfc,
Hill, Eri J., Pfc,
Hill, Eugene, Pfc,
Hill, Hendrick, S., Pfc,
Hill, James F., S/Sgt,
Hill, James G., Pfc,
Hill, James H., Pfc,
†Hill, John W., Pvt,
Hill, John W., Ptv,
Hill, Patrick P., Pfc,
Hill, Richard M., Pfc,
Hill, Robert A., Jr., Pfc,
Hill, Rolla E., Pvt,
Hill, Thomas E., Pvt,
Hill, Walter A., Jr., Pvt,
Hillaker, Delvin L., Pfc,
Hillebrand, Richard J., Pfc,
Hiller, Harland R., Pfc,
Hilliard, Claude H., T/4,
Hillner, William J., Pvt,
Hillyard, Nathan F., Sgt,
Hiltgen, Thomas C., Pvt,
Hilton, James N., Jr., 2nd Lt,
†Himel, Ramon E., Cpl,
Himmel, Sol, Pvt,
Himmelsbach, Richard K., Pfc
Himmerick, Henry, Jr., S/Sgt,
*Hind, John C., Jr., Pfc,
Hindman, George W., S/Sgt,
Hindman, Lee W., Pvt,
†Hindman, William C., Pvt,
Hinds, Richard F., Pvt,
Hines, Harold J., Pvt,
Hines, Hubert H., Pfc,
*Hines, James E., Jr., Pvt,
Hines, Raymond S., T/4,
Hines, Vernon E., Sgt,
Hingel, Nicholas J., Pvt,
Hinkebein, Gary J., Pvt,
Hinkle, Gene D., Pvt,
§Hinkley, Woodrow D., Pvt,
Hinko, Taras, Pfc,
Hinnrichs, John F., Jr., Pvt,
Hinote, Clyde H., Pfc,
§Hinrichs, Gilbert J., Pfc,
Hinsley, Robbie J., Pfc,
Hinson, Herman, Pfc,
Hinspeter, William C., Pfc,
Hinton, Eugene H., Pvt,
Hinton, Rollo Harrison, Pfc,
Hipple, Tyrus L., Pfc,
Hipsher, Franklin S., Pfc,
Hirsch, Sigmund, Pfc,
Hirschberg, Anton C., Jr., Pfc,
§Hirzel, Howard H., Jr., Pfc,
Hisle, Lynwood M., S/Sgt,
Hite, James F., Pvt,
Hite, Jamie C., Pvt,
†Hite, John E., Pvt,
Hite, Robert E. L., Pfc,
†Hitt, Horace L., S/Sgt,
Hitt, Wright, Capt,
†Hjetland, Orlando L., Sgt,
Hlasta, Edward, Pvt,
Hlatky, John C., Pvt,
†Hlinka, Joseph, Pvt,
Hlvac, Charles H., Jr., Pvt,
Hoadley, Carl, T/5,
Hoague, Joseph H., Pfc,
Hoar, Millard G., T/5,
Hoback, John W., Pvt,
†Hobbs, Francis C., Pvt,
Hobbs, James W., Cpl,
Hobbs, Orville, Pfc,
Hobby, Burnie C., Pfc,
Hobson, Joseph D., Sgt,
Hockberger, Robert N., Pvt,
Hockenberry, Wilbur, Pvt,
Hockett, Claude B., Pvt,
†Hodge, Frank L., Pvt,
Hodge, Joseph J., Sr.,
Hodges, H. L., Pfc,
Hodges, James A., Pvt,
Hodges, Joseph G., Pfc,
Hodgins, Joseph V., T/Sgt,
Hodnett, Junior, Pfc,
Hoefke, Robert C., S/Sgt,
‡Hoefler, Raymond H., Sgt,
Hoellman, Robert M., Pfc,
Hoelzer, Everett C., Pfc,
†Hoey, Frederick E., Pfc,
Hofelich, Richard G., T/Sgt,
Hoffman, Adolph I., Pfc,
†Hoffman, Albert G., Pfc,
Hoffman, Arthur L., Pfc,
Hoffman, Charles M., T/5,
Hoffman, Donald C., Pfc,
Hoffman, John H., Pfc,
Hoffman, Leo, Pvt,
Hoffman, Louis M., Pfc,
Hoffman, Morris, Jr., Pvt,
*Hoffman, Philip B., Sgt,
Hoffman, Raymond P., Pvt,
Hoffman, Rudolph, T/4,
Hoffman, Samuel E., Jr., Pvt,
Hoffman, William D., Pfc,
Hoffmann, Kenneth, T/5,
†Hoffmeister, Walter R., Pvt,
Hoffner, Albert F., Pfc,
Hofstad, Boyd S., Cpl,
Hofto, Neil J., Pfc,
Hogan, Andrew J., Pfc,
Hogan, John P., Pfc,
Hogarth, Robert A., Pfc,
Hoge, David W., Pfc,
Hogg, Ira B., Pfc,
Hogle, Charles H., Pvt,
Hoglund, Robert D., Pfc,
Hogue, Jack Cameron, Pfc,
Hoisington, Ernest G., Pfc,
Hoitomt, Spencer No., Pvt,
†Holaway, Jesse C., Sgt,
‡Holbert, Henry H., Pfc,
Holbrook, Dewey, Pfc,
Holbrook, Dolphia, Pvt,
Holbrooks, Austin H., Pfc,
Holbrooks, John, Pvt,
Holchin, Robert R., Pvt,
Holcomb, Earl W., Pfc,
Holcomb, Frederick C., Pvt,
Holcomb, Ralph R., T/4,
†Holcomb, Sanford G., Pvt,
†Holcomb, Wesley L., Pvt,
Holder, David F., S/Sgt,
Holder, James E., Pvt,
Holderby, Lindsey P., Pfc,
Holevinski, Walter P., Pfc,
§Holick, John, Pfc,
Holicky, John, Pvt,
Hollamby, Donald G., Sgt,
Holland, Clifton E., Pfc,
Holland, Clinton R., Pfc,
Holland, George C., Pvt,
Holland, Herold H., Pvt,
Holland, James E., T/4,
*Holland, Joe, Pvt,
Holland, Lester D., Pfc,
*Holland, Robert E., Cpl,
Holland, Robert L., Pfc,
‡Hollars, Ralph D., S/Sgt,
Hollenbaugh, R. W., 1st Lt,
Holler, Robert W., Pfc,
Holley, Carey W., Pvt,
Holley, Ernest O., Pvt,
Holley, Jessie W., T/5,
Holley, William T., Pfc,
†Holliday, Charles T., Pfc,
Hollier, Edgar, Jr., Pfc,
Hollingshead, Joseph, Pfc,
†Hollinsworth, Don C., Pvt,
Hollis, Hosea I., Cpl,
Hollon, Paul H., 1st Lt,
Hollon, Troy B., Cpl,
Holloran, William J., Pfc,
Holloway, Joseph H., Pfc,
Holloway, Lewis, R., Pvt,
Holloway, Odis A., Sgt,
Holloway, Samuel B., Pfc,
‡Hollowell, LeRoy W., Pvt,
Holman, Edward L., Pvt,
Holmes, Amos G., Pvt,
Holmes, Everett G., T/4,
†Holmes, Richard B., Pvt,
Holmes, Thomas W., Pvt,
Holmes, William J., Jr., Pvt,
Holschen, Clarence J., Sgt,
Holsing, Allan T., Pfc,
Holsinger, Walter, Pvt,
Holst, Arne J., Sgt,
Holt, Clayton L., Pvt,
Holt, Ernest G., Sgt,
Holt, Joe T., Sgt,
Holt, Russell A., Pfc,
Holt, Wayland C., Capt,
†Holton, William C., Jr., Sgt,
Holtsclaw, Irvin, Pfc,
Holtzin, Abraham, Pvt,
†Holtzman, Robert F., S/Sgt,
‡Holyoke, John W., Pfc,
Holzbaur, Clinton R., Pvt,
†Holzer, Charles A., Sgt,
Hom, Bing Y., Pvt,
Hom, Wing N., Pfc,
‡Hom, Wing O., Pvt,
Hommell, Roger C., Jr., Pfc,
Homolish, Michael, Pfc,
Homolka, Stephen, Pvt,
†Honeybell, James H., Pfc,
Hong, Taw S., Pvt,
Honnaker, Claude N., Cpl,
Hoober, Joe M., T/4,
Hood, Frank G., Cpl,
Hook, Carl L., Pfc,
Hook, Ira, Pfc,
Hook, Metro, T/5,
Hooker, William A., 2nd Lt,
Hooks, Gareth L., Pvt,
Hooks, Thomas H., Pfc,
Hooper, Roger A., Pfc,
Hooper, William A., Pvt,
†Hoover, Everett L., Pfc,
Hoover, Herbert C., Sgt,
Hoover, James O., Pfc,
Hoover, Martin L., Pfc,
Hoover, Maurice E., Pfc,
†Hoover, Richard H., Pfc,
Hoover, Willie E., S/Sgt,
Hope, George A., Pvt,
Hope, Orval A., Sr., Pvt,
Hopkins, Ernest A., Pvt,
Hopkins, Freeman H., Pvt,
Hopkins, Olph E., Pfc,
*Hopley, Don W., Sgt,
Hopma, Henry, Pvt,
§Horan, Joseph P., Pfc,
Hord, Roy J., Pvt,
Horn, Bige V., Pfc,
†Horn, Charles F., Pvt,
Hornak, Martin J., Pfc,
Horne, Chevis F., Capt,
Horne, James S., Pfc,
Horne, John, Pvt,
Horne, Truby L., Pvt,
Horner, Robert G., Pfc,
Horning, Jesse O., Jr., Pfc,
Horning, Theodore H., Pfc,
Hornor, Marion F., T/Sgt,
Hornsby, P. G., Pfc,
Horrigan, Donald H., Pfc,
Horrigan, Everett S., Pvt,
Horst, Lloyd K., Pvt,
Horton, Charles I., S/Sgt,
Horton, Clifford M., Pvt,
Horton, Edward R., Pfc,
Horton, Horace V., S/Sgt,
Horton, Lenvil S., Pfc,
†Horton, Melford M., Pfc,
‡Horton, Ralph, Pfc,
Horton, Robert V., Capt,
Horvath, Michael A., Pfc,
Horvatt, John S., Pvt,
Horwath, George, Pvt,
Horwedel, Arnold V., Pfc,
Horwitz, Irving, Pvt,
Horyn, Emil, Pvt,
§Horyt, Edward S., Pfc,
‡Hosey, James W., Pfc,
Hosford, Alonzo, S/Sgt,
Hosie, Clair P., Pvt,
‡Hoskie, Peter, Pvt,
Hoskins, Leonard F., Pfc,
Hosler, Delbert J., Sgt,
‡Hosselton, Clifford C., Pfc,
Hoster, Joseph A., Pvt,
Hotaling, Donald R., Cpl,
Hotkiewicz, Benny, Pfc,
Houck, Clyde E., Pfc,
Houck, Leroy W., Pvt,
†Houde, Raymond A., Pvt,
†Hough, George M., Jr., 1st Lt,
Houghton, Walter Wm., Pfc,
†Houghton, William R., Sgt,
Houk, Elmer W., Pfc,
‡Houlihan, John R., Pvt,
House, Copeland W., Pfc,
House, James I., Pfc,
House, Paul W., T/5,
*Houser, Carson E., Pvt,
Houser, Curtis R., Pfc,
Houser, Lawrence T., Pfc,
*Houting, Lewis D., Pfc,
Houtz, Carl C., Pfc,
Hovan, Elmer C., Pfc,
Hovden, Earl C., S/Sgt,
Hovekamp, Clarence A., Pfc,
Hoven, Daniel L., Pfc,
Hovet, Henry O., Pfc,
Hovis, Guy W., T/Sgt,
Howard, Amon J., Pfc,
Howard, Bill, Pvt,
Howard, Dallas G., Pvt,
Howard, George W., Pvt,
Howard, Gerald R., Pvt,
Howard, Jack, Pvt,
Howard, James E., Jr., Pvt,
Howard, Jay J., T/Sgt,
†Howard, Jobie V., Pvt,
Howard, John W., Pvt,
Howard, Lawrence G., Pvt,
†Howard, Murt M., Pfc,
Howard, Paul W., Pvt,
Howard, Ray, Pvt,
†Howard, Wayne, Pfc,
Howard, Wilford D., Pfc,
Howard, William R., T/4,
Howe, Eddie, Pfc,
Howe, Kimball A., Pvt,
Howe, Samuel G., Cpl,
Howe, Woodrow, S/Sgt,
Howell, Biley W., Pvt,
Howell, Clayton W., Pvt,
Howell, Frank N., T/4,
Howell, George W., Pvt,
Howell, Harold, T/5,
Howell, Lawrence E., Cpl,
Howell, Raymond C., T/Sgt,
Howell, Raymond N., Pfc,
Howey, Rolland R., Jr., Pfc,
Howland, Charles J., Sgt,
Howland, Edward R., Pvt,
Howser, Milton, Pfc,
Howson, Arthur P., Pfc,
Hoy, Hobart M., S/Sgt,
Hoy, James H., Pvt,
†Hoy, Patrick E., T/Sgt,
Hoy, Thomas C., Jr., Pfc,
Hoye, Geoffrey E., Pvt,
Hoyt, Kenneth L., Pvt,
Hoyt, Rollan, Pfc,
Hoza, Rudolph G., Pfc,
Hozian, Michael F., Pfc,
Hreha, Thomas L., Pvt,
Hreniuk, Joseph C., Pfc,
Hricko, Edward E., Pvt,
Hrobak, Charles J., Pfc,
Hromoko, Joseph, Pfc,
Hron, Frank L., Pfc,
‡Hruska, Lambert J., Capt,
Huback, Raymond C., Pfc,
‡Hubbard, Dayton M., Pfc,
Hubbard, Elton G., Pvt,
Hubbard, William J., Pvt,
Hubbart, Clyde V., Jr., Pvt,
Hubbs, Clifford L., S/Sgt,
Huber, Kenneth F., Pfc,
‡Huber, Lothar F., Pvt,
Huber, Paul D., Sgt,
Huberty, David J., Pfc,
‡Huberty, Francis J., Pvt,
Hubsky, Arnold J., Pfc,
†Huck, Lawrence G., Pvt,
Huckeby, Cleatis E., Pfc,
Huckins, Damon W., Pfc,
Huddle, John F., Pfc,
Huddleston, Everett F., Cpl,
†Hudock, Peter, Pfc,
Hudson Carl R., Pvt,
*Hudson, John J., Pfc,
Hudson, Roy, Pvt,
Hudson, Roz Lee, Pfc,
Hudson, Theodore A., Pfc,
Hudspeth, Elert, S/Sgt,
*Hudspith, Robert, Pfc,
Huebner, Joseph F., Pfc,
‡Huebsch, Norman F., Pfc,
Huelsmann, Edwin B., Pfc,
Huerta, Adolph A., S/Sgt,
Hueston, Matthew A., Pfc,
Huey, Septimus A., Pvt,
Huff, Charlie N., Pfc,
Huff, Donald N., Pfc,
Huff, George C., Pvt,
*Huff, George T., Pvt,
Huff, Gerald B., Pfc,
†Huff, Jack B., Pvt,
Huff, John E., Sgt,
‡Huff, Neal H., Pvt,
*Huff, Otis V., Pvt,
Huff, Raymond, T/Sgt,
Huff, Raymond J., Sgt,
Huff, William A., Pvt,
Huff, William G., Pvt,
Huffine, Alton C., Sgt,
Huffington, Ralph V., T/Sgt,
Huffman, Glenn J., Pvt,
Huffman, Joseph L., S/Sgt,
Huffman, Roy E., Pfc,
Hufnagel, Leo J., Pfc,
§Hufnagel, Thomas J., Pvt,
Huge, Robert H., Pvt,
Hugghins, Albert E., Pfc,
Huggins, Mack W., Pvt,
Huggins, Monroe L., Cpl,
†Huggins, Norman S., Pvt,
Hughart, Gordon L., Pfc,
Hughes, Arthur E., T/4,
Hughes, Bernard F., Pvt,
Hughes, Boyd J., T/4,
Hughes, Edward F., Pfc,
Hughes, Gordon D., Pvt,
Hughes, Gwynfor H., Pvt,
†Hughes, Harlin P., Sgt,
†Hughes, Herbert H., Pvt,
Hughes, Irvin, Sgt,
Hughes, James T., Pvt,
Hughes, J. T., Pfc,
Hughes, Lincoln, Pfc,
†Hughes, Marshal V., Pfc,
Hughes, Otis W., Pvt,
‡Hughes, Rex L., Sgt,
Hughes, Ted L., Pvt,
Huisman, Bert, Pvt,
Huisman, Ernest, T/5,
*Huitt, Marvin C., Pvt,
Huizenga, Theodore G., Pvt,
Hulings, Kenneth D., Pvt,
Hull, Alfred H., Pfc,
Hull, Ellis P., Sgt,
Hulse, George C., Jr., Pfc,
Hulse, Millard E., Pvt,
Hulsey, Arthur J., Cpl,
Hulslander, Betram V., Pfc,
Hultquist, Philip R., Pfc,
Humbert, Robert E., Sgt,

† Killed in Action. * Prisoner of War. ‡ Missing in Action. § Died of Wounds.

Humble, John D., Pvt,
Hummel, Harry W., Pfc,
Humpf, Kenneth O., Pvt,
Humphrey, Everett W., Pvt,
Humphrey, Harold L., Pvt,
Humphrey, Isaac J., Pfc,
§Humphrey, Roy W., Pvt,
Humphreys, Leslie L., S/Sgt,
Humphries, Earl C., Pvt,
†Hundrup, Anton W., S/Sgt,
Hundsnurscher, Edwin A., Pfc,
Hungerford, Grover E., Pfc,
Hunnes, Frank G., Pfc,
†Hunt, Bryan G., Pfc,
Hunt, Clint, T/5,
Hunt, James C., Pfc,
Hunt, Leslie E., Pfc,
Hunt, Lloyd, Pfc,
Hunt, Mitchell W., Pfc,
†Hunt, Wilbur F., Pvt,
Hunt, William K., Sgt,
Hunt, William R., Pvt,
Hunter, Charles V., Pfc,
Hunter, Chester L., Pfc,
Hunter, Harper J., Jr., Pvt,
Hunter, Harvey Q., Pfc,
Hunter, James A., Pfc,
‡Hunter, James K., Pfc,
Hunter, James T., Pfc,
*Hunter, John R., Pfc,
Hunter, Lewis M., Pfc,
Hunter, Victor Q., Pfc,
Hunterbrinker, B. W., Pvt,
Huntoon, Orland E., 1/Sgt,
Huntsberger, D. G., Jr., Pvt,
Hupke, John J., T/5,
†Hurd, Donald W., Pfc,
Hurd, John W., Sgt,
†Hurlbut, Edmund A., T/Sgt,
†Hurley, Floyd W., Pfc,
Hurley, Thomas J., S/Sgt,
Hurley, William H., Pvt,
Hurst, Chester J., Pvt,
Hurst, Robert E., Pfc,
Hurt, James R., Pvt,
‡Hurt, Stanley R., Pvt,
Hurtt, Lawrence, Pvt,
†Husing, John C., 1st Lt,
Huskey, Paulas A., Pfc,
Huskins, Joseph M., Jr., Pfc,
Hussey, George B., Pvt,
Hussian, Varoodjan R., S/Sgt,
†Husson, John E., Pfc,
†Huston, Paul K., Pfc,
Huston, Silva L., Sgt,
Huston, Wallace J., Pvt,
Hutchins, Hilton L., Pvt,
Hutchins, Lawrence F., Pvt,
Hutchins, Sherman C., Pfc,
Hutchison, Robert H., Pfc,
Hutsell, Perry, Pfc,
Hutson, Cleo R., Pvt,
†Hutto, Eldridge J., Pfc,
‡Hutto, James H., Pvt,
Hutton, Daniel G., Pvt,
Hutton, Leroy, Pvt,
Hutton, Virgil R., Pvt,
Huzar, Victor, Pfc,
Hyatt, George F., Pvt,
Hyatt, Emmett E., Pfc,
Hyatt, Merle B., Pfc,
Hybbeneth, William F., Pvt,
†Hyde, Edward L., Pfc,
Hyde, Orville E., Pvt,
Hyduck, Steven J., S/Sgt,
Hyler, Robert, Pvt,
Hylton, Frank O., Pvt,
Hylton, Roy W., Pcf,
Hypes, Leste L., Pvt,
Hysell, Albert C., Pvt,
Hyytinen, Reino A., Pvt,

Iacopelli, Vito M., Pvt,
†Iadarola, Leo A., Sgt,
Iadonisi, Henry A., Pvt,
Iannucci, Daniel J., Pfc
Idacavage, Albert L., T/Sgt,
Igliozzi, Annibale, Pfc,
Ignaszak, Ernest J., Pfc,
Ilyes, Paul E., Pfc,
Inch, Major A., Sgt,
Ingersoll, Clarence I., Sgt,
Inghelram, Charles L., Pvt,
Ingling, Robert A., Pvt,
Ingoglia, Vito, Pfc,
Ingraham, Paul S., 2nd Lt,
*Ingram, John W., Pvt,
Inman, Richard H., Pvt,
Innes, Howard L., Pfc,
Insley, Harry T., Pvt,
Inzerillo, Sam C., Pfc,
Inzitari, Francis C., Pvt,
Iorillo, Joseph P., Pfc,
Irdi, Olvino, Pvt,
Irish, Robert J., Pvt,
Irion, Ransom L., Pfc,
†Irons, Alvin J., Pfc,
Irons, Kurt C., Pvt,
†Irvin, Roy D., Pvt,
Irwin, Edward M., Cpl,
Irwin, Howard J., Pvt,
Irwin, Samuel, Jr., Pfc,
Isaac, Ralph W., Maj,
Isbell, Woodrow W., Pfc,
Isenberger, Harold D., Cpl,
Isham, Joseph A., Sgt,
Iskin, Joseph, Pvt,
Isola, William, Pfc,
Ison, Berthel, Pfc,
Isonio, Lino J., T/5,
†Israel, Mark J., Pvt,
Issette, Bernie L., Pfc,
Ivanoff, Steve, Pvt,
Iverson, Vernon F., Pfc,
Ivey, Amerine C., Pfc,
Ivey, Jeroutha, Pfc,
Ivie, Gilbert C., Pfc,
Ivie, Wendell R., Pfc,
Iyoob, John M., Pvt,
Izenour, Frank M., Lt Col,
†Izzo, Carmine J., Pvt,
Izzo, William J., Sgt,

†Jablonowski, Casimir, Pfc,
‡Jablonowski, Thaddeus F., Pvt,
Jablonski, Francis X., Pfc,
Jablonski, Stanley J., Jr., Pvt,
Jaccodine, Xavier W., Pvt,
†Jackson, Arthur W., Pfc,
§Jackson, Bill E., Pfc,
Jackson, Clarence O., Pfc,
Jackson, David P., Pfc,
Jackson, Earl H., Pfc,
Jackson, Edwin T., S/Sgt,
Jackson, Frank L., Jr., 1st Lt,
Jackson, Frank P., Pvt,
Jackson, George P., Pvt,
Jackson, Harold N., T/5,
§Jackson, Henry T., Pfc,
Jackson, Isaac W., Pvt,
Jackson, Lester E., S/Sgt,
†Jackson, Oral B., Sgt,
Jackson, Robert L., Pvt,
Jackson, Russell, Pvt,
Jackson, Vincent J., 2nd Lt,
Jackson, William L., Sgt,
Jaco, James L., Pfc,
*Jacob, John G., Pvt,
†Jacob, Robert J., Sgt,
Jacobs, Ameda E., Pfc,
Jacobs, Bernard H., Pfc,
Jacobs, Bruce K., Pvt,
*Jacobs, Charles E., Cpl,
Jacobs, James A., Pfc,
Jacobs, Thomas B., Jr., Pfc,
Jacobs, Isaac, 2nd Lt,
Jacobson, John, T/4,
Jacobson, Lloyd S., Pfc,
Jacobson, Robert D., Sgt,
Jacoby, Francis M., Pfc,
Jacone, Louis F., Pvt,
Jaffe, Abraham S., 1st Lt,
Jaggears, M. E., Jr., 1st Lt,
Jagiello, James J., Pfc,
Jago, John, Pvt,
Jakubik, John M., Pvt,
Jakuta, George P., Pfc,
Jamerson, William N., Pfc,
James, Charles T., Pfc,
James, Curtis H., Jr., S/Sgt,
James, Donald M., Pfc,
James, John F., Pvt,
‡James, Simon G., Pvt,
Jamieson, Arthur D., Pfc,
‡Jamison, Charles L., Pvt,
§Janaro, Carmine R., Pfc,
†Jandel, Joseph G., Sgt,
Jandzik, Milton S., 1st/Sgt,
Janes, Robert F., Cpl,
Janik, Bronislaus T., Pvt,
Jankowski, Arthur J., 1st Lt,
Jankowski, Ziggie J., Cpl,
Jann, Arthur W., Pfc,
*Jannotto, Louis W., Pfc,
†Janofsky, Isaac, Pfc,
*Janowiak, Raymond G., Pfc,
‡Japp, August W., Pvt,
‡Janscak, Joseph P., 2nd Lt,
Jantz, Alvin, Cpl,
Janulewicz, Edward A., Pvt,
Januszewski, Chester D., Pvt,
‡Jaramillo, Joe C., Pvt,
†Jares, Calvin L., Pfc,
Jarnagin, John W., Pfc,
Jarosh, Alvin B., Pfc,
†Jarrett, Benjamin F., Jr., Pfc,
Jarvie, George H., S/Sgt,
Jarvis, John J., Jr., Capt,
†Jarvis, Walter J., Pvt,
Jaska, Joseph T., Pfc,
Jaskunas, Alphonse S., Pvt,
Jasper, Charles E., Pfc,
Jass, Edward S., Pfc,
Jatho, La Verne L., T/5,
Jatho, Roy K., Pfc,
Javarone, Mario J., Pvt,
†Jay, Clinton H., Pvt,
Jay, John C., Pfc,
Jay, Moses, Pfc,
§Jeanes, Reuben J. W., T/4,
Jeffs, Owen L., T/Sgt,
Jekanowski, Harry J., Pvt,
Jenco, Salvatore M., Pfc,
Jenkins, Edward E., Sgt,
Jenkins, Gerwin, Pfc,
†Jenkins, Grady L., Pvt,
Jenkins, Holman W., Pfc,
Jenkins, Monte D., Cpl,
Jenkins, John R., Pvt,
Jenkins, Odes W., Pfc,
Jenkins, Thomas M., Pfc,
Jenkins, Willard B., Sgt,
*Jenneve, George W., Pfc,
†Jennings, Calvin C., Pvt,
Jennings, Charles E., Pvt,
Jennings, John B., Pfc,
†Jennings, Ralph W., Pvt,
Jensen, James L., Pfc,
Jensen, John D., Pvt,
Jensen, Ward V., 1st Lt,
Jentz, Theodore R., Pvt,
Jentzen, Louis G., Pvt,
Jeppesen, Elmer M., S/Sgt,
Jepsen, Milo, Pfc,
Jerdon, Thurman C., Pfc,
Jerkovitz, Joseph I., Pfc,
Jerman, Neal W., Pvt,
Jernigan, James C., 1st Lt,
Jeske, William R., Pfc,
Jeskey, Maurice J., Pvt,
Jessup, Owen A., T/5,
Jestrab, Elmer J., Pvt,
Jesunas, Alfred V., Pvt,
Jetta, Walfred W., S/Sgt,
Jevsevar, James F., Pfc,
Jewell, Dale F., Pfc,
Jewell, Eric A., T/5,
Jewell, Jesse L., Pvt,
Jewell, Melvin W., T/5,
Jillson, Fred A., Pfc,
Jividen, Denver C., 1st Lt,
Job, Eugene E., Pfc,
Joffeyu, Louis, Pfc,
Johansen, Albert M., Pvt,
Johanson, Tage W., Pvt,
Johndrow, Henry, Pfc,
Johns, Lester, Pfc,
†Johns, Marvin J., Pfc,
Johnsen, Robert, Pvt,
Johnsen, Walter, Pvt,
Johnson, Alfred G., Pfc,
Johnson, Andrew J., Sr., Pvt,
Johnson, Arthur E., S/Sgt,
†Johnson, Calvert, Pfc,
Johnson, Carl I., Pfc,
Johnson, Carl M., Pvt,
Johnson, Charles F., Pvt,
Johnson, Charles H., Pvt,
‡Johnson, Charles M., Pfc,
Johnson, Connell F., Pvt,
‡Johnson, Clyde S., Pvt,
Johnson, David W., Pfc,
†Johnson, Denton D., Pvt,
†Johnson, Donald J., Pvt,
Johnson, Earl A., Pvt,
Johnson, Edwin A., Pvt,
Johnson, Edwin G., 1st Lt,
Johnson, Earle J., Pvt,
Johnson, Earle R., Capt,
Johnson, Edward L., Pfc,
†Johnson, Elnes J., Pvt,
Johnson, Floyd L., T/5,
Johnson, George W., Pfc,
Johnson, Glenworth E., Pfc,
†Johnson, Gordon A., Pvt,
Johnson, Harley F., Pfc,
†Johnson, Harold D., Pvt,
†Johnson, Harry J., Pvt,
Johnson, Harry O., Pvt,
Johnson, Helge O., Pfc,
Johnson, Herbert G., T/5,
Johnson, Howard B., Capt,
Johnson, Howard C., Pvt,
Johnson, Ivy L., S/Sgt,
Johnson, James, Pvt,
Johnson, James L., Pfc,
Johnson, Jerry R., Pfc,
Johnson, Jimmie E., Pfc,
Johnson, Jimmie H., Pfc,
Johnson, John A., Sgt,
Johnson, John B., Pvt,
Johnson, John E., Pvt,
Johnson, John L., Pfc,
Johnson, Joseph H., Pvt,
Johnson, Kennedy B., Pvt,
‡Johnson, Kenneth E., Pfc,
Johnson, Laban S., Jr., T/4,
§Johnson, Lawrence, Pvt,
Johnson, Len, Jr., S/Sgt,
Johnson, Leo P., Pvt,
Johnson, Leonard L., Pfc,
Johnson, Mack C., Pfc,
Johnson, Mansel B., Pfc,
Johnson, Marion L., Pvt,
Johnson, Marvin J., Pvt,
†Johnson, Maurice H., S/Sgt,
Johnson, Maurice S., Pfc,
Johnson, Maynard D., Pvt,
Johnson, McCloyd F., Pfc,
Johnson, Melvin E., Pfc,
†Johnson, Melvin M., Pvt,
Johnson, Merland E., Pfc,
Johnson, Merrill, Pfc,
Johnson, Norman S., Pvt,
Johnson, Olin S., Pvt,
Johnson, Orin L., Pvt,
Johnson, Pallmon A., Pvt,
Johnson, Paul E., Pfc,
Johnson, Percy T., Jr., Sgt,
Johnson, Peter D., Pfc,
Johnson, Robert E., Pvt,
Johnson, Robert K., Pvt,
Johnson, Rawleigh, Pfc,
Johnson, Richard C., Pvt,
Johnson, Robert E., Sgt,
Johnson, Robert E., Pvt,
Johnson, Robert R., Pvt,
†Johnson, Robert T., Sgt,
Johnson, Roy B., Pfc,
Johnson, Rufe T., 1st/Sgt,
Johnson, Samuel, Cpl,
Johnson, Thomas B., Pfc,
Johnson, Thomas C., Pvt,
Johnson, Thomas N., Pvt,
*Johnson, Thomas R., 2nd Lt,
Johnson, Walter H., Pvt,
Johnson, Wilbur C., Pfc,
Johnson, Wilbur O., T/5,
Johnson, Wilburn T., Pfc,
Johnson, William A., 1st Lt,
‡Johnson, William, Jr., Pfc,
†Johnson, William O., Pvt,
Johnson, William T., Jr., Pfc,
Johnson, Winfield G., Sgt,
Johnson, Woodrow S., T/Sgt,
Johnson, Woodrow W., Pfc,
Johnston, Fowler L., Pvt,
Johnston, Henry R., Pvt,
Johnston, Howard C., Pfc,
Johnston, Howard E., T/5,
Johnston, Johney, Pvt,
Johnston, Ralph F., Pfc,
Johnston, Robert P., Pvt,
Johnston, Roy J., Pfc,
Johnston, William P., Pvt,
Johnston, William P., Pvt,
Joiner, Willard C., Pfc,
Jojola, Joseph R., Pvt,
Jolley, R. D., T/4,
Jones, Adrian L., Pfc,
Jones, Arlan L., Pfc,
Jones, Ban T., Pfc,
Jones, Basil E., Pfc,
Jones, Burnell G., Pfc,
Jones, Burton R., Jr., T/5,
Jones, Calvin H., Pvt,
Jones, Charles H., Jr., S/Sgt,
Jones, Charlie D., Pfc,
Jones, Curtis L., Pfc,
Jones, David H., Pfc,
Jones, Edmund J., Pfc,
Jones, Ernest E., Jr., Pfc,
Jones, Hayden W., Pfc,
Jones, James C., Pfc,
†Jones, Jasper H., Pfc,
Jones, Joe B., 2nd Lt,
Jones, John P., S/Sgt,
Jones, John W., Pvt,
Jones, John Z., Pfc,
Jones, Lamar C., T/5,
†Jones, Leonard A., T/Sgt,
Jones, Leonard G., Pfc,
Jones, L. C., Sgt,
Jones, Max E., Pfc,
Jones, Paul, Jr., Pfc,
Jones, Paul R., S/Sgt,
Jones, Raymond, Pvt,
Jones, Riley M., Jr., Pfc,
†Jones, Robert F., Pfc,
Jones, Ross A., Jr., Pvt,
Jones, Ross S., Cpl,
Jones, Rowland P., 2nd Lt,
Jones, Roy C., S/Sgt,
†Jones, Roy E., Pfc,
Jones, Swane A., Pfc,
Jones, Thomas, Jr., Pfc,
Jones, Thomas J., Pfc,
Jones, Thomas L., Pvt,
Jones, Tommy, Sgt,
Jones, Truman D., Pfc,
Jones, Wilber N., S/Sgt,
Jones, William A., T/4,
Jones, William R., 1st Lt,
†Jones, Wilson A., Pvt,
Jones, Wilton R., Pfc,
†Jonkman, Boniface, Pfc,
Jordan, Albert, Sgt,
Jordan, Edward L., Pfc,
Jordan, Elzie W., Jr., Pvt,
Jordan, John D., Pfc,
Jordan, John J., S/Sgt,
Jordan, Lealand G., Pfc,
Jordan, Nicholas, Pfc,
Jordan, Robert C., Pfc,
†Jordan, Roy W., Pfc,
†Jordan, Thomas L., Jr., Pvt,
Jordan, Walter W., Pfc,
Jorgensen, Carlton A., Pfc,
Jorgenson, George H., Pfc,
Joseph, James R., Pvt,
†Joseph, Lee, S/Sgt,
Joswiak, Leo J., Sgt,
Joung, Joe, Pfc,
Joyce, Francis M., Pfc,
Joyce, Frank E., Pfc,
Joyce, James S., Pfc,
Joyce, John S., Pfc,
Joyce, Peter J., Pfc,
§Juarez, Frank M., Pfc,
Juarez, Jesse C., Pfc,
Juarez, Raymond, Pfc,
†Jubinville, Gerald J., Pfc,
†Jude, Charlie, S/Sgt,
†Judge, Samuel, Pvt,
Judge, William J., Pvt,
Juenger, Paul E., Pfc,
Juergens, Gerald L., Pvt,
Jugon, William J., Pfc,
Jukich, Russell J., Pvt,
‡Julian, Ellis L., Pvt,
Jumper, Hayden, S/Sgt,
Juneau, Clarence, Pfc,
Jung, Alden F., Pvt,
Jupin, William, Pfc,
Jurasek, Steve F., Pvt,
Jurczak, Frank, Pvt,
Jurecka, George, Pvt,
Jurgelewicz, Tony J., Pvt,
Jurgens, James A., Sgt,
Jurgensen, Robert H., Pfc,
Jurgeson, Stanley R., T/5,
Jurik, Andy M., Sgt,
Jussila, Clyde F., Pfc,
Just, Edward J., Capt,
Justesen, Jack C., Pvt,
Justice, Jeff W., Pvt,
Jwaskiewicz, Joseph J., Pvt,

Kaatz, Gordon S., Pvt,
Kabelka, Charles W., Pvt,
Kabisch, Sidney, Pfc,
Kacsock, Walter J., Pfc,
‡Kaczmarek, Joseph S., Pfc,
Kaczmarek, Leo P., Pfc,
Kadel, Ralph E., Pvt,
Kader, Jesse G., Pvt,
†Kadra, William J., Cpl,
Kafer, Robert E., Pvt,
†Kafka, William J., Pfc,
†Kagle, Raymond P.,
Kahen, Harry, Pfc,
†Kaiser, Glendon H., Pfc,
Kaiser, Joseph N., Pvt,
Kaiser, John T., Pvt,
Kalafsky, Steve P., Sgt,
Kalakewich, John, Pvt,
Kalb, Gerald W., Pfc,
Kaled, Ernest C., Pfc,
Kalina, Abraham M., Pvt,
Kalinowski, Edward S., Pfc,
Kalisher, Simpson, Pfc,
Kalisiak, Morris, 1st/Sgt,
Kallenberger, Ernest T., Pvt,
Kallestad, Emil A., S/Sgt,
Kallies, Joseph A., Cpl,
Kallin, Harold W., Pvt,
Kalmanowitz, Morris, S/Sgt,
Kalmus, Morris A., T/5,
Kamadulski, Frank, Sgt,
Kamberling, Leo A., Pvt,
Kaminsky, Frank V., Pvt,
Kampe, Louis W., Pfc,
Kamplain, Murray L., Pfc,
Kandel, Sam, Pvt,
Kane, Raymond H., Pfc,
Kaniewsky, Paul Z., S/Sgt,
Kanipe, J. C., Pfc,
§Kannaly, John H., Pvt,
Kanost, Phillip F., Pfc,
Kapacs, John, Pfc,
Kanthack, John R., T/5,
Kanz, William J., S/Sgt,
Kapelka, Chester E., Pvt,
§Kaplan, Benjamin, Pvt,

† Killed in Action. * Prisoner of War. ‡ Missing in Action. § Died of Wounds.

Kaplan, Edward, Pfc,
Kaplowitz, Joseph, Pvt,
Kappel, Donald L., Pvt,
Kappelman, Lester B., 1st Lt,
‡Kappes, Harold E., Pfc,
Karachinsky, Joseph A., Pvt,
Karankiewicz, Lucien W., Pvt,
†Karbosky, Stanley T., T/4,
Karch, Elmer J., S/Sgt,
Kardell, Arthur C., Pvt,
Karels, John, Pfc,
Karier, John A., Pfc,
Karlik, Joseph E., Pvt,
†Karluk, Alex M., 1st Lt,
Karnis, Alexander J., Pvt,
†Karns, Harold, Pvt,
Karol, Morris, S/Sgt,
Karpach, Michael, Pvt,
†Karschnia, Walter G., Pvt,
Karten, Everett, Pfc,
*Karwatka, John S., Pvt,
Kasee, Alva L., Pfc,
Kasisuis, Joseph, Pvt,
Kasko, Lawrence R., Pvt,
Kasserman, John, Jr., Sgt,
‡Kassin, Anton F., Pfc,
Kasupski, Bernard W., Pvt,
‡Kasuba, George J., Pfc,
Katchinska, Archie F., Pvt,
Katz, Daniel, Pfc,
§Katz, Herman, Pvt,
†Katz, Sidney, T/5,
Katz, Walter, Pvt,
Katzer, Emil M., Pfc,
Kauffman, Harry, Pfc,
Kaufman, Bernard S., Pvt,
Kaufman, Louis, Pvt,
Kaul, Charles B., Pfc,
Kavis, Raymond F., Pfc,
Kawa, Henry P., Sgt,
Kay, Earnest C., Pfc,
†Kay, Walker H., S/Sgt,
Kaye, Irving, Pfc,
Kaylor, William W., Sgt,
Kaywin, Louis, 1st Lt,
†Kearney, Aloysius R., T/5,
Kearney, Earl B., Pfc,
Kearns, Edward T., Sgt,
Keasling, George N., Pvt,
Keating, Edward T., Sgt,
Keating, Eugene T., S/Sgt,
Keaton, Russell W., Pvt,
Kecis, Andrew S., S/Sgt,
Keck, Russell F., Pfc,
Keefe, Norman N., Pvt,
†Keefer, Norman R., Pfc,
Keeler, Harvey R., Cpl,
Keeler, John G., T/5,
Keeler, Joseph P., Pvt,
†Keeler, Marcus E., Pfc,
Keeling, George W., Pfc,
Kells, Harry S., Pvt,
Keen, Homer, Pfc,
Keene, Alexander C., Jr., Pvt,
Keene, Earl M., Sgt,
Keener, Laurence, Sgt,
Keener, Walter H., Pfc,
†Keener, William H., S/Sgt,
Kees, Joseph W., Pvt,
Keesee, Floyd J., Pfc,
Keeth, Regan K., Pfc,
Keeve, Lawrence P., Pvt,
Keffner, Robert Lester, Pfc,
†Kehler, Harry G., Pvt,
Keit, John P., Pvt,
Keiper, Andrew R., Pvt,
Keith, Malcolm I., Pvt,
†Kell, Harold E., Pvt,
Kellam, Thelmer L., Pvt,
Kelleher, Edward M., Pfc,
Keller, Charles L., S/Sgt,
Keller, Earl M., Pfc,
Keller, Clarence F., Pfc,
†Keller, Henry J., Pfc,
Keller, James N., Jr., Pfc,
Keller, John, Sgt,
Keller, Johnnie, Pvt,
Keller, Norman, Pvt,
Keller, William W., Pfc,
Kellett, Glenn W., Cpl,
Kelley, Edward R., Pfc,
Kelley, James G., Pfc,
Kelley, Oscar L., Pfc,
Kelley, Raymond J., S/Sgt,
Kelley, Thomas J., Pvt,
‡Kelley, William R., 2nd Lt,
*Kellogg, Espy J., Pvt,
Kelly, Arthur H., Pfc,
Kelly, David, Pfc,
Kelly, Edward J., Cpl,
Kelly, Edwin G., 1st Lt,
Kelly, Ellis D., Pvt,
Kelly, Harold A., Pfc,
Kelly, Harvey F., Pfc,
Kelly, James R., Pfc,
Kelly, James J., Pfc,
Kelly, John J., Sgt,
Kelly, Leonard A., Pfc,
Kelly, Milford F., T/5,
Kelly, Norman R., Pfc,
Kelly, Robert J., Pvt,
Kelly, William H., Pfc,
Kelp, Robert, Pfc,
†Kelch, William R., Pfc,
*Keltne, Harry E., Pvt,
†Kelsey, Adolph E., Pvt,
Kempa, John J., Jr., Pfc,
Kempler, Leonard, Pvt,
Kemppel, Walter, Pfc,
†Kendall, Edwin A., Pfc,
Kendall, James G., Pvt,
Kendall, Paul R., Pvt,
Kendall, Vernon W., Pvt,
Kendy, William, Pvt,
Kenjalo, Eli, T/5,
Kennedy, Benjamin T., T/4,
Kennedy, Charles, Pfc,
†Kennedy, Charles M., Pfc,
Kennelly, Patrick C., S/Sgt,
Kenny, John J., Pfc,
Kenosky, Arthur S., Pfc,
Kent, Clarence W., Pfc,
Kent, Harold D., Pfc,
†Kenter, John W., Pvt,
Keogh, Claude R., Capt,
Kephart, Kenneth E., Pfc,
Keplar, Emmett T., Pfc,
Kepler, Dale D., Pvt,
Kera, Jerome J., Pfc,
Kerekes, Steve A., Pvt,
Kerian, Ernest E., Sgt,
Kerley, Chillies W., Pfc,
Kerley, Samuel R., Sgt,
Kerne, Frank A., Pvt,
Kerns, James E., Pvt,
Kerr, Allan D., Pvt,
Kerr, Homer L., Pfc,
Kerr, Richard L., Capt,
Kerrigan, John T., Pvt,
‡Kersey, Hugh M., Pvt,
†Kersey, Robert L., Pvt,
Kershaw, Rodney E., Pvt,
Kershner, Leo W., Pfc,
†Kerski, Walter J., Pfc,
Keryk, Michael, Pfc,
Kessinger, Hubert, Pvt,
Kessinger, Oscar A., Pvt,
Kessler, Alvin J., Pvt,
†Kessler, Jerome D., Pfc,
†Kesterson, Doyle D., Pfc,
Kesterson, Lawrence L., Pvt,
Keta, Walter T., Pfc,
Ketner, Charles H., Pfc,
Kettler, Arnold C., Pfc,
Kettunen, George E., Pvt,
‡Kewley, Clarence E., Pvt,
‡Key, Jack D., Pvt,
‡Key, Ralph, S/Sgt,
Keylon, Herman E., Pfc,
Keys, Benton A., Jr., Pfc,
Keys, Charles H., Pvt,
Keys, Vernon L., Pfc,
Kicklighter, Hartridge, Pvt,
Kidwell, Paul S., Pvt,
Kidwell, Robert J., Pfc,
*Kiefer, Robert, Pvt,
Kiefer, Robert, Pvt,
Killard, John L., Pvt,
Kiehl, Theodore C., Pvt,
Kielian, Steven, T/Sgt,
Kiernan, Edward P., S/Sgt,
Kierstead, Howard D., Pvt,
Kietman, Richard J., Pfc,
Kigner, David L., Pvt,
Kilgore, Ray F., S/Sgt,
Kilgore, Thurman M., Pfc,
Kilburn, Darrell C., Pfc,
†Kilburn, James R., 2nd Lt,
Killam, Herman S., Pfc,
Killard, John L., Pvt
†Killham, John, Cpl,
Killebrew, James A., Sgt,
†Killen, William L., Pfc,
Kilman, Robert J., Pvt,
‡Kimball, Donald R., Sgt,
Kimball, James L., Pfc,
†Kimble, Everett J., Pfc,
†Kimble, Marion A., Cpl,
Kimbrell, John W., Pfc,
Kimes, Clinton R., Pvt,
†Kimmer, Talmadge J., Pfc,
Kimpland, George E., 1st Lt,
Kimzey, Eldon B., Sgt,
Kinart, William K., T/5,
Kincaid, Clifford B., T/5,
Kinder, Young, Pvt,
King, Alger C., Pvt,
†King, Alvin F., Pfc,
King, Burton J., Pfc,
King, Carl F., Sgt,
§King, Charles L., Pfc,
King, Clarence E., Pvt,
King, Daniel R., Pvt,
King, Delbert W., S/Sgt,
King, Ed, Jr., Pvt,
King, Elmer F., Pvt,
King, Emory O., Pfc,
King, Floyd A., Pvt,
†King, George, Pvt,
King, Harry L., Pvt,
King, Harvey E., 1st/Sgt,
King, James E., Pfc,
King, Lawrence A., Pfc,
King, Lindley D., Sgt,
King, Marvin T., Pfc,
†King, Ray J., Pfc,
King, Raymond J., Cpl,
King, Richard, Pfc,
King, Richard T., Jr., Pfc,
King, Ronald, Pfc,
King, Tom J., Pfc,
King, Travis A., Pfc,
King, William B., Pfc,
†King, William C., Pfc,
King, William G., 1st Lt,
King, William H., Pfc,
Kingery, Charles L., T/Sgt,
Kingery, Hugh L., Pfc,
Kingery, Grover J., Cpl,
†Kiniry, Edward J., Pvt,
Kinlaw, Paul H., Pvt,
Kinnear, Carlton P., Pfc,
†Kinnear, Robert M., Sgt,
Kinney, Kenneth W., Pvt,
Kinney, Paul I., Pvt,
Kinney, Thomas D., Pfc,
‡Kinsman, Claude C., Pvt,
Kintz, Orville A., Pfc,
Kinyig, Ellsworth J., T/Sgt,
Kirby, Earl W., S/Sgt,
Kirby, Edward S., S/Sgt,
Kirby, Myron B., Pvt,
Kirby, Richard J., Pfc,
Kirchner, Andrew J., Sgt,
Kirish, Michael, Pfc,
Kirish, Michael, Sgt,
Kirk, James L., Pvt,
Kirk, John N., 2nd Lt,
Kirkpatrick, John E., Pvt,
Kirkpatrick, John L., Capt,
Kirkpatrick, Mason, Pvt,
Kirkwood, William B., S/Sgt,
Kirsch, Carl R., Pfc,
Kirschner, Arnold W., Pvt,
Kirtz, James L., Pvt,
Kiser, Albert J., Pfc,
Kisiel, Andrew N., Pvt,
Kissell, William H., Cpl,
Kistler, Allen J., Pfc,
Kistner, Edward K., Pvt,
Kitchen, Alva C., Pvt,
Kitchens, Emory H., Pfc,
Kitchin, Joseph, T/4,
Kite, Winfield R., Pvt,
†Kitson, Earl E., Jr., Pfc,
Kittinger, Robert H., Pfc,
Kittle, James B., Jr., Pfc,
†Kittredge, Marvin J., Pvt,
Kitts, Milton F., Pvt,
Kivlehan, Thomas H., Pvt,
†Kizirian, Archie T., Pvt,
Klable, Daniel E., S/Sgt,
Klarmann, Harry A., Jr., Pfc,
†Klassen, Harold R., Pfc,
†Klatte, Ralph C., Pvt,
§Klausman, Walter A., 1st Lt,
Klebusits, Louis J., Jr., Pvt,
Kleeman, Gustav, Jr., Pfc,
Klees, James M., Cpl,
†Kleiboeker, Juvert H., Pfc,
Kleier, William R., Pvt,
†Klein, Bernard, Pfc,
†Klein, Edward A., Pvt,
Klein, Edward H., S/Sgt,
Klein, Frederick A., Pvt,
Klein, Henry L., Pvt,
Klein, Joseph P., Jr., Pfc,
Kleinman, Morris J., Pvt,
*Kleinow, Jack P., Pvt,
Klem, Walter, Pfc,
Kleman, Frederick J., Pfc,
Klemm, Robert O., Pvt,
‡Klepk, Paul R., Pvt,
Kleschick, Frank J., Pvt,
Kleyd, Pete P., Pfc,
Kline, Alfred R., Pvt,
Kline, Edgar, Pvt,
†Kline, James M., Pvt,
†Kline, Leon W., Jr., Pvt,
Kline, Wilbur, Pvt,
Kling, Paul E., Pfc,
Klish, Sylvester, Pfc,
Klintworth, Vern, Pvt,
Klonaick, William C., S/Sgt,
Klosinski, Jon H., Pvt,
Kloskowski, Adam, Pvt,
Klunk, Joseph L., Jr., Pvt,
Klupchak, George, Pfc,
Kmiotek, Steven J., Pvt,
Knadler, Frederick V., Pfc,
Knapp, Frederick W., T/5,
Knight, Billie, Pvt,
Knight, Clarence A., Cpl,
Knight, Frederick R., Cpl,
Knight, James A., Pvt,
Knight, Milton C., Pfc,
Knight, Russell C., Pvt,
Knobel, Roger A., S/Sgt,
Knober, Clarence A., Sgt,
Knohr, Earl L., Sgt,
Knoll, Roy E., Pfc,
Knoop, Ebert B., Sgt,
Knooren, Peter J., Pfc,
Knott, Clarence L., Pfc,
Knotts, Richard E., Pfc,
Knowlen, George B., Pfc,
Knowlton, Harold G., Pvt,
Knox, Lawrence E., Sgt,
Knox, Robert F., Pfc,
‡Knuckles, James L., Sgt,
†Knudsen, Herbert S., Pvt,
Knuth, Kenneth V., Pfc,
Knuutila, Victor M., Pvt,
Kobre, Irving J., Pvt,
*Kobylak, Joe, Pfc,
§Kocac, Paul J., Pfc,
Koczwara, Ralph R., Pfc,
Koeberlein, Frank L., Pfc,
Koehler, Edward F., T/4,
Koehler, Joseph W., Pfc,
Kohlman, Myron M., Pvt,
Kohnhorst, Hubert J., Pfc,
Kohrmann, Virgil H., T/Sgt,
‡Koistinen, Vermont M., Pfc,
Koistinen, Vernon E., Pfc,
Kolacz, Joseph, Sgt,
‡Kolakowski, Alfred S., S/Sgt,
Kolder, Nicholas R., Sgt,
Koleda, Paul J., Pfc,
Koletsos, Dan E., Pfc,
†Kolodziej, Edward M., Pfc,
Kolstad, Richard A., Sgt,
Kolstee, Billy E., Pvt,
Kolton, Ignatius F., Sgt,
Kombrick, Hugh, Pvt,
Komives, James L., T/5,
Konczak, Sylvester A., Pfc,
†Kondart, Teddy S., Pfc,
Kononen, Glen M., T/4,
‡Konopka, Joseph S., Pfc,
Koolpe, Bernard, Pvt,
†Koonce, James E., Pvt,
Kopatich, Louis J., Sgt,
Kopchak, Joseph, Pfc,
Koprivnik, Joe S., Sgt,
Korell, Frank B., Pvt,
Korenbaum, Israel J., 1st Lt,
Korman, Sol, T/5,
Kornafel, Steve, Pvt,
Kornberg, Leonard, Pvt,
Koronka, Sylvester H., Sgt,
†Korpal, Alex, Pvt,
Korsh, Steve J., Pvt,
Kosar, George A., Pfc,
§Kosco, John P., Pfc,
†Kosiba, Joseph, Pfc,
†Kosinski, Bernard S., Pvt,
Koskela, William A., Pfc,
Kosla, Edward T., T/Sgt,
Kosmach, John, Pvt,
Koss, Walter F., Pvt,
Kostow, Alek, Sgt,
Kostryk, Steve, S/Sgt,
Kostuck, George E., Pfc,
Kotarski, Henry J., Pvt,
Kotekas, Charles L., Pfc,
Kotran, Joseph A., Sgt,
*Kotlil, Vincent A., Pfc,
Kotz, Raymond, Sgt,
Kouba, Edward J., T/Sgt,
†Kovacevich, Francis, Pfc,
Kovach, Eugene F., Jr., Sgt,
Koval, August J., Pfc,
Kovaleski, Earl W., T/5,
Kovatch, Merle S., Sgt,
*Kowalski, Mitchell R., Pfc,
§Kowalski, Sam, Pfc,
Kowalski, Vincent J., Pfc,
Kowitz, Herbert, Pfc,
Koyama, Raymond M., Sgt,
Kozikowski, Walter A., Pfc,
Kozimor, Stanley M., Pfc,
Kozol, Stanley, Pvt,
Kozoroff, Solomon, Pvt,
Koyubal, Joseph J., Pfc,
Krafft, Francis M., Pvt,
Kral, Charles E., Sgt,
Kramer, Anselm, Pvt,
Krame, David, Pfc,
Kramer, Henry L., Pfc,
†Krampe, Earl E., 1st Lt,
Kramsack, John, Jr., Pfc,
Krasny, Norman, Pvt,
Krasutsky, Alexander, Pvt,
Kraus, Harold P., Pvt,
Kraus, Stanley I., Pvt,
†Krause, Frederick L., Pvt,
Krause, John, Jr., Pfc,
Krause, Ludwig A., Sgt,
Krause, William C., Pvt,
Krebs, Charles H., Pvt,
Krebs, Leonard E., Pfc,
†Kreft, Lester F., Pfc,
§Krein, Ludwig O., Pfc,
Kreis, Johnnie F., Sgt,
Kremenetz, Joseph, Pvt,
Kremer, Joseph W., Pfc,
Kremser, Frank J., T/4,
Krenk, Alois B., Pvt,
†Krepel, Alphonse A., Pfc,
Krerowicz, George, Pvt,
§Kressal, Donald H. C., Pfc,
Kret, Francis J., Capt,
Kretz, Robert M., Pfc,
Kretzer, George F., Pvt,
Kreuscher, Russell B., T/5,
Kriechbaum, Dale E., Pfc,
Krieg, James W., Cpl,
Krieger, Donald R., Pfc,
Kriel, Ronald H., Pvt,
Krigg, Charles A., Pfc,
Krills, William J., Jr., Pfc,
Krista, Stephen, Pfc,
Kristjanson, Hannes A., S/Sgt,
Kristof, Allen C. J., Pfc,
Krizan, Fred A., Sgt,
Krofczyk, Henry L., Pfc,
Krohn, Oliver H., T/4,
Krok, Chester F., Pvt,
Kroll, Raymond J., Pfc,
Krouse, Rupert B., Pfc,
†Krovchuck, William E., Pvt,
Krueger, Oscar A., Pvt,
†Krueger, Paul A., Pfc,
‡Krueger, Robert W., Pfc,
*Krug, Charles, Pvt,
Krug, Victor L., Pfc,
Kruger, Raymond, Pfc,
Krukonis, Joseph P., Pfc,
†Krumroy, Melbert D., Pvt,
Krumski, Joseph G., Cpl,
Krupe, Robert, Cpl,
Krupienski, Stanley A., Sgt,
Kruppner, Leonard F., Pvt,
Krovos, Joseph F., Sgt,
Kryer, James A., Pfc,
Kubelinas, Anthony G., Pvt,
Kubiak, Ignatius D., 1st Sgt,
Kubitski, Clarence A., S/Sgt,
Kucharczyk, Matthew G., Pvt,
Kuckens, John J., Jr., 2nd Lt,
Kuckkan, Edward H., Pfc,
Kudlack, Frank J., Pvt,
Kudyba, John P., Pfc,
Kueck, Werner F., Pfc,
Kuehn, Cecil C., S/Sgt,
Kuester, Freemond H., Pfc,
Kuffel, Raymond V., Pvt,
Kugler, Alfred E., Pfc,
Kuglin, Leo W., Pvt,
Kuhl, James G., Pvt,
Kuhl, Jobe R., Sgt,
‡Kuhn, J. N., Jr., Pfc,
Kuhn, William K., Cpl,
Kuhnell, Clayton A., Pfc,
‡Kuhnle, John W., Jr., Pvt,
†Kuhns, Harry T., Jr., S/Sgt,
Kuhtenia, Alexander, Pfc,
Kujawa, Vincent A., Pvt,
Kuka, Michael, Pfc,
Kukieza, Rudolph A., Sgt,
Kukis, Anthony J., 1st Lt,
‡Kula, Joseph V., Pfc,
Kulaga, Walter F., Pfc,
Kull, Donald C., Pfc,
Kulp, Harry J., Pfc,
Kulungian, M., O., Jr., Pfc,
Kunkelman, Leroy H., Pfc,
Kuperstein, Abner D., 1st Lt,
Kupiec, Stanley L., Pfc,
†Kurdel, Joseph G., Cpl,
Kurdziel, Frank J., Pvt,
Kuronya, Geza C., Cpl,
Kurtz, Theodore, Pfc,
Kurz, Edwin W., 1st Lt,
*Kushka, Alex, Pvt,
Kushnick, Robert P., Cpl,
Kusiak, Edward J., Pvt,
Kusiak, Zygmont M., S/Sgt,
Kuss, Carl S., Pvt,
Kuss, Robert J., Pvt,
†Kutia, Norman A., Pfc,
§Kuttin, Anton Jr., Pfc

† Killed in Action. * Prisoner of War. ‡ Missing in Action. § Died of Wounds.

Kutzler, William F., Pvt,
Kvass, Martin G., 1st Lt,
Kwiatkowski, Daniel J., Pvt,
†Kwiatkowski, Dominic D., Pvt,
Kzaley, Eli J., Pfc,

Laagus, Felix, Pvt,
§LaBare, Donald H., Pfc,
†Labaun, Edwin W., Pvt,
Laber, Walter J., Pfc,
LaBianco, Frank, Pvt,
LaBrie, Roger P., Cpl,
Labushesky, Leonard A., Pfc,
Lacey, George C., Pfc,
Lacez, Willis A., Pfc,
Lachance, Bertrand A., Pvt,
Lachmund, Herman A., Pfc,
Lackey, Howard H., Pfc,
Lacombe, Conrad L., Sgt,
Lacopo, Dean W., Pvt,
Lacoste, Gaspard T., Pfc,
*Lacy, Morris B., Pvt,
Ladd, Clifford A., T/Sgt,
Ladd, James W., Pvt,
Ladenburger, Kenneth A., Pvt,
Ladner, Emil O., Pfc,
Ladowski, Edward A., Pvt,
Lafata, William, Pfc,
Laferrara, Anthony, Pfc,
Laferriere, Albert C., Pvt,
§Laferty, Floyd, Pvt,
Lafevre, Lawrence C., 1st Lt,
Lafferty, Henry J., Pfc,
LaFlam, Roger E., Pvt,
Lafleur, Jevese M., 2nd Lt,
LaFountaine, T. D., S/Sgt,
Lafromboise, Raymond, Pvt,
Laggis, George, Pfc,
Lagle, Ray, Pfc,
Lagorio, Carl W., Pvt,
†Lahna, Leo E., Pvt,
Laho, Walter, Pvt,
Laing, J. C., Pvt,
Laing, Robert E. L., Pfc,
Laird, Harvey L., S/Sgt,
Laird, Robert L., Pvt,
Laird, William W., Pvt,
Lajoie, Raymond R., Pvt,
Lake, Edward B., Sgt,
Lake, Harold L., Pfc,
Lake, Jefferson T., Pfc,
Lake, Paul R., T/5,
Lake, William, Pfc,
Lakeman, Richard F., Pfc,
Lakey, Ralph H., Pfc,
Lakos, Steven R., Pfc,
Lamaster, Claude, Pvt,
Lamb, Harold B., Sgt,
Lamb, James H., Pfc,
Lamb, Rex B., Pfc,
Lambdin, Harold D., Pfc,
Lambert, Claude V., Pvt,
Lambert, Everett T., Cpl,
†Lambert, James R., Pvt,
Lambert, James W., 2nd Lt,
Lambert, Joseph G., 1st Lt,
Lambert, Riley S., Pvt,
Lambright, Roswell K., Pfc,
Lamedica, Oreste T., Pfc,
Lamm, Cecil A., Pfc,
Lamoria, Ralph E., Pfc,
Lampe, William J., Pfc,
Lamper, Joseph F., 1st Lt,
Lamphear, Karlton G., Pfc,
†Lampkin, Ernest A., Pfc,
Lampton, John S., Jr., Sgt,
Lancaster, Melton B., 2nd Lt,
Lancaster, William, Pvt,
Lance, James O., Pfc,
Lancewicz, Anthony, Pvt,
†Lanciano, Carmin J., Pfc,
Land, Ray N., Pfc,
‡Landa, Anastasido M., Pvt,
Landati, Frank A., Pvt,
Lande, Orin, 1st Lt,
Landers, Lloyd L., S/Sgt,
Landingham, George E., Pvt,
‡Landmark, James B., Pvt,
Landon, Burt M., Pvt,
Landon, Fred L., Pfc,
Landon, Robert L., Pfc,
§Landrus, Raymond J., Pvt,
Landry, Dudley J., Pvt,
Landwehr, Sol, Pvt,
†Lane, Carl, S/Sgt,
*Lane, Martin J., Pvt,
†Lane, Richard J., Pfc,
Lane, Vernon W., Pfc,
Lang, Paul, T/5,
Lang, Wilfred E., 1st Lt,
Langdon, Benjamin C., Pvt,
Langdorf, Elroy E., Pvt,
†Lange, Arthur H., Pvt,
Lange, William P., T/4,
Langevin, Joseph E., Pvt,
Langevin, Joseph G., Jr., Pvt,
†Langfield, Leonard R., Pvt,
Langford, Beverly W., Pvt,
Langlais, Anthony A., Pvt,
Langley, Clyde, Pfc,
Langley, Marion D., Pvt,
Langridge, Norman, Pfc,
Langston, F. A., Pvt,
Langston, Roy, Sgt,
Langwasser, Robert T., Pfc,
Lanier, Charles M., Pvt,
Lanier, Phillip O., Pfc,
Lanum, Clarence W., Pvt,
Lanza, Vito B., Pvt,
Lanzar, Manfred, Pfc,
La Palme, Simon A., Pfc,
La Palermo, Joseph, Pfc,
La Perle, Rene G., Pfc,
Lanphear, Leroy A., T/4,
†La Pierre, Clarence J., Pvt,
Lapinski, Raymond B., Pvt,
Lapkoff, Herbert, Pfc,
LaPlaca, Frank P., Jr., Pfc,
LaPoint, Joseph, T/4,
Laponza, Alfred A., Pvt,
†LaPorta, Charles J., Pfc,
LaPorte, Gordon P., Pfc,
Lara, Daniel E., Pvt,
Lara, Luis, Pfc,
Larabee, Frank D., Pfc,
Larabee, Jack B., Pvt,
†Lararud, Orrin L., Pvt,
Large, Alfred W., Pvt,
†Large, Charles W., Pvt,
Larkin, Thomas A., Pfc,
‡Larkin, Thomas F., Pfc,
Laropoulos, Stanley S., Pvt,
Larsen, John R., S/Sgt,
Larsen, Lawrence R., Pvt,
Larsen, Rudolph, Pfc,
Larsen, Wilhelm, Pvt,
Larsen, William A., Pvt,
Larson, Andrew J., Pvt,
†Larson, Hans L., S/Sgt,
Larson, Howard P., Pfc,
*Larson, Nels H., Pvt,
Larson, Robert B., Pfc,
Larue, Charles P., Pfc,
†Lary, Henry P., S/Sgt,
LaSavage, Peter W., S/Sgt,
Lash, Louis R., Jr., Pfc,
Lashbrooke, Elvin C., Pfc,
Laski, Frank J., Pfc,
Lassiter, Frederick A., Pfc,
‡Lassman, Samuel, Pfc,
Lastohkein, Nicholas, Pvt,
†Lategano, Vincent W., Pvt,
Latham, Jack D., Pvt,
Latham, Ralph M., Pfc,
Latimer, George F., Pvt,
Laton, Richard D., Sgt,
Latorraca, Albert M., Pfc,
Latuska, Walter H., Pfc,
Lau, Albert D., Pfc,
Laube, Henry D., Pfc,
Laube, Howard E., Pfc,
Lauber, Robert L., Pfc,
†Lauderdale, Calvin M., Pvt,
Lauderdale, G. W., Capt,
Lauer, Arthur A., Pvt,
Lauerman, Edward P., Pvt,
Laugerman, Harold W., 2nd Lt
Laurent, Leon L., Pfc,
Laurenti, Frank, Pfc,
Lauria, Herbert J., Pfc,
†Lautenschlager, Russell D., Jr.,
Laux, William A., Jr., Pfc,
†Lavallee, Albert C., Pvt,
Lavery, John H., Pfc,
Lavine, Bernard, Pvt,
Lavoie, Norman H., Pfc,
Lavoie, Richard R., Pvt,
†Lavoie, Roland J., Pvt,
Law, Charles H., Sgt,
Law, Forest M., S/Sgt,
†Lawhon, Jesse E., Pvt,
†Lawler, Harry J., S/Sgt,
Lawless, Joseph L., Pfc,
Lawlor, Joseph J., Pfc,
Lawrence, Alton A., Pfc,
Lawrence, Dwight L., T/5,
Lawrence, Houston R., Pfc,
Lawrence, Howard R., Pvt,
Lawrence, John H., Pvt,
Lawrence, John W., Pvt,
Lawrence, Leo B., Pvt,
Lawrence, Robert C., Pvt,
Laws, Donald E., Pfc,
Lawson, Robert L., Pvt,
Lawton, Earl P., Jr., Pfc,
Lay, Boyd, Pfc,
Layman, Albert P., Pvt,
Layman, Charles E., T/4,
Layne, Edwin L., Pvt,
§Layne, Malcom B., Pvt,
*Layton, Joseph W., Pvt,
Layton, Lionel R., Pfc,
‡Lazansky, Joseph F., Jr., Pvt,
†Lazar, Morris, Pvt,
†Lazar, Philip, Pvt,
Lazaroff, Dimitar A., Pfc,
Lazarowski, Matthew G., Pfc,
Lazrine, Robert, T/Sgt,
Lazzaro, Anthony A., Pfc,
Lazzarotto, Peter,
*Lea, Oliver W., Sgt,
Leach, George, Pvt,
Leach, Harry L., Cpl,
Leach, Oliver D., Jr., Pvt,
†Leach, Paul E., Cpl,
Leaf, Gordon R., S/Sgt,
Leahey, Phillip J., Pvt,
Leahy, John J., Pvt,
†Leahy, Patrick E., Pfc,
Leake, William D., Pvt,
‡Leakey, Ross A., Pvt,
Leamon, William H., Pfc,
Leanos, Tony E., Pvt,
Leap, Donald A., Pvt,
Lear, George A., Pvt,
Lear, Harry A., Pfc,
Leary, Jack A., Pvt,
Leary, L. L., Sr., 2nd Lt,
Leas, John B., 2nd Lt,
Leasener, John F., S/Sgt,
Leasher, Francis M., Pvt,
Leavitt, Wendell D., 2nd Lt,
Lebeduik, Walter, Pfc,
‡Lebey, Clifford S., Jr., Pvt,
Lebron, Fernando D., Pvt,
Leckie, Walter J., Pfc,
LeComb, Donald F., Pvt,
Ledbetter, Clyde, Pvt,
Ledbetter, James, Pfc,
Ledbetter, Jessie B., Pfc,
Ledell, Howard E., Pfc,
Lederhouse, Harold G., T/5,
§Ledesma, Domingo S., Pfc,
Ledford, Galer L., Pvt,
*Ledford, Lester T., Pvt,
Ledford, Ward J., Pvt,
LeDonne, John R., Pfc,
Ledsome, Carl E., Pfc,
†Lee, Alvin J., Pvt,
Lee, Charles J., T/5,
Lee, Chester E., Pfc,
Lee, Clifford A., Pfc,
Lee, Clyde F., Pvt,
Lee, Daniel, Pfc,
Lee, David W., Pfc,
†Lee, Ellis N., Pfc,
Lee, Foster E., Pvt,
Lee, Frank J., Pvt,
Lee, Frank R., Pfc,
Lee, George A., T/5,
Lee, George F., Sgt,
Lee, Harvey G., Pvt,
Lee, Horace H., Pvt,
Lee, Jack L., Pvt,
Lee, Jacob C., Jr., S/Sgt,
Lee, James F., Pfc,
Lee, James H., T/5,
Lee, John A., Pvt,
Lee, Joseph, Pvt,
Lee, Matthew J., Sgt,
Lee, Rio H., T/4,
‡Lee, Robert E., Pfc,
Lee, Robert O., Pvt,
†Lees, John M., S/Sgt,
‡Lefebvre, A. G., Jr., Pvt,
Le Fevre, Max A., Pvt,
Lefkowitz, Szaja, Pfc,
Legat, Paul W., Pfc,
Le Gates, Edward R., Pvt,
Leggett, Richard C., Pfc,
†Le Grand, Leonard M., Pvt,
*Lehman, Edwin R., Pvt,
Lehman, Jack B., 1st Lt,
Lehman, Orville L., Sgt,
Lehr, Ralph, Pvt,
Lehtinen, John R., Pfc,
Leib, William, Pvt,
Leibowitz, Raymond H., Pvt,
Leicht, John P., 2nd Lt,
†Leicy, Harold L., Pfc,
Leidich, Frank H., Cpl,
Leidolph, James E., Pvt,
Leifel, Anthony J., Pfc,
†Leigh, Farris E., Pfc,
Leinbach, Mark K., Pvt,
Leininger, Lewis E., S/Sgt,
†Leininger, Milton M., Pvt,
Leintz, Valentine, Pfc,
Leisinger, Robert E., Pvt,
Leister, Charles T., Pvt,
Leith, Robert E., Pvt,
†Leithauser, Arthur, Pvt,
Leitner, Eric F., S/Sgt,
Leking, Earl H., Pvt,
Lemar, Carl R., Pfc,
Lemar, Dewey C., Pvt,
†Lemaster, Junior, Pvt,
Lemasters, Percy, Pvt,
Lemay, Alfred J., Pfc,
†Lembke, Orlan P., Cpl,
Lemcke, Robert G., Pfc,
Lemerond, Clifford A., Pvt,
Lemieux, Armand G., Pfc,
Lemire, Robert C., Pfc,
Lemke, Walter F., Pvt,
Lemme, Michael, Pvt,
†Lemmert, Ernest E., Pfc,
Lemmo, Nick J., Pvt,
‡Lemonds, Dorrance W., T/5,
Lenahan, Charles C., Cpl,
Lenahan, William M., Pvt,
Lengyel, John, Jr., Pfc,
Lenker, Edwin H., Pfc,
Lenning, Erming D., Pvt,
Lennon, Charles P., Pvt,
Lentz, Robert C., Pfc,
Lenz, Milford O., Pvt,
Lenz, Thomas W., Pfc,
*Leon, Joe E., Pvt,
Leonard, Alton A., Jr., S/Sgt,
†Leonard, James E., Pvt,
*Leonard, James J., Pvt,
Leonard, Leland W., Pvt,
Leonard, Marion H., Pfc,
†Leonard, Ocko F., Pvt,
Leonardi, Albert, Pfc,
§Leone, Cesidio, Pfc,
Leone, Philip A., Pfc,
Leong, George G., Pvt,
Leppar, Frank D., Pfc,
Lepucki, Walter F., Sgt,
Lercher, Leo, Pvt,
Le Roy, Paul G., Pvt,
Leschorn, Harold R., Pfc,
§Leslie, B. F., Pvt,
Leslie, Carl R., Pfc,
Leslie, Robert E., Pvt,
Leslie, Thomas C., Pvt,
Lesmeister, William, Pfc,
Lessick, Albert S., Pfc,
Lesswing, Arthur G., S/Sgt,
*Letnianchyn, Andrew, Sgt,
‡Letourneau, Thomas C., Pfc,
‡Letta, Dominick S., Pvt,
Leuenberger, George F., Pvt,
†Leuze, Ralph E., 2nd Lt,
†Levan, Donald R., Pfc,
‡Levario, Ysidro M., Pfc,
Leventhal, Aaron, Pvt,
Levesque, Edgar L. R., Pvt,
Levesque, Eugene A., Pvt,
Levesque, Leo A., Pfc,
Levesque, Normand, Pfc,
Levi, Burgin, Pvt,
Levi, Paul, Pfc,
Levin, Archie, Pvt,
Levin, Leonard, Pfc,
Levin, Louis, Pvt,
†Levin, Percy, Pvt,
†Levin, Ralph L., 2nd Lt,
Levine, Harold I., Pvt,
Levine, James, Pfc,
Levine, Stanley H., Pvt,
Levis, Lawrence J., Pvt,
Levitch, Sam, 1st Lt,
Levy, Arthur, S/Sgt,
Levy, Eli, Capt,
§Levy, Harry E., Capt,
Levy, Harry, Pfc,
Levy, Murray D., Pvt,
Levy, Sigmund, Pfc,
Lew, Tow S., Pvt,
Lewallen, C. T., Jr., T/Sgt,
Lewallen, William L., T/4,
Lewandoski, Joseph W., 1st Lt,
‡Lewandowski, E. M., S/Sgt,
Lewandowski, Frank, Pfc,
Lewington, Ralph F., Pfc,
Lewinski, John D., Sgt,
*Lewinski, Joseph F., Jr., Pvt,
Lewis, A. J., Pvt,
†Lewis, Clair E., Jr., Pfc,
*Lewis, David H., Pvt,
Lewis, Earl L., Pvt,
Lewis, Edward B., Cpl,
Lewis, Floyd L., Pfc,
Lewis, Francis L., Pfc,
Lewis, Frank T., Pvt,
Lewis, Gilbert, S/Sgt,
Lewis, Glenn L., Pfc,
†Lewis, Harold T., Pfc,
Lewis, Jack, Pvt,
Lewis, James H., Pvt,
†Lewis, James R., Pfc,
Lewis, John M., Pvt,
Lewis, Joseph C., Pfc,
Lewis, Lacy L., Pvt,
Lewis, Lenard, T/Sgt,
Lewis, Marvin D., Pvt,
Lewis, Martin G., Pfc,
Lewis, Paul D., Pfc,
§Lewis, Robert E., S/Sgt,
Lewis, Wesley T., Pfc,
Lewis, Wilfred R., Pvt,
Lewis, William E., Pfc,
Lewis, William V., Pvt,
†Lexsinger, Earl W., Pvt,
Leynes, Robert L., Sgt,
Leyva, Henry O., Pfc,
Licastri, Ciro J., Pfc,
Lichvar, Joseph F., Pvt,
Lickliter, Earnest J., Pvt,
Liddle, Raymond T., Pvt,
Lieban, Ralph G., 1st Lt,
‡Liebelt, Edward F., Pfc,
Lieberman, Abraham, Pfc,
Lieberman, Julius, Pfc,
Liebl, Derold L., Pvt,
Liebo, John W., Pvt,
†Lienerth, Julius A., Pvt,
Liese, Henry J., Pfc,
Lieszewicz, Edward, Pvt,
†Lifschitz, Samuel, Pfc,
Ligarski, Joseph J., Pvt,
Lightcap, George A., Pfc,
Ligon, Julian C., Pfc,
Lilevjen, Hugh A., T/Sgt,
Lillard, Johnnie Y., Pvt,
Lilly, Albert C., 2nd Lt,
Lilly, Daniel T., Pfc,
Lilly, Floyd W., Pvt,
Lilly, Orace, Pfc,
Limbert, Raymond M., Pfc,
§Limmer, Robert A., Sgt,
Limpic, John, 1st Lt,
†Limpp, Albert J., Jr., Pfc,
Limprecht, Hollis J., 1st Lt,
Lincoln, Clarence E., S/Sgt,
*Lincoln, Warren H., Pvt,
Linda, Arnold O., Pvt,
Lindauer, Felix O., Pfc,
†Lindbert, Charles T., Pvt,
‡Lindborg, John H., Pvt,
Lindert, Gordon O., 1st/Sgt,
Lindell, Bernard R., Pfc,
Linden, Harry E., Jr.,
†Lindley, James A., Pfc,
Lindsay, Albrey B., Pvt,
Lindsay, Floyd E., S/Sgt,
Lindsay, Joseph F., Pfc,
Lindsay, Maurice E., Jr., Pvt,
†Lindsay, Max D., Pvt,
Lindsey, Charles W., Jr., Pfc,
Lindsey, Earl L., S/Sgt,
Lindsey, Louis E., Pvt,
Lindsey, Paul D., 1st Lt,
Lindsey, Roy M., Pfc,
Lindsey, William N., Pvt,
Lindstrom, Bernard I., 2nd Lt,
†Lindstrom, Floyd K., Pfc,
Lindstrom, Juniel R., Pfc,
Lingenfelter, Fred D., Pfc,
Lingis, Stanley A., Pvt,
Linker, Grady, Pvt,
†Linker, Paul E., Pfc,
Linn, George M., Pfc,
†Linthicum, Franklin H., Pvt,
Linton, John J., T/Sgt,
Linton, Norman L., Pvt,
Linton, Robert Lee, Pfc,
Lintz, Albert, Pfc,
Lintz, Robert D., Sgt,
†Linville, Paul P., Sgt,
Linzmeyer, Aloys H., T/4,
Lioy, Anthony A., Pvt,
Lipchik, John, Pfc,
Lipka, Leo G., Pfc,
Lipke, Charles F., Jr., Pvt,
Lippert, Leonard G., Pfc,
Lipshultz, George, Pvt,
Liptak, Albert P., Pvt,
Lishetti, John P., Pvt,
‡Liscomb, Ferdie D., Pvt,
Lisenbee, Hassie, Pvt,
Lisiecki, Henry M., Pvt,
Lisowski, Bruno A., Pvt,
‡Liston, Devene B., Pvt,
Litherland, James I., Pvt,
Littell, James F., Sgt,
Little, Blair W., Pvt,
Little, Clyde H., Pvt,
*Little, Hubert L., Pfc,
Little, Kenneth K., Pfc,
Littlefield, Lewis E., Pvt,
Littlehead, George, Pfc,
Litzner, Everett D., Pfc,
Lively, Leslie W., Pfc,
†Livergood, Donald C., Pfc,
*Livingston, Max E., Pfc,
Livingston, William R., Sgt,
†Livolsi, Tony, Pvt,
Lloyd, William Jr., Pfc,
Lobb, Richard V., Pfc,
Lobs, Robert J., Pfc,
Locascio, John, Pvt,

† Killed in Action. * Prisoner of War. ‡ Missing in Action. § Died of Wounds.

Locascio, Peter, Pfc,
‡Lochner, Frederick G., Pvt,
Locke, William Louis, Cpl,
*Lockhart, Clovis E., Pvt,
*Lockhart, Jackson H., Pvt,
†Locklear, Winfred, Pvt,
*Lockling, Robert W., Pvt,
Lockmiller, Lincoln G., Sgt,
Lockrem, Milton E., Pvt,
Lockrey, Stanley E., Pvt,
†Lockwood, Paul R., Pvt,
*Lockwood, Robert E., Cpl,
Lockwood, Russell E., Pfc,
Lodise, Albert J., Pfc,
Lodygowski, V. W., Pvt,
Loewe, Lawrence A., Pfc,
Loewen, Lawrence L., T/5,
Loffer, William J., Pvt,
Lofgreen, Lloyd C., Pfc,
Loflin, George V., T/Sgt,
Loftin, William L., Pvt,
*Loftus, John J., Pvt,
Lofy, Giles G., Pvt,
Logan, Vincent A., Pfc,
Logan, William T., S/Sgt,
Logsdon, Jesse M., Pfc,
Logsdon, John M., Pvt,
†Logue, James F., Cpl,
Logue, Thomas A., Cpl,
Loh, Michael J., Pfc,
‡Lohman, William, Pvt,
Lohn, Frederick, Pfc,
Lohse, Frederick H., Pvt,
Loisel, Louis, Pvt,
Lokers, Raymond J., 1st Lt,
Lomax, Grady L., Pvt,
†Lombardo, Clifford E., Pvt,
Lombardo, Louis T., Pvt,
Lomeli, Paul H., Sr., Pvt,
Londe, Paul M., Pfc,
†Long, Austin M., Pfc,
Long, Charles B., Pfc,
Long, Darell J., Pvt,
Long, Donald F., Sgt,
Long, Elvin A., Pfc,
Long, Floyd A., Pvt,
†Long, Harley W., Pvt,
Long, Howard O., Pvt,
Long, James W., Pfc,
Long, Joe T., Pvt,
Long, Kemmist K., Pvt,
Long, Robert W., Sgt,
†Long, Theodore W., Pvt,
Long, Warren M., Sgt,
Long, William A., Pvt,
Long, William J., Pvt,
Longcrier, Herbert H., T/Sgt,
Longo, Michael J., T/5,
Longsderff, Wilfred H., Sgt,
Loofboro, Elmer L., T/5,
Looking, Elk W., Pfc,
Looman, William D., Pfc,
Looney, Leon P., Pfc,
Looney, Roy L., Pvt,
Loop, Forest W., Pfc,
Loos, John N., Pfc,
†Lopeman, Herbert T., Pvt,
Lopena, Alfredo A., Pfc,
Lopez, Henry, Pvt,
†Lopez, Joe, Pvt,
Lopez, John P., Pfc,
Lopez, Juan A., T/4,
Lo Porto, Carmelo C., Pvt,
Lo Presti, Joseph, Pvt,
Lo Presti, Vittorio U., Pfc,
*Lorber, Hyman, Pvt,
†Lord, Lionel B., Pvt,
Lorden, John R., Pfc,
*Lore, Robert E., Pfc,
Loree, Ralph E., Pvt,
†Lorensen, Wilbert F., Pvt,
Lorentzen, Marvin M., Sgt,
Lorenz, Kenneth W., Pfc,
Lorenzetti, Carlo L., Pfc,
†Lorenzo, Arthur J., Pvt,
Lorerzel, Benedict A., Pfc,
Lorey, Louis J., Pfc,
Lorion, Hector J., Pfc,
Lorsen, Edgar F., Pfc,
Lorton, Don C., Sgt,
Lostumbo, Dominick J., 1st Lt,
Lott, Ray T., Pvt,
Louden, Robert C., Pvt,
Lough, Alfha L., Sgt,
Lough, Gaius H., Pfc,
Loup, Benjamin E., Pfc,
Louris, Jim G., Pvt,
Lovall, Donald, Pfc,
Lovato, Lorenzo, S/Sgt,
Love, George W., Pvt,
*Love, James M., Jr., S/Sgt,
Love, Leonard F., Pvt,
Lovelace, Cole, Pfc,
Lovelace, John H., Sgt,
§Lovell, William R., Pvt,
Loven, Merle L., Pvt,
Lover, Dale H., Pfc,
†Lovett, Joseph G., Pvt,
Low, Ernest B., Pvt,
Lowder, Lorie A., Pfc,
Lowdermilk, John W., Pvt,
†Lowe, Francis L., Pfc,
†Lowe, James D., Pvt,
Lowe, James H., Pfc,
Lowery, Forest C., Pfc,
Lowery, Lewis O., Sgt,
‡Lowery, William B., Pvt,
Lowman, Richard M., Pfc,
Lowrey, Henry, Pfc,
Lowry, Edward J., T/5,
Lowry, Rex D., Pvt,
Lowry, Robert W., Pfc,
‡Loyd, James C., Pvt,
Lozano, Salvador R., Jr.,
Luberski, Stanley G., Pfc,
Lucado, Kyle S., Pvt,
†Lucas, Eckler C., T/5,
Lucci, William L., Pvt,
Lucey, Robert L., Cpl,
Luci, Vincent J., Pfc,
Luciano, John R., Pvt,
Luciano, Vito A., Pfc,
Luck, Lynwood L., Pvt,
Ludtke, John H., Sgt,
†Ludlam, Stephen C., Pfc,
†Luebke, Arden D., Pfc,
Luecken, Robert O., Pvt,
Lugr, Dale D., Pvt,
Luidl, Peter J., Pvt,
Lukasiewicy, Eugene J., Sgt,
Lukenbill, Alfred L., S/Sgt,
Lukin, Basil, 1st Lt,
Lulek, Frank J., Pfc,
Lullo, Joseph P., Pfc,
Luman, Frank A., Pfc,
Lumbert, Henry M., Pvt,
Lumen, Leo A., Pvt,
Lumsdon, William G., Pvt,
Lunetta, Charles S., Pfc,
Lunetta, Patrick P., Pvt,
†Lunetta, Salvatore J., Pfc,
Lunghi, Pete, Pfc,
Lunick, George, Sgt,
Lunogo, Albert D., Pfc,
Lunsford, Lawrence A., Pfc,
Luoma, Leonard, Pfc,
Luoma, Reino A., Pfc,
Lupac, Robert G., Pfc,
Lupinski, Bronislaw S., Pfc,
Lupone, Silvio M., Pfc,
Lusk, Rufna F., Pvt,
Lusky, Alex, Pfc,
†Lussy, Robert H., Pvt,
Luteri, Lawrence J., Pfc,
Lutkemeier, Carl E., Pfc,
Lutterman, Vincent J., T/4,
Luttrell, Lowell M., Cpl,
†Luttrell, Walter C., Pfc,
Lutynski, Joseph J., Pfc,
Luzeiki, Michael, T/5,
Lybarger, Daniel, Pfc,
Lybarger, William H., Pfc,
Lykin, Nicholas, Pvt,
Lynch, Clyde R., S/Sgt,
Lynch, George C., 1st Lt,
Lynch, George R., Pfc,
Lynch, James C., 1st Lt,
Lynch, Lawrence, Jr., Sgt,
†Lynch, Nicholas A., 1st Sgt,
†Lyncha, Steve M., Pvt,
Lynn, Paul F., Pvt,
§Lyon, James A., Pfc,
Lyons, Ballard J., Pfc,
Lyons, Buddy A., Pvt,
Lyons, John R., Pvt,
Lyons, Thomas P., Pfc,
Lyons, Thomas P., Pvt,
Lyons, William J., S/Sgt,
Lytle, Marvin C., Pvt,

Maberry, Hamilton W., Sgt,
Mabry, Horace S., Pfc,
Mabry, Robert E., Pvt,
†Mabuce, Eddie L., Pfc,
Macadie, Donald G., Pfc,
Mac Aulay, Norman D., 1st Lt,
Mac Coole, Herbert L., Pvt,
MacDonald, John K., 2nd Lt,
MacDonald, Kenneth R., Pvt,
MacDowall, John D., Pfc,
Macedo, James, T/Sgt,
Macewicz, Alfred F., Pvt,
Macey, Philip H., Pvt,
†Maceyko, Albert V., Pvt,
Machado, Antone, Pfc,
Machado, Aristides M., Pfc,
Machado, Manuel S., Jr., Pvt,
Macino, Joseph, Pvt,
Machtenberg, Philip, Pvt,
Mack, Roland T., Pfc,
Mack, Walter L., Pvt,
Macke, Andrew J., Pfc,
Mackenzie, William F., Pfc,
Mackersie, Vurl M., Pfc,
Mackes, Nick M., Pvt,
Mackey, Edward K., Pvt,
Mackey, James A., Pfc,
Mackey, Robert L., S/Sgt,
Mackey, Robert L., Sr., Pfc,
Mackie, John O., Pfc,
Macklin, Lenny A., Pfc,
‡Mackrill, Calvin G., Pvt,
MacLean, Robert B., Pfc,
MacNeil, Mark C., T/4,
Macomber, William M., Pfc,
MacPhail, George B., T/5,
MacPherson, Howard, Pfc,
MacPherson, Roy A., Pfc,
Macy, Jack P., Sgt,
†Maczka, Marion J., S/Sgt,
Madar, Steve A., Pvt,
Madden, Darius S., T/4,
Madden, John J., Pfc,
†Maddigan, James P., Pfc,
Maddock, Dore P., Pfc,
Maddox, Bonnie P., Jr., Pfc,
Maddox, Pellon E., Pfc,
Madey, Walter S., T/4,
‡Madore, Francis F., Pvt,
†Madrick, Frank J., Pfc,
Madsen, George F., Cpl,
Maederer, Kenneth A., Sgt,
Maffeo, Domenico, S/Sgt,
†Magaro, Peter M., Pvt,
Magdanz, Myron A., T/4,
Magry, Steven, Pfc,
Magee, Charles L., Cpl,
Magee, James J., S/Sgt,
Maggart, Leo D., Pfc,
Maggio, John, Pfc,
Maglinger, William E., Pfc,
Magnotta, Frank F., Pvt,
Maguire, William H., Capt,
Mahan, Albert R., Pfc,
Mahar, Edward F., 1st Lt,
†Mahar, Edward L., 1st Lt,
Mahar, Harold W., 2nd Lt,
†Maher, James A., Pvt,
Maher, James E., Pfc,
Maher, Miles A., Cpl,
Maham, Ralph E., S/Sgt,
Mahon, Ivan T., Pvt,
Mahony, John E., Jr., S/Sgt,
Mai, Clarence W., Sgt,
Maier, Hans W., Pvt,
Maietta, Nicholas A., Pvt,
†Mailhot, Roland J., Pvt,
Mailloux, George J., Pfc,
†Maimone, John, Pfc,
Main, Emmet L., S/Sgt,
Main, Max B., Pvt,
Mainprize, John R., Cpl,
Maiolini, Herman P., Pfc,
Maisch, Jack A., Pfc,
Maisel, Joseph P., Pvt,
Majchrzak, Leonard R., Pvt,
Majeski, Edward J., Pfc,
Majewski, Joe, Cpl,
Majka, Felix F., T/Sgt,
Major, James E., Pvt,
Major, Lawrence J., Pvt,
Maki, Tauno S., Pfc,
†Makinen, Reino R., Pvt,
Makings, Leslie A., Pfc,
Makos, Charles J., Pvt,
Malandra, Aldine A., Pvt,
Malatesta, Edward R., Sgt,
Malatesta, Ellio A., T/4,
Malek, Steve, Pfc,
Malichio, Michael A., Pvt,
†Malicki, Chester S., Pvt,
Malleos, Nickolas P., Jr.,
Mallinger, Samuel H., 1st Lt,
†Malloy, George, Pvt,
Mallozzi, Donald A., T/5,
†Malochleb, Stanley J., Pvt,
Malone, Earl T., Pvt,
Malone, John P., Pfc,
†Malone, Leo J., Pvt,
Malone, Michael J., Pvt,
Maloney, Gerald N., Pvt,
†Maloney, Robert E., Pvt,
Maloney, William A., Pfc,
Malson, Norman W., Pfc,
Maly, Edward, T/5,
Maly, Stanley J., Pfc,
§Malz, Edward H., Pvt,
Mancuso, Peter A., Pvt,
Mancuso, Vincent J., Sgt,
Mandel, Abraham R., Pvt,
†Mandel, David, Pvt,
Manders, Dennis I., Pvt,
Mandeville, David C., Pfc,
Mandick, John J., 2nd Lt,
Mandoki, Stephen, Pvt,
Maness, Eugene A., Jr., Pvt,
Maness, John S., Pfc,
Manfre, Romolo J., Pvt,
Manfred, James A., Pfc,
Mang, Frankie, Jr., T/5,
Mangan, James J., Pvt,
Mangano, Louis A., Pfc,
Mangiapane, F. P., Pfc,
†Mangigian, Minas G., Pfc,
Mangler, Harold J., T/5,
Mangold, Emil G., Pvt,
Manhart, Ashton H., Lt Col,
Manifesto, Frank C., Pvt,
Mann, Timothy J., Pfc,
‡Mann, Wong, Pvt,
Maniscalco, Anthony, Pvt,
Mankins, John W., Pvt,
Mankowski, Edward F., T/5,
Manley, Harry J., Pfc,
Mann, Lee B., Pfc,
Mann, Roy E., Sgt,
Mannella, Tony, Pfc,
Mannerelli, Thomas A., Pvt,
Mannin, Claude, Pfc,
Manning, Aubrey V., Pfc,
Manning, Thomas O., Pfc,
†Mannino, Angelo, Pvt,
†Manno, George J., Pfc,
Manos, George J., T/5,
Manross, Clifford R., Pfc,
Mansfield, Harold D., Pvt,
Mantzey, Charles D., Pfc,
†Manuel, Francis, Pfc,
Manuel, Wilfred, Pvt,
†Manues, Roy L., Pvt,
Manyak, Andrew, Jr., Pvt,
Manzanares, Miguel R., Pfc,
†Manzo, Canuto M., Pvt,
Mapstone, Jesse O., Pfc,
Marble, Floyd E., S/Sgt,
Marble, Floyd E., 2nd Lt,
Marchese, Peter M., Pvt,
Marchetti, Louis J., Pvt,
Marchione, Anthony J., Pvt,
Marchunsky, Albert J., Pfc,
Marchiano, John, Pfc,
Marciano, Ernest, Pfc,
Marck, Andrew A., 1st Lt,
*Marcklinger, William H., Pvt,
Marcoff, Panaiot G., Pfc,
Marcone, Harold J., Pvt,
†Marcotte, Arthur R., Pfc,
Marcus, Morton R., Pfc,
Marecki, Thomas M., Pvt,
Marella, John J., Pfc,
†Marengo, Clarence L., Sgt,
Marenic, William, Sgt,
*Mares, Pablo,
Marin, Albert G., Pvt,
Margritz, Robert M., Jr., Pvt,
Marin, Victor H., Sgt,
†Marinin, Michael R., Pfc,
Marino, Anthony J., Pvt,
Marino, Frank F., Cpl,
*Marino, Joseph, Pvt,
Marino, Louis A., Pfc,
Marion, Elbert R., Pvt,
Marion, Theodore E., Pfc,
Marker, Thaddeus E., Cpl,
Markes, William, Pvt,
Markham, Daniel V., Pfc,
Markins, Lonnie, Pfc,
Markle, Elwood, Pvt,
*Markley, Carl E., Pvt,
Markley, Donald J., Pfc,
Markovich, Charles, Pvt,
Markowitz, Dan W., Sgt,
Markowski, Emanuel, Pfc,
Marlar, William E., 2nd Lt,
†Marlatt, Chester L., Pfc,
§Marlett, Wilborn, Pvt,
Marlin, Charles W., Jr., S/Sgt,
Marlow, Clifford, Pvt,
Marlow, Edward F., Pvt,
Marlow, Howard L., Pfc,
Marlowe, Timothy V., Pvt,
†Marmarelo, Angelo, Cpl,
Maron, Russell T., Pvt,
†Marone, Michael J., Pfc,
Marple, Frank B., Pvt,
Marquart, Harry V., T/5,
Marquez, Gilbert H., Sgt,
Marrazzo, Frank G., Pvt,
*Marrero, Felix, Pfc,
†Marrero, Gerardo, Pfc,
Marria, Alfred L., T/4,
Marro, Samuel J., Pfc,
Mars, William F., Pvt,
Marsden, Russell R., Pfc,
Marsh, James E., Capt,
Marsh, Raymond R., Pfc,
Marsh, Robert D., Capt,
Marsh, Robert W., Sgt,
Marsh, Ted L., Pfc,
Marshall, Charles F., Jr., Pfc,
Marshall, Clarence H., Sgt,
Marshall, Douglas W., Jr., Pfc,
Marshall, James V., Pvt,
Marshall, James W., Pvt,
Marshall, Otis B., Pfc,
Marshall, Tony P., Cpl,
†Marshall, William H., Pvt,
Marshall, William J., Pfc,
Marson, James D., Cpl,
Marteeny, Ellsworth R., Sgt,
†Martel, Ferdinand J., Pfc,
Martell, Jesse A., Pvt,
Martell, Keith T., Pfc,
Marthers, James M., Pfc,
Marti, William R., Pvt,
Martin, Alfred C., Pvt,
Martin, Alfred D., Cpl,
Martin, Alfred L., T/5,
*Martin, Andrew, Sgt,
Martin, Bunyan F., Pvt,
Martin, Claude H., Pfc,
Martin, Charles J., Sgt,
Martin, Cyrus D., Pfc,
Martin, David L., Pvt,
Martin, Dett A., Pfc,
Martin, Donald A., Pfc,
Martin, Edward L., T/4,
Martin, Elmus J., Pvt,
Martin, Emile H., Pvt,
Martin, Ernest J., Pvt,
Martin, Jack M., Pvt,
Martin, James L., Pfc,
Martin, John F., Pvt,
Martin, John O., Pfc,
Martin, John T., Pfc,
Martin, Joseph B., Sgt,
Martin, Joseph E., Capt,
§Martin, Larmer A., Pfc,
Martin, Loyd J., Pfc,
†Martin, Marvin H., Pfc,
Martin, Oscar H., Pfc,
Martin, Paul L., Pvt,
Martin, Ralph E., Pfc,
Martin, Raymond B., Pvt,
Martin, Raymond D., Pfc,
Martin, Robert L., Pvt,
*Martin, Roger M., Pvt,
Martin, Roy D., Pvt,
Martin, Thomas L., T/5,
Martin, Walter G., Pvt,
Martin, Walter M., Pvt,
Martin, Willard E., Pvt,
Martin, William L., Pvt,
†Martin, Willis G., Pfc,
§Martinez, Basil J., Pfc,
†Martinez, Felipe C., Pfc,
Martinez, Frank P., Pvt,
‡Martinez, John A., T/5,
Martinez, Jose L., Pvt,
†Martinez, Patrocinio, Sgt
Martinez, Paul E., Pfc,
Martinez, Paul G., Pfc,
Martinez, Raul M., Sgt,
Martinez, Stephen S., Pfc,
Martini, John L., Pfc,
†Martini, Reno A., Pfc,
Martino, George D., Jr., Pfc,
Martinson, Ole M., T/Sgt,
Martosko, Stephen A., 1st/Sgt,
Martz, Carl E., T/5,
†Martz, Charles E., Pvt,
†Marunycz, George, Pvt,
Marvin, Robert A., S/Sgt,
Marx, James F., Pfc,
Marx, Joseph J., Pfc,
Marx, Phillip, Pfc,
Marx, Walter S., T/4,
Maryanski, Leo J., Pfc,
†Mascali, Frank, Pfc,
†Masciangelo, Albert W., Pvt,
Masciocchi, Louis A., Pvt,
Mascuillo, Louis, Jr., Pfc,
Masero, Frank J., Pfc,
Masessa, Daniel, Pfc,
Mask, Ira C., Sr., Pvt,
‡Maskell, Jacob J., Jr., Pvt,
Mason, Bruce T., 2nd Lt,
†Mason, Harry S., Pfc,
Mason, John C., Pfc,
†Mason, John F., Pfc,
Mason, Leaborn D., S/Sgt,
Mason, Leslie L., Pvt,
Mason, Lloyd H., Pvt,
Mason, Omer, Cpl,
Mason, Oscar H., Pfc,
§Mason, Russell G., Pfc,
*Mason, Walter J., Pfc,
§Massariello, Paul E., Pvt,
Massaro, Dominick A., Pfc,
Massey, Claernce, T/Sgt,
Masters, Herman, Pfc,
Mastrella, Angelo A., 1st Lt,
Maszezak, Michael J., Pfc,
Matarazzo, Anthony, Pfc,
Matassa, Frank, Pfc,

† Killed in Action. * Prisoner of War. ‡ Missing in Action. § Died of Wounds.

Matchett, Alton C., Pvt,
Matello, Louis, Pfc,
Matheis, Elmer, Pfc,
Mathers, Dwane H., Sgt,
Mathers, Wallace J., Sgt,
Mathewes, Donald F., Pfc,
†Mathias, Ervin M., Pvt,
Mathias, Eugene J., Pfc,
Mathieu, Robert L., Cpl,
Mathile, Gerald D., Pfc,
Mathis, John M., Pvt,
†Mathis, Reese C., Pfc,
Mathison, Norman C., T/5,
Mathusa, William W., 2nd Lt,
Matlack, Edwin W., T/5,
Matlock, James R., Pfc,
Matlosz, Edward J., Pfc,
Matlosz, Roman A., T/3,
†Matosky, Stanley A., Pfc,
†Matriss, Frederick J., Pfc,
†Matsas, Donald, Pfc,
Matsen, Howard W., Pfc,
Matson, Clifford D., Cpl,
Matteo, Albert, Cpl,
Matthew, Joseph L., Sgt,
†Matthew, Wilfred L., Pfc,
Matthews, Arthur E., Jr., Pfc,
Matthews, James W., Pvt,
Matthews, Norval M., Cpl,
Matthews, Richard A., Pfc,
Matthews, William F., Sgt,
*Matthews, William V., Pvt,
Matthias, Stuart J., Pfc,
Matthias, Warren H., Pvt,
Matthiesen, James A., Pvt,
†Mattingly, Sylvester A., S/Sgt,
Mattson, Albert W., Pfc,
Mattson, Ralph W., Pvt,
Matusiak, Joseph, Pvt,
Matusovic, Joseph, Pvt,
Mauceri, Larry E., Sgt,
Maul, Henry, Sgt,
Mauragas, Joe C., Pfc,
†Mauran, Howard J., Pfc,
Maurer, Mathis J., Pfc,
Maurizi, Ernest J., Pfc,
Mawson, William R., Pfc,
Maxey, Perry O., Sgt,
Maxson, Marvin R., Pvt,
Maxwell, Grady A., Pfc,
Maxwell, Nelson S., Pfc,
Maxwell, Robert D., T/5,
Maxwell, Wayne G., S/Sgt,
May, Earnest B., Pfc,
May, George F., Pfc,
May, John A., T/4,
†May, Woodrow, Pfc,
Mayback, Myron E., Pfc,
†Mayberry, Kenneth C., Sgt,
Mayer, Aloysius P., Sgt,
Mayer, Arthur, Pvt,
Mayer, Frank W., Pfc,
Mayer, Kenneth A., Pvt,
Mayer, Lew E., Pfc,
†Mayer, Stanley E., Pfc,
Mayfield, Cullen D., T/Sgt,
Mayfield, Horace, Sgt,
Mayhall, Boyd L., Sgt,
Mayhew, John R., 1st Lt,
Mayhugh, Delbert P., Sgt,
Maynard, Robert S., Pvt,
Mayo, Hugh I., Pvt,
†Mayo, John A., 1st/Sgt,
Mazeski, Bronek F., Pfc,
Maziak, Valentino A., Pfc,
Mazur, Frank T., Pvt,
‡Mazurek, Frank, Pfc,
Mazurkiewiecz, J., Jr., Pfc,
†Mazza, Vincent A., Pvt,
Mazzone, Paul O., Pfc,
McAdams, M. J., Jr., Pfc,
McAfee, James W., Pfc,
McAllister, Ira C., Pfc,
McAllister, Martin S., Pfc,
McAllister, Richard J., Pfc,
†McAloon, Eugene G., Pvt,
McAndrew, Robert N., Pvt,
McAntire, Joseph J., T/5,
McArdle, Robert M., Pvt,
McArthur, William L., Pfc,
McAtee, Benjamin F., Pfc,
McBrayer, Boyd, Pvt,
McBride, Charles I., Pfc,
McBride, Earl L., Cpl,
McBride, Edward H., Pvt,
†McBride, John T., T/5,
McCabe, George E., Pfc,
McCabe, Malcolm G., Pvt,
McCabe, William J., Cpl,
McCain, Dilmus F., Pfc,
McCall, Alexander J., Pfc,
McCall, Alfred, Pvt,
McCall, Cyril F., S/Sgt,
McCall, Raymond E., Pfc,
McCallion, Donald, Pvt,

‡McCampbell, Carroll H., Pfc,
McCann, John P., Capt,
‡McCann, Virgil, Pvt,
*McCarroll, Patrick H., Pfc,
McCarry, Earl J., S/Sgt,
McCarter, Cecil V., Pfc,
†McCarter, D. C., Pvt,
McCarthy, Clarence H., Pfc,
McCarthy, Gerard A., S/Sgt,
McCarthy, James W., Pvt,
McCarthy, Jesse J., Pvt,
‡McCarthy, Paul F., Pfc,
McCarty, Herschel E., Sgt,
McCarty, Marion C., Capt,
McCarty, Millard E., Pfc,
McCarty, Winn, Sgt,
†McCarvell, Herbert D., Pvt,
McCauley, Bradley U., Pfc,
McCauley, Charles, Pvt,
McCauley, Mack S., Pvt,
McCawley, Hese E., Pfc,
McClain, Cecil D., T/4,
McClamma, Willis I., Pfc,
McClanahan, Jeff B., Pvt,
McCleary, Thomas, Pvt,
†McClellan, Harold J., Sgt,
McClelland, Ernest L., Cpl,
†McClendon, Clarence D., Pfc,
McCloud, George P., Pfc,
†McCluckie, Earl C., Pvt,
McClung, Elvan E., Sgt,
*McClure, William C., Jr., Pfc,
†McClurg, Albert, Pvt,
McCombs, Arlie E., Pfc,
McConnell, Hollie B., S/Sgt,
McConnell, John P., 2nd Lt,
McConnell, Raymond W., Pvt,
McCord, Paul H., Pfc,
McCorkle, Douglas E., Pfc,
McCormick James C., 1st Lt,
McCormick, Richard C., Pvt,
†McCormick, Robert D., S/Sgt,
McCormick, Thomas L., Pfc,
‡McCorry, James T., Pvt,
§McCoy, Andrew C., Pvt,
McCoy, James H., Pvt,
†McCoy, James L., Pvt,
McCoy, James R., S/Sgt,
McCoy, Thomas F., Pfc,
McCoy, Robert K., Pfc,
†McCoy, Thornton D., Pvt,
†McCoy, Walter F., S/Sgt,
†McCracken, James H., 1st Lt,
†McCrae, Edwin, Pfc,
McCrea, Paul J., Pvt,
McCready, Richard B., Pvt,
McCrickard, Mack M., Pfc,
McCrory, Bentley M., Sgt,
McCroskey, Clifford I., Pfc,
McCrosson, John E., Pvt,
McCrum, William W., Pfc,
McCuish, John B., Cpl,
McCulloch, Stephen G., T/5,
‡McCullough, James H., Pvt,
McCullough, James W., Cpl,
McCullough, John S., Pfc,
McCurry, Howard H., Pfc,
McCurry, Robert, Pfc,
McCutcheon, Willie A., Pvt,
McDaniel, Charles W., Sgt,
McDaniel, Clarence, Pfc,
McDaniel, Eugene F., Pfc,
McDaniel, Henry A., Jr., Pfc,
†McDaniel, John C., 2nd Lt,
McDaniel, John T., Pfc,
McDaniel, Richard B., Sgt,
McDaniel, Woodford S., Sgt,
McDermott, Byron H., Pfc,
McDermid, Alton J., Cpl,
†McDermott, Edward J., Sgt,
McDermott, Peter J., Pvt,
†McDermott, Raymond J., Pvt,
†McDole, Riley J., Jr., Pvt,
McDonald, James E., Pvt,
†McDonald, Joe V., Pvt,
McDonald, John J., Pfc,
McDonald, John J., Pvt,
McDonald, Milburn L., Pfc,
†McDonald, Vernon W., Pfc,
‡McDonnell, Raymond J., Pvt,
†McDonnell, Robert E., 1st Lt,
McDonough, Andrew J., Pfc,
McDougal, Dewey M., Pfc,
McDowell, Roger G., Pfc,
‡McEldowney, James H., Pfc,
McElhiney, Thomas R., Pvt,
McElreath, Frank, Pvt,
McElroy, Donald E., Pfc,
McElroy, Walter T., Pfc,
†McElveen, Joseph M., 1st Lt,
McEwin, Henry B., T/Sgt,
McFadden, Francis J., Pfc,
McFall, Daniel L., Pvt,
†McFarland, Beryl E., Sgt,
McFerrin, George W., Pvt,

McFiren, Thomas J., Pfc,
McGarry, Timothy J., Pvt,
McGarvey, Harry L., Cpl,
McGath, Irvin R., Pfc,
†McGee, Emery J., Sgt,
McGee, Everett O., Pfc,
‡McGee, Hubert W., Pvt,
McGee, James, T/Sgt,
McGee, Oscar B., Pvt,
†McGhan, Paul V., 1st Lt,
McGill, Horace B., Pfc,
McGinn, Harold J., Pvt,
‡McGinnis, James E., Pfc,
McGinnis, James F., S/Sgt,
*McGinnis, Thomas J., Pfc,
McGinty, William P., Pfc,
McGlinn, Charles H. J., Sgt,
*McGlone, Raymond Q., Pvt,
McGlothin, Russell E., Pvt,
McGlothlin, Carlos M., S/Sgt,
McGovern, Thomas J., Pvt,
McGrath, John P., Pfc,
†McGrath, Joseph E., Pvt,
McGraw, Alton J., Pfc,
McGrath, Joseph F., Pfc,
McGraw, Harry W., Pvt,
McGreevy, Robert H., Pvt,
McGreevy, Thomas P., Pfc,
McGregor, Kenneth C., Sgt,
McGrew, Harold F., Pvt,
McGruder, Richard H., Sgt,
McGuckin, Elmer N., Pvt,
McGuigan, Henry J., Pvt,
‡McGuire, Carl J., Pvt,
McGuire, Edward M., Pvt,
McGuire, George H., Pvt,
McGuire, Joseph L., T/4,
McGuire, Loyd, 1st Lt,
McGurer, Otis C., Sgt,
McHam, John M., Pfc,
McHenry, John P., Cpl,
McHugh, William J., Pfc,
McIlduff, Bernard F., Pvt,
McIntire, Carl R., Pfc,
McIntosh, E. W., Jr., 1st Lt,
McIntosh, Howard A., S/Sgt,
McIntosh, Jackson, Sgt,
McIntosh, James O., T/4,
McIntosh, Jesse, 1st Lt,
McIntosh, John P., Pvt,
McIntyre, James L., S/Sgt,
McIntyre, Philip J., Pvt,
‡McKane, Weston S., 1st Lt,
McKay, John J., Pvt,
McKee, James W., Pfc,
†McKeel, Walter D., Pfc,
McKeithen, William S., 1st Lt,
McKenna, Frank A., Pvt,
McKenna, Gerard P., Cpl,
McKenna, Thomas G., Pvt,
McKennon, Cecil O., Pfc,
McKenzie, Paul W., Pfc,
McKeown, John A., Pfc,
McKibbin, Arlo G., T/Sgt,
‡McKibben, Donald H., 2nd Lt,
McKibben, William J., Cpl,
McKibbin, William S., Pfc,
McKinley, Alfred F., Pvt,
McKinley, James L., S/Sgt,
McKinney, William K., Pfc,
McKinney, Charles E., Pfc,
McKinstry, Clifford B., Pvt,
McKinzie, Carroll, Pvt,
McKinzie, Raymond E., Pvt,
McKirgan, Lowell T., Pfc,
McKnight, James P., T/4,
McKnight, John S., Capt,
§McKnight, Wendell L., S/Sgt,
McKnight, William J., Jr., Pfc,
†McLain, Pearl, Pvt,
McLaren, John F., Pfc,
§McLaughlin, Alvin C., Pfc,
McLaughlin, George W., Pfc,
McLaughlin, Roy V., Pfc,
McLaughlin, Tom, Pfc,
McLean, Marvin D., S/Sgt,
McLean, Parrish M., Pfc,
McLean, Thomas J., Pfc,
McLellan, John W., 2nd Lt,
McLemore, Jessie T., Pfc,
McLeod, Charles A., Pfc,
McMahan, Earl D., Pfc,
McManus, Edward B., T/5,
McManus, Joseph L., Cpl,
§McManus, Warren R., Pfc,
McMath, Arthur S., Pfc,
‡McMichael, Ralph R., Pfc,
McMillan, Edwin W., Pvt,
McMillan, Joe W., Pvt,
McMillan, Reed, Pvt,
McMillen, Earl E., Pvt,
McNally, James, Pvt,
†McNally, Thomas J., Pvt,
McNally, Alexander G., Pvt,
McNamara, Dennis, V., Pvt,

McNamara, Donald J., S/Sgt,
McNamara, Frank J., Jr.,
McNamara, Henry F., Pvt,
McNamara, James D., S/Sgt,
McNamara, John M., Pfc,
McNamara, Martin W., Pfc,
†McNamara, Timothy J., Pvt,
McNamee, Fernley W., Pvt,
McNaughton, H. B., Pfc,
McNee, William W., T/5,
†McNeely, Jeff, 2nd Lt,
McNeill, James E., T/5,
McNeil, Richard J., Pfc,
McNemar, William J., Pvt,
McNew, Arthur L., Pfc,
McNicholas, Thomas E., Pfc,
McNulty, Leo M., Pvt,
McNutt, John A., Jr., Pvt,
McNutt, Robert, Pvt,
McPherron, Leon E., Pfc,
†McPherson, Roland N., Pvt,
McPhetridge, William B., Pfc,
McQueen, James C., Pvt,
McQuerrey, William D., Pfc,
McQuery, Willian N., Pfc,
‡McReynolds, Walter W., Pvt,
†McShane, Francis, Pfc,
McShea, Andrew J., Cpl,
McSpadden, Don H., Pfc,
§McTeer, Cecil H., Sr., Pvt,
McTigue, Thomas, Pvt,
†McVay, George, Pvt,
McVey, Alfred, Pvt,
McWeeny, Charles P., Pfc,
McWhorter, Merselis, Pfc,
†McWilliams, Burnham E., Pfc,
McWilliams, Raymond D., Pvt,
Mead, Clarence O., Pfc,
Mead, Lauren R., Cpl,
Mead, Robert J., Pvt,
Meade, Gene B., Pfc,
Meade, George S., Pfc,
Meade, Woodrow W., Pvt,
Meaders, James H., Pfc,
§Meador, Elmer O., Pfc,
Meadows, Asa R., T/4,
Meadows, Bernard L., Pvt,
Meadows, Henry A., Pfc,
Meadows, Raymond H., Pfc,
†Meadville, Charles E., Pvt,
Mears, Noel N., Pfc,
Mecca, Angelo R., Pfc,
Meccariello, Edward P., Pfc,
Mecklenburg, William J., T/4,
Meckley, William J., T/5,
Medaugh, Vernon L., Pfc,
‡Medbery, William M., Pfc,
Madeiros, Joseph, T/5,
Medford, Hillary H., Pfc,
Medicke, Frederick, Pvt,
†Medina, Alfred M., Pvt,
Medina, Lorenzo, Pfc,
Medina, Rumaldo, Pfc,
†Medlin, William A., Pfc,
Medlock, James C., Pvt,
†Mednick, Milton, Pfc,
Meece, Alton B., Pvt,
Meeker, Aron D., Cpl,
Meeks, Donald G., Pvt,
Meeks, Ira T., Pvt,
Meeks, Isaiah J., Pfc,
†Meeks, Martin L., Pvt,
†Meenan, Joseph R., Pvt,
Megela, Paul, Pvt,
†Megown, John N., Jr., Cpl,
Mehl, William W., Sgt,
Mehrhoff, Lloyd E., Pvt,
Meier, Ferdinand, S/Sgt,
Meilner, Edward S., Pvt,
Mein, Wilmar B., Sgt,
Meinert, William J., Pfc,
§Meininger, Walter W., 2nd Lt,
Meirose, Edgar J., Cpl,
Meister, John H., Pvt,
†Mekruit, John, Pfc,
Melancon, Honora J., Pfc,
Melburn, Clarence M., Pfc,
Melchor, Ysabel, Pvt,
Mele, Anthony P., Pfc,
Melegari, Frank M., Pfc,
†Melella, Carmine L., Pvt,
†Melgard, William J., 2nd Lt,
Melhorn, Robert J., Pvt,
†Melia, Anthony R., Pvt,
Melillo, Anthony C., Pfc,
Meliska, Michael, Capt,
Melle, Otto J., Pfc,
Mellen, Roy P., Cpl,
Melling, Joseph J., Jr., Pvt,
Mellow, George J., Pfc,
Melluzzo, Salvatore A., Pvt,
Melodea, Eliodoro T., Pvt,
Melody, Francis F., 1st Lt,
Melson, Elzie W., S/Sgt,
‡Melton, James D., Pfc,

Melton, Henry H., S/Sgt,
Melton, Perry C., Pfc,
Melton, Robert, T/5,
Melvin, Eugene, Sgt,
Melvin, James L., Jr., Pfc,
Menara, Louis P., Pfc,
Menard, Wilfred J., Sgt,
Mench, Louis E., Pfc,
Menchyk, Frank S., Pvt,
Mendenhall, Elwood W., Pfc,
Mendoza, Julian H., Pvt,
Mendoza, Trinidad R., Pfc,
‡Menninger, Charles W., Cpl,
†Menter, John R., Pfc,
‡Mentges, Emil J., Pfc,
Mentzor, Charles K., Pfc,
Menz, Donald H., Pfc,
Merando, Joseph C., Pfc,
Mercadante, Anthony F., Pvt,
Mercadante, Herman V., Pvt,
Mercer, Joseph A., 1st Lt,
Mercer, Richard S., Sgt,
Merchant, Adrian, Pvt,
Mercier, Maurice V., Pvt,
Mercurio, Alphonse T., Pfc,
Mercurio, Leo, Pvt,
Mercurio, Samuel P., Pvt,
Meredith, Ealon O., Pfc,
Meredith, Robert J., Pfc,
Meredith, William B., Pvt,
Merek, John J., Pfc,
Merkel, Earl R., Pvt,
Merker, Peter C., Jr., Pfc,
Merle, John M., Pfc,
†Merlino, Samuel, Pfc,
Merola, Joseph L., Pvt,
Merola, Peter A., Pfc,
Merrell, James E., Pfc,
Merrick, David F., Sgt,
Merrick, Winston V., Pfc,
†Merrihew, Harry L., Jr., Pfc,
Merrill, Alfred L., Pfc,
‡Merrill, Clement F., Pfc,
Merrill, Fred T., Pvt,
†Merrill, Walter, Pfc,
Merriman, Gerald F., Pfc,
Merrington, Leroy A., Pvt,
Merris, Carl E., Jr., Pfc,
†Merritt, Carl A., Pvt,
†Merritt, Edwin L., Pvt,
†Merritt, Russell E., Pvt,
†Merrow, David A., Pvt,
Mersy, John G., Pfc,
Mertz, Robert C., Sgt,
Merwin, George, Pfc,
Mesnick, Ben, Pvt,
Messenger, Calvin J., Pfc,
Messer, Howard, Pfc,
Messer, James K., Pfc,
Messerly, Melvin C., Pvt,
Messina, Kenneth F., Pfc,
Messina, Vincent, Pvt,
Messner, Wayne L., Cpl,
Mester, John, Pfc,
Metcalf, Bernie W., Pvt,
Metcalf, Carl S., Pvt,
Metcalf, Roger C., Sgt,
Metz, Merle K., Pfc,
Metzger, Russell F., S/Sgt,
Metzler, Robert L., Sgt,
†Meyer, Charles F., Pfc,
Meyer, Donald R., Pfc,
Meyer, Edward J., Pfc,
Meyer, Harlan G., T/5,
Meyer, Henry L., Pfc,
Meyer, Henry M., Sgt,
Meyer, Norbert T., Pvt,
Meyer, Ralph M., Pfc,
Meyer, Raymond, Pvt,
Meyer, Wendel N., 1st Lt,
Meyer, William B., S/Sgt,
Meyers, Clifford C., Sgt,
Meyers, Henry F., Pfc,
Meyers, Howard A., Pvt,
Meyers, Maurice, Pfc,
Meyers, Merle W., Pfc,
Mezers, Robert J., Pfc,
†Miazga, Joseph, S/Sgt,
Miceli, Albert, Sgt,
Miceli, Frank, Pfc,
Michael, Gerty A., Pfc,
Michael, William H., Pfc,
Michak, Andrew A., S/Sgt,
Michalik, Joseph, Pfc,
Michaliszyn, Frank T., Pfc,
Michalowski, Emil, Cpl,
Michel, Victor L., Sgt,
Michell, Frank A., Pfc,
Mick, Ross H., Pfc,
Mickevege, Joseph W., Pfc,
Mickle, Gerald W., Pvt,
Mickus, Robert R., Cpl,
Micucci, Dominic J., Pvt,
Middlebrook, Leonard G., Pvt,
Mider, Robert B., Pvt,

† Killed in Action. * Prisoner of War. ‡ Missing in Action. § Died of Wounds.

Midgett, Peleg D., Pfc,
Miele, Guy J., Pvt,
†Miele, John J., Pfc,
†Mier, Robert C., S/Sgt,
Miers, Raymond H., Pvt,
Mihitsch, Edmund J., Pvt,
Mikita, Peter, Pfc,
Mikkin, Harry O., Pvt,
Miklaunus, Charles J., Pvt,
Miklosi, John B., Pvt,
Miko, John, Pfc,
Mikolajczak, Casimir R., Pvt,
Mikulcek, Joseph, T/5,
Milam, Archie P., Pvt,
‡Milam, Charles N., Pfc,
Milano, Arthur H., Sgt,
†Milbourne, Ronald E., Pvt,
Milburn, Harry C., Pvt,
Milburn, Vernon M., S/Sgt,
Milby, Shirley D., Pvt,
Miles, Bobby M., Pfc,
Miles, Frank, Pfc,
Miles, Richard G., Pfc,
Milkovich, George, Pvt,
‡Milkowski, Stanley P., Pvt,
Millar, Kenneth D., Pfc,
Miller, Albert H., Pfc,
†Miller, Albert L., Jr., Sgt,
Miller, Angel, Sgt,
Miller, Aubry D., T/Sgt,
Miller, Bernard, Pfc,
Miller, Blair, Pfc,
Miller, Carlyle E., Capt,
Miller, Charles W., Pfc,
Miller, Clarence B., S/Sgt,
Miller, Claude, Pfc,
Miller, Claude R., Pfc,
Miller, Claude W., T/4,
Miller, Cole L., 1/Sgt,
†Miller, Claude M., Pvt,
Miller, Darwin W., T/Sgt,
†Miller, Dean A., Pfc,
Miller, Donald E., Pfc,
Miller, Earl G., Pfc,
†Miller, Edward J., Sgt,
Miller, Edward Q., Pfc,
Miller, Elsworth C., Pfc,
Miller, Francis A., Pvt,
†Miller, Frank C., Pfc,
Miller, Frank I., Pfc,
Miller, Galen C., Sgt,
Miller, George, Pvt,
Miller, George E., Pfc,
Miller, George P., Pvt,
Miller, George W., Pvt,
Miller, Harold, Pfc,
Miller, Harold J., Sgt,
Miller, Harold K., Pfc,
Miller, Hubert V., 1st Lt,
†Miller, Hughes E., Cpl,
Miller, Irving N., Pvt,
Miller, Jack, Pfc,
Miller, Jack N., T/5,
Miller, Jackie F., Pfc,
Miller, James F., Sgt,
Miller, Joe, Pfc,
Miller, John B., Pfc,
Miller, John J., Jr., Pfc,
†Miller, John L., Pvt,
Miller, Joseph A., Cpl,
Miller, Joseph C., Pfc,
Miller, Joseph L. Pfc,
Miller, Joseph P., Pfc,
§Miller, Kenneth E., Pvt,
Miller, Leroy E., Pvt,
†Miller, Louis H., Pfc,
Miller, Martin J., Pfc,
Miller, Millard C., Pvt,
Miller, Morris S., Pvt,
†Miller, Orren J., Pfc,
Miller, Orville L., Pfc,
Miller, Paul C., 2nd Lt,
§Miller, Paul J., Sgt,
*Miller, Paul J., Pfc,
Miller, Peter C., Pvt,
‡Miller, Phillip I., Pfc,
Miller, Ralph P., S/Sgt,
†Miller, Raymond J., Pfc,
Miller, Robert A., 2nd Lt,
Miller, Robert D., Pvt,
Miller, Roy E., S/Sgt,
Miller, Russell E., Pvt,
Miller, Sidney, Pvt,
Miller, Talmadge E., T/5,
Miller, Thomas E., Pfc,
Miller, Thomas W., Cpl,
*Miller, Tommy R., Pvt,
†Miller, Walter E., Pvt,
Miller, Walter M., Pvt,
§Miller, Wayne E., Pfc,
Miller, William, Pvt,
Miller, William H., Pvt,
†Miller, William H., Pvt,
Miller, William, Jr., 1st Lt,
Miller, William R., Pfc,

Miller, Willie L., Pfc,
Miller, Woodrow, Pfc,
Millett, Verner D., Pfc,
Millheim, Sylvester A., Pvt,
Milligan, Thomas R., S/Sgt,
Millinder, Jeptha B., Pfc,
Millman, Richard B., Sgt,
Millon, Theodore A., Pfc,
Milloway, Doc L., Jr., Pfc,
Mills, Earl M., Pfc,
§Mills, Earl W., Sgt,
Mills, Eldon E., Jr., Pvt,
Mills, Frank E., Pvt,
Mills, Glenn L., Jr., Pfc,
Mills, Ira O., Cpl,
Mills, James H., Pfc,
Mills, Kenneth C., Sgt,
Mills, Ralph M., Pfc,
Mills, Robert H., Pfc,
Mills, Thomas A., Cpl,
†Mills, Thomas K., S/Sgt,
Mills, Wilbur O., Pvt,
Mills, Woodrow W., Pvt,
‡Millwood, Thomas H., S/Sgt,
Milmore, John F., Jr., 2nd Lt,
Milner, Willard M., T/5,
Miltenberger, Walter W., Jr.,
†Milton, Clyde O., T/Sgt,
Mincer, Howard L., Pfc,
Mineek, Jacob S., Pvt,
Miner, Harold J., Pfc,
Miner, Joseph G., Jr., Pvt,
Minerva Frank D., Capt,
Minica, John L., Jr., Pfc,
Minker, Charles B., Pvt,
Minkler, Robert, T/4,
Minnick, Donald E., Pvt,
Minnick, Lowell M., Pvt,
†Minter, Earnest C., Pvt,
Minton, Clifford S., Pfc,
Minton, Marion E., Pfc,
Mintz, William, Pvt,
Minutolo, Joseph A., Pvt,
‡Mioduski, Henry T., Pvt,
Mionie, Murray, Pvt,
Mirabello, Anthony, Pfc,
Miranda, Joaquin P., Jr., T/4,
Mirandi, Frank V., Pvt,
Miscevich, John, Cpl,
Misch, Carl O., Cpl,
Miscikoski, John A., Jr., Pfc,
†Mishkin, Harry, Pvt,
Misterkiewicz, E. W., Sgt,
Mistretta, Frank J., Pfc,
Mistretta, Onofrio, Pfc,
†Mitchell, Donald B., Pfc,
‡Mitchell, Donald M., Pvt,
†Mitchell, Elmo, Pfc,
Mitchell, Frank M., Pvt,
Mitchell, George A., Pvt,
Mitchell, Harold D., Pvt,
Mitchell, Harry T., Jr., Pvt,
Mitchell, Homer J., 2nd Lt,
Mitchell, Jim, Pfc,
†Mitchell, John C., Sgt,
Mitchell, Joseph M., Pfc,
Mitchell, Julian H., S/Sgt,
Mitchell, Lewis H., Pfc,
†Mitchell, Miles M., Pvt,
Mitchell, Raymond E., Pfc,
Mitchell, Robert E., Capt,
Mitchell, Sylvester L., Pfc,
§Mitchell, Vana F., Pvt,
Mitchell, William G., Pfc,
Mitcheltree, J. F., 1st/Sgt,
†Mitchum, Clarence, Pfc,
Mitrook, Andrew, Pfc,
Mitstifer, Francis R., Pvt,
Mitts, Bliss F., Sgt,
Mitts, Roy E., Sgt,
Mize, James B., Pvt,
Mizell, Ralph C., Sgt,
Mizerka, Clarence G., Pvt,
Mizerski, Walter A., Pvt,
Mlinek, Robert J., Pfc,
Mobley, Kenneth E., Pfc,
Mobley, Thomas A., Pfc,
Mobley, Virges A., Pvt,
Mocabee, Jules G., Pfc,
Mock, Merle J., Pfc,
Mock, Neal A., Pfc,
Moczygemba, Chester V., Pfc,
Modugno, Ralph A., Pfc,
Moe, Vernon H., S/Sgt
Moebius, Warren D., Pfc,
§Moede, Owen F., Pvt,
Moehringer, Harold W., Pfc,
Moekevicius, Edward A., Pfc,
‡Moegelin, Walter M., 2nd Lt,
Moffatt, Rowland D., Pfc,
Moffett, Charles F., Sgt,
Moffitt, Lee, S/Sgt,
Mogavero, Frank A., Pfc,
†Mohler, Glover C., Pvt,

Mohwinkel, William G., T/3,
Moldenhauer, Heinz D., Pvt,
Mole, Joseph P., Pvt,
Moler, John V., Sgt,
Molinowski, Edward W., Pvt,
Moll, Marvin H., Sgt,
Mollen, Ray A., Pvt,
Moller, Carl R., Pfc,
Mollette, David, Pvt,
Molloy, Thomas J., Jr., Pvt,
Molloy, Paul F., T/Sgt,
Molnar, Charles P., Pfc,
†Molnar, Frank, Pfc,
†Molyneaux, John M., Pvt,
Monaco, Thomas, Pfc,
Monaghan, James E., S/Sgt,
Monaghan, John K., Sgt,
Monahan, George W., Pvt,
Monarch, James L., 2nd Lt,
†Monasterio, Fidel, Pfc,
Monat, Jack S., T/5,
Moncrief, Christophur I., Pvt,
Mondelli, Hugo J., 1st Lt,
Monfrino, John A., Pfc,
Mongold, Fred O., S/Sgt,
Moniz, Wilbur J., Cpl,
Moniz, William O., Pfc,
‡Monkiewicz, Raymond J., Pfc,
Monks, Milton, Pfc,
Monowicz, Karl, Pvt,
Monroe, Fred A., Pfc,
Monroe, James H., Pfc,
Monroe, Zack R., Cpl,
†Monrreal, Margarito, Pvt,
Monsour, James R., Pvt,
Montag, Walter M., Pvt,
Montagano, Frank F., Pvt,
Montalvo, Manuel C., Pfc,
†Montalvo, Martin, Pvt,
Montano, Jose A., Pfc,
Montano, Jose D., Pfc,
Montano, Porfirio, Cpl,
Montecalvo, Nicholas J., Pfc,
‡Monteiro, John J., Pfc,
Monteith, John W., Pfc,
Montello, Nicholas A., Pvt,
Montemurno, Vincent, Pfc,
†Montes, Raymond G., Pfc,
Montfort, Charles M., Sgt,
Montgomery, Howard E., Pfc,
Montgomery, John C., Pfc,
†Montgomery, John F., Pfc,
Montgomery, Joseph B., Sgt,
Montgomery, Lawrie, Pfc,
Montgomery, Lowell L., Pvt,
Montgomery, Robert F., Pvt,
Monticelli, Peter P., Pvt,
Montijo, Octavio M., Pfc,
†Montoya, Alex, Pfc,
Montoya, Anthony N., Pfc,
*Montoya, Joe C., Pvt,
Montoya, Oscar, Pfc,
‡Monyok, Stephen, Pvt,
Monz, Clifford V., Pfc,
†Moody, Ted R., 2nd Lt,
†Moon, Chiles W., Pvt,
†Mooney, George E., Pfc,
†Mooney, Wayne D., Pfc,
Mooney, William J., Cpl,
Moor, Curtis, Pfc,
Mooradian, George, Jr., Pvt,
Moore, Carl E., Pvt,
Moore, Carlisle C., Pfc,
‡Moore, Charles H., Pfc,
Moore, Charles W., Pvt,
Moore, Clarence E., Pvt,
Moore, Clarence H., Pvt,
Moore, Daryl D., Sgt,
‡Moore, David J., Pfc,
Moore, Duward H., S/Sgt,
Moore, Edward L., Pvt,
Moore, Francis, Pvt,
§Moore, Frank C., Pvt,
Moore, George D., Jr.,
Moore, Hugh, Pvt,
Moore, James F., Pfc,
Moore, James H., Pvt,
Moore, James M., Pfc,
†Moore, Kenneth D., Pvt,
Moore, Kenneth J., Pfc,
†Moore, Marion E., Pfc,
Moore, Miles O., Pvt,
Moore, Morris C., Pfc,
†Moore, Ralph W., Pfc,
†Moore, Richard D., Pfc,
Moore, Richard H., Sgt,
Moore, Roy E., Lt Col,
Moore, Samuel G., 2nd Lt,
Moore, Walter L., S/Sgt,
Moore, Waymon C., Pfc,
Moore, William H., Pfc,
Moore, William H., Pvt,
†Moorhead, Richard A., Pvt,
Moorman, Elmer H., Pvt,

Moose, Donald I., Pfc,
†Morales, Joe, S/Sgt,
Morales, Jose I., Pvt,
Moran, Claude L., Pfc,
Moran, Francis H., Jr., Pvt,
Moran, Michael P., Pvt,
Moran, Thomas E., Pfc,
Moreaux, Keith C., Pfc,
Moreno, Joseph A., Jr., 1st Lt,
Moreno, Julian W., Pvt,
Moreno, Wallie J., Pvt,
†Mores, Stephen E., Pvt,
†Moreschi, William, Jr., Pfc,
Morey, William F., Pvt,
Morgan, Arthur C., Pvt,
Morgan, Chancy E., Pvt,
†Morgan, Coy L., Capt,
Morgan, Elvin R., 1st Lt,
Morgan, Fred M., Pvt,
Morgan, Gaston L., Pvt,
Morgan, Howard, Jr., Pvt,
Morgan, Jack L., Pvt,
†Morgan, James C., Sgt,
Morgan, James F., Pfc,
Morgan, James H., M/Sgt,
‡Morgan, Luther, Pvt,
Morgan, Marian P., Pvt,
Morgan, Nelson M., Pfc,
Morgan, Richard C., Jr., Pvt,
Morgan, Samuel T., Pfc,
Morgan, Saul, Pvt,
Morgan, William A., Pfc,
Morian, Ray W., Sgt,
Moriarty, Wilbur B., Pvt,
Morillo, Albert, Pvt,
†Morin, Clifford J., Pfc,
†Morley, Maynard R., Pfc,
Morman, Robert J., Pfc,
Morowski, Walter L., Sgt,
Moroz, Victor L., Pvt,
Morreal, John A., Pfc,
†Morrett, James A., Pvt,
Morrill, Clyde D., Jr., Pfc,
Morris, Bernard, Pvt,
Morris, Bernard H., Pfc,
Morris, Bernard W., Pfc,
Morris, Edward L., 2nd Lt,
Morris, Edward W., Pfc,
Morris, Elmus, Pfc,
Morris, Francis J., Pvt,
Morris, Frank, Pfc,
Morris, George R., Pvt,
Morris, George V., Pvt,
Morris, Isaac, Pfc,
Morris, James W., T/4,
Morris, Jim H., Pfc,
Morris, Louis T., Pfc,
Morris, Patrick M., Pfc,
Morris, Robert C., Pvt,
†Morris, Sherman, Pvt,
Morris, Victor M., Capt,
Morris, William F., Pvt,
Morris, Wilton, Pvt,
Morrish, Irving W., Pvt,
Morrison, Almond C.,
†Morrison, Archie J., Pvt,
Morrison, Brenton J., Pfc,
§Morrison, Carl K., Pfc,
Morrison, John, Jr., Pvt,
Morrison, John E., S/Sgt,
Morrison, John G., Pfc,
Morrison, Lewis W., Pvt,
Morrison, Lyle F., Pvt,
Morrison, Oscar J., Jr., Sgt,
*Morrison, Robert E., Pvt,
Morrison, Walter D., Pvt,
Morrissey, George A., Pfc,
Morrow, Daniel D., Cpl,
Morrow, Edward J., Pvt,
Morrow, Ethan M., Pfc,
Morrow, John L., Cpl,
Morrow, Lawrence, Pfc,
‡Morrow, Mack D., Pvt,
Morse, James, Pfc,
*Morse, Ralph W., Pvt,
Morseon, Walter F., Pvt,
Mortensen, Olaf H., Pfc,
Mortillite, Samuel A., Pvt,
Mortland, Virgile, T/5,
Morton, Alfred W., Pvt,
Morton, Howard C., Pvt,
†Morton, Howard E., Pfc,
†Morton, James R., Sgt,
Morton, Okrey, Pfc,
Morton, Robert H., Pvt,
Morton, William F., Pfc,
Moryl, John, Pfc,
‡Moschitto, Augie, Pvt,
*Moseley, Clifford T., Pvt,
Mosey, Robert P., Cpl,
Mosher, Francis C., 2nd Lt,
Mosko, George A., Jr., Pfc,
Mosley, Cecil E., Sgt,
Mosley, W. C., S/Sgt,

Mossey, Thomas R., S/Sgt,
Mosshart, Frederick W., Pvt,
Mossop, John C., Cpl,
*Mostkiewicz, Chester, Pfc,
Mote, Roy V., Pfc,
Motes, Clyde, Pfc,
‡Motes, Guy F., Pvt,
Motteberg, Melvin, S/Sgt,
Mougeotte, Paul E., Pfc,
‡Mougey, John T., 1st Lt,
Moumblow, William P., Pfc,
Mount, William, Pfc,
§Mounts, Mason W., Pvt,
Moura, Theodore L., Pvt,
Mourer, Richard L., Pfc,
Mowry, Barlow B., S/Sgt,
†Moyer, Glenn A., Pfc,
Moynihan, Francis D., Pfc,
Mozden, Bernard S., Pvt,
*Mozeika, Felix P., Pfc,
Mozzola, Domenic, Pfc,
Mrozowsky, Donald B., Pfc,
Mucha, Henry J., Pfc,
†Muchmore, R. P., 2nd Lt,
Mudd, Earnest G., Cpl,
Mudd, James L., Jr., Pfc,
Mudry, Metro, T/Sgt,
Mueller, Walter A., T/5,
Muha, Frank P., Pvt,
†Muhar, Andrew J., Pfc,
Muir, Edward G., Pvt,
Mulcahey, Joseph E., T/5,
Mulcahy, John J., Pfc,
Mulconrey, George T., Pfc,
Muldoon, Stephen J., Pvt,
Mulford, Wilmer W., Sgt,
Mulholiam, Edgar A., Pfc,
Mull, Atlas J., Pvt,
Mull, William J., Pvt,
Mullady, William J., Pfc,
Mullan, Thomas J., Pvt,
Mullen, Clyde F., Pfc,
Mullennix, Dale I., Pfc,
†Muller, James E., Pvt,
Muller, L. D. H., Pfc,
†Muller, Roy G., Pvt,
Mulligan, Clifford W., Pfc,
Mulligan, George T., Pfc,
Mulligan, Joseph E., Pvt,
Mullins, John J., Pfc,
Mullins, William K., Pfc,
Mulrain, John J., Pfc,
Mulrooney, Walter S., 2nd Lt,
Mulvaney, Max K., Pvt,
Mulvaney, Mourise B., Pfc,
Mulvey, James J., Pfc,
Mumaw, William O., Pfc,
Munderville, Peter T., Pfc,
Mundt, Henry W., Jr., Pfc,
†Mungay, William, Pfc,
Munkittrick, Irving G., Pfc,
Munn, James, Pfc,
Munn, William M., Sgt,
Munro, John P., Jr., Pvt,
Murck, Harold O., Pvt,
Murchak, John, Pfc,
Murden, Edwin J., Jr., Pvt,
Murdoch, Samuel H., Pvt,
†Murdock, David N., 1st Lt,
Murnaham, Oscar, Jr., Pfc,
Mure, Louis, Pvt,
Murphey, Delta L., Pfc,
Murphy, Albert W., Sgt,
Murphy, Alonzo L., Pfc,
Murphy, Charles F., Pvt,
Murphy, Donald W., Sgt,
Murphy, Edward F., Pfc,
Murphy, Elton, Pvt,
†Murphy, Ernest G., Pfc,
Murphy, Francis W., Pfc,
Murphy, George P., Sgt,
Murphy, Harold W., T/Sgt,
Murphy, James J., Pvt,
Murphy, John E., Pfc,
†Murphy, John E., Pvt,
†Murphy, John G., 2nd Lt,
Murphy, John J., Pfc,
Murphy, Loyd, Pfc,
Murphy, Murray J., Pvt,
Murphy, Norman, Pvt,
Murphy, Patrick L., Pfc,
†Murphy, Paul C., 1st Lt,
Murphy, Ralph G., Pfc,
Murphy, Robert, Pvt,
Murphy, Robert J., Pfc,
Murphy, Russell C., Pfc,
Murphy, Thomas M., Pfc,
Murphy, William A., Pfc,
†Murphy, William G., Pvt,
†Murray, Donald J., Pfc,
Murray, Durl T., Pfc,
Murray, Frank L., Pfc,
Murray, Frank, Sr., Pfc,
Murray, Gaylord L., Pfc,

† Killed in Action. * Prisoner of War. ‡ Missing in Action. § Died of Wounds.

Murray, Howard K., S/Sgt,
Murray, James M., Pvt,
Murray, James O., Pvt,
Murray, James R., Pfc,
Murray, Leland G., Pvt,
Murray, L.E., Jr., 1st Lt,
†Murray, William J., Pvt,
Musacchia, James V., Pvt,
Musak, Floyd S., Pvt,
Musano, Jerry, Pfc,
Muscanero, James B., Pfc,
Muse, John R., T/4,
Muse, Raymond W., Jr., Pfc,
Muselin, Frank, Sgt,
Musgraves, Amos, Pvt,
Mushalko, Andrew, Pvt,
Music, Ardie, Pvt,
Musick, Avery B., Pfc,
Musicus, Dennis E., Pfc,
Muskin, Ira L., 2nd Lt,
Muskey, Eugene T., S/Sgt,
Musser, John, Pvt,
Mustain, Rhoads, Capt,
Musto, Frank, Pvt,
†Muther, Donald, Pvt,
Mutz, Theodore M., Pfc,
Mydland, Didrick B., Capt,
Myers, Alfred T., Pfc,
Myers, Cleo L., Pfc,
Myers, Elwood W., T/5,
Myers, Ernest F., Pvt,
Myers, Floyd H., Pvt,
Myers, Forrest E., Pfc,
Myers, George F., Cpl,
Myers, George R., Sgt,
Myers, Gerald A., Pvt,
Myers, James A., Pfc,
Myers, Ralph E., Pvt,
Myers, Richard F., Pfc,
Myers, Robert J., Pfc,
Myers, Wayne N., Pfc,
Myhra, Norman L., Pvt,
†Mylek, Frank J., Pfc,
Myres, Delvin C., Pvt,
Myslowski, Adam J., Pfc,

Nabors, Charles R., Pfc,
Nacey, Elmer J., Sgt,
§Nadel, Arnold, Pvt,
Nader, George J., Pvt,
Nadler, Abraham, T/Sgt,
Nadler, Bernard, T/Sgt,
Nadler, Harry, Pfc,
Nadolny, Virgil F., Pvt,
Nadridge, Sam, Pfc,
Nagy, Frank J., Pfc,
†Nail, Leo, Pvt,
Naimoli, Joseph, Pvt,
Nair, Lewis C., T/3,
Najera, Benito A., Pfc,
†Naktenis, George M., Pvt,
†Nalbone, Angelo C., Pvt,
Nallie, Omer H., Pfc,
†Nance, Robert D., Pfc,
Nanegos, Willard, Pfc,
Nania, Edward A., Pfc,
Nannini, John A., Cpl,
Nanson, Raymond J., Pfc,
Napier, James W., Pfc,
Napier, Orville, Pfc,
Napoli, Louis M., Pfc,
Napoli, Philip J., Pfc,
Napolitano, Alfred J., Pfc,
Napolitano, Ralph F., Pvt,
Napolitano, Salvatore J., Pfc,
†Nappi, Anthony, T/5,
Naranjo, Henry G., Pfc,
Nardi, Bruno P., Pfc,
Narehood, Charles R., Pvt,
Narodzonek, Frank A., Pvt,
Nasca, Angelo J., 1st Lt,
Nash, Thomas J., Pvt,
Nash, William, Pvt,
Nast, Robert A., Pfc,
Nastari, Augustus, T/Sgt,
Natale, Anthony J., Pfc,
Nathanson, Benjamin, Pfc,
†Nations, Elmer D., T/5,
Naumburg, Bernard F., Pvt,
Nauss, Jerry M., Sgt,
Navarra, Daniel A., Pfc,
Navarro, Jose, Pfc,
Navarro, Rudolph J., Pfc,
Naylor, Earl, Pvt,
§Neal, Donald, Cpl,
Neal, Edgar V., Sgt,
Neal, Leslie, Pvt,
Neal, Raymond A., Pfc,
Neal, Vearl W., Pfc,
†Neal, William T., Pfc,
†Neary, Jerome A., Pfc,
Nebbia, Roland J., Pvt,
Nebel, James H., 2nd Lt,
Needham, George W., Sgt,

Needham, James E., Pvt,
Needles, Frank, Pvt,
†Neels, Milton I., Pvt,
Neely, Murphy E., Cpl,
Neely, Paul C., Pfc,
Neese, George R., Pfc,
†Negless, La Verne L., Sgt,
†Neidermyer, Richard J., Pfc,
†Neidlinger, George R., Sgt,
Neikirk, Ray F., Pfc,
Neil, Julien A., Pfc,
Neiswenter, Ronald B., Pfc,
Neitzel, Clarence E., Cpl,
Nejdlik, John, S/Sgt,
†Nellinger, Ernest, Jr., Pfc,
Nelms, William C., Pvt,
†Nelsen, Eric, Pvt,
†Nelsen, Fred P., Pvt,
‡Nelsen, James D., Pvt,
†Nelsen, Leroy N., Pfc,
Nelson, Albert L., S/Sgt,
‡Nelson, Alfred N., Pfc,
†Nelson, Arnold G., Cpl,
†Nelson, Chris H., Pvt,
Nelson, Clifford F., T/5,
†Nelson, Donald E., Pvt,
Nelson, Donzal L., Pvt,
Nelson, Earl W., Pfc,
Nelson, Edward T., T/4,
Nelson, Enoch, Sgt,
‡Nelson, Enoch N., Pvt,
Nelson, George H., Pvt,
Nelson, Harold A., S/Sgt,
Nelson, Howard O., S/Sgt,
Nelson, John A., Pvt,
Nelson, Philip E., Jr., Pfc,
Nelson, John D., Pfc,
Nelson, Kenneth L., Pfc,
Nelson, Lawrence R., Pfc,
Nelson, Orville O., Pfc,
Nelson, Paul A., 1st Lt,
Nelson, Ralph, Pfc,
*Nelson, Robert S., Jr., Pvt,
Nelson, Roy H., Pvt,
Nelson, Van A., T/4,
Nelson, William J., Pvt,
Nelson, Winston R., Sgt,
Nemec, Joseph C., Jr., Pfc,
Nemeth, Stephen J., Pfc,
Nemitz, Ernest A., Pfc,
Nemser, William J., Pfc,
Neri, Salvatore A., Pvt,
Nesbitt, Merton, M., T/4,
Neshem, Clifford E., Pfc,
Nesmith, Francis S., Pvt,
Nessman, William B., Cpl,
‡Nestor, Stanley L., Pfc,
†Nestler, Fred, Pfc,
†Nett, Ralph H., Pvt,
Nettestad, Chester O., T/4,
*Netz, Herman G., Sgt,
Neu, Charles W., Pvt,
Neuman, Irving W., Cpl,
†Neumann, Earl R., Pfc,
Neurauter, Henry L., Pfc,
Neuschaefer, B. W., Pfc,
†Neuwirth, Julius, Pvt,
†Nevad, Thomas C., Pvt,
Nevers, Herman F., Pvt,
§Neville, Ben W., 2nd Lt,
†Neville, Thomas J., Pfc,
†Newall, Alfred R., Jr., Pfc,
Newberry, Edwin W., Pfc,
Newberry, Homer C., Pvt,
Newberry, Ira, Pvt,
Newbold, Frederic W., Pfc,
†Newbury, Russell W., 1st Lt,
Newby, Darwin K., Pfc,
Newcomb, Rollo T., Pfc,
‡Newhall, Bernard F., Pfc,
Newman, Charles E., Pfc,
Newman, Floyd A., Pfc,
Newman, George L., Pvt,
Newman, James J., Pfc,
Newman, Johnny L., Pvt,
Newman, Kenneth, Pvt,
*Newman, Paul J., Pvt,
†Newman, Robert C., Pvt,
Newman, Samuel, Pvt,
Newman, Samuel A., Pfc,
†Newman, Wayne L., Pvt,
Newsom, Ernest L., Pvt,
Newsom, Robert H., Pvt,
Newsome, Cleve T., Pvt,
Newton, Dallas N., Pfc,
Newton, Jess L., Pvt,
*Newton, William, Cpl,
Ng, Chong G., Pvt,
Niader, Ralph R., T/4,
Niblock, Loren H., Pfc,
Nicastro, Joseph P., Pfc,
Nicchitta, Vincenzo, Pvt,
Nichols, Andrew F., Jr., Pfc,
†Nichols, Edgar A., Pvt,
Nichols, Edward F., Jr., Pfc,

Nichols, Freeman J., Pvt,
‡Nichols, Hoyt H., Sgt,
‡Nichols, Jacob R., Pfc,
Nichols, James, Pfc,
Nichols, John J., Pvt,
Nichols, Loyd T., Pfc,
Nichols, Ralph A., Pvt,
Nichols, Robert R., Pfc,
Nichols, William E., Sgt,
Nichols, Wilton D., Pvt,
†Nicholson, George E., Pfc,
†Nicholson, William C., Pvt,
Nichter, Edward F., T/4,
Nickens, Ardell S., Pvt,
Nicks, William T., Pvt,
†Nicoletti, Paul, Pvt,
Nicols, Lawrence A., Pfc,
Nieber, Ernest W., Pfc,
Niedner, Malcolm B., Pfc,
†Niedzwiecki, Chester J., Pfc,
Nielsen, Hans E., Pvt,
†Nielsen, Ross D., S/Sgt,
§Nielsen, Robert K., Pfc,
Nielson, Vernon H., Pvt,
Niemer, Hall G., Sgt,
Niemeyer, William A., S/Sgt,
Niemi, Wilbert M., Pfc,
Nienow, Erwin C., T/5,
*Niezgoda, Chester E., Pvt,
Nigre, Ralph A., Pvt,
Nigro, Alexander C., S/Sgt,
Niles, Charles S. F., Pvt,
Nilsen, Louis W., Pvt,
Nilsson, Wendell L., Pfc,
Nippes, Kenneth B., Pfc,
Nisi, Frank J., Jr., 1st Lt,
Nishnic, Michael F., Pfc,
Nitzpon, Frank L., Pvt,
†Nix, Robert W. III, 1st Lt,
Nixon, Donald O., Pfc,
Nixon, Willard H., Sgt,
Noack, Nick S., Pvt,
Noble, Donald H., Pfc,
Noble, Floyd, Pvt,
Noble, John F., Pvt,
§Noble, Montie P., S/Sgt,
Noe, Guy, Pvt,
Nocal, Henry E., 1st Lt,
Noel, John M., Jr., Pfc,
Nogues, Ralph J., T/5,
Nolan, Charles E., Pvt,
Nolan, John T., Pfc,
†Nolan, William M., Pvt,
Nolen, J. T., S/Sgt,
‡Nolley, James H., Pfc,
Noon, James R., Pvt,
Nordstrom, Ernest S., Pvt,
Nordyke, Peter, Pvt,
Norelius, George W., Pvt,
Noreuil, Louis O., S/Sgt,
Norfolk, Robert G., Sgt,
Noriega, Joe, Pvt,
†Norland, Archie, Sgt,
†Norling, Sven R., Pfc,
Norman, Willys L., Pfc,
Norquist, Peter J., T/5,
Norris, Cecil L., Sgt,
Norris, Clarence L., Pfc,
Norris, George R., Pfc,
Norris, William C., S/Sgt,
Norrish, Frank W., 1st Sgt,
Nortem, John R., Pfc,
Northam, Wallace A., Pfc,
Northcutt, Carroll E., Pfc,
Norton, Harry E., Sgt,
Norton, John F., Pvt,
Norton, Lowell D., Pfc,
Norve, Lester H., 1st Lt,
†Norwood, Harold W., Pvt,
‡Nosis, William H., Pvt,
Novak, Alfred F., Pvt,
Novak, George L., Pvt,
Novak, John, Pvt,
Novak, John F., Sgt,
Nove, Anthony J., Pvt,
Noviello, James, Pvt,
Novoselich, John, Pvt,
Nowakowski, Dorsey L., Pvt,
Nowakowski, Thomas M., Pfc,
Nowicki, Andrew S., Sgt,
Nowinski, Stephen, Pvt,
Nowosielski, Casimer F., Pfc,
*Noyes, Clarence A., Pfc,
Nuccio, James S., Pvt,
Nudi, Gust, Pvt,
Nunez, Frank, Pfc,
Nunn, Joel L., S/Sgt,
Nuovo, James H., Pvt,
Nussbaum, Melvin F., Sgt,
Nutt, Arden O., Pfc,
†Nuttall, Peter, Pvt,
†Nutter, Jack C., Pfc,
Nydegger, Frederick, Pfc,
Nystrom, Cecil N., Pfc,

Oakes, Alton K., S/Sgt,
Oakes, Howard D., Pvt,
Oakland, Gordon S., T/4,
Oakley, John H., Pfc,
Oaks, Jack, Pfc,
Oates, Raymond R., Pfc,
Obara, Andrew E., Pvt,
Obelleire, Ferdinand E., Pfc,
Obermeier, Frederick F., Sgt,
†Oberndorf, Leo G., Capt,
Oberstein, Harold, Pvt,
Obert, Norman E., Pvt,
Obold, John A., Pvt,
Oboril, Michael P., T/4,
Obregon, George R., Pfc,
O'Brien, Cyril P., Sgt,
O'Brien, Eugene F., Pfc,
O'Brien, Paul Q., Sgt,
O'Brien, Raymond J., Pvt,
O'Brien, Robert W., Pfc,
†O'Brien, Stephen B., Pfc,
†Obush, Martin, Pfc,
Ocasio, Frank, Pfc,
Ocello, Jerome, Pfc,
Ocepew, John, Pfc,
Ocheltree, Denzil, Pfc,
Ochmanowicz, John A., Pvt,
†Ochs, Roy W., Pfc,
Ochsenhirt, Jerome E., Pvt,
Ockinga, Alvin C., Pfc,
O'Connell, Laurence J., Pvt,
O'Connell, Joseph C., 2nd Lt,
O'Connell, Thomas P., Pvt,
O'Connor, Charles F., T/5,
O'Connor, Harold J., Pvt,
O'Connor, James G., T/Sgt,
O'Connor, Joseph R., 2nd Lt,
O'Connor, Richard P., 1st Lt,
O'Connor, Thomas A., Pvt,
O'Connor, William J., Pfc,
Odegard, Oscar, Pfc,
Odehnal, Anton H., T/Sgt,
O'Dell, Cecil A., Pfc,
O'Dell, Clarence, Pfc,
O'Dell, Elward F., Pvt,
O'Dell, Harry L., Sgt,
O'Dell, Joseph P., Pvt,
Odessky, Paul, Pfc,
Odom, Hubert R., T/5,
Odom, Tommy B., Sgt,
†O'Donnell, John E., Pfc,
†O'Donnell, William J., Pvt,
O'Donnell, William P., 1st Lt,
O'Dwyer, Thomas L., 1st Lt,
Oelrich, Carl A., S/Sgt,
Oelrich, Christie B., Pfc,
Oetting, Arthur F., Sgt,
Oft, Harold L., Cpl,
Offsey, Sol, Pvt,
O'Gara, William T., Pfc,
Ogas, Ernest P., Pfc,
Ogden, Harvey L., T/5,
Ogden, Ralph G., Pfc,
Ogle, Walter I., Jr., T/4,
†O'Hanlon, Arthur F., Pfc,
O'Haire, James W., Pvt,
O'Hara, W. F., S/Sgt,
Ohlemacher, Russell, T/4,
Oistacher, Bernard, Pvt,
O'Kane, Robert M., S/Sgt,
O'Keefe, James A., Pfc,
§Olaeta, Laurence, Pfc,
Olcott, Frank W., T/5,
Oldaker, Willard, Pfc,
†Oldham, Alderson G., Pfc,
O'Leary, Edward G., Pvt,
Olenik, Andrew B., Pfc,
Olien, Lyle C., Pvt,
Oliff, Clarence L., Pfc,
Olin, Anthony J., Cpl,
Oliphant, Chas. F., Jr., 2nd Lt,
Oliphant, Donald P., Cpl,
†Olive, Edward J., Pfc,
Olive, Harry, Pvt,
Oliveira, Charles B., Pfc,
Olivera, Alfred, Pfc,
§Oliver, Clyde H., Pfc,
Oliver, Coy E., Pvt,
Oliver, Dixie T., Pvt,
Oliver, Eugene M., T/5,
Oliver, Harold M., Cpl,
Oliver, Hugh D., Pfc,
Oliver, James M., Pfc,
Oliver, Raymond L., S/Sgt,
Oliverio, Patsy, Cpl,
Oliveti, Joseph P., Pvt,
O'Loughlin, Michael J., Pfc,
Olsen, Edwin O., S/Sgt,
Olsen, John V., Pvt,
†Olsen, Norbert L., S/Sgt,
Olsen, Robert A., S/Sgt
†Olsen, Stanley K., Pvt,
Olson, Alfred S., Pfc,
*Olson, Alvin D., Pfc,

*Olson, Arne H., Pfc,
Olson, Arthur K., Pfc,
Olson, Beuford L., T/5,
Olson, Carl I., Pfc,
Olson, Chester I., Pvt,
*Olson, Dave C., Sgt,
Olson, Gordon E., T/5,
Olson, Gordon R., Pfc,
Olson, Robert H., Pfc,
†Olson, Truman O., Sgt,
Olstad, John L., Sgt,
†Olvis, Harvey E., S/Sgt,
Oman, Walter, S/Sgt,
O'Mary, Willie J. L., Pvt,
O'Meara, Forrest C., Pfc,
Omen, Homer E., Pfc,
O'Mohundro, Wiley H., Col,
Onarato, Louis J., Pvt,
Onder, Joseph E., Pfc,
Ondrus, Steve, Pfc,
O'Neal, Bill, S/Sgt,
O'Neal, Elmo W., Pfc,
O'Neal, Ralph B., Pfc,
O'Neal, Virgil N., Pvt,
O'Neil, John W., Pfc,
O'Neil, Thomas J., Jr., Pvt,
O'Neill, Charles C., Pfc,
O'Neill, Hugh A., Capt,
O'Neill, Joe S., Pfc,
O'Neill, Paul J., Pvt,
O'Neill, Robert K., Sgt,
§Oney, Teddy R., Pvt,
Onofrietti, Philip, Pfc,
Opel, Harry E., Sgt,
Oppio, Santino, S/Sgt,
Ordonez, Rafael, Pfc,
Ordos, George M., Pfc,
O'Reilly, Charles P., 2nd Lt,
Orem, James E., Sgt,
Orfanos, George C., Pvt,
†Organis, John S., Pfc,
†Orleski, Stanley, S/Sgt,
Orloske, Harry J., Pfc,
Ornelas, Julian A., Pfc,
Ornstein, Joseph M., Cpl,
*Oros, John M., Pfc,
O'Rourke, John J., Pvt,
Orr, George R., Pfc,
Orr, John G., Pvt,
§Orr, Leonard W., Pfc,
Orros, Edgar M., S/Sgt,
‡Orsborn, Enoch W., Pfc,
Ortega, Ernesto, Pvt,
Ortega, Manuel W., Pfc,
Ortega, Margarito M., Cpl,
Ortega, Zackary, S/Sgt,
Ortenzi, Nicholas J., Pfc,
†Ortiz, Joseph, Pvt,
Ortiz, Manuel V., Pfc,
†Ortiz, Michael J., Pfc,
†Ortiz, Vevo, S/Sgt,
†Osborn, Delbert, Pfc,
Osborn, John C., Sgt,
Osborne, Alda, Pfc,
Osborne, Donald D., Pfc,
Osborne, Elmo L., Pfc,
Osborne, Joseph H., Pvt,
Osborne, Ottis W., Pfc,
Osborne, Paul E., T/Sgt,
Osburn, Raymond H., T/4,
Osgood, Donald A., Pfc,
†Osipoff, Michael, Pvt,
Oson, Harold W., Pvt,
O'Steen, Tom R., Jr.,
Osterberg, Henry G., Pfc,
Osterbur, Herman J., Pfc,
Osterheldt, Kenneth A., Pfc,
Osterhout, Wilbur G., Sgt,
Osterlund, Carl, Jr., Cpl,
Ostmeyer, Charles H., 2nd Lt,
Ostrand, Robert C., Sgt,
Ostrosky, Eruno J., Pfc,
O'Sullivan, Daniel J., Pvt,
Othoudt, Ray T., Sgt,
Ott, Kenneth E., Pvt,
Otten, Virgil L., S/Sgt,
Otto, Raymond, Sgt,
Otto, Richard D., Sgt,
Oubre, George D., Pfc,
Oudsema, La Verne B., Pvt,
Ouellette, Alfred V., S/Sgt,
Ours, Harry F., Pvt,
Outerbridge, Robert L., Pfc,
†Outlaw, Stewart C., Pfc,
Overcash, Brown D., Pvt,
†Overholt, James L., Pvt,
Overholts, Howard L., Pvt,
Overman, Robert F., Pvt,
Overton, Ben G., Pfc,
Overton, Mays G., T/Sgt,
Overton, Willard L., Pfc,
Overturf, Tom A., Pfc,
Oviatt, Dee, Cpl,
Owen, John A., Jr., T/5,
Owen, Johnnie M., Pvt,

† Killed in Action. * Prisoner of War. ‡ Missing in Action. § Died of Wounds.

Owen, Thomas C., Pfc,
Owens, Chester M., S/Sgt,
Owens, Frank J., Pfc,
Owens, Jessie L., Jr., Pvt,
*Owens, Jim H., Sgt,
Owens, June M., Pvt,
Owens, Paul O., Pvt,
Owens, Tench P., 1st Lt,
Owens, Theo W., Pfc,
Owsinski, Joseph, Sgt,
Oyler, Wayne N., Pfc,
Ozimina, Alein, Pfc,

Pacchera, Mario D., Pvt,
Paccione, Joseph A., Pfc,
*Pace, George B., Pvt,
Pacheco, Frank H., Cpl,
‡Pachucki, Michael J., Sgt,
†Pacion, Frank A., Pfc,
Paciotti, James, Pfc,
Pack, David D., Pfc,
Padgett, John N., Pvt,
*Padgett, Joseph E., Pvt,
Padgett, Max G., Pvt,
*Padgett, Orval J., Pvt,
Padgett, Ozzie, T/5,
Padgett, Ray, Pfc,
Pado, John, Pfc,
Paduchak, Michael, Pfc,
*Padurano, Frank P., Pfc,
Paesch, Joseph M., Pfc,
Page, Aucie E., Sgt,
Page, Frank P., S/Sgt,
Page, Ralph R., Pfc,
Page, Roy C., Pvt,
Pagel, Donald E., T/Sgt,
Pahut, Stanley J., Pfc,
Paidle, John J., Jr., Pvt,
†Paige, Clarence W., Pvt,
Paige, Elder L., Cpl,
Paigo, James J., Pfc,
Pakarow, William, Capt,
Palashuk, Walter, Pvt,
Palczreski, Peter B., Pvt,
Palenbaum, Morris, Pfc,
†Palladinetti, Pasquale L.,
Palladino, Julian R., Pvt,
Palley, Harold I., Pfc,
Palmer, Alfred L., Sgt,
Palmer, Harold J., Pvt,
Palmer, James R., 2nd Lt,
Palmer, Jay A., Pfc,
Palmer, John L., Pvt,
Palmer, Joseph E., Pvt,
†Palmer, Mack L., Pfc,
Palmer, Marlin L., Pfc,
Palmer, Paul H., Cpl,
Palmer, Rupert P., Sgt,
Palmero, Frank, Pfc,
*Palmero, Tony, Pfc,
Palmieri, Mario F., Pvt,
Palmisciano, Antonio, Pfc,
Pals, Carl, S/Sgt,
Palubicki, David H., Pfc,
Paluch, Bruno F., Pfc,
Palyszeski, George, Pfc,
Panagos, Harry G., Pvt,
Pancake, Leroy E., Pfc.
Pandora, Ben, Cpl.
Pangel, Seymour, Pfc,
Pangallo, Michael J., Pfc,
Panico, Carlo D., Pfc,
‡Pankonien, Willie R., Pfc,
Pantaleo, Salvatore, Pfc,
Pantanella, Roland E., Pfc,
Papa, Joseph F., Pfc,
Papanek, Carl P., 1st Sgt,
Papas, Christos P., Pvt,
Papas, James, T/5,
Papasotirin, Sam G., Pvt,
Pape, Carmen, Pfc,
Pape, Richard E., Sgt,
Pape, Sigfried, Pvt,
Papp, Joseph S., Jr., Pvt,
Pappalardo, Mario S., Pvt,
Pappaterra, James H., Pvt,
‡Paquette, Charles E., Cpl,
‡Paquette, Donald R., Pvt,
Parachini, Mario A., Pfc,
Paradis, Romeo A., Pvt,
Paradise, Wilfred J., Pvt,
Pardoe, Kenneth E., Pvt,
Pardur, Albert, Sgt,
Parent, Frank R., 1st Lt,
Parent, Fred T., Cpl,
Parent, Joseph A., Jr., 2nd Lt,
Parent, Leo E., Pfc,
†Parimuha, John, Pfc,
Parish, Lynn G., Jr., Pfc,
Parish, Newton B., Pfc,
Parisi Carlo A., Pfc,
Parisi, Clifford J., Pfc,
Parisi, Daniel T., Pfc,
Parisi, Joseph A., T/5.
Pariso, Nicholas W., Pvt.

Park, Floyd D., Pfc,
Parker, Brandon E., S/Sgt,
Parker, Donald R., Cpl,
Parker, Earl, Pvt,
Parker, Edward L., Pfc,
‡Parker, Elmo D., S/Sgt,
Parker, Everett W., Pvt,
Parker, Frank M., M/Sgt,
Parker, Harry T., Pvt,
Parker, Henry G., Pfc,
Parker, Henry H., Cpl,
†Parker, Herbert D., Pfc,
†Parker, Ivan H., Pvt,
Parker, John P., Pfc,
Parker, Lewis C., Pfc,
*Parker, Loyd, Pvt,
Parker, Perham S., Pfc,
†Parker, Preston M., Sgt,
Parker, Sherman, Pfc,
Parker, Troy, Jr., T/5,
Parkhurst, Raymond, Pfc,
‡Parkison, Arthur L., Pvt,
Parks, Alfred W., Jr., Pfc,
Parks, James S., Pfc,
Parks, John M., T/Sgt,
Parks, Willie A., Pvt,
Parmenter, Billy B., Pvt,
Parmenter, Charles E., Cpl,
Parris, Harry G., Pfc,
Parrish, Benjamin F., Pfc,
Parrish, Buil, Pfc,
†Parrish, Clarence S., 1st Lt,
Parrish, Henry R., Pvt,
Parrish, Graeme F., 1st Lt,
Parrott, John L., Pvt,
Parry, Francis W., Pvt,
Parson, Dennis, Pfc,
Parson, Robert L., Pvt,
Parsons, Clifford H., Pfc,
Parsons, Donald D., Pfc,
Parsons, Eugene B., Pfc,
Parsons, Leonard L., Pfc,
Parsons, Norman E., T/4,
Parsons, Virgil L., Pfc,
Parsons, Walter W., Pfc,
Partain, Charles T., Pfc,
Partelow, Irving K., 2nd Lt,
§Parth, Donald R., Pvt,
†Partin, George W., S/Sgt,
Partin, John T., T/Sgt,
Paryl, Martin F., Pvt,
Parzewicz, Joseph G., Pfc
Pascoe, Albert B., Pfc,
Pashko, James M., Pfc,
Pasko, Andrew, Pvt,
Pasqual, Andrew S., Pfc,
Pass, John J., Pvt,
Passione, Vincent D., Pvt,
Pastell, John D., 2nd Lt,
Pastor, Joseph J., Pfc,
Pastorine, Carmine T., Pfc,
Pataki. Ernest, Pfc,
Pate, Robert L., Jr., Pfc,
‡Paterson, William A., Pvt,
Patin, Ewerin, Pvt,
Patinella, Andrew, Pvt,
Patrician, Frank T., Pfc,
Patrick, Billy, Pfc,
Patrick, Charles J., 2nd Lt,
Patrick, Henry M., Jr., Pfc,
Patrick, Hiram D., Pfc,
Patrick, James, Jr., Pfc,
†Patricki, John, Pfc,
Patrizio, Vincenzio, Pfc.
Patterson, Clyde F., Cpl,
Patterson, Drue, S/Sgt,
Patterson, Eldon D., Pvt,
†Patterson, Elwyn D., Pfc,
Patterson, Harry E., 2nd Lt,
Patterson, John D., Pvt,
†Patterson, Orville J., Pfc,
Patterson, Otis E., Pfc,
Patterson, Paul, Pfc,
Patterson, Willis, Pvt,
†Patton, Robert D., Jr., Pvt,
Paukst, Joseph J., S/Sgt,
Paukst, Walter J., Pfc,
Paul, Andrew D., Pvt,
Paul, Clinton D., 1st Lt,
Paul, Donald M., Pvt,
Pauley, William H., Pfc,
Paulison, Arthur W., Pfc,
Paulson, George J., Pfc,
Paulson, Kermit P., T/5,
Paun, John P., Sgt,
Pavelka, Charles W., Pfc,
Pavik, Andrew M., Pfc,
‡Pavlick, Joseph J., Pfc,
Pavlock, Bernard R., Pfc,
Pavuk, George, Pfc,
§Pawlak, Edward J., Pvt,
†Pawlak, Raymond J., Pvt,
Pawlen, Joseph E., Jr., T/5,
Pawlicki, Aloysius J., Jr., Pvt,
Payne, Charles A., S/Sgt,

Payne, Charles D., Pfc,
‡Payne, Delbert W., Sgt,
Payne, Jack H., Pfc,
Payne, Martin L., Pvt,
Payne, Ralph W., 1st Lt,
Payne, Raymond E., Pvt,
Payne, Thomas J., Pfc,
Paynter, Robert F., Pfc,
Paynton, Frederick C., Pvt,
Payton, William A., Cpl,
Paz, Michael M., Sgt,
‡Peabody, Vincent D., Pfc,
Peace, Carlton R., Pvt,
Peacock, George, Jr., Pfc,
Peake, Stephen L., Pfc,
Pearce, William H., T/4,
Pearlman, Sidney, Sgt,
Pearman, James N., Jr.,
†Pearo, Richard J., Pvt,
Pearson, Charley T., Pfc,
Pearson, David H., Jr., T/5,
Pearson, Davis, Pfc,
†Pearson, Ernest E., 1st Sgt,
Pearson, Leslie P., Pfc,
*Pearson, Richard G., Pvt,
Pearson, Warren S., Pfc,
Pecar, Anthony C., S/Sgt,
*Peck, Harry, Pvt,
Peck, Herbert M., Pvt,
Peck, Solle, Pvt,
Pecorari, Frank, Pvt,
Pecoriello, Vincent, Pvt,
Pecsenye, Steven, S/Sgt,
Pederson, Elmo F., S/Sgt,
†Pederson, Henry R., Pfc,
†Pederson, Selmer L., Pvt,
Peek, Arnold H., Pvt,
Peet, Lawrence J., T/4,
Peine, Louis P., T/5,
Pekar, Joseph, Pfc,
Pelle, James L., S/Sgt,
Pellegrino, James P., Pfc,
Pelley, Harlan O., Pvt,
Pellicciari, Nicholas, Lt,
Pellis, Alexander, S/Sgt,
Pelton, Raymond C., Pfc,
†Pelton, Robert C., Pfc,
Pelton, Stanley C., Pvt,
Pemberton, Charles E., Pvt,
Pemberton, Hinson E., Pfc,
Pemberton, Norman Y., Pfc,
Pempek, Leonard S., Pvt,
Pena, Manuel B., Pfc,
†Pena, Ysidro, T/4,
Pendergast, Raymond G., Pvt,
Pendergrass, Burnett E., Pfc,
Pendleton, Verl L., S/Sgt,
Penepacker, Fredrick H., Pfc,
Penington, Isaac, Pvt,
Penix, Lloyd F., Pfc,
Pennatto, Pat J., Sgt,
Pennell, Arnold E., Pfc,
Pennell, Clyde W., S/Sgt,
Pennell, Howard A., Pvt,
†Pennington, Billy N., Pvt,
Pennington, Sherwin D., Pvt,
†Pennisi, Joseph S., Pvt,
Pentiak, Peter R., S/Sgt,
†Peoples, Donald J., Pvt,
Peppard, Harley F., Cpl,
Peppers, Green L., Sgt,
†Peppiatt, Gordon A., Sgt,
Percell, George, Pfc,
Perchan, Harold W., Sgt,
Percuoco, Ralph, Pvt,
Perello, Amedio D., Pfc,
Perez, Antonio, Pvt,
Perez, Hugh A., Pvt,
Perez, Manuel, Pfc,
Perez, Manuel P., Pfc,
*Perez, Vincent C., Pvt,
Perfetto, Jerry D., Pvt,
Perhach, Vincent J., Pfc,
Peribonis, Andrew D., Pvt,
Peris, Edward C., Pvt,
Perisich, Charles M., Pfc,
†Perkins, John D., Jr., Pfc,
Perkins, Lee H., S/Sgt,
Perkins, Marvin R., Pvt,
Perkins, Raymond T., Pfc,
†Perkins, Thomas J., Pfc,
Perko, Stanley J., Sgt,
Perlowitz, Harry, Pvt,
†Perodeau, Vincent J., Pvt,
Peron, Peter F., Pvt,
Perrault, Leo H., Pfc,
Perreault, Maurice F., S/Sgt,
Perrin, Le Roy, Pvt,
Perron, Andrew C., T/Sgt,
Perrone, Paul L., Pvt,
†Perry, Carl E., Pvt,
Perry, Merle T., T/5,
Perry, Morton H., Capt,
Perry, Orrize E., Pfc,
§Perry, Richard C., Pvt,

†Perry, Vernon C., Pfc,
Perry, Weldon, S/Sgt,
Perry, William P., Pvt,
Person, Edward F., Pfc,
Peruch, John, Cpl,
Perygin, William E., Pvt,
‡Perzak, Milton, Pvt,
‡Pesko, Alphonse E., Pvt,
Pesqueira, Alfonso T., Pfc,
Pesta, John A., Cpl,
Peterman, Daniel V., Sgt,
Peters, Charles H., S/Sgt,
Peters, Charles J., Cpl,
Peters, Clarence J., Pfc,
Peters, Edgar E., Cpl,
†Peters, George M., Pvt,
Peters, George W., Pfc,
†Peters, Harry A., Pvt,
Peters, Ralph C., Pvt,
Peters, Ralph T., Pvt,
Peters, Raymond S., 2nd Lt,
Peters, Roy E., Pfc,
Petersen, Earl V., Sgt,
Petersen, Joe F., Pvt,
Peterson, Celon A., Capt,
‡Peterson, Harry A., Pvt,
Peterson, Henry L., Sgt,
Peterson, Hilding T., Pfc,
Peterson, James C., Pfc,
Peterson, Louis E., Pfc,
Peterson, R. M., Jr., Pvt,
Peterson, Raymond G., Pvt,
Peterson, Raymond O., Pfc,
Peterson, Robert, T/5,
Peterson, Robert G., Pfc,
Peterson, Russell A., Pfc,
Peterson, Stanley G., Pvt,
Petite, Raymond L., Pvt,
Petosa, John A., Cpl,
Petoskey, Joseph B., Cpl,
Petracone, Dominic P., T/4,
Petrella, Michael L., Pvt,
†Petrey, Edgar, S/Sgt,
Petrie, Russell J., Pvt,
Petrie, William B., Cpl,
Petrigac, John J., T/4,
Petrolia, Paul J., Pfc,
Petroni, Leonard R., Pfc,
†Petropolis, Stanley, 2nd Lt,
Petroski, Aloize, Pvt,
Petruzel, Frank, Capt,
Petry, Charles D., Cpl,
Pettit, Chester A., Cpl,
Pettit, Jacob E., Pvt,
*Pettit, William E., Pfc,
Pettitt, Millard G., Pfc,
†Pettograssia, Fred J., Pvt,
Pettus, Frank, Pfc,
Pevoski, Joseph J., Pfc,
Peyton, Kenneth F., Pfc,
Peyton, Robert L., Pvt,
Pfeifer, Clarence P., Pfc,
Pfeiffer, Paul E., Pfc,
Pfiester, Herman G., T/Sgt,
Pfuhlmann, Gustav A., T/5,
Phalp, William A., 1st Lt,
Phelps, Conrad O., Pvt,
Phelps, Jasper H., Pvt,
Phelps, Orville, Pfc,
Phelps, Terrance R., Pvt,
Phillips, Amos, Pfc,
Phillips, Andrew J., Pfc,
Phillips, Bill D., Pfc,
Phillips, Clair O., Pfc,
Phillips, Elmer W., Pfc,
Phillips, Eugene G., Pvt,
Phillips, Frederick J., 1st Lt,
Phillips, Gus R., 1st Lt,
Phillips, Guy F., Pfc,
Phillips, Jack H., Pfc,
Phillips, James F., Sgt,
Phillips, James M., Pfc,
Phillips, James T., Jr., Sgt,
Phillips, Kellis F., Pvt,
Phillips, Lester E., Pfc,
Phillips, Lewis G., Pfc,
Phillips, Lloyd E., Pfc,
Phillips, Malcolm H., 1st Lt,
†Phillips, Murray S., Jr., Pvt,
Phillips, Pearce H., Sgt,
Phillips, Sidney C., Pvt,
†Phillips, William, Pvt,
Philmlee, Stephen D., T/5,
Philo, Seymour S., Capt,
Phinisey, Gordon T., Pvt,
Phippin, William F., Pvt,
Phipps, Jack L., Pfc,
Phipps, Junia J., Pvt,
Photos, John T., Cpl,
Piacentine, Jerry E., Pfc,
Piazza, Anthony G., Pfc,
Picardi, Vincent M., Pvt,
Picco, Jacob J., Pvt,
Picco, John M., Pfc,
Piccolo, Salvatore J., Pfc,

Pick, Oscar, Pvt,
Pickard, Paul A., Pfc,
Pickelsimer, Richard B., Jr.,
Pickerel, Lawrence, Pvt,
Pickering, John C., Pfc,
Pickett, John K., Pfc,
Pickford, Norman W., Pvt,
Pickthal, Thomas W., Jr., Capt,
Picone, Joseph, Pvt,
Picone, Joseph S., Pvt,
*Picou, Harry S., 2nd Lt,
Picton, Dean C., 2nd Lt,
†Pie, Justin A., 2nd Lt,
Piechowski, Stephen J., Pvt,
Pieczara, Edward L., Pfc,
Piegat, Walter P., Sgt,
Pier, Robert S., Pvt,
Pieracci, Andrew T., Pfc,
Pierce, Bennie W., Jr., Pfc,
Pierce, Claud H., T/Sgt,
Pierce, Frank B., Pvt,
†Pierce, Frank C., Pvt,
Pierce, John W., Pvt,
Pierce, Milton A., Pvt,
*Pierce, Robert D., Pvt,
†Pierce, Wilber R., Pvt,
Pierce, Winston F., S/Sgt,
Pierno, Michael, Pfc,
Pierog, Walter, Pfc,
Pierson, Floyd E., Pvt,
†Pierson, J. C., Pvt,
Pierson, John V., Sgt,
Pietrowski, Edward J., Pfc,
Pietruszka, Frank J., Pvt,
Pietrzak, Edward J., Pvt,
Pigott, Bernard F., Pvt,
Pilarski, Clarence A., Pfc,
Pilkinton, Jesse B., Pfc,
†Pinard, Raymond F., Pfc,
Pinchbeck, Bernard C., Pvt,
Pincus, Louis, Pvt,
Pindyxki, Michael J., Sgt,
Pingitore, August L., Pvt,
Pinnella, Enrico, Pvt,
Pinner, Isic W., Pvt,
Piller, Emery J., Pvt,
Pinsker, Samuel, Pvt,
Pinson, James M., Pvt,
Pintar, William, Pfc,
§Pinto, Joseph, Pfc,
Pinto, Tony J., Pvt,
Pion, Louis J. B., Pvt,
Piotrowski, Zygmuth S., Pfc,
†Pipa, Louis, Pfc,
Piper, Philip H., T/5,
Piper, Raymond F., T/4,
Pires, Frank R., S/Sgt,
Pirozzi, Frank G., Pfc,
Pirschel, Bill A., Pvt,
Pirtle, George S., Sgt,
Pisarsky, John W., Pfc,
Pistilli, John J., Pfc,
Pistone, Frank J., S/Sgt,
Pitcamer, Stanley P., Pfc,
Pitchell, George E., Pfc,
Pitera, Charles J., Pvt,
Pitkow, Benjamin E., Pfc,
Pitman, Hurbert H., 2nd Lt,
Pitman, Russell A., Pfc,
Pitonyak, William C., Pfc,
Pittala, James J., Pvt,
Pittaluga, Joseph A., S/Sgt,
Pittman, James W., Pfc,
Pittman, Robert G., Pfc,
Pittman, William H., Pfc,
Pitts, Donald L., Pfc,
Pittullo, Glen, Pfc,
Pitzer, Lyndell W., Pfc,
Pixley, Erwin W., Pvt,
Pizzaferrato, Salvatore L., Pvt,
Plagg, Wilbert J., Pfc,
Plaks, Harry, Pvt,
Plamondon, Leonard J., Pfc,
†Plantier, Eugene G., Pfc,
Plaquet, Carroll A., Major,
Plate, William R., Pfc,
Platts, Edmund M., Jr., Pvt,
Pleasant, Wallace W., Pfc,
Plemmons, Thomas W., T/4,
†Pless, Joseph W., Pfc,
Pletzke, George C., T/Sgt,
Plius, Albert B., Pfc,
Plott, Noah S., Pvt,
Plummer, Howard R., Pfc,
Plummer, James O., Pvt,
†Plyler, Edward L., Pvt,
Podczervinski, Edward B., Pvt,
Podejko, Walter J., Pvt,
Podolak, Walter J., Sgt,
†Poff, Henry E., Pvt,
Poffenroth, John E., 1st Lt,
Pogoncheff, Carl G., Pvt,
Pogue, Amos E., Pvt,
Pogue, Lawrence J., Pvt,
Pohler, Heinz, Pfc,

† Killed in Action. * Prisoner of War. ‡ Missing in Action. § Died of Wounds.

†Poidmore, Frank J., Pfc,
Poinsett, Edgar H., Capt,
†Points, Otto L., Pfc,
Pokriefke, Eldred R., Pvt,
Pokrwinski, Harry D., Pvt,
Polachek, Rudolph, Pvt,
Poland, Jack L., Sgt,
Polcyn, Floyd J., Pvt,
Polensky, Frank, Pvt,
Polhmaus, George J., T/4,
Poli, Constantine J., Pfc,
Poliakoff, Pavel, Pfc,
Police, Louie, Pvt,
Polivka, Frank, Pvt,
†Pollack, Samuel, Pvt,
Pollard, Fred R., T/5,
Pollard, Robert E., S/Sgt,
Pollard, Samuel W., Sgt,
Poller, Lawrence P., Pvt,
Polley, Everett, Pfc,
Pollock, William J., Cpl,
Polomsky, Daniel L., Sgt,
Polsinelli, Argentino S., Pvt,
Polson, Elliva A., Pfc,
Polson, Henry S., Jr., 2nd Lt,
Polster, Henry G., Pvt.
Pomietlasz, F. J., Jr., Pfc,
†Pompei, Daniel R., Sgt,
Pompey, Leonard A., Pvt,
†Pomponio, Mario, Pvt,
Pond, Edson H., Pfc,
Ponder, Amos L., Jr., 2nd Lt,
‡Ponieski, Emil T., Pfc,
Ponikvar, Louis J., Pvt,
Pontarelli, Anthony C., T/3,
†Ponticelli, Glen P., Pvt,
Pool, Lynn, Pvt,
Poole, Benjamin F., S/Sgt,
Poole, Clyde A., Pfc,
*Poole, James R., Pfc,
Pooler, Joseph W., Pfc,
Pooley, Raymond D., Pvt,
Poore, David T., Pfc,
Poorman, Donald J., Pfc,
Pope, Edward H., Pfc,
Pope, Ross B., Pfc,
Popick, Nicholas, Pvt,
Popovich, George, Pfc,
Popp, Robert E., Sgt,
Porch, Harold M., Pfc,
Poricky, Karel, Pvt,
Porter, Alfred R., Pfc,
Porter, Alton J., Pvt,
†Porter, John M., Pvt,
Porter, Kenneth D., Pvt,
Porter, Leo, Pvt,
Porter, Norman L., Pvt,
†Porter, Russell H., Pfc,
Porter, Vernon A., Pvt,
Porter, Wiley M., Pfc,
Porterfield, Edwin G., Sgt,
Portman, John C., Pfc,
Poss, Wilbur L., Pfc,
Post, Clifford L., Pfc,
†Post, Harlan, Pfc,
Post, Robert B., Pfc,
Postovit, Arnold E., Sgt,
Poteat, Parks H., T/4,
†Poteete, Elmer F., Pvt,
†Potisuk, Stephen, Sgt,
Potkoski, Bruno, Pfc,
Potocki, Louis J., S/Sgt,
Potratz, George W., Pfc,
Potter, Clyne H., Pfc,
Potter, George E., Pfc,
Potter, Harold F., T/Sgt,
Potter, Leroy A., Pvt,
Potter, Paul F., 2nd Lt,
Potter, Robert E., Pvt,
Potter, Roy E., Cpl,
Potter, Vernice, Sgt,
†Potter, William P., Pfc,
Potts, Charles E., 1st Sgt,
Potts, Garland H., 1st Sgt,
Potts, Gilbert E., Pfc,
Potts, Phillip R., Pfc,
Potwora, Edward, Pfc,
Poulios, Nicholas M., Pfc,
Powell, Cleveland L., Pfc,
*Powell, Edward J., Pfc,
Powell, Elzie F., Pvt,
Powell, James F., Capt,
Powell, James T., Pfc,
Powell, Monroe V., Pfc,
Powell, Philip J., S/Sgt,
Powell, Samuel C., Jr., Pfc,
Powell, Tommie L., T/Sgt,
Powell, Troy N., M/Sgt,
Powell, Walter H., Jr., 2nd Lt,
Powers, Charles B., Pvt,
Powers, James C., Pvt,
Powers, Leo, Pvt.
†Powers, Milford F., Pfc,
Powers, Ralph, Pvt,
Poythress, James L., Pfc,
Pozzolano, Clement S., Cpl,
Prario, Henry S., 2nd Lt,
Prater, William H., T/Sgt,
Prather, Frederick E., Pvt,
Prather, Herman R., Pvt,
Pratico, Vincent A., Pvt,
Pratt, Clarence W., Pvt,
Pratt, Ernest A., 2nd Lt,
‡Pratt, Lawrence F., Pvt,
Pratt, Maurice I., Pvt,
Pratt, Sherman W., Capt,
Praught, Daniel C., Pfc,
Preffer, John A., Jr., T/5,
Prentice, Vern A., Pfc,
Prentiss, Shirley R., Pvt,
Prescott, Earl D., Pfc,
‡Prescott, Hubert, S/Sgt,
Presnell, Elvin P., Pfc,
Pressell, Malcolm R., Pvt,
Pressley, Charles L., Pfc,
Prestage, Bryce, S/Sgt,
Prestage, George E., Pvt,
†Preston, Bascom E., Pvt,
†Preston, Charles E., Jr., Pfc,
Preston, Charles R., T/5,
Preston, George C., 1st Sgt,
Preston, Mike, Jr., Pvt,
Preston, Willis W., Pvt,
§Pretkiewicz, August J., Pvt,
‡Prezioso, Nicholas A., Pfc,
Pribble, William T., T/4,
Pribis, Alex, Cpl,
Price, Billy, Pfc,
Price, Brice E., Pvt,
Price, Charles C., Pvt,
Price, Douglas G., Pvt,
Price, Fred J., Pfc,
Price, Herbert S., Jr., M/Sgt,
Price, James E., Pvt,
§Price, James W., Pvt,
Price, John M., Pfc,
Price, Myron W., Cpl,
Price, Paul J., Pvt,
Price, Peter G., Pfc,
Price, Richard B., Pvt,
Price, Roy M., Pfc,
‡Price, Stanley P., Pvt,
Price, Stephen W., 2nd Lt,
†Principe, Raymond E., T/5,
Prickett, Charles G., Sgt,
†Pridemore, Albert T., Pfc,
†Primmer, Donald B., Pvt,
Prince, Donald P., T/5,
Prince, Edward F., S/Sgt,
Prince, Lonnie R., Pfc,
†Pristas, Joseph, Pfc,
Pritchett, Donald E., Pvt,
†Pritchett, George H., Pfc,
Pritchett, Walter W., Pvt,
Privett, Charlie A., Pfc,
Prochot, John J., Pfc,
Proctor, Albert D., Jr., Pfc,
Proctor, Edward F., Pvt,
Procyson, Paul, Pvt,
§Proffit, Evan W., Pfc,
Proffitt, Aster C., Pfc,
†Proia, Albert, Pfc,
Prokes, Adrian B., Pvt,
Proo, Salvator G., Pfc,
Proper, Monte E., Pvt,
Propst, Homer E., 1st Sgt,
Prosser, Earnest E., Pvt,
Provenzano, John D., Pfc,
Pruitt, Ernest A., Pfc,
Prunty, Edward P., Pvt,
Pruticka, John, Pfc,
Pryde, Robert J., T/Sgt,
Pryor, Ellis A., Pfc,
†Pryor, Muriel G., Pfc,
Przybylski, Edwin S., Pvt,
Pucino, Toby, Pfc,
Puckett, Claude R., Pfc,
Pudder, Forest B., Pvt,
Pueschel, Carl E., Pfc,
Pufall, Walter L., Pfc,
†Pugh, Eugene, Pvt,
Pugh, George W., T/5,
Pugh, Raymond W., Pvt,
Pugh, Robert E., T/5,
§Puglia, Carlo, Pfc,
Pugliese, Leonard, Pfc,
Puig, Eddie, Pfc,
Pulawski, Joseph W., Pvt,
Puleo, Charles J., Pvt,
†Pulver, Bernard L., 2nd Lt,
†Pundt, Arthur R., Pvt,
Punches, William E., Sgt,
Punska, Joseph, T/Sgt,
Purcell, Frank A., Pvt,
Purcell, Joe W., Pfc,
Purcher, Stephen, Pfc,
Purdue, Paul M., Pfc,
Purdun, Kenneth C., Pfc,
*Purks, Heighter L., 2nd Lt,
Purser, Edward W., Pvt,
Purvis, Ernest W., Pvt,
Purvis, Floyd L., Sgt,
†Pusey, Walter W., Pvt,
Putis, John W., Pfc,
†Putman, John E., 1st Lt,
Putnam, James W., Pvt,
Putnam, Robert S., Pfc,
Putnam, William F., Jr., Pfc,
Pyatt, Miles K., S/Sgt,
Pye, Warner W., T/5,
Pyle, Wilborn F., T/5,
Pyplatz, Joseph P., T/4,
Pyrtko, Nicholas, Cpl,

Quackenbush, James A., Pvt,
Quakenbush, Robert D., 1st Lt,
Qualin, Frank P., Pfc,
Qualls, James C., Pfc,
Quan, Fong, Pfc,
Quandt, Claus J., Pvt,
Quarandille, Louie P., Pvt,
Quattrocki, Anthony J., Pfc,
†Quesenberry, Henry, Pvt,
Quick, Edsel R., Pvt,
Quick, Eugene J., Pfc,
Quick, James T., Pfc,
Quick, Lester C., Pfc,
Quilico, Pete, Pvt,
*Quillen, Aaren F., Pfc,
Quimby, William D., Sgt,
Quinehan, James H., Pfc,
†Quinlan, James R., Pvt,
Quinlan, Robert E., Pfc,
Quinn, Hugh, Pfc,
Quinn, James D., Cpl,
Quinn, Joseph J., T/5,
Quinn, Raymond A., Pvt,
Quinn, Raymond F., Pvt,
Quinn, William H., Jr., Sgt,
Quinn, William J., Pvt,
Quinney, Kenneth E., Pfc,
Quinonez, Manuel A., Pfc,
*Quintero, Demetrio M., Pfc,

Raatz, Carl G., Pfc,
Rabalais, Ivey E., Pvt,
Rabinowitz, Edward A., Sgt,
Race, Claude R., Pfc,
Rachiele, Frederick O.,
Raczynski, John, Pvt,
*Raddo, Arthur J., Pvt,
Rademacher, Clarence J., Pfc,
Rader, Clark A., Pfc,
Radmer, Alfred O., S/Sgt,
Radomski, John A., Pfc,
Radtke, George R., T/4,
Radzikowski, Eugene, Pvt,
Rae, John E., Pfc,
Raferty, Vincent P., Pfc,
Ragaisis, John A., Pfc,
Rager, Clifford J., Pfc,
Ragsdale, Charles R., Jr., Pfc,
Ragusa, Samuel A., Pvt,
Rahmer, George A., T/5,
Rahne, Barth M., Pfc,
Raimo, Carl A., Pfc,
Raines, James H., Pfc,
†Rains, Onis L., Sgt,
Rainville, Merrlen J., Pvt,
Rainwater, Boyd T., Pfc,
Rainwater, Claud L., Sgt,
Rainwater, Julian G., S/Sgt,
Raishel, Joseph H., Pvt,
Rajchel, Fred R., Pvt,
§Rake, Edward J., Pvt,
†Rakowski, Frank H., Pfc,
Raksi, James F., Cpl,
Raleigh, Albert W., Cpl,
Rall, Clarence E., T/5,
Rall, Gerard V., Pfc,
Rallis, James P., Pfc,
Ralls, Daniel W., Pvt,
Ralls, Ottie E., Pvt,
Ralls, Willis G., Sgt,
Ralston, B. W., 2nd Lt,
§Ramacker, Harold F., Pvt,
Rambeaut, Aldridge, Pvt,
Ramer, Herman, Capt,
Ramer, Herman, 1st Lt,
Ramer, Tonsie, Pvt,
Ramirez, Ernest, Jr., S/Sgt,
†Ramirez, Jesse M., Sgt,
Ramirez, Jose, Pfc,
Ramirez, Salvador, Pfc,
Raml, Victor M., Pfc,
Ramlow, Bertram A., Pvt,
§Ramnick, Raymond, T/5,
Ramon, Jesus, Pvt,
Rampino, Louis S., Pvt,
Rampola, Bernard, S/Sgt,
Rampy, Leroy, Pfc,
Ramsey, Frank T., T/Sgt,
†Ramsey, Bill, Pvt,
Ramsey, Henry M., Cpl,
Ramsey, Hershel L., Sgt,
Ramsey, Lloyd B., Lt Col,
Ramsey, Walter B., Pfc,
†Rancourt, Augustin C., Pfc,
Rancourt, William H., Pfc,
Randall, Frank E., T/5,
Randazzo, Anthony M., Pfc,
Randisi, Joseph A., Pvt,
Randle, Jesse T., Pfc,
Ranelli, Dominick A., Pvt,
†Raney, John S., 1st Lt,
Rankin, Lester M., Pfc,
†Rankin, Robert W., 1st Lt,
Rao, Louis F., Pfc,
Raphael, Earl C., T/4,
Raposa, August, Pfc,
Rappaport, Ned, Pvt,
Rapsinski, George, Pvt,
Rardin, Walter E., Pfc,
Rasch, Erling R., Pvt,
Raskosky, John M., Sgt,
†Rasmussen, Donald W., Pvt,
Rasmusson, Eddie K., Sgt,
Ratcliff, Cecil D., Pfc,
Ratcliff, Donald R., Pvt,
Rathbun, Glenn E., Maj,
Rathburn, John H., Pvt,
Rathnow, Ray M., Pvt,
Ratliff, Don L., Pfc
Raul, Albert I., Pvt
Raum, Herbert E., Pfc,
Rauschenberg, Robert L., Pfc,
*Ravine, Frank M., Sgt,
Rawlings, Howard W., Sgt,
Rawls, Benjamin R., T/5,
Rawson, Clifford A., Pfc,
Ray, Bernard W., Pfc,
Ray, Clyde W., Jr., Sgt,
Ray, Elmer J., Pfc,
‡Ray, John F., Pvt,
Ray, Kurt E., Pfc,
Ray, Leroy G., Pfc,
Ray, Roy R., Pvt,
Ray, Von W., T/4,
Raykowicz, Carl, Pfc,
Raymer, Alvin, Pfc,
Raymer, Victor W., Pfc,
Raymond, Leo G., T/5,
Raymond, Mark O., Pfc,
†Raymond, Nomand E., Pfc,
Raymond, William W., 2nd Lt,
Rayner, Charles F., Cpl,
Raynes, James L., Pvt,
‡Raynor, Colon, Pfc,
Raynor, Forrest, Pfc,
Rea, Michael G., Sgt,
Read, George F., Pfc,
Reagan, L. J., Pfc,
Reavis, Willis A., T/5,
Reader, Norman J., Jr., S/Sgt,
Reagan, Richard E., Pfc,
Ream, Charles F., T/5,
Ream, Jack D., Cpl,
Reardon, James A., Pfc,
Reardon, John G., Pfc,
Reasor, Woodrow, T/4,
Reaves, Bennie O., Pvt,
Reaves, Darrell W., Cpl,
Reavis, Ira W., Pfc,
Reavis, Randall A.,
Rebovich, George, S/Sgt,
Rebovich, George, 2nd Lt,
‡Recchia, John, Pvt,
Rechert, Lawrence L., Pfc,
Reck, John, Pvt,
Reckinger, William J., Pvt,
Records, James E., Pfc,
†Red, Alvin W., Sgt,
Redden, Norman H., Pvt,
Reddick, John R., T/Sgt,
†Redding, Clarence D., Pvt,
Redding, Francis L., Pfc,
*Redmond, Wilbur H., Pfc,
§Reece, Charles E., Pvt,
Reece, Jap L., Pfc,
Reed, Allen E., Pfc,
Reed, Arpha E., Pfc,
§Reed, Cecil R., Pvt,
Reed, Clarence E., Pfc,
Reed, Clarence L., Pfc,
Reed, Frank L., Pfc,
Reed, Freeman E., Pfc,
Reed, George W., Pfc,
Reed, Harold L., Pvt,
Reed, Howard J., Sgt,
Reed, James H., Pfc,
Reed, Laverne E., Pvt,
Reed, Ralph A., Capt,
Reed, Robert E., Pfc,
†Reed, Russell F., Cpl,
Reed, Wayne P., Pfc,
Reeder, Albert A., S/Sgt,
Reeder, James E., Pvt,
Reekie, Wilbur H., Pvt,
Reesing, Sidney E., Pvt,
Reeve, Arnold M., 1st Lt,
Reeves, Alzie C., Pfc,
Reeves, Ernest F., Pfc,
Reeves, Horace J., Cpl,
Reeves, Jack, Pvt,
Reeves, John D., 2nd Lt,
Reeves, John J., Pvt,
‡Reeves, William E., Pfc,
Refalskey, Tony, Pfc,
Regan, Alex, Jr., Pfc,
Regan, Joseph J., Cpl,
‡Regan, Joseph M., Pvt,
Reagan, Michael, Jr., S/Sgt,
Regan, William S., Pvt,
Regher, David D., Sgt,
Reger, William M., Jr., Pfc,
†Register, William J., Pvt,
Rehak, Joseph F., Pvt,
Rehak, Thomas A., Cpl,
Rehus, James C., Pvt,
Reich, Benjamin W., Pfc,
‡Reichlin, Karl, Pfc,
Reid, Elijah, Pfc,
Reid, Enoch B., Pfc,
Reid, Floyd E., Pfc,
Reid, Francis W., Pvt,
†Reid, Frank A., Pvt,
Reid, Troy L., S/Sgt,
Reidy, William F., 1st Lt,
Reider, Emil G., Pfc,
Reif, Hans G., Pfc,
‡Reiff, William H., Pfc,
Reighard, Ralph J., Pvt,
†Reighter, William A., Pvt,
Reilly, George F., Jr., T/5,
Reilly, Thomas J., Pfc,
Relyea, Wilbur T., Cpl,
†Reinertsen, Paul A., Sgt,
†Reinertson, Stanley T., Pvt,
Reinhard, Richard L., Pvt,
Reinhart, George J., Jr., Pvt,
†Reinig, Walter H., Sgt,
‡Reinke, Howard C., Pvt,
‡Reinstatler, Sylvester A., Pfc,
*Reise, Earl D., Pfc,
Reisig, Gerald R., Pvt,
Reitan, Earl A., Pfc,
Reitemeier, Joseph H., S/Sgt,
Reitzel, Walter D., Pvt,
Rejniak, Edward P., Pvt,
Rekowski, Bruno S., Pvt,
‡Re, Michael A., Pvt,
Remer, Leland F., Pvt,
†Remetta, Edward, Pfc,
†Remick, William C., Pfc,
Remines, Luther J., Pfc,
Remington, Ernest E., Pfc,
Remmers, Loyal H., Pfc,
Rempala, John J., Pfc,
Renfro, Wallace A., Pfc,
Renfrow, Earnest D., Pvt,
†Reno, Sterling, Sgt,
Rennert, Arthur, Pfc,
Rentas, George C., 1st Lt,
Rentfrow, William C., Pfc,
Rentz, Richard E., Pfc,
Renwick, Dick F., T/5,
Renzi, Settimio A., T/5,
Renzo, John, Pfc,
Reo, Carl F., Pvt,
Resheske, Leo F., Pfc,
Resko, Louis F., Pvt,
Resnikoff, Eli, Sgt,
Respondeck, Ronald G., Pfc,
Restive, Andrew P., Pvt,
Restivo, Dominic J., Pfc,
Restivo, Joe J., Pfc,
Restivo, Peter, Pvt,
‡Retas, Louis G., Pvt,
Retherford, Carl E., 2nd Lt,
Revier, John P., Sgt,
†Rewers, Joseph F., Pfc,
Reyes, Domingo G., Pvt,
†Reyes, Richard J., Pvt,
†Reynolds, Blair V., Pvt,
†Reynolds, Buren V., 1st Sgt,
†Reynolds, Earle G., Sgt,
Reynolds, Edwin A., Pfc,
Reynolds, Floyd O., Jr., Pvt,
Reynolds, Joe B., Pvt,
†Reynolds, John E., Pfc,
Reynolds, Oscar, Pvt,
Reynolds, Ralph G., Pvt,
†Reynolds, Robert H., Sgt,
Reynolds, T. G., Pfc,
Reynolds, Uless A., Pvt,
Reynolds, Victor D., 1st Lt,
Reynolds, William E., Pvt,
Rhead, Wallace M., Pfc,
Rhoads, Francis P., Pfc,
Rhoades, Lawrence B., T/Sgt,
Rhoades, Leo E., Pfc,
Rhoades, Pearl D., Sgt,
Rhodes, Alexander A., Pfc,
‡Rhodes, Byrd, Pvt,
Rhodes, Chester P., Pfc,

† Killed in Action. * Prisoner of War. ‡ Missing in Action. § Died of Wounds.

Rhodes, Clinton C., Pvt,
Rhodes, Leighton C., Pfc,
†Rhodes, Roy, Pfc,
Rhodes, Russell R., S/Sgt,
Rhodes, Samuel L., T/Sgt,
Rhodes, Walter E., Pfc,
Ribail, Joe D., Pfc,
Riccio, John A., Pfc,
Riccio, Nicholas J., Pfc,
Rice, Budd, 1st Sgt,
Rice, Clyde E., Pvt,
Rice, Danie E., Pfc,
Rice, George, S/Sgt,
Rice, Robert L., Pvt,
Rice, Roy, Pfc,
†Rice, Timothy, Pfc,
Rice, Walter M., 1st Lt,
Rice, William W., T/4,
Rich, James B., Jr., Capt,
†Rich, Ordway K., Pvt,
Rich, Robert M., Pvt,
Rich, Wayne V., Pfc,
Richard, Arnold E., Pfc,
Richard, Harry H., Pfc,
Richard, Reginald E., Pfc,
Richards, Donald H., Pvt,
Richards, George E., S/Sgt,
Richards, Walter, S/Sgt,
Richardson, Arthur K., 2nd Lt,
Richardson, Charles D., Pfc,
Richardson, Darrell E., Sgt,
Richardson, Dennis H., Pfc,
Richardson, Douglas W., Pfc,
Richardson, Elvin C., Pfc,
Richardson, George R., T/4,
Richardson, George W., Pfc,
Richardson, John W., Pfc,
Richardson, Nolan L., T/5,
Richardson, O. T., Jr., Pvt,
Richardson, Richard L., Cpl,
Richardson, Robert L., Cpl,
Richardson, Shirlie R., Pfc,
Richey, Malcolm F., Pvt,
Richey, Otto P., Pvt,
Richkus, Stanley A., Pfc,
†Richmond, Burl G., Pvt,
§Richmond, Carson D., Pvt,
Richmond, Robert F., Pvt,
Richter, Alfred E., Pvt,
Rickershauser, John F., 1st Lt,
Rickert, John W., Jr., Pfc,
Ricketts, George E., Pvt,
Ricketts, Paul S., Pvt,
Rickles, Jack W., 2nd Lt,
Riddle, Arthur D., Jr., Pvt,
Riddle, Edward C., Pvt,
Rider, Clarence J., Pfc,
Ridge, Henry F., Pfc,
Ridgel, Orrin W., Pvt,
Ridge, Thurman L., Cpl,
Ridner, Arvel L., Pfc,
Riegler, Michael J., Pvt,
Riendeau, Roland E., Pfc,
§Rienks, Louis M., Pfc,
Rierson, George W., Pvt,
Riese, Gilbert E., Pfc,
Riester, Eugene E., Pfc,
Riffle, Charles E., S/Sgt,
§Rigg, Bennie E., S/Sgt,
Riggin, B. F., Jr., 2nd Lt,
Riggin, Lee P., Cpl,
Riggins, Herman F., Pfc,
Riggs, Frank, Pvt,
Riggs, James A., Pfc,
Riggs, Joel T., Pfc,
Riggs, John E., Sgt,
Riggs, Robert E., Pfc,
†Rigney, Anthel M., T/5,
†Rigsbee, Archie, Pvt,
Riha, John D., 2nd Lt,
Rihn, John C., Pfc,
Riley, Clarence, Pfc,
Riley, James T., Pfc,
Riley, John M., Pfc,
*Riley, Lewis C., Pvt,
Riley, Reino P., Pfc,
Riley, William A., Pvt,
Riley, William M., Pfc,
Rill, Theron E., Pfc,
Rimington, Weston F., T/5,
Rinaldi, Francis O., Pvt,
Rinaldo, Anthony J., Sgt,
Rinchuso, Johnnie T., Pfc,
Rinda, Robert E., Pfc,
Rinehart, Hugh T., Pvt,
Rines, Harold G., Pfc,
Rines, Samuel M., Pfc,
Ringle, Clifford V., Sgt,
Rinkenberger, M. J., S/Sgt,
Rinkevich, Edward, Pvt,
Rinn, James P., Jr., Pvt,
Rion, Charles B., Pvt,
Rion, Robert H., Pfc,
‡Riordan, Eugene T., 2nd Lt,
Ripley, Merritt N., S/Sgt,
Rippee, Vernes E., Pvt,
†Risalvato, Joseph C., Pvt,
Riscinto, Nathaniel J., Pfc,
Risdale, Carrol S., T/Sgt,
Risk, Noel W., Pfc,
†Ristich, Michael P., Pvt,
Ritchie, Daniel, Pfc,
Ritchie, Evoy M., Pfc,
Ritchie, Harvey E., Sgt,
Ritchie, Willard, Pvt,
Ritenour, Roy W., Pfc,
Ritchard, Adam M., S/Sgt,
Rithmire, John, Jr., Pfc,
†Rittenhouse, Stanley, Pfc,
†Ritter, Raymond W., Pvt,
Ritter, Rex S., Pvt,
Ritter Rudolph R. T/5,
Ritter, Thomas P., Pfc,
†Rivera, Edward A., S/Sgt,
*Rivera, Teodoro, Pfc,
Rivera, Zoilo F., Sgt,
Rivera-Lopes, Juana J., Pvt,
Rivers, Anthony A., Sgt,
Rivers, Gerald F., Cpl,
Rivet, Joseph L., Pvt,
Rizzatti, Raymond, Pfc,
Rizzo, Ernest J., Pvt,
Roach, Hayes W., Pvt,
Roach, James E., Pvt,
Roach, John C., Pfc,
Roach, John W., S/Sgt,
Roach, Russell, Pfc,
Roach, William C., Pfc,
Roan, Ralph W., Pvt,
Robb, David J., 2nd Lt,
Robb, John H., Pfc,
§Robbins, Alvin J., Pvt,
Robbins, Charles, Jr., T/5,
Robbins, Fred J., Pfc,
Robbins, James H., Pfc,
Robbins, Lee R., Pvt,
‡Robbins, Loyd, Pfc,
Robbins, Maynard O., Pfc,
Robbins, Omer E., Pfc,
Robbins, Ralph E., Pvt,
Robbins, Ray J., T/5,
Robbins, Sam B., Pvt,
†Robblee, Peter L., Pvt,
Roberson, Glen E., Pfc,
†Robertelli, Pasquale A., Pvt,
‡Roberto, Jerry J., Pvt,
Roberts, Alfred J., Pfc,
Roberts, Arthur R., Pvt,
†Roberts, Buford J., Pfc,
Roberts, Burton B., Cpl,
Roberts, Carl E., Jr., Pvt,
Roberts, Carter, Pfc,
Roberts, Cecil E., Pfc,
Roberts, Charles W., Pfc,
Roberts, Edwin B., Pvt,
Roberts, Ernest I., Sgt,
Roberts, George C., Pfc,
Roberts, Gordon, T/Sgt,
†Roberts, Gordon W., Pfc,
†Roberts, Isaac D., Pfc,
Roberts, Jesse J., Pfc,
§Roberts, Laverne F., Pvt,
‡Roberts, Lee R., Pvt,
Roberts, Ray E., Pvt,
Roberts, Reginald G., Pvt,
Roberts, Richard, Pfc,
Roberts, William A., Pfc,
Robertson, Gerald D., Pvt,
Robertson, Henry G., Pfc,
Robertson, Ian, Pfc,
Robertson, James H., Pfc,
†Robertson, Lemuel C., Sr., Pfc,
Robertson, Ollie O., Sgt,
Robey, Robert L., Jr., T/5,
Robin, Simon E., Pfc,
Robinson, Bunnie, Pfc,
Robinson, Calvin E., Pvt,
†Robinson, Darol M., Pfc,
*Robinson, Donald B., Pvt,
Robinson, Donald F., Pvt,
Robinson, Earnest R., Pfc,
Robinson, Edward A., Pvt,
Robinson, Glenn H., Pfc,
Robinson, Henry G., Pfc,
Robinson, Kenneth W., T/5,
Robinson, Leon, Pvt,
Robinson, Lewis H., Pfc,
Robinson, Max W., Cpl,
Robinson, Melvin J., Pfc,
Robinson, Price, Jr., Pvt,
Robinson, Simeon R., Pfc,
Robinson, William A., Pfc,
Robison, Albert E., Cpl,
Robitailie, Dosithe J., Pfc,
Robitaille, Bertrand A., Pfc,
Robitaille, Joseph L., Pfc,
Robitaille, Raymond, Pfc,
Robowski, Raymond H., Capt,
Roby, Reynold G., Pfc,
Rocca, Joseph C., Pvt,
Rocca, Thomas F., Pvt,
†Rocchiccioli, Ralph, 1st Lt,
Rocha, John A., Sgt,
Roche, George D., Sgt,
Rockett, William C., Pvt,
Rockman, Marvin W., Pfc,
Rockwell, Edward F., Pfc,
Rockwell, Lee S., Sgt,
Rodal, Millard L., Pfc,
Roddy, Robert C., 1st Lt,
Roderick, Tom G., Jr., Pfc,
Rodger, Rutherford E., T/5,
Rodgers, Edwin, Pfc,
Rodgers, Gerald L., Pvt,
Rodgers, Robert G., Pfc,
Rodgers, Robert W., Pvt,
§Rodgers, William H., T/5,
†Rodkey, George L., T/5,
Rodman, Bert A., T/Sgt,
Rodrigue, Peter R., Sgt,
Rodrigues, Joao, Pvt,
Rodriguez, Alfred S., Pfc,
Rodriguez, Eleuterio, T/4,
Rodriguez, Frank M., Pvt,
‡Rodriguez, Louis P., Pvt,
Rodriguez, Ramon M., Cpl,
Rodriguez, William, T/5,
Rodvold, Marvin R. C., T/5,
Roe, Curtis W., Pfc,
Roe, James R., Pvt,
Roe, Kenneth E., Cpl,
Roeper, Lawrence A., Pvt,
Rogers, Buddy, Pfc,
†Rogers, Burl, Pfc,
Rogers, Dempsie O., Pvt,
Rogers, Frank S., Capt,
Rogers, Frank H., Jr., Pfc,
Rogers, Fred P., Pfc,
Rogers, Homer C., S/Sgt,
Rogers, James P., Pfc,
Rogers, Kenneth K., Pfc,
Rogers, Laurence B., 1st Sgt,
Rogers, Louis E., Pfc,
Rogers, Robert, Pvt,
Rogers, Wallace W., Sgt,
Rogers, William S., T/Sgt,
Rogowski, Leonard J., Pfc,
†Rohan, Samuel G., Pfc,
Rohde, George E., Sgt,
†Rohling, Gilbert L., Sgt,
Rohr, Joseph J., Pfc,
Rohrer, Donald W., Pfc,
Rojas, Donato, Jr., Pvt,
Rokes, Harold W., Pfc,
Roland, James T., Pvt,
Rolez, Everett A., CWO,
Rolinitis, Joseph A., Pfc,
†Rolke, William A., T/5,
Roller, Robert C., 2nd Lt,
Rollins, Walter E., Pvt,
†Roman, Michael, Pvt,
Roman, Rodolfo C., Cpl,
†Romano, Anthony J., Pvt,
Romano, Attilio, Pfc,
Romano, Dante, Pfc,
†Romano, Frank J., Pfc,
Romano, John J., T/4,
Romano, John J., Pfc,
Romanot, Peter P., Pvt,
Romanowski, Daniel, Pfc,
Romeo, Joseph, Cpl,
Romer, Alfred A., Pvt,
Romer, John, Pfc,
†Romero, Fred I., Pfc,
Romero, Pete G., Pfc,
‡Romero, Ralph L., Pvt,
Romero, Thomas F., Pfc,
Romo, Eilif, Sgt,
Roncevich, Tony A., Sgt,
Rondello, John, Pfc,
Ronneberg, Otmar S., Pfc,
Rood, Walter J., Pfc,
Rook, Franklin H., T/5,
‡Rooks, Gary C., Pvt,
Rooks, R. D., Pfc,
†Rooney, Walter F., Pfc,
Root, George L., Pfc,
Root, Landon E., Pvt,
*Ropp, Curtis M., Pfc,
†Rorer, David P., Jr., Pfc,
†Rosa, Nicholas J., Pfc,
Rosado, John, Pvt,
Rosales, Lupe C., Pvt,
Rosario, Antonio, Pfc,
Rosas, Franco A., Pfc,
Rosasco, Clyde E., Pfc,
Roscart, Charles W., Pvt,
Rosche, William A., Pvt,
†Rose, Arthur C., M/Sgt,
Rose, Bernard E., Sgt,
Rose, Earl M., Pfc,
Rose, Felix D., Pfc,
*Rose, Harry H., Pfc,
Rose, John H., Pvt,
Rose, Robert E., 2nd Lt,
Rose, Vernon E., Pfc,
†Rose, William E., Pfc,
Rosema, George J., Pfc,
†Rosema, Theodore A., Pvt,
Rosen, Morris, Pvt,
Rosen, Seymour, Pvt,
Rosenbaugh, Gerald R., Pfc,
Rosenberg, Philip, T/Sgt,
Rosenblatt, Louis, Pvt,
Rosenfelt, Guy A., Pvt,
Rosenheimer, Herbert, Pvt,
Rosenzweig, Harry, Pvt,
Rosetto, Charles P., Pvt,
Rosinski, Henry J., Pfc,
†Roslof, James H., Sgt,
Rosner, Arthur O., Pfc,
Rosplock, Joseph F., 1st Lt,
Ross, Addison L., 1st Sgt,
Ross, Alzie, Cpl,
†Ross, Carl, Pvt,
Ross, Dudley L., Pfc,
Ross, Ernest L., Pvt,
†Ross, Ernest N., Pfc,
Ross, Herschel I., Cpl,
Ross, James E., Pvt,
Ross, James J., Pvt,
Ross, John, Pfc,
Ross, Lester W., Pvt,
Ross, Robert H., Pfc,
Ross, Robert J., Pvt,
Ross, Sidney F., T/5,
Ross, Wade H., Pfc,
Rossi, James E., Pfc,
Rossi, John P., Pvt,
Rossi, Paul A., Pfc,
Rossilli, Acquilino P., Pvt,
Rossman, Kurt T., Pvt,
§Rossomondo, Angelo, Pvt,
Rosson, William B., Lt Col,
Rotell, William F., Pvt,
Roth, Albert C., Pvt,
†Roth, Randall C., Pvt,
Roth, Robert B., Pfc,
Rothberg, Jacob, Pfc,
Rothenberg, Jacob, Pfc,
Rothenberg, Max, Pvt,
†Rothermund, Darl R., Sgt,
‡Rothman, Julius, Sgt,
Rothrock, Frank P., Pvt,
Rotoli, Alfonse V., Pvt,
Rotrock, Frank, Cpl,
Rotter, David, Pvt,
Rouch, Wayne F., Pfc,
Roufs, Lee A., Sgt,
Roukas, George M., Pvt,
Rouse, Robert H.,
†Roush, Jacob R., Jr., Pfc,
Rousseau, Leon F., 2nd Lt,
Rousseau, Normand J., Pfc,
Rousseau, Ronald A., Pfc,
†Roux, Adrien J. P., Pvt,
Rovas, Joseph A., Pvt,
‡Rowan, George J., Pvt,
Rowan, Milton, Pfc,
Rowe, Joe, Pfc,
Rowe, John C., T/Sgt,
Rowe, Perry E., Capt,
Rowe, Ralph M., Pfc,
Rowett, Albert E., Pvt,
Rowland, Charles L., Pvt,
§Rowland, Edward R., Pfc,
§Rowland, William H., Pfc,
Rowland, William H., Pfc,
Rowles, Donald F., Pfc,
Roy, Raymond J., Pfc,
†Royer, Eugene J., Pfc,
Rozanel, Samuel, Pvt,
Rozier, William R., Jr., Pvt,
Rozniak, Joseph S.,
Ruark, Ernest W., Pfc,
Ruark, Walter R., T/5,
Rubano, Alfred N., Pfc,
Rubeia, Nello J., Pfc,
Rubeo, Ralph, Pfc,
Rubicky, Martin J., Sgt,
Rubin, Herbert, 2nd Lt,
Rubin, Hyma N., Pfc,
Rubin, Irving M., Pfc,
Rubin, Leonard, Sgt,
Rubino, Ciro, Pvt,
Ruby, Harold S., Pfc,
†Ruby, Howard M., Pvt,
Ruby, Hubert E., Pvt,
Ruby, John F., Sgt,
Rucker, Lee B., Pfc,
Rudar, Thomas J., Jr., Pvt,
Rudisill, Thomas R., Sr., Pfc,
Rudolph, John J., Pfc,
†Rudquist, George E., Pfc,
Ruff, Glenn R., Pfc,
§Rugen, Harold P.,
Ruggiero, James L., Pfc,
†Ruggiero, Rafael A., Pvt,
Ruggiero, Rocco M., Pvt,
Ruggiero, Vincent J., Pvt,
Ruggles, Stanley E., Pvt,
Ruh, Charles R., Pfc,
Ruhle, Gustave F., Pvt,
Ruhmann, Victor V., T/4,
Rule, Lester A., Jr., Pfc,
Rumbaugh, Harry B., Pfc,
Ruml, John B., Pfc,
Runberg, Rune, Pfc,
Runci, Michael F., T/5,
Runge, Warren C., Pfc,
Runnels, George W., Pfc,
Runion, William M., Pvt,
Runkle, Luther H., Pfc,
Runyan, Leo W., Pvt,
Ruoff, Edmund C., Pfc,
Ruotolo, Pasquale, Jr., Pfc,
Ruotolo, Renaldo J., Pvt,
Rupp, Harold, S/Sgt,
Ruscetta, Robert H., Pfc,
Rusert, Fred W., Pvt,
‡Rush, Gaston L., Pvt,
*Rush, Thomas D., Capt,
‡Rusher, James, Pvt,
Rusinek, Walter A., Pfc,
Rusis, Joseph N., Pfc,
Rusnak, John, Pfc,
Rusnak, John, Pvt,
Russ, Kenneth L., 2nd Lt,
Russeau, Lawrence R., Pfc,
†Russel, Alexander H., 1st Lt,
*Russell, Arthur A., Pvt,
Russell, Arthur W., Pvt,
Russell, Everett R., Pvt,
Russell, Floyd W., Pvt,
†Russell, Geran W., S/Sgt,
Russell, James E., T/Sgt,
Russell, James V., S/Sgt,
Russell, John A., S/Sgt,
Russell, John A., Pvt,
Russell, John H., Pfc,
Russell, L. B., 1st Lt,
Russell, Marcell K., Pvt,
Russell, Ray, Pvt,
Russell, Robert E., Pvt,
Russell, Roy L., Pvt,
Russell, William L., Pfc,
Russillo, Michael J., S/Sgt,
Russo, Anthony M., Pfc,
Russo, Anthony R., 2nd Lt,
Russo, Battiste P., Pfc,
Russo, Biagio J., Pvt,
Russo, Dominick, Pfc,
Russo, Frank J., Cpl,
Russo, Joseph, Pvt,
Russo, Michael C., Pvt,
‡Russo, Rocco J., Pvt,
Rutecki, Charles A., Pvt,
Rutherford, Fred, Pvt,
Rutherford, Ottis, Pfc,
‡Ruthledge, Vance B., Pvt,
Rutkin, Max, Pfc,
†Rutledge, Robert G., Pvt,
Ruvane, John A., Pfc,
Ruvarac, George, Pfc,
Ruvo, Sam P., Pfc,
Ruvolo, Michael, Pfc,
Ryan, Bernard J., Pfc,
Ryan, Clarence J., Pvt,
Ryan, Clifford A., Pfc,
Ryan, Edward J., Pfc,
Ryan, James C., 2nd Lt,
Ryan, Robert W., 1st Lt,
Ryan, Vincent G., Pfc,
Rybka, Jack J., Pvt,
Rychlak, Joseph A., Pvt,
Rychwalski, Joseph, Cpl,
Ryden, Carl F., Pfc,
Ryder, Lawrence J., S/Sgt,
Rydvall, August E., Pfc,
‡Ryley, Earl C., Pvt,
Rymer, John F., Pfc,
†Rynka, Gerard E., Pvt,
Ryon, Richard B., Pvt,
Rys, Eugene M., Pvt,
Rys, Winibald J., Pfc,
†Ryser, Cornelius J., S/Sgt,
Ryzinski, Stanley T., Cpl,

Sabatini, Armando A., Pfc,
Sabatino, Dominick, Pvt,
§Sabelic, Mike, Pvt,
Sabelia, Vincent A., Pvt,
Sabella, Gasper C., Pfc,
‡Sabetto, Angelo, Pvt,
Sabitino, Daniel, Pvt,
Sabre, Hollis L., Pvt,
Sackel, Sol, Pfc,
Sade, Albert L., Pfc,
Sadowski, John J., Pvt,
*Safdia, Abe, Pfc,
†Saffell, Richard J., Pfc,
Safiey, Robert H., 2nd Lt,
Sage, Herbert W., Jr., Pfc,
Sager, Roderick C., 2nd Lt,
Sailer, Alfred O., Pfc,

† Killed in Action. * Prisoner of War. ‡ Missing in Action. § Died of Wounds.

Saine, George R., Pvt,
Sainz, John R., Pfc,
§Sakocius, George C., Pfc,
Sakser, David P., Pvt,
Salach, Henry J., Pfc,
Salas, Alejandro L., Pvt,
Salatino, Pasquale J., Pvt,
‡Salazar, Jorge, Pvt,
Salazar, Manuel P., Pfc,
Salazar, Toby, S/Sgt,
‡Saldana, Jose M. Pvt,
Salee, Howard A., Pfc,
Salhany, George, Pvt,
‡Salicinski, Chester, Pfc,
Salipante, Nick, Pfc,
Salisbury, Oakley, Jr., S/Sgt,
Salitros, Stephen B., Pfc,
†Sallee, George C., Pvt,
Sallee, Orville C., M/Sgt,
Salley, Dan N., Pvt,
†Salmon, Thomas J., Pvt,
Salo, Oscar, Pfc,
Saltkill, Lewis C., Pfc,
Saltman, Elias, Pfc,
Saluskin, William, Sgt,
Salvagno, James V., Pvt,
Salvatto, Joseph, Jr., Pfc,
†Salveta, Leo, Pvt,
Salvi, Mario A., Pvt,
Salvo, Anthony, Pfc,
‡Salyers, Alfred, Pvt,
Samberg, Max, Pvt,
Sampieri, Orlando S., Pvt,
Sampieri, William S., Pvt,
Sampler, Herman F., Pvt,
†Samples, James V., Sgt,
Samples, John L., S/Sgt,
Samsky, Joe, Jr., Pvt,
Samson, James, S/Sgt,
†Samuels, John H., Pfc,
Samuelsen, Edward O., Cpl,
Samuelson, Gilbert F., Pfc,
‡Samuelson, Robert E., Pvt,
Sanchez, Antonio P., Pfc,
Sanchez, Christopher P., Pfc,
Sanchez, Conrado J., Pfc,
Sanchez, Jose C., Pvt,
†Sanchez, Regino B., Pfc,
Sand, Helge M., Pvt,
Sandback, Glenn E., Pfc,
Sanders, Archie R., Pfc,
Sanders, Claude H., Sgt,
Sanders, Edwin F., Pfc,
†Sanders, Henry, Pfc,
Sanders, Heston E., Pfc,
Sanders, James H., Pfc,
Sanders, John D., Pfc,
Sanders, Lloyd A., Pvt,
Sanders, Marvin C., Pfc,
Sanders, Robert W., Capt,
Sanders, Wilburn, Pvt,
Sanderson, Ellsworth R., Pvt,
Sanderson, Glenn E., Pfc,
Sandgkoski, Louis F., T/5,
‡Sandidge, Taylor W., Pfc,
Sandler, Harold H., 2nd Lt,
Sandonato, Henry L., Pvt,
†Sandusky, Joseph G., Pvt,
Sanfillippo, Paul P., Pvt,
§Sanford, Lewellyn, Pfc,
Sanicki, John C., Pfc,
Sank, Michael, Pfc,
Sanko, George, Pvt,
†Sannicandro, Rudolph A., Pvt,
Sansen, Karmer C., Pfc,
Santalone, John J., Pvt,
Santa Maria, Frank, Cpl,
Santancelo, Joseph, Pfc,
Santee, Eugene G., Pfc,
Santell, Saverio S., S/Sgt,
Santer, Joseph V., Pvt,
Santigago, George, Pfc,
Santilli, Anthony A., Pvt,
†Santillo, Joseph J., Pfc,
Santo, Joseph A., Pfc,
†Santonacita, Lewis, Pvt,
Santoro, Carmen P., S/Sgt,
Santos, Anthony G., Pvt,
Santos, Carlos, Pvt,
‡Sapia, Joseph P., Pfc,
Sapolin, Sidney, Pfc,
Sarao, Joseph J., Pvt,
Sarazin, Charles H., Jr., Pvt,
†Sardo, Pasquale, Pfc,
Sargent, James T., T/5,
†Sargent, Marvin, Pvt,
Sarkett, James, Pfc,
Sarsfield, William J., Pfc,
Sasala, Samuel L., Pfc,
‡Sasges, Francis J., S/Sgt,
Sasser, Henry H., Pvt,
†Sasso, Frank, Pfc,
‡Satiri, Lino, Pvt,
*Satterfield, Edward E., Pfc,
Satterfield, Joe M., Pfc,
‡Satterthwaite, Paul F., Pvt,
Satterthwaite, Richard D., Pvt,
Satterwhite, John F., Pfc,
Satterwhite, William, T/5,
Saucedo, Pedro L., Pfc,
Saunders, Robert P., Pvt,
Sauers, Roy R., Pfc,
Sausedo, Leo R., Pfc,
Savacool, John K., Cpl,
Savage, Lawrence S., Pfc,
†Savage, Raymond E., Pvt,
Savard, Ralph L., Pfc,
Saville, Walter C., Pvt,
Sawula, John W., Pfc,
‡Sawyer, Austin D., Pfc,
Sawyer, Clayton L., Pvt,
§Saylor, Leonard H., Pvt,
Sbernini, Emil, Pvt,
*Scaglione, James A., Pvt,
Scala, Anthony, Pvt,
Scalera, Peter V., Pfc,
Scalzo, Arthur O., Pvt,
Scammacca, Alfio, Pfc,
Scarano, Leo, Pvt,
Scarborough, Roger D., Pfc,
Scarbro, James D., Pfc,
Scardina, Leonard F., Sgt,
‡Scarf, John J., Jr., Pvt,
†Scarfo, Vincent, Pvt,
Scarpellini, Giziano J., Pvt,
‡Scarpinato, Joseph A., Pfc,
†Scates, Edward R., S/Sgt,
Scattum, Arthur H., Pfc,
Scepaniak, William, Pfc,
Schadel, Fred, Pfc,
Schaefer, Clifton H., Pfc,
Schafer, Ralph E., T/5,
Schaeffer, Dave, S/Sgt,
Schaffer, George F., Pfc,
Schaffer, Rueben E., Jr., T/5,
Schaeneman, Roy C., S/Sgt,
†Schaffer, Thomas A., Pfc,
Schake, Howard, Jr., Pfc,
Schaller, Roland, Pvt,
Schan, Charles C., Pvt,
Schander, Charles E., Pvt,
Schapp, Marvin, T/Sgt,
Scharich, Casper, Pvt,
†Schatz, Louis, Pvt,
Schaub, Harry, Pvt,
Schedler, Adolph H., Pvt,
Schehr, Charles F., Jr., Pfc,
Scheider, Edward R., Pvt,
‡Scheidler, Leroy C., Pvt,
Schell, Clarence H., Pfc,
Schell, James T., S/Sgt,
Schell, Nicholas P., Pfc,
Schemer, Philip, T/5,
†Schepkowski, T. V., S/Sgt,
Scheppman, Harold J., Pfc,
§Scherer, Arthur H., Pvt,
Schemenk, Bertrand J., Pfc,
Schepperd, Louis M., Pfc,
†Scherger, Thomas M., Pfc,
Schiare, Julius J., Pfc,
Schiavone, Samuel C., Pvt,
Schiefer, Edward, Pfc,
Schiele, Bert B., Sgt,
Schiff, Leon, Pvt,
Schihl, Clarence R., Pfc,
†Schindel, Fred J., Pvt,
Schipper, James A., Pfc,
Schiro, George A., Pfc,
Schkerke, Robert E., T/5,
†Schlaanstine, F. R., Sgt,
Schlapp, Charles F., T/4,
†Schlechte, Edwin J., Pvt
Schlegel, Carl H., S/Sgt,
Schlegel, Charles K., Pfc,
Schlegel, Walter N., Sgt,
Schleig, Daniel M., Pfc,
Schlichting, Glenn T., Pfc,
Schlindwein, John T., S/Sgt
Schlipstein, Solomon, Pvt,
Schloss, John, Pfc,
Schlotterbeck, Lloyd E., Cpl,
Schmer, Jacob, Pfc,
†Schmer, Wayne D., Sgt,
Schmerr, Andrew G., Jr., Pfc,
Schmickler, David, Pfc,
Schmid, Joseph H., Sgt,
Schmidt, George S., Sgt,
Schmidt, Gerald M., Pfc,
Schmidt, John N., 1st Lt,
Schmidt, William Pvt,
§Schmitt, Anthony P., Pvt,
Schmitt, David P., Pfc,
Schmitz, Walter H., Sr., Pfc,
Schmukler, Jerome H., Pfc,
Schnee, Harold A., Pvt,
Schneider, Joseph M., Cpl,
Schnitzler, James C., Pvt,
Schnitzler, Walter D., Pvt,
Schoeffler, Cecil R., Pfc,
Schoen, John J., Pvt,
†Schoenfeld, Melvin E., S/Sgt,
Schoenfeld, Woodrow J., Pfc,
Schoenk, William A., Pfc,
Schoenly, David H., Pfc,
Schoeny, George E., T/5,
Scholl, Wayne H., Pvt,
Schorg, Harold L., Pvt,
Schorgl, James J., Jr., Pvt,
Schott, Elwood T., Pvt,
Schreckengost, Thurl, Pfc,
Schreiber, Edward E., Pvt,
Schreiber, Paul R., Sgt,
Schrenk, Elmer C., S/Sgt,
Schrepfer, Glen C., Pvt,
Schroder, Wilfred H., Pvt,
Schroeder, Ralph E., Pfc,
Schroeder, Ernest H., Jr., Pvt,
§Schryver, Albert K., Pfc,
Schubert, Joseph, S/Sgt,
Schubert, Otto J., Pfc,
Schubowsky, Mike, Pvt,
Schuettenberg, William E., Pvt
Schuler, Robert R., Pfc,
†Schulman, Philip, Pvt,
Schulp, Cornelius G., Pfc,
Schulte, Elmer H., Pvt,
Schultz, Edward W., Sgt,
†Schultz, Ernest C., Sgt,
Schultz, Erwin M., 1st Lt,
Schultz, Gustav A., Pvt,
†Schultz, Harold A., 1st Lt,
Schultz, James W., Pfc
*Schultz, Wilfred R., Pvt,
Schultz, Willard R., Pvt,
Schumacher, Dale L., Pvt
Schumacher, James F., Pfc,
†Schumacher, John L., Pvt,
Schumacher, Robert D., S/Sgt,
Schurz, Robert A., Pfc,
Schuss, John A., Pvt,
§Schuster, John W., Pfc,
†Schuster, Joseph, Jr., Pfc,
†Schutt, Melvin J., Jr., Pfc,
Schutt, Merle E., Pvt,
Schuurman, Kenneth A., Pvt,
†Schwab, William, T/Sgt,
Schwan, Richard D., Pfc,
Schwartz, Arthur, Pvt,
Schwartz, Carl C., T/5,
Schwartz, George A., Pfc,
Schwartz, Louis H., Pvt,
Schwartz, Louis H., Pfc,
Schwartz, Max, Pfc,
Schwartz, Raymond, Pfc,
Schwarze, Clarence R., Sgt,
Schwebel, Louis H., Pvt,
Schweinfurth, William R., Pvt,
Schweitzberger, Wm. T., Pvt,
†Schweitzer, Harold A., Pfc,
Schwiers, Henry O., Pfc,
†Sciabarra, Carlo, Pvt,
Sciabica, Joseph C., Pvt,
‡Scillion, Floyd E., Pfc,
Scimeca, Vincent, Pvt,
Sciullo, Jack, Pfc,
Sclinick, Joseph H., Pvt,
Scoggins, Arthur F., Pvt,
Scolopio, Emilio M., Pfc
§Scothorn, George M., Pvt,
Scott, Alexander, Pvt,
Scott, Anthony L., Jr., Pfc,
Scott, Charles W., Pvt,
Scott, Dave F., Sgt,
Scott, Donald L., Cpl,
Scott, Donald L., Pvt,
Scott, Donald Y., Pfc,
‡Scott, Elwood, Pfc,
Scott, Ervin, T/5,
†Scott, Fred A., Pvt,
†Scott, George W., Pfc,
Scott, Glenn H., Pfc,
Scott, Irving, Pfc,
Scott, James A., Pfc,
Scott, James J., Pvt,
Scott, Lloyd W., Pvt,
Scott, Marion H., Sr., Pfc,
Scott, Raymond L., Pvt,
*Scott, Spencer J., Pvt,
Scott, Thomas H., Cpl,
Scribner, David P., Pfc,
Scroggin, Ralph, Pfc,
†Scroghines, Raymond, Pfc,
Scull, Charles R., Pvt,
‡Scully, Paul, 1st Lt
†Scully, Thomas H., 2nd Lt
†Sea, Sidney C., Pfc,
Seacatt, Hendricks H., Cpl,
Seagraves, Walker M., Pfc,
Seal, Millard V., Pfc,
‡Search, Lewis H., Pfc,
†Sears, Edwin C., Pvt,
Sears, Herman F., Pfc,
Sears, James H., Pvt,
Sears, Merle W., Pfc,
Seaton, Thomas W., 1/Sgt,
Seay, Furman R., 2nd Lt,
Secchiutti, Mario, Pvt,
Seckman, John P., Sgt,
Seculo, Joe, S/Sgt,
Sedlak, Michael J., T/5,
Sedwick, Richard J., Pfc,
†See, Barnett J., Sgt,
See, Charles B., Sgt,
See, Deforest M., Pfc,
‡See, Preston A., Pvt,
Seek, Richard R., Jr., Pvt,
Seely, John W., Pfc,
*Seelye, Floyd W., Sgt,
Seeman, Myron L., Pvt,
Seems, Lenard L., T/4,
Seen, Wong G., T/5
Seevers, George I., 2nd Lt,
Seewer, Albert E., Pfc,
Seft, Joseph F., Pvt,
Segel, Peter, Pfc,
Seger, George G., T/5,
‡Segler, Charles E., Jr., 2nd Lt,
Segroves, Rupert L., Pfc,
Seguine, Charles W., Sgt,
Segura, Leonardo L., Pvt,
Seibert, Harold K., Pvt,
Seibert, James P., Pfc
Seibert, William J., Pfc,
†Seif, Paul F., Pvt,
Seid, Rubin, Pvt,
Seifarth, Charles K., 1st Lt,
Seifert, Joseph M., Pfc,
Seim, Morris, Pvt,
Seitz, Davis B., Pfc,
Seitz, James E., S/Sgt
†Sekusky, Harold E., Pfc,
Self, Charles H., T/5,
Self, Harmon E., T/Sgt,
§Self, Loise J., Pfc,
Self, L. V., Pfc,
†Sell, Gerhardt W., Pvt,
Selland, Arents B., Pfc,
Sellini, Sam, Jr., Pvt,
†Seltenright, John R., Pfc,
Selvog, Samuel J., 1st Lt,
Semanik, Rudolph R., Sgt,
Semple, Lynn J., Pvt,
†Senatore, Frank, Pvt,
Seneca, Mario A., Pfc,
Senek, John, Jr., Pvt,
Senic, George, 1st Lt,
Sennett, Conrad L., Pvt,
Sennezy, Leon, Pfc,
‡Sensenbach, George G., Pfc,
Sentell, Philip H., Pfc,
Senti, Florian D., Pfc,
Sequin, Louis J., Pfc,
Sercos, Francisco, Pvt
Sereno, Francis C., Cpl,
Serrano, David G., Pvt,
Servidio, Sam, Pfc,
Sesma, Raymond H., Pfc,
Sessamen, Scott W., Pfc,
Setterbo, Lawrence B., Pvt,
Settle, Dorsey E., Pfc,
Settles, Edward L., S/Sgt,
§Setzkorn, Irvin R., Cpl,
Seubert, Gustave E., Pfc,
Severi, Claude, Pfc,
Severn, Keith L., Pfc,
Sevier, Thomas H., Pfc,
Sevigny, Henry J., Pfc,
Sevigny, Raymond A., Pfc,
Seward, Patrick M., Pvt,
Sewell, James R., T/Sgt,
†Sexton, Earl, Pvt,
Sexton, Edward V., Pfc,
Sexton, Elmer C., Pvt,
Sexton, Howard S., Pvt,
Seyller, Marlowe E., Pfc,
Seymour, Guy B., Pvt
Seymour, Warren J., Pfc,
Seymour, Willard K., S/Sgt,
Seymoure, Everett E., Pvt,
Shack, Michael, Pvt,
Shadle, Malcolm B., Pfc,
Shafer, Calvin M., Pvt
Shafer, William, Pvt,
Shaffer, Clyde W., Pfc,
Shaffer, Herbert M., T/4,
Shaffer, John J., Pfc,
†Shaffer, Robert H., S/Sgt,
Shaffner, Aaron, Pvt,
Shain, Joseph, Pvt,
Shakir, Shakir, Pfc,
Shalf, William A., Pfc,
Shallenberger, Vinton C., Pfc,
†Shemirian, Shamir, Pvt,
Shanahan, Robert C., Pfc,
Shanaman, Milton A., Pvt,
Shaner, William A., Jr., Pfc,
†Shank, Earl L., Pvt,
Shank, Orlando J., Jr., Pvt,
Shannon, Glenn L., Pvt,
Shannon, Robert, Pfc,
Shannon, Robert M., 1st Lt,
Shannon, Vincent J., S/Sgt,
†Shannon, William A., Jr., Pfc,
Shapansky, John E., T/5,
Shapiro, Bernard, Sgt,
†Shapiro, Bernard M., Pvt,
Shapiro, Sidney, Pvt,
Shapiro, William, Pfc,
Shapro, Peter S., Pvt,
Sharbono, Leonard J., Pfc,
†Sharol, Teddy W., Sgt,
*Sharp, Edward A., Pvt,
Sharp, James B., Pfc,
Sharp, Robert J., Pfc,
Sharpe, Barney E., Pfc,
Shater, George, Pvt,
*Shatzer, John A., Pfc,
Shaw, Charles D., Pvt
Shaw, Earl P., Pfc,
Shaw, Hubert M., T/5,
Shaw, James G., Sgt,
Shaw, James J., Pfc,
Shaw, Kenneth D., Pfc,
Shaw, Lawrence V., Pfc,
Shaw, Norman, T/Sgt,
Shaw, Robert W., Pfc,
Shaw, Travis P., Pfc.
Shawver, Ralph N., Pfc,
Shawver, Thomas B., Pvt,
†Shay, Everett A., Pfc,
Shea, John E., Pfc,
Shea, John H., Jr., Pfc,
Sheaffer, Kenneth M., Pvt,
Sheaffer, Leon M., T/4,
Shean, Frank R., Pvt,
‡Sheats, James B., T/5,
Shedd, Roy L., Pvt,
†Sheehan, John J., Pvt,
Sheehan, Lawrence E., Pvt,
Sheffield, James R., Pvt,
*Sheffield, Robert E., Sgt,
Sheidow, Carlton R., Jr., Pvt,
Sheldon, Glen E., Pvt,
Shell, Rodger W., Pvt,
Shell, Thomas E., Pfc,
Shelley, James B., Pvt,
Shelley, Martin J., Pfc,
Shellito, Joseph E., Pfc.
Shelton, Charles T., Pvt,
Shelton, Elmer J., Pfc,
Shelton, Joseph P., Pvt,
†Shelton, Simon P., S/Sgt,
Shendock, John E., T/5,
Shepard, Joseph E., 1st Lt,
Shepard, Russell D., Pfc,
Shephard, Dennie V., Sgt,
Shepherd, Edwin W., 2nd Lt,
Shepherd, Elmer V., T/4,
Shepherd, James C., Sr., Pfc,
‡Shepherd, Julian, Pfc,
Shepherd, Keith A., Pvt,
Shepherd, Warren R., Pfc,
Sheppard, Earl R., Sgt,
Sherba, John, Pvt,
Sherbondy, Herbert L., Pvt,
Sherbondy, Wilbur E., Pfc,
Sherd, Leonard F., Pfc,
Sheridan, Lloyd M., S/Sgt,
Sherman, Alfred A., Pvt,
Sherman, Burton L., Pfc,
Sherman, Ellsworth M., Pvt,
Sherman, George A., Cpl,
Sherman, Harry B., Col,
Sherman, Joseph J., Jr., Pvt
Sherman, Joseph R., Pfc,
Sherman, Thomas J., 1/Sgt,
Sherrill, Charles H., Pfc,
Sherrod, Homer D., Sgt,
Shick, Wayne L., Pfc,
Shields, David G., Pvt,
Shields, James, Pvt,
Shields, Maxel, Pfc,
Shields, Robert F., Pvt,
†Shiepko, Anthony T., Pfc,
‡Shiffman, Sidney B., 2nd Lt,
Shimko, John A., Jr., S/Sgt,
Shimp, Lewis L., Pfc,
Shiner, Alfred J., Pvt,
Shinn, Frank M., Pfc,
Shinnamon, George E., Sgt,
Shinsky, Paul E., Pfc,
Shipe, James M., Pfc,
Shipley, Clarence T., 1st Lt,
Shipley, James R., Jr., Pfc,
Shipley, Woodrow, Pfc,
Shipman, Donald O., Pfc,
Shipp, Gaines, Pvt,
Shipp, James R., S/Sgt,
Shipp, Loyd L., Pfc,
Shippell, Raymond J., Sgt,
Shippen, Russell R., Pfc,
Shirey, James F., Pfc,
Shirey, Ralph T., Pfc,
Shirk, Clarence B., Pfc,
Shirk, Howard J., Pfc,

† Killed in Action. * Prisoner of War. ‡ Missing in Action. § Died of Wounds.

Shirk, Martin R., 2nd Lt,
Shives, William C., S/Sgt,
†Sholley, Glenn L., Pfc,
Shocklee, Richard A., Pvt,
Shoemaker, Brooke G., Pfc,
Shoemaker, Warren A., Pfc,
Shomin, Nick N., Pfc,
Shook, Gordon C., Pfc,
Shook, James F., Pfc,
Shook, Perry L., Pfc,
Shook, William E., Pvt,
Shor, Jacob, Pvt,
Shore, Robert J., Pfc,
Shores, Archie L., Pvt,
Shorey, Fred L., T/4,
§Short, Glenn E., Sgt,
†Short, Harlan, Pfc,
†Short, Willard A., Pvt,
Short, William M., Pfc,
Shortencarrier, Leo F., Pfc,
Shotts, V. A., Cpl,
Shoup, Claude A., Pvt,
†Showers, Leroy B., Pfc,
Shows, James, T/Sgt,
Shreve, Merrill E., T/5,
Shriver, Charles I., Pfc,
‡Shryack, Charles E., Pvt,
†Shuey, Thomas G., Pvt,
Shuler, Herman L., Pfc,
Shuler, Oran D., Pvt,
Shulik, Saul M., Pvt,
†Shull, Elmer J., Pfc,
†Shull, Homer P., Pfc,
Shultz, Albert L., Sgt,
Shultz, Albert E., S/Sgt,
Shultz, Arthur P., Pfc
Shumway, Howard H., T/5
Shupe, James H., Pvt,
Shure, David L., Pfc,
Shyock, Howard, Pvt,
Sibich, Nicholas R., Pfc,
Sichau, Albert G., Pfc,
Sicley, Robert J., Pfc,
*Sidel, Charles L., Pvt,
‡Sidener, Emmett P., S/Sgt,
Sider, Louis E., Pvt,
‡Sideri, Pasquale P., Pvt,
Siderio, Alfred C., Pfc,
Siders, William M., Pvt,
Sides, Louie H., Pfc,
Sidwell, Carl C., Pfc,
Siebrasse, Albert L., Pvt,
Siefert, Walter R., Pfc,
†Siegel, Martin, Pfc,
Siegel, Marvin, Pfc,
Siegel, Meyer, 2nd Lt,
Siegel, Murray M., Sgt,
Siegel, Morris, Pvt,
Siegel, Rueben A., S/Sgt,
Siegel, Sanford, Pfc,
Siegel, Theodore, T/4,
Siegel, Franz, 2nd Lt,
Siegeltuch, Martin W., Pvt,
Siffling, Albert, Pvt,
Sigler, Donald L., Pvt,
†Sigmon, Lewis E., Pvt,
Sigmon, Maymon E., Sgt,
Signorelli, Vito J., Pvt,
Sikora, Frank S., Pvt,
Silberman, Arthur I., Pvt,
Silberman, Jack, Cpl,
†Silberstein, Norman, Pfc,
Silkowitz, Harry, Pfc,
Sills, Charlie E., Pfc,
†Silovich, Joseph M., Pvt,
Silva, Albert H., Pvt,
Silva, Antone, Pfc,
Silva, Antonio Lima, Pvt,
Silvas, Jose M., Pfc,
Silvas, Ygnacio E., Pvt,
†Silveira, Joseph G., Pfc,
Silver, Warren L., Pfc,
Silverman, Frederick, Sgt,
Silvers, Nathaniel M., T/4,
Silvey, Chester L., Pvt,
Silvey, Donald S., T/5,
†Silvia, John H., Pvt,
Simcic, Rudolph J., Pfc,
†Sime, Richard C., 2nd Lt,
Simigliano, Joseph J., Pvt,
Simmerman, Charles R., Pfc,
Simmerman, W. C., Jr., Pfc,
Simmons, Boyd L., T/5,
Simmons, David F., Pvt,
Simmons, Guy L., Jr., Pvt,
Simmons, Frank F., Pfc,
*Simmons, Irwin E., Pfc,
*Simmons, Jesse E., Pvt,
†Simmons, Marcus A., Sgt,
Simmons, Max L., Pfc,
Simmons, Merlin J., Pfc,
Simmons, Rayford, Pvt,
Simmons, Robert W., 2nd Lt,
Simms, Charles T., Pvt,
Simokauskas, W. F., Pfc,
†Simon, Harold J., Pvt,
Simon, Henry J., S/Sgt,
Simon, Irving J., Pfc,
Simon, Isidore M., Pfc,
Simon, Paul A., Pvt,
‡Simonds, Cleo J., Pfc,
Simonds, Clyde, Pfc,
Simoneaux, Norman J., Pfc,
Simonelis, Peter A., Sgt,
Simons, Fowler E., Pvt,
Simpson, Daniel E., T/5,
Simpson, David R., Pfc,
Simpson, George W., Jr., Pfc,
Simpson, James M., Pfc,
Simpson, James V., T/Sgt,
Simpson, Kenneth C., Pfc,
†Simpson, Leonard F., Pfc,
§Simpson, Leonard P., Pfc,
Simpson, William R., Jr., Cpl,
Simpson, Willis J., Pvt,
Sims, Charles H., Pfc,
Sims, Howard W., Pvt,
Sims, James F., Pfc,
Sims, James M., Pvt,
Sims, William T., Pfc,
Sinclair, Edmund B., Maj,
Sinclair, Victor E., Lt Col,
Singer, Earl H., Capt,
Singer, Edward B., Pfc,
Singer, Harry, Pfc,
Singleton, Mark, Pfc,
Singo, Oran R., Pfc,
Sinkler, Bruce R., Cpl,
‡Sinon, Cornelius M., Pvt,
Sinsel, Frank C., Maj.,
Sinyakovich, John, Pvt,
†Sipe, Warren H., Pfc,
Siperstein, Herbert B., Pfc,
Sipple, Valen R., Pfc,
Siqueiros, Peter B., Pfc,
Sites, Willard D., S/Sgt,
Sitton, Elmer F., T/5,
Sitzle, Sidney D., Pvt,
Sivak, Michael, Pvt,
Siwek, Charles, Pfc,
Sizemore, Ernest B., Pfc,
Skaggs, Francis E., T/5,
Skallerup, James R., Pvt,
Skarwecki, Joseph J., 2nd Lt,
Skea, Edward I., Pfc,
Skeen, Harold H., Pvt
Skeff, George J., Pfc,
Skeldon, Harold M., Pvt,
Skettini, Edward, Pfc,
Skibicki, Caszmir V., Pvt,
Skibinski, George P., Pfc,
Skibitsky, Fred, T/5,
‡Skidmore, George W., Pvt,
Skidmore, William, Jr., Pfc,
Skinner, Ivon L., Pfc,
Skipper, Herbert C., M/Sgt,
†Skiver, Delielle, Pfc,
*Skladzien, John S., Pvt,
Sklodowski, Anthony E., Pfc,
Skoglund, Albert B., Pfc,
Skovley, Gehard L., Pfc,
‡Skowronski, Louis F., Pvt,
Skryantz, John J., Pvt,
Skrypko, Andrew J., Pvt,
Skrzypek, John S., Pfc,
†Slape, Raymond W., Pvt,
Slatt, Tom, Pvt,
Slatylak, Joseph, Pvt,
Slaughter, J. E., Pvt,
Slaughter, Robert B., Sgt,
†Slavick, Joseph A., Pvt,
Slavik, Francis A., T/5,
Slavin, Paul, Pvt,
Slavinski, John W., Pfc,
Slaw, Paul A., 1st Lt,
Slawkowski, Ignatius J., Cpl,
Slay, James W., S/Sgt,
Sledge, Hugh F., Pvt,
Slemp, William E., Sgt,
Slezak, Johnnie, Pfc,
*Slice, Alvin J., Pvt,
Slier, Andrew, Pvt,
Slish, John F., Pfc,
Sliva, Robert J., Pvt,
Sloan, Arthur M., T/5,
§Sloan, William J., Pvt,
‡Sloane, John C., Pvt,
Slobin, Jacob I., Pvt,
Slobodian, William S., Pvt,
†Slockbower, Edward W., Pfc,
Slone, Clinen, Pfc,
Slowikowski, Zdzislaf I., S/Sgt.
Sluder, Martin C., Pfc,
Smadley, George A., Pfc,
Smail, William J., Pfc,
Smalec, Stanley J., Pfc,
Small, Max A., Cpl,
Small, Thomas R., Sgt,
Small, Thomas S., Pvt,
Smallen, Cooper, Pfc,
Smalley, Paul A., Pfc,
Smallwood, Harry M., Sgt,
Smarr, Grover C., Pfc,
Smart, Alvin L., Pfc,
Smart, William Taylor, Sgt,
Smartt, James E., T/5,
Smedley, Richard E., Pfc,
Smeenge, Gerald H., Pfc,
Smeltzer, Lafean S., Pvt,
Smerillo, Michael J., Sgt,
Smetak, Robert A., S/Sgt,
Smey, Peter, Pvt,
Smith, Aaron E., Pfc,
Smith, Alexander, Pvt,
‡Smith, Arlie L., Pvt,
†Smith, Arnold, Pvt,
Smith, Arnold F., Pvt,
Smith, Arthur J., Jr., Lt Col
Smith, Bill, Pvt,
Smith, Bernell, Cpl,
†Smith, Boyd, Pfc,
Smith, Casper A., Jr., Pvt,
Smith, Cecil C., Pvt,
‡Smith, Cecil H., Pvt,
†Smith, Charles A., Jr., Pvt,
Smith, Charles E., Pvt,
†Smith, Charles E., Pvt,
Smith, Charles W., Pfc,
Smith, Charles W., Pvt,
Smith, Clarence C., Pfc,
§Smith, Clifford B., T/5,
Smith, Clinton E., Cpl,
†Smith, Corwin J., Pvt,
Smith, Cyril E., Cpl,
Smith, David J., Pfc
Smith, Dee, Pvt,
Smith, Dewey E., Pfc,
Smith, Donald E., Pfc,
Smith, Donald F., Pfc,
Smith, Donald G., Pvt,
Smith, Donald K., T/4,
Smith, Donald V., Pfc,
Smith, Douglas, Cpl,
Smith, Earl A., Pfc,
Smith, Edgar J., Pvt,
Smith, Edward E., Pvt,
‡Smith, Edward W., Pfc,
Smith, Elbert M., Pvt,
Smith, Emerald M., T/4,
Smith, Eugene, Pfc,
Smith, Eugene F., T/4,
Smith, Floyd D., Pvt,
Smith, Frank S., Cpl,
Smith, Fred A., Sgt,
Smith, Fred M., Pfc,
Smith, Freddie R., S/Sgt,
Smith, Forrest L., Jr., Cpl,
Smith, George A., Pfc,
Smith, George E., Pfc,
Smith, George W., Pfc,
Smith, Gerald H., Jr., Pfc,
†Smith, Gilbert L., Pfc,
Smith, Glen E., Pfc,
Smith, Grover C., Jr., Pfc,
Smith, Guy W., Pvt,
Smith, Harold C., Sgt,
Smith, Harold E., Pfc,
§Smith, Harold L., Pfc,
Smith, Harry B., Pfc,
Smith, Herbert E., Pfc,
Smith, Herbert G., Pfc,
Smith, Herbert T., Pvt,
Smith, Hiram B., Pvt,
Smith, Hoke L., Pvt,
Smith, Howard A., Pfc,
Smith, Howard B., Pvt,
Smith, Howard G., Pvt,
Smith, Howard L., Pvt,
Smith, Hugh D., 1st Lt,
*Smith, Jack E., Pfc,
Smith, James C., 2nd Lt,
Smith, James E., T/5,
Smith, James E., Pvt,
†Smith, James E., Pfc,
Smith, James G., S/Sgt,
Smith, James S., Pfc
Smith, James M., Pvt,
†Smith, James V., Sgt,
Smith, James W., Pfc,
‡Smith, Jerome I., Pfc,
Smith, Jesse L., Sr., Pfc,
Smith, Joe C., Pfc,
‡Smith, John C., Pvt,
Smith, John F., Pvt,
Smith, John H. E., Cpl,
Smith, John L., Pfc,
Smith, John R., Pvt,
Smith, John T., Pfc,
†Smith, John W., Pvt,
Smith, Johnnie A., Pfc,
Smith, Joseph V., Pfc,
Smith, Joyce M., Pfc,
Smith, Karl E., Pvt,
Smith, Kelsie F., Sgt,
Smith, Kenneth, Pvt,
Smith, Kenneth D., T/4,
Smith, Kyle S., Jr., Cpl,
Smith, Lanceford W., Pfc,
§Smith, Lawrence O., Pfc,
Smith, Lawrence R., Pfc,
Smith, Lee R., Pfc,
Smith, Leonard P., T/5,
Smith, Lewis B., T/5,
Smith, Lloyd L., Pfc,
Smith, Mack H., Pfc,
Smith, Mannie G., Jr., 1/Sgt,
Smith, Marion N., Sr., Pfc,
Smith, Merlin J., Pvt,
Smith, Murlan F., Capt,
†Smith, Nevin K., Pfc,
Smith, Noble M., Pvt,
Smith, Noland H., Pvt,
†Smith, Norvel C., Sgt,
‡Smith, Pat H., Jr., Pvt,
‡Smith, Paul E., Pfc,
Smith, Ralph H., S/Sgt,
*Smith, Raymond W., 2nd Lt,
Smith, Reno, Pfc,
Smith, Richard A., Maj,
†Smith, Richard E., Pvt,
Smith, Riley, Sgt,
Smith, Robert C., Sgt,
†Smith, Robert E., Pfc,
Smith, Robert R., 2nd Lt,
Smith, Rock, Pfc,
Smith, Rome F., Pfc,
Smith, Roscoe R., Sgt,
Smith, Roy E., Pfc,
Smith, Roy L., Pvt,
Smith, Rufus R., Sr., Pfc,
Smith, Russell E., Pfc,
Smith, Sidney L., Pvt,
†Smith, Stanley E., Pfc,
Smith, Stanley L., Pfc,
Smith, Terrell G., Pfc,
Smith, Thomas G., Pfc,
Smith, Thomas H., T/Sgt,
‡Smith, Thomas J., Pvt,
Smith, Thomas T., Pfc,
Smith, T. W., T/5,
Smith, Victor Q., Pfc,
Smith, Virgil W., Jr., 1st Lt,
†Smith, Wallace R., Pfc,
Smith, Walter, Pvt,
Smith, Walter J., Pvt,
Smith, Walter, Jr., Pfc,
Smith, W. C., Pfc,
Smith, Wesley G., Pfc,
†Smith, Wilbur L., Pvt,
Smith, William H., 2nd Lt,
Smith, William L., Sgt,
Smith, William R., T/5,
Smith, William T., Pvt,
Smith, Zay D., S/Sgt,
†Smitherman, Robert W., 1st Lt,
Smithhart, James G., Pfc,
Smithson, Kenneth L., Sgt,
Smoak, Dan E., Pvt,
†Smock, Burdt W., S/Sgt,
Smolen, Edward W., Pvt,
Smolik, Milan S., Pfc,
Smolk, John F., Sgt,
Smrtic, William H., Pfc,
Smulck, John J., Pfc,
Snair, Earl C., Pvt,
Snarsky, Henry L., Pvt,
†Snead, Ernest H., S/Sgt,
Snead, Joseph S., S/Sgt,
†Sneckenberger, Robert J., Sgt,
Snell, Joseph A., Pvt,
Snell, Robert B., Sgt,
Snellenborger, Lenn A., T/Sgt,
Snellina, Joseph E., Pvt
†Snidarich, John F., Pvt,
†Snider, Wilburn S., Pvt,
Snow, James S., Pvt,
‡Snow, Kinzer M., S/Sgt,
Snow, Peter F., Pvt,
Snow, Richard L., Sgt,
‡Snow, Robert B., S/Sgt,
Snowden, Willard A., Pvt,
Snyder, Arthur D., Pvt,
†Snyder, Carl J., Pvt,
Snyder, Edwin D., Cpl,
§Snyder, Frederich P., 1st Lt,
Snyder, Harold G., Sgt,
Snyder, James R., Pfc,
Snyder, Joseph J., Pvt,
Snyder, Kenneth E., S/Sgt,
Snyder, Lowell R., Pfc,
‡Snyder, Morris F., T/Sgt,
Snyder, Myron R., Pfc,
Snyder, Norman, Pfc,
Snyder, Richard A., T/5,
Snyder, Robert L., Pfc,
Snyder, Verlin K., Pfc,
Snyder, Warren, 1st Lt,
Sobatka, John J., Sgt,
Sobel, Wilbur, Pvt,
Sobiesiak, John, Pfc,
Sobin, Thomas J., Pfc,
Soblesky, James P., Pfc,
Sobolewski, Frank, 1st Sgt,
Sobuta, Edward A., 2nd Lt,
Soccio, Angelo T., Pvt,
Sochacki, Edward A., Pfc,
Socie, George R., Sgt,
Sodano, Thomas C., Cpl,
Soderberg, Robert G., T/5,
Soderberg, Wendell V., Pvt,
Soderholm, Edward J., Pvt,
Soderman, Robert M., Pfc,
Soderquist, Sven F., Pvt,
Soen, Pete, Pvt,
Soffriti, Arrigo A., Pvt,
Sofia, Joseph, Pvt,
Sofranek, Joseph, Pvt,
†Soja, Edward F., Pfc,
Sokal, Andrew, Pfc,
Sokal, Anthony, Sgt,
Soland, Raymond T., T/5,
Solarz, Albert F., T/5,
†Soley, William L., Pvt,
Solivoda, Joseph, Pfc,
Solomon, Milton A., T/5,
Solomon, Warren M., Capt,
Soltis, John B., Cpl,
†Solver, Richard A., Pvt,
Solvith, Marvin, Cpl,
Sombs, Carl J., Pfc,
Somerville, Donald P., Pvt,
§Somma, Albert C., Pfc,
†Sondelski, Zig J., Sgt,
Sonner, Thomas G., Pvt,
Sons, Newton E., Pfc,
Soos, Joseph, Jr., Pfc,
Sopestal, Charles G., Pfc,
Sopkwiak, Edward L., Pvt,
†Sorber, George W., Pvt,
Sorenson, William M., Sgt,
Soro, John F., Pvt,
Soroka, Harry G., Pvt,
Soskil, Morris, Pfc,
Sosnowski, Alexander, S/Sgt,
Soto, Clarence E., T/5,
†Soto, Hector M., Pvt,
Soto, Lawrence F., Pfc,
Soucy, Leo L., Pvt,
Soules, John H., Jr., 1st Lt,
Soulliere, Richard R., 1st Lt
Soult,Harold L., Pvt,
South, Lloyd K., S/Sgt,
Southards, Harrison, Pvt,
Southey, Maurice B., Pvt,
Southmayd, Gale E., Pfc,
Southworth, Tommy G., Sgt,
‡Souza, Charles R., Pfc,
Sowers, Walter E., Pvt,
Soyster, Russell J., Sgt,
Space, Paul Jerome, S/Sgt,
Spadavecchia, Albert B., Pvt,
‡Spading, Robert L., Pvt,
†Spadoni, Reynold L. J., Pfc,
Spaeth, Dean W., S/Sgt,
Spagano, Anthony, Pvt,
Spahn, Earl H., Pvt,
Spahr, Rolfe A., Sgt,
Spain, Joe, Pvt,
Spain, Richard E., Sgt,
†Spallina, Joseph E., Pvt,
Spangler, Arvil D., Sgt,
Spanhake, George W., S/Sgt,
Spanovich, Mike M., Pfc,
Sparacio, Anthony J., Pfc,
§Spark, Albert J., Sgt,
Sparkman, Jess T., Pfc,
Sparks, Don O., Pfc,
Sparks, Frank W., Pfc,
Sparks, Richard M., Sgt,
Spaulding, Edward A., Pvt,
Spaziano, Umberto, Sgt,
Spazo, Edward G., Pvt,
Spear, Vernon D., Pfc,
†Spearing, Everett J., Sgt,
Spears, Bredua D., Pfc,
Spears, Bryant, Pvt,
Spears, Eugene E., S/Sgt,
Spears, Georgie, Pfc,
Spears, James M., Pfc,
Speciale, Anthony J., 2nd Lt,
Speckman, Raymond A., Pfc,
†Spector, Bernard, Pvt,
Spector, Reuben, Pfc,
Speedy, Malverne E., Pvt,
Speer, Willibie D., Pfc,
Spellman, Henry M., Pvt,
†Spence, Elmer R., Pvt,
†Spence, John T., Pfc,
Spence, Harold E., Pfc,
†Spencer, Albert L., Pvt,
†Spencer, Edward S., S/Sgt,
Spencer, James M., Pfc,
†Spencer, Leslie V., Pfc,

† Killed in Action. * Prisoner of War. ‡ Missing in Action. § Died of Wounds.

IN WORLD WAR II 473

Spencer, Ralph E., Jr., Pfc,
Spencer, Raymond M., Pfc,
Spencer, Rodrick B., Pfc,
Sperati, Carmen R., Pfc,
Spernyak, George E., Pfc,
Sperry, Gerald R., Pvt,
Spetland, Carl, Pvt,
‡Spicer, McElroy, Pfc,
†Spidle, Jack D., Pfc,
Spiegle, Harry, Jr., Pvt,
Spiess, Gordon H., Pvt,
Spilde, Le Verne H., Sgt,
Spilker, Carl J., S/Sgt,
Spiller, Frank, Pvt,
Spillman, John A., Jr., Pvt,
Spindanger, Thomas E., 2nd Lt
‡Spindler, Kenneth C., Pvt,
Spindler, Russell M., Pfc,
Spingola, Frank, Jr., Pfc,
Spinks, Frank J., Pvt,
Spinrad, Walter I., Capt,
Spire, Julius G., Pvt,
Spires, Clyde J., S/Sgt,
Spires, Frank N., Pfc,
Spisak, Stephen G., Pfc,
Spitale, Basil, T/5,
Spitler, Charles H., Pfc,
Spitzer, Irwin S., Pvt,
Spitzkopf, Albert J., Pvt,
†Splain, Francis T., Jr., Pfc,
Spoelstra, Gael G., Pvt,
Spolarich, Steve, Pvt,
Spooner, Stanley E., T/5,
‡Spoonmore, Maxwell L., Pvt,
Sporleder, Wilbur F., T/4,
Spott, Albert J., Pvt,
Spott, William A., Jr., T/5,
Spotts, Paul F., Pfc,
‡Spratt, Charles E., Pvt,
Spratt, Raymond E., Pvt,
Spriggle, Benjamin F., Jr., Pvt,
‡Spriggs, John H., Pvt,
Springer, Billy, Pfc,
Springer, Robert R., 2nd Lt,
Springer, Wilbur D., Sgt,
Sprinkle, Archie E., Pvt,
Sprong, Ernest R., S/Sgt,
Sprott, John W., Jr., Pfc,
Spruell, Henry W., Pfc,
Spruill, Benton M., Pfc
Squirlock, Paul P., Pfc,
Sramkoski, Leo F., Cpl,
Sromovski, Andrew A., Pfc,
Stacey, Edward, Pfc,
Stachera, Joseph R., Sgt,
Stachowicz, Henry J., Pfc,
Stack, John J., Pfc,
Stacy, Carmel, Pfc,
Stadheim, Kenneth, Sgt,
Stafford, Carl N., Pvt,
Stafford, Forrest H., Pfc,
Stafford, John R., Pvt,
Stafford, Winford J., Pfc,
‡Staffrey, Dominic, Pfc,
Stage, Shirley E., S/Sgt,
Staggs, Dewey V., Pvt,
*Stahl, Harold A., Pfc,
Stahl, Kenneth H., Pvt,
Staiano, John, Pfc,
Staley, Calvin, Pvt,
Staley, Edward W., Cpl,
Staley, Eldon L., T/5,
Stall, Earle R., Jr., 1st Lt,
Stallings, Wilton L., Pfc,
Stalls, Paul F., Pfc,
Stallsworth, Lawrence, Pfc,
Stambaugh, Earl M., Pfc,
Stamen, Samuel, Sgt,
Stamey, J. B., Pvt,
Stamos, Christie J., Pvt,
Stamp, Michael H., Pfc,
‡Stamper, Charlie, Pvt,
*Srancato, Frank J., Pfc,
Stanczak, Joseph J., Pvt,
Standefer, Ralph A., Pvt,
Standley, Charles L., Pvt,
Stanek, John J., Pvt,
Stanfield, Albert P., Pfc,
Stanford, Lester W., Pfc,
Stanford, Ralph J., Sgt,
Stanhope, Edward G., Pfc,
Stanich, Edward G., Sgt,
Staniford, Archie V., Pvt,
Stanislav, Joe, Jr., Pfc,
Staniszewski, Stanley F., Pfc,
Stankaitis, Algard A., Pfc,
†Stankoch, Jerome L., Pfc,
‡Stankowski, Joseph, Pvt,
Stanley, Harry D., 2nd Lt
Stanley, Joseph F., 1st Sgt
Stanley, William G., Pvt,
†Stansberry Ray, Pfc,
Stanton, James C., Pvt,
Stanton, John H., S/Sgt,
‡Stanton, Ronald H., Pvt,

Staples, Albert R., Pfc,
Staples, Burton E., Pvt,
Staples, Harry H., T/Sgt,
Stark, Harry L., Pvt,
Stark, Howard L., Pfc,
Stark, Ivan N., Pvt,
Starnick, Rudy, 1st Sgt,
Starysky, Tom P., Pvt,
Starzyk, Stanley J., Pvt,
Starzynski, Edward F., Pvt,
Staunton, William H., Jr., Pvt
Stavropulos, Chris, Pvt,
Stavros, Peter S., T/5,
†Stawiarski, Stanley, Pfc,
St. Clair, Gilbert C., Capt,
§St. Cyr, George, Pvt,
Steading, Horace F., Sgt,
Stec, Edward, Sgt,
Stec, Joseph, Pvt,
Stecker, Roland H., Pfc,
Steckroth, Paul C., Sgt,
Steele, David, Pfc,
Steele, Frederick M., Pvt,
‡Steele, Harry, Pfc,
Steele, Johnnie R., Pvt,
Steele, Norman E., Pfc,
Steelman, Roy M., Pvt,
Steenberg, Roy J., S/Sgt,
Steese, Clark F., Pfc,
Steeves, William J., Pfc,
†Stefanini, Peter P., Pfc,
†Stefek, Emil, Jr., Pfc,
§Steffan, Elmer E., Pfc,
Steffans, Sylvester M., Pfc,
*Steffey, Richard J., Pfc,
Steffy, Lester S., Pvt,
Steffy, Richard S., Pvt,
†Stefoin, Vincent W., Pvt,
Steging, John H., Pfc,
Stegman, Calvin H., Pvt,
Stegmann, Donald F., 1st Lt,
Stegnerski, Henry J., Pfc,
Stehr, Edward R., Pvt,
Steig, Carl J., Pfc,
Steimer, William A., Pvt,
Stein, Charles V., Pfc,
Stein, Gilbert B., Pfc,
Stein, Joe, Pvt,
Stein, John, Pfc,
†Stein, Joseph N., Pfc,
Stein, Pete, Pvt,
Stein, William H., Pvt,
Steinbach, Kurt, Pfc,
Steinbeck, Frederick W., Pfc,
†Steinberg, Albert J., Pvt,
Steinberg, Saul I., Pvt,
Steinborn, Ralph F., Pfc,
Steiner, Charles E., S/Sgt,
Steiner, James F., Capt,
†Steiner, John H., S/Sgt,
Stellisch, William A., Pfc,
Stelmachowski, C. L., Pvt,
Stelmack, Carl, S/Sgt,
Stelton, Earl E., Pfc,
Stemle, Linus A., Cpl,
Stemple, Lyle H., Cpl,
Stengel, Carl E., Pvt,
Stephan, Paul G., T/5,
Stephens, Clarence H., T/5,
Stephens, Cleo D., Pfc,
Stephens, Earnest E., Pvt,
Stephens, Ewell T., Pfc,
†Stephens, John R., Pfc
Stephens, Ledford, Pfc,
†Stephenson, Dalton O., Pvt,
Stephenson, McCarty, Cpl,
Stephenon, Warren G., Pfc,
Steponik, Frank, Pvt,
Sterling, James N., Pvt,
Stern, Douglas A., 1st Lt,
‡Sternberg, Charles W., Pvt,
Sternberg, Raymond L., Pfc,
Sterner, Russell K., Pfc,
†Sternfield, Bernard, Pvt,
Sternfield, Max, Pvt,
Sterrett, Elmer L., Sgt,
Stetson, James W., Pvt,
Stetz, Ernest J., Pvt,
Stevenback, Oscar W., S/Sgt,
†Stevens, Bennie A., Pfc,
Stevens, Donald H., Pvt,
Stevens, Edwin, Pfc,
Stevens, Ernest L., Pfc,
Stevens, Henry M., Jr., Pfc,
Stevens, Howard L., Pfc,
Stevens, Jesse C., Sgt,
Stevens, John, Pfc,
Stevens, Judge, Jr., Pfc,
Stevens, Ransom H., Pvt,
Stevens, Victor B., Pfc,
Stevenson, Earl K., Pvt,
Stevenson, James L., Pvt,
Stevenson, Robert T., Jr., Pfc,
Steward, Dean, Pfc.
Steward, Glen W., Pfc,

Steward, Irvin W., Pfc,
Steward, Louis E., Pfc,
§Steward, Robert L., Jr., Pvt,
Stewart, Charles G., Pfc,
Stewart, Charles H., Jr., Pfc,
†Stewart, Connie B., S/Sgt,
Stewart, Graham, S/Sgt,
Stewart, Harry R., Pfc,
Stewart, Hugh K., Pfc,
Stewart, James B., Pvt,
Stewart, James C., Pfc,
Stewart, John J., Pfc,
Stewart, Melvin L., Pfc,
Stewart, Raymond H., Pvt,
Stewart, Robert E., Sgt,
Stewart, Samuel C., Pfc,
§Stewart, Samuel E., Pfc,
†Stewart, Wayne S., Pvt,
Stewart, William B., Capt,
Stewart, William J., Pvt,
†St. Germain, Francis F., Pvt,
†St. Hilaire, Andrien J., Pvt,
Stidham, Alber B., Pfc,
Stieff, Jack, Pfc,
†Stierman, John E., Pvt,
Stigers, James A., Pfc,
Stigger, Clifford T., Jr., 2nd Lt,
†Stiles, Arthur R., Pfc,
Stiles, James A., Pvt,
†Stiles, Leslie E., 1st Lt,
Still, Clyde M., Pvt,
Still, Merton J., Pvt,
†Stillings, George V., Pvt,
Stillman, Adee, Pvt,
†Stillwell, Clarence E., Sgt,
Stimac, Rudolph V., Pfc,
Stimmerman, Carl D., Pfc,
†Stine, Daniel A., Pvt,
Stinnett, Grady C., Pfc,
Stinson, Warren A., Cpl,
Stinson, Dennis F., Jr., Pfc,
Stinziano, Joseph J., Pfc,
Stires, William T., Pvt,
Stitely,Thomas B., Sgt,
Stitt, Hugh P., Cpl,
St. Jacque, John S., T/4,
St. John, Elmo A., Pfc,
†St. Laurent, Laurence V., Pvt,
St. Marks, Peter J., Pvt,
Stock, Burdeen N., Pfc,
Stock, William S., Pvt,
Stocker, Earl G., Pfc,
Stocker, George F., Jr., Pvt,
Stockman, Perry J., 1st Lt,
Stockton, Robert H., Sgt,
Stoddard, Richard E., 1st Lt,
†Stoessel, Carl A., Cpl,
Stoffer, Clyde C., Cpl,
Stoffer, Leonard D., Pvt,
Stogadill, James W., Pvt,
Stokes, John H., S/Sgt,
Stokes, Weldon O., Pfc,
Stoliker, Charles K., Pvt,
Stoll, Freeland E., Pvt,
Stoller, Morris, Pfc,
‡Stolowski, Edmond F., Pfc,
Stolte, William C., Pvt,
Stomel, Samuel, Pfc,
Stone, Audrey W., Pvt,
Stone, Clifford J., Pfc,
Stone, Emmett R., S/Sgt,
Stone, John H., Pfc,
†Stone, John T., Pvt,
Stone, Joseph E., Pvt,
Stone, Lamar O., Pfc,
Stone, Ralph W., Pfc,
Stone, Rommie S., Sgt,
Stone, Sidney P., Sgt,
Stone, Thomas D., Pvt,
Stonebrook, Richard A., Cpl
Stoner, George M., Pfc,
Stonesifer, Harry E., Pvt,
Stonestreet, James R., Pfc,
Stonge, Stephen L., Pfc,
Storbeck, Orville H., Pfc,
Storer, Carey M., T/5,
Storey, Maynard, Jr., Pvt,
Storey, Robert L., Pvt,
Storm, Kenneth R., Pfc,
Story, Robert J., Pfc,
Stotesberry, Leslie C., Pvt,
†Stouffer, Ralph S., Pvt,
Stough, Chester J., Pvt,
Stoughton, William R., Pfc,
Stout, Bob S., Pvt,
Stout, Don E., T/5,
Stout, Erman, M/Sgt,
Stout, Lesley D., Cpl,
Stout, William A., T/5
Stoutenburg, Lauren L., Pfc,
Stover, Edward F., Pfc,
Stover, George B., Jr., Capt,
Stover, Ivan L., Pfc,
Stover, Morris, Cpl,
Stover, Ortie L., Pfc,

‡Stover, Robert F., Pfc,
Stowe, Robert W., Jr.,
St. Pierre, Ervin E., Pfc,
St. Pierre, Leo L., Pvt,
St. Pierre, Peter A., Sgt,
St. Pierre, Philip T., Pvt,
Strader, William H., Sgt,
Straight, Leroy O., 2nd Lt
Strain, Russell L., Pfc,
Straka, Frank J., Pvt,
Straley, Roger R., Pfc,
†Strange, Robert E., Pvt,
‡Strange, Thomas J., Jr., S/Sgt,
Strasser, Godfrey G., T/Sgt,
†Stratton, Jesse, S/Sgt,
Strawn, Charles W., Sgt,
Strawser, Marion L., Pvt,
Strayer, Paul K., Pfc,
Strebe, Richard W., T/4,
Strecker, Alec, T/5,
†Strecker, Leonard J., Sgt,
Street, Claude G.,
Street, Homer F., Pfc,
Street, Ralph C., 2nd Lt,
†Streeter, William H., Pfc,
†Strehle, Frank, 2nd Lt,
Strehle, Frederick W., Pvt,
Strickland, Melvin C., Pfc,
Strickland, Robert W., 2nd Lt,
Strickler, Robert R., Pvt,
Strickler, William C., Pvt,
Stricklin, R. D., S/Sgt,
Stringfellow, Martin, Pvt,
Stringfellow, Richard D., Pfc,
Stripp, George E., 1st Lt,
Strish, William T., Pfc,
Strohm, Earl R., Jr., Pvt,
Stromeyer, Wolfgang H., Pfc,
Strong, Victor M., Pvt,
Stroth, Arthur C., T/5,
Stroud, Rondall B., 1st Lt,
‡Stroup, Arnold H., Sgt,
‡Stroupe, Edwin J., Cpl,
Stroyick, William R., Cpl,
Struber, Gilbert, Pvt,
†Struber, Isaac, Sgt,
Struck, George R., Pfc,
†Stuard, Warren G., Pfc,
*Stuart, Omar J., Pfc,
Stuart, Virgil A., Pfc,
Stuber, Carl E., Jr., Pfc,
Stuckey, Jo, T/5,
Studerus, Walter L., Pfc,
Stuhltrager, John A., Pfc,
Stults, Thomas C., Sgt
Stultz, Jesse B., Pfc,
Stumbo, Frank C., S/Sgt,
Stumne, Lester H., Pvt,
†Stump, Charles W., Jr., Pvt,
†Stump, Robert W.,
Sturdevant, Cecil D., Pvt,
Sturgeon, Wilber L., Pfc,
Sturgill, Willie, Pfc,
Sturley, Eric A., 1st Lt,
†Stutchbury, Bruce F., Pfc,
St. Vrain, Hyman S., S/Sgt,
Styer, Neil E., Pfc,
Styles, Eugene L., Pvt,
Stymus, Edward J., Pvt,
Styron, Ralph G., Pvt,
Suarez, Domingo, Pvt
Succheralli, James, Pvt,
Such, Walter J., Pfc,
Suchara, Thaddeus W., 2nd Lt,
Suchovolsky, Manuel M., Pfc,
Suddeth, Frank W., Pvt,
Sudduth, Chester V., 2nd Lt,
Sudduth, Vinson, Pfc,
Sudhalter, Mason L., T/5,
Suelzle, Wilbert, Pfc,
Sugalski, Stephen J., Jr., Sgt,
Sule, William, Pfc,
Sulham, Maurice A., Pvt,
Sulik, Stephen C., T/5,
Sulinski, John W., Sgt,
Sullins, James H., Jr., Pvt,
Sullivan, Clifford M., Pfc,
Sullivan, Cornelius A., Pvt,
Sullivan, Garland C., 2nd Lt,
Sullivan, James C., Pvt,
Sullivan, James J., Pfc,
Sullivan, James K., Sgt,
Sullivan, James W., Pvt,
Sullivan, John J., Sgt,
Sullivan, Stephen L., Jr., Pvt,
Sullivan, Thomas J., Sgt,
†Sullivan, Warren J., Pfc,
Sullivan, William P., Pvt,
Sullo, Arizo J., Pvt,
Suman, Kenneth L., Pfc,
Sumien, Louis Y., Pfc,
Summers, Ernest, Jr., Pfc,
Summers, Ralph W., Pfc,
Summers, William B., Pvt,
†Sumner, Guy W., Cpl,

Sumner, Omer R., Pfc,
Sumner, Victor C., Pvt
Sumner, William W., Pfc,
Sumpter, Eugene D., Pfc,
Sumrall, Edward D., Pfc,
Sundberg, Hugo J., Pfc,
Sundby, Harold R., S/Sgt,
Suppes, John J., Pfc,
†Surean, Lyle N., Pfc,
Surman, Anton I., T/3,
Surratt, Joseph W., Pvt,
Susor, Wallace R., Pvt,
‡Susral, Richard A., Pfc,
Susser, Gilbert, S/Sgt,
Sussman, Harold H., Pfc,
Sutalski, Richard J., Pfc,
Sutera, August J., Pfc,
Sutfin, William A., Pvt,
Sutherland, Donald C., Pvt,
Sutherland, Donald H., T/5,
Sutker, Leonard, Sgt,
†Sutphin, James E., Pvt,
Sutter, Edwin M., Cpl,
Sutton, George E., Pfc,
Sutton, Jesse L., Pvt,
‡Sutton, Russell H., Sgt,
*Sutton, Tommie C., Pvt,
Suvada, Edward, Pfc,
†Svalina, John M., Pvt,
Svoboda, James F., Pfc,
Swadley, Virgil H., Sgt,
Swagler, Cleal L., Pfc,
Swails, Armstrong C., Capt,
Swain, Charles, Pfc,
Swain, Howard R., Pfc,
Swan, Kenneth E., Pfc,
Swan, Kenneth O., Pfc,
Swan, Walter J., Pvt,
Swanger, Alfred J., S/Sgt,
†Swank, Robert E., Pvt,
Swank, Ross A., T/4,
Swanson, Arthur M., Sgt,
Swanson, Chester R., T/Sgt,
Swanson, Curtis W., Pfc,
†Swanson, Earl E., Capt,
§Swanson, Elston A., Cpl,
Swanson, George E., Pfc,
Swanson, James A., Sgt,
Swanson, James C., Pfc,
Swartout, Donald F., Pvt,
Swartz, Alvin J., Cpl,
Swartz, Glenn R., Pvt,
Swartz, Henry E., Cpl,
Swaters, David J., Pfc,
Swauger, Robert Thorton, Pvt,
†Swayne, Robert J., Sr., Sgt,
Swearingen, John N., Jr., Pfc,
Sweat, Arnold L., Sgt,
Sweeney, Francis S., Pvt,
Sweeney, John A., 1st Lt,
Sweeney, Terrence M., Pfc,
Sweeny, Daniel H., Pvt,
Sweet, Edward F., Sgt,
Sweetwood, Milton, 2nd Lt,
†Sweigard, Harold H., Pvt,
Sweitzer, William A., Jr., Pfc,
†Swett, Roy A., Pvt,
Swesey, Roy, Sgt,
Swetland, George L., Pfc,
Swiatecki, Joseph A., Pvt,
Swiatek, Stanley E., Jr., 2nd Lt
Swiatkowski, Aloysius A., Pfc,
Swiatly, William W., Pvt,
Swickard, Walter D., Pvt,
Swift, Charles F., Pvt,
Swift, Willie J., Pvt,
Swineford, Harry P., Pfc,
Swinehart, Leland E., Pfc,
Swinford, Charles C., Pvt,
Swink, Ralph M., Pvt,
Swinton, Bernard G., S/Sgt,
Switzer, Nelson W., Pfc,
Swol, Stanley W., T/5,
Swon, Richard G., S/Sgt,
Swontec, Stanley A., S/Sgt,
Swope, Howard L., Pfc,
†Sykes, Charlie W., Pfc,
Sylte, Irving J., Pfc,
Sylvanowicz, Benjamin, Pvt,
Sylvester, Delbert E., Pvt,
Symonds, Arthur L., Pfc,
Syreika, Stanley C., T/5,
Syrek, Leo V., Pfc,
Syrett, Boyd, Pvt,
§Szabo, Anthony, Pfc,
Szabo, Anthony L., T/5,
Szappanos, Frank, Jr., Pvt,
Szarek, Joseph F., Pvt,
Szarmach, Anastazy, Pfc,
Szczebak, Frank E., Pfc,
Szczepkowski, Henry S., Pfc,
†Szczepanski, Charles J., Sgt,
Szczesniak, Casimir J., Pfc,
Szczesniak, Vernon J., Pvt,
Szekeres, John G., Pfc,

† Killed in Action. * Prisoner of War. ‡ Missing in Action. § Died of Wounds.

Szemacs, Elmer J., S/Sgt,
Szili, Henry J., Pvt
Szladek, Frank J., Capt,
†Szukalski, Teddy J., Pfc,
Szymanik, Frank S., Pfc,
‡Szymanska, Joe, Pvt,
Szymanski, Felix J., Pvt,

Tabbutt, Robert A., Pfc,
Taber, Howard L., Cpl,
Taber, Richard, Pfc,
Tabor, Emil T., Pvt,
Tabor, William C., Pfc,
‡Tackett, Harold L., Pfc,
Tadec, Fred, Pvt,
Tadie, Joseph G., Pfc,
Taft, William J., Pvt,
Taggart, Donald G., 1st Lt,
†Tagler, Leroy V., Pvt,
Taglialatela, Benjamin A., Pvt,
Tagliareni, Dominick, Pfc,
Tague, Edwin P., Pfc,
Tait, Ernest E., Pfc,
†Takacs, John J., Jr., Pvt,
Talbot, Benjamin M., Pfc,
Talbot, Claude J., Pvt,
Talbott, Charles J., Pfc,
Talkington, Eugene E., Pfc,
Tallent, Gene R., Pvt,
Tallent, Max, Pfc,
Talley, Chester W., Jr., 1st Lt
Talley, Freeman, Pfc,
Tallman, Robert B., 1st Lt,
Tallon, Leo R., Pfc,
Tamaroff, Alex H., Pfc,
Tamburelli, Anthony S., Pfc,
Tamburello, Joseph, Pfc,
†Tamburine, Albert J., Pvt,
†Tancin, George, Pvt,
Tancos, Michael G., Pfc,
Tanella, Joseph L., Pvt,
Tankersley, Charles D., Pvt,
Tannehill, Chester L., 1st Lt,
Tanner, George O., S/Sgt,
Tanner, Kenneth D., Pvt,
*Tanner, Odis, Pfc,
Tanner, Virgil L., T/Sgt,
Tanne, Ward D., Pfc,
Tanous, Frederick, Pvt,
Tanzy, Edward F., Pfc,
†Taormina, Vincent J., Pvt,
Tapley, John A., Pfc,
Tapp, Gus M., 2nd Lt,
Tapp, Ralph E., T/5,
Tarasek, Chester, Pvt,
Tarasiuk, Michael, S/Sgt,
Tarbell, John R., Pvt,
Tardy, Lawrence L., Pvt
Taghetta, Nicholas, T/5,
†Tarleton, Francis G., Pvt,
Tarlton, Olin N., Pfc,
Tarpenning, Leland C., Pvt,
Tarr, James, Pvt,
Tarrance, James P., Pfc,
Tarrant, Hugh L., Pfc,
Tarsa, John F., Pfc,
†Tartaglia, Frank, Pfc,
Tarwater, Walter, Jr., T/4,
Tatalone, Samuel A., Pfc,
†Tate, Raymond E., Pfc,
Tatman, William, Pfc,
Tatro, Howard U., Pfc,
†Tatum, Jack M., 2nd Lt
Tatur, Stanley, A., Pvt,
†Tauchen, Robert T., Pvt,
‡Tauriaianen, Robert E., Pvt,
Tax, Murray M., Pvt,
Tayerle, Frank J., Cpl,
†Taylor, Albert, Pfc,
†Taylor, Arbury R., Pfc,
†Taylor, Bruce K., Pvt,
Taylor, Charles A., Pvt,
†Taylor, Charles A., Pvt,
Taylor, Charles P., T/Sgt,
Taylor, Charles R., Pfc,
Taylor, Denzil L., Pvt,
Taylor, Donald F., Pvt,
Taylor, Edward W., S/Sgt,
Taylor, Frank S., Pfc,
Taylor, Fred A., Pfc,
Taylor, Fred C., 2nd Lt,
Taylor, George E., Pvt,
Taylor, Glendon H., Pfc,
†Taylor, Harold, T/5,
Taylor, Jack, S/Sgt,
Taylor, James P., Pfc,
Taylor, Jay, E., Sgt,
Taylor, Jessie, Pvt,
‡Taylor, John C., Pfc,
†Taylor, John C., Sgt,
Taylor, John F., Pvt,
Taylor, John L., Pfc,
Taylor, Kenneth S., T/4,
Taylor, Lester C., S/Sgt,
Taylor, Lloyd W., Pvt,

Taylor, Loran G., Pfc,
Taylor, Lyle, Pfc,
Taylor, Marvin W., Pfc,
†Taylor, Marwood S., 1st Lt,
Taylor, Paul M., Pvt,
Taylor, Richard H., Pfc,
Taylor, Rinaker D., Pvt,
Taylor, Robert, Sgt,
Taylor, Robert E., Pvt,
Taylor, Robert P., Pfc,
‡Taylor, Ronald L., Pvt,
‡Taylor, Samuel H., Pfc,
†Taylor, Shuba W., Pfc,
Taylor, Theodore F., Pvt,
Taylor, Walter E., Pfc,
Taylor, Walter J., Pfc,
Taylor, William, Pvt,
†Teague, Emmett R., Pfc,
Teague, James H., Pfc,
Teague, Norris M., Jr., 1st Lt,
Teal, Ezekal, Pvt
Tebloff, Albert, Pvt,
Tebo, Robert, Pfc,
Teckett, Walter A., Pvt,
Tedder, Gilbert D., Pvt,
Tedeschi, Marino C., Pvt,
Teehan, Harry P., Pvt,
Teekell, Milan J., 1st Lt,
†Teicher, Max, Pvt,
Telleck, Anthony, 1st Lt,
Temple, Samuel, Pvt,
Temple, William W., Pfc,
Tencate, William R., Pvt
Tennis, Murray D., Pfc,
Terczak, Raymond F., Pfc,
Teri, Gasper, Pfc,
‡Terral, William J., Pfc,
Terrel, Henry A., Pfc,
Terrell, James L., Pfc,
Terrell, William E., Pfc,
Terrill, Mathew H., Pfc,
Terry, Eugene, Pfc,
Terry, Philip T., Capt,
Terry, Thomas J., Cpl,
Terry, Vardaman J., Sgt,
†Terry, Wirt B., Pfc,
Tesch, Lawrence A., T/4,
Tesmer, John A., Pfc,
Tessler, Louis, Pvt,
†Testa, Charles F., Pfc,
†Tester, Charles L., Pvt,
Tester, Jackson T., Sr., Sgt,
Tetrault, Robert H., Pfc,
†Tetreault, Albert J., 2nd Lt,
Thacher, Clifford J., Pvt,
Thacker, Fred O., Pfc,
Tharp, Howard C., Sgt,
Tharp, Lewis W., Pvt,
Thatcher, Kenneth B., Pfc,
Thayer, Edwin A., Pfc,
‡Theberge, Archelas G., Pvt,
Theis, Norbert A., T/Sgt,
Theodore, Teddy E., T/5,
Theriault, Joseph H., Pvt,
Theuken, Raymond E., S/Sgt,
Thibodeau, Antonio J., Pfc,
Thiel, John M., Pfc,
†Thielbar, Edward T., Jr., Pvt,
Thierolf, Dwight R., S/Sgt,
Thiesen, Charles D., Pvt,
Thiessen, Harold T., Pfc,
Thinelk, Marvin T., Pvt,
Thobro, Clayton C., Lt Col,
Tholey, Edward P., Pvt,
Thomas, Alpha P., Pvt,
Thomas, Alvin J., Pfc,
Thomas, Arthur L., Pfc,
Thomas, Charles P., Pvt,
‡Thomas, Clarence, Jr., Pvt,
†Thomas, Clifton C., Pfc,
Thomas, Clinton W., Pvt,
†Thomas, Doyle H., Pfc,
Thomas, Edward, Pvt,
Thomas, Ernest E., Pvt,
†Thomas, E. L., Pfc,
Thomas, Franklin L., Pfc,
Thomas, George P., Pfc,
Thomas, George R., Pvt,
Thomas, Horace E., S/Sgt,
Thomas, Jack E., Sgt,
Thomas, Jess F., Lt Col,
Thomas, John, Jr., Pfc,
†Thomas, John E., S/Sgt,
Thomas, Joseph A., Pvt,
Thomas, Kenneth A., Pvt,
Thomas, Kenneth D., Pfc,
Thomas, Kenneth O., Sgt,
Thomas, Lester, Pfc,
†Thomas, Lester D., Pvt,
Thomas, Nichol G., Pfc,
Thomas, Odis A., Pfc,
†Thomas, Philip L., Pvt,
Thomas, Quentin C., Sgt,
Thomas, Rawlin L., Pfc,
Thomas, Richard E., S/Sgt,

Thomas, Robert E., Pvt,
Thomas, Robert H., Sgt,
Thomas, Robert S., Pvt,
Thomas, Virgus C., Pfc,
Thomas, Walter A., WOJG,
Thomas, Ward L., Pfc
Thomas, Warren W., Pfc,
Thomas, William L., Pvt,
Thomas, Wilmer D., S/Sgt,
‡Thomason, Gordon K., Pfc,
Thomason, Joseph L., Pvt,
Thomason, Walter D., Sgt,
Thome, John J., Pfc,
Thompson, Carl R., Pfc,
†Thompson, Charles E., Pvt,
Thompson, Charles J., Jr.,
Thompson, Charles S., Sgt,
Thompson, Charles W., Pfc,
Thompson, Clarence E., Pfc,
Thompson, Clarence P., Pvt,
*Thompson, Clifford F., Pvt,
Thompson, Clint, S/Sgt,
Thompson, Clyde C., Pfc,
Thompson, David S., Pvt,
Thompson, Ernest D. C., Pfc,
Thomley, Vester G., 2nd Lt,
Thompson, Alfred D., Pfc,
Thompson, Calvin C., Pvt,
†Thompson, Glenn O., Cpl,
Thompson, Herbert R., Pvt,
Thompson, Hilton E., Pvt,
Thompson, James M., Pfc,
§Thompson, John W., Pfc,
Thompson, Joseph H., Sgt,
Thompson, Julius C., Pfc,
Thompson, Kenneth G., Pvt,
†Thompson, Kenneth J., S/Sgt,
Thompson, Leonard B., Pvt,
Thompson, Leonard L., Pvt,
†Thompson, Lloyd E., Pvt,
†Thompson, Melville L., Pvt,
Thompson, Morris C., Sgt,
Thompson, Richard G., T/5,
Thompson, Robert E., Pvt,
Thompson, Robert H., Pvt,
†Thompson, Robert R., Pfc,
Thompson, Roy L., Pvt,
Thompson, Theodore F., Jr.,
Thompson, Walter M., Pvt,
Thompson, William A., Sgt,
§Thompson, William B., Pfc,
Thompson, William O., Pvt,
Thomsen, Kjekd H., Pfc,
Thomsen, Roy M., S/Sgt,
Thomson, Gerald S., Pfc,
†Thornburgh, Joseph W., Pfc,
†Thornburg, Kenneth K., Pvt,
Thornburg, Raymond J., Pfc,
Thornhill, John H., S/Sgt,
Thorne, John F., Pvt,
Thorne, Joseph E., Pvt,
Thornton, John B., Pfc,
Thornton, John M., Pvt,
Thornton, Ralph G., Pfc,
†Thornton, Samuel W., Pfc,
†Thorpe, Harry R., Jr.,
Thorpe, James C., Pfc,
Thorsen, Lars M., Pvt,
Thorstenson, Melvin L., Sgt,
Thrall, Leo, Pvt,
Thrash, James R., Pvt,
Thristino, Ralph, Pfc,
Thorolson, Donald A., Pfc,
‡Throne, Marion F., Pfc,
Thrower, Emerson L., T/5,
Thurber, Orville B., Cpl,
Thurber, William G., Pvt,
Thurman, James P., Pfc,
Thurman, Ralph, Cpl,
Thurman, Robert W., Pfc,
†Thurmond, John E., Jr., S/Sgt,
*Thurston, Albert F., Pvt,
Thurston, William J., Pfc,
Thying, Lunsford, 1st Lt,
Tianen, Roger E., Pfc,
*Tibbs, Louie D., Pfc,
‡Tiberio, Aldo P., Pvt,
Tice, Sam R., T/5,
Ticer, Lloyd L., Pfc,
Tidd, Glenn V., Pvt,
Tidwell, Benton, Pvt,
†Tiedeman, George R., Pvt,
Tierney, Albert J., Pfc,
Tifal, Charles G., Pfc,
†Tiffany, Willard H., Pfc,
‡Tighe, Michael J., Jr., Pvt,
Tiferina, Nicholas, Cpl,
Tijerina, Charles T., Pvt,
†Tilden, William T., Pvt,
Till, Edward E., Pvt,
Till, Herold A., Pfc,
Tillery, Robert L., Pfc,
Tilley, Virgle A. B., Pvt,
Tillman, Marion J., Jr., Pfc,

Tillman, Robert L., 2nd Lt,
Tilseth, Orle H., S/Sgt,
Timander, Clarence C., Pfc,
Timmer, Howard E., Pfc,
Timmerman, Walter W., Pfc,
Timmons, Leonard L., Pvt,
Timon, Harry W., Pfc,
Timoney, Joseph L., Pvt,
Tinnel, Herold O., Pfc,
†Tinnell, Clarence, Pvt,
Tinsley, Loy A., Pfc,
Tipling, Kenneth C., 2nd Lt,
Tippit, Floyd, S/Sgt,
Tipswork, Harley A., Pfc,
Tipton, Denville, Pvt
Tipton, Donald R., Pvt,
Tipton, Lawrence C., Pvt,
Tipton, Ralph D., Pfc,
Tirko, John, T/5,
Tironte, Bernard C., Pvt,
†Tischler, Albert J., Pvt,
Tiscione, Serafino E., Pvt,
Tisdale, Henry L., Cpl,
Tisone, Savina V., Pvt,
Titsworth, Alvin W., Pfc,
Titus, Ernest F., S/Sgt
†Titus, Everett G. N., Jr., Pvt,
Titus, William L., Pfc,
Tkaczyk, John, Pfc,
Toal, Mark A., Pfc,
Tobias, Cecil J., Pfc,
Toczylowki, Henry J., Pfc,
Todd, Joseph E., Cpl,
Todd, Lucian B., S/Sgt,
Todd, Stuart E., Pfc,
†Todesco, Pasquale A., Pvt,
Toemmel, William J., Pvt,
Toenges, William H., Pfc,
†Toffey, John J., Jr., Lt Col,
Toft, Carl N., Jr., Pvt,
Togninalli, Reno J., Cpl,
†Toineeta, Jeremiah, Pfc,
Tokarek, Charles R., Cpl,
Tokarski, Thaddeus T., Pvt,
Tokarski, Walter J., Pvt,
Tokarz, Chester S., Pfc,
Toland, Charles R., Pfc,
Toland, Herbert, WO,
*Tolbert, Jack B., Pfc,
Tolbert, Joseph E., Pfc,
†Tolbert, Raymond W., Pvt,
Tole, John R., Pfc,
†Tollefson, Arthur G., Pfc,
§Tomaka, Henry J., Pvt,
Tomaino, Anthony G., Pfc,
Tomaino, Frank, Pfc
Tomao, Thomas J., Pvt,
†Tomaski, Stanley, Pvt
Tomasko, Henry J., Pvt,
Tomaszewski, T. R., T/5,
‡Tomes, Gilert D., Pvt,
Tomszak, Edward C., S/Sgt,
Tomkus, Joseph, Pvt,
Tomlinson, Herbert J., Pfc,
Tompkins, Kermit A., Pfc,
†Tompkins, Robert J., Pfc,
Tomsic, Frank, Pvt,
†Toner, Raymond K., Pvt,
Toney, James D., Pvt,
Toney, Malcolm B., 1st Lt,
Tong, Fat, Pfc,
Tonini, William J., Pfc,
Tonucci, Romolo, T/5,
Tonzello, Umberto J., Pfc,
Toomer, Harold K., 1st Lt,
Toomey, John F., Pvt,
Toomey, William J., Pvt,
Torcivia, Paul, Jr., Pfc,
Torgerson, Martin H., Pvt,
†Tori, John A., Pfc,
Torres, Epitacio C., Jr., Pfc,
Torres, Lupe M., Pvt,
Torres, Jesus A., Jr., Pvt,
Torretto, Frank A., T/5,
Torrez, Manuel A., Pfc,
Torros, Cirilo C., Pfc,
Torten, Archie C., Pfc,
Tortorello, Anthony E., Pvt,
Tortorici, Benjamin J., Pvt,
†Toskos, Sotiris, Pvt,
Tosky, Robert F., Pfc,
Tostenson, Milo A., Pfc,
Tosti, Frank P., Pfc,
Toth, George, Pvt,
Toth, John J., T/5,
Towe, Forrest O., Pfc,
Towles, Arthur E., Sgt,
Townsend, George R., 1st Lt,
Townsend, Harvey B., Pfc,
Townsend, Ross A., Pfc,
§Townsend, Verl F., Pfc,
Trabulsi, Philip L., 2nd Lt,
Tracey, Justus H., Pvt,
Trachte, Kurt, Pfc,

Tracy, Bernard C., Cpl,
†Tracy, Lawrence J., Jr., 2nd Lt,
Tracy, Orrin A., Capt,
Trader, Robert E., Pfc,
Trambley, Walter J., Pvt,
Trammell, James H., Pvt,
Trammell, Joe A., Pvt,
Trapp, Ernst W., T/5,
Trapp, James H., Jr., Pfc,
Trask, Maurice W., Pvt,
Traub, Edward R., Pfc,
Trauman, Nathan N., Pfc,
Trautman, Edward H., Pvt,
Travers, Joseph A., Pvt,
Travis, Elton K., Pvt,
Travis, Ray F., Pvt,
Travis, Walter L., 2nd Lt,
Travoska, Joseph J., Pvt,
Traylor, Willie E., Sgt,
Trbovich, Michael, Pvt,
Treadway, Charles L., Capt,
†Tredway, Herman L., Cpl,
Treece, Louis D., Pfc,
‡Trefry, John E., Pfc,
Tregan, John, Pvt,
Trent, Charles W., Pfc,
†Tressler, Donald V., Cpl,
Trezza, Salvatore A., Pfc,
Tribitt, Victor H., Jr., Pvt,
Triden, Fred A., Sgt,
Trier, Jack P., 1st Sgt,
Trigueros, George A., Pfc,
Trimmer, Earl N., Pvt,
Trina, Anthony M., Pfc,
Trine, Jerry B., Pfc,
Tringale, Sam, Cpl,
Triplett, Oral L., Pfc,
Tripp, George D., Pvt,
Tripp, Russell M., Pfc,
Trippett, Thurman, 2nd Lt,
Triska, Stanley, Pfc,
Trizzino, Paul T., Pvt,
Trlla, Joseph, Pvt,
Troch, John J., Pvt,
Trofino, William H., Pfc,
Troglin, Tip I., T/4,
†Trojak, Joseph W., Pvt,
Trojanowski, Francis T., Pvt,
†Trollinger, Charles G., Pfc,
‡Tron, Paul J., 1st Lt,
*Troper, Ralph, Pvt,
Troskowski, Joseph P., Pfc,
Troth, Thomas A., Pvt,
§Trotter, Morris L., Pfc,
§Trousil, John, Pvt,
Troutt, Louie J., T/4,
Trovato, Jack, Pfc,
Troy, John H., Pfc
†Troy, Thomas M., Pvt,
Troyer, Orve J., T/Sgt,
Truax, Edward, S/Sgt,
*Truby, Walter A., Pfc,
Tresdell, William A., Pvt
Trumpl, Bertram D., 2nd Lt,
Trunzo, Natale J., Pfc,
†Trupiano, Dominick J., Pfc,
‡Truskey, Pete J., Jr., Pvt,
Trzeciak, Edward J.,
Tschida, Lawrence, Pvt,
Tubos, Robert F., Pvt,
Tubman, James J., Pfc,
Tucci, Raymond, Pvt,
Tucker, Alfred V., Cpl,
Tucker, John W., Pvt,
Tucker, Laurenc V., Pfc,
*Tudor, John E., Pvt,
*Tuffs, Lawrence W., Pfc,
Tully, Charles J., Pfc,
Tumblison, James R., S/Sgt,
Tumblson, John W., Pvt,
‡Tumminello, Lawrence, Pfc,
Tuozzo, Richard K., Pfc,
Turchetta, Vincent F., Pvt,
Turchi, Floyd J., Cpl,
Turchi, Nano J., S/Sgt,
*Turcotte, Sylva J., Pfc,
Turk, Wilson C., Pfc,
Turkovich, Francis, Pvt,
Turley, Guy, Pfc,
Turner, Alex, Jr., Pfc,
Turner, Antoni A., Pvt,
Turner, Clarence V., T/4,
Turner, Clyde, Pfc,
Turner, Edwin C., Pvt,
Turner, Gibson G., Pfc,
‡Turner, Harry A., Pvt,
Turner, James H., Pvt,
Turner, James T., Pvt,
‡Turner, Milton L., Pfc,
*Turner, Osie O., 1st Lt,
Turner, Samuel D., Pfc,
Turner, Thomas G., Pfc,
Turner, Wesley J., Pfc,
Turner, William R., S/Sgt,
†Turney, Orville, Pfc,

† Killed in Action. * Prisoner of War. ‡ Missing in Action. § Died of Wounds.

Turningbear, Frederick, Sgt,
Turo, Leo P., Pfc,
Turowski, Stanley, Pfc,
Turpen, Joseph L., T/5,
†Turpin, Theodore E., Pvt,
Tursi, Ralph H., Pvt,
*Turvin, Howard E., Pvt,
Tusin, Arthur W., Pvt,
Tussey, Joe W., S/Sgt,
Tweddle, Edward R.,
Twining, Donald A., Pvt,
Two Bears, Gilbert, Pvt,
Two Hearts, Steven, Pfc,
Twombly, Bowden E., Pfc,
Twoududky, Lawrence F., Pfc,
Tyczka, Walter J., S/Sgt,
Tylenda, Joseph, S/Sgt,
Tyler, Claude E., Pfc,
Tyler, Gordon O., Pfc,
Tyle, Wendell F., Pfc,
Tylke, John, S/Sgt,
Tyner, Donald W., Pvt,
Tyo, Joseph H., Pfc,
Tyus, Jefferson D., Pfc,

Uecher, John G., T/4,
Uehlinger, Gerard P., Pvt,
Uhler, Eugene C., Pvt,
Uhram, Joseph J., Pvt,
†Uhrich, Clarence A., 1/Sgt,
Uidl, John A., S/Sgt,
Ulmer, Gilbert F., T/4,
§Ulmer, Nevin R., Cpl,
Ulvog, Gilbert J., Pfc,
Umberger, Harold C., Pvt,
*Umbreit, Ralph H., Pvt,
Underbakke, Stanley L., T/4,
Underdown, A. W., Jr., Pfc,
†Underhill, F. M., Jr., Pfc,
Underwood, Cecil, Jr., Sgt,
†Ungar, Joseph, Pfc,
Unger, George G., Pfc,
Unmuth, James S., Pfc,
Unruh, Freeman, Pfc,
Upholt, Murle E., T/4,
Upton, Leonard F., Pvt,
‡Upton, William B., Cpl,
†Urba, Walter, Pfc,
Urban, Bernard A., Pfc,
Urban, Joseph J., Pfc,
Urban, Simon F., Pvt,
†Urban, William C., Pvt,
Urbani, Angelo P., Pvt,
Urbanowicz, John J., Pvt,
†Urbanowski, Stanislaus J., Pvt,
Urbanski, Raymond, Pvt,
Urdahl, Eidor E., Pfc,
Uretsky, Ely, Pfc,
Urff, William A., Pvt,
Uri, Raymond E., Pfc,
Uribe, Victor M., Pfc
Urick, John A., Pvt,
Urick, Nick, Pfc,
†Urso, Charles J., Pfc,
Urso, Louis B., Pfc,
†Uschmann, Raymond B., Pfc,
Uschold, Raymond C., Pfc,
Uthoff, Jesse C., T/5,
Utley, James R., Pfc,
†Utley, John D., Pfc,
Uthe, Theodore H., Cpl,
Utt, Ewell D., Pvt,
Uytterbroek, Richard L., Pfc,

Vaccaro, Andrew A., Pvt,
Vaccaro, Charles L., Pfc,
Vaccaro, Dominic, Pvt,
Vahaly, George M., Pfc,
Vaile, Earl C., Sgt,
†Vaillancourt, Ernest J., Pfc,
Valancius, Walter J., Cpl,
Valcanis, Ernest N., Pvt,
Valderrama, Robert S., S/Sgt,
Valdez, Ausencio, Pfc,
Valdez, Fares, Pfc,
§Valdez, Jose F., Pfc,
Valdez, Lorenzo G., Pvt,
Valdez, Thomas P., Pvt,
Valek, Michael J., Pfc,
Valente, Rocco J., Pvt,
Valenti, Isadore L., T/4,
Valentin, Emilo D., Pfc,
Valentine, Elmer, Jr., Pvt,
Valentine, James W., Pfc,
Valentine, Harold A., Pfc,
†Valentino, Joseph J., Pvt,
†Valentino, Nicholas E., S/Sgt,
Valenzuela, Olegario L., S/Sgt,
†Valeri, Ernest, Sgt,
Valerio, Nicholas, Pvt,
Valish, Fred T., Pfc,
†Valkovich, Joseph C., Jr., Pvt,
Vallero, Joseph R., Pvt,
Vanacore, Joseph A., Pvt,
Van Anda, Carroll A., Sgt,
Vanatta, Elmer L., Pfc,
†Vanberg, Alvin B., Pfc,
Van Blargan, Herbert M., Pvt,
Van Breeman, Paul V., Pfc,
Van Buren, Julian, Pvt,
Van Buskirk, G. F., Sr., Pfc,
Van Buskirk, Hal, Pfc,
Vanca, George, Pfc,
Van Camp, Claude N., Pfc,
Van Campen, B. H., Pfc,
Vance, Albert R., T/5,
Vance, Alma E., T/Sgt,
Vance, Winifred C., Sgt,
†Van Cleave, John T., Pfc,
Van Cleave, W. F., Jr., S/Sgt,
Vandelinder, Francis C., Pvt,
Van Demark, Kenneth R., Pfc,
Van Denover, Gerald D., Pfc,
Vanderberg, Vernon L., Pvt,
*Vanderbilt, Frank H., S/Sgt,
Vander Jagt, Isaac C., Pfc,
†Vanderhoof, Victor S., Jr., Pvt,
Vanderkooi, George D., Pfc,
Vanderpool, James W., Pfc,
Vandervort, Francis H., S/Sgt,
Van Dine, Albert H., Pfc,
Vandivier, Guy C. D., Jr., Pfc,
†Van Eck, William R., Pfc,
‡Van Etten, Gordon E., Pvt,
Vangos, Costas A., Pfc,
Van Hewyk, John, Pvt,
Van Hoose, Peter R., Pfc,
Vanhorn, Robert M., Sgt,
Van Horn, Roy M., Pfc,
Van Houwe, Robert L., Pfc,
Vanhoy, Louis R., Capt,
‡Vanicek, Robert M., Pfc,
Vanik, John L., Sgt,
Van Kouwenberg, Jacob J., Pvt
Van Loon, James N., Pfc,
Van Lue, Clarence I., T/5,
Vann, Louis, Cpl,
Van Pelt, Delbert, Cpl,
‡Van Pelt, Harry, Jr., Pfc,
†Van Scoyoc, C. W., Jr., 2nd Lt,
Van Sloten, Henry, Pfc,
Van Steenburg, Perry A., Cpl,
Van Teyens, Nicholas, Pvt,
Vanusek, Joseph, Pfc,
Van Wey, Everett R., Pvt,
Van Wey, William S., Capt,
†Varga, Steve J., Sgt,
Vargas, Richard G., Pfc,
Vargo, Frank, Pvt,
Vargo, Michael J., Pfc,
Varle, Cyrille, Cpl,
Varnadore, Robert T., Pvt,
Varner, Jack R., Pfc,
Varner, Oliver T., S/Sgt,
Varnes, Elmer W., Sgt,
Varns, Lewis A., Pvt,
Vaslinek, John T., Pvt,
Vasquez, Federico, Pvt,
Vasquez, Gilbert E., Pfc,
*Vasquez, Jose, Pvt,
Vasquez, Remedios, Pvt,
Vassallo, John, Pfc,
Vasser, William V., Pvt,
Vastino, Nicholas A., Pfc,
†Vastola, Sam M., Pvt,
Vatter, John H., Pfc,
Vaughan, Harry R., Pfc,
Vaughan, James F., Pfc,
Vaughan, Hermon L., Pvt,
§Vaughn, Alfred D., Pvt,
Vaughn, James C., Jr., Cpl,
Vaughn, Marion E., Cpl,
Vaughn, Thomas G., Pvt,
Vaughn, Thomas R., S/Sgt,
Vaughn, J. Wilbur, Pvt,
Vaughn, William H., Pvt,
Vaught, John H., Pfc,
Vavrek, Luke C., Pvt,
Veatch, Floyd L., S/Sgt,
Veasey, Charles D., Pvt,
†Veilleux, Frenand L., Pvt,
Veldhuizen, Bernard, Pfc,
Velsor, Charles P., Pfc,
Veltri, Joseph P., Pvt,
*Velykis, Peter, Pfc,
Venable, Robert H., S/Sgt,
Venckus, Edward J., Pfc,
Vendetti, Ronald, T/4,
Venezia, Anthony A., Pfc,
†Venezia, Michael C., Sgt,
*Vent, Dale F., Pfc,
Ventola, William, Pvt,
Ventriglio, Nicholas, Pfc,
Verburg, James A., Sgt,
Vergari, Raymond D., Pfc,
†Ver Meulen, Edward F., Pfc,
Vermillion, Max R., Pfc,
†Vernon, Glenn O., Pfc,
†Vernon, Phillip H., Pvt,
Verrilli, Louis C., Pfc,
Verzilli, Anthony A., Sgt,
Vesci, Anthony T., Pvt,
Vesloski, Chester W., Pvt,
Vessella, Alphonse T., Pvt,
§Vestal, Edwin J., Pfc,
Vezzetti, Renato G., Pfc,
Vicario, Vincent F., Pfc,
†Vicic, Frank J., Pvt,
Vick, Charles W., Pfc,
Vickers, Lonnie F., T/4,
Vickner, Francis C., Pvt,
Vicko, Paul, Jr., Pvt,
Victor, Paul, Pvt,
Vieira, John, Jr., Pfc,
Viele, Donald F., Pfc,
Viera, Louis D., Pvt,
Vierth, Arthur W., Pfc,
Vietor, Hendrick W., Pvt,
§Vigil, Gilberto, Pfc,
Vigil, Gilbert S., Pfc,
Vigil, Maxiamo O., Pvt,
Vignati, Joseph, Pfc,
†Vilcot, Jules P., T/5,
Villane, Alphonse J., Pfc,
Villasenor, Frank, Pfc,
Villota, Joseph J., Pfc,
Vilt, Edward J., Pfc,
Vincelette, Claude A., Pvt,
Vincent, James T., Pvt,
Vincent, Loren E., Sgt,
Vines, Luther M., Sgt,
Vingelen, George K., T/5,
Vint, Raymond E., Capt,
Vinton, Frank H., Pfc,
†Viola, James V., Pfc,
†Vipperman, James L., Pvt,
†Viramontes, John G., Sgt,
Vires, Harvey, Pfc,
Visconti, Daniel M., Pfc,
Visconti, Lino L., Pfc,
†Vise, Radis A., Pvt,
Visga, Anthony P., Pvt,
Visich, Chester W., Pvt,
Vislocky, Nicholas, Jr., Pvt,
Visor, Leonard D., Pvt,
Vita, Joseph J., Jr., Pvt,
Vitale, John, Pfc,
Vitale, Joseph M., Pvt,
†Vitale, Prisco A., Pvt,
Vitek, Frank J., Pfc,
Vito, Anthony T., Pfc,
Vizzuso, Benjamin, Pfc,
Vockeroth, Earl P., Pvt,
‡Vogel, Abe, Pvt,
Vogel, Robert B., 1st Sgt,
†Vogt, Glennon J., Sgt,
†Vogt, Lawrence A., Pfc,
Vogt, Nelson W., Pfc,
Vogt, Oswald R., Pfc,
Voigts, Walter E., Sgt,
*Vojtash, Valentine G., Pvt,
Volant, Harry A., Sgt,
Volchok, William, Pvt,
Volenski, Frank, Pvt,
Volk, Charles, Pvt,
Volk, Ellsworth O., T/5,
Volk, John F., Pvt,
Volkmar, Walter H., Jr., Cpl,
†Vollmar, Chester G., Pvt,
Volpe, Anthony J., Pvt,
Volpe, Ralph, Pfc,
Volsen, Arthur J., 1st Lt,
Von Ins, August A., Pfc,
†Voorhees, Darryl V., Pvt,
Voss, Don J., Pvt,
Voss, Howard R., T/Sgt,
Votruba, Kenneth E., T/4,
Vough, Alvin L., Pvt,
Vowell, Earl P., S/Sgt,
Vrataric, Nicholas C., Sgt,
Vreeland, Edward L., Sgt,
Vronka, Edward J., Pfc,
†Vukmirovich, Nick, Pvt,
Vyskocil, Francis J., Pvt,

Wable, Richard E., Pvt,
Wade, James L., Pfc,
Waddell, Clarence W., Pfc,
Wade, Dee A., Sgt,
Wadkins, Emanuel F., Sgt,
Wady, Victor A., Pfc,
†Wagener, Jewel E., Pfc,
Waggoner, Lester T., Pvt,
Wagner, Aubrey M., Pvt,
Wagner, Bernard K. G., Pvt,
‡Wagner, Fred F., Pfc,
†Wagner, Herman E., Capt,
Wagner, Howard M., Jr., Pfc,
Wagner, Jacob, Pvt,
Wagner, Robert J., Pvt,
‡Wagner, Wiley W., Sgt,
Wagner, Willard F., S/Sgt,
Wagoner, Donald A., Sgt,
†Wagoner, John V., Pfc,
Waid, Ronald H., Pvt,
Wainstock, Louis, Pfc,
Waire, Calvin C., Pfc,
Waite, Calvin M., Pvt,
Waite, Lawrence C., Pfc,
Wakeman, Frederick, Pvt,
†Walbert, George, Pvt,
†Waldie, Alexander S., Pfc,
Waldner, Stanley C., 2nd Lt,
Waldo, George F., Pvt,
Waldron, Ralph W., Pfc,
Waldrop, Claud D., Pvt,
Waldrop, Eugene, Pvt,
Waldrop, James C., T/5,
Waldrop, Renoldo C., Pfc,
†Wale,, Albert J., Pvt,
Walek, John R., Pfc,
Walker, Bennett O., S/Sgt,
Walker, Carl E., T/5,
†Walker, Charlie R., Pfc,
Walker, Floyd H., Pvt,
*Walker, Guy C., Pvt,
†Walker, Herbert L., Pfc,
Walker, Joe Eugene, Pvt,
Walker, John R., Pfc,
Walker, Olen E., S/Sgt,
†Walker, Raymond T., Pvt,
Walker, Robert E., S/Sgt,
Walker, Robert E., Pvt,
Walker, Robert T., Pvt,
Walker, Robert W., Pvt,
†Walker, William C., Pvt,
Walker, William E., Pvt,
Walker, William R., Pvt,
Wall, Cornelius E., Pfc,
Wall, Edmon C., Pvt,
Wall, Fay A., Pfc,
†Wall, John P., Pvt,
Wall, Lloyd P., Pvt,
Wall, Stephen J., S/Sgt,
Wall, Truman H., T/Sgt,
Wallace, Charles C., Pfc,
Wallace, Charles R., Pvt,
Wallace, Dillon, Pvt
Wallace, Earl W., Cpl,
Wallace, Edwin L., Pvt,
Wallace, Eugene, Pvt,
Wallace, Floyd J., Jr., Pvt,
Wallace, Garland L., Pfc,
†Wallace, Glenn M. E., Pvt,
Wallace, Jacob S., Sgt,
†Wallace, John, Pfc,
Wallace, John A., Pvt
Wallace, Kenneth W., Lt Col,
Wallace, Mitchell M., Sgt,
Wallace, Robert E., Pvt,
Wallace, Thomas W., Pvt,
Wallace, William G., Pvt,
Wallace, William P., T/4
Wallace, William W., Pfc,
Wallar, Donald L., Pvt,
Wallin, Alfred M., Pvt,
†Wallin, John H., Pfc,
‡Wallingford, Howard T., Pvt,
*Wallis, Howard S., 1st Lt,
Wallis, Wilbert S., Pvt,
Walls, Charles D., Pvt,
Walls, Henry T., Pvt,
Walls, Joseph A., T/5,
Walmsley, Thomas D., Jr., Pfc
†Walsh, Carl N., Pvt,
†Walsh, Charles R., Pfc,
‡Walsh, Edward P., Jr., T/Sgt,
Walsh, Martin R., S/Sgt,
Walsh, Thomas P., Pvt,
Walsh, William E., T/5,
Walter, David, Sgt,
Walter, Michael, Cpl,
Walter, Robert O., Cpl,
†Walters, Arthur A., Pvt,
Walters, Charles L., Pfc,
Walters, Frank, Jr., Pfc,
‡Walters, John T., Pfc,
†Walters, Paul M., Pfc,
Walters, William F., Pfc,
Walters, William R., Pvt,
Waltman, William H., Sr., Pvt,
Walton, James H., Pfc,
‡Waltzer, Herbert, Pvt,
Wampler, Johnnie R.,
Wamsley, Glen M., Pvt,
Wandycz, Frank J., 2nd Lt,
Wang, Laverne E., Sgt,
Wangen, Arnold L., Pfc,
Wanless, Earl R., T/5,
Wannemacher, Maurice R., Pfc
Wanner, William, A., T/5,
Warachowski, Francis A., Pvt,
†Warbeck, Stephen S., Pfc,
†Ward, Christopher C., Pfc,
Ward, Earl, Pfc,
Ward, Elmer L., Pfc,
Ward, Elmer V., Pvt,
Ward, Ernest L., Pvt,
Ward, Gerald H., Pvt,
Ward, Holt R., Pvt,
Ward, James E., Jr., Pfc,
Ward, James H., Pfc,
Ward, Lendon, Pvt,
Ward, Marvin W., Cpl,
§Ward, Maysill E., Pvt,
§Ward, Melvin L., Pfc,
‡Ward, Robert E., Pvt,
Ward, Walter S., Pvt,
Wardell, Carl A., S/Sgt,
Warden, John W., Pvt,
Ware, Cecil A., Pvt,
Ware, Thomas J., T/5,
Ware, Wayne L., Jr., Pfc,
Warfel, David P., Pvt,
*Warger, Myon, Pvt,
Warholic, Joseph, Cpl,
Warming, Stanford L., Cpl,
Warmeth, James L., Sgt,
Warne, William H., Pvt,
Warner, Ernie O., S/Sgt,
Warne, Everett L., Pfc,
Warner, Floyd E., Sgt,
Warner, John H., Sgt,
Warner, Paul E., Pfc,
Warnke, Gustave O., Pvt,
Warnock, Walleyn M., Pfc,
†Warr, Robert L., Sgt,
Warra, Fred M., 2nd Lt,
Warren, Bill R., Cpl,
†Warren, Cleveland A., 2nd Lt,
Warren, Frederick T., Pvt,
Warren, G. T., Pfc,
Warren, James, Jr., Sgt,
Warren, Kenneth E., Pfc,
Warren, Samuel, Pfc,
Warren, Thomas R., Pvt,
Warren, Tom, Pfc,
Warren, Virgil L., Pfc,
Warren, William J., Pfc,
Warren, William W., Sgt,
†Warrington, Stanley R., Pfc,
Wartella, Henry O., T/5,
Warus, Otto M., Cpl,
Waseleski, Edward, Pvt,
Wash, Wirt L., Pvt,
Washburn, Murray A., Pfc,
†Washineski, John L., Pvt,
Washnock, Michael J., Pfc,
Wasilick, Michael C., Jr., Sgt,
*Wasnick, John, Pfc,
Wasserstein, Hyman, Pfc,
Wasson, Carl H., Pfc,
Wasson, Lawrence B., Pvt,
Waterman, Frederick K., Pvt,
†Waters, Robert A., Sgt,
Waterworth, Earl L., Pfc,
Watkevitch, Peter M., Pfc,
Watkins, Albert L., Sgt,
Watkins, Herbert V., Pvt.
Watkins, Kenneth W., Pfc,
Watkins, Matthew F., Jr., Pvt,
Watkins,Oscar C., Pvt,
Watkins, Ralph L., Pfc,
Watkins, Russell L., Pfc,
Watkins, Wayne, Pfc,
Watson, Albert G., Pfc,
Watson, Allen B., Pvt,
†Watson, Donald P., Pvt,
Watson, Earl, Cpl,
Watson, John A., Pvt,
Watson, Lloyd C., Pfc,
Watson, William R., Pvt,
Watt, Archie, Pvt,
Watts, Albert G., Pfc,
Watts, Austin J., Pfc,
§Watts, Franklin L., Pvt,
Watts, Oscar W., Pvt,
Wayne, Ainsley C., 1st Lt,
Wayrynen, Reino W., Pfc,
†Wazny, Casimir P., Pvt,
†Weakley, Alvin W., 2nd Lt,
†Weakley, Luther R., Pvt,
‡Wear, Homer W., Pfc,
Weatherford, Thomas H., Pfc,
Weatherley, Carl, Sgt,
Weatherman, Paul L., Pfc,
Weathers, Norton W., Pfc,
Weaver, Alexander J., Sgt,
Weaver, Charles E., Pfc,
Weaver, Charles W., Pfc,
Weaver, Horace J., Sgt,
Weaver, James T., Sgt,
Weaver, John V., Cpl,
Weaver, Noah H., Pfc,
†Weaver, Robert E., Sgt,
†Weaver, Robert L., Pvt,
Weaver, Roy H., Pvt,
Weaver, William G., Pfc,
‡Weaver, William H., Pfc,
Webb, Aden D., Pvt,
Webb, Burgess, Pfc,
Webb, Carl V., Pfc,
Webb, Charles L., Pvt,
Webb, Charles W., 1st Lt,
Webb, Charles H., Pvt,

† Killed in Action. * Prisoner of War. ‡ Missing in Action. § Died of Wounds.

Webb, Cloise B., Pfc,
‡Webb, Duke M., Pfc,
Webb, Edward F., Pvt,
Webb, Elmer E., Pfc,
Webb, Floyd L., S/Sgt,
Webb, Gordon S., Pfc,
Webb, Joe F., Pvt,
Webb, Leslie S., Pfc,
†Webb, Richard F., Pvt,
Webb, Thomas C., Pfc,
Webb, William C., Pfc,
†Webb, William P., Pfc,
Webb, William P., Pfc,
*Webb, William W., Pfc,
Webber, Coy R.,
Webber, Donald E., Pfc,
Weber, Chester E., Pfc,
Weber, Martin, S/Sgt,
Weber, Martin J., Pvt,
Weber, Stanley, T/Sgt,
Weber, Vincent P., Pvt,
†Webster, Charles H., Pvt,
Webster, Donald H., Cpl,
Webster, Paul K., Pfc,
Webster, Richard S., Pfc,
Webster, Shelton, Pfc,
Weddell, James R., Capt,
Wedding, Albert, Pfc,
‡Wedding, Vincent D., 1st Sgt,
Wedel, Milford N., Pfc,
Wedoo, Robert O., Pfc,
Wee, Erling L., Pfc,
Weeks, Alton L., Sgt,
Weeks, Vernon C., Pfc,
Wehlage, Victor F., Pfc,
Wehmann, Henry, Pvt,
*Wehr, Clarence E., Cpl,
Wehrenberg, F. W., Pvt,
Weidenkopf, Leo F., S/Sgt,
Weigand, Julius F., Pvt,
Weigle, Paul L., Pfc,
Weikle, Calvin S., Pvt,
Weikle, Lamar A., Pfc,
†Weilacher, Emden L., Pvt,
Weimaster, Floyd V., Sgt,
Weiner, Max, Pvt,
Weingarden, Alfred, T/Sgt,
†Weingarden, John R., Sgt,
Weinger, Stanley L., Pfc,
Weinrich, Henry J., T/4,
Weinstein, Louis, Pvt,
Weinstein, Philip L., Pfc,
Weipert, Harley L., Pfc,
Weir, Lyle E., Pvt,
Weishuhn, Clarence A., Pfc,
Weiss, Edward R., Pfc,
Weiss, Fred R., S/Sgt,
Weiss, Melvin F., Pfc,
Weiss, Paul, Pfc,
†Weiss, Seymour, Pvt,
Weisser, James J., S/Sgt,
Weissler, Benjamin, Pvt
Weitl, George H., S/Sgt,
Weitz, Joseph F., Pfc,
Weitzel, William A., Lt Col,
Weitzman, William, S/Sgt,
Welch, Albert A., Pfc,
Welch, John D., Pfc,
Welch, John F., Jr., Pvt,
Welch, Leonard, Pvt,
Welch, Stephen H., Sgt,
Welch, Thomas J., Pfc,
†Weldon, Lloyd M., Pvt,
Welhaf, George L., Pfc,
Welker, William, Jr., Pfc,
Wellens, Harold L., T/5,
†Wellingtham, Alan H., Cpl,
Wellington, Wallace W., Cpl,
Welliver, Clyde N., Cpl,
Wells, Dorsie S., Pfc,
Wells, George W., Sgt,
Wells, Richard F., S/Sgt,
Wells, Robert E., Pfc,
Wells, Willard W., Pvt,
Welsch, Alvin H., Pfc,
Welsh, David, Jr., Pfc,
Wendlowsky, Paul F., Pvt,
†Wendt, Herman A., Pfc,
Wentworth, Harold C., T/5,
†Werbie, Thomas J., Pfc,
Werner, Erwin H., S/Sgt,
Weronki, Stanley F., Pvt,
Werth, Robert J., Pfc,
Wertman, Harry F., Pfc,
§Werzbicki, Walter F., Pfc,
‡Wesack, Everett H. M., Pfc,
‡Wescott, Ernest E., Pvt,
Weselowski, John C., Pvt,
Weselowski, Joseph, Cpl,
Wesenberg, Daniel W., Pvt,
Wessel, Warren G., Pfc,
Wessen, Talmadge C., Pfc,
West, Boyd C., Pvt,
West, Carmez, Pfc,
§West, Coolidge T., Pvt,
West, Dan H., Sgt,

West, Edward O., Cpl,
‡West, Glenn U., Pvt,
West, Harold R., Pfc,
West, James M., Pfc,
West, Jesse J., Pvt,
West, John A., Pvt,
West, John R., Jr., Pvt,
West, Marlow H., Pvt,
West, Marvin R., Pvt,
West, Robert T., Pvt,
‡West, Ross, Pvt,
West, William J., Pvt,
West, Zane, Pvt,
Westenhefe, William, Pvt,
Westercamp, James H., Sgt,
‡Westerfield, William, Pvt,
Western, Cyril C., Pvt,
Westover, Clark R., Pfc,
Westwood, Harold, Pvt,
Wettergreen, Carl L., Pfc,
§Wetzel, Orville, Pfc,
Weverstad, Stanley W., Sgt,
Wewer, Alphons J., Sgt,
Whalen, John F., Pvt,
Whalen, Michael R., Pfc,
Whall, Winston G., Capt,
Wharton, Samuel N., Pvt,
Wheatley, Carson, S/Sgt
Wheeler, James S., Pvt,
Wheeler, Norman L., Pvt,
Wheeler, Orin J., Pvt,
‡Wheeler, William J., S/Sgt,
Wheeler, William J., Pvt,
Wheeley, Leroy S., Pvt,
Wheelock, George A., Pvt,
Whelchel, Henry L., Sgt,
§Whetton, Frank J., Pvt
Whitby, Harry F., Pfc,
Whitacre, Leon F., Pvt,
Whitaker, Charlie B., Pfc,
Whitaker, Ford, Pvt,
Whidby, Nathaniel, S/Sgt,
Whitcomb, Bruce T., Pfc,
Whitcomb, Ralph O., Cpl,
White, Allen H., Pfc,
§White, Alvin G., Sgt,
White, Amasa T., Pvt,
White, Arthur I., Pvt,
White, Basil A., Pvt,
‡White, Charles D., Pvt,
†White, C. L., Jr., 2nd Lt,
White, Clarence H., Jr., Maj,
White, David E., Cpl,
White, Dorsey L., Pfc,
White, Ernest F., Pfc,
White, Floyd E., Cpl,
White, Frank L., Pfc,
White, George W., Jr., T/5,
†White, Gilmer W., Jr., Pvt,
White, Guy E., Pvt,
White, Henry T., Cpl,
White, Jack C., Pfc,
White, James B., T/4,
White, James D., Pfc,
White, James J., Pfc,
White, James V., Pfc,
White, Joe D., Pfc,
White, John T., Pfc,
White, Joseph T., Pfc,
‡White, Kenneth T., Pvt,
White, Morton, Pvt,
White, Nathan W., 1st Lt,
White, Paul R., Pvt,
White, Radford C., Sgt,
White, Robert A., Pvt,
†White, Robert A., S/Sgt,
†White, Roger K., 2nd Lt,
White, Sheff O., Pfc
White, Sylvester F., Jr., Cpl,
White, Ted C., Pvt,
White, Troy R., S/Sgt,
†White, William O., S/Sgt,
White, Wylie F., Pvt,
Whitecotton, Arthur A., Pfc,
‡Whited, Johnnie W., Pfc,
Whitehead, Earl W., Pfc
Whitehead, George, Jr., Pfc,
Whitehead, Grant, Pvt,
†Whitehead, V. O., Pvt,
†Whiteknact, George N., Pvt,
Whiteman, William J., Sgt,
Whitesell, Donald R., Pfc,
Whitfield, Charles L., Jr., Pvt,
Whitfield, Emery O., S/Sgt,
Whiting, Charles B., Pvt,
†Whitley, Adam, Pvt,
Whitley, Alton C., Pvt,
Whitley, Clifton O., Sgt
Whitley, Donald W., Pvt,
†Whitley, William C., Jr.,
Whitlow, Malon L., Pvt,
Whitmer, Harry J., Pfc,
Whitmire, Crockett, Pvt,
Whitmore, Don E., Pvt,
†Whitney, Donald R., Pfc,
Whitsett, Joe E., Pfc,

Whitson, Harold A., Pvt,
‡Whittemore, Frank J., Pfc,
†Whittington, Albert E., Pvt,
Whittle, Roger L., Pfc,
Whyte, Robert N., Pvt,
Wiant, Jerry L., Pfc,
Wicherts, Lawrence H., Pvt,
Wicka, Henry L., Pfc,
Wicker, Loren E., S/Sgt,
Wickham, Norbert R., Jr., Pfc,
Wicklein, Andrew E., Pfc,
Widejkis, Staley J., Pfc,
Widmayer, Edward J., Pfc,
†Wiede, Walter G., Sgt,
‡Wiederholt, Wilbur F., Pfc,
Wiedow, Harry R., Pfc,
Wiese, Alvin J., T/4,
‡Wiese, Elroy J. A., Pfc,
Wiese, Emil C., T/4
Wiese, Kenneth D., Pfc,
Wiest, Francis J., Pfc,
Wiest, Irving G., T/5,
Wigetman, Harold, Capt,
Wiggins, Lloyd, J., S/Sgt,
Wigley, James C., Pfc,
Wiik, Toivo V., Pfc,
Wikoff, Wayne V., Pvt
Wiksstrom, Charles M., Pfc,
Wilber, Charles M., Pfc,
Wilcox, Alonzo A., Sgt,
Wildesin, Raymond C., Pfc,
Wilde, Edwin T., Pfc,
Wilder, Fred B., Sgt,
Wilder, Oliver D., Pfc,
Wildesin, Raymond C., Pfc,
†Wildrick, Andrew A., Pfc
Wilensky, Sidney R., T/Sgt,
Wiles, Erle, W., Sgt,
Wiles, James T., Pfc,
Wiles, Jesse E., Pfc
Wiley, George C., Pfc,
Wiley, Lyle J., Pfc
Wilhelm, Woodrow E., Pfc,
Wilk, Paul F., Pvt,
Wilk, Toivo V., Pfc,
Wilk, Walter, Sgt,
Wilke, Loren W., Pfc,
Wilkerson, Donald R., Sgt,
†Wilkerson, Robert A., Pvt,
Wilkerson, Roy L., Pvt,
Wilkie, William C., Pfc,
Wilkins, Charles T., Pfc,
†Wilkins, Chester O., Pvt,
Wilkins, Harry E., 1st Lt,
†Wilkins, Johnnie W., Sgt,
Wilkins, William C., Pvt,
†Wilkinson, Earl, Pfc,
Wilkinson, Robert C., Pvt,
Wilkinson, William H., Pvt
Wilks, Harry C., T/5
Willbanks, Robert R., Sr., Pvt,
Willett, Harry, Pvt,
Willett, John W., Pvt,
Willett, Wilson E., Sgt
Willey, Albert N., Pfc,
Willhite, Otis M., Pvt,
Williamon, James B., Pvt,
Williams, Bill W., Pfc,
Williams, Billy B., Pvt
‡Williams, Calvin P., Pvt
Williams, Carvis P., Pfc,
†Williams, Charles, Pvt,
Williams, Charles P., Pvt,
Williams, Charlie C., Pfc,
Williams, Clifford O., Pvt,
Williams, Clyde E., Pfc,
Williams, Earl C., Pfc,
Williams, Eddie H., Pvt,
Williams, Edward, Pvt
Williams, Eugene W., Pvt,
†Williams, Floyd E., Jr., Pfc,
‡Williams, Francis B., Pvt,
Williams, Frank L., Capt,
Williams, Freddie L., S/Sgt,
Williams, Harry A., Pfc,
†Williams, Harry L., Pvt,
Williams, Hazel, Pfc,
Williams, Henry T., S/Sgt,
Williams, Howard J., S/Sgt,
Williams, Howard M., Pvt,
Williams, Hubert S., Pvt,
†Williams, James B., Pvt,
Williams, James M., Pvt,
Williams, John D., Pvt,
Williams, John E., Pfc,
Williams, John L., Pfc,
†Williams, John O., Lt Col,
Williams, L. C., Sgt
Williams, Leland A., Pfc,
Williams, Leo A., Pvt,
Williams, L. O., S/Sgt,
Williams, Kenneth O., Pfc
Williams, Lloyd T., Pfc,
Williams, Manford, Pvt
§Williams, Marvin D., T/5,

Williams, Maurice L., S/Sgt,
Williams, Ralph H., Pfc,
Williams, Raymond C., Pvt,
†Williams, Raymond H., Pvt,
Williams, Robert C., Jr., Maj,
Williams, Robert E., Pvt,
†Williams, Robert J., Sgt,
Williams, Roy, Pvt,
‡Williams, Simon B., Pfc,
Williams, Thomas O., Pvt
†Williams, Warren B., S/Sgt,
†Williams, William S., Pfc
Williamson, Aubrey L., Sgt.,
Williamson, Brycel L., Pvt,
†Williamson, Charles R., Pvt,
Williamson, Elwin, E., Pfc,
Williamson, Floyd E., Sgt,
Williamson, Gerald, Cpl,
Williamson, James H., S/Sgt,
Williamson, John W., Pfc,
Williamson, Robert E., Pfc,
Williamson, Russel T., Pvt,
Willick, Lyle A., Pvt,
Willigar, Lawrence H., Sgt
Willingham, George H., Pfc,
Willis, Claude, Cpl,
Willis, Clifford E., Pvt,
Willis, Emerson C., Pfc,
Willis, Emery, Pvt,
†Willis, John E., Pvt,
Willoughby, Donald E., Pfc,
Willoughby, Fitzhugh L., Pfc,
Willoughby, Wayne F., Pvt,
Wills, Bill R., Pvt,
*Wills, Edward, Pvt,
Wilmot, Basil A., 2nd Lt,
Wilmoth, Eli J., Sgt,
Wills, James P., Pvt,
Wilson, Albert W., Pvt,
Wilson, Arley E., Pfc,
Wilson, Arthur L., Cpl
§Wilson, Bassy M., Pfc,
Wilson, Carlyle G., Pfc,
Wilson, Carlyle H., 1st Lt,
Wilson, Charles A., Pfc,
Wilson, Charles A., S/Sgt,
Wilson, Charles F., Pfc,
Wilson, David A., Sgt,
Wilson, Edwin H., Pvt,
Wilson, Forest E., Pfc,
Wilson, Francis A., Pfc,
Wilson, Garnet A., Sgt,
Wilson, Glen, Sgt,
Wilson, Gwyn E., Pfc,
Wilson, Harold, Pfc,
Wilson, Harry, Pfc,
Wilson, Harry C., Pfc,
Wilson, James B., Pfc,
Wilson, James M., Pfc,
Wilson, James R., Pvt,
Wilson, Joe, T/5,
Wilson, Joseph O.,
Wilson, Joseph W., S/Sgt,
Wilson, Lee W., Pfc,
Wilson, Maurice V., Sgt,
Wilson, Millard, Pvt,
Wilson, Naaman N., Pfc,
Wilson, Ollie R., Pvt,
Wilson, Rex E., Pfc,
†Wilson, Robert, Pfc,
Wilson, Robert E., Cpl,
†Wilson, Robert T., Jr., S/Sgt,
†Wilson, Roy W., Pfc,
Wilson, Royl K., Cpl,
*Wilson, Sidney A., Pfc,
Wilson, Sidney L., Pfc,
Wilson, Soule R., Pfc,
Wilson, Virgil, Sgt
Wilson, Virgil L., Pfc,
Wilson, William, Pvt,
Wilson, William L., Pfc,
Wilund, Patrick, 1st Sgt,
*Wimberly, Cathey G., Sgt,
Wims, John J., T/3,
†Wimsett, Forrest L., Pfc,
Winans, Richard, S/Sgt,
Winchell, E. H., Jr., S/Sgt,
Winden, Warren E., Pvt,
Winders, George, S/Sgt,
Windsor, David L., Pvt,
Winegar, Johnny W., Pfc,
Wineman, Arthur E., Pfc,
Wines, George E., Pfc,
Winey, Charles W., Pfc,
Wing, Earl E., Pfc,
Wingard, Clifton W., Pfc,
Wingard, Liss A., Pvt,
Wingard, Nevin W., Pfc,
Winger, Arthur L., S/Sgt.,
Wingo, James W., Pvt,
Winiarski, Edward T., Pfc,
Winkle, Frank N., Jr., Pfc,
Winkleman, George H., Pfc,
Winkler, Russell J., Cpl,
Winn, Alvin, T/5,
Winn, William W., M/Sgt,

Winscher, Kenneth W., Pvt,
Winslow, Donald L., S/Sgt,
Winslow, Edward M., Pfc,
Winter, Charles H., Jr.,
Winter, Richard E., S/Sgt,
†Winter, Virgil W., Cpl,
‡Winters, Charles R., Pvt,
Winters, Gilmer F., Pvt
Winters, John, T/5,
‡Winters, Robert V., Pfc,
Wirth, Donald J., Pvt,
Wirzbioki, Joseph S., Pfc,
Wise, David A., Pfc,
Wise, Marion C., Pvt,
†Wise, Samuel G., Pfc,
Wisnewski, Walter S., Pvt,
Wisniewski, Casmir J., Pfc,
Wisniewski, Chester G., Pfc,
Wisniewski, Frank A., Pvt,
Wissehr, Emil L., T/5,
Wissman, Harry, Pvt
Witbeck, Allan A., 1st Lt,
Withers, Lawrence E., Pfc,
Withers, Thomas E., S/Sgt,
Withey, John J., Sgt,
Witkowski, Edward L., Pfc,
†Withowski, Frank A., Pfc,
Witt, Charles M., Pfc,
*Witt, George A., Pfc,
Witt, Joseph W., Pvt,
Witt, Paul W., Pfc,
Witte, William A., Pfc,
Wiloczewski, Walter B., Sgt,
Wiodarczyk, Emil F., T/5,
†Wixon, Thomas S., Pvt,
Wnorowski, John J., Pfc,
Wnuk, Walter J., Pfc,
Wodzinski, Edward A., Pvt,
Wohrman, Harry E., Pvt
Woitas, Harold E., Pfc
Woith, Ralph E., Pfc,
Wojciechowski, B. W., T/5,
Wojewoda, Thad J., Pfc,
Wojnarowski, Anthony B., Pvt,
Wojtowicz, Eugene H., Pfc,
Wojturski, William J., Pvt,
Wolak, Charles J., Pfc,
†Wolaver, David A., Pfc,
Wolever, William H., 2nd Lt,
Wolf, James L., Cpl,
Wolf, Thomas E., Pfc,
Wolf, Vernon L., Pfc,
*Wolfe, Alexander, Pvt
Wolfe, Emmett S., Pvt,
Wolfe, George D., T/3,
Wolfe, John, Pfc,
Wolfe, John M., Pfc,
Wolfe, Olin, Cpl,
Wolfe, Robert J., Pfc,
Wolfe, Walter J., T/4,
‡Wolfe, Harvey A., Pvt,
Wolfen, Haywood M., Sgt,
Wolff, Frank D., Pvt,
Wolford, Rufoe N., Pfc,
Wolfson, Henry, Pvt,
Woltz, Paul F., Pfc,
§Wolven, Llewellyn R., Pvt,
Womack, Harold O., Pvt,
Wonderley, Percy W., Jr., Pfc,
Wonderling, Eugene, Pfc,
Wong, Ming K., Pvt,
Wong, Roland C., Pfc,
†Wong, Sing, Pfc,
Wong, Theodore S., Pvt,
†Wong, William Y., Pvt,
Woo, Sun V., T/5,
‡Wood, Arthur E., Sr., Pfc,
Wood, Burl L., Pfc,
Wood, Edward J., Sgt,
Wood, Floyd S., Pvt,
Wood, George E., S/Sgt,
‡Wood, George E., Pfc,
Wood, Leonard H., T/4
Wood, Ralph E., 1st Sgt,
Wood, Roy M., Pfc,
†Wood, William D., Pvt,
Wood, William F., Jr., S/Sgt,
Wood, Willis, T/4,
Woodall, Jack L., Sgt,
Woodward, Clifford J., Pfc,
Woodward, Maldwyn G., Pfc
Woodward, Ras M., Pfc,
Wooddell, George P., Sgt
Woodford, Clair G., Pvt,
Woodley, Herbert D., Pvt,
Woodman, Wilbur J., Pfc,
Woodruff, Charles M., Pvt,
Woods, Frank E., Pfc,
Woods, James C., Pfc,
Woods, Lawrence F., Pvt,
Woods, Leo W., Jr., Pvt,
Woods, Michael J., 1st Sgt,
Woods, Nolan E., Pfc,
Woods, Rene E., Pvt,
Woods, Roy M., S/Sgt,
Woods, Thomas M., Pfc,

† Killed in Action. * Prisoner of War. ‡ Missing in Action. § Died of Wounds.

Woods, Warren C. H., Pvt,
Woods, Warren D., Sgt,
†Woodson, Waldo, Sgt,
Woodward, Lowell D., Pvt,
Woodward, Willard N., Pfc,
Woodworth, Alva E., Sgt,
Woolcott, Harry, Jr.,
Wooldridge, Robert B.,
Wooley, Ray O., Pfc,
Woolfe, Philip, Cpl,
Woolums, Robert W., Pvt,
†Woolwine, Carl H., Pfc
Woome, Billy, Pvt,
Woosley, Hassel, Pfc,
Wooster, Forrest A., Pfc,
Wooten, J. D., Pfc,
Wooten, Robert M., Pvt,
†Worden, Frank, Jr., Pvt,
Worden, Walter, Jr., Pvt,
Worebey, John, Pfc,
Workman, Mathew R., Pvt,
Worley, Jess D., Pfc,
Worley, Roy T., Pvt,
Worrall, John A., Pfc,
Worthen, Hal R., Pfc,
Worthington, Elbert T., Pfc,
Wosniak, C., Pfc,
Woyniak, John A., Jr., Pfc,
Woytowicz, Theodore, Pvt,
†Wozneak, Joseph G., Pvt,
Woznicki, John J., Pfc,
Wozniczka, Walter J., Pfc,
‡Wray, Bert H., 1st Lt,
Wray, John W., Pfc,
Wrenn, Calvin C., Pvt,
Wrenn, Eugene L., Jr., T/5,
Wright, Clay W., T/4,
Wright, Edward G., Pfc,
Wright, Elbert C., S/Sgt,
‡Wright, Harold R., Pvt,
Wright, James M., Pfc,
Wright, Joe B., Pfc,
Wright, John H., Pfc,
Wright, Lawrence C., Pfc,
Wright, Robert C., S/Sgt,
Wright, Robert E., T/5,
‡Wright, Robert S., Pvt,
Wright, Seymour C., 1st Lt,
Wright, William T., 1st Lt,
Wroble, Vincent, Sgt,
§Wroe, Edmund, Jr., 1st Lt,
Wrona, Theodore W., 2nd Lt,
‡Wrote, Fred W., Sgt,
Wubbels, Lester R., Pfc
†Wubbens, Vernon L., Pvt,
Wuchte, Emil R., Sgt,
Wudarski, Theodore D., Pfc,
‡Wunderler, Walter P., Pfc,
Wurgler, William W., Cpl,

Wurpel, Clifford A., Pfc,
Wurtsbaugh, Leroy A., Pfc,
Wyatt, Billy G., Sgt,
‡Wyatt, Guard, Pfc,
†Wyatt, Henry J., Jr., Pfc,
Wyatt, Loyd T., S/Sgt,
Wyatt, Richard, Pvt,
Wyatt, Robert H., T/5,
Wyckoff, Donald G., Cpl,
Wyeth, Irving R., Capt,
Wykoff, Gordon N., T/5,
*Wyman, J. C., Pfc,
Wynn, Harold E., Pvt,
Wynn, Harvey E., Cpl,
Wyse, David W., Pvt,

Xavier, Joseph, Pvt,

‡Yakubec, John, Pfc,
Yancey, Floyd C., T/4,
Yandora, Michael B., Cpl,
†Yanish, William G., S/Sgt,
Yankee, Arlen, Pfc,
Yankowski, Joseph P., Pvt,
Yannon, Anthony, Pfc,
†Yannuzzi, Nicholas, Pvt,
Yanoski, Edward, Pfc,
Yarbrough, Glynn N., Pfc,
Yarbrough, Jerrell, Pfc,
Yarbrough, Marshall F., Pfc,
Yarbrough, Riley L., S/Sgt,
Yarcheck, Steve, A., S/Sgt,
Yarger, Willard A., Pvt,
Yarlett, Joseph C., Pvt,
Yarnall, George W., Capt,
Yarrow, Donald L., Pfc,
Yarusawych, George, Pvt,
Yates, Arthur E., S/Sgt,
Yates, Eugene, Pvt,
Yates, Glen C., Pfc,
Yates, Martin C., Pfc,
Yates, Ralph, Capt,
Yates, Robert C., Pvt,
Yaunk, Donald C., Pvt,
†Yavaniski, John J., Pvt,
Yawn, Thomas D., Pvt,
Ybarronde, Vincent A., Pfc,
Yeager, Doane, Jr., Pfc,
Yeager, Harold J., Cpl,
Yeager, Harvey A., T/4,
Yeager, Howard D., T/5,
Yearwood, John K., Pfc,
Yecko, George F., Pfc,
Yelle, John W., T/5,
‡Yepsen, Forrest B., Pvt,
†Yerardi, Salvatore C., S/Sgt,
‡Yetter, Charles F., 1st Sgt,

§Yetter, Howard I., Pfc,
†Yingling, David M., Pfc,
Yoakum, John D., T/Sgt,
Yochum, Philip T., Pfc,
Yohn, Ernest W., Pfc,
Yoho, Clarence J., S/Sgt,
York, Chase B., Sgt,
Yorkovich, Anthony, Pfc,
Yorty, Sherwood L., T/5,
Yost, James H., Pfc,
Yost, Lester E., Cpl,
Young, Archibald R., Pvt,
Young, Billy M., Pfc,
§Young, Carl W., Pfc,
Young, Clinton F., Cpl,
Young, Clyde, Pvt,
Young, Darmond W., Pvt,
†Young, Donald L., S/Sgt,
Young, Donald R., S/Sgt,
Young, Elmer C., Cpl,
Young, Francis B., 1st Lt,
Young, Joe A., Pvt,
Young, Joseph C., Pvt,
Young, Kin H., T/4,
Young, Lawrence D., Pfc,
Young, Lester T., Sgt,
Young, Lionel F., Pfc,
Young, Richard B., Pfc,
Young, Richard T., Maj,
†Young, Vernon W., 2nd Lt,
Young, Vincent E., Pvt,
Young, Wah H., Pvt,
Young, William, T/5,
Young, William, Cpl,
Youngquist, L. L., Pfc,
†Yturri, John, Sgt,
†Yuengert, George R., Pfc,
Yuknavich, Andrew J., Pfc,
Yunger, John F., Jr., M/Sgt,
Yunker, Joseph A., Pfc,
Yurek, Carl J., T/5,
*Yurek, John P., Pfc,
Yurisich, Harold M., Pfc,
Yurkevicy, Benjamin G., Pvt,
Yurkovich, Rudy M., Pfc,
Yurosko, Andrew, Pfc,
†Yusko, Andrew J., Pfc,
Yusko, John L., Jr., Pfc,
†Yutzy, Kenneth J., S/Sgt,

†Zabarsky, Herbert, Pfc,
Zacara, Michael, Pvt,
Zachara, John F., Pfc,
†Zachrich, Nelson R., Pvt,
Zachwieja, Joseph S., Pfc,
Zackeroff, Paul, Pfc,
Zagleskie, John, Pvt,

Zagornik, Henry J., Sgt,
Zahradka, Robert L., Pfc,
Zakas, Edward J., Pfc,
Zaki, John, Pvt,
Zakreski, Henry L., Sgt,
Zaleneski, Tony, Sgt,
Zaletel, John V., Pfc,
‡Zalewski, Constantine J., Pvt,
§Zalka, Louis J., Pfc,
Zambri, Michael J., Pfc,
Zambrzycki, Stanley J., Pfc,
Zampogna, Joseph F., Pfc,
Zanardi, Daniel J., Pvt,
Zandy, Mario J., Pfc,
Zapka, Steve, Pfc,
†Zappile, Charles C., Pvt,
Zappulla, Sebastian, Pfc,
Zaremsky, Sam, Pfc,
Zartarian, Vaughn M., Pvt,
Zarzecki, Bruce, Pfc,
Zasada, Stanley J., Pfc,
Zatovich, William, Pvt,
Zavarise, Louis, Pvt,
Zawacki, Anthony G., Pfc,
‡Zawacki, Joseph J., Pvt,
Zawacki, John H., Pfc,
Zawacky, Chester P., Pfc,
†Zawada, Stanley J., Pvt,
Zawadski, Alfred J., Pfc,
Zawojski, Bernard, Pvt,
Zazzaro, Frank S., Pfc,
Zazzera, Frank L., S/Sgt,
Zdanowicz, Walter V., T/4,
†Zdimal, Albert W., Pvt,
Zealer, Martin E., Pvt,
Zebro, Frank J., Pfc,
Zech, Richard L., Cpl,
Zecha, Ferdinand, Jr.,
Zeckowski, Edward, Pvt,
Zedayke, Michael, T/5,
Zeifman, Sol S., Cpl,
Zeiger, Alfred A., T/4,
Zeigler, Merle A., Pvt,
Zeiler, Leonard A., Pvt,
Zeliff, Grandion V., Pvt,
Zelitsky, Morton, Pfc,
Zell, William R., Pfc,
‡Zemba, Michael, Pvt,
Zene, Michael R., Pfc,
Zepeda, Pedro B., Pvt,
Zetomer, Ivan, T/3,
Ziarko, Paul P., Pfc,
Ziccarelli, Jack, Pfc,
Ziegler, Fred E., 1st Lt,
Ziek, Arthur R., Pvt,
†Zielinski, Frank H., Sgt,
Zielinski, Joseph M., Pvt,

Ziemba, John D., Pvt,
Ziemba, Thaddeus F., Pvt,
Zierolf, Robert E., S/Sgt,
Zieziula, Walter J., Pfc,
Zilka, Raymond J., Pfc,
Zillgitt, Emery D., S/Sgt,
Zimmerle, Charles, Jr., Pfc,
Zimmerman, Charles D., Pvt,
Zimmerman, George H., S/Sgt,
Zimmerman, James N., S/Sgt,
Zimmerman, Robert C., Cpl,
‡Zimmerman, Vincent S., Pvt,
†Zinda, Jake E., Pfc,
†Zinda, Oliver J., Pvt,
Zink, Dee J., Pfc,
Zink, Virgil L., Pfc,
*Zinsmeister, Edward J., Pfc,
Ziolkowski, Vincent T., Pvt,
Ziolo, William J., Pfc,
*Ziomek, Leonard J., Pvt,
Zipf, Robert L., T/4,
Zirgibel, William J., Pvt,
Zirilli, Frank G., S/Sgt,
†Zisner, Irving, Pvt,
Zito, Michael R., Pvt,
Zito, Rocco A., Pvt,
Zoellner, Richard K., Pfc,
Zofrea, Joseph J., Pvt,
Zoltowski, Theodore J., Pvt,
Zoppa, Jerry T., S/Sgt,
Zorn, Leslie J., Pvt,
Zorn, Niles C., Pfc,
Zorna, Joseph R., Pfc,
†Zubal, Leroy J., Pvt,
Zuber, Robert P., T/5,
Zuehlke, Raymond, Pfc,
Zukauskas, Albert A., Pfc,
Zukauskas, Thomas E., Pvt,
§Zullo, Michael A., Pvt,
Zunino, John W., Pfc,
Zunner, Edward B., Pvt,
Zupan, Vincent A., Pfc,
Zupancich, John J., Pvt,
†Zupo, William L., Pfc,
Zur, Francis W., Pvt,
Zuraw, Leon, S/Sgt,
Zurawski, Joseph, Pfc,
Zurek, Edwin J., Pvt,
Zurzola, Nicholas, Pfc,
Zvonik, Frank J., Pvt,
Zweck, Charles H., Pfc,
†Zwierz, Walter J., Pfc,
‡Zwiker, John A., Pvt
Zwilling, Albert, S/Sgt,
Zych, Edward J., Pfc,
Zylko, Walter C., Pfc,
Zyski, Leonard M., Pvt,

† Killed in Action.   * Prisoner of War.   ‡ Missing in Action.   § Died of Wounds.

15TH INFANTRY REGIMENT

The "Can-Do" regiment, for 26 years a guardian of peaceful Chinese citizens and of American property in China, is one of the oldest fighting units of the United States Army.

The 15th Infantry first went into action in the War of 1812, against the British. It was organized in 1812 as a volunteer unit and its record in that first conflict set a brilliant standard for soldiers of later years.

On May 27, 1813, the 15th participated in the capture of Fort George, Upper Canada. When defeat followed the initial victory the regiment covered the American retreat, and although 50 per cent of its strength were casualties, not a single soldier of the 15th surrendered.

Mexico came next, the regiment again was mustered into service as a volunteer organization and sailed for Vera Cruz as part of General Winfield Scott's punitive expedition. In that campaign the regiment saw action at Vera Cruz, Plan del Rio, Cerro Gordo, Churubusco, Las Animas, Jalapa, Chapultepec and Mexico City. When peace returned the regiment was disbanded.

When the Civil War broke out the 15th again was mustered into service and has seen active duty ever since. On May 4, 1861, it was organized as part of the Regular Army. During the Civil War, as a unit of the Western Army, it engaged in the battles of Shiloh, Stone River, Murfreesboro, Chickamauga, Missionary Ridge, Atlanta and numerous small engagements.

Following the Civil War the regiment was stationed at various posts in the south and west. It participated in the campaign against the Ute Indians in New Mexico, and composed a part of the expeditionary force in the war with Spain in 1898.

The 15th Regiment first went to China in 1900 during the Boxer Rebellion, taking part in the bloody work of pacification until ordered to the Philippine Islands. From 1903 until 1912 the regiment was in the United States at Monterey, Calif., where it built barracks and had its last taste of peaceful United States garrison life. In January, 1912, it sailed back to China for the mission of protecting the Pekin-Mukden railroad between Tientsin and Chinwangtao.

During the next 26 years the 15th protected American lives and property in spite of never-ending civil conflict and the later Sino-Japanese "incidents." The regiment was presented with a tablet of gratitude by the Chinese citizens of Tientsin for the protection afforded them against marauders.

In expression of its long and successful service in China and as representative of its confident attitude toward all tasks the regiment adopted as its motto, the Chinese pidgin English expression "Can Do."

On March 2, 1938 the 15th Infantry returned to the United States and joined the 3d Division, of which it remained a component throughout World War II.

15TH INFANTRY*

Regimental Commander

(Highest rank held)	Held pos. from	To	(Highest rank held)	Held pos. from	To
Col. Thomas H. Monroe		16 May 1943	Lt. Col. Ben Harrell	5 Feb 1944	5 Feb 1944
Lt. Col. Brookner W. Brady	22 May 1943	6 June 1943	Lt. Col. Roy E. Moore	6 Feb 1944	13 Mar 1944
Col. Charles R. Johnson, Jr.	7 June 1943	31 Aug 1943	Col. Richard G. Thomas, Jr.	14 Mar 1944	3 May 1944
Lt. Col. Ben Harrell	1 Sept 1943	6 Sept 1943	Lt. Col. Roy E. Moore	4 May 1944	9 May 1944
Col. William L. Ritter	7 Sept 1943	5 Oct 1943	Col. Richard G. Thomas Jr.	10 May 1944	2 Oct 1944
Brig. Gen. William W. Eagles	6 Oct 1943	20 Oct 1943	Col. Hallett D. Edson	3 Oct 1944	
Lt. Col. Ashton H. Manhart	21 Oct 1943	4 Feb 1944			

Regimental Executive Officer

(Highest rank held)	Held pos. from	To	(Highest rank held)	Held pos. from	To
Lt. Col. Harry B. Sherman		21 Feb 1943	Lt. Col. Roy E. Moore	14 Mar 1944	3 May 1944
Lt. Col. Brookner W. Brady(Actg)	22 Feb 1943	27 Feb 1943	Lt. Col. Hallett D. Edson	4 May 1944	2 Oct 1944
Lt. Col. Brookner W. Brady	28 Feb 1943	6 May 1943	Lt. Col. Michael Paulick	8 Oct 1944	10 Nov 1944
Lt. Col. Brookner W. Brady	7 June 1943	10 Aug 1943	Maj. Kenneth B. Potter	12 Nov 1944	14 Nov 1944
Capt. Charles M. Everhart (Actg)	11 Aug 1943	6 Sept 1943	Lt. Col. Michael Paulick	15 Nov 1944	6 Dec 1944
Lt. Col. Ben Harrell	7 Sept 1943	14 Oct 1943	Maj. Kenneth B. Potter	7 Dec 1944	26 Dec 1944
Lt. Col. Joseph B. Crawford	15 Oct 1943	24 Oct 1943	Lt. Col. Keith L. Ware	27 Dec 1944	6 Feb 1945
Lt. Col. Ben Harrell	25 Oct 1943	27 Oct 1943	Lt. Col. Michael Paulick	7 Feb 1945	18 Mar 1945
Lt. Col. Joseph B. Crawford	28 Oct 1943	31 Oct 1943	Lt. Col. Keith L. Ware	19 Mar 1945	31 Mar 1945
Lt. Col. Joseph B. Crawford	16 Nov 1943	9 Mar 1944	Lt. Col. Thomas R. Davis	1 April 1945	
Lt. Col. John J. Toffey, Jr.	10 Mar 1944	13 Mar, 1944			

1st Battalion Commander

(Highest rank held)	Held pos. from	To	(Highest rank held)	Held pos. from	To
Maj. Arthur W. Gardner		27 Dec 1942	Lt. Col. Hallett D. Edson	24 Dec 1943	7 April 1944
Lt. Col. Brookner W. Brady	28 Dec 1942	27 Feb 1943	Lt. Col. Michael Paulick	8 April 1943	15 April 1944
Maj. Raymond H. Giles	28 Feb 1943	27 May 1943	Lt. Col. Hallett D. Edson	16 April 1944	3 May 1944
Lt. Col. Leslie A. Prichard	31 May 1943	4 Oct 1943	Lt. Col. Michael Paulick	4 May 1944	7 Oct 1944
Lt. Col. Thomas R. Davis	5 Oct 1943	6 Nov 1943	Lt. Col. Keith L. Ware	8 Oct 1944	26 Dec 1944
Lt. Col. Michael Paulick	12 Nov 1943	23 Dec 1943	Maj. Kenneth B. Potter	27 Dec 1944	

2d Battalion Commander

(Highest rank held)	Held pos. from	To	(Highest rank held)	Held pos. from	To
Lt. Col. William H. Billings		31 July 1943	Maj. John O'Connell	12 Sept 1944	18 Sept 1944
Maj. Frank J. Kobes, Jr.	1 Aug 19433	25 Aug 1943	Lt. Col. Eugene A. Salet	19 Sept 1944	6 Feb 1945
Lt. Col. William H. Billings	26 Aug 1943	29 Aug 1943	Lt. Col. Keith L. Ware	7 Feb 1945	18 Mar 1945
Lt. Col. Charles E. Frederick	30 Aug 1943	15 Sept 1943	Maj. Burton S. Barr	19 Mar 1945	31 Mar 1945
Lt. Col. John J. Toffey, Jr.	16 Sept 1943	9 Mar 1944	Lt. Col. Keith L. Ware	1 April 1945	
Lt. Col. Thomas R. Davis	10 Mar 1944	11 Sept 1944			

3d Battalion Commander

(Highest rank held)	Held pos. from	To	(Highest rank held)	Held pos. from	To
Lt. Col. Ashton H. Manhart		10 Aug 1943	Maj. Robert L. Feiling	28 Oct 1943	31 Oct 1943
Maj. Kenneth W. Kirtley	15 Aug 1943	19 Sept 1943	Maj. Kenneth W. Kirtley	1 Nov 1943	7 Nov 1943
Lt. Col. Charles E. Frederick	20 Sept 1943	20 Oct 1943	Lt. Col. Joseph B. Crawford	8 Nov 1943	14 Nov 1943
Maj. Robert L. Feiling	22 Oct 1943	24 Oct 1943	Lt. Col. Frederick W. Boye, Jr.	15 Nov 1943	2 Oct 1944
Lt. Col. Joseph B. Crawford	25 Oct 1943	27 Oct 1943			

*The names and positions held apply only from Nov. 8, 1942 to May 8, 1945 (V-E Day). Neither opening nor closing dates of service are listed.

15TH INFANTRY REGIMENT

Abbott, George R., Capt,
Abbott, Raymond A., T/5,
Abel, Peter A., Pvt,
Abelt, William A., Pfc,
Abernethy, Fred E., Pvt,
Abisala, Edward, Pvt,
Ably, Chester M., Pvt,
Abmeyer, Erwin O., Pvt,
Abner, William, Jr., Pfc,
Abramowitz, William, Pvt,
Abramski, Anthony J., Pfc,
Abramson, Melvin, Pvt,
Abramson, Merle R., Pfc,
†Abundes, Joseph P., Pfc,
Accorsi, Richard J., Pfc,
Accorsi, Robert, T/Sgt,
†Acker, Kenneth C., 2nd Lt,
Ackerman, Frederick A., Pvt
†Ackerman, Morris, Pvt,
Acord, Norman P., Pvt,
Acosta, Gabriel S., Pvt,
Acunzo, Joseph, Pfc,
Adair, Claude L., Cpl,
Adamec, George, Pvt,
Adametz, Vincent E., Jr., Pfc,
†Adams, Charles E., Capt,
Adams, Charles E., S/Sgt,
Adams, Clarence E., Pfc,
Adams, Edward I., S/Sgt,
Adams, Edwin K., Pfc,
†Adams, Furman E., Pvt,
Adams, Gerald W., Pfc,
Adams, Henry H., Pfc,
Adams, Howard M., Cpl,
Adams, James H., Pfc,
Adams, John G., Pvt,
†Adams, Lawrence A., Pvt,
Adams, Lewis E., Pfc,
Adams, Leslie E., Pvt,
†Adams, Preston, S/Sgt,
Adams, Reggie G., Pvt,
Adams, Robert F., Pvt,
Adams, Walter D., Pfc,
Adams, Willis W., Pfc,
Adamson, Virgil C., Pfc,
Addiege, Vincent W., Pvt,
Addison, William C., S/Sgt,
Adelman, Milton, Pvt,
Adkins, Benwood, Pfc,
Adkins, Billy, Pvt,
Adkins, Jessie G., Pvt,
†Adkins, Pleasant O., Pvt,
Adkins, Ross, Jr., Pvt,
†Adleman, Julian S., 1st Lt,
Adolphson, Harlan, Pvt,
Adriansen, Thell D., Pvt,
Affield, Herman A., Pvt,
Agius, Charlie, T/5,
Agnich, Frank J., Pfc,
Aguas, Manuel D., Pvt,
Aguiar, Anthony G., Pfc,
†Aguilar, Alfredo V., Pvt,
Ahlers, John H., T/5,
Ahlgrin, Herbert J., Pfc,
Aiello, Joseph, T/5,
Aiken, John D., Pvt,
Aimola, Alfred M., Cpl,
Airey, Robert L., Pvt,
Airheart, Onclo M., Pfc,
†Aivish, William, Pvt,
Aker, Prince L., Jr., Pvt,
Akerblom, Sidney P., Pfc,
Akers, Clarence W., Pvt,
*Akins, Jim A., Pfc,
Aks, Leroy R., Sgt,

Akus, Julian, Cpl,
Alaimo, Benny J., Pfc,
Alayoki, Elmer H., Pfc,
Alberico, Marco J., Pfc,
Albin, Paul H., Pfc,
Albrandt, Alexander, Jr., Pfc,
Albright, Kenneth, T/5,
*Alcamo, Louis P., Pvt,
Alcorn, Henry E., Pfc,
Aldrich, Robert C., S/Sgt,
Alejandro, Celestino S., Pvt,
Alexa, John J., Pvt,
†Alexander, Cecil G., S/Sgt,
Alexander, Clarence L., Pfc,
Alexander, Darrell H., T/4,
Alexander, Francis C., T/5,
Alexander, Henry, Pvt,
†Alexander, James C., Pvt,
*Alexander, James M., Pvt,
†Alexander, Lewis M., Sgt,
Alexander, Walter H., Pvt,
Alfano, Anthony, Jr., Sgt,
Alkazoff, Gregory, Pfc
Allan, Harvey T., Sgt,
Alldredge, William B., Pfc,
Allen, August A., Pvt,
†Allen, Charles E., Pvt,
Allen, David B., Pvt,
Allen, Delbert H., Pvt,
Allen, Frank H., Jr., Pvt,
Allen, Glen D., Pvt,
‡Allen, Herbert W., Pfc,
Allen, Homer D., Pfc,
Allen, Howard O., T/4,
†Allen, James C., Pvt,
Allen, Larkin A., Pvt,
Allen, Lawrence J., Jr., 1st Lt,
*Allen, Matthew E., Pfc,
Allen, Paul D., Pfc,
Allen, Pearl J., Pvt,
Allen, Raymond S., Sgt,
Allen, Robert, S/Sgt,
†Allen, Robert A., Pfc,
Alley, Roy, Pfc,
†Allgood, Edwin B., Pvt,
Allgood, Robert E., Pvt,
Allison, Leo G., Pvt,
Allison, Orville W., Pvt,
Allmann, Donald S., S/Sgt,
Alloway, William, T/5,
Allred, Sherwin R., T/Sgt,
Alojoki, Elmer H., Pvt,
†Alred, Thomas A., Pvt,
Alsobrooks, Louis, Pfc,
Althouse, Walter H., Pfc,
Altman, John B., Pvt,
Alto, Charles J., Pfc,
Alva, Roberto, Cpl,
Alvarez, Louis M., Pfc,
Alvarez, Vincente O., Cpl,
Alvee, Manuel M., Jr., Pfc,
Amado, Eugene H., Pfc,
Amaral, Arthur P., Pvt,
Amata, Todd S., Pvt,
Amato, Joseph, Pvt,
Amaya, Francisco E., Pfc,
Amberg, Wilson B., Pfc,
Ambrose, Meredith J., Pfc,
Amburgey, Haymond, Pvt,
Amedo, Peter, Pfc,
†Amend, Adam J., Pfc,
Amendolea, Frank, Pvt,
†Amendolia, Anthony G., Pfc,
Amerine, Maurice D., Pvt,
Amerjan, Lawrence A., Pfc,

Ames, James L., Sgt,
Amick, Allen E., S/Sgt,
Amos, Able T., Pvt,
Amos, Woodrow L., Pfc,
Amrich, Michael M., Sgt,
Amundson, Oscar M., S/Sgt,
Amundson, Russell I., S/Sgt,
Amundson, Willis O., Pfc,
Anagnostou, Harry H., Pvt,
Anastasio, John J., T/5,
Ancel, Lawrence, Pvt,
Anderson, Alfred C., Jr., S/Sgt
Anderson, Burdette C., Pvt,
Anderson, Carl B., Pfc,
Anderson, Cecil H., S/Sgt,
Anderson, Charles J., Sgt,
Anderson, Charles M., Pvt,
Anderson, Charles W., Pfc,
Anderson, Donald L., T/5,
§Anderson, Elmer, T/5,
Anderson, Elmo A., Pfc,
Anderson, Everette R., 2nd Lt,
Anderson, George E., 1st Sgt,
Anderson, Harold E., T/4,
Anderson, Herman D., Pvt,
Anderson, Ivan L., T/5,
Anderson, Jack T., Pfc,
Anderson, James A., Pfc,
Anderson, James E., Pvt,
†Anderson, James R., 2nd Lt,
Anderson, Jesse L., S/Sgt,
§Anderson, John A., Pvt,
Anderson, John F., T/4,
Anderson, Kenneth A., Cpl,
Anderson, Leroy, Pvt,
Anderson, Marvin H., Cpl,
Anderson, Maurice D., Cpl,
Anderson, Maurice R., Sgt,
Anderson, Richard W., Pvt,
Anderson, Robert C., Pfc,
Anderson, Roy A., Sgt,
†Anderson, Russell E., Sgt,
Anderson, Solomon, Pfc,
†Anderson, Verner E. A., Pvt,
Anderson, Walter A., Pfc,
Anderson, Walter E., Pvt,
Anderson, Wayne, Pfc,
Anderson, William O., Pfc,
Anderton, James H., Pfc,
Andrade, Jesus, Pvt,
Andrade, Tom, Pfc,
Andress, Robert A., Pfc,
Andrews, Daniel B., S/Sgt,
Andrews, Donald B., Sgt
Andrews, Francis J., Pfc,
Andrews, George E., Pvt,
Andrick, Willard C., Pvt,
Androwick, Henry, Pfc,
Andrychowski, Stanley A., Pfc,
Andrzejewski, Adolph, Pvt,
Andrzejewski, John, Pvt,
Andy, Leo, 1st Sgt,
Anes, Joseph, Pvt,
Angel, Louis G., Sgt,
Angel, Thomas J., Pfc,
Angeles, Carlos C., Pfc,
Angell, William W., Pfc,
Angileri, Joe, Sgt,
Anglada-Perez, Walter, Cpl,
Angle, Chesley S., Cpl,
Angle, Gladish D., Pfc,
Anglin, Jess W., Pfc,
Ankele, William D., Pfc,
Annis, Franklin P., Sgt,
Annunziata, John A., Pfc,

Anselm, Donald V., Sgt,
Anselmi, Gino A., Pfc,
Anstey, Jack W., Pfc,
Antel, Robert R., Pfc,
Anthony, Frederick H., Pfc,
Anthony, Robert E., Pvt,
*Antico, John, Pvt,
Antishin, Joseph T., Sgt,
Anto, Abraham, Pvt,
†Antolak, Sylvester, Sgt,
Antonacci, Vito J., Pvt,
Antonelle, Patsy P., Pvt,
Antonine, Michael J., Pfc,
Antonsen, Alfred L., Pvt,
Antosh, Louis S., Pfc,
*Apalategui, Joe H., Pfc,
Appel, Donald A., T/5,
Appelbaum, Jack, Pvt,
Aramanda, Michael C., Pvt,
Aravich, Joseph M., Pvt,
Archer, Edward P., Sgt,
†Archer, John C., Pvt,
Archkavage, Louis B., Pfc,
Archuleta, John J., Pfc,
Archuletta, Albert R., Pvt,
Ard, Herbert, Pvt,
Ardelean, George, Pfc,
Ardito, Stephen S., Pvt,
†Ardolino, Nickolas K., Pvt,
Arentsen, Guy E., Pvt,
Arentshorst, John, Pvt,
Argentieri, Aldo, Pfc,
Arhur, Robert T., S/Sgt,
Armbruster, Ernest J., T/4,
Armelling, John G., Pfc,
†Armetta, Sam M., S/Sgt,
Arminas, Alfred, Pfc,
Arminino, Ernest J., Pfc,
Arminio, Anthony F., Pfc,
Armstrong, Burton, Pfc,
Armstrong, Carl M., Pfc,
Armstrong, George V., T/4,
Armstrong, Joe R., T/4,
Armstrong, John B., Capt,
Armstrong, Lionel, Pfc,
Arnold, Joseph H., Pvt,
Arnold, Otis N., Pvt,
Arnold, Vincent E., Pvt,
Arnold, Walter R., Pfc,
Arnold, William D. R., Pvt,
Arnow, Aaron, T/5,
†Arrance, Edwin S., Pfc,
Arsenault, Francis F., Pfc,
Arsenault, James A., Pvt,
Artana, Leo R., Pfc,
Artea, Felipe C., Pfc,
Arthur, Clyde D., Pvt,
Arthur, Neil L., T/Sgt,
Artko, Steve C., Pfc,
†Arvia, James F., Pvt,
Ash, Herbert E., Jr., Cpl,
†Ashburn, Doyl B., Pvt,
Ashcraft, Gordon, Cpl,
Ashcraft, Harry, Jr., Pfc,
†Ashcraft, Leland J., S/Sgt,
Ashman, Milton A., Pfc,
Ashmun, Garland R., Pvt,
Asquith, Robert A., Sgt,
†Assey, Joseph, Pvt,
Atha, Charles J., Pfc,
Atkins, Levi, T/5,
Atkins, Louis H., Pfc,
Atkinson, Elldredge T., Pfc,
Atkinson, Frank, Pfc,

†Atkinson, Mell V., Pvt,
Atkinson, William H., Pvt,
Atwater, William E., Pfc,
Atwell, Cecil S., Pfc,
Aubin De Paradis, P. P., Pvt,
Aubol, Clarence A., Sgt,
Aubrey, Albert F., Pfc,
Aubut, Lionel H., Pfc,
†Aucker, William N., Pfc,
Auclair, Melvin, Pvt,
Aud, Carl E., Pvt,
†Audette, Eugene F., Pvt,
Auer, Weikko K., T/5,
Auerbach, Max, Pfc,
Auger, Arthur J., Pfc,
Augustine, William H., 2nd Lt,
Auld, Henry C., Jr., Capt,
Auld, Thomas, Pfc,
Aulisio, Anthony, S/Sgt,
Ault, John W., 1st Lt,
Austin, Charles W., Pfc,
Austin, Garry R., T/5,
Austin, Henry T., Pfc,
Austin, Hubert L., T/5,
Austin, James E., Jr., Pfc,
Austin, Orville W., T/5,
Autrey, William C., Pvt,
†Autry, Virgil R., S/Sgt,
Avalle, Joseph P., Pvt,
Avery, Donald S., Sgt,
Avery, Thompson, Sgt,
Avey, Dalton K., Pfc,
†Axenty, Thelmur, Sgt,
Axlerod, Harold D., Pvt,
‡Axton, Roy D., Pfc,
Ayala, Frank V., Cpl,
Aycock, William B., 1st Lt,
Azbell, J. W. G., Pfc,
†Azevedo, John V., Jr., Pfc,
†Azling, Ernest A., Pfc,
Azzorpardi, Anthony, Pvt,
Azzorpardi, Joe, Pvt,

Babanoff, George L., Pvt,
Babcock, Earl P., Pfc,
Babcock, Robert F., 2nd Lt,
Babin, Richard H., T/5,
Babinski, Stanley J., T/4,
Babiyan, Andrew L., Pfc,
Babjak, Joseph A., Pfc,
Baca, Manuel A., S/Sgt,
Bach, Ermin, Pfc,
Bachert, Hadley J., Pfc,
Bachman, Robert H., Sgt,
Bacon, Lawrence A., Pfc,
Bacon, Norris G., Pfc,
Badalamento, Sam, T/Sgt,
Badey, Thomas J., S/Sgt,
Badger, David D., Pvt,
Badorek, Charles J., Pfc,
Baehler, George L., T/5,
Baer, Eugene, Pfc,
*Baer, John G., Pvt
Baese, Clyde E., Pfc,
Bagent, Gilbert E., Pvt,
†Baggett, Richard V., Sgt,
Bagley, Charlie D., Pfc,
Bagley, John E., Pvt,
Bagwell, Forine B., Pfc,
Bahman, Clifford, Pvt,
Bahr, John W., Cpl,
Baiersdorfer, Theodore, S/Sgt,
Bailey, Frank, Pfc,
†Bailey, Gilbert P., 2nd Lt,
Bailey, Herman J., Pvt,

† Killed in Action.   * Prisoner of War.   ‡ Missing in Action.   § Died of Wounds.

Bailey, James R., Pfc,
†Bailey, John T., Jr., T/5,
†Bailey, Joseph T., Pvt,
‡Bailey, Robert L., Pvt,
Bailey, Robert W., Pfc,
Bailey, Ulysses G., Pvt,
Bailey, Van B., T/5,
Bailey, William W., Jr., Pfc,
Baines, Larry, S/Sgt,
†Bair, Roger H., S/Sgt,
Baird, Alva D., Sgt,
Baird, Carl W., Cpl,
Baird, Frank J., Pvt,
Baker, Cedric C., Pvt,
Baker, Elmer D., Pfc,
Baker, George G., Sgt,
†Baker, Gerald F., Pvt,
Baker, Grover L., Pfc,
Baker, James E., Pvt,
Baker, James W., Sgt,
Baker, Leonard W., Pfc,
Baker, Levi, Pfc,
Baker, Oswell K., Pvt,
Baker, Paul D., Pvt,
Baker, Robert E., Sgt,
Baker, Robert P., Pfc,
Baker, Robert L., Pvt,
Baker, Virgil L., Pfc,
Baker, Watt, Pvt,
Baker, William H., Pfc,
†Baker, Woodrow W., Pvt
Balcerzak, Joseph J., Pvt,
Baldassare, David, Pvt,
Baldino, Gerald M., Pvt,
†Baldwin, Eugene W., Pfc,
§Baldwin, Rodner J., Pvt,
Baldwin, Walter L., Pvt,
Bales, Riley H., Pvt,
Balestrieri, Dominick, Pfc,
Balestrieri, Edward B., Pvt,
†Balfanz, Gerald E., S/Sgt,
Balfe, Philip E., S/Sgt,
Balkenbush, Adrian F., Pvt,
Balkus, Joseph W., T/5,
‡Ball, Carl D., Pfc
Ball, Floyd E., Pvt,
Ball, Orville, Pvt,
Ballantyne, Joseph J., Sgt,
Ballard, Ernest M., Pfc,
Ballato, Frank, Pvt,
Ballenger, Benjamin H., Pvt,
Ballestero, Manuel, Pfc,
Ballestros, Martin A., Sgt,
Balliet, Orville R., T/3,
Balogh, Eugene J., T/5,
Balte, Gottlieb J., S/Sgt,
Balun, Vincent W., Pfc,
Baluta, Edward J., Pfc,
Balzano, Daniel V., Pvt,
Balzer, Harold K., Pvt,
Bambace, Felix S., Major,
Bamford, Edwin, S/Sgt,
Banach, Theodore M., Pfc,
†Bandy, Martin E., Pvt,
Bane, Ralph E., Pvt,
†Banek, Stanley C., S/Sgt,
Bangert, Jacob L., Sgt,
Bankowski, Stephen, Pvt,
Banks, Donald H., Pvt
Banks, Harvey E., Pvt
Banks, Horace C., Pvt,
§Banner, John G., Pvt,
Bannon, James H., Pfc,
Baran, Zigmund H., Sgt,
Baranko, William, Pfc,
Baratko, Alexander, Pfc,
Barbaz, George, Pvt,
Barber, Arthur N., Pfc,
Barber, Dormand O., Pfc,
Barber, Eric, Pvt,
Barber, Frederick R., Pvt,
Barber, William R., Pfc,
Barbosa, Joaquim D., Pvt,
Barbosa, Louis H., Cpl,
Barbrey, Robert J., Pfc,
Barchesky, Lester V., Pvt,
Barclift, James M., Pfc,
Barco, Maurice C., Jr., Pvt,
Barcosky, John, Sgt,
Bard, Calvin M., Pfc,
Barden, Roy C., Pvt,
Bardes, Herbert C., 1st Lt,
Bardon, Ralph G., Pvt,
Bardsley, Robert H., Jr., Pvt,
Bare, Ted, Pfc,
Barefield, Aubrey J., Pvt,
Barfield, Jess R., Pvt,
Barfield, Tommie L., Pvt
Bargas, Roberto, Pvt
Barham, William C., Pfc,
†Barker, Cecil E., Pvt,
Barker, Elmer E., T/5,
Barker, Henry N., Pvt,
Barker, Millard, Pfc,
Barkhaus, Anthony L., T/5,
†Barlow, James B., 1st Lt
Barlow, William P., Pvt,
Barna, David A., Pfc,
†Barnaba, Louis J., Pfc,
§Barnao, Bartolo, Jr., Pfc,
Barnes, Albert L., Pvt,
Barnes, Charles D. M., Pfc,
Barnes, Donald H., Pvt,
Barnes, Harvey, Pvt,
Barnes, John A., Sgt,
Barnes, Murphy L., Pfc,
Barnes, Ray J., Pvt,
Barnes, Russell E., T/Sgt,
Barnes, Wilbur A., Pvt,
Barnes, Woodrow W., Pvt,
†Barnett, Billy L., Pvt,
Barnett, Garnet S., S/Sgt,
Barnhart, Robert P., T/4,
Barnshock, Bernard J., Pvt,
Baron, Henry S., Pvt,
Barone, Llewellyn C., Pfc,
Barr, Burton S., Major,
Barr, Charles R., Pvt,
Barr, Donald L., S/Sgt,
Barr, Robert C., Pvt,
Barrasso, Antonio V., Pvt,
Barreiro, Joseph, Pvt,
Barrera, Javier M., Pvt,
Barrett, Carl J., Pvt,
Barrett, John O., Pfc,
Barrett, Lee J., Pvt,
Barrett, Robert S., Pvt,
Barrett, Thomas J., Pfc,
Barrett, William C., Jr., Pvt,
Barrick, Lewis M., Pfc,
†Barron, Everette E., Pfc,
Barrows, Warren A., Pfc,
Barry, Gerard D., Pfc,
Barry, Joseph F., Sgt,
†Barry, Richard W., Pvt,
Barry, Robert R., Pvt,
Barry, Thomas J., Pvt,
Bartels, William J., Pfc,
Barth, Clifford U., T/Sgt,
Bartholomay, Philip B., Pvt,
Bartlett, Irving E., Pvt,
Bartlett, Ora A., T/4,
†Bartlett, Woodrow L., Pvt,
Bartnikowski, John S., Pfc
Barton, Daniel S., Pfc,
Barton, Dorris J., Pfc
Barton, George A., Sgt,
Barton, George E., S/Sgt,
Barton, Harold L., Pfc,
†Barton, James H., Pvt,
Barwick, Gregory B., T/5,
Basca, Stephen, Pfc,
†Basham, Raymond E., Pvt,
Basile, Anthony T., Pvt,
Basile, Jack B., Sgt,
Basilio, Joseph P., Pfc,
Baskin, Carl C., S/Sgt,
Baskins, Shaffer G., Pvt,
Bass, Fred W., Pfc,
Bass, James E., T/Sgt,
Bass, Jesse, S/Sgt,
Basso, Frank, Pvt,
Basso, Louis L., S/Sgt,
Bastian, Henry G., Pfc,
Bastien, John K., Pfc,
Bastura, Stanley, Pvt,
Bataglia, Willard H., Pfc
Batchelor, Raymond R., Pfc,
†Bateman, Mark L., Sgt,
Bates, Arthur R., Pfc,
Bates, Harry J., Pvt,
Bates, Howard E., Sgt,
Bates, John W., Pvt,
Bates, Roy A., Pvt,
Bath, William Y., Jr., Pvt,
Batrez, Anastacio, Pfc,
†Batsakis, James, Pvt,
Battani, George J., Pvt,
Batterton, Clifford O., Pvt,
†Batts, Robert J., S/Sgt,
Bauer, Albert F., Sgt,
Bauer, Clarence F., Pvt,
Bauer, Emanuel R., Pfc,
Bauer, Everett E., Pvt,
Bauer, John W., Pfc,
†Bauer, Norman P., Pfc,
Bauer, Raymond P., Pfc,
Bauerle, James, Pvt,
Baugh, Ernest W., Pfc,
Baugh, William M., Pfc,
Baughman, Robert, Jr., Pvt.
Baum, William F., Jr., Pvt,
Bauman, Lawrence C., Jr., Sgt,
Bauman, Louis H., Pvt,
Baumann, Kurt E., Pfc,
Baumann, William E., Pfc,
Baumgaertner, Cyrus R., Sgt,
Baumgarden, Roger N., Pvt,
Bauschka, Wilbert A., Pfc,
Baxter, John S., Sgt,
Bay, Walter A., Pfc,
Bayer, Daniel, S/Sgt,
Bayes, James E., Pfc
Bayliss, Lindsay E., T/Sgt,
§Baynes, Charles F., Jr., Pvt,
Bayo, Manuel J., T/5,
Bayus, Raymond, Pvt,
Bazo, William, Pfc,
Beal, Lloyd S., Pfc,
Beale, Elmer J., Pfc,
Beamer, Edwin J., 1st Lt,
Bean, Robert H., Pfc,
Bean, Roy R., Pfc,
Beard, Clarence J., Jr., Pfc,
Beasley, Brady H., Pfc,
Beasley, Lee A., T/4,
Beasley, Richard D., Pvt,
Beaston, John R., S/Sgt,
Beathard, Francis L., T/4,
Beatrice, Carmine A., Pvt,
Beattie, James L., 2nd Lt,
Beatty, Myron S., S/Sgt,
Beatty, Roy J., Pfc,
†Beauch, Harvey L., Jr., Pvt,
Beaupre, George A., Pfc,
†Beaven, Lawrence N., Cpl,
Beaver, Clifford R., T/Sgt,
*Beaver, Leonard F., Pvt,
Beavers, Robert M., Pfc,
Becht, Robert L., Pvt,
Bechtold, Roy S., Jr., Pvt,
Beck, Clennon A., T/5,
Beck, Gordon C., Sgt,
†Beck, Harold P., Pfc,
Beck, John J., T/Sgt,
Beck, LeRoy D., Pfc,
Beck, Ralph W., Pfc,
Beck, Raymond M., Pfc,
†Beck, Raymond P., Pfc,
Beck, Wilbur, S/Sgt,
Becker, Bernard J., Jr., Pvt
Becker, Carl E., Pfc,
Becker, Clayton H., Pfc,
Becker, Edward P., Sgt,
Beckett, George, Pfc,
Beckley, John H., Jr., Capt,
Beckley, John W., Pfc,
Beckman, Gordon L., Pvt,
Becknard, Walter S., Pfc,
Becnel, Henry S., S/Sgt,
Beczynski, Anthony S., Pfc,
Bedau, Richard A., Pvt,
Bedell, Thomas M., Pvt,
Beder, Melvin, Pvt,
Bedi, James J., Pfc,
Bedow, Richard N., 1st Lt,
†Beeler, Charles W., Pfc,
Beeler, Forest B., Pfc,
Beer, Leslie W., Pfc,
Beerman, Elmer E., Pfc,
Beeson, Allen C., Pvt,
Beggs, Lyle J., Pfc,
Begley, Ralph B., Pvt,
Behovitz, Frank S., Pfc,
Behr, Edward A., Pfc,
§Beirne, Walter F., Pfc,
Bekker, Peter W., Pfc,
Belair, George M., Pfc,
Belanger, Albert J., T/5,
Belanger, Jacques J. M., Pfc,
Belcastro, John, Pfc,
Belenke, Stephen, Pvt,
†Belford, Donald E., Pvt,
Bell, Charles O., Pfc,
†Bell, Harold E., Cpl,
Bell, James W., Pfc,
Bell, Lawrence A., Pfc,
†Bell, Owen D., Pfc,
Bell, William, Pvt,
Bell, William J., Pfc,
Bellamy, Ronald C., Pvt,
Bellantino, Santo A., Pfc,
Bellew, Glenn A., S/Sgt,
Bellina, Salvatore J., Pvt,
Belling, Olaf C., Pvt,
Bellington, George R., Pvt,
Belliveau, Arthur E., Pvt,
Bello, Joseph, Pvt,
Bellrose, Walter C., Jr., Pvt,
Bellucci, Americo J., Pvt
Belluomini, John J., T/5,
Belmont, Dante C., Sgt,
Beltz, Paul D., Sgt,
Beltz, Russell P., T/4,
Beltz, Walter C., Pvt,
Beltz, William J., T/Sgt,
Bench, Harold D., S/Sgt,
*Bender, Francis H., Sgt,
Bender, John A., Cpl,
Benham, Roy L., Pfc,
Bendian, Nishan G., Pvt
Bendzinski, Victor J., Pfc,
Benedetti, Albert, Pvt,
Benedetti, Manlio, S/Sgt,
Bengston, Earl H., T/5,
Benick, George F., Pvt,
†Beninati, Harry F., Pvt,
Benish, Charles A., Pfc,
Benkiser, Egon, Pfc,
Bennert, William H., 1st Lt,
†Bennett, Ballard A., Sgt,
†Bennett, Clifford E., Pvt,
Bennett, Earlin S., Pfc,
Bennett, George W., Sgt,
Bennett, James B., Pvt
Bennett, John S., S/Sgt,
Bennett, Keith N., Pvt,
†Bennett, Leamon J., Pvt,
Bennett, Marshall W., Pfc,
Bennett, Robert E., T/5,
Benoschek, Jay K., Pvt
†Benoure, Thomas J., Pfc,
Bensch, Edward E., Pfc,
Benson, Raymond L., S/Sgt,
Bensonhaver, Lawrence, Pvt,
Bent, Carl D., 1st Lt,
†Bentley, Arnold, Sgt,
Bentzel, Donald M., M/Sgt,
Benzer, Jack F., Jr., S/Sgt,
Berardi, Pasquale, Pfc,
Berardo, Alfred, Pfc
Berasi, Angelo J., Pfc,
Berdot, Raymond A., Pvt,
Beres, William E., Pvt,
Berezowski, Stefan, Pvt
Berg, Morris S., T/5,
Berg, Robert R., Pvt,
Berg, William K., S/Sgt,
Bergandi, Ernest, S/Sgt,
†Bergdorf, Edward, Capt,
Berger, Alphonse, Pfc,
†Berger, Isidore, Pvt,
Berger, Meyer, Pvt,
Berger, Vernon S., S/Sgt,
Bergeron, Albert, Pfc,
Bergeron, Harry J., Sgt,
Bergh, Rolfe, Pvt,
Bergman, Antone A., Pfc,
Bergman, Henry C., Sgt,
Bergquist, Norbert C., Pvt,
Bergsten, Boyd T., T/4,
Bergstrom, Carl G., Pfc,
Berick, Everett D., Pfc,
Berka, Albert, Jr., S/Sgt,
Berkau, Paul F., Sgt,
Berke, Ralph, 1st Lt,
Berkow, Bori, 1st Lt,
Berkshire, Donald A., T/5,
Berlin, Enoch E., Pvt,
Berlin, Frederick, Pvt,
Berline, James H., 1st Lt,
Bernhardt, Robert, 1st Lt,
Bernstein, Charles, T/5,
†Bernstein, Lawrence L., Pvt,
Bernstein, Louis, Pvt,
†Bernstein, Morris M., 2nd Lt,
Bernstein, Morton J., Sgt,
Bernt, John H., T/5,
Berreman, Everett E., Pfc,
Berringer, Eugene J., Pfc,
Berry, John, Jr., Pfc,
Berry, William, Jr., Sgt,
Bersch, Robert L., Pvt,
Berte, Angelo, Pvt,
Bertolini, Michael, Cpl,
Bertsch, Emil A., Pvt,
Bertsch, John H., Pfc,
†Besch, Philip M., Pvt,
Bessau, Frederick J., Pvt,
†Bessert, William F., Jr., Sgt,
Best, Irving, Pfc
Bestecki, John D., Pfc,
Bestol, Arthur W., Pvt,
Bethea, Admiral D., Jr., Pvt,
Bethke, Walter H., Sgt,
Bettis, Kempton N., Pvt,
Betteley, Paul J., Pvt,
Beuth, Philip J., Pfc,
Bevan, Andrew M., Cpl,
Bever, Lawrence H., Pfc,
Beyer, Anthony K., Pfc,
Beyer, Wesley H., Pvt,
Bezilla, John J., Pvt,
Biagini, Leroy, Pvt,
Bianchi, Geno, Pfc,
Bianchi, Leo A., Sgt,
Bibbs, Charles R., Pvt,
*Bibeau, Joseph V., Pvt,
†Bica, Gus J., Sgt,
Bickel, Hillary H., Pvt,
Bicker, Herbert E., Sgt,
Bickmore, Allan O., T/Sgt,
Biddle, Charles A., Pfc,
Bidstrip, Richard O., Pfc,
Bielawa, Florian J., Cpl,
Bielic, Benedict M., Pfc,
Bielenberg, Robert E., 1st Sgt,
Bienert, Ben W., T/Sgt,
†Bieniek, Vincent J., Pvt,
Bienkiewicz, John P., 2nd Lt,
Bierchen, Theodore F., Sgt,
Bierman, John G., Pfc,
Bigelow, Alvin M., Pfc,
Biggerstaff, Rex, Pvt,
Big Hair, Michael P., Pvt,
Bigler, Arnold, T/5,
*Bigos, Albert L., Pvt,
Biles, Thomas C., Pvt,
Billing, Edward, T/4,
Billings, William H., Lt Col,
Billington, James, Sgt,
Bilotta, Carl A., Pfc,
Bilsky, Gerald, Pvt,
Bilter, Richard E., Pfc,
§Binder, Donald J., T/Sgt,
Binder, Howard W., Pfc,
Binford, Robert M., Cpl,
Binger, Alfred E., S/Sgt,
Bisek, Robert E., Pfc,
Bink, Charles F., Pvt,
Bioty, Max W., Pvt,
Bircher, James G., Pvt,
Bird, Charles E., Pfc,
Bird, Luman A., Pvt,
Bird, Oscar C., Pfc,
Bires, Julius, Pfc,
Birenbaum, Harry, Pfc,
Birgam, Leroy L., T/4,
Birkhead, William E., Pfc,
†Bisbee, Eldon R., T/Sgt,
†Bisceglia, James V., Pfc,
Bischoff, Glenn W., Pvt,
Bisel, Kenneth B., Pfc,
Bishop, Albert L., T/4,
Bishop, Edward G., Pfc,
Bishop, Harvey H., Pvt,
Bishop, Hubert A., Pfc,
Bishop, James E., Pvt,
Bishop, Joseph B., Pvt,
Bishop, Melvin T., S/Sgt,
*Bishop, Paul R., Jr., Pvt,
Bishop, Ronald C., Pvt,
Bishop, Seymour, Pvt,
†Bishop, William M., Sgt,
Bissell, Herbert P., Pfc,
†Bisson, Joseph L., Pvt,
Bisson, William T., Cpl,
†Bitar, Emil S., Capt,
Bittman, Mike, T/4,
Bittman, Philip L., Pfc,
Bittner, Chester H., T/5,
Bittner, Glenn H., Pfc,
Bjordahl, Carroll O., Sgt,
Black, Albert W., 2nd Lt,
Black, Albert W., S/Sgt,
Black, Dale R., Pfc,
Black, Lonnie M., 2nd Lt,
Black, Maurice H., Pvt,
Black, Myron, Pfc,
Black, Raymond S., Pfc,
Blackburn, Clinton, S/Sgt,
Blackburn, James O., Pfc,
Blacker, Irving, Pvt,
†Blacketer, Vern L., T/5,
Blackford, Robert, Pfc,
Blackley, Donald L., T/5,
Blackmon, Wilbur H., Pfc,
†Blacksher, David F., Sgt,
Blackwelder, Homer, Pfc,
Blackwell, Fred A., Pfc,
Blackwell, James W., Pvt,
*Blackwell, Tomas A., Jr., Pvt,
Blackwell, Tullie E., Pvt,
†Blackwood, Joe B., Pvt,
§Blades, Gordon A., Pvt,
†Blair, Allyn M., Pvt,
Blair, Arthur T., Pfc,
†Blair, Gerald D., Pvt,
Blair, Leonard, Pvt,
Blair, Russell G., Pfc,
Blair, Thomas J. W., Pfc,
Blair, William L., Pfc,
Blake, Fred S., 1st Lt,
Blake, James G., Cpl,
Blake, James J., Sgt,
Blake, John F., Pfc,
Blake, Raymond H., Pfc,
Blakeney, Roscoe C., Pfc,
†Blaker, Howard R., Sgt,
Blakesley, Loren H., Pvt,
Blanchard, Bruno J., Pvt,
†Blanchard, Charles E., Jr., Sgt,
†Blanchard, Ellis J., Jr., Pvt,
Blanchard, Francis R., Pfc,
Blankenship, Chester, Sgt,
Blankenship, Floyd R., S/Sgt,
Blankenship, Horace N., Pfc,
Blanton, Edward W., Pvt,
Blanton, Ernest W., Pfc,
Blasingame, Harold B., Pfc,
Blasko, Anthony J., Pfc,
†Blaszczyk, Anthony J., T/5,
Blaurock, Henry, Sgt,
Bledsoe, Raymond L., Pfc,
Bledsoe, Robert B., Pfc,

† Killed in Action. * Prisoner of War. ‡ Missing in Action. § Died of Wounds.

Bledsoe, Walter C., Jr., Pvt,
Bletcher, Clarence E., Pfc,
Bletsas, Leonidas G., Pvt,
Blevins, Buford Y., Pfc,
Blevins, Estel S., Pfc,
Blevins, George K., Pfc,
Blevins, Robert H., Pvt,
Bliss, Arthur G., Jr., Pfc,
Blitz, Stanley E., Pfc,
Blixt, Rudolph E., Pfc,
Blizzard, Bardon, Pfc,
Block, Henry L., Sgt,
Bloom, Frank, Pvt,
Bloom, Henry C., 2nd Lt,
Bloom, Jack W., Pvt,
Blount, George W., S/Sgt,
Blount, Oscar B., Pfc,
Blount, Roscoe F., Pfc,
Blucher, Harry L., S/Sgt,
†Blum, Louis A., Pvt,
Blume, Holcombe H., Pvt,
Blume, Lyndon L., S/Sgt,
Blumenfeld, Hyman, Pvt,
Blumhagen, Robert F., 1st Lt,
Bluthardt, Daniel A., Pvt,
Blythe, Harold C., Pvt,
Blythe, Melvin V., S/Sgt,
†Boag, James E., S/Sgt,
Boardman, Foster, 2nd Lt,
Boatman, Lawrence M., Pvt,
Boaz, Lawrence E., Pfc,
Bobby, Robert J., Pfc,
Bobo, Paul O., Sgt,
Bobrowicz, Charles L., Pfc,
Bochenek, Stanley I., Pfc,
Bociek, Peter J., Sgt,
Boden, Ernest J., Pvt,
§Bodenhamer, Ralph B., T/5,
Bodkin, William G., S/Sgt,
Bodle, Naysmith, Pfc,
Bodnar, John, Pfc,
Boeckman, Roman G., T/Sgt,
Boehm, Hans E., 1st Lt,
Boerner, Fred W., M/Sgt,
Bogden, Vincent J., Pfc,
Boggs, Edwin B., Pfc,
Boggs, James H., Jr., Pvt,
†Boggs, William P., Pvt,
Bogner, Milden E., S/Sgt,
Bogus, Clemens, T/Sgt,
Bohatch, George J., Pfc,
Bohonas, Benny B., T/5,
Bolchalk, Joseph T., Pvt,
Bolda, John E., Cpl,
Boleman, William D., Pfc,
Bolen, Rudy W., Pvt,
Boles, Jesse E., Sgt,
Boles, John R., Pvt,
Boles, Paul H., Pfc,
Boles, Romayne E., T/5,
Boley, Samuel J., Pvt,
Bolick, Rosel C., Pvt,
Bolin, Marvin, Pvt,
Boline, Elwood K. F., S/Sgt,
Boling, Odus C., Pfc,
†Bolinski, Leonard, S/Sgt,
†Bollinger, Andrew L., Pvt,
Bolton, Durwood R., Pfc,
Bomberger, William H., Pvt,
Bommarito, Peter, Sgt,
Bonaccorsi, Samuel E., Pfc,
Bonamarte, Stephen M., Pfc,
Bonasera, Gesualdo J., Pvt,
Bonavita, Raul, Sgt,
Boncore, Angelo, Pvt,
Bond, Chester E., Pfc,
Bond, James I., Pfc,
Bone, Robert C., Sgt,
Bonifante, Rocco F., Pvt,
Bonlie, Glenn M., T/Sgt,
Bonneau, Clement F., Pvt,
Bonnema, Harry I. H., Jr., Pvt,
†Bonnett, Rheinhold E., Pfc,
Boody, William C., Jr., Pvt,
Booker, Jessie C., Pvt,
Bookholz, Ralph W., Sgt,
Boone, Henry L., Jr., Pvt
Boone, John F., Sgt,
Boone, Walter L., Cpl,
§Boone, William E., Pvt,
†Boos, Orville J., Pvt,
Booth, Harry, Pvt,
Boothe, James O., Pfc,
Boreali, Patsy, Pvt,
Borecki, Chester J., Pvt,
†Borek, Richard W., Pfc
Borden, Howard A., Pfc,
Borders, Clinton K., Pvt,
Borgias, Mike P., S/Sgt,
Borino, James V., Pvt,
Borish, Meyer G., Pfc,
§Borisic, Mehila, J., Pvt,
Borkowski, Edward J., Sgt,
Borkowski, Jesse J., Pfc,
†Bornander, Edwin A., Capt,
Borowski, Edwin C., Pvt,
†Borowski, William R., Pvt,
Borradaile. Thomas E., Pvt,
†Borsheim, Arthur C., Pvt,
Borton, Harry L., Pfc,
†Borum, Charles H., Pvt,
Bos, Emerson, T/4,
Bosack, Thomas A., Cpl,
Bosch, Edward, Pfc,
Bosowski, Stanley J., T/5,
Boss, Richard F., Pvt,
Bost, Claude B., Pvt,
Boston, Walter O., Pfc,
§Boswell, Cleveland, Pfc,
Bosworth, LeRoy E., Pvt,
Bothman, Lewis J., Pvt,
Botka, Edward N., T/5,
†Botteri, Guido M., Pfc,
Bottge, Walter W., Pvt,
Botti, Leon J., Pvt,
Botticelli, Dominick P., Pfc,
Bottier, Ernest J., Sgt,
†Botting, Edward J., Pvt,
Bouer, Allie, Pvt,
Bouchard, Percy J., Pvt,
Boucher, William E., Jr., Pvt,
Bouchneau, Robert E., Pvt,
Boudreaux, A. J., Pvt,
Boughn, Lynn W., Pvt,
†Bougie, Alfred, Pfc,
Boulais, Ernest J., Pvt,
†Boulton, Frank M., Pvt,
Bourbina, Jesse R., Pfc,
†Bourgoin, Donald, Pfc,
Bourguet, Napoleon M., Pvt,
Bourque, Joseph S., Pfc,
Bousquet, Edward O., Pfc,
Bova, Thomas D., Pvt,
Bove, Michael J., Pvt,
Bowen, Burl B., Pfc,
Bowen, Chester H., Sgt,
Bowen, Houston H., Sgt,
Bowen, James E., Pvt,
Bower, Walter E., Pfc,
Bowers, Jack H., Pvt,
Bowers, Willard R., Pfc,
Bowers, Wilson F., T/4,
Bowles, Carl, Pfc,
Bowles, William C., Pvt,
Bowling, Lacey S., Pvt,
†Bowman, Donald M., T/Sgt,
Bowman, James E., Pfc,
Bowman, James J., Pfc,
†Bowman, Rayford D., Pfc,
Bowman, Robert L., Pvt,
†Box, Malcolm O., Jr., 2nd Lt,
Boy, Glen L., T/4,
Boyce, Eugene S., Pvt,
Boyd, Bill, Pfc,
Boyd, Kenneth W., S/Sgt,
Boyd, Randall V., Cpl,
Boyd, Thomas L., Pvt,
Boyd, Waymond L., Pfc,
Boye, Frederick W., Jr., Lt Col,
†Boyer, Floyd M., Sgt,
Boyer, James O., Pvt,
Boyer, Robert H., Pvt,
†Boyer, Robert L., Pvt,
Boylan, Joseph S., Pvt,
Boyle, Cornelius D., Pfc,
Boyle, William F., Pfc,
Boylen, James E., Pfc,
Boyles, Kemp A., Pfc,
Boysen, Bernhard E., Pfc,
Bozajian, Constantine E., Pfc,
Braak, John A., T/3,
Brach, Stanley W., Sgt,
Bracken, Edward T., Pvt,
Brackett, Marion M., 1st Lt,
Brackett, Wm. E., Jr., 1st Lt,
Bradberry, Watkins C., S/Sgt,
†Bradbury, Charles W., Pfc,
Braden, John E., Pfc,
Braden, Robert M., Pvt,
Brader, Wayne B., Pfc,
Bradford, Dan L., Pfc,
Bradford, Harold E., Pvt,
Bradford, Richard F., Pfc,
Bradley, Glenn J., Pfc,
Bradley, Glenwood T., Pfc,
Bradley, Harry G., Pfc,
Bradley, James L., Pvt,
Bradley, Lester F., T/5,
Bradshaw, Chas. A., Jr., S/Sgt,
Bradshaw, William, Pfc,
Brady, Brookner W., Lt Col,
Brady, James H., Pfc,
Brady, John J., Jr., 2nd Lt,
Brady, Quentin I., Pvt,
Braganza, Jose D., Pvt,
Bragg, Clifford L., Jr., Pfc,
Bragg, Douglas E., T/4,
Bragg, James D., Pvt,
†Brake, John J., Pvt
Brakenbury, Arnold R., T/5,
Bram, Jack H., Pvt,
Bramble, Clarence P., Pfc,
Bramble, Carl M., Jr., Pfc,
Branagan, John T., Pfc,
Branca, Anthony, Pvt,
Branch, Leo B., Pfc,
†Branch, Winfred B., Pfc,
Brandeberry, Howard D., Pfc,
†Brandon, Van P., T/Sgt,
Brandt, Donald J., Pvt,
Branham, Wesley M., Pvt,
Branscome, Joel D., Pfc,
Branson, Loren D., Pfc,
Branson, Wilbert B., Pvt,
Brant, Wallace E., Pvt,
†Branthaver, Edward L., Pfc,
Branting, Willard C., Pfc,
Branton, Levi L., T/Sgt,
Branyan, Paul F., Pfc,
Brasch, Raymond F., Pfc,
Brase, Edmund B., Pfc,
Brashears, Charlie, Pfc,
†Brassell, Robert J., Pfc,
Bratkowski, Edward J., Pfc,
*Braun, Charles K., Pvt,
Braun, Robert E., Pvt,
†Braun, Theodore L., Pvt,
†Brautlecht, Robert A., Pvt,
Braverman, Eugene D., T/5,
Brawley, Elmer C., S/Sgt,
Bray, William F., Pvt,
†Breau, Hormidas J., Sgt,
‡Breazeale, Leo, Pvt,
Breden, Marven E., Pfc,
§Breed, Newell C., Sgt,
Breeden, Wilbert, Pfc,
Breese, Grover C., Jr., Pfc,
Breese, John L., Pvt,
†Brege, Marvin J., Pfc
Breger, Jacob, Pvt,
Bregman, Philip, Pvt,
Breiner, Roland G., Pfc,
Brendel, Philip H., Jr., Pvt,
Brennan, James A., 1st Lt,
Brennan, Thomas J., T/4,
Bresher, Harold R., Pvt,
†Bress, Louis, Pfc,
Brett, John J., Pfc,
Bretton, Leonard C., Pvt,
Brewer, Clyde E., Pfc,
†Brewer, George W., Pvt,
Brewer, Perry J., S/Sgt,
Brewer, Ralph, Pvt,
Brewster, Warren L., Pvt,
Breyer, Robert G., 2nd Lt,
Bridges, Linue L., Jr., Pvt,
Bridges, Willie, T/Sgt,
†Bridgewater, William E., Pfc,
Briganti, James M., Pfc,
Briggs, Arnold G., Pfc,
Briggs, Chauncey P., Pvt,
Briggs, Ervin W., S/Sgt,
Briggs, William N., Pfc,
Brignac, Woodrow W., Pfc,
Brill, Abe W., T/5,
Brimer, S. T., Pfc,
†Brinson, Logan G., T/Sgt,
†Briody, Christopher, Jr., Pvt,
Briski, Joseph L., Pfc,
Brissette, Frederick F., Pfc,
Bristol, Frank L., T/Sgt,
Britt, Elmo E., Pfc,
Britt, Joseph, Pvt,
†Brittain, Jack P., Pvt,
Britton, Leonard C., Pfc,
†Britvec, John G., Pfc,
Broad, Stanley D., Pvt,
Broadwater, Charles A., Pvt,
Brock, Ferdinand, Pfc,
Brock, Stanley J., Pvt,
Brockelsby, Warren C., Pvt,
†Brod, Elmer L., 1st Lt,
Brodd, Kenneth V., Pfc,
Broderick, Raymond J., Pfc,
Brodeur, Paul E., Sgt,
Brodfuehrer, Richard E., Pvt,
Brogden, James E., Jr., Pvt,
Broic, George, Pfc,
Bronson, Lloyd W., Pfc,
Bronstein, Meyer, Pvt,
Brooks, Bert, Jr., Sgt,
Brooks, Conda R., Pfc,
Brooks, Herbert, Pvt,
Brooks, James L., Pvt,
Brooks, Jess S., Cpl,
Brooks, Marvin G., Pfc,
†Brooks, Norwood O., Pfc,
Brooks, Samuel, Jr., Pfc,
Brooks, William D., Pvt,
†Broome, Raymond E., Pfc,
Brose, Howard A., Pfc,
Brossig, Ramico G., T/5,
Broughton, Charlie, Pvt,
Broussard, Reese R., Pvt,
Brouwer, Peter, S/Sgt,
†Brown, Arthur A., Sgt,
Brown, Arthur I., Pvt,
Brown, Bartholomew E., Pvt,
Brown, Clifton, Pvt,
Brown, Clyde, Pfc,
Brown, Donald J., Pvt,
Brown, Elvin L., Cpl,
Brown, Francis R., S/Sgt,
Brown, Fred J., Pfc,
Brown, Fred O., Jr., Pfc,
*Brown, Garland L., Pfc,
Brown, George A., Pvt,
Brown, George E., Pfc,
Brown, George W., Pvt,
Brown, Harley L., Jr., Pvt,
Brown, Harold A., S/Sgt,
Brown, Howard A., Pvt,
Brown, Howard G., Pfc,
*Brown, Howard W., Pvt,
*Brown, Hubert J., Pfc,
Brown, Jack D., Pvt,
Brown, James H., Pvt,
Brown, James L., Sgt,
†Brown, Jerrold W., Pfc,
Brown, John C., Pfc,
†Brown, Joseph M., S/Sgt,
Brown, Leonard F., Pvt,
Brown, Lora E., Pfc,
Brown, Marshall L., Pfc,
Brown, Merle A., S/Sgt,
Brown, O. J. W., Pfc,
Brown, Otis H., Pfc,
Brown, Philip C., Pfc,
†Brown, Raymond L., Pvt,
Brown, Richard, 1st Sgt,
Brown, Robert S., 1st Sgt,
Brown, Russell, Pvt,
Brown, Stanley V., S/Sgt,
†Brown, Thomas A., Pvt,
Brown, Victor C., Pvt,
†Brown, Vivian G., Pvt,
Brown, Walter T., Jr., Cpl,
Brown, William C., Cpl,
Brown, William E., Pvt,
Brown, William E., Pvt,
†Brown, Willis E., Pvt,
Browne, George E., Pfc,
Browning, Cecil L., Pvt,
Brownlee, Basil E., Pfc,
Brownold, William E., Pvt,
Brozovich, Edward G., T/5
Brubaker, Wilbur K., Pfc,
Bruce, Charles W., Sgt,
Bruce, John F., Pvt,
†Bruce, Johnnie C., Pvt,
Bruce, Lewis E., Pfc,
Bruckner, Frank J., S/Sgt,
Brueski, Joseph S., Sgt,
Bruff, Harry A., Sgt,
Brumfield, Roy A., Pfc,
Brumfield, William B., Pvt,
Bruner, Hugh H., Capt,
Brunk, Woodrow H., Pvt,
Bruno, Aloysius J., Pfc,
Bruno, Anthony J., Pvt,
Bruno, Arnold D., Pfc,
Bruno, Michael R., 2nd Lt
Brunotte, Henry H., Pvt,
Brustad, George H., Sgt,
Bruton, Bill B., T/Sgt,
Bruton, David, Pfc,
§Brutto, Carl R., Pvt,
Brutto, Eugene J., Jr., Pvt,
Bryan, Charles W., Pvt,
Bryan, Richard E., Pvt,
†Bryant, Albert, Pfc,
Bryant, Donald H., S/Sgt,
†Bryant, Evander C., 1st Lt,
Bryant, James D., Pvt,
Bryant, Ollie W., Pfc,
Bryant, Robert G., Pvt,
Bryant, Wilbert P., Pfc,
Bryce, Keith S., S/Sgt,
§Bryk, Stanley J., Pfc,
Bryner, Wesley E., Pfc,
Bryson, Charles M., Pfc,
Brzezinski, Marion V., S/Sgt,
Brzycki, Thaddeus T., Pfc,
†Bubb, Ralph R., Sgt,
Bucelle, Pascal M., Pfc,
Buchanan, Clifford, Pfc,
Buchanan, David F., Pvt,
Buchanan, Henry T., Pvt,
Buchanan, Jay E., Pvt,
Bucharelli, Albert J., Pvt,
Bucher, Walter C., Pvt,
Buchhorn, Carle, Pfc,
Buchthal, Fitz, S/Sgt,
Buck, Alvin J., Pfc,
Buckley, John P., T/5,
Buckley, Thomas P., S/Sgt,
Buco, Anthony J., Pvt,
Budd, Everett W., Pvt,
Budner, William D., Pfc,
Budness, Frank M., Pvt,
†Buelna, Ralph C., Pvt,
Buelow, Harold C., Cpl,
Buemi, Sam E., Pfc,
Buensch, Albert W., Pfc,
§Buerger, John F., Pfc,
Bufano, Eugene C., Pvt,
Buff, Roy M., Pfc,
Buffman, Howard S., Pfc,
Bugar, Rudolph, Pvt,
Bugawijan, Martin J., Pvt,
Buhro, Robert J., Cpl,
Bujarski, Aloysius, T/5,
Bulak, Felix, Pvt,
Bulger, Fred J., Pvt,
Bulla, Steve F., Pfc,
Bullard, Russell C., Pfc,
Bullaro, John J., Pvt,
Bullinger, Lawrence, T/Sgt,
†Bullington, Oakley A., T/Sgt,
Bullock, Berry L., T/4,
Bullock, McCauley O., Pfc,
Bulmash, Ira, Pvt,
Bumbera, Emery J., Pvt,
Bumgarner, Carl N., Pfc,
Bumgarner, James D., Pfc,
Bumgarner, William M., Pfc,
§Bunce, Clyde C., Pfc,
Bunda, Bohdan, Pvt,
Bunge, Karl F., Pfc,
Bunger, Robert C., Pvt,
Bunnell, Darrel A., S/Sgt,
Bunte, August H., T/Sgt,
Bunting, Thomas A., Pfc,
†Buonovolonta, Adolfe O., Pfc,
Burch, Rufus H., Pfc,
Burchett, John T., Pfc,
Burdette, Garnet A., Pvt,
Burford, Walter L., Pfc,
Burger, Carl J., T/4,
§Burgett, Robert E., Pvt,
Burgess, Arthur L., Pvt,
Burgess, Clarence T., Cpl,
Burgess, Orval W., Pvt,
Burgess, Samuel M., Jr., Pvt,
‡Burgess, William A., Pfc,
Burgoin, Donald G., Pfc,
Burgos, Antonio, Pvt,
Burk, Charles M., Pfc,
Burke, Bud M., 1st Lt,
Burke, Frank, 1st Lt,
Burke, Henry, Jr., Pvt,
Burke, James P., Pvt,
Burke, Lawrence G., Pvt,
Burke, Paul J., T/5,
Burke, Richard P., Pfc,
Burke, Thomas, Pfc,
†Burkes, James M., Sgt,
Burkett, Francis T. J., Pvt,
Burkett, John C., T/4,
Burkhardt, Clarence J., Pvt,
Burkhardt, Ray E., Sgt,
Burkit, William C., Pfc,
Burks, George S., 1st Lt,
Burley, Orville B., Pvt,
Burness, Harry L., Pvt,
Burnett, Byron L., Jr., Pvt,
Burnette, Corbin P., T/5,
Burnette, Lawton M., Jr., T/5,
Burnette, Melvin K., Pfc,
Burns, Delmus B., Pvt,
Burns, Earl F., Pfc,
Burns, Edward J., Pvt,
Burns, John J., Pfc,
Burns, Robert G., Pfc,
Burns, Thomas P., Pvt,
Burns, Virgil T., Pvt,
Burr, Eugene H., Pvt,
†Burrage, Ronald P., Jr., Pfc,
†Burrett, Jack D., Pvt,
Burris, Clyde E., Pfc,
Burrow, James E., Pfc,
Burry, Bernard J., Pfc,
Burt, Donald L., Cpl,
Burton, Burgin, Pvt,
Burton, Charles W., Pvt,
Burton, George L., T/5,
Burton, James E., Pfc,
Burton, James H., Pvt,
Burton, John R., Pfc,
Burton, Joseph A., T/Sgt,
Burton, Walter R., Sgt,
Burud, William N., Capt,
Buscang, Irving, Pvt,
Busch, Leo A., Sgt,
Buscher, Louis E., 1st Sgt,
†Busco, James V., Pvt,
†Bush, Donald F., Pvt,
Bush, Kenneth R., Pfc,
Busha, Vance E., Pvt,
Bushey, Edmond M., Pvt,
Bushey, Orval T., Pfc,
Bushey, Richard L., Pfc,
Buss, Clarence A., Pvt,
Buss, William J., T/5,
Butala, Stanley E., Pfc,

† Killed in Action. * Prisoner of War. ‡ Missing in Action. § Died of Wounds.

IN WORLD WAR II 483

§Butcher, Phillip, Sgt,
Butler, Charles P., Capt,
Butler, Dorson A., Pfc,
Butler, Edwin, Pvt,
†Butler, Frederick L., Pfc,
Butler, James J., 1st Lt,
Butler, Joseph C., Pvt,
Butler, Paragon D., Pvt,
Butler, Robert B., Sgt,
Butler, William E., Pfc,
Butler, William H., Pvt,
Butner, Harvey A., Pfc,
Butterworth, Andrew, Pfc,
Buttimer, John B., Pvt,
†Buttram, Edgar R., Jr., Pvt,
Butwin, George, Pvt,
Bux, William E., Pvt,
Buxton, Roland R., Pfc,
Buzek, Paul, Sgt,
Byder, John L., Pfc,
Byerly, Phillip J., S/Sgt,
Byers, Paul E., T/Sgt,
Byham, Richard B., Pvt,
Byington, Edwin A., Pvt,
§Byler, Ernest T., Pvt,
Bynum, Claud R., Pfc,
Byrd, Curtis, Pfc,
Byrd, Frank A., Pfc,
Byrd, James T., Pvt,
Byrd, James W., S/Sgt,
Byrd, Malcolm A., Pvt,
Bytnar, Joseph, Pfc,

Cabadas, Jose, Pfc,
§Caboor, Raymond J., Pvt,
Caborne, Thomas W., Pfc
Cabral, Alfred T., Pvt,
§Cabral, Wilfred M., Pfc,
Caccard, Charles J., Pvt,
Cada, Henry L., Pvt,
Cadarette, Albert J., Pvt,
Cadden, John D., Pvt,
Cafagno, Nicholas A., Pvt,
Caffarella, Edward P., Sgt,
Cagle, Grover C., Pfc,
Cagle, Willie B., Pvt,
Cahan, Murray, Pvt,
Cain, James W., Pfc,
Cain, O. W., Pvt,
Caine, Clair B., Pfc,
Calabro, Dominic, Pvt,
Calabrese, Angelo A., Pvt,
Calabrese, Phillip, Pfc,
Calamari, George J., Pfc,
Calder, Paul H., Pvt,
†Caldera, Howard M., Pvt,
Calderon, Ralph, Pfc,
Caldwell, Boone H., Pfc,
Caldwell, Harold E., Pvt,
Caldwell, Ray G., Pvt,
Caldwell, Wiley H., Pvt,
Cales, Lloyd G., Pvt,
Calfee, William A., 2nd Lt,
Caliguire, Thomas J., Pfc,
Calhoun, Robert O., T/5,
Calipare, Joseph, Pfc,
Calfo, Ross C., Pvt,
Calkins, Merritt R., Pvt,
Call, Forrest E., Pfc,
Callaghan, Richard I., Cpl,
Callahan, Carl C., Pvt,
Callahan, Ernest O., Pvt,
§Callahan, Eugene J., Pvt,
Callahan, Ernest M., Sgt,
Callahan, Francis L., T/5,
Callahan, Peter E., Capt,
Callahan, Robert E., Pvt,
Callaway, James R., Pfc,
Callicott, Henry C., Pfc,
Callihan, James P., Pvt,
Callis, Buell B., Pvt,
†Calloway, Alton L., Pfc,
Calloway, John, Cpl,
Calmes, Eldon C., Pvt,
Calo, Patsy J., Pvt,
Calos, Constantine T., Pfc,
†Calva, Rafael, S/Sgt,
Calvert, Roy C., S/Sgt,
Calvert, William W., T/Sgt,
Camarde, Dominick, Pfc,
Cameron, Clifford, S/Sgt,
Cameron, John A., Pfc,
Cameron, Robert C., Cpl,
†Camp, Ernest M., S/Sgt,
Camp, Frank H., Pfc,
Camp, Perry, Cpl,
Campagna, Robert A., 1st Sgt,
Campana, Carl J., Sgt,
Campanaro, Joseph L., Pvt,
Campanaro, Paul J., Pvt,
Campanelli, Vincent M., Pfc,
Campbell, Charles S., Jr., Pvt
Campbell, Clarence W., Pvt,
Campbell, Clyde R., Pvt,
Campbell, Donald F., Pfc,
Campbell, Edward J., Pfc,
*Campbell, Ernest M., Pfc,
Campbell, Eugene F., Pfc,
Campbell, George A., S/Sgt,
Campbell, James A., Pfc,
Campbell, Jimmy J., T/5,
Campbell, John H. J., Pvt,
†Campbell, Joseph O., Pfc
†Campbell, Michael G., Sgt,
Campbell, Richard C., S/Sgt,
Campbell, Rudolph Q., Pvt,
Campbell, Roy R., Pfc,
Campbell, Vincent A., S/Sgt,
Campi, William, Cpl,
Canadeo, Daniel F., Pvt,
Canale, Joseph E., Pvt,
Cancel, Joaquin, Pvt,
Candelaria, Trancito J., Cpl,
Candler, William W., 2nd Lt,
Canfield, Harry W., Sgt,
Cannaday, Harvey C., S/Sgt,
Cannipp, William A., Pfc,
Cannon, Curtis J., Pfc,
Cannon, Ezra L., S/Sgt,
Cannon, James O., S/Sgt,
Canter, Guy M., Pfc,
Canterbury, Willie A., Pvt,
Cantinieri, Fiorvante V., Pfc,
†Cantwell, Louis, Pvt,
Caouette, Lawrence A., Pfc,
Capalong, Nicholas A., Pvt,
Capell, Albert, Pfc,
Caperton, William, Pfc,
Caplan, Aben S., Pvt,
Caplinger, Milton E., S/Sgt,
Capobianco, Michael A., Pvt,
Caponera, John J., Pfc,
Caponigri, John R., Pvt,
Capp, Michael, Pvt,
Cappozzoli, Louis, Pfc,
Capps, Curtis H., T/Sgt,
Capps, Everett, Cpl,
Cappucci, Frank J., Pvt,
Capuano, Louis J., Pvt,
Capuano, Martin E., Pvt
Caputo, Patsy A., Pvt,
Caracino, Frank J.,
†Caranci, Manfred L., Pfc,
Caraway, James B., Pvt,
Carazo, Joseph, Pfc,
†Carbaugh, Daniel S., Pfc,
Card, Edgar W., Pvt,
Card, Ralph L., Jr., Pfc,
Cardelli, Pat J., Pfc,
Cardi, Franesco, Pfc,
Cardias, John J., Pfc,
Cardillo, Albert, Pvt,
Cardillo, Dominic, Pvt,
Cardonick, Albert, Pvt,
Cardoso, Manuel, Sgt,
Cardoza, Edmund, Pvt,
Cardoza, Joaquin I., Pfc,
Carelle, Premo M., Sgt,
Carello, Rocco V., Pvt,
Carey, Jacob J., Pvt,
Carey, Joseph J., T/5,
Carey, William J., Jr., Pvt,
Carico, Charles C., Pfc,
Carini, Earl P., Pfc,
Carland, Fred J., Pvt,
Carlile, William M., Jr., Sgt,
Carlin, Benjamin, 2nd Lt
Carlsen, Harold D., Sgt,
†Carlsen, Stanley S., Pfc,
Carlson, Calvert L., Sgt,
Carlson, Carl E., Pfc,
†Carlson, Duane K., Pvt,
Carlson, Einar H., Pvt,
Carlson, Kenneth J., Pvt,
Carlson, Norman A., Pfc,
Carlson, Philips, Pfc,
†Carlson, Robert A., Pfc,
Carlyle, Deo G., Pfc,
Carmany, Earl J., T/Sgt,
†Carnegie, Lee J., Pvt,
Carnes, Ned E., T/4,
Carney, Lindell, Pvt,
Carney, James P., Pvt,
Carney, Stephen A., Pfc,
Carney, Thomas W., Pvt,
Carns, Vernon L., Pfc,
Carocci, Albert A., Pvt,
†Carollo, Anthony J., Pvt,
†Caron, Emilein D., Pvt,
Carothers, Francis E., Cpl,
Carpenter, Benedict G., Pfc,
Carpenter, Charles D., Pfc,
†Carpenter, Charles E., Sgt,
†Carpenter, Gordon E., Pvt,
†Carpenter, Harold R., Pvt,
Carpenter, Joe K., Pfc,
Carpenter, Lewis C., Jr., Cpl,
Carpenter, Plynn Q., Pfc,
Carr, Clifford J., Pvt,
Carr, Henry O., Pfc,
Carr, Jacob V., Pfc,
Carr, James J., Jr., Pvt,
Carr, Joseph T., Pfc,
Carr, Rudolph L., Pfc,
*Carr, Samuel H., Pvt,
Carr, William E., S/Sgt,
Carranza, Jose M., Pfc,
Carreirs, Manuel, Pvt,
Carreon, William, Pvt,
Carrese, Angelo O., Pvt,
†Carrico, Dempsey J., Pfc,
Carrier, Curley, Pvt,
Carrillo, Rafael, Pfc,
Carroll, Alex B., S/Sgt,
Carroll, Aubrey L., S/Sgt,
Carroll, Charles W., Sgt,
Carroll, Famon G., Pvt,
Carroll, Floyd, S/Sgt,
§Carroll, John F., Pvt,
Carroll, Samuel W., Pfc,
Carroll, Sheridan M., Pvt,
†Carscaddon, Henry B., Pfc,
Carsella, John J., Cpl,
Carson, Cecil A., Pvt,
Carta, Harold A., Pfc,
†Carte, Samuel B., Jr., Pfc,
Carter, Alonzo W., Pfc,
†Carter, Charles E., Pfc,
Carter, Frank D., Pfc,
Carter, George L., Pfc,
†Carter, George L., Jr., Pfc,
Carter, Harvey, Jr., Pvt,
Carter, James E., Pfc,
Carter, Joe H., T/Sgt,
Carter, Joseph T., Pfc,
Carter, Kenneth P., Pfc,
Carter, Marvin C., Pfc,
Carter, O'Brien, Pvt,
Carter, Owen J., Pvt,
Carter, Paul E., Pfc,
Carter, Raymond W., Sgt,
Carter, Richard C., Jr., Pvt,
Carter, Robert W., Jr., Pvt,
Carter, William W., Jr., Pfc,
Cartier, Roland A., Pfc,
Carver, David M., Pvt,
Carver, Irving F., Pfc,
†Carver, John A., Jr., Pfc,
Carver, John S., Jr., 2nd Lt,
Carver, Marvin R., Pvt,
Carver, Romaden R., Pvt,
Carvalho, Henry J., Pvt,
Cary, Lester J., Pfc,
Cary, John B., Pvt,
Casa, Ralph J., Pvt,
Casci, Fred J., T/5,
Casciero, Anthony J., Pvt,
Cascioli, Robert R., Pvt,
Casciotti, Harry V., Pvt,
Case, Vernon W., Pfc,
Casey, Francis T., Pfc,
Cash, Jimmie, Sgt,
Cash, Louis A., Pfc,
Casiano, Carlos, Pfc,
Caso, George F., Pfc,
Cason, Henry D., Pvt,
Casper, Emmett C., Pfc,
Cassel, Douglas F., Pvt,
†Cassese, Nicholas J., Jr., Pvt,
†Cassetta, Henry, Pvt,
Cassidy, Joseph G., Pvt,
Cassizzi, Joseph M., Pvt,
Cast, Richard E., Pfc,
§Castalluzzo, Angelo J., Pvt,
†Castanon, Juan R., Pvt,
Castellaw, Delbert W., Pfc,
Castelli, Eugene A., Pvt,
Castillo, Alejandro R., Pfc,
Castillo, Angelo, Pvt,
Castillo, Simon S., Jr., Pvt,
Castilow, John E., Pfc,
Castle, Richard H., Pfc,
Castruita, Richard A., Pfc,
Casucci, Dominick P., Pfc,
†Catalano, Frank T., Pfc,
Catalano, Santo, J., S/Sgt,
Cataldo, Thomas J., Pvt,
†Catauro, Dominic, Sgt,
Catlett, Alvin J., Pvt,
Catoe, Henry J., Jr., Pvt,
Caton, June C., 1st Lt,
Catron, Paul C., Pvt,
Caudell, Jack G., T/4,
Caudell, Roy C., Pfc,
Caudill, James W., Pfc,
Caudle, Frank A., S/Sgt,
Cautillo, Michael A., Pfc,
Cavanaugh, John P., 1st Lt,
Cavanaugh, Thomas S., Pfc,
Cavazos, Miguel, Pvt,
Caviglia, Simon E., Pfc,
Cavin, Bomar H., Pvt,
Cawley, Elwood C., Pfc,
Ceccucci, Randall C., Pvt,
†Cecere, Henry S., Pvt,
Cecil, Raymond, Pfc,
Ceizyk, Gasimer J., Pvt,
†Ceimo, Alphonse J., Pfc,
Center, George M., Pvt,
Ceraso, Joseph A., Pvt,
Cericola, Nicholas J., Pvt,
Cerny, David, Pfc,
†Cero, Eddie M., Pfc,
Cetnarski, John S., Pvt,
Ceverha, Melvin G., T/5,
Chabot, Wayne A., Pfc,
Chacham, Sol, Pvt,
Chacon, Joseph J., Pvt,
Chacon, Tony G., Pvt,
Chaize, William E., Pvt,
Chambers, Charles A., Pfc,
Chambers, Charles F., Pvt,
†Chambers, Clarence R., Pfc,
Chambers, David L., Pvt,
§Chambers, Harold M., Pfc,
Chambers, William L., Sgt,
Chamberlain, Armand M., Pvt,
Chamberlain, Stanley W., Pfc,
Chamberlain, Willard, Pvt,
†Champ, William M., Pvt,
†Champagne, Richard, Pvt,
Champion, Charles H., Pvt,
†Champlin, Harvey L., Pvt,
Chancey, Maynard E., Pfc,
Chandler, Chalmer C., Pfc,
Chandler, Hoyte W., Pvt,
Chandler, Joseph W., Capt,
Chandler, Paul, Pfc,
Chandler, Robert E., Sgt,
Chandler, Vernon V., Pfc,
Chaney, Arthur C., Jr., Pfc,
Chanin, Abraham S., T/5,
Channel, Floyd A., Pvt,
Chapdelaine, Charles A., S/Sgt,
§Chapman, Arnold W., Pfc,
Chapman, Arthur L., Pvt,
†Chapman, Daniel O., Cpl,
Chapman, Ernest G., Pfc,
Chapman, Fletcher, T/5,
Chapman, George H., Pfc,
Chapman, James E., Pvt,
Chapman, James H., Pfc,
Chapman, Walter W., S/Sgt,
Chapman, Willard H., T/4,
Chappell, Donald C., Pvt,
Chappell, Lloyd, Pfc,
Chappell, Thomas A., Pvt,
Charifson, Charles, Pfc,
Charlton, Delno L., Pfc,
Charney, John G., Pvt,
Charron, Francis A., Pvt,
Charron, Hector J., T/5,
Charest, James R., Sgt,
Chase, John P., Pvt,
Chase, William A., Jr., S/Sgt,
Chastain, Eugene R., S/Sgt,
Chatfield, Philip H., Cpl,
Chatt, Leon P., Pvt,
Chattin, Sherman L., Pvt,
Chaudron, David L., Pfc,
Chavarria, C. A., Jr., Pfc,
Chavez, Jesus A., Pvt,
Chavis, Talmadge, Pvt,
Chawluk, Walter C., Pvt,
Chazon, George, Pfc,
Chee, Joe M., Pvt,
Chemeleski, Edward R., M/Sgt.
Cheney, Everett B., Sgt,
Cheney, Homer G., Cpl,
Chenoweth, John J., Pfc,
Chepell, William P., Pvt,
Cheramie, Camille A., Pfc,
Cherinka, John, Jr., Pfc,
†Chernoff, Granum, Pvt,
Cherny, Oscar D., Pfc,
Cherry, Paul L., Sgt,
Chew, Art F., T/5,
†Chiamack, Christopher C., Pfc,
†Chiarlitti, Pio, Pvt,
Childers, Eldridge, Pvt,
Childress, James E., T/5,
Childress, Thomas A., Pfc,
Childs, Harold D., Pfc,
†Chilson, Cheston M., Pvt,
Chin, Lun, Pfc,
Chipka, Joseph J., Pvt,
Chipman, Edwin E., Sgt,
Chirco, Sam J., T/5,
Chism, Jack P., T/5,
Chittendan, Frederick M., Pfc,
Cholish, Leonard, Pfc,
Chorzemba, John, Pvt,
Chouinard, John P., T/5,
Christensen, Andrew H., S/Sgt
Christensen, James, Pfc,
Christian, Clarence A., Pvt,
Christian, Edward S., S/Sgt,
Christian, Harold W., Pfc,
†Christian, Herbert F., Pvt,
Christian, Trelvie, T/5,
Christie, Ellery C., Pfc,
Christopher, Enderl W., Pvt,
Chromey, Raymond E., Pfc,
Chrostowski, Robert F., Pvt,
Chunko, Andrew, Pfc,
Chunn, Paul E., Pvt,
Church, Herbert H., Pvt,
Church, Paul W., Pvt,
Churchill, Crawford E., Pfc,
†Chvilicek, William P., Pfc,
Chyrklund, Franklin J., T/Sgt,
Ciabattoni, Guido A., Pvt,
Ciadella, Peter M., Pvt,
Ciancanelli, Arco A., S/Sgt,
Cianci, Louis, Pvt,
†Ciarlo, Corado A., Pfc,
Cicallelli, John F., Jr., Pvt,
†Cichoracki, Raymond M., Pfc,
Cieslak, Chester V., Pvt,
Cifrodella, Angelo A., Pvt,
Cioffi, Ralph, T/4,
Cimadon, Sam A., Pvt,
Cioyacco, Vincent V., Pfc,
Cipri, Joseph, Pvt,
†Ciupaki, Joseph, Pfc,
Claiborne, Wilbur W., Pfc,
Clapper, Eldred W., Pvt,
Clapper, John M., Pfc,
Clark, Alan K., 1st Lt,
Clark, Albert M., S/Sgt,
Clark, Ceacle H., Pvt,
Clark, Clarence T., Pfc,
Clark, Forest D., Sgt,
Clark, Granville L., Pvt,
Clark, H. W., Pfc,
†Clark, Howard F., Pvt,
†Clark, James B., S/Sgt,
Clark, Jessie E., Pvt,
Clark, Leslie E., Pfc,
Clark, Lewis G., Pfc,
Clark, Lloyd L., Pvt,
†Clark, Lorin G., Pfc,
Clark, Milton C., Pvt,
Clark, Richard, Pvt,
Clark, Robert L., 1st Lt,
Clark, Worthington, Cpl,
Claussen, Harmand O., Pfc,
Clavelle, Alfred, Pfc,
Clay, Lyle E., Pvt,
Clayton, Irvin N., Pvt,
Clayton, J. C., 2nd Lt,
†Clayton, Roy O., Pfc,
‡Clemons, Clark F., Pvt,
Clement, Laurian T., S/Sgt,
Clement, Ernest D., Sgt,
Clemens, James M., T/Sgt,
Clemens, William C., Pfc,
Clemmer, Kenneth D., Pvt,
Cleveland, Emery F., S/Sgt,
Cleveland, Harry A., Pvt,
Cleveland, Wilson L., Pfc,
†Clevenger, Eugene E., Pvt,
Clevenger, John H., Pvt,
Clifford, Dennis J., Pfc,
Clifford, Jackson A., Pfc,
Clifford, John R., Pfc,
Clift, Redford W., Pvt,
Clifton, Woodrow D., Pvt,
Climer, Leslie R., Cpl,
Cline, Alfred L., Pfc,
Cline, William W., Pfc,
Clingan, Glenn P., Pfc,
Clippinger, Glenn B., Pfc,
Cloninger, Floyd R., 2nd Lt,
Clontz, William D., Pfc,
‡Clopper, Thomas S., Jr., Pfc,
Clopton, Hal, Jr., Pvt,
Closmore, Alfred G., Sgt,
†Clotfelter, Lee M., Pvt,
Cloud, Clyde R., Pvt,
Clough, Oakleigh D., Pvt,
Cmorey, Andrew B., T/Sgt,
Coakley, Fred R., Cpl,
Coapstick, Ronald B., Pvt,
Cobb, Charlie W., Pfc,
†Cobb, Corwin B., Pvt,
Cobb, T. C., T/5,
Cobb, Thomas D., Pfc,
Coblitz, Lawrence S., Pfc
Coburn, Elton W., Pfc,
Cochran, Carl K., Pfc
Cochran, James M., Pvt,
Cochran, James W., Pvt,
Cochran, John C., Pvt,
Cochran, Obe R., Pfc,
Cochren, Carl K., Pfc,
Cock, Edward W., Pvt,
Cockerham, Clyde C., Sr., Pfc,
Cockerill, Ernest F., Cpl,
Cockrell, Monroe C., Pvt,
Cocozello, Donato M., Pvt,
Cody, Arthur A., Pvt,
Cody, Calvin C., Pvt,
†Cody, Rodney F., Pvt,
Coe, William F., T/4,

† Killed in Action. * Prisoner of War. ‡ Missing in Action. § Died of Wounds.

Coffee, Henry G., Pvt,
Coffey, Michael J., Pvt,
Coffman, Donald, Pfc,
Coffy, Anthony F., Sgt,
Coffindaffer, Doyle V., Pvt,
‡Cofield, Coolidge D., Pfc
Cogan, John M., 2nd Lt,
*Cogbill, Charles L., Jr., Capt,
Cogdell, Herman B., T/5,
Cogswell, Frederick J., Pfc,
Cohen, Abraham, Pvt,
Cohen, Benjamin, Pvt,
Cohen, Benjamin, Pvt,
Cohen, Bernard L., Pvt,
Cohen, Jack M., Pfc,
Cohen, Marvin, Sgt,
Cohen, Morton, Pfc,
Cohen, Sol, Pfc,
Cohenour, Carl R., Pvt,
Cohn, George G., Capt,
Coker, Leon J., S/Sgt,
Colandro, Thomas L., Pfc,
†Colangelo, Charles C., Pvt
Colbert, Dale R., Pfc,
Colburn, Edward L., Pfc,
Colburn, James L., Pfc,
Colburn, Kenneth D., S/Sgt,
Coldewe, Eugene L., T/5,
Cole, Arthur B., S/Sgt,
§Cole, John P., Pvt,
Cole, John S., Capt,
Cole, William C., Pvt,
Coleman, Alfred L., S/Sgt,
Coleman, Cosby L., Pvt,
Coleman, Floyd F., Pfc,
Coleman, George R., Pfc,
Coleman, Henry D., Pvt,
Coleman, Herbert D., Pvt,
†Coleman, Roy J., Pfc,
†Coleman, Seymour I., Pvt,
Coles, James W., Capt,
Colfer, John H., Pfc,
†Collette, Donat J., Pvt,
Collette, Leonard E., Pfc,
Colletti, Salvatore P., Pfc,
Colley, Rollen A., Pvt,
Colley, William B., Pfc,
Collier, Hillmus A., Pvt,
Colligan, James H., Pvt,
Collingsworth, James, Pvt,
Collins, Fred, Pfc,
Collins, Henry, Jr.,
Collins, Jack L., Pvt,
Collins, Paul H., Pfc,
Collins, Paul O., Pvt,
Collins, Richard D., Jr., T/3,
Collins, Thomas W., Sgt,
Collins, William G., Pfc
Collinsworth, David C., Pvt,
Collinsworth, Robert C., Pvt,
†Collison, Robert O., Sgt,
‡Collura, Angelo J., Pvt,
Colucci, Rudolph, Pvt,
Colvinjohn A., Jr., Pvt,
Combest, Louie E., Pvt,
Combs, Alfred B., Jr., Pvt,
Combs, Foster H., Pfc,
Combs, Leo F., Pvt,
Comeau, Victor M., Pfc,
Comer, Russell S., Pvt,
Comitino, Lawrence J., Pvt,
Como, Vincenzo J., Pfc,
Compofelice, Nicholas, Pvt,
Compton, David W., Capt,
Compton, Thomas E., Pfc,
Comrie, Russell M., Maj,
†Comstock, Charles A., Jr., Pfc,
Comstock, Verne E., Capt,
†Comte, Albert J., Pfc,
Conahan, Patrick J., Pfc,
Conant, Karl W., Sgt,
Condes, Pete D., Pfc,
Condon, Gurnsey R., M/Sgt,
Condon, James L., Pvt,
Condren, Charles E., Pfc,
Confalone, Joseph A., Pvt,
Conger, Neal F., S/Sgt,
Conklin, Donald J., Pvt,
Conklin, Edward S., Pvt,
Conklin, Joseph A., Pfc,
Conley, Arlos C., Pvt,
†Conley, Frank J., Pfc,
Conley, Grover C., Jr., Pfc,
Conly, Bert, Pvt,
Conlon, Francis X., Pvt,
Connell, Horace N., Pfc,
Conner, James F., Sgt,
Connett, George C., Pvt,
Connolly, Joseph S., 1st Lt,
Connor, Daniel K., Sgt,
Connor, Frank W., Jr., 2nd Lt
Connor, James F., Sgt,
†Connor, Thomas J., Jr., Pvt,
Connors, John E., Jr., Pvt
Conover, Harry E., Jr., Pfc,
Conover, Lewis J., 1st Lt,
Conquest, Guy T., Pvt,
Conrad, James R., 1st Sgt,
Conrad, John L., Pvt,
†Conrad, Francis, Pvt,
†Conrath, Francis J., Pvt,
Constantin, James M., Sgt,
Constantino, Andrew N., Pvt,
Converse, Edward E., Pfc,
Conway, Denzel B., Sgt,
Conway, Edward J., Pvt,
Conway, George R., Pfc,
Conway, John J., Pfc,
†Conwell, Walter O., Sgt,
Cook, Charles O., S/Sgt,
Cook, Don W., 1st Lt,
Cook, Donald J., Cpl,
Cook, Edward W., S/Sgt,
Cook, Freeley B., 2nd Lt,
Cook, Gerald A., Sgt,
Cook, Glain H., T/5,
Cook, Gordon G., S/Sgt,
Cook, Grat W., Jr., Pfc,
Cook, Harlan B., Pfc,
Cook, Jack C., Pvt,
Cook, John R., Pvt,
Cook, Ned M., Pvt,
Cook, Norman L., S/Sgt,
Cook, Robert B., Pfc,
Cook, Robert E., Pfc,
Cook, Stanley J., Pvt,
Cooke, Carl M., Cpl,
Cookis, Jacob, S/Sgt,
Cooley, Charles A., Pfc,
Cooley, Mervin J., Pfc,
Coon, David C., Pfc,
Coons, Gerald R., Pfc,
Coons, Maynard, Pvt,
Cooper, Clarence H., Pfc,
Cooper, General G., Pvt,
Cooper, Harold L., Pvt,
Cooper, James G., Cpl,
Cooper, James H., Pfc,
Cooper, Robert, Pfc,
Cooper, Robert L., Pfc,
Cooper, William, Pvt,
Cooper, William T., 1st Lt,
Copeland, Clarence D., Cpl,
Copeland, Fondrel, Pvt,
†Copeland, Henry P., Pvt,
Copeland, Joe H., Jr., T/4,
Copeland, Leonard E., S/Sgt,
Copeland, Robert L., Pfc,
Coppola, Louis J., Pvt,
Coppolo, Nicholas, Pvt,
Corbett, Edward J., Pvt,
†Corbett, Glenn W., Pvt,
Corbett, Walter S., Pfc,
Corda, John, Pvt,
Cordell, Wilbur L., Pfc,
Cordell, Robert H., Pvt,
Corder, Henry B., Pvt,
Cordova, Alonzo J., Pvt,
Cordova, Manuel O., Pvt,
Cordray, Lawrence A., Pvt,
Corl, Harold F., S/Sgt,
Corley, Warren M., Pvt,
†Cormanick, Michael W., S/Sgt,
Cormier, George A., T/5,
†Cormier, Thomas J., Pvt,
Corn, Claude F., Pfc,
Cornelison, John A., Pfc,
Cornett, Oscar C., Pvt,
Cornish, Robert E., Pvt,
Corona, Anastacio T., Pvt,
Cornoni, Henry L., Pvt,
Cornwall, George C., Pvt,
Correa, Gabriel S., Pvt,
Correia, Manuel D., Pfc,
Correia, Tony E., T/5,
Corrigan, Charles B., Cpl,
Corrigan, Edward M., Sgt,
Corrigan, Thomas L., Jr., Pfc,
Corrow, Otis D., Pvt,
Corse, George W., Pfc,
Corsi, James J., Pvt,
Cortner, Sidney G., Jr., Pvt,
Cortez, James E., Pfc,
Corvi, Guiseppe, Pfc,
Cosentino, Frank M., T/5,
Cosgrove, Clarence E., Pfc,
Cosgrove, Robert F., Pvt,
Cossari, Andrew T., Pvt,
Cossey, Paul E., T/5,
Cossey, Thomas O., Pvt,
†Costa, James, Pvt,
Costa, Joseph, Pfc,
Costabile, Angelo S., Pfc,
Costanza, Michael C., Pvt,
Costley, Lloyd J., Pfc,
Costardo, Joseph J., T/5,
Costello, Joseph J., T/Sgt,
†Costello, Michael, Pfc,
Cote, Max V., Pvt,
Cote, Melvin N., Pvt,
Cotoia, Frank J., Cpl,
Cotter, William H., Sgt,
Cotter, Kenneth, S/Sgt,
Cotter, Lloyd H., 1st Lt,
Cotter, Pierce J., Sgt,
Cotton, Sanford S., Pvt,
†Cottrell, Daris L., Pvt,
Couchman, John D., Pvt,
Coughlin, Allen O., Sgt,
Coulter, John F., T/4,
†Council, Carlyle C., Jr., Pvt,
Council, Claude A., S/Sgt,
Council, William E., Jr., Pvt,
†Counihan, Morris J., Cpl,
Countryman, John C., Pfc,
Courtney, Daniel C., Pfc,
Courtney, Donald M., T/5,
‡Courtney, William J., 1st Lt,
Courture, Maurice A., Pfc,
Cousins, Basil W., Pfc,
Covello, Americus, 1st Lt,
Cover, Frank C., Jr., Pvt,
Covey, Johnnie L., S/Sgt,
Covington, Rueben L., Pfc,
Covington, Ross L., 2nd Lt,
†Cowan, Bruce D., Sgt,
Cowan, James W., Pvt,
Coward, Eugene A., Cpl,
†Cowell, Albert J., Pvt,
Cowhorn, John B., Pvt
†Cox, Carl, Sr., Pvt,
†Cox, Earl F., Pvt,
Cox, Ernest P., Sgt,
Cox, Eugene D., Pfc,
Cox, Francis C., T/4,
Cox, George E., Jr., Sgt,
Cox, Harold L., Pfc,
Cox, Jewell F., Pvt,
Cox, Mauyer E., Pfc,
Cox, Spencer E., Pfc,
Cox, Troy D., Pfc,
Coy, Guadalupe D. L. S., Pfc,
Coyle, James T., Pfc,
Coyle, William F., Pvt,
Coyne, John L., Pvt,
Cozzi, Thomas, Pvt,
Crabb, John S., Sgt,
Crace, Peter J., Pfc,
Craft, Ira E., Pfc,
Crafton, Edward A., Pvt
Craig, Clayton C., Capt,
Craig, Earl J., Pvt,
Craig, Eugene A., Pvt,
Craig, Harvey D., Pfc,
Craig, Herman, Pvt,
Craig, Howard W., Pfc,
Craig, Jeame W., Pvt,
Craig, LeRoy R., Pfc,
Craig, LeRoy W., Pvt,
Craig, Paul E., Cpl,
†Craig, Robert, 2nd Lt,
Craig, Robert J., T/4,
Craig, Thomas J., Pvt,
Craig, Warren A., Pfc,
Cramblitt, Earl E., Pfc,
Cramer, William E., T/5,
Cramer, William F., Pvt,
Cramton, Malcolm F., Capt,
Crandall, Donald H., Pfc,
Crandall, Lloyd R., T/5,
Crandall, Robert W., Maj,
Crane, Wilber E., Pfc,
Crary, Keith G., Pfc,
Craven, Daniel S., Pvt,
Crawford, Adelbert, Pvt,
Crawford, Everett E., Pvt,
Crawford, Herman C., T/Sgt,
Crawford, Jay G., T/4,
Crawford, Joseph B., Lt Col,
Crawford, Richard E., Pvt,
†Crawford, Sammie L., Pvt,
Crawford, Theodore L., Pfc,
Crawford, W. H., Pvt,
*Crayton, David L., Pfc,
Crean, Donald J., Pvt,
Creason, Henry D., Pvt,
Creasy, Douglas E., Pfc,
Creasy, Fred M., Pvt,
Creciun, Cornell, Pfc,
Credno, Joseph J., Pvt,
Creel, Edward L., Pfc,
Creeley, Matthew W., Pvt,
Creighton, James M., Pvt,
Cress, Donald, Pfc,
Cretaro, Ernest R., Pvt,
Cretaro, Ignatius E., Pfc,
Crews, William B., Pfc,
†Crider, William L., Pfc,
Crim, Hyman R., Pvt,
Crimi, Nicholas J., Pvt,
Cripe, Bruce, Jr., Pfc,
Crisp, Oliver C., Pvt,
Crispin, Raymond C., Sgt,
Crissman, S. S., Jr., 1st Lt,
Crites, William D., Pvt,
Crittenden, Forest D., Pfc,
†Crnic, Thomas L., Sgt,
Crochetierle, N. P., 2nd Lt,
Crocker, Rex P., Pvt,
Crockett, Rupert L., Pfc,
Crocker, Bradford S., Pvt,
Cromer, William A., Pvt,
†Croney, James E., Pvt,
†Cronin, Charles E., Pvt,
Cronin, John T., Pvt,
Crook, James L., Jr., Pfc,
Cropp, Albert E., Jr., T/Sgt,
Crosby, Elmore T., 2nd Lt,
Crosby, Elmore L., T/Sgt,
Crosby, William P., Pfc,
Crosier, Edwin, Pvt,
Crosier, William H., Jr., Pfc,
Crosley, Leonard D., Pvt,
Crosley, Willard D., Sgt,
Cross, Austin C., S/Sgt,
Cross, Eugene M., Sgt,
Crossley, Martin E., Jr., 1st Lt,
Crothers, Richard W., Pfc,
†Crouch, Clifton H., S/Sgt,
†Crouch, Clinton W., Pfc,
Crouch, Dale B., Pvt,
Crouch, Jack A., 2nd Lt,
Crouch, Jack B., Pvt,
Crow, William H., Pfc,
Crowder, Earl F., Pvt,
§Crowe, William J., S/Sgt,
Crowell, Christopher J., S/Sgt,
Crowley, Cornelius A., Cpl,
*Crowley, Henry F., Jr., Pfc,
Crowner, Walter G., T/4,
Crum, George D., Pvt,
Crum, Regis J., Pvt,
Crumpler, Joseph S., Pvt,
†Crumpler, Woodward W., Pvt,
Crupp, Albert E., Jr., T/Sgt
Crutchfield, Carl T., Pfc,
Cruz, Raphael P., Pfc,
Cryar, Joseph H., Pvt,
Cubbon, Robert T., Pvt,
Cuifo, Sylvester A., S/Sgt,
†Culbertson, Walter E., Pvt,
Cullen, John A., T/4,
Cullen, William R., Pvt,
Culley, Levi C., T/Sgt,
Cullins, Cowen W., Pvt,
Culp, Johnnie W., Pvt,
Culver, Ligo C., Pfc,
Cumby, Charles S., Pfc,
Cummings, George E., Pfc,
†Cummings, Lee W., Sgt,
Cummins, John, Jr., Pfc,
Cunerty, James R., Pvt,
Cunningham, Alan W., Pvt,
Cunningham, E. S., Jr., Capt,
Cunningham, Edgar W., Pvt,
Cunningham, Ervil L., Pfc,
†Cunningham, H. P., Jr., Pfc,
Cunningham, Louis D., Cpl,
‡Cunningham, Thomas K., Pvt,
Cunningham, William J., Pvt,
Cunzeman, George H., Pfc,
Curavo, Otto M., S/Sgt,
Curbow, Grafton L., Pfc,
Curcio, Philip, Pvt,
Curcuroto, Sam, Pvt,
Curella, Charles A., Pvt,
Curkendall, William P., Pfc,
Curran, James F., Pfc,
Curran, John J., Sgt,
Curran, Francis C., Pvt,
Currence, Howard P., Jr., Pvt,
Currie, James R., Pfc,
Currin, Clifford C., Pfc,
Curro, James A., Pfc,
Curry, Osborn D., Pvt,
Curry, Thomas F., Pvt,
Curtin, Joseph F., Pvt,
Curtis, John D., Pfc,
Curtis, John L., Pfc,
Curtis, William C., Jr., Pfc,
Cusack, James V., Pfc,
Cusenza, Anthony G., Pvt,
Cushman, Stanley, Pvt,
Cusick, Alvania, S/Sgt,
Custead, John W., Pvt,
Custer, Jack A., Pfc,
Custer, Leland S., T/Sgt,
Cuthill, John, Jr., Pvt,
Cwerenz, Arthur J., Pvt,
Czaplicki, Edward J., Pfc,
‡Czarnecki, Harry J., Pvt,
Czechowski, Stanley J., Pfc,
Czeck, Stanley S., 1st Sgt,
Czerna, Stephen, Pfc,

Da Bell, John F., Cpl,
D'Acunto, Anthony J., Pfc,
*Dacus, James E., Pvt,
Daddazio, Marc J., Pfc,
Daeche, Raymond S., Pfc,
Daeger, Edmund J., Pfc,
Daher, Thomas A., T/5,
†Dahl, Eugene E., Pvt,
†Dahl, Richard H., S/Sgt,
Dailey, Charles E., Pvt,
Dailey, Gerald E., Pfc,
Dailey, Leonard K., Pfc,
Dalbey, Donald E., S/Sgt,
Dale, William J., Jr., Sgt,
D'Alessio, August, Pvt,
§Daley, Charles A., Jr., Pvt,
Daley, Daniel J., Pvt,
Daley, Raymond E., Pvt,
Dalimonte, Anthony C., Pvt,
Dallacqua, Oscar D., Pvt,
Dalli, Harvey E., Cpl,
Dalton, James J., S/Sgt,
Daly, John W., S/Sgt,
†Daly, Joseph P., Pvt,
Daly, Michael J., Capt.,
Dam, George R., Pfc,
Damaso, Meday V., Pfc,
Damato, Daniel F., Pfc,
D'Ambro, Salvatore J., Pfc,
D'Ambrosio, Nicholas A., Pfc,
Dame, John E., T/5,
Damon, Eugene E., S/Sgt,
Dampier, Alvin L., Sgt,
Dana, Robert R., Pfc,
Dandrea, Charles J., T/5,
Danemen, Max, Pvt,
D'Angelo, Frank J., Pfc,
Daniel, Samuel S., Jr., T/5,
Daniel, William E., Jr., Pfc,
Danieli, Robert J., Pfc,
Daniels, Cecil E., Pvt,
Danielson, Harley, Cpl,
‡Danielson, Reuben L., Pfc,
Dann, Albert B., Pvt,
Danish, Peter, Pvt,
D'Anthony, Nick H., Pfc,
Dare, Hoon, Pvt,
Dare, Robert H., Pvt,
†Darkow, Herman O., Pvt,
Darling, Howard L., Pfc,
Darling, Lloyd A., Pvt,
Darnell, Arthur J., Pfc,
Darnell, Clark L., Pvt,
Darrah, Chester L., Sgt,
Darrah, William A., Pvt,
Dasch, Stanley E., T/4,
Dash, Chester A., Pvt,
Dashen, John, Pvt,
Daso, Leon J., Pfc,
Dates, Frederick W., Pfc,
Datko, Joseph J., T/5
Dattolo, Joseph A., Pvt,
Dauby, Gervase F., S/Sgt,
Daughepbaugh, Neil W., Pfc,
Daugherty, Mark E., Pfc,
Daugherty, Willie G., Pvt,
D'Auria, Ralph, Pfc,
Dauser, Frederick E., Pvt,
Davenport, Charles L., Pfc,
Davenport, Conway R., Pfc,
Davenport, Ernest H., Pfc,
Davenport, Harland J., Pfc,
Davenport, Roy L., T/Sgt,
Davey, Francis F., Pvt,
§David, Bernard J., Sgt,
David, Horace L., Pvt,
Davidow, Benjamin, Pvt,
Davidowitz, Jack, Pvt,
Davidowitz, Max, Pvt,
Davidson, Bennie E., Pvt,
Davidson, Carl L., Cpl,
†Davidson, Clyde R., T/4,
Davidson, Floyd O., Pfc,
Davidson, James E., Pvt,
Davidson, John C., Pvt,
†Davidson, William G., 2nd Lt,
Daviduk, Walter, Pvt,
Davies, David J., Pfc,
Davies, David K., Pfc,
Davies, David L., Cpl,
Davila, Rafael, Pvt,
Davis, Albert P., T/4,
†Davis, Andrew, Jr., Pfc,
Davis, Archie F., Cpl,
Davis, Arnold E., Pfc,
Davis, Arnold R., S/Sgt,
Davis, Arvel L., Pvt,
Davis, Bernard F., Pvt,
†Davis, Bernard L., Pvt,
Davis, Calvin C., Pvt,
Davis, Carl H., Pvt,
Davis, Chester H., Pfc,
Davis, Constantinos W., Pfc,
Davis, Daniel T., Pvt,
†Davis, David E., Sgt,
Davis, Donald R., Pvt,
Davis, Earl E., Sgt,
†Davis, Emmett W., Pfc,
†Davis Ernest E., Pvt,
Davis, George J., Pvt,

† Killed in Action. * Prisoner of War. ‡ Missing in Action. § Died of Wounds.

Davis, Harold W., Pfc,
Davis, Harry C., Pvt,
Davis, Henry I., Pfc,
Davis, James B., Pfc,
Davis, James H., Pfc,
Davis, Jefferson, T/5,
Davis, Joe L., Pfc,
†Davis, John C., Pfc,
Davis, Lemuel C., 2nd Lt,
Davis, Leslie E., Pfc,
Davis, Luther, Jr., Pfc,
Davis, Mayden J., T/Sgt,
†Davis, Melvin F., Pvt,
†Davis, Moffett D., Pvt,
Davis, Neal A., S/Sgt,
†Davis, Norman, Pfc,
Davis, Oscar, Pvt,
Davis, Owen A., Pfc,
Davis, Quinton D., S/Sgt,
Davis, Reece O., Pvt,
Davis, Richard C., S/Sgt,
Davis, Roscoe L., Pfc,
Davis, Thomas M., Pvt,
†Davis, Robert P., Sgt,
Davis, Thomas R., Lt Col,
Davis, Warren R., Pfc,
†Davis, Wilfred F., Pvt,
Davis, William A., Pfc,
Davis, William E., Pvt,
Davis, William R., Pvt,
†Davison, George A., Jr., 2nd Lt,
Davison, John J., Pvt,
Davison, Perle A., Cpl,
Davisson, Melvin F., Pfc,
Dawson, Aubrey F., Pvt,
Dawson, William E., Pfc,
Day, Alva H., Pfc,
Day, Horace L., Pvt,
Day, Kenneth L., Capt,
†Day, Mervin W., T/5,
Day, Robert A., Pvt,
Day, Stanley A., T/5,
Dayton, William B., Cpl,
†Daywalt, William T., Pfc,
Deahl, Charles J., III, 2nd Lt,
*Deal, George, Pfc,
Dean, George E., Pfc,
Dean, James O., Pvt,
Dean, Leon L., Pvt,
Dean, Norman F., Pvt,
Dean, William B., Pvt,
Dear, Douglas A., S/Sgt,
Dearmont, John W., Pfc,
Dearstone, Robert E., Pfc,
Deater, Reynold T., Cpl,
Debarthe, William H., Cpl,
De Benedetto, Martin, Pfc,
Debonis, Joseph, Pfc,
De Brown, Warren C., Pvt,
Dechiaro, Lowus J., Pfc,
†Decker, John R., Pvt,
Decker, Melvin, Pfc,
Decker, Oliver, Pfc,
De Clarence, B., S/Sgt,
DeCoste, Russell E., Pfc,
Dedmon, A. F., Sgt,
Dedrick, Edward P., Pfc,
Deeb, Frederick E., Pvt,
†Deeds, Allen A., Pvt,
Deeds, Raymond I., T/5,
Deeley, Donald, Pvt,
Deen, Claude D., Pfc,
Deering, Fred, T/5,
Deering, Stanley J., Pfc,
Dees, William P., S/Sgt,
Deese, Daniel T., Pfc,
Deffebach, Elbert E., T/4,
Defilippi, Armando P., Pfc,
De Flavis, Arthur, Pvt,
De Francisco, Albert A., S/Sgt,
De Gaetano, Antonio, Pvt,
De George, Joseph N., Pvt,
Degier, Allen G., Pvt,
DeGroat, Don L., Pvt,
De Hart, Harold K., Pfc,
Deibert, Charles W., Pvt,
Deidrich, Glenn F., Pvt,
†Deimling, George J., Pvt,
Deitrich, Kenneth A., T/5,
†De Jongh, Norman W., Pvt,
De Knipner, Donald J., Pvt,
De Lade, John H., Pvt,
Delamater, Clifford J., S/Sgt,
Delamater, Clifford, S/Sgt,
Delamater, Schuyler W., Cpl,
†Delaney, Jerry E., Pvt,
Delaney, John V., Pvt,
Delaney, Morris L., Pvt,
Delaney, Woodrow E., Pvt,
Delano, Mario, Pfc,
Delauder, William G., Pvt,
Delaughter, Richard H., Pvt,
De Lay, Daniel E., Pfc,
De La Zerda, A. P., S/Sgt,
Del Campo, Anthony C., Pvt,
Deleault, Armand R., Pfc,
Delegnam, Emile J., 2nd Lt,
Delen, Louis, T/5,
De Leon, Armando, Jr., Pfc,
†De Leon, Pedro, S/Sgt,
†De Leon, Victor, Pvt,
Delgado, Luis A., Pvt,
De Lima, John B., Pvt,
De Lisle, Allen J., Pfc,
Dellaport, Norman, 2nd Lt,
Della Posta, Anthony R., Pvt,
Del Latte, Joseph S., Pvt,
Dellinger, Lewis A., 1st Lt,
*Dellorco, Albert P., Pfc,
Delmonico, Dominick, S/Sgt,
Del Monte, Fileno L., Pfc,
De Long, Ora D., Pvt,
De Looze, Thomas P., Pfc,
§De Lorne, Norbert, Pvt
Delozier, Allen W., Pfc,
†Del Pilar, Francisco, Jr., Pfc
Del Prete, Anthony F., Pvt,
Del Re, Isadore, Sgt,
*Del Rossi, Frank, Pfc,
De Luca, Charles J., Pvt,
§De Luca, George C., Pvt,
De Lucca, Robert J., Pfc,
De Lucia, Theodore E., Cpl,
De Luna, Eligio, Pvt,
De Lung, Alvin W., Pvt,
Del Vecchio, John, Pvt,
Demarco, John, Pvt,
De Marco, Joseph, 1st Lt,
De Maria, Russell S., Pfc,
De Mayo, Dominic J., Pvt,
Dembek, John, Pvt,
De Ment, Theodore R., Pfc,
†Demetriou, Fotios D., T/Sgt
Demitro, Joseph, Pfc,
*Demko, Michael, Pvt,
Demko, Stanley P., Pvt,
Demnarter, John J., Pfc,
DeMorro, Dominick P., Pvt,
Dempsey, Robert L., Pvt,
Demsky, Theodore R., T/4
DeMuynck, Paul, T/4,
De Muzio, Gus J., Pvt,
Denbow, Lewis D., Sgt,
Denike, Edward D., Pvt,
De Nise, Cobert W., Pvt,
†Denison, John M., Pvt,
Denney, Charles E., Pvt,
Denney, Elmer H., S/Sgt,
Dennis, Joe R., T/5,
Dennis, Lloyd T., Pvt,
Dennis, Paul R., Pvt,
§Dennison, Dwaine, Pvt,
Denny, Harvey T., S/Sgt,
Denny, Robert A., Pvt,
Denny, Samuel A., T/5,
Densmore, Archie R., 2nd Lt,
Denson, John D., Pfc,
Dent, Henry E., Pvt,
Denton, Dwight D., Capt,
Denton, Merle W., Pfc,
Denton, Ralph S., Pfc,
De Palma, Joseph, Pvt,
Depoe, James, Pfc,
De Pooter, Robert A., Pfc,
De Prodocini, Bruno A., Pfc,
Derick, Neil E., Pfc,
Derifield, Harvey K., T/Sgt,
Derreckson, Wayne R., S/Sgt,
†De Roche, Albert R., Pvt,
De Roo, William, Pvt,
De Rosia, Harold E., Pfc,
§Derr, Raymond F., Pfc,
Derrick, Carl S., Sgt,
Derrick, Levi H., Pvt,
Derrickson, Wayne R., S/Sgt,
Derrough, Rodger A., 2nd Lt,
Derryberry, William A., Sgt,
Dersch, Derrill R., T/Sgt,
Derus, Norbert S., S/Sgt,
Derus, Walter G., Pfc,
Desanti, Michael, Pfc,
De Santis, Carmen J., Pvt,
Desanto, Albert N., Pvt,
De Santolo, Anthony M., Pvt,
†De Sharlo, Robert F., Pfc,
Deshazer, Thomas J., T/5,
Deskins, Francis M., Pfc,
†Desmond, Lawrence T., Pvt,
De Soto, Francis A., Pvt,
De Spain, C. B., S/Sgt,
De Spain, Weston G., Pfc,
Desrosier, Norman W., T/5,
Desselle, Hanley M., Pvt,
Destanay, Robert L., Pfc,
De Stefano, Emilio C., Pfc,
§Detmer, Leonard H., Pfc,
Dettman, Richard M., Pfc,
Deuth, Gerald Q., Pvt,
Deutsch, Walter H., Sgt,
De Vaney, Frederick E., Cpl,
†Devereaux, Thomas V., Pvt,
Devine, James E., Pvt,
Devine, James F., T/5,
Devito, James V., Pvt,
Devoid, Kenneth E., T/4,
Devore, Dave J., Pvt,
Devore, Meyer R., Pvt,
Dewey, Billy Y., Pfc,
De Witt, Robert L., Pvt
De Witt, William, Pfc,
Deyo, Ralph R., 1st Sgt,
Deyon, William J., Sgt,
De Young, Bogart J., Pvt,
†De Young, Cornelius F., Pvt
Deyton, James W., Pvt,
Dial, Ernest E., Pfc,
†Diamond, Seymour A., Pvt,
Diasparra, Vincent J., Pfc,
Diaz, Efren, T/Sgt,
Diaz, Joseph J., Pvt,
Di Bari, Louis A., Pfc,
Di Benedetto, Nicholas J., Pfc,
Di Bias, Charles J., Pvt,
Dice, Arthur C., Pvt,
†Dick, Bernard W., Pfc
Dick, Homer H., Pvt,
Dick, John A., 1st Lt,
Dickensauge, Cesar, Pvt,
Dickerson, Chester W., Pvt,
Dickerson, Emmett, Pvt,
Dickerson, Herbert A., Pvt,
Dickey, Carl E., Jr., Pfc,
Dickinson, Harold, T/5,
Dickson, Billy, Pfc,
Dickson, William A., 1st Lt,
Diderickson, Eugene M., Pfc,
Dieckman, William F., Pvt,
Diedrich, Alfred H., Jr., T/4,
*Diedrich, Herman J., Pvt,
Diehl, Philip J., Pfc,
Diem, Henry W., Pvt,
Dietlein, Ernest C., Jr., Pvt,
Dietrich, John J., Pfc,
Detrich, Kenneth A., T/5,
De Tour, Donald G., Pvt,
Di Franco, Constantine, Pfc,
Di Giacomo, Ernest, Pvt,
Di Giovanni, Joseph C., Pfc,
†Di Giovanni, Vincent L., Pvt,
Di Girolamo, Edward J., Pvt,
Dignam, Bernard P., Pfc,
†Di Guiseppe, Luigi, Pfc,
Di Gregorio, Dominic, Pvt,
Diiro, Orval W., Pvt,
Di Laura, Feraldo P., Pvt,
†Dill, William B., Pvt,
†Dillard, Leonard E., Pvt,
†Dillard, Lester C., Pfc,
Dillard, Oval G., Pfc,
Dillard, Oval G., Pfc,
Dilley, Delmar C., S/Sgt,
Dillie, Luther, Sgt,
Dillman, George W., Pfc,
Di Maggio, Emil A., Pfc,
Di Mica, Phil, Pvt,
†Dimmitt, Ellsworth A., Capt,
Di Mondi, Bruni, Pvt,
†Dimsdale, Ted, Pfc,
Di Mura, Philip, Pvt,
†Di Napoli, John L., Pfc,
Dineen, Dennis J., Pvt,
†Dinklocker, Robert C., Pvt,
Dins, Richard G., Pvt,
Di Nucci, John J., Sgt,
Diomands, Diomand P., T/5,
Dionisio, John F., Pfc,
Diorio, Jack A., Pvt,
Di Paolo, Leonard, Pvt,
Di Pinto, Alfred, 1st Sgt,
Di Russo, Armondo A., Pvt,
Di Salvo, Henry A., Pvt,
Discenza, Carmen T., Pvt,
†Di Sciscio, Nicholas, Pvt,
Di Sena, Natale, Pvt,
Dishong, John T., Pfc,
Dismukes, Houston L., Pvt,
Dison, Loas, S/Sgt,
Distante, Joseph L., Pvt,
Di Stefano, Emanuel, Pvt,
Di Stefano, Romeo, Pfc,
Distler, Jodie M., Cpl,
Ditcharo, Anthony, Pfc,
Ditterline, Hollace E., Pvt,
†Dittmer, Francis H., Pvt,
Dittoe, George H., Jr., S/Sgt,
Dix, Edwin D., Pfc,
Dix, Jean V., Pvt,
†Dixon, John C., Sgt,
Dixon, Lyle D., Pvt,
Dixon, O'Dell C., Pvt,
†Dixon, Robert A., Pvt,
Dixon, Tom H., Pfc,
D'Med, Vincent S., T/5
Doak, James W., Pvt,
†Dobbins, William H., Pvt,
Doble, Charles K., Jr., Pfc,
Dockery, Ervin W., Pvt,
Dodd, John H., Pvt,
Dodd, Marcus W., 1st Lt,
†Dodd, Marvin L., Sgt,
†Dodderidge, James H., 2nd Lt,
Dodge, Robert E., Pfc,
Dodson, James O., Pfc,
Dodsone, Virgil B., Pvt,
Dogoda, John J., Pvt,
Doherty, Timothy J., Pvt,
Doke, Norris R., Pfc,
Dolan, John W., Pfc,
Dolan, Walter A., Pvt,
Dolaway, Chester W., S/Sgt,
Dolezal, Frank W., Sgt,
Dolinsky, Michael J., Pvt,
Dolliver, Earl N., Pfc,
Dolphin, Joseph, Pvt,
Dombroski, George L., Pvt,
†Dombrowski, Stanley J., Pvt,
Domingos, Alfred L., Pfc,
Dominguez, Valentine, T/5,
Dommer, Carl E., T/5,
Domokos, Beni, Jr., Pfc,
Dompierre, Jerome E., Pvt,
Donahoo, Lacy C., Sgt,
Donahoo, Robert A., Pfc,
Donahue, George R., Pvt,
Donahue, James W., Pfc,
Donahue, Eugene, Pfc,
Donahue, Daniel A., Pvt,
Donaldson, Charles K., Pfc,
Donaldson, Kenneth D., Pfc,
Doneshefsky, Benjamin, Cpl,
Dongara, Joseph J., Pvt,
Donham, Oliver K., S/Sgt,
Donigan, James W., Sgt,
†Donish, William J., Sgt,
Donnella, George F., Sgt,
Donnelly, John P., Pfc,
Donnelly, Thomas J., Pvt,
Donnely, Wilbert L., Sgt,
Donovan, Robert W., Pvt,
Donovan, Russell L., Pvt,
Donovan, Timothy J., Pfc,
Dooley, Paul P., Pvt,
†Doolin, James T., Pfc,
Doornbos, Derk, T/4,
Dorak, Andrew A., Pfc,
Doran, James R., Pvt,
Dorcey, John M., Pvt,
Doria, John T., Pvt,
Dority, William A., Pvt,
Dorough, Dewey H., Pvt,
Dorr, James J., Sgt,
Dorris, Lee A., Sgt,
Dorrough, Richard P., Capt,
Dorsch, Paul M., Pfc,
Dorsek, Stephen, Pfc,
Dorsey, James M., Jr., 1st Lt,
Dory, Donald M., T/4,
Doss, Marvin D., Pfc,
Dotson, Howard B., Pvt,
Dotson, Lloyd H., Pvt,
Doty, Paul L., 2nd Lt,
Doubet, Harold D., Pvt,
Doucette, Albert L., Pvt,
Doucette, William L., Jr., Pvt,
Dougall, Leslie P., Jr., Pvt,
Dougan, Mark E., Pvt,
Dougherty, George W., T/Sgt,
Dougherty, Ira, Pfc,
Dougherty, Robert J., Pvt,
Douglas, E. J., Pvt,
Douglas, Eugene A., Pfc,
Douglas, Horace G., Pfc,
Douglas, Selton R., Pfc,
Dowd, Nicholas C., Jr., Pfc,
Dowdy, Willie H., Pfc,
Dower, Michael J., Pvt,
Dowgil, Michael E., Pvt
Dowlen, Madison B., T/5,
Downard, Donald E., Major,
†Downey, Francis J., Pvt,
Downey, James P., Pvt
Downing, John S., Jr., Pfc,
‡Downing, Theodore C., Pvt,
Downs, John W., Pfc,
Downs, Wesley, S/Sgt,
Doyle, Chester, Pvt,
Doyle, Hubert C., Sgt,
Doyle, James E., Jr., S/Sgt,
Doyle, John R., S/Sgt,
Doyle, Leonard M., Sgt,
Doyle, Thomas G., Pvt,
Drach, Frank W., Pvt,
Dragneff, Nicholas W., Capt,
Dragoo, Marshall L., T/5,
Drake, Harris B., Capt,
Draper, William D., Pfc,
Dreizbach, Carl, Pfc,
Dreizen, Lawrence, Sgt,
Drennan, Harold, Cpl,
†Drenner, Jesse E., Pfc,
†Drewniak, Thaddeus F., S/Sgt,
Dreyer, Ruben H., S/Sgt,
Driggers, Hurshel L., 1st Sgt,
Driggers, Irvin L., Pvt,
†Driggs, Jack H., Pfc,
Driscoll, Hector A., Pvt,
Driscoll, William J., Jr., Pvt,
Drotos, Fred N., Pfc,
Drouin, Arthur F., Pfc,
Druckemiller, Richard D., Pvt,
†Druckmiller, Robert D., Pvt,
Drudge, Maurice D., Pvt,
Drulard, Rex E., Pvt,
Drumheller, Clyde R., Pfc,
Drumm, Kenneth B., Pvt,
Drummond, Angus, Pfc,
Drungil, Walter J., Pvt,
Drury, Philip M., 1st Lt,
Drury, Richard E., Pvt,
Drury, Stanley, Cpl,
Dry, G. W., Jr., Pvt,
Drzyzga, Theodore, Sgt,
Dual, Richard L., Pfc,
Dubcak, Edward T., S/Sgt,
Dubiel, Peter J., Pvt,
Dubois, Use J., Pfc,
†Dubon, Francis J., T/5,
Du Bose, Wade L., Pfc,
Dubovitz, Edward W., Pfc,
†Du Bray, James L., Pfc,
Duch, Raymond A., Pvt,
†Duchesne, George L., Pfc,
Duckworth, Earl L., Pfc,
Duckworth, Herman V., Pvt,
†Dudarenke, Gustave F., Sgt,
‡Dudash, Paul J., Pfc,
Dudish, Peter, Sgt,
Duemler, Robert W., Sgt,
†Duff, Robert T., Pvt,
Duffy, Bernard F., Pfc,
‡Duffy, Bernard L., Pvt,
†Duffy, Daniel L., Pvt,
Duffy, Raymond T., 2nd Lt,
Duffy, William C., Pvt,
Duffy, William H., Pfc,
†Dufrane, George F., Jr., Pvt,
Dugan, Michael F., Pvt,
Dugan, Donald J., Pfc,
Dugan, Raymond J., Pfc,
Duggan, John H., Jr., Pvt,
Dugger, Troy R., T/5,
Duhaime, Maurice W., Pvt,
Duis, Elmer H., Sgt,
Dukes, Russell H., Pfc,
Duket, Joseph E., Sgt,
Dulac, Richard R., Pfc,
Dulgar, Roscoe E., Jr., Pfc,
Dulin, Hardy B., Pvt,
Dulin, William, Pfc,
Dumas, Joseph H., Pvt,
†Dunaway, Carl, Pvt,
Dunbar, Burton L., Jr., T/4,
Duncan, Bobbie J., Cpl,
Duncan, Henry C., Pvt,
Duncan, William J., Pvt,
Duncan, William R., Pvt,
Duncavage, Frank C., Pfc,
†Dunford, Eugene L., Pfc,
†Dunham, George H., Pvt,
†Dunlap, John A., Pvt,
Dunlea, David J., Pvt,
Dunmire, Alfred J., Pfc,
Dunn, Albert O., T/Sgt,
†Dunn, Charles E., Pvt,
Dunn, Ernest J., Pvt,
Dunn, Michael P., Pvt,
Dunn, Norman W., Pfc,
Dunn, William G., Pfc,
Dunnam, Warren F., Cpl,
Dunne, James F., Pvt,
†Dunning, Raymond, Sgt,
Dunning, Robert M., Pfc,
Dunton, Earle N., Pvt,
Dupras, Richard W., Pfc,
†Dupre, Abbey J., Pfc,
Dupree, Paul R., Pvt,
Dupris, Peter, S/Sgt,
Durante, Amidio, Pfc,
Durbin, Harry E., Sgt,
Durecki, Robert J., Pfc,
Durfee, Charles W., 1st Lt,
Durfee, George H., Pvt,
Durga, Charles A., Pvt,
Durigon, Lawrence, Sgt,
Durik, Michael J., S/Sgt,
Duris, John J., Pvt,
Durkin, Leo A., Pvt,
Durkin, Philip, Pfc,
†Durrstein, Harlan L., Pvt,
†Durst, George I., T/5,
Dusak, George, Pfc
Dutko, Edmund A., Pvt,
Dutton, Virgil W., T/5,
Duttry, Blake K., Pvt,
Duverny, Leo D., Pvt,

† Killed in Action. * Prisoner of War. ‡ Missing in Action. § Died of Wounds.

Duwe, Vernon D., Pfc,
Dwight, Norman C., Pfc,
Dwy, Ervin J., T/5,
Dwyer, William J., Pfc,
Dyar, James G., Pvt,
Dybala, Wilbert, Pvt,
Dybalski, Jack N., Pfc,
Dye, William L., Pvt,
Dyer, J. R., Pvt,
Dyer, John W., Pfc
Dyer, Leland H., Pvt,
Dyer, William M., Pvt,
Dyke, Franklin L., Pvt,
Dykeman, Elmer H., Pvt,
Dylewski, Chester J., Pfc,
Dysard, Kenneth E., Pfc,
Dyttmer, Raymond N., Pvt,
Dzurjak, Michael, Pfc,

Eagen, Albert A., Pfc,
*Eagle, Joseph N., Pvt,
Eagles, William W., Brig Gen
Eagleton, Jonnie A., Pfc,
Earl, Lloyd E., Pfc,
Earles, Joseph T., Pvt,
Earley, Ralph K., Sr., Pvt,
Early, Howard V., Pvt,
Early, William H., Jr., Pfc,
Eason, Victor, Cpl,
East, Harold A., Pfc,
Eastberg, James E., Pvt,
Easter, Wilton R., Pvt,
Easterling, Lonnie G., S/Sgt,
†Eastwood, Horace A., Jr., Pfc,
†Eastwood, Kenneth W., Sgt,
Eaton, Arthur M., 2/Lt,
Eaton, Delford A., Jr., Pvt,
†Eaves, Gerald, Pfc,
†Eaves, Joseph A., Sgt,
Ebbert, Walter P., S/Sgt,
Ebberts, Jack, Pfc,
Ebberts, Lewell E., Pfc,
Ebberts, W. W., Jr., T/Sgt,
Ebbets, Gerard A., Pvt,
Eberhardt, Donald L., Pvt,
Eberhardt, Oliver, Pvt,
Eberling, John, Pvt,
†Ebert, Donald E., Pfc,
Echerd, Bill R., Pvt,
Echeverria, Oscar C., Sgt,
Eckel, Robert W., Pvt,
Eckhardt, Lawrence, Pfc,
Eckman, Carl E., Cpl,
Eckman, Donald B., Pvt,
Eckstein, Louis, Pvt,
†Eckstrom, Richard D., Pvt,
Eddinger, Floyd R., Pvt,
Eddington, Lysle A., Cpl,
Eddy, James E., Pfc,
Eddy, Paul M., Sgt,
Eddy, Walter A., Pvt,
†Edens, Edgar A., Pvt,
Edens, Floyd R., Pvt,
Eder, John N., Sgt,
Eder, Philip A., Sgt,
Edgell, Robert E. Lee, Pfc,
Edick, Arthur C., Pfc,
Edick, Lawrence R., Pfc,
Edmond, Walter L., Pfc,
Edmundson, Lawrence H., Pvt,
Edmondson, William K., 1st Lt
Edmonson, Fred S., Cpl,
Edmunds, Fred C., Pfc,
Edson, Hallett D., Col,
Edwards, Alfred O., Pfc,
Edwards, Cecil, Pvt,
Edwards, Claudie D., Pvt,
Edwards, Eugene, T/Sgt,
Edwards, E. W., Sgt,
Edwards, Harvey L., Pvt,
Edwards, Hjalmer, Pfc,
Edwards, Isaac C., Jr., Pfc,
Edwards, Merle L., Pvt,
Edwards, Paul I., Pfc,
Edwards, Robert B., 2nd Lt,
Edwards, Roland L., Pvt,
Edwards, Roscoe E., Pfc,
Edwards, Russell C., Pvt,
Edwards, Sidney L., 1st Sgt,
Edwards, Walter A., Pvt,
Edwards, William J., Jr., Pfc,
§Edwin, Raymond J., Pvt,
Eft, Sheldon E., Cpl,
Egan, Thomas F., Pvt,
Eggers, Frederick G., Pvt,
Eggers, Wiley A., Pfc,
Eggleston, Francis L., Pvt,
Eggleston, Slias W., Pfc,
Ehlke, Arlan H., Pfc,
†Ehmke, Eugene E., T/5,
Ehrenreich, Joel H., Pvt,
†Ehret, Robley W., 1st Lt,
Ehrich, Robert H., T/4,
Eichler, William C., Pvt,
Eier, James M., T/5,

Eifler, Oliver W., Pvt,
Eike, Maurice E., Pfc,
Eikenberry, Edward H., T/5,
*Eikenberry, Ray E., Pvt,
Eilers, Albert A., T/5,
Eisenbaugh, John R., Pfc,
Eisenhut, Jack S., Pvt,
Eiter, Albert L., Pvt,
Eke, James E., Pvt,
Ekovich, Samuel, Pvt,
Elam, Pearl, Pvt,
†Elberson, Robert M., Pfc,
Elder, Gene O., Pvt,
Elder, Jack F., S/Sgt,
Elder, Marvel J., Pfc,
Eldridge, Leroy, Pvt,
Eldridge, Roy M., Pfc,
Elgestad, Carl, Pfc,
Elgot, Calvin C., Pfc,
†Elias, Abram O., Pvt,
Eliott, William H., Pvt,
Elkins, James E., T/5,
†Elkins, Troy L., Sgt,
Elling, James C., Pfc,
Ellington, Richard M., Cpl,
Elliot, Henry P., 2nd Lt,
Elliot, Lead D., Sgt,
Elliott, Charles, Sgt,
Elliott, Charles W., Pvt,
†Elliott, Claude D., Pfc,
Elliott, Clayton F., Pvt,
Elliott, Francis R., Pfc,
Elliott, Harley E., Pvt,
†Elliott, Lloyd H., Pfc,
Elliott, Gerald L., Sgt,
Ellis, Andrew, Pvt,
†Ellis, Francis, Pvt,
Ellis, Joe, Pfc,
Ellis, Lonzo E., Pvt,
Ellis, Marion, Pfc,
Ellis, Richard G., Pvt,
Ellis, William, Pvt,
Ellis, William T., Pvt,
Ellwanger, Richard L., Pfc,
Elmendorf, Thorval H., Pfc,
Elowitz, Martin, Pvt,
Elrod, Ben J., Pfc,
Elrod, Henry G., Pvt,
Elston, Robert B., T/Sgt,
Ely, Homer D., Cpl,
Emerick, Charles, Pfc,
Emerson, Allen R., Cpl,
Emert, Harold L., Pfc,
Emery, Harold E., Pfc,
Emery, Raymond L., Pvt,
Emmert, Albert J., Pfc,
Emmett, Leo A., Pvt,
Emrick, Edward T., T/4,
Emwright, Wesley P., Sgt,
Endecott, William R., Pvt,
Engberg, William M., Pvt,
†Engel, Herman W., T/5,
Engel, James D., Pfc,
England, Claude E., Sr., Pvt,
Engle, Howard R., Pvt,
Engle, Ralph T., Pvt,
Engler, Robert V. G., Pvt,
Englert, Louis D., Sgt,
Engles, Ervin D., Pfc,
Englese, Peter, Pfc,
English, Bercue, Pvt,
Engman, Carl D., Pfc,
Enis, Vert, Jr., Pfc,
Enochs, Aubrie E., Pvt,
†Enos, Albert A., Pfc,
Enquist, Clarence C., Pvt,
†Entrekin, Delma L., Capt,
Entwistle, Sherwood R., 1st Lt,
Enzor, Winsome, Pfc,
§Enzweiler, Albert J., Pvt,
Eosefow, John, Pvt,
Epperson, Walter E., S/Sgt,
†Eppsoepps, Calvin B., 2nd Lt,
Epstein, Joseph, Pvt,
Erb, Elmer, Pvt,
Ercolano, Thomas, Sgt,
Erdlen, Frank R., Pvt,
Erfourth, Leonard I., Pfc,
Erhardt, Calvin A., Pfc,
Erickson, Bernard C., T/Sgt,
†Erickson, Leo H., Sgt,
Erickson, Roy E., Pfc,
Erickson, Samuel E., Pfc,
Ernest, Bernard L., Pvt,
Erno, George L., Jr., T/5,
Ernst, Adam, Sgt,
Ernst, Wayne C., Pvt,
Erpelding, Charles W., Sgt,
Errickson, Edwin P., Pfc,
Ervin, Albion G., Cpl,
Ervin, Eugene M., Cpl,
Erwin, William, Jr., Pvt,
Eschenbauch, Donald J., Pvt,
†Escobar, Ruben, Pvt,
Eskay, Paul R., Pvt,

Espana, Manuel, Pvt,
Esperance, John P., Pvt,
Espinosa, Eugene, S/Sgt,
Esposito, Ernest, Pvt,
†Esposito, James S., Pfc,
†Esposito, Jerry, Pvt,
Essenmacher, Donald E., Pfc,
†Esterly, William M., Pfc,
Estes, Ambrose C., Capt,
†Estes, Dock K., Sgt,
Estes, Hayden R., Pvt,
Estess, Melvin, Pfc,
Essary, William P., Pfc,
†Estrada, Gilbert C., Pvt,
Ethen, John F., S/Sgt,
Etre, Alphonse V., Pvt,
Ethredge, Everett O., Sgt,
Etzel, George, Jr., Pvt,
Eulett, Carl, Pfc,
†Eurick, George E., T/Sgt,
Evancho, Andrew, Jr., Pvt,
Evans, David A., Pfc,
Evans, Doyle H., Pfc,
Evans, Durwood H., Pvt,
Evans, Edward O., Pvt,
Evans, Frank, Pvt,
Evans, Fred L., Pfc,
Evans, Gerald L., Sr., Pvt,
†Evans, James, Pfc,
Evans, Jesse G., Jr., Pvt,
Evans, Lionel N., Pfc,
Evans, Mack, Pvt,
†Evans, Owen W., Pfc,
Evans, Robert E., Pvt,
Evans, Robert N., Pvt,
Evans, Thurman R., Pfc,
Evans, Vaughn G., S/Sgt,
Evans, Willard D., S/Sgt,
Evelyn, Robert C., S/Sgt,
†Evansky, Peter, Pfc,
Evener, Joseph R., Pvt,
Evenson, Merle E., Pvt,
Evenson, Walter P., Pfc,
†Everding, Hubert P., Pvt,
Everetts, Orval N., Pvt,
Everhart, Charles M., Major,
Everhart, Robert A., Pfc,
Everingham, John P., Pvt,
Evert, Robert, Pvt,
Everts, George D., Pfc,
Ewell, Vivian S., Pfc,
Ewers, Leo E., Pvt,
Ewers, Thaerle H., Pvt,
Ewertowski, Norbert J., Pfc,
Ewig, Otto R., Pfc,
Ewing, Lyle D., Jr., Pvt,
Ewoldt, Leland W., T/Sgt,
Eyerman, Robert F., Pfc,
Eyler, Thomas R., Pfc,
Eyman, John F., Pvt,
Eyler, Richard G., Pvt,
Eytchison, Albert R., Pvt,

Fabbio, Pasquale J., Pvt,
§Fabian, Michael, Pfc,
Facemyre, Doil O., Pfc,
Faggione, Joseph, Pvt,
Faherty, Maynard E., Pfc,
Fahlen, Alfred G., Pfc,
Faile, Joseph S., Jr., Pvt,
Fair, Gordon N., Pfc,
Fair, Walter C., Pfc,
Fairclo, Carrol E., Sgt,
§Fairgrief, Elbert K., Pfc,
Falcon, Juan A., S/Sgt,
Falcone, Carl E., Pvt,
Falk, Carl E., Cpl,
Falk, Lyle W., Sgt,
Falk, Marshall, Pvt,
Falkenberg, Walter R., Sgt,
Fallon, George F., S/Sgt,
Fallon, Joseph T., Pfc,
Fallowfield, Victor L., Pvt,
Falls, Eldred C., Pfc,
Famighetti, Alfred, Pfc,
Famolaro, Salvatore, Jr., Pvt,
Fanella, Sisto, Pvt,
Fankhauser, Walter C., 1st Lt,
Fanning, Eugene H., Pfc,
Fant, Walter P., Pvt
*Farace, Bernard H., Pvt,
Faracles, Anthony N., 1st Lt,
Farber, John C., Pvt,
Fargier, Boyd, Pvt,
Farmer, Jack F., Pvt,
Farmer, Jason M., Pvt,
Farmer, Lonnie E., Pvt,
Farnack, Frank T., Pvt,
†Farnum, William R., Pvt,
Farrell, Archie J., Pvt,
†Farrell, John, Pvt,
Farrell, John C., Jr., T/5,
Farrelli, Thomas, Sgt,
Farris, Darrell O., Pvt,
Farris, Delbert E., Pfc,

Farris, Henry A., Pvt,
Fasciana, Salvatore, Pfc,
Fasig, Robert S., Pvt,
Fasone, Joseph, Sgt,
Fattorusso, Thomas L., Pfc,
Faubion, Albert J., T/5,
Faucette, Steven S., Pvt,
Faucher, Oliver J., Lt Col,
Faught, John, Pfc,
Faul, James F., Pfc,
Faulkner, Robert M., S/Sgt,
Faull, Truran M., 1st Lt,
Faust, Donald L., Pfc,
Faust, Perry, Jr., Pfc,
Fay, Joseph A., Pfc,
Fazel, Alfred R., Pfc,
Fazio, Patrick F., Pvt,
Feagine, Clarence S., Sr., Pvt,
Fearns, Frank W., Pfc,
†Feaster, Claude E., Sgt,
Feaster, James F., Pvt,
Feather, Lyall J., 1st Lt,
†Fecho, Leopold E., Sgt,
Feddersen, Richard T., Pfc,
Federici, Dante A., Pfc,
Federmeyer, Bernard P., T/Sgt
Fedler, George W., Pfc,
Fee, James B., Sgt,
Feeley, James P., Pvt,
Feeney, Elmer T., S/Sgt,
Feete, Amos B., Pvt,
Fegelman, Julius, T/Sgt,
Fehr, Lynn J., T/5,
Feibelman, Jack H., Pvt,
Feider, Albert W., S/Sgt,
†Feil, Roland E., Sgt,
Feiling, Robert L., Major,
Feldman, Herbert, Pvt,
Feldman, Rowland A., Sgt,
Feldman, Sol, Pfc,
Feldmann, Ervin J., Pvt,
Felerski, Russell P., 1st Lt,
Feley, Lloyd R., Sgt,
Felio, Randolph G., Pfc,
Fell, Alvin S., Pfc,
Feller, Abe R., Pfc,
Felletter, Raymond T., Pvt,
Fells, Charles E., Pfc,
Felton, Paul W., Pvt,
Felty, Robert E., Pvt,
†Fencik, Joseph, Pfc,
Fennel, Ernest, Sgt,
Fenner, John B., Major,
Fennessy, Francis J., Pfc,
Fenoglio, Emilio J., T/3,
Fenster, Louis J., Pvt,
Fenstermacher, A. E., S/Sgt,
Ferderer, Edmund M., Pvt,
Ferdon, Laverne A., Pfc,
†Ferguson, Edgar A., 2nd Lt,
Ferguson, Fred, Pvt,
Ferguson, George H., Pvt,
Ferguson, George X., 1st Lt,
Ferguson, Harold M., Sgt,
Ferguson, Lacy D., Pfc,
Ferguson, Quentin J., S/Sgt,
Ferguson, Robert R., Pfc,
Ferguson, Smith E., S/Sgt,
Ferguson, Thomas R., Pvt,
Ferguson, Victor E., S/Sgt,
Ferguson, William H., S/Sgt,
Ferguson, William R., Sgt,
Ferguson, Woodrow W., Pfc,
Ferkovich, Raymond A., T/5,
Fern, Clifford E., Sgt,
Fernandez, Daniel, Pvt,
Fernandez, Daniel J., Pvt,
Fernandez, Manuel P., Pvt,
Ferrante, Angelos S., Pfc,
Ferrante, Anthony, Pvt,
Ferrante, Robello A., Pfc,
Ferrara, Arnold V., Pvt,
Ferrara, Pasquale, Pfc,
Ferrara, Salvatore A., Pvt,
Ferrari, Alexander J., Pvt,
Ferrari, Frank J., Pvt,
Ferreira, August, Pvt.
Ferreira, Manuel L., Pfc,
Ferrell, William G., Pfc,
Ferrick, Donald R., Pvt,
Ferrier, Martin L. Pvt,
Ferriero, Angelo A., Sgt,
Ferrill, Harold A., Pvt,
Ferris, Calvin M., Pvt,
Ferris, John L., 2nd Lt,
Ferro, Joseph P., Sgt,
Ferry, Morris A., Pfc,
Festine, Armond J., 2nd Lt,
Fetter, Robert P., Pvt.
Fetterly, Irvan F., Pvt,
Fetto, August F., Pvt,
Fetzer, Christian W., Pvt.
Ficarelli, Anthony F., Pvt,
Ficek, John J., S/Sgt,
Fick, Bernard J., Pfc,

Fickbohm, Louis F., Cpl,
†Fickey, Cecil E., Cpl,
Fiebiger, Donald W., Pfc,
Fiedler, Harold E., Pfc,
Field, Harold G., Jr., Pfc,
Field, William D., Jr., Pvt,
Fielding, James W., Pvt,
Fields, Carl, Pfc,
Fields, Lestin, Pvt,
Fields, Roy E., Pvt,
Fields, Royce L., Pvt,
Fieldstein, Maurice, S/Sgt,
Fiello, Anthony F., Pvt,
†Fiess, Emanuel, T/Sgt,
Fife, James R., Sgt,
§Fifer, Richard E., Pfc,
†Fiffick, Emil J., Pfc,
†Fik, Stephen, Pvt,
Filaccio, Salvatore, Pvt,
Filander, Charles N., Pvt,
File, Charles A., Pfc,
Files, Cleo, Pvt,
Filippidis, George, Pfc,
Filipowski, Frank J., Pvt,
Fillingworth, Robert W., Pfc,
Fillmore, Powhatan F., Pfc,
Filosi, Michael F., Pvt,
Finamore, Emedio T., Pvt,
Finegan, Thomas P., Pfc,
Finch, George C., Pfc,
Finch, Phillip D., Pfc,
Finders, Irwin W., Pfc,
Finger, Marvin S., Pfc
†Fink, Charles J., Pvt,
Fink, Nathan, Pvt,
Finke, Fred W., Pvt,
Finkel, Murray I., Pvt,
Finley, Joe W., Pfc,
Finley, John L., Pvt,
†Finn, John T., S/Sgt,
Finnegan, Daniel R., T/5,
†Finnerty, Edward T., 2nd Lt,
Finney, David D., Pvt,
Finney, Paul A., Pfc,
Finney, Samuel W., Sgt,
Fiorella, Michael, Pvt,
Fiscella, Thomas G., Pvt,
Fisch, Jerome J., Sgt,
†Fischer, George, S/Sgt
Fischer, Herbert M., Pvt,
†Fischer, Paul M., Pvt,
Fischer, Walter, Pvt,
†Fisco, Edward T., Pvt,
Fish, Glenn M., S/Sgt,
Fish, Richard I., Pfc,
Fisher, Albert E., Pvt,
†Fisher, Albert N.,Pvt,
Fisher, Clyde D., Pfc,
Fisher, David F., Pfc,
Fisher, Donnell G., Jr., Capt,
Fisher, Foster G., Pvt,
Fisher, George, S/Sgt,
Fisher, George W., Sr., Pvt,
Fisher, Jesse W., Sgt,
Fisher, Marvin J., Sgt,
Fisher, Mayburn E., Pvt,
Fisher, Roy W., T/4,
Fisher, Tommy D., Jr., Pfc,
Fisher, Vaughn C., Sgt,
Fisher, Virgil D., Pvt,
Fisher, Virgil S., Pvt,
Fisher, Wendell H., Jr., Sgt,
Fishman, Louis, Pvt,
Fisk, Lester P., Pvt,
Fisk, Loron M., Pfc,
†Fiske, Warren, Pvt,
Fitzgerald, Athel B., Sgt,
§Fitzgerald, Berard, Pfc,
Fitzgerald, James J., Pfc,
Fitzgerald, John L., T/Sgt,
Fitzgerald, Paul H., Pfc,
Fitzgerald, Thomas J., Jr., Pvt,
Fitzgerald, Thomas W., Pvt,
Fitzpatrick, Leo E., Cpl,
Fitzpatrick, Walter D., Pvt,
Fitzsimmons, Donald W., Pfc,
Fix, Paul A., Pvt,
†Flagg, Dwight A., Pvt,
Flaherty, Edward J., Sgt,
§Flaherty, Kenneth W., Pfc,
Flanagan, Gerald F., Sgt,
Flanagan, Glen C., Pvt,
Flanagan, Patrick J., Pfc,
Flanders, Frank D., Pvt,
Flanders, Harry H., Pfc,
Flatley, Russel J., Pvt,
Flatuer, Moritz J., Pvt,
Flaum, Leo, Pfc,
Fleet, Oscar W., Pfc,
Fleetwood, Howard E., Pvt,
Fleischer, Henry C., Pvt,
Fleischman, Benjamin, Pfc,
Fleischmann, Ervin C., T/4,
†Fleming, Albert, Cpl,
Fleming, Ben J., Cpl,

† Killed in Action. * Prisoner of War. ‡ Missing in Action. § Died of Wounds.

Fleming, James S., Sgt,
†Flemming, Ralph L., Pvt,
Fler, Glen P., T/Sgt,
Fletcher, Eldridge B., Pfc,
Fletcher, Orville K., 1st Lt,
Fletcher, William B., Pfc,
Flick, Warren E., Pvt,
Flickinger, Ray M., S/Sgt,
Flinn, Glenn H., Pvt,
Fliss, Walter, S/Sgt,
Florentino, Cayetano, T/4,
Florez, Frank L., Pvt,
Florian, Joseph J., Pvt,
Floring, Ernest T., Pfc,
§Flory, Gennaro R., Cpl,
Floto, Kenneth B., 1st/Lt,
Flowers, Ernest E., Pfc,
Flowers, George W., Pvt,
Flowers, James W., S/Sgt,
Floyd, Charles L., Pvt,
Floyd, Ora A., Pfc,
Flynn, Basil, Pvt,
Flynn, Bernard G., Pvt,
Flynn, Francis H., Pfc,
†Flynn, Noble J., 1st/Lt,
*Flynt, Glyndon D., Pfc,
†Fockler, Harvey D., Pfc,
Fodi, Martin, Pfc,
Fogg, William H., Pfc,
Foggia, Alexander R., Pvt,
Folck, Robert F., T/5,
Foley, Estel, S/Sgt,
Foley, John, Pvt,
Foley, Michael P. G., Pvt,
Folger, Edward A., Pfc,
Fones, Dale L., Pvt,
Fonfora, Robert J., Pfc,
Fontanelli, Henry B., Pvt,
Fontenot, Joseph H., Pfc,
Fontenot, Lawrence, Pfc,
Fontenot, Nelson J., Pvt,
Fontenot, Zema J., Pfc,
Fonville, William H., Pfc,
Foon, Ngai Y., Pfc,
Foor, Charles E., Pfc,
Ford, Arthur W., T/5,
Ford, Forest B., Pvt,
Ford, Henry, Pfc,
Ford, James P., Pvt,
Ford, John, Jr., Pfc,
Ford, Joseph A., S/Sgt,
Ford, Richard W., Pvt,
Foreman, Elmer P., Pvt,
Foreman, John A. E., Pvt,
Forester, Clarence, Pvt,
Forester, Johnny C., Pfc,
Forgach, Paul, Pfc,
Forman, William, Pvt,
Fornarotto, Raymond A.,
Forrest, Thomas A., Pvt,
†Forst, James, Pfc,
Forster, Alfred T., Pfc,
Forsythe, Carl W., Pfc,
†Forsythe, William J., Sgt,
Forte, Daniel A., Pfc,
†Fortier, Clyde E., Pvt,
Fortney, Forrest, Pvt,
Fortney, Harry F., Pfc,
†Fortunato, Frank J., Pvt,
Fortune, Albert W., Pvt,
Forwood, Charles F., Jr.,
Fossa, Arnold C., Pvt,
Foster, Carl, Pvt,
Foster, Cecil, Pvt,
Foster, Charles G., Capt,
Foster, John G., Pfc,
Foster, Max L., Pvt,
§Foster, Roger M., Sgt,
Foster, Stanley C., Pvt,
†Fotopoulos, John R., Cpl,
Fotta, John J., T/4,
†Fountain, Kenneth F., Pvt,
Fouts, Clyde, Pfc,
Fowler, Charles E., 1st Lt,
Fowler, Clifford W., Pfc,
Fowler, Dewey E., Pfc,
Fowler, Joseph L., Pvt,
†Fowler, Morris L., Pvt,
Fowler, Victor O., Jr., Pvt,
‡Fowler, William O., Pfc,
Fox, Charles E., Pvt,
§Fox, Ervin A., Pvt,
Fox, Jack H., Pfc,
Fox, Lloyd R., 2nd Lt,
†Fox, Morris O., Sgt,
Fox, Odell M., Pfc,
Fox, Peter, Pfc,
Fox, Rex, Pvt,
Foy, George F., Pfc,
Frabizzio, Mario J., Pfc,
Frady, Louey O., Pvt,
Frady, Richard J., Pfc,
France, James L., Pfc,
France, Ray M., Pvt,
Francis, Thomas A., Jr., Sgt,

†Franco, Anthony J., S/Sgt,
Franco, Horatio R., Pvt,
Frank, Carl G., Pfc,
Frank, Charles E., Jr., Pvt,
Frank, Lawrence, Capt,
Frank, Lawrence R., Sgt,
Frank, Robert A., Sgt,
Frank, William A., Sgt,
Franke, Benjamin F., Pvt,
Frankel, Woodrow J., Capt,
Franklin, Dell W., Sgt,
Franklin, Laurence G., Pvt,
Franklin, Lillard C., Pfc,
§Franko, Joseph, Cpl,
Franks, James D., Pfc,
Franks, James D., Pvt,
Frantz, Lawrence W., Pvt,
Frasher, Vencil L., Pfc,
Frasl, Clarence, Pvt,
Frates, Francis, T/5,
Frattini, James A., Pvt,
Frazee, Ralph M., Pfc,
Frazer, John, Jr., Pfc,
Frazier, Ervin S., Pvt,
Frechette, Eprem J., Pfc,
Freda, Luigi A., Pfc,
Freda, Richard A., Pvt,
†Frederick, Charles E., Lt Col,
Frederick, Floyd W., Pvt,
Frederick, Frank J., Pfc,
Frederick, John J., Sgt,
Frederick, Lloyd A., Pfc,
Frederick, Vera L., Pvt,
†Fredole, Robert H., 2nd Lt,
Fredt, Michael N., Pvt,
Freed, Oscar E., Pfc,
Freeman, Charles M., Pvt,
Freeman, Charles T., Pfc,
Freeman, Elmer W., Pvt,
Freeman, Fred M., Cpl,
Freeman, Frederick L., Pfc,
Freeman, Irvin A., Pvt,
*Freeman, John H., Pvt,
Freeman, John W., Pvt,
Freeman, William O., Cpl,
Freese, Lloyd F., Pvt,
Freidlander, Courtney G., Pfc,
Freije, Fred G., Sgt,
Freilich, Albert, Cpl,
Frelin, Felix M., Jr., Sgt,
French, Harold, Pvt,
French, Everett S., Pvt,
French, James E., Pvt,
French, Lester E., T/4,
French, Russell S., Pvt,
Frendy, Anthony D., T/5,
Frenette, Archie A., Jr., Pvt,
Fretlose, James L., Pfc,
Fretwell, John D., Cpl,
Frey, Clark E., Pfc,
Frey, George A., T/4,
§Fridley, Harry J., Pfc,
Friedes, Jacob, Pvt,
Friedman, Louis, Pfc,
Friedman, Max, Pvt,
Friedman, Mortimer I., Pvt,
†Friend, Charles S., T/5,
Friery, Michael G., Pvt,
Friesen, Levi M., Pfc,
†Frieze, Martin E., Sgt,
*Fritchey, Reeves P., Pfc,
Fritz, Frank J., 2nd Lt,
Frix, Clarence R., Pfc,
Frizzle, Roger R., Pvt,
Frohman, Warner B., 1st Lt,
Frolich, Steve J., T/5,
*Fromelt, Bernard L., T/Sgt,
Froncillo, William A., Pvt,
Fronek, Joseph, Jr., Pfc,
Froom, William D., Pvt
Frost, Albert E., Pfc,
Frost, Eugene A., T/Sgt,
Frost, Harold L., Pfc,
Frost, Robert F., Pvt,
Frost, Victor A., Pvt,
Fry, Ernest H., Pfc,
Fry, Harry M., Pvt,
Frye, Henry L., Pfc,
Frye, Paul F., Pvt,
Fuchs, Charles F., S/Sgt,
Fuchs, Herbert B., Pvt,
Fuhrman, Walter C., Pvt,
Fuhs, Vincent J., Pvt,
Fulara, John J., Cpl,
Fularczyk, August C., Pfc,
Fulde, Karl F., T/Sgt,
§Fulk, Paul R., Pvt,
Fulkerson, Floyd G., T/5,
Fulks, Robert L., T/5,
Fuller, Edward, Sgt,
Fuller, Enoch H., Pvt,
Fuller, Glenn K., T/Sgt,
Fuller, Harold E., T/4,
Fuller, Raymond R., Pfc,
Fuller, Walter M., Pfc,

Fuller, William E., Pvt,
Fullerton, Adrian H., Pvt,
Fullerton, Robert B., Pfc,
Fulton, Harper G., Pfc,
Fulton, Joseph B., Pvt,
Fulton, William K., T/Sgt,
Funk, Omar M., Pvt,
Funkhouser, Donald E., Pvt,
Funtal, Carl A., Pfc,
Fura, Alfred D., Pvt,
Furlong, Russell E., T/4,
Futter, Roy N., Pfc,

Gabbard, Ralph, Pvt,
Gabel, Donald F., S/Sgt,
Gable, Edwin A., Pfc,
Gable, Myron L., Pvt,
Gabor, Peter, Pvt,
Gabriele, Anthony Q., Pvt,
Gaddy, Paul E., Pfc
Gadke, George M., Pfc,
†Gadomski, Stanley, Pvt,
Gadsky, Alfred F., Pvt,
Gaffney, David E., Pfc,
Gaffney, Robert F., Cpl,
†Gagliano, Dominic T., Pfc,
†Gagliardi, Russell A., Pfc,
Gagliardo, Salvatore S., Pfc,
Gagnon, Edward A., Pfc,
Gagnon, Norbert R., Sgt,
Gaillard, George M., Pvt,
Gaitan, Trinidad S., Pvt,
Gaither, Calvin C., Pfc,
Gaither, Herbert L., Pvt,
Gaines, Thomas V., Pvt,
Gainey, Woodrow, Pvt,
Gajewski, Frank A., Pvt,
Galbraith, John B., Cpl,
Gale, Walter C., Pfc,
Galemore, Alva A., Pfc,
Galesk, Bernard, Pvt,
Galewski, George A., Pvt,
Galey, Robert D., T/5,
Galgocy, George J., Pfc,
Galiano, James B., Pfc,
Galiano, Richard B., Pfc,
‡Galica, Andrew A., Pvt,
Gall, Carl J., Pvt,
Gallagher, Joseph, Pvt,
Gallagher, Melvin T., T/4,
Gallagher, Robert L., 1st Lt,
Gallant, Amos, S/Sgt,
‡Gallaway, Marlin R., Pfc,
Galler, Harry, Pvt,
Galliani, Joseph A., Pfc,
Galligan, James K., Pfc,
Gallimore, Clifton, Pvt,
Gallina, Felix M., Pvt,
Gallinoto, Michael R., 1st Lt,
Gallon, Arnold, Pfc,
†Galloway, Alfred L., Pvt,
Galloway, Ross L., Pvt,
Gallucci, Andrew A., Pvt,
Gallucci, Leonard J., Pfc,
Galonsky, Max, Pfc,
Galpin, Albert G., Pfc,
Galvan, Wendell L., Pvt,
Galvin, Donald W., Pfc,
Galvin, Walter S., Pfc,
Gambino, Vincent, Pvt,
Gamble, William T., Pvt,
Gammage, Dewey D., Pfc,
Gammage, Henry, Sgt,
†Gammage, Henry O., S/Sgt,
Gamski, Stanley T., Pvt,
Gandy, Howard W., Pfc,
Gangos, Thomas, Pvt,
Gann, Brent L., 1st Lt,
Gannon, James A., 1st Lt,
Gannon, James J., Pfc,
Ganos, Thomas, T/3,
†Gansarz, William J., Pfc,
Gant, Fred F., S/Sgt,
Gaouette, Albert L., Pfc,
Garaffa, Bartholomew J., Pvt
Garas, Marion L., Pvt,
Garbarini, Andrew L., Pvt,
Garbow, Sam, Pfc,
†Garcia, Alexander T., Pfc,
†Garcia, Andrew A., S/Sgt,
Garcia, Chris, Pfc,
†Garcia, Cruz, Pvt,
†Garcia, Fernando F., Cpl,
†Garcia, Jose V., Pvt,
Garcia, Lionor, Pfc,
Garcia, Michael, Pfc,
Garcia, Nash A., Pfc,
Garcia, Pedro C., Pvt,
Garcia, Victor S., Cpl,
Gardels, Filmore C., S/Sgt,
Gardenshire, Harold R., Pvt,
Gardner, Arthur W., Major,
Gardner, Dean W., Pvt,
‡Gardner, Elon F., Pvt,
Gardner, Hoyle C., Pvt,

Gardner, James C., Pfc,
Gardner, James R., Pvt,
Gardner, Park L., Pfc,
Gardner, Paul, Pvt,
Gargano, Philip J., Pfc,
Garguiolo, Frank L., Pfc,
Garie, Louis, Jr., Pvt,
Garin, Frank W., Pvt
Garing, Robert F., 1st Lt,
Garland, Clint, Pfc,
Garland, Frank C., Pvt,
Garland, Forrest L., Pfc,
Garland, Harold W., Pvt,
Garland, John A., Pfc,
Garland, Robert M., Pfc,
Garlitz, Lloyd C., Pfc,
†Garner, Joseph D., Pfc,
Garnett, Willie J., Pvt,
Garoch, Paul M., Pfc,
Garrett, Clyde W., Pfc,
Garrett, Farris S., Pvt,
Garrett, Thomas A., Pfc,
Garrett, Thomas H., Pvt,
Garrett, William D., Pfc
Garringer, Jesse R., Pfc,
Garrison, Charles W., Pvt,
Garrison, Donald L., 2nd Lt,
Garrison, Leland J., Pfc,
Garrison, Manuel H., 1st Sgt,
Garrison, Woodrow W., Pfc,
Garvy, Andrew C., Jr., Capt,
Gary, Sidney, Jr., Pfc,
Gasaway, Chletis D., Pfc,
Gaskill, Jess R., Pfc,
Gates, Carrol F., Capt,
Gates, Charles W., Pvt,
Gates, Harley L., T/4,
Gatkin, Louis, Pfc,
Gatley, Leroy C., Pfc,
Gau, Urban C., Pvt,
Gaudet, John M., Sgt,
Gaudio, Anton, Pfc,
Gauette, Albert L., Pfc,
Gaul, Richard P., Pfc,
Gaunt, Donald E., T/5,
Gauthier, Napoleon W., Pvt,
†Gauthreaux, Louis J., Jr., Pvt,
†Gautreaux, Edward B., Pfc,
Gay, Marshall E., Pfc,
Gayda, Mike, T/5,
Gaydos, Albert A., Sgt,
Gaydos, Michael, Pfc,
Gaydos, Michael J., Pfc,
Gaylor, Oscar, Pvt,
Gazarian, Edward, 1st Lt,
Gearhart, Robert C., Pvt,
Gebo, Earl J., Pfc,
Gebo, Ivan E., Pfc,
Gee, Gordon E., Pfc,
Geer, Edmond T., Sr., Pvt,
Geerken, George E., Pfc,
Geffrey, William E., Pfc,
Gehlhoff, Robert M., Pfc,
Gehrmann, Carl W., Pfc,
Geibel, Gerald J., Pfc,
Geiger, Charles L., Pfc,
Gelber, Frederick, Pvt,
Geller, Henry, Pfc,
Gengler, Alphonse J., 1st/Sgt,
Geller, Stanley, Pvt,
†Gemeiner, Richard W., Pvt,
Gemp, James E., Pfc,
Gendron, Henry F., Pfc,
Gendron, Joseph A., Sgt,
Genna, Anthony T., Pfc,
Gensler, Donald W., 1st Lt,
†Gentile, Alexander P., Pfc,
Gentile, Michael J., Pvt,
Gentry, Fred H., Pfc,
Gentry, Paul R., Pfc,
Gentry, Raymond E., Pvt,
Gentry, Vernon C., Sgt,
Gentry, Willard F., Pvt,
Gentry, William E., Pvt,
George, Alfred M., Pfc,
†George, Edward L., Cpl,
George, George L., T/5,
George, Ira, Jr., Pvt,
George, Judson H., S/Sgt,
George, Mahlon, Pvt,
George, Oswald C., Sgt,
George, Wilburn W., Capt,
Georgio, Gerald J., Pvt,
Georgudis, Arthur P., T/5,
Geosits, John J., Pfc,
Geraghty, George B., Pfc,
Gerard, Clarence N., T/4,
Gerard, Robert D., Pfc,
Gerber, Joseph J., S/Sgt,
Gerber, Vernon, Cpl,
Gerdes, Alfred A., S/Sgt,
Gerety, John H., Major,
Gerg, Robert H., 1st Sgt,
German, Harry L., Pvt
Germans, Kenneth D., Pvt,

Gerovac, John G., T/Sgt,
†Gerrol, Marvin M., Pfc,
Gervasoni, Fred R., Pfc
Gervol, Victor J., Pfc,
Geyer, Thomas H., Pvt,
Geysen, Joseph F., Pvt,
Ghareeb, Naiff E., Pvt,
Gheen, William H., Pfc,
Giacopelli, Russell, Pvt,
Giandalone, Frank J., Pvt
Giannini, Gene L., Pfc,
Giannini, Leo A., Pvt,
Giannola, Leo, Pvt,
Giardinetto, Anthony, Jr., Pfc,
Giardullo, Fidele, Pvt,
Gibb, Keith W., Pfc,
Gibbons, Edward G., Pfc,
Gibbs, Carroll C., Pfc,
Gibbs, Frank R., Pvt,
Gibbs, Rex W., T/5,
†Gibbs, Theodore H., Pvt,
Gibilaro, Joseph P., Pvt,
†Giblin, Michael T., Pfc
†Gibson, Byron N., Pfc,
Gibson, Edward H., Pvt,
Gibson, Edwin G., T/5,
Gibson, Floyd, Pvt,
Gibson, Gordon P., Pfc,
Gibson, Harold D., Pvt,
†Gibson, Pete, S/Sgt,
Gibson, Shirley J., Pfc,
Gibson, Thomas H., Pvt,
Giddings, Abbot E., Pfc,
†Giddings, Arthur R., 2nd Lt,
Giemzik, William J., Sgt,
†Gier, Eldon D., Pvt,
†Giermann, A. H., Jr., 2nd Lt,
Giesiking, James A., Pfc,
Giessinger, I. F., Jr., Pfc,
Giessinger, Paul D., Pvt,
Gifford, Charles H., Sgt,
Gigante, George A., Pfc,
§Giglio, Leonard J., Pvt,
Gigliotti, Frank J., Cpl,
Gilberg, Ragner F., Pfc,
Gilbert, Clarence L., Capt,
Gilbert, Durwood E., Pfc,
Gilbert, James J., Pvt,
§Gilbert, Joseph H., Jr., Pfc,
Gilbert, Loyd M., Pfc,
†Gilbert, Walter F., Pvt,
†Gilbrech, Omer V., Sgt,
Giles, Elmer J., Pvt,
Giles, James V., Pfc,
Giles, Raymond H., Major,
Giles, Samuel R., Pvt,
Gilfillan, Andrew B., Jr., Pvt,
Gill, Edward J., Pvt,
†Gill, Thomas P., Pvt,
Gillen, Hugh W., Pvt,
Gillen, James F., Sgt,
Gillen, John F., Pfc,
Gillentine, William T., Pfc,
Gillespie, George R., Pfc,
Gillespie, Henry, Sgt,
Gillespie, William R., Pvt,
Gillette, Harold R., Pfc,
Gilliam, Brownlow B., Pfc,
Gilliland, John L., S/Sgt,
Gilliland, William I., Pfc,
Gillim, Arthur D., Pvt,
Gillingham, Willard, Jr., Pvt,
Gillispie, Acie W., Pvt,
Gillispie, Paul C. Pvt,
Gillum, Clinton, T/5,
Gilmer, Ralph E., Pfc,
Gilroy, George, Pfc,
*Gilroy, William J., Pvt,
Gilstrap, John M., Pfc,
Ginsberg, Jerry, Pvt,
Ginsberg, Morris, Pvt,
Ginter, Andrew, Jr., S/Sgt,
Ginter, Edward C., Pfc,
Ginter, Maynard B., Pvt,
Ginwright, Wilson L., S/Sgt,
Giordano, Anthony V., 1st Lt,
†Giorgi, Dominick, Pvt,
Giorgio, Joseph F., Pvt,
Giovannetti, Dina M., Pfc,
Giovanni, John, Pvt,
†Giovinazzo, Dominic, Pvt,
Gipson, Joseph R., Pvt,
Gipson, Wess H., Pvt,
Girard, Marcel R., Pfc,
Girardin, Oliver J., Pfc,
Girdick, Ralph, Pfc,
Girdley, James D., Pvt,
†Gish, Burger S., Pvt,
Gish, Roger E., Pfc,
Gittleman, Nat, Pvt,
Giuliani, Richard A., Pfc,
Giusto, Guy, Pfc,
Gladney, Winston T., Pfc,
Gladding, Arthur J., Pfc,
Gladu, Edward G., Pfc,

† Killed in Action. * Prisoner of War. ‡ Missing in Action. § Died of Wounds.

Gladwin, Jay, 2nd Lt,
Glaser, Bertram, Pfc,
Glaspie, Samuel J., Pvt,
†Glass, Earle W., Pvt,
Glass, Francis C., Pfc,
Glasscock, Dale H., Pvt,
Glassgow, James C., Pvt,
Glavey, James, Pvt,
Glazar, John, Jr., Pvt,
Glaze, Tommie W., Pvt,
Glazer, Andrew P., Pvt,
Gleason, Edward C., Pvt,
Gleeson, Frank J., Sgt,
Glegg, James J., Pfc
Glen, Augustus G., T/5,
Glen, John A., Pvt,
Glen, William, Pvt,
Glenn, Burl D., Pvt,
Glenn, Charles D., Pfc,
Glenn, Sollie S., Pfc,
Glisson, Ellie D., Pfc,
Glivar, Andrew A., Pfc,
Globerman, Morris M., Pfc,
Glochau, George E., Pfc,
Glover, Alfred W., Cpl,
Glover, Frank R., Pfc,
Glover, Russell R., Pfc,
Glowacki, Theodore A., Pvt,
Glowczewski, Florian J., Pvt,
Gluse, Stephen, Pfc,
Glynn, James C., Pvt,
Gnadt, Charles L., 1st Sgt,
Goad, Curtis D., Pfc,
Gobbi, Michael J. Pfc,
Gobis, Anthony J., Pfc,
†Goble, David E., Pfc,
Goble, Lee W., Pvt,
Gochnour, Dwain, T/Sgt,
†Goddard, James O., Pvt,
Godesky, Frank F., T/4,
Godfrey, Floyd R., T/5,
Godfrey, George P., Pvt,
Godfrey, Tom F., Sgt,
Godfried, Leo, Pfc,
‡Godines, Ignacio, Pvt,
Goding, Harold F., Pfc,
§Godwin, Bud B., Pfc,
Godwin, Ransom M., Sgt,
†Godwin, Warren S., Pfc,
§Goede, Ervin H., Sgt,
Goehl, George E., T/Sgt,
†Goehring, Edward H., Sgt,
Goekler, Clarence L., Jr., Pfc,
Goerk, Paul J., Pvt,
Goers, Russell E., Pvt,
Goettsch, Charles J., Pvt,
Goetz, Marshall G., Pfc,
†Goetze, Joseph F., Pfc,
Goewert, Orville O., Pvt,
Goff, Curtis B., Sgt,
Goff, Glen G., Pfc,
Goff, Olden M., Pfc,
Goff, William B., Pfc,
Gogets, John, Pvt,
Goguen, Robert O., Pfc,
Goicoechea, Ben, Pfc,
Goida, Michael, Pvt,
Goike, Edward J., Pfc,
†Goin, Darwin E., Cpl,
Going, William T., Sr., Pfc,
Goins, Wendell R., Pvt,
Goke, Herman F., Cpl,
Gokey, George, S/Sgt,
Gold, Harry, Pfc,
Golden, Harry A., Pfc,
Golden, Loynes R., Pvt,
Goldbach, Regis J. J., Cpl,
Goldbaum, Harry A., Pfc,
Goldbaum, Herman, Pvt,
Goldberg, Al M., Pfc,
Goldberg, Eugene, Pvt,
Goldberg, Irving, Pvt,
Goldberg, Jack, Pvt,
Goldberg, Martin, Pfc,
Goldberg, Philip, Pfc,
‡Goldberg, Sheldon A., Pvt,
Goldman, Howard W., Pvt,
†Goldman, Milton M., Pvt,
Goldman, Rubin M., Pfc,
Goldrick, Bernard V., Pvt,
Goldstein, Barney, Pvt,
Goldstein, Herbert, Pvt,
†Goldstein, Frederick, Pvt,
Goldstein, Joseph, Sgt,
Goldstein, Julius L., Pvt,
Golemba, Stanley, Jr., Pfc,
Golias, Joseph J., Pfc,
Golizio, John J., Pvt,
Golman, Francis J., Pfc,
Golnik, Gustav R., Pfc,
Golson, Cobb M., 1st Lt,
Goman, Ray G., Pfc,
†Gomich, Nicholas M., Pfc,
Gomillar, Frank F., Sgt,
Gondek, Gilbert J., T/5,
Gondek, John A., T/5,
Gondini, John H., Pvt,
Gonet, Mitchell F., Pfc,
Gonzales, Abelardo, Sgt,
Gonzales, Angelo J., Cpl,
Gonzales, Benito V., Pfc,
†Gonzales, Benny G., Pvt,
Gonzales, Fred, T/5,
Gonzales, Joseph, Pfc,
Gonzales, Lucio F., Pvt,
Gonzales, Lupe E., Pvt,
Gonzales, Manuel R., Pvt,
Gonzales, Manuel V., Sgt,
Gonzalez, Antonio M., Pfc,
†Gonzalez, Benny G., Pvt,
Gonzalez, Ceferino R., Pvt,
Gonzalez, Esteban, Pfc,
Gonzalez, Frank D., Pvt
Good, Ernest A., Pvt,
Goodbread, Anthony C., Pfc,
Goodhines, Carl P., Pvt,
Goodin, Levi E., Sgt,
Goodley, Ranzle, Pvt,
Goodliffe, Rulon C., T/5,
Goodman, Marion E., Sgt,
Goodner, Melvin D., Pvt,
†Goodnight, Tommie A., Pvt,
Goodrich, Floyd L., Pfc,
Goodridge, Robert J., Pfc,
†Goodsell, Carol E., Sgt,
Goodsell, Wallace W., Pvt
Goodson, Garlan M., Pvt,
Goodson, Hoyt R., Pvt,
Goodson, Thomas J., Pfc,
Goodwin, Leslie E., Pfc,
Goodwine, Leo G., S/Sgt,
Goolsby, George P., T/5,
Goosey, Dillard, Pvt,
Goralczyk, Leo, Pfc,
Gordian, Andrew, S/Sgt,
Gordon, Morris, Pvt,
Gordon, Patson, Pvt,
Gordy, Richard S., Pfc,
Gore, John B., Pfc,
Gorecki, Edward J., Pfc,
Gorgas, John A., Pvt,
§Gorham, Phillip J., Sgt,
Gorka, George J., Pvt,
Gorman, Andrew J., Pfc,
Gorman, Herman J., Pvt,
Gorman, Howard G., Pfc,
Gorman, James H., Pfc,
Gorman, John C., Pvt,
Gorman, Peter J., Pvt,
Gormsen, Clarence G., Pfc,
Gorzelany, Edmunds, Pfc,
Goskoski, Peter V., Pvt,
Goss, Albert A., Pfc,
Goss, Gunther F., Pvt,
Gosselin, Eugene P., Sgt,
Gossiaux, Tony, Pfc,
§Gotay, Reinaldo, Pfc,
Gothe, William A., Pvt,
Gott, William B., Pvt,
§Gottlieb, George J., Jr., Pvt,
Gottschalk, Edward A., Pfc,
Gottschalk, George, Jr., Pvt,
Gouge, Glen, Pvt,
Gough, William T., Pfc,
†Gould, David, Pfc,
Gould, John W., S/Sgt,
Gould, Ralph G., Pfc,
Goulds, Felix W., Pvt,
Gowdy, Joseph R., 2nd Lt,
Gowin, Francis S., Pvt,
Goyett, Edwin W., Pfc,
Graban, Nicholas, Cpl,
*Grabowski, Nicholas, Pvt,
*Grace, Gordon C., Pfc,
Grace, Thomas J., 2nd Lt,
Gracia, Jose J., Pvt,
Graeber, Peter F., Pfc
Graham, Alvin T., Pfc,
Graham, Frank R., 1st Lt,
Graham, Harry L., Pfc,
Graham, Jesse A., Cpl,
Graham, John B., Pfc,
Graham, John J., Pvt,
Graham, Lowell A., Pfc,
Graham, Robert A., Pfc,
Grammer, Kenneth W., Pvt,
Grampp, Lowell R., Pfc,
Grancy, Robert L., Cpl,
Grandstaff, Loren, Pfc,
Graneri, Daniel F., Pvt,
†Graney, Robert L., Cpl,
Granger, Wallace D., Cpl,
Granice, Antonio J., T/5,
Granstaff, William V., Pfc,
Grant, James A., 1st Lt,
Grant, Robert C., Pvt,
Grant, Thurman B., Jr., Sgt,
†Grantham, Audry, Sgt,
Graptatin, John W., Capt,
†Grasso, Charles J., Pvt,
Grasso, Constantine, Sgt,
Grata, Walter L., Pfc,
Grasso, Frank, Pvt,
Grauman, Herman, T/5,
Gravel, Edgar J., Pfc,
Gravenish, Lawrence T., Pfc,
Graves, Phillip, Pfc,
†Graves, Ralph J., Pvt,
Gray, Cornelius L., Pfc,
†Gray, Elvin W., T/4,
Gray, Fred, Jr., Pvt,
Gray, Fred H., Pfc,
Gray, George C., Sgt,
Gray, George E., S/Sgt,
Gray, Leo H., Pvt,
Gray, Leo P., Pvt,
Gray, Orie E., Pvt,
Gray, Richard A., Pvt,
Gray, Theodore J., Pvt,
Gray, William A., Pvt
Gray, William C., Pfc,
Graybill, Clarence J., Pvt,
Grayson, Richard W., Pfc,
Graziano, Rocco L., Pfc,
Greco, Dominic P., Pvt,
Green, Albert E., Pvt,
Green, Alvin L., Pfc,
Green, Arthur, Pfc,
Green, Arthur F., Pfc,
Green, Charles W., Pfc,
Green, DeWitt H., Pvt,
Green, Eldon M., Pfc,
Green, Elisha P., Cpl,
Green, George C., Pvt,
Green, Glenn S., Pvt,
Green, Ira N., Pvt,
Green, James, Pfc,
Green, Jesse, Sgt,
Green, Jesse H., Pfc,
Green, John F., Pvt,
Green, Leon C., Pvt,
Green, Lloyd L., Pvt,
Green, Louis A., Cpl,
Green, Robert D., Pfc,
Green, Robert H., T/5,
Green, Theron K., Pfc,
Green, Wilburn S., Pvt,
†Greenberg, Hyman, Pvt,
Greene, Charles W., Pvt,
Greene, Edward W., Jr., Pfc,
†Greene, Ellis P., Jr., Pvt,
Greene, Harry A., T/5,
Greene, Roy C., Pvt,
Greene, Rufus W., Pvt,
Greene, Theodore J., Pvt,
Greenhalgh, Ray E., Pfc,
Greenhut, Solomon, Pvt,
Greenlee, Arthur A., Capt,
Greenlee, Frank S., 1st Lt,
Greenlee, William E., Pvt,
Greenlund, Hilbert L., Pfc,
Greenman, Clyde, Pfc,
Greentree, James P., Pfc,
Greenwald, Kearney W., Pfc,
Greenway, Joe W., Pvt,
Greenwood, Charlie L., Pvt,
Greenwood, John F., Pfc,
Greer, Carl, 1st Sgt,
Grefe, John H., Sgt,
Gregg, Ancil F., Jr., S/Sgt,
Gregg, Charles A., Pfc,
Gregg, George H. H., Pvt,
†Gregg, Paschal J., T/Sgt,
†Gregoire, Leo P., Pvt,
Gregoire, Robert W., T/5,
Gregory, Alden G., Pvt,
Gregory, Bernard G., Pfc,
Gregory, Ernest B., Pvt,
Gregory, Fay C., Pfc,
Gregory, James A., Pfc,
†Gregory, James L., Sgt,
Gregory, Leslie S., Cpl,
Gregory, Loyd P., Pvt,
Gregus, Leo J., Sgt,
Grehl, Frederick H., Pfc,
Greiner, David B., Pfc,
Greitzer, Sam, Pfc,
Greive, Bernard J., Pvt,
†Grell, Earl E., Pfc,
Grenier, Ralph J., Pfc,
Gresham, John B., T/4,
Gresham, Luther B., Pvt,
Grey, Lee, T/5,
†Grider, Richard W., Pfc,
Grider, Russell G., Pfc,
Griebel, Floyd H. W., S/Sgt,
Griek, Glen D., 1st Lt,
†Griesemer, William F., Jr., Cpl,
Grieser, Leo E., Pvt,
†Grieshaber, Russell J., Sgt,
Grifasi, Francis V., Pfc,
Griffin, Alfred T., Pvt,
Griffin, Cecil J., Pfc,
Griffin, Charles T., Pfc,
†Griffin, Jack W., Pfc,
Griffin, James P., Sgt,
Griffin, Leonard H., T/4,
Griffin, William E., Pvt,
Griffis, John W., Pvt,
Griffith, Clyde, Pvt,
Griffith, George J., Pvt,
Griffith, Harold S., S/Sgt,
Griffiths, John W., Pfc,
Griffiths, William D., Jr., Pvt,
Grifo, James C., Pvt,
Griggs, George H., Pvt,
Grigsby, Robert W., 2nd Lt,
Grimes, Jack J., Pfc,
Grimmett, Russell E., Pvt,
Grimpe, Arnold, Pvt,
Grinde, Alfred, Pvt,
Grindle, R. D., S/Sgt,
Grindstaff, Howard S., Pfc,
Griswold, Claude G., Pfc,
Griswold, Lawrence, Pvt,
Grizzell, Jack B., Pvt,
*Groen, John A., 1st Lt,
Groetsch, Andrew J., Pvt,
Groff, Howard W., Pfc,
Groff, James A., Pvt,
Groff, Roy, S/Sgt,
Groffenhurst, Rudolph F., Pvt,
†Groh, Edward R., Pvt,
Groman, Dale E., Pfc,
Grondin, Olien C., Pfc,
‡Groome, Arthur C., Pfc,
Grorich, Alvin E., Pvt,
Grose, Jack B., Sgt,
Gross, Harold R., Pvt,
†Gross, Jacob, Pfc,
Gross, Julius, Pvt,
Gross, Walter H., Pvt
Grosser, Herbert G., T/4,
Grosshans, Eugene, Pvt,
Grossman, Martin M., 2nd Lt,
Grossman, Robert E., Pvt,
Grossman, Robert L., Sgt,
Grossman, Max W., Pvt,
Groves, Howard P., Pvt,
Groves, Walter E., Pvt,
Gruba, John J., Pvt,
Grubaugh, Cecil R., Pfc,
Grubb, Edgar L., Pfc,
Grubb, Thomas F., Pvt,
†Gruben, Alvin L., Pfc,
Grubich, Victor T., Pfc,
Gruhler, Robert, Pvt,
Grundon, George K., Pfc,
†Grunza, Michael, Pvt,
Gruszczynski, Anthony P., Pvt,
Gruszka, Edwin T., Pfc,
Gruszkiewicz, Bruno, Pfc,
Grutadaurio, Cataldo, Pvt,
Gruwell, Roy A., Jr., Sgt,
Grygorewicz, Stanley F., Pvt,
Grzyboski, Paul C., Pfc,
Grzybowski, James F., Pfc,
Guanill, Juan A., Pfc,
Guarneri, Joseph J., Pvt,
Guarracino, Nicholas J., Pfc,
Guastella, Leonard J., Pvt,
Guay, James D., Pfc,
*Guenther, George A., Pvt,
Guerra, Michael, Pfc,
Guevara, Fernando, Pvt,
Guffy, Herschel B., Pvt,
Guice, Otis, Pvt,
†Guider, John J., 1st Lt,
†Guiliano, Simone S., Pvt,
Guillebeau, Charles H., Pvt,
Guilliams, Evelin H., Sgt,
Guimond, Richard R., S/Sgt,
Guinn, Amon T., Pfc,
Gulassa, Andrew J., Pvt
Guldseth, Edward W., T/5,
Gullacci, James J., Pfc,
Gullefer, Herbert C., Pfc,
Gullo, Guiseppe, Pfc,
Gulzow, Albert L., Sgt,
Gumz, Paul A., Jr., Pvt,
Gunderson, Chester B., Cpl,
Gunn, Keith W., Pfc,
†Gunn, Robert E., S/Sgt,
Gunst, Otto E., Capt,
Guntow, George B., Pfc,
Gurley, Arley B., Pfc,
Gurley, Charles, Jr., Pfc,
Gurrieri, Michael A., Pvt,
Gurske, Arthur A., T/5,
Gussman, Robert B., Cpl,
†Gust, Paul B., Pfc,
Gust, Louis A., Pvt,
Gustafson, Carl J., Jr., Pvt,
Gutch, Frank W., Jr., T/5,
†Guthrie, David H., Pfc,
Guthrie, Robert L., Pvt,
Gutierrez, Angel, Jr., Pfc,
Gutierrez, Henry, Pvt,
Gutierrez, Manuel D., Pfc,
Gutowski, Bronislaus, Pfc,
Gutowski, Edwin S., Pfc,
†Guy, George W., 2nd Lt,
Guy, Herbert S., Jr., Pvt,
Guy, Joseph G., Jr., Pfc,
Guzman, Albert M., Pvt,
Guzman, John R., Cpl,
Gwaley, Alfred A., 2nd Lt,
Gwin, William, Pfc,
Gwinn, Oliver T., Pfc,
Gydesen, Stanton E., Pvt,

Haager, Ossie R., Pfc,
Haas, Aloysius H., 1st Lt,
Haas, Howard F., Pvt,
Habbestad, Arthur L., Pfc,
Habermeyer, H. H., S/Sgt,
Hackbarth, Elmer A., S/Sgt,
Hackbarth, Samuel E., Pfc,
Hackenberg, Paul A., T/5,
Hacker, Edmund W., S/Sgt,
Hackett, Daniel E., Pfc,
Hadler, Robert F., Pfc,
Hadsell, James A., Sgt,
Haegerty, Patrick D., Pfc,
Haffey, Richard F., Pvt,
†Haffling, Abram H., Pfc,
Hagan, Dallas G., Pvt,
†Hagan, Edward C., Pvt,
Hagel, Clarence J., 1st Lt,
Hagen, Ernest O., Pfc,
Hagen, George E., Pvt,
Hagenberg, Andrew B., T/Sgt,
†Hagens, Wesley S., Pvt,
Hagerdon, Ray B., Pfc,
†Haggard, William E., Pvt,
Haggerty, George E., S/Sgt,
Haggstrom, Alton A., Pfc,
Hagstrom, Ralph A., Pfc,
Hague, John J., Pvt,
Hahn, Arthur D., Pfc,
Hahn, Frederick G., T/5,
Hahn, Manfred, Pvt,
Hahn, Philip, Pvt,
Hahn, Robert W., Capt,
Hahn, Theodore J., Pvt,
Haik, Mitchell H., Pvt,
Hain, Marion A., Jr., Pfc,
Hain, Russell L., Pfc,
Haines, Garwood C., Pvt,
Haines, Harold H., Capt,
Haines, John R., Pvt,
†Hair, Raymond C., Pvt,
†Hajj, Charles, Pvt,
Hale, Gordon R., S/Sgt,
Hale, Kenneth L., Pvt,
Hale, Paul M., Pfc,
Halenda, Harry J., Sgt,
Halerz, Emil C., T/5,
Haley, Calvin J., Pvt,
Halford, Ira H. E., T/5,
Halik, Michael, Pfc,
Hall, Allen E., T/5,
Hall, Ambrose, Pfc,
Hall, Arthur L., Jr., 2nd Lt,
Hall, Clarence W., Pvt,
Hall, Cleo B., Pfc,
†Hall, Cloyse E., Pfc,
Hall, Dale D., Sgt,
Hall, Edward, Pvt,
Hall, Elmer, Pfc,
Hall, Eugene, Pvt,
†Hall, Foster, Pfc,
Hall, Frank T., T/5,
Hall, Fred E., T/Sgt,
†Hall, George L., S/Sgt
Hall, Gerald W., T/4,
Hall, Harold T., Pfc,
Hall, Herman R., Pfc,
Hall, James D., Pfc,
†Hall, James G., Pfc,
†Hall, John A., Pvt,
Hall, John L., T/4,
Hall, Julian P., Pvt,
Hall, Larry B., Pvt,
†Hall, Linwood F., Pvt,
Hall, Mark J., Sgt,
Hall, Merlin, Sgt,
Hall, Noah B., Pfc,
Hall, Paul M., T/Sgt,
Hall, Ralph D., Sgt,
†Hall, Robert L., Capt,
Hall, Robert P., 1st Lt,
Hall, Russell C., Pfc,
Hall, Wayne, Pvt,
Hall, William H., Sgt,
Hall, Wilson A., Cpl,
Hall, Woodrow W., Pvt,
Hallet, Sheldon W., Pfc,
Halliday, William D., T/5,
§Hallstrom, Edwin W., Pvt,
Halmo, Roald M., Pfc,
Halpern, Nathan, Pfc,
Halpern, Robert H., Pfc,
Hals, Ernest E., Cpl,
Halstead, Kenneth B., Pfc,

† Killed in Action. * Prisoner of War. ‡ Missing in Action. § Died of Wounds.

Halvorson, Lloyd C., Pfc,
Halvorson, Thomas A., Pvt,
Hamad, Cemil, Pfc,
Hamaker, Raymond L., Pfc,
Hambelton, Frank E., Pfc,
†Hamblin, David, Jr., Sgt,
Hambright, Jefferson D., Pfc,
Hamby, Charles T., Pvt,
Hamby, Hubert L., Pvt
Hamby, Jack M., Pvt,
Hamilton, Berger W., Capt,
Hamilton, Charles W., Pvt,
Hamilton, Donald R., Pvt,
Hamilton, Douglas, Pvt,
Hamilton, Francis E., Cpl,
Hamilton, George W., Pfc,
†Hamilton, Mose N. J., Pvt,
Hamilton, Robert B., Jr., Pvt,
Hamilton, Robert C., Pfc,
Hamilton, William J., Pvt,
Hamilton, William L., Pvt,
Hamlet, Clentis B., Pfc,
Hamlett, John D., Pvt,
§Hamlin, Elmer A., Pfc,
Hamm, Herman R., Pfc,
Hamm, Walter S., Pfc,
Hammen, Amlin O., Pfc,
Hammer, Daniel, Pvt,
Hammer, Francis, Pvt,
†Hammersten, Henry L., Pvt,
Hammes, Francis J., Pfc,
Hammock, E. G., Sr., Pvt,
Hammond, Carl E., Jr., Pvt,
Hammond, Carl N., Cpl,
Hammond, Harold N., T/4,
Hammond, Henry O., Pvt,
Hammond, John Q., T/Sgt,
†Hammond, Lowell C., T/Sgt,
Hammond, Robert S., Pfc,
§Hammond, Walter, Pfc,
Hammond, Walter F., Pvt,
Hammons, Arsel, Pfc,
Hammons, John S., Pfc,
Hampton, Wallace R., Pvt,
Hampton, William J., Pvt,
Hancher, Carl M., Pfc,
Hancock, Stanley M., 2nd Lt,
Hancock, William A., Jr., Pvt,
†Hand, Everett J. F., Pvt,
Hands, Frank, 1st Sgt,
Handy, Noble R., Sgt,
Haneline, Norman E., S/Sgt,
Hanes, Gilbert A., Pvt,
Hanes, Lee A., Jr., Pfc,
Haney, Charles L., Pfc,
Haney, Charlie C., Pfc,
Haney, Donald, S/Sgt,
Haney, George B., WOJG,
Haney, Sigsby C., Pfc,
§Hansen, Fred E., T/5,
Hansen, Melvin O., T/5,
Hansen, Russell, Pvt,
Hansen, Ted L., Pvt,
Hansen, Wayne G., Pfc,
Hansen, Willard B., Pfc,
Hanson, Fred H., Pvt,
Hanson, Harold J., Pfc,
Hanson, Hartwick E., Pvt,
Hanson, William C., Jr., Pfc,
Hantz, Robert D., Pvt,
Hapak, Stanley H., Pfc
†Hapgood, Llewellyn, Pvt,
Harbeson, George W., Pfc,
Haney, Warren F., Pfc,
Hanisits, William P., Sgt,
Hanko, Joseph, Pvt,
Hanlon, Roy, Pvt,
Hanmer, Douglas R., Pvt,
Hanna, Grover J., Pvt,
Hanna, James H., Pfc,
Hannah, Alvin H., Pfc,
*Hannah, Trumen, Pvt,
Hannah, Walter W., Pvt,
Hannappel, Henry C., Pfc,
†Hannum, Joseph W., Pvt,
Hanrihar, Edward, Pvt,
†Hans, Peter R., Pfc,
†Hanscom, Russell A., Pfc,
Hansen, Charles J., Pfc,
Hansen, Clarence E., Sgt,
Hansen, Clifford L., Pvt,
Hansen, Dean L., Pfc,
Hansen, Edwin L., Pfc,
Hansen, Frank R., Sgt,
Harcourt, Arthur L., Pvt,
*Hard, Clyde H., Pvt,
Hardee, Elton J., Pvt,
Hardenbrook, William G., Pvt,
Harder, Fitzgerald F., Pfc,
Hardesty, Bert L., Pfc,
Hardin, Paul B., Pfc,
Harding, Donald M., Pvt,
Hardman, Harry I., S/Sgt,
†Hardt, Harold H., Pfc,
Hardwich, Percy R., S/Sgt,

Hardy, Frank A., Pvt,
Hardy, John J., Sgt,
Hardy, Sam N., Pfc,
†Hare, Alton R., Pfc,
†Hare, David F., Pfc,
Harford, Robert C., Pvt,
Hargis, George E., Cpl,
Hargrave, Buster, Pfc,
Hargrave, Coleman L., Pfc,
Hargrove, Wiley W., S/Sgt,
Harjo, Babe, Pvt,
Harkinish, Michael, Pvt,
Harkrider, Sherman W., Pvt,
Harlan, George V., Cpl,
Harley, Stanley F., 2nd Lt,
Harlow, Charles W., Cpl,
Harman, Richard L., Pvt,
Harman, Walter N., Pfc,
Harmon, Charles F., Pvt,
Harmon, Ernest H., Cpl,
†Harmon, Leland L., T/5,
Harmon, Lucas C., Pvt,
†Harmon, Thomas A., Pvt,
Harmon, Ulna, Pfc,
Harold, Norman A., Pvt,
Harper, Charles W., Jr., Pfc,
†Harper, Charlie E., Pfc,
Harper, Ralph E., Pvt,
Harper, William E., Pvt,
Harphant, Albert L., Pvt,
Harrell, Allen W., Pvt,
Harrell, Ben, Lt Col,
Harrell, Clyde T., Pfc,
Harrell, Notley R., 1st Lt,
Harrell, Wylie L., Jr., Pfc,
Harrington, Daniel C., T/5,
Harrington, John B., Cpl,
Harrington, William, T/4,
Harris, Allen L., Pvt,
Harris, Arthur G., Pfc,
Harris, Bernarr C., Pvt,
Harris, Earl W., Pfc,
Harris, Elmer G., S/Sgt,
Harris, Floyd C., Pvt,
Harris, George J., Pvt,
Harris, Glenn W., 1st Lt,
Harris, Hilmer C., Pfc,
Harris, Jack S., 1st Lt,
Harris, John, Jr., Pvt,
†Harris, John C., Pvt,
†Harris, Lawrence H., Pfc,
†Harris, Paul G., Capt,
Harris, Paul L., Pfc,
Harris, Ralph J. R., Pvt,
Harris, Ray A., 2nd Lt,
Harris, Roy C., Pfc,
Harris, Taylor E., Jr., Pvt,
§Harris, Walter J., T/Sgt,
Harris, Walter J., Jr., Pvt,
Harris, Warner F., Pfc,
Harris, Willard, Pfc,
Harris, William R., Pfc,
Harrison, Alvan L., Jr., Pfc,
Harrison, Claude J., Pvt,
Harrison, Ernest E., Pvt,
Harrison, Francis E., Pvt,
Harrison, Frank L., Capt,
Harrison, Fred W., 1st Lt,
§Harrison, George T., Jr., Pvt,
†Harrison, James A., Pfc,
†Harrison, James O., Pvt,
Harrison, John J., Pvt,
Harrison, Joseph P., Pvt,
Harrison, Olin C., 1st Lt,
Harrison, Paul R., Pvt,
Harrison, Robert B., T/5,
Harrison, William H., S/Sgt,
Harroff, Charles C., Jr., Pvt,
Harroll, John T., Pvt,
Harrop, Frederick J., Pvt,
Harsh, John J., Pvt,
Harsh, Roy L., Pvt,
Harshbarger, Allen H., Pvt,
§Harshbarger, Clyde N., Pvt,
Harshman, Elmer B., Sgt,
Hart, Arnold H., Pvt,
Hart, Charles J., Pfc,
Hart, Clarence R., Pvt,
§Hart, James, Pvt,
Hart, James A., Pvt,
Hart, James H., S/Sgt,
†Hart, James S., Pfc,
Hart, Leon M., Capt,
Hartdegen, William H., Cpl
Harter, Ellis W., Pvt,
Harter, Jack E., Pfc,
†Harter, John A., Pfc,
Harter, LeRoy E., Pvt,
Hartle, Gerald C., Pfc,
Hartman, George A., Pfc,
Hartman, John A., Pfc,
Hartman, Philip, Pvt,
Hartman, Seymour, 2nd Lt,
Hartman, William R., Pvt,
Hartnagle, Paul F., T/Sgt,

Hartnett, Michael J., Pfc,
†Hartshorn, Winthrop L., Pfc,
Hartstein, George H., Pfc,
*Hartzell, Joseph E., Pvt,
Hartzog, Simon T., Jr., Pfc,
Harvell, Woodrow A., S/Sgt,
§Harvey, Arthur J., Pfc,
Harvey, Charlie M., Pfc,
Harvey, John S., Capt,
§Harvey, Revista J., Pvt,
§Harvey, Russell P., Pvt,
Harville, Connie, Pvt,
Harville, Kenneth L., Pvt,
Harwell, Edward M., 1st Lt,
Harwell, James G., Pfc,
Harwell, Joe A., Pvt,
Harwood, Joseph T., Pvt,
Haschka, Thomas R., Pvt,
†Hasenbin, Albert A., Pvt,
Hashem, Tufie, Pfc,
Haskett, Roy M., T/Sgt,
Haskins, Richard D., Pvt,
Haskins, William T., Pvt,
Haslett, George R., Pfc,
Hassa, John F., Pvt,
Hasse, Arnold V., Pfc,
Hasselmann, Arnold W., T/5,
Hastings, Richard N., Pvt,
Hastings, Robert W., Cpl,
§Hatch, Leland, S/Sgt,
Hatch, Robert C., Pvt,
†Hatchell, James W., Pfc,
Hatcher, Robert, Pfc,
Hatfield, Charles A., Pvt,
Hatfield, James E., Cpl
Hatfield, Shirley M., Pvt,
†Hathcox, James A., Pfc,
‡Hatley, Marion F., Pvt,
Hatosy, Ferdinand, Pvt,
Hatten, Sam, Pfc,
Hattula, Henry R., Pfc,
Hatzenbuehler, George G., Pfc,
Hatzinger, Howard J., Pvt,
Haugen, Fred, T/5,
Haugen, George V., 1st Sgt,
Hauser, Leslie W., Pvt,
†Hausler, Joe F., Cpl,
Hausler, Joseph A., Pfc,
Havel, William H., Pfc,
Havens, Clinton L., Cpl,
Havens, Dean S., Pfc,
Havick, Arthur H., Pfc,
Hawbaker, Dale, Pvt,
Hawes, Richard F., T/Sgt,
Hawker, Paul J., Pvt,
†Hawkins, Jesse H., Pfc,
†Hawkins, John W., Pvt,
Hawkins, Robert L., Capt,
Hawkins, Thomas W., Pvt,
Hawkins, William, Jr., Pvt,
†Hawkins, Willis H., Pvt,
Hawkinson, Nels E., Pfc,
Hawley, Hiram R., S/Sgt,
Haworth, James J., Pvt,
Haworth, Ray, Pvt,
Hawthorn, Folyd C., Pfc,
Hawthorne, Willie M., Pfc,
Haycock, Eugene R., Jr., Pfc,
Hayden, Caskie V., Pvt,
Hayden, Richard C., Pvt,
†Hayduck, Michael G., Pfc,
Hayes, Arnold B., Pvt,
†Hayes, Bruce, Pfc,
§Hayes, Charles, Pvt,
Hayes, Edward R., WOJG,
Hayes, Frank A., Jr., Pvt,
Hayes, Harrison O., T/5,
Hayes, James H., Pfc,
Hayes, John J., Jr., S/Sgt,
Hayes, Martin A., Pvt,
†Hayes, Woods E., Pvt,
Haygood, Robert W., Pvt,
Haynes, Edward P., Pvt,
Haynes, J. R., Pvt,
Haynes, Medlie J., Pfc,
Hays, Edgar N., Pvt,
Hayslett, LeRoy B., T/4,
Hayton, Donald W., 1st Lt
Hayward, Bernard L., Pfc,
‡Hayward, Douglas R., Pvt,
Hayward, Harold D., Capt,
Hayward, John L., Pfc,
†Hazel, Robert K., Pfc,
Hazelton, Charles, Pfc,
Head, Clarence L., Pvt,
Headle, James L., Pvt,
Heafner, Mikel L., Sr., Pvt,
†Heagerty, John F., 2nd Lt,
Heagerty, Patrick D., Sgt,
Healy, James, Pvt,
Healy, John N., Pvt,
Heard, William C., Sgt,
Hearing, James M., Cpl,
Heath, Donald D., Pfc,
Heath, Lloyd M., Pvt,

Heaton, Melvin E., T/5,
Heaton, Timothy F., Pvt,
Heavner, Gordon W., Pfc,
Hebbler, Carl F., Pvt,
Hebda, Edward W., T/Sgt,
Heberbrand, Ralph C., Pfc,
Heben, John J., Jr., Pvt,
Hebner, Robert H., Pfc,
Heckman, Elmer A., Pfc,
Hedemark, George B., Pvt,
Hedger, Marion F., Jr., Pfc,
Hedges, Harold C., Pvt,
Hedges, Leonard O., Pfc,
Hediger, Charles W., Pvt,
Hedrick, Howard, Pvt,
Hedrick, Ned E., Pvt,
§Hedtky, Robert R., Pfc,
Heegard, Cloyce H., Pvt,
Heerschap, Peter, Jr., Pvt,
Hefferan, Cedric E., Jr., Pvt,
†Heffner, Johnnie H., Pvt,
Heflin, Elwyn P., Sgt,
Hegedus, Louis S., Pfc,
Heidel, Martin L., Pvt,
Heifitz, Jack, Pvt,
Height, George C., Pvt,
Height, William A., Pvt,
Heil, Thomas H., Jr., S/Sgt,
Heilman, Russell E., Pvt,
Heiman, Kenneth C., 2nd Lt,
Heimbigner, Leo D., Cpl,
Heimbuch, Howard W., T/4,
Hein, Albert, Cpl,
Heine, Carl F., Pfc,
Heinicke, Edward D., Pvt,
Heinz, Sylvester H., Cpl,
†Heiser, Daniel J., Pfc,
Heisler, Jesse W., Pfc,
†Heistein, Sidney I., Pvt,
Hejduk, Nelson S., Pvt,
Helber, George S., Pvt,
Held, Anton F., Pvt,
†Held, Leslie J., T/Sgt,
Heldman, Selli, Pvt,
Helfand, Sidney S., 1st Lt,
Helfont, Raymond J., Pfc,
Helgeson, Donald V., 1st Lt,
Heller, Joseph, Pvt,
Heller, Paul E., Pfc,
Heller, William, Pvt,
Hellinger, Peter J., S/Sgt,
†Helme, Francis L., Pvt,
Helmin, Daniel H., Pvt,
Helms, Graden H., Pfc,
Helms, Raymond C., Pfc,
Helms, Wayne W., Pvt,
Helowicz, Stanislaus D., S/Sgt,
Helsel, Conrad F., Pfc,
Helt, Lawrence L., Pfc,
*Helton, Joseph, Jr., Pfc,
Helton, Virgil M., Pvt,
Hembd, Paul E., Pvt,
Hemmingsen, Peter M., T/Sgt,
Hemner, Loren E., Pfc,
Hemric, Harvey E., Pfc,
Hencinsky, Charles K., Pfc,
Hendershot, Robert H., Pfc,
Henderson, Arthur P., Sgt,
Henderson, Fred L., Pvt,
†Henderson, Harlin L., S/Sgt,
Henderson, James B., Pfc,
Henderson, Leon A., S/Sgt,
*Henderson, Norman, Pvt,
Henderson, Robert F., Pvt,
†Henderson, Rufus M., Pfc,
†Henderson, Walter C., Pfc,
Henderson, Warren J., Pfc,
Hendon, Max R., 1st Lt,
Hendrick, Albert C., Sr., Pvt,
Hendricks, Emil E., Pvt,
Hendricks, John R., Sgt,
†Hendricks, LaVern L., Pfc,
Hendricks, Robert E., Pfc,
Hendricks, Victor W., Pfc,
Hendricks, Walter W., Pfc,
Hendrickson, James C., T/Sgt,
Hendrickson, Lloyd G., Pvt,
Hendrickson, Roy C., T/5,
Hendrix, Clifford H., Pvt,
Hendrix, Gerroy, Pvt,
Hendrix, James B., T/Sgt,
Hendrix, Oval, Pfc,
Hendrix, Robert L., Pfc,
Hendrixson, Waldo, S/Sgt,
Hendry, Donald G., Pvt,
Hendry, Joseph J., Cpl,
Heneberry, Roger J., 1st Sgt,
†Henegar, Claude C., Pvt,
†Henley, Charles L., Pfc,
Henningsen, Edward J., Pfc,
†Hennrikus, Walter F., Pfc,
*Henry, Emerson J., Pvt,
Henry, Emmett W., Pfc,
Henry, Emmitt, P., Pfc,
Henry, Guy L., Pvt,

Henry, Paul R., Pfc,
†Henry, Ray M., Sgt,
Henry, Robert, Pfc,
Henry, Thomas L., Pfc,
†Henry, Walter, Sgt,
Henry, Wilfred E., Pfc,
Henry, William O., T/5,
*Hensey, Arlie C., Sgt,
Hensler, A. A., Pvt,
Hensley, Gabe, Pfc,
Hensley, Keller B. M., Pvt,
§Hensley, Noah P., Pfc,
Hensley, Orval A., Pvt,
Hensley, Russell W., Sgt,
†Hensley, Theodore, P., Cpl,
Henson, Carl, Pvt,
Henson, Clarence G., Pvt,
Hensen, Kenneth C., Pvt,
Hentges, John C., Pvt,
Hepp, Joseph P., Pfc,
Heptinstall, Paschal P., T/5,
Herack, Frank, Cpl,
Herbert, Chester D., S/Sgt,
Herbert, Roy, Pvt,
Herbst, Arthur C., Pfc,
Heretik, Charles J., Pvt,
Heriford, Carl D., Pfc,
Herink, James W., Pvt,
Herling, Arthur F., Pfc,
Herman, Edwin H., Capt,
Herman, John J., Pvt,
Hernandez, Dan G., Pvt,
Hernandez, Frank, Pvt,
§Herndon, Alvin S., Pvt,
Herndon, Byron M., Pfc,
‡Herndon, William B., Jr., Sgt,
Herr, Aldus J., Pfc,
*Herre, Edwin T., Sgt, Pvt,
Herren, Robert K., T/4,
Herrera, Gilbert F., Pvt,
Herrera, Richard, Jr., T/5,
Herrick, Lynn O., Cpl,
Herrin, James S., Sr., Pvt,
§Herrin, Richard A., Pfc,
Herring, Garvin B., Pfc,
Herring, Paul R., Pvt,
Herring, Willard L., Pfc,
Herrlich, Philip W., Cpl,
Herron, Edward D., Jr., Pvt,
Hersey, Leon J., Pvt,
Hersh, Harry D., Pfc,
Hershey, Galen C., Pvt,
Hershey, William G., Pfc,
Hershock, Nelson W., Pvt,
Herst, Donald L., T/5,
Hert, William, Pfc,
Hertel, Elroy L., Pvt,
†Hertzog, William J., Pvt,
Hescock, Carroll H., Pfc,
Hescock, Paul G., Pfc,
Heshler, William F., T/5,
Hespen, Charles B., Pfc,
Hess, Cyril D., Pvt,
Hess, Francis J., Jr., Sgt
†Hess, Herbert, Pfc,
Hess, Kenneth H., T/Sgt,
Hess, Norbert A., Cpl,
Hess, Ralph T., Pfc,
Hess, Richard A., Sgt,
Hesse, F. W., Jr., 2nd Lt,
Hession, Edward, Pvt,
Heter, Wylie T., Pfc,
†Hetrick, Albert L., Pfc,
Hetrick, Reed A., Pvt,
Hetzer, Harold G., Pfc,
Heuer, Fred W., Pvt,
Heusser, Gail V., T/4,
†Hewlitt, Robert J., Pvt,
Hey, Robert J., Pvt,
Heyd, Henry L., Pvt,
Heymann, Henry, Pvt,
Hibbits, William C., Pvt,
Hice, Harry D., Pfc,
Hickerson, Jessie O., S/Sgt,
Hickey, John P., Pfc,
†Hickey, Keith S., Pvt,
Hickey, Thomas H., Pfc,
Hickman, Claude H., Pfc,
Hickman, John L., Pfc,
Hickman, Raymond J., Pfc,
†Hickman, Richard D., S/Sgt,
Hicks, Alfred R., Pvt,
Hicks, Archie, S/Sgt,
Hicks, Dudley E., Pfc,
Hicks, Elmer V., Pfc,
Hicks, Everett L., Pvt,
†Hicks, Harry L., Pvt,
†Hicks, Lawrence M., Cpl,
Hicks, Mayhew E., Pvt,
Hicks, William E., Pvt,
Hickson, Edward L., 2nd Lt,
Hidalgo, Roman C., Pvt,
Hielkema, Anno, Pvt,
Higginbotham, Ernest R., Pvt,
Higgins, Alfred, Pvt,

† Killed in Action. * Prisoner of War. ‡ Missing in Action. § Died of Wounds.

Higgins, Carl H., Pfc,
Higgins, Daniel E., Pvt,
†Higgins, Francis J., Pvt,
†Higgins, Jack O., Pfc,
§Higgins, James A., Pvt,
Higgins, Martin B., Pvt,
Higgins, Willard D., Pfc,
High, Robert L., Pfc,
Hight, Joe P., Pvt,
†Hight, Reese C., Pvt,
‡Higuera, Joe M., Pvt,
Hilbert, Ralph D., Pfc,
Hilborn, Millard J., Pvt,
Hilburn, Thomas J., 1st Sgt,
Hilderbrand, James E., Pfc,
Hildreth, Lyle C., T/5,
Hileman, Myron W., Pvt,
Hiles, George E., T/3,
Hill, Charlie O., Pvt,
Hill, Clarence L., Pfc,
Hill, Clyde C., Pvt,
Hill, Edward T., Pfc,
Hill, Fred T., Pvt,
Hill, Herman O., Pfc,
Hill, Hugh M., Pvt,
Hill, James E., Cpl,
Hill, Jesse J., S/Sgt,
Hill, John, Pvt,
Hill, John J., Pvt,
Hill, Lester B., Pfc,
Hill, Paul G., Pvt
Hill, Ray C., Pvt,
Hill, Raymond E., Pfc,
Hill, Robert M., Sgt,
Hill, Robert T., Pvt,
Hill, Roy S., Pfc,
Hill, Wayne R., Capt,
Hill, William, Pfc,
Hill, William C., S/Sgt,
†Hilley, Jack, Pvt,
†Hillman, Charles R., Pvt,
Hillmer, Ralph G., Capt,
Hilt, Elmer T., Pvt,
Hilton, Johnnie M., Pvt,
Hilton, Thomas H., Pfc,
Himebaugh, Coin F., Pfc,
Himes, Albert A., Pvt,
Himes, Robert A., 2nd Lt,
Himmelfarb, Joseph, T/5,
Himmelheber, Eugene L., Pfc,
Hinds, Harry E., Pfc,
†Hindsley, Leonard F., Jr., Pvt,
Hine, Donald, S/Sgt,
†Hiner, Laverne E., Pfc,
Hines, Daniel C., Sgt,
Hines, Earl F., Pfc,
Hines, Ray D., Pfc,
Hingle, Sidney M., Pvt,
Hinkel, Clayton L., Jr., Pfc,
Hinkle, Chancey D., Pvt,
Hinkle, Richard S., Pvt,
Hinkley, Raymond W., Pfc,
Hinkofer, Jerome J., Pfc,
Hinrichs, Carl B., S/Sgt,
Hinsey, Louis E., Capt,
Hinson, Herbert J., Pfc,
†Hinton, Clifford A., Pvt,
Hinton, Rollo H., Pfc,
Hinton, Virgil V., Pfc,
Hinzman, Lawrence, Pfc,
Hinzman, Reuben A., Pfc,
†Hirschl, Edward I., 2nd Lt,
Hirschl, Milton, Pfc,
Hirth, Milo W., S/Sgt,
Hite, Warren G., Pvt,
Hites, Joseph D., Pvt,
Hitt, Marion B., Pvt,
Hitt, Rubert G., Pfc,
Hitt, Wright, Capt
Hixson, Ross E., Pfc,
‡Hoard, John C., Pfc,
Hoare, Willis N., Pvt,
Hoback, Richard H., Pfc,
Hobbs, David E., Pfc,
Hobbs, Earl B., 1st Lt,
Hobbs, James M., S/Sgt,
Hobbs, William A., Pvt,
Hoberman, Joe E., Pfc,
Hobson, Raymond A., Pvt,
Hobson, Roland E., Pfc,
Hoch, Daniel C., Sgt,
*Hockenberry, Eugene W., Pvt,
Hockin, Russell, Jr., Pvt,
Hockman, William L., Pvt,
Hodgdon, Fred, Capt,
Hodgdon, George E., 1st Lt,
Hodge, Jerry J., Pfc,
Hodge, Robert H., Pvt,
Hodges, James M., Pvt,
Hodges, Lawrence L., Pvt,
Hodgkins, William G., III, Pvt
Hodgson, LeRoy E., Pfc,
Hoedebeck, Norbert W., Pvt,
Hoeltzer, Walter H., Pvt,
Hoerstman, Robert W., Pfc,

Hoey, Frederick E., Pfc,
Hoey, Harold T., Pvt,
‡Hofacker, Harold E., Pfc,
Hoff, Joseph O., Pvt,
Hoff, Louis R., T/3,
Hoffer, Emerson H., Pvt
Hoffman, David, Pfc,
†Hoffman, Francis E., Pfc,
Hoffman, George A., Pfc,
Hoffman, Helmut P., Pfc
Hoffman, John M., Pvt,
Hoffman, Richard, Pfc,
Hoffmann, Ferdinand F., Pvt,
Hoffner, Hugh L., Pfc,
Hogan, Charlie G., Pfc,
Hogan, Everett, Pfc,
Hogan, George E., Pfc,
Hogan, Harry W., Pfc,
Hogan, Thomas C., Pvt,
Hogan, Walter J., Jr., Pfc,
Hoganson, Charles F., Pvt,
Hogge, James L., S/Sgt,
Hogile, Wirt K., Pvt,
Hoh, Victor W., S/Sgt,
Hohl, Raymond R., Pvt,
Hoidal, William J., Pfc,
Holcomb, George R., T/Sgt,
Holcomb, Robert B., Pvt,
Holcomb, Robert E., Pfc,
Holcombe, William L., Sgt,
Holda, John A., Pfc,
Holden, Paul D., Pvt,
Holder, William M., Pvt,
§Holderness, Harley H., T/Sgt,
Holdner, Edward W., Pfc,
Holeman, Orlyn M., Pfc,
Holguin, Dolores, Pvt,
Holisky, John R., Pfc,
Holland, Alvis W., Jr., Pvt,
Holland, Dale, Cpl,
Holland, Irwin G., Pvt,
†Holland, Walter L., Jr., Pvt,
Holland, William F., Cpl,
Holleman, Phillip M., Pfc,
Holleman, Sam L., Pvt,
Hollen, Norman, S/Sgt,
†Hollerman, Francis L., Pvt,
†Holley, Julian S., Pvt,
Holley, William, Pvt,
Holley, William T., Pvt,
Holliday, Arthur E., S/Sgt,
Holliday, G. F., Jr., 1st Sgt,
Hollifield, Rass., Pvt,
Hollingsworth, Eugene L., Pvt,
Hollingsworth, Forrest B., Pvt,
†Hollins, Clinton R., Pvt,
Hollis, Hubert L., Pvt,
Holloway, Guy L., S/Sgt,
Holloway, Estelle, Pfc,
Holloway, Lynn A., Pfc,
Hollowell, Jean, Pfc,
Holm, Roy S., Cpl,
Holman, Allen C., Pfc,
Holmen, Victor G., Pfc,
Holmes, Arthur A., Sgt,
Holmes, Clarence A., T/4,
Holmes, Douglas A., Pvt,
Holmes, Edwin J., Pvt,
Holmes, George L., Pfc,
Holmes, Loyd E., S/Sgt,
Holmes, Preston N., Pvt,
†Holmquist, George V., T/Sgt,
Holovnia, Sylvester J., Pfc,
Holstein, Louis C., T/4,
Holt, George G., Pvt,
Holt, Guy D., S/Sgt,
Holt, Howard L., Sgt,
†Holt, Hughes L., Pvt,
Holt, J. D., Pfc,
‡Holthaus, Clarence A., Sgt,
Holtman, Francis H., Pfc,
†Holtry, William H., Pvt,
Holtz, Amiel F., Sgt,
Holtz, Earl J., Pvt,
†Holuta, George, Pvt,
Holwegner, Donald F., T/5,
Holz, Charles W., Pfc,
Holzer, Norman V., Cpl,
Holzmueller, Oscar W., Capt,
Holzschuh, William T., Pvt,
Homan, John, Pfc,
Homolish, John, T/Sgt,
Homsey, Michael P., Jr., Pvt,
Homsher, Earl V., Pfc,
Honald, Jim D., Pvt,
Honas, William A., Pvt,
Honeycutt, Alvin C., Pfc,
Honeycutt, Aubrey P., Pfc,
Honeycutt, James V., Pvt,
Honke, Martin A., Sgt,
‡Honnies, Ora F., Pvt,
Hoobs, Robert E., Sgt,
Hood, Emory E., S/Sgt,
Hood, Max V., Pvt,

Hood, Thomas H., Pfc,
Hook, Walter B., Pfc,
Hooker, Phineas H., Jr., T/Sgt,
Hooks, Oscar L., Jr., Pfc,
Hoopengarner, Thomas P., Pvt,
Hooper, Dixon, Pfc,
Hooper, Frankie J., S/Sgt,
Hooper, James N., Pvt,
Hooper, John W., Jr., 2nd Lt,
Hoose, Kenneth A., Pfc,
Hoover, Charles S., Pvt,
Hoover, Edwin L., Pvt,
Hoover, Joseph W., Pfc,
Hoover, Paul, Pfc,
Hoover, Walter L., Pvt,
†Hopfer, Emerson H., Pvt,
Hopkins, Harry E., Pvt,
Hopkins, Robert R., Pvt,
Hopkins, Willie W., Pvt,
Hopper, Frank A., Jr., Pfc,
Hopper, Russell H., Pfc,
Hopper, Russell J., Pvt,
Hoppes, Merrill W., Pvt,
Horan, Francis J., Pvt,
Horan, Percy G., Pvt,
Horbiansky, Joseph, Pvt,
Hordzwick, Charles K., 2nd Lt,
Horenstein, Milton S., Pvt,
Horien, Howard J., Pfc,
Horn, Harvey E., Pvt,
Horn, James F., Pvt,
Horn, Myron D., T/Sgt,
Horn, Paul, Pfc, Hode, Ky.
Horn, Raymond H., Pvt,
Horn, Roger C., Pfc,
Hornak, Edward J., Sgt,
Hornbacher, Henry R., Pfc,
Horne, Ashley, Pfc,
Horne, James W., Pfc,
Horner, Benjamin A., Pfc,
Hornsby, Cyrus E., Jr., 1st Lt,
Hornung, John J., Pvt,
Horrobin, Thomas E., Jr., Pfc,
Horstman, Wilbur R., Pvt,
Horswill, Ernest, Jr., T/5,
Horton, David R., Pvt,
Horton, Harley P., Pvt,
Horton, John W., Cpl,
Hortsman, Carl, S/Sgt,
†Horvath, Anthony J., Pfc,
Horvath, William, Pvt,
Horvath, William S., 2nd Lt,
Horwen, Cyrus, S/Sgt,
Horwood, Harold, Pfc,
Hosea, Ernest W., S/Sgt,
†Hosterman, Reed E., Pvt,
Hotaling, Perry R., 1st Lt,
†Hotson, Kenneth J., Pfc,
Hottinger, William E., Pvt,
Hotz, John, Jr., T/5,
Houchin, Wayne R., Pvt,
Houck, Walter W., T/4,
Houfek, Donald J., Pfc,
Hough, Audie F., Pvt,
§Hough, Charles E., Pvt,
Houghtaling, C. G., Jr., Pcf,
Houghtaling, Reid L., T/Sgt,
Houghton, Argyle W., Pvt
†House, Eugene P., Pvt,
House, Leo R., Pfc,
House, Reedie H., Pvt,
Houseknecht, Lewis S., Pvt,
Housenick, Douglas M., Pvt,
Houston, Johnnie A., Pvt,
Houston, Odis C., Pfc,
†Houtte, Edmund V., Pfc,
Hovan, Elmer G., Pfc,
†Hovancak, Steve P., Pvt,
Hovanecz, Joseph S., Sgt,
Hovda, Roger H., WOJG,
Hovenden, Thomas R., 1st Lt,
Hovern, Alton A., M/Sgt,
Hoversland, Reinert A., T/5,
Hovet, Dennis C., T/4,
Hovey, Charles F., Pvt,
Howard, Charles E., Jr., Pfc,
Howard, David F., Pfc,
Howard, Earl R., T/Sgt,
Howard, Elizah, Pvt,
†Howard, Estill, Pfc,
Howard, George E., Pvt,
†Howard, George V., Pvt,
Howard, Grant L., Cpl,
Howard, James, Pvt,
Howard, Larry J., S/Sgt,
†Howard, Melvern R., Pfc,
Howard, Walter C., Pvt
Howard, Wayne A., Pvt,
Howard, William C., Pvt,
Howard, Willis C., T/5,
‡Howarth, Milton B., T/4,
Howcroft, William R., Pvt,
†Howden, Benjamin E., S/Sgt,
Howe, Clayton C., T/5,
†Howe, Dale F., T/5,

‡Howe, Richard T., Pvt,
Howe, Russell P., Pfc,
*Howell, Cecil R., Pvt,
Howell, Clyde, Pfc,
Howell, Harley L., S/Sgt,
Howell, Horace S., Pvt,
Howell, John C. A., Pfc,
Howell, Joseph, Pvt,
†Howell, Louis W., Pfc,
Howell, Orus M., Pfc,
Howell, Rawleigh R., Pvt,
Howell, Robert D., Pvt,
Howes, Russell K., Pvt,
Howey, Calvin J., S/Sgt,
Howey, Harold G., 1st Sgt,
Howland, Carlton F., Pvt,
Howland, Henry U., Capt,
Howland, Jack L., Pvt,
†Howland, Richard S., Pfc,
Howland, Walter C., Sgt,
Howley, William P., Pfc,
Hoy, Vernon R., Cpl,
Hoyer, Clarence P., Pvt,
Hoyt, Clair F., Pvt,
Hoyt, Milton E., Pfc,
Hrabosky, Leonard O., Pvt,
Hribar, Stanley J., Pvt,
Hriber, Felix J., Pfc,
Hricak, Michael G., Pvt,
Hrin, Edward, Pfc,
Hrin, Paul, Pfc,
Hrinya, George M., Pfc,
Hubbard, Chester, Pfc,
Hubbard, Clyde E., Pvt,
†Hubbard, Elmer L., Pfc,
Hubbard, Wayne D., T/5,
Hubbell, Merle E., Sgt,
Hubble, Roy, Pvt
Hubbs, Donald H., 1st Lt,
Huber, Carl F., Sgt,
Huber, Elmer C., Pvt,
Huber, William C., T/5,
Hubner, Joseph C., Pfc,
Huck, Frederick R., 1st Lt,
Huckabba, Martin V., Pfc,
Huculak, William, Pfc,
Hudak, Paul R., Pvt,
Huddleston, Harlie A., Pvt,
Huddleston, Robert A., Pfc,
Hudek, John J., Pvt,
Hudgins, Johnnie, Pvt,
Hudik, Joseph, Pfc,
Hudler, William R., Pvt,
Hudson, Floyd, Pvt,
Hudson, Forrest E., Pfc,
Hudson, George F., Pvt,
Hudson, Irvin L., Pfc,
Hudson, Leonard H., Pfc,
Hudson, Lewis L., Pvt,
§Hudson, Ray S., Pvt,
Hudson, Raymond J., Pvt,
Hudson, Stancil E., Pfc,
Huene, Joseph R., Pfc,
Huenemeyer, John A., Pvt,
Huether, Ralph A., Pfc,
†Huff, Earl S., Pvt,
Huff, Ernest E., S/Sgt,
Huff, Franklin W., Pfc,
Huff, Henry H., Pvt,
†Huff, Starrett A., Pvt,
†Huffacker, Elmer L., Pfc,
Huffer, Gilbert R., Pvt,
Huffman, Edmund W., Pfc,
Huffman, Neil D., Sgt,
Huffman, Ralph E., Pvt,
Huffman, Willard R., T/4,
†Huggans, Charles L., Pvt,
Huggins, Elbert P., Pfc,
Hughers, Edward P., Pvt,
Hughes, Chester, Pfc,
Hughes, Eugene L., Pfc,
Hughes, Francis P., S/Sgt,
Hughes, George W., Capt,
†Hughes, Homer D., T/5,
Hughes, James, Pvt,
Hughes, John F., S/Sgt,
*Hughes, Leo, Pvt,
Hughes, Mose S., Pvt,
Hughes, Paul, T/5,
Hughes, Raymond E., Pvt,
Hughes, Robert V., Cpl,
Hughes, Samuel W., S/Sgt,
Hughes, William E., Pvt,
Hughes, Williford G., Sgt,
Hughett, Earl H., T/4,
Hulberg, Edward B., Pfc,
Hulbert, Gerald W., Pvt,
Hulbert, Walter G., Cpl,
Hull, Fay O., Pvt,
†Hull, Harold C., Pfc,
Hull, Henry R., Pvt,
Hull, Richard A. J., T/5,
Hull, Robert E., Pfc,
Hull, Walter F., Pvt,
Huls, John E., Cpl,

Hultgren, Willard L., Pvt,
Hulton, Edwin A., Pfc,
Hum, Nan F., Cpl,
Humes, Ollie A., T/5,
Hummel, Clarence J., Pfc,
Hummel, David H., S/Sgt,
Hummer, John, Pvt,
Humphrey, Charlie R., Pfc,
Humphrey, David R., Pfc,
Humphrey, Wallace L., Pvt,
§Humphreys, Victor H., Sgt,
Hunger, Leonard J., Pvt,
Hunn, Charles J., Pvt,
Hunn, Gale G., T/5,
Hunnell, Paul B., Pvt,
Hunolt, Robert A., Pvt,
Hunt, Elmond L., Pfc,
Hunt, Emile, Pfc,
Hunt, James F., Pfc,
Hunt, Norbert L., Sgt,
Hunt, Paul, Pfc,
Hunt, Thomas D., Cpl,
*Hunt, Walter, Pvt,
Hunt, Walter L., T/5,
Hunt, William N., Pvt,
Hunter, Joe B., Pvt,
Hunter, John T., Sgt,
Hunter, Lee K., Pfc,
Hunter, Robert E., Pfc,
Hunter, Wendell B., Pvt,
Huntington, LaVerne J., Pvt,
Huntley, Clifford H., S/Sgt,
Huot, Leo H., Pvt,
Hupence, Frank, Pfc,
Huppert, Henry J., S/Sgt,
Huppi, Melvin, T/5,
Hurd, Stanley R., Pvt,
†Hurd, Walter C., S/Sgt,
Hurdelbrink, Michael W., Capt
Hurley, James R., Jr., Pvt,
Hurst, Hugo, Pfc,
Hurst, Irwin M., Pvt,
Hurt, Albert, Pfc,
Hurtado, Robert E., Cpl,
Hurwitz, Herman B., Pvt,
Hurwitz, Samuel, Pvt,
Huskey, Kenneth J., T/Sgt,
Huss, Fred E., Pfc,
Hussey, William J., T/5,
Hussey, Willie T., Pfc,
Husted, Richard L., Pvt,
Hutchens, Chester L., Pvt,
†Hutchens, Lacy T., Pvt,
Hutchins, Harvey E., Pfc,
Hutchins, Henry V., S/Sgt,
Hutchinson, Carlon R., Pvt,
Hutchinson, Clarence G., Pvt,
Hutchinson, Donald H., Pfc,
Hutchinson, James F., Sgt,
§Hutchinson, Robert, Pvt,
Hutchinson, Verdan N., Pvt,
Hutchinson, William E., Pvt,
Hutlock, Joseph J., Pvt,
Hutson, Samuel R., Pfc,
§Hutton, James R., Pfc,
Huzar, Joseph A., Pvt,
Hyatt, Broadus H., Pfc,
Hyatt, Manuel, Pfc,
Hyden, Henry F., Pvt,
Hyder, Beryl V., Pvt,
Hyder, Harold A., Pvt,
Hyder, Morris D., Pfc,
Hyman, Rogene, Pfc,
Hynd, John A., T/5,
§Hynes, Harold T., Pvt,
Hynes, John A., Pfc
Hyrne, Homer, Pvt,
Hyson, Charles L., Jr., Pfc,

Jablonowski, Casimir, Pvt,
Jablonski, Robert E., Pfc,
†Jacabowitz, Leo A., Pfc,
Jack, Ray W., Pfc,
Jack, Walter P., Pfc,
Jackson, Carlis B., Sgt,
Jackson, Cedric, Cpl,
Jackson, Duane W., Pvt,
Jackson, Howard L., Pfc,
Jackson, Hugh A., Pfc,
Jackson, James A., Pvt,
Jackson, John A., Pfc,
Jackson, John W., Pvt,
§Jackson, Johnnie, Pfc,
Jackson, Joseph L., Pvt,
Jackson, Joseph S., Jr., Pfc,
Jackson, Joseph T., Pvt,
Jackson, Leroy P., Pvt,
Jackson, P. Q., Sgt,
Jackson, Ray E., Pvt,
Jackson, Raymond C., Pfc,
Jackson, Raymond M., Pvt,
§Jackson, Ross M., Pfc,
§Jackson, Stanley C., Pfc,
Jackson, Walter, Pfc,
Jackson, Walter E., Pvt,

† Killed in Action. * Prisoner of War. ‡ Missing in Action. § Died of Wounds.

Jackson, Wilbur J., Pvt,
Jackson, William H., 2nd Lt,
Jackson, Willie K., Pvt,
Jacob, Joseph, Pfc,
Jacob, Vincent R., Pfc,
Jacobs, Arthur W., Pvt,
Jacobs, Edward G., T/5,
Jacobs, Raymond E., Pfc,
Jacobs, Robert L., Pvt,
Jacobsen, Eugene W., Pvt,
Jacot, Donald R., Cpl,
Jacques, Edwin D., Jr., Pfc,
Jacques, Robert E., Sgt,
Jadin, Kenneth R., T/5,
Jaeckel, George T., Pvt,
Jaeger, Carl G., 2nd Lt,
†Jaeger, Frederick W., Pfc,
Jaffee, Oscar C., Pfc,
Jagger, Richard S., Pfc,
Jaggers, Clifton B., Pvt,
Jakobowiski, Edward J., Pvt,
Jaks, Leonard B., Pfc,
Jakubczyk, John A., S/Sgt,
Jamerson, Robert S., Pvt,
James, Charles H., Cpl,
James, David A., Pvt,
James, Chester L., Pvt,
James, George C., Pvt,
James, Herman F., Pvt,
James, Gilbert I., S/Sgt,
James, Homer C., Cpl,
James, Isaac, 1st Sgt,
James, Jessie, Pvt,
†James, Ray, Cpl,
James, Ronda J., S/Sgt,
James, William C., Sgt,
Jamieson, Harvey, Cpl,
Janczuk, Anthony, Pfc,
Janeway, Ralph P., Pfc,
Janik, Albert P., Pvt,
Jankowski, George, Pvt,
§Janosek, George J., Pvt,
Janski, Roger J., Sgt,
Janton, James, Pvt,
Jantz, Rudolph A., S/Sgt,
†Jaramillo, Joe J., Pvt,
Jarasek, Joseph J., Sgt,
†Jarl, Clifton E., Pfc,
Jarowski, Anthony M., Pvt,
Jarrett, Harold L., Pvt,
Jarrett, Clifton E., Pfc,
Jarrett, Thomas E., Pfc,
†Jarvais, Leo N., Pvt,
Jarzynka, Theodore A., Pfc,
Jasinski, Edward I., S/Sgt,
Jaskolka, Stanley L., Pvt,
Jaworowski, Stanley J., Pfc,
Jay, Byron, 1st Sgt,
Jay, Leonard W., 1st Sgt,
Jaynes, Lloyd B., Pvt,
‡Jeanminette, Joseph, Pfc,
Jeannot, Robert A., Pvt,
§Jeantete, Feliberto P., Pfc,
Jech, Robert W., Pfc,
Jeffers, Nelson, Pvt,
†Jeffries, James E., Pvt,
Jeffries, John B., Pfc,
Jeffries, William A., Pfc,
Jenezon, Jack, Jr., Pvt,
Jenkins, Earl G., Cpl,
Jenkins, Frank G., Pvt,
Jenkins, George S., Pvt,
Jenkins, Kenneth W., Pvt,
Jenkins, Lee Roy, T/4,
Jenkins, Robert T., Pvt,
Jenkins, Perry M., Pvt,
Jenkins, Roye, Cpl,
†Jenkins, Sterlin C., Pfc,
§Jenning, George C., Pvt,
Jennings, Frank R., Sgt,
Jennings, George, Pvt,
Jens, Wayne E., Pfc,
Jensen, Carl C., Pvt,
§Jensen, Christian B., Pvt,
Jensen, Eugene F., Pfc,
Jensen, Folmer E., Pvt,
Jensen, Herman, Pfc,
Jensen, Joseph J., Pfc,
Jensen, Lavern A., T/5,
Jensen, Orlo R., Pfc,
†Jenson, George, Jr., T/Sgt,
Jerelos, Gust J., Pfc,
Jeruzal, Thomas E., Pvt,
Jeske, Louie W., Pvt,
Jeske, William R., Pvt,
Jesse, Lester F., Pfc,
Jessee, Kenneth S., Sgt,
Jessen, Walter J., Pvt,
Jett, Harold L., Cpl,
Jillson, Merton H., Jr., Pvt,
Jillson, Merton H., Jr., Sgt,
Jimenez, Jose S., Pfc,
‡Jivery, Leonard A., Pvt,
*Jobe, Carl K., Pfc,
†Jobe, William L., Pfc,

Joe, Young, Pvt,
Johansen, Gordon R., Pvt,
John, Sam, Pfc,
Johnides, George, Pvt,
Johns, Kenneth W., T/Sgt,
Johns, William L., Pfc,
Johnson, Aaron H., Jr., Pfc,
*Johnson, Adam L., Pvt,
Johnson, Albert J., Pvt,
Johnson, Alden E., Sgt,
†Johnson, Arthur L., Pfc,
Johnson, Arthur L., Pfc,
Johnson, Buddie E., Pfc,
Johnson, C. W., Pfc,
Johnson, Carl E., Pfc,
Johnson, Carl E., Pvt,
Johnson, Carl L., Pvt,
†Johnson, Charles A., Sgt,
Johnson, Charles A., Pvt,
Johnson, Charles E., Pvt,
†Johnson, Charles H., Pfc,
Johnson, Charles I., Pfc,
Johnson, Charles R., Jr., Col,
Johnson, Chris J., Pvt,
†Johnson, Donald A., Pvt,
Johnson, Donald C., Pfc,
Johnson, Donald V., Pvt,
Johnson, Duane E., Pvt,
Johnson, Earl V., S/Sgt,
Johnson, Ed, Pvt,
Johnson, Edward L., T/4,
†Johnson, Elden H., Pvt,
Johnson, Ellis D., Jr., Pfc,
Johnson, Elmer G., 1st Lt,
Johnson, Emmett L., Pfc,
Johnson, Erick E., Pvt,
Johnson, Ernest E., Sgt,
Johnson, Everett, 1st Sgt,
Johnson, Floyd H., Pvt,
Johnson, Frank J., Pfc,
Johnson, Fred M., Pfc,
Johnson, Frederick W., Pvt,
Johnson, Gilbert, Pfc,
Johnson, Glen V., Pvt,
Johnson, Glenn D., Pvt,
Johnson, Gordon L., Pfc,
§Johnson, Gunnar, Pfc
Johnson, Gustave H., Pvt,
Johnson, Harold C., Pfc,
Johnson, Harold E., Pfc,
Johnson, Harold L., Pfc,
Johnson, Herbert, Pvt,
Johnson, Herman, Pvt,
Johnson, Irving R., Pfc,
Johnson, James T., Pvt,
Johnson, James W., S/Sgt,
Johnson, J. C. W., Pvt,
Johnson, John A., Pfc,
Johnson, John D., Pfc,
Johnson, John J., Pfc,
Johnson, John P., Sgt,
Johnson, Johnny O., Pvt,
Johnson, Joris O., S/Sgt,
Johnson, Joseph K., Pvt,
Johnson, Kenneth H., Pfc,
Johnson, Kenneth N., Pfc,
Johnson, Leo B., T/4,
Johnson, Leo F., Pvt,
Johnson, Lester M., Pvt,
Johnson, Levi F., Pvt,
Johnson, Ludwig J., Pfc,
Johnson, Lyle A., Pfc,
Johnson, Nevin D., Pfc,
Johnson, Nickolas, Pfc,
§Johnson, Norbert C., Pvt,
Johnson, Oliver, Jr., Pfc,
Johnson, Paul H., Pfc,
†Johnson, Ralph G., Sgt,
Johnson, Ray B., Pvt,
Johnson, Ray M., T/5,
†Johnson, Raymond C., 1st Lt,
Johnson, Robert A., S/Sgt,
†Johnson, Robert B., Pvt,
Johnson, Robert L., Pvt,
Johnson, Roy, Pfc.
Johnson, Roy E., T/Sgt,
Johnson, Sam A., Pfc,
Johnson, Stanley O., Pfc,
Johnson, Ted, Pfc,
Johnson, Walter T., 2nd Lt,
†Johnson, Wayne G., Pfc,
Johnson, Wilbur C., Pfc,
Johnson, Wilbur F., Pfc,
Johnson, William N., Sgt,
Johnson, Willie A., Pfc,
†Johnsrude, Luther O., Pfc,
‡Johnston, Buford G., 2nd Lt,
Johnston, Ralph W., Pfc,
Johnston, Richard C., Pfc,
Johnstone, Robert I., Pvt,
Joiner, Carra G., Pfc,
Joines, Jesse L., Pvt,
Jolly, Avery M., Pfc,
Jolly, William J., Pvt,
Jones, Alfred R., Pvt,

Jones, Abraham R., Pfc,
Jones, Carl E., Pvt,
Jones, Carl L., Pvt,
Jones, Charles E., Pvt,
Jones, Clarence H., S/Sgt,
Jones, Clarence L., Pvt,
Jones, David L., Pfc,
†Jones, Donald C., Pvt,
Jones, Douglas L., Pvt,
Jones, Earl C., Sgt,
Jones, Frank P., 1st Lt,
Jones, Glen R., S/Sgt,
Jones, Harry D., Pfc,
Jones, Harry S., Sgt,
Jones, Hayden H., Pfc,
Jones, Herbert D., S/Sgt,
Jones, J. B., Pvt,
Jones, James A., Sgt,
Jones, James C., Pfc,
Jones, James E., Pfc,
Jones, James F., Pvt,
Jones, James T., Pvt,
Jones, Jessie R., Pvt,
Jones, John E., T/4,
Jones, Kenneth R., Pfc,
Jones, Lawrence C., Pfc,
Jones, Leslie H., S/Sgt,
Jones, LeVern W., S/Sgt,
†Jones, Morris E., 2nd Lt,
Jones, Ottis M., Pfc,
Jones, Paul D., T/5
Jones, Paul E., Pfc,
†Jones, Ralph C., Pfc,
Jones, Ray D., Sgt,
Jones, Robert G., Pfc,
Jones, Robert L., Sgt,
Jones, Robert V., Sgt,
Jones, Roy W., Pvt,
Jones, Thomas B., Pvt,
†Jones, Thomas L., Pvt,
Jones, Warren H., Pfc,
Jones, William C., Pvt,
Jones, William D., Sr., Pvt,
Jones, William E., Pfc,
Jones, William H., Pfc,
Jones, William J., Pvt,
Jones, William L., Pvt,
‡Jones, William N., Jr., Pvt,
Jones, William R., Pvt,
Jones, Woodrow W., Pfc,
Joos, Leo W., Pfc,
Joost, Frederick D., Pvt,
Joppa, Andrew, 1st Sgt,
Jordan, Eli F., Pfc,
Jordan, Elihu, Pfc,
Jordan, Jack H., Sgt,
Jordan, Nicholas, Pvt,
Jordan, Robert E., Pfc,
§Jordan, Thomas H., S/Sgt,
Jordon, Clarence E., Pfc,
Jorgensen, Edward M., T/5,
Joseph, Abraham, Pvt,
Joseph, John C., Pvt,
Josten, Thomas W., Pfc,
Journey, Jack, Pfc,
Joy, Charles J., T/4,
Jozwiak, Robert G., Pvt,
Juarez, Santos J., Pfc,
Judge, Patrick E., Pfc,
†Judy, George F., S/Sgt,
Juisto, Emilio E., Pvt,
Jukich, Russell J., Pvt,
Jukick, Russell J., Pfc,
†Julian, Jeremiah C., Pvt,
†Juliano, Frank L., Pfc,
Julig, Edward P., S/Sgt,
Julius, Virgil R., Pvt,
Jumper, Herchel G., Pvt,
Juner, Oscar W., Pvt,
Junkin, Sam H., Pfc,
Juopperi, Walter W., Pfc,
†Jurgens, Bertus J., Pfc,
Jurievecz, Peter J., Pfc,
Jusseaume, Andre A., S/Sgt,
Justice, Russell, Pvt,
Juston, Thomas M., Pfc,
Justus, Cletus J., Pvt,
Juzwiak, Frank, Pvt,

Kacala, Casimer E., Pfc,
Kachelmier, Joseph, T/5,
Kaercher, Robert J., Pfc,
†Kagle, Wilbur C., 1st Lt,
†Kaiser, Joseph, Pvt,
Kaiser, Wilbur C., Pvt,
Kalafus, Peter P., Pvt,
Kaledo, Charles G., Pvt,
Kaletski, Leo J., Pvt,
Kalinofski, W. J., Jr., S/Sgt,
Kalinowski, Frank P., Pvt,
Kalinski, John, Pfc,
Kallio, Frank J., Pfc,
Kamenetzky, Joel J., Pvt,
Kaminski, Stanley, Cpl,
Kaminski, Stanley A., Pfc,

Kaminsky, Frank A., Cpl,
Kammer, Joseph W., Pfc,
Kammerer, Peter F., Pfc,
Kamp, Warren L., Pfc,
Kamys, Thaddeus J., Pvt,
Kanarek, Seymour S., Pvt,
†Kandle, Victor L., 1st Lt,
Kanduk, John, Pvt,
Kane, John D., Pfc,
Kane, Morris M., T/5,
Kane, William H., Jr., Pfc,
Kane, William J., Jr., Cpl,
†Kanecki, William T., Sgt,
Kania, Stephen, Pvt,
Kanipe, William H., Pfc,
Kann, Robert M., Pfc,
Kantor, Irving S., Pvt,
Kapinos, Rudolph A., Pfc,
Kaplan, Alfred, Pvt,
Kaplan, Benjamin, Pvt,
Kaplan, Myron H., Pfc,
Kaplanis, John, Pfc,
Kapler, Louis C., Sgt,
Kapp, Ervin J., 1st Sgt,
Kaptein, Eugene D., Pfc,
Kapuscinski, Joseph J., Pfc,
Karabatsolis, Nick J., Sgt,
Karasinski, Joseph J., Pvt,
Karbowski, John R., Sgt,
Karch, Philip, Pfc,
Kari, Ernest M., Pfc,
Karinska, John, Pvt,
Karintie, Edward, Pfc,
Karl, Ludwig L., Jr., Pvt,
Karley, Ralph K., Sr., Pvt
Karls, Sylvester C., Sgt,
Karnes, John E., Pfc,
Karnik, Joe F., Pvt,
Karolak, Joseph, Sgt,
Karpe, Harold W., Pvt,
Karr, Clifford L., Pvt,
Karriker, Lewis T., Pvt,
Karst, Frederick W., Sgt,
Kartevold, Obert, S/Sgt,
Kartz, Edmund D., Pfc,
Karvonen, Arthur G., Pfc,
Karwowski, Eugene L., T/4,
Kasco, Johnnie, Pvt,
Kash, Marvin A., Pfc,
Kasinger, Hoy C., Cpl,
Kasitz, Louis J., Pfc,
Kaska, LeRoy, Sgt,
Kaspar, Ervin H., Pfc,
Kasprzak, Joseph J., Pfc,
Kassiotis, Peter E., Pfc,
Katchur, George J., Pvt,
Katz, Arthur, Pvt,
Katz, Calvin, Pvt,
Katz, David, Pfc,
Kauffman, Herbert K., Pfc,
Kauffman, James O., Pvt,
Kaufhold, John A., Pfc,
Kaufman, Alois J., 1st Sgt,
Kaufman, Earl J., Pvt,
Kaufman, Irving N., T/5,
Kaufman, John G., Pfc,
Kaufman, Norbert A., Pvt,
Kaufman, Virgil M., Pvt,
Kauramaki, Chester A., Pfc,
Kausch, Walter R., 2nd Lt,
Kautz, Theodore, Sgt,
Kavachevich, Leo M., Pfc,
Kaveny, Charles, Pvt,
Kawa, Charles C., Pfc,
Kawecki, Harry S., Pvt,
Kay, Carl W., Pvt,
Kay, Robert W., Pvt,
Kaylor, Ray R., Pfc,
Kazierczak, Henry J., Pfc,
Kaznowski, Alfred R., S/Sgt,
Keady, Charles R., 2nd Lt,
Keane, Daniel F., Pfc,
†Kearney, Franklin G., Pvt,
Kearney, John E., T/4,
Kearse, Rufus H., Pfc,
Keating, Edward F., Pfc,
Keator, Harry D., T/Sgt,
Keats, Harry D., T/Sgt,
Kee, Albert J., Sr., Pfc,
Keeler, Joseph P., Pvt,
Keeler, Thomas F., S/Sgt,
Keeley, Theodore C., Pfc,
Keen, Marvin H., Pvt,
Keenan, Chester H., Pfc,
Keenan, James F., Pvt,
Keenan, Robert B., T/4,
Keenan, Robert E., 1st Lt,
Keene, Robert M., S/Sgt,
Keener, Garlin P., Pfc,
Keeth, Regan K., Pvt,
Keeton, Cephus M., Pfc,
Keeton, James H., Pfc,
Keeton, Richard F., Pvt,
Keffer, Bernard R., S/Sgt,
†Kefurt, Gus J., S/Sgt,

†Kehm, William A., Pvt,
Kehr, Alvon, Pfc,
Keihl, Willis P., Sgt,
†Keim, Robert L., Pfc,
Keith, Elmer M., S/Sgt,
†Keithley, Henry C., Pfc,
Kelieher, John P., Pvt,
Kell, Leonard L., Pvt,
Kellander, Richard, Pfc,
Kellas, William W., Pfc,
Kelleher, John, Pvt,
Keller, Albert J., 1st Sgt,
Keller, Charles L., Pfc,
Keller, Everett W., Sgt,
Keller, Fred, Pfc,
Keller, Frederick A., Pvt,
Keller, Hall R., Pvt,
Keller, Harold, Pvt,
Keller, Harold W., Pfc,
Keller, Harvey G., Jr., T/Sgt,
Keller, James E., T/Sgt,
Keller, Raymond C., Pfc,
†Kelley, Andrew, S/Sgt,
*Kelley, Francis J., Pvt,
Kelley, Irving B., S/Sgt,
Kelley, Irving F., Pvt,
Kelley, Martin L., S/Sgt,
Kelley, Samuel J., Pfc,
Kelley, William F., S/Sgt,
Kelley, Willie E., Pfc,
Kellogg, Bernard D., Pvt,
Kells, Bernard R., Pfc,
†Kellum, William L., Pvt,
Kelly, Arthur L., Pvt,
†Kelly, Carl E., Pvt,
Kelly, Charles F., Pvt,
Kelly, Hardy H., Pvt,
Kelly, Horace, Pfc,
Kelly, Hubert W., Pfc,
Kelly, John J., Pfc,
Kelly, John W., 1st Sgt,
Kelly, Joseph J., Cpl,
Kelly, Lynn L., Pvt,
Kelly, Ranald, Pfc,
†Kelly, Robert E., Pvt,
Kelly, Sammie O., Pvt,
Kelly, William F., Pvt,
Kelm, Gustave C., Pvt,
Kelsey, Henry J., Pfc,
†Kelsey, Philander, Jr., 1st Lt,
Kelton, Allen W., Pfc,
Kemmerer, P. W., 2nd Lt,
Kemp, John W., Pvt,
Kemp, Richard L., Pfc,
Kemper, Sylvester H., Jr., Pfc,
Kendall, Carl L., Pfc,
Kendall, John F., Pvt,
Kendall, Maurice W., 1st Lt,
Kendzior, Alexander F., T/Sgt,
Kenel, Frank J., Pfc,
Kenepp, Elmer G., Jr., S/Sgt,
Kenik, Frank A., Sgt,
Kennedy, Edward B., Pvt,
Kennedy, Francis M., Pvt,
Kennedy, Frank E., Pfc,
†Kennedy, Gordon H., Pfc,
Kennedy, Harold M., Capt,
Kennedy, Howard S., Pfc,
†Kennedy, John O., Pvt,
Kennedy, Johnnie J., S/Sgt,
Kennedy, Merrill H., Pvt,
†Kennedy, Thomas L., Pfc,
Kenneke, Gerard F., Pvt,
Kennelly, Edward J., Pfc,
Kennerson, Herbert F., Pvt,
†Kenneson, Donald K., Pvt,
Kenney, Barrett L., Pvt,
Kenny, James T., Pfc,
Kensinger, Donald R., Pfc,
†Kent, Edward A., Pfc,
Kent, George B., Sgt,
Kent, Royal P., 1st Lt,
†Kent, Vincent F., Pvt,
Keohane, Francis G., Pvt,
Keown, Robert L., Pfc,
Keough, John P., Pvt,
*Keough, Joseph W., T/Sgt,
†Keogh, Richard P., Pfc,
†Kepner, Walter E., Pvt,
Kerber, Ralph D., Pvt,
Kerchner, Donald L., Pvt,
Kerekes, Andrew A., Pvt,
Kerins, Francis E., Pvt,
Kerkes, Henry P., Pfc,
Kern, Dale W., Sgt,
Kerner, Gerald J., Sgt,
Kerns, William C., Pfc,
Kerr, Charles W., Pfc,
Kerr, Jack B., Pvt,
Kerr, Willis E., Pvt,
‡Kersey, Edgar, Pvt,
Kershaw, Horace M., Pvt,
†Kershaw, Paul E., 1st Lt,
*Kerstetter, Irvin L., Pvt,
Kerzmann, Elvin M., Pvt,

† Killed in Action. * Prisoner of War. ‡ Missing in Action. § Died of Wounds.

Kesner, Wyman L., Pfc,
Kessel, Harry W., Pfc,
Kessinger, Jack D., Pfc,
Kessler, Albert F., Pvt,
Kessler, Lucian W., S/Sgt,
Kessler, Ralph G., Pvt,
Kestell, Thomas A., Pfc,
Ketcher, Clyde, Pvt,
Ketchum, Charles M., Sgt,
Ketron, Ivan, S/Sgt,
Ketron, Ralph R., S/Sgt,
†Ketzko, Alexander G., Pvt,
†Keyes, Lester S., Pvt,
†Keyes, Orville F., Sgt,
§Kibert, Joseph D., Pfc,
Kibit, Edward, Pvt,
Kickhaefer, William A., Pfc,
Kicklighter, Ryloh, Pfc,
†Kidd, Cauley N., Pvt,
Kidd, Elmer C., Pvt,
Kidd, Hubert C., Pfc,
Kidd, Uriah, Pvt,
§Kidd, William F., Pvt,
†Kidwell, Robert N., Pvt,
Kiedaisch, Charles T., Pfc,
Kieffer, Carl J., Cpl,
Kiehl, Willis P., T/Sgt,
Kielar, Edward O., Pfc,
†Kielb, Joseph F., Pfc,
Kielian, Steve, Pfc,
Kieliszewski, Arthur J., Pfc,
§Kiely, Joseph J., 1st Lt,
Kiggins, Harry R., Pvt,
†Kilen, Theodore N., Sgt,
Kilgore, Andrew J., Jr., Pvt,
Kilgore, Connie G., Pfc,
Kilgore, James G., Pvt,
Kilgore, Roy J., S/Sgt,
Kilkenney, Thomas M., Pvt,
*Killebrew, Ellington, Pfc,
Kilpatrick, Johnnie T., Jr., Pvt,
Kimball, Dwight W., Capt,
Kimberlin, William H., Pfc,
Kimble, Harold J., S/Sgt,
Kimbrell, Donald L., S/Sgt,
†Kimbrelle, Otto E. L., Pfc,
†Kimbril, Levi, S/Sgt,
Kimmage, Michael, Jr., Pfc,
Kimple, Herman L., Jr., Cpl,
Kincade, Philip F., Pvt,
Kincaid, Lonnie S., Pvt,
Kincaid, Olney B., Pvt,
Kincaid, Robert W., Pvt,
Kinder, Carroll E., T/4,
Kinderman, George T., Pfc,
Kindlarski, Joseph, Cpl,
Kindle, Carlin D., Jr., Pfc,
†Kindt, Karl M., Jr., T/4,
King, Andrew L., Pvt,
King, Benny R., Pvt,
King, Buck N., 1st Lt,
King, Charles D., Pfc,
King, Clyde W., Pvt,
King, Donald J., Pvt,
King, Ector, Cpl,
King, Floyd A., Pfc,
King, Frank S., Pvt,
§King, Frederick A., Pvt,
King, George P., Cpl,
King, Homer, Pfc,
King, John E., 1st Lt,
King, John H., Pvt,
King, Lantie N., Pfc,
King, Marion E., Pvt,
King, Patrick J., Pvt,
King, Perry C., Pvt,
†King, Raphael W., S/Sgt,
†King, Raymond D., Sgt,
†King, Reuben W., Pvt,
King, Robert T., Pvt,
King, Sidney R., 1st Sgt,
King, Talmage M., Pfc,
King, William D., Pfc,
Kingan, Joseph W., S/Sgt,
†Kink, Albert J., Pvt,
Kinkelaar, Leo T., Pfc,
Kinne, James T., Pfc,
Kinney, William J., Pvt,
†Kinsella, Robert A., Pfc,
†Kinsley, John A., Pfc,
Kinter, Kenneth E., 2nd Lt,
Kinyon, Vern H., M/Sgt,
Kinz, Joseph W., Pfc,
†Kinzel, Charles L., Cpl,
†Kiphart, William A., 1st Sgt,
Kippert, Robert J., Pvt,
Kirby, Broadus E., Jr., Cpl,
Kirby, Donald G., Pfc,
Kirby, Paul, Pvt,
Kirby, William J., Pvt,
Kirchgessner, Nicholas T., Pfc,
†Kirchmeier, Paul A., Pvt,
Kirchoff, Lawrence L., Pvt,
Kirk, Arthur T., Pvt,
Kirk, Earl W., Jr., Pfc,
‡Kirk, Eugene P., 2nd Lt,
Kirk, Forrest A., Pfc,
Kirk, Johnny M., Pvt,
†Kirk, Junior I., Pfc,
Kirk, Leslie, Pfc,
‡Kirk, Raymond J., Sgt,
Kirkendall, Claude A., Pvt,
†Kirkland, Benjamin C., Pvt,
Kirkland, Homer D., Sgt,
Kirkland, James J., Pfc,
Kirkland, Robert W., Pfc,
Kirkland, Rufus C., Pfc,
Kirkland, William F., Pfc,
Kirkpatrick, Charles C., Pvt,
§Kirkpatrick, E. J., Pvt,
†Kirkpatrick, Robert A., Sgt,
Kirkpatrick, William C., Pfc,
*Kirschner, Richard B., Pfc,
†Kirtley, Kenneth W., Maj,
Kiser, Edgar R., T/5,
Kiser, Homer M., T/5,
Kishefsky, Gerald R., T/5,
Kissel, Marvin, Pvt,
Kissen, Martin D., Capt,
Kitchen, Cleth V., Cpl,
Kitchen, Earl M., Pfc,
Kitchen, Irvin A., Pvt,
Kitchen, Thomas E., Pvt,
Kitchens, Donald R., Pfc,
Kittleson, Delbert M., Pfc,
Kiwakowski, Walter, Pvt,
Kizer, Lee T., Sgt,
Kjorness, Robert F., Sgt,
Klancnik, Joseph, Pvt,
Klapp, James M., Pfc,
Klarman, Herman, Pvt,
Klass, John J., Pfc,
Klaus, Earl R., 1st Lt,
Klaus, Gerhardt, C., Pvt,
§Kleber, Charles E., Pvt,
Kleiman, Louis J., Pvt,
Kleiman, Morris M., Pvt,
Klein, Edward B., Cpl,
Klein, Harold E., Pvt,
Klein, Herman, Pvt,
Klein, Homer R., Pvt,
Klein, Wayne A., Cpl,
Kleinman, Forrest K., Capt,
Kleinschmidt, Robert J., T/Sgt,
Klemick, Daniel, Pfc,
Klemm, Joseph A., Pvt,
†Klimasz, Milton J., Pvt,
Klimaszewski, Joseph, Pvt,
Klimek, Thaddeus M., T/5,
†Klimock, Frank T., Pvt,
Kline, Franklin C., Pvt,
Kline, Henry J., Pvt,
†Kline, John J., Pvt,
Kline, Junior L., Pfc,
Klingaman, Boyd G., Pvt,
Klingenstein, Max, Pvt,
Klinger, George E., Sgt,
Klinger, George J., Pfc,
†Klinger, Stephen J., Cpl,
Klingler, Leroy L., Pvt,
Klingman, David B., Pvt,
*Klinkenborg, Ray J., 1st Lt,
Kloecker, Robert M., Pfc,
Klonkowski, Laurel G., Pfc,
Klonsky, Israel, Pvt,
Klont, Balfour N., Pfc,
Klopotek, Joe F., Pvt,
Kloss, John F., Pvt,
Kloster, Valentine J., Pfc,
Klous, Howard H., Pvt,
†Klovdahl, Carl J., Pfc,
Kluck, Joe, Pvt,
Kluttz, Homer G., Pfc,
Klysa, Michael, S/Sgt,
Kmetz, Joseph, Pvt,
Kmiec, Charles G., Pfc,
Knapp, Robert L., Pfc,
Knauer, Joseph, Pfc,
†Knaus, Gerald J., Pvt,
Kness, Donald E., Pfc,
‡Kniceley, Rendal M., Sr., Pvt,
§Knight, Albert H., Pfc,
Knight, Clarence E., Pfc,
†Knight, Eugene H., Pvt,
Knight, John L., Pfc,
Knight, Kenneth L., Pvt,
Knight, Richard, T/5,
Knight, Robert E., Pfc,
Knight, Robert K., S/Sgt,
Knight, Robert M., Pfc,
Knight, Robert, S/Sgt,
Knighton, John R., Pvt,
Knobloch, Henry W., Pfc,
Knobloch, Lawrence J., Pvt,
Knodel, Harry H., S/Sgt,
†Knoll, Arthur A., Jr., 2nd Lt,
Knoll, Elmer J., Pfc,
Knoll, Robert F., Pvt,
Knopfel, Carl F., Jr., T/5,
§Knotts, L. V., Pvt,
Knowles, James J., S/Sgt,
Knowles, Lynn J., T/5,
Knowles, Wilbur R., Pfc,
Knudsen, Carl C., Jr., Pvt,
Knutson, Andrew T., Pvt,
Knutson, Lester L., Pfc,
†Knutson, Severt, T/5,
Kobak, Peter P., Sgt,
Kobas, Victor D., Pvt,
Kobes, Frank J., Jr., Major,
†Kobistek, Charles M., Pfc,
Kobrinski, Edward J., Pvt,
Kobus, Chester A., Pvt,
Kobylak, Joe, Pfc,
†Koch, Albert P., S/Sgt,
Koch, Edward, Pfc,
Kochera, Joseph T., T/Sgt,
Kochevar, Jack, Pfc,
Kochinski, Julius, Pfc,
Kocken, Cornelius, S/Sgt,
Koczman, Gustave P., T/5,
Koehn, Elton S., Pfc,
Koenig, Edward H., Pfc,
Koepke, Richard A., 1st Lt,
Koeppel, Edouard J., Pfc,
Koering, Arthur C., T/4,
Koger, Donald Lavelle E., Pfc,
Kokoszka, Louis J., Pfc,
Kolanko, Bernard, Pfc,
Kolb, George J., Pvt,
Kolbe, Alfred C., Pfc,
†Kolerus, James H., Pvt,
§Kolesar, Michael, Pvt,
Kolski, Clarence C., S/Sgt,
Kolka, Donald J., Pfc,
Koller, Francis J., Pvt,
Kolodziej, Edward J., Pvt,
Kolodzieski, Benjamin M., Pvt,
Koloski, Harry C., Pfc,
Kolsun, Peter, Pfc,
Kolva, Paul E., S/Sgt,
Komar, Raymond F., Cpl,
Komlanc, Joseph F., Pvt,
Koncar, John C., Cpl,
Konchesky, Stanley, Sgt,
Konik, Walter M., Pvt,
Konopko, Conrad, Pvt,
Kooperman, David, Pvt,
§Koorie, Louis K., Pvt,
‡Kopcheck, John J., Pvt,
Kopchik, Alexander, T/4,
Kopelman, Herbert, Pvt,
Kopelman, Sidney, Sgt,
Koprowski, Mitchell J., Capt,
Korb, Dale O., Pvt,
†Kordon, William I., Pvt,
Korinek, Frank T., T/5,
Korischar, George P., Pfc,
Korkin, Abraham, Pfc,
Korosec, Joseph J., Pvt,
Korzeniowski, Michael F., Pvt,
Koscielski, Valentine B., Pvt,
Kosel, Ernest R., Pfc,
†Koshkin, Eugene S., 2nd Lt,
†Kosicki, John, Sgt,
Kossow, Leo F., S/Sgt,
†Koste, Albert L., Pvt,
†Kostick, George J., Pvt,
Kostrzewski, Stanley T., Pvt,
†Kostus, Louis L., Pvt,
†Kotash, John S., Pfc,
Kotchey, Robert C., Pvt,
Kotchka, Nick, Pfc,
Kotowich, Adam, Sgt.
Kouba, Franklin J., Pfc,
Kouba, Richard G., Pvt,
Koukal, Earl W., S/Sgt,
†Koutnik, Russell E., Pfc,
†Kovacevich, Dan, Pfc,
Kovach, John, Pfc,
Kovacs, Anthony F., Pvt,
Kowalchick, Metro, Sgt,
Kowalcyn, William J., Pvt,
Kowalik, Michael, Jr., M/Sgt,
Kowalkowski, R. P., Pfc,
Kowalski, Frank T., Pvt,
Kowalski, Mickey S., Pvt,
Kowalski, Theodore L., Pfc,
Kowalski, William F., Pfc,
Kozak, John M., Pvt,
†Kozicki, John, Sgt
Kozlik, Joseph F., Jr., Pfc,
Kozloski, Chester P., Pfc,
Kozma, Albert, Pvt,
Kozma, Joseph, Pfc,
Kraft, Christian W., Pfc,
Kraft, Leo C., Pvt,
Kraft, LeRoy A., Pvt,
*Krainz, Joseph H., Pvt,
Krajcech, Joseph, T/4,
Krajewski, Bennie, Pfc,
Krajewski, Emole, Pvt,
Krakowski, Leonard J., Pvt,
Kralian, Aaron, Pvt,
Kralj, Joseph, Jr., Pfc,
Kram, Benjamin, Pvt,
†Kramer, Dickie V., Pvt,
Kramer, Leon A., Pvt
Kramer, Lynn D., Sgt,
Kramer, Oscar D., Pvt,
Kramlich, Ewold, S/Sgt,
Krammes, Glenn L., Pfc,
Kranz, Robert C., Pvt,
Krasner, Sidney, Pvt,
Krason, Melvin S., Pfc,
Kratochvil, Ben, Pfc,
Kratzar, Floyd D., Pvt,
Kraucalis, Joseph J., Pvt,
Krause, Archie C., Pvt,
Krause, Bernard J., Pfc,
Krause, Edward F., Pfc,
Krause, Edwin F., S/Sgt,
Krause, Harry F., Sgt,
Krause, Henry C., Pvt,
Krause, Robert F., Pvt,
Krebs, Earl R., Sgt,
Krebs, Robert C., Cpl,
Krecker, August W., Pfc,
Kreckler, Paul V., Pvt,
Kreidberg, Marvin S., Maj,
Krell, Henry O., Jr., Pvt,
Krepitch, Michael, Pvt,
Kreten, Henry P., S/Sgt,
Krichbaum, Milo D., 1st Lt,
Krieger, Alfred R., Cpl,
Krieger, Wilbert E., T/Sgt,
Kreigisch, Leonard C., T/5,
Krill, Albert J., Pvt,
Kring, Robert E., Pvt,
†Kristoff, Steve J., Pfc,
†Krivtz, Rudulf, Jr., Sgt,
Kroger, Paul, Pvt,
Krok, John S., S/Sgt,
Krolick, Frank J., S/Sgt,
Krolikowski, Anthony G., Pfc,
†Krolikowski, Sylvester L., Pfc,
†Kroll, Robert F., Pvt,
Krom, Arthur D., Jr., Pvt,
Kropp, Walter H., Capt,
*Kroviak, Richard C., Pvt,
Krpata, John, S/Sgt,
†Krpata, Leo, Jr., S/Sgt,
†Kruck, Bohdan, Pvt,
†Kruder, Robert G., Pvt,
Krueger, Daniel, Pvt,
Krueger, William G., Sgt,
Kruger, Louis F., Pfc,
‡Krum, Max R., Pvt,
Krumweide, Darnell M., Pfc,
Krupansky, Stephen F., Pvt
‡Krupp, Wilbur R., Sgt,
Kubin, Frank, Pfc,
Kucera, Joe W., Sgt,
Kuczynski, Casior S., Pvt,
Kudelich, George, Pvt,
Kuehn, Walter H., S/Sgt,
§Kuehner, John P., Jr., Pvt
Kuester, George, Pvt,
§Kuhaneck, Vernie J., Pvt,
†Kuhl, Edward L., Jr., Pvt,
Kuhl, William L., Pfc,
Kuhlker, Henry G., Pvt,
Kuhlmann, Oto R., Pvt,
Kuhn, Marshall L., Pvt,
Kuhn, Robert A., Pvt,
Kuhn, Roy A., T/5,
Kuhnel, George C., Pfc,
Kujanpaa, Toivo J., Pfc,
Kujawa, Vincent A., Pfc,
Kulesa, Joseph, Pvt,
Kukilausaks, William C., Pvt,
†Kulisich, Bernard J., Pvt,
Kulnis, Edward R., S/Sgt,
Kulon, Mathew, Pfc,
†Kummer, James A., Sgt,
Kuner, Martin, Pfc,
Kunert, George C., S/Sgt,
Kunes, Kenneth P., T/5,
§Kunsaltis, Frank L., Pvt,
Kuntz, Stanley S., S/Sgt,
Kunz, Melvin C., Pvt,
Kurgan, Frederick P.,
Kurkewich, LeRoy J., Pvt,
Kurkland, Paul, Pfc,
Kurtz, Roy A., 1st Sgt,
Kurzen, Arnold, Sgt,
Kushner, Lucus, Pfc,
Kusmiak, Eugene, CWO,
Kuta, Alfred M., S/Sgt,
Kutcher, James, Pfc,
Kuti, John P., Pfc,
§Kutz, Max J., Pvt,
Kuzia, Francis B., Pfc,
†Kuzmich, William, Pfc,
Kvaka, John J., Pvt,
Kvasnyak, Alexander, Pvt,
Kwiatkowski, Edmund, Pfc,
Kwilinski, Florian H., Pfc,
Kyle, Kenneth L., Pfc,
Kyle, Woods B., Jr., 1st Lt,

Laabs, Paul L., Pvt,
La Barbera, Vito J., Pvt,
La Barge, Raymond J., Pvt,
La Bell, Alfred J., Pfc,
La Bella, Verdi P., Pfc,
La Blanc, Gerald C., S/Sgt,
Laboch, Harry, Pfc,
LaBonte, Leo W., Pvt,
Laborde, Lawrence C., Pvt
Labowski, Stephen, Pvt,
LaBrack, Earle F., T/5,
Labrum, Walter W., Pvt,
LaBruno, Alfonso J., Pvt,
LaButa, George J., S/Sgt,
Lacey, George E., S/Sgt.
Lach, John E., Pfc,
LaChance, Fred J., Pvt,
Lacher, Albert V., Jr., Pfc,
Lackey, Fred, Pfc,
Lackman, James W., 1st Lt,
LaCorte, James W., Pvt,
Lacy, John R., Pvt,
Laczenski, Stephen A., Pfc,
Ladd, Bob H., Pvt,
Ladd, Clifford A., T/Sgt,
Ladd, Warren S., Pfc
Laffere, Charles J., Pfc,
†LaFlash, David E., Pfc,
§Lafler, Lonnie R., Sgt,
LaFleur, Raymond F., T/5,
La Fontaine, Arthur J., Pvt,
La Fountain, Raymond L., Sgt,
La Francois, Rene J., Pvt,
†LaGace, Raymond G., Pvt,
LaGana, Ferdinand J., Pvt,
‡Lagonterie, Albert L., Pvt,
†Lagozzino, Mike, T/5,
Lahmann, Kenneth R., Pvt,
Lail, Terrell M., Pfc,
Laino, Anthony, Pvt,
Lair, Raymond R., Pvt,
†Laitres, Alfred J., Pfc,
Lake, Davis R., Pfc,
Lalaian, Suren J., Pfc,
Lalima, Salvatore T., Pvt,
Lalomio, Angelo J., Pfc,
Lamaack, Roy H., Pvt,
LaMar, Raymond J., Cpl,
Lamb, Donald E., Sgt,
Lamb, Rex B., Pfc,
Lambert, Ellwood R., 2nd Lt,
Lambert, Joseph A., Pfc,
Lambert, Walter E., Pfc,
Lamberth, William I., Pfc,
Lambranakes, Louis, Pvt,
Lambson, Richard C., Pvt,
§Lamm, Willis L., Pfc,
§Lamma, David O., Pvt,
†Lamonica, Joseph, Pfc,
LaMont, Jack L., Sgt,
Lamotte, Walton L., Pvt,
LaMountain, Raymond P., Pvt,
LaMoureux, Raymond O., Pfc,
Lamp, Alvin H., Jr., Pfc,
†Lamster, Alfred C., Jr., Pfc,
Lancaster, John D., Pfc,
Lancaster, John R., Jr., Pvt,
Lanclos, Lois J., T/5,
Lancour, Alexander C., Pvt,
Lancucki, Marion T., Cpl,
Land, William F., Pvt,
Landekil, Norman T., Pfc,
Lander, Irvine, Pvt,
Lander, Luther E., T/5,
Landers, Calvin H., T/5,
†Landers, Thomas J., Pvt,
Landesberg, Samuel L., Pfc,
Landingham, George E., Pvt,
Landis, Clair E., Pvt,
Landis, Walter R., S/Sgt,
§Landon, Ralph R., Sgt,
Landrum, Ernest C., Pvt,
Landrum, Gussie, Pvt,
Landry, Vernard B., Pvt,
Landwer, Clifford H., Pfc,
Lane, Alvin R., Pfc,
Lane, David B., Pvt,
Lane, Franklin K., T/5,
Lane, James A., Pfc,
Lane, Samie C., Pvt,
Lane, Victor K., S/Sgt,
Lane, William Y., Pvt,
†Laneri, Angelo P., Pfc,
Lang, Joseph P., Pvt,
Lang, Robert, Pvt,
Lang, Roy H., Pvt,
Lange, Edward F., Pvt,
Lange, Maynard A., S/Sgt,
Lange, Robert A., Pvt.

† Killed in Action. * Prisoner of War. ‡ Missing in Action. § Died of Wounds.

Langford, Glenn A., Pvt
Langford, John C., Pfc,
Langlois, Paul G., Pvt,
Langhorst, William J., Pfc,
Langille, Cletus A., Pfc,
Lanier, Albert L., Pvt,
Lanier, Irvin R., Pvt,
Lanier, Robert M., Pvt,
†Lanigan, Neal, S/Sgt,
Lankford, James M., Pvt,
Lankford, Jonathan H., Pfc,
*Lano, Salvatore J., Pfc,
Lansky, Alen I., Pvt,
Lant, Carroll D., Pvt,
Lanter, Loren E., T/4,
Lanzaro, Daniel, Pfc,
Lapeyrouse, Nestor G., Sgt,
LaPidus, Howard P., Pvt,
Lapin, Frank J., Pfc,
LaPlante, Clarence A., Pvt,
La Point, Leo A., Pvt,
La Point, Peter R., Pfc,
LaPolla, Salvatore C., Pvt,
LaPorte, Alphonse F., Pfc,
Lara, Candelario, Pvt,
Larabee, Louis H., Pvt,
Larence, Robert J., Pfc,
Large, William E., Cpl,
Largo, Pablo, Pvt,
Larkin, Arthur V., Pvt,
Larochelle, Armand J. H., Pfc,
†LaRocque, Maurice T., Pfc,
†Larounis, John, Pvt,
Larrimer, James C., S/Sgt,
Larsen, Alfred E., Pvt,
Larsen, Allen D., Pvt,
Larsen, Chester V., Cpl,
Larsen, Harry R., Pfc,
Larsen, Leonard, Pvt,
Larsen, Thomas A., 1st Lt,
Larsen, Tommie, J., Pvt,
Larson, Andrew J., Pfc,
Larson, Arthur G., Pvt,
Larson, Harold F., Pvt,
Larson, Louis A., Pfc,
Larson, Lowell D., Pvt,
Larson, Melvin F., Pfc,
Larson, Milton E., Pfc,
Larson, Odin M., Pvt,
Larson, Reuben C., 1st Sgt,
Larson, Stanley M. D., Pfc,
Larson, Trygive G., Pvt,
Larson, Ward, Pvt,
LaRussa, John J., T/5,
Larweck, Franklyn A., Pvt,
Lasater, J. W., Pvt,
La Shance, Donald E., S/Sgt,
Lasiter, Donald T., Pvt,
Lasko, Arthur S., S/Sgt,
Laskowski, Casimer J., Pvt,
Laskowski, Edward F., Pfc,
Laskowski, Leo A., Sgt,
Laskowski, Theodore J., Sgt,
Lasley, Edgar, Pvt,
Lasley, Ernest M., Pvt,
†Laster, Charles F., Pfc,
Lastinger, M. D., Pfc,
Laston, Donald J., Pfc,
LaTender, Sylvester J., Pfc,
Latham, Royal W., Pfc,
Latraverse, Robert J. P., Pfc,
‡Lattanzio, Theodore, Pfc,
Laubach, Glen E., Pvt,
Lauble, Raymond H., Pvt,
Laudato, Carl E., T/Sgt,
Lauer, Charles E., Cpl,
Lauer, John F., Pvt,
Laughlin, V. W., Jr., Pvt,
Laughlin, Virgil V., Maj,
Laughner, Frank B., Pfc,
Laura, Henry E., Pvt,
Lauria, Albert, Pvt,
Laurie, Eugene C., Pvt,
Lautzenhiser, Glen G., Pfc
Lauzon, Martin E., Pfc,
LaValle, Albert L., Pfc,
LaValle, John R., T/5,
Lavandor, Edward J., Pfc,
†Lavelle, John E., T/5,
Lavender, Oliver E., Sgt,
Lavigne, Norman E., Pvt,
Lavin, John L., Pfc,
LaVoie, Lawrence, Sgt,
LaVoie, Lionel C., Pfc,
LaVoie, Ovila J., Pfc,
Law, Bobby L., Pvt,
Law, Russell S., Pfc,
†Lawless, Michael F., Jr., Pvt,
†Lawley, James J., T/5,
Lawlor, John H., Pfc,
Lawrence, Alvin E., Pvt,
Lawrence, Harry A., Jr., Pvt,
Lawrence, Robert B., 1st Lt,
Lawrence, Russell E., Pvt,

Lawrence, Wallace E., T/Sgt,
Lawrence, William C., Cpl,
Lawrence, William J., Pvt,
Lawrie, John, Pfc,
Laws, Billy C., Pvt,
Lawson, Arthur L., Jr., Pvt,
Lawson, Charles J., Pvt,
Lawson, James, Pfc,
Lawson, Reed H., Pfc,
Lawson, Roney L., Pvt,
Lave, John E., Pvt,
Layne, Harry, Sgt,
Layton, Eugene B., Pfc,
Lazenby, Lester S., Pvt,
Lazowski, Anthony, S/Sgt,
Lazzari, Gino L., Pfc,
Lazzell, Sidney W., Pvt,
Leach, Francis M., T/Sgt,
Leach, John T., Pvt,
Leach, Gerald D., Pvt,
Leaf, Roy F., T/4,
Leake, Ernest C., 2nd Lt,
†Leake, William J., S/Sgt,
Leal, Augustine C., Cpl,
Leal, Robert M., Pvt,
†Leaman, William F., Cpl,
Leaming, Andrew W., Capt,
Lear, Robert L., Pfc,
Lebahn, John E., Sgt,
Lebiak, Peter, Pfc,
LeBlanc, Bernard J., S/Sgt,
Leblanc, George A., Pfc,
LeBlanc, Gerald C., T/Sgt,
Lebowitz, Julian L., S/Sgt,
†Lebrecht, Alfred W., Pvt,
LeBrun, LeRoy J., S/Sgt,
LeClair, Raymond R., Pfc,
LeClair, Wilbra J., Pvt,
LeCocq, Warren, Pvt,
Leddy, Martin P., Pvt,
Ledford, Clifford A., 1st Sgt,
Ledford, Oscar L., Pfc,
Ledford, William, Jr.,
Leduc, Roland P., Pvt,
Lee, Alton, Cpl,
Lee, Charles J., Pvt,
Lee, Clarence, Pvt,
*Lee, Dennis C. L., Pvt,
Lee, Edward M., Pfc,
Lee, Everett L., Pvt,
Lee, George G., Sr., Pvt,
Lee, Gordon M., Pvt,
Lee, Harvey G., Pfc,
Lee, James E., Pfc,
Lee, Leonard J., Pfc,
Lee, Leonard W., Pvt,
Lee, Lester E., T/5,
Lee, Roger W., Pfc,
§Lee, Russell J., Pfc,
Lee, William W., Pfc,
Lee, Wilmer L., 1st Lt,
Leech, Andrew R., Pvt,
Leerhoff, Victor D., Pvt,
Lees, Donald G., T/5,
Leese, John H., Pfc,
Lefchich, John, Pfc,
LeFevere, Alfonse G., Pfc
LeFevre, Robert C., Pvt,
LeFore, Aaron, T/5,
Legault, Harvey V., Pfc,
†Leger, Eugene H., Pvt,
Legere, Cline F., Pvt,
Legere, Maurice A., Pfc,
†Legerides, Efstrauor, Pfc,
Legg, Paul W., S/Sgt,
Legg, Robert L., Capt,
Leggio, Vincent N., Pvt,
Legrange, Clifford J., Pfc,
Lehman, Ralph A., Jr., Pfc,
†Lehman, Walter, Pfc,
Lehotsky, Herman S., Pvt,
Leiby, Warren H., Pfc,
Leichty, Raymond, T/5,
Leigh, John L., Pfc,
Leikvoll, Reynold E., Pvt,
Leinen, Loren F., Sgt,
Leiner, Gerhard P., Pvt,
Leipold, William C., 1st Lt,
Leitch, Russell O., Pvt,
Leithner, Joseph W., Jr., S/Sgt
Leizear, Lownes S., Pfc
Lela, Frank, Pvt,
Lelak, Steven C., T/Sgt,
Lem, William Q. H., Pvt,
Lemanski, Joseph P., Pvt,
†LeMaster, Ross C., Pvt,
Leming, Donald, Pvt,
Lemmerz, Olof L., Pvt,
Lemons, Jay L., Cpl,
Lempert, Jacob A., Pvt,
Lempicki, Joseph, T/Sgt,
Lenahan, Daniel W., Jr.,
Lendway, Stephen J., Pfc,
Lengele, Arthur V., Cpl,

Lenhart, Elmer F., Pfc,
Lenhart, John J., Cpl,
Lenius, Carl J., Pvt,
Lennander, Leroy C., Pfc,
Lenninger, George, Pvt,
Lenz, Floyd A., Pvt,
Lenz, George A., Pfc,
Lenzen, Raymond A., Pfc,
†Leo, Francis F., Pfc,
Leon, Neil, Pvt,
Leonard, Clare J., Jr., Pfc,
Leonard, George W., Pvt,
Leonard, James D., Pvt,
Leonard, Norman H., Pfc,
Leonard, Pierce J., Pfc,
Leonard, Robert H., Jr., Pfc,
†Leonard, William F., T/5,
Leone, Peter A., Pvt,
Leong, George G., Pfc,
Leotta, Salvatore A., Pfc,
LePage, Eli F., Pfc,
Lepper, Jack D., Pvt,
Leptien, Albert W., Pvt,
Lerman, Nat, Pvt,
Leshiewski, A. A., T/4,
§Lesko, Rudolph P., Pfc,
Leslie, Dallard, Pfc,
Lessard, Eugene A., Pvt,
Lessard, Joseph E., Pvt,
Lesse, John H., Pfc,
Lester, Donald T., T/5,
Lester, Mike J., Pvt,
Lester, Thomas D., 1st Lt,
Lester, William F., Pvt,
Letcavage, Lewis A., Pfc,
†Letcher, Marion M., Pfc,
Letson, Fred L., Pvt,
Leuthold, William F., Pfc,
Levi, Heinz, 1st Lt,
Levin, Abraham, Pvt,
Levin, Hyman S., Pvt,
Levin, Joseph I., Pfc,
Levin, Raphael A., 1st Lt
Levine, Arthur, Cpl,
Levine, Bernard P., Pvt,
†Levine, David I., Pvt,
Levine, Joseph, Pvt,
Levine, Joseph, Pvt,
Levine, Milton, S/Sgt,
Levine, Sidney, Pvt,
†Levine, Stanley I., Pvt,
Levinson, Irwin T., Pvt,
Levy, Irvin, Sgt,
*Levy, Samuel, Pvt,
Lew, Tow S., Pfc,
Lewandowski, Chester W., Sgt,
Lewandowski, Wallace L., Pvt,
Lewellen, Joseph C., Pvt,
Lewis, Barney L., Pfc,
Lewis, Byon P., T/Sgt,
Lewis, Clyde L., Pfc,
Lewis, Creslie W., Cpl,
Lewis, Donald E., Pfc,
Lewis, Donald W., Pvt,
†Lewis, Fred, Pvt,
Lewis, Harold E., 1st Lt,
Lewis, Henry, Pfc,
Lewis, James H., 1st Lt,
Lewis, Joseph M., Pfc,
Lewis Kenneth D. T/4,
Lewis, LeRoy, Cpl,
†Lewis, Michael B., Pfc,
Lewis, Norman S., Pvt,
Lewis, Ralph W., T/4,
†Lewis, Robert L., Pfc,
Lewis, Robert N., Pfc,
Lewis, Roy A., Pvt,
Lewis, Virgil L., Lt Col,
Lewis, William D., Sgt,
Lewis, William H., Pfc,
Lewis, William L., Pvt,
Lewis, William R., M/Sgt,
Lewter, Ralph J., Pfc,
Lezaj, William J., Pvt,
L'Herbier, Harry, Pvt,
L'Heureux, Henry G., Pvt,
†Lian, Leonard T., Pvt,
Lian, Luverne J., Pfc,
Liane, Leo C., Pvt,
Libby, Ralph D., Cpl,
Libecap, Charles H., Pfc,
Liberman, Marvin J., Pfc,
Liberto, Joseph P., Pfc,
Librizzi, Joseph, Pfc,
Lichtle, Paul A., Pfc,
Liddell, Clyde R., Pfc,
Liddick, Harold J., Pvt,
Liebe, Albert V., Pfc,
Liebe, Donald H., Major,
Liebenow, Charles A., Pfc,
Lieberman, Alex, Pvt,
Lieberman, Carl E., Pvt,
Lieberman, Harry G., Capt,
Liebman, George R., Cpl,

Lien, Chester L., T/5,
Lien, Robert B., Cpl,
Lieske, LeRoy E., Pfc,
†Lifschitz, Harry, Pvt,
Ligarski, Stanley, Jr., Pfc,
Light, Harry A., Pvt,
Light, Raymond D., Pvt,
†Light, William E., Pvt,
Lightfoot, John A., Pfc,
Ligon, Marvin L., Pvt,
Ligosky, Dimitri A., T/4,
Ligouri, Anthony J., Pvt,
Ligouri, Leonard A., Pfc,
Likovich, William J., Jr., Pvt,
Lilak, Joseph C., Pfc,
Liles, Roy M., Pfc,
Liles, Samuel, Pvt,
Lillejord, Henry M., Pfc,
Lillie, Roy L., Pvt,
Lilly, Clarence H., T/5,
Lilly, Milton E., Pvt,
Limbaugh, James M., Cpl,
§Limoncelli, Matthew G., Sgt,
Linam, Marvin G., Pfc,
Lind, Harold, Pvt,
Lind, Nels E., T/5,
Lindaas, Donald W., Pvt,
Lindberg, Edward M., Pfc,
Lindberg, Wesley G., Pvt,
Lindbohm, Bernard A., T/5,
Lindenberg, Alfred C., Pfc,
Lindenberg, Wilbert H., Pvt,
Linder, Jesse L., Pvt,
*Lindh, George P., Pvt,
Lindley, Elmer H., S/Sgt,
†Lindley, Raymond A., Pfc,
Lindner, William J., T/5,
Lindsay, John E., 1st Lt,
Lindsey, Frank E., Pvt,
Lindsley, Merl C., 1st Lt,
Lineback, Roy M., Pfc,
Liner, James H., Pfc,
Ling, Norman C., T/4,
†Lingle, George, Pfc,
Linker, Henry, Pvt,
†Linker, Morrison L., Pvt,
Linkey, Jerry D., Pvt,
Linley, Robert L., Pfc,
†Linn, Howard C., Pvt,
†Linneman, John J., 2nd Lt,
Lint, Lawrence H., Pvt,
Linton, Joseph B., Jr., Pvt,
*Linville, Wayne A., Cpl,
Linzmeier, Louis J., Pvt,
Lipinski, Stanley J., Pvt,
Lipkind, Marvin L., Pvt,
Lipowski, Bernard, Cpl,
Lippencott, Bert N., T/5,
Lippincott, Frank J., Pfc,
†Lippstreuer, Robert F., T/5,
Lipschitz, Milton I., Pvt,
Lis, Florian, S/Sgt,
Lisby, William R., Pfc,
Lisinichia, Nicholas, Pvt,
Lisowski, Walter, Cpl,
Lissauer, Hans J., Pvt,
Litson, Garland D., Sgt,
Little, Robert I., Pfc,
Littlebird, Harry P., Pvt,
Littleton, James G., Pvt,
†Litwak, Hyman, Pfc,
Litz, Edmund R., Pvt,
Livas, Theodore S., Pfc,
Lively, Robert L., T/Sgt,
Livermore, Edward D., Pvt,
Livingston, Ralph E., Pvt,
Livingstone, Daniel W., Pvt,
Livorsi, Marlo J., Pvt,
Livsey, Maitland, T/5,
Lizzo, Benjamin J., Pvt,
†Llamas, Jesus S., Sgt,
Llewellyn, Coleman H., Pfc,
§Llorens, Oswaldo A., Pvt,
Lloyd, Frank H., Pfc,
Lloyd, James H., Pvt,
Lloyd, Thomas D., S/Sgt,
Loane, Joseph T., Jr., Pfc,
Lochmann, Roger R., Pvt,
Lockaby, Louis, Pfc,
Locke, Elwood H., Pfc,
Lockett, Andrew J., Cpl,
Lockett, William H., Jr., Pvt,
Lockhart, J. C., T/5,
Lockhart, Lother T. J., Pvt,
Locklear, William G., S/Sgt,
Lockridge, John W., Pvt,
†Lockwood, Francis T., Pfc,
Lockwood, Richard M., Pfc,
Loeffler, Kurt E., Pfc,
Loethen, Harold L., Pvt,
Loewe, Lester A., Pvt,
†Lofaso, Frank J., Pfc,
Loff, Lewis M., S/Sgt,
Loforti, Frank J., Pvt,

Loft, John W., Pvt,
Loftin, William D., Pvt,
†Loftis, Howard D., S/Sgt,
Logan, Fred F., Pvt,
Logan, George, T/Sgt,
Logan, Lawrence, Pvt,
Logan, Lewis A., Pvt,
Logan, Roy K., Pfc,
Lo Giudice, Vincent P., Pfc,
Logsdon, James B., Pfc,
Lohmann, Harvey W., T/5,
Lollar, Hardy A., Pfc,
Lomison, John G., Pfc,
Lommori, Joseph P., Capt,
Lonergan, Edmond F., Jr., T/5,
Lonero, Ralph A., Pvt,
Lones, Bert J., S/Sgt,
†Long, Adolph E., Sgt,
Long, Homer D., Pvt,
Long, Huey L., Pvt,
†Long, Joe, Jr., Pfc,
Long, Joseph V., S/Sgt,
Long, Lawrence G., Sgt,
†Long, Lawrence L., Pfc,
Long, Louis G., Pvt,
†Long, Luther B., Pvt,
Long, Murray B., Pfc,
Long, Oscar, Pfc,
Long, Robert M., Pfc,
Long, Roland J., 1st Lt,
Long, Roy R., Pfc,
Long, William A., Sgt,
Long, William G., 1st Lt,
Longeor, Roland E., Pfc,
Longo, Carmen, Cpl,
*Longoria, Guadalupe G., Pvt,
Longoria, Jesus, Pfc,
Lookenbill, Roy E., Pfc,
Loomis, Everett L., Pfc,
Looney, J. C., Pfc,
Loos, John N., Pvt,
Lopata, Zalman A., Pvt,
Lopes, Albert V., 1st Sgt,
Lopes, Peter, Pfc,
Lopez, Anthony, Pvt,
Lopez, John C., Pvt,
Lopez, Roy S., Pfc,
Lo Presti, John P., Pvt,
Lopristi, Sam S., Pvt,
Lord, William A., Pvt,
Lorenz, Harry, Pfc,
Lorenzana, Mike D., Sgt,
Lorusso, Daniel P., Pvt,
†Losey, James E., Sgt,
Lossing, Ernest J., Sgt,
Lotarski, Walter R., Pfc,
Lothrop, Jack W., 2nd Lt,
Lotito, Nicholas, Pfc,
†Lotspeich, Dave C., Pvt,
Lott, Charles R., Pfc,
Lottridge, Allen K., S/Sgt,
Loud, Daniel J., Pvt,
Loudermilk, George T., Pfc,
Loudin, Milford G., Sgt,
Lough, Hugh G., Pvt,
Loughlin, James J., Sgt,
Loughman, Francis X., Pvt,
Louisell, Robert W., Pfc,
Loundy, Abe, Pfc,
Louser, Russell E., Pfc,
†Lousignont, Vernon F., Pfc,
Lovallo, Joseph G., Pfc,
Lovallo, Vito G., Pfc,
†Lovascio, James J., Pfc,
Lovato, Fred, Pvt,
Love, Ben, T/4,
Love, Clyde V., Pfc,
Love, Herman A., Pvt,
Love, John R., Pvt,
Love, Lawrence W., Pfc,
Love, Leroy E., Pvt,
Love, Robert A., T/Sgt,
Loveall, John P., Jr., Pfc,
Loveday, Milton, Pfc,
Lovejoy, Myrle H., Sgt,
Lovelace, Fred, Sgt,
Loveless, Gilbert C., S/Sgt,
Lovell, Atlas A., Pfc,
Lovelock, Joseph F., Pvt,
†Lovino, Benjamin L., Pvt,
Lovoy, Henry A., Pvt,
Lowen, James M., Pvt,
Lowery, Arlen W., Pfc,
Lowery, Carl A. B., Pvt,
‡Lowery, Herman M., Pfc,
Lowery, Kenneth J., Pfc,
Lowery, Roye L., Pfc,
Lowrey, Edd F., Pvt,
†Lowrey, Johnnie P., Pfc,
Lowrey, William M., Pvt,
Loy, James E., Sr., Pvt,
Loyd, Herman C., Pvt,
Lozano, Leopoldo C., Pfc,
Lozier, Edward H., Pfc,

† Killed in Action. * Prisoner of War. ‡ Missing in Action. § Died of Wounds.

Luba, Archie D., Pvt,
Lubas, Leo J., Sgt,
Lubbers, Paul R., Pvt,
Lubbes, Charles B., T/5,
Luca, Angelo N., Pfc,
Lucas, Albertus, Pvt,
Lucas, Benjamin F., Pvt,
Lucas, Floyd J., Pfc,
Lucas, Grady F., T/4,
Lucas, Howard R., Pvt,
Lucas, Thomas E., Pvt,
Lucas, William E., Pvt,
Lucero, Jose S., Pvt,
Lucia, Felice F., Sgt,
Lucido, Samuel J., T/5,
Lucisano, Frank A., Sgt,
Ludemann, John, Pfc,
Ludwig, Daniel E., Pvt,
Ludwig, Norman L., T/5,
Ludwig, Roland F., Cpl,
Ludy, Roland R., Pfc,
Luebeck, John A., T/4,
Luecht, Robert E., S/Sgt,
Lukaszewski, Edmund R., Pvt,
Lukatch, John J., Pfc,
Lukosevicius, Bronis A., Pfc,
Lule, Luis T., Pfc,
Lummis, Cyrus R., Pvt,
Lump, Frank C., Pvt,
Lunder, Robert T., Pvt,
Lundquist, Richard J., Pvt,
Lundquist, Roy W., 1st Lt,
Lundstedt, Ralph N., Pvt,
Lundy, Grant A., Pfc,
Lundy, Roscoe L., Pvt,
Lundy, William R., Pvt,
†Lunsford, Frank J., T/Sgt,
Lupachino, Carl M., Pvt,
Luparella, Joseph, Pfc,
Lupo, Pontaleo, Pvt,
Lusby, Joseph C., 2nd Lt,
Lusk, Earl G., Pvt,
Lusk, John S., Pfc,
Luss, Irving C., Pfc
Lutgen, Orville F., Pfc,
†Luttrel, John E., Cpl,
Luttrell, James A., 2nd Lt,
Luttrell, James R., Pfc,
Lutz, John A., T/4,
Lutz, William D., Pvt,
Lybarger, Franklin R., 1st Lt,
†Lybrand, Carl M., Sgt,
Lykins, Eugene C., Pfc
Lyles, Richard D., Cpl,
Lynah, Joseph F., Pvt,
Lynas, Ward D., Pvt,
†Lynch, Arnold, Pfc,
Lynch, Charles J., S/Sgt,
Lynch, Gerald G., Sgt,
Lynch, Harrison R., Cpl,
Lynch, Henry N., Pvt,
Lynch, John J., Pvt,
Lynch, Kenneth D., Pfc,
†Lynch, Leo E., T/5,
Lynch, Leo E., T/5,
Lynch, Leonard M., Pfc,
Lynch, Robert C., Pfc,
Lynch, Robert E., Cpl,
Lynch, Rodger W., Pfc,
Lynn, James L., Pfc,
Lyon, Ray, Pvt,
Lyon, Raymond C., T/5,
Lyons, Cecil J., Pfc,
Lyons, Cornelius M., Jr., T/5,
Lyons, Lauren O., Pvt,
Lyons, Melvin M., Pvt,
Lyons, Orland W., Pvt,
Lytle, Hallam J., Pfc,
Lytle, Virgil L., Pfc,

Mabry, James L., Pvt,
Mabry, Joseph M., Pfc,
Macak, Arthur A., Pvt,
MacArthur, K. R., Capt,
§Macca, Rosario, Pvt,
Maccarone, Peter F., Pvt,
†MacDonnell, Charles J., Pvt
Mace, Dewey, Pfc,
†Macejka, Anthony, Pvt,
Macey, Ivan J., T/4,
MacGregor, Donald E., Pfc,
Machette, David J., Pfc,
Macht, Adam N., Pfc,
MacIntosh, Cletus J., Cpl,
MacIntosh, Harry C., Pvt,
MacIntyre, Norman J., T/Sgt,
†Macio, Patsy, Pvt,
Mack, Bernard L., Pvt,
Mack, Charles R., Cpl
Mack, Floyd D., Cpl,
Mack, Robert S., 2nd Lt
MacKercher, John A., T/Sgt,
Mackey, Eino, Sgt,
Mackey, Norman G., Pvt,
†Mackie, Robert D., Pvt,
†Mackiewicz, Arthur S., 1st Lt,
Mackiewicz, Eugene T., Cpl,
MacKinnon, John C., Pvt,
Mackintosh, Ronald G., Cpl,
Macklem, Carl H., Pfc
Mackowiak, Stanley J., Cpl,
MacKowsky, Arnold L., 2nd Lt,
†MacLean, Herbert G., Jr., Cpl,
MacNamara, Edward, Pvt,
MacNamee, Fernley W., Pvt,
†MacNeil, John W., Pvt,
MacPherson, Robert A., Pvt,
Madaj, Edwin J., T/5,
Madden, Francis J., 1st Lt,
Madden, Michael V., Sgt,
†Madden, Norman E., Pfc,
Madden, Walter J., Jr., Pfc,
Maddox, Earl E., Pfc,
†Maddox, James R., Pvt,
Maddox, Joe T., Pfc,
Maddox, Robert C., S/Sgt,
Madeiros, John S., T/Sgt,
Madernini, Alfred J., Pvt,
Madigan, Kenneth G., Cpl,
Madonia, Charles, Pfc,
Madrid, Joseph, S/Sgt,
Madrid, Nestor R., Pfc,
Madrigal, Victor M., Pfc,
Madsen, Harold, T/Sgt,
Madsen, Melvin J., Cpl,
Magaletta, Americo M., Pfc,
Magart, Robert E., Pvt,
Magee, Fred M., Sgt,
Magee, John H., 1st Lt,
Magina, Frank, Pfc,
Magnison, Harold E., Pfc,
†Magnusen, Edwin L., S/Sgt,
Maguire, George E., Pvt,
Maguire, Michael J., Cpl,
Mahaffey, Thomas O., Pvt,
Mahalic, Edward P., Pvt,
Mahalick, Louis J., Pfc,
Mahan, Emett R., T/4,
Mahan, Paul, Pvt,
Mahan, Roy W., Pfc,
Mahan, William L., Pvt,
Mahan, William M., S/Sgt,
Maher, James J., Pfc,
Mahfouz, Tophie J., Pfc,
Mahoney, Gerald L., Sgt,
Mahoney, Richard J., Pvt,
Mahoney, William M., Pvt,
Mahoney, William P., Pfc,
†Maier, Alvin, Sgt
Maier, Joseph E., Sgt,
†Main, Evert I., Pvt,
Main, Robert R., 1st Lt,
†Maines, Harvey E., Jr., Pvt,
Mains, Charles E., Pvt,
Mair, Alex, T/5,
Mair, Victor A., Pvt,
Maj, Frank S., Pfc,
Majerczak, Stanley J., Pvt,
Majerek, Henry J., Pvt,
†Majewicz, Casimir T., T/Sgt,
Majewski, Frank, Pvt,
Majewski, Lawrence L., T/Sgt,
Majewski, Thadeus, Pvt,
Majewski, Walter J., Pvt,
†Major, Claud P., Pvt,
†Major, Donald R., Pvt,
Maki, Toivo A., S/Sgt,
Makowski, Anthony W., Pvt,
Makransky, Murray J., 1st Lt,
Malaney, Edward J., Pvt,
Malaussena, James F., S/Sgt,
†Malcolm, Darrel N., Pvt,
Malec, Frank J., Pfc,
Malecha, Leonard L., Pfc,
Malencik, Jack W., Pvt,
Maley, Harry J., Jr., Pvt,
Malkowski, Anton, Pfc,
Malkowski, Arthur J., Pfc,
Mallard, R. E., Pfc,
Malleck, Lester A., Pfc,
Malley, Joseph A., Pvt,
Malliat, Warre H., Pvt,
Mallick, Albert P., Pfc,
Mallin, Richard R., Pfc,
Mallory, Maxwell R., Pfc,
Malloy, Frank J., Pfc,
Malloy, George, Pvt,
Malloy, John P., Pvt,
Mallozzi, Anthony J., Jr., Pvt,
Malone, Austin C., Pfc,
Malone, James, S/Sgt,
Malone, Joe, Pfc,
Malone, John P., Sgt,
Maloney, Joseph B., 2nd Lt,
Maloney, Joseph G., Pfc,
Maloney, Robert J., Pvt,
Maloney, Ronald J., Pvt,
†Maloney, Thomas F., Pvt,
Maloney, Walter R., Pvt,
Maloney, William D., Pvt,
Maltby, James A., Pfc,
Mamet, Maurice C., Pvt,
Mamone, Frank A., Pfc,
Mancini, Louis R., Pvt,
Mancini, William M., Pvt,
Mancusi, Italo V., Pfc,
§Mancuso, Nelson W., Pfc,
Mandak, John, Jr., Pvt,
Mandela, Anthony E., Pfc,
Mandelkorn, Sidney R., Pvt,
Mandernini, Alfred, Pvt
Manderscheid, John H., T/4,
Mandeville, Romeo R., S/Sgt,
†Mandit, Joseph, T/5,
Mandrafino, Alexander, Pvt,
†Mandzuk, John M., Pvt,
Maness, Oran L., Pfc,
†Mangels, Darrell J., Sgt,
Mangerpan, Paul J., Pvt,
Mangiacapra, Joseph, Pfc,
Mangin, Joseph J., Pvt,
†Mangione, Raymond P., Pvt,
Mangler, Harold J., Pfc,
Manhart, Ashton H., Lt Col,
Manijak, Frank J., Pfc
Manion, John, Pvt,
Manion, John J., Pvt,
Manion, Lawrence, Jr., Pvt,
Manista, Frank K., Pvt,
Mank, Walter J., Jr., Pfc,
Mankey, Robert L., Pfc,
Mankin, Dossie C., Pvt,
Mankin, Ernest B., Pvt,
Mankowski, Leo J., Pfc,
Manley, Francis C., Pfc,
Manley, John G., 2nd Lt,
Mann, Archie L., Pfc,
Mann, Bernett E., Pfc,
Mann, Charles B., Pvt,
Mann, Edward N., S/Sgt,
Mann, Freddie J., Pvt,
Mann, George E., Pfc,
Mann, Harold, Pfc,
Mann, Henry, Pfc,
Mann, Loren J., Capt,
Mann, Roland D., Pvt,
Mann, Stanley D., Pvt,
Mann, Travis, Jr., Sgt,
Manney, Irving, Pvt,
Mannine, Pat, Pvt,
Manning, Garnett C., Pfc,
Manning, Howard T., Pvt,
Manning Malcolm M., Pfc
Manning, Phillip H., Jr., Pfc,
†Manning, Richard, Pfc,
Mannion, Joseph S., Pfc
Mannon, Lester R., Pvt,
Manns, Edward M., Pfc,
Manriquez, Frank M., Pvt,
Mansfield, Richard E., S/Sgt
Mansfield, Vincent P., Pvt,
Manson, Robert L., Pfc,
Mantalis, Thomas J., T/Sgt,
Manthie, Otto F., Jr., Pfc,
Manzo, Rocco, Pfc,
Mapes, Lawrence E., Pfc,
Maple, Lawrence A., Pfc,
Mappa, Pasquale, Pfc,
†Maraio, Michael E., Pvt
Marasco, Frank L., Pfc,
Marberger, Harold F., Pfc,
Marble, Carroll F., Pvt,
Marcais, Earl T., T/5,
Marcantin, Amiel L., Pfc,
Marcelle, Alphonse S., Pfc,
Marchant, Julian M., 2nd Lt,
Marchese, John F., Pvt,
Marchetti, Fred, Pvt,
Marchetti, Matthew, Sgt,
†Marchetti, Raymond, S/Sgt,
Marchinsky, John R., Pfc,
*Marciezyk, Charles J., Pvt,
Marcinek, George H., Pfc,
Marcinkiewicz, Anthony, Pvt,
Marcocci, Albert, Pfc,
Marcouillier, Joseph R., Pfc,
Marcum, Donald, S/Sgt,
Marczak, John J., T/5,
Marecic, Albert W., Pvt,
Marek, Delfin E., 2nd Lt,
Marenche, Edward A., Pfc,
†Marentette, Phillip L., Pvt,
Margheim, Edwin P., T/5,
Margolis, Ruben, Pvt,
Mariani, Leo L., Pfc,
Marich, Andrew J., Cpl,
Maricich, John D., Pvt,
Marincel, John K., Pvt,
Marinelli, John A., Pfc,
Marini, Antonio, Pfc,
Marino, Joseph S., Pvt,
Marion, Clement, Pvt,
Marion, Grady W., Pfc,
Marker, Dale M., Pfc,
†Markese, Samuel J., Pvt,
Markham, Harold C., Pfc,
Markin, Stanley G., 2nd Lt,
Markle, Clarence R., Cpl,
Markley, Marvin J., Pvt
Marko, Michael, Jr., Pvt,
Markowitz, Abe, Pvt,
Marks, Harris C., Pvt
†Markwell, Eddie B., Pfc,
Marley, Walter F., Pvt,
Marmillion, Norman J., 1st Lt,
Marmon, Arthur C., Pvt,
Marmor, Marvin, Pvt,
Maron, Ernest J., 2nd Lt,
Maroney, Frederick B., Pfc,
Maroni, Francis M., 1st Lt,
Marostica, Louie B., Pfc,
Marotta, Antonio R., Pvt,
Marquez, Jose O., Pfc,
Marr, William P., Pvt,
*Marra, John, Pvt,
Marren, Charles P., Sgt,
‡Marroni, Dominic M., Pvt,
Mars, Earl C., Sgt,
Mars. John L., T/4,
Marsh, Daniel M., Pvt,
Marsh, Kenneth E., Pfc
Marsh, Lewis K., S/Sgt,
†Marsh, Luther E., Pvt,
Marshall, Albert J., Pfc,
Marshall, Axel J., Pvt,
Marshall, Calvin C., Pfc,
Marshall, Everett O., Pfc,
Marshall, Gordon R., Pfc,
Marshall, James T., Sgt,
Marshall, Kenneth H., Pfc,
Marshall, Ralph S., Pvt,
Marshall, Robert J., Pfc,
Marshall, William O., Pfc,
Marszalek, Walter M., Pfc,
Marte, Raymond J., Pfc,
Martel, Albert, Pfc,
Marten, Lowell M., Pfc,
Martin, Carl E., Pfc,
Martin, Conrad, Pvt,
Martin, Curtis W., Pvt,
Martin, Ernest J., Pfc,
Martin, J. W., Pfc,
Martin, Jerome A., Sgt,
Martin, Joe, Pvt,
†Martin, John H., T/5
Martin, John R., Pfc,
Martin, Kenneth L., Pfc,
§Martin, Kenneth M., Pvt,
Martin, Manuel H., Pfc,
Martin, Max A., 1st Lt,
Martin, Michael M., Pvt,
Martin, Orbin F., Pvt,
Martin, Paul A., Pvt,
†Martin, Quinton L., S/Sgt,
†Martin, Richard L., Pvt,
Martin, Robert N., Pvt,
Martin, Roy I., Pvt,
Martin, Stanley V., S/Sgt,
Martin, Thomas O., Cpl,
Martin, Virgil M., Pfc,
Martin, Virlyn R., S/Sgt,
Martin, Wallace B., 1st Lt,
Martinez, Antonio, Pfc,
Martinez, Charlie L., Pvt,
Martinez, Jesse P., T/5,
Martinez, Leopoldo, Pfc,
Martinez, Ruben, Pfc,
Martinez, Santiago M., T/Sgt
Martini, John E., Pvt,
Martino, Frank, Pvt,
Martinson, Edward, Pfc,
Martinson, Glenn R., Pfc
Martley, Raymod V., Pfc,
Martof, John F., Pfc,
Martowicz, Casimer S., Pfc,
Marvel, Everett M., Pvt,
Marx, Frank F., Pvt,
Marx, Wallace W., W., Pfc,
Marz, Arthur G., Pvt,
†Marzec, Stanley J., Pvt,
Marzullo, Frank J., Pfc,
†Mascari, Frank C., Pfc,
Maser, Edwin W., Pfc,
Masi, Alfred, Pfc,
Maslanki, Michael, Pfc,
Maslek, Edward, Pvt,
Masley, Steve, Jr., Pfc,
Masocco, Diarius, S/Sgt,
Mason, Andrew S., Cpl,
Mason, Charles R., Cpl,
Mason, Eugene V., Pfc,
Mason, Harold J., Pfc,
Mason, James W., Pfc,
Mason, Marion A., 1st Sgt,
†Mason, Murice J., T/S
Mason, Walter A., Pfc,
Masor, Nathan, Pvt,
Massari, Michael, T/5,
*Massaro, Joseph, Pvt,
Masse, Edgar F., Pfc,
Massey, Biddle, Jr., Pvt,
Massey, Burrell T., Pfc,
§Massey, John H., Jr., Pvt,
‡Massey, John W., Sr., Pfc,
Massie, Cyrus T., Pfc,
*Massier, Arnold M., Pvt,
Massingale, Ernest, Pfc,
Massone, Michael, Pvt,
Massong, John J., Sgt,
Massoni, Frank J., Sgt,
†Massow, Nicholas, Sgt,
†Mast, Arthur T., Pfc,
Mast, Marvin E., Pvt,
Masterman, John F., Pvt,
Masters, Isaac T., Pfc,
Mastin, Crawford L., Sgt,
Mastin, Marion G., Cpl,
Mastne, James D., Pvt,
Mastrati, John A., Pvt,
Masur, George J., Jr., Sgt,
Matarese, Charles R., Pfc,
Matay, Louis J., Pvt,
‡Matchett, Willard B., S/Sgt,
Mategrand, Victor, Pvt,
Mateo, Richard, Pfc,
Matheny, Delbert J., Pvt,
Mathews, Ben J., Pvt,
Mathews, Russell A., S/Sgt,
†Mathias, Ernest F., Sgt,
*Mathieu, Ernest R., Pvt,
Mathieu, Henry J., Pvt,
Mathis, Garner W., Pfc,
Mathis, John W., Pvt,
Matlack, Neil A., Pvt,
Matney Ted F., Pfc,
Mattei, James V., Pvt,
Matthes, Leonard W., T/Sgt,
†Matthews, Jack, S/Sgt,
Matthews, John V., Pfc,
‡Matthews, Johnie N., Pvt,
Matthews, L. C., Jr., Pfc,
Matthews, Monroe L., Pfc,
†Matthews, Robert L., Pvt,
Matthews, Russell L., Pfc,
Mattingly, James B., Pvt,
‡†Mattione, John A., Pfc,
Mattos, George, Pfc,
†Mattox, William W., Sgt,
Mattson, Walter L., Pfc,
Matuszewski, Louis, Pfc,
Matuszewski, S. M., S/Sgt,
Matwiejczyk, Henry A., Sgt,
‡Matza, Morris, Pvt,
Mauck, Russell W., Pfc
Mauer, Frank G., Pfc,
Mauff, Otto J., Pvt,
Maugans, James W. E., 1st Lt,
Mauldin, Drew M., Jr., S/Sgt,
Mauldin, Frank S., Pvt,
Mauldin, Sam D., M/Sgt,
†Maxfield, Robert J., S/Sgt,
Maxey, Fred O., Pvt,
Maxwell, Carroll E., Sgt,
Maxwell, Raymond F., Pvt,
†Maxwell, Willie T., Cpl,
May, Eugene, S/Sgt,
May, Fred R., Pfc,
May, Fred V., S/Sgt,
May, Harlan J., Pfc,
May, Harold H., Pfc,
May, Joe T., Pfc,
May, Lester L., T/5,
May, Robert A., Pvt,
May, Thomas E., Pfc,
May, William J., Pfc,
Maya, Lorenzo P., Pvt,
Mayer, Henry A., Pvt,
Mayer, John J., Pfc,
Mayes, William D., Pvt,
Mayhall, Boyd L., Pfc,
†Mayhew, Martin D., Pvt,
Mayhew, Kenneth A., Cpl,
Mayhew, Ralph E., T/Sgt,
†Maynard, Carl H., Pfc,
Maynard, Earle G., Pfc,
†Maynard, Melvin A., Pvt,
Mayo, Coy D., Pvt,
Mayo, Jack W., Jr., Pfc,
†Mayo, Richard N., Pvt,
Mayotte, Richard J., Pfc,
Mazal, Arthur, Jr., Pfc,
Mazhawa, Theodore A., Pvt,
Maziarz, Walter M., Pvt,
Mazolli, George J., Pvt,
Mazuik, Stanley, Pfc,
†Mazur, Stanley P., Pvt,
Mazziotti, Leonard J., Cpl,
Mazzola, Philip J., Pvt,
McAllister, Joe E., Sgt,
McAllister, Mack V., Pvt,

† Killed in Action. * Prisoner of War. ‡ Missing in Action. § Died of Wounds.

IN WORLD WAR II 495

McAlister, Arthur J., T/Sgt,
McAllister, Daniel E., Pvt,
McAnally, George C., Pvt,
†McAnulty, John F., Pfc,
McArdle, Harley E., Pfc,
McArthur, Jack, T/5,
McAteer, Michael J., Pfc,
McAuley, Robert J., T/Sgt,
McBane, Jesse W., Pvt,
McBride, James L., Pfc,
McBride, Joe J., Sgt,
†McBride, John E., Pvt,
McBride, Maurice R., Cpl,
McBride, R. J., T/Sgt,
McCabe, Arthur T., 1st Lt,
McCaffery, Elmer J., Pfc,
McCalip, Cleo M., Pvt,
McCalister, Roy L., Pfc,
McCall, Russell W., Pfc,
McCall, Edward L., Pvt,
McCalmont, Paul M., Pfc,
McCammon, William P., Pfc,
McCampbell, John T., Sgt,
McCarley, John J., Pfc,
McCart, John A., Pvt,
McCarter, Monroe I., Pvt,
McCarthy, Donald E., Pfc,
McCarthy, Edward K., Pfc
McCarthy, Felix P., Pvt,
McCarthy, Florence A., Pvt,
McCarthy, Howard F., Pvt,
McCarthy, John J., Pfc,
McCartney, Clarence W., Pfc,
McCarty, Richard I., Pvt,
McCash, George G., T/4,
McCauley, Sam, Jr., Pvt,
†McChrystal, Charles E., Cpl,
McClain, Paul E., S/Sgt,
McClanahan, Carl E., Pvt,
McClaren, Peter, Pvt,
†McClay, Dean E., Sgt,
McCleary, Homer C., Sgt,
McClellan, Ralph G., Pvt,
McClendon, Gene W., Pfc,
McClesky, Edward, Pfc,
McClory, Joseph A., Pvt,
McCloud, Howard S., Pvt,
McCloud, James C., Pvt,
McClung, Leonard D., Pvt,
†McClure, Donald S., Pfc,
McClure, Frank W., Pfc,
McClure, George O., Pfc,
McClure, N. G., Sr., Pvt,
†McCluskey, Hugh C., Pfc,
†McCollum, George M., Pvt,
McCollum, Howard A., Pvt,
McComber, Hester F., Pfc
McCombs, Charles L., Pfc,
†McConnell, Ernest W., Pfc,
McConnell, Henry, Pfc,
McConnell, Leland F., Pfc,
McConnell, Raymond L., Pfc,
†McCord, Earl T., Pvt,
McCormick, Dallas W., Pfc,
McCormick, Edward A., S/Sgt,
McCormick, John F., Pvt,
†McCormick, Levi G., Pvt,
McCormick, Owen J., S/Sgt,
McCormick, Rodney F., Cpl,
McCosh, Oakley D., Pvt,
McCown, Deward E., Sgt,
†McCoy, Alan D., Pvt,
†McCoy, Alvie S., Pvt,
McCoy, Henry M., Pvt,
†McCoy, James W., Pvt,
McCoy, John N., Sgt,
McCoy, Oliver R., Pfc,
McCoy, Richard L., Pvt,
McCoy, William V., Pvt,
McCrady, John E., Pvt,
‡McCray, Lloyd E., Pfc,
McCray, Robert P., T/5,
McCrea, Charles P., Pfc,
McCrisaken, J. R., Jr., Pfc,
McCrory, Leslie M., Pfc,
McCrory, Wayne C., Pfc,
McCue, Gilbert J., Pvt,
McCullen, John J., Sgt,
McCullers, William E., Pfc,
McCullough, Hubert F., Pfc,
McCullough, Raymond P., Pfc,
McCurdy, Guy O., Pvt,
‡McCutcheon, Johnson L., Pvt,
McDade, Edward W., Pvt,
McDade, Paul E., Pvt,
McDaniel, George B., Pvt,
McDaniel, Harry C., Pvt,
McDaniel, Lee, Pvt,
McDede, William B., Pvt,
McDermott, John M., Pvt,
McDermott, Peter L., Pvt,
†McDermott, Philip F., Pfc,
McDermott, William P., Pfc,
McDevitt, Edward F., Pfc,
McDonald, Berthold E., Sgt,
McDonald, Boyd W., Pfc,
McDonald, Clarence E., Pvt,
McDonald, Earl F., Pfc,
†McDonald, George W., Pvt,
†McDonald, George W., Pvt,
McDonald, John G., Pvt,
†McDonald, Kenneth J., Pvt,
McDonald, Oliver L., Pvt,
McDonald, Thomas, Jr., S/Sgt,
McDonald, Wilburn, Pvt,
†McDonell, John L., Jr., 2nd Lt,
McDonnell, Donald A., Pfc,
McDonnell, Francis L., Pfc
McDonnell, Martin, Pvt,
McDonough, Clyde H., Sgt,
McDonough, George A., Pvt,
McDonough, William H., Pfc,
McDonough, William J., Sgt,
McDougall, Herbert F., T/5,
McDougall, John J., Pfc,
McDowell, Charles E., Pvt,
McDowell, George J., 1st Sgt,
McDowell, Henry C., Pvt,
McDowell, Louie B., Pvt,
†McEachern, Norman J., Pvt,
McEldowney, Patrick P., Pvt,
McEldowney, Paul L., Pvt,
McElhone, Russell N., Pvt,
McElroy, James J., Jr., Pfc,
McElroy, John I., T/4,
McEntire, Ernest F., Pvt,
McEwan, Gordon A., Pfc,
McEwen, M. W., T/5,
†McFalls, Richard F., Pvt,
McFarland, Arthur R., Pvt,
McFarland, Leslie H., Pvt,
McFarland, Robert C., 1st Lt,
McFarlane, Lester W., S/Sgt,
McFarlin, George I., Pfc,
McFate, Alvin F., S/Sgt,
McFerrin, George W., Pvt,
McGahan, Joseph D., Cpl,
McGahey, William A., S/Sgt
McGann, William P., Pfc,
McGary, Walter, Pvt,
McGee, Austin J., Pvt,
McGee, Francis P., Cpl,
‡McGee, Henry H., Jr., Pfc,
McGee, Russell B., T/4,
†McGee, Thomas J., Pvt,
McGhee, Gerald W., Sgt,
McGiffin, James A., Jr., Sgt,
McGill, Carlton, Pfc,
McGill, Patrick, Pfc,
McGinns, John E., Jr., Pfc,
‡McGinty, Anthony F., Pvt,
McGinnis, Stanley E., T/5,
†McGlocklin, William A., Pvt,
McGlone, Charles F., Pfc,
McGlynn, James C., Capt,
†McGlynn, John H., Pvt,
McGonaghy, James G., Pvt,
McGonagle, Ralph D., Pfc,
McGough, Lowell T., Pvt,
McGowan, Jack L., Pfc,
McGowan, Robert F., 2nd Lt,
McGowin, William, Pvt,
McGrane, Adrian H., Pvt,
McGrath, John J., Pvt,
McGrath, Joseph F., Pvt,
McGrath, Paul S., Pfc,
McGrew, Elmer H., Pvt,
McGrew, Ralph A., Pfc
McGrory, James P., Jr., Pvt,
McGruer, James A., Pvt,
McGuire, Clarence N., Pvt,
McGuire, Dennis, Pvt,
McGuire, Francis J., T/5,
†McGuire, Howard A., Pfc,
McGuire, James T., Jr., Pvt,
McGuire, Joseph E., Pvt,
McGuirk, John E., Pfc,
McGuirt, Isaac L., Pvt,
McGurk, Daniel F., Pfc,
McGurk, Robert, Pvt,
McHugh, Patrick J., Pvt,
McIlhoney, John J., Pfc,
McInerney, Thomas J., Pfc,
McIntire, Charles R., Pvt,
†McIntire, Elmer E., 1st Lt,
McIntosh, Roy R., Pfc,
†McKaig, Jay L., Pvt,
McKane, Robert L., Pvt,
McKean, Kenneth L., Sgt,
McKee, Clifford W., 2nd Lt,
McKee, Doyle L., Pfc,
McKeen, Herbert W., Pfc,
McKeithen, Vanne, Capt,
McKellips, Lindsay J., Sgt,
McKelvey, Kenneth E., Pvt,
McKenna, John J., Pvt,
McKenzie, Stanley J., Cpl,
McKeone, Charles P., 1st Sgt,
†McKeown, Arthur L., 1st Lt,
McKim, Ernest E., Pvt,
McKinley, Elliot L., Pfc,
McKinley, Irvin R., Pfc,
McKinley, Thomas E., Pvt,
McKinnon, Henry L., Pfc,
McKinney, Herman E., Pfc
McLain, Carroll H., Pfc,
McLain, Charles, Pfc,
McLallen, Lewis C., 1st Lt,
McLarney, Clifford, Pfc,
McLarney, Thallows, Pvt,
McLaughlin, Charles P., Pfc,
McLaughlin, Edward J., S/Sgt,
†McLaughlin, Frank J., Pvt,
McLaughlin, Francis J., Pfc,
McLaughlin, James A., Pfc,
McLaughlin, Richard E., Pvt,
McLaughlin, Richard J., T/5,
McLaughlin, William R., T/5,
McLean, Clifford S., S/Sgt,
McLean, Delmar A., Pvt,
McLean, Ruel A., Pfc,
McLean, Vernon E., Pvt,
McLellard, Robert, Pvt,
McMahan, Hampton, Pvt,
McMahon, Donald F., Pvt,
†McMahon, William E., 1st Lt,
McMamomy, Leon, Cpl,
‡McManus, Thomas, Pvt,
McMaster, George W., Pvt,
McMillan, Jack E., S/Sgt,
McMillan, Laurence, Pfc,
McMillan, Laverne S., Pvt,
McMillan, Thomas R., Pfc,
McMillan, William L., T/4,
McMillen, Jack, Pvt,
†McMillen, Richard E., Pvt,
McMullin, William B., T/5,
McMurray, Carroll K., T/5,
McMurty, Samuel T., Pvt,
McNamara, Edward J., Jr., Pfc
*McNamara, Joseph H., Pvt,
McNamara, Thomas J., Pfc,
McNamara, William W., Pfc,
McNeel, Merton J., Pvt,
McNeil, Albert J., Pvt,
§McNeil, Haskell H., Pfc,
McNelly, Edward A., Pvt,
McNerney, John A., Pvt,
McNulty, Bernard J., Jr., Pvt,
McNulty, John D., Pvt,
McNutt, Winston E., Pfc,
McPherson, Arthur G., Cpl,
McPherson, Clar. M., T/Sgt,
McPheters, Seth P., Pvt,
†McQueen, Eldon A., Pfc,
McQueen, Ned P., Pvt,
McQuiston, Guy K., Pvt,
McSherry, William J., Pvt,
†McSwain, Lewis D., Pvt,
McVay, Ray R., Pvt,
McVay, Ward L., Pvt,
†McVoy, Kenneth L., Pfc,
McWilliams, John W., Pfc,
†McWilliams, Leslie W., 2nd Lt,
Mead, Charles W., Pvt,
Mead, Lonnie, T/5,
Meade, Winfred, Pvt,
Meadlock, Rolen R., Pvt,
Meador, Howe, Sgt,
Meador, Roy L., Pfc,
Meadows, Homer M., Pfc,
Meadows, Ralph B., Pfc,
Means, Clark E., Pvt,
Means, Harold W., S/Sgt,
Mears, Roy A., Jr., Pvt,
Meceros, John D., T/5,
†Mechikoff, Morris A., Cpl,
Mecler, Robert L., Pfc,
Medeiros, John S., T/Sgt,
Mederos, John D., T/5,
Medford, Francis G., T/Sgt,
Medford, Fred J., T/4,
Medina, Jose D., Pfc,
Medinger, John L., Pvt,
Medwid, Steve, Pfc,
Mee, James H., Pfc,
Meehach, Wilbur L., Pfc,
Meehan, Dennis J., Pvt,
Meehan, John V., Pvt,
Meehan, Philip A., Pvt,
Meek, William H., Pfc,
Meeker, Melvin J., Pvt,
Meeler, Robert L., S/Sgt,
Mees, Arthur C., Sgt,
†Mefford, James C., Pvt,
Meier, Dean F., Pvt,
Meierle, Paul L., Pvt,
Meinecke, Earl W., Pfc,
Meinertz, Bernard C., Pvt,
Moiselman, Leonard, Pvt,
Meisinger, Matthew, Jr., Pfc,
Meisner, Fred, Pvt,
Meissner, Anton J., Pfc,
Meka, Michael, Pvt,
Mele, Joseph, Pfc,
Meleshka, Alexander N., Pvt,
Melhorn, Robert J., Pvt,
Melissare, Frank J., Pfc,
†Melkent, Tony A., Pfc,
†Mellas, Victor J., Pvt,
Mellor, Richard A., Pvt,
Melnik, Chester, Pvt,
Melnyk, Michael, Pvt,
Melone, Dominick A., Sgt,
Melone, Romeo R., Sgt,
Melton, John G., Pfc,
†Melton, Ruben A., Jr., Pfc,
Melvin, George W., Pvt,
Mendenhall, Jess R., S/Sgt,
Mendez, Lazaro A., Pvt,
Mendis, Peter J., Pfc,
Mendoza, Alex, Pvt,
Mendoza, Reyes T., Pvt,
Meneses, Primo J., T/4,
Mengel, Jay R., Cpl,
Mercado, Francisco M., Sgt,
†Mercier, Normand C., Pvt,
Mercuri, Frank A., Sgt,
Merk, Dave, Pfc,
†Merkl, Lawrence J., Pfc,
†Merrell, Joseph F., Pfc,
Merriman, Howard C., Pfc,
Merritt, Ralph D., Jr., Pfc,
Merritt, Willard L., Pfc,
Merrival, Floyd J., Pfc,
Merrow, Floyd A., Pvt,
†Merrow, Robert E., Pfc,
Mershon, George B., Pvt,
Mertz, Calvin C., Pfc,
Merwin, Douglas, Pvt,
Mesa, Rosonda, Pfc,
Meskunas, William L., Pfc,
Mesna, Erwin C., Pfc,
Messier, Francis L., Pfc,
Messina, Angelo L., Pfc,
Messmer, Kurt W., 1st Lt,
Messmer, Louis B., Pvt,
Mestemaker, Robert H., 2nd Lt,
Meszaros, Frank, Pfc,
Meszaros, Stephen W., Pvt,
Metaxa, Dodge P., Pfc,
Metelko, Joseph H., Pfc,
Meth, Fred M., Pvt,
Metrick, Stephen M., Pfc,
Metz, George W., Jr., Cpl,
Metz, Ivan R., Sgt,
Metz, Louis D., Sgt,
Metz, Wilfred W., Pvt,
‡Metz, William W., Pvt,
Metzel, Robert E., Pfc,
Metzker, William V., S/Sgt,
Meyens, Archie F., Pfc
Meyer, Alfred C., Pfc,
Meyer, Alvin F., Jr., Cpl,
Meyer, Earl W., Pvt,
Meyer, Frederick, Pvt,
Meyer, Harlan G., Pfc,
Meyer, Jack D., Sr., Pvt,
Meyer, Paul L., T/Sgt,
†Meyer, Walter C., Pfc,
Meyer, Warren J., Pvt,
Meyer, William F., Pvt,
Meyerdirk, Alvin R., 1st Sgt,
Meyerhoffer, John P., Pfc,
Meyerowitz, Simon, Pvt,
Meyers, George M., Pvt,
Meyers, Henry F., T/5,
Meyers, Howard A., Pvt,
Meyers, Jesse A., Pfc
Meyers, Mark W., Pfc,
Meyers, Vernon L., Pfc,
Micciche, Joseph M., Pvt,
Micetich, Laddie A., Pfc,
†Michael, Charles R., Pfc,
Michael, Charles W., 2nd Lt,
Michaels, Garth C., Pvt,
Michaels, Joseph N., S/Sgt,
Michalek, Clemmence J., T/4,
†Michalski, Joseph L., Pvt,
Michaluk, Peter, Jr., Pfc,
Michaud, Philemon A., Pvt,
Michiewicz, Ralph A., T/Sgt,
†Mick, William E., Jr., Pvt,
Middendorf, Arnold J., Pvt,
Middlebrook, Jack W., Pvt,
Middlemas, John W., Cpl,
Middleton, George H., Cpl,
Midkiff, Robert E., S/Sgt,
Mieczkowski, Raymond F., Pvt,
Mietelski, Wladyslaw T., Pvt,
Miglora, Gerard G., Pvt,
Miguel, Ernie, Pvt,
‡Mihok, Michael J., Pvt,
†Miholik, Joseph J., Pvt,
Mikicinski, Armand W., Pfc,
†Miklush, John J., Pvt,
Mikolajczyk, John E., Cpl,
Mikovich, Ivan, Cpl,
†Mikridge, John, Pvt,
Mikulak, Stephen, Pfc,
Milam, Othal, Pvt,
Milanowycz, Joseph A., Pvt,
Milburn, Lendall N., Pfc,
Milde, Edward L., 2nd Lt,
Miles, Donald C., Pvt,
Miles, James E., Pvt,
Miles, James W., Pvt,
†Miles, Joseph E., S/Sgt,
Miles, Willard L., Pvt,
Milewski, Frank Jr., Pfc,
Milian, Francis W., Pvt,
Millar, Robert A., T/Sgt,
Millard, Harvey H., Pvt,
Millard, John F., Pvt,
Millard, John M., Sgt,
Millen, Richard E., Pvt
Miller, Adam C., Sgt,
Miller, Carlyle E., Capt,
Miller, Charles J., Pfc,
Miller, Charles W., Pfc,
Miller, Clarence J., Pvt,
Miller, Clyde C., Pfc,
Miller, Clyde J., Pfc,
Miller, Dale M., Pfc,
†Miller, Dallas W., Sgt,
Miller, Earl E., Pvt,
Miller, Earl G., Pfc,
Miller, Edward J., Cpl,
Miller, Edward V., Pvt,
Miller, Elmer H., S/Sgt,
†Miller, Emil E., Pvt,
Miller, Floyd W., Pfc,
Miller, Francis, T/4,
Miller, Frederick H., Pfc,
Miller, George H., Pfc,
Miller, George W., Pfc,
Miller, Gordon T., 1st Lt,
Miller, Harlan D., Pvt,
†Miller, Harry J., Pvt,
Miller, Herbert C., Cpl,
Miller, James E., Sgt,
Miller, James T., Pfc,
Miller, James T., Pvt,
Miller, Joe B., Pfc,
Miller, John B., Pvt,
Miller, John R., Pvt,
Miller, Keith R., Pfc,
§Miller, Lon V., Pfc,
Miller, Maurice W., T/5,
Miller, Melvin L., Sgt,
Miller, Melvin R., S/Sgt,
Miller, Merritt V., Pfc,
†Miller, Milton E., S/Sgt,
Miller, Nolen J., Pvt,
Miller, Oscar P., Cpl,
Miller, Philip, Pfc,
Miller, Ray A., Pfc,
Miller, Raymond C., S/Sgt,
Miller, Richard A., 2nd Lt,
Miller, Richard B., Pfc,
Miller, Robert A., Pfc,
Miller, Robert L., Pfc,
Miller, Robert W., Pfc,
Miller, Robert W., Pfc,
Miller, Roland E., Pfc,
Miller, Stephen T., Pfc,
Miller, Sylvester L., Pvt,
Miller, Vic H., Pfc,
†Miller, Vincent F., Pfc,
Miller, Virgil H., Pvt,
Miller, Walter W., T/4,
†Miller, Willis J., Pfc,
Miller, Youland D., Pfc,
Millevoi, Casimiro, Pvt,
Milligan, Thomas R., Pvt,
Milliken, Eugene V., Pfc,
Million, Arthur T., Pfc,
Millis, Galen E., Pfc,
Mills, Cecil K., Pvt,
Mills, Gilbert R., Pfc,
Mills, James D., Pvt,
Mills, James H., Cpl,
†Mills, John W., Pvt,
Millwood, Raymond, T/Sgt,
Millwood, William H., S/Sgt,
Minch, Fred, Pfc,
Mincemoyer, Earl H., Pvt,
†Mincin, Severio P., Pvt,
†Miner, Elbert F., Pfc,
Miner, Howard K., Pfc,
Minerva, Frank D., Capt,
Minieri, Salvatore R., Pfc,
Minkowich, Louis, S/Sgt,
Minkowich, Thomas, Pvt,
Minner, Charles O., Pfc,
Minner, William D., Pfc,
Minnetto, John F., Pvt,
Minnie, William, Pfc,
Minor, Paul H., Pvt,
†Minotto, Dominic, T/5,

† Killed in Action. * Prisoner of War. ‡ Missing in Action. § Died of Wounds.

Minter, William E., Pvt,
Minton, Ambrose J., Jr., Pfc,
Minton, Maurice W., Pvt,
Mirda, Joseph, S/Sgt,
Mireles, Nick M., Pvt,
Mirisciotti, Anthony J., Pvt,
Mironchik, Alexander J., T/5,
Mirucki, John J., S/Sgt,
Misero, Lawrence, Pvt,
Misitano, Joseph P., Pvt,
Misiur, Mathew J., Pvt,
Miskinis, Pete F., Sgt,
Mislevets, Chester S., Cpl,
Missey, Hairm L., Pvt,
Mistishen, John, Pvt,
Misurda, John, S/Sgt,
Mitchell, Archie B., 1st Lt
†Mitchell, Charlie J., Pfc,
Mitchell, Damon L., Pvt,
Mitchell, Ernest F., Sgt,
†Mitchell, Frank E., Pfc,
Mitchell, Henry C., Pvt,
Mitchell, Houston, Pvt,
Mitchell, Howard E., Pfc,
Mitchell, Ingram I., Pfc,
Mitchell, Jack, Pvt,
Mitchell, Raymond J., Pfc,
Mitchell, Robert G., Pvt,
Mitchell, Roy H., Sgt,
Mitchell, Rupert C., Capt,
Mitchner, Charles E., Pvt,
Mitten, William A., S/Sgt,
Mitzkus, Martin, Pfc,
Mixer, Granville I., Pvt,
Mize, Orval O., Sgt,
†Mizera, Francis, Pfc,
Mlakar, Theodore, Pfc,
*Moberg, Jonas W., Sgt,
Mobley, David H., T/5,
Mobriant, Joseph, Pfc,
Mock, Fred G., Pvt,
Moe, Erland O., Pfc,
Moeller, Aloysius W., Pfc,
Moen, Claud M., Pfc,
Moen, John O., Pfc,
†Moen, Midle A., Pfc,
Moffat, James R., Pfc,
Moffett, Walter L., Pfc,
Moffitt, Raleigh, Sgt,
Moga, Adrian F., T/4,
†Mognett, Raymond L., Pvt,
Mogstad, Richard L., Pfc,
Mohl, William B., Pvt,
Mohr, George W., 1st Lt,
Moisan, Herve J., Pvt,
Moison, Theodore E., Pvt,
Moken, Francis W., Pvt,
Mokew, Walter W., T/4,
Mokis, Michael, Pvt,
Moleksy, John, Pfc,
†Molina, Jesus P., Pvt,
Molina, Ralph P., T/4,
Molinaro, Joseph A., Pvt,
Moline, Donald L., Pfc,
Mollenkopf, John R., S/Sgt,
Mollette, William R., Pfc,
Molloy, James T., Sgt,
Molloy, Paul N., Pfc,
Molnar, Julius, Sgt,
†Molson, Joseph, Pfc,
Momjian, James H., Pvt,
Monasco, William F., Pfc,
†Moncrief, Charles W., Jr., Pfc,
Mondt, William A., Jr., Pvt,
Money, Byron A., Pfc,
†Monfils, Henry N., Pvt,
Mongan, Thomas, Pvt,
Mongold, Elza D., Sgt,
Monk, Jesse E., Pfc,
Monk, Raymond, Pfc,
Monks, Richard J., Pfc,
Monneypenny, Joseph A., Pfc,
Monnin, Francis C., Sgt,
Monnot, Charles A., Pvt,
†Monroe, Norval A., Pfc,
Monroe, Thomas H., Col,
Montag, Philip J., Pfc,
Montague, William H., Pvt,
Montague, William P. F., Pfc,
Montalbano, James A., Pvt,
Montano, Vivian A., Pfc,
Montanye, Arthur R., Pvt,
Montejano, Ezequiel C., Pvt,
Montemagno, John, Pfc,
Montemayor, Nemecio S., Pfc,
Montemurno, Vincent, Pfc,
Monteneri, Vincent, Pfc,
Montesano, Anthony, Pvt,
Montgomery, Claude E., Pfc,
Montgomery, Earl E., Pfc,
Montgomery, James A., Pfc,
Montgomery, James R., Pvt,
Montgomery, Richard E., Cpl,
Monti, Ralph, Cpl,
‡Montie, Thomas M., Pvt,

Montieth, Noel R., Pfc,
Moock, Peter G. A., Pvt,
Moody, Fred J., Pvt,
Moody, Forrest A., Pfc,
Moody, Jasper G., Sgt,
§Moody, Roy L., Pfc,
Moon, James W., 1st Lt,
Moon, John W., Pvt,
Mooney, Charles L., Pfc,
Mooney, Ernest W., Jr., Pfc,
Mooney, Jesse E., Pfc,
Mooney, Joe, Pvt,
Mooney, William C., 2nd Lt,
Moore, Alfred W., Pvt,
Moore, Alvin S., Pfc,
Moore, Arlie M., Pvt,
Moore, Aubrey T., S/Sgt,
†Moore, Bert, Pfc,
Moore, Cecil C., Pfc,
Moore, Charlie G., Sgt,
†Moore, Dan, Pvt,
Moore, Daniel, Pvt,
Moore, Denis G., Capt,
Moore, Douglas L., Sgt,
Moore, Elmer E., Pfc,
Moore, Elvis L., Pvt,
Moore, Elwood J., Pvt,
Moore, Fate, Jr., Pvt,
†Moore, George E., Pfc,
Moore, George H., Cpl,
Moore, George K., Pfc,
Moore, George L., Pvt,
Moore, Harold W., Pvt,
Moore, Harry E., Pvt,
Moore, Homer R., Pvt,
†Moore, Jack W., Sgt,
Moore, Jackie C., Pfc
†Moore, James A., Sgt,
Moore, James C., Pfc,
Moore, John C., S/Sgt,
Moore, John D., Cpl,
Moore, John F., Sgt,
Moore, Joseph E., Jr., Capt,
Moore, Joseph W., T/5,
Moore, Lloyd E., Pfc
Moore, Odist E., Pvt,
Moore, Paul, Pfc
Moore, Raymond E., Pfc,
Moore, Robert W., Pfc,
Moore, Roy A., Pvt,
Moore, Roy E., Lt Col,
Moore, Wallace R., Pfc,
Moore, Walter F., Sgt,
Moore, Wilson L., Sgt,
Moorehead, William E., Pvt,
Moores, Ernest E., Pvt,
Moorhead, William R., Pvt,
Morales, Mariano, T/Sgt,
Moran, Frank J., Jr., S/Sgt,
Moran, John D., Pfc,
Moran, Thomas M., Pfc,
Morbillo, Frank, Pfc,
Moree, Edgar A., Pfc,
†Morehouse, George F., Pvt,
Moreland, Norman P., Pfc,
†Moreno, David C., Pvt,
Moreno, Manuel R., S/Sgt,
Moreschi, Bruno G., Pfc,
†Moreton, William S., Sgt,
†Moretz, Walter D., Pvt,
†Morey, Milford A., Pvt,
Morford, Wilbur A., S/Sgt,
Morgan, Charles E., Capt,
Morgan, Dale L., Pfc,
Morgan, Jerry J., Pvt,
Morgan, John L., Pfc,
Morgan, John P., Pvt,
Morgan, Marion P., Pfc,
†Morgan, Melvin O., Pvt,
Morgan, Norman B., 1st Lt,
Morgan, Shelton S., T/5,
Moriarty, John M., Pvt,
Morin, Joseph H., Pfc,
Morisgn, Stanford N., Jr., Pvt,
Morrell, Raymond E., Pfc,
Morrelle, William J., Cpl,
Morrietta, John G., Pfc,
Morris, Arol G., Pvt,
Morris, Astor A., 1st Lt,
Morris, Burley B., Pfc,
Morris, Carl B., Pvt,
Morris, Clair B., Pvt,
Morris, Daniel R., Pfc,
Morris, Dean, Pvt,
Morris, Everett J., Pvt,
Morris, Frank A., Pvt
Morris, Frank E., Pvt,
†Morris, James H., Pvt,
Morris, James M., 1st Lt,
Morris, James W., Pvt,
Morris, John A., 1st Lt,
Morris, John R., Pvt,
§Morris, Kenneth J., T/5,
Morris, Louis J., Pvt,
Morris, Recil M., Pvt,

Morris, Russell G., Pvt,
Morris, Russell M., Pvt,
Morris, Sam W., T/5,
†Morris, Thomas E., Pfc,
†Morris, Warren P., Pvt,
Morris, William D., Pvt,
Morris, James G., Pvt,
†Morrison, Boyd A., Pvt,
Morrison, Ernest C., Pvt,
Morrison, Frank L., Pvt,
Morrison, Fred L., Pvt,
Morrison, James H., Pfc,
Morrison, Joe B., Cpl,
†Morrison, Joe F., Pvt,
Morrison, Robert N., 1st Lt,
Morrison, Robert W., Sgt,
Morrissette, Edgar J., Pvt,
Morrissey, James P., Pfc,
Morrongiello, Sal. J., S/Sgt,
Morrow, Floyd A., T/4,
Morrow, Glen L., Pfc,
Morrow, James W., Pfc,
Morrow, Lawrence, Pvt,
Morse, Clarence, T/Sgt,
Morse, George, Pfc,
Morse, James O., T/5,
Morse, Ralph W., Pvt,
†Morse, Richard H., Pvt,
Morse, Richard L., T/4,
Morseth, Harris R., Pfc,
Morski, Rudolph, Pvt,
Mortimer, Roxford F., Pvt,
†Morton, Eugene V., Pvt,
†Morton, Jack A., Pvt,
Morton, Kenneth W., Pfc,
Morton, Leonard F., Pfc,
Morton, Robert J., Pfc,
Moseley, John H., Pfc,
Moses, James T., Pfc,
Mosher, Vernon E., T/5,
Mosier, Ford, Pvt,
Moskowitz, Seymour L., 2nd Lt
Mosley, Willie, Pvt,
Mosnot, Nick, Pfc,
Mosqueda, Jose T., Pfc,
†Moss, Bertie V., Pfc,
Moss, William F., Jr., T/5,
Mostachetti, Armando, Cpl,
Mote, Albert J., T/Sgt,
Mothershead, Francis, Pfc,
Motichka, Cyril P., Pvt,
Motley, William N., Pvt,
Motta, Joseph, Pfc,
Mottern, William E., Sgt,
Motto, Frank, Pvt,
Mottola, Ralph C., Jr., Pvt,
Mottor, Arthur F., S/Sgt,
Moulton, Lloyd C., Pfc,
Mount, Henry F., Jr., Cpl,
†Mountain, Carl F., S/Sgt,
Mountford, John W., Jr., Pfc,
Moutray, Fennel S., Pvt,
Movia, Octavio, Pvt,
§Mowen, Roy E., Jr., Pvt,
Mowery, Harlan R., Pfc,
Moya, Louis S., Pfc,
Moya, Guadalupe J., Pfc,
‡Moyer, Albert W., Pvt,
Moyer, Daniel A., T/5,
Moyer, Gordon B., Pvt,
Moyer, Kermit C., Pvt,
Moyer, Ralph D., Pvt,
Mozzer, Thotant J., Jr., Pfc,
Mrowca, Charles, Pfc,
Mrowiec, Constantine G., Pfc,
Mrozek, John J., Pvt,
Mucciarone, Coradino L., Pvt,
Mucciolo, Frank P., Pfc,
Mueller, Arthur J., 1st Lt,
Mueller, Wilbur V., S/Sgt,
Mueller, Wilson D., Pfc
Muellersman, John R., Pvt,
†Mueth, Clement S., S/Sgt,
Mugerdichian, Frank, Pfc,
Muir, James F., Pfc,
Muir, Robert H., Pvt,
§Mulderig, John J., Pvt,
Muldoon, Thomas H., 2nd Lt,
Mule, Salvatore F., S/Sgt
Mulhern, Charles E., T/5,
†Mull, Harold L., Pvt,
Mullaly, Lawrence J., S/Sgt,
Mullan, Henry H., Pfc,
Mullarky, Patrick, Pfc,
Mullen, Arthur B., Pfc,
Mullen, Edward J., Pvt,
Mullen, John B., Pvt,
Mullen, Orval H., Sgt,
Mullen, Walter H., Pvt,
Mullen, Whitney P., Pfc,
Mullen, William E., Pvt,
Mullenberg, Charles T., Pvt,
Muller, George K., T/4,
Muller, Henry R., Pvt,
Mulligan, Gerald J., Pvt,

Mulligan, John F., Pfc,
Mullickin, Robert L., Pvt,
Mullin, John, Cpl,
Mullins, James W., 2nd Lt,
Mullins, Ledford, Pvt,
Mullins, Samie, T/5,
†Mullins, Thomas, Pfc,
Mulraney, John F., Pvt,
Mulry, Daniel B., Pvt,
Mumford, Earl E., Cpl,
Mundt, Charles A., Jr., Pfc,
Muniz, Frank, Pvt,
Muniz, Sherman A., T/3,
Munn, Earl C., Pfc,
Munn, Treffle, Pfc,
Munos, John M., Pvt,
Munos, Thomas J., Pfc,
Munoz, Ben C., Pvt,
†Muntan, George F., Pfc,
Munz, Frederick N., Pfc,
Murch, James E., 2nd Lt,
Murie, Charles, Pfc,
Murk, Edward J., 1st Sgt,
Murkerson, James A., Pfc,
Murkowski, Thomas A., Sgt,
†Muro, Manuel L., Pvt,
Murphy, Albert W., Pfc,
Murphy, Audie L., 1st Lt,
Murphy, Charles, Pfc,
Murphy, Charles E., Sgt,
Murphy, Cornelius J., Pvt,
Murphy, Dale, Pfc,
Murphy, Frank J., Pvt,
Murphy, George E., Pfc,
Murphy, Henry E., Pvt,
Murphy, James P., Pfc,
Murphy, James V., T/4,
Murphy, James W., Cpl,
Murphy, John J., Pvt,
Murphy, John P., Pfc,
Murphy, John R., 1st Lt,
Murphy, Mark E., Pfc,
Murphy, Melvin P., Pvt,
Murphy, Patrick R., Pvt,
Murphy, Phil G., Cpl,
†Murphy, Raymond P., Pvt,
Murphy, Robert E., Cpl,
Murphy, Wilbert D., Pfc,
Murphy, William H., T/4,
*Murphy, William H., 2nd Lt
Murray, Alfred, Pfc,
Murray, Charles H., Pfc,
Murray, Elmo P., Pfc,
†Murray, Everett L., Sgt,
Murray, Henry W., Pfc,
Murray, James T., Pfc,
Murray, Lawrence E., Pfc,
Murray, Louis H., Pfc,
Murray, Vernon H., Pfc,
†Murray, William H., Pfc,
Murray, William J., Jr., Pvt,
†Murie, William E., Sgt,
Murtagh, John E., Capt,
†Murtha, John J., 2nd Lt,
Murvin, Garland G., 1st Lt,
Musciano, Orlando J., Pvt,
Muse, William F., Pfc,
Mushalio, Michael, Pfc,
Mushock, Michael, Pfc,
Musick, Harley R., S/Sgt,
Muskopf, Loren H., S/Sgt,
Musselman, Boyd L., Pfc,
†Musselman, Wilbur H., Pvt,
Musser, Clayton, Pvt,
Mutaw, Frank A., Jr., Pfc,
Mutschler, Edward C., Pfc,
Myatt, Elvin E., 1st Sgt,
Mydler, Louis C., S/Sgt,
Myers, Delvin C., Pfc,
Myers, Eugene P., Pfc,
Myers, Francis J., Pvt,
Myers, Harry T., T/5,
†Myers, Lewis D., Pvt,
Myers, Lewis H., Pfc,
Myers, Oliver M., Pvt
Myers, Paul D., Pvt,
Myers, Raymond C., S/Sgt,
Myers, Raymond N., Pvt,
Myers, Richard L., Pfc,
Myers, Robert J., Pfc,
Myers, Robert L., Pvt,
Myers, Robert L., Pvt,
Myers, Thomas R., Pfc,
Myers, Thorvald G., Pvt,
Myers, Willard C., Pvt,
Mynarski, Peter P., Pfc,

†Nadal, Vincent, Pvt,
Nafe, John D., 2nd Lt,
Nagel, Clarence H., Pfc,
Nagy, Frank, Pfc,
Nagy, John S., Pvt,
Nagy, Joseph, Pvt,
Nagy, Julius J., Pvt,
Nahorny, Thomas J., Pvt,

†Nalesnik, William, Pvt
†Nalewajk, Stanley H., Cpl,
†Nam, Leong Q., Pvt,
Nametka, Bernard N., T/5,
Nanchoff, Thomas E., Pvt,
Nanegos, Willard G., Pvt,
Nappi, Joseph J., Pvt,
Napier, Donald D., Cpl,
Napier, William E., Pvt,
Naples, Nick, Pfc,
Nardella, Jack, Pfc
Nardelli, James V., Pfc,
Nardozzi, Mark E., Pfc,
Nardone, Cosmo D., Pfc,
Nase, Clarence, Pfc,
‡Nash, Loren H., Pvt,
Nason, Gilson J., Pfc,
†Nassar, Teufie, Pvt,
Natale, Anthony P., Pvt,
‡Naudusas, Anthony J., Pvt,
Naukam, Robert A., Pfc,
Navarette, Richard B., Pvt,
Nawalaniec, Edward A., Cpl,
§Naylor, Joseph L., Sgt,
Naylor, Richard A., 2nd Lt,
Neal, Dixie B., Jr., Pfc,
Neal, Richard K., Capt,
Neal, William C., Pfc,
†Neal, William F., Pfc,
Neale, Thomas R., 1st Lt,
Neary, William S., Pvt,
Neavor, John D., Pvt,
Nebbia, Ercole, Pvt,
‡Nee, Colman J., Pvt,
Needles, Clinton A., Pfc,
Needles, Frank, Pfc,
Neel, Marion E., Pvt,
Negley, Paul W., T/5,
Needham, Rollie T., Pfc,
Neelands, Marshall W., T/Sgt,
Neeley, Sammy I., Pvt,
Neely, Arthur J., Pfc,
Neely, Robert L., Cpl,
Neff, Richard F., Pfc,
Neff, William J., Pfc,
Negri, Dominick A., Pvt,
Neidig, Alvin W., Pvt,
Neikark, Vernon C., 2nd Lt,
Nell, Lucian V., Pvt,
Neilson, Harry S., Sgt,
Neilson, Pete S., Pvt,
Neilson, Alden, Pfc,
Nelson, Bill E., Pfc,
Nelson, Charles, Pfc,
Nelson, Clyde E., Pfc,
Nelson, Donald N., 1st Lt,
§Nelson, Einar H., Sgt,
Nelson, Einar W., Sgt,
Nelson, Ernest L., Pvt,
Nelson, Evert A., Pvt,
Nelson, Fred, T/5,
Nelson, J. B., Pvt,
Nelson, Jesse W., Sgt,
Nelson, John E., Pvt,
Nelson, John M., Pfc
Nelson, John W., Pvt,
Nelson, Kenneth L., Pfc
Nelson, Marion W., 1st Lt,
Nelson, Merle A., Pfc,
†Nelson, Milton M., Cpl,
Nelson, Osceola P., Jr., Pvt,
Nelson, Percy K., Pvt,
Nelson, Robert B., Pfc,
*Nelson, Roy A., Pvt,
Nelson, Russell J., Pfc,
Nelson, Sylvester C., S/Sgt,
Nelson, Vernon, T/4,
Nelson, Wade A., Pvt,
Nelson, Wallace E., S/Sgt,
†Nelson, William H., Pfc,
Nemmers, Eugene G., Pfc,
Nerhus, Orville M., Pfc,
Neri, Eufemio S., Sgt,
Nesbitt, Earl H., Pvt,
Nesbitt, Robert J., Pfc,
Nescot, Paul, Pvt,
Nesheim, Vernon L., Sgt,
Nesheim, Ernest B., S/Sgt,
Nesmith, Keene W., Sgt,
Nesselroad, Sherman E., Pvt,
Neswoog, Olaf K., S/Sgt,
†Nettles, Herber E., Jr., Pvt,
†Netzer, Emil S., S/Sgt,
Neu, James, Pvt,
Neu, Philip L., Pfc,
Neuberger, Leonard E., Pfc,
Neuharth, Edward H., Pfc,
Neuman, Lawrence, Pvt,
†Neuman, Louis J., Pvt,
Neumann, John G., Pvt,
Neuner, Joseph C., Pfc,
Neville, Charles G., Pfc,
New, Fred, Pfc,
Newberry, Gene O., Pvt,
Newby, William J. T., Pvt,

† Killed in Action. * Prisoner of War. ‡ Missing in Action. § Died of Wounds.

IN WORLD WAR II 497

Newell, Clell A., Jr., Pfc,
Newell, Donald G., Pvt,
Newell, John D., Pvt,
Newkirk, Ralph E., Sgt,
Newlander, Leon G., S/Sgt,
Newlove, Clyde P., Pfc,
Newman, Eugene, Pfc,
Newman, Howard, Pvt,
Newman, Richard N., Pvt,
Newman, Rushton M., Sgt,
Newman, Wallace W., Pvt,
Newman, Wayne L., Pvt,
Newrocki, Thomas J., Pvt,
Newsome, William F., Sgt,
Newton, Arien S., T/Sgt,
Newton, Earl, Pfc,
†Newton, Robert E., Sgt,
Neyens, Archie F., Pfc,
Nezerski, Edward J., Pvt,
Ng, Chong G., Pfc,
Ng, Wo K., Pfc,
Nicastro, Dominick L., Pvt,
Nicholas, James F., Pfc,
Nicholls, Hugh M., 1st Lt,
Nichols, Carlos C., Pvt,
Nichols, Dudley S., T/4,
†Nichols, Earnest, Pfc,
Nichols, Elbert, Pvt,
Nichols, Elmer T., Sgt,
Nichols, Harry E., Pvt,
†Nichols, Herbert H., Sgt,
Nichols, James R., Pvt,
Nichols, Leonard R., Sgt,
Nichols, Monroe, 1st Sgt,
Nichols, Oliver D., 2nd Lt,
Nichols, Sidney L., Jr., Pvt,
Nichols, Wiley L., T/5,
Nicholson, Birvin F., Pfc,
Nicholson, Chester T., Pfc,
†Nicholson, Howard E., 1st Lt,
Nick, Helmuth, Pvt,
Nickelson, Tom N., Pvt,
Nickerson, Jack C., 2nd Lt,
Nickerson, William T., 1st Lt,
Nickol, John J., Pvt,
Nicolette, Nicholas, Jr., Pvt,
Nicolosi, Henry C., Pvt,
Nieboer, Alfred J., Sgt,
Niedens, Leo F., Pfc,
Niehoff, Richard G., Pfc,
Niemela, Paul W., Pvt,
Niemeyer, Harvey A., Pvt,
Niemi, Mathews J., Pvt,
Niemiec, Edwin P., Pfc,
Nieminen, Edward W., Pfc,
Niestuchowski, Edw. F., 1st Lt
Niggeling, James P., Pfc,
Nigro, Filadelfo, Pfc,
Nigro, Louis, Pvt,
Nigro, Louis B., Pfc,
Nimick, John F., Pvt,
Ninkovich, Nick, T/5,
Nino, Frank, Jr., Pvt,
Nipper, Earl G., Pfc,
Nisonger, Paul C., Pfc,
Nissen, Burnell J., Pvt,
Nix, Otis, Pfc,
Nixon, Claude E., Cpl,
Nixon, Wayne M., Pfc,
Noble, Edward J., Pvt,
Noble, French, Pfc,
†Noble, Harold J., Pfc,
Noble, Ray H., Pfc,
Nocera, Dante A., Pfc,
§Nock, Edwin B., S/Sgt,
Noe, J. C., Pvt,
Noe, Thomas E., Sgt,
Noehren, Albert H., Pfc,
Noel, Herbert, Pfc,
Noel, Jack W., Cpl,
Noel, Jack W., Sr., S/Sgt,
Noel, Thomas L., Pvt,
Noftsger, William E., Jr., Cpl,
†Noin, Fernando, Pfc,
Nolan, William T., Cpl,
Noland, Daniel B., Pvt,
Noles, Weldon, Pvt,
‡Nonamaker, Harold L., 1st Lt,
Noonan, David A., Pfc,
†Nopio, Louis, Pfc,
Norbury, Garnet T., Pfc,
Nord, Leonard A., Pfc,
Norfolk, Albert A., Pfc,
†Norman, Arthur B., Pvt,
Norman, Lee, T/5,
Norred, Bennie, Pfc,
Norrick, Joseph T., T/Sgt,
Norris, Carlos Q., Pvt,
Norris, Everett L., Pvt,
Norris, Harold W., Pvt,
Norris, John D., Pfc,
Norris, Leland C., Pvt,
Norris, Marvin H., Pfc,
Norris, William C., Jr., S/Sgt,
Norrod, Claud B., Pvt,

Northover, Edward E., Sgt,
Northrip, Ray E., 2nd Lt,
Norton, Harry G., Pfc,
Norwood, Furman E., Pfc,
Nothe, William F., Pvt,
Nothwehr, Ruben H., Pvt,
Nottke, Edwin H., 1st Lt,
Novacek, Edwin J., Pvt,
Novack, Harry H., Pvt,
Novack, Joseph, T/4,
Novack, Michael E., Pvt,
Novak, Benedict, Sgt,
Novak, Louis V., T/5,
Novak, Michael L., Pvt,
†Novick, Joseph, Pvt,
Novicki, Walter R., Sgt,
Novinske, Francis T., Pvt,
Novotny, Edward J., T/5,
†Nowak, John W., Pvt,
Nowak, Stephen T., Pfc,
Nowicki, Raymond S., T/5,
Nowlan, Charles S., Pvt,
Nugent, Francis J., 2nd Lt,
Nunes, Antonio D., Pfc,
Nunes, Arthur, Pfc,
Nunn, Chester B., Sgt,
Nuno, Jose J., Pfc,
†Nussbaum, Edward, Jr., 1st Lt,
Nussbaum, Sam, Pfc,
Nusser, William J., Sgt,
Nutter, Jack O., 1st Lt,
Nutter, Joseph C., Pvt
Nutter, Walter H., Jr., Pvt,
Nyemscek, George, Pfc,
Nygaard, Arthur K., Pfc,
Nyman, Carl O. T., Pvt,

Oakes, Edward G., S/Sgt,
†Oakes, Ernest N., Jr., Pvt,
Oakley, Edward N., Pvt,
Oakley, Everett E., S/Sgt,
Oakley, Ivan B., Pfc,
Oakley, John H., Pvt,
†Oakley, Melvin J., Pvt,
Oberdick, Charles J., Pfc,
Oberduster, Lewellyn C., Pfc,
Oberlander, Ellis R., Pfc,
Oberster, Howard J., 2nd Lt,
Obert, Norman E., Pvt,
Oberti, Frank A., Jr., Pvt,
Oborne, Walter M., Pfc,
Obrembalsky, Rudolph, Pfc,
O'Brien, Arthur G., Pvt,
*O'Brien, David P., Pvt,
§O'Brien, Donald D., Sgt,
O'Brien, Donald G., Sgt,
Obrien, Francis T., Pfc,
O'Brien, John J., Pvt,
†O'Brien, John P., Pfc,
O'Brien, Joseph A., T/5,
O'Brien, Thomas D., Pvt,
O'Bryan, Bruce W., Pvt,
O'Bryant, Jack W., Pfc,
Obst, Arthur H., Pfc,
O'Byrne, Paul J., Pvt,
Ochs, Jack, Pvt,
Ockay, John F., S/Sgt,
O'Connell, James J., Pvt,
O'Connell, John, Lt Col,
O'Connor, Benson M., Pfc,
†O'Connor, Crescent W., Pvt,
O'Connor, John J., Pfc,
O'Connor, William J., Pvt,
Oddson, Marlin S., Pfc,
Ode, Elling P., Cpl,
O'Dell, Charles, S/Sgt,
O'Dell, Clarence E., Pfc,
O'Dell, Giles R., Pfc,
O'Dell, Merlin L., Pfc,
Odens, Baldwin E., Cpl,
Odess, Samuel L., 2nd Lt,
Odom, Garland W., Pfc,
Odom, James W., Pfc,
Odom, Sol R., S/Sgt,
§Odom, William P., Pvt,
O'Donnell, Michael J., Pvt,
O'Donnell, Robert H., Pvt,
O'Donnell, Robert J., Pvt,
O'Donnell, William J., Sgt,
Oelrich, Carl A., S/Sgt,
Oertel, Earl V., Pvt,
O'Farrell, Theodore W., S/Sgt,
Offenback, Vincent H., Pvt,
Ogburn, Ernest R., Pvt,
Ogle, Ben L., Cpl,
Ogle, Edward W., Pvt,
Ogletree, Lee H., Pfc,
O'Hanian, Andre W., Pvt,
O'Hearn, Paul F., Pvt,
Ohlson, Wendell B., Pvt,
Ohm, Dwight D., Pfc,
Okey, Benjamin M., Pvt,
O'Keefe, Albert D., Pfc,
O'Keefee, James E., Pvt,
Okonski, Raymond P., Pvt,

Olaker, Robert L., T/4,
Oldani, August, T/5,
O'Laughlin, George E., Pvt,
Olawski, Alfred, Sgt,
Oldefest, Willis H., Pvt,
*Oldfield, John H., Pvt,
O'Leary, George A., 2nd Lt,
O'Leary, Thomas J., Jr., Pvt,
†Oledzinski, Felix A., Sgt,
Oleska, Leonard M., Pvt,
Oleson, Raymond F., Pvt,
Olevich, Victor J., Pvt,
Oleynek, Fred, Pfc,
Olger, Chester F., Pvt,
Oliasz, Stanley C., Pfc,
Oliveira, George, Pfc,
†Olivencia, Santiago, Pfc,
Oliver, Harry J., T/5,
Oliver, James, Pfc,
Oliver, John M., Pfc,
Oliver, William H., Pvt,
Oliver, Dick J. S., Pfc,
Oliveri, Joseph P., Pvt,
Oller, Paul D., Pvt,
†Olling, Donald L., Pvt,
Ollinger, Robert J., Pvt,
Olmstead, Carl A., Pfc,
Olmstead, Clayton W., Pvt,
Olmstead, Earl V., T/5,
Olmstead, William C., Pfc,
Olney, Cyrus C., Pvt,
Olsen, Lincoln T., Pfc,
Olsen, Richard R., S/Sgt,
Olsen, Robert A., Pvt,
†Olson, Arlo L., Capt,
Olson, Arthur E., Pfc,
Olson, Arthur R., Sgt,
Olson, Dewey A., S/Sgt,
Olson, Donald J., Pvt,
Olson, Donald W., Pfc,
Olson, Elmer C., Cpl,
Olson, Elmer O., Pfc,
Olson, Elwin N., Sgt,
Olson, Emmons L., Pfc,
†Olson, Fred, Pfc,
§Olson, Gordon B., Pvt,
Olson, Leonard M., Pfc,
Olson, Warren H., Pfc,
Olszanowski, John E., Pfc,
Olszewski, John S., Pfc,
Oman, Walter, Pfc,
Ondeck, Method E., Pvt,
Ondrasik, William, 1st Lt,
O'Neal, Aaron N., Pfc,
O'Neal, Bill, Pvt,
O'Neal, Ephraim, Pvt,
O'Neal, Le Roy, Pfc,
†O'Neal, John R., Pvt,
O'Neil, Bernard, Pfc,
O'Neil, Charles M., Pfc,
†O'Neil, James M., Pfc,
O'Neil, Thomas G., 1st Lt,
O'Neil, Walter E., Pvt,
O'Neil, Wilfred B., Pvt,
O'Neil, Robert J., Pvt,
O'Neill, William A., S/Sgt,
Ooten, Chester A., Pvt,
†Opheim, Johan S., Pfc,
Oppel, Joseph L., Pfc,
Oppedahl, Eldo H., Pfc,
Oquist, Walter G., Pvt,
Oray, Leonard G., S/Sgt,
Ording, Lowell H., Pfc,
Oreb, John, Jr., Sgt,
Orfanos, George G., Pvt,
Oric, John L., Pfc,
O'Riordan, Denis, Pfc,
Orlando, Dominick J., 2nd Lt,
Orlowski, Theodore J., Pvt,
Orluk, Alphonse J., 2nd Lt,
†Ormsby, Robert, Pvt,
Orndorff, Coyd W., S/Sgt,
Orofino, Joseph S., Pvt,
Orona, Paul, Pvt,
O'Rourke, Robert J., Pvt,
Orphanos, John L., Pfc,
†Orr, Howard E., Pvt,
Orr, Jack W., T/Sgt,
Orell, Cletis G., Pfc,
Ortiz, Dominick, Pfc,
Ortiz, Henry H., Pvt,
Ortiz, Jesse A., Pfc,
Ortiz, Toribio E., Pvt,
Ortmeier, Harvey C., Sgt,
Orton, Garry V., Jr., Pfc,
Orton, James M., Pfc,
Orts, Norman M., Pvt,
Orzechowski, Joseph G., Pvt,
†Orzechowski, Joseph L., Pvt,
Osbeck, Harry C., Pfc,
Osborn, Chase S., T/5,
Osborn, John R., T/5,
Osborne, Benjamin F., Pvt,
Osborne, Donald E., S/Sgt,
Osborne, John W., S/Sgt,

Osborne, Nathan W., Pfc,
Osborne, Oliver M., Pvt,
Osborne, Thomas W., Pfc,
†Osborne, William H., Pfc,
Osby, Lloyd A., Pvt,
Osepchuk, Phillip, Pfc,
*Oseth, Olger J., S/Sgt,
O'Shaughnessy, R. C., Pfc,
Oshio, Joe, Pvt,
Osler, Theodore G., Pfc,
Osment, Johnnie H., Pvt
Osment, Walter P., S/Sgt,
Osment, Welton R., Pfc,
Osofsky, Herman, Pvt,
Osowski, Francis, Pfc,
Ossler, William A., Pvt,
Ost, Edward, S/Sgt,
Osterberg, Donald W., Pfc,
Osterbuhr, Dick U., Pfc,
Osterhout, Harold W., Pvt,
Osterloh, Walter K., Pfc,
Ostiguy, Thomas E., Jr., Pvt,
Ostlund, Eric G., Sgt,
Ostrem, Theodore C., Pvt,
Ostrom, Frederick S., Sgt,
Osuna, Arturo F., Pfc,
Otero, David J., Cpl,
Otey, Matthew A., Pvt,
Otis, James E., Pvt,
Otos, Allan R., Pvt,
*Ott, Fred A., Pvt,
Ott, Howard C., S/Sgt,
Ott, John E., Pfc,
Ottinger, Lloyd M., Pfc,
Otto, Frank, Jr., Pvt,
Otto, Raymond, Pvt,
‡Otto, Victor B., Pvt,
Ouchi, Harry M., Pfc,
Ouellette, Herman R., Pfc,
Ouelette, Melvin C., T/5,
Ouillette, Theodore A., Pvt,
Outland, Carlton M., Cpl,
Overbay, Thomas J., Pvt,
Overholtzer, Richard B., Pfc,
Overman, Julian J., Pfc,
Overmyer, Robert D., Pvt,
Overskei, Ernest O., Pvt,
†Overton, Jay E., Pvt,
†Overton, Tom, Pvt.
Owen, Alfred W., T/5,
Owen, Charles L., Pfc,
Owen, Floyd R., Pvt,
Owens, Charles H., Pvt,
Owens, Herman G., Pfc,
Owens, John B., Pvt,
†Owens, Oscar, Pfc,
Owens, Robert E., Pvt,
Owens, Rufice H., Pvt,
Owens, Walter, Pvt,
Owsley, Floyd T., Pfc,
Ozog, Walter J., Pfc,

Pace, Cecil C., Cpl
Pace, George H., Pvt,
Pace, John W., Pvt,
Pacella, Carmen J., Pfc,
Pacheco, Alfred, Pfc,
Pacheco, Alfred M., S/Sgt,
Pacheco, Louis, Pfc,
Pacheco, Seledonio G., Pvt,
§Pacine, Augustus A., Pfc,
Pack, Harley J., Pvt,
Pack, James O., Pvt,
Pacourek, Robert D., Pvt,
Paden, Herbert R., Sgt,
Paderta, John J., Pvt,
Padgett, Ernest L., Pvt,
Padgett, J. C., Pfc,
Padilla, Azerio, Pfc,
Padleski, Edward J., Sgt,
Page, Clyde P., Pvt,
Page, Lester R., Jr., S/Sgt,
Page, Mathew, Pvt,
Page, Thomas F., Sgt,
Page, Travis, 1st Sgt,
Page, Woodrow P., Pfc,
Pagenkopf, Charles A., S/Sgt,
Pagliuca, Philip A., Pfc,
Paige, Leonard H., Pfc,
Painter, Jasper O., Pvt,
Painter, Lester M., Pvt,
Pairgin, Alvin B., Pfc,
†Pais, Joe B., Pvt,
Pajari, Raymond K., Pfc,
Pajich, Paul, Pvt,
Paky, Charles K., Pfc,
Palandri, Pete S., Pfc,
†Palencher, Andy P., Pvt,
§Palette, Fred W., Pvt,
Palm, Curtis G., Pfc,
Palm, Stanley J., Pfc,
Palmer, Arthur H., S/Sgt,
Palmer, Harry O., Pvt,
Palmer, John F., T/Sgt,
Palmer, Robert P., Pvt,

Palmer, Rollie E., Sgt,
Palmer, Thomas J., S/Sgt,
Palmer, Warren E., S/Sgt,
Palmer, Woodward K., Pfc,
Palmieri, Joseph A., Pvt,
Palmiotti, Edward, Pvt,
Palmquist, Runo W., Pvt,
Palo, Arthur C., Pfc,
Palocy, Charles J., Pvt,
Palone, Louis, Sgt,
Palonka, Ladislaus J., Pvt,
Palumbo, Anthony P., Pfc,
Palumbo, Michael A., Pfc,
Paluscio, Joseph B., Pfc,
Paluzzi, Peter M., Pvt,
†Pampena, Peter J., Pvt,
Panagakos, William L., Pvt,
†Panagelis, Peter, Pfc,
Pandolfi, Gerald J., Pvt,
Panettiere, Samuel, Pvt,
Panice, Tobey, Pvt,
Panicko, Stanley, Pfc,
Panneman, R. E., Jr., Pfc,
†Pansarasa, Joseph J., Pfc,
Pantle, Harley R., Pvt,
Panuska, John M., Pvt,
Paoletto, Vincent C., Pfc,
Paolitto, Peter J., Pvt,
Papagelis, Peter, Pfc,
Papaleo, Jerry F., Pfc,
Papanu, Nicholas J., Pvt,
Papex, Joe, T/Sgt,
Papiccio, Anthony N., Pfc,
Papke, Robert B., Pvt,
Papp, Alex T., Cpl,
Papp, Charlie L., Pvt,
Papp, Geza, Pfc,
Pappas, Nick J., Pvt,
‡Papsidero, Ralph, Pvt,
Paradis, Arthur J., S/Sgt,
Paradis, Hubert L., Pfc,
Paridiso, Amelio N., Pfc,
Parfitt, Frederick E., 2nd Lt,
Parham, Donald E., 1st Lt,
Parise, Michael, Pvt,
Parish, John L., Pvt,
Parizo, Norman R., Pfc,
†Park, Alfred H., Pvt,
Parker, Calvin C., Pfc,
‡Parker, Edward H., Jr., Pvt,
Parker, George A., Sgt,
Parker, Henry, Sgt,
Parker, Jerimiah D., Pvt,
Parker, John A., S/Sgt,
Parker, John W., Pvt,
Parker, Johnson A., Pfc,
Parker, Ralph J., Pvt,
Parker, Ray J., Pvt,
Parker, Richard C., Pvt,
Parker, Seaborn K., Pvt,
Parker, Waldin F., Pvt,
Parker, Warren G., Pfc,
Parker, William C., T/5,
Parkes, Allen F., Pvt,
†Parkins, Daymon L., Cpl,
Parkinson, Frank, Jr., Pvt,
Parks, James W., T/Sgt,
Parks, Robert T., S/Sgt,
Parks, Walter H., T/5,
†Parlag, Michael J., Pvt,
Parlo, Charles N., Pvt,
Parmeter, Bernard W., 2nd Lt,
Parnell, Oaggle A., Pfc,
Parone, Anthony J., Pvt,
Parr, Chester E., Pvt,
Parra, Alvaro H., Pvt,
Parra, Justo C., Pvt,
Parra, Sabino, S/Sgt,
Parrin, Savy W., Pvt,
†Parrish, Edward W., Pvt,
Parrish, Herbert R., Sgt,
Parrott, Louis R., S/Sgt,
Parslow, Clifford D., Pfc,
Parsons, Phil E., T/5,
Parsons, Raymond E., Sgt,
Parsons, Walter W., Pfc,
Parsons, William C., Pvt,
Patricella, Sam A., Pfc,
Partridge, Buddy F., Cpl,
Parziale, Charles J., Capt,
Pasca, Anthony A., Pfc,
Pascente, Joseph F., Pvt,
Pascocello, Sylvester, Pfc,
Pasek, Stanley E., Pfc,
†Pashley, Fred C., Pvt,
Pasierbowicz, Edward S., Pvt,
Paske, Edward O., T/Sgt,
Paskiewicz, Alfred W., Pfc,
Pasnick, Nick, Jr., Pvt,
Pasquariello, Carmen V., Pvt,
Pasquini, Oreste J., Sgt,
Passman, Fletcher, Pvt,
Passwaters, Charles T., Pvt,
Pasternack, Carl, Pfc,
Pastorino, Carmine T., Pvt,

† Killed in Action. * Prisoner of War. ‡ Missing in Action. § Died of Wounds.

Pastrano, Manuel A., Cpl
Patchin, Henry A., Sgt
Pate, Henry, Pvt
Pate, L. D., Pfc
Pate, Robert F., Pfc
Pate, Samuel T., Pvt
Path, Emil J., 1st Lt
Patnoe, Tuffield T., T/Sgt
Paton, Lyman N., Pvt
Patriarco, John A., Pfc
Patrick, Billy, Pfc
Patrick, Cary E., Pvt
†Patrick, Edward S., Pfc
Patrick, Jack B. E., Pfc
Patrick, James J., Pfc
Patrick, Lewis, Cpl
†Patrick, Richard B., S/Sgt
Patrunak, George, T/Sgt
Patterson, Charles C., Pvt
Patterson, Dale M., Sgt
Patterson, Delmar P., S/Sgt
Patterson, Earl F., Pfc
Patterson, Earl N., Pvt
Patterson, Elwyn D., Pfc
†Patterson, Glen I., S/Sgt
Patterson, Harold M., 1st Lt
Patterson, James H., Sgt
Patterson, Lawrence E., Pfc
Patterson, Maynard L., Pvt
Patterson, Quincy G., Pfc
Patterson, Robert P., S/Sgt
Patterson, Samuel J., Pfc
Patterson, Thomas E., Sgt
Patton, Charlie Y., Jr., Sgt
Patton, Elmer J., Pfc
‡Patton, Leo J., Pvt
Patton, Leonard C., Pvt
†Patton, Vence H., Pvt
Patty, Thomas L., Pfc
Paul, Frank S., Jr., T/5
Paul, James B., Pfc
Paul, John J., Pvt
‡Paul, Joseph P., Pvt
Paul, Oscar P., S/Sgt
Paul, Robert F., Pvt
Paul, Thomas C., 2nd Lt
Paul, Walter R., Pfc
Pauley, David D., Pfc
Paulick, Michael, Lt Col
Paull, Joseph T., 1st Lt
‡Paullus, Ted, Pfc
Paullus, Rex, Pvt
Paulsen, Randolph F., 2nd Lt
Pavenski, Peter A., Sgt
Pavlas, Hubert J., Sgt
Pavlovic, Anthony, Pvt
Pavlovich, Elroy G., 1st Lt
Pavlovich, William E., T/4
Pavonetti, Pardo A., T/5
Pawlak, Thaddeus W., Pfc
Pawlik, Mike, Cpl
Pawlowski, John R., Pvt
Pawluk, Harry, Pfc
†Payer, Conrad, Pfc
Payer, Steve, T/Sgt
Payette, George N., Pfc
Payne, Carl B., Pvt
Payne, Charles T., Pvt
Payne, Clifford A., Pfc
Payne, Coleman, Pvt
Payne, Dayton, Pvt
Payne, Fred, Pvt
Payne, James R., Pfc
Payne, John H., Pfc
Payne, Joshway, Cpl
Payne, Leland B., Pfc
Payne, Paul R., Pvt
Payne, Perry E., Pfc
Pazek, Theodore G., Pfc
Pazick, Joseph F., Pvt
Peachey, Brazh, Pvt
Pearce, Francis M., 2nd Lt
Pearce, Robert V., Sgt
Pearce, Thomas M., Pvt
†Pearl, Joseph, 1st Lt
Pearless, John H., T/5
Pearson, Bennie L., Pfc
Pearson, Burton L., Pfc
Pearson, Carl R., Sgt
Pearson, Cecil, Pfc
†Pearson, Leroy, Pfc
Pearson, Oscar W., Pfc
Pearson, Percy M., Pfc
†Pearson, Robert L., S/Sgt
Pearson, Roy E., Pvt
Peart, Jack H., Pvt
Pebler, George W., Pfc
Pechacek, Paul F., T/5
Pecheck, Robert R., T/4
Pechin, Frederic W., 1st Lt
Pecinovsky, Bernard J., Pvt
Peck, Earl, Pfc
Peck, Francis A., Pvt
Peck, George W., Cpl
Peck, Gerald E., Pvt
Peck, Raymond I., Cpl
Peck, Vernon H., Jr., Pfc
Peck, William H., Capt
Peckham, Harry L., Pvt
Peckham, Herbert M., Pfc
Peckham, Walter G., Sgt
†Pedersen, Erling W., Pvt
Pedersen, Jack E., Pvt
Pederson, Ernest J., Pfc
Pederson, James F., Pfc
Pedigo, Leland A., 2nd Lt
Pedregon, Augustin G., Pvt
Peed, Harold E., 1st Lt
Peedigo, Ernie, T/5
Peel, Alfred R., Capt
Peeples, Clifford A., Sgt
Pegausch, Robert S., Pfc
Peil, Hans R., Pvt
†Peirce, John J., Pvt
Peirson, Stewart D., Pvt
†Pekala, Frank L., Pfc
Pekala, Sigmund B., Pvt
Pekar, Martin J., Jr., Pfc
Pelcner, Edsel, Pvt
Pelino, Igino G., Pvt
Pelis, John J., Jr., Pfc
Pellerin, Alphonse, Pvt
Peloquin, Edward G., Pvt
Peloquin, Joel D., Pfc
Pelz, Darwin K., T/Sgt
Pelz, Raymond L., S/Sgt
Pelzer, Harold J., Sgt
Pena, Inez, Pvt
†Pence, Earl L., Pvt
Pendarvis, Jack J., Pvt
Pendergroft, Carlyle H., Pvt
Pendergrass, W. F., S/Sgt
†Pendleton, Edward E., Pvt
Pendley, John W., Pfc
Peninger, Coy W., Pvt
Penix, Mose L., Pfc
Penix, Townsel, T/5
Penna, Carmine J., Pfc
Penna, Denver T., Sgt
Pennacchio, Anthony M., Pvt
Pennell, Cubbie C., Pvt
Pennell, Donald N., Pfc
†Pennell, Frank J., S/Sgt
Pennella, Michael, Capt
Penniber, Jerry, Pfc
‡Pennington, William R., S/Sgt
Pennino, Seraphine, Jr., Pfc
Peno, Arthur C., Pvt
§Penzkofer, Gilbert C., Pvt
Peot, Francis P., Pfc
Pepchinski, Bonivent J., Pfc
†Perales, Angel R., Pvt
Peralta, Juan C., S/Sgt
Perch, Adam A., Pvt
Perdue, Ervine E., Pvt
Perea, Robert, Pvt
Perez, Alexander, Pvt
Perez, Guadalupe, Pvt
†Perez, Ignacio R., Pvt
Perez, Jose G., Pvt
Perez, Mario G., Pvt
Perge, Alexander J., Pfc
Perkins, Arthur J., Pvt
Perkins, Bernard B., Pvt
Perkins, Claud E., 2nd Lt
Perkins, Fletcher A., Pfc
Perkins, Glenn D., Pfc
Perkins, Horace A., Pfc
Perkins, Lawrence E., Pvt
Perkins, Lester W., Pvt
Perkins, Richard E., Cpl
†Perkins, Sanford T., Pvt
Perkowich, Anthony J., Pfc
Perkowski, Frank J., 2nd Lt
†Perlos, Nicholas, Pvt
Perlson, Edward, Sgt
Pero, Frank E., Jr., Pfc
Perrier, Roy B., Pvt
Perrin, Robert L., Pvt
Perrin, Savy W., Pvt
Perrine, Edward C., Pvt
Perrine, Joseph T., Pfc
Perrotti, Frank A., Pvt
†Perry, Donald F., Pvt
†Perry, Don O., Pvt
Perry, Edward W., Pvt
Perry, Floyd M., Pvt
Perry, Frank L., Pvt
Perry, Garland, Pfc
Perry, Henry, Pfc
Perry, Lester C., Pvt
Perry, Merrill I., Sgt
Perry, Rainne O., Pfc
Perry, Robert G., Pvt
Perry, Warren S., 2nd Lt
Perry, William N., Pvt
Perry, William S., Pvt
Perry, Woodrow, Pvt
Persaud, Gary, Pfc
Perslin, George J., Pfc
Person, Hilding, Pfc
Persson, Harold P., Pfc
Pesall, George H., T/5
Peshak, Eugene F., Pvt
Petak, Emil S., Pvt
Petechuk, John, Pvt
Peters, Donald H., Pfc
Peters, George R., Pfc
Peters, Harold P., Pvt
Peters, John E., Pvt
Peters, Lloyd C., Pfc
†Peters, Michael, Pvt
Peters, Ralph G., Pvt
Peters, Roy, Pvt
Peters, Roy F., Pfc
Peters, Wilbert I., Pvt
Petersen, Paul P., T/4
Petersen, Thomas L., T/5
Petersohn, Henry F., Pvt
†Peterson, Donald E., Cpl
Peterson, Earl S., Cpl
†Peterson, Edward A., Pvt
Peterson, Edwin R., Pvt
Peterson, Francis J., Pvt
Peterson, Harold E., Pvt
Peterson, Harold O., Pvt
Peterson, Harold Roy, Pvt
Peterson, Harold W., S/Sgt
Peterson, Irvin C., Pfc
Peterson, John, 2nd Lt
Peterson, Lyle E., S/Sgt
Peterson, Melville, Pfc
Peterson, Palmer O., Pfc
Peterson, Percy A., Cpl
Peterson, Ray A., 1st Lt
Peterson, Raymond R., Pvt
Peterson, Robert J., Pfc
Peterson, T. J., Pfc
Peterson, Vernon E., S/Sgt
†Peterson, Victor O., Pvt
Peterson, Vincent L., Pfc
Petito, Albert, Pfc
Petito, Guy W., Jr., Pvt
Petito, John J., Pvt
Petkavich, John P., Pvt
Petker, Herman G., Pvt
Petko, Roger F., Pfc
*Petranovich, Frank, Pfc
Petras, Tony, Pvt
Petrash, John S., Pfc
Petree, Jessie C., Pfc
Petree, Robert G., T/5
Petrella, Patrick J., S/Sgt
Petri, Joe, Jr., Sgt
Petrick, Clarence J., Cpl
Petrick, Michael, Pfc
Petricka, John W., Pfc
Petrie, Earl, Pfc
Petriello, Charles J., Pvt
Petriello, Vincent J., Pvt
Petrillo, Arthur I., Pfc
Petrini, James, Pfc
†Petrizzi, Marico P., Sgt
Petrizzo, John J., Pvt
Petrizzo, Joseph, Pfc
†Petrone, Carl A., Pfc
†Petrone, Charles A., Pfc
Petrongola, Michael A., Cpl
Petroni, Leonard L., Pfc
Petropoulos, Nickolas L., Pfc
§Petroski, Frank E., Pfc
Petrovich, John J., Pvt
†Petrozzi, Evo F., Cpl
Petruccelli, Salvatore S., Cpl
Petruzzelli, Carl V., Pvt
Petry, Lloyd J., Pfc
Pettelle, Joseph H., Sgt
Pettibone, Stephen G., Cpl
†Pettigrew, John S., Pvt
†Pettigrew, Aubrey W., 2nd Lt
Pettit, Joseph T., Pfc
Pettit, William, Pfc
Pettygrove, G. C., Jr., 2nd Lt
Petzel, Anthony, Pfc
Petzke, Theodore W., Pvt
Peuse, Delton R., Pfc
Pevy, Charles E., Pvt
Pewitt, Robert L., Pvt
Peyton, Levi G., Pfc
Pfeifer, John R., Pfc
Pfeiffer, Joseph N., Sgt
Pfeiffer, Milton C., Pfc
Pfeuffer, Arthur M., Pvt
Pfister, Joseph V., Pfc
Pfisterer, Edwin M., Pfc
Pflam, John A., Pfc
Pfotenhauer, Robert J., Pfc
Pfunk, Arthur F., Pfc
Phaff, Wilbert, Pvt
Phalen, James B., S/Sgt
Phaling, Edward W., Pvt
Phegley, Lloyd D., T/3
†Pheil, Julian C., Pfc
Phelps, Chester F., Pvt
Phelps, Kermit C., Pvt
†Phelps, Noah L., Pfc
Phifer, Bert G., Pvt
Philamalee, Earl D., Pfc
†Phillippi, James S., Pfc
*Phillips, Barton E., Pvt
Phillips, Clayton G., Pvt
Phillips, Clifford L., S/Sgt
Phillips, Dexter C., 1st Lt
Phillips, Frank A., Pvt
Phillips, George M., Jr., Pvt
Phillips, George W., Pfc
Phillips, Glen J., Pvt
Phillips, Grady R., S/Sgt
Phillips, Hubert L., Pfc
†Phillips, Hurley M., S/Sgt
†Phillips, James E., Pvt
Phillips, James F., T/5
Phillips, James V., Pvt
Phillips, Ralph S., Pvt
Phillips, Roger N., 1st Lt
Phillips, Ross E., S/Sgt
Phillips, Thomas R., Pfc
Phillips, William J., Pvt
†Phillips, Wayne L., Sgt
Phinisey, Gordon T., Pvt
Phinos, Andrew J., Sgt
Phipps, Charles H., Pvt
Phipps, Dallas A., Pvt
Phipps, Madison J., Pfc
Picchi, John, Pvt
Picchiello, Victor A., 2nd Lt
Piccirillo, Peter, T/5
Piccoli, Vincent J., Pvt
†Pick, Alfred F., 2nd Lt
Pickard, Archie L., Pfc
Pickard, Floyd J., Pfc
Pickard, Frederick C., Pvt
†Pickett, Alonzo I., Pvt
Pickett, Leonard W., Pvt
Pickett, Samuel R., S/Sgt
†Pickrell, James, Jr., Pvt
§Picman, Anthony P., Pvt
Picus, Arthur S., Pfc
Pidgeon, Henry W., Pfc
Piehuta, Joseph E., Sgt
Pieper, Jerry F., Sgt
Pier, Gerald L., Pfc
Pierce, Albert R., T/4
Pierce, Bernard P., Pfc
Pierce, Cecil M., Pvt
Pierce, Charles A., Jr., T/5
Pierce, Curtis B., Pvt
†Pierce, Edgar L., Sgt
Pierce, Erven B., S/Sgt
Pierce, Frank B., Pfc
Pierce, Glarice C., Pfc
Pierce, James P., Sgt
†Pierce, Lester C., Pvt
Pierce, Richard O., S/Sgt
Pierce, Robert E., Pvt
Pierce, Samuel P., Cpl
Pierce, William W., Pvt
Pieretti, Alfred, Pvt
Pierini, Angelo R., Pfc
Pierson, James W., Pfc
Pierson, Lester L., T/5
Pierson, Stewart D., Pfc
Pierzchalski, Steven S., Pfc
Piescki, Charles W., Pfc
Pietruszewski, Valerian, Pfc
Pietryka, Joseph A., Pvt
Pifer, Elmer, Pvt
Pigg, David F., Pvt
†Pignetti, Erminio, Pfc
Pike, Walter A., Pfc
Pike, William B., Sr., T/5
Pilcher, Ben, Pfc
Pilgrim, James, S/Sgt
Pilk, Paul J., Cpl
Pilkington, James S., Pvt
‡Pillars, Curtis A., Pfc
Pilnick, Louis, Pvt
Pilone, Alfred J., Pfc
Pills, Robert B., Pvt
Pimental, James H., Cpl
Pina, Abel, Pvt
Pinali, Gino, Pvt
Pinder, Raymond C., Pfc
Pindris, Andrew, Pvt
Pinkhard, Calvin M., Capt
Pinkerton, Robert E., Pfc
†Pinkley, John R., Pvt
Pinkova, Jerry S., Pvt
Pinter, Martin M., Pvt
Pinto, Joseph J., Pvt
Pinto, Stanley, T/4
Piombino, Joseph S., Pvt
Pipitone, Giacchimo, Pvt
Pipkins, James D., Pfc
†Piquet, Paul K., Pvt
Piquette, Henry A., Pfc
Pirilla, Henry E., Pvt
Pirozzi, John Louis, Pvt
Pirro, Carmen Joe, Pvt
Pirtle, Thomas R., Pfc
Pisarczyk, Edmond, Pfc
Piscitelli, Luca, Jr., Pfc
Piskor, Stanley T., T/4
Pistohl, George C., Sgt
Pitcher, Elmer B., Jr., Pvt
Pitelli, Peter E., Pfc
Pitman, General F., Pfc
Pitman, Steve M., Jr., Pfc
Pitsonbarger, James W., Pfc
Pittelkow, Eric J., Pfc
Pittman, Harold F., Pvt
Pittman, Sam C., Pfc
Pitts, Frederick S., Sgt
Pitts, Robert S., Pfc
Pitts, William R., Pfc
Pixley, Erwin W., Pvt
Pizza, Thomas M., Pfc
†Place, Lloyd C., Jr., Pvt
Placenza, Vito F., Pvt
Plaep, Erwin R., Pfc
§Plano, Paul P., Pvt
Plantz, William N., T/5
Plaska, Theodore, Pvt
Plasky, Andy, Pfc
Plaster, Everett A., T/4
Platt, Kenneth C., Pvt
Platt, Louis I., Pvt
Plaud, Roger A., Sgt
Plawski, Casimir, Pfc
Player, Benjamin, Pfc
Player, Ervin B., Pvt
Pledger, Henry L., Pfc
Plegge, Willard, S/Sgt
Pletz, Kenneth E., Sgt
Plisko, Louis M., Pfc
Ploskonka, Joseph L., Pfc
Plouff, Neil F., Pvt
Plowden, Evans J., Jr., Pvt
Plumeau, Earl C., T/Sgt
Plummer, Earl H., Jr., Capt
Plunkett, Robert L., T/Sgt
Plyler, Millen K., Pvt
Pocchigian, Albert, Pvt
Podenski, Ervin, T/Sgt
†Podgorny, Rudolph V., Pfc
†Podsadowski, John K., Pvt
Poepperling, Paul F. W., Pvt
Poepping, Dominic J., Pvt
Poff, Edward C., Pvt
†Poggioli, Paul P., Pvt
Pogorelc, Anthony J., Pfc
Poindexter, Horace B., Pvt
Poindexter, Roy L., Pfc
§Pointer, Woodrow W., Pfc
Poirier, Marcel J., Pfc
Poklis, Charles, Pfc
Pola, Orlando M., Pfc
Polejewski, Eugene M., Pvt
Polenini, Ensio, Pvt
Poletti, Arthur J., Pvt
Polewarczyk, Walter, Pfc
Polich, George B., T/Sgt
Polin, Edward, Pvt
Politowski, John J., Sgt
Polk, Tom R., Jr., Sgt
Polly, Willis R., T/4
*Polocko, Matthew F., Pvt
†Polonsky, Louis, Pfc
Polt, John, Jr., Pvt
Polt, Milton L., Pvt
Polte, Frank A., Pvt
Pomeroy, Clifford L., Pvt
Pomietlass, Frank J., Jr., Pvt
Pommier, Lester J., Pfc
Pompey, Leonard A., Pvt
Ponder, Caleb, F., Pvt
†Pontbriand, Robert G., Pfc
†Pontecorvo, Franklin E., Pvt
†Pontes, Anthony J., Sgt
Poochigian, Albert, Pfc
†Pool, Braxton, Sgt
†Poole, Arthur J., Pvt
Pore, Henry, Pvt
Porlier, Roy G., T/5
Poore, Otto, Pvt
Poort, Oran J., Pvt
Pope, Carl C., Pfc
Pope, Joseph L., Jr., Pfc
Pope, William C., T/5
†Popenhagen, Louis E., Pfc
Popoloski, Albert, Pfc
Poplawski, Edward J., Pfc
Popow, Stanley, Pvt
Popowicz, Theodore, Pfc
Popp, Gordon C., Pvt
Poppe, Clarence E., Pvt
†Popper, Henry, Pvt
Popple, James C., 1st Lt
Poppleton, Richard J., Sgt
Popsuj, Henry J., Pvt
Poralla, Albert G., Pfc
Porambo, Jacob S., Pvt
Porco, Ralph R., Pfc
Poremba, James N., Pfc
Porter, Cedric E., S/Sgt

† Killed in Action. * Prisoner of War. ‡ Missing in Action. § Died of Wounds.

Porter, Clarence I., Jr., S/Sgt,
Porter, Floyd W., Pfc,
Porter, Granville G., Pvt,
Porter, Harding S., Pvt,
†Porter, Joseph F., Jr., Pfc
†Porter, Kenneth R., Pfc,
Porter, Leonard C., Pvt,
†Porter, Mark F., Pvt,
Porter, Ralph L., S/Sgt,
Porter, Vincent J., Pfc,
Porter, Wayne A., Cpl,
Portillos, Pete, Pvt,
†Portiner, Everett L., Pfc,
Portman, Fred J., Jr., T/Sgt,
Portugal, Othmel W., Capt,
‡Porucznik, Stanley A., S/Sgt,
*Posner, Ralph, Pvt,
Poss, Urban M., Pfc,
†Post, Simon, Pfc,
Posta, Arne H., Pvt
Poston, Richard H., Pvt,
Potaczek, Alois J., S/Sgt,
Potak, George A., T/4,
Poteet, William G., Sgt,
Potkovick, William, Pfc,
†Potter, Clarke M., Jr., Pfc,
Potter, Cleo, Pvt,
Potter, Earl V., Pfc,
Potter, Kenneth B., Maj,
Potter, Worden F., Pfc,
Potterfield, Arthur B., Pvt,
Potts, Bernard L., Pfc,
Potts, Charles D., Pfc,
†Poulin, Gerald F., Pvt,
Pound, Guiles R., Pfc,
Pounds, Ralston A., Pfc,
Povlsen, Svend E., Pvt,
Powell, Adolphus H., Pfc,
Powell, Dean L., Pfc,
Powell, Elias D., Jr., Pfc,
Powell, Elmer A., Pvt,
Powell, Harry A., Pfc,
Powell, Howard, Jr., Pvt,
Powell, Howard S., Pfc,
Powell, Levi A., Sr., Pvt,
Powell, Maynard S., Jr., Pfc,
Powell, Raymond L., Pfc,
Powell, Roy C., Pfc,
Powell, Stanley W., Pvt,
Powers, George G., Pfc,
Powers, Joe M., Pfc,
Powers, John P., Pfc,
Powers, Sam, Pfc,
Powlus, John M., Pfc
Poythress, Sam J., Jr., 1st Lt,
Praeger, Raymond C., Pfc,
Prange, Arnold L., T/5,
Pranulis, Joseph A., Pfc,
Praskevich, Michael, Pfc,
Pransicki, Arthur G., Sgt
†Prassas, Constaninos, T/4,
Prata, Manuel N., Pvt,
Prather, Herman R., Pvt,
Prato, Albert E., Pvt,
Pratt, Clifford L. R., Pvt,
Pratt, Daniel W., 1st Lt,
Pratt, Dillard, Pvt,
†Pratt, Douglas D., Pvt,
Pratt, Leonard M., S/Sgt,
Preece, Harrison H., S/Sgt,
Premetine, George A., Pfc,
Premo, Edward F., Pfc,
Prentice, Claude W., Pvt,
Prentice, Luther S., Pfc,
Presant, Sidney, Pvt,
†Prescott, Arthur W., Pvt,
Perscott, William S., Pvt,
Presensky, John, Pvt,
Presinzano, M. P., Pfc,
Preski, Stanley, Pvt,
Presley, Jenks T., Cpl,
Press, Eli, Pvt,
Press, Isadore, Pfc,
†Presson, Durward E., Sgt,
Preston, Daniel, Pfc,
Preston, John L., Pfc,
†Preston, Morgan O., 2nd Lt,
Presutti, Anthony J., Pfc,
Pretty Bird, Luther, Sgt,
Pretzer, David, Pvt,
Preuss, Frederick H., Pvt,
Previte, Joseph P., Pfc,
Prezio, Palmer, Pvt,
Pribis, Alex, Cpl,
Price, Coker N., Pfc
Price, James A., Pvt,
Price, Jeffrey F., Pfc,
Price, Lloyd K., Sgt,
Price, Redman T., Jr., Pvt,
Price, Thomas, Pfc,
Price, Walter J., S/Sgt,
§Price, Warren, Sgt,
Price, Wilfred J., Sgt,
Price, William J., Pvt,
Prichard, Harley D., Pfc,
Prichard, James M., Pfc,
Prichard, Leslie A., Lt Col,
Priddey, Alfred S., Pfc,
†Priest, George W., Pvt,
Priest, Patrick A., Pfc,
§Priester, Norris J., Pfc,
Prigge, Ray W., Sgt,
Primrose, Douglas F., Pfc,
Prince, Jacob J., Pvt,
Prince, Robert M., Pvt,
†Principio, Dominic W., S/Sgt,
†Prine, Ervine W., Pvt,
Prinkey, Jesse C., Pvt
†Prinzo, Ralph, Pfc
†Prior, Richard G., Pvt
†Prisaznik, Michael, Pvt,
Prislupsky, Michael, T/5,
Pritchard, Harold, Pfc,
Pritchard, Thomas J., Pfc,
Pritchard, Woodrow W., Pfc
Pritt, Raymond L., Sgt,
Pritt, Robert, Pfc,
Pritzel, Gilbert V., Cpl,
Privett, Charlie A., Pfc,
Privette, Hazel R., Pfc,
Privitera, Frank J., Pvt,
Proce, Benedetto, Pfc,
Prochazka, Frank A., S/Sgt
Prochownik, Walter A., Pfc,
‡Procopio, Anthony, Pfc,
Procopio, John W., Pvt,
Proctor, Leslie L., S/Sgt,
Proctor, William W., T/Sgt,
Proegler, Walter H., Jr., Pfc,
Prosser, Harry C., Pvt,
Proto, Anthony, Pvt,
Proulx, Leo J., Pvt,
Provancher, Arthur E., Pvt,
Provard, Ray C., Pvt,
Provengana, Peter J., S/Sgt,
Provolt, Ora O., Pvt,
Prucha, Otto, Pfc,
Pruden, Ellis R., Pfc,
Pruett, Robert D., Pfc,
†Pruitt, Donal C., Pfc,
Pruitt, Wilmer W., Sgt,
Prunier, Henry S., S/Sgt,
Pruser, William, Pvt,
†Prusia, Wesley B., Pfc
Prusinski, Stanley F., Pvt,
Pryor, James A., Pfc
Pryor, Joseph E., Pfc,
Pryor, Richard W., Pvt
†Przeslak, Adam C., Sgt,
Przyblski, Joseph, Pvt,
Przytarski, Edward R., Pvt,
Psaila, George R., Pfc,
Pscolkowski, John M., Pfc,
Psomas, Harry P., 1st Lt,
Ptaszynski, John H., T/Sgt
Pucci, Stephen J., Pfc
Puchlerz, John J., Pfc,
Puckett, Henry C., Pfc,
Puddister, George J., Pvt,
Pudik, Phillip, Sgt,
Puffer, Lavern M., Pvt,
Pugh, Lewis J., S/Sgt,
Pugh, Ralph W., Pfc,
‡Pugliano, Anthony F., Pvt,
Puhala, Cyril J., T/5
Puhl, Harold P., Pvt,
Pulaski, Charles J., Pvt,
Puliafico, Samuel R., Pfc
Pulkowski, Leon F., Pvt,
Pullin, James E., Pvt, Pt.
Pupello, Anthony F., Pvt,
†Puppe, Elmer A., Pvt,
†Puppe, Lester W., S/Sgt,
Purcell, Thomas F., Pvt,
Purdy, Carl H., Pfc
Purdy, Kenneth E., S/Sgt,
Purnell, William S., Pfc,
Pursley, Ralph J., Pvt,
Pustay, Clyde, Pvt,
Puszko, John A., Sgt,
Putman, Loyal L., Pfc
Putnan, Nelson J., S/Sgt,
Puzder, John M., Pvt,
Puzio, George M., Pvt,
Puzyk, Stephen, Sgt,
Pyeatt, Jewel, W., Pfc,
Plye, Clyde T., Pvt,
Pyles, Albert L., S/Sgt,
Pyles, Payton N., Pfc

Quaale, Joseph, S/Sgt,
Quaccia, Laurence D., Pfc,
Quaglia, William A., Pfc,
Quail, Gordon A., Pfc,
Quale, John O., T/4,
Qualeatti, Carl M., Pfc,
Qualey, Joseph P., Pfc,
Quarry, Robert K., Pfc,
Quast, Raymond M., Pfc,
Queen, Carl S., Pvt,
Queener, Arthur L., Pfc,
†Querry, Charles, Pvt,
Quick, Earl C., Pvt,
Quick, Russell W., T/5,
†Quiel, George A., Pfc,
Quier, Marvin P., Sgt,
Quigg, Vincent F., Pfc,
Quillen, Isaac L., Pfc,
Quinby, Richard E., Pfc,
‡Quinlisk, Francis M., Pvt,
Quinn, Clyde E., Jr., Pfc,
Quinn, Fred H., Pvt,
Quinn, Harold C., Pfc,
Quinn, John F., Pfc
Quinn, Thomas J., Pfc
Quintana, Salvator A., Pfc
Quirk, Edward A., T/5
†Quiroz, Simon S., Pfc,
†Quon, William J., Pvt

Raab, Arthur, Pvt,
†Raab, Frederick E., Pvt,
Raas, Alan C., 2nd Lt
Rabago, Felix C., Pvt
Rabe, William M., S/Sgt,
Raber, Merle R., Pvt,
§Rabern, Harvie E., Pvt,
Rabil, Emil P., Pvt
Rabinowitz, Joseph, Pvt,
†Raccuia, Anthony, Pfc,
Rachac, Arthur, T/5,
Rachor, Glenn R., T/5
Rackley, William F., Pvt,
Radack, Sigmond J., Pfc,
Radcliff, Eugene F., Pfc
Radcliffe, Irving A., Pfc,
Radde, Walter R., Pfc,
Rader, Charles, Pfc
Rader, Harold E., Pvt,
†Rader, William H., Cpl
Radigan, Joseph W., Pvt
Radford, Charles T., Pfc
Radomski, Henry F., Pvt,
Radosevich, John J., Pfc
Raduechel, Robert A., Cpl
†Radzevich, John, Pfc
Radzik, Edward S., Pfc,
Raemon, Fred R., Pvt,
Raeth, Ervin F., Sgt,
Raezer, Donald C., Cpl,
Rafferty, Albert F., S/Sgt,
§Rafferty, Hilary A., Pfc,
Raffile, Howard M., Pfc,
Rager, Alfred E., Pvt,
Ragland, Bourland T., Pfc,
Ragsdale, Carl E., Pvt, St.
Raham, Abraham, Pvt,
Raia, Carmine, Pvt,
Raiche, Donald J., Pfc,
Raines, Richard G., Pfc,
Rainey, Joseph V., Jr., Sgt,
Rainwater, Hugh P., Pfc,
Rainwater, Isaac H., Pvt,
Rak, Eugene J., Pvt,
†Rakes, Loyd A., Sgt,
Rakestraw, Doyal B., Pfc,
Rakosnik, E. J., Jr., Pvt,
Rakowski, Albert J., Cpl
Raley, Robert W., Pfc,
Ralston, Robert L., Pfc
Ramas, Agustin, Pfc,
Rambo, Joseph E., Jr., Pfc,
Ramirez, Jose M., Pfc,
Ramme, Donald R., Pvt,
*Ramos, Carlos L., Pvt,
Ramos, Rudolph A., Pvt,
Ramowski, Edward L., Sgt,
Ramsdell, Arthur F., S/Sgt,
*Ramsey, Emuel L., T/Sgt,
Ramsey, Gerald A., Pfc,
Ramsey, Henry M., Pfc,
Ramsey, Homer F., Pvt,
Ramsey, John L., Pfc,
Ramsey, Lloyd B., Maj,
*Ramsey, Ralph W., S/Sgt,
Ramsey, Robert C., S/Sgt,
Ramsey, Roger W., Pvt,
Ramsey, Roy L., S/Sgt,
Ramsey, William, Pvt,
†Ranallo, William A., Cpl,
Ranck, Mike M., T/Sgt,
Rand, Herbert, Pvt,
Rand, William K., Pfc,
Randall, Elton R., Pfc,
Randall, Harold J., Pfc,
Randall, Winstead D., Pfc,
Randle, William M., Pvt,
Randleman, Merl L., Pvt,
Randolph, Blaine P., Pvt,
Randolph, Dionysus, Pfc,
Randolph, Estus, Pvt,
Randolph, Hubert K. Pvt,
Randolf, Joseph L., Pvt,
Raney, George O., Pvt,
Ranford, Paul J., Pfc,
†Rangel, Juan, Pfc,
Rangel, Martin, Cpl,
Ranke, Joseph J., Cpl,
Rankin, Charlie E., Pvt,
Rankin, James W., Jr., Pvt,
Rankin, Marcus R., Pvt,
Rankin, Murphy D., Pvt,
Rankin, Richard T., Pvt,
Rankin, Robert V., Cpl,
Rankin, Vernon H., Capt,
§Ranney, Malcolm L., S/Sgt,
Ransom, Henry R., Maj,
Ransom, William H., Pvt,
Ransom, Willis D., Pfc,
Ranta, Arnold J., Pvt,
†Rants, Allen E., Cpl,
Rapchik, Joseph, Pvt,
Rapert, Halbert R., Cpl,
Ras, Earl, T/5,
Rasch, Erling R., Pvt,
Raschke, Clarence A., Pvt,
Raskauskas, John K., Pvt,
Raskosky, John M., Pvt,
Rasmussen, Donald E., Pvt,
Rasmussen, Elmer L., Pfc,
Rassler, Jay M., T/4,
Ratajczak, Walter T., Pfc,
Rath, Dale B., Pfc,
Rath, Edward F., Pfc,
Rathman, Francis W., Pvt,
†Ratini, John B., 2nd Lt,
Ratliff, James A., Jr., Sgt,
Ratte, Edward, T/3,
Ratzloff, Alfred W., Pvt,
Raty, Seimons E., Pvt,
Raughton, Marvin T., Pvt,
Raup, Domer A., Pvt,
Rautio, Arni T., T/5,
Rautio, Weikko O., Pfc,
Rava, David, Pvt,
Ravenscroft, Earl H., S/Sgt,
†Ravsten, Alvin V., Pfc,
‡Rawlings, Kenneth, Pfc,
Rawlingson, John W., Cpl,
†Rawlins, Earl, Pfc,
†Rawlins, Raymond B., Pvt,
Rawls, Benjamin, Pfc,
Rawls, Wallace G., Pfc,
Ray, Robert D., Pvt,
Ray, Thomas S., 2nd Lt,
Ray, Walter A., T/5,
Rayfield, Vinson S., Pfc,
Raymond, Arnold S., Pvt,
Raymond, Edward A., Pfc,
Raymond, George E., Pvt,
Raymond, Montelle J., Pvt,
Raymond, Robert J., Pvt,
Rea, Mike Q., S/Sgt,
†Reagan, Herbert C., Cpl,
Reagan, Homer L., 1st Lt,
†Reagan, James R., Pvt,
Reagan, Tom R., Pvt,
Reagle, Jay R., Pfc,
†Reamy, Carl E., S/Sgt,
Reardon, Edward J., Pfc,
Reasner, David B., Jr., Pvt,
†Reasoner, Ralph B., 2nd Lt,
Reaves, Charles E., Pvt,
Reaves, Charles E., Pvt,
Rebelak, Edward J., Pfc,
Reca, Charles J., Pvt,
Recchion, Russell W., Pfc,
†Reckner, Clarence V., Pvt,
Recio, Manuel O., Pvt,
Recore, Kenneth R., Pfc,
Rector, Walter H., Pvt,
†Reda, Pasquale J., Pvt,
Redden, Hugh D., Pfc,
Reddick, Dudley, E., Pfc,
Redding, Ollie J., Pfc,
Redemske, Luther, Pvt,
Redling, Arthur A., Pfc,
*Redman, John R., T/Sgt,
Redman, Joseph E., Sgt,
Redpath, Paul R., T/5,
†Reece, Bennie G., 1st Lt,
†Reece, Carl R., Pvt,
Reece, J. A., Pvt,
Reece, Jethro, Sgt,
Reed, Andrew W., Pfc,
Reed, Darrell D., Sgt,
Reed, Dexter R., Pvt,
Reed, Gerald F., Pvt,
Reed, Howard B., Pvt,
Reed, James L., T/5,
Reed, Lewis A., S/Sgt,
Reed, Malcolm H., Pfc,
Reed, Milford, L., Pfc,
Reed, Orvill S., S/Sgt,
Reed, Paul A., Pvt,
Reed, Raymond D., Pfc,
‡Reed, Virgil L., Pvt,
Reed, William, Pfc,
Reeder, Raymond L., Pvt,
Reeder, William T., 1st Sgt,
Reedy, Emil, Jr., Pfc,
Rees, Donald E., S/Sgt,
Reese, Babe B., Pfc,
Reese, Delmer L., Pfc,
Reese, Fred J., Pfc,
Reese, Joseph R., Pvt,
Reese, Marvin K., Pfc,
Reese, Ulas E., Sgt,
Reeves, Cledith G., Pvt,
§Reeves, Earl R., 2nd Lt,
Reeves, Harold L., Pvt,
Reeves, Robert G., Capt,
Reeves, Willard H., Capt,
Rega, Vito J., Pfc,
Regalado, Ernest G., Pfc,
Regan, Dewey C., Pfc,
Regan, Harold T., 2nd Lt,
Regan, Robert E., 2nd Lt,
Rehak, Henry F., Pfc,
Rehder, Emil C., Pvt,
Rehling, Caryl M., Pfc,
Rehloff, Edward A., Pfc,
Rehm, Edward C., Pfc,
Rehwalt, LeRoy W., Pfc,
Reich, Robert J., Pfc,
Reichert, Henry, Pvt,
§Reichert, Walter A., 2nd Lt,
Reichmuth, Andrew I., T/5,
Reid, Calvin J., Pfc,
Reid, Clarence, Pvt,
Reid, Francis W., S/Sgt,
Reid, Robert L., Pfc,
Reidenbach, Robert C., Pfc,
†Reider, Levere J., Pfc,
Reidy, John C., Pvt,
Reidy, William T., Pvt,
Reihe, Clarence W., Pvt,
Reihing, Elmer V., Pfc,
Reil, Francis J., Pfc,
Reilly, Eugene J., Cpl,
Reilly, Martin J., Pvt,
Reilly, Robert E., Sgt,
Reilman, John D., S/Sgt,
Reimer, Abe A., Pfc,
Reimer, Harold E., Pvt,
Reimers, Karl H., T/5,
†Rein, Herman F., Pfc,
§Rein, John E., Pvt,
Rein, William J., Jr., Pvt,
Reinhert, John, S/Sgt,
‡Reinhackle, Walter F., Pfc,
Reinhardt, Victor E., 2nd Lt,
Reinsfelder, Frederick A., T/5,
Reis, Gregory P., T/5,
Reisdorf, Raymond J., Pfc,
Reisdorf, Wandell E., Pvt,
Reish, Frank, T/4,
Reisinger, Belere R., Pvt,
†Reisner, Berl L., Pfc,
Reiss, Edwin J., T/4,
†Reitz, Max, Pvt,
Reitzel, Billy J., Sgt,
Rekowski, Bruno S., Pfc,
Remetch, Alvin F., Pfc,
Remington, Dwayne R., S/Sgt,
Remolino, Louis, Pvt,
Renard, Ronald, Pvt,
Renaud, Edward J., Pvt,
Rende, Frank F., Pvt,
Rendon, Mauro M., Pfc,
Renk, Roman J., 1st Lt,
Renko, Alexis, Pvt,
Renna, William A., Pvt,
Rennar, Dominick J., Pvt,
Rennhack, Russell R., Pfc,
Renninger, Robert J., Pvt,
Renteria, Gregorio U., Pvt,
†Renton, Vaughan J., Pvt,
Reoh, Harold E., Pvt,
†Reschke, Emil W., Pfc
Resnick, Abraham, Pfc,
Rester, Daniel W., Pfc,
Retberg, Alfred R., Sgt,
†Rettew, Donald B., Cpl,
Rettig, Clyde E., Cpl,
Rettig, Irving D., Cpl,
†Reschke, Emil W., Pfc,
Reubsamen, Dorrell L., Pvt,
Reuter, Willard R., Pvt,
Reyell, Harold R., Pfc,
†Reyerson, Robert E., Pvt,
Reyes, Richard J., Pvt,
Reynolds, Charles W., Sgt,
Reynolds, Clarence A., Pvt,
†Reynolds, Clarence W., Sgt
Reynolds, David B., Pfc,
‡Reynolds, Donald F., 1st Lt,
Reynolds, Gerard K., Pfc,
Reynolds, James A., Jr., Pfc,
Reynolds, James E., Cpl,
Reynolds, John E., Sgt,
Reynolds, John T., T/4,
Reynolds, Morris C., Pvt,
Reynolds, Robert M., Pvt,
Reynolds, William F., Pfc,

† Killed in Action. * Prisoner of War. ‡ Missing in Action. § Died of Wounds.

†Reynoso, Salvador H., Pfc,
†Reynwald, Charles J., Cpl,
Rezente, Louis, Pvt,
Rezsnyak, Ernest O., Sgt,
Rhash, James F., Sgt,
Rhoades, Gene M., Pvt,
Rhoades, Lavern A., Pvt,
Rhodes, Gleeson W., Sgt,
§Riakosky, Walter P., Pfc,
†Riaza, Manuel P., Pfc,
Rice, Calvin A., Pvt,
Rice, Elmer J., Pvt,
Rice, Francis C., Pfc,
*Rice, Donald L., Pvt,
Rice, John D., Pfc,
Rice, Melvin M., Pfc,
Rice, Orvil W., Pfc,
Rice, Roy, Pvt,
Rice, Ralph W., Pfc,
§Rice, Sargent G., Pfc,
Rich, Donald F., Pfc,
Rich, Leon, Pfc,
Richard, Charles J., Pvt,
Richard, David A., Jr., Pfc,
Richard, Lawrence P., Pfc,
Richards, John W., Pvt,
Richards, Lee M., Pfc,
Richards, Paul, Pvt,
Richards, Raymond M., Pfc,
†Richards, Rodney, Pvt,
Richards, William D., S/Sgt,
†Richards, William L., Pvt,
Richardson, Albert L., Sgt,
Richardson, Bert L., Pvt,
Richardson, Byron J., Pfc,
Richardson, Dio P., Capt,
Richardson, Donald R., Pvt,
†Richardson, Emery E., S/Sgt,
Richardson, George T., S/Sgt,
Richardson, Harold R., S/Sgt,
Richardson, Harry K., S/Sgt,
Richardson, James F., Pvt,
Richardson, Norman R., Pfc,
†Richardson, Paul E., Pvt,
Richardson, Robert J., Pfc,
Richardson, Robert W., Pfc,
Richardson, Roy C., Pvt,
Richardson, Thomas C., Pfc,
Richerson, Loal H., Pfc,
Richey, Elmer G., Pfc,
Richter, James C., Pvt,
Rickard, Franklin L., Pvt,
Ricker, Edward, Pvt,
Rickless, Nathan, Pfc,
Ricks, Sanford C., Pvt,
Rico, Joe M., Sgt,
Rico, Luis L., Pfc,
Riddle, Clarence, Pvt,
Riddle, Thomas L., Jr., 2nd Lt,
Ridel, Adam S., Pfc,
Rider, Bill, Pvt,
Rider, Edward R., T/Sgt,
Richmond, Tom, Pfc,
Rider, George W., T/5,
†Rider, Guy C., Pfc,
Rider, Robert D., Pvt,
Ridgeway, Robert D., Pfc,
Ridolphi, Eli, Cpl,
Riecken, George J., Pvt,
†Riedel, Arnold W., Pvt,
Riedel, Robert J., Pvt,
Rieger, Carl M., Sgt,
Rieke, Burrell E., Pfc,
Riemensnider, Max B., S/Sgt,
Rife, Byron B., Pvt,
Rigby, Archie A., Pfc,
Riggan, Hiram D., Pfc,
Riggins, Charlie C., Pvt,
Riggins, Robert O., S/Sgt,
Riggs, Dennis W., 2nd Lt,
Riggs, Eugene, Pvt,
Riggs, Glenn J., Pvt,
Riggs, Vernon A., Cpl,
Riggsbee, William A., Pvt,
Rigling, Roy S., S/Sgt,
Rigsby, Lenard M., Pvt,
Rilen, Louis L., T/5,
Riley, Cleo J., Pvt,
Riley, Francis A., Pvt,
†Riley, Robert J., Pfc,
Riley, Russell I., Pfc,
Rimer, Hugh H., Pfc,
†Rinaldo, Alfred, Pvt,
Rinard, Cecil M., Pvt,
Rinehart, John M., S/Sgt,
Ring, Charles O. E., T/4,
Ringwelski, Walter A., Pvt,
Rinker, Alden E., S/Sgt,
Rioni, Alfred E., Pfc,
Riordan, Harold W., Pfc,
Rios, Abel, Pfc,
Ripley, Harold J., Pvt,
Riportella, Joseph C., Sgt,
Rippentrop, Roy R., Pvt,
Rippy, Jesse J., Pfc,
Risdell, Kenneth J., Pvt,
Risley, Edward M., Pvt,
Ristaino, Daniel A., Pfc,
Ritchey, Charles P., Pfc,
Ritchey, Robert P., Sgt,
Ritten, George J., Pfc,
Rittenhouse, David E., Pfc,
Rittenhouse, James W.,
Ritter, Arthur R., Sgt,
Ritter, John H., Pfc,
Ritter, Maurice A., Pfc,
Ritter, William L., Col,
Ritti, Tony A., Pfc,
Riutcel, Lloyd A., Maj,
Rivera, Arturo S., Pvt,
‡Rivera, Ernestino, Pfc,
Rivera, Max J., Pvt,
Rivers, John A., Pfc,
†Rivers, Roger W., Pvt,
Rivet, Gordon, Pfc,
Rivet, Peter C., Pfc,
Rizo, Barbarito M., T/Sgt,
Rizulo, Frank, Jr., Pfc,
Rizzi, Rocco L., Pvt.
Rizzo, John, T/4,
Roach, Bobby M., Pfc,
†Roark, Berry, Pvt,
Roark, Ellis, Pvt,
†Roark, James F., Pvt,
†Roark, Samuel E., Pvt,
Robachinski, Zigmund J., Sgt,
Roback, Martin, T/Sgt,
†Robasciotti, Roy K., Pfc,
Robb, Ernest W., S/Sgt,
Robbins, Calvin M., Pvt,
Robbins, George P., Pvt,
Robbins, William A., Pvt,
Robedee, Thomas A., Pfc,
Robel, Frank G., Pvt,
Robello, Abel A., Pvt,
Roberson, James J., Jr., Pvt,
Roberson, Verlon T., Pvt,
Robertazzi, Anthony F., Pvt,
§Robertazzi, Rosario M., Pfc,
Roberts, Archie H., Pfc,
Roberts, Charles F., Pvt,
Roberts, Clayton, Pfc,
Roberts, Edward C., Pvt,
Roberts, Elmer E., Sgt,
Roberts, Herbert G., Sgt,
Roberts, James B., Pfc,
†Roberts, John, Pfc,
Roberts, John C., Pfc,
Roberts, John E., Cpl,
Roberts, John F., Pfc,
Roberts, John H., Pfc,
Roberts, Merrill H., Pfc,
Roberts, Peyton H., Pfc,
Roberts, Samuel H., Capt,
†Roberts, Vernon E., Sgt,
§Roberts, Virgil E., Pvt,
Roberts, Walter B., Pfc,
Roberts, Walter E., Pfc,
Roberts, William H., 1st Lt,
†Robertson, Buster D., Pfc,
Robertson, Clifford L., Pfc,
Robertson, Elliott V., Sgt,
Robertson, George L., T/5,
Robertson, Milton D., Pfc,
Robertson, Verlon T., Pvt,
Robertson, W. J., Jr., Sgt,
Robin, Charles M., T/5,
Robinette, John H., S/Sgt,
Robinette, Lonnie G., Pfc,
Robinette, William J., T/5,
Robinson, Adrian J., Pvt,
Robinson, Albert L., Pvt,
Robinson, Carel G., Pvt,
Robinson, Charles A., Pvt,
Robinson, Donald E., Pfc,
Robinson, Earl J., Pvt,
Robinson, Eugene, T/5,
Robinson, Floyd A., Pvt,
Robinson, Frank J., Jr., Pfc,
Robinson, Glenn H., Pvt,
Robinson, Harold J., S/Sgt,
Robinson, Hugh, Pfc,
Robinson, James D., Pfc,
Robinson, James M., Pvt,
Robinson, John L., T/4,
Robinson, John T., Pvt,
†Robinson, LeRoy, Pvt,
Robinson, Lewis H., Sgt,
Robinson, Millard, Pvt,
Robinson, Raymond M., Cpl,
Robinson, Richard A., S/Sgt,
Robinson, Robert B., Pvt,
Robinson, Wayne, Pvt,
Robinson, William E., Pfc,
Robinson, William J., Pvt,
Robinson, Woodrow, 1st Lt,
Robitaille, Napoleon M., Pfc,
†Robledo, James R., Cpl,
†Robles, Frank, Pvt
‡Robnett, Charles R., Sgt,
Robnett, Elmer R., S/Sgt,
Robustelli, Joseph A., T/4,
Roccabruna, Mario F., Sgt,
Rocco, Guy T., Sgt,
Rocco, Jerry A., Pfc,
Rocheleau, Richard L., Pfc,
Rockwill, George W., Pvt,
Rod, Fred C., Pvt,
Rodack, John L., Pfc,
Roddy, Jack F., 1st Sgt,
Roden, Milford L., Pvt,
Roden, Ralph P., Pvt,
Roderer, Robert G., Pvt,
Rodger, Patrick J., Pfc,
Rodgers, Bernard J., S/Sgt,
Rodgers, Everett L., Cpl,
Rodgers, James A., Pfc,
Rodgers, John E., Pfc,
Rodgers, Nelson J., Pfc,
Rodier, Henry G., Pfc,
Rodin, Frank G., Pfc,
Rodino, John P., T/5,
Rodkosky, Edward J., Pfc,
†Rodley, Orville M., S/Sgt,
Rodriguez, Carmelo G., Pfc,
Rodriguez, Florencio A., Sgt,
Rodriguez, Frank, Pvt,
Rodriguez, Henry, Pfc,
Rodriguez, James R., Pvt,
Rodriguez, Manuel B., Pvt,
Rodriguez, Margarito, Pfc,
†Rodriguez, Mervin E., 2nd Lt,
Rodriguez, Placido E., S/Sgt,
Rodriguez, Rudolfo E., Pfc,
Rodriguez, Salvador, S/Sgt,
Roe, Charles M., Sgt,
Roe, Michael J., Pfc,
Roebuck, Richard, Sgt,
Roed, Peter J., Pvt,
Roedler, Edward J., Pvt,
†Roehl, Daniel J., T/Sgt,
Roehrig, George F., 2nd Lt,
Roemig, Gilbert, Pvt,
Rofrano, James L., Pvt,
Rogalsky, Hubert, Pvt,
Rogers, Corliss L., Sgt,
Rogers, Ewell A., Pvt,
Rogers, Frederick G., Pfc,
Rogers, George F., Pvt,
Rogers, James E., Pfc,
Rogers, James O., Pvt,
Rogers, John E., Pvt,
Rogers, Joseph E., 1st Lt,
Rogers, LeRoy A., Sgt,
Rogers, Paul J., Pvt,
Rogers, Rufus N., Pvt,
Rogers, Sidney T., Jr., Pvt,
Rogers, Willard L., Pvt,
†Rogerson, Bernice L., Pvt,
Roget, Gordon B., 2nd Lt,
Rognlie, Philip A., Capt,
Roguso, Frank, Pvt,
Rohan, Milton J., Pvt,
Rohde, Alvin D., Pvt,
Rohkar, Charles H., Cpl,
Rohlopf, Edward A., Pfc,
*Rohme, Woodrow W., Pvt,
Rohs, Andrew R., Pvt,
Rokash, Edwin A., Pvt,
Rolek, Adolph, Pfc,
Rolen, Andrew, Pvt,
Rollman, Carl P., 1st Lt,
Roman, Joseph J., Sgt,
†Romano, Joseph, Pvt,
Romano, Louis, Pfc,
Romano, Vincent, Pvt,
Romans, William R., Sgt,
Rome, Thomas G., Pvt,
Rome, William W., Pfc,
†Romero, Alcee, Jr., Pvt,
Romero, Herberto G., S/Sgt,
*Romero, Pablo H., Sgt,
Romero, Richard J., Pvt,
Rominski, Anton T., Pfc,
Rommal, George W. G., Pvt,
Rommell, Henry O., Pvt,
Romo, Juan M., Pvt,
Romolo, Nicholas L., Pfc,
Ronchetto, John, Pfc,
Rondeau, Howard J., S/Sgt,
Roneker, Harris W., Pvt,
Rono, Leo J., Pvt,
Ronquillo, Juan, T/4,
Rons, Edgar A., Pvt,
‡Rood, Homer J., Pfc,
†Rook, John, Pvt,
Rooney, John C., S/Sgt,
Root, George, Pfc,
Root, George L., Pfc,
Rootovich, Dominic C., Jr., Pfc,
†Ropchak, William, Pfc,
Rorvik, Carl J., Pvt,
Rosadini, Joseph W., Pvt,
Rosano, Alfred P., Pvt,
Rosas, Steven O., S/Sgt,
Rosati, George, S/Sgt,
Rosborough, Cyril F., S/Sgt,
Roscoe, Lloyd E., Pfc,
Rose, Earl, Pfc,
Rose, Edward C., Pvt,
Rose, Frank, S/Sgt,
Rose, George F., Pfc,
Rose, Henry B., Pvt,
Rose, Henry P., Pfc,
Rose, Horace E., Pfc,
Rose, Kermit J., Pvt,
Rose, Millard, Jr., Pvt,
§Rose, Robert J., Pfc,
Rose, Wiley, Pvt,
†Rose, Willie B., Pfc,
Roselund, Robert C., Pvt,
‡Rosen, Samuel J., Pvt,
Rosen, Victor, Pvt,
Rosenberg, Burton, Sgt,
Rosenberg, Leonard Y., S/Sgt,
Rosenlund, Dean W., Pfc,
Rosenstein, Leonard A., Pvt,
Rosenthal, Eli A., Pvt,
†Rosenwasser, Adolph S., 1st Lt,
Rosenzweig, Millard E., Pfc,
Rosenzwog, Harold W., Pvt,
†Rosh, Emory E., S/Sgt,
Rosholt, Norman L., Pvt,
Ross, Bert B., Pvt,
Ross, Clyde A., Pfc,
Ross, Donald C., Pfc,
Ross, Gerald, Pfc,
Ross, James A., Pvt,
Ross, James E., Pvt,
Ross, Joseph, Pvt,
Ross, Joseph R., Sgt,
Ross, Lawrence B., Sgt,
Ross, Vincent, Pvt,
†Ross, Robert A., 2nd Lt
Ross, William R., Pfc,
Rose, Louis J., Pvt,
Rossi, Charles, Sgt,
Rossi, George A., Pfc,
Rossi, Harry L., Pvt,
Rossi, Robert V., S/Sgt,
†Rostad, Bennie N., Pfc,
Rotelli, Donald R., S/Sgt,
Roth, David J., 1st Lt,
Roth, Emanuel M., 2nd Lt,
Roth, George H., Pfc,
Roth, Samuel P., Pvt,
Roth, Stanley B., Pvt,
Rothbard, Mitchel, 1st Lt,
Rothgeb, Jay L., T/5,
Rothschild, Walter B., Pvt,
Rothstein, Robert C., Pfc,
†Rotundo, Louis J., Pvt,
Roubison, Joseph E., Pvt,
Roudi, William C., Pvt,
Rouse, James H., Pvt,
Rousseau, Joseph R., Pfc,
Rousseau, Paul E., Pfc,
§Routier, Cinna C., Jr., S/Sgt,
Routt, James S., Pfc,
Rovas, Edmund J., Sgt,
Rowe, Carlis T., Sgt,
Rowe, Cecil B., T/5,
Rowe, George E., Cpl,
Rowe, Jesse B., Pvt,
†Rowe, Leon W., Pfc,
Rowe, Lloyd M., Pfc,
†Rowe, Rolland R., Sgt,
†Rowell, C. J., Pfc,
Rowell, James P., T/Sgt,
Rowland, Earl L., Jr., Pfc,
Rowland, Herman J., Sgt,
Rowland, Orvin C., S/Sgt,
‡Rowlands, Leslie, Pvt,
Rowlands, Thomas E., Pvt,
Rowlen, Joseph R., 2nd Lt,
Rowley, Charles V., Pfc,
Rowley, Lester L., Sgt,
Roy, Hercule A., T/4,
Roy, James H., Pfc,
Roy, Joseph L., Sgt,
†Roy, Roger F., Pfc
Royal, Alonza, Pfc,
Royall, James H., Sr., Pvt,
Royster, Robert R., Pfc,
Rozzi, Edward A., Cpl,
Ruba, Michael, Pfc,
Rubinfeld, Allen J., Pvt,
†Ruby, Bruce E., Pvt,
Ruby, Fred A., Pfc,
Ruby, Hubert E., Pvt,
Ruda, William, Pfc,
Ruddle, Ralph H., Pfc,
†Rudeseal, Joseph R., Pvt,
Rudisill, Lester M., Pvt,
Rudnick, Leonard, Pvt,
†Rudolph, Henry, Pvt,
Rudovitz, Stephen, Pfc,
Rudow, Ferdinand E., Pfc,
Rudow, John E., Pfc,
Ruehle, George E., Pvt,
Ruelle, George J., Pvt,
Rufener, Delbert H., Pvt,
Ruff, Arthur R. J. B., T/4,
Ruffner, Harry C., Pvt,
Ruffner, Walter E., Pfc,
Ruggeri, James J., Pfc,
Ruggiero, Arnello F., Pvt,
Ruggiero, John, S/Sgt,
Ruggiero, Pasquale, Pvt,
Ruggio, Murray L., Pvt,
Ruggles, Claude R., Pfc,
Rugroden, Roger R., Pvt,
Ruhle, Adolph J., Pvt,
†Ruiz, Gilbert, Pvt,
Rule, Orville R., 1st Lt,
†Rumrill, Herman F., Sgt,
Running, Arthur W., Pfc,
Runsvold, Rolf C., Pfc,
Runyon, William T., Pvt,
Ruotolo, Frank J., Pvt,
Ruper, William, Pfc,
Ruport, LeRoy A., Pvt,
*Rupp, Charles E., Pvt,
Rusetski, Peter, Pfc,
†Rush, Alfred A., 2nd Lt,
†Rush, Emil E., Pfc,
Rush, Harold L., Pfc,
Rush, Lloyd N., Pfc,
Rushing, Marion D., Jr., Pfc,
Rusk, Joseph, Pvt,
Russell, Jay N., Pfc,
‡Russell, James B., S/Sgt,
Russell, John A., Pvt,
Russell, Lewis E., T/Sgt,
Russell, Loyce B., Pvt,
Russell, Lloyd L., Pvt
§Russell, Marvin L., Pvt,
†Russell, Peter P., Pfc,
Russell, Ralph E., Pvt,
Russell, Rex L., T/5,
Russell, William F., T/Sgt
Russo, Biagio J., Pvt,
Russo, Frank P., Pfc,
Russo, Raymond J., Pvt
Russoniello, Savino J., Pfc,
Russum, Robert J., Pvt,
Rust, Ben O., Pvt,
†Rutherford, Marvin A., Pvt,
Ruthiewicz, Louis J., Pfc,
Rutter, Howard G., Pfc,
Ruxton, Donald F., Pfc,
Ruybal, Theodore S., Pfc,
Ryan, John J., Pfc,
§Ryan, Leo T., T/5,
Ryan, Paul, Pfc,
†Ryan, Paul T., 2nd Lt,
Ryan, Ralph J., Pvt,
Ryan, Raymond P., Pfc,
Ryan, Thomas P., Pfc,
Ryan, William E., Jr., 1st Lt,
Ryan, William J., 1st Lt,
Ryba, Steve W., Pvt,
Rybicki, Raymond, Pvt,
Ryckman, Bernard C., Pfc,
Ryder, Claude J., Pfc,
Ryder, Gerald C., Pfc,
Rydzowski, Louis P., Pfc,
Rye, Aubey N., Cpl,
†Rye, Casper, Jr., Pfc,
§Rye, John R., Jr., Pvt,
Rylee, Clarence M., T/5,
Ryman, Elmer E., Pfc,
§Rymarski, Kasnuerz, Pfc,
Rzomp, Stanley J., Pfc,

Saari, Richard, Pfc,
Sabatini, Alexander N., Pvt,
Sabatino, Daniel D., Pfc,
Sabol, Paul E., Pvt,
†Sabourin, Bernard A., Pvt,
*Sabovik, Charles T., Pvt,
Saccaro, Theodore, Pvt,
Sacco, Anthony T., Pvt,
Sackett, Allen L., Pvt,
Sadley, Ludwig G., Pfc,
Sadowsky, Frank C., Pvt,
Safarik, Charles A., Pfc,
Safford, Erie C., Pvt,
Safrit, Raymond L., Pvt,
Safstrom, Norman W., T/5,
Sage, Marvin C., T/Sgt,
Sager, John W., Pvt,
Sahaydak, Peter, Pfc,
Sain, James W., Pfc,
Sajec, Louis V., Pvt,
Salanik, Mike, Pvt,
Salaske, Allan L., Pfc,
Salciccia, Renato, Pvt,
Salerno, Joseph F., Pfc,
Salet, Eugene A., Lt Col,
Salgado, John S., Pvt,
Salinas, Dionisio G., Pvt,
†Salisbury, Donald R., Pvt,
Salkind, Harold, Pvt,
Sallee, James G. O., Pfc,

† Killed in Action. * Prisoner of War. ‡ Missing in Action. § Died of Wounds.

Sallette, William F., Jr., S/Sgt,
Salley, Clarence E., S/Sgt,
Salmans, Martin W., Pfc,
Salmon, Daniel J., Pfc,
Salmon, William M., Pvt,
Salter, Melvin R., Pfc,
‡Saltzman, Norman L., Pvt,
Salvadori, Adolf, Pvt,
†Salvatore, Leonard A., Pvt,
†Salvo, Domenic, T/Sgt,
†Salvo, Dominick A., Pfc,
Salzarulo, Mike A., Pvt,
Sambursky, Milton, Pvt,
Samolinski, Edward F., Sgt,
Samolowitz, Jacob, Pfc,
Sams, Berlin W., Pfc,
Sams, Layton H., Pvt,
Samu, John J., Pfc,
Samu, Joseph I., Pvt,
†Samuels, Patrick G., Sgt,
Sanak, William A., Pfc,
Sanchez, Billy, T/4,
Sanchez, David C., T/5,
Sanchez, George V., Sgt,
Sanchez, Mario, Pvt,
Sanchez, Miguel R., Pvt,
Sanchez, Peter, Pvt,
Sancoff, James, Pfc,
Sandberg, Lathom W., Pfc,
Sandefur, Lynwood S., Pvt,
Sanders, Alfred, Pfc,
Sanders, Alvin P., Pfc,
Sanders, Clyde, Pvt,
Sanders, Harold W., Pvt,
Sanders, Jasper P., Pvt,
Sanders, Jerry P., Pvt,
Sanders, Joe, T/5,
Sanders, Joseph J., Pfc,
Sanders, Junior L., Pfc,
Sanders, LeRoy J., Pfc,
Sanders, Robert C., Pfc,
Sanders, Roy M., Sgt,
Sanders, William G., Pvt,
Sanderson, Arthur H., Pvt,
Sanderson, Walter G., Pfc,
Sanderson, Wilfred E., Pfc,
Sandgrin, Roland B., 1st Sgt,
Sandidge, Taylor W., Pvt,
Sandlin, Mack M., Pvt,
Sandoval, Eloy J., Pfc,
Sandow, Carl O., T/4,
Sandstrom, Alfred J., Pfc,
Sane, John B., Pvt,
Sanford, Marvin F., Pvt,
Sanford, Robert H., Sgt,
Saniuk, Adolph J., Sgt,
Sansom, Louis E., Pvt,
Sansone, Frank J., Pvt,
Santa Cruz, Tony, Pfc,
Santaniello, Anile H., Pvt,
Santeford, Harold E., Pfc,
Santerre, Delphis J., Pfc,
Santiago, Juan R., Pvt,
†Santiago, Julio H., Pvt,
Santoro, Anthonio, Pvt,
Santoro, Frank, Pvt,
Santos, Dominigo A., S/Sgt,
Santucci, Armando L., Pfc,
Sanuk, John, Pvt,
San Vito, James A., 2nd Lt,
Sapinski, John J., Pfc,
Sapir,Philip, Pfc,
Sapiro, Saul J., Capt,
Sarabok, Stephen, Pvt,
Saracco, Elmer J., Pfc,
Sardelich, Peter J., Pfc,
†Sargent, Ruffus V., Sgt,
Sarkissian, Kerrigan D., Pfc,
Sarsgard, Richard S., Pvt,
Sartain, Nelson R., Sgt,
Sarver, Harry W., Pfc,
Sauer, Herbert R., Sgt,
†Sass, John, Pvt,
Sass, Paul F., T/5,
Satemia, Joseph, Pvt,
Sature, Andrew, Pvt,
Saubel, Joseph F., Jr., Pvt,
Sauceda, Louis H., Pvt,
Saucer, Thomas M., Pvt,
Saulin, Peter A., Pfc,
Saunders, Floyd R., Pfc,
Saunders, Lee R., Pvt,
Sauter, George J., S/Sgt,
Sauvageau, Dorick T., Pvt,
Savage, Carl H., Pfc,
Savage, John R., Pfc,
Saveliff, Alex J., T/4,
Savenchek, Alexander, Pvt,
Savene, Nicholas J., Pfc,
Saville, Junior C., Pfc,
Savino, John G., Pvt,
Savio, Frank T., Pvt,
Savol, Cyril, T/4,
Sawa, John J., Pvt,
Sawicki, John T., Pfc,
Sawley, William, Jr.,
Sawyer, Edward ., Pfc,
Sawyer, Floyd A., Pvt,
Sawyer, Lynn K., T/5,
Sawyer, William K., Pvt,
Sax, Robert E., Pvt,
Sayers, Claude M., Cpl,
Sayeski, John J., Pvt,
Sayler, Roy B., Pvt,
Saylor, Donald J., 2nd Lt,
Saylor, Ronald G., Pvt,
Saylor, Tommie E., Pfc,
Saylors, Isaac D., Sgt,
Scaccia, Anthony L., Pfc,
Scales, Howard A., Pfc,
Scalizi, alvatore C., Pvt,
Scancarella, Lester S., Pvt,
Scanlon, Bernard, Pvt,
Scanlon, James H., Pfc,
‡Scanlon, Robert C., Pfc,
Scanlon, William N., Pvt,
Scanlon, William R., Pfc,
Scannel, Edward T., Pfc,
Scannell, Bernard F., Pfc,
†Scarbrough, Charles E., Sgt,
Scarpa, Fred, S/Sgt,
Scarpelli, Thomas, T/4,
Scavo, Joseph, Pfc,
Schaafs, Lawrence A., T/3,
Schaefer, George I., Pvt,
Schaefer, Herman B., Pvt,
†Schaeffer, Carl E., Pfc,
‡Schaeffer, Harold A., Pvt,
†Schaible, Albert R., Pvt,
Schalch, Herman A., Pct,
Schalow, Herman F., Pvt,
§Schamberger, Richard, Pvt,
†Schamerloh, Carl, Pfc,
Schanafelt, John J., 2nd Lt,
†Schanz, Allen C.,Pfc,
Schanz, Charles G., Sgt,
Schapiro, Morton, Capt,
Scharper, Harold A., S/Sgt,
Schatz, Lawrence M., Pvt,
Schauer, Henry, T/Sgt,
Scheel, Frank C., Jr., Pvt,
Schechter, Louis L., Pvt,
Schechter, Morris, Pvt,
Scheer, Joseph J., Pvt,
Scheffler, Bernard B., Pfc,
†Schell, Alexander, Pfc,
Schell, Harold M., Pfc,
Schemik, Russell J., Pfc,
Schenck, Walter R., Jr., T/4,
Schenk, Joseph E., Pvt,
†Scherbak, Michael S., Pvt,
Scherer, John W., Jr., T/5,
Scherer, Norman W., Pfc,
Scherer, Sherman J., Pvt,
Schermbeck, Robert E., 2nd Lt,
Schernik, Curtis L., Pvt,
Schettler, Richard C., 2nd Lt,
Schexneider, Malton A., Pvt,
Schcik, Earl O., Pfc,
Schick, Louis T., 2nd Lt,
Schickling, Richard R., Pvt,
Schiering, Harry C., T/5,
Schiers, Robert A., 2nd Lt,
Schiffman, Dave, Pvt,
Schilke, Arthur W., Pfc,
Schiller, Charles J., Cpl,
†Schilz, Leonard J., S/Sgt,
Schimmel, Kenneth C., Sgt,
Schindler, Alexander P., Pvt,
Schindler, Alvin J., Pfc,
Schlacter, John A., Pfc,
Schlatweiler, Harold W., Cpl,
Schlee, Henry J., Sgt,
Schleicher, John S., Pvt,
Schlesinger, Dayton K., 2nd Lt,
Schlichter, Robert J., 1st Lt,
Schlosser, Anthony J., Pfc,
Schlumbohn, John W., Pvt,
Schmeckebier, Glenn F., Pfc,
Schmidt, Alexander N., Pvt,
Schmidt, Arthur H., Pfc,
Schmidt, Frank A., Cpl,
Schmidt, Howard C., Pvt,
Schmidt, John, S/Sgt,
†Schmidt, Joseph N., T/5,
†Schmidt, Kenneth A., Pvt,
Schmidt, Paul J., Pfc,
Schmidt, Victor E., T/5,
Schmidt, Walter E., Pvt,
Schmidt, William E., T/Sgt,
Schmidtke, Leo W., S/Sgt,
Schmieder, Francis W., Pfc,
Schminkey, Samuel C., S/Sgt,
†Schmitt, Emmett R., Pfc,
Schmitz, Charles, Pfc,
Schmoe, Herbert L., Jr., Pfc,
Schmuhl, Wayne H., S/Sgt,
Schnabel, Rudolph C., Sgt,
Schnabel, William F., Pfc,
Schnall, Louis, Pvt,
Schneid, Louis A., Pfc,
Schneider, Albert F., Sgt,
†Schneider, Albert H., Pfc,
Schneider, Carl P., Pfc,
Schneider, Edward J., Pfc,
Schneider, Edward P., Pfc,
Schneider, Fred D., Jr., 2nd Lt,
Schneider, Jacob, Sgt,
Schneider, Joseph M., Pvt,
Schneider, William H., Pfc,
Schneider, William V., Pfc,
Schneidkraut, Jack, Pvt,
Schneld, Louis A., Pfc,
Schnelle, Anthony W., Pfc,
Schnitman, Edward P., Pfc,
†Schnitzer, Miles O., Pvt,
Schodel, Rolf K., Pfc,
†Schoengold, Morton, 2nd Lt,
Schoening, Ernest E., Pfc,
Schoepke, Frederick, Pfc,
Schoessew, Cpl,
Schoessew, Earl H., Pfc,
Scholl, James A., Pfc,
Scholl, John P., Pvt,
Schomburg, Lawrence D., Pfc,
Schonwald, Wallace J., Pfc,
Schoolcraft, James R., T/Sgt,
Schoolcraft, Kenneth D., Pfc,
Schoolcraft, Pete M., Sgt,
Schoonover, Jack N., Pfc,
Schoppe, William G., Pfc,
Schorkopf, William M., Pfc,
Schottler, Fred W., Pfc,
Schrab, Harvey, Pvt,
Schrader, Arthur F., T/Sgt,
Schram, Fritz, Pfc,
Schrepfer, Glen C., Pvt,
§Schriver, Robert W., Pvt,
Schroder, Charles J., Pvt,
Schroedel, Roy P., Pfc,
Schroeder, Louis W., Pvt,
Schroeder, Philip L., Pvt,
Schroeder, Roger N., Pfc,
Schroer, John A., Cpl,
Schuette, Raymond L., 2nd Lt,
Schulenburg, Willard A., T/4,
Schulte, Elmer H., Pfc,
Schulte, George H., Sgt,
†Schulte, Leroy A., Pfc,
Schulte, William C., Cpl,
Schulz, Adolph H., T/4,
Schultz, Edward W., Pvt,
†Schultz, Gussie, Pfc,
Schultz, John R., T/5,
Schultz, Kenneth, Pvt,
Schultz, Thomas P., S/Sgt,
Schultz, Vernon B., T/5,
Schultz, Walter C., Pvt,
Schumann, Edward C., Pfc,
†Schumikowski, K. J., Jr., Pfc,
Schumm, Harold P., Pvt,
Schure, Robert, Pfc,
Schuster, Howard G., 2nd Lt,
Schutt, Norman J., Pvt,
Schutte, Willis C., S/Sgt,
Schuttler, Carl L., Pvt,
Schwab, Albert J., Pfc,
Schwab, Donald K., 1st Lt,
Schwaber, William, Sgt,
Schwalen, Elmer C., Pfc,
Schwarten, Raymond D., T/5,
Schwartz, Eugene, Pfc,
Schwartz, Isadore, T/5,
Schwartz, John A., Pfc,
Schwartz, Lester R., Pvt,
Schwartz, Morris, Pvt,'
Schwartz, Nathan, Pvt,
Schwartz, Philip R., Pvt,
Schwartz, Robert J., 2nd Lt,
Schwartz, Robert L., 2nd Lt,
Schwartz, Sam, Pvt,
Schwartz, Seymour, S/Sgt,
Schwebel, Norman J., Cpl,
Schweickhardt, Walter, Pvt,
Schweider, Edward J., Pfc,
Schweikert, H. A., Jr., 2nd Lt,
†Schweitzer, Seymour S., Pvt,
Schweizer, William T., Pvt,
Schwenk, Charles C., Pvt,
Schwier, Monroe C., Pfc,
‡Schwikert, Ralph A., Pfc,
Schwinn, Murrow D., Sgt,
Sciarillo, Michael P., Pvt,
Sciarrino, Vito, Pvt,
Scienski, Steve J., Pfc,
Scigliano, Dominick, Pvt,
Scimemi, Elio, Pfc,
Scipper, Edward T., Pfc,
Scuillo, John J., Pfc,
Scooee, Peter, Sgt,
Scorsone, Nunzio P., Pvt,
Scott, Bernice L., Pfc,
Scott, Clifton G., Sgt,
Scott, Donat E., Pfc,
Scott, Edward C., Pfc,
Scott, Edwin M., Pfc,
Scott, Elmer L., Pfc,
Scott, George, T/5,
Scott, George G., Pfc,
Scott, James E., Pvt,
†Scott, Joseph P., Cpl,
Scott, Kendrick V., Pfc,
Scott, Kenneth N., Pfc,
Scott, Leo E., Pfc,
Scott, Lowell S., Pfc,
Scott, Max G., S/Sgt,
Scott, Milton A., Pvt,
Scott, Monk, Pvt,
Scott, Peter S., Pfc,
Scott, Raymond L., Pvt,
Scott, Richard F., 2nd Lt,
Scott, Robert H., Pvt,
Scott, Ross A., Pfc,
Scott, Thomas W., T/5,
Scott, Walter C., Pfc,
Scott, Walter R., Pvt,
Scott, William L., 2nd Lt,
Scott, Wilson C., Pfc,
Scripsick, Robert Q., Pfc,
Scrivani, Alfred, Pfc,
Scrogg, Orlando, Pfc,
Sclifo, Victor C., Pvt,
Scura, Sunday, Pfc,
Seago, Ben M., Pfc,
Seagraves, Leslie P., Pvt,
Seagrove, William C., Pvt,
Seal, William E., Pvt,
Seale, Merritt L., Jr., Pvt,
Seaman, Pearley H., Pvt,
Seanez, Manuel C., Pvt,
Sear, Louis P., Sgt,
Sear, Stanley L., Pvt,
Searles, Warren L., Pvt,
Searls, Sidney F., T/4,
Searls, Pearl E., S/Sgt,
Sears, Edward J., Pfc,
Sears, Paul R., Sgt,
Sears, William F., Pfc,
Seavey, Mayhew D., Pfc,
†Seay, Thomas E., Pvt,
Sebastianelli, Nick, Pvt,
Sebastiano, Joseph, Pvt,
†Seblom, Jack B., Pvt,
Seboe, Arthur J., Pfc,
Sebring, George, Pvt,
Secchuitti, Mario, Pfc,
Secor, Morris H., Pvt,
Secrest, Lester P., Pfc,
Secrist, Harold C. Pfc,
Sedita, Nicholas S., Pvt,
Sedlak, Henry J., Pvt,
Sedlmaier, Sigmund, Sgt,
‡See, Adrian C., Pvt,
See, Walter J., Cpl,
Seegitz, Robert, Pfc,
Seehafer, Erwin C., 2nd Lt,
Seek, Harry E., Pfc,
Seelman, Ervin W., Pfc,
Seely, Perry E., Jr., Capt,
Seeman, William E., Sgt,
Seery, Spencer W., Jr., Pfc,
Seffick, Charles R., Jr., Pvt,
Segar, John J., Pfc,
Segrest, Willie P., Pfc,
Segura, Donald, Pvt,
Seiberlich, Albert J., Jr., Pvt,
Seida, Richard F., Pvt,
Seidel, Victor E., Sgt,
Seidner, Alvin, Pvt,
Seifert, Ernest, Pvt,
Seifert, Milton E., Pfc,
†Seipt, Edward, Pvt,
Seitz, Glenn L., Cpl,
Seitz, James E., S/Sgt,
Seitz, Otto C., Pvt,
Sekki, Rudolph O., Pfc,
Selby, Luther D., Jr., Pvt,
Self, Carl F., Pfc,
Selin, Erik T., Pvt,
Seline, Lester R., Pfc,
Sell, Edward E., Pfc,
Sellman, Howard W., 1st Lt,
Sells, Henry C., Pvt,
Selmer, Hollis K., S/Sgt,
Seltman, Frederick J., Jr., Pfc,
Semande, Herman V., Pvt,
†Semingson, Milfred D., S/Sgt,
Sempkowski, Leon P., T/5,
Semrad, Adolph R., Pvt,
Semrau, Leo W., Pvt,
Senecal, Maurice L., Pvt,
Seng, William S., Cpl,
Senger, Frank B., Jr., 1st Lt,
Sentell, Philip H., Pvt,
†Sepik, Francis J., Pfc,
Seppala, Oliva W., Pvt,
Serafini, Albert, Pfc,
Sergeant, Harold E., Pfc,
†Sergi, Anthony P., Pvt,
†Serocki, Joseph, Pvt,
Serpe, Gerald F., Pvt,
Serrano, David G., Pvt,
Serven, Francis R., Pfc,
Sessoms, Harvey R., Pfc,
Sessums, Irvan W., S/Sgt,
Sethman, William O., T/5,
Setter, James T., Pfc,
Settlemir, W. J., Jr., Pvt,
Severson, Clifford V., Sgt,
Sevier, James C., Pvt,
†Seward, Walter A., Pvt,
Sexton, Elmer C., Pvt,
Sexton, Howard R., Pfc,
†Seyfried, Donald O., T/5,
Seymore, James H., Pvt,
Seymour, Roy J., Pvt,
Sfraga, Sebastiano B., Pvt,
Shaak, Paul W., T/Sgt,
Shackleford, Dorsey D., Pvt,
Shackleford, Thomas T., S/Sgt,
Shafer, Bill, Pfc,
Shaff, Ralph M., Pvt,
†Shaffer, Clyde L., Jr., Sgt,
Shaffer, Grover W., Cpl,
Shaffer, John J., Pfc,
Shaffner, Donald C., Pvt,
Shalbert, Anthony, Pfc,
Shall, Stanley V., T/5,
Shalow, Stanley, Pfc,
Shank, Donald L., Pvt,
†Shank, Ray, Pfc,
Shankweiler, Harold S., Pvt,
Shannon, Claud A., Pvt,
Shannon, Grady L., Pvt,
Shannon, James J., Jr., T/5,
Shannon, John D., S/Sgt,
Shapiro, Abraham, Cpl,
Shapiro, Bernard M., Pvt,
Shapiro, Earl, T/Sgt,
Shapiro, Henry H., Pvt,
Shapiro, Herman, Pfc,
Shapiro, Howard E., Capt,
Sharber, Benson D., T/5,
Sharet, Paul, Pvt,
Sharkey, Hugh E., Pfc,
Sharoff, Robt. H., Capt,
Sharp, Forest J., Pvt,
†Sharpe, Herbert W., Pvt,
†Sharpe, Noah H., Pvt,
Sharpe, Wilson, Pfc,
Sharpe, Winford L., Pfc,
Sharrie, Lester, Jr., Pfc,
Shartzer, Clyde C., Pfc,
Shatley, Isaac M., Pfc,
Shaughnessy, Harry, Jr., Pvt,
†Shaughnessy, John P., Jr., Pvt,
§Shaver, Robert L., Pvt,
Shaver, Wilburn E., Pfc,
Shaw, Marvin S., Pfc,
Shaw, William C., Pvt,
Shawver, Ralph N., Pvt,
Shay, Ralph E., Pvt,
†Shea, Edward P., Jr., S/Sgt,
Shea, Richard J., S/Sgt,
Shedd, Roy L., Pvt,
Sheehan, Walter J., Pfc,
Sheehy, John B., Pfc,
Sheeley, Johnnie R., Pfc,
Sheen, Glen J., T/Sgt,
Sheeran, John F., Pvt,
Sheeran, Thomas J., Pvt,
†Sheets, Edward J., Pfc,
Sheets, Fred R., Pfc,
*Sheets, James A., Pvt,
Shefchik, Harry F., Sgt,
Sheffield, Harold C., Pvt,
Shefko, Raymond, S/Sgt,
Sheil, Edward J., S/Sgt,
Sheil, William R., Sgt,
Shelafoe, Joseph F., Cpl,
Sheldon, Clyde L., Pvt,
Shellenberger, Arthur G., Pvt,
Shelton, Arthur H., Pfc,
Shelton, Randall H., Pfc,
Shelton, Varnell, Pfc,
Shelton, William E., Pfc,
Shelton, Willie A., Pfc,
Shenkle, John W., Pvt,
†Shepard, Harold V., Pvt,
Shepard, Louis, T/5,
‡Shepherd, Charles S., S/Sgt,
Sheldon, Clyde L., Pvt,
Shepherd, Joe S., Pvt,
Shepherd, Justice J., 2nd Lt,
Shepherd, Nicholas T., S/Sgt,
Shepherd, Ralph W., Sgt,
Sheppard, Jacob L., Pfc,
Sheppard, Vernon A., Pfc,
Sherbula, Nicholas J., Pvt,
†Sherburne, Arthur W., Pvt,
Sherd, Leon F., Pfc,
Sheremetta, John J., Sgt,
Sheriff, George, Sgt,
Sherk, Harry E., Pvt,
Sherlin, George L., Jr., Pfc,

† Killed in Action. * Prisoner of War. ‡ Missing in Action. § Died of Wounds.

†Sherman, Charles R., Pvt,
Sherman, Ellsworth, Pvt,
Sherman, Harry B., Lt Col,
Sherman, Jack R., Pvt,
Sherman, Jack W., Pvt,
Sherman, Joseph, Pfc,
Sherman, Richard L., Pvt,
Sherman, Stanley L., Pfc,
Sherp, Henry, Pfc,
Sherrill, James B., Pfc,
§Sherrill, Samuel H., Pvt,
Sherry, Gus, Pvt,
Shertzer, Robert S., Jr., T/5,
†Sherwood, Robert F., Sgt,
Shettini, William B., Pfc,
Shevock, Michael P., Pvt,
Shields, Ernest, Pvt,
†Shields, George N., 2nd Lt,
Shields, George P., Pfc,
Shields, Paul R., 1st Lt,
Shields, Robert F., Pfc,
Shiels, Robert H., T/4,
Shiley, Arthur H., Pvt,
Shilo, Henry M., Pfc,
Shilow, Melvin W., Pvt,
Shimek, Albert J., Pvt,
†Shimer, Paul S., Jr., Sgt,
Shimkus, Frank S., Pfc,
Shimon, Joseph J., S/Sgt,
Shimota, Robert E., Pfc,
†Shinn, Lewis S., Pfc,
Shipley, Arless R., S/Sgt,
Shirey, Daniel H., Pfc,
Shirley, Frank D., T/4,
Shirley, John B., 2nd Lt,
Shirley, Reuben L., 2nd Lt,
Shirley, Richard J., Pvt,
Shirley, Silas H., Pvt,
Shively, Clair C., Pvt,
Shiver, Julius W., Pfc,
Shivers, Kenneth, Pvt,
Shockley, Dewey D., Pfc,
Shoe, Arthur H., Jr., Pfc,
Shoe, Martin L., Pfc,
†Shoemaker, Clarence E., Pvt,
Shoemaker, Gilbert A., Pfc,
Shoemaker, John M., Pfc,
Shoemaker, Lewis, Pvt,
Shoemaker, Myrl W., Pfc,
Shoemaker, Roy J., Pfc,
†Shoen, Gordon M., Pvt,
Shoff, Edwin S., Pfc,
Shoffner, Freeman, Pvt,
Sholly, Francis P., T/Sgt,
Shomin, John A., Pvt,
Shook, Benjamin M., Pfc,
†Shook, Hiram, Jr., Pvt,
Shook, William R., Pfc,
†Shoop, Charles W., Pvt,
Short, Paul T., Pvt,
†Shoultz, Eugene D., Cpl,
Showalter, Clyde W., S/Sgt,
†Shradnick, Leonard, 1st Lt,
†Shreffler, Walter O., Pfc,
Shriver, Amos M., Cpl,
Shrout, Edgar A., Jr., Pvt,
†Shroyer, Thomas G., Pfc,
Shrzpcyk, Ladislaus, Pvt,
†Shubert, Vincent D., S/Sgt,
Shugrue, John J., Pvt,
Shuker, Walter H., Pvt,
Shuksteris, Allan A., Pfc,
Shulkatis, Daniel J., 2nd Lt,
Shull, Norris W., Pvt,
Shults, Clyde A., Sgt,
Shultz, Clive W., Pvt,
Shultz, Gregory D., Pvt,
Shumaker, L. H., T/Sgt,
Shuman, Preston N., Pvt,
Shupe, Joseph P., S/Sgt,
Shurin, Harry R., Pvt,
Shurts, William H., Pvt,
Shushereba, John, Pfc,
Shute, James J., Pvt,
†Shutters, Charles D., Sgt,
Siddall, Bernard, Pvt,
Sides, Garth D., Pvt,
Sidlauskas, Albert A., S/Sgt,
Sidler, Edwin, Jr., Pfc,
Sidney, Wilbur A., Pvt,
Sidor, Leonard J., Sgt,
Sieber, Lawrence H., Pvt,
Siebert, George L., Pvt,
Sieczek, John J., Cpl,
Siegfried, Delbert C., Sgt,
Siegiel, Steve A., Pvt,
Siegler, Alex G., Pvt,
†Sieja, Joseph, Pfc,
Siemborski, Peter C., Pfc,
Siemion, Edward A., Pfc,
Siermala, Toivo B., Pvt,
Siers, Willis C., Pfc,
Sietsema, William F., Pvt,
Sievert, Harvey J., Sgt,
Sigillo, Salvatore, Jr., Pfc,

Sigler, Nevin O., Pfc,
†Sigrist, Donald R., Sgt,
Sikkenga, Clarence D., Pfc,
Silberberg, Martin, Pvt,
Silcox, Jack, Pfc,
‡Siler, Robert H., T/5,
Silk, Jack, Sgt,
Sillitto, Dominick, Pvt,
†Silski, Anthony, Pvt,
Silva, John B., Pfc,
Silva, Lawrence C., Jr., Sgt,
Silver, William W., 1st Lt,
Silverman, Arthur, Pfc,
Silverman, Irving, 2nd Lt,
†Silvernail, Carl W., Pvt, St.
†Silverstein, Earl, Pfc,
Silvia, Antone M., Pfc,
Similewich, William J., Pfc,
Simkins, Earl D., Pfc,
Simkins, Henry B., Sgt,
Simko, George B., T/5,
Simkovic, John F., Jr., Sgt,
Simmers, Raymond L., Pfc,
Simmons, A. C., S/Sgt,
Simmons, Alva J., Pfc,
Simmons, Elbert E., Pvt,
Simmons, George D., Pvt,
Simmons, George R., Pfc,
Simmons, Herman L., Pvt,
†Simmons, James U., T/Sgt,
Simmons, John W., Pfc,
Simmons, Lee D., Pfc,
Simmons, Lucius H., S/Sgt,
Simmons, Osbyn G., Pfc,
Simmons, Milton L., 2nd Lt,
‡Simmons, Robert, Pvt,
Simms, James J., Pvt,
†Simon, Daniel L., Pvt,
Simon, Michael A., S/Sgt,
Simon, Stephen, Pfc,
Simons, Raymond G., Pvt,
†Simpson, Arthur R., Pvt,
Simpson, Charles E., Pvt,
Simpson, Herbert R., T/4,
Simpson, James G., 1st Lt,
†Simpson, Kenneth E., Pvt,
Simpson, Leland H., Cpl,
Simpson, Ora E., Pfc,
Simpson, Wilbert R., Pvt,
Sims, Alvin L., Pvt,
Sims, Dale M., Cpl,
†Sims, Harry W., T/5,
Sims, Sammy E., Pfc,
Sims, Willis D., T/5,
Singer, Benjamin, 1st Lt,
Singer, Melvin S., S/Sgt,
Singer, Samuel, Sgt,
Singletary, Vernon L., 1st Sgt,
Sink, Paul J., Pfc,
Sinkevicz, Edward L., Pfc,
†Sinkovitz, Albert, Pvt,
Sinks, Robert E., Sgt,
Sinn, Lyle D., T/5,
Sinnett, Murray M., Pvt,
†Sinnott, John F., Sgt,
Sipple, James W., Pvt,
†Sipsy, Aaron H., Pvt,
Sirabella, Ericardo, Pfc,
Sirbaugh, Elza V., Sgt,
Sires, Duane E., Sgt,
Sirmons, Oliver K., Pfc,
Sisel, Donald J., Pfc,
*Sisk, James R., T/5,
Sisson, Dana M., Pvt,
§Sitko, George A., Pvt,
Sittard, Nicohlas J., Pfc,
Sitter, Ora, T/Sgt,
Sivee, Raymond, Pfc,
Siviglia, Nicholas F., Pvt,
Six, Clyde P., Pvt,
Sjolin, Nels D., T/Sgt,
Skaare, Richard H., Pfc,
Skaflectad, Ingolf, Pvt,
Skaggs, Bennie C., Pfc,
§Skaggs, Boyce G., Pvt,
Skala, Lawrence, Cpl,
Skalski, Walter P., Pfc,
Skean, Philip A., Pvt,
Skeese, Lawrence E., Sgt,
Skelton, Curtis B., Pfc,
Skelton, Ira W., Cpl,
†Skelton, Jack N., Pfc,
Skenadore, Henry I., Pvt,
Skerl, Vincent G., Pfc,
Skibo, Michael A., Pvt,
Skierski, Edmund W., Pvt,
Skila, Mike, Pfc,
Skinner, John F., Pfc,
‡Skjefte, Arley, S/Sgt,
Skjerven, Harvey F., Pvt,
†Skoler, Seymour, Pvt,
Skolil, Stephen V., Pfc,
Skovenski, Chester R., Pvt,
Skowronski, Edward, Pfc,
Skrocki, Frank J., Pfc,

Skubiak, Joseph P., Pfc,
Slack, Henry T., Jr., Pfc,
Slack, Kenneth E., Pvt,
Slack, Lloyd R., Pfc,
Slack, Zigmund C., S/Sgt,
Slakish, Vincent V., Pfc,
Slanski, Mike W., Pvt,
Slate, Lawrence K., Cpl,
†Slate, Wayne, Pvt,
†Slater, Charlie L., Pvt,
†Slaton, James E., Pvt,
†Slattery, Donald J., Pfc,
Slattery, Thomas H., Pfc,
Slatus, Marton H., Pvt,
†Slawter, Oliver J., Sgt,
Slininger, William M., Pvt,
Slivinski, Frank, Sgt,
Sliwinski, Edward M., 2nd Lt,
Sliwinski, Henry J., Pfc,
Sloan, Bob J., Jr., Pfc,
Sloan, Paul B., Pfc,
Slomba, Edward, Pvt,
Slone, Lennie G., T/4,
‡Sloppy, Jack E., Cpl,
Sludock, Andrew J., Pvt,
Slusser, John B., S/Sgt
Smagala, Edward H., Pfc,
Smaida, Edward J., Pvt,
Small, Delmar H., Pvt,
Small, Edward C., Pvt,
Smalley, Ernest R., Pvt,
†Smalligan, Garret P., Pfc,
Smallwood, Julius L., Pfc,
Smarslok, Paul A., Pfc,
Smart, Robert A., Pfc,
Smathers, Earl E., Pfc,
Smeatin, Francis A., Pvt,
†Smee, Robert W., Pfc,
†Smegel, Frank C., Pvt,
Smelts, James E., T/5,
Smerek, Frederick D., Sgt,
Smid, Paul R., Pvt,
§Smiertelny, John J., Pvt,
Smiley, Anthony B., Pvt,
Smiley, William H., Pvt,
Smith, Abner J., Pvt,
§Smith, Albert, Pvt,
Smith, Albert C., Cpl,
Smith, Albert L., Pfc,
Smith, Arnold W., Pvt,
Smith, Bazzle C., Pfc,
Smith, Benjamin F., Pfc,
Smith, Benjamin H., 2nd Lt,
Smith, Burnie G., Pfc,
Smith, Burton E., Pvt,
Smith, Byron L., Pfc,
Smith, Calvin C., Pfc,
Smith, Carl H., Pvt,
Smith, Carlos F., Pfc,
Smith, Carson M., Pvt,
Smith, Cecil C., Pfc,
Smith, Cecil C., Pvt,
Smith, Charles M., Pvt,
Smith, Charles W., Pfc,
Smith, Cicaro E., Pvt,
Smith, Claude E., 1st Sgt,
Smith, Clay, Pvt,
Smith, Clifford W., Pvt,
Smith, Cyril E., Pfc,
†Smith, Daniel K., Pvt,
†Smith, Daniel T., Pvt,
Smith, David R., Pfc,
Smith, Dan R., Pfc,
Smith, Dennie L., S/Sgt,
*Smith, Don P., Pvt,
Smith, Donald F., Pvt,
Smith, Donald G., Pvt,
Smith, Douglas J., Pvt,
*Smith, Duane, 2nd Lt,
Smith, Edward E., Pfc,
Smith, Edward J., Pvt,
Smith, Ellsworth B., Pfc,
†Smith, Ellsworth L., Pvt,
Smith, Elvin B., Pvt,
†Smith, Emden F., Cpl,
Smith, Ernest E., Sgt,
Smith, Floyd M., S/Sgt,
Smith, Francis, Pvt,
Smith, Frank H., Pfc,
†Smith, Franklin M., Sgt,
Smith, Fremont, Pfc,
Smith, George F., Pvt,
Smith, Glenn B., Pvt,
Smith, Grover C., Jr., Pfc,
Smith, Grover N., Pvt,
Smith, Gus R., Pvt,
Smith, Guy W., Pvt,
Smith, Harmon I., Pvt,
Smith, Harold J., Pfc,
Smith, Harold R., Pfc,
Smith, Harry M., Sgt,
Smith, Harry P., Pfc,
Smith, Harry W., Pvt,
Smith, Herald J., Sgt,
Smith, Hillard E., Pvt,

Smith, Hollis J., Pvt,
Smith, Horace W., Pvt,
Smith, Howard L., Pvt,
Smith, Howard N., T/5,
Smith, Howard S., Pvt,
Smith, Howard W., Pfc,
Smith, Hozzie, Sgt,
Smith, Hugh S., T/4,
Smith, Irvin E., Pfc,
Smith, Jack N., 2nd Lt,
Smith, Jack W., Pfc,
Smith, James A., Pfc,
†Smith, James R., Pfc,
Smith, Jerome W., Pvt,
Smith, Jesse H., 2nd Lt,
Smith, Jewell L., Pvt,
Smith, John B., T/4,
Smith, John E., T/Sgt,
†Smith, John F., Pvt,
Smith, John R., Sgt,
Smith, John W., Sgt,
Smith, Joseph N., Pfc,
Smith, Joseph R., Jr., Pfc,
Smith, Junior, Pvt,
Smith, Kingsley J., S/Sgt,
Smith, Lawrence A., S/Sgt,
Smith, Lawrence J., Pfc,
Smith, Leigh P., Pvt,
Smith, Leonard V., Pvt,
Smith, Lesley L., Pfc,
Smith, Lloyd R., Jr., Pvt,
Smith, Loman E., Pvt,
Smith, Lowell C., Pvt,
‡Smith, Martin R., Pvt,
Smith, Max, Pfc,
Smith, Nick, T/5,
*Smith, Ollie, Jr., Pvt,
Smith, Orba D., Pfc,
†Smith, Ozro J., Pvt,
†Smith, Paul, Pfc,
†Smith, Paul V., Pfc,
Smith, Raeford J., Pfc,
*Smith, Ralph C., Pfc,
Smith, Ralph V., Jr., Pvt,
Smith, Ray E., Pvt,
Smith, Raymond, Pvt,
†Smith, Raymond L., Pfc,
Smith, Raymond O., S/Sgt,
Smith, Raymond P., Pvt,
§Smith, Richard L., Pvt,
Smith, Robert N., Pvt,
Smith, Roland, T/4,
Smith Roland C., Sgt,
Smith, Roy S., Pvt,
Smith, Ruice N., Pvt,
Smith, Thomas J., Jr., Pvt,
Smith, Thomas T., Pfc,
†Smith, Tryon Y., Pvt,
Smith, Walter G., Pvt,
Smith, Walter J., Pvt,
Smith, Warren C., Pfc,
Smith, William A., T/5,
Smith, William A., Jr., Pfc,
Smith, William H., Pfc,
Smith, William H., Pfc,
Smith, William H., Pvt,
Smith, William L., Pvt,
Smith, Woodrow O., S/Sgt,
Smithers, Charles E., Pvt,
Smithingell, Lloyd G., Pvt,
Smithson, Douglas B., Pvt,
Smithwick, Ernest E., Sgt,
Smoak, Joseph T., S/Sgt,
Smock, Charles, Cpl,
Smock, Frank, Pfc,
Smolinski, Frank E., Sgt,
Snape, Earl S., Pfc,
†Snarski, Frank, Pfc,
Sneck, Albert G., Pfc,
Snedden, Ned W., Pvt,
Sneed, Charles L., Pfc,
Snider, James M., Pfc,
Snider, Leo L., T/3,
§Snider, Paul S., Pvt,
Sniezek, Ray A., Pvt,
Sniffin, Maurice A., Pfc,
Snipes, Vivian M., Pvt,
‡Snodgrass, Robert L., Pvt,
Snofke, Carl R., Pvt,
Snow, Glenn H., 2nd Lt,
Snow, James L., Pvt,
Snow, Richard, Pvt,
Snowden, James C., Pfc,
Snowden, Willard A., Pfc,
†Snyder, Arthur E., Jr., Pfc,
Snyder, Bernard R., S/Sgt,
Snyder, David J., Pvt,
Snyder, Dean T., Pfc,
Snyder, Glenwood B., Pvt,
Snyder, Harrison, Pfc,
Snyder, Jesse V., Pvt,
Snyder, John M., Pvt,
Snyder, Leroy J., Pfc,
Snyder, Ralph L., Pvt,
Snyder, Richard K., Pvt,

Snyder, Robert C., 1st Lt,
Snyder, Stuart F., Pvt,
Snyder, Thornton T., Pvt,
*Soares, John, Jr., Pvt,
Socha, Leopold J., Pfc,
Sochinsky, Ephraim, Pfc,
Sochor, Robert A., Pvt,
Soderquist, Richard W., Capt,
Soderstrom, Harold O., Pvt,
Soderstrom, Roald M., Pvt,
Soemo, Howard K., Pvt,
†Sofilkanich, Andrew T., Pfc,
Sofranko, Raymond J., T/5,
Sokoll, Frank J., Pvt,
Sokoloski, Leon D., Pvt,
†Sokoloski, Leonard H., Cpl,
Solch, Joseph W., Capt,
Solderitch, Joseph F., Pvt,
Solhan, Anthony M., Pvt,
Solnosky, Frank D., Pvt,
Solock, Edmund J., Pvt,
Solomita, Albert, Pvt,
Solomon, Jasper A., Jr., Pvt,
Solomon, Max, Cpl,
†Solomon, Melvin C., Pfc,
Solomon, Stephen J., Pfc,
Solowij, Joseph, Pvt,
Soltis, John G., Pfc,
Soltis, Peter, Pvt,
Sommer, Everett W., Pvt,
Sommers, Lester C., Cpl,
Somppi, John B., Sgt,
Sonberg, Alfred A. J., Pvt,
Sondgeroth, Raymond J., Pfc,
Sondej, Joseph J., Pfc,
Sone, Jacob, Pvt,
Sonefelt, John F., Pfc,
Soper, Arthur L., Pfc,
Sopik, John S., Pfc,
Sorbero, Anthony S., Pfc,
Sorensen, Hans C., Pfc,
§Sorensen, Paul H., Pfc,
Sorkness, Harry A., Cpl,
Sorrell, Curtis K., M/Sgt,
Sorrells, Jack J., S/Sgt,
Sorrells, T. C., Pfc,
Sorrentino, Angelo J., Pfc,
Sosanko, Mike, Pfc,
Soss, John W., Pfc,
§Sotelo, Hector, Pfc,
Soto, Peter S., Pfc,
Sottilaro, Rocco J., Pvt,
Soucy, Marcel J., Pvt,
Souleyret, James C., Pvt,
Soulia, Nelson M., Pvt,
South, Raymond C., Pfc,
Southall, Joe B., Jr., Pfc,
Southard, Leroy, Pvt,
Southards, Harrison, Pvt,
Southern, Jack, Pfc,
Southern, Lewis E., Pvt,
Southworth, Joseph E., Capt,
Southworth, Laurence R., Pvt,
Sovern, Elmer, Jr., Pvt,
Sowa, Stephen J., T/Sgt,
Soza, Frankie E., Pfc,
†Spaanderman, Adrian J., Pfc,
Spacek, John A., 1st Lt,
Spain, Eugene J., Pfc,
Spain, Paul T., Cpl,
Spain, Wilbur J., Pvt,
Spainhour, Robert, Pvt,
Spalding, Charles H., Pvt,
Spalding, Edward R., Pvt,
Spangler, Albert J., Pvt,
Spangler, Christopher, Jr., Pfc,
†Spanier, George J., Pvt,
Spano, Anthony O., Pfc,
Spardy, Leo R., Pvt,
Sparks, John P., Pvt,
Sparks, Roy A., Pvt,
Sparks, William R., Pvt,
†Sparling, Charles C., S/Sgt,
Spatafora, Louis C., Pvt,
Spataro, Albert, Pvt,
Spaziani, August A., Pfc,
Spears, William, Pfc,
Speas, William E., Pfc,
Specht, Jack W., Pvt,
Specht, Joseph F., Pfc,
Speciale, Victor, Pfc,
Speckmeyer, Roland N., Pfc,
Speegle, James C., Sgt,
Spence, Henry N., Pfc,
Spence, Walter E., S/Sgt,
Spencer, Elvyn P., 1st Lt,
Spencer, James A., Pfc,
Spencer, Rollen, S/Sgt,
†Spencer, William, Pvt,
Spencer, William A., S/Sgt,
Spevak, Sidney, Pvt,
Spiceland, Wayne B., Pvt,
Spicer, Walter W., Pvt,
Spiegel, David, Pvt,
Spieker, Bernard, Pvt,

† Killed in Action. * Prisoner of War. ‡ Missing in Action. § Died of Wounds.

IN WORLD WAR II 503

Spiller, Frank, Pvt,
Spillers, John M., Pfc,
Spillman, Thomas H., Pfc,
Spina, Epifianio, Pvt,
Spina, Nicholas T., Pvt,
Spindler, Edward A., S/Sgt,
Spitler, Seth J., Capt,
Spittler, John H., Pvt,
Spitz, Jerome, Pvt,
†Spitzley, Ronald W., Cpl,
Spivy, Ples D., Sgt,
Spokis, Alphonse J., Pvt,
Spomer, Victor H., Cpl,
†Spoo, Lawrence J., Pfc,
Spores, Andrew J., Pfc,
Spoul, Riley L., Pvt,
Spracher, Andrew R., T/4,
Sprague, Wilbur F., Pvt,
Spratt, William C., Pvt,
†Sprimont, Leonard F., Pvt,
Springer, Frank W., Pfc,
§Sproul, Riley L., Pvt,
Sprouse, James W., Pvt,
Spruill, Charles, Pfc,
Spurgeon, Alan R., Pfc,
Spurgeon, Herbert C., Sgt,
Spurlin, Wesley J., Jr., T/4,
Spurlock, Eldred F., S/Sgt,
Spurlock, Major L., Pvt,
Spurway, Thomas D., Jr., Pvt,
Sroda, Edward F., Pvt,
§Sroka, Arthur B., Pfc,
Staab, Charles F., T/5,
Staats, Garrett R., S/Sgt,
Stacey, Alton E., Pvt,
Stacey, Robert F., Pvt,
Stack, Paul A., Sgt,
Stacy, Forrest G., Pfc,
‡Stacy, Russell E., Pfc,
Stadlberger, Walter J., Pvt,
Staffen, Edward, Pvt,
§Stafford, Clarence E., Pvt,
Stafford, Elmer A., S/Sgt,
Stafford, Gaines W., Pvt,
†Stafford, Marvin E., T/5,
†Stage, Leon L., Pfc,
Stageberg, Milton L., Pfc,
Staggs, Henry O., Pfc,
Stahle, Charles N., Pfc,
Stair, Tom R., 2nd Lt,
†Stakley, Donald L., Cpl,
Stalcup, Gene C., Pfc,
Staley, Basil, Pvt,
Stallard, Walter A., Pfc,
Staller, Meyer, Pvt,
Stallings, Adrian C., Pvt,
Stallings, George M., Pvt,
Stallsmith, Lewis E., T/4,
Stam, John G., Pvt,
Stamper, Joseph N., Pvt,
Stamper, William C., Jr., Pfc,
Stamps, James H., Sgt,
Stancampiano, Vincent J., Pfc,
†Stancevicz, John F., Pfc,
Stancil, James M., Pvt,
Standard, John R., Pvt,
Standen, Orill R., Pvt,
Standerfer, Robert J., 1st Lt,
Stanek, George F., Pvt,
Stanfield, Avery, Pvt,
†Stankus, Joseph, Pfc,
Stanley, Alvin W., T/5,
Stanley, Frederick W., Pvt,
Stanley, Harold C., T/5,
Stanley, Herbert E., T/4,
Stanley, Howard E., T/Sgt,
Stanley, John A., Pvt,
Stanley, Noah W., Pvt,
Stanlos, Anthony, Pfc,
Stanton, Charlie H., Pvt,
Stanton, Roy E., Pfc,
Staples, Burton E., Pvt,
Stapp, Otto A., Sgt,
Starck, Lester C., T/4,
Starcznski, Joseph L., T/4,
Stariha, John M., Pfc,
Stark, David D., Pvt,
Stark, Mike J., T/4,
Stark, Oran P., T/Sgt,
Stark, Wilfred, Pfc,
Starke, Paul H., Pvt,
Starkey, William, Pvt,
Starkey, William H., Pfc,
Starnes, Henry E., Pvt,
Starnes, Joe, Pvt,
Starnes, Lewis M., Pvt,
Starnes, Virgil E., Pfc,
Staroscik, Louis V., T/4,
Starr, Edmund S., Jr., Pvt,
Starry, Clarence E., Pvt,
Startzman, Roy I., Pfc,
Starzyk, Joseph J., Pvt,
Stasiak, Chester W., Pfc,
Stasik, Albert J., 1st Lt,
Stasing, Charles F., Pvt,

Stathis, Theodore P., Pvt,
Staton, William H., Pvt,
Statter, Severin F., Jr., Pvt,
§Stauffer, Mathew R., Pvt,
Stayola, John D., Pfc,
St. Clair, George H., Sgt,
St. Clair, Jack A., 2nd Lt,
‡Stead, Fred G., Pvt,
Stead, Robert L., T/Sgt,
Steadman, Robert A., Sgt,
Stebbins, Milford L., Pvt,
Stebbins, Roy S., Pvt,
Steck, Casimer L., Cpl,
Steel, Bertram N., Pfc,
Steele, Chester A., Pvt,
Steele, Othel S., Pvt,
Steele, Robert H., Cpl,
Steelman, Alvin, Pvt,
Steelman, Roy M., Pvt,
§Steere, Raymond J., 1st Lt,
Stefan, Joseph E., Pfc,
Stefancic, Milan M., Pvt,
Stefanski, Edward J., Pvt,
Steiber, Duane P., S/Sgt,
Steiger, James J., T/4,
Steinbach, Walter A., Pvt,
Steinborn, Herman J., Pvt,
Steinbrecher, Arthur W., Pfc,
Steiner, George A., Cpl,
Steinhardt, John G., Pvt,
‡Steinhauer, George G., Pvt,
Steinhoff, Leighton H., Pfc,
Steinhouse, Delmer G., S/Sgt,
Steinkamp, Albert F., Pfc,
Steinke, John F., Pfc,
Steinman, Vernon A., Pvt,
Steinwand, George J., Pfc,
Stellato, Joseph J., Cpl,
Stempel, Samuel, Pfc,
Stempke, George H., Pfc,
Stenhouse, Joe L., Capt,
Stensrud, Edwin L., Pfc,
Stephens, Jake, Pvt,
Stephens, John M., Pfc,
Stephens, Wallace J., Pvt,
†Stephens, Wayne W., Sgt,
Stephens, Wilfred R., Capt,
Stepp, Arthur L., Pfc,
Sterenberg, Louis, Pvt,
Stern, Charles, Pvt,
Stern, John, Sgt,
Stern, Norman P., Pfc,
Stern, Sidney, Pvt,
Sternberg, Marcus D., Pvt,
Sterricker, Charles I., Pvt,
Stetson, Rudolph E., Sgt,
Stetzel, Jesse J., Pvt,
Stevenback, Oscar W., Pvt,
Stevens, Aaron R., Pvt,
Stevens, Dan W., Pfc,
Stevens, Donald R., Pfc,
Stevens, Francis J., Pfc,
Stevens, James A., Jr., T/5,
Stevens, James E., Cpl,
Stevens, James W., Pfc,
Stevens, Jesse, Pvt,
Stevens, John S., Pfc,
Stevens, Leon E., Pvt,
Stevens, Linden J., Pfc,
Stevens, Paul A., Pvt,
‡Stevens, William F., Pvt,
†Stevens, William L., Pvt,
*Stewart, Albert B., Pfc,
Stewart, Albert H., Pfc,
Stewart, Buford A., S/Sgt,
Stewart, Carl W., Jr., Pvt,
Stewart, Charles D., Pvt,
Stewart, Donald E., Pfc,
Stewart, Glen E., Pfc,
†Stewart, Harvey R., Pfc,
Stewart, James H., Pvt,
Stewart, Jay T., Pfc,
†Stewart, Lawrence A., Pvt,
Stewart, Matthew C., Capt,
Stewart, Paul R., Pvt,
Stewart, R. T., Pvt,
Stewart, Revis C., S/Sgt,
Stewart, Roy J., Jr., Pfc,
Stewart, Thomas L.,Pvt,
Stewart, Walter F., S/Sgt,
Stewart, William R., T/5,
Stezar, William A., T/Sgt,
St. George, Joseph D., Sgt,
St. Hilaire, Jean Paul L., Pvt,
Stibor, Thomas L., Pfc,
Stichweh, Perry A., Cpl,
Stickney, Norman B., Pvt,
Stidham, Cecil R., Pvt,
Stidham, Earl G., Pvt,
Stiefel, Wilbur L., S/Sgt,
Stieferman, Arthur M., Pvt,
Stieg, Carl J., Pfc,
Stiers, Ronald E., Pvt,
Stiffler, Kenneth V., Pfc,
Stiffler, Richard F., Cpl,

Still, Albert A., Pvt,
Still, Thomas Y., Pfc,
Stillphen, Clyde A., Pvt,
†Stimac, John T., Pfc,
Stimmel, Ernest G., Pfc,
Stiner, Benjamin, Jr., T/Sgt,
Stines, Charles P., Cpl,
Stinson, Cecil E., T/5,
Stiritz, Theodore C., S/Sgt,
Stirling, Ellis C., Pfc,
†St. Jeor, Francis D., Pfc,
St. Leve, Edwin H., Pvt
Stobart, John H., Cpl,
Stock, Charles J., Pfc,
Stock, Michael A., Pfc,
Stock, Robert J., Pfc,
Stockinger, Michael G., 2nd Lt,
Stockton, Billie M., Pvt,
Stockton, Paul E., Pfc,
Stockton, Ray M., T/5,
Stodulski, Joseph S., Pfc,
†Stoecker, Albert H., 2nd Lt,
Stoffel, Florian P., Pfc,
†Stoiber, Louis R., Jr., Sgt,
Stoika, Robert J., Pvt,
Stoker, Merlin C., Capt,
†Stokes, Earl E., Pfc,
†Stokes, Fred H., T/5,
Stokes, Harold J., Pvt,
Stokes, Jack W., Pvt,
Stoleson, Floyd C., Sgt,
Stolin, Anthony J., Pfc,
Stolle, John W., Pfc,
Stolle, Wilmer J., S/Sgt,
Stoller, Sam, 2nd Lt,
Stolpe, Fred M., Pfc,
Stolte, William C., Pvt,
Stone, David L., Pvt,
Stone, Frederick R., Pfc,
Stone, George F., T/5,
Stone, Henry B., Pvt,
Stone, Hugh D., S/Sgt,
Stone, Jack H., Pfc,
Stone, James C., Sgt,
Stone, Lester L., Pvt,
Stone, Walter L., T/5,
†Stone, Wilfred M., Pfc,
Stone, William B., 2nd Lt,
Stonebraker, F. J., Jr., 1st Lt,
Stoneking, John D., Pvt,
Stoner, Robert J., Pvt,
Stoneski, Walter A., Pfc,
†Stonier, Eugene H., Pvt,
Stoodley, Robert P., S/Sgt,
Storckman, Robert L., Pvt,
Storek, Warren L., Cpl,
Storie, Howard, Pfc,
Storm, Ralph J., Jr., 1st Lt,
†Storzinski, Walter, Pvt,
Stough, John L., Cpl,
†St. Ours, Harold J., Pvt,
Stout, Charles A., Pfc,
Stout, Lawrence L., Pvt,
Stout, Rudy, Jr., Pfc,
Stover, Lenzie H., Pvt,
Stowell, Robert G., Pvt,
†Straccia, Julius, Pfc,
Stracke, Charles J., Pvt,
Strada, Joe, Pvt,
Stradling, Floyd M., Pfc,
Strait, John S., T/Sgt,
Strand, Lester P., Pvt,
Strange, Leroy A., Pvt,
†Strangstalien, Gordon W., Pfc,
†Stransky, Albert F., Sgt,
Straub, Lindley H., Pfc,
Strawser, Harold L., Pvt,
Strayhorne, Thornton B., Pvt,
Strech, Fritz W., Pvt,
Streeter, Leroy, Pvt,
†Streger, David, Pfc,
Striani, Bernard L., Pvt,
Strickland, Dave L., Pvt,
Strickland, Lloyd G., Pvt,
Strickland, Marion M., S/Sgt,
Strickland, Tim E., Pvt,
Striebich, John, Pfc,
Striedl, Joe, Pfc,
Striegl, Andrew W., Pfc,
†Strife, William L., Pvt,
Striker, Joseph W., Pvt,
Strilich, Thomas F., Pfc,
Stritzei, Edwin P., Sgt,
Strizziere, Felix J., Pvt,
Strnad, Anthony J., T/4,
Strohmeyer, Everett E., S/Sgt,
Strom, Kenneth G., Pfc,
Stroud, Fred M., 1st Sgt,
Stroud, James W., Jr., Pfc,
Stroud, McDonald, Pfc,
Strub, Victor W., Cpl,
Struck, Jose S., Pfc,
Struck, Theodore R., Pfc,
Struckmeyer, Fred C., 1st Lt,

Strukel, Matt J., Pvt,
Strumwasser, Stanley P., Sgt,
Stryk, John, Cpl,
Stryker, Herbert H., Jr., Pfc,
Strysharz, John S., Pvt,
Stuard, James M., Pvt,
†Stuart, Henry M., Sgt,
Stuart, Jerome P. F., Pvt,
Stuart, Warren M., Capt,
Stubbs, Jeff, Pfc,
Stucke, Henry W., Pvt,
Studzinski, Zygmunt J., Pfc,
*Stumf, Joseph E., Pvt,
Stumpf, Frederick, Pvt,
Sturgis, Russell K., 1st Sgt,
Sturgis, Willard E., Pvt,
Sturm, Jack L., Pvt,
Stutes, Glenn E., Sgt,
Stutman, Helman, 1st Lt,
Stutts, Durwood K., 2nd Lt,
Stuve, Evan K., Pfc,
*Styles, John D., Pvt,
Styndl, Albert J., T/4,
Suckus, William S., Pfc,
Suddreth, Bill D., Pvt,
Sudol, Walter, Pvt,
Sugars, Richard H., 2nd Lt,
Sugg, Raymond M., Cpl,
Suhayda, Sylvester E., S/Sgt,
Suhow, Michael, Pvt,
Suhr, Alfred H., Pfc,
Suits, Franklin M., Pfc,
Sullenbarger, George E., Pfc,
Sullivan, Clarence E., Pvt,
Sullivan, David E., Pvt,
Sullivan, Francis V., Pvt,
Sullivan, George M., Pvt,
Sullivan, George M., Pvt,
Sullivan, James C., Sgt,
Sullivan, John F., T/4,
Sullivan, John J., Jr., Pfc,
*Sullivan, John P., Cpl,
Sullivan, Robert M., Pvt,
Sullivan, Timothy, Pvt,
Sullivan, Vernon F., T/5,
Sullivan, Vincent C., Pvt,
Sulyok, Paul P., T/4,
Sumerall, Randolph M., 1st Lt,
Summers, Ernest, Pfc,
Summers, Howard D., Pvt,
Summers, Marion A., T/5,
§Summers, Roy L., Pvt,
Summers, Rush C., Pfc,
Sumner, Lawrence R., Pfc,
Sunday, Earl K., Pvt,
Sunday, Levi, Pfc,
Sunderland, Roy L., Jr., Pfc,
Sunderly, Louis G., Pfc,
Sunkin, David F., Capt,
Sunyogh, Eli J., T/5,
†Supinski, Stanley, Pvt,
Suppes, George J., Pvt,
Suriano, Samuel, Pvt,
Surma, Stephen P., Pvt,
Surowic, Chester, Pvt,
Suter, Frank, Pvt,
Suter, Irvin M., Pfc,
Sutherland, William, Pvt,
Sutlic, Steve J., Pvt,
Sutterfield, Fred C., Pfc,
Sutton, Carl S., Pvt,
†Sutton, Charles W., 1st Lt,
Sutton, Claude R., Pfc,
Sutton, Daniel F., Pfc,
Sutton, Harold W., Sgt,
†Sutton, Ray, Jr., Pvt,
Sutton, William H., Pfc,
Svaton, James M., Pfc,
Svee, George N., Pfc,
Sveva, John J., Pfc,
Svitavsky, Leo E., 2nd Lt,
Svolos, George J., Pvt,
Swacina, Howard G., S/Sgt,
Swader, Alfred A., Pvt,
Swadish, Howard W., Pvt,
Swafford, Johnnie H., T/5,
Swaggard, Richard B., Pfc,
Swagler, Donald E., Pvt,
Swaim, Allan L., 1st Lt,
Swain, Woodrow W., Pvt,
Swan, Harlan H., 1st Lt,
Swan, Thayne J., T/5,
§Swanberg, Charles, Jr., Major,
Swanson, Clarence E., S/Sgt,
Swanson, Harry C., Pfc,
Swanson, Leonard E., S/Sgt,
Swanson, Louis W., Pfc,
Sunkin, David F., Capt,
Swanson, Roy O., Pfc,
Swanson, Willis E., Pfc,
Swarner, Robert L., Pfc,
Swarthout, Glendon F., Pvt,
Swayne, Seward S., Pfc,
Swearengin, Cyrus, Pvt,

Sweat, Lloyd J., T/5,
§Sweatman, Carlisle A., Pvt,
Sweatt, Willie M., Sgt,
Swed, Louis, Pvt,
Swee, Richard J., Sgt,
Sweeney, Nelson L., 1st Lt,
Sweeney, William A., Pfc,
Sweeney, William L., Pfc,
Sweet, Earl L., Pvt,
Sweigart, Thad. W., 2nd Lt,
Sweikow, John A., Pvt,
Swenson, Charles E., Pfc,
Swerdlin, Israel, Pfc,
Swetnam, Michael M., Sgt,
Swiatkowski, Edward J., Pvt,
†Swiderski, Stanley, Pfc,
*Swienton, Edmund J., Pvt,
Swihart, Edward O., T/5,
Swink, Jerre F., T/3,
§Swintek, Louis J., Pvt,
Switzer, Fletcher S., Pfc,
Swogger, Harry E., Sgt,
Sword, Sidney C., T/4,
Sychowski, Leonard J., Pvt,
Sykes, Arthur G., 1st Lt,
Sykes, James W., Pvt,
Sykes, John G., Pvt,
Sykes, Stanley M., Pvt,
Sylke, Walter J., Pfc,
Sylvain, Harold P., Pvt,
Sylvester, James A., Pvt,
Sylvis, Cecil A., Sgt,
Symczak, Walter J., Capt,
Sypolt, Paul E., Pvt,
Szabaga, Peter P., Sgt,
†Szala, Carl S., T/4,
Szatkowski, Alfred S., Pfc,
Szczesek, William F., Pfc,
Szczesniak, Walter F., T/5,
Szczesny, Edward T., Pvt,
Szelina, John A., T/4,
*Szeszol, John F., Pfc,
Szetela, John S., Pfc,
Szmelc, Edward L., Pvt,
Szumlanski, Henry V., Pvt,
Szurley, Scott V., Pfc,
Szwed, Anthony L., Pfc,
Szymanski, Stanley J., Sgt,
Szymanski, Stanley P., Pfc,
Szymczak, Rudolph, Sgt,
Szyperski, Israel A., Pfc,

Tabarracci, Leonard, Pfc,
†Taber, Jesse L., Pfc,
Taber, William, Sgt,
§Tack, Peter, Pfc,
†Tacker, Calvin R., Pvt,
Tackett, George R., Sgt,
†Tackle, Edmund, 2nd Lt,
Taggert, Donald G., 1st Lt,
Taglialetela, Jeremio, Pfc,
Taglialatela, Ralph V., Pfc,
Tait, Arnold C., Capt,
Tait, George E., Pvt,
Takach, William, Pfc,
Takacs, Albert F., Pfc,
Talbert, Howard,Pfc,
Talbert, James, Cpl,
Talbot, Guy R., Pfc,
Talbot, Henri J., Pfc,
Talkowski, Alphonse, Pfc,
Talley, Robert C., Pvt,
Tallman, George T., Pfc,
Tallman, Robert L., Pfc,
Tallotta, Anthony P., Pfc,
Talmadge, Daniel W., 2nd Lt,
Talmadge, Wilson E., T/5,
Tamboli, Carlo, Pfc,
Tamraz, Joesph, Pvt,
Tangalos, John H., Pfc,
Tangemann, John C., Pfc,
†Tanner, Clyde, Pvt,
Tanner, Harvey S., Pfc,
Tanner, James L., Pvt,
†Tansey, Leonard V., Pfc,
†Tapley, Arthur L., Jr., Pfc,
Tapp, Samuel J., Pfc,
Taragano, Irving, Pfc,
Tarczon, Joseph A., Pfc,
Tarnowski, Charles F., Pfc,
Tartaglia, Carl F., Pvt,
Tarte, Julian K., Jr., Pvt,
Tarvin, John D., Sgt,
Tastad, Ervin E., S/Sgt,
Tatara, Edward F., Pfc,
Tatazovich, Nick, Pfc,
Tate, Glen F., Sgt,
Tate, John W., Pfc,
Tate, Olen D., Sgt,
§Tatroe, Lloyd C., Sgt,
Tatteff, George, Cpl,
Tatum, John R., Pvt,
Tatum, Lynwood E., Jr., Pvt,
Taurino, Romeo M., Sgt,

† Killed in Action. * Prisoner of War. ‡ Missing in Action. § Died of Wounds.

Tavano, Charles, Pvt,
Tavares, Manuel C., Pfc,
Tavares, William, Pvt,
†Taverni, Frank J., Pvt,
§Tawes, Jack K., Pfc,
Taylor, Alva L., Cpl,
Taylor, Blaine E., Sgt,
Taylor, Charles W., Pvt,
†Taylor, Clarence I., Pvt,
Taylor, Clayton F., Pvt,
Taylor, Cloys A., Pvt,
Taylor, Dallas P., Pfc,
Taylor, Edward J., Pfc,
Taylor, Frank M., Pvt,
Taylor, Harold J., T/4,
Taylor, J. C. R., Pfc,
†Taylor, James S., Pvt,
Taylor, Jason E., Pvt,
Taylor, Kenneth R., Pfc,
Taylor, Lloyd V., Pvt,
Taylor, Mahlon C., Pfc,
Taylor, Marion P., Pfc,
Taylor, Norman W., Pvt,
Taylor, Oliver E., Pfc,
Taylor, Ray B., T/Sgt,
Taylor, Robert J., Sgt,
Taylor, Robert L., Pfc,
Taylor, Ross P., Pfc,
Taylor, Russell M., T/4,
Taylor, Thomas M., S/Sgt,
Taylor, Wilber W., Pvt,
Taylor, William H., Pvt,
Taynor, James T., Pvt,
†Tayse, Carles C., Pvt,
§Teachout, James E., Pvt,
Teague, Dearl N., T/5,
Teague, Henry C., Pvt,
†Teague, William H., Pvt,
Teasley, Robert W., Pvt,
Teat, Winston D., Pvt,
†Tedesco, Alphonse A., Pvt,
Teetaert, Curiel V., Pfc,
Teets, Francis, T/5,
Tegan, Warren A., Major,
†Tegtmeier, Jack D., Pfc,
Teisberg, Robert C., Pfc,
†Teixeira, John, Pfc,
§Teixeira, Manuel G., Sgt,
Telford, Bennie B., T/4,
Teller, Howard W., Pfc,
Tellstrom, A. T., Jr., T/Sgt,
Temby, Clarence E., S/Sgt,
†Tempkin, Morris, Pvt,
Temple, Calvin C., Pvt,
Temple, Douglas E., Cpl,
Temple, James M., Pvt,
Temple, Lymand, Pfc,
Tencza, Bronislaw M., S/Sgt,
Tenhundfeld, Ralph G., 2nd Lt,
Tenney, Flao L., Pfc,
Teoxeora, John, Pfc,
Terceiro, Joseph T., Pvt,
Terlecky, John C., Pfc,
Termini, Stephen J., Pvt,
†Terracino, William M., Pvt,
Terrarosa, Elmund A., Pfc,
Terrell, Herschel H., 1st Lt,
Terrett, John E., Jr., Pfc,
Terry, Edison S., Pfc,
Terry, Milford A., S/Sgt,
Tesch, Roy R., Sgt,
Teske, Karl O., 1st Sgt,
Tessier, Ernest W., 1st Lt,
Testa, Falco A., S/Sgt,
Teter, John G., S/Sgt,
Tetterton, Herbert, Sgt,
Tettoni, Matthew, Pvt,
Tew, Jesse H., Pfc,
Tews, Glen A., 2nd Lt,
Thacker, Stanley F., Cpl,
Thacker, Vester I., Pvt,
Thaggard, James D., Jr., Pvt,
Thalmann, William G., Major,
Thatcher, James L., Pvt,
Thayer, Franklin B., Pvt,
Theis, Edmund M., S/Sgt,
Theisen, Frank L., T/5,
Theiss, Walter G., Sgt,
Thesen, William C., Pvt,
†Thevenin, Shirl B., Pvt,
Thibeault, Lucien J., Pfc,
Thibodeau, Victor, Pvt,
†Thigpen, Joseph W., Pfc,
Thoma, Andrew L., Pfc,
Thomas, Albert J., Pvt,
Thomas, Alfred R., T/4,
Thomas, Arthur W., Pfc,
Thomas, Carl W., Sgt,
Thomas, Carl W., 2nd Lt,
Thomas, Chester A., Pfc,
Thomas, Dewey D., Pvt,
Thomas, Elmer R., Pfc,
Thomas, Floyd, Pfc,
Thomas, Fred R., Pfc,
Thomas, Harry B., Pvt,
†Thomas, Jack A., Pvt,
Thomas, James R., Sgt,
†Thomas, John E., Pvt,
Thomas, Josiah W., Pvt,
Thomas, Kenneth L., Pfc,
Thomas, Leo, Pfc,
Thomas, Rahn W., Pvt,
Thomas, Richard G., Jr., Col,
Thomas, Robert E., Pfc,
Thomas, Robert L., Sgt,
Thomas, Tierce C., Pfc,
Thomas, Wiley H., Cpl,
Thomas, William L., Pvt,
Thomas, William R., Pvt,
Thomas, William S., Pvt,
Thomaswich, John, Pvt,
Thomison, Charles L., Pfc,
†Thompson, Ben M., S/Sgt,
Thompson, Budwin G., Pfc,
†Thompson, Chester E., Pfc,
Thompson, Clarence L., Pfc,
Thompson, Darwin S., Pfc,
Thompson, Donald W., T/Sgt,
Thompson, Edgar L., Pfc,
Thompson, Edwin W., Pvt,
Thompson, Elmo C., Pfc,
Thompson, Ernest D., Pvt,
Thompson, Floyd L., S/Sgt,
Thompson, George M., T/Sgt,
Thompson, Harold M., T/4,
Thompson, James N., Pvt,
Thompson, Joseph, Pvt,
Thompson, Joseph C., Sgt,
Thompson, Leonard M., Pfc,
Thompson, Neal M., Pvt,
†Thompson, Ned W., Pfc,
Thompson, Otis L., Pvt,
Thompson, Patrick H., Pvt,
Thompson, Ralph E., Pfc,
Thompson, Renick B., Jr., Pvt,
Thompson, Richard T., Pfc,
Thompson, Robert C., Pvt,
†Thompson, Russell L., S/Sgt,
*Thompson, Thomas A., Pvt,
†Thompson, Thomas O., Pvt,
Thompson, William K., S/Sgt,
Thompson, William R., Pfc,
Thomson, Chester D., T/5,
Thomson, Wade C., Sgt,
Thorn, Clyde R., 2nd Lt,
‡Thorn, James I., Sgt,
Thornburg, Leon, Pfc,
†Thornbury, Lester L., 1st Lt,
Thornsberry, Robert, Pfc,
Thornton, Arthur T., T/5,
Thornton, Claude F., Cpl,
Thornton, Henry C., Pfc,
Thornton, J. B., Pfc,
Thornton, James E., Sgt,
Thornton, Milton M., 2nd Lt,
Thornton, Patrick J., Pvt,
†Thornton, Truett, Pvt,
Thorpe, Frank O., Pvt,
Thorpe, George, Cpl,
Thorsted, Edward L., 2nd Lt,
†Thralls, William E., Pfc,
Thralow, Walter M., S/Sgt,
†Thrap, Everton L., S/Sgt,
Thrash, Hiram, Pfc,
Throckmorton, Arnold J., Pfc,
Throckmorton, Elmon L., Pfc,
Throssell, Charles W., Capt,
Thrower, Dee R., Pfc,
Thrun, Arthur J., Pfc,
Thurn, Theodore, Cpl,
Thweatt, Leonard S., S/Sgt,
Tibbetts, Alvah G., Pfc,
Tibbitts, Jack E., Pfc,
Tibbitts, Kenzie H., Pvt,
§Tice, John C., Pvt,
Tickett, Edward F., Cpl,
Tickle, Edward L., Pvt,
Tidd, Edward F., Jr., Pfc,
Tidmarsh, Henry F., Pvt,
†Tidwell, Charlie H., Pvt,
†Tierney, Richard A., Pvt,
Tiffany, Timothy C., Pvt,
Tiffey, Lawrence W., Pfc,
Tighe, Michael J., Jr., Pvt,
Tilford, Vernon D., Pvt,
Till, Franklin L., Pvt,
Tilley, Benjamin F., Pfc,
Tillinghast, Frank J., Jr.,
Tillison, Edmund J., Cpl,
Tillman, Henry J., Cpl,
Tillman, John W., Pvt,
Tillotson, Marvin L., Pvt,
Tilton, James G., Pvt,
Timberlake, Norman E., Pfc,
Timkovich, Steve, T/4,
Timlick, Robert R., Pvt,
Timmerman, James E., Pvt,
Timmons, Homer L., Pfc,
Timperio, Nicholas J., Pvt,
*Tinker, Alva E., T/Sgt,
Tinley, Clifford A., Pfc,
Tinsley, Calvin H., Pfc,
†Tinsley, William J., Pvt,
Tippett, Douglas T., Sgt,
†Tippett, Norman D., T/5,
Tipsword, Harley A., Pvt,
Tipton, Gilbert C., Pfc,
†Tipton, Lattie, Pfc,
Tirelli, Frank S., Pvt,
Tirrell, Alden A., Pfc,
Tischler, Irving, Pvt,
Titchenell, Carl E., Pvt,
Titiev, Matthew, Pvt,
†Titorenko, Jonah, Jr., Pvt,
Titterington, Hugh H., Pfc,
Titus, Clarence, Cpl,
Titus, Lewis F., Pfc,
Titus, Theodore P., Pfc,
Tizzano, Joseph A., Pvt,
Tober, Wilburt A., Pvt,
Tobias, John H., Pvt,
Tobin, Thomas F., Jr., Pfc,
Tobin, William P., Pfc,
Toczylowski, Henry J., Pvt,
Todd, Archie, Pvt,
Todd, Frederick J., Pfc,
Todd, Graves C., Pvt,
Todd, Merl H., T/Sgt,
Tofanelli, Emlo F., Capt,
Toffey, John J., Jr., Lt Col,
Tolbert, Ralph C., Pfc,
†Tolbert, Robert L., Cpl,
Tollefson, Vernon L., T/Sgt,
Tolman, Glen H., Pvt,
Tolmie, Robert, Pfc,
Tomaiolo, Angelo J., Sgt,
*Toman, Homer R., Pfc,
Tomaskovic, Albert E., Pfc,
Tomaszewski, Frank S., Pvt,
†Tomberg, William R., Pvt,
Tombs, Jewel T., Pfc,
Tomczak, Theodore J., Pvt,
Tomec, William R., Pfc,
Tominac, John J., 1st Lt,
Tomkins, Elliott M., Pvt,
Tomlinson, John W., Pfc,
Tomlinson, Harold H., Pfc,
†Tomlinson, Herbert P., T/5,
Tomlinson, Roy, Sgt,
Tomminelli, Peter S., Pvt,
Tompkins, Chester E., Pfc,
Tompkins, Gerald C., Pvt,
Tompkins, Harold L., Pvt,
Toney, Ellis R., T/4,
Toney, James, Sgt,
Tongish, Roy A., T/Sgt,
Toole, Frederick W., 1st Lt,
Toole, John H., 1st Lt,
Toomey, Jacob C., Pfc,
Toomey, William J., Pvt,
Toot, Dean A., Sgt,
Toothman, Elmer D., T/5,
Tope, William F., Sgt,
Topolsky, Milton, Pfc,
Torba, Frank J., Pfc,
Torcivia, Michael, Pvt,
Torman, John, Pfc,
§Torrance, Alexander, Pvt,
†Torrence, Norman M., S/Sgt,
Torres, Bennie L., Pfc,
Torres, Caesar R., Jr., S/Sgt,
Tortorici, Benjamin J., Pvt,
Toscano, Rosario V., Pvt,
Tosh, Henry C., Pvt,
Tosteson, Anthony M., Pfc,
Tosto, George T., Jr., Pvt,
†Toth, Joseph B., 1st Lt,
Toth, Robert M., Pvt,
Toth, Stephen, Pvt,
Toth, Stephen R., Pfc,
Totte, Richard N., Pfc,
Totten, John O., Jr., 2nd Lt,
Touchstone, Prentiss, Pfc,
Touri, Don E., Cpl,
Tournier, Alexis M., Cpl,
†Towhill, William H., Pvt,
Towler, Joseph C., Jr., Pvt,
Townsend, Aubrey S., Pfc,
Townsley, William P., Pfc,
Tozier, George P., Pvt,
Tozzi, Anthony F., Pfc,
Trachimowicz, W. H., 2nd Lt,
Trahan, Howard J., Sr, Pvt,
Trahan, William L., Pfc,
Trainer, William A., Pfc,
Tramantono, Frank M., Pfc,
Traister, Harold E., T/4,
Tranor, Charles E., Jr., 2nd Lt,
Tranum, Joseph, Jr., Pvt,
Trasko, Fred, Cpl,
Trautman, Emil J., 1st Sgt,
Trautwein, George R., Pvt,
Trauzettel, Edward O., Pfc,
Travagliante, Sam, Pvt,
Traywick, Otis A., Pfc,
Travi, George G., Pvt,
†Travis, Lester W., S/Sgt,
Travis, Regan W., Sgt,
Travis, Walter F., Pvt,
Traxinger, Albert A., Pvt,
†Travah, Charles J., Pvt,
Trebian, Arthur C., Pvt,
Treftz, Samuel, Pvt,
Tremblay, Arthur J., Pfc,
Tremblay, John C., Pvt,
Trendler, Charles J., Pfc,
Trenkamp, Edward J., Sgt,
†Trent, William L., Jr., Pfc,
Treon, George F., Pfc,
Trepasso, Dominick L., Pfc,
Tretick, Alexander, Pfc,
Trevethan, Edward W., Pfc,
Trezza, Cono J., Pfc,
Tribble, Carl, T/5,
Tricola, Charles A., Pfc,
Trimble, Dewey C., Pfc,
Trimigliozzi, Fred G., Pvt,
Trinka, Robert, Pfc,
†Tripp, Floyd E., T/5,
Trippel, Herman, Pfc,
Trisolini, Anthony, Sgt,
†Trocki, Bernard A., Pvt,
Trogdon, Joseph P., Pfc,
Troilo, Joseph F., Pfc,
Trompke, Ernest E., Pfc,
Trone, Russell W., Pvt,
Tronziger, John E., Pvt,
Trophenbaum, Frank J., Pvt,
Trout, Merle E., Pvt,
Trout, Morris A., Pvt,
†Troutt, Lloyd E., Pvt,
Troxel, Theron O., Pfc,
†Troyer, Ward A., Pfc,
Truckenbrodt, Edmund P., Pvt,
†Trude, Lamar S., Pfc,
True, Sammy R., Pfc,
Truhan, Arthur, Pfc,
Trujillo, Jose A., Pfc,
Trujillo, Ruben, Pfc,
†Trujillo, Tom T., Pvt,
†Truman, Patrick W., Pfc,
†Trumbull, Gerald S., Pfc,
Trumbull, John C., Pvt,
Trump, Quentin M., Pvt,
Trunk, Lloyd W., Pfc,
Trupia, Joseph P., 1st Lt,
†Tsairsis, Achilles A., Pvt,
Tuarock, Frank J., S/Sgt
Tubb, Robert L., 1st Lt,
†Tuberman, Frank, Pvt,
Tucarella, Anthony P., Pfc,
Tuchscherer, Christian W., Sgt
Tucker, Arthur L., Pfc,
Tucker, Coley W., Pvt,
†Tucker, Darrell D., Pvt,
Tucker, Euzell L., Pfc,
†Tucker, Gordon I., 1st Lt,
Tucker, James H., Pvt,
Tucker, L. J., Pvt,
Tucker, Lester E., Pvt,
†Tucker, Travis C., T/5,
Tucker, Walter J., Pvt,
Tucker, William F., Pvt,
†Tuder, Ralph, Pvt,
Tuenge, Arthur A., T/4,
Tufarolo, Liberino, 1st Lt,
Tulak, Frank, Pvt,
Tuley, Jack C., Pvt,
†Tumlin, A. D., Pvt,
Tumminello, Peter J., Pfc,
Tumulty, Vincent A., T/Sgt,
Tunno, Ferdinand, Cpl,
Tunstall, Herbert L., Sgt,
Tupay, Frank J., Pvt,
Turco, Ernest N., Pfc,
Turcotte, Raymond L., T/5,
†Turetsky, Murray, Pfc,
Turf, Maurice F., Sgt,
Turk, Edward M., 2nd Lt,
Turk, Harold E., Pfc,
Turkovich, Albert P., Pvt,
Turlin, Howard J., 1st Sgt,
Turnbough, Charles E., Cpl,
Turnbull, Joseph W., Sgt,
Turnbull, Robert T., Pfc,
Turner, Albert L., Pfc,
Turner, Bill O., Pvt,
Turner, Brady E., Pfc,
Turner, Charles W., Pvt,
Turner, Donald C., Pfc,
Turner, Henry P., Pfc,
Turner, Herbert M., Pvt,
Turner, Herman, Sgt,
Turner, Houston L., Pvt,
†Turner, Nathan T., Pfc,
Turoczi, Benjamin, Sgt,
Turowski, Frank J., Pvt,
Turpin, John E., Pfc,
Turro, Michael A., Pvt,
Turver, William, Pfc,
Tutino, Joseph S., Pfc,
Tutterow, Alva M., Pvt,
Tuttle, Simon, Pvt,
Twedt, Morgan J., Sgt,
Tweed, Van T., Pfc,
Twing, Robert C., Pvt,
Twitchel, Greely A., Pvt,
Tyack, William R., Pfc,
Tyler, James P., CWO,
†Tyler, Max G., Pvt,
Tyler, Robert V., S/Sgt,
Tyrreel, Sheldon C., Pvt,
Tyson, Harry A., 2nd Lt,
Tyson, Thomas G., S/Sgt,

Udell, Charles H., Pfc,
Uecker, Daniel R., Pfc,
Uekert, Verne L., Pvt,
Uhres, Joseph J., S/Sgt,
Uitti, Clarence T., Sgt,
Ujcic, John L., Pvt,
Ulrich, Wayne T., S/Sgt,
Ulshoefer, Walter A., Pvt,
Umlauf, Charles R., Pvt,
†Umphlett, Willie T., Pvt,
Umphryes, Everett G., Pvt,
Underwood, Clyde, Pvt,
Underwood, Richard E., Sgt,
Ungar, Ernest N., Pvt,
Updike, L. D., Sgt,
Upole, Carl D., Pvt,
†Upton, George D., Pvt,
Upton, Wayne, Pvt,
Urban, John, Pvt
Urban, Michael A., Pvt,
Urick, John A., Pvt,
Urspruch, John H., Pfc,
†Urtado, Frank F., Pfc,
Usinski, Joseph J., Pvt,
Utke, Lawrence J., Pfc,
Uttecht, Huben A., Pvt,
†Uzee, Ernest M., Pfc

Vaghini, Carl, Pfc,
†Valencic, Rudy, Pvt,
Valente, Raymond J., Pfc,
Valentine, George, Pvt,
Valina, Alfred J., Pvt,
Valko, Martin, Jr., Pvt,
Vallelonga, Joseph T., Pvt,
Vallet, Charles, T/5,
Valley, Edward J., Pvt,
Vallinch, John S., Pvt,
Vammer, Philip O., T/5,
Van Asdall, Roy W., Pvt,
Van Bemelen, Clyde V., Pfc,
Van Camp, Raymond D., Pvt,
Van Campen, Benjamin, Pvt,
Vance, Charles R., Pvt,
Vance, Isaac N., Pfc,
Van Cleef, Joseph T., Pfc,
Van De Gejuchte, W. M., Pvt,
Van Deraa, Andrew, Jr., Pvt,
Vanderberg, Thomas P., Pvt,
†Vander Galien, Cornelius, Pvt,
Vandergriff, Bernard, Pvt,
Vandergrift, Arthur E., Pvt,
Vanderheyden, George B., Pvt,
†Vanderloop, Raymond J., Cpl,
Vanderpool, Monroe, Pvt,
Vander Vate, Jacob, Pfc,
Vanderwalde, Herbert, Pvt
Van De Velde, R. G., S/Sgt,
Vandewater, Clar. H., 1st Lt,
Van Dorien, Charley, Pvt,
Van Dusseldorp, Jacob S., Sgt,
Van Duyne, Richard J., Pvt,
Van Dyke, Paul E. F., Pvt,
†Van Dyke, William O., Pvt,
Van Dyne, Vinton L., Pfc,
Vanebo, John E., T/Sgt,
Van Fleet, Ralph, Pvt,
Van Horbeck, Joseph E., Pfc,
Van Horn, Boyd, S/Sgt,
Van Horn, Harry E., Jr., Pvt,
Van Horn, John, Pvt,
Vanier, Gelson A., 1st Lt,
Vaniquette, Myron E., Pfc
§Van Loy, Alphonse A., Pvt
Vann, Michael, Pvt,
Vannamann, Oliver N., Pfc,
Vannice, Willard W., Pfc,
Van Os, George J., T/4,
Vanover, Jesse L., Pvt,
Van Pelt, Jissie K., Pfc,
Van Popering, Lee F., Pvt,
Van Riper, Leonard N., Pfc,
Van Schoiack, Ralph H., Cpl,
Van Sickle, Robert E., 2nd Lt
†Van Stedum, Howard, Pvt
Van Stone, Kenneth T., T/Sgt,
Van Wort, Hubert E., Pvt,

† Killed in Action. * Prisoner of War. ‡ Missing in Action. § Died of Wounds.

IN WORLD WAR II 505

§Varalli, Daniel M., 1st Lt,
Varamo, Michael J., Pvt,
Varga, John P., Pvt,
Vargas, Ralph A., Sr., Pfc,
Varner, Virgil J., Pvt,
Vase, Arthur F., Pfc,
Vasilakis, Thomas, S/Sgt,
Vasos, Stephen B., Pfc,
Vasquez, Antonio B., Pfc,
Vass, George H., Pfc,
Vass, Julius A., Pvt,
†Vatalaro, Liberate, Pfc,
Vaugham, Roy T., T/5,
Vaughan, George B., Pfc,
Vaughn, Charles E., Pvt,
Vaughn, John E., Pfc,
Vaughn, Melvin G., S/Sgt,
Vaught, Eugene F., Pfc,
Vavdik, Joe J., Pvt,
Vayssie, Robert R., 2nd Lt,
Veach, James L., T/5,
Veach, Johnny H., Pvt,
Veach, Kenneth G., Pfc,
Veach, Leslie A. J., Pvt,
†Veazey, Cecil, Pvt,
Velper, Ralph N. Pvt,
Venable, James E., Pfc,
Venne, Gerald M., Pvt,
Ventimiglia, Frank, Pvt,
Ventresca, William A., Pfc,
Ventura, Julian A., Pvt,
Verbeke, Cyril, Pfc,
Verbert, Roger A., Pvt,
Verdugo, Aniseto S., Pvt,
Ver Meer, Henry, Pfc,
Vernstrom, Adelbert G., Pfc,
Versdahl, Adolph C., T/5,
†Verzyl, C. S., Jr., Pfc,
Vesey, Francis L., Jr., Pfc,
†Vest, Irvin F., Jr., Pfc,
Vest, Maurice R., Pfc
Vestal, Joe K., Pfc,
†Vetor, Robert F., Sgt,
Vetter, Leonard H., Pvt,
Vetter, Richard M., T/5,
Vhugen, Jack S., T/5,
Via, Herbert W., Pvt,
Viales, Gonzalo, H., Pvt,
Vice, Milton, Sgt,
Vickers, Charles E., Pvt,
Vickers, Louis B., Cpl,
Vickery, Raymond E., Sgt,
Vidovic, Nick T., Pvt,
Vieira, John, Jr., Pvt,
Viera, Frederick L.,
Vietmeier, Robert W., Pvt,
Viglione, Edmund, Pfc,
Vigue, Gerald B., Pfc,
Villa, Frank R., Pfc,
Villani, Alfred C., Cpl,
Villanueba, Urbano M., Pvt,
Villella, Louis, Pfc,
Vimmerstedt, Richard A., Pfc,
§Vincent, Albert T., Pvt,
Vine, Paul J., Pvt,
Vines, Henry O., Pvt,
Vinson, Louis B., Pfc,
Vinton, Raymond J., Pvt,
Visser, Peter, Pvt,
†Vitaioli, Albert P., Pfc,
†Vitek, Frank J., S/Sgt,
Viteo, Stephen, Pfc,
Viveiros, Jesse F., Pvt,
Vivian, Donald J., Pfc,
Vivolo, Louis P., Pvt,
Vocco, Fred, S/Sgt,
Voellinger, Elmer W., Pvt,
Vogel, Mitchell M., Pfc,
Vogel, Paul E. J., 1st Lt,
Vogelsang, Henry, Pfc,
†Vogt, Raphael L., Pvt,
Vogtmann, Roy C., Cpl,
Voigtsberger, Robert G., Pfc,
†Voiland, Aime L., Pvt,
Voirol, Herman J., Pvt,
Vojtek, Emil J., Pfc,
Volksdorf, Ralph J., Pvt,
Vollert, Everett L., Sgt,
‡Voorhees, Albert C., Pvt,
Vorpahl, George A., Cpl,
Voulo, Salvatore, Pvt,
Vowels, Samuel I., Pfc,
Voyer, Charles E., Pfc,
§Vrable, Michael J., Pvt,
Vrbosky, Steve, T/Sgt,
Vrtacnik, Jack W., Pfc,

Wachtler, Herman, T/Sgt,
Wack, George W., Pfc,
Wacker, Philip F., Pvt,
Waddell, Otis J., S/Sgt,
Waddell, William E., Capt,
Wade, Jack A., Pvt,
Wade, John E., Jr., 1st Lt,
Wade, Norman R., Sgt,
Wade, Victor E., Pfc,
Wade, Winiford W., 1st Lt,
Wadsworth, Clarence C., Cpl,
Waggoner, Dallas L., T/5,
Waggoner, Samuel D., Pvt,
Wagner, Adolph, Pfc,
Wagner, Bernard L., Pfc,
Wagner, Carlos L., Sgt,
Wagner, George F., Pvt,
Wagner, Norvell E., S/Sgt,
Wagner, Oscar J., Pvt,
Wagner, Ray J., Jr., Pfc,
Wagner, William G., Pvt,
Walaski, Bruno E., Pvt,
Walat, Edward, Pfc,
Walberg, Ruben C., Pvt,
Walburn, Ralph H., Pfc,
Walczak, Joseph J., Pfc,
Walden, Kenneth B., Pfc,
Walden, L. R., Jr., S/Sgt,
Waldman, Henry C., Pfc,
Waldner, Stanley C., 1st Lt,
Waldon, Abe, Pvt,
Waldon, Walter B., S/Sgt,
Waldron, Louis, Pvt,
Waldron, Ralph W., Pfc,
†Waldrop, James D., Pvt,
Waletzki, Anton A., Pvt,
Walker, A. C., Pfc,
†Walker, Ballon E., Pfc
Walker, Bennett O., Pvt,
†Walker, Burle R. D., Pvt,
Walker, Earl L., T/Sgt,
Walker, Ernest E., Pfc,
Walker, Floyd E., 2nd Lt,
Walker, Frank E., Jr., T/Sgt,
Walker, George A., Pvt,
Walker, John C., Pfc,
Walker, John H., Pvt,
Walker, John J., Pfc,
Walker, John W., Pvt,
Walker, Kenneth E., Pvt,
Walker, Lloyd D., Pvt,
Walker, Lyle L., Sgt,
Walker, Merlin E., Pvt,
†Walker, Robert E., Cpl,
†Walker, William E., Pvt,
Walker, William W., Cpl,
†Walker, William W., Pfc,
†Wall, Joseph E., Pvt,
Wall, Robert A., Jr., Pfc,
Wall, Robert B., Pfc,
Wallace, Bradley N., Pfc,
Wallace, Elmer J., S/Sgt,
Wallace, James F., Pvt,
Wallace, John H., Jr., 2nd Lt,
Wallace, Lelon, Pvt,
Wallace, Lester E., Pfc,
Wallace, Malcom P., Pvt,
Wallace, Ralph E., Pvt,
Wallach, John Y., Pvt,
Wallack, William F., Pfc,
§Waller, Glenn V., T/Sgt,
Waller, Howard L., Pfc,
Waller, Joseph R., Pvt,
Waller, Oscar L. I., Pfc,
Wallert, Alfred D., S/Sgt,
†Wallin, Olaf J., Pvt,
†Wallingford, Robert G., Pvt,
Wallis, Ernest G., Pfc,
Walls, John, Pfc,
Wallsinger, Nathaniel, Pfc,
Walowitz, Alex, Pvt,
Walsh, Edward L., S/Sgt,
†Walsh, Roy P., Pvt,
Walsh, Dennis, Pvt,
Walsh, Thomas F., Pfc,
Walsh, William D., T/5,
†Walsh, William J., Pfc,
Walter, Francis S., Jr., Pfc,
Walter, Henry R., Pfc,
Walter, Lawrence L., Pvt,
Walter, Ray D., Pvt,
§Walters, Abner W., Pfc,
Walters, Edwin J., Jr., Pfc,
Walters, Formel G., Sgt,
Walters, Franklin G., Pfc,
Walters, Marion T., Pvt,
Walters, Richard T., Pfc,
Walters, Walter C., Sgt,
†Waltner, Paul J., Pvt,
Walton, Homer D., Pvt,
Walton, John P., T/4,
Walton, Leonard, Pvt,
Walton, Lloyd R., T/Sgt,
Walton, Thomas, Pfc,
Walton, William B., Pfc,
Wamsley, William H., Pfc,
Walworth, Jack E., Cpl,
Wanamaker, Clifford M., Pvt,
Wangerin, Leonard F., T/5,
Wann, Robert A., Capt,
*Wanninger, Arden E., S/Sgt
Wappenstein, Carl, Pvt,
Warbeck, Stephen S., Pvt,
Ward, Alan F., Sr., Sgt,
Ward, Bascom Z., Pfc,
Ward, Buel A., Pfc,
Ward, Floyd L., S/Sgt,
Ward, Harry L., Pfc,
Ward, Jack B., Cpl,
Ward, James A., S/Sgt,
Ward, Lee W., Pfc,
Wains, George W., Pfc,
Wainwright, Harold B., Pfc,
Ward, Lester C., Pfc,
Ward, Loyal D., Pfc,
Ward, Russell M., Pvt,
Warden, Carl L., Pvt,
Wardrip, Homer J., Pfc,
Ware, Floyd J., Pvt,
*Ware, Justin J., 1st Lt,
Ware, Keith L., Lt Col,
Ware, Thomas M., Pvt,
Warmouth, George B., Cpl,
†Warmouth, Warren J., Sgt,
Warn, Walter, Pvt,
Warner, Charles F., 1st Lt,
Warner, Clement J., Pfc,
Warner, Dale D., Pvt,
Warner, Delbert F., S/Sgt,
Warner, Granville R., Pvt,
Warner, Harry R., Pfc,
§Warner, Herbert E., Pvt,
Warner, LeRoy L., T/4,
Warner, Marvin W., Pfc,
Warren, Charles W., 2nd Lt,
Warren, Edward C., Pvt,
Warren, George A., Pvt,
Warren, Jefferson E., Jr., Pfc,
Warren, Mondell, Pfc,
Warren, Richard L., Sgt,
Warren, Wesley, Pvt,
†Warren, William A., 1st Lt,
Warszawski, Edward M., Pfc,
Wartzel, Howard, Pfc,
Warzecha, Mitchell, Pfc,
Wash, Joe G., Sgt,
Washburn, Edgar, Cpl,
Wasser, Herbert E., Pvt,
Wassko, Albert J., Pvt,
Wasson, Albert S., Pfc,
Wastier, Lloyd J., Pfc,
Waterman, Francis J., Pvt,
Waters, Harold S., Pfc,
Waters, Solomon E., Pvt,
Waters, William E., Pfc,
Watkins, Cecil E., Pfc,
†Watkins, Floyd L., Pvt,
Watkins, George W., Pfc,
Watkins, Hugh D., Pfc,
Watkins, Mettler M., Pfc,
Watkins, Oscar C., Pvt,
Watkins, Seymour E., T/5,
Watkins, William C., Pvt,
Watkins, William S., T/4,
Watkins, Williard D., Pvt,
Watson, Albert J., Pfc,
Watson, Albert L., Pvt,
†Watson, Bernard V., Pfc,
Watson, Donald P., Capt,
Watson, James P., Pvt,
†Watson, Jesse L., Pvt,
Watson, Joe E., 1st Lt,
†Watson, Joe L., Pfc,
Watson, John A., Pvt,
Watson, John T., 2nd Lt,
Watson, Jules H., Pfc,
†Watson, Oliver F., 1st Lt,
Watson, Richard H., Pvt,
†Watson, Robert, S/Sgt,
Watts, Clarence W., Pfc,
Watts, Donald J., Pfc,
Watts, Paul S., S/Sgt,
Watts, Robert L., 1st Lt,
Watts, Wilbur K., Pvt,
Watts, William E., Pvt,
Watz, Floyd T., S/Sgt,
†Waugh, Clare B., T/5,
Waverek, Anthony A., S/Sgt,
Wawrznski, Henry M., Pvt,
Wawrzyniak, Chester, Pfc,
Wawzinski, Edmund F., Pfc,
†Waxler, Paul G., Sgt,
Way, Harland R., Pvt,
Wayne, William K., T/5,
Weakley, Leonard E., S/Sgt,
Weatherholt, Howard L., Pfc,
Weaver, Arthur G., Pvt,
Weaver, Charles P., Pvt,
Weaver, Cletus R., Pvt,
Weaver, David L., Pfc,
Weaver, Hurley, 2nd Lt
Weaver, Sterling R., Pfc,
Weaver, William C., Pfc,
Webb, Cecil R., Pfc,
Webb, Donald L., Pfc,
§Webb, George L., Pvt,
Webb, James W., Pfc,
Webb, John W., Pvt,
Webb, Kenneth W., M/Sgt,
Webb, Leslie S., Pvt,
Webb, Maurice G., Pfc,
Webb, Ovel O., Pfc
Webb, Raymond T., 2nd Lt,
Webb, William L., Pfc,
Webber, Maxwell S., Pfc,
Webber, William C., Pvt,
Weber, Arthur W., T/5,
Weber, Edward H., Sgt,
†Weber, Francis X., Cpl,
†Weber, George, Cpl,
Weber, Harold R., Pfc,
†Weber, Harry, Pfc,
Weber, Henry, Pfc,
†Weber, Jack I., Pfc,
Weber, Joe J., Pfc,
Weber, John E., Pfc,
Weber, John J., Pvt,
†Weber, Richard R., Pfc,
Weber, Sterl W., Pvt,
Weber, Victor, T/5,
†Webster, Clarence W., Pvt,
Webster, Joseph D., Pfc,
Webster, Norman J., Pfc,
Webster, Reynold C., Pvt,
Webster, Woodrow W., Pvt,
Weed, Malcolm L., Pfc,
Weeks, David M., Sgt,
†Weeks, Franklin L., Cpl,
Weeks, Harvey A., Jr., Pvt,
Weeler, Knolton, Pfc,
Weerts, Erhardt, T/4,
Wefelmeyer, Arthur L., Pvt,
†Wegner, Roland H., Pvt,
Wehr, Donald H., Cpl,
Wehunt, Roy D., Pfc,
Weibel, Leo D., Pvt,
Weiderhoeft, George W., Pfc,
Weidman, Donald C., Pfc,
Weigle, Bernard R., Pvt,
Weil, M. S., Jr., Pfc,
Weiland, Francis J., 1st Lt,
Weiler, Christ A., Cpl,
Weiler, Frederick W., Pfc,
Weinberg, Ernest, Pvt,
Weinberg, William M., Sgt,
Weiner, Abraham, 1st Lt,
Weiner, John, Pvt,
Weinfield, Raymond C., Pvt,
Weingart, Robert B., Pvt,
Weins, Robert E., Pvt,
Weinstein, Harry, Pfc,
Weinstein, John, Pvt,
Weir, Howard J., S/Sgt,
Weir, Jabez A., Jr., Pfc,
Weise, Hugo, Pvt,
Weisman, Edward, Pvt,
Weiss, Herman, Pvt,
Weiss, Robert L., Pfc,
Weisshaar, Gottlieb J., Pfc,
Weitman, Philip, Pvt,
†Weitzsacker, Robert W., Sgt,
Wekkend, Jeffle M., Pvt,
Welch, Frederick G., Pvt,
Welch, Harold F., Pfc,
Welch, Henry F., Pvt,
Welcher, Cecil H., Pfc,
Welker, Paul L., Pvt,
Weller, Arthur, T/4,
Wellfare, Junior M., Sgt,
Welling, Robert G., T/5,
Wellman, Lyle E., Pfc,
Wells, Bert M., Pvt,
Wells, Harry L., Pfc,
Wells, Herbert, Pfc,
Wells, Jesse B., Pfc,
Wells, William C., S/Sgt,
Wells, Woodrow, Pvt,
Welsh, Richard A., T/5,
Welsh, William L., S/Sgt,
Welty, Frank C., Pvt,
Wenda, Gust E., Pvt,
†Wendelowski, John F., Pfc,
Wendschlag, Leonard W., T/5,
Wendt, Lawrence A., Pfc,
Wener, Sidney C., Pvt,
Wengatz, Norman F., Sgt,
Wenk, Edwin J., Pvt,
Wenrich, John G., Sgt,
Wentland, Eugene, T/5,
Wentworth, Paul J., 1st Lt,
Werner, Arthur F., Pvt,
Wernle, Ralph S., T/5,
†Wero, Henry B., Pfc,
Werring, Burt, Sgt,
†Werschkul, Richard H., Capt,
Wert, Wilson, Pfc,
Wertman, Harry F., Pvt,
Wertz, Harold S., Pfc,
Wertz, Ward O., Pvt,
Wesel, Edward H., Pfc,
Wesolowski, Walter, Pfc,
West, Don L., Pvt,
West, Forest D., Pfc,
†West, J. C., Pvt,
West, Jim D., Pfc,
West, John W., Pfc,
West, Thomas J., Pvt,
Westberry, Clifford, Pfc,
Westbrook, George E., Sgt,
Westbrook, James M., S/Sgt,
†Westbrooks, Francis X., Pfc,
†Westburg, John H., Jr., Pvt,
Westcott, Merle E., Cpl,
†Westdahl, Richard E., Pfc,
Westerman, Leroy S., Sgt,
Westphal, Melvin H., Pfc,
Weum, Owen H., Pfc,
Wexler, Howard H., 2nd Lt,
Wexler, Leo A., T/5,
Wexler, Solomon, Pvt,
Weyand, Melvin J., 2nd Lt,
Weyenberg, Jerome H., Pfc,
Weyl, Nathaniel, T/5,
Whalen, Gilbert W., Pvt,
Wharton, Marvin H., Pvt,
Wheat, Ellis F., 2nd Lt,
Wheat, Norwell E., Pfc,
Wheatley, Clifton W., Pvt,
Wheatley, Wilfred G., T/Sgt,
Wheaton, Wendell W., Pfc,
Whedbee, Richard M., Pfc,
Wheeland, Lowell B., Pfc,
Wheeler, Arnic, Sgt,
Wheeler, Knowlton, Pfc,
Wheeler, Melvin O., Pfc,
Wheeler, Morris J., T/5,
Wheeler, Wilbur E., T/5,
Wheeler, William K., 1st Lt,
Wheelock, Abraham J., Pfc,
Whelchel, James W., Pvt,
†Whelchel, Woodrow W., Pfc,
Whipple, Earl J., Pfc,
Whipple, Frederick W., Pvt,
Whisnat, Albert, Pfc,
Whitaker, John M., Pvt,
Whitaker, William G., Pfc,
Whitcomb, Herbert H., Pfc,
Whitcomb, Richard D., Pvt,
Whitcomb, Royland R., Pvt,
White, Arthur F., T/4,
White, Cecil B., Pvt,
White, Edgar L., Sgt,
White, Elvin M., Pvt,
White, Francis W., Pfc,
White, Frank W., Pvt,
White, George M., Pfc,
White, Harry A., Jr., Pvt,
White, Harry S., Pvt,
White, James A., Jr., T/4,
White, James F., Pfc,
White, John A., Pfc,
White, John L., Pvt,
White, John W., Pvt,
White, Joseph H., Jr., Pvt,
White, Kenneth E., Pvt,
White, Luther I., Pvt,
White, Marshall C., Pvt,
†White, Paul O., Pvt,
White, Richard L., Sgt,
White, Robert E., Cpl,
White, Robert H., Pfc,
White, Roland L., Pfc,
White, Standley S., Pvt,
*White, Ted L., 2nd Lt,
White, Walter F., Pfc,
White, Wesley H., Pfc,
White, Whitney C., Pfc,
White, William G., Pvt,
White, William K., Pfc,
Whitefield, Alonza B., S/Sgt,
*Whtehead, Delford B., Pvt,
*Whitehorse, Jerome, Pvt,
Whiteley, Eli L., 1st Lt,
Whiteman, Ernest D., Sgt,
Whiteman, Harold O., Pvt
Whiteside, Willie L., Pvt,
Whiting, Bruce B., 2nd Lt,
Whitley, Clyde, Pfc,
Whitley, James, S/Sgt
Whitley, William L., Pfc,
†Whitlock, John S., Pvt,
Whitman, Francis J., Pfc,
Whitmen, Charles F., Jr., Pfc,
Whitmer, Walter L., Pfc,
Whitmeyer, Gurney W., Pfc,
Whitmire, Clare E., Cpl,
Whitney, Burleigh, Pfc,
Whitney, Willis A., Cpl,
Whitt, Julian G., Pfc,
Whitt, Morris S., Pfc,
§Whittaker, Keith S., Pfc,
Whittehurst, Wilmer C., Pfc.
Whitten, Ernest B., Pvt.

† Killed in Action. * Prisoner of War. ‡ Missing in Action. § Died of Wounds.

Whitten, Willis R., Jr., Pfc,
Whittenburg, Charnel R., Pvt,
Whyte, Robert N., Pfc
Wiant, Jerry L., Pvt,
Wichman, Robert R., Pvt,
†Wick, John, Pvt,
Wick, Roland E., Pfc,
Wickham, William E., Pvt,
Wickler, Ray L., Pfc,
Widmer, Albert J., 2nd Lt,
Wieczorek, Larry R., Pfc,
Wiederhoeft, George W., Pfc,
Wiederlight, Seymour, Capt,
Wieg, Duane O., T/5,
Wielde, James A., Pfc, St.
Wieler, Joseph J., T/Sgt,
Wiersema, Thomas J., T/5,
Wierzalis, Victor A., Pvt,
Wies, Conley D., T/Sgt,
Wiesenhart, Theo. A., S/Sgt,
Wieters, Paul M., Pfc,
Wigby, Edward C., Pvt,
Wiggins, Alton E., Pfc,
Wiggins, Markham D., Pvt,
Wigington, Ralph D., Pfc,
Wigmore, Charles O., 1st Lt,
Wilborn, Earl A., Pvt,
Wilbur, Gola B., Pfc,
Wilbur, Robert J., Pvt,
Wilcox, Oro F., Pvt,
Wilcox, Rolland T., Pfc,
Wilcox, Sherman R., Pfc,
Wilcox, Walter, Capt,
Wilcoxson, Marvin L., Pvt,
§Wilcutt, James H., Pfc
Wilcynski, Thomas R., Pfc,
Wilde, William R., Sgt,
Wilder, Nolan O., Pfc,
†Wilder, Virgil D., Pfc,
Wilds, Orban E., Pfc.
Wiles, Reece O., Pfc,
Wiles, Wilmont C., Pvt,
Wiley, Ora W., T/5,
Wiley, Otho O., Pvt,
Wilhelm, Victor J., Pfc,
Wilinski, John M., Pvt,
Wilk, Andrew, Pfc,
Wilk, Anthony, Pfc,
Wilk, Venceslaw W., Sgt,
Wilken, Roger L., 2nd Lt,
Wilkerson, Edwin E., Pvt,
‡Wilkes, Cecil D., Cpl,
†Wilkey, Arnold E., Pvt,
*Wilkey, Earl, Jr., Pvt,
Wilkins, William, 2nd Lt,
Wilkins, William A., Sgt,
Wilkinson, George S., S/Sgt,
Wilkinson, Ralph E., Pfc,
Wilkinson, Wilbur E., Pvt,
†Willard, Bert F., Pfc,
Willard, Wilmer D., Pfc,
Willen, Isadore, Pvt,
Willert, Charles E., S/Sgt,
§Williams, Alger E., Pvt,
Williams, Berwyn G., Pfc,
Williams, Bobby, Pvt,
Williams, Bruce A., Cpl,
Williams, Cecil L., Pfc,
†Williams, Dewey P., Pvt,
Williams, Earl I., Pvt,
Williams, Earl J., S/Sgt,
†Williams, Edward, Pvt,
Williams, Edwin R., Pfc,
Williams, Frank V., Pfc,
Williams, Glenn H., Pfc,
Williams, Harold E., Pfc,
Williams, Harold J., Capt,
Williams, Harry W., Pvt,
Williams, Hollis G., Pfc,
Williams, Ivan C., Pfc,
†Williams, James E., Pfc,
Williams, James W., Pvt,
Williams, Joe C., Pfc,
Williams, Joe E., Pvt,
Williams, John E., Jr., Pfc,
Willams, John H., Pvt,
Williams, John J., S/Sgt,
Williams, John W., Pfc,
†Williams, Kermit L., Pvt,
Williams, Lawrence J., T/5,
Williams, Lloyd J., Pfc,
Williams, Maurice W., 1st Lt,
Williams, Orlen R., Pfc,
Williams, Ortie L., Pfc,
Williams, Richard C., Jr., Pfc,
Williams, Robert H., Pvt,
Williams, Robert L., Pfc,
Williams, Robert L., Pfc,
Williams, Roger, T/5,
Wlliams, Rolla R., T/3,
Williams, Roy, S/Sgt,
Williams, Roy R., Pfc,
Williams, Stanley D., T/4,
Williams, Stephen G., Pfc,
Williams, Troy K., Pvt,
†Williams, Vinson, Jr., Pfc,
Williamson, Dow E., 2nd Lt,
Williamson, Harris M., Pfc,
Williamson, Thurman, Pfc,
†Williford, Garvey R., S/Sgt,
*Willingham, Albert T., Pvt,
Willis, Ben J., T/4,
Willis, Eston F., Cpl,
Willis, Thomas E., Pvt,
Willis, William L., Pfc,
Williston, Albert, S/Sgt,
Williston, Woodrow, Pfc,
Willkomm, Francis, Pfc,
Willoughby, Curtis G., Cpl,
Willoughby, Walter C., T/5,
Wills, Edward, Pvt,
Wills, George W., Pvt,
†Wilmer, William L., Sgt,
Wilmoth, Lloyd V., T/Sgt,
Wilsford, Aubrey G., S/Sgt,
Wilson, Alonza L., Pvt,
Wilson, Clayton D., Pfc,
†Wilosn, Cecil J., S/Sgt,
Wilson, Clark Z., Pvt,
Wilson, Claude L., Pvt,
Wilson, Earle W., Pvt,
Wilson, Francis E., Sgt,
Wilson, Frank, Pvt,
†Wilson, Frank W., T/4,
Wilson, Franklin M., Pfc,
Wilson, George M., CWO,
Wilson, Glenn M., 2nd Lt,
Wilson, Gordon, Pvt,
Wilson, Grover, Maj,
†Wilson, Henry F., Pfc,
Wilson, Henry F., Jr., Pvt,
§Wilson, Herbert M., Cpl,
Wilson, Jack M., Pvt,
Wilson, James M., Pfc,
Wilson John H., Pfc
Wilson, John O., Pfc,
Wilson, Joseph L., Pvt,
Wilson, Marvin E., Pfc,
Wilson, Ronnie, Pfc,
Wilson, Seth S., Pfc,
Wilson, Stanley, Pvt,
Wilson, Virgil, Pvt,
Wilson, Wallace S., Pfc,
Wilson, Wayne, Pfc,
Wilson, Woodrow K., T/5,
Wilton, Wayne O., Pvt,
Winans, Delbert B., Pvt,
Winans, Loy V., Pvt,
Winchell, Walter H., Pvt,
†Windham, Willie A., Pfc,
Windschitl, Melvin F., Pfc,
Windus, Paul, Pvt,
Wine, Richard R., Pfc,
Wineinger, Clarence, Pvt,
Wing, Carl O., Pvt,
Wingard, Fred J., Pfc,
Wingard, Liss A., Pvt,
Wingle, John H., Pvt,
†Wingle, Lawrence E., Pvt,
Wingness, Manford B., Cpl,
Winn, Perry V., T/4,
Winningham, Carlos G., Pfc,
†Winningham, Haskel D., Pfc,
†Winslow, Joshua E., Pfc,
Winstead, David C., Pvt,
Wint, Carl D., Pfc,
Winter, Roswell C., Pfc,
Winters, Earl M., S/Sgt,
Winters, Vernon C., Pvt,
Winters, William A., Jr., Pfc,
†Wire, Gerald E., Pvt,
Wise, Paul W., Pfc,
Wisecarver, Cornelius, Pfc,
Wiseman, Harold J., Pvt,
†Wiser, James L., Pvt,
Wisinski, Norbert J., 1st Lt,
Wisner, Adolph C., S/Sgt,
†Wisner, Anthony C., S/Sgt,
Wisner, James O., S/Sgt,
Wisneski, Edmund V., Pfc,
Wisniewski, Clarence S., T/5,
Wisniewski, John A., Pvt,
Wisniewski, Matthew W., Pvt,
Wisniewski, Richard F., Pfc,
Wissel, Max J., Pvt,
Wisser, Norman R., Pfc,
Witcher, Willie G., Pfc,
With, Alex H., Jr., T/4,
Witham, Robert L., T/Sgt,
Witherspoon, David C., Pfc,
Withrow, Harry L., Pfc,
Witinski, Joseph, Pvt,
‡Witkowski, Edward J., Pvt,
Witkowski, Richard W., Pfc,
Witkowsky, Vincent J., Pvt,
Witman, Roy W., Pfc,
Witmer, William W., Pvt,
Witt, William E., Pvt,
Wittenberger, Kenneth, Pfc,
†Wittman, Morton, Pvt,
Wittwer, Donald C., Sgt,
Wituszynski, Walter, Pvt,
Wlock, Stanley J., Pvt,
†Woda, Chester J., Sgt,
Wodell, Joseph H., Pvt,
Woelke, Raymond D., Pfc,
Woell, Louis W., Pvt,
Wojtaszek, Thaddeus J., Pvt,
Wojtczak, Frederick S., Pvt,
Wojtczak, Pete F., Cpl,
†Wojtylo, Chester F., Pvt,
†Wolf, Curtis R., Pfc,
Wolf, Edward P., Sgt,
Wolf, Herbert F., 1st Sgt,
Wolf, Theodore J., Pfc,
Wolfangel, Gordon C., Pvt,
Wolfcale, James H., Pvt,
Wolfe, Coy D., S/Sgt,
Wolfe, Elmer S., Pfc,
Wolfe, James J., Pvt,
Wolfe, Jefferson D., Pfc,
Wolfe, Marshall G., 1st Sgt,
Wolff, Ernest G., Pvt,
Wolff, Pete, Pfc,
Wolkow, Sam J., 1st Sgt,
Wollan, Bernard W., Pfc,
Wolski, Bernard M., S/Sgt,
Wolstenholme, Donald, Pvt,
Womack, Charles T., Jr., 1st Lt
Womble, William W., Pvt,
Wonderling, Eugene C., Pvt,
Wong, Sing, Pfc,
Wood, Albert A., Pfc
Wood, Carroll E., Pfc,
Wood, Coy W., T/5,
Wood, Edward S., 1st Lt,
Wood, Eugene, Pfc,
Wood, George C., Pfc,
Wood, George N., Pvt,
Wood, Henry E., Pfc,
Wood, Jack L., T/4,
Wood, James M., Pvt,
Wood, Joseph W., Pvt,
Wood, Levi E., T/5,
Wood, Malcolm L., Pvt
Wood, Paul I., S/Sgt,
*Wood, Richard E., Pfc,
Wood, Richard H., Pfc,
Wood, Robert C., T/5,
Wood, Webster D., 2nd Lt,
Woodall, Edward C., Pvt,
Woodard, Roy D., Pvt,
Woodbury, Donald W., Sgt,
Woodhams, Eugene F., Pvt,
†Woodlan, Frank E., Pvt,
Woodring, Hubert C., Pfc,
Woods, Charles G., Pvt,
Woods, Ernest L., S/Sgt,
†Woods, George H., Pfc,
†Woods, Jesse K., 2nd Lt,
Woods, John F., Capt,
Woods, John F., Pfc,
Woods, Lee R., Pvt,
Woods, Olen F., Pfc,
Woodson, Walter, Jr.,
Woodward, Harry R., Pvt,
‡Woodward, Roscoe, Pvt,
Woody, James D., S/Sgt,
Woodyard, Hillis S., Pvt,
Woolson, Richard C., Sgt,
Wooten, Arthur M., Pvt,
Wooten, Noble J., Pfc,
§Workman, Reavis A., Pfc,
Workman, William C., Pfc,
Works, Walton M., 1st Sgt,
Worley, Herbert R., Pfc,
Worrell, Francis M., Pvt,
Worthington, Julius G., Pvt,
Worthington, William A., Pfc,
Wortkoetter, Robert W., T/5
Wortman, Bobbie V., Pvt,
Wos, Edward A., Pvt,
Wos, Mathew, Pvt,
†Wounaris, Steve W., T/5,
Wozniak, Damian R., Pfc,
Wozniak, Edward S., Pvt,
Wozniak, Philip C., Pfc,
Wozniak, Stanley S., T/4,
Wright, Arthur W., Pvt,
Wright, Cleone H., Pfc,
Wright, Francis O., S/Sgt,
Wright, Francis X., Pvt,
†Wright, George P., Pvt,
Wright, Henry J., Pvt,
Wright, James W., Pfc,
Wright, Junior E., Pfc,
Wright, Millard R., 1st Sgt,
Wright, Millard R., 1st Lt,
Wright, Palmer W., Pfc,
§Wright, Stanley A., Pvt,
Wright, Walter C., Pfc,
*Wright, William E., Jr., 1st Lt,
Wright, William J., Pfc,
Wright, Woodrow J., 1st Lt,
Wriston, Robert, Pfc,
Wrobel, Chester S., Pfc,
Wrobel, Stanley A., Pvt,
Wroblewski, Chester F., Pfc,
Wroblewski, Daniel D., Sgt,
Wrona, John J., Pvt,
Wubbens, Vernon L., Cpl,
Wukich, Samuel, Pfc,
Wunderlich, Edward, 2nd Lt,
Wunderlich, Marvin A., T/5,
Wurm, Robert P., Pfc,
Wurts, Arthur H., Pfc,
Wurtzel, Ralph, Pvt,
Wurzer, Florian J., Pfc,
Wyatt, Homer L., Pfc,
Wyche, Jackie L., Pfc,
Wychoff, Charles S., Cpl,
Wycoff, Raymond O., Pvt,
Wylym, Joseph, Pvt,
Wynn, Julius G., Jr., Pvt,
Wysocki, Edmund J., Pvt,
Wysong, Daniel E., Pvt
Wyszkowski, Edward, Pvt,
†Wytewa, Vincent, Pvt,

Yachna, Harry P., Pvt,
Yackobovicz, Joseph, Pvt,
Yaeger, Richard H., S/Sgt,
†Yaley, Robert E., Pfc,
Yamin, Joseph H., Pfc,
Yarber, Bradford S., Pvt,
Yarborough, George A., Pfc,
Yardley, Ernest M., Pfc,
Yarnall, Harold E., Pvt,
Yarnell, Thomas L., Pvt,
Yarnold, Charles, Pfc,
Yarosz, Charles S., Pvt,
Yarte, Gordon A., Pfc,
Yarussi, Oswald A., Pfc,
Yasher, Joseph R., Pfc,
Yates, Chalmer T., 1st Sgt,
Yates, Clyde A., Pvt,
Yates, Fred D., Pfc,
Yates, Irving, Pvt,
Yates, James B., Pfc,
Yates, John R., S/Sgt,
Yates, Randolph, Pfc,
Yates, Raymond E., Pfc,
§Yaworski, Michael, Pfc,
Ybarra, Lawrence, Sr., Pfc,
Ybarra, Pedro G., Pfc,
Yeager, Roy W., Pvt,
Yeargin, Grady, Pfc,
Yedlinski, John I., Pfc,
Yeend, Howard H., 1st Sgt,
Yendrak, Louis E., T/Sgt,
Yenne, Walter L., T/5,
Yentsch, Paul J., Pfc,
Yeoman, Cloyd F., Pvt,
Yeon, Lee W., Pvt,
Yerby, James D., Sgt,
†Yeruc, Walter P., Jr., Pfc,
Yingling, Henry F., Pvt,
Yip, Wing A., T/4,
Yiskis, Robert, Pvt,
Yoder, Fred W., Pfc,
Yoffe, Benjamin, Cpl,
Yoho, Wilbur O., Pvt,
York, Bertram G., Pfc,
York, Eugene H., Pfc,
†York, Howard J., Cpl,
York, Orville, Pvt,
York, Virgil E., Pfc,
Yost, Tilbert C., 1st Lt,
Yost, William C., Pfc,
Yother, L. B., Pfc,
Youmans, Thomas D., Pfc,
Younce, John J., Cpl,
Young, Albert C., Pvt,
Young, Charlie, Pfc,
Young, Clarence R., Pvt,
Young, Cleo H., Sgt,
Young, Clifford, Pfc,
Young, Dallas J., Pvt,
Young, Daniel W., Pvt,
*Young, Edward L., Pvt,
Young, Elroy G., Pvt,
Young, Grant, Pfc,
Young, Henry E., Pvt,
Young, James E., Pvt,
Young, James M., T/5,
Young, James W., Pvt,
Young, Jim, Sgt,
Young, Joseph K., Pfc,
Young, Kenneth W. L., Pvt,
Young, Milton E., Pvt,
Young, Otis W., Pfc,
†Young, Paul T., Pvt,
Young, Ray W., Pvt,
Young, Richard J., 2nd Lt,
Young, Richard J., S/Sgt,
Young, William M., Pfc,
Young, William W., Pfc,
Youngblood, William E., Pvt,
Youngerman, Philip C., Pfc,
†Youngwirth, Robert L., Cpl,
Younts, Robert E., Pfc,
Yourcak, Stanley, Pvt,
Youst, Keith, Pvt,
Yoxall, Herbert D., Pfc,
Yozie, George, Pvt,
Yuhas, Stephen, Pfc,
Yurkowitz, Harry, Pvt,
Yurosko, Andrew, Pfc,
Yutrzenka, John A., Sgt,

Zaentz, Daniel, Pfc,
Zaffos, Abraham, Pfc,
Zahra, Frank J., T/5,
Zaidinski, Ben L., Pfc,
Zajaczkowski, Adam E., Pvt,
Zalar, Anton L., Pvt,
§Zaleski, Edward J., Pfc,
Zalewski, Anthony, Pfc,
Zalonis, Don G., Pfc,
Zambarbieri, Severino, Pvt,
Zambard, Richard D., Pvt,
Zambri, Michael J., Pvt,
Zampelli, Armand E., Pvt,
Zamperini, Randall R., Pvt,
Zang, Douglas M., Pvt,
Zappa, Attilo R., Pvt,
Zaragoza, William M., Pvt,
Zaretsky, Frank, Pvt,
Zaruba, John M., Pfc,
Zauner, Tobias V., Pfc,
Zavada, George, S/Sgt,
Zaverl, Joseph F., Pvt,
Zavetsky, Andrew W., Pfc,
Zawadski, Stanley F., Pvt,
Zawilinski, John, Pfc,
Zayas, Marcos J., Pvt,
Zeets, Vincent A., Sgt,
Zegarelli, Augustine, 2nd Lt,
Zeidel, Max A., Pvt,
Zehr, William H., Pvt,
Zeitner, Helmet F., Pfc,
Zeliff, Grandine V., Pvt,
†Zelkowski, Tony, Jr., Pfc,
Zeller, Thomas W., Pfc,
Zellner, George S., Pfc,
†Zeltsman, Jacob, Pfc,
Zemaitis, Matthew, Pvt,
Zenk, Norman H., Pvt,
Zentner, Burnell L., T/Sgt,
Zerby, Henry W., Pvt,
Zerilli, Frank M., Pvt,
Zerrenner, Robert J., Pfc,
Zeuli, Anthony M., Pfc,
Zeuli, John P., T/4,
Zielinski, Edward J., 1st Lt,
†Ziemba, Gene F., Pvt,
†Ziemba, John A., Pfc,
Ziemba, John A., S/Sgt,
Zilke, Samuel H., Pfc,
Zimmerman, George F., Pfc,
§Zimmerman, John A., Pvt,
Zimmerman, Richard C., Pvt,
Zimmerman, Robert H., Pvt,
Zimmerman, Rollin K., Pfc,
Zimoski, Joseph A., Cpl,
Zindorf, Cedric W., Pvt,
Zingo, Frank J., Pfc,
Zink, John F., Pvt,
Zinn, Ernest E., T/5,
Zipperer, Wilfred E., Pfc,
Zinser, Robert L., Pvt,
Ziolkowski, Anthony T., Pvt,
Zirkler, Earl H., Pfc,
Zirpoli, Emanuel D., Pvt,
Zito, Richard, Pvt,
Zizzamia, Frank N., Pvt,
Zoellick, Harold F., Pvt,
Zoellner, Richard K., Pfc,
Zollum, Paul, Pvt,
Zombotti, David J., Pfc,
†Zotos, Stephen, Pvt,
Zrudlo, Stanley A., Pvt,
Zubeck, John, Pfc,
Zugg, Maxwell, Pfc,
Zuklie, Stanley J., Pvt,
Zuniga, Mike H., Sgt,
Zuttermeister, F. M., 2nd Lt,
†Zwiazek, Milton H., Pfc,
Zych, Adam T., Pvt,
Zylberberg, David, Pvt.

† Killed in Action. * Prisoner of War. ‡ Missing in Action. § Died of Wounds.

30TH INFANTRY REGIMENT

The 30th Infantry participated in the War of 1812 and with the Union forces in the Civil War, 1861-1865.

The present 30th Infantry was formed by Act of Congress on 2 February 1901 and organized at Fort Logan, Colorado.

From March to August 1901, the regiment trained in San Francisco, California, and then sailed to the Philippine Islands where it participated in the campaign to stamp out the Philippine Insurrection of Aguinaldo and his band. It was at this time that General of the Army (then 2nd Lt.) George C. Marshall, joined the regiment and was assigned to Company "L" as a platoon leader—his first military assignment.

For its actions in the Philippines the regiment was awarded the Philippine Insurrection Battle Streamer. After remaining in the Philippines for three years, the 30th Infantry returned to the United States in 1904.

In the period from 1904 to 1917, the 30th Infantry was stationed successively in Nebraska, along the Mexican border, in Alaska, in New York, in Texas and again at the Presidio of San Francisco.

In 1917 the regiment served under General John J. Pershing in the Mexican border campaign.

The 30th Infantry joined the 3d Division upon its organization in November 1917 at Camp Greene, North Carolina. It was assigned to the 6th Brigade along with the 38th Infantry and the 9th Machine Gun Battalion.

The 30th Infantry went to France as part of the 3d Division in March, 1918.

The Aisne defensive, 1-5 June; the Chateau-Thierry operations 15-17 July; the Aisne-Marne offensive, 18-29 July; the St. Mihiel and Meuse-Argonne offensives from September to November saw the regiment in constant action.

During the Champagne-Marne defensive, 15-17 July 1918, the 30th Infantry wrote a bright page in the history of American arms, and it was in this engagement that the colors of the regiment were decorated with the French Croix de Guerre with palm.

From November 1918 to August 1919 the 30th Infantry joined the 3rd Division in occupation duties in Germany, in the district of Mayen, near Coblenz.

Upon returning to the United States in late August the regiment spent four years in various posts throughout the United States. In 1923 it returned to the Presidio of San Francisco, which became its permanent station.

From 1923 to 1941 the 30th Infantry was stationed at the Presidio where it was often referred to as "San Francisco's Own."

During this 18-year period the regiment developed a reputation of being one of the outstanding "spit and polish" regiments of the United States Army, with a band that was famous for its excellence throughout northern California.

Throughout the thirties the regiment had an annual "Message to Garcia" run from the San Francisco Civic Center to Crissy Field, Presidio of San Francisco Parade Ground. This run was made with full field equipment, each man in a company running five full city blocks.

In 1939 the regiment sent a color guard company to the San Francisco International Exposition on Treasure Island. This color guard demonstrated perfection in close order drill formations.

In 1940 the 30th Infantry worked out in full detail a defensive maneuver for defense of the city of San Francisco against invasion and attack from the sea.

The first inductees joined the 30th Infantry on 21 January 1941 and in April 1941 the regiment was once again returned to the 3rd Infantry Division at Fort Lewis, Washington.

30th INFANTRY*

Regimental Commander

(Highest rank held)	Held pos. from	To	(Highest rank held)	Held pos. from	To
Col. Arthur H. Rogers		19 Oct 1943	Col. Lionel C. McGarr	7 Jan 1945	5 May 1945
Col. Lionel C. McGarr	20 Oct 1943	12 Dec 1944	Lt. Col. James L. Osgard	6 May 1945	
Lt. Col. Richard H. Neddersen	13 Dec 1944	7 Jan 1945			

Regimental Executive Officer

(Highest rank held)	Held pos. from	To	(Highest rank held)	Held pos. from	To
Lt. Col. Lionel C. McGarr		19 Aug 1943	Lt. Col. Richard H. Neddersen	5 Dec 1944	12 Dec 1944
Lt. Col. Fred W. Sladen, Jr.	20 Aug 1943	3 Dec 1943	Maj. Edmund M. Sanders	12 Dec 1944	7 Jan 1945
Lt. Col. Edgar C. Doleman	4 Dec 1943	1 June 1944	Lt. Col. Richard H. Neddersen	7 Jan 1945	20 Mar 1945
Lt. Col. John A. Heintges	2 June 1944	4 Dec 1944			

1st Battalion Commander

(Highest rank held)	Held pos. from	To	(Highest rank held)	Held pos. from	To
Lt. Col. Fred W. Sladen, Jr.		19 Aug 1943	Lt. Col. Oliver J. Faucher	27 Mar 1944	26 May 1944
Lt. Col. Oliver G. Kinney	20 Aug 1943	25 Jan 1944	Lt. Col. Allen F. Bacon	27 May 1944	30 Aug 1944
Lt. Col. Richard H. Neddersen	26 Jan 1944	27 Jan 1944	Lt. Col. Christopher W. Chaney	30 Aug 1944	23 Sept 1944
Lt. Col. Oliver G. Kinney	28 Jan 1944	19 Feb 1944	Lt. Col. Mackenzie E. Porter	23 Sept 1944	6 May 1945
Lt. Col. Richard H. Neddersen	20 Feb 1944	28 Feb 1944	Maj. Kenneth A. Noseck	6 May 1945	
Maj. Edwin A. Nichols	29 Feb 1944	26 Mar 1944			

2d Battalion Commander

(Highest rank held)	Held pos. from	To	(Highest rank held)	Held pos. from	To
Lt. Col. Lyle W. Bernard		28 Aug 1943	Lt. Col. James L. Osgard	15 Dec 1944	9 Feb 1945
Maj. Lynn D. Fargo	29 Aug 1943	15 Sept 1943	Maj. Kenneth A. Noseck	9 Feb 1945	12 Mar 1945
Lt. Col. Lyle W. Bernard	16 Sept 1943	18 Feb 1944	Lt. Col. James L. Osgard	12 Mar 1945	6 May 1945
Lt. Col. Woodrow W. Stromberg	19 Feb 1944	22 June 1944	Maj. Hugh E. Wardlaw, Jr.	6 May 1945	
Lt. Col. Frederick Armstrong	23 June 1944	15 Dec 1944			

3d Battalion Commander

(Highest rank held)	Held pos. from	To	(Highest rank held)	Held pos. from	To
Maj. Charles Johnson	23 Sept 1942	27 Jan 1943	Lt. Col. James B. Bennett	2 April 1944	27 May 1944
Lt. Col. Edgar C. Doleman	28 Jan 1943	3 Dec 1943	Lt. Col. Richard H. Neddersen	28 May 1944	4 Dec 1944
Lt. Col. Richard H. Neddersen	4 Dec 1943	19 Dec 1943	Lt. Col. Christopher W. Chaney	4 Dec 1944	18 Jan 1945
Lt. Col. Hilmer B. Haegelin	20 Dec 1943	19 Feb 1944	Maj. Robert B. Pridgen	18 Jan 1945	31 Jan 1945
Lt. Col. Allen F. Bacon	20 Feb 1944	27 Feb 1944	Lt. Col. Christopher W. Chaney	1 Feb 1945	7 May 1945
Lt. Col. Hilmer B. Haegelin	28 Feb 1944	4 Mar 1944	Maj. Robert B. Pridgen	7 May 1945	
Lt. Col. Allen F. Bacon	5 Mar 1944	1 April 1944			

*The names and positions held apply only from Nov. 8, 1942 to May 8, 1945 (V-E Day). Neither opening nor closing dates of service are listed.

30TH INFANTRY REGIMENT

Aaby, Arthur J. P., Pvt,
Aalbu, Harold A., Pvt,
Aaron, Paul S., Jr., Pvt,
Aaselund, Walter B., Pfc
Abbott, Andrew J., Jr., Pfc,
Abbott, Charles L., Pfc,
Abbott, Curil L., Sr., Pvt,
Abbott, George R., Capt
Abels, Harold E., Pvt,
Abernethy, Charles H., S/Sgt,
Abreu, James W., Pvt,
Abriola, Cono P., Pfc,
Abruzzess, Bartholomew, Pfc,
Abruzzi, Louis, Pvt,
Abshire, Milton J., S/Sgt,
Acampora, George V., Pfc,
Acantora, Nicholas U., Pfc,
Aceves, Richard M., Pfc,
†Ackermann, Frederick A., Pfc,
Ackermann, John E., Pvt,
Ackroyd, William C., Pvt,
Acosta, Felix R., T/Sgt,
‡Acosta, Jesus P., Sgt,
Acosta, Martin U., Pvt,
Acree, Edward W., Pfc,
Acs, Frank P., Sgt,
Adair, William L., Pvt,
Adamick, Raymond F., Pvt,
Adamczyk, Roman R., Pvt,
Adamczyk, Theodore, Pvt,
‡Adams, Afton E., Pvt,
Adams, Albert W., Pvt,
Adams, Arthur L., Jr., Sgt
Adams, Carl S., Pfc,
Adams, Carl W., 2nd Lt,
Adams, Charles D., 1st Lt,
Adams, Charles R., Pfc,
Adams, Connie L., T/Sgt,
†Adams, Emanuel, Pfc,
Adams, Herman, Pvt,
Adams, Howard H., Jr., Pvt,
Adams, Innes L., T/5,
†Adams, James A., Pvt,
Adams, James R., Cpl,
Adams, John A., Pfc,
Adams, John E., Pfc,
Adams, Lawrence K., Pvt,
Adams, Lucien, S/Sgt,
Adams, Martin G., Cpl,
Adams, Melvin P., T/4,
Adams, Newt E., Pfc,
Adams, Omer C., Pvt,
Adams, Paul N., Pvt,
Adams, Robert K., Pvt,
Adams, Roy T., Pfc,
Adams, William E., Pfc,
Adamski, Raymond, S/Sgt,
Adamson, Gilbert E., T/4,
Adamson, McCoy M., Pfc,
†Addington, Mack M., Sgt,
Addison, Harold F., Pfc,
Adelson, Bernard, Pfc,
Ader, William, Sgt,
Adinolfi, Frank R., Cpl,
*Adkins, David C., Pfc,
Adkins, Elmer L., Pfc,
Adkins, Grable R., Pfc,
Adkins, William H., Pfc,
Adkisson, Charles C., T/5,
Adler, Orliff F., Pfc,
Adomitus, Warren H., T/5,
Adornetto, John, Pvt,
Affet, Joseph F., Pvt,
Agatone, Domenico B., Pvt,
Aghbashian, Charles, Pfc,
†Agius, John A., Sgt,
Agostinelli, Lorenzo, Pfc,
Agres, John T., Pfc,
§Ahlroth, John T., 1st Lt,
Airington, James W., Pvt,

Aitken, James T., S/St,
Akers, Eldon R., Pfc,
Akers, Willis B., Pfc,
Akridge, Clifford, Pfc,
Alagna, Gregory A., Pfc,
†Alaniz, Clemente, S/Sgt,
Albert, Claude W., Sgt,
Albrecht, Frederick J., Pvt,
Albrecht, Stuart E., Pfc,
Albrecht, Victor E., Pfc,
*Albright, Harry E., Pvt,
Albright, Robert H., Pvt,
Albritton, James E., S/Sgt,
Albritton, James T., Capt,
Alcantara, Jose M., Pfc,
‡Alcorn, George E., Pfc,
Aldrich, Stewart F., Pvt,
Aldridge, Myron C., Pvt,
Aldridge, Vernon I., Pvt,
Alexander, Charles R., Pvt,
Alexander, Earl B., Cpl,
Alexander, Elbert R., T/5,
Alexander, Hugh N., Pvt,
Alexander, Joe L., Pfc,
Alexander, John D., Pfc,
Alexander, Junior A., Pvt,
Alexander, Lon B., T/5,
Alexander, Mat. M., Sr., Pvt,
†Alexander, Richard J., Sgt,
†Alexander, William E., Pfc,
Alexander, William V., Sgt,
Alexis, Ralph R., Jr., Pfc,
Alfano, Alberto, Pfc,
Alfassa, Morris, Pvt,
Alfieri, Cosmo, Pvt,
Alfieri, Joe, Pvt,
†Alfred, Edward F., Pfc,
Alfree, George M., Pvt,
Alfono, Anniello T., Sgt,
†Alfonso, Joseph R., Jr., Pfc,
Algasso, Joseph, Pvt,
§Alinikoff, Arthur, Pfc,
Aliotto, Jimmy, Pvt,
Allain, Carl N., S/Sgt,
Allard, Maurice A., Pvt,
Allds, Marion T., Pfc,
Allen, Abe I., Pfc,
Allen, Albert H., Pvt,
Allen, Carl J., Sgt,
Allen, Charles C., Sgt,
Allen, Charles E., T/5,
Allen, Clarence B., Pfc,
†Allen, Earley S., Pfc,
Allen, Edward W., Pfc,
Allen, Frank A., Cpl,
Allen, George A., 2nd Lt,
Allen, Glenn E., Pvt,
Allen, Harold E., M/Sgt,
Allen, James C., Pfc,
Allen, John, Pfc,
Allen, Leroy W., Pvt,
Allen, Lon W., Pvt,
†Allen, Louis R., Pvt,
Allen, Purman R., Pvt,
‡Allen, Ray A., Pfc,
Allen, Robert Q., Cpl,
Allen, Vernon N., Pvt,
Allen, William A., Sgt,
Allen, William L., Pfc,
*Allender, Maurice B., S/Sgt,
§Alley, John B., Pvt,
Allinger, Robert V., Pvt,
Allison, Albert E., Jr., Sgt,
Allison, Henry L., Pvt,
†Allison, Odell J., Cpl,
†Allison, Orland E., Pvt,
†Allman, Boyd F., Pvt,
Allman, Walter E., Pvt,
Allred, Eliga R., Sgt,
Almand, John J., Pfc,

Aloutto, Patsy P., Jr., Pvt,
Alpheus, George I., S/Sgt,
Altemus, Ronald A., Pvt,
Altman, Robert, Cpl,
Alton, Clyde J., T/Sgt,
Alton, Vernon, Pvt,
Altringer, Raymond M., S/Sgt,
Altum, Marion L., S/Sgt,
Alvarado, Armando, Sgt,
‡Alvarez, Justo R., Pfc,
Alvarino, Gerald R., Pfc,
Alverez, Ygnacio D., Pvt,
Alvernaz, Edward H., Pfc,
Alverson, Harold A., Pvt,
Alvey, Howard F., Pvt,
Alward, Lavern, Pvt,
†Amalfitano, Nicholas, Pfc.,
†Amaral, Alvaro O., Pfc,
Amatangelo, Alfred L., Pfc,
Ambrose, Kazimer J., Jr., Sgt,
Amendola, Armand J., Pfc,
Amirault, Mark E., Pvt,
Amman, Vincent L., T/5,
Anair, Wilfred J., S/Sgt,
Andersen, Darwin E., Pvt,
†Anderson, Alonzo I., Sgt,
Anderson, Andrew H., Pvt,
Anderson, Ben F., Cpl,
Anderson, Berlin P., Cpl,
†Anderson, Chester, Pvt,
Anderson, Delbert L., Pfc,
†Anderson, Earnest P., Pfc,
Anderson, Edwin R., Sgt,
Anderson, Eugene, Pvt,
Anderson, Fay D., S/Sgt,
Anderson, Fred W., T/5,
Anderson, George E., Sgt,
Anderson, Gilbert, Cpl,
†Anderson, Harry C., Pvt,
Anderson, Herbert C., Pvt,
Anderson, Herman C., Pvt,
Anderson, James J., Pvt,
Anderson, James T., Pfc,
Anderson, Joe, Pvt,
Anderson, John P., Pfc,
Anderson, John P., Cpl,
Anderson, LaVerne P., Pvt,
Anderson, Lonnie, Pvt,
†Anderson, Lucian, Pfc,
Anderson, Lyle E., 2nd Lt,
Anderson, Martin, Cpl,
Anderson, Murrell R., Pfc,
Anderson, Ray W., Pfc,
Anderson, Richard D., Sgt,
Anderson, Robert H., Sr., Cpl,
Anderson, Robert S., S/Sgt,
Anderson, Shelley A., S/Sgt,
Anderson, Thomas, T/4,
Anderson, William J., Pfc,
Andre, Alois J., T/5,
Andreen, Carl E., Pfc,
Andreone, Anthony M., Pfc,
Andreski, Anthony A., Pfc,
Andress, Earl R., Pvt,
Andrew, David W., Pvt,
Andrew, James R., Pvt,
Andrews, Edward C., Jr., Pvt,
Andrews, Edward C., Pfc,
Andrews, Edward J., Pfc,
Andrews, Gordan L., Pfc,
Andrews, Ivan A., Sgt,
Andrews, James P., Pfc,
Andrews, Norbert F., Pfc,
Andrews, Ruddell R., T/4,
Andrews, Walter J., Cpl,
*Andros, James S., Pfc,
Andros, Joseph F., Pvt,
Andrzejczyk, John, Pfc,
Angel, Howard M., Sgt,
Angelone, Louis V., T/5,

Angell, Guy B., Jr., Pvt,
Angelle, Roy P., Sgt,
Angellotti, Anthony B., Pvt,
†Angelo, Ralph J., Pvt,
Angelone, Phillip, Pvt,
Anglin, Doyle L., Pfc,
Anistratenko, Peter P., T/Sgt,
Ankney, Forest E., Pvt,
Anseeuw, Camiel L., Pvt,
†Anselmo, Richard, Pvt,
Anstett, Frederick A., Sgt,
Anstice, Edward, Pvt,
Antaya, Joseph E., Sgt,
Antes, Newton G., S/Sgt,
Anthony, Boyd G., Pfc,
†Anthony, James R., Pvt,
Antone, Peter, Pvt,
Antonelli, Gino J., Pvt,
Antonelli, Joseph I., S/Sgt,
†Anzalone, Angelo, Pvt,
Apalatea, Henry, T/5,
Apecelli, Frank A., Pvt,
Applegate, William I., Pfc,
Apriceno, Louis P., Pvt,
Aquelino, Victor W., Pvt,
Arancio, Edward, Pvt,
Araujo, Clarence L., S/Sgt,
Aravich, Joseph M., Pfc,
†Arbuckle, James W., 1st Lt,
Arcand, George J., T/5,
Arceneaux, Arthur, Pfc,
Arceneaux, Eddie, Pfc,
Archbold, Edgar B., Jr., Pfc,
Arcos, Vincente S., Jr., Pfc,
Arcuri, Carmine J., Pvt,
Ardito, Steven S., Pvt,
Arens, Arthur F., Pvt,
Arensman, Charles R., Jr., T/5,
†Aretino, Dominick C., Pfc,
Arey, Malcolm P., Pvt,
Argadine, Lee, Pfc,
Argo, David D., Cpl,
Arispe, Jesus G., S/Sgt,
†Arjauo, Leonard W., Sgt,
Ark, Huie, Pvt,
‡Arko, Anthony R., Pfc,
Armstrong, Edward H., Pfc,
†Armstrong, Fred R., Lt Col,
Armstrong, John J., S/Sgt,
Armstrong, John R., S/Sgt,
Arndt, Clarence C., Cpl,
Arndt, Howard E., Pfc,
Arneson, Harold, Pfc,
Arnett, James M., Pfc,
Arno, Raymond F., S/Sgt,
Arnold, Billy C., Pvt,
Arnold, Curt A., Jr., Pvt,
†Arnold, Harry L., Pfc,
*Arnold, Kenneth L., T/Sgt,
§Arnold, Lowell E., Pvt,
Arnold, Robert L., 2nd Lt,
Arnond, James N., Pvt,
Aronow, Irving M., T/5,
Arola, William A., Pvt,
Arons, Robert F., Pvt,
Arndsohn, Charles M., 1st Lt,
Aronovitz, Michael, Pvt,
Arp, Arch W., T/5,
Arreguin, Louis M., Pfc,
†Arrington, Fred J., Pfc,
Arrowsmith, Paul, 1st Sgt,
Arroyo, Raymond, Jr., Pvt,
Arruda, John V., Pfc,
Arsenault, Gerard J., Pvt,
‡Arsenault, James F., Pvt,
Arseneau, Rupert R., Pfc,
Artese, Michael, Sgt,
Arwine, Charles K., Pvt,
†Arv, Richard E., Pfc,
Ash, Cloyd, Pfc,

†Ashba, William L., Pvt,
Ashbrook, Merle R., T/5,
Ashby, Allen L., Pfc,
Ashby, James, Pfc,
Asher, William B., Pvt,
†Ashland, William A., Pvt,
†Ashly, Elmer, Cpl,
Asken, Emil F., Pvt,
†Askenas, Marvin F., Pfc,
Asman, Rudolph K., S/Sgt,
Aspinwall, Wilfred, Pvt,
Assman, William R., T/4,
‡Asvestas, James, Pfc,
Atkins, William T., 2nd Lt,
*Atkinson, Guy J., Pfc,
Atkinson, Horace C., Pfc,
Atkinson, Paul C., Pfc,
Atler, Henry D., Jr., Pvt,
Aubin, Arthur J., Pfc,
Aubrey, Richard L., Pfc,
Auburn, Raymond T., Sgt,
Aucion, John T., Pvt,
Auerbach, Sol, Pvt,
Augsburger, Eugene H., Pfc,
Augustini, Joseph G., S/Sgt,
Augustowicz, Casimir J., Pfc,
Ault, Kenneth H., Pfc,
†Aultman, Trenton R., Cpl,
Aupperle, Howard L., Pvt,
Aurand, Norman G., Pvt,
Auriemma, Anthony, Sgt,
Austin, Ben R., S/Sgt,
Austin, Charles A., Pvt,
†Austin, Eugene H., Pfc,
Austin, Harold C., Pvt,
*Austin, Herschel V., Pvt,
*Auten, Wayne M., Pvt,
Authier, George A., Pvt,
†Authier, Joseph A., Pvt,
Autin, Loney J., Pfc,
‡Avala, William J., Pfc,
Avant, Joe R., Pfc,
†Aver, James M., Pvt,
†Averill, Lewis S., T/5,
†Averitt, Wyatt H., Pvt,
†Avila, John H., Sgt,
Axt, Ronald E., Pfc,
Axtetter, Edward J., S/Sgt,
Ayers, Claude, Jr., Pvt,
Ayers, James D., Cpl,
‡Ayres, LeRoy E., Sgt,
Ayotte, Clifford, Pvt,
Azman, Edward C., Pfc,

*Baade, Ray C., Pvt,
Baar, Edward F., Pfc
Babb, Harley G., Jr., Pvt,
Babcock, Charles L., Pvt,
Babcock, Elton H., Pfc,
Babiarczyk, Leslie E., Pvt,
§Babisky, Bernard, Pfc,
Baca, Manuel A., S/Sgt,
Baca, Teofilo R., Pfc,
†Bacas, Charles H., Pfc,
Bacchus, Donald W., Sgt,
Bachand, George H., T/5,
†Bachert, Peter E., Pvt,
Bachta, Stanley A., Pvt,
†Bachusz, Joseph F., Sgt,
Backert, Thomas, Pvt,
Bacon, Allen F., Lt Col,
Baddoes, Richard A., Pvt,
‡Bacon, Victor D., Pfc,
Badtka, Leo W., Pfc,
†Bagacz, John F., Pvt,
†Baggenstroos, Florian H., Pfc,
†Bagnuolo, Daniel M., Pfc,
Bagnuolo, Maurice D., Pvt,
Baha, William C., Pfc,
Bahe, Alfred H., Pfc,

† Killed in Action.   * Prisoner of War.   ‡ Missing in Action.   § Died of Wounds.

Baie, William J., Pvt,
Bailey, Alvin P., S/Sgt
†Bailey, Carroll W., Pvt,
Bailey, Guy M., Pfc,
†Bailey, Howard D., Pvt,
§Bailey, James D., Pfc,
Bailey, James K., Cpl,
Bailey, Jesse, Pvt,
†Bailey, Jewell D., Pvt,
Bailey, Patsey J., Pvt,
Bailey, Ulysses G., Pfc,
Bailey, William R., Pfc,
Bailey, Willie, Pfc,
†Balardo, John, Pvt,
†Baillargeon, Vela P., Sgt,
Bailor, Bruce, E., Pvt,
Bain, John W., Pfc,
Baines, Larry, Sgt,
Baines, Robert A., Pvt,
Baior, Albert, Pfc,
Baird, R. L., S/Sgt,
Baisden, Chester, Pfc,
Bajek, Gelbert W., S/Sgt,
Baker, Jesse R., S/Sgt,
Baker, Kenneth J. D., Pvt,
Baker, Leo L., Pfc,
Baker, Leonard, Pvt,
Baker, Loren F., Pvt,
Baker, Paul, Pfc,
Baker, Virgil W., Pfc,
Baker, Woodrow W., Pvt,
†Bakus, Joseph, Pfc,
Balaban, Michael S., Pvt,
†Balcer, Frank J., Pvt,
Balcom, Lymert S., Pvt,
Baldwin, Brice N., S/Sgt,
†Baldwin, Howard F., Pvt,
Baldwin, Melvin F., Sgt,
Baldwin, Richard R., Pfc,
†Baletine, Billie E., Pvt,
†Balfore, Charles, Pvt,
Balko, Andrew S., Pfc,
Ball, Dexter, Cpl,
Ball, Hubert W., Pvt,
Ball, Lester, Sgt,
Ball, Olan L., Cpl,
Ball, Warren C., Cpl,
Ballah, James M., Pfc,
Ballantine, Robert, Pvt,
Ballard, Claude, Pfc,
Ballard, Homer V., Pvt,
Ballard, Thomas E., Pvt,
Ballati, Armando S., S/Sgt,
‡Balliet, Fred H., Pvt,
Ballinger, Allen H., Pfc,
Balsover, William C., Pfc,
Baltazar, Megdaleno M., Cpl,
Balthazor, Lawrence E., Pfc,
†Baltuskonis, Adam A., Pfc,
Baltzley, Kermit A., Pfc,
Balzano, Nicholas, Pvt,
Bambeck, Roland J., S/Sgt,
†Barals, Edward E., Pvt,
Banasiak, John S., Pvt,
Banaszak, William E., Pvt,
Bancks, Robert W., Pfc,
Banducia, Tony G., Cpl,
Banegas, Fred P., Sgt,
Banghart, Lawrence J., Jr., Pvt
Banks, Brooksher T., 1st Lt,
Banks, Harvey E., Pfc,
Banks, Paul L., Cpl,
†Banks, William B., Pfc,
Banovech, John, S/Sgt,
Baraban, Sidney, Pvt,
Baran, Andrew, T/5,
†Baran, Chester J., Pfc,
Baran, Michael, Pvt,
Baratko, Alexander, Pfc,
†Barbee, Willie B., Pfc,
Barbella, Theodore, Pvt,
†Barber, Alfred M., Pvt,
†Barber, David H., S/Sgt,
Barber, John T., Pfc,
Barber, Ray A., Pfc,
Barber, Steve C., Pfc,
Barbo, Marco R., Pfc,
Barbour, Merle E., S/Sgt,
Barclay, Louis L., Pfc,
Barcroft, Dan C., Pvt,
Bard, Dean C., Pfc,
†Bardill, Wilburn R., Pfc,
Barfield, James R., Pvt,
Barfield, Plas A., Pfc,
Barger, Berl V., Sgt,
Barham, Thomas H., Sgt,
Barke, Arnold O., S/Sgt,
Barker, Carl, Pvt,
Barker, Glenn A., Pvt,
Barker, Wilson D., Sgt,
Barksdale, Edgar E., S/Sgt,
Barleen, Vernon A., Sgt,
Barlow, Bert E., Pfc,
Barlow, Patrick H., Pfc,
Barmore, Fred C., Jr., Cpl,
Barnard, Norman C., Pfc,
Barndollar, Roy E., Pvt,
Barnes, Isidore S., Sgt,
Barnes, Curtis E., Pfc,
Barnes, Elmer L., Pfc,
Barnes, James D., Pfc,
Barnes, James L., Cpl,
Barnes, John W., Pvt,
Barnes, Lecil B., Cpl,
Barnes, Leonard, Pvt,
Barnes, Morris L., Pfc,
Barnes, Myron D., Pfc,
Barnes, Robert J., Pvt,
Barnes, Veldee A., Pfc,
Barnes, Vernon E., Pfc,
Barnes, Wendell H., Pfc,
†Barnett, Frank F., Pfc,
Barnett, Jack A., Pvt,
†Barnett, Lloyd F., Pfc,
Barnett, Octavio, Pfc,
Barnette, Clyde, Jr., Pvt,
Barnette, Earl L., Sgt,
Barney, Basil H., Pfc,
Barney, Harry D., S/Sgt,
Barney, Walter G., Pvt,
Barnhart, Eugene D., Cpl,
Barnhart, Hulon G., Pfc,
Barnhisel, Jack H., Pvt,
Barno, Steven, S/Sgt,
Barnum, Norman L., Pfc,
Baron, Frank, Jr., Pvt,
Baronsky, Dennis J., Pvt,
Baronsky, Henry N., Pvt,
Barr, John R., Pfc,
Barr, Joseph B., T/Sgt,
Barr, Robert L., Pfc,
Barr, William E., Cpl,
Barrecchia, Paul J., Pvt,
Barrerio, Joseph H., Pfc,
Barris, Raymond C., Pvt,
Barrett, Claude A., Pvt,
Barrett, Francis, Pfc,
Barrett, Francis R., Pfc,
Barrett, John A., Pvt,
§Barrett, John P., Pfc,
Barrett, Raymond J., Pvt,
†Barrett, Sheldon C., S/Sgt,
Barrick, Mervin A., Pvt,
†Barringer, Robert L., Pvt,
†Barrow, Benjamin F., Sgt,
Barry, John A., Pvt,
Barry, Kenneth M., Pfc,
†Barstow, Gilbert L., Pfc,
†Barsztaitis, John F., Pfc,
Barta, Frank J., Sgt,
Barton, Robert C., Pfc,
Barthelmy, Jesu, Pfc,
Bartholomew, Loren T., Pfc,
Bartlett, Donald J., Pfc,
Bartlett, Erwin W., T/5,
Bartlett, Fred H., Pvt,
Bartlett, John C., Capt,
†Bartley, Claude, Pvt,
Bartley, Jady C., Pfc,
Bartolotta, Antonio W., Pvt,
Bartolotta, Anthony J., Pfc,
Barton, Jack G., Pvt,
Barton, Roy L., Pvt,
Bartow, Bernard B., S/Sgt,
Bartow, Kenneth W., Pvt,
Bartsch, Harvey A., Pvt,
Bartz, Herbert F., Pfc,
Barzda, Edmund J., Pvt,
†Basel, Harold, Pvt,
Basen, Albert P., Pvt,
Basila, Basil F., Lt Col,
Basina, Frederick, Sgt,
Baskes, Edwin C., Pfc,
Baskin, Maxwell, Pvt,
Bassett, Jack G., Sgt,
Bassett, Louis K., 1st Lt,
Bassette, Arnold W., Pfc,
Basso, Joseph, Pfc,
Bastasic, Daniel, Pfc,
Bastoe, Billy, Pvt,
Batchelor, Chester, Pfc,
*Batchelor, Elmer S., Pfc,
Batdorff, Emerson L., 1st Lt,
Bates, George E., Pfc,
Bates, Louis F., Jr., Pvt,
Bates, Sherrill B., T/5,
Bates, William C., 2nd Lt,
Batic, Albert J., Pvt,
Batstone, Norman V., Pfc,
†Battaglio, Louis, Pvt,
Batte, Bruce H., Sgt,
Batties, John T., Pfc,
†Battin, Harold A., Pfc,
Battison, William M., Pfc,
Battista, John, Pvt,
Batto, Dominic, S/Sgt,
Baugh, William F., T/5,
Baughman, James W., Cpl,
Baughn, Earl D., Pvt,
§Baum, Ernest, Pfc,
Bauman, Jack L., Cpl,
Baumann, Jack, Jr., Pfc,
Baumgart, John E., Pfc,
Baumgartner, Anthony R., Pfc,
Bauml, Anton, Pvt,
Baunach, Joseph R., Jr., Sgt,
†Baurs, Leo G., Pvt,
Baxter, Wiley C., T/Sgt,
Bayerkohler, Alvin E., Pfc,
Bayes, Leonard L., Pvt,
Baylard, Elden D., Jr., T/5,
†Bazillo, Leonard H., Pvt,
Bazzell, William D., S/Sgt,
Beach, William R., Pfc,
†Beahm, Harold W., Pfc,
Bean, Oel L., Sgt,
Beal, Life E., Pfc,
Bealer, John L., T/4,
Beam, James E., T/5,
Beard, Gordon C., Sgt,
Beard, Samuel I., Sgt,
†Bearden, James E., Sgt,
†Bearden, Robert T., Pfc,
Beardslee, Owen C., S/Sgt,
Bearse, Frederick, Pvt,
Beasley, Ellis H., T/5,
Beasley, Harry I., Pfc,
‡Beasley, James L., Pfc,
Beasley, Lee A., T/4,
Beasley, Thomas W., S/Sgt,
Beasley, William K., Pfc,
Beasley, Willie L., Pfc,
Beaton, Donald R., Pvt,
§Beatrice, Armond F., Pfc,
Beattie, Hugh F., Pvt,
Beatty, Earl H., Pfc,
Beatty, Harry E., Pvt,
Beaty, Albert J., T/5,
†Beaudoin, Edgar E., Pfc,
Beauvais, Alfred L., Pfc,
Beaver, Baldwin D., Pfc,
Beaver, Jreman C., Pvt,
†Beaver, Richard F., Pfc,
Beavers, James F., Pfc,
Beaverson, Donald H., Pfc,
Bebee, Robert M., Pfc,
Bebelheimer, Francis A., Cpl,
Beco, Ernest, Pfc,
Beck, Donald E., Pvt,
Beck, Glenn H., Pvt,
Beck, James M., 2nd Lt,
Beck, Ralph C., Pvt,
Becken, William H., Pvt,
Becker, Clarence H., Cpl,
Becker, Dean C., Pvt,
Becker, Harry P., Sgt,
Becker, Peter L., S/Sgt,
Becker, Oscar, Pvt,
Becker, Reginald W., Cpl,
Becker, Richard V., Pfc,
Becker, Stanley C., T/Sgt,
Becker, Walter E., Cpl,
Becker, William C., S/Sgt,
Beckerman, Martin, Pfc,
Beckman, James R., Pvt,
Beckstrand, Wendell E., T/4,
Beckwith, Eugene W., Pvt,
Beckwith, Junior M., Pvt,
Beckworth, Daniel S., Pvt,
Becze, John F., Pfc,
†Bedard, Norman W., Pfc,
Bednar, Joseph P., Pfc,
†Bednarczyk, Anthony S., Pvt,
Bednarski, John, Pvt,
Beebe, Roy, Pfc
Beede, Rolland R., Pfc,
§Beerbower, Chester J., Pvt,
Beeson, Allen C., Pvt,
Beeson, Laurance T., Pfc,
Beeson, William C., S/Sgt,
Begalke, Eldore E., Pvt,
†Begay, Alfred K., Pfc,
Beggs, Lloyd W., 1st Lt,
Behnk, Adolph F., Pfc,
Behr, Alexander T., 1st Lt,
Behrendt, John B., Pfc,
Behrens, Charles, Jr., Sgt,
Behrens, Walter C., T/5,
†Behrens, Walter E., Pvt,
†Behrens, Warren J., Pfc,
Behringer, Joseph D., Pfc,
Beigel, Ralph B., Pvt,
Beisser, William J., Pfc,
Belanger, Roger, T/4,
Belcher, Elton L., Cpl,
Belding, Alvin H., S/Sgt,
Belisle, Daniel E., Pvt,
‡Beljam, George E., Pvt,
Belkin, Samuel, Pvt,
Belknap, Ralph R., Pvt,
Bell, Charles F., Pfc,
Bell, Frederick F., Sgt,
Bell, Harold F., Pfc,
†Bell, Harvey H., Jr., T/Sgt,
Bell, James M., Jr., Pvt,
Bell, John A., Pfc,
Bell, Raymond B., Pfc,
Bell, Robert J., Sgt,
Bell, Wallace A., Jr., 1st Lt,
Bella, Nicholas S., Pfc,
†Bellace, Frank S., Sgt,
Bellanco, John J., Pvt,
Bellina, Joseph, Pfc,
Bellinger, William F., Pfc,
Bellish, John E., T/Sgt,
Bellon, Raymond A., Cpl,
Beltz, Philip B., Pvt,
‡Benavidez, Arturo, Pvt,
Benavidez, Ubaldo C., Pvt,
Bencenti, Ned, Pfc,
Bender, Delbert E., Pfc,
Bender, Albert R., Pvt,
Bender, Harold L., Sgt,
Bender, Robert E., Pvt,
Bendt, Clarence A., Cpl,
Bene, Andrew, S/Sgt,
Benedetto, Aldo R., Pvt,
†Beneman, Frederick M., Pfc,
Beneventi, Joseph, T/5,
Benevides, Louis W., Pfc,
Bengtson, Harold W., Jr., Pfc,
Benko, John F., 1st Lt,
Bennett, Austin P., Pfc,
Bennett, Bryan E., Pvt,
Bennett, Charles A., Sr., Sgt,
Bennett, Charles R., Pvt,
Bennett, Cecil G., T/Sgt,
Bennett, Clifford H., 2nd Lt,
Bennett, Curtis N., Jr., Pfc,
Bennett, Eugene, Pvt,
Bennett, George R., Pfc,
Bennett, Harold E., 1st Lt,
Bennett, Irwin L., Pvt,
Bennett, James B., Lt Col,
Bennett, James W., Jr., Pvt,
Bennett, Lawrence M., Pfc,
Bennett, Thomas A., Pvt
Bennett, Warren G., Pfc,
Bennett, William V., Pfc,
Benninger, Richard K., Pvt,
†Bennis, Charles W., Pvt,
Benny, William H., Pvt,
Bensley, Vernon L., S/Sgt,
†Benson, David L., Pfc,
Benson, Harold W., Sgt,
Benson, Henry C., Pvt,
Benson, John N., Pfc,
Benson, Leonard G., Sgt,
Bentley, Eugene W., S/Sgt
Benton, Donald E., Pvt,
Benzinger, Herbert H., Pvt,
Berardi, Raymond R., Pvt,
Berg, Bennett W., Cpl,
‡Berg, George E., Jr., Pvt,
‡Berg, John W., Pfc,
Berg, Robert F., Pvt,
Berga, Albert, Sgt,
Bergeson, Milfred J., T/5,
Berger, John P., Pfc,
Berger, Roger G., S/Sgt,
Berger, Russell C., T/4,
Berger, Thaddeus R., Cpl,
Bergh, Rolfe R., Pvt,
§Berkheimer, Jack J. C. E., Sgt,
Berkowitz, Irving, Pvt,
Bermal, Jose L., Jr., Pfc,
Berman, Albert, Pvt,
Bernard, Lyle W., Lt Col,
Bernard, Leonard B., Sgt,
Berinato, John J., Pvt,
*Bergholm, George M., S/Sgt,
Bergman, Hyman, Pfc,
Bernard, Felix U., Pvt,
Bernart, Gustave F., Pvt,
Bernasek, Charles, Jr., Pvt,
†Bernheim, Siegfried, Pvt,
Bernhardy, William H., Pvt
Bernick, Norman F., Cpl,
Bernier, Ansel H., Pfc,
Bernier, Ernest T., Pfc,
Bernstein, Bernard N., Pfc
Bernstein, Henry L., Pfc,
Bernstein, Herman, Pvt,
Bernstein, Hyman, Pfc,
†Bernstein, Louis, Pfc,
Berres, Russell T., T/5,
†Berrong, John R., Sgt,
Berry, Carroll C., Pvt,
Berry, Charles J., Pfc,
Berry, Colon O., Pfc,
Berry, Harvey L., Pfc,
Berry, John F., Pfc,
Berry, Lawrence A., Pfc,
Berson, Ira, Pfc,
Berson, Irving, Pvt,
Bertelsen, Norman A., Pvt,
Bertenshaw, Earl, Jr., Pfc,
Bertolozzi, Edward, Pfc,
Bertrand, Duane A., Pvt,
†Bertrand, Joseph, Jr., Pfc,
Bertrand, Kenneth A., Pvt,
Bertsch, Emil A., Pvt,
Berube, Armand J. C., Pvt,
Berube, Edward F., Pfc,
Beson, Dale B., Pfc,
Bess, Eugene G., T/Sgt,
Bester, Anthony V., T/5,
†Bevan, Wallace C., Pfc,
Bevins, Garrett R., Pfc,
Beyes, George H., Pvt,
Bezverchy, John J., Pvt,
Biagini, John, Pvt,
†Bianche, Thomas, Pvt,
Biancosino, Frank J., Sgt,
‡Bianelli, Anthony J., Pfc,
Biase, Anthony J., Pvt,
Bibb, Ellis B., III, Pfc,
†Biberdorf, Gerhard E., T/5,
Bibona, Frank T., Cpl,
Bickel, John, Sgt,
Bickelman, Robert H., Pvt,
Bickett, Francis G., Pfc,
Bickfor, Edwin G., Pvt,
Bickley, Thomas Z., Pfc,
Bickmore, Louis D., Pvt,
Bidgood, Gerald T., Pvt,
Bidlake, Rex W., Pvt,
Bieder, Leonard H., S/Sgt,
Bieganowski, Edwin A., Pfc,
Bielawne, Frank A., Pvt,
Bielich, Daniel, S/Sgt,
Bielmeier, Louis, Pfc,
Bien, John A., Pfc,
*Bierwagen, Joseph G., Pvt,
Bieschke, Norbert J., Pvt,
Biesmann, Marcus C., 1st Sgt,
Bifano, Eugene W., Pfc,
Bigelow, Merrick H., Pvt,
Bigge, James E., Sgt
Bigger, Henry L., Pfc,
‡Bilasz, Stephen, S/Sgt,
Bilby, Kenneth W., Maj,
Bilda, Gerald J., Pfc,
Bileau, Emile M., Pvt,
Bilek, John F., Pfc,
Bill, Robert F., Pvt,
Billerbeck, Verele A., S/Sgt,
Billings, Arthur D., T/5,
†Billings, Paul C., S/Sgt,
Billingsley, Charles E., Pvt,
†Bills, Darrell M., Pvt,
Bilpuch, Paul, Pfc,
Bingham, Romaness, Pvt,
Bingham, William T., 1st Sgt,
Binienda, Joseph, Jr., Pvt,
Binney, Charles A., Pfc,
Binning, William A., Pvt,
Binns, Herschel E., Pfc,
†Birchmier, Robert L., Pfc,
Birdsong, George W., Sgt,
Birkett, Lindley L., Pfc,
† Birnbaum, Abr. W., 2nd Lt,
Bisanti, Paul G., Pvt,
Bischoff, John A., Jr., Pvt,
†Bish, William H., Pvt,
Bishop, Harold C., 1st Lt,
Bishop, Allen C., Cpl,
Bishop, Irvin C., Pfc,
†Bishop, Marvin L., Pvt,
Bisignano, Carl J., Pvt
§Bishop, Lawrence M., Pvt,
Biss, Richard L., T/5,
Bissonette, Ernest E., Pfc,
Bissonette, Ledonia J., Pfc,
*Bittner, Clark B., Cpl,
Bivens, Walter A., Pfc,
Bixby, Lewis F., 1st Lt,
Bizek, Bernard R., Cpl,
Bizzell, David, Pvt,
Bjerke, Rolf N., Cpl,
Bjork, Mike J., S/Sgt,
Bjork, Stanley L., Pvt,
Bjorkman, John D., Pfc,
Black, Donald G., Pvt,
Black, Ed, T/5,
Black, Glenn A., 2nd Lt,
Black, Leslie H., Pfc,
Black, Richard G., Pfc,
*Black, Thurman I., Pvt,
Blackburn, Edward R., Pvt,
Blackburn, Lawrence T., T/4,
§Blackenhorn, C. W., Jr., Pvt,
Blacketer, Charlie S., Pvt,
Blackledge, Thomas H., Sgt,
Blackmon, Charles E., Jr., T/5,
Blackmon, Orbis C., Pvt,
Blackwell, Harold A., Jr.,
Blackwell, James R., Pfc,
Blackwell, Tullie E., Pvt,
Blackwell, William A., Jr., Pvt

† Killed in Action. * Prisoner of War. ‡ Missing in Action. § Died of Wounds.

IN WORLD WAR II 511

Bladow, Roy H., T/5,
Blaha, Henry J., Pvt
Blain, Walter A., 1st Lt,
Blais, Edward E., Cpl,
Blaisdell, Albert L., Pfc,
Blake, Albert J., Jr., Sgt,
Blake, Frank A., Jr., 1st Lt,
Blake, Gerald F., Pfc,
Blakely, Thomas J., Pvt,
Blaker, John W., 1st Lt,
*Blalock, Bennie, Pfc,
Blalock, Jack, Pfc,
Blanchard, Albert J., Pvt,
†Blanchet, Joseph J., Pfc,
Blanchette, Elmer J., Pfc,
Blankenbecler, George D., Pvt,
Blankenship, Floyd O., Sgt
Blanton, Ernest S., Pfc,
‡Blaser, George S., Pfc,
Blass, Adelbert, S/Sgt,
Blaszak, Mathew J., Pvt,
Blechschmidt, Otto C., Sgt,
Bleicker, Frederick E., Pfc,
Bledsoe, Robert J., Pfc,
Bledsoe, Warren E., T/Sgt,
Bleimiester, Frank A., Pfc,
Bleitzhofer, Leo G., S/Sgt,
Blesinger, Raymond J., 1st Lt,
†Bloch, Stewart, 2nd Lt
Block, David, Pvt,
†Block, Robert O., S/Sgt,
Blocker, Donald C. C., Pvt,
†Blodgett, Everett J., Pfc,
Blohm, Gordon H., Pfc,
Blomberg, John L., Pfc,
†Bloms, Fred W., Pfc,
Bloodworth, Wilbur B., Pvt,
Bloom, James D., Pfc,
Bloom, Parvin O., Pvt,
Bloor, Will F., S/Sgt,
Blosser, Edward C., Pvt,
Blossom, Chales C., Jr., 1st
Blue, Gilbert W., Pfc,
Blum, Benjamin, Pvt,
Blumanthal, Rienald H., Pvt,
Blumenthal, William, Pvt,
Blumer, Edgar M., Pvt,
†Blumst, Roland A., Pfc,
Blyshak, John, Pfc,
Blythman, James W., Pvt,
Boatman, Virgil L., Pfc,
Boatwright, Paul F., Pfc,
Boaze, John H., Pvt,
Bobak, Anton, T/4,
Bobar, Chester B., Pvt,
Bobbitt, Frederick, Pvt,
Bobin, Stanley J., Pvt,
Bocchicio, Joseph J., Pfc,
Bockman, Norbert B., T/4,
Boddy, Robert M., Capt,
Bode, Frank J., Pvt,
†Bodnar, Edward L., Pvt,
‡Bodnar, George, Pfc,
Bodnar, Michael J., Pfc,
†Bodner, Ernest L., Pvt,
Bodo, Frank J., Pvt,
Bodziuch, Edward J., S/Sgt,
Boeder, Alexander H., Jr., Sgt,
Boehm, George R., Pfc,
Boehmke, Edward W., Pfc
Boehner, Lawrence W., Pvt,
Boehnlein, George W., Sgt,
Boerstler, Montie H., 2nd Lt,
†Boettcher, Roy M., Pfc,
Boffanie, Clebert B., Sgt,
Bogachov, William T., S/Sgt,
Bogard, Richard H., Pvt,
Bogner, Donald W., Pfc,
Bogue, Wayne L., Pfc,
Bogusz, John M., Sgt,
Bohall, Lee H., Pfc,
Bohannan, Lawson, Cpl,
Bohannan, Virgil, Pfc,
Bohannon, Raymond, S/Sgt,
†Bohanon, Charles E., Pfc,
†Bohaty, Charles D., Pfc,
Bohler, Robert E., Pfc,
Bohlman, Victor R., Pfc,
Bohme, Bert G., Pvt
Bohmer, Howard E., Pfc,
Bohn, Leslie A., Pfc,
Bohnenberger, Francis J., Pfc,
Bohner, Dale A., T/5,
Bohon, Galan E., Pvt,
Bohot, Herbert A., Cpl,
Bohrer, David, Pvt,
Boils, Ernest E., Sgt,
Boisvert, John A., Pvt,
Boland, Stanley R., Pfc,
Bolda, John E., Sgt,
Boles, Sanford R., T/Sgt,
Boles, Savage, Pfc,
Boleyn, Robert F., Pfc
Boling, Louis E., S/Sgt,
Boller, Ewald T., Pvt,
Boller, Kenneth O., S/Sgt,
Bollinger, Francis L., Jr., Pfc,
Bolte, Ervin E., T/4,
Bolte, Lawrence J., Pfc,
Bolte, Willis H. Pfc,
Bolton, Joseph J., Pvt,
Bonazelli, Harry O., Pvt,
Bond, Mager K., Pvt,
Bond, Paul I., Pvt,
Bone, Grady C., Pfc,
Bone, Joseph O., Pvt,
Bonham, Raymond L., Pfc,
Bonito, Gerald G., Pfc,
*Bonito, Salvatore P., Pfc,
Bonneau, Fred, Pvt,
Bonneau, Wilson A., Pfc,
Bonner, David T., Sgt,
Bonner, Francis G., Capt,
Bonner, Howard, S/Sgt,
Bonner, James R., Sgt,
Bonner, William A., Capt,
Bonnes, John, Jr., Pfc,
Bonny, William H., Pvt,
Bonyai, John J., Pfc
Boodry, Ralph E., S/Sgt,
Book, Elmer W., Pfc,
Booker, A. G., Pfc,
‡Booker, Ellis M., Pvt,
Booker, James M., Capt
Boone, Antoine, Sgt,
Boose, Edward D., S/Sgt,
Booth, Carl W., Sgt,
Booth, Frank S., Cpl,
Booth, Fred S., Jr, 2nd Lt,
Booth, George Q., T/Sgt,
Booth, Kay C., Pfc,
Booth, Warren L., Pvt,
Borcheller, Karl H., Pvt,
Borda, William P., Cpl,
Bordelon, Luther J., Sgt,
Borden, Keith D., Pfc,
Borders, Joe B., Sgt,
Borek, Joseph J., Pvt
†Borelli, Joe A., Pfc,
Borello, Thomas F., Pvt,
Borgen, Otto O., Pvt,
Borges, Jack, Pvt,
†Borgese, Joseph, Pvt,
Borgese, Joseph P., Pvt,
Borglin, Richard A., Pfc,
Borgomainerio, Carl F., Pfc,
Borick, John S., Pfc,
Borkowicz, Richard A., Pfc,
*Boroff, Alfred, Pvt,
Boros, Steve P., Jr., T/Sgt,
Borowski, Chester F., Sgt,
Borries, Oscar J., T/5,
‡Borsos, Mike, Jr., Pvt
Borzino, Bernardino, Pfc,
Bosch, Russell P., Pvt,
Bosch, Samuel, Pfc
†Bosel, Fred, Pfc,
Bosler, William D., Pvt
Bosniak, Sidney, T/5,
Boss, Louis W., Pfc,
Bossena, Nelson J., Pvt,
Bostelman, George R., Pvt,
Boston, Willie E., T/4,
‡Bostron, Reinholdt, Pfc,
Botch, Frank, S/Sgt,
Botka, Peter, Pfc,
Botkin, Samson, Pfc,
‡Bott, Lawrence J., Pvt,
Bott, Raymond W., Pfc,
Botti, Mario, Pvt,
Bottolfson, Kenneth G., Pfc,
Bottomley, Leonard, Pvt,
Botzong, Johnny, Pfc,
Bouchette, Murphy L., Pvt,
Boudendistle, Arthur J., Pvt,
Bouder, Charles T., Pvt,
Boudreaux, Claude J., Pvt,
Boudreaux, Clifton J., Pfc,
†Boudreaux, Harry T., T/5,
Boulay, Raymond A., Pfc,
§Bourgoyne, Telesphore J., Pvt,
†Bourn, Richard W., Pvt,
Bouy, Daniel J., Cpl,
Bove, Charles M., Pvt,
†Bove, Thomas E., Pvt,
Bovee, Lester M., Pvt,
Bovio, Clement J., Pvt
‡Bowcutt, Blaine, S/Sgt,
Bowden, Benjamin C., Pfc,
Bowen, Arvo P., Pvt,
Bowen, Charles L., Pfc,
Bowen, Colie, Pfc,
†Bowen, Keith H., Pfc,
Bowen, Robert O., Pfc,
*Bower, Charles E., Pfc,
Bower, Ralph D., Pvt,
Bower, William P., Pvt,
Bowers, Alonzo Q., Pvt,
Bowers, Fay D., Pvt,
Bowers, Fulton B., Pvt,
Bowers, Harold T., Pvt,
Bowers, Robert H., Pvt,
†Bowers, William R., Pfc,
Bowes, Frederick A., Pfc,
‡Bowker, James L., Pfc,
†Bowles, Robert E., Pfc,
Bowling, Lincoln, Pfc,
Bowling, Luther M., Pvt,
Bowman, Basil A., Pvt,
†Bowman, Ray A., Pfc,
Bowman, Robert M., Cpl,
Bowman, William F., Pfc,
Bown, James D., Cpl,
*Bown, John C., Pfc,
†Bown, Martin V., Pvt,
Boyajian, Aram S., Pvt,
Boyce, Edward L., Pvt,
†Boycik, Joseph C., T/5,
Boyd, Alfred O., Pvt,
Boyd, Denver, Pvt,
Boyd, George E., Jr., T/Sgt,
Boyd, James H., Pvt,
Boyer, Billy E., Pvt,
Boyer, James F., Pvt,
†Boyer, Thomas W., Pfc,
†Boyle, Francis P., Pvt,
†Boyle, James F., 2nd Lt,
Boyle, Joseph J., Sgt,
Boyle, Robert R., Pfc,
Boylen, James E., Pfc,
Boylen, James E., Pvt,
Boynton, Roy J., Jr., Cpl,
Box, Johnnie W., Cpl,
Bozek, Walter J., Pfc,
Bozeman, Chas. E., Jr., S/Sgt,
†Bracey, Randolph, 1st Lt,
†Braden, Verne E., Pvt,
Bradford, Charlie P., Pvt,
Bradford, Earl C., Pvt
Bradford, Edgar O., Pvt,
Bradley, Angus, Pvt,
Bradely, Edward F., T/5,
‡Bradely, Wilfred H., Pvt,
Brabson, Robert L., T/5,
Bradshaw, James C., Pvt,
Brady, John P., Pfc,
Brady, Robert J., Pfc,
Bragen, John, Pvt,
Braid, William D., 2nd Lt,
†Braithwaite, George L., Jr., Pvt
Braman, Howard A., Cpl,
Brame, Robert G., S/Sgt,
Brammer, Paul B., Pfc,
Brancale, Armand, Sgt,
Branch, Hoye M., Cpl,
†Branch, Robert L., 2nd Lt,
†Branciaroli, Albert C., 2nd Lt,
†Brand, Frank F., Pvt,
Branda, Patsy J., Pfc,
Brandeis, Robert, Pvt,
Brandenburg, Albert F., Pvt,
Brandt, Earl J., Pfc,
†Brandt, Edward C., Sgt,
Brandt, Gustave F., Pfc,
Brandt, Walter T., Pvt,
Brannock, Milton, T/5,
Brannum, James V., Pfc,
Branscombe, Merlin A.,
Branscum, Lawson, Sgt,
†Branson, Francis M., Pfc,
Branson, James L., Pfc,
Branson, William A., 1st Lt
Branson, William E., Pvt,
Brant, Cletius R., Sgt,
Brant, James R., Sgt,
Brasher, James D., Pfc,
Brass, Robert E., Pvt,
Brassaw, Oscar J., Pfc,
Braswell, James W., Pfc,
Bratzke, Milton F., T/4,
Brauch, Joseph E., T/Sgt,
Braudrick, Thomas J., T/Sgt,
Braun, George J., Pvt,
Bray, George R., Jr., Pfc,
Bray, Joseph S., Cpl
‡Bray, Joseph S., Cpl,
Bray, Wesley C., Pfc,
†Brazelton, Jack M., 1st Lt,
Brazer, Walter J., Pfc,
Brazil, Garson R., Pfc,
‡Brazowski, Joseph, Pfc,
Bread, Hubert S., Pvt,
Brecher, Nicolas, Pfc,
Breidal, Clifford H., Pfc,
Breier, Ben J., Pfc,
Breisinger, Paul H., Jr., Pfc,
Breitling, Clarence A., S/Sgt,
Breneman, Henry G., Jr., Pvt,
†Brenia, Walter J., Sgt,
Brennan, Bernard A., Pfc,
†Brennan, John J., Jr., Pvt,
Brennan, John W., Pvt,
Brennen, Wilfred E., S/Sgt
Breon, Junior L., Pfc,
Brese, Robert B., Pfc,
Bresinski, Louis J., Pvt,
Breske, James J., Pfc,
†Breth, Harold D., Pfc,
Brethauer, Gustave J., Pfc,
Bretschneider, Reuben P., Pfc,
Bretthorst, George P., Cpl,
†Brettin, Charles E., S/Sgt,
Brewer, Andrew J., Pvt,
Brewer, Carl E., Pfc,
Brewer, Clena A., Pfc,
†Brewer, Earlon A., Sgt,
Brewer, Edward J., Pfc,
Brewer, Ellis M., T/Sgt,
Brewer, Grover G., Pvt,
†Brewer, Henry C., T/Sgt,
Brewer, Lester J., Pfc,
Brewer, Robert S., T/5,
Brewer, Robert T., Pfc,
Brewer, Walton E., S/Sgt,
§Brewster, Harry O., Pvt,
Brewster, Philip R., Pvt,
†Breyfogle, Peter H., Pfc,
Bria, Albert S., Pvt,
Briasco, John D., Pvt,
Brickman, Lewis E., Sgt,
Brickner, Richard V., Pfc,
Bridge, William T., Pfc,
Bridges, Charlie L., Pfc,
Bridges, Claude W., Pfc,
Bridges, Joseph K., Jr., Pfc,
Bridges, Robert L., Pvt,
†Bridgman, George H., Pfc,
Briese, Clayton F., Pvt,
Briganti, Anthony V., S/Sgt,
Brigecs, Felton, S/Sgt,
Briggs, Chester W., Pvt,
Briggs, Orland M., Pfc,
Briggs, William R., S/Sgt,
Brigman, Clinton P., Pvt,
Brigman, John B., Pfc,
Brindza, John C., Pfc,
Brinker, Eugene P., Pfc,
Bristol, Frank L., T/Sgt,
*Brill, Irving, Pvt,
Brin, Martin, Pvt,
Britt, John W., Pvt,
Britt, Maurice L., Capt,
Brittingham, Walter M., Pvt,
†Britton, John R., Jr., Pvt,
Britton, Troy, Sgt,
Britton, Walter W., Pfc,
Brletic, Frank J., Pvt,
Broadhurst, Harris, Pvt,
Broadwater, Marvin M., Pfc,
Broadway, Carl C., Pvt,
Broadway, Harry T., Pfc,
Broadway, McDonald, T/Sgt,
Brockman, William F., Jr., Pfc
Broderick, John J., Pfc,
Brogan, Robert G., Pfc,
‡Broge, Frank W., Cpl,
†Brohlin, Edsel K., Pfc,
Broide, Macy I., Cpl,
Bronson, William T., Pvt,
Brooks, David A., Pvt,
†Brooks, George A., Pvt,
Brooks, Gerald E., Pvt,
Brooks, Mosby H. J., Pfc,
Brooks, Robert J., Pvt,
Brooks, Walter A., S/Sgt,
†Brooks, Weslie, Pvt,
Brooks, William H., Pvt,
Brooks, W. J., Pvt,
Brophy, James F., Pvt,
Broskey, Robert H., Sgt,
‡Brosnan, Daniel B., Pfc,
Brost, Leland F., Pfc,
Brothers, Roy C., Cpl,
Broughton, Connie N., S/Sgt,
Brouillette, James E., Sgt,
Broussard, Julian J., Sgt,
Brousseau, Maurice L. R., Pfc,
Browdy, Charles M., Pvt,
Brower, Esker C., Pfc,
Brown, Albert S., S/Sgt,
Brown, Carl J., Pvt,
Brown, Charles B., Capt,
Brown, Charles R., Pfc,
Brown, Clarence, Pfc,
†Brown, Clarence K., Pvt,
Brown, Clyde, Pvt,
*Brown, David H., Pfc,
Brown, Delbert W., Pfc,
Brown, Dutch, Pvt,
Brown, Earl A., Pfc,
Brown, Edwin C., T/4,
Brown, Elson, Pfc,
Brown, George P., Pvt,
‡Brown, Glen, Pfc,
Brown, Homer D., S/Sgt,
Brown, Horace W., Pfc,
Brown, Howard R., Pfc,
Brown, John C., Pvt,
Brown, John W., Pfc,
Brown, Lawrence E., Pfc,
Brown, Marvin N., Pfc,
Brown, Oscar E., Pvt,
Brown, Paul J., Pvt,
Brown, Ralph J., Pvt,
Brown, Roger L., Pvt,
Brown, Robert E., Pfc,
Brown, Robert C., Pvt,
Brown, Robert H., 2nd Lt,
Brown, Rufe, T/5,
Brown, Russell E., Cpl
Brown, Russell J., Sgt,
Brown, Samuel, T/4,
Brown, Virgil W., Pvt,
Brown, Wayne T., Pvt,
Brown, William A., Sgt,
Brown, William B., Pfc,
Brown, W. T., Pfc,
Brownchweig, Mack, Pfc,
Browne, Hughes B., S/Sgt,
Brownfield, Robert C., Pfc,
Browning, John H., T/5,
‡Browning, Robert H., Pvt,
Brownlee, Charles W., Jr., Pvt,
Brownlee, Wilburn, Pvt,
Brozek, William E., Pvt,
Brozowski, John J., Pfc,
Bruce, George M., 1st Sgt,
Bruce, John H., S/Sgt,
Bruce, Robert L., S/Sgt,
Bruch, Harvey W., Pfc,
Brumas, Gus J., Sgt,
§Brumfield, Ray W., Pvt,
Bruneau, Henry S., Sgt,
Brunelle, Arthur E., S/Sgt,
Bruner, Harold H., Pfc,
Brunette, Paul O., Pfc,
Brunetto, Rosario, Pfc,
Bruning, Lawrence E., Pfc,
Brunner, John J., Jr.,Pvt,
Brunner, William D., Pvt,
Bruno, Andrew L., Pvt,
Bruno, Daniel N., Pfc,
Bruno, Victor A., Pvt,
Brusco, Joseph D., Pfc,
Brush, James E., Jr., Sgt
†Brusich, Anthony J., Sgt,
‡Brusin, Gunnar, S/Sgt,
Bryak, Frank J., Pvt,
Bryan, Ben F., Pfc,
Bryant, Calvin W., Sgt,
Bryant, David K., S/Sgt,
Bryant, Ethel L., Pfc,
†Bryant, Hugh E., Pfc,
Bryant, Jack R., Pfc,
Bryant, James M., Pfc,
Bryant, Joe L., Sgt,
†Bryant, John J., S/Sgt,
Bryant, Pearly, 1st Sgt,
Bryant, Walter C., Cpl,
Bryce, Hugh J., Jr., Pvt,
Bryce, Robert A., Pfc,
†Bryden, Adam E., Pvt,
Brylinski, Casimir V., Pvt,
Brzezicki, Joseph J., Pfc,
Bucchio, Frank, Pfc,
Buchinsky, Stanley, Pfc,
Buccini, Oresto, Pvt,
†Buch, Ernest T., S/Sgt,
Buchen, John C., Pfc,
Buchanan, Gerald C., 1st Lt,
Buchanan, Ted R., Pvt,
Bucher, L. D., Pfc,
Buchheit, Floret P., Cpl,
Buckhout, Edward E., Sgt,
‡Buck, Harry W., S/Sgt,
Buck, Marion W., Cpl,
Buczakowski, Peter L., Pvt,
Buczkowski, Xavier W., Pfc,
Budahl, Norman R., Pfc,
Budetti, Genaro, Pfc,
Budser, LeRoy J., Pvt,
Buenzow, Kenneth F., Pfc,
†Buehrer, Cleo F., Sgt,
Buffington, Alfred P., Cpl,
Buginnis, Stanley F., T/Sgt,
Buhl, James G., S/Sgt,
Bukovack, Joseph P., Pfc,
Bulczynski, Stanley J., T/Sgt,
†Buler, Edwin K., Pfc,
Bullard, Oscar H., Pfc,
Bullert, Louis P., Pvt,
Bullins, Kelly D., Sgt,
Bulovcsak, Michael G., Jr., Pvt,
Bump, Ralph O., Pvt
Bunce, Albert E. L., 2nd Lt,
Bunch, Perry V., Pvt,
Buncic, John F., Pfc,
Bundy, Burrell C., Pfc,
‡Bundy, Hulin S., Sgt,
Bundy, William T., Pfc,

† Killed in Action. * Prisoner of War. ‡ Missing in Action. § Died of Wounds.

Bunker, Rufus P., Jr., Pfc,
Bunn, Quentin S., Pfc,
Bunnell, Dwight L., Pfc,
Bunner, Charles M., S/Sgt,
†Bunton, Neal E., Cpl,
Buongiorno, Pietro J, Pvt,
Burazer, Nickolas J., Pfc,
†Burbacher, Charles, Cpl,
Burch, Charles J., Pfc,
Burch, Mitchell, Pvt,
Burchard, Darrel L., S/Sgt,
Burchfield, Billy O., Pvt,
‡Burckhardt, John D., Pvt,
Burdick, George J., Pfc,
Burge, Carry B., T/4,
Burge, Purley P., Cpl,
†Burger, Fred A., Pvt,
Burger, Helmuth C., T/4,
Burger, William J., Pfc,
Burgess, Ira T., Pfc,
Burgess, John D., T/Sgt,
Burgess, Robert W., Pfc,
Burgess, Walter L., Jr., Pfc,
Burgett, Don M., T/5,
Burghardt, Fred C., Pvt,
Burke, Albert, Pvt,
Burke, Charles A., Pvt,
Burke, James H., Pfc,
Burke, John F., Pvt,
Burke, Kenneth E., Pvt,
Burke, Stanley C., Pfc,
Burkhalter, Edward J., Pvt,
Burkhalter, James W., Pvt,
Burkhammer, Ottie A., Pvt,
Burkhardt, Ernest, Pfc,
Burkhart, James F., T/5,
Burkhart, Vernon R., Pfc,
Burkle, Howard J., Pvt,
†Burleigh, Richard C., Jr., Pfc,
Burleson, James A., Pfc,
Burling, Benjamin, Pvt,
Burnasky, Peter, T/Sgt,
Burnett, Glenn E., Pfc,
Burnett, Walter E., Cpl,
Burnette, George S., Pfc,
Burnham, Ellsworth A., Pvt,
†Burns, David W., Pfc,
§Burns, Herman A., Pvt,
Burns, Marlowe J., Cpl,
*Burns, Stanley W., Pfc,
Burns, Virgil E., Pvt,
Burns, Wilber M., Pfc,
Burnside, William D., S/Sgt,
Burrell, William O., Cpl
Burris, Thomas H., Pfc
Burris, Walter A., Pvt,
Burroughs, George C., Pvt,
Burrus, Oscar T., Jr., Pvt,
Burt, Ernest D., 1st Sgt,
Burt, William T., Pvt,
Burton, John P., Pfc,
Burton, Melvin C., S/Sgt,
Burwell, Francis A., Pfc,
Busby, Henry J., Pfc,
Busch, Richard J., Pvt,
Bush, Earl B., 1st Lt,
Bush, Roy J., Pfc,
Bushaw, Charles S., Pfc,
Bushey, Rudolph W., Pfc,
Bushnell, Asa E., Jr., Pfc,
Busk, Grant C., Pfc,
Buskirk, Arthur, Pfc,
Buss, Fred, S/Sgt,
Busse, Herman A., T/Sgt,
Busto, Victor J., Pfc,
Butch, Joseph F., Pvt,
Butcher, Matthew V., Sgt
Butelewski, George, Pvt
Butensky, Walter J., Pfc,
Butera, Charles J., Pvt,
Butera, Samuel F., Pfc,
‡Buthmann, John, Sgt,
Butkus, Walter J., S/Sgt,
Butler, Carl W., Cpl,
Butler, Clyde H., Jr., Pvt,
Butler, Coy, Pfc,
Butler, Dennis H., Pfc,
Butler, Donald A., 1st Lt,
Butler, George K., Capt,
Butler, Harold, T/4,
Butler, Harry W., Pvt,
Butler, James E., Pfc,
*Butler, Marvin, Pvt,
Butler, Milton D., Pvt
Butler, Oscar O., Pfc,
Butler, Raymond E., Cpl,
†Butler, Raymond E., Pfc
Butler, Wallace M., T/Sgt,
†Butor, Adolph, S/Sgt,
†Butrim, George, S/Sgt,
Butt, William M., Pvt,
Butterfield, Lowell R., Pvt,
Butterstein, Arthur F., 2nd Lt,
†Butterworth, Arthur L., Pfc,

Butterworth, Paul R., Pfc,
‡Buttler, Bernard H., Sgt,
Button, William B., 1st Lt,
Butts, Chester E., Pfc,
Butts, Kenneth L., S/Sgt,
†Butts, Russell F., Pfc,
Butz, Frederick W., Pfc,
Butzin, Kenneth E., Pvt,
Buvilo, Joseph C., Pvt,
Buyarski, Walter, Cpl,
Buydaert, Jerome E., Pfc,
Buzzard, Norman L., Pfc,
Byerly, Silas W., Pvt,
‡Byers, John J., Pvt,
Byke, Emil T., 2nd Lt,
Byrd, James E., Pvt,
Byrd, Marvin L., Sgt,
Byrd, Morris L., Pvt,
Byrd, Richard E., Pfc,
Byrd, Rupert H., Pvt,
Byrket, James S., Pvt,

Cabana, Raymond F., S/Sgt,
Cabeen, Joseph E., Pfc,
Cabibi, Dave, Pfc,
†Cable, Ruddell F., Pfc,
Cabral, Francisco, Pvt,
Cacaj, Thaddeus, Pfc,
Caccavale, Philip J., Sgt,
Cade, Robert, T/4,
Cadeau, Raymond A., Pfc,
Caden, Paul J., Pvt,
Cadena, Jose G., T/5,
‡Cadle, William D., Pfc,
†Cadogan, Joseph J., Pvt,
Cadwallader, Arthur N., Pvt,
Cafarelli, Richard J., Pvt,
Cafaro, Joseph A., Pvt,
Cagle, James C., Pvt,
§Cagle, Otis S., Pfc,
Cahill, Arthur M., T/5,
Cahill, Phillip E., T/Sgt
Cahill, Shermann E., T/5,
†Cahill, Thomas A., Jr., Pvt,
Cain, Jessie R., Pvt,
Cain, Lillion W., Capt,
†Caine, Lloyd C., S/Sgt,
Calabrese, Gerard R., Pvt,
§Calahan, Ora T., Pfc,
*Calcagno, John B., Pvt,
†Caldarelli, Frederick, Pvt,
Canan, Richard, Pfc,
Canant, Elmer O., Cpl,
Canastar, Anthony J., Pvt,
Candeleria, Solomon M., Pvt,
‡Canestrale, Pete L., Pvt,
Canfield, Yale M., Pfc,
Cannon, Orvil E., T/4,
Cannon, Ray, Pvt,
Cannon, William H., Pvt,
Cansino, Vernon, Pvt,
Canterbury, Claude, Pfc,
Canterell, Wilson M., Pfc,
*Cantofanti, Angelo, Pvt,
Caparatta, Salvatore F., Pvt,
†Cape, Vernor, Pvt,
†Capenter, Earl G., Pfc,
Caperusso, Rocco A., Pvt,
Capik, Michael, Pvt,
Caplan, Edward, Pvt,
*Caplinger, Harold E., Pfc,
Cappelletto, Antonio, Pvt,
†Caprini, Severino A., Pfc,
Caprio, Raphael, Pvt,
Captain, Louis T., Pfc,
Capuano, Rosario, Pvt,
Capuozzo, Anthony L., Pfc,
Caraberia, Peter G., Pvt,
Caracappa, Mathew A., Sgt,
Caravella, Manuel R., Pfc,
Carbone, Joseph M., Pfc,
Calderon, Isabel, Pvt,
Caldwell, Charles E., Pfc,
Caldwell, Melvin P., Cpl,
Caldwell, Wagner W., Pvt,
†Caley, Robert W., 1st Lt,
‡Calhoun, Arthur P., Pvt,
Caligan, Edward H., Pfc,
†Call, David B., Pfc,
Callahan, David V., Pvt,
Callahan, Eugene E., Pvt,
Callahan, Frank H., Pfc,
Callahan, Harry B., 1st Sgt,
Callahan, John J., Pvt,
Callahan, Marion R., Pfc,
Callens, Albert J., Pvt,
Calloway, Cecil G., Pfc,
Calloway, Stokes, Pfc,
Calsoni, Arthur, Pvt,
Calvert, Emmertore M., Pfc,
‡Calvert, Ross H., Jr., 1st Lt,
Calzetta, John J., Sgt,
‡Camaione, Pete J., Pfc,
Camara, August, Pvt,

Camba, Gumersindo, Pfc,
†Camboni, Armando F., Pvt,
Cambra, Edmund M., Pvt,
Camden, Roy T., Cpl,
Cameron, Clarence A., Sgt,
Cameron, Louis C., T/4,
Camp, Clifford Z., Cpl,
Camp, James T., Pfc,
Camp, Robert L., Pfc,
Camp, Vernon H., Pvt,
Campagna, Joseph M., S/Sgt
Campagnone, Alfred, Pfc,
Campano, Joseph J., Pvt,
Campbell, Albert H., Pvt,
Campbell, Charles H., Pvt,
*Campbell, Frank J., Pvt,
Campbell, Harry V., Pfc,
Campbell, Herbert L., Pvt,
Campbell, John D., Cpl,
Campbell, John H., Pvt,
Campbell, Leonard T., Pvt,
‡Campbell, Lloyd E., Pfc
Campbell, Paul R., T/5,
†Campbell, Robert R., Pvt,
Campbell, Sidney, Pfc,
Campbell, Walter E., Pvt,
Campbell, William D., Sgt,
†Campbell, William E., S/Sgt,
Campbell, William T., Pvt
Campbell, Woodrow P., S/Sgt,
Campell, Charles O., Pfc,
Camren, Clarence C., Pvt,
Camsky, Victor H., T/5,
Camuto, Joseph J., Pvt,
Canady, George M., S/Sgt,
Canady, Joseph C., Pfc,
†Cardea, Tony, Pvt,
Cardello, Joseph L., S/Sgt,
Carden, Carl K., Pvt,
Cardile, John, Pvt,
Carella, Peter T., Pfc,
Carellas, James C., Pfc,
Carey, Richard N., Pvt,
Carey, Robert R., Pvt,
Carfagno, Joseph, Pfc,
Carione, Vito W., Pvt,
Carl, Raymond J., Pfc,
Carlbert, Carl E., Pfc,
Carletti, Gabriel S., Pvt,
Carlin, Francis F., Pfc,
Carlock, William O., Pvt,
Carlson, Alton E., T/5,
Carlson, Carl E., Pfc,
Carlson, Carl G., Pvt,
†Carlson, Charles H., Pfc,
Carlson, Edwin, Sgt,
Carlson, Harold E., Pvt,
Carlson, Ralph E., Pfc,
Carlson, Theodore W., Pvt,
Carman, Jesse L., Pfc,
§Carmichael, Wilbur N., Pfc,
Carmody, Donald P., Pfc,
Carnevale, Thomas J., Pfc,
†Carnevali, Mariano P., Pfc,
Carney, Eugene G., Pvt,
Carnicky, Andrew B., Pfc,
§Caro, William B., Pfc,
Carollo, Leonard, Pfc
Carollo, Tony, Pvt,
Caron, Eugene J., Pvt,
Caron, Roland, 2nd Lt,
Carosella, Arthur A., Pvt,
*Carpenter, Blaine D., Pfc,
Carpenter, C. E., Pvt,
Carpenter, Clarence, C., Pfc,
Carpenter, Donald L., Pvt
‡Carpenter, Earl G., Pfc,
Carpenter, George L., Pvt,
Carpenter, Homer R., Jr., Pvt,
Carpenter, Joe B., Pvt,
†Carpenter, Kenneth L., Pfc,
Carpenter, Leonard E., Pfc,
§Carpenter, Ralph R., Capt,
Carpenter, Wilbur J., Pvt,
Carpentieri, John J., Pvt,
Carr, Edward W., Pvt,
Carr, George M., Sgt,
Carr, Homer, Pvt,
Carr, James A. J., Pvt,
Carr, John W., Sgt,
Carr, William T., Sgt,
†Carragher, Matt, Pvt,
Carraturo, Lorin J., Pfc,
Carrier, Robert, Pfc,
Carriera, Manuel, Pvt,
Carriere, Mark T., Pfc,
Carrillo, Frank C., Pfc,
Carrin, Thomas R., Sgt,
Carroll, Bill W., Cpl
Carroll, Dexter F., Pfc,
Carroll, Eugene P., T/5,
Carroll, James W., Pvt,
Carroll, Jesse L., Pvt,
Carroll, Robert E., Jr., 1st Lt,

Carroll, Roger L., Pvt,
†Carroll, William J., Jr., Pfc,
†Carroll, William W., Sgt,
Carson, Bernard L., Pvt,
Carson, William E., Sgt,
†Carter, Donald S., 2nd Lt,
†Carter, Jake P., S/Sgt,
Carter, John F., Cpl,
Carter, O'brien, Pvt,
Carter, Richard, Pvt,
Carter, Van D., Pvt,
†Carter, Vorel V., Jr., Pvt,
†Carter, Willard L., Pfc,
Carter, William B., Pvt,
Carter, William H., Pfc,
Carter, William M., Pvt,
Cartmill, Thurman E., Sgt,
Cartwright, Aubrey R., Sgt,
Cartwright, George C., Pfc,
Carty, William J., Pfc,
Caruso, Frank P., Sgt,
Carver, David N., Pvt,
†Carver, Lloyd E., Pfc,
Carver, Thomas C., T/5,
§Casada, John R., Pfc,
Cascetta, Luigi, Sgt,
Casella, Stanley A., Pfc,
Casey, David G., Pvt,
Casey, George C., Sgt,
Casey, William F., Pfc,
Cash, Carl U., Sgt,
Cashin, William F., Pfc,
Casidy, Leo B., Jr., Pfc,
Casillas, Bernard J., Pvt,
†Caslow, William R., T/Sgt,
Cason, Homer D., Pvt,
Casper, John J., Sgt,
Cassel, Robert S., Sgt
Cassela, Joseph F., Pvt,
Cassell, Robert S., T/5,
Cassella, William, Pfc,
Cassiday, Roy P., S/Sgt,
Cassone, Giovanni, Pfc,
Castaldo, Raine A., Pvt,
†Castaneda, Edward V., Pfc,
Castelberry, Johnnie W., Pvt,
Castellano, David, Pfc,
Castellaw, Charles R., Pfc,
Casterline, Theo. M., Jr., Pvt,
Castillo, Albert G., Pfc,
Castillo, Alfredo A., Pvt,
Castillo, Irvin J., Pvt,
Castleman, L. C., Sgt,
Castleman, Wm. W., Jr., Pfc,
Castner, Arthur J., Pfc,
Castrechino, Ralph A., Pvt,
Castro, Charles, T/4,
Cataldo, John W., Pfc,
Catallo, John A., Pvt,
Catanzaro, Philip J., Pfc,
Cate, Kenneth P., Sgt,
‡Cathey, Norman D., S/Sgt,
Catlin, Robert A., Pfc,
Caudill, Owen, Pfc,
Caudle, Robert J., Sgt,
Caulder, Carson B., Pfc,
Causey, Alonzo W., Pfc,
Cautillo, Leonard J., Pfc,
Cavalier, George P., Pvt,
†Cavallero, Nunzio J., Pvt,
Cavanaugh, Edgar J., S/Sgt,
Cavariani, Frank, Pfc,
†Caverly, Jack M., Pvt,
Cawley, Robert H., Pvt,
Cawthorn, Paul P., Pfc,
Cayson, Marcus B., Sgt,
Cazares, Benjamin J., Pvt,
Cazeau, Edgar J., Pfc
Cecching, Albert A., Pvt,
Cehovet, Francis B., Pfc,
Cekada, Rudolph J., Sgt,
†Cella, James F., Pfc,
Celento, Benjamin A., Pvt,
Celuh, John J., S/Sgt,
Ceneri, Amerigo, Pfc,
‡Cenko, Steve, Jr., Pfc,
Centi, Larry, Pvt,
Cepale, Louis, Pvt,
Cerasoli, Roland C., Pvt,
Cermely, Valdimir L., Pfc,
Cerny, Carlo G., Cpl,
Cesarek, Joseph A., Pvt,
Cesca, Orlando, Pfc,
Chacho, Frank A., Pvt,
Chackslack, John G., Sgt,
Chadwick, Robert L., Pfc,
Chafee, Charlie, Pvt,
Chaffin, Joseph J., Pvt,
Chaisson, Marshal, Pfc,
Chaklosh, Pete, S/Sgt,
Challinor, Samuel B., Jr., Pvt,
Chambers, Alfred T., Pfc,
Chambers, Douglas W., 1st Lt,
Chambers, Eugene L., Pvt,
Chambers, Hayward R., T/4,

Chambers, James E., Pvt,
†Chambers, Thomas V., Pfc,
Chambers, William E., Pvt,
Chamblee, Francis L., Pfc,
Champion, Delmar C., Pvt,
Chandler, J. T., S/Sgt,
Chandler, Ronald V., Pvt,
Chanevich, Constantine, Pvt,
Chaney, Chris. W., Lt Col,
Chaney, Junior P., Pvt,
Chaney, Willie M., Sgt,
Chaplin, Marvin, Pvt,
†Chapman, Charles M., Pvt,
†Chapman, Kenneth G., Pvt,
Chapman, Sheppard W., Pvt,
Chapman, Wilbert J., Pvt,
†Charcut, Chester S., Cpl,
Charmock, Andrew L., Pvt,
Charron, Bertrand L., S/Sgt,
Chartrand, Oscar A., Pfc,
Chase, Eugene H., Sgt,
Chase, Frank, Pvt,
Chase, James G., Pfc,
Chatterton, Van L., Pvt,
†Chavez, Romolo, Pfc,
Chayka, Reindl F., Pvt
Chebra, Joseph, Pfc,
Cheel, Bobby R., S/Sgt,
Cheesman, Robert E., Pfc,
Cheholtz, Lewis H., Pfc,
Cheman, Paul R., Pvt,
Chenard, Robert A., Pvt,
Chenze, Alfred H., T/5,
Cherne, Fred W., Cpl,
Cherry, William R., Pvt,
Cherven, James A., Sgt,
Chesher, James G., Pvt,
Chesley, Grover H., Pfc,
Chesser, George D., Pfc,
‡Chestnut, Louis L., Pvt,
Chevalier, Normand Z., Pvt,
Chevenicky, Mike, T/5,
Chewning, William B., Pfc,
Chiarella, Joseph, Pfc,
§Chiarelli, Frank, Pvt,
Chiarello, Russell S., Sgt,
Chibici, Elias J., Pvt,
Chichetto, James J., 2nd Lt,
Chick, Steve J., Pvt,
Chidester, Kenneth F., Pvt,
†Chilcoat, Joseph E., Pfc,
Chillura, Nicholas A., Pfc,
†Chilson, Glen L., Sgt,
Chilson, Walter W., T/4,
Chilton, Harold W., T/5,
Chin, Henry W., Pvt,
Chin, Hing Y., Pfc,
†Chinn, Robert C., 1st Lt,
Chioke, Joseph S., S/Sgt,
†Chipley, Clarence L., Pfc,
Chipp, Augustine R., Pfc,
Chism, Harry D., Pfc,
Chitty, William H., Pfc,
†Chizmar, Albert, Pvt,
†Chmara, Andrew, Pvt,
†Chmiel, Walter J., Pvt,
Chojnacki, Edward J., Pfc,
Choka, Andy, S/Sgt,
†Chomicz, Charles, Pfc,
Chomiszewski, Anthony S., Pvt,
Chop, Thomas J., S/Sgt,
Chopman, Donald A., Pvt,
Chrisman, Joseph A., Cpl,
Christ, Bennie S., Sgt,
Christen, Walter W., Pfc,
§Christens, Laverne G., Cpl,
Christensen, Calvin, Cpl,
Christensen, Earl A., Pvt,
Christensen, Edward, 1st Lt,
Christensen, George L., Pfc,
†Christensen, Harold A., Cpl,
Christensen, Martin W., Pfc,
Christensen, Otis M., Sgt,
§Christensen, Walter, Pfc,
Christensen, William G., Pvt
†Christensen, William T., Pvt,
Christian, Clifford E., Pvt
Christian, Donald R., Pvt,
Christian, Frank J., Pvt,
‡Christian, Olice, Pfc,
Christian, Ted H., Pvt,
Christianson, Franklin C., Pvt,
Christie, Ellery C., Pvt,
Christmann, Frank, Sgt,
Christopher, James M., Jr., Pfc
Christovich, William E., Pvt,
Chromek, Paul J., Pvt,
Chrosman, Kenneth W., Pfc,
Chrzanowski, John B., Sgt,
Chrzanowski, Wencel, T/4,
Chupen, Tony P., S/Sgt,
*Chura, Nick, Pvt,
Church, Edwin D., Cpl,
Churick, Pete, Pvt,
Ciaffone, Louis P., Pvt,

† Killed in Action. * Prisoner of War. ‡ Missing in Action. § Died of Wounds.

Ciallella, Joseph, T/4,
Ciampa, Attilio J., Pvt,
*Ciariello, Albert S., Sgt,
Ciavaglia, Gidio, Pfc,
‡Cigarich, George, Pfc,
Cihowski, Edward J., Pfc,
Ciluffo, Alex J., Pvt,
Cimino, Victor, Pvt,
Cimore, Ernest P., Pvt,
Cinci, Frank S., Pfc,
Cioccia, Gennaro J., Pvt,
Ciociola, Louis, Pfc,
Ciolino, Lous J., 2nd Lt
†Cipri, Silvio, Pvt,
†Cipriano, Louis J., Pvt,
Cirando, Frank G., Pfc,
Ciresi, Joseph, Pvt,
Cischke, Donald W., Pvt
Cisero, Joseph, Pvt,
Cissa, Ralph C., Cpl,
†Citronberg, William N., Sgt,
Claire, Roland H., Pfc,
Clantz, Vance S., Sgt,
Clapp, Clyde N., Jr., T/5,
§Clapp, Dean W., Pvt,
Clapp, Jourdan M., Pfc,
Clapper, Ernest W., Pfc,
Clark, Arthur G., Jr., T/5,
Clark, David E., S/Sgt,
Clark, Elvin L., Pvt
Clark, Ernest D., Pvt,
Clark, Frank B., Pvt,
Clark, Fred A., Pvt,
Clark, Gilbert A., Pvt,
Clark, Henry C., Pvt,
Clark, James W., Pvt,
Clark, Joseph A., Pvt,
‡Clark, Joseph H., Pvt,
Clark, Loring T., S/Sgt,
Clark, Martin F., Pvt,
Clark, Martin L., Pvt,
Clark, Max J., Pfc,
Clark, Thomas L., Jr., S/Sgt,
†Clark, Wagner E., Pvt,
Clarke, William J., Pfc,
Clary, Richard T., Pvt,
Clausen, Fred W., Sgt,
Clausen, John H., Pvt,
*Claxton, Daw A., Pvt,
Clayton, Calvin C., Pvt,
‡Clayton, Robert D., Pfc,
Clegg, Elijah, Pvt,
Clem, Earl, Pfc,
Clemens, Maurice D., T/Sgt,
Clemens, Maurice D., 2nd Lt,
Clement, John F., Pfc,
Clementi, Anthony B., Pfc,
†Clements, Dean S., Pfc,
‡Clements, Edward, T/5,
†Clements, Luie L., Pfc,
Cleveland, Wilson L., Pfc,
Click, Loren A., Pfc,
Clift, Lawrence E., 1st Lt,
Cline, Calvin C., Pvt,
Cline, Donald K., Pvt,
Cline, Jacob P., Jr., T/Sgt,
‡Cline, Jerome, Pfc,
Clites, Earl E., Pvt,
†Clore, Walter M., Sgt,
Close, Martin R., S/Sgt,
§Clow, William E., S/Sgt,
Clower, Conlee A., Cpl,
‡Clyde, Benton W., Pvt
Coan, Edward J., Pvt,
Coannt, Lewis T., Sgt,
Coates, Elmer D., Pvt,
Coates, Robert B., Pvt,
†Coats, Clair R., Sgt,
§Coats, Milton E., S/Sgt,
Coaty, Leo V., S/Sgt,
†Cobb, Roy L., Pvt,
Cobden, Nathan D., Cpl,
Cobett, Jasper, Pvt,
Cochran, Andrew H., Jr., Cpl,
Cochran, Howard A., S/Sgt,
Cochran, Marvin G., Pfc,
Cochrum, Floyd, Pvt,
Cocilova, Viro, Pfc,
‡Cocke, Claude S., Pfc,
Cockrell, Clyde D., S/Sgt,
Cockrell, Irby G., Pvt,
Cody, Jeremiah I., Pvt,
Coe, Ernest E., Pvt,
†Coffey, Reginald J., Pfc,
Coffin, Arthur L., Pvt,
Coffman, Charlie S., Pvt,
Cohen, Benjamin, Pfc,
Cohen, Bernard, Capt,
Cohen, Hyman, Pfc,
Cohen, Seymour, Pvt,
Cohn, Morris, Pvt,
Coiro, Vincent M., Pvt,
Coker, Roval L., Pfc,
Coker, William E., Pfc,
Colaizzi, Evaristo A., Pvt,
Colamesta, Thomas, Pvt,
Colannino, Vincent, Pvt,
Colbert, Reford W., 1st Lt,
Colburn, Robert M., Pfc,
Colby, Ernest C., Pfc,
Colby, Robert L., Sgt,
Coldieron, Elmo N., Pfc,
Cole, Bolding J., Pfc,
Cole, Earnest W., Pvt,
Cole, Ferris E., Sgt,
Cole, Jack C., 1st Lt,
Cole, John B., Pvt,
†Cole, John P., Pvt,
†Cole, Quinton O., Pfc,
Cole, Raymond, Pfc,
Cole, Seymour, Cpl,
Coleman, Charles S., 2nd Lt,
Coleman, Clyde J., T/Sgt,
Coleman, James C., Pvt,
‡Coleman, James D., Pfc,
†Coleman, Robert C., Pfc,
Coleman, Warren C., 1st Lt,
Coletti, Henry D., Pfc
†Collazzo, Edward P., Pvt,
Collier, Howard S., Pfc,
Collier, Warren L., Pfc,
Collins, Calvin, Pvt,
Collins, Floyd M., 2nd Lt,
Collins, Guy B., Pvt,
Collins, Henry, T/Sgt
Collins, Howard E., Pfc,
Collins, James J., Pvt,
‡Collins, Owen K., Sr., Pfc,
†Collum, Lloyd D., Pfc,
Colo, Leo J., Pvt,
Colombaro, Natalino A., T/5,
Colonna, Edward A., Cpl,
Colquette, Charles W., Sgt,
Colson, Richard M., S/Sgt,
†Colson, Spencer W., Pfc,
†Coltharp, Arthur G., Pfc,
Coltts, Joseph W., Pvt,
Colvez, Wayne J., Pfc,
Colvin, Alfred C., Pvt,
†Colvin, Earl L., Pvt,
Combs, Earnest A., Pfc,
Combs, Harold J., Pfc,
Combs, William J., Sgt,
Comeau, Henry A., Pfc,
Comer, William H., Cpl,
Commander, Hubert C.,
Compton, Horace L., Pfc,
Comstock, Walter L., Pfc,
Conard, Wayne L., Pvt,
Conary, Harold K., Pvt,
Conaway, Alfred E., Pvt
†Conaway, Elmer L., Pfc,
Concotelli, Frank A., Pvt,
Conder, Boyce L., T/5,
†Condon, James A., Pvt,
Conerly, Monroe W., Pvt,
†Coney, Francis E., Pvt,
Conigliaro, Joseph, Pvt,
Conine, Richard E., Jr., Pvt,
Conklin, Howard L., Jr., Pvt,
Conklin Lloyd E., Pfc
Conklin, Robert E., Pfc,
Conlan, Garrett F., Pvt,
Conley, Glover A., M/Sgt,
Conley, James T., Pvt,
Conley, Wilburn W., Pvt,
Conley, William H., Pfc,
*Conlin, Henry T., Pfc,
Conn, Richard, Pfc,
†Conneely, John F., Capt,
Connell, Everett L., Pvt,
Connell, Gerald H., Pvt,
Connelly, Clyde L., Jr., Sgt,
†Conner, Chester W., Pvt,
Conner, Jewel L., Pfc,
Conner, Lynwood, Pfc,
‡Connon, Lloyd, Pvt,
Connor, Frank W., Jr., 1st Lt,
Conoly, George W., Pfc,
Conrad, Jerry C., 1st Lt,
Conrad, Tom F., Pvt,
‡Conroy, Robert P., Pfc,
Conte, John J., Pvt,
Conte, Joseph F., Pfc,
†Conte, Michael, Pfc,
†Conte, Pasquale A., Pfc,
†Contento, Louis W., Pvt,
Contestabile, Rufino C., Capt,
Conti, John J., Pfc,
†Contreras, Edward D., Sgt,
Contreras, Rudolph, T/5,
Contrino, Fred M., Pfc,
Conway, Andrew S., Pvt,
Conway, Clarence G., T/4,
†Conway, Claude E., Pvt,
Conway, Daniel D., S/Sgt,
Conway, Donald A., Sgt,
Conway, Milton J., Pfc,
Conwell, Robert L., Cpl,
Conyers, Vernon E., S/Sgt,
Conzaman, Steve C., Cpl
‡Cook, Arnold, S/Sgt,
Cook, Clarence E., Pvt,
Cook, Dale, Pvt,
Cook, Ernest D., Pvt,
†Cook, Erven A., Pfc,
Cook, Eugene W., Pfc,
Cook, Guess E., Jr., T/5,
Cook, John R., Pfc,
†Cook, Ova G., Pfc,
Cook, Phil B., T/4,
Cook, Philip, Pvt,
Cook, Walter I., S/Sgt
Cook, William, S/Sgt,
Cook, William R., Cpl,
†Cooke, James W., Cpl,
Cooksley, Alfred J., Cpl,
Cooley, Gerald M., Cpl,
Coon, Richard J., T/5,
Cooper, Bennie F., Pvt,
Cooper, Charles, Pfc,
Cooper, Charles C., Pfc,
Cooper, Donald K., Pvt,
Cooper, George F., Pfc,
Cooper, George W., 1st Lt,
‡Cooper, James T., Pfc,
†Cooper, Joe B., Pvt,
†Cooper, Lance N., Pvt,
Cooper, Norman E., Sgt,
Cooper, Oliver L., Pfc,
Cooper, Robert W., Pfc,
Cope, Russell D., Pvt,
†Cope, Truman, Pvt,
Copeland, James E., Pvt,
Copley, John R., T/Sgt,
†Coppola, Oreste L., Pvt,
Copres, Robert M., Pvt,
Coraci, Jerry, Pfc,
Corbett, Lawrence F., Pfc,
Corbin, Arthur M., Pvt,
Cordell, Alfred T., Pfc,
†Cordero, Jose P., Pfc,
Cardi, Franesco, Pfc,
Cordial, Earl A., Pvt,
Cordova, Jose A., Pfc,
Cordova, Ralph U., T/5,
Cordry, Elmer, Cpl,
Cores, Thomas R., S/Sgt,
*Corgill, Huston R., Pfc,
Corkett, Peter, Pvt,
Corley, Ralph L., Pvt
‡Corliss, James P., Pfc,
Corman, William J., Pvt,
Corn, Lawrence R., Pfc,
Cornatzer, Clinton C., Pfc,
*Cornelius, Alvin O., Pfc,
Cornelius, Harold J., S/Sgt,
Cornell, Clarence A., Pfc,
Cornell, Edward D., S/Sgt,
Cornwall, Charles O., Sgt,
†Cornwell, Howard L., Sgt,
Cornett, Chester, Jr., Pfc,
Corona, Anastacio T., Pvt,
Coronado, Richordo F., Pfc,
Corrado, Benjamin, Pfc,
‡Corrigan, John E., Pfc,
Corrigan, Joseph M., Pvt,
‡Corpron, Edward I., Pfc,
Cortese, Frank A., Pfc,
Cortner, Lester W., T/5,
Corum, Lloyd D., Pfc,
Corvino, Angelo, Pfc,
Corvino, Armando, Pfc,
Corwin, William W., Capt,
Cory, William H., Pfc,
Costa, Alfred N., Pvt
Costa, Joseph V., Pvt,
†Costa, Peter, Pfc,
Costa, Raymond, Pfc,
Costan, Edgar, Pvt,
Costanza, Sam, Cpl,
Costein, James, Pfc,
Costella, Clyde, Pvt,
Costello, Michael, Pvt,
†Costello, Thomas A., Jr., Pvt,
‡Costello, Thomas O., Pvt,
Costello, William J., Sgt,
Costen, John, Sgt,
‡Coston, Cleadis J., Sgt,
Cota, Francis B., Pvt,
†Cote, Wilfred G., Pvt,
Cotnoir, Horacetus E., Pvt,
Cotter, Paul G., T/5,
Cotton, Melvin K., S/Sgt,
Cotton, Sanford S., Cpl
Cottone, Gerald, Pvt,
†Cottrell, Hobert H., Pvt,
†Coty, George E., Pfc,
Couch, John E., Pvt,
Couch, Lester, Pfc,
Coughlin, George G., Pvt,
Coulmbe, Frederick L., Pvt,
Coulson, Edward S., Pfc,
†Coulson, William H., Pvt,
Courtemanche, Hector, Sgt,
Courtemanche, Ray. R., Pvt,
Courtney, John W., Sgt,
Coute, Clarence, Pfc,
Couture, Phelician J., Pvt,
Coutturier, Charles J., Pfc,
Covell, Ralph F., Pfc,
Covert, Henry H., S/Sgt,
Covington, Brian D., 1st Lt,
Covington, Henry S., Jr., Sgt,
Covington, Robert L., Jr., Sgt,
Covoletsky, Victor J., Sgt,
Cowan, Clyde C., Pvt,
Cowgill, Robert E., Sgt,
Cowin, Wren J., Pfc,
†Cowsert, Cecil R., Pfc,
Cox, Alfred F., Pvt,
Cox, Anthony J., Pfc,
Cox, Charlie, Pfc,
†Cox, Ernest L., S/Sgt,
Cox, John S., Pfc,
†Cox, Leslie, Cpl,
†Cox, Orville L., Pfc,
Cox, Richard J., Pfc,
Cox, Robert R., T/5
Cox, Roy, Pvt,
Cox, William M., Pvt,
Coxey, James W., Pvt,
†Coyne, John P., Pfc,
Coyne, Milton, Cpl,
Cozzens, Earl R., Pvt,
Craft, William H., Pfc,
Craghead, Millard O., Pvt,
Craig, Thomas J., Jr., Pfc,
Craig, William R., Pvt,
Cramer, Leward J., Pvt,
Cramp, Edmund L., S/Sgt,
Crandall, Calvin L., Pfc,
Crandall, Melvin F., Pfc,
Crane, Albert L., Pvt,
†Crane, Charles T., Pvt,
Crane, Stanley D., Pfc,
Cravey, David S., Pvt,
Crawford, Arden L., S/Sgt,
Crawford, Charles F., Pfc,
Crawford, Clayton E., T/Sgt,
Crawford, Harry C., Pfc,
Crawford, Harry E., Pvt,
Crawford, John A., S/Sgt,
Crawford, Orla E., S/Sgt,
§Crawford, William R., Pvt,
Creage, James H., S/Sgt,
Creagh, Joseph T., T/5,
Creamer, Harley, Pfc,
Creamer, Roy C., Pfc,
Crecco, Michael, Pvt,
Creech, Timothy T., Pfc,
Creed, Andrew, Pfc,
Creed, Bill, Pvt,
Creel, Marvin W., Pfc,
Creiman, Garry R., 1st Lt,
Crennan, James B., Pvt,
†Creppa, Francis H., Pfc,
‡Cribb, Charles H., Pvt,
Cribby, Edward J., Pvt,
†Crider, Tyrus T., Pfc,
Crigger, Robert M., Pvt,
Crimmins, Robert F., Pvt,
Criner, George W., Pfc,
Crinieri, Joseph L., Pvt,
Crinnin, Frederick T., Pvt,
Criscuolo, Charles W., Pfc,
Crisp, James O., Pvt,
Crisp, Harvey A., Pvt,
Crisp, Virgil G., Pvt,
Crites, Ervin B., Pvt,
Crocker, William C., Cpl,
Crockett, Edwin C., Pvt,
Crooks, Rader K., Capt,
‡Cromer, Earl F., Pfc,
Cromer, Walter A., Capt,
Crosby, Theodore, Pfc,
†Cross, Calvin H., Pfc,
Cross, Francis W., Pfc,
†Cross, Jessie W., Pvt,
Cross, L. B., Pvt,
Crossman, Nathan H., 1st Sgt
Crotts, Huland T., Pvt,
Crouch, John D., Jr., Pvt,
Crouch, Nobel L., Pvt,
Crowder, Charles D., Pvt
Crowe, Robert O., Sgt,
Crozier, Wilfred L., Pfc,
†Cruber, Carson H., S/Sgt,
†Crucis, Guerino, Pvt,
Crumling, Dale E., Pvt,
Crump, William F., Pvt,
Crutchfield, Carl T., Pvt,
Crutchfield, James C., Pvt,
Crutchfield, Roscoe R., S/Sgt,
Cruthirds, Roland L., Pvt,
Cruz, Ermelindo, Pfc,
§Cruz, Manuel L., Pvt,
Csencsits, Paul I., Pvt
Csizmar, John H., T/5,
†Cuellar, Everrardo J., Cpl,
Cuicello, James W., S/Sgt,
Culbane, Thomas J., Sgt,
Culber, Arthur Paul T., T/Sgt,
†Cullen, James J., Pvt,
Culler, Donald R., Pfc,
Cullifer, Leslie B., Cpl,
Cullotta, Harry R., Pvt,
Culotta, Salvatore J., Pvt,
Culp, Clarence L., Pvt,
Culver, Douglas W., T/4,
Cummings, Archie L., T/4,
Cummings, Lloyd A., 1st Lt,
Cummings, Raymond W., Pfc,
‡Cummings, William G., Pvt,
Cundiff, Gordon P., 1st Lt
Cunha, Henry J., S/Sgt,
Cunningham, Abraham H., Pvt,
Cunningham, Ace G., Pvt,
Cunningham, Edwin S., Sgt,
Cunningham, Frank P., Pfc,
Cunningham, George C., Cpl,
Cunningham, Matthew T., Pfc,
Cunningham, Robert J., S/Sgt,
Cunningham, Stanley, Pvt,
Curfman, Merle C., Pvt,
†Curialo, Dominic M., Pvt,
†Curino, Vincent, Pvt,
Curl, Edward C., S/Sgt,
Curley, George J., Pvt,
Curran, Eugene B., Pvt,
Curren, Alfred J., Pfc,
Current, William R., Pfc,
Curreri, Salvatore J., Cpl,
Currie, Elbert H., Jr., 2nd Lt,
Curry, Milton G., Pvt,
Curry, William H., Pfc,
Curtaccio, Dan O., Pfc,
Curtis, Donald, Pvt,
Curtis, Herbert E., Cpl,
Curtis, John N., Pfc,
Curtis, Joseph C., 1st Sgt,
Curtis, Robert M., Pvt,
†Curtis, Robert, Pfc,
†Curts, William J., Cpl,
Curvin, Lymon H., S/Sgt,
Cushing, Cecil W., Pvt,
Cussen, John B., Pvt
†Cutler, Alonza P., Pvt,
Cutler, Isadore E., Pvt,
Cutrona, Rosaria, T/4,
†Cutruzzuia, Frank S., Pfc,
†Cutshall, Kenneth R., 2nd Lt,
Cuvo, Victor J., Pvt,
Cwienk, George T., Pvt,
Cybulski, Constantine A., Sgt,
Cybulski, Edmund D., Pvt,
Cychosz, Clarence, Pfc,
Cylka, Herbert I., S/Sgt,
Cyphers, William E., Pfc,
Cyr, Maurice P., Pvt,
Czachor, Stanley J., S/Sgt,
Czap, Eugene A., Pfc,
‡Czarbuawski, Edward M., Pvt,
Czarnik, Stanley, Pfc,
Czarnik, Walter S., Pfc,
Czeczok, Leroy A., Pfc,
Czemerda, Martin J., Pfc,

Dabney, Charles F., S/Sgt,
D'Achille Vite U., Pfc,
Daczyk, Ambrose, Cpl,
Daeger, Roland G., Pfc,
Daggett, Elmer J., Pvt,
D'Agostino, Louis, Pfc,
Dahl, Richard W., Pvt,
Dahl, Vester, Pvt,
Dahlen, Clarence B., Pvt,
Dahm, Robert L., Pvt,
Daigle, Camille S., Sgt,
‡Daigrepont, Lawrence, Sgt,
Dailey, Jack H., S/Sgt,
Dailey, James, Pfc,
Dakar, George R., Pfc,
D'Alba, James V., Pvt,
Dale, Floyd B., Pvt,
Dale, John L., T/5,
Dale, Richard, Pfc,
Dale, Rush T., Pvt,
Daley, Kenneth J., Pfc,
Dallas, James T., Pvt,
Dalsass, Mario, Pfc,
Dalton, David H., Cpl,
Dalton, Robert G., Pvt,
Daly, Byrone M., Maj,
Daly, John J., Jr., Pvt,
Daly, John L., Jr., Pvt,
Daly, Peter, Pfc,
Daly, William L., Pvt,
Dambrackas, Raymond, Pvt,
Damico, Paul L., Pvt,
Damitz, Irvin F., Pvt,
D'Amora, Hector J., Pvt,
Damm, Marvin C., Pvt,
†D'Andrea, Joseph T., 1st Lt,
Daney, Paul, Pfc,

† Killed in Action. * Prisoner of War. ‡ Missing in Action. § Died of Wounds.

Daneault, Henry J., Pfc,
†Dangelico, Alexander F., Pfc,
Daniel, Carl D., Pvt,
*Daniel, Gerald W., Pvt,
Daniel, Harling E., Pvt,
Daniel, Perry A., Jr., Sgt,
Daniel, Robert J., S/Sgt,
Danielson, Robert E., Pfc,
Daniels, Cecil E., Pvt,
Dann, Dale J., Pvt,
‡Dannic, Edward J., Jr., Pfc,
Dannucci, Joseph D., Pfc,
Danver, Arthur E., Jr., Pvt,
†Daoa, Dionisio, Pfc,
D'Aprilo Michael D., Pfc,
†Daraszkiewics, Edward J., Cpl,
Darby, Carles J., Pfc,
Darchuk, George, T/5,
*Dargie, George A., Pfc,
†Dargush, Anthony V., Pfc,
Darko, Emanuel W., T/5,
Darlak, Peter J., Cpl,
Darley, Donald L., Pfc,
‡Darling, Frederick E., Pfc,
Daronco, Martino G., Pfc,
Darrah, John R., Maj,
†Dart, Kenneth R., Pvt,
Dash, Clarence E., Sgt,
Dash, Walter J., Sr., S/Sgt,
†Daugherty, Floyd, Pvt,
Daugherty, Roy E., Sgt,
Daughtry, William F., Pvt,
Dave, Harold, Pvt,
Davenport, A. P., Sgt,
Davenport, Charles R., Pvt,
Davenport, Francis S., Pfc,
Davenport, Lee H., Pvt,
Davenport, Wilburn L., Pvt,
Davey, Leo C., T/5,
Davey, William J., Pfc,
David, Atule, S/Sgt,
David, George W., Pvt,
†Davidson, Edward D., Pfc,
Davidson, Emmett W., Pfc,
Davidson, Roscoe, Pfc,
Davies, Elwood D., Jr., S/Sgt,
†Davies, Ernest A., Pvt,
Davies, Harold D., Pvt,
Davies, Percvial E., Sgt,
Davies, Robert L., Capt,
Davies, Thomas, Capt,
Davila, Tony A., Pfc,
Davis, Willis H., Pvt,
Davis, Alfred R., Pfc,
Davis, Charles C., Sgt,
Davis, Dean, Pvt,
Davis, Dewey L., Pfc,
†Davis, Boyan, Pfc,
Davis, Elmer I., Pfc,
§Davis, Fletcher T., Pvt,
Davis, George E., Cpl,
Davis, Harry L., Pfc,
Davis, Henry E., Pfc,
Davis, Huston H., Pvt,
Davis, Jack, Pvt,
Davis, Jerome, Pvt,
Davis, Joe, Pvt,
Davis, John D., Pfc,
Davis, John T., Pfc,
§Davis, Kenneth E., Pfc,
Davis, Leland A., Sgt,
Davis, Leo F., S/Sgt,
†Davis, Leo R., Pvt,
Davis, Loy W., Pfc,
Davis, Marshall L., Pfc,
Davis, Maurice L., Pfc,
Davis, Milford W., Pfc,
†Davis, O'Neal E., Pfc,
Davis, Oscar, Pvt,
§Davis, Rayford, Pvt,
Davis, Rondal N., S/Sgt,
Davis, Russell, Sgt,
Davis, Sam, Pvt,
Davis, Thenonie, Cpl,
Davis, Thomas R., Lt Col,
Davis, Thomas V., T/5,
Davis, Walter A., Pvt,
Davis, Wendell E., Pfc,
Davis, Wilburn C., Pvt,
Davis, William A., Pfc,
Davis, William E., Pvt
Davis, William L., Pvt,
Davis, William R., Sgt,
Davis, William T., Pfc,
Davison, Raymond, S/Sgt,
Dawes, Ivan J., S/Sgt,
Dawkins, Howard J., Pfc,
Dawson, Richard C., S/Sgt
Dawson, Theodore J., Pvt,
Dawson, Thomas A., Capt,
Day, Edward R., Cpl,
†Day, Joseph C., 1st Sgt,
Day, Paul H., Pvt,
Day, Vernon R., Sgt,
Daze, David J., 2nd Lt,

Deahl, Fred A., Sgt,
Dean, Benjamin F., Pvt,
†Dean, Donald L., Pfc,
Dean, Ernest A., Pvt,
Dean, Joseph H., Pfc,
Deanda, Peter G., Pfc,
DeAngelo, Patrick P., Cpl,
DeAngleo, Frank R., Sgt,
‡Dears, Anthony M., Pfc,
Deas, Thomas E., Pvt
Deatherage, Birt L., Pvt,
DeAtley, Robert L., Pvt,
Deavellar, Robert, Pvt,
DeBaise, Thomas R., Pvt,
De Bartole, Hansel W., Capt,
DeBerger, Robert L., S/Sgt,
DeBerry, Ralph C., Pfc,
DeBeer, Ralph E., 2nd Lt,
†DeBello, Nicholas A., Pvt,
Debol, Charles J., Pfc,
DeCanio, Sam, Pfc,
DeCarlo, Frank, Jr., Pvt,
Decatur, Harvey B., Pfc,
Decessare, John, Sgt,
Decewicz, Walter J., S/Sgt,
Dechambeau, Maurice H., Cpl,
Decker, Charles E., T/Sgt,
Decker, Elwood R., Pfc,
†Decker, Nicholas E., Pfc,
§Dedes, James E., S/Sgt,
Dedes, James R., S/Sgt,
Dedrich, William F., Pvt,
‡Deemer, William H., Sgt,
Deese, Guy L., T/5,
DeFelice, Albert H., Pvt,
‡Defeo, Joseph C., Pfc,
DeFio, Joseph V., Pfc,
DeForge, Raymond F., Pvt,
DeFurio, Frank A., Pfc,
DeGalbo, Anthony R., Pvt,
‡DeGeorge, Elmer, Pfc,
DeGifford, Samuel D., T/3,
DeFrasse, Norman F., Pvt,
DeHaven, Harry C., Pfc,
Dehls, Tonie C., T/5,
Dehm, Raymond A., Pvt,
Dehmer, Robert T., Pfc,
Dejarain, Robert P., Pfc,
DeJarnett, George A., Pvt,
DeJourdan, William J., Sgt,
Dekens, Michael L., S/Sgt,
Dekmar, Stephen, Sgt,
De Land, Paul K., 1st Lt,
Delaney, James M., Pfc,
Delaney, Paul K., S/Sgt,
Delaney, William B., Pfc,
De Lange, Harold J., Pvt,
Delano, Frank E., Pvt,
Delano, John K., Pfc,
DeLaRosa, Richard Y., Pvt,
Delashmutt, Van R., Pvt,
Delashmutt, Walter R., Cpl,
Delatte, Ferdinand J., S/Sgt,
Del Campillo, Santos R., Pvt,
§Delemo, Alexander J., Pfc,
DeLeon, Santos D., Pvt,
Delehanty, Joseph, Pfc,
Delestewicz, John F., Pvt,
Delgade, Ralph A., Pfc,
†Del Grosso, Nicholas J., Pvt,
Del Guidice, Alfred J., Sgt,
†Delia, John A., Pvt,
§Della, Vecahia Chas C., S/Sgt,
Dellafave, Michael T., Pvt,
Dellaghelfa, John, Jr., Pvt,
Dellisanti, John, Pvt,
Del Monaco, Frank D., Pvt,
†Delo, Charles W., Pfc,
†DeLong, Gerald C., Pfc,
DeLorenzo, Enrico H., Sgt,
DelSignore, Guy J., Pvt,
DeLuca, Alfred, S/Sgt,
DeLueiso, Joseph C., Col,
Del Vecchio, Joseph G., S/Sgt,
Dely, Alex J., Cpl,
‡Demarais, Pete, Pfc,
‡DeMarco, Stephen J., Jr., Pfc
DeMarco, Stephen, Pfc,
DeMarcus, John B., 2nd Lt,
DeMarie, Anthony, Sgt,
DeMario, Louis, S/Sgt,
DeMars, Robert E., Pvt,
DeMartino, John, Pvt,
DeMasse, Stephen P., Pvt,
Demayo, Anthony R., Pvt,
Demers, Fred L., Pfc,
Demers, Harold V., Pvt,
Demetri, Harry C., Cpl,
*Demo, Alexander T., Pvt,
DeMonaco, Henry F., Pfc,
Demonbren, Jimmie D., Pvt,
Demos, Christ, Pvt,
Dempsey, Donald F., Pvt,
†Damsiak, Walter, Pfc,
†DeNinno, Patsy, Pvt,

Denio, Michael, Jr., Pvt,
Denn, William J., Pvt,
Dennehy, Joseph P., Pfc,
*Dennis, Floyd I., Pvt,
Dennis, Lee R., Pvt,
Dennis, Lloyd T., Pvt
Dennis, William F., Pfc,
†Denny, George E., Pvt,
*Dent, Hugh D., Pfc,
DePalma, Anthony V., Pvt,
DePalmo, Anthony, T/Sgt,
Depasquale, Dominick, S/Sgt,
Depasquale, Nicholas, Pfc,
Depe, Abe J., Pfc,
DePietro Salvatore J., Pfc,
Depka, Thomas R., Pvt,
†DeProbert, Norman V., Pfc,
Deptula, Stanley J., Pvt,
DePuy, Francis H., Pvt,
†Derach, Frank E., Pvt,
DeRenzo, Albert C., Cpl,
DeRobertis, Nunzio S., Pfc,
†DeRoche, Francis D., Pvt,
De Rosa, Frank A., Pvt,
DeRosa, Orlando P., Pvt,
Derrick, John J., S/Sgt,
Derrick, Lee, Pvt,
Derringer, Billie, Cpl,
Derringer, Byron I., S/Sgt,
†DeRubeis, Frank W., Pvt,
†Desack, Andrew, Jr., Pfc,
De Santis, Orazio J., Capt,
Desbiens, Albert J., Pfc,
Deshaies, Joseph E., T/5,
DeSimone, John J., Pfc,
Desmarais, Walter W., Pfc,
Desmond, Henry A., Pfc,
Deso, John, Pvt,
Desrosiers, Leo H., Pfc,
Detor, Raymond S., Pvt,
Dettman, Richard E., S/Sgt,
De Valk, Henry, Pvt,
Devaney, John W., Pvt,
DeVeaux, Harold H., Pfc,
†DeVeies, John, Jr., Pvt,
Deverick, Ralph N., Pvt,
Devers, Joseph G., Cpl,
Devine, Robert T., S/Sgt,
Devino, Milton, Pfc,
DeVisch, Kamiel G., S/Sgt,
DeVito, Dominick W., Pvt,
†DeVito, James J., Jr., Pvt,
Devivo, Louis A., Pfc,
Devlin, John J., Pfc,
Devlin, John J., T/4,
De Volk, Henry, Pvt,
DeVries, Martin, Pvt
Dewaters, Arthur P., Pfc,
Dewey, Leonard F., Pvt,
Dewey, William L., Cpl,
‡DeWitt, Walter P., Sgt,
DeWolf, Ray. E., Jr., Sgt,
Dial, James H., Pfc,
Dial, Paul, Cpl,
Diamico, Leonard R., Pvt,
Diamond, Irving, S/Sgt,
†Diamond, Louis, Pvt,
Dias, Imberto, Pvt,
DiBari, Nicholas A., Pfc,
‡DiBello, George G., Pfc,
‡DiCarlantonio, Martin J., Pvt,
†DiCarlo, Salvatore, Pvt,
†DiCarolia, Piorentino J., Pvt,
†Dickens, Lee L., Pvt,
Dickerman, John W., T/5,
Dickerson, Floyd E., Pvt,
Dickerson, Floyd L., Pvt,
Dickerson, George E., Pfc,
‡Dickerson, John Q., Pfc,
Dickerson, Oscar E., Pfc,
Dickey, Freeman, Pfc,
Dickey, John R., S/Sgt,
Dickinson, George H., Pfc,
Dickinson, Thomas A., T/5,
Dickinson, Walter, Sgt,
Dickson, Leslie T., Pfc,
*DiDomenico, Matthew, Pvt,
‡Diechkman, Harold D., Pfc,
Diedrich, Robert C., Pvt,
Diehl, Earl H., Jr., 2nd Lt,
†Diener, Victor F., Pfc,
Dietrich, George W., Pfc,
Dietrich, John J., Sgt,
Dietrich, Robert, Pfc,
Dietz, Dale L., Pfc,
Dietz, Lawrence J., Pvt,
Dietz, William J., Pvt,
DiFilippo, John P., Pfc,
DiFiore, John J., Sgt,
DiGiacomo, Thomas A., Pvt,
*Diggs, Jesse F., III, 2nd Lt,
Diggs, James R., Cpl,
Dignan, William H., Pvt,
DiGuili, Raymond J., Pfc,
Dilday, Willard C., Sgt,

Dill, Andrew J., Pvt,
Dill, Roger L., Jr., Sgt,
Dillan, Henry, Sgt,
Dillard, Herbert A., Pvt,
*Dillard, Wilson M., Pvt,
†Dillenback, Frank A., Cpl,
Diller, Joseph E., Pvt,
Dillin, Claude O., Pfc,
Dillin, William M., Pvt,
Dillion, Robert F., Pvt,
Dillon, Charles M., Pvt,
†Dillon, James N., T/Sgt,
Dillon, John J., Sgt,
Dillon, Milborn, Pvt.
Dillon, Robert E., Pvt,
Dilluvio, Salvatore J., Pfc,
Dilts, James A., Jr., 2nd Lt
DiMarcello, Nicholas A., Pfc,
DiMarco, Salvatore E., Pvt,
DiMarie, Carmen, Pvt,
Dimenno, Vincent L., Pfc,
Dimino, Anthony V., Pvt,
*Dimling, John N., Jr., 2nd Lt,
DiMonte, John, Sgt,
DiMuro, Mario G., Pvt,
Dina, Steve M., Pfc,
Dinehart, Boyd A., Pfc,
Dingfelder, Franklin E., Pfc,
Dinicolas, Salvatore, Pvt,
Dion, Raymond S., Sgt,
†Dionne, Adelard J., Sgt,
DiOrio, Alphonso A., Pvt,
DiOrio, Andrew A., Pfc,
DiPaolo, Nunzio V., Pvt,
DiRenzo, Armand M., Pfc,
Dirienzo, William M., Pvt,
Di Sabatino, Ralph J., S/Sgt,
Disciulle, Samule J., Pvt,
Disdier, Orlando A., Pfc,
Disorbe, Michael J., Pvt,
DiTaranto, Michael J., Pvt,
Ditlefsen, Russell R., Pfc,
†DiTommaso, Lawrence, Pfc,
DiTondo, Charles, Pvt,
Ditzler, William H., S/Sgt,
Diveley, Wilbur R., M/Sgt,
Dix, Dan, Pfc,
Dix, Harold B., Pfc,
Dix, Richard B., Pvt,
†Dixon, George E., Jr., Pvt
Dixon, Milton, Pvt,
Dixon, Robert G., Pvt,
Dixon, Ronald A., Pfc,
Dixon, William B., Pfc,
†Dizer, John W., Pfc,
Dmiczak, Victor F., Pfc,
‡Dobberton, Myron E., Pfc,
Dobbins, John B., Pvt,
Dobbs, Charles E., Pvt,
Dobeck, Henry T., Pvt,
Dobilas, Anthony A., Pvt,
†Dobins, Earl E., Pvt,
Dobinson, William A., Pfc,
Dobrosky, Michael J., Pfc,
Dobrowolski, Theodore E., Pvt,
Dobson, James L., Pvt,
Dobstaff, Gerard, Pvt,
Docherty, William H., Pvt,
‡Dodaro, Anthony G., Jr., Pvt,
†DoDaro, Joseph S., S/Sgt,
Dodd,Leonard Y., Pvt,
Dodd, Paul E., S/Sgt,
†Dodd, Robert, Jr., Pfc,
‡Dodds, James A., Pfc,
†Dodricj, John, Pvt,
Dodril, Fred, Pvt
Dodson, Harvey A., Pvt,
Dodson, Howard H., Pfc,
Doerflein, William J., 1st Lt
Doering, Henry F., T/5,
†Doering, William A., T/5,
Doherty, Paul E., Capt,
Dolan, John T., Pvt,
Doleman, Edgar C., Lt Col,
Dolese, Edmond F., Pvt,
Dolph, Roy, Sgt,
†Dolsen, Fred R., 1/Sgt,
Dombrowski, Waclaw, Pfc,
Domenico, Louis J., S/Sgt,
Domencio, Louis J., S/Sgt,
Dominiak, William W., Cpl,
Dominichetti, Chester L., Pfc,
Dominick, Louis A., Pvt,
Dominick, Luis A., Pfc
Domingues, Mannel V., Pfc,
Dominguez, Robert, Pfc,
Dominski, Tyrus, S/Sgt,
Domzalski, Harry W., Pvt,
Donaghy, James F., Pvt,
†Donahoe, Donald F., Pvt,
Donahue, Harold C., 1st Lt,
†Donatelli, Benjamin N., S/Sgt,
Donatello, Anthony R., Pfc,
Donati, Enrico, Sgt,

Donato, Anthony, Pvt,
‡Donato, John E., Pvt,
Donegan, Winfred S., Pfc,
Donelly, Thomas N., Jr., Pvt,
†Doner, Winfield A., Pvt,
Donlon, Paul A., Jr., Pfc,
Donnel, Lonnie L., Jr., Sgt,
Donnell, Lonnie L., Jr., Pfc,
†Donnelly, John J., Sgt,
Donnelly, Michael J., Pfc,
†Donohue, John A., Pfc,
Donovan Gerard C., Pfc,
Donovan, Robert E., T/5,
Donovan, William P., Pvt,
Donton, Franklin G., Pfc,
Dooley, John F., S/Sgt,
Dooley, Thurman J., Sgt,
Dooling, John B., Pfc,
Doran, James H., Pfc,
Doran, John P., Sgt,
Dorchincez, John, Pvt,
Doring, Edward J., Pfc,
†Dority, Eugene W., S/Sgt,
Dorman, Albert A., Pfc,
Dorman, Jessie O., T/Sgt,
†Dornan, Marlin P., S/Sgt,
Dorn, Albert H., Pvt,
Doros, John S., Pfc,
Dorr, Milton E., Pfc,
Dorrell, Edward L., Pfc,
Dorrico, Anthony F., Sgt,
Dorsey, Cephus P., Pfc,
Dorsey, Clarence J., Pvt,
Dorta, Reinaldo A., Pfc,
Doss, Cornelius B., Sgt,
Dostman, George S., 1st Sgt,
Dostson, Harry J., Sgt,
Dotter, Robert M., Pvt,
Doty, Merle R., Pfc,
Doty, William L., Sgt,
Dotzert, Paul H., Pvt,
†Douestts, James A., Pvt,
Doughherty, William J., Sgt,
*Doughney, John E., Jr., Pvt,
Douglas, Charles R., Pfc,
†Douglas, James B., Cpl,
Douglas, James H., Sr., Pvt,
†Douglas, Martus G., Pvt,
Douglas, Samuel W., Pfc,
Douglass, Kenneth R., Jr., Pfc
†Douglass, Robert H., Pfc,
Douthitt, John, S/Sgt,
Dove, Theodore M., S/Sgt,
Dowd, Graham G., Sgt,
Dowdle, Victor C., Pfc,
Dowdy, Hershel H., Pfc,
Dowhy, John, Pfc,
†Dowling, George E., Pvt,
Dowling, William R., Pvt,
Downer, Robert P., Sgt,
Downey, Robert F., Pvt,
Downs, Jack, Pvt,
Downs, James H., Pvt,
Downs, Morgan L., T/Sgt,
Doxey, Donnie, Sgt,
Doxey, Henry J., Pvt,
†Doxier, William E., Pfc,
Doyle, Charles V., Cpl,
Doyle, George A., Pvt,
Doyle, Ira C., Pfc,
Doyle, James H., Pfc,
Doyle, Johnnie J., Pfc,
Doyle, Lawrence W., Pfc,
Doyle, Leonard, Pfc,
Doyle, Ward, S/Sgt,
Drabczyk, Edward L., Sgt,
Drager, Orville F., Pfc,
‡Dragon, Arthur R., Pvt,
Dragonette, Albert J., Pvt,
Drake, Vyron E., T/Sgt,
Drapeau, John W., Pvt,
Draper, Willard T., 1st Lt,
Draucek, Joseph D., Pfc,
Drega, Henry F., Cpl,
Dreistadt, George A., Pvt,
Drennan, John P., Jr., Pvt,
Drennen, Grover W., Pvt,
Drew, Dale H., Pfc,
†Drew, Jodie A., Pfc,
*Drewnisk, Stanley J., Pvt,
†Dries, Joseph O., Jr., Pfc,
‡Driggers, Edward B., Pfc,
Driscoll, Thomas J., Pvt,
Driver, Roy L., Pfc,
Driver, Wilbert D., Pvt,
Drobats, Andrew J., Cpl,
Drohan, John T., Pvt,
Drohman, Vown A., Pvt,
Drohman, Vown A., Pfc,
Drolet, Donald L., Cpl,
Droll, Robert L., Pfc,
Drolla, Charles P., Sgt,
Droney, Lawrence W., Pvt,
Droogan, Paul J., Pvt,
Drossner, Jacob L., Capt,

† Killed in Action. * Prisoner of War. ‡ Missing in Action. § Died of Wounds.

§Drost, Joseph J., Pvt,
Drozd, Henry R., S/Sgt,
Drozdenko, Constantine, Pfc,
Drozdowicz, Henry, Pfc,
Drucker, Samuel, Pfc,
‡Drum, John C., Pfc,
Drummond, Shannon J., Pvt,
Drye, Hersel R., S/Sgt,
Dua, Leonard W., T/5,
Duarte, Daniel F., Pvt,
Duarte, Robert J., Pvt,
Dubey, Joseph E., S/Sgt,
Dubey, Joseph E., Pfc
Dubois, Bernard H., Pfc,
Dubois, Vernon G., Pfc,
DuBord, George H., Pvt,
Duchemin, Irvin P., Cpl,
Ducker, Saul, Pvt,
Duckworth, James E., S/Sgt,
Duclos, John P., Pvt,
Ducote, Florian A., Cpl,
Ducy, John D., S/Sgt,
Dude, Gerald R., Pvt,
Dudik, Andrew S., S/Sgt,
Dudley, James S., Jr., Pvt,
Due, Paul A., Pfc,
Duenes, Asuncion J., Cpl,
Duenn, Albert E., T/5,
†Duffey, Charles W., Pvt,
Duffy, Donald L., Pvt,
Duffy, John F., 1st Lt,
Duffy, Martin J., Pfc,
‡Duffy, Thomas F., Jr., S/Sgt,
Duffy, William H., Pfc,
Dufour, Anton P., Pvt,
DuFour, Donald L., Pfc,
Dugas, Ernest A., Pvt,
†Dugas, Hayward J., Pfc,
Dugger, Cleamo S., Sgt,
Dugger, Kenneth M., T/4,
Dugger, Robert F., Sgt,
†Dugo, Carl S., Pfc,
DuHamel, Arthur E., Pvt
Duhon, Mabry, Pvt,
Duke, Elmer, Pvt,
Duke, Harvie L., Pfc,
Duke, Rolland W., Pfc,
Duket, Robert L., Pvt,
Duley, Raymond A., Capt,
Dulibain, Alex P., Sgt,
Dulong, George E., T/5,
Dumais, Hampy, Pfc,
Dumanski, Charles A., T/3,
Dumas, Joseph A. R., Pfc,
Dumont, Russell E., Pfc,
DuMouchel, Leo J., S/Sgt,
Dunaway, John A., Pvt,
Dunbar, Kenneth D., Pfc,
Dunbar, Marion E., Pvt,
Duncan, Buell M., 1st Lt,
Duncan, Carl R., Pfc,
Duncan, Charley A., Pfc,
†Duncan, Heath L., Pvt,
Duncan, John C., Pfc,
Duncan, Luther, Pvt,
Duncan, William L., Pvt,
Dunford, James A., Pvt,
Dunham, Arthur W., Pfc,
Dunham, James R., Sgt,
Dunham, Ralph, T/Sgt,
Dunivan, Robert E., Sgt,
Dunkel, Duane I., Pfc,
Dunkin, William W., Pfc,
Dunlap, Fred A., Pvt,
Dunlap, Nelson L., S/Sgt,
Dunlap, Ralph C., Pvt,
Dunlap, Robert J., Pfc,
Dunlap, Walter C., Sgt,
Dunlop, Raymond E., Pfc,
Dunn, Clif A., Pvt,
Dunn, Earl R., Pfc,
†Dunn, French, Sgt,
Dunn, James R., Pfc,
Dunn, Michael J., Pfc,
†Dunn, Paul, Pvt,
†Dunn, Wilburn, H., Pvt,
Dunn, William O., Pfc,
Dunnaway, Floyd, Pfc,
Dunster, Belford B., Pvt,
Dunsworth, Ralph, Jr., Pvt,
Dupont, Joseph J., Pvt,
Dupra, Earl J., Pvt,
Dupy, Thomas S., Pvt,
Duran, Epifanio C., Pfc,
Duran, Joe A., Sgt,
Durham, Russell, T/Sgt,
Durant, Peter A., Pfc,
D'Urbano, Generous, Pvt,
Durda, Walter H., Sgt,
Durden, Eddie J. R., Sgt,
Durkin, John T., Sgt,
Durling, Robert E., Pvt,
Durnil, Lawrence N., Pvt,
Durstock, Donald W., Pfc,
Dusek, Robert J., Pfc,

Dutcher, Eugene, Pvt,
Dutcher, Paul M., Pvt,
Dutka, Leonard J., Sgt,
†Dutko, John W., Pfc,
Dutra, John, S/Sgt,
Dutton, Francis S., Pfc,
†Dutton, William C., Pfc,
Duval, Robert J., Pfc,
Duvall, Claude E., Pvt,
Duvall, Elmer D., Sgt,
Duwe, Arthur E., Jr., S/Sgt,
Duwell, Frederick J., Pfc,
Duzicky, Mike, Pvt,
Dvorak, Clarence J., Sgt,
Dwan, John E., II, Capt,
Dwyer, James R., Pvt,
*Dwyer, Richard F., Pvt,
Dybas, Edward, T/4,
Dye, Clarence, Pvt,
Dye, Willard C., Pfc,
Dyer, Clifford F., Sgt,
Dyer, Samuel N., Pfc,
Dyes, James F., Jr., Pvt,
†Dygert, Claire R., Pvt.
Dykes, Denzil, Pvt,
†Dykes, Samuel, 1st Lt,
Dykman, Conrad, Pfc,
Dysart, James C., Pvt,
Dyvad, Bert H., T/4,
Dziedzic, Edward J., T/4,
Dziurbiel, Joseph, Pvt,
Dzurec, John A., Pvt,
Dzurenda, Joseph A., Cpl,

Eabray, Gene C., Sgt,
†Eades, Emmett K., 1st Lt,
Eagles, Floyd R., Pvt,
Eagles, William F., T/Sgt,
Eailiani, Mario, Sgt,
‡Eakes, Raymond L., Pvt,
Eanes, David C., Capt,
Eanes, James T., S/Sgt,
Eargle, Jesse R., Pfc,
Earles, Raymond H., Pvt,
Earnest, Charles E., Sgt,
Earnest, Francis E., Pfc,
Eastbury, Herbert C., Pvt,
Eastep, W. L., Sgt,
Easterday, Dan C., Capt
†Easterling, Grady L., Pfc,
Easterling, Willie R., Sgt,
Eastin, Robert L., Pfc,
Eastman, Fred V., Pvt,
Eastmond, Frank T., Pfc,
‡Easton, Robert E., Pvt,
Eastwood, John P., Pvt,
Eaton, Charlie B., Pvt,
†Eaton, Franklin C., Pfc,
Eaton, Hamilton D., T/5,
Eaton, Louis, Pfc,
Eaves, Bennie, Pfc,
Ebeling, Robert F., Pfc,
Eberhardt, William H., S/Sgt,
Ebersole, Richard C., Pvt,
Ebert, Arnold L., Sgt,
Ebling, John, Cpl,
Eckel, Joseph A., Cpl,
Eckelberry,Clarence F., Pvt,
Eckels, Louis A., Pvt,
Eckels, William H., Pvt,
Eckerstrom, R. E., Sr., 2nd Lt,
Eckert, Dynwood R., Pvt,
Eckhardt, Lloyd E., S/Sgt,
Eckhart, Lloyd A., Pfc,
Eckman, Albert D., Pfc,
Eckman, Bernard L., Pfc,
Edelinsky, Joseph J., S/Sgt,
Edgar, William F., Pfc,
Edgerton, Edwin J., Pvt,
†Edinger, Donald E., Pfc,
Edmison, Tom L., Pvt,
Edmondson, James T., Sgt,
†Edmonson, Paul J., Pvt,
Edwards, Alton G., S/Sgt,
Edwards, Broudis A., T/4,
Edwards, Cecil, Pfc,
Edwards, Cilie C., Pvt,
Edwards, Calvin R., Pfc,
Edwards, Clifford S., Pfc,
†Edwards, Eddie L., Pfc,
Edwards, Edward R., Pvt,
‡Edwards, Fred R., Pvt,
Edwards, Harry M., Pfc,
Edwards, Irvin J., Sgt,
Edwards, Joseph B., Pvt,
†Edwards, John H., Jr., Pfc,
Edwards, Richard B., Pvt
†Edwards, Robert C., Pfc,
†Edwards, Robert K., Pvt,
Eeds, Broide, Pvt,
Edwards, William L., Sgt,
Egan, Joseph R., Sgt,
Egan, Thomas F., Pfc,
Eggleston, David T., T/5,
Eggleston, Elmer F., Capt,

Eggleston, Henry M., Pfc,
Ehle, Werritt L., Pvt,
Ehlers, Roland A., Pfc,
Ehlert, Theodore M., T/Sgt,
Ehrich, Raymond H., Pfc,
Ehrenreich, James O., Pvt,
*Ehring, Daniel, Pfc,
Ehrhardt, Charles N., Pfc,
Eichelberger, Wilber W., Pfc,
Eichier, Edward R., Pfc,
Eicholtz, Orval G., Pvt,
Eiermann, Herbert C., Pfc,
Eifert, George W., Sgt,
Eilis, Hubert N., S/Sgt,
Eilis, John F., S/Sgt,
Eilis, Lionel G., Pfc,
*Eimen, Loren E., S/Sgt,
Eirhart, Joseph W., Pfc,
†Eirtle, Edward C., Cpl,
Eisenhower, Raymond, Pvt,
Eisenhuth, William C., Pvt,
Eisenzimer, Joe J., T/5,
Eix, Howard W., Pvt,
Elarth, Norman D., Sgt,
Elbin, Herman Z., Pvt,
Elder, Luther B., Pvt,
Eldridge, Russell F., Pvt,
Elevecky, Joseph B., Pvt,
Elevitch, Maurice J., Pvt,
Elfers, Henry J., Pvt,
‡Elffors, Norbert C., Pfc,
Elflein, Oscar, Pfc,
Elfman, William, Pfc,
Elfnan, George C., Pfc,
†Eline, Joseph G., Pvt,
Elixon, J. W., Pvt,
Elke, John A., Sgt,
‡Elkins, Phillip D., Pvt,
‡Ellebracht, Willie L., Pvt,
‡Elledge, Charles R., Pfc,
Elledge, Ernest E., Pvt,
†Eller, Ralph D., Pvt,
Elliot, Earl H., Pfc,
Elliott, Edward M., Pvt,
Elliott, Edward D., Pvt,
Ellinger, Arthur G. W., Pfc,
Ellington, Phillips S., Pfc,
Ellis, Calvin C., 1st Lt,
Ellis, Newton G., T/5,
†Ellis, William, Pfc,
Ellis, Wayne C., Sgt,
†Ellis, William D., Pvt,
Ellis, William L., Cpl,
Ellison, Irving J., 1st Lt,
Ellison, R. L., Pvt,
†Elmore, C. L., Capt,
Elvey, Frederick L., Pvt,
Elwell, John W., Pvt,
Emerich, Arthur L., Pfc,
Emerle, Mathew J., Pfc,
Emerson, Sidney A., Pfc,
†Emilio, Orazio, Sgt,
‡Emmerson, James T., Pvt,
‡Emmons, William F., Pfc,
†Emond, Norman E., Pvt,
Enders, Dennis M., Pfc,
Enders, Theobald L., S/Sgt,
Ends, William E., T/4,
Eneigh, Charles F., Sgt,
Enerson, Harlan S., T/4,
Enes, Clarence L., Pvt,
†Engberg, Robert G., Pvt,
Engebritson, Gisle C., T/5,
Engel, Bert C., 1st Lt,
†Engels, Edward M., Pfc,
England, Donald I., Pvt,
England, Lon L., Cpl,
English, Gordy F., Pfc,
Enke, Lester E., Pfc,
Ennel, John F., Cpl,
Ennis, Clifford J., Pvt,
‡Ennis, George, Jr., Pfc,
†Ensign, Glenn E., Pvt,
Ensley, Albert L., Pfc,
Ensley, John D., Pvt,
Entneier, Charles F., Pfc,
Entwistle, Francis E., Pfc,
Enyart, Edward L., Pvt,
Epperly, Sherman J., Pfc,
Epperson, Thomas N., Jr., Pfc,
Epright, Reeve S., Pfc,
Epstein, Murray, Pfc,
Erauth, Mitchell L., Pvt,
Ericksen, Carl M., Pvt,
Ericssen, Herbert G., Sgt,
Erickson, Svan, Pvt,
†Ermilio, Joseph A., Pvt,
Ernest, Fred W., S/Sgt,
Ernst, Wilbur L., T/5,
‡Erting, Edgar W., Pfc,
†Ertl, Edward R., 1st Lt,
Ertman, Joseph, Cpl,
‡Ervin, Walter R., Pfc,
‡Escontrias, Paul M., Pfc,
Escobar, Francisco S., Jr., Pvt,

†Esenwein, Erich K., Pvt,
Eshelman, John H., Pfc,
Eshbaugh, Raymond C., Sgt,
Esonis, Frank, Pfc,
Espinesa, William C., Cpl,
Esposito, Anthony G., Pvt,
Esposito, James F., Pfc,
Esquibel, Julio G., Pvt,
Essman, John H., Pfc,
Estes, Charlie T., Pvt
Estes, Earl W., Pvt,
Estes, Hayden R., Pvt,
Estes, Luther B., Jr., S/Sgt,
†Estes, Walter R., Pfc,
Estrada, James C., Pvt,
Estrada, Joe, Pvt,
Etheredge, M. B., Jr., Capt,
§Etheridge, Nolain, Pvt,
Etherton, Rudolph D., Pfc,
Ettinger, Harold H., Pvt,
Ettmore, Joseph, Pvt,
Eurolla, Ramon R., T/4
Evanovich, Michael, Cpl,
Evans, Albert J., Pfc,
Evans, Ambross R., Cpl,
Evans, Aubrey J., Pvt,
Evans, Charles E., Pfc,
‡Evans, David L., Pfc,
Evans, Earnest D., Pvt,
Evans, Edgar M., 2nd Lt,
Evans, Edward J., Pvt,
Evans, Everett L., T/4,
†Evans, Glen B., Pvt,
Evans, Harold J., Pvt,
Evans, Henry A., Pfc,
Evans, James L., Pvt,
Evans, Joe D., T/4,
Evans, Kenneth G., Pvt,
Evans, Robert J., Pfc,
†Evans, Thomas R., Pvt,
Evans, William H., S/Sgt,
Evans, Willie C., Pfc,
Eveland, Frank, Pfc,
Everard, James F., Pfc,
Everett, Clyde L., Pvt,
†Everett, Edward A., Pfc,
Everett, James A., Jr., Pvt,
Everett, Joseph P., Pvt,
Everett, Oliver L., Cpl,
Everhart, Harry J., Pfc,
Everhart, Martin, Jr., Pvt,
Evernan, Richard M., Pfc,
Ewald, Harvey H., Pfc,
Ewing, Berwell F., Pfc,
Ewing, Lyle D., Jr., Pvt,
Eyermann, Charles A., Sgt,
Ezell, John M., Pvt,
Ezzi, John L., Pvt,

Fabiano, John N., T/Sgt,
Fabiano, Nicholas E., Pvt,
Fador, Andrew F., Jr., Sgt,
Fagin, James, Pfc,
Fagin, Solomon, Pvt,
Fagon, Charles, Pfc,
Fahnestock, Lee E., Pfc,
*Fahrenbacher, Preis, Pfc,
Fahringer, James A., Pvt,
†Faikowski, Joseph J., Jr., Pvt,
Failas, Francis L., Pvt,
Failer, Frank P., T/5,
Fair, Randall O., Pfc,
*Fairall, Charles L., Pfc,
Fairbanks, Paul L., T/4,
Fairchild, Rila T., Pvt,
†Faires, Harold D., S/Sgt,
Fairlie, George, Pfc,
Faisst, William H., Major,
Fajmon, John R., S/Sgt,
Falco, Joseph P., Pfc,
Falcon, Leslie F., Pfc,
Falcone, Carl, Pvt,
†Falen, Leonard K., Pvt,
Falkner, William E., Pfc,
Fallis, Eddie G., Sgt,
†Fall, Merle R., Pfc,
‡Fallehy, Patrick H., Pvt,
Fallon, Nelson F., Pvt,
Falls, Arne A., Pfc,
Falter, Elwood J., Pvt,
Falvey, Robert E., Pfc,
Falzone, Donald J., Pfc,
Famer, Charles, Pvt
Fancher, Roy E., Pfc,
Fanniff, George J., T/5,
Fannon, Willard A., Sgt,
Faraday, Donald H., Pfc,
†Farber, Abe, Pfc,
Faretto, Raymond J., Pfc,
Fargo, Lynn D., Major,
Faria, George P., Pvt
Faria, Robert C., Pfc,
Farias, John M., Pfc,
Farkas, Eugene J., S/Sgt
†Farley, Herman M., Cpl,

Farley, Thomas, Pvt,
Farmer, Charles W., 2nd Lt
Farmer, Lawrence V., Pvt,
†Farmer, Stanley B., Sgt,
Farnsley, Carl H., Pfc,
Farrell, Addison S., Capt,
Farrell, Charles C., Pfc,
Farrell, Charles H., Pvt,
Farrell, James F., Pfc,
†Farrell, John E., Pvt,
Farrell, Robert, Capt,
Farrell, Warren, Pfc,
Farrell, William, Pfc,
Farrier, Robert F., Pfc,
Farrow, Jimmie L., Pfc,
†Fascett, Frederick N., Pvt,
Fasnacht, Jerome J., Pvt,
Fau, Albert M., Pvt,
Fauber, Buel H., S/Sgt,
Faubion, Driskill S., S/Sgt,
†Fauble, Hollis L., Pvt,
Faucher, Oliver J., Lt Col,
*Faudree, Harry E., Cpl,
†Faught, Robert O., Pvt,
Faulk, Fidele W., Sgt,
Faulkner, Emmett J., Pvt,
Faulks, Lewellyn P., Pfc,
Faunce, Harry F., Sgt,
Faust, Edwin M., Cpl,
Faust, Francis S., Sgt,
†Fausting, Harry J., Pfc
Faver, Wayne B., S/Sgt,
†Fawcett, Harry P., Pvt,
Fay, Robert F., Pvt,
Fazende, Morris J., Pvt,
*Fazida, Alphonse, Pvt,
‡Fazzino, Angelo, Pfc,
Fectman, Robert H., Capt,
†Federico, Frank B., Pvt,
Fegeley, William A., Pvt,
Feehan, William E., Pfc,
Fehr, Charles A., Pfc,
Fehr, Raymond G., Pvt,
Feichtl, John A., Pfc,
Feigelman, Jacob, Pvt,
Feilling, Robert L., Capt,
Feinberg, Louis, Pvt,
Feingold, Albert H., Pvt,
Feinerman, Irving, Pvt.
Feldkamp, Rudolph C., Cpl,
‡Feldman, Harry S., Pvt,
Feldman, John H., Pvt,
Feldt, Alfred V., Sgt,
†Felezzola, Angelo, Pvt,
Felger, Jack E., T/Sgt,
Felix, Leonard G., Pfc,
Feliz, Joseph L., S/Sgt,
Fell, Russell C., S/Sgt,
Fellbaum, Edmund R., Pvt
Feller, Stephen H., T/5,
Felney, John, T/4,
Feltner, Edison L., Pfc,
Felton, Harold J., Sgt,
Felton, James H., S/Sgt,
*Felts, H. C., Pvt,
Feltych, Charles J., Pvt,
Feltz, Levi, Sgt,
Femia, Joseph A., Pvt,
Fennell, Robert P., Sgt,
†Fennesse, James, Pfc,
Fenstermacher, E. W. F., Pvt,
Ference, Steve, Pfc,
Fereshitian, Albert M., T/5,
Feret, Joseph C., Pfc,
Ferguson, Charles R., Pvt,
Ferguson, Douglas R., Pvt
Ferguson, Glen J., Cpl,
Ferguson, Harry C., Pvt,
Ferguson, James C., Pvt,
Ferguson, James P., Pvt,
*Ferguson, Joe D., Pvt,
Ferguson, John A., S/Sgt,
†Ferguson, John W., S/Sgt,
Ferguson, Lloyd G., S/Sgt,
Ferguson, Robert H., Pvt,
Ferguson, Walter A., Pvt,
Ferguson, William H., 2nd Lt,
Ferguson, Worth, Pvt,
Ferioli, Fred B., Pfc,
Fernandez, Cirilo O., Pvt,
Fernandez, Manuel S., Pfc,
Ferner, Daryl A., Pfc
Feroleto, Patrick, Pvt,
Ferranti, Joseph G., Sgt,
Ferrara, Carson, Pvt
Ferrara, Salvatore J., Pvt,
Ferrari, Aldo C., Pvt,
Ferrell, Clyde L., S/Sgt,
Ferrell, Henry A., Pvt,
Ferris, Larry, Pfc,
Ferris, Walter J., Pfc,
Ferro, Samuel J., Pfc,
Ferron, Gordon D., Sgt,
Fertig, Marlin G., Pfc,
†Fetterman, Max W., Pfc,

† Killed in Action. * Prisoner of War. ‡ Missing in Action. § Died of Wounds.

Fetters, Earnest G., Pvt,
Feueknabe, Sheppard, Pfc,
Fiami, Ralph J., Pvt,
Ficheria, John, Pvt,
Fickle, Arthur R., Pfc
Fiddelke, Joseph W., Pvt,
Fidler, Thomas M., Jr., Pvt,
Fiebelkorn, Joseph W., Pfc,
Fiegler, August J., S/Sgt,
Fields, William M., Pfc,
§Fieser, Adolph D., Pfc,
Fife, James R., Cpl,
Fife, Norman T., Pvt,
Fifer, Harry G., S/Sgt,
Fifield, William N., S/Sgt,
Figuly, John, T/5,
Filipek, Walter W., Sgt,
‡Fillipe, Henry L., Pvt,
Finch, Eugene H., Pfc
Finch, Paul J., Pvt,
Finch, Ralph E., T/Sgt,
Fingland, Harold T., Pvt,
‡Fink, Leo J., Pfc,
Fink, Roy C., Pvt,
Finkbeiner, Clifford E., Pfc,
Finkler, Isadore, Pvt,
Finley, Arthur C., T/4,
‡Finnerty, Thomas P., T/4,
Finnessy, Albert C., Pvt
†Finney, Eldon L., Pvt,
Finney, Ralph D., Pfc,
Finnie, Willard, Sgt,
Finnigan, Joseph, Pfc
Fioramonti, Rocco C., Pfc,
Fiore, Durant L., Pvt,
Firlik, James E., Pvt,
Fischer, Aaron Z., Pvt,
Fischer, Fred, S/Sgt,
Fischer, Harold C., Pfc,
Fischer, Joseph B., Pvt,
†Fish, Orman O., 2nd Lt,
Fisher, Alvin E., S/Sgt,
Fisher, Albert, Pvt,
Fisher, Cecil R., 2nd Lt,
Fisher, Donald E., Cpl,
†Fisher, George C., Pfc,
Fisher, James H., Sr., Pfc,
Fisher, Jerome, Pvt,
Fisher, J. L., S/Sgt,
Fisher, Joseph F., Pfc,
‡Fisher, Omer R., Sgt,
Fisher, William A., Pvt,
Fishman, Louis, T/5,
Fisk, Thomas E., Pfc,
Fisk, William P., Sgt,
Fite, Artie E., S/Sgt,
Fite, George P., T/5,
Fite, Oscar S., Pvt,
Fitzgerald, Clifford J., Pvt,
Fitzgerald, David D., Pfc,
Fitzgerald, Olin B., Pfc,
Fitzgerald, Thomas P., Pfc,
Fitzpatrick, Frank, Pfc,
Fitzpatrick, John T., Pfc,
Fitzsimmons, Fred A., Pfc,
Fitzsimmons, Harold S., Pvt,
Fiumara, Matthew J., Pvt,
Fiume, Leonard J., Pvt,
Flack, Adam A., Pvt,
Flach, Curtis L., Pvt,
Flaherty, George M., Pfc,
Flaherty, Michael E., Pfc,
Flamer, Michael J., Pvt,
Flanagan, Daniel R., Pvt,
†Flanagan, Joseph F., Pfc,
Flanary, Homer, Pvt,
§Flanigan, Maynard F., Pvt,
Flanigan, Paul J., Pfc,
Flanigan, Robert F., Pvt,
*Flannery, Thomas A., Pfc,
Flaten, Clifford O., Sgt,
†Flatraker, Peter, Pfc,
Flatt, Willis E., Pfc,
Flattery, John J., Pfc
Flavin, John T., Pvt,
Fleck, Lloyd H. G., Pvt,
Fleeman, Jerome, Capt,
Fleenor, Lon, Pfc,
Fleenor, Paul E., Pfc,
Fleet, Robert L., Capt,
Flehan, Henry, Pfc,
Fleming, Beryl, Pvt,
‡Fleming, Charles D., S/Sgt,
†Fleming, Joseph C., Sgt,
Fleming, Robert L., Pvt,
Flender, Stanley J., Pfc,
Flesher, Allan E., T/5,
Flesher, Walter D., T/5,
†Fleszewski, Edward J., Pvt,
†Fletcher, Horace E., Pfc,
Fletcher, John R., Pvt,
†Fletcher, Mearle E., Pvt,
‡Fleury, Edward P., Sgt,
Flick, Wayne L., Pfc,
†Flickenger, Charles C., Pvt,
†Flinchbaugh, James T., Pfc,
Flis, Joseph S., Pfc,
Floistad, Victor P., Cpl,
Flores, Alberto T., Pvt,
†Flores, Alex, Pfc,
Flores, Camilo, Pfc,
Flory, Lawrence E., Pvt,
Flowers, Claude A., Sgt,
Flowers, Ervin C., 2nd Lt
Flowers, George P., Pfc,
Flowers, Guy L., Pfc,
Floyd, Edmund W., Pvt,
Floyd, Edward C., Pfc,
‡Floyd, James S., Pvt,
Floyd, Vannie O., Pvt,
Fluck, Roger E., Pvt,
Flynn, James J., Pvt,
§Flynn, James P., 1st Lt,
§Flynn, Joe B., Pfc,
Flynn, Louis, Pfc,
Flynn, Patrick H., T/5,
Flynn, Robert L., Pvt,
Flynn, Stephen E., T/5,
†Flynn, Walther J., Pfc,
Fockler, Bryce W., Sgt,
Foell, John E., S/Sgt,
†Foglesong, Harvey V., Pvt,
†Foglia, Reno V., Pfc,
Foister, Shelby, Pfc,
Foisy, Jean E., Pvt,
Foley, Michael, Sgt,
Foley, Ross R., Pvt,
Folio, John J., Pfc,
Follett, Paul M., Pvt,
Follin, Lee M., Pvt,
Foltyn, Theodore P., T/5,
Foltz, Wayne E., S/Sgt,
‡Foncannon, Robert J., Pfc,
Fonda, Lawyer E., Pvt,
Foote, Louie G., Cpl,
Foote, Walter A., Pvt,
Foote, Wells D., Jr., Pvt
Foppe, Robert H., Pfc,
Forastiere, Michael J., Pfc,
§Forbes, LaVerne, Pvt,
Forbis, Edward C., Pvt,
Forcey, Samuel A., S/Sgt
†Ford, Benjamin F., Pfc,
Ford, Clayton S., Pfc,
Ford, George G., Pvt,
Ford, James L., Pfc,
Ford, Lawrence C., S/Sgt
Ford, Rex V., Pvt,
Ford, Thomas J., Jr., Pvt,
Ford, Wilbur A., Pvt,
Ford, William A., T/4,
Forde, Harold I., Pvt,
Fordice, Vane C., Pvt, I
Forehand, Edgar E., T/Sgt,
Foreman, Patrick H., Pvt,
Foret, Harold J., Cpl,
Forgash, Herbert L., Cpl,
Forgety, Ned H., Pvt,
Forkell, Roland A., Pfc,
*Forkin, John V., Pvt,
§Forman, Sidney, Pfc,
Forney, Howard G., Pvt,
Forni, Elmer J., Pfc,
Forni, Louis, Sgt,
Forrester, Boyce L., S/Sgt,
Forrey, Harry D., Pfc,
Forsell, Richard A., Pfc,
Forster, Floyd W., Pfc,
†Forsther, Paul, Sgt,
Forsyth, Claud W., Pvt,
Forte, Edward M., Pvt,
Fortier, Leo C., Pvt,
Fortin, Napoleon, T/5,
†Fortunato, Donald A., Pvt,
Fortunato, Pasquale, Pvt,
Fortune, Dominic R., Pfc,
Fortune, Thomas E., Pvt,
Forzano, Joseph, Cpl,
†Foss, Howard E., Pfc,
†Fossum, Burton H., Sgt,
Foster, Carl G., 2nd Lt,
†Foster, David G., Pvt,
Foster, Eugene H., Pvt,
Foster, James E., T/Sgt,
Foster, Lawrence F., Pvt,
‡Foster, Lloyd G., Pfc,
Foster, Luther E., Pfc,
Foster, Stanley E., Pvt,
Foster, Thomas M., Pvt,
Foster, William T., Pvt,
Foster, Windfield L., Pfc,
Fotis, Spire, T/Sgt,
Fotusky, Edward J., Pfc,
Fouler, Anthony G., Pfc,
Foulkes, Walter C., Pvt,
Fournier, Charles D., Pvt,
Fournier, Edmond P., Pfc,
Foust, Wilbur K., Pfc,
Fowler, Fred A., Pvt,
§Fowler, George E., Sgt,
Fowler, Stephen B., Pfc
Fowler, Thomas L., Pvt,
Fox, Billy C., Pvt,
Fox, Eleston, Pfc,
†Fox, Fred C., Pvt,
Fox, Hubert C., Pfc,
Fox, John M., Pfc,
†Fox, Joseph, Pvt,
Fox, Kenneth E., Pfc,
Fox, Richard K., Jr., Pvt
Fox, Thomas F., Pfc,
Foy, Thomas D., Jr., T/4,
Fraber, John W., Jr., Pvt,
†Frajman, Mark M., Pvt,
Frampton, Lewis J., Pvt,
†France, Benjamin A., Pfc,
France, Howard L., Pfc,
Francis, Doran F., Pvt,
Francis, Edward U., Pvt,
Francis, James M., Pvt,
Francis, Jordon, Pvt,
Francisco, Forrest D., Pvt,
‡Franck, Ralph W., S/Sgt,
Franco, Maurice G., Pvt,
Frank, Henry F., Pvt,
Frank, John W., Pvt,
†Frank, Leon, Sgt,
Frank, Robert C., Pvt,
‡Frankel, Albert, Pvt,
Franklin, Alvie L., Pfc,
Franklin, Carroll C., S/Sgt,
†Franklin, Edward L., Pvt,
Franklin, Robert E., Pfc,
Franklin, Robert E., Pvt,
Franklin, Robert G., Pfc,
†Franklin, Wesley B., Sgt,
Franks, Clarence W., Pfc,
Franks, Dan H., T/4,
Franz, Richard J., 2nd Lt,
†Frappier, Richard E., Pvt,
Fraser, David, Pvt,
Fraser, William J., Pvt,
Frasier, Harold K., Pfc,
Frates, Ernest J., Pvt,
Frates, Francis, T/5,
Frattine, Eugene F., Pvt,
Frazier, Fred W., Pfc,
†Frazier, Gilbert L., Pvt,
†Frazier, Homer L., Cpl,
Frazier, Raymond H., Pvt,
Frechette, Ernest A., 2nd Lt,
Frederick, Edward, Pfc,
†Frederick, John E., Pvt,
Frederick, John J., S/Sgt
Fredine, Raymond D., Pvt,
†Fredrick, Henry P., Sgt,
Fredrick, John J., 1st Lt,
Fredrick, Oscar L., Pvt,
‡Freed, Harry J., Pvt,
Freedman, Maxwell, Pvt,
Freeland, Leonard J., Pfc,
Freeman, Ival E., S/Sgt,
‡Freeman, Jack D., Pvt,
Freeman, John, Pfc,
Freeman, Louis F., Pvt,
Freeman, Robert B., T/5,
Freene, Donald O., T/5,
Freiburger, Walter A., T/4,
Freidman, Francis J., Pfc,
Freiman, Herman L., Pvt,
Fren, John J., Pvt,
French, Charles R., Pvt,
†French, Roscoe G., Pvt,
Frenson, Robert J., Pfc,
Frenzel, William R., Jr., Pfc,
†Freshwater, Clarence B., Pfc,
Frey, Kelvey N., Pvt,
Frey, Leonard J., Pfc,
Frey, Lory M., Jr., Pfc,
Fridgen, Robert J., Pvt,
†Fried, Isadore, Pvt,
Friederich, Lambert P., 2nd Lt,
Friedman, Bernard, Pfc,
†Friedman, Edwin R., Pfc,
Friedman, George M., Pfc,
Friedman, Harry, Pfc,
Friedman, Jacob G., Cpl,
†Friedman, Mart, Sgt,
Friend, James A., Pvt,
†Friends, Edward J., Pfc,
Fries, Fredrick J., 2nd Lt,
Friese, Forest R., Pvt,
Friesen, John D., Cpl,
Fringer, Rodney J., Pfc,
Frink, Charles S., Pvt,
Frisbee, Robert K., S/Sgt,
Frisoli, John A., Pfc,
Fristed, Charles H., S/Sgt,
Frith, Melvin N., Pvt,
†Fritts, Jesse E., Pfc,
Fritz, Francis J., Pvt,
Frizzell, Thomas P., Pvt,
Froeber, Walter A., S/Sgt,
Froehlich, Andrew A., 1st Lt
Froloff, William, T/5,
Fronhofer, Leonard, Jr., Pvt,
Fry, Leonard L., Pvt,
Frye, Joseph M., S/Sgt,
†Fryman, Ernest, Jr., Pvt,
Fudge, Thomas J., Pfc,
Fuentes, Victor, Pvt,
§Fuernisen, Charles H., Pvt,
Fuith, Fred, T/4,
Fulerson, Mervin A., Sgt,
Fulford, Hubert F., Pvt,
Fulkerson, James W., Pfc,
Fulks, Lawrence H., Pvt
Fulks, Oscar L., Pvt,
Fullman, Bernard J., Pfc,
Fuller, Arthur R., Pvt,
Fuller, Loyd W., Pfc,
Fuller, Russell H., T/5,
Fuller, Wayne A., Sgt,
Fuller, Woodrow, Pvt,
Fullman, Gregory P., Pfc,
†Fullmer, Arthur, Pvt,
Fulmer, Norris L., Pfc,
Fulton, Frederick S., Cpl
Fults, Russell W., Pfc,
Funaro, Benjamin P., Pfc,
§Funchion, Kenneth C., Cpl,
Fundakowski, John, Pvt,
†Furgason, David C., Jr., Pvt,
Furgason, Everett W., Pfc,
Furgason, Gordon L., Pvt,
Furlan, Martin, Cpl,
Furlo, Frank A., 1st Lt,
Furman, Michael J., Pvt,
Furry, Robert S., Cpl,
†Furseth, Floyd L., Pfc,
Fusco, Joseph, Pfc,
Fusco, Michael A., Pfc,

Gabally, Joseph E., Sgt,
Gable, George R., T/4,
Gackowski, Gerald J., Pfc,
Gaddis, Carl E., Pvt,
Gadomski, Hendy, Pvt,
Gaffney, Edward J., Pfc,
Gage, Ward E., Capt,
‡Gagnier, Camille A., Pfc,
Gaige, Albert C., T/5,
Gaines, Ben M., T/5,
Gains, Jack E., Cpl,
Gair, Donald O., 2nd Lt,
Gaither, Francis S., Jr., S/Sgt,
Gajda, Cassmer S., Pfc,
Gajewsik, Edward J., Pvt,
Galabis, Tony, Pvt,
Gale, James H., Jr., Sgt,
Gale, William E., Pvt,
Galenti, August S., Pvt,
Galer, Raymond E., Pfc,
†Galgzia, Fred R., Sgt,
‡Galimore, Arnold W., S/Sgt,
Galioto, Steven M., Pvt,
Gall, Frank L., Pvt,
‡Gall, Leo, Jr., Pvt,
Gallagher, Edward J., Pvt,
Gallagher, Neil F., Sgt,
Gallagher, Lesetr D., Pfc,
Gallagher, Loren E., Pvt,
†Gallegos, Joe M., Pfc,
Gallegos, Manuel, Sgt
Gallelli, Albert J., Pfc,
Gallello, Frank A., Pfc,
†Gallipeau, Bernard W., Pvt,
Galliani, Dominic, Pvt,
Gallik, John M., Pvt,
*Gallis, Lawrence V., Pvt,
Gallo, Ralph J., Pvt,
Gallo, John C., Pvt,
†Galloway, Henry J., Pfc,
Galus, Thomas A., Cpl
Galvroath, Duncan H., Pvt,
Gamber, Charles W., Pfc,
Gambill, Arnold, Pvt
Gamble, Charlie P., Pvt,
Gamble, Dale O., Pfc,
†Gamez, Joaquin S., Pfc,
Gane, Donald W., S/Sgt,
†Ganea, John, Pfc,
Gann, Mart J., T/4,
Gano, Carl K., Sgt,
Ganser, Jerome J., T/Sgt,
Gantert, William T., Pvt,
Gantz, Joseph D., Pfc,
Ganz, Sisto A., Pvt,
Garant, George A., Pvt,
Garavailia, Edward, Pvt,
Garber, Max, Pfc
†Garber, Michael, Pfc,
Garber, Robert F., Pvt,
Garcia, Joseph, T/4
Garcia, Paulo R., Pfc,
Garcia, Randolph O., Sgt,
†Gardinello, Peter M., Pfc,
Gardner, Carl C., Jr., 1st Lt,
Gardner, Cecil S., Pvt,
Gardner, Eugene M., Pvt,
Gardner, Gerald L., Pfc,
Gardner, Lawrence C., Pfc,
Gardner, Leslie E., T/Sgt,
Gardner, Lloyd J., Pvt,
Gardner, Madison D., 2nd Lt,
Gardner, Virgil, Cpl,
Garfoot, Lester R., Pvt,
Garganc, Charles J., Pfc,
Gargars, Frank, Pvt
Garland, Kermit R., Sgt,
Garlick, James W., Pvt
Garman Selvic D., Pfc,
Garner, Joseph N., S/Sgt,
Garner, Harold F., Pvt,
Garner, Leslie J., Pfc,
Garo, Louis W., Pvt,
Garofalo, Mario A., Pfc,
‡Garone, Anthony P., Sgt,
Garrard, James B., T/5,
Garre, Gaetano O., Sgt,
Garrett, Ben T., Pvt,
Garrett, Carton R., Pfc,
Garrett, Delbert, Pfc,
Garrett, Everett, Pvt,
†Garrett, Luther, Sgt,
Garrett, Orlow F., Jr., Pfc,
Garrett, Ralph C., Jr., Pfc,
Garrett, Wayne E., Pvt,
Garris, Otha C., Pvt,
Garrison, Ray, Pfc,
Garrison, Winfred, T/4,
Garritano, Nicholas, Pfc,
Gartenlaub, Paul, Pvt,
Gartner, Herbert P., Pvt
Gartin, Lester L., T/4,
Garton, Edgar A., Pvt,
Garver, Leslie A., Pfc
Garvey, Joe V., Sgt,
†Garzo, Anthony J., Pfc,
Case., Eugene J., Sgt,
Gasik, Charles J., Pfc,
Gasmovic, Raymond R., Sgt,
Gaspard, Barney G., Pfc
Gasparro, Arthur A., Pfc,
Gast, Emil O., Pvt,
Gastenguay, Eugene, Pvt,
Gataletto, Dominick J., Pfc,
Gates, Donald H., Pvt,
Gates, William A., Pfc,
Gatlin, Carl R., T/5,
Gatti, Joe, Sgt,
Gatto, John A., Capt,
†Gaubatz, Clifford S., Sgt,
Gaudet, Clarence J., Pvt,
Gaudet, Gerald, Pvt,
Gaudreau, Domina D., Pfc,
Gaulrapp, Richard P., Pfc,
Gauntt, Jesse C., Pfc,
Gaura, Anthony L., Pvt
Gaus, Anthony L., Pvt,
Gausnell Ruben J., Sgt,
Gauthier, Edward A., Pfc,
Gauthier, Felix H., Pvt,
Gavak, Stephen C., Pvt,
†Gavalyas, Louis C., 2nd Lt,
Gay, Aubrey J., Cpl,
*Gay, George H., Pfc,
Gay, Jack D., Pvt
Gaylon, John W., Pfc,
Gaylord, Kenneth H., Pfc,
Gayzur, Vincent J., S/Sgt,
†Gazda, Edward L., Pfc,
†Geades, James, Pfc,
Gebhard, Raymond H., Pvt,
Geckler, Duane H., Pvt,
Gee, Merrill T., Cpl,
‡Geer, Herschel J., Pfc,
Gehret, Kenneth G., Pvt,
Gehrig, Edmund J., Sgt,
Gehrig, Lionel L., Pfc,
Gehrstz, Joseph G., Pvt,
Geible, Harry F., Pvt
Geiger, William C., Pvt,
Geighes, John J., Pfc,
Geil, Edward E., Jr., Pfc,
Geisler, Earl A., Pfc,
Gele, Charles, Pvt,
†Geller, James A., Pfc,
Geller, Robert E., Pvt,
Gelroth, Albert H., Pvt
Geneder, Louis, Pvt,
†Genga, Theodore S., Pfc,
Gener, Edward P., 1st Lt,
Genem, Michael G., Pfc,
Genito, Nicholas H., Pfc,
Geninatti, Raymond C., Pvt,
Gennella, Thomas J., Pvt,
Gentee, Victor, Pvt,
Gentile, Frank, Pfc,
Gentiluomo, Nickolas J., T/4,

† Killed in Action. * Prisoner of War. ‡ Missing in Action. § Died of Wounds.

IN WORLD WAR II 517

Gentry, Edward J., Pvt,
Gentry, Jimmie H., Pfc,
Gentry, Johnnie E., Pfc,
Gentry, Loren J., Pfc,
George, Aubrey L., Pvt,
George, Darrell D., Pfc,
George, Donald F., Cpl,
George, Robert J., Pfc,
Geraci, Gust, Sgt,
Gerahian, Kearny, Pvt,
Gerakaris, Harold J., Pfc,
Gerard, Clarence N., Cpl
Gerdes, John W., T/5,
Geren, Olen C., Pfc,
Gerdis, Laurence G., T/5,
Gerfen, William W., Pvt,
Gergel, Steve P., S/Sgt,
†Gerhardt, Charles P., Pfc,
Gerhardt, John H., S/Sgt,
‡Gericki, Robert H., Pfc,
†Gerken, Edgar H., Pfc,
Gerkins, Eugene B., Pfc,
†Germain, George D., 1st Lt,
*Germain, Robert F., Pfc,
†German, Clifford H., Pvt,
†Gerschutz, Herbert E., Cpl,
Gerster, Jewell R., Pfc,
Gerstein, Sol, Pvt
‡Gerstung, Ralph C., Pfc,
†Gertz, Jack I., T/5,
Gervasoni, Fred R., Pvt,
Getz, Carl W., Jr., Pfc,
†Getz, Roy C., Pfc,
Getzfread, John J., Jr., Pvt
Geyer, Edwin W., Pfc,
†Geyer, Miles R., Pfc,
Gdowski, Joseph L., S/Sgt
Ghierso, Lloyd J., Sgt,
Giacomelli, Joseph P., Pvt,
Giaimo, Rosario J., Pvt,
Giammico, Anthony, T/5,
Giampa, Joseph N., Jr., Pvt,
Giannuzzi, Vincent J., Pfc,
†Giardina, Samuel A., Pvt,
Gibbons, August A., Pfc,
Gibson, Brooks E., Pvt,
Gibson, Charles E., Cpl,
Gibson, Donald S., 2nd Lt,
†Gibson, Edward A., Pvt,
Gibson, Eric G., T/5,
Gibson, Lester D., Pvt,
†Gibson, Stephen V., Pvt,
Giddens, Bradus, Pvt,
†Giear, Francis R., Pvt,
Giergielwicz, Edward J., Pvt,
Gieringer, Warren L., Pfc,
Gieser, William H., Pvt,
Giffes, Costas, Pfc,
Gifford, Coy G., T/Sgt,
‡Gifford, Earl D., Pfc,
Giger, Albert R., Cpl,
†Gilbeck, Marvin O., Pfc,
§Gilbert, Calvin L., Pvt,
Gilbert, Hennon, 1st Lt,
Gilbert, William E., Pvt,
Gilberson, Glen C., Sgt,
Gile, Floyd H., S/Sgt,
Gilfus, Leroy J., Pfc,
Gill, Alfred G., Pvt,
†Gill, John E., Pfc,
Gill, Joseph N., Sgt,
Gill, Robert E., Pfc,
Gill, Stephen, Pvt,
Gill, Walter L., 2nd Lt,
*Gillenwater, Rex E., Pvt,
Gillespie, Paul A., Pvt,
Gillespie, William C., Pfc,
†Gilli, Domenico A., Pvt,
Gilligan, Thomas P., Pfc,
†Gilliland, Vivan C., Pvt,
Gillis, Lawson D., S/Sgt,
Gills, Clarence W., Pfc,
*Gilmore, Harold T., Pvt,
Gilmore, Martin L., Jr., T/5,
*Gilroy, Robert, 1st Lt,
‡Gingrich, Kenneth T., 1st Lt,
Ginn, Doyle L., Pvt,
Ginneman, Thomas J., Pvt,
†Ginnetti, Louis, Pfc,
Ginter, Edward H., Pfc,
†Ginter, Henry W., Pvt,
Ginther, Harold, Jr., Pfc,
Giordane, Salvatore G., Pfc,
Giordano, Nicholas A., Pvt,
Giordano, Alexander J., Pvt,
Giorgo, Peppino, Jr., Pvt,
Giraca, Philip J., Pvt,
Giraitis, Joseph, Pfc,
†Girard, Francis L., Pfc,
Girard, Hervey W., Pvt,
Girvin, Gilbert E., Pvt,
†Githens, George H., Pfc,
Givan, Elmer L., Pvt,
Givens, William R., Pvt,
Giza, Frank J., 1st Lt,
Gladstone, Lyle E., Pvt,
Glantz, Hyman M., Pfc,
Glascock, Paul M., Pfc,
Glaser, Benjamin, Pfc,
Glaser, Frank J., Pvt
Glasgow, John B., Cpl,
Glass, Amos W., Pvt
Glass, Guy V., Pfc,
Glass, Edward B., Pfc,
†Glass, James W., Pvt,
†Glass, William A., Pvt,
Glatt, Lowell D., Pvt
Glatzmaier, Andrew J., T/4,
Glaza, Elmer M., Sgt,
Gleason, Dana W., Pvt,
Gleason, Lawrence W., Pfc,
Gleason, Thomas J., Jr., Sgt,
Gleason, William M., Jr., Pvt,
Gleich, Elmer F., Pvt,
Glenn, Charlie C., Pfc,
Glenn, Loster M., Pfc,
Gleue, Fred C., Cpl,
Gliniewicz, Demund C., Pfc
Glisson, Edgar, Pvt,
Glor, Walter, Pvt,
Glover, Robert L., Pfc,
‡Gluck, Donald E., Pfc,
Glynos, Paul D., Pfc,
Gmurek, Henry W., Sgt,
Gnat, Thomas H., Pvt,
†Gnecco, Robert J., Pfc,
Gniadek, Walter A., T/5,
Goad, Lawrence T., T/5,
Goble, Elvis, Jr., Pvt,
Goble, Wesley E., Pfc,
Goble, William E., Pfc,
Goblinger, Richard B., Pvt,
†Goche, Raymond B., S/Sgt,
Godey, Harold E., Jr., Pfc,
Godfrey, Samuel W., S/Sgt,
Godwin, John J., S/Sgt,
Goebel, Murray J., 1st Sgt,
Goen, Henry J., Pfc,
†Goerlitz, Adam, T/4,
Goetz, Mowry E., Jr., Cpl,
Goff, Arthur, Pfc,
Goff, Duane R., Pvt,
Goff, Hallie L., Pfc,
Goings, Alenzo S., Jr., Pvt,
Goins, Kelso, T/4,
†Gold, Alfred, Pvt,
Gold, Edward L., Pfc,
†Goldberg, Joel H., T/5,
Goldbert, William, Pfc,
†Goldby, Orrin E., Pfc,
Golden, Irving, Pvt,
Golden, James V., Pvt,
‡Goldman, Harold, Pfc,
Goldman, Hyman, Pvt
Goldman, James J., Pfc,
†Goldman, Kenneth E., Pfc,
†Goldman, Levi, Pvt,
Goldman, Lloyd E., Pvt,
†Goldsmith, Chester N., Pfc,
Goldsmith, Edward, Pvt,
Goldsmith, Joseph, Pvt,
§Goldstein, Carman, Pfc,
§Goldstein, Carman, Pfc,
Goldstein, Herbert, Sgt
Goldstein, Joseph, Pfc,
Goldstein, William, Pvt,
Golias, John F., Pfc,
Golightly, James G., Pfc,
Golojuck, Frank H., Pfc,
Golon, John S., Pvt,
Goll, Walter, Pvt
‡Golla, Raymond T., Pfc,
Golles, Leon, Pfc,
Goltrie, James V., Pvt,
Golub, Carl, Pvt
Gombar, George J., Cpl,
†Gombecs, Steven J., Pfc,
Gomez, Domingo, Pfc,
†Gomez, Isador, Pfc,
Gomez, John P., Pfc,
‡Gomez, Ramon V., Pfc,
Gomez, Raymond R., Pvt,
Gomoll, Frederick W., Pvt,
Gondorchin, Peter, Pfc,
Gonzales, Claudio, Pvt,
Gonzales, Conzaglo J., Pfc,
Gonzales, Hector, Sgt,
Gonzales, Henry I., Pfc,
†Gonzales, Jose C., Pfc,
Gonzales, Joseph M., Pvt,
Gonzales, Leopoldo, Pfc,
Gonzales, Oscar T., Pvt
Gooch, Wallace V., Cpl,
Good, Bale V., T/4,
Good, Richard J., Pvt,
Goode, Roy V., Sgt,
Goode, Charles W., Sgt,
Goodell, Arthur E., Pfc,
Goodhart, Merle S., Pfc,
Goodfellow, Frank E., Pvt,
Goodfox, Lawrence, Pfc
‡Goodhines, Carl P., Pvt,
†Goodin, Gale O., Pfc,
Goodier, Donald R., Pvt,
Goodin, Gerald G., Pfc
Goodin, Hayward, 2nd Lt,
Goodin, Martin L., Pvt,
Goodman, James, Pvt,
†Goodman, Linton, Pfc,
Goodman, Robert H., T/Sgt,
Goodman, Solomon, Pvt,
Goodrich, Donald A., Pfc,
Gookin, Ross F., Pvt,
Goran, James, Pfc,
Goranson, Sam, Pvt,
Gordon, Edward T., Pvt,
Gordon, Francis L., Pvt,
†Gordon, Harold W., Pvt,
Gordon, L. E., Pfc,
Gordon, Robert H., Pfc,
Gordon, William E., Pvt,
§Gordon, William H., Pfc,
Gordon, Vance H., Pvt
Gordon, Yates N., Pvt,
Gore, Charles J., Pvt
Gorecki, Edward T., S/Sgt,
Gorelek, Andrew, Pvt,
Gorman, Bartley A., Pvt,
Gorman, Carroll E., Pfc,
Gorman, Harry C., Sgt,
Gorman, Joseph A., Pvt,
Gorman, Louis J., Pvt,
Gorman, Robert A., Pvt,
Gormley, David C., Pfc,
Gorobetz, Milton L., Sgt,
Gorobetz, Seymour, Pvt
Gorrow, Harold R., Pfc
Gorsuch, Ralph E., T/5,
Gorton, Leonard J., S/Sgt,
Gory, Frank A., Pfc,
Goslin, Henry B., Pfc,
Goslow, George H., 1st Lt,
Gosnell, Charlie R., Pvt,
Goss, Billy W., Pfc,
Goss, Robert, Pfc,
Goss, William E., Jr., Pfc,
Gosselin, Leo W., Pfc,
Gossett, Lamar, S/Sgt,
†Gottlieb, Norman H., Pvt,
Gottsacker, Eugene J., Sgt,
Gottschall, Kenneth W., Pfc,
Gould, Charles H., Pfc,
Gould, Roger C., T/5,
Goulet, Lester R., Pvt,
Gourde, Conrad R., Pvt,
Gouty, John L., Pfc,
†Gowans, Neil, Pvt,
*Gowen, John W., Pvt,
Gowin, Frank L., Pvt
Grabert, Donald L., Pvt,
†Grabill, Max D., Pvt,
Graboski, Alfred H., Pvt,
Grabowski, Ralph S., Pfc
Grace, Cornelius J., Jr., Capt,
Grace, Joseph M., Pfc,
Grace, Larry E., Pvt,
Grace, Lawrence, Pvt,
Grace, Ray V., Pvt,
Gracey, George G., Pvt,
Grady, John R., Pvt,
Graefe, Vernon O., Pvt,
Graf, Howard, Pvt,
†Graham, Alfred W., Sgt,
Graham, Alfred W., Pvt,
Graham, Alvin T., Cpl,
Graham, Earl L., Pfc,
Graham, Elmer G., Pvt,
Graham, Eugene B., 2nd Lt,
Graham, Harold E., T/4,
Graham, James H., Pfc,
Graham, Jessie, Cpl,
Graham, John B., Pvt
Graham, Leon F., Pfc,
Graham, Ross S., Pfc,
Graham, Sam B., Pfc,
Graham, Wade, Cpl,
Graham, William T., Pfc
Grainger, Vernon J., T/5,
Grambowitz, Edward W., Pvt,
†Gramsky, Walter, Pfc,
Grandchamp, John J., Pfc,
†Grande, Anthony A., Pvt,
Granger, Elmer W., Pvt,
Granillo, Juan T., Pvt,
Granlund, Warren A., S/Sgt,
Granowski, Stanley A., Pfc,
Grantham, Melton, Sgt,
Grant, Arthur, Pvt
Grant, Earsel M., Pvt,
Grant, Joseph G. H., Pvt,
Grasso, Joseph J., Pvt
Grasso, Peter J., Pvt,
Grates, Sylvester P., T/5,
Gratt, Walter S., T/5,
Gratz, Charles A., Pvt,
Grau, Nelson W., T/5,
Graubman, Harold, Pvt,
Gravely, Thomas B., Pvt
Graves, Jessie M., Sgt,
Graves, Lucein, Pfc,
Graves, Harlow, Jr., Cpl
Graves, Melvyn F., Pfc,
Graves, William C., III, Pfc,
Gray, Bruce E., Pvt,
Gray, Charles E., Pfc,
Gray, Charles G., Pvt
Gray, Clyde M., Pvt
Gray, Edwin G., Pvt,
Gray, Frederick R., Pvt,
Gray, Harold, Pfc,
Gray, Horace W., Pfc,
Gray, Kenneth F., Pvt,
Gray, Robert F., Cpl,
Gray, Thomas F., Sgt,
Gray, William C., Pvt,
Gray, Willie, Pvt,
Graziano, Peter J., Cpl,
Greager, Thomas F., S/Sgt,
Greathouse, Cecil, Pfc,
Greathouse, Marcus S., Pvt,
Greaves, Frank C., T/4,
Grecho, Paul P., Pvt,
Greco, Angelo J., Pvt,
Greco, Frank, Pvt
Greco, Guiseppe V., Pfc,
†Green, Clarence J., T/5,
Green, Claude P., Pvt,
Green, Clifford R., Pvt,
Green, Edward, Pvt,
Green, Garney H., Pvt,
Green, Hugh, T/5,
*Green, James C., Pfc,
Green, James I., Pvt,
Green, Mallory J., Pfc
Green, Purdy H., S/Sgt,
Green, Ralph A., T/5,
Green, Ralph E., Jr., Pvt,
Green, Robert P., Sgt,
†Green, Walter C., Sgt,
Green, William R., S/Sgt,
†Greenberg, Irvin, Pfc,
*Greenberg, Mitchell, Pvt,
*Greene, Donald D., Pvt,
Greene, James H., Capt,
Greene, Kenneth M., 1st Lt,
Greene, Leon, Pvt,
Greene, William C., Pvt,
Greeney, Charles F., Pfc,
Greenfield, William, Jr., Pfc,
Greenholtz, Harold, Pvt,
Greenhouse, Arthur A., Pfc,
Greenman, Leo, Pvt,
†Greenstein, Arthur, Pfc,
Greenwald, Warren A., T/5,
Greenwood, Ben P., 1st Lt,
Greenwood, Charles E., Pvt,
Greenwood, Lawrence W., Sgt,
Greenwood, Lionel H., S/Sgt,
Greer, George, 1st Sgt,
Greer, Harold E., Major,
Greer, Robert B., S/Sgt,
Gregg, Roy A., Pfc,
Gregoire, Florian J., Pvt,
Gregory, Gradon F., Jr., Pvt,
†Gregory, James R., Pvt,
Gregory, Robert B., Sgt,
Greinder, Robert F., Pfc,
Gremillion, Joseph E., Pvt
†Grener, Kenneth, Pfc,
Grenier, Joseph A., Pfc,
Gresdky, David, Pfc,
Gressett, Charles A., Sgt,
Greway, Charles E., Pfc,
Grewe, Walter, Pvt,
Grider, Fredrick J., Pfc,
Gribbs, Molder, Pfc,
Griewski, Bernard F., Pfc,
Griffee, John M., Pvt,
†Griffin, Elliott J., Pvt,
Griffin, Charles L., Pfc,
Griffin, Earl, Pvt,
Griffin, Henry T., Pvt,
Griffin, James W., Pvt,
Griffin, Karl R., Pvt,
Griffin, Lee W., T/4,
Griffin, Loyal E., Pvt,
‡Griffin, Paul D., Pvt,
Griffin, Roy B., Pvt,
Griffis, Thomas E., Jr., Pvt,
Griffit, Joseph R., Sr., Pvt
‡Griffith, Claud, Sgt,
Griffith, Fred W., T/4,
Griffith, George O., Jr., Pvt,
Griffith, Gerald D., Pvt,
Griffith, Roth E., Pvt,
Griffith, Roy E., Pfc,
Griffith, Sylvan W., Pfc,
Griffiths, Hamlet, T/5,
Grigg, Harvey J., Pvt,
Griggins, Anthony J., 2nd Lt
Griggs, Thomas R., S/Sgt,
Grillo, James J., Pfc,
Grillo, Joseph A., Pvt,
Grimm, Edward M., Pvt,
Grimwood, Clyde A., Pvt,
Grindel, Edmond J., Pfc,
†Grindrod, John W., Pvt,
Grindstaff, John L., Sr., Pvt,
Grisham, J. Y., Pvt,
Grissom, Parretson, Pvt,
Griswold, George W., T/5,
‡Griswold, William S., Pvt,
†Grizell, Johnnie J., Pvt,
‡Grochowski, Benny V., Pvt,
Groden, Raymond, S/Sgt
Groemer, Anthony H., Pvt,
Groman, Joseph M., Jr., Pvt
†Gromek, Raymond J., Cpl,
Grondin, Robert J., Cpl,
Groskreutz, Harold A., Pvt,
Gross, Charlie W., Pvt
Grossbaum, Philip, Pvt,
Grosscup, Vernon, Pfc,
Grosse, Alfred R., Pvt,
*Grossi, William E., Pvt,
Grossman, Abraham, Pvt,
†Grossman, Harry M., Pvt,
Grossman, Jack, Pvt,
Grossman, Nathan H., S/Sgt,
Grosso, Joseph, Pvt,
Grotepas, Dirk, Pvt,
Groth, John J., Pvt,
Grotzke, Edward C., Cpl,
Grotzke, Howard F., S/Sgt,
Grove, Kenneth, Sgt,
Grove, Leon H., Pvt,
Grove, Merle, 1st Lt,
Grover, Sam W., Pfc,
†Grover, William K., Pvt,
Grover, Cecil H., Pvt,
Groves, Richard P., Pfc
Grow, Brimson, Sgt,
‡Grubb, Lemuel R., Pvt,
‡Grubb, William E., Pvt,
Gruber, Eugene N., Pvt,
Grumbacher, Ernst, Pfc,
‡Grumka, Michael, Pvt,
Grundy, George H., Sgt,
Gryeswiewicz, Matthew T., Pvt
†Gryfinski, Joseph A., Pfc,
†Gryga, Henry, Pfc,
Grzechowiak, Edward F., Pfc,
Guadagnine, Tullio, Pvt,
Guard, Charles A., Pvt,
†Guccion, Frank J., Pfc,
Guckian, John J., Pfc,
Guenrich, Donald E., T/Sgt,
Guenrich, Ronald H., Sgt,
Guensberg, Gerald, Pfc,
Guerra, Robert, Pvt,
Guerrero, Vicente, Pvt,
Guida, Frank J., Sgt,
Guide, Joseph A., T/5,
Guider, William J., Pfc,
Guido, Salvatore, Pfc,
Guidry, Theorgene F., Pfc,
Guilds, Lewis A., Pvt,
Guilliams, Raymond J., Pvt,
Guinn, Edward R., Sgt,
Guintole, William M., 2nd Lt
Guldbech, Ernest, T/Sgt,
Gulizia, John J., Pfc,
Gully, Harold N., Pvt,
†Gully, Thomas N., Pvt,
Gum, Harold D., Pvt,
†Gumz, Richard, Sgt,
†Gunderson, George E., Pvt,
†Gundze, Charles P., S/Sgt,
Gunn, James W., Pvt,
Gunning, LeRoy, 1st Lt,
Gunter, Hiram O., Pvt,
Guntow, John E., Pvt,
†Guralczyk, Clarence J., Pfc,
Gurganus, Jabie D., Pfc,
Gurin, Sol, Pvt,
Gurnaud, Robert E., Pfc,
Gurtowsky, Lewis L., Pfc,
Gusciora, Thaddeus A., Pvt,
Guskind, Bernard, Pfc,
Gusler, Noel, Jr., Pfc,
Gustafson, Donald A., T/5,
Gustafson, Frederick, Pfc,
Gustafson, Gunnar F., T/4,
Gustin, Lester, Pfc,
Guthier, John W., Pfc,
†Guthrie, Jack, Pfc,
Guthrie, John M., Pfc,
Guthrie, Robert E., Pfc,
†Gutowski, Anthony J., Pfc,
Gutshall, Ferris M., T/4,

† Killed in Action. * Prisoner of War. ‡ Missing in Action. § Died of Wounds.

Guy, Earl M., Pfc,
Guy, Virgel, Pfc,
Guyer, Albert W., T/Sgt,
†Guyette, Fred J., 2nd Lt,
Guzzo, Ralph G., Pfc,
Gwinn, Frank W., Capt,
Gwozdz, John J., Pvt,

Haas, Albert H., Pfc,
Haas, Randle L., Pfc,
Haas, Raymond E., Pfc,
Habeck, Maurice R., Pvt,
Habers, Evert, Pvt,
Habighurst, Edward W., Pvt,
Habina, Paul F., Pvt,
Hacker, Samuel E., Pvt,
Hacker, Samuel E., Cpl,
Hackworth, Vernon, Pvt,
Hadala, Leo J., Pfc,
Hadley, Jack L., T/Sgt,
Hadlock, John D., S/Sgt,
Haegelia, Hilmer B., Lt Col,
Haeussler, Elden L., Cpl,
Haff, William F., Pvt,
Haffener, Clarence E., Cpl,
Haffner, Albert J., Pfc,
†Hafter, David, Pvt,
Hagadorn, Walter F., Pfc,
Hagen, Donald H., Pvt,
Hager, John C., T/5,
Hagerman, Clifford A., Pfc,
Hagerman, Norman, Pvt,
Hagerstrom, Maurice G., Cpl,
Hagelin, Richard H., 1st Lt,
†Haggard, Glen E., Pfc,
Hague, William K., Pfc,
Hahn, George, Pfc,
Hahn, Harry F., Pvt,
Hahn, Vernon T., Pfc,
Haight, Cyril L., Pvt,
Haimowitz, Samuel I., Capt,
Haines, Mervine V., S/Sgt,
Haislop, Walter G., Pfc,
†Haithcock, Herbert J., Pvt,
‡Haithcock, Hugh B., Pfc,
Hajdinovich, Milan, Pfc,
‡Halbakken, Gilman, Pfc,
Halbeck, Charles J., Pfc,
Halford, Aaron T., T/4,
Halford, George C., T/4,
Haldemann, Marvin A., Pvt,
§Haley, Francis E., Pvt,
Haley, Howard D., Pvt,
Haler, Jake, Pvt,
Halle, Martel R., Pvt,
Halford, James W., Sgt,
Hall, Alfred, Pfc,
†Hall, Arthur W., Pfc,
Hall, Charles H., Sgt,
Hall, Charles L., Pfc,
Hall, Dewey D., Pvt
Hall, Francis M., S/Sgt,
Hall, Gordon G., T/5,
Hall, John O., Cpl,
Hall, John R., S/Sgt,
Hall, Joseph H., Pvt,
Hall, Marion F., Pfc,
Hall, Merle J., Pfc,
Hall, Charles F., Pfc,
Hall, Otis W., Pfc,
Hall, Robert W., Pfc,
Hall, Robert A., Pfc,
Hall, Virgil E., Pvt,
Hall, Virgil L., Pvt,
Hall, William C., Pfc
Hall, William M., T/5,
Hallett, Clyde C., Jr., Pfc,
†Halligan, John J., Pfc,
Hallisey, Paul T., Pvt,
Hallstrom, Lincoln A., Cpl,
Halpert, Harold G., Pvt,
Halstad, Anton S., S/Sgt,
Halstead, Forrest, Cpl,
Halsted, Thomas J., Pfc,
‡Haltom, James C., Pfc,
‡Halverson, Clifford B., Pfc,
Halverson, Stanley O., T/5,
*Halverstadt, Eldon M., Pfc,
Hambelton, John A., Sgt,
Hambrick, Ray, Pvt,
Hamburg, Jake, M/Sgt,
†Hamburg, Leo, Jr., S/Sgt,
‡Hamburger, Max, Pfc,
Hamelin, Robert, Pfc,
Hamelink, Paul G., Pvt,
†Hamer, John, Pfc,
Hamill, John M., Pvt,
Hamilton, Andrew T., T/5,
Hamilton, Conrad T., S/Sgt,
Hamilton, Daniel R., Pfc,
Hamilton, Emery, Pfc,
Hamilton, James E., Pfc,
Hamilton, James J., Jr., Pfc,
Hamilton, Martin L., Pfc,
Hamilton, Robert H., Pvt,
†Hamilton, Rudolph A., Pfc,
†Hamilton, Thomas C., Pvt,
Hamilton, Thomas D., Pfc,
Hamlett, Lewis W., Jr., Pfc,
Hamm, Bonham, O., T/5,
†Hammer, Albert L., Pfc,
Hammer, Henry L., Pfc,
Hammerle, Henry J., Pvt,
‡Hammond, Alton W., Pvt,
Hammond, Omer, Pfc,
†Hammonds, Robert W., S/Sgt,
Hampelman, Marvin K., Pvt,
§Hamrick, Alton M., Pvt,
Hamrick, Alger V., Pvt,
Hanaburgh, David H., 1st Lt,
†Hanauer, Henry L., Pfc,
Hance, Robert, Pfc,
Hancherick, Alex, Pvt,
Hancock, Benjamin M., S/Sgt,
‡Hands, William W., Pvt,
†Handy, Daniel H., Pfc,
Handzlik, Lawrence H., Cpl,
Hanes, Gilbert A., Pfc, St.
‡Haney, Glenn C., Pvt,
Hanford, Roy E., Capt,
Hanks, Donald E., T/4,
Hanley, Charles D., Pvt,
Hanley, John F., Capt,
Hanlon, Charles R., Pvt,
Hann, George J., Pvt,
Hannah, Loring A., Pfc,
Hannan, William T., Pvt,
Hannon, James J., Pvt,
†Hanousek, Eugene M., 1st Lt,
Hanrahan, Cornelius P., Pvt,
Hanrahan, Robert L., Pvt,
Hansberry, Charles A., Sgt,
†Hansen, Matthias P., Pvt,
Hansen, Jack W., Pvt,
Hansen, Glenn H. P., Pvt,
Hansen, Ruel M., 1st Lt
Hansen, Verner A., Pvt,
†Hanson, Arnold O., Pfc,
Hanson, Clarence J., Pvt,
Hanson, Clifford G., Pfc,
*Hanson, Marvin D., S/Sgt,
Hanson, Norman A., Pfc,
Hanson, Raymond E., Pfc,
Hantin, Joseph C., Pfc,
Harden, Elmer L., Pvt,
Harden, Gaskell O., 1st Sgt,
Hardiman, Thomas A., T/4,
Hardin, Homer C., Pfc,
Hardin, Lershov H., Pvt,
Hardin, Ray W., Pvt,
Harding, Dallas D., Pvt,
Harding, Delburt W., Pvt,
Harding, Frederick D., 1st Lt
Harding, Luther C., Pfc,
Hardman, William B., Pvt,
Hardt, Anthony A., Pvt,
†Hardy, James C., Pfc,
Hardy, Lester W., Jr., Pvt,
Hargreaves, Joseph P., Pvt,
Haring, Bernard F., Sgt,
‡Harju, Robert L., S/Sgt,
Harken, Donald K., Pfc,
Harkins, George L., Capt,
Harmala, Arthur, Pfc,
Harmanes, Leonard, Sgt,
Harmon, Cortland F., Cpl,
Harmon, Franklin G., Pfc,
Harmon, James L., Pfc,
Harmon, John H., S/Sgt,
Harmon, Lenzy R., Pfc,
Harmon, Wilbur P., S/Sgt,
Harmor, William E., Pvt,
Harms, Jacob I., S/Sgt,
Harold, William R., Pvt,
Harootunian, Zaven, Pfc,
Harper, David N., T/4,
‡Harper, Ivan, 1st Lt,
Harper, Max S., Cpl,
Harper, William W., 2nd Lt
Harrell, Frank H., 2nd Lt,
Harrell, Thomas E., Pfc,
Harrell, Wilbur E., Pfc,
Harrington, Robert H., Pvt,
Harrington, Policar, S/Sgt,
Harris, Bert C., Pvt,
†Harris, Carl L., Pvt,
Harris, Charley J., Pfc
Harris, Charlie T., Pvt,
Harris, Francis L., S/Sgt,
Harris, Franklin C., Pfc,
Harris, Frederick E., Pvt,
Harris, Gene D., Sgt,
Harris, Harley L., Pvt,
Harris, Harry E., Pfc,
Harris, Walter, Pfc,
Harris, Yorel, 2nd Lt,
Harrison, Boyce E., Pfc,
Harrison, George H., Pfc,
Harrison, Howard W., 1st Lt,
†Harrison, Jacob L., Pvt,
Harrison, Vernon F., Pfc,
Harrison, William A., Pvt,
Harrison, Woodrow W., Pfc,
Harrman, Walter P., Pfc,
Harrod, Lester L., Pfc,
†Harrower, Cldye R., Pfc,
Harstick, Orville M., Pfc,
Hart, Darwin S., S/Sgt,
Hart, Elmer, Pvt,
Hart, Harold L., Sgt,
Hart, James D., S/Sgt,
†Hart, John D., Pfc,
†Hart, Laverne A., 1st Lt,
Hart, Lester R., Pfc,
Hart, Marvin S., Pfc,
Hartland, James H., Sgt,
Hartlege, John R., Capt,
Hartlove, Walter A., Pfc,
*Hartman, Elmer, Jr., Pfc,
‡Hartman, Elmer J. H., Pfc,
Hartman, Lester H., Pfc,
Hartman, Reuben G. D., Pvt,
Hartman, Robert F., Pfc,
Hartranft, Glenn F., S/Sgt,
Hartsell, William J., Pfc,
Hartstein, Theodore, T/4,
Hartwig, Herbert C., Maj
Hartz, Charles E.
†Hartzell, Francis J., Pfc,
†Harvey, Daniel J., Sgt,
Harvey, Ernest B., Pvt,
Harvey, Leslie P., Pfc,
Harvey, Millard D., Pfc,
†Harwood, Euell W., Pfc,
Harwood, Leland L., Pvt,
Hash, Ernest G., T/5,
Hash, Wayne L., S/Sgt,
Haskell, Louis Q., Pvt,
Haslach, Joseph, Pvt,
Haslach, Joseph M., Pfc,
Hass, Joseph, Pvt,
†Hassel, Charles E., Pvt,
Hasselberg, Eric G., Pfc,
§Hassell, James O., Pvt,
Hassett, Charles2J., Cpl
†Hassinger, Sanford E., Sgt,
†Haston, Leonard M., Pfc,
Hatchel, Lee A., Pfc,
Hatcher, Daniel W., Sgt,
Hatcher, James O., Pfc,
Hatchett, Barnett P., Pfc,
Hatfield, Lee E., Pfc,
Hatler, Ernest J., Pfc,
†Hatton, Robert J., 1st Lt,
Haug, Emil J., Sgt,
Haugh, Lloyd R., T/5,
Haulk, William M., 1/Sgt,
Hauser, Elmer H., Pvt,
Hautala, Gustave A., Pvt,
Havel, Leonard H., Sgt,
Havens, Wayne L., S/Sgt
Havlin, John W., Pvt,
Hawal, Steve, Pvt,
Hawk, Fambrough, Sgt,
Hawk, Jessie F., T/4,
Hawke, Wilbur C., Pvt,
Hawkins, Alvin L., Cpl,
Hawkins, Charles E., T/5,
Hawkins, Clayson R.,
Hawkins, James D., Pfc,
Hawkins, James R., S/Sgt,
Hawkins, John T., Pfc,
Hawkins, Lonnie G., Pfc,
Hawkins, Paul E., Pfc,
Hawkins, Ralph G., 1st Lt,
Hawks, Lloyd C., Pfc,
Hawks, Wilbur C., Pvt
Haworth, Ray, Pvt,
*Hay, Robert D., Pfc,
Hayes, Charles M., Pvt,
†Hayes, Clavin W., Pvt,
Hayes, Edward J., 1st Lt,
Hayes, Emmett C., Sgt,
Hayes, J. B., Sgt
Hayes, John J., Jr., S/Sgt,
Hayes, Paul L., 1st Lt,
Hayes, Ralph, Pfc,
Hayes, Richard L., S/Sgt,
†Haygood, Wilton S., Cpl,
Hayne, Donald L., Cpl, St.
*Haynes, Cameron G., Pvt,
Haynes, Donald L., 1st Lt,
Haynes, Forest D., Jr., Pvt,
Hays, Callie H., Pvt,
Hays, Carl E., Pfc,
Hazlett, Harry B., Cpl,
*Heacock, William N., Pvt,
Head, Philip N., Pvt,
Head, Virgil G., Sgt,
Head, William O., Sgt
Headle, James L., Pfc,
Healy, James G., Pfc,
Heard, John B., Pfc,
Hebb, Robert G., Pvt
†Hebert, Gabriel P., Pvt,
Hebert, Nolan J., Pfc,
Hebert, Wilson J., Pfc,
†Herbert, Roosevelt, Pfc,
Heck, James W., Pfc,
Heck, Wilbert N., Pvt,
Heckman, Gerald T., 1st Lt,
Hedden, Thomas E., Pvt,
Hedge, Glenn E., Pfc,
Hedrick, Charles E., Pvt,
Heege, Lester J., Pvt,
Heery, John J., Pfc,
Heffner, Raymond G., Cpl,
Hegely, Louis G., Sgt,
‡Hegvick, Louis M., Sgt,
Heick, Harry H., T/4,
Heide, Frederick A., Pfc,
Heideman, Gerald E., Cpl,
Heidenreich, Raymond J., Pvt,
Heil, Howard C., Sgt,
Heil, Raymond F., Pfc,
Heil, Robert F., Pvt,
Heile, Ralph C., S/Sgt,
Heimbuck, Rudolph, Pvt
†Heineman, Arthur H., S/Sgt,
†Heinlein, Floyd L., Pfc,
Heintges, John A., Lt. Col,
Heinze, Eugene F., Pvt
Heipel, Lorne W., M/Sgt,
§Heisel, Herman, Pvt,
Heiss, James T., Sgt,
Heister, Samuel V., Pvt,
Helkkila, Irvin M., Pfc,
Hellbusch, Elton H., Cpl,
*Heller, Leonard J., Pfc,
Heller, Walter S., Pfc,
Hellman, William F., S/Sgt,
Helmer, John G., Pfc,
Helms, James T., Pvt,
Helms, James W., Pfc
Helton, Clyde S., Pfc,
Helton, Willis A., Pfc,
†Heltzen, Walter W., Pfc,
Hembroff, Curtis D., Pvt,
Hemenway, Owen R., Pvt,
§Hemphill, Paul P., Pfc,
Henault, Edward, Pfc,
Hendershot, Sanford, Pvt,
Henderson, Edward K., Pvt,
*Henderson, Elmer L., Pfc,
Henderson, John J., Sgt,
Henderson, Rubin B., Pfc,
Henderson, Torsten E., Pvt,
Henderson, Ulsworth, Pvt,
Henderson, Walter B., Pvt,
†Henderson, William B., Pvt,
Henderson, William C., Pfc,
Hendricks, Milburn L., Pfc,
Hendrix, Mitchell T., Pfc
Hendrix, Rufus O., Pvt,
Hendry, Samuel P., Pvt,
Henke, Henry J., Pvt,
Henley, Delton R., Cpl,
Henneberry, William F., Pfc,
Hennessey, Russell P., Pvt,
Hennessy, Daniel J., Sgt,
Henricksen, Hans, T/5,
Henrotin, Martin F., S/Sgt,
Henry, Glen, Pfc,
Henry, Harold L., Pvt,
Henry, Jasper F., Pvt,
Henry, William, Pfc,
Henry, William P., Pfc,
Henschel, Senus W., Pvt,
Henshaw, Otis H., Sgt,
Hensley, J. H., Pvt,
†Henson, Duard E., Pvt,
Henson, Otha L., S/Sgt,
Henson, Willie R., Pfc,
Heppler, James W., S/Sgt,
Hercog, Frank A., Pvt,
Herdzina, Stanley L., Pvt,
Herman, Adam, S/Sgt,
Herman, Clarence J., S/Sgt,
Hermes, Elroy C., Jr., Pvt,
Hermes, Gerald T., Pvt,
Hern, Joseph F., Pfc,
Hernandez, Arthur A., Pvt,
†Hernandez, Antonio, Pfc,
Hernandez, Concepcion, Pvt,
Hernandez, Dan G., Pfc,
†Hernandez, Francisco, M/Sgt
†Hernandez, Joseph N., Pfc,
Hernandez, John S., Pvt,
Hernandez, Jose D., Pfc,
†Hernandez, Leonardo H., Pvt,
Heron, Ellis C., Pvt,
§Herrara, Brualio P., Pvt,
Herrera, John C., Pvt,
Herrera, Manuel, Pfc,
Herring, Charles J., Pfc,
Herring, J. P., Pfc,
†Herrington, B. F., Jr., Pfc,
Herriott, Robert L., 2nd Lt,
Herrmann, Donald H., Pfc,
Hershatter, Milton A., Pvt,
Hershberger, Joseph M., Sgt,
Hershey, Jack, Cpl,
Hervert, Richard G., Pfc,
Heschke, John D., Pfc,
Hess, John W., Pfc,
Hess, Lynford C., Pvt,
Hester, Donald, Sgt,
Hester, Edward J., Pfc,
Heuer, Edward P., Pvt,
§Hewitt, John R., 1st Lt,
Heyse, Curtis L., T/5,
†Hiatt, William G., Pvt,
Hickey, James B., Pfc,
‡Hickey, Thomas E., Pvt,
Hickman, Alton A., Pfc
Hickman, Edwin L., Pvt,
Hickman, Leo, Pfc,
Hickman, Ralph D., Pfc,
Hicks, Boris A., 1st Lt,
Hicks, Clarence S., Pfc,
Hicks, George E., Pvt,
Hicks, James C., Pfc
Hicks, John P., Pvt,
Hicks, Raymond I., Pfc,
Hicks, Vernon H., Pvt,
Hieber, Eugene J., Cpl,
Hiers, Henry G., Pfc,
Higbee, William U., Pvt,
Higginbottom, Jack, Pvt,
Higgins, Bruce, Pvt,
Higgins, James C., S/Sgt,
Higgins, Leon J., Pvt,
‡High, John J., S/Sgt,
Highland, Charles H., Pvt,
Hightower, Arthur L., Pfc,
Hightower, Leonard R., Pfc,
Higuera, Edward W., Pfc,
†Hildago, Roman C., Pvt,
Hile, Robert, Pvt,
Hill, Albert, Pfc,
Hill, Benjamin H., Pvt,
†Hill, Carl D., Sgt,
Hill, Carl D., Pfc,
Hill, Clarence R., Pfc,
Hill, David D., Pvt,
Hill, John W., Pvt,
Hill, Henry L., Pvt,
Hill, Jack H., Sgt
Hill, James K., Pfc,
Hill, John T., Pvt,
Hill, Louie F., Pvt,
Hill, Maurice, Pfc,
†Hill, Roby C., Pfc,
Hill, Russell M., Pfc,
Hill, William T., Cpl,
†Hillaird, Arthur, Pvt,
†Hillebrand, Harold G., Pvt,
Hilliard, Perry, Pfc,
Hilligass, Charles R., Sgt,
Hilliker, Gordon C., Pfc,
Hilmoe, Roy A., Cpl,
Hilt, Elmer T., Pvt,
Hilton, Edgar L., Pvt
Hilton, Edsel L., Sgt,
‡Hilts, Richard B., S/Sgt,
Hilty, Andrew N., Pfc,
Hilvick, Anthony, T/5,
Hina, Earl W., Pfc,
Hinch, John F., Pfc,
Hinde, John W., Sgt,
Hinds, Henry G., Cpl,
Hines, Charles A., Pfc,
Hines, Ray D., Pfc,
‡Hines, Vernon D., Pfc,
Hingle, Milton J., Pvt,
§Hinkle, Jake S., S/Sgt,
Hinkle, James C., Pvt,
Hinphy, Edward J., Pvt,
†Hipp, Floyd L., Jr., Pfc,
Hird, Robert C., Pvt,
Hirschberg, Martin L., Pvt,
Hisaw, Johnnie M., Pfc,
Hiscock, Merrill A., T/5,
Hisxon, James C., Pvt,
Hittle, Marion F., Pvt,
Hoag, Frederick, Pvt,
†Hoaglin, John R., Sgt,
†Hobbs, Edward C., Pvt,
Hobbs, James R., Sgt,
Hobbs, Leslie R., Pfc,
Hobson, Ambrose G., Pvt,
†Hockenberry, James O., Pfc,
Hocker, Joseph N., Pvt,
Hodapp, Donald W., Pfc,
Hodge, Forrest W., Sgt,
Hodges, Loyd, Cpl
Hodges, Ralph W., Pfc,
Hodges, Robert E., Pfc,
Hodges, Taylor, Cpl,
Hodges, Vaughn S., T/5,

† Killed in Action. * Prisoner of War. ‡ Missing in Action. § Died of Wounds.

Hodges, William K., Pvt,
Hodges, William S., Pfc,
†Hodgson, Edmund, Pfc,
†Hodkinson, Chester R., Pfc,
Hoefle, Royden, Pfc,
Hofercamp, Donald H., T/4,
Hoff, Edward T., Pfc,
Hoffert, Russel W., Pfc,
Hoffman, Bruce A., Pvt,
Hoffman, Burgess L., Pvt
Hoffman, Daniel R., Pvt,
Hoffman, Edward, Pfc,
Hoffman, Ernest R., Pfc,
Hoffman, Frank L., Pvt,
Hoffman, Harry, 1st Lt,
†Hoffman, Howard J., Cpl,
Hoffman, Irving, Pvt,
Hoffman, Oran C., Cpl
†Hoffman, Robert E., Pvt,
Hoffman, Roman W., Pvt
§Hoffmann, Robert W., Pvt,
Hofhines, Ursel, Pvt,
Hogan, James P., Pfc,
Hogberg, Ernest R., Pfc,
Hoge, Charles G., Pvt,
†Hogsberg, Ernest R., Pfc,
Hogsed, Virgil, S/Sgt,
Hogue, Archie F., Jr., Pfc,
Hohlt, LeRoy E., Pfc,
Hohmann, Edward J., T/Sgt,
Hoit, Robert G., Pfc,
Hoke, Glen B., Pvt,
Holbrook, George J., S/Sgt,
Holbrook, Howard C., Pvt,
Holbrook, Karl L., Sgt,
Holden, Herman A., Pfc,
Holder, Oral W., S/Sgt,
Holder, Ralph E., Pfc,
Holder, Sorelle, T/Sgt,
Holder, Walter C., S/Sgt,
Holderbaum, Edward P., Pfc,
Holderfield, Curtis O., Pvt,
Holderman, Charles E., Pvt,
Holicky, John, Pfc,
Holiday, John A., Pvt,
Holk, Melvin L., M/Sgt,
Holland, Bedford, T/5,
Holland, Frank G., Pfc,
Holland, Fred, Pfc,
Holland, John H., Pfc,
Holland, John R., T/5,
Holland, Jonus, Pvt,
Holland, Warren G., Pfc,
Hollar, Raymond L., Pfc,
Hollingsworth, Charles E., Pfc,
Hollis, James H., Pfc,
‡Hollis, John H., S/Sgt,
Hollis, Perley A., Pvt,
†Hollis, Walter R., Sgt,
Hollway, Richard C., Pvt,
†Holm, Robert E., Sgt,
Holman, Dedford A., Pvt
Holme, John, Pfc,
Holmes, Eldon A., T/5,
Holmes, Joseph, Pvt,
Holmes, Owen T., Pfc,
Holsonbake, Fred R., Sgt,
Holt, Everett R., Pfc,
Holt, Fred E., T/5,
Holt, John H., Pfc,
Holt, John W., Pfc,
Holt, Lloyd E., Pfc,
†Holt, Russell D., S/Sgt,
Holt, Warren B., Pfc,
Holtzin, Samuel, T/4,
Holzemer, Raymond J., Pfc,
§Holzer, Harry, Pvt,
Holzman, Edward J., Pvt,
†Hombis, John, Pvt,
Homola, John F., Pfc,
Homsley, L. V., Pfc,
Honaker, James B., Pfc,
†Honaker, John T., Pfc,
Honchul, John D., Pvt,
Hones, Jack A., Pvt
Hones, Luther E., Cpl,
†Honey, William I., Pfc,
Honeycutt, Lobirte, Cpl,
Honig, Irving I., Pvt,
Honkonen, William H., Pfc
Honn, Harry W., S/Sgt,
Hons, Lee F., Pvt,
Hoober, Joe M., T/4
Hood, Jefferson W., Pvt,
Hook, Glen F., Pfc,
Hooker, James H., Jr., Pvt,
Hooks, R. L., Sgt,
Hooten, Troy D., Cpl,
*Hoover, Alton L., Pfc,
†Hoover, James O., Pvt,
†Hoover, Leonard V., Pfc,
‡Hopkins, Austin G., S/Sgt,
Hopkins, Donald E., Pvt,
Hopkins, Ernest J., Pfc,
Hopkins, Martin B., Pfc,
Hopkins, Jack, T/5,
Hopper, Leroy, Sgt,
Hopper, Mitchell C., Pfc,
†Hoppy, William F., Pfc,
Hor, Charles L., Pfc,
Horan, Martin J., Pvt,
Horan, William, S/Sgt,
Horeftis, Theodore J., Pfc,
Horn, Edward W., Pfc,
Horn, Ellis W., Sgt,
†Hornback, Marvin L., Pfc,
Horne, Robert G., Pfc,
Horne, Thomas J., Jr., Pfc,
Horner, William H., Sgt,
†Horney, Eugene, Pfc,
Horowitz, Sam, Pvt,
Horstman, Clarence W., T/Sgt,
Horton, Charlie R., Pfc,
Horton, George H., Pfc,
Horton, Harold H., Pfc,
Horton, Justus S., Cpl,
Horton, Orion V., Pfc,
Horton, Robert L., Pfc,
‡Horton, Walker V., Pfc,
Horvath, George A., Pfc,
‡Hosfelt, Harry H., Jr., Pfc,
Hosmer, Carl L., T/5,
Hoss, Vernon W., T/5,
Hostak, Paul F., Pvt,
Hostetter, John A., S/Sgt,
Hott, Jay W., Pvt,
Houck, Lee R., Pfc,
Houde, Albert J., Pfc,
Houeck, Ernest F., Pvt
Houghton, John W., T/4,
Houghton, Walter W., Pfc,
Houle, Henry J. W., S/Sgt,
Houp, Ben W., Pfc,
House, Guy B., Pfc,
†House, Hubert B., Pvt
Householer, Clyde C., Sgt,
Houser, Palmer R., Sgt,
*Housh, Raymond V., Pfc,
†Houston, Herbert D., Pfc,
†Houston, Lanier W., Pvt,
†Houston, Lovely O., S/Sgt,
Houston, Victor W., S/Sgt,
Hovden, Alvin O., Pfc,
Hove, Joseph W., S/Sgt,
Hove, Arlow H., Sgt,
†Howard, Earnest, Sgt,
Howard, Palmer, Pvt,
*Howard, Raymond L., Pvt,
†Howe, David M., Sr., 1st Lt,
Howe, Edward W., Pfc,
†Howe, Oran W., Cpl,
Howell, Alvin G., Pfc,
Howell, Estel B., Pvt,
Howell, James P., Sgt,
Howell, Joseph E., Cpl,
Howell, Lawrence E., S/Sgt,
Howell, Thomas R., Pfc,
Howells, Myron T., Pfc,
Howery, George W., Sgt,
Hozan, Martin J., Cpl,
Hritz, Steve, S/Sgt,
Hubbard, Buddington S., Pvt,
Hubbard, Clifford W., Pvt,
Hubbard, Harry S., Cpl,
Hubbard, Julian M., Pfc,
Huckelba, Ishmall, Pvt,
Hudak, Mike, Pfc,
Hudak, Nicholas M., Pvt,
Huddleston, Ernest H., Pvt,
†Huddleston, Otis R., Pfc,
Hudek, Joseph P., Cpl,
Hudgins, Ernest M., Pfc,
Hudevsky, John G., Pvt,
†Hudolin, Edward, S/Sgt,
Hudon, Louis L., Pfc,
Hudson, Dewey L., Sgt,
Hudson, Elbert L., Pfc,
Hudson, Harry O., 1st Sgt,
Hudson, Howard D., T/5,
§Hudson, Kendrick B., Pvt,
Hudson, Robert E., Pvt,
Hudson, W. B., Pvt,
Hudson, William H., Pfc,
Huey, Ben M., S/Sgt,
Huey, Delford, Pfc,
Huff, John, Pvt,
Huff, Verne R., Sgt,
Huffam, Richard R., Pfc,
Huffman, Calvin E., Pfc,
Huffman, Dewey L., Pfc,
Hufford, Fred P., Sgt,
Huggins, Harold H., T/5,
Hughes, Ben H., Pvt,
Hughes, Collins M., Pvt,
Hughes, Elwyn, Pfc,
Hughes, George A., Jr., Cpl,
†Hughes, Herbert H., S/Sgt,
Hughes, John P., Pfc,
Hughes, Joseph D., Cpl,
Hughes, Leroy, Pvt,
Hughes, William C., Pvt,
Hughes, William L., T/5,
Hull, Jack E., Pvt,
‡Hull, Raymond C., Pvt,
Hull, William H., Pfc,
Hulsey, Charles E., Pfc,
†Hultsapple, Alfred L., Pvt,
Humbert, Willard, Pfc,
Humbertson, Francis G., Pvt,
Humble, Robert H., Pvt,
Huminsky, Tony, Pvt,
Humiston, Leroy M., Sgt,
Humphery, Denver, Pfc,
†Humphrey, John C., Pvt,
Huml, Gerald J., Pvt,
†Humphrey, John M., Pfc,
Humphrey, Wallace L., Pvt,
Humphreys, Byng B., S/Sgt,
Humphreys, John D., Pfc,
Humphries, Hugh L., Pfc,
Humphries, James O., T/4,
Humting, Nicolas, Pfc,
Hundley, Dan, Pfc,
Hundley, Julius E., Pvt,
Hunsberger, Donald L., S/Sgt
Hunt, Albert L., T/Sgt,
Hunt, Arthur W., Pfc,
Hunt, David, Pvt,
Hunt, Elvis D., Pfc,
Hunt, Emile, Pfc,
Hunt, Francis W., Pvt,
Hunt, George A., Pvt,
Hunt, Gilbert B., Capt,
Hunt, James R., Pvt,
Hunt, James R., Pfc,
Hunt, John J., Cpl,
Hunt, Marshall T., Capt,
Hunt, Ralph A., Pfc,
*Hunt, Terrell, Pfc,
§Hunt, Wilford C., Pfc,
Hunt, William P., Pfc,
Hunter, Carl W., Pfc,
Hunter, Lester C., Jr.,
Hunter, Macon G., Pfc,
Hunter, Richard L., Pfc,
Huntley, Robert M., M/Sgt,
Hunter, Stanley A., Pfc,
Hunter, Wendell B., Pvt,
†Hunter, William F., Pvt,
Huppenthal, Michael A., Pfc,
Hurd, James N., T/5,
Hurd, Ted M., Pfc,
Hurdle, Elwood, Pvt,
Hurl, Charles W., Pvt,
Hurst, Coy K., Pvt,
Hurst, Irwin M., Pvt,
Hurst, Lawrence A., Pfc,
Husek, James H., Pfc,
Husser, George D., Capt,
Huston, Paul V., Pvt,
Huston, Richard K., Pfc,
Huston, William, Pvt,
Huszar, William G., Pvt,
Hutchins, Harvey E., Pvt,
Hutchins, Hugh C., Pvt,
Hutchinson, Virgil C.,
Huth, Walter W., Pfc,
Hutson, Philip L., 1/Sgt,
Huttlinger, Frank D., Pfc,
Hutton, Ralph E., Pfc,
†Huval, Euzebe, Pfc,
Hyatt, George, Pvt,
Hyde, Herbert H., Pfc,
†Hyder, Charles W., Pfc,
Hygema, Roscoe C., Pvt,
Hyman, Willard, Pvt,
Hymann, Harry, Pvt,
†Hynes, James W., Cpl,
Hys, Julian A., Pvt,
Hysell, Glenn G., Pfc,

Iacovelli, Gaetano, Pfc,
Iafelice, Joseph F., Sgt,
Iasnogle, Edgar L., Pvt,
Icard, Jack C., Pvt,
Icard, Robert R., Pfc,
Ide, Edwin, Pfc,
Iezzi, Antonio, Pvt,
Igo, William F., Jr., Pfc,
Ilacqua, Norman S., Pvt,
Ilchisin, Steven, Pfc,
Illich, John E., Jr., Pfc,
Illuzzi, Dominick, Pvt,
Imbriglio, Anthony, Pvt,
Imhoff, Bruce O., Pfc,
Impavido, Charles A., Pfc,
Imperioso, Anthony, Pfc,
Ince, Lowell C., 1st Sgt,
Ingemie, Joseph N., Pvt,
Ingle, Donald B., 2nd Lt
†Ingle, Tricy L., Pfc,
Ingles, Harold S., Pfc,
Ingram, Edgar W., Pvt
Ingram, Robert C., Sgt,
†Ingran, Julius N., Pfc,
Innes, Donald A., Pfc,
Intindola, Nicholas, Pvt,
Introini, Brun J., Sgt,
Ipe, Arthur F., Pfc,
Iralan, Lowell W., Pfc,
Irvin, Bennie T., Pvt,
Irving, James, Sgt,
Irwin, J. D., S/Sgt,
Irwin, Lewis G., Pfc,
Isaac, Edwin A., S/Sgt,
Isaac, Emanuel, Pfc,
Isaac, Frank, Pvt,
Isaac, George D., Pfc,
†Isaacs, Emmett J., Pvt,
†Isaacson, Walter A., Sgt,
Isenberg, Mayes D., Pfc
Isenberger, Raymond, Pfc,
Isenour, Frank M., Maj
Isernhagen, Arnold H., Pfc,
Ishes, James T., Pvt,
‡Ishler, Theodore W., Pfc,
*Ishmale, James B., Pvt,
Isocsky, Stephen J., Pvt,
Italiano, Jasper, Pfc,
Iuliano, Victor A., Pvt,
Ivancie, Frank, Pfc,
†Ivers, Richard H., Cpl,
Iverson, Carl B., 1st Lt,
Iverson, Carl I., T/Sgt,
Ivey, James F., Pfc,
Ivins, Richard, 2nd Lt,
Iwen, Harold W., Pvt,
Izzo, Samuel D., Pfc,

Jachimski, Joseph, Pfc,
Jack, Lloyd E., T/Sgt,
Jackowitz, Adolph J., Pfc,
Jacks, Stephen D., Pvt,
Jackson, Charles L., Pvt,
Jackson, Clarence W., Pfc,
†Jackson, Earl F., Pfc,
Jackson, Eugene A., Sgt,
Jackson, Everett A.,
Jackson, Francis, Pfc,
Jackson, Henry E., Sgt,
Jackson, Herbert V., S/Sgt,
Jackson, James R., Pfc
Jackson, Jessie A., Pvt,
Jackson, Loutis E., Pfc,
Jackson, Raymond P.,
Jackson, Robert F., 1st Lt,
Jackson, Robert L., Pfc
†Jackson, Robert L., Pvt,
Jackson, Robert R., Pvt,
†Jackson, Walter, S/Sgt,
Jackson, Willie P., Pfc,
§Jacob, Robert T., Pvt,
Jacob, Walter H., S/Sgt,
Jacobs, Herbert L., 2nd Lt,
Jacobs, Herman W. E., Sgt,
Jacobs, Leonard L., 1st Sgt,
Jacobs, Julius, T/4,
Jacobs, Thomas A., T/5,
Jacobs, Raymond S., T/4,
Jacobs, Stanley M., Cpl,
†Jacobsen, Theodore M., Pfc,
†Jacoby, Robert S., T/4,
Jacoway, Earl G., Pfc,
Jaddard, William T., Pvt,
Jaeger, Horace W., Pvt,
Jagielski, Walter J., Pvt,
Jagla, Andrew D., Sgt,
Jahn, George A., Pvt,
Jaime, Cesilio A., Pfc,
Jakubowski, Henry, Pvt,
†Jambrosek, Joseph J., Jr., Pfc,
James, Arthur E., Pvt,
James, Carl D., Pvt,
James, Dewey, Pfc,
James, Francis H., Pvt
James, Garland W., Pvt,
James, Howard S., Pvt,
James, Robert E., Pfc,
James, Rufus W., Pvt,
†Jamieson, Thomas S., 2nd Lt,
Jamison, William R., S/Sgt,
Janczak, Lou S., S/Sgt,
Janes, John M., Pfc,
Janiczek, Anthony, Pvt,
Janik, John S., Pfc,
Janisch, Walter J., T/5,
Janke, Jake, Pfc,
Jankowski, Mitchell A., Pfc,
Jankowski, Ollie, Pfc,
Jannone, Michael J., S/Sgt
Janos, John, Pfc,
Janoski, Joseph M., Sgt,
Janousek, George, Pvt,
Janowski, Bernard, Pfc,
†Jansen, Dale C., Cpl,
Jansen, Melvin C., Sgt,
January, Steve, Pfc,
§Janulis, Tony W., Pfc,
Janusek, Gravriel E., Pfc,
Jardanowski, Ervin F., Pfc,
Jarocki, Edmund E., Cpl,
Jaroscak, John J., Pfc,
*Jarosz, Edward A., Pfc,
‡Jarrell, Frank B., Pfc,
Jarrell, Walter G., Jr., Pvt,
Jarvey, Carl W., Pfc,
†Jarvis, Howard E., Sgt,
Jarvis, John I., Pvt,
Jaschek, Otto, Pfc,
†Jasman, Carl P., S/Sgt,
§Jasmer, Elton E., Pfc,
Jasso, Joseph G., Pfc,
Jastrzembski, Chester, Pvt
Jasukonis, John A., Pvt,
†Javanosky, Leonard C., Sgt,
Jaxtimer, Jack A., Cpl,
Jay, Robert E., Pvt,
Jaynes, Orlo, Pvt,
†Jeffcoat, Chester D., Pvt,
Jeffers, Melvin L., Pfc,
Jefferson, Dee N., Pfc,
Jefferson, Peerless, Pvt,
Jeffries, Harlow L., Pfc,
Jelinski, Zigmund J., T/5,
Jendziezyk, Stanley W., Pfc,
Jenkins, Albert S., Pvt,
Jenkins, Alvin R., 1st Lt,
Jenkins, Archie J., Cpl,
Jenkins, Bruce L., Pvt,
Jenkins, Clifford C., Pfc,
Jenkins, Ernest A., Sgt,
Jenkins, Herbert M., Pfc,
Jenkins, James R., Pfc,
†Jenkins, M. L., Pfc,
Jenkins, Robert M., S/Sgt,
Jenks, Charles A., Pfc,
Jenne, Richard O., Pvt,
Jennings, Earl D., Pvt,
Jennings, Edward J., Pfc,
Jennings, Floyd, S/Sgt,
Jennings, Frank L., Jr., Pvt,
Jennings, Harold G., Pfc,
‡Jennings, Jesse M., Pfc,
Jennings, Jesse N., Pfc,
§Jennings, John A., Jr., Pfc,
†Jennings, Randolph T., Pvt,
Jensen, Christian M., T/5,
Jensen, Gilbert A., T/5,
Jensen, Jens R., S/Sgt,
†Jensen, Lyle M., 1st Lt,
Jensen, Verner T., Pfc,
Jenson, Lloyd K., Capt,
Jepson, Ivan, Pfc,
†Jernigan, Alton A., Sgt,
Jerome, Roland H., Pfc,
Jersey, William H., Pfc,
Jeske, Clifford C., Pvt,
Jesse, Edward L., Pfc,
†Jessee, Robert M., Jr., Pfc,
Jessup, Arthur C., M/Sgt,
Jessup, Jeyell E., Pfc,
Jew, Yet H., Pfc,
Jewell, Carolos E., Pfc,
Jewell, Donald B., Pvt,
†Jewell, George A., Pfc,
Jewell, Melvin W., Pvt
Jez, Jarome L., Pvt,
Jezek, George W., Pvt,
Jiminez, Pete, S/Sgt,
Joe, Herbert, Pvt,
†Joergens, Herman T., Pfc,
Joffe, Maxwell S., Pvt,
Jogielski, Stanley, Pvt,
†Johannemann, James G., Pvt,
Johanson, Carl E., Pvt,
Johanson, Karl F., Pfc,
John, Lawrence R., Pvt
Johns, Carl O., Jr., Cpl,
Johns, Julius C., S/Sgt,
Johns, Louis L., S/Sgt,
Johns, Talmage, Jr., Pvt,
Johnson, Albert E., Pfc,
Johnson, Albert I., S/Sgt,
†Johnson, Alex G., Pvt,
Johnson, Alvin L., T/Sgt,
Johnson, Arden E., Pvt,
Johnson, Buddy T., Pvt,
†Johnson, Carroll G., 2nd Lt,
Johnson, Casey O., Pfc,
Johnson, Charles E., Lt Col,
Johnson, Charles E., Pfc,
Johnson, Charles E., Pfc,
Johnson, Charles J., Pvt,
Johnson, Charles P., Pfc,
Johnson, Clarence A., Pvt,
†Johnson, Clarence R., Pfc,
Johnson, Cloid M., Sgt,
Johnson, Clyde L., S/Sgt,
Johnson, David M., Pvt,
†Johnson, David O., Pfc,

† Killed in Action. * Prisoner of War. ‡ Missing in Action. § Died of Wounds.

520 HISTORY OF THE THIRD INFANTRY DIVISION

Johnson, Denver C., Pfc,
Johnson, Ed, Pvt,
Johnson, Edmund H., Pfc,
Johnson, Edwin H., S/Sgt,
†Johnson, Ellsworth E., Pfc,
Johnson, Emil R., Pfc,
Johnson, Eugene F., Pvt,
Johnson, Eugene O., Pfc,
Johnson, Eustace L., Jr.,
Johnson, Frank O., T/Sgt,
Johnson, Franklyn B., Pfc,
Johnson, Gardner, Pvt
Johnson, Gene P., Pvt,
Johnson, Gustaf J., Pfc,
Johnson, Herbert A., Pvt,
Johnson, Herman E., Pfc,
Johnson, Howard T., Cpl,
†Johnson, Howard W., 2nd Lt,
Johnson, James N., Pfc,
Johnson, Joe N., S/Sgt,
Johnson, John H., Pvt
Johnson, Joseph D., S/Sgt,
Johnson, Junior C., Pfc,
Johnson, Kenneth G., Pfc,
Johnson, Kenneth J., T/5,
‡Johnson, Kenneth R., Pfc,
Johnson, Laurence, Pvt,
Johnson, Leslie L., S/Sgt,
†Johnson, Lloyd V., Pfc,
Johnson, Lloyd W., Sgt,
Johnson, Loyal D., Pfc,
Johnson, Norris O., S/Sgt,
Johnson, O. B., 2nd Lt,
Johnson, Omar, Pvt,
†Johnson, Ora L., Jr., Pfc,
†Johnson, Paul M., Pfc,
†Johnson, Peter C., Cpl,
Johnson, Pratt H., Cpl,
†Johnson, Rae D., Pvt,
Johnson, Ray A., Pvt,
Johnson, Ray B., Pfc,
Johnson, Raymond, Pvt,
Johnson, Raymond L., Capt,
Johnson, Richard J., S/Sgt,
Johnson, Robert E., 1st Lt,
Johnson, Robert W., 2nd Lt,
Johnson, Robert W., Pfc,
Johnson, Roland S., Pvt,
‡Johnson, Sam W., Pfc,
†Johnson, Tom B., Sgt,
Johnson, Wallace C., Pfc,
Johnson, Walter, Pfc,
‡Johnson, Walter C., Pvt,
Johnson, Walter J., Sgt,
Johnson, Willard C., 1st Lt,
†Johnson, Willard D., Jr., Pvt,
Johnson, William T., Cpl,
Johnson, Woodrow N., Pvt,
Johnston, Arnold, Pfc
Johnston, Charles E., Pvt,
Johnston, Dean W., Pfc,
Johnston, Robert E., Pvt,
Johnston, Robert L., Pvt,
Johnston, Willie A., T/4,
Johnstone, Frederick E., 1st Sgt
†Joines, John D., Pvt,
Jokiel, Stanley L., Pvt,
†Jolly, Cecil K., Sgt,
Jolly, David L., Jr., Cpl,
Jolly, James E., S/Sgt,
Jones, A. D., S/Sgt,
Jones, Alfred W., T/5,
Jones, Bobby J., Pvt,
§Jones, Burchell D., Pfc,
Jones, Charles E., Pvt,
†Jones, Claude M., Pvt,
Jones, David S., S/Sgt,
Jones, Don C., T/5,
Jones, Eugene V., Cpl,
Jones, Doyle, 2nd Lt,
Jones, Frank E., Pfc,
Jones, Fred J., Pvt,
Jones, George G., Pvt,
Jones, Gerald E., Cpl,
Jones, Harold C., Pfc,
Jones, Harold N., T/4,
Jones, Harry D., Pfc,
Jones, Harry J., Pvt,
Jones, Hence, Pfc,
Jones, Herschel P., Pvt,
Jones, Howard M., Pvt,
Jones, Jack J., 2nd Lt,
Jones, James D., Jr., Pfc,
Jones, James E., Capt
Jones, James E., Pfc,
Jones, James H., Jr., Pfc,
Jones, James W., Pfc,
Jones, J. B., S/Sgt,
‡Jones, Jesse R., Pvt,
Jones, John A., Sgt
Jones, John C., Pvt,
Jones, John H., Pvt,
Jones, Keith A., T/5,
Jones, L. C., Pvt,

Jones, LeRoy, Pfc,
§Jones, Lewis L., Sgt,
Jones, Marshall E., Sgt.
Jones, Murphy C., Pfc,
Jones, Napolon, Pvt,
Jones, Norman D., T/5,
Jones, Omar R., Pfc,
Jones, Orin W., Pvt,
Jones, Orville K., Pvt,
Jones, Paul G., Pfc,
Jones, Paul J., Pvt,
Jones, Ray E., Pvt,
†Jones, Russell F., Pvt,
Jones, Thomas A., S/Sgt,
Jones, Thomas E., Pvt,
Jones, Thomas W., Pvt,
†Jones, Willa, Pvt,
Jones, William A., Pfc,
Jones, William C., Pvt,
Jones, William E., WOJG,
Jones, William H., Pvt,
Jones, William M., Pvt,
Jones, Willie C., Pfc,
Jonnson, Charles R., Pvt,
Jonson, Charles J., Pfc,
Jorczak, John J., Pfc,
Jordan, Cecil B., Pfc,
†Jordan, Hilary R., 1st Lt,
Jordan, Hubert L., Pvt,
Jordan, Hugo J., Pvt,
Jordan, Junior L., Pfc,
Jordan, Vernon C., Pfc,
Jordan, Walter J., Pvt,
Jordan, William C., Pvt,
Jordanek, Andrew J., Cpl,
Jorgensen, Wendell W., Pfc,
Jorgenson, Howard E., Pvt,
Jorgenson, Walter, Pvt,
†Joseph, George P., Pfc,
Josh, Charles F., Jr., Pfc,
‡Joslin, Wilber E., Pfc,
Joslyn, Austin L., Pfc,
Joubert, Harry T., Pvt,
Joy, Wilbur, T/5,
†Joyal, Henry E., Pfc,
Joyce, John F., Pfc,
Joyner, Alton E., Pfc,
Joyner, Ralph J., Pvt,
Judd, Dell P., Pvt,
Judd, Lucian E., Pvt,
Judy, Donald E., Pvt,
Judy, Homer M., Pfc,
Judy, Maurice E., T/4,
Juist, Donald A., S/Sgt,
Juknis, Carl J., Sgt,
Julian, George W., Pvt
Julian, James E., T/4,
‡Julian, Rosaire M., T/5,
Juliano, Jennarine S., T/5,
Jumpe, Donald R., Pvt,
Jumper, William D., T/5,
Juneau, Maxwell A., 2nd Lt,
Junk, Robert N., Pfc,
Jurchenko, Elmer, Pfc,
Jurczak, John, Pfc,
Jurczak, Leo, Pfc,
Jurewicz, Anthony, Pfc,
*Jurgs, Donald W., Pvt,
Jursch, Carl C., Pvt,
Jurss, Clarence W., Pfc,
Jussila, Clyde F., Pfc,
Just, Kenneth G., Pfc,
Justice, Adron, Pvt,
Justice, Clarence H., S/Sgt,
†Justice, Stanley, Sgt,

Kaats, Joseph F., Sgt
Kaczmarek, Roy J., Pvt
Kadaroff, Albert, Pvt,
Kaehler, Herbert W., Sr., Pfc,
Kagin, William, Pfc,
Kaha, Martin, Pfc,
Kahla, George C., Pvt,
†Kaimakais, Peter, Pvt,
Kaiser, Irving A., Pfc,
†Kaiser, Sylvester D., Pfc,
‡Kalata, Harold J., Pfc,
Kalavetinas, Charles, Cpl
Kalemon, Paul, Pvt,
Kaler, John F., Pvt,
†Kaler, Robert L., Pfc,
Kalhagen, Alvin M., Pfc,
Kalina, Gerald W., Pfc,
Kalinowski, Joseph A., S/Sgt,
Kalinowski, Walter J., T/Sgt,
Kalita, John, Pfc,
Kalita, John J., Pfc,
Kall, Robert E., Pfc,
Kallio, Marvin W., Sgt,
Kaltenbrun, Eugene R., S/Sgt,
†Kaminski, Henry J., Sgt,
Kammerer, Paul G., Sgt,
Kampe, Klemens A., Capt
Kanable, George D., Pvt,

Kandrack, Edward A., Pvt
Kandrock, Edward A., Pfc
Kane, James N., Pvt,
Kancy, Terrance S., Pvt,
Kangas, Oliver J., Pvt,
Kania, John J., Pfc,
Kantorski, Anthony, Jr., Pvt,
Kapaun, Ralph O., Pfc,
Kapel, John J., Pfc,
†Kaplan, Louis, S/Sgt.
Kaplan, Maurice B., Pvt,
Kaplan, Walter, Pvt,
Kaplowitz, Sidney, Pfc,
Kappa, Albert, Pvt,
Kappes, John R., Pvt,
Kapsick, Steven N., Cpl,
Karageorge, George, Pvt,
Karasinki, Joseph J., Pvt,
Karasky, Sidney I., Cpl,
Karczewski, Thaddeus, Pvt,
Karnas, Henry P., Pvt,
Karney, George R., Cpl
Karnz, Louis R., Pfc,
Karow, Kenton J., T/4,
Karschnick, Arthur E., Pfc,
Kashieta, John J., Pfc,
Kasmarik, Edward L., Pvt,
Kasoski, Gilbert J., Pfc,
Kasperowica, Walter S., Pvt,
Kasperski, Louis B., Pfc,
Kasten, Raymond G., Pvt,
Kastman, Lester G., 2nd Lt,
†Kasunsky, Seymour, Pfc,
Katen, Ralph S., Pvt,
Katz, Ander, Pvt
Katz, Ander, Pfc
Katz, Charles R., Pvt,
Katz, Edward, T/5,
†Katz, Jerome, Pfc,
†Katz, Joseph, Pvt,
†Katze, Louis, Pfc,
Kauderer, Bernard J., Pvt
Kauffman, Gael F., Capt,
Kaufman, Dexter K., Pvt,
Kaufman, John J., Pvt,
Kauppila, Norman R., Pvt,
†Kauty, Richard, Pfc,
†Kaval, George, Pfc,
†Kavalcik, Edward, Pfc,
Kavanagh, Charles F., Cpl,
Kavanagh, Richard L., S/Sgt,
Kawa, Walter J., S/Sgt,
Kaymiuskim, Thomas W., Pfc
†Kayser, Frank, Pvt,
Kazaren, Emil V., Pvt,
Kerney, Thomas A., Pfc,
Keating, James W., T/5,
Keedy, Vernon L., Pfc,
*Keefe, Wilbert E., Pvt,
†Keefer, Albert D., Pfc,
Keefer, Frank L., Pfc,
Keegan, Edwin F., Jr., Pvt
‡Keel, Richard H., Pvt,
Keel, Victor P., Pvt,
Keeler, Joseph P., Pvt
Keeley, Vermont, Pfc,
†Keeling, Rudolph, Pfc,
Keeman, Joseph J., T/5,
Keen, Leon P., Cpl,
†Keenan, William J., Pvt,
Keene, Andrew J., Jr., Cpl,
Keene, William F., 2nd Lt,
Keener, George M., Pfc,
Keeter, Leo, T/4,
†Kefsizian, Charles, Cpl,
Kehoe, Joseph E., T/Sgt,
Keifer, Sydney M., Cpl,
Keith, Arnold E., Pfc,
†Keith, James G., Pvt,
†Keith, Joseph L., Pfc,
Keith, Lewis F., Pfc
Keith, Oran, T/Sgt,
Keith, Randel, Pfc,
Keithley, Douglas G., Pvt,
Kelland, William, Pvt,
Keller, Albert J., Pfc,
Keller, Charles J., Pvt,
Keller, Harold W., Sgt,
Keller, Joseph, Sgt,
Keller, Louis P., Pvt,
Keller, Robert R., Pvt,
Keller, Walter, Jr., Pfc
Keller, Walter, Jr., Pvt
Kelley, Andrew J., Pfc,
Kelley, Charles R., Pvt,
Kelley, Clarence W., Pvt,
Kelley, Hugh D., Pfc,
Kelley, James E., Pfc,
Kelley, James H., Pfc,
Kelley, Leroy K., Pfc,
Kelley, Loren L., Pfc,
Kelley, Marcus F., Sgt,
Kelley, Newell R., Cpl,
Kelley, Paul H., Pfc,

Kelley, Robert B., Pfc
Kelley, Robert E., Pvt,
Kelley, Silas R., Pfc,
Kellner, Maurice A., Pfc,
Kellog, Olen, Sgt,
Kellogg, Robert F., Pfc,
Kelly, Aron, Pvt,
Kelly, Bentley C., Jr., 1st Lt,
Kelly, Donald H., Pfc,
Kelly, Donald J., Pvt,
Kelly, George W., Sgt,
†Kelly, Harold R., Pfc,
Kelly, Herschel E., Pvt,
Kelly, Hubert F., Pfc,
Kelly, John C., Pfc,
Kelly, John D., Pfc,
Kelly, John W., Pvt,
Kelly, Lawrence J., Pvt,
Kelly, Lawrence J., Jr., Pfc,
Kelly, Michael J., Pfc,
Kelly, Terrance G., Pvt,
Kelly, Wiley, Pfc,
‡Kelman, Victor, Pvt,
Kelsey, Robert M., Pvt,
Kelsey, Walter E., 1st Lt,
Kemmer, Harold C., Pvt,
Kemp, Dennis A., T/5,
†Kemp, Ray, Pfc,
†Kemp, Raymond, Pfc,
†Kemper, William H., S/Sgt,
Kendall, Arnold G., Pvt,
Kendall, James G., Pfc,
Kendall, Lawrence C., Pvt,
Kenaston, Douglas A., T/5,
Kendle, Lawrence D., Pfc,
Kendrick, Loomis C., Pfc,
Kendrick, Robert, Jr., S/Sgt,
Kendzierski, William, Pfc,
Kenne, Frederick E., Pfc,
Kenneally, Francis J., Pfc,
Kenneally, John J., S/Sgt,
Kennedy, Alvan E., Pfc
Kennedy, Alvin E., Pvt
†Kennedy, Cecil J., Pvt,
Kennedy, Charles L., Pvt,
Kennedy, Cyril P., Sgt,
Kennedy, Edward J., Pvt,
Kennedy, Everett W., 1st Lt,
Kennedy, Frank J., T/5,
†Kennedy, Glenn W., Pvt,
Kennedy, Harry E., Jr., Pvt,
Kennedy, James E., Pfc
Kennedy, James E., Pvt
Kennedy, John O., Pvt,
Kennedy, Joseph P., Sgt,
Kenney, Raymond D., Pfc,
Kennison, John H., Pvt,
Kenny, Bernard F., Cpl,
Kenny, Leon E., Sgt
†Kensinger, Stanton W., Sgt,
Kent, David A., Pvt,
Kent, Dillard G., Pvt,
*Kent, James W., 2nd Lt
†Kent, William C., Pfc,
Kenward, Howard R., Pfc,
†Kenyon, Donald D., Pvt,
Keough, George J., Sgt,
Kephart, Albert B., Pfc
Kephart, John W., Pvt,
Kephart, Ralph B., Pvt
‡Kephart, Virgil A., Sgt,
Kephart, Walter G., Pfc,
Keppler, Leo F., Pfc,
Kerbor, Herman W., Sgt,
†Kerby, Earl L., Pfc,
Kercheval, Marion L., 2nd Lt,
Kerchner, Norman E., Pvt,
Kerley, Bernard J., Pvt,
Kermode, Joseph, Pvt,
Kern, Samuel H., Pfc
Kerr, Frederick J., Sgt,
†Kerr, Hugh S., Pvt,
Kerr, Stanley L., Pvt
Kerrigan, Leo J., Pvt,
†Kessler, Albert F., Pfc,
†Kessler, Patrick L., Pfc,
*Kester, Charles A., Pvt,
Kester, Harold J., Pfc,
†Ketchmark, Thomas F., T/5,
Ketchum, William C., S/Sgt,
Ketterling, Edwin, Pfc,
Key, Roy, Jr., S/Sgt,
Kidd, Charles L., Pfc,
Kidd, Ralph M., Cpl,
Kidwell, John W., Cpl,
Kielman, Harold O., Pfc,
Kieliszewski, Lawrence F., Pfc,
Kiessling, Orville C., Pfc,
Kietz, William A., Pfc,
Kiger, Coy N., Pvt,
†Kighlinger, Clifford L., Pfc,
Kiker, George F., Pvt,
Kilar, Ferdinand J., Sgt,
‡Kilduff, Maurice M., Pfc,

Kilduff, Thomas C., Pfc,
Kile, Theodore R., S/Sgt,
Kiley, John D. L., Pvt
Kiley, John J., Pfc,
Killelea, George F., Pfc,
†Killewald, Wilford, Pfc
Killian, Andrew W., Pfc,
Killian, James H., Pfc,
Killian, Leland E., S/Sgt,
Killian, Winston W., Pvt,
Killingsworth, William, Pvt,
Killmer, Chester A., Pfc,
Kilmer, Francis J., Pfc,
Kilner, Paul B., Pfc,
Kilpatrick, Grover S., Pvt,
Kilpatrick, Paul D., Cpl,
Kilroy, Bernard F., Jr., Pvt,
Kimbel, Melville E., T/5,
Kimbrel, Melvin E., Pvt,
Kimbrell, Darrell R., Pvt,
Kimikowski, Stanley J., Pfc,
Kimmel, Donald M., Pvt,
Kinard, Norville F., Pfc,
Kincaid, Onley B., Pvt,
Kinder, Frealy F., Pvt,
King, Arthur E., S/Sgt,
King, Charles R., Pfc,
King, David D., Pvt,
King, Denver W., S/Sgt,
King, Elmer, Pvt,
†King, Elzie O., Pvt,
King, Herman E., Pfc,
King, Jack, Cpl
King, James F., Cpl,
King, John F., Jr., Pvt,
King, Leonard L., Pfc,
King, Lewis C., Pfc,
King, Louis, Pvt,
King, Luther L., Pvt,
King, Myron D., Pvt,
†King, Norman R., Pfc,
King, Robert E., Pfc,
King, Roy V., S/Sgt,
King, Thomas J., Pvt,
King, Warren A., Pfc,
†Kingery, Raymond J., Pvt,
Kinley, John, Pfc,
Kinne, William O., 2nd Lt,
Kinney, Oliver G., Maj,
Kinny, Peter, Pvt,
Kinsala, George W., T/4,
Kinsbrunner, Adolf, Pfc,
Kinsey, Willie W., S/Sgt
Kinsman, Roy A., Pfc,
Kinswa, James, Pfc,
Kirby, Edward P., 2nd Lt,
*Kirby, Everett E. D., Pfc,
Kirby, Thomas P., Pvt,
Kircheval, Robert H., Pfc
Kirchner, Edward R., T/4,
Kirchner, Patrick H., S/Sgt,
Kirchoff, Elroy E., Pfc,
Kirk, Frank M., Pfc,
Kirk, Louis L., Pvt
Kirkland, William C., Sgt,
Kirkley, Luther W., Pfc,
Kirkman, Brady G., Pvt
Kirkpatrick, James M., Pfc,
Kirksey, Dennie F., Pfc,
Kirkwood, Clement W., S/Sgt,
Kirsch, Herbert A., T/4,
Kirschbaum, Lester M., S/Sgt,
Kirschbaum, Robert F., T/5,
Kirsh, Seymour C., Sgt,
Kish, Ernest, Pfc,
Kish, George, T/5,
Kish, Joseph F., Pfc,
Kishton, Mark, Pfc,
Kisner, Drexel D., Pvt,
Kissell, Harry, Jr., Pfc,
Kissinger, Albert, S/Sgt,
Kitchen, Raymond F., Pvt,
Kittleson, Lawrence, Pvt,
Kiwatisky, Nicholas F., S/Sgt,
Klaes, James C., Jr., Sgt,
Klais, John W., Pvt,
Klang, Carl J., Pvt,
Klapan, Joseph G., Pvt,
Klaren, Donald A., Cpl,
Klaren, Edwin M., Pfc,
†Klasinski, Walter J., Pvt,
†Klatt, Walter L., Cpl,
Klaus, Frank A., Pfc,
Klaus, James W., S/Sgt,
Klaus, Robert W., T/5,
Kleaver, Otis, Pvt,
Kleeman, Arthur E., Pfc,
Kloepfer, Herman F., Pvt,
Klein, Edward N., Pfc,
Klein, Rudolfo P., Pvt,
Klein, Seymour H., Pfc,
†Kleiza, John, Pfc,
‡Klejko, Edmund J., Sgt,
Klemenc, Frank J., Pvt

† Killed in Action. * Prisoner of War. ‡ Missing in Action. § Died of Wounds.

Klementowicz, Leon, Sgt,
†Klementowisz, Joseph S., Sgt,
Klemetsurd, Stanley H., Pvt
‡Klemm, Fred W., Pfc,
Klepk, Edwin J., Pvt,
Klett, Ralph A., Pfc,
Kliest, Lloyd E., Pvt,
Kliewer, Eugene L., Pfc,
Klima, Joseph W., Pfc,
Klimbiewicz, Florian C., Pvt
Klimek, Joseph A., Sgt,
Klindworth, John M., Pfc,
‡Kline, Edgar, Pvt,
Kline, Paul E., Sr., Pfc,
Klinkner, Jacob, Pfc,
†Klish, Chester B., Cpl,
Klister, Joseph J., S/Sgt,
Klistzner Saul, Pvt,
Klodzinski, Lawrence J., Pvt
Klombies, Arthur G., Sgt,
Klopovic, Edward, Jr., Pvt,
§Kloss, Julius N., Sgt,
Klug, Earl A., Pvt,
†Klush, Edwin F., Pvt,
†Kluever, Gordon, Cpl,
Klumas, Edward F., Pfc,
Klyder, John, Jr., Pvt,
Knack, John H., T/5,
Knapp, Edgar V., Pfc,
Knapp, Charles E., T/5,
Knapp, Marlin R., Pfc,
Knapp, Vincent M., Pfc,
Knappenberger, Alton W., Pfc,
Knickerbocker, Charles F., Pfc,
Knight, Albert H., 1st Sgt,
Knight, Archie L., Sgt,
Knight, Charles W., Sgt,
Knight, F. M., Sgt,
Knight, Guy, Pvt,
§Knight, Samuel F., Jr., 1st Lt,
Knight, Thurman, Pvt,
Knight, William B., Jr., Pvt,
Kniola, Richard A., Pfc,
Knobloch, Norbel, Pvt,
Knobel, Joseph, Pvt
Knois, Cecil A., Sgt
Knois, Cecil A., Pfc,
§Knoll, Ernest F., Pvt,
Knopf, Walter, Pfc,
Knosp, Wesley E., Cpl,
Knouse, Norval N., Cpl,
Knowles, Berkley St. C., Pfc,
Knowles, Wesley T., Jr., Pfc,
Knupp, Richard J., Pvt,
Knurek, Charles W., Pfc,
Kobernick, John W., 1st Sgt,
Kobneck, Stanley E., T/4,
†Kobischka, Fred F., Pfc,
Koboldt, Harry W., Pfc,
Kobylinski, Michael, Pfc,
Koch, Ettrick A., Pvt,
Koch, Frederick L., Pfc,
*Koch, George, Pvt,
Kochan, Edward R., Cpl,
Kochanski, Walter V., Pfc,
Kocher, Harold W., Pfc,
Kochert, Carroll E., Pvt,
Koczi, Louis A., Pfc,
Koczmerak, Roy J., Pvt
Kodadek, Robert C., S/Sgt,
Koeln, William O., Pfc
Köeneke, Harry C., Cpl,
Koenig, Herman, Pfc,
§Koenig, Richard, M/Sgt,
Koenig, Robert F., T/5,
†Koenis, Jacob J., Pfc,
Koeppelle, Carl J., Pvt,
Koerner, Robert L., 1st Lt,
Koffman, David, Sgt,
Kohl, John P., Pfc,
†Koisa, John S., S/Sgt,
Kolb, Donald D., Pfc,
Kolb, Russell P., Pvt,
Kolkau, Paul J., Jr., Pfc,
Kollar, Louis P., Pvt,
Kollman, Carl A., Pvt,
Kolsahk, Leonard M., Pvt,
Kominsky, Vincent F., Pfc,
Komisarek, Charles F., Pfc,
‡Komorowski, John B., Sgt,
Konanz, Irvin L., Pfc,
Koncilia, Frank W., Pfc,
*Konczal, Joseph A., Pvt,
Kondra, Peter J., Pfc,
Koneski, Theodore M., Pfc,
Konik, Walter M., Pfc,
†Konowalik, Stanley P., Pvt,
†Kontor, Steve, Pfc,
Koolidge, Louis R., Cpl,
Koon, Meredith L., Pfc,
Koonce, Kenneth V., Pvt,
Koope, William T., Pfc,
Kopczynski, Joseph S., Pvt,
*Kopka, John P., Pfc,

Kopp, John S., Pfc,
†Kordek, Walter J., Pvt,
Kordell, Peter, Pfc,
Kordish, Victor A., S/Sgt,
Kordosh, John, 1st Lt,
‡Korman, Stephen C., Pvt,
Kornacker, Joseph A., Pvt,
Kornerich, Anton, Pvt,
Kornexl, Andrew J., Sgt,
Korsianski, Stephen J., Pvt,
Kosh, Emil J., Sgt,
‡Kosko, Joseph F., Sgt,
Kosky, Joseph G., Sgt,
Koslovsky, Stanley, Pvt,
Kosmecki, Stanley J., Pfc,
Koss, Fred, S/Sgt,
Koss, Walter S., S/Sgt,
†Kosse, Roman L., Pfc,
Kostedt, Ervin L., Pvt,
Kostelich, Anton, Pvt
Kostelnik, Joseph F., Pvt,
Kostera, Leonard G., Pvt,
Kostiw, Michael, Pfc,
Kostrisak, John A., Sgt,
Kostuch, Clements H., Pvt,
Kosuda, Joseph R., Pfc,
Kott, Edward, Pvt,
Kottenbrock, Louis H., Cpl,
†Koury, George C., Pvt,
Koutsky, Edward L., Pfc,
§Kovach, Alex, Pvt,
†Kovaciak, Nick R., S/Sgt,
Kovalcik, John A., Pvt,
Kovalycsik, Anthony A., Pfc,
Kowalchik, William, Pvt,
Kowaleski, Joseph T., Sgt,
Kozarshak, Michael, Pvt,
Kozich, Henry, Pfc,
Koziol, Thomas W., Pfc,
Kozloski, John S., 1st Sgt,
Kozma, Louis, Sgt
Kozminski, Charles J., Sgt,
Kradyna, Adam J. J., Pfc,
Kraemer, Arnold, S/Sgt,
§Kraemer, Floyd L., Pfc,
Krajeski, Leonard F., Pfc,
Krajewski, Walter J., Pvt,
†Kral, Charles, Pfc,
Kramer, Charles L., Pvt
†Kramer, Lawrence P., Pfc,
Kramlich, Emil, Pvt,
†Krantz, John P., 2nd Lt,
Krasner, Theodore W., Pvt
†Kratcoski, Edward J., Pvt,
Kratzer, Clarence C., Pfc,
Kraus, Francis H., Pvt,
Kraus, Lawrence, Pvt,
Krause, Earle G., S/Sgt,
Kravetz, Albert T., Pvt,
Kravitz, Hilard L., Capt,
Kredel, Andrew W., Pvt,
Kresie, Harry L., Pvt,
Kreillich, Joseph P., Pvt,
Kreiner, Raymond J., Pvt,
Kreitzman, Lester M., Pfc,
Kremer, William T., Pvt,
Kremholz, Charles A., Pvt,
Kren, Darrel D., Pvt,
Krenn, Arthur C., Pfc,
Krezan, Thomas, Pfc,
Krieg, Lawrence B., Pvt,
Kriesak, Paul H., Pvt,
Krikorian, Charles S., T/5,
Krinke, Leonard A., Pvt,
Krivitsky, Lewis J., Pvt,
Krochmal, Arnold, Lt,
Krol, Anthony J., Pvt,
†Kroll, Robert E., Pfc,
Kroll, Ted J., Pvt,
Kroll, Tygmunt J., Pfc,
Kronst, Paul C., Pfc,
Kropp, Glenn, Pvt,
†Krosch, Oscar A., Cpl,
‡Krotki, Philip T., Pfc,
Krueck, Walter B., Pvt,
Krueger, Edwin, Pfc
Krueger, John A., Pvt,
Krueger, Arnold W., Pfc,
Krueger, Vernon A., Pvt,
Krueger, William C., Sgt,
Krueger, William S., S/Sgt,
Kruep, Theodore H., Sgt,
Krug, Charles E., Jr., S/Sgt,
†Krug, Donald R., Pfc,
§Kruger, Leo H., Capt,
Kruss, Joseph, Cpl,
Kryfka, Edward P., Pfc
*Krzewinski, Edward J., Pfc,
Kubis, Thaddeus A., Pvt,
Kubish, John A., Pvt,
Kucher, Paul, Pfc,
Kucinski, William B., T/Sgt,
Kudey, Frank R., Pfc,
Kudzia, Daniel I., T/4,

Kuehling, Lester G., S/Sgt,
Kuenzer, Lyle E., Sgt,
Kuez, Theodore, Pfc,
Kufel, John M., Pfc,
Kugel, Leonard, Pvt,
Kughn, Melvin R., Pfc,
Kuhl, Dwight P., Pfc,
†Kuhlmann, C. J., Jr., 1st Lt,
Kuhn, Billy L., Pvt,
Kuhn, Frederick A., Pfc,
Kuhn, Hugh L., T/4,
Kuhn, Wallace L., Pfc,
Kukla, Adam J., Pfc,
Kulas, Victor A., Pfc,
Kumpula, Sulo M., Pfc,
Kun, Charles L., Pvt,
Kunellis, Chris E., L/Sgt,
Kunts, Henry J., Cpl,
†Kuntz, Lawrence W., Pfc,
§Kuntz, Lester, Sgt,
Kuntz, William M., Pfc,
‡Kunz, Joseph E., Pvt,
Kurt, Oscar L., Pvt,
Kurtz, Andrew P., Pfc,
Kurtz, Kenneth D., Pfc,
Kuruca, Joseph, Pvt,
Kuryla, Albert W., Pvt,
Kushner, George J., Pvt,
Kussman, Hayden W., T/Sgt
Kustron, Edward J., Pvt,
Kusy, Walter S., Pvt,
†Kutovicz, John R., Pfc,
Kutzelman, Lawrence A., Pvt,
†Kuusenoksa, Arthur K., Pvt,
Kuymandall, Sebron L., Pfc,
Kuzel, John S., Sgt,
†Kuzyk, Myron, 1st Lt
Kwasnik, Max M., Pfc,
Kwiatkowski, William J., Pvt,
‡Kwiatowski, Henry S., Pfc,
Kyle, Archie A., Pvt,
Kyle, Hugh S., T/5,

Laackmann, Herbert H., Cpl,
Labeau, LeRoy B., Pfc,
Labelle, Edward C., 1st Lt,
§Laborde, Sidney J., Pfc,
Labosky, Raymond, Sr., Pfc,
‡Lacey, Edward E., Sgt,
Lach, John E., Pfc,
†LaChance, George B., S/Sgt,
Lachapelle, Wilbrod A., Pvt,
Lack, Henry C., Pvt,
Lackhart, Virgil E., T/5,
Lackman, Elwood E., Jr., Cpl,
‡LaCome, George E., Cpl,
Ladd, Milton R., Pfc,
‡LaDouce, Edward H., S/Sgt,
Laeka, Bicuwa, Pfc,
Laeser, Walter E., S/Sgt,
Lafarier, Ray A., Pvt,
LaFauris, Jacques E., Pvt,
Lafitte, Arthur O., S/Sgt,
LaFon, Opal D., Pfc,
Lafran, Michael J., Pfc,
Lagriola, Alexander, Pvt
Laha, Milburn E., Pfc,
LaHaye, Edmund J., Pvt,
Lahr, Charles, Jr., 1st Lt,
Lahti, Arvid M., S/Sgt,
§Laithinen, John E., S/Sgt,
‡Lake, John W., Pvt,
†Lake, Robert J., Pfc,
Lakowitz, William P., Pvt,
Lallier, Gerard E., Pvt,
LaLonde, Irving W., Pfc,
Lamar, Leo, 1st Lt,
LaMarca, Joseph, Pvt,
LaMarche, Dennis F., Pvt,
Lamb, Robert W., T/5,
Lambert, Monroe H., Pvt
Lambert, Richard T., S/Sgt,
Lambert, Vernon R., Pfc,
Lamberth, Owen G., Cpl,
†Lamberti, Michael F., Sgt,
†Lamica, Emery O., Pvt,
Lamker, Nelson A., T/5,
LaMonica, Bennie, Pfc,
†Lampella, LeRoy, Pvt,
‡Lampi, John T., Pfc,
Lampley, James T., Pfc,
Lanava, Anthony J., Sgt,
†Lancaster, Herbert, Pvt,
Lancaster, Hewlett, Pfc,
†Lander, Norman S., Pvt,
Landers, Charles E., Pfc,
Landfield, David, Pfc,
Landini, Albert, Pfc,
Landman, Henry, Pfc,
‡Landman, John, Pfc,
*Landry, Edward, Pfc,
Landry, Ernest G., Pvt,
Landry, Ulleans J., Pfc,
Landry, Willis P., Sgt,

‡Landsale, Gilbert B., Pvt,
‡Landucci, Oscar J., Pfc,
‡Lane, Donald C., 2nd Lt,
Lane, Guy, Pvt
Lane, Herbert W., Pfc,
Lane, James E., Pfc,
Lane, Leon D., Pfc,
Lane, Thomas A., Pvt
‡Lane, William Y., Pfc,
Lang, William G., Pfc,
Langely, Wallace E., S/Sgt,
Langenbahn, Charles C., Pvt,
Langenberg, Joseph J., Sgt,
Langer, Herbert E., Pvt
Langford, Lloyd E., Capt,
Langley, Albert T., S/Sgt,
Langley, Albert T., Pvt,
†Langley, Dalton O., Pvt,
Langner, James G., Pfc,
Langnes, Benjamin P., Cpl,
*Langnese, Robert T., T/5,
Lanoue, Raymond A., Pfc,
Langone, Edward A., Pfc,
Langowski, Frank D., Pvt,
Langrigan, Clifford W., Pfc,
Langston, Autry, 2nd Lt,
Lanier, Forrest S., Pfc
Lanier, Joe R., Pfc,
Lansdowne, Guy R., T/4,
†Lansing, Dan E., Pvt,
Lansing, George W., Jr., Sgt,
Lantz, Harry L., Pvt,
Lantz, William, Jr., Pfc,
Laperle, Laurent W., Pfc,
‡LaPine, Glenn, S/Sgt,
LaPlant, George L., Pvt,
LaPointe, Paul, Pvt,
LaPointe, James E., Pvt,
LaPore, Fred, Pvt,
LaPorte, Norman H., Pfc,
LaPose, Richard J., Pfc,
Laquerre, Reginald R., Pvt,
Lara, Augustine L., Pvt,
Laraber, Harry M., Sgt,
†Laraia, Alfred J., Sgt,
*Laramore, Willard E., Pfc,
Larence, Jack E., Pvt
Large, Arvle R., Pfc,
Larimore, Philip B., Capt,
Larkin, David F., Pvt,
Larkins, Lawrence E., Pfc,
LaRosa, James V., Pfc,
LaRose, Roland V., Pfc,
Larosee, Romeo P., Pvt,
†LaRossa, John P., Pvt,
Larrabee, Robert A., Pfc,
Larsen, Kenneth C., Sgt,
Larsen, Olef, Jr., Pfc
Larsen, Ward F., T/4,
Larson, Harold G., Pfc,
Larson, Harold R., Pvt,
Larson, John W., Capt
Larson, Joseph L., Pfc,
Larson, Kenneth A., Cpl,
Larson, Lawrence M., T/5,
Larson, Louis L., Pvt,
Larson, Robert G., Pvt,
Larson, Rudolph A., S/Sgt,
Larson, Verlin A., Pvt,
§LaRue, Kenneth E., S/Sgt,
†Larva, Valentina, Pvt,
†Larwa, John J., Pvt,
LaSala, Patsy, Pvt,
Lash, Michael J., Sgt,
Lash, Wesley, Pfc,
Laskowski, Rudolph, T/5,
Lasley, George P., Pfc,
Lasley, Robert J., Pvt,
†Lassiter, Clifford G., Pvt,
Lata, Joseph J., Pvt,
Latart, Allen E., Pfc,
Latham, Arthur A., 1st Lt,
Latiolais, Wiley L., Pvt,
Latour, Albert L., Pfc,
Latremore, Francis D., Pvt,
‡Lattas, Mick, Pfc,
Lattin, Leonard A., T/Sgt,
Latz, Elmer H., Pvt,
Lau, Raymond H., Pvt,
†Lauber, Frank J., Pvt,
†Laubhan, Frederick, Jr., Pfc,
§Laudemann, Charles J., Pvt,
Lauderdale, Bill, Pfc,
†Laufer, Lester, Pfc,
Laug, Vernon J., T/4,
Laughlin, Byron W., Cpl,
Laughlin, William H., S/Sgt,
‡Laurent, Harry E., S/Sgt,
Laurin, Wesley W. C., Pfc,
Lause, Norbert F., Pvt,
LaValley, Alfred, Pvt,
†LaVecehis, John, Jr., Pvt,
Lavelle, Edward C., Pvt,
Lavelle, James I., Pfc,

Lavender, Frank E., S/Sgt,
‡Laverdore, Harry R., Pfc,
Lavery, Michael J., Pvt,
Lavin, Alfred G., Sgt,
Lavin, Frank C., Capt,
Lavner, Nathan, Pfc,
§Lavoie, Gerald, Pfc,
Law, William P., Jr., 1st Lt,
Law, William W., Pvt,
Lawhorne, George, S/Sgt,
†Lawing, Elmer H., S/Sgt,
Lawler, John J., Pvt
Lawler, Lowman T., T/4,
Lawrence, David L., Pfc,
Lawrence, Harry L., Cpl,
Lawrence, Joseph B., Pvt,
Lawrence, Paul E., Pvt,
Lawrence, Robert J., Pvt,
Lawrence, Wallace E., S/Sgt,
Laws, Kenneth O., Pvt,
Lawson, Carl E., Cpl,
Lawson, Carl W., Pvt,
Lawson, Carter E., Pfc,
Lawson, Delbert H., Pvt,
Lawson, Gerald J., Pfc,
Lawson, Haskel V., S/Sgt,
Lawson, John E., Pvt,
*Lawson, Thomas E., Cpl,
Lawyer, Edmund G., Pvt,
Lawyer, Orville, Cpl,
Lay, Fay N., Pvt,
†Lay, Gene F., Pvt,
Laycock, William J., Pfc,
Layne, Glen D., Cpl,
Layton, Carl L., Pvt,
Layton, Jesse, Pvt,
Layton, Robert V., Pvt,
Lazar, Charles J., S/Sgt,
Lazarcheck, John J., Pfc,
Lea, John F., Pfc,
†Leach, Frank L., Jr., Pfc,
Leach, George, Pfc,
Leach, Rowland C., Pvt,
Leadmon, Harry D., Pvt
Lear, Seymour, Pvt,
Leard, Harold R., Pfc,
Learnerd, Weldeon B., Pvt,
Leary, Benjamin F., T/5,
Leary, Wallace E., Sgt,
LeBlanc, Edmond J., Pfc,
LeBlanc, Howard F., Pvt,
LeBlanc, Irvin L., Cpl,
LeBlanc, Louis E., Pfc,
Lebo, William A., S/Sgt,
†LeBouef, Samuel L., Sgt,
†Leboulch, Yves M., Pvt,
LeBrasseur, Clayton J., Sgt,
LeBreton, Raymond R., S/Sgt,
Lecaroz, Benoit R., Pvt,
Lechtanski, Teddy J., Pfc,
Leck, Stanley J., Pvt,
Leckie, Douglas C., S/Sgt,
Leclair, Alphonse J., Pfc,
Leclair, Peter J., Pvt,
Leclair, William M., Pfc,
LeCorno, John F., Pvt
Ledbetter, Leonard, T/4,
§Leddy, Irving, Sgt,
Ledford, Robert, S/Sgt,
Ledgerwood, John L., 1st Lt,
†Ledoux, Gilbert, Pvt,
LeDuc, Donald E., Pvt,
†Ledy, Clayton A., Cpl,
Lee, Andrew J., Sgt,
Lee, Arlie L., Jr., Pfc,
Lee, David, Pfc,
Lee, Herschel E., Pvt,
Lee, James E., 1st Sgt,
Lee, James E., Pvt,
Lee, John D., Pfc,
Lee, Kenneth L., Pvt,
Lee, Malcolm, Pfc,
†Lee, Mallory J., Pvt,
Lee, M. L., Pvt,
Lee, Milton L., Pfc,
†Lee, Paul M., Jr., Pfc,
Lee, Rabun A., S/Sgt,
Lee, Robert H., T/4,
Lee, William G., Pfc,
Leeper, Charles S., T/5,
Lees, Robert A., Pfc,
Leeth, Emmett E., Pfc,
Lefeave, Richard P., S/Sgt,
Lefevere, Alfonse G., Pfc,
†Leffler, Kenneth E., Pfc,
Lefler, Milton R., Pvt,
Legare, Maurice B., Capt,
Leger, Nolton, Pfc,
Legere, Alfred J., Pvt,
Legett, Vernon, Sgt,
*Legge, Robert W., Pfc,
Legler, Peter F., Pvt,
Legrand, John U., Pvt,
Lehman, David L., Pvt,

† Killed in Action. * Prisoner of War. ‡ Missing in Action. § Died of Wounds.

†Lehman, Emmit T., Pvt,
‡Lehman, Mahlon E., Pfc,
Lehna, Carl B., Pfc,
Lehnert, James G., Pfc,
Lehous, Philip E., Jr., Pvt,
Leibley, Howard F., Pfc,
Leibrook, Raymond H., Pvt,
Leicher, Sheldon A., Pvt,
Leidel, Paul A., Pvt,
Leigh, Gene D., Pfc,
Leighton, Earl F., Cpl,
Leinweber, Benedict F., Pvt,
Leisgang, Robert L., Pfc,
Leistner, Jerome G., Pvt,
Leistritz, Kenneth E., S/Sgt,
Leitgeb, John R., Pvt,
Leith, Robert E., Pvt
Leitz, Lawrence W., Pfc,
LeLoge, Herbert F., Pvt,
LeMaster, Robert L., Pvt,
†Lemke, Arvin E., S/Sgt,
Lemke, Herbert R., T/4,
Lemke, Howard D., Pfc,
Lemming, Martin P., Pfc,
*LeMoine, Floyd A., Sgt,
LeMoine, Joseph W., T/Sgt
Lemons, Edgar R., S/Sgt,
Lemoreux, Elmer B., Pfc,
†Lemus, Juan, Pfc,
Lemus, Marco, Pvt,
§Lending, Ralph D., 2nd Lt
Lengyel, William A., Sgt.
Lenke, William J., Jr., Pfc
Lenox, Charles M., Pfc,
Lentfer, Ervin A., S/Sgt,
Lento, John P., Pvt,
Lentz, Wilmer L., Pvt,
Lenz, Milford O., Pvt,
Lenza, William M., Pvt,
Leo, Arman F., S/Sgt,
Leoffler, Layne E., 2nd Lt,
†Leonard, David W., Pvt,
Leonard, Donald W., T/Sgt,
†Leonard, James H., Pfc,
Leonard, Obedish L., Pfc,
Leonard, William F., S/Sgt,
Leone, Joseph J., Pvt,
Leone, Russell, Pvt,
Leone, Salvatore, Pvt,
Leong, Dick M., T/4,
LePage, Nicholas E., Pvt,
†Lepisto, Paul A., Sgt,
Lepisto, Tauno J., Pvt,
‡Leroux, Roger D., Pfc.
Leroy, Clarence G., Pfc,
Lerum, Sanford I., Pfc,
Lesica, Francis R., T/5,
Leslie, John R., Pfc,
Leslie, Paris L., Pfc,
Letendre, Lawrence A., Pfc,
Leto, Herman A., Pfc,
Lettice, Fred E., Jr., 1st Lt,
Letton, Jack A., T/5,
*Leumer, Edward J., Pfc,
Levasseur, Joseph L. M., Pvt,
Levationo, James, Sgt,
§Levenson, Henry H., Pvt,
Leverland, Bernard G., M/Sgt,
Levesque, Francis J., Pfc
Levesque, Lucien A., Pvt,
Levey, Merton D., Pvt,
Levi, Joseph L., S/Sgt,
Levin, Hyman S., Pfc,
†Levine, Daniel I., Pfc,
Levine, Lawrence, Pvt,
Levine, Raymond, T/5,
Levine, William I., S/Sgt,
Levinsky, David, Pvt,
Levy, Meyer, 1st Lt
Lewark, Earl R., Pvt,
Lewicke, George T., Sgt,
†Lewicki, Mack, Pvt,
*Lewin, Joseph, Pfc,
Lewis, Abel, Sgt,
Lewis, Benjamin E., Sgt
Lewis, Bruce A., Pvt
Lewis, Carl J., Pfc,
‡Lewis, Carlton G., Pvt,
Lewis, Clatie F., Pvt,
†Lewis, Curtis E., Pvt,
Lewis, Edward F., Pvt,
Lewis, Edward G., 1st Lt,
Lewis, Floyd J., Capt,
†Lewis, Harry M., Jr., 2nd Lt,
Lewis, Holly E., T/5,
Lewis, James R., Pfc,
Lewis, John H., Pvt,
‡Lewis, Leroy, Pfc,
Lewis, Leslie C., Pvt
†Lewis, Ralph H., Pvt,
Lewis, Robert L., Pfc
Lewis, Ruel H., Capt,
Lewis, Russell I., Pvt,
Lewis, Stanley R., Pvt,
†Lewis, Thomas A., 2nd Lt,
Lewis, Warren R., Pvt,
Lewis, Wilbur F., Jr., Sgt,
Lewis, William R., Pvt,
†Lewman, Lloyd L., T/Sgt,
Leyns, William R., Pfc,
Libera, John M., Pfc,
Liberti, Bart A., Pfc,
Liberto, Joseph P., Pfc,
Librie, Anthony J., T/5,
Licht, Edmund F., Pfc,
†Licka, Eugene M., Sgt,
‡Liddance, William J., Pfc,
Liddon, Byron E., Pvt,
Liebenshoh, Edward, Pvt,
Liebowitz, Irwin, Pvt
Liedkiewicz, Ervin V., Pfc,
†Liephardt, Casper, Jr., Pvt,
Lierman, Gilbert H., T/4,
Lieske, Henry A., Pfc,
Lifshitz, Alvin B., Pvt,
Lifshitz, Boris, Pvt,
Liggett, Delbert E., S/Sgt,
Light, James A., S/Sgt,
Ligon, William W., Pfc,
Lillard, George R., Pvt,
Lillard, Perry A., T/4,
Lima, Wallace F., Pfc,
Lind, Albert, Pfc,
Lindeen, Eskil C., 1st Sgt,
Lindell, Arne T., Pfc,
Lindenbaum, Isadore, Pvt,
†Lindenbaum, Norman T., Pvt,
Lindenaur, Max, Pfc,
Lindholm, James F., Pfc,
Lindquist, John A., Pfc,
Lindquist, Malcolm N., Sgt,
†Lindsay, John A., Pvt,
Lindsay, Morgan C., Pvt,
Lindsay, William G., Sgt,
Lindsey, Harold L., Pfc,
†Lindsey, James W., Pfc,
Lindsey, Philip L., S/Sgt,
*Lindstrom, Pat H., Pvt,
†Linebarger, Sterling F., T/5,
Linhart, Charles, Pvt,
Linicus, George A., Jr., Pfc,
Link, Alfred W., Pfc,
Link, Herbert V., Pvt
Link, Joseph R., Jr., S/Sgt,
Linken, Joseph, Pvt,
Linker, Lewis B., Pvt,
Linstrom, Charles O., Sgt,
Liontonio, Frank A., Pvt,
Lipka, Robert W., S/Sgt,
Lipke, Charles F., Jr., Sgt,
Lippstreuer, Russell G., Pfc,
Lipski, Anthony, Jr., Sgt,
Lipstein, Milton E., Pfc,
†Liscotti, Domenic J., Pvt,
Lisowski, Joe F., Pfc,
‡Lister, Harold, Pfc,
§Lister, Harry, Pvt,
Litchko, Michael T., Pvt,
Litchmann, Solomon, Sgt,
Litteral, Winnie, Cpl,
†Little, Blair W., Pfc,
Little, Dale J., Pvt,
Little, Edgar N., Pvt,
Little, John E., Sgt,
†Little, John R., Jr., Pfc,
Little, Leo, Sgt,
Little White Man,
Litvin, John, Pvt,
†Livers, Lester W., Pfc,
Livesay, Denver H., Pvt,
Livingston, Ewell S., Pvt,
Livingston, Jack, Pfc,
Livingston, Rufus M., Pfc,
Lizak, Andrew S., Pvt,
Lloyd, Arlon L., Pfc,
Lloyd, Clennis J., Pvt,
Lloyd, Henry J., Pvt,
Lloyd, Hershell N., Sgt,
Lloyd, John E., Pvt,
Lloyd, Robert A., Pfc,
Lloyd, Wilkins, Pvt,
†Llufrio, Paul M., Pfc,
†Lobato, Amaranto A., Pfc,
Lochbaum, Earl C., T/5,
Lochman, LeRoy, Pfc,
Lochridge, Odis W., Pvt,
LoCicero, Paul, Pfc,
Lock, George, Pvt,
Lockett, Charles W., Jr., Pfc
Locklear, Edward, Pvt,
Lockrem, Stanley B., Pvt
†Lockrunner, Bernard A., Pfc,
Lockwood, Arthur L., Sgt,
Loden, Lewis E., Pfc,
Loebbaka, Leroy J., T/5,
Loeffers, John H., Pvt,
Loewer, Henry G., Cpl
Loews, Marvin E., T/Sgt,
Lofgren, Paul F., 1st Lt,
Loflin, Jefferson C., Pvt,
Loftin, Earl N., Pfc,
Loftis, Dallas, Pfc,
Loftus, Philip M. C., Pvt,
Logan, Thomas D., 1st Sgt,
Logan, Tony, Pvt,
LoGiudice, Rosario, Pfc,
Logsdon, Leroy, Sgt,
Logsdon, Thomas W., T/Sgt,
Logue, Donald J., Sgt,
†Loheide, Paul B., Pvt,
Lohman, Richard H., Pvt,
Lohner, Roy E., S/Sgt,
Loible, Mathew, Cpl,
Lomax, Ralph W., Pfc,
Lombard, LeRoy L., Pfc,
Lombard, William E., Pfc,
†Lombardi, Louis J., 1st Lt,
Lombardo, Augustine S., Cpl,
London, Harry B., Pvt,
London, Kenneth M., Pfc,
Loney, William R., 2nd Lt,
Long, Albert S., Pvt,
†Long, Billy M., Pfc,
Long, Charles E., Pfc
‡Long, Charles R., Sgt,
Long, Edward E., S/Sgt,
†Long, Hal, Pvt,
Long, Jesse J., Pfc,
Long, Samuel J., Pvt,
*Long, Warren S., Pvt,
Long, William, Sgt,
Long, William F., Pfc
§Longeria, Amos F., Pvt,
§Longmar, Glen, Pfc,
Longo, Vincent D., Pfc,
Longstreth, Ralph L., Pvt,
Look, Carl J., Pfc,
‡Looman, Robert V., Pfc,
Loomis, Paul H., Pfc,
Loomis, Robert C., Sgt,
Loomis, Stanley B., Cpl
Loper, Albert V., Sgt
Loper, E. B., T/Sgt,
Loperfido, Joseph, Pvt,
Lopez, Charlie, Sr., Pfc,
Lopez, Jess S., Pfc
Lopez, John J., Pfc,
Lopez, John O., S/Sgt,
Lopez, Jose G., Pfc,
Lopez, Louis A., Pfc,
†Lopez, Luis, Pvt,
†Lopez, Manuel T., Pvt,
Lopez, Trinidad A., Pvt,
Lopez, Victor E., Pvt,
Lopke, John P., Jr., Pfc,
Loprete, August, Pvt,
LoPrieno, Joseph, Pvt,
Lorah, Henry, Pfc,
Lorda, Clarence R., S/Sgt,
Lorentson, Frederick I., Pvt,
Lorenz, Walter H., T/Sgt,
Lorenze, Joseph P., Pfc,
Lorenzetti, Carlo L., Pvt
Lorincz, Lester, T/4,
Loring, Richard G., Pfc,
Loss, John R., Pfc,
Lothridge, Bennie F., Pfc,
Lott, Ernest L., Jr., Pfc,
Lott, Shelby, 2nd Lt,
Lottmann, Vernon G., T/Sgt,
Lotze, Milton R., Cpl,
Loughlin, Thomas A., Pfc,
Love, Benjamin F., Pvt,
Love, John D., Jr., Pvt,
Love, John P., Cpl,
†Lovig, Howard D., Sgt,
Lovington, Albert E., T/5,
Lovvorn, J. B., S/Sgt,
§Lowe, Alvin M., T/Sgt,
Lowe, Fletcher, Pfc,
Lowe, Howard D., Capt,
Lowe, Otis, Sgt,
Lowe, Winford, Pvt,
Lowenstein, Gilbert A., Pvt,
Lowerr, Robert, Pfc,
‡Lowery, Damon C., Pfc,
Lowery, Donald E., Pvt,
†Lowery, John A., Pvt,
Lowrey, Henry, Pfc
Lowry, Roye L., Pfc,
Lowry, Russell W., Sgt,
Lowther, Hugh T., Pvt,
Loy, Ralph A., Pvt,
Lubas, Michael P., Pvt,
†Lubinski, Chester J., Pfc,
Lucas, Edgar D., T/4,
Lucas, Harold H., Pfc,
Lucas, James S., Pvt,
Lucas, James T., Pfc,
†Lucas, Lee D., Jr., Pfc,
Lucas, Raymond L., Sgt
Lucas, Robert R., Pfc,
Lucas, Roy E., Pfc,
Lucas, Sherley L., Cpl,
Lucas, Stephen, Cpl,
†Luce, Frank W., Pfc,
Luceford, Ernest L., Pfc,
†Lucerna, George, Pfc,
Lucero, Eliseldo J., Pvt,
Lucero, Lucian, Pfc,
Lucero, Ralph, Pvt,
Lucero, Richard, Pfc,
Luchansky, Leon, S/Sgt,
Luchente, Joseph R., Pvt,
Lucido, Mario, Sgt,
Lucietta, Raymond R., Pfc,
Lucke, Harry W., Pvt,
Lucot, Virgil J., Pfc,
†Ludrovsky, Joseph G., Pvt,
Ludwig, Roland F., Sgt
Luebbers, Bernard H., Pfc,
Luebsen, John H., Capt,
Luhrs, Francis H., Pvt,
Lukie, Steven A., Pfc,
Lukomski, Boleslau B., Pfc,
†Lulich, Matthew D., Pvt,
Lumber, Ernest G., Pfc,
†Lunde, Stanley J., Sgt,
Lunore, Laverne L., Pfc,
Lunsford, Forest N., Pvt,
Lunsford, Harold W., Pfc,
Lundstrom, Louis D., Pfc,
Luoma, William H., Pfc,
Luporini, Angelo J., Pfc,
Lurie, Ernest J., 1st Lt,
Luris, Max S., Pvt,
Luruzzo, Jasper, Pvt,
Lusinger, Horace E., Pfc,
Luther, James M., Pfc,
Lutkin, Francis V., Pvt,
Lutz, Reinhardt, Pvt,
†Lutzevitch, Walter J., Pvt,
Lux, Leonard, Pvt,
Lydon, Edmund P., Cpl,
Lye, Arthur F., Pfc,
Lyhene, James L., Pfc,
Lyman, C. H., Sgt,
Lynch, Charles P., S/Sgt,
Lynch, Edward J., Pvt,
Lynch, Edwin L., Pfc,
Lynch, Herbert J., Sgt,
Lynch, John G., S/Sgt,
Lynch, John W., Pfc,
Lynch, Martin, T/4,
Lynch, Thomas J., Jr., Pfc,
Lynch, Wayne W., T/4,
Lynch, Willard H., Pvt,
Lynch, William J., Pfc,
Lynn, Carl D., Pvt
Lynn, Edward F., Pvt,
‡Lyons, Albert A., Pfc,
Lyons, Dean J., Cpl,
Lyons, Harold L., Pfc,
Lyons, Raymond C., Cpl,
Lyons, William L., Pfc,
Lystvedt, Robert M., Sgt,
†Lyttletown, Leslie J., Sgt,

Maag, Howard H., Pvt,
Maager, John T., Pvt,
Maasz, Leroy H., Sgt,
Mabbutt, Allen M., Pfc,
Mabry, Clifford, Pfc,
Mabus, Paul W., Sgt,
MacDougall, Allan H., Sgt,
Machael, Robert E., Pvt,
Machen, Leon H., Pvt,
Machey, Earnest C., 1st Sgt,
Machin, Wilson F., Pvt,
Machka, Joseph E., Pvt,
Machut, Norman H., Pvt,
MacIntosh, Robert P., T/5,
Mackenna, Neil S., Pvt,
MacKenzie, Lloyd G., Pvt,
Mackey, John C., S/Sgt,
Mackey, Norman G., S/Sgt,
Mackiewicz, Deward, Pvt,
†Macklin, Howard W., Pfc
Macko, Edward W., T/5,
MacLean, Angus B., 2nd Lt,
MacLennan, Robert B., 2nd Lt,
Macorig, Alvise M., Pvt,
MacPherson, John, Sgt,
MacPherson, K. W., Jr., Pfc,
MacTavish, Jack W., Pfc,
Macucki, Benny J., Pfc
Macur, Perry P., Pvt,
Maczuga, Jacob, Pfc,
Madaleno, Narciso E., Pfc,
Madon, Bernard H., Pfc,
Maddin, William J., Pfc,
Maddox, Blance T., Pvt,
Maddox, John C., Pfc,
‡Maddox, Lake L., Pvt,
Madeloni, Vito W., Pvt,
Madison, Sydney S., Sgt,
Madison, Walter T., Pfc,
Madrid, Thomas R., T/5,
Madrijan, Frank V., S/Sgt
Madron, Andie M., Pfc,
Madron, Joseph P., Pvt,
Madruga, James S., Pvt,
Maduros, Paul P., Pfc,
Maffee, D. M., Jr., S/Sgt,
‡Maffetone, Nicholas C., Pvt,
Magana, Joe F., Pfc,
Magarl, George, Pfc,
†Magee, George R., Jr., Pvt,
*Magee, Royden W., Pfc,
Magers, Donald J., Pvt,
Maggi, Vincent, Pfc,
Magro, Joseph N., Pvt,
Maguire, Joseph S., Pfc,
Maguire, Robert D., Pvt,
Mahan, James M., Pvt,
‡Mahathey, William B., Jr., Pvt,
Maher, Daniel W., Sgt,
Maher, James H., Pfc,
*Maher, James L., Pfc,
Maher, Kenneth J., Pvt,
Maher, Thomas F., Pvt,
Mahler, George C., Sgt,
Mahony, Robert J., Cpl,
Mahoney, John C., Pfc,
Mahoney, John W., Pfc,
Mahr, Walter J., Pfc,
Maier, Lee M., 2nd Lt,
Mailino, Salvatore, Pvt,
†Main, Donald F., Pvt,
Mains, Charles E., Pvt,
Maizel, Macklin, Pvt,
†Majerczak, Stanley J., Pvt,
Majerus, Joseph F., Pvt,
Majka, Beleslaus W., Pvt,
Major, Wayland E., Pfc,
Makarewicz, Charles P., S/Sgt,
Maki, John F., S/Sgt,
Maki, William E., Pvt,
Maksymowicz, Victor J., Pfc,
Malanssena, Maximilian, Pfc,
‡Malaski, Bernard F., Pvt,
‡Maldin, Lois M., 2nd Lt,
Malik, Rudolph J., Pfc,
†Malinawski, Adam S., Sgt,
Malinosky, Frank, Pvt,
Mallnowski, Adam A., Pvt,
Malito, Louis F., Pvt,
Maljwac, John G., Pvt,
Malko, Russell, Pfc,
Malkovich, George, Pvt,
Mallen, Raymond E., Pfc,
Mallette, John, Pfc,
Malley, Harold E., Pfc,
Mallone, James E., Pfc,
Malloy, Gerard P., Pfc
Malo, Norman F., Pvt,
†Malo, Wilfrid J., Pvt,
Malone, Anthony J., T/4,
Malone, Harold E., Pvt,
Malone, Harry A., S/Sgt,
Malone, Robert F., Pfc,
Malone, Robert J., Pvt,
Maloney, Clarence H., Pvt
Maloney, Harvey L., Pvt,
Maloney, John P., 2nd Lt,
Maloney, Wilbert J., 1st Lt,
Malott, Harlan W., T/4,
Malter, Robert H., Pvt,
Malterer, Raymond S., Pfc,
†Maltese, Philip G., Pvt,
Maly, Joseph, Pfc,
Malyuk, John, Pvt
Mamon, Walter J., Pvt,
Manasco, Simon C., Pfc,
Manasco, Thomas, Pfc,
Manbeck, William W., S/Sgt,
Manco, Santo A., Pfc,
Mancuso, Frank, 2nd Lt,
Mancusso, Ralph P. J., Pvt,
Manda, Daniel B., Cpl,
†Mandell, Aaron, Pvt,
Mandler, Hurly A., Pvt,
Manerio, Joseph A., Sgt,
§Manett, John J., Pfc,
Mangan, William J., Pfc,
Mangione, Joseph S., Pfc,
Mangold, Anthony L., Pvt
Mangum, Roland M., Pfc,
‡Mangum, William W., Pvt,
‡Manikas, William M., Pvt,
†Mann, Frederick E., Sr., Pvt,
Mannon, Grover R., Pvt,
Manone, Henry U., Jr., Sgt,
Manry, John C., 1st Lt,
Manry, Robert B., S/Sgt,
Mansello, Dominic, Pfc,
Manship, Sidney E., Pvt
†Manske, Julius G., Jr., Pfc,
Mansmith, Ralph O., Pvt,
Mantle, Arthur L., Cpl,

† Killed in Action. * Prisoner of War. ‡ Missing in Action. § Died of Wounds.

IN WORLD WAR II 523

Manus, Evan S., Pfc,
Manus, Leo J., T/5,
Manuso, Dominick, Pvt,
Maple, Jack D., Pfc,
Maple, Larry G., Pvt,
Marana, Vincent C., Pvt,
Maranda, Daniel L., Pfc,
Marantonio, Salvatore J., T/5,
Marasco, Joseph, Pfc,
Marcantel, William A., Sgt,
March, William A., Pvt,
Marchel, Benjamin J., Pfc,
Marchetto, Ben P., Pfc,
Marchinana, Lucas A., S/Sgt,
Marcus, Arthur, Pfc,
Marcus, Donald, Pvt,
Marcus, Philip W., Capt,
‡Marder, Samuel, S/Sgt,
Mards, Marvin H., S/Sgt,
§Mare, Levi G., Pfc,
Mares, Andres, Pfc,
Margolin, Leon, 1st Lt,
Marianda, Joseph, Pfc,
Mariani, Adnrew P., Pvt,
Maricick, John D., Pvt,
Marinaro, Tavis B., Pvt,
Marinelli, Carmine D., Pfc,
Mariner, George L., Pvt,
†Marino, Anthony, Pfc,
Markelewicz, Joseph F., Pvt,
Marker, Louis W., Jr., 2nd Lt
Markert, James J., Pfc,
†Markland, Athel, Pvt,
Markovich, George, Pvt,
Markovich, Matt J., S/Sgt,
Markowitz, Fred, Pvt,
Markowski, Edward W., Sgt,
‡Marks, Charles S., Jr., Pvt,
Marks, Earl J., Cpl,
Marks, Earle L., Pfc,
Marks, Lewis, Sr., Pvt,
§Marks, Lilburn, Sgt,
Marks, Robert, 2nd Lt
Marks, William F., T/5,
Marlitt, Gerald, Pfc,
Marmilstein, Benjamin, Pvt,
‡Marodi, Charles, Pfc,
†Maroki, Charles, Pfc,
Marotta, Carmine A., Cpl,
†Marquering, Joseph E., Sgt,
Marquis, Marcial M., Pfc,
Marro, John, Pvt,
Marsh, Charlie A., Pfc,
Marsh, Clifford I., Pfc,
Marsh, David L., Pfc,
Marsh, Frank L., Pfc,
‡Marsh, Glenn E., Pfc,
Marsh, Robert J., Pvt,
Marshall, Albert J., Pfc,
Marshall, Arthur J., Pvt,
Marshall, Calvin C., Sgt,
Marshall, Donall M., Pfc,
Marshall, Edward L., Pfc,
Marshall, Fred E., Pfc,
Marshall, Hardaman E., Pvt,
Marshall, Iris V., Pfc,
Marshall, William C., Pfc,
Marshman, Ashton L., Jr., Pfc,
Marsteller, Donald F., S/Sgt,
†Marston, David J., Pvt,
Marsy, Arthur L., Pvt,
Marszalek, Francis J., Sgt,
Martell, Jesse A., Pvt,
Martin, Alfred L., Sr., Sgt,
Martin, Carmine A., Pvt,
Martin, Charles W., Pvt,
Martin, Chester, Pfc,
Martin, Curtis, S/Sgt,
Martin, Edgar, Pfc,
Martin, Elmer J., Pvt,
Martin, Ernest E., Pvt,
Martin, Frank E., T/5,
Martin, Frank W., Cpl,
†Martin, George, Pvt,
†Martin, George P., Pfc,
Martin, Gilbert, Pfc,
Martin, Harold J., Pvt,
Martin, Harry C., Pfc,
Martin, Henry, Pfc,
‡Martin, Hershel, Pfc,
†Martin, James N., Sgt,
Martin, John D., Pvt,
Martin, John E., 2nd Lt,
Martin, Joseph A., Pvt,
†Martin, Joseph B., Pvt,
Martin, Joseph S., T/Sgt,
Martin, Julius L., Pvt,
Martin, Kenneth C., Pvt
†Martin, Lauchlin H., Pvt,
Martin, Lionel A., Sgt,
Martin, Lucien G., Pvt,
Martin, Melvin, Pvt,
Martin, Morris B., Pvt,
†Martin, Neima E., Pfc,

Martin, Ralph R., Jr., Pvt,
†Martin, Richard D., Pvt,
Martin, Robert, Cpl,
Martin, Roy E., Pvt,
Martin, T. J., Pvt,
Martin, Tom M., Cpl,
Martin, Truman C., Pfc,
Martin, Wayne H., Sgt,
Martin, Wilder F., Pfc,
Martin, William G., Pfc,
Martine, John, Pvt,
Martinez, Alfonso O., Pvt,
Martineau, Charles D., Capt,
Martinez, George T., Pvt,
†Martinez, Joseph F., Pfc,
†Martinez, Joe R., Pfc,
Martinez, Juan, Pfc,
Martinez, Max R., Sgt,
Martins, George E., Pvt,
†Martisch, George S., Sgt,
Martoff, Valent G., Pvt,
Martuch, George J., Pfc,
Maruszewski, E. J., T/Sgt,
Marvel, Roland J., Sgt,
Mary, William D., Pfc,
†Marx, Frederick J., Jr.,
Marzucca, Michael L., Pvt,
Masa, Henry H., T/5,
Masalle, Daniel N., S/Sgt,
*Masaraechia, Frank, Pfc,
†Mascuerquiga, Mateo L., Pfc
Mashoum, Albert A., Pfc,
Mashburn, Clarence, Pvt,
Masi, Eugene E., S/Sgt,
†Masitis, George, T/Sgt,
Maskey, Maurice D., Pvt
Moslak, Victor F., Pvt
Mason, Carl E., Pfc,
Mason, Floyd W., Sgt,
Mason, Hale A., Pvt,
Mason, Joseph, Pfc
Massarci, Durdy P., Pfc,
Massel, George, Pvt,
‡Massengill, Harvey D., Pvt,
‡Massey, George E., Pvt,
Massey, Herman E., T/4,
Massey, Leo D., Pvt,
Massung, George, Pvt,
Masterson, Lennart D., Pfc,
Mastie, Henry F., Cpl,
Mastilak, Nick A., Pfc,
†Maston, Joseph M., Pfc,
Mastroianni, Anthony E., Pfc,
Masty, Floyd J., S/Sgt,
Masuska, Joseph J. J., Pfc,
Mateju, John C., Pfc,
Mathe, Carl J., Pvt,
Mathews, Ralph M., Pfc,
Mathiey, Jerome W., Cpl
Mathis, Alton E., T/4,
Mathis, Edwin W., Pfc,
Mathis, Lon, Pvt,
Mathis, Wade T., Pvt,
Matlock, James, Pfc,
Matson, Bernard R., Pvt,
Matson, Edward E., Pvt,
†Mattel, Neil W., Pvt,
Matteoni, Rene E., Pvt,
Matteta, Oscar H., Pvt,
Matthews, Roy S., Pvt,
Mattison, Walter E., Pvt,
†Mattiuzzo, Louis J., Pfc,
†Mattix, Paul W., Pvt,
‡Mattola, Guglielmo, Sgt,
Matul, Francis G., Pvt,
Matysiak, Casmer A., Pfc
Matzke, William H., T/5,
†Maudlin, Raymond L., Pvt,
Maulshagen, A. J., Jr., S/Sgt,
Mauney, Grover T., S/Sgt,
†Maupin, Herbert E., T/Sgt,
Mauro, Vincent J., Pvt,
Maurogeorge, Plato A., Pvt,
‡Mauser, Curtis N., S/Sgt,
Maxey, Albert L., Jr., Pvt,
Maxfield, Robert, Sgt,
Maxwell, Thomas W., Pfc,
Maxwell, William C., Pvt,
May, Edwin H., Pvt,
†May, James W., Pvt,
May, Joe N., Pfc,
†May, Marks L., 2nd Lt,
May, Peter P., Jr., Pfc,
†Mayberry, David R., Pvt,
Mayberry, Gwyn H., Pvt,
‡Mayer, Ernest J., Pfc,
Mayer, Frank E., Pvt,
Mayer, John J., Capt,
Mayer, Robert J., Pfc,
Mayes, Barney R., Pfc,
Mayfield, Clyde, Pfc,
Maynard, Arthur P., Pfc,
Maynard, Charles K., Pfc,
‡Maynard, Verl A., Pfc,

Mayo, Charles, Pvt,
Mayo, Hershel, Pfc,
Mayo, John H., Pvt,
Mays, George A., Jr., Sgt,
Mays, Julius E., Sgt,
Mazarella, Leroy, Sgt,
Maze, Luther M., Jr., Sgt,
Mazur, Frank T., Pfc,
†Mazur, Joseph J., 1st Lt,
Mazurek, Frank J., Sgt,
Mazziotti, Edward D., Cpl,
†McAleer, Joseph G., T/5,
McAleese, John M., Jr., Pvt,
McAlister, Carl C., S/Sgt,
McAller, Joseph F., Pvt,
McAlliffe, Joseph R., Pvt,
†McAllister, Sylvester J., Pvt,
McAllister, Wallace B., T/Sgt,
McAlpin, Thomas E., Pvt,
McAnany, Donald J., Sgt,
McAuley, John A., Pvt,
McAuley, William J., T/5
McBeain, Raymond A., T/3,
McBee, Roy C., Pvt,
McBeth, Cleo C., Pfc,
†McBride, Albert E., Jr., Sgt,
McBride, Edward R., Pvt,
McBride, Vincent G., Pvt,
McCabe, George F., Pfc,
McCabe, Sylvester A., Pvt,
McCain, Claude E., Pfc,
McCall, Bernice O., Pvt,
McCall, Walter C., Pfc,
McCallum, Garvice, S/Sgt,
McCambridge, Harold, Pvt,
McCamish, John E., T/5,
McCann, William T., Cpl,
McCannany, Donald S., Sgt,
McCanney, Aubrey S., Pvt,
†McCardel, Henry L., Pvt,
†McCarron, Peter J., Pvt,
McCarter, John M., Pvt,
McCarthy, Daniel A., Pfc,
McCarthy, Harry L., Pvt,
McCarthy, Hubert T., Pfc
†McCarthy, William T., Pvt,
McCarthym, Paul F., Pfc,
McCary, Leon E., Pvt,
McCauley, John E., Pvt,
†McCauley, John E., Pfc,
McCauley, William J., T/Sgt,
McClain, Leonard J., Sgt,
†McClain, Mack, Pfc,
McClain, Orris L., Pfc,
McClintock, David J., Pvt,
†McClintock, Jack E., 1st Lt,
McClure, Ray, Pvt,
McClure, Titus D., Pvt,
McConnell, Albert H., T/Sgt,
McConnell, Arthur L., S/Sgt,
McConnell, Claude A., S/Sgt,
McConnell, Gerald L., Pvt,
McConnell, Johnney D., Pfc,
McConnell, Oramel A., Pfc,
McCool, Edward J., Pvt,
†McCoombe, T. V., Jr., Pfc,
McCord, Clarence F., S/Sgt,
McCord, Robert E., Pvt,
†McCormick, Charles W., Pfc,
McCormick, Francis P., S/Sgt,
†McCormick, T. F., Jr., Sgt,
McCormick, Thomas P., T/4,
McCown, John D., Pvt
McCoy, Clarence V., Pvt,
†McCoy, John J., Pvt,
McCoy, Ledford E., Pvt,
†McCoy, Leinster W., Jr., Pfc,
McCoy, Ralph A., Pfc
McCoy, Richard E., Sgt,
McCracken, Clarence E., Pvt
McCracken, Robert S., T/4,
McCracken, Walter S., 1st Lt,
McCrady, Jack R., Pvt,
McCraney, George T., Pvt,
McCraw, Foi, T/Sgt,
McCreight, Allen H., Pvt,
†McCroskey, Raymond R., Pfc,
*McCullough, Addison F., Sgt,
‡McCullough, Harry J., Pfc,
McCullough, John D., 1st Lt,
McCurley, Alfred C., 2nd Lt,
McDade, James E. A., Pvt,
McDanel, Eugene O., Pvt,
McDaniel, A. J., Pfc,
McDaniel, Russell W., Pvt,
McDaniels, Victor, Pfc,
McDavid, Lewis L., Pfc,
†McDermaid, William E., Pfc,
McDermott, Joseph, Pfc,
McDermott, Robert, Pvt,
†McDill, Harry M., Pvt,
McDonald, Albert H., Jr., Pvt
McDonald, Claude D., Jr., 2nd
McDonald, Durward C., Pfc,

McDonald, Jack N., S/Sgt,
McDonald, Richard F., T/Sgt,
McDonald, Roy L., Pvt,
‡McDonald, Victor H., Sgt,
McDonald, William J., Pfc
McDonell, Kenneth J., Pfc,
*McDonough, Albert H., Cpl,
McDonough, Delbert C., Sgt,
McDonough, James G., Pvt
§McDonough, James V., 1st Lt,
McDonough, Robert W., Pvt,
McDowall, William J., Pfc,
McDowell, Joseph C., Pfc,
†McElhaney, Carl D., Pfc,
†McElhose, Harold M., S/Sgt,
McElreath, Ernest N., T/5,
McElroy, Joe A., Pfc,
McEneany, Gerard J., Pvt,
‡McEnroe, Victor R., Pfc,
McEvers, Harold R., Pfc,
McEvers, Richard P., Pvt,
McEvoy, Eugene F., Pfc,
McEvoy, Robert F., Pfc
McFadden, John F., Jr., Pvt,
†McFall, Gerald D., Pvt,
McFalls, Carroll, Jr., Capt,
McFalls, Jack D., Pvt,
McFarland, Clyde N., Pvt,
McFarland, F. R., Sr., Pfc,
McGahey, Melbourne C., Pfc,
McGalliard, Joseph W., Pfc,
McGarr, Lionel C., Col,
McGarrity, Charles L., Pvt,
§McGarry, John F., Pvt,
McGarthy, Paul F., Cpl,
McGarty, John D., Pvt,
McGaughey, Edward, Pfc,
McGee, Frankie J., Pvt,
McGee, Gerard H., Pfc,
McGee, Harry F., 1st Lt,
McGee, James, Sgt
‡McGee, William D., Pvt,
*McGettigan, James D., Pfc,
McGhee, Garrett N., Cpl,
†McGill, John J., Pfc,
†McGill, William R., Pvt,
McGinn, William J., Sgt,
†McGinn, James L., Pvt,
McGinnis, George T., Pvt,
McGinnies, Raymond C., Pvt,
†McGladreym, Cecil, Pfc,
†McGlohon, Herbert H., Sgt,
McGlynn, James C., Capt,
McGonigal, William H., Pfc,
McGourty, Henry J., Jr., Pfc,
‡McGowan, Malcolm, Pvt,
McGrath, Joseph J., Pvt,
McGreevy, John P., Pfc,
McGregor, Charles, Sgt,
McGrew, Claude, Pfc,
McGrew, Russell A., Pvt,
McGuffin, Robert W., Pfc,
McGuigan, Arthur J., Pvt,
†McGuiness, William T., Pvt,
McGuinn, Robert J., Pvt,
McGuire, Daniel A., Pvt,
McGuire, Jim, Cpl,
McGuire, Loyd, 2nd Lt,
McGuire, Ray P., Pvt,
McHan, Euell, Sr., Pfc,
†McHarg, James J., T/Sgt,
†McHenry, John P., Pfc,
McHugh, Edward J., Pfc,
*McIlroy, James F., Pfc,
McInerney, John M., Jr., Pfc,
McIlwain, Billy F., T/5,
McIntire, Charles W., 1st Sgt,
McIntosh, Charles O., Cpl,
McIntosh, Gerald L., Pfc,
McIntosh, Leonard W., Pvt,
†McIntosh, Ray M., Sgt,
†McIntosh, Virgil H., Cpl,
McIntyre, Edward O., Pfc,
McIntyre, William K., Pvt,
McKaig, James W., Pfc,
McKay, Harold F., Pvt,
McKean, Lloyd G., Cpl,
‡McKee, John F., Pfc,
McKee, Lewis F., Pfc,
McKelley, Lawrence C., Pfc,
McKenna, Frank J., Pfc,
McKenna, Homer C., Pvt,
†McKenny, Robert A., Pvt,
McKenzie, Dale, Pvt,
McKeown, William J., Pvt,
†McKexzie, Hugh D., Maj,
McKibben, John C., Sgt,
McKinley, Dale, Pvt,
McKinley, Elliot L., Pvt,
McKinley, Francis L., Pvt,
†McKinley, Robert C., Jr., Pvt,
McKinney, Charles, Sgt
McKinney, Gayle R., Pfc,
McKinney, James L., Pvt,
McKinney, Lee K., S/Sgt,

McKinnon, Howard E., Pvt
McKinstry, Elmer L., Pvt,
McLain, William O., Pvt,
McLaughlin, Edward F., Pvt,
McLaughlin, John J., Pfc,
McLaughlin, Leonard R., Pfc,
†McLaughlin, Robert J., Pfc,
McLaughlin, T. N., 2nd Lt,
McLean, Charles A., Pfc,
†McLean, John R., Pvt,
McLean, Luther C., Cpl,
McLean, Thomas E., Pvt,
McLean, William, Pvt,
McLendonThomas E., Pvt,
McLeod, James P., Pfc,
McLester, Ewell W., Pvt,
McLish, Calvin C., Pvt,
†McMahan, Clifford L., Sgt,
McMahan, Roy S., T/5,
McMahon, Charles E., Pfc
McMahon, Charles P., T/5,
McMahon, Clifford M., Pvt,
McMahon, Joseph F., Pvt,
McMahon, Richard B., Cpl,
McMahon, Robert J., Pvt,
McManis, Alva V., Pvt,
McManis, William F., Pfc,
McManus, Lawrence P., Pfc,
McManus, Leo A., Pfc
McMaster, George W., Pfc,
McMicken, Eugene R., Pvt,
McMillan, John F., Cpl,
McMillian, Henry K., Pvt
†McMinis, Willie M., Pvt,
McMullan, Frank L. Sgt,
McMullen, Asa D., Pvt
†McMunn, Stuart A., Sgt,
McMurty, George M., Pvt
McNally, Daniel P., Jr. Pvt,
McNamara, Edward J., Pvt,
†McNamara, Martin J. Pvt,
†McNamara, Melvin, Pfc,
†McNamera, Francis P., Pvt,
McNealy, Winburn, Pfc,
McNee, Lawrence W., Pvt
McNeel Merton J., Pvt,
McNeeley, Franklin, Sgt,
†McNeil, Francis P., Pfc,
McNeill, Francis C., Pfc,
McNutt, Vance O., Pfc,
McPhaill, James C., 1st Lt,
McPherson Alexander, Pvt,
McPherson, George B., Pfc,
McPherson, James, S/Sgt,
McQuade, Stephen E., Pvt,
McQueen Harry L., T/4,
McQueen, Howard L., 1st Lt,
†McSherry, John B., Pvt,
McSpadden, Frank B., Pfc,
McTee, Lawrence L., S/Sgt,
†McVeigh, William J., Pfc,
McVey, Norman B., T/Sgt,
McWhinney, Tommy, Pfc,
Meachum, Hubert J., 2nd Lt,
Meade, James M., T/4,
†Meadows, Alfred L., Pvt,
Meadows, Ford, Pfc,
Meadows Sanford, Pfc,
Meaghe, Michael J., Cpl,
Mealer, Steve M., Pvt,
Meaney, William J., T/4,
Mecum, Warren L., Pfc,
Medeiros, Manuel J., Pfc,
†Medeiros Alfred, Pvt,
Medeiros, John W., Pvt,
Medina, Daniel C., Pfc,
*Medlar, Warren C., Sgt,
†Medoza, Joseph, Pfc,
Medsker, Ralph, Pvt,
Meeks Harvey, Pfc,
Meeks, Hildred, Pfc,
Meffert, Donald W., Pvt,
Mehuron, Gerald G., 2nd Lt,
Meindl, Albert S., Pvt,
Meinert, Robert, Pvt,
†Meiser Samuel L., Sgt,
Meisner, Robert M., Pfc,
Meiter, Elmer A., T/5,
Meka, Joseph, Sgt,
Melanson, Anthony P., S/Sgt,
§Melanson, Ernest S., Pfc,
Melcher, Donald, Pfc,
Melcher, Elmer R., Pfc,
Mellard, Robert J., T/Sgt,
Mellert, Roger J., S/Sgt,
Mellon, Charles R., Pvt,
†Mellor, John R., 1st Lt,
Mellum Lavern G., Cpl,
Melton, Ray, S/Sgt,
Melville, Alan V., Pfc,
Melvin, Derolad L., Pvt,
Melze, John B., Pfc,
Memoli, Anthony, Pfc,
Menchini Salvatore, Pvt
Mende, Ralph A., T/Sgt,

† Killed in Action. * Prisoner of War. ‡ Missing in Action. **§ Died of Wounds.**

Mendelsohn, Alvin, Pvt,
Mendes, Manuel C., Pvt,
Mendoza, Ralph, Pvt,
‡Menter, Merle W., Cpl,
Mentozos, Paul G. S/Sgt,
Menzel, George E., Pvt,
Menzel, Herman W., 1st Lt,
Mercer, Elroy, Pvt,
Mercer, John B., Pfc,
Merchant, Selah W., Pvt,
Mercurio, Peyer P., T/5,
Merdieth, Archie E., Pfc,
Meredith, Edward J., S/Sgt,
Meredith, George E., Pvt,
Meritz, Martin D., T/4,
†Merkel, Gottfried, Pvt,
†Merling Theodore P., Pfc,
Merlino, Paul F., Pfc,
Merlo, Victor F., Sgt,
Mernaugh, Wilbur J., Pfc,
‡Mero, Thomas F., Pvt,
Merola, Thomas, Jr., Pvt,
Meroshoff, Robert, T/Sgt,
‡Merrick, Charles D., Pfc,
Merrick, George E., Cpl,
Merricks, Joseph G., Pvt,
Merrihew, T. D., Jr., Pvt,
Merrill, Earl, Pfc
Merriman, Russel E., Pfc,
Merritt, Toxie W., Pvt,
†Merritt, William J., Pfc,
Merryman, Russell E., Pvt,
Mersch, Harold J., Pfc,
Mervine, Norman J., T/5,
Meserole, Joseph W., S/Sgt,
†Mesic, Wilford C., Pfc,
Mesich, Frank E., S/Sgt,
Mesich, John J., S/Sgt,
Mesko, John J., Pfc,
§Messer, Clayton, Pfc,
Messick, Charles W., Pvt,
Messina, Anthony F., Pvt,
Messina, Anthony L., Pvt,
‡Messine, Frank A., Pfc,
Messineo, Anthon A., Pvt,
†Meszaros, Martin, Pfc,
Metcalf, Charles E., 1st Lt,
Metcalfe, Rex, 1st Lt,
Methe, George L., Jr., Pvt
Metido, John A., Jr., Pfc,
†Metz, Charles H., Pfc,
Metz, John G., Pvt
Metzcar, R., Maurice, 2nd Lt,
Metzgar, Albert A. R., Cpl,
Metzgar, Lawrence L., Pvt
Metzgar, Matthew G., Pvt
Metzger, Emil E., Cpl,
Metzler, Roland N., Pfc,
Meuris, John J., Pvt,
Meyer, Harby E., Pfc,
Meyer, Harlan R., T/5,
†Meyer, Herbert A., Sgt,
Meyer, Otto C., Pfc,
†Meyers, Walters V., Pfc,
Mezera, Alvin T., Pvt,
Mezydle, Aloysius J., Cpl,
Miceli, Albert, Cpl,
Miceli, Anthony J., S/Sgt,
Michael, Clifford H., S/Sgt,
Michaelis, Edward L., T/Sgt,
†Michaelson, Arnold D., Pfc,
Michalety, John L., Pvt,
Michaud, Louis P., Pvt,
Michand, Renault G., Pfc,
†Michaux, Joseph U., Pvt,
†Michel, Cleo, Pfc,
Michehl, Milton C., Cpl,
†Michell, Clarence L., Pfc,
‡Michelli, Vincent J., Pvt,
Micheloff, George, Pvt,
Michels, John J., Pvt,
†Michling, Frank O., Pfc,
Mickels, William A., Pvt
Mickelson, Richard W., Pvt,
Mickelson, Richard, Pvt,
‡Mickens, Lionel E., Pvt,
Micollef, Angelo J., Pfc,
Middletown, Delford L., Pfc,
§Miesch, Nerbert J., Pfc,
Mielnichji, Walter, Pvt,
Mier, Earl F., Pfc,
Mier, Wayne E., S/Sgt,
†Mietelski, Joseph S., Pvt,
Migliore, Anthony H., Pvt,
Mihalio, John, Pvt,
Mihalopulos, Arthur L., Pvt,
Mihay, Ernest, Pvt,
Mike, Seraphine, Pfc,
Mikesell, Clyde E., Pvt,
Mikill, Marion S., Pvt,
Mikkelson, Warren M., Pfc,
†Mikkola, Sulo A., Pfc,
Mikszewski, Frank, Pfc,
Milam, Irving L., Cpl,
Milardo, Santi S., Pvt,
Milazzo, Joseph, Pvt,
Milburn, George W., Pvt,
†Milby, William L., Pfc,
Milens, Leslie B., S/Sgt,
Miles, George, Pvt,
Miles, James E., Pvt,
Miles, John F., Jr., Pfc,
Milestone, Leon C., T/Sgt,
Milewicz, John J., Pvt,
Miley, William L., Pvt,
Milham, Earl H., Pvt,
Miliczky, George A., T/5,
Milikas, John J., Pfc,
Milines, Alfred W., Pfc
Milisits, Stephen F., Sgt,
Miller, Albert E., Pvt,
Miller, Allen, Pvt,
Miller, Alvin H., Pvt,
Miller, Andrew E., Pfc,
Miller, Arthur B., Pfc,
Miller, Arthur P., Pfc,
§Miller, Bruce M., Sgt,
Miller, Carl E., Pvt,
‡Miller, Cecil E., Sgt,
†Miller, Charles A., Pvt,
†Miller, Charles C., Pvt,
‡Miller, Clair H., Pvt,
Miller, Donald A., Pvt,
Miller, Charles J., T/5,
Miller, Charles P., Pfc,
†Miller, Clarence E., Jr., Sgt,
Miller, Duane M., Pvt,
Miller, Edward C., Sgt,
Miller, Ernest E., Pfc,
Miller, Ethan R., Pfc,
Miller, Floyd F., Pvt,
Miller, Frank L., Pfc,
‡Miller, Fred C., Pvt,
Miller, Gerald E., T/5,
Miller, Glenn E., S/Sgt,
Miller, Harry S., Pfc,
Miller, Herman C., Pvt,
†Miller, Howard C., Pvt,
Miller, Howard F., Pvt,
Miller, Howard W., Pvt,
Miller, Irving L., T/5,
Miller, Jack R., 1st Lt,
Miller, James V., Pvt
Miller, Kenneth G., Pfc,
Miller, Lawrence L., Sgt,
Miller, Lawrence M., Sgt,
Miller, Leward H., Pfc,
Miller, Lilee, S/Sgt,
Miller, Louis, S/Sgt,
Miller, Morris E., S/Sgt,
Miller, Norman B., Pvt,
Miller, Norman, Pvt,
‡Miller, Orville, Pfc,
Miller, Ovie, Pvt,
Miller, Paul C., Capt,
†Miller, Paul N., Sgt,
Miller, Philip, Pfc,
Miller, Raymond W., Pfc
Miller, Richard E., T/4,
Miller, Robert M., Pvt,
Miller, Shelby, Pfc,
Miller, Shirley E., 1st Lt,
Miller, Sidney, Pfc,
Miller, Stanley F., Pfc,
†Miller, Thomas O., S/Sgt,
Miller, Warren N., Pfc,
Miller, Wayne, Pvt
Miller, Wilber, Sgt,
Miller, William D., Pfc,
Miller, Willis J., Sgt,
Millette, Leo A., Pfc,
Millican, Kenneth R., Pfc,
Millikan, William J., Pfc
Million, Glen, Pvt,
Millis, Jack, Sgt
Mills, Ervin, Pvt,
Mills, Frank H., Pvt,
Mills, George R., Pvt,
†Mills, Irving E., Pvt,
Mills, Jack W., Pvt,
*Mills, Lamond L., Pfc,
Mills, Lloyd A., Sgt,
Mills, Roman, Pvt,
Mills, Thomas F., Cpl,
Millstead, James E., Pvt,
Milner, Homer, T/Sgt,
Milno, Morton M., Pvt,
Milward, John N., Pfc,
†Minch, Richard T., Pvt,
Mincielli, Frank J., Pvt,
‡Miner, Francis H., Pfc,
Minet, Harry J., Pvt,
†Miney, John M., Pfc,
Mininni, Hormidas A., Pfc,
Minix, William K., Pvt,
Minjock, Harry, Jr., Pfc,
Minnich, Clarence R., Sgt,
†Minnich, Floyd B., Pvt,
Minnick, Clyde H., Pfc,
Minnick, Donald E., Pvt,
Minter, Clarence C., Pvt,
Minter, Gene, Pvt,
‡Minter, James G., S/Sgt,
Minter, James G., Pfc,
‡Minter, Obie D., Pfc,
Mintz, Edward, Pvt,
Misener, Robert F., Pvt,
Misger, Frank R., Sgt,
Mishakas, Joseph, T/Sgt,
Mishkin, Stephen, Sgt,
Misiaszek, Stanley J., Pvt,
Misiuda, Frank J., Pfc,
Misiuk, Stanley P., Pfc,
Miskowiec, Andrew F., T/4,
Mislak, John A., Sgt,
Misner, John C., Pfc,
Misurac, Marijan, Pvt,
Misurelli, Frank, S/Sgt,
Mitchell, Aburey D., Pfc,
Mitchell, Chandos L., Cpl,
Mitchell, Emmett A., Pfc,
Mitchell, Jasper J., Pvt,
Mitchell, John R., Pvt,
Mitchell, Lonnie, Pvt,
†Mitchell, Peter J., 2nd Lt
Mitchell, Robert B., Pfc,
Mitchell, Robert J., Pfc,
Mitchell, Robert W., Pvt,
Mitchell, Samuel C., 2nd Lt
Mitchell, William R., Jr., Pfc,
Mitchem, Clyde E., Pvt,
Mitchusson, Vernice, Pfc,
Mittelsteadt, Lloyd E., Pfc,
Mixon, S. L., Pvt,
Mizer, Harry E., Pvt,
Mizger, Frank R., Pvt,
Mizinski, Frank R., Sgt,
Mlywarski, Edward J., T/5,
Moakes, James J., Pvt,
Moakler, Howard W., Pfc,
Moats, William F., Pvt,
Mobley, William J., Pvt,
Mockus, Bruno J., Pfc,
Modrigan, Frank V., Sgt,
†Modro, LeRoy T., Pfc,
Modzelewski, Chester M., Pvt,
Moen, Claude M., Pfc,
Moen, Lloyd P., Pfc,
Moergen, Herman A., Sgt,
Moff, Pasquale C., Pfc,
†Moffitt, Orville A., S/Sgt,
Mogielnicki, Walter M., Pvt,
Mohar, Sgt,
Mohne, Leonard C., Pvt,
Mohon, Willis A., Pfc,
Mohrland, Raymond N., Pfc,
Mokina, Jesus C., Pvt,
Moleski, Ramond A., Pvt,
Molesworth, Howard W., Pfc,
Molinar, Jesus L., Pfc,
Molldren, Clifford R., T/Sgt,
Mollers, Lee, Pfc,
†Molloy, Joseph M., Pvt,
Molnar, Louie, Cpl,
Molner, Zigmond, T/Sgt,
Monahan, Robert C., Pvt
Monberg, Bernard M., Pfc,
§Monblow, William H., 2nd Lt
Mondani, Peter, S/Sgt,
Mondragon, Joseph, S/Sgt,
Monette, Arthur L., Pvt,
Monette, Francis E., Pvt,
Mongeau, Dallas, T/4,
Monguia, Albert D., Pvt,
Monis, Francis J., Sgt,
Monk, Robert H., Pvt
‡Monks, Earl A., Pfc,
Monks, James, Sgt,
Monroe, John P., Pvt,
Monroe, John S., Pvt,
Monroney, Dale M., Pvt,
Monsco, Jerry, Pvt,
Montageno, Frank F., Pfc,
Montanari, Edward S., Cpl,
Montaque, Herbert, Jr., S/Sgt,
Montaque, R B., Jr., S/Sgt,
Montasano, John W., Pvt,
Monteleone, Frank N., Pfc,
Montessano, Anthony, Pfc,
Montgomery, Ernest P., Pfc,
Montgomery, Francis R., Sgt
Montgomery, Hugh S., Capt,
Montgomery, Jay T., Cpl,
Montgomery, Neil I., Cpl,
Montgomery, Orel L., S/Sgt,
Montgomery, R. C., Pvt,
Montgomery, Thomas G., Pvt
Montijo, Manuel, Pfc,
‡Montoya, Cesario P., Pvt,
Montoya, Elias, Pfc,
Montoya, Josquin, Sgt,
Motnoya, Manuel F., Pvt,
Monts, George C., Pfc,
Monty, Armen L., Pfc,
Montuoro, Ralph G., Pfc,
Moody, James A., Pfc,
Moody, Joseph H., Pfc,
Moody, Lee L., Cpl,
†Moody, Ralph W., S/Sgt,
Moody, Theodore M., Cpl
Moon, Charles F., Pfc,
Moon, Clarence L., Pvt,
Moon, Donald F., Pfc,
Mooney, Earl S., Capt,
‡Mooney, James E., Pvt,
Mooney, Noel F., Pvt,
Mooney, Raymond, Pvt,
*Moore, Albert M., Pfc,
†Moore, Alfred J., Jr., Pfc,
Moore, Anglis, Cpl,
Moore, Arthur, Pfc,
‡Moore, Billy A., Pvt,
Moore, Clarence H., Pvt,
Moore, Claud L., Cpl,
Moore, Clayton H., Jr., 1st Lt,
Moore, Dalmer H., Pvt,
†Moore, Dewey D., Pvt,
Moore, Donald K., Pvt,
Moore, Edward F., Pvt,
‡Moore, Frank H., Pvt,
Moore, George L., Pvt,
Moore, Harry D., T/Sgt,
Moore, Herbert E., Pfc,
Moore, Hilton O., 2nd Lt
Moore, Howard, Pvt,
Moore, James F., Pfc,
‡Moore, James G., Pfc,
Moore, James H., Pfc,
Moore, Jim B., Pvt,
Moore, Johnnie H., Pfc,
Moore, Joseph A., Pvt,
Moore, Joseph F., Pvt,
Moore, Robert F., Jr., T/5,
*Moore, Russell, Pvt,
Moore, William H., Pvt,
Moore, William T., Pvt,
Moorman, Banks A., Pfc,
Morales, Jesse, Pvt,
Morales, Louis, Pfc,
Moran, Edward J., Pvt,
*Moran, Emil A., Pvt,
Moran, Gordon, T/4,
Moran, Groen T., Jr., Pvt,
Moran, John M., S/Sgt,
†Moravec, Frank J., Pfc,
Moravec, Joe A., Pvt,
More, Antonio, Pvt,
Moreau, Leonard D., Pfc,
Moreland, Herman E., Pvt,
Moreland, James G., Pvt,
Moreland, Paul L., Pfc,
Morelli, Leo M., Pvt,
‡Moren, James L., Pvt,
Morenz, Bernard, Jr., Pvt
Moretti, Frank A., 1st Lt,
Moretz, Millard D., Sgt,
Morey, Kennet D., Pfc,
‡Morford, John C., Pfc,
†Morgan, Daniel C., 1st Lt,
Morgan, Estel H., Pvt,
Morgan, Frank C., Sgt,
Morgan, Frank L., Pfc,
Morgan, Gilbert, Pfc,
Morgan, Howell F., Capt,
†Morgan, John P., Pfc,
Morgan, Leland L., Sgt,
Morgan, Lloyd E., Pvt,
†Morgan, Perry A., Pvt,
Morgan, Stanley, Cpl,
Morgan, Ted, Pvt,
Morgan, Thomas J., 2nd Lt,
Morgan, William H., Pfc,
Morgenstern, Robert, Pvt,
†Moriarity, Edward J., Pfc,
Morin, Alcide R., S/Sgt,
§Morin, Arthur H., Pvt,
Morley, Robert J., Sgt,
Morneau, Henry J., Pvt,
†Moro, Mario, Pfc,
Morphew, Ralph W., Pvt,
Morra, Lawrence L., Pvt,
†Morreale, James J., Pfc,
Morrill, Frederick D., Cpl,
Morris, Billy V., 1st Lt,
Morris, Charles J., 2nd Lt,
Morris, Forrest P., Pvt,
Morris, F. P., Jr., Pvt,
Morris, Gary B., Jr., Pvt,
Morris, Henry G., Sgt,
Morris, John K., Pfc,
Morris, John W., Pvt,
Morris, Lloyd K., Sgt,
Morris, Michael, Pfc,
‡Morris, Myles W., S/Sgt,
Morris, Robert J., Pfc,
‡Morris, Thomas E., Pfc,
Morris, William W., S/Sgt,
Morrison, Alvin A., Pvt,
Morrison, Elis L., Pfc,
Morrison, Fred L., Pfc,
Morrison, George E., 1st Lt
Morrison, Hugh E., 1st Lt,
‡Morrison, William A., Pvt,
†Morrissey, William T., Pfc,
Morrow, Charles L., Pfc,
§Morrow, James L., Pfc,
Morrow, Paul E., Pvt,
Morrow, Robert L., Pfc,
Morrow, Robert M., Pvt,
†Morrow, William C., Maj,
Morse, Charles W., Jr., 1st Lt,
Morse, Harry S., Pfc
Morse, Kenneth Jay, Pvt,
Morse, Raymond, Pfc,
Morse, Robert L., Pfc,
Mortiner, Karl F., Pvt,
Morton, Carl A., Cpl,
Mortto, Salvatore J., Pfc,
†Mortzfelt, Edward E., Pfc,
Moscato, Frank, Pvt,
Moschetti, Joseph V., Pvt,
Moser, Robert G., Sgt,
Moskalski, Albert, Pvt,
Moslak, Victor F., Pvt
Moslander, Woodrow W., T/5,
‡Mosley, George B., Pfc,
Mosley, William L., Pvt,
Moss, Eliot W., Pvt,
Moss, James R., Pvt,
†Mosser, Charles W., Pvt,
‡Mosses, Frank, Pvt,
Mosshart, John W., Pvt,
†Mott, Courtland D., T/5,
Motta, Alfred, Pfc,
Mottola, Anthony J., Pfc,
‡Mottox, Harold W., Pvt,
Motts, Robert C., Sgt,
‡Motz, Philip G., Sgt,
Moughemer, Alroy G., S/Sgt,
Mount, John E., Pfc,
‡Mountcastle, John A., Pvt,
Mourer, Laverne L, Pvt,
Mourtgis, Arthur C., Pvt,
Moussally, Paul, Pfc,
Mowery, Ellis F., Pvt,
Movano, Rafael E., Pfc,
Moyer, Harold R., Pfc
Moyer, John W., Pvt,
Mozal, Kike, Pfc,
§Mozdzierz, Henry J., Pvt,
Mrkonjic, Walter J., Pfc,
‡Mrowka, Francis J., Pfc,
Mrozik, Roman J., Sgt,
Mudd, William C., 1st Lt,
Mudie, Charlie E., Jr., Pfc,
Muelker, Quentin E., Pfc,
Mueller, Leslie F., Pfc,
Mueller, Eugene H., Pfc,
Mueller, Frederick W., Pvt,
Mueller, Leslie F., Pfc,
Mueller, Werner, Pvt,
Mugavero, Charles M., Pfc,
†Mulcahy, John P., Pvt,
Mulherin, Clifford, Pvt,
†Mulholland, Arthur J., Sgt,
Mull, Joe E., Pvt,
‡Mullally, Frank J., Sgt,
*Mulle, Michard, Cpl,
Mullen, Robert, S/Sgt,
Mullenberg, Carl R., Cpl,
Muller, Harvey C., 2nd Lt,
Mulligan, Harold, Pvt,
Mulligan, Joseph D., Cpl,
Mulligan, Robert J., Pvt,
Mullins, Andy J., Cpl,
Mullins, John J., Pfc,
‡Mullins, Lacey, Pfc,
Mullins, Oscar D., Jr., Pfc,
Mullins, Ray M., Pvt,
†Mullins, Ronnie, Pfc,
†Multer, Malcolm E., Pfc,
†Mulvaney, Harry O., Pfc,
Mulvey, Robert J., Pvt,
Mumma, Salman B., Sgt,
Munis, George, Pfc,
Muniz, Hilario, Pfc,
Munro, Robert N., S/Sgt,
Munsey, Giles R., 1st Lt,
Munson, Allan A., S/Sgt
Munson, Ray M., T/4,
Munson, Virgil L., Cpl,
Munzek, Ben, Pvt,
Muratori, Attilio J., Pfc,
Murch, John H., Pvt,
†Murdock, Archie C., Pvt,
Murdock, Corut, Cpl,
Murfitt, Philip J., Pvt,
Murphrec, Samuel R., Cpl,
Murphy, Carl G., Pvt,
Murphy, Francis J., S/Sgt,

† Killed in Action. * Prisoner of War. ‡ Missing in Action. § Died of Wounds.

Murphy, Francis K., Pfc,
Murphy, Frank J., Pvt,
Murphy, Garnett G., S/Sgt,
†Murphy, Jack H., Sgt,
Murphy, John J., Sgt,
†Murphy, Malachey, 1st Sgt,
Murphy, Millard E., Sgt
‡Murphy, Thomas, Pfc,
Murphy, Thomas E., S/Sgt
Murphy, Wilbett, Pvt,
†Murphy, William J., Pvt,
Murr, John D., Pvt,
Murray, Charles A., T/5,
†Murray, Charles J., Pvt,
Murray, Charles P., Jr., Capt,
Murray, Michael W., Pvt,
Murray, Rollo, Pvt,
Muse, Walter W., Pfc,
§Muselli, Alfred J., Pvt,
Musgrove, Morgan W., T/Sgt,
†Muskal, Frances A., Pfc,
§Musller, Henry E., Pvt,
Mustard, Russell V., Pvt
Mustari, Mario J., Pfc,
*Muston, Kenneth H., Pfc,
Muszynail, William J., S/Sgt,
‡Mutter, William W., Cpl,
Mydlach, William D., Cpl,
Myer, Paul E., Pfc,
Myers, Carey, T/5,
Myers, David M., Pvt
Myers, Delbert L., Sgt,
Myers, Edward G., Jr., Cpl,
Myers, Elmer J., Pfc,
Myers, Gerald A., S/Sgt,
Myers, Harold W., Pvt,
Myers, John E., Pvt,
Myers, John J., Pfc,
Myers, Lawrence R., Pvt,
Myers, Peter W., Pvt,
Myers, Rould L., Sgt,
Myers, Roy J., T/4,
Myers, Stanley H., Pvt,
†Myers, William R., Pvt,
‡Myler, Fred S., Pfc,
Myrick, Marcin A., S/Sgt,
Myrick, Neubern G., Pvt,
Mysliwiec, Daniel S., Pfc,
Mytkowicz, John, Pvt,

Naasz, Jacob, T/5,
†Naccarato, Mike, Pfc,
Nacey, John A., Pvt,
Nadean, Hector L., Pvt,
Nadoing, Joseph S., Pvt
Nagle, Donald R., Pvt,
Nagle, Gabriel, Pvt,
†Nagler, George H., Sgt,
Nagorsky, Sol, Pvt,
‡Nagowski, William A., Sgt,
Nagy, Alex, Pfc,
Nagy, Frank J., Pfc,
Nalker, Robert D., Pvt,
Nalle, Charles C., Capt,
Nally, John F., S/Sgt,
Nance, Ernie L., Pvt,
Nann, Anthony F., Sgt,
Naple, Frank, Pvt,
Napolitano, Joseph S., Pvt,
Naquin, Cedric P., S/Sgt,
Narodzonek, Stanley E., Sgt,
Narusis, Walter S., Pfc,
†Naser, Samuel, Pfc,
Nash, Clarence H., Jr., T/Sgt,
‡Natale, Nicholas S., Pfc,
†Naugle, Crawford, Pvt,
†Nault, Benjamin J., Sgt,
†Nault, Lionel J., Sgt,
Naumuk, Wssyl, Pvt,
Navarro, Ramon, Pvt,
Nave, Willis E., T/5,
Naylor, Harry E., T/4,
Neace, Burgess, Pfc,
Neal, Ernest F., Pvt,
Nedbalski, Charles J., Pvt,
Neddersen, Richard H., Lt Col,
Nedna, Edwin C., Pvt,
‡Neel, David W., Pfc,
Neeley, Lawrence C., Pfc,
Neer, James, Cpl,
Negri, Charles A., Pvt,
Neilson, Lavar, Pfc,
Neisler, James L., Cpl,
Nelson, Albert L., Pfc,
Nelson, Alfred W., Jr., 1st Lt,
Nelson, Andrew S., S/Sgt,
†Nelson, Andy A., Pvt,
Nelson, Carl E., T/4,
Nelson, Clarence A., T/5,
‡Nelson, Clarence M., Pfc,
Nelson, Edner J., Maj
†Nelson, Fielding J., Pfc,
Nelson, Gerald A., Sgt,
Nelson, John L., Sgt,
Nelson, Lyle M., Pfc,
Nelson, Marlin E., Pfc,
†Nelson, Myron J., Pvt,
Nelson, Olen, Pfc,
Nelson, Oscar W., Pfc,
Nelson, Osceola P., Pfc,
Nelson, Otis T., Cpl,
Nelson, Sidney, T/Sgt,
Nelson, Warren J., Pvt,
Nelson, William A., Pvt,
Nelson, William L., Pfc,
Nemits, George, Pvt,
†Nenow, Nonie, Pfc,
Neporadny, John C., Pvt,
†Neri, Girard J., Pvt,
Nesaw, Russell, Pfc,
Nesbitt, James H., Pfc,
Nethken, Lloyd H., T/5,
Neudorff, Charles H., Pvt,
‡Neumann, George E., Pvt,
Neumann, Hans, Cpl,
Neumann, Harold B., Pvt,
Neumann, Walter F., Pvt,
Neutze, Melvin A., Pvt,
Nevins, Francis J., Pvt
Nevisu, Ellsworth H., Cpl,
Nevitt, Norman, Pvt,
Nevue, Paul L., S/Sgt,
Newby, Frank E., Pfc,
Newby, Knarf S., Pvt,
Newby, Lexer D., Pfc,
Newby, Louis E., S/Sgt,
Newell, Dwight H., Sgt,
Newell, John R., Pfc,
Newell, Richard, 1st Lt,
Newhouse, Jesse P., 1st Sgt,
Newkirk, Howard D., 1st Lt,
Newland, James E., S/Sgt,
‡Newland, Mark, Pfc,
Newman, Edward F., Pfc
Newman, Edwin T., Pvt,
Newman, Eugene, Pfc,
Newman, Francis A., Pfc,
†Newman, George M., Pvt,
Newman, James E., T/5,
Newman, Leonard, Pvt,
Newman, Norbert, Pvt,
Newsome, John H., Sgt,
Newsome, Pitt, Pvt,
Newsome, Robert G., Pvt
Newton, Arthur C., 2nd Lt,
†Newton, Arthur S., T/5,
Newton, Edward C., Pfc,
Newton, Leslie J., Cpl,
Newton, Robert B., Pvt
Newweiler, Edward M., Pvt,
Nezich, Andrew D., Pvt,
Niccoli, Richard, Pfc,
Nicely, Robert W., Pvt,
Nicely, Roy H., Jr., Pvt,
Nicholas, Frank M., Pfc,
†Nicholls, James W., Pvt,
Nichols, Amos J., Pvt,
Nichols, Carroll E., Pvt,
Nichols, Edwin A., Maj,
†Nichols, Harvey H., Pvt,
Nichols, Homer L., Pfc,
Nichols, James B., Pvt,
Nichols, James M., Pvt,
Nichols, John L., Pvt,
Nichols, Lee R., S/Sgt,
‡Nichols, Richard L., Pvt,
†Nichols, Robert L., Pfc,
Nichols, Walter F., Pvt,
Nichols, William, Pvt,
Nicholson, Harry L., 1st Lt,
Nicholson, Harry M., T/Sgt,
Nicholson, Joseph F., S/Sgt,
Nicholson, Theodore R., Pvt,
Nicholson, Willard, Pvt,
Nichoson, Daniel O., 2nd Lt,
Nickels, William A., Pfc
†Nickerson, Philip E., Pfc,
Nicks, Clifford W., 1st Lt,
Nicoli, Albert L., T/5,
Nicosia, Salvatore P., Pvt,
Nicusanti, Ugo J., Pfc,
Niedringhause, Kimsey R., Pfc,
Nielson, Maltha W., Pfc,
†Nieman, Edward F., Cpl,
Niemann, Earl N., Pvt,
Niemann, Werner F., Pvt,
†Niemela, Nester J., Cpl,
Niemiec, Frank, Pvt,
*Nigh, William J., Pvt,
Nigro, Francesco, Pvt,
Niileksela, Arvo F., Cpl,
Niland, Anthony, Pvt,
Niles, Marvin A., Pfc,
Niles, William, S/Sgt,
Nilles, Bernard H., S/Sgt,
Nine, Leo V., Pfc,
Niovich, Edward, Pvt,
†Nipper, William E., S/Sgt,
‡Nisson, Norman H., Pvt,
Nitzel, Kenneth E., Sgt,
Nix, George E., Pfc,
Nix, James H., Jr., 1st Lt,
Nixon, Albert B., S/Sgt,
Nixon, Thomas P., Cpl,
Niznick, Edward, Pvt,
Nobbs, Arthur W., Pvt,
Noble, Lee B., Pvt,
‡Nodtvedt, Ellert E., Pvt,
Noel, Raymond F., Pfc,
Noethlich, Robert M., Pfc,
Noffsinger, Norman J., Pvt,
Noga, John J., Pfc,
Noivich, Edward, Cpl,
Nolan, Harvey T., Pvt,
Nolan, John W., Pvt
†Noland, Kentis D., Pvt,
Nolen, Elmer H., Pvt,
‡Norbury, Garnet T., Pfc,
Nordeste, Manuel C., Pfc,
Nordquest, Raymond D., Pvt,
*Nordstrom, Reuben A., Pvt,
Noreen, Edward J., Pvt,
Norman, Glen A., T/4,
Norman, Harold L., Pvt,
Norman, James W. Pfc,
Norris, Clarence L., Pvt,
Norris, Grady, Pfc,
Norris, Harry A., Pvt,
§Norris, James W., Pvt,
Norris, John M., Pfc,
Norris, Lovis E., Pfc,
Norris, Mark G., Jr., Pvt
Norris, Seborn D., S/Sgt,
Norris, Warren P., Cpl,
North, Eldon F., 2nd Lt,
North, Ivan E., S/Sgt,
†Northen, Thomas F., S/Sgt,
Northing, John W., Jr., 1st Lt,
Norton, Daniel J., Pfc,
Norton, George E., Cpl,
Norton, Lowell D., Sgt
Norton, Rufus B., Jr., Pvt,
Norton, William A., Pfc,
Norton, William L., Pfc,
Norwood, Leland P., Pfc
Noseck, Kenneth A., Major,
Notis, Joseph G., Pvt
§Nott, Paul H., Pfc,
Nottingham, Lucius S., Jr., Pvt
Novack, Charles P., Pfc,
Novak, Edward, Pfc,
Novak, Leo P., Pfc,
Novak, Louis P., Pfc,
Novak, Marion S., Pfc,
Novak, Michael L., Pvt,
§Nowak, Charles A., Pvt,
Nowak, Frank J., S/Sgt,
†Nowak, Richard S., Pfc,
†Nowak, Stephen I., Pfc,
†Noyes, George F., Pfc,
Noyes, James R., Pfc,
Nunan, Frank J., 1st Lt,
Nunley, Henry, Pfc,
Nunn, James, Pfc,
Nusbaum, Arthur H., 1st Lt,
Nutter, Edward J., Pvt,
Nutter, Kenneth L., Pvt,
Nuutinen, George J., Pfc
Nyahay, Edward, Pvt.
Nyberg, Carl W., Pfc,
Nyberg, Joseph E., Jr., Pvt,
Nylund, Leonard O., Sgt,
Nyquiest, Howard W., Pvt,
Nystrum, Clyde O., Pfc,

‡Oakley, Billy N., Pvt,
‡Oakley, Wilson J., Pvt,
Oakley, Wilton J., Pvt
†Oakman, Michael C., Pvt,
†Oate, Patrick J., Pvt,
Oates, Calvin W., S/Sgt,
Obadowski, Joseph J., 1st Lt,
†Ober, Leroy G., Pfc,
O'Block, Victor J., Pvt,
O'Bora, Chester E., Pvt,
†O'Boyle, Edward J., Pvt,
Obregon, Miguel L., Pvt,
†O'Brian, Edward J., Pfc,
O'Briant, Harold J., Pvt,
O'Brien, Arnold R., Pfc,
O'Brien, Francis W., Pvt,
†O'Brien, Henry A., Cpl,
O'Brien, James D., Pvt,
O'Brien, James J., Sgt,
O'Brien, John F., Cpl,
O'Brien, Patrick J., Pfc,
Ochar, John J., Pvt,
Ochoa, Leopoldo B., Pvt,
Ochs, Thomas V., Pfc,
†Ochs, William C., Pvt,
†Ockene, Bernard A., Pvt,
Ockerhausen, James R., S/Sgt,
Ockman, Andre J., Sgt,
O'Connell, Frank M., Pfc,
†O'Connell, John J., Sgt,
O'Connell, John W., Sgt,
†O'Conner, William F., Pvt,
O'Connor, Alexander V., Pvt,
O'Connor, Frank N., Pfc,
O'Connor, William N., Pvt,
O'Dea, Robert L., Pvt,
Odice, John S., Pvt,
Odien, Christy W., Pvt,
§Odom, Wiley G., T/5,
Odom, William H., Pfc,
O'Donell, Harry T., Pfc,
O'Donnell, Joseph J., Pvt,
†Odum, James W., T/Sgt,
†Oeftger, Donald G., Pfc,
†Oesterle, Eugene C., Pfc,
Oestreicher, Milton B., Pvt,
Offredo, Emil J., Pvt,
Ogilvie, Robert J., Pvt,
Ogilvie, William H., Pfc,
Ogle, Robert E., 2nd Lt,
Oglesby, David H., Jr., 2nd Lt,
Oglesby, Paul, S/Sgt,
Oglesby, Willie H., Pvt,
‡O'Grady, John B., Pfc,
O'Grady, Robert T., Pfc
O'Hagan, James M., Pvt,
O'Halloran, William H., Pfc,
O'Hanian, Benjamin J., Pvt
O'Hara, James A., 2nd Lt,
‡Ohlberg, Renest, Pfc,
Ohlerich, Louis H., Pvt,
Ohmer, Howard E., Pvt,
O'Kal, John J., Jr., Pvt,
O'Keefe, James J., Pfc,
‡O'Keefe, John F., Pfc,
O'Keefe, William L., Jr., Pfc,
Okenquist, Howard, Pvt,
Okey, Leo E., Pfc,
Oldenkamp, Henry, Pfc,
Older, Linden R., Sgt,
Olds, Kendall A., Pvt,
Olds, Paul F., Pfc,
Oldham, Glenn C., Sgt,
‡O'Leary, Daniel F., Jr., 2nd Lt,
O'Leary, Daniel T., Pvt,
O'Leary, Gerald C., Jr., Pfc,
O'Leary, Regis B., Pfc,
Olecki, Joseph F., Pfc,
Olenik, Steve F., T/Sgt,
Olguin, Manuel V., T/5,
Oleck, Ansel, T/5,
Oliveira, Rodolfo A., Cpl,
Oliver, Alfred W., Pvt,
Oliver, Garnet W., 1st Lt,
Oliver, Jack A., Pvt,
Oliver, James A., Pvt,
‡Oliver, John R., Pvt,
Oliver, Joy J., Pfc,
Oliver, Marion A., Pfc,
Oliver, Raymond D., Pfc,
Oliver, Raymond E., Pvt,
Olivera, Louis N., Pvt,
Olkowski, Richard J., Pvt,
Olmeda, Jose A., Pfc,
*Olmsted, Emry C., S/Sgt,
Olnhausen, Kenneth E., Pvt,
O'Loughlin, Joseph A., Pfc,
Olsen, Carl H., Pfc,
Olsen, Cortes C., Pfc,
Olsen, Frank I., Sgt,
Olsen, George W., Pfc,
Olsen, Merlin H., Pvt,
Olsen, Paul S., Pvt,
Olsen, Wallace R., Sgt,
Olson, Carl J., Pvt,
Olson, Charles J., Pvt,
Olson, Emil A., Sgt,
Olson, Gust H., Pfc,
Olson, John, Jr., Pvt
Olson, Lawrence G., Pvt,
Olson, Marlin P., Pvt,
Olson, Phillip J., T/4,
Olson, Raymond F., S/Sgt,
O'Malley, James J., Pfc,
Oman, Alvin N., Pvt,
*O'Mullane, Alland D., Pfc,
O'Neal, Arl F., Pvt,
O'Neal, Bedford H., Pvt,
O'Neill, James C., Pvt,
O'Neill, John R., Pvt,
O'Neill, Peter L., Jr., S/Sgt,
O'Neill, Robert E., Cpl,
Ong, Donald C., S/Sgt,
Oocumma, Andy, Pvt
Oosterhouse, Henry C., Pfc,
†Ooton, Charles H., S/Sgt,
Opachick, Roger S., Pfc,
Opel, Earl C., Pvt,
O'Pelt, Jack D., Cpl,
†Onpedisano, Joseph F., S/Sgt,
Oppek, Florian J., T/3,
Oppenheim, Armand, 1st Lt,
Oppenheim, Irving, Pfc,
Oquin, Louis O., Pfc,
Oravec, Andrew, Pvt,
*Oravitz, Leonard F., Pfc,
Orbach, Manfred, Pfc,
O'Reilly, Richard F., T/5,
Oreskovich, Steve, Pvt,
Orgler, Siegfried F., Pvt,
Oritz, Fernando, Pvt,
Orlando, Jack, Pvt,
Ormsby, William N., Jr., Pfc,
O'Rourke, E. J., Jr., S/Sgt,
†Orstad, Melvin T., Pfc,
Orr, William R., 1st Lt,
Ortallono, Jack G., Pvt,
Ortega, Arthur A., Pvt,
Ortega, Oscar M., Pvt
Orth, Donald R., Pvt,
Orth, James E., Pvt,
Orth, John P., Pfc,
Ortiz, Frank, Pvt,
Orton, William O., Pvt,
Ortu, Joseph E., Pvt,
Osborn, Donald W., Pvt,
Osborn, Edward L., Sgt,
Osborn, Harold E., Pfc,
Osborn, William C., Jr., Cpl,
Osborne, Arthur, S/Sgt,
Osborne, Benjamin F., Pfc,
Osborne, Don W., Pfc,
Osborne, Evan J., Pvt
Osborne, Francis L., Pvt,
†Osborne, James H., Pvt,
Osborne, James R., Pvt
Osborne, Walter B., Sgt,
‡Osburn, Carl J., Pfc,
Osenkowski, John, Sgt,
Osgard, James L., Lt Col,
Osgood, Neal E., Pvt,
O'Shield, Grover N., Pvt,
Osment, James, Pvt,
Osofsky, Herman, Pfc,
Ostaszewski, Stanley J., Sgt,
Osterhout, Carl E., 2nd Lt,
Osterhout, Harold, Cpl,
Ostrander, Frank J., Pvt,
Ostrander, George E., Pvt,
Ostrowski, Julian, Pvt,
Oswald, John M., Pfc,
O'Toole, Aloysius L., Pfc,
†Ott, Alexander, Pfc,
Ott, Daniel B., T/4,
†Ott, Melvin R., Jr., Pvt,
Otterbacher, Wade E., Pfc
Otterson, Orlin J., Pfc,
Ottino, Arthur R., Pfc,
Ouellette, Clement P., T/5,
Ousley, Billy E., Pvt,
Overby, Henry E., Sgt,
Overdorf, Donald K., Pfc,
Overlee, Vernon W., T/5,
*Overly, Warren G., Pfc,
Overmier, Richard A., Pvt,
Overstreet, Marvin E., Jr., Pfc,
‡Overstreet, Ralph L., Pfc,
Overstreet, Robert L., Pfc,
Owen, Earl C., Pvt,
Owen, Hubert R., Pvt
Owen, William H., Pvt,
Owens, Charles E., Pvt,
Owens, Cletus C., T/5,
Owens, Dominic T., Pfc,
*Owens, Edward F., Pfc,
Owens, Gilbert H., Pvt,
Owens, Jennings B., 1st Sgt,
Owens, Joseph G., Pvt,
Owens, Martin P., Pvt,
Owens, Roy E., Pfc,
Owens, Sidney E., Pfc,
Owens, Thomas, Jr., Sgt,
Owens, William A., Pvt,
Owens, William C., Pvt,
†Owyang, Castro Y., Pvt,
Oxfeld, Frank, Pvt,
Oxley, Charles K., S/Sgt,
Oxner, Fred, S/Sgt,
Ozwirk, Joseph F., T/Sgt

Paar, Edward G., Capt,
Pabeschitz, Frank J., Pfc,
†Pacaccio, Ralph J., Pvt,
Pace, Frank S., Pfc,
†Pace, Preston L., Sgt,
Pace, Willie E., Sgt,
Pacheco, Adam, Sgt,
Pacheco, Selinio G., Pfc,
§Pacifico, Thomas C., Pvt,
Pacillo, Angelo A., Pvt,
Pack, Charles H., Sgt,
Packman, James L., Capt,
Packwood, Burleigh T., Capt,
Pacunas, Alban A., CWO,
Padgett, Earl S., Pvt,

† Killed in Action. * Prisoner of War. ‡ Missing in Action. § Died of Wounds.

Padgett, Reuben D., Jr., Pfc,
Padilla, Juan J., Pfc,
Padjen, Nicholas P., Pvt,
†Page, Dalton D., 2nd Lt,
Page, Floyd K. E., T/5,
‡Page, Thomas F., Jr., Pvt,
Page, Warren L., Pvt,
Paklonsky, Gus A., Pvt,
Palangio, Frank M., Pvt,
Palazzola, Frank F., Pfc,
Palencher, Peter G., Pvt,
Palermo, James V., Pvt,
†Palermo, Joseph P., Pvt,
Pallante, Angelo, Pvt,
Paller, Gerald J., Pvt,
Pallone, Albert A., Pvt,
Palma, Robert E., 1st Sgt,
†Palmer, Elliot S., Cpl,
Palmer, Harry C., Cpl,
Palmer, Jack W., S/Sgt,
Palmer, Julian R., Pvt,
Palmer, Merle R., Pfc,
Palmer, Seymour L., Pvt,
Palmer, Walter G., T/5,
Palmerlee, Herman R., Pfc,
Palmieri, Joseph A., Pfc
Palocy, Charles J., Pvt,
Paluda, John C., Sgt,
†Palumbo, Joseph, Pfc,
Pampuch, Narcel A., Pvt,
Pamraning, Elmer W., Pvt
‡Panagakos, William L., Pvt,
Panak, George P., Pfc,
Pandolfo, William, Sgt,
Panek, Jerry A., Pfc,
Panek, Thomas J., Pvt,
Panetta, James L., Sgt,
Panetti, Robert R., Pfc,
Panfil, Bruno A., Pvt,
Panice, Tobey, Pfc,
‡Panich, Michael, Pvt,
†Pankake, Jack O., Cpl,
Panko, Lloyd W., Sgt,
†Pannier, Walter H., Pfc,
Pannullo, Ottilio A., Pfc,
Panse, Arthur F., Pfc,
Pansino, Charles J., Pvt,
‡Paolello, James R., Pvt,
Papa, Joseph G., Pfc,
†Papak, Stanley A., Pfc,
Pappa, Anthony J., T/5,
Papus, John J., Pvt,
Papuzynski, Joe T., S/Sgt,
Paragin, Jesse O., S/Sgt,
Pardo, Raymond, S/Sgt,
Parenteau, Joseph A. D., Pfc,
Parham, James R., Pvt,
Paris, Carlton, Pvt,
Paris, Charles L., Pvt,
Parish, Howard L., Pvt,
Park, Fred, Pvt,
Parker, Alvin M., Pfc,
Parker, Arthur Y., Pvt,
Parker, Carl, S/Sgt,
Parker, Charles B., Pfc,
Parker, Charles W., Pfc,
Parker, Ernest, Pfc,
Parker, Fred, Pfc,
Parker, Harlan H., Cpl,
Parker, Homer W., Pvt
Parker, Howard F., Sgt,
Parker, Howard M., Pvt,
Parker, Raymond E., Pvt
Parker, Sidney, Pvt,
Parker, Tom, Pfc,
Parkin, Wallace H., Pfc,
Parkinson, Gerald D., Cpl,
Parks, Jack, Pfc,
†Parks, Rex E., Pfc,
Parmeter, Bernard W., 2nd Lt,
Parness, Maurice K., 2nd Lt,
†Parr, Chester E., Pfc,
†Parris, Charles L., Pfc,
Parris, Noah, S/Sgt,
Parrish, J. D., Pfc,
Parrott, Clarence L., Pvt,
Parsons, James L., Jr., Pvt,
Parsons, Lowell D., 1st Lt,
Partick, John W., Pfc,
Partin, Frank A., Pfc,
Partin, Fred O., Pfc,
Partridge, Loren B., S/Sgt,
Partridge, Charles H., T/Sgt,
Parzych, Stanley R., Pfc,
‡Pasante, Irving R., Pvt,
Paschich, Lawrence W., T/Sgt,
Pascocello, Sylvester, Pfc,
Pascoe, Frank R., Sgt.
Pascual, Nicolas, 1st Lt,
Pasculli, Vito P., Pvt,
Pase, Arnold R., S/Sgt,
Pashkowski, John, Pvt,
†Pasillas, Jesus, Pfc,
*Pask, Kenneth C., Pvt,

Pasko, Joseph W., Pvt
Passalacqua, Steve, Pvt,
Passino, Frank E., Pvt,
Passmore, Allen E., Pvt,
Pastrana, Joe M., Pfc,
Patchell, Donald, Pvt,
Pate, Robert L., Jr., Pvt,
Patera, Miloslof M., T/4,
Patrem, Charles A., Pfc,
†Patrick, Russell W., Pvt,
†Patry, Jean A., Pfc,
Patson, Edward J., Pvt,
Patterson, Allen O., Pvt
Patterson, Daniel R., Pfc,
Patterson, Howard L., Pfc,
Patterson, Louis F., Pvt
Patterson, Robert E., Pfc,
Pattillo, Robert L., Pvt,
Patton, Burleigh E., Pvt,
Patton, James E., S/Sgt,
Patton, Stewart H., Jr., 1st Lt,
§Patty, Thomas L., Pfc,
Pauker, Arnold, Pvt
Paul, Archie, Pfc,
Paul, Charles A., Pfc,
Paul, Charles E., Pvt,
Paul, Raymond J., Pvt,
Paul, Stanley M., Pvt,
Pauley, Levien C., Cpl,
Pauley, Raymond L., Pvt,
†Paulsen, Albert H., Pvt,
Paulson, Archie L., Pfc,
Paulson, Arthur C., Pfc,
Paulson, Vernon J., Pvt,
Pavlock, Stanley E., Jr., Pvt,
Pavol, Louis, Pfc,
Pawlak, John P., Jr., Pfc,
Paxton, Letser L., Sgt,
Paxton, Victor E., Pfc,
Pyan, Albert, Pfc,
Payne, Clyde L., Cpl,
†Payne, Harold C., Pvt,
‡Payne, Howard T., Pfc,
Payne, Lawrence, Sgt,
Payne, Odis L., Sgt,
Payne, Ray M., Pvt
Payne, Thomas D., Jr., Pvt
Payne, Robert L., Pvt,
Payne, William C., S/Sgt,
Paynter, Paul H., Pvt,
Peachey, George H., Pvt,
*Peak, Jack R., Pfc,
Peal, Robert A., Pvt,
†Pear, Andrew J., Pvt,
Pearce, James H., Pvt,
†Pearce, John A., Pfc,
Pearce, Niel A., 1st Lt,
Pearce, William P., Jr., Pfc,
Pearl, Albert G., Pfc,
Pearson, James F., Pvt,
Pearson, Marvin L., Pfc,
Pearson, Paul A., Pvt
Pearson, Reynold P., Pfc,
Pearson, Richard V., Pfc,
Pearson, Robert W., Pvt,
Pearson, Stanley E., Pfc,
Peatrowsky, Marvin E., Pvt,
Pechaver, Frank J., Cpl,
Peck, Clifford O., Pvt,
Peck, George S., Capt,
†Peck, Millard D., Pvt,
Peckham, Albert F., Pvt,
Peckham, George M., Capt,
Peckinpaugh, Richard B., Capt,
Peckman, Howard W., Pfc,
Pedersen, Walter H., Pvt,
Pedings, John T., Pvt,
Pedregon, Baudelio H., Sgt,
†Pedregon, Eugene H., Pfc,
Peeple, James W., Pfc,
Pegausch, Robert S., Pfc,
Pegos, Michael, Pvt,
Pegram, Mabron F., Pvt
Pegues, Phillip A., Pfc,
Peine, Morris E., Pvt,
Pekarcik, Steve A., Pvt,
Pelino, Anthony V., T/5,
Pell, Gerald O., T/Sgt,
Pella, Joseph J., Pvt,
Pellegrino, Anthony J., Pfc,
Pellegrino, Dominic L., Pvt,
Pelletier, Arthur L., Pfc,
Pellettiere, Michael J., Pfc,
Pelliccio, Anthony P., Pfc,
Pellizzi, Frank J., Pvt,
§Pelton, Robert F., Pvt,
Pelton, Stanley C., Pfc,
Pemberton, Henry C., Pfc,
Pena, Jesus, Pvt,
Pena, John T., S/Sgt,
Pena, Robert, Pvt,
§Pence, Oscar J., Pvt,
Pender, Horace E., S/Sgt,
†Pendergast, Cyril G., Pfc,

Pendlebury, Richard, Jr., Pfc,
Pendley, Eustus H., Pfc,
†Pendolino, Dominick G., Pfc,
Pengk, Louis E., Pvt,
†Pengrin, Wasil, Pvt,
Penland, Walter, Pvt,
Penley, Luther W., Pfc,
Penn, Irwin I., Pfc,
†Penna, Louis, Pvt,
Pennekamp, George C., Pvt,
Pennell, Joseph P., Pvt,
Pennington, Frelon J., Cpl,
Pennuto, Lawrence B., Pfc
Penny, Louis R., T/Sgt,
†Peno, Arthur C., Pfc,
†Pepe, Nicholas J., Pfc,
Peplowski, Stanley E., Sgt,
†Perch, Malcolm P., Pvt,
Perdue, Bonnie L., Sgt,
Perdue, Leo C., Pvt
Peregoy, Charles W., Pvt,
Pereira, Manuel L., Pfc,
Perez, Arthur P., Sgt,
†Perez, Carlos B., Pvt,
‡Perez, Eduardo, Pfc,
Perez, Eloy F., 2nd Lt,
Perez, Pablo, Pvt,
Pergament, Hyman, 1st Lt,
Perino, Thomas D., Cpl,
Perkins, Carl W., S/Sgt,
Perkins, Clifford W., Pvt,
Perkins, James, Pfc,
Perkins, John C., Major,
Perkins, Joseph D., Pvt,
§Perkins, Robert A. Z., S/Sgt,
Perkins, Thomas E., Pvt,
Perkins, Wilson M., Sgt,
Perlino, Ralph A., Sgt,
Perme, Louis, 1st Sgt,
Perpoli, Julius J., Pvt
Perras, Joseph P., Pfc,
Perreault, Lucian B., Pvt,
Perrine, Bernard F., Sgt,
Perrone, Frank P., 1st Sgt,
Perrone, Paul, Pvt,
Perry, Arthur M., Pvt,
Perry, Charles A., Pvt,
†Perry, Clifford E., Pfc,
Perry, Donald C., Pvt
‡Perry, Isadore P., Pvt,
Perry, James E., Pfc,
Perry, Oscar W., Jr., Pvt
†Perry, Richard D., Pvt,
Perry, Victor J., Pvt,
§Perry, Walter E., Pvt,
Perschbacher, Edward H., Pfc,
Persig, Claude L., Cpl,
Persyn, Frank P., Pvt,
Perusich, Paul, T/5,
†Pesha, Vincent A., Pvt,
Peskin, Alexander, Pvt,
Pesmark, Martin J., Pfc,
Pesta, Irving V., Pvt,
Pestle, Chester L., Pvt,
Peszek, Henry J., Sgt,
Peter, William E., S/Sgt,
Peters, David, Pvt,
Peters, George K., Jr., Pvt,
Peters, Herman, Pvt,
Peters, Hugh N., Cpl,
Peters, Richard H., Pfc,
Peters, Robert J., Pvt,
Petersen, Ole J., Pfc,
†Petersen, Stanley M., Pvt,
Peterson, Carl E., Pfc,
Peterson, Charles E., Pfc,
Peterson, Everett L., Pfc,
Peterson, Frank J., Pfc,
Peterson, Franklin E., Sgt,
Peterson, Lester R., Pvt,
‡Peterson, Orville S., S/Sgt,
Peterson, Richard M., Pfc
Peterson, Vernon R., T/3,
Peterson, Virgil F., Cpl,
Peterson, Willis S., T/5
Petrarca, Dominic W., Pvt,
Petre, Earl F., Sgt,
Petree, William H., Jr., Cpl,
Petrelis, Calvin C., Pvt,
Petrella, Daniel D., T/Sgt,
Petrie, Russell J., Pvt,
Petrillo, Peter J., Pfc,
Petro, Andrew J., Pvt,
Petroi, Dometro, Pfc,
Petrone, Emanuel, Pvt,
Petrosky, Albert J., Pfc,
†Petrowski, Edward A., Pvt,
Petrucci, Frank G., Pvt,
Petrucci, Fred J., Pfc,
‡Petruska, John, Sgt,
Petruso, Frank J., Sgt,
‡Petruzziello, Mario, T/Sgt,
Petty, Charlie W., Pfc,
†Peyton, Harold T., T/Sgt,

Pfeffer, Roman L., Pvt,
Pfeiffer, Dennis W., Pvt,
Pfeiffer, George T., Pfc,
Pfeiffer, Willam J., 1st Lt,
‡Pfister, Ralph J., Pvt,
†Pfitzenmaier, Norman M., Pfc,
Pfleeger, Fred H., Pfc,
Phario, Joseph J., Pvt,
†Pharis, Andrew J., Pfc,
Pheil, William C., Pvt,
†Phelps, Asa B., Jr., Pvt,
Phelps, Jim S., Capt,
Phelps, John W., Cpl,
Phelps, Lyle A., Pfc,
Phelps, Robert F., Pvt
Phelps, Thomas O., Pfc,
*Phemister, Howard B., Sgt,
Philbin, Alden R., Pvt,
Philbrick, Wesley A., Pvt,
Philbrook, Arthur C., Pfc,
Philipp, Edward H., T/5,
Phillips, Clinton O., Pfc,
Phillips, Edgar J., Pfc,
Phillips, Edward H., Pvt,
†Phillips, Gaither L., Pfc,
Phillips, George H., Pvt,
Phillips, Guy F., Pfc
Phillips, Hoyt G., 1st Lt,
Phillips, John B., Jr., S/Sgt,
Phillips, John E., Pfc,
†Phillips, John P., Jr., Cpl,
Phillips, John R., T/5,
Phillips, Kenneth R., Pvt,
Phillips, Leo H., Sgt,
Phillips, Melvin E., Pvt,
Phillips, Michael, Jr., Pvt,
Phillips, Michael P., Pfc,
Phillips, Obert L., Pvt,
Phillips, Paul D., Cpl,
Phillips, Paul G., Pvt,
Phillips, Robert A., Pvt,
Phillips, Stanley, Pvt,
Phillips, Wayne A., Pfc,
Phillips, Wendel M., 1st Lt,
Phillips, Wiley W., S/Sgt,
†Phills, Robert D., Pfc,
Phye, Wade V., Pvt,
Pialorsy, Brun, L., Pfc,
†Pian, Seymour R., 1st Lt,
Piantedosi, Alexander, Pvt,
†Piazza, Joseph, Pvt,
Piazza, Vincent R., Pvt,
Pickard, Dorsal L., Pvt,
Pickett, Claudius, S/Sgt,
†Pickett, James W., Cpl,
Picoso, Jose H., Pvt
Piechowiak, Edward F., Pvt,
Piegan, Peter P., Pvt,
Pieper, Harold B., Pvt,
Pierce, Charles L., Sgt,
§Pierce, Albert J., Pvt,
Pierce, Elton R., Pfc,
Pierce, Harold S., Pvt,
Pierce, Joe M., Sgt
Pierce, Joseph A., Pvt
†Pierce, Millard E., T/Sgt,
Pierce, Walter A., Pfc,
Pierson, Paul E., Pfc,
Pietrolongo, Salvatore, Pvt,
Pietrowski, Leonard F., Sgt,
†Pifer, Nevin W., S/Sgt,
Pignanelli, Augustino, Sgt,
†Piha, Emil V., Pvt,
†Pike, John J., Pvt,
Pilgrim, John R., Sgt.
Pillegrino, Anthony J., Pfc,
Pillman, Harry A., Pvt,
Pilski, Alfred P., Pvt,
Pimsner, Edward W., Cpl,
Pinkerman, William, Pfc,
Pinkham, Lawrence P., 1st Lt,
Pinkley, Rex R., Cpl,
Pinkston, James H., Pfc,
Pinkston, James H., Pfc,
‡Pinkston, John R., Pvt,
Pinkowitz, Israel, Pfc,
Pinkowski, Chester T., Pvt,
Pinneo, Willard, Pfc,
Pino, Albert, Pvt,
Pinsky, Edward B., T/5,
Pinson, Joseph J., Pvt,
Pintar, Martin, Sgt,
Pipes, Melvin, Pfc,
Piraino, Dominic M., Pfc,
‡Pirec, Rudolph, Pvt,
Piro, Carmine, Pfc,
Pisani, Rocco M., Pfc,
Pisani, Salvatore E., Pvt,
†Pisano, Joseph, Pvt,
Pisano, Salvatore S., Pfc,
Pisano, Domenic J., Pvt,
†Piscioneri, Salvatore D., Pvt,
Piscitelli, Clemente P., S/Sgt,
Pisello, Bartoli V., Pvt,

Pitcher, Elmer B., Pfc,
Pitstick, Frederick J., T/5,
Pittinger, Nelson M., 1st Lt,
Pittman, Bennie, Pfc,
†Pittman, Edward R., Pvt,
Pittman, Robert T., 2nd Lt
Pittman, Vernon B., Pvt
Pitts, Donald E., Pvt,
Pitts, Floyd E., S/Sgt,
Pivinski, Steve L., Pvt,
Pizana, Ernesto G., Pvt,
Pizzi, Domenick A., Pfc,
†Pizzonia, Albert, Pfc,
Plack, John D., Pfc,
Placke, Lawrence W., Pvt,
Plaga, Walter J., Pfc,
Plahs, Fred J., Pfc,
†Plante, Arthur J., Pfc,
Plaskon, George, Pvt,
Plath, Walter V., Sgt,
Plummer, Richard A., Pvt,
Pocock, Kenneth R., Pfc,
Podgur, Julian, Pfc,
Podobinski, Stanley J., Pvt,
Poe, Herbert, Cpl,
Poe, Martine, Pvt,
‡Poertner, John W., Pfc,
Poetmpa, Raymond A., Pvt,
‡Poetter, Glen T., Pfc,
Pohl, Barton, Jr., Sgt,
Pohlig, William G., Jr., 2nd Lt,
Poine, Paul S., Pvt,
Poinsett, Albert J., Pvt,
Poirier, Paul L., Pfc,
Poissonnier, Arthur, Sgt,
Poitiers, James M., Pvt,
Pokrajac, Peter, Pfc,
Polacek, Joseph S., Pvt,
Polan, Robert N., Pvt,
Poland, Leonard O., Pfc,
Polches, Louis, Pvt,
Polenchar, Joseph E., Sgt,
Polera,Frank, Cpl,
Pollard, J. T., Pvt,
Polley, R. H., S/Sgt,
Pollino, Sam A., Pvt,
Pollitt, John C., Pfc,
Pollock, Clifton M., Pvt,
Pollock, Donald C., Pvt,
Pollock, Donald C., Pfc,
†Polly, Theodore F., Pvt,
Polsin, Charles J., Pvt
‡Polson, Luther B., Pfc,
Poltiske, Anton, T/5,
Pomeres, Juan B., Pvt,
‡Ponicki, Joseph, Pvt,
Pontzer, John J., S/Sgt,
Pontzer, Lloyd L., S/Sgt,
Ponzillo, Anthony, Pvt,
Pool, Merle A., Cpl,
Pool, William, Pvt
Pool, James C., Pvt,
Poole, Joe E., Pfc,
Poole, Joseph L., Pvt,
Poole, Vernon, T/5,
Poole, William F., Pfc,
Poor, Marvin H., Pvt,
Poore, Otto, Pvt,
Pope, Dewy H., Pfc,
Pope, Donald J., T/5,
†Popella, Edwin, Pvt,
†Poplarchek, William M., Pfc,
Poplin, Calvin C., Pvt,
Popoff, Homer W., Pfc,
†Popovich, William, S/Sgt,
†Poquet, Luc L., Pvt,
†Poraczky, John G., Pfc,
Porath, Richard C., Cpl,
†Porch, Harry E., Pfc,
Porebski, Leonard A., Pfc,
Poreheddu, Thomas A., Pvt,
Poris, James, Pvt,
Porta, Robert R., Pfc,
†Porter, Carl R., Pvt,
Porter, Harry, Jr., S/Sgt,
Porter, Len, Jr., Pvt,
Porter, Mackenzie E., Lt Col,
Porter, Morris C., 1st Lt,
Porter, Owen P., Pfc,
†Porter, Vernon A., Pvt,
Porter, Wallace E., Pvt,
Posternack, Saul, Pvt,
Postiglione, Carl J., Pfc,
Post, Benjamin M., Jr., Pfc,
Poston, Clyde L., Pvt,
Potash, Philip, T/Sgt,
Poter, Granville C., Pvt,
Potratz, Chester W., Pfc
†Potter, Clarence W., Pvt,
Potter, Grant A., Sgt,
Potter, Milton E., Cpl,
Potthoff, Ralph F., Pfc,
†Potts, Charles F., Pvt,
Potts, John D., Cpl,

† Killed in Action. * Prisoner of War. ‡ Missing in Action. § Died of Wounds.

†Potts, Fred L., Pvt,
Potts, Ridgway W., Pfc,
†Poudrier, Edward, Cpl,
Poulen, Harold R., Pvt,
Poulin, Alcide G., Pfc,
Pouquette, Frank A., Sgt,
Povolo, James T., Pfc,
Powelkop, Arthur J., Pvt,
‡Powell, Allen T., Jr., Pvt,
Powell, Ashby R., Pvt,
Powell, Gary B., S/Sgt,
†Powell, Herbert O., 2nd Lt,
Powell, Ira M., Pvt,
Powell, Jack C., Pvt,
†Powell, John G., Pvt,
§Powell, Junior F., Pvt,
Powell, Joseph H., Pvt,
Powell, Philip R., Sgt,
Powell, Wilbur E., Pfc,
Powell, William A., Pfc,
Powell, William B., Pfc,
Powell, William C., Pfc,
Powers, Clovis L., Pvt
Powers, John C., Pfc
Powers, John C., Pfc,
Powers, Stanley, Pfc,
‡Poythress, James D., Jr., Pvt,
Poznanovich, Paul, 1st Lt,
Prado, Santos R., S/Sgt,
Prall, Francis L., 2nd Lt,
Pranckunas, Withold, Pfc,
Pranckus, Edward, Pfc,
Praskay, Michael J., Jr., Pfc,
Praskevich, Michael, Pfc,
Prather, Herman E., T/Sgt,
*Pratico, Myles F., Pfc,
Pratt, Harry G., Pvt,
Pratt, Theodore B., 2nd Lt,
Pratt, Vernon R., T/4
Prebush, John F., Pvt,
Preece, Wendell M., Pvt,
†Prego, Tony, Pfc,
Preis, Harry W., Pvt,
Prendergast, Richard J., T/5,
Prendiville, Joseph P., S/Sgt,
†Prepon, Herbert, Pvt,
Prescott, Wayne W., Pvt,
Press, Joseph M., Pfc,
Preston, Neil W., T/5,
‡Prestridge, Robert T., Pfc,
Presutti, Carmen W., Pvt,
Preyers, John M., Pvt,
Pribbenow, Milo L., Pfc,
†Pribila, Michael F., Cpl,
Price, Albert W., Pfc,
Price, Carroll J., T/5,
‡Price, Delbert, Pfc,
Price, Elvin R., Pfc,
Price, Frank B., S/Sgt,
Price, Harland H., Pvt,
Price, James G., Jr., T/5,
Price, Joel D., Pfc,
Price, Marvin P., Sgt,
Price, Robert I., Pfc,
†Price, Robert L., Pfc,
Price, Vonnie L., Pfc,
Price, Walter E., S/Sgt,
Price, William A., Pvt,
Price, William R., Pvt,
*Prichard, Kenneth D., Cpl,
Pridemore, Lawrence E., Pfc,
Pridgen, Harry W., Pvt,
Pridgen, Robert B., Maj,
Prill, William, Pfc,
Prim, Cecil M., Pfc,
Prince, Daniel G., Jr., Pfc,
‡Prince, Floyd E., 1st Sgt,
Pringle, James A., 1st Lt,
Pritchard, Eugene, Pfc,
†Prittchett, Lonzo O., Pfc,
†Procaccini, Eugene J., Pfc,
Proctor, Eugene R., Pvt,
Proctor, James V., Pfc,
Proctor, Marvin H., Pvt,
Proehl, Frank J., Sgt,
Prohme, Rupert, Capt,
Proir, Charles I., Pvt
Prosek, Charles, Pvt,
Prosek, Milton S., Cpl,
Prospero, Albert J., Pfc,
Prosser, Darel E., T/4,
†Protowicz, Theodore, Pvt,
†Proulx, Clement G., Pvt,
Pruden, Harry J., S/Sgt,
†Pruden, John W., Pvt,
Pruitt, Roscoe, Sgt,
Prus, Felix, Pvt,
Proveaux, Jackson W., Jr., Pvt
Pryor, James E., T/5,
†Pryor, Odell I., Pvt,
Pryor, Raymond N., Pvt,
Przekwas, Frank E., Pvt,
Przybek, Matthew J., Pfc,
Przymylski, Sigismund S., Pfc,
Psiropoulos, George M., Pfc,
Psyzbys, Mitchel J., Cpl,
Publido, Jesus H., Sr., Pvt
Pucci, Raymond C., T/Sgt,
Puchalski, Joseph V., Pvt,
Puchko, Steve, Pvt,
Puckett, Herman V., Jr., Pfc,
Puckett, Louis S., Pvt,
Puckett, William C., Pvt,
Puco, Ralph J., Pfc,
Puett, Arthur E., Pvt,
†Pugh, John D., Pvt,
Pugh, John H., T/4,
*Puglia, Anthony F., Pfc,
Puicci, Carl, Pvt,
Puishis, Anthony J., Pvt,
†Pulk, Frank S., Jr., Pvt,
†Pulsipher, Dalton, Pvt,
Pumphrey, Cecil B., Pfc,
Purcell, Fred J., Pfc,
Purcell, John W., Pvt,
†Purcell, John Q., Pfc,
Prussack, Raymond M., S/Sgt,
Purcha, Leo T., Pvt,
Purdy, Melvin J., Pfc,
‡Purdy, Willis H., Pfc,
Purol, Raymond A., Pfc,
Purpora, Anthony, Pvt,
Purser, William A., Pfc,
‡Pursley, James R., Pfc,
Purtle, Bethel, S/Sgt,
Purvis, Eual L., Sgt
*Puskar, Joe G., Jr., Pfc,
†Pyers, Edward W., Pvt,
Pylant, James H., Pvt,
§Pyles, Lester L., S/Sgt,
Pysz, Charles F., Pfc,

Quade, Thomas, Pfc,
Qualls, James D., Pvt,
Quan, Fong, Pfc,
Quast, Clifford A., T/5,
Queen, Arthur K., Pfc,
Queen, Paul C., 1st Lt,
Quenzer, Christian J., Sgt,
Querio, John M., Pfc,
‡Quick, Arthur O., Pfc,
Quick, George B., Jr., Sgt,
Quick, Richard C., Pfc,
Quigley, Charles E., Pvt,
‡Quigley, John J., Sgt,
†Quinby, Ronald W., Pfc,
Quinlivan, George T., Capt,
†Quinn, Daniel H., Pvt,
Quinn, Donald J., 1st Lt,
†Quinn, James E., Pfc,
†Quintanna, Willie, Pfc,
Quistorf, Richard G., Pvt,
Quyas, Ralph, Pfc

†Raabe, Louis, Jr., Pfc,
Raatz, DuWaine R., Pfc,
Raba, Charles A., Pfc,
Rabe, Robert A., Pvt,
Rabideau, Thomas A., Pfc,
Raby, Wheeler J., Pfc,
‡Race, Edward F., Sgt,
Rackez, George H., Pfc,
†Radcliffe, Irving A., Pfc,
Radeck, Gorman R., Pvt,
Radecki, Frank M., Pfc,
Rademacher, Herbert, Pfc,
†Rader, Walter J., Pfc,
Radigan, Joseph V., Pvt,
Radolak, Frank H., Pvt,
Radosevich, M. S., 1st Sgt,
Radvansky, Adam, Pvt,
Radylovich, William J., Pvt,
Radzieski, Vincent V., Pfc,
Rafenstein, Raz M., Pvt,
Raferty, Joseph P., Sgt,
Raff, Morris, Sgt,
Rafferty, James T., Pvt,
Raffin, Albert, Pvt,
Rafuse, Clyde J., Pfc,
Rager, Alfred E., Pvt,
Ragland, Billy N., Pfc,
Rago, Angel A., Pvt,
Raia, Carmine, Pvt,
‡Raiford, Fred W., Pvt,
Raihl, Elmer T., Pvt,
Raines, Alfonso, Pfc,
Raines, Dallas W., Jr., Pvt,
Rainey, Glenn A., Pfc,
Rainey, Raymond E., 1st Lt,
Rainone, Anthony, Pvt,
Rains, Denver C., S/Sgt,
Rains, Lewis V., Pvt,
†Rains, Ralph C., Pfc,
Raitano, James A., Pvt,
Raker, Ruel W., Pfc,
Rakoskie, Alphonso, T/5,
Ralls, Daniel W., Pvt,
Ralph, Albert H., Pfc,
Ramas, Nepolian D., Pvt,
Ramer, Parm A., Pvt,
Ramerez, Fefuaio, Pfc,
Ramirez, Ignaci oP., Pfc,
Ramirez, Julio S., Pvt,
Ramsey, Carl D., Capt,
†Ramsey, Joseph A., Pvt,
Ramsey, Robert W., Pvt,
Ramsier, Ivan F., T/5,
‡Ramstedt, Ernest F., Pvt,
Rancilio, Attilio J., S/Sgt,
Randall, Gilbert L., Pvt,
Randall, Herbert S., Pfc,
Randazzo, Joseph V., Pvt,
†Randolph, Delmus, Pfc,
Randolph, Everette, S/Sgt,
Randolph, George P., Sgt,
Raney, Arthur N., Pfc,
‡Raney, Arthur N., Pfc,
Raney, Ray J., T/5,
Raney, William L., Pvt,
Raniolo, John, Jr., Pvt,
Rankin, Ben F., S/Sgt,
Rankin, W. T., S/Sgt,
Ransdell, William E., Pvt,
Ransom, Alfred M., Pfc,
Rantala, Warner W., Pvt,
‡Raposa, Clement P., Pfc,
Rapoza, Joseph N., Pvt,
Rapoza, Victor, T/Sgt,
‡Rapoze, Charles, Sgt,
Rapsynski, Edward J., Pvt,
†Rash, Walter C., Pfc,
Rasmussen, William F., Cpl,
Raspetnik, Victor L., Pvt,
‡Raster, Joseph F., Pvt,
Ratcliffe, Charlie H., T/Sgt,
†Ratekin, Jason E., S/Sgt,
‡Rath, Anton, Pfc,
Rath, Howard W., 2nd Lt,
Ratcliff, Blaine R., Pfc,
Raterman, Louis J., Cpl,
Ratliff, Clara B., Pvt,
Ratliff, Gerald A., Pvt,
Ratliffe, Paul, Pvt,
Rau, Julian P., Pfc,
Rauch, Francis A., Pvt,
Raulonis, John P., Pfc,
Rauworth, John E., Pvt,
Rawlings, William H., Sgt,
Rawson, Earl A., Pfc,
†Ray, Deamous T., Pfc,
Ray, Clarence R., Sgt,
‡Ray, Edwin D., S/Sgt,
Ray, George R., 1st Sgt,
Ray, James C., Pvt,
Ray, Jim D., Pfc,
Ray, Robert H., Pvt,
Ray, Sidney E., Pvt,
†Rayl, John A., 1st Lt,
Raymond, George E., 1st Lt,
Raymond, William R., Sgt,
Raynor, Leslie R., Pvt,
Re, Frank, Pfc,
Read, Martin O., Pfc,
†Reap, Donald J., Pvt,
‡Reaper, Jack D., Pvt,
Rearick, Ralph E., Pvt,
Reavy, Robert R., Pfc,
Reay, Edwin T., Pvt,
Reber, Charles H., T/5,
Reda, Frank, Pvt,
‡Reddeman, Lawrence C., Pfc,
Redden, Calvin C., Jr., Pvt,
†Redding, Joseph R., Pvt,
Reddish, Joseph M., Pfc,
Redman, Harvey G., Cpl,
Redman, Roy R., T/4,
Redmon, William D., Pfc,
Reece, Billie, Pvt,
Reed, Charles H., Pfc,
Reed, Claude V., S/Sgt,
Reed, Ira D., T/5,
Reed, Junior S., Pvt,
Reed, Paul A., Cpl,
Reed, Robert R., Pfc,
Reed, Toliver E., Pfc,
Reed, William, Pfc,
Reeder, Manny, Pfc,
Reedy, John M., Pfc,
Rees, Walter E., Pfc,
Reeser, Clarence C., Pvt,
Reeves, Alvin D., Pfc,
†Reeves, Elmer J., Pvt,
*Reeves, Fay, Sgt,
Reeves, Harold L., Jr., Pfc,
Reeves, John R., Pfc,
§Reeves, John W., Pvt,
§Reeves, Vernon L., S/Sgt,
Reges, Clarence R., Sgt,
Regi, Merrill R., T/5,
Rehbany, Nicholas, Pfc,
Riech, Eugene, Pvt,
Reich, Joseph, Pvt,
Reichert, George, Pfc,
Reid, Henry L., Pvt,
Reid, James M., Sr., Pfc,
†Reid, Paul J., Pvt,
Reid, William B., 1st Lt,
Reid, Willie V., S/Sgt,
Reiger, Luther R., Pfc,
*Reile, Jacob J., Pfc,
Reilly, Michael, Pvt,
Reilly, Paul S., Pfc,
†Reilly, Thomas V., Pvt,
Reindel, Oswald, Pfc,
Reine, Joseph R., Pfc,
Reine, Philip, Pvt,
Reineger, Donald C., Pfc,
Reiner, Wallace D., Pfc,
†Reinhardt, John H., Pvt,
Reinsch, Frank G., Pfc,
Reinschmidt, Paul J., Pvt,
‡Reinwald, Hubert A., Pvt,
Reise, John J., Pvt,
†Reisman, Adolph J., Pfc,
Reiter, Howard G., Pfc,
†Rembis, Walter S., Pfc,
Rembley, Alfred W., S/Sgt,
Remp, Edwin J., Pvt,
Rempfer, Hugo L., Sgt,
Rempfer, Reinhart O., Pfc,
Remsying, John, Cpl,
Renda, Benjamin, Pfc,
Renfro, Carl T., Pvt,
Rennell, Carl W., Pvt,
Rensford, Charles W., Pvt,
Rensi, Willie, V., Pfc,
§Reppert, Edward C., Pfc,
Restivo, Frank H., Pvt,
Restzloff, Arnold B., Pfc,
Revercomb, George W., Pvt,
Reymere, Richard R., Sgt,
Reynolds, Arthur M., Pvt,
Reynolds, Delwin E., Pfc,
†Reynolds, Elmer D., Pfc,
Reynolds, Edgar E., Sgt,
Reynolds, Fournier H., Pvt,
Reynolds, Roscoe G., T/4,
Reynolds, Samuel M., Pvt,
Reynolds, Wayne C., S/Sgt,
Rezanka, John, 2nd Lt
Reznak, Joseph, Pvt,
Reznikoff, Jay S., Pvt,
Rezzutti, Louie E., T/4,
†Rhoads, George I., Pvt,
Rhoads, George L., T/5,
Rhoads, Halbert D., Pfc,
Rhodes, Edwin J., Cpl,
Rhodes, Forest G., Pvt,
Rhodes, Lawrence E., Pvt
Rhodes, LeRoy, S/Sgt,
Rhodes, Ralph I., Pfc,
Rhodes, Richard L., Pfc,
Rhymes, James R., Pvt,
†Riberto, Manuel G., Pvt,
Ribons, Norman C., Cpl,
Ricci, Domenic, Pvt,
†Ricci, Frank J., Pvt,
Rice, Bruce A., 1st Sgt,
Rice, Frank, Pvt,
Rice, George E., Pfc,
Rice, Harry W., T/Sgt,
Rice, James A., Pvt,
Rice, Joseph, Pvt,
Rice, Vernon W., 1st Lt,
Rice, Walter A., Pfc,
Rich, Arthur I., 1st Lt,
Rich, Earl H., Pvt,
Richaby, Francis H., Sgt,
Richard, David J., T/5,
Richardi, Alfred J., Pfc,
Richards, Clyde A., Pfc,
Richards, Harley W., Pfc,
†Richards, Henry E., Pvt,
Richards, Joseph W., 1st Lt,
Richardson, Bert G., Pfc,
Richardson, Bruce D., Pfc,
Richardson, Edw. G., S/Sgt,
†Richardson, Fred M., Pvt,
‡Richardson, Hancel L., Pfc,
Richardson, Karl A., Sgt,
Richardson, Lon D., Pfc,
Richarik, Stanley E., Pfc,
Richer, Merlin R., T/5,
Richer, Ralph B., Sgt,
Richie, James P., Pvt,
Richinello, Frank J., Pfc,
Richlison, Victor F., Pfc,
Richmond, Harry, Pvt,
Richmond, Herbert, Pvt,
Richnafsky, Albert G., Pfc,
Richoux, Leyman J., Pvt,
Richvalsky, Stephen L., Pfc,
*Rickenbaker, Josia L., Pvt,
Rickert, William E., Pvt,
Ricketts, Blaine D., Pfc,
‡Riddell, Charles G., Pfc,
Riddell, Wade N., Pvt,
†Riddella, Paul, Pfc,
†Riddett, Albert L., Pfc,
Riddlebarger, James W., Pfc,
Rideout, Arthur W., Pfc,
Riddle, Carl J., Pfc,
‡Riddle, Robert W., Pvt,
Rider, Dana A., S/Sgt,
Rider, Walter E., Pfc,
Ridgway, Ralph J., Pvt,
Ridgway, William O., WOJG,
†Ridout, Arnold B., Pfc,
Riebel, Raymond, Pvt,
Riedy, Milton L., T/5,
†Rieke, Chester V., 1st Lt,
†Riel, Francis X., T/5,
Riel, Joseph A., Pfc,
Ries, John R., Sgt,
Rife, Fredrick C., T/Sgt,
Riffitts, John T., Pvt,
Rifkin, Charles, 1st Lt,
Rigby, Shirley C., Pfc,
Riggin, Harry F., Pvt,
Riggs, Donald E., Cpl,
Riggs, Elzia, Pvt,
Riggs, William A., T/5,
Righter, Cyrus H., Sgt,
Rigsby, Orbin, Sgt,
Riha, Raymond E., Pfc,
†Riley, Charles A., Pvt,
Riley, Daniel F., Pvt,
Riley, Robert T., Pfc,
Riley, Ronald K., Pvt,
Riley, Samuel W., 1st Lt,
Rimes, Oran T., Pfc,
†Rimmer, Henry E., Pvt,
Rineer, Clarence E., Pfc,
Rinehart, Lewis M., Pvt,
Riney, Charles E., S/Sgt,
Ring, Creighton F., T/5,
§Ringel, Robert W., Sgt,
†Ringswold, Anthony E., Pvt,
Rini, Victory D., Pfc,
Rinier, Tony A., Pfc,
Rink, Arthur G., Capt,
†Rinker, Harold W., Pfc,
Rio, Francesco S., Pvt,
Ripley, Walton H., Pvt,
Riplinger, Benjamin M., Sgt,
Risban, Clair J., Pfc,
†Risch, Marvin D., Pfc,
†Riseling, Robert E., Pfc,
Riser, Robert T., Pvt,
Risi, Nunzio G., Pvt,
†Risk, Verne O., T/Sgt,
Rispin, Cyril, T/5,
‡Ristuccia, Frank A., Pfc,
§Ritchey, John E., Jr., S/Sgt,
†Ritchey, John W., Pfc,
‡Ritchie, Harry C., Pfc,
†Ritchie, John H., Pvt,
Ritenour, Marvin K., Pvt,
Rittenhouse, James D., Pvt,
Ritter, Fletcher, Pfc,
Rivas, Florencio, Pfc,
Rivera, Alexander, Pfc,
Rivera, Louis A., Pvt,
Rivere, Duffy J., Sgt,
‡Rivet, Roger E., Pvt,
Rivett, Donald I., 1st Lt,
Rizor, Denny L., Cpl,
Rivuad, William C., Pfc,
Rizzardi, Joseph A., Pfc,
Rizzitello, Vincenzo A., Pfc,
Rizzuto, Joseph F., Pfc,
Roach, John P., WOJG,
Roark, John O., Pfc,
‡Roark, John R., Pvt,
Roark, John T., S/Sgt,
Roark, Robert L., Pvt,
Robarge, Harold A., Pfc,
Robart, Arnold W., Pvt,
Robb, Kenneth R., Capt,
Robbelino, Frank, Sgt,
Robbins, Harvey A., Pvt,
Robbins, Ollie C., Jr., Pvt,
Robbins, Willie B., Pfc,
Roberge, Clyde E., Pvt,
Robert, Earl C., Pfc,
†Robert, James D., Pvt,
†Roberts, Alfred L., Pfc,
Roberts, Arthur J., 2nd Lt,
Roberts, Rob, Pfc,
Roberts, Claude E., Sgt,
Roberts, Cloyd O., Pvt,
†Roberts, Edward E., Pvt,
†Roberts, Everett M., Pfc,
†Roberts, Francis E., Pfc,
Roberts, George W., Jr., Pvt,
Roberts, James W., Pvt,
Roberts, Jesse W., Cpl,
Roberts, John P., Pfc,
Roberts, Kenneth, Pvt,
Roberts, Leonard R., T/4,
Roberts, Lionel O., 1st Lt,
Roberts, Louis, Pfc,

† Killed in Action. * Prisoner of War. ‡ Missing in Action. § Died of Wounds.

†Roberts, Melvin R., Pvt,
Roberts, Sam K., Pfc,
Roberts, Vernon N., T/4,
Roberts, Will D., Jr., Pfc,
Roberts, William C., Pfc,
Roberts, William M., S/Sgt,
Roberts, Willie E., Pvt,
Robinson, Edmond T, Pfc,
Robinson, Ernest N., T/5,
Robertson, Ellis R., T/5,
Robertson, Garland R., Pvt,
Robertson, James A., Pfc,
Robertson, Julius B., Pvt,
Robertson, William B., T/Sgt
Robertson, William B., S/Sgt,
Robey, Paul W., Pfc,
§Robich, Andrew, S/Sgt,
‡Robins, Ralph M., Pvt,
Robinson, Elbert M., Pvt,
Robinson, Elmer N., Pfc,
Robinson, George T., Pvt,
Robinson, Harold E., Pfc,
†Robinson, Henry C., Pfc,
†Robinson, Irving F., Pfc,
Robinson, James N., Pfc,
Robinson, Lawrence R., Pvt,
Robinson, Marshall E., S/Sgt,
†Robinson, Ralph B., Sgt,
Robinson, Waldo K., Sgt,
Robinson, William L., Pfc,
Roble, Harry, Cpl,
Robson, Matthew H., Pvt,
Rocha, John K., Pvt,
Rocheleau, Richard L., Pfc,
Rock, John, S/Sgt,
Rockwell, Arthur R., Pvt,
Rodak, Michael, Pvt,
†Rodarte, Leo P., T/Sgt,
Roddy, Thomas J., Pfc,
Rode, John S., 2nd Lt,
Rodecap, Roger E., Pfc,
*Rodeman, Chris C., Jr., Pvt,
Rodemeyer, Michael L., 1st Lt,
Roden, John R., Pvt,
Rodenbough, Francis C., Pvt,
Rodgers, Malcolm W., T/5,
†Rodgers, Thomas R., 1st Lt,
Rodgers, William L., Pvt,
Rodman, William P., T/5,
Rodrigue, Roland G., Pvt,
Rodrigues, Anthony F., Pvt,
†Rodriguez, Felix B., Pvt,
Rodriguez, Fernando, Pfc,
Rodriguez, Gilbert, Pvt,
Rodriguez, Joseph, Pvt,
†Rodriguez, Milton, S/Sgt,
Rodriguez, Raymundo, Pvt,
§Rodriguez, Tulio A., Pvt,
Roedler, Dewitt, Pvt,
Roeske, Raymond C., Pvt,
Roffey, Donald G., Pvt,
Rogala, Edward W., Pfc,
Rogan, James M., Pfc,
Rogan, Richard J., Jr., Pvt,
Rogel, Albert, Pvt,
Rogerleski, Paul A., Pfc,
Rogers, Arthur H., Col,
Rogers, Billie J., Pvt,
Rogers, Clyde H., Pfc,
Rogers, Duell, Pvt,
†Rogers, Dwight R., Pvt,
Rogers, Edgar, Pvt,
Rogers, Edward H., Sgt,
Rogers, Emil, Jr., Pfc,
§Rogers, Gerald V., Sgt,
Rogers, Jack H., Sgt,
Rogers, James N., Pvt,
Rogers, Joseph C., Pvt,
Rogers, Luther, Pfc,
Rogers, Raymond, S/Sgt,
†Rogers, Roland C., Sgt,
Rogers, Stephen J., Capt,
Rogers, Thomas L., Pvt,
Rogerson, Raymond, Pfc,
Roggem, Melvin, Pvt,
†Rogine, Frank P., Pfc,
†Rohach, Michael, 2nd Lt,
Rohan, Milton J., Pvt,
Rohler, Emanuel B., Pvt,
Rohrbeck, Arthur N., T/5,
Rohrer, Wilbur K., S/Sgt,
Rohwedder, Clarence, Pvt,
†Roicem, Jay B., Jr., Sgt,
Roif, Harold, Pvt,
†Roitz, Norman O., Pvt,
Rokosz, Henry, Pvt,
Rolak, Joseph J., Pfc,
Roland, Howard T., Pvt,
†Roland, James E., Pvt,
Rolen, Craig A., Pvt,
Rollins, Otis P., Pfc,
Roman, Elio P., T/5,
Rollf, Frederick, Pvt,
Roman, Victor A., T/5,
Romano, Aime, S/Sgt,
*Romano, Carmelo B., Pfc,
Romano, Ciro J., Pfc,
Romano, Lino N., T/5,
Romano, Salvador J., Pfc,
Romanoski, John T., Sgt,
Romanowski, Robert J., Pvt,
Romberger, Roland R., Pfc,
Romero, Emilio, Pfc,
Romero, Salvatore C., Pvt,
Romine, Jacob D., Pfc,
Romine, Lloyd L., Pfc,
Rominger, Arnold G., Pfc,
Rominger, Arthur D., Pfc,
Rons, Carl E., Pfc,
†Rood, Harold D., T/Sgt,
Rooney, Thomas F., Pvt,
‡Roper, Howard M., Pvt,
Roper, Hubert L., Pvt,
Roper, Robert L., Pfc,
†Roper, William K., Pvt,
Rorrer, Abram A., Pfc,
Rosa, Felix, Pvt,
Rosa, Frisco J., Pfc,
Rosanas, William V., Pfc,
Rosati, Angelo, Pvt,
†Rose, Albert L., Cpl,
†Rose, Arnold P., Pfc,
Rose, David J., S/Sgt,
Rose, Emerson J., Pvt,
Rose, Everett W., Sgt,
Rose, Frederick J., Cpl,
Rose, Frederick, Pfc,
Rose, Harry R., T/4,
Rose, Lewis E., Jr., Pfc,
Rose, Offie L., Cpl,
Rose, Phillip T., Pvt,
Rose, Reginald F., Cpl,
Rose, Willard R., Pvt,
Rose, William B., Cpl,
‡Roseberry, Edford, Pfc,
Rosebury, Richard W., 1st Lt,
Rosemberg, Ralph E., Pfc,
*Rosen, Edward, Pvt,
Rosenbraum, Adolph, Pvt,
Rosenberg, Sam, Pvt,
Rosenberger, Robert L., Pvt,
Rosenblatt, Albert, Pvt,
Rosenblum, Philip, Sgt,
Rosendall, Frank E., Pvt,
Rosenfield, Arthur H., Pvt,
Rosenfield, Solomon, S/Sgt,
Rosenthal, Lawrence, Pfc,
Rosenzweig, Zyman J., Pvt,
Rosevear, Thomas L., Cpl,
‡Rosi, James A., /Sgt,
Rosier, James C., Pvt
Rosner, Adolph C., Jr., 1st Lt,
Rosner, Lawrence J., Capt,
Ross, Andrew J., Pfc,
†Ross, Charlie S., Pvt,
Ross, Frank J., Pvt,
Ross, Franklin P., Pvt,
Ross, Harley P., Cpl,
Ross, Lyle G., Pfc,
Ross, Norman, Pvt,
Ross, Robert A., Pvt,
§Ross, Robert E., Pfc,
Ross, Robert E., Pfc,
Ross, Thomas M., Pvt,
Ross, Vincent, Pvt,
Ross, Wilburn K., Pfc,
‡Rossa, Frank S., Pfc,
Rossi, John G., Pfc,
Rossi, Michael P., Pfc,
Rossi, Pasquale, Jr.,
Rossodivito, Dominic J., Pvt,
Roth, Bernard E., Pfc,
Roth, Harry L., Sgt,
Roth, Richard C., Pvt,
†Roth, Robert F., Pvt,
Rothe, Harry R., Pfc,
Rothman, Bernard S., Pfc,
Rothseid, Maurice, Capt,
Rothstein, Harry L., Sgt,
Rothstein, Harry L., Pfc,
Rotti, Frank A., Pfc,
Rotz, Marshall H., Pvt,
†Roughan, Thomas B., Jr., Pvt,
Roundtree, David M., Pvt,
†Roundtree, Donald A., Sgt,
Rounsaville, James R., S/Sgt,
Rourke, Joseph E., Pvt,
Rousseau, Francis N., Cpl,
†Rousseau, Richard A., Pfc,
†Roussel, Larry J., Pfc,
Rovner, Louis W., Pvt,
Row, Ivan F., Pfc,
Rowcroft, Wenley J., Cpl,
Rowe, Howard B., Pfc,
‡Rowe, James R., Sgt,
Rowe, James R., Pfc,
§Rowell, Alphers R., Pvt,
Rowell, John A., Jr., Pvt,
Rowland, Albert, Pvt,
Rowland, Arlin J., Pvt,
Rowland, Carter J., Pfc,
Rowland, Howard, Pvt,
Rowland, John W., Pfc,
Rowles, Carl E., Sr., Pfc,
Roz, Charles A., Pvt,
Rozanski, Stanley J., Pvt,
Rozer, Norwood L., Pvt,
§Rozinski, Stanley J., 2nd Lt,
Rozzelle, Harry R., Pfc,
†Ruben, David, Pvt,
Rubick, Allan J., T/Sgt,
Rubin, Albert A., Pvt,
†Rubin, Dave, Pfc,
Rubin, Hax, Pvt,
Rubine, William C., Pfc,
†Rubino, Joseph C., Sgt,
Rucinski, Theodore, T/4,
†Ruck, Vernon V., Pfc,
Rucker, Jess W., T/5,
Rudy, Metro, Pvt,
†Rudys, Teddy S., Pfc,
Ruf, William L., Pvt,
Ruff, Arthur, Pfc,
†Ruff, Raymond H., Pfc,
Ruffell, Robert W., T/4,
Ruffennach, Edward I., Pvt,
Rugg, Charles B., Cpl,
Ruggiero, James, Pfc,
Ruiz, John A., Pvt,
Ruiz, Ralph C., Pvt,
Ruka, Albinas P., Pvt,
Rukab, Lupti, Sgt,
Rummells, Vernon W., Pvt,
Rumpler, John E., Jr., Pvt,
Rumsey, Andrew L., Pvt,
†Runyan, Jake, Jr., Pvt,
Runyon, Billie, R., Cpl,
Runyon, Edward, Pvt,
Rupe, Joseph J., Pvt,
Rupkey, James A., Sgt,
†Ruppe, Lynn, Pvt,
Rusciano, Joseph C., Pvt,
†Rush, Edward L., Pvt,
Rush, John C., Pvt,
Rush, Woodrow W., Pvt,
Rushing, Clifton L., S/Sgt,
Rusinko, Nicholas, Pfc,
†Ruskowski, Leo J., S/Sgt,
Russel, Alexander H., 1st Lt,
Russell, Carl J., Pvt,
‡Russell, Charles W., Pvt,
†Russell, George J., Pfc,
Russell, Harris A., S/Sgt,
Russell, Herbert C., Sgt,
Russell, James P., Pfc,
Russell, John M., Pvt,
Russell, Morris L., Pvt,
Russell, Posy W., Pvt,
†Russo, Andrew L., Pfc,
Russo, Charles S., Pvt,
Russo, Dominic J., Pvt,
Russo, Joseph, Pvt,
Russo, Joseph F., Pfc,
†Russo, Joseph R., Pfc,
Russo, Rocco, Pvt,
*Rustici, Herman L., Pfc,
Rutchasky, Edward, Sgt,
Ruth, Robert R., T/4,
Rutherford, Chester M., Pfc,
Rutherford, Glenn W., Pfc,
Rutherford, Lindell S., Pvt,
§Rutkowsky, William M., Sgt,
Rutledge, Clinton, Pvt,
Rutledge, Henry H., Pfc,
Rutledge, William J., T/5,
Rutstein, Clifford, Pvt,
‡Ryan, Daniel J., Pfc,
Ryan, Donald E., Pfc,
Ryan, Daniel F., Sgt,
Ryan, Edward J., Pvt,
Ryan, Edward V., Pfc,
†Ryan, Everett M., Pvt,
Ryan, Grover L., Pvt,
Ryan, Harold F., Pfc,
†Ryan, James F., Pvt,
Ryan, James N. Pvt,
Ryan, Roy C., Pvt,
Ryan, Timothy B., Pfc,
Ryduchowski, E. J., T/Sgt,
Rzechowski, Stanley J., Pvt,

Saban, George J., Pfc,
Sabin, Earl M., Pfc,
†Sabo, William, S/Sgt,
Sabourin, Roger J., Pfc,
Sackett, Richard E., 2nd Lt,
Sacks, Jerome E., T/Sgt,
Sadler, Cleo K., T/5,
†Sadley, John C., Pvt,
Safin, John F., Pfc,
‡Sager, Herbert F., Pvt,
Saine, Harold J., 1st Lt,
Sakaris, John, Pfc,
§Salatino, Rocky A., Pvt,
Salazar, Philbert H., T/Sgt,
Salazar, Raymond L., Pfc,
Salet, Eugene A., Capt,
Salinas, Nick P., Pvt
Saling, Neil E., Capt
Salley, Otis E., Pvt,
†Salsgiver, Howard H., Pvt,
Salts, Lloyd C., Sr., Pvt,
Saltzman, Jacob, Capt,
Salvatore, Joseph F., Pfc,
Sammons, William A., Pvt,
†Samoray, Joseph A., Pvt,
Samples, John L., S/Sgt
Sampson, Richard, Pfc,
Sams, Jesse H., Pfc,
Sams, Miles B., Jr., Pvt,
Samuels, Nat, T/5,
†Sanders, Earl L., Pvt,
Sanders, Edmund M., Major
†Sanders, George, T/Sgt,
‡Sanders, Hobson J., Pvt,
Sanders, John R., Pvt,
Sanders, Raymond T., 1st Lt,
Sanders, Walter L., Pvt,
†Sanders, William R., Pfc,
Sanderson, Lawrence M., Pfc,
Sanderson, Aubrey B., Pvt,
Sandfoss, Arthur J., Pvt,
Sandifer, Carl C., Jr., Cpl,
Sandridge, Ernest R., S/Sgt,
Sands, Albert, Pfc,
‡Sanislo, Frank A., Pvt,
‡Santangelo, Anthony, Pfc,
Santiana, Peter G., Pfc,
Santillo, Russell J., Sgt,
Saper, Herbert, Pfc,
†Saperstein, Harry, Pvt,
Saponara, Sam H., Pfc,
Sapp, Melvin, Pvt,
†Sapp, Ralph, Pvt,
Sarginson, Kenneth J., Pvt,
†Sarten, Edmon L., Pfc,
†Satchwell, Anthony J., Pvt,
‡Sauer, George E., Pvt,
Sauer, Norbert B., Capt,
†Saul, James R., Pvt,
Saunders, Lawrence E., Pvt,
Saunders, Zebulon V., Pvt,
Saurage, Leonard P., Pvt,
Savage, Alva R., Pvt
Savage, Frederick A., Pvt,
Savage, Peter E., Pfc,
Savant, Harold, Pvt,
Savaresy, Richard M., Major,
Saville, Harry G., Pvt,
‡Savitz, Harold D., Pvt,
‡Savraw, Robert J., Pfc,
‡Sawyer, Norman P., Cpl,
Saxton, Cyril M., Pfc,
Sayer, Ralph E., Pfc,
Sayers, Carroll E., T/Sgt,
†Scales, Enoch A., Pvt,
Scalia, George A., T/5,
‡Scalise, James A., Pvt,
†Scallo, Phillip, Pfc,
Scalone, Corradion, T/4,
Scancerella, Joseph, Sgt,
Scandariato, Vincent F., Pvt,
Scebold, Robert R., Pfc,
‡Schaefer, Philip G., Pvt,
Schaeffer, Warren M., Pvt,
†Schaffer, Robert C., T/Sgt,
Schalkle, August M., Pfc
Schank, Clarence V., Pfc,
Schatte, Frederick, 2nd Lt,
‡Schattl, Jacob, Pfc,
‡Schauer, Frank S., Pfc,
Schaut, Aloysius H., Pfc,
Schear, Dwight B., Pvt,
Scheidecker, Frederick A., Pvt,
Scheidt, Edward H., Pvt
†Scheinman, Neil R., Sgt,
Schembri, Anthony F., Pvt,
Schenfeld, Albert J., S/Sgt,
Scherer, Theon L., Pvt
†Scheufele, Norman B., Pfc,
Schieber, Harold J., Pvt,
‡Schildt, Kenneth H., Pfc,
Schiller, Arthur, Pvt,
Schiro, Michael A., Pvt,
Schirrmacher, Walter A., Pfc,
‡Schkoda, Fredrick T., Pfc,
Schlabach, Robert, T/4,
†Schlehuber, Paul A., Pvt,
†Schlemmer, Lawrence V., Pvt,
Schlicher, William R., Pfc,
Schlicht, Raymond J., S/Sgt,
Schloe, Leo J., Pvt,
Schlotterer, George F., T/5,
Schmadel, Delbert C., T/4,
Schmalz, Jason F.,
Schmalz, John L., T/4,
Schmelitsch, Leo F., Pvt,
Schmidt, Anton, Pvt,
Schmidt, Arthur D., 2nd Lt,
Schmidt, Arthur D., T/Sgt,
Schmidt, Charles A., Pvt,
Schmidt, Herman L., S/Sgt,
‡Schmidt, Joseph J., Pfc,
Schmidt, Marvin C., Pvt,
‡Schmidt, Raymond A., Pvt,
Schmitt, Bernard J., T/Sgt,
Schneider, Charles W., 1st Lt,
§Schneider, Devlin A., T/Sgt,
Schneider, Richard J., Pvt,
Schneider, Robert, Pvt,
‡Schnick, Berthold, K. W., Pvt,
§Schohl, Edward N., Pfc,
Scholl, George R., Sgt,
Scholtz, John E., Pfc,
Schoonover, John H., 2nd Lt,
‡Schorle, Carl L., Jr., Pfc,
‡Schowalter, Richard A., Pvt,
§Schrader, Maurice D., Pfc,
Schram, Robert, Pfc,
Schram, Virgil H., Pvt,
Schramm, Luther W., Sgt,
Schranz, Francis M., 1st Lt,
†Schriener, Howard K., Pfc,
Schroader, Jayce, Pfc,
Shroeder, Raymond J., Cpl,
‡Schuld, Nikelaus K., Pvt,
Schultz, Charles A., Pfc,
Schultz, George J., Pfc,
Schultz, James F., 1st Lt,
Schultz, Joseph H., 1st Lt,
*Schultz, Samuel C., Pfc,
Schulz, Robert C., Pvt
†Schulz, Robert G., Pvt,
Schumacher, Donald J., 1st Lt,
Schuman, Sidney, S/Sgt,
Schumann, Joseph R., Pfc,
†Schurman, Eugene F., Pvt,
Schuster, Raymond L., Pfc,
‡Schuttenberg, Frank J., Pvt,
†Schwalbach, James E., Pfc,
Schwarck, Milo R., Pfc,
Schwartz, Alvin G., Pvt,
Schwartz, Harry, Pfc,
Schwartz, Irvin, 1st Lt
Schwartz, James R., 1st Sgt,
§Schwartz, Richard H., Cpl,
Schwartz, Sidney B., Pfc,
Schwartzer, John, Pfc,
Schwarz, Aloysius, Pvt,
†Schwennen, Peter, Pvt,
Schwidde, Jesse T., Capt,
Scialpi, Arcangelo, Pvt,
Scionti, John F., T/5,
Scites, Lloyd T., Sgt,
Sciulli, Umberto, Pfc,
Scofield, Leland J., Pvt,
Scola, Andrew C., Pfc,
Score, Francis B., Pfc,
†Scott, Arthur F., 1st Lt,
Scott, Charles B., 1st Sgt,
Scott, Charles R., T/5,
†Scott, Everett V., Pfc,
‡Scott, George J., Sgt,
†Scott, Gordon W., Pfc,
Scott, Harvey D., S/Sgt,
Scott, Richard W., Pvt,
†Scott, Thomas A., Pfc,
Scott, Thomas L., Pfc,
Scott, Thomas W., Pfc,
Scott, Wilford E., Pfc,
†Scott, William A., Pvt,
†Scott, William H., Pfc,
Scribner, Wilbur L., Sgt,
‡Scruggs, Joseph W., Pvt,
Sculley, Harold F., 1st Lt,
Scuris, Peter C., Pvt,
Sears, George, Pvt,
Sears, Harry C., Pvt,
Seay, Claude T., Pfc,
Sebrowski, Walter P., Pvt,
Secal, Irving, Pfc
Seder, Donald E., 2nd Lt
Sedgeman, Richard T., Pfc,
Sedwick, Harold H., Cpl,
See, Earl R., Jr., Pfc,
See, Gerald J., Pvt,
Seegar, Frank A., Pvt,
†Seelye, Percy W., Pvt,
Seeman, Curtis W., Pfc,
†Seelbinder, Remus L., Jr., Pfc,
Seetin, Samuel E., Capt,
†Seets, John J., Pvt,
Segall, Joseph, Pfc
Segura, Jesse, Jr., T/5,
†Seibal, Anthony, Pvt,
Seibert, Joseph G., Pvt,
Seideward, Richard F., Pfc,
Seiger, Clarence E., Pvt,
Seiger, James P., Pvt,
Seigler, Walter J., T/3,
Seiler, Wilbur J., Pfc,

† Killed in Action. * Prisoner of War. ‡ Missing in Action. § Died of Wounds.

IN WORLD WAR II 529

Seim, Christian A., Jr., Pvt
Sekerka, George J., 1st Lt,
Sellers, James H., Sgt,
Selley, Paul F., T/5,
Sellner, Leonard J., Pfc,
‡Selman, Joe C., Pvt,
Selter, Gordon J., Pvt,
†Seltman, Robert E., Pfc,
†Seman, Thomas, Pfc,
Semancik, Joseph G., Pvt,
Semerjin, Harry, Pvt
Semus, John, Pvt,
Senay, Joseph H., S/Sgt,
Senecal, Joseph S., Pfc,
Seni, Thomas J., Pvt,
†Seniuk, Michael, Pvt,
Serpico, Joseph A., Pfc,
Serra, Lawrence, Pfc,
Serrato, Anthony, Pvt,
†Servant, Roland A., Pfc,
Sessa, Jerry, Pfc,
†Sessa, Silvio J., Pvt,
Sesztak, John, Pvt,
Setinc, Martin W., Sgt,
Severa, John E., Sgt,
†Severinsky, Michael, Pfc,
Seward, Ben B., 1st Lt,
Seward, Millard L., Cpl,
Sexton, Robert M., Pvt,
Shade, Ernest, S/Sgt,
†Shafer, Earlston F., Pfc,
Shaffer, Clarence C., Pfc,
Shaffer, Duane E., Pfc,
Shaffer, Edward L., Pfc,
Shaffer, William O., Jr., Pfc,
Shaheen, Mike, Pfc,
Shainis, Joseph, Pfc,
†Shaker, George J., Pfc,
†Shamp, Arvel W., T/5,
†Shamp, LeRoy J., Pfc,
†Shanahan, Robert D., Pvt,
Shanks, Howard J., T/5,
§Shanks, Joseph K. S., Cpl,
Shanks, Ralph E., Pfc,
Shannon, William J., 2nd Lt,
Shapovnick, Morris, 2nd Lt,
Sharp, Caswell A., Pfc,
Sharp, George, Pfc,
Sharp, Ralph R., T/5,
Shapiro, Montague, Pvt,
Shaughnessy, John J., 2nd Lt
Shaver, Edward H., S/Sgt,
Shaw, Dale E., Pvt,
Shaw, Ferris L., S/Sgt,
Shaw, Frank W., Jr., Capt,
†Shaw, Howard E., Jr., Capt,
†Shaw, Lloyd W., Pfc,
†Shaw, Luther W., Pfc,
Shaw, Robert L., Jr., 1st Lt,
Shealy, Edward C., Pvt,
Sheehan, Eugene H., Pvt,
§Sheele, Raymond L., Pfc,
‡Sheely, John E., Pfc,
‡Sheirich, John M., Sgt,
Sheld, Clarence A., T/5,
Sheldon, Frank W., Pvt,
†Shelton, Alonzo E., Sgt,
Shelton, Arthur E., Pvt,
Shelton, Beverly F., Pvt,
Shelton, Charles D., Pvt,
†Shelton, George C., Cpl,
Shelton, Hubert P., Sgt,
Shelton, Jessie A., Pvt,
Shepard, James D., S/Sgt,
Shepardson, John W., Cpl,
Shepherd, Clifford J., Pvt,
†Shepherd, Robert L., Cpl,
Sherfey, Hall O., Pvt,
Sherrill, Elwood E., 2nd Lt,
‡Sherrod, Jack M., S/Sgt,
Sherwood, Clifford D., Pvt,
Shilling, Robert E., Pfc,
Shimet, George, Pfc,
Shingleton, James H., Pvt,
†Shinoski, Edward J., Pfc,
Shir, Allen, Pvt,
Shires, Nott B., Pvt,
Shirey, Kenneth H., Pvt,
Shirk, John R., Pfc,
†Shirley, Elmer R., Pfc,
Shirley, Richard C., Pfc,
Shirley, Stanley W., Pfc,
Shively, Theodore C., Pfc,
†Shivler, Herman L., Pvt,
Shmidt, Lloyd R., S/Sgt,
Shobe, William V., Pfc,
†Shobert, Samuel A., T/Sgt,
Shoemake, Elbert O., Pfc,
Sholl, Herbert A., 2nd Lt,
Shores, Elmer E., T/3,
Short, Richard C., Pfc,
Short, Willis E., T/4,
Shows, Charles E., T/4,
‡Showers, Howard L., S/Sgt,
†Shouse, James A., Pfc,

Shrader, Royal J., Pvt,
†Shriner, James R., Pfc,
Shrout, James H., Pfc,
†Shubert, Hugh L., Pvt,
Shuck, Roy H., T/Sgt,
Shuey, Floyd R., Pvt,
§Shuey, Loren W., Cpl,
†Shuffield, Richard C., Pfc,
†Shular, William A., Jr., 1st Lt.
Shuler, Glenn, Capt,
Shumaker, Robert F., Pvt,
Shute, Gerald L., Pvt,
Shutt, Samuel W., 1st Lt,
†Shutt, William A., Pfc,
‡Shutts, Donald L., Pvt,
§Sibat, Joseph, Pvt,
Sibert, Russell G., Pvt,
Sicina, Florian S., S/Sgt,
†Sicuro, Frank J., Pvt,
†Siddle, Kenneth M., Pfc,
Siembab, John A., Sgt,
†Sieniewicz, Stanley W., Pvt,
Sigelmier, George C., Pfc,
Siggers, Thomas E., Pvt,
Sigismondi, Michael S., Pfc,
Sikora, Matthew F., Pfc,
Sikorski, Chester S., Pvt,
Silesky, Ralph L., Pfc,
Sillery, Nadean A., Pfc,
Sillito, Frank J., Pfc,
Sillyman, Frank J., Pfc,
Silph, Etheridge B., Pfc,
†Silva, John J., Pvt,
Silva, Joseph, Sgt,
‡Silva, Joseph F., Pfc,
Silver, William, Pfc,
§Silverman, Alfred, Pvt,
Silverstein, George, Pfc,
†Simmler, Robert L., Pvt,
Simmons, Leon G., 1st Lt,
Simmons, James E., S/Sgt,
Simmons, James T., Sgt,
§Simmons, Warren C., 1st Lt,
Simon, Anatole J., Jr., S/Sgt,
‡Simon, Andrew H., Pvt,
Simon, Lawrence, Pfc,
‡Simon, Louis, Pfc,
Simondiski, Charles T., 1st Lt,
Simone, Alfred P., Pfc,
Simons, William W., Pvt,
Simpson, Arley, Pfc,
Simpson, Curtis, Pvt,
Simpson, Glen E., Pfc,
Simpson, John P., Pfc,
Simpson, Leo E., Pvt,
Simpson, Robert A., Pvt,
§Simpson, Walter C., Jr., Pfc,
§Sims, Cleatus L., Pvt,
Sindelar, Otto R., Pvt,
‡Singer, Everett W., Jr., Pvt,
†Singer, Rosario F., 1st Sgt,
Singles, William H., Pfc,
†Singletary, Garland P., Pvt,
Singletary, Madison, Pvt,
Singleton, Clark I., Pfc,
†Singleton, James R., Pvt,
Sinkwicz, Stanley, Pvt,
Sinovich, Michael, Jr., Pvt,
*Sinuch, Vino E., Pvt,
Sir, Kenneth O., Pfc,
Sirna, Samuel A., Pvt,
†Sirois, Gilman M., Pfc,
Sisco, Glen W., Pfc,
Sisk, Norman W., Pfc,
Sisson, Arthur E., Pfc,
Sisson, Thomas M., Jr., Pfc,
*Sites, John W., Pfc,
‡Sitterding, Jack R., Cpl,
Siverling, Barton W., Pfc,
Sivertsen, Elmer T., Pvt,
*Sizemore, Brainard T., Pvt,
Sizemore, Euell E., Pfc,
†Skafar, Tony, Jr., Pfc,
Skeahan, Charles H., Jr., 1st Lt
Skeiber, Stanley C., Capt,
Skelton, Frank O., Pvt,
Skibell, Sol, Pvt,
Skipper, Morris T., Cpl,
Skolik, Alexander A., Pvt,
Skousen, Peter J., T/5,
Skowronski, Leonard G., Pvt,
Skrobacz, Stanley T., Pvt,
†Skrubuten, Richard G., Pvt,
Skrzypczyk, Ladislaus J., Pvt,
Slade, Gordon S., Pvt,
Sladen, Fred W., Jr., Lt Col,
Slagle, Forest P., Sgt,
Slaight, Albert J., Cpl,
Slasor, Robert H., Cpl,
†Slate, Douglas A., 1st Lt
‡Slater, Ernest R., Pvt,
Slatton, John H., Pfc,
‡Slaughter, Leonard D., Pfc,
Slavings, James T., Pvt,

Slawinski, Heinz, J., Pvt,
Sleyster, Raymond J., Pfc,
†Slezak, Roy J., Cpl,
Sliesher, Cecil B., Pvt,
Sliva, Michael J., Pvt
Slopey, Richard O., Pfc,
Slothower, William R., Pvt,
‡Sloup, Milton J., Pfc,
Smedbergh, Edward A., Pfc,
Smedburg, Jon K., Pfc,
Smeltzer, Ernest D., Pvt,
Smetana, Walter A., Pfc,
Smi, Nickolas, Pfc,
†Smiley, Charles W., S/Sgt,
‡Smith, Alan C., Pfc,
†Smith, Allan R., Pvt,
†Smith, Audrey W., Pvt,
Smith, Carl E., Pvt,
Smith, Charles A., T/5,
†Smith, Clarence A., Pfc,
Smith, Clarence R., Pfc,
Smith, Claude F., Pfc,
Smith, Cleo I., S/Sgt,
Smith, Charles E., Pfc,
Smith, Charlie N., Sgt,
Smith, Clifford D., Pfc,
Smith, Ben J., Jr., T/5,
Smith, Bill B., S/Sgt,
Smith, Daniel F., Pfc,
Smith, Dexter D., Cpl,
†Smith, Edward, Pfc,
Smith, Edward J., Pvt,
Smith, Edward W., Pvt,
†Smith, Floyd V., Pfc,
Smith, Francis W., Pfc,
Smith, Frank, Pfc,
†Smith, Frank J., Pvt,
Smith, George W., Pfc,
§Smith, Henry C., S/Sgt,
Smith, Herman A., M/Sgt,
Smith, Herman W., Pfc,
Smith, James C., Pvt,
Smith, James E., Pvt,
Smith, James H., Pvt,
Smith, James M., Pfc,
Smith, James T., T/4,
Smith, Jack W., Pvt,
Smith, John E., Pvt,
Smith, John E., Pfc,
Smith, John R., Capt,
Smith, John R., T/4,
Smith, John W., Pvt,
Smith, Joseph M., Sgt,
Smith, Kenneth E., Pvt,
Smith, Kenneth W., Pvt,
†Smith, Lawton W., Jr., Pfc,
Smith, Leo C., Pfc,
Smith, Leonard, Pfc,
Smith, Leonard F., 1st Lt,
§Smith, Leonard R., Pvt,
Smith, Leslie R., Sgt,
Smith, Louis M., Pvt,
†Smith, Lloyd N. Pfc,
†Smith, Lozelle, F., Pfc,
Smith, Lyle J., Sgt,
Smith, Lyle M., Pvt,
Smith, Mark A., Sgt,
Smith, Marshall A., S/Sgt,
Smith, Nelson S., Pvt,
†Smith, Marvin P., Pfc,
Smith, Orville L., Pfc,
†Smith, Paul A., Sgt,
†Smith, Paul R., Pvt,
Smith, Ralph C., Pfc,
Smith, Randolph, Pvt,
Smith, Robert C., Pvt,
Smith, Robert J., T/5,
Smith, Robert L., S/Sgt,
*Smith, Ronald A., Sgt,
Smith, Roy, Pvt,
Smith, Rudolph, Sgt,
Smith, Sterling W., Cpl,
Smith, Sylvester D., T/5,
Smith, Thomas J., Pfc,
Smith, Thurman L., Pvt,
Smith, Vernon H., Pvt,
Smith, Victor L., Pvt,
Smith, Walter A., Pfc,
*Smith, Walter S., Pvt,
Smith, Wesley, S/Sgt,
Smith, Willard P., S/Sgt,
Smith, William A., 1st Lt,
Smith, William G., Pfc,
Smith, William P., Sr., Pfc
Smith, William R., Pfc,
Smith, William W., Cpl,
†Smith, Wyatt H., S/Sgt,
Smitha, Ralph G., Cpl,
Smithey, James M., Pfc,
Smysor, Eldon R., Pvt,
Smyth, Victor S., Pvt,
Snaer, Bernard A., Capt
Snapp, Ira B., Jr., 1st Lt,
Snead, William B., Pfc,

Sneck, Albert G., Pfc,
Sneddon, John W., Pvt,
Snell, Harry C., Pfc,
Snelson, Clifford W., Pvt,
Snider, Glen W., Pvt,
Snider, Lester E., T/5,
Snowden, Norwood L., Capt,
Snyder, Buis L., Pfc,
Snyder, John F., Jr., Pvt,
Snyder, Merritt W. J., Pvt,
Snyder, Richard J., Pvt,
Snyder, Walter H., S/Sgt,
†Snyder, William C., Pvt,
§Sobocinski, Stanley J., Pvt,
†Sofrin, Robert E., Pvt,
Solomon, Harry L., Pfc,
†Solpa, Melroy H., Pvt,
†Soltis, John A., Sgt,
Somlo, Arthur, Pfc,
‡Soop, Norman G., Pvt,
†Soper, Eugene W., T/5,
†Soper, James A., Pfc,
Sorbo, Glen G., Pvt,
Sordi, Luciano, Pvt,
Sorocco, Frank J., Pfc,
Soroczak, Walter, S/Sgt,
Sorrell, Delbert J., Pvt,
Sos, Paul, Pfc,
†Soth, Charles H., Pvt,
Soto, John A., Jr., Pvt,
Sotterfield, Fred L., Pvt,
Sottile, Frank A., S/Sgt,
Soule, Dalbert, Pfc
South, Hamilton R., Pfc,
‡Sova, Ernest J., Pvt,
Sowers, Alvin P., T/5,
Sowers, Jesse E., 1st Lt,
Spahr, Robert F., Pvt,
Spain, Elmer F., Pvt,
Spangler, George C., 1st Lt,
Span, Manuel O., T/Sgt,
†Spear, Daniel D., Pvt,
Speer, Frederick E., Sgt,
§Speer, Herbert A., Pfc,
*Spencer, Edward P., Pvt,
Spencer, Lawrence A., Pfc,
Spencer, Lawrence R., Pvt,
Spencer, Powell J., Pvt,
Spencer, Richard J., Pvt,
‡Speroer, Arthur, Pfc,
Spicer, Burl C., Pfc,
Spicer, George K., 1st Lt,
Spicer, Kermit B., Pfc,
Spicer, Leonard L., Pvt,
Spieseisen, Benjamin, Pvt,
Spiesman, Harold K., Pfc,
Spiller, William, Pvt,
Spillman, Amiel E., 1st Lt,
Spina, Anthony, Pfc
Spinelli, Rosario F., Pvt,
Spinks, Garlan, Pfc,
†Spires, Clifford L., Pvt,
Spodnick, George L., Pvt,
Spooner, Norman E., T/5,
†Spoor, Ralph E., Pvt,
Sporar, Harold A., Pfc,
†Sporleder, Raymond,
Spota, Anthony F., Sgt
Spoto, Sebastian J., T/Sgt,
Spotts, Lewis R., S/Sgt,
Spotts, Melvin E., S/Sgt,
Sprague, George D., Pfc,
†Sprenkel, Carson E., Pvt,
Spring, Richard T., Pfc,
§Springer, Ruel H., S/Sgt,
Sprinkle, Orjin R., Pfc,
Spruill, Carroll R., Jr., S/Sgt,
Spurrier, Lawrence G., Pvt,
Spuryer, Robert M., Sgt,
†Squires, John C., Sgt,
Staats, Joel F., 2nd Lt,
Staats, Joel F., M/Sgt,
Stacy, Henry E., 2nd Lt,
Stacy, John H., Jr., Pvt,
§Stafford, Bill M., Pfc,
Stafford, Joseph F., Pvt,
Stafford, Roy T., Pfc,
Stainback, William, Sgt,
†Staines, Ira B., Pvt,
Staite, Silvio, Pvt,
†Stake, Eugene C., Pfc,
Staley, Robert A., Pvt,
§Stambaugh, Millard D., Pfc,
St. Amore, Earl L., Pvt,
†Stancil, James C., Pfc,
Stancil, James F., Pfc,
§Standish, Lysle E., Capt,
†Stanek, George E., Pvt,
Stanford, Rolland T., Pfc,
Stanik, Edward, Pvt,
Stanish, Peter C., T/5,
†Stank, Charles R., Pvt,
Stanley, Paul W., Capt,
Stannard, Robert N., Jr., Pfc,
St. Antoine, Fabian A., 1st Sgt,

Stanton, John J., T/3
†Stanton, Loren L., Capt,
Staples, Clarence J., Pfc,
§Stapleton, Arthur, Pvt,
Stapp, Oliver R., Pfc,
†Starc, Robert J., Pvt,
Stark, Harry S., 2nd Lt,
Starke, Frank C., Pvt
Starkey, Carol E., 1st Lt,
Starkey, George C., Jr., T/Sgt,
Starks, Warren A., T/5,
Staron, George A., Pvt,
†Starr, Eskill J., S/Sgt,
Starr, Kenneth E., Pvt,
Starrett, Ernest R., Cpl,
Stastny, Robert A., S/Sgt,
†Staudacker, Carl F., Pfc,
Stauffer, Roscoe M., Cpl,
†Staurt, Lewis R., Pvt,
St. Clair, Jack A., 2nd Lt,
†Stebleten, Bryan M., Pfc,
‡Steel, Rolland E., Pfc,
Steele, Fred M., Jr., Pvt,
Steele, Thomas D., Pvt,
Steele, William D., T/5,
Steelman, Morrison O., Pfc,
Steenberg, Walter J., Pfc,
Stees, George M., Pvt,
†Steet, Richard A., Pfc,
Stefancik, Mike, Pfc,
§Steffen, Robert D., Pfc,
Steimler, Charles F., Pfc,
Stein, Jacob, Pfc,
Steinbach, Edward S., Sgt,
Steinberger, Frank J., T/5,
Steinert, Vernon E., Pvt,
Steltzner, William D., T/4,
Stenberg, Robert L., Pfc,
Stephans, Robert C., Pvt,
‡Stephens, Alexander H., 1st Lt,
Stephens, Charles J., Pfc
‡Stephens, Daniel R., Pvt,
Stephens, Edward L., Pvt,
Stephens, Escar L., Jr., Pfc,
Stephens, Herbert S., 2nd Lt,
Stephens, James F., Pvt,
Stephens, William H., 1st Lt
‡Stephenson, Clifford, Pvt,
†Stephenson, John D., Pvt,
Stephenson, William R., Pvt,
Stepped, Paul, Pvt,
‡Stepping, Joseph J., Pfc,
‡Steranko, Melvin A., Pfc,
Sterner, Gunnar A., Pfc,
†Sterrett, Joseph W., Jr., Pvt,
Steve, Roger J., Pvt,
†Stevens, Ernest A., Sgt,
‡Stevens, George H., Pfc,
Stevens, Harry A., T/5,
Stevens, Howard A., Pvt,
Stevens, James A., T/5,
Stevens, James H., Pvt,
†Stevens, John F., Pfc,
Stevens, Norman C., Pvt,
Stevenson, Lloyd T., Pvt,
Stevenson, Robert L., T/5,
Steward, Charlie G., Pfc,
Stewart, Edgar E., Jr., Pvt,
Stewart, George W., Pvt,
Stewart, Girard E., Pvt,
‡Stewart, James A., Pvt,
Stewart, John A., Pfc,
*St. George, Roland T., Pvt,
†Stichel, Richard W., Pvt,
Stickney, William C., T/4,
Stieber, Alexander, Pvt,
Stiegler, Henry S., Pvt
Stienstra, Floyd O., Pfc,
Stieve, Alfred P., Sgt,
†Still, Edward H., 2nd Lt,
†Stillman, Don A., T/4,
Stiltner, Raymond B., S/Sgt,
‡Stinnett, William A., Pvt,
Stitely, Donald F., Pvt,
Stobaugh, Elbert O., Cpl,
Stockonis, Robert A., Pvt,
Stockwell, Jay A., Pvt,
Stocton, Jesse J., T/4,
Stodolski, Alexander J., Pfc,
Stokes, J. D., Pvt,
Stoller, Jacob, T/4,
Stolp, Harold C., T/5,
Stoltz, Edwin I., Pvt,
Stone, Bernard, Pfc,
Stone, C. B., Pfc
‡Stone, Robert T., Sr., Pfc,
Stone, Roy, Pfc,
‡Stoner, Edward W., Pfc,
Stoner, Maxwell H., Pvt,
Stopar, Michael, Pvt,
Storey, Columbus M., Jr., T/4,
Storros, Steve O., Pvt,
Story, Robert R., Cpl,
Story, Tommie A., Pvt,

† Killed in Action. * Prisoner of War. ‡ Missing in Action. § Died of Wounds.

†Stouffer, James A., Pfc,
Stout, Irvin P., Sgt,
Stovall, Jay C., Pfc,
St. Pierre, Emerson A., 2nd Lt,
St. Pierre, Gerald E., Pvt,
Strand, Carl M., Pvt,
Strand, Philip O., Pvt,
‡Strang, Arthur, Pfc,
Strang, Earl R., Pvt,
Strang, George L., 1st Lt,
Stranz, George O., Pvt,
Stranhan, Herbert B., 1st Lt,
Strauss, Daniel, Sgt,
†Strauss, Ernest, Pvt,
Strauss, Raymond C., Pfc,
†Strauss, Werner M., Pvt,
Strausser, Charles, Pvt,
Streb, Claude R., Capt,
Stresnak, Richard T., Pvt,
Stressel, Philip H., Pvt,
Strickland, Brice, Pvt,
Strickler, Ivan C., Pfc
§Strine, Marvin C., Pfc,
†Stripling, Gordon A., Pfc,
Strohl, Robert R., Pfc,
Stromberg W. W., Lt Col,
Strong, Clarence, Pvt,
Strong, Harry W., Pfc,
Strong, Max, Pfc,
Stroud, Olah H., Pvt,
Struck, Elmer P., Pvt,
Struck, Lester C., Pfc,
†Strunk, William L., T/Sgt,
†Stuart, Frank C., 2nd Lt,
Stucky, William G., Capt,
Studebaker, Milton R., Sgt,
Studer, Walter C., Pvt,
Stueflaten, Paul H., Pvt,
‡Stumbaugh, Lester, Pvt,
Sudell, Edward J., Pvt,
Suek, Sylvester C., S/Sgt,
Sugerman, Robert N., Pfc,
Suits, James T., Pvt,
Sullivan, Francis C., WOJG,
†Sullivan, Howard P., Pvt,
§Sullivan, James D., Sgt,
Sullivan, John, Pfc,
Sullivan, John J., Pvt
Sullivan, John T., Pvt,
Sullivan, Walter G., S/Sgt,
*Sulser, Garlan E., Pfc,
Sumner, Ledford, Pfc,
Sumner, William A., 1st Lt,
Sumpter, Charles, Jr., Pfc,
Surdo, Bruno P., Pvt,
Suronen, Oiva, Pfc,
Suter, Joseph A., Pvt,
†Suter, Robert D., Pvt,
‡Sutherland, Blaine G., Pfc,
Sutherland, John O., T/5,
Sutherlin, William H., Pvt,
†Sutt, John S., Jr., Pfc,
†Sutton, Myles L., T/Sgt,
Sutton, Robert B., Pfc,
Svaco, John, Pvt,
Svitanek, James C., Jr., Pfc,
†Svoboda, Frederick A., Jr., Pfc,
Svoboda, Joseph S., Pvt,
Swackhammer, Howard E., Pvt
Swaim, Allan L., 2nd Lt,
Swan, William J., Pvt,
Swanberg, Charles, Jr., Capt,
Swanberg, Harold A., Cpl,
†Swank, Mathias J., Pfc,
Swann, James B., Pvt,
Swanson, Carl B., Cpl,
Swanson, Carl E., Pvt,
Swanson, John W., Pfc,
Swanson, Ralph B., Pvt,
Swary, Vincent J., Pfc,
†Swatzburg, Gerald H., 2nd Lt,
†Sween, Clyde V., Pfc,
Sweeney, Frank E., Jr., S/Sgt,
Sweeney, Hugh A., 1st Lt,
Sweeney, Walter L., Pfc,
Sweeney, William J., Jr., Cpl,
Sweet, Donald, Sgt,
‡Sweet, Russell C., Pvt,
†Swenson, Albert O., Pvt,
Swertzer, Ralph L., Pvt,
†Swiatek, Stanley J., Pfc,
Swicegood, Jacob H., Pvt,
Swickerath, Carl H., Capt,
†Swiech, Edward A., Pfc,
Swigonski, Edward, Pvt,
Swinney, Leon T., T/5,
Swinney, Monor C., Pvt,
Swisher, Edward F., Pvt,
†Switzer, Darl A., S/Sgt,
†Sykes, Donald J., Pvt,
Sykes, Eldon C., Pvt,
‡Sykora, William, Pvt,
†Sylvester, Arthur, S/Sgt,
Sylvester, Arthur, Sgt,

Syms, William M., Jr., Pfc,
§Syslo, Emil G., Cpl,
‡Szcyerbinski, C. A., Pfc,
Szczepanowski, Karol, S/Sgt,
Szczepanski, Stanley, S/Sgt,
Szczygiel, Chester P., Pfc,
*Szematowicz, Anthony V., Pvt,
Szotek, Walter L., Pfc,
Szymanski, Marcell, 2nd Lt,
‡Szymezak, Anthony E., Pfc,

Tabler, Grover P., Pvt
‡Tackett, James O., Pvt,
Tacy, Roger H., Sgt,
Tafel, Robert H., Pfc,
§Tafoya, Leo H., Pvt,
Taft, Russell A., Sr., Pvt,
Taggart, George B., Pvt,
Tagles, Alfonso, Pvt,
Tait, Ernest E., Pfc,
Tait, George R., Jr., Pfc,
Tait, William S., Sgt,
Takacs, William J., S/Sgt,
†Takala, Earl E., Pvt
Talarico, Harry G., Pvt,
Talarico, Vincent J., Pvt,
Talbert, Earl H., Pfc,
Talbert, James, Pfc,
Talgo, George L., Sgt,
§Talkington, Isaac L., Jr., Pvt,
†Tall Chief, Timothy, Pfc,
†Talley, William D., Pfc,
Tallman, Richard E., Pfc,
§Tally, Stewart D., Pvt,
Hamagni, Charles A., Pfc,
Tampas, Peter, Pfc,
Tancredi, Vincent A., Cpl,
†Taninatz, Joseph, Pvt,
Tannatt, Willard C., Pfc,
†Tannebaum, Joe, Pvt
Tannehill, Rupert I., Pvt,
Tanner, Clair W., Pfc,
Tanner, James W., S/Sgt,
Tannous, Don W., Pvt,
Tanori, Ramon B., Pvt,
†Tapley, Elbert, Sgt,
‡Tarknaski, Frederick J., Pfc,
Tarkowski, Chester J., Pfc,
†Tarpley, George, Pvt,
Tarpley, William H., Pfc,
Tarte, Roy, Pfc,
Tashman, Richard A., Pfc,
Tasso, Joseph M., T/Sgt,
Tatar, Robert W., Pfc,
Tatum, Alonzo E., Pfc,
†Tatlock, Eric W., 1st Lt,
Tatko, Walter A., Pfc,
Tarver, Jessie R., Pvt,
Tassainari, Raymond L., Pvt,
Tauss, Theodore W., Sgt,
Tautkas, Edward A., Pfc,
Tavares, John, Jr., Sgt,
Taylert, Paul J., Pvt,
Taylor, Alfred, Pvt,
Taylor, Bertram G., Pvt,
*Taylor, Cecil, Pvt,
Taylor, Dallas F., Pfc,
Taylor, Dean W., Pvt,
Taylor, Edward J., Pfc
Taylor, Erving J., Pfc,
Taylor, Eugene M., Pfc,
Taylor, Floyd B., Pfc,
Taylor, Frank J., Pvt,
†Taylor, George T., Pfc,
Taylor, Henry E., Pvt,
†Taylor, Jack E., Pvt,
Taylor, Jackson C., Pvt,
Taylor, James O., Pfc,
Taylor, John D., Pfc,
Taylor, John E., S/Sgt,
Taylor, Keith L., 1st Lt,
Taylor, Kenneth W., Cpl,
§Taylor, Lamar C., Pvt,
Taylor, Lawrence A., Pvt,
Taylor, Lawrence L., Pvt,
Taylor, Leonard E., Cpl,
Taylor, Myron D., Pvt,
Taylor, O. E., Pvt,
Taylor, Olin L., Pfc,
†Taylor, Paul L., Sgt,
Taylor, Ray A., T/Sgt,
Taylor, Roy D., Pfc,
†Taylor, Robert L., Pvt
Taylor, William C., Pvt,
Taylor, William E., Pvt,
Taylor, William L., Pfc,
†Taylor, Walter C., Pfc,
†Taylor, Willis E., 2nd Lt,
Teakell, Weldon A., Pfc,
Tebbats, Charles E., Pvt,
Tebo, Charles L., Pvt,
Tecco, Robert, Pvt,
Teder, Isadore, Pvt,
Tedrow, Odell, S/Sgt,

Tee, Wilbert M., S/Sgt,
Tegland, Harold L., Pfc,
†Teitelbaum, Milton A., Pfc,
Tekavec, Albert, Pfc,
Teklinski, Stanley F., Pfc,
Teller, Claude K., S/Sgt,
Teller, Howard W., Pfc,
Telles, John, Jr., Pvt,
Tellier, Joseph L., Pvt,
Templeton, Edward L., Pfc,
Templeton, Joffree, Pvt,
*Teng, Wei H., Pvt,
Tengren, Rune W., Pfc,
Tennant, Virgil D., Pfc,
Tenney, Edward P., Pvt,
Terifay, Joseph M., Pvt,
Terling, Anthony F., Pvt,
Terpstra, Edwin H., Pfc,
†Terpstra, Theodore, Pvt,
†Terrebonne, Junior J., Pfc,
Terrinoni, William E., Pvt,
Terrone, John, Pvt,
Terry, David, Pvt,
Terry, Gerald C., Pfc,
Terry, Wayne B., Pfc,
Terwilliger, Stanley C., Sgt,
Tesdall, John W., Pvt,
Testa, Angelo L., Pvt,
†Testa, Phillip, Pvt,
Tetrick, Tusca H., Pfc,
Tews, Raymond F., Pvt,
Thacker, Harold E., Pfc,
Thacker, John L., Sgt,
Thacker, Noah J., Pfc,
‡Thaler, Fred, Pvt,
Tharp, Harry L., Pvt,
Tharp, Robert A., 2nd Lt,
Them, Kilian F., Jr., Sgt,
Thebaud, Edward R., Pfc,
Theoharres, Paul, Pvt,
Thibodeau, Henry, Sgt,
Thill, George J., S/Sgt,
Thimis, Timmy G., Pvt,
Thimmes, James G., T/4,
Thoftne, George C., Pfc,
Thomas, Alexander J., Pvt,
Thomas, Boyce M., Pvt,
Thomas, Bruce H., T/4,
Thomas, Carl M., Pfc,
Thomas, Charles B., Jr., Pfc,
Thomas, Charles W., T/Sgt,
Thomas, Curtis J., Pfc,
Thomas, Dewey D., Cpl,
Thomas, Donald L., Pfc,
Thomas, Edward, Cpl,
Thomas, Everett M., Pfc,
Thomas, George W., Jr., Sgt,
Thomas, James C., Pfc,
Thomas, John L., S/Sgt
Thomas, John W., Pvt,
Thomas, Kermit W., T/4,
Thomas, Laben E., Pfc,
Thomas, Lester, Pfc,
Thomas, Maxwell H., T/5,
Thomas, Nelson W., Pvt,
†Thomas, Norman O., Cpl,
Thomas, Robert E., Pfc,
Thomas, Robert G., Pfc,
Thomas, Truman E., Sgt,
Thomas, Toy, Pvt,
Thomas, Wilbur, Cpl,
Thomas, William B., Pvt,
Thomas, William E., Pvt,
Thomasson, James R., Pfc,
Thomasson, Paul E., Pfc,
Thome, Paul I., Jr., Sgt,
Thompason, Lee L., Pvt,
Thompson, Bernice L., Pfc,
Thompson, Carl T., Cpl,
Thompson, Bufort G., Pvt,
Thompson, Clarence M., Pvt,
Thompson, Clifford A., Pfc,
Thompson, Dale G., Pfc,
Thompson, Eddie C., Pfc,
Thompson, Ernest W., Pvt,
Thompson, Ernest G., Pfc,
Thompson, Fred, Pvt,
‡Thompson, Frederick C., Pfc,
Thompson, Gaylor B., Pvt,
Thompson, George D., Cpl,
Thompson, Gerald, Pfc,
Thompson, Herbert R., Pfc,
Thompson, Herbert M., Pfc,
Thompson, James S., Pvt,
Thompson, James T., S/Sgt,
§Thompson, John B., Cpl,
Thompson, Joseph D., Sr., Pfc,
Thompson, Mancil L., Pvt,
Thompson, Marion E., Pfc,
Thompson, Paul E., Pfc,
Thompson, Ray, Pfc,
Thompson, Ray H., Pfc,
Thompson, Theodore J., Pfc,
†Thompson, William A., Pfc,

†Thompson, William B., Pfc,
Thompson, William F., Pvt,
Thompson, William K., Pvt,
Thompson, Winston, Pvt,
Thompston, Edward C., Pvt,
Thoms, Harold W., Pfc,
Thorn, Henry W., Pfc,
‡Thornton, Billy R., Pfc,
Thornton, Clyde W., T/5,
Thorsen, Ralph L., Pvt,
Thrall, Leo, Cpl,
Thrasher, Orville C., Pfc,
Thruman, Russell K., Pfc,
Thuilliez, Raymond R., Sgt,
Thurber, Harlow, Cpl,
Thurman, James J., Pfc,
Thurman, Richard K., T/Sgt,
Thurston, Thomas D., Pfc,
Tibbals, George A., Pfc,
Tice, Cecil R., Pvt,
Tickler, Peter A., Sgt,
†Tidwell, Jack M., 1st Lt,
Tierney, Richard W., Pfc,
Tiffany, Hiero G., 1st Lt,
Tilghman, Marion E., Pvt,
Tiller, Jack B., Sgt,
Tillery, Charles L., Pvt,
†Tilley, Charles E., Pfc,
Tilley, Roy L., Pvt,
Tillis, John, Pvt,
†Tillis, Wiley M., Pfc,
Tillman, John W., Sgt
Tilton, Gale E., Pfc,
Tilton, William H., Pvt,
†Tilvikus, George H., S/Sgt,
Timberlake, Howard G., Pvt,
Timberlake, J. C. P., 1st Lt,
Timon, Ervin A., T/4,
Tina, Joseph, Pfc,
Tindell, James R., Pfc,
†Tindle, Houston E., Pvt,
†Tindle, John F., Pfc,
Tinker, Samuel M., S/Sgt,
Tinsman, Oliver L., Pvt,
Tintera, Jerry J., Pvt,
Tinti, George J., Sgt,
§Tippy, Kenneth H., Sgt,
Tipton, Alva W., Pfc,
Tipton, Eugene W., Pfc,
Tirpak, John, T/5,
Tisdale, Robert E., 2nd Lt,
Tiska, Leo S., Pfc,
Tittle, William A., Pvt,
Titus, Robert L., Pfc,
Tkach, Joseph F., S/Sgt,
Tobin, Frank, Pfc,
†Todd, Jack A., Pfc,
Todd, James G., Cpl,
Todd, James H., Sgt,
Todd, Jimmie L., Pfc,
Todd, Robert L., Pvt,
Tokarczyk, Michael A., T/4,
Tokarz, Edward J., Pvt,
‡Tokarz, Frank J., Pvt
Tolar, Douglas S., 1st Lt,
Tolberd, Robert S., Pvt,
†Toledo, Anthony C., Pvt,
†Tollefson, Martin T., Pvt,
Tolley, Willard G., Pvt,
Tolliver, W. E., Pvt,
Tomaselli, John B., Pfc,
Tomasetta, Philip P., T/3,
Tomasini, James C., Pfc,
Tomaszewski, Edward J., Sgt,
Tomaszewski, Stanley E., Pvt,
Tomczak, Henry A., Pvt,
Tomczak, Walter L., Pfc,
Tomel, John J., Sgt,
Tomlin, Jack L., 2nd Lt,
Tomlinson, Carl H., Pfc,
†Tomlinson, Jack R., Pvt,
Tomlinson, Russell C., Pfc,
Tompkins, Cordell L., Pvt,
Toolan, Edward M., Pfc,
Topalian, Harry V.,
Topie, Carl P., Pvt,
Torcellini, James V., T/5,
Torell, Ray E., Pfc,
Torgerson, Lief T., T/4,
Torkelson, Raymond F., 2nd Lt,
Torno, Otto F., Jr., Pfc,
Torrens, Floyd W., Pvt,
†Torres, Esteban, Pvt,
Torres, Harding, Pfc,
†Torres, Rosendo, Pfc,
Torretta, Peter J., Pfc,
Torza, Camille W., Pvt,
Totera, Frank R., Pvt,
Totton, Hurstle M., Pfc,
Touchstone, Henry T., Pvt,
‡Touma, Joseph A., Pvt,
*Towezuk, James, Pvt,
Towner, Ferdy T., S/Sgt,
Towner, Raymond E., Pvt,

Townsend, John T., Pfc,
‡Townsend, J. R., Pvt,
Townsend, Nelson R., Pfc,
Townsley, Robert, Cpl,
†Trach, Joseph F., S/Sgt,
Trachman, Sol, Pvt,
†Tracy, John F., Pfc,
Tracy, Leonard J., Pvt,
Trad, John P., Sgt,
Traester, Lewis R., Pfc,
Trainello, Reginald, Pvt,
Trainor, John E., Pfc,
†Trapani, Charles, Sgt,
†Trapani, Frank A., Pvt,
Trapp, John A., Pvt
Trasatti, Gabriel F., Pfc,
Traski, Stefan, Pvt,
Treadwell, Chandler H., Pvt,
Treece, Louis W., Pfc,
Trees, Robert A., Pfc.
Treise, Warren F., Pvt
Tremayne, William J., Pfc,
Trembienski, Florian F., Pvt
Tremplay, Telesphor C., 2nd Lt
Trent, Clayton J., Cpl,
Trevillian, Denzil E., Pvt,
Trevino, Domingo, Pvt,
Trevinor, Alfredo, Pfc,
Tribukait, Henry A., Pvt,
Tribus, Steven, Pfc,
Triebwasser, Luverne V., Pvt,
†Trimbell, LaVerne E., Cpl,
*Trimble, Leo J., Pfc,
Trimble, Lloyd, Pvt,
Trimboli, Anthony, Pvt
Trimpe, Clifford H., Pfc,
Triolo, Bertola A., Pvt,
Triolo, Erasmo F., Pvt,
Triona, Charles E., T/Sgt,
Triplett, Taylor, Cpl,
Tritico, Louis A., 1st Lt,
Troff, William, Cpl,
Troik, Edmund J., S/Sgt,
Tronnes, Henry O., T/4,
Tronson, William H., Cpl,
Troop, Charles A. L., Pvt,
Troski, Edward M., Pvt,
Trost, Louis R., 1st Sgt,
Trotta, Rocco J., S/Sgt,
Trout, Harold E., Pfc,
Trout, Meredith L., Pvt,
Trout, Merle E., Pvt
Troutman, Leonard R., Pfc,
Troxel, Joseph A., S/Sgt,
Troxel, William H., Pvt,
Truax, Garrel E., Pfc,
Trudelle, Ernest L., Pvt,
Truhan, Emery, S/Sgt,
Trujillo, Benjamin M., Pvt,
Trujillo, Jack R., Pfc,
Trujillo, Manuel, Pfc,
Trujillo, Manuel, Cpl
Trulock, Loren C., Pfc,
Truta, Milenko, Pfc,
Trynor, Edward E., Pvt,
Tschudy, Leroy P., Pvt,
Tuck, George C., Pfc,
Tuck, Maynard, Pfc,
Tucker, Bernard C., S/Sgt,
Tucker, Bob J., S/Sgt,
Tucker, Charles J., Jr., Pfc,
Tucker, Edward E., Cpl,
§Tucker, Floyd T., Pvt,
Tucker, James P., Pvt,
Tucker, Raymond F., Pvt,
Tucker, Van V., Pvt,
Tucker, Wager E., Pvt,
Tuffs, Lawrence W., Pvt,
Tuggle, James E., Pfc,
Tuladziecki, Anthony J., Pvt,
Tulchinsky, Arthur A., Pvt,
Tuley, Robert F., Pvt,
Tulik, Joseph S., T/5,
Tuma, Arthur A., Pfc,
Tumis, Frank, Cpl,
Tunnicliff, Leslie J., Pfc,
Tuomie, Toivo T., Pvt,
Tupa, Leonard E., Pfc,
Turegano, Fernando A., Pvt,
Turk, Frank B., Pvt,
Turley, Robert M., Pvt,
Turmail, Weldon J. W., Pvt,
Turman, Arlie A., Pfc,
Turnage, Carson, Pvt,
Turner, Alton, Pvt,
Turner, Alvin, Pvt,
Turner, Carl, Pfc,
‡Turner, David H., T/5,
Turner, Deward B., Pfc.
Turner, Eugene B., 1st Lt,
Turner, Hiram, T/5,
Turner, J. B., Pvt,
Turner, Lillard D., Pvt,
Turner, Ralph Q., Pvt,

† Killed in Action. * Prisoner of War. ‡ Missing in Action. § Died of Wounds.

IN WORLD WAR II 531

Turner, Thomas J., Pvt
‡Turner, Timothy D., Pvt,
Turner, Wayne H., Pfc,
†Turtis, Jacob L., Pvt,
Tuthill, Fred T., Jr., Pvt,
Tyler, Clarence N., T/5,
Tyndall, Ronald N., Pvt,
Tyrer, David P., Pvt,
Tyrrell, Francis E., 2nd Lt,
Tyska, Edward W., Pfc,
Tyson, Robert G., Pvt,
Twardzik, John F., Pvt,
Tweedel, Frank R., Pvt
‡Twist, Dan, Pfc,

Ubert, Gilbert, T/5,
Udowski, Frank J., Sgt,
Uelman, Nicholas T., Pfc,
Ugalde, Jesse G., Capt,
Ugalde, Prudencio, Pfc,
Uhl, Earnest, Pfc,
Uhler, George W., Pvt,
Ulanski, Chester, S/Sgt,
Ulbriokson, Charles F., T/4,
Ulloa, Atanasio, Pvt,
Underwood, G. S., Jr., Pvt,
Underwood, John C., Pvt,
Underwood, John W., Pvt,
Underwood, Ray E., Pvt,
Underwood, Raymond, Pvt
Ung, Charles A. W., Pfc,
Unger, Willard S., Pfc,
Unnone, Michael, Pfc,
Unsicker, Harold I., S/Sgt,
Uomoleale, James P., Pfc,
†Uplinger, Lawrence E., Pvt,
Upp, John C., Pvt,
Uptgraft, Donald W., Pvt,
Urban, John, T/Sgt,
Urbanik, John J., Pvt,
Urbanovitch, Joseph J., Pvt,
Urdsick, Leo, Pvt,
Uribe, Francisco I., Pvt,
Urnetta, Jerolawo, Pvt,
Urquizu, Pedro, Pvt,
Usher, Charles H., Pfc,
Usher, James E., Pfc,
Usry, Harry E., Sr., Pvt,
Utermohlen, Emil E., Pvt,
‡Utley, Curtis W., Pfc,
Utz, Charles E., 2nd Lt.

†Vaccaro, James, Pvt,
Vachon, Albert L., Pvt,
Vadnais, Lawrence M., Sgt,
Vail, James M., Pfc,
Vaillancourt, Lee, Pvt,
Valdivia, Roger C., Pvt,
Valent, Charles J., Cpl,
Valentine, James L., Pvt,
Valenzuela, Frank, Pfc,
Vales, Happy D., Pfc,
Valgoi, Martin, T/5,
Valine, Arthur, Pfc,
Valla, Leo B., Pvt,
Vallanto, John, Pvt,
Vallery, Gordon, Pfc,
Valley, Auguste P., Jr., Pfc,
Valverde, Samuel A., Pvt,
Vance, Dexter L., Pvt,
Vance, Elmer, Pvt,
†Vance, Frederick S., Pfc,
‡Vance, Henry G., Pvt,
Vance, Marion C., Cpl,
Vancil, David T., Pfc,
Van Cleve, Harley W., Cpl,
Vandalsen, Willie M., Pfc,
Vanden, Louis H., Pvt,
Vandenberg, Alphons E., Pvt,
Vandenberg, Frank B., Pfc,
Vandenbosch, Walter H., Pvt,
Vander Ende, C. T., S/Sgt,
Vander Kolk, Lewis J., Pvt,
Van Der Meer, Martin, Pvt,
Vanderver, Ruvle E., Pvt,
Van Dieron, Hans M., Pvt,
Van Dyke, Leslie L., Pfc,
Vane, Rudolph F., Sgt,
Van Etten, Richard, Pfc,
‡Van Euwen, Matthew G., Pfc,
Van Gilder, Kenneth C., Cpl,
‡Van Horne, Alton J., Pvt,
†Van Horne, John P., Pfc,
Van Hyning, Edward R., Pvt,
‡Van Keen, Jacob M., Pfc,
Van Lerberghe, K. C., Pfc,
Van Matre, James H., T/5,
Van Meter, Jack E., Pvt
Van Meter, Rollin E., Pvt,
Van Name, Abram A., Pvt,
Vanne, Orval F., Pvt,
Van Nest, Norman O., Pvt,
Van Nice, Alfred L., Pvt,
Vann, Martin F., Pvt,
Vanore, Louis S., 1st Lt,

Vanover, Vernon, Sgt,
Vanover, Ralph E., S/Sgt,
†Van Son, John H., Pfc,
Vansco, Philip J., Sgt,
Van Troyer, William, Pfc,
Van Vleet, Richard J., Pvt,
Van Vliet, Walter R., Pfc,
‡Van Wyk, Robert D., Pvt,
Varela, Arthur O., Pvt,
Varela, Julio B., Pfc
Varga, John, Pvt,
Vargo, William Z., S/Sgt,
Vario, Joseph, Pfc,
Varley, Thomas S., Pvt,
Varner, Daniel H., Pvt,
†Varner, William R., Cpl,
Varney, Paul J., Pvt,
†Varrella, Peter, Pvt,
Vasconcellos, Oscar, Pfc,
Vasil, Joseph T., Pfc,
Vasilchak, George J., Pfc,
*Vasiliadiz, Michael C., Pfc,
Vasilko, John, Pvt,
Vasion, Daniel P., Pfc,
†Vasos, Nick G., Sgt,
†Vasser, Lester E., Pfc,
Vatland, Albert K., Pvt
Vatland, Albert L., Pvt,
Vatne, Carsten, Cpl,
†Vauclain, James L., S/Sgt,
Vaughan, Harvey L., Pvt,
*Vaughan, Howard A., Pfc,
Vaughan, Jim C., Pvt,
Vaughan, Milburn L., Pfc,
Vaughan, Robert J., Pfc,
Vaughan, William T., Pfc,
Vaughn, William J., Pvt,
†Veach, Raymond E., S/Sgt,
Veach, Warren J., Pfc,
Vedel, George J., Pvt,
‡Vela, Amador, Pfc,
‡Vela, Juventino C., T/5,
‡Veleno, Nicholas A., Pvt,
Vella, Joseph S., Pvt,
Vellano, Daniel, Pvt,
Venable, Clarence A., Cpl,
Venable, Everette, Pvt,
†Venable, James E., Pvt,
Venchenko, Armenio, T/5,
Vendemia, Pete A., Pvt,
Venegas, John M., Pfc,
Veneto, Bruno J., Pvt,
Vennettilli, Armenio, Pvt,
Ventimiglia, Benedetto, 1st Sgt,
Ventrello, Pasquale, Pvt,
Ventura, Joe, Pvt,
†Venzwieten, John, 2nd Lt,
Veometti, Robert C., Pvt,
Verab, Eugene F., Pfc,
Vercellone, Joseph, T/Sgt,
†Verdegan, John A., Jr., Pvt,
Verderame, Pasquale S., Pvt,
Verdile, Rocco, Pvt,
‡Verga, Charlie D., Pvt,
Vergobbi, Leonard A., Pvt
Verhague, Russell B., Pvt,
Verhoven, Ben G., Pfc,
Verkine, Roy L., Jr., Pvt,
Vermette, Herman W., Pvt,
Vernarelli, Arnold F., 1st Lt,
Verneris, Arthur H., Pvt,
Vernon, Reed F., Sgt,
Vernon, Walter E., Pvt,
Verrecchia, Albert, Pfc,
Verta, Frank M., Sgt,
Vertefeuille, Roland M., Pfc,
Verwoert, Robert H., 2nd Lt,
Vesco, John J., Sgt,
Vest, Osie M., Pvt
‡Vestal, Robert J., Pvt
Veto, Eugene A., Pvt,
Vetrone, Robert J., Pvt,
Vezza, Salvatore, Pfc,
Via, Ivan V., Pfc,
Vial, Joseph R., S/Sgt,
Viau, Albert J., T/5,
Viavatine, James R., Pvt,
†Vibart, Albert L., S/Sgt,
†Vicars, Charles W., Pfc,
Vick, William J., Jr., Sgt.
Vickerman, Howard O., Pfc,
Vickers, Burton J., Pvt.
Vickers, Henry F., S/Sgt,
Vicknair, Alton H., Cpl.
Vickroy, Wilbur E., T/5,
Victor, Edward J., Pfc
†Videtich, John A., Sgt,
Viehland, Hugo A., S/Sgt,
Vierke, Harold C., Pfc,
Viers, Lewis, Pvt
Viers, Walter W., Pfc,
Vigue, Rosaire J., Sgt,
Viherek, Stephen J., Pvt,
Villa, Anthony, Pvt,
Villano, Anthony M., Pvt,

*Villarreal, Evslie F., Pvt,
Villarreal, Reynaldo J., Pvt,
Villemarette, Ray, Pvt
Viero, Frank T., Pvt
Vincent, Gillis E., Pfc,
Vincent, Wilbur T., Pvt,
Vinci, Gregory J., Pfc,
Vinciguerra, Charles A., Pfc,
Vinicki, Joseph S., Pfc,
Vires, James V., Cpl,
Virgin, Lydon L., Pfc,
†Virzi, Frank J., Pfc,
Visaggi, Ralph, Pvt,
Visconti, Louis T., Pvt,
Viscount, Edward, Pfc,
Viscuso, Carmelo R., Pfc,
Vital, Arthur R., Pfc,
Vitale, Joseph P., Pvt,
Vivian, William H., Pvt,
Vizzi, Salvatore S., Cpl,
Vizzone, Frank J., Pvt
Vladika, Joseph, Pfc,
Vogel, Albert, Pvt,
*Vogel, Felix, Pfc,
Vogel, Frank J., Pvt,
Vogel, George C., Pvt,
Vogt, Robert W., Pfc,
Vogt, William O., S/Sgt,
Vonder, Charles J., Pvt,
Voltaggio, James J., Pvt,
Vojtek, Robert, Sgt,
Von Dreele, N. F., Jr., S/Sgt,
Vong, Leonard E., T/5,
Voutsaras, Theodore S., T/Sgt,
Von Holtz, Edward F., Pvt,
Von Kahle, Vancino A., Pfc,
Vorhis, Phallis J., Pvt,
Voss, Glenn R., Pfc,
Voss, James R., 1st Sgt,
Votta, Charles C., Pvt,
Vought, William I., Pfc,
Voulgaris, Alexandros A., Pfc,
†Vuletich, Robert, Sgt,
Vowell, Lommie, Pvt,
Vrana, Randolph L., Sgt,
Vrban, Joe F., Pvt,
Vreeland, Chester M., Pvt,

Waasdorp, Jacob J., T/Sgt,
Waasdorp, John J., S/Sgt,
Wabbel, Carl L., Pvt,
Wach, Daniel E., Pvt,
Wachowiak, Florian T., Jr., Pvt
*Wachter, Joseph C., Pvt,
Waddell, Bryant E., S/Sgt,
Waddell, William E., Pfc,
†Waddell, William E. G., Pvt,
Waddington, Charles C., Pfc,
Waddington, Harry A., Pfc,
‡Waddle, Charles W., Pvt,
†Wade, Charley J., Pfc,
Waddell, Samuel J., Jr., Pvt,
Wadhams, Robert D., Pvt,
Waeltz, Robert G., Jr., Pvt,
Waggenspack, Laville L., Pvt,
Waggner, William J., Pvt,
‡Wagner, Carl D., Pfc,
Wagner, Clarence J., Jr., Pvt,
Wagner, Clyde O., Pvt,
Wagner, Fred D., Cpl,
Wagner, George F., T/5,
Wagner, Herbert J., Pfc,
*Wagner, John P., Pfc,
Wagner, Leo W., Sgt,
Wagner, Otto W., Pfc,
‡Wagner, Richard H., Pfc,
Wagner, Russell D., Pfc,
Wagner, Sherman J., T/4
†Wagoner, Lloyd S., Pvt,
Wagonmaker, Edward G., Pvt,
Wahl, Robert W., Pvt,
‡Waintroop, Saul B., Pvt,
Waite, Clyde A., Pvt,
Wakeman, Roland C., Pvt,
Walaitis, Wilham B., Pvt,
Walberg, Alf H., Pfc,
§Walden, John T., Pvt,
Walder, Harry F., Cpl,
Waldren, Albert C., Pfc,
†Waldron, Ray P., Pfc,
Waldrop, Robert L., Pfc,
Waldvogel, Willard B., Pvt,
Walen, Michael W., Pvt,
Walenga, Richard A., 2nd Lt,
Walker, Arthur, Cpl
Walker, Bobby C., Pfc,
Walker, Charlie M., Jr., Pvt,
Walker, Darwyn E., 1st Lt
Walker, David L., Pvt,
Walker, Earl L., Sgt,
‡Walker, Floyd P., Pvt,
Walker, George W., Jr., S/Sgt,
Walker, Howard G., Sgt,
Walker, James M., S/Sgt,

Walker, Joseph L., 1st Sgt,
Walker, Mardie W., T/5,
‡Walker, Patrick, Jr., Pvt,
Walker, Paul O., Sgt,
Walker, Merle D., Pfc,
Walker, Raful E., Cpl,
Walker, Robert J., 2nd Lt,
Walker, Russell D., Pvt,
Walker, Tommie J., Sgt,
Walker, Warren W., Sgt,
Walker, William J., Pvt,
Walker, William J., Pfc,
†Wall, Laral W., Pfc,
Wall, Ralph A., Pfc,
Walla, Louis J., Sgt,
Wallace, Arthur S., Pvt,
Wallace, Elmer L., Pvt,
Wallace, Glenn D., Pfc,
†Wallace, Harold J., Pfc,
Wallace, James W., Pvt,
Wallace, Kenneth L., Pfc,
Wallace, Lawrence L., T/5,
Wallace, Leonard, T/5,
Wallen, Howard A., Pvt,
†Wallen, J. D., Pvt,
Waller, Guy B., Pvt
Waller, John, Pvt,
*Waller, Virgil A., Pfc,
Walling, Harvey, Pvt,
Walls, Ernest, Pvt,
Walls, Everett A., Pfc,
Walsh, Edward J., Pfc,
Walsh, Dominick J., Pvt,
Walsh, James J., Pfc,
Walsh, James T., Sgt,
Walsh, John J., Pvt,
Walsh, John P., T/5,
Walsh, Laurence J., Pvt,
Walsh, Leneus E., T/4,
Walsh, Robert E., T/Sgt,
†Walsh, Thomas F., Pvt
Walsh, William F., Pfc,
Walston, Stanley B., Pvt,
Walter, Aaron L., Pvt,
Walter, Isaac F., Sgt,
Walter, Raymond C., S/Sgt,
Walter, William B., Pfc,
†Walters, Fayette M., Pfc,
Walters, Harry P., Pvt,
Walters, Henry J., Sgt,
Walters, James C., Pfc,
†Walters, John G., Pvt,
Walters, John T., Pvt,
Walters, Robert E., Pvt,
Walthers, Charles W., Pvt,
Walton, Finis M., Pfc,
Walton, Frank J., Pfc
Walz, Bernhard, Pfc,
Walz, Ora F., Cpl,
Wampler, Roy H., Pvt,
Wang, Lawrence E., Cpl,
Wanger, Harold C., Pvt
Wanner, John K., Pfc,
Wanogaitis, Paul P., Pvt,
Ward, Albert, Pvt,
Ward, Donnie W., Pfc,
†Ward, Herbert B., Jr., Pvt,
Ward, Herschal O., Pfc,
†Ward, Jessie J., Pvt,
†Ward, James C., Pvt,
Ward, M. T., Pvt,
Ward, Norvle, Pvt,
Ward, Murrell R., Pfc,
Ward, Silas J., S/Sgt,
Ward, Talbot C., Cpl,
Wardell, William T., 1st Lt,
Wardlaw, Hugh E., Maj,
Ware, Robert L., Pfc,
†Warfield, Walter H., Pvt,
Warley, William G., Pfc,
Warman, Edgar F., Pfc,
Warner, Alval, 1st Sgt,
Warner, Calvin J., S/Sgt,
Warner, Edward P., Cpl
‡Warner, Edwin F., Pvt,
Warner, Kenneth D., Cpl,
Warr, Flavel H., Pvt,
Warren, Arnold E., S/Sgt,
Warren, Ben, Pfc
Warren, Elwood V., Pvt,
Warren, Eugene H., Pvt,
Warren, James R., Pvt,
Warren, John R., Pvt
Warren, Odell H., Pvt,
Warren, Paffard W., Pfc,
Warren, Ralph J., Sgt,
Warrener, John F., Jr., Pvt,
Warrenfeltz, LeRoy O., T/Sgt,
Warro, Alex W., Pfc,
‡Warthman, Loren A., Pvt,
Warwick, Earl L., Pvt,
Warwick, Robert D., Pfc,
Wasco, Casimir W., Pfc,
Wasdin, Simon, Pfc,

Washburn, Raymond, Pvt,
Washington, Wilson S., Jr., Pfc
Washko, Edward, Pvt,
Wasilinin, John J., Sgt,
†Wasmund, Edward, Pfc,
Wassel, Raymond P., 2nd Lt,
*Wasselle, Richard, Pvt,
Waste, Richard J., Pvt,
Wasurczak, Walter, Pfc,
Water, Thomas W., Pvt,
Watermen, Andrew J., Pvt,
Waters, Ernest J., Cpl,
Waters, Paul R., S/Sgt,
Waterworth, Robert E., S/Sgt,
Watkins, James F., Cpl,
Watkins, LeRoy, Sgt,
Watkinson, George, Pvt,
Watsabaugh, Warren L., Pfc,
Watson, David M., Pvt,
Watson, Edward L., Pfc,
†Watson, Harry, Sgt,
†Watson, Herman O., Pfc,
†Watson, John F., Jr., Pfc,
†Watson, John W., Pvt,
‡Watson, John W., Pvt,
Watson, Phillip D., Pfc,
Watson, Robert, Sgt,
Watson, Robert G., Sr., Pvt,
Watson, Thomas J., 1st Sgt,
Watson, Zack W., Pfc,
Watters, David J., S/Sgt,
Watts, Geater, Pfc,
Watts, James F., Cpl,
Watts, Otis, Pfc,
Watts, Preston L., Pfc,
Wax, Earl R., S/Sgt,
Way, Harold A., 1st Lt,
Waycaster, Herman H., Sgt,
Wdowiak, Thomas, Pfc,
Weatherford, George M., Pvt,
§Weatherford, Wilburn R., Pvt,
Weatherhead, Charles L., Pfc,
Weathermon, Lee E., Pfc,
Weathersby, Frank R., Sgt,
†Weaver, Clifton, Pvt,
Weaver, Ervin E., Pfc,
Weaver, Hershel H., S/Sgt,
Weaver, Howard E., Sgt,
Weaver, Joseph A., Pvt,
Weaver, Kenneth G., Pvt
Weaver, Leland E., Sgt,
Weaver, Michael S., Pvt,
Weaver, Neal O., Pvt,
‡Weaver, Roland F., Sgt,
Weaver, Roy M., S/Sgt,
Weaver, Will R., Pvt,
Weaver, William W., T/4,
Webb, Archie, 1/Sgt,
Webb, Robert A., Pfc,
Webb, William T., Pfc,
Weber, Edwin T., S/Sgt,
Weber, George, Jr., Cpl,
Weber, Harold F., Sgt,
Weber, John, 2nd Lt,
Weber, Joseph M., Pvt,
†Weber, Leo F., Pvt,
Weber, Mathew J., Pfc,
†Weber, Ralph E., Pvt,
Weber, Stanley L., Pvt,
Weber, Thomas M., Pvt,
Webster, Alfred M., Sgt,
Webster, Billy B., Pfc,
§Webster, Chester F., Pfc,
†Webster, Ernest M., Pfc,
Webster, Mahlon J., S/Sgt,
†Weddle, Mack E., Pfc,
Wedlake, Glenn W., Cpl,
Weeber, Thomas R., Pfc,
Weeden, David M., Pvt,
Weeks, Harvey A., Pvt
Weeks, Lawrence D., Pfc,
Weeks, Seneca J., Pvt,
Weeks, Walter L., S/Sgt,
Weese, Albert P., Pfc,
Weese, Floyd, Pfc,
Wegford, Wayne G., Pvt,
Wegrzyn, Casimir P., Pvt,
Wehmeier, Ernest F., T/4,
Wehr, Harold C., Pvt,
Wehrley, Leroy G., Pvt,
Weider, James F., Pfc,
Weidner, Earl L., Pfc,
Weidner, Walter E., Pfc,
Weil, Harold U., Sgt,
Weiler, Richard B., S/Sgt,
Weimar, David P., Sgt,
Weinberg, Isadore, Pfc,
Weindorfer, Frank P., Pvt,
Weiner, Hymie, Pvt,
Weiner, Samuel, Pfc,
Weinik, Leonard B., Pfc,
Weinstein, Albert, Pvt,
Weinstein, Murray W., Cpl,
Weir, Charles W., S/Sgt,

† Killed in Action. * Prisoner of War. ‡ Missing in Action. § Died of Wounds.

Weir, Dick, T/4,
Weisback, John L., Pfc,
Weiser, John, Pvt
Weisman, Simon A., S/Sgt,
Weisner, Gordon R., Pvt,
Weisner, Herbert L., Pfc
Weiss, Berthold, Pfc,
Weiss, Edwin, Pvt,
‡Weiss, Howard T., Pfc,
Weiss, Hyman M., T/5,
‡Wekford, Ronald V., Pfc,
Welborn, Lee H., Pvt,
Welborn, Rufus H., Pfc,
Welch, Charley E., Pfc,
Welch, Fred C., Sgt,
Welch, George F., Pvt,
Welch, James A., Pvt,
Welch, Lowell T., Pvt,
†Welch, William H., Pfc,
Welch, Wilfred, Pvt,
Welchko, Laurence M., Pvt
Weldman, Frederick R., T/5,
Weldon, Arthur W., Pfc,
Weldon, Lester W., Sgt,
Weldon, Urban T., S/Sgt,
Welford, James C., Pvt,
Wellendorf, Dale E., Pvt,
Wells, Calvin C., Pvt,
†Wells, Delbert G., Sgt,
Wells, Edward, Pvt,
Wells, Franklin E., Jr., Pvt,
Wells, George E., Pfc,
Wells, Herbert E., Pfc,
Wells, Isaac A., T/5,
†Wells, Robert M., Pfc,
Wells, Walter B., Pfc,
§Welton, William N., Pfc,
Weltz, Lawrence J., Cpl,
Wendland, Richard H., 1st Lt,
Wendt, John G., Sgt,
Wenner, George A., Pvt,
Wentovich, Paul, Pvt,
Wenz, Harold A., Pvt,
Wenzel, William, Pvt,
Wenzel, William F., Sgt,
Weprin, Charles W., Pvt,
Werkheiser, Raymond T., Pvt,
Wern, Donald R., Pvt,
Wertman, Willard A., S/Sgt,
Wesler, Leonard S., Pvt,
Wesley, Kirby C., Pfc,
Wesley, Victor, Pfc,
Wesolowski, Casimir J., Cpl,
Wessels, Robert D., Pvt,
West, Harvey G., Pvt,
West, John H., Capt,
West, Kenneth A., Pvt,
West, Lawrence A., 1/Sgt
West, Luther, Pfc,
†West, Melvin W., Pfc,
West, Orby L., Pvt,
West, Woodrow W., T/5,
Westcott, Ralph H., Pfc,
Westcott, Theodore P., Sgt,
Westmeir, Edward J., Pfc,
Westmorlan, Leroy, Pvt,
Wetzel, Paul R., S/Sgt,
Wexler, Jerome N., Pvt,
†Weyhing, George E., Cpl,
Weylandt, W. A. V., S/Sgt,
Whalen, Eldon, Pvt,
Whaley, Leslie A., Pvt,
Whear, Clayton H., T/5,
Wheat, James O., Pvt,
Wheat, Paul G., Sgt,
Wheatley, Laurence E., Pvt,
Wheaton, Gabriel D., Pvt,
§Wheaton, Rendall L., Pfc,
Wheeler, Dalton W., S/Sgt,
Wheeler, Howard O., Pfc,
Wheeler, Ivan E., Cpl,
Wheeler, James B., Pvt,
Wheeler, Lawrence A.,
Wheeler, Splint V., Pfc,
†Wheeler, Walter O., Pvt,
Wheeler, William L., Pvt,
Wheldon, John W., Pvt,
Wheliss, John A., Pfc,
Whicker, Clell A., Sgt,
Whipple, Frederick W., Pvt,
†Whisner, Walter H., Pfc,
Whitaker, Otis T., Pvt,
Whitaker, Robert P., Pvt,
Whitall, Charles H., Sgt,
†Whitby, Charlie L., Pfc,
§White, Albert W., Pvt,
White, Archie J., Pvt,
White, Ben E., Pvt,
White, Bernard F., Pvt
White, Buford A., Pvt,
White, Charles E., Jr., S/Sgt,
‡White, Charles E., Pvt,
White, Clarence E., Sgt,
White, Clyde, Pvt,
White, Danil R., Jr., Pvt,
White, David A., T/5,
‡White, Erman, Pfc,
White, Francis L., T/Sgt,
White, Franklin, Pvt,
White, George M., Pfc,
§White, Gerald S., Cpl
White, Gordon B., 2nd Lt,
White, Harvey H., Pfc,
White, Jason S., Sgt,
White, John C., Pvt,
White, John C., Pvt,
White, John E., Pvt,
White, John W., Pvt,
White, Joseph B., Pvt,
White, Leland P., S/Sgt,
White, Lloyd G., Pfc,
White, Murray C., Pvt
White, Newman J., Pvt,
White, Ralph, Pvt,
White, Raymond V., Pvt,
†White, Roy M., Pvt,
White, Roy W. Pvt.,
White, William C., Pfc,
Whited, Curtis, Sgt,
Whitehead, Fred W., Pvt
Whitehead, James E.,
Whitehead, John H., S/Sgt
Whitehead, Ottis, R., Pvt,
Whitehorn, Raymond B., Pfc,
Whitehouse, John F., Sgt,
Whiteside, William T., Pvt,
†Whiteworth, Ralph W., Pvt,
†Whitler, Frank L., Pvt,
Whitley, Harson, Pfc,
Whitlock, Earl C., Pfc,
Whitlock, Lee D., Cpl,
‡Whitlock, Tommie C., Pfc,
Whitman, Arnold L., Jr., Pfc,
Whitman, Bert E., Pvt,
Whitney, Myron E., Pvt,
Whitsett, James T., Pfc,
Whittaker, George E., Pvt,
Whitten, A. J., Pfc,
Whittington, Fred F., Cpl,
Whittington, James K., S/Sgt
Whittington, Joe, Pvt,
Whittington, Julius, Sgt,
Whittle, John H., S/Sgt,
†Whittle, Robert E., Pfc,
†Whyte, Virgil D., Sgt,
Whyte, William E., T/5,
Wiatr, Thomas R., Pvt,
†Wick,Joseph F., Sgt,
Wickard, Clarence M., S/Sgt,
‡Wickey, Jack M., Pvt,
*Wickham, Raymond E., Pfc,
Wicklein, Carl H., Pfc,
Wicknich, Albert, Pvt,
Widger, Bernard J., Pvt
Widman, Albert A., S/Sgt,
Wieczorek, Ferdinand, Pfc,
Wieczorek, William J., T/5,
Wiedyk, Ernest M., Pfc,
Wieg, Dwain O., Pvt
Wiegman, Dale H., Pvt,
Wiener, Jack, Pvt,
Wiener, John, Pfc,
Wiener, Melvin H., Pfc
Wienke, Melvin E., Pfc,
Wierczbowski, Chester J., Pvt,
Wierschem, Joseph F., S/Sgt,
†Wiese, Hans, Pvt,
‡Wiese, Rockley F., Pvt,
Wieyel, William J., Cpl,
‡Wiggington, Vincent, Pvt,
Wiggins, Cecil W., T/Sgt,
Wiggins, Kowell O., Pfc,
Wiggins, Lee E., T/5,
Wigington, Claud L., Pfc,
Wigington, Letcher, Jr., Capt,
Wikson, Jess, Pfc,
*Wik, Thomas J., Pvt,
Wiland, George C., Sgt,
Wilbanks, Cletis A., Pvt,
Wilbanks, Curtis C., Pvt,
Wilbur, Albert A., Pvt,
Wilbur, Jerome E., Pvt,
Wilcox, Edward F., 2nd Lt,
Wilcox, Edward J., Pfc,
†Wilcox, Stanton, Pvt,
Wilcoxon, William J., Pvt,
†Wilczek, John, Pfc,
Wild, Stanley D., Pfc,
†Wilder, George M., Pfc,
Wilder, Woodrow W., Sgt,
‡Wiles, Charles J., Pfc,
‡Wiley, Donald B., Pfc,
*Wiley, Hugh T., Pvt,
Wiley, James O., Pfc,
Wilhelm, Gail E., Pvt,
Wilhelm, George J., Cpl,
Wilhoit, Edgar H., Pvt,
Wilke, LeRoy W., Pvt,
†Wilkes, Harrison W., Pvt,
†Wilkey, James H., Pvt,
Wilkins, Lawrence W., Pvt,
Wilkins, Floyd H., Pvt,
Wilkinson, Robert A., Pfc,
Wilkinson, Thomas C., 2nd Lt,
†Wilkinson, William H., Sgt,
Wilkinson, Woodrow W., Pvt,
Willaford, Irvin, Pvt,
†Willard, Charles H., Pfc,
Wille, Byron J., Sgt,
Willeford, Lloyd E., Sgt,
†Willem, Donald W., Pvt,
Willems, John T., T/5,
†Willenbaker, Robert G., Pvt,
Willey, George O., Pfc,
Wilks, Albert H., Pvt,
Wilkosz, Theodore F., Pfc,
Willey, Duane, E., S/Sgt,
William, Marvin E., Pvt,
Williams, Alfred, Pfc,
Williams, Alonzo H., Pfc,
Williams, Bennie F., Pfc,
Williams, Billy R., Pfc,
Williams, Burl, T/Sgt,
Wiliams, Calvin, Pvt,
Williams, Carl H., Pfc,
Williams, Charles H., Pvt,
Williams, Charles S., Capt,
Williams, Charles, Pvt,
Williams, Charleston C., Pvt,
Williams, Clarence, Pvt,
†Williams, Clifford L., Pvt
Williams, Clifford S., Pvt,
Williams, Clyde R., Pvt
Williams, Colie W., Pfc,
§Williams, Curtis L., Pvt,
Williams, Derrel R., Jr., Pvt,
†Williams, Donald, Pvt,
Williams, Donald R., Pvt,
Williams, Earl J., Pvt,
Williams, Earl R., S/Sgt,
Williams, Elwood, Pvt,
Williams, Foister, Pfc,
‡Williams, Fred D., Pvt,
Williams, George M., Pvt,
Williams, Glenn F., S/Sgt,
Williams, Grover, Pfc,
Williams, Grover C., Sgt,
Williams, Guy E., Pvt,
Williams, Harold, Pfc,
‡Williams, Harold R., Pvt,
†Williams, Harry, Pvt,
‡Williams, Harry D., Pfc,
Williams, Irving B., 1st Lt
Williams, James D., Pfc,
Williams, James F., Pfc,
Williams, James F., Pfc,
†Williams, James H., Pvt,
Williams, Joe W., Pvt,
Williams, John G., Pfc,
Williams, John H., Pfc,
Williams, John L., Pvt,
Williams, John R., Pvt,
Williams, John W., Pvt,
Williams, Joseph C., Cpl,
Williams, Julius E., Pfc,
Williams, Kenneth L., Pfc,
Williams, Leon B., Pvt,
Williams, Leonard F., Pfc,
Williams, Leroy R., Pvt,
†Williams, Mervin R., Pvt,
Williams, Metton F., Pvt,
Williams, Milton O., Sgt,
Williams, Norval R., Pvt,
Williams, O. N., Pfc,
Williams, Orlo, Pfc,
Williams, Pat, Pvt,
§Williams, Philip J., Pfc,
†Williams, Ray P., Cpl,
Williams, R. L., S/Sgt,
Williams, Robert, Pvt,
§Williams, Robert B., Sgt,
†Williams, Robert D., Pvt,
Williams, Robert M., Pvt,
Williams, Robert O., Pfc,
†Williams, Robert P., Pvt,
Williams, Robert V., Pfc,
Williams, Robert W., Pvt,
Williams, Roland F., Pvt,
†Williams, Rual H., Cpl,
Williams, Sam G., Pfc,
Williams, Sylvester B., Pvt,
Williams, Tharmon L., S/Sgt,
Williams, Thomas L., S/Sgt,
Williams, Thomas S., Pfc,
§Williams, Valdon, Pvt,
*Williams, Vern L., Pvt,
Williams, Warren B., S/Sgt,
Williams, Wilbert F., S/Sgt,
Williams, William J., Pfc,
Williams, William W., Pvt,
Williams, Winston W., T/5,
†Williamson, Ben, Pvt,
Williamson, Elwin E., Pfc,
§Williamson, Eugene, Pfc,
Williamson, Lewis C., Pvt,
†Williamson, Louis W., Sgt,
Williamson, Paul A., Cpl,
†Williamson, Paul G., Pvt,
†Williamson, William H., Pvt,
Willis, Cecil W., Pfc,
Willis, Charles C., Pvt,
Willis, Robert C., Jr., Pvt,
†Willis Earl T., Pvt,
*Willis, Louis G., Pvt,
Willis, Robert E., Pvt,
Willis, Robert W., Pfc,
Willis, Vernon, Pvt,
Willis, William R., Pvt
Willis, Wayne C., Pvt,
Willmore, Pyford C., Pvt,
Willmore, Maurice G., Pvt,
Willmot, Perry T., Pvt,
Wills, Elmer H., Pfc,
Wills, Frank H., Pvt,
Willyard, Shirley, Pvt,
Wilmot, George W., Pvt,
Wilmoth, Leo H., Pvt,
Wilson, Albert G., Pfc,
§Wilson, Alert R., Pfc,
Wilson, Allen A., Jr., Pfc,
Wilson, Avery W., Pvt,
Wilson, Charles W., S/Sgt,
Wilson, Cola, Pvt,
Wilson, Daniel E., 1st Sgt,
Wilson, Earl S., Pvt,
Wilson, Edward F., Cpl,
Wilson, Edward W., Pvt,
Wilson, Evan K., Pvt,
Wilson, Felix W., Pvt,
Wilson, Francis C., Pfc,
†Wilson, George F., Pvt,
Wilson, George L., Pvt,
Wilson, Glen W., Capt,
Wilson, Glenn, Pvt,
Wilson, Henry O., Jr., Pfc,
Wilson, Herman W., Pvt,
Wilson, Howard A., Pfc,
Wilson, Howard F., Pvt,
Wilson, Hueston L., T/4,
Wilson, Hyman, Sgt,
Wilson, Ira E., 2nd Lt,
Wilson, James W., Pfc,
Wilson, John G., Pvt,
Wilson, John G., Pvt,
Wilson, John G., Pvt,
†Wilson, John W., Sr., Pvt,
Wilson, Joseph F., S/Sgt,
Wilson, Joseph H., Pvt,
‡Wilson, Kenneth R., Pfc,
Wilson, Loraine S., Cpl,
Wilson, Moel A., 1st Lt,
Wilson, Orie A., Pvt,
‡Wilson, Oscar D., Sgt,
Wilson, Quentin B., Pfc,
Wilson, Richard J., Pvt,
Wilson, Robert L., Pvt,
‡Wilson, Sidney H., S/Sgt,
Wilson, Wade W., S/Sgt
Wilson, Walts M., Pvt,
Wilson, William H., 2nd Lt,
Wilson, William H., T/Sgt,
Wilson, William H., Pvt
Wilson, William L., T/5,
Wilson, Woodrow W., Pvt,
Wiltsie, Floyd H., Pvt,
†Wilusz, Edward J., Pvt,
Wimmer, Ray E., S/Sgt,
Winchester, Samuel G., Pvt,
†Winchester, Edward M., Pfc,
Wind, William P., Pfc,
Windal, Donald O., Cpl,
Winder, William D., Pvt,
Windholz, Edgar, Pfc,
Windle, John P., Sgt,
Winecoff, Huber D., Pfc,
Winegar, Charles A., Pfc,
Winer, Sidney J., Pvt,
Winfrey, George M., Pfc,
Wing, Martin A., Pvt,
Wingate, Curtis L., Pfc,
Wingate, Jacob D., Pvt,
Wingert, John W., Pfc,
‡Wingfield, Bas S., Jr., Pvt,
Wingo, Elmer E., Pfc,
Winkle, Lemar J., Pvt,
Winkler, Emil, Pvt,
Winkler, Melvin J., Sgt,
Winkler, Russell E., Pvt,
Winkler, Thurston N., Pvt,
*Winner, Russell, Cpl,
†Winsten, Harry E., Pfc,
Winter, Arthur A., Pvt,
†Winter, Hyman L., Pvt,
Winters, George P., Pvt,
‡Winters, Lloyd E., Pfc,
Wirebaugh, Lloyd E., Jr., Pvt,
Wirgau, Wilmer C., Pfc,
Wirth, Frank, Pvt,
Wisdom, Joseph, S/Sgt,
Wisehard, Max H., Pvt,
Wiseley, George W., Sgt,
†Wiseman, Billy B., Pvt,
*Wiseman, William H., Pvt,
Wiseman, Willis, T/4,
Wisnieski, John S., Pvt,
Wisniewski, Athew W., Pfc,
Wist, Sulo, Pfc,
Wisurik, Leslie W., Pfc,
Witbeck, Allen B., Pfc,
Witham, Eugene B., Pvt,
Withelms, John E., T/5,
Wither, Gordon H., S/Sgt,
‡Withman, Louis W., S/Sgt,
Witinski, Joseph, Pvt
Witkosky, Herman O., Pvt,
Witkovich, Thomas J., Pvt,
Witt, Billy H., Pvt,
Witt, Carlton R., Pvt,
Witt, Robert E., Pvt,
Witter, Clinton W., Cpl,
Witz, Leslie K., Pfc
Witzel, Cecil L., Pfc,
*Wix, James E., Pvt,
Woefert, Robert W., Pvt,
Woelpern, Frederick R., S/Sgt,
Wojciak, Casimir A., Pfc,
†Wojewada, Louis, Pvt,
Wojewodka, Bernard V., Pfc,
†Wojtanowski, Walter J., Pvt,
Wokcik, Edwin S., Pvt,
Wolcott, Nelson J., Pvt,
Wolf, Elmer C., Pvt,
Wolf, James T., Pvt,
Wolf, Leroy, T/5
Wolf, Murray M., Cpl,
Wolf, Owen J., Pfc
Wolf, Vincent V., Pvt,
†Wolf, William J., Pvt,
Wolfe, Beacher, T/Sgt,
Wolfe, Charles A., 2nd Lt,
Wolfe, Earnest W., Pvt,
Wolfe, Edward M., Pvt,
Wolfe, Howard D., Pfc,
*Wolfe, John H., Pvt,
Wolfe, Lester E., Pvt,
Wolfe, Regis E., Pfc,
Wolfe, Roland E., Sgt,
Wolfkill, Albert C., Pvt,
Wolford, Richard E., Pvt,
Wolinsky, Steve, Pfc,
†Wolka, Alfred G., Sgt,
Wollaber, Clyde G., Pvt,
Wollyung, William J., Pvt,
Wolovlek, John, Jr., Pfc,
Wolpers, John A., 1st Lt,
Wolski, Floyd S., Pfc,
Wolski, Raymond S., Pvt,
Wolverton, Harry A., Pvt,
Womack, Dewitt, Pvt,
Wondrack, Andrew R., Pvt,
Wong, John L., T/4,
Wood, Brennan C.,1st Lt,
Wood, Charles V., Pfc,
Wood, Clarence W., Pfc,
Wood, David F., Pvt,
†Wood, Elbert G., Jr., Pfc,
Wood, Elmer W., S/Sgt,
Wood, George C., Pvt,
Wood, George T., Jr., Pvt,
Wood, Hal B., Pfc,
Wood, Hiley D., Sgt,
Wood, Huey E., Sgt,
Wood, Hulet D., Sgt,
§Wood, Irial E., Pfc,
Wood, Irving A., Pfc,
Wood, James A., Pfc,
Wood, James R., Pvt,
Wood, J. C., Pvt,
Wood, Jedd O., 2nd Lt,
Wood, John W., S/Sgt,
Wood, Kenneth M., Pvt,
Wood, Kenneth P., Pvt,
‡Wood, Lewis E., Pvt,
Wood, Mark H., Cpl,
Wood, Paul K., T/4,
Wood, Percy M., Pvt,
Wood, Thomas N., Pvt,
‡Wood, Walter T., Jr., Pfc,
Wood, Wayne E., Pfc
Woodard, Ambrose A., Pvt,
Woodard, Creighton H., Pfc,
‡Woodard, Edward W., Pfc,
Woodard, Tommie L., Pfc,
Woodard, Vern C., Pvt,
Woodbury, James A., Pfc,
Wooden, F. A., Pfc,
Woodfore, James R., Jr., Pvt,
†Woodruff, Carson A., Pvt,
Woods, Charles C., Pvt
Woods, Jack R., T/5,
Woods, Kelly O., T/5,

† Killed in Action. * Prisoner of War. ‡ Missing in Action. § Died of Wounds.

Woods, Richard S., Pfc,
Woods, Roy E., T/5,
Woods, Thomas W., Jr., Sgt,
Woods, Woodrow, Pfc,
Woodson, William C., Pfc
Woodsworth, Roy W., Pvt,
Woodsworth, Walter J., Pvt,
Woodul, Finley, Pfc,
*Woody, Rufus F., Pfc,
Woodyatt, Richard, Jr., 2nd Lt
Woolery, Danford K., S/Sgt,
Woolf, Joseph A., Pvt
Woolridge, Gerald V., Pfc,
Woolridge, Noah, Pvt,
Woolsey, Charles E., Pfc,
Woolsey, Dennis L., Sgt,
Wooten, Clyde G., Sgt,
Wooten, Homer P., Jr., Pvt,
Wooten, Joe F., Pvt,
Worden, Fred A., Pvt,
Workman, William C., Pvt,
Worley, James H., Sgt,
Worstman, Sam, Pvt,
Wotherspoon, S. G., T/Sgt,
Worthington, Ralph B., Pvt,
*Worthy, Thomas E., Pvt,
Wozniak, Chester J., Pfc,
Woznicki, Lawrence, Pvt,
Wray, Vergil E., Pfc,
Wray, William G., Pvt,
Wren, James L., Pvt,
†Wrensch, Lawrence S., Pvt,
Wright, Arthur A., Sgt,
Wright, Arthur W., Pvt,
Wright, Calvin D., Pvt,

‡Wright, Calvin D., Pvt,
Wright, Calvin F., Pfc,
†Wright, Carlton O., Pvt,
Wright, Chester O., T/Sgt,
Wright, Clarence D., M/Sgt,
Wright, Claude A., Sgt,
Wright, Donald, Pfc,
*Wright, Donald E., Pfc,
Wright, Edward E., Pfc,
Wright, Elam W., Jr., 1st Lt,
Wright, Eugene D., Pvt,
Wright, Eugene N., Pfc,
Wright, George F., Pvt,
‡Wright, Guy G., Pfc,
†Wright, Harold C., Pfc,
†Wright, Henry E., Pfc,
Wright, Herman L., Pfc
Wright, James H., Pfc,
Wright, Joe B., Pvt,
Wright, Joe, Pvt
†Wright, John H., Cpl,
Wright, Joseph E., Pvt,
Wright, Lee, Pvt,
Wright, Max O., Pvt,
Wright, Robert F., T/Sgt,
Wright, Thomas L., Pvt,
Wright, Thomas M., T/Sgt,
Wright, Thomas W., Pfc,
Wright, Walter L., 1st Lt,
Wright, Will B., Pvt,
†Writer, John M., Pvt,
Wuis, Thomas R., WOJG,
‡Wulfeck, Walter R., Jr., Pfc,
Wunder, Robert J., Pfc,
Wurscher, Vernon E., T/5,

Wurth, Edward M., Pvt,
Wyant, Daniel, Pvt,
Wyatt, Carl R., 1st Lt,
Wyatt, Earl, Pfc,
Wyatt, Elisha D., Pfc,
†Wyehrauch, Arthur J., Pvt,
Wyllie, Robert H., Pvt,
Wypijewski, Matt R., T/5,
Wyrick, Robert E., Pvt,
Wyrick, Samuel E., Pvt,
Wysocarski, Stanley M., Pvt,
Wysoglad, Vincent J., Pfc
Wyss, Maurice, 1st Lt,

Xiques, George M., Pvt

†Yablonski, Alexander, Pfc,
Yaciuk, Nick, Pvt,
Yager, Harold D., Pfc,
Yandall, David R., 2nd Lt,
Yannerilla, Martin R., Pfc,
Yanni, Alfred P., Jr., Pvt,
Yannitelli, Frank J., Pfc,
Yanofsky, Seymour, Pfc,
Yantis, Roy N., Pvt,
Yarbrough, Raymond H., Pvt,
Yarnall, George W., Pvt,
Yaro, Tony, Pfc,
†Yarusinsky, Edward J., Cpl,
Yates, Elmer G., Pfc,
Yates, Ernest, Sgt,
Yates, Garland P., Pvt,
Yates, Howard M., Pfc,
†Yates, Thomas R., Pvt,
Yates, Jack F., T/5,

Yates, William J., T/3
Yavornicki, Gregory, Pfc,
Yavorsky, Fred C., Pvt,
Yaworski, Joseph, Pfc,
Yazzie, Shorty, Pvt,
Ybarra, Mike M., Pvt,
Yeates, Merlin D., Pfc,
Yeatts, Claude A., Pfc,
Yeckley, John E., Pvt,
Yenglin, Merle L., Pfc,
‡Yerusavage, Joseph M., Cpl,
†Yerxa, Renfrew A., 2nd Lt,
Yochum, Earl C., Pfc,
Yocum, Marvin P., Pvt,
Yodis, Albin M., Pfc,
Yodis, Joseph V., Pvt,
Yoh, Jonathan A., Pvt,
Yokley, Andrew J., Pvt,
Yoncuskey, John H., Pfc,
Yoo, Louis J., Pfc,
§York, James W., Pvt,
†York, Joe, Sgt,
York, Leon E., Cpl,
York, Thomas L., Cpl,
York, Tommy W., Pfc,
Yorke, John, Jr., Cpl,
Yosay, John, Pvt,
Yossett, Charles G., Pfc,
Yost, Thernom, Pvt,
Youd, Wayne C., Pfc,
*Young, Albert A., Pvt,
Young, Charles R., Sgt,
†Young, Earl R., 1st Sgt,
Young, Edward R., Pvt,

*Young, E. B., Pvt,
Young, Frederick W., Pfc,
Young, George D., Pfc,
Young, Grady L., Cpl,
Young, Herbert, Pvt,
Young, Jack, 1st Lt,
Young, James E., Cpl,
Young, James L., Pvt,
Young, Leonard, S/Sgt,
Young, Melvin C., 1st Lt,
Young, Oscar E., S/Sgt,
Young, Ray, Capt,
†Young, Richard C., Pvt,
Young, Robert G., Pfc,
Young, Robert L., Pvt,
Young, Robert L., Pvt,
Young, Thomas E., Pvt,
†Young, Thomas L., Pvt,
Young, Walter H., S/Sgt,
Young, Walter L., Pfc,
†Young, Warren K., Sgt,
Young, William M., Pfc,
Young, Willie L., Sgt,
†Younger, Clarence, Pfc,
‡Youngman, Murrell F., T/Sgt,
Younkin, Glenn, S/Sgt,
Younkin, Kenneth D., Pvt,
Yourey, Michael, Pfc,
Yourison, Frank B., Sgt,
Yourkstovich, Alex E., Pvt,
Yowell, William E., S/Sgt
Yowler, Charles E., Pvt,
Yurik, Martin A., Pfc,
Yusko, John A., Cpl.

† Killed in Action. * Prisoner of War. ‡ Missing in Action. § Died of Wounds.

HEADQUARTERS AND HEADQUARTERS BATTERY
3D INFANTRY DIVISION ARTILLERY

Division Artillery, composed of four battalions—the 9th, 10th, 39th and 41st—attained a position of greatest respect and admiration with infantry of the 3d Division for its accomplishments during World War II.

Artillery and infantry were an inseparable team. Many an infantryman owes his life to the accurate, rapid answer to his request for fire. Artillery, for example, was credited with the major role in repelling the two great attacks by the Germans against 3d Infantry Division positions on the Anzio Beachhead on February 16-17 and February 29-March 3, 1944.

Artillery forward observers, consisting usually of one officer and three men with a radio, walked in the infantry team and usually were required to be present with the most advanced element of the infantry battalion to which they were attached. Their casualty figures were proportionate to those of rifle platoon leaders.

American artillery in World War II was considered by many experts, both Allied and enemy, the best in the world. The 3d Infantry Division Artillery was second to none.

Commanding General

(Highest rank held)	Held pos. from	To
Brig. Gen. William A. Campbell		22 June 1944
Brig. Gen. William T. Sexton	23 June 1944	

Executive Officer

Col. Paul C. Boylan		3 Nov 1943
Lt. Col. Kermit L. Davis	6 Nov 1943	20 June 1944
Col. Christopher C. Coyne	21 June 1944	

Abrams, Robert E., Pvt,
Adams, Morgan K., Capt,
Adams, Raymond A., Cpl,
Ansell, Dale W., Capt,
Althoetmar, August P., T/5,
Aman, Otto, T/4,
Anderson, Alex H., Jr., T/5,
Anderson, Clarence C., M/Sgt,
Anderson, Earl W., T/4,
Anderson, Lester K., M/Sgt,
Anderson, Merrill N., M/Sgt,
Anderson, Merritt W., T/5,
Anderson, Orland A., T/5,
Anderson, Richard W., Pvt,

Barnes, Cortlandt V., S/Sgt,
Barone, Roy T., T/4,
Beau, Wesley J., Jr., Pfc,
Becker, John W., 1st Lt,
Berg, Charles L., Pvt,
Berg, Harold R., T/4,
Berys, Elmer, Pvt,
Blakeley, William E., 1st Sgt,
Boe, James E., S/Sgt,
Bogner, Charles, Major,
Boisvert, Herbert L., Pvt,
Bouler, Donald E., Pvt,
Bourguet, Napoleon M., Pvt,
Boylan, Paul C., Col,
Brown, James F., S/Sgt,

Bryant, Gilbert K., Pfc,
Burnett, Thomas E., Pvt,

Campbell, William A., Brig Gen
Cassella, William H., S/Sgt,
Chancellor, William H., Pvt,
Chase, Kenneth W., Pfc,
Chellis, Ellwood C., Pvt,
Chin, Hing Y., Pvt,
Ciolina, Louis C., 1st Lt,
†Clark, Archie V., T/5,
Clark, Fred B., T/5,
†Clark, Richard J., Capt,
Claussen, Glenn M., Pfc,
Clifford, Frederick C., Cpl,
Cobb, Francis W., T/5,
Cobb, Leonard G., S/Sgt,
Comstock, Harold A., Pvt,
Cooperman, Fred W., Pvt,
Cornelius, Leonard P., T/4,
Corporon, Jack F., T/4,
Coyle, Bernard R., Pvt,
Coyne, Christopher C., Col,
Cross, Luther A., Pfc,
Custer, George W., T/3,
Cunningham, Louis E., Pvt,

Dahnieu, Edwin C., Pvt,
Daires, John N., Pvt,
Davis, Audubon R., Cpl,

Davis, Kermit L., Lt Col,
Davis, Paul O., T/4,
Daniels, Arthur J., Jr., Pvt,
DeMartini, Loring A., Capt,
De Munbrun, Roland R., T/4,
Devlin, Raymond J., Cpl,
Dillenbeck, John F., Pvt,
Dunne, Frank A., Jr., Pfc,
Dupee, Sam, Pvt,
Dziura, Joseph F., 1st Lt,

Edkins, John J., T/5,
Egan, Joseph F., T/5,
Ellis, Calvin C., Maj,
Ellis, Victor C., S/Sgt,
Elmore, Robert R., 1st Sgt,
English, Glenn R., Pvt,

Fargusson, Ralph M., S/Sgt,
Ferguson, Kenneth H., Pvt,
Finch, Harold K., Pvt,
Flowers, Russell F., Jr., T/5,
Foley, Ronan, Capt,
Fuhrer, John, Pfc,

Gaitan, Manuel, Pvt,
Galer, Stanley R., Pvt,
Garver, David H., 1st Lt,
Geist, Glenn W., T/5,
Georgelas, John G., Maj,

Gjestreen, Benny N., T/5,
Goldberg, Harry, Pvt,
Gorelet, Robert R., T/5,
Grammont, Willard C., S/Sgt,
Grant, Davis B., Capt,
Graves, Donald P., Pvt,
Green, Max, Pfc,
Gribinas, John, T/5,
Griswold, Claude G., Pvt,
Griswold, James W., S/Sgt,
Guinn, Theodore J., T/5,
Gusk, Douglas J., T/4,
Guzek, Frank J., Cpl,

Haag, Arthur W., Pfc,
Hamilton, Jean A., 1st Sgt,
Hamilton, Robert B., Cpl,
Hannay, Robert D., Cpl,
Harbin, Perry K., Pvt,
Hargrave, Virgil H., Pvt,
Harrison, Glenn, Jr., T/5,
Harrison, Merrill S., Pfc,
Hartman, John H., Pvt,
Heizer, Carl R., Pvt,
Helgeson, Orrin C., Pfc,
Hellsteu, Bernard R., Pvt,
Henderson, Marvin J., CWO,
Herdeck, Rudolph, T/4,
Hetrick, Harry L., T/4,
Hines, Charles F., Pfc,

Hogan, Dennis D., Capt,
Hurrle, Charles H., Pvt,
Hurysz, John C, Pfc,

Infelise, Thomas A., T/5,
Isaacson, Ronald T., T/4,

James, Robert G., T/4,
Jaque, Ellsworth P., Pfc,
Jehling, Gilbert, S/Sgt,
Jilka, Frank A., S/Sgt,
Johnson, Herbert E., T/5,
Johnson, Houston L., Pvt,
Joubert, Emilton S., S/Sgt,
Joubert, Emilton S., 2nd Lt,
Jurek, Sylvester, T/5,

Kaufman, Loren R., Cpl,
Keegan, Francis A., Pvt,
Kerwin, Walter T., Lt Col,
King, Dick A., Maj,
King, Wallace E., T/5,
Kitzke, Jerome F., Pfc,
Kloskowski, Adam, Pvt,
Koenig, William P., Pfc,
Kreutz, Fred W., T/5,
Krohn, Fred W., S/Sgt,
Kucks, Anthony S., Pfc,

Lacey, Victor E., M/Sgt,

† Killed in Action. * Prisoner of War. ‡ Missing in Action. § Died of Wounds.

†Lang, Leslie S., S/Sgt,
Large, William E., Cpl,
Latella, Dominick V., Pvt,
Lawrence, Hazen G., T/4,
LeBlanc, Charles L., T/4,
LeDue, Louis V., Jr., T/4,
Lee, George C., T/5,
Leseman, Jack F., T/4,
Lewis, Glenn L., Pvt,
Ley, Robert P., T/5,
Lindgren, Leslie J., T/4,
Lonigro, Jack J., Pfc,
Ludgate, John W., Pfc,
Lusby, Orville L., Pfc,
Lusby, William D., Pfc,

Machristie, Stanley, Pfc,
Mack, Edward B., 1st Lt,
Mandell, Phillip L., T/5,
Mann, Leonard L., T/5,
Marut, Michael, Pvt,
McDowell, Harvey E., T/5,
McElroy, John I., Pvt,
McIlvain, Mose, Pfc,
McIntyre, William C., Maj,
McIsaac, Frank A., Pvt,
McMordie, William A., Pfc,
McStravick, Walter, Sgt,
Mednia, Peter P., Pfc,
Meeks, Willie W., Pfc,
Miller, Charles N., Pfc,
Mitchell, Ralph D., Pfc,

Mitchell, Stephen W., T/5,
Mollison, John C., Pfc,
Monti, Joseph, Pvt,
Morrow, Vincent I., T/4,
Mull, William J., T/5,
Myers, Harlan A., T/5,

Nardi, William A., Cpl,
Nattinger, Kerlin E., Pvt,
Newberry, Chester E., Pvt,
Newman, Charley W., Pfc,
Newman, Earl L., Pvt,
Nielsen, Hans, Pvt,
Nordstrom, Edward C., S/Sgt,

O'Hara, John F., T/5,
Olson, Chester L., Pvt,
Omundson, Vern G., T/5,
Oppenheimer, John S., 1st Lt,
Oringer, Max, Pfc,
Osborn, George G., Cpl,
Osipowicz, William S., Pvt,
Oswald, Raymond C., Capt,
Oudemolen, Herman, Pvt,

Parkinson, Peter A., CWO,
Paluer, Thomas W., Pvt,
Payette, Francis B., Pvt,
Pelon, Virgil F., Sgt,
Perkins, William J., Pvt,
Perry, Robert H., T/5,
Peterson, James M., Pfc,

†Phillips, Kenneth H., Pfc,
Pirrone, John B., T/4,
Pinkard, Calvin M., Capt,
Pribble, Harry M., Sgt,
Procanin, Theodore J., Sgt,

Quinlivan, George, Capt,

Reichow, Howard R., 1st Lt,
Reis, Warren T., 2nd Lt,
Reppert, Jack, T/5,
Richeson, Eugene, Cpl,
Richmond, Gordon R., Cpl,
Rigney, Lester V., Pvt,
Riley, Cleo J., Pfc,
Robbins, Ray, Pfc,
Robinson, Gordon R., T/5,
Roderer, Robert G., Pvt,
Romeo, Vincent J., T/4,
Rose, Frank R., Pvt,
Rosensteel, David R., T/5,
Rosner, Erwin, 1st Lt,
Russell, Claude, T/5,
Royston, Theodore J., T/Sgt,

Sack, Richard F., T/Sgt,
Sampson, Jack, Pfc,
Samuels, Everett, Pfc,
San Filippo, Sam, Pvt,
Santomero, Anthony T., Pfc,
Scheer, Chester A., Pfc,

Scheppler, Clifford K., S/Sgt,
Schnettler, Alton E., T/Sgt,
Schuldt, John C., Pfc,
Schultz, Alfred W., Capt,
Scordino, Paul A., 1st Lt,
Sebion, Raymond A., Pfc,
Sevits, Kenneth R., T/5,
Sexton, William T., Brig Gen,
Sharp, William D., T/4,
Sheppard, Byron E., S/Sgt,
Shiering, Harry C., Sgt,
Smith, Ralph J., Major,
Smith, William W., Pvt,
Snider, John, T/4,
Snitchler, John M., Jr., S/Sgt,
Snow, George L., II, Capt,
Sogue, Pedro A., T/4,
Sopp, John, T/Sgt,
Spreyer, Frederick C., 1st Lt,
Stamler, Maurice, Major,
Stefanski, Frank J., T/5,
Stevens, Frank A., T/4,
Stevens, James A., Jr., Pvt,
Stevens, James D., Cpl,
Strand, Donald A., T/4,
Surratt, Joe F., Lt Col,
Swope, Howard L., Pvt,

Tanner, Norman C., Major,
Teisberg, Robert C., Pfc,
Termer, William, T/Sgt,

†Tilghman, Merrill L., 1st Lt,
Tong, Fat, Pfc,

Vaughn, Albe L., T/5,
Volpicella, Leonardo, T/5,

Wagenhofer, Anthony S., T/5,
Walker, Eugene P., T/5,
Wamsley, Harry A., Pfc,
Ward, Earl, T/5,
Weaver, Kenneth G., T/3,
Weise, Harold H., T/5,
Weisiger, William B., 2nd Lt,
Weller, Wenner W., T/5,
Wencus, Bert J., T/5,
Wendt, James R., Jr., Lt Col,
Wentworth, Jack, 2nd Lt,
Wentworth, Paul J., T/Sgt,
Westover, Martin W., T/5,
Whitaker, James B., Cpl,
White, Joseph F., 1st Lt,
Whitelock, Kenly W., Capt,
Wielgus, Edwin J., Sgt,
Wilbanks, Scurlock W., T/5,
Wilson, Charles E., T/5,
Woltring, Rex O., T/4,
Woodbury, Clyde D., Jr., T/5,
Wynn, Clarence L., T/5,

Youngquist, Fredolph W., Pfc,

Zobrist, Ernest E., Pvt.

† Killed in Action.   * Prisoner of War.   ‡ Missing in Action.   § Died of Wounds.

9TH FIELD ARTILLERY BATTALION (MEDIUM)

The 9th Field Artillery Regiment—now a battalion—was organized at Schofield Barracks, Oahu, T.H., in 1916. It bore the double distinction of being the first completely motorized field artillery regiment in the world, and the only regiment of field artillery ever to be organized overseas.

Commanding Officer

(Highest rank held)	Held pos. from	To
Lt. Col. Christopher C. Coyne		20 June 1944
Lt. Col. Wendell J. Coates	31 June 1944	19 July 1944
Lt. Col. Karl Conner	20 July 1944	22 Mar 1945
Maj. Beryl L. Boyce	23 Mar 1945	

Adamek, Walter R., Pvt,
Adams, J. T., Pfc,
Adams, John D., Cpl,
Adams, Lewis E., Pfc,
Addy, Walter M., Pfc,
Ahlstrom, Allen P., S/Sgt,
Albro, Robert W., T/5,
Alcorn, Thomas R., Jr., Sgt,
Alger, John W., Pvt,
Allchin, Floyd E., Pfc,
Allecher, Arthur, Pfc,
Allen, James B., Jr., Sgt,
Allen, John W., Pfc,
Alm, Theodore A., T/4,
Alveraz, Louis A., T/5,
Anderson, Arnold L., Cpl,
Anderson, Corbett B., Pvt,
Anderson, Gerald K., T/5,
Anderson, Harold K., 1st Sgt,
Anderson, James E., T/5,
Anderson, Vernon A., 1st Lt,
Anderson, Vincent M., Cpl,
Andrews, Gordon L., Pvt,
Andrews, Lawrence E., Pfc,
Ansell, Dale W., Capt,
Anthony, Robert E., Pvt,
Apecelli, Frank A., Cpl,
Argeras, Harry P., Pvt,
Armbrust, Martin J., Jr., T/5,
Armijo, Alberto, Pvt,
Arthur, Woodrow W., Cpl,
Ashmun, Garland R., Pfc,
Aumock, Earl B., Cpl,
Austin, John H., Pfc,
Axtell, James S., T/4,
Azevedo, Tony L., T/4,

Babcock, Russell A., Pvt,
Backiel, John, Pvt,
Bailey, Charles A., Sgt,
Bailey, Reid S., T/4,
Baker, Allen K., T/5,
Baker, Howard J., Pfc,
Baldwin, Robert A., T/4,
Ball, Orville, Pvt,
Balser, William, Pvt,
Bancroft, Ardell, T/5,
Barco, Ernest T., Jr., Capt,
Barioni, Qurrino P., Pfc,
Barnes, Donald L., Sgt,
Barnes, Edwin O., Cpl,
Barnes, George F., Pfc,
Barry, Henry J., Pfc,
Battease, Homer E., Pfc,
Battle, Marion S., Jr., Pvt,
Beal, Ivan W., T/4,
Beard, Charles C., Cpl,

Beasley, Homer E., Pfc,
Beauford, Harry J., Jr., Cpl,
Decker, Oswald, Pfc,
Bell, Robert E., Pvt,
Belsey, Bernard G., Pfc,
†Benbo, Harvey E., T/4,
Bender, Robert R., Pfc,
Benoit, Harvey L., T/4,
Benson, Martin E., Pfc,
Bentley, John H., T/5,
Berdahl, Benny O., Pvt,
Berger, Leonard A., Pvt,
Berju, Gunther J., Pvt,
Berkawitz, Solomon I., Pvt,
Bernhardt, Chester W., Pvt,
Betts, John, Pvt,
Betzer, Clifford R., Cpl,
Bickar, Francics J., Pvt
Billiet, Leslie P., T/5,
Billman, Paul W., S/Sgt,
Binstock, Ernest W., Cpl,
Bird, Paul H., Pfc,
Birgin, Lowell B., S/Sgt,
Birt, Harvey C., Pvt,
Bisacquino, Benny M., Cpl,
Bishop, James A., Pfc,
Bishop, James W., Pfc,
Blair, Douglas W., Pvt,
Blais, Donald R., T/4,
Blake, Ray, S/Sgt,
Blanchette, Ralph F., Pfc,
Bleitner, Francis K., Pvt,
Boerner, Robert E., Pvt,
Boling, Thomas, Pvt,
Bond, Chester E., Pfc,
Bonigut, Martin G., Pfc,
†Boone, Hubert A., 1st Lt,
Bork, Harold K., Pfc,
Borowski, Felix S., Pfc,
Borson, Oscar, T/4,
Boskovich, Steven M., Sgt,
Bost, John W., Jr., Sgt,
Bottoms, Cyril E., Pfc,
Bowman, Roy J., Pfc,
Boyce, Beryl L., Major,
†Boyer, Francis A., 2nd Lt,
Brackey, Helmer O., Cpl,
Bradshaw, James J., T/5,
Brazell, Roy E., Cpl,
Breaux, Oscar C., Pvt,
Brenner, Stephen A., Pfc,
Brewer, Ira V., S/Sgt,
Brice, Paul O., Cpl,
Bristow, Ivan P., S/Sgt,
Broske, Richard H., Pfc,
Brough, Ferris T., Pvt,
Brown, Clifford C., Sgt,
Brown, Isaac W., S/Sgt,

Brown, James F., S/Sgt,
Brown, Jessie C., Cpl,
Brown, Norton L., Pvt,
Brown, Robert J., Pvt,
Brown, Rubin, Pvt,
Brown, Walter H., Pfc,
Bruce Robert J., Pvt,
Bruno, Frank P., Sgt,
Bryson, Grant L., Pvt,
Buber, Donald J., Pvt,
Buchanan, Walter T., Pfc,
Buchbinder, Edwin W., Pfc,
Bucholt, Joseph L., 1st Lt,
Buck, Warren W., Pvt,
Buckley, Joseph M., Cpl,
Budreau, Harold L., T/4,
Bugher, Myron H., Cpl,
Bukowski, Donald J., S/Sgt,
Buller, Daniel W., Pfc,
Burchell, James, Sgt,
Burich, Johnny, Pfc,
Burke, John L., S/Sgt,
Burkell, James S., Pvt
Burns, Clifford C., Pvt,
Bussey, Godfrey C., Cpl,
Buzzard, Raymond A., Pvt,

Caldwell, DeWitt W., Cpl,
Caldwell, Warren L., Pfc,
Campbell, James P., Cpl,
Campos, Angelo J., T/4,
Canton, Robert W., Pvt,
Carney, James P., Cpl,
Carr, Seigle A., Pvt,
Carroll, William, Pvt,
Carter, James W., 2nd Lt
Casanova, Joseph C., S/Sgt
Cash, Daniel S., Pvt,
Cassady, Michael L., Pvt,
Cassell, William H., S/Sgt,
Castellano, Samuel, Jr., T/4,
Castle, William G., Pfc,
Cate, Austin J., Capt,
Cavalieri, Sam P., Pfc,
Cespiva, Edward, T/Sgt,
Chain, Frank D., Pfc,
Chambley, Ray T., Pvt,
Chase, Paul B., Pfc,
Chingman, Louis, Cpl,
Chives, Bernard S., Pfc,
Christensen, Victor A., Pfc,
Chupko, William, Pfc,
Cihla, Henry, T/5,
Cimaroli, Alexander C., Pfc,
Clancey, Donald L., 1st Lt,
Clark, Daniel C., Cpl,
Clark, Merwin R., Sgt,
Clark, Richard J., Pfc,
Clark, Richard J., Capt,

Clarkson, Thomas L., Pvt,
Clay, Irvin, Pvt,
Clayton, John W., Pvt,
§Clemison, William, Jr., Pvt,
Clifcorn, Earl T., Pvt,
Cline, Henry, Pvt,
Clutts, Clyde, S/Sgt,
Coleman, James E., Pfc,
Coleman, Stuart H., T/5,
Collins, John D., Sgt,
Condon, Avard L., S/Sgt,
Conerly, Fred H., T/4,
Connor, Karl, Lt Col,
Connors, Robert C., T/4,
Cooke, Harold O., Cpl,
Coombes, Alfred R., S/Sgt,
Cooper, Henry H., T/4,
Corso, George, S/Sgt,
§Cory, Robert W., Cpl,
Costas, George C., 2nd Lt,
Cox, Mont, Cpl,
Crandall, Raymond K., T/4,
Crawford, Clarence E., Pfc,
Croal, Charles R., T/3,
‡Croce, Mario, Jr., Pvt,
Crosby, Richard N., Sgt,
Croslon, Wesley T., Sgt,
Cross, Monroe, T/5,
Cross, Paul H., Pvt,
Crouch, Ervon D., Pfc,
Crump, John H., 1st Lt,
Cruse, Gilbert G., T/5,
Cubbage, Sherman R., Pfc,
†Culver, George B., Pfc,
Curran, Allen B., Pvt,
Curran, James F., Pfc,
Curtis, Vincent V., S/Sgt,
Cutler, Neal T., Pvt,
Cyrus, William F., Cpl,
Cziok, Arthur F., Cpl,

Dahms, Virgil H., 1st Lt,
Dana, Robert R., Pfc,
Dangora, Harry G., Cpl,
Daniel, Everette L., Pfc,
Dark, Melville L., T/4,
Daum, Walter A., Pfc,
Davenport, Thomas A., Pvt,
Davenport, Walter A., Pvt,
Davies, Alva C., Pvt,
Davies, Leonard D., S/Sgt,
Davies, William S., Pvt,
Dawson, Woodrow W., Pfc,
Day, Noble C., Jr., Pfc,
De Angelis Paul E., Pvt,
Dean, Enoch, 1st Sgt,
Deal, Robert E., Capt,
Deere, Lewis F., Pvt,
Defenbaugh, Harry, Pfc,

De Filippo, Casper W., Pfc,
Delacy, Edward M., Pvt,
Deluco, Francis M., Pvt,
DeMersseman, Donald, T/5,
DeMoine, Arthur L., Pfc,
Denham, Hubert, Pvt,
Dennis, Frank G., Pfc,
Dennis, James, Pvt,
Dennison, Arthur, S/Sgt,
Densmore, Richard J., Cpl,
Derrick, George L., Pvt,
DeSteal, Norbert T., Sgt,
Dettman, Thomas L., Pvt,
Dextrom, Albert J., Pfc,
Dickey, William A., Pvt,
Dieball, Harold E., T/5,
Diefenbach, Walter L., T/4,
Dietz, John F., Jr., Pfc,
Dinneny, Francis X., Pfc,
Dodini, Edward F., Pfc,
Doering, Charles J., Jr., Pfc,
Donato, Joseph W., Pfc,
Dorado, Alejandro, Pvt,
Downer, George G., T/5,
Doyal, Eugene P., T/4,
Drazen, Arnold G., Cpl,
Drenon, Lloyd C., Pfc,
Droz, Frank A., Sgt,
Drummond, James L., S/Sgt,
Dubin, David, Pvt,
Duco, Louis P., Pfc,
Du Frane, George F., Jr., Pvt,
Dugan, Raymond P., Pvt,
Duke, Robert J., Pvt,
Dulitus, Bronie, T/4,
Dunn, Carl R., Pvt,
Dworkowitz, Ben, Pvt,
Dziak, Theodore A., Pvt,
Dziak, Thomas F., Pvt,
Dziura, Joseph F., 1st Lt,

Eckles, Carl J., Jr., Cpl,
Ecklund, Daryl L., Pfc,
Edwards, Elwood, T/5,
Elledge, Ernest, Pvt,
Ellison, Robert B., Capt,
Emmerick, Jack P., Pvt,
Endsley, Horace S., Pfc,
Epps, Arthur G., Pvt,
Erato, Joseph F., Pfc,
Erickson, Paul, Pvt,
Erickson, Robert G., Pfc,
Essex, Arthur W., Cpl,
Espeland, Arthur M., Capt,
Evans, Thomas W., Pvt,
Evenson, Robert L., Cpl,

Fabiano, Florindo A., Pfc,
Faranda, Anthony, Pfc,

† Killed in Action.   * Prisoner of War.   ‡ Missing in Action.   § Died of Wounds.

IN WORLD WAR II 537

Farck, Edward D., T/5,
Faris, Ronald, T/5,
†Farland, Romeo L., Pfc,
Farnham, Robert H., 2nd Lt.
Fatto, Vito P., Pfc,
Fawdi, Harland E., Pvt.
Fereire, Leo J., Jr., T/5,
Ferrara, James A., Pvt,
Ferris, Gerald E., Pvt,
†Ferris, Warren J., Pvt,
Fiene, Rudolph D. C., Pfc,
Figlar, Joseph P., Pfc,
Filipski, Stanley G., Pfc,
Filtz, Clarence S., T/5,
Firestein, Norris, Pvt,
Fish, Omar R., Sgt,
Fisher, Alvin H., Pfc,
Flowers, June C., Pvt,
Fly, Benjamin G., Pvt,
Foard, Robert W., Pfc,
Folsom, Virgil C., Pfc,
Fontaine, Edward J., Pfc,
Ford, Daniel J., Pfc,
Ford, Haynes S., S/Sgt,
Forfia, Bastista, E., Sgt,
Forgue, William E., Cpl,
Forsman, Frank B., Pfc,
Fowler, Louis H., T/5,
Freeman, Herman E., Pfc,
†Freeman, Julian H., 1st Lt,
Freemore, Robert E., Pvt,
†Fritts, Frederick G., Sgt,
Frizzell, Burt J., Capt,
Fugich, John, 1st Sgt,
Fuller, William J., Cpl,
Fulmer, Dale D., 1st Lt
Furry, Howard W., Cpl,
Fusco, Domenic, Cpl,
Fuston, William H., T/5,

Gadney, George W., Cpl,
Gaines, Melvin E., Pfc,
Gaitskill, Thomas M. J., T/4,
Gallups, Henry H., Sgt,
Gamble, Frank, Pvt,
Gansz, George F., Cpl,
Gardunia, Orville C., Pvt,
Garner, Irby, Sgt,
Gardner, Kenneth L., 2nd Lt
Garrett, James W., Cpl
Garrisi, Gerome B., Pvt,
Garvey, Andrew C., Jr., Capt,
Garza, Benito, Pvt,
Gasser, James E., Sgt,
Gayron, Charles R., Pvt,
Gebhard, James E., Pfc,
Gee, James A., Pfc,
Gelderman, Carl F., Sgt,
Gentry, James S., Cpl,
Gentry, Jodie M., Pfc,
George, Norman A., Cpl,
Gettinger, Daniel W., 1st Lt,
Ghiggeri, John J., Pvt,
Giannotti, Joseph, Pfc,
Giddens, Jack, Pvt,
Gifford, Dale F., Sgt.
Gilgenbach, Harold I., Cpl,
†Gilliam, Paul J., Pfc,
Glasser, Raymond N., Cpl,
Glatin, Lawrence D., Pvt,
Glynn, Edward R., Pvt,
Gnatek, Stanley W., Sgt,
Golnick, Kenneth A., T/5,
Gonzalez, Juan, Pfc,
Gooch, Wallace V., Cpl,
Goodman, Owen F., Capt,
Goodmiller, Emil, Pvt,
Goodwin, Chester R., Pvt,
Goss, Albert, Cpl,
Graham, Charles E., Pfc,
Grant, Arnold S., Cpl,
Grant, William R., Pvt,
Grass, Joseph A., Pvt,
Graves, Walter F., Cpl,
Green, Merele R., Pfc,
Greene, Philip M., Sgt,
Greenhut, Bernard N., Pfc,
Greer, Elzie F., Pvt,
†Greer, Harold L., Pvt,
Grege, Michael, Pfc,
Greiser, Bruce E., Pvt,
Grinnell, Sidney G., Pfc,
Gross, Joseph A., Pvt,
Guhter, Vincent D., Cpl,
Gustafson, Frank O., S/Sgt,
Guthrie, Henry F., S/Sgt,

Habercorn, Lester J., T/4,
Hadle, Joseph C., Pfc,
Hadler, Robert, Pvt,
Hall, Raymond J., S/Sgt,
Hall, William L., Pvt,
Halladay, Thomas, 1st Lt,
Halperin, Dan M., Pvt
Halter, Richard O., Pfc,
Hamill, Alfred D., Pvt,
Hamilton, Franklin, Pvt,
Hammett, John W., S/Sgt,
Hanninen, Elmer E., T/5,
Hansen, Clifford C., T/4,
Hansen, Edward, T/5,
Hansen, John D., Pfc,
Hansen, Ted A., Pvt,
Hanssen, Peter F., Pfc,
Harbarger, Forest D., T/5,
Harkness, Otis W., Jr., Pfc,
Harman, Earl K., Cpl,
Hart, Walter D., S/Sgt,
Hartlove, Walter A., Pvt,
Hartman, Henry M., Cpl,
Hartsock, William B., Pvt,
Haslam, Clarence H., Jr., Pfc,
Hatch, Charles D., Pvt,
Hawk, Arthur A., Pvt,
Hawthorne, Willie M., Pfc,
Haynes, Lawrence G., Pvt,
Hazelgrove, Lee F., Pfc,
Head, Warren A., Pvt,
Healy, John W., Cpl,
Heath, Harry, Pvt,
Heath, Ralph S., Jr., Capt,
Heath, Robert J., Pvt,
Heathcoe, Edwin J., T/4,
Heck, Merrit E., Pvt
Hegberg, Paul R., Cpl,
Heikkila, Norman W., Pvt,
Hein, Frederick C., T/5,
Heiser, Raymond B., T/5,
Henderson, Aubie C., Pvt,
Henderson, John W., Sgt,
Hendricks, Harry S., Pfc,
Hendricks, Herman W., Pfc,
Hendricks, Leo O., Pfc,
Henry, John E., Pvt,
Herbert, Elmo J., Pfc,
Hernandez, Frank B., Cpl,
Hess, Raymond L., Pfc,
Heynen, Vance J., T/4,
*Hiatt, Bruce A., T/5,
Hiatt, James S., Pfc,
Hicks, Marvin P., Pvt,
Hilderbrand, James C., Pvt,
Hill, Edgar M., 1st Lt,
Hill, Sterling L., Capt,
Hill, Walter A., Jr., Pfc,
Hillman, Preston W., T/5,
Hites, Louis G., T/5,
Hoalcraft, Raymond C., Pfc,
Hodges, Wayne E., T/4,
Hodin, Joseph, Pfc,
Hoffman, Edward J., Sgt,
Hoffman, Wilford G., Cpl,
Hoffman, William N., Pvt,
Hoffmeister, Donald E., Maj,
Hogan, Woodrow W., Pfc,
Hogeland, David F., Pfc,
Holicky, John, Pvt,
Holland, Olivir G., Pvt,
Hollstein, Harry H., T/3,
Holshue, Edward, Pvt,
Holtje, Arthur M., Pvt,
Homer, Allan V., Pvt,
Homyak, Frank T., Pfc,
Hookway, Hugh E., 1st Lt,
Hopkins, Albert C., Pfc,
Hornell, Jack L., Sgt,
Horrall, Junior H., Pfc,
Hostetler, Richard L., Sgt,
Howard, George C., Pvt,
Howard, Warren H., Pfc,
Howarka, John H., Cpl,
Howarth, Olan H., Pvt
Howell, Dewey, Pfc,
Howell, Denver D., Pfc,
†Hoye, Geoffrey E., Pvt,
Hubbard, Harry S., Pfc,
Huddleston, Charles A., Pfc,
Hudson, Horace B., T/5,
Hudson, Thomas R., Pvt,
Huff, Gordon G., T/5,
Huffman, Dave E., Pvt,
Hupfer, William M., Jr., Pvt,
Hupp, Edward F., T/5,
Hyder, Mack, Pfc,

Iacovino, John S., Pvt,
Irby, Lester J., T/4,
Irvine, Dale E., Pfc,

Jaber, Edward F., Sgt.
Jablonski, Charles J., Pfc,
Jack, Roy E., T/5,
Jaco, Ora G., S/Sgt,
Jamieson, Dale W., S/Sgt,
Jankowski, William C., Pvt,
Jasinski, Felix J., Cpl,
Jaworski, Edmund L., Pvt,
Jaynen, John T., Pvt,
Jenson, Vernon, Pvt,
Jewell, Grover C., T/5,
Johansen, Thorwald L., Jr, Pfc,
Johnson, A. J., Jr., WOJG
Johnson, Burdette R., Pfc,
Johnson, Clyde W., Pfc,
Johnson, Edward W., T/5,
Johnson, Harry S., Pvt,
Johnson, Mack, Pfc,
Johnson, Novis F., Cpl,
Johnson, Paul R., 1st Lt,
Johnson, Vernon V., T/5,
Johnston, Charles J., Pfc,
Johnston, Dale B., Cpl,
Johnston, George F., Cpl,
Johnston, William P., Cpl,
Johnstone, Gerald L., Pfc,
Jolly, Woodrow W., Pfc,
Jones, Alvin J., T/5,
Jones, Irvin L., T/5,
Jones, James F., Cpl,
Jones, Leonard F., Cpl,
Jones, Melvin R., Cpl,
Jones, Samuel C., Cpl,
Jones, William H., Cpl,
Jordan, Joseph H., Pvt,
Joseph, Edward W., Pvt,
Josephson, Harold W., Pvt,

Kachler, Bernard F., Pfc,
Kaderka, Joe, Pfc,
Kahla, Charles G., Pfc,
Kane, Preston C., Jr., Pvt,
Kangeter, George I., T/5,
Kaplowitz, Benjamin B., Pvt,
Kasel, Joseph H., Cpl,
Katzman, Oscar, Pfc,
Kazda, James C., S/Sgt,
Kazmierczak, Ervin G., Pfc,
Keefe, Thomas J., T/5,
Kehoe, Erwin T., T/4,
Kehoe, Joseph S., Pfc,
Kellar, Harold W., 1st Sgt,
Kemp, William W., T/4,
†Kempf, Elmer A., Sgt,
Kendall, James G., Pvt,
Kennedy, Silas B., Jr, Pfc,
Kepler, Dale D., Pvt,
Kestory, Leonard, Pvt,
King, George E., T/5,
King, Grover W., T/4,
King, Lewis E., Pvt,
Kinsey, Kemmel, T/5,
Kirchner, Dewey R., Pvt,
Kirk, Edward T., Pfc,
Kirkland, Edwin E., Cpl,
Kiser, Ollie L., T/5,
Klein, George P., Jr., Pfc,
Klein, Robert E., S/Sgt,
Kleinemas, George J., Cpl,
†Klipfel, Myles H., S/Sgt,
Knapp, Calvin A., Pvt,
Kneissel, Edward M., T/Sgt,
Knepper, Arnold W., T/5,
Kniefel, Harvey J., T/5,
Knutson, Elmer, Pvt,
Knutson, George R., Pvt,
Koetting, Ernest M., T/4,
Korber, John F., Cpl,
Kostikos, John Z., Pfc,
Kovacic, Joseph E., Pvt,
Kovar, Joe C., Pfc,
Kowalczyk, Walter E., Pfc,
Kozari, Steve, Jr., Pfc,
Kozlek, John W., Pfc,
Kozlowski, Chester R., Cpl,
Kraus, John C., Jr, Capt,
Krar, John F., T/5,
Kratzke, Edward C., T/5,
Krebbs, George E., Pvt,
Kresbach, Henry J., Pfc,
Krey, Henry J., T/5,
Kriechbaum, Dale E., Pvt,
Krusyga, Floyd J., Sgt,
Kull, Karl F., Pfc,
Kunde, Robert P., Pfc,
Kunz, Melvin C., Pvt,

Laisure, Doyle L., S/Sgt,
Lamb, Thomas H., Cpl,
Lampson, Harold L., Cpl,
Landson, Peter A., Pfc,
Lane, Elijah H., T/4,
Langella, Harry A., T/4,
Langenmayr, Robert, Pfc,
Langworthy, Robert, Pvt,
Lanning, Virgil E., T/4,
Larson, Carl W., Cpl,
Larson, Leroy W., Cpl,
Larson, Sterling E., Capt,
Lathrop, William H., Pfc,
Lauria, Joseph A., Pfc,
Lawrence, John E., Pfc,
Lawson, James, Pfc,
Lay, Elmo L., T/5,
Leach, John T., Pvt,
Leathem, James T., Pfc,
Lee, Hilton W., Pfc,
Lefler, Milton R., Pvt,
Lemacher, Charles A., 1st Lt
Lemmon Thain T., Cpl,
Lenherr, Burnell W., Cpl,
Lennie, Eugene T., Pvt,
Lerche, Carl J., Pfc,
†Leverich, Edward K., Pvt,
Lewis, Junior, Pfc,
Lewis, William P., CWO,
Lewitt, Monte, Pfc,
Lidwin, Chester J., Cpl,
Lincoln, Roy L., Pvt,
Lingelback, Ray A., T/4,
Link, Wilmot J., Pvt,
Livesay, Wesley R., T/4,
Livingston, Robert B., T/4,
Lockwood, Morris G., Pvt,
Loeser, Edgar C., Pfc,
Long, Runar A., Cpl,
Longino, Bert P., Pfc,
Lovell, Edward R., Capt,
Lowdermilk, John W., Pvt,
Lulek, Frank J., Pvt,
Lumbard, Billie A., Pvt,
Lumpkin, Raymond M., Pfc,
Lumpp, Charles A., Pvt,
Lundahl, Milo, Pfc,
Lupinaccio, Francis A., Pfc,
Lybarger, Charles W., Pfc,
Lynn, Orval R., Cpl,

MacNaughton, Charles C., Pvt,
Maczowski, James C., Pfc,
Madrid, Armando G., Sgt,
Manetta, Joseph J., Pvt,
Mandrel, Harlan E., Pvt,
Markland, Gearge, Cpl,
Marochi, Greno J., Pfc,
Marsh, Charles O., 1st Sgt,
Martin, Arthur J., Pvt,
Martin, Lyle W., Sgt,
Martineau, Harvey R., T/4,
Mascali, Frank, Pvt,
Massey, Herman E., T/4,
Masurka, Elmer, Cpl,
Mathews, Jasper H., Pfc,
Matthews, John M., Cpl,
Matuszak, Alphonse J., Cpl,
Mauro, Joseph A., Pfc,
Mayerle, Jack L., Pvt,
Mayo, James W., Pvt,
Mayock, Peter P., Pfc,
†Mazurek, Harold H., Pvt,
McCallum, Donald J., Pfc,
McClanahan, Maurice W., T/5,
McClelland, Charles R., Pfc,
McClung, Lonnie E., Pvt,
McCoy, Bert, Pvt,
§McCrite, William C., S/Sgt,
McCutcheon, W. T., Jr., Pfc,
McDonnell, Joseph J., Jr., Cpl,
McDowell, James C., Pfc,
McElroy, Orval J., S/Sgt,
McGinty, William P., Pvt,
McGough, Robert L., Pvt,
McGuirl, Maurice E., S/Sgt,
McHenry, Dewayne C., Sgt,
McIllice, Foster E., Pfc,
McInerney, Henry B., 1st Lt,
McKay, Ed., Pfc,
McKee, Delbert R., S/Sgt,
McKinley, Thomas E., Pvt,
McKinney, Marion D., Pfc,
McKray, Robert H., S/Sgt,
McLean, Glenn W., Pfc,
McMahan, Alfred, Pvt,
McMillan, Vincent R., Pfc,
McNutt, John T., S/Sgt,
Meglich, John F., Pfc,
Mein, Wilmar B., Sgt,
Mejak, Edward, Pvt,
Melby, Arnold O., S/Sgt,
Melchert, John W., Pvt,
Mellady, Joseph A., Cpl,
Menczywor, John J., T/5,
Menetti, Samuel N. Pfc,
Menker, Bernard H., Sgt,
Mercurio, Salvatore, Pfc,
Meschino, Michael A., S/Sgt,
Meyer, Walter W., Pvt,
Meyerick, Grant T., T/5,
Michael, Monroe H., Pfc,
Michels, Robert J., T/4,
Michelson, Daryle E., Sgt,
Michener, Edwin C., S/Sgt,
Mickelson, Richard A., T/5,
Mickevich, Edmund R., Cpl,
Mickley, Theodore J., Pvt,
Mikacevich, Jerry J., T/4,
Mikos, Theodore W., Pfc,
Milburn, George W., Pvt,
Miles, Earnest, Pvt,
Miller, Arthur F., Cpl,
Miller, Howard C., Pvt,
Minges, Arthur H., Pfc,
Minoletti, Stephen L., T/5,
Minton, Martin T., Pvt,
*Mires, Robert W., Pfc,
Minsky, Sidney A., Pvt,
Mitchell, Frank G., Sgt,
Mitchell, Frank W., Pvt,
Mitchell, William F., Pfc,
Mitchem, Deck, Pvt,
Mizger, Frank R., Pvt,
Mole, Joseph P., Pvt,
Monkmon, Bruce N., T/5,
Monson, John H., T/4,
Moore, Arthur L., Jr., Cpl,
Moore, Leonard, Pvt,
Moore, Sherman A., Pvt,
Moore, Wesley W., Pvt,
Montgomery, Jay R., Pvt,
Morales, Juan G., Pvt,
Morgan, James A., Cpl,
Morgan, James T., Cpl,
Morris, Albert F., Pvt,
Morris, Francis J., Pvt,
Morton, Charles R., Pfc,
Moss, Robert D., Cpl,
Mostachetti, Armando, Cpl,
Mountford, John W., Jr.,
Mowery, John A., 1st Lt,
Moyle, Clarence R., Cpl,
Mullen, Edward J., Pvt,
Munro, George A., Pvt,
Murray, Thomas E., Sgt,
Myers, Harold, S/Sgt,
Myrick, Charles N., Jr., Sgt,

Nasca, Michael R., Pvt,
Nash, Max H., T/4,
†Natale, Joseph J., Pvt,
Nattinger, Kerlin E., Pvt,
Nauss, James B., Pvt,
Neidlinger, Craig N., Pfc,
Neese, Wilford D., Pfc,
Nemphos, James T., Pfc,
Nerebecki, Henry, Pfc,
Neumann, Robert D., Pfc,
Newell, Richard C., Cpl,
Nolan, Jack T., Cpl,
Nollsch, Harry E., T/3,
Nord, Albert S., 1st Sgt,
Norman, Clarence A., Sgt,
Norris, Johnnie M., Pfc,
Nosko, Mike R., Pfc,
Nowak, Thomas M., Pfc,
Nunnery, Oscar J., Pfc,

Oben, Leon L., T/4,
O'Boyle, Joseph O., Pfc,
Ochs, Joseph J., Pvt,
†Odquist, Ronald E., T/5,
§Oelzen, Walde, Pfc,
Offenbach, Vincent H., Pvt,
Olinsky, John, Pfc,
Olivas, Mike A., Pvt,
Olson, Albin W., Pfc,
Olson, Clyde W., Pvt,
Olson, Morril S., Pfc,
Olson, Walter, Cpl,
Opper, Millard B., Pfc,
Oren, Milton A., Pfc,
Ott, Francis R., T/5,
Ottaviani, Armando, Pfc,
Over, Frederick T., Pvt,
Owens, Jack D., Pfc,
Owens, Thomas C., Pvt,

Padlo, Stanley T., Pfc,
Pagel, Harry, T/4,
Painter, Robert A., Pvt,
Palik, George J., Jr., Pvt,
Palmer, Charley D., Pvt,
Palmer, William H., Pvt,
Palocy, John J., Pfc,
Parke, Charles T., T/4,
Parker, Garcier, Pvt,
Parks, Bennett B., Pvt,
Parks, Thomas E., Pfc,
Parsons, Arthur J., Pfc,
Parzynski, Chester C., Cpl,
Pate, Herbert, T/5,
Patt, Louis, Pfc,
Patton, Leonard H., Pvt,
Patton, Marion L., Pfc,
Paynter, Charles A., S/Sgt,
Pearman, Allen C., Pvt,
Pearson, George T., Pfc,
Pellas, George A., Pfc,
Penson, Herbert N., Jr., Cpl,
Pepper, Gerald E., Cpl,
Peregrin, Joseph A., Pvt,
Perella, Albert A., Pvt,
Perez, Angel R., Pfc,
Perez, Richard M., Pfc,
Perlino, Ralph A., Sgt,
Perrin, John L., Pvt,
Perry, Donald F., Pvt,
Person, Hilding, Pfc,
Peters, Frederick, Pfc,
Peters, John J., 2nd Lt
Peters, Leo W., Pvt,
Peterson, Andrew J., Cpl,

† Killed in Action. * Prisoner of War. ‡ Missing in Action. § Died of Wounds.

Peterson, Edward L., T/5,
Peterson, George E., Pvt,
Peterson, Melville, Pfc,
Petterson, Palmer, T/5,
Pflanzer, Edwin J., Cpl,
Phair, Herbert R., Jr., Pvt
Phelps, Clyde L., M/Sgt,
Phillips, Carlos E., Pfc,
Phillips, John T., T/5,
Phillips, Thomas H., Pfc,
Pielin, Anthony V., Pfc,
Pierri, Jack A., Pfc,
Pierro, Joseph G., Pfc,
Pikl, Anton F., Pvt,
Pilcher, Luther L., Sgt,
Pillow, James H., Pvt,
Pitkin, Raymond B., Pvt,
Pittman, William L., Pfc,
Platt, Walter, Pvt,
§Poirier, Joseph T., T/5,
Polina, John, Pvt,
Poole, John H., Pvt,
Poole, Tim F., Sgt,
Poore, Archie D., T/5,
Porath, James J., Sgt,
Porter, Carl K., T/5,
Porter, Paul M., Pfc,
Portier, Lawrence, Pfc,
Portis, Archie R., Pvt,
Possehl, Alfred J., Pfc,
Precht, Harold L., T/5,
Price, James R., Pvt,
Prim, Charles W., Pvt,
Prority, Wesley J., T/5,
Pucciarelli, Ellis, Pfc,
Purcell, Joe W., Pvt,
Purdy, Roy E., Sgt,
Putman, Hawley R., T/5,

Quinn, Herbert J., Pvt,
Quinn, William A., Pfc,

Raleigh, Robert R., Pfc,
Ramirez, Martin M., Pvt,
Ratcliff, Elzber R., Pvt,
Rathburn, Frank P., Pvt,
Ratledge, Gordon V., Pfc,
Ratzow, Harold W., T/5,
Raynor, Robert W., T/4,
Razwick, Frank A., Pvt,
Reed, James, Pvt,
Reed, Wayne P., Pfc,
§Reiker, Earl C., Pvt,
Reith, Arthur L., Pvt,
Rembish, John A., Pfc,
Remiszewski, Edward D., T/5,
Renfro, Horace A., Pfc,
Retherford, James R., Pfc,
Rhodes, Charles R., 1st Lt,
Rice, Charles H., Capt,
Richardson, Harry, Jr., Pvt,
Richardson, Lewis W., Cpl,
Rickards, Cecil R., Sgt,
Rierson, Phillip V., Cpl,
Riggs, Elbert H., Sgt,
Riggs, Gilbert E., Pvt,
Riley, Eugene, 2nd Lt,
Riley, Max E., 1st Lt,
Rimmer, Ralph W., Pvt,
Rincon, Roberto G., S/Sgt,
Rinelli, Walter J., Pfc,
Ring, William H., Cpl,
Ritchey, Charles P., Pfc,
Roach, Raymond C., Pfc,
Roark, Morris, Cpl,
Robedeaux, Clifford A., 1st Lt,
Roberts, Bruce P., Pvt,
Roberts, George P., T/5,
Roberts, James A., Jr., Pfc,
Robinson, F. D., Pfc,
Robinson, Robert C., Pfc,

Robinson, Walter A., Pvt,
Roddy, James O., Pfc,
Rode, Arthur E., Cpl,
Rodriguez, Manuel R., Pvt,
Rogers, Paul I., Pvt,
Roman, Anthony, Pvt,
Romano, Frank J., Pvt,
Roode, Ray E., Cpl,
Rook, Donald W., Pfc,
Ross, Alzie, Pvt,
Ross, Dorsey C., T/5,
Ross, Elmer J., Pfc,
Ross, Harry L. R., S/Sgt,
Ross, Phillip E., S/Sgt,
Rowland, Herbert J., Pvt,
Roy, Lionel E., T/5,
Roy, Leo F., Pvt,
Rubincan, Benjamin L., Pfc,
Runge, Lawrence E., T/4,
Russell, Walter L., Pvt,
Russell, William K., Capt,
Russon, Raymond S., Sgt,
Rutters, Richard C., Pfc,
Ruud, Edwin H., T/4,
Ryan, John, Pvt,

Sabatella, Louis J., Pvt,
Sabino, Michael J., Pfc,
Sain, Dick M., 1st Lt,
Salazar, Daniel, Pfc,
Salge, Steven J., Pvt,
Sallie, Edward F., Cpl,
Salpeter, Louis, Pvt,
Sampson, Robert E., T/Sgt,
Sanders, Henry H., Pvt,
Sanders, Achad, 1st Lt,
Sarles, Harold E., T/5,
Satter, Wesley W., Cpl,
Saucedo, Rudy H., Pvt,
Sawoscinski, Leo P., Pfc,
Sawtell, William T., Pvt,
Sayler, Willard P., Pfc,
Schaefer, John, Pfc,
Schaffer, Walter A., Sgt,
Schartz, Lawrence N., Pfc,
Scheid. Milford L., Pvt,
Schell, John W., T/4,
Scheppleck, Leonard M., Pvt,
Schilling, Milew W., T/5,
Schirmer, Carl F., Sgt,
Schiro, Samuel H., 1st Lt,
Schlecht, Gideon, T/5,
Schlueter, Douglas G., T/5,
Schlumbohm, George H., Pfc,
Schmalz, Edwin H., Cpl,
Schmidt, Alvin L., Cpl,
Schmidt, Cecil R., T/Sgt,
Schmidt, Jacob, Pfc,
Schmidt, Peter W., Pfc,
Schneider, John E., S/Sgt,
Schottenbauer, Elmer J., Pfc,
Schrader, Earnest, Sgt,
Schraer, Lloyd G., Pvt,
Schriver, Herschel R., Jr., Pvt,
Schroeder, Donald S., Sgt,
Schwagel, Arved P., Pfc,
Schwartz, Meyer, T/5,
Schwartz, Michael J., Pvt,
Schwartz, Robert, Pfc,
Schwartz, William A., 1st Sgt,
Scott, Filmore R., Pvt,
Scovill, Carl T., S/Sgt,
Seawell, George D., Pvt,
See, John S., Pvt,
Seeman, John H., Pvt,
Seems, Chalmer J., Pfc,
Semler, Roland S., Pvt,
Sersante, Albert, T/5,
Serva, Caesar J., 1st Sgt,
Shaddeau, Robert D., T/5,
Shankles, Samuel W., T/5,

Shannon, Richard E., Pfc,
Sharp, Marion C., Pvt,
Sharp, William D., T/5,
Shattuck, William J., Pfc,
Shaughnessy, Thomas E., Capt,
Shaw, Lawrence V., Cpl,
Shea, John H., Pvt,
Shellhammer, Lloyd T., Pfc,
Shelley, Joseph W., Pvt,
Sherping, Wallard H., T/5,
Shockman, Melvin, Pfc,
Shoden, Eric A., Pvt,
Shryock, Louis D., Jr., S/Sgt,
Shuey, Daniel W., Pfc,
Sicinski, Stanley J., Cpl,
Sidell, Charles H., Pvt,
Sides, Roscoe E., Pvt,
Sider, Louis, Pvt,
Siegel, Louis, Pfc,
Sievers, Herbert L., Pfc,
Simerly, Howard S., T/5,
Simmons, Coys O., Pfc,
Simon, Minor A., Pfc,
Simpson, Lowell C., Cpl,
Sims, Ernest A., Sgt,
Sinchak, Alexander C., Pfc,
†Singer, Milton, Pvt,
Sissel, George W., Pfc,
Skapik, Steve, Pvt,
Skroski, Vincent, Pvt,
Sloan, William J., Pvt,
Smith, Ernest, Pvt,
Smith, James A., Jr., Cpl,
Smith, James M., Sgt,
Smith, Leonard R., T/4,
Smith, LeRoy T., T/4,
Smith, Robert A., Pvt,
Smith, Walter G., Pvt,
Smith, William A., 1st Sgt,
Smith, William J., Pfc,
Sneed, Charles E., Cpl,
Snelgrove, M. G., T/5,
Snook, William R., T/5,
Snow, George L., Capt,
Snyder, William H., Cpl,
Somers, David D., T/4,
Sommer, Lawrence G., Pvt,
Soos, Frank W., S/Sgt,
Sorensen, Ib, Pfc,
Sowder, Kenneth I., Pfc,
Spadafora, Frank, Pvt,
Spears, Douglas W., Pfc,
Spears, James H., Jr, Pfc,
Specker, Thomas W., Pvt,
Splinter, Earl E., S/Sgt,
Spreigal, Clarence T., S/Sgt,
Spreyer, Frederick C., 1st Lt,
Spriggs, Robert L., 1st Lt,
Stanovich, Peter E., Pfc,
Stanton, Clayton P., T/5,
Stanton, George W., Cpl,
Steplas, Frank E., Cpl,
Stebbins, Thomas J. V., T/5,
Stein, John F., Maj,
Steinman, Donald V., Pfc,
Stevens, David W., Pfc,
Stewart, Paul R., Pvt,
Stiles, Arthur R., Pvt,
Stinnett, Andrew L., Cpl,
Stocks, Edward A., Pfc,
Stone, Albert K., T/5,
Stoop, Alfred G., Pfc,
St. Paul, David, T/5,
Strandberg, Howard G., T/5,
Strasser, Godfrey P., Pvt,
Strouf, Ladislav E., Pvt,
Stumpf, Robert R., T/5,
Suchanek, John F., S/Sgt,
Suitter, Gilbert H., Pfc,
Sullivan, James A., M/Sgt,
Sullivan, John D., Pvt,

Sullivan, Richard J., 1st Lt,
Sustarich, John W., T/5,
Sutphin, Malcolm I., Pvt,
Swanson, Oliver C., Cpl,
Sweatt, Roy E., S/Sgt,
Swopes, Joseph F., T/5,
Sykotnicki, John S., Cpl,
Szabados, Jesse, Pfc,
Szelepski, William, T/5,
Szpyrka, Marion A., T/5,

Talmage, John W., Pvt,
Tassone, Frank, T/5,
Taylor, Burdette F., Pfc,
Taylor, Everett, Pfc,
Taylor, Herbert A., Pfc,
Taylor, Hubert, Pvt,
Taylor, James W., 1st Lt,
Taylor, Leo E., T/5,
Taylor, Lester D., Pvt,
Taylor, William A., 1st Lt,
Teat, George C., Pfc,
Teller, Charles, 1st Sgt,
Tenneriello, Ciro M., Pfc,
Ternet, Clifford O., Pfc,
§Terry, Ivan D., Pfc,
Terry, James W., 1st Lt,
Thedens, George J., T/5,
†Therrien, Donald T., T/5,
†Thiel, Lloyd L., Pvt,
Thompson, Barney H., Pfc,
Thompson, Calvin F., T/4,
Thompson, Floyd W., Pfc,
Thorell, Clarence M., Pfc,
Thorndyke, Donald G., Cpl,
Thorson, Alton I., T/5,
Threet, Bernard H., Cpl,
Thull, Herbert J., Sgt,
Ticknor, Arthur R., T/5,
Tiegen, Adry A., Pfc,
Tobias, Robert C., Pvt,
Todd, Charles S., T/4,
Tomczyk, Chester J., Pfc,
Tondryk, Joseph M., Pfc,
Toomey, Johnnie F., Pfc,
Tornensis, Carl E., Pfc,
†Torok, Earnest V., T/4,
Travis, Raymond J., T/5,
Treadway, Robert E. L., Cpl,
Trepp, Hans A., Pvt,
Trickel, Maurice D., Pvt,
Troxell, Billy F., Pfc,
Tunnell, Guy J., Sgt,
Turnbull, Robert T., Pvt,
Turner, Fred A., T/5,
Twigg, Lloyd J., Pfc,

Udell, Lee E., Pfc,
†Ulrey, Wayne L., Pfc,
Underwood, Thurman E., Pvt,
Urbanik, Edward W., 1st Lt,
Urmetz, Elmer A., Cpl,

Vallett, Charles, T/5,
Valley, Robert W., S/Sgt,
Van Brunt, Billie V., T/5,
Vanderhoof, Russell E., Pfc,
Van Pembroke, William A., Sgt
Van Ryswyk, Vernon P., T/5,
Vento, Carl J., Pvt,
Villines, Alfred D., T/5,
Vincent, James G., T/5,
Vomacka, John, T/5,
Voss, Arthur H., Pvt,

Wages, Bonnie C., Pvt,
Wagner, Charles R., T/5,
Wagner, Ernest, T/5,
Wakefield, Robert L., Sgt,
Walding, John W., Pvt,
Walker, Carl E., 1st Sgt,

Walker, Carl E., Pfc,
Wall, John L., Pvt,
Walls, William, Pvt,
Wallner, Gilbert F., Pfc,
Walsh, Roger J., S/Sgt,
Walraven, Raymond K., T/4,
§Walter, Archie R., Pvt,
Walter, John W., Pfc,
Ward, Jack B., Cpl,
Ward, James, Pvt,
Ward, Houston R., Pvt,
Warner, George E., Sgt,
Warner, William R., Pvt,
Warzecha, Anthony J., Pfc,
Washburn, Lawrence E., Pfc,
Watkins, Oscar C., Pvt,
Weaver, Alfred G., Pvt,
Weaver, Littleton M., Pfc,
Webb, Earl E., S/Sgt,
Webb, William R., Pvt,
Weber, James L., 1st Lt,
Weir, Robert L., Capt,
Weitzer, Joseph L., S/Sgt,
Welling, Donald L., Pvt,
Wells, Francis M., Pvt,
Wells, Harold J., Pvt,
Welke, Clayton, T/4,
Wendt, Raymond W., Pfc,
West, George N., T/4,
Westlake, Bernard P., Pfc,
Weston, Ward W., Cpl,
Wheeler, Wesley L., Sgt,
Whipps, John A., Jr., Capt,
Whitley, Albert J., Pfc,
Whyte, William, Sgt,
Wilcox, Vernon A., Pfc,
Wilfong, James M., Pfc,
Wilhite, Joseph J., Jr., Pfc,
Wilkinson, John F., Pvt,
Wilks, Harry A., T/4,
Willard, James F., Pfc,
Williams, James F., Pfc,
Williams, Harold J., Pvt,
Williams, Robert, Cpl,
Wilm, Mathew M., Sgt,
§Wilson, Lester, Pvt,
Wilson, William R., Pvt,
Winters, Gilmer F., Pvt,
Winters, Harry E., Pvt,
Wirth, Victor, Pfc,
Wise, Kenneth, Pfc,
Wiste, Theron C., Pfc,
Wojcik, Ted, Pfc,
Wolfe, Frank W., 1st Sgt,
Wolff, Robert C., Cpl,
Wolford, Harry, Pvt,
Wolford, Ore C., T/4,
Wolford, Wilbur W., T/5,
Wolovlek, John J., Pvt,
Woolard, Leo D., T/4,
Wootan, LeRoy A., Pvt,
Worden, Irving C., Cpl,
Wright, Robert C., 1st Sgt,
Wrobel, Adam J., Pfc,
Wurm, Frank A., Cpl,
Wybronski, Steve, Cpl,

Yager, Malcolm D., Pvt,
Yanovich, Nick, Pfc,
Yelle, John W., Pvt,
Young, Edward R., Pvt,
Young, John H., S/Sgt,

Zambick, John S., Pvt,
Zeiger, Alfred A., Pvt,
Zeisler, Dan H., Cpl,
Ziegelmeyer, Clarence J., Pfc,
Zielinski, Charles, Pvt,
Ziff, Nathan, Pfc,
Zimmerle, Berman B., Cpl,
Zimmerman, James N., Cpl,
Zohns, Charles D., Pvt,

† Killed in Action.   * Prisoner of War.   ‡ Missing in Action.   § Died of Wounds.

10TH FIELD ARTILLERY BATTALION (LIGHT)

The 10th Field Artillery, organized in 1917 at Douglas, Arizona, soon became part of the 3d Field Artillery Brigade, 3d Division, and was sent to France in World War I where it engaged in five major operations: Champagne, Champagne-Marne, St. Mihiel and Meuse-Argonne. The 10th won its right to the motto, "The Rock's Support," in the famous stand of the 3d Division on the Marne River. In recognition of its services the regiment—now a battalion—was awarded the Croix de Guerre by Marshal Petain.

Commanding Officer

(Highest rank held)	Held pos. from	To
Lt. Col. Kermit L. Davis		18 July 1944
Lt. Col. Donald E. Hoffmeister	5 Nov 1943	

Achelpohl, Donald A., Pvt,
Adameczyk, Roman R., Pvt,
Adkisson, Willard J., Cpl,
†Aiosa, Anthony M., Pvt,
Albaugh, Gordon E., Pfc,
Alday, Albert, Pvt,
Aldrich, Lester B., T/5,
Aldrich, Marvin E., Pfc,
Allen, Wilbur E., Sgt,
Allevi, Roger A., Pfc,
Alsum, Milton R., T/5,
Amdahl, Lorin P., T/5,
Amidon, Eugene L., T/5,
Anderson, Albert E., Pvt,
Anderson, Edward L., T/4,
Anderson, Elmer C., Sgt,
Anderson, John C., Pvt,
Anderson, Louis, T/Sgt,
Anderson, Martin E., T/4,
†Anderson, Warren E., Capt,
Anderson, William R., Pfc,
Andreasen, Stanley C., T/5,
Armet, Lawrence E., Pfc,
Attlesey, Thomas M., T/4,
Ayres, William A., Pvt,

Baack, Lutz W., T/3,
Baars, Donald A., T/5,
Baer, Jacob, T/4,
Baer, Joe M., S/Sgt,
Bailey, Lewis T., T/5,
Bair, John H., Pfc,
Bairski, Benjamin S., T/5,
Baker, Richard E., T/5,
Ballard, Vance C., Pvt,
Ballentine, Talmadge F., T/5,
Ballou, Merlyn N., T/5,
Balser, William, Pvt,
Baltagis, Edmund L., S/Sgt,
Barber, Harry L., Cpl,
Barker, John E., Pfc,
Barnes, Sewell A., Cpl,
Barrick, Stacy T., Pfc,
Barrow, Ernest J., Pfc,
Bartels, Carl H., T/5,
Bartholomew, James G., T/5,
Bartlette, Eugene W., Cpl,
Basta, John A., T/4,
Bates, Edward N., Sgt,
Bautch, Frank D., Sgt,
Baynes, Owen K., Pfc,
Bays, Charles E., T/5,
Bean, Roy R., Pvt,
Beard, Billy D., T/4,
Bearden, Cecil M., Pfc,
Becker, Henry L., T/5,
Bedell, Glenn O., Pvt,
Bedwell, Jack, Pfc,

Beecher, Howard I., S/Sgt,
‡Belcher, Charles C., Pfc,
Bennett, Clifford E., T/5,
Bennett, Thomas W., Cpl,
Benson, Clarence M., S/Sgt,
Benson, Oster A., Sgt,
Beran, John A., Pvt,
Berglund, Sidney E., Sgt,
Bergvig, Earl A., Pfc,
Berklacich, Johnny, S/Sgt,
Bernard, Raymond P., T/5,
Bernard, Rodner, Sgt,
Berretta, Joseph S., Pfc,
Besher, Floyd R., Pfc,
Bettelyoun, Joseph, Pfc,
Betzer, Clifford R., Sgt,
Bevil, Ben S., T/5,
Bierstedt, Harold A., Sgt,
Bilansky, John M., T/5,
Billman, Paul W., Sgt,
Binder, Quentin A., Pvt,
Bisbing, Herbert S., Jr., Pfc,
Bisher, Russell W., T/5,
Bjoralt, Harly T., Pfc,
Blair, Jesse C., Pfc,
Blair, Samuel J., Sgt,
Bless, Herman E., Sgt,
Bligh, Allan E., S/Sgt,
Blucher, Harry L., Cpl,
Blum, Arthur S., Sgt,
Boehm, Fred, Pvt,
Boggs, Cecil C., Pfc,
Boike, Leroy B., Cpl,
Bonnell, Donald M., Sgt,
Booker, James M., Capt,
Borel, Edward, T/5,
Bossert, Truman O., Pvt,
§Bothwell, Eugene E., T/5,
Boullion, Harold J., Pvt,
Bowen, Hubert E., Jr., 1st Lt,
‡Bowers, Reuben M., Cpl,
Boyd, Samuel P., Sgt,
Boyle, George, Pfc,
Boyle, Sanders C., Jr., Pvt,
Brant, Benjamin, T/5,
Brantley, William C., Pvt,
†Breuninger, Fred, Sgt,
Brilla, John C., T/4,
Broadston, Merle D., S/Sgt,
Brode, William E., Jr., Pvt,
Brooking, Morris M., T/5,
Brooks, Calvin, Sgt,
Brouillette, Albert W., Pvt,
Brown, Donald E., Pvt,
Brown, Jadie, Pvt,
Brown, Jennings E., T/5,
Brown, Leonard E., Pvt,
Brown, Vergil G., Pvt,
Brown, Walter J., Jr., Sgt,

Browning, John W., Jr., Sgt,
Broyles, Jesse E., Pvt,
Brumfield, Chester F., Cpl,
Brunell, Loren J., Pvt,
Brzoska, John W., Pvt,
Buckley, Joseph M., S/Sgt,
Burcham, Harley S., Pfc,
Burgess, Sheldon G., Pfc,
Burkart, George A., Pfc,
Burr, Leonard W., T/5,
Bush, Bernice E., Cpl,
Butler, Richard P., T/4,
Buzzard, Eldon C., T/5,
Buzzell, Frank R., Pvt,
Byerly, Emery F., Pfc,

Cadorette, Francis R., Pfc,
Cahill, Eamon P., Pfc,
Cameron, John K., Capt,
Cannon, Meril, Jr., T/5,
Cararie, Anthony, 1st Lt,
Card, Ray S., Cpl,
Cardwell, Glenn S., T/Sgt,
‡Carey, James K., T/5,
Carlsen, Edwin H., S/Sgt,
Carr, Clifton M., Jr., Pfc,
Carrington, Joseph F., T/5,
Carter, Earl F., Pfc,
Carter, Granville E., Pvt,
†Cassidy, James D., Pfc,
Castaldi, Raymond, Pfc,
Casto, Noah, Pvt,
Castro, Max C., Cpl,
Caudell, Edwin C., Pfc,
Cessna, George E., Pfc,
Chambley, Roy T., Pvt,
Chank, Ernest A., Pfc,
Charbonneau, Robert J., Pvt,
Cheaney, Louis B., Jr., Pvt,
Chee, Joe M., Pvt,
Chesser, James H., T/5,
Chicanich, Emil, Pvt,
Chilson, Thearn R., T/4,
Chin, Lum, Pvt,
Choate, John D., Capt,
Christensen, Victor A., Sgt,
Christoph, Will J., T/5,
Ciccone, Philip V., Pfc,
Clark, Joseph F., Capt,
†Clark, Richard J., Capt,
Claypool, George F., Pvt,
Clifton, Glenn A., Pfc,
Clinton, Murell W., Cpl,
Cloutier, George R., Pvt,
Clutts, Clyde, Pfc,
Coady, Francis C., Sgt,
Cocker, George A., Pfc,
Cohrac, George T., Pvt,

§Colby, Ray S., Pfc,
Coleman, Robert, Pvt,
Collier, Howard, Pvt,
Collins, Archie B., Pvt,
Connizzo, Joseph, Pvt,
Conrad, Walter F., Pfc,
Conway, Archie C., Pvt,
Cook, Donald E., Pvt,
Cooper, Bernon J., Pfc,
Coppini, Elvin C., Cpl,
†Corbeille, Maxsum E., T/4,
Corporon, Jack F., S/Sgt,
Corrigan, Emmett D., Pvt,
Cossman, Leonard F., Pfc,
Cote, John R., Pvt,
Coughlin, Robert J., T/5,
Craft, Arthur L., Pfc,
Craig, John W., Pfc,
Cretacci, George J., Pvt,
Cristiano, John J., Pfc,
Crook, James L., Pfc,
Crouch, Dennis A., Pvt,
Cubbage, Emery N., T/5,
Cummings, Julian W., 1st Lt,
Cummings, Richard H., 2nd Lt,
Czubinski, John, Cpl,

Dachtler, Jacob H., 1st Sgt,
Dack, Virgil U., Pfc,
D'Alessandro, Fred, Pvt,
Dalton, Jesse N., Pfc,
Daugherty, Melvin A., Pvt,
Davidson, Harry S., Pvt,
Davidson, Robert F., Pfc,
Davidson, Thomas A., Jr., Sgt,
Davies, Alva C., Pvt,
Davis, Delbert A., T/5,
Davis, Floyd L., Pvt,
Davis, Johnnie H., Pvt,
Davis, Kermit L., Lt Col,
‡Davis, Richard E., 2nd Lt,
Davison, Boyd L., Pfc,
Davy, William G., S/Sgt,
Day, Rollan, S/Sgt,
Dea, Wing J., Pvt,
Dedon, William L., Pfc,
Deere, Lewis F., Pvt,
DeJaro, Paul P., Pfc,
Del Costello, Herman B., Pvt,
Demiterchik, Joseph, Pfc,
Denbo, William C., Pfc,
Dennis, Raymond C., Sgt,
Dethman, Frank E., 1st Sgt,
Dewberry, John W., Sgt,
Diaz, Joseph, Pvt,
Dickerson, Kenneth L., T/Sgt,
Dickinson, Connie C., Pfc,
Dietz, Adolph, Pfc,

DiStasi, Michael A., 1st Lt,
Dohm, George E., T/5,
Doig, Robert, T/4,
Dolson, Lee R., Pfc,
Domincovitch, Frank, Sgt,
Donohoo, Joe H., Pfc,
Doran, James K., Pvt,
Dorough, James S., Pfc,
Downing, James J., Pvt,
Doyle, Vincent P., Cpl,
Dragoo, Harrison M., T/5,
Drenon, Lloyd C., T/5,
Drkanic, Frank, Pfc,
Duchatel, Ernest L., Pvt,
DuChene, Raynald J., Pfc,
Dulinski, Charles J., Pfc,
DuMarce, Mitchell A., Pvt,
Dumbeck, Charles A., S/Sgt,
Duncan, Robert S., T/5,
Dunnagan, William L., Sgt,
Durant, James L., Pfc,
Durr, William F., Pvt,
Dye, Earl W., Pvt,
Dysart, Maurice S., 1st Lt,

Easley, Alvin L., T/4,
Eddy, Elmer R., Pfc,
Edo, Dominick V., Pvt,
Eggert, George E., Pvt,
Egizio, Florie, Sgt,
Eickhoff, Harry C., Cpl,
Elder, Elmore D., Pfc,
Ellis, Malcolm D., WOJG,
Ellis, Rynal, Pvt,
Elmore, Robert R., Sgt,
Elsen, Herman J., T/4,
Elton, Amos S., Pvt,
Emerson, Ralph, Pfc,
Emery, Dennis R., Cpl,
Emmons, Ray V., Pvt,
England, Robert L., Pfc,
Engle, Ned O., Capt,
Enquist, Robert E., Pvt,
Erickson, Herbert J., Cpl,
†Erwin, James R., Pvt,
Esquibel, Alarindo, Pvt,
Ettestad, Elmo L., T/4,
Evans, Eldon D., T/5,
Evans, Robert J., Pvt,
Ewell, Byron L., Pvt,

Fahnestock, Furman, Pvt,
Fairchild, Earl F., T/4,
Fairchild, Phillip C., T/5,
Farmer, John J., Pfc,
Farrow, Alfred V., Pfc,
Farwell, Arthur E., Pvt,
Faubion, Donald E., T/5,
†Fay, John A., Pfc,

† Killed in Action.   * Prisoner of War.   ‡ Missing in Action.   § Died of Wounds.

Fedorczyk, Mitru, Pvt,
Feight, Merle D., Pfc,
Fennell, Gordon W., T/5,
Fennell, Winfred E., Pfc,
Ferderer, George L., Pfc,
Feuer, Abe, Pfc,
Field, Earl O., 2nd Lt,
Field, James E., Pvt,
Finegan, Peter J., Pfc,
†Finney, Jack L., T/5,
§Firlet, Henry L., T/5,
Fisher, Arnold H., T/5,
Fitzgerald, Robert G., Pvt,
Flaherty, Francis J., Pfc,
Fleck, Paul J., Pfc,
Florek, John R., Pvt,
Flores, Joseph D., Pfc,
Foch, Francis M., Cpl,
Fogle, Joseph G., Pfc,
Footer, Joseph C., Pvt,
Ford, Michael N., Pfc,
Foreman, Avery L., Pfc,
Fortier, Gilbert J., Jr., 1st Lt,
Forys, Walter S., Pfc,
Foster, Charles C., Cpl,
Foster, Flavus M., Cpl,
Foster, James S., Pvt,
Fouche, James P., Sgt,
Fought, Kenneth G., Sgt,
Founds, John S., Sgt,
Francillo, William A., Pvt,
Franco, Joseph R., Cpl,
†Frank, Raymond R., Pvt,
Franklin, Chester V., 2nd Lt,
Frederick, Jack F., Pfc,
Freeman, Julian H., 1st Lt
Freeman, Walter C., Cpl,
Freeman, Willard L., Pfc,
Freese, Allen R., Pvt,
Frick, Walter C., Pfc,
Fricke, Earl H., T/4,
Frizzell, Burt J., Maj,
Fucci, Charles C., T/4,
Fuentes, Fidel V., Pvt,
Fulla, Anthony, Pvt,
Fulton, Richard A., Pvt,
†Furey, Charles R., T/5,

Gabel, Paul V., Sgt,
Gabriel, Harold M., Pfc,
Gadbaw, George M., T/5,
Gale, Robert C., 1st Lt,
Gallagher, James J., Cpl,
Gange, John, Pfc,
Gange, Pius, Pvt,
Gann, Howard J., Cpl,
Garcia, Fernando B., T/5,
Garcia, Juan T., Pfc,
Garcia, Lawrence V., Sgt,
Garrett, Clarence W., Pvt,
Garrett, James M., Pvt,
Gaydosh, John A., Pfc,
George, Harold P., Pvt,
†Gerard, Carmine J., Pvt,
German, Wilbert B., Pfc,
Gersetich, Albert E., Sgt,
Getzlaff, Raymond A., T/5,
Ghiggeri, John J., T/5,
Gibson, Robert, Pvt,
Gilbert, Robert W., S/Sgt,
Glass, Loren H., Pfc,
Glazier, Thomas G., Sgt,
Gnagy, Williard J., T/4,
Goforth, Ralph C., Sgt,
Golda, Peter A., T/Sgt,
Golden, George A., Pfc,
Gonzales, Amado, Pfc,
Gonzales, Frederick L., Pfc,
Gonzales, Macedonio, T/5,
Gonzales, Reinaldo, Jr., Pvt
Goodman, Owen F., Capt
Gordon, David, T/4,
Gori, Albert F., Cpl,
Goss, Albert H., Jr., Cpl,
Goure, Albert C., S/Sgt,
Gowin, Dale Y., Pvt,
Grand, Frank, T/4,
Graniere, John, Pfc,
Graves, Vance E., T/5,
Graziosi, John N., Cpl,
Greeley, Alexander J. D., T/4,
Green, Enos E., Pfc,
Greenberg, Benjamin, Pvt,
Gress, Leslie I., Sgt,
†Griggs, Caston E., Pfc,
Grimm, Marin H., T/5,
Gross, Raymond L., T/4,
†Grotzinger, Henry C., Pfc,
Guetel, Frank A., Pvt,
Gurley, James E., T/5,
Gurney, James R., Pfc,
Gustafson, Elmer W., Cpl,

Hagood, Lillian, Pvt,
Hagstrom, Richard E., Sgt,
Hainley, Paul F., T/5,
Hall, Arthur W., Pfc,
Hallsten, Erland A., Cpl,
Hamby, James E., T/5,
Hammer, Benjamin F., Pvt,
Hanna, Albert M., Pvt,
Hansen, Vernon C., Pfc,
Hanson, Kenneth R., Pvt,
Hardman, John R., T/4,
†Harker, Harvey A., Pfc,
Harper, George A., Pvt,
Harrell, Bill F., Cpl,
Harrington, Milo E., Pvt,
Harrison, Henry A., Jr., 1st Lt,
Harrison, Norman L., Pvt,
Harrold, Hugh, Jr., 2nd Lt,
Hart, Kenneth P., Pvt,
Hartley, Joseph H., Pfc,
Hartsock, William B., Cpl,
Hartwig, Jack, Jr., T/5,
Hartzell, Clifford E., Pfc,
Hathcote, Mark B., Pvt,
Hazelgrove, Lee F., Pfc,
Hazelton, Floyd S., S/Sgt
Head, James, Sgt,
Heimkes, Orlando L., Cpl,
Heins, Jerome J., Capt,
Heirman, Alois D., T/5,
†Helm, William L., T/5,
Hemker, Joe E., Pfc,
Henry, Thomas F., Cpl,
Hester, William L., T/4,
Hevezi, Alex, T/5,
Hawk, George W., Jr., Pvt,
Hayes, Harold J., Cpl,
Hayes, Jerome K., Cpl,
Highes, William L., Pvt,
Hildenbrand, Francis E., Pfc,
Hill, Chester W., 1st Lt,
Hill, Stanley F., S/Sgt,
Hillstrom, George H., Pvt,
†Hines, Raymond S., T/4,
Hinrichs, Keith F., Pfc,
Hipple, Robert E., T/5,
Hissong, Kenneth G., Pfc,
Hobbs, William E., Pvt,
Hodlik, Chester J., Pvt,
Hoffman, Eugene E., T/5,
Hoffmann, Matthew, Pvt,
Hoffmeister, Donald E., Lt Col,
Hohage, Carl, Pvt,
Holbrook, Samuel G., Pvt,
Holder, Robert N., Pvt,
Holland, Alfred J., Pvt,
Holland, Basil, Pfc,
Holt, Ernest G., Sgt,
Holton, Julian R., Pvt,
†Hoover, Virgil F., Pfc,
†Horner, Donald M., T/4,
Hornick, Frank, Sgt,
Hoskins, Orange F., S/Sgt,
Hostetler, Richard E., Sgt,
Hotavis, Donald J., Pvt,
Hotchkiss, Melvin L., Cpl,
Howe, Vernon R., T/5,
Howe, Wilson D., T/5,
Howes, Leo J., T/4,
Hromada, Michael, Pvt,
Hudson, Thomas R., Pvt,
Hughes, Donald E., Pvt,
Hull, Frank W., Jr., Pfc,
Hunter, George A., Cpl,
Huse, John L., Pfc,
Huseman, Lawrence J., Cpl,
Hutcherson, Otis L., Sgt,
Hutchison, John T., S/Sgt,

Iffert, Sylvester C., Cpl,
Ifft, Gale E., Pvt,
Igleheart, William D., S/Sgt,
Ingino, James J., Pfc,
*Isabell, Walter T., T/4,
Isaac, Lee, Major,
Ivester, Jack, Capt,

Jackson, Walter, T/5,
Jacobs, Charles H., Pfc,
Jaeger, Jack J., 1st Sgt,
Jamieson, Russell A., 1st Sgt,
Jefko, Boleslaw, Pvt,
Jelinek, John A., Pvt,
Jenkins, Samuel A., T/5,
Jensen, Harold G., Pfc,
Jensen, Max H., T/4,
§Jensen, Richard E., Sgt,
†Jesevich, Peter, Pfc,
John, William K., WOJG,
Johnson, Charles W., Pvt,
Johnson, Chester T., S/Sgt,
Johnson, Clyde W., Pfc,
†Johnson, Elver S., T/5,
Johnson, Harold D., Pfc,
Johnson, Henry A., Pvt,
Johnson, Lawrence L., Sgt,
†Johnson, Morris T., Pfc,
Johnston, Charles S., Pfc,
Jones, David E., Pvt,
†Jones, Jenkin R., 1st Lt,
Jones, Lloyd H., 1st Lt,
Jones, Richard W., Pvt,
Jordan, Clinton A., Pvt,
*Jordan, James W., 1st Lt,
Joseph, Donald H., Cpl,
Joseph, Robert D., Pvt,

Kaiser, Richard J., T/4,
Kamrath, Wilfred E., Pvt,
Kana, Paul, Pvt,
Kaplan, David, Pvt,
Kardos, Ernest F., Pfc,
Kasper, Adolph H., Pvt,
Kath, Victor H., S/Sgt,
Kedzior, Casimer J., 1st Lt,
Keenom, Loyd R., Pfc,
Keller, Melvin D., Pvt,
Kellerman, Henry B., Cpl,
Kelsey, Grover C., Pvt,
Kerbs, Dave, Sgt,
Kerby, Kenneth E., Capt
Kerr, Paul G., Cpl,
Kershaw, William E., S/Sgt,
Kessler, John M., Pvt,
Kildare, William, Cpl,
King, Wallace E., T/5,
Kinney, Richard W., T/4,
Kinsley, James A., Pvt,
Kinzie, Donald H., WOJG,
Kirk, Edward A., Cpl,
Kirk, Edward T., Pfc,
Kirk, Lewis V., Pfc,
Kirtley, Cave J., Pvt,
Kiser, Ollie L., T/5,
Kitchens, John D., Pvt,
Kitt, Clyde Jr., Cpl,
Kitts, Arthur C., T/5,
Kling, John P., T/4,
Knight, Lawrence L., Pfc,
Knisey, Glenn C., Pfc,
Knoll, Raymond J., 1st Lt,
Knutson, Marvin E., T/5,
Knutson, Richard O., Pfc,
Kobylar, Stanley, Pvt,
Kollock, Mark A., Jr., T/5,
Kopco, Albert P., Pvt,
Kos, Edward, Sgt,
Kockuba, Merrill J., T/4,
†Kostreba, Valentine A., T/4,
Kozlowski, Walter A., Pfc,
Kramer, Howard F., Cpl,
Krullich, Frank, Pvt,
Kubacki, Jacob S., Pvt,
Kuciej, Edward T., Pfc,
Kuhn, Walter J., Capt,
Kulhavy, Jerry, Pfc,
Kulp, Robert A., T/Sgt,
Kuntz, Harold J., T/5,
Kury, Math, Pvt,
Kycia, Bruno, Pfc,
Kyle, Ernest J., Pvt,
†Kyte, George J., Jr., 1st Lt,

Lalk, Edwin O., Cpl,
Lalli, Joseph, Pfc,
Lambertz, Laverne A., S/Sgt,
Lanagan, William D., T/5,
‡Lane, Ernest, Pfc,
Langeliers, Leslie J., T/5,
Langstrom, Robert A., Pfc,
Lannigan, George W., Pvt,
La Plante, Allan F., Cpl,
Laporte, Norman N., Pfc,
Larsen, Ralph M., Pfc,
Larson, Herbert D., Pfc,
Larson, Roy G., S/Sgt,
Larson, Sterling, E., Capt,
Lashua, Russell D., Sgt,
Latham, Carl K., Sgt,
Leach, Lewis G., Pfc,
Leary, William F., Pvt,
Leatherman, Thomas E., T/5,
Lee, Robert M., Capt
Lee Toy, Charles, Pfc,
Le Fever, John B., Pvt,
†Legako, Roman, T/Sgt,
Legg, Hugart O., Pfc,
Legrand, Bill, Pvt,
Lenherr, Burnell, Sgt,
Leon, Lawrence K., Pfc,
Leon, Robert S., Capt,
Leonard, William A., Sgt,
Lewis, Gerald A., Pfc,
Lewis, Robert L., S/Sgt,
Lewis, William J., Maj,
Lillis, Donald R., Pfc,
Lippert, Robert, Pvt,
Little, John E., T/5,
†Liuzzi, Donato L., 2nd Lt,
Locke, Charles, Pvt,
Locke, Newton, Pvt,
Long, Donald L., T/5,
Long, George B., Cpl,
Long, Phillip F., Pvt,
Long, Robert F., Pvt,
Long, Robert H., Cpl,
Loper, J. E., Pfc,
Lorenz, Donald S., S/Sgt,
Lott, Cletis, Pfc,
Loubier, Lionel J., Pvt,
Lovelady, John R., T/5,
Lozier, Raphael E., Pvt,
Lum, Yet S., Pfc,
†Lyon, Ralph F., Pvt,
Lyons, Emmett F., Pvt,
Lyons, John S., Capt,
Lyons, Richard F., T/5,

McAdoo, Archie, Pfc,
McBee, Vance B., Pvt,
McCann, James H., Pfc,
McCathron, Fred, Pfc,
McClure, Clifford, 1st Lt,
McCormick, W. E., Jr., Pvt,
McCoy, Benjamin C., Pvt,
McCoy, Gerald J., Cpl,
McDaniel, Dan M., Pvt
McDaniel, Orman N., Pvt,
McDonald, Harry, Pvt,
McDonald, Robert J., Pvt,
McDonald, William A., Cpl,
McFarland, Malcolm H., Pfc,
McGovern, Robert J., Pfc,
McGree, Thomas P., Cpl,
McGuire, Russell A., Sgt,
§McIntosh, Park, Pfc,
†McKenny, Ramon J., Pfc,
McKinney, Charles L., Pfc,
McLain, Keith W., T/5,
McLaughlin, Arthur J., Pvt,
McLaughlin, Fred W., S/Sgt,
McLaughlin, William M., Pvt,
McLean, Kenneth B., T/5,
McMahon, Ralph H., 2nd Lt,
McNamara, Joseph R., T/4,
McNeal, Paul T., Pvt,
Machia, Richard V., M/Sgt,
MacKay, Charles A., Pvt,
Mackland, Jack F., Pvt,
Magee, George B., Pfc,
Magolis, William V., Pvt,
Magon, Arthur G., Pfc,
Maison, Leonard B., Pvt,
Major, Charles V., Pvt,
Mandrell, Roy C., Pfc,
Mangler, Harold F., Pvt,
Marcoux, Bertrand, Cpl,
Marier, Daniel J., Cpl,
Marker, Albert, S/Sgt,
Markham, Albert R., T/5,
Markus, Bernard H., S/Sgt,
Martin, Albert R., Pfc,
Martin, Gene P., Pvt,
§Martin, William R., T/5,
Martin, William W., S/Sgt,
Marut, Michael, Pvt,
Mascagni, Joseph R., T/5,
Mason, Fred S., Pvt,
Matchett, Billy L., Sgt,
Matey, Edward W., Jr., Cpl,
Matheny, Charles A., Pfc,
Mathews, Jasper W., Pfc,
Mathis, George E., Pfc,
Matthews, Paul J., Jr., 1st Lt,
Mattucci, George D., Pvt,
Maxon, Max D., Pfc,
Maxon, Wayne L., Pvt,
Mayne, Woodrow, Pvt,
Mazich, Nicholas, T/5,
Meade, Herbert D., Pfc,
Meade, Roy A., Pvt,
Meanor, Wayne H., Pfc,
Medrano, Ramon, Pvt,
Mejak, Edward, Pvt,
Mekus, Peter E., Cpl,
Menchaca, Oliveros L., Pfc,
Menetti, Samuel N., Pfc,
Menkel, Carlson B., Capt,
Mercurio, Salvatore, Pfc,
Meredith, Peyton W., T/5,
Metz, Robert L., 1st Lt,
Meyer, Herbert W., Cpl,
Meyer, Wilbur H., S/Sgt,
Michael, Monroe H., Pfc,
Michelsen, Louis A., Capt,
Mikkelson, Lars S., Cpl,
Mikulencak, Daniel C., Cpl,
Milanese, Edward J., Pvt,
Milburn, James H., Pfc,
Miller, George, Pvt,
†Miller, Henry C., Pvt,
Miller, Jack D., Pvt,
Milligan, John C., Pvt,
Milton, Malcom J., Pvt,
Minisci, George E., Pvt,
Minson, Roscoe T., Capt,
Minster, Norton, S/Sgt,
Mitchell, Raymond P., S/Sgt,
Mitinck, Israel, Pvt,
Modesto, Vito, Pvt,
Monson, John H., T/4,
Montague, Marvin R., T/5,
Montuoro, Joseph P., T/5,
Mooradian, Mose M., M/Sgt,
†Moore, Earl H., Sgt,
Moore, William L., Pvt,
Mootz, Alphonse E., Pvt,
Morello, Joe M., Pvt,
Morgan, Letcher V., Pfc,
Morgoch, Theodore, Pvt,
Morissette, Henry W., Pvt,
†Mormanis, Kris D., Cpl,
Morris, Hubert G., 2nd Lt,
Morris, Raymond R., Pfc,
Morrison, Harry G., Pfc,
Morrison, Joseph F., 1st Lt,
Moscoe, Ernest L., Pfc,
Muellemann, Robert E., Pvt,
Muhlhauser, Raymond B., Cpl,
Munro, John P., Jr., Pvt,
Musgrove, William E., Pfc,
†Musulin, Tony, Pvt,
Myers, Charles W., Cpl,

Naill, Doyle O., T/5,
Najarr, Sabas G., Pfc,
Nation, Luther A., Cpl,
Neal, Willard C., Cpl,
Nebel, Elmer E., Cpl,
Neely, Howard F., S/Sgt,
Nehus, Charles H., Jr., Pfc,
Nelson, Donald N., S/Sgt,
Nelson, Harry R., T/5,
Nelson, Leon, T/5,
Nelson, Lester E., T/5,
Nelson, Raymond T., Cpl,
Nelson, Wesley C., Pvt,
Nemecek, Howard O., 1st Lt
Ness, Leonard F., T/4,
Neutzling, Alvin C., Cpl,
Newcomb, Robert B., Pvt,
Newton, Ernest F., Pvt,
Nordine, John W., Sgt,
Nordstrom, Lawrence K., Cpl,
Nork, Albert S., 1st Sgt,
Norman, Valientin, Pvt,
Norris, Herbert F., Pfc,
†Novak, Herman E., Pfc,
Nugent, Robert H., T/3,

†Oblad, Briant O., Capt,
O'Connor, Frank R., Pvt,
O'Dell, Edward J., Pfc,
Odland, Clifford, Pfc,
O'Donnell, Fred J., Jr., T/4,
O'Donnell, Gerald B., Pvt,
O'Hara, Wallace B., Sgt,
Olds, Francis C., Pvt,
Olson, Arthur G., S/Sgt,
Olson, Vernon O., S/Sgt,
Olson, Wallace V., Pvt,
O'Malley, Edward J., Pfc,
Omelina, George J., Pvt,
O'Neal, Jasper W., Pvt,
Orlick, Thomas S., Pfc,
Orr, Delmar D., Pvt,
Orton, Lucius R., Jr., 1st Sgt,
Osborne, James H., S/Sgt,
O'Sullivan, Basil J., T/5,
Outland, Ralph M., Pfc,
Owens, Charles E., Cpl,
†Owens, Merlin L., Pvt,

Paconowski, Edward C., Pfc,
Page, George H., Capt,
Page, Joseph B., Jr., T/5,
Page, Robert P., Pfc,
Palazzo, Jerome J., Pvt,
Papendick, John R., Jr., Pfc,
Papes, Vincent C., Pvt,
Pardis, Duane L., Pfc,
Park, Delos M., Pfc,
Parker, George C., WOJG,
Parmelee, Luke W., T/5,
Partridge, Oscar R., M/Sgt,
Passon, Walter, Pfc,
Patterson, Gayther N., T/5,
Patterson, James A., Cpl,
Patton, Frank C., T/5,
Pawlak, Edward P., Pvt,
Peacher, Russell P., Cpl,
Peak, Cecil B., Pvt,
Pearson, George T., Pfc,
Peck, Thomas A., T/5,
†Peden, Forrest E., T/5,
Pederson, Henry M., Sgt,
Pelon, Virgil F., S/Sgt,
Pentz, Charles F., Pvt,
Percifield, Charles F., Cpl,
Perkins, Howard L., Pfc,
Perkowski, Robert J., T/5,
Pershall, Edd W., Pfc,
Personius, Delbert L., Pvt,
Pestka, Raymond B., Pfc,
Peters, John I., 2nd Lt,
Petersen, Earl E., T/4,

† Killed in Action. * Prisoner of War. ‡ Missing in Action. § Died of Wounds.

IN WORLD WAR II

Peterson, Bernard J., S/Sgt,
Peterson, Harold A., Cpl,
Peterson, Raymond L., Pfc,
Peterson, Robert N., 1st Lt,
Peterson, Theodore A., S/Sgt,
Petrowsky, Leo H., Pfc,
Petrozzello, Thomas J., T/5,
Petteys, George E., T/5,
Phillips, Everett L., T/5,
Picard, John C., Pfc,
Pierce, Burrell W., Pvt,
Pietrowski, Edward, Pvt,
Pilgrim, Billy E., Pvt,
§Pinianski, Paul, Jr., Pvt,
Pinter, William A., T/4,
Pirtle, William E., Pvt,
Pistone, Frank J., S/Sgt,
Placek, Edward G., 1st Lt,
Policandriotes, Spero J., Sgt,
Poprac, Lukas J., Pfc,
Porras, Roberto, T/5,
†Porth, Harold J., T/5,
Prado, Carlos A., Pfc,
Pratt, Charles B., Pvt,
Pratt, Delby L., Cpl,
Prentice, John P., Pvt,
Prentiss, Augustus C., Pfc,
Preston, Ralph B., T/5,
Preston, Roy D., Pvt,
Price, Vernon G., Jr., Pfc,
Prigitano, Frank S., Pfc,
Priske, Charles C., Pvt,
Proffitt, Frank E., Cpl,
§Provost, Thomas F., Pvt,
Prucha, Edward J., T/4,
Pruitt, Thermon E., Pfc,
Pugh, Earl R., Pvt,
Pugh, Melvin L., 2nd Lt,
†Pulkkinen, Oiva L., Pfc,
Pulver, John M., Cpl,
Purdy, Willis H., Pvt,
§Pytko, Steve J., Pfc,

†Quinn, Aubrey, Pfc,
Quirion, Adelbert, Pvt,
Quirple, Robert W., Pvt,

Rake, Harry O., Jr., Pvt,
Ramirez, Fernando, Pfc,
Ramuta, William R., Sgt,
Ranson, Bruce M., T/5,
Ranta, Rudolph, Pfc,
Rauenzahn, Bruce F., Pfc,
Rauh, John, Pvt,
Rawls, Cyrus A., Pvt,
Ray, Albert H., Pvt,
Ray, Ernest D., Cpl,
†Ray, Lloyd B., Pvt,
Rayburn, Richard R., Pvt,
Redfern, John H., Cpl,
Reece, Fred H., Pfc,
Reed, Eugene, Cpl,
Reed, Robert H., S/Sgt,
Reid, Ernest J., Pvt,
§Reid, John W., Pfc,
Reidner, Lyle L., Cpl,
Reife, Irving N., Pvt,
†Reimers, Frederick R., 2nd Lt,
Reis, Warren T., 2nd Lt,
Reiss, Lyle P., T/5,
Remington, James A., Pfc,
Remington, Lloyd C., T/5,
Resch, Donald F., Cpl,

Revels, Vernon V., Sgt,
Reyes, Andres R., Pvt,
Reyes, Concepcion, Pfc,
Reynolds, Cecil R., Pvt,
Riccio, Eli A., Pvt,
Richwine, Arthur M., T/4,
Rickman, Johnny U., T/4,
Riebold, Raymond J., Pfc,
Rieks, Wilbert W., T/5,
Riggins, Vernon J., Pfc,
‡Rinehart, Edmon L., 1st Lt,
†Ritland, Lester G., Pvt,
Roal, August L., Pvt,
Roberts, Ronald K., T/5,
Robertson, James H., Pvt,
Robertson, Norman H., Cpl,
Robertson, William D., T/5,
Robienczak, Benny E., Pvt,
Robinson, John D., Pfc,
Rodriguez, Mike M., Pvt,
Roesner, Carl A., T/4,
Rogenski, Stanley, T/4,
Rogers, William M., T/5,
Romo, Henry J., Jr., Capt,
Ronning, George A., T/4,
Rork, James R., Pfc,
‡Rosal, John J., Cpl,
†Roscia, Vincent, Pfc,
Rosenwinkel, Edgar W., Sgt,
Rosko, Edward, T/5,
Rosner, Erwin, 1st Lt,
Ross, Marcel A., Pfc,
Ross, Marvin H., Pvt,
†Rossell, Berton L., T/4,
Rossi, Frederick N., Pvt,
Roth, Albert R., 1st Sgt,
Rowe, James W., Pvt,
Roybal, Cruz H., Pfc,
Rozzik, Angelo A., Sgt,
Rubin, Leo, Pfc,
†Ruby, Donald A., Pvt
Rudolph, John B., T/5,
Rudy, John R., T/5,
Russo, Joseph G., Cpl,
Rust, Claude E., Cpl,
Rutter, Charles W., Pfc,
Ryan, LaMar F., Cpl,

Sack, Richard F., S/Sgt,
Sa Franko, Nicholas, Cpl,
Sager, Luther W., Pfc,
Sakariason, Martin O., Sgt,
Salazar, Eulojio, Pfc,
Samsel, Edward J., Pvt,
Samuels, Everett, Pfc,
Sandiford, Raymond W., Pfc,
Sandor, Anthony J., Pfc,
Sanfilippo, John, Pvt,
Sanko, Michael A., Sgt,
Sapone, Frank, Cpl,
Sapp, Jack W., S/Sgt,
Sauastano, Ralph J., Pfc,
Scala, Thomas C., Pfc,
Scharf, Edmund P. R., 1st Sgt,
Schechter, Benjamin H., Pvt,
Scheckel, LeRoy A., Pfc,
Schepker, Dietrich, Jr., Pfc,
†Scheuch, Henry F., 2nd Lt,
Schlueter, Wilbert M., Pfc,
Schlueter, Dean A., S/Sgt,
Schmidt, Edward E., Jr., Pvt,
Schmidt, Henry, T/5,

*Schmitz, Rafael J., T/4,
Schneider, Emanuel, Pvt,
Schnettler, Alton, T/3,
Schroeder, Paul R., Pvt,
Schuerer, Ernest R., S/Sgt,
†Schultz, Emmett E., T/4,
Schultz, George H., Pfc,
Schultz, Henry J., 1st Lt,
Schuppert, Stanley O., Pvt,
Schwamm, Howard R., Pfc,
Scoggins, William H., Pvt,
Scribner, John T., Pvt,
Seay, Furman R., S/Sgt,
Sefzik, Raymond C., Pfc,
Selfridge, Richard J., S/Sgt,
Seminara, Michael M., Pfc,
Sepulvado, Wilburn, Pfc,
Sergakis, Emanuel, Sgt,
Serpento, Santino T., T/5,
Sesto, Anthony, Pfc,
Severe, Henry W., T/5,
Shadleck, Arthur L., Pvt,
Shaw, Donald B., Pfc,
Shaw, Lawrence V., 2nd Lt,
Shaw, William E., Pvt,
Sheehan, John L., T/4,
Shenkel, Robert D., Pfc,
Sheppard, Alvin L., Cpl,
Sheppard, Harold W., Pvt,
Shertel, John R., Pvt,
Shumaker, Johnny W., Pfc,
Shuster, Harry F., Pvt,
Sigfrid, Gene E., Pvt,
Sikes, Edgar D., Pvt,
‡Silbernagel, Joseph, Sgt,
Siler, Carl J., Pvt,
Silvi, Dominic P., Pfc,
Silvola, Edwin F., Sgt,
Simon, Floyd W., T/5,
Simonich, Louis A., Pvt,
Simpson, Thurston B., Pvt,
Skaff, Paul E., T/5,
Skelton, Glen E., Sgt,
Skinner, Duayne E., Pvt,
Skinner, John A., Pvt,
Skinner, Paul V., Cpl,
Sklar, Norman J., T/4,
Sladky, Robert C., Pvt,
Sloothaak, Willard G., Pfc,
Smith, Charles G., 1st Lt,
Smith, Clay, Pvt,
Smith, Clifford D., Sgt,
Smith, Francis W., M/Sgt,
§Smith, James T., Jr., S/Sgt,
Smith, John D., T/5,
Smith, Hilman D., Pfc,
Smith, Merle L., Sgt,
Smith, Merlin F., T/4,
Smith, Toliver R., S/Sgt,
Smith, Waldren W., Pvt,
Smith, William E., T/4,
Smrdel, Ludwig J., Pfc,
†Snyder, Glenn H., T/5,
Sogge, Osmund A., Cpl,
Someroff, Phil S., Pfc,
Somers, David D., Cpl,
Sommer, Lawrence G., Pvt,
†Sorensen, Ralph C., Capt,
Spence, Samuel G., Pvt,
Spickler, Stanley J., Cpl,
†Sornoso, Sylvester J., Pvt,
Spodnick, Paul P., Pvt,

Springer, Edward J., Pvt,
Squazzo, Francis L., T/4,
Squire, Elmer E., T/5,
Stanley, Irving J., T/5,
Stanovich, Peter E., Pfc,
Stansky, John J., Pvt,
Stark, Orville W., T/5,
Start, Earl T., T/4,
Steele, William H., Pvt,
Stefanski, Frank J., Pfc,
Steinle, Carl H., Capt,
†Stergos, James P., Sgt,
Stewart, James C., Pfc,
Stewart, Thomas J., Pvt,
Stilley, Glenn E., T/4,
St. Louis, Edward O., Pvt,
Stockton, Frederick E., S/Sgt,
Stookey, Guy J., Pvt,
Storley, Laverne E., Pvt,
Streeter, Allen L., Pvt,
Strickland, Randall J., Pvt,
Sullivan, Jerome E., T/5,
Summers, Aaron T., T/5,
Summers, Robert W., Capt,
Sunquist, Dean R., Cpl,
Sutton, Charles L., Pvt,
§Swan, Leland, T/5,
Swanbom, Luther E., Pvt,
Swanson, Gordon W., S/Sgt,
Swanson, John E., Pvt,
Swart, John W., Pfc,
Swendsen, Paul O., S/Sgt,
Swenson, George O., T/4,
Swiderski, Adam J., Pfc,
Swisher, Carl W., Pfc,
Symionow, Nick, T/5,

Tacito, Antonio, Pfc,
Talbott, John M., Pvt,
Tardy, Lawrence L., Pvt,
Taylor, Delworth J., Pvt,
Taylor, Horace, Pfc,
Teigland, Lucas W., Cpl,
Terock, John, Pfc,
Terry, Charles B., Pvt,
Terry, James L., Pvt,
Terry, Vernon E., Pfc,
Tesine, Joseph, Pvt,
Thane, Louis B., Pfc,
Thelen, Alphonse A., S/Sgt,
Therrien, Alfred J., Pvt,
Thiel, Louis H., Jr., Pvt,
Thien, Leonard G., Pfc,
Thiesse, Clarence H., Cpl,
Thirstrup, James N., Pfc,
Thomas, Calvin N., Pfc,
Thompson, Berthal F., Pvt,
Thompson, Marion G., Pvt,
Tiernan, John J., Pvt,
Tierney, Richard W., Pfc,
Timmerman, Willis B., T/4,
Timmons, William J., Jr., Pfc,
Todnem, Theodore M., S/Sgt,
Torvinen, Edward O., Pfc,
Tow, Warren M., T/5,
Tracy, Wilbur D., T/4,
Tschoerner, Anthony R., T/4,
Tupaj, Stanley, Pvt,
Turini, Louis S., Pvt,
Turner, Roy R., Pvt,
Twelkmeyer, V. N., 1st Sgt,
Tykson, Lawrence M., Pfc,

Tyson, George J., Cpl,

Usrey, James D., S/Sgt,

Valashinas, John A., T/4,
Valdespino, Emilio J., Cpl,
VanEverey, William G., Cpl,
VanHorn, William C., Pvt,
Van Hyning, Dale, 1st Lt,
Van Keirsbulck, L. R., 1st Lt,
Vecchitto, Frank J., Pfc,
Vervella, Louis B., T/5,
Vilican, George, Jr., 1st Lt,
Vincent, Edward E., Pvt,
†Vodlick, John, Jr., Cpl,
Vrieze, Elwyn F., T/4,

Waldron, John L., Pfc,
Walton, Curtis R., Jr., 1st Lt,
Warkala, Vincent F., 2nd Lt,
Wasik, Anthony, Pvt,
Watkins, Herbert V., Pvt,
Watts, Frank M., T/5,
Weaver, Gilbert D., Pvt,
Weaver, Jesse R., Cpl,
Webb, Alonzo F., Cpl,
Webb, Lawrence V., S/Sgt,
Webster, Robert A., Pfc,
Wedger, Wilbur L., 1st Sgt,
Weeks, Robert B., Sgt,
Weidemann, LeRoy I., Sgt,
Weiland, Emmett G., Cpl,
Weir, Robert L., Capt
†Wiesen, Donald, T/4,
Weisenburg, L. E., Jr., Capt,
†Weisiger, William D., 2nd Lt,
Wendt, James R., Jr., Maj,
Wenger, Henry R., T/5,
Westlin, Darrell E., Pfc,
Weygant, Vincent R., Cpl,
White, Robert J., T/5,
Wightman, Thomas H., Pvt,
Wiley, Robert W., Pfc,
Wilhelm, Eldon E., T/4,
Williams, David J., T/4,
Williamson, John B., 1st Lt,
Willis, Don L., Sgt,
Wilson, Arlie L., Pfc,
Wilson, Arthur B., Pfc,
Wilson, Donald J., Capt
Wilson, Edward P., Pfc,
Wilson, Emerly L., Pvt,
Wilson, Harold, Pvt,
Wilson, James M., Jr., 1st Lt,
Wilson, Leon J., Pvt,
Wilson, Webster W., 1st Lt,
Winters, Harry D., Cpl,
Wisneski, Albin J., Cpl,
Wisniak, Henry, Pvt,
§Wittkopp, Arthur, Pfc,
Wobeter, William C.,
Wojcik, Walter K., Capt,
Wood, James A., Pfc,
Wortzkey, Edgar N., Pvt,

Yamond, Joseph R., Pvt,
Yrigoyen, Joe, Pfc,

Zavodnik, Edward F., 2nd Lt,
Zemke, Clarence A., S/Sgt,
Zimmerle, Berman B., Cpl,
Zupan, Edward A., T/4.

† Killed in Action.   * Prisoner of War.   ‡ Missing in Action.   § Died of Wounds.

39TH FIELD ARTILLERY BATTALION (LIGHT)

The 39th Field Artillery Battalion was activated at Fort Lewis, Washington, on October 1, 1940, the same post on which its predecessor of World War days was organized. The original 39th Field Artillery, then a regiment, was organized at Camp Lewis in 1918 and was demobilized in 1919. Cadre for the 39th Field Artillery was supplied by the 10th Field Artillery Regiment.

Commanding Officer

(Highest rank held)	Held pos. from	To
Lt. Col. John D. Byrne		18 July 1944
Lt. Col. Wendell J. Coates	19 July 1945	

Abell, James P., Pfc,
Adams, Edward, T/5,
Adman, Karl E., T/5,
Aho, Douglas R., T/5,
Albertson, Robert M., Cpl,
Albrewczynski, Joseph S., Pvt,
Alcorn, Robert A., Sgt,
Alden, Warren H., Capt,
Aldridge, Marion G., Cpl,
Alexander, Horace A., Pfc,
Alexander, Rober P., Pvt,
Alexander, Warren G., S/Sgt,
Alfstad, Laurence F., Pfc,
Allen, Charles W., Sgt,
Allen, Water P., 1st Sgt,
Allyn, Melvin L., T/5,
Aloisio, Louis, Pvt,
Alton, O'Neil R., Pfc,
Anderson, Albert G., T/5,
Anderson, Clark, Jr., Pvt,
Anderson, Gordon W., Pvt,
Anderson, John W., Capt,
Anderson, Roy C., Pvt,
Andrews, Edgar, Pvt,
Anglin, Homer C., Pvt,
Anthony, Louis R., Pfc,
§Antonino, Patrick C., Pfc,
Aquilina, Anthony G., T/5,
Arata, Benjamin L., Pfc,
Arias, Jose R., Pfc,
Arsaga, Frank C., Pvt,
Ask, Myran M., S/Sgt,
Ault, Holland A., T/5,
Austin, Lovell D., T/4,

Bach, Archie C., Sgt,
Bailey, Lester R., Sgt,
Baker, William K., T/3,
Bakken, Arthur O., T/4,
Bakshis, Frank J., Pvt,
Bailey, Roland W., Jr., Capt,
Ballman, Herman F., Sgt,
Banks, Harvey E., Pfc,
Banovich, Vincent E., Pvt,
Barker, George A., Pfc,
Barretta, Louis, Pvt,
Barron, Eugene D., T/5,
Barrows, Henry R., Cpl,
Bartley, Ralph E., Pfc,
Baum, Donald A., Cpl,
Beaird, Frank D., Pfc,
Bedford, Henry R., Pfc,
Belanger, Joseph W., Pvt,
Bell, Roy, Pvt,
Bellefeuille, Raymond G., Pvt,
Benedict, Gerald L., Sgt,
Bensing, Floyd A., S/Sgt,
Benson, Roy D., Pvt,
Benstine, Donald H., S/Sgt,
Berg, Ole H., Pfc,

Berndt, Alvin D., S/Sgt,
Bernstein, Abraham, Cpl,
§Berry, Raymond M., Pvt,
Berwick, Bertram E., Pvt,
Binstock, Louie, Pfc,
Birchell, Weldon D., T/Sgt,
Birchall, William E., Pfc,
†Bischoff, Leon F., Pvt,
Bishop, Delbert N., Pvt,
Bishop, Raymond P., Pvt,
Bishop, Willis A., T/5,
Bishop, Woodrow W., S/Sgt,
Bless, Paul E., Pvt,
Blish, Rexverd C., Cpl,
Bliss, Alfred, T/5,
Blum, Ralph G., T/4,
Bodzin, Hyman, Capt,
Boettiger, Allen R., Pfc,
Boland, Roy C., S/Sgt,
Bonafide, Sylvestero, Pvt,
Bonner, John W., Pfc,
Bonsignore, Louis, Pvt,
Borchers, Victor D., Pvt,
Bosshart, Lester E., Pfc,
Bossier, Jasper R., Pvt,
Bottesi, Marvin J., Pvt,
Bottoms, Ary T., T/4,
Bouchard, Gordon W., Cpl,
Bourelle, James L., Cpl,
Bowers, George E., Jr., Pfc,
Boyce, Beryl L., Capt,
Boyd, Jackson, Pfc,
§Boyke, Martin, Pfc,
Boykin, Lynch D., Jr., Pfc,
Brack, Albert L., Pfc,
Brainerd, Ben V., T/4,
Bramowski, Ignatius J., Cpl,
Brazil, Leonard A., Pvt,
§Breaux, Oscar C., Pvt,
Breitmeier, John F., T/4,
Brennan, William G., Pvt,
Breuninger, John T., Pvt,
Brezeale, Everett L., CWO,
Brinkworth, Donald A., Pfc,
Brittos, George, T/5,
Brooks, Fellice O., Pvt,
Brown, Arthur H., Sgt,
Brown, Claude F., Pvt,
Brown, Ernest, T/5,
Brudnicki, Edward J., Cpl,
Brunstad, Irving O., Capt,
Bruyere, Patrick D., Cpl,
Bryant, James A., Pvt,
Bryant, James E., Pvt,
Bucci, Frank T., Pfc,
Buckley, William H., T/5,
Buday, Joseph C., Pfc,
Buillian, Henry E., Pfc,
Burchfield, Glenn E., Cpl,

Burke, James E., Pvt,
†Burke, Robert W., T/5,
Burns, Clifford C., Pfc,
Burns, Francis X., Cpl,
Burns, Wilbur M., Pvt,
Burns, Willard R., T/5,
Buckley, William P., Sgt,
Burrill, Henry W., Pfc,
Burton, Robert C., S/Sgt,
Burton, William W., Pvt,
Bushaivsky, Harold, Pvt,
Buskett, Bruce D., 2nd Lt,
Butler, Bryan, Pfc,
Byrd, David A., Pfc,
Byrne, John D., Lt Col,

Caballero, Delfino, Pfc,
Cable, William N., T/4,
Calabria, Anthony F., Pvt,
Caldwell, Tom R., Pvt,
Campbell, Robert J., Cpl,
Carr, Harrel, Pfc,
Cartee, James C., Pvt,
§Castello, Joe, Pfc,
Catlin, Arthur W., Pvt,
Cerrone, John R., Pvt,
Chamberlin, Orval S., Pfc,
Champ, Harry W., Cpl,
Chaplin, Arthur E., Cpl,
Chapman, Clinton D., Pfc,
Chase, Russell A., Pvt,
Chastain, William L., Pvt,
Chavez, Daniel S., Sgt,
Chichura, Michael, 1st Sgt,
Chismar, Andrew E., Pvt,
Chowning, Dale E., T/4,
§Christy, Kenneth L., S/Sgt,
Cichoski, Raymond F., Pfc,
Cichy, George S., Pfc,
Cioffi, Dante L., Cpl,
Cipriani, Ralph, T/4,
Clapham, Noel, Pfc,
Clark, Irvin L., Pfc,
Clark, Richard J., Cpl,
Clark, Robert W., Pfc,
Clarkson, Thomas L., Pvt,
Clasen, Robert E., Cpl,
Claypool, Russell B., T/4,
Clelland, Paul G., Cpl,
Clifford, Leonard W., Pvt,
Cloutier, Ernest A., Pvt,
Cluka, William R., Pfc,
§Clukey, Julian P., T/5,
Coats, Wendell J., Lt Col,
Cohen, Ned M., T/Sgt,
Colagrossi, Joseph W., Pvt,
Cole, John E., Pvt,
Cole, Rupert A., Pvt,
Coletta, Peter, Pvt,

Combs, George N., Pfc,
Compagnoni, Peter, Pvt,
Conchieri, Ernest L., T/5,
Conley, John P., 1st Lt,
Connor, Arthur B., Pvt,
Conway, Gerald T., Pfc,
Cook, William E., T/4,
Cooklin, Clarence J., S/Sgt,
Corn, Charles E., Cpl,
Cornett, Floyd C., T/5,
Corson, Woodrow O., Pvt,
Couch, Carl V., Pfc,
Covey, Edwin O., 1st Sgt,
Cox, Jesse H., Pfc,
Cox, John L., T/5,
Creech, Colvin H., Pvt,
Crespin, Jose, Pvt,
Cristall, Richard T., Pfc,
Crittendon, Alpheus, Pvt,
Cromartie, John D., T/4,
Crowl, Gerald H., T/5,
Crutchfield, Carl T., Pfc,
Cubbage, Sherman R., Pfc,
Cumings, Floyd M., Pfc,
Cunningham, Francis J., Pfc,
Cunningham, Theodore R., Pfc,
Cushman, Norman J., T/5,

Dailey, Waldon M., Pfc,
Daley, Edward J., Pvt,
Dalpiaz, Joe, Pfc,
Dalton, Harold E., Pfc,
Danskey, Edmond, Pvt,
Darby, Andrew J., Jr., 2nd Lt,
Darden, Jesse C., Pfc,
Darnall, Ray E., Pfc,
Daumen, Kenneth P., Pvt,
Davenport, Wesley A., Pvt,
Daves, Charles L., T/5,
Davidson, Lonnie A., M/Sgt,
Davis, Charles L., Pfc,
Davis, Lawrence P., S/Sgt,
Davis, Ralph E., 1st Lt,
Davis, Ted T., T/5,
Deack, John, Pfc,
Dean, Elza B., Pvt,
DeAngelo, Frank, Pfc,
DeCoster, Joseph J., T/5,
Delgado, Manuel L., Pvt,
DeLuca, Bart J., T/5,
Deluca, Orfeo G., T/5,
Delucia, John F., Pfc,
Deluco, Francis M., Pvt,
Denham, Walter E., Pvt,
Derda, Joseph A., Pvt,
Derhaag, Albert W., Sgt,
Derr, Howard H., Pfc,
Desput, Frank, Pfc,
Destenay, Robert L., Pfc,
Devol, Brenton A., Jr., Capt,
Dibbert, Orin H., Pfc,

Dickerson, Howard G., Pvt,
Diem, Raymond H., Pfc,
Dillman, Albert J. A., Pvt,
Dillon, William P., Cpl,
Diprizio, Jerry, Pvt,
Disco, Michael T., Pfc,
*Dix, Harold C., 1st Sgt,
Dubbs, Henry T., Pfc,
Dodd, William O., Pvt,
Doeskin, George, Sgt,
Dolinka, William, T/4,
Dooley, Thomas A., Pfc,
Dornan, Joseph F., Pfc,
Downey, Jerome, Pfc,
Doze, Franklin J., Cpl,
Drennan, Vincent J., Pfc,
Drennan, William E., Jr., Pvt,
Drinka, Simon W., Pvt,
Drury, Raymond E., Cpl,
Dubin, David, Pvt,
Ducharme, Joel U., Pfc,
Ducharme, Paul L., Pfc,
Duckworth, Gordon L., Pvt,
Dudley, Johnnie, Sgt,
Dunbar, John C., S/Sgt,
Dunbar, Paul B., Pfc,
Duncan, Elmer S., Pfc,
Dunkin, Oscar B., Pfc,
Dunn, Leroy W., Pvt,
Duranleau, Robert J., Pvt,
Durham, Weldon T., Pfc,
Dvorak, Wesley G., S/Sgt,

Eaddy, Heston A., Pvt,
Edmunson, Tom F., S/Sgt,
Edwards, Ollie C., Pvt,
Egan, Pono P., Sgt,
†Eikens, Irvin J., S/Sgt,
Eilers, Eugene, S/Sgt,
Eldridge, James W., Jr., Pfc,
†Ellerbruch, Ernest E., Sgt,
Elliott, Howard N., T/5,
Elliott, Turner L., T/4,
Ellison, Donald C., Cpl,
Elrod, Louis C., Cpl,
Elsesser, George E., Pfc,
Emery, Norman D., T/4,
Engelhardt, John, Pvt,
Engelhardt, Michael T., Cpl,
§English, Bert L., 1st Lt,
Engom, Arthur C., Sgt,
Epperson, Olin W., Sgt,
Ercolini, John A., Pfc,
Erickson, Evarts C., Pfc,
Eschner, Ernest W., Pfc,
Escott, James F., Cpl,
Estes, Dewey K., Pvt,
Evans, Evan P., 1st Sgt,
Everhart, James E., Sgt,
Eyles, Robert R., 1st Lt,

† Killed in Action.   * Prisoner of War.   ‡ Missing in Action.   § Died of Wounds.

IN WORLD WAR II 543

†Fagan, Boyd J., Cpl,
Fagan, Lewis W., Pfc,
Falls, Eino E., S/Sgt,
†Fanella, Michael, Pvt,
Fannin, Hubert V., Pfc,
Farnsworth, George H., Cpl,
Fasano, James, Pfc,
Faulk, James R., Cpl,
Faulk, Roy L., Pvt,
Fenner, William B., Pvt,
Ferguson, Charles R., Pvt,
Filipek, George, Cpl,
Finley, Calvin C., Pvt,
Finley, Jack D., Sgt,
Fisher, Charles H., Pfc,
Fishman, Ruben R., Pvt,
Fitzgerald, Roland J., S/Sgt,
Fleming, Bernard T., T/5,
Flesik, Martin, Jr., Pfc,
Fochesato, Roger A., T/4,
Fonseca, James V., Pfc,
Forman, Chester D., T/4,
Fortin, Alphonse L., S/Sgt,
Foster, Ernest A., Pfc,
Foster, Gerald L., Cpl,
Foster, Russell J., 1st Lt,
Fourcade, Martin E., Pvt,
Fox, Garold L., Cpl,
Fraime, Guy L., Pfc,
Francese, Anthony J., Pvt,
Frank, Joseph N., 2nd Lt,
Frankiewicz, Chester R., T/5,
Frederick, Robert E., Pfc,
Fredrickson, Albin, Sgt,
Freidag, Wallace H., Pvt,
French, William C., 1st Lt,
Fritzgerald, Patrick J., Pvt,
Fronk, Edwin A., Jr., Capt,
Frye, Donnelle C., Pfc,
Fueglein, Donald C., Pvt,
Fuller, Blackwood, Pfc,
Fuller, Curtis A., Pfc,

Gaeta, Torino C., Pvt,
Galarza, Samuel G., Pfc,
Galbicka, Joseph A., Pfc,
Galbraith, Alexander, 1st Lt,
Gambrell, R. D., Jr., Capt,
Gamon, Willis D., Pvt,
Ganguin, Henry J., Pvt,
Garcia, Antonio, Pfc,
Gaul, Manford M., Cpl,
Gavigan, Russell R., Pvt,
Gavin, John W., T/4,
Gawart, Herman F., Pvt,
Gerace, George, T/4,
Gervasoni, Fred R., Pfc,
Giaudrone, Aldo, Cpl,
Gibbons, James M., Pfc,
Gibson, Warren B., 1st Lt,
Gillespie, Johnnie L., Sgt,
Gillespie, Willam S., Pvt,
Gilliam, Clyde, Pfc,
Gilliland, Robert L., Cpl,
Gills, Edward A., 2nd Lt,
Gipson, Chester W., Pvt,
Gizzo, Frank C., Pfc,
Glasrud, Baldwin G., Cpl,
Gondoly, John T., Pvt,
Gonzales, Mercedes E., Pvt,
Goodrich, Don I., Pvt,
Gordon, Marten D., Pvt,
Gosnell, William, Pvt,
Goss, Edward H., Pvt,
Graefe, Wayne A., Pvt,
Graham, Archie L., Sgt,
Graves, Francis P., Jr., 1st Lt,
Gray, Wilbur O., Pfc,
Greb, Howard J., Pfc,
Greene, Donald D., Pvt,
Greene, Joseph, Pfc,
Greenfield, John, Pfc,
Griffiths, Jack D., 1st Lt,
Griffiths, William D., Pvt,
Griffith, William L., Cpl,
Griffy, Marion D., T/5,
Griggers, Claude G., Sgt,
Grossett, Jack N., Pvt,
Gruber, David P., 1st Lt,
Guillory, Thomas F., Pvt,
Guillotte, Bernard E., Pfc,
Guiseppe, James, Pvt,
Gunderson, Morris R., T/5,
Gunderson, Orville A., S/Sgt,

Haas, Wayne N., Sgt,
Habura, Leon T., Pvt,
Haddon, Arvell D., Pvt,
Hagar, Carl A., Pfc,
Haglund, Wesley E., T/5,
Hale, Walker M., Pvt,
Hall, Frank W., Pvt,
Halverson, Orvin M., T/4,
Hamill, Alfred D., Pfc,
Hammons, Ned, Pvt,
Hancock, Charles E., Pvt,
Hansen, Richard C., Capt,
Hanson, Emil, T/5,
Hanucak, George M., Pfc,
Happ, Richard C., T/5,
Harbin, Perry K., Pvt,
Harbour, David E., Sgt,
Hardy, Axel O., S/Sgt,
Hardy, Douglas W., Capt,
Hardy, Francis W., Cpl,
Harkey, William T., T/4,
Harkins, John P., Pfc,
Harland, Earl J., Pvt,
Harless, Richard A., Cpl,
Harper, Audie N., 1st Lt,
Harris, Lloyd V., Pfc,
Harris, Robert R., Pfc,
Harrison, Earl E., Cpl,
Harten, Francis P., Pvt,
Haselwood, Ray, Pvt,
Hatch, Floyd G., Capt,
Haupert, Paul E., T/5,
Hauser, Frank C., Jr., Pvt,
Haydel, Ottis J., Cpl,
Hayes, Glenn L., Sgt,
Healy, John P., Pvt,
Healy, William P., Pvt,
Heaslet, Thomas T., Pvt,
Heath, Herman B., Pvt,
Hebert, Wills J., Pfc,
Heil, Howard R., Pvt,
Heinen, John N., Pvt,
Heistand, Joseph T., Pfc,
Helkey, Russell L., Pfc,
Heller, Ralph E., T/5,
Henderson, John T., Pfc,
Henley, Charles R., 2nd Lt,
Henley, Dewey E., Pfc,
Henning, Robert E., Cpl,
Henrickson, Monroe B., T/5,
Henry, George E., Cpl,
Henry, Kenneth H., Cpl,
Hensen, Wilford H., T/3,
Henson, Carl W., Pfc,
Herbert, Herbert, M/Sgt,
Herman, Walter E., Pvt,
Hermanson, Abram, Cpl,
Hertlein, John A., Pfc,
Hester, Edward J., S/Sgt,
§Hestley, Charles S., Pfc,
Heydeman, John J., Cpl,
Hickey, Laurence H., Pfc,
Hill, Charles W., Pfc,
Hill, Chester W., 2nd Lt,
Hinrichsen, Robert L., 1st Sgt,
Hinton, Paul R., 1st Lt,
*Hirmer, Philip G., 1st Sgt,
Ho, Ronald W., T/5,
Hoffmann, Albert J., Pvt,
Holka, Robert F., Pfc,
Holmes, William N., Pfc,
Honzik, Paul A., S/Sgt,
Hopkins, Galen G., Pfc,
Hopkins, Thomas M., Jr., Pvt,
Horner, Walter R., 2nd Lt,
†Horton, William H., 1st Lt,
House, Lawrence H., T/4,
§Hovland, Martin J., T/4,
Howard, Lewis G., Pfc,
Howard, Ned S., 1st Sgt,
Hubbard, John F., Jr., Pfc,
Hudgins, George V., Sr., Pvt,
Hudlow, Leon F., Pvt,
Hudson, Ira A., Pfc,
Hudson, Russell, Pfc,
Huff, John, Pfc,
Huffman, Murray J., Pvt,
Hughes, William R., Pvt,
Humphreys, Roy S., T/5,
Hunt, Emile, Pfc,
Hunter, Claude, Cpl,
Huntington, John B., Cpl,
Hurt, Ray T., Pvt,
Hutchens, Daniel C., Pfc,
Hyland, William, Pvt,

Iantorno, Ernest M., Pvt,
Ilchman, Carl, Pfc,
Ingraham, Arthur C., Pfc,
Isler, Harry, T/5,
Ivankovich, Floyd D., T/5,
Iverson, Alvin J., Sgt,

Jablonski, Charles J., Pfc,
*Jacobs, Billie E., Pfc,
James, Ralph L., Pfc,
James, Ronda J., S/Sgt,
Janicki, Leonard C., WOJG,
Jankowski, Walter S., Pfc,
Jaschek, Otto, Pfc,
Jaskiewicz, Henry J., Pfc,
Jeffrey, John A., Pvt,
Jeffries, James M., Pfc,
Jeffries, William, 2nd Lt,
Jenkins, Wilburn D., T/5,
†Jensen, Erik L., Sgt,
Jensen, William V., T/4,
Jepsen, Paul A., Pvt,
Jester, Thomas H., Pfc,
Jimenez, Raul C., T/5,
Joens, Cornelius J., T/4,
Johnson, Arnold C., Pfc,
Johnson, Carl A., S/Sgt,
Johnson, George W., Pfc,
Johnson, John R., Pfc,
Johnson, Oliver T., S/Sgt,
Johnson, Orin M., Cpl,
Johnson, Oscar, Pfc,
Johnson, Richard M., Pfc,
†Johnson, Thomas W., Pvt,
Jones, Cary E., Jr., Cpl,
†Jones, Glen A., Pfc,
Jones, Robert F., Pvt,
Jones, Robert M., 1st Lt,
Jordan, Warren G., Pfc,
Joseph, Alfred A., 1st Lt,
Joswiak, Joseph, Cpl,
Judd, Jack L., T/5,
Just, Frank C., Pfc,

Kabza, Raymond A., Pvt,
Kane, Francis C., Capt,
Katcher, Glenn W., Pfc,
Katschta, Carl J., Pvt,
Kauffman, Zane E., Pfc,
Kazmierczak, Henry J., Pfc,
Keaiser, Clayte S., Sgt,
Keane, John V., Pfc,
Kearney, Louis, Pvt,
Keener, Lewis C., Pvt,
Keil, Ira O., Pvt,
Kelly, Joseph L., Sgt,
Kelly, Wesley W., T/4,
Kemp, Robert M., Pfc,
Kennedy, Donald J., Sgt,
Kern, Fred O., T/4,
Kicak, Mike, Pvt,
Kijek, Walter A., Pfc,
King, John H., Jr., Pfc,
King, Richard T., Jr., Pvt,
†Kirkpatrick, Seba W., 1st Lt,
Kirkpatrick, Thomas W., Cpl,
Kitchel, Ralph R., Cpl,
†Klang, Bernard, 1st Lt,
Knecht, Robert C., Pfc,
Knopsnyder, Ralph H., Pvt,
Knudson, Harold A., Sgt,
Knutson, Neil I., S/Sgt,
Kohl, William G., Cpl,
Kolaczewski, Thomas C., Sgt,
Kollock, Fred C., T/5,
Konkel, Raymond H., Pvt,
Kopec, Joseph T., Pfc,
Kowsh, George P., Pvt,
Kozacki, Stanley V., Pfc,
Krause, Robert A., Pfc,
Krebs, George E., Pvt,
Kress, Oscar, Pfc,
Krieter, Benjamin, Cpl,
Kruempel, Robert W., Cpl,
Krystofiak, Ted M., Cpl,
Kubuske, Leonard F., 2nd Lt,
Kuhn, John P., Cpl,
Kumm, Donald C., T/5,
Kunz, William J., Sgt,

Labonte, Germain O. D., Pfc,
Lacy, Robert J., Cpl,
Lagana, Ferdinand J., Pvt,
LaGreide, Arvid B., Sgt,
Laity, Oliver J., Pvt,
Lamoureaux, Calvin J., T/4,
Landau, Richard E., Cpl,
Landrus, Glenn L., Pfc,
Lane, Robert C., Pfc,
Lane, Warren A., Pfc,
Lang, Clarence W., T/4,
Langenbeck, Oscar B., Pvt,
Langenberg, Henry F., Pfc,
Lantzer, Paul, T/5,
Lara, John H., T/5,
Larson, Gilbert L., Pfc,
LaTorre, Frank, Pfc,
Lazar, John, Pfc,
Lebsock, Clarence V., T/4,
Lee, Hilton W., Pvt,
†Lehman, Ralph J., Pfc,
LeMay, Emile J., Pvt,
Lentz, Ralph V., Pfc,
Lerum, Leonard W., Pfc,
Letson, Alonzo A., Pfc,
Levin, Ralph I., Pfc,
†Lewis, Hume B., S/Sgt,
Lewis, Marvin D., Cpl,
Lewis, Russell L., S/Sgt,
Liggenstoffer, Richard A., T/5,
Lile, William W., S/Sgt,
Linder, General W., Pfc,
Lindsey, Theodore A., Cpl,
Linn, John, Pvt,
Lloyd, William E., T/5,
Lodato, John J., Capt,
Loftus, Milton R., T/5,
§Logan, George E., T/5,
Logsdon, Johnnie C., Pvt,
Long, Runar A., Cpl,
Lonski, Frank J., 1st Lt,
Looney, James R., Pvt,
†Lorch, Arthur F., Pfc,
Lorenz, Marvin P., T/Sgt,
*Lorenzen, Harry F., 1st Lt,
Lorusso, Daniel P., Cpl,
Losh, Elmer E., T/5,
Love, George G., T/4,
Lovegren, Walter E., Cpl,
Lubas, George M., Pvt,
Lumpkin, Raymond M., Pfc,
Lundsten, Roy D., Pfc,
Lytle, William P., Pvt,

MacFarlane, Iver R., Pfc,
Maciel, Frank H., 2nd Lt,
Mackenzie, George F., T/4,
Madamba, Edward F., 1st Sgt,
Madrid, Armando G., Sgt,
Magatelli, Mike, T/5,
Mages, John E., T/5,
Mainer, Chester L., Pfc,
Maloney, Kenneth H., Cpl,
Maniscalco, Joseph F., Pvt,
Mantoani, Ugo, Cpl,
Mapes, Terrance S., Cpl,
Marchsteiner, Gordon F., Pvt,
Marek, Roger V., Jr., Pfc,
Marks, Robert L., Cpl,
Marmo, Charles A., Pvt,
Marshall, John A., Pfc,
Marshall, Robert P., Sgt,
Martin, James A., Pfc,
Martin, LaVerle M., T/5,
Martin, Maurice C., T/5,
Martinez, Augustine, Pfc,
Martinez, John, Pfc,
Mason, Harry, Pvt,
Mason, Louis E., Sgt,
Massett, Allen W., Pvt,
Massey, Burrell T., S/Sgt,
*Matheson, Marvin M., 2nd Lt,
Matlock, Henry A., Capt,
Matta, Arnold A., T/5,
Maupin, Clarence W., Pfc,
Maves, Arthur H., T/Sgt,
Maybee, Dale F., T/5,
Mayo, James W., Pvt,
Mays, Julius E., Pfc,
Mazepa, Walter J., Pfc,
Mazor, John V., T/4,
McCabe, Willard R., Pvt,
McCallum, William A., S/Sgt,
McClung, George R., Cpl,
McCormick, James M., Pfc,
McCutchan, Charles O., 1st Lt,
McDonald, Emmett E., Pfc,
McElvain, Floyd E., Pfc,
McGaffigan, Charles F., Pfc,
McGee, Robert C., Pvt,
McGowan, John, Pvt,
McGrath, Donald B., Cpl,
McGraw, Melvin, G., Pvt,
McGregor, James R., 1st Lt,
McGroarty, Frank J., Pvt,
McIntyre, W. C., Jr., Maj,
McLaughlin, Selden M., Cpl,
McLewee, Robert C., Pfc,
McMillen, James M., M/Sgt,
McTeer, Andrew G., Pfc,
Medvinsky, Louis, Pfc,
Meeks, Burl E., Pvt,
Meese, Harry L., T/5,
Mehl, William R., T/4,
Mehmen, William, T/5,
Meister, Earl O., Pfc,
Melius, Carl R., Pvt,
Mellinger, Leonard, Pfc,
Mendoza, Xavier, Pvt,
Mercauto, Jerry, Pvt,
Merkel, Arthur L., Pvt,
Merrell, James E., Pfc,
†Merson, Richard B., Cpl,
Mertsching, Frank R., Cpl,
Mesa, Trinidad J., Pfc,
Metcalfe, Elmer E., Pfc,
Meyer, Leonard F., Pvt,
Miceli, Joseph J., Pvt,
Mikos, Paul, Pfc,
Miles, Donald C., S/Sgt,
Miller, Carl C., Pfc,
Miller, Dale N., Cpl,
Miller, Machull, T/4,
Miller, Philip, Cpl,
Miller, Ramon A., T/5,
Miller, Willam O., Pfc,
Milligan, George F., Pfc,
Millot, Morse, Sgt,
Milner, Grant A., Cpl,
Minetti, Plinio J., Pvt,
Mirosh, Peter, Pvt,
Mitchell, Hobart V., Pvt,
Mitchell, Stephen W., S/Sgt,
Mitchem, Plato C., S/Sgt,
Mockus, Bruno J., Cpl,
Monico, Vincent T., Pfc,
Montalbano, Anthony J., Pvt,
Moody, Chester E., T/5,
Moody, Henry E., T/5,
Moore, Peter, Pvt,
*Morales, Jose I., Pfc,
Moreno, Rodolfo M., Pvt,
Morgan, Leon J., Sgt,
Morris, Aaron E., T/4,
Morris, Anthony J., Pfc,
Mortenson, Theodore M., Pfc,
Moss, Flem, Jr., Pfc,
Motise, Anthony G., Pvt,
Mullen, Richard D., 1st Lt,
Mulvaney, Edward M., Pfc,
Murphy, James R., T/5,

Nardozzi, Donato A., Pvt,
Naylor, Robert J., Pvt,
Neidert, Charles H., Pfc,
Neidlinger, Craig N., Pfc,
Nelson, Donald N., 2nd Lt,
Nelson, Earl R., Sgt,
Nelson, John R., T/5,
Nettleton, John W., Pvt,
Neuens, Joseph L., Pfc,
§Nevarez, Augustine U., Pfc,
Newell, Richard C., Cpl,
Newell, Richard C., Pvt,
Newlen, Kenneth W., Sgt,
Nezich, George J., Pfc,
Nichols, Harold E., 1st Lt,
Nicholson, P. L., Jr., T/5,
Niemeyer, Clifford H., T/4,
Niemi, Arvid B., Pfc,
Nievar, Paul E., Pvt,
Noland, Richard P., T/5,
*Nold, Louis F., Cpl,
Nooner, Marion G., Pfc,
Normoyle, Benedict F., T/5,
Norton, John J., Jr., Pfc,
Norvell, William J., Pfc,

O'Brien, Mark P., T/4,
O'Brien, Robert J., Pfc,
O'Hara, Hugh J., Pfc,
Olthoff, Simon C., Cpl,
O'Malley, John J., Pvt,
O'Meara, Philip G., S/Sgt,
O'Neil, Joseph T., Pfc,
O'Neill, Thomas J., Pvt,
Oppenhimer, John S., 1st Lt,
Opperud, Raymond, T/5,
O'Rourke, John J., Pfc,
Osborn, James W., T/5,
O'Shaughnessy, Francis J., Pfc
Oswald, Raymond C., 1st Lt,
Owen, Charles B., Pfc,
Owon, Jack L., Cpl,

Pagni, Albo, Pfc,
Pajity, Stephen, T/4,
Palmenters, Vito, Pvt,
Palmer, Robert G., Pvt,
Palumbo, Sam, Pfc,
Papin, Gerald J., Cpl,
Parker, Lynn A., Pfc,
Parlegreco, Thomas A., Sgt,
Parrish, Henry R., Pfc,
Pater, John, Pfc,
Patsey, Edward G., T/5,
Patterson, Donald M., Pfc,
Paulsen, Lawrence T., T/5,
Payne, Richard M., Jr., Pfc,
Peasgood, Robert L., Pvt,
Pecanas, Emil M., T/5,
Pederson, Odd P., Sgt,
Pendleton, Donn W., Pvt,
Penn, Kenneth L., Pfc,
Pentz, Edward J., T/5,
Perrott, Eddie C., Pvt,
Perry, Buster, Cpl,
Perry, Joe, Pfc,
Peters, William B., Cpl,
Peterson, Julius E., S/Sgt,
Peterson, Stanley N., Sgt,
Peterson, Warren O., S/Sgt,
Phillips, George O., Pvt,
Phillips, Warner E., Pfc,
Phinney, Lester H., Cpl,
Phipps, Herchell E., T/5,
Pichot, Emil, Pvt,
Pieretti, Guido, T/4,
Pineau, Robert N., Cpl,
Piona, Steve, Pvt,
Pitts, Dallas, Pfc,
Pointer, Grant, Cpl,
Polek, Michael P., S/Sgt,
Poling, Andrew W., M/Sgt,
Ponchetti, Louis, Pvt,
Poole, Benjamin F., Jr., S/Sgt,
Porath, James J., Sgt,
Porter, Paul M., Pfc,

† Killed in Action. * Prisoner of War. ‡ Missing in Action. § Died of Wounds.

Portera, Richard J., Pfc,
§Posch, Andrew J., T/5,
Posch, Arthur S., Cpl,
Posner, Julius L., Pvt,
Powell, Audie E., Pvt,
Powell, Hallie F., Pvt,
Poy Fair, Nelson E., Pfc,
Primavera, Anthony, Pvt,
Primmer, Donald B., Pfc,
Prenosil, Loddie E., T/4,
†Presley, James M., Cpl,
Pruitt, William H., Pvt,
Przada, Julian J., Cpl,
Pueschel, Earnest E., Cpl,

Quaife, Harold A., T/4,
Quigley, William J., Pvt,

Rabe, Charles H., Pvt,
Ramsey, Henry M., Pfc,
Ramsey, Willie, T/5,
Randall, Oliver E., Pfc,
Rapach, John D., 2nd Lt,
Rathbun, Frank P., Pvt,
Ratzer, John S., Pfc,
Reck, Howard M., Pfc,
Reio, James J., Sgt,
Reno, James E., Pvt,
Retman, Clarence R., Pvt,
Retzlaff, Robert E., Pfc,
Reuwsaat, Clarence H., 1st Sgt,
Rhodes, Jake R., Pfc,
Rice, Al, T/5,
Richards, William A., 1st Lt,
Richardson, Robert R., Pvt,
Riechers, Harold J., T/5,
Rigby, Paul T., Major,
Rittner, John F., Sgt,
Roark, Dalmer D., Pvt,
Robbin, Burdette C., S/Sgt,
Robbins, Howard M., T/4,
Robbins, John G., Pvt,
Roberts, James N., Pfc,
Roberts, Joseph M., Pvt,
§Roberts, William H., T/3,
†Robinett, Clarence I., S/Sgt,
Robinette, Virgil, Pvt,
Robinson, Richard B., Cpl,
Rodgers, James E., Pfc,
Rodrique, Ernest L., Pfc,
Roesslein, Theodore A., 1st Lt,
Rogers, Arnold W., Cpl,
Rogers, Hans L., Pvt,
Roller, Alvin H., Pfc,
Roman, Paul P., Pvt,
Rose, Offie L., Cpl,
Rosen, Morris, Pvt,
Rosenberg, Norman, Pvt,
Rosensteel, David R., Pvt,
Rosenthal, Louis, Pvt,

Rosenwinkle, Edmund H., T/5,
Rosenzwog, Harold W., Pfc,
Rosner, Erwin, 2nd Lt,
Ross, Elwood R., T/4,
Rossi, Frank, T/5,
Rowell, John A., Jr., Pfc,
Rowland, Earl E., Cpl,
Royston, Theodore J., Sgt,
Rudd, Donald J., Pvt,
Rudman, Mitchell, T/4,
Rundin, Joseph C., T/5,
Rundle, C. O., Jr., T/4,
Rupert, J. V., S/Sgt,
Rutter, Lee M., T/4,
Rychnosky, Anton J., Jr., Pvt,

Sabo, William B., Pvt,
Sackman, Berthold E., Cpl,
Sandreczski, Max, Pfc,
San Roman, Emilio, Pvt,
Santos, Rafael G., Jr., Pfc,
Sarkilahti, Segyrd W., S/Sgt,
Satalich, Simon C., Pvt,
Schear, Dwight B., Pfc,
Schefter, Leonard W., Cpl,
Scheibner, Alfred A., Pvt,
Schenck, Sanford R., Pvt,
Schlaps, David, Sgt,
Schneider, Anton J., S/Sgt,
Schnettler, Alton E., T/5,
Schroeder, Frederick C., Pvt,
Schuch, Ivan C., Pfc,
Scott, Thomas G., Pvt,
Seger, Raymond J., Pfc,
Selle, Harvey H., Pvt,
Sette, Philip R., Pvt,
Shadle, John N., Pvt,
Shanks, Don E., Pfc,
Sharp, Jim C., T/Sgt,
Sharp, Marion C., Pvt,
Sheehan, Edwin P., Pvt,
Sheftick, Michael A., Pfc,
Sheldon, Duane L., T/5,
Sheldon, William P., T/4,
Shell, John R., 1st Lt,
Sheppard, Bryon E., S/Sgt,
Schultz, Edward S., Pfc,
Schwartz, Sol S., Pfc,
Shultz, Earl L., T/4,
Shurgalla, John S., Pfc,
Sicinski, Stanley J., Pfc,
Sidock, Leonard S., Pfc,
Sieber, Elmer, Pvt,
Siemrzuch, Stanley F., T/4,
Siewert, Forrest A., Sgt,
Sifuentes, Emmett M., Pvt,
Silva, Jose, Pvt,
Silveira, Frank H., Pfc,
Simmons, Oscar F., Pfc,
Simonds, George E., Sgt,

Simonds, Herbert, T/4,
Simone, Alfred P., Pvt,
Simonson, Kenneth R., 1st Lt,
Sinclair, Gordon M., Pfc,
Siskaninetz, Frank, Pfc,
Sissel, George W., Pfc,
Sitzler, Sidney D., Pfc,
Siverston, Harlon W., T/4,
Skopkowski, Stanley S., Cpl,
Slocum, Edwin J., T/5,
Smetak, Robert E., Pfc,
Smiley, Alfred F., Pfc,
Smilovitz, Seymour, Pfc,
Smith, Barton C., Sgt,
Smith, Clyde O., Pvt,
Smith, Keith A., T/4,
Smith, Marion I., Pvt,
Smith, Robert C., Pvt,
Smith, Sam W., T/Sgt,
Smith, Sid, Cpl,
Smith, William E., Cpl,
Smith, William J., T/5,
Smithingell, James W., Pvt,
Sneck, Albert G., Pfc,
Solomon, Harry, Pvt,
Spencer, Halbert H., Pvt,
Spencer, Lawrence R., Pvt,
Spencer, Norman M., Pvt,
Spinnato, Jack J., Pfc,
Spolar, Jasper J., Jr., T/4,
Sportsman, Charles O., T/5,
Spotts, Wayne L., T/5,
Spratt, Earl E., T/4,
Stanek, James R., Pfc,
Stanley, Villis L., S/Sgt,
Starkweather, Chester K., Pfc,
Steffen, George E., Pfc,
Steger, James R., T/4,
Steigberg, Ole S., M/Sgt,
Steik, Robert J., Pfc,
Stetter, Severin F., Jr., Pfc,
Stevens, Fred P., Capt,
Stewart, Daniel J., S/Sgt,
Stewart, Gordon R., Cpl,
Stinson, Paul, Cpl,
Stobart, Louis C., Pfc,
Stofko, Edward R., Pfc,
Stoll, James W., S/Sgt,
Stool, Henry W., Cpl,
Stover, Charles W., Pvt,
Stranko, Joseph, Pfc,
Strasser, Leo J., Pvt,
Streid, Delmar, Sgt,
Strietzel, Lester R., T/4,
Stroyan, Jacob L., Pfc,
Sturk, George A., Pfc,
Sturzl, Budd F., Capt,
Sudlow, Robert D., Pfc,
Summers, Amos L., T/4,
Swanson, Alvin A., T/4,

Swida, Barney P., Pvt,
Swider, Charles A., Pfc,
Sykora, George, Pfc,

Talanian, Kay, Pfc,
†Talbert, Clyde L., T/5,
Tamayo, Andrew S., Pfc,
Tambussi, Frank J., Pfc,
Tarrant, Robert M., S/Sgt,
Terranova, Edmund, Pvt,
†Terry, William O., Cpl,
§Testerman, David, Pvt,
Thatcher, Carl W., Pvt,
Theisen, Edmund E., T/4,
Thomas, Cecil B., Jr., 1st Lt,
Thomas, Robert E., Pfc,
Thompson, Phillip, Pfc,
Tierney, George A., T/5,
Tigue, Robert T., T/5,
Timperley, John H., Cpl,
Tomlinson, LeRoy H., Sgt,
Toombs, Jack J., Cpl,
Tourville, Arthur J., S/Sgt,
Townley, Roe H., Pfc,
Trapani, Rosario J., Pfc,
Truax, Charles W., Cpl,
Trethewey, Thomas G., T/5,
Trevino, Gustave G., Pvt,
Trojanowski, Thomas J., T/5,
Truitt, William O., Cpl,
Trujillo, Manuel, Pvt,
Trupukka, Walter H., T/5,
Tudor, Charley L., Pfc,
Turner, Cecil S., Pvt,

Unger, Harold, Cpl,
Upton, Charles G., Pvt,

Valenzuela, Efren, Cpl,
Vargo, John, Pvt,
Varley, Ray B., Pvt,
Vasey, Johnnie E., 2nd Lt,
Vash, Eugene C., Pfc,
Vaughan, Jesse L., 1st Lt,
Vela, Raymundo, Pvt,
Venn, Robert J., Cpl,
Vest, Stanley H., Pfc,
Villareal, Melchor, Jr., Pvt,
Virdin, Brice H., Pvt,
Voorhees, Kenneth B., Pfc,
Voss, Allan R., S/Sgt,
Vriesman, Roy J., Pvt,

Wake, Arthur H., Jr., Pvt,
Walker, Frederick W., Pfc,
Walsh, Joseph J., Pvt,
Ward, Walter W., Cpl,
Warden, William H., Pvt,

Watts, Jefferson R., 1st Lt,
Webb, Walter D., Jr., Lt Col,
Wedger, Wilbur L., 1st Sgt,
*Wegner, Mervin A., T/5,
Weinzierl, Carl E., Cpl,
Weispfenning, W. W., 1st Lt,
Wellons, Julius A., Pfc,
§Wendland, John J. W., Cpl,
Wennersten, Sheldon D., Pvt,
Wentworth, Paul J., S/Sgt,
West, Harold F., S/Sgt,
Wheeler, William R., T/5,
Whisnant, Hubert O., Pfc,
White, Barney D., Major,
Whitecomb, David, Jr., 1st Lt,
Whitelock, Kenly W., Capt,
Whiteside, William O., Pvt,
Widener, Carl M., Pfc,
Wiemerslage, Fremont F., Sgt,
§Wiener, Raymond, 1st Lt,
Wiese, Walter W., T/5,
Wilberger, Roy C., Cpl,
Wilhelmson, Rognald A., S/Sgt,
†Wilkins, Paul N., Pfc,
Wilkinson, Edward L., Capt,
Williams, Lewis M., Pvt,
Williams, Raymond B., Pvt,
Williamson, Louis B., Pvt,
Wilson, Blaine R., Cpl,
Wilson, Clarence, T/4,
Wilson, Howard R., Cpl,
Wilson, James M., Cpl,
Wilt, Robert T., Pvt,
Winkler, Herbert A., Pvt,
Wirtz, Louis T., Cpl,
Witmer, Roy H., Pfc,
Woerthmann, John J., Pvt,
†Wojdan, Aloysius, Pvt,
Wolfe, Cecil H., T/5,
Wolfert, Dave I., Pfc,
Wood, David D., Pvt,
Woodruff, Arthur N., Pvt,
Wooley, Clyde G., T/5,
Woolums, Eldon A., Cpl,
Wright, Edwin C., Pvt,
†Wright, Orville A., T/5,
Wright, William K., Sgt,

Ybanez, Gilberto, Cpl,
Yeager, William A., T/5,
York, Charles H., Sgt,

Zapata, Ruben P., Pfc,
Zavala, Frank M., Pvt,
Zickefoose, George O., Pvt,
Ziegler, Elwood W., 1st Lt,
Ziff, Nathan, Pfc,
Zimmerman, Fritz, Cpl,
Zrioka, John, Sgt,

† Killed in Action.   * Prisoner of War.   ‡ Missing in Action.   § Died of Wounds.

41st FIELD ARTILLERY BATTALION (LIGHT)

The 41st Field Artillery Regiment—now a battalion—was first organized at Camp Custer, Michigan, in August, 1918, and was demobilized there in February 1919. It was reconstituted and consolidated with the post-war regiment in 1936, and activated as the 41st Field Artillery Battalion on October 1, 1940. Personnel for the 41st Battalion came from the old 10th Field Artillery Regiment.

Commanding Officer

(Highest rank held)	Held pos. from	To
Maj. Walter D. Webb, Jr.		8 Jan 1943
Maj. Edward C. Robertson	9 Jan 1943	17 Jan 1943
Lt. Col. Mercer C. Walter	18 Jan 1943	14 July 1943
Maj. Edward C. Robertson	15 July 1943	9 Aug 1943
Lt. Col. James R. Wendt, Jr.	10 Aug 1943	1 Dec 1944
Lt. Col. Barney D. White	2 Dec 1944	

Abernathy, Joseph B., T/4,
†Abney, Floyd R., Pvt,
Abrahamson, Fred R., Cpl,
Ackerman, Floyd S., Sgt,
Adam, Gottfried H., S/Sgt,
Adams, Frank L., Cpl,
Adams, Morgan K., Capt,
Aho, Arthur M., T/4,
Ahrens, Richard B., 2nd Lt,
Albright, Slocum L., Sgt,
Allen, Kenneth P., Pvt,
Allen, Thomas, T/5,
Allenby, Ray L., Pvt,
Alpert, Paul, 1st Lt,
Alston, Dee L., Pfc,
Amos, Ray C., Pvt,
Anderson, Carl A., S/Sgt,
Angaretis, Nick M., Pvt,
Angerhofer, Martin W., Pfc,
Anker, Walter, S/Sgt,
Antonelli, Basil, 2nd Lt,
Arena, Louis L., Pfc,
Armstrong, Blair L., 1st Lt,
Asche, Fred, Pvt,
Ashook, George W., Pfc,
Austin, Wilbur R., Pvt,
Azevedo, Lawrence P., Pfc,

Baca, Edward E., Pvt,
Bailey, Carl W., Pvt,
Baird, George A., T/Sgt,
Baker, Richard F., Pvt,
†Baker, Victor W., Pvt,
Balmes, Donald W., Pvt,
Balsley, Richard L., 1st Lt,
Baran, Joseph S., Pfc,
Barco, Barney M., 1st Lt,
Barker, Witt H., 1st Lt,
‡Barr, William J., 1st Lt,
Barsh, George E., Pvt,
Barrett, Fred L., S/Sgt,
Basquez, Manuel, Cpl,
Bates, Walter M., Pfc,
Beal, Robert J., Pfc,
Bean, William W., Pfc,
†Beatrice, Louis, Pfc,
Beck, Dwight, Cpl,
Beck, James R., Cpl,
Benner, Christ, Sgt,
Bennett, Joe R., Pvt,
Benning, Gerald L., 1st Sgt,
Berger, Mike, Cpl,

Bergman, Herman A., T/4,
Berk, Morris, T/5,
Bernstein, Maurice L., Pvt,
Berry, David O., T/4,
Berry, James H., Pvt,
Best, Walter J., Sgt,
Bettenhausen, Roy H., Sgt,
Biasotti, Louis M., T/4,
Bigone, John P., Pfc,
Biles, Denzil E., Pvt,
Billman, Frederick C., 1st Lt,
†Billman, Jay D., 1st Lt,
Birsch, Edwin T., Pvt,
Blackwell, Henry W., Pvt,
Blake, John A., Sgt,
Blakewood, Norman R., Pvt,
Blatti, George G., T/5,
Blaufuss, Mathew, Cpl,
Blaziek, Alvin J., Sgt,
Blue, Valentine B., Pfc,
Bly, Stanley E., T/4,
Board, Oliver P., 1st Lt,
Bogner, Charles, Maj,
Boland, Albert A., Pvt,
Bonogofsky, Jacob J., S/Sgt,
Bonviso, Fiore, Pvt,
Boos, Richard O., S/Sgt,
Borton, Truman W., Pvt,
‡Boucher, Wilfred M., 1st Lt,
Bouck, Charles A., Cpl,
Bowen, Clarence A., Pvt,
Bower, Harold C., 2nd Lt,
Bowers, Raymond E., Pfc,
†Bradford, James C., Pfc,
Bradybaugh, Nathan C., Pvt,
Branaugh, Frank J., Sgt,
Brandt, Tabor D., T/5,
Brettell, Jack E., Pfc,
Briggs, James E., Pvt,
Brimmer, Marvin L., 1st Sgt,
Brittain, Noel, Pfc,
Broom, Paul T., Pfc,
Brossard, Wayne A., S/Sgt,
Brown, Albert L., Pfc,
Brown, Raymond D., T/4,
Brownfield, Milton C., Pfc,
Brownlee, Henry, 1st Lt,
Brunk, Forrest D., T/5,
Bryant, Charles R., Pfc,
Buchanan, Walter T., Pfc,
Bue, Sigurd M., Pfc,
Bufkin, J. R., Pfc,

Bulich, Robert, S/Sgt,
Buntin, William A., 2nd Lt,
Burden, Phillip, Pvt,
Burkick, La Valla, Pvt,
Burk, Ezria A., Pvt,
Burke, Uless S., Pvt,
Burnett, Thomas E., T/4,
Burtchett, James H., Pvt,
Bury, Frank M., S/Sgt,
Burzynski, Eugene S., Sgt,
Busbee, James E., T/4,
Butler, Arthur L., Pvt,
Butler, William H., 2nd Lt,
Buzzard, Raymond H., Pfc,
Byrd, Elmo F., T/4,

Cable, Norman V., Capt,
Cahill, Robert, Pvt,
Cahoone, William H., Pfc,
†Caldwell, Paul D., Capt,
Calvin, Warren B., Pvt,
Camano, Raymond, Pfc,
Campbell, John R., 1st Lt,
Candela, Anthony J., Pvt,
Carlotta, Joseph F., Cpl,
Carmany, Clifford E., Pfc,
Carpenter, Donavon V., T/5,
Carrizales, Gustavo T., T/4,
Carroll, Cornelius E., Pvt,
Carson, Homer G., T/5,
Carter, Charles O., T/5,
§Carter, Harold J., Pfc,
Castro, Porfirio, Pfc,
Catuna, Ernest H. F., T/5,
Cavicchia, Louis A., Pvt,
Chaffin, James H., T/5,
Champigny, Albert L., Pfc,
Chapkowski, Chester J., Pvt,
Chapman, David P., Pvt,
Checotah, Clinton, Pvt,
Cherion, John, T/4,
Chick, George H., T/3,
Cholger, Alvin M., Pvt,
Christianson, Albert A., Pfc,
Chrobak, John S., Pfc,
Cijka, Felix P., Pvt,
Ciolino, Louis J., 1st Lt,
Clapham, Noel, Pvt,
Clarence, William, Sgt,
Cark, Clifford J., Pvt,
Clark, Daniel C., Cpl,
Clark, Howard L., T/4,

Clark, James R., Pvt,
Clark, John V., Pfc,
Clark, Murrel R., Pvt,
Clemente, Samuel P., Pvt,
Coble, John D., Jr., Cpl,
Cockrell, William M., T/5,
Coffin, Robert E., Capt,
Coffman, Jarvis D., Pfc,
Cohn, Julius, Pvt,
Colbaugh, James F., Pvt,
Cole, Roert J., Cpl,
Coleman, Mark S., Pfc,
Collier, James J., Pfc,
†Collins, Paul H., Pvt,
Collins, Virgil M., Pfc,
Combs, Bill, Pvt,
Comer, Jack C., Pfc,
Comerford, Vincent P., S/Sgt,
Compton, Howard L., S/Sgt,
Condon, Jack F., Pvt,
Conley, Brooks M., Pfc,
Conley, John P., 1st Lt,
†Cook, Forrest N., Pfc,
Coraggio, Anthony, Pvt,
Cordova, Alfonso G., Pfc,
Cornelius, James F., 1st Sgt,
Coronel, Rudolph J., Pfc,
Correa, Walter, Pfc,
†Corso, Americo, 1st Lt,
Costas, George C., 1st Lt,
Cousland, John A., Sgt,
Coventry, Jack R., Pvt,
Cozad, S. C., Pfc,
Craft, Ennis C., Pvt,
†Cross, Eldon C., Sgt,
Cross, Ernest L., T/5,
Cummings, Mark C., Sgt,
Curnick, William E., T/4,
Curutolo, Joseph, Pvt,
Custer, George W., T/3,
Czar, Joseph F., Pfc,
Czywczynski, Carl, Pfc,

Dagon, Willis F., Jr., Pfc,
Daisey, Edward B., Pvt,
Daley, Joseph T., Pfc,
D'Alicandro, Frank W., Pvt,
D'Amato, Silvio W., T/4,
Daniels, John E., T/4,
Daschal, Joseph A., Cpl,
Daum, Walter A., Pfc,
Davis, Arthur L., Cpl,

Davis, Ervin L., S/Sgt,
Davis, Gordon H., Pfc,
Davis, John N., T/5,
Dawson, Aaron S., Pfc,
Dealy, Harold W., Pvt,
DeBord, Everett G., Cpl,
Dechman, John M., Cpl,
Deck, Thomas W., Pvt,
Deerkop, Bernal J., Pfc,
DeFalco, Joseph N., Pvt,
DeGooyer, Louis C., Capt,
Deitz, Edwin A., Pvt,
DeJonckheere, Maurice A., Pvt
Delmolino, Everett J., Pvt,
Dempsey, Christopher T., Pfc,
DePaul, Samuel, Pfc,
Derine, William J., Pvt,
DeRosa, John J., Pfc,
Depula, Joseph N., Pfc,
Derschon, Anton, Pvt,
Deutsch, Frederick E., T/5,
Dever, Eugene C., 1st Lt,
Diaz, Francisco A., Pfc,
Dickey, Albert T., Pvt,
Dickson, Marshall L., Pvt,
†Dietrich, Roy L., Sgt,
Dietz, George J., Pfc,
Dillenburg, Linus V., Pfc,
Dockins, John T., Pfc,
Doebert, Wallace H., Pfc,
§Doherty, John E., Capt,
†Doherty, Joseph C., 1st Lt,
Dolan, Thomas J., 1st Lt,
Donaldson, Otis L., Pvt,
Donnelly, Lester, Pfc,
Dossey, Harold D., Sgt,
Doxrud, Norman E., T/5,
Doyle, Michael R., Cpl,
Drake, Coley E., Pvt,
Drayler, Daniel E., Pvt,
Drinkard, Malcom T., Pfc,
Droz, Frank A., Sgt,
Druskin, Benjamin, Pvt,
DuBois, Wilfred F., Pfc,
Ducay, John J., Pfc,
Duckloe, Howard W., Pvt,
Duda, Felix A., Cpl,
Duncan, Bille J., Pvt,
Duncan, Roger E., Cp,
Dunn, Harry R., Pvt,
Dunne, John J., Pvt,
Dunnell, Merle J., T/5,

† Killed in Action.　　* Prisoner of War.　　‡ Missing in Action.　　§ Died of Wounds.

Duree, Loren J., 1st Sgt,
Durfey, James F., S/Sgt,
Durnell, Clyde W., T/4,

Eberle, Fred I., T/4,
Eccles, Alfred E., Pfc,
Eckenrode, Ray L., Pfc,
Eckhardt, Glenn, Pvt,
Edinger, Melvin R., Pfc,
Edstrom, Albert R., Cpl,
Edwards, George F., Pfc,
Egge, Dale W., T/5,
Ehrlich, Martin M., Pfc,
Eisele, George W., Pvt,
Eliott, James E., T/4,
Elkins, Emuel, Pfc,
Elliott, Walter L., T/5,
Ellis, Richard G., T/5,
Elmer, Garth C., T/4,
Ericsson, Carl W., T/5,
Evans, Eugene R., S/Sgt,
Evans, Howard D., Major,
Ewoldt, Albert H., Pfc,

Fader, Phillip, Pfc,
Fay, George F., Pfc,
Fehrer, Raymond A., Pfc,
Feldman, Barnet, Pfc,
Femling, Frank C., Pfc,
†Fernandez, Raymond F., S/Sgt
Ferraris, Henry L., Cpl,
Fiene, Rudolph D. C., Pfc,
Fik, Edwin F., Pvt,
Fincher, Wilson M., Pvt,
Finn, Edward W., Pfc,
Fiss, David B., T/Sgt,
Flanigan, Patrick E., Pfc,
Flatt, William M., Pfc,
Fleming, John F., Pfc,
Flint, Charles, Pvt,
Foland, Floyd D., T/5,
Folkstad, Maurice H., Cpl,
Fong, Foo, Pvt,
Forlines, Clarence G., Pfc,
Forsythe, Ivan, Pfc,
Fowler, Harlan E., Pvt,
Frahm, Howard L., Pfc,
Franco, Joseph V., Cpl,
Frandsen, Victor C., T/4,
Frank, John J., Cpl,
Frederick, Clyde E., Pfc,
Frediani, Fred J., S/Sgt,
Frohnfoeffer, Lawrence, Pfc,
Frye, Willard M., Pfc,
Fuchs, William P., Pfc,
Fuqua, Jack C., Cpl,
Fuller, Robert E., Cpl,
Fullmer, Ferrol, T/5,
Funderburk, Jennings H., Pfc,
Furgerson, James H., Pvt,

Gage, Charles D., 1st Lt,
Gaines, Boyd, Pvt,
Gaitan, Manuel, Pvt,
Gaitskill, Thomas M., Jr., T/4,
Galas, Oscar, T/5,
Gallegos, Joe V., Jr., Pfc,
Gance, Grant E., T/4,
Garren, Clarence W., Pvt,
Gaughan, Charles E., Pfc,
Gauldin, Lester F., T/5,
Georgias, John G., Capt,
Gestone, Robert C., Pfc,
Gilbert, Cecil D., Pvt,
Gillette, Earl W., Sgt,
Glasson, Crist A., Pvt,
Glerum, Cornelius, 1st Lt,
Glibert, Clinton E., Cpl,
Glovka, Edward G., 2nd Lt,
Glynn, William P., Sgt,
Godbout, Joseph D., Pvt,
Goddard, Roy W., Sgt,
Godjos, Frank, T/5,
Goldberg, Harry, Pfc,
Goode, Frederick M., Sgt,
Goodman, Owen F., Capt,
Gordan, Luther L., Pfc,
Gorelik, Justin S., T/4,
Gowin, Robert, T/5,
Graham, John J., Pfc,
Graham, Warren A., Pfc,
†Greene, Garland A., S/Sgt,
Grenier, Arthur J., T/5,
Griebe, Kenneth W., Pfc,
Griggs, Albert T., Pvt,
Grigsby, John P., Pfc,
Grubbs, Walter F., Pvt,
Grygiel, Stanley, Pfc,
Guerin, Thomas J., Pvt,
Guthrie, Robert W., T/4,
Gutzmer, Henry E., Cpl,

†Hager, Earl H., T/4,
Hahn, Elmer O., Pfc,
Hale, Charles D., Pfc,
Hall, Russell B., Pfc,
Hall, Quince S., Capt,
Hallahan, Charles J., Pvt,
†Haller, Glenn E., Pvt,
Hamblen, Edward G., Pvt,
Hamilton, Alexander M., 1st Lt
Hannah, William C., Pfc,
Hansen, Carl W., Pfc,
Hanson, Elmer J., T/4,
Hanson, Norman A., Sgt,
Hanson, William W., S/Sgt,
Harbaugh, Willard W., Cpl,
Harbin, James R., Pfc,
Harris, Umphry C., Pvt,
Harrison, Jefferson O., Cpl,
Harrison, Jessie D., Cpl,
Hartlove, Walter A., Pvt,
Harvieux, Maurice W., Pfc,
Hastings, Donald K., Pvt,
Hastings, Earle G., Jr., Capt,
Hatcher, Paul D., Sgt,
Hatfield, Joe L., Pfc,
Haugh, Charles E., Pfc,
Heater, McClellan D., Pvt,
Heath, Donald F., Pvt,
Heath, Ralph S., Jr., Capt,
Heath, Robert J., Pvt,
Hebert, Elmo J., Pfc,
Hebert, Jessie M., Pfc,
Hedberg, Arthur J., T/4,
Hedrick, Harry T., Pvt,
Heil, Arthur J., Pfc,
†Heller, Martin, 2nd Lt,
Hemel, Julian S., Pfc,
§Hemingway, James W., S/Sgt,
Henderson, Carl, Pfc,
Hendrickson, Emila, Pfc,
Henkel, Andrew J., Pvt,
Hertel, Clarence A., Pvt,
Hertz, Riehnold, T/4,
Hibbing, Harold H., WOJG,
Hill, Walter, Pfc,
Hills, Albert E., Pvt,
Hindman, Paul L., T/5,
Hintz, Frederick, Jr., Pvt,
Hoar, Maurice J., Cpl,
Hofstad, Halvor, T/5,
Hogan, James P. F., Pvt,
Hohmann, Edward J., T/Sgt,
Holka, Robert F., Pvt,
Holland, Oliver G., Pvt,
Honn, Edward F., Pvt,
Hoover, Samuel T., Pvt,
Horn, William A., Cpl,
Hornsby, Earl E., Pfc,
Hotz, Theodore, Pfc,
Hourihan, Daniel B., Sgt,
House, Percy L., Pvt,
Housley, Eugene, 1st Sgt,
Howard, Arthur E., Pvt,
Howarth, Robert M., Pvt,
Howe, Robert G., Pfc,
Huber, Randolph, Cpl,
Hudgins, Earl H., Pvt,
Huff, Vester E., Pvt,
Hull, Vernon J., Pfc,
Humpreys, Julian W., S/Sgt,
Hupert, Kamil J., Pvt,
Hurley, William E., Pvt,
Huston, Doran A., Capt,
Hutchins, Eugene W., Pfc,
Hutchinson, Louis E., Pvt,
Hutson, Marvin L., Pvt,
Hutson, William T., Pvt,
Hylton, Curtis, Pfc,

Inglis, Walter, CWO,
Iruin, William B., Cpl,
Isert, Joseph F., Sgt,
Isgrig, Eddie A., S/Sgt,
Ivie, Wendell R., Pfc,

Jackson, George J., 1st Sgt,
Jackson, Harry R., 1st Lt,
Jacobs, Loren D., Sgt,
Jacobsky, Anthony J., Pvt,
Jacobson, Alfred A., Pvt,
Jakovich, Raymond F., T/4,
Janssen, William G., S/Sgt,
Jarnecke, Lawrence, Cpl,
Jaske, Donald L., S/Sgt,
Jeanetta, Bonnie J., Jr., Pfc,
Jeffcoat, Frank M., Pfc,
†Jensen, Bernard, Pvt,
Jensen, Ingeman A., Sgt,
Johnsen, John E., Cpl,
Johnson, Carl A., Pvt,
Johnson, Clarence T., Cpl,
Johnson, Gustave W., Cpl,
Johnson, Herschel L., Pfc,
Johnson, John R., Pvt,
Johnson, L. V., Pfc,
Jones, Benjamin, Jr., Pfc,
Jones, Ernest O., Pfc,
Jones, Kingsmill, Pfc,
Jordan, George R., Capt,
Jordan, Joseph H. H., Pvt,
Jordan, Layton G., Pfc,
Joseph, Robert D., Pvt,
Jozwiak, Alex C., Pfc,

Kadrmas, William B., Cpl,
Kaiser, Herbert E., Pfc,
Kalata, Andrew J., Pvt,
Kane, Michael, 1st Lt,
‡Kasper, Carl J., 2nd Lt,
Kasza, John J., T/5,
Kauyman, Arnold E., Pvt,
Kaywin, Louis, Capt,
Kean, Edward J., Pvt,
Kee, Sammie R., T/5,
Keeler, John R., Pvt,
Kelly, Thomas P., Pfc,
Kendall, Francis J., Sgt,
Kennedy, Oran J., 1st Lt,
Kenvin, James, Pvt,
Ketterling, Harold, T/5,
Kienle, Helmut O., Pfc,
Kimball, Burrell R., Cpl,
Kirby, Olen P., Pvt,
Kirkland, Edward J., Pfc,
Kirschman, Edward, S/Sgt,
Kittel, Edwin W., T/5,
Kitzrow, Glenn H., T/5,
†Kleinsasser, Benjamin B., Pvt,
Klinger, Erwin O., Sgt,
Kluk, Stanley, Pvt,
Knight, Roy D., T/4,
Kondartino, Peter, Pvt,
Koons, Ernest L., Pvt,
Kramer, William H., Pfc,
Kratochvil, Mark W., Pfc,
Kraynick, John, Pfc,
Krupski, Stanley, Jr., T/5,
Kukoff, Jack, Pvt,
Kurpatwa, Fred E., Pfc,
Kuzbecki, Frank H., T/5,

Ladanyi, Frank, Pvt,
LaDuke, Russell O., T/5,
Ladwig, Charles P., T/5,
Lampe, Nathan C., S/Sgt,
Lampert, Lauren D., 1st Lt,
Lane, Erman, Pvt,
Lang, Leslie S., T/3,
LaPointe, Francis J., Cpl,
Larkin, Francis J., T/Sgt,
Larsen, Hans W., M/Sgt,
Lashua, Melvyn G., Cpl,
Lattyak, Edward J., Pvt,
Laurent, Edward, M/Sgt,
Laverty, James E., Pvt,
Lawhon, Ira, Pvt,
Lawson, Sam B., T/5,
†Lawwill, Elmer P., Pfc,
Lembicz, Stephen M., S/Sgt,
Lennon, Alfred A., Sgt,
Lent, Robert P., T/5,
Lesneski, Stanley A., Pvt,
Lewin, Robert C., 2nd Lt,
Lewis, Jessie O., S/Sgt,
Lieblich, Sidney, Pvt,
Ligot, Canuto M., T/5,
Lile, William W., S/Sgt,
Lipinski, Jerome E., Cpl,
Lloyd, Warren H., Pfc,
Lockey, Beuyord H., Pfc,
Loftin, Clarence D., T/5,
Lohmann, Albert, Jr., Pfc,
Loncala, Walter, Pvt,
Long, Raymond, Pvt,
Lovstad, Henry R., T/4,
Lowrie, Floyd, T/5,
Lowry, Nason E., Pvt,
Lucero, Antonio R., Pvt,
Lucima, Jerome, Cpl,
Lugert, Lawrence C., Cpl,
Lumpkin, William T., Jr., Sgt,
Lunde, Kenneth H., T/4,
Lynch, Milford S., Pfc,
Lyons, Lyle E., Pfc,

MacDonald, John A., T/4,
Mack, Leonard D., Pfc,
Mackey, Charles N., Pfc,
MacQuarrie, James S., Pvt,
Madrid, David, Jr., Pvt,
Maher, Thomas F., Pvt,
Mahoney, Rodney E., Sgt,
Maiello, Michael A., Pvt,
Maikai, Calvin W., Pfc,
Maleski, Joseph L., Pvt,
Malone, Henry L., Pvt,
Marek, Joseph E., Pfc,
Margavich, Walter T., Pfc,
Marks, Gerald J., Cpl,
Marlow, Earl S., Pvt,
Marsh, Wesley, W., Cpl,
Marshall, Derby E., Pvt,
Martin, Don A., T/4,
Martin, Harold R., Pfc,
Martin, Howard E., Cpl,
Martin, John W., Pfc,
Martin, Leonard P., Pvt,
Martinez, Ramon G., Pvt,
Martinez, Wenceslado, Cpl,
Martinson, Frank L., T/5,
Mashburn, Clarence, Pvt,
Mason, Warren F., Pfc,
Mathewson, Kenneth C., Pvt,
Matson, Arno M., T/5,
Mattis, Russell B., Pfc,
Mattox, Calvin A., Pvt,
Matzko, Mike, Pfc,
May, Russell C., Pvt,
Maynard, Robert E., Capt,
Mayo, Henry W., Jr., Capt,
Mays, James C., Pvt,
McConnell, Russell B., Capt,
McCourt, Thomas J., Pvt,
McDermott, Thomas M., Pfc,
McDurman, Jack H., T/5,
†McFadden, James E., Pvt,
McGee, Ennis P., Pfc,
McGorvin, Raymond, Pfc,
McGraw, Harry W., Pvt,
McGregor, Richard W., S/Sgt,
McGuirl, Maurice E., S/Sgt,
McIntosh, William D., Pfc,
McKenney, Harold S., S/Sgt,
McKeown, Gordon, T/5,
McLaughlin, John J., Pfc,
McLaughlin, Philip J., Pvt,
McLaughlin, Thomas R., T/5,
McPeek, Robert W., Cpl,
McQuinn, Robert J., Pvt,
Medlen, Ahmon C., T/5,
Mephee, Michael, S/Sgt,
Merkens, John L., T/4,
Merritt, James L., T/5,
Mershak, Andrew G., T/5,
Michelsen, Virgil V., Pfc,
Miedlar, Edward W., Pfc,
Mills, Herbert, Pfc,
Minar, LeRoy B., T/4,
Minton, Willie A., S/Sgt,
Mollison, John C., Pvt,
Money, Herman G., Pfc,
Monroe, James R., Pvt,
Montoya, Albert, 1st Lt,
Moodey, Edward W., Pvt,
Moore, George H., S/Sgt,
Moore, Harold J., Pfc,
Moore, Kenneth E., Pfc,
Morgan, David E., Pvt,
Morgan, Lawrence C., Pvt,
Morgan, Walter D., T/5,
Morris, James F., Pfc,
Morris, Lewis L., Pfc,
Mortensen, Vincent A., T/5,
Mousseau, Lyle C., Sgt,
Mulik, Mike, Pvt,
Muller, Edmund W., Pvt,
Muller, Edward J., Pvt,
Mullet, Doty K., S/Sgt,
Mullin, John E., Cpl,
Murach, Andrew J., Pfc,
Murray, James R., 1st Lt,
Myer, Thomas L., 1st Lt,
Myers, Bennie L., Pvt,

Nalewajka, Erwin, Pvt,
Needles, Clinton A., Pfc,
‡Neinas, Elmer, Pvt,
Nelson, Arthur M., T/Sgt,
Nelson, John L., Cpl,
Nelson, Lloyd N., T/4,
Nelson, Palmer C., Cpl,
Nicholas, Paul, Pfc,
Nickle, Lewis F., Cpl,
Nieborsky, Henry, T/4,
Niemeyer, Alvin, Sgt,
Nieminski, John J., Cpl,
Nobles, James K., Pfc,
Nolen, Tommy A., Pfc,
Norris, Clyde G., Cpl,
Norris, Shelby O., Pvt,
Novak, Clifford P., Pfc,
Nowacki, Jerome L., Pfc,
Nuttall, Ralph L., Capt,
Nuggard, Walter F., T/5,

Odom, William T., Pfc,
O'Hara, John F., Pvt,
Olsen, Grover T., Pvt,
Olter, Donald M., Pvt,
Opolka, Joseph V., Pfc,
Osborne, Alfred E., T/4,
Osborne, Vernon L., M/Sgt,
Osterberg, John A., Sgt,
Overland, John P., T/4,
Owens, Roger W., Cpl,
Owsiany, Edward, T/5,

Page, James F., Cpl,
Palocy, John J., Pfc,
Papeck, Michael T., Cpl,
Pardue, Charles E., T/5,
†Parete, Anthony G., Pvt,
Parini, William T., Pfc,
Parker, James W., Pvt,
Parker, Robert J., Cpl,
Parnell, Kenneth A., Sgt,
Parulski, Walter S., Cpl,
Pashkowski, John, Pvt,
Patz, Harold W., Pvt,
Paulson, Bernard D., T/5,
Payne, Arthur M., Pfc,
Payne, Harry W., Pvt,
Peairs, Douglas D., 1st Lt,
Pearson, Ernest J., Sgt,
Peasley, Martin H., Pvt,
Pederson, Francis W., Sgt,
Pellagrini, Nadzarini, Pfc,
Pelliteri, Santo, Pfc,
Pennanen, Wilho E., T/5,
Perez, Pedro, Cpl,
Perkins, Lester O., Cpl,
Perkins, William, T/4,
Perry, Kenneth M., Pvt,
§Person, Claude A., S/Sgt,
Peru, Charles O., Pfc,
Peters, James, Pfc,
Peters, John I., 2nd Lt,
Petersen, Marvin L., Cpl,
Peterson, Lloyd M., Pfc,
Peterson, Lyman K., Capt,
Petroski, Peter P., Pvt,
Philips, Wendell, 2nd Lt,
Phillips, Kenneth C., T/4,
Phillips, George F., Pvt,
Phillips, Jack W., Sgt,
Pinelli, Thomas E., Pvt,
Pinkerton, Stanley B., Sgt,
Pirc, Fred A., Cpl,
Pitz, Harlan W., T/4,
Pomante, Daniel J., Pfc,
Pomerantz, Milton, Pfc,
Pospieszny, Raymond F., Pfc,
§Powell, Joseph P., Sgt,
Presley, Marshall T., Pfc,
Preis, Irving P., Pvt,
Prentice, Elmer R., Pvt,
Presley, Marshall T., Pvt,
Price, Loyd A., 1st Lt,
Prigge, Eugene P., Pfc,
Pruitt, William H., Pfc,
Pruitt, Wilton E., Pfc,
Pullin, Leslie C., Pfc,

Quarles, Lee W., Pfc,
Quast, Clifford A., Cpl,
Quattrochi, Andrew A., Cpl,
Quick, Daniel M., Pvt,

Rabcow, Theodore H., Pvt,
Race, Abrum H., Jr., Pvt,
Rapp, Alfred W., Pfc,
Rattiner, Morris, Pvt,
Raty, Theodore E., Pfc,
Ratzow, Harold W., T/5,
Rawstern, Elias Y., S/Sgt,
Ray, Walter J., Pvt,
Raynor, Howard D., T/5,
†Read, Howard K., Capt,
Reichert, Leon H., Sgt,
Reichwein, Robert F., Sgt,
Reinhardt, Otto L., Cpl,
Reiser, David A., Pvt,
Renaud, Albert A., Sgt,
Renville, Joseph S., Pfc,
Replogle, Oliver D., Pfc,
Rew, Welby L., Cpl,
Reynolds, Maiben C., Capt,
Reynolds, Richard E., Pvt,
Rhodes, David M., Cpl,
Rihner, Philip O., T/5,
Richard, Lloyd C., Cpl,
Richardson, Kenneth J., S/Sgt,
Rigby, Paul T., Maj,
Riniker, John P., T/5,
Ritter, Carl J., Cpl,
Ritter, Harold W., T/4,
Robards, John T., T/5,
Roberson, Thurman W., Pvt,
Robertson, Anderville, Pvt,
†Robertson, Edward C., Maj,
Robertson, Leo W., Pfc,
Robinson, Edward C., T/4,
Robinson, Grady H., Pvt,
§Robinson, William D., Pfc,
Rock, Sylvester B., Sgt,
Rodrigue, John J., 1st Lt,
Rodriques, Amelio E., Pvt,
Roelofs, Bernard, T/5,
Roemer, David H., 1st Lt,
Rogers, Arthur L., Cpl,
Romo, Henry J., Jr., 1st Lt,
Ronning, Eugene R., Pvt,
Rose, John J., Pfc,

† Killed in Action. * Prisoner of War. ‡ Missing in Action. § Died of Wounds.

Rose, William B., Sgt,
Rosenauer, Otto, Pvt,
Rouwhorst, Gerald, T/5,
Running, Arnold M., Pvt,
Rupert, J. V., S/Sgt,
Russell, Edgar B., Pfc,
†Ryan, Donald A., Cpl,
Ryan, Matthew B., Jr., T/5,
Ryan, John L., Pfc,
Rychwalski, Frank S., Cpl,
Rydzewski, Edwin W., T/4,
Rygh, Wilhelm, Pfc,
Rubin, Ralph L., Pvt,

Saenz, Jose A., T/5,
Salley, Arnold, Pfc,
Salmenson, Lester, Pfc,
Sampson, Ernest, Pvt,
Samsa, John E., 1st Lt,
Sandberg, Paul R., Pfc,
Sandoral, Anastacio C., Pfc,
Sandrik, Lester L., Pfc,
Sands, Ralph B., T/4,
Santiago, Nicholas, Cpl,
Sarber, Willard E., Pvt,
Saunders, Edward L., Jr.,
Sawyer, Hadwin E., Pvt,
Saye, William E., Pfc,
Sayler, Oscar, T/5,
Schaaf, Larry L., T/5,
Schaeffer, Samuel C., 1st Lt,
Schelkoph, Leonard L., Pfc,
Schellenberg, Robert E., T/4,
Schiller, Matthew J., T/5,
Schmidt, Albert, Cpl,
Schneider, Eugene E., 1st Lt,
Schraeder, Edward H., T/5,
Schreiner, John W., Pfc,
Schultz, Donald J., T/5,
Schultze, Arthur A., Pfc,
Schwabland, Howard J., Pfc,
Schwappe, Elmer H., T/4,
Scobie, Robert F., Sgt,
Selemon, Nicholas, Pfc,
Sermuszyn, Andrew S., Pvt,
Sessler, Jacob G., T/5,
Shadel, Marvin C., Pfc,
Shaffer, J. D., S/Sgt,
Shears, Adolph L., Cpl,
Shepp, Clarence J., Pvt,
§Shinn, Tom E., Sgt,
Shook, Herman E., Pvt,
Shook, Ollo K., Jr., Pvt,
Shorey, Daniel W., Pvt,

Shows, Clinton, Pfc,
Sichmeller, Stanley F., Sgt,
Sides, Joe W., Sgt,
Siebieda, Matthew L., Pvt,
Sievers, Orville H., Cpl,
Sikes, Earlie E., Pfc,
†Silvers, Kelly D., Cpl,
Simonich, Walter A., T/5,
Simpson, Arthur A., Pvt,
Simpson, Norman, Pvt,
†Singleton, Harvey C., T/Sgt,
Skain, Walter W., Jr., Pvt,
Skehen, John F., Pfc,
Skipper, Morris J., Cpl,
Sleisher, Everett J., Sgt,
Slides Off, Owen N., Pvt,
†Slocum, George W., Pfc,
Smart, Estle G., Pfc,
Smetana, Jerry J., T/5,
Smith, Bruce P., Pvt,
Smith, Don E., Pvt,
Smith, Herbert W., Pvt,
Smith, Omen J., Pfc,
Smith, Robert A., Pfc,
†Sneed, Frank J., T/5,
Snowden, Norward L., 2nd Lt,
Sochacki, Henry J., T/4,
Solomon, Irving, Pvt,
Solomon, Irving I., T/5,
Somers, George A. W., Pfc,
Sommer, Arnold E., Pfc,
Southern, Hulen, Sgt,
Soyka, Stephen, Pvt,
Spadayora, Frank, Pvt,
Spaide, James L., Pvt,
Spangenberg, Harold J., T/4,
Spaulding, Roy, Pvt,
Spence, Artis P., T/4,
Spencer, Verdon V., S/Sgt,
Sperling, Sidney, Pvt,
Speros, Theodore S., S/Sgt,
Splichal, Albert A., Pfc,
Sponsler, George L., Pfc,
Spotto, Joseph P., Pvt,
Sprague, Fred M., Sgt,
Stackhouse, C. L., Jr., 1st Lt,
Stallings, Ernest E., T/4,
Stamler, Maurice, Capt,
Stanek, Millard J., Capt,
St. Arnaud, Albert J., Pfc,
Stave, Jacob, Cpl,
Steekal, Melvin E., Pfc,
Stein, Harry H., Pfc,

Steinbach, Martin A., Sgt,
Steinman, Edward W., Pfc,
Stender, Ray B., Cpl,
Stepanski, Eugene F., Pfc,
Stevens, Billie M., Pfc,
Stirek, Louis, T/4,
Stone, Arthur W., Pvt,
Stone, Loren F., Capt,
Stiner, Edward A., Pfc,
Storace, Nicholas, Pvt,
Stout, Kale, T/5,
Streator, William H., T/5,
Streible, Joseph A., Sgt,
Strenge, Dick E., Sgt,
Strizak, Mike, T/5,
Strzempek, Ted J., S/Sgt,
Stuart, Richard W., Cpl,
Stuchlik, Edward, Cpl,
Stuy, Cornelius, T/5,
Stych, Henry, T/3,
Suetter, Earl D., Pfc,
Suski, John J., 1st Lt,
Swan, John E., Pvt,
Swanger, Stanley T., T/5,
Swatske, Jack J., Pfc,
Sweeney, Carl C., Sgt,
Swinney, Jacob M., T/4,
Switzer, Charles B., Pfc,

Tait, James A., Pvt,
Talbott, Niel P., T/5,
Tarasenko, Ernest E., T/5,
Taylor, Elijah, 1st Sgt,
Taylor, Keith E., 1st Sgt,
Templeton, Charles B., Sgt,
Terry, Alvin, T/5,
Thomas, Carlton J., Pfc,
Thomas, Jasper, Pfc,
Thomas, Stuart M., Pvt,
†Thompson, Allen N., T/4,
Thompson, Arnold J., Pfc,
†Thompson, Earl J., Cpl,
Thompson, George M., Cpl,
Thompson, Harold V., T/5,
Thompson, Roger G., S/Sgt,
Thone, Frederick W., Pvt,
Thorson, Stanley H., Cpl,
Thress, Arnold H., Sgt,
Tilley, Norman F., Pvt,
Tilson, Glen L., T/5,
Titus, Howard W., Pvt,
Toivonen, Lauri E., Sgt,
Tollerude, Julian A., T/5,

Trotter, Robert T., Pfc,
Trujillo, Johnnie H., Pvt,
Tucro, James W., Pvt,
Tudor, Benjamin R., Cpl,
Tuggle, Cornelius J., M/Sgt,
Two Stars, John, Pfc,

Underation, James C., T/4,
Underwood, Jack R., T/5,
Utter, Harley D., S/Sgt,

Van Asselt, Alvin W., Sgt,
Van Bogart, Bernel, Pfc,
Van De Graaf, Anthony, Pfc,
Vanhaus, Arthur B., T/5,
Van Winkle, Hiram, Pfc,
Vargas, Cruz T., Pfc,
Vassello, Frank W., Pvt,
VeKens, Philemon, Pvt,
Vergano, Frank D., S/Sgt,
Villagran, Edward, S/Sgt,
Villard, Angelo, J., T/5,
Villarreal, Jose, Pfc,
Vogds, Wallace J., Pfc,
Vuyancih, Michael, Pvt,

§Wagner, Arthur, Pfc,
Walker, Carl L., Pvt,
Walls, Ralph W., Pfc,
Walter, Mercer C., Lt Col
Wandler, Marcus D., S/Sgt,
Wanta, Louis L., Pfc,
Warnke, Edwin M., T/Sgt,
§Warren, Leo E., Pfc,
Warwick, William R., Pfc,
Warzenski, Edward S., Pfc,
Wasco, John, Cpl,
Watson, Donald E., Pfc,
Wauters, Albert J., Pvt,
Weaver, Andrew F., Pvt,
Webb, Walter D., Lt Col,
Webber, Robert M., Capt,
Weber, Lawrence J., Cpl,
Weber, Thomas R., Pfc,
Weimer, Gottfried, T/5,
Weirick, William A., T/Sgt,
Weischedel, Walter C., Cpl,
Weiss, Ralph B., Cpl,
Weissberg, Homer J., Pfc,
Wellhausen, Walter F., Pfc,
Welsh, Harry E., T/4,
Wendt, James R., Jr., Lt Col,
Werdick, Robert E., Pfc,
†Werry, William C., Pfc,

Westlund, Bernard T., S/Sgt,
Westman, Clifford M., Pvt,
White, Barney D., Lt Col,
White, Clifton, Cpl,
White, Clyde, T/4,
White, Edwin S., Pvt,
Whited, James W., Pfc,
Whittier, Floyd J., Pfc,
Wieclaw, John J., Pvt,
Wiede, Walter A., Cpl,
†Wientjes, Raymond C., T/4,
Wilkins, Alfred H., T/4,
Willard, Wiley, Pvt,
Williams, Andrew P., T/4,
Williams, Edward B., 1st Lt,
Williams, David C., Cpl,
Williams, Eugene S., Cpl,
Williams, James F., Pfc,
Williams, Lummie, Pvt,
Williams, Melvin J., Pvt,
Williamson, Richard H., Sgt,
Wilson, Leland N., T/5,
Wilson, Leonard F., Pvt,
Wilson, Lloyd C., T/5,
Wilson, Ray, Pfc,
Wilson, Robert, Pvt,
Wing, Clinton H., 2nd Lt,
Wojcicki, Chester J., Pvt,
Wold, Richard C., Pvt,
§Wood, Jedd J., 2nd Lt,
Woods, Bernard G., Pfc,
Woods, Eugene S., Cpl,
Worott, Francis E., Pvt,
Wright, Roy J., T/5,
Wybranoski, Steve, Pfc,
Wylie, Ivan E., T/5,

†Yancey, Robert A., 2nd Lt,
Yeddis, Lewis, Pfc,
Yesefski, Raymond A., Pfc,
Yeske, Joseph B., T/5,
Young, Charles B., T/4,
Young, Willard B., 1st Lt,
Yucius, Florentine V., Cpl,

Zanardi, Daniel J., Sgt,
Zerebny, Peter, Pfc,
Zimmerman, George J., Sgt,
Zinn, George, T/5,
Zielke, Alvin A., Jr., Pfc,
Zlatin, Sam J., Pfc,
Znidersic, Ignatz K., Pfc,
Zuck, Robert E., Sgt,
Zucker, George C., Pfc.

† Killed in Action.   * Prisoner of War.   ‡ Missing in Action.   § Died of Wounds.

3D RECONNAISSANCE TROOP

The 3d Reconnaissance Troop was activated on August 20, 1940 at Fort Lewis, Washington in accordance with the Tables of Organization and Tables of Basic Allowances of a triangular division. Its cadre was supplied by the 4th Cavalry Regiment. Its Tables of Organization and Tables of Basic Allowances were changed frequently throughout peacetime training in an attempt to adapt it to the mission it was to execute. At different periods in the war it served as a specially-organized task force in addition to its normal function.

Commanding Officer

(Highest rank held)	Held pos. from	To
Capt. R. W. Crandall		26 Jan 1943
1st Lt. A. D. Meyer	27 Jan 1943	1 May 1943
Capt. A. T. Netterblad, Jr.	2 May 1943	27 Dec 1943
1st Lt. Harry B. Evans, Jr.	28 Dec 1943	25 Apr 1944
Capt. John O'Connell	26 Apr 1944	30 Aug 1944
1st Lt. Allen R. Kenyon	31 Aug 1944	

Apecelli, Frank A., Cpl,
Agnen, Joseph A., Pvt,
Asselin, Joseph E., Pvt,
Arnold, Robert H., Pfc,
Acosta, Gabriel S., Pvt,
†Asche, Fred, Cpl,
Archuleta, Esquiel Z., Pvt,
Adams, James R., Sgt,
Alton, O Neal R., Sgt,
†Amicone, Albert F., Pvt,
Anderson, Russell C., Pvt,
Applegate, Clifford A., T/5,
†Albright, Donald C., Pvt,

Balser, William, Pvt,
Bisher, Russell W., Pvt,
Boyd, Jackson, T/5,
Bennett, Eugene, Pvt,
Blankenburg, William L., Pvt,
Barringer, Harold G., Pfc,
Ballantini, Bruno J., Sgt,
Boucher, Ernest E., Pvt,
Buikema, John, Jr., Pvt,
Bickford, David G., T/5,
Bennett, Samuel H., Pvt,
Brytos, Girard T., Cpl,
†Ball, Earl, Pfc,
Ballard, Carl R., Pvt,
‡Burinskas, Robert I., Pvt,
‡Bickers, Walter H., Pvt,
Ball, William J., Pvt,
Brown, Russell, Cpl,
Burns, Virgil E., Pfc,
Bushely, Ernest A., Pfc,
Bailey, William R., Pfc,
Blankenship, Floyd R., S/Sgt,
Broad, Stanley D., Pvt,
Bennett, Robert E., Pvt,
Bowen, Donald E., Pvt,
Brown, Byron C., Pfc,
Bankes, Edgar E., Pvt,
*Beale, Joe R., Pvt,
†Bond, Jerold R., Pvt,
Bray, Lewis M., Pfc,
†Bradford, Edgar O., Pvt,
†Berge, Karl, Jr., Pvt,
Bernabei, Louis, Sgt,
Berger, Richard H., T/4,
Baker, Ivey, T/5,
Beno, Walter T., T/5,
Blissit, Charley N., T/5,
Bloom, George A., T/5,
Buchanan, Milton O., T/5,
Beck, Vernon H., Pfc,
Boltjes, Herman, T/5,

Baker, Leo S., Pfc,
Blair, George E., Pvt,
Bryner, Homer G., Pvt,
Bunch, Dean, T/5,
Busching, Harold H., T/5,
Blinco, Richard M., T/5,
Bromley, James S., Pfc,
Beason, William H., Pvt,
Begovich, John C., 2nd Lt,
Bickers, Melvin H., T/5,

Cotton, Sanford S., Cpl,
‡Christensen, Ernest C., T/4,
†Campbell, Emery D., Pvt,
†Carr, Kenneth L., Pfc,
†Caliesch, Peter J., Pvt,
Courcier, William A., Pvt,
Carter, Orcal L., Pvt,
Cordell, Alfred T., Pfc,
Canada, Linro H., S/Sgt,
Chipman, Charles J., Pvt,
Carney, Lindell, Pfc,
Camren, Clarence C., Pvt,
Cash, Daniel S., Pvt,
Campbell, Herbert L., Pvt,
†Culver, George B., Pfc,
†Carvalho, Henry J., Pvt,
Cox, Jewell F., Pvt,
Campbell, Howard E., Pvt,
Curry, Charles F., Sgt,
Caruso, Angelo A., Pfc,
Castiglione, Joseph P., T/5,
Caldwell, Dewitt W., Sgt,
Cosper, J. B., T/5,
Cohen, Paul, Cpl,
Champion, Marshall H., Pfc,
Craft, Norman M., Pfc,
Caldwell, Boone H., Pfc,
Cooley, Lester C., Pfc,
Cooper, Arthur, Pfc,
Crews, William B., Pfc,

Dehmer, Robert T., Pfc,
Dailey, Jack H., Pvt,
Dahm, Walter J., T/5,
Dann, Dale J., Pvt,
Davis, Gardner, Pvt,
Dority, William A., Pvt,
DeSantold, Anthony M., Pvt,
Davis, James, Pvt,
Dingle, Jack G., Pvt,
†Duffy, Bernard F., Pfc,
Discenza, Carmen T., Pvt,
Dyer, William M., Pfc,

Daughtry, M. L., T/4,
Deater, Clifford J., Cpl,
DeKuiper, Donald J., T/5,
*Dickinson, Edgar M., Pvt,
Delgado, Inocencio, Pvt,
DelRicci, John J., Pfc,
Dumm, Elmer N., Pfc,
‡Dutkowski, Clarence N., 2nd Lt
Dubbery, Jack, Pfc,

Elms, Harold B., Pfc,
Edwards, Eugene, S/Sgt,
Estes, Clyde G., Pvt,
Eckhout, Donald C., Pvt,
Ellwanger, Richard L., Pfc,
Eddy, Walter A., Pvt,
Eastburg, Herbert C., Pvt,
Ellison, Donald C., Pfc,
Ewell, Vivian S., Pfc,
Ellis, Lonzo E., Pfc,
Engle, Donald R., T/4,
Edwards, Phillip H., Sgt,
Eller, Fred A., Pfc,
Epps, Arthur G., Pfc,
Erb, Jack W., Pfc,
Ezzi, John L., Pfc,
Eaton, Douglas B., 2nd Lt,

†Focht, John V., Pvt,
Farmer, Dwight M., Cpl,
Fischer, Laurence M., Pvt,
Fortenberry, Willaim M., Pvt,
Freeland, Robert E., Pvt,
†Feaster, Franklin A., Pvt,
Freese, Donald O., Pfc,
Flick, Warren E., Pvt,
†Flatt, William M., Pfc,
Fankhauser, Edward, S/Sgt,
French, George T., Pvt,
Forsyth, Ira R., 1st Sgt,
Fenstad, Arthur E., Pfc,
Furrow, Alvin M., T/4,
Frazel, George O., T/5,
Fauerbach, Roscoe F., Pvt,
Fisher, Edward K., T/4,
Flynn, William M., Pfc,
Fraber, John W., Pvt,
Fromhart, Wilbur B., Pfc,
Fowler, Clifford W., Pfc,
Fredrick, John J., 1st Lt,

Graves, Phillip, Pfc,
†Gerard, Clarence N., Cpl,
Good, John L., Pvt,
‡Gamble, Earl S., Pvt,

Gilarski, Eugene B., Pvt,
Gannucci, Edward H., Pfc,
Gancos, Steve M., S/Sgt,
Gross, Lewis, S/Sgt,
†Glanovsky, Joseph G., Pvt,
†Griffin, Robert E., Pfc,
Gilchrist, Clifford C., Pfc,
Groninger, Carl H., Pfc,
Griswald, Glenn C., Sgt,
Gates, Drollinger W., S/Sgt,
Goetz, Mowry E., Cpl,
†Gorman, Harry C., Sgt,
Gebhard, James E., Pvt,
Gleeson, Joseph J., Pvt,
†Gooding, Francis X., Pvt,
Griffee, John M., Pvt,
Griffith, Sylvan W., S/Sgt,
Grizzell, Jack B., Pvt,
Gross, Joseph A., Pfc,
Greene, Frank A., Sgt,
George, Bernard T., Sgt,
Greenfield, Edgar J., Cpl,
Gardner, Eugene M., T/5,
Good, Elmer J., T/5,
Gillett, Robert W., T/5,
Goff, William B., Pfc,
Gay, Lawrence R., Pfc,
Gravely, Thomas W., Pfc,
‡Gill, Walter L., 1st Lt,
Gallo, James V., Pfc,

Hubbard, Harry S., Cpl,
Huff, Ernest E., S/Sgt,
Hurt, James R., Pvt,
Holmes, Douglas A., Pvt,
Haskens, Eugene W., Pvt,
Hansen, Harry C., Pvt,
Hansen, Robert J., T/5,
Halverson, Julian C., Pvt,
Hancock, John, Pvt,
Handy, John, S/Sgt,
Hyland, Jeremiah J., Pvt,
‡Herout, John S., Pfc,
Hartman, Merle E., Pvt,
Huitt, Vernon J., Pfc,
‡Howden, Robert J., Pfc,
Hoffman, Oran C., Cpl,
Hutchinson, Clarence G., Pvt,
Howell, Joseph E., Pvt,
Hamby, James E., T/5,
Hudak, Nickolas M., Pvt,
Hertz, Leonard B., Pvt,
Harp, Walter P., Pvt,
Hall, Henry F., Cpl,
Henderson, Leroy, Cpl,

Horvath, William, Pvt,
†Haddock, Wayman J., Pvt,
†Hawkins, Willis H., Pvt,
Hernandez, Leonard G., Pvt,
Huttman, Frank, T/4,
Hetzner, Herbert J., T/5,
Hund, Joseph C., T/5,
Huxtable, Charles C., T/5,
Hedges, Leonard O., Pfc,
Heitzman, Robert T., Pfc,
Hall, Roger S., Pvt,
Hardy, Francis W., Pvt,
Head, Worley L., Pfc,
Herron, Ralph H., T/5,
Higgins, Jess W., Pvt,
Hughes, Gordon D., Pvt,
Holliday, James L., Pfc,
Haas, Kenneth L., Pfc,

Ingraham, Burl V., Pfc,
Ivey, Walter F., Pvt,
Ivie, William D., Pfc,

Johnson, Herman E., Pfc,
Jacuk, Michael, Pfc,
†Johnson, Paul V., Pvt,
†Janus, Joseph, Pvt,
Johnson, Wilbur C., Pvt,
Johnson, Charles L., T/5,
Johnson, John W., T/5,
Jones, Edward A., T/5,
Jones, Frank E., Pfc,
Jones, Melber J., Pvt,
Jones, James C., Pfc,
Jones, John A., 2nd Lt,

Kaser, Arnet G., Pfc,
Klebs, Earl M., T/4,
Kline, Alvin L., T/5,
‡Kutza, John J., Pvt,
Kosakowski, Charles T., Pvt,
†Kralian, Arron, Pvt,
Kerber, Ralph D., Pvt,
Kepco, Albert P., Pvt,
Kitzrow, Glenn H., T/5,
Kreiter, Benjamin, Pvt,
Kreiner, Raymond J., Pvt,
Kalina, Abraham M., Pvt,
Keeler, Joseph P., Pfc,
Krok, George B., Pfc,
Keinath, Elmer A., T/4,
Krueger, Manvil H., T/4,
Kittle, Orville O., T/5,
King, Arvel M., Cpl,
Kelleher, John, Pvt,

† Killed in Action.   * Prisoner of War.   ‡ Missing in Action.   § Died of Wounds.

Kanowitz, Seymour, Pvt,
Knapp, Herbert A., Pfc,
Kenyon, Allen R., Capt,

Lacombe, Conrad L., Pfc,
Lewis, Richard T., Cpl,
Langmack, Jack E., Pvt,
Lile, Irvin M., Sgt,
Linunen, Raino H., Pfc,
Light, Paul B., Cpl,
Lynch, James C., Cpl,
Lutz, Kenneth N., Cpl,
Ladowski, Edward A., Pvt,
LeBrun, Harold W., Pvt,
Lundblade, Albert G., T/5,
Larson, Andrew J., Pfc,
Lee, Clifford A., Pvt,
Lowery, Carl A. B., Pvt,
Law, William W., Pvt,
†Ludwig, Roland F., Pfc,
Lay, Fay N., Pvt,
Leas, Robert L., Pvt,
Lopez, Victor E., Pvt,
Logue, Donald J., Pvt,
Long, William A., Pvt,
Laagus, Felix, Pvt,
Lewis, Marvin D., Cpl,
Lennon, Thomas P., Pvt,
†Longest, Alvin, Pvt,
Lindsey, Marvin H., Pvt,
Larsen, Gilbert E., 1st Sgt,
Lynch, Carl J., S/Sgt,
Levin, Sidney B., S/Sgt,
Ladd, Bob H., Pvt,
LaRose, Murray K., T/5,
Leavitt, Edwin, Pfc,
Leslie, Fredrick W. G., Pvt,
Lintz, John T., S/Sgt,

Mottweiler, Richard H., 1st Lt,
McCloskey, John J., 1st Lt,
McGee, James, 1st Lt,
‡Mahoney, James J., Pvt,
Meyer, Fredrick, Pvt,
Miller, Kermit B., Pvt,
McManus, John J., Pvt,
Mensen, Leonard H., Pfc,
†Munn, Franklin W., Pvt,
†Magit, Harold, Cpl,
‡Matranza, Vincent G., Cpl,
Medlock, Norman C., T/5,
McCaffery, John F., T/5,
Marcum, Sebern J., Pvt,
McGonagle, Ralph D., Pfc,
Meskunas, William L., Pvt,
McCallie, John R., S/Sgt,
Myers, David M., Pvt,
Merril, Fred T., Pvt,
Merkel, Arthur L., Pvt,
Maddox, James R., Pvt,
‡Meglich, John F., Pfc,
McCoy, William V., Pvt,
Masurka, Elmer, Cpl,

Moore, Elmer E., Pfc,
Mason, James W., Pfc,
Mills, Ervin, Pvt,
Muller, Roy G., Pvt,
Mathieu, Jerome W., Cpl,
Maness, William H., S/Sgt,
Marsh, Ted L., Pvt,
Mancusi, Italo V., Pfc,
Martoff, Val G., Pvt,
McGinniss, Raymond C., Pvt,
Mills, Woodrow W., Pvt,
Murphy, Albert W., S/Sgt,
McKay, John W., 1st Sgt,
Marchesin, Enrico, Sgt,
†Marvin, Robert J., Sgt,
McRae, Clayton, Sgt,
†McCaffrey, John E., T/4,
Maple, Roger P., Cpl,
McCaw, Laurence R., T/5,
Mittelstadt, Levurn H., T/4,
Moore, John J., Sgt,
Maack, Burdell H. F., Pfc,
Mastorine, Stanley, T/5,
Mazur, Frank T., Pfc,
McFeeley, Charles J., T/5,
†Metzinger, Sylvester M., Pfc,
Manion, Jack E., T/5,
Maple, Robert M., T/5,
McLeod, George M., T/4,
Magrath, Paul F., Pfc,
Mehan, Robert J., Pfc,
Mejia, Elliot, Pfc,
‡Marshall, Kenneth R., Pfc,

Newland, Harold G., Pfc,
Nelson, Clarence E., Pvt,
Neace, Burgess, Pvt,
Nicholis, Russell A., Cpl,
Needles, Frank, Pvt,
Neal, Dixie B., Pfc,
Newton, William B., T/5,
Naylor, Robert J., Pfc,
Newland, Harold B., Pvt,
Norton, Lowell D., Sgt,
O'Dooley, Emmet J., Pvt,
O'Sickey, Benjamin H., Pvt,
Olszewski, Leon T., T/4,
Oaks, Troy W., Pfc,
Ogas, Ernest P., Pfc,
O'Neal, Bill, Pvt,
Ooten, Chester A., Pvt,
Olson, Arthur B. T/4,
Osmundson, George R., Cpl,

Palmer, Paul H., Pvt,
†Paradise, Raymond L., Pvt,
Pardo, Raymond, Cpl,
‡Parke, William F., Pvt,
†Parker, William C., 1st Lt,
Paul, Harry, T/5,
Pawlicki, George J., Pvt,
Pecora, Louis, Jr., Pfc,
Pennell, Clyde W., S/Sgt,

Perry, Merle T., Pvt,
Perry, Francis S., T/4,
Pesnell, Cecil G., S/Sgt,
Peterson, Robert W., T/4,
Phillips, James F., Pvt,
Pill, Irving J., Pvt,
Piper, Marvin M., S/Sgt,
Platt, Walter, Pvt,
Plumb, William C., T/5,
Pollock, Robert S., Pfc,
Porter, Earl V., Pvt,
Potty, Joseph C., Pfc,
Pray, Ronald E., T/5,
†Probert, Robert R., T/5,
†Purser, Edward W., Pvt,

Quackenbush, James A., Pvt,
‡Quick, Daniel M., Pvt,

Raymond, Robert M., Pvt,
Ripke, Robert W., Pvt,
Ritcher, Alvin A., Pvt,
‡Rasch, Harold J., Pfc,
Robinson, Raymond C., Pvt,
Roenfeldt, Harry F., S/Sgt,
Reang, Robert R., Pvt,
Richard, Reginald E., Pvt,
Robinson, Lewis H., Sgt,
Ross, Alzie, Pvt,
Ramsey, Robert W., Pvt,
Roberts, Archie M., Pvt,
†Rainwater, Isaac H., Pvt,
Reith, Arthur L., Pfc,
Reed, Junior S., Pvt,
Reuter, Willard R., Pvt,
Rhoda, Leo L., T/5,
Ralls, Ottie E., Pvt,
Roberts, George W., Pvt,
†Rossi, Frank, T/5,
Reynolds, Francis A., Pfc,
Riddle, Robert F., Pfc,
Risdahl, Magnus, T/Sgt,
Roy, Erle G., T/5,

Samples, John L., S/Sgt,
Sims, Richard G., Pvt,
Slayden, Jack A., Pvt,
Singer, Edward, Pvt,
Sushak, Stanley J., Pfc,
†Sexton, William L., Pfc,
Spurling, William G., Pvt,
†Stabler, Robert D., Pvt,
Sumers, Pete A., S/Sgt,
Saxer, Harry W., Pfc,
‡Stivison, Morton V., Pvt,
‡Shelafeau, George P., T/5,
‡Scerni, Attilia J., Pfc,
Scepniak, Edward J., Pvt,
Shafer, William, Pvt,
Shattuck, George M., Pvt,
Shofner, Virgil O., Pvt,
Studdard, Louis B., Pvt,
Stritzl, Edwin P., Pvt,

*Stump, Albert H., T/5,
Schaffer, Silas H., Cpl,
Sweeney, William A., Pfc,
Sherman, Burton L., Pvt,
Sessman, Scott W., Pfc,
Schuller, William J., Pvt,
Strasser, Leo J., Pvt,
Sturgeon, Donald W., Pvt,
Stanlos, Anthony, Pvt,
Salkind, Harold, Cpl,
†Swanson, Stanley M., Pvt,
Spencer, Raymond M., Pfc,
Silva, Antonio L., Cpl,
Skallerup, James R., Pfc,
Smith, Harry C., S/Sgt,
Schwetke, William E., S/Sgt,
Siske, Wilmoth W., Sgt,
Settle, Russell C., T/4,
Schmitt, Robert G., Cpl,
Sinclair, Tony S., T/5,
*Sallander, Gordon N., Pfc,
Smith, William M., Pfc,
Smith, Murl D., T/5,
Steffen, Walter O., T/5,
Schram, Burton P., Pvt,
Schwarz, Horace W., Pfc,
Seymour, Ernest A., Pfc,
Skaptauckas, Robert P., Pfc,
Smith, Charles J., T/5,
Smith, Paul S., Pfc,
Smith, Robert N., Pvt,
Solarz, Andrew D., Pvt,
Starkey, Elvyn H., Pfc,
St. John, Carroll A., Pfc,
†Stover, Edward F., Pfc,
Strzyz, George, T/5,
†Stillings, George V., Pvt,
Schoppe, William C., Pfc,
Shelder, Lloyd W., Pfc,
Spruill, Benton M., Pfc,

Tillman, John W., Sgt,
Tennyson, George R., Pvt,
‡Thomas, Donald H., Pvt,
‡Temple, William H., Pvt,
Thompson, Roger S., T/5,
Tucker, Euzell L., Pvt,
Tolley, Willard G., Pvt,
Tellier, Joseph L., Pvt,
Troskowski, Joseph P., Pvt,
Tannehill, Robert I., Pvt,
Tambussi, Frank J., Pvt,
‡Thompson, Bethal F., Pvt,
Thomas, Odis A., Pvt,
Taylor, Charles P., T/Sgt,
Toomey, William J., Pvt,
Trujillo, Manuel, Cpl,
Tusing, Arthur W., Pvt,
Taylor, Edward J., Pfc,
Thomas, Kenneth O., Sgt,
Tardy, Lawrence L., Pvt,
Thomas, Lester, Pvt,
Tatum, Alonzo B., T/5,

Thompson, Garnet E., T/4,
Thompson, Leslie W., Pfc,
Thornbrough, L, W., Pvt,
Trenton, Robert L., Pfc,
‡Tidwell, Jack N., 1st Lt,

Ulery, Charles H., T/5,

*Votaw, Abner E., Cpl,
Vascik, Steve M., Cpl,
Visaggi, Ralph, Pvt,
Van Hevel, Albert E., T/4,
Van Handel, Raymond J., Cpl,
Vires, Harvey, Pfc,
Vaskas, Joseph B., Pfc,
Vanezo, John E., T/Sgt,

Wallis, Guy W., 1st Lt,
Wisemore, Doyle E., T/4,
†Wells, Stanley M., T/5,
Wissman, Vernel C., Sgt,
Woodworth, Walter J., Pvt,
Williams, Richard H., Pvt,
Woodward, Vern C., Pvt,
White, John C., Pvt,
‡Whiteside, Willie L., Pvt,
Whitaker, John M., Pvt,
Woodbury, Donald W., Sgt,
Wiezorek, Lawrence A., T/5,
Windish, Frank J., Pfc,
‡Whitlock, Earl C., Pvt,
Wilson, James B., Pfc,
Waddington, Harry A., Sgt,
Wampler, Johnnie R., Pfc,
Wissman, Harry, Pvt,
†Wong, William Y., Pvt,
†Waybur, David C., 1st Lt,
Wolfe, Roy W., 2nd Lt,
Wojtcsak, Fredrick S., Pvt,
Wolfe, John M., Pfc,
Ward, Robert E., T/4,
Weiss, Homer L., T/4,
Winfrey, Theodore R., T/4,
Werth, John F., T/4,
Witte, Arnold E., Cpl,
Wohlgemuth, Glen J., S/Sgt,
Weinman, Abraham, T/5,
White, Marshal C., T/5,
Williams, Nolin E., T/4,
Wahl, Ervin H., Pfc,
Weeks, Loyz B., Pfc,
Welch, Harry K., T/5,
Wilkinson, James W., Sgt,
Wilson, William, T/5,
Wilson, Willys L., Pfc,
West, John W., Pfc,

Yasgar, John M., Pvt,
Yee, Wing S., Pfc,

Zielinski, Joseph M., Pvt
Zoeller, Louis G., S/Sgt.

† Killed in Action.   * Prisoner of War.   ‡ Missing in Action.   § Died of Wounds.

10TH ENGINEER COMBAT BATTALION

The 10th Engineer Battalion, formerly the 2d Battalion, 6th Engineer Regiment, bore the distinction of being a part of the first unit of the 3d Division to sail for France in 1917. After having been assigned to duty with British forces, the regiment performed the feat of constructing 16 bridges in 40 days.

As a *combat* engineer battalion in World War II, the unit engaged in infantry fighting with distinction at several periods—notably during certain periods on the Anzio Beachhead. Its primary work there of laying wire and mines, however, was more hazardous, since the men had to go ahead of the infantry front lines.

The 10th Engineer Battalion's most widely-publicized single feat in World War II was its construction of the bridge at Cape Calava on the north coast of Sicily.

During the long push up the Italian peninsula the battalion was extremely busy spanning blown bridges and removing German mines. Its other functions, simultaneously or during "rest" periods, were road-building, construction of command posts, mosquito control and removal of mines in areas over which practice amphibious landing maneuvers were to be conducted.

Commanding Officer (Division Engineer)

(Highest rank held)	Held pos. from	To
Lt. Col. Leonard L. Bingham		10 Sept 1943
Lt. Col. Charles F. Tank	11 Sept 1943	18 Sept 1944
Lt. Col. Robert L. Petherick	19 Sept 1944	

Abramovitz, Seymour, Pvt,
Abrams, Daniel, Sgt,
Acheson, Robert F., Jr., Pfc,
Ackroyd, Cleveland M., Pvt,
Acosta, Luke C., Pfc,
Adjatzik, Walter H., Pvt,
Agresta, Dominic, Pvt,
Ahrens, Edwin F., T/5,
Albritton, John L., T/5,
Alden, Jake, Pvt,
§Aldridge, Stanley H., T/5,
Alexander, Charles C., Capt,
Alexander, Jerome G., T/5,
*Alexander, William A., 1st Lt,
Allen, Kenneth C., Cpl,
Allen, Vesten, Pfc,
Allgire, Howard R., T/5,
Allingham, Emmett M., Sgt,
Alsteen, Raymond W., T/4,
Altiere, Ferdinando, Pfc,
Ambro, Paul E., Sgt,
Amos, Clark M., T/5,
Amos, Theodore B., Pfc,
Amicone, Albert F., Pvt,
Amundson, Arthur O., Pfc,
Andenno, Anthony J., T/5,
Anderson, Albert, T/5,
Anderson, Phillip A., Pvt,
Anderson, Robert, T/4,
Anderson, Wilson L., T/5,
Anglin, Homer C., Pvt,
Archbald, George D., T/5,
Armstrong, Harold A., Pvt,
Armstrong, Ray C., Pfc,
§Artz, Beryl E., 2nd Lt,
Atterbury, John H., T/5,
Azzopordi, John, Pfc,

Babelewski, Brun J., Pfc,
Back, Herschel P., T/5,
Badali, Vincent A., T/4,
Badger, Harold H., Pvt,
Badzinski, Harry R., T/4,
Bailey, Joseph L., Pfc,
Baker, Jesse C., Pfc,
†Baker, Wallace B., Pfc,
Baker, Wilburn D., Pfc,
Balko, John P., Jr., Pfc,
Ball, John G., Sgt,
Bangert, Robert L., Capt,
†Barabas, Ted, Cpl,
Barabee, Roland E., Pfc,
Barben, Charlie W., T/5,
Barker, Forrest W., T/5,
Barnett, James M., T/5,
Barney, Charles E., T/5,
Barrett, Alfred H., Pvt,
Barrett, David J., Pvt,
Barringer, Alfred Z., Pfc,
Barrow, Willard E., S/Sgt,
Barson, Joseph, Pvt,
Bartelli, Osmero L., Pfc,
Barton, Willis H., Pvt,
Basquez, Julian J., S/Sgt,
Bass, Charlie G., Pfc,
†Bassett, Wyatt D., Sgt,
†Batlotte, Louis, Pfc,
Baughn, Earl D., Pfc,
Bauman, Armond J., T/5,
Baxter, Virgil W., Pfc,
Bear, Clarence L., Pvt,
Bear, Jack, Pfc,
Beasley, Richard D., Pfc,
Beauford, Harry J., Jr., Cpl,
§Beck, Harley D., T/5,
Becker, Dean C., Pvt,
Beckerleg, John, S/Sgt,
Beddoes, Richard A., Pfc,
Beers, Karl A., Pvt,
Bell, Lawrence A., Pfc,

Bell, Marlin J., Pvt,
Bell, Robert J., Pvt,
Beller, Raymond T., Pfc,
Bellows, Dean K., Pfc,
Belmont, Aloysius, Pfc,
Benjamin, Robert P., Cpl,
Bennett, Fred W., Sgt,
Benson, Atwood O., Cpl,
Bentley, Burnell E., T/5,
§Berckefeldt, Roy, Pvt,
Berger, Virgil E., Pfc,
Bergren, Albert L., Cpl,
Bernal, Alex M., Pvt,
Bernhardt, Victor J., Pfc,
Berninger, Robert W., Pfc,
Berry, Francis E., T/5,
Berry, Harold K., Pvt,
Bertoldo, Ignacio N., T/4,
Bestermann, William, Pvt,
Bialek, John A., Sgt,
Bieder, Chester, Sgt,
Biganski, Vincent F., Pfc,
Bingham, Leonard L., Lt Col,
Bird, Luman A., T/5,
Bischoff, Glenn W., Pvt,
Bishop, Wilder W., Pfc,
Bizon, Walter E., T/5,
Blackman, Ollie C., Pfc,
Blair, Floyd W., T/5,
Blair, George T., Pfc,
Blair, Kenneth, T/5,
§Bland, George L., Sgt,
Bockenhauer, Ethan E., T/4,
Bogenschutz, Edwin A., S/Sgt,
Boire, Elmond, Pvt,
Bolden, George C., Pvt,
Bonadona, Nick J., Pfc,
Bonner, Forrest L., Sgt,
Borchers, Victor D., T/5,
Borriello, Joseph F., T/4,

Borsse, Anton A., Pvt,
Bortugno, Raymond, Pvt,
Boss, George E., T/5,
Bottles, Guy H., Pfc,
Boutin, Alexander J., Pfc,
Bowen, Paul H. M., 1st Lt,
Bowen, Paul H., T/5,
Bowers, Truman A., Pvt,
Boyer, James C., Pfc,
Boyett, Roy M., Pfc,
Bradley, Walter G., WOJG,
Braden, Roy A., Cpl,
Bramwell, Arthur, Cpl,
Branstetter, Robert H., S/Sgt,
Brauer, John L., Jr., Pfc,
Braunschweig, Arthur W., Sgt,
Breaux, Leroy S., Pfc,
Breskovic, Andrew, T/Sgt,
Brewer, Dayton, Pvt,
Brewer, Harold W., CWO,
Bridges, Charles H., S/Sgt,
Briggs, Walter E., Pfc,
Bright, James M., Jr., T/5,
Brinkman, Carl A., T/5,
Britton, Donald K., Pfc,
Brogan, Emmett B., Pfc,
Brooks, George, T/5,
Brooks, Marshall S., Pfc,
§Brothers, Vernon W., Sgt,
Brown, Byron C., Pfc,
Brown, Clifton H., T/5,
†Brown, Earl D., Pfc,
Brown, George W., Sgt,
Brown, Harce M., Pvt,
Brown, Julian W., Pfc,
Brown, Leslie E., S/Sgt,
Brown, Perry S., Sgt,
Browning, William C., T/5,
Bruce, Lester M., Jr., Pvt,
Bruenig, Norbert C., Pfc,

Bruns, Charles F., T/5,
Bryan, James E., T/5,
Bryan, John E., Pvt,
Budz, Theodore J., Cpl,
Buerger, Fred W., Jr., S/Sgt,
Bugden, William E., Pfc,
Bullard, Curtis C., T/5,
Bullard, Harold C., T/5,
Buller, Daniel W., Pvt,
Burchett, John W., Pfc,
Burchett, Samuel J., Pvt,
Burdick, La Valla, Pvt,
Buresh, Emil, T/5,
Burke, Chester A., Pfc,
Burke, James J., Jr., Pfc,
Burkenhiser, Chester, Pvt,
Burkle, Clifford J., T/5,
Burns, Egbert, Sgt,
Burress, Waymon, Pfc,
Busch, William J., Cpl,
Bush, Rob O., Cpl,
Bush, Thomas R., Pvt,
Butts, Norris D., T/4,
Byers, George I., T/5,
Byrne, Arthur J., Pfc,

Caldwell, James T., 2nd Lt,
Caligiuri, Joseph V., T/5,
Callsen, Chester R., Pfc,
Cameron, David W., S/Sgt,
*Campanella, Salvatore, Pvt,
Campbell, Dexter, Cpl,
Camponeschi, Philip A., Pvt,
Cancelliere, Albert P., Pvt,
Candy, Nathan E., M/Sgt,
Captain, Constant, Pfc,
†Carecchio, George J., Pvt,
Carley, Kenneth E., Sgt,
Carlisle, Glenn E., Pvt,
Carlson, Bertil V., Capt,

† Killed in Action.   * Prisoner of War.   ‡ Missing in Action.   § Died of Wounds.

Carlson, Gordon J., T/5,
†Carlson, Richard, Pvt,
Carpenter, Horace E., Pvt,
Carrasco, Conrado D., Pfc,
Carroll, Charles A., Capt,
Carter, John D., Pfc,
Carter, Myron M., Pvt,
Carter, William N., Pvt,
Carver, John H., T/5,
Case, Marvin H., T/5,
Casoria, Anthony G., Pvt,
Cassidy, Robert E., Pfc,
Castelunovo, Eugene B., Pfc,
Castillo, Pedro, Pfc,
Castonguay, Lucien J., Pfc,
Castro, Porfirio, Pvt,
Casullo, John, Jr., Pvt,
Catania, Vince F., T/5,
Caudill, Lloyd R., Pfc,
Causer, Russell K., Jr., Pfc,
Cavanough, Francis W., Pfc,
Cavarretta, Vester, S/Sgt,
Cawhorn, John B., Pfc,
Ceglar, Rudolph J., Pfc,
†Cellmer, Emil J., Cpl,
Chamberlain, Robert E., T/5,
Chapman, Cinton D., Pfc,
Chapman, Gorman M., Pfc,
Chapman, Leon A., Jr., Pfc,
Chappell, Lawrence D., S/Sgt,
Charecky, Morris, Sgt,
Charvat, Martin J., T/4,
Chase, Thomas P., Pvt,
Chastain, Fred L., Pfc,
Chenger, Paul P., Sgt,
§Chevalier, Cyril J., T/5,
Chipman, Charles J., Pvt,
§Chisnell, Ransler E., Pvt,
Choate, William D., Pvt,
Christensen, James, T/5,
Christian, Francis M., Pfc,
Christie, Elmer W., Pfc,
Christy, Boyde L., Pvt,
Churchill, Harlan R., Pvt,
Ciaramitaro, Sam, Pfc,
Ciesla, Theodore, Pfc,
Clark, Kenneth C., Pfc,
Clews, William R., CWO,
Cobas, George M., Pvt,
Cockrell, Earnest E. V., T/5,
Cockrell, James D., Pfc,
Cogdill, Lewis E., Pfc,
Cohagan, John R., 1st Lt,
Cohen, Nathan M., 1st Sgt,
Cohen, Paul, Pvt,
Cohrac, George T., Pvt,
Cole, Charlie W., T/5,
Cole, John D., T/4,
Cole, Paul D., Pfc,
Collier, Roy R., Pfc,
Collins, Frank J., Pfc,
Collins, Harry C., Pvt,
Collins, Harry F., Pfc,
Colpitts, Everett M., Jr., Pvt,
Conca, Thomas D., Pfc,
Condon, Darrell K., Pfc,
Conkle, Thomas E., Pvt,
Conley, Berton B., Pfc,
Constance, Mike, Pvt,
Cook, Albert H., Capt,
Cook, Frederick A., T/5,
Copeland, William M., 2nd Lt,
Corbett, Robert J., Pfc,
Corbin, Willie L., T/5,
Cordova, Anthony C., Pvt,
Cornwell, Ralph L., Pfc,
Cosat, John W., Pfc,
Cossey, Doward, Pfc,
Costanzo, Raphael J., Pvt,
Cott, Edward, Pvt,
Council, William E., Jr., Pfc,
Cox, James E., Pvt,
Cozatt, Perry C., Jr., Pvt,
Craddock, Bryan E., Cpl,
Cramer, Bernnie L., Sgt,
Cramer, Harold G., Pfc,
Crane, Jess, Jr., Cpl,
Crane, John T., Pvt,
Crawford, George M., Pvt,
Crawford, Lawrence R., T/Sgt,
Creasy, Fred M., Pvt,
Crenshaw, Lawrence A., Sgt,
Crescenzi, Columbo E., Pfc,
Crew, Theodore R., Pvt,
Crocker, Anison C., Pvt,
Crow, Ned A., Pfc,
Crowley, James H., Pvt,
Crutchley, James H., Pvt,
Cuicello, James W., S/Sgt,
†Culbertson, James W., Sgt,
Culkins, Robert V., Pfc,
Culp, Woodrow W., T/5,
Cundy, Donald T., Capt,
Cunningham, Douglas J., Pfc,
Cunningham, Robert L., Sgt,

Curtis, Leo J., Pfc,
Cushman, Walter W., S/Sgt,
‡Cwynar, Leonard F., Pvt,

Daenens, Albert A., Pfc,
Dahler, Jack A., Pvt,
Dailey, James H., Pfc,
Dakauskas, Leon V., T/5,
Dalmonego, Albin A., Pfc,
Daly, James E., Pfc,
Daly, James J., S/Sgt,
Danbury, Hildon H., Pvt,
†Dann, Eugene H., Pvt,
Dashiel, Charles F., Pfc,
Daugherty, Howard R., Pfc,
Davenport, James E., T/5,
Davenport, Lawrence M., Pvt,
Davenport, Macdonald, Pvt,
Daves, Kenneth W., T/4,
David, Michael, T/5,
Davis, Albert H., Cpl,
Davis, Clarence W., Pvt,
Davis, Elmer L., Pfc,
Davis, Henry A., Sgt,
†Davis, James W., Pfc,
Davis, John M., T/4,
Davis, Lee, Pfc,
Davis, Roland H., Pfc,
Davis, Wesley N., 1st Sgt,
Davis, William J., Pvt,
Dazey, William W., 2nd Lt,
Deane, Harold T., Pfc,
DeCesare, Daniel, Sgt,
Decker, Elwood R., Pfc,
Decorah, Melvin, Pfc,
DeFelice, Dominic J., Pvt,
Dellinger, Paul F., Pfc,
Demmel, Ivan H., Sgt,
Dennis, Charlie E., T/5,
Dennison, William K., Jr., Capt
Depner, Arthur J., Cpl,
†DeStefano, Edward J., Pfc,
Deutsch, Edward A., Pvt,
†DeVita, Joseph, T/5,
DeVoss, Albert A., Cpl,
Dewhurst, Elton E., T/5,
Diabo, Matthew, Pvt,
Diaz, Joe, Pvt,
Dickerson, Clyde C., 1st Lt,
Dignan, William J., Pvt,
Dinkel, Ralph L., Pfc,
Distler, John S., T/5,
Dittemore, Carl F., T/5,
†Dobbins, Robert H., Pfc,
Doherty, John J., Pfc,
Donini, Raymond A., Pvt,
Doty, Vernon H., T/5,
Dougan, Robert O., Jr., Pfc,
Doyle, Thomas E., Pvt,
Drake, Coley E., Pvt,
Drennon, Paul U., Sgt,
Drescher, Lawrence E., S/Sgt,
Drinkwine, Leo H., T/5,
Driskill, Sylvester L., Pfc,
Drof, Joseph J., Pfc,
Dryburg, William, Pfc,
Duckworth, Frederick E., Pvt,
Duco, John P., Pfc,
§Dudek, Joseph, Pvt,
Dunbar, Alexander S., Pvt,
Dunn, Charles E., Pvt,
Dunn, Guy F., Pvt,
Durack, Walter L., Pfc,
Durgen, John, T/5,
Durham, Tafus L., S/Sgt,
Dutcher, Ray W., T/5,
Duty, Hoyt C., Pfc,
Dye, Denver W., Pfc,
Dyer, Sam E., Cpl,

Eadie, Harold J., T/5,
Earnheart, Richard L., Maj,
Eberle, George H., Pfc,
Eden, Frank, Pvt,
Edmonds, Kermit M., Pvt,
Edwards, Doyle F., Pfc,
Edwards, James H., Pvt,
Eenigenburg, Donald M., T/5,
Eggers, William M., Pvt,
Eisenhardt, John J., Pvt,
Elkins, Charles W., Pvt,
Ellis, Harry F., Sgt,
Ellwanger, Richard L., Pfc,
Elmer, Morris R., S/Sgt,
Elmore, Lester C., 2nd Lt,
Elsesser, George J., Pvt,
Elwell, Charles W., T/5,
†Embrogno, Joseph A., Pfc,
Emerick, Frank J., T/5,
†Engle, Robert A., Pvt,
English, Bercue, Pvt,
Erfourth, Raymond E., Pfc,
Erickson, Oscar C., Pvt,
Ernstes, Herman C., Sgt,
Espelien, Clarence K., Cpl,

Etsell, Norman W., Cpl,
Evans, Lloyd G., T/5,
Evans, Samuel G., T/4,
†Evans, Vernon H., 1st Lt,
Even, Francis A., Capt,

Fabrick, Walter A., Pvt,
Faerber, Milton V., 2nd Lt,
Fahey, Robert W., Pfc,
Faltinson, Gilbert E., Pfc,
Famiglietti, Vito, Pvt,
Farmer, Fred E., Pfc,
Farmer, Leonard C., 1st Sgt,
Farnham, Bertram C., Jr., Pfc,
Farnsworth, George E., Pvt,
Faulkner, Edward L., Pfc,
Feinstein, Morris, T/5,
Feister, Elmer W., S/Sgt,
Ferber, Charles S., Cpl,
Ferraro, Frank, Pfc,
Ferriola, Charles F., Pvt,
Fidroeff, Wilford E., Sgt,
Fields, Joseph W., Pfc,
Fields, Mason M., Pvt,
Filippone, Ray, T/4,
†Fillmore, Robert J., Pfc,
Finken, Stillman W., T/5,
Finley, Calvin C., Pvt,
Fisher, Albert J., Pfc,
Flaharty, Henry W., Pvt,
Flanagan, Thomas J., Pvt,
Flanigan, William A., Jr., Pfc,
Flannery, Clyde E., Pfc,
Flehan, Henry, Pfc,
Flynn, Martin L., Pfc,
Fogde, Roy E., Pvt,
Follette, Melvin S., T/5,
Foltz, Lyle E., T/5,
Foraker, Lewis F., T/5,
Ford, Charles M., Pvt,
Ford, Martin J., T/5,
Foreman, Eldridge J., Pvt,
Forrest, Melvin, S/Sgt,
Forte, Guerrino J., Pfc,
Foster, George R., Pfc,
Fowler, Hurl J., Pfc,
Fowles, Fred L., Pfc,
Fraijo, Leandro R., T/5,
Frailey, Louis H., Pvt,
Frank, Charles, Jr., Pvt,
Franklin, Clyde D., T/5,
Franko, Joseph C., Pvt,
Freeburg, Dewey E., Pfc,
Freiberg, Louis E., T/5,
†French, Leo W., Jr., 2nd Lt,
Frentress, Billie L., Pvt,
Fromdahl, Earl R., S/Sgt,
Froncilo, William A., Pvt,
Fuhrer, John G., Pvt,
Fuhs, Vincent J., Pvt,
Fuller, Chester J., Pfc,
Fundine, Linden E., Pfc,
Funk, Clifford L., Pvt,
Funke, Irvin N., Pfc,
Furrow, James W., Pvt,

Gaabo, Rudolph A., Pfc,
†Gabriel, Paul E., Pvt,
Galligar, Isaac M., S/Sgt,
Games, Richard E., Pfc,
Garcia, Victoriano, Jr., Pvt,
Gardner, George, 1st Sgt,
Garner, Casey, Pvt,
Garres, James, Pfc,
Gaska, Joe A., T/5,
Gavron, Joseph, Pvt,
George, Roy T., Pfc,
Gersh, Samuel, Pfc,
Gesicki, Lawrence J., T/5,
Giese, Clayton O., S/Sgt,
§Giesken, Joseph M., Pfc,
Gilbert, Paul F., Pfc,
Gilley, Frank C., T/5,
Gillis, Herman, T/5,
Gilmore, Robert K., Pfc,
Ginsbach, Joe V., T/4,
Glade, Leonard F., S/Sgt,
Glasscock, B. A., T/4,
Glasford, Delbert O., Sgt,
Glaze, Jacob H., Pfc,
Glenn, Cap A., Cpl,
Glibert, Clinton E., T/5,
Gochis, Anthony, Pfc,
Goellar, Charles O., T/5,
Goldfarb, Keva, Pvt,
Goldman, Paul E., Pvt,
Goldsworthy, Robert B., T/4,
Goldusky, Frederick J., Sgt,
Gomez, Salvadore, Pfc,
Gonzales, Max, Pfc,
Gonzales, Dionicio, Pvt,
Good, George E., Pvt,
Goodman, Elmer C., T/5,
Gottschalk, Walter J., T/4,
†Graff, Harlan L., Sgt,

Graham, Albert, Cpl,
Grahovac, Louis A., Pfc,
Granado, Thomas D., Pvt,
Grande, Gilbert B., T/5,
Grant, Charles I., Sgt,
Grant, James A., 1st Lt,
Gray, Herbert L., T/4,
Gray, William A., Pvt,
‡Graybeal, James R., Sgt,
Greathouse, Cecil, Pfc,
Green, William A., Pvt,
†Greencrow, Harvey, Pvt,
Greenhalgh, Clarence, Sgt,
Grieger, Noel W., S/Sgt,
Griffith, Gordon J., Capt,
Griffith, Uriah, Pvt,
Grincavitch, William J., Pfc,
Griswold, James W., T/3,
Grittner, Victor L., M/Sgt,
Groomer, Claude G., T/5,
Grosch, Francis J., T/5,
Gross, Charles H., Pvt,
Gross, Nick, Sgt,
Grubb, Ernest H., Pfc,
Grubb, J. C., Pfc,
†Grzyb, Stanley J., T/5,
Guerra, Pilar L., Pvt,
Gumieny, Edmund J., T/5,
Gurtner, William H., T/4,
†Guski, Stance, Cpl,
Guzdowski, John F., Pfc,
Gwinn, Fred G., Pvt,

Haberek, Peter A., T/5,
Hackney, Odes E., Pvt,
Hadjuk, William R., T/5,
Hadley, Fred C., T/5,
Haenny, George M., T/5,
Haggerty, James, Pvt,
Haggerty, James J., Pfc,
Hain, Carl E., Pfc,
Hainley, Arthur P., Pfc,
Halik, Casimir S., Pfc,
Hall, Eugene S., Jr., Pvt,
Hall, Malcolm E., Pfc,
Hamby, Hubert L., Pvt,
Hamilton, John H., Pvt,
Hamilton, Virgil J., T/5,
Hammond, George F., Pfc,
Hancock, Geston E., T/4,
Handy, Claude H., Pvt,
Hannum, Lynn M., T/5,
Hansen, Olaf C., Sgt,
Hanson, Arthur C., Pfc,
Hanson, Elmer J., T/4,
Hanson, Fred L., T/5,
Hapak, Stanley H., Pfc,
Hapanowich, Paul, T/5,
†Hardy, William H., Sgt,
Harkey, William C., Pvt,
Harney, William M., Pvt,
Harris, John, Jr., Pvt,
Harris, Lamar D., Pvt,
Harris, William R., Pfc,
Harshbarger, Paul E., Pvt,
Hart, John F., Pfc,
Hart, Leland J., S/Sgt,
Hartley, Joseph H., Pvt,
Hartman, Joseph, Pvt,
Hartosh, John A., Pvt,
Harvey, Russell A., Pfc,
Harvey, William J., S/Sgt,
Hash, Porter G., Pvt,
Hasz, Roland J., Pfc,
Hatfield, Ralph W., Pvt,
Hatton, James W., Pfc,
Hawthorne, Harold J., T/5,
Haydel, Ottis J., Cpl,
Hayden, James E., Maj,
Hayes, Jerome K., Cpl,
†Hazy, Mike, Pfc,
Head, Harry W., Pvt,
Heil, Louis J., Pfc,
Heinen, John N., Pvt,
†Heller, Lawrence A., Sgt,
Henderson, Eugene B., Sgt,
Hennek, Leonard P., Pfc,
Herrara, Marshal P., Pvt,
Herrin, Richard J., Pvt,
Herrman, Jerome F., S/Sgt,
Hielkema, Anno, Pvt,
Hightree, Kenneth E., Sgt,
Hilkey, Robert E., Cpl,
Hill, Charles J., Pvt,
Hill, Elbert A., Pvt,
Hill, John M., Pvt,
Hilla, Cortland C., T/5,
Hilliard, Claude E., Pvt,
Hinrichs, Evan G., Sgt,
Hirsbrunner, Glenn H., Pfc,
Hitchcock, Oren W., Cpl,
Hite, Daniel P., T/5,
Hix, Frank W., Pvt,
Hobson, Ambrose G., T/5,
Hodge, Ernest D., Pvt,

†Hodge, John M., Pvt,
Hodgson, Ralph, T/5,
†Hoffmann, Alfred G., T/5,
†Hohensee, Melvin E., T/5,
Hohman, George C., Capt,
Hollamon, David T., T/5,
Holland, George C., Pvt,
Hollingsworth, Hubert W., Pfc,
Hollister, Eugene A., Pvt,
Holmes, Thomas W., Pvt,
Holzemer, John, Pfc,
Honovich, William, Pfc,
Hood, William L., Pfc,
Horner, Orval Q., Pfc,
Hotz, Russell R., Pfc,
†Houlihan, Thomas J., Pvt,
Houseman, David P., Cpl,
Howard, Walter R., Pvt,
Howell, Lester E., Pfc,
Howle, Caleb A., Pvt,
Huckeba, Lloyd W., Jr., Pvt,
Hughes, Albert E., Pfc,
Hulstine, Quinton L., WOJG,
Humphrey, Charles C., Pfc,
Hunter, John W., M/Sgt,
Huntington, Howard S., Pvt,
Huot, Leo H., Pfc,
†Hupert, Kamil J., Pvt,
Huskin, Donald E., Pfc,

Iacuzzi, Joseph T., T/4,
Idell, George A., Pfc,

Jablonski, Harry A., T/5,
Jackson, Edwin C., Pvt,
Jackson, James A., Pvt,
Jacobs, Edwin J., Cpl,
Jacobsen, Calvert H., Pvt,
James, Lawrence A., Sgt,
James, Lawrence J., Pfc,
Jankowski, Fred V., Pfc,
Jannone, Michael J., S/Sgt,
Jelen, Walter S., Pfc,
Jensen, Clarence H., T/5,
Jensen, Joseph L., T/4,
Johanon, Paul G., Sgt,
Johansen, Victor C., Pvt,
Johnson, Charlie H., Pvt,
Johnson, Chester T., T/4,
Johnson, Clyde I., S/Sgt,
†Johnson, Cullie B., S/Sgt,
Johnson, DeLoyd R., T/5,
Johnson, James B., T/5,
Johnson, James J., T/5,
Johnson, Malcolm R., Pfc,
Johnson, Parnell P., Pfc,
Johnston, Orville J., T/5,
Jones, Alvin F., Pfc,
Jones, Burt C., Pfc,
Jones, Doyle, 1st Lt,
Jung, Raymond A., T/5,
Jones, Fred J., 1st Sgt,
Jones, Howard, Pvt,
Jones, Hutsell B., T/5,
Jones, Jack D., 1st Lt,
Jones, Louis H., Pvt,
Jones, Paul F., Pfc,
Jones, Robert C., Sgt,
Jones, William W., Sr., Pvt,
Jorgenson, Edward C., T/5,
Josephs, Clarence E., T/3,
Joslin, Morris B., Capt,
Judge, Frederick J., Pvt,

Kaffman, Harold L., Pvt,
Kaluza, Anthony J., Sgt,
Kaluza, Ludwig, T/5,
Kalvelage, Arthur J., Pfc,
Kapchunas, William J., Pvt,
†Karst, Edwin W., Sgt,
Kasprzyk, Stanley, Pfc,
Katsogiannis, James T., Pfc,
†Katz, Arthur, Pvt,
Keating, Henry L., Pvt,
Keene, Jerald J., T/5,
Keiper, Ernest F., T/4,
Kellogg, Daryl B., T/5,
Kelly, Donald P., Pvt,
Kelly, Donald T., Pvt,
Kelly, Myron, Pfc,
Kelpy, Ronald P., Pvt,
Kendziorski, Sylvester L., T/5,
Kennedy, Luke R., T/5,
Kenny, William J., Pvt,
Kent, Golden E., Sgt,
Kenyon, Francis R., Pfc,
Kerchinski, Frank F., Pfc,
Kertes, Jay A., Pvt,
Keryk, Michael, Pfc,
Keslinke, Joseph S., T/4,
Kessel, Lawrence W., T/4,
Kesten, Joseph M., Pvt,
Kesterson, Wayne N., S/Sgt,
Kidner, Niles C., Pfc,
Kiepke, Richard E., T/5,
Killinger, John L., Pvt,

† Killed in Action. * Prisoner of War. ‡ Missing in Action. § Died of Wounds.

Kimbrough, James, Pfc,
Kincaid, George C., Pfc,
†King, George B., Pvt,
King, Milton L., Pfc,
Klappich, Walter S., 1st Lt,
Kleinfeld, Joseph H., T/5,
Knapp, Robert F., Pvt,
Knight, Carlton A., Jr., Cpl,
Knisley, Harold D., Cpl,
Koberstein, Henry K., Maj,
Kocourek, Andrew, S/Sgt,
Koenig, Karl J. R., Sgt,
Kolencik, Gabriel T., Pvt,
Kolodziej, Teddy J., Pvt,
Kolpack, Marvin E., Pfc,
†Komanekin, Joseph G., T/5,
Komarowski, Edwin F., T/5,
Kondracki, Sam T., Pfc,
Kosakowski, Charles T., Pvt,
Kotek, John, Pfc,
†Kotar, Edward A., T/5,
Kotleski, John W., S/Sgt,
Kovach, Louis L., Pvt,
Kowalski, Leonard P., Pvt,
§Kraemer, Leonard T., T/5,
Kraska, Stanley J., Pvt,
Krause, William J., T/5,
Kregel, Earl J., T/5,
Kress, Floyd D., Pvt,
Krintz, Lloyd C., T/5,
Krueger, Alvin A., Cpl,
†Krueger, Harold C., Pfc,
Kubik, Edwin F., T/4,
Kubow, Frederick A., Cpl,
Kucera, Arthur J., T/5,
Kucinskas, Charles J., Pvt,
Kunde, Arthur A., S/Sgt,
Kurcharski, Stefan, Pvt,
Kuss, Fred W., T/4,
Kusnetzow, Samuel, Cpl,

LaBelle, John P., Pfc,
LaFontaine, Wilfred P., Pfc,
Laguna, Crispo, T/Sgt,
Lakari, Tovio T., Pfc,
Lambie, James A., Pfc,
Lamothe, Arthur S., Pvt,
Land, Pervin H., Jr.,
Lane, Clifford R., Pfc,
Langner, John D., S/Sgt,
Langstaff, Kenneth D., Pvt,
Langston, Roger W., T/5,
Larcher, Albert F., Pvt,
Larson, Herbert D., Pfc,
†Larson, Stanley E., Capt,
LaTart, Alan E., Pfc,
Lauffer, William P., T/5,
Lavallee, Lawrence J., T/5,
Lavoie, Edmond D., Pvt,
†Lawson, Edward W., 2nd Lt,
Lawson, Preston, Pvt,
Leage, Vincent C., Pvt,
§Lear, Melvin C., Pvt,
Leary, Lewis W., Pfc,
Lebeau, Earl H., T/5,
§Le Duc, Lawrence E., Pfc,
Lee, Robert E., T/5,
Lefler, Homer M., Capt,
Leh, Paul L., Pfc,
Leiby, Warren H., Pfc,
Leith, Donald, Pfc,
†Lenta, Mario, Pfc,
Lente, Arne U., T/5,
Leon, Robert J., 1st Lt,
Leopold, Lewellyn E., Pvt,
Lesniewski, Raymond, T/5,
Levesque, Adelard, WOJG,
Levine, Murray, Pvt,
Levins, Roy M., T/5,
Lewandowski, A. J., S/Sgt,
Lewis, Earl F., Pvt,
Limoges, Georges E., T/5,
Lindley, Robert B., 1st Lt,
Link, Glennie W., Pfc,
Little, Ralph L., Pvt,
Litton, John W., 2nd Lt,
†Livezey, Robert H., Pfc,
Livinghouse, Frederick J., Pvt,
Loaney, Robert C., Cpl,
Lodermeier, Louis J., Pfc,
Logan, Bruce G., Pvt,
Long, Ernest L., Pvt,
Long, James L., Pfc,
Long, James R., T/5,
§Loomis, Neil Pvt,
Lopez, Albert V., Sgt,
Lordan, George W., Pvt,
Louderback, Earl L., Pvt,
Loumakis, Nikolas, Pvt,
Love, Allen T., Pfc,
†Love, George W., Pvt,
Lovejoy, Norman D., Pfc,
Lowden, Steve, Pfc,
Lowry, Clifton E., T/5,
†Lubin, Austin P., Pfc,

Lucere, Daniel H., Pfc,
†Luebke, Edwin G., T/4,
†Lugtigheid, Harold, T/5,
Lundell, Frank J., T/4,
Lutman, Raymond E., Cpl,
Lyons, Thomas E., Pvt,
Lyons, Richard W., Pfc,

Mackintosh, Ronald G., Pvt,
Maddalozzo, John, Pfc,
Madsen, Chester A., 1st Sgt,
Magnuson, Conrad I., Pfc,
Mahalic, Louis D., Sgt,
Mahoney, Paul J., Pfc,
Maier, Alfred, T/5,
Majka, Theodore J., Sgt,
Majors, Wiley J., T/4,
Makepeace, William R., 1st Lt,
Malamazian, John, T/4,
Malloy, George F., T/5,
Malmo, Ralph I., Pvt,
§Manchester, Stuart C., Pfc,
Mangelsen, John E., Cpl,
Manna, John, Pfc,
†Marcantonio, Joseph N., 1st Lt,
Marciszewski, Steve A., Pfc,
Mariani, Alfred, Sgt,
Marion, Carl D., T/4,
Marion, Elbert R., Pfc,
Marion, George W., Pvt,
Mariotti, Deno G., Pvt,
Marks, Gerald J., Pvt,
Marlar, John M., Pvt,
Marquardt, Hugo S., Pfc,
Martens, Floyd, T/5,
Martin, Arthur J., Pvt,
†Martin, Grant H., Pfc,
Martin, Paul A., Pfc,
Martin, Robert J., S/Sgt,
Martin, Roy D., Pvt,
§Martinsen, Melvin G., T/Sgt,
Maruska, Peter, Pvt,
Maselek, Stanley J., Pvt,
Mason, Richard L., T/5,
†Massey, Walter F., Pvt,
Massung, George, Pfc,
Mattzela, Andrew P., Pvt,
Maturo, Albert N., Pfc,
Maunoir, Malcolm F., Pvt,
Maxhimer, Leroy, Pvt,
Mazany, Florian L., Pvt,
Mazurchik, Jacob, Pvt,
Meade, Vernon L., T/5,
Meek, William H., Pfc,
Meek, William R., Sgt,
Meeks, Jim L., T/5,
Melgard, Howard A., T/5,
†Merdalo, George J., Pvt,
Michael, William E., T/Sgt,
Mickles, Albert J., Pvt,
Miller, Joseph S., Cpl,
Miller, Robert E., Pfc,
Miller, William J., Pvt,
Minchella, John R., Pvt,
Miner, Vere W., T/5,
Minnerly, Vincent, Pvt,
Miramontes, Salvador C., T/5,
Mitchell, Arthur, Pvt,
Moe, Oscar G., T/4,
Moeller, Robert E., Pfc,
Montijo, Victor M., Pvt,
Montville, Frank J., T/5,
Moore, Earl, Pvt,
Moore, Glen H., Sr., T/5,
Moore, Harland A., Pvt,
Moore, Homer R., Pvt,
Moore, Jesse R., Pfc, C
Morel, Arthur F., Pvt,
Morelli, Leo M., Pvt,
Morfitt, Winfield C., 1st Sgt,
Morgan, Paul R., 1st Lt,
Morina, Louis, Sgt,
Morris, Earl, Pvt,
Morris, Sam W., Jr., T/5,
Moskovitz, Norman, Pfc,
Mosley, Leo B., T/4,
Moszner, James C., Pvt,
Moy, Baker, Pvt,
Mrasak, Edward J., Pfc,
§Muir, Robert E., Pfc,
Mullen, Joseph, Pfc,
Mullin, Donald M., Pfc,
Mullins, Lonzo, Pvt,
Munday, Edward W., Pfc,
Munro, Edward J., 2nd, T/5,
Munson, Erland K., T/5,
Munson, John D., T/5,
Murphy, Marion W., T/5,
Murray, John J., Pfc,
Murray, Roy L., Pfc,
Myers, Oliver M., Pvt,
Myrvik, Lloyd E., T/4,
McCall, Alfred, Pfc,
§McCall, Bernice O., Pvt,
McCanney, Aubrey J., Pfc,

McCaron, William V., Cpl,
McCarther, Glen, Cpl,
†McCarty, Robert E., Pvt,
McCauley, Marco A., Pfc,
McClain, Earl F., Pfc,
McCormick, Harry T., Pvt,
McCoy, John E., Pvt,
McCue, Gilbert J., Pfc,
McCullock, Richard A., Pfc,
McDermott, Robert J., S/Sgt,
McDonald, Walter J., T/5,
McElroy, Francis C., Pfc,
McGary, Walter, Pvt,
McGee, Robert C., Pvt,
McGreger, Jacob F., Pfc,
McGrory, Paul J., Jr., Pvt,
McHann, William E., Pvt,
McIntyre, Lester J., T/5,
McKay, Charles H., Pfc,
McKinley, John D., T/5,
†McKinney, Lloyd J., Pvt,
McLellan, William H., 2nd Lt,
McLeod, Everett W., Pfc,
McMahan, Charles F., Cpl,
McNally, Lawrence, Pvt,
McSwain, Earl, T/5,

Nabors, Charles R., Pfc,
Nachtigal, James J., T/4,
Napier, John B., Pfc,
Napolitano, Salvatore A., Pvt
Nardini, Freddie J., Pfc,
Nash, Donald A., 1st Lt
Nawrocki, Andrew W., M/Sgt,
Neeson, George F., T/5,
Neino, John, Pvt,
Nelson, Leo C., Pvt,
Nelson, Donald V., Pfc,
Nelson, Wayne, Pvt,
Nelson, William S., 1st Lt,
Nestell, Robert E., Cpl,
Newgren, Conrad D., Pvt,
Newman, Maurice J., Pvt,
Neumeister, Clarence J., Pfc,
Nickelson, Howard B., T/5,
Nicholson, Philip, T/4,
Nicpon, Stanley, Pvt,
Nilsen, Lyder M., T/4,
Norman, Ray E., Pfc,
Norris, William E., T/4,
Norton, Clair W., Pfc,
Nunn, Herbert M., Pfc,
Nutter, Joseph C., Pfc,

Obler, Edward I., 1st Lt,
O'Brien, Francis X., Pvt,
O'Brien, John G., Pfc,
OBrien, Michael J., Pvt,
Ochava, Jesus F., Pvt,
Odegard, Arnold B., S/Sgt,
†Odegard, Gustave, T/5,
Odegard, Peter, 1st Sgt,
O'Dell, George L., Pfc,
Odom, Garland W., Pfc,
Ohanian, Andrew, Pvt,
O'Hara, Robert F., Pvt,
Oliver, Frank, T/5,
Oliver, Robert J., Pvt,
Olson, Ernest A., Pvt,
Olson, Einar, Pfc,
Olson, Russell I., T/5,
Olter, Donald M., Pvt,
O'Malley, George V., Pvt,
Oneto, John L., Jr., T/5,
§Ordonez, Rafael, Pfc,
Orlando, Tony, T/5,
Ortega, Peter, Cpl,
O'Shea, William L., Jr., Pvt,
†Ostmeyer, Earl H., 2nd Lt,
O'Toole, Francis R., T/5,
Owen, Dan, S/Sgt,
Owens, Leonard W., Pvt,

Pace, Willie, T/5,
Paez, Armando M., Pfc,
Palmer, Allan L., S/Sgt,
Pagan, Rudolph L., T/5,
Palmer, Horace C., Pvt,
Palmer, Thomas W., Pvt,
Pappe, Simon C., S/Sgt,
Parks, Walter L., Pvt,
Parrish, Ben J., Pvt,
Parzych, Chester C., T/5,
Pasanen, Hubert O., T/Sgt,
Patake, Harry W., Pfc,
Patyk, Emil, Pfc,
Paul, Bernard, Pvt,
Paul, Charles A., Pfc,
Paul, Charles E., Pvt,
Peacock, William E., Pvt,
Peck, Gerald E., Pvt,
†Pedersen, Willy, Pfc,
Peeler, Zeb, T/5,
Peluso, Paul J., Pvt,
§Pereira, Joseph C., Pvt,
Pernice, Peter C., Sgt,

Perrine, Foster, Pvt,
Perrott, Eddie C., Pvt,
Perry, William S., Pfc,
Peters, Frederick, Pvt,
Peterson, Archie C., Pvt,
Peterson, Robert L., Pfc,
Petherick, Robert L., Lt Col,
Petokas, Daniel B., M/Sgt,
Pfister, Alfred J., Pvt,
Phillips, Frank, Jr., Pfc,
Pickard, Archie L., Pfc,
Pickett, Claudius A., S/Sgt,
Pierson, Julius B., Pfc,
Pigg, David F., Pvt,
Pina, Tony D., Jr., Pvt,
Pinnow, Arthur W., Pvt,
Pinson, Jack L., Pvt,
Pinto, Tony J., Pfc,
Pisano, Anthony R., Cpl,
Pitt, Charles F., T/4,
Pittman, Vestel, Pvt,
Pitts, William D., Pfc,
Platts, Godfrey, Pfc,
Plummer, James R., 1st Lt,
Poeppe, Ambrose A., T/5,
Pollock, Samuel D., 1st Lt,
Pomnichowski, Thaddeus, Pfc,
Pop, Ignatius, Pvt,
Porfilio, Albert P., S/Sgt,
Posthuma, Peter H., Pfc,
Predoehl, Walter F., Cpl,
Preston, Roy D., Pvt,
Priamiano, Pete R., Pfc,
Priebe, Harold F., Pvt,
Prince, Cecil E., T/5,
Printy, Thomas, Pfc,
Pritchett, Donald H., T/4,
Proctor, William D., T/5,
Provenzola, Anthony, Cpl,
Provost, Clifford J., Pvt,
Przybyl, Felix, Pfc,
Przybyliski, Aloize, T/5,
Pullman, Samuel, Pfc,
Pyrz, Joseph S., Pfc,

Quaglia, Alphonso, Pvt,
Quigg, Russel H., T/5,
§Quinnan, Ralph W., Pvt,

Radosevich, Branko, Pvt,
Rahne, Victor A., T/5,
Rainville, Merrlen J., Pvt,
Rake, Lawrence W., T/5,
Rambo, Charles F., Pvt,
Ramirez, Jesse B., Pvt,
Rankin, Richard T., Pvt,
Ranson, Woodrow L., Pvt,
Rayfield, Billie L., Cpl,
Raymer, Lawrence L., Sgt,
Raymond, Daniel A., Capt,
Rebello, Albert C., Pvt,
Rechtman, Irving, T/5,
Rechterman, Walter G., Sgt,
§Redmond, Thomas J., T/5,
Reed, Clatis L., Pfc,
Reeves, Carl R., T/5,
Reeve, Harold O., Pvt,
Register, Harvey, Pvt,
Reid, Gilmore W., 1st Lt,
Reiff, Fred H., T/5,
Reisenauer, Anton A., T/5,
Reitz, John G., T/5,
Renaud, Albert A., Pvt,
Renda, Gus J., Pvt,
§Renfro, James M., S/Sgt,
Rennhack, Russell R., Pfc,
Renzullo, Arnold J., Pvt,
Retzack, Charles A., Pfc,
Reynolds, James A., Jr., Pfc,
Rhodes, Harold, 2nd Lt,
Rhoads, Paul M., 1st Lt,
Rice, Harold D., T/5,
Rice, Harold E., Pvt,
Richards, Kenneth W., Sgt,
†Richardson, Archie E., Sgt,
Richgels, Ray A., T/5,
Richland, Irvin J., T/4,
Richmond, Thomas D., Pvt,
Richtar, Joe, Pfc,
Richter, James C., T/5,
Richter, Julius, Jr., Pfc,
Rickard, Vaughn T., Jr., Pvt,
†Rickman, Woodford L., Pvt,
Riley, Albert D., T/5,
Riley, Charles H., Sgt,
Rinkle, Elton W., Cpl,
Roberts, Cleatus L., T/4,
Roberts, Frank, S/Sgt,
Roberts, Raymond A., Pvt,
Robertson, Alexander, 1st Lt,
Robinson, Lloyd J., T/5,
Robinson, Neal T., Pvt,
Robinson, Paul T., T/5,
Roden, Milford L., Pvt,

Rodgers, Clyde R., Pfc,
Roesener, Howard J., Pfc,
Rogers, Alfred T., T/4,
Rogers, Fred, Pfc,
Rogers, John F., Pfc,
§Rogers, Lawrence, Pvt,
Rogers, Paul J., Pvt,
Rooney, Joseph A., Pvt,
Rorick, Robert W., Pvt,
Rosbruch, Nathan, Pvt,
Ross, Delmas D., T/4,
Ross, Jessie C., Pvt,
Rota, Alfred J., Pvt,
Roush, Davis C., Pfc,
Routzahn, Robert H., Cpl,
Roux, Roland J., Pfc,
Rowson, Roy W., T/Sgt,
Royer, Frederick E., T/5,
Rude, Charles D., Pfc,
Rudert, Royal E., Pvt,
Rudnick, Joseph, Pfc,
Ruggirello, John J., Pvt,
Ruggless, Dwight M., Pvt,
†Ruiz, Gustave, Pvt,
Rukab, Lutfi A., Sgt,
Rumple, Cleo E., Pvt,
Russell, John P., Capt,
Russell, Walter L., Pvt,
Ruzicka, John, Pfc,
Ryan, James P., Pfc,
Ryan, John, Pfc,
Rygh, Arthur, Cpl,
Rzadkowolski, Arnold J., T/5,
Rzepecki, Burno B., Pfc,

Sakellariou, Nick,
Salagi, Joseph P., Pvt,
Salazar, Eloy S., Pfc,
Saleski, William, Pvt,
Salisbury, Carroll D., Cpl,
Salisbury, William W., Sgt,
Saltz, Martin, Pfc,
Salvador, Antone, Pfc,
Sama, Gerardo N. P., Pfc,
Sampson, Jack, Pvt,
Sanborn, William A., T/5,
Sanchez, Joe A., Pvt,
Sander, Ralph J., Sgt,
Sanders, David L., Pvt,
Sarvet, Paul W., Pvt,
†Sasse, LeRoy F., 1st Lt,
Sassin, Raymond F., Pvt,
Satterlee, Vernon L., Pfc,
Saunders, Warren C., Jr.,
Savastano, Ernest A., Pfc,
Saylor, Ray, Pvt,
Scalise, Rocco, Pvt,
Schepker, Dietrich, Jr., Pvt,
Scheuerman, Lester R., T/5,
Schierman, Ruben, S/Sgt,
Schladweiler, Raymond J., Sgt,
Schleifer, Lavern C., Sgt,
Schmid, Joseph L., Jr., Pvt,
Schmidt, Donald F., S/Sgt,
Schmidt, Francis J., Pvt,
Schmidt, Lawrence A., Pfc,
Schneider, William R., Pfc,
Shneidt, Paul F., T/5,
Schoenberg, George J., Jr., Pfc,
Schouest, Vorest A., Jr., Pvt,
Schram, Cecil L., Pfc,
Schultz, Leo L., Pvt,
Schumacher, Rueben A., Cpl,
Schumann, Edmund D., T/5,
Schutt, George L., Pvt,
Schwarz, Ralph T., Pvt,
Schweiger, Clarence W., Cpl,
Sciotto, Francesco, Pfc,
†Scott, Glen W., Sgt,
Seagle, Astor R., Pfc,
Seal, Clyde E., Pfc,
Sears, Elmer, Pvt,
Sebastian, Clay, Sgt,
Self, Charles W., Pvt,
Selkey, George, T/5,
§Selph, Israel E., Sgt,
Seppala, Oiva W., Pvt,
Seta, Lawrence, Pvt,
Seward, John H., Pfc,
Seyfang, Harry R., Pfc,
Seys, Oscar, T/5,
Shaon, William V., Pfc,
Sharp, Thomas C., Pvt,
†Shattuck, Amos W., Pvt,
Shaw, Donald B., Pvt,
Sheatz, Elmer A., Pvt,
Sheldon, John E., Sgt,
Shelley, Wallace J., T/5,
Shepard, Howard J., Pfc,
§Shepherd, Grover G., Cpl,
Sheridan, James J., Pvt,
Siebieda, Matthew L., Pvt,
Siegfried, Granville H., T/4,
Siese, Joseph L., Sgt,

† Killed in Action. * Prisoner of War. ‡ Missing in Action. § Died of Wounds.

Silverman, Robert, Pfc,
Simmons, Earl C., Pfc,
Simons, Raymond G., Pvt,
Simpson, John B., Jr., Pfc,
Sims, Bernard R., Pvt,
Singleton, Albert B., T/5,
Siobert, Albert, Pfc,
Sippe, Carol F., Pvt,
Sizemore, Carl E., T/5,
Slade, Albert H., Pfc,
Sladky, Ernest E., Pfc,
Slattum, Ralph E., Pfc,
Slay, Donald L., Pvt,
Sleeth, Robert K., 1st Lt,
Sloan, Paul B., Pfc,
Slubowski, George A., Pvt,
Smetana, Jerry J., T/5,
Smiley, Lester B., Sgt,
Smith, Allen R., Sgt,
Smith, Armel E., Pfc,
Smith, Everett J., Pvt,
Smith, Francis E., Pfc,
Smith, Fred D., Pfc,
Smith, Fred W., T/5,
Smith, James N., Pfc,
Smith, Loy E., Pfc,
Smith, Robert C., S/Sgt
Smith, Tom C., S/Sgt,
Smith, William G., Pvt,
Smith, William T., Pvt,
Snyder, Martin Lee, T/5,
Sokol, Steve O., Pfc,
Sokoloff, Philip, Pvt,
Sokolowski, Julius, T/4,
Solberg, Harold L., Pvt,
Solie, Marshall R., S/Sgt,
Somers, Robert T., Pfc,
Sontag, Samuel, Pfc,
Sorensen, Clarence, Pfc,
Sorenson, Earl M. P., Pvt,
Sorrell, Charles H., Pvt,
Sorrells, Urel, Pfc,
Sotak, William J., Pvt,
Spanbauer, Lawrence M., Pfc,
Spielman, Robert F., Pvt,
Spooner, Henry H., Sgt,
Sporleder, Andrae B., Pfc,
Springmeyer, Robert L., 1st Lt,
Spurgeon, Hubert C., Sgt,
Squires, Weller J., Cpl,
Stadler, Robert J., Pfc,
Staggs, Charles T., T/5,
†Stamp, Ernie E., S/Sgt,
†Standish, Fred C., Cpl,
Staples, Willard, Pvt,

Stefanoski, Francis J., Pfc,
Stegall, Deward H., T/5,
§Steinberger, Arthur W., Pvt,
Stephens, Clifton W., Pfc,
Stevens, Kenneth E., Pfc,
Stevens, Thomas M., Pvt,
Stewart, Roy J., Jr., Pfc,
St. Louis, Edward O., Pvt,
†Stokes, Rex F., Pfc,
Stone, Paul S., Pvt,
†Stoner, Kenneth A., Sgt,
Storms, Ralph D., Pfc,
Stover, Glenn C., 1st Sgt,
Stubblefield, Clifford B., Pvt,
Studebaker, Johnnie V., Pfc,
Sturdivant, Leonard H., T/5,
Stuffelbeam, Herschel E., T/5,
Suhajda, Vincent P., Cpl,
Summers, Aaron T., Cpl,
Summers, Chadwick J., T/4,
Sutyla, Julian F., Pfc,
Swanson, Quentin D., S/Sgt,
Swartz, Francis C., Pfc,
Sweat, John D., S/Sgt,
Sweat, Lomis P., Cpl,
Swift, Edwin M., Capt,
Sweigart, Franklin L., Pvt,
Syddall, George E., Pvt,
Szczygiel, Philip J., T/5,

Tagnon, Alexander J., Cpl,
Talmer, Henry J., T/5,
Tank Charles F., Lt Col,
Tanner, Elbert L., Sgt,
Tapia, Joseph M., S/Sgt,
Tarnowski, Staley J., Pvt,
Taylor, Harvey D., S/Sgt,
§Taylor, Jack H., T/4,
Taylor, Oscar C., Pvt,
Taylor, Roy C., T/4,
Taylor, William B., Pfc,
Tebbe, Bernard J., Cpl,
Theodaskis, George G., T/4,
Theophile, John ., Pvt,
Terwelp, Andrew P., T/5,
Teske, Elmer J., Pvt,
§Theurer, George F., T/5,
Thomas, Harold C., Pvt,
§Thomas, Odis A., Pfc,
Thomas, Robert M., T/4,
Thomas, Roger C., T/5,
Thomas, Travis L., Pfc,
‡Thomas, William A., 2nd Lt,
Thomas, William H., Pfc,
Thompson, Kenneth J., Pvt,

Thompson, Norman E., T/5,
Thurston, Loren H., S/Sgt,
Timberlake, J, C. P., 1st Lt,
Tobin, Joseph V., Sgt,
Tolliver, Alvin, Jr., T/5,
Tomes, Grady D., Pvt,
Tortorice, Anthony, Pvt,
†Tosh, Donald N., Sgt,
Toth, Stephen J., T/5,
Toto, Nicholas C., Pvt,
†Towslee, Donald J., Pfc,
Tracy, Lyle C., T/4,
Trammell, James D., Pfc,
Tramontano, Biagio B., Pfc,
†Trasatti, Guido D., Pvt,
Treece, Hobart M., Jr., Pfc,
Tresko, Earl J., Pvt,
Trickel, Maurice D., Pvt,
Troje, Bernard M., WOJG,
Trottner, Joseph A., Pfc,
Truesdale, William B., T/4,
Trumbley, Bert E., Pvt,
Tuchberry, Malcolm L., Pvt,
Tucituch, Stephen, T/Sgt,
Tuinman, Wallace, Pvt,
Tully, Harold L., Pfc,
Turnbull, Wendell L., Pvt,
Turriff, Thomas J., T/5,
Tutsch, Rodney J., Capt,
Tyson, Carlos L., Pfc,

Underhill, Arthur F., T/4,
Unser, Edgar, T/5,
Uram, Peter W., Pfc,
Uttech, Gordon C., T/5,

Vahl, Henry A., Pfc,
Van De Wyngarde, M. J., S/Sgt,
Van Orden, Clark O., Capt,
Van Werven, Herman, Pfc,
Vann, Michael, Pfc,
Vannelli, Robert J.,
Vasquez, Raymond J., Pfc,
Velky, Joseph E., Pfc,
†VerMeer, Peter, T/4,
Vermillion, Eugene, Capt,
Vetter, Henry J., Sgt,
Viger, Archie H., Pvt,
Villa, Mario H., Pfc,
Viola, John J., T/5,
Voors, Carl W., Pfc,

Wachal, James W., Jr., Pvt,
Wachowicz, Steve, S/Sgt,

Wagner, Charles E., T/5,
Wagner, Clarence R., Pvt,
Wagner, John E., Pfc,
Wagner, Stanley R., Pfc,
Waldrop, Oliver P., T/5,
Wallace, Charles C., Pfc,
Wallace, Willard C., T/5,
†Walter, Dorvall J., Pfc,
Walton, Bobbie R., Pfc,
Wambold, Howard C., Pvt,
Wandersee, Lorrain L., Pvt,
Ward, Herbert A., Pfc,
Ware, Homer W., Pvt,
Warner, Calvin J., S/Sgt,
Warner, Charles R., Pvt,
Warner, Edwin L., Pvt,
Watkins, Garvin A., Pvt,
Watters, Joseph A., T/5,
Wattles, Charles R., Cpl,
Watts, Kenneth P., Pfc,
Wayne, Ainsley C., 1st Lt,
Weaver, Melvyn W., Pfc,
Webb, Russell L., Pfc,
Weber, Victor D., T/5,
Webster, John E., Pvt,
§Weems, Leon J., T/5,
Wehnes, Melvin H., T/5,
Weichert, Rogus W., Pfc,
Weinzierl, Carl E., Cpl,
Weir, Reino A., S/Sgt,
Weisensel, Roman A., Pfc,
Weitz, William F., Jr., Pvt,
Welch, James D., M/Sgt,
Welch, Walter M., Pvt,
Weldon, Charles E., Pct,
Wellman, Kleon B., S/Sgt,
†Werner, Albert J., Sgt,
Werner, Earl D., Pfc,
Werner, Leonard L., Cpl,
West, Otis P., Pfc,
†West, Robert, Pvt,
White, Basil A., Pvt,
White, Eugene D., 2nd Lt,
Whitehead, Thomas A., Sgt,
Wichman, Edmund, 2nd Lt,
Wiegand, Wallace S., Pfc,
Wieting, Earl K., T/4,
Wilborn, Earl A., Pvt,
Wilfong, Chester D., T/4,
Wilhelm, John, Pvt,
Wilkerson, Earl E., Pfc,
Willers, Carl A. H., Pvt,
Williams, Dewel W., Pvt,
Williams, F. B., Jr., 1st Lt,
Williams, Joe E., Pvt,
Williams, Leroy N., Pvt,

Williams, William D., T/5,
Williams, William F., Jr., Pfc,
Williamson, Floyd N., S/Sgt,
Willsey, Frank M., 1st Lt,
Wilson, Buster B., Pvt,
Wilson, Doyle O., Pfc,
Wilson, Emery L., Pvt,
Wilson, William R., Pvt,
Winsor, Kenneth M., Pfc,
Wirtz, Louis T., Cpl,
Witt, Victor B., Cpl,
Wittig, Richard M., Pfc,
Wilusz, Edward J., Sgt,
†Wilusz, Fred E., Pvt,
Woelk, Albert, Sgt,
Wojtalewicz, Alex, T/5,
Wolfe, Emmett S., Pvt,
Wolfe, Frank E., Pfc,
Wolfe, Nicholas, Jr., Pvt,
Wolfe, Robert L., Pvt,
Wolfskill, John M., Pfc,
Womack, Joseph P., Pfc,
Wood, Frederick O., Pvt,
Wood, William F., Pfc,
Woodson, C. N., Jr., M/Sgt,
†Workman, Carl J., Pfc,
Workman, Clayton E., Pvt,

Yancey, Clarence H., Jr.   Pvt,
Yario, Joseph M., Cpl,
Yeager, Cecil B., Pfc,
Yeager, Clarence J., T/5,
Yefchak, John, Jr., T/5,
Yelton, Wilmer E., Cpl,
Young, Frederick L., 1st Lt,
Young, Lester C., Pfc,
Young, Willie M., Pfc,
Yurkowitz, Harry, Pvt,

Zackavec, George, T/5,
Zagorski, Casimir L., Cpl,
Zaremba, Edward C., T/5,
Zaszczuzrynski, Ted J., T/Sgt,
Zelinski, Walter, T/4,
Zemrowski, Joseph F., T/5,
Ziffino, Tony J., Pfc,
Zimpel, Earl, Pvt,
Zinkus, Joseph, Pvt,
Zirkel, Robert R., T/4,
Zitlow, Wyman R., Sgt,
Zivoder, Charles, Pfc,
Zizzo, Matt, T/5,
Zuka, Joseph F., Pvt,
Zulishy, Henry, Pfc,
Zwerin, Irving, Pvt,

† Killed in Action.   * Prisoner of War.   ‡ Missing in Action.   § Died of Wounds.

3D MEDICAL BATTALION

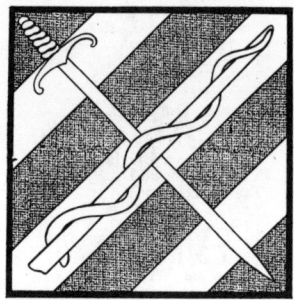

The 3d Medical Battalion was originally organized as the 3d Sanitary Train in 1917. During World War I, it served with the 3d Division and distinguished itself in the battles of the Aisne, Champagne, Champagne-Marne, Aisne-Marne, St. Mihiel and Meuse-Argonne. The 3d Sanitary Train was re-organized as the 3d Medical Regiment in 1921 and as the 3d Medical Battalion in 1939.

Commanding Officer

(Highest rank held)	Held pos. from	To
Lt. Col. William J. McCarthy		9 Oct 1944
Maj. Murl O. Anderson	10 Oct 1944	30 Oct 1944
Lt. Col. Hubert L. Binkley	1 Nov 1944	

Abrahams, Albert R., T/4,
Acton, William R., Pfc,
Adam, Gustave G., Pfc,
Adams, Morgan K., Capt,
Adams, Paul H., Pvt,
Adkins, Estle L., T/5,
Agne, Herbert G., 1st Lt,
Alberhasky, Donald D., T/4,
Albrecht, Clarence, T/5,
Alden, Warren H., Capt,
Amnan, Robert E., Pfc,
Anderson, Howard O., Pfc,
Anderson, Lester B., Pfc,
Anderson, Murl O., Maj,
Anderson, Neal K., T/5,
Andreas, Harry K., Pvt,
Arnold, Hubert E., Pvt,
Aronsohn, Charles M., 1st Lt,
Ashe, Louis, Pvt,
Atkins, Clarence E., Cpl,
Austin, Robert W., Pvt,
Austin, Vaughn H., Pvt,

§Bader, Frederick W., Jr., Sgt,
Baer, Henry A., Pfc,
Bailey, Donald A., T/5,
Baines, Sanford J., T/5,
Baker, Virgil D., Sgt,
Bakula, Richard, Pfc,
Balkus, Joseph W., Pvt,
Baltzer, Walter E., Pfc,
Barnes, John E., 1st Sgt,
Barnish, John D., T/4,
Barr, J. Y., S/Sgt,
Barrett, James A., Pfc,
Baskins, Shaffer G., Pvt,
Bateman, John F., S/Sgt,
Beck, Joseph C., S/Sgt,
Bell, John T., Pfc,
Berger, William H., S/Sgt,
Berkowitz, Louis, S/Sgt,
Bialk, Max J., Pvt,
Biggs, Edwin E., Cpl,
Binkley, Hubert L., Lt Col,
Biskup, Alfred J., T/4,
Blakley, Richard E., Pfc,
Blanchard, Elbert W., Pvt,
Bixler, Herbert D., Pvt,
Blanken, Walter H., Pfc,
Blankenship, Herman L.,
Blume, Stanley I., S/Sgt,
Blyseth, Lloyd W., Pfc,
Bobrosky, David, Pvt,
Bohannon, Farmer, Jr., Sgt,
Bolla, Andrew J., Pfc,
Bonnanni, John, Sgt,
Bondeson, Arnie G., T/5,
Bonkowski, Gerald F., T/5,
Booker, James M., Capt,
Born, Clifford A., T/5,
Botwin, Elliot, Pfc,
Bowen, Bascomb, 1st Sgt,

Bowen, Donald E., Pvt,
Bowyer, Carl F., Pfc,
Boyd, Wallace L., 2nd Lt,
Branson, Herbert R., Pfc,
Brenneise, Samuel H., T/4,
Brewer, Emmett E., Pfc,
Brewster, Ralph B., T/5,
Brignall, William J., Cpl,
Brill, Frank L., Sgt,
Brinkmeyer, Edward J., Pvt,
Brown, John K., T/4,
Brown, Kenneth W., 1st Lt,
Bruce, Arnold B., T/5,
Brunetti, Andrew S., Pfc,
Bullock, Orville D., Pvt,
Bunk, Donald J., T/4,
Burk, William F., Pfc,
Burke, Harvey K., Jr., Cpl,
Burke, Kenneth E., Pfc,
Burns, Robert C., Pfc,
Bush, Floyd O., Pfc,
Butler, William S., Pfc,
Byrd, Jack, T/4,

Cain, Jessie R., Pvt,
Calabria, Salvatore C., T/4,
Calloway, Jack F., Sgt,
Cane, Edward M., Capt,
Cantor, Homer D., Jr., Pfc,
Cap, Joseph R., Sgt,
Carbone, Louis S., T/5,
Carevic, Andrew F., Pfc,
Carlock, William O., Pvt,
Carlson, Carl G., T/3,
Carlson, Harold E., Pfc,
Carney, Grover, Jr., Pfc,
Carranza, Florentino M., Pvt,
Carswell, Elmer E., Pfc,
Carvoski, John, Pfc,
§Carwin, John J., Pvt,
Casady, Phineas M., Capt,
Casteel, Earl S., Pfc,
Castleberry, Roy E., Pfc,
Castro, Charles, Pvt,
Cavallo, Francis E., Pfc,
Cavallone, Joseph A., Pfc,
Charboneau, Bert M., T/4,
†Chersonsky, Harry, Pfc,
Chiapella, Karl J., Major,
Chiccino, Victor, Pvt,
Childre, Saunders G., Pvt,
Childs, Denver V., Pfc,
Childs, Elwood M., S/Sgt,
Chilko, Louis, Pfc,
Christon, Sam, T/4,
Chytracek, Frank A., T/5,
*Clampitt, Raymond V., Pfc,
Clark, Doyle S., 2nd Lt,
Cloud, Noble H., T/3,
§Clydesdale, Russell K., Pvt,
Cohen, Stanley, 1st Lt,
‡Cohoon, John H., Pvt,

Cone, Wallis D., Capt,
†Conley, John A., Pfc,
Contestabile, Rufino C., Capt,
Collier, Carroll, T/5,
Cook, Hal B., T/4,
Cook, Perry A., Pfc,
Cooke, Stanley J., Capt,
Corbin, Charles F., Pfc,
Cotton, James C., T/5,
Cox, George E., T/4,
Crawford, William E., Cpl,
Cross, Homer V., Capt,
Cross, Keith W., Pvt,
Cross, Milton P., Pvt,
Crotinger, Clarence R., Pfc,
Crump, John H., Capt,
Cunningham, Nicholas R., Pfc,
Cuny, Theodore E., T/5,

Daft, Edward L., Sgt,
Dally, Ardell T., Sgt,
Daneke, Frank W., Pfc,
Davila, Guadalupe, Pfc,
Davis, Harvey J., Pfc,
Davis, Wilfred H., T/4,
Dea, Wing J., Pvt,
Dean, Lloyd L., T/4,
Debartolo, Hansel M., Capt,
Decker, Gerald E., Pfc,
Deitzler, Forrest M., Pfc,
†Deletis, Patsy, Pvt,
Delisle, George O., Pfc,
Dell, Joseph, 1st Lt,
Delonais, Donald J., T/4,
Demaris, Loren H., T/4,
Dercher, Frank, T/4,
Deso, John, Pvt,
Devaal, Peter A., T/5,
Devoogd, Gerald, Pvt,
Devore, Raymond H., Pfc,
Diener, Samuel, Capt,
Diomandes, Diamond A., T/5,
Dosenbach, Robert S., Sgt,
Douglas, Fred N., Pvt,
Dowling, Robert S., Pfc,
Drake, Harry A., Pfc,
Drum, Charlie, T/5,
Duffy, Michael E., Pfc,
Duke, Elmer, Cpl,
Dupre, George F., M/Sgt,
Duval, George F., Jr., Pvt,
Dvorak, Leonard T., Pfc,
Dvores, Morton, Pvt,
Dyal, Herbert R., Pvt,
Dye, Elmont E., T/5,

Earhart, Emory W., Jr., M/Sgt
Eastman, James O., Pfc,
‡Ecker, Frank G., T/5,
Edwell, Alfred M., Capt,
Ek, Manfred L., T/4,
Elliott, William H., Pfc,
Ellingwood, Dail M., Pfc,

Elmore, Ralph L., Pvt,
Elofson, Carlton B., Pfc,
Erne, Walter F., 2nd Lt,
Ertman, Carl W., Pfc,
Estes, Ambrose C., Capt,
Etier, David E., Sgt,
Evans, Edward, Jr., Pvt,
Everett, Edward L., Pfc,
Eyerdam, John W., Capt,

Fagan, Charles B., Pfc,
Farnham, Richard L., Pvt,
Farnsworth, Jerry D., T/5,
Farrowe, Carl D., Pvt,
Faust, John E., 1st Lt,
Ferguson, Allen L., Pvt,
Ferguson, Hal, Capt,
Fesbinder, Abraham, Pfc,
Fickett, Merle P., Pfc,
Fields, James F., T/4,
‡Figura, Edward J., T/5,
Filip, Mitchell J., Pvt,
Finlay, George E., Sgt,
Finley, Maynard C., Cpl,
Fisher, Adam O., Pfc,
Fitzgerald, John J. W., Pvt,
Fleeger, Lewis X., Pvt,
Fogata, Robert, Pfc,
Foley, Vincent S., S/Sgt,
Fore, James M., Sgt,
Fortune, James L., Pfc,
Foster, Walter C., 1st Sgt,
Fowler, Don F., Sgt,
Frady, Norris L., Pvt,
Francis, Harry A., Cpl,
Frankel, Woodrow J., Capt,
Franklin, Clyde D., Pfc
Freed, Marion J., S/Sgt,
Freed, Westley J., T/4,
Freeman, Robert B., Pfc,
Freiss, Mearle V., Pfc,
Frerking, Herman F., Sgt,
Fuller, Robert G., Pfc,
Fyhrie, Lambert W., T/5,
Fyten, Donald W., T/5,

Galik, Stanley T., Pfc,
Gall, Norbert V., S/Sgt,
Gallagher, Leroy, Pvt,
Gangle, Leonard H., T/4,
Gannon, Thomas J., Pvt,
Gaponoff, Gordon, Pfc,
Gardner, Carl C., Jr., Capt,
Gaskin, Hubert, T/Sgt,
Geary, Thomas C., Capt,
Gemma, James A., S/Sgt,
Gilbertson, Melvin G., Pfc,
Gill, Robert E., Pfc,
Gillaspie, Robert E., 1st Lt,
Givens, Jay E., Pvt,
Glenn, Johnnie H., Sgt,
Gody, Thomas C., Pvt,

Goforth, Eugene G., Capt,
Goldsmith, George, Pvt,
Goldkoski, Frank R., Pfc,
Gomez, Adam S., T/5,
Goodman, Herbert, Pfc,
Gordon, Meyer, T/5,
Gould, Ernest H., Capt,
Grasser, Lester S., Pfc,
‡Green, Philip S., Sgt,
Green, Richard R., T/5,
Greengard, David R., Pfc,
Griffin, Everett G., Pfc,
Griffin, Melvin F., T/4,
Griffith, Frederick W., Sgt,
Griffith, Lyman R., Pfc,
Grimm, Lawrence E., T/5,
Grimmitt, Billy T/5,
Grinsunas, Alphonse, Pfc,
Gross, Reno A., Pfc,
Gruenhagen, Alfred F., Cpl,
Guajardo, Vincent G., Pfc,
Guber, Alfred M., Pvt,
Guercio, Paul J., S/Sgt,
†Guerrera, Joseph, Pvt,
Guiffreda, Sam, Pvt,
Guy, Harold C., Pfc,
Gwyn, Lester L., Pvt,

Haase, Clement L., Jr., 1st Lt,
Habeck, Oswald W., T/5,
Hall, Robert P., Pfc,
Hall, William C., Pvt,
Hall, William T., T/3,
Halsted, Harry C., 1st Lt,
Hamann, Leroy E., Pfc,
Hamel, Edward E., Sgt,
Hamilton, Loyd G., Sgt,
Hamilton, Marvin C., T/5,
Hanford, Roy E., 1st Lt,
Hannah, William G., T/5,
Happel, Fergus E., Pfc,
Hardman, Lawrence B., Sgt,
Hardeman, Raymond O., S/Sgt
Hardy, Max C., Pfc,
Harrenga, John H., Sgt,
Harris, John E., Jr., S/Sgt
Harrop, Joseph K., 1st Lt,
Hastings, Clyde F., Pvt,
Haustein, Karl D., T/5,
Hausmann, Louis H., T/4,
Hawkins, James C., Pfc,
Hawkins, Collins W., Sgt,
Hayes, Raymond G., Pfc,
Hayton, Donald W., 1st Lt,
Hed, Vernon M., T/5,
Hedrick, John F., Pfc,
Heidenfelder, John J., Jr., Pvt,
Helfman, Richard C., Sgt,
Helton, Luther C., T/4,
Henderson, Gaylord A., Cpl,
Hermanson, Albert M., Pfc,
Herrera, Paul, Pfc,

† Killed in Action.   * Prisoner of War.   ‡ Missing in Action.   § Died of Wounds.

IN WORLD WAR II 555

Hilborn, Donald W., Pfc,
Hilbourn, Carl C., Pvt,
Hill, Dee M., Pfc,
Hilner, William J., Pvt,
Hines, Vernon J., Pvt,
§Hirsch, Sam, T/5,
Hirshkovitz, Jacob J., Cpl,
Hivner, Elbert T., Pvt,
Hlatky, John C., Pvt,
Hoard, Kenneth K., Pfc
Hockens, Perry L., T/4,
Hodgson, Vernon E., S/Sgt,
Hoerr, Edward G., Pfc,
Hoffman, Donald P., S/Sgt,
Hojara, Benjamin S., T/4,
Hohman, George C., Capt,
Holcomb, Jack W., Sgt,
Hoots, Carl F., Pfc,
Hopkins, Ellis D., Pfc
Hopkins, Melvin F., Pfc,
Hosmer, Rawson F., Capt,
Houston, David L., Jr., Pvt,
Howard, William, Pvt,
Hudson, Clifford L., Pfc,
‡Huebner, Joseph H., Pfc,
Hughes, John R., Pvt,
Hughes, Harold F., Capt,
Hull, Edward A., Pvt,
Hunchak, Michael, Pvt,
Hungerford, Grover E., Pvt,
Husted, Robert G., 1st Lt,
Hutson, Lawrence E., S/Sgt,

Ingham, Walton C., Capt,
Irwin, Don R., Pfc,
Isham, Herbert B., T/4,

Jackson, Claude A., Capt,
Jackson, Maynard M., T/4,
Jacobs, Thomas A., Pvt,
Jarman, Hugh, S/Sgt,
Jenko, Joseph J., Pfc,
Jodts, Emil R., Pfc,
John, Lawrence R., Pfc
Johnson, Andrew M., T/4,
†Johnson, Arthur A., Pfc,
Johnson, Curtis W., Pvt,
Johnson, Jack, Pfc,
Johnson, Marcellus A., Capt,
Johnson, Veron M., Pfc,
Jones, Charles I., Pfc,
Jones, Steven G., Pfc,
Jones, William H., Pfc,
Jongeling, Clarence H., T/5,
Jose, Patrick O., Cpl,
Juarez, Paz M., Pfc,
July, Gordon F., Pfc,
§Juske, Paul H., Pvt,

Kampe, Klemens A., Capt,
Kane, Francis C., Capt,
Katz, Joseph, Pfc,
Katz, Norman, Cpl,
Kaywin, Louis, Captain,
Kelil, Richard C., Cpl,
Kelly, Vincent P., T/5,
Kelly, William A., Cpl,
Kennedy, Charles D., S/Sgt,
Kerber, Karl K., T/3,
Kerby, Kenneth E., Capt,
Kern, Samuel H., Pfc,
†Kershner, David N., Pfc,
Kilpatrick, William A., T/5,
Kinderman, John H., Cpl,
†King, Edward T., Pfc,
Kingston, George R., Maj,
Kirkpatrick, George E., T/Sgt,
Knotz, John V., Pfc,
Knowles, Marion E., Pvt,
Kocian, Erwin I., T/5,
Kohoutek, Edward A., Pfc,
Kornblatt, Arthur, Pvt,
Kosavich, Bernard S., Cpl,
Kovalcik, Paul M., T/4,
Kraft, Lelan R., T/5,
Krauth, Joseph, Pfc,
Krening, Daniel W., S/Sgt,
Krohn, William M., Pfc,
Kromer, Joseph J., Pfc,
Kryger, James A., Pvt,
Kubisztal, Matthew J., Pvt,
Kucks, Anthony S., Pvt,
Kuhns, Edwin C., Cpl,
Kumpf, Elmer H., Pfc,
Kuss, Robert J., Pfc,
Kuzma, John J., S/Sgt

La Barba, Vincent C., T/5,
Lacey, Leonard, T/5,
Ladner, Emil O., Pvt,
La Fata, Frank M., S/Sgt,
Lakoma, Thaddeus P., Sgt,
Lambros, Louis P., Sgt,
†Lamken, Russell, Pvt,
Landfried, Louis E., Pfc,
Landowski, Alexander T., Sgt,
Langreck, Edmund J., Pvt,

Larkin, Herbert J., Pfc,
Larrabee, Robert A., Pvt,
Larson, Amos C., Pfc,
Larson, Kenneth V., 1st Sgt,
Larson, Gunard A., 1st Sgt,
Lauck, Arthur S., S/Sgt,
Laude, Lester D., Pfc,
Laufer, Henry F., Pfc,
Laughlin, Bennie B., Pfc,
La Valla, Clifford F., Pfc,
Leavitt, Edwin, Sgt,
Lee, Robert M., Capt,
Lee, Theodore L., Pfc,
Legg, Robert L., Capt,
Leibowitz, Gerald, T/5,
Leonardi, Rosario J., Pfc,
Leoutsakos, George T., T/5,
Lewis, Arthur L., Cpl,
Lewis, Leslie D., S/Sgt,
Licata, Sam J., Pvt,
Liddane, William J., Pfc,
Lieberman, Harry G., Capt,
Liekhues, George H., T/5,
Lincoln, William H., Pfc,
Little, Joe E., S/Sgt,
Lofgren, William H., T/4,
Lonergan, John M., Pfc,
Long, Eddie L., Pfc,
Longyear, Cornwell B., Cpl,
Lord, Lionel B., Pvt,
Lovaas, Bernie V., T/5,
Love, Lucian R., Pfc,
Lucero, Daniel H., Pvt,
Luckett, Charles L., Capt,
Ludema, Joe, T/5,
Lunt, Donald E., S/Sgt,
Lusk, Chester C., T/3,
Lutcavish, Robert E., Pfc,

McCarty, Haze J. M., S/Sgt,
McCarty, William J., Lt Col,
McClurg, Albert, Pvt,
McCorkle, Douglas E., Pvt,
McCrary, James B., Pfc,
McCrary, James B., Pfc,
McCready, John R., Pvt,
McCready, John R., Pvt,
McDonald, Wm. A., Pvt,
McGaugh, Sidney R., Pvt,
McGinnis, Carl M., T/3,
McGoff, John P., Pfc,
McGreevey, James E., Capt,
McGuire, Loyd, 1st Lt,
McLaughlin, Ted J., Sgt,
McLeod, Charles W., Pfc,
McMahon, Martin T., Pvt,
McNemar, Howard D., S/Sgt
Mack, Ross D., Pfc,
Magnuson, Glen W., Pfc,
Magnuson, Otto E., Pfc,
Mahloch, Arnold H., Pfc,
Makarewicz, Harry V., Pvt
Mallinger, Eugene A., Pfc
Malone, Homer L., T/5,
Malott, Vernon C., T/4,
Mammen, Leonard M., T/4,
Mangeli, John R., Pvt,
†Manning, Gerald D., Pfc,
Markham, Otto, T/5,
Markley, John D., Sgt,
Marsh, Raymond G., Cpl,
Marshall, Donald F., Capt,
Marthers, James M., Pvt,
Martin, Horace N., Pvt,
Martinez, Manuel, Pvt,
Martinez, Narciso J., Pfc,
Mason, Clyde, T/4,
Massicotte, Albert Pfc,
Matusik, Walter M., Pfc,
Mauk, William H., Capt,
Maxwell, John E., Cpl,
Mayfield, Charley B., Pvt,
Mayo, Gilbert H., Pfc,
Mayo, Henry W., Jr., Capt,
Meadows, James I., T/5,
Meek, Bernard F., T/5,
Mehlhoff, Frederick P., T/4,
Menkel, Carlson B., Capt,
Merrell, David W., Pfc,
Merrill, William B., 1st Sgt,
Messina, Salvatore S., Pfc,
Messine, Frank A., Pvt,
Michlitsch, William, Pfc,
Milam, Hays, Sgt,
Miller, Bernard H., Pfc,
Miller, Billy H., T/5,
Miller, William H., Capt,
Millhauser, Leonard, Pfc,
Milne, Merton M., Pvt,
Mincey, Randolph, Pfc,
Minerva, Frank D., Capt,
Miracle, Milton H., Pfc,
Mirda, Joseph, T/5,
Mitchell, Andrew F., Pfc,
Mitchell, Joe E., T/5,
Mitrisin, Andrew, Pfc,
Mittleider, Fred, Pfc,

Mooney, William H., Pfc,
Moore, Clarence H., Pvt,
Moore, Richard T., Pfc,
Moore, Thomas C., T/3,
Moran, Peter, Pvt,
Morley, James E., Pfc,
Morris, Wythe C., Pfc,
Morrissey, Edward J., Pfc,
Moss, Lloyd D., T/5,
§Motter, Francis W., Pfc,
Mueller, Henry B., Pfc,
Muilenburg, Maynard A., Pfc,
Muir, William R., Pvt,
Mullens, James S., T/5,
Muller, Norman J., Pvt,
Munchak, Steven E., Pvt,

Naugle, George F., S/Sgt,
Navarro, Ralph, Pfc,
Neary, Robert N., T/3,
Nelson, Alfred E., Pfc,
Nelson, Archie L., Pfc,
Nelson, Enoch N., Pvt,
Neubauer, Alfred F., Pvt,
Newcomb, Ollie, Pfc,
Nichol, Fred J., Pvt,
Nitsch, Adolph H., Jr., Pfc,
Nordstrom, Clarence V., Pfc,
Nosko, John P., Pfc,
Nottingham, Donald A., Capt,
Nowicki, Frank P., Pfc,
Null, Farrell P., Pfc,
Null, Leonard R., T/5,
Null, Richard S., T/5,
Numainville, Woodrow W., T/4

Oak, Gunnar E., Pvt,
Ober, Ralph E., Pvt,
O'Brien, John, Pvt,
O'Callaghan, Jack, Pfc,
O'Dell, Joseph A., T/Sgt,
O'Donnell, Charles L., Sgt,
O'Leary, Edward J., T/5,
Omundsen, William J., Pfc,
Ondrasik, William, 1st Lt,
O'Neail, Earl E., Pvt,
O'Neill, Hugh A., Capt,
‡Orr, John W., Jr., Pvt,
Orville, B., Pfc,
O'Shea, Patrick J., Pfc,
Otis, Charles E., Pvt,
†Overby, Clarence H., Pvt,
Owens, Charles E., Pfc,

Paciejewski, Steve S., Pfc,
Page, Nobel W., 1st Lt,
Parr, John J., Pfc,
Patten, Frank L., Pfc,
Paul, Frank D., Pvt,
Pavlock, Stanley E., Jr., Pfc,
Peake, John H., Pvt,
Peck, Allen R., Pvt,
Peppe, Edward A., Pfc,
Perrotta, John J., Pfc,
Perrucci, Alphonse T., Cpl,
Pesota, Raymond, T/5,
Peterson, Dale W., S/Sgt,
Peterson, Silas L., Pvt,
Peterson, Roy, T/5,
Pfeifle, Fred, T/4,
Philo, Seymour S., Capt,
Pierce, Maurice E., Pfc,
Pierog, Walter, Pvt,
Pietrus, Chester S., T/4,
Pincherri, Joseph A., Pvt,
Pipe, Willard J., Pfc,
Pittala, James J., Pvt,
Podobinski, Stanley L., Pfc,
Poindexter, Chester L., T/4,
Pollard, Alvin R., Pvt,
Polsfuss, Vern L., T/5,
Potelunas, Clement B., Capt,
Power, Jeffrey M., Pvt,
Prato, Louis A., Pfc,
Preece, Wendell M., T/5,
Preziotte, John A., Pfc,
Prock, Luther C., Pfc,
Proctor, Elward F., Pfc,
Profera, Louis, Cpl,
Proud, Harry S., Capt,
Pryor, James E., T/5,
Putnam, George A., Pvt,
Putney, Morris R., Pfc,

Quinn, Daniel C., Pfc,

Rafferty, Thomas F., T/5,
Raines, Ralph J., Cpl,
Ramotowski, Alexander J., Pfc,
Ranalla, Frank H., Sgt,
Raney, Everett W., Sgt,
Raphael, Earl C., Cpl,
Rappold, Buell E., Pfc,
Rasmusson, Lyle V., Pfc,
Ratcliff, Robert, S/Sgt,
Ray, Russell J., Pfc,
Reddick, Ernest L., Pfc,
Reed, Ross E., Pvt,

Reitano, Joseph G., Pfc,
Rello, Nicholas, Pvt,
Riddle, Robert D., T/3,
Ripkoski, Herman W., Pfc,
Rivers, Troy B., Sgt,
Roar, Cledith, Pfc,
Robello, Alfred J., Pvt,
Roberts, Albert N., Pfc,
Robiadek, Edward, Pfc,
Robinson, Connie D., Pvt,
Roebuck, James P., Pfc,
Rogers, John C., Pvt,
Rohan, Bernard R., Pfc,
Roper, Hubert L., Pvt,
‡Rose, Ralph D., Pvt,
Rowan, Harold W., Pfc,
Roy, Bernard, T/5,
Roy, Robert E., S/Sgt,
Rubino, James C., Pfc,
Rudar, Charles F., S/Sgt,
Rudd, Louie G., Pvt,
Rumfield, Henry M., Pfc,
†Rummell, Robert A., Pvt,
Ruocco, Alphonso F., Pvt,
Russo, Joseph, Pvt,

Sakal, John S., Pvt,
Salter, De Witt, Pfc,
Salvas, Gerard A., Pvt,
Sambursky, Nathan, T/5,
Sanchez, Juan D., Pfc,
Santucci, Dominic, Pfc,
Sarabia, Ben V., Pvt,
Schaefer, Lawrence J., T/4,
Schaffer, Oscar D., Pfc,
§Schaller, Joseph A., Pvt,
Schepker, George, Pfc,
Scherman, Joseph P., Sgt,
Schlegel, Charles J., S/Sgt,
Schleifman, Philip, Pvt,
Schmidt, Robert, T/4,
Schneider, Edward J., T/5,
Schneider, Ernest R., Jr., Pfc,
Schneidewind, C. A., S/Sgt,
Schuldinger, Max W., Pfc,
Schultz, Michael A., Pvt,
Schuster, Raymond O., Pfc,
Schwab, Charles W., Pvt,
Schwidde, Jesse T., Capt,
Scott, Edward O., Pfc,
Scrogg, Orlando, Pvt,
Seeley, Leroy W., Pvt,
Seems, Lenard L., T/4,
Sellers, Homer W., Pvt,
Sentell, Philip H., Pfc,
Shadle, Harold C., Pfc,
Shadley, Miles L., Jr., S/Sgt,
Sharoff, Robert L., Capt,
Sharp, Lewis E., Pvt,
Shaw, Sol, Pfc,
Shaw, Victor K., T/3,
Sheldon, Daryl L., S/Sgt,
Shelton, Arthur E., Pvt,
Sherman, James W., Pfc,
Sherman, Warren L., Pfc,
Shipp, Ernest L., Pfc,
Shotkoski, Alex A., T/4,
Simmons, Walter F., T/5,
Simokonis, John C., Pfc,
Sims, Lloyd H., Pfc,
Sioris, John L., Pfc,
Skeel, George F., T/3,
Skinner, Duane E., Pvt,
Smith, James B., T/5,
Smith, John H., Pfc,
Smith, Lewis B., Sgt,
Smith, Lewis M., Pfc,
Smith, John R., Pfc,
Smith, Payton J., T/5,
Smith, Tommy C., Pvt,
Smith, Wilson R., Pfc,
Snider, Carroll L., T/4,
Sonnier, Adam, Sgt,
Soos, Joseph, Pfc,
Spencley, Earl E., S/Sgt,
Spinrad, Walter I., 1st Lt,
Spotten, Robert J., Pfc,
Spratt, Robert W., Pfc,
Spratt, Vaughn J., S/Sgt,
Stacy, Henry D., 1st Lt,
Stafki, Joseph W., Pfc,
Stahl, Paul, Jr., Pvt,
Stark, Orville B., Pfc,
Stedman, Alfred B., Jr., T/4,
Steiwig, Cleve, Pvt,
Stewart, Donald E., Capt,
Stiewel, Robert C., 2nd Lt,
Stroth, Thomas R., Pvt,
Strother, Richard G., Pfc,
Strykowski, Francis J., Pvt,
Stubstad, Stuart C., T/5,
Stupic, Edward W., Pfc,
Summers, Marion A., T/5,
Surguy, William W., Pfc,
Swalley, Bert C., Pvt,
Swanovski, John, T/5,
Swayze, Ralph E., T/5,
Sweatt, Joseph H., T/5,

Swigert, James H., Jr., Pfc,
Syintsakos, Peter, Pvt,
Sypniewski, Edward J., T/5,
Shein, Rubin, Pfc,
Smart, Harry T., S/Sgt,
Szladek, Frank J., Capt,

Taar, Frank J., Pfc,
Taber, Alden R., T/5,
Tackett, Carl D., 2nd Lt,
Tallman, Richard E., Pvt,
Tapper, Egon F., Jr., Pvt,
Taylor, Birket F., Jr., Pfc,
Teer, Henry E., Pfc,
Terrell, Chester E., Pfc,
Thalmann, William G., Capt,
Thomas, Bub, Pfc,
Thomas, Calvin E., S/Sgt,
Thomas, Denton B., Pvt,
Thomas, Richard L., Pfc,
Thomas, William E., T/5,
Thompson, Lawrence A., S/Sgt
Thornton, Dell S., Pfc,
Tiberio, Patsy J., Pfc,
Tito, Joseph B., Pfc,
Tolas, Carl D., Pfc,
Tomey, Waitman E., Pfc,
Tosches, Nicholas, Pfc,
Traweek, Max E., Pvt,
Trevizo, Pablo, Cpl,
Trimble, William J., Pfc,
Trinka, Anton J., T/5,
Tuomie, Toivo T., Pvt,
Tuscher, David A., Pfc,
Two Bears, Gilbert, Pfc,
Twomey, Albert J., Pvt,

Uecke, William R., Pfc,
Uffelman, David, T/4,
Ulrich, Earl R., Pfc,
Underwood, William L., Pfc,
Urban, Edwin J., Pfc,
Utley, Richard E., Pfc,

Valdez, Augustine, Cpl,
Vallejo, Frank D., Pvt,
Vanasse, Eugene A., T/5,
Van Cleave, Lissol S., Pvt,
Vaughn, Johnny W., Sgt,
Vilaramos, Manuel, Pvt,
Vincino, Rosario A., Pfc,
Vanderkwast, John, Pvt,
Vitley, Antonio D., Pfc,

Wadsworth, Ray E., Pvt,
Waite, Ralph N., T/5,
Wallace, George W., Jr., Cpl,
Wallace, Winford B., Sgt,
†Walsh, William J., T/5,
Walters, James T., Pfc,
Wamsley, John D., Pfc,
Ward, Carrol A., WOJG,
Ward, Marcus L., Pfc,
†Warden, Homer O., Pvt,
Wasmund, Edward, S/Sgt,
Watson, Clifford O., Cpl,
Watterson, Claud M., Pfc,
Watts, Frank M., T/5,
‡Webb, James R. L., Pvt,
Wedell, James R., Capt,
Westerlund, Basil C., T/4,
Wheeler, Donald B., T/Sgt,
Whitaker, Darwin E., T/4,
White, Forest B., S/Sgt,
Wickman, Arthur J., Pfc,
Wielinski, Louis, T/4,
Wildman, James D., Pvt,
Wilkens, Ross E., Pfc,
Wilkins, Lewis D., Pfc,
Wilkinson, Lyle B., T/5,
Williams, James M., Pfc,
Williams, Sidney L., S/Sgt,
Wills, Edward, Pvt,
Wilson, Donald J., Capt,
Wilson, Ernest B., Pfc,
Wilson, Gregie O., Pvt,
Wilson, Joseph P., Pfc,
Wisdom, Robert L., Pfc,
Wisner, Robert L., Pfc,
Witty, Melvin L., T/Sgt,
Wojtowicz, Stanley, Pfc,
Wolff, Herbert H., Sgt,
Wood, Fay L., Pvt,
Wright, Leon, T/4,
Wright, Truman H., Pfc,
White, Harvey W., Pfc,
Walters, Charles L., Pvt,
Welker, Paul L., Pfc,

Yannette, Anthony, Pfc,
Yasgar, John M., Pfc,
Yates, Maurice C., Pfc,
Yorty, Theron E., Pfc,
Young, Leonard E., T/4,
Young, Loey S., Pfc,
Young, Orphus R., Pvt,

Zimmerman, Raymond E., Pfc,
Zuccarini, Amerigo G., Sgt.

† Killed in Action. * Prisoner of War. ‡ Missing in Action. § Died of Wounds.

3D SIGNAL COMPANY

The 3d Signal Company, successor to the 5th Field Signal Battalion of World War I, has a distinguished history of its own. Throughout the first war the 5th served with the 3d Division in the Aisne Defensive, Champagne-Marne Offensive, Marne Offensive, St. Mihiel Offensive and the Meuse-Argonne battle. In 1921 the re-organized battalion became the 3d Signal Company.

Commanding Officer

	(Highest rank held)	Held pos. from	To
Capt.	Daniel A. Chinlund		28 Aug 1943
1st Lt.	George A. Fezell	29 Aug 1943	15 April 1944
Capt.	LeRoy M. Northrup	16 April 1944	

Adams, David L., 1st Lt
Affsprung, Harold E., T/5
Akagi, Joseph, Pvt,
Alberic, Bartholomeo J., T/4,
Alexander, George, Pfc,
Alexander, Joseph L.,
Allen, Hugh E., Sr., Pvt,
Allen, Roy E., T/Sgt,
Allgood, Robert E., Pvt,
Amble, Everett A., Pvt,
Anderson, Reid S., T/4,
Andrews, Harry, Pfc,
Andrus, Alton L., M/Sgt,
Atterbery, David L., Pvt,
Aubuchon, Jesse W., T/4,
Ausmus, Robert P., Pfc,

Bacon, James C., Pvt,
Bakken, Harold C., T/4,
Baldwin, Donald S., T/5,
Balog, William L., T/4,
Barber, John P., T/5,
Barbosa, Ellis S., Pfc,
Barsh, George E., Pvt,
Bartelli, Osmero L., Pfc,
Beasley, George R., Pvt,
Beck, Otto J., T/Sgt,
Bell, Clifton, Pfc,
Bell, Jack N., T/4,
Bennett, Eugene F., Pfc,
Berg, Ralph J., T/3,
Bickel, Maynard E., Pvt,
Bingham, Jack E., Pfc,
Biwer, Raymond C., T/4,
Bjornson, Bjarni S., Pfc,
Blackburn, Goeffrey L., Pfc,
Blackshear, Jimmie, Pvt,
Blaustein, Alfred, Cpl,
Blaylock, Furman G., Sgt,
Bobp, Ralph D., M/Sgt,
Boden, Clarence C., T/5,
Boden, J. B., Pvt,
Boleyn, Robert F., Pfc,
Bolen, Lloyd H., Pvt,
Bone, Samuel E., Pfc,
Boone, James F., T/4,
Borchardt, Howard L., M/Sgt,
Borchardt, Oscar W., T/Sgt,
Borucki, Arthur A., Pvt,
Boschult, William D., Pvt,
Bowen, John M., Jr., Pvt,
Bowles, Earl, Pfc,
Bowman, George M., T/5,
Brady, George C., Jr., T/5,
Branom, Arthur P., Pfc,
Brettell, Jack E., Pfc,
Brewer, Elto H., WOJG,
Brooks, James F., Jr., Lt Col

Brophil, Edward F., Sgt,
Brown, George R., Sgt,
Brown, Joe, S/Sgt,
Brown, William D., Pvt,
Brown, William P., Jr., Pfc,
Bshara, Farah, Pvt,
Buckalew, Jay R., S/Sgt,
Burgett, Paul M., Pfc,
Buriak, John, Sgt,
Burke, John G., Pfc,
Burks, Delbert L., T/5,
Burns, George R., T/4,
Burnside, William R., Cpl,
Butler, Denton L., T/5,
Byrum, Harry L., T/4,

Caling, Chester L., Pfc,
Campbell, William T., Pfc,
Carani, Angelo V., T/5,
Carden, Jessie H., Pvt,
Cardiff, Frank J., T/Sgt,
Carter, Loyal D., Jr., Sgt,
Carter, William R., T/4,
Cartwright, Phil, Pvt,
Caruso, Michael Jr., Pvt,
Casadona, George J., Sgt,
Cedrone, Arduino H., T/5,
Chapman, Donald E., T/5,
Chatnnet, B. D., 1st Sgt,
Cheever, Jack M., T/5,
Chinlund, Daniel K., Capt
Chrisman, George L., T/Sgt
Christy, Russ J., II, 1st Lt
Churchill, David R., 1st Lt,
Clawson, Harry C., Sgt,
Clover, Nelson R., Pfc,
Cohrac, George T., T/5,
Cole, Edward W., Pfc,
Cole, John D., T/3,
Coleman, Ross O., S/Sgt,
§Comer, John P., T/5,
Cook, Jack B., S/Sgt,
Cornell, Ralph E., T/5,
Corriveau, Joseph P., T/Sgt,
Cortinas, Esteban, Jr., Pvt,
Couch, Dillard G., T/4,
Counts, James A., Cpl,
†Cousino, Ernest C., T/4,
Cowan, Watt L., 1st Lt
Craig, Harvey L., 1st Sgt,
Crawford, George E., Pvt,
Crooks, Raymond M., T/5,
Croston, Warren L., T/5,
†Crotts, Lawrence L., T/5,
Csencsits, Paul I., Pfc,
Cunningham, Charles, T/5,
Curcio, Daniel A., Pfc,
Curdie, James A., Pfc,

Cushman, Stanley, Pvt,
Cussen, Jack B., T/5,

Dalton, Winfred E., Pvt,
Daly, Joseph P., Pvt,
Darby, A. D., T/4,
Darst, Homer C., Pvt,
Daub, David L., 1st Lt,
Davis, Ottice A., 1st Lt
Day, Lyle H., T/4,
Dayton, William E., Pfc,
Deeds, Robert L., T/5,
Demianycz, Harry, T/5,
Dennis, Loyd T., T/5,
§Dennis, Arthur N., T/4,
DeOra, John V., Pfc,
DePeel, Victor E., T/4,
DeSantis, Peter P., Pfc,
DeWandeler, James O., T/5,
DeYoung, Ward L., Pfc,
Diden, John S., Pfc,
Dietz, Marvle D., T/4,
DiLaura, Anthony, 1st Lt
Divis, Richard C., Pvt,
Dockter, Henry, Pfc,
Donahue, Garland E., Pfc,
Dotzler, Francis J., Cpl,
Dryden, Phillip A., Pvt,
Dubinsky, Edward A., T/3,
Duckett, Cecil W., T/5,
Duhamel, Arthur E., Pfc,
Dundee, Morris G., 1st Lt,
Dvores, Morton, Pvt,

Earl, John J., Pvt,
Easley, James H., S/Sgt,
Ebbets, Gerard A., Pfc,
Ebeling, Robert F., Pvt,
Edmunds, Lacy B., T/3,
Eggleston, Francis L., T/4,
Eidelman, Robert, Pvt,
Eisenstein, Harold L., Pfc,
Elder, William H., T/Sgt,
Ellis, Donald S., T/5,
Ellison, Charles N., T/Sgt,
Elwood, Clyde E., Pfc,
Emery, James B., Sgt,
Epstein, Robert B., Pvt,
Erickson, Alton G., T/5,
Esaary, William P., Pvt,
Eveland, Robert D., T/5,
Ewaskio, 1st Lt

Fallon, Robert J., Pvt,
Farlaino, Jakie, T/5,
Ferrelli, Francis, Pfc,
Fezell, George H., Lt Col
Fiddelke, Kenneth W., Pvt

Fields, Mason M., Jr., Pvt,
Fiello, Anthony F., Pvt,
Finley, Calvin C., Pvt,
Flaherty, Martin J., Pvt
Flock, Jack A., S/Sgt,
Foell, John E., Pvt,
Ford, Arnold J., T/4,
Forsyth, Claude W., Pvt,
Fox, Richard K., Jr., Pvt,
Freeland, Robert E., Pfc,
French, Eugene F., S/Sgt,

Gabrione, Joseph N., Pvt,
Galowich, Joseph J., Pvt,
Ganaway, Elto H., Pvt,
Garrow, Edward D., Pvt,
Garry, Gilbert C., T/Sgt,
Gasiewski, Albin J., Sgt,
Geiss, Oliver E., T/Sgt,
Gerber, Sam, Sgt,
Ginder, Hubert J., T/Sgt,
Gleason, Thomas J., Jr., Pvt,
Goodridge, Llewellyn E., Pfc,
Gordon, Martin D., Pvt,
Gould, Gerald J., T/5,
Granger, Robert A., T/5,
Griffith, Woodrow W., Pfc,
Groessel, Arthur F., T/5
Gutowski, Julius P., T/4,
Gwynn, Walter G., T/5,

Haines, John T., Sgt,
Hale, Jack, T/4,
Hall, Sherwood, B., Pvt,
Hanson, Arthur C., T/5,
Hanson, Lowell M., T/5,
Hardy, Thurman L., Pvt,
Harley, Francis A., Pvt,
Harner, Joseph L., Pvt,
Harrington, Russell D., Pvt,
Harris, Aaron G., Capt,
Harris, Ace, Pvt,
Hart, John B., Pfc,
Hawblitzel, Joseph R., T/4,
Hawk, Grover C., Pfc,
Hebb, Robert G., Pvt,
Hegedus, Gene J., T/5,
Helgerson, Lester R., T/4,
Heller, William, T/4,
Helmholz, V. Eugene, S/Sgt,
Henderson, Max H., T/5,
Hennie, John J., T/5,
Herman, Henry C., Pfc,
Herring, Earl A., T/4,
Higdon, Francis H., Pfc,
Hill, Charles J., Pvt,
Hill, Dennis H., T/4,
Hillman, Preston W., Pvt,

Hinderliter, Jay, S/Sgt,
Hingson, George D., T/Sgt,
Hinshaw, Clavis J., Pvt,
†Hinton, David G., Pfc,
Hirak, John, Pfc,
Hoalcroft, Raymond C., Pfc,
Hochron, Joseph, T/4,
Holeman, Jay B., T/5,
Hollingsworth, Robert F., T/5,
Hopf, Julian G., Pvt,
Hopfer, William M., Jr., T/5,
Hornbach, Frederick H., Pfc,
Horwich, Howard T., T/5,
House, Arthur L., T/3,
Howard, Warren D., T/5,
Hudy, Joseph D., T/5,
Hungerberger, William A., T/5
Hurst, Grady, T/5,
Hurst, Herman F., T/5,
Hymers, Stuart C., T/5,

Ivey, Charlie J., Pfc,

Jameson, Edward R., Jr., Pvt,
Janulevicus, Anthony J., T/5,
Jastrzembski, Chester, Pfc,
Javins, Rexford R., 1st Lt,
Jeffcoat, Otis, Pfc,
Jencarelli, James A., Jr., Pvt,
Jerger, Martin L., Sgt,
Jewell, Melvin W., T/5,
Johannes, Leland C., T/5,
Johnson, Burt, Jr., Sgt,
Johnson, John H., Pvt,
Jones, Leslie R., T/3,
Julian, George W., T/5,

Kaatz, Gordon S., Pvt,
†Kachelmier, Joseph J., T/5,
Kaczmarek, Roy J., Pvt,
Kandrack, Edward A., T/5,
Kaszewicz, Edward F., S/Sgt,
Katseles, Gregory G., Sgt,
Katz, Andor, Pvt,
Kauderer, Bernard J., Pvt,
Keegan, Edwin F., Jr., Pvt,
Keegan, John R., Cpl,
Keilbach, Russell J., T/5,
Keith, Sam, T/5,
Keller, Walter, Jr., T/5,
Kennedy, James E., Pfc,
Kelly, Donald E., T/5,
†Kemp, James L., 2nd Lt.
Kendricks, Tillman E., Pvt,
Kennedy, Alvan E., Pfc,
Kennedy, Edward H., CWO,
Kenner, Winfred W., Pfc,
Kephart, Alfred B., T/5,

† Killed in Action. * Prisoner of War. ‡ Missing in Action. § Died of Wounds.

Kerdaffret, Joseph, Pfc,
Kerr, Jack, Pfc,
Kiess, Rudolph, T/4,
Kilwien, James J., T/4,
Kleszics, Stephen, Pvt,
Kohl, Pat W., Pvt,
Kolbe, Raymond F., S/Sgt,
Koski, William A., T/5,
Kosseff, Jerome W., Sgt,
Kovach, Jerome P., Pfc,
Kramer, Oscar D., Pvt,
Kuhn, Marshall L., 1st Sgt,
Kukol, Edward J., Pfc,
Kussman, James R., Pfc,
Kutil, William F., Pfc,

Laboda, Joseph Jr., Pvt,
Lambert, Monroe H., Pvt,
LaMoia, Pasquale L., Pfc,
Landers, Charles L., T/4,
Lane, Thomas A., T/5,
Langer, Herbert E., Pfc,
Lapka, Russell J., Jr., T/5,
LaRoy, Wallace M., Cpl,
Larsen, William A., Pvt,
Lau, Frederick G., T/3,
§Lawson, Fred E., Pvt,
Leden, Wilbur, T/Sgt,
Lee, James H., T/5,
Legg, Burton C., Pfc,
Leith, Robert E., Pfc,
Lewis, Russell L., Pfc,
Libich, William J., T/5,
Linder, Bernard A., Sgt,
Lindsey, William N., Pvt,
Link, Herbert V., T/5,
Little, Edward K., Jr., Pfc,
†Little, Samuel G., Jr., Pvt,
Lizzi, Michael R., Pvt,
Locascio, Joe, T/5,
Lorenzetti, Carlo L., Pfc,
Lossing, Lawrence W., T/4,
Louden, Robert C., Pvt,
Lovell, Ottice, Sgt,
Loyd, Charles W., Pvt,
Lucas, Ormond R., Pfc,
Lundry, Earl D., T/4,
†Lunt, Richard D., Pvt,
Lynch, Eugene W., Pvt,
Lyons, Robert L., T/5,

†Maas, Robert F., Pfc,
†MacGregor, Don B., Pvt,
Machinski, Stanley J., T/4,
Mackey, Maurice D., Pfc,
MacQuarrie, James S., Pfc,
Magnison, Harold E., Pfc,
†Maguire, Robert D., Pvt,
Maher, Kenneth T., Pfc,
Mahoney, James T., T/4,
Mailloux, George J., Pfc,

Mancuso, Leonard O., T/4,
Maners, Earl W., T/5,
Mankey, Wilbur J., Pvt,
Marlitt, Gerald, Pfc,
Marshman, Glen E., Pfc,
Martin, Chester R., Cpl,
Martin, Gene P., Pvt,
Martin, Kenneth C., Pfc,
Marusiak, Joe S., Cpl,
Mascoe, Arthur E., T/5,
Mason, J. K., 2nd Lt,
Mast, Lester I., Pfc,
Maupin, Raymond C., T/4,
Maxwell, Louis J., T/Sgt,
McCabe, James J., Pvt,
McClellan, Kenneth M., T/5
McCloud, George W., T/5,
McConnell, Robert C., Pfc,
McDonald, Gerald D., T/5,
McDonald, William C., T/4,
McDowell, Leonard E., T/5,
McGillivray, Francis J., T/4,
McKinley, William R., Pfc,
†McKinney, Jack D., Pvt,
McKnight, John F., Pvt,
McLeod, George M., Pfc,
McQuade, Clarence E., T/5,
Meekins, Roger O., T/5,
Messenger, Virgil B., Pfc,
Metzgar, Laurence L., T/5,
Metzger, Matthew G., Pfc,
Michel, Fredrick J., Pfc,
Miller, Albert F., Jr., Pvt,
Miller, Donald J., Pvt,
Mist, Ellis H., 1st Lt,
Moats, Richard H., Sgt,
Moll, Arthur, T/Sgt,
Monahan, Robert C., Pvt,
Monfrino, John A., Pfc,
Montgomery, Clarence M., Pfc,
Montpetit, Dan H., T/5,
Moore, Franklin D., Pvt,
Morales, Robert R., T/4,
Motisi, Anthony L., Pvt,
Mulhollem, Dean E., M/Sgt,
Munkittrick, Charles, Jr., Pfc,
Murphy, John J., T/5,
Murphy, Vaughan E., Pfc,
Muscio, Edward G., T/5,
Musser, John, Pvt,
Myers, David M., T/5,
Myers, Paul E., Pfc,

Neibert, Raymond E., Pfc,
Nelson, Bedford F., S/Sgt,
Nelson, Edward S., T/3,
Nelson, Wallace L., Pvt,
Nester, Gilbert C., 1st Lt
Nevins, Francis J., T/5,
Newyear, Harold W., M/Sgt,
Nicholson, Jack L., T/4,
Nickelson, Howard B., T/5,
Northrop, LeRoy M., Capt,

Northrup, Robert L., T/4,
Nurnberger, Roy N., S/Sgt,

Orlob, Carl E., Sgt,
O'Reilly, Richard F., Pvt,
Ortega, Manuel W., Pfc,
Osborne, Evan J., Pfc,
Oswalt, Virgil L., Sgt,

Palmer, Leroy W., T/5,
Parkinson, Gilbert N., 1st Lt,
Paskievitch, John H., Pfc,
Pedinoff, Murray N., Pfc,
Peeler, Zeb, Pvt,
Peterson, Sheldon C., T/5,
Pierce, Cecil M., T/4,
Pinkerton, Leo C., T/5,
Pool, Beverly G., S/Sgt,
Porter, George I., M/Sgt,
Postlethwaite, George J., T/4,
Potier, Joe E., S/Sgt,
Prenter, James A., Pvt,
Prevo, Randall M., T/4,
Pudlo, Van S., Pvt,
Pugh, Joe J., Pfc,
Pyle, Earnest L., Pvt,

Rahm, Ben, Pfc,
Randazzo, John A., Pfc,
Rasmussen, August C., Pvt,
§Rasmussen, Carl, T/5,
Rath, Louis F., S/Sgt,
Rathbun, Vaughn C., Pfc,
Ratliff, Britton A., T/Sgt,
Rauba, Edward J., T/5,
Reed, Jesse W., Pfc,
Reiber, Harry E., S/Sgt,
Reighard, Lester G., T/5,
Reinschmidt, Paul J., Pvt,
Resko, Louis F., Pvt,
Rich, Eric S., Pfc,
Ring, Alex, Pfc,
Ripple, Emmit V., Pfc,
Roberts, John A., Pvt,
Roberts, Louis J., T/4,
Rodgers, Robert E., T/5,
Rodney, Frederick H., Cpl,
Rogers, John C., T/5,
Rogers, Robert L., T/5,
Rogowski, John P., S/Sgt,
Roland, James T., Pvt,
Romain, William B., Sgt,
Ronningen, Melvin, T/4,
Rose, Thomas G., 1st Lt,
Rosebaugh, Ray C., Pfc,
Rosenbaum, Harry A., WOJG,
Roy, Lester E., S/Sgt,
Rubow, Alfred B., Cpl,
Rugg, Walter B., T/4,
Russell, Ralph E., Pfc,
Rutherford, Lloyd, Jr., T/4,
Ryan, Edward J., T/5,
Ryan, Michael J., T/4,
Rydell, Guinard H., T/5,

Sarnese, Joseph A., Pvt,
Scheibner, Alfred A., Pvt,
Scheider, John T., T/4,
Scheiner, Louis E., Pfc,
Schmit, Roland A., Jr., T/5,
Schollar, Manuel D., T/4,
Schroeder, Roger N., T/5,
Schuffler, William L., Pvt,
Scifo, Joseph A., T/5,
Scoles, Isaac F., Jr., Pfc,
Scott, Lawrence J., Pvt,
Scott, Raymond L., Pvt,
Seesock, Robert S., Pfc,
Selhaver, Loren E., T/5,
Selles, Jules J., T/4,
Serena, Joseph V., T/5,
Shaffer, Francis, M., S/Sgt,
Shampine, Delbert L., Pfc,
Shattuck, George M., Pfc,
Sherry, Nicholas R., T/5,
Short, Charles L., T/4,
Shumaker, Johnny W. T/5,
Shuman, Charles D., Pvt,
Sicinski, Stanley J., Cpl,
Silver, Fred N., T/5,
Simmonds, Ray E., T/Sgt,
Simone, Nicholas J., S/Sgt,
Simpson, Richard B., Pfc
Skibby, Edward N., S/Sgt,
Smeloff, Thomas, T/4,
Smith, Earl H., S/Sgt,
Smith, Leonard R., T/Sgt,
Smith, Oscar D., T/5,
Smith, Perry L., Jr., S/Sgt,
Smith, T. W., T/5,
Snyder, Bernard L., Pfc,
Snyder, Harry B., T/4,
Sokolow, Henry A., T/5,
Sommer, Elmer C., Pvt,
Somers, Francis C., Cpl,
Sowers, Woodrow M., T/5,
Spanier, William J., Sgt,
Speakman, Noah J., T/5,
Spears, Alvin B., Pvt,
Spruill, Charles, Pfc,
Stanislowski, Delbert, Pfc,
Stavinoha, Freddie L., T/4,
Stearns, Ben M., Pfc,
Stegnick, Stanley P.,
Steiner, Earl F., T/Sgt,
Stewart, Frank T., Sgt,
Stewart, Jack A., M/Sgt,
Stewart, Owen E., T/4,
Stocker, John A., Sgt,
Stone, Richard B., T/5,
Stranan, John P., T/Sgt,
Suchodolski, Joseph, Sgt,
Summers, Chadwick, J., Pvt,
Swaney, Myron E., T/5,
Swart, Frederick T., T/5,
Szymanski, Stanley F., T/4,

Tannehill, Rupert I., Pfc,

Taylor, Albert E., Pvt,
Taylor, Frank M., Pvt,
Teilmann, Walter S., T/5,
Terry, Rex E., Pfc,
Teske, Lawrence H., T/4,
Thomas, Jesse F., Lt Col,
Thomas, Robert W., Cpl,
Thompson, Dale D., Sgt,
Thornton, James A., T/5,
Toler, Lewis L., Pvt,
Toomey, William J., Pfc,
Topping, Patrick J., Pfc,
Torgerson, Lief T., T/3,
Trapp, John A., T/5,
Trembienski, Florian F., T/4,
Trieger, Seymour, Pvt,
Troske, John J., Pvt,
Trout, Merle E., Pfc,
Trybom, Victor H., Sgt,
Tschappat, Clarence I., T/4,
Tuck, George T., Pfc,
Tuholski, Edmund J., T/5,
Tuholski, Raymond C., T/5,
Turekian, Samuel, S/Sgt,
Turner, Herbert M., Pfc,
†Turo, Michael A., Pvt,
Tyska, Frank W., T/5,

Van Alstine, Robert W., Pfc,
Vance, Albert R., T/5,
Van Valkenburg, John J., T/3,
Vigil, Ernest, S/Sgt,
Volkman, Wilfred E., S/Sgt,

Wallace, Vincent W., T/5,
Warde, Vernon D., T/5,
Weeks, Harvey A., Jr., Pfc,
Wegrzyn, Stanley G., Pvt
Welch, Frederick C., Pfc,
Westenberg, Roger E., Pvt,
Whitney, Homer C., Jr., T/3,
Whittaker, James C., Pvt,
Wiebelt, Frederick R., 2nd Lt,
Wieg, Dwain O., T/5,
Wilhelm, Joseph H., Pfc,
Williams, George W., Jr., Pfc
Williams, Richard G., Jr., Cpl,
Willingham, Harold L., 2nd Lt,
Willis, Alfred H., T/5,
Wilson, James W., T/Sgt,
Witinski, Joseph, Pfc,
Witmer, William W., T/4,
Wobbe, Fremont M., Cpl,
§Woebkenberg, E. F., M/Sgt,
Woods, Charles C., Pfc,
Wright, John H., Jr., Pvt,
Wyatt, Billy G., Pvt,

Yeager, Verol F., Pvt
Young, Kenneth W. L., Pfc,
Youngson, William, T/5,

Zwawadski, Stanley F., Pfc,
Zynda, Edwin G., Pvt.

† Killed in Action.   * Prisoner of War.   ‡ Missing in Action.   § Died of Wounds.

3D QUARTERMASTER COMPANY

The 3d Quartermaster Company has been organized since October 12, 1939. It was formed from units of the 3d Quartermaster Regiment, which in turn was created from the old 3d Division Quartermaster Train. By authority of the War Department, the 3d Quartermaster Company has assumed the history, battle honors and coat-of-arms of its World War I and peacetime predecessors.

Commanding Officer
(Highest rank held)

Capt. Max Ware
Capt. Clifford Milnar
Capt. Raymond Schwab
Capt. Leland F. Sanford
Capt. John A. Newsom

Abernathy, Omer M., Pfc,
Abromski, Stanley, T/4,
Adams, Lewis E., Pfc,
Adams, Ralph E., Pfc,
Akins, Clayton T., Pfc,
Allen, Louie C., Pfc,
Anagnos, Menelaos, Pfc,
Androsian, Sarkis, Pfc,
Ankrom, Leonard G., Pfc,
Archuleta, Ernesto J., Pfc,
Ashby, Tuell D., Pfc,
Attaway, Homer E., Pfc,
†Avender, Steve, Pvt,

Badgett, Karlton D., T/4,
Baier, Joseph J., Pfc,
Banks, Harvey E., Pfc,
Barnes, Luther, T/5,
Barnhouse, John H., T/5,
Basch, Clinton W., Pfc,
Bass, Grover T., Cpl,
Batchelder, William L., S/Sgt,
Baukair, Akle N., T/5,
Beasley, William H., Pvt,
Beaushaw, Merrill D., T/5,
Beck, Thomas L., Pvt,
Beck, William A., Pfc,
Bedel, Norbert F., T/5,
Best, Irving, Pfc, New
Betz, Joseph H., Sgt,
Birt, Robert J., Pfc,
Blach, Alois S., Pfc,
†Blackburn, Elijah P., Pvt,
Blaine, Billy M., T/5
Blevins, Edward B., Pvt,
Blevins, George H., Pvt,
Bogden, Stanley W., Pvt,
Boldon, Dallas, Pfc,
Borosky, John J., T/5
Bouton, Vernon W., W.O.,
Bowen, Joseph F., T/Sgt,
Bowhay, Victor N., T/5,
Boyce, Charles E., T/5,
Bozaich, Fred J., Cpl,
Brenke, Edwin H., Pfc,
Bridges, Frank L., Sgt,
Brigham, Laurence F., Sgt,
Broadstock, Clarence E., Pfc,
Brookshire, James E., Pfc,
Bucco, Clement F., Cpl,
Buettner, Edwin C., Cpl,
Burgess, Clyde C., Pvt,
Burnes, Edward J., T/5
Burton, George L., Pvt,

Campbell, John B., Pfc,
Cappadona, Anthony D., Pfc,
Carley, Charles M., Pfc,
Carraway, William D., T/5,
Cason, Daniel L., Pvt,
Chamberlain, Robert L., Pvt,
Chambers, George B., T/5,
Chapman, Wilburn P., Pvt,
Chenoweth, John M., Jr., Pvt,
Chesler, Maurice P., 2nd Lt
Childers, Lyle R., T/5,
Chin, Lun, Pvt
Churchman, John E., Pfc
Clark, Floyd W., Pfc,
Clark, Ralph L., Pfc,
Clark, Robert W., Pfc,
Clippinger, Glenn B., Pfc,
Cloud, Paul V., Pfc,
Clouse, Harry, Pfc,
Cogar, Manfred E., T/5,
Cook, Charles H., Pvt,
Corcoran, John L., T/Sgt,
Cowing, Claude J., Jr., Pvt,
Cox, Robert W., T/5,
Crepage, Charles, S/Sgt,
Crook, James L., Jr., Pfc,
Culbertson, John L., Pvt
Cundiff, Gordon P., 1st Lt,
Curtin, Stanley J., S/Sgt,
Cyphers, Paul W., Cpl,

D'Alesio, Umberto G., Pfc,
Davenport Robert J., Pvt,
Davis, William J., 2nd Lt,
Dederich, Francis A., T/4,
Deinas, Victor E., T/5,
Dennington, James J., 1st Lt
Destenay, Robert L., Pfc,
Dettlaff, Frank J., Jr., Pfc,
Diehl, William O., T/Sgt,
Digilio, Frank T. A., Pfc
Dodini, Edward F., Pfc,
Doerrer, Donald L., Pvt,
Dolezal, Joseph W., Cpl,
Dougall, Leslie P., Pfc,
Douglass, Lyman M., Pvt,
Drenner, Jesse E., Pfc,
Ducharme, Paul L., Pvt,
Dunn, Carl R., Pfc,
Dupuis, Joseph, Jr., T/5

Eakin, John K., WO,
Eckwert, Vernon P., Pfc,
Edwards, James L., Pvt,
Eilers, Norbert B., T/5,
†Endres, Robert J., Sgt,
†Engholm, Waldo L., Pfc,
Erbstoesser, James L., Pvt,

Farrington, Wm. G., Jr., Pfc,
Ference, George C., Pvt,
Ferguson, Quentin J., T/4
Flynn, Francis M., T/5,
Folds, David P., Pvt,
Fonner, Edwin G., T/5,
Foreman, Howard F., Cpl,
Forner, Harold J., T/5,
Fraczak, Stanley L., 1st Sgt,
Fronek, Joseph Jr., Pfc,
Frye, Benny, Pvt,
Fuller, Allen E., Cpl,

Gabig, Jack F., T/5,
Gallagher, Donald J., Pvt,
Garrison, William E., S/Sgt,
Geoghan, Harry R., Pvt,
Gervasoni, Fred R., Pfc,
Gessleman, B. F., Jr., 2nd Lt,
Gilbertson, Gilbert L., T/5,
§Gilliland, James L., Pvt,
Giordano, Nicholas W., Cpl,
Golden, Doyle J., Pvt,
Gomez, Ignacio H., T/5,
Gonring, Eugene M., Pfc,
Goodwin, Benjamin F., Lt Col,
Gould, Orville E., T/5,
Gresham, Luther B., Pfc,
Griffith, Elmer S., Pvt,
Griwatch, Clarence H., T/5,
Grobelny, Edward V., Pfc,
Guadagno, Vincent A., Pfc,
Guapo, Manuel J., T/5,
†Guardabascio, Joseph, Jr.,
Gullett, Franklin W., Pfc,
Gunter, Millege W., Pfc,

Haase, Robert S., T/Sgt,
Hadley, Joseph J., Pvt,
Halloran, Joseph P., T/5,
Hamback, F. J., Sgt,
Hamburger, Max, Pvt,
Hamby, Kirby S., T/5,
Hamilton, James W., Cpl,
Hanback, Brunce T., T/5,
Harris, Hilmer C., Pfc,
Harris, James G., Pvt,
Haycox, Floyd J., Pvt,

Heimes, Charles M., Sgt,
Heitmanek, Ernest, T/5,
Hill, Earnest J., T/5,
Hill, Joseph E., T/5,
Hillard, Earl W., Pfc,
Hilman, Kenneth W., Pfc,
Hilton, Marion D., T/5,
Hocking, Alvin H., Pvt,
Hoffman, Donald E., Pvt,
Hoflund, Arnold M., Pvt,
Homko, Nick, Pfc,
Homola, Elmer P., 2nd Lt
House, Jesse R., Pfc,
Howe, Clyde F., 1st Lt,
Huls, John E., Cpl,
Husereau, Rosario J., Pvt,

Iannacone, Saverio, Pvt
Inzenga, Gesualdo A., Pvt,

Jackson, James, Pvt,
Jacobson, Carnes K., Sgt
James, Boyce M., Col
James, Wilbur E., Pfc,
Jasinski, Stanley, Pfc,
Jewett, William B., Pvt,
Joensen, Walter H., Pfc,
Johnson, Clifford S., Pfc,
Johnson, Everett, Pvt,
Johnston, Bruce D., Pvt,
Jolly, James I., Cpl,
Jones, Earl W., Jr., Pfc,
Jones, William E., 2nd Lt
Jordan, Grady M., T/5,
Junemann, Theodore M., Pfc,
Jung, Raymond A., T/4,
Juskiewicz, Julius E., Pfc,

Kalamon, John, Pfc,
Kaufman, Charles E., T/5,
Kay, Joseph H., Pvt,
Kazmierczak, Henry J., Pfc,
Kees, Joseph W., Pfc,
Kelly, Elwin E., Pfc,
Kemmerer, Warren H., T/5,
Kennedy, John, Pvt,
Keno, Leland, T/5,
†Kilgarriff, Joseph J., Pvt,
Kirkpatrick, Gerald R., T/5,
Koch, George A., Pfc,
Kolota, John, Pfc,
Kon, Dov, Pvt,
Kortte, Ferdinand C., Sgt,

Krepky, Morris, Pvt,
Kress, August, 1st Sgt,
Kurtz, Theodore, Pfc,

Laffey, James P., Pfc,
LaFramboise, A. B., Pfc,
Lamb, Amos F., Pfc,
Lamonna, Vito, Pfc,
Lancy, Clarence P., Pfc,
Lanning, Donald W., T/5
Larsen, Leonard J., Pvt,
Lauck, Arthur E., S/Sgt,
Lauritsen, Donald E., M/Sgt,
Ledlie, John P., 2nd Lt
Lenahan, Daniel W., Jr., Major
Leonard, George W., Jr., Pvt,
Lerner, Joseph, Capt,
Lester, William J. E., Pfc,
Lewis, Earl J., T/5,
Lieberman, Abe, Pfc,
§Lilienstein, Ernest A., Pvt,
Longstreth, Oscar D., 1st Lt,
Lovrenchick, Adam H., T/Sgt,
Lucotti, Frank, Pfc,
Luongo, Albert D., Pfc,
Lynch, Edward J., Pfc,

Malecki, Anthony, Pfc,
Malinowski, Joseph W., Pvt,
Marcantin, Amiel L., Pfc,
Margoliash, Jacob S., 1st Lt
Marquette, Richard A., T/4,
Marshall, James A., Pvt,
Martin, Kenneth G., 1st Sgt,
Matechak, John, Pvt,
Matuszewski, Benny J., Pfc,
Mauldin, Owen O., Pfc,
Mayer, Roy H., Sgt,
Meade, Lester G., Cpl,
Melquist, Glenn W., Pvt,
Meyer, William E., Pfc,
Mielke, Alvin A., Pfc,
Milnar, Clifford F., Capt
Minagro, Michael J., Sgt,
Minish, Stoy, T/5,
Minkus, Samuel M., Pvt,
Monarch, James L., Jr., 2nd Lt
Monett, Lester L., Cpl,
Mongeon, Francis A., Pfc,
Montgomery, J. B., Jr., Sgt,
Moon, John V., Cpl,
Moore, Richard D., Pfc,

† Killed in Action.   * Prisoner of War.   ‡ Missing in Action.   § Died of Wounds.

Moore, Tom P., Pfc,
Moore, Vernon E., Pvt,
Moran, Sylvester, Pvt,
Moretti, Edward P., Cpl,
Morong, Henry M., T/5,
Morse, Arthur J., Pvt,
Morton, Dudley W., Pfc,
Mowry, Harold W., 1st Sgt,
Moyer, Adam R., Pfc,
Mulcahy, William P., T/5,
Mullen, Paul E., Pvt,
Muller, Charles J., Pfc,
Munroe, John P., Jr., Pvt,
Murphy, Mark E., Pfc,
Murray, Charles, Sgt,
McClimate, Paul L., Pfc,
McDonald, Orlan E., T/5,
McKinley, Elliott L., Pvt
McLaren, John F., Pfc,
McNabb, Paul R., S/Sgt,
McNeal, Gilbert J., Pvt,
McPherson, Alan W., Pfc,

Neumeyer, Donald R., Pfc,
Newman, Melvin S., 1st Lt
Newsom, John A., Capt
Nichols, Wilkie F., T/5,
Nichols, William H., Pvt,
Nieman, Clarence F., T/5,
Noah, Hugo E., Pvt,

Norelius, George W., Pvt.
Notte, Joseph N., Pfc,

O'Brien, Edward E., S/Sgt,
Odor, Charles, Pfc,
O'Hara, William J., T/5,
O'Leary, Thomas, Cpl,
Olson, William H., T/5
Orlando, John, Pvt,
Osborn, Fred E., Pvt,

Panopoulos, Mike, Pfc,
Paradis, Sylvio A., Pvt,
Parker, Oliver F., Major
Parrett, Sherman, T/4,
Paslowsky, John, Pvt,
Peacock, Byron C., T/5,
Pearman, James N., Jr., Capt
Peterson, Ernest G., Pvt,
Phillips, Harold M., Pfc,
Pijoe, Wiley J., Pvt,
Pilewski, Alexander A., Pvt,
Plant, Robert B., Pvt
Poling, Andres W., 1st Sgt,
Porzel, Edward P., Pfc,
Powell, Edward F., Sgt,
Pregont, Kermit M., Pfc,
Prestenback, Morris J., Cpl,
Proffitt, Harold, Pvt,
Pryor, Delbert, Pfc,
Pucciarelli, Anthony A., Pvt,

Ramsey, Henry M., Pfc,
Randall, Oliver E., Pvt,
Rather, Wilburn E., Pfc,
Rawls, Robert L., 2nd Lt
Reardon, Edward J., 1st Lt,
Redford, Joseph O., T/5,
Reese, Francis G., S/Sgt,
Reeves, Victor L., Sgt,
Reid, Floyd E., Pvt,
Rice, Sam J., Pvt,
Richardson, Linnie, Cpl,
Rico, Luis L., Pfc,
Rollf, Dale J., S/Sgt,
Rosenfeld, Frank, Pvt,
Roth, Walter J., Cpl,
Rowland, Ballard E., Pvt,
Rucker, Robert I., Pvt,
Ryan, Joseph M., M/Sgt,

Sabo, Carl W., Pfc,
Sanders, Joseph J., Pvt,
Sanderson, Thomas A., Pvt,
Sandor, Sandor A., Sgt,
Sanford, Leland F., Major
Santora, Thomas, Pfc,
Satterwhite, Luther D., Pfc,
Sauter, George J., S/Sgt,
Saveski, Vincent W., Pvt,
Schellenberger, Arthur G., Pvt,
Schnitman, Edward P., Pfc,

Schwab, Raymond H., Capt,
Scott, Thomas H., Jr., Capt,
Seesock, Robert S., Pvt,
Seriven, Clarence F., Pvt,
Shaw, Lester R., S/Sgt,
Shaw, Robert C., Capt,
Sherman, Harry, T/5,
Shoemaker, Hiram I., S/Sgt,
Simmons, Guy H., Pfc,
Smith, Hobert C., 1st Lt,
Southward, Esker D., Pvt,
Spurrier, Paul J., T/5,
Starr, George W., Jr. Sgt,
Stillman, Edgar, Jr., Pvt,
Stingley, Ferrill, Pvt,
Strong, Clyde E. T/5,
St. John, James D., Pvt,
Strupp, Paul T., T/4,
Stubelik, Paul S., Pvt,
Sumski, Alexander A., Pfc,
Supek, Stanley F., Pfc,
Swayne, Dale H., Pfc,
Swink, William S., Jr., Pvt,

Tait, Arnold C., Capt
Tait, Terence P., Pvt,
Taptich, John, Pfc,
Taylor, Walter J., T/5,
Taylor, Walter V., Pfc,
Teutschlander, George W., Sgt,

Tibbatts, Daniel G., Pvt,
Tillison, Edmund J., T/5,
Toll, Vincent M., Pfc,
Troje, Bernard M., S/Sgt,
Tylinski, Stanley A., Cpl,

Walk, Richard L., 1st Lt,
Walker, Arthur, Pfc,
Ware, Max E., Capt,
Warner, Alva L., 1st Sgt,
Watkins, Floyd R., 2nd Lt,
Watkins, Herbert V., T/5,
Webb, Edwin I., S/Sgt,
Weiss, Robert L., Pfc,
Wende, William E., Pvt,
Werner, Darrell E., T/5,
West, Gordon L., T/4,
Whelan, Francis J., Pvt,
Williams, Duart M., S/Sgt,
Wilson, Gordon P., Pvt,
Witcher, Clarence V., Sgt,
Wolfer, Frederick F., Lt Col,
Woods, Dave L., Pvt,
Worthington, Philip W., T/4,
Wounaris, Steve W., T/5,
Wray, Carlton L., Pfc,

Yanbrek, Steve, T/5,
Yarnall, Clifford, Pvt,

Zarzecki, Bruce, T/5.

† Killed in Action.   * Prisoner of War.   ‡ Missing in Action.   § Died of Wounds.

703D ORDNANCE COMPANY

In the fall of 1942, automotive maintenance was transferred from the Quartermaster Corps to the Ordnance Department, and the Ordnance Section of the Division headquarters and the automotive elements of the 3d Quartermaster Battalion were taken from their parent units and combined to form the 703d Ordnance Company. It was activated September 25, 1942.

The company did not participate in the Fedala landing, although Maj. James McGehee, Division Ordnance Officer, and six enlisted men landed on D-Day (Nov. 8, 1942), and experienced considerable difficulty in establishing adequate ammunition dumps and in supplying the troops because of the lack of transportation.

The company followed in December, 1942, and after that time rendered excellent service in close support of operations. Apart from regular duties, notable contributions of the company include preparing skillfully executed armor-plated command vehicles and the manufacture of Maj. Gen. John W. O'Daniel's invention, the "battle sled," on the Anzio Beachhead.

Commanding Officer

(Highest rank held)	Held pos. from	To
Capt. Harold B. Benedict		16 Mar 1944
Capt. O'Berlin J. Evenson	17 Mar 1944	31 Dec 1944
Capt. Graham L. Patterson	1 Jan 1945	

Achelpohl, Henry J., T/5,
Alford, James S., Pvt,
Allen, Jack H., M/Sgt,
Allen, Jesse J., T/5,
Amistadi, John J., S/Sgt,
Anderson, Evelyn H., T
Applegate, Hilton H., T/4,
Arnost, Albert, T/3,
Atwood, Dean L., S/Sgt,
Aubertine, William J., T/5,
Awen, Joseph H., S/Sgt,

Baca, Gregorio, T/5,
Backert, George H., T/5,
Baer, Bernard C., T/5,
Baie, William J., T/5,
Baister, Louis E., Pvt,
Bartell, Stanley F., Pfc,
Bauer, Carl G., T/4,
Bean, Roy R., Pvt,
Becke, Mark G., T/4,
Belekanic, Michael, T/5,
Benedetti, Philip J., T/5,
Benedict, Harold B., Capt,
Benton, Sam, T/4,
†Berkowitz, Fred N., T/5,
Bernal, Jose L., Jr., Pfc,
Berry, Clarence W., T/Sgt,
Bishop, William N., T/5,
Bixler, Herbert D., Pvt,
Blackwood, Edward C., Jr., Pfc
Block, George W., T/4,
Bohrer, Charles P., T/3,
Boyda, Henry A., T/3,
Brieden, Otis G., 1st Sgt,
Bright, Luzerne R., WOJG,
Brown, Eugene D., T/3,
Brown, Grover L., T/4,
Burke, Thomas J., Pvt,

Campbell, Jimmie J., T/5,
Canzoneri, Anthony P., T/5,
Carpenter, Ralph E., T/3
Carter, Jack G., Pvt,
Caruso, Michael, Pvt,
Cavalieri, Sam P., Pvt,
Chulak, Robert J., T/5,

Church, Edwin D., T/5,
Clark, Robert B., T/5,
Cohen, Philip S., T/5,
Cole, Albert J., T/4,
Cole, Harold N., T/5,
Coupland, John R., Capt,
Cowley, Walter E., Pvt,
Crawmer, Marion A., T/5,
Crittenden, Eldon F., T/4,
Crowley, Frederick J., Pfc,
Crowley, John S., Pvt,

Daniels, Erle H., T/4,
Dawson, John C., 1st Sgt,
Dekett, L.D.G., Pfc,
DeLong, Ora D., S/Sgt,
DeRose, Joseph, T/5,
Detz, Charles J., Sgt,
Dolge, Lyle W., T/5,
Duffy, William J., T/5,
Dye, Donald J., T/3,

Eggelston, Joseph H., Pvt,
Elliott, Leroy J., T/4,
Erickson, Wendell D., T/5,
Evenson, Oberlin J., Major,

Fall, Jack T., T/4,
Farrell, Noel R., T/5,
Feinerman, Irving, T/5,
Fiutem, Lawrence P., Pvt,
Frederick, Robert W., S/Sgt,

Gamon, Willis D., Pvt,
Garberich, Donald J., T/3,
Garrison, Elmer A., T/5,
Garves, Edward A., Pfc,
Geller, Paul, T/3,
Gonzales, Heron, T/5,
Goucher, John M., T/4,
Graney, Francis P., 1st Lt,
Grant, Roy J., T/5,
Grant, William T., T/4,
Gray, Joe H., T/4,
Gross, Thomas A., Pvt,
Groves, Cleburn F., Pvt,
Gualco, Reynold J., S/Sgt,
Gurule, Everett, T/4,

Hall, Robert P., T/3,
Hamaker, Charles O., T/3,
Harris, David, T/5,
Heckman, Ray H., T/5,
Hensel, Robert H., T/5,
Hetrick, Harry E., Pvt,
Higgins, Carl H., T/5,
Hugghins, Albert E., Pfc,
Huntsman, Kenneth, T/4,

Ingrim, Mervyn H., Pvt,

Jankowski, Walter J., Pvt,
Jackson, Edward D., T/Sgt,
Johnston, Robert J., T/Sgt,
Justus, Calvin W., T/5,

Kadow, Fred W., T/4,
Kaler, John F., Pfc,
Kaune, Arnold F., T/5,
Kilwein, Carl P., T/5
Krubsack, Harvey C., T/4,
Kuntz, Harold J., T/5,
Kuznia, Henry S., S/Sgt,

LaDam, George W., Cpl,
Larson, Louis L., Pvt,
Lash, Leslie A., T/4,
Lau, Ellwood A., T/4,
Lawrence, Duane R., Sgt,
Lindblom, Tillman O., S/Sgt,
Lipchik, John, T/5,
Lipkin, Isidore, T/4,
Loudy, Robert D., Pfc,

Mashburn, Clarence, Pvt,
Massanova, Joseph F., T/5,
Massey, Burrell T., Pvt,
McCafferty, James I., T/5,
McEntire, Donald N., T/5,
McGehee, James L., Lt Col,
McMillin, William I., T/4,
Meehan, Edward A., Pvt,
Melfi, Michael A., Sgt,
Meyer, Adolf, Cpl,
Milanowski, A. D., S/Sgt,
Miller, Elder G., T/5,
Miller, Ralph E., T/4,
Minton, Clifford S., T/5,

Moedinger, Gerald T., T/Sgt,
Molongowski, Joseph J., T/5,
Moore, Avery L., T/4,
Morell, Frank E., Jr., 1st Lt,
Moyer, Adam R., T/5,
Murr, Clyde E., T/Sgt,
Myers, George C., T/5,

Naylor, Clarence A., T/3,
Nelson, Jimmie L., T/5,
Newland, Richard M., T/3,
Nix, George W., Jr., Pfc,
Nowc, Clarence A., S/Sgt,
Nye, John G., T/3,

Obbink, Marvin B., T/5,
Oberle, August L., T/5,
Orosz, Emery J., T/4,

Parker, William F., T/4,
Partridge, Loren B., Jr., Pvt,
Paterson, Graham L., Capt,
Peak, John J., III, T/5,
Pedersen, Walter K., T/5,
Personeni, John L., T/Sgt,
Peyton, Lee O., T/5,
Pine, Ray A., T/5,
Poduska, John M., Pfc,
Pond, Charles M., Pfc,
Puccinelli, Angelo J., T/5,

Reid, Ralph E., T/3,
Rhodes, Norman H., Jr., T/3,
Ritchey, John R., T/5,
Robinson, Thomas H., T/5,
Rogers, Elbert G., T/5,
Rogers, Hardin W., Pvt,
Romanoski, John T., Pfc,
Rufo, Joseph J., T/4,
Ryan, John F., S/Sgt,

Schaffer, Clarence H.,
Schell, John A., T/5,
Schimke, Rudolph, T/3,
Schreiber, Walter H., T/5,
Schulz, Donald W., M/Sgt,
Schunk, William J., 1st Sgt,
Sefer, William J., T/4,
Seibt, Lawrence H., Pfc,
Shelton, Crowell B., Capt,

Shew, Roger I., Cpl,
Slater, Jesse L., S/Sgt,
Snowden, Wayne H., Major,
Somplack, Paul A., T/4,
Spadafora, Frank, Pvt,
Stead, Jack M., T/4,
Stoffregen, Frederick W., Sgt,
Stowers, John G., T/3,
Swihart, Edward O., T/5,
Tauber, Howard R., Capt,
Tees, Frederick M., Pvt,
Terrell, Clarence W., Pfc,
Todoroff, James G., Pfc,
Tomlinson, Richard E., Pfc,
Trail, Raleigh L., T/Sgt,
Truszkowski, John J., T/5,
Turnipseed, Francis M., Pvt,

Ungerer, Frederick W.,

Valacich, Albert M., S/Sgt,
Vana, Joseph J., S/Sgt,
Vanderheid, William J., T/5,
Vandermark, Robert L., T/5,
Vavricka, Louis M., Jr., T/4,
Vitek, Frank J., T/5,
Vockeroth, Earl P., T/5,
Vogan, Adam E., Pfc,

Wade, Henry, T/4,
Wasson, Carl H., Pvt,
Weber, William E., T/3,
Wegrzyn, Stanley G., Pfc,
Weissberg, Homer J., Pvt,
Wheeler, Leroy G., 1st Sgt,
§Wheeler, Wilbur E., Pvt,
Whitehead, George J., T/4,
Williams, Courtland A., T/4,
Williams, Earl M., T/5,
Wilson, Kenneth L., 1st Lt,
Winkler, Emil P., T/5,
Wise, Wilford O., S/Sgt,
Woinoski, Stanley A., 1st Lt,
Woodman, Charley E., T/5,
Workman, Arthur L., T/3,
Wright, Blair W., T/5,
Wuis, Thomas R., M/Sgt,
Young, Charles W., S/Sgt,

Zink, Richard R., T/4,

† Killed in Action. * Prisoner of War. ‡ Missing in Action. § Died of Wounds.

3D INFANTRY DIVISION BAND

When the 3d Division went overseas, there were three bands: that of the 7th Infantry, 15th Infantry, and Division Artillery. All rendered fine service with their organizations during the campaigns in Africa, Sicily, and Southern Italy. Late in 1943, the War Department directed that infantry divisions have one band, to be formed from two existing bands. Accordingly, the Division Band was activated on 1 January 1944, at Pozzuoli, Italy. The best men were taken from the three bands, and the balance transferred out in February. The new organization came under the leadership of Chief Warrant Officer Eugene Kusmiak of the 15th Infantry Band and Warrant Officer Junior Grade Milton L. Bronstein, of the 7th Infantry Band. The Sergeant Major from activation throughout the war was Technical Sergeant—later Master Sergeant—William Feigel, who had served more than five "hitches" in the 7th Infantry Band.

Initially a small ensemble was sent to the Anzio beachhead to entertain the troops, but eventually the entire band came there, and after that the band remained close to the Division, playing at formations and ceremonies and providing music at rest camps, hospitals, and social affairs.

Baul, Roque C., T/4,
Beck, Ralph W., Pfc,
Beckwith, Eugene W., Pfc,
Beltz, Russel P., T/4,
Berys, Elmer, Pfc,
Billman, Frederic C., 2nd Lt,
Boisvert, Herbert L., Pvt,
Bourguet, Napoleon M., Pvt,
Bronstein, Milton L., WOJG,

Carl, Victor D., Pfc,
Closmore, Alfred G., Sgt,
Comstock, Harold A., Pvt,
Cooperman, Fred, Pvt,
Cornelius, Leonard P., T/4,
Corporon, Jack F., T/5,
Cox, Chester H., T/5,
Cunningham, Louis E., Pvt,

Davis, Paul O., T/4,
Deffebach, Elbert E., T/4,
Di Gregorio, Oscar, Pfc,
Dott, Albert R., S/Sgt,
Dudley, Joseph L., T/5,
Dunbar, Burton L., T/4,

Feigel, William, M/Sgt,
Feigley, William B., Jr., CWO,
Ferkovich, Raymond A., T/5,
Floring, Ernest T., Pfc,

Galer, Stanley R., Pfc,
Gaimmatteo, Robert, S/Sgt,
Grammont, Willard C., T/Sgt,
Green, Robert D., Pfc,
Griffiths, Robert A., T/5,
Griswold, Claude G., Pfc,
Gusk, Douglas J., T/4,

Harris, Wendell W., T/4,
Harrison, Glenn, Jr., T/5,
Hayes, Harrison O., T/5,
Hegedus, Gene J., Pvt,
Hetrick, Harry L., T/5,
Holt, Joe T., T/4,
Houghton, Walter W., Pfc,
Hughett, Earl H., T/4,
Hysell, Albert C., Pvt,

Isaacson, Ronald T., T/5,

Johnson, Edward L., T/4,

Jones, Hayden H., Pfc,
Jussila, Clyde F., Pfc,

Kincaid, Clifford B., T/5,
Kitzke, Jerome F., Pfc,
Kloskowski, Adam, Pvt,
Kusmiak, Eugene, CWO,

LaMoria, Ralph E., Pfc,
Lavandor, Edward J., Pfc,
Leckie, Walter J., Pfc,
LeDuc, Louis V., Jr., T/4,
Leseman, Jack F., T/4,
Lester, Donald T., T/5,
Lewis, Glenn L., Pfc,
Ligosky, Dimitri A., T/4,

Maccarone, Peter F., Pfc,
Marshall, William C., Pfc,
Martin, Edward L., T/4,
Masero, Frank J., Pfc,
Mayes, William D., Pfc,
McElroy, John I., T/4,
McMullin, William B., T/4,
Meeker, Aron D., Pvt,
Mollison, John C., Pfc,

Moon, John W., Pfc,
Morales, Mariano, T/Sgt,

Niader, Ralph R., T/4,

Olson, Gordon E., T/5,
Ording, Lowell H., Pfc,

Paliani, Ubaldo S., T/5,
Palm, Stanley J., Pfc,
Peterson, James M., T/5,
Psaila, George R., Pfc,

Randolph, Blaine P., Pfc,
Riley, Cleo J., Pvt,
Ripley, Merritt N., S/Sgt,
Robinson, William C., T/5,
Rodriguez, Eleuterio, T/4,
Roderer, Robert G., Pvt,
Ruark, Walter R., Jr., T/5,

Schiffman, Dave, Pfc,
Shertzer, Robert S., Jr., T/5,
Silvey, Donald S., S/Sgt,
Simpson, David R., Pfc,
Skeen, Harold H., Pfc,

Small, Max A., Cpl,
Stancampiano, Vincent J., Pfc,
Standard, John R., Pfc,
Stevens, Frank A., S/Sgt,
Stevens, James A., Jr., T/5,
Strebe, Richard W., T/4,
Swope, Howard L., Pfc,
Szabo, Anthony L., T/5,

Teisberg, Robert C., Pfc,
Thomas, Edward, Pfc,
Timmons, Leonard L., Pfc,
Turcotte, Raymond L., T/5,

Ulrich, Wayne T., S/Sgt,

Vallet, Charles, T/5,

Weise, Harold H., T/5,
Weller, Wenner W., T/5,
Welsh, Richard A., T/5,
West, Harold R., T/5,
Williamson, Elwin E., Pfc,
Wilson, Arthur L., Cpl,
Woltring, Rex O., T/4,

Zeuli, Anthony M., Pfc.

† Killed in Action. * Prisoner of War. ‡ Missing in Action. § Died of Wounds.

441st ANTIAIRCRAFT ARTILLERY BATTALION (SP)

By General Order No. 36, dated June 1, 1942, Headquarters Antiaircraft Training Center, Camp Stewart, Georgia, the 441st Separate Coast Artillery Battalion (AA) was activated. The enlisted cadre was formed from several other antiaircraft units at the camp. The Battalion was made mobile prior to its change of station to Camp Carrabelle (later Gordon Johnston), Florida, where it conducted amphibious training with the 38th Infantry Division.

The Battalion arrived at Camp Pickett, Virginia, on January 26, 1943, to commence training with the 45th Infantry Division. It moved with the 45th from a final staging at Camp Patrick Henry, Virginia, on May 26, 1943, and embarked at Newport News, Virginia on June 8. By this time it was designated 441st AAA AW Battalion (SP). The Battalion participated throughout the Sicilian Campaign with the 45th Division.

The 441st was first attached to the 3d Division on September 15, as the Division was in the act of moving to Salerno.

The first major kill made by the Battalion was at the Volturno River, where seven out of 30 enemy planes were destroyed on October 15, despite the strength and intensity of the air attack, which caused several casualties in the outfit. One man received the Silver Star for his gallantry in this action.

It was at Anzio, following the Southern Italy campaign, however, that the 441st really proved its mettle. Enemy air raids during January and February were numerous and determined. In the first 17 days on the Beachhead the 441st shot down 23 German planes, and several "probables."

To protect Division Artillery observation planes, the Battalion set a "cub trap" in the forward areas. Pilots under duress were instructed to swoop low over an area in which there were four camouflaged half-tracks. The trap was sprung on two occasions, netting one enemy plane.

During the 3d's rest periods in the "pine forest," the 441st provided protection. It moved right along with the Division on the attack to Rome, and the subsequent landings in France and north to the Vosges Mountains.

Early in October, after some preliminary experimentation, it was found that light antiaircraft weapons were of great value in aiding foot troops in the attack. This marked a turning point for the battalion. This sort of firing, in addition to utilizing the half-tracks for evacuation of wounded, undoubtedly prompted the first statement that the 441st was "Anti Anything Anywhere."

At Remiremont the Battalion began converting from M-13's to M-16's by exchanging the twin .50 cal. machine guns of the M-13's for turrets with quadruple .50 cal. guns, doubling the original fire power.

The Battalion performed its greatest ground-support role in the attack to wipe out the Colmar Pocket, supporting the attack, repelling counterattacks and firing at the first enemy jet-propelled planes on January 29. In its support mission on the Colmar Canal crossing, B Battery expended 22,000 rounds, and C Battery 16,000 rounds of ammunition. On February 2, the Battalion shot down an ME-262 jet plane.

In the last phase of the war, the 441st had one more field day against its primary targets, following the fight at Nurnberg. This was at the Dillingen bridgehead, at that time very important to the Germans. When the 12th Armored seized the span, the *Luftwaffe* showed up in strength. Six enemy planes were shot down, with about five more "probables."

The 441st AAA Battalion (SP) remained with the Division until some time after V-E Day.

Commanding Officer

(Highest rank held)	Held pos. from	To
Lt. Col. Harry W. Lins	21 July 1942	9 Jan 1943
Lt. Col. Clifton L. MacLachlan	10 Jan 1943	12 Oct 1943
Lt. Col. Thomas H. Leary	13 Oct 1943	

Abbott, Royal L., Sgt,
Ackley, William, Pfc,
Acquavia, James P., T/5,
Adams, Vernon L., T/5,
Aiken, William H., T/5,
Alberts, Raymond J., Capt,
Albertson, Robert N., T/5,
Allen, George W., Jr., WOJG,
Allen, Harry M., T/4,
Allen, Jack L., Pvt,
Altman, Frank B., Pfc,
Alvarez, Pedro A., Pfc,
Alverson, William B., Sgt,
Anderson, Arthur W., T/4,
Annis, William W. S/Sgt,
Arata, George T., Sgt,
Archer, Odell G., Pvt,
Archibald, William J., Sgt,
Arel, Harry R., T/5,
Armato, Bernard J., S/Sgt,
Armstrong, James L., S/Sgt,
Arnett, Oliver W., T/5,
Arnold, Charles C., 1st Lt,
Ashley, Robert F., Pvt,
Ashton, John T., T/5,
Ayres, Landon S., Cpl,

Baber, John W., Pfc,
Bailey, Irving J., T/5,
Baker, Ervin E., T/5,
Baker, Robert M., Cpl,
Baker, Ronald L., 1st Lt,
Baker, Russell L., T/5,
Bakow, Harry, T/5,
Balf, Thomas E., T/5,
Balko, John, T/5,
Ballor, Elda C., T/5,
Barbella, Albert, Pfc,
Barlow, Ernest J., T/5,
Barnhart, Howard A., Pvt,
Barnes, Dempsey J., Jr., Pvt,
Barontuch, Saul B., Sgt,
Barrett, William E., Pvt,
Barrick, Ashton M., T/4,
Basarab, John, Cpl,
Basile, Frank P.,
Bates, Norman R., Pfc,
Battaglia, Gennaro F., Pfc,
Bauer, Roy E., Sgt,
Bauer, Wayne G., T/5,
†Bauer, William, Sgt,
Bean, Jesse, Pfc,
Bean, Robert W., Pvt,
Beaver, Sherman M., T/5,
Bechtold, Paul C., Pvt,
Beecher, Edward W., T/5,
Bell, George E., Pfc,
Bellingham, Joseph R., Pvt
Bellrose, Walter C., Pfc,
Benson, Charles F., T/5,
Berard, Joseph L., T/5,
Berkowitz, John T.,
Beshires, James O., T/4,
Bickel, George H., T/5,
Billiot, Orville J., Cpl,
Birmingham, Enos S., Cpl,
Bishop, Raymond J., Pvt,
Blackwell, Robert J., T/4,
Blackwell, William A., Pvt,
Blalock, John R., T/5,
Boeer, Walter H., Sgt,
Boiko, Morris A., Pvt,
Bojanek, Walter J., T/5,
Bornes, Walter, T/5,
Boros, Henry L., T/5,
Bostic, George W., Pfc,
Bourbeau, George N., T/4,
Bournival, Leo E., T/5,
Bourque, Dewey, Pfc,
Bovender, Lonnie W., T/5,
Bowman, William F., Pvt,
Boyd, Robert E., S/Sgt,
Boyce, James W., Pvt,
Bradley, Joseph J., Pfc,
Brady, Joseph D., Capt
Braidich, Henry M., Cpl,
Bramwell, Gordon, Cpl,
Bray, Edgar L., T/5,
Brewer, James C., T/5
Briggs, Stanley M., T/5,

Brine, Francis C., Sgt,
Brosnan, Bernard J., S/Sgt,
Brown, Clyde, Cpl,
Brown, Oval J., T/5,
Brown, Rex, T/5,
Bruemmer, Gerhard C., T/5,
Bryant, James S., 1st Lt,
Bumgardner, Howard F., Pvt,
Burke, William A., Pvt,
Burress, Earnest N., T/5,
Burton, Teddy J., Pvt,
Bush, Bernard D., Cpl,
Byram, Theodore H., Sgt,
Byrd, Malcolm A., Pfc,
Byrd, Reecie R., T/5,
Byrne, Martin P., Sgt,
Byrne, Thomas E., Cpl,

Cadena, Luciano C., Cpl,
Cagle, Willie B., T/5,
Callahan, Harold V., Sgt,
Campbell, Claude C., T/Sgt,
Canty, William P., 1st Lt,
Cargile, Flem, T/5,
Cargill, William, Jr., 1st Lt,
Carpenter, Rovert L., T/4,
Carr, Almon E., S/Sgt,
Carson, Edward J., Pvt,
Carswell, Arthur L., Sgt,
Carter, Samuel M., Sgt,
Carty, Edwin F., T/5,
Caruso, Joseph R., T/5,
Casatelli, Thomas D., T/4,
Casertano, Angelo J., Cpl,
§Casey, James J., 1st Lt,
Cassidy, Victor E., T/5,
Catterlin, Jack B., T/5,
Caughman, William E., Cpl,
Chahl, John M., Cpl,
Challener, John E., Cpl,
Chambers, Francis S., T/5,
Chambers, James L., Pfc,
Chaney, Edwin J., T/5,
Chastian, Lloyd W., T/5,
Chesnavich, Vincent J., Sgt,
Chipkin, Louis, Pfc,
Christ, Charles L., T/5,
Church, George E., Pfc,
Church, Harold C., Pfc,
Cipkowski, John J., Pfc,
Cipperly, Arthur R., T/5,
Citara, Fred A., Cpl,
Ciulac, Theodore A., T/5,
Clack, William L., Cpl,
Clark, Harry G., T/5,
Clark, Robert M., 1st Lt,
Clark, Wade J., Pfc,
Clauss, Arthur L., T/4,
Clayton, Wyman W., Pfc,
Clementi, Frank, T/4,
Cloud, George E., Cpl,
Coats, Paul M., T/4,
Cohen, Max M., Pvt,
Cohen, Morris G., Pvt,
§Cole, Eugene E., T/5,
Collins, Herman E., Cpl,
Commerford, Robert D., T/5,
Condon, Paul L., Pfc,
Conlon, John G., Pvt,
Connick, Aloysius A., Pvt,
Conrad, Walter A., T/5,
Constantine, Paul J., Cpl,
Convertino, Frank J., Cpl,
Coogan, Donnall F., Pfc,
Cook, Raymond, T/5,
Cooley, Arlie, Pfc,
Cooney, Thomas J., Cpl,
Coots, Harold N., Pfc,
Copeland, Henry, Pvt,
Corbo, Ignazio J., Pfc,
Corr, Joseph J., 1st Lt,
Corrigan, Newton W., T/3,
Costa, Joseph, Pfc,
Costan, George A., Capt,
Costello, Emmett M., M/Sgt,
Cote, Roger G., T/5,
Coughlin, Thomas R., T/5,
Counsellor, Russell L., T/5,
Courtney, George, Cpl,
Cox, Aaron, Pvt,

Cox, James E., Pfc,
Cox, Robert F., Pfc,
Craft, Jettie E., Cpl,
Craig, John O., Jr., Pfc,
Crane, David, T/5,
Crapps, John W., T/5,
Crawford, George W., Pvt,
Crawford, Maurice H., Pfc,
Cressotti, Caro B., T/5,
Cromnick, Alex, S/Sgt,
Cron, William F., S/Sgt,
Cronan, Joseph D., 1st Lt,
Crumley, Leonard R., Pfc,
Crounk, Samuel M., Sgt,
Cullen, James T., Jr., Sgt,
Cupo, Carmine, T/4,
Currin, Paul S., Pvt,
Czartolinski, Bronislav T., Cpl,

Dailinger, Francis E., S/Sgt,
Daley, Joseph T., T/5,
Dancha, Peter, Pfc,
Danner, Edgar L., T/5,
Davenport, Carter G., Cpl,
Davenport, Thomas M., Pfc,
Davis, Joseph, Cpl,
Davies, Percival E., Sgt,
Dawes, Claude L., T/5,
DeAngelis, Raymond, Pvt,
Deaton, Colman J., Pvt,
Definis, Michael J., T/4,
Delapa, William, T/5,
DeLacerda, William L., Pfc,
DeLeon, Fulgencio, Pfc,
DeLibero, Frank C., Sgt,
Del Mar, Wilson B., Pvt,
Delmontague, Joseph, 1st Sgt,
§DeNapoli, James P., Cpl,
De Nuccia, Louis L., 1st Sgt,
De Paolo, Patsy, T/5,
De Pasquale, Thomas F., Pfc
DeRienzo, Leonard, Jr., T/5,
De Vito, James V., M/Sgt,
Dickerson, Wm. E., Jr., 1st Lt,
DiBartolo, Joseph V., Pfc,
Di Maio, Paul, S/Sgt,
Di Meglio, Benedetto J., Pfc,
Donaldson, Edgar L., T/5,
Donley, William J., Pvt,
Dorcus, John C., T/4,
Doris, Thomas, Cpl,
Driggers, Julius, T/5,
Drone, William C., T/3,
Du Bois, Frederick, Pfc,
Duchnyak, Stephen, T/5,
Dugay, John E., Pvt,
Duncan, Robert F., Pfc,
Dunlavey, Francis J., Cpl,
Dunne, Martin H., Cpl,
Dwyer, Thomas W., T/5,
Dysert, Russell C., Sgt,
Dziuban, Eugene J., T/4,

Economon, Christopher B., T/5,
Edmunds, Ray C., Pvt,
Edwards, Eugene R., Pvt,
Edwards, William T., T/5,
Einhorn, Joseph, Pfc,
Elder, George A., Pfc,
Emery, Chester F., T/5,
Emmi, Daniel, T/5,
†Endres, Herman A., Jr., Cpl,
Endweiss, Daniel M., Capt,
Engardio, Frank J., T/5,
Engels, Arthur E., T/4,
Epstein, Nathan, Pfc,
Esposito, Patsy, Pvt,
Estep, Kenneth P., T/5,
Etchison, Roy F., Cpl,
Etheridge, Wade M., Sgt,
Evans, Hardy V., Pfc,
Evans, Lonnie O., T/5,
Evasick, Edward J., Pfc,

Faig, Harold L., Pfc,
Fair, Eldon G., Pfc,
Falardeau, Roland L., Cpl,
Falls, Eino E., 1st Sgt,
Farmer, Howard F., Pvt,
Farr, Edward W., Pfc,

§Farrington, Edward A., Sgt,
Farrington, William H., Pvt,
Favata, Clemente B., Sgt,
Fellows, Kenneth E., Sgt,
Felton, Paul W., Pfc,
Ferguson, Homer K., Sgt,
Fiduccia, Dominick, T/5,
Filka, John, S/Sgt,
Finch, Leonard F., T/4,
Finney, Dale C., T/4,
Firman, Myron C., Pfc,
Fischlein, Otto J., S/Sgt,
Florschutz, Henry A., Cpl,
Flowers, Walter L., 1st Sgt,
Fluitt, Carol D., T/5,
Forest, Jacob, Pfc,
Foulds, Robert A., Capt,
Fournier, Ernest J., Pvt,
Fox, Thomas J., Pfc,
Frabizzio, Mario J., Pfc,
Franceskina, Primo P., Pfc,
Fratiz, George W., T/5,
Frederick, Harley W., Pvt,
Freistuhler, Gerald E., Pfc,
Fren, John J., Pvt,
Frey, Harold W., Cpl,
Frias, Domingo, Pfc,
Friscia, Gasper, Pfc,
Froelich, Howard O., Pfc,
Frye, David W., Pvt,
Fudali, Joseph B., Pfc,
Fugo, Anthony, S/Sgt,
Fuller, Vernie L., T/5,

§Galletly, William, Pfc,
Gallis, Max, Cpl,
Gallucci, Vincent J., T/5,
Gandolfo, David N., S/Sgt,
Gangi, Peter, Sgt,
Ganley, John A., T/5,
Garcia, Raul V., Pfc,
Gardner, Carl C., Capt,
Gardner, William K., S/Sgt,
Garland, Henry J., T/5,
Garner, Clark W., T/5,
Garwood, William, Jr., T/4,
Gaul, George W., Pfc,
Gavalas, John P., T/5,
Gazda, Adolf, Pvt,
Gellis, Abner, Pvt,
Geraghty, Frank J., Pfc,
Giannotti, Robert, T/4,
Gilliland, William E., Pfc,
Gibson, Hassel S., Pvt,
†Ginicola, William V., Pvt,
Gilles, Louis J., Pfc,
Glass, Carl A., Sgt,
†Goadby, Warren W., Pfc,
Goldstein, Edward, Pfc,
Goldstein, Jacob, Pfc,
Goodling, Victor A., T/5,
Goot, Lionel D., T/5,
Gordon, Clyde A., Pvt,
Gordon, Oscar, S/Sgt,
Goretskie, Albert A., Pfc,
Goretsky, Paul L., Sgt,
Gorman, John J., 1st Sgt,
Gosa, John M., T/5,
§Grainer, Joseph A., Cpl,
Grant, Robert E., T/5,
Grasso, Paul, Sgt,
Grassifulli, Carmello, Pfc,
Graves, Earl C., T/5,
Graves, John E., T/5,
Gray, Hargis, Pvt,
Gray, Samuel L., Cpl,
Green, Saul, T/5,
Gregorchuk, Philip D., Cpl,
Griesbach, Theodore H., Pfc,
Grimsley, Ples T., T/5,
Grindstaff, Thomas, T/5,
Grothmann, Henry H., 2nd Lt,
Growcock, Walter, Jr., S/Sgt,
Gruhler, Robert, Pfc,
Guilmain, Homer M., T/5,
Gunderman, Donald M., T/5,
Gutierrez, Pedro, Pvt,

Haas, Charles H., T/5,
Haggart, Jerome A., S/Sgt,
Hamilton, Roy M., Sgt,

Hammerstrom, R. S., T/4,
Handler, Herbert S., S/Sgt,
Haneline, Jack M., Pfc,
Hankins, Wallace M., T/4,
Hanlen, Don F., 1st Lt,
Hanly, John R., T/5,
Hannover, Ardell R., Cpl,
Harris, Marshall F., T/5,
Hart, Charles E., T/5,
Hartmeyer, Herbert, Pvt,
Harvey, Frederick W., T/5,
Hauch, Walter A., Pvt,
Hawk, Hiram P., Capt,
Hawkins, Alfred, Cpl,
Hawrylak, Nicholas, T/5,
Hayden, Thomas B., Pfc,
Heafner, Lloyd E., T/5,
Heifetz, George J., T/5,
Hemenway, Lewis H., Cpl,
Henderson, Willard R., Cpl,
Henkelman, Edward G., T/5,
Henson, William E., Pfc,
Hepper, Melvin R., T/5,
Herlihy, John P., 1st Lt,
Herrera, Lurencio, T/5,
Hershey, Galen C., Cpl,
Hess, Frank P., Jr., 1st Sgt,
Hess, John L., S/Sgt,
Heydon, William T., Cpl,
Higgins, Charles B., T/5,
Hilberger, Hilson G., S/Sgt,
Hilton, Charles D., Capt,
Hird, John A., Pfc,
Hirschhorn, Solomon, Cpl,
Hochstetler, Merrill O., Pfc,
Hockaday, Robert L., Pvt,
Hoffman, William P., T/5,
Hohl, Raymond R., Pfc,
Holen, Elias, Jr., Pfc,
Holton, John J., Cpl,
Hone, Bernard J., Pvt,
Hoover, James B., T/4,
Hoover, Samuel E., T/5,
Hopkins, Gilbert W., Pvt,
Houle, Harvey M., T/5,
Houston, Wilbert E., Pvt,
Hounshell, Anderson H., Cpl,
Howe, Robert J., Pvt,
Huberty, Martin W., 1st Sgt,
Hughes, Raphael E., Sgt,
Hughes, Samuel J., Pfc,
Hull, George A., T/5,
Hung, Wong, Pfc,
Hunkin, Alfred J., 1st Lt,
Hunt, William R., Pfc,
Hunter, John E., T/5,
Hurley, Jesse C., Cpl,
Hutton, Walter A., Sgt,

Isaacson, Eino R., Pfc,
Israel, Karlton, T/5,

Jackson, Daskell E., Pvt,
Jackson, Frank, S/Sgt,
Jackson, John, Jr., S/Sgt,
Jackson, William A., T/5,
Jardine, Leslie B., T/5,
Jarrell, Herman F., Pvt,
Jesunas, Alfons A., Pfc,
Johnson, Henry T., Sgt,
Johnson, Judson L., Pvt,
Johnson, Lyle R., Pfc,
Johnson, Raymond J., Pvt,
Johnson, Waldo E., Cpl,
Johnson, Willie, Pvt,
Jones, Albert K., Pvt,
Jones, D. (i. o.) C., Pfc,
Jones, Earl L., Sgt,
Jones, Edward L., Pfc,
Jones, Frederick C., Pfc,
Jones, Lee B., T/5,
Joyner, Edwin P., Cpl,
Judd, Lewis L., T/5,

Kainer, Lester F., Pfc,
Kalom, Lawrence, Capt,
Kaplan, Jack S., Pvt,
Kaploniak, Charles E., Cpl,
Karachin, Anthony, T/3,
Karlo, Edward L., Pvt,
Karns, George F., T/5,

† Killed in Action.   * Prisoner of War.   ‡ Missing in Action.   § Died of Wounds.

Karyczak, Joseph, T/5,
Katz, David, Pfc,
Keeler, Robert C., Pfc,
Keith, Barney C., Sgt,
Kelley, Merritt W., T/4,
Kells, Harold C., T/5,
Kelly, Gerad V., Pvt,
Kelly, William J., T/5,
Kempsky, Johnnie A., T/5,
Kennard, Homer M., Pvt,
Kennedy, Edward, Jr., Pvt,
Kennedy, John A., 1st Lt,
Kesselschmidt, Abraham, Cpl,
Ketron, Curtis J,, T/5,
Kidd, David H., T/5,
Kierst, Adam J., T/5,
Killen, John J., Pvt,
Killian, Stanley, Cpl,
Killough, Willis J., T/5,
Kinde, Harold, Cpl,
King, Joseph V., Cpl,
Kinney, Gerald, Cpl,
Klinzing, Harry F., Pfc,
Klos, Walter F., T/5,
Knapp, Nelson C., Pfc,
Koen, Carl E., T/5,
Kolucki, George J., Cpl,
Konieczny, Leonard M., Pvt,
Kontorchik, Stanley L., T/5,
§Korn, Paul E., Cpl,
Kozlevcar, Stanley J., Cpl,
†Kratovil, William A., T/4,
Krause, Gibert, Pvt,
Kravitz, Michael, Sgt,
Krieger, Isadore, Pfc,
Kriete, William H., 1st Lt,
Kroleski, Edward J., Pfc,
Kruzycki, Raymond A., Pvt,
Kubicek, Edward, T/5,
Kuehl, Hans A., Cpl,
Kuligowski, Carl V., Sgt,
§Kulikauskas, Edmund J., T/4,
Kurylo, Walter, T/5,
Kutylowski, Walter, T/5,
Kuzma, Michael J., Cpl,
Kwizola, Joseph J., Pfc

Labay, Valentine C., Cpl,
Ladouceur, Louis J., Pvt
Ladzinski, Joseph S., T/5,
Lagoda, John J., Pfc,
Lail, Ivey T., S/Sgt,
Lake, Clarence J., Pfc
Lambert, Jacob I., T/5,
Landers, Joseph L., Pvt,
Lange, Ervin A., Pfc,
Langel, Charles Y., Jr., Pfc
Lanza, John L., Pvt,
Lardirei, Peter C., Pfc,
Larger, Charles, Jr., Sgt,
Larson, August J., Pfc,
Larson, Edwin, Sgt,
Larson, Leonard, Pfc,
Lastayo, Lester H., Cpl,
Latham, William R., Cpl,
Lazzaro, John E., Sgt,
Leabold, Lester C., Pfc
Leary, Thomas H., Lt Col,
Le Clair, Francis F., Pfc,
Ledanski, Wesley, T/5,
Ledden, Allen P., Pfc,
Leedy, Charles R., S/Sgt,
LeGrand, Glen E., Pvt,
Lemons, Wendell G., T/5,
Lengyel, Joseph J., Pfc,
Lewis, Andrew O., Sgt,
Lewis, Thomas M., Cpl,
Liccardi, Charles P., T/5,
Lichtenegger, Seibold, 1st Lt,
Lieberman, Henry, 1st Lt,
Lifsey, Julian, Pvt,
Lindsay, George T., 1st Lt,
L'Italien, Henry, T/5,
Lincoln, Richard L., T/5
Lindsey, J. C., Pfc,
Linehan, Robert W., Pfc,
Lipscomb, George T., Pfc,
Littell, Harold D., T/5,
Lodle, Elwood G., 1st Lt,
Lo Grande, Salvatore D., Cpl,
Lombardo, Dominic, Pvt,
Lopez, Thomas F., Pvt,
Lott, Chester D., Pfc,
Love, Leamon B., T/4,
Loveland, Francis J., T/5,
Lowe, Lionel D., Pfc,
Lucarelli, Anthony, T/5,
Lucier, Theodore, Pfc,
Ludwig, Fred A., T/5,
Lummis, Cyrus R., Pfc,
Lundkvist, David A., Pfc,
Lyden, John J., Pfc,

Macias, Robert, Pfc,
MacKernan, William F., Pvt,

Mahoney, John J., S/Sgt,
Malanaphy, Joseph F., Pfc,
Malec, Frank, Cpl,
Malinowsky, Vladislaus, T/5,
Mallon, William J., T/5,
Maltz, Harry, Pfc,
Mangum, David B., T/5,
Maney, Cecil L., T/5,
Manniello, Frank E., S/Sgt,
Marchak, Joseph T., T/5,
Marcinkevitch, Joseph G., Pfc,
Marhefka, Stanley E., T/5,
Marimpietri, Dominick, T/4,
Marks, John W., Sgt,
Marley, Albert L., T/5,
Marshall, Gerald F., Pfc,
Martin, Albert E., Maj,
Martinez, Senovine H., Pfc,
Martino, Vincent A., T/5,
Maruca, Harry B., T/4,
Martorelli, Angelo, Jr., Pfc,
Mass, Louis, Pfc,
Matarese, Daniel B., Pvt
Matthews, Joel H., T/5,
Matthews, Marion J., Cpl,
Maxwell, Kenneth, T/5,
Mazziotto, Joseph, T/5,
McAuliffe, John J., Sgt,
McCann, Thomas G., T/5,
McCann, Thomas J., Sgt,
McCelland, George E., T/4,
McClendon, Lennie C., Pvt,
McCoy, William V., Pfc,
McCrady, John E., Pfc,
McDonald, Lee R., Cpl,
McDowell, William I., T/5,
McFadden, Arthur W., T/5,
McGee, Walter D., 2nd Lt,
McGinn, Charles R., T/5,
McGovern, James F., Capt,
McGroerty, Harry J., Cpl,
McMahon, Edward M., T/5,
McNeely, James R., T/5,
McNeil, Albert J., T/5,
†McNeil, Hector, Cpl,
McPhate, Baker N., S/Sgt,
Meade, Raymond, Pfc,
Mealey, Arthur S., Pfc,
Mecca, Anthony J., T/5,
Medders, Ernest M., Pfc,
Meehan, Harold C., Pvt,
Meister, Herbert A., T/5,
Melton, Thomas B., T/5,
Melvin, Earl E., Pfc,
Mercoun, William S., Jr., Cpl
Merritt, Russell B., T/5,
Meyer, Jack D., Sr., Pvt,
Meyerowitz, Simon, Pfc,
Miceli, Albert, T/Sgt,
Michalski, Raymond J., Pvt,
Mickelson, Leroy E., Pvt,
§Miculka, Clarence J., T/5,
Mielcarz, Alexander J., Cpl,
Mierek, Joseph C., Pvt,
Milbert, Anthony S., S/Sgt,
Miller, Earle W., T/Sgt,
Miller, Harry, T/4,
Miller, Henry J., Cpl,
†Miller, Jerome S., Pvt,
Miller, John S., S/Sgt,
Miller, Luther C., T/5,
Miller, Thomas G., Pvt,
Millican, Burr, Capt,
Millician, Horace, T/4,
Millraney, Joe B., Pfc,
Mitchell, John B., T/5,
Mitchell, Pheston, Cpl,
Model, George, T/5,
Mohr, Roy, Capt,
Mole, Robert A., 1st Lt,
Mondanaro, Antonio, Pvt,
Monti, Ernest G., T/4,
Moore, Mark D., 1st Lt,
Morgan, Curtis E., T/5,
Morreale, Charles A., T/5,
Morris, Bennie, T/5,
Mosakowski, Tony E., T/5,
Morissette, Joseph E., Pfc,
Mott, Harold, Pfc,
Moyer, Marvin S., Pfc,
Muething, Gerald F., Capt,
Mullins, Harold J., Cpl,
Munger, Henry J., Pfc,
Murin, John, Jr., Pvt,
Murphy, James C., T/5,
Mutek, Wendell A., Pvt,
Muzzy, Edward J., Sgt,

Nakonechny, Andrew, Pfc,
Nali, Melvin J., Pfc,
Nett, Paul N., Cpl,
Nevill, Dariel B., Pfc,
§Newton, William H., Pvt,
Nickerson, Ernest H., Sgt,
Noble, Clair A., Pvt,

Noeske, William C., Pvt,
Noraig, Kastant, Pfc,
Norris, John A., T/4,
Novak, Frank, Pfc,
†Novarro, Elmer A., Sgt,
Nugent, James I., Pfc,

Ochocki, John J., T/4,
Oliver, John, T/5,
Olsen, Gerald R., CWO,
O'Neill, John J., Cpl,
Opthof, John, Jr., T/5,
Orlando, Samuel L., Sgt,
Orseno, Joseph, Pfc,
§Orrell, Robert, Pvt,
Osar, Joseph F., Pfc,
Osgood, Fred E., T/5,
Oskirko, Edward, T/5,
Ostrowski, Walter J., Pfc,
Ottenthal, Philip G., Pvt,
Owen, Stewart B., Cpl,

Pagragan, Francis III, Pfc,
Pannozo, Clinton C., Pfc,
Pantaleo, Joseph V., Cpl,
Parmeter, Burton E., T/5,
Paronett, Robert J., T/4,
Parr, Louie A., Pfc,
Parsons, George R., T/5,
Pascucci, Ernest M., T/4,
Pascuzzi, Charles A., Pvt,
Patterson, William E., Pfc,
Peagler, Vernie L., Pfc,
Peele, Oscar H., Jr., T/5,
Peltz, Samuel P., Pvt,
Penny, Peter, Cpl,
Peraset, Charles, T/4,
Pereira, George A., Cpl,
Perez, Frank P., Pfc,
Perrotta, Ralph J., T/5,
Perusek, Stanley F., Cpl,
Pesich, Peter, T/5,
Petaja, George J., Pvt,
Petitta, Patsy, T/5,
Petrak, James H., Sgt,
Petrovich, Joseph J., Jr., T/5,
Petty, H. (i. o.) T., Pvt,
Pfeffer, Phillip W., Pfc,
Phipps, Dallas A., Pvt,
Picciano, John J., Sgt,
Pickard, James H., Pvt,
Pickett, John E., T/5,
Piper, John H., T/4,
Pixley, William F., T/5,
Plyman, Norman O., Pfc,
Pointer, Joseph L., T/5,
Pollak, Albert J., S/Sgt,
Polzin, Edward J., Jr., Pvt,
Pontius, Park B., S/Sgt,
Poor, George A., Cpl,
Porcaro, Emilio R., Cpl,
Porter, Harold A., T/5,
Porth, John F., Pfc,
Potter, Charlie G., Pfc,
Posaski, Chester, Pfc,
Posluszny, Edward, Pvt,
Powell, James A., S/Sgt,
Preda, Teddy, Pfc,
Prescott, Arthur M., T/5,
Price, Myles A., Pfc,
Pritchett, Claude E., T/5,
Pruett, James R., Pvt,
Proft, Frank J., Cpl,
Pruitt, Algie G., Pvt,
Pruitt, Roy T., T/5,
Prutsman, Aronld L., Cpl,
Puckett, Raymond E., Cpl,

Radcliffe, Burdette C., T/5,
Ragland, Joel M., S/Sgt,
Rasey, John F., Pfc,
Rasnick, Sidney O., T/5,
Raymer, Clarence G., Pfc,
Reber, Austin W., T/5,
Recchia, Edward A., Pvt,
Reed, Hardy W., Pfc,
Reeg, Leonard J., Pfc,
Reese, Robert A., T/5,
Rehak, John J., Pvt,
Reitz, Henry G., Sgt,
Renavitz, Andrew, Pfc,
Rexroad, Lloyd E., T/5,
Reynolds, Fred E., T/5,
Reynolds, Michael F., Cpl,
Reynolds, Robert H., T/5,
Richard, Francis L., Cpl,
Richards, John W., Pfc,
Richardson, John N., Jr., Pfc,
Rigelon, Joseph, Sgt,
Roan, James M., T/5,
Robbins, Clarence W., Pfc,
Roberts, Gilbert B., T/5,
Roberts, Oscar B., 1st Lt,
Robinson, James S., S/Sgt,
Robinson, Robert L., T/5,

Rodda, James D., T/5,
Roddy, Francis J., Major,
Rodenstein, Gerson, Pfc,
Rodriguez, Oscar R., S/Sgt,
Rogers, Francis F., Capt,
Rogers, Hardin W., Pvt,
Rogers, Herschel E., T/5,
Rogers, Roy W., Pfc,
Rohde, John W., Pfc,
Roll, Jacob E., Sgt,
Rollston, Arthur E., T/5,
Rongo, Gennaro P., Pvt,
Rosenfeld, Sam J., T/5,
Ross, James A., Cpl,
Ross, John L., Pvt,
Roy, Allen L., Sgt,
Royal, Richard R., T/Sgt,
Rubendall, Nelson E., T/4,
Rudge, Frederick R., Sgt,
Runkle, Benjamin G., Sgt,
Russell, Jessie, Pvt,
Russell, John W., T/5,
Ryan, Warren J., Pfc,

Saddler, John T., T/5,
Salerno, John J., Pfc,
Salvagio, Louis T., Pfc,
Sampsel, Lester W., Pfc,
Sanders, Bascom, T/5,
Sansone, Robert P., T/5,
Sante, Anthony, T/5,
Satuloff, Sanford M., 1st Lt,
Schaefer, William F., S/Sgt,
Schanck, Robert S., Sgt,
Schaub, Charles R., Pvt,
Scheflo, Ove H., S/Sgt,
Schiedel, Herbert E., 1st Lt,
Schinderle, John J., T/4,
Schlegelmilch, Donald W., T/5,
Schnackenberg, Earl M., T/5,
Schnorenberg, Bernard L., T/3,
Schroer, William, Pfc,
Schultz, Edward J., Pfc,
Schweighardt, Andrew F., T/5,
Scott, George F., T/5,
Scott, George R., Pfc,
Scott, Willis, Cpl,
Scraper, Jasper S., T/5,
Sedlak, Andrew P., Sgt,
Segala, Henry, T/5,
Segvich, Jerry J., Pfc,
Selich, Edward, Pvt
Senlak, Anthony B., T/5,
Seulowitz, Isidore T., Pfc,
Shane, Charles S., Cpl,
Sharp, John M., T/5,
Sharpe, Thomas W., Pf
Shaw, John Y., Jr., T/5,
Shea, John D., Sgt,
Shea, William E., Sgt,
Shears, Adolph L., Pvt,
Sheeman, Charles B., Pvt,
Shields, Edward J., Pvt,
Shields, George D., Jr., T/Sgt,
Shiles, William G., T/5,
Shoemaker, Edgar C., Cpl,
Showell, Ralph, T/5,
Shumway, Charles N., Pfc,
Shuster, Clare M., Major,
Sibley, Archie E., Pvt,
Sifford, Howard A., Pfc,
Sigler, Kenneth J., Pfc,
Silvestri, Thomas, Pfc,
Simi, Roy J., 1st Lt,
Simmons, George D., Cpl,
Simmons, James U., T/Sgt,
Simon, Edward D., Pvt,
Simon, Harry P., T/5,
Simpson, Albert, Pvt,
Simpson, Charles B., Jr., Pfc,
Simpson, J. B., Pvt,
Slavinsky, Edwin A., Capt,
Smith, Elvin, Jr., 1st Lt,
Smith, Herbert, Pvt,
Smith, Hermit S., T/5,
Smith, J. D., Pvt,
Smith, James T., Sgt,
Smith, John J., Cpl,
Smith, Oliver W., Pvt,
Smith, Walter S., T/5,
Smith, William H., T/5,
Smyth, Richard E., Sgt,
Snell, Hugh F., T/5,
†Snell, Parker C., 2nd Lt,
Soliz, Guadalupe, Pfc
Soulier, Philip B., T/5,
Sowden, Harvey E., Pfc,
Spak, Tadous, Pvt,
Sparrow, Sam B., Pfc,
Spilman, Berle B., Pvt,
Stadler, Louis, T/5,
Stafford, Lawrence V., T/4,
Stahnke, John L., Pfc, St.
Stalker, John P., 2nd Lt,
Stamper, John E., T/5,

Stanford, Edwin G., T/4,
Stanton, Floyd E., T/4,
Stranger, Earl R., T/4,
Stasion, Henry, T/5,
Steeb, John, Sgt,
Steinitz, Henry J., Cpl,
Stevens, Arthur V., Pfc,
Stevens, George R., Pfc,
Stieber, Arthur M., Pvt,
Straight, Leroy O., 2nd Lt,
Strand, Erick R., Pvt,
Strecok, Steve, T/5,
St. Sauveur, Leodore, Pfc,
Stubblefield, Charles B., Pfc,
Suber, Harold C., T/4,
Suckley, George A., Sgt,
Super, Alexander, T/5,
Surakus, John A., Jr., Cpl,
Surma, Henry S., Pfc,
Sutter, George H., WOJG,
Sykes, Jesse T., Sgt,
Sykes, Richard H., Pvt,

Taffit, Morton A., Pfc,
Tagge, Peter H., S/Sgt,
Taggart, James R., T/5,
Tanski, Steven F., Pvt,
Tate, William H., Sgt,
Taylor, Robert L., 1st Sgt,
Taylor, Solon L., T/5,
Tecza, John J., Sgt,
Tees, Frederick M., T/4,
Tem, Edward, Pvt,
Ten Eyck, John F., T/Sgt,
Terborg, Henry L., Pfc,
Tesser, Jack, Pvt,
Thaw, William B., T/5,
Thomas, Daniel W., 1st Lt,
Thomas, Glenn, Cpl,
Thomas, Josiah W., T/5,
Thompson, Curtis T., Pfc,
Thompson, Harold C., Pfc,
Thompson, Henry M., Pvt,
Thompson, Lucious A., Cpl,
Tichnell, Walter C., T/5,
Tittsworth, Everett T., T/5,
Todoroff, Donald S., T/5,
Trabucci, Samuel J., Pfc,
Tracey, Bernard C., Cpl,
Trail, David, Pvt,
Trumpf, William H., Jr., Cpl,
Truscello, Gaston, Pvt,
†Tschaekofske, Leo, Pvt,
Tubek, Edward J., Sgt,
Tucker, Buford L., Jr., T/4,
Tucker, Edward D., Pvt,
Tumolo, Stephen P., Cpl,
Tunstall, Elmer I., Pvt,
Tweedale, George T., T/4,
Tyree, Nelvin M., Cpl,

Uliana, Nisio F., S/Sgt,
Underwood, William M., Cpl,
Upchurch, Pershing E., Pfc,
Upchurch, Woodrow B., Pfc,
Utterback, Howard C., Cpl,

Vail, Ralph J., T/5,
Vallero, Sam L., Cpl,
Vandermay, Walton B., Pfc,
Van Horn, Charles R., Sgt,
Van Meeteren, William A., Cpl,
Van Scoy, Roscoe H., Pfc,
Vargas, Joaquin R., Jr., T/5,
Varrone, Anthony E., T/5,
Vasquez, Reynaldo, T/5,
Vaughn, William H., T/4,
Vay, Henry M., S/Sgt,
Verrelli, Rocco J., Pfc,
Villanueva, Santiago E., Pfc,
Villegas, Ben C., Pvt,
Visceglio, Nicholas, Pvt,

Wade, Edward B., Pvt,
Wade, Levi L., Cpl,
Wagenhoffer, Stephen H., T/5,
Wagner, Joe, Pvt,
Waite, Joseph F., Pfc,
Walker, Roy F., Pvt,
Wallace, Floyd A., T/5,
Wallin, Tage H. S., S/Sgt,
Walsh, Edwin J., Pfc,
Walter, Harry, Cpl,
Ward, James, T/5,
Wasyluk, Joseph, Pfc,
Waters, Denver C., Cpl,
Watkins, Oscar R., Pvt,
Watkins, Roney, Pfc,
Watland, Clarence, T/5,
Wawrzyniak, Leonard J., Pfc,
Weatherford, Linwood H., Pvt,
Weaver, Elijah E., Pfc,
Weber, Frank J., Pvt,
Weinhold, Franklin I., Sgt,
§Weinpel, Frank J., T/5,

† Killed in Action. * Prisoner of War. ‡ Missing in Action. § Died of Wounds.

Weisman, Robert J., Pvt,
Werth, Leonard J., M/Sgt,
Werner, Erich M., Pfc,
Wescott, Lawrence A., Cpl
Westerman, Homer, T/5,
White, Charlie C., Pfc,
White, Ernest W., Cpl,
White, Otis, T/5,
Whiteman, Alvin W., Pfc,
Whitley, James A. G., Jr., Sgt,

Whitelock, Lawrence E., Sgt,
Wiggins, Howard ., Sgt,
†Wildmann, George A., Capt,
Willi, Joseph P., Cpl,
Williams, George, Pfc,
Williams, George E., Pfc,
†Williams, Robert A., Pfc,
Willis, Alton C., T/5,
Wilson, Charles A., Pvt,
Wilson, Harry T., Cpl,

Wilson, Thomas, S/Sgt,
Winchell, Donald C., 1st Lt,
†Wiseman, Louis, 1st Lt,
Witunsky, Frank J. W., Pvt,
Wojciechowsky, Wm. E., Pfc,
Wood, Arthur W., Pfc,
Wood, Raymond J., Pfc,
Woolston, Buell M., T/5,
Woonsook, Dwight, H., Pvt,
Wragg, Alben H., Cpl,

†Wray, Granville H., T/5,
Wright, Henry J., Pfc,
Wrobelwski, Anthony, Pvt,
Wyatt, Leon F., T/5,

Xaiver, Anthony, Pfc,

Yazel, William R., Cpl,
Yeagley, Kenneth B., Pfc,
Yount, Joseph H., T/5,

Yuska, Anthony J., Cpl,

Zablidowsky, Theodore, Pvt,
Zakrzewski, Martin, Pvt,
Zanoline, David E., Cpl,
Zapp, Alfred M., S/Sgt,
Zaucha, Joseph W., T/4,
Zenone, John J., T/5,
Zoyac, Stanley, Pvt,
Zweisdak, George, T/5.

† Killed in Action.   * Prisoner of War.   ‡ Missing in Action.   § Died of Wounds.

601ST TANK DESTROYER BATTALION

The 601st Tank Destroyer Battalion was attached to the 3d Infantry Division for so many months that its men and officers felt almost as though their unit was an organic part of the Division—a feeling that was heartily reciprocated by the infantry.

The Battalion was activated August 19, 1941 as a part of the 1st Infantry Division and left the United States for England with the 1st Division on August 2, 1942.

In North Africa the Battalion participated in the battles of Ousseltia Valley, Sbeitla, Kasserine Pass, El Guettar (for which it was awarded the Presidential Unit Citation for destroying 37 tanks in 24 hours) and Mateur, operating with the 1st, 9th and 34th U. S. Infantry Divisions and the 76th British Division, II U. S. Corps and XIX French Corps.

It landed at Salerno on D-day, September 9, 1943, with the 36th Infantry Division and 1st Ranger Battalion and remained attached until September 30, 1943, when it was attached to the 3d Division, with which it remained until the end of the war.

The 601st went far beyond normal expectation in its performance of duty in combat. The Standing Operating Procedure for tank destroyer units is to destroy enemy tanks. The 601st was called upon, in addition, to engage various other ground targets, such as pillboxes and other enemy fortifications or possible strongpoints in close support of the attacking infantry. Enemy infantry was also considered a prime target.

During the Anzio Beachhead period the 601st destroyed 42 enemy tanks and killed a large number of enemy personnel, at the same time losing only two tank destroyers to enemy fire. During the 16-day battle at Colmar the Battalion succeeded in destroying 18 enemy tanks or tank destroyers and many enemy fortifications.

In the Division's attack against the Siegfried Line the Battalion played an important role, using direct assault fire against enemy pillboxes. During the latter days of the German campaign, the 601st Reconnaissance Company ranged far ahead of the infantry and helped keep the disorganized remnants of the German army within our zone of advance from consolidating and re-organizing.

Commanding Officer

(Highest rank held)

Lt. Col. Walter E. Tardy

Colonel Tardy commanded the Battalion during the major portion of the 601st's attachment to the 3d Infantry Division.

Abbott, James F., Sgt,
Adams, Marlin A., Pfc,
Adamus, Valentine B., Pvt,
Adcock, Jesse J., Pfc,
Africano, Salvatore J., T/4,
Agaglia, Robert R. V., Pvt,
Agnes, Angelo J., T/5,
Agnew, Morris W., T/5,
Aimone, Otto T/5,
Akridge, William T., Pvt,
Albensi, Joseph W., T/5,
Aldridge, Howard L., Cpl,
Alexander, A. J., Jr., Sgt,
Alexander, Stanley J., T/4,
Alexander, Virgil R., Cpl,
Alexander, William E., T/4,
Alexson, Isidor A., T/5,
Alfredo, Jose T., Pfc,

Allen, Lemuel D., T/Sgt,
Alston, Edward D., T/5,
Altman, Abraham, Pvt,
Altschuld, Max, Sgt,
Amadio, Rocco J., Pvt,
Amaro, John F., Pvt,
Amato, John, Pfc,
Amerine, Maurice D., Pvt,
Amos, Ambrose C., T/5,
Anders, John V., Cpl,
Anderson, Gustaf R. K., Pvt,
Anderson, Henry, 1st Lt,
Anderson, Mose, Cpl,
Anderson, Norman L., T/Sgt,
Andress, Max A., Sgt,
Anold, Austin J., Cpl,
Ansell, Earl G., T/5,
Antel, Robert R., Pfc,

Anton, Carmen, T/4,
Apodaca, Victoriano A., Pvt,
Appling, Hugh S., T/5,
Aquilino, Vincent J., T/5,
Archambeau, Leonard C., T/4,
Arnold, Lawton E., Pfc,
Arvonia, Biagio V., T/4,
Ashe, William C., Pfc,
Asinof, Coleman D., Capt,
Askew, Matthew C., Cpl,
Atherton, Charles S., Cpl,
Au, Daniel S., Cpl,
†Auderer, Joseph A., Pvt,
Augustine, Michael, Pvt,
Austin, Edward L., Maj,
Ayers, Harmond N., T/4,

†Babcock, Albert M., Jr., Pfc,

Babcock, George S., Sgt,
Baca, Carlos G., Pfc,
Bachen, Robert S., Pfc,
Baddorf, George E., Cpl,
Badeau, George R., S/Sgt,
Bagley, William D., Jr., 1st Lt,
†Bailey, Mason E., Pvt,
Bailey, Richard K., Sgt,
Bailey, Warren J., Pfc,
Bailey, William E., Sgt,
Bakasy, Andrew V., Sgt,
Baker, Elmer M., T/5,
Baker, Herschel D., Lt Col,
Baker, Homer, T/4,
Baker, Sydney A., Pfc,
Bakey, Russell F., Capt,
†Baldwin, Robert L., Pvt,
Baldwin, Wilbur F., T/5,

Bales, Leonard, Capt,
Ball, James R., T/5,
Ballantini, Elmer, Pfc,
Ballou, Warren E., S/Sgt,
Baran, John S., Sgt,
Barker, Joseph O., Jr., T/4,
Barnard, Marvin E., Pfc,
Barnell, Robert D., Pvt,
Barnes, John H., T/5,
Barnes, William C., Pfc,
Barnett, Earl, Pfc,
Barney, Linwood, Pvt,
Baron, Peter, T/5,
†Barone, Gregory, T/4,
Barr, James M., T/5,
Barrett, Robert J., Cpl,
Barry, Alfred R., 1st Sgt,
Bartels, Howard W., S/Sgt,

† Killed in Action.   * Prisoner of War.   ‡ Missing in Action.   § Died of Wounds.

IN WORLD WAR II 567

Barth, Edward J., S/Sgt,
Bartlet, Robert L., Pvt,
Bartling, Herman C., S/Sgt,
Bartnikowski, Stanley P., Pvt,
Barten, August J., Pfc,
Bartruff, Cecil P., T/4,
Bass, Robert M., Pvt,
Battaglia, Consolato C., Pvt,
Baxter, Cecil G., Pvt,
†Beal, George M., T/5,
Beall, William A., Cpl,
Beard, Howard A., Pvt,
Beard, William E., Pvt,
Becci, Joseph J. A., T/5,
Beck, Elwood F., Pvt,
Beck, John W., S/Sgt,
Bednarz, Louis J., S/Sgt,
Beebe, Frederick S., Cpl,
Begy, John W., Pfc,
†Behrendt, Paul C., Pfc,
Behr, Louis, Pfc,
Beitler, John R., Cpl,
Bell, Charles R., 1st Lt,
Bell, Clayton R., Cpl,
Bencher, Donald J., T/5,
Benesch, Werner K., Cpl,
Beneze, Jesse A., Pvt,
Benigno, James V., T/5,
Benjamin, Howard F., T/5,
Bentley, Frederick J., T/4,
Benwell, William H., Pfc,
Berendes, Anton J., Cpl,
Berg, Julius M., Pvt,
Berggren, Sophus T., T/4,
Berner, Lester L., T/4,
Bernett, James A., T/Sgt,
Bernstein, Barnard, Cpl,
Betsch, Walter, Pvt,
Bettem, Robert E., T/5,
Betters, Herbert D., Pfc,
Bevins, George M., Pvt,
Bianchi, Anthony J., 1st Lt,
§Bianconi, Orland J., T/5,
†Bickford, Lawrence R., Cpl,
Biladeau, James E., Pfc,
Billings, Howard B., T/5,
Billington, Coy P., Pvt,
Bishop, Burl F., T/5,
Bishop, Charles L., Pvt,
Bissette, Roy R., Pvt,
Bixby, Allen J., 1st Sgt,
Bixby, George E., Jr., Pvt,
†Blackburn, Beverly S., 2nd Lt,
Blackin, Sidney, T/Sgt,
†Blair, Harold N., Pvt,
*Blair, Roy M., T/5,
Blais, Raymond L., Pvt,
Blake, John P., Cpl,
Blasi, Michael, Pvt,
Blaumuller, George J., T/5,
Blayney, Charles E., Pvt,
Blevens, Virgil S., Pfc,
†Bliss, George L., Sgt,
Bloore, Albert G., Pvt,
Blum, Harvey R., T/Sgt,
†Blumberg, Paul O., T/4,
Blundo, Frank, T/5,
Bobarsky, Chas. J., Pfc,
Beck, Reinhold G., Cpl,
Boehm, John W., Pvt,
Boelhower, Joseph J., Pvt,
Boes, John J., T/5,
Boente, Norman, Cpl,
Boles, Clifton H., Pfc,
Boster, Gerald J., Pfc,
Bolton, Keith D., T/5,
*Bond, John W., Pvt,
*Bond, William E., Sgt,
Bonner, Vincent H., 1st Lt,
Booker, James M., Capt,
Borders, Forest E., T/5,
Bornhoft, William H., Jr., T/5,
Borowy, Peter, Pfc,
Boskovich, Stephen, Pvt,
Bosley, Charles R., Pvt,
Bottenfield, Arlie G., Pvt,
Bove, Frank A., S/Sgt,
Bowman, Allen H., Pfc,
Bowman, William A., 2nd Lt,
Boyce, Charles E., T/5,
Boykin, James C., Pvt,
Boyer, George C., Cpl,
Boyer, Lester W., Pvt,
Boyle, Hugh P., T/4,
Bradbury, Charles E., S/Sgt,
Bradley, Ralph J., Pvt,
Brady, Raymond L., T/5,
Bramack, William K., Pfc,
*Brault, Albert R., Sgt,
Bray, Otis, Pfc,
Brdar, Vincent J., Pfc,
Brecky, John, Pfc,
Breed, Allen L., S/Sgt,
Breiten, Louis A., Pvt,
Brennan, Kevin F., Pvt,

Brenot, Edward L., T/5,
Brew, Edward W., Pvt,
Bridgers, Alfred D., Pfc,
†Bridgers, Wilson R., Cpl,
Brigante, Vincent E., S/Sgt,
Briggs, Geary E., Pvt,
Brin, Andrew, T/5,
Bronson, Lloyd W., Sgt,
Brookler, Paul E., T/5,
Brooks, George P., T/5,
†Brooks, Willard E., T/5,
Broughton, John D., Pvt,
Brown, Frank F., Jr., Cpl,
Brown, Franklin C., Pvt,
Brown, Howard N., Pfc,
Brown, Paul R., Pvt,
Brown, Ralph, Jr., Pvt,
Brown, Thomas B., Jr., T/4,
†Brown, William B., T/5,
Brown, William L., Cpl,
Brucchieri, Vito M., Pfc,
Bruce, Ludwell H., Pvt,
†Bruske, Otto J., Pfc,
Bryan, Harold V., Cpl,
Buchman, Arthur H., Cpl,
Buckley, Benjamin A., S/Sgt,
Buckley, Robert A., Cpl,
Budgio, John J., Pvt,
Budrevich, Joseph E., Sgt,
†Buffkin, Eddie F., T/5,
Burdetle, Clarence A., Pvt,
Burleigh, Alexander J., Cpl,
Burnett, Jimmie F., Pvt,
Burnett, Paul G., Pfc,
Burnette, Robert S., Pvt,
Burnham, Hazen A., Pfc,
Burns, Virgil A., Pfc,
Burrell, Robert L., T/4,
Burris, Joe B., T/4,
Burton, Aberm S., Pfc,
Burud, William N., Cpl,
Bush, Donald G., T/5,
Bush, Edward D., Cpl,
Butindaro, Salvatore, Pfc,
Butler, Arthur L., Pfc,
Butler, Lavon H., Pfc,
Butler, William T., Pfc,
Buttner, Ernest L., T/5,
Byrd, Willard C., Sgt,
Buzzell, Frederick P., Sgt,
Bzdak, Stanley J., T/5,

Caccamise, John J., T/4,
Cacciatore, Leonard P., T/5,
Cadugan, Woodrow H., T/5,
†Call, Clelland C., Cpl,
Callahan, Cloyd, Pvt,
Callahan, Lloyd E., T/4,
Campbell, Alvin W., S/Sgt,
Campbell, Earl, Sgt,
Campbell, John A., 1st Lt,
Campbell, Thomas R., Pvt,
Capotosto, Anthony J., T/5,
Cappiello, Dante, Sgt,
Carano, Frank, Pvt,
Carballeira, Maniel J., Capt,
Card, Jack H., 1st Lt,
Carden, Billie J., T/4,
Cardona, Louis A., T/5,
*Cardone, Anthony, Pfc,
†Cardosi, Cyrus J., Pfc,
†Cardoza, Verne P., Pfc,
Carey, Frederick D., Pfc,
Carey, Joseph J., T/5,
Caristo, Michael J., Pvt,
Carlson, Edmund P., Pfc,
Carlton, Kenneth D., Pvt,
Carlucce, Tony, T/5,
Carpenter, Clarence R., T/4,
Carpenter, Daniel M., Pfc,
Carpenter, Samuel J., T/5,
Carr, Edward W., T/5,
Carreiro, Leonard, T/5,
Carriero, William, Pfc,
Carroll, James E., Jr., S/Sgt,
Carroll, Patrick J., T/5,
Carroll, Rodger W., T/5,
Carver, Marvin R., Pvt,
Carst, Jesse C., Jr., Pfc,
Casario, Albert, T/5,
Casner, Milan J., Pvt,
Castranovo, Girlando J., T/4,
Caswell, George S., Pvt,
Cates, Harold G., Cpl,
Catoe, Reece B., Pvt,
Cerasuolo, Joseph H., T/5,
†Chamberlain, Paul A., Sgt,
Chambers, Robert G., Pvt,
Chamblee, Frank R., Cpl,
Chamnese, Murray E., Pvt,
Chance, Odas W., T/Sgt,
Chaney, Marvin L., Sgt,
Charles, Herman D., S/Sgt,
Chastain, Olen B., Pfc,
Chichelo, Jack F., T/5,

Cheramie, Edward J., Pvt,
Chicketti, Stephen W., S/Sgt,
†Childers, James C., Sgt,
Choate, Clyde L., S/Sgt,
Choate, Joe H., S/Sgt,
Christiaen, Albert J., Pfc,
Christian, John D., 2nd Lt,
Christmas, Clyde E., T/5,
Church, William C., T/4,
Ciancotta, Michael, T/4,
Cibulka, Howard F., Pvt,
Cimoch, Stanislaw, S/Sgt,
Cickiewicz, Nick S., T/4,
Cipowski, Michael D., Pfc,
Citro, Thomas, T/4,
*Ciuk, Stanley W., Pfc,
Clark, Robert R., Pfc,
Clark, Thomas W., Sgt,
Clarke, Leonard J., Pvt,
Clarkin, Leonard C., T/5,
Claycomb, Harold K., Cpl,
†Clayton, Eugene C., S/Sgt,
Cleary, Dean A., Sgt,
Clemens, Clyde E., T/5,
Cobb, Cyrus W., 2nd Lt,
Cofer, Howard C., Pvt,
Coffey, Robert, T/5,
Cohan, Abraham S., Pfc,
Cole, Ralph E., M/Sgt,
Colelli, Ernest C., Pfc,
Coleman, Richard T., S/Sgt,
Collier, Dale L., Pfc,
Collins, John H., S/Sgt,
Colprit, Charles W., Sgt,
Coltey, Glenn G., Cpl,
Combs, Adam A., Pvt,
Concannon, Edward M., Pfc,
Condon, John F., Pvt,
†Condos, William G., Pfc,
Conklin, Ray C., Cpl,
Connelly, Joseph P., Pfc,
Conner, Thomas R., Pfc,
Connor, Charles F., Pfc,
Conway, John J., Sgt,
Cook, Donald E., Pvt,
Cook, John J., T/5,
Cook, Leo G., Sgt,
Cook, Richard C., T/4,
Cook, William C., Pvt,
†Cookson, Craig E., Cpl,
*Cooper, Willam T., Pvt,
Coppens, Cyril A., Pvt,
Coppenger, Francis J., Pvt,
Core, Elzie J., Pvt,
Corliss, Russell E., Pfc,
Corn, Ernest, Pfc,
Cornell, Gene M., Cpl,
Cornell, Harry A., Sgt,
†Corthell, Richard C., Pvt,
Costello, John M., T/5,
Cote, Marcel, T/5,
Cotten, Leonard E., T/5,
Coughlin, John F., Jr., Pfc,
†Covarrubias, Jesus V., Pfc,
Covert, Junior, 2nd Lt,
Coveliski, Charles J., Pvt,
Cox, Kenneth W., Pvt,
Crane, Chester, Pvt,
Cranford, Coy, Pvt,
Craycraft, Howard G., Sgt,
Crehan, John M., Pvt,
Crisco, Connie C., Pfc,
Cristofoletti, Renato A., Pvt,
Cromer, Charlie S., Pfc,
Crone, Ford S. T., Pfc,
†Cronin, Michael J., Pvt,
Cross, Recie S., T/4,
Crowe, Valentine, Pvt,
Croze, Clarence E., Pfc,
Culberson, James R., Pvt,
Cullen, John R., Pvt,
Cummings, Charles P., Cpl,
Cummings, Davis, Pvt,
Cunning, John N., S/Sgt,
Cunningham, Buford Z., Pvt,
Cunningham, Charles G., Pvt,
Cupriniski, Walter J., Pvt,
†Curatolo, Alfred F., Pvt,
Curtis, John J., Pfc,
Cusack, Thomas M., Pvt,

§Dabulas, Edward A., Pvt,
Dailer, John W., Pfc,
Daley, John R., Pfc,
†Dalrymple, Evan S., T/4,
Damms, Bernard V., Pfc,
D'Andrea, Victor J., Pfc,
Danahy, Joseph P., T/5,
Dangott, Fred R., Pfc,
Darcy, Thomas F., Pfc,
Dargush, Vincent B., 1st Lt,
Darnley, George, Pvt,
Davey, Jasper F., T/4,
Davila, Roman R., Pvt,
Davis, Arthur V., S/Sgt,

Davis, Dale L., Sgt,
Davis, Ernest E., Pvt,
Davis, Raymond W., Pfc,
†Davis, Robert B., Pvt,
Davis, Russell F., Pvt,
Davis, Stanley L., Pvt,
†Davis, Thomas, Pfc,
Davis, William G., T/5,
Davis, Wilton, Pvt,
Dearborn, Earl L., Pfc,
DeBlaere, Julian, T/4,
Decker, Peter F., Pvt,
Defosses, Philippe R., Cpl,
DeGrosa, Michael J., T/4,
DeJulius, Joseph M., T/5,
Dekowski, Peter F., Cpl,
Delach, George F., Pvt,
Delamater, Clarence E., T/5,
DeLay, James W., S/Sgt,
Delgado, Joe W., Pfc,
Delia, Franklin F., T/5,
Dellinger, Marvin J., Sgt,
Demarais, Ernest A., T/5,
Deminck, John, Pvt,
Dempsey, Horace L., Cpl,
Dennin, Robert A., Cpl,
Denny, Charley W., T/5,
Densmore, William F., Sgt,
Densmore, William P., T/4,
DeRose, Henry W., T/5,
Derryberry, Hugh C., Sgt,
Derwoyed, Stanley, T/5,
DeSalvo, Charles, Pvt,
Desforge, William V., 1st Lt,
DesJardins, Anthony J., T/5,
DeStefano, Anthony N., Pvt,
DeTienne, Earl L., Sgt,
Deutsch, Harry L., T/4,
Deutsch, Sidney, T/5,
Dexter, George B., Pfc,
Diamond, Morton C., T/5,
Diaz, Frank, Cpl,
Dickerson, Joseph H., Pfc,
Dickson, Richard A., Pfc,
Diebold, Kenneth G., S/Sgt,
Dietz, George J., Sgt,
Dillard, Milton H., Pvt,
DiMatteo, Pasquale A., Pfc,
Dinapoli, Frank, Pvt,
Dineen, Francis P., Pvt,
Dinsmore, Robert O., Pvt,
Dinsmore, William P., T/4,
Dionne, Arthur J., Pfc,
Divers, Edward, Pvt,
Dobsky, Clarence C., Cpl,
Dockery, Willard J., T/5,
Dolan, James W., Sgt,
Dolezal, George J., T/5,
Dominichetti, Lester L., Pfc,
Domoslay, Joe, T/4,
Donahue, John, M/Sgt,
Donaldson, Albert C., Sgt,
Doney, Daniel E., Sgt,
Donovan, Joseph E. R., M/Sgt,
Doren, Simon, Pvt,
Douglas, Lester D., Pvt,
Douville, Francis A. E., Cpl,
Dowling, William D., S/Sgt,
Downing, Vernon E., T/5,
Doyle, Harvie, Pvt,
Dragon, Michael, S/Sgt,
Drake, Silas B., Sgt,
Dreadfulwater, Levi, Pfc,
Dreistadt, George A., Pfc,
Drew, Raymond F., Pvt,
Drew, Samuel, Pvt,
Dudek, Alexander, T/5
Duffy, Robert N., Sgt,
†Duggan, Thomas F., Pvt,
DuHaime, Robert A., Pfc,
Dulowski, Chester J., Pvt,
Dumont, Alfred A., Pfc,
Dumphy, Lawrence J., Pvt,
*Dupcavitch, Leonard J., T/5,
Dusterhoft, Edward J., T/Sgt,
Dwyer, Hugh D., T/5,
Dye, Diamond A., T/4,
Dyer, Alfred L., 1st Lt,
Dykstra, Peter, Cpl,

Early, Thomas F., Pfc,
Eaton, Harry F., T/4,
Eaton, James E., T/4,
Eaton, Walter G., Cpl,
Eberle, George E., Pfc,
Eberly, John H., Pvt,
Eckmayer, Peter, T/4,
Eddy, J. S., T/4,
Edelon, Carl H., 1st Lt,
Edick, Kenneth G., 1st Lt,
Edwards, James R., Pfc,
Edwards, Sylvester T., Pvt,
Egan, James J., T/4,
†Egloff, Kenneth F., Sgt,
Einfalt, Martin A., T/5,

Elchak, Nicholas T., T/4,
Elder, Arthur J., Pvt,
Elenbark, William R., Pvt,
Elias, Norman, Pvt,
Eller, Jack M., Pvt,
Ellington, William K., Cpl,
Elliott, George S., Pvt,
Elliott, Gordon A., T/5,
†Elliott, Lewis P., 1st Lt,
Elliott, Okla H., Pfc,
Elliott, Owen W., Pfc,
Ellis, Edward J., Pvt,
Emigh, Frank, Pfc,
England, Earl R., Pvt,
Engledahl, Warren O., Pvt,
Englehart, Walter S., T/5,
Ennis, Samuel J., Pfc,
Enser, Edward W., T/5,
Epstein, Herman, T/5,
Erickson, Gunnar, T/4,
Erle, William, Pvt,
Ernst, Dale O., Pvt,
Ershan, Leonard, Cpl,
Erwin, Daniel M., Sgt,
Eskridge, Tilford H., 1st Lt,
Esser, Alfred M., Pfc,
Esposito, John, Sgt,
*Esposito, Joseph J., Pfc,
Esten, Walter E., Pvt,
Ethridge, Cecil O., S/Sgt,
Evans, Stuart A., M/Sgt,
*Everett, James C., Sgt,
Ezzell, James C., Sgt,

Faber, Irving, Cpl,
Fabrizi, Angeo A., Pvt,
Facchini, Ralph S., Pfc,
Faircloth, O. H., Pfc,
Faram, James W., T/5,
Farber, Nathan, Pvt,
Farfaglia, Leonard, Pvt,
Farish, Robert J., Pfc,
Farmer, Walker C., Pfc,
Farr, Connard T., Pvt,
Farrelly, James P., Cpl,
Farris, Norman F., Cpl,
Faucett, Carl G., T/5,
Fein, Irving F., S/Sgt,
Feinne, Walter C., T/5,
Feldstein, Daniel W., Pfc,
Ferando, Salvatore, Pfc,
Ferguson, Cecil J., Pfc,
Ferguson, James C., 1st Sgt,
Ferri, Victor, Pfc,
Ferretti, Fiorino A., T/5,
Festa, Mike, T/5,
Fett, Steven A., Pvt,
Fields, John L., Cpl,
Fienberg, Seymour, Pvt,
Fife, George T., Pvt,
Fillion, Norbert P., Cpl,
Finley, Herve A., S/Sgt,
Finley, William W. III, 1st Lt,
Finn, Thomas J., Pfc,
Finnegan, Robert P., Pvt,
*Finstein, Ernest S., T/4,
Fisher, Gradean C., T/5,
Fithian, William K., Pvt,
Flynn, Joe B., Pvt,
Foor, Max O., T/5,
Foote, Haven L., T/5,
Forchino, Joseph L., T/5,
Forlines, Woodrow W., Pfc,
Fotopoulos, Anthony P., T/5,
Fountain, William M., Pfc,
Frades, Harold J., Cpl,
Francis, Franklyn W., Pfc,
Franco, Angelo L., Pfc,
Free, Virgil O., Pvt,
Freed, Orville W., T/5,
†Freeman, Melvin F., Pfc,
Freer, Edward A., Cpl,
Frericks, Arthur R., Pvt,
Frick, Harold G., Pfc,
Fritz, Melvin H., T/5,
Fritzen, Robert F., Pfc,
Full, Elliott D., T/5,
Fuller, Benjamin A. G., Maj,
Fuller, Eugene, T/5,
Futuluyohuk, Steve, S/Sgt,

Gaddis, Woodrow, Pvt,
Galanos, John, Sgt,
Galanopoulos, Thomas C., T/5,
Galion, David M., T/5,
Gallant, Joseph A., S/Sgt,
Gallo, Louis A., T/4,
Galvin, John T., Cpl,
Gantz, Davis E., S/Sgt,
Garbo, Joseph, Pfc,
Garcia, Cristobal S., Pvt,
Garcia, Frank M., Cpl,
Garcia, Roberto, Pfc,
Gard, Carl A., T/5,
Garner, Kenneth P., T/4,

† Killed in Action. * Prisoner of War. ‡ Missing in Action. § Died of Wounds.

Gary, James R., Pvt,
*Gaskin, Joseph A., Sgt,
Gates, William O., S/Sgt,
*Gauquier, Anthony J., S/Sgt,
Gauthier, Conrad A., Sgt,
Gawron, Felix J., Pfc,
Gee, Merrill T., Pvt,
Geffken, Robert C., T/5,
Gelade, Benjamin, Sgt,
†Gelbstein, Theodore P., Pfc,
Gentile, Dominick J., T/5,
Gentile, Luigi A., T/5,
Gentle, Lloyd, T/4,
George, Clarence E., S/Sgt,
Gessleman, B. F., Jr., 2nd Lt,
Gettier, Russell W., T/5,
Giaclone, Peter J., T/5,
Gibbs, Roy C., Pfc,
†Gibeau, John A., Pfc,
Gibeau, Leon J., Pvt,
Gibson, Curtis C., Cpl,
Gilbert, Frank E., Pvt,
Gilbert, Nelson R., T/5,
Gilhaney, John J., T/4,
Gill, Donald R., Pvt,
Gill, Norman A., Pvt,
Gilleece, Hugh J., Sgt,
Gillespie, Samuel J., T/4,
Gillman, Joseph, T/5,
Gilmore, Loyd T., Cpl,
Gioia, Joseph A., Capt,
Giordano, Nicholas W., Cpl,
Giuliani, Alpidio P., Pvt,
Glazier, Frank X., M/Sgt,
Glembeski, Joseph, Jr., T/5,
*Glisson, Thomas W., Cpl,
Glover, William H., T/4,
Goble, Claude W., T/5,
Godlewski, Henry E., Sgt,
Godstrey, Herbert H., T/Sgt,
Golden, David E., Sgt,
Golden, Howard V., Pfc,
Goldsmith, James F., Sgt,
Golembski, Joseph, Cpl,
Gomberg, Oscar, Pfc,
*Gomez, Concepcion R., 1st Sgt,
Gonter, Charles C., T/5,
Gonza, John, Pfc,
Goodman, Donald H., Pfc,
Gorek, Gustave A., T/5,
Gorman, George G., Pfc,
Gott, William R., T/4,
Grager, David A., Pfc,
Grawe, George B., Pvt,
Gray, John J., Pfc,
Gray, William C., Pvt,
Grechowski, Stanley, Pvt,
Green, Daniel H., Jr., T/4,
Green, Russell D., Cpl,
Greene, Joe T., Pvt,
Green, Paul A., Pvt,
Greene, Robert L., S/Sgt,
Greenspon, Ben, Pvt,
Greggos, Thomas, Sgt,
Grembi, John J., T/5,
Griffis, Thomas E., Jr., T/5,
†Griffith, Robert D., Cpl,
Griffiths, Earl E., Pvt,
Grigiss, Charles P., Pfc,
Grimes, James C., Capt,
Grosch, Wilbur E., T/5,
Grover, George E., T/5,
Grubich, Daniel E., T/5,
Gruenberg, Rudolph F., T/4,
Grumelot, Ivan M., Cpl,
Guarino, Frederick J., Pvt,
Guenther, Charles T., Cpl,
Gunsalus, Lester N., Pvt,
Gustaferro, Louis R., Pfc,

Haden, Julius C., Pfc,
Hadju, James S., Pfc,
Hafner, Donald L., Pfc,
Hagood, Lillian J., Pvt,
Hagwood, Ruben S., T/5,
†Hale, William P., T/5,
Hall, Bert, Jr., Pfc,
Hall, Charles W., T/5,
Hall, Edgar L., Pfc,
†Ham, Clarence L., Pvt,
Hamel, Victor T., Sgt,
*Hamer, Walter, Cpl,
Hamilton, Howard S., T/5,
Hamond, James A., Cpl,
†Hammond, Richard G., Sgt,
Hamstra, Fred A., Sgt,
Hancharik, Michael, Pfc,
Hanf, Frederick E., Pvt,
Hankins, William A., T/5,
Hanners, Harry E., Jr., T/4,
Hanson, Arvin M., Pvt,
Harbo, Howard W., Pvt,
†Hard, Carl W., T/5,
*Hardenberg, James, T/5,
Hardman, Ralph B., T/4,
Hardman, William B., Pfc,
Hare, Earl W., Pfc,
Hargens, George A., Sgt,
Harles, Martin G., Pvt,
Harper, Bill R., S/Sgt,
Harple, Kenneth L., T/5,
Harrelson, Egbert G., Pvt,
Harrington, Charles R., Pvt,
Harris, Harold E., T/5,
Harris, John T., Cpl,
Harris, Richard H., Pvt,
Harrison, Harry, Jr., T/5,
Harrison, William R., Maj,
Hart, John R., Sgt,
Hartman, Harry M., Pvt,
Hartman, Lyman B., Pvt,
Harvey, Anthony G., T/5,
Hasher, Joseph F., Pfc,
Hasselbach, Ralph, Pvt,
Hatch, James K., Pvt,
Hatch, Robert W., T/5,
Hathcock, Dueward B., Pfc,
Hawes, George W., Pfc,
Hawks, Robert A., Sgt,
†Hays, Tolbert, Jr., 1st Lt,
Healy, Burton J., Pvt,
Healy, Frank D., Pvt,
Hearn, Leonard E., S/Sgt,
Heath, Donald E., Pvt,
Heberle, Gerald J., T/4,
Heiman, Frederick, Pfc,
Heischuber, Elias, Pvt,
Hemby, Lavaughn, Pvt,
Hemer, Claude, T/5,
Henderson, Charles, Pfc,
*Henderson, Thomas R., Pvt,
Henderson, Winston S., Pfc,
Hendra, Harry B., S/Sgt,
Hendricks, Joseph F., T/5,
Hendricks, Richard P., Pfc,
Hendrickson, Francis J., Pfc,
Henry, Harold D., Pfc,
Henry, Thomas W., T/5,
Henry, Jules J., Pfc,
Herbaly, Neal B., Pvt,
Hernandez, Mario G., Pvt,
Heron, Edwin R., T/5,
Hickman, Rufus B., T/5,
Hill, Calvin K., Cpl,
Hill, Eugene R., T/4,
Hill, Joe A., Sgt,
Hill, William, T/Sgt,
Hiller, John W., Cpl,
Hillis, Carroll T., T/5,
Hines, Joplin J., Pvt,
Hines, Robert C., Cpl,
Hinman, Daniel S. T., Maj,
Hinojosa, Jacinto L., Jr., Pvt,
Hinson, Homer, Pfc,
†Hird, Charles M., Pfc,
*Hobbs, David H., Pvt,
Hodge, Frederick W., Maj,
Hogue, Thomas F., Pvt,
†Hoffman, Alfred, Sgt,
Hoffman, George, Pfc,
Holden, Clyde L., Cpl,
Holden, James A., Pvt,
Hollandsworth, Troy M., T/5,
Holman, Otis H., Pfc,
Holmes, Roger A., T/5,
Holmes, Stuart P., T/5,
Holloway, Gradey, Sgt,
Holstein, Ernest B., Sgt,
§Homan, Virgil O., Pfc,
Hon, Gerald T., T/5,
Honea, Hoyt T., Pfc,
Hood, Johnnie W., T/5,
Hood, Richard, Jr., Pfc,
Hopkins, Ernest N., Pvt,
Horan, Edward C., T/4,
Horan, Patrick J., Pvt,
Horaney, George R., Cpl,
Horne, Ammie W., Pfc,
Horne, James G., Sgt,
Hornsby, P. G., Cpl,
Houle, Raymond A., T/4,
House, Lester W., T/5,
Hovey, Walter R., T/4,
Howk, Kenneth J., Pfc,
†Hritchkewitch, Austin A., T/4,
Hubler, David S., Pvt,
Hudson, Chester L., Cpl,
Hughes, Leigh P., Pfc,
Hughson, David N., 1st Lt,
Hummer, John E., Sgt,
Humphrey, Lucian L., Pfc,
Humphries, Ames T., Pfc,
Hunley, Jesse N., Jr., 1st Lt,
Hunsucker, Everette E., Pfc,
†Hunt, Henry H., Jr., Pfc,
Hutchings, George E., Sgt,
Hutto, Cecil, T/5,
Hyde, Robert A., Pvt,

Iaci, Anthony, T/5,
Iagulli, Raffael, S/Sgt,
Ielapi, Joseph A., Pfc,
Iovino, John E., T/5,
†Iovino, Patsy M., Cpl,
Indelicato, Vincent S., T/4,
‡Ingram, Irving A., Pfc,
Irving, Joseph L., Cpl,
Isaac, Lewis S., T/5,
Isham, Harold E., Pvt,
Iturrino, Joseph, T/4,
Ivey, Wiley C., Cpl,
Iwanicki, Stanley J., T/5,

Jablonski, Edward C., T/4,
Jablonski, Walter M., Pfc,
Jacobs, Cesary, T/5,
Jacobs, Nicholas, Pfc,
Jacoby, Bernard L., Pfc,
Jagels, Fred H., 2nd Lt,
Jakober, Charles A., Pvt,
Jamerson, Jessie L., Pfc,
James, Francis H., Pvt,
Jancich, Stephen F., Pfc,
†Jarrett, Harold B., Sgt,
Jayne, Frank L., Pvt,
Jefferies, Arthur A., Jr., T/Sgt,
Jendre, James W., Sgt,
Jenkins, James A., Pfc,
Jensen, Ward V., 1st Lt,
Jerzyk, Theodore J., Sgt,
Johannes, Edward, Pvt,
Johnson, Carl G., S/Sgt,
Johnson, Donald L., T/5,
Johnson, Henry H., Sgt,
†Johnson, Nathan P., Pfc
Johnson, Roger M., Pfc,
*Johnson, Robbie E., T/5,
Jones, Emanuel W., T/4,
Jones, Harry J., T/5,
Jones, Milton G., T/5,
Jones, Robert N., Sgt,
Jordan, Keith, T/4,
Josowitz, Edward L., 1st Lt,
Joyce, Arthur C., Pfc,
*Julian, Lionel G., Pfc,

Kabel, Garland W., Pvt,
Kafka, Paul A., T/5,
Kalata, Frank J., T/4,
Kale, Mack, T/4,
Kaleyias, Spiros M., Pvt,
Kalish, Harold A., T/5,
Kalwite, Kenneth D., Sgt,
Kaminski, Michael B., 1st Lt,
Kamiskie, Bronislaw, Pvt,
Kaplan, Frank S., T/5,
Kappen, William G., S/Sgt,
Karolewski, Chester J., Sgt,
Kascius, Adolph A., Pvt,
Kasparovich, Eugene, 1st Lt,
Kaufman, Huber L., Pfc,
Kawejsza, Edward J., Pvt,
Keefer, Edward W., T/5,
Keenan, Forest L., Pfc,
Keim, Fred F., T/5,
Keleman, John, Cpl,
Kelley, Arthur L., Jr., T/4,
Kelley, Shelton P., T/4,
Kelly, Raymond P., Cpl,
‡Kelly, Samuel H., Pfc,
Kelly, Thomas J., 1st Lt,
Kemery, George R., T/5,
Kennedy, Cecil H., Cpl,
Kennedy, James E., Pfc,
Kenney, Raymond A., Sgt,
Kenser, Mel B., Pvt,
Kent, Donald B., T/5,
Kerkove, Howard G., Pfc,
Keyes, Robert R., Jr., Pfc,
†Kielar, Walter J., Sgt,
Killian, Harry, S/Sgt,
Killough, Henry R., S/Sgt,
Kindall, Joseph J., S/Sgt,
*King, Edwin C., Pfc,
Kinney, Verner F., Sgt,
Kirk, Kenneth M., T/5,
Kirk, Robert J., Cpl,
Klank, Frank C., Pvt,
Klein, Joseph, T/5,
Klenk, Julius J., Pvt,
Klizek, Henry F., Pfc,
Knadler, Eugene L., Sgt,
Knishkowy, Emanuel S., 1st Lt,
Kociencki, Henry J., T/4,
Koeneman, Walter A., T/4,
Koenig, Herman B., Pvt,
Konopka, Frank S., T/4,
Kontorchik, Simon J., T/4,
†Kordana, Theodore S., T/5,
Korpela, Leslie A., T/4,
Koschak, John A., Pfc,
Koslo, Joseph W., Pfc,
Koterba, Frank M., T/5,
Koziuk, Joseph, Pfc,
Kozlowski, Chester J., T/4,
Kozlowski, Stanley J., T/4,
Krietzer, Harry W., Pvt,
Kressin, Edwin R., T/5,
Krey, Francis J., WOJG,
Krieger, Benjamin C., T/5,
Kristoff, Henry P., T/5
Kudryk, Joseph S., T/5,
*Kufta, John W., Pfc,
Kukuo, Edward J., Cpl,
Kulesza, Theodore W., Pvt,
Kunash, Charles J., T/5,
Kupco, John P., Pfc,
Kunz, Philip H., Pvt,
Kyzar, Bertram E., T/4,

Lacefield, Marvin R., Pvt,
Lacina, Walter F.,
Lacy, Ray S., Pfc,
LaCoste, Leo P., Sgt,
LaDuke, Franklin R., Sgt,
LaFlamme, Joseph L., Pfc,
LaFrance, Omer, Pfc,
†Lalla, Emanuel D., Pfc,
Lamb, Leonard H., Sgt,
Lambert, Francis X., Capt,
Lamp, Edward F., S/Sgt,
Landou, Ralph, Pfc,
Lane, Erman, Pfc,
‡Lane, Earl C., Pfc,
Lane, Walter F., S/Sgt,
Lang, Ralph K., S/Sgt,
Langan, Thomas L., Sgt,
Langelotti, Joseph F., Pvt,
Langley, Emitt R., Pfc,
Langleis, Milford D., Sgt,
Langstaff, William J., Pfc,
Lanich, Clyde C., Cpl,
Langston, Autry, 2nd Lt,
Large, Henry, T/4,
†LaRocca, Albert, Pvt,
Larsen, Alfred J., Pfc,
Larson, Rudolph E., Sgt,
Latta, Raymond E., Sgt,
Latz, Mack L., Pfc,
Lavin, Douglas E., Pfc,
Lawler, Arley B., Pfc,
Lawrence, George E., Pfc,
Layton, Donald W., T/5,
Lazar, Bernard, Pvt,
Lazzari, George G., Pfc,
Leach, Carl M., Pfc,
†LeBlanc, Paul R. J., Pvt,
Lebo, Leonard, 1st Lt,
Lebowitz, Victor, Pvt,
LeBrun, Joseph L., T/5,
Leedom, John O., Pfc,
Lees, Donald G., Cpl,
Legg, Robert L., Capt,
Leitner, Paul S., T/5,
LeMay, Emile J., Pfc,
Lemoine, Alven P., T/5,
Lenihan, William F., Pvt,
Lesh, Thaddeus E., T/4
Lewis, Alvin R., Pvt,
Lewis, William E., T/5,
Lindsay, Harry K., T/5,
Linkey, Ernest W., 2nd Lt,
Linsay, Jack E., Pfc,
Linser, Edward J., S/Sgt,
Liona, Walter A., T/5,
Littleton, Emory E., Pfc,
Lizotte, Albert J., Pvt,
Lockwood, James C., T/5,
Lokey, William H., Maj,
Lombardi, Serverino S., S/Sgt,
Long, Hobart E., Pfc,
Long, Norland E., Pfc,
†Lopacki, Joseph, T/4,
†Loper, James L., Pfc,
Lopez, Willie, Pvt,
Lorenzo, Anthony J., Pfc,
Loschke, Homer L., Pfc,
Loughrey, James, Pfc,
Love, John B., Pvt,
Loveitt, Richard C., Cpl,
Lovelace, Bruce M., Pvt,
Lowenbach, M. R., Jr., Pfc,
Lundell, Emil A., T/5,
Lundquist, Harold E., Pfc,
Lustig, Henry, Pvt,
Luthi, Robert A., 1st Lt,
Lydiard, Charles W., Capt,
Lykins, LeRoy L., Pvt,
Lyman, Matthew J., Sgt,
Lynch, Arthur, Sgt,
†Lynch, Kenneth, S/Sgt,
Lyons, Brian V., Sgt,

Macklin, George F., Capt,
MacLean, Clifford E., Sgt,
MacNeil, John J., T/5,
Macri, Vincent J., Pfc,
Mader, Merrill T., T/5,
Magdali, O'Neil, Pvt,
Magerka, Walter, T/5,
Magolis, William V., Pvt,
Mahon, William F., Pvt,
Mahoney, James P., Capt,
Maiorano, Joseph, Pvt,
Major, Joseph J., S/Sgt,
Makhoul, Nicholas, E/5,
Makrai, Joseph Cpl,
Maksimowich, Walter, T/5,
Male, Roy R., Jr., Sgt,
Malone, Richard C., Pfc,
Mancini, Adolph, Pvt,
Maningo, Joseph, Pfc,
Manley, Dorrence C., T/5,
Mann, Wiley, Sgt,
Manning, Henry G., Sgt,
Marcus, Lawrence R., 1st Lt,
Margiewicz, Edmond P., Pfc,
†Markel, James E., Cpl,
†Markowski, Benjamin J., Sgt,
Marks, Thomas, S/Sgt,
Maroney, Henry S., Pfc,
Marquez, Ignacio, Jr., Pvt,
Marshall, Stanley, Pvt,
Martell, John W., Sgt,
Martell, Lawrence W., T/5,
Martin, Arnold W., T/5,
Martin, John A., Sgt,
Martin, Walter E., Pvt,
Martinez, Guillermo, Pvt,
Marvin, Charles B., T/4,
Masters, William, S/Sgt,
Masterson, John P., Cpl,
Mathews, Charles C., Pfc,
Mathewson, Kenneth C., Pfc,
Matte, Cecil J., Pvt,
Matter, Lester D., Jr., Capt,
Mattis, Benjamin, J., T/5,
Mattys, John, T/5,
Mauer, Milton L., Pfc,
*Maymon, Herbert L., Pfc,
Maynard, Robert A., Capt,
Mayne, Woodrow, Pvt,
Maxey, Ralph W., Cpl,
Mazur, John M., S/Sgt,
Mazzola, Nicholas C., Sgt,
McAvoy, Philip A., Pfc,
McAninch, Carl C., Pfc,
McAndrew, Robert N., Pvt,
McBreen, James J., T/5,
McBride, Jasper H., T/5,
McBroom, Burt E., T/5,
McCarthy, John M., Sgt,
McClellan, Thomas W., Pfc,
McClure, Edward S., T/5,
McClusky, Archie M., Pfc,
McCormick, Vincent A., Pfc,
MDermott, Robert J., Sgt,
McDermott, Robert M., Pvt,
†McDonough, Michael E., Pvt,
McElroy, Robert C., S/Sgt,
McEvans, Lincoln J., T/4,
McFarland, Allen G., T/Sgt,
McGowan, Joseph M., Pvt,
McGrath, Robert J., Pvt,
McGrath, William A., T/5,
McGuirk, Leo, Pvt,
McIntyre, Albert J., Pfc,
McLaughlin, Edward J., Sgt,
McLean, Frank B., Jr., Sgt,
McLemore, Harold E., Pvt,
McNeal, Paul T., Pvt,
McNeely, Richard C., M/Sgt,
McPhee, Ellsworth B., Pfc,
Meczywor, Longin M., Cpl,
Medeiros, Jose, Cpl,
†Meeks, Burl E., Pvt,
Mehl, John F., S/Sgt,
Meister, Elmer A., T/5,
Mejeur, Garritt, Pfc,
Mello, Antone J., Sgt,
Mendez, Ralph M., Pfc,
Merget, Anthony J., T/5,
Merrill, Gilbert R., Pfc,
Merritt, Charles W., Pvt,
Messina, Anthony, Pvt,
Meyers, Paul C., Pvt,
Miceli, Louis C., Cpl,
Michelli, Thomas D., Pfc,
Migliaccio, Salvatore H., T/Sgt
Milanovich, Michael, Pfc,
Milbery, James M., Sgt,
Milburn, George W., Cpl,
Milke, William J., Cpl,
Millard, Alfred J., T/5,
Miller, Arthur, Pvt,
Miller, Calvin E., T/5,
Miller, Francis E., T/4,
Miller, Francis L., Pfc,
Miller, Henry J., Jr., Cpl
Miller, James E., T/5,
Miller, John B., 1st Lt,
Miller, Joseph, Pfc,
†Miller, Walter, Pvt,
Miller, William J., Pvt,
Miller, William J., T/5,

† Killed in Action. * Prisoner of War. ‡ Missing in Action. § Died of Wounds.

Mills, Charles S., Pfc,
Mills, John E., 2nd Lt,
Mills, John H., Cpl,
Mills, Warren E., Jr., Cpl,
Minard, David E., T/5,
Miner, Frederick C., Maj,
Minogue, Thomas J., T/5,
Miranda, Louis O., T/4,
Misulich, Joseph, Cpl,
†Mitchell, Charles A., Cpl,
Mitchell, Henry E., Capt,
Mitchell, Joseph H., Cpl,
Mojsl, Rudolph G., Pfc,
Molloy, Troys M., Cpl,
Monahan, Joseph W., T/5,
Montgomery, Melvin G., Pvt,
Moody, Grady, Pfc,
Moon, George R, Jr., 1st Lt,
Moon, Walter C., Pfc,
Mooneyham, Clifton W., 1st Lt.
Moneymaker, Charles A., Pvt,
Moore, Charles C., Pfc
Moore, Donald J., T/5,
Moore, Everett S., Sgt,
†Moore, Robert H., Cpl,
Moore, Robert L., 1st Sgt,
Moore, Rollin O., 1st Sgt,
Morano, Dominick T., T/5,
Morehart, Cecil C., Pvt,
Moreland, Merle R., Jr., Pfc,
Moreland, Walter, Pfc,
Morey, Frank M., Sgt,
Morgan, Frederick H., Pfc,
Morgan, Norman L., Pfc,
Moriarty, Edward C., T/4,
Morone, Angelo P., S/Sgt,
Morrison, Thomas E., T/5,
Morrissey, Edward F., Sgt,
Morse, Raymond C., T/5,
Morvant, Robert J., Sgt,
Moses, Joseph A., Pvt,
Mosier, Edson E., T/5,
Moyer, Myron R., T/4,
Mulcahy, John J., S/Sgt,
Mulkey, James O., Pvt,
Mullen, John W., 1st Sgt,
Mullen, Robert, T/4,
†Muller, Clayton F., Cpl,
Mullins, Edward T., Pvt,
Mullins, Theodore F., T/5,
Mullis, Don J., Sgt,
Munn, Charles N., 1st Lt,
†Murphy, Charles J., Pvt,
Murphy, Francis T., Pvt,
Murray, Joseph F., Sgt,
Muse, Raymond W., Jr., Sgt,
Mutchler, Donald J., Pfc,
†Myers, Robert E., 2nd Lt,
Myrick, William H., Cpl,

Nabywaniec, Joseph S/Sgt,
Nagurka, John E., Pvt,
Naparty, William, Cpl,
Napier, Basil, Pfc,
Nash, Bernard L., T/5,
Natoli, Bartolo, Pvt,
Neary, Thomas A., S/Sgt,
Neikirk, Ray F., Cpl,
Nelson, Carl M., T/5,
Nelson, Hayden A., T/Sgt,
Nelson, James, T/5,
†Nelson, Oucie, Pvt,
Nemenz, Richard C., Pfc,
Nerthing, Carl H., Sgt,
Nesmith, Willis B., Sgt,
Nevers, Philip O., S/Sgt,
Newcom, Willie B., Pvt,
Newton, Gilert R., T/5,
Nickeson, Rudolph F., Pfc,
Niliba, Stanley J., Pfc,
Nolan, Michael R., T/5,
Norman, Walter I., Pvt,
Novak, Stephen J., Jr., T/4,
Novich, Steve, Pfc,
Nowak, John, Sgt,

O'Brien, James F., S/Sgt,
*O'Brien, Harold L., S/Sgt,
Oden, John K., Pvt,
O'Donnell, John C., Cpl,
Oglenski, Leonard, Pfc,
O'Hara, John J., Pvt,
O'Hare, Francis J., Pvt,
O'Kane, Thomas R., Pvt,
O'Keefe, James E., Pfc,
Olish, Adam R., Pfc,
O'Neil, John A., Pvt,
O'Neil, John J., Pvt,
Opperman, Nelson M., T/4,
Orlinski, Joseph J., Pfc,
Orr, Delmar D., T/5,
Orsini, Andrew J., T/4,
Osbun, Earl, Pvt,
Ostrobinski, Stanley J., T/4,
Osuchowski, William W., Sgt,

Owen, John C., T/5,
Owen, William T., T/4,
Ozment, Charley C., T/5,

Paino, John, Pvt,
Palmer, Edward J., Sgt,
Panico, Ralph, Sgt,
Panier, Edgar V., Pfc,
Panther, George B., Pvt,
Pappas, Alexander M., Pvt,
Parent, Joseph A., Jr., T/4,
Parent, Roger L., Pvt,
Parente, Nunzie P., Pfc,
Parkhurst, Myron K., Sgt,
Parkhurst, William G., Sgt,
Park, Jacob M., Jr., Pvt,
Parker, Clarence G., Pvt,
Parks, Roy E., T/5,
Parks, Walter M. C., T/5,
Parson, John W., Pfc,
Parman, Raymond, Pfc,
Parobeck, Henry J., S/Sgt,
Patronski, Benjamin W., Pvt,
Patterson, Ted L., Pvt,
Pattie, William, Pfc,
Paul, Donald M., Pvt,
Paulick, Michael, Capt,
Pearson, Freddie H., T/5,
Pearce, Henry N., T/5,
Peck, Walter L., T/4,
Peifer, Wilbur A., Cpl,
Pellegrini, Emanuel A., Pfc,
Pelletier, Frederick J., S/Sgt,
Penhollow, Frank, Cpl,
Penn, Charles N., Jr., 1st Sgt,
†Pennington, Johnny H., Pvt,
Penny, William J., T/3,
Penski, Philip, Pvt,
Peranio, William J., Pvt,
Perry, Howard E., Pvt,
Perry, John C., Capt,
Perry, Steven A., Pfc,
Peters, Ralph G., Pfc,
Peterson, Arnold K., Pfc,
Peterson, Ralph L., Pvt,
Petitbon, Leo A., 1st Lt,
Pettee, Frederick R., Pvt,
†Petteruto, Alphonse J., T/4,
Pfalzgraf, George H., Pvt,
Ffeifer, Arthur J., Pvt,
Pfleger, Jack F., T/5,
Pfleger, Robert G., T/5,
Phallen, Charles W., T/Sgt,
Phelps, Roswell F., Sgt,
Phillips, Richard D., Pvt,
Philipovich, George, 1st Lt,
Philip, Philip, T/4,
Philson, George H., Pfc,
Piaggi, Francis E., Pfc,
Picard, Ovila H., Sgt,
Piccitto, Salvatore, T/5,
Picotte, Clarence E., Pfc,
†Pierce, Alvin L., Sgt,
Pierce, Daxton, Pfc,
Pierce, Oren A., Pvt,
Piland, John, Pvt,
Pinkham, Woodrow W., Pfc,
Piper, Edward A., Cpl,
Pisacane, John A., Pfc,
Pivarski, Vincent, Pfc,
Pizzi, Anthony F., Pfc,
Poff, Kenneth S., Cpl,
Pohanick, Michael G., T/5,
Poindexter, Robert A., T/4,
Polakoff, George J., Pfc,
Poler, Erwin C., Pfc,
†Pollet, George, Sgt,
Polokoski, Joseph F., Pfc,
Poore, Henry B., T/4,
Poore, Lewis C., T/4,
Poorman, Paul K., Sgt,
Poretz, Bernard, T/5,
Porter, Floyd J., T/5,
Porter, James M., Pvt,
Porter, Ralph R., Cpl,
Porter, William H., T/4,
Porterfield, Claude F., Pfc,
Posey, Adrian H., T/5,
Potter, William G., Pfc,
Poulson, Ralph C., Pvt,
Povanda, Spencer A., T/5,
Powell, Burley F., T/5,
Powers, Edward L., T/4,
†Powers, Forrent F., Cpl,
†Powers, William C., T/5,
Pratt, Howard J., T/4,
†Prauman, Earl L., S/Sgt,
†Prevo, Lloyd J., Pvt,
Price, Edward A., Pvt,
Price, Leonard W., Pfc,
Prichard, Marvin, Pvt,
Preziosi, Alphonse A., Pfc,
Privitera, Samuel F., T/5,
Provenzano, Ralph J., Pvt,
Pruitt, Pleamon H., T/Sgt,

†Pruse, Thomas J., Pfc,
Puchta, John H., Pfc,
Puckett, Leo J., T/5,
Puckett, Woodrow W., Sgt,
Pursley, Elwood C., Pvt,
Purvis, Howard L., T/5,

Quanstrom, Clyde E., T/4,
Quinn, John J., Pvt,
Quinney, Lywood, Pfc,

Raiti, Frank J., Pvt,
Rambo, Ralph R., Pfc,
Rasner, Ernest C., Pfc,
Ratner, Joseph M., Pfc,
*Rauchwarger, Abe, Pfc,
Raymond, Adolph I., S/Sgt,
Raymond, Leo O., T/5,
Redding, Laven, Pvt,
Rees, Harold S., Pfc,
Reese, Robert C., Pfc,
Reimer, Clayton A., T/5,
Reis, Charles D., T/5,
Reschke, Fred J., Jr., Pfc,
Rhodes, Edward J., T/5,
Rice, Carmon H., T/4,
Rice, Walter R., Pvt.
Richards, E. N., Jr., 1st Sgt,
Richardson, Samuel G., Capt,
Rickard, James F., Cpl,
Riddleberger, Patrick W., Capt,
Riedel, Warren F., T/5,
Riler, Ernest, Pvt,
Riley, Richard E., Pvt,
Ring, Martin R., Pvt,
Ringer, Frank, Pvt,
Riordan, Daniel F., Sgt,
Ritchie, Harry J., Sgt,
†Ritso, John C., S/Sgt,
Rivers, Francis J., T/5,
Roberts, Archie J., Cpl,
Roberts, Harry E., Pfc,
Roberts, James W., Pfc,
Roberts, Raymond J., 1st Lt,
Robertson, Edgar J., Sgt,
Robertson, John B., Pvt,
*Robinson, Charles T., Pfc,
Robinson, Frederick N., Pfc,
Robinson, Marion, T/5,
Robinson, Walter W., Pfc,
Rodeffer, Rudolph Y., T/5,
Rodgers, John H., Jr., T/5,
Rodriquez, Demetrio T., Pvt,
Rogers, Curtis H., T/Sgt,
Rogers, Otis R., 1st Lt,
Rogers, Jackson A., Sgt,
†Rogers, Jefferson S., Pvt,
Rogove, Harry, Pfc,
Rogowski, Frank J., Pfc,
Rolli, Aldo,
†Rosenfeld, David, T/5,
Rosick, Michael, Cpl,
Rothenberg, Harry L.,
Rothgeb, James W., Pfc,
Rothstein, Allen M., Pvt,
Rotkiewicz, Edward C., T/5,
Rottmann, Nicholas G., Sgt,
Rouse, Patrick L., Pfc,
Rowe, Thomas G., Pvt,
Roy, Eugene F., Pvt,
Rubin, Max, Pfc,
Ruderman, Barney B., 1st Lt,
Rudy, John V., T/4,
Russell, Elmer, Pvt.
Russell, James E., Pvt,
Ryan, John F., Sgt,
Rychlik, Lee, Pvt,
Rybski, Alexander J., T/5,
Ryder, Emmett R., T/5,
Rysz, Edmund P., Sgt,
Ryznar, Anthony J., T/5,

†Sabala, John S., Sgt,
Sackett, John H., Cpl,
Sadlier, Robert N., T/5,
Sakowski, John J., T/5,
Salanitri, Vincent, Pvt,
Saling, Albert J., Pvt,
Salfen, Ambrose G., Capt,
Sanders, Kenneth V., Pvt,
Sanders, Ryndal L., 1st Lt,
Sanders, Walter B., Pfc,
†Sandoval, Toney T., Pvt,
Sanford, Ernest R., T/5,
Santasiera, Michael A., S/Sgt,
Santelli, John, Pvt,
Santoro, Anthony, T/4,
Sargent, Cone J., T/4,
Sasso, Anthony, Pvt,
Satterfield, Ralph E., T/5,
‡Sauklis, John, T/5,
Saul, Henry, Sgt,
Saunders, Clyde W., Pvt,
Savitski, Augustine W., T/4,
Sawyer, James W., Pvt,

Sawyers, Glenn A., T/5,
Scarpitti, Peter J., S/Sgt,
Schara, Charles A., T/5,
Scharlach, Robert M., Pvt,
Scheer, Hamilton, Pvt,
Schirmer, Charles W., Sgt,
Schmelz, Leo E., Pfc,
Schmidt, Charles D., T/5,
Schmitt, August A., Pfc,
Schneider, Eugene J., Pfc,
Schneider, John P., 1st Lt,
Scholl, Eugene F., Pfc,
Schools, Thomas C., Cpl,
Schroader, Joyce, Sgt,
Schwartz, Carl F., T/4,
Schwartz, Eugene, Pvt,
Schwartzman, Francis, T/5,
†Schwebach, Clarence J., Pfc,
†Schweizer, John J., Pfc,
Scofield, James J., Pvt,
Scoggins, Joseph W., Sgt,
Scott, Clarence V., Pvt,
Scott, Herbert C., T/5,
Scott, Lloyd, Pvt,
Scott, Robert, T/4,
Scott, William W., T/5,
Seaman, John J., T/5,
See, Raymond W., T/5,
Segit, Joseph A., 2nd Lt,
Seider, Camilla H., Sgt,
Seiffert, Frank H., 1st Lt,
Sells, Maurice, T/4,
Senuta, Adam W., Sgt,
Sepanski, Michael J., Sgt,
Seward, Charlie C., Pfc,
Shaffer, William G., T/5,
Shaheen, Ralph, T/Sgt,
Shanker, Ruben, T/5,
Shapter, Peter L., Sgt,
Sharp, James L., Cpl,
*Sharpe, Albert E., T/5,
Sheets, Maxwell C., Cpl,
Shell, John G., Pvt,
Shelton, Arthur N., Pfc,
Sheppard, Gerald J., Cpl,
Shields, Blain, Pfc,
Shimak, Stanley H., Cpl,
Shinnick, Jeremiah F., Cpl,
Shipton, Richard, Pvt,
Shively, Jay W., T/4,
Shoemaker, Clyde, T/4,
Shope, William A., Jr., Pfc,
Schrader, Leslie H., T/5,
Shumate, Kemper F., Pfc,
Shumchenia, Michael, S/Sgt,
Shupe, Paul B., T/5,
Sicard, Robert H. W., Cpl,
Sieg, Francis X., Pfc,
Siegil, Arnold, Pvt,
Silva, Antonio, T/Sgt,
Silva, George G., T/4,
Silverfarb, Harold, Pfc,
Silveria, William D., 1st Sgt,
†Silverstein, Morris, Pvt,
Simms, Dale, Pfc,
Sinclair, Milton R., Pfc,
Skarren, Norman C., T/4,
Skeens, Charles W., Pfc,
Skelton, Carl M., Pfc,
Slater, Joseph M., T/5,
Small, Bernard E., T/5,
Smart, Perry W., T/5,
Smedley, Richard E., Cpl,
Smiley, Stewart D., Pvt,
Smith, Arthur R., Pvt,
Smith, Cleatus, T/5,
Smith, Clinton E., Pfc,
Smith, Curtis A., Pvt,
Smith, Delbert W., T/4,
Smith, George E., T/5,
Smith, Hugh B., Pvt,
Smith, James E., Pfc,
Smith, James N., Pvt,
†Smith, John A., Sgt,
‡Smith, John F., Sgt,
Smith, Lynwood A., Cpl,
Smith, Malon W., Pfc,
†Smith, Richard T., Pvt,
Smith, Russell W., T/5,
Smith, Warren A., Sgt,
Smith, William G., Pvt,
Smith, Willie G., T/5,
*Smoot, Charlie E., Pvt,
Snailer, Matthew J., Pvt,
†Snowden, Chester E., Pfc,
Snyder, Harold A., Cpl,
Solon, Lewis L., Sgt,
Soper, Robert S., T/4,
Sorrells, Gladis W., Pvt,
Spear, Clarence, T/4,
Spear, John J., Pvt,
Spears, Gilbert, Cpl,
Speedling, William, Pvt,
Spence, Theodore F., Pvt,
Spence, Scott, T/5,

Specciati, Emil C., Pfc,
†Spicer, Lynn A., Cpl,
‡Spielberger, George, 1st Lt,
Springer, Alex, T/Sgt,
Springer, John H., Pvt,
Sprouse, Richard J., T/5,
Squire, David P., Pfc,
Stainback, Henry, Jr., Pvt,
Stancliff, Walter S., T/5,
Stansill, LeRoy M., S/Sgt,
Stark, Julius F., Pvt,
Stark, Kenneth B., 1st Lt,
Stassun, Henry C., T/5,
Steele, Donald P., 1st Lt,
†Steele, Robert N., Capt,
Steere, Lyle N., T/4,
Steese, Donald R., Sgt,
Steies, John N., Pfc,
Steinhauer, Charles T., Pvt,
Stepelewick, Joseph W., Pvt,
Stephenson, Vernie O., Cpl,
Stevens, Daniel A., T/5,
Stevens, James R., T/5,
Stevenson, Fred P., Sgt,
†Stevenson, George E., Capt,
Stevenson, Richard V., Capt,
Stewart, James C., Cpl,
Stewart, John, Pvt,
Stima, Michael W., S/Sgt,
Stinson, Milton T., Pvt,
St. Jean, Robert L., Pvt,
Stockley, Russell H., T/4,
Stokes, Joe C., S/Sgt,
†Stone, Kenneth H., S/Sgt,
Storey, Ernest M., Pfc,
*Stotts, Wilcher C., 2nd Lt,
Stow, Russell A., 1st Sgt,
Strack, John H., Pfc,
Strange, Carl H., Cpl,
Streshenkoff, Nick J., T/5,
Strickland, Dorsey R., T/5,
Strickland, Garland, Pvt,
Strickland, James C., Pvt,
*Strickland, James W., T/5,
Strisco, Michael J., 1st Lt,
Strunk, Clifford, S/Sgt,
Strzepek, Stanley A., T/5,
Stuart, Anthony L., Pvt,
Stuart, Thomas, Sgt,
Stuart, Thomas M., Jr., Pvt,
Stuart, William N., T/5,
*Sturak, Mike, Pvt,
Sudol, Edward J., Pvt,
Sullivan, Jeremiah, Pvt,
Sullivan, Latson P., T/4,
Summer, Joseph, Pvt,
Summers, Charles J., T/4,
Summerville, Harold R., T/4
Sunderland, Roy L., Jr., Pfc,
Sundstrom, Herbert E., Capt,
Surgenti, Matthew A., Pvt,
Suter, Joseph A., Pvt,
Swartz, Fred E., Sgt,
Swasta, Michael, Pfc,
Swearingen, Jasper T., T/5,
Swigert, John J., Cpl,
Switzer, Arthur, Pvt,
†Swygert, Henry R., Pvt,
Sykes, James M., Jr., Pfc,
†Syrko, Michael, Pvt,
†Szczotka, John F., T/5,

Taggart, George, T/5,
Taitz, Harold, Pfc,
Tanguay, Joseph E., Pvt,
Tannenbaum, Joseph S., Pfc,
Taphorn, Francis J., Sgt,
Tardif, Joseph M., Sgt,
Tardy, Walter E., Lt Col,
Tarolli, Joseph R., T/5,
Taylor, Alton W., T/5,
Taylor, Billy C., Pfc,
Teachman, Lawrence E., S/Sgt,
Tedesco, Salvatore J., Pvt,
Teets, Fred J., T/4,
†Teff, Robert P., Pfc,
Telecky, Richard C., Sgt,
Telesco, Peter J., T/5,
Tench, Ray, S/Sgt,
Tennison, Tom L., Pvt,
Tenorio, Crescencio, Pfc,
Thoele, Joseph G., Jr.,
Thomas, Daman L., T/Sgt,
Thomas, David P., Cpl,
Thomas, Henry R., Pvt,
†Thomas, Joseph, T/4,
Thompson, Clifford B., 1st Lt,
Thompson, Earl E., Jr., Sgt,
Thompson, Henry H., Pfc,
*Thompson, James H., Cpl,
Thompson, John W., T/[illegible].
Thornton, Herman L., Pfc,
Tibbets, Donald, Pvt,
Tijerina, Nicholas, T/5,
Tilley, J. R., Sgt,

† Killed in Action. * Prisoner of War. ‡ Missing in Action. § Died of Wounds.

Timmer, Albert, Jr., T/5,
Tobiczyk, John E., T/5,
Tomb, Frederick J., Pvt,
Tompkins, James T., Pfc,
Toplitz, Irving A., Pfc,
Trump, John W., Jr., Pvt,
Tryon, Raymond N., Pfc,
Tucker, Taylor E., Sgt,
Tuley, Lester B., Pfc,
Tulis, Edwin J., T/5,
Tullos, Steven W., T/5,
†Turano, Philip J., Cpl,
Turner, Charles J., Pfc,
Turner, Marvin E., Pvt,

†Uhlinger, George R., Pfc,
Ullrich, Emil A., Pfc,
Upton, Charles G., Pvt,
Utter, William H., Sgt.

Vagg, Byron W., Pvt,
Vancheri, Samuel J., Pvt,
Van Der Mark, George W., Sgt,
†Van Elk, Gilbert J., Pfc,
Van Kuren, Francis, S/Sgt,
Van Renssalaer, Philip M., Cpl,
†Vargo, Frank A., Cpl,
‡Vargo, John C., 2nd Lt,

Vellucco, Louis, Cpl,
Verolini, Armondo A., Pfc,
Vickerelli, Peter M., Pfc,
Villegas, Jesus M., Pfc,
Villeman, Marietz, Pvt,
Vita, Stefano, Sgt,
Vogt, Louis P., Pvt,

Wade, Willie A., Pfc
Wagner, Frank W., CWO,
Walker, Ernest L., Pvt,
Walker, John W., Cpl,
Walkowski, Edward H., T/4,
Walkup, Walter B., T/4,
Wallack, George L., 1st Lt,
Wallack, Julius A., Pfc,
Walls, William M., Sgt,
Ward, Armon B., Pvt,
Ward, Joseph P., S/Sgt,
Ward, Thomas, S/Sgt,
Ward, Willard D., Cpl,
Wardwell, Walter I., Capt,
Waren, Kenneth D., Pvt,
Warren, Louis W., Pfc,
†Wasilk, Francis J., Pfc,
Wasko, Mike, Sgt,
Waters, John, Pvt,
Waters, William J., T/4,

Watrous, Arthur H., Pvt,
Watson, William F., Pvt,
†Watters, Richard, Pfc,
Watwood, Acy C., T/5,
Way, Robert E., Pvt,
Waymire, Harry F., Pvt,
Weatherwax, James A., T/5,
Weber, Ralph R., Pfc,
Weber, Sterl W., Pvt
Webster, Theodore R., Sgt,
†Wedell, Wilbur M., Pvt,
Weedman, Jean W., 1st Lt,
Weidner, John V., T/5,
Weier, William M., Cpl,
Weintraub, Morris, Pfc,
Welch, Thomas P., 1st Lt,
Wells, Earl, T/5,
Westberry, Artise, Pvt,
Wharton, George E., Pfc,
Wheeler, Roscoe M., Pfc,
Whiddon, Elzie A., Pfc,
White, Carl C., Pvt,
White, Harvey L., T/4,
White, Norwood C., Pvt,
White, Stafford T., Sgt,
White, Ted C., Pvt,
Whitehair, Gilbert T., Pfc,
Whitson, Mansfield E., Pfc,

Whittingham, Norman J., T/4,
Wilby, Albert, S/Sgt,
Wilczyz, Steve S., Pvt,
Wilkins, Oliver L., Jr., Pfc,
Willey, Reid, Pfc,
Williams, Carl H., T/5,
Williams, Carl P., Cpl,
Williams, Paul H., Pfc,
Williamson, Deltha J., Pvt,
Williamson, John T., Sgt,
Wilson, Barnett, T/5,
Wilson, Frank F., Sgt,
Wilson, James E., Pvt,
Wilson, James E., Pfc,
Wilson, Virgil J., T/5,
Wilson, Warren W., Pfc,
Winters, Leo W., Pvt,
Winters, Troy E., Pfc,
Wise, Earl L., Cpl,
Wisnewski, John B., Pfc,
Wolowicz, Anthony M., Pvt.
Wood, Everett F., Pvt,
Woodall, James E., Pfc,
Woods, John F., Sgt,
Woods, Loren A., Pfc,
Worley, Harry E., Pfc,
Wray, James A., T/5,
Wright, Roy G., T/5,

Wright, Troy, Pvt
Wrona, Joseph K., T/5,
Wurst, Christian E., Pvt,

†Yadaresto, Dominic, Pvt,
Yaggle, Lester R., Pvt,
Yancek, Joseph J., Pfc,
Yerg, Joseph M., Pfc,
Yielding, John D., Pvt,
York, James O., S/Sgt,
Young, Forest L., Pfc,
Young, Karl R., Sgt,
Young, Robert R., Pfc,
Young, Wilmer A., Pvt,
Youngblood, Billy R., S/Sgt,
Yowell, John D., 1st Lt,

Zadnik, William, T/5,
Zafron, Joseph H., Pvt,
Zamora, Geronimo, Pvt,
Zemrose, Louis, Pvt,
Zerley, Bernard R., Pfc,
†Zielewicz, Joseph S., S/Sgt,
Zielinski, Charles, Pvt.
Zwilling, Sol, Pfc,
Zylstra, Harold W., Pfc,
Zyskowski, Leo, Pfc.

† Killed in Action.   * Prisoner of War.   ‡ Missing in Action.   § Died of Wounds.

756TH TANK BATTALION

Another of the 3d Infantry Division's long-time major attachments was the 756th Tank Battalion. The spirit of this organization is reflected by the fact that two of its members were posthumously awarded the Congressional Medal of Honor for actions performed during the passage of the Vosges Mountains.

The 756th was activated as a light tank battalion on June 1, 1941, at Fort Lewis, Washington. The battalion received its first training at Fort Lewis as part of IX Corps. It first joined the 3d Infantry Division after it left Fort Lewis on August 4, 1942, at Fort Ord, California, and it was there it took its first amphibious training.

At Camp Pickett, Virginia, Company A (reinforced) was attached to the 7th Infantry, and Company C (reinforced) was attached to the 30th Infantry. The remainder of the battalion went to Fort Dix, New Jersey on November 28, 1942, for further staging. Companies A and C landed with the 3d Division at Fedala and assisted the Division in establishing and exploiting one of the first beachheads in the North African theater.

The remainder of the Battalion rejoined its units at Port Lyautey in February, 1943. It was relieved of attachment to the Division on May 7 and moved to Pont du Cheliff, Algeria under control of I Armored Corps. Its next move was to Petit Port in May and to Magenta, Algeria early in June, where it trained with elements of the Fifth Army Tank Destroyer school.

The first combat commitment of the 756th was at Paestum on September 17, attached to the 45th Infantry Division. It was re-attached to the 34th Infantry Division on October 1, after having supported the 45th in action, and continued in this mission until October 20, when it reverted to VI Corps control.

After numerous combat missions, the unit was re-designated from 756th Tank Battalion (L) to 756th Tank Battalion by authority of General Order No. 107, Headquarters Fifth Army, dated December 15, 1943.

The Battalion supported the 34th Division on the first and second attempts at crossing the Rapido River, the second of which, on January 29, was successful. The 756th was the first Allied unit into Cassino. The Battalion continued in close support of the 34th Division until February 22, when it was relieved after having suffered heavy casualties in personnel and tanks.

During the period from May 11, 1944 to June 10 the Battalion was attached no less than eleven times, each one for combat. It participated in all phases of the drive on Rome. It was not relieved until June 10, six days after the fall of Rome.

The 756th Tank Battalion was attached to the 3d Infantry Division at Qualiano, near Naples on June 19, as the Division was preparing for its part in the invasion of southern France.

Except for two brief periods with the 103d Infantry Division, the 756th remained with the 3d Division for the rest of the war. Its hardest fight came during the Colmar Pocket battle, in which accurate enemy *panzerfaust,* bazooka and tank destroyer fire accounted for much of its armor. The Battalion in turn, however exacted a heavy toll in enemy armor and personnel.

From D-day, August 15, 1944, until May 8, 1945, the Battalion was continuously in action except for one ten-day period.

Commanding Officer

(Highest rank held)	Held pos. from	To
Lt. Col. Harry W. Sweeting		2 Mar 1944
Maj. Welborn G. Dolvin	2 Mar 1944	13 Mar 1944
Lt. Col. Glenn F. Rogers	13 Mar 1944	14 Feb 1945
Maj. Oscar S. Long	14 Feb 1945	13 April 1945
Maj. Edwin Y. Arnold	13 April 1945	

Abbott, Harvey, 1st Lt,
Abrahamson, Arthur, 1st Lt,
Abshire, Carl E., T/5,
Ackerman, Walter R., S/Sgt,
Adams, Ervan I. M/Sgt,
Adams, Roy L., Pfc,
Adams, Steve, Pfc,
Addeo, Samuel J., Pvt,
Adkins, Drury C., Cpl,
Adlard, Ithel R., S/Sgt,
Admoites, Paul P., Pfc,
Akers, Howard L., T/5,
Alderman, Samuel I., 1st Lt,
Alee, Harry W., Pvt,
Alfieri, Patsy, Pvt,
Allard, Howard A., Pvt,
Allen, Charles B., Capt,
Allen, William M., Sgt,
Alonge, Sam F., T/5,
Ambroziak, John, T/4,
Ames, Thomas P., S/Sgt,
Amorello, Philip G., Pfc,
Anders, William E., Pvt,
Andersen, Paul C., Pfc,
Anderson, Donald L., S/Sgt,
Anderson, Harley, Sgt,
Anderson, Roy L., S/Sgt,
Andreoli, Americo, Pfc,
Andrew, Thomas H., T/5,
Andrews, William H., Sgt,
Andring, Ted H., Sgt,
Andrus, Gerald C., Pfc,
Anfuso, Frank P., Pvt,
Angerer, Bennie B., T/5,
Angle, Frank P., S/Sgt,
Anglin, Suel C., S/Sgt,
Annichiarico, Vincent, Pvt,
Aragon, Filimon, Pvt,
Arbini, Joseph M., T/4,
Armstrong, Donald O., Pfc,
Arndt, Daniel, Cpl,
Arnold, Edwin Y., Maj,
Arrendale, Roscoe, Pfc,
Arruda, Lewis E., T/5,
‡Atkins, Clyde L., Cpl,
Attello, Joseph A., T/4,
Auer, John J., Sgt,
Austin, Richard L., Pfc,
*Avetttant, Edward A., T/4,
Aycock, George, Pfc,
Ayers, Edgar P., T/5,

‡Bacha, John F., Pvt,
Baer, Robert S., Pvt,
Balaban, George L., Pvt,
Ballard, Russell W., Pvt,
Bandera, Kenneth E., Pvt,
Banham, LeRoy F., T/Sgt,
Barber, Thomas M., T/5
†Barger, James R., Sgt,
Barger, Ralph L., T/5,
Barker, Robert D., Cpl,
Barnard, Ernest P., T/4,
Barnes, Lee P., Sgt,
Barnes, Ralph, T/5,
Barnett, Charles E., Cpl,
Barney, Jose L., Pfc,
†Baron, William J., Cpl,
Barry, Charles A., Pvt,
Bart, J., T/5,
Basham, Leverett J., T/5,
Basich, Antone G., 1st Sgt,
Bates, Samuel C., T/4,
†Bates, Stuart M., Pfc,
Battaglino, Tony J., T/5
†Bayless Herman J., T/4,
Beal, Abe C., T/5,
Beam, Roy, T/5,
Bearden, Neal E., Pfc,
Beavers, Ernest E., T/5,
Beck, Everett L., T/4,
Beckwith, John P., 2nd Lt,
†Behymer, Harold M., Sgt,
Bell, Everett N., Cpl,
Benadom, Max, S/Sgt,
Benedict, Julian, T/5,
Bentancour, Ignacio V., Cpl,
Berg, Arvid, Cpl,
Bergbower, Roy J., T/5,

Bergheger, Louis H., T/5,
Berkouski, John E., 1st Sgt,
Bernhard, George W., Sgt,
Berry, Glen W., T/Sgt,
Bettis, Nathan W., Sgt,
Bigler, Mont L., 1st Sgt,
Bikelites, Poll, Cpl,
Bindas, Nick, Pvt,
Birmingham, Jesse E., Pfc,
†Birtinen, Joseph P., Pvt,
Blackwell, James H., Sgt,
Blair, Milton E., Pfc,
Blakely, Richard C., Cpl,
†Blanchard, Thomas A., Cpl,
Blanco, Stanley C., Pfc,
Blanford, Forrest M., 1st Lt,
Blankenship, Glen J., Pfc,
Blankenship, John C., T/4,
Blose, Donald E., Pfc,
Blosser, Lamar C., T/4,
†Blythe, Winston L., 2nd Lt,
Boenzle, Arthur C., Cpl,
Bogart, Elmer K., T/5,
Bogart, Robert C., Pvt,
†Bohland, Robert A., Pvt,
Bonora, Phillip, T/5,
Boose, Isaac J., Cpl,
Borsock, Andrew J., Pvt,
Bosmay, John C., Pfc,
Boston, William W., Sgt,
Bostwick, John J., T/4,
Botts, Clie L., S/Sgt,
Bouch, William F., 1st Lt,
Boucher, Charles J., Cpl,
Boutilier, George A., S/Sgt,
Bowden, John N., Cpl,
Bowerman, David H., Jr., Pvt,
Bowers, Howard J., T/4,
Bowles, Earl H., Pfc,
Bowman, Johnnie E., Sgt,
Bowser, Gerald E., Pfc,
†Boyer, William R., T/5,
Boyle, Andy E., S/Sgt,
Bradburn, Morin, S/Sgt,
Bramblett, Simon, Sgt,
Brant, Quin E., Cpl,
Braswell, Walter B., Pfc,
Braun, Robert L., T/4,
Brenneman, Raymond V., T/5,
†Brewer, Charles R., T/5,
Brewer, James E. Cpl,
Brody, Michael, S/Sgt,
Brooks, Merle E., T/5,
Brown, Bedford M., T/4,
Brown, Jack H., Sgt,
Brown, James B., T/5,
Brown, Joseph W., Cpl,
Brown, Orus M., T/5,
Broz, Otto L., Cpl,
Brustuen, Reider, Pfc,
Bryant, Walter J., T/5,
Buckley, Robert C., Pfc,
Buczynski, Joseph, Pvt,
Budreckis, John A., T/5,
Buford, Fred C., Pvt,
Buisset, William H., Pvt,
Bulen, Bertie L., T/4,
†Bullock, Raymond W., Sgt,
Bungay, Edward A., T/5,
Burcham, Harding, Pvt,
Burdette, Roy C., T/Sgt,
Burg, Walter E., Cpl,
Burger, Jack E., T/5,
Burgio, Carmelo L., T/5,
Burt, Phillip N., S/Sgt,
Butler, Granger L., Cpl,
Buys, Roland L., Sgt,

Cafaro, Modestino A., T/4,
Cain, Leonard B., Sgt,
Calhoun, Harvey F., Sgt,
Callis, Edwin E., Pvt,
Cameron, Clyde M., Pfc,
Cameron, Weston W., Pfc,
Campbell, Clinton E., T/5,
*Campbell, Leland P., Sgt,
Camperlengo, Patrick J., Pvt,
Cappucci, Armond T., T/5,

†Cardullo, Paul N., Pfc,
Cardwell, Ross, S/Sgt,
Carlson, Stanley E., Pfc,
Carman, Charles E., Pvt,
†Carmello, Frank, Pfc,
Carpino, Michael J., T/5,
Carter, Allan B., T/4,
Carter, John R., Pfc,
Carter, John S., Pvt,
†Carter, Watson O., T/4,
Cartier, Leonard W., Pvt,
Case, William D., T/5,
Casper, Frank J., Pfc,
Castagnola, George P., Pfc,
Castiglione, Arthur, Pvt,
Cates, Victor L., Sr., Pvt,
Cavazos, Raul E.,
Cecilione, Ralph J., Sgt,
Cejka, Frank J., Pvt,
Channel, Clarence E., Pfc,
Chapman, Richard L., Pvt,
Chavez, Ernesto A., Sgt,
Cheever, Francis L., 2nd Lt,
Chiarelli, Peter F., 2nd Lt
Chirico, Angelo, Cpl,
Chisenhall, Preminto E., T/5,
Chotin, Gerald C., Pvt,
Christiansen, Vernon E., Pvt,
Christie, James L., Pvt,
‡Chuba, Bernard T., Pvt,
Cilente, Joseph J., Cpl,
Clapp, Edgar W., T/4,
Clark, Edward J., Sgt,
Clayson, Clark J., Pfc,
Clayton, Elmer H., Jr., Pfc,
†Clayton, Norval N., Pfc,
Clemente, Celestine A., Cpl,
Clerico, David E., Pvt,
†Clow, Dean R., Cpl,
Cobb, Kenneth, Cpl,
Cochran, Harry C., T/4,
Cochran, Thomas E., Sgt,
Cochrane, William R., T/5,
Cockerill Frank R., Jr., S/Sgt,
Cody, Doyle K., Sgt,
Cogdill, Clyde F., Sgt,
*Coleman, Charles H., Cpl,
Coller, Theodore, Cpl,
Colley, Raymond W., S/Sgt,
Collins, George R., Pfc,
Collins, Howard F., T/5,
Collins, Lawrence E., T/5,
Collins, Patrick J., Pfc,
Collins, Roy, 2nd Lt,
Conklin, Donald W., Pfc,
Colvin, Ansel M., Sgt,
Conaway, John G., Sgt,
Conn, Robert W., Pfc,
‡Connor, Charles W., Pfc,
Coody, Everest C., Cpl,
Cook, George W., T/5,
Cook, Norris M., T/5,
Cooke, Cloyce L., Cpl,
Coombs, Richard S., T/5,
Corak, Nick, Sgt,
†Corbitt, Mack N., Sgt,
Corboy, Thomas, Pvt,
Corcoran, George F., T/5,
Cornell, Roger W., Pvt,
†Corson, Melville E., Sgt,
Cory, Richard S., Pfc,
Cothren, Glendon A., Cpl,
Cottongim, Randolph, Cpl,
†Cottonware, Louis E., Pfc,
Cowan, Lynn F., T/4,
Cowley, Kenneth C., Pvt,
Cox, Ned S., T/4,
Cox, Robert B., T/5,
Cox, William T., T/4,
Coyle, Richard G., Cpl,
Crabtree, Edd A., Cpl,
Cramer, Albert C., Pfc,
Cramer, Leonard S., T/5,
*Crawford, Carl T., S/Sgt,
Crenshaw, Oscar T., S/Sgt,
Cristofono, Louis J., Pvt,
†Criswell, Coy H., Sgt,
Crouse, Glen J., Cpl,

Crowe, Valentine, Pvt,
Crumm, William H., T/4,
Culler, William O., Cpl,
Culver, Milton A., Pvt,
Cundiff, John L., Pfc,
Cunningham, Earl W., T/4,
Cunningham, Lionel J., 2nd Lt,
†Current, George A., 1st Lt,
Cutrone, Joseph, Cpl,
Cuzzo, Joseph J., T/5,
Cyr, Rene E., Sgt,
Czapla, Mathew V., Pfc,
Czekala, Henry S., T/4,
Czerkas, Joseph, Cpl,

Dalton, James C., M/Sgt,
Damsey, Robert T., Pfc,
†Danby, Edgar R., 1st Lt,
Daniels, John T., S/Sgt,
Daniels, Walter C., Pfc,
Daniels, Walter R., Sgt,
Danner, Robert B., Sgt,
†Daufeldt, Marvin G., Pvt,
Daugherty, Donald F., T/4,
Daugherty, Donald V., Pfc,
Daugherty, William A., T/4,
Davenport, John C., T/5,
Davis, Edgar F., T/5,
Davis, George C., Pfc,
Davis, John, Pvt,
†Davis, John W., Cpl,
Davis, Kenneth H., Pvt,
Davis, Marion A., Cpl,
Davis, Ross E., Pvt,
Davis, Walter J., Jr., Pfc,
†DeCiero, Roy, S/Sgt,
Deenihan, John J., Cpl,
DeHermidia, Eugene A., 1st Lt,
Deicken, Henry L., Cpl,
Deicken, John L., Cpl,
Delany, William J., Pvt,
D'Elia, Nunzio J., T/5,
DeMars, Joseph E., Sgt,
Demartini, John E., T/5,
Demipoulos, Peter T., Pvt,
Demitropoulos, N. P., T/4,
Denton, Clarence W., Sgt,
DePalmo, Andrew, Pfc,
Deputy, Frank A., Sgt,
DeRensis, Raymond, T/5,
DeSio, Meiro, Pvt
Desmett, George L., Pvt,
DeTrempe, Richard L., Pvt,
Devando, Edward P., T/5,
DeVido, Edward P., S/Sgt,
Devlin, Thomas F., T/5,
Diaz, Louis A., Cpl,
Dick, Andrew M., Pfc,
Didio, John R., Jr., T/4
DiRocco, Louis P., Cpl,
†Dishner, Dual F., Pvt,
Doby, Bunvon M., Jr., Pvt,
Doell, Jr., Emil C., Pvt,
Dolvin, Welborn G., Major,
Donelson, Billy J., Sgt,
Donley, Ralph, Sgt,
Donnelly, Earl F., Sgt
Donohue, John J., Jr., Pvt,
Dooley, John H., Sgt,
Doolittle, Leroy, T/4,
Dorsey, George R., T/5,
†Draughn, Harvey G., Cpl,
Dufalla, John, T/5,
Duffner, William, T/5,
Duffy, William L., T/5,
Duggan, Thomas V., T/Sgt,
‡Dugger, George C., Cpl,
Duncan, Robert L., Pvt,
Dungate, Edward P., 1st Lt,
Duran, Simon M., T/5,
Durham, Edward D., Cpl,
Durrant, Lawrence, T/5,
Durrant, Benjamin L., T/4,
Duvinski, Chester A., Sgt,
Duzan, Orval L., Pfc,
Dwyer, John D., T/4,
Dymond, William H., Pfc,

Easley, Charles A., Jr., Capt,
Eaton, Calvin E., T/5,
Eaton, Floyd D., Pvt,
Eckerle, Myron J., Pfc,
Eddy, Charles W., 2nd Lt,
Edwards, Elmo M., T/4,
Edwards, William A., Pfc,
Egliori, Livio W., Pvt,
‡Elder, James M., Pvt,
Ellenwood, Russell O., Pvt,
Ellis, Raymond E., T/5,
Ellis, Sidney E., Pfc,
Ellison, Tommy R., Cpl,
Elrod, Cecil E., T/4,
Elrod, J. S., Pvt,
Emery, Elmer H., Cpl,
Engfer, William R., 1st Sgt,
Ergott, Chester, T/4,
Erickson, Carl E., T/4,
Erickson, James A., Pvt,
Erkoboni, Virino J., T/4,
Eshbaugh, William K., Pfc,
‡Esparza, Ascencion, Pfc,
Essv, Victor M., T/4,
†Estkowski, Chester L., S/Sgt,
Eureyecko, Michael, T/5,
Evans, Loren E., Cpl,
Evans, William L., 2nd Lt,
Everett, Herman H., T/4,
Evola, Phillip, Pfc,

Faedtke, Vernon E., Cpl,
Fahey, Bernard D., S/Sgt,
Falkoski, Zigmund S., T/4,
Farley, Ed, Sgt,
Farley, Henry J., Pvt,
‡Farrell, Edward F., Cpl,
Farrow, Inman, Pfc,
Faulkins, Raymond D., T/5,
Favor, Frank J., Pfc,
Fawcett, Robert M., Capt,
Fazendin, Roger A., 1st Lt,
†Feeney, James F., Cpl,
Feese, Gerald, T/5,
Felegy, George, Jr., Pfc,
Fennell, Gerald T., 2nd Lt,
†Ferguson, Alfred, Pfc
Fernandez, Orlando, Pvt,
Ferone, Peter D., Pvt,
Ferraiulo, Carmine A., T/4,
Ferrante, Rinaldo V., T/5,
Fick, George F., Cpl,
Fink, Bernard, Cpl,
Finn, Leroy G., 1st Lt,
Finnestad, Donald R., 1st Sgt
Fischer, Donald W., T/4,
Fischer, Francis A., T/4,
Fisher, Lloyd R., Pvt,
Fisher, Louis H., Sgt,
Fitch, Clint D., 1st Sgt,
Fitzgerald, John W., Pvt,
†Fodor, William S/Sgt,
Fogel, William A., Sgt,
Folchi, Marion A., T/5,
Folino, Angelo A., Pvt,
Ford, Albert F. Sgt,
Ford, Robert E., T/5,
Foss, Charles M., Jr.,
Fowler, Arnold C., Jr., Pvt,
Fredrick, Cloyd, T/4,
Free, Melvin L., Pvt,
Free, Virgil O., Pfc,
Freeman, Donald A., Sgt,
Freeman, Frank, T/5,
Freeman, Raymond C., T/5,
Frensdorff, Hans K., Cpl,
Fricke, Anton C., Pvt,
Fries, Ruben F., T/5,
Frigulti, Anthony, Sgt,
†Froneberger, Leonard D., Sgt,
Fronning, Norris H., Pvt,
Fuchs, Norbert E., Pvt,
Fugger, Earl W., T/4,
Fuller, Grady P., Pfc,
Fuller, Hartwell L., Pvt,
Fuller, Jack W., Sgt,
†Fuller, Norman C., S/Sgt,

† Killed in Action.   * Prisoner of War.   ‡ Missing in Action.   § Died of Wounds.

Fuller, Ralph, Pvt,
Fullmer, Gaylen H., Cpl,
†Furnell, David S., Jr. Sgt,
Furness, Charles L., Pvt,

Gabin, Herman L., Cpl,
Gabner, William W., Pvt,
Gackstatter, Paul T., Pfc,
Gaddy, Charles H., Pvt,
†Galbraith, Raymond V., Sgt,
Gallo, Donald A., T/4,
Gallo, Joseph F., Pvt.
Galvin, Benito, Pvt,
Ganas, Benjamin C., T/4,
Garcia, Eusebio, T/5,
Garcia, Martin, T/5,
Garcia, Tomas S., Sgt,
Gardner, Floyd H., 1st Sgt,
*Garramone, Joseph C., Jr., Pvt,
Garza, Telesforo F., T/5,
Gaugler, Bernard H., 1st Lt,
§Gautieri, Michael, T/5,
Gavenda, George F., Jr., T/5,
Gaylord, Herbert F., T/5,
Geraghty, John F., T/5,
Gerhold, LeRoy A., Pfc,
Getz, Raymond S., Cpl,
Giesige, Earl V., T/5,
Gilbert, Robert F., Cpl,
Gilden, Bert D., 2nd Lt,
Giles, Joseph M., 2nd Lt,
Gilkerson, James H., Sgt,
Gill, Robert W., Pvt,
Gillick, Thomas, Sgt,
Gillispie, George M., S/Sgt,
Gillispie, William W., Pvt,
†Gilman, Robert L., 1st Lt,
Glasener, Robert O., Cpl,
Glenn, D. W. L., T/5,
Glogosky, Michael J., T/5,
Ghode, Henry E., Sgt,
†Gober, Albert T., T/5,
*Goddard, Jeff D., T/5,
Goldsberry, Vincent B., T/5,
Golightly, Otto M., T/4,
Gonzalez, Porfirio, T/5,
Goodloe, Charles N., S/Sgt,
Gordon, Glenn R., T/4,
Gorman, Richard J., T/5,
Gough, Francis L., Pvt,
Gourley, Donald F., Capt,
Graffagnini, Charles J., Sgt,
Graham, Samuel A., Cpl,
Granzig, William G., Pvt,
Grass, Bedford B., Sgt,
Grate, David L., Jr., Sgt,
Grau, Clifford A., Pfc.
Greene, Walter L., 1st Lt,
Gregory, Allan T., Pfc,
†Grigsby, Dennis W., S/Sgt,
Grimes, John F., Pfc,
Groft, Donald L., T/5,
Grosso, James, S/Sgt,
Guarino, Giacomo J., T/5,
Gudell, Albert, Pfc.
Guild, Clyde W., Cpl,
Guillen, Espiridion, T/4,
Guillen, Robert M., Pfc,
Gundelach, Ted W., T/5,
Gursky, Edward S., Pvt,
Guzman, Robert D., T/5,
Gwinn, Frank W., Capt,

Habenicht, Hugh M., Pvt.
Hagan, Harry J., T/5,
Hagan, Lilburn L., T/5,
Hagenberg, Francis J., Pvt,
Hall, Denzil E., Pfc,
Hall, Willard C., Pvt,
Hallford, Jimmie L., Pvt,
Hallman, Edgar M., T/5,
Hamilton, John M., 1st Lt.
Hamlin, Lewis R., Pfc,
†Hammar, Elvert H., T/5,
‡Hammer, William M., 1st Lt,
Hamp, Louis F., Pfc,
Hance, Charlie R., Pvt,
Hancock, Charles A., Pvt,
Hanlon, John P., Jr., T/5,
Hannan, Denis T., T/5,
Hannon, Thomas J., T/5,
†Hanson, John D., 2nd Lt,
†Hanson, Ralph L., 1st Lt,
Harding, James H., T/5,
Hardy, Norman L., T/5,
Hargrove, R. J., T/4,
Haritos, George, Pvt,
Harley, Howard M., Jr., 1st Lt,
Harmon, Charles W., Pvt,
Harmon, John F., 1st Lt,
Harper, Ernest C., Pvt,
Harris, Charles W., S/Sgt,
Harris, Clarence, T/4,
†Harris James L., 2nd Lt,
Harris, Reese T., Sgt,

Harris, Wilbur L., Pvt,
Harrison, Howard A., S/Sgt,
Hartline, Taylor N., Sgt,
Hartman, Marcus, T/5
Haspel, James E., 2nd Lt,
Hastings, Thomas E., Pvt,
Hatch, Smith E., T/5,
Havnar, Cline J., Sgt,
Haycraft, Wilbert O., Sgt,
Hayner, Gerald A., Pfc,
Headley, Sylvester P., S/Sgt,
Heafy, Harold F., Pvt.
Heard, John W., Capt,
Heidrick, Benny J., T/5,
Helit, Francis K., Sgt,
Hendrzak, Albert J., Pvt,
Henige, Robert F., Pvt,
Herrmann, James P., Cpl,
Herron, Raymond J., T/5,
Herschkell, William R., Pvt.
Hershey, George E., Pvt,
Hervitz, Morris, Pfc,
†Heuer, August C., T/4,
Hicks, Marzell D., T/4,
Highfield, Frank, T/5,
Hildebrandt, Lewis G., S/Sgt,
Hill, Girdon H., Pvt,
Hill, Howard, T/5.
Hill, William L., Jr., 1st Lt,
Hines, Horace H., 1st Lt,
Hirschensohn, Gerald, Sgt,
Hirt, Alfred A., Sgt,
Hoar, John J., T/4,
Hockersmith, Herschel W., Pvt
Hodges, James R., Cpl,
Hoercher, Loren W., S/Sgt,
†Hogan, Jack, 2nd Lt,
Holguin, Esteban P., Pvt,
Holland, Marion D., Pvt,
Hollon, Earl, T/4,
†Holloway, Robert J., Sgt,
Holm, Howard L., T/5,
Holmlund, James O., 1st Lt,
†Holmquist, Edwin, Sgt,
Holton, William F., Sgt,
Hood, Oscar S., S/Sgt,
Hood, Willis M., Pvt,
Horan, Lawrence T., T/5,
Hornsby, Henry C., Pfc,
Horvath, Stephen J., Cpl,
Howard, Jessie R., Pfc,
Howell, Alma A., Pfc,
Howell, Clifton, T/Sgt,
Howell, Ottest V., Pfc,
Hubbarth, David J., Jr., T/5,
Hudgins, Wallace R., Pvt,
Hudson, Charles E., 2nd Lt,
†Hudspeth, James R., S/Sgt,
Huff, Charles W., Sgt,
Huffman, Alexander L., Cpl,
Huffman, Donald K., T/5,
Hughes, Kenneth L., S/Sgt,
Hull, Levi F., Jr., Pvt,
Hultz, James W., T/5,
Humble, Willard, Jr., Pvt,
Hunsaker, Horace D., T/4,
Hunter, Jewett L., Cpl,
Hunter, Roland V., 2nd Lt,
Hutchison, Morvylle J., Pvt,
Hyles, Otis E., T/5.

Ihm, Paul R., T/4,
Isham, Harold E., Pfc,

Jackson, Burton T., Jr., Pvt,
Jackson, Charles B., Jr., T/5,
Jackson, Thurman S., T/4,
Jacob, Clyde T., T/5,
Jacobson, Meyer J., Cpl,
Jaime, David H., Pvt.
Jaksys, Albert A., Cpl,
James, Thomas F., S/Sgt,
James, Wallace L., T/4,
Jamison, John F., Jr., S/Sgt,
Jankowski, John, Pvt,
Janssen, Glen W., T/5,
Jaramillo, Alejandro, Pvt,
Jaroski, Joseph, 1st Sgt,
Jarrett, John W., Pvt.
Jarvis, Louis J., Sgt,
Jewell, Louis J., T/5,
Jimenez, Ignacio P., Pfc,
Johannesen, Oric W., S/Sgt,
†Johns, Charles R., Pvt,
Johnson, Cecil O., Sgt,
Johnson, Charles W., T/5,
Johnson, Clarence L., T/5,
Johnson, Donald D., Jr., 2nd Lt
†Johnson, Glen D., T/5,
Johnson, Lewis D., T/4,
Johnson, Raymond T., Cpl,
Johnson, Roy C., S/Sgt,
Johnson, Roy L., Pfc,
Jolly, Coy E., Pfc,
Jones, Anthony J., T/5,

Jones, Earl L., Pvt,
†Jones, Ferris G., Pfc,
Jones, Grover Q., T/5,
Jones, Harold A., Sgt,
Jones, James V., Jr., T/4,
†Jones, Lee R., T/5,
Jones, Marvin D., Cpl,
Jones, Ralph D., Pfc,
Jones, Raymond J., Pvt,
Jones, Willie, Pfc,
†Jordan, Lewis, Pfc,
Jorgenson, Carl H., T/4,
†Juarez, Maurice A., Sgt,
Judge, Vincent P., Pvt,
Judy, Vernon D., Pvt,
†Juliano, Alfred B., T/5,
Junker, Charles E., Pfc,
Justa, Stanley B., Pfc,

Kania, Casimir J., T/5,
Kanode, Richard R., T/5,
Karpinski, Stanley, Sgt,
Kartheiser, Theodore A., S/Sgt
Kartis, Frank S., T/5,
Kasey, Altie T., Jr., T/4,
Katz, Leon, Pvt,
Kaufmann, Herman J., 1st Lt,
Kea, Joe S., T/4,
Kearns, Edward D., Cpl,
Keefer, Marshall R., Pvt,
Keith, William M., T/5,
Keller, Norman W., Pfc,
Kempf, Marvin E., Cpl,
Kendrick, Carsel, Pvt,
Kennedy, Kenneth M., T/Sgt,
Kent, Charles D., Pvt,
Kent, William K., Sgt,
Kerby, William H., T/5,
Kerns, Wilbur F., T/4.
Kerwood, William J., Sgt,
Kidd, Jack P., 2nd Lt,
Kilgore, Earl C., Pfc,
‡Kimball, Harold W., Pfc,
Kimbro, Arvil W., Jr., Pvt,
Kincaid, Karl K., Pvt,
King, Marvin E., Sgt,
King, Robert L., Sgt,
†Kinney, Burdette W., T/4,
§Kinsworthy, Luther A., Sgt,
Kirk, Emery W., Pvt,
Kirk, Homer R., T/5.
Kirkland, Clifford E., Cpl,
Kirkpatrick, Hobert J., Sgt,
Kirtley, Herman C., S/Sgt,
Klingshirn, Richard J., T/5,
Knight, Kenneth B., Pvt,
Koback, Stanley L., Pvt,
Koch, Julius J., Pfc,
Kommel, Alfred, Pvt.
Kosanke, Roy R., T/4,
Kotarski, Stanley J., Pfc,
Kozub, Walter J., T/5,
Krasner, Harvey M., Pvt,
Kratzer, Robert E., T/5,
Kreckel, Patrick F., Sgt,
Kremer, Robert F., Capt,
Kreusiger, Paul H., Pvt.
Kristal, Max M., Cpl,
†Kriz, Virgil V., Cpl,
Krugh, Howard W., Cpl,
Krum, George C., Pvt,
†Kudick, Merlin A., Pvt,
Kuhry, Wilfred A., Cpl,
Kujava, Thomas J., Pfc,
Kujawski, Anthony P., Jr., Pvt.
Kuklis, Martin, Pfc,
Kupriance, Lotka U., Cpl,
Kyle, Edward H., Pvt,
Kyser, Jack G., Sgt,

Labisch, Albert A., Pfc,
†Ladue, Donald E., Cpl,
*Laliberty, Louis A., T/5,
Lamb, William V., Pvt.
Lancaster, James A., Pvt,
Landgraf, Charles E., S/Sgt,
Lang, Lawrence J., 2nd Lt,
‡Langham, Verus M., 1st Lt,
Langone, Egnazio A., Pvt,
Lansdale, Clay B., Pfc,
Laston, Leo R., Pfc,
Laurent, Edward F., Cpl.
Lavinski, Chester, T/5,
Lawlor, James L., T/5,
Layher, Raymond G., Pvt,
Lazarus, Paul E., Pvt,
Lechner, Leo W., Sgt,
Ledet, Charles J., Pvt,
Lee, William, Jr., T/5,
Lehr, Leonard H., T/5,
Leonard, Raymond L., Pvt,
†Levengood, John C., Sgt,
Levy, Harold, 1st Lt,
Lewis, French G., Major
Lewis, Lawrence A., S/Sgt,

Liberto, Sam A., T/5,
Lieberman, Fred, Pvt,
†Lierl, Anthony M., Pfc,
Lightell, Ambrose, Cpl,
Limbaugh, Woodrow S., Pvt,
Linderman, Frank H., Cpl,
Lindow, Norman S., S/Sgt.
Lipman, Maxwell G., Pvt,
Liskoff, Frederick M., T/4,
Little, Carl E., Pvt,
Littreal, Jacob D., S/Sgt,
†Lobas, Harry, Cpl,
Loeb, David, Capt,
Logue, Leonard E., T/4,
Logullo, John, Pvt.
Lohnes, Richard C., T/5,
Lombardo, Anthony, Cpl,
Long, Marion E., Sgt,
Long, Oscar S., Major,
Longobardi, Nunziando, Pvt,
Longtin, Bertrand W., Pvt,
Look, Oliver R., T/5,
Loring, Charles W., Cpl,
Lotz, James C., Pfc,
Lovell, John G., Cpl,
Love, David, Cpl,
Lozano, Jose R., T/4,
Lozano, Timothy R., T/5,
Lukaszek, Edward M., Pvt,
Lundblad, John P., 2nd Lt,
Lutes, Charles E., Pfc,
Lutz, Christian C., T/4,
Lynch, Jesse L., Pfc,

Mackert, Paul W., S/Sgt,
Maddox, John W., Pvt,
Madriaga, W. H. D., M/Sgt,
Madsen, Chester A., 1st Sgt,
Magurany, William A., 1st Lt,
Mahler, Calvin E., Sgt,
Makynen, Richard F., Pfc,
Maloney, Bob E., Sr., T/5,
Malsom, Tony J., T/5,
Manak, Frank C., T/4,
Mancini, Alfred W., Jr., Sgt,
Mancini, Orlando J., Sgt,
Mandalski, Frank J., Pvt,
Mandel, Edward S., Capt,
Mangione, Thomas S., T/5,
Mann, Raymond A., Jr., Pvt,
Mann, Weyman R., T/5,
Manning, Rodney A., Pvt,
Manzo, Joseph A., Cpl,
‡Mapes, Reuben B., T/4,
Marcell, Edward V., Pfc,
Margro, Anthony P., Pfc,
Marine, Maynard T., Pvt,
Mariana, James, T/5,
Marin, Rufus P., T/4,
Marini, Loreto, Sgt,
†Markus, Gus T., T/4,
Marquis, Andrew J., Pvt.
Marrocco, Frank, Pvt,
Martel, Aime L., T/5,
Martin, Courtney K., Jr., T/5,
Martin, Douglas M., Jr., T/Sgt,
Martin, James W., Cpl,
Martin, Owen J., Pfc,
*Martinez, Melesio, Pvt,
Martinez, Nazario, Cpl,
Masciola, Albert A., T/5,
Mathies, Harold H., T/5,
Matthews, Eugene M., Pfc,
Maude, Glee H., Jr., Sgt,
Maurer, Richard E., Pvt,
Mawhiney, Thomas E., Pfc,
Maxwell, Ruben L., Cpl,
†Mayfield, Marion F., T/5,
Mays, Howard A., S/Sgt,
Mazurkewiz, Edward W., Pvt,
Mazza, Ralph D., Pvt,
McAlinden, Bernard W., Pfc,
†McCarthy, Thomas P., Sgt,
McCarver, James W., Pvt,
McCloskey, John H., Pvt,
McConaghey, David L., T/4,
McCune, James L., Sgt,
McEntire, Oscar W., Pvt,
McInrue, William J., Sgt,
McIntosh, Neal L., Cpl,
McIntyre, Delmar P., Cpl,
McIntyre, Donald C., Pvt,
McGuire, James B., Pfc,
McGuire, James R., Pvt,
†McGuire, Thomas P., Sgt,
McKee, Doyle M., T/4,
McLear, James, Cpl,
McNamara, James A., T/5,
McPhearson, Warren L., T/5,
Mearian, Robert M., Sgt,
Medcalf, Handy L., Pfc,
Meisinger, Norwood H., T/4,
‡Mekus, John D., Pfc,
‡Melfi, Anthony F., 2nd Lt,

Melragon, Gilbert R., Capt,
Mercer, Ernest, Pvt,
Merchant, George C., Pvt,
Merna, James J., Pfc,
Merritt, Leo R., Pfc,
Mesa, Treno C., Pvt,
Michel, Harold C., Pvt,
†Mielcarski, Frank W., Sgt,
Mikucki, James V., T/5,
Miles, John W., Pfc,
Miller, Armond W., Pfc,
Miller, James W., Jr., Sgt,
Miller, Jessie T., T/Sgt,
Miller, John R., T/Sgt,
Miller, John T., Cpl,
†Mills, Walter J., Pfc,
Minarik, Stephen P., T/4,
Minnick, George W., Jr., Sgt,
Minter, Bobby J., Pvt,
Mittge, Merrill L., T/5,
Mize, Edward R., T/4,
Molinaro, Albert A., Pvt,
Molnar, Victor J., Cpl,
Monkelbaan, Joseph R., T/5,
Montgomery, George A., S/Sgt,
Montemarano, Joseph R., Pfc,
Montijo, Frank, Cpl,
Moor, Merrill L., Pfc,
Moore, Charlie L., T/4,
Moore, Clarence E., T/4,
Moore, Dale, T/4,
Moore, Edwin R., Sgt,
Moore, Erple W., 2nd Lt,
Moore, Jessie D., T/4,
Mootz, Gilbert J., Cpl,
Moralez, Joe A., Pvt,
Morano, Frank J., T/5,
Morgan, Leonard D., 2nd Lt,
Morris, Arthur R., T/5,
Morris, John J., Pfc,
Morris, Leldon L., Pvt,
Morrison, Donald W., Pfc,
Morrison, Leroy, Pfc,
Morrissey, Robert E., Cpl,
Moseman, Martin R., Pvt,
Moser, Frank D., T/4,
Mostransky, Nicholas, Pvt,
Motto, Nicholas P., T/5,
Mras, Carl A., T/4,
Mullen, Ira C., S/Sgt,
†Mulraney, John M., S/Sgt,
Murchison, James F., Pfc,
Murchland, Steve J., WOJG,
Murray, Leo H., Cpl,
Murray, Robert P., Cpl,
†Musil, Elmer R., T/5,
Myler, Donald V., T/5,

Nall, Rex D., Sgt,
Nalley, Bert L., Pfc,
Nappen, Elvin L., Pvt,
Nash, Charles O., T/4,
Natalini, Albert, Jr., T/5,
Neal, Charles R., Sgt,
Nelson, Kenneth S., 1st Lt,
Neuburger, Edward F., T/5,
Neuman, Albert A., Pfc,
Neumann, Walter F., Pfc,
†Newman, William H., 1st Lt,
Nicholas, Hillard M., T/5,
*Nicholas, James M., T/4,
Nichols, John S., T/4,
†Nicholson, Melvin W., Pfc,
Nicklaw, Millard D., Pvt,
Nickovski, Charles V., Pfc,
Noch, Joseph C., Pvt,
Norris, Raymond, Sgt,
Northey, Howard T., T/5,
Notaroberto, Anthony L., Cpl,
Nowlin, Carl R., Pfc,
Nowosielski, Frank, T/5,
Null, John C., T/4,
Nusz, Alvin, 1st Sgt,

Oakes, Wheeler R., Cpl,
Oakley, James W., T/4,
O'Connell, William J., Pvt,
Odoms, Richard G., T/5,
Oestreicher, Carl L., Sgt,
Offerman, Cletus J., Cpl,
Ohmberger, Arthur F., T/4,
†Olbyk, Joseph J., Cpl,
O'Leary, Calvin J., Cpl,
Oliva, Philip A., T/5,
Oliver, Haskell O., S/Sgt,
Ollis, Charles K., Cpl,
Olsen, Louis D., T/4,
Olson, Charles M., T/5,
Olson, Edwin B., Capt,
O'Malley, Vincent P., Cpl,
Onusko, Edward, Cpl,
†Orient, Andrew D., 2nd Lt,
†Osganian, Robert, Sgt,
†Overton, James E., Sgt,
Owens, Melvin V., T/5,

† Killed in Action. * Prisoner of War. ‡ Missing in Action. § Died of Wounds.

Padgett, Robert E., Pfc,
Padillo, Diego G., T/5,
Page, Lewis G., S/Sgt,
Palazzolo, Vito, Pvt,
Palumbo, Gene, T/5,
Palzkill, Charles P., Sgt,
Pantoja, Baldemar S., Cpl,
Parkus, Walter J., Pfc,
Parr, John S., Cpl,
Parrish, Millard J., Pvt,
Patsch, Gene W., T/4,
Patten, Moultrie, 1st Lt,
Patty, James B., T/5,
Paxton, Lewis, Pvt,
‡Payne, Francis, Pfc,
‡Payne, William T., Cpl,
Pearson, Lial B., Cpl,
Peckham, Julian F., Jr., T/5,
Pelley, Charles H., Pfc,
Peluso, Rocco, T/4,
Pena, Yrieno H., Cpl,
Pendergrass, Norris S., T/4,
Penick, Marvin L., T/5,
†Pennetta, William F., Pvt,
Pennington, Donald L., Sgt,
Perdue, Randolph H., T/4,
Perkins, Gordon E., 1st Lt,
Perry, Frank B., Pvt,
Perry, John H., Pvt,
Perry, Richard D., T/4,
Pesso, Joseph J., Cpl,
Peters, Herbert D., Sgt,
Peters, Reynold, Cpl,
Peters, Rudolph J., Sgt,
Peterson, Alvin R., Sgt,
Petrarca, Ernest, Pvt,
†Petronis, Edward I., Pvt,
Petrucci, John J., Cpl,
Pettijohn, James A., T/Sgt,
Petty, Leo, 1st Sgt,
Pflugrad, Winton M., Sgt,
Pickett, Roy V., Pvt,
Pickelsimer, John E., Pvt,
Pidich, Michael, Cpl,
Pieper, Harvey W., T/5,
Pierre, Joseph F., Pfc,
Pillow, Lenard W., T/4,
Pineda, Pablo, T/4,
†Pinkstaff, Thomas W., Cpl,
Piotrowski, Frank E., 1st Lt,
Pisacane, John A., Pfc,
Pitman, Richard E., Pfc,
Plagge, Leland H., T/5,
Poe, Willard S., S/Sgt,
Pokstis, Bruno J., Cpl,
Pollock, William A., Cpl,
Pompey, Daniel, S/Sgt,
Pompilio, Vincent E., T/5,
Pope, Carl H., Sgt,
Pope, George W., 1st Lt,
Porter, Richard P., Pvt,
Posik, Arthur J., T/5,
Potter, William J., Jr., T/4,
Powell, Charles R., Pvt,
Powell, John O., Pvt,
Powell, R. L., Pfc,
Powell, Reid H., T/5,
†Precise, William T., Cpl,
Preddy, Chester D., T/4,
Preli, Dominick J., T/5,
†Presto, Frank C., Pfc,
Preston, Curtis J., Pvt,
Preston, John E., T/5,
Pruett, Hershell E., Pvt,
Preuss, Charles W., 2d Lt,
Prianti, Michael, Pvt,
Pribyl, Edward J., Cpl,
Puhr, Walter E., Pvt,
Purvis, Walter T., T/5,
Puskarich, Mike, Jr., Pvt,
Pyka, Ralph J., T/5,
Pytelewski, John J., S/Sgt,

Quarrels, James C., Jr., T/5,
Querback, Robert A., Pfc,

Rabago, Jesus, T/5,
Rachel, Leonard, T/5,
Radzikowski, Eugene, T/5,
Rafferty, Terrance J., Pfc,
Rafter, Edward A., T/5,
Rainwater, Elbert, T/5,

Raio, Antonio, T/5,
Raio, John M., Pvt,
Ralston, Donald L., Pfc,
Rand, John D., Pvt,
Randazzo, Joseph A., Pfc,
Randolph, Bernard L., Pfc,
Ranspach, Paul M., Jr., Cpl,
Ray, Covie L., Pfc,
Reas, Eugene A., S/Sgt,
Rebock, Stephen J., Cpl,
Redle, David D., Capt,
Reed, Alex P., Pvt,
†Reed, Donald E., Pvt,
Reedy, William E., Cpl,
Regnier, Earl A., Sgt,
Reid, Douglas, Pfc,
Reid, Robert E., Sgt,
Reimers, Alfred H., Sgt,
Renfrew, John R., T/5,
Rest, David, Pvt,
†Rhoden, Victor H., T/5,
†Richardson, O. A., Jr., Capt,
Richiuso, Natale, Pfc,
Richter, Arthur F., 1st Lt,
Rickart, Elmer, Sgt,
Rickerson, Jesse B., Jr., T/4,
Ricketson, William L., T/3,
Riley, James M., S/Sgt,
†Rittenbach, Edwin R., Cpl,
Robbins, Alfred C., Pvt,
Robbins, Dorman L., Pvt,
Roberts, Charles A., T/5,
Robertson, Cenery E., Pfc,
Robinson, Cline J., S/Sgt,
Robinson, Ottie C., T/5,
Robison, J. T., S/Sgt,
Rodgers, Arthur J., T/5,
Rodgers, Clovis E., Pfc,
Rodgers, George F., Pfc,
Rodriguez, John, Pvt,
*Rodriguez, Philip, Cpl,
Rodriguez, Tito F., T/5,
Rogers, Glenn F., Lt Col,
Rogers, J. C., Cpl,
Rosen, Eli, Pvt,
Ross, Dominic R., 2nd Lt,
Ross, Eugene R., Cpl,
Roth, Joel M., T/5,
Roth, John M., T/4,
Rovelli, Anthony J., Pfc,
Rowley, Carl R., Pfc,
Rule, Eugene H., Cpl,
Rummel, Arthur P., Sgt,
Ruscheinsky, Frank P.,
Russell, Edward J., Pvt,
Rustek, Stanley A., Cpl,
Rutledge, John M., 2d Lt,
Rutzen, Ralph A., Sgt,
Ryan, John A., Pfc,
Rydman, Robert H., Capt,
Ryndak, Edmund P., Pfc,

†Saale, Paul A., T/5,
Sabler, Joseph, T/5,
Sadowski, Edward J., T/5,
Safranek, Clifford G., Pvt,
Saladonis, Michael E., T/5,
Salvatore, Joseph E., Pvt,
Samberg, Abraham, T/5,
Sams, Menard E., Pvt,
Sanders, Murray W., Cpl,
Sanders, Thomas W., Cpl,
†Sandona, Eugene F., T/4,
*Sanislow, Henry J., Sgt,
Sapinsky, Louis, T/4,
Sapp, Joe F., Pfc,
Sarno, Anthony M., Capt,
Savaloja, Rueben A., T/4,
Saxon, Eric D., Pfc,
Saxon, Jeffrey D., Pvt,
†Schafer, Frank M., Sgt,
Schaefer, Ralph M., 2nd Lt,
Schaffer, Virgil C., T/5,
†Schipper, Reuben C., T/4,
†Schleicher, Ray V., Sgt,
Schmall, Albert C., Cpl,
Schmidt, Fred L., Capt,
Schnall, Nathan, Pvt,
Schneider, Michael F., 2nd Lt,
Scholz, Victor W., Pfc,
Schommer, Leonard A., Pfc,
Schuder, Max E., Pvt,

Schumacher, Kenneth F., T/5,
Scognamillo, Anthony, Cpl,
Scott, Hubert L., Pfc,
Scovil, Robert R., Pfc,
Scruggs, Horace W., Pvt,
Secor, Donald F., T/5,
Seel, Harlow W., T/5,
Seelye, Dillman E., T/5,
Self, Harry E., Pvt,
Semerdjian, Maridious, Sgt,
Senior, John H., T/4,
Septak, Joseph, Jr., Cpl,
Serdan, William M., S/Sgt,
Sessions, Keith L., Pfc,
Shannon, Joseph W., Cpl,
Shapiro, Irving F., T/5,
Shapiro, Maxie, Pvt,
†Sharbutt, Randolph A., T/5,
Shaver, Ralph J., T/5,
Shaw, James E., Jr., Pfc,
Shaw, Ralph L., 2nd Lt,
Shea, Edward C., Pfc,
Sheehan, Charles P., Cpl,
Sheffield, Guy H., T/4,
Shelton, William H., Pfc,
Shepherd, Stephen S., T/5,
Sheridan, William A., Pvt,
Sherlock, John P., Pfc,
*Shew, Hubert S., T/5,
Shew, John W., Pvt,
Shind, Isaac S., Sgt,
Shirley, Gene B., S/Sgt,
Shirlock, George F., Pvt,
Shonka, Donald G., Cpl,
Shue, Bernard J., Pfc,
Sichak, Mike, Pvt,
Silva, Edward, T/5,
Simon, Bernard J., T/4,
Simon, Theodore E., Pfc,
Simpson, James W., T/5,
Sing, Shue W., T/5,
Sipe, Ray M., T/5,
Slate, Calvin C., Pvt,
Skinner, Edward C., Pfc,
Slusser, Ralph E., T/5,
Small, Jay H., T/4,
Smith, Frank, Jr., Cpl,
Smith, Edmund, 2nd Lt,
†Smith, Hamilton A., S/Sgt,
Smith, Horace M., T/5,
Smith, John P., Pvt,
Smith, Joseph W., Sgt,
†Smith, Malcolm L., T/4,
Smith, Robert A., Cpl,
†Smith, Walter F., Pvt,
Smock, Donald R., T/4,
Smolensky, Joseph J., Pfc,
Smullin, Orville W., Pvt,
Smykowski, Benjamin A., T/5,
Spillard, Albert F., 2nd Lt,
Soetebier, Charles F., Jr., Sgt,
Solberg, Walter P., Pvt,
Souden, Frank P., Pfc,
Sowers, Woodrow W., T/5,
Sprague, Warren P., Pfc,
Sprattler, Werner G., Sgt,
Sprich, Carl G., Cpl,
Squillante, Thomas F., Pfc,
Staake, Hugo E., 1st Lt,
†Staege, Dale R., Pfc,
Stajdl, Frank J., Pvt,
Stamper, Ben, Cpl,
Stanley, Lewis E., T/5,
Starr, Herbert L., Capt,
St. Denis, Maurice A., Pvt,
Steadman, Vern A., T/5,
Steele, Frederick W., T/5,
Steger, Edwin R., Cpl,
Stenholm, Arthur E., T/4,
Stephens, Ben T., Capt,
Steves, Lionel R., T/4,
Stiles, William E., S/Sgt,
Stilwell, Harold R., Cpl,
Stinn, Alfred J., Pfc,
Stone, Charles H., S/Sgt,
Stone, Clifford W., Pvt,
†Stone, Donald R., Pfc,
Stone, Eugene, Pvt,
Stout, Everett L., Cpl,
Stout, Lloyd R., Sgt,
Strand, Arne, Sgt,
Stroud, Paul B., T/5,

Stuber, Robert A., Pvt,
Stubbings, Gordon G., T/5,
Stubbs, J. T., T/5,
Sudvary, Mike, Jr., Cpl,
Sullivan, Marvin B., Pvt,
*Sullivan, R. C., 2nd Lt,
Sulantich, Mike J., T/4,
†Sundahl, George A., T/5,
Supinger, Verne M., T/Sgt,
Suplee, Bertraum P., Pvt,
Suste, John G., Pvt,
Sutro, Edgar D., Pfc,
†Swanson, Swan J., Pfc,
Swartz, Milton, Pfc,
Sweeting, Harry W., Lt Col,
Swift, Royal F., S/Sgt,
Swinton, William W., Cpl,
Switzer, Daron E., Pvt,
Szkutak, Raymond S., Cpl,

Tacy, Francis L., Pvt,
Taft, Joseph, Cpl,
†Taloney, Ryland E., T/5,
Tarrant, Orval J., Pfc,
Taylor, Frank C., Pvt,
Taylor, Jim U., Sgt,
Taylor, LeRoy G., T/4,
Taylor, Paul L., Pvt,
Taylor, Walter A., 2nd Lt,
Taylor, Wilfred J., Pfc,
†Taylor, Walter C., Sgt,
Tazzi, Anthony M., Pvt,
Tenpas, Rexford W., Pfc,
Terry, William, Sgt,
Thanel, William F., Pfc,
Tharp, Price, Sgt,
Thayer, Robert H., Sgt,
Thiel, Louis C., Pvt,
Thomas, Lloyd L., T/4,
Thompson, Morris B., T/Sgt,
Thompson, Willard, T/4,
Thrasher, Alfred E., T/4,
Tidwell, Phillip S., Sgt,
Tikkanen, Emil A., T/4,
Tikkanen, Ernest W., Cpl,
†Tirpak, Paul P., Cpl,
Toler, William B., Sgt,
Tomashewski, Edward P., Pvt,
Tomasik, John T., Jr., T/5,
Tomaszerski, Edward, T/5,
Tominello, Sidney, Pfc,
*Tompkins, Erwin E., T/4,
Torchia, Joseph R., T/4,
Tortomasi, Joseph S., T/5,
Tower, Osgood, Capt,
Trafton, Willis A., Jr., 1st Lt,
Traversa, Tony M., Pfc,
Treadwell, Clyde A., Pvt,
Trimble, Claude, Pvt,
Tropea, Benny S., T/4,
Truxal, David H., Pvt,
†Tucker, Harmon E., Pfc,
Tumio, Anthony, Cpl,
Turek, William J., Pvt,
Turpin, Herman L., Sgt,
Turtainen, Armas, T/4,

Ulsh, John R., Pfc,
Ulvestad, Olaf I., Pvt,
Uren, John R., Pvt,

Vader, Maynard W., Cpl,
Valante, Benny, Pfc,
Van Emmerick, Wynand, Sgt,
†Vargo, Steve, Cpl,
Vasquez, Refugio M., Pfc,
Vaughn, Frank W., T/5,
*Vaughn, James T., Sgt,
Veilleux, Eugene J., Pfc,
VeKasky, Paul P., S/Sgt,
Veley, Donald L., T/5,
Vera, Emidio B., Pfc,
Vernillo, Jerry J., Sgt,
Vidrine, Louis O., Jr., T/5,
Vignolo, Armando V., Sgt,
Virelli, Louis J., Cpl,
Voegele, Albert C., Sgt,
Votto, Patrick J., Pvt,
Vucurovich, Pete L., S/Sgt,

Wagner, Wilbur W., T/5,

Waldron, Charles P., Capt,
Walker, Don E., T/4,
Wall, Norbet, T/Sgt,
†Wall, Willie, Jr., S/Sgt,
Wallace, George D., Pvt,
Waller, Jesse L., Pvt,
Walling, Hubert, T/5,
Walters, Jack E., Sgt,
Walsh, Daniel G., Pvt,
†Wammes, Bernard C., T/4,
Ward, Cullen B., T/4,
Ward, Earl C., T/4,
Ward, Sylvanus W., T/4,
Ward, Thomas S., Cpl,
Ward, William E., Sgt,
Ware, Frank M., Cpl,
Wawrzyniak, Fred S., T/4,
‡Weatherwax, Merton E., Pvt,
Weil, Berthold F., Sgt,
Weimer, Robert L., T/5,
Welch, Francis L., Pvt,
Welsh, Kenneth R., T/4,
Wenzel, Donald R., T/5,
Werth, Herbert W., Pvt,
Wesol, Stanley J., Pvt,
Werthman, Edward H., Cpl,
Wessels, John, T/5,
Whisenand, Guy H., Sgt,
White, John, T/5,
Whitcomb, Elwood S., T/5
Whiting, Lyle O., Pfc,
Whittle, Glen. T/5,
Widener, T. F., Jr., 1st Sgt,
Wierzbicki, Raymond S., Pvt,
Wilander, Thomas E., T/5,
Wilcheck, Casimer A., T/5,
Wilcox, James H., Sgt,
Wilkerson, George B., Pvt,
*Wilkinson, C. M., Jr., Capt,
Willette, William L., 1st Lt,
Williams, Howard E., S/Sgt,
Williams, Robert H., Cpl,
Williamson, John R., Pvt,
Willis, William M., Jr., Pvt,
Wills, Richard E., T/4,
Wilson, Leon W., Pfc,
Wilson, Louis W., T/4,
Winlock, John R., 2nd Lt,
Wise, Merlin W., T/4,
Wisniewski, Eugene, T/5,
Witulski, John J., Cpl,
Wojcik, Albert A., Pvt,
Wolfe, Lauren E., Pfc,
Wolfe, Lawrence M., T/5,
Wood, Alvin H., Sgt,
†Wood, John J., Pvt,
Wood, Raymond, Cpl,
Workman, Terry E., T/Sgt,
Wright, Edward J., Pvt,
†Wright, Joe K., T/4,
†Wunderlich, Eugene K., S/Sgt,
Wyatt, Rawleigh A., T/5,
Wyonbradnik, Nicholas, T/5,

Yancey, Joseph B., Pvt,
Yasosky, Stephen J., T/5,
Yates, Lee, T/5,
Yeatts, Clarence E., T/4,
Young, Loys R., M/Sgt,
Young, Richard E., Cpl,
Young, William V., Pvt,
Younker, Christian A., Pfc,
Yuengal, Walter G., T/4,
Yurko, Peter P., T/5,

Zabinski, Leo S., Sgt,
Zajac, Tony A., Pfc,
Zamora, Geronimo M., Pvt,
Zank, Meredith J., Pfc,
Zanoni, Mario, T/5,
Zeek, James F., Pvt,
Zehe, Frederick H., Sgt,
Zehl, Louis P., Jr., Pvt,
†Zentz, Ervin E., Cpl,
Zimdars, Clarence A., S/Sgt,
Ziemba, Theodore T., Pvt,
Zinsmeister, John G., T/5,
Zoilo, John T., T/5,
Zurita, Lawrence J., Pfc,
†Zussman, Raymond, 2nd Lt,
Zwirn, Edward M., T/5,
Zyloney, Edward J., T/5.

† Killed in Action.   * Prisoner of War.   ‡ Missing in Action.   § Died of Wounds.

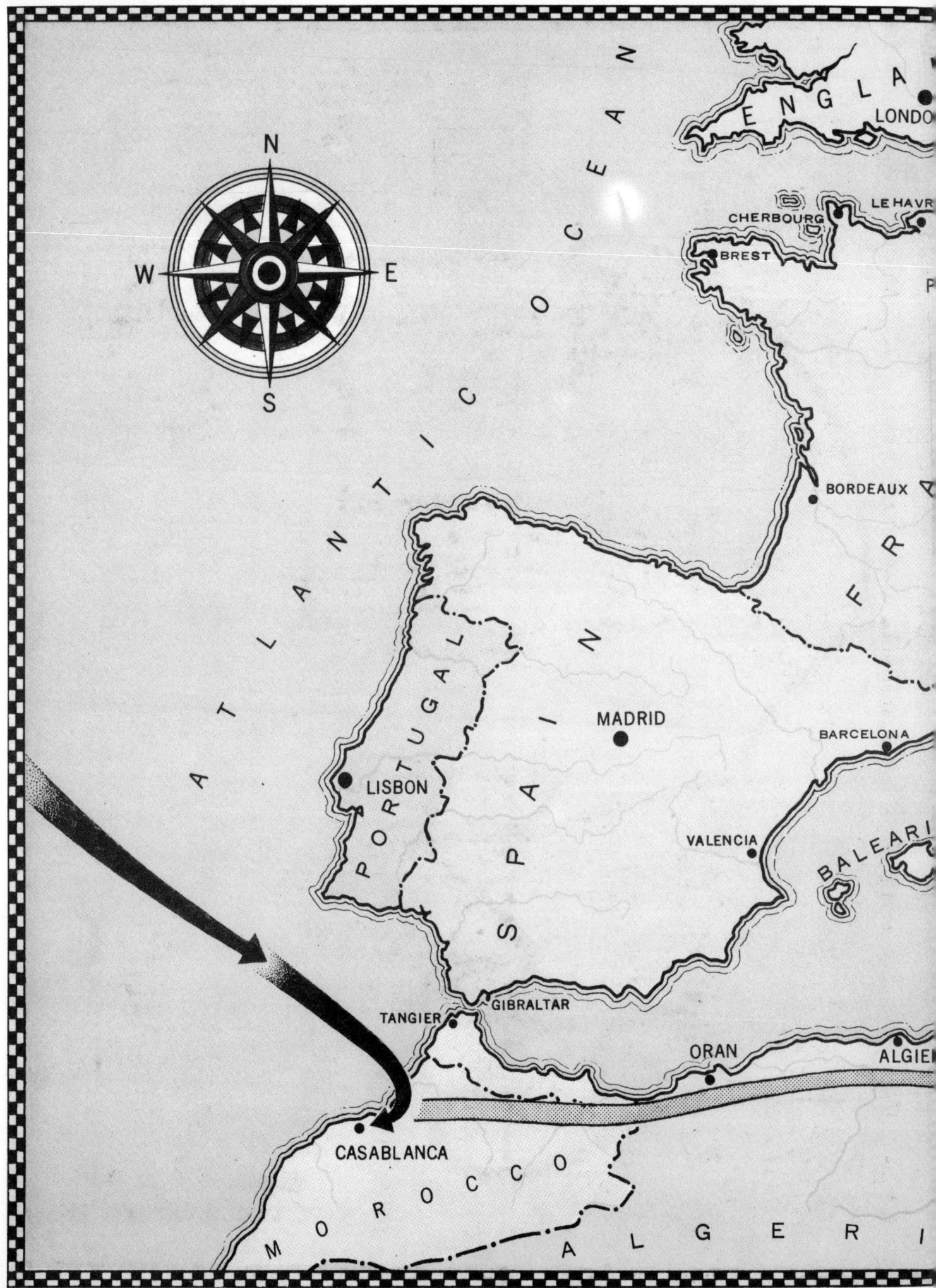